Presented

to

~~HAMMERMILL LIBRARY~~
~~MERCYHURST COLLEGE~~

In memory of

MARION SHANE

WILLIAM SHAKESPEARE

A TEXTUAL COMPANION

WILLIAM SHAKESPEARE

A TEXTUAL COMPANION

BY
STANLEY WELLS AND GARY TAYLOR
WITH
JOHN JOWETT AND WILLIAM MONTGOMERY

CLARENDON PRESS · OXFORD

1987

Oxford University Press, Walton Street, Oxford OX2 6DP
London New York Toronto
Delhi Bombay Calcutta Madras Karachi
Petaling Jaya Singapore Hong Kong Tokyo
Nairobi Dar es Salaam Cape Town
Melbourne Auckland
and associated companies in
Beirut Berlin Ibadan Nicosia

OXFORD *is a trade mark of Oxford University Press*

Published in the United States
by Oxford University Press, New York

© *Oxford University Press 1987*

All rights reserved. No part of this publication may be reproduced,
stored in a retrieval system, or transmitted, in any form or by any means,
electronic, mechanical, photocopying, recording, or otherwise, without
the prior permission of Oxford University Press

British Library Cataloguing in Publication Data
Wells, Stanley
William Shakespeare: a textual companion.
1. Shakespeare, William: criticism and interpretation
I. Title   II. Taylor, Gary
822.3'3   PR2976
ISBN 0-19-812914-9

Library of Congress Cataloging in Publication Data
Wells, Stanley
William Shakespeare, a textual companion.
1. Shakespeare, William, 1564–1616—Criticism, Textual.   I. Taylor, Gary.   II. Title.
PR3071.W44   1986   822.3'3   86-8474
ISBN 0-19-812914-9

Computerized typesetting by Oxford University Press
Printed in Great Britain
at the University Printing House, Oxford
by David Stanford
Printer to the University

PREFACE

THIS volume has been written in conjunction with editorial work on the text of the Complete Oxford Shakespeare, which was published in modern-spelling and original-spelling versions in 1986. This has been a highly collaborative labour, initiated in 1978 by Stanley Wells and, soon afterwards, Gary Taylor who, starting as Assistant Editor, quickly assumed the responsibilities of co-General Editor. They were joined in 1981 by John Jowett and in 1984 by William Montgomery. The editing of each of Shakespeare's works was assigned primarily to one member of this team; another member had particular responsibility for scrutinizing his colleague's work; initials at the end of each Textual Introduction identify the editor or—in a few cases—editors (unbracketed) and the scrutinizer (bracketed). The editor also compiled a glossarial commentary (at present unpublished). The General Introduction (with the exception of 'Editorial Procedures') and the sections on Canon and Chronology have been written by Gary Taylor.

In addition to those individuals and institutions whose assistance is acknowledged in the Complete Oxford Shakespeare, the authors are grateful for help received from B. Brainerd; Peter Brown; Susan P. Cerasano; Inga-Stina Ewbank; Beth Goldring; Thomas Halton; Gwen Hampshire; William Hodges; Bernice Kliman; Anne Lancashire; Leley Le Claire; William Long; Jerome J. McGann; Scott McMillin; Laurie Maguire; David Maskell; Jeremy Maule; Thomas Merriam; Felix Pryor; Julian Roberts; Alan Sinfield; Eliot Slater; Kristian Smidt; Glynne Wickham; Gary Jay Williams; the staff of the Boston Public Library; the staff of the John Rylands Library, Manchester; the staff of Edinburgh University Library.

Linda Agerbak was of immense assistance in co-ordinating the text origination, proofing, and provision and checking of line numbers for this volume; the very considerable labour of putting the book into final shape has been undertaken with great devotion by Christine Avern-Carr.

S.W.W.   G.T.
J.J.   W.L.M.

CONTENTS

LIST OF ILLUSTRATIONS	ix
GENERAL INTRODUCTION	1
THE CANON AND CHRONOLOGY OF SHAKESPEARE'S PLAYS	69
SUMMARY OF CONTROL-TEXTS	145
ATTRIBUTIONS TO COMPOSITORS OF THE FIRST FOLIO	148
EDITORIAL PROCEDURES	155
WORKS CITED	158
Commendatory Poems and Prefaces (1599-1640)	163
The Two Gentlemen of Verona	166
The Taming of the Shrew	169
The First Part of the Contention (2 Henry VI)	175
Richard Duke of York (3 Henry VI)	197
Titus Andronicus	209
1 Henry VI	217
Richard III	228
Venus and Adonis	264
The Rape of Lucrece	265
The Comedy of Errors	266
Love's Labour's Lost	270
A Midsummer Night's Dream	279
Romeo and Juliet	288
Richard II	306
King John	317
The Merchant of Venice	323
1 Henry IV	329
The Merry Wives of Windsor	340
2 Henry IV	351
Much Ado About Nothing	371
Henry V	375

CONTENTS

Julius Caesar	386
As You Like It	392
Hamlet	396
Twelfth Night	421
Troilus and Cressida	424
Sonnets and 'A Lover's Complaint'	444
Various Poems	449
Sir Thomas More	461
Measure for Measure	468
Othello	476
All's Well That Ends Well	492
Timon of Athens	501
King Lear	509
The History of King Lear (Quarto)	510
The Tragedy of King Lear (Folio)	529
Macbeth	543
Antony and Cleopatra	549
Pericles	556
Coriolanus	593
The Winter's Tale	601
Cymbeline	604
The Tempest	612
All Is True (Henry VIII)	618
The Two Noble Kinsmen	625
LINEATION NOTES	637
INDEX TO NOTES ON MODERNIZATION	666
A SELECTIVE INDEX	668

ILLUSTRATIONS

1. From *The Tragicall Historie of Hamlet* (1604–5), sig. H2ᵛ *The British Library*	5
2. A page from a playwright's foul papers *Melbourne Gardens Charitable Trust*	8
3. 'By me William Shakspeare'; signature on his last will and testament *Public Record Office*	10
4. 'The Booke of Sir Thomas Moore' (MS Harley 7368), fol. 9ᵃ *The British Library*	11
5. 'The Second Maiden's Tragedy' (MS Lansdowne 807), fol. 55ᵇ *The British Library*	13
6. 'The Witch' (MS Malone 12), p. 88 *Bodleian Library*	21
7. An alternative version of Sonnet 2: Westminster Abbey, MS 41, fol. 49ᵃ *Dean and Chapter of Westminster*	24
8. Verses attributed to Shakespeare, from the Stanley tomb at Tong *Joint School of Photography, RAF Cosford*	25
9. Page of an almanac, with a manuscript entry relating to the burning down of the Globe theatre *Bodleian Library*	29
10. Extract from a letter from Henry Bluett to Richard Weekes, relating to the burning down of the Globe theatre *Somerset Record Office, Taunton*	29
11. A ballad relating to the burning down of the Globe theatre *West Yorkshire Archives Service, Bradford*	30
12. Extract from a letter from Henry Wotton to Edmund Bacon, relating to the burning down of the Globe theatre *Bodleian Library (shelfmark Vet. A 3.f. 137)*	30
13. The permutations of dramatic manuscripts	31
14. The Stationers' Register entry for the Shakespeare First Folio *Stationers' Hall, by permission of the Worshipful Company of Stationers and Newspaper Makers*	32
15. The title-page of the first edition of *King Lear* *Trinity College, Cambridge*	35
16. A quarto sheet, showing the disposition of the pages	40
17. A quire of three folio sheets, showing the disposition of the pages	41
18. *The Chronicle History of Henry the fift* (1619), sig. F4ᵛ *Trinity College, Cambridge*	42

LIST OF ILLUSTRATIONS

19. The final page of *Much Ado About Nothing*, from *Comedies, Histories, and Tragedies* (1623)   44
    The British Library

20. The arrangement of type in the upper and lower case   46

21. The original setting of sig. xx6^v, a page of *Antony and Cleopatra*, marked for stop-press correction by the Folio proof-reader   48
    By permission of the Folger Shakespeare Library

22. A conjectural reconstruction of a portion of the foul papers of *2 Henry IV*   50

23. The permutations of printed editions   51

GENERAL INTRODUCTION

ANYONE preparing a new edition of Shakespeare's works will be asked, eventually if not immediately, 'Why?' or 'What does that mean, exactly?' These questions are obvious and simple; the answers are complex and far from self-evident. Perhaps for this reason, editors are imaginatively imprisoned in two contradictory, but equally derogatory, stereotypes. According to one popular caricature, editors spend preposterous sums of public money and private time fussing over whether to use a colon or semicolon, whether to spell 'O' or 'Oh', whether an author wrote 'toward' or 'towards'—tinkering with minutiae of no conceivable import to writers or their readers. According to the alternative caricature, editors labour to undermine the foundations of our cultural heritage, restlessly crawling over the surface of great works of art, seeking an excuse to deface what every sensible critic and reader intuitively recognizes as the handiwork of genius. These twinned stereotypes are a classic double bind, a catch-22, for editors can only escape the charge of inconsequentiality by risking the charge of over-ambitious cultural vandalism. Editing might therefore be provisionally defined as a total waste of time which periodically reconstructs our image of the past.

If Socrates had been an editor, and had been asked 'Why edit Shakespeare?', he might have responded by posing a question of his own: 'How do we know what Shakespeare wrote—the works he composed, and the words of which those works were composed?' The answer is, we don't know. Both stereotypes—the editor as pedantic drudge, the editor as cultural hooligan—presuppose that we all already know perfectly well what Shakespeare wrote. ('What Shakespeare wrote is what we read when we were at school.') Hence, editors really have nothing to do, and so must invent a function for themselves. But in fact, since we do not *know* what Shakespeare wrote, someone has to *decide* what Shakespeare wrote, on the basis of the evidence available at a particular time. Editors are the people who decide. This book attempts both to define and defend: to explain and justify the decisions of the editors of the 1986 Oxford University Press text of Shakespeare's *Complete Works*, and also, more generally, to describe the materials upon which all editors of Shakespeare must base their decisions.

Editorial Mediation

All texts of Shakespeare are editions; all have been edited; all have been mediated by agents other than the author. This complicating limitation applies as much to the earliest extant editions as to the most recent. We can only read Shakespeare's discourse through the filter of earlier readers, who have 'translated'—handed over, transmitted, transmuted—his texts to us. To translate is, notoriously, to betray; to communicate is to corrupt. Shakespeare's texts have thus inevitably been betrayed by the very process of their transmission even before they are betrayed—no less inevitably—by their critical and theatrical interpreters.

None of Shakespeare's own literary manuscripts survives. Three pages in the British Library manuscript of the play *Sir Thomas More* may be an exception; but whether those three pages constitute an exception depends upon whether Shakespeare wrote them, and hence our reading of those three pages is mediated by an editorial decision that Shakespeare did or did not write them, and that they do or do not belong among his collected works. The exception, if it does exist, is thus no true exception: the text of those pages is not unmediated, but simply mediated in a different fashion from the rest of the canon.

All Shakespeare's undisputed works survive only in print. Because (unlike William Blake) Shakespeare was not himself a printer, the work of translating his singular manuscripts into multiple copies of a printed edition was left to a number of publishers and printers, using the technologies and the working practices then current. Half of Shakespeare's plays were not printed until after his death, and for those works he could not have influenced or controlled the ministrations of the middlemen who posthumously published his corpus. But because (unlike Ben Jonson) Shakespeare himself does not seem to have undertaken to oversee the printing of his plays, even during his lifetime, from the perspective of his printers the author was effectively 'dead' to his work even before he physically deceased. So far as the essential conditions of their transmission are concerned, all but two of Shakespeare's works were, actually or metaphorically, posthumed.

The two exceptions are *Venus and Adonis* (1593) and *Lucrece* (1594): poems written to be published, politely introduced to us by authorial prefaces, and soon after they were written printed in the shop of a prestigious stationer (Richard Field) who happened to come from Shakespeare's home town. Here, we might think, Shakespeare speaks to us, his readers, directly. But even here Field stands between us and Shakespeare, and the degree of interference can be seen in two other works also printed by Field in the 1590s: *Orlando Furioso* (1591) and *The Metamorphosis of Ajax* (1595), both by Sir John Harington. For both, Harington's own manuscripts survive (as Shakespeare's do not), and the manuscripts differ from the printed texts in literally thousands of features: visual presentation, punctuation, spelling, wording.[1]

Moreover, *Venus and Adonis* and *Lucrece* are both dedicated to Henry Wriothesley, Earl of Southampton. The poems are 'letters' (collections of alphabetical symbols; literature; personal epistles) 'addressed' to Wriothesley; we only overhear one half of an exchange between Shakespeare and his patron. Of course, this triangular relationship is deeply ambiguous: one might as reasonably say that the dedications express a desire/hope/expectation that the chosen patron will overhear a conversation between poet and public. But whether the poet is transmitting his message to us or through us, the fact remains that each poem is a discourse between two parties overheard by a third—and as such subject to the misinterpretations of any other form of eavesdropping.

In *Venus* and *Lucrece* the dedications—which, curiously, are excluded from concordances of Shakespeare's works, as though they somehow did not belong with his other artificial fictions—make this triangular relationship explicit, but such a relationship in fact affects the text of all his works. Obviously and similarly so in the Sonnets; differently and less obviously in the plays. But in the narrative poems and sonnets the concept of an overheard transmission is a conceit, and however much it affects our interpretation of those poems it has little or no discernible effect upon their 'text', as editors normally use that term: that is, we can establish which signs Shakespeare put down on paper, without paying much attention to the way in which the signification of those marks on paper might be influenced by the intended direct or indirect audience. But in the plays the triangular relationship between one writer and two different sets of readers becomes all-important to establishing what constitutes the text itself. For the manuscripts of Shakespeare's plays were not written for that consortium of readers called 'the general public'; they were written instead to be read by a particular group of actors, his professional colleagues and personal friends, who would in turn communicate the plays through performance to a wider public. He could rely on this first special readership to 'edit' his manuscript, at least mentally and perhaps physically, as they read it. In the first place, he could count on their ability (through prolonged familiarity) to decipher his handwriting—more successfully, at least, than most of the hapless printers were able to do. He could also rely on those readers to bring to their reading much specialist knowledge about the conditions and working practices of the contemporary theatre, and the circumstances of the specific company to which they and he belonged. The written text of any such manuscript thus depended upon an unwritten para-text which always accompanied it: an invisible life-support system of stage directions, which Shakespeare could either expect his first readers to supply, or which those first readers would expect Shakespeare himself to supply orally. The earliest editions of the plays all fail, more or less grossly, to supply this unwritten text; modern editions, more or less comprehensively, attempt to rectify the deficiency, by conjecturally writing for him the stage directions which Shakespeare himself assumed or spoke but never wrote. To fill such lacunae is necessarily hazardous: necessary, if we are to relish the texts as scripts for theatrical performance, but hazardous, because the filling which modern editors concoct might not always be to Shakespeare's taste.

Shakespeare intended his words to be acted: to be heard, not read. Shakespeare's plays thus stand midway between Homeric epic (orally composed to be aurally apprehended) and modern novels (written to be read). *Loues labors lost* was written to be heard; the text is a score for several lost voices. As with music, so with drama, different techniques for scoring vocal performances have prevailed in different periods. Modern scores and scripts are generally more precise and prescriptive than their Renaissance counterparts, which relied to a far greater extent upon authorial presence—not the fictive 'presence' implicit in any text, but the corporeal presence of the author, as a living appendage to his text. Thus, even if we could confidently strip away the interference of subsequent scribes and compositors, and arrive at a script whose spelling and punctuation were entirely the author's, those authentic signals might tell us little (if anything) about how Shakespeare expected *Loues labors lost* to sound. Shakespeare's punctuation would not have been anything like the precise notation of, for instance, Samuel Beckett or Harold Pinter. Moreover, although Elizabethan spelling was probably more indicative than modern spelling of phonetic practice, like the spelling of all languages in all periods it must have been an uneven compromise between representation and convention. In Shakespeare's period this perennial uncertainty is compounded by the variety of spellings current for any single word.

Later in the seventeenth century strenuous attempts were made to regularize and systematize English usage. We are the heirs of that linguistic reformation. Consequently, the indefinition of Renaissance spelling and punctuation has become for us inadvertently prescriptive. We read either 'Love's Labour's Lost', or 'Loves' Labour's Lost', or 'Love's Labours Lost', or 'Loves' Labours Lost', where Shakespeare expected us to hear three words which could be interpreted in any and all of these ways. We read 'travel' or 'travail', where Shakespeare expected us to hear both. We confront this problem whenever we read the plays in any text, in old or in modern spelling: the text in either case offers us only one spelling, which will for a modern reader usually have a fixed meaning as a fixed form of a particular word. Shakespeare's words have been mediated irremediably by time: our perception of them is necessarily affected by changes in theatrical practice, in punctuation, in pronunciation, in the meaning and spelling of words, in their obscurity or familiarity or social register. We can—and indeed should, if we wish to gain the most from our encounters with his art—familiarize ourselves with the conditions of Shakespeare's time, try to think like Elizabethans; but we will always remain moderns, acting the part of Elizabethans.

But the texts have been mediated by time in other ways, too. Almost all literary works evolve, and these evolutions are incarnated in a procession of separate scripts: rough notes, draft fragments, a sustained first draft, subsequent copies containing a greater or lesser degree of authorial reshaping. But for most of Shakespeare's work only a single layer of this textual continuum is extant: time has 'edited' the multiplicity of textual forms down to a single exemplar. For a few texts, this single layer/document is sporadically supplemented by excerpts from another layer/document; in a very few, two authoritative documents are available in full. For no work do we possess more than two reliable layers/documents. The text of Shakespeare which we read is therefore confined by the accidents of survival: most of the editing has already been done for us, invisibly, by 'deuouring Time'; we read, the modern editor edits, only Shakespeare's remains.

An unmediated text of Shakespeare is therefore unattainable; we can only choose which mediator(s) to accept. As R. B. McKerrow declared in the opening sentence of his great *Prolegomena*, 'There can be no edition of the work of a writer of former times which is satisfactory to all readers, though there might, I suppose, be at least half a dozen editions of the works of Shakespeare executed on quite different lines, each of which, to one group of readers, would be the best edition possible'.[2] McKerrow's successor, Alice Walker, admitted that 'a definitive text of Shakespeare will never be established—except by Act of Parliament'. She perhaps exaggerated the power of Parliament. No edition of Shakespeare can or should be definitive. Of the variety of possible and desirable undefinitive editions, one asks only that they define their own aims and limitations: that they be self-conscious, coherent, and explicit about the ways in which they mediate between writer and reader.

Thus, photographic facsimiles of early editions are for some purposes and to some persons indispensable, but they nevertheless constitute modern 'editions', shaped—like all others—by the assumptions of a scholarly intermediary. An editor must choose which copies of which editions of which works to photograph; whether to reproduce a single extant copy, or to compose an 'ideal' copy using either formes or pages from several copies; whether to photograph corrected or uncorrected states of press-variant formes; which photographic process to use; what apparatus to provide. Such facsimiles may be reliable[3] or unreliable;[4] may offer separate texts of individual works[5] or collections of many;[6] may even provide parallel photographic facsimiles of different editions of a work.[7] Moreover, photography itself, like any other medium, communicates its own message: that what you see is real, accurate, genuine. Facsimiles compound the modern technological authority of photography with the original historical authenticity of 'documents'; but both these claims prove, upon examination, questionable. And of course, even if the facsimile imported no such invisible assertions, it could do no more than reproduce the editing of earlier agents of transmission.

Variorum editions also serve many valuable purposes: our own task would have been greatly simplified if more (and more up-to-date) variorums had been available. But even if we ignore the inevitable failures of execution in individual editions, all variorums appear to secure objectivity by multiplying subjectivities: as though many simultaneous intermediaries were necessarily better than one. Inevitably, in a variorum the opinions of Shakespeare's many previous editors and commentators effectively crowd out Shakespeare's own text(s). And even if the variorum umpires never intruded personal judgements about the relative merits of competing opinions, they must inevitably select which opinions to record, at what length, in what place; that process of selection itself imposes a further intermediary, influencing our view of the views of earlier intermediaries. Most variorum editors (if not all) do explicitly intrude their own views, and in the process enter the fray which they claim objectively to survey. Moreover, any variorum commentary must be keyed to a variorum text; whether a photographic facsimile, a transcript of a particular copy of a single edition, or a conventionally edited text, any such text will itself carry its own assumptions.

But Shakespeare is most often read not in facsimiles, or transcripts, or variorums, but in individual editorial reconstructions: texts prepared by one or more editors, who attempt to correct errors of transmission in the earliest available documents, and who present the results of those individual decisions in modern typography, in old or modern spelling, with or without commentary, with or without textual apparatus. Our own edition is of this kind, and like all such editions it is inevitably not only fallible but arbitrary. Not one of the four editors agrees with every editorial decision. But even in the impossible event that someone agreed with each decision to emend or not to emend, the resulting text of Shakespeare could be produced in many different formats—'each of which, to one group of readers, would be the best edition possible'. Thus, in the old-spelling text we have retained the original typographical conventions for the use of i, j, u, and v, but have not preserved ſ, or indicated ligatures (except for œ and æ); some editors would prefer to modernize the use of i, j, u, and v, while others would wish to retain ſ and all ligatures. Likewise, an editor might accept our reconstruction of Shakespeare's text in old spelling, but wish to modernize more or less conservatively than we have done. We have in fact changed our own minds about some of these decisions during our eight years of work on this project. But one edition cannot be all editions. Equally, though, all editions should not be the same, and we do not wish to pretend that our own manner of proceeding is the only responsible course.

The aims and limitations of the Oxford edition will be defined more specifically elsewhere in this introduction, but something should first be said about the character of all such 'individual editorial reconstructions'. In practice, such editions have invariably combined two functions which are nevertheless logically distinct. With one hand, they attempt to reconstruct the characteristics of lost, specific, real documents: the autograph manuscripts of Shakespeare's plays and poems, which must once have existed. In pursuit of this aim editors emend individual words and punctuation marks, in order to remove a layer of intervening corruption. But with the other hand editors want to supply a layer of ideal para-text which was never present in those early documents: necessary stage directions, consistency of speech-prefixes, regularity and readability of format. The first aim makes a text more accurate; the second makes it more 'legible' (in the broadest sense). For example, a passage in the 1604/5 edition of *Hamlet* may be reproduced photographically like this:

> *Quee.* Nor earth to me giue foode, nor heauen light,
> Sport and repofe lock from me day and night,
> To defperation turne my truft and hope,
> And Anchors cheere in prifon be my fcope,
> Each oppofite that blancks the face of ioy,
> Meete what I would haue well, and it deftroy,
> Both heere and hence purfue me lafting ftrife,   *Ham.* If fhe fhould
> If once I be a widdow, euer I be a wife.   breake it now.
>   *King.* Tis deeply fworne, fweet leaue me heere a while,
> My fpirits grow dull, and faine I would beguile
> The tedious day with fleepe.
>   *Quee.* Sleepe rock thy braine,
> And neuer come mifchance betweene vs twaine.   *Exeunt.*
> *Ham.* Madam, how like you this play?
>   *Quee.* The Lady doth proteft too much mee thinks.
> *Ham.* O but fhee'le keepe her word.
>   *King.* Haue you heard the argument? is there no offence in't?

1. (*above*) From *The Tragical Historie of Hamlet* (1604–5), sig. H2ᵛ.

This differs markedly from a conjectural reconstruction in print of the autograph manuscript of these lines:

Quee	nor earth to me giue foode, nor heauen light	
	fport and repofe lock from me day and night	
	to defperation turne my truft and hope	
	an Anchors cheere in prifon be my fcope	
	each oppofite that blancks the face of ioy	
	meete what I would haue well, and it destroy	
	both heere and hence purfue me lafting ftrife	Ham if fhe fhould
	if once a widdow, euer I be a wife	breake it now
King	tis deeply fworne, fweet leaue me heere a while	
	my fpirits grow dull, and faine I would beguile	
	the tedious day with fleepe	
Quee	fleepe rock thy braine	
	and neuer come mifchance betweene vs twaine	Ex
Ham	madam how like yᵒᵘ this play	
Quee	the lady doth proteft too much mee thinks	
Ham	O but fhee'le keepe her word	
King	haue yᵒᵘ heard the argument? is there no offence in't	

In such a manuscript, the speech-prefixes would occupy a distinct column to the left of the dialogue, and stage directions a similar column to the right. Longer prose speeches (like the last in this passage) would extend into the right-hand column; in a verse passage, this column would provide a convenient space for a marginal addition such as Hamlet's aside. Each speech would be followed by a short horizontal rule. Capital letters would not be usual at the beginning of verse lines, and punctuation would be considerably lighter than in the printed text. In the fourth and eighth lines, this reconstruction corrects what were probably compositor's errors. The printed text's '*Exeunt.*' where just one character leaves is taken to be a misinterpretation of 'Ex' for 'Exit' in the manuscript.

An alternative editorial treatment would be to take the same passage and, without emending its dialogue at all, offer a more readable, 'ideal' text of the 1604/5 edition:

> PLAYER QUEEN
>   Nor earth to me give food, nor heaven light;
>   Sport and repose keep from me day and night;
>   To desperation turn my trust and hope,
>   And anchor's cheer in prison be my scope;
>   Each opposite that blanks the face of joy
>   Meet what I would have well, and it destroy;
>   Both here and hence pursue me lasting strife,
>   If once I be a widow, ever I be a wife.
> PRINCE HAMLET If she should break it now!
> PLAYER KING (*to Player Queen*)
>   'Tis deeply sworn. Sweet, leave me here awhile.
>   My spirits grow dull, and fain I would beguile
>   The tedious day with sleep.
> PLAYER QUEEN   Sleep rock thy brain,
>   And never come mischance between us twain.
>   *The Player King sleeps. The Player Queen exits*
> PRINCE HAMLET (*to Queen Gertrude*) Madam, how like you this play?
> QUEEN GERTRUDE The lady doth protest too much, methinks.
> PRINCE HAMLET O, but she'll keep her word.
> KING CLAUDIUS Have you heard the argument? Is there no offence in't?

Because they are edited on distinct principles, the two texts differ in verbal detail; neither is identical to the original- or modern-spelling versions of the Oxford edition, which is edited on yet different lines. Either rendition of this passage fulfils a real, if limited, need; for scholarly purposes, certainly, it would be useful and interesting to have some examples of the first kind of exercise—though the experiment need not be conducted on the entire canon. But most readers assume that editions both recover the readings of Shakespeare's lost manuscripts and add a conventional format and apparatus for the readers' better understanding of the text. There is no harm in the combination so long as the preparers, readers, and critics of such editions appreciate the distinction between its two functions.

Those who prepare such editions should, ideally, examine all the available documents; familiarize themselves with any aspect of textual transmission or theatrical practice which might affect individual texts; acquire a comprehensive knowledge of the verbal usage of the author and the period; and scrutinize the available text(s) in detail with all this information in mind, simultaneously and comprehensively. This ideal is, of course, unattainable; but editors nevertheless try to attain it, individually and collectively, and by means of whatever attainment they have managed they set out to identify and correct errors and inadequacies in earlier editions (including the earliest). By editing Shakespeare, they essay to un-edit him, to compensate for the deficiencies and biases of previous intermediaries who were less informed or less careful or less interested or less dis-interested. In short, they spend prodigious stretches of time and effort trying to determine exactly what an author wrote, so that other people, with less time to spend, can read those words, and enjoy or interpret them as they wish.

An editor, like Oedipus, is thus a pragmatist, a believer in the efficacy of practical action, who is confronted with corruption, and undertakes to cure it; but, like Oedipus, the editor is also an idealist, believing that hidden truths can be dis-covered, that the lost past can be recovered (and not merely re-covered). Editors may take heart from the knowledge that Oedipus succeeded—but only at the cost of recognizing his own incest. Though editors properly aspire to an objective perception and perceptive distance, the nature of the organism they essay to cure always critically sabotages the application of a merely scientific procedure. Editors claim to serve, wish to serve, only as the invisible presenters of an author's 'work'; but editors can only perform their own 'work' by becoming, at some stage, and perhaps at every stage, authors themselves, re-creating what the first author created.

This dilemma by no means transfixes editors alone: it defines and circumscribes the activity of all literary scholarship, and indeed of all literature. In trying to establish the real identity of the 'fathers' of a culture, the editor or critic or author inevitably, to a limited extent, finds that he has taken the father's place. The authority of scholars derives from their capacity or their claim to recover and interpret the revered texts of such cultural 'fathers'; like priests, they tell us what the father meant; by doing so, they earn the affection of their 'mother' (the Church; or its secular equivalent, the university).

Dr Johnson affected not to comprehend why the disputes between editors generated such vituperative intensity.[8]

It is not easy to discover from what cause the acrimony of a scholiast can naturally proceed. The subjects to be discussed by him are of very small importance; they involve neither property nor liberty; nor favour the interest of sect or party. The various readings of copies, and different interpretations of a passage, seem to be questions that might exercise the wit, without engaging the passions. But, whether it be, that 'small things make mean men proud,' and vanity catches small occasions; or that all contrariety of opinion, even in those that can defend it no longer, makes proud men angry; there is often found in commentaries a spontaneous strain of invective and contempt, more eager and venomous than is vented by the most furious controvertist in politicks against those whom he is hired to defame.

Perhaps the lightness of the matter may conduce to the vehemence of the agency; when the truth to be investigated is so near to inexistence, as to escape attention, its bulk is to be enlarged by rage and exclamation: That to which all would be indifferent in its original state, may attract notice when the fate of a name is appended to it. A commentator has indeed great temptations to supply by turbulence what he wants of dignity, to beat his little gold to a spacious surface, to work that to foam which no art or diligence can exalt to spirit.

In our own commentary, we have tried to heed Johnson's plea for moderation. But Johnson himself, in deploring the polemic of his predecessors, is simply perpetuating an alternative polemical ploy: his own 'observation, with extensive view,' surveys the eccentric behaviour of other editors 'from China to Peru' (or Rowe to Warburton), and by a trick of Olympian perspective persuades us that he has risen above their internecine squabbling. Johnson's complacent admonition had, predictably, no effect upon the practice of his immediate successors. Nor can such editorial acidity be dismissed as an academic by-product of the satirical tone of Enlightenment culture: witness the ferocity of the nineteenth-century controversies surrounding Collier,[9] the noisy battles between Halliwell and Furnivall,[10] the triumphant righteousness of Greg and Bowers. These periodic exchanges of enfilading editorial fire should make it clear that more is at stake than the advisability of adopting particular readings: these editors are fighting for cultural authority. As George Orwell said (in relation to a more systematic editorial project), 'He who controls the present controls the past; he who controls the past controls the future.' Editorial controversy, like all other forms of discourse, is an instrument of power. If poets are, as Shelley claimed, 'the unacknowledged legislators of the world', textual critics are the unacknowledged civil servants who promulgate and administer their legislation. Editors are the pimps of discourse.

Like biography, historiography, or archaeology, the editing of works of literature is an attempt to understand the past, and to make that past more accessible to our own contemporaries. And the necessary first step in understanding the works of an author is to understand the circumstances in which and the means by which those works were first composed and then transmitted to us.

And I should wronge ye iudgment of ye highest pr[ince]
the world adores. See my Alphonso goe
leave us alone Are, my deare cosen,

(stage direction) so prince with discourse: Alphonso goes
And all withdraw.

Alp: As your highnesse wills soe
must bee S. motion.   Endimi:

Prince. Why yf death weare heere,
And sett wide ope his iawes I would not shunne
The chamber for ye griesly monsters companie
Not iuie bearded Soldiers with lesse feare
Dares see the Canon fired, they will find sir
Much he his Cannon in the resounding awe
And heare his thundring whistle then I dare
Encounter Danger, though that danger hads
Death for his Pagen attendant Death.

Lor: By heaven my Lord
Not all ye witt I am commander off
Can make mee the Oedipus and unvoile
The mysteries of ye Sphinx: I came
To bee ye happie messenger of ye
approaching happinesse

Prince.   Good good intelli...
Abroad   And can theare bee an happier state
Before man meetes with his last fate.

Lov: what are you learnt Epictetus, or have you read Boethius
de Consolatione or have you read Catos statuts, or is it
is a commendable thing in a Prince to hope you
will in tyme write bookes, that the whole world may
laugh at you: If you gives bookes wee must all
turne schollers and every one buie his lordes booke. nay
those who are wedded may gett obtaine such volumes by
deed of gift, without troubling ye statute. when Doming studied Iacondio, I dare
say not a Courtier but walked with his Iacobb staffe

GENERAL INTRODUCTION

From Plot to Prompt-book

If Shakespeare was like other authors, in composing a play what he probably first committed to paper was a 'plot', a preliminary outline of the sequence of scenes. We know of plots by Ben Jonson, John Day, Robert Daborne, and Nathan Field;[11] a plot for a scene of *The Faithful Friends* (anonymous, c.1620s) survives in manuscript, with the text of the scene itself;[12] an unfinished plot for an anonymous lost play (c.1625-50) is also extant.[13] Passages of a play might have been roughed out and/or drafted on odd scraps of paper; John Day wrote some verse lines of a speech from an unknown play on the back of a loose sheet preserved among the financial records of the theatrical entrepreneur Philip Henslowe.[14] For Shakespeare we possess no examples of or references to either plots or scraps, though they probably existed, and have sometimes been cited as explanations for peculiarities in certain printed texts.

A Caroline book-keeper refers to '*the fowle papers of the Authors*', contrasting these with '*the booke where by it* [i.e. the play] *was first Acted*';[15] Robert Daborne, a Jacobean playwright, similarly refers to 'the foule sheet' of a scene, contrasting it with 'ye fayr' sheet.[16] In early theatrical usage, 'foul papers' were thus distinguished both from the official prompt-book and from an author's own fair copy, and the phrase usefully serves as a label for an author's first complete draft of a play. Such manuscripts have seldom survived. Today, holograph manuscripts are prized by collectors as the relics of cultural saints; in Renaissance England they had no such numinous value. The manuscripts which have survived tend to be either prompt-books (preserved initially for legal reasons) or private transcripts (hoarded in the personal libraries of aristocratic families). We reproduce here a single page of a folded 'foul sheet' from the Melbourne manuscript, recently discovered, of an unknown play (Illustration 2); the two sheets of these foul papers have survived solely because they were treated as waste paper and used as the wrapping for a bundle of other, more important, manuscripts.[17] Such texts are often characterized by loose ends, false starts, textual tangles, unresolved confusions, and duplicated alternative versions of particular passages; by extensive inconsistency in the designation of characters in speech-prefixes and stage characters; by 'ghost' characters called for in stage directions, who never speak and are never spoken to; by extreme deficiences in stage directions, particularly by repeated failure to provide entrances for characters; by the use of an actor's name (instead of the character's) in stage directions and speech-prefixes.[18] Moreover, as the term itself implies, foul papers must have been less legible than a fair copy made by the author or by a professional scribe, and texts printed from such manuscripts usually contain an exceptional number of obvious errors apparently caused by the misreading of difficult handwriting.[19] (In making a fair copy, theatrical scribes would sometimes leave blanks when they could not decipher words, to be filled in by the author, or by someone else more familiar with the text: this practice can be seen in the manuscript of *Orlando Furioso*.[20])

The fragments of handwriting most reliably attributed to Shakespeare are signatures on legal documents (see Illustration 3). He probably wrote his plays and poems in a mixed English secretary hand.[21] The most common misreadings generated by this hand are minim errors, affecting the letters formed by minim strokes (c, i, m, n, r, u, v, w). A copyist can easily misinterpret the number of strokes, and authors themselves—as demonstrated by Hand D of *Sir Thomas More* (reproduced in Illustration 4)—sometimes ink one stroke more or less than they intend. The dangers of confusion multiply when words combine two or more such letters in sequence: hence, in Q2 of *Hamlet* we find the nonsensical reading 'arm'd' (4.7.22/2826), apparently in error for 'a wind' (the reading of the Folio text). Moreover, in Shakespeare's

---

2. (*facing*) A page from an unidentified playwright's foul papers, preserved by its use as a wrapper for other documents at Melbourne Hall; Webster and Shirley are among suggested authors. The handwriting mixes secretary and italic forms (compare 'his' in lines 25 and 31). Some letters are malformed through haste (for instance 'pp' in 'happinesse', line 22). Abbreviated word-forms are used, as in line 21; the first might be 'y^e' (the) or 'y^t' (that). In contrast with many play manuscripts, the first letter of most verse lines is capitalized. The writer made a double false start to line 24 and introduced a *currente calamo* correction at line 32; he made a marginal addition at line 4, and interlined corrections in lines 19 and 27 and an addition at line 33. Speech-prefixes vary between the full word 'Prince' and three-letter abbreviations for longer names. The one stage direction 'Exeunt' (line 7) is misleading: it is intended to apply to Alphonso and others but not to the Prince and Lorenzo.

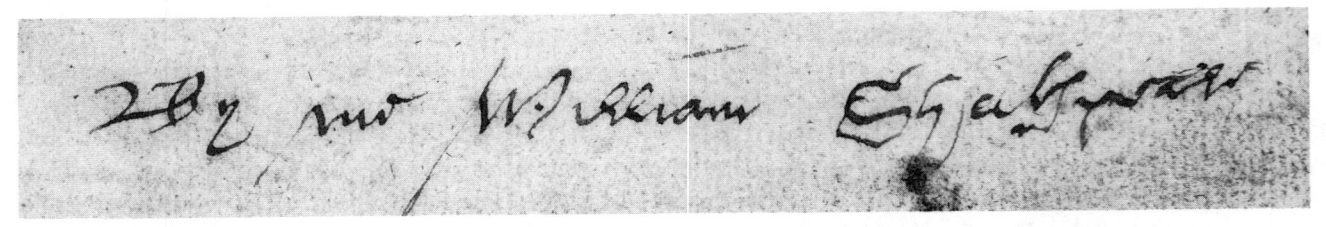

3. 'By me William Shakspeare'. Shakespeare's signature, enlarged × 1½, from sheet three of his last will and testament, 25 March 1616 (Public Record Office, Principal Probate Registry, Selected Wills, Prob. 1/4). Photographic reproductions of all the known Shakespeare signatures—authenticated, doubtful, or spurious—are included in S. Schoenbaum, *William Shakespeare: Records and Images* (1981).

signatures, and in Hand D of *Sir Thomas More*, 'a' can also be confused with a minim letter, leading to such absurdities as 'dimme' (Q2 *Romeo* 3.2.79/1661) for 'damnd' (Q4). Other common cases of confusion include: a/o, c/t, d/l, e/d, e/l, e/o, e/t, e/y, f/ſ, k/l, k/t, l/t, r/s, s/t. The probability of these misreadings varies, both with the individual hand and the specific position of the letters; moreover, in some circumstances, other misreadings are also possible. None the less, the canon contains many examples of unsatisfactory readings which are made satisfactory (either by conjecture, or by the testimony of another document) by the assumption of one of these categories of misreading; on this basis one may reasonably deduce that Shakespeare normally wrote in an English secretary script which strongly resembled that in the Hand D pages of *Sir Thomas More* (whether or not he wrote those pages).[22]

The pages of *Sir Thomas More* also illustrate other features characteristic of the dramatic manuscripts of the period. Verse lines do not begin with an initial majuscule letter; in the printed editions, the use of initial capitals to identify verse is almost universal, the sole erratic exception being the first edition of *The Merchant of Venice*. Speech-prefixes are generally placed in a separate column of the left-hand margin and speeches are separated by a horizontal line; in print, by contrast, a new speech is usually marked by indenting the line to the right, and setting the speech-prefix in italics just before the first words of the new line (as in Illustration 1). Stage directions also sometimes occur in the margins. The Hand D passages have virtually no punctuation at the end of verse lines, and little medial punctuation.[23]

All Shakespeare's works must, at some time, have existed in such an authorial manuscript, which could have been more or less 'foul' depending upon the number of earlier part-drafts which preceded it, Shakespeare's difficulty in composing it, and his care in copying it. His plays, if they were ever to be performed, must also have taken, at some time, the form of a prompt-book. The contemporary technical theatrical term for a prompt-book was, simply, 'the booke' (as in 'The Booke of Sir Thomas Moore', written on the wrapper of that manuscript); 'prompt-book' is potentially misleading, because an Elizabethan or Jacobean theatrical 'book' bore little similarity to the detailed prompt-books of modern institutions like the Royal Shakespeare Company or the British National Theatre. Nevertheless, 'booke' is, in the context of textual criticism, unhelpfully ambiguous, and we will therefore continue in this volume to call such manuscripts 'prompt-books'.

The defining characteristic of a prompt-book was legal: it contained the authorization of the Master of the Revels (an official subordinate to the Lord Chamberlain), who licensed plays for performance.[24] The licence afforded the company legal protection, and its cost rose from seven shillings in the 1590s to one pound in the 1620s; the prompt-book was thus valuable by virtue of its mere existence, quite apart from any functions it might serve in the theatre. But—although absolute proof is unobtainable—it seems likely that the prompt-book did actually regulate performances, directly or indirectly, in three ways. First, it was certainly sometimes (and probably all the time) directly used, as in later theatrical practice, by a

4. (*facing*) Anthony Munday and others, 'The Booke of Sir Thomas Moore' (British Library, MS Harley 7368), fol. 9ª. This is the most legible of the pages believed to be in Shakespeare's hand. For a transcript of these pages, see pp. 463–7. The altered speech-prefix (3), and the heavier deletion lines (2), are in the hand and ink of a scribe; smaller deletions are authorial (1).

and to add ampler matyere to this
and that not only, but lose yt alsoe that this yo^u had found
this thronge this proseed, but hym selfe hath bene wronge
tall^d theire God on earth, what do you thincke
in suffring this, that you^e had God hym selfe beinge offended
but ryse against god, what do yo^u to yo^u^r sowles
in doinge this o desperat as you are
wa?h your fowle mynds with teares and those same hands
that yo^u lyke rebells lyft against the peace
lift vp for peace, and your vnreuerent knees
make them your feet to kneele to be forgyven
is safer warrs then euer you can make
~~in in to yo^u^r obedienc~~
~~whose discipline is ryot; why euen yo^u^r warrs hurly~~
~~cannot pceed but by obedienc~~ what rebell captaine
as mutynes ar incident, by his name
can still the rout who will obay the traytor
or howe can well that pclamation sounde
when there is no adde^d but to obedienc
to quallefy a rebell, tell me but this
what you haue gott; Ile tell yo^u, yo^u had tought
how insolenc and strong hand should preuayle
how ordre should be quelled, and by this patterne
not on^e of yo^u should lyve an aged man
for other ruffians as their fancies wrought
w^t sealf same hand sealf reasons and sealf right
would shark on yo^u and men lyke ravenous fishes
woold feed on on^e another
do^o but marke the kinge of heauens messengers
let but to hym say, yt to yo^u what kinge woold yo^u haue
whither woold yo^u goe
what countrey by the nature of yo^u^r error
should gyve yo^u harber go yo^u to ffraunc or flanders
to any Iarman province, to spane or portigall
nay any where ~~why yo^u~~ that not adheres to Ingland
why yo^u must needs be straingers, woold yo^u be pleasd
to find a nation of such barbarous temper
that breaking out in hiddious violence
woold not afoord yo^u, an abode on earth
whett their detested knyves against yo^u^r throtes
spurne yo^u lyke doggs, and lyke as yf that god
owed not nor made not yo^u, nor that the elaments
wer not all appropriat to the^r Comforts
but chartered vnto them, what woold yo^u thinck
to be thus vsd, this is the strangers case
and this yo^u^r mountainish inhumanyty

all   ffayth a saies trewe letts ds as we may be doon by
Linco   weele by gud m^r moore thoule stand our
moore   Submyt yo^u to theise noble gentlemen
        entreate their mediation to the kinge
        geve vp your self to forme obay the magestrat
        and thers no doubt but mercy maie be found yf yo^u so seek

book-keeper who would 'holde the booke'[25] to prompt actors who had forgotten their lines or business. Secondly, it was probably the manuscript which was copied in order to produce each actor's 'part' (a manuscript containing all the speeches and cues for one character). Thirdly, it was probably the manuscript from which the book-keeper extracted a 'plat'—a synopsis of the play's entrances, exits, properties, and sound effects, which was used to regulate rehearsals or performances (or both).[26] Contemporary examples of both 'parts' and 'plats' survive, and although we possess no direct testimonials on how they were normally prepared, it would seem natural—and perhaps would be necessary—to derive both from the prompt-book (rather than 'foul papers').[27]

A number of early prompt-books survive, and Illustration 5 reproduces a page from the earliest such manuscript which can be unequivocally associated with Shakespeare's company. The typical features of such a manuscript are implicit in its function. It may contain alterations and instructions from the Master of the Revels, who was responsible for censoring scripts before licensing them. Stage directions tend to be more systematically supplied, in order to help regulate (directly or indirectly) offstage sounds, to ensure the readiness of actors backstage so that they can enter on cue, and to call attention to necessary properties. Directions tend to be placed more systematically in the margins (where they are easily spotted), rather than contained in the body of the dialogue; they tend also to be more practically, and laconically, worded. In some prompt-books, entrances are signalled in the margin some while before they occur: such advance notification presumably served as a warning to the book-keeper, and hence to the actor, to be ready for the upcoming entrance. The names of particular actors—generally, of those playing small, transient parts—were sometimes noted marginally in stage directions. Characters tend to be more consistently identified in speech-prefixes. In general, the entire presentation of the text is more legible.[28] To all of these generalizations occasional or partial exceptions can be found, and for all of them the standard of consistency is relative;[29] but these general characteristics are directly related to the functions of any such manuscripts, and hence can be identified to a greater or lesser degree in all of them.

The simplicity of this schematic distinction between foul papers and prompt-books can, however, easily harden into a misleading dichotomy which conceals the many permutations of dramatic manuscripts in this period. To begin with, the author's foul papers might themselves be marked up to serve as a prompt-book (as perhaps happens in Thomas Heywood's *The Captives* and the anonymous play *The Wasp*);[30] in such cases there would exist not two different manuscripts, but one manuscript in two different states at different times. In other cases—like *Sir Thomas More* itself—an authorial fair copy marked up for use in the theatre by both a scribe and a censor contains within it the 'foul sheets' of additional or adapted passages; these 'foul sheets' have then been themselves marked up by a theatrical scribe.

Another potential manuscript category which blurs the distinction between pure foul papers and pure transcript is the so-called 'intermediate transcript', much favoured by Fredson Bowers and his school.[31] Such a manuscript would be a scribal copy of authorial foul papers, from which another copy—the true prompt-book—was in turn made. No clear examples of such manuscripts have been found, and their existence is an inference, used to explain the features of certain printed texts. The whole category seems to us (as it did to Greg) suspect, being almost inevitably based upon a subjective conviction that a certain text is not clean enough, not consistent enough, not thorough enough, to have served as the 'official' company prompt-book. The study of official company prompt-books quickly disabuses us of such idealistic expectations. Moreover, transcripts cost money. That theatrical companies found it worth paying for a scribal transcript which could serve as prompt-book is demonstrated by the King's Men's manuscripts of *The Second Maiden's Tragedy* (1611) and *Sir John van Olden Barnavelt* (1618), among others; but it seems extravagant to imagine a theatrical company paying for two separate transcripts, rather than simply

5. (*facing*) Thomas Middleton (?), 'The Second Maiden's Tragedy' (British Library, MS Lansdowne 807), fol. 55[b]. The change of dialogue, marked by a cross in the margin (1), was made by Sir George Buc, Master of the Revels, who examined and licensed the play on 31 October 1611. The text appears to be a scribal copy; the 'florish' in the left margin (3) was added by another scribe, clearly associated with the playhouse. Vertical lines in the left margin (2) indicate deletions of dialogue.

                        to pcy thee harder
          Spiritt   my truest loue
                     liue euer honourd here, and blest aboue.
Enter   Tir.   oh is ther be a hell or flesh and spirrit
Nobles   tis built within this bosome: my Lordes treason
           Gou.   now death, giue me hye, wellcome
           Ty.   a kinges guerdon I am poisoned
           Memph.   the king of heauen be prais'd for't
           Ty.   lay hold on him
                     on Gouianus
           Memph.   een with the best loues
                     and truest hartes that euer subiects owde
                                               all
           Ty.   how's that, I charge you laie handes on him
Enter   Memph.   look you my lord yo^u will shalbe obaide
Helvetius   Heere comes another, wee'l haue his hand too.
           Hel.   you shall haue both mynes, if that worke you forward
                     beside my voice and tuike
           Ty.   Heluetius? — then my destruction was conferrd amongst em
                     premeditation wrongst it: o my tormentes:
florish   All   liue Gouianus longe our vertuous kinge
           Tyr.   that thunder strikes me dead
           Gou.   I cannot better
                     reward my Ioyes then with astonisht silence
                     for all the wealth of wordes is not of powre
                     to make vp thankes for yo^u my honord Lordes:
                     Iust like a man pluckt vp from many waters
                     that neuer lookt for helpe, and are strongly set
                     vpon this cheerfull mountaine where prosperitie
                     shootes forth her richest beame
           Memph.   longe in weede lord
                     the tyrannye of his actions grew so weightie
                     his life so vitious:
           ——   to wish this is vertue
                     Monster in sinne, this, the disquieted bodye
                     of my too resolute childe in Honors warr
           ——   that he became as hatefull to our myndes
           ——   as death's vnwellcome to a spouse of pittyes
                     or what can more expresse it
           Gou.   well sirs goe
                     and all the kingdomes ills perish with him
                     and furre the bodie of that vertuous Ladie
                     is taken from her rest, for memorie
                     of her admired mistris, 'tis our wills
                     it receiue honour dead, as it tooke partie
                     with vs in all afflictions when it liu'de:
                     her place shee in this throane neer her our Quene
                     the first and last that euer we make ours
                     her constancy strikes so vnmouedly in vs :
                     that honor donne let her be solempnly borne

marking up the first, as they thought necessary or fit. We have therefore sought to avoid presuming the existence of intermediate transcripts, and in no case do we propose that a printed text is set from one. Occam's famous warning against the multiplication of unnecessary entities is in the case of Renaissance dramatic manuscripts strengthened by financial considerations; for most plays, probably only two manuscripts ever existed.

With the exception of *Sir Thomas More*, the issue for Shakespeare's editors is not to identify the nature or function of an extant manuscript, but to try to identify the nature or function of a lost manuscript which served as the printer's copy for an extant edition. Even if the distinction between foul papers and prompt-books were wholly untroubled by permutations and complications, it might be impossible to distinguish between the two categories of text when we can only see them through the filter of an intervening printed edition. In fact, we believe the distinction can be discerned, but the difficulties in discerning it have sometimes been underestimated. The distinction is clearest when we can compare two texts of a single play. Thus, the first edition of *Much Ado About Nothing*, printed in 1600, shows every sign of having been printed from authorial foul papers: it omits many necessary entrances, it calls for entrances which do not occur, it uses actors' names in speech-prefixes, it seems to have been set from a very lightly punctuated manuscript in a handwriting remarkably similar to that of Hand D. The 1623 edition of the play is, for the most part, a simple reprint of the 1600 edition; but it alters a number of details, chiefly affecting stage directions and speech-prefixes, presumably by reference to a manuscript, now lost. These changes, though by no means systematic, all move the text in the direction of what we expect of a prompt-book. Relative to one another, the lost manuscript behind the first edition looks even more like foul papers, and the lost manuscript consulted for the second edition even more like a prompt-book. We find exactly the same situation when we compare the 1623 texts of *Love's Labour's Lost*, *The Merchant of Venice*, *A Midsummer Night's Dream*, *Richard II*, and *Titus Andronicus* with the first editions of each. Moreover, in each case we seem actually to be dealing with two different manuscripts, and not simply with the same manuscript in a different condition at different times. All these works were composed some time before they were first printed, and we would expect most of the prompt-book-like alterations visible in the 1623 edition to have been made on the occasion of the first production. Some of the changes could have been, or certainly were, the result of later revivals; but most seem to arise naturally from any attempt to put the play on to the stage. We may therefore reasonably deduce that such alterations were made in the prompt-book at an early date, and the fact that these alterations do not appear in the first editions suggests that the first editions were indeed printed from authorial foul papers, which were at some point and by some person copied in order to produce a fairer manuscript which served as the prompt-book.

From such examples it seems that Shakespeare's foul papers were normally copied. We have no way of knowing, to start with, who copied them. In the extant manuscripts of the period, fair copies are sometimes made by the author himself, sometimes by a scribe. It is likely enough that, during the course of his career, both methods were occasionally used for Shakespeare's plays; certainly, it is unwise to be dogmatic about the company's normal procedure. An author's own fair copy does not have to be paid for, and it allows the author another opportunity to polish his composition. On the other hand, Shakespeare was a leading actor and shareholder in the company;[32] and it might sometimes have seemed sensible to himself and the company to free his time for acting, managing, and writing by paying someone else to copy his scripts. Given the normality of copying (by author or scribe), we can easily explain why most of the authoritative early editions of Shakespeare's plays were apparently printed from his foul papers: once his draft manuscript had been copied, it had only a secondary value (as an insurance against loss of the prompt-book), and might therefore be sold to a publisher. Publishers usually paid 40 shillings for the manuscript of a pamphlet, and the same rate evidently prevailed for plays;[33] any such payment would help to defray the expense of having Shakespeare's foul papers copied, on that or some other occasion, or would be an extra source of income for the company. Finally, for the opposite reason, we can explain why so few of the editions of Shakespeare's plays — or of public theatre plays generally, printed before the closing of the theatres in 1642—were printed from prompt-books. Such manuscripts were extremely valuable to a theatrical company, constituting as they did the material proof of the company's ownership of and licence to perform a play; the owners might reasonably be reluctant to sell or lend such manuscripts to a printer. Thus, even the 1623 edition of plays like *Much Ado* was not printed directly from a prompt-book, but only from an earlier printed edition which had been marked up by reference to that prompt-book.

Presuming, then, that we can legitimately distinguish editions based upon foul papers from editions based upon prompt-books, what difference does the distinction make? Prompt-books clear up confusions which editors will usually clear up anyway; they add information—about actors, for instance—which editors will usually ignore. Many features which help to distinguish the two kinds of manuscript are, in themselves, of minimal editorial interest. But although in some respects the nature of its engagement with an audience has already been determined, foul papers represent the text in an as yet individual, private form; the prompt-book is a socialized text, one which has been communally prepared for communication to a wider public.[34]

Either category of text has its uses. As students of modern literature are aware, the study of authors' manuscript (or typescript) drafts can often illuminate their methods of composition, their personal and artistic preoccupations, their strengths and weaknesses. It would be possible—indeed, desirable—to prepare an edition of some at least of Shakespeare's works which struggled to reproduce as exactly as possible the first draft. Modern authors have become aware of the potential financial and intellectual value of such drafts, and often preserve them in the expectation that they will someday be studied; in such cases—as has long been true of literary letters and diaries—the allegedly private text has a perceived public future, even as it comes into its present existence. Shakespeare by contrast devoted his life to the theatre, and dramatic texts are necessarily the most socialized of all literary forms. Where matters of verbal and theatrical substance are involved, we have therefore chosen, in our own edition, to prefer— where there is a choice—the text closer to the prompt-book of Shakespeare's company. We do not wish to pretend that this is the only rational choice; but we do insist that a choice has to be made, and that editors and readers must live with the consequences of either decision.

Nevertheless, one may usefully distinguish between two kinds of modification which a text may undergo in its progress from a private to a socialized mode. Some changes an author can control; other changes he cannot. Most obviously, Shakespeare could not veto or influence any changes imposed upon his plays in the theatre after his death. Fortunately, the economics and mechanics of the pre-Restoration repertory system made it impractical to reshape a play every time it was revived;[35] when later adaptation did occur, it usually involved the addition of discrete chunks of material.[36] Therefore the number of changes affected by such intervention should be small, and those interventions that do occur should be extensive enough to be detectable. Unfortunately, such changes are, even after they have been identified, difficult to repair. It seems to us reasonably clear that the Folio texts of both *Macbeth* and *Measure for Measure* have suffered from posthumous theatrical adaptation; but we possess no other substantive text of either play. We have drawn readers' attention to the uncertain status of both works; we have identified certain features of each which seem to belong to the adapted rather than the original version; in the case of *Measure* we have even offered conjectural reconstructions of two episodes. But we cannot magically produce the lost, unadapted text.

Posthumous adaptation may have occurred occasionally; censorship did occur systematically.[37] Prompt-books are, by definition, manuscripts submitted to and approved by the Master of the Revels; against such changes as the censor might choose to impose, Shakespeare had no recourse. Such changes can often be identified and repaired, and where possible the Oxford edition has restored the uncensored text. Thus, we know that Sir John Falstaff was, in *1 Henry IV*, originally called Sir John Oldcastle, and that the change was forced upon Shakespeare after the play's first performances; certain variants in the texts of *Richard II*, *Merchant*, *Merry Wives*, *2 Henry IV*, *The Tragedy of King Lear*, and *Pericles* also seem to be due to political interference. More generally, Parliament in May 1606 passed 'An Acte to Restraine

Abuses of Players', which forbade the use of God's name in theatrical performances.[38] Those of Shakespeare's plays written after that date are virtually bare of profanity; more seriously, some plays written before that date were retrospectively stripped of objectionable oaths and allusions. We have, wherever possible, put such profanities back in Shakespeare's mouth.

Most readers will, we feel sure, want to read Shakespeare in an unexpurgated and uncensored text; but anyone who wishes to consider Shakespeare's works *as performed* in his lifetime will need to take account of ways in which the political authorities influenced the object presented to the public.[39] Shakespeare's conflicts with the censors—those places where he tried to get certain sensitive material past them, but did not succeed—are, in themselves, of considerable political interest to readers and critics; the Textual Introduction to each play apparently affected by censorship draws attention to the relevant passages.

Over matters of government censorship, or posthumous adaptation, Shakespeare as author obviously had no control; his personal responsibility for certain other changes is more debatable. As a rule, we have not held him responsible for textual variants which seem to derive from general changes of circumstance which he could not anticipate when writing the play. Thus, *Julius Caesar* as originally conceived requires two actors of a noticeably 'lean and hungry look' (Cassius and Ligarius); in some later performances, only one such actor seems to have been available, and the text was apparently accommodated to this dearth of thin talent; so far as possible, we have restored the original text. Likewise, it seems clear that, during the course of Shakespeare's career, his company, under the pressure of theatrical competition, changed its practice in respect to intervals or intermissions during performance: for most of his writing life, plays for the public theatre were performed without interruption, but from c.1608, when the King's Men acquired the indoor Blackfriars playhouse, performances were divided into five acts by four musical interludes.[40] Such act divisions were also restrospectively imposed on plays originally designed for continuous performance. When the new act divisions coexist with other authorial revisions (as in *Titus Andronicus* and *King Lear*) or with extensive posthumous adaptation (as in *Measure for Measure* and *Macbeth*) they have been retained in our text because of the difficulty of disentangling the revised performance structure from the rewritten text; but in most cases the divisions have simply been inserted in the prompt-book, without any other attempt to reshape the play. Shakespeare himself may have determined the placing of some of these divisions, just as he may in some cases (particularly *2 Henry IV* and *Othello*) have determined which exclamations or interjections should be substituted for the profanities made illegal by the 1606 legislation. But the need for any change at all came from outside the play; it did not arise as part of an effort by the author, or his theatrical colleagues, to realize the original artistic intention as fully and powerfully as possible. Such variants do not properly belong to the play's transition from a private to a socialized script; they belong instead to the afterlife of a text, to the history of its modification by subsequent interpreters under the pressure of subsequent conditions.

But although a text printed seven years after the author's death from a manuscript influenced by theatrical practice may, in the foregoing respects, contain accretions or transformations which misrepresent the author's own intentions, such interference can affect only certain texts, in certain particular, recognized ways. By contrast, the author's own contribution to the socializing of his play can affect any part of any text in any way. An essential difference between foul papers and fair copies is that the latter may contain further authorial revisions. Like other writers, playwrights habitually change their minds during the long process of composition. Modern editors have generally accepted that, even within the foul papers, Shakespeare sometimes had second thoughts: major examples of such revision can be seen in the Additional Passages for *Titus Andronicus*, *Love's Labour's Lost*, and *A Midsummer Night's Dream*; briefer instances will be found among the textual notes for *Romeo and Juliet* (1.4.56-92/514-50, 2.1.232/963, 3.2.76/1658, 3.3.40-3/1765-8, and 5.3.108/2798), *Hamlet* (3.3.374-6/2102-4), and *Timon* (5.4.2/2213). Such revisions will only survive into a printed text if the compositor fails to perceive that one reading is meant to replace another, and we can be sure that Shakespeare's foul papers contained many more examples successfully suppressed by the printer (as the author would have wished them to be). Hand D's contribution to *Sir Thomas More* contains verbal substitutions, additions of words and phrases and speeches, deletions of words, and a change of speech-prefix. Very few, if any, of these changes would be apparent if we possessed only an early edition printed from the British Library manuscript.

Though willing enough to accept that Shakespeare changed his mind from one moment to the next within the same manuscript, editors have been much more reluctant to concede that Shakespeare could have changed his mind between one manuscript and the next. The distinction between these two kinds of revision (intra-text and inter-text) is of cardinal importance for an editor, but of venial moment to an author. Revision between manuscripts occurs as often among poets and playwrights as revision within manuscripts. Despite the paucity of material literary evidence which survives from the classical period, we know that both Aristophanes and Euripides each, on one occasion at least, reworked a play even after it had been performed;[41] such reshaping also occurred among the Roman comic dramatists.[42] Calderón, Lope de Vega, Corneille, Racine, and Molière all revised;[43] so did Strindberg, Ibsen, and Chekhov.[44] Authorial revision is thus a constant feature of the work of the great dramatists of the European tradition; in general, the more evidence we possess of an author's processes of composition, the more authorial variation we see.

Shakespeare's artistic peers in other countries revised; Shakespeare's countrymen did so too. Even if we ignore anxiously meticulous poets like Tennyson, Yeats, Housman, and Eliot, we discover the same phenomena in writers whose profiles better match Shakespeare's own: middle-class poets, like Keats and Burns, who never went to university, who spelled and punctuated erratically, who possessed great verbal facility and imaginative sympathy.[45] And we find the same variation in the work of the English playwrights of Shakespeare's lifetime: in self-conscious poets like Ben Jonson, George Chapman, Francis Beaumont, and John Fletcher (glancing over their shoulders, anxious to ensure that and what posterity would think of them), but also in unpretentious journeymen professionals like Thomas Dekker, Thomas Heywood, and that 'base fellow' Thomas Middleton (glancing over their shoulders too, anxiously anticipating the debt-collector).[46] The roll-call of Shakespeare's revising contemporaries would no doubt be larger if more evidence had survived.

In these writers and others, from Euripides to Stoppard,[47] authorial revision takes every form available to authorial composition: substitutions, additions, deletions, transpositions, inventive restructuring, inconsequential fiddling. Nothing is sacred. Revisions sometimes improve, sometimes debase, and sometimes make no discernible difference whatever. Nothing is predictable, beyond the mere fact of unpredictable variation. The only constant is authorial inconstancy.

For much of Shakespeare's canon, the possibility of authorial revision is only a ghost which haunts the extant text; for twenty-one of his major works, we possess only a single substantive printed edition. But for three plays—*2 Henry IV*, *Hamlet*, and *Othello*—we are blessed with two substantive editions, each set from a different manuscript; for each play, the two texts differ in hundreds of readings, including the presence or absence of extended passages. For another three plays—*Richard II*, *Troilus*, and *King Lear*—the Folio edition was apparently prepared by marking up the first edition with readings taken from an independent manuscript; all three reveal a similar pattern of textual instability, including the presence or absence of extended passages. In addition, four short poems survive both in the 1609 edition of *Shakespeare's Sonnets* and in another, independent text; all four alternative texts contain sensible verbal variants. Thus, the Shakespeare canon includes six major and four minor works which survive in two independent substantive sources, both apparently authoritative; all ten manifest the same multiplicity of variation. Such variation cannot be convincingly attributed to error or sophistication introduced by agents of transmission, because these ten works were transmitted over a period of a quarter of a century by different compositors and different scribes, who were elsewhere guilty of relatively little interference. The only agent of transmission common to all ten texts is Shakespeare himself.[48]

Editors and critics have nevertheless long resisted the obvious conclusion, that Shakespeare occasionally—perhaps, if we could only see it, habitually—revised his work. The reasons for this reluctance are many and complex. The Folio preface claims that Shakespeare's 'mind and hand went together: And what he thought, he vttered with that easinesse, that wee haue scarse receiued from him a blot in his papers'. This encomium has often been cited as evidence that Shakespeare never revised. But scholars do not normally pay such reverence to a commendatory blurb written about a dead friend.[49] Even the blurb has the honesty to qualify its praise: as Touchstone might say, 'much virtue in *scarse*'. Nor need a scarcity of blotting signal a paucity of revision. If an author copies his work, he may change his mind as he copies, without blotting at all; indeed, the embargo on blotting has more relevance to revision within a single manuscript (which editors already concede) than to revision between manuscripts (which editors have resisted). Finally, the testimony of the Folio preface is directly contradicted by the most impressive testimonial in the Folio preliminaries, Ben Jonson's panegyric, which affirms that Shakespeare *did* 'strike the second heat | Vpon the *Muses* anuile' (ll. 60-1).

Editorial resistance to the evidence that Shakespeare revised his work cannot be founded upon the ambiguous oracles of the First Folio, nor upon historical norms, nor upon literary parallels; the motives for that resistance are not logical, but ideological and sociological, rooted in convictions about the nature of art and in the working practices of the editorial profession. Editors are aware—and should be aware—of the propensity of copyists occasionally to misinterpret, alter, transpose, omit, or interpolate words; any single example of variation between two texts often can be plausibly explained as an example of such error. Unfortunately for an editor, many of the changes revising authors make cannot, in isolation, be distinguished from those which corrupting copyists make, and the nature of a textual apparatus encourages editors to examine variants one by one, in isolation.[50] The nature of their work, and the format in which that work is recorded, thus tend to discourage editors from seeing the two characteristics which distinguish authorial variants from transmissional errors: the very (objective) bulk of variation, and the (subjectively perceptible) thematic or dramatic or structural relationship between separated variants. Moreover, much of an editor's work is necessarily adversarial. When confronted—as so often in Shakespeare—with only one substantive text, an editor must judge over and over again whether a specific word is corrupt, and if so which of several available conjectures most probably restores the intended word. This judgemental mode of thought, this lifetime of weeding goats from sheep, is not easily abandoned when the editor moves into the unfamiliar and uncertain terrain of a work which survives in two texts: faced with two sheep, it is all too easy to insist that one *must* be a goat.

When authors write two versions of a line or speech or sentence, the variations they create only permit two interpretations: either one reading is superior to its alternative, or both readings are equal. If one reading is perceived as inferior, it immediately qualifies itself as a candidate for excommunication from the authentic canon, on the grounds that, being inferior, it must result from deterioration in transmission (whichever the text in which it occurs). On the other hand, if the variants are indifferent, it can be claimed, with equal plausibility, that the functionaries of transmission often introduce such immaterial alternatives, and that the author can have had no discernible motive for making such functionless changes. Thus, however an author alters a text, revision can look like error, in one text or the other.

Editors—like other critics and readers—wish to find in literary texts both permanence and perfection. But the perfection of permanence is unattainable if the text itself was never fixed, if the author has left us only 'bifold authority', if we can only experience what 'is and is not Cressid' (or is and is not *Troilus and Cressida*). Likewise, the permanence of perfection, of a transcendental ideal, of the one true text, is denied us when we discover that even the author regarded so many of the components of the artefact as disposable or interchangeable, when we see for ourselves that the same thing can be said in so many different ways, none beyond praise or reproach. The dilemmas created by the instability of texts touch the central beliefs of our culture about the nature of language and of the world:

> and my Soule akes
> To know, when two Authorities are vp,
> Neither Supreame; How soone Confusion

>   May enter 'twixt the gap of Both, and take
>   The one by th'other.
>   (*Coriolanus* 3.1.111-15/1556-60)

In literature as in politics, the counter-claims of competing authorities can affectively and effectively undermine the legitimacy of both. Political pluralism and textual polytheism both require a tolerance of opposed possibilities.

Such editorial and critical distortions of perspective have affected the text of Shakespeare more than that of any other author. The absence of authorial manuscripts, or even of publications overseen by the author personally, has permitted the hypothesis of massive corruption in transmission to flourish. The gradual elevation of Shakespeare within the hierarchy of English and then of world literature has transformed him into the central exemplar of literary permanence and perfection, an artist somehow apart from all others, who demonstrates the pure potentiality of language. The use of Shakespeare in education throughout the English-speaking world has demanded a fixed and stable artefact of study and instruction. Finally, Shakespeare's own bifold nature, as poet and dramatist, has permitted an editorial bifurcation of the textual evidence: one set of readings represents the author's own intentions, preserved in the privacy of his foul papers, while the alternative set represents what happened to this innocent text after it left his protection to be violated and debased in the theatre.

A prejudice against the theatre is not confined to editors; it has infected European culture throughout the Christian era (always visible, sometimes virulent).[51] But anyone who shares this prejudice would be best advised not to bother with Shakespeare at all. The acknowledged genius of his work resides in its marriage of verbal and theatrical talents; if both powers operated in the initial phases of composition, both should also have operated in subsequent phases, and in practice multiple verbal and 'literary' variants always coexist with 'theatrical' variants affecting staging, pace, the shape of a scene, the character of an entrance or exit. One would hardly suppose that Shakespeare devoted less mental energy to theatrical problems the closer a play got to its first performance; if anything, he might have become more concerned with that aspect of his craft as the realities of enactment drew nearer.

Playwrights do, to varying degrees, lose control of their scripts once a play is handed over or sold to a theatre. But Shakespeare was the most successful playwright of his era, and the only playwright of that era who was also an actor and shareholder in the company which performed his plays—the most stable, long-lived, and prosperous company in the pre-Restoration English theatre. One would not expect the views of such a person, such a valuable commercial property, to be lightly or consistently overruled by his colleagues and friends. The three leaders of the company—Richard Burbage, John Heminges, and Henry Condell—were the only London acquaintances singled out for mention in Shakespeare's will; Burbage died in 1619, but the other two were responsible for the collected edition of Shakespeare's plays published in 1623, without which our knowledge of his work would be disastrously foreshortened. No other playwright was paid the compliment of having his work posthumously collected by his fellow actors. In the circumstances it seems reasonable to suppose that Shakespeare personally suggested many or most of the alterations made in rehearsal, and that he acquiesced in others. Most writers show their work to a few friends or colleagues before it faces a larger public; they gratefully accept or develop some suggestions, and simply ignore others. For instance, Racine added a scene in one play and deleted a scene in another, both on the basis of his friend Boileau's criticism; Humphrey Moseley tells us that when Beaumont and Fletcher's '*Comedies* and *Tragedies* were presented on the Stage, the *Actours* omitted some *Scenes* and Passages (with the *Authour's* consent) as occasion led them; and when private friends desir'd a Copy, then they (and justly too) transcribed what they *Acted*'.[52] In preparing the Oxford edition we have assumed that Shakespeare behaved, in this as in other respects, like other writers, and that in accepting the suggestions of other people he assumed responsibility for them. If, in the judgement of some readers, he was occasionally weak or foolish in doing so, then an editor cannot save him from his weakness or his folly.[53]

Beyond the Prompt-book

All Shakespeare's acted plays must once have existed in both a foul paper and a prompt-book incarnation (even if the two phases occurred at different times in the life of a single manuscript). These two categories of manuscript are essential; others are accidental, and may or may not have arisen in particular instances. As Moseley tells us, an unpublished play might be transcribed in order to provide a copy for an individual reader or 'private friend'; since such transcripts were expensive, such readers must either have been able to pay for such a copy themselves (and hence wealthy) or important enough for the company to wish to court their favour (and hence wealthy). Humphrey Moseley's preface to the Beaumont and Fletcher Folio of 1647 excused the 'Chargeablenesse' of the printed book by comparing its price with that of private transcripts:[54]

Heretofore when Gentlemen desired but a copy of any of these *Playes*, the meanest piece here (if any may be called Meane where every one is Best) cost them more then foure times the price you pay for the whole *Volume*.

The number of such private copies must have been small. Plays could be enjoyed in the theatre; once a play had been published it could be bought cheaply in printed form. The only play which we know was transcribed more than once is Thomas Middleton's phenomenally popular and topical *A Game at Chess* (1624), the stage production of which was closed down by the political authorities after nine performances—creating a situation in which exceptional demand could only be met, at first, by the circulation of private transcripts. Anyone who wanted such a manuscript, moreover, would probably approach the playwright or the theatre directly; most extant transcripts were made by the author himself, or by a scribe connected with the relevant theatrical company, and seem to have been copied directly from the foul papers or the prompt-book.

Although the Shakespeare canon affords no extant example of such manuscripts, the work of other playwrights supplies several. The most interesting of these were prepared by Ralph Crane. Crane, a professional scrivener, worked mostly for the legal fraternity, but eight manuscripts of dramatic works that he prepared between 1618 and 1625 survive.[55] He is also thought to have supplied the printer's copy for John Webster's *Duchess of Malfi* (1623) and the third edition of Middleton's *A Game at Chess* (1625). But his interest to editors of Shakespeare arises from the fact that he apparently prepared the manuscripts from which were printed the Folio texts of *The Tempest*, *Two Gentlemen*, *Merry Wives*, *Measure*, *Winter's Tale*, and (probably) *Cymbeline*.[56]

All of the plays which Crane transcribed were performed by the King's Men—an association with Shakespeare's company he confirmed in the preface to his one published work:[57]

> *And some imployment hath my vsefull* Pen
> *Had 'mongst those ciuill, well-deseruing* men,
> *That grace the* Stage *with* honour *and* delight,
> *Of whose true honesties I much could write,*
> *But will comprise't (as in a Caske of Gold)*
> *Vnder the* Kingly Seruice *they doe hold.*

Crane does not seem to have been employed as the company book-keeper, though his transcript of *Barnavelt* was annotated, by another hand, to serve as prompt-book. His other transcripts were explicitly or inferentially prepared for a patron's private reading.

Crane's transcripts visually resemble a contemporary printed play more than a theatrical manuscript. (See Illustration 6.) The first page of *The Witch*, for instance, announces the play's genre, title, company, and author; then, under a rule, Crane writes 'The Sceane Rauenna', over a double-columned list of 'The Persons'. Most of the characters are given pocket labels: '*Contracted to Isabella*', '*a fantasticall Gentleman*'. In the text itself, Crane abandons the defined columns of a theatrical manuscript. Speech-prefixes, regularly italicized, protrude only slightly to the left of the text; consequently the first line of a speech is

6. Thomas Middleton, 'The Witch' (Bodleian Library, MS Malone 12), p. 88; transcribed by Ralph Crane between 1619 and 1627. The top of the page includes the ending of the song 'Black Spiritts, and white', also used in *Macbeth* 4.1.

indented right. Prose does not extend markedly farther into the right margin than does verse; when combined with Crane's habit of not capitalizing the initial word of verse lines, this practice can make verse visually indistinguishable from prose.

Three of the Folio texts apparently set from Crane transcripts—*Two Gentlemen*, *Merry Wives*, and *Winter's Tale*—mass the directions for entrances, listing all the characters who appear in a scene in a single initial direction, without any indication of exactly when during the course of the scene they should enter. Such an arrangement, though as inconvenient for readers as actors, would probably have been regarded as neo-classical, garnishing the dramatic text with the literary authority of antiquity. The same procedure prevails in the Bodleian manuscript of *A Game at Chess*, and in the first edition of *The Duchess of Malfi*. Elsewhere Crane provided normal mid-scene entrances, squeezing them (and other directions) into the right margin. Directions often had to be split into two or more lines; he usually tried to place such directions so that they ended at or just before the point where the action should occur.

As the massing of entrances demonstrates, Crane did not shy from interfering with stage directions. He habitually made minor changes of wording, and sometimes altered their substance. Such changes occasionally reduce the information content of a direction; more often, they increase it. Their motive seems to have been a solicitude for the reader, who is supplied with details based upon Crane's own knowledge of the play in performance. Consequently the stage directions of a Crane transcript leave few clues to the nature of the stage directions in the manuscript he was copying.

Crane also, as a rule, imposes his own spelling and punctuation on the text. His punctuation is particularly remarkable for its heavy use of parentheses, hyphens, and apostrophes. He hyphenates words idiosyncratically: 'hangs ore-me', 'barkes-out' (*Demetrius* 2909, 2934), 'come-vp to two-Cock-broth' (*Witch* 472). His apostrophes usually indicate elision, either substituting for the elided letters in the normal way (I'me, y'are) or coexisting with them (I'am, you'are). Sometimes an apostrophe draws attention to an ellipsis in colloquial speech: 'pray, at' back-dore, 'Morrow, with' (for 'with the'). At other times the positioning of apostrophes, or their very presence, defies logical explanation (do'st, Sha's, hee'rs, ha'st, not'within hearing, thinck yo^w'). This fussy but erratic marking of elisions obviously creates possibilities for confusion, particularly in verse. Crane may also have been responsible for some expurgation of profanity. But in other respects he was an accurate copyist. His elegant secretary hand, interspersed with modified and Italianate letters, was far more legible than Shakespeare's seems to have been.

Another scribe thought to have affected the transmission of at least one Shakespearian text is 'Mr. Knight', a book-keeper for the King's Men named in two memoranda of Sir Henry Herbert, Master of the Revels, on 12 October 1632 and 21 October 1633. On 27 December 1624 an exemption order signed by Herbert lists twenty-one attendants of the King's Men; an 'edward Knight' is listed first, an 'Anthony Knight' sixteenth. The book-keeper was probably 'edward'.[58] Knight's hand has been identified in three theatrical manuscripts belonging to the King's Men; he also prepared an undated private transcript of *Bonduca*. The 1634 Quarto of *Two Noble Kinsmen*, printed from a manuscript which apparently reflects a revival of 1625/6, contains stage directions probably penned by Knight.[59]

Whether Knight influenced any of the manuscripts used as copy for the First Folio has not been established. Although the first extant documentary link between Knight and the King's Men postdates publication of the Folio by thirteen months, his handwriting shows up in documents of March 1615/16 and May 1623 which make it clear that his connection with the theatre began much earlier.[60] Knight sophisticated the presentation and incidentals of manuscripts less visibly than Crane, and his presence would be correspondingly difficult to detect behind a printed text. Equally difficult to identify through the veil of print would be the one scribe that we know worked for Shakespeare's company in Shakespeare's lifetime: the anonymous scribe who prepared the manuscript of *The Second Maiden's Tragedy* (1611)—or, for that matter, the anonymous book-keepers who annotated in the theatre that transcript and Crane's of *Barnavelt*. Nevertheless, it would be useful to know more about both Knight and the unnamed *Second Maiden's* scribe, so that the possibility of their influence upon the Folio could be systematically investigated. One would also like to know more about 'one *Thomas Vincent* that was a Book-keeper or prompter at the Globe play-house nere the Banck-end in Maid-lane'.[61]

Private transcripts of poems are, in the literature of Elizabethan and Jacobean England, far more common than presentation copies of whole plays. Much of the poetry of the period circulated in manuscript long before it reached print.[62] Francis Meres testified in 1598 that Shakespeare's 'sugred Sonnets' were passed 'among his priuate friends' over a decade before the entire sequence of *Shakespeare's Sonnets* was published in 1609.[63] Although none of these early manuscripts is known to survive, we do possess later copies of several sonnets, and some of these appear to derive from earlier manuscripts, independently of the printed tradition (see Illustration 7). Shakespeare's miscellaneous and occasional poems would also probably have been written for private circulation rather than publication, and private transcripts survive of several such poems attributed to Shakespeare. Likewise, songs from a dramatic text might be excerpted and circulated separately as short lyrics. Several of Shakespeare's songs made their way into seventeenth-century manuscripts. In other cases Shakespeare's poetry achieved the textual fixity which critics so desire: he apparently wrote several epitaphs which were carved in stone upon a tomb. As Shakespeare knew, not marble nor the gilded monuments of princes will outlive a pow'rfull rhyme, and his epitaphs have sometimes outlasted the tombs for which they were composed, but in two cases—his own epitaph, and the verses on the Stanley tomb at Tong (Illustration 8)—the original stone survives.

Private transcripts may heavily sophisticate the texture of a work, but they leave its text basically intact. Memorial reconstructions, by contrast, fundamentally mis-transmit the text. Prompt-books and other transcripts were made by taking an existing text and copying it, word by word, line by line; as the copyist moved his eye back and forth between the two pieces of paper, he had to carry in his head the words to be copied, but only a few words at a time were held in this mental suspension. The limitations and deficiencies of the human memory wreak their usual havoc, even in these circumstances, but such a process of textual reproduction effectively minimizes the damage, by limiting the load which the memory must carry and the distance it must traverse. But by contrast with this normal mode of textual transmission, a memorial reconstruction results from the attempt to remember and write down an entire play, without any access at all to a written copy.

It may seem surprising that anyone ever attempted so impossible a task, but mere impossibility has seldom deterred human need, greed, and ingenuity. Richard Sheridan's *The School for Scandal* was illegitimately reconstructed by such means in 1777; John Bernard, who compiled the reconstruction, has left an account of how he did it. Sheridan's *The Duenna* also appeared in a pirated text, as did Macklin's *Love à-la-Mode*; and a pirated reconstruction of *Le Mariage de Figaro* formed the basis of the first English adaptation.[64] In Spain, Lope de Vega complained about the pirating of his plays as early as 1603, in the Prologue to *El Peregrino en su Patria*, and often thereafter.[65] In another Prologue, in 1620, he criticized

> the stealing of comedias by those whom the vulgar call, the one *Memorilla*, and the other *Gran Memoria*, who, with the few verses which they learn, mingle an infinity of their own barbarous lines, whereby they earn a living, selling them to the villages and to distant theatrical managers; base people these, without a calling, and many of whom have been jail-birds. I should like to rid myself of the care of publishing these plays, but I cannot, for they print them with my name while they are the work of the pseudo-poets of whom I have spoken. Receive then, Reader, this Part, corrected as well as it was possible to do it, and with my good will, for the only interest it has is that you may read these comedias with less errors, and that you may not believe that there is anyone in the world who can note down a comedia from memory, on seeing it represented.

In 1630 an eyewitness (Suarez de Figueroa) described the practice of one of these play-pirates, who 'takes from memory an entire comedia on hearing it three times, without the slightest variation either in plot or verses. The first day he devotes to the general disposition of the plot, the second to the variety of the composition, and the third to the exactness of the verses'. Memorial transmission of this kind, however peculiar or deplorable it may seem to the age of the photocopier, is familiar enough to historians. For instance, in 1601 Londoners could buy a pamphlet containing 'A Declaration of the Practises &

Death & this man were long at Stand
Bycause hee was still in the mendinq hand
At length comes death in very fowle weather
And ripps of his soule from the vpper leather./

An Epitaph on Mr Hen: Boling

If gentlenesse could tame the fates, or witt
Delude them, Bolinge had not perisht itt
But hee that condemns death in iudgment giue
And sayes our sinns are stronger then o^r witts.

On an old woeman

Sibla is toothlesse, yet when shee was young
Shee had both teeth enough & too much tongue:
what shall I now of toothlesse Sibla say?
But that her tongue hath worne her teeth away.

To one y^t would dye a Mayd.

When forty winters shall besiege thy [brow]
And trench deepe furrowes in y^t lovely feild
Thy youths faire liuery so accounted now
Shall bee like rotten weeds of no worth held
Then being askt where all thy bewty lyes
Where all ye lustre of thy youthfull dayes
To say within those hollow sunckden eyes
Were an all-eaten truth & worthlesse prayse
O how much better were thy bewtyes use
If thou couldst say this pretty child of mine
Saues my account & makes my old excuse
Making his bewty by succession thine
This were to bee new borne when thou art old
And see thy bloud warme when thou feelst it cold.

7. Westminster Abbey, MS 41, fol. 49. The manuscript is a poetical miscellany owned by George Morley, and compiled in the 1620s and 1630s. This page contains the most reliable of eleven manuscripts of an alternative version of Sonnet 2.

GENERAL INTRODUCTION

8. Verses attributed to Shakespeare, from the Stanley tomb in the Collegiate Church of Saint Bartholomew, Tong, Shifnal, Shropshire. The upper photograph shows a detail from the east end of the tomb, where the verses appear between the heads of the reclining effigies (above and below); the lower, the corresponding detail from the west end of the tomb, at the feet of the effigies.

Treasons attempted and committed by *Robert* late Earle of *Essex*' which included 'The speaches of Sir *Chr. Blunt*, at the time of his death, as neere as they could be remembred'.[66] The proceedings of Parliament were similarly reported, surreptitiously, until late in the eighteenth century.

Such techniques undoubtedly have a bearing on the publication of some play texts from Shakespeare's period. Thomas Heywood, in a prologue first published in 1637 but probably written *c.*1626, alleged that one of his plays had been published in a pirated text.[67] The play was being revived, but on the occasion of its first performances, in 1605, spectators

> Did throng the Seats, the Boxes, and the Stage
> So much; that some by Stenography drew
> The plot: put it in print: (scarce one word trew:)

In 1608, in an address 'To the Reader', Heywood complained[68]

> some of my plaies haue (vnknowne to me, and without any of my direction) accidentally come into the Printers handes, and therfore so corrupt and mangled, (coppied onely by the eare) that I haue bene as vnable to know them, as ashamde to chalenge them. This therefore I was the willinger to furnish out in his natiue habit: first beeing by consent, next because the rest haue beene so wronged in beeing publisht in such sauage and ragged ornaments.

In 1612 George Buc, the Master of the Revels, wrote of one shorthand system 'by the meanes and helpe therof (they which know it) can readily take a Sermon, Oration, Play, or any long speech, as they are spokĕ, acted, & vttered in the instant'.[69] Buc's description seriously exaggerates the capacities of the available shorthand systems, but it does link such surreptitious means of copying to plays which are 'acted'—a subject with which Buc was uniquely familiar. And sermons were indeed published actually advertising that they had been printed from manuscripts composed by such methods.[70]

All these allusions establish that in Shakespeare's lifetime a method or methods existed by which plays—like sermons, scaffold speeches, and Parliamentary debates—could be illegitimately transmitted by someone who had heard them performed one or more times. This context provides an obvious explanation for the claim, in the preface to the Folio, that

> (before) you were abus'd with diuerse stolne, and surreptitious copies, maimed, and deformed by the frauds and stealthes of iniurious impostors, that expos'd them: euen those, are now offer'd to your view cur'd, and perfect of their limbes; and all the rest, absolute in their numbers, as he conceiued thĕ.

Heminges and Condell cannot be referring to all of the earlier quarto editions of Shakespeare's plays, for they recognized the authority of some of those texts by reprinting them almost verbatim in their own collection; moreover, they explicitly distinguish 'euen those' from 'all the rest'. But they do claim that some of Shakespeare's plays, like some of Heywood's, were published in texts which were disastrously corrupt. Most modern editors agree that the texts to which Heminges and Condell refer were the first editions of *The First Part of the Contention* (1594), *Richard Duke of York* (1595), *Romeo and Juliet* (1597), *Richard III* (1597), *Henry V* (1600), *Merry Wives* (1602), and *Hamlet* (1603). *Pericles* is another example, though in its case no authoritative and reliable text was ever published. To this list some scholars would add *The Troublesome Reign of King John* (1591) and *The Taming of a Shrew* (1594), but these examples are altogether more problematic. Critics have also conjecturally identified such corrupt texts in the canons of other dramatists.[71] Such texts inexplicably stop being published after 1609. Their disappearance may be related to the fact that in 1606 the Master of the Revels, long responsible for licensing plays for performance, also took responsibility for approving their publication; in 1610 Sir Edmund Tilney was officially suceeded by Sir George Buc, who had acted as his deputy since at least 1606.

The corrupt texts of the Shakespeare canon were probably not taken down by shorthand, or by spectators with exceptionally capacious memories.[72] None of the few complaints about the practice actually names the culprits—either because the 'impostors' were unknown, or because members of the theatrical profession did not wish to foul their own nest by accusing other members of the theatrical profession. For the agents of transmission seem to have been actors—actors who, like Bottom, attempted to play the parts of all the characters. Some recognition of the part unscrupulous actors might play in the surreptitious transmission of texts is suggested by a passage in Robert Tailor's *The Hog Hath Lost His Pearl* (1614: BEPD 321), in which a playwright shows a player—called 'M. Change-coate'—a text of his new jig, and then, afraid that he is going to be cheated of his just reward, says 'I feare you haue learned it by heart, if you haue powdred vp my plot in your sconce, you may home sir and instruct your Poet ouer a pot of ale, the whole methode on't' (sig. B3). Actors, of course, make a living from their capacity to remember parts of plays, and in the Jacobethan repertory system they were expected to learn new parts rapidly and to revive old parts at even shorter notice. An actor's memory of his own speeches, and their cues, might therefore be exceptionally accurate. His memory of the rest of the play would be erratic. The character and quality of a memorially reconstructed text therefore depend upon (*a*) the number of actors engaged in the reconstruction, and (*b*) the parts they played.[73] The actors with the greatest motive for preparing such a text would be those with no economic or personal loyalty to the company which owned and performed the play: either major actors who had moved to another company, or 'hired men' who worked for companies on a freelance basis, and who usually played several small parts.[74]

The texts which seem to us to have been created by memorial reconstruction have, since 1725, sometimes been explained by an alternative hypothesis: that they represent earlier versions of the plays, which Shakespeare later 'extreamly improved' or 'entirely new writ'. This hypothesis has recently been restated by several scholars and, given our own views about authorial revision, we have examined it with some sympathy.[75] Nevertheless, like other modern editors we have, in the end, found it fundamentally untenable. It ignores the substantial early historical evidence, from this period and others, of such aural and memorial methods of transmission; generally, it isolates for discussion individual passages in individual texts, rather than surveying each text or the whole group of texts in their entirety.[76] The 'early versions' in question differ drastically from the genuine cases of authorial revision elsewhere in the canon, where both texts exist in reliable editions. The quality of the memorial reconstruction soars and plummets, so that the resulting verbal texture cannot be convincingly assigned to any one period of Shakespeare's career. All these texts, if authorial, have to be relegated to an earlier period than any of the extant authoritative texts, even though some of the plays—like *Merry Wives*, *Henry V*, and *Hamlet*—are either not mentioned at all or not attributed to Shakespeare until much later. The fluctuations in style and verbal confidence coincide, not with any discernible artistic motive, but with the presence or absence of certain characters played by certain actors. Finally, for *Contention*, *Duke of York*, *Richard III*, and *Henry V*, the later authoritative text draws closely upon known historical sources; the earlier suspect text in each case regularly and demonstrably confuses and misinterprets this historical material. All these anomalies can be explained by the single, simple hypothesis that such texts derive from a process of aural transmission similar to that alluded to and documented in this and other periods.

Such texts will be of limited use to an editor. What aural and memorial transmission do to a text can be seen from the transcript of the United States Senate 'Watergate' hearings of 4 October 1973. Videotape preserves Senator Sam Ervin's accurate rendering of the following lines:

> Good name in man and woman, dear my lord,
> Is the immediate jewel of their souls.
> Who steals my purse steals trash: 'tis something, nothing;
> 'Twas mine, 'tis his, and has been slave to thousands:
> But he that filches from me my good name
> Robs me of that which not enriches him,
> And makes me poor indeed.

The official stenographic report—compiled in much more favourable circumstances than an Elizabethan memorial reconstruction—transforms this into

> Good name in man and woman, dear lord, is the immediate juror of their souls;
> Who steals my purse steals trash;
> Tis something, nothing.
> Twas mine,
> Tis his, and has been a slave to thousands.
> But he that filches from me my good name,
> Robs me of that which not enriches him and makes poor indeed.

Nor can such errors be attributed to the modern stenographer's unfamiliarity with Jacobean English. Comparable omissions, interpolations, and substitutions can be found in the manuscript commonplace book of Edward Pudsey (1573-1613), which quotes a number of passages from *Othello*. As the play was not printed until almost a decade after Pudsey's death, those quotations almost certainly record (imperfect) memories of the play in performance.[77]

Editors have been understandably reluctant to make much use of a text prepared by such means. Nevertheless, this commendable caution can easily lead to a dogmatic tendency to ignore the memorial reconstructions altogether. Sometimes a reliable text transmitted in the normal way differs from a suspect text memorially transmitted only in readings that could easily have been corrupted by a scribe or compositor: a variant which could be due to misreading, an omitted word, adjacent transposed words, an added article or preposition. In such cases the 'unreliable' text might preserve the authorial intention—especially if the line in question was spoken by an actor who helped to reconstruct the text.[78] Memorial texts printed before 1606 also sometimes preserve profanities excised from otherwise reliable texts printed later, or titles altered by the systematizing tendencies of the Folio editors. (Actors will seldom forget the title of the play they are performing.)

Equally important, memorial texts represent—however imperfectly—the performance script of a play. Often these scripts have been much abbreviated, always by the foreshortening and compression of memory, sometimes because they report an abridged text used or intended for use on provincial tours.[79] Their omissions, though of some interest, generally cannot be trusted by editors.[80] But in other respects a memorial reconstruction may represent a more finished, dramatic, socialized phase of the text than that preserved in an edition printed from Shakespeare's foul papers. Thus, the memorial text of *Richard III* contains an additional passage (4.1.101-19/2424-42) so good that all editors have incorporated it. Memorial reconstruction and authorial revision should not be regarded as incompatible alternatives, as proponents of either hypothesis have tended to assume. Textual critics ask, 'Did Shakespeare revise, or were some of his texts badly transmitted?' One might as well ask, 'Was Shakespeare irascible, or did he ever have toothache?' One condition does not guarantee immunity from the other. Each text, with different combinations of revision and/or reporting, creates different problems and opportunities. The Oxford edition takes memorial reconstructions much more seriously than its predecessors, recognizing the potential value of these texts in preserving corrections and revisions.

Memorial reconstructions attempt to report the entire text of the play as performed; other documents haphazardly report on particular details. Ben Jonson complains about a regrettable piece of writing in *Julius Caesar*; the line does not appear in the Folio text. Simon Forman records, in a private notebook, his visit to an early performance of *Cymbeline*; his brief account of the plot corresponds with the text as we know it, except in respect to the play's title and the heroine's name. For both details Forman appears to be right, and the Folio wrong. One of Shakespeare's last plays was being performed when the Globe theatre burned down; as a result an exceptional number of spectators recorded the event, and all agreed that the play being performed was *called* 'All Is True', and was *about* 'The Life of King Henry the Eight'. (See Illustrations 9-12.) The Folio, by contrast, transforms the play's subject matter into its title, bringing the text into conformity with its arrangement of plays dealing with recent English history. Editors of Shakespeare have in practice ignored these external witnesses, though similar 'indirect' testimony has been put to widespread use by the editors of classical and biblical texts.[81]

Shakespeare's editors have also in practice ignored the miscellaneous poems preserved in stone and manuscript, the manuscript evidence for the censorship of *1 Henry IV*, the manuscript versions of Shakespeare's sonnets, and almost the entirety of the text of the memorially reconstructed editions. This conspiracy of inattention and inaction testifies to the human desire for simplicity. Editors try whenever possible to reduce the multiplicity of competing voices to a single, clear, wholly reliable oracle of authenticity, whose utterances they need do no more than reverentially reproduce. When witnesses proliferate, editors must choose between them; choosing is difficult, because uncertain; uncertainty requires the exercise of personal judgement; personal judgement interposes the editor conspicuously between a dead author and living readers; conspicuous exposure makes editors uncomfortable. (We, too, dislike it.) Nor should such discomfort be regarded as wholly undesirable. Even W. W. Greg confessed

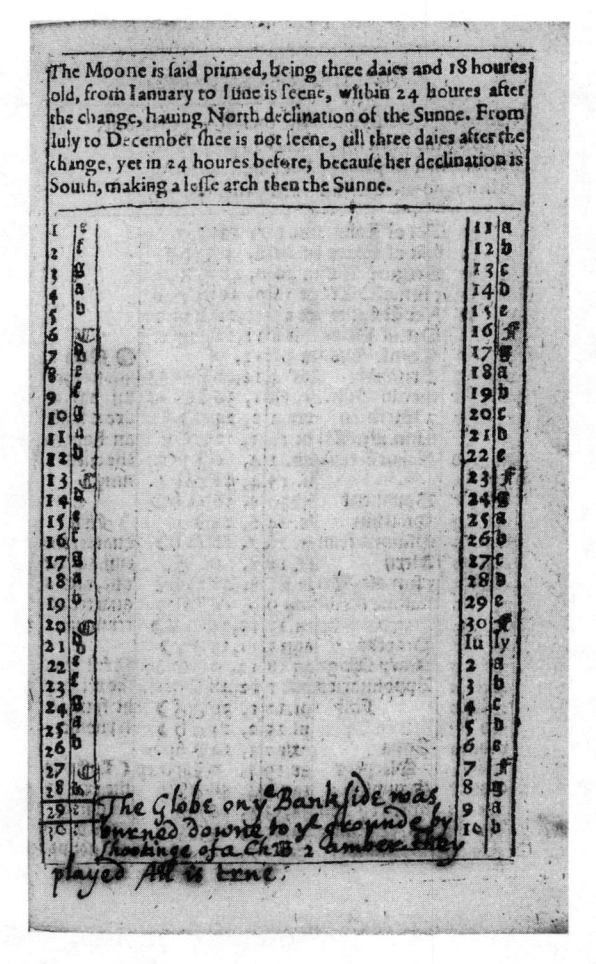

9. Part of a page from an almanac by Arthur Hopton (STC 461; in Bodleian Library, MS Ashmole 66), sig. B2. The manuscript entry for 29 June, written by Matthew Page, reads, 'The Globe on the Bank-side was burned downe to the grounde by shootinge of a Chamber. they played All is true.' (See H. R. Woudhuysen, *Notes and Queries*, 229 (1984), 217–18.)

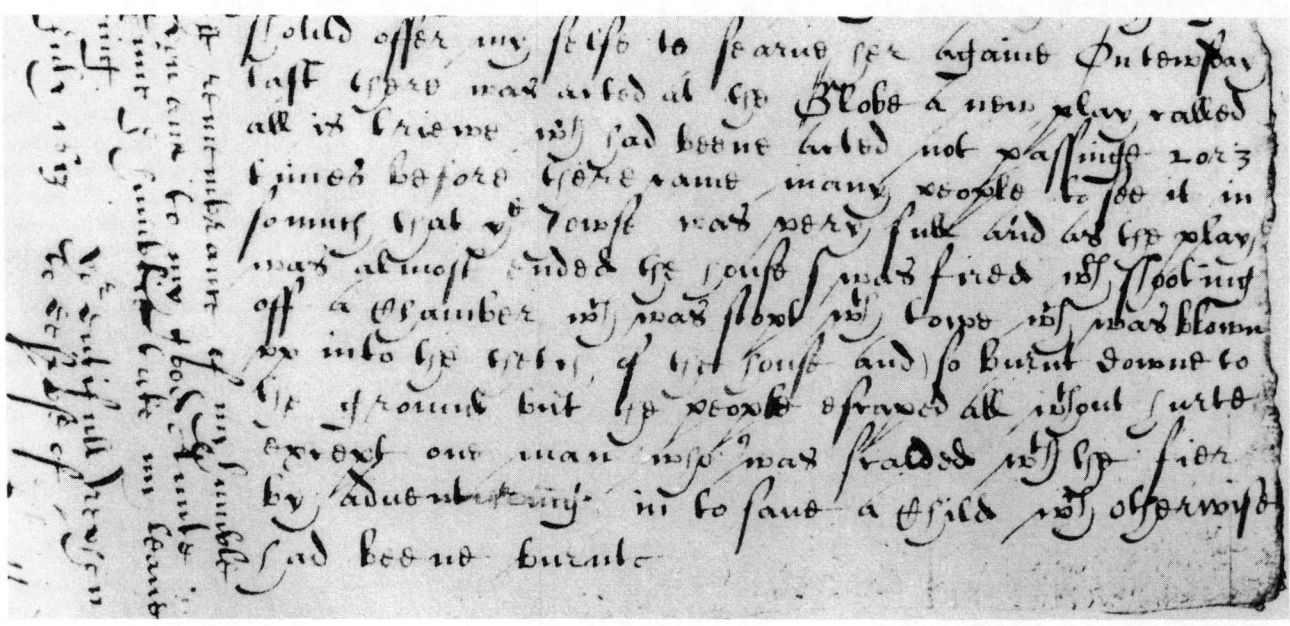

10. Extract from a letter from Henry Bluett to Richard Weeks, 4 July 1613 (formerly in the Somerset Record Office, Taunton). The relevant sentences read, 'On tewsday last there was acted at the Globe a new play called all is triewe wch had beene acted not passing 2 or 3 times before there came many people to see it in so much that ye howse was very full and as the play was almost ended the house was fired wth shooting off a Chamber wch was stopt wth towe wch was blown vp into the thetch of the house and so burnt downe to the ground'. The 'tewsday last' would have been 29 June. (See Maija Jansson Cole, *Shakespeare Quarterly*, 32 (1981), 352.)

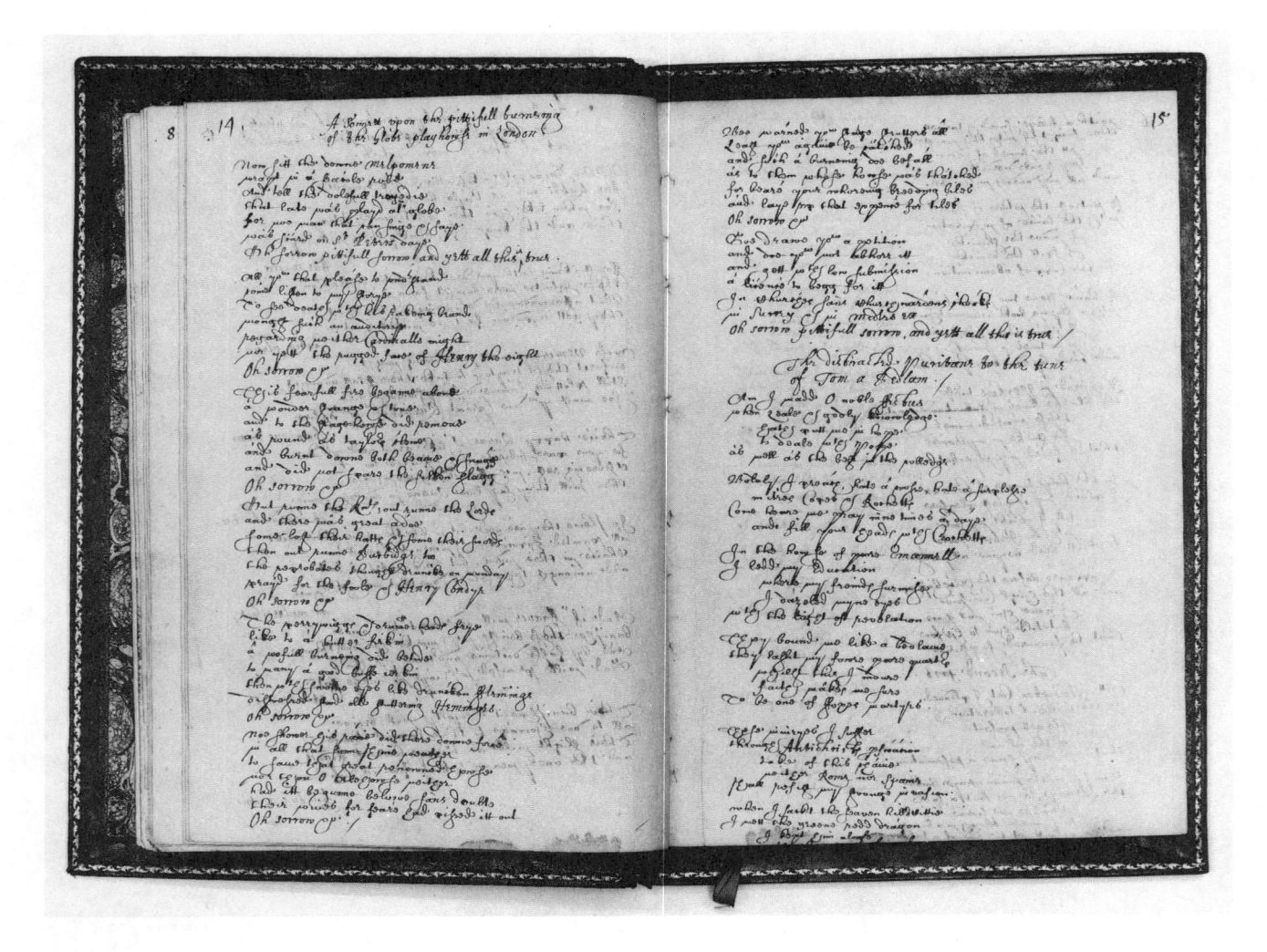

11. (*above*) A ballad (West Yorkshire Archives, Hopkinson MSS, Vol. 34, pp. 14-15). The ballad was first reprinted from this manuscript in *The Gentleman's Magazine*, 86 (February 1816), p. 114; the manuscript was presumed lost, and its authenticity questioned, until the rediscovery of the Hopkinson manuscripts by Peter Beal (*Notes and Queries*, 222 (1977), 543-4). Beal drew attention to the ballad itself in 1986. As he observes, the ballad was also noticed in the *Third Report of the Historical Manuscripts Commission* (1872), Appendix, p. 299.

12. Extract from a letter of 2 July 1613, as first printed in *Letters of Sir Henry Wotton to Sir Edmund Bacon* (1661), pp. 29 ff. Though the letter has been known to Shakespeare scholars since the eighteenth century, the 1661 printing seems not to have been transcribed until 1974.

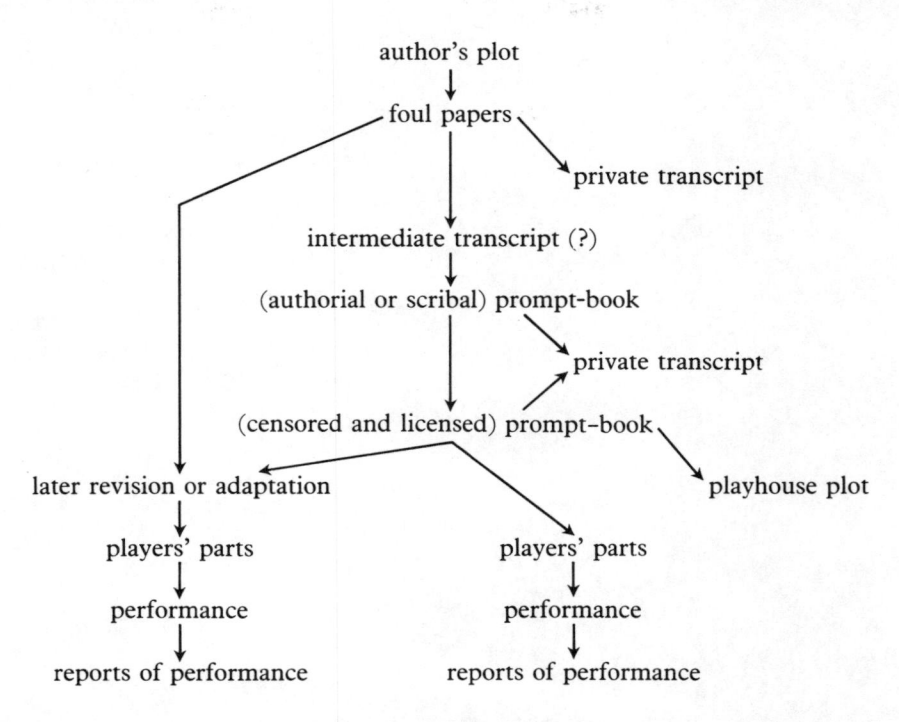

```
                        author's plot
                             ↓
                  ┌──── foul papers ────┐
                  │         ↓           ↓
                  │                  private transcript
                  │         ↓
                  │   intermediate transcript (?)
                  │         ↓
                  │   (authorial or scribal) prompt-book
                  │         ↓           ↘
                  │                      private transcript
                  │         ↓           ↗
                  │   (censored and licensed) prompt-book
                  │      ↙       ↘
                  ↓                          playhouse plot
        later revision or adaptation
                  ↓                    players' parts
            players' parts                   ↓
                  ↓                     performance
            performance                      ↓
                  ↓                  reports of performance
        reports of performance
```

13. The permutations of dramatic manuscripts.

that 'a mechanical rule that affords release from constant embarrassing judgements may appeal to the modesty of an able editor as well as to the laziness of an incompetent'.[82] These sentiments perhaps explain why Greg devoted his long, varied, and brilliant career to bibliography, meticulous transcription, photographic reproduction, and the formulation of rules of editorial practice: he never actually 'edited' a play, in the conventional sense of that multifarious verb. Nevertheless, as A. E. Housman—who did edit—recognized, 'the application of thought to textual criticism' is not only unavoidable but desirable.[83]

But the general absence of attention to the manuscript evidence must also be attributed, in part, to the tyranny of print: the fixity and security and authority of the printed word has suppressed the messiness of barely legible scraps of manuscript scattered here and there. And since most of Shakespeare's work survives only in books produced by Gutenberg's technology, anyone interested in Shakespeare's text must understand how the multiple incarnations of script (see Illustration 13) are transformed into print.

From Author to Compositor

In the mid fifteenth century Johann Gensfleisch zum Gutenberg developed, through a series of related technical innovations, a practicable process by which books could be 'printed and accomplished without the help of reed, stylus, or pen, but by the wondrous agreement, proportion, and harmony of punches and types'. The new technology became operational in the early 1450s, its most conspicuous early product being the 'Gutenberg Bible' (1455-6). William Caxton, diplomat and humanist, printed the first book in English in 1474, and the first in England in 1477. During the following century the twin trades of publishing and printing expanded prodigiously, in England as elsewhere, feeding themselves by feeding the public with books practical and polemical, secular and divine, trivial and eternal. The potentially subversive power of such a widespread dissemination of knowledge and opinion was not overlooked by the ecclesiastical and political authorities, and as printing expanded its freedom shrank, confined both by explicit legislation and by the self-regulation of an oligarchic trading guild, the Company of Stationers.

3° Noue[m]bris 1623 A° Jac: 21°   69

Roger Jackson. Entred for his Copie under the handes of mr Bill warden A booke called A Daylie exercise of Pietie divided into 4 partes, viz: Confession of Sinnes. Thankes giuinge prayers. Observation written in latine by John Gerard and translated into English prouided he bringe further authoritie before it be printed   } vjd

12° Feb. 1624   me mr Doll. Heathe hath assigned ouer his booke to mr Jackson

Mr Blounte
Isaak Jaggard.
Entred for their Copie under the handes of mr Doctor Worrall and mr Cole warden mr William Shakspeers Comedyes Histories & Tragedyes soe manie of the said Copies as are not formerly Entred to other men. vizt   } vij s

Comedyes.
  The Tempest
  The two gentlemen of Verona
  Measure for Measure
  The Comedy of Errors
  As you like it
  All's well that ends well
  Twelfe night
  The winters tale

Histories
  The thirde parte of Henry ye sixt
  Henry the eight

Tragedies.
  Coriolanus
  Timon of Athens
  Julius Cæsar
  Mackbeth
  Anthonie & Cleopatra
  Cymbeline

11° Nouembris

Nath: Newburie. Entred for his Copie under the handes of mr Doc. Heathe and mr Cole warden A booke called A sweet posie for gods saints to smell on conteyninge manie suettle and choise flowers.   } vjd

Nath: Butter. Entred for his Copie under the handes of mr Cottington and mr Cole warden A booke called The Wonderfull resignation of Mustapha and the advancem[en]t of Amurath a yonger brother of the latelie dispos[s]ed Osman   } vjd

14° Nouember

Mr Jackson. Entred for his Copie under the handes of mr Doc. Gorie and mr Islip warden A booke called An Exposition vpon the ten Comandem[en]ts by mr Peter Harket minister at Shor[e]ham in kent shire   } vjd

In the 1580s stationers responded to the growing popularity of the theatres by beginning to print plays; but publication of plays only became frequent c.1593-5, no doubt due to the severe disruption of London's theatrical companies caused by the plague of 1592-3. The publication of Shakespeare's poems (1593-4) and the first publication of any of his plays (1594) were both almost certainly a consequence of the plague. Plays never constituted a very significant part of the total book trade; though now among the most prized publications of the period, they seem to have been regarded by most printers as ephemera. In some sense the printers were right, for these early editions provided readers—who had no newspapers, magazines, radio, or television—with 'news' of an ephemeral event, the performance of a play in one of London's theatres. (For reasons of economics and government control, the professions of player and printer were concentrated in the capital.)[84]

The first edition of a work generally agreed to have been written by Shakespeare was published in 1593, and in the century that followed such editions multiplied. For editorial purposes these books can be intellectually divided into two categories: substantive editions (based upon access to a manuscript of some sort) and derivative editions (which simply reprint an existing printed text, with or without editorial corrections). Although for two centuries much editorial labour was expended on distinguishing these two categories, the distinctions are now in all but a few cases secure, and we will in this volume devote little attention to the derivative editions. The substantive editions can, in turn, be conveniently divided into two categories: quarto (a small cheap book, produced by folding each printed sheet of paper twice) and folio (a larger, more expensive book, produced by folding each printed sheet of paper once). In the Shakespeare canon there are many substantive quartos, all but one printed by 1622; there is only one substantive folio, the collected edition of Shakespeare's *Comedies, Histories, and Tragedies* published in 1623.

The beginning of a play's transmission into print is its acquisition by a publisher or printer. When a playwright sold a play to a company (for, usually, £5 to £8) he lost his rights in it, and in the normal course of events lost physical possession of at least one and perhaps all of his manuscripts of it.[85] A theatrical company preferred Londoners to pay their money for entry to the theatre rather than for purchase of a book; nor did it want other companies to acquire the text of a play (for which it had paid), and so become able to perform it in the provinces. Consequently, playwrights were theoretically unable, and companies theoretically unwilling, to sell play scripts to publishers. In such circumstances illicit methods of transmission flourish: a demand for the texts of plays was deliberately frustrated by 'the grand possessors' wills'. In other times and places, where authors rather than publishers enjoyed the legal protection of copyright (as in the nineteenth and twentieth centuries) or where plays were published soon after their first performances (as in the heyday of French classical drama), either the economic incentive or the legal opportunity for such piracy disappeared.

But although the theatrical companies of Shakespeare's time generally discouraged publication, authoritative texts of plays none the less made their way into print. Thomas Heywood in 1608, assuring us that 'It hath beene no custome in mee of all other men . . . to commit my plaies to the presse', nevertheless admitted that 'some haue vsed a double sale of ther labours, first to the Stage, and after to the presse' (*The Rape of Lucrece*, sig. A2). On other occasions the company itself may have wished to raise capital by selling plays: an exceptional number of texts owned by the Chamberlain's Men seem to have been sold around the time of their move into the Globe Theatre in 1599-1600.[86]

Since Shakespeare was both a playwright and a major shareholder in a theatrical company, we do not know whether he personally or the company collectively profited from the sale of his manuscripts, but only twelve of his plays appeared in authoritative quartos during his lifetime. One (*Titus Andronicus*) was written before the Chamberlain's Men came into being, and was owned by a succession of companies, so we can only guess who sold it to the publisher; another (*1 Henry IV*) may have been published under

14. (*facing*) The Stationers' Register entry for the Shakespeare First Folio: 8 November 1623, Register D, p. 69 (Stationers' Hall). The entry lists only those plays 'not formerly entred to other men'.

pressure from the political authorities; in another (*Troilus*) the preface alludes to 'the scape' which the play 'has made' in being published at all; four were probably sold to raise capital for the new Globe. Cumulatively, these circumstances suggest that Shakespeare normally took little interest in the dissemination of his plays on paper. This inference receives further support from the contrast between his two narrative poems (excellently printed, and supplied with authorial prefaces) and his plays (poorly printed, and devoid of authorial ornament).

Until 1709 copyright was held not by authors but by stationers, and a publisher's claim to a book was established by entering it (for a fee) in the Stationers' Register. Fortunately, this register survives. Some quarter to a third of all books published were apparently not entered. Accordingly not every Shakespeare edition appears in the register, but most do, beginning with *Venus and Adonis* on 18 April 1593.[87] These entries can be of considerable value in dating plays, and they are sometimes of interest in establishing the circumstances of publication. The relevant entries for individual plays are transcribed, and where necessary discussed, in our Introduction to each work; the entry of sixteen previously unprinted plays anticipating their publication in the 1623 Folio is reproduced as Illustration 14.

After a stationer had acquired a manuscript, but before it could be printed, it had to be licensed. In 1586 authority for licensing all books for publication was vested in the Archbishop of Canterbury and the Bishop of London, who in 1588 delegated the task to a panel of deputies. But these regulations were aimed at, and for a decade chiefly affected, only controversial political and religious tracts. In 1593 a Puritan polemicist complained that 'a good booke' was often delayed or rejected, while 'other bookes full of all filthines, scurrilitie, baudry, dissolutenes, cosonage, cony-catching, and the lyke . . . are eyther quickely licensed, or at least easily tollerate, without all denyall or contradiction whatsoeuer'.[88] In 1599, in part as a response to Nashe's scandalous lost play *The Isle of Dogs*, the Archbishop directed 'That noe playes be printed excepte they bee allowed by suche as haue aucthoritie'; thereafter, the entry of plays in the Stationers' Register became more cautious, publication sometimes being conditionally dependent upon 'better Aucthority'.[89] Such ecclesiastical censorship, or anticipation of it, seems to have affected the first editions of *Richard II* and *2 Henry IV*.

Sometimes the stationer who owned the copyright on a work printed it himself; sometimes he paid another stationer to manufacture the book. Printing shops in this period were small businesses, with only one or two hand-presses, employing a minimal number of press-men and compositors; the quantity of their output was limited, and its character often a reflection of the entrepreneur himself.[90] The amount and nature of the preparation which a manuscript received before typesetting began must have varied, but in all cases it may be divided into two processes. The manuscript might be copy-edited and it might be cast off.

For most quartos 'copy-editing' probably consisted of nothing more than preparing copy for the title-page. Title-pages needed to advertise the play and publisher, and in most cases their format and content owe more to the publisher than to the author. (The head title, on the first page of the text proper, probably comes closer to the author's intentions.) The publisher might also write a preface (*Othello*, 1622), or commission one (such as, perhaps, that to *Troilus*, 1609), or solicit and gather commendatory verses (*Shakespeare's Poems*, 1640). In other respects, derivative quartos might be copy-edited in order to make them look substantive. The 1628 quarto of *Othello* took readings from both the 1622 quarto and the 1623 Folio texts, thereby initiating the practice, since followed by many editors, of conflating two entirely separate versions of a work. *Shakespeare's Poems* (1640) brought together poems from various printed sources and rearranged them in order to pass itself off as a new and authoritative collection. The second edition of *Titus Andronicus* (1600) was copy-edited for similar reasons: the exemplar of the 1594 edition from which the printer worked was defective, and someone was therefore compelled to invent occasional words, phrases, and lines in order to fill the otherwise indecent lacunae.[91] Editing in such cases occurs only because of the absence of anything better. The most significant and confusing instance of such copy-editing involves a group of quartos printed in 1619 by William Jaggard for Thomas Pavier, apparently as part of an attempt to bring out a collection of Shakespeare's plays.[92]

> # M. William Shak-fpeare:
>
> ## HIS
> True Chronicle Hiftorie of the life and death of King LEAR and his three Daughters.
>
> *With the vnfortunate life of* Edgar, *fonne* and heire to the Earle of Glofter, and his fullen and affumed humor of TOM of Bedlam :
>
> *As it was played before the Kings Maieftie at Whitehall vpon* S. Stephans *night in Chriftmas Hollidayes.*
>
> By his Maiefties feruants playing vfually at the Gloabe on the Bancke-fide.
>
> LONDON,
> Printed for *Nathaniel Butter,* and are to be fold at his fhop in *Pauls* Church-yard at the figne of the Pide Bull neere S*t*. *Auftins* Gate. 1608.

15. The title-page of the first edition of *King Lear*. By contrast, the head title reads only 'M. William Shak-fpeare | *HIS* | Hiftorie, of King Lear.' The prominence given to Shakespeare's name in both places may reflect the bookseller's desire to distinguish this play from the anonymous *Chronicle History of King Leir* (1605: STC 15343). The reference to performance at court misleadingly suggests that it occurred during the Christmas holidays of 1607; in fact it took place in 1606, as the publisher knew. (See the Stationers' Register entry, transcribed in the Introduction to *The History of King Lear*.) On printers' copy for title-pages generally, see Blayney, *The Texts of King Lear*, i. 259-62.

			Collation
1, 2	*The Whole Contention*	'Printed at London, for T. P.'	A–Q4
3	*Pericles*	'Printed for T. P. 1619.'	Tit., R–Aa4, Bb1
4	*A Yorkshire Tragedy*	'Printed for T. P. 1619.'	Tit., A–C4, D1–3
5	*The Merchant of Venice*	'Printed by I. Roberts, 1600.'	A–K4
6	*The Merry Wives of Windsor*	'Printed for Arthur Iohnson, 1619.'	A–G4
7	*King Lear*	'Printed for Nathaniel Butter, 1608.'	A–H4
8	*Henry V*	'Printed for T. P. 1608.'	A–G4
9	*1 Sir John Oldcastle*	'London printed for T. P. 1600.'	A–K4
10	*A Midsummer Night's Dream*	'Printed by Iames Roberts, 1600.'	A–H4

All these editions are reprints. Three of these plays were excluded from the Folio altogether; one (*Oldcastle*) is definitely not by Shakespeare, and another (*Yorkshire Tragedy*) has been generally regarded as the work of another writer. Four of the remainder—*The Whole Contention* (containing both *Contention* and *Richard Duke of York*), *Merry Wives*, and *Henry V*—derive from editions based upon memorial reconstruction. As the right-hand column above shows, the first few plays were given page signatures as for a single volume. Most of the volumes were, in the event, sold separately, but they were also sold as a set, and two such sets survive in their original bindings. On 3 May 1619 the Court of the Stationers' Company recorded consideration of a letter 'from the right ho^ble the Lo. Chamberleyne' which led them to the conclusion that 'It is thought fitt & so ordered That no playes that his Ma^tyes players do play shalbe printed w^thout consent of some of them'.[93] The letter itself does not survive, but its contents are probably recapitulated in another to the same effect written on 10 June 1637, which among other complaints observes that the books contain 'much corruption to the iniury and disgrace of the Authors'.[94] There can be no doubt that the King's Men were responsible for the Lord Chamberlain's intervention, either because their plans for the Folio were already under way, or because Pavier's attempt persuaded them that they should oversee the publication of Shakespeare's work personally.

In the 1623 Folio, copy-editing becomes both more important and more problematic. To begin with, we cannot be sure who did the editing. John Heminges and Henry Condell, senior members of the King's Men who had been with the company since its founding about thirty years before, appended their names to both the Dedicatory Epistle and the preface addressed 'To the great variety of readers';[95] a colophon states that the volume was 'Printed at the Charges of W. Jaggard, Ed. Blount, I. Smithweeke, and W. Aspley' (bbb6).[96] It was printed in the shop of William Jaggard. Ben Jonson, who contributed two conspicuous poems to the preliminaries, was, like Heminges and Condell, an old associate of Shakespeare; other commendatory verses were contributed by Hugh Holland (a friend of Jonson), and by Leonard Digges and James Mabbe who, like Jonson, formed part of the literary circle of Edward Blount.[97] Any of these people could have contributed to the preparation of the collection, and it seems unlikely that all the work was shouldered by Heminges and Condell—old men, with many other responsibilities, and with more experience of the theatre than of publishing. In so far as the King's Men did oversee the volume, the detailed work was probably delegated to their book-keeper (Knight?) and any other scribes who (like Crane) regularly worked for the company.

As a collected volume, the Folio presented problems of preparation which individual quarto editions did not. In the first place, someone had to decide what to include. That decision must have been left entirely to Heminges and Condell, who were better qualified than anyone else to make it. Their judgement has been vindicated by subsequent centuries of scholarship. No extant play excluded from the Folio has ever been convincingly attributed in its entirety to Shakespeare; no play included in the collection has ever been convincingly attributed in its entirety to someone else. About collaborative plays Heminges and Condell were less consistent, but collaborative plays reduce even modern editors to inconsistency. If we compare the contents of the 1623 Shakespeare Folio with those of the 1647 Beaumont and Fletcher Folio, Heminges and Condell emerge as models of scholarly responsibility.[98]

Having decided what to include, the Folio editors had to decide how to arrange it. The 1616 Folio edition of Ben Jonson's *Works* presented the plays in their order of composition, and identified the date of each; the 1623 Shakespeare Folio did not. Perhaps Heminges and Condell could not remember, or could not be bothered to check, when all the plays had been written; though they could certainly have given dates for some plays, perhaps they preferred to be systematically but unobtrusively unhelpful, rather than glaringly inconsistent. Perhaps they thought Jonson's provision of dates was pretentious; or perhaps they recognized that some of the plays had been revised or adapted in ways that would make a single 'date of composition' actively misleading. Whatever their reasons, they did not provide dates, and this omission has had critical consequences which can hardly be overestimated. For a century and a half after the publication of the First Folio no one even attempted to divine the chronology of the Shakespeare canon. Dryden thought that *Troilus and Cressida* was one of Shakespeare's 'first endeavours of the Stage';[99] this conviction no doubt resulted from, and in turn influenced, his almost total incomprehension of the play's manner and conduct.

If one does not know the order of composition of an author's works, one cannot form any notion of his artistic development; if one has no notion of his artistic development, it becomes fatally easy to acquire the notion that (artistically) he did not develop, but instead sprang, like Athena, full-grown from the forehead of the nearest available Muse. In Shakespeare's case this myth was abetted by the First

Folio's prominent inclusion of Ben Jonson's prefatory panegyric. Jonson was an immeasurably more important artist than any of the others who contributed metrical blurbs, and his offering is predictably the most brilliant and the most memorable—and, less predictably, one of Jonson's most generous creations. From the particular perspective of Ben Jonson, William Shakespeare did undoubtedly possess '*small* Latine *and lesse* Greeke'; nevertheless, this statement of relative fact easily coupled with the absence of a chronology for Shakespeare's work to father the doctrine of Shakespeare's untutored genius. Jonson at least knew Shakespeare; Milton of course did not, and in terms of textual derivation Milton's 'warbling his native wood-notes wild' is merely a late and corrupt recension of '*Sweet Swan of Auon*'.[100] Milton was even more formidably learned, and even more formidably brilliant, than Jonson, and these two facts in conjunction explain both the error and the influence of Milton's judgement. To the poetic testimony of the Jonson–Milton axis was added, in 1767, that of a Cambridge classicist, Richard Farmer. Farmer's monograph, *An Essay on the Learning of Shakespeare*, proved that Shakespeare's knowledge of Greek and Latin was, beyond a doubt, less than would be expected of any eighteenth-century English nobleman, scholar, or poet. Farmer's estimate of the paucity of Shakespeare's learning remained orthodox for 180 years.[101]

When Farmer published his monograph, Edward Capell was still at work on the first systematic attempt to establish a chronology of the Shakespeare canon. Capell unfortunately did not live to publish his findings, and no such conjectural chronology was available until Edmond Malone supplied one in 1778. Capell assigned *1 Henry VI* to 1600 and *Twelfth Night* to 1607; Malone dated *All Is True* '1601' and *Twelfth Night* '1614' (as Shakespeare's last work); both thought that *Othello* was written in 1611, and *Caesar* in 1607 or 1608.[102] Two centuries later, thanks in part to the haphazard discovery of documents, we can see much more clearly than Capell or Malone the general shape of the progress of Shakespeare's art from early to late; but the damage to Shakespeare's reputation had, by the late eighteenth century, already been done. Whole traditions of exegesis and criticism were founded upon assumptions generated by the non-chronological arrangement of the first collected edition of his work.

The First Folio's failure to date Shakespeare's work did not so much reshape his canon as unshape it. Upon the resulting shapeless assortment the editors then imposed an artifical tripartite division which itself obscured rather than illuminated the structure and nature of the plays. The book which modern scholars familiarly call 'the First Folio' was of course in its own time known as *The Comedies, Histories, and Tragedies of Mr. William Shakespeare*. This unwieldy title itself probably resulted from some sort of publishing compromise. The 1616 'First Folio' of Jonson had unabashedly named itself *The Works*, a title which was immediately ridiculed.[103]

> *To Mr. Ben. Johnson demanding the reason*
> *why he called his playes works.*
>
> Pray tell me *Ben*, where doth the mystery lurke,
> What others call a play you call a worke.
>
> *Thus answer'd by a friend in Mr.*
> *Johnsons defence.*
>
> The authors friend thus for the author sayes,
> *Bens* plays are works, when others works are plaies.

Shakespeare was only the second public playwright to be honoured with a collection of his work in folio, and the controversy over the title of the first such collection created an unenviable dilemma for the editors of the second.[104] If they called it '*Works*', they would subject Shakespeare to the same ridicule visited upon Jonson—and (perhaps) impose upon him a label of self-importance which misrepresented the nature of the man they knew. A desire not to appear pretentious or pedantic seems evident in the failure to supply dates and in the tone of the prefatory matter; in any case the unavailability of the author made impossible the exacting attention to substance and presentation apparent in Jonson's volume. On the other hand, 'Plays' could be interpreted either as a rebuke to Jonson (who was clearly involved in the volume's preparation) or as a confession of Shakespeare's intellectual inferiority ('others works are plaies'). *Comedies, Histories, and Tragedies* successfully navigates between the Scylla and Charybdis of *Works* or *Plays*, while at the same time confidently advertising the range of Shakespeare's output—as successful in three genres as Jonson had been in one.

The organization of the volume in three sections may well have arisen as a consequence of the decision about its title. That organization of course betrays the plays, which are characterized by fluidity not consistency of genre, by a continual mixing of modes. The very table of contents of the first collected edition of Shakespeare's plays—'A CATALOGVE of the seuerall Comedies, Histories, and Tragedies contained in this Volume'—suggests the author's allegiance to strict distinctions of genre which the plays themselves disregard, and this palpable discrepancy between form (of the Folio) and content (of Shakespeare's actual plays) surely contributed to the subsequent fruitless centuries-long critical preoccupation with decorums of genre. This malaise of classification affected the whole canon, but for some plays the damage was particularly acute. *Cymbeline* and *Troilus and Cressida* were both badly misplaced, with lamentable consequences for subsequent interpretation. *Richard II* and *Richard III* became Histories, though each was described on the title page of the first edition as a Tragedy; both *Lear* and *Macbeth* became Tragedies, though based on the same chronicle sources as the English history plays. Only plays dealing with 'English' (as opposed to 'British') monarchs were included among the 'Histories', and all were given titles which identified them, in formulaic terms, with a particular reign. More generally, the disposition of the histories by chronology of reign, rather than chronology of composition, inevitably created a sequence of two 'tetralogies', spanning the period from the death of Woodstock to the death of Richard III—an accident of juxtaposition which continues to inhibit a proper sensitivity to the individuality of the eight plays huddled in this anachronistic chronological ghetto.

Having explicitly divided Shakespeare's work into three categories, the First Folio implicitly, by exclusion, created a fourth: the poems. The poems were probably omitted for a number of interlocking reasons. The King's Men had no claims on them; *Lucrece* and *Venus and Adonis* were Shakespeare's most popular quartos, and Roger Jackson and William Barnett, who held the copyrights, were not members of the Folio syndicate, and would probably not have relinquished their rights. Thomas Thorpe, who owned the copyright on the Sonnets, was not a member of the syndicate either. Whatever the reasons, the omission relegated Shakespeare's non-dramatic poetry to a critical limbo from which it did not begin to emerge until Malone's edition of the Sonnets (1780) and Coleridge's praise of the early narrative poems (1817).[105] Moreover, in limiting themselves to the plays Heminges and Condell left the Shakespeare canon only half-defined. The Folio had effectively doubled the size of the dramatic canon, excluded some items falsely attributed to Shakespeare in print, and provided better texts of several works hitherto available only in seriously corrupt editions. An authoritative collection of the poetry might have reshaped our perception of the non-dramatic canon just as fundamentally. But no such collection ever appeared. In 1640 John Benson, recognizing the lacuna, tried to exploit it with the publication of *Shakespeare's Poems*. This collection adds nothing of value to the historical record, but its derivative and unauthoritative character was not recognized until Malone published his work on the Sonnets, so that for almost a century and a half Benson's mangled hodgepodge was an accepted repository of Shakespeare's lyric verse. Our understanding of Shakespeare's non-dramatic poetry can only be secured by a thorough investigation of manuscript sources, and of the authority of printed attributions (particularly those in *The Passionate Pilgrim*); the Oxford edition contributes to this process, but a great deal of work remains to be done.

Having decided to exclude the poems, and to group the plays by genre, the Folio editors still needed to arrange the items within each genre. For the 'Histories' historical sequence was an obvious possibility, obviously in practice adopted. For the other genres the problem did not so easily solve itself. *The Tempest*, first in the volume, was—so far as we know—the last play Shakespeare wrote without a collaborator; *Cymbeline*, last in the volume, was—according to our chronology—the penultimate play Shakespeare wrote without a collaborator. Both were, we believe, printed from manuscripts prepared by the same scribe, who had a close working relationship with the King's Men. The volume begins with '*A tempestuous noise of Thunder and Lightning*' and ends with 'Feasts' and 'Peace';[106] the contrast may be fortuitous, but it reflects with surprising sensitivity the preoccupations which critics have discerned in Shakespeare's work, particularly at the end of his career. Just as the last written of the Comedies is printed first, so the last written of the Tragedies (*Coriolanus*) begins that section. In both sections the last example of the genre is followed—in our chronology—by the very first (*Two Gentlemen*, *Titus Andronicus*).

But such considerations of theme and chronology will not account for the ordering of most of the plays in the Comedies and Tragedies sections. That order seems to have been governed, to some extent, by the nature of the copy being given to the printer. All three sections begin and end with plays never before printed. In the Comedies, the first four plays were all set from Ralph Crane transcripts; the sixth, seventh, eighth, and ninth essentially reprinted available authoritative quartos. In the Tragedies too, *Coriolanus* (set, we believe, from a scribal transcript) was to have been followed by three plays which essentially reprint available authoritative quartos: *Titus*, *Romeo*, and *Troilus*. (In the event *Troilus* was moved, and now appears between the Histories and Tragedies; it was replaced by *Timon*.) Beyond these runs of similar copy, the order seems fortuitous.

Unlike the publishers of individual quartos, the Folio syndicate probably had some choice in the copy from which plays were to be printed, since they had access to the manuscripts accumulated by the King's Men. In general, they clearly preferred transcripts (seventeen) or existing editions (eleven). Only eight Folio texts were, we believe, set from foul papers; noticeably, several of these are very early plays (*Errors*, *Shrew* (?), *Contention*, *Richard Duke of York*, and *1 Henry VI*), and one seems to have been an addition to the original plan (*Timon*). No text was certainly set from a prompt-book, though prompt-books were clearly consulted in order to supplement some of the plays reprinted from earlier editions. When reprinting or consulting quartos, the Folio editors consistently favoured recent reprints over earlier first editions. But this policy may reflect availability rather than choice: as any collector knows, old first editions are harder to find than new reprints. The compilers did use earlier editions for *Merchant* (Q1), *Richard II* (Q3), and part of *Richard III* (Q3), although in each case more recent reprints were at hand.

Beyond deciding on the contents, arrangement, and copy, the Folio editors seem to have interfered little with the texts. They were once thought to have imposed literary act divisions, but most of these seem in fact to derive from late theatrical practice.[107] Only in *Shrew* and *Henry V* do the divisions seem wholly editorial; thereafter the editor (or printer) apparently abandoned the attempt to ensure that every text was parcelled into five acts. Most of the expurgation of profanity also apparently reflects late theatrical practice—though the printer was likely to remove on his own initiative oaths by 'God's wounds' or 'God's blood', which were considered particularly offensive.[108]

As a rule, then, the editors did not personally expurgate the plays, or divide them into acts; they simply supplied to the printer manuscripts in many of which such things had already been done. From this selection of manuscripts emerges a Shakespeare less profane, and less political, than the original. A choppier Shakespeare too: his *œuvre* divided into three genres, his scripts divided into five acts, his syntax divided into innumerable clauses and parentheses and modifiers by the heavy punctuation of the Folio compositors and of the scribal transcripts from which they usually worked. And a modernized Shakespeare, his texts beginning already to be subtly reshaped to reflect changing theatrical conditions, changing legal restraints, changing standards of spelling and punctuation and grammar.

In the degree of editorial attention they received from the publishers, quartos and Folio differ dramatically; but the preparation by the printers was much the same. A printer needs to know the extent of a text in order to estimate how much paper and labour will be needed to manufacture the book, and in order to decide how to distribute work among the available workforce. A quarto might be set into type—as, for instance, the first edition of *Much Ado* apparently was—by a single compositor who began with the first word and continued until the last. Alternatively, and more commonly, the setting was divided between two or more compositors (or two or more printing houses).[109] If more than one compositor was

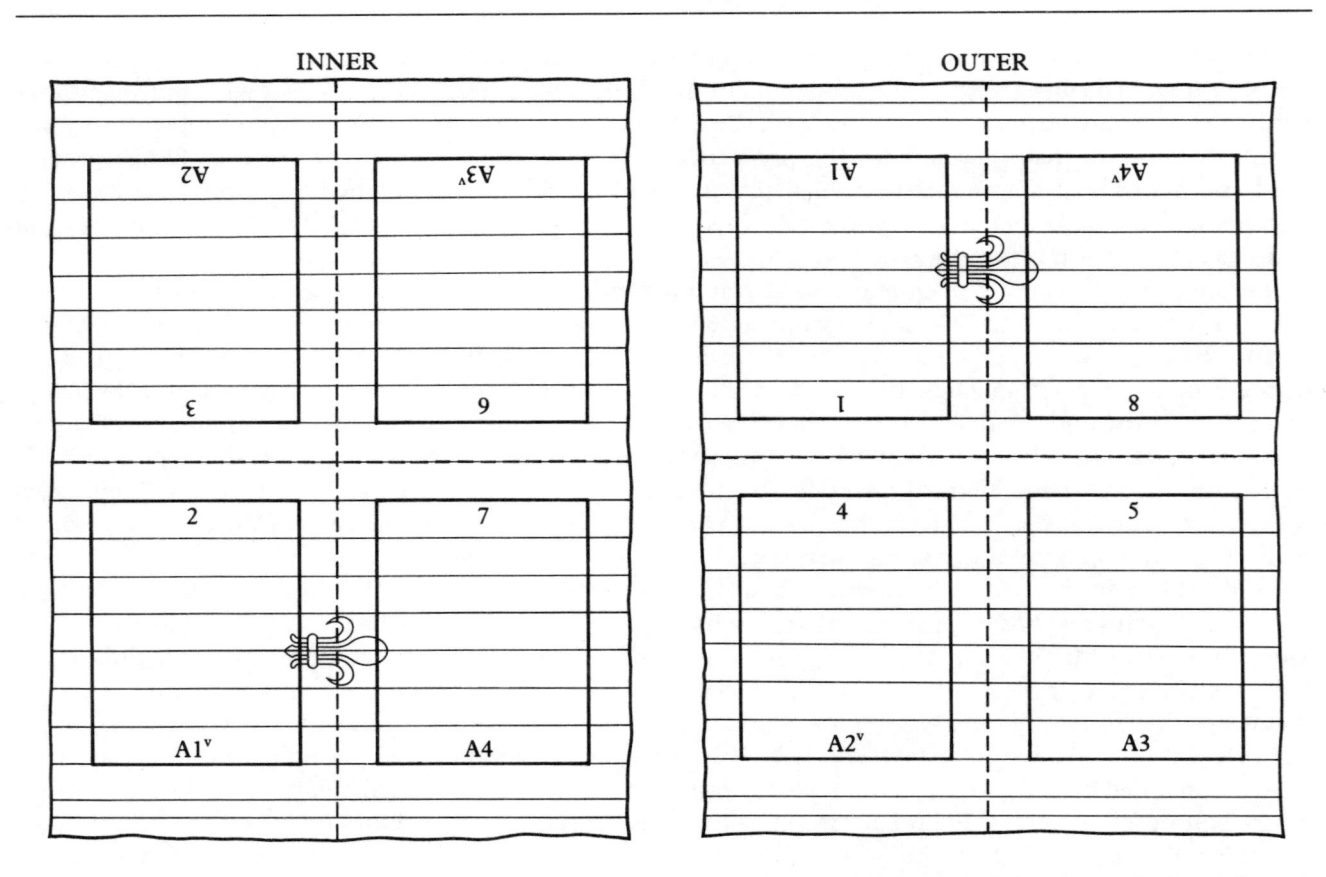

16. A quarto sheet, showing the disposition of pages on the inner and outer formes (opposite sides of a single sheet of paper). The sheet is folded twice (along the dotted lines) to produce four leaves, or eight pages, of the printed book.

working on the text at the same time, then the copy had to be divided up between them in advance. The need to divide up the copy would be even greater if, as was usual, the text was not set into type 'seriatim', from first word to last, but instead by formes. In seriatim setting, pages are set in the sequence in which they appear in the finished book (1, 2, 3, etc.); in setting by formes, all the pages which will appear on one side of a sheet of paper are set, and then all the pages which will appear on the other side. In a quarto format, this sheet of paper will eventually, after printing, be folded twice; as can be seen from Illustration 16, pages 1, 4, 5, and 8 (or A1, A2^v, A3, and A4^v) appear on the so-called 'outer' forme, and pages 2, 3, 6, and 7 (or A1^v, A2, A3^v, and A4) appear on the 'inner' forme. For setting by formes, compositors must know before they begin work which portion of the manuscript will correspond to which pages of the printed book; consequently someone must go through the manuscript beforehand, 'casting off'—defining exactly where page-breaks will fall in the printed book.[110] These marks—which sometimes consist only of uninked creases or indentations—can be seen in some of the few surviving manuscript examples of early printer's copy.[111] In the Folio the mechanics of estimating the extent of the text and marking page-breaks would have been the same as for a quarto, but the layout of cast-off pages in the eventual printed book was different. Because a folio sheet was only folded once, a forme consisted of only two pages. For almost the whole of the 1623 Folio, three sheets of paper were folded in half and interleaved, creating a quire which consisted of six leaves, or twelve pages. (See Illustration 17.)

Like any other detail of the mechanics of textual transmission, the practice of casting off concerns an editor only when it goes wrong. If someone underestimates the amount of space a passage of manuscript will consume in print, the compositor may run out of room. In the right circumstances—for instance, when setting E1^v of the inner forme of a cast-off quarto—he may be able to push the excess material on to another page (E2); but this solution may only postpone the problem. If the outer forme has already been set into type and printed, then E2ᵛ will begin with a particular phrase ('story of lust and foul thoughts'), and by the end of E2 the compositor has to reach the words which precede it ('Index and prologue to the hi-'). If not, there will be a gap in the text. As Illustration 19 demonstrates, a compositor in solving such problems might employ a variety of expedients, some involving matters of mere layout, others incidental matters of spelling and punctuation, others—particularly in the work of Jaggard's Compositor B—more material matters of actual verbal and dramatic substance.

Alternatively, the compositor may find himself with too much space. Usually such problems can be overcome by various formal expedients for wasting space; sometimes they lead to deliberate mislineation;

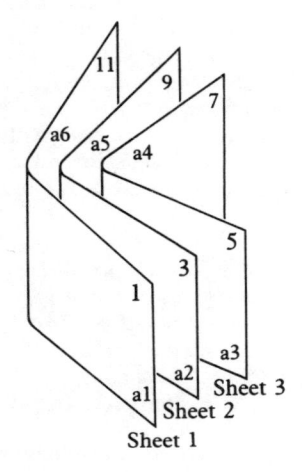

17. A quire of three folio sheets, showing the disposition of pages.

sometimes they precipitate actual verbal additions to the text. Compositor B probably set the page shown in Illustration 18;[112] he also set passages in *Richard II*, *2 Henry IV*, *Contention*, *Hamlet*, and *King Lear* where problems with casting off apparently led to deliberate expansion of the text. Such problems arise most often in pages with a large proportion of prose, which is harder than verse to cast off; they are less likely to occur in simple reprints than in texts set either from manuscripts or from an earlier printed text supplemented by extensive alterations and additions from a manuscript.

From Compositor to Reader

A printed book is manufactured in three stages: composition (the setting of the text into type), press-work (the imprinting of a visual pattern produced by inked types on to multiple sheets of paper), and binding (the folding and stitching together of sheets of paper in a predetermined order so as to produce an intended sequence of text). Mistakes can and do happen at each stage, but the mistakes which occur in composition matter most to an editor. Composition is done by compositors, who are to printed transmission what scribes are to manuscript transmission: the human medium which links two pieces of paper, the electrical impulse which leaps between material nerve-endings.

Like scribes, compositors vary in their habits and abilities, and over the last three decades much work has been expended in discriminating and identifying the compositors who set substantive editions. The process actually began in 1920, when Thomas Satchell first described two patterns of spelling in the Folio text of *Macbeth*, and interpreted those patterns as symptomatic of the work of two compositors, labelled 'A' and 'B'.[113] Sixty-six years later, Satchell's division of *Macbeth* remains intact, having been confirmed by a wide range of evidence spotted by subsequent bibliographers. Compositor B in fact contributed to the setting of 35 of the 36 plays included in the Folio, and is the single most important

18. *The Chronicle History of Henry the fift*, 'Printed for T.P. 1608' (actually 1619), sig. F4ᵛ. The amount of wasted space around directions (1, 3, 8) and in the right margin itself suggests that the compositor was deliberately stretching the text. In Fluellen's third speech (2), two lines in the compositor's copy ('Ancient . . . appetite') have been rearranged as three; similarly expansive mislineation affects three consecutive speeches in the middle of the page (5). A stage direction has been added (8), as have seven words within eight lines: 'But in the' (4), 'it is enough' (6), and 'too' (7). Cumulatively, such expedients waste ten type lines on this page.

transmitter in the history of the communication of William Shakespeare's text. By a curious coincidence, B's name may have been John Shakespeare.[114]

Current attributions of Folio pages to specific compositors are summarized below, and the introductions to individual works record current opinion on the compositors who set specific quartos. All such attributions are conjectural; some are more conjectural than others. The Folio has been screened for compositorial habits by many investigators over many decades; individual quartos have been studied by one or two scholars for months or at most a few years. Moreover, the basic unit of composition is a page; folio pages, being larger than quarto pages, always contain more evidence on which to base attribution to a particular workman. The Folio also contains more pages than a quarto: 36 plays (plus preliminaries) instead of one. The 1623 Folio represents a large proportion of the work done in William Jaggard's printing shop in 1622-3, and the book can therefore be more confidently understood in the context of the printer's business for those months. For the quartos we must deal with smaller bibliographical units, fewer bibliographical units, and (usually) less understanding of the production context. Compositor attributions in the quartos are as yet, and perhaps for ever, intrinsically less reliable than those in the Folio.

Some sceptics would contest the reliability even of the Folio attributions, and question the very effort to discriminate compositors at all.[115] Certainly, a layman's confidence is not encouraged by the spectacle of accomplished bibliographers achieving fundamentally different results from the study of the same quarto (*Love's Labour's Lost, Richard III*). But scientists too sometimes simultaneously announce contradictory conclusions, and one does not in consequence infer that science is bunk, but only that one scientist or the other is wrong—or that both are wrong. Our understanding of the manufacture of early books, like our understanding of other aspects of the physical world, becomes progressively more complicated and exact. Satchell saw only two compositors in the Folio, where we now see seven or eight. The pace of progress in bibliographical research is slow, because human and financial resources are limited, because society (rightly) gives a limited priority to such studies. But the progress of bibliographical research is as dialectical and cumulative as the progress of other studies which society values more highly.

The leap from patterns of composition in printed books to the identification of individual human compositors remains, of course, only an inference. But from the perspective of textual criticism, that identification matters less than the establishment of patterns of compositional homogeneity. If we know that certain pages share features of layout, orthography, punctuation, typography, lineation, and error, it hardly concerns us whether such similarities result from the presence of a specific human body, or from the complex dance of warring atoms, or from divine intervention. We may instead operate on the working assumption that, the more known features two pages share, the more likely it becomes that their similarities arise from some cause, and that the cause in question will generate further similarities. In short, the greater the number and variety of shared features, the greater the probability of similarity in other features. We may therefore reasonably pass from the identification of certain areas of compositional homogeneity to the cataloguing and analysis of error in the stints of hypothetical workmen.[116] Many of the errors identified by such means could have been committed, on occasion, by any compositor (or scribe); a catalogue of the errors in a variety of books during a given period can be helpful to any editor of a work from that period.[117] More specifically, some compositors (like some scribes, like other human beings) have a propensity for particular kinds of error, and an awareness of such propensities can be useful to an editor.

Every compositor, however, repeatedly performed certain simple functions. He would first look over the manuscript and read (or decipher) a few words—by no means always an easy business, when confronted with what apologetic authors identified as their own 'bad writing', and what frustrated printers called 'ragged Written Copy'.[118] Having determined the sense, the compositor had then to decide how to spell and punctuate the intended meaning; it was '*a task and duty incumbent on the* Compositor . . . *to discern and amend the bad* Spelling *and* Pointing *of his Copy, if it be in English*'.[119] He would then take the necessary types from his type case and insert them one by one into his composing stick. When the composing stick held four or five full lines of type, he would transfer its contents on to the galley—a wooden tray which held the equivalent of a page of type. The compositor would then set up another line of type in his composing stick, and so continue until the page was complete. He would then supply the headline at the top of the page, and at the bottom the catchword (the first word of the following page) and, on the recto of some leaves, the page signature. After the first sheet or two of a book, the compositor reused headlines from the pages of a sheet already printed. He would also eventually need to distribute into his case all of the type from formes once they had been printed, in order to replenish the diminishing supply.[120]

In their efforts to reproduce the words of a manuscript, compositors can commit any of the errors to which all copyists are liable: misreading, eyeskip, dittography, haplography, transposition, sophistication, substitution, simple omission, simple interpolation. But they add to these errors others specific to the medium of print. In retrieving types from the type-case, they may accidentally reach into a compartment adjacent to the one intended, consequently setting a type which bears no visual resemblance to the manuscript form. The same error may arise from a different process if a compositor, when distributing type back into his type-case, accidentally returns a type to the wrong compartment, or overfills a

Much adoe aboat Nothing. 121

Then this for whom we rendred vp this woe. *Exeunt.*

Enter Leonato, Bene. Marg. Vrsula, old man, Frier, Hero.

Frier. Did I not tell you she was innocent?

Leo. So are the Prince and Claudio who accus'd her,
Vpon the errour that you heard debated:
But *Margaret* was in some fault for this,
Although against her will as it appeares,
In the true course of all the question.

Old. Well, I am glad that all things sort so well.

Bene. And so am I, being else by faith enforc'd
To call young *Claudio* to a reckoning for it.

Leo. Well daughter, and you gentlewomen all,
Withdraw into a chamber by your selues,
And when I send for you, come hither mask'd:
The *Prince* and *Claudio* promis'd by this howre
To visit me, you know your office Brother,
You must be father to your brothers daughter,
And giue her to young *Claudio*. *Exeunt Ladies.*

Old. Which I will doe with confirm'd countenance.

Bene. Frier, I must intreat your paines, I thinke.

Frier. To doe what Signior?

Bene. To binde me, or vndoe me, one of them:
Signior *Leonato*, truth it is good Signior,
Your neece regards me with an eye of fauour.

Leo. That eye my daughter lent her, 'tis most true.

Bene. And I doe with an eye of loue require her.

Leo. The sight whereof I thinke you had from me,
From *Claudio*, and the *Prince*, but what's your will?

Bened. Your answer sir is Enigmaticall,
But for my will, my will is, your good will
May stand with ours, this day to be conioyn'd,
In the state of honourable marriage,
In which (good Frier) I shall desire your helpe.

Leon. My heart is with your liking.

Frier. And my helpe.

Enter Prince and Claudio, with attendants.

Prin. Good morrow to this faire assembly.

Leo. Good morrow Prince, good morrow Claudio;
We heere attend you, are you yet determin'd,
To day to marry with my brothers daughter?

Claud. Ile hold my minde were she an Ethiope.

Leo. Call her forth brother, heres the Frier ready.

Prin. Good morrow *Benedike*, why what's the matter?
That you haue such a Februarie face,
So full of frost, of storme, and clowdinesse.

Claud. I thinke he thinkes vpon the sauage bull:
Tush, feare not man, wee'll tip thy hornes with gold,
And all *Europa* shall reioyce at thee,
As once *Europa* did at lusty *Ioue*,
When he would play the noble beast in loue.

Ben. Bull *Ioue* sir, had an amiable low,
And some such strange bull leapt your fathers Cow,
A got a Calfe in that same noble feat,
Much like to you, for you haue iust his bleat.

Enter brother, Hero, Beatrice, Margaret, Vrsula.

Cla. For this I owe you: here comes other reckings.
Which is the Lady I must seize vpon?

Leo. This same is she, and I doe giue you her.

Cla. Why then she's mine, sweet let me see your face.

Leon. No that you shal not, till you take her hand,
Before this Frier, and sweare to marry her.

Clau. Giue me your hand before this holy Frier,
I am your husband if you like of me.

Hero. And when I liu'd I was your other wife,
And when you lou'd, you were my other husband.

Clau. Another *Hero*?

Hero. Nothing certainer.
One *Hero* died, but I doe liue,
And surely as I liue, I am a maid.

Prin. The former *Hero*, *Hero* that is dead.

Leon. Shee died my Lord, but whiles her slander liu'd.

Frier. All this amazement can I qualifie,
When after that the holy rites are ended,
Ile tell you largely of faire *Heroes* death:
Meane time let wonder seeme familiar,
And to the chappell let vs presently.

Ben. Soft and faire Frier, which is *Beatrice*?

Beat. I answer to that name, what is your will?

Bene. Doe not you loue me?

Beat. Why no, no more then reason.

Bene. Why then your Vncle, and the Prince, & Claudio, haue beene deceiued, they swore you did.

Beat. Doe not you loue mee?

Bene. Troth no, no more then reason.

Beat. Why then my Cosin *Margaret* and *Vrsula*
Are much deceiu'd, for they did sweare you did.

Bene. They swore you were almost sicke for me.

Beat. They swore you were wel-nye dead for me.

Bene. 'Tis no matter, then you doe not loue me?

Beat. No truly, but in friendly recompence.

Leon. Come Cosin, I am sure you loue the gentlemā.

Clau. And Ile be sworne vpon't, that he loues her,
For heres a paper written in his hand,
A halting sonnet of his owne pure braine,
Fashioned to *Beatrice*.

Hero. And heeres another,
Writ in my cosins hand, stolne from her pocket,
Containing her affection vnto *Benedicke*.

Bene. A miracle, here's our owne hands against our hearts: come I will haue thee, but by this light I take thee for pittie.

Beat. I would not denie you, but by this good day, I yeeld vpon great perswasion, & partly to saue your life, for I was told, you were in a consumption.

Leon. Peace I will stop your mouth.

Prin. How dost thou *Benedicke* the married man?

Bene. Ile tell thee what Prince: a Colledge of witte-crackers cannot flout mee out of my humour, dost thou think I care for a Satyre or an Epigram? no, if a man will be beaten with braines, a shall weare nothing handsome about him: in briefe, since I do purpose to marry, I will thinke nothing to any purpose that the world can say a-gainst it, and therefore neuer flout at me, for I haue said against it: for man is a giddy thing, and this is my con-clusion: for thy part *Claudio*, I did thinke to haue beaten thee, but in that thou art like to be my kinsman, liue vn-bruis'd, and loue my cousin.

Cla. I had well hop'd y wouldst haue denied *Beatrice*, y I might haue cudgel'd thee out of thy single life, to make thee a double dealer, which out of questiō thou wilt be, if my Cousin do not looke exceeding narrowly to thee.

Bene. Come, come, we are friends, let's haue a dance ere we are married, that we may lighten our own hearts, and our wiues heeles.

Leon. Wee'll haue dancing afterward.

Bene. First, of my vvord, therfore play musick. *Prince*, thou art sad, get thee a vvife, get thee a vvife, there is no staff more reuerend then one tipt with horn. *Enter. Mes.*

Messen. My Lord, your brother *Iohn* is tane in flight,
And brought with armed men backe to *Messina*.

Bene. Thinke not on him till to morrow, ile deuise thee braue punishments for him: strike vp Pipers. *Dance.*

L *FINIS.*

compartment so that the types later spill into an adjacent box; in either event, the error lies in wait until the (wrong) type is picked up from the (right) compartment. The textual consequences arising from both categories of error—of retrieval and distribution—are governed by the layout of the type-case, or 'lay of the case'. (See Illustration 20.) Such mechanical errors—which editors generally refer to as 'foul case'—for the most part produce combinations of letters which readers instinctively reject as nonsensical, like 'faiendship' (for 'friendship') or 'onby' (for 'only'); many such errors are documented in our lists of emendations of incidentals. But at other times the same process generates recognizable words: not the word intended by the author, or appropriate to the context, but a word nevertheless, like 'them' (for 'then') or 'hut' (for 'nut'). Errors of distribution can also occur because of the similar appearance or width of types (o/e, e/c, u/n, t/r) rather than proximity of compartments.

For a compositor words consist of types, not letters: 'fiſt', for instance, has four letters but only two types. Types which print more than one letter are called ligatures, and the ligatures available in this period include æ, ct, fi, ff, fl, ffi, ffl, œ, ∞, ſb, ſi, ſl, ſſ, ſt, ſſi, ſſl, and italic *as*, *is*, *us*, and *ll*. Other single typepieces represented abbreviations for words whereby, in manuscript, the initial letter would be followed by a superscript ('wᶜ' for 'which', 'yᵘ' for 'thou'); on the typepiece the raised letter was placed directly over its antecedent. Not every printer had all of these in every typeface, and the supply of some of the less common letter combinations might be limited. Naturally, if a compositor did not have a ligature, he had to use the separate types for the two letters. For the vowel combinations, or 'ct', the use of two types instead of one meant more work for the compositor, but did not in itself create any technical difficulties. The other ligatures, however, were designed to solve a problem created by the shape of the letters 'f' and 'ſ'. Both letters 'kern': that is, part of the letter extends off the body of the typeface, and hence runs the risk of running into another letter. This problem still exists for the letter 'f', and if you examine the text of this introduction you will find that the letter 'i' lacks its dot when preceded by an 'f', and that the letters ff and fl are joined. The identical problem created by 'ſ' has been solved in modern typography simply by abandoning the letter-form altogether, and using 's' (once reserved for terminal positions) universally. The same expedient, now adopted everywhere, is by Renaissance printers adopted locally: the shortage or unavailability of ligatures might lead compositors to anticipate modern practice by setting 'ask', 'husband', 'permiſsion' (rather than 'aſk', 'huſband', 'permiſſion'), for instance.

Subtleties of typography make no difference to the content of the linguistic sign, though for a bibliographer they may produce important clues to the printing process. In other cases, however, compositors might remedy a shortage of ligatures by spelling words differently: 'Creſſeid', for example, instead of 'Creſſid'. Moreover, since what forces a compositor to such shifts is the kern, the same problems and solutions might be precipitated by other kerning letters, for which no ligature was ever available. Italic founts kern more letters than roman ones: the '*e*' in '*Quickely*' or the hyphen in '*Shake-speare*' avoids a clash between an italic '*k*' (which kerns forward, below the line) and the italic '*y*' or '*ſ*' (which kern backward, below the line). In print, spelling is sometimes a function of typography.[121]

Error can also be a function of typography. Because compositors deal in types, a single mistake in distribution or retrieval can lead to the printing of two or even three letters instead of one ('Siſterſtood' for 'Siſterhood'). Equally, a compositor's use of a ligature, or failure to use one, can sometimes demonstrate that he set a word quite deliberately, and so discredit emendations accepted by editors inattentive

---

19. (*facing*) *Comedies, Histories, and Tragedies* (1623), sig. L1 of the Comedies: the final page of *Much Ado About Nothing*. As evidence of crowding, notice: the absence of white space around entrance directions (1, 3, 4); the abbreviation of names in stage directions (1, 11); the omission of a line of verse, 'Heere comes the Prince and Claudio' (2); the alteration of '*and two or three other*' to '*with attendants*' (3); the shortening of speech-prefixes, from '*Clau.*' to '*Cla.*', in order to avoid turnovers in verse lines (5); the setting of verse, which would have required three type lines as prose, requiring only two (6); the omission of 'that' (7), 'that' (8), and 'such' (9), in order to avoid turnovers in verse lines; the use of tildes and abbreviations in tightly set lines (10); the treatment of an entrance direction as though it were an exit (11); the setting of '*FINIS*' in the space usually reserved for catchwords (12). Cumulatively, such expedients save up to seventeen type lines on this page.

20. The arrangement of type in the upper and lower case, derived from Plate 1 of Joseph Moxon's *Mechanick Exercises on the Whole Art of Printing* (1683-4). Moxon describes the lay of the case illustrated here as 'the most common', but notes that the cases 'are not in every *Printing-House* disposed alike'. Moxon's is the earliest illustration of an English case; for early continental models, and an eighteenth-century English one, see Philip Gaskell, *A New Introduction to Bibliography* (1972), figs. 21-3.

to typography. For example, 'chaft' in the 1600 edition of *Merchant* (2.9.47/1104) is unlikely to be a compositor's mis-setting of 'chaff' because 'ft' required two pieces of type where 'ff' was a single ligature.[122]

In most cases, a compositor successfully retrieves the type he desires from the type-case; in most cases, he successfully transfers it to the composing stick. Sometimes, though, he will put the type into the stick upside down, a simple mechanical error which makes 'u'/'n' and 'p'/'d' interchangeable. So, with a turned 'u', 'you' looks like 'yon'; with a turned 'n', 'denote' seems to read 'deuote' (*devote*). Alternatively, working as he does from left to right, the compositor may set two types in the wrong order, so that the last shall be first, and the first last, resulting usually in palpable nonsense ('fegin'd' for 'feign'd'), but occasionally in less obvious varieties of nonsense ('bouldy' for 'bloudy', *Richard II* 3.2.36/1339, where some editors have emended 'boldly').

Finally, unlike a scribe, a compositor must not only set certain letters side by side; he must also ensure that they *remain* side by side (something a scribe can take for granted). The type must be wedged tightly enough together that individual types do not become loose and so fall out or shift. Just as any system of language requires a neutral filler (silence, blank space) which can separate and distinguish signifiers (letters, sounds, words), so the system for disseminating written languages developed by Gutenberg requires a neutral filler (uninked types) which can hold together and hold apart the signifiers (inked types). In both prose and verse, the compositor must fill every line of his composing stick. If the words of the text do not fill it, he must supplement them with spaces; if the words of the text will not fit, he must reduce the amount of uninking type or move some of the inking type on to another line. But a Renaissance compositor, unlike his modern counterpart, could solve the problem of filling every type line—a process called 'justification'—not only by the addition or subtraction of uninking spaces, but also by the addition or subtraction of inking letters. The variety of contemporary orthography gave compositors considerable freedom in spelling words, and some spellings filled more of the type line than others. Spelling is thus often a function of justification—particularly in prose.[123] Although verse lines also had to be justified, this could in general be done easily enough by filling out the rest of the type line with however many blank spaces were needed. However, sometimes the amount of space available to a compositor in setting verse is less than appears to the untrained eye, for in setting verse compositors sometimes 'indent the stick' in order to reduce their measure. In such cases the compositor has to squeeze the words into a space considerably narrower than the printed page, and may need to compress the text accordingly.[124]

After the compositor has set type for all the pages of a forme, the forme will be machined and a first (or 'foul') proof will be run. This proof will then be checked, normally against copy; corrections will be marked on it, and it will be returned to a compositor for the indicated corrections to be made in the type. In Shakespeare's age, as in ours, proofs might be checked by the author. Among playwrights, Thomas Nashe, George Chapman, and Ben Jonson all proof-read at least some of their works.[125] Shakespeare probably read the proofs of *Venus and Adonis* and *Lucrece*, but either he did not read proofs of the early editions of his plays, or he was an abysmal proof-reader. Given the quality of the setting of the narrative poems, and the other evidence that he took little interest in the printing of his dramatic work, the probability that he did not read proof for the plays is so high that it may be treated, in practice, as a certainty. For the posthumous quartos of *Othello* and *Kinsmen*, and the entire Folio, he could not have read proof, even if it had been his custom to do so. The poor quality of the text of some of the plays has led some scholars to conjecture that foul proofs were not pulled or checked at all, but the historical evidence for the normality of foul proofs is overwhelming.[126] Cheap play texts may not have been proof-read with the same care as the Bible, or works of classical scholarship, but even the worst of them is too well printed not to have been proofed at all. The Folio, in any case, was not a cheap play text, but an expensive and prestigious volume. In the words of William Jaggard himself, 'it touches a Printer as much to maintaine his reputation in the Art he liues by, as a Herald in his Profession'.[127] Indeed, who would be foolish enough to begin printing copies of a text—at a cost in paper, ink, and manpower, quite apart from reputation—which had not even been looked at, and might contain spectacular and grotesque errors?

After the foul proofs had been checked, and the type corrected, printing would begin. As a forme was being printed, a sample sheet would be pulled, and the text would be checked again, while printing went forward. If mistakes were spotted, the press would be stopped and the type corrected; then printing would continue. This process might be repeated several times. The formes already printed, which contained the errors spotted in this further round (or rounds) of press correction, would not be thrown away, but bound up in copies of the book which would eventually be put on sale. No attempt was made to compose individual copies entirely from corrected or from uncorrected formes; instead, each copy would contain a mixture of states. Consequently, the text of an early edition can only be properly established by collating every extant copy of that edition, noting the variants between them, and determining which reading represents the corrected and which the uncorrected state of the text. Needless to say, this is a considerable task, and seldom a rewarding one textually, for the 'stop-press' corrections left to this stage of manufacturing are usually few and trivial. On the other hand, until an edition has been collated, we cannot be sure how important or trivial might be the press variants it contains. Less than a quarter of the known surviving copies of the Folio have been checked; most, but not all, of the substantive quartos have been collated at least once.

No foul proofs of a Shakespeare edition have been discovered (though they exist for other books of the period), but several proof sheets from the stop-press stage of correction survive.[128] (See Illustration 21.) The examination of these proofs, and of those from other books of the period, confirms what anyone who has proof-read a modern book will know: not every correction called for gets made, and of those acted upon, a proportion result in miscorrection, which may take the printed text even further away from what stood in the manuscript. Sometimes miscorrection results in further corruption of the poor word which the proof-reader had asked to have corrected; at other times, the original error is left standing, and some innocent bystander, intact in the proof, suffers the correction intended for another word, and so becomes fortuitously corrupted. At other times, the proof-reader corrected apparent errors intuitively, without consulting the manuscript again; such 'corrections', even when properly executed, may do no more than further corrupt the text. Proof-readers also occasionally 'improve' the grammar or spelling or punctuation of a text in proof, according to standards of their own, which may move the *hould my performance perish.

Rom. Thou hast *Ventidius* that, without the which a
Souldier and his Sword graunts scarce distinction: thou
wilt write to *Anthony*.

Ven. Ile humbly signifie what in his name,
That magicall word of Warre we haue effected,
How with his Banners, and his well paid ranks,
The nere-yet beaten Horse of Parthia,
We haue iaded out o'th Field.

Rom. Where is he now?

Ven. He purposeth to Athens, whither with what hast
The waight we must conuay with's, will permit:
We shall appeare before him. On there, passe along.

Exeunt.

Enter Agrippa at one doore, Enobarbus at another.

Agri. What are the Brothers parted?

Eno. They haue dispatcht with *Pompey*, he is gone,
The other three are Sealing. *Octauia* weepes
To part from Rome: *Caesar* is sad, and *Lepidus*
Since *Pompey's* feast, as *Menas* saies, is troubled
With the Greene-Sicknesse.

Agri. 'Tis a Noble *Lepidus*.

Eno. A very fine one: oh, how he loues *Caesar*.

Agri. Nay but how deerely he adores *Mark Anthony*.

Eno. *Caesar*? why he's the Iupiter of men.

Ant. What's *Anthony*, the God of Iupiter?

Eno. Spake you of *Caesar*? How, the non-pareill?

Agri. Oh *Anthony*, oh thou Arabian Bird!

Eno. Would you praise *Caesar*, say *Caesar* go no further.

Agr. Indeed he plied them both with excellent praises.

Eno. But he loues *Caesar* best, yet he loues *Anthony*:
Hoo Hearts, Tongues, Figure,
Scribes, Bards, Poets, cannot
Thinke speake, cast, write, sing, number: hoo,
His loue to *Anthony*. But as for *Caesar*,
Kneele downe, kneele downe, and wonder.

Agri. Both he loues.

Eno. They are his Shards, and he their Beetle, so:
This is to horse: Adieu, Noble *Agrippa*.

Agri. Good Fortune worthy Souldier, and farewell.

Enter Caesar, Anthony, Lepidus, and Octauia.

Antho. No further Sir.

Caesar. You take from me a great part of my selfe:
Vse me well in't. Sister, proue such a wife
As my thoughts make thee, and as my farthest Band
Shall passe on thy approofe: most Noble *Anthony*,
Let not the peece of Vertue which is set
Betwixt vs, as the Cyment of our loue
To keepe it builded, be the Ramme to batter
The Fortresse of it: for better might we
Haue lou'd without this meane, if on both parts
This be not cherisht.

Ant. Make me not offended, in your distrust.

Caesar. I haue said.

Ant. You shall not finde,
Though you be therein curious, the least cause
For what you seeme to feare, so the Gods keepe you,
And make the hearts of Romaines serue your ends:
We will heere part.

Caesar. Farewell my deerest Sister, fare thee well,
The Elements be kind to thee, and make
Thy spirits all of comfort: fare thee well.

Octa. My Noble Brother.

Anth. The Aprill's in her eyes, it is Loues spring,
And these the showers to bring it on: be cheerfull.

Octa. Sir, looke well to my Husbands house: and

Caesar. What *Octauia*?

Octa. Ile tell you in your eare.

Ant. Her tongue will not obey her heart, nor can
Her heart informe her tougue.
The Swannes downe feather
That stands vpon the Swell at the of full Tide:
And neither way inclines.

Eno. Will *Caesar* weepe?

Agr. He ha's a cloud in's face.

Eno. He were the worse for that, were he a Horse, so is
he being a man.

Agri. Why *Enobarbus*:
When *Anthony* found *Iulius Caesar* dead,
He cried almost to roaring: And he wept,
When at Phillippi he found *Brutus* slaine.

Eno. That yeare indeed, he was troubl'd with a rume,
What willingly he did confound, he wail'd,
Beleeu't till I weepe too.

Caesar. No sweet *Octauia*,
You shall heare from me still: the time shall not
Out-go my thinking on you.

Ant. Come Sir, come,
Ile wrastle with you in my strength of loue,
Looke heere I haue you, thus I let you go,
And giue you to the Gods.

Caesar. Adieu, be happy.

Lep. Let all the number of the Starres giue light
To thy faire way.

Caesar. Farewell, farewell. *Kisses Octauia.*

Ant. Farewell. *Trumpets sound. Exeunt.*

Enter Cleopatra, Charmian, Iras, and Alexas.

Cleo. Where is the Fellow?

Alex. Halfe afeard to come.

Cleo. Go too, go too: Con e hither Sir.

Enter the Messenger as before.

Alex. Good Maiestie: *Herod* of Iury dare not looke
vpon you, but when you are well pleas'd.

Cleo. That *Herods* head, Ile haue: but how? When
Anthony is gone, through whom I might commaund it;
Come thou neere.

Mes. Most gratious Maiestie.

Cleo. Did'st thou behold *Octauia*?

Mes. I dread Queene.

Cleo. Where?

Mes. Madam in Rome, I lookt her in the face: and
saw her led betweene her Brother, and *Marke Anthony*.

Cleo. Is she as tall as me?

Mes. She is not Madam.

Cleo. Didst heare her speake?
Is she shrill tongu'd or low?

Mes. Madam, I heard her speake, she is low voic'd.

Cleo. That's not so good: he cannot like her long.

Char. Like her? Oh *Isis*: 'tis impossible.

Cleo. I thinke so *Charmian*: dull of tongue, & dwarfish
What Maiestie is in her gate, remember
If ere thou look'st on Maiestie.

Mes. She creepes: her motion, & her station are as one.
She shewes a body, rather then a life,
A Statue, then a Breather.

Cleo. Is this certaine?

Mes. Or I haue no obseruance.

Cha. Three in Egypt cannot make better note.

Cleo. He's very knowing, I do perceiu'r,
There's nothing in her yet.

printed text even further from the author's intentions. References to the 'uncorrected' and 'corrected' state of a press-variant text therefore mean 'the text before press-correction' and 'the text after press-correction', always with the understanding that the later state may be worse, and that textual criticism must begin with the earliest available state of the printed text.

Stop-press correction might also occur on the title-page of an edition, sometimes deliberately creating two distinct versions: the second quarto edition of *Hamlet*, for instance, is dated '1604' in some copies and '1605' in others. In two other quartos the variation is so extensive that it creates what is generally regarded as a second issue of the edition. In the quarto edition of *Troilus*, some copies have a variant title-page and a preface; in the quarto of *2 Henry IV*, the title-page remains unchanged, but the second half of sheet E (4 pages) has been replaced with a new full sheet (8 pages) in order to accommodate a scene which was not included in the first issue. In both cases, the correction seems to have been made very shortly after printing of the first issue was completed.

During proof-reading and proof-correction, the composition phase of manufacturing overlaps with the printing phase. The printing phase proper, though sometimes of interest to the bibliographer, seldom impinges directly upon the work of editors or the pleasure of readers. Individual types may slip, so that they fail to ink properly, or begin to move across the page, creating different readings in different copies of a book; but these apparent press-variants do not result from deliberate interference in the printing process, and being of a purely mechanical origin usually leave no one in any doubt about the correct state of the text. Individual types may also suffer damage during the course of printing, so that the word 'wife' is gradually transformed, between different copies of the Folio, into the word 'wife' (*Tempest* 4.1.123/1579).[129] Such direct textual relevance in the damage to a type is rare; more usually progressive damage simply enables us to determine which reading in a press-variant text represents the later stage of correction, or to trace the recurrence of a particular type and so determine the sequence of printing.[130]

What happens to the type itself during printing is incidental and accidental; the true substance of the printing phase is that the inked types come into contact with paper. For the first readers, the quality of the paper used, and the binding, said something about the character of the book and its contents—as they continue to do today. In 1633 a Puritan diatribe against the theatre complained that Shakespeare's works were 'printed in the best Crowne paper, far better than most Bibles'.[131] (For like-minded readers, 'Crowne'—which technically refers to the watermark of the paper—may itself have carried connotations of royal extravagance or decadence.) Moreover, the quality of the paper and the binding contributed mightily to the price. The traditional price of a quarto was sixpence; the Folio upon publication probably cost a pound. (A schoolmaster in 1621 might earn only £10 a year—which was at the very top of the pay scales for London workmen.)[132]

The paper itself was hand-made, and different stocks of paper are identifiable by means of their watermarks and chain-lines.[133] Partly on the basis of such evidence, Pollard, Greg, and others were able to determine earlier this century that several seventeenth-century quarto editions were misdated.[134] An edition dated '1600' on its title-page contains a watermark dated '1608'; in another, the '1608' of the title-page is contradicted by a watermark dated '1613' (or '1617', or '1619').[135]

Partly by the study of paper, it has also been possible to demonstrate that the second issue of the quarto of *2 Henry IV* was set and printed almost immediately after the first.[136] This demonstration in turn makes it necessary to explain why the scene added by the second issue (3.1/Sc. 8) had been omitted in the first issue. The study of printing alone does not solve that problem, but it defines the terms which any solution must satisfy. The study of dramatic manuscripts suggests, in turn, that the scene would have been omitted most easily if it were a late authorial addition to the foul papers, written on both sides of an interleaved sheet of paper: the compositor might well have failed to notice the proper point for its intended insertion, and so when he came upon the interleaved sheet failed to set its contents. (See

21. (*facing*) The original setting of sig. xx6ᵛ of the 1623 Folio, a page of *Antony and Cleopatra*, marked for stop-press correction by the proof-reader.

Illustration 22.) A purely bibliographical problem (the date of the second issue), solvable by bibliographical evidence (the identification of paper), by such reasoning opens a window on a feature of Shakespeare's foul papers, and hence of his processes of composition. The textual critic may then notice that the second edition of *2 Henry IV*—that printed in the Folio—contains several long passages not present in the first, and that these passages are related in theme and content to the scene apparently interleaved in the foul papers. The seeming coherence of these facts may be a delusion, of course, but all textual criticism—all literary criticism, all human hypotheses—proceeds by creating narrative plots which link and relate certain fixed points. The plot inevitably suggested by these fixed points has Shakespeare finishing a first draft of the play, deciding that certain aspects of the story need further development, adding as a consequence a new scene on an interleaved sheet, and then preparing a fair copy in which those features are further developed by related expansions. In other words, the study of paper leads to an explanation for the vexed textual problems of *2 Henry IV*, an explanation which links 'intra-text' revision to 'inter-text' revisions, as part of a continuous process of authorial shaping.

The second issue of the 1600 edition of *2 Henry IV* might be described as a second edition of one sheet, bound with copies of the first edition of the other sheets. The new sheet (leaves E3-6) is itself of mixed authority, consisting as it does of a mere reprint of the original half-sheet E3-4 into which is inserted an entirely new text of one scene taken from a manuscript authority. The canon of substantive editions of Shakespeare's plays contains a number of texts of such mixed parentage. The 1608 quarto of *Richard II* (Q4) is for the most part a mere reprint of a reprint of a reprint, but it also publishes for the first time a text of one passage—the 'abdication episode' (4.1.145-308/1977-2140)—which had been omitted from previous editions because of censorship. The text of that episode which it prints apparently results from memorial reconstruction, but that text is nevertheless substantive, because the printer must have had access to a manuscript of some sort. The second editions of both *Romeo and Juliet* and *Hamlet* are printed

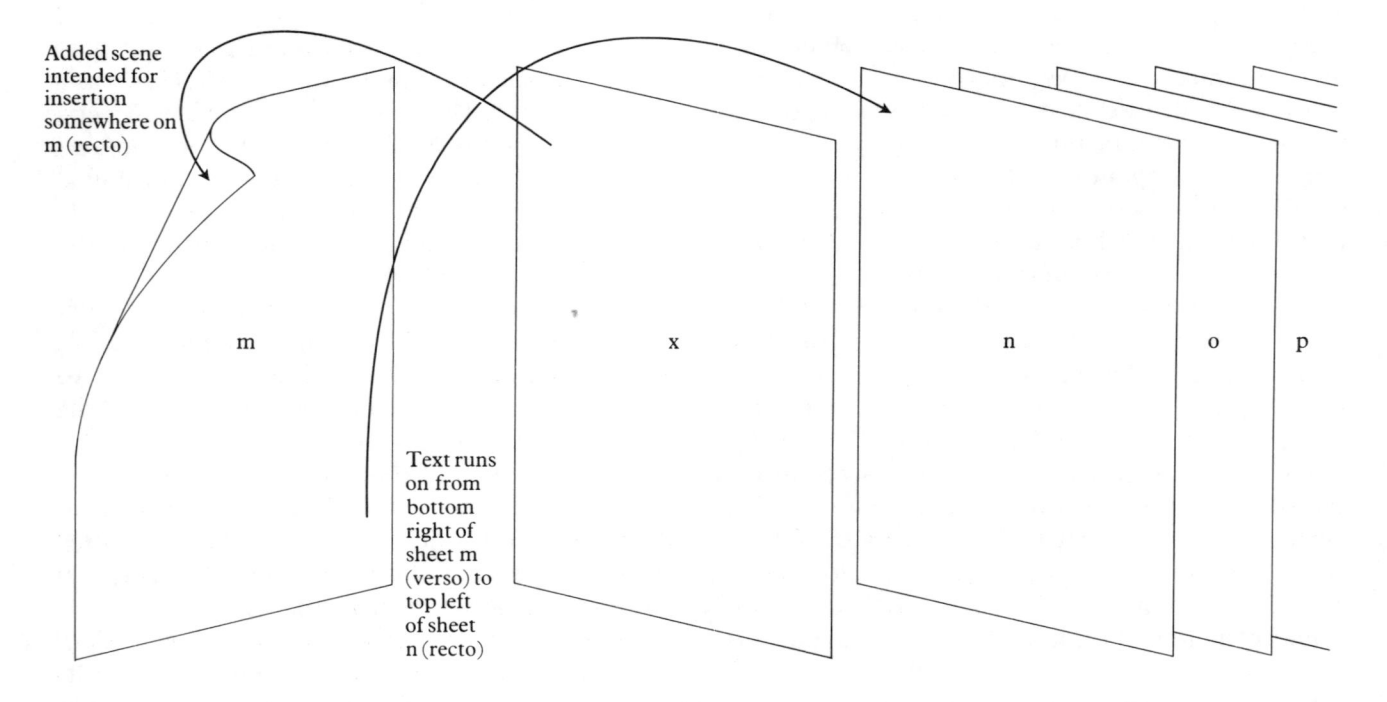

22. A conjectural reconstruction of a portion of the foul papers of *2 Henry IV*. If the added extra sheet X contained revised material which should have been inserted on the recto of sheet M, the compositor could easily have failed to discover X until he reached the bottom of the verso of sheet M; he would then conclude that X was out of place, and continue setting at the top of sheet N. By this process 3.1/Sc.8 could have been omitted in the first issue of the 1600 Quarto.

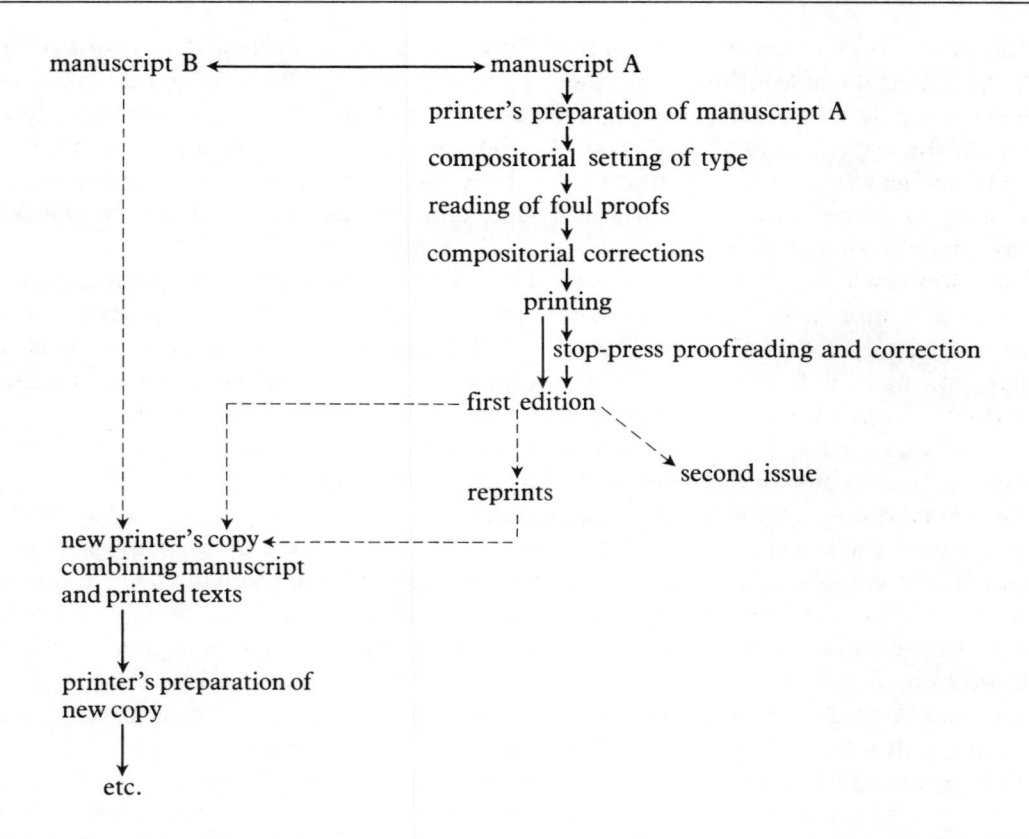

```
manuscript B ←─────────────→ manuscript A
         │                        │
         │                        ↓
         │           printer's preparation of manuscript A
         │                        ↓
         │             compositorial setting of type
         │                        ↓
         │               reading of foul proofs
         │                        ↓
         │              compositorial corrections
         │                        ↓
         │                     printing
         │                        ↓
         │           stop-press proofreading and correction
         │              ↓         ↓
         │     ┌────────── first edition ╲
         │     │               ↓            ╲
         │     │                              ↘ second issue
         │     │            reprints
         ↓     ↓
   new printer's copy ←─────────────┘
   combining manuscript
   and printed texts
         │
         ↓
   printer's preparation of
   new copy
         │
         ↓
        etc.
```

23. The permutations of printed editions. This summary illustrates only features which occur in the Shakespeare corpus. All texts go through the stages from manuscript to first edition; second issues, reprints, and new editions of mixed authority are optional.

for the most part from authoritative manuscripts, but both in certain respects clearly derive from an earlier edition.

But most such texts of mixed authority occur in the Folio. Eleven plays in the collection were printed from annotated copies of an earlier printed text. The degree of annotation varies considerably. The four reprinted comedies—*Much Ado*, *LLL*, *Midsummer Night's Dream*, and *Merchant*—were reprinted with little change except to stage directions and speech-prefixes. Because such features would have been placed in the margins of a theatrical manuscript, they would be easiest for a scribe to check against a printed text. In *Richard II*, the manuscript was more thoroughly compared with a printed text, so that dialogue readings were sporadically altered, in addition to the systematic alteration of stage directions and speech-prefixes. This policy continued in *1 Henry IV*, and reached a peak in *Richard III*, where both dialogue and stage directions were systematically collated, and the degree of annotation involved was enormous, necessitating the use of two different printed texts in order to provide the base on which corrections could be made. *Romeo* was little changed, and in *Titus* corrections were almost entirely restricted to stage directions, speech-prefixes, and the addition of a single extra scene. The same procedure was originally envisaged for *Troilus*, but the plans for this play had to be abandoned; when it was finally set into type—after the Folio preliminaries (left to the end, as usual) had already been printed—the quarto the editors had chosen to reprint had been extensively annotated by reference to a manuscript. Such collation seems also to have been undertaken for *King Lear*. Noticeably, all of the plays reprinted with minimal alteration were either in the copyright of members of the syndicate which published the Folio, or the copyright was derelict; by contrast, the syndicate did not own the copyright to any of the five texts which were more extensively annotated. Three of the five—*Richard II*, *1 Henry IV*, and *Richard III*—were in the copyright of Matthew Law (the only works in the volume which he could claim); *Lear* was the sole item held by Nathaniel Butter; and the change of plans for *Troilus* has been widely attributed to problems with the copyright held by Richard Bonian and Henry Walley. It appears that the decision whether or not to heavily annotate a reprint depended on whether such a cumbersome labour was necessary in order to circumvent the copyright of some other publisher.[137] We may be thankful that the syndicate was driven to such subterfuges.

An earlier edition was often directly used as the copy (annotated extensively, minimally, or not at all) from which a new edition was printed; in such cases a modern textual critic at least knows what to expect. More disturbing, because less predictable, is the occasional consultation of an earlier edition when setting primarily from manuscript. Although the first quartos of *Romeo and Juliet* and *Hamlet* were only directly used as copy for the second quartos in a small proportion of the text, the earlier quarto was undoubtedly available in the shop where the new quarto was being printed, and it seems clear that compositors occasionally consulted it when baffled by the manuscript. In such circumstances *any* reading shared by the two editions *might* result from contamination of the second by the first—a prospect made especially worrying by the fact that the first edition was in each case based upon memorial reconstruction. In the Folio such sporadic consultation demonstrably or probably took place in *Henry V*, *Contention*, and *Richard Duke of York*; in each case, the earlier edition consulted was a derivative reprint of a memorial reconstruction. Consultation is also likely to have affected the Folio text of *Hamlet*—creating an unfortunate situation in which the second edition is haphazardly contaminated by the first, and the Folio haphazardly contaminated by a reprint of the second. Such procedures may have simplified the task of a Renaissance compositor, but they do not make the task of a modern editor any easier.

Printed editions not only influenced the preparation of other printed editions; they also influenced the preparation of some manuscripts. We know, for instance, that theatrical companies sometimes used available editions as prompt-books.[138] Shakespeare's company, which already had the manuscript prompt-book, would not normally have needed a printed text for such purposes. But if one of their manuscripts became for any reason defective, it might well be patched by recourse to an edition; this apparently happened to the prompt-book of *Richard II*, one passage of which seems to have been copied, at some date, from the 1615 quarto edition. In such cases, the impact of a printed text upon a manuscript one can be precisely delimited. But at other times scribes could, like compositors, use a printed edition as a crib to help them decipher a manuscript; the scribe who prepared the manuscript from which the Folio text of *2 Henry IV* was printed may have used a copy of the 1600 quarto in this way. Finally, an author sometimes uses an existing edition as the base on which to undertake a later revision (as Montaigne did with his *Essais*); Shakespeare apparently began reworking *King Lear* on a copy of the 1608 quarto. The permutations of print can be as complicated, and as bewildering, as those of manuscript (see Illustration 23).

After 1623

The Folio was entered in the Stationers' Register on 8 November 1623; it was probably available in bookstalls by late November or early December. With its publication the substantive history of Shakespeare's dramatic texts virtually comes to an end. In 1634 *The Two Noble Kinsmen* was published for the first time in an authoritative quarto which attributed it (correctly, most modern scholars believe) to John Fletcher and William Shakespeare. Every other edition published after 1623 was derivative.

Manuscripts of many of Shakespeare's works must still have existed in 1623, but by the eighteenth century, when editors and antiquaries began to take an interest in acquiring such manuscripts, none was to be found. Shakespeare's last direct descendant, his granddaughter Elizabeth, died in 1670. She had been married to Thomas Nash in 1626 and, after his death, in 1649 to John (later Sir John) Bernard of Abington Manor in Northamptonshire.[139] Any of Shakespeare's private papers or books might have passed to Elizabeth from her parents, who had inherited most of Shakespeare's estate; in 1742 a tradition is recorded that she carried away with her from Stratford many of her grandfather's papers. Another, less plausible, anecdote, first reported in 1729, has them destroyed in the fire which burned down much of Warwick in 1694.[140]

Fire certainly played the part of chief villain in destroying the many manuscripts in Shakespeare's hand, or referring to him, which stayed behind in London. His play scripts no doubt remained in the possession of the King's Men until 1642, when the theatres were closed; at that time certain of the actors are said to have seized the company's apparel, hangings, and 'books', and to have converted them to their own use.[141] The value of manuscripts of plays already widely available in print would have been limited. Some manuscripts apparently survived into the Restoration; Davenant, for instance, clearly had access to a source of *Macbeth* in addition to the Folios. Probably some manuscripts perished in the Great Fire of 1666. A manuscript of *Cardenio* survived until late in the eighteenth century, presumably because the play had never been printed, which made the manuscript commercially valuable enough to preserve; it probably perished in a fire.[142] The papers of Sir George Buc, Master of the Revels from (effectively) c.1606 to 1622, were destroyed by fire according to Sir Henry Herbert, who succeeded him after a brief interregnum of a few months; most of Herbert's papers, too, are lost, presumed burnt.[143]

While the manuscripts went the way of all ash, printed texts went forth and multiplied. Quartos of the more popular plays and poems continued to be printed separately until the Restoration; thereafter some, like *Hamlet* and *Caesar*, were issued in so-called 'Players' Quartos', purporting to represent the text as acted by the Restoration companies. In 1632 a second edition of the Folio was published, based upon a copy of the 1623 edition which had been 'corrected' by an unknown editor who knew Latin and French, and who displayed a special sensitivity to metre, grammar, and stage directions.[144] In 1663 a third edition appeared, with a second issue (in 1664) which added *Pericles* and six apocryphal plays: *The London Prodigal*, *Thomas Lord Cromwell*, *Sir John Oldcastle*, *The Puritan*, *A Yorkshire Tragedy*, and *Locrine*. A fourth folio was published in 1685. These derivative seventeenth-century folios were used—as quartos had once been—to prepare prompt-books for theatrical companies which lacked access to Shakespeare's manuscripts. Some of these early prompt-books survive, and can be of interest as records of early revivals, but have no textual authority.[145] The later folios occasionally, by guesswork, correct the text, but more often they corrupt it, and these corruptions often survived unnoticed well into the eighteenth century.

A proper history of the editing of Shakespeare from 1709 to 1790 would encompass much of the literary and intellectual history of England in the eighteenth century. Even a list of dramatis personae—Jacob Tonson, Nicholas Rowe, Alexander Pope, Lewis Theobald, William Warburton (who became the Bishop of Gloucester), Samuel Johnson, Edward Capell, George Steevens, Edmond Malone, James Boswell the younger—establishes the importance which the English literary Enlightenment attached to the editing of Shakespeare. The conception of his canon formed by their collaborative shaping remains—to a remarkable degree, by turns exhilarating and depressing—the conception still current today. Two of the four great collections of primary Shakespearian documents—at the Bodleian (Oxford) and Trinity College (Cambridge)—are based chiefly upon the private collections of Malone and Capell respectively; a third, that of the British Library (London), has its origin in David Garrick's concern with Shakespeare's text. Only the Folger Library (Washington) has been similarly shaped by the obsessions of a single subsequent collector. The mental and physical geography of modern Shakespeare scholarship was formed in the eighteenth century.

The editing of Shakespeare began with the publication of the first editions of his work in the 1590s, but literary historians usually regard Nicholas Rowe as Shakespeare's first editor, perhaps because he is the first we can confidently name.[146] Rowe was himself a playwright, best known for his *Fair Penitent* (an adaptation of *The Fatal Dowry*, by Philip Massinger and Nathan Field) and *Jane Shore* (written 'in imitation of Shakespeare's style'). The editorial virtues of his text derive in large part from his theatrical background. He provided dramatis personae lists and act divisions for all the plays not so adorned in the Folio, and he systematically supplied most of the entrances and exits required by the dialogue but omitted from the Folio text. He also modernized the spelling, punctuation, and grammar as he saw fit—as, indeed, did all editions in the seventeenth and eighteenth centuries. Textually, the 1709 edition was a reprint of the 1685 folio, transferred to a more manageable multi-volume quarto format. Rowe made almost no use of the 1623 Folio, or of the early substantive quartos, though he was aware of the existence of at least some of them. He reproduced, or conjecturally emended, many derivative readings contained in the fourth folio. But, being a poet himself, he did successfully eliminate most of the problems of mislineation in the Folio, and he did restore sense to many passages by means of obvious emendations. Making use in large part of theatrical contacts, he also added an invaluable introduction, containing the first extended biography of Shakespeare.

Alexander Pope was not only a better poet than Rowe, but also a better editor. He excluded from the canon all the apocryphal plays added in 1664, and made extensive use of the early quartos.[147] He also, as a poet, further corrected the lineation of the seventeenth-century texts: Rowe and Pope between them are responsible for most of the relineation accepted by all modern editors. But Pope's gifts as a poet were also the cause of his undoing as an editor, for he assumed that Shakespeare shared the dominant aesthetic principles of the eighteenth century, and that apparent departures from those principles in the early texts must therefore result from corruption by scribes or printers; despite his claim that he had carried out 'the dull duty of an Editor . . . with a religious abhorrence of all Innovation', he made hundreds of emendations to restore decorum. Many of these emendations are sensible, but most result from a misunderstanding of the pronunciation, metrical principles, and stylistic decorums of Shakespeare's period. As a result, Pope became the first of Shakespeare's editors to learn from experience that success in conjectural emendation will be taken for granted, and failure unforgivingly taken to task. Three years after the publication of his edition, he became the target of a relentless, sarcastic, often scholarly and accurate attack by Lewis Theobald, whose *Shakespeare Restored* (1728) was the first book entirely devoted to the textual problems of the Shakespeare canon—but also, more practically, a successful bid to nominate himself as the man best equipped to replace Pope's edition. Pope counter-attacked with *The Dunciad*. It might reasonably be maintained that, if the history of the editing of Shakespeare had contributed nothing to our understanding of Shakespeare himself, it would still be justified by the mere fact that it stimulated the composition of so brilliant a poem. Nevertheless, though Pope wrote the more permanent and memorable polemic, he lost the argument: Theobald was the better scholar, and indeed remains one of the finest editors of the last three centuries. His collection of early quartos was larger than Pope's, his knowledge of Shakespeare's period wider, his enthusiasm for the task greater, his aesthetic preconceptions less obviously anachronistic.[148] Of his contemporaries, only 'the learned and ingenious' Dr Styan Thirlby, of Jesus College, Cambridge, could match his understanding of Shakespeare and of the nature of editing; but Thirlby never completed an edition, and consequently exerted only a dislocated subterranean influence upon the editorial tradition, as his orphaned conjectures were adopted (often without acknowledgement) by others.[149]

Hanmer's edition (1744), the first published at Oxford, was one of the worst in the eighteenth century, despite its elegant bindings, fine typography, and original illustrations: 'very pretty volumes, Mr Hanmer; but you must not call it Shakespeare'. Warburton had contributed many conjectures to Theobald's edition, and Theobald had adopted the best of them; Warburton's own edition (1747) does nothing more than publish the detritus, and Warburton's reputation as an editor would be greater if he had never published a text of his own. But his edition did the world the service of provoking Thomas Edwards to publish *The Canons of Criticism* (1748), another abusive but just polemic on the editing of Shakespeare. Edwards's first two Canons of Criticism should perhaps be prominently displayed, like a Government health warning, on the front of all works of textual criticism:

I. A Professed Critic has a right to declare that his Author *wrote* whatever He thinks he *ought* to have written, with as much positiveness as if He had been at his Elbow.

II. He has a right to alter any passage which He does not understand.

Dr Johnson's edition (1765), the first to be published after Edwards's celebrated exposure of Warburton, refrains from too much positiveness. It contains many judicious notes, which draw upon the linguistic knowledge Johnson accumulated in compiling his *Dictionary*, and upon his own considerable common sense; but its text does not mark any very noticeable advance on previous editions. The famous Preface is the best thing in it.[150]

All these editions share certain weaknesses. To begin with, each is a modified reprint of its immediate predecessor.[151] This practice perpetuates error; worse, it perpetuates assumptions. Each of these editions is a descendant, more or less modified, of the 1685 reprint of the 1623 collection: the tyranny of the First Folio, first established in the seventeenth century by the quantitative and qualitative decline in quartos after its publication, was continued and confirmed by the intellectual imprimatur of a succession of eighteenth-century editors. None of these editors knew much about the circumstances of performance or the mechanics of textual transmission in Shakespeare's time; none had a coherent textual theory; what theory did govern their practice was borrowed from the very different models applicable to the editing of classical texts. Moreover, because the first editors knew least, and because each editor worked from the text of his immediate antecedent, much of the time and energy of subsequent editors was devoted to abusing their predecessors. The rhythms of polemic ensured that more attention was paid to eighteenth-century editions than to those from the Elizabethan and Jacobean period. The editing of Shakespeare became ingrown before it had even grown up.

Edward Capell escaped from at least one of the intellectual prisons built for itself by the editorial tradition:[152] he did not simply reprint an earlier eighteenth-century text, or even revert simply to the First Folio itself, but meticulously transcribed by hand the early substantive quartos, and (where available) made them the basis for his own text. His text (1768) was the first collected edition ever published based upon the earliest authoritative documents. This edition should have been hailed as a revolutionary achievement; instead it was pilloried as a pedantic eccentricity. Subsequent editors stole from it silently while abusing it shamelessly. But Capell escaped from the tyranny of the Folio only by seeking to establish, in its place, an alternative tyranny, in which the quartos were to be worshipped, and the Folio condemned wherever possible.

Johnson's edition was revised by Steevens (1778), whose chief innovation was to indent the second half of a verse line shared by two speakers, in order to indicate the metrical structure visually.[153] But, by one of the recurrent curiosities of intellectual history, Steevens's edition was again less important than the reaction it provoked. Edwards's *Canons of Criticism* professed to be 'A Supplement to Mr. Warburton's edition of Shakespear'; Edmond Malone in 1780 published, with Steevens's blessing, *A Supplement to the Last Edition of Shakespeare*. This two-volume supplement contributed more to the understanding of Shakespeare than the ten volumes of the Johnson–Steevens edition. Malone's own edition, published a decade later, synthesized, climaxed, and canonized the eighteenth-century tradition. Malone's life has never been properly written, but he was one of the greatest intellectuals of the English Enlightenment, the most talented and influential of all scholars to have dedicated his energies to the explication of Shakespeare's life and work.[154] Unlike Rowe, Pope, Theobald, and Johnson, Malone was not a poet (major or minor); nor was he, like Warburton, a theologian, devoted to the propagation of eternal verities. Malone, like Capell, was an historian. But Malone's range as an historian was greater than Capell's: Capell is chiefly remarkable as an historian of texts, where Malone perceived that the history of those texts could not be properly understood outside the encompassing history of the author, the institutions in which he worked, the times which shaped him and which he helped to shape.

In the nineteenth century, editions proliferated, freed from the restraints of copyright, feeding the demand created by increasing literacy and education. Many of these editions made minor contributions to the text, by conjectural emendations accepted and recorded by subsequent editors, or by explications of obscure passages accepted silently by subsequent editors. But few are of major intellectual importance. Boswell's edition, though published in 1821, may legitimately be regarded as the last of the eighteenth-century editions, for its chief importance derives from the inclusion of material Malone had left unpublished at the time of his death. Moreover, like all the other eighteenth-century editions except Capell's, Boswell's is a variorum edition, recording the comments of previous editors (except Capell, who continues to be paid the compliment of silent expropriation); much of the eighteenth century's editorial legacy is entombed in its twenty-one volumes. Malone's 1790 text was piously reproduced by other editors for half a century, until its hegemony was broken by the innovative first editions of Knight (1838-43) and Collier (1842-4). In the next decade the German critic Tycho Mommsen—younger brother of the great classicist Theodor Mommsen—published studies of *Hamlet*, *Romeo and Juliet*, and *Pericles* which in textual sophistication surpassed the work of any English editor of the Victorian period.[155] Indeed, German critics (Schlegel, Tieck, Gervinus) and scholars (Delius, Schmidt) were for much of the century more rigorous and original than their English cousins.

But the most important nineteenth-century edition, perhaps the most important edition in the post-Folio era, was the Cambridge edition, published in nine volumes in 1863-6, edited by W. G. Clark, W. A. Wright, and J. Glover. In 1864 its text was also published in a single-volume, popular format, without textual collations, known as the Globe edition. In 1948 the American publisher Harcourt, Brace and Company conducted a poll of professors of English to determine whether to reprint the familiar Globe text or to print a new text based upon the latest scholarship; the octogenarian text won a landslide victory.[156] The most esteemed and influential British edition of the twentieth century, edited by Peter Alexander and published in 1951, retained the line numbering of the Globe edition (at considerable cost to coherence). For ninety years after its publication, most works of criticism and reference were keyed to the Cambridge text or its Globe alter ego.

The Cambridge edition owes its influence in part to its own scholarly virtues. It was the first edition to provide collations of the readings in all known sixteenth- and seventeenth-century editions of the plays and poems, and by means of such collations to establish (with a few exceptions) which editions were derivative and which substantive. It also recorded the conjectures and emendations accumulated in the century and a half since 1709. For its collations alone the Cambridge edition deserved the acclaim it garnered. In that respect the edition's contribution to our collective understanding of Shakespeare's texts was both fundamental and permanent.

Capell's contribution had also been fundamental and permanent, but it never received the reward it had earned. In fact, the reasons for the immediate and sustained influence of the Cambridge edition are as much sociological as logical, as much rhetorical as real. The Cambridge edition, as its cognomen declares, was the first academic edition of Shakespeare. Shakespeare had until then been edited by poets, barristers, aristocrats, clerics, journalists: in a word, amateurs. With the Cambridge edition the professed professionals took over, announcing that Shakespeare was a fit subject for professional academic research. The Cambridge edition, prepared by three fellows of Trinity College, was nourished by and in turn nurtured the intellectual imperialism of the Universities throughout the Victorian period.[157] Moreover, the Cambridge editors recorded variants and conjectures, but, unlike their predecessors, did not explain why they chose one reading and rejected others. Like the tablets brought down from the mountain, the text of Shakespeare came down from Cambridge, and the world was invited to accept its authority. Readers may criticize the logic or challenge the evidence of an explanation; if you offer none, your explanation can never be refuted. Nor can you give offence to living scholars who favour the reading you reject: silence may obscure, but it will seldom insult. The eighteenth-century variorum tradition had left textual criticism open to the scrutiny of any reader; the Cambridge editors distanced themselves from the traditions of editorial polemic, so seeming to stand above petty squabbling, and to arbitrate upon it from a position of omniscient objectivity and tolerant wisdom. The Globe text intended for the general public did not even provide collations. In this strategic reticence about editorial procedures they applied to Shakespeare norms already established in nineteenth-century editions of the classics, particularly by the great and influential German textual critic Karl Lachmann (1793-1851). Textual criticism became, as it has largely remained, a private club. As a result, as Housman complained of textual criticism generally, 'error and folly are subject to very little correction from outside'.

GENERAL INTRODUCTION

The domination of Trinity College continued into the twentieth century. In the 1890s two Trinity undergraduates, R. B. McKerrow and W. W. Greg, plotted a revolution in the editing of English Renaissance texts, and then for the first half of the twentieth century proceeded to put their undergraduate ambitions into practice.[158] W. A. Wright, the last surviving editor of the Cambridge triumvirate, was instrumental in having Greg appointed as Trinity College Librarian in 1907. Greg never attempted to edit Shakespeare; McKerrow died before he could publish even the first volume of the edition to which he devoted the last decade of his life. Like T. S. Eliot's critical preoccupation with Shakespeare's contemporaries, the life work of Greg, McKerrow, and the lesser luminaries of the 'new bibliography' was a flanking movement so vast that it never succeeded in turning the enemy's flank. In both cases, the real object of interest and attention was Shakespeare (his style, or his text); but Shakespeare was too formidable a problem to be tackled directly, and could only be approached through a comprehensive mastering of his context. For Greg and McKerrow the required context was the transmission of manuscripts and the printing of books in the century before the Restoration. Meanwhile, in another part of the forest, the compilers of the Oxford English Dictionary in one stroke rendered obsolete most of the philological commentary accumulated in two centuries of Shakespeare editions, by setting Shakespeare for the first time in the vast linguistic context of the English of his era. For the first half of the twentieth century British scholars dominated and revolutionized the study of Shakespeare; but in the post-war period, in scholarship as in politics, British hegemony waned. Hinman and Bowers, both from the United States, succeeded McKerrow and Greg.[159] The sweep of textual criticism narrowed to a preoccupation with technical problems, but at the same time bibliographers escaped from their previous exclusive concern with Renaissance plays to consider the implications for theory and practice of the evidence from other periods and genres.

In so summary a survey of editorial history justice cannot be done to the achievements of individual editors, and it would be ungenerous to haul up for public ridicule examples of individual failure. In a given period—our own as much as any other—the range of options open to editors will be limited by the intellectual, economic, and social conditions in which they work. Eighteenth-century editors had to create from scratch a new historical discipline; the period is characterized by a steady accumulation of knowledge about the past, to which every major edition contributed, to a greater or lesser degree. Every edition is judged, and found wanting, by the very standard of achieved knowledge which it helped to create. In the nineteenth century, editions multiplied rapidly but the pace of intellectual progress slowed. Interest in Shakespeare actually grew, but the focus of that interest shifted from editorial to critical and biographical issues. Where advances were made in knowledge of the texts, the new details were simply slotted into an intellectual framework inherited from the eighteenth century. The Cambridge edition owed much of its authority to the fact that it did not in any way disturb the assumptions of its readership. Although the received text had been altered in hundreds of readings, the structure remained consistently familiar. This pattern has persisted into the twentieth century. The thorough reconsideration of minutiae assures readers of the conscientious accuracy and scrupulousness of a new edition; at the same time, the perpetuation of all matters of substance, structure, and critical significance asserts the essential identity of the new edition and the old, which strengthens confidence in both.

The twentieth century has been characterized by an explosion of information relevant to the editing of texts, and by a fundamental revision of the intellectual frameworks which govern editorial thought. But these developments have not been matched by correspondingly radical changes in the character of editions themselves. Although individual modern editions have improved in detail, as a whole the editing of Shakespeare in this century has failed to come to terms with the legacy of the previous century: the unstoppable, burgeoning multiplicity of editions. Many of these editions make no original contribution to the investigation of textual problems; even Variorum editors have systematically ignored them. Yet this invisible army of undistinguished popular editions has for almost two centuries exercised an inestimable influence by institutionalizing Shakespeare's texts in fixed and unquestioned versions. As editions multiplied, each became less important, and all became more alike. Notoriously, excess of supply causes a decline in unit value, and the multiplicity of Shakespeare editions has led to a general intellectual devaluation of any individual edition. The sheer mass of available and similar editions, most of them intended to serve a common educational purpose, has created a strong psychological pressure towards conformity. To the weight of this cumulative tradition succeeding editors succumb and in turn contribute. Moreover, new editions continue to be generated, as in the eighteenth century, by marking up and modifying the text of a recent predecessor. Even justly admired editors like Peter Alexander and G. B. Evans—editors to whom, as our collations show, we are often indebted—have perpetuated this practice.

As the twentieth century has progressed, a tension has become increasingly apparent between editorial theory and practice. While agreeing on the need for reliable old-spelling texts, editors have continued to clone modern-spelling ones; while agreeing that particular act or scene numbers are mistaken, they continue to use them. A lack of confidence is visible in both publishers and editors. Publishers wish to maximize their share of the market by printing editions which will appeal to the largest number of readers, and hence hesitate to risk offending some readers by tampering with the product. Most editors are employed primarily as teachers and literary critics, expected to edit Shakespeare in their spare time, and lack the confidence, in face of the growing technicality of bibliographical studies, to put new ideas into practice.

Proliferation of editions has been matched by an increase in the number of works of criticism and reference which must be keyed to editions. The Cambridge-Globe edition sustained its pre-eminence for so long largely because of its value as a fixed point of reference. The Cambridge editors for the first time numbered every line of the text of Shakespeare (as they defined it). Shakespearians need a way of referring to specific places in the canon in such a way that other Shakespearians will be able to locate the passage in question. As editions multiply—all with different numbers of lines, based upon the twin determinants of editorial decisions about the text and printers' decisions about typeface and page-size—the availability of a single agreed standard of universal reference becomes all the more important. If new editions cannot simply reproduce this standard of reference, they can at least try not to alter the text fundamentally, for such changes would reduce the ability of readers using the (new) text to apply it to the (old) system of reference. The more texts and the more critics, the greater the imperative of interchangeability of reference. Errors in the text of Shakespeare are thus preserved in order not to disturb scholarly convenience and convention. The tail wags the dog.

The need for and absence of a reliable old-spelling edition has haunted editors of Shakespeare for half a century. Greg, for instance, could refer to the modernizing of 'vild' to 'vile' as 'sheer perversion'.[160] In order to palliate their sense of guilt about continuing to produce the modernized texts which publishers want to publish, some editors have modernized the text grudgingly and half-heartedly, producing hybrids of Renaissance and modern orthography which satisfy the needs neither of scholars nor of common readers. However much we admire the proponents and accomplishments of the 'new bibliography', we must also recognize that the movement had some unfortunate side-effects, including a schizophrenic attitude towards modernization and an increasing dissociation of bibliographical research from practical editing. Greg insisted, rightly, that an editor must understand the basic circumstances of transmission before a text can be properly edited. But at some point, having determined these circumstances, the editor must still sit down and edit the text, and familiarity with the process of transmission will not solve all editorial problems.

Earlier editors devoted their labours almost exclusively to problems of emendation, with scant regard to the circumstances of transmission; modern textual critics have, for the most part, simply reversed the prejudice. Like so much else, this practice begins with the Cambridge edition. W. A. Wright decreed that 'Vanity and Ignorance are the fruitful parents of conjectural emendation'. Vanity and ignorance are indeed fruitful parents, but conjectural emendations are not their only children; conjectural glosses and conjectural conservatism can also often be traced to their loins. Wright himself did not believe his own edict, for he and his colleagues—like all other editors of Shakespeare—accepted many conjectural emendations. But with very few (and insignificant) exceptions, the conjectures which the Cambridge editors accepted were the conjectures of other people, not their own. Logically, someone else's old conjecture is no more authoritative than your own new conjecture; but a choice between pre-existing conjectures can, in the format of textual collation, appear indistinguishable from a choice between variant documentary readings. Editors in this way promulgate the notion that editing is no more than a matter of judicious *selection*; they obscure the fact that it also depends upon judicious *invention*. The intellectual authority of the Cambridge edition derived in part from its being so barren of new pride. This Victorian repression of the need for and the fact of editorial fertility has been perpetuated by the finest textual critics of our age. Bibliography aspires to the status of a science; at the least it can claim to be an archaeology of texts. Emendation is, by contrast, all too obviously an art—an art for which the despised poet-editors of the eighteenth century might have been rather better equipped, in some respects, than their sophisticated academic twentieth-century successors. Perhaps for this reason, the twentieth century has produced little fruitful discussion of the theory and practice of emendation in Shakespeare's text.

Greg's British Academy lecture on 'Principles of Emendation in Shakespeare', for instance, confines itself to the sound but minimal proposition that all emendation must be governed by a knowledge of the circumstances of transmission.[161] A natural corollary of this postulate is that some texts in the Shakespeare canon will require more emendation than others. Yet editors almost invariably divide into those (like McKerrow) who in practice always emend sparsely and those (like Alice Walker) who in practice always emend generously. Though in neither case will the reasoning behind particular choices be discredited, the practice of emendation in either case must have more to do with the emendation-threshold of the individual editor than with the corruption-quotient of the individual text. If a translator rendered Herodotus and Thucydides, or Aeschylus and Euripides, so that they sounded stylistically indistinguishable, we should be certain that one author or the other was being misrepresented; we can be equally certain that editors who are conjecture-happy or emendation-shy in all circumstances are doing an injustice to half the texts they edit. Some plays in the Oxford edition—*Hamlet* and *Othello*, for instance—are edited more conservatively than usual; others—like *Pericles*—are edited less conservatively than usual; in each case the frequency and kind of emendation reflects our understanding of the text's transmission. Of course the Oxford editors are not immune from individual prejudice towards conservative or liberal emendation, but we hope that the collaborative nature of the edition will have acted as a check on such prejudice.

Just as different kinds of text require different policies of emendation, so different kinds of error occur in every text. Most editors are either constitutionally interventionist or constitutionally non-interventionist; likewise most of them favour particular forms of intervention, and neglect others. Housman observed that classical editors prefer whenever possible to postulate palaeographical error, and a similar fondness for misreading can be discerned in most modern editions of Shakespeare. This predisposition was actively encouraged by the laudable efforts of the 'new bibliography' to establish the characteristics of different Elizabethan and Jacobean hands. But—as Hinman, among others, often insisted—scribes and compositors also commit other sorts of error.[162] 'An emendator with one method is as foolish a sight as a doctor with one drug.'[163] Most modern editors have, nevertheless, remained loath to accept substitution, transposition, interpolation, or (especially) omission as the explanation of a textual difficulty. On the evidence of their work in reprints, we would expect the Folio compositors to have omitted a few entire verse lines from every play, and we have no reason to suppose that the compositors who set Shakespeare's plays in quarto were any less fallible.[164] Such losses can seldom be repaired, but it seems reasonable to admit from time to time that a line has probably been lost, by marking a lacuna.

Words and phrases, too, can be omitted. Editorial reluctance to concede this possibility can often be related to the modern hesitation to make emendations which restore metrical regularity. Just as eighteenth-century editors sometimes anachronistically supposed that Shakespeare shared their own ideals of strict metrical decorum, so twentieth-century editors sometimes anachronistically suppose that Shakespeare shared their own ideals of metrical irregularity and rhythmical freedom. Our own practice has been based upon a study of metrical norms in individual texts, and governed by certain simple propositions about the logic of metrical emendation. For instance, the more often a metrical pattern or licence recurs in different texts, the less likely is it to result from corruption; conversely, corruption is more likely if a metrical anomaly coincides with difficulties of sense or syntax.[165] No doubt our application of these principles—as of all others—has been at times imperfect, but such failures of execution do not invalidate the general utility of the principles themselves, or the desirability of a coherent and articulated policy towards issues of metre.

Contemporary literary practice influences modern editing in more ways than in its attitude to metre. As many critics have observed (approvingly or disparagingly), twentieth-century literature has been characterized by difficulty, by conspicuous obscurity, by a conviction that complex worlds cannot be uttered in simple words. One might share this aesthetic without believing that it prevailed in all periods. Nevertheless, modern editors of Shakespeare have sometimes advocated readings or variants which presuppose that the playwright aspired to be unintelligible. This tendency has been abetted by a misunderstanding of the classical editorial preference for *difficilior lectio*, 'the more difficult reading'. In fact, even in classical practice, *difficilior* does not mean 'more difficult to understand', but only 'more difficult to explain as an error'. That principle was originally formulated by editors of biblical texts, and then applied to the literary works of antiquity; but Shakespeare's plays were transmitted in different conditions by different technologies. For Shakespeare—and 'modern national scriptures' generally—the more relevant rule is *praestat insolitior lectio*, 'prefer the rarer reading'. 'Rarer' does not mean 'occurring in fewer textual witnesses', but rather 'lexically more unusual, verbally less commonplace'.[166] Even this rule must be tempered by an awareness that revising authors sometimes deliberately replace an arcane word (like 'crants', in the second quarto of *Hamlet*, 5.1.226/3197) with a more comprehensible one (like 'Rites' in the Folio).

All propositions about the practice of emendation assume that emendation is itself a legitimate practice. That central assumption could be disputed. Philosophically, no emendation is logically defensible. It may be said that the text at a particular point does not make sense; but perhaps it was not meant to make sense; perhaps the character was meant to be mad, or incoherent; perhaps the passage has a private meaning; perhaps it has a meaning which would have been understood then though not now; perhaps its meaning is evident, even now, to some other reader. No emendation is 'necessary'; all emendations depend upon an individual assessment of probability and a subjective inference about intention.

In a famous passage in Harold Pinter's *The Homecoming*, Lenny the pimp memorably and at length describes his encounter with a woman who was 'falling apart with the pox'. At the end of his story, the listener asks, 'How did you know she was diseased?' Lenny answers, 'I decided she was.'[167] An editor, in emending, decides that a text is diseased; such decisions may be mistaken. But we know that every early printed edition of Shakespeare's plays is more or less diseased: every compositor and every scribe commits errors. Corruption somewhere is certain; where, is uncertain. We also know that Shakespeare's texts were composed on paper by an author before they were composed in type by a compositor. The lost manuscripts of Shakespeare's work are not the fiction of an idealist critic, but particular material objects which happen at a particular time to have existed, and at another particular time to have been lost, or to have ceased to exist. Emendation does not seek to construct an ideal text, but rather to restore certain features of a lost material object (that manuscript) by correcting certain apparent deficiencies in a second material object (this printed text) which purports to be a copy of the first. Most readers will find this procedure reasonable enough; those who do not would be best advised to read Shakespeare only in photographic facsimiles, or—preferably, from a materialist point of view—in the surviving copies of the original editions.[168]

Our own decisions about emendation are no more infallible than anyone else's. Moreover, our edition too, like any other, reflects the limitations and opportunities of a particular time and place. Unlike other modern editors, who have to squeeze time for research into a day already dense with obligations, we have been specifically employed by a major international publisher in order to complete the research necessary to prepare this edition. We have been provided with computers, with clerical help, with financial support for research expenses which seemed to us necessary. Despite the scale of investment involved, the publisher has not tried in any way to influence our editorial decisions. As editors we have been uniquely fortunate in receiving such support, and in being able to work as a team in the closest possible collaboration. Any virtues of the Oxford edition reflect the privileged circumstances of its editors, and no doubt other editors if blessed with such opportunities would have exploited them to equal or greater avail. But even in such circumstances, where fundamental research was not only made possible but actively encouraged, it would have been impossible to continue work until every problem in the Shakespeare canon had been resolved to our own and everyone else's satisfaction. We have learned from the misfortune of our predecessors, McKerrow and Walker, that an ambition to answer every question leads in practice to the answering of none, and that the pursuit of a definitive edition only results in an edition indefinitely postponed. We have therefore concentrated our finite resources—temporal, fiscal, and mental—upon certain jobs, and left other jobs undone. For instance, we have made no attempt systematically to collate, or recollate, early editions in order to identify press-variants. This is a fault, and one which we hope will be remedied by other scholars. We have not provided historical collations of seventeenth-century editions, or select collations of major editions since 1709, though such collations would no doubt be useful for certain purposes.[169] We have not undertaken collateral investigations of the practices of the printers of individual quarto editions, or new technical studies of the setting and manufacture of such quartos. We have laboured to be honest about what we have left undone, but other scholars will no doubt notice other opportunities and obligations which we could and ideally should have pursued, but did not. We have aimed, particularly, to consider afresh the whole process of modernizing spelling and punctuation; to explore in detail the textual consequences of the theatrical origins and intentions of the great bulk of Shakespeare's work; to determine the nature of the manuscript or printed copy which lies behind each substantive edition; to investigate the possibility of authorial revision; to begin a re-examination of the non-dramatic canon, and of manuscript sources generally; and to reconsider problems of collaboration in a few plays of disputed authorship.

If our circumstances have furnished unique opportunities, they have also created corresponding risks. The collaboration of four editors, many assistants, and (at different times) three different computers, has made the work possible; but it has also, no doubt, despite our best efforts, produced inconsistencies which might not have occurred in the work of a single editor. An exaggerated estimate of our own resources has occasionally tempted us to commence lines of enquiry which in the event we could not pursue to a satisfactory conclusion. An awareness of the Press's considerable investment of trust and money in our work has generated in us a corresponding sense of obligation to finish our work expeditiously, especially as publishing deadlines approached; the demands of urgency and adequacy are not always comfortably reconcilable.

Oxford University Press's willingness to publish our text in both old and modern spelling has spared us one onerous choice, but in other cases we have had to make decisions in which advantages cannot be disentangled from disadvantages. This *Textual Companion*, for instance, enables us to record and explain our editorial decisions in greater detail than would be possible if collation and text cohabited in a single volume; moreover, by opening both books it should be possible to make text and collations simultaneously available (which cannot be done when collations are placed at the back of a text and can only be reached by flipping back and forth). Yet we realize that many readers of the Oxford *Complete Works* may not buy the Oxford *Textual Companion*, and that as a consequence our edition will perpetuate the segregation of textual critics from common readers. Likewise, although we prepared a commentary for each text as it was edited, those commentaries have not been included in the initial publication of the text; this publishing procedure may serve the needs of different markets, but it will leave the editors' understanding of certain difficult passages unexplained to readers of the plain text. It may also suggest a belief—implied in some recent critical editions of Renaissance dramatists—that an editor can establish a reliable text without constructing a commentary. Our analytical presentation of the textual apparatus—separating substantives, incidentals, stage directions, and lineation into distinct categories—seems to us helpful and unambiguous in the great majority of cases, but it does make it more difficult to reconstruct the wholly unemended text of a given passage, and it does occasionally impose upon us uncertain decisions about classification (particularly in distinguishing substantive from incidental emendations). Any careful perusal of our Editorial Procedures will reveal other such options, where any decision about format and presentation will inevitably foreclose possibilities and secrete assumptions.

Whatever the value of our personal contribution, we hope at least that the Oxford edition may serve as a useful synthesis of the disparate work of many fine scholars over recent decades. A summing up before moving on. Such a synthesis in itself provokes and makes possible future progress, by identifying unsolved problems and undeveloped opportunities. A successful work of scholarship stimulates the very research which will make it obsolete, and, with our own task now behind us, we look forward to our future obsolescence.

GARY TAYLOR

---

[1] See Ludovico Ariosto, *Orlando Furioso*, trans. Sir John Harington (1591), ed. Robert McNulty (1972); W. W. Greg, 'An Elizabethan Printer and his Copy', in *Collected Papers* (1966), 95-109. Randall McLeod is engaged in a thorough examination of Field's treatment of the manuscript copy for both works.

[2] *Prolegomena for the Oxford Shakespeare: A Study in Editorial Method* (1939), 1.

[3] Charlton Hinman's Norton Facsimile (1968) of the First Folio; the Shakespeare Quarto Facsimiles edited by Greg (1939-58) and Hinman (1964-75).

[4] The quarto facsimiles prepared by Charles Praetorius, 1880-9; facsimiles of F1-4 published by Methuen, 1904-10 (see J. H. P. Pafford, 'The Methuen Facsimile, 1910, of the First Folio, 1623', *N&Q* 13 (1966), 126-7).

[5] John Dover Wilson's series of facsimiles of First Folio plays (1928-31); the Scolar Press facsimiles of Q1, Q2, and F1 *Hamlet* (1969).

[6] *Shakespeare's Poems: A Facsimile of the Earliest Editions*, ed. James M. Osborn, Louis L. Martz, and Eugene M. Waith (1964); *Shakespeare's Plays in Quarto: A Facsimile of Copies Primarily from the Henry E. Huntington Library*, ed. Michael J. B. Allen and Kenneth Muir (1981).

[7] Michael Warren's *The Complete King Lear* (forthcoming from the University of California Press).

[8] Preface to Shakespeare, 1765, in *Johnson on Shakespeare*, ed. Arthur Sherbo (1968: vols. vii and viii of the Yale edition of Johnson's *Works*), vii. 59-113, 108.

[9] For an account of the controversies (biased in Collier's favour) see Dewey Ganzel, *Fortune and Men's Eyes: The Career of John Payne Collier* (1982).

[10] S. Schoenbaum, *Shakespeare's Lives* (1970), 429-30, etc.

[11] *Henslowe's Diary*, ed. R. A. Foakes and R. T. Rickert (1961), fol. 43ᵛ, 3 December 1597, fol. 51ᵛ, 23 October 1598; *Henslowe Papers*, ed. Greg (1907), p. 57, 4 June 1601 (?) and p. 84, June 1613.

[12] *The Faithful Friends*, ed. G. M. Pinciss and G. R. Proudfoot, MSR (1975), ll. 2815-35.

[13] J. Q. Adams, 'The Author-Plot of an Early Seventeenth-Century Play', *The Library*, IV, 26 (1945), 17-27.

[14] Reproduced in Greg, *English Literary Autographs, 1550-1650* (1932), plate V.

[15] John Fletcher, *Bonduca*, ed. Greg, MSR (1931), ll. 2377-9.

[16] *Henslowe Papers*, Article 89, p. 78.

[17] See Felix Pryor, *John Webster: The Duke of Florence* (auction catalogue: Bloomsbury Book Auctions, 20 June 1986) for a description, transcript, and photographic reproduction of all four pages. Pryor's attribution of the manuscript to Webster, and his dating (c.1606-9), are speculative.

[18] Greg, *Folio*, 114-21. As Greg points out, an author would *substitute* an actor's name for a character's name; actors are also named in some prompt-books, but typically in added notes which create a *duplication*.

[19] See *Henry V*, ed. Taylor (1982), 17-18.

[20] Greg, *Two Elizabethan Stage Abridgements: 'The Battle of Alcazar' and 'Orlando Furioso'* (1922); the manuscript is reproduced—along with many others—in Greg's *Dramatic Documents from the Elizabethan Playhouses*, 2 vols. (1931).

[21] For a description of letter forms and confusabilia in such hands see R. B. McKerrow, *An Introduction to Bibliography for Literary Students* (1927), and W. S. B. Buck, *Examples of Handwriting, 1550-1650* (1973). Photographic reproductions of typical hands from the period are available in Greg, *English Literary Autographs*; Giles E. Dawson and Laetitia Kennedy-Skipton, *Elizabethan Handwriting 1500-1650: A Manual* (1966); and Anthony G. Petti, *English Literary Hands from Chaucer to Dryden* (1977).

[22] See *Shakespeare's Hand in the Play of Sir Thomas More*, ed. A. W. Pollard (1923); J. D. Wilson, *The Manuscript of Shakespeare's 'Hamlet' and the Problems of its Transmission*, 2 vols. (1934), i. 106-14; Giles Dawson, 'Theobald, *table/babbled*, and *Sir Thomas More*', in *TLS*, 22 April 1977, p. 484.

[23] See also Peter Alexander, 'Shakespeare's Punctuation', *Proceedings of the British Academy*, 31 (1945).

[24] For discussion of the Master of the Revels and his role in playhouse regulation, see Gerald Eades Bentley, *The Profession of Dramatist in Shakespeare's Time, 1590-1642* (1971), 145-96.

[25] Thomas Nashe, *Summer's Last Will and Testament*, in *Works*, iii. 290, ll. 1819-21: 'I pray you holde the booke well, we be not *non plus* in the latter end of the play'. Further

[25] references to prompting are conveniently gathered in G. E. Bentley, *The Profession of Player in Shakespeare's Time, 1590-1642* (1984), 80-6.

[26] On the function of the 'plat' see David Bradley, *The Ignorant Elizabethan Author and Massinger's 'Believe as You List'* (1977).

[27] For examples and discussion of 'plats' and 'parts' see Greg, *Dramatic Documents*. In the Restoration theatre 'parts' were called 'sides'. Scholars normally call the plats 'plots', but this creates considerable confusion with authorial plots.

[28] Greg, *Dramatic Documents*, and *Folio*, 141-2.

[29] See William B. Long, 'Stage-Directions: A Misinterpreted Factor in Determining Textual Provenance', *TEXT*, 2 (1985), 121-38.

[30] *The Captives*, ed. Arthur Brown, MSR (1953); *The Wasp*, ed. J. W. Lever, MSR (1976, for 1974). Neither manuscript contains a licence by the Master of the Revels, and scholars have accordingly been divided over whether they actually served as prompt-books; but they were certainly heavily worked over by a theatrical scribe.

[31] Bowers, 'The Texts and their Manuscripts', in *On Editing Shakespeare and the Elizabethan Dramatists* (1959), 3-32. See also our individual introductions to *Julius Caesar*, *As You Like It*, and *Twelfth Night*. Bowers's position develops a conjecture by Alice Walker, which was effectively dismissed by Greg (*Folio*, 168 and 467-8).

[32] See S. Schoenbaum, *William Shakespeare: A Documentary Life* (1975), 147-50, 154-5. Subsequent statements about Shakespeare's life and career may be presumed to derive from this biography.

[33] See *The Three Parnassus Plays*, ed. J. B. Leishman (1949), 247-8; Nathan Field, *A Woman is a Weathercock* (1612: BEPD 299), sig. A3; John Stephens, *Cynthia's Revenge or Menander's Ecstasy* (STC 23248; 1613), sig. A2ᵛ; George Wither, *The Scholar's Purgatory* (STC 25919; 1624), sig. I1ᵛ, p. 130; *Aubrey's Brief Lives*, ed. O. L. Dick (1949), 23.

[34] For the socialization of the text, see Jerome J. McGann, *A Critique of Modern Textual Criticism* (1983). In part McGann is reacting against the work of Fredson Bowers, and particularly against Bowers's interpretation and application of Greg's enormously influential article, 'The Rationale of Copy-Text' (*SB* 3 (1950), 19-36; reprinted in *Collected Papers*, ed. J. C. Maxwell (1966), 374-91); see in particular Bowers's article 'Greg's "Rationale of Copy-Text" Revisited', in *SB* 31 (1978), 90-161.

[35] Roslyn L. Knutson, '*Henslowe's Diary* and the Economics of Play Revision for Revival, 1592-1603', *Theatre Research International*, 10 (1985), 1-18.

[36] John Kerrigan, 'Revision, Adaptation, and the Fool in *King Lear*', in *Division*, 195-245.

[37] The most thorough survey is Janet Clare's 'Art made tongue-tied by authority: a study of the relationship between Elizabethan and Jacobean drama and authority and the effect of censorship on the plays of the period' (unpublished Ph.D. thesis, University of Birmingham, 1981). See also Chambers, *Stage*, i. 277-307 and ii. 318-28; Bentley, *Profession of Dramatist*, 145-96; *The Dramatic Records of Sir Henry Herbert*, ed. J. Q. Adams (1917); Mark Eccles, 'Sir George Buc, Master of the Revels', in *Thomas Lodge and other Elizabethans*, ed. C. J. Sisson (1933), 409-506.

[38] 3 Jac. I, c. 21 (reprinted in Chambers, *Stage*, iv. 338-9). For the effect of this act upon the Shakespeare canon see Taylor, 'Zounds'.

[39] See for instance Annabel Patterson, *Censorship and Interpretation* (1984).

[40] Wilfred T. Jewkes, *Act Division in Elizabethan and Jacobean Plays, 1583-1616* (1958); Taylor, 'Act Intervals'.

[41] See Aristophanes, *Clouds*, ed. K. J. Dover (1968), lxxx-xcviii; Euripides, *Hippolytos*, ed. W. S. Barrett (1964), 10-45.

[42] See R. L. Hunter, '*Eubulus*': *The Fragments* (1983), 146-7. For revision by other Roman authors—including Ovid, with whom Shakespeare has often been compared—see L. D. Reynolds and N. G. Wilson, *Scribes and Scholars: A Guide to the Transmission of Greek and Latin Literature*, second edition (1974), pp. 23, 194, 248.

[43] Molière, *Œuvres Complètes*, ed. Georges Coutin, 2 vols. (1971); Corneille, *Œuvres Complètes*, ed. Georges Coutin, 2 vols. (1980-4); Racine, *Œuvres Complètes*, ed. Raymond Picard, 2 vols. (1950-1); Pedro Calderón de la Barca, *En la Vida Todo es verdad y todo mentira*, ed. Don William Cruickshank (1971) and *The Prodigious Magician/El Mágico Prodigioso*, ed. and translated Bruce W. Wardropper (1982); Lope de Vega, *El Piadoso Aragonés*, ed. J. N. Greer (1951) and *La Desdichada Estefania*, ed. Hugh W. Kennedy (1975). See also Gay McAuley, 'The Spatial Dynamics of *Britannicus*: Text and Performance', *Australian Journal of French Studies*, 20 (1983), 340-60. In *Britannicus* a cut which was undoubtedly authorial creates an inconsistency in the text (not usually noticed by audiences or readers); a similar inconsistency is created by a cut made in 3.1 of the Folio version of *King Lear*.

[44] See Michael Meyer, *Strindberg: A Biography* (1985), 32, 39, 52, 60, 67, 188, 504; Meyer, *Ibsen: A Biography* (1971), 481, 512, 524-5, etc.; *The Oxford Chekhov*, ed. R. Hingley, vol. iii (1964), esp. 310-12.

[45] Honigmann, *The Stability of Shakespeare's Text* (1965), 47-77.

[46] Honigmann, *Stability*, 47-77; John Kerrigan, 'Revision, Adaptation, and the Fool in *King Lear*', in *Division*, 194-239; Greg, 'The Escapes of Jupiter' (1925; reprinted in *Collected Papers* (1966), 156-83); *If You Know Not Me You Know Nobody, Part II*, ed. Madeleine Doran, MSR (1935, for 1934), pp. xi-xix.

[47] Philip Gaskell, in *From Writer to Reader* (1978), 245-62, describes in detail the progress of the script of Stoppard's *Travesties*.

[48] This paragraph condenses an argument developed and documented at length in Gary Taylor, 'Revising Shakespeare', forthcoming in *TEXT*, 3 (1987).

[49] For evidence of the conventionality of this phrase see Honigmann, *Stability*, 22-6. The poetaster Matthew in Jonson's *Every Man In His Humour* claims to have written his verses '*extempore*, this morning' (Folio text, 4.2.65).

[50] For the dangers of apparatus formats, see Randall McLeod, 'Gon. No more, the text is foolish.', in *Division*, 157-71.

[51] J. A. Barish, *The Antitheatrical Prejudice* (1981). For an intriguing analysis of the relationship between such attitudes and the editing of texts see Timothy Murray, 'From Foul Sheets to Legitimate Model: Antitheater, Text, Jonson', *New Literary History*, 14 (1983), 641-64.

[52] Louis Racine, quoted in Jean Racine, *Les Plaideurs*, ed. Jean Fabre (1963), 13-14, p. 13; Jean Racine, *Œuvres Complètes*, i. 30-2; *Comedies and Tragedies Written by Francis Beaumont and John Fletcher* (1647), sig. A4.

53 The 'integrity of the work of art' derives from 'those intentions which are the author's, *together with those others of which he approves or in which he acquiesces*': James Thorpe, 'The Aesthetics of Textual Criticism', *PMLA* 80 (1965), 465-82; reprinted in *Art and Error: Modern Textual Editing*, ed. Ronald Gottesmann and Scott Bennett (1970), 62-101.

54 *Comedies and Tragedies* (1647), sig. A4. Moseley, of course, had motives for exaggerating the price of manuscripts, and was writing three decades after Shakespeare's death, during a period when printed books were becoming commoner and cheaper, manuscript copies rarer and more expensive.

55 Ben Jonson, *Pleasure Reconciled to Virtue* (1618), Chatsworth MS; John Fletcher and Philip Massinger, *The Tragedy of Sir John van Olden Barnavelt* (1619), British Library Add. MS 1865; Thomas Middleton, 'Song in Several Parts' (1622), PRO MS State papers domestic, v. 129, doc. 53; Thomas Middleton, *A Game at Chess* (1624), Folger MS 7045, British Library MS Lansdowne 690, Bodleian MS Malone 25; Thomas Middleton, *The Witch* (1624-5), Bodleian MS Malone 12; John Fletcher, *Demetrius and Enanthe* (1625), Brogyntyn MS 42. For all these texts except *Barnavelt*, 'Song in Several Parts', and *The Witch* alternative early texts survive, enabling us to compare Crane's work with another authoritative textual witness.

56 For Crane's influence on the first five texts, see especially T. H. Howard-Hill, *Ralph Crane and Some Shakespeare First Folio Comedies* (1972). See also the Introduction to *Cymbeline* below. Crane was first identified as scrivener to the King's Men by F. P. Wilson, in 'Ralph Crane, Scrivener to the King's Players', *The Library*, IV, 7 (1926), 194-215.

57 *The Works of Mercy* (1621: STC 5986), sig. A6.

58 G. E. Bentley, *The Jacobean and Caroline Stage*, 7 vols. (1941-68), ii. 494-5.

59 *The Honest Man's Fortune* (Victoria and Albert, Dyce MS 9: licensed 8 February 1624/5), *Believe as You List* (British Library MS Egerton 2828: licensed 6 May 1631), and *The Soddered Citizen* (c.1632-3), ed. J. H. P. Pafford, MSR (1936, for 1935). For *Bonduca* and *The Honest Man's Fortune* alternative texts survive in the 1647 Beaumont and Fletcher Folio, thus making possible some evaluation of Knight's merits and deficiencies as a scribe.

60 Bentley, *Jacobean and Caroline Stage*, ii. 495; Johan Gerritsen, ed., *The Honest Man's Fortune* (1952), pp. xxi ff.

61 John Taylor, *Taylor's Feast* (1638: STC 23798), sig. E4^v, p. 66. Taylor's anecdote associates Vincent with the actor John Singer, who was dead by 1609.

62 See *Index of English Literary Manuscripts*, Volume I. *1450-1625*, ed. Peter Beal (1980).

63 *Palladis Tamia* (1598: STC 17834), 281^v-282.

64 Richard Brinsley Sheridan, *Dramatic Works*, ed. Cecil Price, 2 vols. (1973), i. 4 and 214-15; Thomas Holcroft, *Memoirs*, ed. W. Hazlitt (1816), ii. 54-8; L. B. Wright, 'A Note on Dramatic Piracy', *Modern Language Notes*, 43 (1928), 256-8.

65 H. A. Rennert, *The Spanish Stage in the time of Lope de Vega* (1909), 175-6. See also Arnold G. Reichenberger, 'Editing Spanish *Comedias* of the XVIIth Century: History and Present-Day Practice', in *Editing Renaissance Dramatic Texts*, ed. Anne Lancashire (1976), 69-96.

66 Francis Bacon, *A Declaration . . .* (1601: STC 1133), sig. Q1. The phrase 'as neere as they could be remembered' also occurs on sig. K3.

67 *Pleasant Dialogues and Dramas* (STC 13358), sigs. R4^v-5, 248-9. The prologue is to 'the Play of Queene Elizabeth as it was last revived at the Cock-pit', evidently the same play as, or the basis of, *If You Know Not Me*, to which the prologue was added in the eighth quarto of 1639 (*BEPD* 215).

68 *The Rape of Lucrece* (1608: *BEPD* 273a), sig. A2.

69 Sir George Buc, *The Third University of England* (1612), in John Stow's *Annals* (1615: STC 23338), sig. Oooo1^v, Cap. 39: 'Of the Arts of Calligraphie, Brachygraphie, Steganographie, Arithmetik, and Cyphering'.

70 In 1589 a sermon by Stephen Egerton (STC 7538), and in 1590-1 two sermons by Henry Smith (STC 22693, 22664), were printed in editions which claimed that the text had been 'taken by characterie' or 'taken as it was vttered by characterie'.

71 Leo Kirschbaum's 'A Census of Bad Quartos'—*RES* 14 (1938), 20-43—is overly enthusiastic in identifying texts as 'bad', but his list provides a useful summary of editions sometimes suspected of memorial transmission.

72 For decisive refutations of the shorthand hypothesis see G. N. Giordano-Orsino, 'Thomas Heywood's Play on "The Troubles of Queen Elizabeth"', *The Library*, IV, 14 (1933-4), 313-38; W. Matthews, 'Shorthand and the Bad Shakespeare Quartos', *MLR* 27 (1932), 243-62, and *MLR* 28 (1933), 81-3; W. Matthews, 'Shakespeare and the Reporters', *The Library*, IV, 15 (1934-5), 481-98; G. I. Duthie, *The 'Bad' Quarto of Hamlet* (1941) and *Elizabethan Shorthand and the First Quarto of 'King Lear'* (1949).

73 Gary Taylor, 'Three Studies', 124-64. We are grateful to Mrs Laurie E. Maguire for calling our attention to the passage in *The Hog Hath Lost His Pearl*, ed. G. R. Proudfoot, MSR (1966), lines 166-9.

74 Taylor, 'The Transmission of *Pericles*', *PBSA* 80 (1986), 193-217.

75 See Pope's edition (1725), I, viii; more recent exponents of this minority view include C. T. Prouty, *The Contention and Shakespeare's '2 Henry VI': A Comparative Study* (1954); Hardin Craig, *A New Look at Shakespeare's Quartos* (1961); Albert B. Weiner, ed., *Hamlet: The First Quarto, 1603* (1962); Random Cloud [Randall McLeod], 'The Marriage of Good and Bad Quartos', *SQ* 33 (1982), 421-31; Steven Urkowitz, '"Well-sayd olde Mole": Burying Three *Hamlets* in Modern Editions', in *Shakespeare Study Today*, ed. Georgianna Ziegler (1986), 37-70; '"I am not made of stone": Theatrical Revision of Gesture in Shakespeare's Plays', in *Renaissance and Reformation/Renaissance et Réforme*, 10 (1986), 79-93.

76 For a statistical analysis of the vocabulary of the allegedly memorial texts, which clearly distinguishes them from the authentic canon, see Alfred Hart, *Stolne and Surreptitious Copies: A Comparative Study of Shakespeare's Bad Quartos* (1942).

77 The Senate transcript was cited by Paul Bertram, *White Spaces in Shakespeare* (1981), 19. For Pudsey see Juliet Mary Gowan, 'An Edition of Edward Pudsey's Commonplace Book (c.1600-1615) from the Manuscript in the Bodleian Library' (unpublished M.Phil. thesis, University of London, 1967); Shakespeare Birthplace Trust Record Office, MS ER 82; *The Times* (25 June 1977), p. 14.

78 For a full discussion of the potential value of memorially reconstructed texts in relation to different categories of verbal variant, see Taylor, 'Three Studies', 124-64.

79 For 'London Companies on Tour' see Bentley, *Profession of Player*, 177-205. Our knowledge of theatrical activity in the

provinces is rapidly expanding due to the efforts of the Canadian *Records of Early English Drama* project.

[80] Taylor's Oxford edition of *Henry V* (1982) contains an annotated list of all passages not present in the Quarto text (Appendix F). We have not here attempted any systematic recording and discussion of such omissions.

[81] See for instance Bruce Metzger, *The Text of the New Testament*, second edition (1968), 86-92; S. Timpanaro, *Maia* 22 (1970), 351-9.

[82] *Editorial Problem*, p. xxix, note 3.

[83] A. E. Housman, 'The Application of Thought to Textual Criticism', *Proceedings of the Classical Association*, 18 (1921), 67-84, reprinted in *Classical Papers*, ed. J. Diggle and F. R. D. Goodyear, 3 vols. (1972), 105-69, and in *Art and Error*, ed. Gottesman and Bennett, 1-16. Unless indicated otherwise, subsequent quotations from Housman refer to this essay.

[84] Two useful introductions to the rise of printing, both with helpful bibliographies, are George Walton Williams, *The Craft of Printing and the Publication of Shakespeare's Works* (1985), and D. F. McKenzie, 'Printing in England from Caxton to Milton', in *The Age of Shakespeare*, ed. Boris Ford (revised edition, 1982), 207-26.

[85] For contractual relations between playwrights and acting companies, see Bentley, *Profession of Dramatist*, esp. 62-144.

[86] In 1599-1600 *A Warning for Fair Women* (BEPD 155), *Every Man out of his Humour* (BEPD 163), *Romeo* (Q2), *2 Henry IV*, *Much Ado*, *Dream*, *Merchant*, and *Every Man in his Humour* (BEPD 176), all owned by the Chamberlain's Men, were published in authoritative editions. By contrast, in 1594-8 only three plays owned by the company were printed in such editions (*Love's Labour's Lost*, *Richard II*, and *1 Henry IV*)—of which the third may have been printed by demand of the political authorities.

[87] The fullest discussion for the canon as a whole remains Leo Kirschbaum's polemical *Shakespeare and the Stationers* (1955), as corrected by his 'The Copyright of Elizabethan Plays' (*The Library*, V, 14 (1959), 231-50) and C. J. Sisson's 'The Laws of Elizabethan Copyright: The Stationers' View' (*The Library*, V, 15 (1960), 8-20). In general early claims of publishing piracy seem to be seriously exaggerated, and plays need to be set in the context of entries for less prestigious non-literary works, which have hitherto received less meticulous attention. For further discussion of individual entries see the relevant Introductions below. All the entries pertinent to the Shakespeare canon are reproduced in S. Schoenbaum, *William Shakespeare: Records and Images* (1981), 201-45.

[88] Philip Stubbes, *Motive to Good Works* (1593: STC 23397), sigs. N5v-6, pp. 186-7.

[89] For licensing generally see Greg, *Some Aspects and Problems of London Publishing between 1550 and 1650* (1956), and *Licensers for the Press, &c. to 1640* (1962).

[90] See for instance A. E. M. Kirwood, 'Richard Field, Printer, 1589-1624', *The Library*, IV, 12 (1931-2), 1-39; W. Craig Ferguson, *Valentine Simmes* (1968); Akihiro Yamada, *Thomas Creede: Printer to Shakespeare and His Contemporaries* (1981); Blayney, *The Texts of 'King Lear' and their Origins*, vol. i, *Nicholas Okes and the First Quarto* (1982); Gerald D. Johnson, 'Nicholas Ling, Publisher 1580-1607', *SB* 38 (1985), 203-14; 'John Trundle and the Book-Trade 1603-1626', *SB* 39 (1986), 177-99; and 'John Busby and the Stationers' Trade, 1590-1612', *The Library*, VI, 7 (1985), 1-15.

[91] The explanation for Q2's variants was first pointed out by Joseph S. G. Bolton, 'The Authentic Text of *Titus Andronicus*', *PMLA* 44 (1929), 776-80, and independently by R. B. McKerrow in 'A Note on *Titus Andronicus*', *The Library*, IV, 15 (1934), 49-53. The fullest account can be found in Joseph Quincy Adams's introduction to the facsimile of the 1594 edition (1936), 23-8.

[92] For a summary of this complex problem see Greg, *Folio*, 11-17. Important work on the Pavier quartos since 1955 includes D. F. McKenzie, 'Compositor B's role in *The Merchant of Venice* Q2 (1619)', *SB* 12 (1959), 75-90; W. S. Kable, *The Pavier Quartos and the First Folio of Shakespeare* (1970); John F. Andrews, 'The Pavier Quartos of 1619: Evidence for Two Compositors' (unpublished doctoral dissertation, Vanderbilt University, 1971); Peter W. M. Blayney, '"Compositor B" and the Pavier Quartos: Problems of Identification and Their Implications', *The Library*, V, 27 (1972), 179-206, and 30 (1975), 143-5; Richard Knowles, 'The Printing of the Second Quarto (1619) of *King Lear*', *SB* 35 (1982), 191-206. Also valuable are editions of two non-Shakespearian plays included in the Pavier collection: *Sir John Oldcastle* in Michael Drayton, *Works*, ed. J. W. Hebel *et al.*, 5 vols. (1931-41); and *A Yorkshire Tragedy*, in *The Shakespeare Apocrypha*, ed. C. F. Tucker Brooke (1908). Both collate the 1619 edition; Brooke's collations should be supplemented by the account of press variants in the Malone Society Reprint of the 1608 edition (1973, for 1969), ed. Sylvia D. Feldman and G. R. Proudfoot.

[93] Court-Book C, 3 May 1619; see *Records of the Court of the Stationers' Company 1602 to 1640*, W. A. Jackson (1957), 110.

[94] Public Record Office, L.C.5/134, pp. 178-9; transcribed in *Collections*, Vol. II, Part iii, MSR (1931), 384-5.

[95] The documentary record for Heminges's and Condell's careers is conveniently gathered in Chambers, *Stage*, ii. 310-11, 320-3, and Bentley, *Jacobean and Caroline Stage*, ii. 410-13, 465-9.

[96] For Jaggard see E. E. Willoughby, *A Printer of Shakespeare: The Books and Times of William Jaggard* (1934). Neither Aspley nor Smethwick has been the subject of detailed study; essential information can be gleaned from *A Dictionary of Printers and Booksellers in England, Scotland and Ireland, and of Foreign Printers of English Books 1557-1640*, ed. R. B. McKerrow (1910); McKerrow, *Printers' & Publishers' Devices in England & Scotland 1485-1640* (1913); P. G. Morrison, *Index of Printers, Publishers and Booksellers ... 1475-1640* (1961).

[97] For the Blount circle see Honigmann, *Stability*, 34-5; Arthur W. Secord, 'I. M. of the First Folio Shakespeare and other Mabbe Problems', *Journal of English and Germanic Philology*, 47 (1948), 374-81; Leslie Hotson, *I, William Shakespeare* (1937), 238-50, 255; Sidney Lee, 'An Elizabethan Bookseller', *Bibliographica*, 1 (1895), 474-98. For Holland, see Mark Eccles, 'Brief Lives: Tudor and Stuart Authors', *SP* 74 (1982), 67-73.

[98] See particularly Cyrus Hoy, 'The Shares of Fletcher and his Collaborators in the Beaumont and Fletcher Canon', *SB* 8 (1956), 129-46; 9 (1957), 143-62; 11 (1958), 85-106; 12 (1959), 91-116; 13 (1960), 77-108; 14 (1961), 45-68; 15 (1962), 71-90.

[99] *Troilus and Cressida* (1679), in *The Works of John Dryden*, vol. xiii (1984), ed. George R. Guffey, 225.

[100] Seventeenth-century characterizations of Shakespeare are conveniently collected in *The Shakspere Allusion-Book: A Collection of Allusions to Shakspere from 1591 to 1700*, ed. C. M.

Ingleby *et al.*, 2 vols. (1932). The commentaries are now out of date, and various additional allusions have been recorded in the last half-century.

101 It was finally overturned by T. W. Baldwin with *William Shakspere's Small Latine & Lesse Greek*, 2 vols. (1944).

102 Capell's chronology, though earlier, was not published until his posthumous *Notes* (1783), II. ii. 183-6; Malone's 'An Attempt to ascertain the Order in which the Plays attributed to Shakspeare were Written' is included in the Steevens edition of 1778 (i. 269-396). Malone's chronology draws heavily upon Capell's.

103 Jonson, *Works*, ix (1950), 12.

104 Jonson's *Works* (1616: STC 14751) had been preceded by Samuel Daniel's (1601-2; STC 6236), which were expanded and published again in 1623 (STC 6238). Several of the dramatic pieces in the 1623 collection are dated.

105 Malone's *Supplement* (1780) to Steevens's edition (1778); Coleridge, *Biographia Literaria*, Chap. 15.

106 We owe this observation to John Pitcher. On the thematic importance of tempests and music see especially G. Wilson Knight, *The Shakespearian Tempest* (1932).

107 Taylor, 'Act Intervals'.

108 Taylor, 'Zounds'.

109 For the frequency of editions shared by more than one printer, see Peter W. M. Blayney, 'The Prevalence of Shared Printing in the Early Seventeenth Century', *PBSA* 67 (1973), 437-42, and Blayney, *Texts of 'King Lear'*, *passim* (indexed on 732-3).

110 Joseph Moxon, *Mechanick Exercises on the Whole Art of Printing* (1683-4), ed. Herbert Davis and Harry Carter (1962), 239-44; George Walton Williams, 'Setting by Formes in Quarto Printing', *SB* 11 (1958), 39-53; and Hinman, *passim* (see Index).

111 For surviving examples of early printer's copy see Percy Simpson, *Proof-reading in the Sixteenth, Seventeenth, and Eighteenth Centuries* (1935), as supplemented by Carol M. Meale, 'Wynkyn de Worde's Setting-Copy for *Ipomydon*', *SB* 35 (1982), 156-7.

112 In the Pavier edition of *Henry V* all the significant expansions and alterations of the text, which have puzzled scholars, can be attributed to such causes. We have not undertaken a systematic study of the relation between casting off and textual variation throughout the Pavier collection.

113 'The Spelling of the First Folio', *TLS*, 3 June 1920, p. 352.

114 Hinman, ii. 513. A 'John Shakespeare', son of a Warwickshire butcher, was apprenticed to Jaggard in 1610, and finished his apprenticeship in 1617. For other Jaggard apprentices see D. F. McKenzie, *Stationers' Company Apprentices 1605-1640* (1961), 19.

115 See especially D. F. McKenzie, 'Stretching a Point: Or, The Case of the Spaced-out Comps', *SB* 37 (1984), 106-21. McKenzie's key example has not been the subject of such extensive, independent, and interlocking investigation as the 1623 Folio. See also McKenzie's influential, sceptical 'Printers of the Mind: Some Notes on Bibliographical Theories and Printing-house Practices', *SB* 22 (1969), 1-75.

116 Alan Craven, 'Simmes' Compositor A and Five Shakespeare Quartos', *SB* 26 (1973), 37-60; John O'Connor, 'Compositors D and F of the Shakespeare First Folio', *SB* 28 (1975), 81-117; Werstine, 'Compositor B'; Werstine, 'Folio Compositors'.

117 J. O. Halliwell-Phillipps compiled *A Dictionary of Misprints* (1887), based upon contemporary errata, but unfortunately he did not identify his sources. Blayney includes full listings of errata (1604-9) and press-variants (1607-8) in books produced in one printer's shop in *Texts of 'King Lear'*, 559-629.

118 Thomas Nashe, in *Works*, ii. 203; Isaac Jaggard's epistle 'To the Reader' in vol. ii of the *Decameron*, 2 vols. (1620: STC 3172).

119 Moxon, 192; see also the editors' note on 381. The study of reprints, and of editions printed from extant manuscripts, confirms that this practice prevailed in Shakespeare's time.

120 For an introduction to composition see Philip Gaskell, *A New Introduction to Bibliography* (1972), 40-56.

121 See Randall McLeod, 'Spellbound', in *Play-Texts in Old Spelling*, ed. G. B. Shand and Raymond C. Shady (1984), 81-96.

122 Pointed out by Alice Walker, in her unpublished textual note for the Oxford Shakespeare.

123 T. H. Howard-Hill, 'Spelling and the Bibliographer', *The Library*, V, 18 (1963), 1-28.

124 D. F. McKenzie, '"Indenting the Stick" in the First Quarto of *King Lear* (1608)', *PBSA* 67 (1973), 125-30; Antony Hammond, '*The White Devil* in Nicholas Okes' Shop', *SB* 39 (1986), 135-76.

125 See Simpson, *Proof-reading*, 5, 10, 12-13.

126 See Blayney, *Texts of 'King Lear'*, 188-205.

127 Augustine Vincent, *A Discovery of Errors* (1622: STC 24755.8), sig. ¶¶1.

128 See Tucker Brooke, 'Elizabethan Proof Corrections in a Copy of *The First Part of the Contention* (1600)', *Huntington Library Bulletin*, 2 (1931), 87-9; for those in the Folio, Hinman, i. 233-5; Hinman, Norton Facsimile, Appendix A, VIa and VIIa; Blayney, *Texts of 'King Lear'*, 234-44. Another dramatic example survives in Chapman's *Monsieur D'Olive* (1606): see W. W. Greg, 'A Proof-Sheet of 1606', *The Library*, IV, 17 (1937), 454-7.

129 Jeanne Addison Roberts, '"Wife" or "Wise"—*The Tempest* l. 1.786', *SB* 31 (1978), 203-8.

130 For the use of damaged types to determine the order of printing, see especially Hinman; Blayney, *Texts of 'King Lear'*, 89-150; and Hammond, '*White Devil*'.

131 William Prynne, *Histrio-Mastix* (1633: STC 20464), 'To the Christian Reader', fol. 1ᵛ.

132 For evidence of the price of the 1623 edition see Greg, *Folio*, 454-5. For the schoolmaster's salary see Bentley, *Profession of Dramatist*, 95-7. For wages in London in this period see Ann Jennalie Cook, *The Privileged Playgoers of Shakespeare's London, 1576-1642* (1981).

133 For watermarks see C. M. Briquet, *Les Filigranes. Dictionnaire historique des marques du papier dès leur apparition vers 1282 jusqu'en 1600*, 3rd edn., ed. Allen Stevenson (1968); W. A. Churchill, *Watermarks in Paper in Holland, England, France . . . in the XVIIth and XVIIIth Centuries* (1967); Allen Stevenson, *Observations on Paper as Evidence* (1961).

134 W. W. Greg, 'On Certain False Dates in Shakespearian Quartos', *The Library*, II, 9 (1908), 113-31, 381-409; A. W. Pollard, *Shakespeare Folios and Quartos: A Study in the Bibliography of Shakespeare's Plays, 1594-1685* (1909), 81-107; William J. Neidig, 'The Shakespeare Quartos of 1619', *Modern*

Philology, 8 (1910), 145-63; A. W. Pollard, 'False Dates in Shakespeare Quartos', *The Library*, III, 2 (1911), 101-7.

¹³⁵ Allen Stevenson, 'Shakespearian Dated Watermarks', *SB* 4 (1951), 159-64.

¹³⁶ John Jowett and Gary Taylor, 'The Three Texts of *2 Henry IV*', forthcoming in *SB* 40 (1987).

¹³⁷ The pattern of annotation in the Folio is discussed at greater length in John Jowett and Gary Taylor, 'Sprinklings of Authority: The Folio Text of *Richard II*', *SB* 38 (1985), 151-200.

¹³⁸ See C. J. Sisson, 'Shakespeare Quartos as Prompt-copies', *RES* 18 (1942), 129-43; the Chicago copy of *A Looking Glass for London and England*, Q4 (1604?), described by C. R. Baskerville in *Modern Philology*, 30 (1932), 29-51, and MSR, ed. Greg (1932); W. A. Jackson, *The Carl H. Pforzheimer Library*, 3 vols. (1940), i. 367. Conversely, a defective printed book might be patched by transcription from a prompt-book; though such procedures do not apparently influence any Shakespeare text, see for an example Thomas Dekker's *Blurt, Master Constable*, ed. Thomas L. Berger (1979), p. 10.

¹³⁹ For Shakespeare's descendants see G. R. French, *Shakespeareana Genealogica* (1869); French traces the descendants of the families into which Shakespeare's daughters married.

¹⁴⁰ Schoenbaum, *Shakespeare's Lives*, 125-6.

¹⁴¹ Bentley, *Jacobean and Caroline Stage*, i (1941), 69. The company seems to have maintained a skeletal existence till c.1647-8.

¹⁴² On the fire see Brean S. Hammond, 'Theobald's *Double Falsehood*: An "Agreeable Cheat"?' *N&Q*, NS 31 (1984), 2-3.

¹⁴³ N. W. Bawcutt, 'New Revels Documents of Sir George Buc and Sir Henry Herbert, 1619-1662', *RES*, NS 35 (1984), 316-31, and 'Craven Ord Transcripts of Sir Henry Herbert's Office-Book in the Folger Shakespeare Library', *ELR* 14 (1984), 83-94; and Eccles, 'Sir George Buc'.

¹⁴⁴ Matthew W. Black and Matthias A. Shaaber, *Shakespeare's Seventeenth-Century Editors, 1632-1685* (1937).

¹⁴⁵ See the Smock Alley and Padua prompt-books reproduced in G. Blakemore Evans, *Shakespearean Prompt-Books of the Seventeenth Century* (1960-); see also C. H. Shattuck, *The Shakespeare Promptbooks. A Descriptive Catalogue* (1965).

¹⁴⁶ Rowe has attracted little independent study. See Alfred Behrend, *Nicholas Rowe als Dramatiker* (1907); R. B. McKerrow, 'The Treatment of Shakespeare's Text by his Earlier Editors, 1709-1768', *Proceedings of the British Academy*, 19 (1928), 147-216, reprinted in *Studies in Shakespeare: British Academy Lectures*, ed. Peter Alexander (1964); D. Nichol Smith, *Shakespeare in the Eighteenth Century* (1928), 30-3; Brian Vickers, ed., *Shakespeare: The Critical Heritage*, 6 vols. (1974-81), i. 2, 15.

¹⁴⁷ Maynard Mack, *Alexander Pope: A Life* (1985), 418-26. When Pope's edition was reissued in 1728, a ninth volume (containing the apocrypha) was published simultaneously, but Pope's name does not appear on its title-page, and since it simply reprints Rowe's edition, Pope presumably bears no responsibility for it.

¹⁴⁸ Richard Foster Jones, *Lewis Theobald* (1919), is the most recent biography. For a full history of the Pope-Theobald controversy, see also Thomas R. Lounsbury, *The Text of Shakespeare* (1906).

¹⁴⁹ John Hazel Smith, 'Styan Thirlby's Shakespearean Commentaries: A Corrective Analysis', *SSt* 11 (1978), 219-41.

¹⁵⁰ Arthur Sherbo, *Samuel Johnson, Editor of Shakespeare*, Illinois Studies in Language and Literature, 42 (1956). For a critically sophisticated deconstruction of Johnson's editorial principles see Christopher Norris, 'Post-structuralist Shakespeare: text and ideology', in *Alternative Shakespeares*, ed. John Drakakis (1986), 47-66.

¹⁵¹ See McKerrow, 'The Treatment'; for a physical specimen of the procedure, see Richard Corballis, 'Copy Text for Theobald's "Shakespeare"', *The Library*, VI, 8 (1986), 156-9.

¹⁵² Alice Walker, 'Edward Capell and his Edition of Shakespeare', *Proceedings of the British Academy*, 46 (1960), 131-45, reprinted in *Studies in Shakespeare*, 132-48; Vickers, vi. 32-3.

¹⁵³ Capell's manuscripts show that he too was concerned with this problem, though his system was cumbersome and did not reach print: see Paul Werstine, 'Edward Capell and Metrically Linked Speeches in Shakespeare', *The Library*, VI, 7 (1985), 259-61; Richard Knowles, 'Capell's Lineation of Shakespeare's Verse', *The Library*, VI, 7 (1985), 354-5.

¹⁵⁴ James Prior's *Life of Edmond Malone, Editor of Shakespeare* (1860) remains the only biography. J. O. Halliwell-Phillipps edited and published Malone's correspondence with John Jordan (1864) and with James Davenport (1864); A. Tillotson edited the *Correspondence of Percy and Malone* (1944); but most of his correspondence remains unpublished. Schoenbaum, in *Shakespeare's Lives*, 162-248, makes some use of the manuscript material.

¹⁵⁵ *Neue Jahrbücher für Philologie und Paedagogik*, 72 (1855), 57, 107, 159; *The Athenaeum*, 7 February 1857, p. 182, reprinted in the New Variorum *Hamlet*, ed. H. H. Furness, 2 vols. (1877), ii. 25-6; *Romeo und Julia* (parallel text, 1859). Mommsen also published (1857) an edition of George Wilkins's *Painfull Aduentures* (1608: STC 25638.5), with important notes on its relevance to *Pericles*.

¹⁵⁶ The episode is recounted in G. B. Harrison's preface to his edition of *Shakespeare: Major Plays and the Sonnets* (1948).

¹⁵⁷ See Chris Baldick, *The Social Mission of English Criticism, 1848-1932* (1983); D. J. Palmer, *The Rise of English Studies* (1965); Terry Eagleton, *Literary Theory: An Introduction* (1983), 17-53.

¹⁵⁸ For an illuminating brief history of the movement they personified, see F. P. Wilson, *Shakespeare and the New Bibliography*, rev. by Helen Gardner (1970); also instructive are W. W. Greg, 'Ronald Brunlees McKerrow, 1872-1940', *Proceedings of the British Academy*, 26 (1942); John Dover Wilson, 'Alfred William Pollard, 1859-1944', *Proceedings of the British Academy*, 31 (1945); W. W. Greg, *Biographical Notes 1877-1947* (1960).

¹⁵⁹ Hinman's influence was concentrated in two books (*Printing and Proof-Reading*, and his 1968 Norton Facsimile of the Folio); he did not live to complete his edition of Shakespeare's *Works*. Bowers has exerted more influence as the teacher of a generation of distinguished bibliographers; as editor for four decades of *Studies in Bibliography*, and of standard editions of Dekker, Marlowe, and the Beaumont and Fletcher canon; see also his collected *Essays in Bibliography, Text, and Editing* (1975).

¹⁶⁰ *Editorial Problem*, pp. l-li.

¹⁶¹ *Proceedings of the British Academy*, 14 (1928); reprinted in *Aspects of Shakespeare* (1933).

¹⁶² 'Shakespearian Textual Studies: Seven More Years', in

Shakespeare 1971, ed. Clifford Leech and J. M. R. Margeson (1972), 37-49.

[163] A. E. Housman, ed., *M. Manilii Astronomicon Liber Primus* (1903), p. liv.

[164] On omissions generally see Gary Taylor, 'Inventing'.

[165] These principles are discussed in greater detail, with examples, in Gary Taylor, 'Metrifying'. Housman has some useful remarks on 'Prosody and Method' (*Papers*, iii. 1114-26).

[166] See Gary Taylor, '*Praestat*'.

[167] Harold Pinter, *The Homecoming* (1965), p. 31.

[168] For attempts at a critique of the whole activity of editing see for instance Randall McLeod, 'UnEditing Shakespeare', *Sub-stance*, 33/34 (1982), 26-55; Jonathan Goldberg, 'Textual Properties', *SQ* 37 (1986), 213-17; Terence Hawkes, *That Shakespeherian Rag* (1986), 73-91.

[169] For a debate on the merit of historical collations, see Paul Werstine, 'Modern Editions and Historical Collation in Old-Spelling Editions of Shakespeare', *AEB* 4 (1980), 95-106; and Fredson Bowers, 'The Historical Collation in an Old-Spelling Shakespeare Edition: Another View', *SB* 35 (1982), 234-58.

THE CANON AND CHRONOLOGY OF SHAKESPEARE'S PLAYS

LIKE children, works of art acquire a being independent of those who conceived them. We may judge and interpret and enjoy a poem or person, without knowing the author or the father. But poems, like persons, come in families: they have progenitors and siblings, contexts and consequences. Some critics discipline themselves, democratically, to regard each work on its own terms, or on their terms, or on any terms other than those imposed upon it by the accidents of birth and place. Such critics would ideally encounter works one by one, separately bound, in a material solitude which embodies the intellectual integrity the critic seeks. But other kinds of critical curiosity are less easily satisfied; like Coriolanus, some find it impossible to act as if a work were author of itself, and knew no other kin. For 'the biological school' of literary criticism, individuals cannot be fully or properly understood without some knowledge of the family and the culture to which they belong; such critics would ideally encounter works in groups, in collections bound together instead of apart, so that we might appreciate the similarities which foil and counterpoint their differences. In this sense a 'Complete Works' is the literary equivalent of a family reunion, the gathering of a clan of siblings born of the fruitful union of a unique artist and a unique society. In recognizing the existence of such literary families, we need not accept any exaggerated theoretical estimate of the power of one parent—the 'author'—to impose successfully and consistently his or her intentions upon the children: we simply accept that each parent had some influence, often unconscious, commonly unpredictable, upon the maturing of each individual creation. And in understanding the relationships within such a family (or any other), it will help to know the order of birth of the offspring.

In Shakespeare's case, no such family reunion occurred until after the death of both parents. Shakespeare did not personally oversee the publication of a collected edition of his works, and no autograph manuscripts survive of works attributed to him in his lifetime. The contents and chronology of his canon—the number of his literary children, and their order of birth—therefore remain, and will for ever remain, a matter of dispute. Editors must decide, because Shakespeare did not decide for them, what to include and how to arrange it; the decisions of any collected edition—from that printed by William Jaggard in 1623, to that published by Oxford University Press in 1986—are fallible, and may be challenged by those with better evidence or better judgement.

Scholars base their judgements about the date and authorship of works of art upon two kinds of evidence. 'External evidence' consists of early documentary witnesses: manuscripts and printed books which assert, for instance, that author X composed work Y. 'Internal evidence' consists of features of workmanship in the object itself: tricks of usage in work Y which betray the hand of author X. If you think of a work of art as a tin of food, 'external evidence' is the label around the tin, describing its contents; but sometimes such labels are missing, or misleading, and then we resort to 'internal evidence', opening the tin and testing its contents, by methods which range from simple taste to complicated chemical analysis. Both types of evidence have their value and their limitations.

Authorship: External Evidence

The chief external evidence for the works of William Shakespeare is the folio volume of *Mr. William Shakespeares Comedies, Histories, & Tragedies*, published in 1623 (STC 22273). This volume contains a dedication and an epistle (reproduced among 'Commendatory Poems and Prefaces' in the Oxford edition) signed by John Heminges and Henry Condell. Along with Richard Burbage (who died in 1619), Heminges and Condell were the only London figures mentioned in Shakespeare's will. Both were members of the Chamberlain's Men, later the King's Men, the theatrical company of which Shakespeare was a member from 1594 to his death in 1616. The Chamberlain's Men are first mentioned in June 1594, in the records of the theatrical entrepreneur Philip Henslowe; the first inkling of the company's membership occurs in the Accounts of the Treasurer of the Queen's Chamber, which records a payment on 15 March 1595 to William Shakespeare, William Kempe, and Richard Burbage for two performances by the company during the preceding Christmas season (reproduced in Schoenbaum, *Documentary Life*, p. 136). Heminges is first named as a member of the company in a document of December 1596, and Condell in one of 1598. The company must always have consisted of more than the three men named on 15 March 1595 as its representatives, and it has been widely and reasonably assumed that Heminges and Condell belonged to the company from its beginnings. It is even possible that they knew Shakespeare before the formation of the Chamberlain's Men; for that company seems to have taken over most of its members from Strange's Men. Heminges is named among members of Strange's Men in May 1593; less reliably, the plat of *2 Seven Deadly Sins*, which has been conjecturally dated in 1590-1, refers to an actor named 'Harry', who might have been Condell (see Greg, *Dramatic Documents*). Three of Shakespeare's plays are associated with Strange's Men in the early 1590s. The 1623 Folio also includes prefatory material by

Ben Jonson—who knew Shakespeare by 1598, and who later said 'I lov'd the man, and doe honour his memory (on this side Idolatry) as much as any' (*Discoveries*, ll. 654-5, in *Works*, viii. 583-4)—and by Leonard Digges, the stepson of Shakespeare's friend Thomas Russell (also mentioned in his will). Those associated with the 1623 edition thus possess exemplary credentials as witnesses to Shakespeare's dramatic output from at least the middle of 1594 on. Moreover, no one at the time objected to their choice of plays, in the way that Aston Cokayne complained about the Folio collection of *Comedies and Tragedies Written by Francis Beaumont and John Fletcher*: in *A Chain of Golden Poems* (1658: Wing C4894), Cokayne claimed that the 1647 collection included much work by Philip Massinger and little by Beaumont. Since Shakespeare's plays were collected only seven years after his death, at a time when the theatres were still thriving, someone would probably have objected if the collection were objectionable. We must assume, as the initial premiss of any investigation of the Shakespeare canon, that any play included in the 1623 Folio must have been written by Shakespeare in whole or at least part; equally, the claims of any play Heminges and Condell did not include must be treated with some scepticism.

We can evaluate the credentials of the 1623 edition in part because we know who was responsible for its contents. A number of other individuals, about whom we know a great deal, attest the authenticity of particular plays. John Weever (1599) testifies to Shakespeare's authorship of *Romeo* and of another play in which a character named 'Richard' featured prominently—presumably either Richard II or Richard III (see Honigmann, *Lost Years*, 50-8). Gabriel Harvey (1598-1603) testifies to his authorship of *Hamlet* (see Stern), Ben Jonson (1619) to his authorship of *The Winter's Tale* and *Julius Caesar* (*Conversations with Drummond*, ll. 208-10, *Works*, i. 138; *Discoveries*, ll. 662-5, *Works*, viii. 584). Weever and Jonson certainly, and Harvey probably, attributed these plays to Shakespeare before any edition was published bearing his name. Leonard Digges attributed to Shakespeare *Romeo, Henry IV, Much Ado, Caesar, Twelfth Night,* and *Othello*; although the poem in which he makes these claims was not printed until after 1623, given his personal connection with Shakespeare he probably had access to sources of information other than the First Folio itself. Likewise, a manuscript by Richard James which attributes *1 Henry IV* to Shakespeare post-dates the Folio, but James clearly had access to unpublished information about the play's original composition, and so constitutes an independent witness to the play's authorship (see Taylor, 'Richard James').

The most important such witness is Francis Meres. His *Palladis Tamia* was entered in the Stationers' Register on 7 September 1598, and published in an edition dated 1598 (STC 17834). Meres tells us that

the sweete wittie soule of *Ouid* liues in mellifluous & hony-tongued *Shakespeare*, witnes his *Venus* and *Adonis*, his *Lucrece*, his sugred *Sonnets* among his priuate friends, &c.

As *Plautus* and *Seneca* are accounted the best for Comedy and Tragedy among the Latines: so *Shakespeare* among the English is the most excellent in both kinds for the stage; for Comedy, witnes his *Gentlemen of Verona*, his *Errors*, his *Loue labors lost*, his *Loue labours wonne*, his *Midsummers night dreame*, & his *Merchant of Venice*: for Tragedy his *Richard the 2. Richard the 3. Henry the 4. King Iohn, Titus Andronicus* and his *Romeo and Iuliet*.

Meres must have relied upon independent sources of information, for at least six of the works he mentions had not yet been printed, and of those in print only five named Shakespeare as author. Three of those five editions—*Love's Labour's Lost, Richard II,* and *Richard III*—were published in 1598, and therefore might post-date Meres's testimony. (For Meres, see Allen.)

It does not seem likely that Heminges and Condell were influenced in their choice of plays for the 1623 collection by a knowledge of Meres's comments, in an obscure book a quarter of a century old, or by Weever's equally old and equally unimportant poem, or by Harvey's manuscript jottings. These witnesses are apparently independent, and they corroborate one another. None of them has any obvious motive for dishonesty. Such personal attributions—by Weever, Harvey, Jonson, Digges, James, and Meres—ascribe to Shakespeare seventeen of the thirty-six plays included in the Folio.

A third category of documentary evidence is less secure. Shakespeare's name appears on a number of editions of individual works before the collected edition of 1623. It first occurs in print appended to the dedications of *Venus* (1593) and *Lucrece* (1594); in neither edition is it advertised on the title-page—which suggests that the publisher did not expect the author's credentials to increase sales. Shakespeare's name first appears on the title-page of a play in 1598, when it occurs in the three editions mentioned above—each a reprint of an earlier text. In all, nineteen of the thirty-six plays included in the 1623 collection were printed in separate editions before that date; those first printed after 1600 invariably named Shakespeare as author. Those title-page ascriptions are, however, of uncertain value. In the 1590s, when Shakespeare was a relatively obscure playwright, and when consequently the motive for falsely attributing works to him was slight, his plays were usually published anonymously; in the 1600s, when he had become famous, printed plays were frequently attributed to him, but those attributions might represent only the dishonest efforts of publishers to exploit his name.

Such scepticism is justified by the fact that the 1623 collection does not include every play attributed to Shakespeare in editions printed before that date: it excludes *The London Prodigal* (first attributed to Shakespeare in the edition of 1605), *A Yorkshire Tragedy* (1608), *Pericles* (1609), *1 Sir John Oldcastle* (1619), and *The Troublesome Reign of John, King of England* (1622). These disparities increase our confidence in the 1623 collection, and decrease our confidence in the testimony of individual editions before 1623. If Heminges and Condell had included every work previously attributed to Shakespeare in a separate edition, we might suspect that they merely accepted the assertions of earlier publishers. Their rejection of several such items confirms the independent value of their inclusion of others. Noticeably, all the works which they exclude were first attributed to Shakespeare early in the seventeenth century, when his reputation created incentives to dishonesty, and before the Folio itself ended the market for such fraudulence by providing the public with a reliable dramatic canon.

In evaluating the testimony of an early edition a great deal depends upon the evidence of authorial involvement in the publication. Epigraphs, dedications, prefaces, and commendatory poems by friends all demonstrate an author's active engagement in preparation of the work for print; so does extensive correction and revision of the text in proof—as we find for instance in editions of some of Ben Jonson's plays, or in Barnaby Barnes's *The Devil's Charter* (1607: BEPD 254). But of works attributed to Shakespeare, only the narrative poems contain dedications signed by the author, and only the first of those sports an epigraph; those two poems were also better printed than any other work attributed to him, and must presumably have been proof-read with greater care than any of the editions of his plays. The absence of such proof of authorial presence deprives most of the early editions attributed to Shakespeare of any commanding authority, and forces an investigator back upon the testimony of the 1623 Folio. Of course, many of the attributions made in early editions are confirmed by the Folio; but if the Folio did not exist, we could not distinguish—without resorting to stylistic evidence—between the documentary testimony for *King Lear* (1608) and the documentary testimony for *A Yorkshire Tragedy* (1608): both look equally valid, and hence both are equally worthless.

Finally, one category of documentary evidence must be mentioned only in order to lament its absence. Theatrical companies kept records of their financial affairs, including the sums of money paid to playwrights for composing particular plays; the survival of such records from the theatrical entrepreneur Philip Henslowe establishes the authorship of many plays—including *1 Sir John Oldcastle*. Shakespeare's company must have possessed similar records, and indeed the ledger in which they were kept probably appeared on stage in performances of Philip Massinger's *Believe as You List*, which contains a stage direction calling for the use of 'the great booke: of Accomptes'. If this book survived it would presumably solve all our problems in determining what Shakespeare wrote, and when, from mid-1594 to 1616. Although Heminges and Condell almost certainly had access to such a book when determining what to include in the 1623 collection, that source apparently did not survive beyond the interregnum. Nor did the records of Sir Edmund Tilney or Sir George Buc, who were successive Masters of the Revels from 1579 to 1621, and who had to license every play before it could be performed. The only comparable theatrical document which does survive, naming the authors of certain plays, is a manuscript from the Revels Accounts of 1604-5, which specifies Shakespeare as the author of *Errors*, *Merchant*, and *Measure*. This document (PRO, Audit Office, Accounts, Various, A.O. 3/908/13; reproduced by Schoenbaum, *Documentary Life*, pp. 200-1) was once considered a forgery; its authenticity was defended by Chambers and Stamp, but has recently been challenged again by Hamilton (1985). Giles Dawson (privately) rejects Hamilton's palaeographical argument, and we have accepted the document as genuine.

In practice the 1623 Folio solves most of the canonical problems faced by Shakespeare's editors. However, no document is an island; no document stands alone, and even the Folio must be interpreted in the light of other literary and theatrical records of the period. In determining the contents of the Shakespeare canon, editors have acted upon two principles: (1) all works included in the 1623 collection should be included in any subsequent collection, and (2) any work excluded from that collection should be excluded from any subsequent collection. The first principle commands more confidence and has in practice commanded more allegiance than the second. For the reasons outlined above, we can and indeed must assume that any play included in the 1623 collection was written in whole, or at least substantial part, by Shakespeare, and any such work must be represented in a responsible edition of his complete works. When the Folio speaks, we must echo it; but when the Folio is silent, its silence cannot be so confidently interpreted or obeyed. Bibliographical analysis of the Folio has demonstrated that *Troilus and Cressida* was almost omitted, apparently because of problems over copyright; in consequence, *Timon* was included, although it may not have formed part of the original plan. All scholars accept that both plays belong among Shakespeare's works. *Pericles*, likewise, has been accepted as genuine since the late eighteenth century, though the Folio excludes it. An increasing majority of scholars in the twentieth century has accepted the evidence for Shakespeare's authorship of part of *The Two Noble Kinsmen*, and of three pages in the manuscript of *Sir Thomas More*, both excluded from the Folio. The Folio also omits two lost plays, *Love's Labour's Won* and *Cardenio*, which there is good reason to believe that Shakespeare wrote, in whole or part. Such exceptions, grudgingly accepted by the community of scholars over three centuries, collectively demonstrate that the mere absence of a play from the 1623 collection does not and should not irrevocably exclude it from the Shakespeare canon.

Nevertheless, the burden of proof rests upon any new candidate for inclusion in the dramatic canon. Of the exceptions catalogued above, *Timon*, *Pericles*, *Kinsmen*, *More*, and *Cardenio* all appear to have been collaborative works; only *Troilus* and *Love's Labour's Won* were, certainly or probably, entirely by Shakespeare. Of these, *Troilus* was, after all, fitted in, though at the very last minute—a measure, surely, of the scrupulousness of the 1623 editors. About the sole remaining exception, *Love's Labour's Won*, we know only two things: it was an early play, and it was in print by 1603. Either fact might explain its exclusion. Possibly the copyright belonged to a recalcitrant stationer, unwilling to relinquish it to the Folio syndicate; or perhaps, because the play had been written early in Shakespeare's career, Heminges and Condell could not locate a manuscript of its text. Of these two explanations, the first can be incorporated in the second, for if Heminges and Condell possessed a manuscript they could have printed the play from it, even without the consent of that hypothetically recalcitrant stationer—as they apparently did with *Troilus*, and other plays.

Two factors can thus be reasonably invoked as an explanation for exclusion of a 'Shakespearian' play from the 1623 collection: collaboration, or early composition. By the Jacobean period Shakespeare's verbal style had become so distinctive that, in any extended passage, it should be recognized. Although he could have contributed a few lines or a single speech to other men's plays without our being able to detect his presence, it seems highly unlikely that he wrote even as much as a scene in any extant Jacobean play other than those included in the Oxford edition and long recognized by scholars as probable or certain examples of his work. In practice, then, there seems little prospect of any significant addition to Shakespeare's Jacobean dramatic canon. But we cannot be so confident about the situation at the other end of his career. The authority of Heminges and Condell diminishes the further back into the sixteenth century we go. *Love's Labour's Won* probably post-dates *Love's Labour's Lost*, and hence belongs to the mid-1590s; nevertheless, it failed to find a place in the Folio. The Folio certainly does include plays which Shakespeare wrote before 1594, when the Chamberlain's Men was formed; but we cannot be sure that Heminges and Condell knew every play that Shakespeare wrote in that earlier period, or would have been able to secure copies of every play they remembered. The plays that Shakespeare wrote for the Chamberlain's Men became and remained the property of that company, which survived without interruption until the publication of the 1623 Folio. But although that company clearly acquired some of the scripts that Shakespeare wrote before the company's formation, nothing in Elizabethan theatrical practice guarantees that they would have acquired all of them. The plays were not Shakespeare's property; he could not automatically bring them with him, when he moved into a new company—even if he had written the whole play. His claim upon collaborative early plays would be even more tenuous. If Shakespeare were a sharer in a company which broke up, he might ask for his proportion of the company's remaining assets to be paid in playscripts; but we have no evidence that he was a sharer in any early company. Shakespeare might well have written, early in his career, whole plays or parts of plays, lost or extant, which were not included in the 1623 collection.

The Folio cannot be relied upon to contain all Shakespeare's collaborative plays, or all his dramatic work from the late 1580s and early 1590s. Nor should we assume, as though it were an article of faith guaranteed by divine revelation, that the Folio excludes all collaborative plays. In evaluating the authority of the Folio in this regard we must answer two separate questions: did Shakespeare ever collaborate, and if so did the Folio editors on principle exclude such works?

It has often been assumed or asserted that Shakespeare did not collaborate. Leonard Digges praised him because he did not beg 'from each witty friend a Scene | To peece his Acts with' (Commendatory Poems, p. xlvi/lxii, ll. 16–17). But this claim must be understood in its context: a poem repeatedly contrasting Shakespeare with the most admired playwrights of the 1620s and 1630s. Digges elsewhere in the poem explicitly contrasts Shakespeare with Jonson, and here by implication contrasts him with Fletcher, who wrote almost entirely in collaboration with other playwrights. Of Fletcher one might reasonably say that he borrowed from 'each' witty friend a scene. Shakespeare collaborated less frequently, and with fewer partners, and by comparison to Fletcher (or most of the playwrights of Fletcher's generation) Shakespeare deserved Digges's praise. But that praise must be understood in relative terms. After all, Digges also claims that Shakespeare never borrowed material from Greek, Latin, or foreign authors, and never plagiarized from his own countrymen— claims which we know to be exaggerated.

It has been estimated that as many as half the plays written for the public theatres during Shakespeare's writing life were collaborative (Bentley, 199); in the companies which worked for Henslowe, the proportion is nearer two-thirds. According to contemporary documentary evidence, Greene, Marlowe, Nashe, Lodge, and Peele all collaborated; so did Jonson, Middleton, Webster, Tourneur, Chapman, Marston, Dekker, Beaumont, Fletcher, Massinger, Rowley, Heywood, Drayton, Chettle, Munday, Daborne, Field, and indeed every public playwright about whom we know anything. Shakespeare, recognized from the beginning of his career as a 'Johannes fac totum', seems intrinsically unlikely to have differed in this respect from all his contemporaries. We have no reason to believe that he shared Jonson's élitist classical disdain of collaboration—and even Jonson, who disdained it, did it. Those who advertised and those who bought the 1634 edition of *The Two Noble Kinsmen* apparently found nothing odd in the suggestion that Shakespeare might work alongside another playwright. Any objective perusal of Shakespeare's theatrical context strongly suggests that he must occasionally have collaborated—even if such collaborations are all lost. Anyone who wishes to assume otherwise must provide compelling evidence for that assumption, and no such evidence has ever been delivered.

But the near certainty that Shakespeare collaborated tells us nothing about the Folio's policy toward such collaborations. The absence of *Pericles*, *Cardenio*, and *Kinsmen* suggests that the Folio editors generally excluded late collaborative romances. Of course, such evidence is only relevant if one accepts that those plays were written in part by Shakespeare. Scholars who deny that Shakespeare wrote any of those works, or that any was a collaboration, cannot claim that the Folio excludes collaborations, for they have dismissed all the potential examples of such exclusion. But if we accept the growing consensus favouring collaboration in those three works, we must also accept that Heminges and Condell apparently excluded some works solely because Shakespeare was not sole author.

It does not follow, however, that they excluded any play which had been written in collaboration. One of the plays in which collaboration seems most certain, *Timon of Athens*, was apparently a stopgap addition to their original plan. Two others—*1 Henry VI* and *All Is True*—are chronicle plays, needed to round out the sequence of 'Histories' which forms one-third of the 1623 volume. Shakespeare's success in that genre distinguished him from most of the playwrights of the Jacobean period, and the Folio editors might reasonably have felt that Shakespeare's survey of English history represented a distinctive and coherent whole. The editors were apparently willing to change the titles of plays in order to present that section of the volume as a tidy survey of the reigns of English monarchs; it does not stretch the imagination to suppose that they were also willing to include plays in that genre which Shakespeare had written in collaboration. At least, we cannot assert that such conduct would be unthinkable or irresponsible. Like Shakespeare, Heminges and Condell, as veteran theatrical professionals, almost certainly did not regard dramatic collaboration as a crime against art.

In the case of late plays, Heminges and Condell must have known whether Shakespeare worked alone or had a partner. About early plays we can credit them with no such omniscience. Noticeably, with the exception of *Timon* (a stopgap) and *All Is True* (the culmination of the sequence of English history plays), all the Folio plays seriously suspected of dual or multiple authorship were written before the formation of the Chamberlain's Men: *Shrew*, *Contention*, *Duke of York*, *1 Henry VI*, and *Titus*. These plays all appear to pre-date Robert Greene's famous attack on Shakespeare as an 'vpstart Crow, beautified with our feathers' (September 1592). None of the plays that Shakespeare wrote in the twelve years following that attack can be seriously suspected of multiple authorship; then around 1604, with *Sir Thomas More* and *Timon of Athens*, he again begins collaborating. This pattern does not seem to us fortuitous. Certainly, it would have been difficult for any young playwright, trying to establish himself in the professional public theatre of the late 1580s and early 1590s, to avoid writing collaborative plays. After a playwright had made his reputation, he might—like Jonson, or Shakespeare—generally avoid collaboration; but an apprentice could hardly afford such scruples. It therefore seems likely that some of Shakespeare's earliest works, like some of his latest, were written in collaboration. The very period of his career in which he was most likely to collaborate is also the period for which Heminges and Condell must have had the least information and the dimmest memory.

Heminges and Condell themselves do not explicitly tell us what attitude they adopted toward collaborative work; nor does any contemporary. We must therefore interpret their actions on the basis of what we know about attitudes toward dramatic authorship in the period. Even in the case of reputable editions of single plays, like *1 Honest Whore* (*BEPD* 204), the title-page identifies only the main author (Dekker), though theatrical documents demonstrate that he had a junior partner (Middleton). Shakespeare wrote, at a conservative estimate, at least 90 per cent of the words included in the Folio; the remainder was shared out between at least two major nameable dramatists and perhaps several minor unnameable ones. In the circumstances no one would have objected to the title, or the credentials, of the volume. We cannot say for certain, on the basis of the external evidence alone, that Heminges and Condell did include some collaborations, or that they did not include any. They might have included one or two collaborative plays in exceptional circumstances (*Timon, All Is True*); they might also have included others from Shakespeare's early period, not being sure of his sole authorship, but confident that he did write at least part of a play, and anxious 'to lose no drop of that immortal man' (as David Garrick wrote in the Prologue to his adaptation of *The Winter's Tale*). Sometimes, as with *1 Henry VI*, both motives might overlap. Of course, in a modern critical edition we would expect the editors' policy toward collaboration to be made clear, with any instance of collaboration explicitly labelled. But the Folio is not a modern critical edition, and no one in 1623 would have expected it to supply the pedantry of marginalia and apparatus to a collection of popular entertainments.

If the editors did not automatically or consistently exclude wholesale collaborations, they would be even less likely to eschew texts that had undergone minor theatrical adaptation. The Folio text of *Macbeth* calls for a song at 3.5.33/1200 and for another at 4.1.43/1334; the two specified songs appear in a manuscript of Thomas Middleton's play *The Witch* (Bodleian MS Malone 12). This manuscript contains a dedication by Middleton himself, and was apparently copied from his foul papers. Two reliable documentary witnesses therefore contradict each other as to the authorship of those two songs. In *Measure for Measure* the Folio prints one stanza of a song at 4.1.1-6/1647-52; the same song appears, with an additional stanza, in two independent editions of *Rollo, Duke of Normandy; or, The Bloody Brother* (1639, 1640: *BEPD* 565),

attributed on the title-pages to John Fletcher and others. Again, an appeal to 'external evidence' cannot determine who wrote the song, for the external evidence contradicts itself. We know that songs were sometimes added to plays on the occasion of a revival. Did Shakespeare write the songs in *Measure* and *Macbeth*, or were they interpolated for a posthumous revival? Editors cannot solve such problems by invoking the authority of Heminges and Condell, for the authority of Heminges and Condell in such cases is the very point at issue. In *Measure*, the song and the passage of dialogue that links it to the rest of the play contain 196 words, out of 21,269: the suspect passage thus represents less than 1 per cent of the text printed in the Folio. In *Macbeth*, again, the suspect passages in the two scenes that call for the songs represent less than 2 per cent of the Folio text. In *Timon of Athens*, by contrast, Thomas Middleton appears to have written about one-third of the play. The Folio editors would be even more likely to accept adapted texts than collaborative ones. After all, assuming that they had no other text of *Macbeth*, would we thank them if they had decided to omit it altogether, just because the text they possessed had added a few speeches and a little extra spectacle, had transposed a scene or two, and made a few cuts? Shakespeare might have made similar changes himself, if he had lived to supervise the revival. Would it be better to print a cut text, or to cut the entire play out of Shakespeare's corpus? Obviously, in admitting *Macbeth* into the Shakespeare canon Heminges and Condell did a greater service to their dead friend's reputation, and a greater service to truth, than they would have done by omitting it.

In considering such possibilities the documentary evidence of the Folio itself must be interpreted in the light of other documentary evidence of theatrical practice in the period. We know, from reliable witnesses, that songs were sometimes added to plays on the occasion of a revival; so were epilogues and prologues (Bentley, 235-63). Other 'new additions' might expand the role of a clown, or introduce superfluous minor characters, or elaborate a scenic effect. Generally such adaptation did not interfere with the detail of the existing dialogue; it worked instead by means of discrete and substantial chunks—whole scenes or speeches or characters added or transposed or cut (*Division*, 195-205). The more successful the playwright, the more likely that his plays would be revived, and hence that some of them would undergo such adaptation. Shakespeare was the most successful playwright of his era.

Nevertheless, the amount of such adaptation has sometimes been exaggerated (Knutson, 1985). And until his retirement Shakespeare himself could have revised or adapted his own plays. Hence, when we find a scene added to *Titus Andronicus*, or a detachable monologue for the Fool added to *King Lear*, that fact does not in itself constitute evidence of posthumous adaptation. Indeed, in such cases we know that Heminges and Condell had access to an unadapted text, for one was already in print in a quarto edition; we cannot, as with *Macbeth*, excuse their inclusion of an adapted text by conjecturing that no other text was available. Since the clearest examples of posthumous theatrical interpolation occur in plays first printed in the Folio (*Measure* and *Macbeth*), and since Heminges and Condell's inclusion of such texts is best excused by the hypothesis that they possessed no other, we might reasonably surmise that such interpolation is unlikely to explain the variants in Folio texts (like *Titus* and *Lear*) that had already been printed in quarto.

In summary, every play printed in the 1623 collection must be included in the Shakespeare canon; but it does not follow that Shakespeare wrote every word of every play so included. Some allowance must be made for collaboration and for late theatrical adaptation. The number of texts in either category will probably be small, and in adapted texts the number of lines not written by Shakespeare undoubtedly will be small. The 1623 collection presumably includes every Jacobean play that Shakespeare wrote on his own; but it probably omits a number of collaborative plays, and it also probably omits some dramatic material written by Shakespeare before about 1595. Our capacity to repair such omissions with confidence varies. Any edition of a play written after 1600 of which Shakespeare wrote a major share would almost certainly have advertised the fact; consequently the range of candidates for the Jacobean period can be limited to anonymous manuscript plays, or to printed plays attributed to Shakespeare. In both cases we are searching only for collaborative works. Within the range of works so defined, Shakespeare's presence should be easy to identify on the basis of internal evidence, because of the distinctiveness of his later style. But in searching for early dramatic work by Shakespeare, we face severe handicaps. Fewer plays from the 1580s and 1590s reached print, and Shakespeare himself had not yet achieved a reputation which would especially encourage publication of his plays. His early work is more likely than his late work to have perished. Even if such work survives, we might lack any external evidence linking it to Shakespeare. Plays published before 1598 almost certainly would not have identified him as the author, for such attribution occurs in none of his known plays printed before that date. Francis Meres is not known to have resided in London before 1597, and he was in Oxford until at least 1593; he does not mention four plays included by the Folio editors, and all four—*Shrew*, *Contention*, *Duke of York*, *1 Henry VI*—apparently belong to the period before 1593. All four may be collaborative, too. Like Heminges and Condell, Meres is least reliable for very early plays, especially early plays written in collaboration. Such limitations in the documentary record ensure that we will always know less, and be less confident of what we do know, about Shakespeare's beginnings than about the period of his artistic maturity.

Such limitations also ensure that our knowledge of the non-dramatic canon will always be less secure than our knowledge of the plays. The 1623 collection of *Mr. William Shakespeares Comedies, Histories, & Tragedies* does not include any of his narrative and lyric poems. The absence of a collected edition therefore forces an editor to rely upon potentially unreliable attributions in individual editions and manuscripts. The authenticity of the two narrative poems can hardly be challenged, given the clear evidence of authorial involvement in their preparation. But the immediate and sustained popularity of the two narrative poems created in publishers an incentive to dishonest attribution of poetry to Shakespeare before such an incentive existed for plays. Strange as it may now seem, Shakespeare was initially more famous among the reading public as a poet than a playwright. After the success of *Venus* and *Lucrece*, the next book of non-dramatic poetry attributed to him is almost certainly an example of publishing fraud: *The Passionate Pilgrim* (published in 1599, or earlier) contains twenty poems, of which four are attributed to other poets in other, apparently more reliable documentary sources. Another three had already appeared in print in *Love's Labour's Lost*, in an edition attributed to Shakespeare printed in 1598—leaving only two which are independently ascribed to Shakespeare in later sources. These facts induce considerable scepticism about the authorship of the eleven undistinguished poems which are included in editions of Shakespeare solely on the testimony of *The Passionate Pilgrim*. Shakespeare's name was again taken in vain in 1612, when an expanded edition of *The Passionate Pilgrim* added nine poems by Thomas Heywood. Heywood complained about the theft, and noted that Shakespeare himself was not very happy about it (*An Apology for Actors*, 1612: STC 13309; sigs. G4–G4ᵛ):

Here likewise, I must necessarily insert a manifest iniury done me in that worke, by taking the two Epistles of *Paris* to *Helen*, and *Helen* to *Paris*, and printing them in a lesse volume, vnder the name of another, which may put the world in opinion I might steale them from him; and hee to doe himselfe right, hath since published them in his owne name: but as I must acknowledge my lines not worthy his patronage, vnder whom he hath publisht them, so the Author I know much offended with M. *Iaggard* (that altogether vnknowne to him) presumed to make so bold with his name.

The publisher subsequently inserted a correction attributing the relevant poems to Heywood; even so, Shakespeare's name alone remained on the title-page. In 1640 an edition of *Shakespeare's Poems* (STC 22344) included the Heywood pieces as Shakespeare's. Some years later, a collection called *Cupid's Cabinet Unlocked* was published under Shakespeare's name: it does not contain a single authentic poem.

Obviously, the attribution of poems to Shakespeare in print after 1594 has little or no automatic value as evidence of his authorship. By contrast, manuscript attributions of poems to Shakespeare have, potentially, much greater value. Manuscript attributions may be honestly mistaken, but they need not be suspected of deliberate commercial fraud. Moreover, printed attributions of poems and plays are often contradicted by other, more reliable attributions; genuine manuscript attributions seldom, and perhaps never, are—the two potential exceptions may both be nineteenth-century forgeries (see Introduction to 'Various Poems', below). The manuscript attributions can be corroborated, in a satisfying number of cases, by biographical evidence: the miscellaneous poems on Alexander Aspinall, the Stanleys, Ben Jonson, Elias James, John Coombe, and King James all involve persons Shakespeare knew personally or professionally, and most of those connections cannot have been public knowledge in the 1630s. On the other hand, no exceptional knowledge of Shakespeare was required in order to attach his name in the late 1590s to 'sugred Sonnets' written on the theme of *Venus and Adonis*—his most popular printed work.

Whether or not all the manuscript attributions are correct, as a class they deserve far more respect than the attributions in *The Passionate Pilgrim*. Nevertheless, in the past printed attributions have generally been respected by editors, and manuscript attributions ignored. In part this tendency derives from the application to the non-dramatic canon of habits acquired in editing the dramatic canon, which constitutes the bulk of Shakespeare's work (and of an editor's). As a class, dramatic works either reached print, or they did not survive at all; very few from the period of Shakespeare's working life are extant in manuscript. Of those few, only a small part of one may be by Shakespeare, and even in that case a decision must be based entirely upon internal evidence, for the manuscript itself does not identify its authors. By contrast, the lyric poetry of the period circulated more freely in manuscript than in print. The poetry of Sidney, Ralegh, Donne, Davies, Beaumont, and many others was never published in a collected edition by the author, and most of it was never printed at all until after the author's death. For Shakespeare's plays editors can rely upon a pre-constructed canon which they may supplement cautiously from other printed sources; for the poems they must, instead, retrospectively *construct* a canon, drawing entirely upon scattered printed and manuscript sources. Any editor will regret that situation, but regret does not relieve us of the necessity to survey the evidence and make choices as responsible as possible in the circumstances.

Hitherto, we have considered only documentary evidence which explicitly attributes a work to 'William' (or 'W.') 'Shakespeare' (in a variety of spellings). Such witnesses may be reliable or not, but at least we know what they mean. More difficult to evaluate are attributions to 'W.S.' Shakespeare was not the only man of his time with those initials. William Stanley (1561-1642), the sixth Earl of Derby, maintained a company of players from 1594 to 1618, and had written plays of his own by 1599 (Chambers, *Stage*, ii. 127, iii. 495). Wentworth Smith pops up among the financial records of Philip Henslowe in April 1601; over the next two years Henslowe paid him for two plays, and for part of thirteen others. Henslowe's records are interrupted in March 1603, and after that date we know nothing certain of Wentworth Smith. None of William Stanley's or Wentworth Smith's plays is known to survive. In 1615 the title-page of *Hector of Germany* (BEPD 329) tells us it was 'Made by W. Smith'; the author in an epistle mentions 'a former play' he had written, 'called the Freemans Honour, acted by the Now-Seruants of the Kings Maiestie'. This 'W. Smith' therefore wrote on occasion for Shakespeare's own company. He may be 'Wentworth Smith', but we cannot be sure. Warburton claimed to possess a lost manuscript play called *St. George for England*, written by 'Will Smithe', of uncertain date (Greg, 1911). Sir Henry Herbert licensed on 28 November 1623 a lost play called *The Fair Foul One* by one 'Smith', of unknown Christian name (Adams, p. 26). William Sampson is known to have written the lost play *The Widow's Prize*, completed in 1625, and *The Vow Breaker*, printed in 1636 (BEPD 510); he also collaborated in *Herod and Antipater* (BEPD 382), published in 1622 (see G. E. Bentley, *The Jacobean and Caroline Stage*, v. 1042-7).

A play attributed to 'W.S.' might belong to any of these claimants, and the initials cannot be taken as external evidence for Shakespeare's authorship. Such attributions might be honest, or might be half-hearted attempts to capitalize upon Shakespeare's reputation. However, the reference to 'W.S.' in *Locrine* (1595) can hardly represent false advertising, for Shakespeare's name did not appear on the title-page of a play until 1598. After 1600, any published work actually written by Shakespeare would presumably say so unambiguously. The use of the initials on title-pages in 1602 (*Cromwell*), 1607 (*Puritan*), and 1611 (*Troublesome Reign*) suspiciously suggests Shakespeare, without actually perpetrating fraud. No play previously attributed to 'W.S.' was included in the 1623 collection, and for the dramatic canon the initials do not have much significance (Maxwell, 1956, pp. 1-21).

For the poems, as always, matters are more complicated. One of the manuscripts of Shakespeare's second sonnet explicitly, and another arguably, attributes it to 'W.S.' (see Taylor, 'Some Manuscripts'). The initials must in this instance stand for 'William Shakespeare', and they attribute the poem correctly. Furthermore, the use of initials to indicate authorship occurs far more commonly in manuscripts of poetry than on the title-pages of printed plays. The initials therefore intrinsically deserve more editorial attention when appended to a poem than when advertised at the front of a play, and given the uncertainty surrounding Shakespeare's non-dramatic canon such texts should be studied intensively and systematically. Unfortunately, no such survey has ever been attempted.

As with the plays, so with the poems the initials 'W.S.' might conceal a number of artistic personalities. William Smith wrote a sonnet sequence called *Chloris, or The Complaint of the passionate despised shepherd*, published in 1596 (STC 22872); his known works have been edited by Sasek (1970). William Strachey wrote occasional poems from about 1604 to his death in 1621; what we know of his life and work has been collected by Culliford (1965). William Strode, chaplain to the Bishop of Oxford and later a canon of Christ Church, Oxford, was one of the most popular minor poets of the Caroline period; his poems circulated extensively in manuscript, and were collected and edited by Dobell (1907). The playwright William Sampson (see above) had his long poem *Virtus Post Funera Vivit, or Honour Triumphing over Death* printed in 1636 (STC 21687), while a second, 'Love's Metamorphosis, or Apollo and Daphne', apparently disappeared without achieving publication. The Bodleian includes a manuscript poem by a William Snelling (c.1650; Crum N570) and others by Walter Stonehouse (c.1656?; Crum H571, N316). Most of the poems attributed to 'W.S.' can safely be attributed to a particular owner of those initials. For instance, the card index of manuscript attributions in the Folger Shakespeare Library catalogue includes 76 poems initialled 'W.S.' in one or more manuscripts; but in three of those (V.a.339, fols. 185^v, 197, 197^v) the initials are Collier forgeries, appended to poems from *The Passionate Pilgrim*. Another 71 of those poems are attributed to 'W.S.' in one or both of two particular manuscripts, with strong Oxford connections (V.a.170, V.a.245); almost all of the 71 can be confidently attributed, on the basis of other external evidence, to William Strode, and since the compilers of both miscellanies clearly used 'W.S.' to identify Strode we must take those initials as evidence that they thought (rightly or wrongly) that the remainder were also by Strode (and not by any other poet with the initials 'W.S.'). Thus, of 102 occurrences of the initials 'W.S.' in Folger manuscripts, only two may be regarded as genuinely ambiguous. Neither, in fact, could be by Shakespeare. One was written by Strode (V.b.43, fol. 16; Crum G120); the second is an epitaph on a man who died on 'Aprill the 18 1622' (V.a.103, Pt. I, fol. 22). Thus, on the evidence of its card index, the Folger apparently does not contain a single poem genuinely attributed to 'W.S.' which can be assigned to Shakespeare. In her index of Strode poems Crum notes another sixteen 'W.S.' attributions, in the Bodleian or the British Library (B79, B251, F508, I430, L413, L415, M12, M333, P427, S215, S714, T2455, T2712, T2933, W1611); thirteen of these, again, occur in only two manuscripts (MS Eng. poet. 3. 97, MS Rawlinson Poet. 199). All but two (T2712, T2933) are attached to poems also attriuted to 'W.S.' in the Folger.

Any particular manuscript attribution to 'W.S.' must first be tested against the unambiguous documentary evidence for the poetic canons of Sampson, Smith, Snelling, Stonehouse, Strachey, Strode, and Shakespeare. The corpus of ambiguous 'W.S.' attributions could thus be whittled down to a small number of cases where those initials constituted our only documentary evidence. Those poems would then have to be compared, stylistically, with the known works of all contemporary 'W.S.' poets, in order to determine which canon (if any) should most probably receive it. Even then, allowance would have to be made for the existence of other 'W.S.' poets about whom we know nothing, or for the possibility that a playwright named William or Wentworth Smith might occasionally write poems—as other playwrights certainly did. The final decision would have to be based upon internal evidence; but the external warrant of the initials 'W.S.' at least provides us with an indication of which poems merit further investigation. The Bodleian, for instance, contains three poems attributed in manuscript to 'W.S.' which Crum could not confidently assign, on the basis of other external evidence, to a specific writer.

The sources we have mentioned account for 82 poems attributed to 'W.S.' in manuscript. Foster says there are nearly one hundred such poems; we have not attempted to duplicate his unpublished survey, and a proper examination of the additional 'W.S.' poems he has found must fall to future scholars. But it is already clear that, if we exclude the two manuscripts in the Folger and the two in the Bodleian (which by any criteria represent a special case), 'W.S.' attributions of poems in miscellanies are not at all common, and genuinely ambiguous cases are rare indeed.

Easier to locate than manuscript attributions are those which occur in print. STC and Wing include dozens of non-dramatic works attributed to 'W.S.' Most of those works were written too late or too early, or their subject-matter discourages attribution to Shakespeare; but at least one long poem was published under those initials during his lifetime, and at least three short poems so attributed occur in various collections. We have included a brief notice of all such printed attributions known to us, and of the three ambiguous manuscript attributions in the Bodleian, among 'Works Excluded', below.

Finally, it remains likely that some—perhaps many—of Shakespeare's poems survive in manuscripts, or even in printed collections, which do not attribute them at all. Most of the manuscript texts of the sonnets, or of excerpts from the plays, do not identify their author. In general, most manuscripts do not declare the authorship of most of the poems they contain. The law of averages suggests that some of Shakespeare's poems, circulating in manuscript, survive only in such anonymous contexts. On the evidence of those poems which did reach print, most of Shakespeare's non-dramatic writing comes from the early and middle 1590s. Some of that poetry must have been lost, because it never reached print; some of it survived only in ambiguous ('W.S.') or anonymous texts. Such gaps in our understanding of Shakespeare's non-dramatic canon occur in the very period for which our understanding of his dramatic canon is also least secure.

Authorship: Internal Evidence

Like anyone else, Shakespeare had tricks of style which distinguish him from his fellow artists. In part he shared such proclivities with his contemporaries. The music or the poetry of one century can easily be distinguished, by any practised critic, from the music or the poetry composed one or two centuries later. The distinctions between two writers of the same epoch are less broad, but no less real. External evidence is a label attached to a literary product, identifying the mind in which it was manufactured; labels can be attached to the wrong product, fraudulently or accidentally. Internal evidence, by contrast, is inconspicuous but incorruptible. The title-page of the Pavier edition of *A Midsummer Night's Dream* is external evidence; it states that the edition was 'Printed by Iames Roberts' in '1600'. But the study of internal evidence—of paper, recurring type, ornaments, headlines—established that the edition was in fact one of several printed by William Jaggard for Thomas Pavier in 1619 (see General Introduction, pp. 34-6). The bibliographer and the student of authorship both want to know who 'composed' a book, and when; both recognize that title-pages cannot always be trusted. Likewise, on 17 November 1595 Queen Elizabeth was entertained at Essex House by an interlude or dramatic 'device'; the Pierpont Morgan Library contains a manuscript (MA 1201, fols. 12-21ᵛ) attributing the speeches to 'Mr Cuffe seruant to the Earle of Essex'. But the speeches also survive in a rough draft (Lambeth Palace MS 936, No. 274) and a fair copy (Lambeth Palace MS 933, No. 118), both in a handwriting identifiable as that of Francis Bacon (Beal, BcF 308, 309, 314). In such cases the internal evidence decisively contradicts and refutes the external evidence. Unfortunately, the relationship between the two categories of evidence does not always produce such satisfyingly final resolutions.

All modern editions of Shakespeare's works include *Pericles*; none include *A Yorkshire Tragedy*. But the explicit documentary evidence for Shakespeare's authorship is almost identical for the two plays. *A Yorkshire Tragedy* was entered in the Stationers' Register on 2 May 1608, attributed to 'Wylliam Shakespere'; a quarto text appeared later that year, claiming on the title-page that the play had been 'Written by W. Shakspere'. *Pericles* was entered in the Stationers' Register on 20 May 1608; the entry does not name Shakespeare. But the first edition, which appeared in 1609, assigned the play to 'William Shakespeare'. Though omitted from the 1623 First Folio, both plays were added to the second issue of the Third Folio (1664).

Both plays were thus explicitly attributed to Shakespeare during his own lifetime, at a period when he was still actively engaged in London theatrical life. That attribution was never explicitly denied. *A Yorkshire Tragedy* was described as Shakespeare's in the Register as well as on the title-page of the first edition; there is nothing irregular about the Register entry or the subsequent history of the play's publication or the text published. By contrast, *Pericles* was printed (after some delay) in an execrable text, by a different publisher from the one who entered it. Moreover, the copyright for *A Yorkshire Tragedy* was owned by Thomas Pavier, who was not part of the syndicate of publishers which brought out the 1623 Folio, but who had instead attempted to bring out a rival Shakespeare collection in 1619. *A Yorkshire Tragedy* might therefore have been omitted from the 1623 Folio for legal, personal, or commercial reasons. If we confine ourselves to documentary evidence, *A Yorkshire Tragedy* has a claim at least as good as, and arguably better, than *Pericles*.

We do not mean to suggest that Shakespeare wrote *A Yorkshire Tragedy*, or to cast doubt upon his authorship of part of *Pericles*. We wish only to emphasize that both the inclusion of one, and the exclusion of the other, from modern collected editions rest in essence upon internal evidence. To most of us, parts of *Pericles* 'sound' like Shakespeare, and like Shakespeare only; *A Yorkshire Tragedy* does not. Such intuitions can be articulated, quantified, and verified, in ways subject to scholarly scrutiny. And if, on the basis of such internal evidence, editors are willing to accept some documentary claims and to reject others, then such internal evidence must be credited in other cases, too. One cannot concede that internal evidence distinguishes two styles in *The Two Noble Kinsmen*, without also conceding that the same kind of evidence distinguishes two styles in *All Is True*. One cannot accept the stylistic evidence when it concerns minor plays by minor dramatists, and then reject it when the same scrupulous methods, scrupulously applied, challenge traditional attributions of masterpieces like *The Revenger's Tragedy* and *Timon of Athens*. Editors must either blindly accept all documentary attributions, or they must accept the validity of internal evidence in evaluating external claims; and once the validity of internal evidence is granted, its application to other cases cannot be avoided.

These simple and obvious propositions must be articulated at the outset, because for the past several decades internal evidence has been regarded with some suspicion. During the late nineteenth and early twentieth century much of the Shakespeare canon was conjecturally redistributed among other playwrights on the basis of a little evidence and a lot of imagination. (Schoenbaum (1966) acidly chronicles the history of those follies.) Such speculation was magisterially rebuked by E. K. Chambers, who memorably characterized such efforts as 'The Disintegration of Shakespeare' (1924). Chambers set in motion a reaction which, like many reactions, went too far in the other direction. The fact that some Victorian and Edwardian scholars sometimes used little evidence, poorly defined and inconsistently applied, does not mean that studies of internal evidence conducted a century later will invariably be subject to the same criticisms. Acceptance of the cumulative modern evidence for Middleton's authorship of a third of *Timon of Athens* will not lead us to the pre-modern *reductio ad absurdum* in which 'Shakespeare' became an empty receptacle for the work of other playwrights. Internal evidence can only be accumulated and evaluated if one first accepts the validity and stability of a core of work of unquestioned authenticity, established by reliable external evidence and by its own stylistic integrity. Most of the plays contained in the 1623 Folio clearly belong in that category, as do the Sonnets and the two narrative poems. Around this radiant core circles a penumbra of less certain status. The individual works in that borderland are judged by criteria established by the acknowledged central works.

All studies of internal evidence, in any art form, depend upon the fact that artists repeat themselves. The more predictable and idiosyncratic the repetition, the greater its value as evidence of an author's presence. Such evidence can be conveniently divided into a number of discrete categories. The more categories which support a particular attribution, the stronger the attribution.

Biographical evidence cannot often be found, but cannot easily be dismissed when present. Connections with Stratford tend to confirm Shakespeare's hand in *Shrew* (the Induction), *1 Henry VI* (Sir William Lucy), *Richard III* (Sir James Blunt), *Venus and Adonis* and *Lucrece* (both printed by Shakespeare's fellow-Stratfordian Richard Field). Sonnet 145 apparently puns on 'Hathaway' (Shakespeare's wife's maiden name). Kerrigan notes a parallel between Shakespeare's own successful petition for a coat of arms and *The Tragedy of King Lear* 3.6.9–14/1856–61 (*Division*, pp. 227–8). However, much of Shakespeare's biography remains conjectural, and biographical conjectures—that Shakespeare was a lawyer, or that Chapman was the rival poet, for instance—cannot provide a secure foundation for further conjectures about authorship.

Palaeographical evidence may be direct or indirect: direct when a work survives in manuscript, indirect when the character of the handwriting of a manuscript is inferred by characteristics of a printed text. Obviously the former justifies more confidence than the latter. However, only six generally authenticated Shakespeare signatures survive, all from later in his life; Hamilton (1985) attempts to multiply this evidence by claiming that many other extant manuscripts are holograph, but he has not initially convinced specialists in Renaissance palaeography. Given the paucity in the direct control sample, controversy remains inevitable about its significance for disputed cases (most noticeably *Sir Thomas More*).

Theatrical provenance is sometimes established by title-pages, or by theatrical documents of other kinds, but it can also be conjectured on the basis of internal evidence: the presence of certain scribal hands, specification of certain actors' names, presumption of a certain size of cast, roles or spectacle characteristic of certain actors or companies. For those years when we know that Shakespeare was a sharer in the Chamberlain's/King's Men, attribution of a play to some other company would contradict its attribution to Shakespeare. Such evidence has recently become a focus of debate in relation to *Sir Thomas More*. The combined external and internal evidence that *The Puritan* was performed by a company of boys reinforces other evidence that Shakespeare did not write it; but in other disputed cases such evidence seems inconclusive. The internal evidence for attribution of theatrical provenance is in general less varied and less reliable than the internal evidence for authorship itself, and conjectural provenance provides an insecure foundation for conjectural attribution.

Chronological evidence consists of the variety of internal evidence—discussed below—which links a work, or part of a work, to a particular period of Shakespeare's personal stylistic development. Gross disparities in such evidence within a play, such as those between different parts of *Timon* and *Pericles*, demonstrate either (*a*) that the work was written at one date, and that part of it was thoroughly revised at another date, or (*b*) that it was written in collaboration. In general, the second hypothesis should always be favoured over the first, because it better reflects the practical norms of the Renaissance theatrical system. In practice, such ambiguous evidence will almost always be seconded by other evidence which decisively favours composite authorship, or will be self-contradictory: for instance, the metrical characteristics of the parts of *All Is True* usually assigned to Fletcher are in some respects characteristic of Shakespeare's earlier work, and in others characteristic of his very latest work.

Vocabulary can distinguish one writer from another, so long as attention focuses upon the overall structure and distribution of vocabulary, rather than upon individual words. Thus, the fact that the word 'palliament' (*Titus* 1.1.182/182) is only recorded elsewhere in the work of George Peele cannot be taken as reliable evidence that Peele wrote the first scene of *Titus Andronicus*. On the other hand, Hart demonstrated that Shakespeare's acknowledged plays consistently contain a larger vocabulary than works of similar length by other dramatists, and that Shakespeare is also unusual in his relative fondness for neologisms, certain kinds of compounds, and *hapax legomena*. Such criteria tend to confirm Shakespeare's authorship of *Kinsmen* and *A Lover's Complaint*—and *Edward III*. Such data can be rigorously defined, isolated, and verified; individual words might be imitated by other poets, but the whole pattern of vocabulary could not be. On the other hand, such methods may not always be able to distinguish a play entirely by Shakespeare from one which he wrote in collaboration. Thus, three playwrights, all with smaller individual vocabularies than Shakespeare, would also have vocabularies which differed from each other; if those three playwrights collaborated, the gross vocabulary of the resulting play would be artificially higher than the usual vocabulary of any one of the three contributors. If Shakespeare were himself one of the contributors, a mere vocabulary count would be unlikely to distinguish such a collaborative play from one of single Shakespearian authorship. Thus, more faith can be placed in Hart's evidence for Shakespeare's share of part of *Kinsmen* than in his evidence for Shakespeare's authorship of the entirety of the three 'Henry VI' plays. In *1 Henry VI*, such conclusions are further compromised by the fact that the chief contender for the authorship of Act I (Thomas Nashe) himself had one of the largest Elizabethan vocabularies outside Shakespeare.

Oaths and exclamations constitute a special sub-category of a playwright's vocabulary. Lake (1975) and Jackson (1979) have demonstrated that some Jacobean playwrights can be consistently distinguished by the type and frequency of such oaths found in their plays. Shakespeare's use of oaths, and their treatment in sixteenth-century plays, have not been systematically investigated.

Imagery cannot be defined so easily as some of the preceding categories. Spurgeon, in the first systematic study of the imagery of Shakespeare, claimed that in certain respects it differed consistently from the work of his contemporaries—for instance, in the frequency of images of natural and rural life drawn from personal observation (not simply imitated from previous authors). Waldo and Herbert have made similar claims about his use of musical imagery and terminology; as early as the eighteenth century, Malone noticed his exceptional fondness for legal terms. Unfortunately, most such claims, however valid, have never been systematically substantiated, making it difficult to evaluate the exact weight which should be accorded to the presence in a play (or a scene) of a certain number of a certain type of image. Moreover, unlike other kinds of internal evidence, images can be imitated. Such evidence supports Shakespeare's authorship of the whole of *Shrew*, and to the same degree supports theories of collaboration in *Contention*.

Image clusters were first identified and discussed by Armstrong, who was not a literary critic but a psychologist. Rather than count mere categories of image, Armstrong observed the irrational associations between one image and another: thus, a goose often appears in Shakespeare's acknowledged works as part of a chain of associated ideas including disease, bitterness, culinary seasoning, and restraint. Such patterns of association can be identified as a 'cluster' of images, dependent upon an idiosyncratic process of imaginative reflex. The more complex, irrational, tightly packed, and frequent the cluster, the greater its value as evidence of Shakespeare's hand. Such clusters confirm Shakespeare's authorship of part of *Kinsmen* and of all of *A Lover's Complaint*—and of *Edward III*. Several such clusters have been found in Shakespeare's share of *Timon*; none in the share attributed to Middleton. The weakness of such clusters, as positive proof of Shakespeare's hand, is that scholars have been more assiduous in tracing their recurrence throughout Shakespeare's work than in systematically surveying the work of his contemporaries for possible examples. Jackson (1963), for instance, noted an occurrence of the 'beetle' cluster in Shelley. However, the Romantic poets read and studied Shakespeare so assiduously that their works teem with conscious and unconscious echoes (Bate); a parallel from the Romantics does the evidence of image clusters less harm than would similar parallels from the Renaissance. Although we can say with confidence that these particular clusters seldom occur outside the Shakespeare canon, we would like to be able to say that they never occur outside that canon. Moreover, we would like to know what idiosyncratic image clusters characterize the work of other playwrights, so that the presence of a collaborator might be spotted not only by the absence of Shakespearian clusters but by the presence of (say) Fletcherian or Middletonic clusters. Finally, in evaluating the evidence of clusters one must beware of elastic definitions of the key terms of the cluster, and of expansion of the field in which such terms occur—a field of ten lines obviously constituting better evidence than a field of two hundred.

Verbal parallels have been used, misused, and abused more often than any other species of internal evidence. As a scientific method for determining authorship, they have two great disadvantages: they cannot be mechanically counted or measured (what qualifies as a parallel?), and they may be due to causes other than shared authorship (imitation, coincidence, joint derivation from some third source). Despite these weaknesses, their utility should not be casually dismissed. In his edition of the apocryphal plays Malone seized upon *Pericles* as the only Shakespearian text solely on the evidence of verbal parallels—a conclusion which has never been seriously challenged, and which has subsequently been supported by other tests. A large part of the evidence which links three pages of *Sir Thomas More* to the Shakespeare canon consists of verbal parallels, and Littledale (edn., 1876; 1885) first made a persuasive case for Shakespeare's share of *Kinsmen* on the basis of such parallels. Holdsworth convincingly reinforces other evidence for Middleton's share of *Timon* by analysing systematically verbal parallels in both canons. In such cases parallels have been trusted because most informed readers have accepted that the parallels are both genuine and plentiful; that their presentation is scrupulous and (within the limits of the technology of the time) systematic; that they seem unlikely to result from sustained imitation or from the mere exploitation of commonplaces of the period. The conviction resulting from such communal subjective assessments cannot be statistically measured, but it is nevertheless real.

One weakness of verbal parallels specific to the Shakespeare canon has not been paid as much attention as it deserves. Shakespeare, unlike most of his contemporary playwrights, was an actor; he therefore acted in many plays which he never wrote. An actor must memorize speeches, and Shakespeare must therefore have memorized many lines written by other dramatists. A verbal parallel between a work attributed to Shakespeare and a play attributed to some other writer, in which Shakespeare might have acted, is therefore of no conceivable significance in undermining Shakespeare's claim to the work conventionally assigned to him. Early efforts to disintegrate the Shakespeare canon usually overlooked this simple principle, which is particularly relevant to Shakespeare's early work—written at a time when he probably did more acting, and when we are less sure of the relationship between Shakespeare, an acting company, and its repertoire. Many of the parallels between Shakespeare's early plays and the canons of Greene, Peele, Marlowe, Kyd, etc., might be due to such causes. (Later in his career Shakespeare acted less, and his probable collaborators—Fletcher and Middleton—wrote more for other companies, and wrote many plays after Shakespeare's retirement and death, which Shakespeare consequently could not have imitated.) On the other hand, playwrights who were not actors would have no reason to remember multitudes of lines from Shakespeare's plays. Just as one should be naturally suspicious of the use of verbal parallels from other men's plays in efforts to disintegrate the early Shakespeare canon, so one should be equally suspicious of claims that other men's plays show everywhere the signs of intimate familiarity with and imitation of Shakespeare's work. This caveat applies, again, particularly to the early period, when Shakespeare's plays were not in print and he had not yet achieved a pre-eminent reputation.

Structural parallels were pioneered in an effort to reclaim several early plays for Shakespeare. Sampley showed that the acknowledged plays of George Peele consistently displayed weaknesses of structure absent from *Titus Andronicus*, and hence concluded that Peele could not have been the author of that play; Price showed that parallels could be found in acknowledged works of Shakespeare for the structure of certain episodes and characters in *Titus* and other disputed early plays. Although this technique of analysis was pioneered as an alternative to verbal 'parallelography', if anything it suffers from greater weaknesses than the study of verbal parallels. Larger patterns of structure and organization may be remembered by a spectator, and hence may consciously or unconsciously influence another playwright, far more easily than minutiae of phrasing. Jones has demonstrated that Shakespeare exploited and echoed the structure of scenes from early plays, like *James the Fourth*, which no one imagines that he wrote. We also know, from Henslowe's records and from other theatrical documents, that the scenario for a play might be written by one playwright, even though the play itself was shared out among two or more collaborators (Bentley, p. 239): even if we could be confident that Shakespeare designed a play or a scene, that would not prove that he actually executed it. In any case, what constitutes 'structure' is as problematic as what constitutes a 'parallel'. This method has usually been founded upon the critical premiss that a successful structure implies the presence of Shakespeare, while the presence of any other playwright implies an inadequate structure—a shaky syllogism upon which to base an attribution. One would have more confidence in the method if it discerned different techniques of scene construction, both equally valid, but associated with different playwrights: attribution must depend upon methods of analysis which are descriptive, not normative.

Metrical evidence has generally fallen out of favour, because some metrical characteristics are not easily defined, and because poets may consciously vary their metrical technique. Despite these theoretical and practical objections, some metrical evidence commands assent. Timberlake demonstrated that in respect to feminine endings (one of the most easily defined of all metrical phenomena in Renaissance blank verse) Shakespeare can be readily distinguished from most of his Elizabethan contemporaries. Oras, using three independent measures of mid-line pause, demonstrated a similar individuality in Shakespeare's treatment of the placing of syntactical breaks within verse lines. Similar techniques have proven useful in identifying spurious classical works, and Jackson (1979) shows that metrical evidence isolates certain features of *The Honest Man's Fortune* (*BEPD* 662) when linguistic evidence fails. Although unusual metrical features in very small areas of text may result from artistic choice or from the natural fluctuations which in total comprise any norm, anomalies sustained over hundreds of lines cannot be so explained: the unusual mixtures of rhyme, irregular verse, and prose in the suspect scenes of *Timon*, or the metrical disparity between the two parts of *Pericles*, or the two verse styles evident in *All Is True* and *Kinsmen*, resist rationalization. The availability of computerized Shakespeare data bases could overcome earlier objections that metrical tables present only conclusions, without documenting the individual choices and identifications on which they depend; in future, scholars should be able to define metrical characteristics more precisely, and signal specific licences systematically on computer-readable texts. Such procedures would permit detailed constructive criticism (which stimulates improved research), in place of the prevailing abstract scepticism (which inhibits it).

Linguistic evidence depends upon the writer's use of certain variant but indifferent verbal forms: *ye* instead of *you*, *has* instead of *hath*, *between* instead of *betwixt*, contractions of pronouns and auxiliary verbs (*you'll*, *I'm*), and so forth. Such evidence can be strictly defined and reliably tabulated; it cannot be explained away as the result of deliberate—or even unconscious—literary imitation. Evidence of the relevant linguistic practices of most Jacobean playwrights has been accumulated (Hoy, Lake 1975, Jackson 1979); it confirms that most of those playwrights can be distinguished by their treatment of such minutiae. One weakness of such evidence is its occasional susceptibility to sophistication by certain scribes; however, this explanation can only be invoked when the presence of a scribe is established by independent textual or bibliographical evidence, and when the pattern of distribution of that evidence is compatible with scribal interference. The presence of some such markers in isolated speeches might theoretically reflect a deliberate effort at characterization; however, this explanation can only be invoked for certain variables, and would need to be substantiated both by the pattern of distribution and by collateral evidence of the 'characterizing' effect of such linguistic forms. In practice, neither limitation affects many cases. Unfortunately, such evidence has not been systematically collected for Elizabethan playwrights, and it will probably be less useful in discriminating them, simply because their exploitation of colloquialisms and contractions was less varied and adventurous.

Stage directions share with linguistic evidence the advantage that they can easily be isolated and counted, and that their peculiarities cannot be dismissed as the consequence of literary imitation. Unfortunately, the nature of stage directions permits few idiosyncratic variables; but when such variables can be identified they may provide exceptionally reliable evidence. Holdsworth has tabulated throughout the drama of the period occurrences of directions in the form '*Enter* X *meeting* Y'; this formula distinguishes Middleton from almost all other dramatists of the English Renaissance. Taylor ('Shakespeare and Others') has tabulated occurrences of '*here*' in stage directions in plays of the 1580s and early 1590s; the adverb is rare outside the work of Thomas Nashe. Other formulas which might repay systematic investigation are '*aside*' (almost non-existent until the mid-1590s, and indicated by a variety of phraseology before then) and '*to* X', signalling to whom a speech is addressed (almost non-existent in the Shakespeare canon, except for its repeated appearance in one scene of *Duke of York*). Theoretically, the treatment of stage directions might be influenced by book-keepers or scribes, but such interference cannot explain the sustained presence (or absence) of idiosyncratic forms in the work of one playwright, or the concentration of such forms in one part of a play but not another.

Stylometry attempts to define a system of individual word usage which can be statistically measured and evaluated. In fact, several of the foregoing types of evidence satisfy this ambition; but 'stylometry' is strongly and specifically associated with the methods and disciples of Morton. Morton's techniques and conclusions in the analysis of Biblical texts have been seriously challenged (see Kenny); they are subject to particular objections in relation to the Shakespeare canon. For instance, tests based upon a word's initial or terminal position in a sentence depend upon the definition of a sentence—not a difficult matter in inflected languages, or in modern texts based upon holograph manuscripts, but impossibly inexact when applied to the modern punctuation in (variant) modern texts of Shakespeare, or even when applied to the (compositorial) punctuation in early substantive editions. Whatever the theoretical usefulness of such traits in distinguishing authors, statistical analysis proves nothing when based upon masses of unreliable data. ('Garbage in, garbage out.') The statistical procedures have themselves been challenged by professional statisticians (Smith), and hitherto have been founded upon a severely constricted sample. One cannot base reliable conclusions about Shakespeare's habits upon the evidence of one short play (*Caesar*) and two of disputed authorship (*Titus*, *Pericles*), especially when they lead to such patently absurd conclusions as the attribution to Shakespeare of the entirety of *Sir Thomas More*, despite the presence in the manuscript of the handwriting of five different playwrights. Nevertheless, although such teething troubles make it impossible to place any reliance upon current stylometric studies, they do not justify wholesale dismissal of the potential validity of such analyses. The limited samples hitherto employed can easily be enlarged, the statistical methods refined, and the tests restricted to characteristics not affected by the vagaries of Renaissance textual transmission. The study of collocations—*and* followed by *the* or *a*, *by* followed by *the*, etc.—might well distinguish writers in ways subject to reliable measurement and statistical evaluation. Such unconscious habits, sustained over large areas of text, could hardly be the result of imitation or deliberate artistic choice.

Function words satisfy most of the criteria emphasized by the champions of stylometric analysis, but they are subject to fewer objections. In a classic study of the Federalist Papers, Mosteller and Wallace demonstrated that the known work of Alexander Hamilton could be readily distinguished from the known work of James Madison by the relative frequency with which each used certain common words: articles, adverbs, conjunctions, prepositions. By means of this test they were able to establish the authorship of most of the unattributed Federalist Papers. Jackson (1979), in a preliminary examination of thirteen such words in the Middleton canon, showed that such tests are potentially of great value in discriminating Middleton from most other Jacobean dramatists.

In the hope that they might prove useful in solving certain problems in the Shakespeare canon, we asked Dr Marvin Spevack to provide us with relative frequencies, averages, and standard statistical deviations for 25 such common words: *all, as, at, but, by, for, from, how, if, in, it, most, much, never, no, nor, not, now, or, out, so, some, such, than, that, the, then, there, these, this, to, upon, what, when, where, which, who, why, with*. This information was derived from computer transcripts of the Riverside edition, from which Spevack had generated his *Concordance*. On the basis of the data Dr Spevack supplied, we selected ten words for which Shakespeare's usage was most consistent. That consistency can be—indeed, must be—expressed and evaluated mathematically. Consistency is defined by the relationship between the average and the standard statistical deviation: the greater the proportion of the average represented by the standard statistical deviation, the more variable Shakespeare's practice, and the less reliable the average as an indicator of Shakespearian authorship.

The ten function words selected, with averages and standard statistical deviations (s.s.d.), are listed in Table 1. The figures in this chart, and in our initial data from Spevack, are based upon a minimal definition of the Shakespeare canon, excluding all works of doubtful or collaborative status: *Shrew, Contention, Duke of York, 1 Henry VI, Titus, A Lover's Complaint,* the various uncollected poems, *Sir Thomas More, Timon, Macbeth, Pericles, All Is True,* and *Kinsmen*. We have in fact included all these works in our edition, and the degree of doubt attaching to them varies enormously, as can be seen from our detailed notes on 'Works Included' (below). However, in establishing a reliable Shakespearian norm one must begin with an uncontroversial core of undisputed works. This core data base demonstrates Shakespeare's consistency in using certain words with a certain frequency. In Table 1, the ten words are listed in alphabetical order; the first line of figures gives the arithmetic mean, or average frequency (per 100 words) with which each is used in the 31 works of the core canon; the lower line gives the standard statistical deviation. In a normal distribution 95 per cent of the individual figures will fall within two standard deviations of the arithmetic mean, and 99.7 per cent will fall within three standard deviations. Thus, *but* occurs 0.78 times per 100 words in the minimally defined Shakespearian corpus; in 95 per cent of Shakespeare's works *but* should occur with a frequency within the range 0.58 to 0.98 (= two standard deviations on either side of the mean), and in 99.7 per cent of his works it should occur with a frequency within the range 0.48 to 1.08 (= three standard deviations on either side of the mean).

Having identified ten function words which Shakespeare uses relatively consistently, we can then determine what proportion of the total vocabulary of a work those ten words normally constitute, and how frequently they occur relative to one another. This information is provided in Table 2. The words are again listed in alphabetical order. In this case, however, the values for each word represent its percentage of the total number of occurrences of all ten words. Thus, the word *but* accounts for 6.28 per cent of the total occurrences of the ten function words in *The Tempest*. After the ten words, below 'total', we record the proportion of the total vocabulary of the play which these ten function words represent: thus, in *The Tempest* they account for 11.14 per cent of the entire play. In Table 2, these relative frequencies are shown for all 31 works of the core canon; below them are given the arithmetic mean (average) and the standard statistical deviation. The figures for any play which lie outside two standard deviations are printed in bold italic. Such figures occur 15 times among the 341 values (= 4.4 per cent). Only one figure in Table 2 has a value of three standard deviations from the mean: the frequency of *not* in *Lucrece*, which is 3.17 deviations from the arithmetic mean. This does not mean that *Lucrece* was written by someone other than Shakespeare; it means that, in a homogeneous population, it should not surprise us to find one item out of 341 (= 0.29 per cent, or less than one third of one per cent, of the population) with a standard deviation of three.

The evaluation of statistical populations in terms of standard deviations is one of the easiest but most generally reliable of statistical procedures. For our purposes, we have regarded any value of two standard deviations or greater as potentially significant evidence, and any value greater than three as highly suspicious. Not being mathematicians, we have not attempted the more sophisticated multivariate statistical procedures employed by Mosteller and Wallace; but such analyses could, and we hope will, be undertaken in future, by those qualified to do so.

Most literary scholars will immediately recoil in horrified disbelief at the suggestion that Shakespeare's artistic personality is summarized by a statistical table. Such scepticism is entirely justified. Other writers might share this pattern of distribution with Shakespeare: it does not explain his greatness, it does not define his uniqueness. Nevertheless, it does represent an undeniable pattern in the uncontested works of Shakespeare's authorship. From that perspective, Shakespeare's acknowledged writing constitutes a homogeneous statistical population. Any candidate for inclusion in that population can be judged statistically, in order to measure the degree to which it fits that pattern.

This test is more useful in establishing that a work does *not* belong in the Shakespeare canon than in establishing that a work *does* belong. One might say that in judging the merits of an individual work, the test errs on the side of mercy: it would rather include a few bastards than exclude any legitimate children. In order to use this test as positive proof of Shakespeare's authorship, we would need to establish that no other writer of the period ever used these ten words with the same relative frequency as Shakespeare. Such conclusions could only be justified by a comprehensive examination of the occurrence of these words throughout all literary works written between 1580 and 1620. We have not attempted any such Herculean survey, in part because it seems likely only to prove what any reasonable person would expect: that other writers do sometimes use these words in frequencies which overlap with Shakespearian norms.

Nevertheless, we have run the function-word test on a sampling of works from the Elizabethan and Jacobean period. These works were chosen simply because of their availability in computerized concordances, or in the archive of literary texts at the Oxford University Computing Service. Each of the items in Table 3 was individually tested against the norms established by the Shakespearian core canon, using figures taken from Ule's Marlowe concordance. ('Deviation' gives the number of standard statistical deviations, rather than the value of the s.s.d.) The use of function words clearly distinguishes Shakespeare from Marlowe. Of the eleven Marlowe works tested, four have values in excess of three deviations; in fact, three of the four have *two* such values. Each of those four works also contains several additional values in excess of two deviations. We can declare, with absolute confidence, that the person who wrote the 31 works of the Shakespeare core canon did not write either of the two parts of *Tamburlaine* or the translations of Ovid and Lucan. If we look at the Marlowe canon as a whole, 36 of the 121 values (= 34 per cent) exceed two standard deviations; this contrasts unmistakably with the Shakespeare canon, where such anomalous figures constitute only 4.4 per cent of the total—exactly according to statistical expectation. Every single work in the Marlowe group contains at least one value in excess of two deviations. One would think that such evidence should for ever put an end to theories that Shakespeare was Marlowe—were it not

TABLE 1
Function words: frequency as a percentage of total vocabulary

	but	by	for	no	not	so	that	the	to	with
AVERAGE	0.78	0.47	0.93	0.47	1.06	0.64	1.41	3.28	2.26	0.91
SSD	0.10	0.06	0.15	0.08	0.15	0.09	0.19	0.43	0.24	0.15

TABLE 2
Function words: frequency relative to one another

	but	by	for	no	not	so	that	the	to	with	TOTAL
Tempest	6.28	4.13	7.45	4.85	8.71	4.76	11.40	28.10	16.97	7.36	11.14
Two Gentlemen	6.98	3.81	*10.79*	3.81	9.44	5.23	*14.43*	*18.08*	20.46	6.98	12.61
Merry Wives	5.63	4.46	7.86	4.07	9.41	4.46	9.89	27.16	18.82	8.24	*10.31*
Measure	7.14	4.15	8.37	3.46	8.53	4.22	11.52	24.65	20.66	7.30	13.02
Errors	6.31	4.69	9.55	3.32	9.47	4.13	12.78	24.11	18.37	7.28	12.36
Much Ado	6.90	3.91	8.81	5.24	9.98	5.49	12.22	22.86	16.96	7.65	12.03
LLL	5.95	4.40	8.65	3.32	7.95	5.41	10.89	31.04	16.60	5.79	12.95
Dream	6.19	3.63	7.43	4.46	8.75	5.95	9.58	28.24	17.09	8.67	12.11
Merchant	6.88	3.95	8.54	3.48	8.30	4.43	9.96	30.67	16.84	6.96	12.65
As You Like It	7.17	3.27	7.81	*5.34*	9.40	5.10	12.99	25.10	16.65	7.17	12.55
All's Well	6.90	3.49	7.48	3.82	9.23	5.57	12.72	26.02	19.37	5.40	12.03
Twelfth Night	7.14	3.90	8.39	*5.32*	9.80	5.48	12.38	23.34	17.03	7.23	12.04
Winter's Tale	6.96	3.90	7.19	3.98	9.48	6.04	10.55	26.30	19.42	6.19	13.08
K. John	6.06	4.01	6.14	2.70	7.62	5.24	12.45	27.85	19.98	7.94	12.21
Richard II	5.67	3.45	7.64	3.53	7.72	4.85	10.76	26.79	21.04	8.55	12.17
1 Henry IV	6.41	4.33	7.71	4.16	9.35	5.63	9.61	29.61	16.10	7.10	11.55
2 Henry IV	5.41	3.58	6.66	3.58	7.57	5.49	9.82	31.11	18.22	8.57	12.02
Henry V	5.25	3.33	8.33	2.67	6.58	4.83	10.58	*33.83*	16.83	7.75	12.00
Richard III	5.46	4.58	8.03	3.29	7.39	4.90	12.45	26.51	20.32	7.07	12.45
Troilus	6.79	3.52	6.10	4.47	10.57	4.81	11.00	27.92	18.04	6.79	11.64
Coriolanus	5.48	3.01	7.02	3.78	8.26	*3.94*	9.88	30.79	20.29	7.56	12.96
Romeo	6.44	4.21	7.98	3.69	9.27	5.24	12.62	32.52	18.63	8.41	11.65
Caesar	6.09	4.20	7.65	4.03	11.03	6.10	12.43	24.53	17.78	6.26	12.15
Hamlet	7.03	3.13	6.64	3.67	8.36	5.16	10.78	29.06	19.38	6.80	12.80
Lear (QF)	*4.42*	2.95	*5.29*	5.29	9.63	4.68	12.32	30.44	18.47	6.50	11.53
Othello	7.13	3.69	7.63	3.36	10.40	5.20	12.84	23.99	18.96	6.80	11.92
Antony	6.37	3.60	6.62	3.86	9.22	4.95	10.73	29.42	18.78	6.45	11.93
Cymbeline	6.68	3.66	7.00	3.98	8.51	6.21	11.30	27.37	19.09	6.21	12.57
Venus	6.79	4.33	6.37	3.57	6.88	5.94	9.76	29.63	16.47	*10.27*	11.78
Lucrece	5.56	4.74	6.54	3.16	*4.59*	5.64	12.41	26.09	20.45	*10.83*	13.30
Sonnets	7.49	4.27	7.89	3.62	7.73	*6.68*	*14.81*	20.37	18.76	8.37	12.42
AVERAGE	6.35	3.88	7.60	3.90	8.68	5.21	11.54	26.92	18.48	7.43	12.19
SSD	0.71	0.48	1.07	0.70	1.29	0.63	1.37	3.36	1.42	1.16	0.61
RANGE	4.93–	2.93–	5.45–	2.50–	6.11–	3.95–	8.80–	20.21–	15.63–	5.11–	10.97–
(±2 SSD)	7.78	4.83	9.75	5.30	11.26	6.48	14.28	33.63	21.32	9.75	13.41

for the fact that those who entertain such theories are impervious to refutation.

But although the function-word test can clearly distinguish between the Shakespeare canon as a whole and the Marlowe canon as a whole, and although it can clearly eliminate certain specific works (*Tamburlaine*, the translations from Ovid and Lucan), it cannot discriminate so securely between the Shakespeare canon and other individual works. For instance, *Dido* and *Edward II* and *The Jew of Malta* each contain only one figure in excess of two deviations. If we were evaluating any one of those plays individually, the presence of one figure in excess of two deviations might make us pause, but it would hardly constitute decisive negative proof: after all, nine of the 31 works in the Shakespeare core canon contain at least one figure in excess of two deviations, and for all we know *Dido* or *Edward II* or *The Jew of Malta* might be yet another example. If we were called upon to admit too many such dubious works, we could reasonably object; but considered one at a time, we could not be so sure. We could not even reject out of hand *The Massacre at Paris*, though it contains three figures in excess of two deviations—because so does *The Two Gentlemen of Verona*. However, one needs no statistician come from the grave to tell us that, on the basis of these figures, *The Massacre at Paris* is a much more dubious candidate for admission than *Edward II*. Roughly, one might say that it is nine times more dubious: nine works in the Shakespeare core canon contain at least one deviation greater than two, but only one such work contains three. But it would take statistical methods far more complicated than those we have attempted in order to evaluate precisely the degree of probability that *Massacre at Paris* should be excluded from the Shakespeare canon. For the moment, we can say only that this test rather strongly discourages its inclusion, but cannot rule it out utterly.

In making such observations I do not mean to raise seriously the possibility that Shakespeare wrote *Edward II*; I am merely discriminating between two uses of the function-word test. If you take the Marlowe canon as a unified group, you can confidently say that the group is statistically incompatible with the Shakespeare group. On the other hand, if you consider some of the works in the Marlowe group individually, you could not prove, on the basis of this test alone, that Shakespeare did *not* write them. The function-word test can eliminate a group of works decisively; it can eliminate some individual works decisively; about other works it can only create suspicion.

Table 4 records the results of the application of the function-word test to a disparate group of fifteen works from the archive of the Oxford Computing Service, based upon

TABLE 3
Function words: Marlowe canon tested against Shakespeare norms

	but	by	for	no	not	so	that	the	to	with	TOTAL
Dido	0.07	0.03	0.07	0.03	0.09	0.04	0.12	0.25	0.19	0.11	11.19
Deviation	1.19	0.80	0.41	1.41	0.26	1.64	0.01	0.63	0.32	**2.60**	1.55
Edward II	0.07	0.03	0.08	0.03	0.09	0.05	0.11	0.29	0.18	0.08	12.41
Deviation	0.79	**2.42**	0.57	1.25	0.04	0.83	0.48	0.59	0.24	0.53	0.35
Faust (A)	0.07	0.03	0.08	0.04	0.08	0.04	0.12	0.27	0.19	0.09	11.15
Deviation	0.76	**2.38**	0.43	0.31	0.87	**2.09**	0.60	0.05	0.18	1.48	1.60
Faust (B)	0.06	0.03	0.08	0.03	0.07	0.04	0.12	0.30	0.18	0.08	11.49
Deviation	0.24	**2.50**	0.77	1.40	0.97	**2.01**	0.58	0.87	0.08	0.56	1.11
Hero	0.07	0.04	0.07	0.02	0.05	0.05	0.10	0.30	0.20	0.10	11.68
Deviation	0.56	0.41	0.14	**2.52**	**2.44**	0.15	0.90	0.83	1.17	1.68	0.81
Jew	0.09	0.03	0.10	0.05	0.09	0.06	0.10	0.25	0.17	0.06	12.30
Deviation	**2.73**	1.10	1.80	1.44	0.20	1.22	0.75	0.62	1.01	1.05	0.17
Lucan	0.04	0.04	0.04	0.02	0.04	0.04	0.09	0.43	0.14	0.11	11.43
Deviation	**2.54**	0.12	**3.02**	**2.48**	**2.88**	**2.20**	1.57	**3.66**	**2.63**	**2.82**	1.20
Massacre	0.06	0.03	0.07	0.02	0.05	0.04	0.13	0.32	0.21	0.08	12.63
Deviation	0.99	**2.37**	0.22	**2.09**	**2.56**	1.95	0.91	1.35	1.41	0.67	0.70
Ovid	0.06	0.06	0.05	0.04	0.07	0.04	0.08	0.26	0.21	0.13	10.47
Deviation	0.06	**3.55**	**2.48**	0.02	1.07	1.90	**2.30**	0.36	1.50	**3.74**	**2.48**
1 Tamburlaine	0.04	0.04	0.07	0.01	0.04	0.04	0.10	0.33	0.20	0.13	12.31
Deviation	**2.82**	0.04	0.63	**3.05**	**2.87**	**2.32**	0.87	1.76	0.75	**3.57**	0.19
2 Tamburlaine	0.04	0.03	0.06	0.02	0.05	0.03	0.09	0.38	0.18	0.12	12.16
Deviation	**2.78**	1.35	1.21	**2.60**	**2.72**	**3.05**	1.45	**2.76**	0.04	**2.98**	0.05

TABLE 4
Function words in miscellaneous works

	but	by	for	no	not	so	that	the	to	with	TOTAL
Anon: *Famous Victories*	0.09	0.02	0.07	0.04	0.08	0.04	0.10	0.29	0.18	0.07	11.22
Deviation	**3.26**	**2.79**	0.51	0.53	0.23	**2.01**	0.98	0.67	0.02	0.33	1.50
Anon: *Leir*	0.07	0.03	0.10	0.03	0.06	0.06	0.09	0.22	0.27	0.07	12.20
Deviation	0.73	1.81	**2.17**	0.75	1.72	1.05	1.62	1.47	**3.96**	0.46	0.01
Anon: *Woodstock*	0.06	0.04	0.08	0.04	0.07	0.06	0.09	0.28	0.21	0.08	10.65
Deviation	0.85	0.71	0.52	0.07	1.22	0.79	**2.01**	0.39	1.57	0.15	**2.27**
Barnes: *Sonnets*	0.07	0.04	0.09	0.03	0.05	0.04	0.10	0.18	0.20	0.19	9.96
Deviation	0.65	0.28	1.53	1.60	**2.39**	1.21	0.92	**2.26**	0.89	**4.84**	**3.02**
Daniel: *Rosamund*	0.04	0.03	0.06	0.04	0.06	0.07	0.14	0.29	0.20	0.08	13.09
Deviation	**2.47**	0.90	1.26	0.54	**2.04**	**2.07**	1.38	0.59	0.89	0.30	1.40
Dekker: *Match*	0.06	0.03	0.07	0.06	0.11	0.05	0.09	0.26	0.21	0.06	10.28
Deviation	0.09	0.96	0.28	**2.45**	1.35	0.69	1.89	0.28	1.79	1.32	**2.69**
Dekker, etc.: *Witch of Ed'ton*	0.08	0.03	0.08	0.06	0.11	0.05	0.08	0.23	0.23	0.06	10.57
Deviation	1.72	1.15	0.03	**2.38**	1.55	0.89	**2.14**	1.23	**2.89**	1.22	**2.36**
Fletcher: *Demetrius*	0.09	0.03	0.08	0.05	0.12	0.04	0.11	0.22	0.20	0.06	7.13
Deviation	**2.80**	**2.28**	0.11	1.55	**2.58**	**2.07**	0.13	1.39	0.89	0.82	**4.60**
Fletcher: *Thomas*	0.08	0.04	0.10	0.07	0.10	0.07	0.10	0.19	0.19	0.07	9.87
Deviation	1.88	0.48	1.99	**3.42**	1.16	**2.25**	1.20	**2.11**	0.04	0.29	**3.10**
Fletcher: *Valentinian*	0.08	0.02	0.10	0.05	0.11	0.05	0.11	0.24	0.20	0.05	11.52
Deviation	**2.09**	**2.63**	1.84	1.20	1.47	0.68	0.50	0.81	0.72	1.85	1.06
Middleton: *Game at Chess*	0.05	0.05	0.10	0.03	0.05	0.03	0.12	0.35	0.16	0.06	11.50
Deviation	1.09	1.92	1.77	**2.24**	1.40	**2.58**	**2.63**	0.20	**2.15**	1.59	0.98
Middleton: *Ghost*	0.02	0.05	0.05	0.01	0.02	0.03	0.13	0.41	0.18	0.10	11.81
Deviation	**3.91**	1.54	**2.07**	**3.01**	**3.85**	**3.27**	1.00	**3.33**	0.25	**2.02**	0.61
Middleton: *Rev. Trag.*	0.07	0.03	0.07	0.03	0.08	0.05	0.13	0.25	0.21	0.07	10.29
Deviation	0.88	1.53	0.11	0.69	0.47	0.20	0.84	0.48	1.42	0.37	**2.68**
Middleton: *Witch*	0.06	0.03	0.09	0.04	0.10	0.05	0.12	0.23	0.22	0.06	10.77
Deviation	0.20	1.61	1.41	0.52	0.94	0.88	0.02	1.04	**2.03**	1.23	**2.12**
Nashe: *Summer's*	0.07	0.03	0.09	0.05	0.07	0.04	0.11	0.27	0.21	0.06	12.05
Deviation	1.38	**2.30**	1.22	**2.06**	1.21	1.24	0.72	0.11	1.66	1.21	0.23

figures generated by the Oxford Concordance Program. As can be seen, all these works contain at least one figure which falls outside two standard deviations of the Shakespearian mean; fourteen of the fifteen include more than one such figure, six contain at least one figure outside three standard deviations, and two contain one figure outside four deviations. Even without other evidence, we could deduce on the basis of these figures that most of the works in Table 4 were not written by Shakespeare. On the other hand, as we would expect, a few individual items are, in their distribution of function words, statistically indistinguishable from Shakespeare: one has only one deviant figure, and another six have only two. Such results should not encourage speculation that Shakespeare had a hitherto unsuspected hand in those works: yet again, it simply confirms that the function-word test, as presently defined, rules works out more reliably than it rules them in.

Finally, we can evaluate the extent to which the test might be influenced by, or might help to identify, textual corruption. Individual compositorial or scribal error can obviously have no effect upon a test dealing with such high frequencies of common words; memorial reconstruction, however, might be expected to result in a significantly aberrant distribution of function words. We therefore tested individual texts suspected of memorial reconstruction against the norms established by the Shakespearian data base, using figures from Spevack's *Concordance*; the results are presented in Table 5.

Noticeably, three of the texts generally regarded as 'bad quartos'—the first editions of *Romeo*, *Henry V*, and *Hamlet*—do not contain a single figure which exceeds two deviations. Either these texts were not produced by a process of memorial reconstruction, or memorial reconstruction did not always have a significant effect upon the pattern of distribution of these words. As memorial reconstructions differ greatly among themselves (see Taylor, *Three Studies*), the second explanation seems to us the more plausible. However, the function-word test by itself cannot resolve the problem. The test can, however, demonstrate that neither the first edition of *Merry Wives* nor that of *Duke of York* is likely to be a genuine, normally transmitted work by Shakespeare. *Merry Wives*, the least reliable of all the bad quartos textually, is also the most deviant in its treatment of function words. *The Taming of a Shrew* and *The Troublesome Reign of John, King of England* differ noticeably both from the Shakespearian norm and from the recognized memorial reconstructions. We can therefore be entirely confident that (despite claims to the contrary by Sams and Everitt) Shakespeare wrote neither work, and reasonably confident that neither work is an ordinary memorial reconstruction of a play by Shakespeare. Both plays resemble 'bad quartos' less than they do plays like *King Leir* and *The Famous Victories of Henry the Fifth* (Table 4), which served as sources for plays by Shakespeare. We seem to be dealing, in the two *Shrew* plays and the two on King John, with derivative works rather than derivative texts. This conclusion does not

TABLE 5
Function words in suspected memorial texts

	but	by	for	no	not	so	that	the	to	with	TOTAL
Contention (1594)	0.08	0.03	0.10	0.03	0.06	0.04	0.13	0.28	0.18	0.06	12.28
Deviation	1.71	0.93	**2.12**	1.21	1.85	1.36	0.94	0.39	0.28	1.04	0.14
Duke of York (1595)	0.06	0.03	0.10	0.04	0.06	0.04	0.11	0.27	0.22	0.08	12.43
Deviation	0.44	1.48	1.72	0.28	**2.10**	**2.07**	0.14	0.01	**2.08**	0.52	0.38
Romeo (1597)	0.07	0.04	0.08	0.03	0.09	0.05	0.13	0.23	0.20	0.07	11.56
Deviation	1.23	0.56	0.49	0.61	0.11	0.37	0.83	1.08	0.74	0.14	1.00
Henry V (1600)	0.05	0.04	0.09	0.04	0.07	0.04	0.10	0.34	0.17	0.06	11.16
Deviation	1.75	0.42	1.22	0.19	1.00	1.25	1.06	1.87	1.22	0.82	1.59
Merry Wives (1602)	0.05	0.05	0.10	0.04	0.08	0.06	0.10	0.23	0.22	0.07	9.75
Deviation	1.37	1.27	1.85	0.29	0.67	1.42	1.33	0.99	**2.37**	0.39	**3.21**
Hamlet (1603)	0.07	0.04	0.08	0.04	0.08	0.04	0.11	0.28	0.19	0.06	11.81
Deviation	1.14	1.06	0.02	0.70	0.36	1.47	0.62	0.20	0.63	0.98	0.61
Reign (1591)	0.05	0.03	0.08	0.02	0.06	0.05	0.09	0.32	0.23	0.08	13.47
Deviation	1.71	**2.27**	0.11	**2.32**	1.72	1.05	1.84	1.36	**2.73**	0.56	1.93
A Shrew (1594)	0.07	0.02	0.14	0.02	0.08	0.06	0.11	0.20	0.23	0.07	11.54
Deviation	0.79	**2.98**	**4.02**	**2.59**	0.60	0.51	0.45	1.88	**2.83**	0.02	1.03

help in establishing whether Shakespeare was the borrower or the lender, but it does usefully narrow the range of possibilities.

So far, the conclusions generated by this test are neither startling nor, in a way, very useful. Although Pitcher has argued for Shakespeare's authorship of *Famous Victories*, and similarly eccentric claims have been made for a few of the other works included in Tables 3–5, such conjectures have not been taken very seriously, and can hardly be counted among the incendiary issues of modern scholarship. However, we take it as one merit of this test that its conclusions agree so remarkably with the common sense of the last three centuries. It demonstrates, with some statistical precision, that the 31 works most securely assigned to Shakespeare are statistically homogeneous; that Shakespeare did not write the works of Marlowe, or vice versa; that he did not write a number of other dramatic and poetic works of the period; and that at least some (though not all) texts long suspected of massive textual corruption are indeed anomalous. Such conclusions will reassure the great majority of Shakespeare scholars, and may even persuade them that statistical tests may have something intelligent and intelligible to say about the limits of the Shakespeare canon.

But the primary interest of the function-word test, and our motive in developing it, is its possible value in arbitrating on Shakespeare's share in works of collaborative or disputed authorship. Because it deals in statistical probabilities, it cannot be applied straightforwardly to very small samples, like the 1,387 words attributed to Shakespeare in *Sir Thomas More*, or the two brief Hecate passages allegedly interpolated into *Macbeth* (303 words, not counting the songs), or the individual lyrics which we have gathered together among 'Various Poems'. But it should be of some use in evaluating long poems, or large chunks of full-length plays. We therefore tested, individually, each of the suspected works or part-works in Table 6 against the norms established by the Shakespearian core canon.

As can be seen, the totals for *Shrew*, *Contention*, and *Duke of York* contain no figure in excess of two deviations. However, in themselves such results cannot rule out the possibility of dual authorship in those works. As Tables 3 and 4 demonstrate, whole works by other authors sometimes fall within an acceptable 'Shakespearian' range, and it should therefore not surprise us if plays written in part by Shakespeare also fall within such a range. In such circumstances the collaborator's preferences would have to be very different from Shakespeare's in order for the discrepancy to be apparent in the figures for the play as a whole. The disparity would have to be even greater if Shakespeare wrote a larger proportion of the play than his colleague, or if the play were split up among more than two collaborators, whose individual styles would tend to even out the disparities between them. Without further investigation, we cannot be sure of Shakespeare's sole authorship of these three early plays; but the function-word test does nothing to discountenance that hypothesis.

By contrast, the figures for *Macbeth* and 'A Lover's Complaint' arouse some anxiety. Those for *Macbeth* exclude the Hecate material; the high deviance for the word *by* suggests that the remainder of the play may also have been affected verbally by adaptation. Only three figures out of 341 in the core canon have a deviance higher than this 2.82 registered in *Macbeth*. 'A Lover's Complaint' contains three figures in excess of two deviations: 3.25 (*no*), 2.79 (*by*), and 2.64 (*that*). However, in the core canon five of the fifteen deviations greater than two occur in the non-dramatic work: one-third of the high deviations fall in one-tenth of the sample. This suggests that Shakespeare's usage was less consistent in the poetry than in the plays, and in relation to the poetry the figures for 'A Lover's Complaint' are not exceptionally anomalous: *Lucrece*, for instance, has anomalies of 3.17 and 2.93 deviations. Moreover, 'A Lover's Complaint', with only 2,563 words, is the smallest sample we have tested, and the figures may be slightly distorted by its relative brevity. The function-word test casts more doubt upon the integrity of *Macbeth* than upon Shakespeare's authorship of 'A Lover's Complaint'.

The function-word test distinguishes with remarkable clarity between the two shares of both *Timon of Athens* and *Pericles*. In both plays, the share assigned to Shakespeare by other tests does not contain a single figure in excess of two deviations. By contrast, the share of *Timon* assigned to Middleton contains three deviations in excess of three (3.47, 3.40, 3.32), and another in excess of two. Shakespeare is more likely to have written *Tamburlaine* than to have written those scenes of *Timon*. To put it another way: Shakespeare is less likely to have written the suspect material in *Timon* than he is to have written anything else in editions of his Complete Works. Likewise, the first nine scenes of *Pericles* contain one figure in excess of three (3.76), and another of two (2.00). Although the spread of anomalies is not so great in *Pericles*, the highest deviance is even higher than any in *Timon*. No work in the Shakespeare core canon contains a single deviance as high as any of the four highest in the suspect portions of *Timon* and *Pericles*. Nor can the disparity in *Pericles* be explained as the result of memorial corruption. In the first place, such an explanation does not account for the disparity between the two parts of the play: why should memorial reconstruction have left the proportion of function words intact in three-fifths of the play, while seriously distorting it in the other two-fifths? Memorial reconstructions almost always deteriorate toward the end of a play, yet in *Pericles* the more Shakespearian distribution occurs in the last three acts. In the second place, the disparity in the suspect portion of *Pericles* is greater than in any of the bad quartos catalogued in Table 5. The contrasting figures for the two parts of *Timon* and *Pericles* cannot be reconciled with Shakespeare's unassisted authorship of both plays. Even if we had no other evidence—and of course we have a great deal of other evidence—the function-word test in itself establishes that Shakespeare did not write parts of those two plays.

Unfortunately, the picture is not so clear in the other suspected collaborations. In *Titus*, both the suspect scenes (2.55) and those more confidently assigned to Shakespeare (2.05) contain one deviation in excess of two; noticeably, the figure for the suspect material is higher, but not so as to be statistically significant. The figures throw a little doubt upon Shakespeare's authorship of all of *Titus*, but the doubt is not compelling, nor—at this stage—does it discriminate very usefully between different parts of the play. Likewise, in *Kinsmen* both the Shakespeare portion (2.28) and the Fletcher portion (2.49) contain one anomalous figure, though again the figure is a little higher in the suspect share. In *All Is True* the picture

Table 6
Function words in disputed works

	but	by	for	no	not	so	that	the	to	with	TOTAL
Contention	0.06	0.04	0.09	0.03	0.07	0.04	0.10	0.30	0.19	0.08	12.22
Deviation	0.63	0.27	1.04	0.76	1.40	1.21	1.15	0.88	0.41	0.36	0.05
Duke of York	0.07	0.04	0.09	0.04	0.07	0.04	0.11	0.26	0.20	0.09	12.53
Deviation	0.37	0.43	1.66	0.32	1.40	1.91	0.32	0.17	0.84	1.05	0.54
The Shrew	0.06	0.03	0.10	0.04	0.10	0.06	0.10	0.21	0.22	0.08	11.28
Deviation	0.08	1.86	1.93	0.25	1.00	1.85	1.02	1.61	1.98	0.09	1.42
Macbeth	0.06	0.02	0.05	0.93	0.08	0.05	0.12	0.34	0.18	0.07	12.64
Deviation	0.79	**2.82**	1.97	0.80	0.53	0.84	0.01	1.95	0.14	0.53	0.72
Complaint	0.06	0.05	0.06	0.01	0.08	0.05	0.16	0.26	0.21	0.06	11.39
Deviation	0.76	**2.79**	1.30	**3.25**	0.85	0.05	**2.64**	0.35	1.81	1.07	1.26
Timon (S)	0.06	0.04	0.06	0.03	0.10	0.04	0.12	0.29	0.18	0.08	10.97
Deviation	0.04	0.48	1.55	0.61	0.95	1.53	0.16	0.50	0.48	0.80	1.85
Timon (M)	0.07	0.02	0.09	0.05	0.09	0.08	0.12	0.17	0.25	0.06	11.69
Deviation	1.34	**3.40**	1.31	1.00	0.55	**3.32**	0.43	**2.61**	**3.47**	1.20	0.80
Pericles (S)	0.08	0.04	0.08	0.04	0.07	0.04	0.09	0.29	0.20	0.07	11.69
Deviation	1.56	0.06	0.48	0.43	1.12	1.76	1.42	0.53	1.10	0.07	0.80
Pericles (W)	0.06	0.05	0.09	0.02	0.07	0.05	0.10	0.24	0.26	0.05	12.61
Deviation	0.34	**2.00**	1.29	1.99	1.10	0.58	0.77	0.77	**3.76**	1.99	0.67
Titus (S)	0.05	0.03	0.10	0.04	0.07	0.04	0.11	0.27	0.20	0.09	11.59
Deviation	1.56	1.53	1.92	0.26	1.56	**2.05**	0.48	0.08	1.32	1.54	0.95
Titus (?)	0.04	0.05	0.09	0.03	0.09	0.05	0.14	0.22	0.20	0.09	11.94
Deviation	**2.55**	1.90	0.93	1.43	0.09	0.10	1.62	1.37	0.93	1.65	0.40
Kinsmen (S)	0.06	0.03	0.07	0.03	0.07	0.04	0.13	0.31	0.18	0.08	12.00
Deviation	0.71	**2.28**	0.70	1.23	1.07	1.57	1.20	1.12	0.16	0.41	0.31
Kinsmen (F)	0.07	0.04	0.08	0.04	0.08	0.06	0.13	0.25	0.18	0.07	10.46
Deviation	0.73	0.67	0.74	0.70	0.57	0.51	0.83	0.63	0.02	0.63	**2.49**
True (S)	0.04	0.05	0.07	0.04	0.08	0.03	0.11	0.29	0.23	0.06	11.86
Deviation	**2.61**	**2.23**	0.24	0.33	0.70	**3.06**	0.30	0.70	**2.54**	1.53	0.53
True (F)	0.06	0.04	0.09	0.04	0.06	0.06	0.12	0.26	0.21	0.07	10.69
Deviation	0.12	0.29	0.99	0.09	1.69	1.31	0.04	0.38	1.58	0.67	**2.22**
True	0.05	0.04	0.07	0.04	0.07	0.05	0.12	0.29	0.21	0.06	11.61
Deviation	1.97	0.87	0.10	0.39	1.33	1.00	0.31	0.64	1.83	1.23	0.92
1 Henry VI (N)	0.05	0.03	0.06	0.03	0.07	0.04	0.07	0.32	0.22	0.10	9.82
Deviation	1.41	1.25	1.49	1.16	0.94	1.83	**2.99**	1.57	**2.06**	**2.22**	**3.15**
1 Henry VI (S)	0.05	0.06	0.07	0.05	0.08	0.04	0.10	0.28	0.18	0.09	10.07
Deviation	**2.15**	**3.40**	0.14	1.32	0.49	1.96	0.86	0.29	0.62	1.55	**2.91**
1 Henry VI (V)	0.05	0.04	0.09	0.04	0.07	0.07	0.10	0.22	0.23	0.10	12.20
Deviation	1.67	0.73	1.20	0.52	0.98	**2.72**	0.98	1.49	**2.63**	1.86	0.01
1 Henry VI (?)	0.06	0.03	0.07	0.03	0.07	0.06	0.09	0.27	0.21	0.09	10.27
Deviation	0.17	0.96	0.09	0.82	1.03	1.25	1.64	0.04	1.86	1.03	**2.70**
1 Henry VI	0.06	0.04	0.08	0.04	0.07	0.05	0.11	0.27	0.19	0.09	11.88
Deviation	0.17	0.19	0.02	0.16	1.08	0.01	0.73	0.10	0.61	1.30	0.50

is even more confusing: Fletcher's share contains only one anomaly (2.22), while Shakespeare's contains four (3.06, 2.61, 2.54, 2.23). We should not be too surprised that the function-word test cannot isolate Fletcher's share in either play: after all, Fletcher's *Valentinian* only contains two anomalously high deviations (2.09, 2.63), and if we tested more Fletcher plays we would probably find others that fell even more comfortably within Shakespeare's range. It would take little if any 'contamination' by Shakespeare in order to push such Fletcher figures into the ranges visible in *All Is True* and *Kinsmen*. More disturbing is the anomalous profile of the material assigned to Shakespeare in *All Is True*. Such results suggest that the problem of collaboration in *All Is True* has not yet been resolved (see 'Works Included', below).

Equally confusing is the pattern in *1 Henry VI*. (In Table 6, N = Act 1, attributed to Nashe, V = Act 5, S = passages attributed to Shakespeare, ? = passages attributed to someone other than Shakespeare.) Act 5, which has been isolated by other criteria (Taylor, 'Shakespeare and Others'), contains two anomalous deviations (2.63 *to*, 2.72 *so*), which in itself would look suspicious. However, the Shakespeare share isolated by Taylor contains even more anomalies (3.40 *by*, 2.91 *total*, 2.15 *but*). Act 1, attributed to Nashe on other grounds (Wilson, edn., 1952; Taylor; Thiele), is also anomalous, though in a different way (2.70 total). Not surprisingly, if we combine all these disparate patterns and take only the reading for the play as a whole, the anomalies cancel one another out: the complete play does not contain a single suspiciously high deviation. We can only conclude that, in its present state, the function-word test can discriminate successfully with some collaborations, but not others. More sophisticated applications and developments of the test in future may be successful in sorting out these remaining puzzles—but then again they may not. Lavatch thought he had found an answer which fitted all questions, but we do not expect to find a single tool which solves all authorship problems.

However, the function-word test does usefully discriminate between three anonymous plays which have been seriously proposed as candidates for inclusion in Shakespeare's early dramatic canon (Table 7). The figures for *Arden of Faversham* and *Edward III* are taken from texts in the Oxford Archive; raw data for *Edmond Ironside* were privately supplied by Eric Sams, using a computer-generated concordance prepared for him by Louis Ule. Of the three plays, *Ironside* is least likely to be Shakespeare's: its three highest deviances (3.65, 2.74, and 2.55) are higher than any in either *Edward III* or *Arden*. Its worst anomaly is more deviant than any figure in the Shakespeare canon except the un-Shakespearian portion of *Pericles*, and its other anomalies are greater in both number and value than those in *Pericles*. No single complete text in the Shakespeare canon, whether good or bad, whether of single or dual or disputed authorship, is in its overall totals as anomalous as *Ironside*. Many works in Tables 3 and 4 are more likely to be Shakespeare's than is *Ironside*.

The evidence for *Arden* and *Edward III* is more ambiguous. *Arden* has only one anomaly, but its deviance (2.55) is greater than either in *Edward III* (2.27, 2.32). The anomaly in *Arden* might, however, be explained on the hypothesis that the printed text represents a memorial reconstruction. Even without such a hypothesis, the single anomaly in *Arden* is lower than six anomalies in the Shakespeare core canon. Of the 25 works tested in Tables 3 and 4, only one has a function-word profile more Shakespearian than *Arden*: Marlowe's *Edward II*. In *Edward III*, the anomalies might be due to collaboration; however, two proposed definitions of Shakespeare's share, assuming he wrote only part of the play, do nothing to make the function-word profile any tidier. In any case, the figures for the play as a whole are better than those for *Two Gentlemen*, *Lucrece*, *Lear*, or the Sonnets. Either play might belong in the Shakespeare canon; neither can be decisively endorsed or vetoed by this particular test.

The fact that, on the evidence of the function-word test, we can be more confident about excluding *Ironside* than about including *Arden* or *Edward III* reflects a limitation of most forms of internal evidence. If we want to establish that Shakespeare *did* write a play, or part of it, we have to prove that it contains a whole range of features characteristic of all his other work, features not subject to deliberate imitation, and not present (in combination) in the known work of any of his contemporaries. Not surprisingly, such criteria are difficult to

TABLE 7
Function words in three apocryphal plays

	but	by	for	no	not	so	that	the	to	with	TOTAL
Arden	0.08	0.03	0.10	0.04	0.09	0.05	0.11	0.25	0.17	0.08	11.15
Deviation	**2.55**	1.13	1.74	0.06	0.22	0.71	0.37	0.53	0.92	0.31	1.60
Edward III	0.07	0.03	0.07	0.03	0.05	0.04	0.13	0.30	0.20	0.08	12.71
Deviation	1.49	1.16	0.83	1.04	**2.32**	**2.27**	0.69	0.91	0.97	0.43	0.83
Edward III (S + B)	0.08	0.04	0.07	0.03	0.06	0.03	0.13	0.30	0.21	0.07	13.23
Deviation	1.68	0.10	0.92	1.58	**2.22**	**2.84**	1.08	0.83	1.67	0.66	1.60
Edward III (S)	0.07	0.04	0.06	0.03	0.06	0.03	0.14	0.29	0.22	0.07	13.15
Deviation	0.98	0.31	1.15	1.84	**2.01**	**2.74**	1.44	0.64	**2.01**	0.63	1.49
Ironside	6.98	4.07	9.64	1.86	9.64	5.04	7.16	22.10	25.46	8.05	11.31
Deviation	0.86	0.39	1.77	**2.55**	0.72	0.27	**2.74**	1.37	**3.65**	0.52	1.37

satisfy. With the exception of *Sir Thomas More*, no anonymous work has ever been successfully elevated into the Shakespeare canon. Even those pages remain a matter of controversy, after more than a hundred years of study. Moreover, the stylistic evaluation of those pages can be supplemented by palaeographical evidence, which is not available for most anonymous plays, simply because most of them survive in print rather than in manuscript.

On the other hand, if we want to establish that Shakespeare did *not* write a play, or part of it, we need only prove that it does not contain an idiosyncrasy characteristic of all his other work. If such idiosyncrasies crop up consistently, invariably, in every single one of his acknowledged works, without regard to date or genre or mode or theme or character or style, then we may reasonably infer that they are subconscious constants, imprinted patterns of association beyond the author's control, ruts in the roadways of his mind. The authors of *Ironside*, or of parts of *Timon* and *Pericles*, moved in a different rut from Shakespeare's.

One limitation of this test, and indeed of most others, is that as the verbal sample gets smaller, the verbal evidence gets less reliable. We have already noticed the possibility that this factor may distort the figures for 'A Lover's Complaint' (2,563 words); it might also account, in part, for some of the discrepancies in Shakespeare's share of *1 Henry VI* (3,846 words). The suspect portions of *Timon* (6,538 words) and *Pericles* (7,906)—more than a third of a play of average length—should not be affected by sample size; and, of course, Middleton's share of *Timon* and Wilkins's share of *Pericles* harbour deviances greater than any in the smaller samples. But when we move from whole plays, or large fractions of plays, to scenes, or poems, statistical evaluation becomes increasingly difficult, and perhaps impossible. Ule (1979, 1982), using a battery of such tests, increases existing doubts about Marlowe's authorship of 'I walked along a stream for pureness rare'; but although his methods display a statistical sophistication sadly lacking in most studies of the Shakespeare canon, in their application to a sample so small they remain open to serious objection.

Consequently, in judging Shakespeare's claims to short poems we are at present, and perhaps for ever, forced back upon kinds of internal evidence which resist confident statistical formulation or evaluation: primarily, verbal parallels, imagery, and certain formal features—all subject to imitation, or to conscious artistic variation in lyric contexts. About such matters differences of judgement cannot be banished, or resolved. If we except poems called forth by private and public occasions (chiefly epitaphs), most of Shakespeare's short poems were probably written in the 1590s, before his verbal style had achieved the rich particularity evident in the seventeenth-century plays and in such late poems as *The Phoenix and Turtle* or 'A Lover's Complaint'. Even the Sonnets, though no doubt mostly written in the 1590s, seem to have been revised at a later date, and if we want a true measure of Shakespeare's lyric style in his first decade we must look instead at sonnets incorporated in the dialogue of *Love's Labour's Lost*, *Romeo*, and *Henry V*, or at the apparently unrevised first versions of some sonnets, or at songs and lyric passages in the early plays. This is a small body of poetry, and not a particularly distinguished one. Shakespeare worked best with dramatic materials, or with narratives which could be treated dramatically; what distinguishes the Sonnets as a sequence is the unfolding dramatic and psychological relationship between the principals. Shorn of such support, relatively few of Shakespeare's poems capture in isolation that singular wholeness and finish visible in the verse of some of his contemporaries. The fact that the rather mediocre poems in *The Passionate Pilgrim* continue to be included in editions of Shakespeare testifies to the difficulty of identifying his early verse: for either he did write those poems (in which case he demonstrably could write weakly), or he did not write them (in which case his admittedly genuine verse is not so different from such weak poems that we can distinguish genuine from spurious).

When evidence runs out, opinion runs in, and in the case of Shakespeare opinion will generally equate accomplishment with authenticity. But arbitrary taste cannot be made the arbiter of authorship. One may admire Act 3 of *Timon of Athens*, or disdain Act 1 of *Titus Andronicus*, without believing that such critical judgements, however confident, however warranted, have any pertinence to the problem of who wrote either. The poems, far more than the plays, still attract such critical pronouncements, only because we lack the kind of reliable multiple internal evidence which might replace them. More such stylistic evidence has been accumulated in support of Shakespeare's authorship of 'Shall I die?' than for any other short poem in the canon; yet, in spite of it, most critics apparently remain sceptical, simply from an intuitive conviction that the poem does not 'sound' like Shakespeare. The sceptics may be right in their disparagement of the available internal evidence, but if so one can only conclude that in the study of Shakespeare's uncollected poetry internal evidence remains, as yet, a tool too crude to trust. Where we cannot trust internal evidence, we have little choice but to credit external evidence. The Oxford edition accordingly includes all those poems—and only those poems—attributed specifically to 'William Shakespeare' in contemporary documents which are not contradicted by other contemporary documents. As editors, we can only modestly defer to the testimony of the extant witnesses, when we lack any other evidence more substantial than our own aesthetic judgement.

Chronology: External Evidence

The same categories of documentary evidence which establish authorship may also establish date of composition. A play must have been written before it could be printed or performed. The publication of a text, or even the entry of a text in the Stationers' Register, proves that it existed by that date. Explicit references to a play, or records of its performance, serve the purpose equally well, so long as the play we mean is the play our informants meant—an equation by no means always so evident as editors would wish.

Such documentary evidence suffers from two abiding and insuperable weaknesses: paucity and incompleteness. We do not have enough of it, and it tells us only half of what we need to know. We can identify the first performances of only two plays: *All Is True* and *1 Henry VI*—the latter depending upon a disputable interpretation of the word 'ne', combined with an equally disputable identification of 'harey the vi'. If more theatrical records of the period had survived, we would know on which day each play was completed by the author(s), handed over to the company, and paid for; but the meagre documents in our possession in some cases do not even specify which decade. Even when explicit references to a play do survive, they only fix one end of a chronological continuum: a closing bracket, without an opening one. The knowledge that a person had been born by 1598 does not tell us that person's age in 1598, and references to a play usually only establish its existence, not its age. As a result, we can always say 'not later than' more confidently than we say 'not earlier than'.

Beyond these general weaknesses, particular species of external evidence create particular kinds of difficulty. Titles, for instance, are sometimes mentioned in early documents, and then appear later affixed to printed texts; one naturally assumes that the text attached to the title in an edition is the text implied by that title in the documentary allusion. That assumption is usually justified, but plays were sometimes adapted, and the published edition might represent a play in its post-adaptation or pre-adaptation form, depending on the kind of manuscript from which it was printed. Since we can only determine the kind of manuscript which lies behind an edition by examining certain minutiae of its text, our interpretation of the chronological significance of the 'external' evidence of an edition's existence will depend upon the 'internal' evidence afforded by bibliographical and textual analysis. Alternatively, the same abbreviated title might be affixed to more than one play of the period. We know that the Admiral's Men in November 1595 performed a 'ne[w]' play which Henslowe's records identify as 'harey the v'; no one supposes that it was the play on the same subject, written by Shakespeare, which was later performed by the Chamberlain's Men; but a reference to 'Henry the Fifth', out of context, could refer to either. Similar ambiguities arise, more contentiously, in relation to two texts which dramatize the taming of 'a' or 'the' shrew: the variant article seems designed to signal inconspicuously a difference which the identity of the rest of the title conspicuously conceals—a subterfuge no doubt designed to tease or deceive audiences, and which continues to bemuse scholars.

Francis Meres helps fix the chronology of the early dramatic canon as well as its contents. *Palladis Tamia*, in which he mentions twelve of Shakespeare's plays by name, was entered in the Stationers' Register on 7 September 1598; hence, those twelve plays must have been written before that date. Elsewhere in his book Meres mentions Edward Guilpin's *Skialetheia* (STC 12504), entered in the Stationers' Register eight days after *Palladis Tamia* itself; scholars often take Meres's knowledge of Guilpin's book as proof that his summary of Shakespeare's canon was similarly up-to-date. But the two cases are not similar: Guilpin's book might have circulated in manuscript before its sale to a publisher, but Shakespeare's plays would become known only through public performance. In terms of performance, the exact date of the entry of *Palladis Tamia* matters less than the pattern of London theatrical seasons.

The London season, in Shakespeare's time and for centuries after, usually coincided with the legal calendar, running from the beginning of Michaelmas Term in the autumn to the end of Trinity Term in early summer. During the summer the smart set left London for their country estates; indeed, by law landowners were required to spend a certain amount of time each year on their estates. Queen Elizabeth chose the summer months for her periodic progresses through the country, and for similar reasons the actors toured the provinces then: during the summer the weather was better, and better weather made for easier transportation and larger audiences in the makeshift provincial venues. The exact dates no doubt fluctuated—as the end of term did—but we know of no public performances in London by any company with which Shakespeare was associated after 29 June (*All Is True*) or perhaps 3 July (Chambers, *Shakespeare*, ii. 322-3), and of none before 13 September (*Shakespeare*, ii. 328). For mid-September to June we have records of many performances in London or at court (in and around London). By contrast, if we ignore times of plague, the summer months account for almost every datable reference to a provincial performance by a London company with which Shakespeare was—or may have been—associated. Moreover, accounts of provincial performances by Strange's Men (1591-3) and the Chamberlain's/King's Men (1594-1613) have been found for almost every year of Shakespeare's professional career. (For performance records see Chambers, *Shakespeare*, ii. 303-45; his account of provincial records has since been supplemented by Malone Society Collections II.3, VII, VIII, IX, XI, and REED volumes for Chester, Coventry, Cumberland, Gloucestershire, Newcastle-upon-Tyne, Norwich, Westmorland, and York.) John Aubrey also recorded (in 1681) that Shakespeare returned home to Stratford each year, and since the trip took three days each way he would probably not have made it frequently, or for short stays, and the summer interims would have provided the most natural opportunities for a prolonged stay in Stratford. Although we cannot often be certain of Shakespeare's whereabouts, what evidence we have does not discourage the assumption that he left London when the company did, during the summers: he to go home, they to tour. He was undoubtedly in London on 15 March 1595 and 1603, on 10 and 31 March 1613, on 11 May 1612, and on 15 October 1598; all these dates fall within the regular London theatrical season. His presence at Stratford is harder to demonstrate because we do not know how many of his business dealings were executed by his father, mother, wife, or friends. However, he was involved in major business transactions finalized at Stratford on 1 May 1602, 4 May 1597, 24 July 1605, and 11 September 1611; his daughter Susanna was married on 5 June 1607. Noticeably, only in early May is there any overlap between these Stratford dates (May to mid-September) and the London dates (mid-October to mid-May). Of course, the dates of Shakespeare's Stratford visits, like the limits of the London season itself, must have fluctuated slightly, but it is reasonable to assume that Shakespeare was usually in Stratford for July and August at least. The company would not be likely to rehearse one of his new plays in his absence, nor would they be likely to open a new play in the last week of the season, and consequently it would be safest to assume that none of his plays was given a first performance in July, August, or the first half of September.

At some time after the acquisition of the Blackfriars indoor playhouse (August 1608), this pattern apparently changed: James Wright in his *Historia Histrionica* (1699) claimed that, before the closure of the theatres, the King's Men owned 'The Black-friers, and Globe on the Bankside, a Winter and Summer House'. Once the company had acquired two theatres, it could use the more comfortable indoor venue during the 'season', when it depended upon a wealthier clientele, and the cheaper, more popular, open-air Globe during more temperate months. However, in April 1610 Prince Lewis Frederick of Württemberg saw *Othello* at the Globe, and in April 1611 Simon Forman saw two plays there: if the Globe had already become a 'summer' house, 'summer' was liberally defined. It seems likely that Wright was describing developments which post-dated Shakespeare's retirement from the theatre.

This evidence from Shakespeare's own company may be supplemented, cautiously, by evidence from Henslowe's records of companies at the Rose playhouse. In 1595, 1596, 1599, and 1600 gaps in Henslowe's records indicate a break in London playing over the summer. In 1594 no such break occurs—which is hardly surprising, given the fact that plague had prevented public performances in London for most of the preceding two years. For 1597 and 1598, however, playing also appears to have continued during the summer, for reasons which are harder to fathom. We know that the Chamberlain's Men broke for the summer in 1597, because we have records of provincial performances at Faversham in August and Bristol in mid-September. But 1598 is one of the few years for which we do not (yet) have positive evidence of a summer tour by the Chamberlain's/King's Men; so it is possible that they stayed in town, along with their rivals at the Rose. On the one hand, Henslowe's records tend to confirm that companies usually toured in the summer. On the other hand, the long season of 1594-5 reminds us that touring was a matter of custom and convenience, not law; during the early years of James I's reign, when plague so often foreshortened the regular season, we should not assume that the King's Men automatically left London in the summer, if mortality rates were low enough to allow them to play in the capital.

The shape of the London seasons affects inferences about dating throughout Shakespeare's writing life. To return to the example which prompted this digression: because *Palladis Tamia* was entered on 7 September, during the usual interim between London seasons, Francis Meres could hardly have anticipated the new plays of the autumn season. Thus, unless the Chamberlain's Men uncharacteristically stayed in London in the summer of 1598, Meres's mention of *The Merchant of Venice*, though printed in a book entered on 7 September, actually sets an earlier limit than the play's own entry in the Stationers' Register on 22 July.

Scholars dispute the significance of Meres's omissions. For instance, he does not mention *Shrew* or the *Henry VI* plays, which all modern editors place early in Shakespeare's career. Such gaps might be explained by the fact that Meres was still in Oxford in 1593 (when he took his MA), and is first recorded as living in London in 1597. But Meres does mention other plays which most modern scholars place in the same early period; Honigmann, indeed, would assign to those years over half the plays which Meres does name (*Lost Years*, 128-9). In the list as it stands Meres includes six comedies and six 'tragedies' (serious plays, including four based upon English chronicles); symmetry may have mattered more than comprehensiveness. But Meres could have added *Shrew* as a comedy, and *Henry VI* as a tragedy, without disturbing the balance of his encomium. The omission of those plays may have more to do with their authorship than their chronology. On the other hand, no one seriously doubts Shakespeare's sole authorship of *Merry Wives*, *Much Ado*, *As You Like It*, or *Julius Caesar*, and no one believes that these plays were written at the beginning of Shakespeare's career, and so Meres's failure to include them must have other causes. Honigmann proposes that the three comedies were new, and that Meres could not find room for three more comedies without fatally unbalancing his symmetries (*Impact*, p. 76). But surely anyone facing such a rhetorical dilemma would jettison an old play, never remarkably popular, like *Two Gentlemen*, in favour of a new, immediately and perennially successful play like *Much Ado*. We therefore suppose, as have most other scholars, that Meres does not name *Much Ado* and its companions because he did not know them, and that he did not know them because they had not yet appeared on the London public stage.

Finally, the items Meres does mention create some ambiguities. We cannot be sure whether '*Henry the 4.*' covers one play or two; 'his sugred Sonnets' may allude specifically to poems of fourteen lines, arranged in a particular rhyme scheme, or more generally to 'a short poem or piece of verse; in early use especially one of a lyrical and amatory character'—a wider definition 'very common' between 1580 and 1650 (*OED* sb. 2). '*Loue labours wonne*' probably identifies a lost play, but conjecture has happily attached it as an alternative title to almost every other comedy. Curiously, Meres enumerates the comedies in a sequence which corresponds to our own chronological arrangement—a coincidence we only noted after deciding upon our own order, and to which we attach no overwhelming significance. However, his catalogue of the non-dramatic poems also obeys what we know of the chronological sequence, moving from *Venus* to *Lucrece* to the Sonnets. On the other hand, his list of 'Tragedies' cannot plausibly be wrested into any semblance of chronological coherence. He begins with four English histories, followed by two foreign tragedies; the two tragedies do, coincidentally or not, appear in the order in which all scholars would agree they were written (*Titus* before *Romeo*). But the list of English chronicle plays does not correspond with historical chronology or chronology of composition or even alphabetical order: instead it seems organized by an irrational numerical progression, from 'Richard the *second*' to 'Richard the *third*' to 'Henry the *fourth*' (our italics), with the numberless *King John* tacked on at the end. Alternatively, the first three histories might have been listed in their order of publication, followed by the as yet unpublished *King John*. Whatever the logic that led Meres's pen, it cannot help us to determine the order in which Shakespeare composed his histories.

Meres, almost comprehensively, defines the boundaries of Shakespeare's early period, but he does not map for us the territory within those boundaries: he collects, but does not arrange. This deficiency is compounded by a peculiarity in the distribution of the other external evidence. In the period after 1598, we have records of specific performances for *Caesar* (1599), *Twelfth Night* (1602), *Measure* (1604), *Othello* (1604), *Lear* (1606), *Pericles* (1606-8), *Macbeth* (1611), *Winter's Tale* (1611), *Cymbeline* (1611), *Tempest* (1611), *Cardenio* (1612-13), and *All Is True* (1613). In some cases those performances took place several years after we believe that Shakespeare finished the play, but in every case they preceded publication or any other explicit reference to the play. By contrast, for works written before 1598 we know of such performances of only four: *1 Henry VI* (1592), *Titus* (1594), *Errors* (1594), and *Love's Labour's Lost* (1597?). The interpretation of all four is disputed. For the later period, performance records are plentifully and evenly distributed, creating in themselves a minimal chronological gradation; for the earlier period, the same records are hard to find and hard to interpret.

The same lopsidedness afflicts the record of publication. The first publication of a play included in the 1623 collection did not occur until 1594 (*Titus* and *Contention*), though Shakespeare was mentioned as a playwright in 1592 and can hardly have begun his career later than 1591. Another dramatic publication followed in 1595 (*Duke of York*), then three in 1597 (*Romeo*, *Richard II*, *Richard III*). Before the watershed year of 1598, although Shakespeare must have been writing for at least seven years, only six of his plays had reached print, and those publications are weighted heavily toward the later end of the scale. By contrast, after 1598 records of works published or entered for publication multiply and diversify: *2 Henry IV* (1600), *Much Ado* (1600), *Henry V* (1600), *As You Like It* (1600), *Merry Wives* (1602), *Troilus* (1603), *Hamlet* (1603), *Lear* (1608), *Antony* (1608), and *Pericles* (1608)—and the list would be longer if we included works mentioned by Meres but not published until afterwards. Such sources dry up again at the very end of Shakespeare's career, but the presence of performance records compensates for their absence. Indeed, by an uncanny felicity all too rare, in the second half of Shakespeare's career publication records almost invariably plug the holes in performance records, and vice versa: every play after 1598 except *All's Well*, *Timon*, and *Coriolanus* is covered by one sort of document or the other. No such luck operated in preserving documentary references to his early work.

In those few records which do survive from the 1590s, two suffer from the apparent ambiguity of 'ne'. Henslowe affixed those letters to the records of certain performances, and they have been naturally interpreted as a spelling of the word *new*. However, this interpretation, though it will satisfy the overwhelming majority of cases, is embarrassed by two occasions on which the play in question appears not to be, in the usual senses of that word, 'new' (*Henslowe's Diary*, pp. xxx-xxxi). It might, at such times, mean 'newly adapted' or 'newly submitted to the censor'—in which case, 'ne' would in fact on some occasions mean 'old', for only an old play can be newly adapted. It contributes little to the solution of chronological problems to be confidently informed that a play is 'either new or old'. However, the number of apparent exceptions to the straightforward interpretation of 'ne' has been exaggerated, and few plays were heavily adapted for the purposes of revival (see Knutson, 1985). We therefore incline to take 'ne' literally, as 'new'. But for Henslowe, as for modern metropolitan managements, 'new' means 'new in London': a play that had been touring the provinces for eighteen months might still be news to Londoners.

Of course, plays normally began their theatrical life in London; but at times the acting companies were driven out of London by plague. A severe outbreak closed the London theatres for all but a few weeks from June 1592 to May 1594. The plague then subsided until just after the death of Queen Elizabeth, but from June 1603 until December 1610 it seriously and consistently curtailed the annual London season, in some years probably abolishing it altogether (Barroll). At such times the acting companies became increasingly dependent upon private patronage, at court or at the Inns of Court, and to the same degree upon provincial audiences, before whom—in the absence of a London season—they would have to try out and perfect the plays which they would eventually offer at court. During such periods, interpretations of the documentary record must always take account of the constricted theatrical season. Indeed, although for the most part new external evidence is discovered only by chance (and increasingly infrequently), our knowledge of the shape of theatrical seasons in London will expand systematically in the coming years, as a result of the continuing survey of provincial theatrical records: we know the Chamberlain's Men were not in London when we find them in Oxford or Dover.

The shape of the London season may have affected Shakespeare's own patterns of composition as much as it affects our interpretation of the documentary record. John Ward (1629-81), who was vicar of Stratford in the last twenty years of his life, recorded in a notebook from the years 1661-3 that Shakespeare 'supplied ye stage with 2 plays every year' (Schoenbaum, *Documentary Life*, p. 155). A simple calculation of the length of Shakespeare's career and the number of his plays produces roughly the same figure. But his productivity must have fluctuated. However we arrange the evidence, in the Jacobean period he wrote fewer plays, and of those few wrote more in collaboration. A certain relaxation often enough attends age and success; a corresponding excess of energy may accompany youth, indigence, and ambition. Shakespeare might have been particularly industrious in the first years after the Chamberlain's Men was formed, laying the foundations of the stability and prosperity of the new company to which he had allied himself. The Admiral's Men, who were in a comparable position after the reopening of the theatres, put on twenty-one new plays in 1594-5, nineteen in 1595-6, and only fourteen in 1596-7. A comparable bunching of new work in mid-1594 to 1596 can be seen in our proposed chronology for Shakespeare's plays. But the plays written in this period are, besides being more frequent, shorter: *Errors* is Shakespeare's shortest play, *Dream* comes third in the brevity stakes, *King John* is the most compact of the histories, and as a group the seven plays which precede *1 Henry IV* have only about as many words as the next six. Moreover, *King John* uncharacteristically takes over the plot of another play, scene by scene—a labour-saving method of composition employed, so far as we know, nowhere else in the canon.

Shakespeare's patterns of composition must have been influenced by the commercial needs of his company, perhaps at all times, but especially after he became a leading member of the Chamberlain's Men. Chambers (1930), Evans (edn., 1974), and indeed most other scholars assume a sequence of four early history plays (the 'first tetralogy'), uninterrupted by comedies or tragedies; Gurr, in his edition of *Richard II* (1984), presumes that it immediately preceded the two Henry IV plays; most critics assume that all four final romances belong to an undisturbed chronological group. We think such prolonged indulgence in a single genre unlikely. We know that *Henry V* was separated from the other plays of the 'second tetralogy', and written four years after *Richard II*; in 1598-1600, when we can discern the sequence of composition with unusual clarity, we see a remarkable mixing of comedy, English history, classical and Christian tragedy; a similar variety proclaims itself in the so-called 'lyrical' group (*Love's Labour's Lost*, *Richard II*, *Romeo*, *Dream*), which seem to belong—in no certain order—to the same year or two. Like actors, dramatists of the period were expected to turn their hand to any genre, depending on the demands of the current repertoire. Consequently, although we have not wantonly disrupted generic groupings when we find no reason to do so, we have not respected them when the little evidence in our possession encourages an alternative order. Where we keep them—as in the 'Henry VI' plays, or the three 'Sir John' plays, or the two narrative poems—we do so by default, not design.

On at least one occasion, we know that Shakespeare did not have a new play available when the company wanted one. Walter Cope, in a letter to Robert Cecil endorsed '1604' (old style), wrote that 'Burbage ys come, & Sayes ther ys no new playe that the quene hath not seene, but they have Revyved an olde one, Cawled *Loves Labore lost*, which for wytt & mirthe he sayes will please her excedingly. And Thys is apointed to be playd to Morowe night at my Lord of Sowthamptons'; other documents make it likely that this performance took place between 8 and 15 January 1605 (Chambers, *Shakespeare*, ii. 331-2). *Othello* had been played at court on 1 November 1604, and *Measure* on 26 December 1604; otherwise, between November 1604 and February 1605 the King's Men only performed old plays at court (*Errors*, *Love's Labour's Lost*, *Merchant*, *Merry Wives*, and *Henry V*). We do not know what play they 'provided And discharged' on 3 February 1605. *Othello* and *Measure* are the only named plays from this court season which could be new, and since it is likely enough that Shakespeare had written two plays during the year since the last court season, it seems reasonable to assume that both were indeed brand new—a conclusion in any case independently warranted by other evidence. Cope's letter, in conjunction with other documentary evidence, thus virtually establishes that Shakespeare completed only two plays between the end of the previous court season (19 February 1604) and the beginning of January 1605. By fixing Shakespeare's output for one year, it creates a watershed, on either side of which the Jacobean canon must be distributed. With the exception of *Sir Thomas More*, every play which precedes *Measure* in the Oxford edition (and the following chronology) can be confidently fixed before February 1604. Of those which follow *Measure* and *Othello* in the Oxford chronology, only five might theoretically precede February 1604: *All's Well*, *Timon*, *Antony*, *Winter's Tale*, and *Cymbeline*. Of these five, only the first two seem at all possible as candidates for such an early date—and neither, in our judgement, is likely. We do not know which plays the King's Men offered the court in their nine performances between 2 December 1603 and 19 February 1604, although *Dream* was apparently one of them; the fact that, in the next court season, the company had to reach back to a series of plays written before 1600 suggests that in their first court season for the new monarch they offered their most successful plays of 1600-3. But the Oxford chronology—like that of Chambers—leaves 1603 empty of new plays: between the completion of *Troilus* (before 7 February 1603) and the completion of *Measure* and *Othello* in 1604 only a minor contribution to *Sir Thomas More* seems probable. For most of that year, the death of Queen Elizabeth and then plague closed the London theatres, and the accession of James I meant that plays already seen by the old monarch could now be shown again to the new. It is tempting to suppose that during this interim, as in the previous interim of 1592-3, Shakespeare briefly turned his attention to non-dramatic poetry.

Chronology: Internal Evidence

The internal evidence can be divided into two categories: relationships between the canon and things outside it, and relationships within the canon itself.

Theatrical provenance can help to establish a play's date, if the company to which a play belonged was born or died at a known time. Since after mid-1594 Shakespeare's plays were all written for a single company, such evidence affects the chronology of his canon only (*a*) for the early plays, or (*b*) when the name of his company changed, due to a change of patron, or (*c*) when the text calls for a particular actor, known to have died, or to have left the company, or to have joined it, at a particular time. But Shakespeare's early theatrical affiliations themselves remain obscure and conjectural, and the movements of particular actors cannot always be traced with the exactitude which chronological nicety requires.

Quotations from a play, or unmistakable allusions to its characters or scenes, or parodies of it, establish its existence as clearly as does explicit documentary evidence. However, scholars have disagreed, and will always disagree, about what constitutes a genuine or unambiguous allusion; there can be no consistent standard of validation.

Echoes can be roughly distinguished from quotations: authors assume or desire that readers will recognize the source of a quotation or allusion, but authors either remain unconscious of an echo, or consciously wish readers to remain unconscious of it. By definition, echoes are harder to spot, and to the same degree easier to imagine. Alleged echoes in allegedly memorial texts should be regarded with particular suspicion. In the first place, memorial texts are not easily identifiable unless an alternative authoritative text exists, and outside the Shakespeare canon such clarifying duplication seldom occurs. Nor can memorial texts easily or confidently be identified if we do not know the play's author, or alternatively if we know the author but possess little or none of his work in authoritative texts; in either situation, we cannot define defective texts by comparison with whole ones. Even in the Shakespeare canon, where the conditions for identifying memorial texts might be considered ideal, a minority of scholars continues to deny their existence, or denies the applicability of the hypothesis to particular individual texts. By characterizing a text as a memorial reconstruction, scholars create a presumption that it echoes Shakespeare, as a result of its imperfect method of transmission; but that imperfect method of transmission itself remains a hypothesis, and sometimes a rather wobbly one. In the second place, the alleged echoes have seldom been collected or tested objectively. Those who collect them always know Shakespeare's works better than they know the works of his contemporaries, and sometimes they go to such sources specifically seeking echoes of a particular play or plays. Not surprisingly, they often find what they seek, but having found it they do not bother to check whether it might be an echo of some Elizabethan or Jacobean work less familiar than Shakespeare's play, or consider that it might be an echo of one of the multitude of plays from the period which are now lost. Fuzzy parallels randomly piled upon a wobbly foundation do not a proof construct.

In determining the direction of influence (who echoes whom?), critics sometimes argue for Shakespeare's priority on the grounds that his use of an image or idea is 'apter' or 'more original' than its corresponding use by another writer. Such arguments can never be trusted. Shakespeare often improved what he stole.

Sources, when they can be securely identified, establish more clearly than any other evidence the earliest date by which a work can have been written. But in some cases we cannot be sure whether Shakespeare was influenced by, or himself influenced, another work; in others, the books which Shakespeare pillaged were written many years before the plays themselves, and hence provide only a distant chronological horizon.

Topical allusions within the work to events outside the work create a presumption that the passage in question was written after the event in question. Some passages unmistakably refer to specific identifiable contemporary persons or events outside the text; others unmistakably refer to such extra-textual matter, but the specifically intended referent remains unclear, or cannot itself be confidently dated; in other cases, we cannot even be sure whether the text does or does not allude to anything outside its fictional world. Even when we can be sure of an allusion, we can seldom fix a date by which it would have ceased to be topical.

The foregoing categories of internal evidence—which might be called 'extrinsic', because they point outside the canon itself—usefully narrow the range of chronological possibilities. But all require the exercise of judgement, and all can be abused. The same obvious limitation applies to the remaining categories of internal evidence—which might be called 'intrinsic', because they depend upon the relationships of one canonical work to another. Intrinsic evidence does not determine a work's date in relation to the world's date (a certain number of years after the hypothetical birth of Christ), but instead defines an ideal order among and between works, a sequence of relationships based upon measurements of affinity and dissimilarity, charting the movement of a mind and the evolution of a style. Such studies have a value all their own, beyond chronological utility, in alerting us to the detail and maturing of Shakespeare's art; they should interest us even if we knew the very day and hour, place and weather, when each of Shakespeare's compositions was conceived or completed. But in the absence of such certainties, they can, in compensation, offer probabilities, probabilities no less (if no more) trustworthy than those generated by sources, echoes, and topical allusions.

As in problems of authenticity, such stylistic evidence can only usefully be applied to problems of chronology if we already possess a core of reliable external evidence. If we know the actual relative order of some works, we can extrapolate from them patterns of development, and then relate works of unknown or uncertain date to those patterns. If we know the real historical dates of A, C, and E, we can create a line of development, and fix on to that line the appropriate positions for B and D; we may then conjecture that the stylistic pattern corresponds with an historical one, and that B came between A and C in the world's sequence, as well as the canon's.

In order for such reasoning to carry conviction, our anchor points in the external evidence must be not only securely dated, but securely attributed. Since we are tracing patterns of stylistic development in a single author, that pattern could be confused, or distorted, if the evidence included matter from another mind. In fact, such stylistic evidence often helps us to isolate a collaborator's contribution; but in establishing our initial profile of Shakespeare's habits, we must first eliminate any material of dubious authenticity. This restriction, unfortunately, affects the beginnings of the Shakespeare canon most severely. In our present ignorance, we must suspect collaboration (or at least countenance such suspicions) in several early plays, without being able to isolate the other author confidently, as we usually can in the late collaborations. Such suspicions further deplete the already sparse external signposts to the early chronology.

As in so many other respects, the early canon creates special problems of its own in the evaluation of stylistic evidence. After 1598 there are enough fixed points in the relative dating of Shakespeare's works for it to take little effort to construct or to justify a skeletal chronology from which to extrapolate stylistic trends. Among the earlier works such fixed points are hard to find. In the following summary, we have set out the minimum framework, established by external evidence and by convincing 'extrinsic' internal evidence, upon which must be stretched any stylistic analysis of Shakespeare's early canon. Works of uncertain authorship are followed by a query; a group of works, all demonstrably later (or earlier) than another, but of uncertain relationship to each other, is bracketed together. Thus, *Duke of York* and *1 Henry VI* may both be collaborative, but both are certainly earlier than *Venus and Adonis*, which is certainly earlier than *Lucrece*, which is certainly earlier than *Richard II* or *Henry IV*.

1. (*Duke of York?*, *1 Henry VI?*) ⇨ *Venus* ⇨ *Lucrece* ⇨ (*Richard II*, *Henry IV*)
2. *Titus?* ⇨ *Lucrece*, or *Titus?* = *Lucrece*
3. (*Titus?*, *Duke of York?*, *1 Henry VI?*, *Shrew?*, *Errors*, *Venus*) ⇨ (*Dream*, *Merchant*)

Although the traditional assumption rests on precious little external evidence, it also seems probable that *Contention*, *Duke of York*, and *Richard III* were written in a sequence which corresponds to the historical sequence of their subject-matter, and that this group of plays was followed by another group, from *Richard II* to *Henry V*, also written in historical sequence. We might therefore add the following proposition:

4. *Contention?* ⇨ *Duke of York?* ⇨ *Richard III* ⇨ *Richard II* ⇨ *1 Henry IV* ⇨ *2 Henry IV* ⇨ *Henry V*

If we accept this proposition, among the histories only the relative positions of *1 Henry VI* and *King John* remain uncertain.

The limited value of these conclusions should be obvious. Although we know the relative position of most of the histories, that knowledge tells us little about their actual time of composition, because so few of the individual histories can be confidently dated: we know that the first two were probably written between 1587 and 1592, and that *Richard II* and *1 Henry IV* were written between 1595 and 1598, but that only tells us that *Richard III* comes between 1588 and 1595. What is worse, this limited knowledge of the sequence of the histories cannot be related to the sequence of the comedies and tragedies. The history sequence can be related chronologically to the narrative poems, but that knowledge may not produce reliable internal evidence of stylistic development, because differences of genre may distort the results. Brainerd (1979) has shown that even the frequencies of very common words can be affected by genre. Such disparities seem to matter less in Shakespeare's later work, when his verbal style had settled down to a certain assured homogeneity; but they can hardly be ignored in the early work, and they further weaken our confidence in the little evidence we possess. The most confidently datable of all the early works are the narrative poems; yet they also differ most obviously from all the others.

Given these limitations, it should hardly surprise us that editors have, over the centuries, disagreed radically about the distribution of the early canon: about the relative order of the early comedies, about the relation between the composition of works in different genres, about the year when Shakespeare began writing plays. Without the discovery of more external evidence, such disputes will never end. Nevertheless, without exaggerating the level of appropriate complacency, we may acknowledge that the shape of the problem is perhaps better understood now than it has been in the past, and that modern editors have at their disposal the gleanings of evidence and ingenuity accumulated by their predecessors. Several categories of evidence and reasoning have influenced the chronology of the early plays adopted in the Oxford edition.

The size of cast envisaged by a script usefully divides Shakespeare's plays into two groups. *The Taming of the Shrew*, *Titus Andronicus*, and the three plays on the reign of Henry VI all—even with the doubling of actors normal in the Elizabethan and Jacobean theatre—presuppose casts much larger than those required to perform the remaining plays. Noticeably, all five plays can be assigned, on reliable external evidence, to the period before 1594; all were performed, or at the very least might have been written in whole or part, before the closure of the theatres in mid-1592. Such large casts are also presumed in some other plays of this pre-plague period (McMillin, 'More'). It therefore seems reasonable to suppose that these plays were written at a time when a playwright could count, as a matter of course, upon a company larger than the later Chamberlain's Men. This change in company structure cannot easily be dissociated from the devastating effects on the London acting profession of the long interregnum caused by plague. Of course, not every play written before mid-1592 required a large cast. But it does seem to us significant that Shakespeare's later histories and tragedies, though they dramatized similar sorts of material, call for smaller casts than the demonstrably early histories and tragedies (Ringler), and we assume that those later plays therefore post-date 1592. Honigmann (*Impact*; 1985) wishes to push *Richard III* and *King John* back to 1591; but we do not see why Shakespeare should, in that year, suddenly have started writing history plays for a smaller company. It seems more economical to relate the change of theatrical requirements to a change in theatrical opportunities.

The use of rhyme was taken by Malone, in one of the first attempts to apply internal evidence to chronological problems, as a symptom of early composition. If we understand this proposition in relation to the canon as a whole, it is obviously true: the plays with a high proportion of rhymed verse cluster conspicuously in the first decade of Shakespeare's career. But it by no means follows that Shakespeare's *earliest* plays contain the *most* rhyme. Indeed, that proposition seems to be self-evidently false, for none of the plays which can be confidently placed before the 1592 interregnum contains much rhyme. Columns 1-3 in Table 8 give the proportions of rhymed verse to total verse in Shakespeare's plays; these proportions are displayed visually in Graph 1. In both the table and the graph, the plays are listed in the chronological order adopted here; but that order was in fact chosen before its relevance to the pattern of rhyme was realized. What causes the sudden increase in the use of rhyme? Apparently, the event which immediately precedes that increase is the composition of the 1,194 rhymed lines of *Venus and Adonis*, followed within the year by composition of the 1,855 rhymed lines of *Lucrece*; at about the same time Shakespeare probably began writing large numbers of rhymed sonnets. No other explanation so readily and naturally accounts for Shakespeare's fondness for rhyme in comedies, histories, and tragedies, all most probably dating from the years 1594-5. The composition of that large quantity of non-dramatic rhymed verse has, in turn, a natural source and origin in the prolonged suspension of theatrical activity caused by the London plague of 1592-3. The plague for a time made Shakespeare rhyme for a living, just as it made him write plays for a smaller company.

Biographical evidence offers another explanation for the pattern of distribution of the early plays. On 20 September 1592 *Greene's Groatsworth of Wit* was entered in the Stationers' Register; it was published in an edition dated 1592 (STC 12245), and contains the first explicit reference to Shakespeare as a member of the theatrical profession:

there is an upstart Crow, beautified with our feathers, that with his *Tygers hart wrapt in a Players hyde*, supposes he is as well able to bombast out a blanke verse as the best of you: and beeing an absolute *Iohannes fac totum*, is in his owne conceit the onely Shake-scene in a countrey.

The exact purport of this attack, and even its author, have been disputed for two centuries, and any interpretation must remain speculative. But this passage occurs in the context of a warning '*To those Gentlemen his Quondam acquaintance, that spend their wits in making plaies*', and Shakespeare is one of the persons of whom the author warns them to beware. We can confidently assign only five plays in the Shakespeare canon to the period before publication of *Greene's Groatsworth of Wit*: *Shrew*, the three plays on Henry VI, and (less confidently) *Titus*. In all five reasonable modern scholars have suspected collaboration. Such doubts can be reasonably entertained for no other play earlier than 1603-4. One need not believe that all five early plays where collaboration is

Table 8
Rhyme and prose

	Verse lines	Rhymed lines	Rhymed (%)	Prose (%): Spevack
Two Gentlemen	1,638	128	8	25
Shrew	2,022	151	7	18
Contention	2,611	96	4	16
Duke of York	2,901	128	4	0
1 Henry VI	2,675	318	12	0
Titus	2,482	130	5	1
Richard III	3,536	152	4	2
Venus	1,194	1,194	100	0
Lucrece	1,855	1,855	100	0
Errors	1,533	378	25	12
LLL	1,734	1,150	66	32
Richard II	2,757	529	19	0
Romeo	2,567	466	18	13
Dream	1,544	798	52	20
K. John	2,570	132	5	0
Merchant	2,025	142	7	23
1 Henry IV	1,683	76	5	45
Merry Wives	240	26	11	87
2 Henry IV	1,492	72	5	52
Much Ado	720	76	11	72
Henry V	1,562	58	4	42
Caesar	2,301	32	1	8
As You Like It	1,143	217	19	57
Hamlet	2,579	135	5	27
Twelfth Night	938	176	19	61
Troilus	2,251	186	8	30
Measure	1,666	89	5	39
Othello	2,631	103	4	19
All's Well	1,482	279	19	47
Timon (S)	1,056	37	4	
Timon (M)	617	123	20	
Timon	1,673	160	10	23
Lear (QF)	2,403	169	7	25
Macbeth	1,800	64	4	7
Antony	2,772	40	1	8
Pericles (S)	803	22	3	(30)
Pericles (W)	802	197	25	(15)
Pericles	1,605	219	14	17
Coriolanus	2,577	28	1	22
Winter's Tale	2,166	59	3	28
Cymbeline	2,729	122	4	15
Tempest	1,509	64	4	20
True (S)	1,160	6	1	(1)
True (F)	1,532	20	1	(5)
True	2,692	26	1	2
Kinsmen (S)	1,074	24	2	(5)
Kinsmen (F)	1,486	44	3	(6)
Kinsmen	2,560	68	3	6

Notes: Figures for total verse lines and for rhymed lines are taken from Chambers, *Stage*, ii., App. H; they exclude verse which Chambers characterized as 'external' (prologues, epilogues, choruses, interludes, masques, Pistol's bombast and the play's speech in *Hamlet*). Spevack's figures for total verse lines include such material, and also count many incomplete verse lines separately, thus consistently producing larger totals. By contrast, Spevack's figures for prose are based upon the number of words of prose, a more accurate measurement than the number of lines, since it is not affected by differences in page or column width. Percentages in brackets, for parts of collaborative plays, are taken from Chambers; comparable Spevack figures are not available.

suspected were indeed collaborative, in order to grant that there is good evidence of *some* collaboration before Greene's posthumous attack, and no good evidence of *any* collaboration for a full decade after. Again, the shape of Shakespeare's early career seems to have been determined by events in 1592: by abandoning collaboration, and writing a serious classical narrative poem, Shakespeare demonstrated that he did not need to adorn himself with anybody else's feathers.

The foregoing interpretation of Shakespeare's biography is, and will always be, conjectural; it cannot withstand contradiction by any convincing external or internal evidence. But in the absence of better evidence, we believe that the interrelationship of these three factors—the change in company size apparently caused by the plague, the turn to rhyme apparently caused by the plague, and the attack on Shakespeare coincident with the plague—do establish that the second half of 1592 represented a watershed in Shakespeare's career. The Henry VI plays, *Shrew*, *Titus* almost certainly, *Two Gentlemen* perhaps, were written before that watershed; everything else, after. This conclusion is not contradicted by any of the existing stylistic evidence, which instead tends to reinforce it; moreover, unlike other stylistic evidence, it cannot be distorted by the possibility of collaboration in certain early plays, for neither the relatively large casts nor the relative paucity of rhyme in the earliest plays can be attributed to collaborators.

Rhetorical evidence supports the same arrangement of the early canon. Studies of internal evidence have generally been confined to vocabulary (which words the author uses) or to metre (the verse forms into which he fits those words); but an author's style is also shaped by rhetoric (the tropes by which he arranges words). Clemen, in a study instantly recognized as a classic, described *The Development of Shakespeare's Imagery*, and Mincoff, in a series of investigations of early plays, worked out in detail some of the chronological implications of Clemen's analysis, tracing Shakespeare's use of extended similes, compound adjectives, and other rhetorical schemes. Such studies—and Brooks's related discussion, in his edition, of the style of *Dream* and the other so-called 'lyrical' plays— demonstrate in detail that Shakespeare did not begin his career writing rhetorically and artificially, and then by a steady and uninterrupted progression become more and more 'naturalistic'; instead, in certain respects the verse in Shakespeare's middle plays is more artificially and self-consciously patterned than anything we find in the earlier work. *Errors*, *Love's Labour's Lost*, *Richard II*, *Romeo*, and *Dream* are, like the narrative poems, displays of virtuoso verbal exhibitionism.

By such interrelated criteria, combined with the existing external evidence and the 'extrinsic' internal evidence, we can define two distinct groups of early plays: *Shrew*, the Henry VI plays, and *Titus*, on the one hand, and on the other *Errors*, *Love's Labour's Lost*, *Richard II*, *Romeo*, and *Dream*. *Richard III* seems clearly to belong between the two groups; only *Two Gentlemen* and *King John* remain—as yet—ambiguous. Unfortunately, we still cannot discern with any confidence the chronological relationship *between* the items in each group.

However, this structuring of the early canon does take us some distance toward locating the source of Shakespeare's Nile, the beginnings of his dramatic career. If Shakespeare had written only five, or at most six, extant plays by 1592, it would be rather surprising if he had been writing plays since 1586, as Honigmann believes. Of course, many plays from that earliest period might be lost; but if we confine ourselves to the surviving work, we have little reason to suppose that Shakespeare began writing in 1586. Moreover, Honigmann's alternative 'early chronology' creates a number of general problems, beyond those incident to the dating of particular plays (discussed below, under 'Works Included'). First, Honigmann supposes that *The Troublesome Reign of John, King of England* was written in 1590-1, then published in 1591. Why was it published, anomalously, so soon after its composition? Because, he tells us, the Queen's Men were in trouble. But *Troublesome Reign* is the only play belonging to the Queen's Men published at that time; several were published in 1594. *Troublesome Reign* thus becomes the only evidence for the alleged cause of its own case, the sale of new plays to publishers by a financially troubled company. Secondly, Honigmann's chronology, by pushing back the traditional dating of the early histories, creates a large gap between *King John* (early 1591) and *Richard II* (1595), in which Shakespeare purportedly wrote no history plays at all—a genre which, on Honigmann's account, he had created almost single-handed, and which had been the staple of his early success. Likewise, after resounding and early successes in tragedy (*Titus* 1586?, *Romeo* 1591?), we are to suppose that Shakespeare did not write another tragedy for eight years. All of Shakespeare's histories, with the possible exception of *Contention*, must postdate publication of Holinshed's *Chronicle* (1587: STC 13569), and most scholars have believed that the sudden popularity of the genre owes something to the swell of nationalism associated with the defeat of the Spanish Armada (August 1588). In pushing Shakespeare's beginnings back to the mid-1580s Honigmann must therefore fill the gap with plays which cannot be confidently dated on the basis of their sources: *Titus Andronicus* (1586?), *Two Gentlemen* (1587?), *Shrew* (1588?), and *Errors* (1589?). It is suspiciously convenient to suppose that Shakespeare confined himself, in the 1580s, to plays which could not be confidently dated by their dependence upon recent materials, and which therefore permit any investigator to date them as early as he likes; it would be more plausible to suppose that such undatable materials were more evenly scattered through his writing life. Finally, Honigmann's early dating asks us to believe that Shakespeare was not mentioned by name in any surviving document for the first seven years of his playwriting career—years in which he allegedly dominated theatrical life, writing a series of plays so successful that they were busily echoed and pillaged by all his elders and contemporaries. Most young writers imitate older writers; in Shakespeare's case, Honigmann asks us to believe that, unnaturally, age knelt to youth, and the upstart crow was lionized.

Curiosity abhors a vacuum, and the urge to push Shakespeare's first play farther and farther back into the 1580s is palpably designed to fill the black hole of our ignorance about those years; but since we must then spread the same number of plays over a larger number of years, by filling one big vacuum in the 1580s we simply create other vacuums elsewhere. Moreover, by a kind of artistic gravity, the power of any single great reputation tends to attract, absorb, and eclipse lesser reputations, and consequently Shakespeare's unquestionable artistic brilliance leads easily to the assumption that he can be credited with every accomplishment of his

THE CANON AND CHRONOLOGY OF SHAKESPEARE'S PLAYS

GRAPH 1
Percentage of rhyme to verse

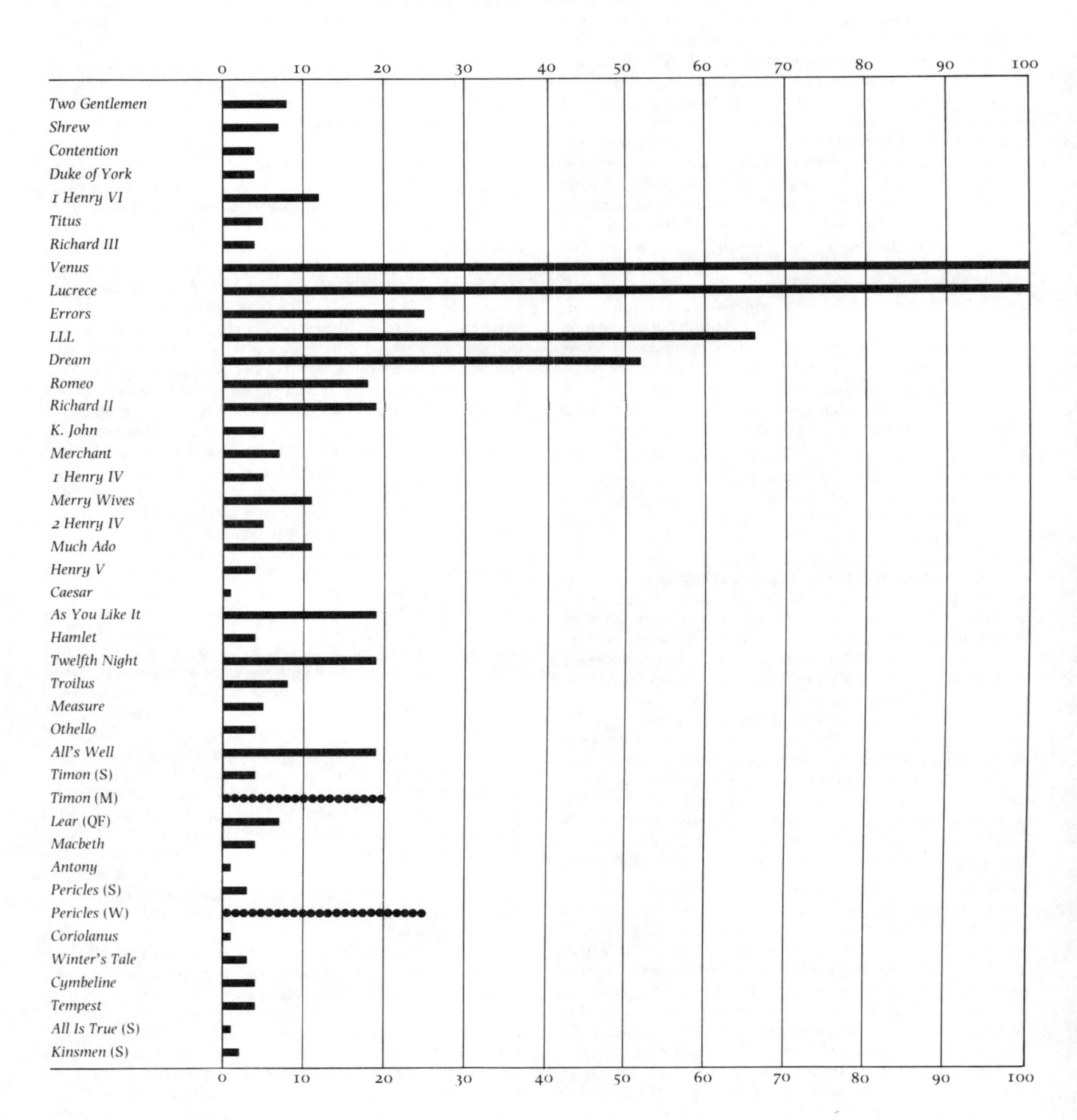

GRAPH 2
Colloquialisms

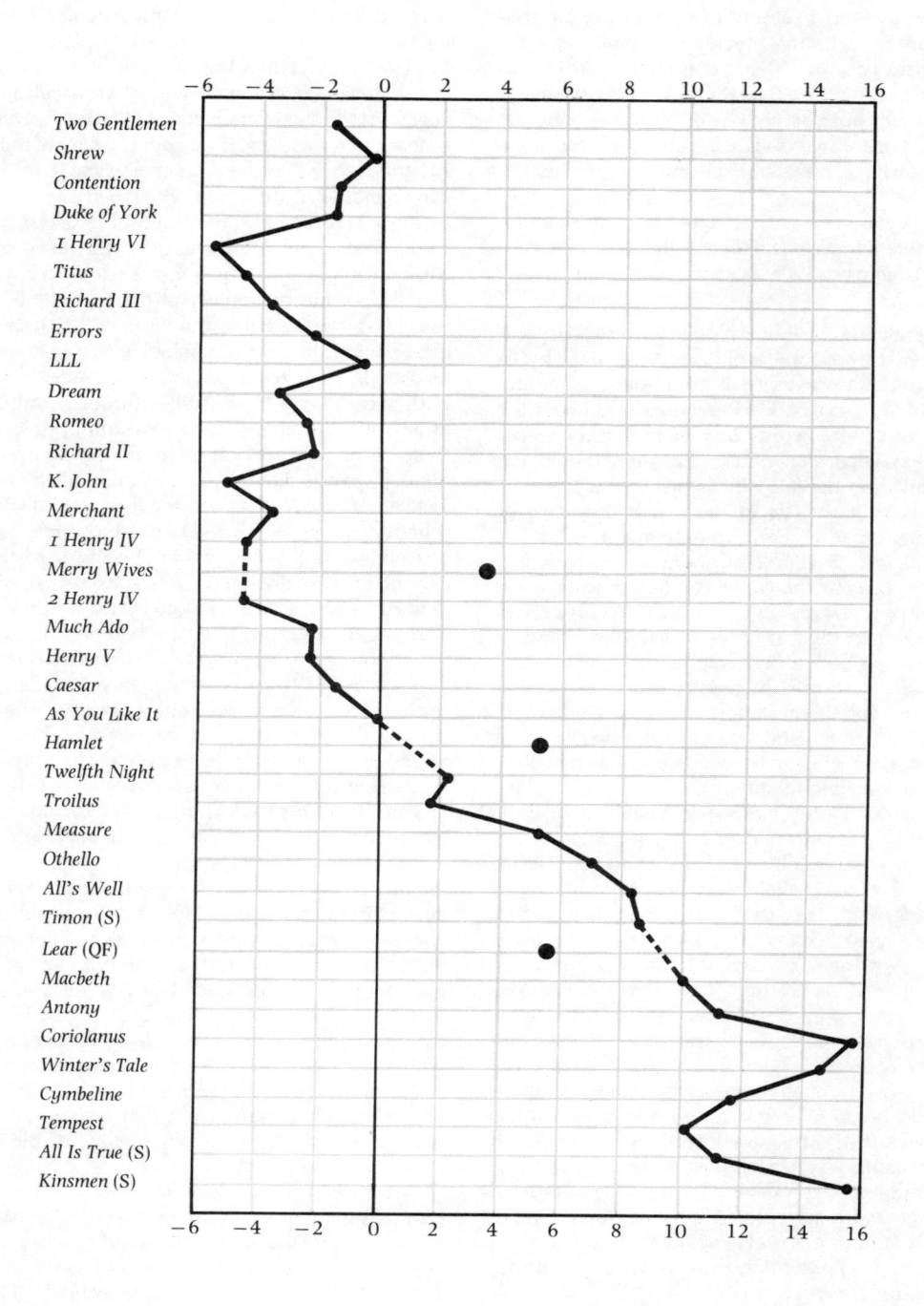

```
                -6  -4  -2   0   2   4   6   8  10  12  14  16
Two Gentlemen
Shrew
Contention
Duke of York
1 Henry VI
Titus
Richard III
Errors
LLL
Dream
Romeo
Richard II
K. John
Merchant
1 Henry IV
Merry Wives
2 Henry IV
Much Ado
Henry V
Caesar
As You Like It
Hamlet
Twelfth Night
Troilus
Measure
Othello
All's Well
Timon (S)
Lear (QF)
Macbeth
Antony
Coriolanus
Winter's Tale
Cymbeline
Tempest
All Is True (S)
Kinsmen (S)
                -6  -4  -2   0   2   4   6   8  10  12  14  16
```

period, reducing the chaos of talent in the late sixteenth century to a comfortingly regular system, with a handful of lesser planets circling and reflecting the solar glory of Shakespeare. This system suspiciously duplicates the curriculum of modern universities, in which 'Shakespeare's contemporaries' are defined by reference to him. It seems to us more likely that Shakespeare began by imitating others, older and more experienced and better educated than himself; it seems to us that Greene's attack stings with the bitterness of recent rivalry from an unexpected quarter. Such impressions and assumptions hardly constitute 'evidence', and we offer these prejudices of our own only as viable alternatives to the prejudices of others.

Once we pass beyond the earliest quarter of the canon, quantifiable stylistic evidence offers more guidance in the construction of a chronology. Such evidence comes in several species.

Vocabulary may indicate chronology, if a writer's usage of certain words follows a predictable pattern. One might hypothesize, for instance, that proximity of composition generates similarity of vocabulary, so that works composed at about the same time will have more words in common than works composed at widely separated times. This hypothesis was tested, and confirmed, in the late nineteenth century by Sarrazin, using words which occur in the canon only two or three times. It has recently been tested, much more systematically, by the late Dr Eliot Slater, who surveyed words of up to ten occurrences in the canon. Slater defined 'word' carefully, and evaluated the results statistically, first in a series of individual articles and then in an extended thesis. Slater's body of information will often be noted in the discussion of 'Works Included', because it is the best evidence we have of vocabulary overlap; but its limitations must be recognized. In the first place, other factors besides chronology clearly influence the proportion of shared vocabulary. For instance, *King John* shares an exceptional amount of 'rare' vocabulary with (in order of decreasing correspondence) *Richard II*, *Richard III*, *1 Henry IV*, *Contention*, *2 Henry IV*, *Romeo*, and *Henry V*. Six of these seven plays are, like *King John* itself, histories, and one can hardly avoid the conclusion that genre affects the results as much as proximity of composition. Which histories share the most vocabulary with one another may help us to determine their relative position, but the mere statistical predominance of history plays does not in itself mean much. On the hypothesis of a purely random distribution, the excess correspondence between *King John* and *Romeo* does not pass the threshold of statistical significance; but it clearly matters more than the correspondences with *Contention*, *2 Henry IV*, and *Henry V*, for unlike them it cannot result from genre: *Romeo* is the only tragedy or comedy with which *King John* shares any remarkable proportion of 'rare' vocabulary, and that correspondence probably results from composition at approximately the same time. Such complications could be, but have not yet been, analysed statistically; consequently we can call attention to such warping without being able to measure it precisely.

Slater divided *Pericles* into the two traditional parts, and his data confirm the presence of two authors. But he did not take account of the possibility of collaboration in the three Henry VI plays, *Titus*, *Shrew*, *Timon*, or *All Is True*; he did not include *Kinsmen* at all, or the passages of *Sir Thomas More* commonly attributed to Shakespeare. By including material possibly written by a collaborator, and by excluding some dramatic material probably written by Shakespeare, Slater endangered the validity of his results. As with all other stylistic tests, reasonable conclusions about chronology can only be reached if we are first reasonably sure about authorship. This limitation applies most obviously to Slater's study of *Edward III* (1981). By comparing the distribution of rare vocabulary in the Shakespeare canon with that in *Edward III*, Slater believed that he had demonstrated Shakespeare's authorship of that anonymous play. If we could be sure of the date of *Edward III*, and if the stylistic evidence applicable to the Shakespeare canon indicated the same date, then the coincidence of the external evidence and the internal (Shakespearian) evidence could contribute to an argument for Shakespeare's authorship: we might say, 'Surely no other author would have been using the same vocabulary at the same time.' Or if we knew that Shakespeare wrote the play, an analysis of stylistic evidence applicable to the Shakespeare canon could help to fix its date. But when we cannot be sure of either the date or the authorship, stylistic evidence cannot simultaneously determine both. Variables have no meaning, unless we can relate them to at least one fixed term; in the case of *Edward III* neither term is fixed. If we confine ourselves to external evidence, *Edward III* floats on a current of interdeterminate authorship, blown by a wind of indeterminate date; Slater tried to stabilize its position, by anchoring it to the Shakespeare canon. But his anchor attached itself to a shifting bottom. *Edward III* shares more 'rare' vocabulary with *1 Henry VI* than with any other play in the Shakespeare canon. But since Shakespeare probably wrote only a fraction of *1 Henry VI*, the correspondence between the two plays raises new questions without answering the old ones. And since both plays are chronicle histories, the correspondence might owe as much to genre as to authorship or date.

Although Slater separately investigated the 'rare' vocabulary in the poems (1975), he did not include the poems in his larger survey of the canon, and the data of the two separate investigations cannot be easily or simply combined. Shakespeare's vocabulary in the poems might theoretically have differed from that in the plays; but Slater's study of the poems does not encourage that assumption, and in any case it would have been better to test the assumption by including the poems in the larger data base. Slater's bifurcation of the canon—besides omitting yet more Shakespearian matter from the vocabulary he analysed—deprives us of stylistic evidence where we most need it. The poems are the only fixed points, in terms of both date and authorship, in the early canon, and it would be extremely useful to know exactly how the vocabularies of the early plays relate to the vocabularies of those two fixed points.

Slater went farther than any previous investigator in analysing systematically and statistically the chronological implications of vocabulary distribution; but we need to go farther yet before we can be wholly confident that we have squeezed all the right meanings from the data at hand. A professional statistician could have subjected Slater's evidence to more sophisticated and rigorous tests than any he employed. Ule (1979, 1982), for instance, developed a programme to determine which conjectural sequence of Marlowe's works would produce the maximum amount of shared vocabulary between adjacent compositions. The logic behind this method is simple, and will be familiar to anyone who has ever had to calculate, in school or in earnest, the shortest route through seven cities. In Shakespeare's case we need to find the shortest route through forty cities, which makes the problem more cumbersome but (for a computer) no less practicable. On the other hand, Ule's definition of 'vocabulary' is cruder than Slater's, for Ule takes no account of differences in meaning or grammatical function. Moreover, Ule's test incorporates all vocabulary, while Slater's confines itself to 'rare' vocabulary, on the principle that 'rare' words slip in and out of a writer's active vocabulary, and hence may be a better measure of chronology. We will not know which method produces more accurate results until both have been thoroughly tested against the external evidence.

Statistically, the most sophisticated analysis of Shakespeare's vocabulary in relation to chronology is the study by Brainerd (1980), which tested 120 lemmata for their correlation with what we know of the sequence of composition. Twenty such lemmata—including related forms of certain words—had chronological correlations with an absolute value greater than 0.4. (An absolute value of 0 describes a purely random association; an absolute value of 1 describes a 100 per cent positive correlation.) By combining these twenty lemmata with certain other chronological variables he produced an 'omnibus predictor of date of composition'. Brainerd's test suffers, however, from a few questionable assumptions about the dating of certain plays in his control sample. He dates *Two Gentlemen* in 1594, *Measure* in 1604, *As You Like It* in 1599, and *Cymbeline* before *Winter's Tale*. Proponents could be found for all these dates, but they can hardly be considered certain, and we believe that all of them are wrong. A stylistic test can hardly help us to determine the relative dating of *Cymbeline* and *Winter's Tale* if we select data on the assumption that the former precedes the latter; the test will simply return us the answer we have already predetermined in our formulation of the question.

Linguistic evidence can be applied to problems of chronology as well as authorship, and it has the same advantages and limitations in both cases. Conrad drew attention to a chronological progression to Shakespeare's use of obsolescent syllabic -ed inflections in verse; Estelle Taylor documented a similar progression in the use of -eth inflections; Waller tabulated similar fluctuations in the use of a number of other linguistic variables. We have combined and supplemented this evidence to produce a colloquialism-in-verse test for the entire canon (Table 9). In evaluating the suitability of a variable we simply determined whether it occurred much more or much less frequently in works composed before *As You Like It*, or works composed after *As You Like It*. *As You Like It* serves as a useful median, because it falls almost exactly in the middle of the canon, and because scholars actively agree about which plays come before and after it. Only *Merry Wives* might fall on either side, and in our initial selection we simply ignored *Merry Wives*. All features which significantly increased after *As You Like It* were assigned a positive value (columns 1–21); features which decreased were assigned a negative value (columns 23–6). The negative subtotal (column 27) was subtracted from the positive subtotal (column 22) to produce a colloquialism total (column 28), which was then subdivided by the number of words of verse in each work (column 29), to produce a colloquialism quotient (column 30).

As in studies of authorship, such linguistic evidence might be affected, occasionally, by an interfering compositor or scribe. We have found no clear instance of such high-handedness with these particular variables in the Shakespeare canon, although *The Shrew* may well be an example (see 'Works Included'). On the other hand, memorial transmission, which so often cannot get the words right, can hardly be expected to preserve incidental linguistic preferences, as *Pericles* demonstrates. We would also predict that the presence of a second author could distort the figures, and such distortions can be seen in *Timon*, *1 Henry VI*, and to a lesser degree *All Is True* and *Kinsmen*.

As can be seen in Graph 2, for most of the canon the colloquialism quotient produces a steady curve which can be easily interpreted. From *King John* to *Coriolanus* Shakespeare's verse becomes more and more colloquial, in a progress clearly related to what we know (or think we know) about the dating of individual plays and poems. Only three plays are anomalous: *Merry Wives* (which earlier scholars often dated after 1600), *Hamlet*, and *Lear*. After *Coriolanus* we must assume a bend in the curve: no one supposes, or reasonably could suppose, that the last three romances all pre-date *Coriolanus*. Shakespeare's reversion to an antiquated dramatic form apparently coincides with some backsliding toward a less colloquial poetry. The final collaborations with Fletcher begin to reverse this movement, but even so *All Is True* and *Kinsmen*, in part or whole, remain less colloquial than *Coriolanus*. For the final period as a whole we see a large dip in the curve, from *Coriolanus* to Shakespeare's share of *Kinsmen*.

The dip in the curve at the end of the canon creates no difficulties of interpretation, because the other external and internal evidence makes the pattern easy enough to understand. We can also see that some bending must be assumed at the beginning of the canon: no one supposes that *King John* and *1 Henry IV* are earlier than all the other plays mentioned by Meres, or all the others which precede them in the Oxford edition (and other editions). *King John* is Shakespeare's least colloquial uncollaborative play; although it abandons the high proportion of rhyme characteristic of the 'lyric' period, it carries forward and even extends certain other features of the consciously 'poetic' style of those plays.

Ideally, *King John* should represent the nadir of a tidy curve. It does not. The evidence would be easy to interpret if Shakespeare began writing with some colloquialism, gradually used less and less until the turning-point represented by *King John*, and thereafter used more and more. We can see the outlines of such a pattern in the earlier histories: the figures fall from *Contention* to *Duke of York* to *Richard III* to *King John*. *1 Henry VI* must, in any case, be dismissed as anomalous: the play as a whole differs wildly from its companion dramatizations of the reign of Henry VI, and the discrepancy arises almost entirely from the scenes apparently written by some playwright(s) other than Shakespeare. But *Richard II* can hardly fall between *Duke of York* and *Richard III*, as its colloquialism quotient indicates; nor will many critics find tempting the supposition that *Romeo* precedes *Titus*. The fact that the colloquialism index would put all of the early comedies before *Richard III* might be dismissed as a consequence of genre, but the disparities in *Richard II* and *Romeo* cannot be so easily

Table 9
Colloquialism in verse

	1 't	2 i'th'	3 o'th'	4 th'	5 'em	6 'll	7 'rt	8 're
Edward III	1	—	—	—	—	8	—	—
Two Gentlemen	5	—	—	3	—	11	—	—
Shrew	15	1	1	—	2	17	2	2
Contention	25	1	1	5	—	19	—	—
Duke of York	7	—	—	3	—	27	—	—
1 Henry VI	4	—	—	4	—	18	—	—
1 Henry VI (S)	—	—	—	1	—	9	—	—
1 Henry VI (?)	4	—	—	3	—	9	—	—
Titus (S)	1	—	—	2	—	8	—	—
Titus (?)	—	—	—	—	—	4	—	—
Richard III	6	—	—	10	—	4	—	—
Venus	—	—	—	2	—	—	—	—
Lucrece	—	—	—	7	—	—	—	—
Sonnets	3	—	—	12	—	—	—	—
Errors	1	1	—	3	—	12	—	1
LLL	7	1	—	7	—	6	—	—
Richard II	5	—	—	1	—	7	—	—
Romeo	11	—	—	7	—	15	—	—
Dream	4	1	—	2	—	11	—	—
K. John	7	1	—	7	—	6	—	—
Merchant	3	1	—	2	—	9	—	—
1 Henry IV	3	—	—	1	—	8	—	—
Merry Wives	1	2	—	2	—	9	—	—
2 Henry IV	2	—	—	1	—	1	—	—
Much Ado	2	—	—	1	—	6	—	—
Henry V	3	2	—	22	1	18	—	—
Caesar	6	1	—	4	6	13	—	—
As You Like It	2	2	—	5	—	13	—	—
Hamlet	61	8	1	42	—	12	1	1
Twelfth Night	9	1	1	5	—	3	—	1
Troilus	11	4	—	18	—	18	—	1
More	—	—	—	3	—	1	—	—
Measure	27	5	1	23	—	9	1	3
Othello	83	4	6	23	—	15	—	5
All's Well	30	6	—	19	—	11	—	3
Timon (S)	24	1	8	23	2	9	2	2
Timon (M)	20	2	—	5	9	—	2	2
Lear (Q)	37	12	5	12	2	14	—	8
Macbeth	40	14	13	31	5	13	1	—
Antony	76	24	18	34	3	24	5	2
Pericles (S)	17	3	—	10	1	9	1	3
Pericles (W)	11	—	—	2	—	13	—	1
Coriolanus	56	31	13	103	12	34	1	4
Winter's Tale	90	16	21	36	2	20	—	4
Cymbeline	68	20	36	52	1	31	—	8
Tempest	31	13	20	24	16	8	—	—
True (S)	36	15	20	41	18	8	—	7
True (F)	11	3	4	4	39	7	—	12
True	47	18	24	45	57	15	—	19
Kinsmen	55	19	30	36	52	35	—	8
Kinsmen (S)	28	9	21	22	15	3	—	2
Kinsmen (F)	27	10	9	14	37	32	—	6

DIFFERENCES in spelling (o'th', a'th'; 'em, 'um; etc.) and the absence of apostrophes in contracted forms are ignored. Column 1 omits occurrences of *'tis*, *'twas*, and *'twere*; column 6 omits occurrences of *I'll*; column 19 ignores contractions of 'is' after *here, there, where, what, that, how, he, she,* and *who*. These excluded contractions, common throughout Shakespeare's career,

TABLE 9. Colloquialism in Verse (*cont.*)

	9 'd/'ld	10 'lt/'t	11 'st/'ve	12 I'm	13 'as	14 this'	15 'a'/ha'	16 a'
Edward III	—	—	—	—	—	—	—	—
Two Gentlemen	2	—	1	—	—	—	—	—
Shrew	—	—	—	1	—	1	2	4
Contention	—	—	—	—	—	—	—	1
Duke of York	1	—	—	—	—	—	1	—
1 Henry VI	—	—	—	—	—	—	—	1
1 Henry VI (S)	—	—	—	—	—	—	—	—
1 Henry VI (?)	—	—	—	—	—	—	—	1
Titus (S)	—	—	—	—	—	—	—	—
Titus (?)	—	1	—	—	—	—	—	—
Richard III	—	—	—	—	—	—	—	—
Venus	—	—	—	—	—	—	—	—
Lucrece	—	—	—	—	—	—	—	—
Sonnets	—	—	1	—	—	—	—	—
Errors	—	—	—	1	—	—	—	3
LLL	—	—	—	—	—	—	1	4
Richard II	—	—	—	—	—	—	—	3
Romeo	—	—	—	—	—	—	—	8
Dream	—	—	—	—	—	1	—	—
K. John	1	—	—	—	—	—	—	—
Merchant	—	1	—	—	—	—	—	—
1 Henry IV	—	—	—	—	—	—	—	1
Merry Wives	—	—	—	—	—	—	—	—
2 Henry IV	—	—	—	—	—	—	—	—
Much Ado	—	—	—	—	—	—	—	—
Henry V	—	—	—	—	—	—	—	2
Caesar	—	—	1	1	—	—	1	—
As You Like It	—	—	—	—	—	—	—	—
Hamlet	—	2	1	—	—	—	3	3
Twelfth Night	1	—	1	—	—	—	—	—
Troilus	5	1	1	—	—	—	—	1
More	—	—	—	—	—	—	—	—
Measure	5	—	—	—	1	1	—	—
Othello	7	—	1	—	2	—	—	—
All's Well	2	—	—	1	—	—	—	4
Timon (S)	3	3	1	—	—	—	—	3
Timon (M)	4	—	—	3	3	—	—	—
Lear (Q)	11	2	—	—	—	1	—	1
Macbeth	2	1	1	—	—	—	—	—
Antony	2	—	—	—	—	—	2	2
Pericles (S)	2	—	—	—	1	—	—	3
Pericles (W)	2	—	—	—	2	1	—	1
Coriolanus	10	1	2	—	2	—	1	24
Winter's Tale	12	—	—	—	—	—	2	—
Cymbeline	8	2	1	1	—	—	1	—
Tempest	2	—	—	—	—	—	—	—
True (S)	1	—	—	—	—	—	1	1
True (F)	2	—	6	4	3	—	—	1
True	3	—	6	4	3	—	1	2
Kinsmen	2	—	—	—	—	—	—	1
Kinsmen (S)	1	—	—	—	—	—	—	—
Kinsmen (F)	1	—	—	—	—	—	—	1

display no significant chronological bias. Column 25 tabulates the frequency of obsolescent pronunciations of unaccented syllables for metrical purposes, comparable to the disyllabic pronunciation of the -ion suffix (column 24), as in trisyllabic *ocean*, *patient*, *marriage*, etc.

TABLE 9. Colloquialism in Verse (*cont.*)

	17 o'	18 's (us, his)	19 's (is)	20 has	21 does	22 POSITIVE	23 -eth	24 -ion
Edward III	—	—	3	—	—	12	14	4
Two Gentlemen	1	—	7	1	1	32	10	11
Shrew	—	—	4	5	6	63	20	8
Contention	—	—	4	1	—	57	13	20
Duke of York	—	—	6	1	1	47	18	13
1 Henry VI	—	—	5	—	—	32	34	17
1 Henry VI (S)	—	—	1	—	—	11	2	4
1 Henry VI (?)	—	—	4	—	—	21	32	13
Titus (S)	—	—	—	—	—	11	2	9
Titus (?)	—	—	—	—	—	5	8	2
Richard III	—	—	—	1	—	21	18	24
Venus	—	—	—	—	—	2	53	2
Lucrece	—	—	—	—	—	7	34	3
Sonnets	—	—	2	—	—	18	14	—
Errors	—	1	1	—	—	24	5	11
LLL	2	1	2	—	—	31	8	5
Richard II	—	—	4	—	1	21	13	10
Romeo	—	—	8	—	—	49	9	11
Dream	—	—	1	—	—	20	8	10
K. John	—	1	4	—	1	28	11	30
Merchant	—	1	2	—	—	19	19	14
1 Henry IV	—	—	—	1	3	17	9	26
Merry Wives	—	—	1	1	1	17	—	—
2 Henry IV	—	—	3	1	—	8	7	27
Much Ado	—	1	—	—	—	10	2	8
Henry V	—	—	3	—	—	51	2	24
Caesar	—	1	3	3	4	44	7	21
As You Like It	—	—	3	2	—	27	4	7
Hamlet	—	3	4	3	22	167	4	4
Twelfth Night	1	—	2	1	8	34	3	3
Troilus	—	—	9	2	4	75	4	13
More	—	—	—	—	—	4	—	—
Measure	2	2	18	2	4	104	1	4
Othello	—	2	26	6	12	192	3	6
All's Well	—	4	20	10	13	123	—	—
Timon (S)	—	—	14	4	6	105	—	1
Timon (M)	—	1	8	13	12	84	—	1
Lear (Q)	1	10	19	4	10	149	2	1
Macbeth	—	5	15	16	21	178	1	3
Antony	—	11	20	21	29	273	3	4
Pericles (S)	—	1	3	2	7	63	—	1
Pericles (W)	—	1	18	5	3	60	6	6
Coriolanus	1	19	13	17	14	358	1	9
Winter's Tale	3	16	14	18	22	276	—	4
Cymbeline	—	20	23	6	8	286	2	4
Tempest	1	2	13	6	12	148	1	2
True (S)	1	9	8	32	13	211	—	10
True (F)	2	—	1	9	4	112	—	13
True	3	9	9	41	17	323	—	23
Kinsmen	2	10	24	44	13	331	—	2
Kinsmen (S)	—	5	13	15	6	140	—	—
Kinsmen (F)	2	5	11	29	7	191	—	2

TABLE 9. Colloquialism in Verse (*cont.*)

	25 other	26 -ed	27 NEGATIVE	28 TOTAL	29 WORDS	30 RATIO
Edward III	1	56	75	-63	19,533	-3.23
Two Gentlemen	2	28	51	-19	12,692	-1.50
Shrew	12	28	68	-5	16,736	-0.30
Contention	4	50	87	-30	20,656	-1.45
Duke of York	8	47	86	-39	23,277	-1.68
1 Henry VI	6	89	146	-114	20,454	-5.57
1 Henry VI (S)	1	8	15	-4	3,846	-1.04
1 Henry VI (?)	5	81	131	-110	16,608	-6.62
Titus (S)	5	55	71	-60	13,122	-4.57
Titus (?)	6	13	29	-24	5,910	-4.06
Richard III	9	75	126	-105	27,862	-3.77
Venus	—	17	72	-70	9,730	-7.19
Lucrece	—	72	109	-102	14,548	-7.01
Sonnets	—	62	76	-58	17,520	-3.31
Errors	2	34	52	-28	12,712	-2.20
LLL	—	27	40	-9	14,278	-0.63
Richard II	5	43	71	-50	21,809	-2.29
Romeo	10	73	103	-54	20,796	-2.60
Dream	4	41	63	-43	12,859	-3.34
K. John	7	84	132	-104	20,386	-5.10
Merchant	4	43	80	-61	16,167	-3.77
1 Henry IV	7	33	75	-58	13,064	-4.44
Merry Wives	2	6	8	9	2,647	3.40
2 Henry IV	2	26	62	-54	12,388	-4.36
Much Ado	5	9	24	-14	5,748	-2.44
Henry V	5	56	87	-36	14,879	-2.42
Caesar	7	37	72	-28	17,668	-1.58
As You Like It	1	14	26	1	9,082	0.11
Hamlet	4	44	56	11	21,433	5.18
Twelfth Night	—	11	17	17	7,427	2.29
Troilus	3	22	42	33	17,948	1.84
More	—	1	1	3	977	3.07
Measure	1	30	36	68	13,077	5.20
Othello	5	30	44	148	20,972	7.06
All's Well	1	25	26	97	11,997	8.09
Timon (S)	2	21	24	81	9,453	8.57
Timon (M)	2	3	6	78	4,303	18.13
Lear (Q)	4	40	47	102	18,155	5.62
Macbeth	1	17	22	156	15,344	10.17
Antony	3	23	33	240	21,777	11.02
Pericles (S)	—	24	25	38	7,674	4.95
Pericles (W)	—	11	23	37	7,073	5.23
Coriolanus	4	16	30	328	20,732	15.82
Winter's Tale	1	10	15	261	17,791	14.67
Cymbeline	1	14	21	265	22,878	11.58
Tempest	1	12	16	132	12,812	10.30
True (S)	—	15	25	186	16,613	11.20
True (F)	—	2	15	97	6,684	14.51
True	8	17	48	275	22,743	12.09
Kinsmen	5	19	26	305	22,062	13.82
Kinsmen (S)	1	7	8	132	8,355	15.80
Kinsmen (F)	4	12	18	173	13,707	12.62

explained. We must therefore presume—not a simple change of direction in the curve, but (again)—a dip in the curve. The colloquialism quotient falls, briefly rises, falls again, and then after *King John* begins a sustained rise which will take it through *Coriolanus*.

Unfortunately, this seeming dip in the curve deprives us of any secure bearings on the very plays where bearings would be most welcome: those written before *1 Henry IV*. We cannot tell, on this evidence, whether *Shrew* belongs before *Contention*, or at about the same time as *Love's Labour's Lost*, or between *Caesar* and *As You Like It*. We cannot relate the order of composition of the early comedies to that of the early histories. However, we do get a steady progression if we assume—as the graph does—that the four 'lyrical' plays were written in the order *Love's Labour's Lost*, *Richard II*, *Romeo*, and *Dream*. We possess no evidence which would contradict this order; recent editors of *Romeo* (Evans, 1984) and *Dream* (Brooks, 1979) have advanced fragile but believable reasons for supposing that *Dream* post-dates *Romeo*; and our own investigations of external and extrinsic evidence had driven us to date all of the last three in or just after 1595. Therefore, although the Oxford edition adopts a different order (*Dream*, *Romeo*, *Richard II*), I would now be inclined to reverse that sequence. It is a measure of the uncertainty surrounding the early canon that such changes of mind can occur in the year between giving the publisher the order of printing for an edition and giving the publisher this essay.

We do not wish to exaggerate the value of this test, simply because we developed it ourselves. Shakespeare's style, as measured by this evidence, does not display the uniformity of development a mathematician would prefer. Like metrical tests, it only measures verse; unlike some metrical tests, it does not depend upon debatable decisions about scansion or versification, but it may be subject to some distortion by agents of transmission. The presence of some obvious anomalies (*Hamlet*, *Lear*), for which we have as yet no explanation, should alert us to the possibility of other, less obvious ones. This test simply gives us a little more information about Shakespeare's style, which may be of value—as often—when we have nothing better.

Verbal parallels were dismissed by Chambers (*Shakespeare*, i. 255), prematurely. He objected that no scholar 'can claim the gifts of observation and memory required to assemble out of thirty-six plays all the parallels of thought and sentiment for which verbal clues are lacking'. We may accept the pragmatism of this claim, in regard to the canon as a whole; but it loses much of its force when applied to specific cases. Such parallels for the three disputed pages of *Sir Thomas More* were exhaustively accumulated by R. W. Chambers, and they support other evidence in suggesting that the passage belongs to the seventeenth century. A scholar studying intensively a single poem or play might reasonably attempt such a survey for that work, particularly if its dating remained a matter of dispute; and over a period of time individual studies of that kind might contribute to a larger pattern. As in other respects, Chambers magisterially discouraged further research simply because it lay outside the bounds of his own interest or patience. He noted that the only such study hitherto published, of *Twelfth Night*, was 'very far from complete', citing a review which supplemented it; but by means of such criticisms we arrive, collectively, gradually, at a more reliably comprehensive account. If such studies were published electronically, they could be continually assessed and updated.

Moreover, although parallels of thought cannot be mechanically collected, purely verbal parallels can be, by 'the patient exploitation of a concordance'. Chambers dismisses the effort by objecting that such parallels might arise from similarity of situation, or from a revival which brought old phrases back to mind; indeed they might, theoretically, but we cannot know if such factors do indeed influence the results until we look. Chambers asserts that even if most parallels resulted from proximity of composition, they could not take us beyond a rough chronological grouping of the plays. It is hard to guess how he could know this, even before such a tabulation had been made. Chambers cautions that verbal parallels cannot be treated (as 'rare' words can) as 'convertible counters', susceptible to statistical treatment. But the validity of such criticisms depends entirely upon the definition of 'verbal parallel' employed by an investigator. If 'verbal parallel' is strictly and arbitrarily defined as the repetition of two or more words in conjunction, then such parallels can legitimately be treated as 'convertible counters' of uniform value. Such parallels—like 'proud insulting' (*Duke of York* 2.1.168/750, 2.2.84/875, *1 Henry VI* 1.3.117/315), or 'insulting tyranny' (*1 Henry VI* 4.7.19/2036, *Richard III* 2.4.50/1404)—are more frequent than most people realize; and, as these examples suggest, their distribution does correspond strongly with what we know about the chronology of Shakespeare's works. We could also limit an investigation to 'rare' collocations (those which occur no more than ten times in the canon), thereby discounting commonplaces, just as we do when studying 'rare' vocabulary. Taylor ('Shakespeare and Others') has undertaken a preliminary survey of such parallels in the passages of *1 Henry VI* attributed to Shakespeare, and (using a looser definition of 'parallel') in the two versions of Sonnet 2 ('Some Manuscripts'); a more comprehensive survey could be useful.

Metrical tests are known better, and trusted less, than any other form of stylistic evidence. Chambers provides a useful survey, summary, and critique of such work up to 1930. On the one hand, any reader will sense that Shakespeare's blank verse suffers a sea change, rich and strange, between the early and late plays; on the other hand, that change has proven difficult to measure in terms which will satisfy every carping critic. Chambers dwells upon the deficiencies within and contradictions between individual tests of different verse features; such objections can to a large degree be overcome by combining individual tests into an 'omnibus predictor' of metrical development. Shakespeare's blank verse style, created by the interaction of a variety of metrical techniques, is best described by a test which synthesizes the measurement of several features. Such a comprehensive measurement was independently developed by Gray, and (more satisfactorily) by Wentersdorf (1951). Wentersdorf's final 'metrical index' combines feminine endings, alexandrines, extra mid-line syllables, extra syllables, overflows, extreme overflows, unsplit lines with pauses, and split lines. However, Fitch cogently objects that the treatment of pauses, in the tests upon which Wentersdorf draws, is 'open to serious statistical objection'. It depends upon the assumption that the frequency of pauses remains constant from play to play; in fact the frequency fluctuates considerably: *Romeo and Juliet* has, in Fitch's count, approximately 71 sense-pauses per 100 lines, as against only 63 in *As You Like It*. 'The only satisfactory method, therefore, is to express the number of sense-pauses occurring within the line as a percentage of the total sense-pauses for the play' (Fitch, 299). Unfortunately, Fitch provides such figures for only eight plays. His figures usefully place *Romeo* between *Richard II* and *King John*, and *As You Like It* after *Henry V* (p. 300); but for most of the canon they leave us in the dark. Consequently, we have simply removed 'unsplit lines with pauses' from Wentersdorf's test, and recalculated the metrical index. The results can be seen in column 2 of Table 10.

As with other tests, the results are easier to interpret after *1 Henry IV*, when we can see a fairly regular progression. Wentersdorf observed that 'the indices of the historical plays are in general relatively lower than those of the other pieces' (p. 186), and consequently he separated them into a distinct curve. But this does not help much in the earlier part of the canon, where a fall from *Contention* to *Duke of York* precedes a rise to *Richard III*, and where *King John* belongs to the same period as *Contention*; the alleged distinction between the histories and other plays does not affect Shakespeare's share of *All Is True*, and need not be assumed with *Richard II* if it were the last (or first) of the 'lyrical' group, and need not be assumed with *Henry IV* if both plays preceded rather than followed *Merchant*, and need not be assumed with *Henry V* if it preceded *Much Ado*. Wentersdorf's premisses may be correct, but they are a shaky rule by which to interpret the figures, since they predetermine the very issues which the test itself is meant to help resolve.

The figures for the early plays are such a jumble that little relevant information can be derived from them. *1 Henry VI* has the lowest figure, but since it is almost certainly collaborative, the anomaly cannot be easily interpreted. If we assume a dropping curve we can put the 'lyrical' plays in the order *Richard II* (12), *Love's Labour's Lost* (9), *Romeo* (9), *King John* (9), *Dream* (8); if we assume a rising curve we get a very different order. The drop from *Contention* to *Duke of York*, and the low figures for both, might be due to the presence of a collaborator; but the order of plays in the Oxford edition produces a steady decline from *Two Gentlemen* to *1 Henry VI* and *Titus*. When so much depends upon guesswork, anybody's guess is as good as anybody else's.

Fitch invalidated without replacing previous tests of the frequency of mid-line pauses; but Oras supplied a measurement, not of the simple frequency of such pauses, but of their relative distribution within the verse line (Table 10). The character of a verse line is determined not only by the number of pauses within it, but by where they fall: after the first, or second, or whichever of the ten syllables of a pentameter. Using three separate criteria—any pauses (Oras A), strong pauses (Oras B), and changes of speaker (Oras C)—he tabulated all the works of Shakespeare and many by his Elizabethan and Jacobean contemporaries. These figures not only differentiate Shakespeare from many other poets of his time, but also reveal a clear development in his own usage. Although these three criteria agree in the broad pattern of development, the most reliable figure seems to be the most comprehensive (Oras A), and in our analysis of individual plays we have accordingly given it greater weight. In each case, Oras's figures listed here give the proportion of pauses in the first half of the line, which steadily decreases. Moreover, unlike many other stylistic tests, these do throw some light on the sequence of Shakespeare's early plays.

Although all these metrical tests are expressed in numbers, they only record simple proportions, and do not subject those results to statistical evaluation. Yardi made a rather inept attempt at statistical interpretation of the data; Brainerd (1980), more reliably, included the relative frequency of split verse lines among the variables in his 'omnibus predictor of date of composition'. Brainerd's article points the way forward to a more sophisticated interpretation of stylistic evidence; but that advance must be accompanied by a more sophisticated collection of metrical data.

Since Chambers summed up and put down the study of internal evidence, advances in the study of Shakespeare's style have come largely from the periphery of the international Shakespeare industry: from devoted amateurs (like Armstrong and Slater), from statisticians (like Brainerd, Morton, Yardi), from countries other than England and North America (Clemen, Jackson, Lake, Mincoff, Spevack, Wentersdorf). Yet the last half-century has seen enormous progress in statistical analysis, and in the availability of resources—like concordances and computers—which make such studies more practicable, reliable, and verifiable than they were before 1930. Only by the combined efforts of professional Shakespearians (who know the limitations and complexities of the data) and professional statisticians (who know the limitations and complexities of the interpretation of data) can we expect to do better than our predecessors in arriving at some reasoned hypothesis about the gradations of Shakespeare's stylistic development.

Although minor ambiguities remain about the order of particular plays, we can be reasonably confident about the shape of the canon after about 1597. The early years remain perplexing. In terms of authorship, our external evidence is least reliable for those years; lost plays, collaborative plays, and uncollected non-dramatic verse probably cluster in that period; less study has been devoted to the stylistic discrimination of the playwrights active in those years; Shakespeare's own apprentice style would have been less developed, more derivative, less immediately identifiable than it later became. In terms of chronology, for the early plays we have less theatrical and publishing evidence; Shakespeare's theatrical affiliations are unclear; he made less use of topical allusions which we can trace; his style fluctuated more radically in sympathy with genres; and stylistic tests which seem to work well for other parts of the canon are ambiguous, or break down altogether. We can only hope that the next half-century will begin to map an order in that chaos.

But in recognizing that more remains to be done we should not lose sight of what has already been accomplished. Tests of internal evidence, whether of authorship or chronology, to a remarkable degree reinforce one another. No one has devised a way to measure their combined force, but they cohere into something of great constancy. We dwell, naturally enough, upon the limitations of the evidence, because those limitations frustrate us: we want to know the very line when Fletcher took over from Shakespeare, or which of two plays written in one year was written first, and the evidence cannot (always) answer our questions with quite the certitude we

TABLE 10
Verse tests

	Metrical index (Wentersdorf)	Metrical index (revised)	Sense pauses (Fitch)	Pause patterns Oras A	Oras B	Oras C
Two Gentlemen	12	12	—	64.1	65.0	66.7
Shrew	13	10	—	68.2	65.9	59.0
Contention	9	9	—	63.6	64.5	63.6
Duke of York	9	8	—	67.3	66.5	58.3
1 Henry VI	7	7	—	67.6	72.9	46.7
Titus	9	8	—	69.2	65.8	66.7
Richard III	12	12	19.7	62.5	64.3	75.0
Errors	12	10	—	61.6	57.1	58.3
LLL	10	9	—	62.2	63.5	73.5
Richard II	13	12	23.2	60.2	57.8	63.3
Romeo	13	9	30.9	62.1	62.0	48.5
Dream	11	8	—	60.6	57.9	53.8
K. John	11	9	28.2	58.7	59.8	60.0
Merchant	17	16	—	51.7	58.0	37.5
1 Henry IV	12	13	—	53.5	53.0	46.9
Merry Wives	19	19	—	56.2	52.3	61.5
2 Henry IV	15	14	—	56.1	50.5	36.7
Much Ado	18	17	—	54.0	43.9	40.7
Henry V	16	16	32.1	49.4	43.5	46.2
Caesar	17	16	—	51.8	43.1	46.9
As You Like It	18	17	35.7	52.5	47.7	34.5
Hamlet	22	20	—	47.8	42.1	42.3
Twelfth Night	19	17	—	46.2	42.6	47.7
Troilus	23	22	—	54.6	51.9	52.1
Measure	25	24	—	42.2	36.8	31.9
Othello	26	24	—	49.2	50.9	43.9
All's Well	28	26	—	34.5	26.8	22.5
Timon	28	26	—	39.1	31.3	28.5
Lear (QF)	29	27	—	39.1	33.0	26.8
Macbeth	31	29	—	35.3	27.7	21.1
Antony	35	33	64.1	29.6	23.9	18.9
Pericles (S)	28	24	—	31.4	27.8	25.0
Pericles (W)	—	—	—	50.7	56.8	29.4
Coriolanus	35	34	66.3	29.8	22.0	14.6
Winter's Tale	35	32	—	31.2	25.3	20.2
Cymbeline	38	34	—	30.0	23.9	20.0
Tempest	36	34	—	33.6	24.6	19.0
True (S)	37	34	—	25.2	20.4	14.8
True (F)	—	—	—	32.6	23.5	—
Kinsmen (S)	—	—	—	25.8	15.7	15.7
Kinsmen (F)	—	—	—	32.0	22.8	—

require or desire. But the fact that our questions have become so particular, so precise, is itself a tribute to the cumulative researches of the last two centuries. Consider *Pericles*. Apparently printed from a memorial text, it should, by one of the cardinal rules for the interpretation of internal evidence, offer no foothold for the student of authorship (Schoenbaum, 1966). Yet since the eighteenth century it has been clear to almost all scholars that the play had two authors—an intuition confirmed by its imagery, its rare vocabulary, its treatment of function words, its collocations, its use of rhyme, its verbal parallels with the canons of Shakespeare and Wilkins, its verse technique, its omission from the 1623 Folio. In the case of *Pericles*, we can see more than we are supposed to be able to.

But *Pericles* also illustrates the necessity for textual criticism, for certain peculiarities in the text of that play can only be explained in terms of its transmission. Hence the inclusion of an essay of this kind in a book otherwise devoted to textual and bibliographical problems. The study of authorship and of chronology begins and ends in editing. Editors must establish the words and the credentials of a document before we know what to make of the evidence it contains—whether internal or external. And editors determine, or decide upon, a canon and a chronology in order to fix the table of contents in a real or hypothetical collected edition: we try to discover what Shakespeare wrote, and when he wrote it, in order to influence what readers read, and the order in which they read. Some readers will find pleasure in following the guide's advice, and others will, just as surely, and no less legitimately, enjoy ignoring it.

WORKS INCLUDED IN THIS EDITION

The last sustained synthesis and assessment of evidence for authorship and chronology throughout the canon was undertaken by Chambers in 1930 (*Shakespeare*, i. 205-576, ii. 397-408). McManaway (1950) reviewed chronological studies undertaken in the next two decades. In a succession of articles Mincoff struggled with problems of chronology in the early canon, chiefly on the basis of a sensitive and detailed analysis of definable stylistic features; these investigations were revised and synthesized in a book (1976) which, having been published in Bulgaria, has not received the attention it deserves. Honigmann (*Impact*; 1985) has also attempted a reassessment of the early canon, chiefly in order to push the beginning of Shakespeare's career back into the mid-1580s. Evans (edn., 1974) provides a skeletal summary of 'Chronology and Sources'. Most of the substantial work on problems of chronology and authorship since Chambers has occurred in scattered notes and articles, or in editions of individual plays. We have not attempted to provide here a complete bibliography of such studies, but have mentioned any which seem to us significant. Editions of individual works are here identified only by editor and date; fuller information will be found in the relevant Introduction, below.

The Two Gentlemen of Verona 1590-1

Mentioned by Meres (1598); printed in 1623. One passage (3.1.294-358/1313-79) seems indebted to Lyly's *Midas*, 1.2.19-67; this indebtedness may result from witnessing a performance (c.1588-9) or reading the first edition (1592: BEPD 106). Several passages are influenced by Arthur Brooke's *The Tragical History of Romeus and Juliet* (1562: STC 1356.7). This influence has often been taken to suggest composition at about the same time as *Romeo and Juliet*, but Shakespeare sometimes made use of the same sources at widely separated periods, and appears to have been familiar with Brooke at least as early as the composition of *Richard Duke of York* (5.4.1-31/2594-2624). The play could belong to any year in the decade before Meres mentioned it. Wells (1963) showed that in terms of basic dramatic technique the play is more naïve than anything else in the canon. Independently of Wells, Leech (edn., 1967) persuasively argued, on the basis of the relative density and sophistication of comparable dialogues, that *Two Gentlemen* is earlier than *Errors* (pp. xxxii-xxxiv), and that some of its confusions may result from composition at about the same time as *Shrew* (p. xxxii). Mincoff follows Chambers in treating *Two Gentlemen* as Shakespeare's third comedy, but betrays more uncertainty about the play than about the relative priority of *Shrew* and *Errors*: he notes for instance that 'no writing in *The Comedy of Errors* is so flat and apparently imitative as we meet with in some scenes' of *Two Gentlemen* (pp. 174-5). He thinks the play later almost solely because Lance is a greater comic creation than the comic servants in the other early comedies (p. 175); but he admits that Lance is at bottom a static and undramatic figure, a stand-up comic minimally integrated into the plot (p. 180). Leech indeed thought that Lance could easily be a late addition to the play's structure. Honigmann (*Lost Years*, 128) regards the play as Shakespeare's first comedy, preceded only by *Titus*, and conjecturally dated 1587.

In rare vocabulary *Two Gentlemen* has most links with *Shrew* and *Richard III*, and to a lesser extent with *Titus*; its colloquialism figure is closest to *Contention*; metrically it falls between the figures for *Errors* and *Richard III*. These figures are not of much use, though they might suggest a slightly later dating than we have given the play. However, Oras's pause test would place it before *Richard III*, or any play later than *Richard III* in the Oxford edition. Brainerd (1980) unwisely chose *Two Gentlemen* as one of his 'unambiguously dated' test plays, assuming a date of '1594'; however, of the nineteen plays in this control, *Two Gentlemen* proved anomalous in both checks on the stability of his data (pp. 225-6). The obvious conclusion, which Brainerd fails to draw, is that the play was misdated to begin with.

The Taming of the Shrew 1590-1

A play called *The Taming of a Shrew* was entered in the Stationers' Register on 2 May 1594 and published in an edition dated 1594. The relationship between this text and the text entitled *The Taming of the Shrew*, first published in 1623, remains problematic, but it may safely be assumed that one text in some way imitates or derives from the other. It has generally been assumed that either title might be used for either play; this cannot be proven, but the obvious possibility makes it difficult to evaluate the documentary allusions. Henslowe recorded a performance of 'the Tamynge of A Shrowe' on 11 June 1594, at Newington Butts, in a short season by 'my Lord Admeralle men & my Lorde Chamberlen men' (*Henslowe's Diary*); Henslowe's carelessness about titles makes it difficult to repose complete confidence in his use of the indefinite article, and we cannot even be sure who performed the play, because his ambiguous head-note may refer to joint or to alternating performances by the two companies.

In either event, the date of *A Shrew* is important to the date of *The Shrew*. Lines present in *A Shrew* but not *The Shrew* seem to be satirized in Robert Greene's *Menaphon* (1589: STC 12272), and in Thomas Nashe's prefatory epistle to that work; but since *A Shrew* lifts whole passages from other plays, one cannot determine whether the lines satirized in *Menaphon* are themselves original to *A Shrew*, or plagiarism from some earlier work now lost. The title-page of the 1594 edition claims that *A Shrew* belonged to Pembroke's Men, a company last heard of in August 1593, when they were bankrupt. It has been plausibly suggested that the 'Simon' inexplicably listed in a stage direction at Sc.iii.21 was Simon Jewell, an actor buried on 21 August 1592 (see Edmond and McMillin). If accepted, this identification pushes composition of *A Shrew* back another year. On the other hand, *A Shrew* must be later than Marlowe's *Doctor Faustus* (BEPD 205), which it quotes several times. Unfortunately, the date of *Faustus* is itself disputed. If we accept the tendency of recent scholars to place it after publication of the lost or extant translation of the *Faust Book* (both in 1592: STC 10711), the *Faustus* allusions and the 'Simon' direction in conjunction would date *A Shrew* firmly in 1592. If we do not accept either conjecture, then *A Shrew* could belong to any year from c.1587 to 1593. (Lancashire and Levenson (1973) provide an annotated bibliography of studies of *A Shrew*.)

The Shrew must be later than Kyd's *Spanish Tragedy* (BEPD 110), which it quotes; unfortunately, the date of *The Spanish Tragedy* (c.1582-91) is even less certain than that of *Doctor Faustus*. Freeman's judgement—which is the most recent, and seems to us plausible—is that, on the basis of the tone of its Spanish allusions, it predates the Armada (1588). If we disregard the allusions to 'The Taming of a Shrew', as being of uncertain reference, the earliest explicit allusion to the Folio title occurs in S. Rowlands's *Whole Crew of Kind Gossips* (1609: STC 21413): 'The chiefest Art I haue I will bestow, | About a worke cald taming of the Shrow' (sig. E1). But as Moore first observed, *The Shrew* must be earlier than 1593, in which year Antony Chute published his poem *Beauty Dishonoured, Written Under the Title of Shore's Wife* (1593: STC 5262; Stationers' Register 16 June 1593): Chute's line, 'He calls his Kate, and she must come and kisse him' (p. 21; sig. C3) can refer to either of the last two scenes of *The Shrew*, where the kissing is explicit and climactic. *A Shrew* contains nothing comparable. Since the theatres closed (after a brief reopening) in February 1593, Chute must have seen the play before then. Moreover, this evidence is supported by several echoes in *A Knack to Know a Knave* (1594: BEPD 115), first performed in June 1592 (*Henslowe's Diary*). These parallels, collected by Proudfoot (MSR, 1963) and Thompson (1982), echo a number of passages common to *A Shrew* and *The Shrew*, which could be used for dating either; but *Knack* twice echoes passages only in *The Shrew*. Whether these echoes belong to the original 1592 text of *Knack* or to a memorial reconstruction which lies behind the 1594 publication, they establish the existence of *The Shrew* before the closure of the theatres after the brief season in January 1593, and probably before June 1592. Sams, in order to deny this evidence, has to imagine that the passages extant in *The Shrew* once belonged to *A Shrew*, but were cut from the published text—a procedure which could explain anything. By such reasoning one could, for instance, assert that *The Shrew* pre-dates *Menaphon*.

If the two texts are evaluated independently of one another, they occupy an almost identical range: from the beginning of Shakespeare's career to 1592-3. There is more reason for dating *A Shrew* late in this period (on the basis of the *Faustus* quotations) than for so dating *The Shrew*; if this late dating is correct, and if *A Shrew* is the earlier text, then both plays must have been written within about a year. It is by no means clear why Shakespeare should have reworked someone else's play so soon after its first performance. On the other hand, if *The Shrew* is the earlier text, the two plays might be separated by several years, and the composition of *A Shrew* would fit logically into our picture of the activities of Pembroke's Men c.1592-3.

In fact we believe, as have most recent scholars, that *A Shrew* imitates *The Shrew*, and we are not persuaded by Sams's efforts to reverse this order. Sams—dismissing the Chute allusion—argues that *The Shrew* dates from c.1604, a date impossible by every stylistic criterion. In Oras's pause test both *The Shrew* and *Two Gentlemen* are earlier than *Richard III*, *Errors*, and *Love's Labour's Lost*. In rare vocabulary *The Shrew* has exceptional links with no play later than 1596; it has strong links with both *Contention* and *Richard Duke of York*, as do they with it. On a random distribution the two histories should share only 126 rare words with *Shrew*; instead they share 166 (chi-square = 12.6). Since these links cannot be due to similarity of genre or theme, they are most likely to be due to chronological proximity. Mincoff's analysis of imagery and rhetoric also places it in the same period as the two histories. *Shrew*'s metrical figure is lower than any play after *King John*. Even the colloquialism-in-verse test, which is thrown off by an anomalously high proportion of *has* and *does*, puts *The Shrew* earlier than 1599. (*Has* and *does* appear eleven times in the play, but no play before *Caesar* has more than six, and six of the occurrences in *Shrew* occur in a mere 180 lines of the text: 2.1.213-364/1021-1172, 5.2.37-62/2438-63.) Although this stylistic evidence does not pinpoint the play's composition precisely enough to determine the direction of influence between *A Shrew* and *The Shrew*, it does establish that the play must have been in existence by 1598, when Meres published his list of Shakespeare plays.

Sams does, however, usefully insist upon the real difficulty created by the reference to 'Soto' (Ind.1.81-7/81-7). This allusion seems to fit the circumstances of John Fletcher's *Women Pleased* (BEPD 664). The same passage identifies the actor who played 'Soto' by the speech-prefix 'Sincklo', a prefix which appears nowhere else in this play. John Sincklo is named in other dramatic documents, some of which may date as early as the late 1580s, another as late as 1604, so the name in itself cannot help in dating *The Shrew* (see Introduction, below). However, we are made suspicious by the unique appearance of the name in a passage which (*a*) is utterly superfluous and (*b*) topically alludes to a Jacobean play—a play, moreover, written by John Fletcher. Fletcher also wrote a sequel or response to *The Shrew*: *The Woman's Prize; or, The Tamer Tamed* (BEPD 660), conjecturally dated 1611 in the the most recent edition (Beaumont and Fletcher, *Works*, iv). Noticeably, the text of *Shrew* would be perfectly intelligible if the lines were omitted ('So please your lordship to accept our duty.—Well, you are come to me in happy time.'); of the seven suspect lines, two are metrically irregular. It is possible, then, that the Soto allusion may reflect a Jacobean revival of *The Shrew*, planned to coincide with performances of *The Tamer Tamed*, and accordingly touched up for the occasion. (The high frequency of *has* and *does*, mentioned above, also suggests that the text may have been altered in some respects at a later date.) If we consider the Soto allusion as evidence of interpolation, rather than of original composition, it could be much later than the rest of the play. The traditional dating of *Women Pleased*, on the basis of its cast list, is 1620; however, that date is uncertain, and seems too late for Sinclo, otherwise last heard of sixteen years before.

Morris (edn., 1981) regards *The Shrew* as the earliest of Shakespeare's comedies, and perhaps his earliest play; but this conclusion relies excessively on the Warwickshire allusions in the Induction, which need not indicate composition soon after Shakespeare left Stratford. In rare vocabulary it is most strongly linked with *Love's Labour's Lost*; its colloquialism figure is also closest to *Love's Labour's Lost*; its metrical figure is closest to *Errors*. These figures might be taken to support composition in 1594-5, just after publication of *A Shrew*: Chambers dated the play in 1594. However, as elsewhere with the early plays these figures may be skewed by genre, illustrating no more than the play's links to Shakespeare's other early comedies. Mincoff points to a number of more specific verbal features suggesting stylistic immaturity, especially in relation to *Errors*; he regards *Shrew* as Shakespeare's earliest play. The size of its cast associates it with the other pre-plague plays (*Contention*, *Richard Duke of York*, *Titus*, and *1 Henry VI*).

Meres does not include *Shrew* in his 1598 list of Shakespeare's works, and it was first attributed to him by inclusion in the 1623 Folio. Chambers is only the most respected of several scholars who have regarded the play as collaborative (*Shakespeare*, i. 322-8). Chambers, on the basis of 'a general stylistic impression from which I cannot escape', gave the Bianca sub-plot to a collaborator, and assigned to Shakespeare the Induction/0-271, 2.1.1-38/809-47, 2.1.114-320/922-1128, 3.2/Sc. 7, 3.3.22-124/1456-1558, 4.1/Sc. 9, 4.3/Sc. 11, 4.6/Sc. 14, 5.2.1-184/2402-2585, and possibly 1.2.1-114/527-640. This view has been discredited less by dispassionate consideration of the internal evidence than by a general wave of scepticism about studies of authorship. Morris approvingly cites essays by Kuhl (1925) and Wentersdorf (1954, 1972); but of these Kuhl had not succeeded in persuading Chambers, while Wentersdorf's first effort depends upon the play's use of isolated imagery which could be paralleled in other Elizabethan dramatists, and his second finds the clearest example of an idiosyncratic cluster of Shakespearian imagery in 4.1, a scene already attributed to Shakespeare by Chambers. More impressive is the study of musical terms by Waldo and Herbert (1959), which suggests not only the homogeneity of the play but its correspondence with Shakespeare's early comedies. But in opposition to such conclusions one must note Mincoff's judgement that 'if one were compelled to prove Shakespeare's authorship of the play on the basis of the style and poetry alone, one would be very hard put to it' (p. 156). The function-word test for the play as a whole does not encourage the hypothesis of collaboration; but we have not tested Chambers's divisions separately. Given the weakness of the case for disintegration as it has hitherto been presented, we have assumed that the play is Shakespeare's throughout, but this conclusion is not as secure as one would wish. The evidence of cross-purposes and revision (discussed in the Introduction, below) might be accounted for by collaboration, or by later adaptation and interpolation, or by a messy authorial first draft.

Finally, although it seems likely that *Shrew* belongs early in Shakespeare's career, it might easily have been written after *Contention* and *Richard Duke of York*, or between them; but in the absence of anything which might generate conviction, we have placed it with *Two Gentlemen* before the initiation of the histories sequence.

The First Part of the Contention 1591

Entered in the Stationers' Register on 12 March 1594 and published in an edition dated 1594. Our dating of the play presumes that the 1594 edition represents a memorial reconstruction, and hence that the original composition predates the 1594 publication (see Introduction, below). Because plague closed the London theatres for all but a month from 23 June 1592 to January 1594, the play presumably dates from 1592 or earlier. All scholars agree that its composition preceded that of *Richard Duke of York* (see below), and many believe that both plays preceded composition of *1 Henry VI* (see below). Our own chronology presumes that *Contention* was the first written of the three plays, which had all been completed by March 1592; in this scenario, it cannot be earlier than 1591. *Contention* is the only one of the canonical history plays which is not demonstrably indebted to the second edition of Raphael Holinshed's *Chronicles* (1587: STC 13569). However, this fact seems more important to the relative order of composition (*Contention* before the other histories) than to actual date (*Contention* before 1587): even Honigmann dates it 1589 (*Lost Years*, 128). Most critics would accept that it post-dates Marlowe's *Tamburlaine* (BEPD 94-5; composed 1586-7?), which by its great success seems fortuitously to have initiated a fashion for two-part plays on historical themes. It also seems indebted to Spenser's *Faerie Queene*, Books 1-3 (STC 23080; Stationers' Register, 1 December 1589, in print by January 1590). Although some parts of Spenser's poem were circulating in manuscript as early as 1587-8, we think it unlikely that Shakespeare, as a relatively unknown minor actor and playwright, would have seen the poem in manuscript, though that possibility cannot be conclusively ruled out.

The play is first attributed to Shakespeare in the unauthorized 1619 Pavier reprint. Meres (1598) does not include any of the three *Henry VI* plays among Shakespeare's works. The omission may be fortuitous, but many scholars have doubted Shakespeare's authorship of the whole play. Hart (edn., 1909), largely on the basis of verbal parallels, believed that the play was a collaboration by Shakespeare, Peele, Marlowe, Greene, and possibly Nashe or Lodge, and that it was later thoroughly revised by Shakespeare, in whole or part. However, this hypothesis was based in part upon a view of the 1594 edition which few scholars now accept (see Introduction, below). Wilson (edn., 1952) argued that Shakespeare revised a text by Greene, Nashe, and perhaps Peele. Wilson saw little evidence of Shakespeare's hand in 1.2/Sc. 2, 1.4.24/616-end of scene, 2.2.1-53/880-932, 2.3/Sc. 7, or 2.4/Sc. 8. He found Act 3 (Sc. 9-11) the most clearly Shakespearian. Mincoff, beginning with a presumption of Shakespeare's authorship of the entire play, was nevertheless forced to recognize that Act 3/Sc. 9-11 was 'a remarkable achievement in dramatic verse' (p. 88), quite unlike most of the rest of the play; along with 5.3.31-65/3067-3101 and 5.5.5-9/3125-9 ('of . . . occasion'), it seemed to him explicable only if it belonged to an entirely different period of Shakespeare's writing. (Mincoff reached identical conclusions about *1 Henry VI*, on the basis of disparities which have since been shown to result from multiple authorship.) Brainerd (1980) found *Contention* statistically deviate relative to his ten tested variates (p. 227). Waller noted the anomalously high frequency of 'ye' (twenty occurrences; only one in Act 3). Unfortunately, serious investigation of the problem of authorship in *Contention* has for centuries been bedevilled by the textual problems posed by the relation between the 1594 and 1623 texts. Most earlier theories of collaboration were based upon the presumption that the 1594 text represented an early version of the play, later revised; but to conclude (as most modern scholars do) that the 1594 text results from a memorial reconstruction by no means establishes that Shakespeare was sole author of the original play. Nor do recent critical claims that the play has a satisfying dramatic unity create a presumption of single authorship. However, the problem cannot be solved without a thorough reconsideration of authorship throughout the dramatic output of the 1580s and early 1590s. Until such time, the question of the authorship of the bulk of *Contention* should be regarded as open.

Richard Duke of York 1591

Published in an edition dated 1595. Our dating of the play presumes that the 1595 text represents a memorial reconstruction, and hence that the original composition must pre-date its publication (see Introduction, below). A line from the play (1.4.138/539), present in both the 1595 and the 1623 texts, was parodied in *Greene's Groatsworth of Wit* (STC 12245; entered in the Stationers' Register on 20 September 1592, and allegedly written shortly before Robert Greene's death on 3 September 1592). As the public theatres were closed between 23 June and the composition of the pamphlet, the allusion almost certainly dates performances of the play before June 1592. The play—like all Shakespeare's subsequent histories—must be later than 1586, for it clearly draws upon Holinshed's *Chronicles* (1587). It seems to echo Spenser's *Faerie Queene* (January 1590): see *Contention*, above. It must post-date *Contention*, and must pre-date *Richard III*; it seems likely that it pre-dates *1 Henry VI* (see below). Honigmann (*Impact*, 80) collects alleged echoes of it in *The Troublesome Reign of John, King of England* (1591: BEPD 101-2); he dates it in 1590 (*Lost Years*, 128). In our chronology it could hardly be much later than late 1591.

The play is first attributed to Shakespeare in the unauthorized 1619 Pavier reprint. Meres (1598) does not include any of the three *Henry VI* plays among Shakespeare's works. This omission may be fortuitous, but many scholars have doubted Shakespeare's authorship of the entirety of *Richard Duke of York*. Hart (edn., 1910), largely on the basis of verbal parallels, believed that the play was originally a collaboration of Marlowe with Shakespeare, subsequently revised by Shakespeare. This hypothesis was in part based upon a view of the 1595 edition which few modern scholars would accept (see Introduction, below). Wilson (edn., 1952) argued that Shakespeare revised a text by Greene and possibly Peele. Wilson saw little or no evidence of Shakespeare's hand in 2.6.44-110/1220-86, 3.3/Sc. 13, or Act 4/Sc. 14-23. The speech directions in 3.3/Sc. 13 ('Speaking to Bona', etc.) are certainly uncharacteristic of Shakespeare. Brainerd (1980) found *Richard Duke of York* statistically deviate relative to his ten tested variates (p. 227). The problem here closely resembles that in *Contention* (see above), and pending further investigation Shakespeare's responsibility for every scene of the play should be regarded as uncertain.

1 Henry VI 1592

Meres (1598) does not mention *Henry VI* at all, and most editors since Theobald have doubted Shakespeare's authorship of the entirety of *Part One*. Brainerd (1980) found *1 Henry VI* statistically deviate relative to his ten tested variates (p. 227). The spelling of unusual proper names and of the exclamation 'oh', the erratic marking of scene divisions, the frequent use of 'here' in stage directions, and a variety of linguistic preferences and verse tests all indicate the presence of more than one author, and assign to Shakespeare 2.4/Sc. 12 and 4.2.0-4.7.32/1751-2049. These are the passages also most often attributed to him on the basis of verbal parallels and the quality of the writing. Shakespeare's collaborators cannot be so confidently identified, but Thomas Nashe probably wrote most of Act 1 (Sc. 1-8); more conjecturally, there are a number of links between *Locrine* (see 'Works Excluded', below) and the author of Act 3 and the bulk of Act 5. For a detailed analysis of the problem of authorship see Taylor, 'Shakespeare and Others'; for independent evidence of Nashe's presence, see Thiele.

Part One makes use of the 1587 edition of Holinshed. Nashe clearly alludes to the play in *Pierce Penniless* (entered in the Stationers' Register on 8 August 1592): 'How would it haue ioyed braue *Talbot* (the terror of the French) to thinke that after he had lyne two hundred yeare in his Tombe, hee should triumphe againe on the Stage, and haue his bones newe embalmed with the teares of ten thousand spectators at least (at seuerall times), who, in the Tragedian that represents his person, imagine they behold him fresh bleeding' (*Works*, i. 212). Since London theatres were closed because of plague from 23 June until January 1593, Nashe's allusion dates the first performance no later than June 1592. *Henslowe's Diary* identifies a 'Harey the vj', first performed at his Rose Theatre on 3 March 1592, and marked as 'ne'. Henslowe's regular practice, when referring to multi-part plays, was to identify a 'Part I' simply by the main title, indicating the part only when referring to a 'Part II' or 'Part III' (see Knutson, 1983); hence, 'Harey the vj' could be *1 Henry VI*, but could not be the play which the Folio identifies as *3 Henry VI* (= *Richard Duke of York*); it also seems unlikely to be the play which the Folio identifies as *2 Henry VI*, which was either the first part of *The Contention* or the second part of *Henry VI*, but which we have no reason to believe was ever called the first part of *Henry VI*. The play, belonging to Strange's Men, was performed thirteen or fourteen times during the spring and early summer, with exceptionally good receipts; most critics accept that Nashe alludes to the same play which Henslowe records (see especially Born). Wilson (edn., 1952) pointed to a number of departures from the play's historical sources which coincide with features of the English campaigns in Normandy in the winter of 1591-2; most subsequent critics have accepted the evidential value of those parallels. We therefore accept, as did virtually all critics before Alexander (1929), that *1 Henry VI* is Henslowe's 'harey the vj', which is thus the most securely dated of all Shakespeare's early work.

Internal evidence has suggested to most editors that *Part One* assumes an audience's familiarity with *Contention* and *Duke of York*, which in turn require no familiarity with *Part One*. Rare vocabulary in the portions most securely attributable to Shakespeare link them most strongly (in order) with *Duke of York*, *Richard III*, *Titus*, and *Two Gentlemen*; statistically comparable figures are not available for the poems. Rare phrasing—verbal collocations of two or more words, which occur less than eleven times in the canon—link Shakespeare's portion most closely with *Venus*, *Duke of York*, *Richard III*, and *Titus* (see Taylor, 'Shakespeare and Others').

Titus Andronicus 1592

A play which Henslowe identified as 'titus & ondronicus' was performed by the Earl of Sussex's Men on 24 January 1594 (*Henslowe's Diary*, where it is marked 'ne'). John Danter entered in the Stationers' Register two weeks later, on 6 February, 'a booke intituled a Noble Roman Historye of Tytus Andronicus' and also 'the ballad thereof'; Danter published an edition of the play dated 1594. The 1594 performances can hardly have been the first, for the 1594 title-page indicates that the play had belonged to three different companies: 'As it was Plaide by the Earle of *Darbie*, Earle of *Pembrooke*, and Earle of *Sussex* their Seruants'. (Derby's Men were also known as Strange's, and are so identified, for clarity, throughout this discussion of chronology.) We are unpersuaded by George's attempt to interpret this statement as a reference to performance by the three companies combined on 23 January 1594. Consequently, in the most natural interpretation of the title-page, it must have belonged to the three companies in sequence. Sussex's Men owned it at the end of this sequence, and in any case had been an entirely provincial company before that season; we must therefore assume that it originated with either Strange's or Pembroke's Men.

An apparent allusion to *Titus* occurs in *A Knack to Know a Knave*, first performed by Strange's Men on 10 June 1592 (*Henslowe's Diary*):

> as welcome shall you be ...
> As Titus was unto the Roman senators,
> When he had made a conquest on the Goths,
> That in requital of his service done,
> Did offer him the imperial diadem.

Unfortunately, our earliest text of this play (Stationers' Register, 7 January 1594: *BEPD* 115) is allegedly a memorial reconstruction, and hence this allusion (sig. F2^v) might result from a 1594 memory rather than a 1592 one (see Bennett). Alternatively, the lines might refer to a lost source of *Titus*, rather than the play itself. The lines in *A Knack* cannot easily be interpreted as an advertisement for a play already in (or about to enter) the repertoire of Strange's Men. We have a full record of that repertoire from 19 February to 22 June 1592 (*Henslowe's Diary*)—and it does not include *Titus Andronicus*. If *Titus* was so old that Strange's Men did not even perform it once among the twenty-four plays they offered that season, it seems unlikely that they would bother to advertise it in a new play, or fail to revive it after the opening of that new play. If, on the other hand, *Titus* were a new play, in progress or about to enter the repertoire, they might choose not to open it at the very butt-end of the season, or it might not have been quite ready; but then why does it not appear in the company's repertoire among the twenty-nine performances they gave in the winter of 1592-3? That repertoire includes a 'Titus' (6, 15, and 25 January), but the ambiguous title almost certainly refers to 'Titus and Vespasian', from the company's 1592 repertoire: Henslowe did not mark it as 'ne', or distinguish it with a full and unambiguous title, as he did 'titus & ondronicus' the following year. *Titus Andronicus* must have belonged to Strange's Men either long before 1592, or not until after January 1593. Either explanation makes the *Knack* allusion difficult to explain as a deliberate advertisement originating in performances of June 1592. It must therefore originate from memorial confusion in the 1594 text, or indicate that the story of *Titus Andronicus* was well known to London audiences by mid-1592.

So far as the theatrical evidence takes us, then, the performances by Strange's Men must belong on either side of the period February 1592–February 1593. If they belong to the later range, *Titus* could have been 'new' in London in January 1594, and Henslowe's 'ne' can be interpreted literally. On the other hand, Pembroke's Men were apparently bankrupt by August 1593 (Chambers, *Shakespeare*, ii. 314); if the play passed from Strange's to Pembroke's Men then Strange's Men must have relinquished it very quickly. However, Pembroke's Men may have been an offshoot of Strange's, which would account for the transfer (McMillin, 1972).

Unfortunately, Pembroke's Men are the most obscure of the companies associated with Shakespeare's name. They performed at court on 26 December 1592 and 6 January 1593, and are otherwise traceable only in the provinces. However, they can hardly have sprung from oblivion into the accolade of two court appearances, and since the London theatres were closed that summer and autumn we can probably assume that they had a London base in the first half of 1592, and again for the month of playing in January 1593. That base may have been the Rose, if Pembroke's Men are just an offshoot of Strange's. If Pembroke's Men are not a splinter of Strange's, then *Titus* might have been playing somewhere else in London in spring 1592, when Strange's Men were at the Rose—thus accounting for the allusion in *Knack*. But this interpretation leaves Henslowe's 'ne' difficult to explain, except as an indication that the play had been adapted for Sussex's Men. If, however, Pembroke's Men did not acquire the play until January 1593, the London theatres might have been closed again before they could perform it in the metropolis.

An early date is supported by Ben Jonson's Induction to *Bartholomew Fair* (1614: BEPD 455): 'Hee that will sweare, *Ieronimo*, or *Andronicus* are the best playes, yet, shall passe vnexcepted at, heere, as a man whose Iudgement shewes it is constant, and hath stood still, these fiue and twentie, or thirtie yeeres' (Induction, 106-9, in *Works*, vi. 16). Scholars dispute the degree of precision which should be accorded Jonson's statement, especially given his motives in context for exaggerating the age of *The Spanish Tragedy* and *Titus*. If taken literally, Jonson would date *Titus* between 1584 and 1589; Honigmann places it in 1586, as Shakespeare's first play (*Lost Years*, 128). We are inclined to interpret Jonson more loosely, as of uncertain value in arbitrating between the late 1580s or early 1590s as its most probable period of composition.

At this time no confidence seems attainable about the play's original theatrical affiliation or its date of composition. In placing it where we do we have been impressed by (*a*) the fact that, like *Richard III* and *1 Henry VI*, it can be linked to Strange's Men, and (*b*) the large size of its cast, which associates it with the pre-plague plays. If Shakespeare's contribution to *1 Henry VI* was finished by mid-February 1592, then we would expect him to have begun another play before the closure of the theatres late in June, and that play would have assumed the size and shape of cast available at that time. That play might well not have been finished when the theatres closed for the summer. In these circumstances the play's subsequent theatrical history, between its completion in summer 1592 and its first recorded performance in January 1594, might be as complicated and obscure as the history of the theatrical companies themselves during that period, and the play itself might well have been literally 'new' to London audiences when Sussex's Men performed it at the Rose. The only feasible alternative would be to assume that *Titus* belongs to the very beginning of Shakespeare's career, and hence that it was written in 1590 or before. Either scenario seems preferable to our earlier assumption, reflected in the order of the plays in the Oxford edition itself, that *Titus* immediately preceded *1 Henry VI*.

Stylistically, Slater's vocabulary test links *Titus* most strongly with (in order) *Contention*, *Duke of York*, *Richard III*, *1 Henry VI*, and *Shrew*. We might expect a stronger link with *1 Henry VI*, on our proposed chronology; but Slater's figures reflect the entire play, of which Shakespeare wrote only a part. All these plays belong to the pre-plague group, except *Richard*, which we believe followed *Titus* (see below). If the two narrative poems are grouped together, they have stronger links with *Titus* than with any other play; although this association no doubt to some extent reflects shared classical subject-matter, it does not encourage the supposition that *Titus* was written, as Honigmann proposes, seven full years before the poems (1593-4). This vocabulary evidence, and Mincoff's analysis of the play's verbal style, support the assumption that *Titus* belongs toward the end, rather than the beginning, of Shakespeare's pre-*Venus* period.

However, the value of such stylistic evidence depends in part upon our assumptions about the play's authorship. Meres (1598) included *Titus* in his list of Shakespeare's works, and his authorship was not explicitly doubted until Edward Ravenscroft's preface to his own adaptation of the play in 1687, in which Ravenscroft claimed to 'have been told by some anciently conversant with the Stage, that it was not Originally his, but brought by a private Author to be Acted, and he only gave some Master-touches to one or two of the Principal Parts or Characters; this I am apt to believe, because 'tis the most incorrect and indigested piece in all his Works; It seems rather a heap of Rubbish then a Structure'. Ravenscroft had ulterior motives for denying Shakespeare's sole responsibility, and his late testimony in any case cannot challenge Meres's early attribution of the play to Shakespeare, in a list which contains no other item which can be seriously doubted. The external evidence strongly supports the play's authenticity, and later critical disparagement must be weighed against its early popularity.

Nevertheless, a number of stylistic anomalies have suggested that the play may be a collaboration between Shakespeare and another writer. Brainerd (1980) found *Titus* statistically deviate relative to his ten tested variates (p. 227). *Titus* has even more alliteration than (the collaborative) *1 Henry VI*, which is otherwise the most alliterative play in the canon (Hill). Suspicion has in recent years concentrated upon Act 1. Maxwell (1950) observed a grammatical construction (a possessive adjective or pronoun as antecedent to a relative clause) rare in Shakespeare but common in Peele which appears 'six or seven' times in the play's first scene; Mincoff notes that this trick of style 'is comparatively unobtrusive', and hence 'less likely to be imitated' (p. 131). Jackson (1979), drawing upon earlier work, noted a remarkable discrepancy between the low frequency of feminine endings in three scenes of the play (1.1, 2.1, and 4.1/Sc. 1, Sc. 2, and Sc. 7) and the high, typically Shakespearian frequency elsewhere. Jackson has also noted, in a contribution to *Shakespeare Newsletter* (1979, pp. 43-4), that the suspect scenes contain a much higher frequency of *and* than any other play, an anomaly entirely due to the play's first two scenes (or one scene, as originally written). Waith (edn., 1984), quoting Taylor, objected that these three scenes are linked by no narrative or formal logic; but in fact the first two scenes are, in the 1594 edition (and so presumably in the first version of the play), a single uninterrupted scene; the scene division was created by a change of staging associated with an act division. In the original division of labour between putative collaborators, the first 626 lines might well have been regarded as a single unit. In a collaborative play one writer might well be given responsibility for a single act, and for another scene elsewhere; in this instance, Act 1 initiates the play as a whole, and 4.1/Sc. 7 initiates the counter-action. The division suggested by feminine endings is thus compatible with patterns of collaboration in the drama of the period, and it rests upon the most easily and reliably identified of all metrical criteria—criteria for which we possess comprehensive data for plays up to 1595 (Timberlake). Jackson showed that this division corresponds to a significant disparity in rare vocabulary links with other plays; he also notes disparities in imagery and in the use of compounds. Hill's analysis of a variety of features of the play's rhetoric and verbal style forced him to conclude that it was either (*a*) collaborative, or (*b*) Shakespeare's earliest surviving play. But the hypothesis of an early date conflicts with other stylistic evidence suggesting a later period. Jackson does not attempt to reconsider Hill's evidence in the light of his own conjectural division. Defenders of Shakespeare's sole authorship repeatedly claim that influence or imitation can account for the parallels with Peele in the first scene; in itself, this explanation is satisfactory, but it is harder to explain why such parallels should concentrate so heavily in one part of a play. The parallels suggest that the first scene was written by either Peele or an imitator of Peele; but the rest of the play seems to have been written by neither.

The function-word test does not decisively support single authorship or collaboration (see above). The colloquialism-in-verse test reveals some difference between the two parts, but the disparity is not significant; in the complete absence of any comparable studies of other dramatists, the figures cannot be taken as evidence of Shakespeare's sole authorship. (The colloquialism figures do, however, suggest—along with other evidence discussed above—that *Titus* belongs after the first two comedies and the *Henry VI* plays.) Metz (1985) deploys stylometric evidence in defence of Shakespeare's sole authorship; but such tests are, at present, unreliable (see above). If anything they weigh against Peele, as a particular alternative, more successfully than they support Shakespeare. Arguments from construction (Sampley, Price) are also unreliable, and at most suggest that Shakespeare wrote the 'plot', from which he—and possibly someone else—worked. As yet, the internal evidence mustered in defence of single authorship is inconclusive or unreliable. The matter merits further investigation. One possibility which seems not to have been considered is that the changes of plan evident in the first scene (discussed at length by Wells, *Re-Editing*) result from Shakespeare tidying up and improving the work of his collaborator: the apparently late addition of the Mutius material, for instance, contributes strongly to the structural patterning which critics have praised as characteristically Shakespearian.

Finally, 3.2/Sc. 6 creates its own problems of both authenticity and chronology. The scene does not appear in the quarto editions of the play, and first appeared in print in the 1623 Folio. Bibliographically, the scene shows every sign of being a late addition, though how much later than the rest of the play cannot be said. Kramer, in the most extended study, concluded that it was a much later interpolation by another playwright; his hypothesis would be supported by the way in which the added scene requires an immediate re-entry of several characters, a licence made possible by the act-break—which was probably only added after 1608 (see Taylor, 'Act Intervals'). If the scene is Jacobean in origin, it can hardly be Shakespeare's. However, most critics have believed that the scene is Shakespeare's, and it could have been added on the occasion of a revival in the 1590s. It is possible that such an addition could account for Henslowe's description of the play as 'ne' in 1594. Examined separately, the added scene is most closely linked with the four early comedies, while the rest of the play is most strongly associated with the first tetralogy (*Division*, p. 463). Metrically, too, the scene contains proportionally more licences than the rest of the play, suggesting a somewhat later period of composition. Given the scene's brevity, its authorship may be indeterminable upon purely stylistic evidence; it seems safest to assign it to Shakespeare.

Richard III 1592–3

Entered in the Stationers' Register on 20 October 1597, and printed in an edition dated 1597; mentioned by Meres (1598), and attributed to Shakespeare in the reprint of 1598. We believe that the first edition is a reported text (see Introduction, below); if so, then if we allow time for the play to be performed and a report compiled, the original composition could hardly be later than early 1597. Taylor ('*Richard III*'), developing a suggestion by earlier scholars, proposes that the report was communally compiled when the Chamberlain's Men were on a provincial tour in the summer of 1597, and had left their prompt-book behind—something perhaps unlikely to happen if the play were new. The play makes use of the 1587 edition of Holinshed, and at 4.5.11/2985 it alludes unhistorically to 'Sir' James Blunt: the Blunt family owned land in Stratford, were related by marriage to Shakespeare's acquaintances the Coombes, but were first knighted in 1588 (see Shanker). The play can therefore be confidently dated in the period 1589–96. Like the plays on the reign of Henry VI, it is indebted to Spenser's *Faerie Queene* (Brooks, 1979); if we accept that this influence would probably only have occurred after Spenser's poem reached print, then *Richard III* cannot have been written before January 1590.

Critics have always agreed that the play post-dates *Contention* and *Richard Duke of York*; as Mincoff astutely argued, the remarkable difference in dramatic power and stylistic control between *Richard Duke of York* and *Richard III* suggests that the latter did not immediately follow completion of the former. In particular, Mincoff suggested that the tragic structure and Senecan detail of *Richard III* owed much to Shakespeare's composition of *Titus* in the interim, and we have acted upon this suggestion in our ordering of the plays. Taylor ('Shakespeare and Others') shows that the Shakespearian portions of *1 Henry VI*, which seem confidently datable to early 1592 (see above), are closely associated verbally with *Titus* and *Richard III*. Both *Titus* and *1 Henry VI* are linked by documentary evidence to Strange's Men; Honigmann, collecting and adding to previous discussions, persuasively argues that the treatment of Derby in *Richard III* rearranges history in order to flatter Derby's descendant, the patron of Strange's Men (*Lost Years*, 63–4). However, *Richard III* differs from *Titus* and *1 Henry VI* (and *Duke of York*, and *Shrew*) in that no documentary evidence, or certain allusion, dates it in the pre-plague period—a silence which seems to us remarkable, given the play's evident later popularity and impact. Moreover, it differs from all the certain pre-plague plays in requiring a smaller cast, of the size normal in all Shakespeare's plays after *c.*1592. For this reason we have placed it after *1 Henry VI* and *Titus*, assuming that it was not begun until after the theatres were closed in June 1592. This conclusion accords well with the supposition, reasonable though not demonstrable, that the publication of *The True Tragedy of Richard the Third* (1594: BEPD 126) was designed to exploit the success of Shakespeare's play—a supposition rather more difficult to credit if *Richard III* had been in existence since 1590-1.

Our dating coincides with Chambers's (though Chambers gives no reasons for it); but it cannot easily be reconciled with Brooks's conclusion that *Richard III* is echoed in *Edward II* by Marlowe, who died on 30 May 1593. Although the evidence for Marlowe's indebtedness to *Contention* and *Duke of York* seems to us persuasive, we find the alleged parallels with *Richard III* unconvincing. By the admission of both Brooks (1968) and Hammond (edn., 1981), most of the verbal parallels are commonplaces or could result from influence in either direction, or from sources which both authors consulted; what Brooks and Hammond emphasize as the key parallel (*Edward II* 5.4.56-63) depends upon no more than Machiavellian hypocrisy masquerading as a 'bashfull puretaine'—a notion hardly unique to Shakespeare, or unattractive to Marlowe. Even less conclusive are the parallels between *Richard III* and *The Troublesome Reign of John, King of England* (1591: BEPD 101-2), summarized by Honigmann (*Impact*, 80-1). Given the continuing disagreement over the relationship between that play and Shakespeare's *King John* (see below), it seems impossible to arbitrate, on the basis of connections far fewer and less certain, whether *Richard III* lent to or borrowed from that text.

Cairncross (1960) and Wentersdorf (1977) attempt to link the 1597 edition of *Richard III* to the reported texts associated with Pembroke's Men; if this connection could be established it would firmly place the play before summer 1593. But the late date of Q1's publication militates against their conjecture, and Taylor ('*Richard III*') challenges the verbal parallels on which it is based. Brainerd's statistical test (1980) suggests that the play is later than the Riverside edition placed it (before *Titus*, *Two Gentlemen*, and *Shrew*); but this conclusion is of more value in suggesting that the three other plays are dated too late than that *Richard III* itself has been dated too early. In the colloquialism test, *Richard III* is closest, among the early histories and tragedies, to *Titus*; in Oras A and B it follows all the plays which precede it in the Oxford edition; in rare vocabulary it is linked most closely, predictably, to the three *Henry VI* plays and—perhaps more significantly—to *Titus*. The only comedy with which it has exceptional links is *Errors*.

Venus and Adonis 1592-3

Entered by Richard Field (a native of Stratford-upon-Avon) on 18 April 1593, and published in an edition dated 1593, with a dedication signed 'William Shakespeare'. Most scholars agree that it was written during the enforced idleness which followed closure of the theatres in July 1592. It would not have been immediately obvious, to Shakespeare or anyone else, how long that interim would last; composition of *Venus* is unlikely to have begun in earnest before autumn 1592. The dedication's description of the poem as 'the first heire of my inuention' has sometimes been taken to imply composition in the 1580s, before any of the plays; but 'heire' probably means 'legitimate offspring', contrasting the poem favourably with the 'bastard' products of his theatrical career. If Shakespeare had intended to imply priority of composition, one would have expected him to say 'first fruits' (which are traditionally offered up to a protector/deity): compare for instance the preface to T.H.'s *Oenone and Paris* (1594: STC 12578.5), which describes that poem as 'the first fruits of my indeuours and the Maiden head of my pen'. In any case it would be odd to advertise that one's offering to a patron was an immature work dredged up from the past.

In Slater's rare vocabulary test (1975) *Venus* is linked, among the plays, most closely to *Dream*, *Titus*, and *Two Gentlemen*. These associations may be of limited chronological significance, however, since they could be due to shared classical or romantic subject-matter.

The Rape of Lucrece 1593-4

Published in an edition dated 1594, with a dedication signed 'William Shakespeare'. This edition was printed by the same stationer and dedicated to the same patron as *Venus*, and *Lucrece* is generally taken to be the 'graver labour' promised in the dedication to the earlier poem. It is probable that composition of the Sonnets began in the interim between the two narrative poems (see below), and likely too that Shakespeare worked on one or more plays during this period, but in the absence of certainty we have for convenience grouped the narrative poems together in our edition.

In Slater's rare vocabulary test (1975) *Lucrece* is linked, among the plays, most closely with *Titus*, *1 Henry VI*, *Richard III*, and *Romeo*. These associations are clearly influenced by genre, but the prominence of *Richard III* (as opposed to *Richard II*, 1595) is perhaps significant, and might reinforce arguments in favour of a relatively late date for *Titus*, *1 Henry VI*, and *Richard III* (see above). Moreover, the presence of *Richard III*, and its absence from the comparable list for *Venus and Adonis*, suggests that *Richard III* might post-date *Venus*.

The Comedy of Errors 1594

Performed at Gray's Inn on 28 December 1594; mentioned by Meres (1598). The play has often been treated as the first of Shakespeare's works, but such a dating has little to do with external or internal evidence; it reflects a judgement that the play's classical and farcical character is uncharacteristic of Shakespeare's mature comedy, and a prejudice that Shakespeare should logically have moved from imitation of classical models to development of his own 'romantic' forms. The play's only certain topical allusion (3.2.125-7/850-2) must have been written after 1584, but such allusions persist for several years after the truce of July 1593. Another, less certain allusion may exist in Dromio's comparison of the kitchen maid to a terrestrial globe (3.2.116-44/841-69): Emery Molyneux's globes, the first to be made in England and the first made by an Englishman, were put on the London market in 1592, and immediately became both popular and famous (see Wallis). Although continental globes existed before 1592, the passage in *Errors* would certainly be especially appropriate in or after 1592. None of this evidence for dating the play is very secure, and we date it as late as we do largely because we 'find it difficult to believe that the gentlemen of Gray's Inn would have entertained their guests on a grand night in 1594 with a play staled by five years on the public stage' (McManaway). In this connection, it is worth recalling that *Richard II*, which can hardly be earlier than 1595 (see below), was regarded as an 'old play' in January 1601—so old that the Essex conspirators had to pay the Chamberlain's Men to revive it for one performance in a public theatre.

In rare vocabulary, *Errors* is most closely linked to *Shrew* (which we regard as the previous comedy), *Richard III*, and *Romeo*; the two latter associations, which cannot be explained by similarity of genre or theme, seem the more significant chronologically, and are difficult to account for on the assumption that *Errors* belongs to the 1580s. Its colloquialism-in-verse figure associates it most closely with *Richard II* and *Romeo*. The heavy use of rhyme suggests composition in the lyrical period initiated by *Venus*. Mincoff, in the most detailed analysis of its style in relation to other early plays, places it after the first tetralogy, *Titus*, and *Shrew*, but before *Love's Labour's Lost*; he is less confident of its relation to *Two Gentlemen*.

Love's Labour's Lost 1594-5

Mentioned by Meres (1598). The first extant edition (which attributes the play to Shakespeare) is dated 1598, but the 1598 title-page makes it clear that an earlier edition has been lost. The nature of that earlier edition is disputed (see Introduction, below), but it seems likely to have been published before 1598. In the cases of other memorial texts replaced by authorial ones (*Romeo* and *Hamlet*), there is a gap of one or two years; nor is there any parallel in the Shakespeare canon of a work given two quarto editions in one year and none thereafter. We can therefore be reasonably confident that the play dates from 1597 or earlier. This supposition is corroborated by the title-page declaration that the play 'was presented before her Highnes this last Christmas', which almost certainly refers to the Christmas season of 1597-8, if not to that of 1596-7. Lever (1952) argued that 5.2.880-97/2632-49 could not have been composed before the publication of Gerard's *Herbal* (1597: STC 11750); but this contention has been disproven by Kerrigan (1982).

Stylistically, there has been widespread agreement that the play is earlier than *Dream* and *Romeo* (see below). Oras's pause test would place it after *Richard III*; in rare vocabulary it is linked most closely, predictably, with other comedies, but the strong link with *Romeo* cannot be explained as the consequence of genre. The heavy use of rhyme suggests composition in the lyrical period initiated by *Venus*. Innumerable topical allusions have been discerned in it; these are conveniently gathered, and for the most part dismissed, by David (edn., 1951). We find most plausible the suggestion that the masque of Muscovites (5.2/Sc. 9), and Biron's remarks at 5.2.461-3/2210-12, allude to the Gray's Inn revels of December 1594 (see *Errors*, above). Since both these links come late in the play, its composition might have been well advanced by the end of 1594. Bullough argues plausibly that the King of Navarre would be an unlikely subject from July 1593 to autumn 1594, the period of greatest English annoyance with him (i. 428-9); but the play could have been composed on either side of this range, and its satire of Navarre's perjury favours the later date. After his release from prison in 1604, Southampton entertained the royal family at his house with a performance of the play, and it seems plausible—though not certain, or necessary—to associate the play's composition with the period of Shakespeare's known intimacy with Southampton.

Love's Labour's Won 1595-6

A play by this title is included by Meres (1598) among Shakespeare's works. No text of this play is known to survive, but a bookseller's catalogue compiled in August 1603 demonstrates that an early edition was printed. The same catalogue makes it clear that 'Love's Labour's Won' cannot be simply an alternative title for *Shrew*, as has sometimes been proposed (see Baldwin). No other comedy by Shakespeare survives from the period before 1598 to which the title could be applied; of all the candidates *As You Like It* has perhaps the greatest number of links with *Love's Labour's Lost*, and Knowles catalogues various conjectures which have linked that play with Meres's title (edn., 1977). But the difference in titles remains very difficult to explain, as does the fact that *As You Like It* was entered in 1623 among 'plays never before printed', even though a play with its alleged alternative title (*Love's Labour's Won*) had definitely reached print. We therefore interpret Meres's allusion as a clear reference to a play now lost. That play could belong to any year from the beginning of Shakespeare's career to 1598; alliteration suggests that *Love's Labour's Lost* is the earlier of the two plays, and *Love's Labour's Won* a sequel, but the sequel need not have followed immediately. Wickham notes the repeated emphasis, at the end of *Love's Labour's Lost*, upon completion of the story after a 'twelvemonth'; he suggests that this would fit well with a performance of the first play at the Inns of Court, with the promise of a sequel during the next year's holiday season.

Richard II 1595

Entered in the Stationers' Register on 29 August 1597, and published in an edition dated 1597; listed by Meres (1598), and attributed to Shakespeare in the 1598 edition. The play must be later than Holinshed's *Chronicles* (1587), on which it draws. It has usually been assumed that the play is referred to in a letter of 7 December 1595 by Sir Edward Hoby to Sir Robert Cecil (Hatfield MS xxxvi.60; printed in full in Chambers, *Shakespeare*, ii. 320-1): 'I am bold to send to knowe whether Teusdaie may be anie more in your grace to visit poor Channon rowe where as late as it shal please you a gate for your supper shal be open: & K. Richard present him selfe to your vewe.' This interpretation of the letter has been challenged (see Shapiro and Bergeron); but a new play still seems more likely than an old one (*Richard III*), or a book, or a painting. Moreover, the play is probably indebted to Samuel Daniel's *The First Four Books of the Civil Wars* (STC 6244; Stationers' Register, 11 October 1594, and published in an edition dated 1595). Some connection between the two works seems indisputable: Ure (edn., 1956) expressed considerable diffidence about the direction of influence, but the case for Shakespeare as the borrower has been confirmed by Logan. We are also in part swayed by a suspicion that, in this period of their respective careers, Shakespeare was more likely to borrow from a prestigious courtly poet like Daniel than Daniel to borrow from a public playwright.

In rare vocabulary *Richard II* is most strongly linked to *Richard III* and *Titus*, and to a lesser degree with the three *Henry VI* plays; its links with *King John*, though statistically significant, are weaker, and with the exception of *King John* it has no links with any play we date later than 1593-4. In its use of rhyme, and its 'lyrical' style, it seems to belong to the period of *Love's Labour's Lost*, *Romeo*, and *Dream*, but such affinities cannot inform us whether it belongs to the end, middle, or beginning of that group. Slater's vocabulary evidence suggests that it belongs at the beginning; the colloquialism index supports an order which would place it after *Love's Labour's Lost* but before *Romeo* and *Dream*; the metrical tests, though less certain, can also support that interpretation. In the absence of any evidence to the contrary, it seems best to accept these fragile indications (which also have the merit of separating *Richard II* from the stylistically very different later histories).

Romeo and Juliet 1595

The play was mentioned by Meres (1598), and appeared in an edition dated '1597'. The fourth edition (undated) is the first with a title-page which attributes the play to Shakespeare. Weever (1599), like Meres (and perhaps following him), states that the play was Shakespeare's. The title-page of the 1597 edition claims that it was 'Printed by Iohn Danter', and that the play had 'been often (with great applause) plaid publiquely, by the right Honourable the L. of *Hunsdon* his Seruants'. Shakespeare's company ceased to be known by that name on 17 March 1597; Danter's shop was raided at some time between 9 February and 27 March 1597; his presses were seized (and later destroyed). Although Danter printed only the first four sheets (A-D), these facts establish that printing of those sheets must have been completed by 27 March 1597 at the latest. Since the first edition appears to be a memorial reconstruction, by March 1597 the play had been 'often . . . plaid', and a memorial reconstruction made, sold to a printer, and at least partly printed. It would be difficult, in this scenario, for Shakespeare to have finished the play any later than December 1596 (see Lavin). Lever (1953) plausibly argues that two passages (3.5.1-7, 19-22/1935-41, 1953-61) are indebted to poems by du Bartas published in John Eliot's *Ortho-Epia Gallica* (1593: STC 1574); Gibbons (edn., 1980) and Evans (edn., 1984) note several parallels suggesting the influence of Samuel Daniel's *Complaint of Rosamund* (1592: STC 6243.2). These parallels suggest a date in 1593 or later.

The Nurse specifies that ''Tis since the earthquake now eleven years' (1.3.25, 37/377, 389), and her insistence upon both the earthquake and its timing has led scholars since the eighteenth century to suspect a topical allusion. The only two earthquakes to which this might reasonably refer are those of 1580 and 1584; the earlier of these was the more significant, but Shakespeare himself may have had a special interest in the latter (see Thomas). If the passage is an allusion, then the play was composed either in 1591 or 1595, and the apparent parallels with Eliot and Daniel favour the later date. So do two links, noted by Bradbrook, between the play and the family of the Earl of Southampton, with whom Shakespeare developed an association between 1593 (*Venus*) and 1594 (*Lucrece*). George Gascoigne wrote a masque in 1575 for a double marriage in the Montague family (that of Southampton's mother), featuring the 'ancient grudge' between the Montagues and Capulets; in October 1594 Southampton sheltered Sir Charles and Sir Henry Danvers, who had killed another man in a family feud. The Southampton, Eliot, and Daniel evidence, in conjunction, tilts us toward the 1595 interpretation of the earthquake allusion. The 1591 date would have to be reconciled with the dating evidence for several other plays, for *Romeo* seems stylistically to belong in the same period as *Love's Labour's Lost*, *Dream*, and *Richard II*. Moreover, it remains possible that no allusion is intended, and without such an allusion there would be no reason at all to date the play so early as 1591. In the colloquialism test it is closest to *Errors* and *Richard II*; in Oras A and B it would follow *Love's Labour's Lost* and precede *Dream*; Slater's rare vocabulary test links it most closely to *Love's Labour's Lost*, *Titus*, *1 Henry IV*, and *Richard III*. Even Honigmann would agree that the first and third of these items belong to the mid-1590s; the link with *Titus* may be based upon genre. These tests therefore confirm the evidence of rhyme and rhetorical technique in putting the play in the mid-1590s.

Evans (edn., 1984) disagrees with most scholars in placing *Romeo* in the second half of 1596, basing his argument heavily upon Tobin's contention that the play is indebted to Nashe's *Saffron Walden*. Jackson (1985) disposes of these arguments. One may also note that, even if we assume that *Romeo* is the last of the 'lyrical' plays, the second half of 1596 is already rather crowded (see below).

A Midsummer Night's Dream 1595

Listed by Meres (1598), and ascribed to Shakespeare in the first edition (1600). Scholars have generally agreed that *Merchant* and both parts of *Henry IV* post-date *Dream*, and that all three must have been written by September 1598 (see below); at the very least this would push composition of *Dream* back to early 1597 or before. At the baptismal feast of Prince Henry, on 30 August 1594, a chariot was drawn in by a blackamoor: 'This chariot should have been drawne in by a lyon, but because his presence might have brought some feare to the nearest, or that the sights of the lights and the torches might have commoved his tameness, it was thought meete that the Moor should supply that room.' An account of this incident was published in *A True Reportary* (Stationers' Register, 24 October 1594; *Somers Tracts*, 4 vols. (1748), ii. 179), and it bears a remarkable resemblance to the action of Bottom and his fellow actors, who, planning an entertainment for their sovereign, likewise anticipate the fear that might be produced by bringing in 'a lion among ladies', and adjust their scenario accordingly. Rather than a 'topical allusion' which the dramatist intended to communicate to the audience, this incident instead seems to have served as a source for his construction of part of the plot.

Composition soon after 1594 is also suggested by a few other details. The reference to 'the death | Of learning, late deceas'd in beggary' (5.1.52-3/1752-3) seems to us relatively unlikely to refer to any specific individual, but Greene had died in 1592, Marlowe in 1593, and Kyd in 1594: the years 1592–4 were disastrous for the men who had dominated the English stage in the 1580s. Tasso died in April 1595; whether the author and audience thought of native drama or continental epic, the lines would be most telling in 1594–5. At 5.1.195–8/1896–8 Hero and Leander, Cephalus and Procris are referred to in rapid succession, as types of classical love: poems on both couples were entered in the Stationers' Register in 1593. Finally, on 17 September 1594 the Admiral's Men were performing a 'ne' play called *Palamon and Arcite* (recorded in *Henslowe's Diary*); it seems likely that both companies were offering the public a Theseus play at about the same time. The allusion to unseasonable weather (2.1.82–117/437–72) would fit the second half of 1594, 1595, or 1596, and hence is of little value in narrowing the range of composition. Most scholars would agree that, given the extraordinary parallels between them at every level of style and structure, *Dream* and *Romeo* were written at about the same time, though there is no consensus about which came first: Brooks (edn., 1979) and Evans (edn. of *Romeo*, 1984) both give plausible grounds for placing *Romeo* first, pointing to its influence on Shakespeare's departure from his sources for the Pyramus and Thisbe story. More generally, *Dream* belongs stylistically to a group of plays which includes *Romeo*, *Love's Labour's Lost*, and *Richard II*: the verbal characteristics of this group are well analysed by Brooks (edn., 1979).

Many scholars have believed that *Dream* was written to celebrate a particular aristocratic wedding. This hypothesis seems to us unnecessary: see Wells (edn., 1967, pp. 12–14). The first play known to have been written specifically for such an occasion was Samuel Daniel's *Hymen's Triumph* (1614: STC 6257), in a period when court entertainments had become more elaborate. However, we do know that plays were sometimes performed at private houses during the 1590s, and it is not inconceivable that a new play might have been requested for such a performance by a company's patron. If such an occasion is sought, the only two likely candidates are the marriage between Elizabeth Vere and the Earl of Derby (26 January 1595) and that between Elizabeth Carey and Thomas Berkeley (19 February 1596). Elizabeth Carey's grandfather and father were successively patrons of the Chamberlain's Men from 1594 to 1603; by contrast, Shakespeare's connection with Strange's Men (patronized by the previous Earl of Derby) had ended at least eight months before the 1595 marriage. Hunter (1983, 1985) shows that a literal astronomical interpretation of the play's opening lines also favours the 1596 date.

King John 1596

Listed by Meres (1598), and undoubtedly later than Holinshed's *Chronicles* (1587). It could be, and has been, dated in any year of the decade between these two termini. The play is certainly related to *The Troublesome Reign of John, King of England*, an anonymous two-part play published in 1591 (BEPD 101–2). Most scholars believe that *Troublesome Reign* is a major source of *King John*; this view has been cogently restated by Smallwood (edn., 1974). But Honigmann argued, in his edition of 1954 and in *Shakespeare's Impact* (1982), that *Troublesome Reign* is an imitation of Shakespeare's play, influenced by memories of *King John* in performance. Even so, however, he is forced in 1982 to concede a direct link between the wording of two stage directions in *Troublesome Reign* and those in *King John*, which could not be due to memorial transmission and would normally be interpreted as clear evidence that Shakespeare worked in composing *King John* directly from a text of *Troublesome Reign*; he averts this conclusion only by supposing that the Folio compositors sporadically consulted an edition of *Troublesome Reign* when setting from the manuscript of *King John* (*Impact*, p. 62). Given the fact that the two plays have only one full line in common, we find this supposition highly improbable.

In rare vocabulary *King John* is most strongly linked to *Richard II*, and to a lesser degree to *Richard III* and *1 Henry IV*. Noticeably, all these plays are histories, and genre may be skewing the figures, but even so this vocabulary test puts *King John* with *Richard II* in between *Richard III* and *1 Henry IV*. The only non-history play with which it has exceptional vocabulary links is *Romeo*. Likewise, the colloquialism-in-verse test puts *King John* closest to the two *Henry IV* plays, and Oras A puts it later than anything up to *Richard II*, and closest to that play. Even Honigmann places *Richard II* and *1 Henry IV* in 1595–6, and their strong links with *King John* are difficult to explain on his hypothesis. Brainerd's statistical test (1980) forcefully corroborates a late date, leading him to conclude (pp. 228–9) that the Riverside edition placed the play too early in assigning it to a period before *Dream*, *Romeo*, and *Richard II*. Recent editors who accept that Shakespeare's play post-dates *Troublesome Reign* have nevertheless tended to place it before *Richard II*, but this preference simply expresses a desire to keep the 'tetralogies' together, with *King John* as a divider. All the stylistic evidence, and the play's relatively infrequent use of rhyme, place *King John* after *Richard II*, and in the absence of good evidence to the contrary we have accepted that order (as did Chambers).

The Merchant of Venice 1596–7

Entered in the Stationers' Register on 22 July 1598, and mentioned by Meres (September 1598), although not published until 1600, in an edition which attributed it to Shakespeare. Holmer notes that Shylock's use of the story of Jacob and Laban (1.3.70–89/387–406) is almost certainly indebted to Miles Mosse's *The Arraignment and Conviction of Usury* (1595; Stationers' Register, 18 February 1595; STC 18207). The reference to 'wealthy Andrew' (1.1.27–9/27–9) apparently alludes to a Spanish vessel, the *St. Andrew*, captured in the Cadiz expedition of 1596; news of the capture apparently reached England on 30 July 1596, and the ship continued to arouse interest until the summer of 1597 (Brown, edn., 1955, pp. xxvi–xxvii). Stylistically, its metrical figure would place it just after *Henry IV*, while the colloquialism-in-verse figure would place it either before *King John* or after *Henry IV*. Such evidence, and Oras's pause test, reinforce the Andrew allusion in linking the play to the period of *Henry IV*; in placing it early within this spectrum we have been influenced by our belief that its handling of imagery and verse is less mature than in *Part Two*. By placing it before *Part*

One we make the second half of 1596 relatively crowded; if instead it followed *Part One*, the history play could have been completed by mid-summer. Our grouping of the three 'Sir John' plays together owes more to convenience than conviction.

1 Henry IV 1596-7

Entered in the Stationers' Register on 25 February 1598, and published in an edition dated 1598; Meres (1598) includes 'Henry the 4.' among Shakespeare's plays, and the title-page of the 1599 edition attributes it to him. The play's probable indebtedness to Daniel's *Civil Wars* (1595), and the fact that it must post-date *Richard II*, effectively narrow the date of composition to 1596 or 1597. It must be earlier than *Merry Wives*, which the consensus of recent opinion dates in spring 1597 (see below). Taylor ('Richard James') argues that the circumstances of the change of the name Oldcastle strongly suggest that the play was censored in connection with a court performance, possibly during the Christmas season of 1596-7.

The Merry Wives of Windsor 1597-8

Entered in the Stationers' Register on 18 January 1602, and published in an edition dated 1602, which attributes it to Shakespeare. It must post-date the composition and censorship of *1 Henry IV* (see above). Chambers and most earlier scholars assigned the play to 1600-1; both the colloquialism-in-verse and the metrical tests would support this interpretation. However, verse represents an exceptionally small proportion of this play, and the verse may also have been composed at exceptional speed; we are therefore inclined to place relatively little reliance on verse tests in this instance. In 1931 Hotson suggested that the play was written for the Garter Feast held at Whitehall on 23 April 1597, at which the patron of the Chamberlain's Men was inaugurated into the Order of the Garter; this view has won widespread acceptance (see Green and Roberts). Moreover, Slater's rare vocabulary test (1975) strongly associates the play with the same period as *Henry IV*. A late seventeenth-century tradition reports that Shakespeare wrote the play in two weeks, at the command of Queen Elizabeth; such circumstances would explain certain peculiarities of its form and style. Its composition may have interrupted work on *2 Henry IV* (see below).

Hotson's dating of *Merry Wives*, though plausible, remains conjectural, and by pushing the composition of *1 Henry IV* back into 1596 it further cramps the chronology for 1595-6, and leaves 1597-8 by comparison relatively empty. If we abandon the 1597 Garter Feast as the play's origin and occasion, then *1 Henry IV* could have been written in 1597 (after the death of William Brooke, Lord Cobham, briefly Lord Chamberlain, whose title descended from Oldcastle), and performed at court early in the Christmas season of 1597-8 (where the Chamberlain's Men played on 26 December, 1 and 6 January). The censorship could have occurred at that time, and Queen Elizabeth's request for a play on Falstaff in love could have been made in anticipation of a later court performance that Whitehall season (on 26 February). The officially instigated publication of *1 Henry IV*, in order to advertise the change of Sir John's name, would then have followed very soon after the censorship itself. *Merry Wives* could, on this interpretation, have recollected, rather than anticipated, the Garter ceremonies of spring 1597; the play would still have been written with a court performance in mind, honouring by allusion the company's patron, and satirizing by contrast Henry Brooke, the new Lord Cobham, who would have been instrumental in the censorship of *1 Henry IV*. Shakespeare's composition of *2 Henry IV* would have been interrupted by the request for *Merry Wives*, and *2 Henry IV* as a consequence would not have been completed until spring or early summer of 1598. This scenario produces the same order of plays, but it eases their timing.

2 Henry IV 1597-8

Entered in the Stationers' Register on 23 August 1600, and published in an edition dated 1600; both attribute it to Shakespeare. Meres's allusion (1598) to 'Henry the 4.' is ambiguous, but the play must be earlier than *Henry V* (late 1598-early 1599); Justice Silence is referred to in Jonson's *Every Man Out of his Humour* (1599: BEPD 163). When *1 Henry IV* was entered in the Stationers' Register on 25 February 1598, it was not identified as 'Part One', nor was it so identified on the title-page of the 1598 edition; though not decisive, this conspiracy of silence has suggested to most scholars that *Part Two* had not by February 1598 been performed. It must in its entirety post-date *1 Henry IV*; several recent scholars have been attracted by the conjecture that work on *Part Two* was interrupted during composition of 2.2/Sc. 5, in order to write *Merry Wives* (see Oliver's edn., pp. lii-lv). Taylor ('Richard James') provides further evidence for that inference, and also argues that the treatment of Sir John suggests that the Oldcastle surname had been censored in *1 Henry IV* before Shakespeare had written much if anything of *Part Two*. The reference to Amurath at 5.2.48/2822 apparently alludes to the accession of Muhammad III to the Turkish Sultanate in late February 1596.

Much Ado About Nothing 1598

Mentioned in the Stationers' Register on both 4 August and 23 August 1600, and published in an edition dated 1600. The second Register entry and the title-page both attribute it to Shakespeare. The 1600 edition, apparently set from foul papers (see Introduction, below), makes it clear that Shakespeare expected William Kempe to play the role of Dogberry; Kempe left the Chamberlain's Men early in 1599 (Chambers, *Stage*, ii. 326). The fact that the play is not mentioned by Meres (September 1598) is usually interpreted as evidence that it had not been performed by mid-1598, thus fixing the date precisely (see above). In rare vocabulary *Much Ado* is most closely linked to *Love's Labour's Lost*, *2 Henry IV*, *Hamlet*, and *Henry V*; the last three all belong to 1597/8-1600, and the concentration of links with non-comedies in this brief period cannot be discounted statistically. The play also seems clearly to belong to Shakespeare's prose period, stretching from *1 Henry IV* to *All's Well*. In the metrical test *Much Ado* ranks higher than any preceding play except *Merry Wives*; but its figure is identical to that for *As You Like It*, which is sometimes placed before it. However, the colloquialism-in-verse test clearly places *Much Ado* earlier than *As You Like It*. Although this cumulative stylistic evidence cannot determine whether *Much Ado* belongs to late 1597 or 1598, it does suggest that its position relative to surrounding plays can be fixed with some confidence.

Henry V   1598-9

Mentioned in the Stationers' Register on 4 August and 14 August 1600, and published in an edition dated 1600. It was first (implicitly) attributed to Shakespeare by inclusion in the projected Pavier collection of 1619. Evidence for dating is most fully discussed by Taylor (edn., 1982). The play must post-date *2 Henry IV* (see above); it probably post-dates George Chapman's *Seven Books of the Iliads of Homer* (entered in the Stationers' Register on 10 April 1598, and published in an edition dated 1598). *Henry V* is not mentioned by Meres (September 1598). The allusion to Essex's expedition to Ireland (5.0.29-34/2750-5) could have been written as early as November 1598, though it probably belongs to a time closer to Essex's departure on 27 March 1599. It has generally been assumed that the allusion dates completion of the play before midsummer, when it became clear that Essex was unlikely to return victoriously; Brown has, however, pointed out that the allusion could fit July or August, with the dramatist and his audience hoping against hope, and with Essex's predicament resembling Henry's before Agincourt. Nevertheless, this later dating of *Henry V* creates problems for the dating of *Caesar* (see below). If Shakespeare were writing *Henry V* during the summer break, he should have been cautious about inserting an allusion which could be obsolete by the play's first (autumn) performances. In any event, the play must have been finished before Essex's return on 27 September 1599; it was probably imitated in *1 Sir John Oldcastle* (*BEPD* 166), completed on 16 October 1599 (*Henslowe's Diary*).

Julius Caesar   1599

First published in 1623, but also attributed to Shakespeare by Jonson and Digges. It was not mentioned by Meres (September 1598), but a performance was witnessed by Thomas Platter on 21 September 1599. Schanzer objected that this might have been a play performed by the rival Admiral's Men at the Rose, but Henslowe's records for that year give no indication of any such play in their repertoire; one must therefore assume that the play Platter saw was Shakespeare's. The Platter allusion is also supported by two apparent allusions to the play in Jonson's *Every Man Out of his Humour*, 3.4.33 and 3.1.77 (1599: *BEPD* 163). The play may be indebted to Samuel Daniel's *Musophilus* (in *Poetical Essays*, STC 6261; entered 9 January 1599; first edition dated 1599) and to Sir John Davies's *Nosce Teipsum* (STC 6355; entered 14 April 1599, first two editions both dated 1599): see Taylor, 1984. The allusion to Rome at *Henry V* 5.0.26-8/2747-9 suggests that Shakespeare was influenced towards the end of that play by his primary sources in writing *Caesar*; although it is impossible to be sure whether that allusion anticipates or recollects *Caesar*, it agrees with other indications that the two plays belong together. In rare vocabulary *Caesar* has most links with *Hamlet* and *Troilus* (the next two tragedies); metrically, it is closest to *Henry V*, and must be later than *Henry IV*; the colloquialism-in-verse test places it between *Henry V* and *As You Like It*.

As You Like It   1599-1600

Mentioned in the Stationers' Register on 4 August 1600; a setting of 'It was a lover and his lass' (5.3.15-38/2465-88) was published in Thomas Morley's *First Book of Airs* (1600: STC 18115.5). Morley's book was apparently written in the summer of 1599 or the summer of 1600. The play must be later than the publication of its principal source, Thomas Lodge's *Rosalynde* (STC 16664), written in 1586-7 and published in 1590. In judging that the play belongs to 1599-1600 scholars can rely on no documentary evidence beyond the absence of mention by Meres (September 1598). Knowles (edn., 1977) surveys the alleged topical allusions which have been detected in the text, finding most of them dubious. However, we would repose less faith than he seems willing to do in the assumption that Marlowe's *Hero and Leander* (Stationers' Register, 28 September 1593) was not printed until 1598, the date of the first extant edition (STC 17413); even if that assumption is justified, it does not warrant the further assumption that Shakespeare's allusion to the poem (3.5.82-3/1803-4) post-dates its publication. Of alleged references to contemporary events we find most plausible (1) the interpretation of 'the little wit that fools have was silenced' (1.2.84-5/249-50) as an allusion to the burning of satirical books in June 1599, and (2) the conjecture that Jaques' 'All the world's a stage' (2.7.139/1062) alludes to the motto of the new Globe theatre, which was occupied by 21 September 1599 at the latest, and perhaps as early as 16 May 1599. It does not seem to us at all clear that Shakespeare wrote Touchstone's part for Robert Armin, who seems not to have joined the Chamberlain's Men until early in 1600.

Oras's pause test clearly places *As You Like It* in the period after *King John*, as does its high proportion of prose. The metrical test would place it after *Henry V* and *Caesar*; this is valuable in indicating that the play belongs at about the turn of the century, but since the same test would also put *Much Ado* in the same position we cannot press it too hard as a measure of relative composition. The colloquialism-in-verse test places it after *Much Ado*, *Henry V*, and *Caesar*, which is where most scholars have been inclined to put it. However, Slater's rare vocabulary test places the play rather earlier, linking it most strongly to *Love's Labour's Lost*, *Shrew* and *Much Ado*: this might be taken to support conjectures that it originally went by the title *Love's Labour's Won* (see above). But Slater's figures are probably skewed by genre, and the vocabulary links with *Henry V* are a better indication of date.

The Stationers' Register entry of 4 August 1600 associates *As You Like It* with other plays belonging to 'my lord chamberlens men', but it was first attributed to Shakespeare by inclusion in the 1623 Folio. Knowles surveys and rejects various theories of interpolation. Glynne Wickham suggests (privately) that 2.4.41-55/788-803 bear all the marks of a later addition, since Rosalind's speech at 2.4.41-2/788-9 exactly repeats the substance of that at 2.4.56-7/804-5, and the intervening material could easily be a later expansion by the clown. The suspected interpolation could, however, have been Shakespeare's own: Honigmann ('Revised Plays') cites comparable examples of authorial repetition produced by late additions to the dialogue. The song at 5.3.15-38/2465-88 might not have been written by Shakespeare, whether or not *As You Like It* post-dates Morley.

Hamlet, Prince of Denmark 1600-1

The evidence for dating the play of this name included in our edition is repeatedly complicated by the existence of an earlier play of the same name (see *Hamlet*, in 'Works Excluded', below). A *Hamlet*, 'latelie Acted by the Lord Chamberleyne his seruantes', was entered in the Stationers' Register on 26 July 1602, and printed in an edition dated 1603, which because of its title-page allusion to Shakespeare's company as 'his Highnesse seruants' must post-date 19 May. Both the 1603 edition and that of 1604/5 attribute the play to Shakespeare. If we accept that the 1603 edition represents a memorial reconstruction of the play later printed in editions of 1604/5 and 1623 (see Introduction, below), then that play must antedate July 1602. An edition of *Merry Wives*, apparently representing a memorial reconstruction, includes the line 'What is the reason that you use me thus?' (l. 1188 in Greg's edn.), which is not present in the authoritative 1623 text of that play, but does occur in texts of *Hamlet* (5.1.287/3257); this probably represents an actor's memory of *Hamlet*, which would thus have had to exist before entry of *Merry Wives* in the Stationers' Register (18 January 1602). Both these pieces of evidence for dating the play before 1602 depend upon the validity of the hypothesis of memorial reconstruction. Such dating in turn presumes that the play's indebtedness to John Florio's translation of Montaigne's *Essays* (1603: STC 1804) results from access to the translation in manuscript. Florio's translation was entered in the Stationers' Register on 20 October 1595 and again on 4 June 1600, and clearly existed in manuscript years before it was published.

On a blank half-page of his copy of Speght's 1598 edition of Chaucer (British Library Add. MS 42518, fol. 394ᵛ; renumbered 422ᵛ), Gabriel Harvey notes that 'The younger sort takes much delight in Shakespeares Venus, & Adonis; but his Lucrece, & his tragedie of Hamlet, Prince of Denmarke, haue it in them, to please the wiser sort'. The note is not dated, and conjectural dates have ranged from 1598 to 1606. It seems to us, as to most other scholars, that the note antedates the elevation of Lord Mountjoy to Earl of Devonshire on 21 July 1603, and probably antedates the execution of Essex on 25 February 1601 (see particularly Honigmann, 1956). However, even if these probabilities are accepted, their relevance to the dating of the play printed in 1604/5 depends upon the assumption that Shakespeare himself did not write the ur-*Hamlet*. If Shakespeare did write the earlier play, and if the interpretation of Q1 as a memorial reconstruction is rejected, then the Hamlet play reproduced in our and other editions of Shakespeare's works is not unquestionably referred to until 1604. Some copies of Q2 are dated '1604', and Anthony Scoloker's *Daiphantus* (1604: STC 21853) clearly alludes to that text.

The text printed in 1604/5 draws upon Thomas Nashe's *Pierce Pennilesse* (1592), and thus must post-date the Hamlet play to which Nashe alluded in 1589. Meres does not include *Hamlet* among Shakespeare's works (September 1598). Two superfluous allusions to the materials from which Shakespeare constructed *Julius Caesar* (Additional Passage A.6-13; 3.2.99-100/1826-7) strongly suggest that *Hamlet* post-dates composition of that play, of about mid-1599 (see above). A passage alluding to the 'little eyases' (2.2.339-62/1269-92) cannot have been written before Michaelmas 1600, when a troupe of boy actors established itself at the Blackfriars theatre; but that passage occurs only in the 1623 edition, and probably represents a later addition (although 'later' may mean days, rather than years). Another passage, alluding to the 'inhibition' upon the players' activities which results from 'the late innouation' (2.2.332-3/1262-3) has usually been interpreted as a reference either to (1) the abortive Essex uprising of 8 February 1601, or to (2) a Privy Council decree of 22 June 1600, restricting London playhouses to two and performances to twice weekly (reprinted in Chambers, *Stage*, iv. 331-2). Hibbard (edn., 1987) rightly objects that the passage requires no such topical interpretation, and that London companies were often affected by innovations or inhibitions; but the proximity of the two incidents to the period of *Hamlet*'s composition makes it difficult to rule out the possibility of some extra-dramatic referent. Wilson (edn., 1936) argued that the discussion of Fortinbras's campaign against Poland (Additional Passage J) alluded to the siege of Ostend, beginning in July 1601. This conjecture was rejected by Chambers (1944) and Honigmann (1956); but Goldring observes that the lines would much better fit the English victory at Nieuport, under Sir Francis Vere, on 22 June 1600. The battle was fought on a narrow strip of sand between two sets of dunes, and approximately 6,000 people were slain: see Harrison, pp. 95-7, and contemporary reports in STC 16671, 17679, and 11029. Noticeably, all these topical connections locate the play near the turn of the century.

Other attempts to pinpoint the date of composition within the range afforded by this external and internal evidence depend upon the play's relationship to two other plays: John Marston's *Antonio's Revenge* (BEPD 285; composed winter 1600-1; entered 24 October 1601) and Thomas Dekker's *Satiromastix* (BEPD 195; entered 11 November 1601). However, although in both cases the resemblances with *Hamlet* can hardly be coincidental, scholars continue to disagree over the direction of influence.

The metrical test puts *Hamlet* earlier than *Troilus* and all subsequent plays, but later than any play which we place before *Troilus*. In rare vocabulary its strongest links are with *Troilus*, *Othello*, and *Lear* (the three subsequent tragedies), and to a lesser degree with *Henry V* and *Macbeth*; these figures are obviously skewed by genre, and for that reason the link with *Henry V* is perhaps most significant. But in both the colloquialism-in-verse test and the pause tests it could be as late as *Measure* and *Othello*; and Brainerd's statistical test (1980) also predicts a later date (p. 229). Although all these criteria agree in placing *Hamlet* early in the seventeenth century, they do not agree with one another precisely enough to enable us, on their testimony, to place it in 1600 rather than 1601 (or 1603).

Twelfth Night, or What You Will 1601

First printed, and attributed to Shakespeare, in 1623. John Manningham's memorandum book (British Library MS Harley 5353, fol. 10) describes a performance at the Middle Temple on 2 February 1602. That the play is later than 1598 is suggested by: (*a*) the fact that Meres does not mention it in that year among Shakespeare's plays; (*b*) the two references to the Sophy (2.5.174/1158; 3.4.271/1748), which probably reflect topical interest in the visit of Sir Anthony Sherley to the Persian court, between summer 1598 and the end of 1601; (*c*) an apparent allusion (3.2.24-6/1370-2) to the Arctic voyage of William Barentz in 1596-7, first described in an English translation of Gerrit de Veer's account, entered in the Stationers' Register on 13 June 1598 (STC 24628; earliest surviving edition dated 1609); (*d*) Maria's allusion to 'the new map with the augmentation of the Indies' (3.2.74-5/1422-4), which is generally agreed to refer to a map first published in 1599 (in Hakluyt's *Voyages*, STC 12626; reproduced in *Shakespeare's England*, i. 174). On this evidence the play can be no earlier than 1599. The snatches of songs in 2.3/Sc. 8 are taken from songs which first occur, to our knowledge, in Robert Jones's *First Book of Songs or Airs* (1600: STC 14732). Feste's avoidance of the phrase 'out of my element' because the word element 'is ouerworn' (3.1.57-8/1242-3) has been plausibly interpreted as an indication that *Twelfth Night* post-dates Dekker's *Satiromastix* (BEPD 195; Stationers' Register, 11 November 1601), which had been performed at some time in 1601 by Shakespeare's company, and which three times pokes fun at the expression 'out of [one's] element' (1.2.134-6, 1.2.186-8, 5.2.324-7). Finally, the Chamberlain's Men performed an unidentified play at court on 6 January 1601 (Twelfth Night), on which occasion Queen Elizabeth's guest of honour was Don Virginio Orsino, Duke of Bracciano. Hotson (1954) contended that *Twelfth Night* was performed on that occasion; like most other scholars we regard this conjecture as unlikely, but Shakespeare was probably influenced by the occasion in choosing the name of his protagonist, which appears in none of the play's possible sources. Cumulatively such evidence suggests that the play was composed in 1601, and hence was at least relatively new when Manningham saw it.

In rare vocabulary *Twelfth Night* is closest to *Hamlet*, *Lear*, *Troilus*, and *Winter's Tale*; the metrical test places it just before *Hamlet* and *Troilus*, but the colloquialism-in-verse test puts it after *Troilus*. Although this stylistic evidence justifies linking it to the period of *Hamlet* and *Troilus*, it cannot determine relative priority of composition.

Troilus and Cressida 1602

Entered in the Stationers' Register on 7 February 1603, and first attributed to Shakespeare in the edition of 1609. The play is indebted to Chapman's *Seven Books of the Iliads of Homer* (STC 13632; entered 10 April 1598), and is not mentioned by Meres (September 1598). Henry Chettle and Thomas Dekker were writing a play on the same subject in April 1599, which was probably completed by May (*Henslowe's Diary*), but as this play only survives in a fragmentary plat (British Library Add. MS 10449, fol. 5) we cannot determine the direction of influence, if any. The 'prologue arm'd' (Pro.23-4/23-4) probably alludes to Jonson's *Poetaster* (1601: BEPD 186); the prologue only appears in the 1623 text, and may be a later addition, but we would not expect it to post-date the rest of the text by much. In the epilogue (Additional Passage B) Pandarus promises that 'Some two months hence my will shall here be made'; Palmer (edn., 1982) ingeniously interprets the 'two months' as an allusion to the interim between Twelfth Night (the last day of the Christmas holidays, on which he conjectures that the play was originally performed) and Ash Wednesday (the beginning of Lent). Of possible dates of composition, this interim fits only the year 1603, and hence would suggest composition in 1602. We record this conjecture without reposing much faith in it (see the textual note to the passage). Honigmann ('Date and Revision') conjectures that the play was written in the first half of 1601, and that it remained unacted because of fears that it might be interpreted as a political allegory about the Earl of Essex. One might accept this explanation for the play's suppression without crediting Honigmann's date: alleged allusions to Essex were being detected by ingenious censors as late as 1604-5. In rare vocabulary the play is linked most closely to *Hamlet*, and to a lesser degree *Henry V* and *Macbeth*. In Oras's pause tests it is later than *Henry IV* but earlier than *Othello*, but could be anywhere in between. If we ignore *Hamlet* (which is anomalous: see above), the colloquialism-in-verse test puts it later than *As You Like It* or any preceding play, and earlier than *Twelfth Night* or any subsequent play. The metrical test puts it after *Hamlet* and before *Measure* or *Othello*; but would also put it after, rather than before, *Twelfth Night*. The degree of consensus in these figures certainly suggests composition in 1600-2, but cannot determine whether the play precedes or follows *Hamlet* or *Twelfth Night*.

Sonnets 1593-1603

On 3 January 1600 the Stationers' Register records an entry for 'A booke called *Amours* by I.D., with certen oyr [i.e. other] sonnetes by W.S.'; this could refer to Shakespeare's sonnets, or to those of William Smith, who published a sequence in 1596. 'Shakespeares Sonnets' were entered in the Stationers' Register on 20 May 1609, and printed in an edition dated 1609. Meres refers to Shakespeare's 'sugred Sonnets among his priuate friends' (1598), and two sonnets were included in *The Passionate Pilgrim* (second edition dated '1599'; earliest edition fragmentary, and date uncertain). Some of the sonnets existed by this date, but there is no evidence that they yet constituted a sequence, and the scattered distribution of the sonnets in manuscript—along with the publication of only two in *The Passionate Pilgrim*—suggests that they circulated separately.

It has generally been agreed that Shakespeare's sonnets were probably begun in the period after the 1591 publication of Sidney's *Astrophil and Stella* (STC 22536), which initiated a vogue for sonnets, with contributions by Daniel (1591-2) and Spenser (1595), among others. In Slater's rare vocabulary test (1975) the Sonnets as a whole are linked most closely with *Henry V*, *Love's Labour's Lost*, *Dream*, and *Richard II*. The chronological clustering of the last three of these plays is difficult to ignore. Such internal evidence strongly confirms the supposition, encouraged by Meres, that most of the sonnets were written in the 1590s, probably the mid-1590s. But we find persuasive the arguments of Wilson (edn., 1966), reiterated and strengthened by Kerrigan (edn., 1986), that Sonnet 107 dates from spring 1603, alluding to the death of Elizabeth and the accession of James I. The sequence as we know it could not, in this interpretation, have been completed until 1603, and this conclusion agrees with the independent evidence for dating *A Lover's Complaint* (see below). Finally, the variation in the texts of four sonnets (reproduced among Additional Passages) suggests that Shakespeare at some point revised the poems, and the revisions in Sonnet 2 particularly suggest that the revision was relatively late and was related to the organization of the separate sonnets into a sequence (see Taylor, 'Some Manuscripts'). Our positioning of the Sonnets does not reflect the date of original composition of most of the poems, but the earliest date by which the poems could have achieved the state represented by the 1609 edition.

A Lover's Complaint   1603-4

Although not mentioned in the Stationers' Register entry or the title-page, this poem was included in the 1609 edition of *Shakespeares Sonnets*, beginning on the page after Sonnet 154 ('A Lovers complaint. | BY | WILLIAM SHAKE-SPEARE.'). Shakespeare's authorship was doubted by most earlier editors, but Muir (1964) and Jackson (1965), in independent and complementary studies, vindicated its authenticity, citing among much other evidence its use of compounds, neologisms, and imagery. Both Duncan-Jones and Kerrigan (edn., 1986), developing hints by earlier critics, have defended its position at the end of the Sonnets, by analogy with codas to other Elizabethan sonnet sequences.

On the basis of its imagery and of specific verbal parallels both Muir and Jackson dated the poem's composition early in the seventeenth century; Slater's rare-word test (1975; including words of up to fifteen occurrences) confirms this conclusion, linking it most clearly with *All's Well*, *Lear*, and *Hamlet*. If anything such evidence would date the poem, and hence finalization of the sonnet sequence, somewhat later than we place it. Assignment of a position for a sequence developed over a decade or more is inevitably arbitrary, and in assigning it to 1603 we have been influenced by the parallel case of the narrative poems, which originated in the interregnum of playing caused by plague. The similar, though less prolonged, interregnum in 1603-4 would have afforded an opportunity and incentive to tidy up the collection of poems which Shakespeare probably began writing during the plague of 1592-4. (Southampton's release from prison in 1603 could also be relevant.)

Various Poems   1593-1616

The date and authenticity of the miscellaneous poems collected under this heading are individually discussed in the Introduction to each. The poems apparently range in date from the mid-1590s to 1616. While more logical, it would have been less convenient to scatter them throughout the volume on the basis of their apparent individual dates of composition, and we have instead placed them all near the middle of their range, in proximity to the other lyric poetry (and to the disputed pages from *Sir Thomas More*).

Shakespeare's lost *impresa* for the Earl of Rutland would have been included among 'Various Poems' if it had survived. The evidence for its existence and for Shakespeare's composition occurs in the 'Account' of Thomas Screvin, steward to Francis Manners, sixth Earl of Rutland (H.M.C. Rutland MSS iv. 494): 'Itm 31. M^{r}tij [1613]. to m^r Shakspeare in gold. about my Lorde Impreso—xliiij^s / To Rich Burbadge for payntjng & making yt / in gold xliiij^s.' (The manuscript is reproduced in part by Schoenbaum, *Documentary Life*, p. 220, and discussed by Chambers, *Shakespeare*, ii. 153.) This *impresa* was for the tilt upon the King's accession day, 24 March 1613. Burbage received payment for a similar function on 25 March 1616.

Sir Thomas More   1603-4
(Addition II.D; Addition III)

British Library MS Harleian 7368 is an undated dramatic manuscript in several hands. For purposes of analysis it is conventionally divided into two parts. The original play is throughout in the hand of Anthony Munday; on this original are comments by Sir Edmund Tilney, Master of the Revels from 1579 to 1610. This original was probably written between autumn 1592 and mid-1595, probably by Munday and Henry Chettle (see the entry for *Sir Thomas More*, among 'Works Excluded'). To this original script have been added a series of 'additions', in several hands. 'Hand A' is that of Chettle; 'Hand E' is Thomas Dekker; 'Hand B' is probably Thomas Heywood; 'Hand C' is a professional theatrical scribe, who transcribed some material and annotated other passages, in both the original and the additions. 'Hand D' is the passage which has aroused most interest, and which is believed to be Shakespeare's autograph.

Simpson first proposed Shakespeare's authorship of three of the additions—including II.D and III—in 1871. The history of scholarly debate since then is conveniently charted by Metz ('Voyce and Credyt'). Most of the great palaeographers of the twentieth century have concurred that Hand D bears a remarkable resemblance to the handwriting of Shakespeare's attested signatures and to the handwriting implied by errors in printed editions of his work. This conclusion has been endorsed by E. Maunde Thompson (1923) and W. W. Greg (1923), C. J. Sisson (edn., 1954), Harold Jenkins (MSR, 1961), Peter W. M. Blayney (1972), G. B. Evans (edn., 1974), the late P. J. Croft (privately), R. E. Alton (privately), Charles Hamilton (1985), and Giles Dawson (forthcoming). Since palaeographical judgements are based upon experience as much as science, such testimony is not easily dismissed. On the basis of its handwriting Addition II.D cannot be attributed to any other dramatist of the period whose handwriting has survived. The only dramatist who seems capable of composing the passage whose autograph is not certainly extant is John

Webster, and Chillington offered him as an alternative candidate on that basis; but Taylor ('Date and Auspices') and Forker demonstrate, on the basis of verbal parallels, orthography, and misreadings, that Webster is far less likely to have written it than Shakespeare. If the Melbourne manuscript (see General Introduction, Illustration 2) is indeed in Webster's hand, then Webster is certainly not Hand D (see General Introduction, Illustration 3). The palaeographical evidence for Shakespeare's authorship of Addition II.D has been buttressed by investigations of its orthography (by Wilson) and of its patterns of thought and imagery (by R. W. Chambers in particular). Cumulatively such internal evidence has persuaded us, as it has most scholars, that Hand D is Shakespeare. The status of Addition III is less certain, because it exists only in a transcription by Hand C, leaving us wholly dependent upon verbal parallels in a much briefer passage. No one who doubts Shakespeare's authorship of II.D will be persuaded by the meagre evidence for attributing Addition III to him. However, if one accepts his presence among the adapters, he seems more likely than the other available candidates to have written the speech.

The additions must be later than the original; how much later is uncertain. All scholars are agreed that the additions make no serious attempt to respond to Tilney's objections; nevertheless, the use of the word 'Lombards' on two occasions (Addition II.B.82, 104) suggests that at least that addition was written after Tilney saw the play, for Tilney had insisted on precisely that change in the identification of the aliens (ll. 364, 368). Moreover, the complete absence of Munday's hand in the additions, and the fact that they are written on different paper from the original, make it clear that the problem of dating the additions must be considered separately from the problem of dating the original. McMillin believes that D's addition belongs to the same period as the original composition, but Melchiori's study of the paper encourages the traditional assumption that all the additions belong to a single period.

The additions collectively contain twenty-seven profanities of a kind forbidden by the Act to Restrain Abuses of Players (3 Jac. I, c. 21: May 1606), and since these occur in all of the additions it seems clear that composition of the added material antedates the legislation. The allusion to the scouring of Moorditch (Addition IV.215-16) would best fit 1595 or 1603. Several passages in Addition I (lines 12-16, 23-7, 58-61) allude to the court, the King, and 'Lord Spend-alls Stuart's' in a way which would be appropriate after the accession of James I. Several parallels between Addition II.D and Chettle's *The Tragedy of Hoffman* (1631: *BEPD* 438; composed between 29 December 1602 and c.1604) suggest that Chettle was influenced by that addition when writing the play. Lake (1977) demonstrates, on the basis of stylistic evidence, that Dekker's contribution must post-date 1599. The political circumstances which forbade production of the play after mid-1595 ceased to exist when Elizabeth I died, in March 1603; moreover, on 21 June 1603 Sir George Buc was granted the reversion of the Revels office. The prospects for resubmission of the play must have looked better in mid-1603 than at any time for eight years or more, and the first years of the seventeenth century had already seen a series of successful plays on early Tudor themes: *Thomas Lord Cromwell* (*BEPD* 189), *Cardinal Wolsey*, Parts I and II (*Henslowe's Diary*), *Lady Jane*, Parts I and II (*Henslowe's Diary*). Chettle was involved in all four Henslowe plays. We therefore regard 1603-4 as the likeliest date for the projected revival, and for composition of all the additions. The evidence for this conclusion is presented in full in Taylor's 'Date and Auspices'. Taylor there contests the orthodox assumption that the additions were written soon after the original. McMillin independently shows that the theatrical demands of the additions suggest a revival c.1603-4 (though he and Taylor disagree on the company which prepared it).

If Addition II.D was written by Shakespeare, then the internal evidence points strongly to a date in the early seventeenth century. Jackson shows that the linguistic evidence, the vocabulary, and the distribution of pauses in verse lines all place it in the period from *Twelfth Night* to *Macbeth*. Although the passage contains a predictable number of parallels from crowd scenes scattered throughout Shakespeare's career (*Contention*, *Caesar*, and *Coriolanus*), outside such parallels dictated by the subject-matter its most striking verbal resemblances are with *Hamlet*, *Troilus*, *Othello*, and *The History of King Lear*. The colloquialism-in-verse test places it unmistakably in the seventeenth century, just after *Troilus* and *Twelfth Night*. This internal evidence for dating Addition II.D corresponds remarkably well with the evidence for dating the additions generally c.1603, and we believe that in doing so it strengthens Shakespeare's claim to authorship of the passage. In fact, if the passage could on other grounds be confidently dated in 1595 or earlier, the attribution to Shakespeare would need to be seriously re-examined.

The only obstacle to a Jacobean date for the additions has been the presence of Hand C, who has hitherto been identified in only two theatrical documents: the plat of *2 Seven Deadly Sins* (Dulwich College MS xix: Strange's Men, c.1589-91?) and that of *2 Fortune's Tennis* (British Library Add. MS 10449, fol. 4: Admiral's Men, c.1597 or c.1602). Both manuscripts are reproduced in Greg, *Dramatic Documents*. Although Shakespeare can plausibly be associated with Strange's Men in the early 1590s, there is no evidence of his association with the Admiral's Men, or Henslowe, or any company beside the Chamberlain's/King's Men after 1594. However, Hand C does not appear in any of the voluminous Henslowe documents of 1597-1602; nor does Thomas Goodal, the actor whose name is written in the margin opposite the beginning of Addition V. Their presence in the additions therefore does not impede attribution of the play to the King's Men. Even if the play at some stage belonged to Henslowe, it could at another stage have belonged to the King's Men, and our ignorance of the detail of the operations of the King's Men should not encourage dogmatism about the relationship between provenance and authorship in such a case. After all, our only knowledge of anyone who acted as book-keeper for Shakespeare's company before 1609 (Thomas Vincent) is an anecdote in which he fraternizes with the actor John Singer, the principal comedian of the rival company (see General Introduction, note 61).

Measure for Measure 1603

According to a Revels Account document now in the Public Record Office (Audit Office, Accounts, Various, A.O. 3/908/

13), the play was performed at court on 26 December 1604; however, Hamilton (1985) has recently revived early suspicions of the document's authenticity. 1.1.67-72/67-72 apparently allude to King James I's distaste for crowds, which was evident as early as June 1603; but the passage could be a late addition to the play. Plague closed the theatres from 19 May 1603 to 9 April 1604, so that even if the play were finished in early summer 1603 its London premiere could not have occurred until April 1604. Lever (1959) discerned a plausible parallel between 2.4.20-30/939-49 and *The Time Triumphant* (STC 7292), entered in the Stationers' Register on 27 March 1604. Lever assumed that the pamphlet influenced Shakespeare; but Walker reasonably objected that the pamphlet, written in whole or part by Robert Armin, might as easily have been influenced by *Measure*. Lever (edn., 1965) also interpreted Pompey's reference to the proclamation (1.2.84-8/165-9) as an allusion to a proclamation of 16 September 1603; this seems to us most unlikely. But the later statement that 'the olde Women were all dead' (4.3.8/1938) is naturally interpreted as a reflection of the great mortality caused by plague, which became serious in mid-May 1603; likewise, the severe punishment of Lucio for 'Slandering a Prince' might reflect King James I's strong views on defamation. *Measure* also seems to belong to a group of 'disguised ruler' plays associated with the start of the new reign (Marston's *The Malcontent* and *The Fawn*, Middleton's *The Phoenix*: BEPD 203, 230, 243). If we accept such cumulative indications of Jacobean composition, the play could belong to any time from summer 1603 to November 1604.

Stylistic evidence supports this dating. Both the colloquialism-in-verse and the metrical tests place *Measure* after *Troilus* and *Twelfth Night* but before *All's Well*. In rare vocabulary it is linked most strongly to *Winter's Tale*, *All's Well*, and to a lesser degree *Hamlet* and *Troilus*; the link with *Winter's Tale* is difficult to explain, but the others all fit the apparent chronology.

Jowett and Taylor, developing hints from previous scholars, argue at length that the 1623 text represents a posthumous adaptation of the play. The song 'Take oh take those lips away' (4.1.1-6/1647-52) also occurs, with another stanza, in *Rollo, Duke of Normandy*, also known as *The Bloody Brother* (1639: BEPD 565), by John Fletcher and others. *Rollo* is most plausibly dated in mid-1617, and the song seems to us to have originated in Fletcher's play, not Shakespeare's. It occurs in a context which has long been suspected of textual dislocation, which can be explained as the consequence of interpolating the act-break, the song, and the dialogue immediately following it. Also suspect is the episode with Lucio and the two anonymous gentlemen at the beginning of 1.2/Sc. 2. This passage is again associated with textual dislocation, and as a superfluous expansion of the clown's role is characteristic of late interpolations. On stylistic grounds, too, it seems less characteristic of Shakespeare than of a writer like Thomas Middleton. Overdone's complaint at 1.2.80-2/161-3 better fits the circumstances of 1619-21 than of 1603-4; the reference to the King of Hungary at 1.2.2-5/85-8 would have been particularly topical in 1621-2, and 'the sanctimonious Pirat' of 1.2.7/90 would also have been especially pertinent in 1621. Although none of these apparent topical allusions can be regarded as certain, they do suggest that the passage could date from 1621 or early 1622.

Othello 1603-4

Attributed to Shakespeare in the edition of 1622. According to a Revels Account document now in the Public Record Office (Audit Office, Accounts, Various, A.O. 3/908/13), the play was performed at court on 1 November 1604; however, Hamilton (1985) has recently revived early suspicions of the document's authenticity. *Othello* is also probably echoed in Dekker and Middleton's *The Honest Whore, Part 1* (BEPD 204); Henslowe had made an earnest payment for the play by 14 March 1604 at the latest, and it was entered in the Stationers' Register on 9 November. Hart (1934) contended that the 1603 edition of *Hamlet* included a handful of words and phrases which resulted from an actor's memories of *Othello*; but none of these parallels is as striking as that which assists in the dating of *Hamlet* itself (see above), and none seems to us convincing. Wells (1984) pointed out that the play's apparent indebtedness to Richard Knolles's *History of the Turks* (1603: STC 15051) for details of the movement of Turkish galleys in 1.3 points to a date of composition in late 1603 or 1604: Knolles's book contains an epistle dated 'the last of September, 1603'. If accepted this evidence fixes the play's composition in the year before its recorded court performance. Jackson (1985), attempting to reconcile Hart's evidence with Wells's, notes that the 1603 edition of *Hamlet* cannot have been printed before 19 May, and may date from late in the year; but since the London theatres were closed for most of 1603, he thinks the *Hamlet* reporter 'could hardly have achieved his familiarity with *Othello* had *Othello* not reached the stage by early 1603 at the latest'. But since reporters were usually hired men, a reporter could have become acquainted with *Othello* during provincial performances later in 1603. The King's Men were in Oxford in 1603-4, and if the 1603 edition of *Hamlet* were compiled and published late in that year both its title-page allusion to Oxford performances and its alleged echoes of *Othello* might be a consequence of the same plague-induced touring. If so, then *Othello* would probably pre-date *Measure* (as it might in any case). However, on balance it seems to us more probable that the few similarities of phrasing between *Othello* and *Hamlet* Q1 are coincidental.

In rare vocabulary *Othello* is most strongly linked to *Hamlet*, *Troilus*, and *Henry V*. The metrical test places it with *Measure* but before *All's Well*; the colloquialism-in-verse test places it after *Measure* but before *All's Well*.

All's Well That Ends Well 1604-5

First mentioned in 1623, in the Stationers' Register entry for F. It has often been suggested that the play was originally called *Love's Labour's Won* (see above), and that the text we possess constitutes a later, re-titled revision. There is no evidence for this conjecture, and if the text was revised internal evidence demonstrates that the revision was so thorough that it constitutes in effect a new play. Most critics have agreed that Lavatch belongs to the series of clown roles which Shakespeare created for Robert Armin, who joined the company c.1600, after the departure of William Kempe. In rare vocabulary *All's Well* is linked most closely (in descending order) to *Measure*, *Troilus*, *Othello*, and *Coriolanus* (see Slater, 1977).

The colloquialism-in-verse test puts it after *Measure* and *Othello*, and Oras's pause tests locate it between *Macbeth* and *Antony*. Its metrical figure places it after *Othello* and before *Lear*; a more detailed analysis of the metrical characteristics of the text by Lowes puts the play in the period 1606-8. Brainerd's statistical test (1980) would also place the play in that period (p. 229). Fitch's more reliable redaction of the 'sense-pause' test puts *All's Well* somewhere between *Measure* and *Lear* (p. 300).

This internal evidence not only rules out identification of *All's Well* with the lost play mentioned by Meres in 1598; it also points to a date of composition somewhat later than is usually supposed. Malone assigned the play to 1606, but modern editors have generally assumed that it pre-dates *Measure*. The two plays are related in many ways, but priority is not easily established. Shakespeare may have imported the bed-trick into *Measure* because of its use in the source for *All's Well*; but even if that were—as it is not—demonstrably so, Shakespeare might have read Boccaccio's story years before he decided to dramatize it. The tendency to date *All's Well* earlier than *Measure* is founded upon little more than a critical prejudice that *Measure* is 'the less uncertain achievement'. We do not share that belief, and even if we did would regard it as an inadequate argument for dating. Critically, one can plausibly relate *All's Well* to the romances as well as to the 'problem plays'. Every stylistic test places *All's Well* after *Measure*; Walker, independently of such evidence, observed that the names of major characters in *Measure* recur as incidental figures in *All's Well*, again suggesting that *Measure* is the earlier play. At 2.1.93/652, Helen is apparently disguised or muffled, and Lafeu says 'I am Cresseds Vncle, | That dare leaue two together'; in *Troilus*, when Pandarus does bring two together (3.2.205/1781), Cressida is veiled. The allusion in *All's Well* is more naturally explained if the play post-dates *Troilus* (as most scholars have assumed). We therefore feel confident in placing *All's Well* after *Troilus* and *Measure*, but less confident about its exact place in the period 1604-7. If *Othello* pre-dated *Measure*, then *Measure* and *All's Well* might be juxtaposed; but Shakespeare might have been influenced by his previous comedy even if it were not his immediately previous play.

There are few topical allusions to assist in dating composition. Wilson (edn., 1929) related 1.3.92-3/396-7 to the controversial enforcement of the surplice in 1604; less plausibly, he saw allusions to the Gunpowder Plot (late 1605) at 1.1.118-20/119-21 and 4.3.20/1958.

Timon of Athens 1605

First mentioned in the Stationers' Register entry for the 1623 collection. No convincing topical allusions have been discerned in the text: 3.3.31-3/984-6 do not seem to us at all likely to refer to the Gunpowder Plot (late 1605). *Timon of Athens* may or may not draw upon the anonymous play *Timon*, written c.1602 (Victoria and Albert, Dyce MS 52; best studied in the MSR, ed. J. C. Bulman and J. M. Nosworthy, 1980 for 1978); it does draw upon Plutarch's 'Life of Antony', in North's translation. This was also a primary source of *Antony and Cleopatra*, but Shakespeare refers to material on Antony in *Macbeth*, too, and had already made extensive use of North's translation for *Caesar*. Moreover, Shakespeare's interest in Timon could have been stimulated by the twenty-eighth novella in William Painter's *Palace of Pleasure* (1566: STC 19121); Painter's thirty-eighth novella provided the primary source for *All's Well*. These sources are of little value in fixing the play's date, though they do intimate—as does, very strongly, its style—that the play belongs to the seventeenth century, and probably to the reign of James I. Beyond that, the play's date must be decided entirely on the basis of stylistic evidence, and such evidence cannot be properly evaluated until the problem of authorship has been resolved.

Knight (edn., 1838) suggested that Shakespeare might not be the sole author, and this conjecture stimulated many competing attempts to assign the collaborator(s) a name. Partly in reaction against such theories, Chambers and Ellis-Fermor argued that the play was unfinished. This conjecture grew out of Chambers's belief that Shakespeare's failure to finish the play resulted from a mental breakdown, and his related belief that *Timon* was the last of the tragedies, abandoned before a revived and spiritually whole Shakespeare began composing the romances. These biographical speculations represent a wholly uncharacteristic lapse from Chambers's usual standards of good sense, and they illustrate the lengths to which conjecture is driven in the effort to resist the evidence of collaboration. Both the metrical test and Slater's rare-word test (1978)—linking the play most strongly with *Lear*, *Hamlet*, *Troilus*, and to a lesser degree *All's Well* and *Coriolanus*—discourage the very late date which Chambers favoured. Even in the saner formulation of Ellis-Fermor, the 'unfinished play' hypothesis presupposes working methods which seem uncharacteristic of Shakespeare and of other writers; nor does it explain the play's most striking stylistic inconsistencies. Oliver (edn., 1959), attempting to attribute some of these features to scribal interference, proposed that parts of the play were transcribed by Ralph Crane; this hypothesis, implausible in itself, does not survive even the most cursory examination of Crane's habits. These theories all place great weight upon the absence of direct evidence for contemporary performances of the play, and this lacuna is now often cited as evidence that the play was never performed. But we also possess no contemporary evidence that *As You Like It*, *More*, *Troilus*, *All's Well*, or *Antony* were performed; our only evidence for performances of *Two Gentlemen* and *King John* is Meres's familiarity with them; apparent verbal echoes by two of Shakespeare's personal friends constitute our only evidence that *Coriolanus* was performed (see below). Such theories also emphasize loose ends and inconsistencies in the text, but in our judgement these are no more considerable than those found in other foul paper texts—especially in the foul papers of two collaborators, who have not yet prepared a fair copy which irons out incompatibilities in their artistic conceptions.

Hinman's study of the printing of the Folio demonstrated two things pertinent to the authorship problem: (a) *Timon* appears where it does in the Folio only because plans for *Troilus* had to be altered, and thus might not have been included at all if the troubles with *Troilus* had not occurred; (b) the text was set by one compositor, thus making it impossible to attribute textual inconsistencies to printing-house influence. Although subsequent scholarship has attributed one page of *Timon* to a second compositor, this minor revision does nothing to weaken the force of Hinman's conclusion. It has been widely recognized that the Folio text is anomalous in its lineation, an anomaly hitherto unexplained by proponents of single authorship; it is also anomalous in its treatment of pronouns (Brainerd, 1979, p. 14, Fig. 2). Developing a conjecture by Wells (1920) and Sykes (1924), Lake (1975), Jackson (1979), and Holdsworth have provided extensive, independent, and compelling evidence that approximately a third of the play was written by Thomas Middleton. This conclusion is based in each case upon studies of the entire Middleton canon, set in the context of surveys of relevant evidence in the entire corpus of Jacobean drama. Specifically, Middleton's presence in *Timon* is indicated by the distribution of (*a*) linguistic forms, (*b*) characteristic oaths and exclamations, (*c*) function words, (*d*) rare vocabulary, (*e*) characteristic stage directions, (*f*) verbal parallels, (*g*) spellings, (*h*) inconsistencies of plotting, (*i*) rhyme. Holdsworth's investigation of verbal parallels for the first time comprehensively compares every phrase in an entire play with the complete corpus of both candidates for authorship; although, as might be expected, each author occasionally uses phrases which occur in the other's works, the great bulk of the verbal parallels, and all of the most striking ones, fall into distinct patterns, corresponding to the division of authorship already established on other grounds. The consistency of all these independent forms of evidence cannot be plausibly dismissed.

If we accept these divisions, the colloquialism-in-verse test puts Shakespeare's share of the play just after *All's Well* and before *Macbeth*. Middleton's portion, by contrast, has a figure higher than any accepted work of Shakespeare. Jackson (1979) also re-examined the distribution of rare vocabulary on the basis of this division: Shakespeare's share falls in the period 1604–5, while the rest of the play—if by Shakespeare—would have to be dated 1594–5, which seems clearly impossible. If Middleton's conjectured share is related to Middleton's works, it fits most comfortably, according to Holdsworth, in the period 1604–6. Such conclusions not only reinforce the evidence for collaboration; they agree in juxtaposing Shakespeare's share of *Timon* with composition of *Lear*. Most critics have felt that these two plays are as strongly related as *Dream* and *Romeo*, or *Measure* and *All's Well*. Which came first is, in this instance, even more difficult to determine, given the complications introduced by collaboration.

The History of King Lear 1605–6

Attributed to Shakespeare in the Stationers' Register (26 November 1607) and first edition (1608). Performed at court on 26 December 1606, and clearly influenced by Samuel Harsnett's *Declaration of Egregious Popish Impostures* (1603: STC 12880). The Jacobean date demonstrated by the influence of Harsnett is confirmed by a cluster of apparent topical allusions to James I and his court in Sc. 4. To the examples discussed in *Division*, 102–5, should be added the line 'If thou be as poore for a subiect, as he is for a King, thar't poore enough' (4.20-1/515-16), which would have been uncomfortably pertinent to the financial difficulties which James soon encountered; the use of the third person pronoun makes such an allusion even more likely. In total these allusions could hardly be earlier than mid-1604. Shakespeare makes extensive use of the anonymous play *King Leir* (1605: BEPD 213), entered in the Stationers' Register on 8 May 1605. *Leir* itself probably dates from *c*.1590; Greg (1939) conjectured that Shakespeare knew it in manuscript, and that its publication was an attempt to capitalize on the success of *Lear*. But *Lear* was also apparently influenced by *Eastward Ho* (BEPD 217: first three editions all dated 1605), written by George Chapman, Ben Jonson, and John Marston in early 1605, and entered in the Stationers' Register on 4 September 1605 (see Taylor, 'New Source'). Moreover, the reference to 'These late eclipses in the Sunne and Moone' (Sc. 2.103/400) almost certainly alludes to the eclipses of 17 September and 2 October 1605. The play may also be indebted to George Wilkins's *Miseries of Enforced Marriage* (BEPD 349), which cannot have been written earlier than mid-1605. The fourth scene might be echoed in Edward Sharpham's *The Fleer* (BEPD 255, entered on 11 May 1606), but the parallels cannot be confidently evaluated.

The stylistic evidence is affected to some degree by the problem of revision; previous investigations have conflated the two versions of the play. Taylor's re-examination of the rare vocabulary evidence in the two separate texts put *The History of King Lear* between *Othello* and *Macbeth*, either just before or just after *Timon* (*Division*, pp. 388–90, 452–68). Both the metrical test and the pause test, although based on conflated texts, give *Lear* the same position; the revision is unlikely to have affected these figures much, although they must be used with some caution. See also *The Tragedy of King Lear*, below.

Macbeth 1606

First printed in 1623. Simon Forman saw a performance at the Globe on 20 April 1611 (Bodleian MS Ashmole 208, X, fols. 207-207^v). His note on the play is reproduced in the Introduction, below. The choice of a Scottish and demonic subject, and the prophetic reference to King James (4.1.127.1-140/1418.1-31), make it clear that the play was written after James I's accession. James was touching for 'the king's evil' (4.3.144/1691) as early as November 1604. The reference to equivocation coupled with treason at 2.3.8-11/622-5 very probably alludes to the trial of the Gunpowder Plot conspirators (January–March 1606). The reference to 'the Tiger' (1.3.6-24/84-102) may allude to the terrible voyage experienced by a ship of that name which arrived back at Milford Haven on 27 June 1606 and at Portsmouth Road on 9 July, after an absence which lasted almost exactly 'Wearie Seu'nights, nine times nine' (see Loomis). Paul makes a circumstantial case for the play's performance before James I on 7 August 1606, during the visit of King Christian of Denmark; although this is likely, it should by no means be taken as proven, or as reliable evidence for dating the play, since the plausibility of the conjecture largely depends upon a prior assumption about dating. Allusions to Banquo's ghost have been plausibly detected in *The Puritan* (1607: BEPD 251) 4.3.89, and in Beaumont and Fletcher's *Knight of the Burning Pestle* (BEPD 316; composed 1607?) 5.1.26-12.

The metrical test and the colloquialism-in-verse test both place *Macbeth* after *Lear* and *Timon* but before *Antony*. Oras's pause tests also place it after *Lear* but before *Antony*. The rare-word test links it most closely to the earlier tragedies *Hamlet* and *Troilus*, and to *Lear*. The allusion to Antony at 3.1.58/859 suggests that *Macbeth* and *Antony* belong to the same period, but cannot determine which came first (see *Antony*, below).

It has been known since the late eighteenth century that the two songs called for in *Macbeth* appear in Middleton's play *The Witch* (Bodleian MS Malone 12; best studied in the MSR, ed. W. W. Greg and F. P. Wilson, 1948). W. G. Clark and W. A. Wright (edn., 1869) proposed that the songs were a late interpolation into Shakespeare's play. This conjecture has been widely accepted. Nosworthy attempts to argue that the late adaptation was Shakespeare's own, *c*.1611, but his efforts are not convincing. The songs draw upon Scot's *Discovery of Witchcraft* (1584: STC 21864), an important source for Middleton's play, but not otherwise used in *Macbeth*, or in Shakespeare's other Jacobean plays. Holdsworth provides further evidence for Middleton's authorship of the Hecate passages (3.5, 4.1.38.1-60/1329.1-1351, 4.1.141-148.1/1432-39.1) in which the songs appear. Since Middleton was apparently collaborating with Shakespeare at about the time *Macbeth* was written (see *Timon*, above), his presence in the play might theoretically result from collaboration rather than late adaptation; but the character of his contribution does not seem to us to encourage that possibility. The Hecate passages—spectacular, dispensable, written in a different style and introducing a new character—are typical of 'new additions': see Kerrigan in *Division*, pp. 195-205. And Forman does not mention the Hecate passages, though they might be expected to interest him.

It is difficult to determine in what other ways adaptation may have affected the text. (1) Clark and Wright suspected Middleton's hand in much of the play, but the likeliest candidate for extended writing by him is 1.2. Wilson (edn., 1947) argued for his presence there, and Holdsworth provides further evidence of a connection between that scene and the Middleton canon. Muir (edn., 1951) does not even discuss the possibility of Middleton's presence in this scene, simply asserting that Shakespeare was deliberately writing in an uncharacteristic 'epic' style. (2) Dislocation of 3.5, which comes between the two Hecate scenes, has been suspected; but any rearrangement seems to have affected the text to such a degree that it is impossible to sort out what the original was like. Muir's edition contains the fullest discussion. (3) The weird sisters might originally have been 'feiries or Nimphes', as Forman describes them, and as Holinshed suggests; if they initially appeared as beautiful figures, rather than 'filthy hags' (4.1.131/1422), this would better fit the play's insistence that 'Fair is foul, and foul is fair'. In the original conception the witches might have been initially as morally ambiguous as Hamlet's ghost. The Folio text's insistence upon the weird sisters' hideousness better fits the antimasque convention initiated by Jonson's *Masque of Queens* (2 February 1609: BEPD 280). One's impression of their initial appearance is entirely created by Banquo's speech at 1.3.37-45/115-23, which might be an addition, or a substitution for a Shakespearian original. (4) Amneus suggests, on the evidence of Forman and of contradictions in the text, that a scene has been lost between 3.3 and 3.4; in this lost scene the murderers reported to Macbeth on the assassination of Banquo. This change apparently affected the text of both 3.2 and 3.4. (5) Independently of Forman, Coghill conjectured that an appearance by King Edward the Confessor formed part of the original text of 4.3. There may also have been other cutting, although the mere brevity of the text is inadequate evidence for such an assumption. The whole issue of adaptation requires further investigation, based in part upon a more thorough examination of the links between *Macbeth* and the Middleton canon.

Antony and Cleopatra 1606

First printed, and attributed to Shakespeare, in 1623. Entered in the Stationers' Register on 20 May 1608. Samuel Daniel's revision of *Cleopatra*, published with a title-page dated 1607 (STC 6240), is probably indebted in a number of details to Shakespeare's play; Barroll argues plausibly that Daniel must have seen Shakespeare's play before December 1607 in order to be influenced by it. (John Pitcher, at work upon an edition of Daniel's works, informs us privately that he disputes Barroll's analysis of the details of the printing and publication of Daniel's collection, but that his differences do not seriously affect the argument.) As the theatres were closed because of plague for most of 1607, that inference pushes performances of *Antony* back to March 1607. Shakespeare's play also seems related to Barnaby Barnes's *The Devil's Charter* (1607: Stationers' Register, 16 October 1607: BEPD 254), performed by the King's Men at court on 2 February 1607. However, the printed text of Barnes's play advertises itself as 'renewed, corrected, and augmented by the author' since its court performance, so that even if we could be sure of Shakespeare's influence it might have been exerted later than the original composition of Barnes's play. Nevertheless, it seems to us (as to Barroll) unlikely that Shakespeare's influence on Barnes occurred during post-performance literary revision; Pitcher feels that Daniel's familiarity with the play is less likely to originate in public performances than in private ones, at court or at the Inns of Court, presumably in the Christmas season of 1606-7. Barroll rightly observes that acceptance of Shakespeare's influence on Barnes may push *Antony* back to a period very close to the court performance of *Lear* on 26 December 1606; in terms of external evidence we cannot be sure which was the earlier play. But Barroll's key piece of evidence for Barnes's indebtedness to Shakespeare is the episode in which Cleopatra treats the adder as though it were a baby at her breast. A similar episode occurs in George Peele's *Edward I* (BEPD 112; 1593, reprinted 1599), Sc. 15 (sig. I2^r), in which a woman is murdered by an 'Adder' which is described as her 'Babe' at 'her brest', and she as its 'Nurse'. Barnes's treatment resembles Peele's more closely than it does Shakespeare's.

All stylistic tests—rare vocabulary, metre, pauses, colloquialism-in-verse—concur in placing *Lear* before *Antony*; even if they were performed at court in the same season, Shakespeare seems to have written *Lear* first. (It must also have been performed first at court, for 26 December was the first performance of the 1606-7 winter season.) It is harder to be confident about the relative priority of *Macbeth*. We possess no external evidence for dating it so early as *Lear* and *Antony*. But the stylistic tests are also resolutely consistent in giving *Macbeth* priority over *Antony*. If we accept this unanimity of stylistic evidence, we must assign the completion of all three tragedies to the fifteen months following September 1605. On the other hand, it is possible that the stylistic figures for *Macbeth* are being slightly warped by the hand of an adapter; if so, *Macbeth* could be placed somewhat later.

Pericles 1607

The title-page of the first edition (1608) claims that the play was written 'By William Shakespeare'; nevertheless the play was excluded from the 1623 collected edition. This combination of conflicting external evidences puts *Pericles* in a class of plays which includes *The London Prodigal* (1605) and *A Yorkshire Tragedy* (1608). The company which *Pericles* keeps does not encourage confidence in Shakespeare's sole authorship, and the first edition appears to be irregular, legally and textually (see Introduction, below). Moreover, because *Pericles* remained popular into the 1620s, the King's Men must have possessed a text which they could have supplied to, or copied for, the printer and publishers of the 1623 Folio.

Most scholars since Malone (1780) have nevertheless accepted that Shakespeare contributed to the play. By *c.*1606-8, Shakespeare's poetic style had become so remarkably idiosyncratic that it stands out—even in a corrupt text—from that of his contemporaries, and approximately the last three-fifths of the play (Sc. 10-22) betray clear evidence of his presence. Equally clearly, Sc. 1-9 show little or no evidence of Shakespearian authorship. Edwards's attempt to attribute the differences in style and quality to the methods of two different reporters has been generally discredited (see Introduction, below). Moreover, in the rhyme test Sc. 1-9 differ remarkably from Sc. 10-22; they have more rhyme than any play except *Dream* and *Love's Labour's Lost* (see Table 8). This disparity can hardly be attributed to differences in reporting.

It has been suggested that Sc. 1-9 were written early in Shakespeare's career, while the rest of the play represents a late rewriting of early material; but apart from the intrinsic improbability of such a procedure, it leaves unexplained much of the internal evidence (and simply ignores the play's exclusion from the Folio). Brainerd (1980) found *Pericles* statistically deviate relative to his ten tested variates (p. 227); he did not attempt to divide the play into two shares, but if both shares were by Shakespeare the figures for the whole play should not be deviate. The function-word test more precisely confirms the Shakespearian status of Sc. 10-22 while denying Shakespeare's authorship (at any period) of Sc. 1-9; so does Smith's analysis of stylometric collocations. In rare vocabulary the first nine scenes are most strongly linked with *Titus* and *1 Henry IV*. Although the association with *Titus* might encourage those who believe in an early version, the link with *1 Henry IV* is harder to justify, and the association probably originates in the popularity of both plays; *1 Henry IV*, in particular, was clearly familiar to many readers, and echoes of it can be found in many writers. By contrast, Sc. 10-22 are most strongly linked, in vocabulary, with *The Tempest*. The first nine scenes actually have only 54 links with the last three romances, instead of the 65 which would be produced by a merely random distribution; by contrast, the last thirteen scenes have 153, instead of an expected 106. This disparity can hardly be accidental, and it strongly supports either collaborative authorship, or—less plausibly—composition in different periods.

The probable author of Sc. 1-9 is George Wilkins, the undoubted author of *The Painful Adventures of Pericles, Prince of Tyre* (1608: STC 25638.5), a novella which attempts to cash in on the play's success. Lake (1969) identified a series of peculiarities in rhyme technique in which the first nine scenes of *Pericles* correspond more closely with the work of Wilkins than of any other candidate; earlier scholars had pointed to a surprising number of parallels between *Pericles* and Wilkins's (few) other works. Further internal evidence for the Wilkins attribution will be provided by MacDonald P. Jackson's forthcoming Oxford Shakespeare edition. The external evidence of *Painful Adventures* (associating Wilkins with the play a year before Shakespeare's name was linked to it), when combined with such internal evidence, seems to us sufficient to establish Wilkins's claim to a part-share.

Wilkins was a minor free-lance dramatist, and *Henslowe's Diary* demonstrates that such authors would often have presented theatrical companies with a plot, and/or one or more acts, in hopes of advance part-payment. Shakespeare, as sharer and company dramatist, must have been involved in such transactions, regularly or occasionally, and could have decided to contribute to (or take over) a play initiated by someone else. Wilkins had recently scored a popular success with *The Miseries of Enforced Marriage* (King's Men, *c.*1606: BEPD 349), so the company's interest in his work would not be surprising; Shakespeare's interest is easily explicable in terms of the preoccupations evident in his other late plays. Basically, Wilkins appears to have written Sc. 1-9, and Shakespeare Sc. 10-22; there may have been some shared writing within these larger blocks, or Shakespeare may have rewritten some material drafted by Wilkins, but the confused textual situation makes the detailed character of the collaboration difficult to identify. However, this caveat applies with less force to the speeches of Gower (for reasons explained in the Introduction, below): we see no evidence of Shakespeare's presence in the epilogue (22.108-25/2374-91), and little in Sc. 18.

These problems of text and authorship make it impossible to use internal evidence to date *Pericles* precisely, relative to Shakespeare's other Jacobean plays, though it is clear that Sc. 10-22 belong among the late plays. (Oras's pause test puts Shakespeare's share in the vicinity of *Macbeth* and *Antony*.) We are thus thrown back upon the meagre external evidence. The play must have existed by 20 May 1608, when it was entered in the Stationers' Register; Wilkins's novella, which is based on the play and which uses the play's names for the characters, is dated 1608; the Venetian ambassador witnessed a performance at some time between 5 January 1606 and 23 November 1608 (*Venetian State Papers*, xi. 193, xiv. 600). Since the ambassador paid 'more than 20 crowns' for attendance by himself and three others, he cannot have been witnessing a court performance; plague closed the London theatres in the summer and autumn of 1608, so he must have seen the play by May or June at the latest. Given the play's demonstrable early popularity, it seems unlikely that it was very old at the time of these earliest allusions; most editors have therefore dated it in 1607 or early 1608. Since plague apparently closed the theatres from April to December 1607, and since 1606 is already very full (see *Lear*, *Macbeth*, and *Antony* above), the play is unlikely to have been performed in London before late December 1607 (though it might have been completed a few months before); it probably made its initial impact in the first five months of 1608.

Coriolanus 1608

First referred to in the Stationers' Register entry for the 1623 Folio. It is probably indebted to Camden's *Remains* (1605: STC 4521). Stylistic tests uniformly place the play after *The History of King Lear*, *Macbeth*, and *Antony*. The 'coale of fire vpon the Ice' (1.1.171/169) probably glances at the great frost of December 1607–January 1608, and the choice and treatment of subject-matter is strikingly pertinent to the Midlands riots of 1607-8. An allusion has often been detected in 3.1.99-100/1544-5 to Hugh Middleton's project for bringing water into London (February 1609, but known for some time before). Cumulatively such internal evidence suggests a date no earlier than spring 1608. The play must have existed by 1609, when 2.2.101/1124 was echoed at 5.4.224-5 of Ben Jonson's *Epicoene* (BEPD 304; composed late 1609) and 1.1.210-11/210-11 was echoed in the address 'Ad lectorem' to Robert Armin's *The Italian Tailor and His Boy* (1609: STC 774; entered in the Stationers' Register on 6 February 1609): 'a strange time of taxation, wherein euery Pen & inck-horne Boy, will throw vp his Cap at the hornes of the Moone in censure' (sig. A4). It may also be significant that the Folio text contains regular act divisions: the King's Men apparently only began to make habitual use of act intervals after they acquired the Blackfriars in August 1608 (see Taylor, 'Act Intervals').

Most editors place *Coriolanus* before *Pericles*, but that arrangement seems based upon nothing more than a desire to lump the romances together in a single chronological sequence: it presupposes the latest possible date for *Pericles* and the earliest possible date for *Coriolanus*, while leaving 1607 uncharacteristically empty.

The Winter's Tale 1609

First printed in 1623; also attributed to Shakespeare by Jonson. Simon Forman witnessed a performance at the Globe on 15 May 1611 (Bodleian MS Ashmole 208, fols. 201ᵛ-202), and it was performed at court on 11 November 1611. The dance of twelve satyrs at 4.4.340.1/1947.1, which apparently makes use of material performed at court on 1 January 1611, seems to us a later interpolation (see Introduction, below); it is thus of no value in dating the original composition, except in so far as it suggests that the play was completed before the end of 1610. At 4.4.784-92/2393-2401 the play makes use of material from Boccaccio's *Decameron* (Day 2, Tale 9), which is also exploited in *Cymbeline*; critics have usually taken this borrowing as evidence that *Cymbeline* preceded *Winter's Tale*; though it may suggest proximity of composition such a parallel cannot determine priority of composition. Pafford (edn., 1963) demonstrates Shakespeare's indebtedness to Plutarch for several incidental features (pp. 142-3, 153-5), which suggests that *Winter's Tale* was written in or not long after the period of the classical tragedies. All stylistic tests place it in Shakespeare's late period. In rare vocabulary its strongest links are with (in descending order) *Measure*, the Shakespearian portion of *Pericles*, and *The Tempest*; in Oras's pause test it is closest to Shakespeare's portion of *Pericles*; the colloquialism-in-verse test puts it after *Coriolanus* and before *Cymbeline*; its metrical figure is closest to *Antony*'s. Although we lack hard evidence which enables us to fix a *terminus post quem*, most critics agree that the play should be paired with *Cymbeline* (see below).

The Tragedy of King Lear 1610

Printed in 1623. Although for convenience we have printed the two versions of *Lear* side by side, the revision appears to post-date the original composition by some time. The revision apparently began on a copy of the 1608 edition of *The History of King Lear*, and it makes no use of the sources of the original version. It may have been influenced by details of Plutarch's 'Life of Marius' (echoed in *Coriolanus*) and of George Puttenham's *The Art of English Poesy* (1589: STC 20519; echoed in *Winter's Tale*). The rare vocabulary unique to the Folio version does not have statistically significant links with the plays from *As You Like It* to *Othello*, as the Quarto version does; its strongest links are instead with *Winter's Tale*, *Cymbeline*, *Tempest*, and *All Is True*. Moreover, the language of *Lear* seems to have re-entered Shakespeare's active vocabulary at about the same time as *Cymbeline*; *Lear* and *Cymbeline* are also linked by many similarities in sources and preoccupations. 'No heretics burn'd' (3.2.84/1612) is unlikely to have been written after 14 December 1611, when Edward Wightman was condemned to death for heresy; he and Bartholomew Legate went to the stake in March 1612. The foregoing evidence is discussed at length in *Division*, 351-468, 485-6. In addition Taylor ('Act Intervals') argues that the revision presumes the use of act intervals, and hence post-dates the purchase of the Blackfriars in August 1608.

Stone conjectured that Philip Massinger was responsible for the Folio alterations; *Division* presents linguistic evidence which rules out every plausible candidate but Shakespeare. The type and distribution of rare vocabulary, verbal parallels, clusters of imagery, sources, and chronological evidence are all compatible with Shakespeare's authorship, and we see no serious evidence of posthumous or unauthoritative adaptation. The only passage sometimes isolated as a theatrical interpolation is the Fool's prophecy (3.2.79-96/1607-24); but the grounds for the allegation are wholly subjective, and we do not share the distaste of some critics for the passage. Honigmann ('Revised Plays') and Wittreich provide further arguments for its authenticity.

Cymbeline 1610

Printed in 1623. Simon Forman witnessed a performance, probably between 20 and 30 April 1611, and obviously before his death on 8 September 1611 (Bodleian MS Ashmole 208, fol. 206). The play's composition probably dates from the period of or after *Macbeth*, for 5.3 is based upon a minor incident in Holinshed's 'History of Scotland', which Shakespeare seems to have consulted only in relation to *Macbeth*. In rare vocabulary its strongest links are with *Hamlet*, *Macbeth*, *Lear*, *Winter's Tale*, *Tempest*, and to a lesser degree *Coriolanus*; with the exception of *Hamlet*, all of these date from 1605 or later.

Moreover, the play is clearly related in some way to Beaumont and Fletcher's *Philaster* (1620: BEPD 363), which Gurr convincingly dates in 1609; whatever the direction of influence, the two plays almost certainly were written at about the same time. Judgements of their relative priority have, we believe, too often been characterized by a desire to exonerate Shakespeare of any indebtedness to the lesser playwrights. *Philaster* was apparently their first great success; *Cymbeline* does not seem to have been especially popular, if we may judge from the dearth of references to it. Beaumont and Fletcher could only have been influenced by Shakespeare's play through performance, and the London theatres were closed because of plague until at least December 1609, and perhaps until January or February 1610. Since *Philaster* had been read by John Davies before October 1610, in order to be influenced by *Cymbeline* the play must have been written in the first half of 1610. This conclusion conflicts with Gurr's evidence that 'the new platform' (5.3.3) alludes to an event hotly topical in May 1609; although that reference would make sense in the next few months, there would be less reason to introduce it almost a year later. By contrast, as sharer and primary dramatist for the King's Men Shakespeare would almost certainly have seen the manuscript of *Philaster* before it was performed; he would have had the opportunity to read the entire text, without being dependent on memories of performance. Moreover, he might have seen the text months before it was performed, as plague continued to delay the reopening of the London theatres. This scenario seems to us better to account for the character of the similarities between the two plays, and to suggest that *Philaster* preceded *Cymbeline*. If so, *Cymbeline* can hardly have been completed before the beginning of 1610.

Forman does not specify at which theatre he saw *Cymbeline*; it may well have been performed at both the Globe and the Blackfriars, but in its style and theatrical requirements Shakespeare seems to have had in mind the resources and audience of the indoor theatre.

Cymbeline's verbal mannerisms have persuaded most critics that it belongs to the final period of Shakespeare's career, and that it was relatively new when Forman saw it; the essential difficulty has been whether to place it before or after *Winter's Tale*. Most critics have placed it before, on the grounds that *Winter's Tale* is the more mature achievement. This does not seem to us either true or relevant. Unlike *Pericles* (Jackson, 1975) and *Winter's Tale*, *Cymbeline* contains no verbal echoes of Plutarch, which suggests that it was written at a greater distance from the period of *Timon*, *Antony*, and *Coriolanus*. The cumulative rare vocabulary evidence puts *Cymbeline* later than *Winter's Tale*; so does the colloquialism-in-verse test. The metrical and pause tests are ambiguous. Although the evidence is not so conclusive as for the relative priority of *Measure* and *All's Well*, it does favour *Cymbeline* as the later play.

Furness (edn., 1913) and Granville-Barker attributed much of the play to an unidentified collaborator; these theories depended on little evidence, and have won little support. The vision in 5.4 has been more widely condemned as an un-Shakespearian interpolation, and it does satisfy the criteria for such interference, being a discrete and spectacular scene involving a new set of characters which occurs in a text apparently set from a late manuscript. But its integrity has been persuasively defended on grounds of imagery and style by Meyerstein, Knight, Craig, and Nosworthy (edn., 1955); we would add that in performance its old-fashioned fourteeners can achieve an impressive oracular authority.

The Tempest 1611

Performed at court 1 November 1611. Malone claimed to possess evidence that the play existed by the middle of 1611 (Boswell's edition, xv. 414), but the basis for this claim has never been discovered. The play is indebted to sources which were not available before September 1610: William Strachey's manuscript of the *True Repertory of the Wrack and Redemption of Sir Thomas Gates*, dated 15 July 1610 in Virginia (first printed in 1625: STC 20509); Sylvester Jourdain's *A Discovery of the Bermudas* (title-page dated 1610, with a dedication dated 13 October: STC 14816); and the Council of Virginia's *True Declaration of the Estate of the Colony in Virginia* (1610: STC 24833; Stationers' Register, 8 November). Shakespeare thus must have written the play within a year of its first court performance. According to Simon Forman's journal, Shakespeare had also completed *Winter's Tale* by 15 May 1611, and *Cymbeline* no later than September (see above). Unless all three plays were written at extraordinary speed, it seems certain that *The Tempest* post-dates *Winter's Tale*, and likely enough that it post-dates *Cymbeline*. In rare vocabulary its closest links are with Shakespeare's share of *Pericles*, and to a lesser degree *Winter's Tale* and *Cymbeline*; its total rare vocabulary emerges as later than all three. In Oras A and the colloquialism-in-verse test it also emerges as last of the four romances, if we assume a bend in the curve at about the time of *Coriolanus*. The metrical test is ambiguous in this area. Although we cannot be positive that it followed *Cymbeline*, that does remain the most probable interpretation of the data at our disposal.

The masque in 4.1 has sometimes been regarded as an interpolation, written for a performance of the play at court in the winter of 1612–13, between the betrothal and marriage of Princess Elizabeth and the Elector Palatine (see Wilson, edn., 1918, and Smith). The King's Men were paid in May 1613 for fourteen plays performed during this period, *The Tempest* being one of them. Although interpolation cannot be proven, it also cannot be disproven; the conjecture seems to us unnecessary and improbable, but it would not in any case affect the text, since an addition at that date could have been written by Shakespeare himself.

Cardenio 1612–13

This lost play apparently derives from *Don Quixote*, first published in English translation in 1612 (STC 4915). On 20 May and 9 July of 1613 the King's Men were paid for court performances of a play variously spelled 'Cardenno' and

'Cardenna'. On 9 September 1653 Moseley entered 'The History of Cardenio, by Mr Fletcher & Shakespeare' in the Stationers' Register, but appears not to have published it. In 1728 Theobald published a play, called *The Double Falsehood*, claiming that it was an adaptation of a play by Shakespeare which he possessed in manuscript. Theobald refers to this manuscript several times (see Frehafer). In 1770 a newspaper account stated that the manuscript still survived, in the library of Covent Garden playhouse; the playhouse burned down in 1808 (see Hammond). Frazier makes a concerted effort to deny that Theobald ever possessed a manuscript of the play; but her arguments are not wholly convincing, and even if we accepted them they would not disprove Shakespeare's part-authorship of a lost play, but only Theobald's access to that work.

Although Theobald's adaptation betrays little verbal evidence of a Shakespearian source, this is hardly surprising given the character of other post-Restoration adaptations: Shakespeare's late style was far more likely than Fletcher's to have suffered excision and recasting. Muir (1960) discerns evidence of Shakespeare's imagery through the intervening haze, and Frey convincingly relates the pattern of the play's plot to the preoccupations of Shakespeare's late romances. Moseley can hardly have been aware of the court payments, which independently attribute the play to Shakespeare's company at the very time when he was collaborating with Fletcher on *All Is True* and *Kinsmen*. Although Moseley could have known of the claim of collaboration on *Kinsmen*, he could not have dated it, and there is no evidence that Fletcher's share in *All Is True* was common knowledge in the seventeenth century.

All Is True 1613

The Globe Theatre burned down during a performance of this play on 29 June 1613, and a letter of 4 July 1613 (reproduced as Illustration 10 in the General Introduction, above) reports that the play had not been acted more than two or three times before. This documentary evidence, recently discovered, renders obsolete previous speculation—summarized and endorsed by Foakes (edn., 1957)—that the play might date from a somewhat earlier time.

If the date of this play can be fixed with unusual precision, its authorship remains disputed. The only contemporary testimony to its authorship is its inclusion in the 1623 Folio. Spedding (1850) first proposed that the play was a collaboration between Shakespeare and John Fletcher; this conjecture has been widely, but by no means universally, accepted. An annotated bibliography of significant essays on both sides of the question is provided by Humphreys (edn., 1971, pp. 50-4). Spedding assigned the Prologue, 1.3, 1.4, 2.1, 2.2, 3.1, 3.2.204-460.1/1697-1953, Act 4, 5.2, 5.3, 5.4, and the Epilogue to Fletcher. Spedding felt that Act 4 might be the joint work of Beaumont and Fletcher; he also suggested that 3.2 may be either Shakespeare revising the work of another, or another revising Shakespeare. Hoy (1962), as part of a thorough investigation of attribution problems in the Beaumont and Fletcher canon, gave Fletcher a much smaller share of the play: full details are given in the Introduction, below, but essentially Hoy gives back to Shakespeare 2.1, 2.2, all of 3.2 and Act 4, in each case allowing for the possibility that Fletcher touched up Shakespeare's work. Though Hoy's work is now nearly a generation old, no one has yet attempted to reconcile his conclusions (based on the evidence of linguistic forms characteristic of Fletcher) with those of Spedding (based on literary and stylistic arguments). Not only are their cases built on differing kinds of evidence, but their approaches to the question are different. Spedding aims to identify what is not by Shakespeare, and his attribution of these non-Shakespearian portions of the play to Fletcher (and Beaumont) is done casually, and remains always incidental to his main argument. Hoy, by contrast, aims to identify those portions of the play written by Fletcher. When Fletcher's linguistic thumb-print is absent, Hoy assigns a scene to Shakespeare—not because he has found persuasive evidence for Shakespeare's hand, but simply by default. Hoy's methods have not persuaded everyone: Schoenbaum (edn., 1967) cannot accept Shakespeare's responsibility for 2.1 and 4.1. Although debate has for some time focused entirely upon Fletcher and Shakespeare as the only candidates, Spedding's original suspicion of a third hand may well be justified, and deserves reconsideration. Hoy had earlier pointed out (1958) that Beaumont is sometimes impossible to identify on the basis of linguistic evidence—an elusiveness he shares with Shakespeare. In dealing with collaborations between Beaumont and Fletcher, Hoy was forced to identify Beaumont not positively, but by default—by the absence of markers pointing to Fletcher. This procedure does not enable us to discriminate, in *All Is True*, between two authors (Beaumont and Shakespeare) who are both identifiable only by default. Those portions of the play where linguistic evidence rules out Fletcher, but stylistic evidence rules out Shakespeare, might well be by Beaumont. The matter deserves further study; it cannot be resolved solely on the basis of the available linguistic evidence.

Such disarray over the precise limits of Shakespeare's contribution should not be allowed to obscure the fact that both stylistic and linguistic evidence, accumulated over a century, assigns to Fletcher at least a quarter of the play. Foakes characteristically attempts to dismiss the internal evidence, by ignoring much of it and misrepresenting much of the rest; subsequent attacks on the hypothesis of collaboration, by Clayton and Dominik, are no more convincing. These arguments for single authorship are no stronger than those Bertram deploys in discussing *Kinsmen* (see below). Brainerd (1980) finds *All Is True* statistically deviate in relation to his ten tested variates; he does not divide the play into authorial shares, but if the entire play were by Shakespeare it should not be deviate. As Partridge (1949) and Hoy (1962) demonstrate, certain portions of the play are anomalous in their treatment of orthographical and linguistic forms. Verbal parallels between these passages and other plays connect them more often and more closely to Fletcher's canon than to Shakespeare's. Jackson (1979) observes that the same passages have an abnormally low frequency, for Shakespeare, of rare vocabulary. Slater's rare-word test did not discriminate between different parts of the play, but Jackson shows that the 'Shakespearian' portion of the play, by Spedding's division, belongs according to such criteria at the very end of the canon; the 'non-Shakespearian' portion by contrast would have to be dated—impossibly—at the turn of the century.

Oras's pause-test (1960) confirms the traditional division of the play, which is also supported by the earlier metrical tests surveyed by Chambers, by Langworthy's analysis of the relationship between sentences and verse lines, by Jackson's study of affirmative particles (1962), and by Oras's study of 'extra monosyllables' (1935). Hart, on the basis of his studies of vocabulary distribution, concluded that *All Is True*—like *Pericles* and *Kinsmen*—could not be entirely from Shakespeare's hand (1943, p. 133). There is also a noticeable discrepancy between the two parts of the play in the colloquialism-in-verse test (see above). Merriam (1981), in the only published stylometric test based upon the entire Shakespeare canon, showed that the distribution of proportional pairs (*them* in relation to *they* and *their*) is wildly anomalous in *All Is True*, and that the anomaly is accounted for by one part of the play. No less remarkable, though harder to quantify, are the disparities in complexity and idiosyncrasy of syntax and imagery. The scenes assignable to Shakespeare display consistently the kinds of grammatical muscularity characteristic of his late style (see Burton and Clemen); those assignable to Fletcher or Beaumont do not, demonstrating instead the verbal ease and digestibility for which those writers were most famed in their own era and most criticized in ours. On the basis of such interlocking evidence it seems reasonable to conclude that Shakespeare did not write the entire play, and that at least part of it was written by Fletcher.

The Two Noble Kinsmen 1613-14

Entered in the Stationers' Register on 8 April 1634, and published in an edition dated 1634; both the entry and title-page attribute the play to 'William Shakespeare and John Fletcher'.

The morris dance in 3.5 was apparently borrowed from Francis Beaumont's *Inner Temple and Gray's Inn Masque* (1613: BEPD 309), performed on 20 February 1613 and entered in the Stationers' Register a week later; it seems too integral to the plot to represent a later interpolation. The prologue's reference to 'our losses' is plausibly interpreted as an allusion to the burning down of the Globe on 29 June 1613, and it has been often assumed that *Kinsmen* was the first play performed in the rebuilt theatre (completed by June 1614). Jonson's *Bartholomew Fair* (first performance 31 October 1614) twice sarcastically alludes to 'Palamon' (4.3.70, 5.6.83-4), in a way which suggests that *Kinsmen* would be fresh in the spectators' minds.

Bertram claimed the whole play for Shakespeare, but his arguments were decisively refuted by Hoy (1969). Brainerd (1980) found *Kinsmen* statistically deviate relative to his ten tested variates; he did not attempt to divide the play into authorial shares, but if Shakespeare were sole author it should not be deviate. Moreover, if Shakespeare were sole author, the play should have been included in the Folio.

Most discussion of authorship has turned, not on whether Shakespeare wrote all the play, but whether he wrote any of it. The play's omission from the Folio can easily be explained by the collaborative authorship asserted on its first publication. Although publishers' attributions of plays to Shakespeare before 1623, or after the closing of the theatres, must be regarded with considerable scepticism, *Kinsmen* is the only play attributed to him in the two decades between the Folio and the Civil War, and the only play before the Restoration attributed to him as part-author. In 1619 the Lord Chamberlain insisted, in a letter to the Court of the Stationers' Company, that in future no plays belonging to the King's Men should be printed without their consent; between this date and the closing of the theatres only two plays were printed in first editions which attributed them to Shakespeare: *Othello* (1622) and *Kinsmen* (1634). The attribution is supported by the fact that it occurs in the Stationers' Register as well as the first edition, and by the hypothesis that the text was printed from a manuscript annotated by the book-keeper of Shakespeare's company (see Introduction, below). Finally, the independent external evidence for *Cardenio* and internal evidence for *All Is True* (see above) establishes that Shakespeare was probably collaborating with Fletcher at the time when *Kinsmen* was composed—a fact of which the publishers of *Kinsmen* can hardly have been aware. The external evidence for Shakespeare's part-authorship of *Kinsmen* therefore appears to be reliable.

Studies of vocabulary by Hart (1943), of imagery by Armstrong, Mincoff (1952), Muir (1960), and Hobday, of linguistic evidence by Hoy (1962), of verbal parallels by Littledale (edn., 1876; 1885), of pause-patterns by Oras, of the treatment of sources by Thompson (1978), and of metre (summarized by Chambers), all corroborate the external evidence, discriminating two stylistic patterns in the play, one remarkably congruent with late Shakespeare, the other equally congruent with middle Fletcher. Metz (1982) provides a useful bibiliography of these and other studies.

WORKS EXCLUDED FROM THIS EDITION

The following alphabetical list does not attempt to discuss every play or poem ever attributed to Shakespeare. Hubbel counts 75 plays excluded from the 1623 Folio which have at one time or another, by one person (and sometimes no other), been conjecturally nominated for inclusion in the canon. We have restricted ourselves to printed works ascribed to Shakespeare, or to 'W.S.', in the sixteenth or seventeenth century, and to four anonymous early plays (*Arden of Faversham, Edward III, Edmond Ironside,* and *Sir Thomas More*). In selecting anonymous works we have been guided by two quite different criteria. *Arden* and *Edward III* have been seriously entertained for two centuries, and to have ignored them would have left the record miserably incomplete, for those two plays have a better claim to attention than anything else in this list. By contrast, Shakespeare's authorship of parts of the original of *Sir Thomas More* and of all of *Edmond Ironside* has been proposed so recently that no final sifting of the evidence has yet taken place; we include them not from any belief in the probability of the attributions, but simply as an acknowledgement of the current scholarly debate. By contrast, we

WORKS EXCLUDED FROM THIS EDITION

have been more systematic in recording external evidence, however dubious, in the belief that such early attributions, even when demonstrably wrong, constitute a part of the historical record more important than the forgotten follies of subsequent enthusiasts. Most of these attributions originate in early quartos, or in late Stationers' Register entries, or in unreliable lists of plays printed after the closing of the theatres. Edward Archer's 1656 play-list, in addition to works discussed below, attributes to Shakespeare Peele's *Arraignment of Paris*, Fletcher's *The Chances*, Chettle's *Hoffman*, Kyd's *Spanish Tragedy*, Massinger's *Roman Actor*, and Middleton's *Trick to Catch the Old One*. (For a comprehensive discussion of the play-lists see Greg, 1946.)

The apocryphal poems have never been collected or edited; the first collection of apocryphal plays was published in 1664, when seven plays were added to a second issue of the 1663 Third Folio (*Cromwell*, *Locrine*, *London Prodigal*, *Oldcastle*, *Pericles*, *Puritan*, *Yorkshire Tragedy*). All seven had previously been attributed to Shakespeare in some other source, but only *Pericles* has been accepted into the canon. Brooke (1908) provided edited old-spelling texts of fourteen plays; of these, *Kinsmen* and parts of *More* have since found their way into editions of the Complete Works. G. R. Proudfoot is currently at work upon a new edition of the dramatic apocrypha. Chambers discussed most of the apocryphal plays (*Shakespeare*, i. 532-42).

Ad lectorem, de Authore

A four-stanza, twenty-four line commendatory poem, signed 'W.S.', prefaced to Nicholas Breton's *The Will of Wit* (1599: STC 3706), sig. A4^v. It begins 'What shall I say of Gold, more then tis Gold? | Or call the Diamond, more then precious?' Breton's book was entered in the Stationers' Register in 1580, and transferred to Creede on 20 October 1596; the earliest extant edition is dated 1597 (STC 3705), but both known copies are fragmentary. Grosart compared the opening to *King John* 4.2.11/1632, and would 'gladly accept' the initials as Shakespeare's (ii. 63); but we see little reason to assign the poem to him.

Arden of Faversham

Entered in the Stationers' Register on 3 April 1592, and published anonymously in 1592 (*BEPD* 107). Another edition, also printed in 1592, was confiscated, and no copies survive (Stationers' Register, 18 December 1592). Greg (1946) speculated that the 1656 play-list (*BEPD* 766; see iii. 1330, l. 14) attribution to Shakespeare of Peele's *Arraignment of Paris* might have been a compositor's error, and that the name should have been placed opposite *Arden*; but the play-list is, in any case, unreliable. The play was first attributed to Shakespeare by Edward Jacob (edn., 1770), and was included in Brooke's *Apocrypha*; Lancashire and Levenson (1973) provide a bibliography. It is indebted to Holinshed's *Chronicles*, probably in the 1587 edition, and apparently alludes to John Lyly's *Endymion* (*BEPD* 99; performed at court 2 February 1588; Stationers' Register 4 October 1591). M. L. Wine, in the most thorough modern edition (Revels Plays, 1973), concludes that 'of all the cases presented for and against various known playwrights that for Shakespeare emerges as the strongest' (p. lxxxviii). Cases have also been made for Kyd and Marlowe. The function-word test is ambiguous (see above); in Oras's pause test the play is closest to *Contention*. The evaluation of internal evidence is complicated—and perhaps permanently defeated—by uncertainty over the text of the 1592 edition: Hart (1942), Jackson (1963), and Wine agree that it represents a memorial reconstruction.

The Birth of Merlin

First published by Francis Kirkman in 1662 (*BEPD* 822), as having been 'Written by *William Shakespear*, and *William Rowley*'. Brooke includes the play in his *Apocrypha*, but in this century only Dominik has taken the Shakespeare half of the 1662 attribution seriously; Dominik's comparisons of thought and phrasing are wholly unconvincing, and he postulates an unparalleled form of collaboration in which Shakespeare is solely responsible for no isolable portion of the text. There is no evidence that Rowley had any connection with the King's Men before 1623. Jackson (1979) surveys commentary on authorship, and demonstrates that Middleton cannot have been Rowley's collaborator; linguistic evidence also clearly rules out Fletcher.

Thomas Lord Cromwell

Entered in the Stationers' Register on 11 August 1602, and published that year in an edition (*BEPD* 189) claiming that it had 'beene sundrie times publikely Acted by the Right Honorable the Lord Chamberlaine his Seruants. Written by W.S.' The play was included in the 1664 Folio and in Brooke's *Apocrypha*; Lancashire and Levenson (1975) provide a bibliography. The external evidence is weak, and the internal evidence tells strongly against Shakespeare's authorship of all or part; no one this century has supported attribution to Shakespeare. Maxwell (1956) argues on the basis of echoes of *Henry V* and *Caesar* that the play post-dates 1599; he plausibly sees evidence of collaboration in the unevenness of the play's structure and texture, and on the basis of its sources and their treatment thinks it likely that the collaborators may have included one or more of the dramatists connected with *Sir Thomas More* (Munday, Chettle, Heywood, Dekker) or Henslowe's lost plays on *Cardinal Wolsey* (Munday, Chettle, Wentworth Smith). Participation of the latter would explain the title-page ascription to 'W.S.'

Cupid's Cabinet Unlocked

The title-page of this undated duodecimo volume does not indicate when or by whom it was printed, but describes it as 'Cupids Cabinet Unlock't, OR, THE NEW ACCADEMY OF COMPLEMENTS. Odes, Epigrams, Songs, and Sonnets, Poesies, Presentations, Congratulations, Ejaculations, Rhapsodies, &c.' written 'By W. Shakespeare'. Neither STC nor Wing records this item, nor does it appear in the British Library Catalogue. We have been able to trace only two copies, both defective: Folger C7597a lacks leaf G11, and

Boston Public Library G.176.62 lacks leaves I1-3. On the basis of the signatures (G8-12, H12, I1-3) it would appear to be an extract from a larger work; but no such work has as yet been identified, the pagination is regular (1-38), and p. 38 concludes with a 'FINIS.' The Folger copy is a separate item. The Boston copy is bound with a work with the running title 'The New Accademy of Complements', beginning on sig. K1 (p. 57); it therefore lacks the entirety of sheet I, which must have contained the join between the two works. This 'New Academy' is not the 1669 volume of that title (Wing N529-531). Both these works are bound with a fragment of *The Art of Courtship* (beginning with sig. C1, p. 21). It seems likely that *Cupid's Cabinet Unlocked* post-dates Benson's edition of *Shakespeare's Poems* (1640), and the title probably exploits an allusion to the pamphlet *The King's Cabinet Opened* (Wing C2358; dated 14 June 1645), which marked a turning-point in the Civil War. In the political pamphlet, 'cabinet' is a pun, referring both to the chest of papers captured by the Parliamentarians, and to the inner workings of the King's cabinet; no such pun operates in the 'Shakespeare' volume, which is therefore probably the later work. The allusion implies that a treasure-chest of Shakespeare's poems has been found, comparable in importance to the chest of Charles I's papers published in June 1645. Although this allusion establishes that the volume dates from 1645 or later, similar titles can be found as late as 1679. We have not attempted to date the volume more precisely on the basis of its type. The few visible watermarks seem unlikely to be of value in determining its period.

The volume has received little attention. It was first mentioned by Britton (1814), who remarks 'I have seen a rare little volume, called *Cupid's Cabinet Unlocked*, in the possession of James Parry, Esq. with his [Shakespeare's] name; but it has no other characteristic of the great author, whose name is thus prostituted' (p. 22). In the 'Catalogue of the Valuable Library of the late Benjamin Heywood Bright' (Sotheby's, 1845) it appears as item 5116, being described as 'a piece of a book'. This is presumably the Folger copy, which was owned by Halliwell-Phillipps and then by William Augustus White; the Boston copy belongs to the Thomas Pennant Barton collection, and according to a slip pasted inside the front cover it was acquired for £5 5s. in a sale in which it was the first item. The description of the volume in this sale catalogue states that 'from the general appearance of its type, the lines round the letter-press, and some other circumstances, it is probable that it was published about 1645, by Humphrey Moseley, bookseller, in St. Paul's Churchyard, who, sometime before the year 1653, printed an edition of Shakespeare's *Poems*, in octavo'. This statement about Moseley is unfounded, and based upon a misinterpretation of the fact that he bought up the unsold stock of Benson's edition (*BEPD* iii. 1176; Separate List IV, item 91); but it finds its way into Jaggard's *Bibliography* (1910). Bartlett (1922), who knew only the Folger copy, listed it as item 157, and Alden (1964) mentioned the volume among interesting items in the Barton collection. So far as we can trace, these are the only references to *Cupid's Cabinet Unlocked*.

This lack of attention is hardly surprising, for the thirty-three poems in the volume do not include a single item elsewhere attributed to Shakespeare, or plausibly attributable to him. It does include two poems by Milton, both first published in 1645: the first ten lines of 'L'Allegro' (p. 2) and 'On a May Morning' (p. 17). These texts have hitherto been overlooked by Milton scholars: Shawcross does not mention them. It attributes one poem ('Sweetest, thy name to me doth promise much', pp. 17-20) to 'R.H.', and another ('Since 'tis my fate to be thy slave', pp. 11-12) to 'K.D.' There are many poets of the period with the initials 'R.H.', but 'K.D.' is rare, and suggests Sir Kenelm Digby (1603-65). The late date of the volume's publication, its surreptitious character, its inclusion of poems demonstrably by other authors, and the abysmal quality of the remaining verse all confirm its unauthoritative character. However, it has some importance both in relation to Shakespeare's seventeenth-century reputation as a non-dramatic poet, and as a potential check on manuscript attributions which might be discovered in the future: any poem attributed to Shakespeare (or 'W.S.') in manuscript which was also included in this collection would probably have derived its attribution from the (worthless) printed source.

Edward III

Entered in the Stationers' Register on 1 December 1595, and anonymously printed in an edition of 1596 (*BEPD* 140), which states only that it '*hath bin sundrie times plaied about the Citie of London*'. First attributed to Shakespeare in Rogers and Ley's 'An exact and perfect Catalogue of all *Playes* that are Printed' (1656: *BEPD* 761; see iii. 1323, l. 138), which in the same place assigns to him Marlowe's *Edward II* and Heywood's *Edward IV*; Shakespeare's authorship was first seriously proposed by Capell (*Prolusions*, 1760). The play was included in Brooke's *Apocrypha*, and of all the non-canonical plays has the strongest claim to inclusion in the Complete Works. Shakespeare certainly, at the very least, knew the play, for his reference to King David of Scotland in *Henry V* (1.2.160-2/293-5) follows *Edward III* in a unique historical error. Shakespeare's responsibility for all or part of *Edward III* has been supported by studies of the size and shape of vocabulary by Hart; of imagery and structure by Wentersdorf (1960), Koskenniemi, Osterberg, and Muir (1960); of rare words by Slater (1981). Earlier arguments are conveniently summarized in the old-spelling edition by Fred Lapides (1980) and in Proudfoot's lecture (1985); Metz (1982) provides a useful annotated bibliography. It was once generally thought that Shakespeare was responsible only for the Countess scenes, but most recent studies of vocabulary and imagery conclude that the play is of single authorship. The collaborator theory orginally arose from a belief that the romantic plot had a different source (William Painter's *Palace of Pleasure*, 1575) from the historical one (Holinshed's *Chronicle*); but Smith demonstrated that the chief source for both plots was Lord Berners's translation of *The Chronicle of Froissart* (1523: STC 11396). In some ways the dispute over whether Shakespeare was sole or part author is irrelevant, and has served to obscure the consensus of investigators that *Edward III* deserves a place in the Shakespeare canon.

The play clearly post-dates the defeat of the Armada (August 1588). A German academic play about King Edward III and the Countess of Salisbury might have been prompted by an English play on the same theme, performed by English actors on tour in Gdansk at some time in or before 1591 (see Limon). Such evidence—which is accepted by Lapides—would place *Edward III* c.1589-90, making it perhaps earlier than any of the *Henry VI* plays, and those who favour Shakespeare's authorship generally presume such an early date. Wentersdorf (1960) concludes that the metrical tests independently support such a dating, if we assume Shakespearian authorship; but his conclusions cannot be given much weight, for metrical evidence at the very beginning of the canon is bedevilled by inconsistencies, and by the problems created by possible collaboration. In the colloquialism-in-verse test, *Edward III*'s figure places it closest, among the history plays, to *Richard III*; unless *Contention* and *Duke of York* are collaborative plays, by this test *Edward III* belongs after them, not before. Jackson (1965), on the basis of alleged echoes in apparently memorial texts, concludes that the play belonged at some stage to Pembroke's Men. This evidence is weaker than one would desire, and the play's company affiliations remain uncertain. The casting pattern would fit the Chamberlain's Men as readily as the pre-1590 Admiral's, or what we conjecture about Pembroke's. Indeed, the size of cast does not resemble any Shakespeare play which we place before June 1592 except *Two Gentlemen*, which cannot be dated with any certainty. The references to Lucrece (987-91) and to Hero and Leander (947-51), and the presence of a line (786) which also occurs in the Sonnets (94.14), would also suit a rather later date. Osterberg's analysis of parallels favours composition c.1592-4. Timberlake's study of feminine endings supports attribution of the play, in whole or part, to Shakespeare, but puts it closest to the middle plays (*Love's Labour's Lost*, *Dream*, *Romeo*, and *John*). Muir's comparison (1960) of the Countess scenes with Edward IV's wooing of Lady Elizabeth Gray (in *Duke of York*) also suggests that *Edward III* is the more mature, and therefore later, achievement. The early dating depends upon acceptance of the (shaky) Gdansk evidence; but even if we take that to imply an English play on the subject, *Edward III* might easily have inspired more than one play in the patriotic post-Armada period. (Compare the three or four plays on Henry V from the 1580s and 1590s.)

We have excluded *Edward III* in part because of uncertainties about date, in part because Shakespeare's share of the early plays is itself problematic: for instance, Slater's rare vocabulary test links *Edward III* most closely to *1 Henry VI*, of which Shakespeare only wrote about 20 per cent (see above). The function-word test is ambiguous (see above). The stylistic evidence for Shakespeare's authorship of *Edward III* is greater than that for the additions to *Sir Thomas More* (excluding the palaeographical argument); if we had attempted a thorough reinvestigation of candidates for inclusion in the early dramatic canon, it would have begun with *Edward III*.

An Epistle to Mr. W— Fellow of Trinity College in Cambridge. In praise of an University Life

A 67-line poem, attributed in Bodleian MS Rawlinson poet. 173 (fol. 167ᵛ) to 'W.S.' It begins 'Now thou, dear Will, and every Friend's withdrawn, | How do I loath the pleasures of the Town!' Crum (N576) could not identify an author, but the subject-matter is less characteristic of Shakespeare than of the University poets who people such miscellanies.

Eurialus and Lucretia

A lost play, included by Robert Scott in a Stationers' Register entry on 21 August 1683 of 26 titles attributed to 'Shakespeare'. The attribution presumably originated in confusion with Shakespeare's very popular *Lucrece*.

Fair Em

First published in an undated quarto (*BEPD* 113), which states that it 'was sundrie times publiquely acted in the *honourable citie of London, by the right honourable* the Lord Strange his seruants'. This company existed only from 1589 to 1593; Lord Strange became Lord Derby on 25 September 1593. Standish Henning, in the most thorough edition available (1980), convincingly argues that the quarto was printed at some time in the twelve months after August 1592, and that it was printed from a memorial reconstruction. Neither that edition nor the 1631 reprint names an author; the play was bound with *Mucedorus* and *Merry Devil* in a volume of Charles II's library entitled 'Shakespeare. Vol. I.', but Edward Phillips (*Theatrum Poetarum*, 1675) attributed it to Robert Greene. However, two lines in the final scene are ridiculed in Greene's *Farewell to Folly* (1591: STC 12241). Brooke included the play in his *Apocrypha*, but no one this century has taken seriously the very weak external evidence linking the play to Shakespeare. Henning, who summarizes and extends previous discussions of authorship, thinks that Anthony Munday is the likeliest candidate. Lancashire and Levenson (1973) provide a bibliography.

A Funeral Elegy

An elegy, almost 600 lines long, 'In memory of the late Vertuous Maister William Peter of Whipton neere Excester', attributed on the title-page to 'W.S.' (1612: STC 21526); the same initials sign the Epistle. It begins 'Since Time, and his predestinated end, | Abridg'd the circuit of his hope-full dayes'. It seems not to have attracted critical attention, perhaps because it survives in only two copies (both at Oxford); but its style does not encourage us to believe that it could represent a product of Shakespeare's maturity. The author more than once refers to his 'youth' (sigs. B1, C3ᵛ), and 'W.S.' seems likely to have been a young friend of the deceased, who was not, or did not become, a professional poet.

Hamlet

Thomas Nashe alluded to a play on the Hamlet story in 1589: 'hee will affoord you whole *Hamlets*, I should say handfuls of Tragicall speeches' (*Works*, iii. 315-16: preface to Robert Greene's *Menaphon*). Another allusion, locating performances of the play at 'yᵉ Theator' (owned by the Burbages), occurs in Thomas Lodge's *Wit's Misery* (1596: STC 16677, p. 56); a performance of the play is recorded in June 1594, by the Admiral's Men, or the Chamberlain's Men, or both performing together (*Henslowe's Diary*). There is universal agreement that this play cannot be the one printed in collected editions of Shakespeare's works since 1623, or a similar text printed in

1604-5: stylistically, these later texts cannot belong to the years before 1590. An undated Gabriel Harvey memorandum, alluding to Shakespeare's *Hamlet*, is ambiguous, and might refer to either play (see above, under 'Works Included'). The other early allusions do not explicitly specify the authorship of the early play, though Shakespeare editors from Malone (1790) to Jenkins (1982) have felt that Nashe's context points to Thomas Kyd. It has sometimes been contended that the text of this early play is preserved in an edition entered in the Stationers' Register on 26 July 1602 and printed in 1603, attributed to 'William Shakespeare'; however, like most other scholars we believe that the 1603 text instead represents a memorial reconstruction of the later play (see Introduction, below). If so, then the text of the early play is lost, and its authorship cannot be determined.

Henry I, Henry II

Entered by Moseley in the Stationers' Register on 9 September 1653, as 'by Wm. Shakespeare and Robert Davenport'. The plays are lost, but Davenport's *History of Henry the First* was licensed by Sir Henry Herbert for performance by the King's Men on 10 April 1624, eight years after Shakespeare's death. Equally suspect are *The History of King Stephen*, and *Duke Humphrey, a Tragedy*, and *Iphis & Ianthe, or a marriage without a man. a Comedy*, all lost, and all entered by Moseley on 29 June 1660, bracketed as 'by Will: Shakespeare'. Four of these titles reflect the strong association of Shakespeare's name with English chronicle plays, an association which presumably accounts for the attribution to him, in an unreliable play-list of 1656 (*BEPD* 761; see iii. 1323, ll. 137, 139), of Marlowe's *Edward II* and Heywood's *Edward IV*.

Edmond Ironside

Included as the fifth item in the collection of plays in British Library MS Egerton 1994; it is best studied in the MSR (ed. E. Boswell, 1928). Lancashire and Levenson (1975) provide a bibliography. The play, which in the manuscript is undated and anonymous, was first attributed to Shakespeare by Everitt (1954); this attribution has been elaborately championed by Eric Sams (edn., 1985), who dates the play c.1588. Everitt (1954) claimed that the manuscript was in Shakespeare's hand throughout; Hamilton (1986), a more considerable palaeographer, has supported this claim; but the attribution depends upon acceptance of his controversial views on a number of other alleged autographs (1985)—views which are too recent to have been subjected to thorough scholarly scrutiny. Sisson, who reviewed Everitt's book, did not accept the identification; neither Greg (1931) nor Boswell believed that the manuscript was autograph. The Shakespeare attribution is only plausible if the play can be dated earlier than any play included in the 1623 Folio; Sams's dating is possible, but certainly not certain, and probably not probable. Sams accumulates numerous indiscriminate parallels with early plays in the Shakespeare canon, but the value of these parallels in determining authorship is weakened by uncertainty over Shakespeare's sole authorship of the three *Henry VI* plays and *Edward III*, and by the possibility of Shakespeare's influence on *Ironside*, or *Ironside*'s influence on Shakespeare. Martin concludes that *Ironside* has been influenced by *Venus and Adonis*, and that it shows a familiarity with Holinshed's treatment of the Wars of the Roses, as filtered through the three plays on Henry VI. Although these conclusions might in themselves be compatible with Shakespearian authorship, they force one to date the play in 1593 or later—a dating fatal to the plausibility of the attribution. The function-word test also argues strongly against Shakespeare's authorship (see above). Sams makes no attempt to test his parallels against the work of other dramatists of the late 1580s and early 1590s. The material and arguments accumulated by Sams vary widely in their reliability; however, irritation at Sams's tone and the erratic conduct of his argument should not obscure the real verbal similarities between *Ironside* and Shakespeare's early work. The whole subject merits further investigation.

Locrine

Entered in the Stationers' Register on 20 July 1594, and printed in an edition dated 1595 (*BEPD* 136), with a title-page ambiguously declaring it to be 'Newly set foorth, ouerseene and corrected, | By *W.S.*' It was included in the 1664 Folio, and in Brooke's *Apocrypha*. The play is best studied in the MSR (ed. R. B. McKerrow, 1908), or in Gooch's edition (1981); Lancashire and Levenson (1973) provide a bibliography. One copy of the 1595 edition (Bodmer Library) contains a marginal note, apparently in the handwriting of George Buc and initialled 'G.B.', claiming that the play had been written by 'Char. Tilney' (died 1586); the subject is discussed by Berek. *Locrine* is clearly related in some way to *Selimus* (1594: *BEPD* 130), and has clearly been revised: see Maxwell (1956) and Berek.

The London Prodigal

First published in 1605 (*BEPD* 222), 'As it was plaide by the Kings Maiesties seruants. By William Shakespeare'. It was included in the 1664 Folio, and in Brooke's *Apocrypha*; Lancashire and Levenson (1975) provide a bibliography. No serious scholar has taken the attribution seriously; but no convincing alternative has been offered. Maxwell (1958) and Jones-Davies make a case for Dekker as author or collaborator; Wilkins and Middleton have also been mentioned.

The Merry Devil of Edmonton

Entered in the Stationers' Register on 22 October 1607, and published anonymously in an edition dated 1608 (*BEPD* 264), which states that it had '*beene sundry times Acted, by his Maiesties Seruants, at the Globe, on the banke-side*'. This attribution to the King's Men is supported by a Revels Account entry of 15 May 1618. None of the six seventeenth-century editions names an author; the play was bound with *Mucedorus* and *Fair Em* in a volume in Charles II's library entitled 'Shakespeare's Works. Vol. I.', and attributed to Shakespeare in a Stationers' Register entry by Moseley (9 September 1653) and in the unreliable play-lists of Archer

(1656: *BEPD* 766; see iii. 1334, l. 372) and Kirkman (1661: *BEPD* 820; see iii. 1347, l. 413). This external evidence is very weak, and the internal evidence strongly contradicts it. The play must be earlier than 1604, when Middleton referred to it in his *Black Book* (STC 17875; Stationers' Register, 22 March 1604); since the theatres were closed due to plague from 17 May 1603 to April 1604, Middleton must be referring to performances in the spring of 1603 or earlier. Brooke included the play in his *Apocrypha*; Abrams (edn., 1942) makes a strong case for composition in 1601-2 by Thomas Dekker, the only candidate to have achieved any currency. There has been no investigation of the linguistic evidence, which might clinch or disprove this attribution. Lancashire and Levenson (1975) provide a bibliography.

Sir Thomas More

The play is best studied in Greg's transcription (MSR 1911; rev. 1961), or in the modernized text prepared by Harold Jenkins for Sisson's edition of Shakespeare's *Works*. The original play of *Sir Thomas More* must be later than 1579, when Sir Edmund Tilney was appointed Master of the Revels, and earlier than 1607, by which date Henry Chettle was dead. Tilney made comments upon the play, and Chettle wrote some of the additional matter. Jowett has also convincingly demonstrated that Chettle probably wrote several scenes of the original. The extent and vehemence of Tilney's objections to the play strongly suggest that it was submitted to him at a time when its subject-matter was particularly sensitive, and three such times have been proposed: the anti-alien riots of 1593, the riots of 1595, and the Essex rebellion. Thompson (1915-17) contended that Munday's handwriting more closely resembles that in his *John a Kent and John a Cumber* (Huntington Library: 1589-96?) than that in his *The Heaven of the Mind* (British Library Add. MS 33384: 1602); this observation has probably been paid more attention than it deserves, for *The Heaven of the Mind* is, unlike the other two, a formal manuscript in an italic hand. However, the anti-alien rioting of 1593-5 does seem a more likely explanation of Tilney's attitude than the (absence of) rioting during Essex's abortive rebellion. We may thus rule out the third of these proposed occasions. Pollard plausibly contends that the savage executions after the anti-alien riots of June 1595 would have made it impossible for anyone to contemplate writing such a play thereafter; Anthony Munday, a part-time government spy, was especially unlikely to do so. It has thus seemed to most scholars that the original play antedates June 1595; it might be as early as September 1592, for Blayney shows that the hysterical xenophobia which sparked the 1593 riots had been noticed as early as the previous autumn. If the play was written after the autumn of 1592, then its composition might well have coincided with the closure of the theatres because of plague; this fact, combined with Tilney's objections, could easily explain why the play was laid aside for some time.

Merriam (1982) conjectured that Shakespeare wrote the entire play, including all the additions; but the stylometric evidence for this conclusion is crude, and does not take account of the palaeographical and stylistic evidence for multiple authorship. More seriously, McMillin ('*More*') conjectures that Shakespeare's addition dates from the same period as the original composition, hence opening up the possibility that Shakespeare did indeed write one or more scenes of the original—particularly the scene replaced in part by Addition II.D. McMillin convincingly contends that the original, in its casting requirements, must have been written for Strange's Men. Shakespeare might well have collaborated on a play written for that company *c*.1592-3, and his collaboration on the original would explain his contribution of one of the additions; but there is no convincing internal evidence to link him to any substantial extant portion of the original. We have therefore included in our edition only the two passages among the additions which there is good reason to suppose that Shakespeare wrote (see the discussion under 'Works Included').

Mucedorus

Transfer is recorded in the Stationers' Register on 17 September 1618. The first extant edition is dated '1598' (*BEPD* 151); the third extant edition (1610) includes 'new additions' and states that the play was acted 'By his Highnes Seruants usually playing at the Globe'. Charles II's library included *Mucedorus*, *Edmonton*, and *Fair Em* in a volume described as 'Shakespeare. Vol. I.'; *Mucedorus* was also attributed to Shakespeare in Edward Archer's wholly unreliable play-list of 1656 (*BEPD* 766; see iii. 1334, item 375). The additions apparently post-date 1603, and Shakespeare as company dramatist might have written them: Jackson (1964) notes stylistic and dramatic similarities to his acknowledged work. Lancashire and Levenson (1973) provide a bibliography.

A notable description of the World

A 16-line poem, signed 'W.S. *Gent*.', in *The Phoenix Nest* (1593: STC 21516), sigs. L3-L3ᵛ. It begins 'Of thick and thin, light, heauie, dark and cleere, | White, black, & blew, red, green, & purple die'. An anonymous reviewer in *The North British Review*, 52 (1870), pp. 280-1, suggested that the poem could be by Shakespeare; but Shakespeare was not a 'gentleman' in 1593. Hyder Rollins (edn., 1931) assigns the poem to William Smith; but Sasek doubts that attribution.

'Oft when I look, I may descry'

A 6-line poem, which is headed 'To his Mrs' and which begins 'Oft when I look, I may descry | a little face peepe throughe that eye', is attributed in British Library MS Sloane 1446 (fol. 23ᵛ) to 'W.S.' Crum (O219), who notes another copy in Bodleian MS Rawlinson poet. 142 (fol. 15ᵛ), could not identify the author.

The First Part of Sir John Oldcastle

Entered in the Stationers' Register on 11 August 1600, and printed in an edition dated 1600 (*BEPD* 166); a second edition, also dated '1600' on the title-page but in fact printed in 1619 for Thomas Pavier, claims that it was 'Written by

William Shakespeare'. The play was included in the 1664 Folio, and in Brooke's *Apocrypha*. It can be studied in the MSR (ed. Percy Simpson, 1908), in Hebel's edition of Drayton's *Works* (1961), or in Rittenhouse's modern-spelling edition (1984). *Henslowe's Diary* demonstrates that the play was written by Anthony Munday, Michael Drayton, Robert Wilson, and Richard Hathway, and completed on 16 October 1599. It was presumably attributed to Shakespeare because 'Oldcastle' was the original name of 'Falstaff' in *1 Henry IV* (see Introduction, below).

The Puritan; or, The Widow of Watling Street

Entered in the Stationers' Register on 6 August 1607, and published that year in an edition (*BEPD* 251) which claimed it had been 'Acted by the Children of Paules. Written by W.S.' The play was first attributed to Shakespeare in Archer's play-list of 1656 (*BEPD* 766; see iii. 1335, l. 450); it was included in the 1664 Folio and in Brooke's *Apocrypha*. The declared company—supported by internal evidence—in itself argues against interpretation of 'W.S.' as Shakespeare; Maxwell (1956) demonstrates that the play is larded with topical allusions which can hardly have been written before 1606. Most investigators up to and including Maxwell (1956) assigned the play to Thomas Middleton, on the basis of verbal and structural parallels with his other early plays; Lake (1975) and Jackson (1979) have provided convincing linguistic confirmation of Middleton's authorship.

The Second Maiden's Tragedy

Included in British Library MS Lansdowne 807; best studied in the MSR (ed. Greg, 1910) or in Anne Lancashire's modernized edition (Revels Plays, 1978); Lancashire and Levenson (1975) provide a bibliography. The play belonged to the King's Men and was licensed on 31 October 1611. At the end of the manuscript three later hands attribute the play successively to 'Thomas Goff' or 'George Chapman' or 'Will Shakespeare'. The latter attribution has been taken seriously only by Everitt. Lake (1975) and Jackson (1979) strongly corroborate earlier conjectures that the play is by Thomas Middleton; so does Lancashire's edition.

The Troublesome Reign of John, King of England

First published anonymously in 1591 (*BEPD* 101-2); the second edition (1611) claims that it was 'Written by W. Sh.', and the third (1622) expands this to 'W. Shakespeare'. Presumably on the basis of this edition the play is also assigned to Shakespeare in an unreliable play-list of 1656 (*BEPD* 766; see iii. 1333, l. 290), in Gerald Langbaine's *Account of the English Dramatick Poets* (1691), and by Pope (edn., 1725), who attributed the play to Shakespeare and 'W. Rowley'. Pope was perhaps thinking of *The Birth of Merlin* (see above); William Rowley's first known play was published in 1607. Samuel Rowley would be a likelier candidate. The play was included in Brooke's *Apocrypha*; it is best studied in J. W. Sider's edition (1979). Neither regards the Shakespeare attribution as a serious possibility; in this century only Everitt seems to have credited it. It probably results from or dishonestly exploits confusion with *King John*, not published until 1623 (see *King John*, among 'Works Included'). For a bibliography see Lancashire and Levenson (1973).

'Vpon the vntimely Death of the *Author* of this ingenious *Poem*, S^r. THO: OVERBVRY Knight, poysoned in *the Towre*'

A 66-line commendatory poem, signed 'W.S.', added to the first of the three 1616 editions of Sir Thomas Overbury's *Wife* (STC 18909). It begins 'So many *Moones* so many times gone round, | And rose from *Hell*, & *Darknesse*, vnder ground'. Another commendatory poem in the same edition is initialled 'W. St.', and was probably written by William Strachey (see Culliford).

'What worldly wealth, what glorious state'

A 4-line translation of Latin verses, attributed in Bodleian manuscript Top. gen. e. 29 (fol. 65) to 'W.S.' Crum (W796) was unable to identify an author, but such translations are less characteristic of Shakespeare than of the University poets who provided most of the material for such miscellanies.

A Yorkshire Tragedy

Entered in the Stationers' Register on 2 May 1608, and published that year (*BEPD* 272); both entry and title-page attribute the play to Shakespeare. It was included in the Pavier collection of 1619, the 1664 Folio, and Brooke's *Apocrypha*. The play has been often reprinted; it is best studied in the MSR (ed. Sylvia D. Feldman and G. R. Proudfoot, 1973 for 1969) or the Revels edition (ed. A. C. Cawley and Barry Gaines, 1986). Lancashire and Levenson (1975) provide a bibliography. The 1608 title-page claims that it was 'Not so New as Lamentable and true'; it cannot be earlier than the publication of its sensational source (STC 18288; Stationers' Register, 12 June 1605), and Maxwell (1956) convincingly argued that it was probably finished before the fate of its protagonist became known: he was executed on 5 August 1605. Its use of oaths certainly suggests composition before the Act to Restrain Abuses (May 1606). This date argues strongly against the attribution to Shakespeare, whose remarkable late style is nowhere in evidence. Lake (1975) provided clear evidence for Thomas Middleton's authorship of most of the play, but thought Shakespeare might have been responsible for the first scene; Jackson (1979) independently confirmed Middleton's authorship of the bulk of the play, and argued strongly against the need to suppose a second author for scene 1; Jackson's conclusions are further supported by Holdsworth. The attribution to Shakespeare is probably, in this instance, deliberately dishonest. However, the head title identifies the play as 'All's One, or, One of the foure Plaies in one, called a York-shire Tragedy'; the brevity of the text supports this claim that it formed one of several short dramatic entertainments presented on a single occasion, a genre which survives in the titles of other extant and lost texts. If so, Shakespeare might have written one of the other 'foure Plaies in one' presented on that occasion; such a 'collaboration' with Middleton in 1605 would not be surprising (see *Timon*, above), and would explain how Shakespeare might have been honestly if mistakenly credited with *A Yorkshire Tragedy*.

GARY TAYLOR

WORKS CITED

Adams, Joseph Quincy, ed., *The Dramatic Records of Sir Henry Herbert* (1917)

Alden, John, 'America's First Shakespeare Collection', *PBSA* 58 (1964), 169-73

Alexander, Peter, *Shakespeare's 'Henry VI' and 'Richard III'* (1929)

Allen, Don Cameron, ed., *Francis Meres's Treatise 'Poetrie'* (1933)

Amneus, D. A., 'A Missing Scene in *Macbeth*', *Journal of English and Germanic Philology*, 60 (1961), 435-40

Armstrong, Edward A., *Shakespeare's Imagination* (1946; rev. 1963)

Baldwin, T. W., *Shakspere's 'Loves Labours Won'* (1957)

Barroll, J. Leeds, 'The Chronology of Shakespeare's Jacobean Plays and the Dating of *Antony and Cleopatra*', in *Essays on Shakespeare*, ed. Gordon Ross Smith (1965), 115-62

Bartlett, Henrietta C., *Mr. William Shakespere: Original and Early Editions of his Quartos and Folios* (1922)

Bate, Jonathan, *Shakespeare and the English Romantic Imagination* (1986)

Bennett, Paul, 'An Apparent Allusion to *Titus Andronicus*', *N&Q* 200 (1955), 422-4, and 'The Word "Goths" in *A Knack to Know a Knave*', 462-3

Bentley, G. E., *The Profession of Dramatist in Shakespeare's Time, 1590-1642* (1971)

Berek, Peter, '*Locrine* Revised, *Selimus*, and Early Responses to *Tamburlaine*', *Research Opportunities in Renaissance Drama*, 22 (1980), 33-54

Bergeron, David M., 'The Hoby Letter and *Richard II*: A Parable of Criticism', *SQ* 26 (1975), 477-80

Bertram, Paul, *Shakespeare and 'The Two Noble Kinsmen'* (1965)

Blayney, Peter W. M., 'The Booke of Sir Thomas Moore Re-Examined', *Studies in Philology*, 69 (1972), 167-91

Born, Hanspeter, 'The Date of *2, 3 Henry VI*', *SQ* 25 (1974), 323-34

Bradbrook, M. C., *Shakespeare: The Poet in his World* (1978)

Brainerd, B., 'Pronouns and Genre in Shakespeare's Drama', *Computers and the Humanities*, 13 (1979), 3-16

—— 'The Chronology of Shakespeare's Plays: A Statistical Study', *Computers and the Humanities*, 14 (1980), 221-30

Britton, John, *Remarks on the Life and Writings of William Shakespeare* (1814)

Brooke, C. F. Tucker, ed., *The Shakespeare Apocrypha* (1908)

Brooks, Harold F., 'Marlowe and Early Shakespeare', in *Christopher Marlowe*, ed. Brian Morris (1968), 65-94

—— ed., *A Midsummer Night's Dream*, Arden (1979)

—— '*Richard III*: Antecedents of Clarence's Dream', *SSu* 32 (1979), 145-50

Brown, Keith, 'Historical Context and *Henry V*', *Cahiers Élisabéthains*, 29 (1986), 77-81

Burton, Dolores M., *Shakespeare's Grammatical Style* (1973)

Cairncross, Andrew S., 'Pembroke's Men and Some Shakespearian Piracies', *SQ* 11 (1960), 339-40

Chambers, E. K., 'The Disintegration of Shakespeare', British Academy Annual Shakespeare Lecture, 1924, reprinted in *Shakespearean Gleanings*

—— *Shakespearean Gleanings* (1944)

Chambers, R. W., 'Some Sequences of Thought in Shakespeare and in the 147 Lines of *Sir Thomas More*', *Modern Language Review*, 26 (1931), 251-80

—— *Man's Unconquerable Mind* (1939), 204-49

Chillington, Carol, 'Playwrights at Work: Henslowe's, not Shakespeare's, *Book of Sir Thomas More*', *English Literary Renaissance*, 10 (1980), 439-79

Clayton, Thomas, review of Schoenbaum, *Internal Evidence*, *SSt* 4 (1968), 350-76

Clemen, Wolfgang H., *The Development of Shakespeare's Imagery* (1951)

Coghill, Nevill, '*Macbeth* at the Globe, 1606-1616(?): Three Questions', in *The Triple Bond*, ed. Joseph Price (1977), 223-39

Conrad, Hermann, ed., *Shakespeare's Macbeth* (1907)

Craig, Hardin, 'Shakespeare's Bad Poetry', *SSu* 1 (1948), 51-6

Crum, Margaret, *First-Line Index of English Poetry 1500-1800 in Manuscripts of the Bodleian Library Oxford*, 2 vols. (1969)

Culliford, S. G., *William Strachey 1572-1621* (1965)

Dawson, Giles, 'Hand D is Shakespeare's Hand' (seminar paper, Shakespeare Association of America conference, 1982; revised and expanded version forthcoming)

Dobell, Bertram, ed., *The Poetical Works of William Strode* (1907)

Dominik, Mark, *William Shakespeare and 'The Birth of Merlin'* (1985)

Duncan-Jones, Katherine, 'Was the 1609 Shake-speares Sonnets really Unauthorized?', *RES* 134 (1983), 151-71

Edmond, Mary, 'Pembroke's Men', *RES* 25 (1974), 129-36

Edwards, Philip, 'An Approach to the Problem of *Pericles*', *SSu* 5 (1952), 25-49

Ellis-Fermor, Una, '*Timon of Athens*: An Unfinished Play', *RES* 18 (1942), 270-83; reprinted in her *Shakespeare the Dramatist* (1961), ed. Kenneth Muir

Everitt, E. B., *The Young Shakespeare: Studies in Documentary Evidence* (1954)

Fitch, John G., 'Sense-Pauses and Relative Dating in Seneca, Sophocles, and Shakespeare', *American Journal of Philology*, 102 (1981), 289-307

Forker, Charles, 'Webster or Shakespeare? Style, Idiom, Vocabulary, and Spelling in the Additions to *Sir Thomas More*', in '*Sir Thomas More*': *The Play and the Problem*, ed. T. H. Howard-Hill (forthcoming)

Foster, Donald, letter to the *TLS* (24 January 1986)

Frazier, Harriet C., *A Babble of Ancestral Voices* (1974)

Freeman, Arthur, *Thomas Kyd: Facts and Problems* (1967), 70-9

Frehafer, John, '*Cardenio*, by Shakespeare and Fletcher', *PMLA* 84 (1969), 501-13

Frey, Charles, '"O sacred, shadowy, cold, and constant queen": Shakespeare's Imperiled and Chastening Daughters of Romance', in *The Woman's Part: Feminist Criticism of Shakespeare*, ed. C. R. S. Lenz, G. Greene, and C. T. Neely (1980), 295-313

George, David, 'Shakespeare and Pembroke's Men', *SQ* 32 (1981), 305-23

Goldring, Beth, 'Eyases, Essex, and Ostend' (unpublished seminar paper, Shakespeare Association of America conference, 1982)

Gooch, J. L., ed., *The Lamentable Tragedy of Locrine: A Critical Edition* (1981)

Granville-Barker, Harley, '*Cymbeline*', in *Prefaces to Shakespeare*, Second Series (1930)

Gray, H. D., 'Chronology of Shakespeare's Plays', *Modern Language Notes*, 46 (1931), 147-50

Green, William, *Shakespeare's 'The Merry Wives of Windsor'* (1962)

Greg, W. W., 'The Bakings of Betsy' [1911], in *Collected Papers*, ed. J. C. Maxwell (1966), 48-74

—— 'Shakespeare's Hand Once More' [1927], in *Collected Papers*, 192-200

—— *Dramatic Documents from the Elizabethan Playhouses*, 2 vols. (1931)

—— 'The Date of *King Lear* and Shakespeare's Use of Earlier Versions of the Story', *The Library*, 20 (1939), 377-400

—— 'Shakespeare and *Arden of Faversham*', *RES* 21 (1945), 134-6
—— 'Authorship Attributions in the Early Play-Lists, 1656-1671', *Transactions of the Edinburgh Bibliographical Society*, 2 (1946), 305-29
Grosart, A. B., ed., *The Works in Verse and Prose of Nicholas Breton*, 2 vols. (1879)
Gurr, Andrew, ed., *Philaster*, by Francis Beaumont and John Fletcher, Revels Plays (1969)
Hamilton, Charles, *In Search of Shakespeare* (1985)
—— views on *Edmond Ironside* quoted in Don Caruthers, 'Much Ado: A Shakespearean Whodunnit', *Dramatics*, 58 (1986), 14-19
Hammond, Brean S., 'Theobald's *Double Falsehood*: An "Agreeable Cheat"?', *N&Q* 229 (1984), 2-3
Harrison, G. B., *A Last Elizabethan Journal* (1933), 95-7
Hart, Alfred, *Shakespeare and the Homilies* (1934)
—— *Stolne and Surreptitious Copies* (1942)
—— 'Vocabularies of Shakespeare's Plays', *RES* 19 (1943), 128-40
—— 'The Growth of Shakespeare's Vocabulary', *RES* 19 (1943), 242-54
Hebel, J. William, ed., *The Works of Michael Drayton* (1931; rev. 1961)
Hill, R. F., 'The Composition of *Titus Andronicus*', *SSu* 10 (1957), 60-70
Hobday, C. H., 'Why the Sweets Melted: A Study in Shakespeare's Imagery', *SQ* 16 (1965), 3-17
Holdsworth, R. V., 'Middleton and Shakespeare: The Case for Middleton's Hand in *Timon of Athens*', unpublished Ph.D. thesis, University of Manchester, 1982 (forthcoming)
Holmer, Joan Ozark, '"When Jacob Graz'd His Uncle Laban's Sheep": A New Source for *The Merchant of Venice*', *SQ* 36 (1985), 64-5
Honigmann, E. A. J., 'The Date of *Hamlet*', *SSu* 9 (1956), 24-34
—— 'Shakespeare's Revised Plays: *King Lear* and *Othello*', *The Library*, VI, 4 (1982), 142-73
—— *Shakespeare's Impact on his Contemporaries* (1982)
—— 'The Date and Revision of *Troilus and Cressida*', in *Textual Criticism and Literary Interpretation*, ed. Jerome McGann (1985), 38-54
—— *Shakespeare: the 'lost years'* (1985)
Hotson, Leslie, *Shakespeare versus Shallow* (1931)
—— *The First Night of 'Twelfth Night'* (1954)
Hoy, Cyrus, 'The Shares of Fletcher and his Collaborators in the Beaumont and Fletcher Canon', *SB* 8 (1956), 129-46; 9 (1957), 143-62; 11 (1958), 85-106; 12 (1959), 91-116; 13 (1960), 77-108; 14 (1961), 45-68; 15 (1962), 71-90.
—— review of Paul Bertram, *Modern Philology* 67 (1969), 83-8
Hubbel, L. W., *Note on the Shakespeare Apocrypha* (1977)
Hunter, William B., 'The Date and Occasion for *A Midsummer Night's Dream*', in *Milton's Comus: Family Piece* (1983)
—— 'The First Performance of *A Midsummer Night's Dream*', *N&Q* 230 (1985), 45-7
Jackson, MacD. P., 'Affirmative Particles in *Henry VIII*', *N&Q* 107 (1962), 372-4
—— 'Material Toward an Edition of *Arden of Faversham*', unpublished B.Litt. thesis, University of Oxford, 1963
—— 'Shakespeare and *Edmund Ironside*', *N&Q* 208 (1963), 331-2
—— 'Edward Archer's Ascription of *Mucedorus* to Shakespeare', *Journal of the Australasian Universities Language and Literature Association*, 22 (1964), 233-48
—— *Shakespeare's 'A Lover's Complaint': Its Date and Authenticity* (1965)
—— '*Edward III*, Shakespeare, and Pembroke's Men', *N&Q* 210 (1965), 329-31
—— 'North's Plutarch and the Name "Escanes"', *N&Q* 220 (1975), 173-4
—— 'Linguistic Evidence for the Date of Shakespeare's Additions to *Sir Thomas More*', *N&Q* 223 (1978), 155-6
—— *Studies in Attribution: Middleton and Shakespeare* (1979)
—— 'Hand D of *Sir Thomas More*', *N&Q* 226 (1981), 146
—— 'Editions and Textual Studies', *SSu* 38 (1985), 245-6
—— 'Some Thoughts on the "Shakespearian" Additions to *Sir Thomas More*' (forthcoming)
Jaggard, William, *Shakespeare Bibliography* (1910)
Jones, Emrys, *Scenic Form in Shakespeare* (1971)
—— *The Origins of Shakespeare* (1977)
Jones-Davies, M. T., *Un peintre de la vie londonienne, Thomas Dekker*, 2 vols. (1958)
Jowett, John, 'Henry Chettle and the Original Text of *Sir Thomas More*', in *Sir Thomas More: The Play and the Problem*, ed. T. H. Howard-Hill (forthcoming)
—— and Taylor, Gary, '"With New Additions": Theatrical Interpolation in *Measure for Measure*', in Jowett and Taylor, *Shakespeare Re-shaped, 1606-23* (forthcoming)
Kenny, Anthony, *A Stylometric Study of the New Testament* (1986), 'Sentence Length and Positional Stylometry', pp. 101-15
Kerrigan, John, '*Love's Labour's Lost* and Shakespearian Revision', *SQ* 33 (1982), 337-9
Knight, G. Wilson, *The Crown of Life* (1947)
Knutson, Roslyn L., 'Henslowe's Naming of Parts', *N&Q* 228 (1983), 157-60
—— 'Henslowe's Diary and the Economics of Play Revision for Revival, 1592-1603', *Theatre Research International*, 10 (1985), 1-18
Koskenniemi, Inna, 'Themes and Imagery in *Edward III*', *Neuphilologische Mitteilungen*, 65 (1964), 446-80
Kramer, Joseph E., '*Titus Andronicus*: The "Fly-Killing" Incident', *SSt* 5 (1969), 9-19
Kuhl, E. P., 'The Authorship of *The Taming of the Shrew*', *PMLA* 40 (1925), 551-618
Lake, David, 'Rhymes in *Pericles*', *N&Q* 214 (1969), 139-43
—— *The Canon of Middleton's Plays* (1975)
—— 'The Date of the *Sir Thomas More* Additions by Dekker and Shakespeare', *N&Q* 222 (1977), 114-16
Lancashire, Anne, and Levenson, Jill, 'Anonymous Plays', in *The Predecessors of Shakespeare: A Survey and Bibliography of Recent Studies in English Renaissance Drama*, ed. Terence P. Logan and Denzell S. Smith (1973)
—— 'Anonymous Plays', in *The Popular School: A Survey and Bibliography of Recent Studies in English Renaissance Drama*, ed. Terence P. Logan and Denzell S. Smith (1975)
Langworthy, Charles, 'A Verse-Sentence Analysis of Shakespeare's Plays', *PMLA* 46 (1931), 738-51
Lavin, J. A., 'John Danter's Ornament Stock', *SB* 23 (1970), 21-44
Lever, J. W., 'Three Notes on Shakespeare's Plants', *RES* 3 (1952), 117-29
—— 'Shakespeare's French Fruits', *SSu* 6 (1953), 79-90
—— 'The Date of *Measure for Measure*', *SQ* 10 (1959), 381-4
Limon, Jerzy, *Gentlemen of a Company: English Players in Central and Eastern Europe, 1590-1660* (1985)
Logan, George M., 'Lucan-Daniel-Shakespeare: New Light on the Relation Between *The Civil Wars* and *Richard II*', *SSt* 9 (1976), 121-40
Loomis, F. A., 'Master of the Tiger', *SQ* 7 (1956), 457
Lowes, John Livingston, unpublished metrical analysis of *All's Well*, Harvard University Archives (summarized in Hunter's edn., 1959)
McManaway, James, 'Recent Studies in Shakespeare's Chronology', *SSu* 3 (1950), 22-33
McMillin, Scott, 'Casting for Pembroke's Men', *SQ* 23 (1972), 141-59
—— 'The Plots of *The Dead Man's Fortune* and *2 Seven Deadly Sins*: Inferences for Theatre Historians', *SB* 26 (1973), 235-43
—— 'Simon Jewell and the Queen's Men', *RES* 27 (1976), 174-7
—— 'The Book of *Sir Thomas More*: Dates and Acting Companies', in '*Sir Thomas More': The Play and the Problem*, ed. T. H. Howard-Hill (forthcoming)
Martin, Randall, 'Critical Editions of *Edmond Ironside* and Anthony Brewer's *The Lovesick King*', unpublished D.Phil. thesis, University of Oxford, 1986
Maxwell, Baldwin, *Studies in the Shakespeare Apocrypha* (1956)
—— 'Conjectures on *The London Prodigal*', in *Studies in Honor of T. W. Baldwin*, ed. Don Cameron Allen (1958), 171-84
Maxwell, J. C., 'Peele and Shakespeare: A Stylometric Test', *Journal of English and Germanic Philology*, 49 (1950), 557-61

WORKS CITED

Melchiori, Giorgio, 'The Book of Sir Thomas More: A Chronology of Revision', SQ 37 (1986), 291-308

Merriam, Thomas, 'Henry VIII and the Integrity of the First Folio', The Bard, 3 (1981), 69-73

—— 'The Authorship of Sir Thomas More', Association for Literary and Linguistic Computing Bulletin, 10 (1982), 1-8

Metz, G. Harold, Four Plays Ascribed to Shakespeare (1982)

—— 'Disputed Shakespearean Texts and Stylometric Analysis', TEXT, 2 (1985), 149-172

—— '"Voyce and Credyt": the Scholars and Sir Thomas More', in 'Sir Thomas More': The Play and the Problem, ed. T. H. Howard-Hill (forthcoming)

Meyerstein, E. H. W., 'The Vision in Cymbeline', TLS (15 June 1922), 396

Mincoff, Marco, 'The Authorship of The Two Noble Kinsmen', English Studies, 33 (1952), 97-115

Mincoff, Marco, Shakespeare: The First Steps (1976)

Moore, William H., 'An Allusion in 1593 to The Taming of the Shrew?', SQ 15 (1964), 55-60

Morton, Andrew Q., Literary Detection (1978)

Mosteller, F., and Wallace, D., Inference and Disputed Authorship: The Federalist (1964)

Muir, Kenneth, Shakespeare as Collaborator (1960)

—— '"A Lover's Complaint": A Reconsideration', in Shakespeare 1564-1964: A Collection of Modern Essays by Various Hands, ed. Edward A. Bloom (1964); revised in Muir, Shakespeare the Professional (1973), 204-19

Nosworthy, J. M., Shakespeare's Occasional Plays (1965)

Oras, Ants, 'Extra Monosyllables in Henry VIII and the Problem of Authorship', Journal of English and Germanic Philology, 52 (1935), 198-213

—— Pause Patterns in Elizabethan and Jacobean Drama: An Experiment in Prosody, University of Florida Monographs, Humanities, 3 (1960)

Osterberg, V., 'The "Countess Scenes" of Edward III', Shakespeare Jahrbuch, 65 (1929), 49-91

Partridge, A. C., The Problem of 'Henry VIII' Re-opened (1949)

—— Orthography in Shakespeare and Elizabethan Drama (1969)

Paul, H. N., The Royal Play of 'Macbeth' (1950)

Pitcher, Seymour, The Case for Shakespeare's Authorship of The Famous Victories (1961)

Pollard, A. W., 'Introduction', in Shakespeare's Hand in the Play of 'Sir Thomas More' (1923), 1-40

Price, Hereward T., 'The Authorship of Titus Andronicus', Journal of English and Germanic Philology, 42 (1943), 55-81

—— Construction in Shakespeare (1951)

Proudfoot, G. R., 'The Reign of King Edward the Third (1595) and Shakespeare', British Academy Annual Shakespeare Lecture, 1985 (forthcoming)

Ringler, William A., Jr., 'The Number of Actors in Shakespeare's Early Plays', in The Seventeenth-Century Stage, ed. G. E. Bentley (1968), 110-34

Rittenhouse, Jonathan, ed., A Critical Edition of 1 Sir John Oldcastle (1984)

Roberts, Jeanne, Shakespeare's English Comedy: 'The Merry Wives of Windsor' (1979), 41-50

Sampley, A. M., 'Plot Structure in Peele's Plays as a Test of Authorship', PMLA 51 (1936), 689-701

Sams, Eric, 'The Timing of the Shrews', N&Q 230 (1985), 33-45

Sarrazin, G., 'Wortechos bei Shakespeare', Shakespeare Jahrbuch 33 (1897), 121-65, and 34 (1898), 119-69

Sasek, Lawrence A., ed., The Poems of William Smith, Louisiana State University Studies, 20 (1970)

Schanzer, Ernest, 'Thomas Platter's Observations on the Elizabethan Stage', N&Q 201 (1956), 466-7

Schoenbaum, S., Internal Evidence and Elizabethan Dramatic Authorship: An Essay in Literary History and Method (1966)

Shanker, Sidney, 'Shakespeare Pays Some Compliments', Modern Language Notes, 63 (1948), 540-1

Shapiro, I. A., 'Richard II or Richard III or ... ?', SQ 9 (1958), 204-6

Shawcross, John T., Milton: A Bibliography for the Years 1624-1700 (1984)

Simpson, Richard, 'Are there any Extant MSS. in Shakespere's Handwriting?', N&Q 183 (1 July 1871), 1-3

Sisson, C. J., review of Everitt, SQ 6 (1955), 456

Slater, Eliot, 'Word Links Between Poems and Plays', N&Q 220 (1975), 157-63

—— 'Word Links with The Merry Wives of Windsor', N&Q 220 (1975), 169-71

—— 'Word Links with All's Well that Ends Well', N&Q 222 (1977), 109-12

—— 'Word Links Between Timon of Athens and King Lear', N&Q 223 (1978), 147-9

—— 'Word Links from Troilus to Othello and Macbeth', The Bard, 2 (1978), 4-22

—— 'The Problem of The Reign of King Edward III, 1596: A Statistical Approach', unpublished Ph.D. thesis, University of London, 1981

Smith, Irwin, 'Ariel and the Masque in The Tempest', SQ 21 (1970), 213-22

Smith, M. W. A., 'The Authorship of Pericles: Collocations Investigated Again', The Bard, 4 (1983), 15-21

—— 'An Investigation of Morton's Method to Distinguish Elizabethan Playwrights', Computers and the Humanities, 19 (1985), 3-21

Smith, R. M., 'Edward III: A Study of the Authorship of the Drama in the Light of a New Source', Journal of English and Germanic Philology, 10 (1911), 90-104

Spedding, James, 'Who Wrote Shakespeare's Henry VIII?', The Gentleman's Magazine, NS 34 (August 1850), 115-23

Spurgeon, Caroline, Shakespeare's Imagery and What It Tells Us (1935)

Stamp, A. E., The Disputed Revels Accounts (1930)

Stern, Virginia P., Gabriel Harvey: his Life, Marginalia, and Library (1979)

Stone, P. W. K., The Textual History of 'King Lear' (1980)

Sykes, Dugdale, Sidelights on Elizabethan Drama (1924), 1-48

Taylor, Estelle W., 'Shakespeare's Use of s/th Endings of Certain Verbs', unpublished Ph.D. thesis, Catholic University of America, 1969

Taylor, Gary, 'A New Source and an Old Date for King Lear', RES 132 (1982), 396-413

—— 'Musophilus, Nosce Teipsum, and Julius Caesar', N&Q 229 (1984), 191-5

—— 'Some Manuscripts of Shakespeare's Sonnets', Bulletin of the John Rylands University Library of Manchester, 68 (1985), 210-46

—— 'Shakespeare and Others: The Composition of Henry the Sixth, Part One', forthcoming in Medieval and Renaissance Drama in England

—— 'Richard III': The Nature and Preparation of the Folio Copy (forthcoming)

—— 'William Shakespeare, Richard James, and the House of Cobham', RES, NS 38 (1987), 334-54

—— 'The Date and Auspices of the Additions to Sir Thomas More', in 'Sir Thomas More': The Play and the Problem, ed. T. H. Howard-Hill (forthcoming)

Thiele, Joachim, 'Untersuchung der Vermutung J. D. Wilson über den Verfasser des ersten Aktes von Shakespeares "King Henry VI, First Part" mit Hilfe einfacher Textcharakteristiken', Grundlagenstudien aus Kybernetik und Geisteswissenschaft, 6 (1965), 25-7

Thomas, Sidney, 'The Earthquake in Romeo and Juliet', Modern Language Notes, 64 (1949), 417-19

Thompson, Ann, Shakespeare's Chaucer: A Study in Literary Origins (1978)

—— 'Dating Evidence for The Taming of the Shrew', N&Q 227 (1982), 108-9

Thompson, E. Maunde, 'The Autograph Manuscripts of Anthony Munday', Transactions of the Bibliographical Society, 14 (1915-17), 324-53

—— 'The Handwriting of the Three Pages Attributed to Shakespeare Compared with his Signatures', in Shakespeare's Hand in the Play of 'Sir Thomas More', ed. A. W. Pollard (1923), 57-112

Timberlake, Philip W., The Feminine Ending in English Blank Verse (1931)

Tobin, J. J. M., 'Nashe and the Texture of Romeo and Juliet', Aligarh Journal of English Studies, 5 (1980), 162-74

—— 'Nashe and Romeo and Juliet', N&Q 225 (1980), 161-2

Ule, Louis, *Concordance to the Works of Christopher Marlowe* (1979)
—— 'Recent Progress in Computer Methods of Authorship Determination', *Association of Literary and Linguistic Computing Bulletin*, 10 (1982), 73-89

Waldo, T.R., and Herbert, T.W., 'Musical Terms in *The Shrew*: Evidence of Single Authorship', *SQ* 10 (1959), 185-99

Walker, Alice, 'The Text of *Measure for Measure*', *RES*, NS 34 (1983), 1-20

Waller, Frederick O., 'The Use of Linguistic Criteria in Determining the Copy and Dates for Shakespeare's Plays', in *Pacific Coast Studies in Shakespeare*, ed. Waldo F. McNeir and Thelma N. Greenfield (1966), 1-19

Wallis, Helen M., 'The First English Globe: A Recent Discovery', *The Geographical Journal*, 117 (1951), 275-90

Wells, Stanley, 'The Failure of *The Two Gentlemen of Verona*', *Shakespeare Jahrbuch*, 99 (1963), 161-73
—— 'Dating *Othello*', letter to *TLS* (20 July 1984)

Wells, William, '*Timon of Athens*', *N&Q* 112 (1920), 226-9

Wentersdorf, Karl, 'Shakespearean Chronology and the Metrical Tests', in *Shakespeare-Studien*, ed. W. Fischer and K. Wentersdorf (1951)
—— 'The Authenticity of *The Taming of the Shrew*', *SQ* 5 (1954), 11-32
—— 'The Authorship of *Edward III*', unpublished Ph.D. thesis, University of Cincinnati, 1960
—— 'Imagery as a Criterion of Authenticity: A Reconsideration of the Problem', *SQ* 23 (1972), 231-59
—— '*Richard III* (Q1) and the Pembroke "Bad" Quartos', *English Language Notes*, 14 (1977), 257-64

Wickham, Glynne, 'To Fly or Not to Fly? The Problem of Hecate in Shakespeare's *Macbeth*', in *Essays on Drama and Theatre: Liber Amicorum Benjamin Hunningher*, ed. P. Binnerts *et al.* (1973), 171-82
—— 'Reflections upon two recent productions of *Love's Labour's Lost* and *As You Like It*' (forthcoming)

Wilson, John Dover, 'Appendix: The Spellings of the Three Pages, with Parallels from the Quartos', in *Shakespeare's Hand in the Play of 'Sir Thomas More'*, ed. A. W. Pollard (1923), 132-41

Wing, Donald, *Short-Title Catalogue . . . 1640-1700*, 3 vols. (1945-51; rev. 1972-)

Wittreich, Joseph, '*Image of that Horror*': History, Prophecy, and Apocalypse in '*King Lear*' (1984), 47-74

Yardi, M. R., 'A Statistical Approach to the Problem of Chronology of Shakespeare's Plays', *Sankya*, 7 (1945), 263-8

SUMMARY OF CONTROL-TEXTS

We here summarize our choice of control-text(s) for the works included in the Oxford edition, and briefly recount our view of the nature of the copy, usually a manuscript, which stands immediately behind each control-text. Further information is provided in the Introductions to individual works, below.

W.L.M./(S.W.W.)

WORK	CONTROL-TEXT	NATURE OF UNDERLYING COPY	COMMENT
The Two Gentlemen of Verona	F	Crane transcript of either holograph (foul papers) or a manuscript prepared for use in the theatre	F's text is expurgated.
The Taming of the Shrew	F	Possibly holograph (foul papers); possibly a scribal transcript of them	The manuscript seems to have been annotated for the theatre.
The First Part of the Contention	F and Q1 (1594); additional matter from Q1	F: holograph (foul papers) Q1 (additional matter): report of a revised prompt-book	Five passages in F (see introduction) seem to have been set from a copy of Q3 (1619); for these passages Q1, Q3's copy, serves as our control-text. We also adopt other matter from Q, absent from F, which appears to derive from a revised version of the play.
The True Tragedy of Richard Duke of York	F	Holograph (foul papers)	The Folio compositors seem also to have consulted Q3 (1619).
Titus Andronicus	Q1 (1594); additional matter from F	Q1: holograph (foul papers) F (additional matter): prompt-book	The principal copy for F, Q3 (1611), was supplemented by reference, probably, to a prompt-book.
1 Henry VI	F	Holograph (collaborative foul papers)	The manuscript seems to have been annotated for the theatre.
Richard III	F for substance; Q1 (1597) for incidentals	F: annotated Q3 (1602) and Q6 (1622) Q1: communal report	——
Venus and Adonis	Q1 (1593)	Holograph (fair copy)	——
The Rape of Lucrece	Q1 (1594)	Holograph (fair copy)	——
The Comedy of Errors	F	Holograph (foul papers)	
Love's Labour's Lost	Q1 (1598)	Lost earlier quarto (Q0), set from holograph (foul papers)	The copy for F, Q0 or Q1, seems to have been annotated from a theatre manuscript.
A Midsummer Night's Dream	Q1 (1600)	Holograph (foul papers)	The copy for F, Q2 (1619), was annotated from a prompt-book.
Romeo and Juliet	Q2 (1599); Q1 (1597) for one passage	Q2: holograph (foul papers) Q1: report	For one passage (1.2.52–1.3.36/301–88), Q2 seems to have been set from a copy of Q1; for this passage we adopt Q1 as our control-text. The copy for F, Q3 (1609), may have been lightly annotated from a theatre manuscript.
Richard II	Q1 (1597); additional matter from F	Q1: holograph F (additional matter): prompt-book	The principal copy for F, Q3 (1598), was supplemented by reference, probably, to a prompt-book.
King John	F	Transcript, made by two scribes, possibly of foul papers	F's text is expurgated.
The Merchant of Venice	Q1 (1600)	Holograph (fair copy), or perhaps a scribal transcript of it	The copy for F, Q1, appears to have been annotated from a prompt-book.

SUMMARY OF CONTROL-TEXTS

WORK	CONTROL-TEXT	NATURE OF UNDERLYING COPY	COMMENT
1 Henry IV	Q1 (1598) for one section; Q2 (1598) elsewhere	Q1: scribal transcript of authorial papers Q2: Q1	Only the one section of Q1 survives. The copy for F, Q6 (1613), appears to have been annotated, perhaps from a transcript of a prompt-book.
The Merry Wives of Windsor	F	Crane transcript, possibly of a post-1606 prompt-book	Q1 (1602) is evidently based on a report. F's text is expurgated.
2 Henry IV	Q1 (1600); additional matter from F	Q1: holograph (foul papers) F (additional matter): scribal transcript of holograph (fair copy) used as prompt-book	F's text is expurgated.
Much Ado About Nothing	Q1 (1600)	Holograph (foul papers)	The copy for F, Q1, appears to have been influenced by a prompt-book.
Henry V	F; additional matter from Q1 (1600)	F: holograph (foul papers) Q1 (additional matter): report of revised prompt-book	The Folio compositors seem also to have consulted Q3 (1619).
Julius Caesar	F	Prompt-book, or a transcript of it	There is little to indicate whether the copy was holograph or scribal.
As You Like It	F	Prompt-book or a literary transcript	There is little to indicate the precise nature of the copy.
Hamlet	F for substance; Q2 (1604) for incidentals	F: scribal transcript, which may have been used as a prompt-book, of a revised holograph (fair copy) Q2: holograph (foul papers)	Q2 was influenced by Q1 (1603), a report; the Folio compositors may also have consulted Q3 (1611).
Twelfth Night	F	Scribal transcript of uncertain origin	——
Troilus and Cressida	F for substance; Q1 (1609) for incidentals	F: Q1 Q1: holograph (foul papers)	The copy of Q1 from which F was set appears to have been extensively and systematically annotated from a prompt-book
Sonnets, and 'A Lover's Complaint'	Q1 (1609)	Transcript of author's revised manuscript	——
Various Poems:			
'A Song'	Rawlinson poet. MS 160, fols. 108^v–109^v, a transcript	An earlier transcript of unknown provenance	——
'Upon a pair of gloves'	Shakespeare Birthplace Trust Records Office MS ER.93, p. 177, a transcript in the hand of Sir Francis Fane	Unknown	——
The Passionate Pilgrim	1599^1; additional matter, 1599^2	1599^1: a transcript of unknown provenance 1599^2: 1599^1	Only a fragment of 1599^1 survives.
'The Phoenix and Turtle'	Robert Chester's Loves Martyr (1601), sigs. Z3^v–Z4^v	Unknown	——
'Verses upon the Stanley Tomb'	Stanley tomb at Tong	Unknown	——
'On Ben Jonson'	Bodleian MS Ashmole 38, p. 181, a transcript, probably in the hand of Nicholas Burgh	Unknown	——
'An Epitaph on Elias James'	Stowe's Survey of London (1633), p. 825	Transcript of tombstone	——
'An extemporary epitaph on John Combe'	Folger MS V.a.147, fol. 72^r, a transcript, probably in the hand of Robert Dobyns	Combe's tomb (?)	——
'Another Epitaph on John Combe'	Bodleian MS Ashmole 38, p. 180, a transcript, probably in the hand of Nicholas Burgh	Unknown	——
'Upon the King'	James I's Works (1616), frontispiece	Unknown	——
'Epitaph on Himself'	Shakespeare's grave at Stratford	Holograph (?)	——
Sir Thomas More	BL MS Harley 7368: Add.II.D (fols. 8^r–9^r), holograph (foul papers); Add.III (fol. 11*^{v}), a scribal transcript (of foul papers?)	——	——
Measure for Measure	F	Crane transcript of a prompt-book reflecting late, non-authorial adaptation	F's text is expurgated.

SUMMARY OF CONTROL-TEXTS

WORK	CONTROL-TEXT	NATURE OF UNDERLYING COPY	COMMENT
Othello	F for substance; Q1 (1622) for incidentals	F: scribal transcript of Shakespeare's revised manuscript Q1: scribal transcript of foul papers	F's text is expurgated.
All's Well That Ends Well	F	Holograph (foul papers)	The foul papers may have been annotated by a book-keeper.
Timon of Athens	F	Holograph (foul papers) of both Shakespeare and Middleton	——
The History of King Lear	Q1 (1608)	Holograph (foul papers)	——
The Tragedy of King Lear	F	Q2 (1619), annotated from either holograph or scribal transcript of holograph	Spelling and punctuation of F are heavily influenced by Q2.
Macbeth	F; additional matter from Thomas Middleton, *The Witch*, a Crane transcript (Bodelian MS Malone 12)	F: scribal transcript (a prompt-book) Middleton: uncertain	F's copy may itself have been the prompt-book, or a transcript of it.
Antony and Cleopatra	F	Holograph (foul papers) or a scribal transcript of it	——
Pericles	Q1 (1609), with additional matter based on George Wilkins's *The Painful Adventures of Pericles, Prince of Tyre* (1608)	Q1: report Wilkins: holograph	——
Coriolanus	F	Scribal transcript (possibly of a prompt-book)	——
The Winter's Tale	F	Crane transcript (possibly of authorial fair copy, and probably a prompt-book)	The satyr dance seems to be a slightly later theatrical addition.
Cymbeline	F	Scribal transcript, probably by Crane, of a manuscript in two hands	It is difficult to say much about the manuscript that the scribe copied.
The Tempest	F	Crane transcript (of foul papers?)	Crane seems to have been influenced by memories of performance.
All Is True	F	Scribal transcript of uncertain origin	——
The Two Noble Kinsmen	Q1 (1634)	Probably holograph (fair copy?) of Shakespeare and Fletcher, but possibly a scribal transcript of such a document	The copy for Q1 appears to have contained at least two layers of theatrical annotations; the later of these was probably by Edward Knight.

ATTRIBUTIONS TO COMPOSITORS OF THE FIRST FOLIO

The foundation of modern studies of the composition of the 1623 Folio was laid by Charlton Hinman's *The Printing and Proof-Reading of the First Folio of Shakespeare* (1963). Primarily on the basis of recurring types, and of the spelling of three common words (*do, go,* and *here*), Hinman identified five compositors: A, B, C, D, and E. Hinman's work remained unchallenged for a decade. Then T. H. Howard-Hill split Hinman's Compositor A into two workmen, A and F, and on the basis of a wider survey of evidence redistributed a number of pages in the Comedies ('The Compositors of Shakespeare's Folio Comedies', *SB* 26 (1973), 62-106); Howard-Hill's conclusions were themselves sophisticated by John S. O'Connor ('Compositors D and F of the Shakespeare First Folio', *SB* 28 (1975), 81-117). Howard-Hill has accepted most of O'Connor's revision of his hypothesis, but he has privately supplied us with additional evidence which supports the attribution of column b of F1 and column a of F1^v to Compositor D rather than C. Hinman's type-recurrence evidence was re-examined, with particular implications for compositor assignments in quires G, H, and I, by Paul Werstine ('Cases and Compositors in the Shakespeare First Folio Comedies', *SB* 35 (1982), 206-34). Howard-Hill also investigated the integrity of Compositors E and B, first in two privately circulated monographs ('Compositors B and E in the Shakespeare First Folio and Some Recent Studies' (1976) and 'A Reassessment of Compositors B and E in the First Folio Tragedies' (1977)), then in 'New Light on Compositor E of the Shakespeare First Folio' (*The Library*, VI, 2 (1980), 156-78). These studies resulted in some modification of Hinman's attributions, particularly in assigning to Compositor E a greater share of the Tragedies. Howard-Hill expressed doubts about Compositor E's responsibility for pp6 and pp6^v of *Hamlet*, but has not yet provided an explanation or defence of those doubts; we have accordingly queried E's presence, but not reattributed the pages to B. Howard-Hill's new attributions in the Tragedies conflict at several points with Hinman's case identifications; the discrepancies have not yet been explained, but Werstine is at work on a re-examination of recurring types in the affected texts (unpublished seminar paper, Shakespeare Association of America, 1982). Gary Taylor, focusing primarily upon attributions with which Hinman himself was dissatisfied, further diminished Compositor A's share of the volume by identifying three new minor compositors: H, I, and J ('The Shrinking Compositor A of the Shakespeare First Folio', *SB* 34 (1981), 96-117). Of these identifications, H and I are most secure, and seem to have been generally accepted, but J remains problematic. The identification is tentatively supported, and the distinction between B and his partner in the *Henry IV* plays solidified, by S. W. Reid ('B and "J": Two Compositors in Two Plays of the Shakespeare First Folio', *The Library*, VII, 2 (1985), 126-36). Paul Werstine, however, believes that the pages Taylor assigns to J were set by A; his argument has not yet been published, but in deference to it we have queried all attributions to J, below. Jeanne Roberts has questioned the existence of F, noting that almost all the evidence used to distinguish that putative compositor from D consists of spellings which could be due to the influence of manuscript copy prepared by Ralph Crane: F has been identified only in four plays believed to have been set from Crane manuscripts ('Ralph Crane and the Text of *The Tempest*', *SSt* 13 (1980), 221). Roberts's suggestion has been taken up and extensively documented by Werstine, in a forthcoming article. We find Werstine's evidence compelling, and have hence substituted 'D?' for 'F' in the relevant pages of *The Tempest, Two Gentlemen, Merry Wives,* and *Measure* in Table 11, below; in Table 12, however, we identify these pages as the work of 'D? (F?)', to enable readers to locate the disputed passages. In addition to these major studies, other investigations, not primarily devoted to compositor identification, have clarified the attribution of particular disputed pages. John Jowett's 'Ligature Shortage and Speech-prefix Variation in *Julius Caesar*' confirms Compositor B's responsibility for the second column of ll3 (*The Library*, VI, 6 (1984), 244-53; 252 n. 9); Gary Taylor's 'The Folio Copy for *Hamlet, King Lear,* and *Othello*' throws doubt on the attribution to either B or E of dd3^v of *Titus* (*SQ* 34 (1983), 45), and those doubts are confirmed by Paul Werstine, 'Folio Editors, Folio Compositors, and the Folio Text of *King Lear*', in *Division*, p. 262. Taylor also, in *Three Studies*, offers reasons for supposing that the setting of h5 preceded that of h2^v (p. 64), thus reversing the order tentatively suggested by Hinman (ii. 17). In 'Folio Compositors and Folio Copy: *King Lear* and its Context', Taylor notes the lack of clear evidence as to whether B or E set the bottom of column a of rr1^v (*PBSA* 79 (1985), 46-7).

After a quarter-century of further research, the great bulk of Hinman's work remains intact, and has been supported by the collection of much new evidence. Although we do not expect the attributions summarized here to remain in every particular unchallenged, we shall be surprised if the next quarter-century much alters the fundamental pattern. Hinman's type-recurrence evidence must some day all be re-examined, and supplemented by more intensive studies of the kind already undertaken for certain Jacobean quartos; computerized concordances to the Folio should make possible more systematic analysis of spelling patterns, which may clarify certain attribution problems. The following summaries will, we hope, prove useful to future investigators.

Hinman's conclusions were summarized in a chart (ii. 514-

ATTRIBUTIONS TO COMPOSITORS OF THE FIRST FOLIO

18), on which Table 11 is modelled. We have corrected some errors in Hinman's own summary, omitted his identification of the case from which each compositor worked, and taken account of the modifications of his hypothesis by subsequent investigators (detailed above). A slash (/) in Table 11 indicates that two or more compositors set a single page; most commonly, the first compositor named set the first column ('*a*', in Table 12) and the second the second ('*b*'). However, pages were sometimes divided within columns, rather than between them; Table 12 identifies such stints with the abbreviation '*pt*' (for 'part of a page'). Square brackets mark blank pages (hh6^v). Of the pages referred to as *gg2^v–5, *gg2^v (the penultimate page of *Romeo*) was reimposed (but not reset) as gg2^v (and so appears twice in Table 11, once with its original forme-mate, *gg5, and once with its later forme-mate, gg1); *gg4 and *gg4^v were salvaged as the pages immediately following those referred to as χ1–1^v (the Prologue and first page of *Troilus*); pages *gg3 and *gg3^v (the original last page of *Romeo* and first of *Troilus*) were cancelled (the cancelland is reproduced in *The Norton Facsimile: The First Folio of Shakespeare* (1968), pp. 916, 918); no copy of page *gg5 survives, though there can be no doubt that it was composed, and little doubt that the workman was Compositor E (Hinman, ii. 237 ff.). Table 11 gives the order of composition, forme by forme, for the entire Folio; Table 12 lists the Folio plays in the order in which they appear in that volume, subdividing them into the shares set by the different compositors. It should be noted that plays were not set in the order in which they appear in Table 12, and that work on them might be interrupted by work elsewhere: the fact that a compositor set a number of sequential lines in a play does not mean that he set those lines sequentially. Line references in Table 12 are keyed both to the through line numbering (TLN) supplied by Hinman to *The Norton Facsimile* and to the continuous line numbering of the Oxford original-spelling edition (1986).

G.T./(W.L.M.)

TABLE 11

COMPOSITOR ATTRIBUTIONS BY PAGE

THE COMEDIES

B B	D? B	B B	B B	C D?	C D?	D? C	C D?	C D?	
A1:6^v	A1^v:6	A3^v:4	A3:4^v	A2^v:5	A2:5^v	B3^v:4	B3:4^v	B2^v:5	
C D?	D? C	D? C	C D?	C D?	C D?	C D?	C D?	C D?	
B2:5^v	B1^v:6	B1:6^v	C3^v:4	C3:4^v	C2^v:5	C2:5^v	C1^v:6	C1:6^v	
D? C	D? C	C C	C C	C C	C C	B B	D? B	B D?	
D3^v:4	D3:4^v	D2^v:5	D2:5^v	D1^v:6	D1:6^v	E3^v:4	E3:4^v	E2^v:5	
B B	B B	B B	C C	D C	D C/D	C/D B	D/C B	C/D C	
E2:5^v	E1^v:6	E1:6^v	F3^v:4	F3:4^v	F2^v:5	F2:5^v	F1^v:6	F1:6^v	
B C/D?	B D?/C	B C	D?/C D?	B D?/C	B/C/B D?/C	D C/D	C/D B	C B	
G3^v:4	G3:4^v	G2^v:5	G2:5^v	G1^v:6	G1:6^v	H3^v:4	H3:4^v	H2^v:5	
D/C D/C	C/D B	C B	D C	B C	B C	B C	B C	B C/B	
H2:5^v	H1^v:6	H1:6^v	I3^v:4	I3:4^v	I1^v:6	I2^v:5	I1:6^v	I2^v:5	
C B	C C	D C/B	C D	C D	C D	C C	C D	C D	
K3^v:4	K3:4^v	K2^v:5	K2:5^v	K1^v:6	K1:6^v	L3^v:4	L3:4^v	L2^v:5	
D D	C D	C D	C B	C B	C B	C B	C B	C B	
L2:5^v	L1^v:6	L1:6^v	M3^v:4	M2^v:5	M3:4^v	M2:5^v	M1^v:6	M1:6^v	
C D	C D	B D	C C	B D	B D	B B/C	C D	C B/C	
N3^v:4	N3:4^v	N2^v:5	N2:5^v	N1^v:6	N1:6^v	O3:4^v	O2^v:5	O3^v:4	
C D	C D	C D	D C	D C	D C	D C/B	C/D/C B	D B/C	
O2:5^v	O1^v:6	O1:6^v	P3^v:4	P3:4^v	P2^v:5	P2:5^v	P1^v:6	P1:6^v	
C B	C D	C D	B C/D	C D	C B	B C	B C	B C	
Q3^v:4	Q3:4^v	Q2^v:5	Q2:5^v	Q1^v:6	Q1:6^v	R3^v:4	R3:4^v	R2^v:5	

ATTRIBUTIONS TO COMPOSITORS OF THE FIRST FOLIO

B C	B C	B B	B B	B B	B B	B B	B B	B B
R2:5ᵛ	R1ᵛ:6	R1:6ᵛ	S3ᵛ:4	S3:4ᵛ	S2ᵛ:5	S2:5ᵛ	S1ᵛ:6	S1:6ᵛ
B B	B B	C D	C D	C D	C D	D C	D C	B B
T3ᵛ:4	T3:4ᵛ	T2ᵛ:5	T2:5ᵛ	T1ᵛ:6	T1:6ᵛ	V3ᵛ:4	V3:4ᵛ	V2:5ᵛ
B B	B B	B B	B B	B B	B B	B B	B B	B B
V2ᵛ:5	V1ᵛ:6	V1:6ᵛ	X3ᵛ:4	X3:4ᵛ	X2ᵛ:5	X2:5ᵛ	X1ᵛ:6	X1ᵛ:6
B B	B B	C C	C C	C C	C C	C C	B B	B B
a3ᵛ:4	a3:4ᵛ	a2ᵛ:5	a2:5ᵛ	a1ᵛ:6	a1:6ᵛ	b3ᵛ:4	b3:4ᵛ	b2ᵛ:5
B B	B B	B B	B B	B B	B B	B B	B B	B B
b2:5ᵛ	b1ᵛ:6	b1:6ᵛ	Y3ᵛ:4	Y3:4ᵛ	Y2ᵛ:5	Y2:5ᵛ	Y1ᵛ:6	Y1:6ᵛ
B B	B B	B B	B B	B	B B	B B	B A	B A
Z3ᵛ:4	Z3:4ᵛ	Z2ᵛ:5	Z2:5ᵛ	Z1:[6ᵛ]	Z1ᵛ:6	c3ᵛ:4	c2ᵛ:5	c3:4ᵛ
B A	B A	B A	A B	A B	A A	A A	A A	A B
c2:5ᵛ	c1:6ᵛ	c1ᵛ:6	Aa3ᵛ:4	Aa3:4ᵛ	Aa2ᵛ:5	Aa2:5ᵛ	Aa1ᵛ:6	Aa1:6ᵛ
B B	B A	B A	B A	B A	B A	A	A B	
Bb3ᵛ:4	Bb3:4ᵛ	Bb2ᵛ:5	Bb2:5ᵛ	Bb1ᵛ:6	Bb1:6ᵛ	Cc1:[2ᵛ]	Cc1ᵛ:2	

THE HISTORIES

B B/A	B A	A A	A A	A A	A A	A A	A B	A B
h3ᵛ:4	h3:4ᵛ	h5:2ᵛ	h2:5ᵛ	h1ᵛ:6	h1:6ᵛ	i3ᵛ:4	i3:4ᵛ	i2ᵛ:5
A A	A A	A B/A	A A	A A	A A/B	A A	A A	A A
i2:5ᵛ	i1ᵛ:6	i1:6ᵛ	k3ᵛ:4	k3:4ᵛ	k2ᵛ:5	k2:5ᵛ	k1ᵛ:6	k1:6ᵛ
B B	A B	A A	A B	A B	A B	B A	B A	B A
l3ᵛ:4	l3:4ᵛ	l2ᵛ:5	l2:5ᵛ	l1ᵛ:6	l1:6ᵛ	m3ᵛ:4	m3:4ᵛ	m2ᵛ:5
B A	B A	B A	A B	A B	A B	A B	A B	A B
m2:5ᵛ	m1ᵛ:6	m1:6ᵛ	n3ᵛ:4	n3:4ᵛ	n2ᵛ:5	n2:5ᵛ	n1ᵛ:6	n1:6ᵛ
B A	B A	B A	B A	B A	B A	B B	A B	A B
o3ᵛ:4	o3:4ᵛ	o2ᵛ:5	o2:5ᵛ	o1:6ᵛ	o1ᵛ:6	d3ᵛ:4	d3:4ᵛ	d2ᵛ:5
A B	B B	A B	B J?	B J?	B J?	B J?	B J?	B J?
d2:5ᵛ	d1ᵛ:6	d1:6ᵛ	e3ᵛ:4	e3:4ᵛ	e2ᵛ:5	e2:5ᵛ	e1ᵛ:6	e1:6ᵛ
J? B	J? B	J? B	B B	J? B	J? B	B B	B J?	B J?
f3ᵛ:4	f3:4ᵛ	f2ᵛ:5	f2:5ᵛ	f1ᵛ:6	f1:6ᵛ	g3ᵛ:4	g3:4ᵛ	g2ᵛ:5
B J?	B J?	B J?	B B?	J? B?	J? B	J? B	J? B	J? B
g2:5ᵛ	g1ᵛ:6	g1:6ᵛ	χgg1:8ᵛ	χgg1ᵛ:8	χgg4ᵛ:5	χgg4:5ᵛ	χgg3ᵛ:6	χgg3:6ᵛ
J?/B/J? B	J? B	B A	B A	B A	B B	B A	B A	
χgg2ᵛ:7	χgg2:7ᵛ	p3ᵛ:4	p3:4ᵛ	p2ᵛ:5	p2:5ᵛ	p1ᵛ:6	p1:6ᵛ	
A B	A B	A B	A B	A B	B B	B B	B B	B B
q3ᵛ:4	q3:4ᵛ	q2ᵛ:5	q2:5ᵛ	q1ᵛ:6	q1:6ᵛ	r3ᵛ:4	r3:4ᵛ	r2ᵛ:5

ATTRIBUTIONS TO COMPOSITORS OF THE FIRST FOLIO

B A	A A	B A	A B	A B	A B	A B	A A	A B
r2:5ᵛ	r1ᵛ:6	r1:6ᵛ	s3ᵛ:4	s3:4ᵛ	s2ᵛ:5	s2:5ᵛ	s1ᵛ:6	s1:6ᵛ

THE TRAGEDIES

B A	B B	B A	B A	? E	B A	E E	B B	E E
aa3ᵛ:4	aa3:4ᵛ	aa2:5ᵛ	aa2ᵛ:5	dd3ᵛ:4	aa1ᵛ:6	dd3:4ᵛ	aa1:6ᵛ	dd2ᵛ:5
A/B B	B E	B E	B B	B E	B E	B B	B E	A B
bb3ᵛ:4	cc1:6ᵛ	cc1ᵛ:6	bb3:4ᵛ	cc2:5ᵛ	cc2ᵛ:5	cc3:4ᵛ	cc3:4ᵛ	kk3ᵛ:4
A B	A B	E E	B B	B B	B B	E E	B B	B B
kk3:4ᵛ	kk2ᵛ:5	dd2:5ᵛ	kk2:5ᵛ	kk1ᵛ:6	kk1:6ᵛ	dd1ᵛ:6	ll3ᵛ:4	ll3:4ᵛ
E E	B B/A	E E	B B	B A	B A	B E	A/B B	B B
dd1:6ᵛ	ll2ᵛ:5	ee3ᵛ:4	ll2:5ᵛ	ll1ᵛ:6	ll1:6ᵛ	ee3:4ᵛ	bb2ᵛ:5	bb2:5ᵛ
B E	A B	A B	E E	A B/A	A A	E E	A A/B	B/A B
ee2ᵛ:5	bb1ᵛ:6	bb1:6ᵛ	ee2:5ᵛ	mm3ᵛ:4	mm3:4ᵛ	ee1ᵛ:6	mm2ᵛ:5	mm2:5ᵛ
A B	E E	A B	B B	E E	B B	B B	B B	E E
mm1ᵛ:6	ee1:6ᵛ	mm1:6ᵛ	nn3ᵛ:4	ff3ᵛ:4	nn3:4ᵛ	nn2ᵛ:5	nn2:5ᵛ	ff3:4ᵛ
B I	E E	B I	E E	B I	B I	B I	B I	E E
nn1ᵛ:6	ff2ᵛ:5	nn1:6ᵛ	ff2:5ᵛ	t3ᵛ:4	t3:4ᵛ	t2ᵛ:5	t2:5ᵛ	ff1ᵛ:6
B I	B I	I B	I B	B B	I B	E E	I B	I B
t1ᵛ:6	t1:6ᵛ	v3ᵛ:4	v3:4ᵛ	v2ᵛ:5	v2:5ᵛ	ff1:6ᵛ	v1ᵛ:6	v1:6ᵛ
B E	B I	B I	E E	E E	B I	B I	I B	B B
*gg3ᵛ:4	x2ᵛ:3	x2:3ᵛ	*gg4ᵛ:3	*gg2ᵛ:5	x1ᵛ:4	x1:4ᵛ	oo3ᵛ:4	oo3:4ᵛ
E E	B B	I B	I B	I/B B	B B/I	E E	B I	B E
gg1:2ᵛ	oo2ᵛ:5	oo2:5ᵛ	oo1ᵛ:6	oo1:6ᵛ	pp3ᵛ:4	gg1ᵛ:2	pp3:4ᵛ	pp2ᵛ:5
B E	B E?	B E?	B E	E E	E B	B E	B E	B E
pp2:5ᵛ	pp1ᵛ:6	pp1:6ᵛ	qq3ᵛ:4	qq3:4ᵛ	qq2ᵛ:5	qq2:5ᵛ	qq1ᵛ:6	qq1:6ᵛ
B B	E B	B B	E B	E/B B	E B	B B	E B	B B
rr3ᵛ:4	rr3:4ᵛ	rr2ᵛ:5	rr2:5ᵛ	rr1ᵛ:6	rr1:6ᵛ	Gg3ᵛ:4	Gg3:4ᵛ	Gg2ᵛ:5
B B	B B	B B	B B	B	B B	B B	E E	B B
Gg2:5ᵛ	Gg1ᵛ:6	Gg1:6ᵛ	hh3ᵛ:4	hh1:[6ᵛ]	hh3:4ᵛ	hh1ᵛ:6	ss3ᵛ:4	hh2:5ᵛ
B B	E E	E E	E E	E E	E B	B B	E B	E B
hh2:5ᵛ	ss2ᵛ:5	ss3:4ᵛ	ss2:5ᵛ	ss1ᵛ:6	ss1:6ᵛ	tt3ᵛ:4	tt3:4ᵛ	tt2ᵛ:5
E B	E B	E B	B B	E B	E B	E B	E B	E B
tt2:5ᵛ	tt1ᵛ:6	tt1:6ᵛ	vv3ᵛ:4	vv3:4ᵛ	vv2ᵛ:5	vv2:5ᵛ	vv1ᵛ:6	vv1:6ᵛ
E E	B E	B E	B B	B E	B E	B B	B B	B B
xx3ᵛ:4	xx3:4ᵛ	xx2ᵛ:5	xx2:5ᵛ	xx1ᵛ:6	xx1:6ᵛ	yy3ᵛ:4	yy3:4ᵛ	yy2ᵛ:5
B B	B B	E B	B B	B B	B B	B B	B B	B E
yy2:5ᵛ	yy1ᵛ:6	yy1:6ᵛ	zz3ᵛ:4	zz3:4ᵛ	zz2ᵛ:5	zz2:5ᵛ	zz1ᵛ:6	zz1:6ᵛ

ATTRIBUTIONS TO COMPOSITORS OF THE FIRST FOLIO

B B	E B	B B	B B	E B	B B	B B	B B	B B
3a3^v:4	3a3:4^v	3a2^v:5	3a2:5^v	3a1^v:6	3a1:6^v	3b3^v:4	3b3:4^v	3b2^v:5

B B	B	B B	B H	B H	B H	B H	B H	B H
3b2:5^v	3b1:[6^v]	3b1^v:6	¶3^v:4	¶3:4^v	¶2^v:5	¶2:5^v	¶1^v:6	¶1:6^v

H B	H B/H	H H	H H	H H	H H	H	B H
2¶3^v:4	2¶3:4^v	2¶2^v:5	2¶2:5^v	2¶1^v:6	2¶1:6^v	3¶1:–	χ1:1^v

TABLE 12

COMPOSITOR ATTRIBUTIONS BY FOLIO ORDER

The Tempest (A1–B4)   TLN   CLN

- B: A1   1–87   0.1–72
- A3–A4^v 484–1006   413–880
- A6–A6^v 1257–1512   1117–1347.1
- D? (F?): A1^v 88–219   73–185
- A5–A5^v 1007–1256   881–1116
- B1–B1^v 1513–1769   1347.2–1564
- B3^v 2160–2291   1906–2018
- C: A2–A2^v 220–483   186–413
- B2–B3   1770–2159   1565–1905
- B4   2292–2341   2019–2062.1

The Two Gentlemen of Verona (B4^v–D1^v)

- D? (F?): B4^v–B5^v 1–349   0.1–334
- C4–C6^v 1358–2101   1307–2017
- C: B6–C3^v 350–1357   335–1306
- D1–D1^v 2102–2298   2018–2201.1

The Merry Wives of Windsor (D2–E6^v)

- C: D2–D2^v 1–231   0.1–232
- D4–D6^v 480–1243   486–1269
- D? (F?): D3–D3^v 232–479   233–485
- E3   1755–1882   1796–1918
- E5   2257–2383   2285–2409
- B: E1–E2^v 1244–1754   1270–1795
- E3^v–E4^v 1883–2256   1919–2284
- E5^v–E6^v 2384–2729   2410–2733

Measure for Measure (F1–G6^v)

- C: F1a   1–46   0.1–40
- F1^{v}b–F2a   157–285   145–261
- F3^v–F5a   601–1046   550–961
- F6^v 1372–1503   1258–1390
- G1pt   1570–1591   1454–1475
- G2b   1828–1887   1700–1752
- G4a   2274–2329   2105–2153
- G4^{v}b–G5   2457–2653   2255–2438
- G6b   2851–2916   2619–2680
- G6^{v}pt   2938–end   2702–2702.1, dramatis personae
- D: F1b–F1^{v}a   47–156   41–144
- F2b–F3   286–600   262–549
- F5b   1047–1112   962–1023
- D? (F?): G2a   1768–1827   1646.1–1699
- G4b–G4^{v}a   2330–2456   2154–2254
- G5^v–G6a   2654–2850   2439–2618
- G6^{v}pt   2917–2929   2681–2693
- B: F5^v–F6   1113–1371   1024–1257
- G1a   1504–1569   1391–1453
- G1pt–G1^v 1610–1767   1492 (for)–1646
- G2^v–G3^v 1888–2273   1753–2104
- B? C?: G1pt   1592–1609   1476–1492 (detected)
- ?: G6^{v}pt   2930–2937   2694–2701

The Comedy of Errors (H1–I2^v)

- C: H1–H1^{v}a   1–164   0.1–160
- H2b–H3a   289–549   278–535
- H4a   743–808   683–746
- H5^{v}pt   1235–1254   1146 (And)–1165
- D: H1^{v}b–H2a   165–288   161–277
- H3b–H3^v 550–742   536–682
- H4b   809–874   747–807
- H5^{v}pt   1128–1234   1051–1146 (dam)
- B: H4^v–H5   875–1127   808–1050
- H6–I2^v 1255–1919   1166–1778

Much Ado About Nothing (I3–L1)

- B: I3   1–99   0.1–97
- I5b   553–617   543–607
- K4   1779–1910   1762 (How)–1893
- K5b   2103–2167   2088–2145
- D: I3^v 100–230   98–225
- K2^v 1392–1523   1380–1514
- K5^v–K6^v 2168–2552   2146–2517
- C: I4–I5a   231–552   226–542
- I5^v–K2   618–1391   608–1379
- K3–K3^v 1524–1778   1515–1762 (for)
- K4^v–K5a   1911–2102   1894–2087
- L1   2553–2684   2518–2645.1

Love's Labour's Lost (L1^v–M6^v)

- C: L1^v 1–99   0.1–94
- L2^v–L4   230–740   216–713
- M1–M3^v 1370–2144   1278–1987 (gall)
- D: L2   100–229   95–215
- L4^v–L6^v 741–1369   714–1277
- B: M4–M6^v 2145–2900   1987 (Gall)–2667.1

A Midsummer Night's Dream (N1–O3^v)

- B: N1–N1^v 1–218   0.1–205
- N2^v 348–472   330 (mus)–452
- O3   2003–2129   1899–2040

ATTRIBUTIONS TO COMPOSITORS OF THE FIRST FOLIO

C:	N2	219–347	206–330 (for *Pira-*)
	N3–N3^v	473–727	453–703
	N5^v	1110–1237	1068–1192
	O1–O2^v	1501–2002	1436–1898
	O3^v	2130–2222	2041–2132
D:	N4–N5	728–1109	704–1067
	N6–N6^v	1238–1500	1193–1435

The Merchant of Venice (O4–Q2^v)

B:	O4a	1–47	0.1–43
	O4^{v}a	95–160	86–151
	P5^{v}b–P6^{v}a	1938–2197	1841–2088
	Q2	2517–2646	2385–2504
C:	O4b	48–94	44–85
	O4^{v}b	161–224	152–216 (meaning)
	P1^{v}pt	862–875	827 (last)–841 (come)
	P1^{v}b	924–982	883–935
	P4–P5^{v}a	1493–1937	1426–1840
	P6^{v}b–Q1^v	2198–2516	2089–2384
	Q2^v	2647–2738	2505–2589
D:	O5–P1	225–861	216 (chooses)–827 (Monday)
	P1^{v}pt	876–923	841 (I will goe)–882
	P2–P3^v	983–1492	936–1425

As You Like It (Q3–S2)

C:	Q3–Q3^v	1–228	0.1–223
	Q5^{v}a	609–674	584–647 (Deere)
	R4–R6	1725–2351	1680–2280
B:	Q4	229–357	224–348
	Q6^v–R3^v	853–1724	816–1679
	R6^v–S2	2352–2796	2281–2714.1
D:	Q4^v–Q5	358–608	349–583
	Q5^{v}b–Q6	675–852	647 (Show)–815

The Taming of the Shrew (S2^v–V1)

B:	S2^v–S6^v	1–1139	0.1–1063
	T3–T4^v	1654–2175	1572 (greater)–2069
	V1	2689–2750	2538–2595
C:	T1–T2^v	1140–1653	1064–1572 (no)
D:	T5–T6^v	2176–2688	2070–2537

All's Well That Ends Well (V1^v–Y1^v)

B:	V1^v–V2^v	1–345	0.1–321 (manie)
	V5–Y1^v	864–3078	809 (I)–2860.1
D:	V3–V3^v	346–602	321 (of)–564
C:	V4–V4^v	603–863	565–809 (answer)

Twelfth Night (Y1–Z6)

B:	Y2–Z6	1–2579	0.1–2503

The Winter's Tale (Aa1–Cc2)

A:	Aa1–Aa3^v	1–754	0.1–656
	Aa5–Aa6	1005–1387	867–1210
	Bb4^v–Cc1^v	2411–3319	2153–2972
B:	Aa4–Aa4^v	755–1004	657–866
	Aa6^v–Bb4	1388–2410	1211–2152
	Cc2	3320–3369	2973–3018

King John (a1–b5^v)

C:	a1–a2^v	1–480	0.1–454
	a5–a6^v	997–1507	949.2–1427
	b3^v–b4	2147–2397	2034–2273
B:	a3–a4^v	481–996	455–949
	b1–b3	1508–2146	1428–2033
	b4^v–b5^v	2398–2729	2274–2573.1

Richard II (b6–d5)

B:	b6–c4	1–1111	0.1–1071
	d1^v	1865–1990	1779–1894
	d3^v–d5	2374–2849	2264–2699.1
A:	c4^v–d1	1112–1864	1072–1778
	d2–d3	1991–2373	1895–2263

1 Henry IV (d5^v–f6)

B:	d5^v–d6^v	1–344	0.1–338
	e1–e3^v	345–1108	339–1079 (you)
	f2	2120–2243	2031–2143
	f4–f6	2616–3180	2482–3004.3
J? (A?):	e4–f1^v	1109–2119	1079 (that)–2030
	f2^v–f3^v	2244–2615	2144–2481

2 Henry IV (f6^v–^{x}gg8)

B:	f6^v–g4	1–988	0.1–1003
	^{x}gg1	1613–1742	1601 (whereby)–1729
	^{x}gg2^{v}b	2081–2115	2060–2089
	^{x}gg5–^{x}gg7^v	2643–3322	2564–3197
B?:	^{x}gg8	3323–3350	3197.1–3230.1
J? (A?):	g4^v–g6^v	989–1612	1004–1601 (being)
	^{x}gg1^v–^{x}gg2^{v}a	1743–2080	1730–2059
	^{x}gg2^{v}c–^{x}gg4^v	2116–2642	2090–2563

Henry V (h1–k2)

A:	h1–h2^v	1–479	0.1–460
	h4b–i4	809–2425	784–2324
	i5^v–i6	2678–2933	2559–2802 (make)
	i6^{v}b–k2	2999–3381	2867–3243
B:	h3–h4a	480–808	461–783
	i4^v–i5	2426–2677	2325–2558
	i6^{v}a	2934–2998	2802 (you)–2866

1 Henry VI (k2^v–m2)

A:	k2^v–k5a	1–673	0.1–596
	k5^v–l3	729–1742	641–1556
	l5	2126–2253	1918–2039
B:	k5b	674–728	596.1–640
	l3^v–l4^v	1743–2125	1556.1–1917
	l5^v–m2	2254–2931	2040–2674

2 Henry VI (m2^v–o3^v)

B:	m2^v–m3^v	1–354	0.1–338
	n3^v	1762–1891	1626–1751
	n4^v–o3^v	2021–3355	1873–3158
A:	m4–n3	355–1761	339–1625
	n4	1892–2020	1752–1872

3 Henry VI (o4–q4^v)

A:	o4–o6^v	1–731	0.1–657
	p4–p5	1502–1891	1388–1732
	p6–p6^v	2022–2275	1851–2061
	q1^v–q3^v	2397–3021	2166–2717
B:	p1–p3^v	732–1501	658–1387
	p5^v	1892–2021	1733–1850
	q1	2276–2396	2062–2165
	q4–q4^v	3022–3217	2718–2904.1

ATTRIBUTIONS TO COMPOSITORS OF THE FIRST FOLIO

Richard III (q5–t2^v)

B:	q5–r1	1–595	0.1–538
	r2–r5	728–1595	667–1445
	s4–s5^v	2707–3222	2451–2867
	s6^v–t2^v	3341–3887	2969–3450.1
A:	r1^v	596–727	539–666
	r5^v–s3^v	1596–2706	1446–2450
	s6	3223–3340	2868–2968

All Is True (t3–x4^v)

B:	t3–t3^v	1–209	0.1–169
	v2^v	1350–1481	1073–1191 (depart)
	v4–x2^v	1740–3017	1418–2442
I:	t4–v2	210–1349	170–1072.23
	v3–v3^v	1482–1739	1191 (The)–1417
	x3–x4^v	3018–3433	2443–2817

Troilus and Cressida (χ1–1^v, *gg4–4^v, ¶1–3¶1)

B:	χ1	1–32	0.1–31
	¶1–¶3^v	391–1178	375 (lookes)–1136
	2¶4–2¶4^{v}a	2740–2937	2613–2797
H:	χ1^v	33–125	31.1–122
	¶4–2¶3^v	1179–2739	1137–2612
	2¶4^{v}b–3¶1	2938–3592	2789–3341.1
E:	*gg4–*gg4^v	126–390	123–375 (*Hectors, and now hee*)

Coriolanus (aa1–cc3^v)

B:	aa1–aa3^v	1–743	0.1–628
	aa4^v	868–991	731–850.1
	aa6^v	1377–1507	1178–1297
	bb2	1768–1899	1525–1637 (*Sicinius*)
	bb2^{v}b–bb3	1966–2163	1686–1847
	bb3^{v}b–cc3^v	2230–3838	1905–3343.2
A:	aa4	744–867	628.1–730
	aa5–aa6	992–1376	850.2–1177
	bb1–bb1^v	1508–1767	1298–1524
	bb2^{v}a	1900–1965	1637 (*Heare*)–1685
	bb3^{v}a	2164–2229	1848–1904

Titus Andronicus (cc4–ee2^v)

B:	cc4	1–91	0.1–70
	ee2^v	2651–2708	2447–2500.1
E:	cc4^v–dd3	92–1364	71–1231
	dd4–ee2	1491–2650	1354–2446
?:	dd3^v	1365–1490	1232–1353

Romeo and Juliet (ee3–gg2^v, Gg1)

B:	ee3	1–96	0.1–105
	Gg1	3108–3185	2922–2999
E:	ee3^v–gg2^v	97–3107	106–2921

Timon of Athens (Gg1^v–6^v, hh1–5^v)

B:	Gg1^v–Gg2^v	1–351	0.1–295
	Gg3^v–hh5^v	478–2607	417–2309.1
E:	Gg3	352–477	296–416

Julius Caesar (kk1–ll5^v)

B:	kk1–kk2	1–354	0.1–326
	kk4–ll5a	739–2610	668–2345
	ll5^v	2675–2730	2400–2450.1
A:	kk2^v–kk3^v	355–738	327–667
	ll5b	2611–2674	2346–2399.1

Macbeth (ll6–nn4)

A:	ll6–mm1^v	1–456	0.1–385 (*Ermites*)
	mm2b–mm3^v	519–947	438–778 (so:)
	mm4b–mm5a	1007–1252	823–1024.1
B:	mm2a	457–518	385 (Where's)–437
	mm4a	948–1006	778 (to)–822
	mm5b–nn4	1253–2529	1024.2–2146.1

Hamlet (nn4^v–qq1^v)

B:	nn4^v–nn5^v	1–352	0.1–320
	oo1b	677–742	615–674
	oo2^v–oo3	1001–1257	913–1146
	oo4–pp4a	1389–3015	1271 (fashion)–2812
	qq1–qq1^v	3735–3906	3489 (giue)–3625.2
I:	nn6–oo1a	353–676	321–614
	oo1^v–oo2	743–1000	675–912
	oo3^v	1258–1388	1147–1271 (the)
	pp4b–pp4^v	3016–3211	2813–2993
E:	pp5–pp5^v	3212–3473	2994–3244
E?:	pp6–pp6^v	3474–3734	3245–3489 (worne:)

The Tragedy of King Lear (qq2–ss3)

B:	qq2	1–94	0.1–89
	qq3^v	353–484	327–462 (mis)
	qq5	735–863	711–824
	rr1^{v}b	1426–1491	1333–1386
	rr3^v–rr6^v	1862–2738	1725 (with)–2489
E:	qq2^v–qq3	95–352	90–326
	qq4–qq4^v	485–734	462 (|chief)–710
	qq5^v–rr1^{v}pt	864–1409	825–1317
	rr2–rr3	1492–1861	1387–1725 (not)
	ss1–ss3	2739–3302	2490–2942.1
?:	rr1^{v}pt	1410–1425	1318–1332

Othello (ss3^v–vv6)

E:	ss3^v–ss6	1–731	0.1–663
	tt1–tt3	855–1495	772–1366 (issue)
	vv1–vv3	2388–3026	2143–2717
B:	ss6^v	732–854	664–771
	tt3^v–tt6^v	1496–2387	1366 (will)–2142
	vv3^v–vv6	3027–3685	2718–3278.1

Antony and Cleopatra (vv6^v–zz2^v)

B:	vv6^v–xx3	1–743	0.1–631
	xx5^v	1267–1394	1071–1187
	yy1^v–zz2^v	1788–3636	1508–3016.2
E:	xx3^v–xx5	744–1266	632–1070
	xx6–yy1	1395–1785	1188–1507

Cymbeline (zz3–3b6)

B:	zz3–zz4	1–334	0.1–282
	zz5	467–590	415–524
	zz6	717–842	628–737 (Apes,)
	3a1	968–1096	855–966
	3a2–3a2^v	1223–1471	1067–1277
	3a3^v–3b6	1596–3819	1394–3292.1
E:	zz4^v	335–466	283–414
	zz5^v	591–716	525–627
	zz6^v	843–967	737 (most)–854
	3a1^v	1097–1222	967–1066
	3a3	1472–1595	1278–1393

EDITORIAL PROCEDURES

EACH subsequent section of this volume offers information about the text (or texts) that it covers. First comes an Introduction giving basic information about early publication and discussing the work's overall textual problems. When we accept orthodox views, we refer to standard treatments of the subject; when we have new information or theories, we develop our case at greater length.

The basic function of the Textual Notes is to record substantive departures from the control-text, along with the more plausible emendations that we have not accepted. The aim has been to ascribe all emendations to the edition (identified in small capital letters, e.g. ROWE) in which they first appeared. When the emendation can be ascribed to someone other than the editor who first adopted it, the originator is identified in parentheses, e.g. THEOBALD (Thirlby). References in the left-hand column are to both the original- and the modern-spelling text except when a note refers only to one or the other, when only a single reference is provided. The case for well-founded and long-accepted emendations is not argued; in the interests of economy, we often refer without discussion to published work (such as other editors' notes). Modernizations are noted only when it seems desirable to draw attention to ambiguity in the control-text, or in conspicuous departures from standard practice. Substantive press-variants are recorded, e.g. Qa (first state), Qb (second state), Qc (third state).

The section headed Incidentals records non-substantive departures in the original-spelling edition from the copy-text (other than those noted below as being silently changed). It also records non-substantive press corrections in dialogue, except for those affecting matters (such as wrong-fount type) listed below as not recorded.

The stage directions in the control-text (and in other substantive texts where relevant) are reproduced in full as they appear in those texts. The reference is to the point in our texts at which a corresponding direction occurs. Changes of placing are noted. All directions not listed here may be taken to be editorial.

All departures to the lineation of verse, and changes of verse to prose and prose to verse, are recorded in the Lineation Appendix. The head-note to this appendix explains the procedures and principles which have governed our emendation and recording of lineation.

Original-Spelling Edition

We follow the edition which we believe to be closest to Shakespeare's manuscript in spelling, punctuation, capitalization, and italicization except when we believe these to be mistaken by the standards of the period, or of the text itself. Long s (ſ) and ligatures (except for æ and œ in classical names) are not retained, but are indicated in the textual notes in citations from the control-text of words emended. Original stage directions are retained in so far as they accurately indicate action required by the dialogue. They are modified, and additional directions are provided, in an attempt both to supply directions for necessary action and to clarify the play's original staging. (These matters are discussed in Wells, *Re-Editing Shakespeare*.) Such changes are not automatically indicated; broken brackets indicate directions (and speech-prefixes) whose substance and/or location are, in the editors' opinion, not confidently to be inferred from the dialogue, however likely they may appear.

Abbreviated titles and Christian names in dialogue are not normally expanded; when an identifying character name is abbreviated in a direction (e.g. '*Enter Glo.*') or in dialogue it is expanded and (in dialogue) recorded among incidental changes. Contractions (y^u, y^t, etc.) are retained, as are ampersands except at the start of a verse line relined from justified prose. Commas and colons at the ends of speeches are retained if they seem intended to indicate interrupted speech. Numerals are not spelled out. In adding words to directions or dialogue, we attempt to imitate the orthographical conventions of the copy-text (and, where possible, of the compositor). Speech-prefixes are expanded and regularized, normally to the form most common in the copy-text; generic designations (e.g. CLOWNE, LADY) are in general retained if they are used more consistently than the personal name. Speech-prefixes are printed above the line for verse (except for unassimilated part-lines), on the line for prose. Potentially ambiguous forms (e.g. 'of', 'off', 'to', 'too', 'two') are normally retained, but 'two' meaning 'too' and 'thee' meaning 'the' are emended. In foreign language passages, only what seem to be scribal or compositorial errors are emended.

Alterations that are recorded

Substantive alterations are recorded in the Textual Notes, as are corrections to literal errors when these result in a known word, however inappropriate in context (e.g. 'loueliness' for 'loneliness').

Non-substantive errors are recorded as Incidentals. They include:

(*a*) non-substantive errors of punctuation (e.g. omission of punctuation at the end of an uninterrupted speech)

(*b*) non-substantive literal errors

(*c*) erroneous italics (e.g. '*Naples*' meaning 'napless')

(*d*) alteration of syllabic and non-syllabic past-participial endings (-ed, 'd) in verse. Original forms are changed when they violate a convention established by the text itself; the normal convention is that '-ed' is sounded when it follows a sounded consonant (including 'r', but not 'w').

(*e*) alteration for metrical reasons of syllabic and non-syllabic -est/'st in the verbal inflection.

Alterations that are not recorded

1. Full stops are removed from the ends of stage directions and speech-prefixes.
2. Stage directions are italicized throughout (except for a few occurring within passages of italic type).
3. Exit directions are printed to the right unless they form part of a longer stage direction.
4. Directions for action (other than exits) within a speech which form a complete sentence are placed on a line of their own and indented.
5. Music cues are normally placed at the beginning of a direction or speech.
6. Disguise names are added to entry directions.
7. Ornamental letters, etc., are not indicated; copy capitals after an ornamental letter are normalized.
8. Wrong-fount type is corrected.
9. Minuscule letters at the start of speeches and verse lines are capitalized. When passages wrongly printed as verse are changed to prose, and in realigned verse, capitals at the beginnings of lines are reduced unless the practice of the copy requires them. Capitalization is not otherwise altered except when it is actively misleading, when the change is recorded.
10. Songs are indented, as are alternating rhymed lines (except in the Sonnets). Refrains of songs are given in full on each occurrence.
11. A hyphen at the end of a justified line is removed unless the word could normally be hyphenated (e.g. 'Grand-father').
12. Spaces are closed within words and inserted between words except when linked words form a legitimate period compound (shalbe) and when words now linked were acceptably separated (to morrow).
13. Turned-over lines (in which the turned-over words are often marked by a single parenthesis) are not indicated except when the lineation has been otherwise altered.
14. Scene references, and act and scene references, are inserted in arabic numerals. (Unusual scene breaks are recorded and discussed.)

15. Speeches beginning on the same line as another speech are placed on a line of their own.

16. Headings such as 'Song', 'Epilogue' are placed above lines to which they refer instead of to the left of the first line.

17. Errors of inking are not normally noted unless there is doubt about the reading intended.

18. Literal errors in stage directions (retained in the stage direction lists) are not recorded in the notes; literal errors in speech-prefixes (not retained in our format) are recorded only if there is doubt about the reading intended.

The Modern-spelling edition

Spelling and punctuation are modernized; the basic principles are discussed in Wells, *Modernizing Shakespeare's Spelling*. Foreign-language passages and names are normally presented in their modern equivalents (e.g. Anthonio, Petruchio, and Iachimo become Antonio, Petruccio, and Giacomo). Syllabic -ed endings which would not usually be sounded in modern pronunciation are marked by a grave accent (damnèd, savèd).

In the interests of clarity and intelligibility, stage directions are treated a little more freely than in the original-spelling edition in so far as, for example, pronouns or articles may be added (e.g. *Enter the Queen* for *Enter Queene*, *A trumpet sounds* for *Sound trumpet*), and certain technical terms of the Elizabethan theatre (e.g. *discovered* (for 'revealed') and *manet*) are reworded.

Speech-prefixes of a generic type are usually replaced by a personal name (FESTE, LADY MACBETH) except when a character's function is all-important (e.g. SOOTHSAYER in *Cymbeline*).

Words in a foreign language are italicized. Elisions in verse (e.g. 'stolne') are indicated ('stol'n') when marked in the copy-text when their observance is metrically desirable.

References

In the original-spelling edition, the lines of the play are numbered from beginning to end; a whole line of verse shared by two or more speakers, or an unassimilated verse line, counts as a single unit. The public theatres of Shakespeare's time seem not to have observed act divisions until late in Shakespeare's career: about the time of the extension of the King's Men's activities to the Blackfriars, in 1609. The natural theatrical unit, then, would have been the scene, so we number each scene consecutively throughout the play, adding, for convenience of reference, the act-scene divisions of our modern-spelling edition. This practice does not apply to the late plays (from *Coriolanus* onwards), or to *Titus Andronicus*, *The Comedy of Errors*, *Measure for Measure*, *The Tragedy of King Lear*, and *Macbeth*, in which act divisions are observed, for reasons discussed in the relevant Introduction.

In the modern-spelling edition, act-scene references are provided (relatively unobtrusively, since in most plays the action seems to have been continuous), and the line-numbering is by scenes.

In cross-references to the Shakespeare canon we have drawn upon a variety of reference tools: Marvin Spevack's *Complete and Systematic Concordance to the Works of Shakespeare*, 9 vols. (Hildesheim, 1968-80), T. H. Howard-Hill's series of old-spelling *Oxford Shakespeare Concordances* to the copy-texts of individual plays (Oxford, 1968-73), and concordances to the stints of individual Folio compositors specially generated for us at the Oxford University Computing Service. Facilities at the Computing Service have also enabled us to search the unedited canon for verbal collocations of various kinds. We have in general not acknowledged these sources, but it may be assumed that our knowledge of the presence or absence of parallels derives from one or all of them. All cross-references reflect the line-numbering of our own text.

WORKS CITED

EDITIONS OF SHAKESPEARE

F	Comedies, Histories, and Tragedies (1623)
F2	Comedies, Histories, and Tragedies (1632)
F3	Comedies, Histories, and Tragedies (1663)
F4	Comedies, Histories, and Tragedies (1685)
Alexander	Peter Alexander, *Works* (1951)
Bevington	David Bevington, *Complete Works* (1980)
Boswell	James Boswell, *Plays and Poems*, 21 vols. (1821)
Brooke	C. F. Tucker Brooke, ed., *The Shakespeare Apocrypha* (1908)
Bullen	A. H. Bullen, *Works*, 10 vols. (1904-7)
Cambridge	W. G. Clark and W. A. Wright, *Works*, 9 vols. (1863-6)
Cambridge 2	William Aldis Wright, *Works*, 9 vols. (1891-3)
Capell	Edward Capell, *Comedies, Histories, and Tragedies*, 10 vols. (1767-8)
Chambers	E. K. Chambers, *Works*, 39 vols. (1904-8)
Collier	John Payne Collier, *Works*, 8 vols. (1842-4)
Collier 2	John Payne Collier, *Plays* (1853)
Collier 3	John Payne Collier, *Comedies, Histories, Tragedies, & Poems*, 'The Second Edition', 6 vols. (1858)
Collier 4	John Payne Collier, *Plays and Poems*, 8 vols. (1875-8)
Collier MS	Manuscript emendations in J. P. Collier's copy of F2 (the 'Perkins Folio'), probably by Collier himself
Cowden Clarke	Charles and Mary Cowden Clarke, *Plays*, 3 vols. [1864-8]
Craig	W. J. Craig, *Works* (1891)
Craig-Bevington	*Works*, ed. Hardin Craig (1951), revised by David Bevington (1973)
Delius 2	Nicolaus Delius, *Werke*, 7 vols. (1854-[61])
Dyce	Alexander Dyce, *Works*, 6 vols. (1857)
Dyce 2	Alexander Dyce, *Works*, 9 vols. (1864-7)
Dyce 3	Alexander Dyce, *Works*, 9 vols. (1875-6)
Gildon	Charles Gildon, *Poems* (1710)
Gildon 2	Charles Gildon, *Poems* (1714)
Globe	W. G. Clark and W. A. Wright, *Works* (1864)
Halliwell	James O. Halliwell, *Works*, 16 vols. (1853-65)
Hanmer	Thomas Hanmer, *Works*, 6 vols. (1743-4)
Harness	*Dramatic Works*; with notes . . . By the Rev. William Harness, 8 vols. (1825)
Henley	W. E. Henley, *Works*, 10 vols. (1901-4)
Hudson	H. N. Hudson, *Works*, 11 vols. (1851-6)
Hudson 2	H. N. Hudson, *Works*, 20 vols. (1880-1)
Johnson	Samuel Johnson, *Plays*, 8 vols. (1765)
Keightley	Thomas Keightley, *Plays*, 6 vols. (1864)
Kittredge	George Lyman Kittredge, *Works* (1936)
Knight	Charles Knight, *Comedies, Histories, Tragedies, & Poems*, Pictorial Edn., 55 parts [1838-43]
Knight 2	Charles Knight, *Comedies, Histories, Tragedies, & Poems*, 12 vols. (1842-4)
Knight 3	Charles Knight, *Works*, Pictorial Edn., 'The Second Edition, Revised', 8 vols. (1867)
Malone	Edmond Malone, *Plays and Poems*, 10 vols. (1790)
Marshall	Henry Irving and F. A. Marshall, *Works*, 8 vols. (1887-90)
Munro	John Munro, *The London Shakespeare*, 6 vols. (1958)
Neilson	W. A. Neilson, *Complete Dramatic and Poetic Works* (1906)
Neilson-Hill	William Allan Neilson and Charles Jarvis Hill, *Complete Plays and Poems* (1942)
Pope	Alexander Pope, *Works*, 6 vols. (1723-5)
Pope 2	Alexander Pope, *Works*, 10 vols. (1728)
Rann	Joseph Rann, *Dramatic Works*, 6 vols. (1786-94)

WORKS CITED

Reed	Isaac Reed, *Plays*, 21 vols. (1803)
Reed 2	Isaac Reed, *Plays*, 21 vols. (1813)
Riverside	G. B. Evans (textual editor), *The Riverside Shakespeare* (1974)
Rowe	Nicholas Rowe, *Works*, 6 vols. (1709)
Rowe 2	Nicholas Rowe, *Works*, 6 vols. (1709)
Rowe 3	Nicholas Rowe, *Works*, 8 vols. (1714)
Singer	Samuel W. Singer, *Dramatic Works*, 10 vols. (1826)
Singer 2	Samuel W. Singer, *Dramatic Works*, 10 vols. (1856)
Sisson	Charles J. Sisson, *Complete Works* (1954)
Staunton	Howard Staunton, *Plays*, 3 vols. (1858-60)
Steevens	Samuel Johnson and George Steevens, *Plays*, 10 vols. (1773)
Steevens 2	Samuel Johnson and George Steevens, *Plays*, 10 vols. (1778)
Steevens-Reed	Samuel Johnson, George Steevens, and Isaac Reed, *Plays*, 10 vols. (1785)
Steevens-Reed 2	George Steevens and Isaac Reed, *Plays*, 15 vols. (1793)
Theobald	Lewis Theobald, *Works*, 7 vols. (1733)
Theobald 2	Lewis Theobald, *Works*, 8 vols. (1740)
Verplanck	Gulian C. Verplanck, *Plays*, 3 vols. (1847)
Warburton	William Warburton, *Works*, 8 vols. (1747)
White	Richard Grant White, *Works*, 12 vols. (1857-66)
White 2	Richard Grant White, *Comedies, Histories, Tragedies, & Poems*, 3 vols. (1883)
Wordsworth	Charles Wordsworth, *History Plays*, 3 vols. (1883)

OTHER WORKS

Abbott	E. A. Abbott, *A Shakespearian Grammar*, 2nd edn. (1870)
AEB	*Analytical and Enumerative Bibliography*
Beal	Peter Beal, *Index of English Literary Manuscripts: Volume I: 1450-1625* (1980)
Blackstone	William Blackstone (contributed conjectures to Steevens-Reed)
BEPD	W. W. Greg, *A Bibliography of the English Printed Drama to the Restoration*, 4 vols. (1939-59)
Binns	J. W. Binns, 'Shakespeare's Latin Citations: the Editorial Problem', *SSu* 35 (1982), 119-28
Blayney	Peter W. M. Blayney, *The Texts of King Lear and Their Origins*, vol. i, *Nicholas Okes and the First Quarto* (1982)
Brook	G. L. Brook, *The Language of Shakespeare* (1976)
Bullough	Geoffrey Bullough, ed., *Narrative and Dramatic Sources of Shakespeare*, 8 vols. (1957-75)
Capell, *Notes*	Edward Capell, *Notes and Various Readings to Shakespeare*, 3 vols. (1783)
Cartwright	Robert Cartwright, *New Readings in Shakespeare* (1866)
Cercignani	Fausto Cercignani, *Shakespeare's Works and Elizabethan Pronunciation* (1981)
Chambers, *Stage*	E. K. Chambers, *The Elizabethan Stage*, 4 vols. (1923)
Chambers, *Shakespeare*	E. K. Chambers, *William Shakespeare: A Study of Facts and Problems*, 2 vols. (1930)
CLN	Continuous Line Numbering (to the Oxford original-spelling edition)
Dekker	*The Dramatic Works of Thomas Dekker*, ed. Fredson Bowers, 4 vols. (1953-61); *Blurt Master Constable*, ed. T. L. Berger (1979)
Dessen	Alan C. Dessen, *Elizabethan Stage Conventions and Modern Interpreters* (1984)
Division	*The Division of the Kingdoms: Shakespeare's Two Versions of 'King Lear'*, ed. Gary Taylor and Michael Warren (1983)
Dobson	E. J. Dobson, *English Pronunciation 1500-1700*, 2nd edn., 2 vols. (1968)
EDD	*The English Dialect Dictionary*, ed. Joseph Wright, 6 vols. (1898-1905)
Edwards	Thomas Edwards, *The Canons of Criticism*, 7th edn. (1765)
Elze	Karl Elze, *Notes on Elizabethan Dramatists with Conjectural Emendations of the Text* (1880, 1884, 1886)
Franz	Wilhelm Franz, *Shakespeare-Grammatik* (1924)
Greg, *Folio*	W. W. Greg, *The Shakespeare First Folio: Its Bibliographical and Textual History* (1955)
Greg, *Problem*	W. W. Greg, *The Editorial Problem in Shakespeare: A Survey of the Foundations of the Text* (1942, rev. 1951, 1954)
Hall	Edward Hall, *The Vnion of the Two Noble and Illustre Famelies of Lancastre and York* (1548)
Heath	Benjamin Heath, *A Revisal of Shakespear's Text* (1765)
Henslowe	*Henslowe's Diary*, ed. R. A. Foakes and R. T. Rickert (1961)
Hinman	Charlton Hinman, *The Printing and Proof-Reading of the First Folio of Shakespeare*, 2 vols. (1963)
Holinshed	Raphael Holinshed, *The Third Volume of Chronicles* (1587)

WORKS CITED

Howard-Hill	T. H. Howard-Hill, *Ralph Crane and Some Shakespeare First Folio Comedies* (1972)
Hulme	Hilda Hulme, *Explorations in Shakespeare's Language: Some problems of word meaning in the dramatic text*, 2nd edn. (1977)
Jackson	Zachariah Jackson, *Shakespeare's Genius Justified: Being Restorations and Illustrations of Seven Hundred Passages in Shakspeare's Plays* (1819)
Jonson	Ben Jonson, *Works*, ed. C. H. Herford and P. and E. Simpson, 11 vols. (1925-52)
Jowett and Taylor	John Jowett and Gary Taylor, 'With New Additions: Theatrical Interpolation in *Measure for Measure*', in *Shakespeare Reshaped, 1606-1623* (forthcoming)
Kellner	Leon Kellner, *Restoring Shakespeare: a Critical Analysis of the Misreadings in Shakespeare's Works* (1925)
Kinnear	B. G. Kinnear, *Cruces Shakespearianae* (1883)
Kökeritz	Helge Kökeritz, *Shakespeare's Pronunciation* (1953)
Lettsom	W. N. Lettsom, 'New Readings in Shakespeare', *Blackwood's Edinburgh Magazine*, 74 (August 1853), 181-202. Conjectures also recorded in Cambridge, Dyce 2, W. S. Walker.
Marlowe	Christopher Marlowe, *Works*, ed. Fredson Bowers, 2 vols. (1973)
Mason	John Monck Mason, *Comments on the Last Edition of Shakespeare's Plays* (1785)
Massinger	*The Plays and Poems of Philip Massinger*, ed. Philip Edwards and Colin Gibson, 5 vols. (1976)
Modernizing	Stanley Wells, 'Modernizing Shakespeare's Spelling', in Stanley Wells and Gary Taylor, *Modernizing Shakespeare's Spelling, with Three Studies in the Text of 'Henry V'* (1979)
MSR	Malone Society Reprint
N&Q	*Notes and Queries*
Nashe	*The Works of Thomas Nashe*, ed. R. B. McKerrow (1904-10) ... With supplementary notes ... by F. P. Wilson, 5 vols. (1958)
ODEP	*Oxford Dictionary of English Proverbs*, 3rd edn., ed. F. P. Wilson (1970)
OED	*The Oxford English Dictionary, being a corrected re-issue ... of A New English Dictionary on Historical Principles*, 13 vols. (1933), and Supplements 1-3 (1972, 1976, 1982)
OET	Oxford English Texts
PBSA	*The Papers of the Bibliographical Society of America*
Re-Editing	Stanley Wells, *Re-Editing Shakespeare for the Modern Reader* (1984)
RES	*Review of English Studies*
Ritson	Joseph Ritson, *Remarks, Critical and Illustrative, on the Text and Notes of the Last Edition of Shakespeare* (1783). Also contributed conjectures to Steevens-Reed 2.
SB	*Studies in Bibliography*
Schäfer	Jürgen Schäfer, 'The Orthography of Proper Names in Modern-spelling Editions of Shakespeare', *SB* 23 (1970), 1-19
Schmidt	Alexander Schmidt, *A Shakespeare Lexicon*, 3rd edn. (revised by G. Sarrazin), 2 vols. (1902; reprinted 1962)
Schoenbaum	S. Schoenbaum, *William Shakespeare: A Documentary Life* (1975)
SEL	*Studies in English Literature 1500-1900*
Seymour	E. H. Seymour, *Remarks ... upon the Plays of Shakespeare*, 2 vols. (1805)
Shakespeare's England	Sidney Lee and C. T. Onions, eds., *Shakespeare's England: An Account of the Life and Manners of his Age*, 2 vols. (1916)
Sipe	Dorothy L. Sipe, *Shakespeare's Metrics* (1968)
Sisson, *New Readings*	Charles J. Sisson, *New Readings in Shakespeare*, 2 vols. (1956)
Spevack	Marvin Spevack, *Complete and Systematic Concordance to the Works of Shakespeare*, 9 vols. (1968-80)
SQ	*Shakespeare Quarterly*
S.R.	Stationers' Register
SSt	*Shakespeare Studies*
SSu	*Shakespeare Survey*
STC	A. W. Pollard and G. R. Redgrave, *A Short-Title Catalogue of Books Printed in England, Scotland, & Ireland, and of English Books Printed Abroad, 1475-1640*, revised by W. A. Jackson, F. S. Ferguson, and Katharine F. Pantzer, 2 vols. (1976, 1986)
Sugden	Edmund H. Sugden, *A Topographical Dictionary to the Works of Shakespeare and his Fellow Dramatists* (1925)
Tanselle	G. Thomas Tanselle, 'External Fact as an Editorial Problem', *SB* 32 (1979), 1-47
Taylor, 'Act Intervals'	Gary Taylor, 'The Structure of Performance: Act Intervals in the London Theatres, 1576-1642', in Gary Taylor and John Jowett, *Shakespeare Reshaped, 1606-1623* (forthcoming)
Taylor, 'Inventing'	Gary Taylor, 'Inventing Shakespeare', *Jahrbuch 1986*, 26-44
Taylor, 'Metrifying'	Gary Taylor, 'Metrifying Shakespeare', forthcoming in *SSt*
Taylor, '*Praestat*'	Gary Taylor, '*Praestat Difficilior Lectio*: *All's Well that Ends Well* and *Richard III*', forthcoming in *Renaissance Studies*

WORKS CITED

Taylor, 'Three Studies'	Gary Taylor, 'Three Studies in the Text of *Henry V*', in Stanley Wells and Gary Taylor, *Modernizing Shakespeare's Spelling, with Three Studies in the Text of 'Henry V'* (1979)
Taylor, 'Zounds'	Gary Taylor, 'Zounds Revisited: Theatrical, Editorial, and Literary Expurgation', in Gary Taylor and John Jowett, *Shakespeare Reshaped, 1606-1623* (forthcoming)
Thirlby	Styan Thirlby's unpublished conjectures (mainly manuscript annotations in his copies of contemporary editions) influenced Theobald and Johnson, and possibly others.
Tilley	M. P. Tilley, *A Dictionary of the Proverbs in England in the Sixteenth and Seventeenth Centuries* (1950)
TLN	Through-Line-Numbering to the First Folio: conveniently available in *The First Folio of Shakespeare: The Norton Facsimile*, prep. by Charlton Hinman (1968)
TLS	*The Times Literary Supplement*
Tyrwhitt	Thomas Tyrwhitt, *Observations and Conjectures upon Some Passages of Shakespeare* (1766)
Vaughan	H. B. Vaughan, *New Readings and Renderings of Shakespeare's Tragedies*, 3 vols. (1878-86)
W. S. Walker	W. S. Walker, *A Critical Examination of the Text of Shakespeare*, ed. W. N. Lettsom, 3 vols. (1860)
Werstine, 'Compositor B'	Paul Werstine, 'Compositor B of the Shakespeare First Folio', *AEB* 2 (1978), 241-63
Werstine, 'Folio Editors'	Paul Werstine, 'Folio Editors, Folio Compositors, and the Folio Text of *King Lear*', in *Division*, 247-312
Wing	Donald Wing, *Short-Title Catalogue: 1641-1700*, 3 vols. (1945-51)

COMMENDATORY POEMS AND PREFACES (1599–1640)

TEXTUAL NOTES

Ad Gulielmum Shakespeare

John Weever, *Epigrammes in the oldest cut, and newest fashion* (1599: STC 25224), Epig. 22 (E6). For text and commentary see R. B. McKerrow, ed., Weever's *Epigrammes* (1911); *The Shakspere Allusion-Book*, ed. C. M. Ingleby *et al.*, rev. E. K. Chambers, 2 vols. (1932), i. 24; E. A. J. Honigmann, *Shakespeare: the 'lost years'* (1985), pp. 53–6.

5   Rose-cheekt] Roſ-checkt Q
9   *Romeo*] *Romea* Q

A neuer writer, to an euer reader

See the Introduction to *Troilus and Cressida*.
4   *y*ᵗ] MALONE; *your* Q

To our English Terence

Iohn Davies, *The Scourge of Folly* (n.d.; S.R. 8 October 1610; STC 6341), Epig. 159 (pp. 76–7). For discussion see *Allusion-Book*, i. 219; Chambers, *Shakespeare*, ii. 214; Schoenbaum, 148, 205.

To Master W. Shakespeare

Thomas Freeman, *Runne and a Great Cast* (1614: STC 11370), Epig. 92 (K2ᵛ). Freeman was of Magdalen College, Oxford.

10   Whence] When Q
11   Then] Thence Q

Inscriptions

For discussion see *Allusion-Book*, i. 267; Chambers, *Shakespeare*, ii. 182–5.

1   SOCRATEM] SOPHOCLEM Steevens (*conj.*)
7   SITH] SIEH

On the death of William Shakespeare

This elegy was enormously popular, surviving in a multitude of manuscripts, and printed in three different collections before the Civil War. We have searched for manuscript copies in the Bodleian, British Library, Folger, Harvard, Huntington, Rosenbach, and Yale collections; most of the manuscripts listed below were unknown to earlier investigators. No doubt a further search would uncover further copies. For discussion see William Basse, *Works*, ed. R. W. Bond (1893); *Allusion-Book*, i. 286–9; Chambers, *Shakespeare*, ii. 226. (In the following list of sigla, we have identified where possible the items known to the *Allusion-Book*.)

B1   British Library, Add. MS 10309, fol. 119ᵛ
B2   British Library, Add. MS 15227, fol. 77
B3   British Library, Harleian MS 791, fol. 63ᵛ
B4   British Library, Lansdowne MS 777, fol. 67ᵛ
B5   British Library, Sloane MS 1792, fol. 114 (*Allusion-Book* 7)
F1   Folger MS V.a.103, Pt. I, fol. 3ᵛ (apparently the manuscript from which the poem was printed in Fennell's *Shakespere Repository* (1853), p. 10; *Allusion-Book* 2)
F2   Folger MS V.a.125, Pt. II, fols. 8–8ᵛ
F3   Folger MS V.a.232, p. 32
F4   Folger MS V.a.262, p. 57
F5   Folger MS V.a.275, p. 174
F6   Folger MS V.a.319, fol. 6
F7   Folger MS V.a.322, p. 189
F8   Folger MS V.a.345, p. 74
FBP   Francis Beaumont, *Poems* (1653), sig. M1
HP1   Halliwell-Phillipps, ed., *The Marriage of Wit and Wisdom* (1846), p. 92
HP2   Halliwell-Phillipps, Catalogue of the Halliwell Collection of printed Proclamations and Broad-sides in the Chetham Library, Manchester (1851), item 2757
JDP   John Donne, *Poems* (1633), sig. Y3
N   Nottingham, PW V 37
O1   Bodleian, Ashmole MS 38, p. 203 (*Allusion-Book* 9)
O2   Corpus Christi, Oxford, MS CCC 328, fol. 59
O3   Bodleian, MS Eng.poet.c.50, fol. 59ᵛ
O4   Bodleian, MS Eng.poet.e.14, fol. 98ᵛ
O5   Bodleian, MS Malone 19, fol. 40
O6   Bodleian, MS Rawlinson poet.117, fol. 16ᵛ (*Allusion-Book* 6)
O7   Bodleian, MS Rawlinson poet.160, fol. 13ᵛ (*Allusion-Book* 5; noted by Malone)
O8   Bodleian, MS Rawlinson poet.199, fol. 184
R1   Rosenbach, MS 239/22, fol. 19ᵛ
R2   Rosenbach, MS 239/23, p. 187
R3   Rosenbach, MS 1083/17, p. 7
SP   *Shakespeare's Poems* (1640), sig. K8ᵛ
WR   *Wits Recreations* (1640), sig. AA2
Y1   Yale, MS Osborn b.197, p. 48
Y2   Yale, MS Osborn fb 143, p. 20

Title   *On the death of* William Shakespeare] An Epitaph vpon Poet Shakespeare B1; An Elegie vpõ yᵉ Death of Mʳ Wilyam Shakespeare B2; *untitled* B3; On Mʳ Wᵐ. Shakespeare he dyed in Aprill 1616 B4; Vpon Shackpeare B5; Epitaphium Gulielmi Shakspeare B6; On Mʳ William Shakspeare, FBP, WR, F1; Vpon Poet Shakespeare F2; An Epitaph prepared for Shakspeare, if hee had been buryed at Westminster. F3; An Epitaph vpon William Shakspeare F4; An Epitaph F5; On Mʳ Shakspeare F6; On Mʳ Willm. Shakespeare who dyed in April 1616 F7, HP2, R2; An Epitaph on mʳ Shakespeare F8; *On Shakespeare. Basse.* HP1, R1; On Mʳ Shak-speare O1; An Epitaph on Shakespeare yᵉ Poet O2; On Mʳ Wᵐ Shakepeare. Apr. 1616 N, O4; Basse his Elegie on Shakspeare O3; Basse his Elegie one Poett Shakesear, who died in April 1616 O5; Basse his Elegye of Shakespear O6; Shackspeares Epitaph O7, Y1; On Shakespeare's death O8; An Epitaph on Will: Shakesphear (By William Basse [*added in a later hand*]) R3; On Willᵐ Shakespear bury'd att Stratford vpon Avon, his Town of Nativity. Y2; *On the death of* Williamn Shakespeare, who died in Aprill, Anno. Dom. 1616 SP. Given this variety of titles, it seems impossible to determine which was Basse's own;

COMMENDATORY POEMS AND PREFACES (1599–1640)

we have adopted an abbreviated version of SP, since this was the first appearance of the text as a commendatory poem. (The identity of title in O7 and Y1 is explained by the derivation of both manuscripts from the same source; see Introduction to 'Shall I die' among Various Poems.)

1 *Spenser*] Chaucer B3, JDP, O2
1 lie a thought more nigh] a thought nearer lie B5
1 nigh] neere F6, O1
2 learned *Chauser*] rare *Beaumond* JDP, O2
2 *Chauser*] Spencer B3; Beaumont F1, HP1, O2, R1, R3, N, O4
2 rare] learned JDP, O2
2 rare *Beaumount* lie] thou Beaumont rare F6
3 neerer] nere O2
3 *Spenser*] Chaucer F1, HP1, R1, R3, N, O4
4 foure-fold] foure B5
5 lodge] lye O2
5 all foure in one bed] in one bedd, all 4 O5
5 one] owne O2
6 Vntill Doomes-day] Vntill Dommes-day SP; Till Doomes day F4, O1; Till day of doome F5; For vntill Doomesday hardly B3, JDP, O2
6 hardly will a fift] hardly shall a fift SP; hardly will fift F1; I hardly thinke a fift B1, B6, F4
7 Betwixt this day and that] Between this day and that F8; betwixt this and that O7; Betwixt this, & y^t day B1, F5; Betwixt this and that time F3; Twist this, and that tyme shall F4, O1; Betwixt this time and y^t F6; Twixt that and this day shall B6
7 by Fate be slaine] be slaine by fate F8; be euer slayne O2, O3; be slaine, JDP
7 Fate] fates F3, F4, O1, Y2, FBP, WR
7 slaine] seen B3
8 your] the B2, B6, F1, F2, N, O3, HP1, R1
8 Curtaines] curtaine F6, HP1, R1
8 need] may SP, B2, B3, B4, B5, B6, O5, O6, O8, R2, WR, F2, F5, F7, F8, FBP, Y2; shall F1, F3, HP1, N, R1, O4; should F6; will Y1, O7; needs O2
9–16 But if . . . by thee] *not in* F6
9 but if] All texts except F1, F5, and R1 read 'If your'.
9 in death doth barre] of death goe ba⟨re⟩ F4 (corrected to 'barre'); of death doth barre JDP, O2
9 doth] doe B3, B6, F1, F2, FBP, N, O1, O4, R3, WR, Y1, Y2; goe F4; *not in* O3
10 your] that B1, B3
10 place in your sacred] to have place in your B5
11 Vnder this] In this F1, N, O4; In an HP1, R1; Then underneath this F3
11 carved] caruen F5; sacred FBP, SP, WR, Y2; sable B5; vncarved F1, HP1, N, R1; *not in* F3; curled JDP, O2; incarved O4
11 thine] thy SP, F1, F7, O3
12 Sleepe . . . sleepe] Lye . . . lye R1, HP1
12 rare] braue F1, F2, F8, N, O4, HP1, R1
12 Tragedian] Comœdian O7, Y1
13–14 Thy . . . Graue] *not in* F3, JDP, O2
13 Thy] thine R3
13 Thy unmolested] Thine immolested B5
13 peace] F1 ? rest N, HP1, O4, R1
13 unshared] in an unshar'd FBP, SP, WR, Y; thy unshared F4; vnshaded B1
13 Caue] haue O3. B3 ? craue R1 (?), O6
14 of] to B3, F1, F4, F8, N, O1, O4, O7, R1, Y1, HP1
14 thy] ye B2, R3
15 us, or others] others F1, R1, HP1, N, O4; others, or us F2
15 or] and SP, B1–4, F3, F4, F8, FBP, O1, JDP, O2, R2, R3, WR
In this F1 N, O4; In an HPL, R1 Then underneath this F3
15 be] counted be F1, R1, HP1, O4
16 laid] lay O2
16.1 William Basse] SP (W.B.), B4, F1, F7, HP2, O3, R1, R2, Y1; Dr Doone JDP, O1

The Stationer to the Reader

From *Othello* (1622), A2. See Introduction to *Othello*.

1623 Preliminaries

For F1 see the General Introduction. Ben Jonson's 'To the Reader' (here reproduced as our frontispiece beneath a copy of the engraving to which it refers) in F1 also served as a frontispiece, opposite the engraving (which occurred on the title-page). We therefore do not reproduce it among those commendatory verses; we also omit F1's title-page, and its table of contents ('CATALOGUE').

To the memory of my beloued

29 didst] didſtſt

To the memorie of M. W. Shake-speare

Iames Mabbe] I.M. F1. Of the other plausible candidates John Marston seems ruled out by style, Jasper Mayne and John Milton by age: Arthur W. Secord, 'I.M. of the First Folio Shakespeare and other Mabbe Problems', *Journal of English and Germanic Philology*, 47 (1948), 374–81; Leslie Hotson, *I, William Shakespeare* (1937), 238–50, 255; E. A. J. Honigmann, *The Stability of Shakespeare's Text* (1965), 24–5, 34–5.

The Names of the Principall Actors

5 Kempe] Kempt

An Epitaph on the admirable Dramaticke Poet

First printed in F2 (1632), which we adopt as copy-text; then in *Shakespeare's Poems* (1640), in *Poems of Mr John Milton* (1645), in F3 (1664), and in *Poems, &c. Upon Seueral Occasions* (1673). F3 reprints F2, as 1673 does 1645. The poem's date of composition is identified in 1645. See R. M. Smith, *The Variant Issues of Shakespeare's Second Folio and Milton's First Published Poem* (1928), and *The Poems of John Milton*, ed. John Carey and Alistair Fowler (1968), pp. 122–4. Although the later texts published in Milton's lifetime probably contain authorial revisions, we have adhered to the text first printed as prefatory material to an edition of Shakespeare.

1 neede] need'st SP; needs 1645
4 starre-ypointing] star-ypointed F2 (uncorrected state)
6 dull] weak SP, 1645
8 lasting] liue-long SP, 1645
10 hart] part F2, F3
13 herself] ourself SP; itself 1645
15 Dost] doth SP

On Worthy Master Shakespeare and his Poems

63 But] Bnt
65 Lawne,] ~.

Vpon Master WILLIAM SHAKESPEARE

Digges died on 7 April 1635.

7 say,] ~)
46 Cataline] Catalines
65 Shakespeares] Sheakſpeares

In remembrance

Sir William D'avenant, *Madagascar, with other Poems* (1637: STC 6304), p. 37.

COMMENDATORY POEMS AND PREFACES (1599-1640)

An Elegie

Poems (1640: STC 22344: S.R. 4 November 1639), L1. The reference to Jonson shows that the poem was written by 1637.

To *Shakespeare*

Thomas Bancroft, *Two Bookes of Epigrammes* (1639: STC 1354), Epig. 118, 119 (D2).

To **Mr. William Shake-spear**

Witts Recreations Selected from the finest Fancies of Moderne Muses (1640: STC 25870: S.R. 15 October 1639), Epi. 25.

To the Reader

Poems: written by Wil. Shake-speare (1640: STC 22344: S.R. 4 November 1639). For this volume see Introduction to *Sonnets*.

Of M.ʳ *William Shakespeare*

3   Benson's] *Allusion-Book*; *not in* SP

Title   The Workes of William Shakspere] F (*subs.*). This half-title appears on the last recto [πB2] before the plays begin (on A1, with *The Tempest*); the intervening verso is blank. F spells the name 'Shakeſpeare', as usual; but 'Shakspere' is used in five of the six authenticated signatures, and the fifth ('Shakspeare') agrees in omitting the traditional 'e' after 'k'.

THE TWO GENTLEMEN OF VERONA

The Two Gentlemen of Verona was first published in the 1623 Folio (F) and was included in the Stationers' Register entry for plays new to that volume. It exhibits some of the peculiar features which distinguish other plays printed early in the volume, in which it is placed second. Notable among these are the grouping together at the head of a scene of the names of all the characters taking part in the scene, whether they should enter there or not (probably in partial imitation of classical practice) and the absence of any other stage directions except exits. These and other idiosyncrasies have resulted in the belief that the play was printed from a transcript made by Ralph Crane, a professional scribe known to have worked for the King's Men (see pp. 20–2). We cannot be sure of the precise nature of the script that he was copying. The play contains inconsistencies, loose ends, and apparent confusions which may suggest that it had not undergone final revision, and so that Crane used Shakespeare's working papers. On the other hand, the naming of the characters in speech-prefixes exhibits none of the variability that seems often to have been present in Shakespeare's foul papers, which might suggest either that Crane used a manuscript prepared for the theatre, or that he himself was careful to make such details consistent.

Crane is known to have imposed his personal habits of spelling and punctuation upon the manuscripts he transcribed. The result is that such incidental features of the text as capitalization, hyphenation, and the marking of elisions are less likely to represent Shakespeare's own practice than in plays printed from non-scribal manuscripts.

In our modern-spelling text, the marking of elisions is preserved when it conforms to our general principles, but not otherwise. Thus, we print 't'exchange' (2.6.13/899), where the slurring is required by the metre (even though Shakespeare may have written the words out in full), but 'blackest' (for 'black'st') in 3.1.281/1300, as this is a prose passage. Apostrophes before 'save' (1.1.70/70), 'fool' (1.2.53/200), 'give' (2.1.92/473), and 'Pox' (3.1.368/1389) indicating that another word is notionally omitted are not retained.

The division into acts and scenes, found in F, may derive from Crane, as may a list of 'The Names of all the Actors' printed at the end. However, the act divisions might derive from late theatrical practice. A late revival would also account for the almost complete absence of profanity from the text, which is uncharacteristic of Shakespeare's work before 1606. (See Taylor, 'Zounds'.)

One page in F (sig. C4) has an exceptional number of press-corrections. Hinman shows that the readings of the 'corrected' state in some cases almost certainly represent a reversion to copy, but other variants seem to result from typical printing-house sophistication.

S.W.W./(G.T.)

WORKS CITED

Bond, R. Warwick, ed., *The Two Gentlemen of Verona*, Arden (1906)
Leech, Clifford, ed., *The Two Gentlemen of Verona*, Arden (1969)

TEXTUAL NOTES

Title *The Two Gentlemen of Verona*] F (*head title*); *The two Gentlemen of Verona* F (*running titles, table of contents*); *The two gentlemen of Verona* S.R.

1.1.26   swam] F (fwom). Leech spells 'swum' on the grounds that 'F's "swom" represents this form of the word: cf. Franz, p. 164'; but the variants were indifferent in Shakespeare's time, whereas 'swum' would now be ungrammatical.

1.1.43/43   doting] This edition; eating F. See *Re-Editing*, pp. 43–4.

1.1.65/65   leaue] POPE; loue F

1.1.66   metamorphosed] F (metamorphis'd). The *-ise* spelling had a comparatively short life simultaneously with the *-ose* form which has become standard. In Shakespeare the word occurs only here and in *Kinsmen* (5.5.84/2586). There seems no point in retaining the obsolete spelling.

1.1.76/76   a Sheepe] F2; Sheepe F1

1.1.138/139   testern'd] F2 (*subs.*); cestern'd F1

1.1.141   wreck] F (wrack)

1.2.49/196   *Exit*] Leech instructs Lucetta to drop the letter here. This seems wrong, since Julia has to call her back so that she can read it. The alternative is for Lucetta to drop the letter on her re-entry (1.2.130.1/277.1), and this is strongly supported by the corresponding passage in *Diana*, where the maid 'of purpose ... let the letter closely fall, which, when I perceived, What is that that fell downe? (saide I), let me see it. It is nothing, Mistresse, saide she ...' (Bullough, i. 231).

1.2.62   angerly] F. Formed from the noun, not from the adjective. The spelling 'angrily' is not found in early texts of Shakespeare; the 3 occurrences of 'angerly' are in F; 2 of them, at any rate, mean 'as if in anger' rather than 'being angry', but it is unlikely that this distinction was felt.

1.2.83/230   o' Loue] THEOBALD; O, Loue F

1.2.97/244   your] F2; you F1

1.2.99   bauble] F (babble). 'Both "babble" and "bauble" could be spelt "bable" in the sixteenth century' (Wilson). 'Bauble' makes better sense in the context.

1.2.122   ragged] F. Probably from the same root as *rugged*, but *OED* keeps the forms distinct, and *ragged* has several meanings not included in modern *rugged*.

1.3.0.1/287.1   *Panthino*] The name occurs, in full, 6 times in F, as 'Panthino' in 1.3.0.1, 1.3.1, 763/276.1, 288, 363, and as 'Panthion' in 2.2.18.1, 2.3.0.1/563.1, 565.1, and in 'The Names of All the Actors'. The traditional preference for 'Panthino' is supported by the fact that this is the only form occurring in dialogue, since the directions all appear to be scribal in phrasing.

1.3.50/337 Oh] F2; Pro⟨teus⟩. Oh F1
1.3.88/375 Father] F2; Fathers F1
1.3.91/378 Exeunt] F2; Exeunt. Finis. F1. Presumably F1's peculiar Finis is a remnant of, or means, Finis Actus Primus, a formula found in a number of Jacobean and Caroline plays, but occurring nowhere else in Shakespeare except in Twelfth Night and Folio LLL.
2.1.95 and she] Maybe and means 'if' (an).
2.1.106 stead] F (fteed)
2.1.133/514 What, are] This edition; What͵ are F. It would be possible to retain F's punctuation, but elsewhere Shakespeare seems to use 'reason with' only as an intransitive verb.
2.3.0.1 Lance] F and editors spell 'Launce'. This 'may be the Christian name "Lance", a short form for Lancelot, or may signify "lance", the weapon or the surgical instrument' (Schäfer). There is no reason to retain F's spelling.
2.3.27/593-4 mou'd woman] This edition; would-woman F. See Re-Editing, p. 36.
2.3.49/615 thy Taile] F; my tail HANMER. Leech accepts Hanmer's reading without discussion, but it is anatomically difficult. Cambridge punctuates 'thy tail!', implying that Panthino turns the remark back on Lance with a ribald pun; he might alternatively speak it as a bewildered repetition.
2.4.7/631 Many editors give Speed an exit, as he has no more to say. This may be right; but as Valentine's page, he could remain in silent attendance.
2.4.60/683 knew] F. Hanmer's emendation to 'know' is quite possible.
2.4.106/729 worthy] ROWE; worthy a F
2.4.113.1/736.1 Enter a Seruant | SERUANT] THEOBALD; Thur⟨io⟩. F. As Thurio is on stage, his knowledge of the Duke's wishes is implausible; and Silvia's reply may seem addressed to two different people. Nevertheless, the error may have arisen in the process of transcription; or F may represent accurately what Shakespeare, however ineptly, wrote.
2.4.162 braggartism] F (Bragadifme). Editors spell 'braggardism', but this is an indifferent variant.
2.4.164/787 makes] F2; make F1
2.4.194/817 Is it] F2; It is F1
2.4.194/817 mine eye, or] THEOBALD; mine, or F. Many other emendations have been suggested; none seems more satisfactory, though 'eyes' or 'eyen' are also possible. Many editors also emend 'Valentines' to 'Valentinus'', but a mid-line pause gives weight to the antithesis. G.T. conjectures 'Valentine his'.
2.5.1/836 Milan] POPE; Padua F. 'Padua, nursery of arts' (Shrew, 1.1.2/276) had a famous university.
2.5.8 shot] F. The spelling 'scot' is tempting (cf. scot-free) but OED keeps the forms distinct and gives slight evidence to suggest that shot was used specifically for payments due at taverns.
2.5.37/872 that] F2; that that F1
2.5.45/880 wilt,] KNIGHT; wilt͵ F
2.6.1, 2/887, 888 forsworne;] THEOBALD; ~? F
3.1.81/1100 of Verona] HALLIWELL; in Verona F. Probably Shakespeare is responsible for the anomaly, which may be a remnant of an early draft; the simple alteration, like that at 2.5.1/836, avoids confusion.
3.1.153 Phaëton, for . . . son] F (Phaeton (for . . . fonne))
3.1.204/1223 you—] THEOBALD; you. F
3.1.227/1246 pale,] This edition; ~͵ F. The point is that the natural pallor of her hands is as laudable as it would be if it had only just come upon them, and had been caused by her woe, not as if they might have been 'pale for woe' at any time, but have just become so.
3.1.271 catalogue] F's 'Cate-log' is usually retained as 'a pun on the girl's name ("Kate-log", a record or account of Kate)' (Bond). But the girl is not elsewhere named, and 'log' in this sense is not recorded till 1679 in the expression log book, and 1825 independently. F's capital C and hyphen may be compositorial or scribal.
3.1.271/1290 Conditions] F4; Condition F1. All the citations for 'catalogue of' in OED are followed by a plural.

3.1.291/1310 try] Fb; thy Fa
3.1.299/1318 sew] F (fowe)
3.1.314/1333 followes] Fa; follow Fb. For the acceptability of Fa's inflection see Abbott, 335.
3.1.316/1335 be broken short] This edition (G.T.); be F; be kissed ROWE. Our reading, meaning 'be tamed with' moving into 'be intimately conferred with' (OED break, v. 22.a and b), supposes a pun on 'breakfast'.
3.1.323/1343 talke] Fb; Fa take
3.1.325/1345 villaine] Fb; villanie Fa
3.1.332/1352 loue] Fb; lone Fa
3.1.343/1363 haire] Fb; haires Fa
3.1.346/1366 last] Fb; not in Fa
3.1.349/1369 be. Iie] THEOBALD (subs.); be ile F
3.2.13/1406 PROTHEUS] Fb (Pro.); not in Fa
3.2.14/1407 grieuously] Fb; heauily Fa
3.2.25/1418 I] F1; I doe F2 (other possibilities: as I; omit And also)
3.2.49/1442 weede] F. Several emendations have been suggested; Leech makes a good case for 'wind' (first adopted by Keightley), but 'weed' seems possible, if not very good; cf. 'weed my vice and let his grow', Measure 3.1.526/1634.
4.1.34/1524 I had beene often] COLLIER; I often had beene often F1. Editors usually follow F2 in omitting the second 'often', but Collier's version scans better.
4.1.44/1534 awfull] F. The required sense is not precisely authenticated, and Hawkins's suggestion, 'lawful', may be correct.
4.1.47/1537 An heire and neere͵] THEOBALD; And heire and Neece͵ F
4.1.56/1546 want—] THEOBALD; want. F
4.1.72/1562 Crewes] F; caves SINGER. F's reading, though possible (Crewe meaning a 'band of outlaws') is doubtful, both because the plural seems unnecessary and because the speaker and his companions already form a Crewe in themselves.
4.2.81.2/1645.2 aboue] Silvia's inability to recognize Proteus and her failure to see the musicians have lent support to the belief that she should appear at a stage window or on an upper level.
4.2.110/1674 his] F2; her F1
4.3.4.1/1705.1 aboue] The direction seems consistent with Silvia's entry in the previous scene and with the knight's calling to her, though the action could take place on the level.
4.3.17/1718 abhors] HANMER; abhor'd F. Leech defends F, but the error is an easy one and the probable omission referred to in the following note suggests a compositor prone to error.
4.3.37-8/1738-9 grieuances, | Which] F. The use of which is warranted as a connective particle without antecedent; see note in Taylor's Oxford Henry V to 3.2.46, and Chettle's Hoffman (MSR) 489. The construction has caused difficulty: Keightley suggested a missing line 'And sympathize with your affections'.
4.4.54/1802 Hangman boyes] SINGER; Hangmans boyes F. Schmidt, defending F, says, 'probably the servants of the public executioner', but we can find no evidence that dogs were hanged by the public hangman.
4.4.60 on end] F (an end)
4.4.68/1816 thou] F2; thee F1
4.4.72/1820 to] F2; not F1
4.4.170 beholden] F (beholding). 'Beholding' is 'an ancient error . . . now obsolete' (Fowler, Modern English Usage), and with no independent significance.
5.2.7/1969 IULIA] COLLIER (Boswell); Pro⟨teus⟩. F
5.2.13/1975 IULIA] ROWE; Thu⟨rio⟩. F
5.2.17/1979 Leech follows Pope in punctuating as a question; but to follow F in treating as a statement is more in keeping with Thurio's complacency.
5.2.18/1980 your] F3; you F1
5.2.31/1993 saw] F1; saw Sir F2
5.2.42/2004 stand,] F2; ftand, F1
5.3.7 Moses] F (Moyfes). Leech, describing 'Moyses' as a 'fairly common' form of Moses, says 'There seems no need to modernize it here.' There seems even less need to retain it in a modern-spelling edition.
5.4.48/2078 oathes,] F4; ~͵ F1

THE TWO GENTLEMEN OF VERONA

5.4.67/2097 trusted] F1. Editors often regularize the metre by adopting F2's 'trusted now', but this seems an example of a 'silent stress', as at e.g. 2.4.165, 3.1.212/788, 1231. Proudfoot conjectures 'one's own right hand'.

5.4.83 in Silvia] F; 'e'en Silvia' is a possible interpretation, perhaps supported by F's placing the phrase between commas.

5.4.127/2157 Verona] F. 'Milan' seems to be required (see note to 3.1.81/1100). Probably another sign of unrevised copy; the correction cannot be made without damaging the metre, though in performance 'This Milan' or 'Our Milan' could be substituted.

5.4.128/2158 Touch—] STEEVENS; Touch: F. The line, which seems to have passed without explicit comment, makes sense only as an interrupted threat, though many editors, including Cambridge, Bond, and Leech, have retained F's colon without attempting to interpret it. Warburton placed a dash after the following line, which has much the same effect and is an acceptable alternative.

5.4.151 endowed] F (endu'd). Discussed in Taylor's Oxford *Henry V* at 2.2.136.

5.4.158/2188 include] F; conclude This edition *conj*. This is *OED*'s only instance of the required sense.

INCIDENTALS

11 Sweet] Fb; ſweet Fa   47 Loue,] Fb; ~ ; Fa   68 naught] Fa; nought Fb   107 louer.] ~ ₐ   233 it.] ~ ,   363 *Panthino*] *Panthmo*   429 well-fauourd.] ~ ?   501 mouingly.] ~ :   504 so.] ~ :   546 *Iulia*.] ~ :   569 Sonne] F (*text*); ſonne F (*c.w.*)   656 off.] ~ ₐ   693 bestow,)] ~ .)   814 another,] ~ .   831 dazeled] dazel'd   876 me.] ~ ,   982 Madam.)] ~ ₐ)   1025 your] yonr   1111 her.] ~ ,   1153 Lord.)] ~ ₐ)   1201 be,] ~ ;   1211 'tis] t'is   1239 banished?] baniſh'd?   1240 offer'd] offered   1297 Sea.] ~ :   1319 *so* ?] Fb; ~ . Fa   1336 breth] Fa; breath Fb   1366 mine, twice,] ~ ₐ ~ ,   1379 impossible —] ~ .   1388 long,] Fb; ~ , Fa   1388 going ₐ] Fb; ~ , Fa   1394 you,] Fa; ~ , Fb   1405 gon?] Fb; ~ . Fa   1646 euen] eu'e   1660 returne,] ~ ₐ   1807 stay'st] ſtayeſt   2013 *Siluias*] *Siluas*   2036 distresses] diſtreſtes   2098 periur'd] periured

FOLIO STAGE DIRECTIONS

1.1.0.1/0.1   *Valentine: Protheus*, and *Speed*.
1.1.62/62   *Exit*.
1.1.146/147   *Exit*.
1.2.0.1/147.1   *Enter Iulia and Lucetta*.
1.2.49/196   *Exit*.
1.2.140/287   *Exeunt*.
1.3.0.1/287.1   *Enter Antonio and Panthino. Protheus*.
1.3.91/378   *Exeunt. Finis*.
2.1.0.1/378.1   *Enter Valentine, Speed, Siluia*.
2.1.126/507   *Exit. Sil*.
2.1.165/545   *Exeunt*.
2.2.0.1/545.1   *Enter Protheus, Iulia, Panthion*.
2.2.20/565   *Exeunt*.
2.3.0.1/565.1   *Enter Launce, Panthion*.
2.3.58/624   *Exeunt*.
2.4.0.1/624.1   *Enter Valentine, Siluia, Thurio, Speed, Duke, Protheus*.
2.4.189/812   *Exit*. (after 'haste')
2.4.212/835   *Exeunt*.
2.5.0.1/835.1   *Enter Speed and* Launce.
2.5.51/886   *Exeunt*.
2.6.0.1/886.1   *Enter Protheus solus*.
2.6.43/929   *Exit*.
2.7.0.1/929.1   *Enter Iulia and* Lucetta.
2.7.90/1019   *Exeunt*.
3.1.0.1/1019.1   *Enter Duke, Thurio, Protheus, Valentine,* | *Launce, Speed*.
3.1.372/1393   *Exeunt*.
3.2.0.1/1393.1   *Enter Duke, Thurio, Protheus*.
3.2.97/1490   *Exeunt*.
4.1.0.1/1490.1   *Enter Valentine, Speed, and certaine Out-lawes*.
4.1.74/1564   *Exeunt*.
4.2.0.1/1564.1   *Enter Protheus, Thurio, Iulia, Host, Musitian, Siluia*.

4.3.0.1/1701.1   *Enter Eglamore, Siluia*.
4.3.47/1748   *Exeunt*.
4.4.0.1/1748.1   *Enter Launce, Protheus, Iulia, Siluia*.
4.4.202/1950   *Exeunt*.
5.1.0.1/1950.1   *Enter Eglamoure, Siluia*.
5.1.12/1962   *Exeunt*.
5.2.0.1/1962.1   *Enter Thurio, Protheus, Iulia, Duke*.
5.2.54/2016   *Exeunt*.
5.3.0.1/2016.1   *Siluia, Out-lawes*.
5.3.14/2030   *Exeunt*.
5.4.0.1/2030.1   *Enter Valentine, Protheus, Siluia, Iulia, Duke, Thurio,* | *Out lawes*.
5.4.171/2201   *Exeunt*.

[Printed after the play]

The names of all the Actors.

Duke: Father to Siluia.
Valentine. } *the two Gentlemen.*
Protheus.
Anthonio: father to Protheus.
Thurio: a foolish riuall to Valentine.
Eglamoure: Agent for Siluia in her escape.
Host: where Iulia lodges.
Out-lawes with Valentine.
Speed: a clownish seruant to Valentine.
Launce: the like to Protheus.
Panthion: seruant to Antonio.
Iulia: beloued of Protheus.
Silvia: beloued of Valentine.
Lucetta: waighting-woman to Iulia.

THE TAMING OF THE SHREW

A PLAY specifically attributed to Shakespeare and entitled *The Taming of the Shrew* was first printed in the First Folio (F), by Compositors B, C, and D. However, on 2 May 1594 an item with a rather similar title was entered in the Stationers' Register:

Peter Shorte / Entred vnto him for his copie vnder mr warden
    Cawoode hande / a booke intituled
    A pleſant Conceyted hiſtorie called
    the Tayminge of a Shrowe

In 1594 Short printed for Cuthbert Burby, in quarto, 'A Pleasant Conceited Historie, called The taming of a Shrew. As it was sundry times acted by the *Right honorable the Earle of* Pembrook his seruants' (*BEPD* 120a). This short play (made up of fewer than 1,550 lines) was reprinted in 1596 and 1607. On 11 June 1594, Philip Henslowe recorded receipts of nine shillings for a performance of 'the tamynge of A shrowe' by the Lord Admiral's and Lord Chamberlain's Men at Newington Butts (*Henslowe's Diary*, p. 22). The text printed in 1594 differs so drastically and systematically from that printed in 1623 that the former must be considered a distinct entity. The relationship between these two texts, and whether Henslowe recorded a performance of the text printed in 1594 or that printed in 1623, remain matters of fundamental dispute: *A Shrew* may be a source for *The Shrew*, or Shakespeare's own earlier play, later completely reworked as *The Shrew*, or a 'bad quarto' of *The Shrew*, or a derivative play influenced by *The Shrew*. But the controversy does not much impinge upon the editing of *The Shrew*, because—as with *The Troublesome Raigne* and *King John*—the differences between the two texts are so great that one can hardly assist the editor of the other.

One particularly intriguing feature of *A Shrew* is its continuation and rounding-off of the Christopher Sly framework, which ceases in the Folio text at the end of 1.1/Sc. 1. The author of *A Shrew* is generally supposed to have invented the additional passages, or to have derived them from a common original, now lost. But there is another possibility, not so far explored. It is perfectly possible that the play as acted by Shakespeare's company included a continuation and rounding-off of the Sly framework written by Shakespeare himself at a later stage of composition than that represented by the Folio text, and that the corresponding episodes in *A Shrew* derive from these. For this reason, we print these episodes as Additional Passages.

The printer's copy for F has been disputed. It seems relatively unlikely that F was set from a prompt-book: as Greg and Oliver note, it has deficiencies, errors, and inconsistencies which would be unusual in such a manuscript, even by the standards of the time. Wilson thought the copy was a scribal transcript of foul papers, but this theory was heavily dependent upon the (disputable) quantity of alleged omissions of single words, which might be due as well to a combination of authorial and compositorial carelessness. It remains true, nevertheless, that the number of such omissions is almost certainly greater than usual. The heavy preponderance of 'oh' spellings, in defiance of Shakespeare's apparent preference, might be due either to scribal interference or to an early date of composition. (See John Jowett and Gary Taylor, 'With New Additions'.) Scribal copy, or some combination of scribal and autograph copy, cannot be ruled out. Some annotation in the theatre is also possible. It is easy enough to imagine Shakespeare himself using the name of a particular and physically striking actor—Sinclo—as the speech-prefix for one of the Players (Ind.1.86/86), just as he does in Quarto *2 Henry IV*. It is more difficult to explain why the author should specify '*Nicke*' as the speech-prefix for a Messenger (3.1.80/1296); on the other hand, the book-keeper who annotated the manuscript of *Sir Thomas More* added only one actor's name in the margin—for a messenger (MSR, V.1-2). Likewise, the peculiar prefixes '*Fel.*' (4.3.63/1942) and '*Par.*' (4.2.73/1830), for Haberdasher and Pedant respectively, may be explained in a number of ways, but it is possible that actors are being specified. What encourages suspicion is the number of such anomalies in a single play. Shortly before the odd prefix '*Nicke*' occurs a little cluster of speech-prefix errors (3.1.46, 49, 50, 52/1262, 1265, 1266, 1268), which suggests some kind of irregularity in the manuscript; but the traditional corrections are not disputed; nor are they at 4.2.4, 6, 8/1761, 1763, 1765, where errors have apparently resulted from someone's use of *Li.* or *Lit.* (= *Lisio*) as a prefix for Hortensio, misunderstood by someone else as *Lu.* or *Luc.* (= *Lucentio*). Responsibility for the error is impossible to attribute confidently, though Shakespeare himself seems most likely to be the agent who started labelling Hortensio by his disguise name 'Lisio'.

There are signs of revision which we believe to have been undertaken during composition, though others regard it as being of a later date; H. J. Oliver, indeed, supposes it to have occurred after the performances seen by the compiler of *A Shrew*. The most problematic scenes are 3.2/Sc. 7 and 4.4/Sc. 12. It is generally agreed that the speeches assigned to Tranio in 3.2/Sc. 7 were originally given to Hortensio, to whom they are far more appropriate in his capacity as Petruccio's old friend. It has been generally assumed that an entry for Lucentio was carelessly or accidentally omitted at the beginning of the scene, but his presence is not required till 3.3.1/1435, and we assume rather that an entry has been omitted at that point, and that it would have marked the start of a new scene (see note to 3.3/Sc. 8 below).

4.4/Sc. 12 is more problematical. The opening line firmly locates it before Baptista's house; but the later part of the scene makes better sense if thought of as taking place before Tranio's lodging (see e.g. 4.4.50, 54, 57, 67/2123, 2127,

2130, 2140). There is an obvious anomaly in the double entrance for the Pedant, 4.4.0.1/2073.1 and 4.4.18.1/2091.1. The problem is resolved if we suppose (with Wilson) that Shakespeare wrote the second part of the scene first, then added the first eighteen lines, failing to locate them properly and to correct adequately the direction at 4.4.18.1/2091.1. At 4.4.67.1/2140.1 is a mysterious 'Enter Peter'. We suppose that Shakespeare originally ended the scene here, and that this is a misexpansion of an uncancelled remnant of a direction for the entry of Pet⟨ruchio⟩ (or Petr⟨uchio⟩) and others, probably for the episode which now begins at 5.1.7/2266.

At 4.4.61/2134, in F1, Baptista says 'Cambio hie you home...'; there is no exit at the end of his speech for 'Cambio' (Lucentio); the following line is spoken by Biondello, followed by Exit, though the next line, Tranio's 'Dallie not with the gods, but get thee gone' is obviously addressed to him. Clark and Wright assumed that Cambio was a mistake for Biondello. We assume rather that Shakespeare originally intended to dispatch 'Cambio' but substituted Biondello while omitting to change the name at this point. This makes still better sense if we suppose that in the scene as originally written—i.e. before the addition of the initial episode—Biondello was not present at all. The only likely objection to this hypothesis is the allusion to him in Tranio's 'My Boy shall fetch the Scriuener presentlie' (4.4.58/2131), but this does not require the boy (Biondello) to be on stage. The exit-line 'I praie the gods she may with all my heart' comes even better from Lucentio than Biondello, to whom nevertheless it seems clear that Shakespeare transferred it. This leaves Lucentio with nothing to say in the scene, but traces of his presence remain in the following episode when Biondello says to him 'You saw my Master winke and laugh vpon you...' (4.5.3-4/2147-8). There is evidence here of conflicting intentions, as if Shakespeare meant to write Lucentio out of the scene but did not sustain his intention. So it seems best to keep him in it, marking an exit for him at 4.4.65.1/2138.1 and one for Biondello at 4.4.67.1/2140.1.

A problem remains with the scene's final episode (from 4.4.71/2144). F1 clears the stage with an Exeunt, then directs Enter Lucentio and Biondello; yet a few lines later Biondello says 'my Master...[hath] left mee here behinde'. The only way of resolving this contradiction would be to restore Biondello at 4.4.71/2144; this seems contrary to the purpose of Shakespeare's revision and leaves awkwardness in Lucentio's rapid, unexplained re-entry (about which there would be no difficulty if Shakespeare had not included an allusion to Lucentio's presence during the preceding dialogue). We do what we can to ease the situation by marking a new scene-break at 4.4.71/2144, justified both because the stage has been cleared and because the consequent suggestion of a possible time-gap increases the plausibility of the subsequent, essentially expository, conversation.

Another vexing problem, which may or may not be related to others, is caused by Ind.1.86/86: 'Sincklo. I thinke 'twas Soto that your honor meanes.' The speech-prefix 'Sincklo' presumably refers to the actor John, identified elsewhere in the plot of The Seven Deadly Sins (c.1591?), the Folio text of Richard, Duke of York (1623; composition c.1591), the Quarto of 2 Henry IV (1600; composition c.1597), and the Induction to the King's Men's adaptation of The Malcontent (1603-4). Unless W. W. Greg's dating of The Seven Deadly Sins can be discredited, the identification of Sinclo in this prefix is of little help in dating the play, or the line in question. The question of date arises because the only character of that name in an extant play occurs in John Fletcher's Women Pleas'd, where he is indeed 'a Farmers eldest sonne' (Ind.1.82/82) who might be said to have 'woo'd the Gentlewoman' (Ind.1.83/83)—though that interpretation has been disputed. Fletcher was not born until 1579; his earliest known work for the stage dates from 1605-6; he seems to have written at first primarily and perhaps exclusively for the children's companies. The only evidence for dating Women Pleas'd itself is the cast list printed in the 1679 Beaumont and Fletcher Folio, which cannot belong to a performance earlier than c.1620; such cast lists usually relate to the first performance, but in this instance might not. Eric Sams (N&Q, NS 32 (1985), 33-45) arbitrarily dates Women Pleas'd c.1604, assumes that at this early date Fletcher was already writing for the King's Men, and concludes that the entirety of the Folio text postdates Fletcher's play. This conclusion is wildly at odds with all the stylistic evidence, which points to a much earlier period of composition. Even if we could be confident that F alludes to Women Pleas'd, the allusion might be a late interpolation, authorial or not: lines Ind.1.81-6/81-6 could be omitted without damage to the surrounding text, and Sinclo is identified only in the one prefix at Ind.1.86/86. One might also conjecture that the evidence of revision in 3.1-3.3/Sc. 6-Sc. 8 and 4.2/Sc. 10 belongs to the same period; such a hypothesis might explain other puzzling features of the text, most notably its combination of the characteristics of a transcript and of foul papers. However, it is not certain that the Folio reference to Soto alludes to Fletcher's play. Elizabethan and Jacobean plays often took over or adapted the plots of earlier plays, and most editors have assumed that the Folio alludes to a lost Elizabethan play later adapted by Fletcher. We suspect this explanation is correct, but in the nature of the case it could never be proven (or disproven). Alternatively, it is even possible—if unlikely—that Shakespeare invented the fictitious Soto, and that Fletcher (who wrote a sequel to Shakespeare's play before it was published) simply expanded the hint into a character in one of his own plays.

The Folio text might therefore derive from Shakespearian foul papers, or from a transcript which had undergone some minor theatrical adaptation at a later date. It might also derive from collaborative foul papers (see the section on 'Canon and Chronology'). Dual authorship might account for some of the evidence of textual cross-purposes and revision. However, in the absence of a reliable and thorough investigation of authorship one must assume that the whole play is Shakespeare's.

In some respects Shrew is the most problematic play in the canon, textually; the provenance of the Folio text remains radically uncertain. The Folio has not been expurgated. It marks 1.1/Sc. 1 (at the beginning of the entire play), Act 3 (as in our text), 4.1/Sc. 9 (at our 4.3/Sc. 11), and Act 5 (at 5.2/Sc. 16). Pope first used the term 'Induction' for the Sly scenes; other scene divisions (to which we suggest modifications below) derive from eighteenth-century editors. The Folio act division seems too incompetent to reflect theatrical practice at any period, and is probably of printing-house origin.

A quarto, dated 1631, contains a text of *The Shrew* (*BEPD* 120e). Collier suggested that this edition dated from 1607-9, that F was printed from a copy of it, and that the 1631 title-page was added later as a cancel; the Cambridge editors (vol. iii, Preface) showed that this is bibliographically impossible, and subsequent editors have accepted that the 1631 edition is merely a derivative reprint of F.

S.W.W./(G.T.)

WORKS CITED

Hibbard, G. R., ed., *The Taming of the Shrew*, New Penguin (1968)
Hosley, Richard, ed., *The Taming of the Shrew*, Pelican (1964)
Oliver, H. J., ed., *The Taming of the Shrew*, Oxford (1982)
Thompson, Ann, ed., *The Taming of the Shrew*, New Cambridge (1984)
Wilson, John Dover, ed., *The Taming of the Shrew*, New (1928, rev. 1953)

TEXTUAL NOTES

Title *The Taming of the Shrew*] F (*head title, running titles, table of contents*)

Ind.1.1/0.1, etc. SLIE] F (*Beg⟨ger⟩.*)

Ind.1.10/10 Headborough] F; third-borough POPE 2 (Theobald)

Ind.1.15/15 Breath] SISSON (Mitford); Brach F

Ind.1.62/62 he is] F; he's Sly WILSON 1928 (Johnson). Wilson withdrew his reading because the lord 'had not so far heard Sly's name'—not a necessary objection, as Sisson says. But Sisson is over-dismissive of the interpretation 'he is, must be, lunatic now, if he thinks he hears such nonsense correctly' (Oliver).

Ind.1.80/80 A PLAYER] F (*2. Player; this line seems appropriate to the leader of the group*)

Ind.1.86/86 ANOTHER PLAYER] HANMER (*subs.*); Sincklo F

Ind.2.2/138 Lordship] Q 1631; Lord F

Ind.2.26/162 is it] F; it is ROWE

Ind.2.52 wi'th'] F (with). ALEXANDER's interpretation.

Ind.2.72/208 Christopher] F1; Christophero F2

Ind.2.92/228 Greete] HOSLEY (Halliwell); Greece F

Ind.2.99-136, 1.1.250/235-72, 524 BARTHOLOMEW] F (*Lady., La.*)

Ind.2.124.1/260.1 *Enter a Messenger*] F. Hibbard's conjecture that the lord brings the message is attractive.

Ind.2.133/269 will let] F1; will. Let F3. F1's reading suits Sly's growing lordliness.

Ind.2.133/269 play it, is] CAPELL (play't—Is); play, it is F1; play; is it F4

Ind.2.134 gambol] F (gambold: *excrescent '-d'; an indifferent variant*)

1.1.3 fore] F (for); from THEOBALD; in CAPELL (Heath). Many editors retain F's 'for', glossing 'in', but this is not paralleled elsewhere in Shakespeare.

1.1.13/287 Vincentio] HANMER; Vincentio's F

1.1.17-18/291-2 studie, | Vertue and] F; study | Virtue, and COLLIER

1.1.25 *Mi perdonate*] Capell's regularization of F's '*Me Pardonato*' seems desirable in a modernized text.

1.1.33/307 Ouid,] F3; Ouid; F1

1.1.47.1 Katherine] Four forms of the complete name occur in F— Katerina, Katherina, Katerine, Katherine—distributed among the four compositors. The name occurs in four other plays of Shakespeare, always, in the texts nearest to holograph, with a 'th', never ending in '-a'. The 't' and 'th' evidence may be insignificant, as they were partially interchangeable (Cercignani, p. 330), so we standardize to 'th'. The '-a' ending provides a useful metrical variant (cf. Isabel-Isabella) which cannot be ignored in dialogue. Shakespeare may have regarded it as Italianate (Caterina), but it is recorded in medieval English (E. G. Withycombe, *Oxford Dictionary of English Christian Names*, 1945; 3rd edn. 1977). We ignore it in directions, standardizing to 'Katherine'.

1.1.47.3/321.2 suter] F2; *sifter* F1

1.1.75 said—Bianca] CAPELL; faid, Bianca F

1.1.106/380 you: Their loue] F1; you: there loue Q 1631; you: Our love F3; you. Your love MALONE (*conj.*); you there. Love SISSON *New Readings*

1.1.160/434 captum] F2; captam F1

1.1.209/483 Sir] F; good sir POPE

1.1.209/483 sith it] F; sithence it DYCE 2; sith y^t it G.T. *conj.*

1.1.233 I sir?] F (I sir,); Ay, fir, ROWE

1.1.237/511 could] F1; would F3

1.1.237/511 'faith] F; faith MCKERROW (galleys; *presumably interpreting* 'utter on my word of honour, swear', *OED faith, v.*)

1.1.242/516 your] F2; you F1

1.1.246.2/520.2 speake] ROWE; *speakes* F

1.2.0.1 Petruccio] F's 'Petruchio' clearly represents the Italian name.

1.2.18/544 masters] THEOBALD; miftris F

1.2.24/550 Con tutto] THEOBALD; Contutti F

1.2.24/550 il] THEOBALD; le F (*probably Shakespeare's error*)

1.2.24 cuore] F (core)

1.2.24/550 ben] THEOBALD; bene F

1.2.24 trovato] F (trobatto)

1.2.25/551 ben] F2; bene F1

1.2.25/551 molto] THEOBALD; multo F

1.2.25/551 honorato] F2; honorata F1

1.2.29-30 service—look you, sir:] F (feruice, looke you fir:); service! Look you, sir: OLIVER (Perring); service, look you, sir. HUDSON

1.2.33 pip] F (peepe)

1.2.45 this'] F (this; *a contracted form*)

1.2.51/577 growes. But . . . few,] HANMER; growes but in a few. F

1.2.72/598 me, were] STEEVENS; me. Were F. Riverside's 'Wher'er she is as rough . . . seas', an interesting attempt to rethink a traditional emendation, seems unsupported by *OED*.

1.2.72/598 as] Q 1631; is as F

1.2.111/637 rope trickes] F; rhetricks (*Grumio's corruption of* rhetorics) SISSON

1.2.119/645 me and other more,] CAPELL; me. Other more, F

1.2.133/659 least] F; last HOSLEY

1.2.171/697 helpe me] ROWE; helpe one F

1.2.189/715 Antonios] ROWE; Butonios F

1.2.190/716 his fortune] This edition; my fortune F. F makes poor sense, and the mistake is easy. See *Re-Editing*, 41-2.

1.2.213/739 ours] THEOBALD (Thirlby); yours F

1.2.223/749 he *Biondello*] F; he *Biancas* father *Biondello* G.T. *conj.* Mention of Bianca's name seems necessary to account for Gremio's 'her', and the compositor's eye could easily have skipped from *Bianca* to *Biondello*.

1.2.224/750 her to—] F; her to woo HALLIWELL (Malone); her too? DELIUS 2 (Tyrwhitt)

1.2.251/777 aske] F1; to ask F2

1.2.267/793 feete] ROWE; feeke F

1.2.276/802 contriue] F; convive THEOBALD (*recorded only in* 'Troilus')

1.2.282/808 Ben] F2; Been F1

2.1.3/811 goods] F; gawds THEOBALD

2.1.8/816 thee] F2; *not in* F1

2.1.60 Licio] F's 'Lisio' (4 times) and 'Litio' (3 times) apparently represent the Italian name.

2.1.75-6/883-4 wooing. Neighbor] THEOBALD; wooing neighbors F

2.1.79/887 vnto you] CAPELL (Tyrwhitt); vnto F

2.1.104/912 Pisa, by report,] ROWE; Pifa by report, F

2.1.110.2/918.2 *Biondello following*] He may remain till 168/976.

Gremio and Tranio also are present with nothing to say during this time.
2.1.141/949 shakes] F1; shake F2
2.1.203/1011 light.] F; light— ROWE
2.1.206 Should be?—should buzz.] F (Shold be, fhould: buzze.). Many interpretative variants are possible.
2.1.242 askance] a fconce F (*a possible spelling*)
2.1.326/1134 in] ROWE 2; me F
2.1.347 cypress] F (Cypres)
2.1.351/1159 belongs] F; belong ROWE
2.1.371 Marseilles] F's 'Marcellus' appears also at *All's Well* 2561.
3.1.4/1219 this *Bianca* is,] This edition (G.T.); this is, F. See *Re-Editing*, 51-2.
3.1.28, 32, 41/1243, 1247, 1257 sigeia ... Sigeia ... sigeia] F3, F2, F2; figeria ... Sigeria ... figeria F1
3.1.46/1262] *continued to Hortensio*, ROWE 2; *spoken by* Luc⟨entio⟩., F
3.1.49/1265 BIANCA] POPE 2 (Theobald); *continued to Lucentio* F
3.1.50/1266 LUCENTIO] POPE 2 (Theobald); Bian⟨ca⟩. F
3.1.52/1268 BIANCA] POPE 2 (Theobald); Hort⟨ensio⟩. F
3.1.79/1295 change] F2; charge F1
3.1.79/1295 odd] THEOBALD; old F
3.1.80/1296 MESSENGER] F (*Nicke.*)
3.2.0.1/1306.1 *Tranio*] His speeches in this scene are far more appropriate to Hortensio, to whom they were probably originally assigned.
3.2.0.2/1306.2 *Bianca*] She has no specific function in the scene, though Shakespeare may have desired a full stage. Editors usually take her off with Katherine (3.2.26/1332).
3.2.8/1314 KATHERINE No] F ('*Kate.* No' *text*); No F (*c.w.*)
3.2.14/1320 man,] ROWE; ~; F
3.2.16/1322 them] MALONE; *not in* F. Many editors follow F, but the fact that Shakespeare does not elsewhere use *invite* intransitively combined with the metrical deficiency supports emendation.
3.2.29/1335 thy] F2; *not in* F1
3.2.30/1336 olde newes] CAPELL; *not in* F. Some emendation seems required by 3.2.32/1338 and 3.2.42/1348, and Capell's seems as good as any that have been offered. In F the speech ends with a comma, which may suggest that words have been omitted at the end of the sentence.
3.2.33/1339 heare] Q 1631; heard F
3.2.54/1361 Waid] F; sway'd HANMER
3.2.55-6 half-cheeked] F (halfe-chekt), *sometimes interpreted as* 'half-checked'
3.2.58/1364-5 now repaired] F; new-repaired DYCE 2 (W. S. Walker)
3.2.91/1398 not] KEIGHTLEY; *not in* F. Riverside, not emending, adds at the end of the line '*Pretending great excitement*' (following Elze's conjecture '*Imitating a coxcomb*', recorded by Cambridge). We interpret as an unfinished sentence which Petruccio himself interrupts. The negative improves both metre and sense.
3.3/Sc. 8] Usually undifferentiated, though awareness of awkwardness is shown e.g. by Capell's direction 'Tranio follows; but is beckon'd back by Lucentio, who converses a while apart'. But F has no entry for Lucentio anywhere in the scene; editors follow Rowe in bringing him on at the start of 3.2/Sc. 7, but this means that he is silent till this point. Tranio must be present earlier, since he is addressed (as 'Lucentio') in the first line. There is no evidence that Shakespeare ever intended Lucentio to be present before this point. By adding him to the direction, editors create the awkwardness of his silent presence till 3.3.11/1445, of his being addressed by Tranio as if they had already been talking, and of Gremio's re-entry implausibly rapidly since he describes the wedding which he left to see only 21 lines before. McKerrow, on his galley proofs, marked a new scene at this point, and we follow him because to do so removes the difficulty of Lucentio's silent presence earlier, justifies the mid-conversational tone of Tranio's first line, and suggests a time gap which adds plausibility to Gremio's re-entry. There is residual awkwardness in Tranio's immediate re-entry, but convention seems to have permitted this when the re-entering character is in new company.
3.3.1/1435 sir, to Loue] KNIGHT; to her love WHITE; fir, Loue F
3.3.3/1437 I] POPE; *not in* F
3.3.39/1473 vicar] This edition (G.T.); wench F. F's metrical irregularity arouses suspicion, and editors often follow F2's 'rose up' (for 'rose'). But there is no particular reason to introduce Katherine at this point, and 'wench' is a conceivable misreading of 'vicar'.
4.1.23/1582 CURTIS] Q 1631; Gru⟨mio⟩. F
4.1.37/1596 wilt thou] F1; thou wilt F2
4.1.42/1601 the white] F1; their white F3
4.1.56/1615 'tis] F; is ROWE 2
4.1.81 sleekly] F (slickely). *Sleek* and *slick* are closely related, and *OED* records this as its only instance of *slickly* meaning 'sleekly'. It seems improbable that Shakespeare would have recognized any distinction.
4.1.104/1664 GRUMIO] F3; Gre⟨mio⟩. F1
4.1.128/1688 Soud, soud, soud, soud.] F (Soud, foud, foud, foud.); food, food, food, food. WILSON. It seems unlikely that the compositor would have replaced the common word by such an unusual one.
4.1.134/1694 of] F; off ROWE
4.2.4/1761 HORTENSIO] F2; Luc⟨entio⟩. F1 (see Introduction)
4.2.6/1763 LUCENTIO] F2; Hor⟨tensio⟩. F1 (see Introduction)
4.2.7/1764 you, first,] THEOBALD; you firft, F
4.2.8/1765 LUCENTIO] F2; Hor⟨tensio⟩. F1
4.2.8/1765 reade that I professe,] ROWE; reade, that I professe, F
4.2.11-13/1768-70] The lines are metrically anomalous, to no apparent purpose, and strained in sense. F's 'Now tell me' permits ironic emphasis on 'Now'; metre is easily regularized by Capell's 'Tell me now'. In 4.2.12/1769, G.T. conjectures 'swear it, that'; omission would have been easy, and restoration would give a basically iambic line, require no strain on the sense of 'tell', and point the common Shakespearian distinction between 'tell' (or 'say') and 'swear'. 4.2.13/1770 is iambic if 'in the' and 'well as' are syncopated. Error is certain in 4.2.13/1770 (see next note), and a cluster of corruption is not improbable. But the irregularities may represent the unpolished state of the manuscript.
4.2.13/1770 none] ROWE; me F
4.2.31/1788 her] F3; them F1
4.2.64/1821 Marcantant] F; *mercatante* CAPELL
4.2.72/1829 *continued to Tranio*, F2; *ascribed to 'Par.'*, F1. There is no obvious explanation though '*Par.*' may represent a false start or marginal correction misinterpreted as a speech-prefix.
4.2.72/1829 in] THEOBALD; me F
4.2.72.2/1829.2, etc. *Pedant*] F; *Merchant* THOMPSON (Hosley). Ann Thompson remarks that the character appears to be a merchant; but Hortensio calls him 'a Marcantant, or a pedant', and even if F was, as Thompson supposes, printed from a transcript, it is difficult to imagine a scribe changing all occurrences of the designation, in prefixes and directions, merely because he did not understand 'Marcantant'. While Shakespeare gives the character some characteristics of a merchant, he seems to have thought of him primarily in relation to the type-character of the pedant (or schoolmaster), perhaps under the influence of Italian comedy.
4.3.63/1942 HABERDASHER] ROWE; Fel. F (presumably = Fellow)
4.3.81/1960 a] Q 1631; *not in* F
4.3.88/1967 like a] Q 1631; like F
4.3.93/1972 nor cap] This edition; neither cap F
4.3.179/2058 account'st] ROWE; accountedft F
4.4.0.1-2/2073.1-2] F duplicates the entrance for the Pedant at 4.4.0.1-2/2073.1-2, and 'booted and bare headed', 4.4.18.1/2091.1 (see Introduction).
4.4.1/2074 Sir] THEOBALD; Sirs F
4.4.19/2092 TRANIO] F; *spoken by Pedant*, THEOBALD. Most editors follow Theobald, but Tranio's completing of the prepared speech (perhaps in unison with the Pedant) shows that it is part of the plot.
4.4.32/2105] Metrically deficient. F2 prints 'I sir upon'; Keightley,

'agreement, sir'. G.T. conjectures 'sure agreement'. But this may simply be rough writing.

4.4.65-7/2138-40] See Introduction.

4.4.67.1/2140.1] F's *Enter Peter*, difficult to explain, may be a mistaken interpretation of an abbreviated entry for Petruccio, a false start that remained uncancelled in the manuscript. (See Introduction.)

4.4.71/2144 *Exeunt*] Some editors leave Lucentio on stage: see Introduction.

4.5/Sc. 13] This edition's division. See Introduction.

4.5.6 he's] F (has)

4.5.18/2163 except] F2; expect F1. F1 could be supported by *OED* 6, glossing 'suppose', but the easy error seems probable.

4.5.29/2174 t'attend] This edition; to come F. See *Re-Editing*, 42-3.

4.6.14/2193 And if] F; An if COLLIER

4.6.19/2198 is] Q 1631; in F

4.6.23/2202 so it shall be still] SINGER 2 (Ritson); fo it fhall be fo F

4.6.27/2206 Company] F; what company STEEVENS-REED 2 (Ritson)

4.6.39/2218 where is] F2; whether is F1

4.6.79/2258 be] F2; *not in* F1

4.6.80/2259 to be] F; *omitted* OLIVER

5.1.5/2264 masters] CAPELL; miftris F

5.1.27/2287 from *Padua*] F; to Padua POPE; from Pisa MALONE (Tyrwhitt); from Mantua HALLIWELL (Malone). Oliver defends F, while admitting that it is 'perhaps not the best of jokes'. Conceivably the Pedant remembers being told that Mantuans are proscribed from Padua (4.2.82-6/1839-43).

5.1.47/2307 Masters] F2; Miftris F1

5.1.60 copintank] F (copataine). The word, of obscure origin, exists in many variant forms.

5.1.84.1/2344.1 *Enter an Officer*] *not in* F. Capell directed *Enter one with an officer*, but 'one' is not needed unless he first exits. The dialogue does not fully provide for the necessary stage actions.

5.1.101/2361 and—] CAPELL; and, F

5.2.2/2403 done] ROWE; come F

5.2.39 thee, lad] F2; the lad F1

5.2.47/2448 better] F; bitter CAPELL (Theobald)

5.2.47 two] F (too; *a recorded spelling*)

5.2.67/2468 sir] F1; for F2. See Thompson.

5.2.91/2492 better] F; a better CAPELL

5.2.111/2512 wonders] HUDSON (Lettsom); a wonder F

5.2.133/2534 a] CAPELL; fiue F (*probably misreading* a *as* v)

5.2.137 you're] F (your)

5.2.153/2554 maintenance, commits] CAMBRIDGE; maintenance. Commits F

INCIDENTALS

133 peasant.] ~,   154 Slies] Sies   244 Ladies.] ~,   260 blood.] ~,   272 a] a a   280 companie,] ~.
288 brought] brough   372 kinde, and liberall,] kinde, and liberall,   364 resolud] refould   479 Coulord] Conlord   499 time.] ~,   571 twixt] twixr   700 belou'd] beloued   701 Belou'd] Beloued   758 streets] ftreers   909 great.] ~:   926 better'd] bettered   1025 Gentleman.] ~,   1058 then] rhen   1145 strife.] ~,   1188 world.] ~,   1208 wither'd] withered   1243 hic] hie   1258 steterat] F2; ftaterat F1   1264 yet.] ~:   1337 of.] ~,   1429 Bride,] ~?   1460 grumbling] grumlling (*an easy foul-case error*)   1686-7 Where ... those?] (roman)   1688 Soud ... soud] (roman)   1767 proue] ptoue   1792 forsworn.] ~,   1793 oath,] ~.   1823 countenance] eountenance   1929 lou'st] loueft   2052-3 Larke ... beautifull?] Larke? ... beautifull.   2065 And] Aud   2082 'Twere] ,Twere   2137 arriu'd] arriued   2165 *priuilegio*] (F2) *preuilegio*   2165 *solum*] (F2) *folem*   2167 for] fot   2197 then] theu   2231 trauell'st] trauelleft   2244 grieu'd] grieued   2299 brought] brough   2319 doublet] doubtlet   2372 brau'd] braued   2390 dough, but] doug, hbut   2397 No] Mo   2401 then neuer] then ueuer   2439 office.] ~,   2443 Head and but,] Head, and but,   2445 awakend] awakened   2542 threatning] thretaning   2590 wee'le] weee'le

Additional Passages

C.3 sending,] ~,

FOLIO STAGE DIRECTIONS

Ind.1.0.1/0.1 *Enter Begger and Hostes, Christophero Sly.*

Ind.1.13.1/13.1 *Falles asleepe.*

Ind.1.13.2-3/13.2-3 *Winde hornes. Enter a Lord from hunting, with his traine.*

Ind.1.71.2/71.2 *Sound trumpets.*

Ind.1.74.1/74.1 *Enter Seruingman.*

Ind.1.76.1/76.1 *Enter Players.*

Ind.1.102.1/102.1 *Exit one with the Players.*

Ind.1.128.1/128.1 *Exit a seruingman.*

Ind.2.0.1-3/136.1-3 *Enter aloft the drunkard with attendants, some with apparel, | Bason and Ewer, & other appurtenances, & Lord.*

Ind.2.34/170 *Musick* (after 'plaies,')

Ind.2.98.1-2/234.1-2 *Enter Lady with Attendants* (after Ind.2.97/233)

Ind.2.124.1/260.1 *Enter a Messenger*

1.1.0.1/274.2 *Flourish. Enter Lucentio, and his man Triano.*

1.1.47.1-3/321.1-3 *Enter Baptista with his two daughters, Katerina & Bianca, | Gremio a Pantelowne, Hortentio sister to Bianca. | Lucen. Tranio, stand by.*

1.1.101/375 *Exit.*

1.1.104/378 *Exit*

1.1.143.1-2/417.1 *Exeunt ambo. Manet Tranio and Lucentio*

1.1.218.1/492.1 *Enter Biondello.*

1.1.246.1-2/520.1-2 *Exeunt. The Presenters aboue speakes.*

1.1.252.1/526.1 *They sit and marke.*

1.2.0.1/526.2 *Enter Petruchio, and his man Grumio.*

1.2.17.1/543.1 *He rings him by the eares*

1.2.19.1/545.1 *Enter Hortensio.*

1.2.135.1/661.1 *Enter Gremio and Lucentio disgused.*

1.2.216.1/743.1 *Enter Tranio braue, and Biondello.*

1.2.281/808 *Exeunt.*

2.1.0.1/808.1 *Enter Katherina and Bianca.*

2.1.22/830 *Strikes her* (after 'so.')

2.1.22.1/830.1 *Enter Baptista.*

2.2.29.1/837.1 *Flies after Bianca*

2.2.30/838 *Exit.*

2.2.38.1-4/846.1-4 *Enter Gremio, Lucentio, in the habit of a meane man, | Petruchio with Tranio, with his boy | bearing a Lute and Bookes.*

2.1.108/916 *Enter a Seruant.*

2.1.141.1/949.1 *Enter Hortensio with his head broke.*

2.1.168/976 *Exit. Manet Petruchio.* (after 2.1.167/975)

2.1.181.1/989.1 *Enter Katerina.*

2.1.217.1/1025.1 *she strikes him*

2.1.269.1/1077.1 *Enter Baptista, Gremio, Trayno.*

2.1.320.1/1128.1 *Exit Petruchio and Katherine.*

THE TAMING OF THE SHREW

2.1.395/1203   Exit (after 1202/2.1.394)
2.1.399/1207   Exit.
2.1.407.1/1215.1   Exit.
3.1.0.1-2/1215.2-3   Enter Lucentio, Hortentio, and Bianca.
3.1.79.1/1295.1   Enter a Messenger.
3.1.90/1306   Exit.
3.2.0.1-2/1306.1-2   Enter Baptista, Gremio, Tranio, Katherine, Bianca, and o-|thers, attendants.
3.2.26.1/1332.1   Exit weeping.
3.2.29.1/1335.1   Enter Biondello.
3.2.84.1/1391.1   Enter Petruchio and Grumio.
3.2.123.1/1430.1   Exit.
3.2.127/1434   Exit.
3.3.21.1/1455.1   Enter Gremio.
3.3.55.1/1489.1   Musicke playes. (after 3.3.56/1490)
3.3.56.1-2/1490.1-2   Enter Petruchio, Kate, Bianca, Hortensio, Baptista.
3.3.111.1/1545.1   Exeunt. P. Ka.
4.1.0.1/1558.1   Enter Grumio. Exeunt.
4.1.10.1/1569.1   Enter Curtis.
4.1.93.1/1653.1   Enter foure or fiue seruingmen.
4.1.105.1/1665.1   Enter Petruchio and Kate.
4.1.125.1/1685.1   Ex. Ser.
4.1.128.1/1688.1   Enter seruants with supper.
4.1.135.1/1695.1   Enter one with water.
4.1.164/1724   Exeunt.
4.1.164.1/1724.1   Enter Seruants seuerally.
4.1.166.1/1726.1   Enter Curtis a Seruant. (after 4.1.167/1727)
4.1.173.1/1733.1   Enter Petruchio.
4.1.197/1757   Exit
4.2.0.1/1757.1   Enter Tranio and Hortensio:
4.2.5.2/1762.2   Enter Bianca.
4.2.59.1/1816.1   Enter Biondello.
4.2.72.2/1829.2   Enter a Pedant.
4.2.122/1879   Exeunt.
4.3.0.1/1879.1   Enter Katherina and Grumio.
4.3.32/1910.1   Beats him.
4.3.35.1/1941.1   Enter Petruchio, and Hortensio with meate.
4.3.60.1/1939.1   Enter Tailor.
4.3.62.1/1941   Enter Haberdasher (after 4.3.61/1940)
4.3.166/2045   Exit Tail.
4.4.0.1-2/2073.1-2   Enter Tranio, and the Pedant drest like Vincentio.
4.4.7.1/2080.1   Enter Biondello.
4.4.18.1/2091.1   Enter Baptista and Lucentio: Pedant booted | and bare headed.
4.4.66/2140.1   Exit.
4.4.67.1/2140.1   Enter Peter.
4.4.71/2144   Exeunt.
4.5.0.1/2144.1   Enter Lucentio and Biondello.
4.5.30/2175   Exit.
4.5.34/2179   Exit.
4.6.0.1/2179.1   Enter Petruchio, Kate, Hortentio
4.6.27.1/2206.1   Enter Vincentio.
4.6.77.1/2256.1   Exeunt.
4.6.80.1/2259   Exit.
5.1.0.1-2/2259.1-2   Enter Biondello, Lucentio and Bianca, Gremio | is out before.
5.1.3/2262   Exit.
5.1.6.1-2/2264.1-2   Enter Petruchio, Kate, Vincentio, Grumio | with Attendants.
5.1.12.1/2271.1   Knock.
5.1.13.1-2/2273.1   Pedant lookes out of the window.
5.1.35.1/2295.1   Enter Biondello.
5.1.50.1/2310.1   He beates Biondello.
5.1.55.2-3/2315.2-3   Enter Pedant with seruants, Baptista, Tranio.
5.1.98.1/2358.1   Enter Biondello, Lucentio and Bianeu.
5.1.102.1-2/2362.1-2   Exit Biondello, Tranio and Pedant as fast as may be.
5.1.103.1/2363.1   Kneele.
5.1.127/2387   Exit.
5.1.128.1/2388.1   Exit
5.1.129.1/2389.1   Exeunt.
5.1.141/2401   Exeunt.
5.2.0.1-5/2401.1-4   Enter Baptista, Vincentio, Gremio, the Pedant, Lucentio, and | Bianca. Tranio, Biondello Grumio, and Widdow: | The Seruingmen with Tranio bringing | in a Banquet.
5.2.39.1/2440.1   Drinkes to Hortensio.
5.2.50.1/2451.1   Exit Bianca.
5.2.83/2484   Exit.
5.2.85.1/2486.1   Enter Biondello.
5.2.92.1/2493.1   Exit. Bion.
5.2.94.1/2495.1   Enter Biondello.
5.2.101/2502   Exit.
5.2.105.1/2504.1   Enter Katerina.
5.2.125.1/2524.1   Enter Kate, Bianca, and Widdow.
5.2.194.1/2593.1   Exit Petruchio

THE FIRST PART OF THE CONTENTION
(2 HENRY VI)

This play (*BEPD* 119) survives in two versions, one shorter by about a third, and in other ways variant from, the other. It was in connection with the publication of the shorter version that the play was entered, on 12 March 1594, in the Stationers' Register:

Thomas Myllington / Entred for his copie · vnder the handes of bothe the wardens/ a booke intituled, the firste pte of the Contention of the twoo famous houſes of york and Lancaſter wᵗʰ the deathe of the good Duke Humfrey and the baniſhement and deathe of the duke of Suff' and the tragicall ende of the prowd Cardinall of wincheſter / wᵗʰ the notable rebellion of Iack Cade and the duke of yorke firſt clayme vnto the Crowne

Three editions of the shorter version, all quartos, were published. The earliest, dated 1594 (Q1), bears essentially the same title as the S.R. entry (see the Title textual note); it was printed by Thomas Creede for Millington. G. W. Williams has argued that this edition was probably set from a single set of cases by one compositor who, working faster than his press, set the text partly seriatim and partly by forme. A second quarto edition was printed, again for Millington, in 1600 (Q2) by Valentine Simmes from a copy of Q1. On 19 April 1602 Millington transferred his rights in the play to Thomas Pavier who, in 1619, brought out an undated, edited third quarto edition (Q3) as part of a collection of ten plays, all printed by the Jaggards, and all allegedly by Shakespeare (see the General Introduction, pp. 34-6). Q3 appears to have been set chiefly from a copy of Q1. The longer version of the play first appeared in the First Folio, and was there entitled 'The ſecond Part of Henry the Sixt, | with the death of the Good Duke | HVMFREY'.

In the 1920s Peter Alexander and Madeleine Doran demonstrated independently of one another, and to the satisfaction of most scholars, that Q, formerly believed to be either Shakespeare's source for F or an early version partly or wholly by him of the play he later revised to F, was instead a memorial reconstruction of F—one of the so-called 'bad quartos'. The linchpin of Alexander's argument, never plausibly refuted, lies in his explanation of a single variant passage, 2.2.9-52/889-931, in which York states his claim to the crown (Alexander, p. 62):

York had to prove that, although descended from the fifth son of Edward III, he was, because of his father's marriage with a descendant of the third son, more in the direct line of succession than the heirs of the fourth son. The Quarto writer by making him declare his ancestor the Duke of York to be the second son to Edward III renders further argument superfluous; he had now no need to claim the throne through a daughter of the third son as he proceeds to do.

The point is not whether the Q version of the speech is historically accurate, for an author as well as a reporter could garble the facts. The point is, rather, that, as it stands, there is no dramatic reason for the Q speech to continue past its fifth line: yet it does continue, and for a further twenty-one lines. No one who understood what he was writing—that is, no author—could have made this error, but someone parroting someone else's work, of which he himself had but a dim understanding—that is, a reporter—easily could. Once having established that part of Q is clearly a report, it is natural to suppose that the rest of the text—which is open to alternative explanations—is also a report.

To this central argument, Alexander added several shoring observations, the most persuasive of which, upon which Alfred Hart and others have built, is that Q contains a number of echoes of other plays, by Shakespeare and others, which are absent from F. In the context of the bad quarto hypothesis, these echoes in Q are easily explained as the reporters' interpolations from other plays they knew; in its absence, they must be explained, less probably, as deliberate excisions from F.

Alexander's hypothesis plausibly and economically accounts for the Q text, and we accept it, with but slight qualification.

Alexander believed the report to be of the full F text, and that its comparative brevity, like its other variants, resulted from a failure of memory. Doran, on the other hand, suggested that Q reports an abridged and possibly otherwise revised version of the F text. This view, most recently developed, first, by McMillin, and later, by Montgomery, we find the more probable.

Alexander also believed that the reporters responsible for Q had at their disposal manuscript fragments of the official text with which they supplemented their memories. This qualification to his general hypothesis he found necessary in order to account for several instances of agreement between Q and F of a kind for which memorial reconstruction was an inadequate explanation; he mentioned, but rejected, the alternative possibility that these close correspondences could have resulted from Q having been used intermittently as copy for F. We accept the alternative hypothesis, and discuss it more fully later.

We do not know with any certainty who was responsible for the reporting of Q, though several candidates have been advanced. Alexander thought two reporters, both actors, one

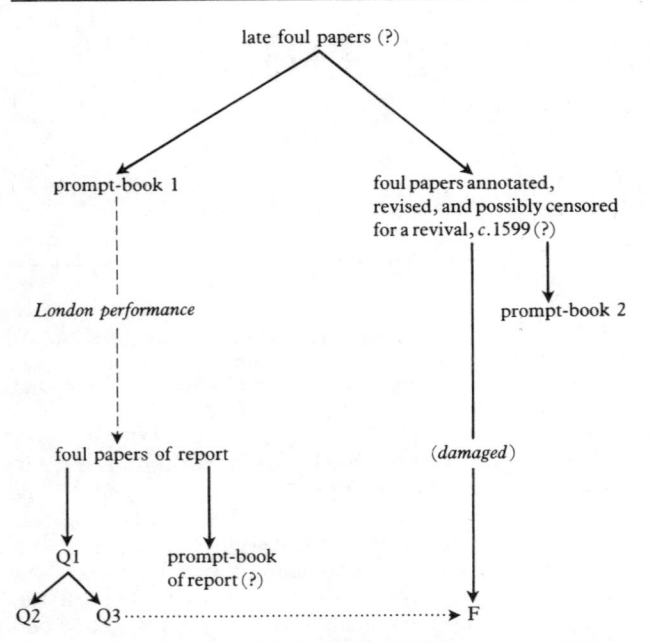

```
                    late foul papers (?)
                    ╱              ╲
                   ╱                ╲
         prompt-book 1      foul papers annotated,
              │             revised, and possibly censored
              │             for a revival, c.1599 (?)
    London performance │              │
              │                       │
              │                  prompt-book 2
              ▼
      foul papers of report        (damaged)
         ╱        ╲
        ▼          ▼
       Q1      prompt-book
      ╱  ╲     of report (?)
     ▼    ▼
    Q2    Q3 ·················▶ F
```

playing Warwick, the other doubling Suffolk and Lord Clifford, had collaborated on it; Chambers (*Shakespeare*, i. 283) suggested the book-keeper, but has been challenged by Jordan (1105-8; the idea of book-keeper reporters is now generally discredited: see Greg, *Problem*, 60, and *Modernizing*, page 129, note 1); Doran tentatively proposed that the report was a group effort, put together by a number of actors, a hypothesis which McMillin has developed. The matter requires further study. Whoever the reporter(s), it seems certain from McMillin's and Montgomery's work that the production reported was a London one, and not, as Doran had suggested, one given on a provincial tour.

The whole of the play may not be by Shakespeare (see 'Canon and Chronology'). Various features of the Folio text, however, suggest that the manuscript which served as its principal copy was authorial foul papers: imprecise directions, including unmarked necessary entrances (e.g. Somerset's 1.3.103.2/469.2, and Stanley's 2.4.17.5/1087.5) and unmarked necessary exits (that of the Duchess 2.3.16.1/977.1, her fellow prisoners 2.3.8.1-2/969.1-2, and Buckingham 5.1.114.1/2930.1); uncertain ('*Bolingbroke or Southwell reades*' 1.4.23.2/615.2) or descriptively vague staging ('*Fight at Sea. Ordinance goes off*' stage directions list 4.1.0.1-2/2012.3-4); variety of character designation (Duke Humfrey-Gloster-Protector, Beauford-Cardinall); and vague ('*infinite numbers*' 4.2.32.2-3/2190.2, '*Multitudes*' 4.8.9.1/2691.1) or summary designations ('*state*' 2.3.0.1/961.1, '*others*' stage directions list 4.1.0.3-6/2011.4-8) all point to this. So, too, does an apparent undeleted authorial false start (see the note to 5.1.109/2925). Greg, who also thought the manuscript probably autograph, believed it a fair copy, chiefly because he felt the survival of foul papers from so early a date and from another company not likely (*Problem*, p. 55). He may be right. He also thought that the manuscript had been annotated by the prompter, either so that a prompt-copy could be prepared from it (*Folio*, p. 183) or so that it might itself be used as a prompt-book (*Problem*, p. 55). Again, he may be right, but his position (*Folio*, p. 182) rests on two features of F, neither of which constitutes very strong evidence of the prompter's hand. Firstly, he points to the 'very full provision of noises', and secondly, to the introduction of actors' names for minor characters ('*Beuis, and Iohn Holland*' note to 4.2.0.1/2160.2, and probably also '*Michael*' note to 4.2.109.1/2270.2, '*George*' note to 4.7.21.1/2477.1, and '*Iohn*' note to 4.7.7/2465). The noises do not seem so numerous as to be inconsistent with authorial origin, and the use of actors' names for minor characters, as Wilson (*Third Part*, p. 117 ff.) argued—though Greg rejects him out of hand (*Folio*, p. 183, note 10)—seems to us quite plausibly the author's own. We take F as our principal control text.

Cairncross argued (pp. xxv-ix) that the manuscript underwent some censorship before it reached the Folio compositors; he may be right, but the arguments he adduces—principally based on differences between Q and F—are not very strong. The differences to which he alludes may as easily, and perhaps more probably, be explained as revisions which occurred between the (early) state of the play represented by the manuscript behind F, and the (later) prompt-book, from which Q, indirectly, derives. However, his point that the allusion to the Cardinal's bastardy in the Q scene corresponding to our 2.1/Sc. 5 (see the note to 2.1.38-43/700-5) metrically fits into F, and thus suggests late excision from it, has some force. It may be that the editors of F themselves lightly censored the manuscript, or it may be, the original licensed prompt-book having been lost in the tumult and change of companies in the early 1590s, that the Chamberlain's Men by perhaps the late 1590s found themselves in possession of only the foul papers, which they submitted for relicensing, and that some censorship occurred then. It is difficult to be certain.

There can be little doubt, however, that this manuscript was not the only copy employed for F: some recourse clearly was had to a copy of some edition of Q, probably Q3, though the extent and frequency of consultation is uncertain. McKerrow ('Note') first developed this hypothesis, arguing for limited Q contamination of F: he suggested that the manuscript was in some places damaged, and that only for these indecipherable passages did the Folio compositors turn to Q. Cairncross, taking as his starting-point the premiss that compositors prefer printed copy, even heavily marked-up printed copy, to manuscript, developed a hypothesis of extensive Q contamination. Montgomery, after an examination of Cairncross's arguments, concluded that for only five passages can it be demonstrated that Q copy was used, but that further contamination, in the form either of use of Q as principal copy for longer F passages or of occasional consultation of Q for isolated readings, remains possible. We accept Montgomery's findings: for the five demonstrable instances of Q contamination (1.1.55-59, 2.1.70.1-3, 2.1.117-55.3, 4.5.0.1-4.6.0.2/55-9, 732.1-3, 779-817.4, 2427.2-40.3, and most of 2.3.58.1-2.4.0.2/1019.1-1070.4) we take Q as our only substantive text, adopt its incidentals, and treat any departures from it—including those which we adopt from F—as emendations. We assume there probably was occasional consultation elsewhere, and edit the text on this basis, but since no further use of Q as principal copy has been demonstrated, we suppose that none was made, and nowhere else adopt Q as our control text.

Montgomery shows that Q3 was set principally from a copy

of Q1, but that its compilers had recourse on perhaps six occasions to some other authority, possibly a chronicle for the defective genealogy and some form of supplementary report for the five other extensive variants. Q3 appears to have been the edition used by the Folio compositors. Cairncross believed that both Q2 and Q3 had been used as copy for F, but none of his evidence in support of this hypothesis withstood Montgomery's scrutiny; Montgomery himself, however, cited the following variant direction, which occurs within one of the passages of certain Q contamination of F. Q1–2 read 'Enter the Lord *Skayles* vpon the Tower | walles walking. | Enter three or foure Citizens below' (G1r); Q3 omits altogether the line referring to the Citizens ('Enter ... below'); F prints '*Enter Lord Scales vpon the Tower walking. Then enters | two or three Citizens below*' (TLN 2613–14). Montgomery pointed to the curious variation in the number of citizens directed to enter. If F had been set from Q1 or Q2, it would be difficult to account for its alteration of 'three or four' to 'two or three'. One might suggest that the copy of Q1 or Q2 employed by the F compositors had served as a prompt-book at some point, and that this variation was penned in it by the prompter, but this is improbable: a prompter might well alter 'three or four' to 'four', 'three', or 'two', but he would not, if he were bothering to make an alteration at all, change one indefinite direction to another. But if Q3 had been F's copy here, it would be manifest to the F editor that the Q3 direction is incomplete: Scales does not enter alone; some 'Citizens'—for so he would surmise from the Q3 speech-prefix '1. *Citizen*', which at once identifies the character and reveals there to be more than one of them—enter with him. Scales enters 'on the Tower' (i.e., above) and his dramatic situation is defence of the Tower from the rebels (4.5.8–9/2435–6); the citizens' dramatic situation is to beg aid of Scales to defend the city (4.5.4–6/2431–3): dramatically, therefore, they enter to Scales from elsewhere in the city; they are thus outside the Tower, and therefore, 'below'. It would be an easy matter for the F editor to translate inferences similar to these into the succinct stage direction '*Then enters two or three Citizens below*'. That this part of the F direction is an interpolation is to some extent corroborated by the un-Shakespearian '*enters*': the form occurs in stage directions only seven times elsewhere in the canon (quarto and Folio *Contention* 2.4.58.3/1019.3, quarto *1 Henry IV* 5.3.0.1/2736.2, Folio *Hamlet* 3.2.129.1/1857.1, quarto *Othello* 1.2.52.1/238.1, *Timon* 3.1.0.3/802.3, *Coriolanus* stage directions list 1.8.0.1–3/605.1–3, and *Tempest* 5.1.57.1/1776.1). Q *Contention* is a bad quarto, and for this direction we believe F is dependent on Q; quarto *1 Henry IV*, Folio *Hamlet*, quarto *Othello*, *Coriolanus*, and *The Tempest* are, in our opinion, all set from scribal transcripts; and the *Timon* direction comes in a part of that play which we assign to Middleton.

Montgomery has isolated 176 substantive variants between Q3 and its copy, Q1. Twenty-five of these agree with F against Q1: each of these we have considered as a potential Q3 contamination of F, and where we conclude this probably to be so, we usually adopt Q1's reading. Those unique Q3-F agreements which we do not believe to be instances of contamination, and which we therefore do not emend, we record among the textual notes. Further contamination probably also occurred in passages where Q3 is invariant from Q1, so we have regarded every instance of Q-F agreement, especially when it occurs in the midst of otherwise not well reported passages, with suspicion.

If in instances of agreement between Q and F we believe it probable that F has been contaminated by Q, we record our view by attributing the reading to 'Q, F'—that is, we cite Q first; if, on the other hand, we feel that the probabilities favour F's independence of Q, and that the agreement is the result of accurate reporting, we attribute the reading to 'F, Q'. However, we do not routinely record instances of the latter.

The quarto, as we have seen, appears to derive from a performance: its ultimate authority is therefore the prompt-book, which represents a later stage in the play's development than the foul papers manuscript which probably was used for F. This means that while it will, no doubt, corrupt much of the text it reports, it may also preserve, perhaps in garbled form, authorial alterations—revisions—made subsequent to the play's early draft, and thus absent from F, but in time to have been incorporated in the prompt-book. On a number of occasions we believe that precisely this happened in *The Contention*. Accordingly, we adopt a number of Q passages or arrangements usually excluded from edited texts of this play. These we discuss individually in the textual notes.

Still other Q variants may represent neither corruption nor revision, but rather the preservation of readings which have become corrupted in the transmission of the F text. For this reason, other Q readings, normally excluded, we have accepted in our text. A number of Q readings which may fall into this category, but of which we are sufficiently uncertain that we do not adopt them, we list separately among 'Rejected Quarto Variants'.

We frequently adopt stage directions from Q, or construct directions on the basis of action implicit in Q's dialogue, because, as a bad quarto, Q seems to us to have special authority in this regard. In general, if Q seems to expand or clarify a vague direction in F, or if it specifies or hints at action not mentioned in F but not inconsistent with F, or if it seems to represent a probably authorial restaging of a sequence from that represented in F, we adopt Q, and record that we have done so. Since, however, Q may derive from an abridged adaptation of the prompt-book performed under circumstances different from, and perhaps more constrained than, those for which the original prompt-book was prepared (see McMillin and Montgomery), we do not observe cuts which appear to have been made to the text which Q reports, nor do we adopt Q variants which may have been necessitated by cast limitations. In this way we hope to recapture as nearly as we can the original prompt-book, without incorporating into our text alterations subsequent to that original prompt-book which Q may also reflect. Some of Q's cuts, however, may be authorial; we note the more interesting of these.

The quarto's 'The First Part of the Contention of the Two Famous Houses of Yorke & Lancaster' is probably closer to the title by which the play was contemporarily known than the Folio's 'ſecond Part of King Henry the Sixt'. The reporter(s) who put together Q probably would not have forgotten the play's title, nor is it easy to see a reason why either they or Millington would have deliberately altered it. Millington's object in publishing the play was to sell copies—it was in his interest to make sure that it carried a title which the book-buying public would recognize. The Folio's 'ſecond Part' cannot have been the play's original title, if, as we believe, the 'firſt Part' was written after it (see the Introduction to *1 Henry VI*).

Neither Q nor F is divided into acts and scenes. We accept the traditional divisions with a few exceptions. For the reasons discussed in the note to 4.7.154-5/2613-14 we continue 4.7/Sc. 18 to include what is usually 4.8, and renumber the remaining scenes in this act accordingly: 4.9 becomes our 4.8/Sc. 19, and 4.10 our 4.9/Sc. 20. To the customary three scenes of Act 5 we add two, at points where, in our view, the stage is cleared. We regard the battle between Richard and Somerset and the passage dealing with King Henry's flight—both traditionally part of 5.2—as separate scenes. The former we detach from its Folio context and place it, on the evidence of Q, immediately after 5.1/Sc. 21 as our 5.2/Sc. 22. What remains of the traditional 5.2 thereby becomes our 5.3/Sc. 23. Henry's flight, which ends the traditional 5.2, we mark as our 5.4/Sc. 24. The traditional 5.3 thus becomes our 5.5/Sc. 25.

Unless otherwise indicated, references to McKerrow in our notes are to the commentary to his Oxford edition of the play, which had reached an advanced state at the time of his death, and references to Walker are to marginal comments made by Alice Walker to McKerrow's edition.

W.L.M./(G.T.)

WORKS CITED

Alexander, Peter, *Shakespeare's 'Henry VI' and 'Richard III'* (1929)
Cairncross, A. S., ed., *The Second Part of King Henry VI*, Arden (1957)
Doran, Madeleine, *Henry VI, Parts II and III: Their Relation to the Contention and the True Tragedy* (1928)
Hart, Alfred, *Stolne and Surreptitious Copies: A Comparative Study of Shakespeare's Bad Quartos* (1942)
Hart, H. C., ed., *The Second Part of King Henry the Sixth*, Arden (1909)
Jordan, John E., 'The Reporter of *Henry VI, Part 2*', *PMLA* 64 (1949), 1089-1113
McKerrow, R. B., 'A Note on the "Bad Quartos" of *2* and *3 Henry VI* and the Folio Text', *RES* 13 (1937), 64-72
McMillin, Scott, 'Casting for Pembroke's Men: The *Henry VI* Quartos and *The Taming of A Shrew*', *SQ* 23 (1972), 141-59
Montgomery, William, ed., 'The Contention of York and Lancaster: A Critical Edition', vol. ii (unpublished D.Phil. Thesis, University of Oxford, 1985)
—— ed., *The First Part of the Contention 1594*, MSR (1985)
Sanders, Norman, ed., *The Second Part of King Henry the Sixth*, New Penguin (1981)
Turner, Robert K. and George Walton Williams, eds., *The Second Part of King Henry the Sixth*, Pelican, revised (1969)
Williams, George Walton, 'Setting by Formes in Quarto Printing', *SB* 11 (1958), 39-53
Wilson, John Dover, ed., *The Second Part of King Henry VI*, New (1952)
—— ed., *The Third Part of King Henry VI*, New (1952)

TEXTUAL NOTES

Title *The . . . Lancaster*] This edition (Q running title, *subs.*); THE FIRST PART OF THE CON-|TENTION OF THE TWO FAMOVS | Houſes of *Yorke* & *Lancaſter*, with the death of | the good Duke *Humphrey*. Q (*head title*); THE | Firſt part of the Con=|tention betwixt the two famous Houſes of *Yorke* | and *Lancaſter*, with the death of the good | Duke *Humphrey*: | And the baniſhment and death of the Duke of | *Suffolke*, and the Tragicall end of the proud Cardinall | of *Wincheſter*, with the notable Rebellion | of *Iacke Cade*: | And the Duke of Yorkes firſt claime vnto | the Crowne Q (*title-page*), S.R. (*subs.*, except 'of' is substituted for Q's 'betwixt'); The firſt . . . pts of henry the vi^t S.R. *transfer*; The ſecond Part of Henry the Sixt, | with the death of the Good Duke | HVMFREY F (*head title*); *The ſecond Part of Henry the Sixt*. F (*running title*); *The Second part of King Hen. the Sixt*. F (*table of contents*). See the Introduction.

1.1.0.1-7/0.1-7 *Enter . . . Earles . . . Warwicke*] Q (. . . *Earle* . . .). The F version of this direction (see the stage directions list) has Salisbury and Warwick enter with the King, and Somerset and Buckingham enter with the Queen, Suffolk, and York. It also does not direct that 'others' enter with the King, and it implies that the order of entrance through the second door is Queen, Suffolk, York, rather than Q's York, Suffolk, Queen. We take Q here to reflect performance.

1.1.8/8 twenty] F, Q3; then the Q1-2

1.1.24-9/24-9 Th' . . . *King*] Q; *not in* F. The F version of this speech is very different (see Additional Passage A). This scene is in general well reported in Q, however, especially this earlier part of it. Since there is nothing in the Q version of the speech which suggests memorial interpolation, either from elsewhere in this play, or from the other plays which the reporter(s) appear to have known, we suppose Q here reflects a revised version of the speech made in the preparation of the prompt-book (see the Introduction). Many of the following notes cite parallels with Shakespeare's acknowledged work and show that, allowing for memorial error, there is nothing inconsistent with the suggestion that Shakespeare was responsible for the revision.

1.1.24/24 excess of] This edition; exceſſiue Q; *not in* F. Shakespeare uses *excessive* only once (*All's Well* 1.1.53/54), but *excess of*, for which *excessive* would be an easy memorial slip, five times (*Two Gentlemen* 3.1.219/1238, *Henry V* 2.2.42/649, *Twelfth Night* 1.1.2/2, *Othello* 4.1.98/2225, and *Kinsmen* 1.3.4/385).

1.1.25/25 lauish of my tongue] Q; *not in* F. The phrase *lavish tongue* occurs in *1 Henry VI* 2.5.47/1000, a play there is no reason to believe the reporter knew (but in a part of that play which appears to be not by Shakespeare).

1.1.26/26 beseemes] Q; *not in* F. With one exception ('beseeming', *Cymbeline* 5.6.411/3217) Shakespeare used this word, or forms of it, only in the 1590s; during this period, however, he uses it not infrequently ('beseem' *Two Gentlemen*, *Shrew*, *Duke of York*, *Errors*, *Richard II*, *Sonnets*; 'beseems' *Duke of York*, *1 Henry VI* (twice), *Lucrece*, *K. John*; 'beseemeth' *LLL*; 'beseeming' *Two Gentlemen*, *1 Henry VI*, *Romeo*, *Richard II*).

1.1.27/27 suffice] Q; *not in* F. The word occurs throughout the canon, but it is more frequently used in earlier plays.

1.1.27/27 blisse] Q; *not in* F. Frequently used throughout the canon.

1.1.27/27 liking] Q; *not in* F. Frequently used in this sense throughout the canon.

1.1.28/28 nought] This edition; nothing Q; *not in* F. The Q line is unmetrical: *nothing* would be an easy memorial substitution for *nought*. An alternative emendation—'Nothing' for Q's 'And nothing'—is equally plausible as a memorial error, but the reading is less attractive because it juxtaposes 'Nothing' with 'liking', which ends the previous line.

1.1.35/35 LORDS (*kneel*)] This edition; *All kneel*. F

1.1.38/38 contracted] F; contract G.T. *conj*. In support of the conjecture see *OED ppl. a.* and *Richard III* 3.7.169/2159.

1.1.41-54/41-54 Inprimis . . . read on] F. This passage may have been set from Q.

1.1.41 Imprimis] F (Inprimis), Q

1.1.45/45 *Reignier*] F; *Raynard* Q. For Q's form see *Duke of York* and *1 Henry VI*.

1.1.48/48 *It . . . them*] Q (roman); *not in* F. The omission may be explained as resulting from eyeskip (*Item* to *them*). Line 1.1.55-

6/55 confirms Q, for both readings of the document should be identical.

1.1.50/50 deliuered] F; deliuered ouer Q

1.1.50/50 *fa*] Q (roman); *father* F. Q probably records performance here, and F could easily be a 'correction' of what was thought to be an error or abbreviation.

1.1.50.1/50.1 *Gloster lets the paper fall*] Q (*Duke Humphrey lets it fall.*); *not in* F

1.1.55-71/55-71 Item . . . performde] Q. This passage was set from Q. We adopt Q as our control text, and follow its incidentals.

1.1.56-7/56 *Duchy of Aniou and the County of*] CAIRNCROSS (*subs.*); *Duches of Aniou and of* Q1, Q2 (*Dutches . . .*); *Dutcheſſe of Aniou and* F, Q3 (*. . . and of*); *Dutchies of Anjou and* ROWE. F has been contaminated by Q here: the Cardinal's reading should be identical with Gloucester's.

1.1.57/57 deliuered] CAIRNCROSS; deliuered ouer Q, F (*italic*)

1.1.59/59 without dowry] Q (roman); without hauing any Dowry F

1.1.61/61 thee] Q; thee the F

1.1.64/64 I'th] F; in the Q

1.1.66/66 *and Buckingham*] Q; *Buckingham* F

1.1.71.2/71.1-2 [*Duke Humphrey of Gloster staies*] *all*] Q (*and Duke Humphrey ſtaies all*); *Manet* F

1.1.90/90 had] GRANT WHITE; hath F. 'Retaining "hath" we must presumably read the phrase as "And hath mine Vnckle *Beauford*, (and myselfe) crowned his Highnesse in Paris in his infancie?", which involves the assumption of an awkward inversion of order in the original, but is not impossible. The fact that in F1 the final h of "hath" appears to be slightly high to paper perhaps suggests correction in proof. An original "hat" (for "had") might easily be miscorrected to "hath"' (McKerrow).

1.1.98 Razing] F (Racing)

1.1.106 roast] F (roſt), Q (roaſt). Tilley R 144 confirms *roast* as an acceptable variant form of the proverb. *Roost* is more common nowadays.

1.1.142/142 But . . . speake] Q; *not in* F. The Q line fits the F context better than its own. It was probably inadvertently omitted by the F compositor.

1.1.142/142 But ile] Q; *not in* F; So ile This edition *conj*.; I will This edition *conj*. Q would be an easy memorial slip for either of our conjectures.

1.1.166 all together] F (altogether)

1.1.167 hoist] F (hoyſe)

1.1.176/176 Protector] Q; Protectors F

1.1.184/184 o'th'] F, Q3 (of the); of Q1-2

1.1.190 thee] F (the). An alternative modernization would be 'the'; Q, however, reads 'thee'.

1.1.197-8/197-8 The . . . command] Q; *not in* F. The Q phrases probably are not memorial interpolations: they do not echo anything in F, but they do explain why Salisbury, too, is important for the success of Warwick and York.

1.1.208/208 Then lets away] This edition (G.T.); Then lets make haſt away F; Come ſonnes away Q; Then let's make haste POPE. Cairncross follows Pope, on the assumption that Q was printer's copy, and was imperfectly corrected. But this speech occurs near the bottom of column b of a cast-off Folio page (m3ʳ), set by Compositor B. In order to stretch his copy, B appears to have mislined the preceding speech and the first line of the following one; in neither case was the mislineation caused by exigencies of justification. Moreover, here and in the following speech B uses uncharacteristically unabbreviated speech-prefixes, presumably in order to disguise the unusually short lines of dialogue. One must therefore suspect that B interpolated the redundant and extrametrical 'make haſt', not present in Q, for the same reason. (Although *make haste* occurs 31 times elsewhere in the Shakespeare canon, *make haste away* occurs nowhere else.) For similar alteration of copy elsewhere in B's work, see the note to 4.7.154-5/2613-14 and the General Introduction, p. 41.

1.1.236-59/236-59 Anjou . . . downe] F. Probably set from Q. With the exception of one variant, in line 1.1.238/238 (see the list of rejected quarto variants), this passage is substantively identical in Q3 and F (Q1-2 read 'graffle' not 'grapple' in 1.1.257/257).

No trace of the first half of the F speech (1.1.214-35/214-35) is in Q. The simplest explanation—that the entire F speech derives from authorial copy, that the production Q reports, as part of a general abridgement (see the Introduction), cut the first half of the F speech, and that Q accurately reports what was left—is not likely, for several reasons. York repeats lines 1.1.237-8/237-8, verbatim, in their Q form (i.e. ending in 'England' rather than 'England's soil') later, at a point in Q where F has York say 'Cold Newes for me: for I had hope of France, | As firmly as I hope for fertile England' (3.1.87-8/1268-9). Their appearance in this first scene in Q thus looks suspiciously like anticipation of that later occurrence, and their appearance here in F looks suspiciously like Q contamination. (That the later F occurrence is authorial is confirmed by the King's 'Cold' (3.1.86/1267), which York's lines echo, and by the general divergence of Q from F there, making F dependence on Q unlikely.) Another reason for doubting that Q is simply an accurate report of what remained of F in performance is the fact that the passage is spoken by York, and in soliloquy. For a soliloquy to be as accurately reported as this, one would have to suppose its speaker was among the compilers of the report. York, however, cannot have been one of the reporters: his part, on the whole, is not well reported, either in this scene or elsewhere in the play, and, moreover, it contains a clear objective instance of serious memorial error—the genealogy in 1.4/Sc. 4, which enabled Alexander to identify Q as a bad quarto.

Alexander suggested that the close QF correspondence here resulted from the reporters having had in their possession a manuscript fragment of the full play (Alexander, p. 87). This, of course, is possible, but the existence of such fragments has been challenged (Chambers, *Shakespeare*, i. 283). This hypothesis leaves unexplained the apparent instance of Q anticipation in F. Folio 1.1.236-59/236-59 was probably set from a copy of Q3, though there is no objective bibliographical evidence to confirm this. One promising clue, 'show' Q1-2; 'shew' Q3-F (1.1.241/241), cannot be interpreted as evidence of Q3 copy, for Compositor B, who set this portion of F, had an overwhelming preference for 'shew'. The only evidence is subjective: the apparent instance of anticipation, 1.1.237-8/237-8.

If we accept this hypothesis of Q3 contamination, we are forced to conclude that the first half of the speech, 1.1.214-35/214-35, was absent from the production Q reports. There are two possible explanations for this. (1) It was simply cut or (2) what survives in Q represents a later, alternative version of York's speech, and F's conflation of these two versions is an error resulting from part use of manuscript copy (1.1.214-35/214-35) and part use of Q3 (1.1.236-59/236-59). It is not possible to determine which of these explanations is true. The second would require the deletion of 1.1.214-35/214-35; the first, the retention of the F version of the speech, with perhaps some emendation (perhaps the deletion of 1.1.237-8/237-8, and possibly also of 1.1.236/236). We assume the first explanation, and retain F; in the absence of hard evidence of Q contamination, we also retain F as our control text for 1.1.236-59/236-59, rather than switch to Q1 for this passage.

1.1.247/247 humors] Q, F; Humour ROWE. The word appears to have been considered singular, describing, probably, the mix of humours which make up Henry's temperament (see Abbott, 333).

1.1.251/251 surfet in the] HANMER; surfetting in Q, F. An easy memorial error.

1.1.256/256 in] Q; in in F

1.1.257/257 grapple] Q3, F; graffle Q1-2. *OED* does not confirm the existence of a word 'graffle'. Q3's 'grapple' is a plausible but probably wholly unauthoritative reading. If Compositor B did set this passage in F from a copy of Q3, then 'grapple' there remains no more than the Q3 editor's guess. It may be right. G.T., however, suggests that what Q1 intended was 'wraffle' (wrestle).

1.2.19/278 houre] CAIRNCROSS (Vaughan); thought F. Vaughan suggested that the error resulted from 'thoughts' in the previous line and 'that *hour*' in this one.

THE FIRST PART OF THE CONTENTION

1.2.22/281 dreame] CAPELL; dreames F. The combination of Q ('troubled with a dreame'), the singular verb 'doth', and the occurrence of 'dreame' in lines 1.2.31/290 and 1.2.52/311 support the emendation.

1.2.26-31/285-90 twaine ... knowes] F; two, and on the ends were plac'd, | The heads of the Cardinall of *Winchester*, | And *William de la Poule* firſt Duke of *Suffolke* Q1-2; twaine, by whom I cannot geſſe: | But as I thinke by the Cardinall. What it bodes | God knowes; and on the ends were plac'd | The heads of *Edmund* Duke of *Somerset*, | And *William de la Pole* firſt Duke of *Suffolke* Q3; two: and on the ends were plac'd | The heads o'th' Cardinall of *Winchester*, | And *William de la Pole* first Duke of *Suffolke* This edition *conj.*

This is the first of five major Q3 departures from Q1 all of which, in varying degrees, resemble F, and all of which depart from passages of Q1 which, when considered without reference to F, do not appear to be in error (for the other four, see the notes to 1.2.62-7/321-6, 1.3.83/449, 2.1.10/672, 3.1.359/1540). Montgomery, in the most recent study of Q, advances three hypotheses to explain these Q3 variants, only one of which has any bearing on the text of F: Q3 contamination of F. The five Q3 lines of the present example are the last lines on A4ᵛ, and may represent an expansion, on the part of the Q3 compositor, of the corresponding three Q1 lines to resolve a problem with cast-off copy. It would be easy for someone in Pavier's shop, if not the compositor himself, to interpolate the additional Q3 matter: Gloucester will be in the Cardinal's care when he is murdered, so the latter might reasonably be viewed as 'breaker' of the former. The interpolation of this whole line, however, led not only to the stretching of the two Q1 half-lines on either side of it (Q1 'two' becomes 'twaine, by whom I cannot geſſe:', while Q1 'and on the ends were plac'd' is prefaced by 'God knowes;'), but to the substitution of Somerset's head for the Cardinal's: the latter could hardly both be breaker of and have his head affixed to the staff. Compositor B, who set this part of the Folio, is known to have elsewhere in the volume emended copy for metrical reasons: if he were here dependent on Q3, the F variations from Q3 are not beyond his powers.

Moreover, the substance of Q1 is in some ways preferable to that of F: if the dream is meant to be an accurate prophecy, one would perhaps expect the heads of the two who die after 'breaking' first, Gloucester's power (his enforced resignation of the Protectorship), and then the man himself, would be the heads displayed on the broken staff.

However, though he advances this hypothesis as a possible explanation of the Q3 variant and its agreement with F, Montgomery concludes that it is not the most probable explanation. The hypothesis he favours, that Q3 somehow had access to a supplementary report not available to those responsible for Q1, in no way undermines F's authority here—rather, it confirms it. We retain F.

1.2.38/297 are] Q; wer F. 'The unusual spelling "wer" in F1 (preserved in F2) seems to be due to a crowded line and does not suggest a misprint; but nevertheless "are" may be correct' (McKerrow).

1.2.62-7/321-6 While ... Pageant] F; But ere it be long, Ile go before them all Q1-2; As long as Gloſter beares this baſe and humble minde: | Were I a man, and Protector as he is, | I'de reach to'th Crowne, or make ſome hop headleſſe. | And being but a woman, ile not behinde | For playing of my part Q3. This is the second of the extended Q3 variants from its Q1 copy which resembles F. As in the earlier example, the Q3 lines come near the bottom of a page, B1ʳ, and may represent copy-stretching which somehow contaminated F, but this seems less likely here. The variation between Q3 and Q1 is more extensive, and therefore less plausibly of the compositor's invention; a theory of contamination would not help us explain how Q3 'I'de reach to'th Crowne, or make ſome hop headleſſe' became F's superior 'I would remoue theſe tedious ſtumbling blockes, | And ſmooth my way vpon their headleſſe neckes': Q3 seems more like a memorial corruption of the two F lines than the F lines a

compositorial revision of Q3. Possibly, as Montgomery suggests, Q3 had access to some kind of supplementary report here. It is perhaps worth noting that both 1.2.26/285 and this example occur on the same Q1 page, B1ʳ.

1.2.70/329 Iesus] F, Q; Jesu CAIRNCROSS

1.2.71/330 thou? Maiesty:] F; ∼ₐ ∼ ? VAUGHAN (*conj.*). Vaughan's conjecture seems plausible, in view of the common use of *what* as equivalent to *why*; compare OED *what*, 19 (McKerrow).

1.2.75 Jordan] F (*Iordane*). There seems little to recommend the more usual modernization, 'Jourdain'.

1.2.75/334 cunning Witch of Eye] ALEXANDER ('... Eie'); cunning Witch F; cunning Witch of *Ely* Q1-2; cunning witch of *Rye* Q3; witch of Eie CAIRNCROSS. Hall (Cxlviʳ; repr. Bullough, iii. 102), Shakespeare's probable source, calls this character 'Margerie Jourdayne surnamed, the witche of Eye' (Grafton and Holinshed agree substantively with Hall here). We presume that Q here preserves a corrupt version of a historical detail added to the text in the preparation of the prompt-book, but absent from the foul papers upon which F is based. See the Introduction, and the notes to 2.1.38-43/700-5, 4.1.0.2-3/2011.4-5, 4.7.106/2564-5 and 4.7.107-8/2566.

1.2.76/335 With *Roger*] F, Q; With CAIRNCROSS

1.2.76/335 Coniurer] F; cunning conjurer CAIRNCROSS. Cairncross does not collate this emendation.

1.3.1/367 let's] F, Q3 (lets); let vs Q1-2

1.3.6/372 I. PETITIONER] F4; Peter. F1. From line 1.3.11/377 it appears that the First Petitioner and not Peter had pressed forward, in his haste mistaking Suffolk for the Lord Protector. The compositor may have misinterpreted manuscript *Pet* (i.e. *Petitioner*) as *Peter*. Sanders, however, defends F1 (Sanders, p. 182).

1.3.13/379 To] F; For CAPELL. If we suppose 'To my Lord Protector' to be written as a heading to the supplication, and that the Queen reads this, Capell's emendation becomes unnecessary.

1.3.27-9/393-5 Against ... Crowne] F. Peter is here either reciting from memory or reading the contents of his petition: the form 'Againſt ... Crowne' precisely parallels what Suffolk earlier read aloud in the petition against himself. Peter may shout this out in a (successful) attempt to divert Suffolk's attention from the Second Petitioner's supplication, without prompting. Though unlikely, it may be that his line was preceded by a question in dumb show from the Queen, put while Suffolk addressed the Second Petitioner. Or it may be, as G.T. suggests, that something is wrong with the F text here (Q is different), and either the staging requires emendation, probably along the lines suggested by Q, or some dialogue is missing, probably in the form of a question put to Peter by the Queen.

1.3.29/395 to] F, Q3; vnto Q1-2

1.3.32/398 Mʳ] WARBURTON (*subs.*); Miſtreſſe F. The F error probably arose from the compositor misreading 'Mʳ' as 'Mʳˢ', leading him to expand the abbreviation wrongly.

1.3.33-5/399-401 vsurer ... vsurper] Q; Vſurper F. The F omission is easily explained as compositorial eyeskip from 'an vſurer' to 'an vſurper'.

1.3.44/410 ALL PETITIONERS] This edition; *All.* F

1.3.46/412 Is this the Fashions] F. OED (*sb.* 8b) confirms that in the plural *fashions* often meant, as here, '"Manners and customs" (of nations), "ways" (of men)'. The singular verb in this context is perfectly regular (Abbott, 335).

1.3.71/437 haught] F1; haughtie F2. The choice of forms of this word, in Shakespeare and other authors, seems entirely dependent on metrical considerations; compositorial substitution could occur easily.

1.3.83/449 She beares a Dukes Reuenewes on her backe,] F, Q3 ('whole reuennewes'); *not in* Q1-2. This is the third of the extended Q3 variants from Q1 which seem to bring it closer to F. While Q3 may derive from some kind of supplementary report, more probably it was set from a variant copy of Q1 which included this line (only three exemplars of this page survive; all of these, however, are invariant). The line resembles one in Marlowe's *Edward II* ('He weares a lords revenewe on his back',

1.4.407), a play which the reporters of Q knew, and from which they interpolated other lines. However, there is no reason to suspect interpolation here: the line works better in its F context than in the variant one of Q3, and the dates of these two plays are sufficiently uncertain relative to one another for either author to have been the borrower. The idea was proverbial (Tilley L 452).

1.3.93/459 their] ROWE; the F

1.3.103/469 Helme.] ROWE (Q); Helme. Exit. F. F's error almost certainly reflects the manuscript; if the play is of divided authorship, the confusion here might be caused by a change of authors.

1.3.103.1–7/469.1–6 Enter ... Duke Humphrey of Gloster, Dame ... Winchester] Q (... Humphrey, Dame ...)

1.3.107 denied] F (denay'd)

1.3.126/492 Since] F, Q3; since that Q1–2

1.3.133 wife's] F (Wiues)

1.3.140.2/506.2 The Queene lets fall her Fanne] Q (... gloue); not in F

1.3.145/511 Ide] Q; I could F

1.3.147/513 will? good King,] Q (subs.); will, good King? F

1.3.148/514 pamper] This edition (conj. McKerrow); hamper F. 'Hamper "appears to have no other sense than the usual one of "fetter", "hinder", and does not seem congruent with the phrase "dandle thee like a Baby", which follows'. Compare Richard III 2.2.88/1271 (McKerrow).

1.3.153/519 Furie] DYCE 2; Fume F. Though OED provides ample evidence of fume meaning 'fit of anger', it is usually part of the prepositional phrase in (a) fume. Dyce's reading is attractive: the minim error involved ('m' for 'ri') is very easy, and the emendation improves the line's metre.

1.3.154/520 farre] F; fast POPE

1.3.184.1/550.1 indicates] This edition; not in F, Q. Some such direction seems necessary in order to clarify the action to a reader. While indicates is anachronistic, its first recorded occurrence not coming until the early 19th c., it nevertheless seems preferable to a contemporary form like points at which, in this context, seems overly prescriptive.

1.3.207/573 iudge by case] CAIRNCROSS (after Q); iudge F. Though the Q context is variant, it is difficult to postulate the reporter inventing the phrase 'by case'. It does not occur elsewhere in the play. Probably it derives from performance and reflects the prompt-book. Since the phrase improves the line's metre, it is possible that it also stood in the manuscript behind F, but was for some reason omitted here.

1.3.213/579 This] F; King. This CAIRNCROSS. Neither Cairncross's solution to the dramatic problem here nor Sanders' defence of F is persuasive. In F, Somerset thanks the King, who has not spoken, and indeed never does comment himself on the Regentship. This is the last line of a Folio page and forme (m4ᵛ); the omission of a short speech is, in these circumstances, not implausible. Certainly, an omitted speech is more plausible than an omitted prefix here. See the next note.

1.3.214/580 KING Then ... of Somerset] Q (subs.); not in F. See the previous note. If something has dropped out of F, it seems most reasonable to reconstruct it on the basis of what stands at the same point in Q. But Q's context has been altered to allow for Somerset's immediate departure (probably for casting reasons); as a result we can accord little authority to the last two lines in Q ('Make haft my Lord, tis time that you were gone, | The time of Trufe I thinke is full expirde'). Moreover, the rest of the speech may be subject to memorial corruption. See the following notes.

1.3.214/580 so.] THEOBALD; ~ₐ Q

1.3.214/580 Somerset,] THEOBALD; ~. Q

1.3.215–16/581–2 We ... foes] This edition (G.T.); We make your grace Regent ouer the French, | And to defend our rights gainft forraine foes, | And fo do good vnto the Realme of France Q; not in F; We make your Grace regent over the French THEOBALD.

The first of these Q lines is metrically unacceptable in ways suggestive of memorial corruption: it contains two reversed feet in the middle of the line, and no caesura. The third Q line, though characteristic enough of Henry, is composed of two phrases ('do good', 'realm of France') which occur elsewhere and might therefore be memorial patchwork here. No such explanation will account for the second Q line, though even this seems to be corrupt, in its syntax if nothing else.

1.3.225/591 be] CAIRNCROSS; fhall be F. Capell was almost certainly right to treat this speech as verse. The King elsewhere speaks verse in this scene; the preceding scene is verse; the final speech of a scene is usually verse; the last sentence of the speech is a wholly regular pentameter; and the rest of the speech is metrical, except for a single extra syllable produced by a grammatically redundant auxiliary verb ('shall'), which could have been unconsciously interpolated by the compositor.

1.3.225/591 the last of the next moneth] F; on the thirtith of this month, | With Eben ftaues, and Standbags combatting | In Smythfield, before your Royall Maieftie Q. The Q version of these lines, spoken by Gloucester, are probably an anticipation of the actual combat, incorporating into the dialogue parts of the reporter's visual memory of it. That the combat should occur in Smithfield, which is not specified in F, alone of the additional Q matter is corroborated by Hall (Clʳ; repr. Bullough, iii. 105), but this could well be a coincidence, Smithfield being a usual location for trials and executions (F has the witch sentenced to be burned there).

1.4.12.1/604.1 She lies downe vpon her face.] Q; not in F

1.4.12.2/604.2 Enter Elianor aloft] placement This edition; follows 'worke', 1.4.13/605, F. The Duchess's line indicates she has overheard at least part of Hume's speech.

1.4.15.1/607.1 Enter Hume aloft] This edition; not in F. Hume's re-entrance, aloft, though clearly required (line 1.4.8/600), is not directed by F. Editors usually have him enter immediately before the Duchess's speech (line 1.4.14/606). This may be right, but does not allow him very much time to leave the stage, ascend, and re-enter above.

1.4.23.2/615.2 Southwell reades] This edition; Bullingbrooke or Southwell reades, Coniuro te, &c. F; Q, which omits the character Southwell altogether, has Bullenbrooke utter a variant incantation. Bollingbroke instructs Southwell at line 1.4.13/605 to read; the latter has no other lines in the play.

1.4.25/617, etc. Asnath] CAIRNCROSS; Asmath F; Askalon Q. Cairncross argues that 'Asnath' is an anagram of 'Sathan'. Q's 'Askalon' may derive from a confusion on the part of the reporter between this spirit and the 'Ascalon' mentioned in the plot of 1 Tamar Cam, a play he may have known.

1.4.33/625 Tell me what] POPE; what Q, F. This and the following note strongly suggest Q contamination of F here. Pope produces better metre, and agrees with F's second reading of the prophecies (2.1.183/845).

1.4.33/625 fate awaits] Q2–3; fates await F; fate awayt Q1

1.4.35/627 betide] Q; befall F. Q here agrees with 2.1.187/849, which repeats the question.

1.4.39–40/631–2 Discend ... auoide] F. The Q version of this speech, an edited version of which we provide as Additional Passage B, is longer; it may reflect lines added in rehearsal to the prompt-book to cover the spirit's descent.

1.4.40.1–2/632.1–2 The Spirit sinkes downe againe] Q (He finkes ...); Exit Spirit F

1.4.41.1–3/633.1–3 Bullingbrooke ... and Southwell] This edition; not in F, Q

1.4.44/636 deepe] ROWE; deepely F. As it stands, F is metrically unacceptable. The alternative emendation to this one, suggested by an unidentified post-1957 marginal conjecture in the McKerrow galleys, would be to read 'deepely debted' instead of 'deepe indebted'. This may be right. But Shakespeare never uses 'debted', though he does use 'indebted' twice elsewhere, once 'much indebted'. Also, 'deep' and 'deeply' are both common, and are synonyms. It would be easy to suppose the compositor substituted 'deepely' for manuscript 'deepe'.

1.4.49/641 He ... Writings] This edition; not in F

1.4.54/646 All away] F; not in POPE. Walker suggests that 'All away' may be a stage direction, duplicating 'Exit'.

1.4.57.1/649.1 Buckingham ... Writings] This edition; not in F, Q

1.4.58-9/650-1 What ... posse] This edition. In F York reads the prophecies aloud at this point; Q transposes this reading to the next scene and assigns it to King Henry. The Q arrangement has considerable dramatic merit. It eliminates the impression of artless redundancy which F's repetition here leaves, and it allows both the King and Suffolk to react to the prophecies regarding them. Since Q derives from a performance, and seems, in this matter, dramatically superior to F, we accept that it here reflects a change made between the foul papers, which stand behind F, and the prompt-book, which stands behind the performance. We adopt the Q arrangement. See the following notes and those to 2.1.178-89/840-51.

1.4.58/650 He Reades the Writings] This edition; Reades. | The Duke yet liues, that Henry ſhall depoſe: | But him out-liue, and dye a violent death. F. See the note to 1.4.58-9/650-1.

1.4.59/651 Æacidā] This edition (conj. Binns); Æacida F; te, Aeacida ROWE

1.4.59 Aeacidam] (Æacidā). See the previous note.

1.4.59/651 poſſe] F2; poſſo F1

1.4.59/651 poſſe.] This edition; poſſo. | Well, to the reſt: | Tell me what fate awaits the Duke of Suffolke? | By Water ſhall he dye, and take his end. | What ſhall betide the Duke of Somerſet? | Let him ſhunne Caſtles, Safer ſhall he be vpon the ſandie Plaines, | Then where Caſtles mounted ſtand F. See the note to 1.4.58-9/650-1.

1.4.60-1/652-3 These ... vnderſtood. Come, come my Lorde,] This edition (anon. conj. in Cambridge (the conjecture retains F's 'Lords')); Come, come, my Lords, | Theſe ... vnderſtood. F; Come, come, my Lords, these oracles are hard, | Hardly attain'd and hardly underſtood G. R. HIBBARD conj. in N&Q 210 (1965), p. 332. This emendation, which improves both the sense and metre, corrects a probable error which easily could have arisen from a misplaced marginal insertion. Hibbard's is a very attractive alternative solution, however.

1.4.60/652 are hardly] THEOBALD; are hardly F. The compositor might not even have recognized any distinction between Theobald's form and F's; even if he did, substitution would be easy.

1.4.61/653 Lorde] This edition; Lords F. Buckingham appears to be the only lord remaining on stage with York: York has already commanded 'All away', and after Buckingham's exit, he has to call within for a servant to deliver his message to Salisbury and Warwick. The graphical error presumed, terminal s/e, is easy and common.

1.4.68/660 Exit Buckingham] Q (Exet Buckingham.); not in F. Though we normally adopt Q1's incidentals when we accept its directions into our text, we depart from that practice with this word: Q1 always spells it with a medial 'e'; we silently normalize it, here and elsewhere, to the usual F form, 'Exit'.

1.4.68/660 Who's within] F, Q; Within CAIRNCROSS

1.4.70.1/662.1 seuerally] Q (Exet Yorke ... Exet); not in F

2.1.0.1-2/662.2 with her Hawke on her fiſt] Q; not in F

2.1.0.3-4/662.3-4 with Faulkners hallowing] F; as if they came from hawking Q

2.1.10/672 Hawkes doe] F, Q3; Hawke done Q1; hawke doe Q2. This and the variants of three of the next four notes constitute the fourth major Q3 departure from its Q1 copy. This complex of variants, perhaps more than any other, suggests that the exemplar of Q1 used as copy for Q3 had been corrected by someone with an imperfect memory of the authorial text. In particular, the Q3 substitution of 'bird can ſore' for Q1-2 'Falkons pitch' in 2.1.14/676, while at the same time leaving the now-weakened 'ſores' (Q1-2 'can ſore') instead of substituting F's 'mounts', suggests this.

2.1.11/673 They know their] F, Q3; He knowes his Q1-2

2.1.11/673 loues to be aloft] F, Q1-2; ſores a Faulcons pitch Q3

2.1.12/674 And ... Pitch] F; not in Q. But see the preceding and the following notes.

2.1.14/676 mounts ... Bird can ſore] F; can ſore ... Falkons pitch Q1-2; ſores ... bird can ſore Q3

2.1.15/677 hee would] F; he'd POPE

2.1.23/685 growne] F; grown so ROWE

2.1.24 caeleſtibus] F (Cœleſtibus)

2.1.25-6/687-8 Good Vncle ... doe it] F; Good vnckle can you doate Q1 ('... dote' Q2; '... do't' Q3); Good uncle, can you dote, To hide such malice with such holiness CAIRNCROSS; Good Vncle can you doe it? | Hide such mallice with such Holyneſſe G.T. conj. The Q arrangement, which G.T. argues makes better sense and metre, suggests to him that 'Hide ... Holyneſſe' is misplaced in F: it may have been a marginal addition intended as a complete line, but whose placement the F compositor got wrong.

2.1.26/688 some] This edition; ſuch F; not in Q. The misreading would be an easy one for the F compositor to make, both graphically and in view of 'such' in the previous line. If the whole clause 'hide ... Holyneſſe' is, as G.T. suggests (see the previous note), a possibly crowded marginal addition, the probability of compositorial misreading is increased.

2.1.29/691 you] F, Q; yourself POPE

2.1.30/692 Lords Protectorſhip] F, Q; Lord-Protectorship CAPELL

2.1.38-43/700-5 GLOSTER ... words] Q; not in F. Cairncross (p. xxvii and note 38 on p. 39) argues that these lines were censored from the manuscript behind F at some time subsequent to their having been performed (and so reported by Q). They may be, however, lines added by the author in the preparation of the prompt-book. They contain additional historical matter (Beaufort's bastardy) unlikely to have been interpolated by the reporter, and of a kind which seems to have been elsewhere similarly incorporated into the prompt-book (see the Introduction and notes to 1.2.75/334, 4.1.0.2-3/2011.4-5, 4.7.106/2564-5, and 4.7.107-8/2566). Both positions, however, favour the inclusion of the lines.

2.1.46 an if] F (And if). F, however, provides a plausible modern-spelling alternative.

2.1.52-3/714-15 Are ... CARDINALL] 'Most editors ... follow Theobald in giving "are ye aduis'd ... Groue" to the Cardinal, supposing him to repeat the appointment to make sure that there is no mistake. "Are ye aduis'd?" is then to be taken as "Do you understand?". But the alteration, though possibly right, seems not strictly necessary. "Are ye advis'd?" may be a sneer of Gloucester's, "Is this prudent in you?". Moreover, in [Q] the place of meeting is mentioned by Humphrey and by him alone.... If we assign the disputed words to the Cardinal, we may, I think, guess that "Cardinall" in [2.1.53/715] is a misunderstood correction, the word being intended to be inserted higher up as a speaker's name and read "Card. Are ye aduis'd? | The East side of the Groue. | Gloſt. I am with you" omitting "Cardinall" from the text. Alternatively, only the words "I am with you" might be assigned to the Cardinal and this distribution of the lines has some slight support from [Q] where the dialogue runs:
    Humph.   the East end of the groue.
    Card. Heres my hand, I will.'   (McKerrow)
We adopt the latter course. See the next note.

2.1.53/715 CARDINALL] CAIRNCROSS (McKerrow); Cardinall, F. See the previous note.

2.1.55/717 Now by Gods Mother, Prieſt] F; Faith Prieſt Q1-2; Gods Mother Prieſt Q3; Now by God's mother CAIRNCROSS

2.1.65/727 tell] This edition (G.T.); and tell F. And is one of the easiest words for a compositor to interpolate.

2.1.70.1-3/732.1-3 Enter ... chaire] This stage direction was set from a copy of Q, probably an exemplar of Q3. We adopt Q1's incidentals.

2.1.70.2/732.2 with Muſicke] Q; not in F

2.1.74/736 ſight] WILSON (Lloyd); his fight F. The compositor may have caught 'his' from the preceding line. The emendation improves both sense and metre.

2.1.84/746 KING] F, Q3; Humphrey. Q1-2

2.1.110/772 Albone] F2 (subs.); Albones F1

2.1.112/774 Red] F, Q3; Why red Q1-2

2.1.115/777 And ... ſir,] Q; What Colour is my | Gowne of? | Simpc⟨oxe⟩. Black forſooth, F. Q probably represents the performing text. The allusion to this episode slightly later in the scene, at a point where F depends on Q ('To name the seuerall colours we doo weare', 'To nominate them all'), requires Q here.

2.1.117-55.3/779-817.4 SUFFOLKE . . . *miracle*] Q. This passage was, in all probability, set from an annotated copy of Q, a view to which McKerrow ('Note', p. 66, note 1) also inclined. We follow Q1's incidentals, and emend on the presumption of memorial error. See the Introduction.

2.1.118/780 before] F; ere Q

2.1.118/780 a many] F; many a one Q

2.1.119/781 WIFE . . . *life*] F; *not in* Q

2.1.120/782 Tell] F; But tell Q

2.1.125-6/787-8 SIMPCOXE . . . *name?*] Q; *not in* F. The F omission could easily have resulted from eyeskip.

2.1.129, 130/791, 792 Symon] This edition; Sander Q, F (Saunder). In a passage absent from Q, Simpcox earlier identifies himself as 'Symon' (2.1.93/755). Tucker Brooke (Yale Shakespeare, 1923) explained the discrepancy as a deliberate one, but he was writing before Alexander showed Q to be a reported text, and before the view was advanced, which we accept, that F here derives from Q. McMillin has argued that an actor named 'Sander' belonged to Pembroke's Men, the company probably responsible for Q, and that he played Simpcox. Q's 'Sander' may thus derive from him, and F's 'Saunder' from Q. We accept 'Symon' as authoritative, and emend what we view as the corrupt 'Saunder' accordingly.

2.1.129/791 Simpcoxe] F; *not in* Q

2.1.129/791 and] Q; and if F

2.1.130/792 thou] CAIRNCROSS; *not in* Q, F; thee KEIGHTLEY

2.1.132/794 our] CAIRNCROSS; all our Q, F

2.1.134/796 distinguish] This edition (*conj.* Cairncross); distinguish of Q, F. Shakespeare never elsewhere uses the idiom 'distinguish of'. (Though Riverside reads 'distinguish' here, the editor privately confirms that this is an error.)

2.1.136/798 Saint] CAIRNCROSS; My Lords, Saint Q, F. The unmetrical phrase, *my lord(s)*, is a common memorial interpolation: the reporter of Q *Richard III* introduces it nine times, and the reporter of this play interpolates it twice elsewhere (at lines 1017 and 1019 of the Malone Society facsimile of Q, which correspond roughly with 3.1.84-6/1265-7 of this edition). Here, however, because F derives from Q, the spurious phrase found its way into F.

2.1.136/798 Albone] F; Albones Q

2.1.137/799 Would] This edition (*conj.* Cairncross); And would Q, F

2.1.137/799 you] Q; ye F

2.1.137/799 his] Q; it, F; that ROWE

2.1.138/800 legs againe] Q, F; legs POPE. Shakespeare prefers *restore* without *again* (29 to 4): *again* may be a memorial interpolation (as it is in quarto *Richard III* 3.7.65/2055).

2.1.139/801 that] F; I would Q

2.1.141/803 Beadles] Q, F; A beadle CAIRNCROSS. The line is metrically acceptable without emendation (defective initial foot); moreover, 'send for one' (2.1.143/805) suggests that Gloucester here asks a general question; the parallelism with 'whips' also supports QF.

2.1.142/804 We haue, my Lord, and if it please your grace] This edition; Yes, my Lord, if it please your Grace Q, F; Yes, my lord CAIRNCROSS. Cairncross's solution seems unnecessarily drastic; moreover, even when combined with his emendation of the next speech (see below), it produces an irregular line.

As an answer to 'haue you not?', 'We haue' would be more idiomatic as well as metrically regular. The question *Have you not?* is posed 19 times altogether in the canon. Aside from this instance, it is directly answered seven times: twice negatively, and five times affirmatively. All five affirmative answers take the form *[pronoun] have* (*Shrew* 2.1.44/852, *Richard II* 2.2.58/974, *Hamlet* 2.1.68/876, *Measure* 3.1.213/1320, *Othello* 1.1.176/177).

'And if' produces a regular caesura, where 'if' does not; the idioms are synonymous, and here easily subject to memorial error. The Mayor's next speech is entirely regular.

2.1.142 an] This edition (and). See the previous note.

2.1.143/805 Then send] Q, F; Send CAIRNCROSS

2.1.145/807 Bring] This edition; Now fetch Q, F. Almost certainly dependent on Q here, the repetitions of 'fetch' from the preceding F line and of 'Now' in the following strongly suggest memorial error. See the next note.

2.1.145/807 stoole] This edition (G.T.); ftoole hither by and by Q, F. The repetition of 'hither' from the preceding line in this reported text suggests memorial error. See the preceding note. *By and by*, though not uncommonly used by Shakespeare to mean *at once* (see Schmidt and *OED*, *adv. phr.*, 3), produces here a poor metre. The phrase is used once elsewhere in the play, at line 1.3.2/368, but it is not in Q at that point. It may therefore here be a memorial interpolation, recollected from 1.3/Sc. 3.

2.1.146/808 ore] This edition (G.T.); ouer Q, F

2.1.147/809 runne away] Q, F; run CAIRNCROSS. 'Runne(s) away' recurs in the stage direction at 2.1.155.2/817.2; but the reporters are unlikely to have remembered the wording of that stage direction, and it seems more likely that their memory of the dialogue influenced their wording of the direction; the direction thus indirectly supports the QF reading here.

2.1.148/810 am not able euen to] This edition (G.T.); am not able to Q, F; cannot CAIRNCROSS

2.1.149.1/811.1 *Enter a Beadle with Whippes*] F; Enter Beadle Q (*after* 'away', in line 2.1.147/809). Q's placement is perhaps to be preferred, with Simpcox's first 'Alaffe maifter . . .' (2.1.147/809) speech a frightened response made upon seeing the armed Beadle.

2.1.150/812 sirrha] CAIRNCROSS; Sir Q, F. 'Sir' is not only unmetrical, but uncharacteristic. Lower-class characters are elsewhere in the play always addressed as 'sirrha', not 'sir'. Simpcox is three times elsewhere called 'sirrah'. It would be an easy memorial error. See the next note.

2.1.151/813 Whip] CAIRNCROSS; Sirrha Beadle, whip Q, F. The unmetrical phrase is probably a verbalized stage direction, indicating that Gloucester addresses the second part of his speech to the beadle; 'sirrha' could easily have been picked up by the reporter from its proper position in the preceding line.

2.1.152-3/814-15 I will my Lord, | . . . Come] Q, F; Come CAIRNCROSS

2.1.154/816 Alas maister] Q, F. The same collocation has already occurred twice elsewhere in Simpcox's speeches. The word 'maister', superfluous here in sense and metre, could be omitted (G.T.).

2.1.154-5/816 am not able to] Q, F; cannot CAIRNCROSS (*conj.*)

2.1.160/822 to the Maior] This edition; *not in* Q, F. That his speech is directed to the Mayor and not the Beadle is suggested by Q, where the Mayor answers 'It fhall be done my Lord'.

2.1.161.1/823.1 *Exit Mayor*] Q; *Exit* F

2.1.178-89/840-51 And . . . *stand*] This edition; As more at large your Grace fhall vnderftand F. Details of the reconstruction are given in the following notes; a discussion of the reasons for undertaking it is given in the note to 1.4.58-9/650-1.

2.1.178/840 And . . . them] Q; *not in* F

2.1.178.1/840.1 *Buckingham . . . King*] This edition; *not in* F, Q. However, in both Q and F it is clear that Buckingham delivers the prophecies to the King. See lines 1.4.66-7/658-9.

2.1.179/841 KING] Q (*subs.*); Yorke. F

2.1.179/841 First . . . of him become] This edition; become of him Q; *not in* F. F does not repeat this initial question in York's reading of the prophecies, although Q does. We accept that Q reflects a later version of the text, but, since it is reported, we do not place much confidence in its verbal particularities. We therefore accept the repetition of this line, after Q, but follow F's earlier version of it, in the conjuration (1.4.30/622), for substance and incidentals.

2.1.180-1/842-3 The . . . death] This edition (*after* Q); *not in* F *here*. Placement of these lines is on the authority of Q; their substance and incidentals are those of F at York's earlier reading (see the notes to 1.4.58-9/650-1 and 1.4.58/650).

2.1.182/844 Gods will be done in all.] Q; *not in* F

2.1.182/844 Well, to the rest:] This edition (*after* F); *not in* Q. The placement of this half line we infer from Q and the part-line in Q, not in F (see the previous note). This part-line itself, however, comes from York's earlier reading of the prophecies in F (see the note to 1.4.58-9/650-1 and the third note to 1.4.59/651).

2.1.183-4/845-6 Tell . . . end] This edition (after Q); not in F here. For substance and incidentals, F; for placement here, Q (see the note to 1.4.58-9/650-1 and the third note to 1.4.59/651).

2.1.185-6/847-8 SUFFOLKE . . . lie] Q; not in F. The direction is editorial.

2.1.187/849 KING] Q (subs.); F assigns to York as part of the earlier reading (see the note to 1.4.58-9/650-1 and the third note to 1.4.59/651).

2.1.187-9/849-51 What . . . stand] This edition (after Q); not in F here. F's substance and incidentals; Q's placement (see the note to 1.4.58-9/650-1 and the third note to 1.4.59/651).

2.2.6/885 out at full] This edition (conj. McKerrow); at full F. The combination of 'o' plus a minim ('ou') could sufficiently have resembled an 'a' for the compositor to skip 'out' to 'at' inadvertently. Capell emended to 'at the' which is harder to explain graphically; McKerrow and Wilson further suggested 'all at', which is plausible.

2.2.7 and if] F; An if w. s. WALKER (conj.).

2.2.9-10/888-9 Then thus: | Edward the third, my Lords] F; Then thus my Lords. | Edward the third Q; Edward the Third, my lords CAIRNCROSS. Since there is no question of Q contamination of F here, agreement confirms F's 'Then thus'.

2.2.16/895 was Thomas] F, Q; Thomas F3. The line as it stands in F is unmetrical, and were it not for Q's agreement, F3 would offer an attractive emendation: 'was' would be an easy interpolation, especially in view of the parallel in the preceding line. But since Q contamination of F is most implausible here, we must view Q as a confirmation of F's 'was'.

2.2.26/905 well] This edition (G.T.); all F; both Q

2.2.28/907 Duke of Yorke] CAIRNCROSS; Duke F. The omission can be easily explained as eyeskip (-ke to -ke). The emendation also produces an attractive contrast with 'Lancaster' (2.2.29/908).

2.2.28/907 told the truth] F; told the very truth HANMER; surely told the truth CAPELL; told the truth in this KEIGHTLEY. None of these conjectures explains the alleged error. See the preceding note.

2.2.35, 49 Phillipe] F (Phillip)

2.2.41 Owain Glyndŵr] F (Owen Glendour). See the textual notes to 1 Henry IV 1.1.40 and 1.3.115.

2.2.45/924 was Sonne] ROWE; was F. This and the following line are unmetrical and nonsensical; one should therefore assume that the two deficiencies are related. Alexander's emendation (see the next note) solves one problem, while ignoring the other, thereby creating a confusingly postponed object to the preposition 'to'. Given the degree of trouble that the author devoted to metrifying these genealogical arguments, there is no accounting for the sudden hiccup here; the normal grammatical position of 'Sonne' (after 'was') would also produce regular metre. The error might have arisen through confusion in the manuscript, miscorrection in foul proof, or even compositorial error. (Compositor A is clearly responsible for the mislineation in this scene.)

2.2.46/925 Sonne] THEOBALD; Sonnes Sonne F; son, son ALEXANDER (Walker). See the preceding note.

2.2.56/935 Iohns] This edition (G.T.); his Q, F; Gaunts This edition conj. Probably an instance of Q contamination of F: though Q and F are very close to one another throughout this speech, only this line is substantively identical in the two texts (the next line is variant only in 'flouriſhes' F/'floriſheth' Q). Sudden agreement of this kind, coupled with an awkward reading, suggests contamination.

2.2.77/956 off] CAPELL; we off F

2.3.0.2-10/961.2-9 King Henry . . . Warwicke] Q (subs.); not in F. The Q direction does not mention the witch, the two priests, or the conjuror, though F clearly requires them. Q does direct the entry of Buckingham, the Cardinal, and Warwick, though none of these characters has anything to say, nor are they addressed, in either Q or F. Q thus seems to confirm the presence of these last three characters.

2.3.3/964 sinnes] THEOBALD; ſinne F

2.3.19/980 graue] CAIRNCROSS; ground F. Cairncross cites a biblical parallel 'then yee shall bring my gray head with sorow vnto the graue' (Genesis 42: 38), and points to a similar error in Hamlet 4.5.38/2594 (F, Q1 'graue'; Q2 'ground').

2.3.30/991 Healme] STEEVENS (Johnson); Realme F

2.3.34/995 erst] Q1-2; ere Q3, F. It is difficult to account for Q3-F agreement in this reading other than by supposing contamination here. Lines 2.3.34-6/995-7 are very close in the two texts, the only substantive variants being this one, 'Father Henry' F/'noble father' Q, and 'willingly' F/'willing' Q. 'Erst' (which Shakespeare uses in Titus (twice), Henry V, As You Like It, Sonnets, Pericles) occurs once elsewhere in this play (2.4.14/1084): Compositor A, who set this line, also set that one, so it is doubtful that he altered the spelling here. Both words work here (ere, adv. A4 = on a former occasion; erst, adv. B2 = in the first place). We assume Q3 contamination and adopt Q1.

2.3.35/996 willing] Q; willingly F

2.3.46/1007 youngest] F; haughtiest STAUNTON (conj.); highest KINNEAR (conj.)

2.3.52 therefor] F (therefore)

2.3.58.1-2.4.0.2/1019.1-1070.4 Enter . . cloakes] Q, F. Much, if not all, of this passage was set from an annotated copy of, probably, Q3. We assume Q was the principal copy for 2.3.58.1-75/1019.1-1036, 2.3.84-90/1045-51, and 2.3.104-2.4.0.2/1065-1070.4, and for these passages take Q1 as our control text, and adopt its incidentals.

2.3.58.3/1019.3 drunken] Q; drunke F

2.3.64/1025 Heres] Q; And here's F. In both texts the preceding speech begins 'And here', making corresponding interpolation of 'And' particularly easy here. 'And' is, in any case, frequently interpolated.

2.3.65/1026 double beere,] Q; ~ ₐ F. See the next three notes.

2.3.65/1026 neighbor,] Q; ~ : F

2.3.65/1026 drinke ₐ] Q; ~ , F

2.3.65/1026 and be merry, and] Q; and F. The F omission could easily have resulted from eyeslip ('and' . . . 'and').

2.3.68/1029 ile] Q; and Ile F

2.3.70/1031 affeard] Q1-2; afraid Q3, F. Probably an instance of either Q3 contamination of F, or independent Q3/F sophistication.

2.3.71-4/1032-5 Here . . . be] Q; Be F. The Q lines probably were not in the foul papers manuscript which served as principal copy for F; we suppose them to have been introduced to the prompt-book, in rehearsal, and so into the performance tradition from which Q derives.

F is here dependent on Q: the lines are in Q, but they are not in F. The F omission may not plausibly be attributed to compositorial eyeskip (Q3 copy does not lend itself to this here), nor can we suppose it to have been made to accommodate problems in cast-off copy (the episode occurs at the beginning of a Folio forme (n outer). If, however, we suppose Q had been collated with the manuscript (or at least with its decipherable portion) and corrected from it, the omission may have been marked in Q because the lines in question were seen not to be in the manuscript. (The absence of a line or two might well be discernible in an otherwise largely illegible manuscript.)

This, of course, has no bearing on the line's authority: if it were a rehearsal addition, it would not be in the foul paper manuscript; but equally (and obviously) neither would it be there if it were a wholly unauthoritative interpolation. There is, after all, nothing in these lines beyond the power of a reporter or an actor to invent. Perhaps slightly favouring their spuriousness is an allusion to 'Clarret Wine' later in F (4.6.4/2444) for which Q substitutes 'red wine': 'Claret' here may be a memorial anticipation of that later, genuine, occurrence, while the very presence of the third apprentice may be an unauthoritative invention made to balance the armourer's third neighbour. But 'Claret-wine' may equally be merely a local memorial corruption.

On the whole, however, we incline to the view that Q here reflects, though perhaps not perfectly, an authorial revision.

2.3.76/1037 refusing the offers of drinke] This edition; not in Q, F. Suggested by Q's 'but ile drinke no more' which agrees with the

THE FIRST PART OF THE CONTENTION

chronicles' accounts of this combat (Hall Bb2ʳ; Grafton Fff4ᵛ; Holinshed Nnn5ᵛ).

2.3.76–83/1037–44 I . . . already] F. Variant in Q. If F were set from Q here, it was from an annotated copy, perhaps corrected by recourse to the foul papers.

2.3.78 an if] F (and if)

2.3.89/1050 that thou] Q; thou F. The F omission may easily be attributed to eyeskip.

2.3.90/1051 well] F; not in Q. F may derive from the manuscript, coming as it does at the very end of one of Q's stints as principal copy.

2.3.91–103/1052–65 Masters . . . right] F. Variant in Q. Like 2.3.76–83/1037–44, if F were set from Q here, it was from an annotated copy.

2.3.97.1/1058.1 Sound . . . Combattants] This edition; as dialogue F

2.3.97.2/1058.2 and Peter hits the Armorer on the head] Q (subs.); not in F

2.3.98.1/1059.1 He dies] Q; not in F. The only evidence that Horner dies here is the Q stage direction and 2.3.105/1066 (which F reproduces verbatim, along with the whole of the King's speech, 2.3.104–9/1065–70, probably because of Q copy). Hall (Bb2ʳ; repr. Bullough, iii. 105) and Grafton (Fff4ᵛ) each have the armourer 'vanquished by his seruannte, beyng but a cowarde and a wretche, whose body was drawen to Tiborne, & there hanged and behedded'. Holinshed (Nnn5ᵛ), to which there is no evidence Q had recourse, has the armourer 'slaine without guilt. As for the false seruant, he liued not long vnpunished; for being conuict of felonie in court of assise, he was iudged to be hanged, and so was, at Tiburne'.

2.3.101/1062 waỹ] This edition (C.A.A-C.); way F. OED records wame to have been a current northern term for belly in the 16th c., one which by the 17th c. had been adopted in southern use as a jocular substitute for belly. York speaks the line, so northern dialect is appropriate.

2.3.102/1063 kneeling] Q (He kneeles downe.); not in F

2.3.102/1063 Enemie] F2; Enemies F1. See 3.2.312/1874.

2.3.109.1/1070.1 Sound a flourish] F; not in Q

2.4.4/1074 abound] F; rebound G.T. conj.

2.4.6/1076 Tenne] F; Almoſt ten Q; 'Tis almost ten LETTSOM (conj.)

2.4.17.1–6/1087.1–6 Enter . . . holbards] Q. See the next note.

2.4.17.4/1087.4 the 2. Sheriffes] This edition (the Sheriffes Q); Sherife F. Two sheriffs appear to have been the rule (Stow, Chronicles); for this reason we are inclined to take seriously Q's plural as reflecting performance (see also 2.4.18/1088), to interpret it, on the basis of Stow, to mean two, and to direct the entry of a second, but mute, sheriff.

2.4.18/1088 Sherifes] Q (Sheriffes); Sherife F. See the previous note.

2.4.21/1091 do'st] F, Q3; doeſt Q1–2

2.4.21/1091 they] F. This and the following allusions in both Q and F suggest that some commons may have entered with the Duchess. Since Q and F agree in not directing their entry, however, and since there is no reason to suppose Q contamination of F here, we take Q as confirmation that they did not enter.

2.4.56/1126 canst] F, Q3; can Q1–2

2.4.74/1144 Exit Herald] Q; not in F

2.4.75, 101/1145, 1171 Sherife] F, Q. The two texts agree that only one sheriff is addressed.

2.4.76/1146 not her Penance] F; her Penance not G.T. conj.

2.4.77, 103/1147, 1173 [1.] SHERIFE] This edition; Sh⟨erife⟩., Sherife. F. Q and F seem to agree that only one sheriff speaks.

2.4.80/1150 here] F; there W. S. WALKER (conj.)

2.4.85.1/1155.1 Gloster begins to leaue] This edition; not in F. Eleanor's comment in the next line suggests this movement.

2.4.104.1/1174 Exit Sherifes] This edition; not in F, Q

3.1.0.1–6/1181.1–6 Enter . . . Warwicke] Q

3.1.46/1227 Life,] POPE; ~ₐ F

3.1.54–5/1235–6 And . . . Lambe] F; not in Q. The cut is an attractive one, for it permits direct transition from 'Water', 'deepe', and 'Brooke' in line 3.1.53/1234 to 'vnfounded' and 'deepe deceit' in line 3.1.57/1238.

3.1.78/1259 Wolfe] ROWE; Wolues F. Plural errors of this kind are common in printing.

3.1.98/1279 Suffolkes Duke] Q; Suffolke F. Though the omission is hard to explain, Q is probably right here. The same collocation is used in line 1.1.121/121. The emendation improves the metre.

3.1.114/1295 my Tryall] F; the iudgement Q. Though Q may be a memorial error, it is in some ways the superior reading, and is possibly connected with the variant at 3.3.27/2005, in that both introduce into the play a Calvinist element (G.T.).

3.1.137/1318 you to] F; thee to Q; to CAPELL. Q confirms F, and the agreement cannot in this case be attributed to contamination. (Cairncross follows Capell.) See the next note.

3.1.137/1318 my good] Q; my F. 'Cardinall' is often divided, in this play (1.3.151/517, 2.1.16/678, 3.2.373/1935, etc.) and elsewhere, into two syllables; Q's line is therefore regular. Even if it were regarded as three syllables, Q produces a hexametre, which is much more acceptable than F's line. Since 'my good Lord Cardinall' appears nowhere else in the play, Q's phrase is unlikely to have arisen from memorial contamination.

3.1.140/1321 suspence] F; suspect CAPELL; suspects MALONE

3.1.182/1363 But] F, Q3; I but Q1; Yea but Q2. (Q2 alters all of Q1's instances of 'I', meaning yes, to 'yea'.)

3.1.188/1369 Sirs] F; Who's within there Q. Q's call for off-stage attendants reflects a variant staging.

3.1.194.1/1375.1 with the Cardinals men] Q; not in F

3.1.211/1392 straỹes] CAIRNCROSS (Vaughan); ſtrayes F; strives THEOBALD. Compare Folio Henry V 3.1.32/1069 (set by the same compositor).

3.1.211 strains] straỹes. See the previous note.

3.1.222.1/1403.1 with Salsbury and Warwicke] Q (Exet King, Salsbury, and Warwicke); not in F

3.1.248/1429 were set] F; set G.T. conj. G.T. observes that F is both metrically and syntactically irregular: '[to] set' would be parallel to 'As [to] place' (3.1.250/1431), whereas F instead yokes a passive ('were set') with an active ('place') construction. This sentence itself provides one of many examples of the omission of a grammatically necessary, implied 'to'; the Folio compositor may have misinterpreted (perhaps unconsciously) the construction and supplied what he took to be the implied word.

3.1.260/1441 Humfrey,] MALONE; ~ₐ F

3.1.260/1441 Reasons] F; treasons HUDSON. Cairncross provides parallels for the alleged error, but is less convincing on the need for emendation: although the nobles call Gloucester a traitor, they cannot prove he is a traitor on the basis of anything he has done: rather, they reason that he must be one (like the fox): reasons here stands in implicit contrast to evidence or witnesses.

3.1.264/1445 conceit] DELIUS 2; deceit F. The error could easily have been caught from the following line, which ends in 'deceit'.

3.1.280/1461 spoke] F; spokẽ HANMER (spoken). As it stands, the F line is acceptable metrically, either as a feminine tetrameter or, joined with the previous line, as a hexameter. 'Have spoke' is common in Shakespeare.

3.1.319–30.1/1500–11.1 Prouide . . . Exeunt] F; see Additional Passage C for Q's staging, which provides Buckingham with a part to play in this portion of the scene. Q may report an authorial revision here, for Buckingham's disappearance in F looks like a foul papers slip which would have been caught in rehearsal. But this whole part of the scene, from Henry's exit, is very different in Q: if there is revision here, it may be very extensive.

3.1.326/1507 Lord Suffolke] F; Suf⟨folk⟩. Lord CAIRNCROSS; QUEENE Lord Suffolke G.T. conj.; SUFFOLKE (aside to the Cardinall) This edition conj.

3.1.329/1510 For] F; Frõ This edition conj. In support of the conjectured for/from error, compare Various Poems: A Song, line 82, Caesar 3.1.286/1373, Hamlet 1.3.120/533, and Coriolanus 3.3.114/2043.

3.1.348 nurse] F (nouriſh). OED records a variety of forms—nourish, nourice, nursh, nurse—all having the same meaning, differing only in the extent to which they have been reduced in pronunciation. Metrically a monosyllable is required here, as at Titus 5.1.84/2016.

3.1.359/1540 Mortimer] F, Q1-2; ~ | (For he is like him euery kinde of way) Q3. This, the fifth of the longer Q3 departures from Q1, is reminiscent of the F lines 'For that *Iohn Mortimer*, which now is dead, | In face, in gate, in speech he doth resemble' (3.1.372-3/1553-4) which are absent from all three editions of Q. Q3 may represent a supplementary report, or it may derive from a copy of Q1 variant from either of the two which survive.

3.1.363 porcupine] F (Porpentine)

3.1.381/1562 coistrill] Q (coystrill); Rascall F. Either word could easily be misread as the other; but whereas *rascal* is very common, *coistrel* (or 'custrel') is a rare word; *OED* records no examples of any form between 1613 and 1783, and most of its examples cluster in the period 1577-1601.

3.2.0.1-3/1564.1-3 *Then . . . him in his bed*] Q; *Enter two or three running ouer the Stage, from the Murther of Duke Humfrey* F. Since Q derives from a performance, we follow its staging of this scene by having Gloucester's murder occur on stage.

Claire Saunders has argued that the Q staging may have been influenced by a parallel episode in *Woodstock* ('"Dead in his Bed": Shakespeare's Staging of the Death of the Duke of Gloucester in *2 Henry VI*', *RES* 36 (1985), 19-34). She may be right—but this argument does not really impinge on the staging's authority, and in any case the date of *Woodstock* is notoriously problematic.

3.2.13/1577 'Tis] F; All things is hansome now Q; 'Tis handsome CAIRNCROSS

3.2.14/1578 *Then . . . gone*] This edition; *Away, be gone* F; *Then draw the Curtaines againe and get you gone* Q. Shakespeare elsewhere uses 'close' as a collocate of 'draw' and 'curtains' (e.g. below, 3.3.32/2010, and *Lucrece* 367, 374). This line, or something like it, is needed to clarify Q's staging, and was probably added at the time the staging was revised. Since the passage, on the whole, is poorly reported, we are not inclined to accept Q dialogue verbatim. See the note to 3.2.0.1-3/1564.1-3.

3.2.14.1-5/1578.1-3 *Exeunt . . . Attendants*] after Q (*Exet murtherers.* | *Then enter the King and Queene, the Duke of Buckingham, and the Duke of Somerset, and the Cardinall*); F directs Suffolk to leave with the murderers, and to re-enter immediately with the King. On this matter, we follow Q. Since, however, Buckingham has no part to play in the following long scene in either Q or F, we assume Q's inclusion of him in the entry direction to be an error, and on this point follow F and exclude him.

3.2.15/1579 *to Suffolke*] after Q (*My Lord of Suffolke*); not in F

3.2.26/1590 Meg] CAPELL; Nell F

3.2.75 leper] F (Leaper)

3.2.79/1643 Queene *Margaret*] This edition; Dame *Elianor* F; Dame *Margaret* ROWE. *Dame* is used of Eleanor seven times, of Margaret only once (when Eleanor is imagining herself as Queen, and Margaret as her subject). *Queen Margaret* occurs three times in this play, and she is regularly identified as *Queen* in stage directions and speech-prefixes.

3.2.79 ne'er] F (neere)

3.2.82 wrecked] F (wrack'd)

3.2.83, 85/1647, 1649 winds] Q; winde F. Q appears to be the more idiomatic form. Compositor B, who set this portion of F, when working from printed copy is known to be guilty of addition or deletion of -s once every two Folio pages; the error would be even easier as a misreading of manuscript copy.

3.2.100/1664 Margaret] ROWE; Elianor F

3.2.107 heart] F (Hart)

3.2.116/1680 witch] THEOBALD; watch F. See line 3.2.119/1683.

3.2.120/1684 Margaret] ROWE; Elinor F

3.2.121.1-2/1685.1 *and Salisbury*] Q; *not in* F. But F requires Salisbury to be present when Warwick addresses him at line 3.2.134/1698. The commons appear not to have entered in the Q staging.

3.2.135.1-2/1699.1-2 *Exit . . . another*] Editors often direct that only Warwick exit, and that Salisbury, with the Commons, stand apart from the rest of the court. This is possible. But later, at 3.2.236/1799.1-2, the 'noise' which Q explains as the Commons crying 'Down with Suffolk' is directed to come from 'within', and later still, Salisbury is directed to enter (3.2.243.1/1805.2-3). A more plausible staging, therefore, would appear to be the one directed here: Warwick exits through whichever door the bed is later thrust out of (3.2.146.2/1710.2), while Salisbury and those Commons who entered with him exit through another.

G.T. suggests that Warwick remain on stage, as he does in Q: Warwick tells Salisbury to 'stay' while he 'goes'; instead, by an inverse convention used elsewhere, Salisbury 'goes' while Warwick 'stays'. But Q contains no speech between Salisbury's exit and the appearance of the bed: if the intervening F speech had been cut from the performance reported in Q (no echo of it occurs there, in an otherwise fairly well-reported scene), the staging would have to be adapted as well, for Warwick could hardly exit and immediately re-enter with the bed. Q therefore seems to represent a variant staging from that of F.

3.2.137/1701 *My thoughts, that . . . soule*] F; *That . . . grieued soule* S.W.W. *conj.* The repetition of 'My thoughts' here seems most un-Shakespearian, and resembles that in Sonnet 146, where the repetition is generally agreed to be accidental. Shakespeare uses *grievèd* to modify *soul* in *Richard II* 1.1.138/138; other possibilities include *troubled* (*Lucrece* 1176), and *inward* (*Lucrece* 1779, *Richard II* 2.2.11, 28/927, 944, *K. John* 3.1.153/1102). But compare *Errors* 4.2.64-5/1093-4 'I am prest downe with conceit: | Conceit, my comfort and my iniury'.

3.2.146.1-2/1710.1-2 *who . . . bed*] Q (subs.). 'As appears from the S.D. of [Q], the curtains of the inner stage are drawn, discovering Gloucester dead in his bed (in his room). The bed is then (according to the Folio) pushed out on to the main stage, as was normally done in such scenes when it was necessary for several persons to gather round' (McKerrow).

3.2.202.1/1766.1 *Exit Cardinall*] Q; *not in* F. Beaufort's and Somerset's silence throughout this scene is a major problem. Each speaks but once (Beaufort, 3.2.31-2/1595-6; Somerset, 3.2.34/1598); Somerset's presence is subsequently ignored, while Beaufort is last addressed at 3.2.183/1747 and last referred to at 3.2.196/1760. Q, which also directs Somerset's entry, and thus confirms his presence on stage for at least part of the scene, omits his single line of dialogue. It does not direct his exit. Q omits Beaufort's single F line of dialogue, but adds one in this vicinity (the texts are variant here), addressed to Warwick: 'But haue you no greater proofes then these?' Q also converts the third-person reference to Beaufort in line 3.2.196/1760 to a direct address.

McKerrow suggested that Beaufort 'may have been represented as becoming ill in the course of the scene' and being helped off stage, we suggest by Somerset, during the altercation of Warwick and the Queen. He dies in bed in the next scene.

Though Somerset may stand silently throughout the scene and leave with the King and Warwick (3.2.303.1/1865.1), Q seems to tell against this, for it specifically directs '*Exet* King and *Warwicke*', and both texts have Margaret say, immediately after the King's exit, 'There's two of you'.

3.2.223 born] F (borne)

3.2.231.1/1795.1 *Exeunt . . . Warwicke*] Q (*Warwicke puls him out. Exet Warwicke and Suffolke*); *Exeunt* F

3.2.236/1799.1-2 *All . . . Suffolk*] Q; *A noyse within* F. See also the note to 3.2.243-3.1/1805.1-3. Q in these instances represents performance, and provides concrete information, while F is just vague about such details, as indeed are many foul papers texts.

3.2.236 COMMONS . . . Suffolk! Down with Suffolk!] This edition (Q). See the previous note.

3.2.243-3.1/1805.1-3 *The . . . Salsbury*] Q (. . . Salbury); *Enter Salisbury* F

3.2.243-3.1 COMMONS . . . commons] This edition (Q). See the previous three notes.

3.2.254/1816 *As . . . liking*] F. 'I do not understand this line. Is it possible that we should read "Albeit" for "As being"? The line may, indeed, perhaps be read with the following one: the fact that he (Suffolk) is thought to be distasteful to you makes them forward in pressing for his banishment. But this seems very awkward, and the word "contradict" seems intended to carry on the sense of "opposite intent"' (McKerrow).

3.2.267   whe'er] F (where)
3.2.272/1834   COMMONS (within)] F (Commons within.)
3.2.281/1843   COMMONS (within)] CAPELL; Within F; The Commons cries Q
3.2.292.1/1854.1   Exit Salisbury] Q; not in F
3.2.303.1-3/1865.1-3   Exit . . . Suffolke] after Q (Exet King and Warwicke, Manet Queene and Suffolke); Exit F
3.2.305   sour] F (fowre)
3.2.312/1874   enemies] Q; enemy F. Q agrees with 'them' in the next line (in both Q and F): the error, 'enemie(s)', is an easy substitution. See the second note to 2.3.102/1063.
3.2.314/1876   Could] Q; Would F. The repetition of 'would' in the next line is suspicious, and may have led the compositor erroneously to substitute 'would' for manuscript 'could' here. Q seems the superior reading.
3.2.322/1884   My] Q; Mine F. The collocation *my hair* is used seven times by Shakespeare (in *Richard III*, *Dream*, *Caesar*, *As You Like It*, *Twelfth Night*, *Lear*, and *Macbeth*); *mine hair* occurs only here.
3.2.322   on] F (an)
3.2.322   distraught] F (distract), Q
3.2.336/1898   turne] ROWE; turnes F
3.2.338/1900   this] Q; the F
3.2.346.1/1908.1   She kisses his palm] This edition; not in F, Q
3.2.348/1910   vpon these lips] This edition (G.T.); vpon these F; on these lips HANMER. Hanmer altered 'vpon' to 'on' to make room, metrically, for 'lips'. This is unnecessary, however, because *by the* could be elided to *by th'*: it is often printed 'by the' even when elision is required. All we need assume is the omission of the single word *lips*.
    McKerrow, however, who believed emendation unnecessary here, observed: 'These lines [3.2.348-9/1910-11] are somewhat obscure, but presumably "these" are the "wofull Monuments" and "whom" is the "Seale" envisaged as the image of the Queen's living lips through which a "thousand sighs" had been breathed. The use of "who" or "whom" of inanimate objects when their verb implied animate action is not unusual'.
3.2.370/1932   no] F; to SINGER 2 (Collier MS); now G.T. conj.
3.2.383/1945   Vaux] Q (Vawfe); not in F
3.2.395/1957   could I] F, Q3; could I, could I Q1-2
3.2.397/1959   his] Q; it's F. *OED*'s first recorded use of *its* as a possessive pronoun dates from 1598. Excepting this line, and *Measure* 1.2.4/88 (which is probably a late interpolation: see the Introduction to that play), the form does not appear in Shakespeare's work before *Winter's Tale* (1.2.159/206, etc.).
3.2.402.1/1964.1   He kisseth her] This edition; not in F, Q
3.2.404/1966   By thee to dye] Q (. . . die); To dye by thee F
3.2.411/1973   out.] F, Q; out. | Away! CAIRNCROSS
3.2.412.1/1974.1   She kisseth him] Q; not in F
3.2.416.1/1978.1   Exeunt seuerally] Q (Exet Suffolke. | Exet Queene); Exeunt F
3.3.0.2-4/1978.2-5   and then . . . madde] Q; to the Cardinal in bed F
3.3.10   whe'er] F (where), Q (whether)
3.3.27/2005   think'st] F; dieſt aſſured Q. See the note to 3.1.114/1295.
3.3.28.1/2006.1   The Cardinall dies] Q; not in F
4.1.0.1-2/2011.3-4   Alarmes . . . sea] Q
4.1.0.2-6/2011.4-8   And . . . Gentlemen] Q (And then enter the Captaine of the ſhip | and the Maiſter, and the Maiſters Mate, & the Duke of Suf-|folke diſguiſed, and others with him, and Water Whickmore)
4.1.0.2-3/2011.4-5   the Captaine of the ship] Q; Lieutenant F. The stage direction 'of the quartos seems clearly to be correct, and as the source used for the scene refers to a Captain ["capitayne" Hall, Clviᵛ; Bullough, iii. 112] the Lieutenant of Ff would seem to be a mere error' (McKerrow). Since the garbled genealogy of 2.2/Sc. 6 in Q is strong presumptive evidence that the reporters did not have access to a chronicle, the Q correction of 'Lieutenant' to 'Captain' must either have been a guess on the part of the reporters (which is possible, the inference deriving from 4.1.107/2118, which is in Q), or it must reflect revision between foul papers and prompt-book (see the Introduction). A number of other historical details (e.g. 1.2.75/334, 4.7.106/2564-5, 4.7.107-8/2566) appear to have been added at this stage. In either case, 'captain' seems clearly to be the correct reading, and 'Lieutenant' the author's error.
4.1.1-7/2012-18   The gaudy . . . ayre] F. 'It seems impossible that the epithets in [4.1.1/2012] should have so little meaning as they appear to have. The first seven lines are not in Qq, and are very suspicious' (McKerrow). By 'suspicious' McKerrow presumably intimates the possibility of interpolation, but it is not clear how such an interpolation would arrive in F.
4.1.6   Clip] F (Cleape); Clap POPE; Clepe WILSON (conj.)
2025, 2043, 2050   Water] This edition (Q); *Walter* F. McKerrow believed F's spelling, 'Walter', was a sophistication. Q consistently has 'Water'. Moreover, 'Water' occurs in F at 4.1.116/2127 (when Compositor B did not realize what he was setting) and at 4.1.140.1/2151.1 (see the list of stage directions). There is a similar sophistication at *Richard III* 5.8.14/3423, where F (set by B) and Q6 independently change Q1 'Water' to 'Walter'.
4.1.20/2031   ⌜WHITMORE⌝ Cut] This edition (conj. Malone 2); Cut F. It does not seem probable that the Lieutenant, who calls Whitmore's aim to kill his prisoner 'rash', and who instead urges him to 'take ransome' (4.1.29/2040) would speak these lines. Neither would the Master or the Mate, both of whom have already settled on their ransom demands. Only Whitmore consistently demands death, so probably he is intended to speak these lines.
4.1.22/2033]   Lacuna marked by this edition. The lines 4.1.21-3/2032-4 as they stand in F are unsatisfactory, and several emendations have been proposed. Malone was the first to suggest a missing line, though he believed it to have been immediately before 4.1.21/2032 rather than, as we suggest, after it. Malone may be right.
    The missing line clearly contained a negative, probably 'cannot', and probably named something inadequately 'counter-poys'd' by such a 2,000-crown ransom.
4.1.23/2034   counter-poys'd] F; vnder-poys'd MCKERROW (conj.)
4.1.32.1/2043.1   Suffolke ſtarteth] Q (He ſtarteth); not in F
4.1.33/2044   thee] CAIRNCROSS (Vaughan); death F
4.1.49/2060   Ioue sometime went disguiſde, and why not I?] Q; not in F
4.1.51/2062   SUFFOLKE] Q (Suf.); not in F. See the note to 4.1.52/2063.
4.1.51/2062   lowsie] F; lowly POPE (Q). Pope's decision to adopt the Q reading is difficult to justify, though many editors have followed it. As McKerrow notes, *OED* records *lousy* to have been a general term of abuse. Sanders (p. 239) notes that the word may have been adopted from Hall's account of Cade's murder of his old acquaintances, lest 'they should blaſe & declare his base byrthe and lowsy lynage' (Hall, Clxᵛ). Foul-case error is out of the question since the compositor used a single typepiece ('ſi') instead of the two typepieces ('l' 'i') Q would require ('lowlie').
4.1.52/2063   The] Q; Suf⟨folke⟩. The. F. See the first note to 4.1.51/2062.
4.1.53/2064   iadie] Q (Iadie); iaded F. Q repeats 'Iadie' at 4.1.130/2141, in place of F's 'Vulgar'; Q thus gives double warrant for a form not otherwise recorded until 1873. F's word, by contrast, is common. We have accepted Q as the rarer reading, of which F might easily be a corruption. See Taylor, 'Praestat'.
4.1.71/2082   CAPTAINE . . . I] ALEXANDER (McKerrow); *Lieu.* Poole, Sir Poole ? Lord, | I F; *Cap.* Yes Poull. | *Suffolke.* Poull. | *Cap.* I Q. McKerrow and Alexander independently supposed that F 'Sir' was a misreading of 'Suf' (probably indicated by 'S' or 'Su') and 'Lord' for 'Lieu' (probably indicated by 'L'). See Alexander, *SSu* 5 (1952), 7-8, and the notes to 4.1.0.2-6/2011.4-8 and 4.1.0.2-3/2011.4-5.
4.1.77/2088   shalt] Q; ſhall F
4.1.85/2096   Mothers bleeding] ROWE; Mother-bleeding F
4.1.93/2104   are] ROWE; and F
4.1.98/2109   our] F. This seems odd in the context, and may be an error.

4.1.108/2119 *Bargulus the strong Illyrian Pyrate*] F; Abradas, | The great Maſadonian Pyrate Q. The Q allusion is not known, though it is probably somehow related to Greene's two uses of this identical phrase (*Menaphon* 5.197.19, *Penelope's Web* 6.77.27). The F version seems to derive from the juxtaposition in Cicero, *De Officiis* 2.11.40, of '*archipirata*' and '*Bardulis Illyrius latro*'. The Q phrase may be a memorial interpolation: if Greene used the phrase twice in prose works, he may have used it a third time, in a play, now lost, but which the reporter knew. Other, identifiable, interpolations from other authors' works are present in Q. See Alfred Hart.

4.1.113/2124 CAPTAINE . . . Rage.] This edition; *not in* F; *Cap.* I but my deeds ſhall ſtaie thy fury ſoone. Q; CAPTAINE I but my deeds shall staie thy Rage as soone G.T. *conj.* Either F has dropped a line which was in its copy, or Q imperfectly reflects a line which was added in the preparation of the prompt-book.

In either case, it seems probable from what remains in Q that a parallelism was intended between this line and the one immediately preceding: Q's 'fury' repeats a word from its version of the previous line, where F has 'Rage', and 'words' in that line is clearly paralleled in Q by 'deeds' in this one. But Q is a report, and as such is prone to memorial error: it would be an easy mistake for the reporter to substitute 'fury' for 'Rage' in the previous line, as comparison with F shows he probably did (the metrical irregularity of Q arising from the substitution of disyllabic 'fury' for monosyllabic 'Rage' argues against authorial revision), and to repeat the error here, where he remembered the word was repeated. But if 'Rage' is simply substituted here for 'fury', the line becomes unmetrical. Our reconstruction attempts to restore both the metre and the parallel.

4.1.114/2125 SUFFOLKE] CAIRNCROSS; *not in* F. See the preceding note.

4.1.116-17/2127-8 CAPTAINE Water: | WHITMORE Come] ROWE (*subs.*); Lieu⟨tenant⟩. Water: W. Come F; Whit⟨more⟩. Come CAIRNCROSS. Cairncross argues that F's '*Lieu.*' is the speech-prefix caught from the omitted line 'Ay . . . soon' (3 lines above: see the note to 4.1.113/2124), and that F's 'Water: W.' constitutes a (unique) speech-prefix ('Water Whitmore').

4.1.118/2129 *Pene*] MALONE; *Pine* F1; *not in* F2-4; *Poenoe* THEOBALD; *Pone* MITFORD (*conj.*); *Iam* WORDSWORTH; *Perii* WILSON (Thomson); *Aque* MCKERROW (*conj.*).

4.1.118 *Paene*] (*Pene*). See the previous note.

4.1.121 daunted] F (danted)

4.1.134/2145 SUFFOLKE Come] HANMER; Come F. See the next note.

4.1.135/2146 That] HANMER; Suf⟨folke⟩. That F. See the previous note.

4.1.138/2149 *Brutus*] F. The final typepiece of F is a turned italic '*us*' ligature, and not the two typepieces 's' and 'n', wrongly set, as recorded by editors.

4.2.0.1/2160.2 *2. Rebels*] TURNER-WILLIAMS; *Beuis, and Iohn Holland* F; *two of the Rebels* Q. 'Beuis' and 'Iohn Holland', which F also employs as speech-prefixes within this scene, have been identified as actors' names. In Q the speech-prefixes for these two characters, not named in the direction, are 'George' and 'Nick', which McMillin has argued also represent actors' names.

Neither *John Holland* nor *Bevis* occurs in Q's stage directions or speech-prefixes, though there is a reference in the dialogue of Q to 'Beuys of South-hampton' which is absent from F (see line 879 in the Malone Society facsimile of Q); aside from the opening of this scene, Bevis and Holland are not mentioned elsewhere in F, though there is a 'Iohn' (4.7.7, 10, 15/2463, 2466, 2471) which editors from Capell onward have identified with Holland.

Editors usually assume Q's 'George' and F's 'Beuis' refer to the same actor, and emend the direction here to 'George Bevis', though there is no external evidence whatever of an actor 'George Bevis'. Our editorial policy, however, is to substitute fictional names for those of actors, and so here, as elsewhere in the Cade scenes, we substitute *rebel* for a name which is not supported in the dialogue.

4.2.0.1, 4.2.32.3/2160.2, 2190.2 *with long staues*] Q; *not in* F. Q's dialogue alludes to the staves: they may reflect performance, therefore.

4.2.30/2188 *Weauer*] F. In the F dialogue three rebels are discussed: Best the tanner (4.2.23-4/2181-2), Dick the butcher (4.2.27/2185), and Smith the weaver (4.2.30/2188). Q's dialogue lists, besides the butcher, 'Robin the Sadler, and Will that came a wooing of our Nan laſt Sunday, and Harry and Tom, and Gregory that ſhould haue your Parnill'.

4.2.34/2192 *to his Fellowes*] This edition; *not in* F. Each of the speeches so directed could be an aside, either to the audience or to a single other character.

4.2.36/2194 falle] F4; faile F1. Compare Leviticus 26 : 8, '& your enemies shall fall before you vpon the sworde'. Cade may be punning implicitly on his name and the Latin verb *cadō, cadere*, meaning *fall*.

4.2.86/2246 Chattam] Q; Chartam F. There is a small place, near Canterbury, called Chartham, but it seems more likely that Chatham, near Rochester, is meant. Editors, however, are about equally divided on which they adopt. Cade's party already has in it the Tanner of Wingham (to the east of Canterbury, line 4.2.24/2182) and the Butcher of Ashford (to the south-west of Canterbury, line 4.3.1/2352). If we suppose that Cade is meant to have accumulated his rabble following as he moved through Kent, roughly towards London, we are led to conclude that he has already passed along a west-south-westerly path through Wingham and Ashford. Chatham is roughly between Ashford and London, lying north-west of Ashford; Chartham lies between Ashford and Canterbury, to the north-east of Ashford. So to suppose that F is correct is to suppose that the rebels retrace their path after Ashford, while to suppose 'Chattam' is the correct reading is to suppose them following a London-bound course from Ashford. The supposed F error, r/t foul case, is common in the work of Compositor B in this play: besides this instance it occurs seven times (all recorded among the Incidentals emendations). In three of these seven instances, 'r', as here, is mistakenly set for 't' (1916, 1970, 2889); in the remaining four instances, 't' is mistakenly set for 'r' (2021, 2394, 2640, 2950).

4.2.91 He's] F (Ha's); hee has Q; Has CAMBRIDGE

4.2.99/2260 y^t] Q (that); it F. The Q reading makes better sense, and it would be easy for the Folio compositor to have mistaken manuscript 'y^t' as 'yt', which he then set as 'it'.

4.2.102/2263 an] F2; a F1. The collocation *an honest* occurs in Shakespeare at least 62 times; *a honest* only here. F1 may be right, however, and reflect a dialectal pronunciation for Cade.

4.2.109.1/2270.2 *a Messenger*] TURNER-WILLIAMS; *Michael* F; *Tom* Q

4.2.110, 112, 117/2271, 2273, 2278 MESSENGER] TURNER-WILLIAMS; Mich⟨ael⟩. F; Tom. Q

4.2.119/2281 *Mortimer*] F; Mortemer, | Is there any more of them that be Knights? | *Tom.* I his brother. | He Knights *Dicke Butcher*. | *Cade.* Then kneele downe Dicke Butcher, | Riſe vp ſir Dicke Butcher Q. Though clearly reflecting a performance, the additional Q matter, which may be authorial, could easily have been interpolated to stretch out, for example, a popular piece of business. Q's version of this scene is different from F's.

4.2.131/2293 was] F, Q3; was but Q1-2

4.2.133/2295 And what] F; What CAIRNCROSS

4.2.134/2296 this:] THEOBALD (*subs.*); ~ₐ F. The punctuation of F, however, may be correct and some previous mention of Roger Mortimer may have been dropped out. In Q Cade says in his previous speech, 'But I come of the Mortemers', which suggests that there may have been something more here. At present the transitions of thought are very abrupt (McKerrow).

4.2.144/2306 and] Q; if F. The substitution of *if* for 'and' (=*an*) is common in F.

4.2.147/2309 testifie] Q1-2 (*subs.*); teſtifie it F, Q3

4.2.160 maimed] F (main'd), Q (maimde)

4.2.189/2351 *Exeunt*] Q (*Exet omnes*); *not in* F

4.3.0.1/2351.1 *excursions*] This edition; *not in* F

4.3.6/2357 Thou] Q1-2; and thou Q3, F

4.3.7/2358 License] Q (licence); a License F

4.3.9.1/2360.1 He ... Armour] HART (subs.); not in F, Q. The chronicles (Fabyan, Hall, Grafton, Holinshed) all agree that Cade thus 'apparells' himself; only Holinshed specifies the armour taken as Sir Humphrey's.

4.4.0.1/2368.2 reading] Q; with F

4.4.0.3/2368.4 with others] Q; not in F. Q is unlikely to add characters, and attendants are normal in such a scene, though often omitted in authorial papers.

4.4.19-24.1/2387-92.1 SAY ... Messenger] F corresponds exactly with Q in this passage, except for one variant: Q 'my loue, if' for F 'me (Loue) if that' in 4.4.22/2390. Given the metrical irregularity of the passage, one must suspect some Q contamination, which may extend to the preceding line.

4.4.20/2388 How now] F, Q; How CAIRNCROSS. See the previous note: Cairncross may be right.

4.4.20/2388 lamenting and mourning] POPE; lamenting and mourning for Q, F; lamenting CAIRNCROSS. F's superfluous preposition 'for' produces an irregular line, and could easily have been interpolated unconsciously by any agent of transmission. However, since F here agrees with Q for the first 10 words of Henry's speech, either F is authoritative, or (more probably) F has been directly influenced by Q. We assume Q contamination.

4.4.23/2391 wouldest not] THEOBALD; would'ſt not F1, Q; would'ſt not halfe F2

4.4.24/2392 No my] F, Q; My POPE; No, CAPELL

4.4.38 Kenilworth] F (Killingworth)

4.4.42/2410 Traitors rabble hateth] This edition (G.T.); Traitors hateth F. As it stands, F is both metrically and grammatically irregular. The grammatical irregularity is not without parallel (e.g. Dream 2.1.90-1/445-6 'fogs ... hath'), but it is rare. Coming, therefore, as it does, in conjunction with a metrical irregularity, it suggests corruption, probably in the form of a lost two-syllable word. G.T.'s emendation renders the line both grammatically and metrically sound, and makes good sense. See the next note.

4.4.42 trait'rous] F (Traitors). OED does not record 'traitors' as a possible spelling of traitorous, though it does record 'traytorsly' (which is early) and 'traytoursly'. F may be wrong, its error in some way connected with the line's dropped word (see the previous note); it may be a rare acceptable spelling of traitorous; or, indeed, it may mean traitor's.

4.4.48/2416 almost] Q; not in F

4.4.57/2425 be betraid] F2; betraid F1

4.5.0.1-4.6.0.2/2427.2-40.3 Enter ... stone] Q. Q is almost certainly principal copy for F here; accordingly, we use it as our control text, and adopt its incidentals. See the Introduction.

4.5.0.1-2/2427.2-3 Enter ... below] Q1-2; not in Q3; Then enters two or three Citizens below F. See the Introduction.

4.5.0.1/2427.2 the Lord] Q; Lord F

4.5.1/2428 Is Iacke Cade] Q, F; Are Iacke Cade and his followers conj. This edition.

4.5.2-6/2429-33 No ... Rebels] Q, F ('craues' instead of 'crueth', line 4.5.4/2431). Probably originally verse (see the lineation notes), these lines have been corrupted in Q beyond confident reconstruction. We treat them as prose.

4.5.2/2429 Lord Scayles] This edition (G.T.); Lord Q, F. Lord Scales is not named in the dialogue as it is reported, but only in stage directions and speech-prefixes. We must suppose, therefore, that the reporter responsible for this passage either knew from an authorial reference in the prompt-book (as, for example, in his part) that the lord who enters was Scales, and that the audience was never intended to know the precise identity of the lord in this scene, or we must suppose (more probably) that the reporter has omitted some dialogue reference to Scales which was originally present.

Our emendation is the least obtrusive change that can be made to render the surviving text theatrically sound.

4.5.3/2430 he and his men] This edition; they Q, F; his men G.T. conj. QF 'they' is weak, and does not follow naturally from Lord Scales's questions about Cade specifically (see, however, the note to 4.5.1/2428 for an alternative conjecture).

4.5.4/2431 did withstand] This edition (G.T.); withstand Q, F; did there withstand This edition conj. The tense of QF seems wrong: an alternative emendation would be 'withstood' (G.T.).

4.5.9/2436 assay'd] F; attempted Q

4.5.10/2437 Get you to Smythfield, there to gather head] This edition; But get you to Smythfield, and gather head Q, F; But get thee into Smithfield, gather head POPE; Get you to Smithfield, and there gather head CAIRNCROSS. The poor metre of QF, coupled with the repetition of 'But' from line 4.5.8/2435 and of 'And' in line 4.5.11/2438, suggests memorial corruption. Our reconstruction aims both to restore the metre and to eliminate these two suspicious words.

4.5.11/2438 will I] F2; I will Q, F1. The F2 reading is metrically superior: the Q transposition, from which F derives, would be an easy error on the part of either the reporter or the compositor.

4.6.0.2/2440.3 sword] Q; ſtaffe F. Q here reflects performance, and agrees with the chronicles: the variant is probably authorial. See 1.2.75/334, 4.1.0.2-3/2011.4-5, 4.7.106/2564-5, and 4.7.107-8/2566 for other instances of historical detail evidently added between the manuscript behind F and the prompt-book. See, however, the note to 4.7.214/2672 among the list of rejected quarto variants, and the textual note to 4.7.219.1-2/2677.1-2 for Q evidence that Cade carried a staff.

4.6.1-4.7.4/2441-60 Now ... word] F. Though there is probably extensive Q contamination here, the two texts are sufficiently different for us to doubt that Q continues to serve as principal copy. We therefore revert to F as our control text, and follow its incidentals.

4.6.6/2446 otherwise] Q; other F. F's variant might be Compositor B's effort to make the line (which he sets as verse) metrical. See the note to 4.6.13-14/2453-4.

4.6.8/2448 Sounes,] Q; not in F. This oath is often removed editorially from the Folio; it only occurs once in the entire volume (K. John 2.1.467/743). See Taylor, 'Zounds'.

4.6.9-10/2449-50 BUTCHER If ... warning] F; not in Q; Weau⟨er⟩. If ... warning. ROWE. See the note to 4.6.11/2451.

4.6.10.1-2/2450.1-2 He takes a paper from the souldiers body, and reades it] This edition (G.T.); not in Q, F. Some such action seems necessary in order to explain the character's knowledge of the dead messenger's news.

4.6.11/2451 My] CAIRNCROSS; Dicke. My Q, F. 'Dicke' is the same character as the butcher, so that this prefix apparently duplicates that at 4.6.9/2449; but 4.6.9-10/2449-50 is not in Q, and since 'But.' is F's usual prefix for the character, and 'Dicke.' is Q's, the duplication seems to result from the use of imperfectly annotated Quarto copy here.

4.6.13-14/2453-4 go on] Q; go F. F is, again, probably Compositor B trying to make 'verse' metrical. See the note to 4.6.6/2446.

4.6.14/2454 a fire] Q1, Q3; on fire F, Q2. Probably independent sophistication on the part of the Q2 and F compositors.

4.7.0.1/2455.2 Excursions, wherein] This edition; not in F. Some such action seems necessary in order for the audience to know that Gough and his men are slain.

4.7.0.1/2455.2 Mathew Goffe] The case here is similar to that at 4.5.2/2429, except that Gough is mentioned once in the dialogue of a previous scene (4.5.11/2438). So once again, either the audience was not intended to know the identity of the soldiers' leader who is here slain, and the reporter was able to identify him either by recalling an authorial reference in his part or in the prompt-book or by recalling the reference in the earlier dialogue, or (more likely) some explicit reference to him here has been omitted from the dialogue by the reporter. G.T. suggests that a theatrical solution to the problem would be to have Gough appear on the walls with Scales in 4.5/Sc. 16 and identified, by a gesture, in 4.5.11/2438.

4.7.0.1/2455.3 of his men with him] Q (with him); not in F. Q clarifies that only Gough and his followers are slain.

4.7.2/2457 Court] F; the Court Q. Compositor B's deletion of 'the' here, though possibly made without reference to any authority, is probably correct. OED provides no evidence of the phrase 'Inns

THE FIRST PART OF THE CONTENTION

of *the* Court', and the interpolation of 'the' would have been an easy memorial error.

4.7.7/2463 IOHN] F; Dicke Q. F's '*Iohn*' may mean the same character as 'Iohn Holland' (see the note to 4.2.0.1/2160.2), whom we call '2. Rebell', though Q, which assigns most of Holland's speeches to a character or actor called 'Nicke', does not corroborate this. We treat John here and at 4.7.15/2471 as a miscellaneous rebel, and retain his name only because he is addressed by it in 4.7.10/2466.

4.7.10/2466 WEAUER] F (Smith). See the note to 4.2.30/2188.

4.7.21.1–158/2477.1–2617 *Enter . . . kill*] This Folio page, o1ʳ, contains several suspicious features. The Butcher's speeches are consistently prefixed 'Dicke' not 'Butcher' (only once elsewhere in F is there a 'Dicke' speech-prefix, at 4.6.11/2451, and that appears to be related to Q copy). Two passages are reported in Q at points which correspond with points on this F page, yet there is no trace of either in F (see the notes to 4.7.122.1–4.7.140.1/2581.1–2599, 4.7.143–6/2602–5). Compositor B found it necessary to stretch his copy as he neared the bottom of the second column (see the note to 4.7.141/2600). Perhaps also significantly, Saye's entrance begins this page, and the Saye episode occupies most of it.

4.7.21.1/2477.1 *a Rebell*] This edition; *George* Q, F. QF agreement in the identification of this rebel looks suspiciously like Q contamination of F. The surrounding F dialogue shows no signs of contamination, yet it does not name this character. If the identification were authorial, like Holland and Bevis, above (see the note to 4.2.0.1/2160.2), but present only in the stage direction, it is not likely that the reporter would know it (but see the notes to 4.5.2/2429 and 4.7.0.1/2455.2). More probable is that 'George' is the reporter's interpolation and that it was picked up from Q by the Folio compositor.

4.7.23 *serge*] F (Surge)

4.7.27 *Dauphin*] F (Dolphine), Q

4.7.44/2501 on] Q; in F. The Q idiom is the correct one: F is wrong (McKerrow). F's error may be a simple misreading.

4.7.49/2506 their shirts] This edition (G.T.); their shirt F. The plural would appear to be required from the parallel 'Doublets' in 4.7.48/2505 and from 'their' here. *OED* records no instance of *shirt* functioning as a generic plural.

4.7.54–7/2511–14 *Bonum . . . inough*] Q; Away with him, away with him, he speaks Latine F. The Q version, though not beyond the interpolative powers of a reporter, seems superior to that of F, giving, as it does, something for some of the other rebels to say who, in F, simply stand about. Q thereby more effectively conveys the sense of an unruly rabble. We assume the Q version represents an authorial revision introduced to the prompt-book.

4.7.58 where] F (wher'e); possibly *where'er*

4.7.61/2518 because] F; beauteous, HANMER; bounteous, VAUGHAN (conj.); pleasant, KINNEAR (conj.); pleteous, CAIRNCROSS (conj.)

4.7.69/2526 But] RANN (Johnson); Kent F

4.7.82/2540 for watching] F1; with ~ F2. G. L. Brook, *The Language of Shakespeare* (1976), 94, shows that *for* can mean 'because of', the sense which seems intended here.

4.7.87/2545 Caudle] F4; Candle F1

4.7.87–8/2545–6 the helth oth] This edition; the help of F; the pap of a STEEVENS (conj.); pap with a CAIRNCROSS (Farmer). F, though possible, is unsatisfactory; Steevens and Cairncross, though proverbial (Tilley P 45), are graphically implausible. 'Helth oth' requires the compositor to have misread manuscript 'th' first as 'p' (or 'pe' which he set as 'p') and then as 'f': difficult, but not impossible, errors, especially if the manuscript were damaged here. Compare *Errors* 1.1.151/151 where Folio 'helpe' appears to be an error for manuscript 'helth'.

Health works in connection with *caudle* (= a gruel for the sick, *sb*. 1), and perhaps puns on *helve* (= handle, *sb*. 1): 'To throw the helve after the hatchet', meaning 'one loss on top of another', was proverbial (Tilley H 413). Cercignani, p. 331, attests to the possibility of the proposed v/ð homophony by observing that, if exact, the *farthest/harvest* rhyme in *Tempest* 4.1.114–15/1570–1 'would have to be explained as depending on v from ð in *farthest* (cf. $f < p$, § 117.1)'.

4.7.90/2548 prouokes] F; provoketh HANMER

4.7.106/2564–5 to the standerd in Cheapeside] Q; not in F. This historical detail, present in the chronicles, was probably added by the author as he revised his foul papers in the preparation of the prompt-book. Q's 'chop' for F's 'strike' may be a related authorial variant made for the alliteration with 'Cheapside'. See the notes to 1.2.75/334, 4.1.0.2–3/2011.4–5, 4.6.0.2/2440.3, the next note, and the Introduction.

4.7.107–8/2566 go to milende-greene,] Q; not in F. Another detail from the chronicles: see the previous note.

4.7.116.1–2/2574.1–2 *Exeunt . . . one or two, with the Lord Say*] Q (subs.); not in F

4.7.116.1/2574.1 *the Butcher and*] This edition. The butcher must re-enter with the Sergeant, line 4.7.125.1/2584.1, in the passage adopted from Q (which does not provide for his exit either).

4.7.120/2578 Married men] Q; Men F. Q makes better sense: the skip involved (from *m* to *m*) would be an easy one for the Folio compositor to make.

4.7.122.1–140.1/2581.1–99 *Enter . . . Sargiant*] Q; not in F. For a variety of reasons it seems probable that Q here reports an authorial addition made in the preparation of the prompt-book, but absent from the earlier foul paper draft upon which F is based. See the Introduction.

Firstly, the news that London Bridge is on fire responds to an order Cade gave, in both texts, earlier; secondly, the addition serves a theatrical function, namely to provide a reasonable pause between the rebels' exit with Saye (4.7.116.1–2/2574.1–2) and their return with the heads (4.7.147.1–2/2606.1–2); thirdly, it is linked to another addition (4.7.143–6/2602–5) by the theme of sexual threat; and finally, it cannot be due to problems of casting or memory. Many of the notes which follow indicate links between this passage and Shakespeare's acknowledged work, which suggest that he was responsible for the addition.

4.7.122.1/2581.1 *a Rebell*] This edition; *Robin* Q

4.7.123/2582 REBELL] This edition; *Robin* Q

4.7.123/2582 London bridge is a fire] Q. This report is a natural development from Cade's earlier order (4.6.14/2454).

4.7.124/2583 Billingsgate] Q. The allusion here fits into a pattern by which Q stresses specific London locations, significant for the play's original audiences, as a means of emphasizing the frightening reality and immediacy of Cade's rebellion. For a related use of London locations in *Richard III*, see Ralph Berry, *Shakespeare and the Awareness of the Audience* (1985), 16–29.

4.7.124/2583 flaxe] Q. Shakespeare alludes to flax as a particularly combustible material later, at 5.3.55/3091, and in *Kinsmen* 5.5.98/2600.

4.7.125/2584 quench] Q3; squench Q1–2. Q1–2's form of the verb does not elsewhere appear in Shakespeare's works; 'quench', though, is frequent.

4.7.125.1/2584.1 *Enter the Butcher and a Sargiant*] Q ('Enter Dicke . . .')

4.7.126/2585 Iustice, iustice] Q. Similar exclamations occur in Shakespeare at *Errors* 5.1.134, 198/1483, 1540, *Merchant* 2.8.17, 21/1021, 1025, and *Measure* 5.1.20, 25/2185, 2190.

4.7.129/2588 rauisht my wife] Q. Two of Shakespeare's earliest works are concerned with a rape (*Titus*, *Lucrece*); he uses the verb *ravish* in this sense 18 times.

4.7.130/2589 rested] Q. Shakespeare uses this aphetic form four times, all in *Errors*.

4.7.131/2590 went and] Q2; went and and Q1

4.7.130/2590 entred my Action] Q. Shakespeare uses both 'enter' and 'action' in the sexual senses punned on here (Colman, pp. 182, 192). The phrase 'entred the action' occurs at *2 Henry IV* 2.1.1–2/612, in a dialogue between a wronged woman (Quickly) and two sergeants, who unsuccessfully attempt to carry out an arrest. The dialogue is full of sexual innuendoes.

4.7.132/2591 proper] This edition (G.T.); paper Q. This would be an easy error. Several senses of *proper* are appropriate: 'very own' (sb. 1), 'private, exclusive; the opposite of *common*' (sb. 2), 'admirable, excellent' (sb. 7), 'honest, respectable (used of women)' (sb. 7b), 'good-looking' (sb. 8), 'apt, suitable, fitting' (sb. 9). Shakespeare uses the word in all these senses, and both early examples of sb. 7b are from his works.

4.7.132/2591 house] Q. (*a*) abode, place of habitation; (*b*) deliberative assembly, of a political, municipal, or religious nature (sb. 4d, 4e); (*c*) vagina. For this last sense, compare *Lear* (*History* 9.27/1547; *Tragedy* 3.2.27/1555): 'The Codpeece that will house', where the penis (= codpiece) is imagined as 'taking shelter, being housed' in a vagina.

4.7.133/2592 follow thy sute] Q. Compare 'I *follow* thus a loosing sute' (*Merchant* 4.1.60-1/1869-70; the italics are ours). *Suit* is, of course, often used of a romantic or sexual proposition, in addition to its legal sense. It is, moreover, probably a homophone of *shoot* (Cercignani, 347), and as such 'Vaguely yet indubitably . . . indicates or insinuates the pointing of the male towards the female generative organ' (Partridge). So, too, may *shoot* (sb.¹ 2c), 'An offshoot; a growth or sprout from a main stock', suggest the penis.

4.7.134/2593 you horson villaine] Q. The identical phrase occurs at *Shrew* 4.1.141/1701; *whoreson . . . villain* recurs at *Errors* 4.4.25/1215 and *2 Henry IV* 2.4.209/1241.

4.7.134/2593 Sargiant] Q. With this description compare Dromio of Syracuse's (*Errors* 4.3.13-41/1107-35). In *Errors* Antipholus of Ephesus is arrested by a sergeant just after his dinner (4.1/Sc. 9).

4.7.135/2594 take any man by the throate] Q. Compare *Othello* 5.2.364/3261: 'tooke bi'th throate'.

4.7.136-7/2595 haue him to prison] Q. For the idiom see *OED have*, v. 16; it does not appear in Shakespeare's acknowledged works. G.T. *conj*. 'hale' for Q 'haue'.

4.7.138/2597 cut out his toong] Q. The fate of Philomele, to whose rape Shakespeare alludes in both *Titus* and *Lucrece*.

4.7.139/2597 cogging] Q; cogging, | *The Sargiant tries to run away* G.T. *conj*.

4.7.140/2598 brane] This edition; Braue Q. The verb *brain* is used three times by Shakespeare (*1 Henry IV* 2.4.22/842, *Measure* 5.1.393/2557, and *Tempest* 3.2.89/1281).

4.7.140.1/2599 *Exit Butcher*] This edition; *Exet* Q

4.7.141/2600 REBELL] This edition; Dicke. F; Nicke. Q. In the passage (4.7.122.1-140.1/2581.1-2599) adopted from Q, Cade specifically tells Dick to take care of the sergeant, so the F attribution of this line cannot stand. Instead of adopting Q's 'Nicke', however, which may well merely name an actor (see McMillin), we assign the line to an unspecified rebel.

4.7.141/2600 My Lord, when] F (My Lord, | When); But when Q; When Q G.T. *conj*. From this point to the end of the page Compositor B wastes space consistently, by setting prose as verse (see the lineation notes) and using blank lines around stage directions: undoubtedly the amount of text o1ʳ could accommodate had been underestimated when its copy was cast off. In this context, the Folio vocative, 'My Lord', which wastes an extra line of space, may be, as G.T. suggests, B's interpolation. But 'My Lord' is often used by the rebels in addressing Cade, so it is difficult to rule out its authority here.

4.7.143-6/2602-5 He . . . smocke] Q; *not in* F. This Q passage probably represents another authorial addition between foul papers and the prompt-book—it cannot be accounted for as having resulted from peculiar deficiencies of cast or performing space, and, moreover, it seems directly related to the earlier addition (see the note to 4.7.122.1-140.1/2581.1-99) in its emphasis on the sexual threat posed by Cade. Q, however, places this passage earlier in the scene, and in this may represent a memorial error. We follow the placement suggested by the F dialogue, between Cade's 'Marry presently' and the Rebels' wonder-struck reply, 'O braue'.

4.7.147.1-2/2606.1-2 *Enter . . . poles*] Q; *Enter one with the heads* F. See the note to 4.7.116.1-2/2574.1-2. Q makes better sense: the author of F clearly has forgotten that the heads were to be brought upon two poles (4.7.109-10/2567-8).

4.7.154-5/2613-14 Away . . . Vp] This edition (G.T.); Away. *Exit* | *Alarum, and Retreat. Enter againe Cade,* | *and all his rabblement.* | *Cade. Vp* F. In Q there is no exit and no re-entrance; after Cade's speech (ending 'let them kiffe togither'), Buckingham and Clifford enter, interrupting the intended exit. Such interrupted exits are a common feature of dramatic texts (particularly Shakespeare's), and the Folio staging violates the 'law of re-entry': Cade and his followers exit and immediately re-enter. Moreover, the '*Alarum, and Retreat*' which apparently makes this re-entry acceptable, is itself highly suspect. At this point Cade has defeated the last of the enemies sent against him (Gough), and is apparently, throughout the preceding scene, in complete control of London. We hear nothing of an enemy coming to meet him, and his speech upon his exit gives no sense of an exit to battle. Moreover, *retreat* is nowhere else used in the directions associated with Cade's battles. One must strongly suspect that the Folio's stage directions and speech-prefix—which waste at least four and possibly five type lines—are an expedient by Compositor B for dealing with inadequately cast-off copy, an expedient suggested to him, perhaps, by Cade's line 'Dare any be fo bold to found Retreat' (4.7.157/2616-17). B has, already, in the preceding lines, set prose as verse (4.7.148-54/2607-13) and possibly added words to the dialogue (4.7.141/2600) to waste space; he sets blank lines around stage directions here (around *Alarum . . . rabblement*) and at 4.7.147.1-2/2606.1-2 and 4.7.156.1/2615.1. The word '*rabblement*', which sounds unusual and hence authorial to modern readers, was common at the time (*OED*), and simply offers a longer form of the word. The direction is thus deeply suspect. Moreover, even if the Folio text is authoritative, it offers an awkward and pointless sequence of staging, improved in the theatrical text of Q. On either of these grounds the staging of Q is to be preferred. We have thus omitted F's direction; as a consequence, we do not mark a new scene here (traditionally, 4.8).

4.7.154/2613 Away.] F. This unnecessary word could easily be a part of Compositor B's interpolation, related to the following *Exit*.

4.7.155/2614 Saint Magnes corner] F. Mentioned in Holinshed at this point (p. 222), and hence authoritative—as is presumably the whole sentence ('Vp . . . Thames').

4.7.157/2616 What noise is this?] This edition (G.T.); What noife is this I heare? F. This is a suspiciously long-winded way of putting the question. *What noise is this?* occurs earlier in this play (at 3.2.237/1800) and at *1 Henry VI* 1.4.15/342, *Richard III* 2.2.33/1216, *Romeo* 1.1.72/86, *Othello* 5.2.95/2992, and *Macbeth* 4.1.122/1413; but there is nothing comparable to F here, which is set as a single verse line. B is probably still stretching copy, and has interpolated these two words to make the question not appear to be a short verse line.

4.7.157-8/2616-17 Dare . . . kill] F. This is suspiciously metrical (F sets it as a single verse line). On the evidence of 4.7.159/2618, Cade must ask a question which contains the word 'dare', and probably the word 'disturb', but Compositor B may have expanded the text to make it metrical. Buckingham's reply would better fit a question like 'Dare any be so bold to disturb me?' (G.T. *conj*.).

4.7.166/2625 rebbel] SINGER (*subs*.); rabble F. Q, whose parallel speech is variant, includes 'Traitor Cade' and 'Rebell'.

4.7.171.1/2630.1 They . . . Cade] This edition; *not in* F; They forfake Cade Q. Line 4.7.168/2627 suggests the bracketed part of the direction.

4.7.188.1/2646.1 *They runne to Cade againe*] Q; *not in* F

4.7.219.1-2/2677.1-2 He . . . away] Q; *Exit* F

4.8.27/2709 stout Irish] COLLIER (Mitford); ftout F

4.8.34/2716 calmd] F4 (*subs*.); calme F1

4.8.37/2719 go] F; to go MALONE; go thou DYCE 2

4.8.42/2724 My Lord, Ile yeelde my felfe to] F; I'ld yield, my lord, to CAIRNCROSS. Cairncross conjectures that 'my lord' was written above 'myself' as a correction in the manuscript, and so printed as a separate line in F. This is possible. More likely, however, is that the error here is related to cast-off copy: this is still Compositor B's stint, and the two F lines (see the lineation notes) come near the bottom of the second column of o1ᵛ. B is probably once again stretching copy, either, as our text assumes, by breaking an acceptable hexameter in two, or perhaps by interpolating the line's introductory 'My Lord,'.

4.9.6/2738 or] HANMER (subs.); on F
4.9.6 o'er] (or). See the preceding note and the note to *Kinsmen* 1.4.45
4.9.15.1/2746.1 *Cade . . . them*] Q
4.9.15.2/2746.2 *and 5. of his men*] Q (and his men); *not in* F. Q, which derives from a performance, here seems to confirm a matter of staging only implicit in the dialogue of F ('and thy fiue men', 4.9.38-9/2770-1). Wilson, however, argued that the F phrase was instead 'Intended, perhaps not to refer to persons present, since Iden certainly enters soliloquizing at [4.9.16/2747], but as an insulting suggestion that this petty squire had but five men on his estate' (his note to 4.10.38-9, p. 193). See our note to 4.9.41-53/2773-85.
4.9.20/2751 waining] ROWE; warning F
4.9.23.1/2754.1 *Cade rises to his knees*] This edition; *not in* F. Suggested by line 4.9.58-9/2791.
4.9.24/2755 Sounes,] Q; *not in* F. See the note to 4.6.8/2448.
4.9.27/2758 Crownes] F, Q. A curious departure from the chronicles, all of which read, with F, Q at 5.1.79/2895, 'marks'.
4.9.41-53/2773-85 *Nay . . . forbeares*] F. Q seems to report imperfectly an abbreviated version of this speech (lines 4.9.41-6/2773-8; no trace of 4.9.47-53/2779-85 appear in Q). This is consistent with our textual hypothesis of Q's origin (see the Introduction). However, the Q version of the speech also implies a variant staging to that of F, one not in any discernible way necessitated by the abridgement, but nevertheless bound up with it to the extent that it is inconsistent with the text of the full F speech.

In Q, Iden's speech ends with an address to his servants, whose presence on stage F only implies (4.9.38-9/2770-1), but which Q makes explicit, first, at Iden's entrance (see the note to 4.9.15.2/2746.2), and next, here: 'Sirrha fetch me weopons, and ftand you all afide'. F, however, has Iden conclude with the line 'Let this my fword report what fpeech forbeares' (4.9.53/2785). In other words, Q had Iden enter unarmed, and then send one of his men for 'weopons', while F has him enter armed. Moreover, there is a critical point to the Q variant—Cade challenges six men while Iden chivalrously has his men 'stand all aside' so that he and Cade can fight alone: the attendants thus magnify both Cade and Iden. But to accept the staging implicit in Q requires that we alter or omit at the very least Folio lines 4.9.52-3/2784-5, so that the attendant can be dispatched to fetch the weapons. If Q were closer verbally to F here, this is the course we would unhesitatingly adopt. As it is, however, we are inclined to be more cautious, and to adopt from Q only 'Stand you all aside'—which makes the critical point, but does not conflict with the text of F.

4.9.41/2773 shall nere] F, Q3 (fhall neuer); neuer fhall Q1-2
4.9.41/2273 stands] F, Q3; doth ftand Q1-2
4.9.42/2774 an Esquire] F, Q; esquire CAIRNCROSS
4.9.52/2784 As for] F; As for mere MASON (*conj.*). 'The line is manifestly corrupt, but no satisfactory emendation seems to have been proposed. The general sense seems to be "As for words—my sword (not my tongue) shall show whose greatness answers his words": "answer's" presumably stands for "answers his", though all modern editors seem to print "answers"' (McKerrow). There is, however, reason to believe the lines were cut from the acting text. See the note to 4.9.41-53/2773-85.
4.9.54/2786 Stand you all aside] Q; *not in* F. See the note to 4.9.41-53/2773-85
4.9.58/2790 God] Q; Ioue F. See Taylor, 'Zounds'.
4.9.59.1/2791.1 *Cade stands*] This edition; *not in* F. That he does not stand earlier is suggested by 4.9.58-9/2790-1.
4.9.59.1/2791.1 *Cade fals downe*] Q; *not in* F
4.9.77 bore] F (bare). Shakespeare used both forms, but preferred 'bore', which increasingly predominated during his lifetime.
5.1.5/2821 who would] F, Q; who'd CAIRNCROSS
5.1.10/2826 sword] CAIRNCROSS (Johnson); soule

5.1.31/2847 *Henry be more weake, and I more strong*] F; thou meete thy fonnes, | Who now in Armes expect their fathers fight, | And not farre hence I know they cannot be Q. Though probably verbally corrupt, Q may nevertheless here report something introduced to the prompt-book: it makes clear to the audience, in a way which F does not, that York's expected strength is that of his sons, and that they are near at hand.
5.1.47.1/2863.1 *Exit souldiers*] Q; *not in* F
5.1.55.1/2871.1 *Enter*] F; But fee, his grace is comming to meete with vs | Enter Q
5.1.66/2882 *Kneeling*] Suggested by Q's dialogue: 'Lo here my Lord vpon my bended knees, | I here prefent'; *not in* F
5.1.69-70/2885-6 *Oh . . . trouble*] F. After a variant version of these lines Q adds: 'A vifage fterne, cole blacke his curled locks, | Deepe trenched furrowes in his frowning brow, | Prefageth warlike humors in his life'.
5.1.72/2888 I wus] This edition (*conj.* Wilson); I was F. Wilson's conjecture (= assuredly, indeed, truly) makes better sense than F, and is supported by Shakespeare's use of the word in three other plays from the 1590s (*Shrew, Richard III,* and *Merchant*). OED confirms that for the word to consist of two particles was not uncommon in the sixteenth century, and cites, among others, the forms 'I wus', 'I wis', and 'I wys'. Of these, the u/a misreading of the first is easiest to imagine, so this is the form we adopt.
5.1.72 Iwis] This edition (I wus). See previous note.
5.1.82/2898 *Exit*] Q; *not in* F
5.1.83/2899 wi'th'] This edition (G.T.); with th' F. 'The' cannot be elided forward, to join with 'Queen'; if elided backward, it becomes indistinguishable from the 'th' at the end of 'with'. As metre requires a single syllable between 'comes' and 'Queene', it seems probable that the contraction wi'th'—used five times elsewhere—was intended.
5.1.109/2925 Sirrah] This edition (S.W.W.); Wold'ft haue me kneele? Firft let me ask of thee, | If they can brooke I bow a knee to man: | Sirrah F. Theobald emends 'thee' to 'these', which almost certainly accurately represents either what was in, or what was intended to be in, the manuscript behind F. But even after this emendation the two lines which we cut do not make sense, since there is no one on stage to whom 'these' and 'they' (in the second line) can refer. Probably these two lines represent a first thought, abandoned when the author realized that York's sons are not yet on stage. This sort of false start is not uncommon in foul paper texts: the lines leave no trace in Q, and probably had been cut from the prompt-book.
5.1.109/2925 sonnes] Q; fonne F
5.1.111/2927 for] F2; of F1
5.1.112/2928 to Buckingham] This edition; *not in* F. See the next note.
5.1.114.1/2930.1 *Exit [Buckingham]*] CAPELL; *not in* F. Buckingham, present in the earlier part of the scene, must exit at some point in order for the King's call at 5.1.190/3006 to make sense. It may not, however, be here that he leaves. The scene is staged differently in Q.
5.1.119.1-2/2935.1-3 *Enter . . . soldiers*] Q; *Enter Edward and Richard* F
5.1.120.1-2/2936.1-2 *At . . . souldiers*] Q; *Enter Clifford* F. Young Clifford needs to arrive on stage by 5.1.209/3025: F provides no entry direction for him.
5.1.122/2938 *kneeling to the King*] Q (and *Clifford* kneeles to *Henry,* and fpeakes); *not in* F
5.1.122.1/2938.1 *He rises*] This edition; *not in* F, Q. Suggested by York's demand that he 'kneele againe' (5.1.125/2941).
5.1.142/2958 *Call . . . braue Beares*] F, Q (~ . . . rough beares). After this line, Q inserts King Henry's call for Buckingham (5.1.190/3006), which in some ways is superior to the F arrangement, and may well reflect a later authorial stage. But that call, in F, is so fully integrated with the surrounding dialogue as to make difficult the reconstruction here, with any confidence, of the Q arrangement.
5.1.145.2-3/2961.2-3 *with Drumme and souldiers*] Q; *not in* F
5.1.147 bearherd] F (Berard). OED assigns Shakespeare's three uses

of 'berard', etc., to *bearherd* rather than to *bearward*, chiefly because he elsewhere uses *bearherd*, but not *bearward*.

5.1.151/2967 suffer'd₍] F; ~, CAIRNCROSS (Vaughan)

5.1.155/2971 CLIFFORD] F (*Clif.*); y⟨oung⟩. C⟨lifford⟩. CAPELL. 'Capell gives these lines to Young Clifford on the ground that his chief characteristic is filial affection and that he would hardly have remained silent until line [5.1.209/3025]. He points out the similarity of these lines to [5.1.213/3029]. But the fact that F1 does not begin to distinguish the two Cliffords as speakers until later [(5.1.193/3009)] is somewhat against the proposed change' (McKerrow). The oversight probably is the author's, and a director may wish to assign some lines—say, 5.1.155-6/2971-2 (son replying to son)—to Young Clifford.

5.1.192/3008 or] ROWE 3; and F

5.1.194/3010 You were] F; you had Q; Thou were CAIRNCROSS. See the next note.

5.1.195/3011 you] Q; thee F. The disagreement in F between 5.1.194/3010 and 5.1.195/3011, in mid-sentence, is highly suspect. Either line could be right, and Q twice endorses 'you'.

5.1.199/3015 houshold] Q; houſed F1; houſes F2

5.1.205/3021 to] Q; io F1 (*or possibly* ſo); ſo F2

5.2.0.1-6.1/3030.2-6.1 *Alarmes ... body*] This edition (after F). F places this encounter later, following 5.3.65/3101; Q, whose version of this speech is different (see the notes to 5.2.1/3031 and 5.2.5-6/3055-6), places it here. Q's transposition of this scene may be related to its variant, more emblematic version of the encounter between York and Clifford (see the note to 5.3.20-30/3056-66.1): by placing, as Q does, Somerset's death before, rather than after, that encounter, King Henry's cause seems to hang decisively on Clifford's success or failure. We retain F for substance and incidentals, but adopt Q's placement.

5.2.0.1-3/3030.2-4 *Alarmes ... Albones*] Q; *Enter Richard, and Somerſet to fight* F. While 'the ſigne of the Caſtle' may have been a stage property employed in this scene, the Q direction may equally be the reporter 'literalizing' for his reader: the dialogue in both texts would make it clear to an audience that Somerset lay dead under the ale-house sign, whether that sign were actually present on stage or not. See the next note.

5.2.1/3031 there] F; there, and breathe thy laſt. | Whats here, the ſigne of the Caſtle? | Then the propheſie is come to paſſe, | For Somerſet was forewarned of Caſtles, | The which he alwaies did obſerue Q. While Q may represent a revised version of this speech—it usefully reminds us of the detail of the prophecy—there is nothing in it that the reporter could not have interpolated. See the previous note.

5.2.5-6/3035-6 Sword ... kill] F; *not in* Q

5.2.6.1/3036.1 Exit] Q; *not in* F

5.3.0.1/3036.3-4 *Alarme again ... alone*] Q; *Enter Warwicke* F

5.3.8/3044 CLIFFORD ... come.] Q (*subs.*); *not in* F. After Warwick's speech ('... armes'), but before York's entry, Q has the following: 'Clifford ſpeakes within. | Warwicke ſtand ſtill, and view the way that Clifford hewes with | his murthering Curtelaxe, through the fainting troopes to finde | thee out. | Warwicke ſtand ſtill, and ſtir not till I come.' Moreover, following the direction, '*Enter Yorke*' (5.3.8.1/3044.1), F prefixes the continuation of Warwick's speech with '*War.*' (5.3.9/3045), duplicating the earlier speech-prefix (5.3.1/3037).

(1) Cairncross took this repetition of the speech-prefix as evidence of Q copy here. He argues that this speech of Clifford's is a Q interpolation, which the Folio editor deleted in the copy of Q from which F would be set, because he noticed that there was nothing corresponding to it in the manuscript. This editor failed, however, also to delete Q's speech-prefix, '*War.*', following the interpolated speech, and this found its way into F, where it appears as an unnecessary duplication. Cairncross's hypothesis, consequently, ascribes no authority to the Q speech.

While the speech repetition may be significant, it is not necessarily so; this sort of thing happens elsewhere in F, and is especially understandable here, where the continuation is of a speech which began in the previous column. However, even if we do choose to view the speech repetition as significant, there is nothing to link it or the surrounding text with Q copy—indeed, Q and F are not even particularly close to one another here.

(2) Possibly something like the Q speech was in the manuscript behind F, but was omitted either deliberately (perhaps because of cast-off copy problems—column b of 03ʳ is very tightly set) or inadvertently (maybe as the result of eyeskip, related to 'Warwicke' which begins QF 5.3.7/3043 and the first and last lines of the Q speech): either of these hypotheses would account for the duplicated F speech-prefix. (3) Or possibly, as elsewhere, the Q speech reflects matter introduced in the preparation of the prompt-book, but absent from the foul papers behind F: this would require us to view the repeated speech-prefix as a coincidence, unrelated to Clifford's Q speech. (4) Or, of course, Q may be an interpolation and also unrelated to the repeated speech-prefix.

Of these four hypotheses, only the first—Cairncross's—and the last ascribe no authority to the Q speech. Since there is no clear evidence of Q copy here, we view Cairncross's position sceptically; though Q may be an interpolation, it seems more probable that it derived from *something* in the prompt-book, though in this we may be mistaken.

The remaining two hypotheses accept that Q reflects, albeit imperfectly, an authorial speech. Since only the last of the Q speech constitutes a complete verse line, we assume it to be more accurately reported than the rest, and adopt it, recognizing that probably something like the rest of the speech also stood in the prompt-book, but that its original form is irrecoverable.

5.3.20-30/3056-66.1 YORKE ... *Yorke*] Q; *not in* F. The F version of this encounter is very different (see Additional Passage C). Cairncross believed it to be a revised version, written in response to late censorship (pp. xxv-xxix): he may be right. We incline to the view that F's emphasis here on the personal encounter between York and Clifford represents the earlier version, and Q's transformation of the encounter into a political emblem of the struggle between York and Lancaster the later revision, made for incorporation in the prompt-book (see the note to 5.2.0.1-6.1/3030.2-6.1). The Q version does not seem plausibly explicable as memorial error. But whether F represents a late revision required by the censor or an earlier version which was discarded in the preparation of the prompt-book, the restoration of Q seems a reasonable editorial course to follow. See the Introduction to this play, and that to *1 Henry IV* (for a discussion of a similar problem with regard to Falstaff/Oldcastle).

5.3.20/3056 Clifford] This edition; Now Clifford Q; *not in* F. The interpolation of 'Now' is an easy and not uncommon memorial error.

5.3.22/3058 know] This edition; now Q; *not in* F. The line as it stands in Q is weak: the substitution of 'now' for 'know' would be an easy error, resulting from either a memorial slip on the part of the reporter, or from a scribe or the compositor dropping the initial 'k'.

5.3.25/3061 not] This edition (G.T.); neuer Q; *not in* F. The repetition of 'neuer' in the next line is suspicious, and suggests memorial error either there or here.

5.3.30.1/3066.2 *Alarmes ... alone*] Q; *Enter yong Clifford* F

5.3.31/3067 YONG CLIFFORD] ROWE (Q); Clif⟨ford⟩. F

5.3.61.1/3097.1 *He ... backe*] Q (*subs.*); *not in* F

5.3.62-5/3098-101 As ... mine] F; And thus as old Ankyſes ſonne did beare | His aged father on his manly backe, | And fought with him againſt the bloodie Greeks, | Euen ſo will I. But ſtaie, heres one of them, | To whom my ſoule hath ſworne immortall hate. | Enter *Richard*, and then *Clifford* laies downe his father, | fights with him, and *Richard* flies away againe. | Out crooktbacke villaine, get thee from my ſight | But I will after thee, and once againe | When I haue borne my father to his Tent, | Ile trie my fortune better with thee yet Q; This edition *conj.* F's 'As ... Nothing ſo heauy as' *followed by a dash and then* Q's 'but ſtaie ... yet'. Q provides a confrontation between Young Clifford and Richard here which may reflect, in perhaps a garbled form, an authorial revision.

5.3.65/3101 Nothing ... mine] F. Following this line F inserts what we treat as 5.2/Sc. 20. See the note to 5.2.0.1–6.1/3030.2–6.1.

5.3.65.1/3101.1   *Exit with the body*] Q (*Exet yoong Clifford with his father*); *not in* F

5.4.0.1–2/3101.2–4   *Alarmes . . . Tent*] Q; *Fight. Excursions* F

5.4.0.3/3101.4   *Alarmes still*] Q; *not in* F

5.4.12.1/3113.1   *yong Clifford*] CAPELL (subs.); *Clifford* F

5.4.13/3114   YONG CLIFFORD] CAPELL (subs.); *Clif⟨ford⟩*. F

5.5.0.2/3120.1   *Edward*] Q3; *not in* F, Q1–2. Q, however, does supply Edward with two lines of dialogue (see the note to 5.5.17.1–19/3137.1–39). It is curious, therefore, that Q1–2 should omit Edward from the entry direction.

5.5.0.2/3120.2   *Richard*] Q; *Richard, Warwicke* F. We follow Q, which derives from a performance, and direct Warwick to enter with his father at 5.5.17.1/3137.1.

5.5.1–4/3121–4   *How . . . rights:*] Q; *not in* F. These lines, which usefully emphasize the significance of the battle just concluded, are probably not a memorial interpolation, but rather an authorial addition made to the prompt-book. Their precise form, however, may have become memorially corrupt.

5.5.5/3125   *Of*] F; *old* Q. The repetition of the preposition *of* in this line, 'Of Salisbury, who can report of him', is a perfectly acceptable Shakespearian construction. Compare, for example, 'In what enormity is Martius poore *in*' (*Coriolanus* 2.1.16/770; our italics), and '*on* vs both did haggish Age steale *on*' (*All's Well* 1.2.29/257; our italics).

5.5.17.1–19/3137.1–39   *Enter . . . Yorke*] Q (subs.); *But Noble as he is, looke where he comes. | Enter Salisbury* F. These lines of Edward's, as indeed Edward's presence in this scene at all, may be the reporter's interpolation. But it seems right, theatrically, that Edward should be on stage with his victorious father in this last scene. Moreover, the lines are related to another Q variant—Salisbury and Warwick's joint entrance (F directs Warwick to enter with York in the scene's opening direction)—and together they emphasize both visually and verbally the importance of these two earls to the York cause. Since the two variants are dependent on one another, and since one of them is purely a matter of staging—an area in which Q, as a reported text, has considerable authority—we accept that Q here reflects performance, and thus probably the prompt-book. However, 'noble father', echoing as it does the beginning of the previous F speech (5.5.11/3131), makes us suspect the verbal accuracy of Q's version of Edward's two lines.

5.5.37/3157   *Drummes*] Q; *Drumme* F

Additional Passages

C.2   gainst] This edition; againſt Q
D.10   oeuures] F2 (subs.); eumenes F1
D.10.1   *Alarmes . . . Clifford*] Q; *not in* F
D.12.1   *Exit Yorke*] Q; *not in* F

REJECTED QUARTO VARIANTS

1.1.3/3   to] for
1.1.8/8   twenty] then the
1.1.9/9   haue perform'd] did performe
1.1.10/10   humbly now vpon] now, moſt humbly on
1.1.10/10   knee] knees
1.1.11/11   Lordly] royall
1.1.44/44   *espouse*] wed and eſpouſe
1.1.49/48–9   *Dutchy . . . the County of*] Dutches . . . of
1.1.73/73   vnload] vnfold
1.1.138/138   ye] you
1.1.159/159   Iesu] Ieſus
1.1.179/179   While] Whilſt
1.1.183/183   the] this
1.1.238/238   Englands soile] England
1.2.59/318   vs] vs I am ſure
1.2.78/337   promised] promiſed me
1.3.23/389   Melforde] long Melford
1.3.29/395   to] vnto
1.4.17/609   silent] ſilence
2.1.26/688   doe it] doate Q1; dote Q2; do't Q3
2.1.31/693   thine] thy
2.1.116/778   of] on
2.1.172/834   against] gainſt
2.4.48/1118   Rascall] raſcald
2.4.56/1126   they'le tangle] they will intangle
2.4.80/1150   protect] conduct
3.1.40/1221   allegation] Alligations
3.1.53/1234   deepe] deepeſt
3.1.99/1280   this] then
3.1.116/1297   taxe] racke
3.1.124/1305   whiles] whilſt
3.1.129/1310   felonious] felonous
3.1.328/1509   I] I wil Q1–2; I'le Q3
3.1.375/1556   House and Clayme] claime and houſe
3.2.29/1593   Lord: *Gloster* is] F, Q2 (subs.); Lord, Gloſter is Q1; Lord of Gloſters Q3
3.2.49/1613   thy] thine
3.2.85/1649   fore-warning] foretelling
3.2.196/1760   Tallons] talants
3.2.207/1771   say] ſay it
3.2.212/1776   into] vnto
3.2.220/1784   Knee] knees
3.2.223/1787   wast] F, Q2; was Q1, Q3
3.2.227/1791   while] whilſt
3.2.228/1792   dar'st] dare
3.2.245/1807   send] ſends
3.2.246/1808   Lord] falſe
3.2.275/1837   Could] Would
3.2.281–2/1843–4   or wee will all breake in] my Lord of *Salsbury*
3.2.351/1913   whiles] whilſt
3.2.362/1924   and] but
3.2.382/1944   cries] cald
4.1.30/2041   George] ring
4.1.65/2076   it] I
4.1.70/2081   thy] thine
4.2.75/2235   on] of
4.2.117/2278   No] No, no hees but a knight
4.2.134/2296   Earle] the Earle
4.3.6/2357   is] was
4.7.23/2479   Surge] George
4.7.26/2482   *Basimecu*] bus mine cue
4.7.107/2565   strike] chop
4.7.109/2567   strike] cut
4.7.109/2567   head] head too
4.7.214/2672   sword] ſtaffe
4.9.38/2770   these] this
4.9.57/2789   the] this
4.9.57/2789   in] into
4.9.59/2791   be] fal into ſome ſmiths hand, and be
5.1.46/2862   Field] fields
5.1.82/2898   vnto] F, Q2; to Q1, Q3
5.1.87/2903   is] proud
5.1.191/3007   hast,] haſt, | Both thou and they, ſhall curſe this fatall houre
5.1.209/3025   Father] Soueraigne
5.1.210/3026   the] theſe
5.3.3/3039   Trumpet sounds alarum] Trompets ſound Alarmes

THE FIRST PART OF THE CONTENTION

INCIDENTALS

55 Item] *italic* Q   55-6 It . . . the] *roman* Q   56 of Aniou and] *roman* Q   56-7 of Mayne . . . deliuered] *roman* Q   57-9 to the . . . dowry] *roman* Q   62 And] F; & Q   66 and] *italic* Q   77 field,] ~:   102 peroration] preroration   102 circumstance?] ~:   183 Cardinall,] ~.   267 Inchac'd] Inehac'd   280 world] worid   282 Lord?] ~,   283 dreame.] ~?   337 promised,] ~₍ₐ₎   482 reason *Buckingham*] reaſon *Buekingham*   534 vnmeet.] ~, (?)   546 accus'd] accused   687 mallice₍ₐ₎] ~:   688 Holyneſſe:] ~₍ₐ₎   700 thee] rhee   709 Groue.] ~:   766 deſir'd] defired   779 I] F; *italic* Q. The substitution of italic for roman capital 'I' is a feature of Q, and is not substantive.   792 lying'ſt] F; lyingeſt Q   794 might'ſt] F; mighteſt Q   803 call'd] F; called Q   818 bear'ſt] beareſt   839 Councell.] ~,   873 dis-honor'd] dis-honored   906 murthred] muthered   1069 murther'd] F; murthered Q   1140 worne.] (*possibly* ~:)   1292 England,] ~.   1399 teares;] ~,   1399 eyes,] ~;   1441 Reasons,] ~₍ₐ₎   1506 spent.] ~,   1514 be;] ~,   1514 art,] ~;   1563 Humfrey,] ~;   1710 Obsequies:] ~,   1711 Image,] ~:   1916 Aduenture] Aduenrure   1970 It] Ir   2021 their] theit   2022 discolour'd] difcoloured   2027 head.] ~,   2061 be.] ~,   2062 blood,] ~.   2123 me.] ~:   2144 more.] ~:   2145 can,] ~.   2150 *Cæsar*,] ~.   2251 in't.] ~₍ₐ₎   2314 this.] ~₍ₐ₎   2323 and] And (*first word of line*)   2386 haue] huae   2394 Southwarke] Southwatke   2412 danger.] (*possibly* ~:)   2424 Rebels.] ~₍ₐ₎   2458 BUTCHER] *Rut.*   2479 ah] Ah (*first word of line*)   2518 Country] Covntry   2526 maintaine₍ₐ₎] ~,   2528 King,] ~.   2540 good.] ~₍ₐ₎   2593 Sargiant,] ~₍ₐ₎ Q   2593 youle₍ₐ₎] ~, Q   2640 Freedome] Fteedome   2889 thou] rhou   2904 imprison'd] impriſoned   2950 arrested] atreſted   2974 selues.] ~:   2989 conſider'd] confidered   3009 true.] ~₍ₐ₎   3049 lou'd] loued   3055 thee] theee   3081 ordained] ordain'd   3137 body.] ~,

Additional Passages

B.1 poule,] ~. Q   B.2 sits,] ~. Q   B.4 Stykes.] ~, Q   B.5 flames.] ~, Q

STAGE DIRECTIONS

Most of the stage directions listed here are those of the Folio, our principal control text for this play. We have, however, occasionally adopted the first quarto as our control text: for these passages we list the Q1 stage directions instead of any directions corresponding F passages may contain, and note that we have done so.

1.1.0.1/0.1   *Flourish of Trumpets: Then Hoboyes.*
1.1.0.1–7/0.1–7   *Enter King, Duke Humfrey, Salisbury, Warwicke, and Beau-|ford on the one side. | The Queene, Suffolke, Yorke, Somerset, and Buckingham, | on the other.*
1.1.36.1/36.1   *Florish*
1.1.71.1–2/71.1   *Exit King, Queene, and Suffolke.*
1.1.71.2/71.2   *Manet the rest.*
1.1.144.1/144.1   *Exit Humfrey.*
1.1.169/169   *Exit Cardinall.*
1.1.177.1/177.1   *Exit Buckingham, and Somerset.*
1.1.213.1–2/213.1   *Exit Warwicke, and Salisbury. Manet Yorke.*
1.1.259.1/259.1   *Exit Yorke.*
1.2.0.1–2/259.2   *Enter Duke Humfrey and his wife Elianor.*
1.2.55.1/314.1   *Enter Messenger.*
1.2.60.1/319.1   *Ex. Hum* (after 1.2.59/318)
1.2.69.1/328.1   *Enter Hume.*
1.2.86/345.1   *Exit Elianor.*
1.2.107/366   *Exit*
1.3.0.1–2/366.1–2   *Enter three or foure Petitioners, the Armorers | Man being one.*
1.3.5.1/371.1   *Enter Suffolke, and Queene.*
1.3.36.1/402.1   *Enter Seruant.*
1.3.39/405   *Exit.*
1.3.42.1/408.1   *Teare the Supplication.*
1.3.44.1/410   *Exit.*
[1.3.103/469]   *Exit.* (after 'Helme')
1.3.103.1/469.1   *Sound a Sennet.*
1.3.103.1–7/469.1–6   *Enter the King, Duke Humfrey, Cardinall, Bucking-|ham, Yorke, Salisbury, Warwicke, | and the Duchesse.*
1.3.140.1/506.1   *Exit Humfrey.*
1.3.141.1/507.1   *She giues the Duchesse a box on the eare.*
1.3.150.1/516.1   *Exit Elianor.*
1.3.154.1/520.1   *Exit Buckingham.*
1.3.154.1/520.2   *Enter Humfrey.*
1.3.179.1–2/545.1   *Enter Armorer and his Man.*
1.3.226.1/592.1   *Flourish. Exeunt.*
1.4.0.1–3/592.2–3   *Enter the Witch, the two Priests, and Bullingbrooke.*

1.4.10/602   *Exit Hume.*
1.4.12.2/604.2   *Enter Elianor aloft.* (after 1.4.13/605)
1.4.23.1–4/615.1–4   *Here doe the Ceremonies belonging, and make the Circle, | Bullingbrooke or Southwell reades,* Coniuro | te, &c. *It Thunders and Lightens | terribly: then the Spirit | riseth.*
1.4.40.1–2/632.1–2   *Thunder and Lightning. Exit Spirit.*
1.4.40.3–5/632.3–5   *Enter the Duke of Yorke and the Duke of Buckingham | with their Guard, and breake in.*
1.4.54.1–4/646.1–4   *Exit.*
1.4.58/650   *Reades.*
1.4.68.1/660.1   *Enter a Seruingman.*
1.4.70.1/662.1   *Exeunt.*
2.1.0.1–4/662.2–4   *Enter the King, Queene, Protector, Cardinall, and | Suffolke, with Faulkners hallowing.*
2.1.61.2/723.1   *Enter one crying a Miracle.*
2.1.70.1–3/732.1–3   (Q) *Enter the Maior of Saint Albones and his brethren with | Musicke, bearing the man that had bene blinde, | betweene two in a chaire.*
2.1.144/806   (Q) *Exet one.*
2.1.149.1/811.1   (Q) *Enter Beadle.* (as in F; after 'away', line 2.1.147/809, in Q). See the textual note.
2.1.155.1–3/817.1–4   (Q) *After the Beadle hath hit him one girke, he leapes ouer | the stoole and runnes away, and they run after him, | crying, A miracle, a miracle.*
2.1.161.1/823.1   *Exit.*
2.1.165.1/827.1   *Enter Buckingham.*
2.1.217/879   *Flourish. Exeunt.*
2.2.0.1–2/879.1   *Enter Yorke, Salisbury, and Warwick.*
2.2.82/961   *Exeunt.*
2.3.0.1–2/961.1–2   *Sound Trumpets. Enter the King and State, | with Guard, to banish the Duchesse.*
2.3.38/999   *Exit Gloster.*
2.3.58.1–7/1019.1–6   (Q) *Enter at one doore the Armourer and his neighbours, drinking | to him so much that he is drunken, and he enters with a drum | before him, and his staffe with a sand-bag fastened to it, and | at the other doore, his man with a drum and sand-bagge, and | Prentises drinking to him.*
2.3.97.1–3/1058.1–3   *They fight, and Peter strikes him downe.*
2.3.109.1/1070.1   (Q) *Exet omnis.*
2.4.0.1–2/1070.3–4   (Q) *Enter Duke Humphrey and his men, in | mourning cloakes.*
2.4.17.1–5/1087.1–5   *Enter the Duchesse in a white Sheet, and a Taper | burning in her hand, with the Sherife | and Officers.*
2.4.70.1/1140.1   *Enter a Herald.*

THE FIRST PART OF THE CONTENTION

2.4.87.1/1157.1   *Exit Gloster.*
2.4.111/1181   *Exeunt*
3.1.0.1-6/1181.1-6   *Sound a Senet. Enter King, Queene, Cardinall, Suffolke, | Yorke, Buckingham, Salisbury, and Warwicke, | to the Parliament.*
3.1.81.1/1262.1   *Enter Somerset.*
3.1.92.1/1273.1   *Enter Gloucester.*
3.1.194.1/1375.1   *Exit Gloster.*
3.1.222.1/1403.1   *Exit.*
3.1.281.1/1462.1   *Enter a Poste.*
3.1.330.1/1511.1   *Exeunt.*
3.1.330.1/1511.1   *Manet Yorke.*
3.1.383/1564   *Exit.*
3.2.0.1-3/1564.1-3   *Enter two or three running ouer the Stage, from the | Murther of Duke Humfrey.*
3.2.4.1/1568.1   *Enter Suffolke.*
3.2.14.1/1578.1   *Exeunt.*
3.2.14.3-5/1578.2-3   *Sound Trumpets. Enter the King, the Queene, | Cardinall, Suffolke, Somerset, with | Attendants.*
3.2.18/1582   *Exit.*
3.2.26.1/1590.1   *Enter Suffolke.*
3.2.32.1/1596.1   *King sounds.*
3.2.121.1-2/1685.1-2   *Noyse within. Enter Warwicke, and many | Commons.*
3.2.146.2/1710.2   *Bed put forth.*
3.2.231.1/1795.1   *Exeunt.*
3.2.236/1799.1-2   *A noyse within.*
3.2.237.1-2/1800.1-2   *Enter Suffolke and Warwicke, with their | Weapons drawne.*
3.2.243.1/1805.2-3   *Enter Salisbury.*
3.2.303.1-2/1865.1   *Exit.*
3.2.370.1/1932.1   *Enter Vaux.*
3.2.383/1945   *Exit*
3.2.416.1/1978.1   *Exeunt*
3.3.0.1-3/1978.2-4   *Enter the King, Salisbury, and Warwicke, to the | Cardinal in bed.*
3.3.33.1/2011.1   *Exeunt.*
4.1.0.1-2/2011.3-4   *Alarum. Fight at Sea. Ordnance goes off.*
4.1.0.3-6/2011.4-8   *Enter Lieutenant, Suffolke, and others.*
4.1.140.1/2151.1   *Exit Water with Suffolke.*
4.1.143.1/2154.1   *Exit Lieutenant, and the rest.*
4.1.143.1/2154.1-2   *Manet the first Gent.*
4.1.143.2/2154.3   *Enter Walter with the body.*
4.1.145/2156   *Exit Walter.*
4.2.0.1/2160.2   *Enter Beuis, and Iohn Holland.*
4.2.32.1-3/2190.1-3   *Drumme. Enter Cade, Dicke Butcher, Smith the Weauer, | and a Sawyer, with infinite numbers.*
4.2.85.1/2245.1   *Enter a Clearke.*
4.2.109/2270.1   *Exit one with the Clearke*
4.2.109.1/2270.2   *Enter Michael.*
4.2.120.1-2/2282.1-2   *Enter Sir Humfrey Stafford, and his Brother, | with Drum and Soldiers.*
4.2.180.1/2342.1   *Exit.*
4.3.0.1-3/2351.1-3   *Alarums to the fight, wherein both the Staffords are slaine. | Enter Cade and the rest.*
4.3.17.1/2368.1   *Exeunt.*
4.4.0.1-3/2368.2-4   *Enter the King with a Supplication, and the Queene with Suf-|folkes head, the Duke of Buckingham, and the | Lord Say.*
4.4.24.1/2392.1   *Enter a Messenger.*
4.4.47.1/2415.1   *Enter another Messenger.*
4.4.59.1/2427.1   *Exeunt.*
4.5.0.1-2/2427.2-3   (Q) *Enter the Lord Skayles vpon the Tower | walles walking. | Enter three or foure Citizens below.*

4.5.13.1/2440.1   (Q) *Exet omnes.*
4.6.0.1-2/2440.2-3   (Q) *Enter Iacke Cade and the rest, and strikes his sword | vpon London stone.*
4.6.6.1/2446.1   *Enter a Soldier running.*
4.6.8.1/2448.1   *They kill him.*
4.6.15/2455.1   *Exeunt omnes.*
4.7.0.1-4/2455.2-5   *Alarums. Mathew Goffe is slain, and all the rest. | Then enter Iacke Cade, with his Company.*
4.7.17.1/2473.1   *Enter a Messenger.*
4.7.21.1/2477.1   *Enter George, with the Lord Say.*
4.7.122.1/2581.1   (Q) *Enter Robin.*
4.7.125.1/2584.1   (Q) *Enter Dicke and a Sargiant.*
4.7.140.1/2599   (Q) *Exet with the Sargiant.*
4.7.147.1-2/2606.1-2   *Enter one with the heads.*
4.7.154.1/2613.1   *Exit*
[4.7.154.3/2613.3]   *Alarum, and Retreat. Enter againe Cade, | and all his rabblement.*
4.7.156.1/2615.1   *Sound a parley.*
4.7.158.1/2617.1   *Enter Buckingham, and old Clifford.*
4.7.219.1-2/2677.1-2   *Exit*
4.7.222.1/2680.1   *Exeunt some of them.*
4.7.224/2682   *Exeunt omnes.*
4.8.0.1-2/2682.1-2   *Sound Trumpets. Enter King, Queene, and | Somerset on the Tarras.*
4.8.6.1/2688.1   *Enter Buckingham and Clifford.*
4.8.9.1-2/2691.1-2   *Enter Multitudes with Halters about their | Neckes.*
4.8.23.1/2705.1   *Enter a Messenger.*
4.8.49.1/2731.1   *Flourish. Exeunt.*
4.9.0.1/2731.2   *Enter Cade.*
4.9.15.2/2746.2   *Enter Iden.*
4.9.59.1/2791.1   *Heere they Fight.*
4.9.75.1/2807   *Dyes.*
4.9.84.1/2816.1   *Exit.*
5.1.0.1-2/2816.2-3   *Enter Yorke, and his Army of Irish, with | Drum and Colours.*
5.1.11.1/2827.1   *Enter Buckingham.*
5.1.55.1/2871.1   *Enter King and Attendants.*
5.1.63.1/2879.1   *Enter Iden with Cades head.*
5.1.82.1/2898.1   *Enter Queene and Somerset.*
5.1.119.1-2/2935.1-2   *Enter Edward and Richard.*
5.1.120.1/2936.1   *Enter Clifford.*
5.1.145.2/2961.2   *Enter the Earles of Warwicke, and | Salisbury.*
5.1.214.1/3030.1   *Exeunt*
5.2.0.2-3/3030.2-3   *Enter Richard, and Somerset to fight.* (5.2/Sc. 22 transposed with 5.3/Sc. 23: see the Introduction)
[5.2.6.1/3036.1]   *Fight. Excursions.*
5.3.0.1/3036.3-4   *Enter Warwicke.* (5.3/Sc. 23 transposed with 5.2/Sc. 22: see the Introduction)
5.3.8.1/3044.1   *Enter Yorke.*
5.3.13.1/3049.1   *Enter Clifford.*
5.3.19/3055.1   *Exit War.*
5.3.30.1/3066.2   *Enter yong Clifford.*
5.4.0.3-4/3101.4   *Enter King, Queene, and others.*
5.4.6.1/3107.1   *Alarum a farre off.*
5.4.12.1/3113.1   *Enter Clifford.*
5.4.19/3120   *Exeunt*
5.5.0.1-3/3120.1-2   *Alarum. Retreat. Enter Yorke, Richard, Warwicke, | and Soldiers, with Drum & Colours.*
5.5.17.1/3137.1   *Enter Salisbury.*
5.5.38.1/3158.1   *Exeunt.*

RICHARD DUKE OF YORK
(3 HENRY VI)

Two versions of this play (*BEPD* 138) survive, one shorter by about a thousand lines than, and in other ways variant from, the other. Three editions of the shorter version were published, all before 1623. An octavo (O), bearing the title-page 'The true Tragedie of Richard | Duke of Yorke, and the death of | good King Henrie the Sixt, | with the whole contention betweene | the two Houſes Lancaſter | and Yorke', was printed in 1595 by P[eter] S[hort] for Thomas Millington. The second edition, a quarto (Q2), was printed by W[illiam] W[hite] in 1600 from a copy of the octavo, again for Millington. In 1602 Millington transferred his rights in the play to Thomas Pavier who published an undated, edited third quarto edition (Q3) in 1619 as part of a collection of ten plays, all allegedly by Shakespeare, and all printed by the Jaggards. This, like Q2, was set from a copy of O. The longer version of the play, entitled 'The third Part of Henry the Sixt, | with the death of the Duke of | YORKE' was first published in the First Folio (F).

In the 1920s Peter Alexander and Madeleine Doran demonstrated independently of one another, and to the satisfaction of most scholars, that O, formerly believed to be either the source for the play printed in F or an early version of it, is instead a memorial report, one of the so-called 'bad quartos'. The linch-pin of Alexander's argument, never plausibly refuted, lies in his explanation of a single variant passage, 4.1.46-56/1892-1902, in which Gloucester and Clarence reproach their brother, King Edward, with preferring his wife's relatives before themselves (Alexander, 63-5). Alexander observed that while the Folio accurately follows the apparent source for the passage, Hall (1548: STC 12721), fol. cxcix^v (reprinted in Bullough, iii. 189), and matches the heiresses of Hungerford, Scales, and Bonville to, respectively, Lord Hastings, the Queen's brother, and the Queen's son, O corrupts the sense, matching the Lord Scales himself with the daughter of someone called Lord Bonfield, and omitting all reference to the Queen's relatives. The point of the chronicle passage, as Alexander explained, which F preserves but which O loses, is that two important heiresses, the daughters of Scales and Bonville, had both been given in marriage to close relatives of the Queen. The octavo, he pointed out, 'mangles history, and has no point of its own'. The corruptions cannot plausibly be attributed to 'a compositor, a transcriber, an abridger, or to their combined efforts', for the error is one of memory, and betrays a reliance on memory to an extent far in excess of that which one would normally expect from any of these agents. 'Here at least', he concluded, 'we are dealing not with a transcript of Shakespeare's (or any other writer's) original, but only with a report of that original'. Once having established that part of O is clearly a report, it is natural to suppose that the rest of the text—which is open to alternative interpretations—is also a report. This hypothesis plausibly and economically accounts for the O text, and we accept it with only slight qualification.

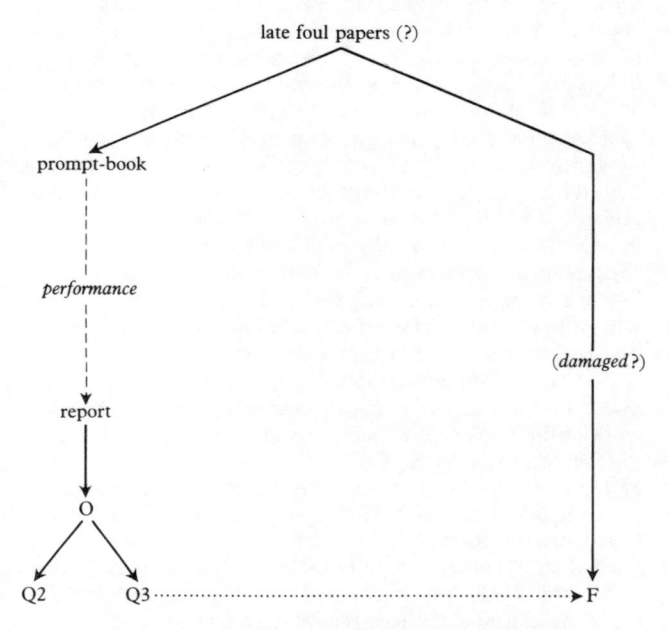

```
                    late foul papers (?)
                    /              \
                   /                \
          prompt-book               \
               |                     \
               |                      \
          performance              (damaged?)
               |                         \
               |                          \
             report                        \
               |                            \
               ↓                             \
               O                              \
              / \                              \
             /   \                              ↓
            Q2   Q3  ··························→ F
```

Alexander believed the report to be of the full F text, and that its comparative brevity, like its other variants, resulted from a failure of memory. Doran, on the other hand, suggested that O reports an abridged and possibly otherwise revised version of the F text. This view, most recently developed by Scott McMillin, we find the more probable.

We do not know with any certainty who was responsible for the reporting of O, though several candidates have been suggested. Alexander believed that the actors who played Warwick and Clifford collaborated on the report; Chambers suggested (*Shakespeare*, i. 283), for both this play and *The First Part of the Contention*, the book-keeper, but this has been challenged, at least with regard to *Contention*, by Jordan (1105-8; the idea of book-keeper reporters is now generally discredited: see Greg, *Problem*, 60, and *Modernizing*, page 129, note 1); Doran tentatively suggested the report was a group effort, put together by a number of actors, a hypothesis more recently endorsed by McMillin.

Two observations suggest that the manuscript behind F, our control text, was authorial, a matter upon which most editors now agree: firstly, F contains a fair number of vague, descriptive stage directions of the kind usually associated with authorial copy; secondly, actors' names have on two occasions crept into both stage directions and speech-prefixes ('Gabriel', 1.2.47.1/321.1, 1.2.49/323; 'Sinklo' and 'Humfrey', 3.1.0.1/1286.2). Greg interpreted the second of these features as evidence of the prompter's hand, but in this has been refuted by Wilson (*The Third Part*, 117 ff.).

The state of the authorial copy, however, and the extent (if any) to which it had been annotated, is less clear. Several inconsistencies of a kind which one might expect of an author in the act of composition, but would not expect in fair copy (much less prompt copy), and which are eliminated in O (and therefore presumably in the acting text from which O ultimately derives), suggest that F derives from foul papers. At least three speeches are clearly misassigned in F (1.1.69/69, 2.2.133/924, 5.7.30/2888). The author's initial and subsequent thoughts on the shape of 2.6/Sc.10 are perhaps discernible from the observation that while '*Montague, & Clarence*' appears to have been appended to the stage direction at line 2.6.30.2-4/1206.2-3 ('*Enter Edward, Warwicke, Richard, and Soldiers, Montague, & Clarence*'), only Clarence is actually used in the following action (the O direction mentions neither Montague nor Clarence, though, as in F, the latter is required on stage: see the note to 2.6.30.4/1206.3). Also probably indicative of the author's shifting views is the duplication, in 2.5/Sc. 9, of the father's entrance. The initial conception appears to have been that of a tableau, with the father and son entering simultaneously, but at separate doors, while the second entrance for the father, immediately before his speech (2.5.79/1116), probably reflects a later stage of the author's thinking. (O follows this later state.) Greg suggested that the father's separate entrance may have been the work of the book-keeper, as he also thought may have been 'the very full provision of noises' throughout the play (*Folio*, 182): he may, of course, be right. Certainly, the number of music cues in this play is well above the usual (see the list of Folio stage directions).

If the play is of divided authorship (see 'Canon and Chronology'), the copy may have consisted of each author's foul papers which one of them revised in an attempt to achieve internal consistency: this would account for the foul-paper-like character of the copy as a whole, and would also explain the annotations which Greg ascribed to a book-keeper, which a revising author's work might occasionally have resembled (see the Introduction to *1 Henry VI*). Additionally, however, this hypothesis could account for the confusion of Montague's relationship to York and Warwick which led both Wilson and Cairncross to suspect different kinds of revision.

We see no reason to accept Cairncross's hypothesis that the manuscript available to the Folio compositors was a scribal transcript (Cairncross, pp. xxxiii–xxxiv): the errors he cites as evidence may be explained just as plausibly and more simply as compositorial in origin. Neither do we find convincing, in the light of recent work by Gary Taylor and William Montgomery on other F texts with regard to which Cairncross advanced similar views, his hypothesis that large portions of F were set from annotated O copy. However, we have recorded in our collations the emendations and conjectures Cairncross made in conjunction with his hypothesis, though according to our usual criteria of selection many of these would not otherwise have been noticed. We do think it probable, though, that the F compositors had a copy of Q3 available for reference, and that they consulted it when they were unable to decipher a word or phrase in the manuscript.

Q3, a Pavier quarto (see the General Introduction, pp. 34-6), appears to have been printed from an extensively edited copy of O. Comparison of the substantive variants between these two editions with F leads us to conclude that the Q3 departures from O are probably editorial or compositorial in origin, without any independent authority (see, for example, the textual note to 5.6.90-1/2854-5, where significant departures from O are made apparently as the result of problems with cast-off copy). About half of Q3's departures from O happen to occur in passages which closely parallel F, enabling us to compare the two versions. This comparison reveals that in over half the instances F agrees with O-Q2 against Q3, and that in the other instances, F agrees with Q3 against O. If the Q3 variants somehow represented authoritative corrections to its copy (deriving, say, from manuscript fragments or a supplementary report) we would expect F and Q3 more often than not to agree against O. That they agree in only about half the instances suggests, rather, Q3 contamination of F. Unless we suppose that the F compositors also had a copy of O or Q2 (and we have found no evidence to support this possibility), those instances in which F agrees with O-Q2 against Q3 increase our confidence in the accuracy of the report. The Q3 departures from O appear to be without authority; these unauthoritative readings appear on a number of occasions to have found their way into F; F's frequent agreement with O-Q2 against Q3 gives us grounds for trusting O's verbal accuracy in these well-reported passages; therefore, when F and Q3 agree against O, and the Q3 reading is not a clear correction of error in O, we have normally emended the F reading to that of O. We list among the textual notes those few instances in which we do not emend readings which agree in Q3 and F against O-Q2.

But what of those instances, which no doubt exist, where the F compositor consulted his copy of Q3 for a reading which is invariant from O? Are we to regard every instance of O-F agreement with suspicion? Potentially, yes. But as we have seen, we have reason to believe that in its well-reported passages, O is often verbally very accurate, so O-F agreement here should cause us little anxiety. Sudden agreement in less well-reported passages, on the other hand, is more suspicious, but on the whole we have adopted a cautious editorial stance even with regard to these, and emended only when O-F seems clearly to be wrong. On the whole, though, Q3 contamination of F seems usually to be localized and limited, the result of occasional consultation by the F compositor.

One passage, however, invariant among the three quarto editions and nearly so in F, requires special attention. McKerrow ('Note') suggested that the opening stage direction and the first eighteen lines of 4.2/Sc. 15 were set directly from one of the three editions of O. There probably is some O contamination of F within these eighteen lines, for they share three instances of apparent common error (i.e. two metrically irregular lines, 4.2.2/1994, 4.2.9/2001; and 'town', 4.2.15/2007, instead of 'towns'), but the extent of the contamination is unclear. Since Warwick, who speaks seventeen of the passage's eighteen lines, may have been one of the reporters of O, we may not take as persuasive evidence of contamination the substantive identity of these lines in the two texts. The directions are not identical (O, D5ʳ 17: '*Enter Warwike and Oxford, with fouldiers*'; F, 4.2.0.1-2/1992.2-3: '*Enter Warwicke and Oxford in England, with French Souldiors*', and, at line 4.2.2.1/1994.1, a direction not in O: '*Enter Clarence and Somerset*'), nor do the speech-prefixes take precisely the same form (O: *War., Cla.*; F: *Warw., Clar.*). The absence of such differences would have offered strong evidence of contamination; their presence, unfortunately, tells us little. On the one hand, they may be viewed as consistent with O copy. Compositor A, who set this part of the Folio text, elsewhere in the volume inconsistently expands copy speech-prefixes; the additional F direction could have been inferred from the dialogue ('But ſee where *Somerſet* and *Clarence* comes', line 4.2.3/1995); the variation in the opening stage direction may be explained by supposing the transcription began immediately after it. But, on the other hand, these differences are not inconsistent with manuscript copy. For this passage the compositor may have followed what appears to have been the usual practice, making good intermittent deficiencies in the manuscript by glancing reference to an exemplar of one of the editions of O (presumably Q3); or, finding in his manuscript intermittent deficiencies or perhaps a major lacuna, as McKerrow ('Note') suggested, he may have resorted to Q3 for the entire passage. In view of this uncertainty, we assume only intermittent contamination. Accordingly, we emend the three instances of shared O-F error, but retain F's incidentals.

The octavo, as we have seen, derives from a performance: its ultimate authority is therefore the prompt-book, which represents a later stage in the play's stemma than the foul-paper manuscript behind F. This makes it particularly valuable to an editor. In well reported passages, the editor must always consider whether variants could be due not to corruption by the reporter, but to changes made to the text—revisions—in the preparation of the prompt-book, or, on the other hand, whether in the case of single variant words, the possibility that O preserves original readings which have become corrupted in F through compositorial mistakes or misguided attempts to improve or modernize the original. The difficulty of this discrimination is compounded in the case of *Richard Duke of York* by the possibility that the O report either is, itself, or reports, an adaptation of the original prompt-book, and does not simply report a performance of that prompt-book (see McMillin). In the light of this difficulty, we have adopted a more cautious editorial approach here than with other bad quarto texts. We accept all octavo stage directions which appear to us merely to amplify F (e.g. 2.4.11.1-2/1035.1, 4.7.0.1-6/2150.1-5). Moreover, when, in a well-reported passage a variant octavo staging seems clearly superior to that of F and not necessarily related to any possible adaptation, we adopt the octavo direction, along with any attendant variations in dialogue or speech assignment which appear to have been necessitated by it (e.g. 5.1.80-3/2483-6). It seems to us that in these matters of staging, O's claim to authority is greatest. We are more cautious in accepting single-word variants which may represent the preservation of original readings which have become corrupted in F. We attempt to identify all such variants and include those which we do not adopt in a separate list of 'Rejected Octavo Variants'.

The play was never entered in the Stationers' Register; editors usually assume that it was covered either by Millington's 1594 entry of *The First Part of the Contention* (see the Introduction to that play) or by his transfer on 19 April 1602 of, among other titles, 'The firſt and Second pte of henry the vjt | ij bookes' (i.e. Folio parts two and three) to Thomas Pavier. ('The thirde parte of Henry ye Sixt' is included in the 1623 collective entry of new plays, but this probably refers to the last-written and last-published of the three Henry VI plays, Folio 'The first Part'.)

The Octavo's head title *The true Tragedie of Richard Duke of Yorke, and the good King Henry the Sixt*, is probably closer to the title by which the play was contemporarily known than either Folio's 'The third Part' or the 1602 transfer entry's 'Second parte'. Those who memorially reconstructed the octavo text probably would not have forgotten the title of the play; nor is it easy to imagine why they would have deliberately altered it. Although York dies at the end of Act 1, this fact need not diminish the authority of O's title: Caesar, for example, dies early in Act 3 of *Julius Caesar*, and the eponymous character of *The Downfall of Robert, Earl of Huntington* (1601: BEPD 179) and its sequel *The Death of Robert, Earl of Huntington* (1601: BEPD 180) is dead by the end of the sequel's fifth scene. Clifford Leech has demonstrated a pattern in two-part plays of the late 1580s and early 1590s whereby a 'second part' shows the fall of a Machiavellian character whose rise has been dramatized in the first. O's title exploits that structural expectation. The double emphasis on York and King Henry, which is common to the Folio main title and the octavo main, head, and running titles, is also paralleled by *The Death of Robert, Earl of Huntington*: the Matilda of that play's subtitle (*Otherwise called Robin Hood of merrie Sherwodde: with the lamentable Tragedie of chaste Matilda, his faire maid Marien, poysoned at Dunsmowe by King Iohn*) like Henry, does not die until near the play's end. The Folio's 'The third Part' cannot have been the original title, if, as we believe, 'The first Part' was not written until later (see the Introduction to *1 Henry VI*); nor is there any reason to assign particular authority to the 1602 'Second parte' in view both of its relative lateness and the simple economy for the Stationer of recording two related plays on the reign of Henry VI as 'the first and second part'. *OED* records no parallel to corroborate the often-stated interpretation of 'whole' in the O title as 'completed'. We therefore adopt O's title, by which almost certainly the play was first (and perhaps always, before 1623) known in the theatre.

Neither O nor F is divided into acts and scenes. We accept the traditional division with two exceptions: following 4.3.27/2048, at a point at which the stage appears to be cleared, we introduce a new scene division (4.4/Sc. 17), and, following a suggestion by P. A. Daniel (p. 321) and substantively adopted by Wilson and endorsed by Norman Sanders, we introduce a new scene division (4.10/Sc. 23) at the end of Act 4.

Unless otherwise indicated, references to McKerrow in our notes are to the commentary to his Oxford edition of the play, which had reached an advanced state at the time of his death, and references to Walker are to marginal comments made by Alice Walker to McKerrow's edition.

W.L.M./(G.T.)

WORKS CITED

Alexander, Peter, *Shakespeare's 'Henry VI' and 'Richard III'* (1929)
Cairncross, A. S., ed., *The Third Part of King Henry VI*, Arden (1964)
Daniel, P. A., *A Time Analysis of the Plots of Shakspere's Plays*, Transactions of the New Shakspere Society, 1877-9, Series 1, part 2 (1879)
Doran, Madeleine, *Henry VI, Parts II and III: Their Relation to the 'Contention' and the 'True Tragedy'* (1928)

Hart, H. C., ed., *The Third Part of King Henry the Sixth*, Arden (1910)
Jordan, John E., 'The Reporter of *Henry VI, Part 2*', PMLA 64 (1949), 1089-1113
Leech, Clifford, 'The Two-Part Play: Marlowe and the Early Shakespeare', *Shakespeare-Jahrbuch*, 94 (1958), 90-106
McKerrow, R. B., 'A Note on the "Bad Quartos" of *2* and *3 Henry VI* and the Folio Text', RES 13 (1937), 64-72
McMillin, Scott, 'Casting for Pembroke's Men: The *Henry VI* Quartos and *The Taming of A Shrew*', SQ 23 (1972), 141-59
Montgomery, William, ed., '*The Contention of York and Lancaster*: A Critical Edition', vol. ii (unpublished D.Phil. Thesis, University of Oxford, 1985)
Sanders, Norman, ed., *The Third Part of King Henry the Sixth*, New Penguin (1981)
Urkowitz, Stephen, ' "Theatrical Revision" in Shakespeare's *3 Henry VI*', Paper delivered in Seminar I: 'Bad Quartos' as Documents of the Theatre, Second World Shakespeare Congress, Stratford-upon-Avon, 3 August 1981
Wilson, John Dover, ed., *The Second Part of King Henry VI*, New (1952)
—— *The Third Part of King Henry VI*, New (1952)

TEXTUAL NOTES

Title The ... Sixt] O (*head title, subs.*); The true Tragedie of Richard | Duke of Yorke, and the death of | good King Henrie the Sixt, | with the whole contention betweene | the two Houſes Lancaſter | and Yorke, as it was ſundrie times | acted by the Right Honoura-|ble the Earle of Pem-|brooke his ſeruants. O (*title-page*); The Tragedie of Richard D. of Yorke, and Henrie the ſixt. O (*running title*); The third Part of Henry the Sixt, | with the death of the Duke of | YORKE. F; The ... Second pte of henry the vjᵗ S.R.

1.1.0.1/0.1 *A Chayre of State*] A state, or raised platform, is required here and in 3.3/Sc. 13. Here it is surmounted by one chair; there, by two or perhaps three. In each case, it may have been 'discovered' on the inner stage, or brought on to the main stage for the duration of the scene; alternatively, it may have been visibly present on stage throughout the play.

1.1.0.3/0.3 *Crookeback*] O; *not in* F

1.1.0.3/0.3 *Mountague*] F, O; Falconbridge CAIRNCROSS (*passim*)

1.1.0.5-6/0.4-5 *with white Roses in their hats*] O; *not in* F

1.1.6/6 himselfe,] ROWE; ~. F

1.1.14/14 Brother] F. Warwick, not York, was Montague's brother, but in view of the fact that York and Montague address one another as 'Brother' on four occasions in the next scene, it seems probable that Malone was right in supposing this speech and lines 1.1.116-17/116-17 were spoken to York. 'Brother' can mean 'brother-in-law', and in this lies one possible explanation of the confusion: York was married to the sister of Richard Neville, who was Montague's father. But if the author confused the Richard Neville-Montague relationship to be not, correctly, father-son, but, incorrectly, brother-brother, then it would be unsurprising for Montague to address his 'sister's' husband as 'Brother'. This anomaly has been cited as evidence of revision during the course of which the character Falconbridge, York's brother, was eliminated and his lines given to Montague. See the note to 1.1.240/240.

1.1.19/19 hape] DYCE (*subs.*); hope F, O

1.1.21/21 I, ... Yorke.] F, O (~ₐ ... ~,); ~ .... ~, THEOBALD

1.1.24/24 Heauen] F, Q3; heauens O, Q2

1.1.34.1/34.1 *The Souldiers withdraw*] This edition (*conj.* Walker). It is difficult to say with confidence precisely when the soldiers leave the stage: that they do leave is clear from their re-entrance at 1.1.170.1-2/170.1-2.

1.1.36 council] F (counsaile)

1.1.43/43 not‿ my Lords:] O; ~, ~ ~ₐ F

1.1.55/55 & you both] F, O; both CAIRNCROSS (*conj.*)

1.1.69/69 EXETER] O (*Exet.*); Weſtm⟨erland⟩. F. O is probably correct here in its assignment of the line to Exeter, given that Henry's next remark appears to be addressed to him.

1.1.76/76 I am thine] F; Thou art deceiu'd: I am thine O. Though O may be right, the metrical irregularity may equally have led, or encouraged, the reporter to a possibly unconscious anticipation of Northumberland's line later in the scene (1.1.156/156).

1.1.78/78 mine] O, Q2; my F, Q3

1.1.83/83 and that's] Q3; and that is O, Q2; that's F

1.1.105/105 Thy] O; My F

1.1.106/106 Grandfather] F, O; grandsire CAIRNCROSS

1.1.120-4/120-4 NORTHUMBERLAND ... king] O; for F see Additional Passage A. Stephen Urkowitz has argued that a different characterization of Henry seems to have been intended in O than in F. This he believes evidence of O's prior composition. If, as McMillin argues, however, O derives from an adaptation of the original prompt-book rather than from that prompt-book itself, the revision may have occurred at that time as part of a process of simplification (and debasement) rather than as one of increased complexity. We take the view, however, that the variant is authorial, and part of the reworking which inevitably occurred between the foul-paper stage of the play, upon which we believe F is based, and the prompt-book. See the Introduction.

1.1.121/121 Yorke] This edition; *Plantagenet* O; *not in* F. O is unmetrical: the word could easily be an anticipation on the part of the reporter of 'Plantagenets' in the next line.

1.1.122/122 both] This edition; both both O; *not in* F

1.1.136/136 Tell me, may] F, O; May CAIRNCROSS (*conj.*)

1.1.138 An] F (And)

1.1.171/171 me] O; *not in* F

1.1.185.1, 187.1/185.1, 187.1 *Exit with his Souldiers ... Exit with his Souldiers*] The placement follows O, but both men could leave at the same time as Clifford, 1.1.189.1/189.1. Moreover, it is uncertain whether they, or Clifford, are accompanied in their departure with soldiers.

1.1.197/197 thine] O, Q2; an F, Q3

1.1.200/200 nor] This edition (G.T.); neyther F. See the textual note to *1 Henry VI* 5.1.59/2172.

1.1.203/203 King Henry] F, O; the king CAIRNCROSS (*conj.*)

1.1.203.1/203.1 ⌈*Yorke descends:*⌉ *Henry and Yorke embrace*] This edition; *not in* F

1.1.207/207 Farewell my gracious Lord, Ile to] F; My Lord Ile take my leaue, for Ile to *Wakefield* | To O; Farewell, my gracious lord; I'll take my leaue, | For I'll to Wakefield to CAIRNCROSS. O may well be a memorial interpolation on the part of the reporter. Wakefield is clearly identified in both texts at 2.1.107/689 as the place at which York is killed. If the reporter associated the present destination with that later identification of it, it would be an easy matter for him to anticipate the identification of it here, as he appears to have done so elsewhere (A7ʳ 12, 23; A7ᵛ 16). Cairncross (in his note to 1.1.212-13) incorrectly observed that 'Wakefield ... is not mentioned elsewhere in this play', and emended partly on this basis.

1.1.207.1-210.1/207.1-210.1 *Exeunt ... with Souldiers*] These sequential exits derive from O: it is possible (though unlikely) that all four parties depart at 1.1.210.1/210.1.

1.1.211.2/211.2 *and Prince Edward*] O (*subs.*); *not in* F

1.1.240/240 *Faulconbridge*] F, O; *Mountague* This edition *conj.* Faulconbridge, York's brother, is not a character in the play as it survives; if, however, as has been argued, he was in some earlier version of the play but later merged with the character Montague (see the note to line 1.1.14/14), this reference to him may be viewed as a vestige of that earlier version which evidently was overlooked in revision and so found its way into the prompt-book (and the performance from which O derives). F and O both have Montague come from and return to the sea (line 1.1.210/210).

1.1.244 seely] F (silly)

1.1.255/255 the vtter ruine] This edition; vtter ruine F. In performance, almost certainly elided to 'th'utter ruin'. F, however, favours the full form, even when elision is necessary, so it is to that form we emend. 'Ruin' was probably disyllabic (Cercignani, p. 291).

1.1.260/260 with] O; not in F
1.1.262/262 from] O; to F
1.1.269 coast] F (cost). 'The spelling is ambiguous. Most modern editors print "cost", accepting Malone's explanation that it is here equivalent to "cost [me]". Johnson, however, followed Warburton in reading "coast", quoting Warburton's gloss "hover over it". Onions glosses under "coast", explaining as "assail, attack". The last explanation seems the most satisfactory; see *O.E.D.* coast v. 9' (McKerrow).
1.1.274.1/274.1 *Flourish. Exeunt*] *Exit.* | *Flourish* F. The misplacement of '*Flourish*' in F may be viewed as evidence that this sound direction was a marginal addition. See line 4.8.70.1/2322.1.
1.2.40/314 to Edmund Brooke] O; vnto my F. The F text probably reflects an instance of late censorship. As it stands, F is unmetrical; O provides extra historical information not likely to have been interpolated by a reporter; and, moreover, the Brooke/Cobham family are known to have been sensitive to their ancestors' appearance in plays. See the Introductions to *1 Henry IV* and *Merry Wives of Windsor*.
1.2.72/346 Vnckles] HUDSON (subs.); Vnckle F
1.3.0.1/349.2 *Alarmes, and then*] Q; *Alarum* F. F places this before the exit direction which ends the previous scene. From Q 'it seems probable that the *Alarum* took place when the stage was empty and represented the noise of a battle off. Capell and later editors give *Alarum* at the end of sc. ii, . . . and add further *Alarums* at the head of sc. iii' (McKerrow).
1.3.1.1/350.1 *Enter Clifford*] O places Clifford's entrance immediately before Rutland's line, 'Ah . . . comes'; F places it immediately afterward.
1.3.7/356 Souldiers, away] F, O; Away CAIRNCROSS (conj.)
1.3.15/364 o're] F, Q3; ouer O, Q2
1.3.37/386 *Kneeling*] This edition (conj. Walker, after Hall)
1.3.52.1/401.1 *and Souldiers*] The stage is cleared at this point: whether or not any soldiers remain on stage to exit here depends on how many entered with Clifford, and of these, how many exited with the tutor (1.3.9.1/358.1). The question, unresolvable, is an important one, for it asks, essentially, whether Clifford's murder of Rutland is witnessed by anyone.
1.4.16-17/417-18 [. . . And cry'de] This edition (conj. Cambridge); And cry'de F; Ned cried COLLIER (conj.); Edward CAIRNCROSS (Lettsom); He cried KINNEAR (conj.); And Edward cried G.T. conj. The Cambridge editors suggest that the lost line referred to Edward.
1.4.26/427 makes] F1; make F2. See Abbott, 247.
1.4.34 Phaëton] F (Phaeton)
1.4.51/452 buckle] O; buckler F
1.4.61.1/462.1 *They [fight, and] take Yorke*] O (subs.); not in F
1.4.64/465 conquer'd] F, Q3; conquered O, Q2
1.4.76/477 where's] F, Q3; where is O, Q2
1.4.82/483 thy] O; the F
1.4.96.1/497.1 *paper*] Though nothing in either O or F indicates the composition of the crown, there is in *Richard III* a clear reference to its having been made of paper: recalling this episode, Richard says to Margaret 'The curse my noble father laid on thee | When thou didst crowne his warlike browes with paper' (1.3.171-2/583-4). Since *Richard III* was written and performed after *Duke of York*, and since one of the chief objectives of much of 1.3/Sc. 3 in the later play seems to have been to remind the audience of the events of the earlier, it is unlikely that Richard's description of his father's humiliation and death, one of the most powerful and memorable images from the earlier play, would have been at variance with the actual theatrical practice.
1.4.108/509 *She knocks it from his head*] This edition. The crown may have been removed later in the scene, at 1.4.165/566.
1.4.121/522 wert thou] F, O; wert CAIRNCROSS (W. S. Walker)
1.4.130/531 knowes] F; wots O, CAIRNCROSS. Cairncross argues that this is an instance of F sophistication. However, Compositor A, who set this line, set 'wot' twice elsewhere in this play (4.8.82,

5.4.71/2334, 2664), and four times elsewhere in the Folio (*1 Henry VI* 4.6.32/1992, *Richard III* 3.2.86/1709, *Richard II* TLN 1169 (2.3.59/1124), and *Henry V* ('wots') 4.1.279/2060). It is difficult to see why he should balk at setting 'wot' here, if that were what his manuscript read, when he does not seem to object to the form elsewhere.
1.4.138/539 Tygres] F. 'The reading "Tygers" in Qq and Green's *Groatsworth* indicates that "tiger's" is intended, not "tygress" as Capell reads' (McKerrow).
1.4.143/544 obdurate] F; indurate O, CAIRNCROSS. Cairncross cites 'obdurate' here as 'the strongest example' (p. xxxix) of Folio sophistication. But 'indurate' never occurs in Shakespeare: 'obdurate' occurs eight times elsewhere, four times in good quartos (*Venus* (1593), *Lucrece* (1594), *Titus* (1594), and *Merchant* (1600)); in *Richard III* its use is confirmed by F and Q (1.3.345/757, 3.1.39/1465). Although Cairncross calls O's form 'more abstruse and obsolescent', *OED*'s examples indicate that the forms are interchangeable in the period.
1.4.151/552 passions moue] O; paſſions moues F; passion moves CAMBRIDGE. Editors usually retain F, citing Abbott, 333. But nowhere else does Shakespeare treat 'passions' as 'singular in thought', and the error would be an easy one for the compositor to make.
1.4.167/568 too cruell hand] F; two cruell hands O, Q2; too cruell hands Q3. O, however, may be right, and F the result of progressive contamination via Q3.
2.1.0.2/582.2-3 *with drum and Souldiers*] O; *and their power* F
2.1.20.1/602.1 *Three sunnes appeare in the aire*] O; not in F
2.1.28.1/610.1 *The three sunnes begin to ioyne*] This edition; not in F
2.1.94.2-3/676.2 *with drum, ancient, and souldiers*] O; *and their Army* F
2.1.94.2 ensign] O (ancient). See Gary Taylor, 'Ancients and Moderns', *SQ* 36 (1985), 525-7
2.1.113/695 And verie well appointed as I thought,] O; not in F
2.1.127/709 Captaines] O (subs.); Captiues F
2.1.131/713 an idle] O; a lazie F
2.1.144/726 his] O; the F
2.1.158/740 make] F1; makes F2
2.1.198/780 Richard,] O; ~ˏ F
2.1.204.1-205/786.1-787 *Enter . . .* WARWICKE] F ('Enter . . . War.' text); War. F (c.w.)
2.1.209 sorts.] F (~,)
2.1.209.1/791.1 *March.*] This edition; not in F. Twice in this scene an entrance is accompanied by a march (2.1.0.1/582.2, 2.1.94.1/676.1); Edward's line (2.1.204/786) strongly suggests that one should be played at this exit.
2.2.0.1/791.2 *Yorkes head thrust out, aboue.*] This edition (G.T.); not in F. The dialogue in this scene, beginning with Margaret's first speech ('Yonders the head . . .'), suggests that the head is visible here. It seems likely that it remains visible until its removal is called for, at 2.6.85-6/1261-2.
2.2.46/837 ill] F, Q3; euill O, Q2
2.2.62/853 Lesson;] F, Q3; leſſon boy, O, Q2
2.2.89/880 GEORGE . . . Since] F1, O (subs.); Since F2. See the next note.
2.2.92/883 our brother out] O; out me F
2.2.105/896 fly] F, Q3; flee O, Q2. This may be an instance of Q3 contamination of F, but since Shakespeare frequently uses 'fly', and only once elsewhere uses 'flee' (*LLL* 3.1.63/796), we assume F to be correct and the Q3 reading to be independent of and only fortuitously coincident with it.
2.2.107/898 droue] F, Q3; that droue O, Q2
2.2.108/899 NORTHUMBERLAND] F (Nor.), O
2.2.116/907 Sunset] F; funne ſet O, Q2; Sun-ſet Q3
2.2.116 sun set] F (Sunſet), O (funne ſet)
2.2.133/924 RICHARD] O; War⟨wicke⟩. F
2.2.142/933 Sham'st thou] F, Q3; Shames thou O; Sham'ſt Q2
2.2.169/960 Or bath'd . . . bloods] F. 'No critic seems to have commented on this odd phrase, which seems to mean "watered thy growth (the increase in power of the house of Lancaster)

with our warm blood"—but I do not think it was usual to speak of "bathing" a plant in the sense of watering it' (McKerrow).
2.2.172/963 deniest] O; denied'ſt F. The proposed misreading, e/ed, is an easy one.
2.2.177.1-3/968.1-3 Flourish . . . another doore] This edition; Exeunt omnes F
2.3.8.1/976.1 George ⌈running⌉] This edition; Clarence F; George O
2.3.13.1/981.1 Richard ⌈running⌉] O; Richard F
2.3.49 all together] F (altogether)
2.4.0.1/1024.1 Alarmes.] O; not in F
2.4.0.1-2/1024.1-2 at one dore . . . at the other] O; not in F
2.4.11.1-2/1035.1 and rescues Richard] O; not in F
2.5.1-54/1038-91 KING HENRY . . . him] F. King Henry's 54-line soliloquy is reduced to 13 lines in O. The abbreviated version may reflect performance practice, but whether the abridgement was authorial or not is uncertain.
2.5.36/1073 So . . . Eane] F; W. S. Walker conjectures a line missing after this one which completed the rhetorical pattern with 'months'. The omission is plausible, compositorial eyeskip being very easy among lines so similar as these. However, 'months' is also missing from the introductory lines (2.5.27-9/1064-6), though it is included in the summary line (2.5.38/1075).
2.5.37/1074 yeares] F; months ROWE. A line may be missing here, either immediately before this line, or as two part-lines, so: ⌈   ⌉ere I shall sheere the Fleece: | So many yeares, ⌈   ⌉. If there is a lacuna, its first element was probably 'So many months'.
2.5.38/1075 Weekes] ROWE; not in F
2.5.54/1091 When] F; Wher This edition conj.
2.5.54.1-2/1091.1-2 Alarum . . . armes] O. The scene appears to have been conceived originally as a tableau, with both father and son entering here. The repetition, however, of the father's entry direction at 2.5.78.1-2/1115.1-2 probably represents a later stage of composition and the actual theatrical practice—with the son entering first, speaking, commented on by King Henry, and then followed on stage by the father's entry, when the scene turns into a tableau. This much would appear to be corroborated by O, which derives from a performance. Their entry at two doors, which only F specifically mentions, though probable, is not certain. See the Introduction.
2.5.60.1, 81.1/1097.1, 1118.1 He remoues the dead mans helmet] This edition (G.T.); not in F
2.5.82/1119 our] F; a COLLIER (conj.)
2.5.113.1, 2.5.122.1/1150.1, 1159.1-2 Exit . . . Exit] These sequential exits derive from O; F marks a single exit, after 2.5.122/1159.
2.5.119/1156 Een] CAPELL (Even); Men F1-3; Man F4; Sad ROWE; Meer MITFORD (conj. in Cambridge); Son DELIUS 2 (Mitford); 'Fore men or To men KEIGHTLEY (conj.); Mang'd BULLOCH (conj. in Cambridge); Main ANON. (conj. in Cambridge); Meet SISSON. The graphical error presumed by Capell's emendation, E/M (or e/m), is difficult to explain, however.
2.5.124.1, 127.1, 133.1/1161.1, 1164.1, 1170.1 Alarums . . . Edward the Prince| . . . Queene Margaret| . . . Exeter] We follow O to the extent that we divide F's single entrance for Prince Edward, Margaret, and Exeter, which it places after 2.5.124/1161, into three separate directions. O, however, has Margaret enter first, followed by the Prince, then Exeter. Each speaks upon entry. Each of these characters speaks in F, too, but in the sequence Edward—Margaret—Exeter, so this is the order in which we direct them to enter: O's transposition of Edward and Margaret's speeches might easily have resulted from memorial error. In O only the first of the three entrances is preceded by alarums—there, it happens to be Margaret's. We have, therefore, retained F's alarums before Prince Edward's entry, but have not added them to accompany either Margaret's or Exeter's.
2.6.0.1-2/1176.1-2 with an arrow in his necke] O; not in F
2.6.6/1182 Commixture] O; Commixtures F
2.6.8/1184 The common people swarme like summer flies,] O; not in F
2.6.24/1200 out] F, Q3; our O, Q2
2.6.30.4/1206.3 Montague] F; not in O. From its unusual position after 'Soldiers', 'Montague, & Clarence' (i.e. 'Montague, & George' in our text) appears to have been added to this entry direction as an afterthought. George, however, is given a part in the scene and is included in O; Montague is a 'ghost' here—he has no lines to speak, nor is he addressed by anyone—and is absent from O. He may well have been deleted from the prompt-book (though, on the other hand, a silent presence on stage would be an easy thing for a reporter to forget).
2.6.42/1218 EDWARD] O; Rich⟨ard⟩. F. F's redistribution of this and the following lines seems to represent a superior staging and probably results from authorial revision between the foul papers, from which F derives, and the prompt-book from which O indirectly derives. See the Introduction.
2.6.43/1219 RICHARD A] O; A F
2.6.44/1220 EDWARD . . . See] O; See F
2.6.44/1220 Richard goes to Clifford] This edition; not in F
2.6.44/1220 And] O; Ed⟨ward⟩. And F
2.6.60/1236 his] O, F2; is F1
2.6.80/1256 buy but] O; buy F. Given that the two words begin identically, the F compositor may be supposed to have skipped the second, mistaking it to be the same 'bu-' word he had just set.
2.6.110.1/1286.1 Yorkes head is remoued] This edition (G.T.); not in F. See the note to 2.2.0.1/791.2. It may be that York's head is replaced with Clifford's (see lines 2.6.85-6/1261-2), but of this we can be less confident than that York's head was displayed. Characters several times remind us by their comments between 2.2.0.1/791.2 and here of York's displayed head; the display of Clifford's head is mentioned only once (2.6.85-6/1261-2).
3.1.12.1/1298.2 disguisde] O; not in F
3.1.17/1303 wast] F3; was F1. Possibly foul case ('s' for 'ſt').
3.1.19 press] F (preaſe)
3.1.24 thee] F (the)
3.1.24/1310 the sower Aduersitie] SINGER 2 (Dyce); the sower Adueſaries F; these sour adversities POPE. 'The chief objection to the reading of F1 is that "adversary" seems very seldom to occur with a stress on the second syllable. In sense it might seem to accord with Matthew v. 25, "Agree with thine adversary quickly", &c., save that no particular adversaries seem to have been in Henry's mind at the moment' (McKerrow). Against this, and in favour of F, we observe that 'sour' can be disyllabic. Still, the emendation seems desirable.
3.1.30/1316 Is] F2; I: F1
3.1.55/1341 thou that] O; thou F
3.1.80/1366 No, for we] F; No, we POPE
3.1.82/1368 sweare] F; sware CAIRNCROSS (Delius)
3.1.96/1382 We] F; and therefore we O. O's 'therefore' fits its context, but not F's: 'for as we thinke | You are our quondam king, K. Edward hath depoſde, | And therefore we charge you'.
3.1.96/1382 in the] This edition (G.T.); the O, F
3.2.3/1389 Lands] O; Land F. O represents the more idiomatic form (as evident, in this scene alone, from its use in 3.2.4, 21, 31, 40, 42, 55, 71, 117/1390, 1407, 1417, 1426, 1428, 1441, 1457, 1503).
3.2.28/1414 whip me then] O; then whip me F. O is metrically superior; F's transposition is an easy and common compositorial error.
3.2.30/1416 and] O, Q2; if F, Q3
3.2.30 an] O (and)
3.2.32/1418 them] O; then F
3.2.119/1505 as] O; your F. F may be explained as the compositor's anticipation of the other 'your' in this line.
3.2.123/1509 honourablie] O (subs.); honourable F. 'O.E.D. accepts the F1 reading as a rare adverbial use of 'honourable'; but there are no parallels of near date and the quartos support this more usual form' (McKerrow).
3.2.161/1547 or an] F1-2; or F3
3.2.183/1569 that which] F, Q3; that that O, Q2. This may be an instance of Q3 contamination of F, but the F line is sufficiently

different from that of Q3 ('I cry content, to that which greeues me moſt') to make us doubt this. We assume that the manuscript behind F read 'that which', that this was corrupted in performance or in the report to O's 'that that', and that the Q3 editor altered this, without authority, to 'that which'. The Q3-F agreement we therefore view as a coincidence.

3.3.0.1/1581.1 2.] A third chair of state may be required for Bona, the French King's sister.

3.3.11/1592 State] DYCE (W. S. Walker); Seat F

3.3.33 An] F (And)

3.3.109/1690 *Edward*, and *Oxford*] F. '*Edward*' may be three syllables (compare line 3.3.140/1721); alternatively, for '*Oxford*', G.T. *conj.* 'Lord *Oxford*'.

3.3.124/1705 eternall] O; externall F. McKerrow, who rejected this traditional emendation, believed 'the sense to be that Edward's love is the outward and visible result of his virtue and Bona's beauty and [could] see no point in "eternal" here, especially as the plant is not exempt from "disdain" even if, as Warburton maintains, there is an allusion to "the plants of Paradise"; see *O.E.D.* external 2'. We, however, prefer O for several reasons. Love is often thought of as 'eternal', an association which is theatrically appropriate here given the rapidity with which it is undercut. Moreover, it is difficult to see how love is any more 'external' than virtue or beauty, or any more an 'outward and visible result'.

3.3.133/1714 tempted] F, O; temper'd CAIRNCROSS (Vaughan)

3.3.140/1721 *Edward*] F. Possibly three syllables (compare line 3.3.109/1690); if so, 'the English' would, when spoken, be elided to 'th'English'.

3.3.156/1737 Warwicke, Peace,] F2; Warwicke, F1. 'All editors from F2 (except Malone) read "Peace" at the end of the line. This is no doubt an improvement, but it has no authority whatever' (McKerrow).

3.3.202 ay] F (I)

3.3.228/1809 Ile] O; I F. The O reading is to some extent confirmed by the post's repetition of it in his otherwise very accurate account of Bona's message. See line 4.1.98/1944.

3.3.233.1/1814 *Exit Post*] F, Q3 (*Exit Meſ.*); *not in* O, Q2

3.3.243/1824 Wedlocke] F, Q3; wedlockes O, Q2. There is no reason to doubt the correctness of F here: *OED* (*sb.* 4a) provides ample evidence of 'wedlock' used, as here, at this time as a simple attributive. Besides this one, it cites two further examples from Shakespeare ('wedlock houres', *Merchant* 5.1.32/2314; 'Wedlocke Hymne', *As You Like It* 5.4.135/2632), and provides a precise, if late, parallel from Milton ('wedlock-bands', *Samson* 986). Q3 may be an independent correction of O-Q2 'wedlockes'. The close correspondence of this speech of Warwick's in the two texts probably should not be viewed as evidence of O contamination of F: Warwick is supposed by some to be one of the reporters who compiled O and, while the rest of this scene is reported with varying accuracy, Warwick's speeches are, on the whole, well reported.

3.3.253/1834 Shall] F, O; Shalt F2

3.3.263/1844 to bring him downe againe] F, O; againe to bring him downe CAIRNCROSS (*conj.*)

4.1.13/1859 our] F; your G.T. *conj.*

4.1.17/1863 you] ROWE; *not in* F

4.1.21/1867 pittie] F, Q3; a pittie O, Q2

4.1.28/1874 my] O, Q2; mine F, Q3

4.1.40/1886 But] F; But all VAUGHAN (*conj.*); But sure G.T. *conj.* G.T. cites *Winter's Tale* 1.2.432/479, 'but I am sure 'tis safer'.

4.1.41/1887 vsing] F; losing VAUGHAN (*conj.*). 'The word is, I think, suspicious, for the sense should be ignoring, lacking or without' (McKerrow).

4.1.46/1892 Lord] F, Q3; the Lord O, Q2

4.1.65 brother's] F (Brothers)

4.1.91/1937 thy] O; the F. O's reading is supported by King Louis having uttered it when instructing the post what message to take to King Edward. See line 3.3.223/1804.

4.1.122/1968 *aside*] This direction could come before 'Not'. The F line division, 'I: | My', however, suggests this arrangement.

4.1.133/1979 neer'st] O (neereſt), Q2; neere F, Q3

4.2.0.1-4.2.18/1992.2-2010 Enter . . . easie] These lines appear to have been influenced by a copy of one of the three editions of O, probably Q3. OF variants are listed among the 'Rejected Octavo Variants'. See the Introduction.

4.2.2/1994 sort] This edition (G.T.); people F, O. This line, identical in O and F, is metrically corrupt. The fact that F and O agree here, and that they agree in error, is one of the chief reasons for supposing that this passage, which in the absence of agreement in error could be explained as an instance of accurate reporting, is, rather, one of O contamination of F. We accept this hypothesis. It follows, then, that the error is memorial in origin, and substitution of the kind which we propose happened here—of the more prosaic 'people' for the less usual 'sort'—is as common a type of memorial error as are transpositions of the type suggested by the rejected emendations of the following note. 'Sort' is used later in the play with reference to the commons, at 5.5.86/2761, and seems to us the superior reading.

An alternative possibility, in view of this line's similarity to line 2.6.8/1184, is that the whole line is a memorial interpolation—an instance of 'recollection' on the part of the reporter—and that the original text is lost; at the very least its form here may have been conditioned by the earlier line.

4.2.2/1994 by numbers swarme to vs] F, O; swarm by numbers to us POPE; swarm to us by numbers HUDSON. Each of these is a plausible alternative to the emendation that we make, and each is consistent with our textual hypothesis of O contamination of F at this point (see the previous note).

4.2.5/1997 Feare] F, O; Fear you CAIRNCROSS (*conj.*)

4.2.12/2004 come] CAIRNCROSS; welcome F, O. The line as it stands in F, O is almost certainly wrong: its irregular metre strongly suggests as much. Given that it occurs within a passage in which F was contaminated by a copy, probably, of Q3, the error may be presumed to be memorial in origin. 'Welcome' for 'come' would be an easy substitution for the reporter to make, especially in view of the two previous occurrences of 'welcome' in this speech, one of which, as here, is associated with Clarence. But 'sweet' elsewhere in the play describes 'Clarence' (5.5.72/2747), which suggests the alternative possibility that its presence here is a memorial interpolation. This, in turn, suggests an alternative emendation to the one we have made: 'But welcome Clarence'.

4.2.15/2007 Townes] THEOBALD (Thirlby); Towne F, O. 'Townes' in line 4.3.13/2034 supports this emendation. This line's similarity to that one also suggests the possibility of memorial anticipation (and hence corruption) here.

4.3.14/2035 keepes] F. The line is metrically deficient: Theobald emended to 'keepeth', Hanmer added 'here' and Vaughan 'out'. All of these are redundant, and Theobald's metrically inferior. G.T. conjectures 'keeps state' (compare *LLL* 5.2.589/2340, *Henry V* 1.2.273/406, *Macbeth* 3.4.4/1028, *All Is True* 1.3.10/483, etc.); W.L.M. conjectures 'keepes close' (*1 Henry IV* 2.5.545/1471, *Henry V* 2.3.57/855, *Hamlet* 4.7.102/2906, etc.) or 'keepes place' (*Merry Wives* 2.1.59/618).

4.3.16/2037 worship, and quietnesse] F; quietnesse, and worship G.T. *conj.*

4.4.0.1/2048.5 *The Drumme . . . sounding*] F. 'Pope, Capell, and recent editors apparently regard the Drum and Trumpet as accompanying the re-entry of Warwick. It seems, however, possible that these are intended to signify a combat "off"' (McKerrow).

4.4.3/2051 The Duke? Why] F, O; Why CAIRNCROSS

4.4.32.1/2080.1 *some with Edward*] O; *not in* F

4.5.4/2089 What?] O; ~, F

4.6.0.2/2120.2 *with Souldiers*] This edition; *not in* F, O. Richard says that King Edward has been told that he will 'finde his Friends with Horse and Men', and when King Edward enters, he addresses 'Gloster, Lord Hastings, and the rest', 'rest' suggesting more than just Stanley.

4.6.4/2124 stands] F2; ſtand F1

4.6.8/2128 Comes] F2; Come F1

4.6.16/2136 Now . . . rest] F. Compare line 4.8.1/2253, which this line suspiciously resembles, but which is metrical, as this line is not.

4.6.22/2142 And] F; *King Edward.* And WILSON
4.6.23/2143 *aside*] This edition (S.W.W.)
4.7.0.1-6/2150.1-5 *Enter ... Tower*] This edition; Enter *Warwicke and Clarence*, with the Crowne, and then king *Henry*, and *Oxford*, and *Summerſet*, and the yong Earle of *Richmond* O; *Enter King Henry the ſixt, Clarence, Warwicke, Somerſet, young Henry, Oxford, Mountague, and Lieutenant* F. O omits altogether the character 'Lieutenant'; the omission of 'Montague' from the O entrance direction, however, is an error, for Warwick addresses him late in the O scene.
4.7.0.4/2150.3-4 *Earle of Richmond*] O; *not in* F
4.7.11/2161 prisonment] HUDSON (Lettsom); impriſonment F
4.7.55/2205 be confiscate] MALONE; confiſcate F1; confiscated F2. McKerrow points out that 'confiscate' was sometimes accented on the second syllable (see *Errors* 1.1.20/20, *Cymbeline* 5.6.325/3131), but the modern accentuation is the more common, the line is a syllable short, and the addition of 'be' is syntactically helpful.
4.7.56/2206 GEORGE OF CLARENCE What else? and] F (*subs.*). Alice Walker believed it odd that this whole line should be assigned to Clarence, and wondered if it might not be divided between two speakers, one to ask the question, 'What else?', and one to reply.
4.8.0.2-3/2252.2 *with a troope of Hollanders*] O; *and Souldiers* F
4.8.1/2253 Lord *Hastings*] F; *Hastings* POPE. See the note to 4.6.16/2136.
4.8.9.1/2261.1 ⌈*Hastings*⌉ *knockes at the Gates of Yorke*] This edition (G.T.); *not in* F
4.8.16.1/2268.1 *He knockes*] This edition (G.T.); *not in* F
4.8.25/2277 *aside*] Possibly '*aside to King Edward*', or '*aside to Hastings*'.
4.8.67-74/2319-26 I ... fight] This edition. O omits line 4.8.70/2322 and the stage direction at 4.8.70.1/2322.1 and assigns the remainder of these lines to Montgomery. F divides them among Montgomery, Edward, and a soldier. While O may reflect revision, the variation is explicable as a combination of memorial error on the part of the O reporter and as an error arising from misinterpretation on the part of either the Folio compositor or whoever prepared the manuscript which lay behind F for the printing house.

Hastings's part in this scene, a small one, is poorly reported in O. It is easy to suppose that the reporter forgot line 4.8.70/2322 and misassigned line 4.8.69/2321 to Montgomery; 'Sound Trumpet, *Edward* ſhal be here proclaim'd' is a perfectly reasonable thing for Montgomery to say at that point in the O context.

The agent of the F error appears to have misinterpreted 'fellow Souldior' (4.8.70/2322) to be a reference to some common soldier rather than, as seems more probable from 'fellow' and the context, one to Montgomery. Since he believed, therefore, that a soldier had been instructed to make the proclamation, he inserted the speech-prefix 'Soul.' before the proclamation. Perhaps the copy speech-prefix for Montgomery was omitted or indistinctly placed; perhaps it was clearly placed, but believed to be wrong. Lines 4.8.73-4/2325-6 must be assigned to Montgomery, as indeed they are in F. Probably any speech-prefix for Montgomery in this vicinity was assumed to belong to these lines alone. But this left line 4.8.72/2324 apparently incomplete: the F '*&c*' may have been interpolated on the assumption that the proclamation was meant to continue in like fashion, much as '&c' following 'Coniuro te, &c' at *Contention* 1.4.23.2/615.2, meant that the conjuration was to continue, but for which continuation no text was supplied in foul-paper copy.

In further support of O's assignment of 4.8.71-2/2323-4 to Montgomery, we refer to the parallel cited by Hart which, though of another occasion, suggests that the formula behind these lines was for the champion to make both the proclamation and the challenge himself: 'At the ſecond courſe came into the hall ſyr Robert Dymmock the kings Champion makyng proclamation, that whoſoeuer would ſaye that King Richard was not lawfull King, he woulde fight with him at the vtteraunce, and threwe downe his gauntlet, and then all the hall cryed King Richard, King Richard.' (Grafton, 'Richard the Thirde', *A Chronicle at Large* (1569: STC 12147), ii. 802 (sig. Aaaa 6ᵛ).)

4.8.70/2322 *To Mountgomerie*] This edition; *not in* F. See the previous note.
4.8.70.1/2322.1 *Flourish*] F (*Flouriſh. Sound*). This looks like a duplicated direction, 'Sound' being original, and 'Flourish' a marginal annotation, possibly of playhouse origin. See line 1.1.274.1/274.1 and the Introduction.
4.8.71/2323 MOUNTGOMERIE] This edition (O); *Soul⟨dier⟩*. F
4.8.72/2324 Ireland,] O; *Ireland, &c.* F. See the note to 4.8.67-74/2319-26.
4.8.73/2325 And] O; *Mount⟨gomerie⟩*. And F. See the note to 4.8.67-74/2319-26.
4.9.0.3/2339.2 *and Oxford*] CAPELL (*subs.*); *Oxford, and Somerset* F. Capell omits Somerset, but includes Exeter. We follow Wilson and introduce Exeter at the beginning of a new scene, 4.10/Sc. 23. See the note to 4.10.0.1/2371.2
4.9.2/2341 hastie] F, O; lusty W. S. WALKER (*conj.*); hardy CARTWRIGHT (*conj.*); huftie MCKERROW (*conj.*)
4.9.12/2351 stirre] POPE (*subs.*); stirre vp F. F is unmetrical, and to interpolate 'vp' after 'stirre' would be easy, especially following the previous line's 'vp'.
4.9.17/2356 belou'd,] HART; ∼, F
4.9.18/2357 Oxfordshire,] HART; ∼ₐ F
4.9.31/2370 *Exit*] This edition (G.T.); *not in* F. Warwick's final line, 4.9.32/2371, directed as it is to 'sweet Lords' appears *not* to be addressed to Henry. Henry's departure here makes his re-entrance at 4.10.0.1/2371.2 easier.
4.9.32.1/2371.1 *Exeunt*] F, O (*Exeunt Omnes*)
4.10.0.1/2371.2 *Enter King Henry and Exeter*] WILSON (Daniel, p. 321); *not in* F. See the note to 4.9.0.3/2339.2.
4.10.18.1/2389.1 *A Lancaster,* ⌈*A Yorke*⌉] This edition; *A Lancaſter, A Lancaſter* F; *A York! A York!* DYCE (Johnson). The F reading may be an instance of dittography, either on the part of the author or that of the compositor. The sense would appear to require some off-stage representation of conflict between King Edward's men and those defending King Henry.
5.1.45/2448 *To Warwicke*] The entire speech may be '*To Warwicke*', and not just this part of it.
5.1.47/2450 *to Warwicke*] The entire line may be '*to Warwicke*', and not just this part of it.
5.1.59.1-2/2462.1-2 *Oxford ... City*] O (*Exit*); *not in* F
5.1.66/2469 *to Oxford, within*] Oxford may enter 'above' at this point, or he may be meant to be 'below', within the city walls (and so out of the audience's view).
5.1.67.1-2/2470.1-2 *Mountague ... City*] O (*Exit*); *not in* F
5.1.68 bye] F (buy); abie O, Q2; abide Q3. *OED* records 'bye' to be an aphetic form of 'aby'. The sense required here, 'to pay for, atone for, make amends for' (*bye, v. obs.* 1) is equivalent to *aby, v.* 2 and indistinguishable from *buy, v.* 3. We choose the more unusual form to avoid possible confusion with *buy, v.* 1 meaning *purchase*.
5.1.72.1-2/2475.1-2 *Somerset ... City*] O (*Exit*); *not in* F
5.1.75/2478 and] O, Q2; if F, Q3
5.1.75 an] O (and)
5.1.78/2481 an] F2; in F1
5.1.80-3/2483-6 GEORGE OF CLARENCE ... WARWICKE] O; *not in* F. O seems so theatrically superior here that we must suppose either that a lacuna occurs in F (possibly the result of eyeskip from the initial 'C' in the manuscript speech-prefix 'Cla⟨rence⟩.' (5.1.80/2483)—in our text, 'GEORGE OF CLARENCE'—to the initial 'C' in the first word caught in F, 'Come' (5.1.83/2486)), or, more probably, that O here reflects revision between the foul papers, which lie behind F, and the prompt-book, from which O, indirectly, derives. See the Introduction.
5.1.84.1-2/2487.1-2 *He ... Warwicke*] O (*subs., and after* 5.1.82.2/2485.2); *not in* F
5.1.94/2497 Iephthah] F1 (*Iephah*); *Jepthah* F3; *Jepthah's* ROWE 3. McKerrow observed that the name, which occurs in Judges 11, is spelt 'Iephthah' in the Bishops' Bible (1568), and 'Iphtah' in

the Authorised Version (1611); the Geneva Bible (1560) reads 'Iphtáh'. He believed there to be no justification for the F3 form, with 'pth'. The error proposed would be an easy one to make, for it would require the compositor to skip from 'p' to the 'h' after 't', thereby omitting the intervening '-ht-'. McKerrow agreed with Rowe 3 to the extent that the grammar requires the possessive, but pointed out that 'this kind of loose construction is not unusual'.

5.1.102/2505 Brothers] O; Brother F. George immediately addresses first one, then the other, of the two brothers to whom he now turns (5.1.103-4/2506-7).
5.1.114/2517 dar'st] F, Q3; darest O, Q2
5.2.7/2526 that?] F, O; ~ ⋀ CAIRNCROSS (Vaughan)
5.2.7/2526 shewes,] F, O; ~ ? CAIRNCROSS (Vaughan)
5.2.44 canon] F (Cannon). 'Most modern editors read "clamour" which is intelligible, but gives a poor sense. I suggest that the word is "canon", in the musical sense, which appears to have been used for a part song . . . the idea being that the hollow reverberations make the words indistinguishable' (McKerrow). See *The New Oxford Companion to Music*, i. 306.
5.3.0.3/2569.4 souldiers] O; *the reſt* F
5.3.24.1/2593.1 *Flourish. March.*] This edition; not in F
5.4.27 raggèd] F (raged)
5.4.35/2628 Yorke] This edition (G.T.); not in F
5.4.82.1-5.5.17/2675.1-92 Alarum . . . ambitious Yorke.] F; for the O version of these lines, see Additional Passage B.
5.5.5.1/2680.1 *Exit Oxford*] O; not in F. See the next note.
5.5.6.1/2681.1 *Exit Somerset*] O (*Exit Sum.*); *Exeunt* F
5.5.33/2708 are all] F, O; are POPE
5.5.49/2724 The] O; not in F
5.5.76-7/2751-2 butcher,] O; butcher *Richard?* F
5.5.77/2752 thou?] F, O; ~, CAIRNCROSS
5.5.78/2753 thy] F, O; thine CAIRNCROSS (*conj.*)
5.5.83/2758 aside] This edition; not in F. 'The chroniclers record, with some conviction, Richard's supposed responsibility for Henry's death in the Tower on 23 May 1471 (Hol. 324, Hall 303), though in a later context (following More) they represent Edward as ignorant of Richard's intentions' (McKerrow). Edward's reply (5.5.85/2760) does seem more appropriate to the news that Richard is hurrying to London than to his intention to murder Henry.
5.6.0.1/2764.2-3 on the Walles] F; *in the Tower* O. 'It is doubtful where this scene is intended to take place. The quartos have "Enter *Gloster* to king *Henry* in the Tower" and this accords better with Henry being at his book than does the Folio location "on the Walles", as indeed does the reference in [5.6.93/2857] to the disposal of the body "in another roome". The Cambridge editors considered that an intentional change of scene had been made to the walls and that the reference in [5.6.93/2857] had been accidentally retained. I suspect that the arrangement is simply a device for indicating that Richard had arrived at the Tower. Probably Henry was shown as reading in his room, represented by the inner stage. Richard then arrives on the walls (i.e. in the gallery) meeting the Lieutenant there and afterwards descends and appears on the main stage' (McKerrow).

Instead of entering to the 'inner stage', King Henry may have entered to the main stage, thereby placing his murder, when it comes, well forward. On the other hand, there may have been some emblematic significance attached to Henry's murder taking place 'above'.

5.6.15/2779 Male] F, O (maile); mate KINNEAR (*conj.*); make G.T. *conj.* 'This seems to make no sense. A father cannot reasonably be described as the male of his son and there seems no point in an allusion to the Queen here. The abnormal spelling 'maile' in Qq seems to suggest that the printer did not understand the word' (McKerrow). The sense required does seem to be 'father' or 'parent', yet *OED* records no instance of 'male' having this meaning, and the parallels Cairncross cites in support of O, F are not persuasive (2.1.42/624, above, 'You loue the Breeder better then the Male', and *2 Henry IV* 3.2.128-9/1653-4, 'so the sonne of the female is the shadow of the male'). If this is an instance of O contamination of F, the original reading may be irrecoverable.

On the other hand, if one does believe 'sweet Bird' to be an allusion to the Queen, then G.T.'s is probably the superior emendation, for it carries both the sense of 'Of animals, esp. birds: A mate' and 'Of human beings: A mate, consort; a . . . wife' (*sb.*¹, 4 & 5). Shakespeare's only other use of 'make' in this sense, however, does not come until 1605 in *History of Lear* (17.35/2237).

5.6.46/2810 Tempests] O (*subs.*); Tempeſt F
5.6.47/2811 rook'd her] F; croak'd CAPELL. 'Rook'd' is usually 'explained as "ruck", i.e. crouch, squat (*O.E.D.*, ruck *v.*¹). Hart maintains that "We want here a noise, a note, or a croak". To "rook" is to "cry as a crow or raven" in Sc. dialect (Jamieson), see *O.E.D.* rook *v.*¹ 6, and the word may have been dialectal elsewhere; but the construction of such a word would hardly be reflexive' (McKerrow).
5.6.62/2826 in] F; into W.L.M. *conj.*
5.6.71/2835 I] F, Q3; That I O, Q2
5.6.75/2839 Jesus] F, O; Jesu CAIRNCROSS
5.6.80/2844 I had no father, I am like no father,] O; not in F. The sense of the O line is of sufficient complexity to make it an improbable memorial interpolation. Since O is otherwise well reported here, and given that this and the following line begin so similarly, we assume eyeskip on the part of the F compositor and adopt O.
5.6.82/2846 [Loue]] F. 'The use of square brackets where we should use quotation marks was frequent, indeed normal, at the time in serious prose, though less often met with in plays' (McKerrow).
5.6.85/2849 kept'st] F (keept'ſt), O (keptſt)
5.6.90-1/2854-5 Henry . . . rest] O (*subs.*), Q2; King *Henry*, and the Prince his Son are gone, | *Clarence* thy turne is next, and then the reſt, F; King *Henry*, and the Prince his ſonne are gone, | And *Clarence* thou art next muſt follow them, | So by one and one diſpatching all the reſt Q3. Q3 expands a single O line ('Henry and his ſonne are gone, thou *Clarence* next') to two complete verse lines. As we explain in the Introduction, our analysis of all the substantive departures by Q3 from its copy, O, leads us to conclude that the Q3 editor had reference to no authority other than his own imagination. In this instance, the Q3 variant is almost certainly related to problems of cast-off copy.

Whoever cast off these final pages of O in preparation for its use as Q3 copy, appears not to have made adequate allowance for the wider measure available to the Q3 compositor, or for the generous white space on O E7ʳ. In several cases text which occupies two typographical lines in O (E6ᵛ 9-10, 14-15, which correspond roughly with lines on Q3 sig. Q3ᵛ; E7ʳ 12-13, 26-27 and E7ʳ 14-15, which correspond with lines on Q3 sig. Q4ʳ) the Q3 compositor set as single lines, while the three-line stage direction on O E7ʳ he set on Q4ʳ as two lines. This tendency alone may have led him to find himself short as he approached the end of Q3ᵛ, but the problem was compounded by his having inadvertently omitted an O line (E6ᵛ 14: 'If anie ſparke of life remaine in thee,') earlier on this same page. Consequently, he padded out his text as he approached the point in his O copy at which he knew he must begin a new page. He interpolated a line six lines from the end of Q3ᵛ, following O E7ʳ 5, 'Vnder pretence of outward ſeeming ill,', and, as we remarked earlier, he expanded the second and third lines from the bottom of Q3ᵛ from a single O line. (He seems to have had a similar problem at the bottom of the next page, the last in the forme, where he found it necessary to expand O's 'Clarence and Gloſter, loue my louelie | Queene' (E7ᵛ 14-15) to 'Brothers of Clarence and of Gloſter, | Pray loue my louely Queene' (the fourth and fifth lines from the bottom of Q4ʳ).)

Ordinarily, variants of this kind in an unauthoritative derivative text would have no significance for an editor, but one of these Q3 expansions seems to have found its way into the Folio. F adopts the Q3 line 'King . . . gone' and combines elements of the next two Q3 lines, 'And . . . reſt', into a single line 'Clarence thy turne is next, and then the reſt,'. We postulate that the manuscript behind F was defective at this point, but not so defective that the compositor could not see that two lines of text were required, the second of which he could perhaps make out ended in 'the rest', or perhaps he assumed that, like in Q3, a rhyme for 'best', in the next line, was required to end this one. He consulted Q3, found, and adopted the whole of the 'King . . . gone' line. (That he did not go back very much further in following Q3 is evident from his not having adopted the spurious Q3 line 'Vnder . . . ill'.) He conflated the next two Q3 lines into one, however, to provide himself with the single verse line ending in 'rest' which he required. These two lines in F, therefore, have no authority.

For them we have substituted the two parallel O lines, with one emendation (see the next note). This whole speech of Gloucester's is in general well reported in O, and therefore, while these two lines may not represent precisely the two lines which the compositor could not make out in his manuscript, they probably come closer to them than those which he substituted. The second line, in particular, has the real attraction of providing a subject, 'I' ('I will difpatch . . . | Counting'), for the following line, a subject which is lost in both Q3 (which substitutes 'difpatching all . . . | Counting') and F.

5.6.90/2854 art] F; *not in* O. See the previous note.
5.7.0.3/2858.3-4 *Richard of Gloster*] F, Q3 (*subs.*); *not in* O, Q2
5.7.0.4/2858.4-5 *with the infant Prince Edward*] O (with the young prince); *not in* F
5.7.5/2863 Renownd] O (*subs.*); Renowne F. The proposed misreading on the part of the F compositor, e/d, is an easy one.
5.7.21/2879 and] O, Q2; if F, Q3
5.7.21 an] O (and)
5.7.25/2883 and] Fb; add Fa
5.7.25/2883 thou] O; that F. The copy may have read 'y^u' ('thou') which was mistaken for 'y^t' ('that').
5.7.25/2883 shalt] F, O; shall BROOKE (Vaughan)
5.7.27/2885 kis] Fb; 'tis Fa
5.7.30/2888 LADY GRAY] O (*Queen.*); Cla⟨rence⟩. F
5.7.30/2888 Thankes] O, F2; Thanke F1
5.7.42/2900 rests] Fb; tefts Fa
5.7.46.1/2904.1 *Flourish.*] This edition (S.W.W.); *not in* F

Additional Passages

B.1 ALL THE LANCASTER PARTY] O (*All.*)
B.1.6 *flourish*] This edition; found O
B.2 Now] F; Lo O
B.5 Goe beare them hence,] F; Awaie O
B.8 *Edward*] F; Now *Edward* O
B.9 stirring vp my Subiects to rebellion] O; stirring my Subiects to rebellion W.L.M. *conj.*; stirring vp my Subiects to rebell W.L.M. *conj.*

REJECTED OCTAVO VARIANTS

1.1.18/18 But] What
1.1.41/41 depos'd] be depofde
1.1.78/78 It was] Twas
1.1.93/93 Yes] No
1.1.134/134 against . . . King] gainft . . . foueraigne
1.1.144/144 Lords] Lord
1.1.145/145 'twere] that were
1.1.145/145 his] the
1.1.198/198 this . . . Warre] thefe . . . | Broiles
1.1.260/260 thou wilt] wilt thou
1.1.265/265 how] her
1.2.38/312 Norfolke] Norffolke ftraight
1.2.55/329 Brother] Cofen
1.3.16/365 asunder] in funder
1.4.36/437 as] like
1.4.113/514 poysons] poifon'd
1.4.116/517 their] his
1.4.121/522 Were] Twere
1.4.146/547 Wind blowes] F; windes blowes O, Q2; windes blow Q3
1.4.152/553 That] As
1.4.152/553 my] mine
1.4.161/562 tell'st] tell
1.4.171/572 should] could
2.1.21/603 See] *Edw.* Loe
2.1.30/612 inuiolable] inuiolate
2.1.32/614 Heauen figures] heauens doth figure
2.1.119/701 Oath] heires
2.1.125/707 her] his
2.1.132/714 strucke] fmote
2.1.144/726 Soldiers] power
2.1.172/754 swore] fware
2.2.174/756 And] But
2.1.182/764 march] march amaine
2.1.190/772 failst] faints
2.2.72/863 are] be
2.2.101/892 the] thy
2.2.112/903 *Clifford*] *Clifford* there
2.2.153/944 to] till
2.2.166/957 hath] haue
2.2.175/966 *Edward*] *Edward* ftaie
2.3.1/969 Fore-spent] Sore fpent
2.5.92/1129 O] Poore
2.5.92-3/1129-30 soone . . . late] late . . . fone
2.6.6/1182 fall, thy] die, that
2.6.9/1185 flye] flies
2.6.41/1217 is] be
2.6.72/1248 While] Whilft
2.6.78/1254 spare] foord
2.6.80/1256 two] an
2.6.96/1272 Coronation] coronation done
3.2.23/1409 Blow] clap
3.2.25/1411 God forbid that] Marie godsforbot man
3.2.25/1411 vantages] vantage then
3.2.132/1518 place] plant
3.3.88/1669 it] that
3.3.89/1670 hath] had
3.3.102/1683 My] mine
3.3.106/1687 while] whilft
3.3.163/1744 these Letters are] this letter is
3.3.165/1746 These] This
3.3.229/1810 are] be
4.1.20/1866 forbid] forefend
4.1.102/1948 are] be
4.2.0.1/1992.2 *in England*] *not in* O
4.2.0.2/1992.3 *French*] *not in* O
4.2.1/1993 Lord] Lords
4.2.2.1/1994.1 *Enter . . . Somerset*] *not in* O
4.2.28/2020 Why] Cla⟨rence⟩. Why
4.4.5/2053 Embassade] embaffage
4.4.18/2066 as] a
4.4.28/2076 Ile follow you, and] Ile come and
4.6.16/2136 Brother of Gloster, Lord Hastings, and] brother and
4.9.3/2342 Hath] Is
5.1.85/2488 my] mine
5.2.10/2529 foe] foes
5.2.44/2563 Cannon] clamor
5.4.75/2668 my eye] mine eies
5.4.80/2673 is] ftandes
5.5.36/2711 are] be

RICHARD DUKE OF YORK

5.5.57/2732　name it] name
5.5.85/2760　comes] come
5.6.15/2780　my] mine
5.6.28/2792　my] mine
5.6.51/2815　indigested and deformed] vndigeſt created
5.6.55/2819　which] that

5.6.56/2820　cam'st—] camſt into the world
5.6.81/2845　Brother . . . Brother] brothers . . . brothers O, Q3; brother . . . brothers Q2
5.6.88/2852　That] As
5.7.44/2902　pleasure] pleaſures

INCIDENTALS

30 dye.] ~:　　116 honor'st] honoreſt　　384 Therefore—] ~ ---　　519 deedes,] ~.　　678 recompt] tecompt　　694 gathred] gathered　　706 Spleene,] ~.　　758 house] houſe　　896 thine.] ~:　　898 your] yout　　1115 griefe.] ~ˌ　　1126 Stratagems] Stragems　　1131 common greefe!] ~ˌ　　1159 murthred] murthered　　1182 fall, thy] ~. Thy　　1195 Had] Hed　　1260 satisfie.] ~ˌ　　1298 past.] ~:　　1366 king.] ~ˌ　　1677 obeydest] obeyd'ſt　　1737 Peace, impudent,] ~, ~,　　2111 informed] inform'd　　2143 meaning.] ~ˌ　　2156 Sou'rains:] ~ˌ　　2160 kindnesse,] ~.　　2481 right,] ~,　　2565 deliuered] deliuered　　2577 arriu'd] arriued　　2675.4 Somerset] Sum.　　2740 off,] ~.　　2755 hence.] ~,　　2767 'Tis]ˌ~　　2768 ˌGood] '~　　2787 Boy,] ~.　　2832 feare.] ~,　　2874 Yong] Fb; Kong Fa

FOLIO STAGE DIRECTIONS

1.1.0.1–5/0.1–4　Alarum. | Enter Plantagenet, Edward, Richard, Norfolke, Mount-|ague, Warwicke, and Souldiers.
1.1.32.1/32.1　They goe vp.
1.1.49.2–4/49.2–3　Flourish. Enter King Henry, Clifford, Northumberland, | Westmerland, Exeter, and the rest.
1.1.170.1–2/170.1–2　He stampes with his foot, and the Souldiers | shew themselues.
1.1.203.1, 1.1.206.1/203.1, 206.1　Senet. Here they come downe. (after 1.1.206.1/206.1)
1.1.211.2/211.2　Enter the Queene.
1.1.274.1/274.1　Exit.
1.2.0.1–2/274.2　Flourish. Enter Richard, Edward, and | Mountague.
1.2.3.1/277.1　Enter the Duke of Yorke.
1.2.47.1/321.1　Enter Gabriel.
1.2.61/335　Exit Mountague.
1.2.61.1/335.1　Enter Mortimer, and his Brother.
1.2.68.1/342.1　A March afarre off.
1.2.75/349.1　Alarum. Exit.
1.3.0.1–2/349.2–3　Enter Rutland, and his Tutor.
1.3.1.1/350.1　Enter Clifford. (after 1.3.2/351)
1.3.9.1/358.1　Exit.
1.3.52.1/401.1　Exit.
1.4.0.1/401.2　Alarum. Enter Richard, Duke of Yorke.
1.4.22.1/423.1　A short Alarum within.
1.4.27.1–3/428.1–3　Enter the Queene, Clifford, Northumberland, | the young Prince, and Souldiers.
1.4.181.1/582.1　Flourish. Exit.
2.1.0.1–2/582.2–3　A March. Enter Edward, Richard, | and their power.
2.1.42.1/624.1　Enter one blowing.
2.1.94.1–3/676.1–2　March. Enter Warwicke, Marquesse Mountacute, | and their Army.
2.1.204.1/786.1　Enter a Messenger.
2.1.209.1/791.1　Exeunt Omnes.
2.2.0.2–4/791.3–5　Flourish. Enter the King, the Queene, Clifford, Northum-| and Yong Prince, with Drumme and | Trumpettes.
2.2.66.1/857.1　Enter a Messenger.
2.2.80.1–3/871.1–2　March. Enter Edward, Warwicke, Richard, Clarence, | Norfolke, Mountague, and Soldiers.
2.2.177.1–3/968.1–3　Exeunt omnes.
2.3.0.1/968.4　Alarum. Excursions. Enter Warwicke.
2.3.5.1/973.1　Enter Edward running.
2.3.8.1/976.1　Enter Clarence.
2.3.13.1/981.1　Enter Richard.
2.3.56/1024　Exeunt
2.4.0.1–2/1024.1–2　Excursions. Enter Richard and Clifford.
2.4.11.1–2/1035.1–2　They Fight, Warwicke comes, Clifford flies.
2.4.13/1037　Exeunt.
2.5.0.1/1037.1　Alarum. Enter King Henry alone.

2.5.54.1–2/1091.1–2　Alarum. Enter a Sonne that hath kill'd his Father, at | one doore:
2.5.78.1–2/1115.1–2　and a Father that hath kill'd his Sonne at ano-|ther doore. (after 2.5.54.2/1091.2)
2.5.78.1–2/1115.1–2　Enter Father, bearing of his Sonne.
2.5.122.1/1159.1–2　Exit
2.5.124.1, 127.1, 133.1/1161.1, 1164.1, 1170.1　Alarums. Excursions. Enter the Queen, the | Prince, and Exeter. (after 2.5.124/1161)
2.5.139/1176　Exeunt
2.6.0.1/1176.1　A lowd alarum. Enter Clifford Wounded.
2.6.30.2–4/1206.2–3　Alarum & Retreat. Enter Edward, Warwicke, Richard, and | Soldiers, Montague, & Clarence.
2.6.41.1/1217.1　Clifford grones
2.6.110.1/1286.1　Exeunt
3.1.0.1–2/1286.2　Enter Sinklo, and Humfrey, with Crosse-bowes | in their hands.
3.1.12.2/1298.2–3　Enter the King with a Prayer booke.
3.1.100/1386　Exeunt
3.2.0.1–2/1386.2–3　Enter K. Edward, Gloster, Clarence, Lady Gray.
3.2.117.1/1503.1　Enter a Noble man.
3.2.123.1/1509.1　Exeunt.
3.2.123.1/1509.1　Manet Richard.
3.2.195/1581　Exit.
3.3.0.1–5/1581.1–5　Flourish. | Enter Lewis the French King, his Sister Bona, his | Admirall, call'd Bourbon: Prince Edward, | Queene Margaret, and the Earle of Oxford. | Lewis sits, and riseth vp againe.
3.3.16/1597　Seats her by him.
3.3.42.1/1623.1　Enter Warwicke. (after 3.3.43/1624)
3.3.46.1/1627.1　Hee descends. Shee ariseth.
3.3.59/1640　Speaking to Bona. (after 'Madame')
3.3.111.1–2/1692.1–2　They stand aloofe.
3.3.131/1712　Speaks to War. (after 'day')
3.3.160.1/1741.1　Post blowing a horne Within.
3.3.162.1/1743.1　Enter the Poste.
3.3.163/1744　Speakes to Warwick, (after 'you')
3.3.165/1746　To Lewis. (after 'Maiesty')
3.3.166/1747　To Margaret (after 'you')
3.3.166.1/1747.1　They all reade their Letters.
3.3.233.1/1814　Exit Post.
3.3.250.1/1831.1　He giues his hand to Warw.
3.3.255.1/1836.1　Exeunt. Manet Warwicke.
3.3.265.1/1846　Exit.
4.1.0.1–3/1846.1–2　Enter Richard, Clarence, Somerset, and | Mountague.
4.1.6.1–4/1852.1–3　Flourish. | Enter King Edward, Lady Grey, Penbrooke, Staf-|ford, Hastings: foure stand on one side, | and foure on the other.
4.1.82.1/1928.1　Enter a Poste.

207

RICHARD DUKE OF YORK

4.1.121.1/1967.1 *Exit Clarence, and Somerset followes.*
4.1.130.1/1976.1 *Exeunt Pembrooke and Stafford.*
4.1.146/1992.1 *Exeunt.*
4.2.0.1-2/1992.2-3 *Enter Warwicke and Oxford in England, | with French Souldiors.*
4.2.2.1/1994.1 *Enter Clarence and Somerset.*
4.2.27.1/2019.1 *They all cry, Henry.*
4.2.29.1/2021.1 *Exeunt.*
4.3.0.1-2/2021.2-3 *Enter three Watchmen to guard the Kings Tent.*
4.3.22.1-3/2043.1-2 *Enter Warwicke, Clarence, Oxford, Somerset, | and French Souldiors, silent all.*
4.3.27.1-3/2048.1-4 *Warwicke and the rest cry all, Warwicke, Warwicke, | and set vpon the Guard, who flye, crying, Arme, Arme, | Warwicke and the rest following them.*
4.4.0.1-5/2048.5-9 *The Drumme playing, and Trumpet sounding. | Enter Warwicke, Somerset, and the rest, bringing the King | out in his Gowne, sitting in a Chaire: Richard | and Hastings flyes ouer the Stage.*
4.4.21.1/2069.1 *Takes off his Crowne.*
4.4.30.1/2078.1 *They leade him out forcibly.*
4.4.32.1/2080.1 *Exeunt.*
4.4.37/2085 *exit.*
4.5.0.1/2085.1 *Enter Riuers, and Lady Gray.*
4.5.35/2120 *exeunt.*
4.6.0.1-2/2120.1-2 *Enter Richard, Lord Hastings, and Sir William | Stanley.*
4.6.13.1/2133.1 *Enter King Edward, and a Huntsman | with him.*
4.6.30/2150 *exeunt*
4.7.0.1-6/2150.1-5 *Flourish. Enter King Henry the sixt, Clarence, Warwicke, | Somerset, young Henry, Oxford, Mountague, | and Lieutenant.*
4.7.68/2218 *Layes his Hand on his Head.*
4.7.76.1/2226.1 *Enter a Poste.*
4.7.88.1/2238.1 *Exeunt.*
4.7.88.1/2238.1-2 *Manet Somerset, Richmond, and Oxford.*
4.7.102/2252 *Exeunt.*
4.8.0.1-3/2252.1-2 *Flourish. Enter Edward, Richard, Hastings, | and Souldiers.*
4.8.16.2/2268.2-3 *Enter on the Walls, the Maior of Yorke, | and his Brethren.*
4.8.29.1/2281.1 *He descends.*
4.8.34.1/2286.1 *Enter the Maior, and two Aldermen.*
4.8.37.1/2289.1 *Takes his Keyes.*
4.8.39.1-2/2291.1-2 *March. Enter Mountgomerie, with Drumme | and Souldiers.*
4.8.50.1/2302.1 *The Drumme begins to march.*
4.8.70.1/2322.1 *Flourish. Sound.*
4.8.74.1/2326.1 *Throwes downe his Gauntlet.*
4.8.87.1/2339 *Excunt.*
4.9.0.1-3/2339.1-2 *Flourish. Enter the King, Warwicke, Mountague, | Clarence, Oxford, and Somerset.*

4.9.32.1/2371.1 *Exeunt.*
4.10.18.1/2389.1 *Shout within, A Lancaster, A Lancaster.*
4.10.19.1-2/2390.1-2 *Enter Edward and his Souldiers.*
4.10.25.1/2396.1 *Exit with King Henry.*
4.10.32.1/2403.1 *Exeunt.*
5.1.0.1-2/2403.2-3 *Enter Warwicke, the Maior of Couentry, two | Messengers, and others vpon the Walls.*
5.1.6.1/2409.1 *Enter Someruile.*
5.1.10.1, 15.1-2/2413.1, 2418.1-2 *March. Flourish. Enter Edward, Richard, | and Souldiers. (after 5.1.15/2418)*
5.1.57.1-2/2460.1-2 *Enter Oxford, with Drumme and Colours.*
5.1.66.1-2/2469.1-2 *Enter Mountague, with Drumme and Colours.*
5.1.71.1-2/2474.1-2 *Enter Somerset, with Drumme and Colours.*
5.1.75.1-2/2478.1-2 *Enter Clarence, with Drumme and Colours.*
5.1.116.1/2519.1 *Exeunt.*
5.1.116.2-3/2519.2-3 *March. Warwicke and his companie followes.*
5.2.0.1-2/2519.4-5 *Alarum, and Excursions. Enter Edward bringing | forth Warwicke wounded.*
5.2.4/2523.1 *Exit.*
5.2.28.1/2547.1 *Enter Oxford and Somerset.*
5.2.50.1/2569.1 *Here they beare away his Body. Exeunt.*
5.3.0.1-3/2569.2-4 *Flourish. Enter King Edward in triumph, with | Richard, Clarence, and the rest.*
5.3.24.1/2593.1 *Exeunt.*
5.4.0.1-3/2593.2-3 *Flourish. March. Enter the Queene, young | Edward, Somerset, Oxford, and | Souldiers.*
5.4.59.1/2652.1 *Enter a Messenger.*
5.4.66.1-3/2659.1-2 *Flourish, and march. Enter Richard, | Clarence, and Souldiers.*
5.4.82.1/2675.1 *Alarum, Retreat, Excursions. Exeunt.*
5.5.0.1-4/2675.2-4 *Flourish. Enter Edward, Richard, Queene, Clarence, | Oxford, Somerset.*
5.5.5.1, 5.5.6.1/2680.1, 2681.1 *Exeunt. (after 5.5.6.1/2681.1)*
5.5.11.1/2686.1 *Enter the Prince.*
5.5.38.1/2713.1 *Stabs him.*
5.5.39.1/2714.1 *Rich. stabs him.*
5.5.40.1/2715.1 *Clar. stabs him.*
5.5.41.1/2716.1 *Offers to kill her.*
5.5.49/2724.1 *Exit.*
5.5.81.1/2756.1 *Exit Queene.*
5.5.89/2764 *Exit.*
5.6.0.1-3/2764.1-3 *Enter Henry the sixt, and Richard, with the Lieutenant | on the Walles.*
5.6.57.1/2821.1 *Stabbes him.*
5.6.60/2824 *Dyes.*
5.6.67.1/2831.1 *Stabs him againe.*
5.6.94.1/2858.1 *Exit.*
5.7.0.1-5/2858.2-5 *Flourish. Enter King, Queene, Clarence, Richard, Hastings, | Nurse, and Attendants.*
5.7.46.1/2904.1 *Exeunt omnes*

TITUS ANDRONICUS

On 6 February 1594 John Danter entered in the Stationers' Register 'a booke intituled a Noble Roman Historye of Tytus Andronicus' along with 'the ballad thereof'. The 'Historye' is not certainly the play, which however Danter printed in that year (*BEPD* 117). Haggard, from an analysis of damaged types, concluded that Q was set from a single case by one compositor; MacDonald P. Jackson has suggested, on the basis of variant spellings, that sheets A–E were set by a different compositor from F–K ('The Year's Contributions to Shakespearian Study: Textual Studies', *SSu 38* (1985), p. 248). This first quarto (Q1) was reprinted in 1600 (Q2) and 1611 (Q3). Q1 is agreed to derive from the author's manuscript ('foul papers') in an unpolished state. The single surviving copy, discovered only in 1904, is in the Folger Shakespeare Library. A facsimile with an introduction by J. Q. Adams appeared in 1936. Q2 was reprinted from a damaged copy of Q1. The lacunae were filled in, most conspicuously and fancifully by a substantially new version of the play's last line, followed by the addition of four extra lines. Some invention was displayed, but the changes (listed by Waith; see his Introduction, pp. 37–8) have no demonstrable authority. There are numerous other substantive changes, many clearly intended as improvements, including the omission of three and a half lines apparently inconsistent with their context (see textual note to 1.1.35/35). Because we know only one copy of Q1, the possibility that Q2 preserves readings from corrected formes not found in this copy is unusually open (for example 5.3.26/2327). Eight substantive Q2 readings are accepted in the present edition. Q3 is a page-by-page reprint of Q2, with some corrections and corruptions. F, printed from a copy of Q3, makes additional minor corrections and corruptions, one obviously the result of censorship (4.2.71/1598). More importantly, certain changes, particularly to stage directions, and the addition of an entire scene (3.2/Sc. 6), indicate that the copy of Q3 used by the printers had been annotated by comparison with another source, probably the prompt-book. As usual, the annotation appears to be unsystematic, but it provides information about staging which is properly incorporated into an edited text, and as some of its variants may be authorial, we list those that we do not accept. There is no reason to question Shakespeare's authorship of the added scene, which probably dates from about 1594 (see Waith). The Folio also adds one probably authentic complete line (1.1.395/395) and a mysterious short one of only two words (see note to 4.1.36/1435), along with act (but not scene) divisions which are probably unauthoritative, but which appear to reflect later stage practice. The division at the end of Act 1 causes Aaron to exit and re-enter instead of remaining on stage; that at the end of Act 3 (after the interpolated 'fly' scene) requires a whole set of characters to re-enter immediately after leaving the stage. Since, therefore, the act divisions must be regarded as integral to the structure of the play in its revised form, we accord them equal prominence to those in the late plays.

As well as the three and a half lines already mentioned, Q1 contains two other passages probably intended for deletion; both are printed as Additional Passages. Staging presents peculiar problems; in an attempt to clarify it we have added more directions than are customary. A discussion of the staging of Act 1 forms Chapter 4 of Wells's *Re-Editing Shakespeare*; it sets out a hypothesis of revision which is acted upon in this edition. The appendix to that book offers an attempted reconstruction of Shakespeare's first draft of Act 1.

The textual notes record such of our additions and substantive alterations to stage directions as are first found in the Folio or in an intermediate quarto. F's non-substantive changes of quarto directions are not recorded. In the dialogue, F's divergences from Q1 are recorded only when adopted, except for a few readings of exceptional interest. As Q1 diverges from the convention of representing syllabic -ed endings in over thirty instances, such endings are not regularized in our old-spelling text. The aside at 1.1.438/438 is apparently signalled in Q1 by indentation of a verse line; that at 4.4.34/1853 is explicitly directed in F.

We are indebted to Professor T. W. Craik for a number of suggestions concerning the text.

S.W.W./(G.T.)

WORKS CITED

Barnet, Sylvan, ed., *Titus Andronicus*, Signet (1964)
Bolton, Joseph S. G., 'The Authentic Text of *Titus Andronicus*', *PMLA* 44 (1929), 776–80
Haggard, F. E., 'The Printing of Shakespeare's *Titus Andronicus*, 1594' (unpublished Ph.D. thesis, University of Kansas, 1966)
Maxwell, J. C., ed., *Titus Andronicus*, Arden (1961, rev. 1968)
Ravenscroft, Edward, *Titus Andronicus; or the Rape of Lavinia* (1687)
Waith, Eugene M., ed., *Titus Andronicus*, Oxford (1984)
Wilson, John Dover, ed., *Titus Andronicus*, New (1948)

TEXTUAL NOTES

Title *The most Lamentable Romaine Tragedie of Titus Andronicus*] Q (*head title; title-page* THE MOST LA-|mentable . . .); The moſt lamentable Tragedie of Titus Andronicus Q (*running titles; sometimes* 'Lamentable'); a Noble Roman Historye of Tytus Andronicus S.R.; The Lamentable Tragedy of Titus Andronicus. F (*head title*); *The Tragedie of Titus Andronicus.* F (*running titles*); *Titus Andronicus.* F (*table of contents, among* 'TRAGEDIES'). F1 follows the title-page of Q3 in omitting 'Romaine' from the title.

1.1.0.1/0.1 Flourish] F; *not in* Q
1.1.0.3-4/0.3-4 at the other] F; *not in* Q
1.1.0.4/0.4 Drum and Colours] F; *Drums and Trumpets* Q
1.1.1/1 SATURNINE] The metrical variant 'Saturnine' preponderates in Q's speech-prefixes and dialogue; 'Saturninus' is more common in directions.
1.1.17.1/17.1 Enter] F; *not in* Q
1.1.17.1/17.1 aloft] F; *not in* Q. Q's centred direction is often interpreted as implying simply that Marcus is here seen to be holding the crown; perhaps that he steps forward with it, or is handed it. But there is no proof that Marcus 'has been on stage with the other Tribunes from the beginning of the scene' (Maxwell), whereas F's additions provide evidence for the alternative interpretation.
1.1.18/18 MARCUS] ROWE; *not in* Q
1.1.35/35 field.] Q1 has an additional three and a half lines, printed as Additional Passage A. The omission, found in Q2 and subsequent editions, is generally held to stem from apparent conflict between the statement that Titus has 'at this day ... Done sacrifice of expiation | And slaine the Noblest prisoner of the *Gothes*' and the fact that this act is portrayed later (1.1.96/96 ff.). We agree with H. F. Brooks (in Maxwell) that '"at this day" *could* conceivably mean "on the day corresponding to this"'; and Q2's omission may have no authority. Nevertheless, the absence of Alarbus' name from the direction at 1.1.69.6/69.6, along with the self-contained nature of the sacrificial episode and the close resemblance between 'the Noblest prisoner of the *Gothes*' and 'the prowdest prisoner of the *Gothes*' (1.1.96/96), justifies the assumption that the episode was an afterthought and so that these lines are redundant.
1.1.40/40 succeeded] CAPELL; fucceede Q. Maxwell, interpreting 'succeed' as an infinitive, supposes that 'the ground of Marcus' appeal to the factions seems to be the respect each of them feels for its own candidate', but this requires him to be addressing 'you' to the groups in 1.1.40/40 and 1.1.42/42 but to individual leaders in (probably) 1.1.43/43 and (certainly) in 1.1.44/44 and 1.1.45/45. The line remains awkward in its use of the past tense, as the leaders still wish to succeed. Riverside takes 'succeede' as a contracted past participle, but this seems incommunicable.
1.1.63.1/63.1 Flourish.] F; *not in* Q
1.1.64/64 CAPTAINE] *not in* Q
1.1.69.2-3/69.2-3 men bearing Coffins] This edition; *two men bearing a Coffin* QF. More than one corpse is to be interred (1.1.83, 87, 89/83, 87, 89). At 1.1.149.2/149.2 F alters Q's 'Coffin' to 'Coffins'; this may reflect consultation of the prompt-book (though the anomaly remains elsewhere); in any case, common sense requires the change.
1.1.69.4-5/69.5 in his Chariot] WAITH (subs.); *not in* QF
1.1.69.8/69.8 Coffins] This edition; *Coffin* QF
1.1.71 freight] Q (fraught)
1.1.78 rites] Q (rights)
1.1.98/98 manes] F3; *manus* Q
1.1.104/104 kneeling] WAITH; *not in* QF. At 1.1.451-2/451-2 Tamora makes clear that (as would be natural) she has knelt here. This provides a dramatic contrast when Titus kneels, to her and Saturninus, at 1.1.422.1/422.1 or 1.1.424.1/424.1.
1.1.110/110 triumphs, and returne,] Q; triumphs and return, THEOBALD
1.1.138/138 his] Q; her THEOBALD. See Waith.
1.1.141/141 quit her] ROWE; quit the Q; quite these CAPELL (conj.)
1.1.143 rites] QF (rights)
1.1.149.1/149.1 ⌜Flourish.⌝ Then sound] F; *Sound* Q. Possibly F unnecessarily duplicates Q's direction; but a 'Flourish' could include drums and horns, so two soundings may be intended.
1.1.149.2/149.2 Coffins] F; *Coffin* Q
1.1.157/157 LAUINIA] *not in* Q
1.1.160/160 obsequies] In the unique copy of Q1 a contemporary hand has substituted 'exequies'.
1.1.226/226 Tytăs] Q2 (Tytans); Tytus Q1
1.1.231-3/231-3 Patricians ... Lord ... And] Q2; *damage to the single copy of Q1 leaves only 'tricians ... d ... d'*

1.1.233.1/233.1 A long ... downe] F; *not in* Q
1.1.242/242 Pāthean] F2 (*Panthæon*); Pathan QF
1.1.264/264 chance] Q2; change Q1
1.1.270/270 Lauinia] Q (text); ~. Q (c.w.)
1.1.275.1/275.1 Flourish] Capell's direction seems necessary.
1.1.275.1-2/275.1-2 Exeunt ... moore] This edition (*after* McKerrow, *galleys*); *not in* QF; *The Emperor Courts Tamora in dumb shew* ROWE (*after* 1.1.279/279); *Saturninus addresses Tamora* CAPELL. The imperial party must leave the stage at some point in order to return 'aloft' at 1.1.294.2/294.2. For the theory that Q misrepresents Shakespeare's final intentions by failing to delete lines intended for omission after the addition of the killing of Mutius, see *Re-Editing*, 100-1.
1.1.280/280 cuique] F2; *cuiqum* Q1; *cuiquam* Q3, F1
1.1.283/283 gard?] This edition (G.T.). QF have 4 lines here (reproduced in Additional Passages). See note to 1.1.275.1-2/275.1-2
1.1.287.1/287.1 Titus kils him] F (*He kils him*); *not in* Q
1.1.294.1/294.1 with Mutius body] This edition (G.T.); *not in* QF. See *Re-Editing*, 103.
1.1.295/295 Follow ... backe] *as here* This edition; *after* 1.1.285/285 QF. For the theory that this line is misplaced, see *Re-Editing*, 101.
1.1.301/301 Was none] Q1; *Was there none els* F2 (*adding of at end of line*)
1.1.313/313 Phebe] F2; *Thebe* Q1
1.1.330/330 Queene Panthean:] POPE (subs.); *Queene: Panthean,* QF
1.1.337.2/337.2 carrying Mutius body] This edition (G.T.); *not in* QF. See *Re-Editing*, 103.
1.1.355/355 QUINTUS *and* MARTIUS] CAPELL; *Titus two fonnes fpeakes* Q; *Martius* WAITH (Bolton)
1.1.357/357 QUINTUS] ROWE; *Titus fonne fpeakes* Q; *Martius* CAPELL
1.1.361 struck] Q (ftroke)
1.1.365/365 MARTIUS] MALONE; *3. Sonne* Q; *1. Sonne* F; *Lucius* ROWE; *Quintus* CAPELL
1.1.366, 368/366, 368 QUINTUS] ROWE; *2. Sonne* QF; *Martius* CAPELL
1.1.384 friends'] Q (friends)
1.1.386/386 ALL ⌜BUT TITUS⌝ (kneeling)] This edition; *they all kneele and fay* QF
1.1.387.1/387.1 Exit ⌜all but Marcus and Titus⌝] Q (subs.); *Exit* F; *no direction* ROWE; *All but Marcus and Titus stand aside* KITTREDGE. Q's direction can be retained by supposing that Titus' sons are the 'others' of 1.1.395.6/395.6 (G.T.).
1.1.395/395 MARCUS] DYCE (Malone); *not in* F
1.1.395/395 Yes ... remunerate.] F; *not in* Q
1.1.395.1/395.1 Flourish.] F; *not in* Q
1.1.395.5/395.5 Lucius, Quintus, and Martius] This edition (G.T.); *others* QF. See note to 1.1.387.1/387.1.
1.1.422.1/422.1 He kneeles] *as here* This edition; *after* 1.1.424/424, BEVINGTON; *not in* QF. It is clear from 1.1.456/456 that Titus kneels, and there is no other convenient opportunity for him to do so. The length of time he is on his knees would be dramatically significant in itself.
1.1.438.1/438.1 Aside] F; *not in* Q
1.1.470.1/470.1 Bassianus] Not usually listed; but he is no less implicated than the others.
1.1.471/471 LUCIUS] ROWE (*after* F); *not in* Q; *All.* Q3; *Son.* F. Lucius normally acts as spokesman (e.g. 1.1.371, 384/371, 384); but more than one son may speak.
1.1.474/474 MARCUS ⌜kneeling⌝] He is usually supposed to kneel with the others at 1.1.470.2/470.2, but Tamora has not mentioned him, he has been with Titus rather than with Bassianus and his followers, and he may effectively kneel in their support.
1.1.482/482 Stand vp] *as here* Q; *as stage direction* POPE
1.1.491-2.1.0.1/491-491.1 ⌜Flourish. Exeunt⌝ | ⌜Enter Aron alone⌝] *after* F (*Exeunt. | Actus Secunda. | Flourifh. Enter Aaron alone.*); *Exeunt. | found trumpets, manet Moore.* Q. Clearly the trumpet call, or flourish, should accompany the *Exeunt*. Shakespeare seems originally to have intended Aaron to remain on stage. F's

new direction is explicitly theatrical, not obviously a simple literary addition of an act-break; it probably reflects late performances of the play. The suggestion of a break in time adds to the plausibility of the action, and would be convenient for the removal of a stage property representing the tomb.

2.1.14/515 mount her pitch] Q. Repetition of 'mount' from the previous line raises suspicion; G.T. conjectures 'fly her pitch', a phrase which occurs at *1 Henry VI* 2.4.11/830, *Contention* 2.1.6/668, and *Caesar* 1.1.73/73. There is no Shakespearian parallel to 'mount her pitch'.

2.1.26/517 yeares wants] Q, F1; years want F2
2.1.26/517 wits wants] Q1; wit wants Q2; wits want WILSON
2.1.69/560 and] Q: an CAPELL (*after* Q)
2.1.93 struck] Q (ſtroke)
2.1.110/601 than] ROWE; this Q
2.1.123/614 with all] F; withall Q
2.1.123/614 what] Q1; that Q2
2.1.136/627 *Per Stigia, per manes Vehor*] F; *Per Styga, per amnes igneos amnes vehor* T. W. Craik (*conj.*). Craik writes: 'i.e. the whole Senecan phrase, but adapted to the present situation by altering *sequar* to *vehor*. The compositor set what he could read—making a transposition error in the process—and omitted the two words he couldn't.' But, as Binns notes (p. 122), Shakespeare seems elsewhere to quote Seneca imperfectly, as if from memory, or to adapt.
2.1.136 *Styga*] Q (*Stigia*)
2.2.0.2/627.2 *and Marcus*] F (*at end of direction*); *not in* Q
2.2.1/628 Morne] Q3; Moone Q1
2.2.14/641 Lords] Q; lord DYCE
2.2.24/651 runne] F2; runnes Q1. Q could be defended, taking 'game' as the subject of 'runnes', but to assume that the simile refers to the 'horse' and that 'runne' is in apposition to 'follow' makes a better parallel with the previous speech.
2.3.13/666 snakes] Q1; ſnake Q3. A northern plural.
2.3.20/673 yellowing] Q; yelping F
2.3.33/686 and] Q2; ann Q1
2.3.63/716 the] QF; thy G.T. *conj*. It was Actaeon's own hounds that attacked him; *the* may have this meaning, but 'thy' would be more pointed, and contrast with '*his* hounds' (2.3.70/723).
2.3.64/717 driue] Q; dine COLLIER 2 (*appropriate to this play, and graphically close to 'driue'*)
2.3.69/722 trie experiments] Q2; trie thy experimens Q1
2.3.72/725 swarte] F (ſwarth); ſwartie Q
2.3.85/738 note] POPE; notice Q
2.3.88/741 haue I] F2; I haue QF. Q can be defended (as by Maxwell) but Tamora is not conspicuously patient.
2.3.115/768 yee not hence forward] This edition (G.T.); yee not hence forth Q; yee not from henceforth POPE; not henceforth CAPELL. The same error occurs in Q2 of *Contention*. Henceforward occurs 6 times elsewhere: in *1 Henry VI*, *Contention* (2), *Duke of York*, and *Romeo* (2)—all early plays.
2.3.118 Ay,] Q (I,)
2.3.117.2/770.2 *Tamora turnes to Lauinia*] This edition; *not in* QF. Some threatening action must provoke Lavinia's words.
2.3.126/779 quainte] This edition; painted QF. Q's sense and metre are both 'awkward' (Maxwell). Many emendations have been proposed, most requiring alteration of two or more words. Alice Walker suggested 'paulled' ('pall'd'), meaning 'weakened' (*RES*, NS 6 (1955), 81). 'Quaint' makes better sense: a compositor finding its initial letters difficult to read might have guessed at 'painte' and turned it into a past participle to fit the context. The sense is not unlike *1 Henry VI* 4.1.102-3/1658-9, 'though he seeme with forged queint conceite | To set a gloſse vpon his bold intent'.
2.3.131/784 ye desire] F2; we deſire Q. Modern editors tend to follow Q (see Maxwell, and Sisson, *New Readings*) but it gives only a strained sense.
2.3.132/785 out liue vs] Q (*modernized by Theobald to* 'out-live, us'); o'er live, us MAXWELL (*conj.*); outliu't, us G.T. *conj*.
2.3.144 sucked'st] Q (ſuckſt)
2.3.153/806 Some] Q2; So me Q1

2.3.158/811 thee: for] THEOBALD; thee for Q
2.3.180/833 satisfie] Q (ſatiſfiee). See Waith.
2.3.186.2/839.2 *and couer the mouth of it with branches*] WAITH; *not in* Q
2.3.191/844 *Exit*] F; *not in* Q
2.3.192/845 ARON] *not in* Q
2.3.210/863 vnhallowd] F; vnhollow Q
2.3.222/875 bereied] WILSON; bereaud Q1; embrewed Q2-3, F1. Q1 has a contemporary, manuscript, alteration of 'bereaud in blood' to 'heere reav'd of lyfe'.
2.3.222/875 in blood] Q1; heere Q2-3, F
2.3.231/884 Piramus] Q2; Priamus Q1
2.3.236/889 Cocitus] F2; Ocitus Q1
2.3.245.1/898.1 *He falls into the pit*] *not in* Q; *Boths fall in.* F
2.3.260/913 gripde] MAXWELL; griude Q
2.3.276/929] The early editions, not printing a prefix at 2.3.268/921, print the prefix '*King.*' (i.e. Saturninus) here.
2.3.291/944 fault] THEOBALD (Ravenscroft); faults Q
2.3.296 father's] Q (Fathers)
2.3.301/954 the] QF; their COLLIER 2
2.3.303/956 *Exit*] This edition (G.T.); *not in* QF. Q fails to provide many necessary directions. Saturninus must not overhear Tamora's words to Titus; though he may not have left the stage, he must be preparing to do so.
2.3.306.1/959.1 *Exeunt*] F; *not in* Q
2.4.10.2/969.2 *Winde Hornes*] F; *not in* Q
2.4.10.2-3/969.2-3 *to Lauinia*] F; *not in* Q
2.4.11/970 MARCUS] *not in* Q
2.4.14/973 If I] Q (text); I Q (c.w.)
2.4.21/980 halfe] Q; have THEOBALD
2.4.27/986 him] ROWE (Ravenscroft); them Q
2.4.30/989 three] HANMER; their Q
2.4.38/997 Philomele] CAMBRIDGE; Philomela Q
3.1.0.3/1016.3 ou^r] WAITH (S.W.W.); on Q
3.1.12/1028 two] This edition (*conj*. Jackson); *not in* QF. Though modern editors tend not to emend, the metre is indefensible; a compositor finding 'two' in an unpunctuated line might have taken it to qualify 'tribunes' and have omitted it as an unlikely mode of address; or it might have been omitted by simple eyeskip.
3.1.15.1/1031.1 *Exeunt all but Titus*] F (*Exeunt, after* 3.1.16/1032.); *not in* Q. Editors take Q's '*pass by him*' as an *exeunt*; F probably derives from the prompt-book, being placed after 3.1.16/1032 because 3.1.15/1031 is long.
3.1.17/1033 ruines] Q; urns HANMER. Sisson (*New Readings*) argues strongly against Hanmer; but Q remains suspect.
3.1.34/1050 if] Q; or if Q2-3; oh if F
3.1.35/1051 must] This edition (*conj*. Maxwell); muſt, | And bootleſſe vnto them Q. Sisson defends Q's line against Maxwell's suggestion, following Wilson, that it is 'a false start which Sh. intended to delete in his MS.', claiming 'The only "difficulty" is a broken line'; but the use of 'bootleſſe' for 'plead bootlessly' is not easy. Cambridge marked a lacuna after 'them'. The short line could be emended (e.g. 'bootleſſe sue vnto them') but this would still have Titus pleading to the tribunes, not the stones. Perhaps Shakespeare intended to write e.g. 'And bootleſſe vnto them bewaile my griefs', but abandoned the line on realizing the need to return to an explanation of why Titus should 'recount [his] sorrowes to a stone'. F (reading 'oh' before 'if', and 'did heare' for 'did marke' in 3.1.34/1050), included 'they would not pittie me' though this, with the remainder of the line, had been omitted from Q3. As Maxwell says, this suggests consultation of the prompt-copy, but does not explain why F still followed Q3 in omitting 'yet pleade I must' as well as 'And bootleſſe vnto them'.
3.1.66/1082 Lauinea] The only copy of Q has a mark resembling an acute accent above the 'e', but Laetitia Yeandle, who has inspected the copy, considers it 'a speck in the paper'.
3.1.146/1162 with his] F4; with her Q
3.1.169 enemy's] Q (enemies)
3.1.215/1231 sorrows] DYCE 2 (*conj*.); ſorrow Q
3.1.224/1240 blow] F2; flow Q1

3.1.229/1245 her] Q; their THEOBALD (conj.) (but 'her' could mean 'their': see Onions)
3.1.239.1/1255.1 Exit] F; not in Q
3.1.259 Rend] Q (Rent)
3.1.280-1/1296-7 And Lauinia thou shalt be imployde, | Beare thou my hand sweet wench betweene thine Armes:] This edition (partly after CAMBRIDGE); And Lauinia thou ſhalt be imployde in theſe Armes, | Beare thou my hand ſweet wench betweene thy teeth: Q. F substitutes 'things' for 'Armes'. CAMBRIDGE conjectured that 'the Author, or some other corrector, to soften what must have been ludicrous in representation, wrote "Armes" above "teeth" as a substitute for the latter'; that the printer of Q1 'took "Armes" to belong to the first line'; and that the scribe responsible for F 'made sense of the passage by substituting "things" for "Armes"'. Munro (followed by Riverside) acted on this to the extent of omitting 'in these Armes', but not of substituting 'Armes' for 'teeth'. We build upon Cambridge by supposing the alteration 'thine Armes' (not just 'Armes'). Malone, adopting F's 'these things', omitted 'And', supposing it to have been accidentally repeated from the previous line, but metrical irregularity can be avoided by stressing 'Lavinia' on the first and third syllables, as seems desirable also at 3.1.66/1082.
3.1.286.1/1302.1 Manet Lucius] F; not in Q
3.1.290/1306 loues] leaues ROWE
3.2/3.2] This scene is first found in F.
3.2.13/1328 with outragious] F2; without ragious F1
3.2.35/1350 no] F; to T. W. CRAIK (conj.). Craik interprets '"Here is something for you to drink", which Lavinia then declines, Titus commenting on her action'. This is plausible, but Titus could be exclaiming at an absence of drink from Lavinia's place at the table.
3.2.38 maſhed] F (meſh'd)
3.2.39/1354 complayner] CAPELL; complaynet F (conceivably representing complainant, Collier's MS reading)
3.2.52/1367 thy] F2; not in F1
3.2.53/1368 Fly.] F2; Flys, F1
3.2.54 thee,] F (the,)
3.2.55/1370 are] F2; not in F1
3.2.60/1375 father, brother?] HUDSON (Ritson); father and mother? F. Most editors follow F, but the emendation improves the metre, removes the discrepancy with 'he' in the following line, and keeps the emphasis appropriately on fathers; Titus elsewhere addresses Marcus as 'brother'. Compositor E, who set this passage, substitutes 'Mother' for 'brother' at Hamlet 5.2.190/3458.
3.2.62/1377 dirges] This edition; doings F; dolings THEOBALD. F is very weak ('An odd phrase', Maxwell), and OED offers little support for 'dolings'; 'dirges' (used in Lucrece and Romeo) is perfect sense and might have been misread as 'doinges'.
3.2.72/1387 my ſelfe] F2; my ſelfes F1
3.2.84/1399 begin] F; begins ROWE 2
4.1.10/1409 MARCUS] HUDSON; continued to Titus, Q. Capell attributed only 4.1.15/1414 to Marcus.
4.1.12 Ah] Q (A)
4.1.17/1416 or] Q; of THEOBALD (conj.)
4.1.36/1435] F adds, as a separate line, What booke?
4.1.42 Metamorphoses] Q (Metamorphoſis)
4.1.69/1468 here] This edition (conj. W. S. Walker); not in QF. The metre is deficient; 'here' might easily have been omitted because of its resemblance to 'have'.
4.1.76/1475] as here Q1; attrib. to Titus, Q3, F1; attrib. to Boy, CAPELL
4.1.77/1476 TITUS] MAXWELL; not in Q
4.1.90/1489 ſware] F3; ſweare Q
4.1.96 wake and ... once.] STAUNTON (after Q); wake, and ... once, Q3, F1; wake; and ... once, THEOBALD
4.1.100/1499 let] Q; let it Q3, F
4.1.114/1513 Shall] Q; Shalt CAPELL
4.2.15/1542 that] POPE; not in Q
4.2.25/1552 Now ... Aſſe] Q. T. W. Craik suggests that only the last two words are spoken aside, and that Aaron assumes the expected conclusion, 'a scholar'.

4.2.51 Good] Q (God)
4.2.68 fair-faced] Q (fairefaſt)
4.2.107 figure] Q1 (vigour). See Re-Editing, 55-6.
4.2.123/1650 yt] Q3; your Q1. Q1 presumably misread yt as yr.
4.2.135/1662 doe ioine] This edition (G.T.); joine Q1; are joind MAXWELL (conj.); all ioine F2
4.2.151/1678 Muliteus] Q1; Muli lives SINGER 2 (Steevens). See Sisson, New Readings.
4.2.177/1704 fat] This edition (conj. Cartwright); feede Q1; feast HANMER. The repetition of both word and construction seems implausible; a baby seems more likely to 'fat' than to 'feast' on curds and whey; Shakespeare uses the verb at 3.1.202/1218, and, intransitively, at Richard III 1.3.312/724.
4.3.14/1720 Metrically irregular, perhaps because Titus is mad; G.T. conjectures 'Deliver him I pray you this petition'.
4.3.26 diſtraught] Q (diſtract)
4.3.27/1733 Lords] Q; Lord F2
4.3.32/1738 But ...] 'But' is the catchword in Q1; it seems that a line has been omitted.
4.3.40/1746 now] HANMER; ſo Q. Q gives poor sense and grammar; the substitution may be by anticipation.
4.3.54/1760 Apollinem] ROWE; Apollonem QF
4.3.57/1763 Saturn, Caius] CAPELL; Saturnine, to Caius Q
4.3.77/1783] continued to Titus, Q2; attributed to Clowne, Q1
4.3.78/1784 Sirra] Q2; Titus: Sirra Q1
4.3.80/1786 Ho] Q; Who? ROWE
4.3.93/1799 After this line, QF print the passage given in our edition as Additional Passage C. We accept, and act upon, Wilson's arguments, adding that Marcus nowhere else speaks prose, and that the Clown's replies to the repeated question are contradictory.
4.3.109/1815 For] Q; So MAXWELL (conj.)
4.3.109/1815 hast made] Q; must hold T. W. Craik (conj.). Craik's conjecture, supposing that the line is addressed to the Clown, is interesting, though the proposed error is not easily explained.
4.4.5/1824 as know] CAMBRIDGE; not in Q
4.4.24, 25/1843, 1844 he ... he] Q; she ... she ROWE
4.4.34/1853 (aside)] F (after the next line); not in Q
4.4.36-7/1855-6 quicke: | ... out,] MAXWELL; quicke, | ... out: Q
4.4.48 by' Lady] Q (be Lady). See Maxwell.
4.4.62/1881 Lords] Q; lord CAPELL (Ravenscroft)
4.4.67/1886 this] Q; his ROWE
4.4.93/1912 feede] Q3; ſeede Q1-2; foode F1
4.4.100/1919 before to be] Q; before, be CAPELL. Maxwell follows Capell; but see Cercignani, 291, for 'be' contracted before a vowel.
4.4.105/1924 on] F4; in Q1
4.4.113/1932 incessantly] CAPELL; ſuceſſantly Q. See Waith.
5.1.0.1/1932.2 Flourish] F; not in Q
5.1.0.2/1932.3 Souldiers] Q; Colours CAPELL
5.1.16 avenged] Q (aduengde)
5.1.17/1949 GOTHS] F2 (Omn.); not in Q, F1
5.1.23 building, suddenly,] Q (building ſuddainely,)
5.1.27 dam] Q (dame)
5.1.46/1978 deafe, what] This edition (T. W. Craik); deafe, Q. As Craik says, 'the natural completion of an incomplete line'.
5.1.46/1978 what not] KEIGHTLEY; not in Q
5.1.53/1985 Get me a ladder] continued to Lucius, THEOBALD; ascribed to Aaron, Q. Signet follows Q, presumably supposing that Aaron stresses his willingness to die provided that his son be saved.
5.1.58 more but 'Vengeance rot you all!'] Q (more, but vengeance rotte you all)
5.1.65/1997 treason,] Q; treasons: MAXWELL (conj.)
5.1.119 swooned] Q (ſounded)
5.1.132/2064] A short line; G.T. conj. 'cillie [i.e. 'seely/silly', innocent] cattle' and an eyeskip error.
5.1.133/2065 haystacks] Q3 (hayſtakes Q2); hayſtalks Q1. See Waith.
5.1.141/2073 But] Q1; Tut Q2
5.1.165/2097 come, away.] CAPELL; come, march away. Q. Q is

metrically awkward; and, as Maxwell notes (though he follows Q), 'The absence of an *Exeunt* in Q1-2 (not known to Capell) tells in favour of his correction.' It seems that the compositor misunderstood the stage direction, and so transposed it.

5.1.165.1/2097.1 *Flourish. Exeunt*] F; *not in* Q. F's direction presumably replaces the manuscript's postulated '*March*', indicating both the music and the movement.

5.2.1 habiliment] Q (habilliament)

5.2.18/2115 it action] F; that accord Q; it that accord POPE. Sisson (*New Readings*) supports Pope, but F seems better sense (see Maxwell) and is not easily seen as 'an improvisation' (Sisson).

5.2.49/2146 Globe] DYCE (Capell); Globes Q

5.2.50/2147 two] ROWE; thee two Q

5.2.52/2149 murderers] CAPELL; murder Q. Sisson (*New Readings*) defends Q, implausibly regarding 'murder' as 'personified and plural in sense'.

5.2.52/2149 caues] F2; cares Q

5.2.56/2153 Hipereons] F2; Epeons Q1; Eptons F. Probably the manuscript used a crossed 'p' for 'per'.

5.2.57/2154 verie] Q; weary WILSON (*conj.*) (*plausible particularly considering the high incidence of error in this passage*)

5.2.61/2158 they thy] F2; them thy Q

5.2.62/2159 Rape] Q; Rapine F

5.2.65 worldly] Q (wordlie)

5.2.91/2188 are. What] POPE; are, what Q

5.2.144 dam] Q (dame)

5.2.153/2250 *Chiron. Demetrius*] Q; Chiron and Demetrius THEOBALD

5.2.203/2300 Ile] Q; I will w. S. WALKER (*conj.*)

5.3.0.1-2/2301.2-3 *Aron, prisoner, ⌈and an attendant with his child⌉*] The child is needed at 5.3.118/2419; Shakespeare seems not to have provided for its entrance; it could be brought on at e.g. 5.3.65.1-2/2366.1-2.

5.3.1/2302 tis] Q; it is THEOBALD

5.3.3/2304 A GOTH] Q (*Got.*)

5.3.15.2/2316.2 *Flourish*] F. Presumably intended to replace Q's '*Sound Trumpets*' at 5.3.16.1/2317.1, which F nevertheless retains.

5.3.25.1/2326.1 *Hoboyes. A Table brought in.*] F; *not in* Q. '*Hoboyes*' substitutes for Q's '*Trumpets founding*'.

5.3.26/2327 gratious] Q2-3, F; *not in* Q1

5.3.27/2328 welcome *Lucius*] Q; *Lucius* welcome CAPELL

5.3.28/2329 all:] F; all, Q1-2; all, Q3

5.3.42/2343 effectuall] HANMER; and effectuall Q

5.3.46.1/2347.1 *He kils her*] Q3, F1; *not in* Q1

5.3.59/2360 *reuealing the heads*] This edition (G.T.); *not in* QF. Though not certain, this seems probable as the climactic horror.

5.3.63/2364 deede] Q; foin G.T. *conj*. Absence of a rhyme for 'point', following 5 couplets, combined with the triple rhyme *deed . . . bleed . . . deed*, arouses suspicion. The compositor might have substituted 'deed' for 'foin' (= 'thrust or push with a pointed weapon', *OED* 1) by eyeskip: for rhymes 'based on loss of final t' see Cercignani, 315.

5.3.65.1/2366.1-2 *Confusion followes. ⌈Enter Gothes. Lucius, Marcus and others goe aloft.⌉*] *after* CAPELL; *not in* QF. The 'confusion' seems called for by Marcus' subsequent lines. Maxwell argues that 5.3.129/2430 ff. do not 'require the speaker and his friends to be visibly higher than their audience', but the following speeches would come well from a raised position (cf. *Caesar* 3.1/Sc. 8), and Maxwell, allowing that 5.3.129/2430 ff. might 'demand some sort of raised position', suggests 'a movable scaffolding'. We do not agree that 'Neither ascent nor descent is here covered by dialogue'; an ascent could easily be made during the confusion following upon Lucius' killing of Saturninus, and Lucius must be on the main stage by 5.3.152/2453.

5.3.72/2373 ROMANE LORD . . .] Capell deleted the prefix and emended 'Let' (5.3.72/2373) to 'Lest'. He was followed by editors up to Maxwell, who admits that this 'does not explain everything'. Sisson (*New Readings*) saw that the speech makes sense if 'But if . . .' (5.3.76/2377) is taken as dependent on 'Let Rome her selfe', but unnecessarily interpreted 'Romane Lord' as Emillius (Riverside follows). The Lord's intervention after Marcus' request to the crowd is explicable on the assumption that Marcus goes unheeded. It is presumably mere clumsiness that the Lord immediately follows his request for attention with an invitation to someone else to speak. 'Roomes deare friend' (5.3.79/2380) is usually interpreted as Lucius, but could be Marcus, especially if we assumed a missing speech-prefix for him before 5.3.87/2388; this would have the advantage of not requiring the Lord to repeat his invitation to Lucius, but is perhaps too speculative to adopt.

F altered 'Romane Lord' to 'Goth', but only 5.3.72-5/2373-6 could conceivably come from an enemy to Rome, and for Marcus to resume at 5.3.76/2377 would require the assumption that the F1 corrector failed to add a necessary prefix and would also scarcely be consonant with Marcus' words at 5.3.118/2419, 'Now is my turne to speake . . .'. The most likely explanation of F's change is that it was made not on authority, but by someone in the printing house who, noting the stop at the end of 5.3.75/2376, and reading no further, considered that no Roman would wish *bane* upon Rome, and so attributed the lines to an anonymous non-Roman.

5.3.75/2376 selfe,] SISSON; (self,); felfe. Q

5.3.78/2379 words.] SISSON; ~, Q

5.3.123 is to witness,] MAXWELL (*after* Q, 'witnes,'); is, to witneſſe F

5.3.123/2424 true.] F; ~, Q

5.3.124/2425 cause] F4; courfe Q

5.3.125/2426 reuenge,] F; ~. Q1-2; ~, Q3

5.3.133/2434 And] Q (*text*); An Q (*c.w.*)

5.3.136/2437 Come come] Q; Come, Marcus, come MAXWELL (*conj.*)

5.3.140/2441 ROMANS] CAPELL; *Marcus.* Q

5.3.141/2442 MARCUS] CAPELL; *not in* QF

5.3.143/2444 adiudgde] Q3; adiudge Q1

5.3.145/2446 ROMANS] CAPELL; *not in* Q

5.3.153/2454 staind] F3; flaine Q

5.3.175/2476 A ROMANE] Q; Emillius DYCE (Ravenscroft)

5.3.191 father's] Q (fathers)

5.3.195 rite] Q (right)

Additional Passages

A.2 yᵉ] CHAMBERS; that Q

REJECTED FOLIO VARIANTS

1.1.5/5 am his] was the
1.1.5/5 ware] wore
1.1.14/14 The Imperiall] Th'Imperiall
1.1.68/68 where] whence
1.1.69.4/69.4 then] After them,
1.1.69.8/69.8 then] They
1.1.94/94 hast thou of mine] of mine haſt thou
1.1.99/99 earthy] earthly
1.1.108/108 sonne] ſonnes
1.1.122/122 their] the

1.1.122/122 your] you
1.1.129.1/129.1 *Titus sonnes*] Sonnes
1.1.131/131 neuer] euer
1.1.132/132 not] me
1.1.134/134 looke] lookes
1.1.154/154 drugges] grudges
1.1.162/162 this] the
1.1.164/164 fortunes] Fortune
1.1.174/174 alike] all alike
1.1.206/206 were] wert

TITUS ANDRONICUS

1.1.214/214	friends] Friend?	
1.1.217/217	peoples] Noble	
1.1.219/219	yee] you	
1.1.223/223	sute] sure	
1.1.224/224	our] your	
1.1.250/250	imperious] Imperiall	
1.1.252/252	thy] my	
1.1.258/258	you] your	
1.1.259/259	your honour] you Honour	
1.1.269/269	you] your	
1.1.280/280	cuique] cuiqum Q; cuiquam F	
1.1.357/357	vouch] vouch'd	
1.1.365/365	with] not in F	
1.1.366/366	till] tell	
1.1.377/377	wise] not in F	
1.1.388/388	drīrie] ſudden F; sullen DYCE conj. (withdrawn)	
1.1.444/444	you] vs	
1.1.474/474	doo I] I do	
2.1.4/495	aboue] about	
2.1.18/509	ſeruile] idle	
2.1.22/513	Nymph] Queene	
2.1.26/517	wits wants] wit wants	
2.1.46/537	yee] you	
2.1.55/546	those] theſe	
2.1.62/553	pettie] pretty	
2.1.64/555	iet] ſet	
2.1.70/561	diſcords] diſcord	
2.1.80/571	I loue] I do loue	
2.1.81/572	Why makes] Why, mak'ſt	
2.1.101/592	That . . . speede] not in F	
2.1.123/614	what] that	
2.1.128/619	and] of	
2.1.131/622	lust] luſts	
2.1.134/625	Sit] Sij	
2.1.134/625	streame] ſtreames	
2.1.135/626	these] their	
2.2.10/637	inspired] inſpir'd. | Winde Hornes.	
2.2.17/644	broad] not in F	
2.2.24/651	like] likes	
2.3.9.2/662.2	alone] not in F	
2.3.13/666	snakes] Snake	
2.3.54/707	quarrels] quarrell	
2.3.55/708	Who] (who); Whom	
2.3.95/748	Ouercome] Ore-come	
2.3.120/773	the] thy	
2.3.201/854	morning] mornings	
2.3.204/857	hurt] not in F	
2.3.220/873	who] how	
2.3.222/875	bereied in blood] bereaud in blood Q; embrewed heere F	
2.3.223/876	to a] to the	
2.3.227/880	this] the	
2.3.229/882	earthy] earthly	
2.2.230/883	this] the	
2.3.245.2-3/898.2-3	Enter . . . Moore] Enter the Emperous and Aron, the Moore. Q; Enter the Emperour, Aaron the Moore. F	
2.3.250/903	sonnes] ſonne	
2.3.256/909	them] him	
2.3.258/910	them] him	
2.4.5/964	scrowle] ſcowle	
2.4.15/974	an] in	
2.4.38/997	Philomele, why] Philomela, why Q; Philomela F	
2.4.41/1000	Cosen hast thou met] haſt thou met withall	
3.1.28/1044	you] not in F	
3.1.34/1050	if . . . marke] oh if . . . heare	
3.1.36/1052	to] bootles to	
3.1.43/1059	Tribunes] Tribune	
3.1.44/1060	soft as] as ſoft	
3.1.55/1071	and] and and	
3.1.57.1/1073.1	with] and	
3.1.58/1074	aged] noble	
3.1.115/1131	them] him	
3.1.121/1137	signe] ſignes	
3.1.125/1141	like] in	
3.1.134/1150	miserie,] miſeries,	
3.1.191/1207	your] you	
3.1.192/1208	my] me	
3.1.196/1212	for] for for	
3.1.208/1224	wouldst] wilt	
3.1.213/1229	possibilitie] poſſibilities	
3.1.224/1240	doth] doe	
3.1.237/1253	griefe] griefes	
3.1.254/1270	hand] hands	
3.1.255/1271	sonne] ſonnes	
3.1.258/1274	thy] my	
3.1.273/1289	hath] haue	
3.1.280-1/1296-7	imployde . . . Armes] imployde in theſe Armes, | Beare thou my hand ſweet wench betweene thy teeth Q; employd in theſe things: Beare thou my hand ſweet wench betweene thy teeth F	
3.1.285/1301	yee] you	
3.1.297/1313	like] likes	
4.1.5/1404	thine] thy	
4.1.9/1408	her] not in F	
4.1.21/1420	for] through	
4.1.36/1435	deede.] deed. | What booke?	
4.1.38/1437	were] was	
4.1.40/1439	for] to	
4.1.71/1470	this] that	
4.1.76/1475	writ] writs	
4.1.96/1495	yee] you	
4.1.100/1499	let] let it	
4.1.105/1504	our] your	
4.1.108/1507	base] bad	
4.2.0.2/1527.2	the other] another	
4.2.8/1535	That . . . newes] not in F	
4.2.9/1536	villaines] villainie's	
4.2.13/1540	bid] bad	
4.2.21/1548	arcu] arcus	
4.2.27/1554	them] the	
4.2.44/1571	your] your	
4.2.58/1585	thy] thine	
4.2.71/1598	Zounds ye] Out you	
4.2.76/1603	Villaine . . . mother] not in F	
4.2.77/1604	her] not in F	
4.2.97/1624	whitelimde] white-limb'd	
4.2.114/1641	ignomie] ignominie	
4.2.117/1644	thy] the	
4.2.138/1665	as] at	
4.2.141/1668	no one] none	
4.2.143/1670	the] the the	
4.2.145/1672	to the] to th'	
4.2.161/1688	you] ye	
4.3.0.4/1706.5	ends] end	
4.3.8/1714	catch] find	
4.3.49/1755	backs] backe	
4.3.67, 79, 84, 85/1773, 1785, 1789, 1790	Iubiter] Iupiter	
4.3.76/1782	his] your	
4.3.93/1799	Emperals] Emperialls	
4.3.99/1805	vp] not in F	
4.4.18/1837	vniustice] Iniuſtice	
4.4.38/1857	Anchor] Anchor's	
4.4.40/1859	Mistriship] Miſterſhip	
4.4.48/1867	be] ber	
4.4.78/1897	your] our	
4.4.93/1912	feede] feede Q; foode F	
4.4.96/1915	eares] eare	
4.4.100/1919	be] not in F	
4.4.103/1922	Euen . . . Andronicus] not in F	
4.4.113/1932	to] for	
4.4.113.1/1932.1	Exeunt seuerally] Exeunt. Q; Exit. F	
5.1.0.2/1932.3	Drums] Drum

TITUS ANDRONICUS

5.1.13/1945	Be bold] Behold	
5.1.43/1975	her] his	
5.1.67/1999	in] by	
5.1.86/2018	to] to to	
5.1.88/2020	and] *not in* F	
5.1.93/2025	hands] hands off	
5.1.107/2039	that] the	
5.1.126/2058	the] few	
5.1.134/2066	their] the	
5.1.155/2087	what's] what	
5.2.31/2128	thy] the	
5.2.32/2129	thy] my	
5.2.40/2137	offender] offenders	
5.2.54/2151	thy] the	
5.2.50/2147	black] as blacke	
5.2.71/2168	humors] fits	
5.2.80/2177	plie] play	
5.2.92/2193	hath] haue	
5.2.97/2194	I will] Ile	
5.2.105/2203	shalt] maift	
5.2.105/2203	thine] thy	
5.2.128/2225	Feast] Feasts	
5.2.137/2234	abide] bide	
5.2.142/2239	knew] know	
5.2.142/2239	supposd] fuppofe	
5.2.155/2252	and] *not in* F	
5.2.160/2257	And . . . crie] *not in* F	
5.2.164/2261	fast.] faft. *Exeunt.*	
5.2.181/2278	Whiles] Whil'ft	
5.2.190/2287	owne] *not in* F	
5.2.201/2298	may] might	
5.2.204/2301	against] gainft	
5.3.7/2308	Empresse] Emperous	
5.3.10/2311	I feare] If ere	
5.3.25.2/2326.2	dishes] meat on the table	
5.3.47/2348	thou] *not in* F	
5.3.51/2352	To . . . done] *not in* F	
5.3.59/2360	this] that	
5.3.67/2368	as] like	
5.3.90/2391	my] my very	
5.3.91/2392	yee] you	
5.3.92/2393	And force you to] Lending your kind hand	
5.3.93/2394	Her's Romes young] Heere is a	
5.3.94/2395	While . . . by] Your hearts will throb	
5.3.95/2396	Then gratious] This Noble	
5.3.96/2397	*Chiron* and the damn'd] curfed *Chiron* and	
5.3.108/2409	I am the] And I am	
5.3.118/2419	the] this	
5.3.127/2428	haue you] you haue	
5.3.129/2430	pleading] now	
5.3.131/2432	hurle our selues] caft vs downe	
5.3.132/2433	soules] braines	
5.3.140/2441	haile] haile to	
5.3.163/2464	storie] matter	
5.3.164-8/2465-9	And bid . . . kisse] Meete, and agreeing with thine Infancie: | In that refpect then, like a louing Childe, | Shed yet fome fmall drops from thy tender Spring, | Becaufe kinde Nature doth require it fo: | Friends, fhould affociate Friends, in Greefe and Wo.	
5.3.170/2471	them . . . them] him . . . him	
5.3.183/2484	Ah] O	
5.3.190/2491	Emperour] Emp.	
5.3.194/2495	rauinous] heynous	
5.3.195/2496	weede] Weeds	
5.3.197/2498	to] of	
5.3.198/2499	beastlie] Beaft-like	
5.3.199/2500	dead . . . pittie] fo, fhall haue like want of pitty. | See Iuftice done on *Aaron* that damn'd Moore, | From whom, our heauy happes had their beginning: | Then afterwards, to Order well the State, | That like Euents, may ne're it Ruinate.	

INCIDENTALS

8 indignitie.] ~,   14 vertue‸consecrate,] ~‸~‸   56 right,] ~.   66 Succesfull in] Succefful lin   96 Gothes,] Gotbes   122 Gothes] Gotbes   266 waie.] ~‸   267 discontent,] ~. (?)   280 iustice] iuftce   356 What] what   359 thee,] ~.   431 forfend,] ~.   445 sinne,] ~.   450 life,] ~.   472 mildlie] mild ie   496 sunne] fuune   552 Gothes] Gotbes   570 a] A   664 doth] dorh   697 chastitie] chafttitie   730 obscure] obfure   759 But] Bu   763 Laciuious] Lauicious   771 Semeramis] Semeranis   785 Let] Q (*text*); Le Q (*c.w.*)   817 brother] brothet   899 here,] ~.   917 writ,] ~.   961 cut] eut   1014 will] wlll   1037 on thy] outhy   1197 care] eare (?)   1207 dispatcht.] ~ ■   1291 about,] ~.   1353 sorrow,] ~:   1353 cheekes:] ~,   1372 brother] broher   1408 meane.] ~,   1448 annoie,] ~,   1449 leaues.] ~,   1451 Philomela] Phlomela   1452 Forcd] Frocd   1456 rapes.] ~,   1457 den,] ~.   1458 Tragedies.] ~,   1462 bed.] ~,   1475 writ.] ~,   1476 Demetrius] Dmetrius   1486 hope] Q (hop *or* l op)   1521 good man] goodman   1523 Marcus] Marous (?)   1548 nec] nee   1621 Alcides] Alciades   1687 Emperour] Lmperour   1859 Emperiall.] ~,   1931 deuises.] ~,   1936 desirous] defirons   1948 Tamora.] ~:   1985 ladder.] ~,   2026 trimming.] ~,   2159 so,] ~.   2240 will] willl   2246 imploid.] ~,   2247 doe.] ~‸   2301 comes.] ~,   2337 Virginius] Viginius   2346 with] wirh   2364 deede.] ~,   2376 selfe,] ~‸

QUARTO STAGE DIRECTIONS

1.1.0.1-4/0.1-4	Enter the Tribunes *and* Senatours *aloft: And then enter* | Saturninus *and his followers at one dore, and* Bassianus *and* | *his followers, with Drums and Trumpets.*
1.1.17.1/17.1	Marcus Andronicus *with the Crowne.*
1.1.55.1/55.1	*Exit Soldiers.*
1.1.63.1-2/63.1-2	*They goe vp into the Senate house.* | *Enter a* Captaine.
1.1.69.1-8/69.1-9	*Sound Drums and Trumpets, and then enter two of* Titus | *sonnes, and then two men bearing a Coffin couered with black,* | *then two other sonnes, then* Titus Andronicus, *and then* Ta-|mora *the Queene of Gothes and her two sonnes* Chiron *and* | Demetrius, *with* Aron *the More, and others as many as can* | *be, then set downe the Coffin, and* Titus *speakes.*
1.1.89.1/89.1	*They open the Tombe.*
1.1.129.1/129.1	*Exit* Titus *sonnes with* Alarbus.
1.1.141.1-2/141.1-2	*Enter the sonnes of* Andronicus *againe.*
1.1.149.1-2/149.1-2	*Sound Trumpets, and lay the Coffin in the* Tombe.
1.1.156.1/156.1	*Enter* Lauinia.
1.1.294.2-4/294.2-4	*Enter aloft the Emperour with* Tamora *and her two* | *sonnes and* Aron *the moore.*
1.1.334.1/334.1	*Exeunt Omnes.*
1.1.337.1-2/337.1-2	*Enter* Marcus *and* Titus *sonnes.*
1.1.355/355	Titus *two sonnes speakes.*
1.1.357/357	Titus *sonne speakes.*
1.1.366.1/366.1	*The brother and the sonnes kneele.*

TITUS ANDRONICUS

1.1.383.1/383.1 *they put him in the tombe.*
1.1.386/386 *they all kneele and say,*
1.1.387.1/387.1 *Exit all but Marcus and Titus.*
1.1.395.1-3/395.1-3 *Enter the Emperour, Tamora | and her two sonnes, with the | Moore at one doore.*
1.1.395.4-5/395.4-5 *Enter at the other doore | Bascianus and Lauinia, | with others. (opposite 1.1.395.1-3/395.1-3)*
1.1.491/491 *Exeunt.*
2.1.0.1/491.1 *sound trumpets, manet* Moore.
2.1.25.1/516.1 *Enter Chiron and Demetrius brauing.*
2.1.45/536.1 *they drawe.*
2.1.136/627 *Exeunt.*
2.2.0.1-3/627.1-3 *Enter Titus Andronicus, and his three sonnes. | making a noise with hounds & hornes.*
2.2.10.1-3/637.1-3 *Here a crie of Hounds, and wind hornes in a peale: then | enter Saturninus, Tamora, Bascianus, Lauinia, Chiron, | Demetrius, and their Attendants.*
2.2.26/653 *Exeuunt.*
2.3.0.1/653.1 *Enter Aron alone.*
2.3.9.2/662.2 *Enter Tamora alone to the Moore.*
2.3.50.1/703.1 *Enter Bascianus, and Lauinia.*
2.3.88.1/741.1 *Enter Chiron and Demetrius.*
2.3.116.1/769.1 *stab him.*
2.3.191.1-2/844.1-2 *Enter Aron with two of Titus sonnes.*
2.3.208.1/861.1 *Exit. (after 2.3.207/860)*
2.3.245.2-3/898.2-3 *Enter the Emperour and Aron, | the Moore.*
2.3.258.1/911.1 *Enter Tamora, Andronicus, and Lucius.*
2.3.267.1/920.1-2 *She giueth Saturnine a letter. | Saturninus reads the letter.*
2.4.0.1-3/959.2-4 *Enter the Empresse sonnes with Lauinia, her handes | cut off, and her tongue cut out, & rauisht.*
2.4.10.1/969.1 *Exeunt.*
2.4.10.2-3/969.2-3 *Enter Marcus from hunting.*
2.4.57/1016 *Exeunt.*
3.1.0.1-4/1016.1-4 *Enter the Iudges and Senatours with* Titus *two sonnes | bound, passing on the Stage to the place of execution, and Ti-|tus going before pleading.*
3.1.11.1/1027.1-2 *Andronicus lieth downe, and the* Judges *passe by him.*
3.1.22.1/1038.1 *Enter Lucius with his weapon drawne.*
3.1.57.1/1073.1 *Enter Marcus with Lauinia.*
3.1.149.1/1165.1 *Enter Aron the Moore alone.*
3.1.184.1/1200.1 *Exeunt.*
3.1.190.1/1206.1 *He cuts off* Titus *hand.*
3.1.190.2/1206.2 *Enter Lucius and Marcus againe.*
3.1.204/1220 *Exit.*
3.1.232.1/1248.1 *Enter a messenger with two heads and a hand.*
3.1.286.1/1302.1 *Exeunt.*
3.1.299/1315 *Exit Lucius.*
4.1.0.1-3/1399.2-4 *Enter Lucius sonne and Lauinia running after him, and | the Boy flies from her with his Bookes vn-|der his Arme.*
4.1.0.3/1399.4 *Enter Titus and Marcus.*

4.1.69/1468 *He writes his name with his staffe and guides it | with feete and mouth. (after 4.1.67/1466)*
4.1.75.1-2/1474.1-2 *Shee takes the staffe in her mouth, and guides it with her | stumps and writes.*
4.1.121.1/1520.1 *Exeunt.*
4.1.128/1527 *Exit.*
4.2.0.1-4/1527.1-4 *Enter Aron, Chiron, and Demetrius at one doore, and at | the other doore young Lucius, and another with a bundle of | weapons, and verses writ vpon them.*
4.2.17.1/1544.1 *Exit.*
4.2.48.1/1575.1 *Trumpets sound.*
4.2.51/1578 *Enter Nurse with a blackamoore childe.*
4.2.144.1/1671.1 *He kils her.*
4.2.170.1/1697.1 *Exeunt.*
4.2.179.1/1706.1 *Exit.*
4.3.0.1-4/1706.2-5 *Enter Titus, olde Marcus, young Lucius, and other gen-|tlemen with bowes, and* Titus *beares the arrowes with letters | on the ends of them.*
4.3.53.1/1759.1 *He giues them the Arrowes.*
4.3.76.1/1782.1-2 *Enter the Clowne with a basket and two pidgeons in it.*
4.3.112/1818 *Exit.*
4.3.113/1819 *Exeunt.*
4.4.0.1-4/1819.1-4 *Enter Emperour and Empresse and her two sonnes, the | Emperour brings the Arrowes in his hand | that Titus shot at him.*
4.4.38.1/1857.1 *Enter Clowne.*
4.4.44.1/1863.1 *He reads the letter.*
4.4.49/1868 *Exit.*
4.4.60.1/1879.1 *Enter Nutius Emillius.*
4.4.107/1926 *Exit.*
4.4.113.1/1932.1 *Exeunt.*
5.1.0.1-2/1932.2-3 *Enter Lucius with an Armie of Gothes with | Drums and Souldiers.*
5.1.19.1-2/1951.1-2 *Enter a Goth leading of Aron with his child | in his Armes.*
5.1.151.2/2083.2 *Enter Emillius.*
5.2.0.1-2/2097.2-3 *Enter Tamora and her two sonnes disguised.*
5.2.8.1/2105.1 *They knocke and Titus opens his studie doore.*
5.2.121.1/2218.1 *Enter Marcus. (after 5.2.120/2217)*
5.2.164.1-2/2261.1-2 *Enter Titus Andronicus, with a knife, and Lauinia, with | a Bason.*
5.2.202.1/2299.1 *He cuts their throats.*
5.2.204.1/2301.1 *Exeunt.*
5.3.0.1/2301.2 *Enter Lucius, Marcus, and the Gothes.*
5.3.15.2/2316.2 *Sound Trumpets. Enter Emperour and Empresse with Tri-|bunes and others.*
5.3.25.1-4/2326.1-4 *Trumpets sounding, Enter Titus like a Cooke, placing the | dishes, and Lauinia with a vaile ouer her face.*
5.3.62.1/2363.1 *He stabs the Empresse.*
5.3.199.1/2500.1 *Exeunt.*

1 HENRY VI

THE first and only substantive text was published in the First Folio (*BEPD* 399). The Stationers' Register entry of seventeen plays first printed in F includes 'The thirde parte of Henry the Sixt'; since the plays which F identifies as *Part Two* and *Part Three* were already in print, and had earlier been identified in the Stationers' Register as *Part One* and *Part Two* (see pp. 175, 199), the 1623 entry of 'The thirde parte' presumably refers to the only unpublished play of the trio, *Part One*.

The traditional view, that *Part One* is a collaborative work written later than the two other plays on the reign of Henry VI, has been restated by Gary Taylor, who provides new evidence of multiple authorship ('Shakespeare and Others'). Taylor proposes the following division of shares:

1.1.1–102/102	Y? (or X)
1.1.103–151/103–51	?
1.1.152–77/152–77	Y? (or X)
1.2.–1.8/Sc. 2–8	Thomas Nashe
2.1–2.3/Sc. 9–11	X
2.4/Sc. 12	Shakespeare
2.5/Sc. 13	X
3.1–3.8/Sc. 14–21	Y
4.1/Sc. 22	X? (or Y)
4.2–4.7.32/Sc. 23–8, 2049	Shakespeare
4.7.33–96/2050–2113	mixed? (Shakespeare and Y?)
5.1–end/Sc. 29–end	Y

The identities of X and Y are unknown, though Y has particular links with *Locrine* (*BEPD* 136), and both have strong similarities to the dramatic writings of Robert Greene and George Peele. The uncertainty about the authorship of large parts of the play makes emendation difficult in those passages, where no standard of comparison for authorial practice is available.

The Folio text appears to have been set (by Compositors A and B) from foul papers. A number of characters are inconsistently identified in speech-prefixes and stage directions: Charles/Dauphin, Joan/Pucelle, Richard/York, Cardinal/Winchester, Pole/Suffolk, General/Captain. Entrances are omitted for the Captain (2.2/Sc. 10), the Porter (2.3/Sc. 11), Vernon and the Lawyer (2.4/Sc. 12), René (3.3/Sc. 16), Alençon (3.5/Sc. 18), Burgundy (3.7/Sc. 20), Vernon and Basset (3.8/Sc. 21), the Captain and Lucy (4.4/Sc. 25), and a French herald (5.1/Sc. 29); three probable entrances of soldiers (see 1.7.26.1, 2.1.39.1, 5.5.84.1/552.1, 634.2, 2324.1) are also omitted. No provision is made for important properties: a rose-bush (2.4/Sc. 12), roses for characters to wear (3.1/Sc. 14, 3.8/Sc. 21, 4.1/Sc. 22), a scroll (3.1/Sc. 14), a paper (5.3/Sc. 31). At 1.7.39.1/565.1 there is an inept direction for off-stage sounds, which probably would have been sorted out in a prompt-book; at 2.1.39.1/635.2 an alarum seems required but is not indicated; at 2.1.78/673 there is an erroneous '*Exeunt*' direction. No actors are identified in speech-prefixes or stage directions. Cumulatively such deficiencies and inconsistencies strongly suggest that the manuscript had not been used in the theatre; nor is it likely to have been a private transcript or scribal fair copy. In particular, we would expect a scribe to have obscured many of the orthographical and linguistic features which distinguish the various authorial shares.

Cairncross, who suspected scribal copy, based his case for the existence of a scribe exclusively upon claims that the text is seriously corrupt, in ways most readily explained by scribal interference. Cairncross's textual hypothesis depended upon, and had the effect of reinforcing, his belief that Shakespeare wrote the entire play: given the poverty of much of the writing, this belief could only be sustained by a corresponding assumption that the Folio text in many places seriously misrepresents the play's intended verbal texture. Like other editors, we are not convinced of the need for so many emendations, or by Cairncross's explanation of those which seem necessary. However, because of the influence of Cairncross's edition and the potential relationship of questions of authorship and textual authority, we have recorded Cairncross's emendations and conjectures (though many of these would not have been given such prominence, according to our normal criteria).

Nevertheless, although the hypothesis of scribal copy can be rejected, certain features of the text do distinguish it from 'normal' foul papers; these led Greg to believe that the manuscript had been 'annotated by the book-keeper and used by the prompter' (*Folio*, 187). The three occurrences of '*Senet*' were almost certainly written later than the rest of the directions in which they appear (see notes to 3.1.190.1/1270.1, 3.8.27.1/1538.1, 5.1.0.1/2113.1); at 4.1.181/1737.1 '*Flourish*' has been misplaced; at 4.1.0.3/1556.2 '*Exeter*' appears to be an addition to the original direction. However, such anomalies can easily be explained by the fact that the foul papers were in this instance collaborative, and had probably been tidied up by at least one of the writers after the various authorial shares had been brought together. Two passages—1.1.103–51/103–51, 2.4/Sc. 12—appear to have been written later than the material around them, by a different hand; disparities between stage directions and speech-prefixes in 3.3/Sc. 16 and 3.5/Sc. 18 suggest that René's part in Acts 1–4 was an afterthought, and that his speeches in those scenes had originally been distributed among the other French nobles; the erroneous '*Exeunt*' at 2.1.78/673 can hardly be explained except on the assumption that 2.1.79–83/673.1–677.1 are an afterthought. As we might expect in a collaboration between four playwrights, a certain amount of stitching and reworking could only be done after the separate foul papers had been combined, and might reasonably be done before a fair copy was prepared. The writer (or writers) responsible for such polishing might equally be responsible for the addition of 'Senet' or 'Exeter' to certain stage directions, or for the late addition of eight lines of dialogue (4.1.174-81/1730-7), which had the effect of making the originally correct positioning of 'Flourish' appear incorrect. (See note to 4.1.173.1/1729.1.) The only other alleged evidence of a prompter's addition is 'Their Drummes beating a Dead March', which Wilson conjectured had been misplaced; but the direction is, we believe, correct. (See note to 2.1.7.2-3/603.2-3.) Consequently, all the features of the Folio text are most economically explained by the hypothesis that the copy was collaborative foul papers, containing last-minute adjustments; there is no need to suspect intervention by scribe or book-keeper.

One inconsistency between the different authorial shares which must have been cleared up before the play was staged had apparently not been cleared up in F's copy. In 1.4/Sc. 4 Winchester is clearly a cardinal; in the remainder of Acts 1-4, he is addressed as a bishop; in 5.1/Sc. 29 he has apparently just been promoted to cardinal (5.1.28-33, 51-62/2141-6, 2164-75); in 5.6/Sc. 34 he is identified as a cardinal in stage direction and speech-prefix (5.6.91.1, 96/2482.1, 2485). This inconsistency could have been dealt with either by altering the dialogue of 1.4/Sc. 4 or by omitting eighteen lines in 5.1/Sc. 29. If the second option had been chosen, the cut might have been signalled in the foul papers by the usual vertical line in the left margin, which might in turn have been ignored by the Folio compositor; this hypothesis would allow us to suppose that the problem had been solved in the foul papers themselves. However, this option leaves Winchester (and Exeter and the ambassadors) without a word to speak or function to perform in 5.1/Sc. 29; as a result, moreover, the rivalry between Winchester and Gloucester, so prominent in Acts 1 and 3, entirely disappears from the last two acts; Winchester's central role in the disgraceful peace treaty of 5.6/Sc. 34 consequently is divorced from his ecclesiastical ambition and his rivalry with Gloucester. The omission of the offending lines from 5.2/Sc. 30 not only sadly weakens the scene itself, but more fundamentally undermines the play's only unifying theme: dissension at home as the cause of defeat abroad. By contrast, the minor alteration of six lines in 1.4/Sc. 4, removing all references to Winchester as a cardinal, would have no appreciable negative effect upon either the scene itself or the structure of the play. (In fact, if Gloucester's taunts about Winchester being a haughty cardinal were replaced by taunts about his being a 'mere bishop', removing the inconsistency could actually strengthen the play's narrative coherence, using the Gloucester/Winchester quarrel as a direct motive for Winchester's eventual elevation.) It therefore seems to us far more likely that the contradiction was in practice resolved by revision of 1.4/Sc. 4; however, this revision—involving the substitution or addition of dialogue, rather than a mere 'deletion' mark, as in 5.1/Sc. 29—should have reached print, if it had stood in the Folio copy. It appears that the foul papers left the matter temporarily unresolved, and since we do not possess a text of the fair copy which presumably resolved it, we must either print a text that is incoherent in its treatment of Winchester or we must conjecturally make the minimum of necessary alterations in 1.4/Sc. 4. Since the play can be made coherent by the omission of two lines and the alteration (mostly obvious) of eight words of dialogue, we have adopted the second of these options. (See notes at 1.4.19/346, 1.4.36/363, 1.4.41/368, 1.4.48/375, 1.4.55/382, 1.4.55.1/382.1, 1.4.78/405, 1.4.83/410.)

Act and scene divisions were also apparently left incoherent in the foul papers. This deficiency is less serious in theatrical terms, but a considerable nuisance editorially. The beginnings of Acts 1-4 are sensibly marked; Act 5 begins, in F, at the beginning of the last scene of the play (5.7/Sc. 35 in this edition). This can hardly be right, and probably reflects misinterpretation of a scene division. The last fifth of the play contains, in addition to the erroneous act division, two scene divisions: 'Scena secunda' (5.1/Sc.29 in this edition) and 'Scœna Tertia' (5.2/Sc. 30 in this edition). It seems reasonable to suppose that these markings indicate scene divisions in an intended Act 5, rather than in Act 4 (which begins almost 600 lines before the said 'Scena secunda', and contains seven scenes according to the normal criteria). Editors since Capell have assumed that the original first scene of Act 5 is lost, and have accordingly renumbered 'Scena secunda' as 5.1/Sc. 29, and so forth. F2 by contrast identified the beginning of Act Five with the entrance of the victorious French 63 lines before the Folio's 'Scena secunda'. But F2's division has the disadvantage that the bodies of Talbot and his son remain on stage between 4.7/Sc.28 and 5.1/Sc. 29: the act division is not, properly, a scene division. We have followed Capell, with misgiving, on the assumption that the original structural intention is irrecoverable, due to revision or the loss of a scene.

The act divisions seem to be literary rather than theatrical in origin. The public theatres seem not to have made use of intervals between the acts before c.1609, and the copy for F seems in any case not to have undergone theatrical annotation. It will be noticed that the division of authorial shares broadly reflects the act divisions, which may well reflect the collaborators' efforts to note the place of their own contribution in a predetermined structure; alternatively, all the divisions might be the work of X and Y alone, or of whoever put the various authorial papers together. We have therefore assumed that they have no theatrical significance.

Equally literary is the division into scenes. Scene divisions are only marked in Acts 3 and 5, and seem to be a mannerism of playwright Y. Moreover, Y does not treat the cleared stage as evidence of a new scene: 3.2-3.6/Sc. 15-19 are all treated as one scene ('Scœna Secunda'), presumably because they all deal with the battle for Rouen, and take place in and around that city. Likewise, 5.2-5.5/Sc. 30-3 contain no scene divisions except the preliminary 'Scœna Tertia', presumably because they all dramatize a single battle sequence. Editors have retained the Folio divisions in Act 3, and only slightly modified those in Act 5; but the principle behind the Folio divisions in both acts conflicts with theatrical practice in the period and with editorial practice in the rest of the canon; moreover, it reflects the literary assumptions of only one of the authors of this collaborative play. We have therefore applied the normal criteria throughout the play, with the result that our divisions depart more than usual from the traditional scene-numbering.

This edition	Traditional	Folio
1.3/Sc. 3	1.2 (continued)	—
1.4/Sc. 4	1.3	—
1.5/Sc. 5	1.4	—
1.6/Sc. 6	1.4 (continued)	—
1.7/Sc. 7	1.5	—
1.8/Sc. 8	1.6	—
3.3/Sc. 16	3.2 (continued)	3.2 (continued)
3.4/Sc. 17	3.2 (continued)	3.2 (continued)
3.5/Sc. 18	3.2 (continued)	3.2 (continued)
3.6/Sc. 19	3.2 (continued)	3.2 (continued)
3.7/Sc. 20	3.3	3.3
3.8/Sc. 21	3.4	3.4
5.1/Sc. 29	5.1	5.2
5.2/Sc. 30	5.2	5.3
5.3/Sc. 31	5.3	5.3 (continued)
5.4/Sc. 32	5.3 (continued)	5.3 (continued)
5.5/Sc. 33	5.3 (continued)	5.3 (continued)
5.6/Sc. 34	5.4	5.3 (continued)
5.7/Sc. 35	5.5	'Actus Quintus'

McKerrow's work on *Part One* had reached an advanced stage, and we have adopted a number of his conjectures; references in the Textual Notes are to his galley proofs, annotated by Alice Walker.

G.T./(J.J.)

WORKS CITED

Cairncross, A. S., ed., *1 Henry VI*, Arden (1962)
Sanders, N. J., ed., *1 Henry VI*, New Penguin (1981)
Tanselle, G. Thomas, 'External Fact as an Editorial Problem', *SB* 32 (1979), 1–47
Taylor, Gary, 'Shakespeare and Others: The Authorship of *1 Henry VI*' (forthcoming in *Medieval and Renaissance Drama in England*)
Wilson, John Dover, ed., *1 Henry VI*, New (1952)

TEXTUAL NOTES

Title *The first Part of Henry the Sixt*] F (*head title, running titles*); *The First part of King Henry the Sixt*. F (*table of contents*); The thirde parte of Henry ye sixt S.R. For the Register entry, see Introduction.

1.1.0.4–5/0.4–5 *Warwicke . . . and the Duke of Somerset*] F. Neither is identified, or takes any part in this scene—or in the play, until 2.4. In a prompt-book they might either have been removed from the scene, or given a proper part in it.

1.1.6/6 King *Henry*] F; *Henry* POPE

1.1.45.1/45.1 *Exeunt Warwicke, Somerset, and Heralds with Coffin*] This edition; *not in* F; *Exit Funeral* CAIRNCROSS. The author may not have worked out when the funeral should leave; but here seems likelier than the end of the scene, partly because it frees extras earlier, for the battle sequence in 1.2. See 1.1.0.4–5/0.4–5: this is the only convenient opportunity for Somerset and Warwick to exit.

1.1.49/49 moistned] F1; moist F2

1.1.50/50 marrish] POPE; Nouriſh F. F produces an awkward repetition, in which mothers nurse their babes with tears and England is also a nurse who nurses with tears; Pope's emendation produces a natural sequence, as the tears of the mothers turn England into a salty marsh populated only by wailing women. An easy minim misreading.

1.1.56/56 bright—] F. Despite numerous conjectures about the intended completion of this sentence, a dramatic interruption is almost certainly intended.

1.1.60 Guyenne] F (Guyen)

1.1.60 Compiègne] F (Champaigne). F follows the spelling in Hall and Fabyan ('the toune of Champeigne').

1.1.60/60 Roan, Rheimes,] This edition; *Rheimes*, F; *Rheimes, Roan*, CAPELL. If 'Roan' has been omitted—as seems almost certain from 1.1.65/65 and the defective metre here—then eyeskip from one initial 'R' to another seems likely, and this explanation suggests that 'Roan' came first. Metrically, either position is possible (especially given our uncertainty about the author's pronunciation of these names, and the uncertainty of metre throughout these scenes).

1.1.60 Rheims] F (Rheimes)

1.1.61 Gisors] F (Guyſors)

1.1.61 Poitiers] F (Poiɛtiers)

1.1.62 corpse] F (Coarſe)

1.1.65 Rouen] F (Roan). See also 1.1.60.

1.1.76/76 third] F1; third man F2; third, he ORGER (*conj. in* Cambridge)

1.1.81/81 *Exit*] WILSON: *not in* F

1.1.83/83 her] F; their THEOBALD

1.1.86.1/86.1 *He remoues his mourning Robe*] This edition (J.J.); *not in* F

1.1.89/89 2. MESSENGER] ROWE; *Meſſ.* F

1.1.92, etc. Dauphin] F (Dolphin)

1.1.94/94 *Reyneir*] ROWE (*subs.*); *Reynold* F. It seems probable that the author intended to refer to Margaret's father, though Wilson points out that a 'Veignold' is mentioned by Hall and Grafton among the French leaders at Orléans. Perhaps the manuscript read 'Reynard' (see note to 4.4.27/1886).

1.1.95/95 Duke of] F; Duke w. s. WALKER (*conj.*). Contamination from the preceding line would have been easy; 'the Duke Alanson' occurs at *LLL* 2.1.61/538 and *Henry V* 4.8.18–19/2613–14.

1.1.103/103 3 MESSENGER] ROWE; *Meſ.* F

1.1.112/112 full scarce] F; scarce full ROWE

1.1.124/124 slew] F (flew); flew ROWE 3

1.1.131 Fastolf] F (Falſtaffe). F's spelling is a variant of 'Fastolf', the name by which historians normally identify the 14th-c. figure. (See Norman Davis, 'Falstaff's Name', *SQ* 28 (1977), 513–15 and George Walton Williams, 'Second Thoughts on Falstaff's Name', *SQ* 30 (1979), 82–4.) Since 'Falſtaffe' occurs in the stints of both Folio compositors, it seems unlikely to be—as Williams contends—a printing-house sophistication, caused by the later fame of Prince Hal's companion; we therefore retain it in the old-spelling text.

1.1.132 vanguard] F (Vauward)

1.1.137 Walloon] F (Wallon)

1.1.141/141 slaine‸ then?] F; ~ ?~‸ THEOBALD 4 (1757)

1.1.157 Fore] F (for). See *Henry V* 3.5.60, *All's Well* 4.4.3, and *Kinsmen* 1.4.49.

1.1.157/157 Orleance] HANMER; Orleance is F. A compositor misled by the preceding ambiguous spelling 'for' could easily interpolate an apparently required 'is'. Hanmer's emendation not only brings this line into conformity with the chronicles and the rest of the play; it also eliminates a contradiction within the scene itself, since 1.1.60/60 and 1.1.157/157 can now be reconciled.

1.1.176/176 steale] SINGER (Mason); ſend F

1.2.0.2, etc. René] F spells 'Reignier' and 'Reignier'; see also notes to 1.1.94/94 and 4.4.27/1886.

1.2.7/184 Otherwhiles] F; The whiles CAPELL. Like F, Capell's emendation has no Shakesperian parallel; the metrical irregularity it eliminates (an extra initial syllable) is acceptable, whoever wrote the passage.

1.2.9 porrage] F (Porredge)

1.2.21 flee] F (fly). Compare *Tragedy of Lear* 2.2.256–8 (the only other instance in the canon where rhyme encourages the 'flee' pronunciation).

1.3.8 Froissart] F (*Froyſard*)

1.3.9/207 bred] ROWE; breed F. F might be defended: Froissart reads 'England's entire population [to be] of the breed of Oliver and Roland' during that time.

1.3.17/215 to be] F; be POPE. Compare *Othello* 2.3.183/1189: Q 'be' (metrical), F 'to be' (unmetrical).

1.3.65/263 which you may] F1; which you F2; you may CAIRNCROSS

1.3.78/276 fiue] STEEVENS; fine F. (Emendation based on chronicles.)

1.3.79/277 Church-yard] F; Church POPE. A feminine line-ending hardly constitutes grounds for emendation, whoever the author; Holinshed has 'church', but F's variant is difficult to explain as an error, and easily explained as deliberate clarification.

1.3.81/279 come] F; come on This edition *conj*.

1.3.82.1, 1.6.79, 1.7.0.2, 1.8.3, 29/280.1, 516, 527.2, 568, 594 le Puzel] ROWE (*la*); de Puzel F. Compositor A was guilty of a number of such errors in *Henry V*, which he set immediately before *1 Henry VI*; all these examples occur in his stints, and once he had made the misreading he would be likely enough to repeat it. He may also have been misled by the correct use of 'de' elsewhere in Act 1 (1.1.80, 1.3.78, 1.6.6/80, 276, 443). The sources agree in treating 'Puzel' as an epithet, not a place name; contrast '*Ione of Aire*' at F 5.6.49/2440. On the evidence of other plays, the distinction of gender between 'le' and 'la' is unlikely to have been observed. See also 5.3.0.1/2196.1.

1.3.92 rites] F (rights)

1.3.104/302 o're] F; over ROWE. If metrical regularity should be restored, it might be preferable to add 'yea' after 'Orleance': the resulting 'yea or no' occurs twice elsewhere in this play (4.1.29, 5.3.36/1585, 2276) and at *Contention* 1.3.110/476, *Errors* 4.2.3/1032, and *Richard III* 4.4.455/2960.

1.3.106/304 Ile] F; I will CAPELL

1.3.110/308 Halcyons] F1; Halcyon F3

1.3.111/309 entred] F1; entred thus F2. McKerrow, noting that Shakespeare did not elsewhere treat F's word as a trisyllable, conjectured emending 'these Warres' to 'these your Warres'.

1.3.119 Mohammed] F (*Mahomet*)

1.3.124/322 reuerently] F; reverent DYCE 2

1.3.127/325 and be] F; be MARSHALL

1.4.4/331 Gloster] F. Here, at 1.4.6/333 and 1.4.61/388, the name must be trisyllabic, if the lines are to be metrically regular; but that pronunciation need not have been indicated orthographically.

1.4.5, 7, 9/332, 334, 336 within the Tower] This edition; *not in* F; *Within* MALONE. The fact that three different characters speak from within the Tower, at such length, suggests that something other than an ordinary 'speech from off-stage' is involved. Perhaps they were intended to appear at a barred window, or 'above', or behind an on-stage structure. Compare *Errors* 3.1.

1.4.5/332 knocketh] THEOBALD; knocks F. F's variant may be due to line-justification.

1.4.15/342, 1.4.18/345 within the Tower] This edition; *and Wood-uile the Lieutenant speakes within* F (continuing the preceding stage direction); *Within* ALEXANDER

1.4.19/346 My Lord] This edition; The Cardinall F. For the confusion over Winchester's rank, see the Introduction. 'My Lord of Winchester' occurs at 3.1.110, 125, 3.1.135, 5.1.28/1190, 1205, 1215, 2141; this produces a tetrameter, but Nashe's scenes are often metrically irregular. Alternatively, and more radically, one might omit this line completely and substitute 'Winchester' for 'him' in 1.5.20/347 (producing a regular pentameter, if 'commandement' were treated as trisyllabic).

1.4.28/355 Or wee'le] F; We'll POPE

1.4.29/356 Visheir] This edition; Vmpheir F; Humphrey THEOBALD. Theobald's emendation has been universally accepted, because it replaces nonsense with sense; but it leaves F's reading almost impossible to explain. In any case, why should Winchester here introduce Gloucester's Christian name? In *Part One*, the name only occurs twice, much later (3.1.3, 5.1.58/1085, 2171), in each case in the formula '*Humfrey* of Gloster'; in *Part Two*, though much more common, it is infrequently used on its own, and not until after it has been carefully established as an alternative to 'Gloster'. For all these reasons—and because both plays strongly prefer medial 'f', not 'ph'—Theobald's emendation seems as implausible critically as palaeographically; one would instead expect from Winchester an abusive epithet, to which Gloster's 'Piel'd Priest' is a reply. As Protector, Gloster is Viceroy, and 'Vizier' (with its Mohammedan associations) would be appropriately insulting, and a noun to which 'ambitious' would naturally apply. It is also—unlike 'Humphrey'—a word unusual enough to cause a compositor trouble. *OED* lists 'viseir' as a contemporary spelling; although we have found no parallels for F's medial 'h', among the various spellings of this foreign word it would not be implausible (especially by confusion of 'Viceroy' and 'heir').

1.4.29 vizier] See preceding note.

1.4.30/357 to be] F; be POPE. See note to 1.3.17/215.

1.4.36/363 If] This edition; Ile canuas thee in thy broad Cardinalls Hat, | If F. See note to 1.4.19/346. The image of the Folio's preceding line depends entirely upon the shape of a cardinal's hat, and can only be omitted or rewritten entirely. But the conditional threat ('If . . . insolence') can be kept.

1.4.36/363 insolence—] This edition; ~. See preceding note.

1.4.41/368 Purple] This edition; Scarlet F. Since a child's christening cloth was white, the image here does not depend upon the colour of Winchester's robes. See note to 1.4.19/346.

1.4.46/373 Tawny Coats] F; tawny POPE

1.4.48/375 Ile] F2; I F1

1.4.48/375 Bishops Mitre] This edition; Cardinalls Hat F. See note to 1.4.19/346. For a bishop wearing his mitre on stage, compare for instance Marlowe's *Edward II* (1591-3), 1.1.188-9 ('Throwe of his golden miter, rend his stole, | And in the channell christen him anew'), where it is clear in context that the Bishop of Coventry must be visibly wearing both stole and mitre.

1.4.51/378 thou wilt] F; thou'lt POPE

1.4.55/382 cloked] This edition; Scarlet F. See note to 1.4.19/346. 'Scarlet', here referring both to the cardinal's robes and to the 'scarlet woman' of Revelation 17: 4 ff., cannot be properly replaced by 'Purple', as at 1.4.41/368. *OED* cites 'cloked hypocricy' in 1526, 1529, and 1555 (see *hypocrisy*; also *cloak, sb.* 3). This substitution supplies a conventional epithet, while retaining both the Folio's emphasis on Winchester's clothing and a parallel to the first half of the line (coats/cloked, in place of tawny/scarlet).

1.4.55.1/382.1 Bishops] This edition; *Cardinalls* F. See note to 1.4.19/346.

1.4.71/398 canst, cry] F; canst. Cry CAIRNCROSS; canst, | Cry CAMBRIDGE

1.4.72/399 OFFICER] HANMER; *not in* F. F indents the line as though it were the beginning of a new speech.

1.4.78/405 Bishop] This edition; Cardinall F. See note to 1.4.19/346.

1.4.80/407 wee'le] F; we will CAMBRIDGE (W. S. Walker)

1.4.83/410 Bishop is] This edition; Cardinall's F. See note to 1.4.19/346.

1.4.86/413 ere] F; ere't be CAPELL

1.5.8/424 Princes spyals] POPE; Princes eſpyals F; Prince' espials CAIRNCROSS. Assimilation (-es es-) would be easy: metrically and euphonically F seems unlikely, whoever the author.

1.5.10/426 Wont] STEEVENS (Tyrwhitt); Went F

1.5.13/429 They may vex vs] F; Vex vs they may CAIRNCROSS (*conj*.); They may vs vex This edition *conj*.

1.5.16/432 haue I watcht] F; watcht CAIRNCROSS (Vaughan). Cairncross conjectures that 'haue I' was interpolated under the influence of the previous line; but 1.5.15/431 (on Folio k4) reads 'I haue', and 1.5.16/432 (on Folio k4v) 'haue I', so that Cairncross must attribute the interpolation to a scribe (since the compositor apparently set k3 in the interim between k4 and k4v) and further assume that 1.5.16/432 *should* have read 'haue I'. This elaborate hypothesis seems unnecessary, merely in order to eliminate a hexameter (which occur often enough in plays of this period). See lineation notes.

1.5.20.1/436.1 *Exit M. Gunner at one doore*] This edition; *Exit.* F (after 1.5.19/435)

1.6.0.3/437.3 among...Glasdale] not in F. For 'Glasdale', see note to 1.6.41/478.

1.6.5/442 Duke] THEOBALD; Earle F. Probably an authorial error; Bedford's rank is not specified elsewhere in scenes attributable to Nashe.

1.6.6/443 Lord] F; Captaine This edition *conj.* Compare 'the valiaunt Captaine, called Poynton of Sanctrayles' (Grafton, pp. 592-3; xth year).

1.6.6 Santrailles] F (*Santrayle*). Though the chronicles spell this name variously, they all agree in giving it a terminal -s, which may have been accidentally omitted by the compositor (Walker, MS).

1.6.11/448 pil'd] F; vild THEOBALD. Theobald's unnecessary emendation creates a parallel with Sonnet 121.1.

1.6.28/465 were] F; was ROWE

1.6.38/475 Grate] F; secret grate DYCE. Hall has 'secret grate'.

1.6.41/478 Glasdale] This edition; *Glanfdale* F. The chronicles agree on 'Glasdale', which is confirmed by 15th-c. sources; one cannot easily discern an authorial motive for F's change, which could result from simple misreading, repeated four lines later by the same compositor.

1.6.43.1/480.1 *They looke through the Grate*] This edition; *not in* F

1.6.44/481 Lou] This edition (conj. Walker, MS); Lords F; Loire MCKERROW (*conj.*). Folio 'Lords' makes feeble sense: why should lords 'stand' at the North Gate, and if they did what difference should that make to the attack? Walker's conjecture, like McKerrow's, assumes compositorial misreading of an unfamiliar proper name taken from this section of the chronicles: Folio 'stands' here seems more natural in relation to a bastille ('the bastile of saint Lou': Holinshed) than to a 'stagnant' part of the river. Neither 'Lou' nor 'loo' was established as an English noun.

1.6.45/482 GLASDALE] This edition; *Glanfdale.* F

1.6.67/504 Beare...bury it.] CAIRNCROSS (Brooks); F *places after* 1.6.64/501. Since Salisbury is alive and gesturing at 1.6.68-72/505-9, and is apparently still on stage at 1.6.88/525, this line cannot refer to him; neither the chronicles nor the play suggest any other victim but Gargrave, and Talbot's conclusion that Gargrave is dead comes more naturally after his attempt to rouse him than before it. Moreover, some provision must be made for removing his body before the end of the scene. Cairncross attributes F's error to 'omission and erroneous insertion' by a scribe; but it is more easily explained by the assumption that the misplaced line was an ambiguous marginal addition, which Compositor A inserted in the wrong place.

1.6.73/510 like thee, Nero,] MALONE; like thee, F1; *Nero-like will* F2; Nero-like POPE; like the Roman, W. S. WALKER (*conj.*). Cairncross follows Pope, conjecturing that the error results from 'omission...and consequent emendation, conjectural'; Malone's emendation produces an equally acceptable reading by simpler means.

1.6.77/514 the] F; this POPE

1.6.85 Pucelle *or* pucelle] F (*Puzel or Puſſel*). The two senses required here—'virgin' and 'slut'—are treated as one word by *OED*, and neither spelling is exclusively associated with one sense. Cotgrave (1611) also gives another meaning, not recognized by *OED* or editors, but clearly relevant here: 'the riuer Pilchard; or a young, or little Shad-fish'. Editors retain F's spelling of the second word, but such inconsistent modernization produces a 'word' not found in any dictionary. The sense 'maid' is last recorded in England in 1575, and is elsewhere used in this play only as a part of Joan's French 'title'; the sense 'slut' survived as English slang until at least the early 18th c. We have treated the 'pure' meaning as a French, and the 'impure' as an English, variant of the same word.

1.6.85 Dauphin] F (Dolphin). Although here—uniquely in the Shakespeare canon—a pun is clearly intended on 'dolphin', the primary reference is to the French heir, mentioned at 1.6.79/516.

1.6.88/525 me] F; we CAIRNCROSS (Vaughan)

1.6.89/526 And then wee'le try] F; and then try CAIRNCROSS (W. S. Walker). Cambridge records 'Then we'll try' (Long MS); Pope omitted 'these', later in the line. Even for Act 1, the metre is unusually awkward.

1.7.3/529 men] This edition (conj. Vaughan); them F. An easy error, under the influence of 'them' in 1.7.2/528.

1.7.6/532 art a] F; arrant CAIRNCROSS (*conj.*)

1.7.14.1-2/540.1-2 *the French passe ouer the stage and enter*] This edition; *enter* F. Alternatively, '*then enter the Towne with Souldiers*' might be an anticipatory description of Joan's exit four lines below (as Capell and Malone assumed).

1.7.16/542 hungry-starued] F; hunger-starved ROWE

1.7.26.1/552.1 *Enter English Souldiers*] This edition; *not in* F. The earlier stage directions, and the character of the action, make it clear that Joan and Talbot engage in single combat on an otherwise empty stage; Talbot's first eight lines after Joan's exit (1.7.19-26/545-52) read like a soliloquy; but at 1.7.27/553 he addresses his 'Countreymen,' and at 1.7.32.1/558.1 English soldiers must be on stage to engage in '*another Skirmish*'. Since an alarum was technically 'a call to arms' (*sb.* 1, 2, 3, 4), it could naturally be followed by the entrance of soldiers, here as often elsewhere.

1.7.29/555 Style] MARSHALL (Dyce); Soyle F; Shield VAUGHAN (*conj.*). If for any reason the tail of an 'h' were obscured, it could easily be misread as 'o' (McKerrow).

1.7.37.1/563.1 *Exeunt Souldiers*] This edition; *not in* F

1.7.39.1-1.8.0.1/565.1-2 *Alarum, Retreat | Flourish.*] F (*Alarum, Retreat, Flouriſh.*). F gives a formula for the course or end of a battle: one army's 'alarum' leads to a 'retreat' and then a 'flourish' for the entrance of the victorious army. In this case part of the formula is inept—fighting has stopped before the end of Talbot's speech, and the French have entered Orléans, so 'Alarum' is pointless—but it no doubt represents what the author called for.

1.8.0.3/565.4 *with Colours*] This edition; *not in* F

1.8.2/567 English] F1; English Wolves F2; English dogs STAUNTON (*conj.*). 'Wolves' seems unfortunate, since wolves had been exterminated in England long before; for 'dogs' see 1.7.25/551 and *Henry V* 2.4.69/925.

1.8.6/571 Garden] F; gardens HANMER

1.8.11/576 out the Bells] F; bells CAIRNCROSS (Steevens)

1.8.21 pyramid] F (Pyramis)

1.8.22/587 of] DYCE (Capell); or F

1.8.25/590 rich-iewel'd Coffer] F; rich jewel-coffer CAIRNCROSS (Steevens). Nashe twice has 'Iuel-Coffer' (i. 359. 8, 9); Puttenham has 'rich iewell coffer'(Dii'); North's *Plutarch* has 'the riche coffer, that was found among king Darius iuells' (iii. 333, marginal note). C. G. Harlow ("The Authorship of *1 Henry VI*', *SEL* 5 (1965), pp. 270-2) claims that this passage is closest to North; but only Nashe and *1 Henry VI* specify that the coffer was carried before the king. The ambiguity about whether the coffer was intended only to carry jewels, or was itself jewelled, easily arises from either North or Puttenham; in the play, it cannot carry jewels (for it has to carry Joan's ashes), so the emphasis must instead fall on the precious character of the coffer itself. Though the Folio hyphenation might well be compositorial, emendation seems unnecessary.

1.8.27/592 France] F; France up-born CAPELL

2.1.5/601 A SENTINEL] CAPELL; *Sent.* F. F is ambiguous (as at 2.1.38/634).

2.1.7.2-3/603.2-3 *Their Drummes beating a Dead March*] F. CAIRNCROSS (following a conjecture by Wilson) omits this direction, transferring it to 2.2.6/683 to cover a (conjectural) funeral procession for Salisbury; RIVERSIDE transposes it to 2.2.0/Sc. 10.0 (for the entrance of the victorious English army!). But see *OED dead, a.* 14 ('muffled'), and for the action compare the anonymous *King Leir* (c.1590), 'a stil march' (l. 2464), the anonymous *Alarum for London* (c.1599), 'a still march' (ll. 319, 321); Heywood's *Rape of Lucrece* (c.1607), and *2 Iron Age* (c. 1612) 'a soft march, without noise'. All these parallels involve—

like this passage—a secret attack, usually clearly occurring at night. Wilson conjectured that a book-keeper was confused by the similarity of directions at 2.1.7.1/603.1 and 2.2.0.1/677.2; but Greg observed that 'a book-keeper, reading through the text, would be very unlikely to misplace his annotations, and would, moreover, simply write "Dead March" rather than "Their Drums beating a Dead March"' (*Folio*, 189).

2.1.24/620 begun—] This edition; ~. F. Editors who retain F emend or disregard the colon at 2.1.22/618; but Talbot's 'Well' would naturally follow an incomplete sentence.

2.1.29 all together] F (altogether). For the contemporary acceptability of F's form see *OED*, *adj*. 2.

2.1.31/627 faile] F; fall CAIRNCROSS

2.1.33.1-2/629.1-2 *Exeunt seuerally Bedford and Burgundy, with some Souldiers*] This edition; *not in* F. The different 'corners' which Bedford and Burgundy attack might be different parts of the tiring-house façade, but it would be more natural—and in theatrical terms more practical—for them to attack off-stage different parts of the city.

2.1.37.1/633.1 *Talbot and his Souldiers scale the Walls*] This edition; *not in* F. See previous note. THEOBALD first added a direction for scaling the walls at this point.

2.1.38/634 SENTINELS] F (*Sent.*) See 2.1.5/601.

2.1.39.2/634.2 *Alarum*.] This edition; *not in* F

2.1.39.2/634.2 *French Souldiers*] This edition; *French* F. Those who 'leape ore the walles' can hardly 'Enter seuerall wayes'; nor need we assume that the second sentence of this stage direction duplicates the first.

2.1.39.3/634.1 *& exeunt*] This edition; *not in* F

2.1.78/673 them.] CAPELL; them. | *Exeunt.* F. F's direction, which contradicts 2.1.79-79.1/673.2, cannot plausibly be attributed to Compositor B, so presumably reflects confusion in the copy. It seems likely that 2.1.78.1-83/673.1-677 are a later addition, either by the author of the surrounding material or by a collaborator tidying up and revising the foul papers. Compare *King Leir* (*c*.1590?), Sc. 28 and 29, where after a French night attack, 'with a stil march', the text calls for '*Alarum, with men and women halfe naked: Enter two Captaynes without dublets, with swords*', asking 'Where are those villaines that were set to watch' etc.

2.2.6 centre] F (Centure)

2.2.6.1/683.1 *Exit one or more*] This edition; *not in* F; *Dead March. Enter with the body of Salisbury* CAIRNCROSS (Wilson). Cairncross's emendation depends upon the assumption that the Folio direction at 2.1.7.2-3/603.2-3 is misplaced: see note. The dialogue gives no indication of the entrance or exit of a funeral procession; but it does seem likely that someone responds to Talbot's order.

2.2.20/697 Arce] ROWE; Acre F; Aire CAIRNCROSS. Cairncross undoubtedly restores the manuscript reading, which occurs in Holinshed and at 5.6.49/2440. But Holinshed's reading is an error, which the author would no doubt have corrected if it had been pointed out to him. For the editorial principle, see Tanselle.

2.2.54/731 'tis] F; it is MALONE

2.3.11/748 Madame ... desir'd] F. CAIRNCROSS omitted 'Madame'; POPE, 'desir'd'. Pope's is the more attractive emendation, since it not only normalizes the metre but removes a duplication in the sense (which could have arisen by *currente calamo* revision).

2.3.21 seely] F (filly)

2.3.60/797 That] F: That, madam, STEEVENS (*conj.*); Lady, that KEIGHTLEY

2.4.41/860 from the Tree are cropt] CAIRNCROSS; are cropt from the Tree F

2.4.57/876 law] CAIRNCROSS (anon. *conj.*); you F. Assimilation to the earlier 'you' probably played as much part as misreading in the error.

2.4.76/895 fashion] F; faction THEOBALD. The two words were to some extent interchangeable—see *OED faction*, *sb*. 1—but as there are no parallels for F's spelling taking Theobald's meaning, modernization to 'faction' seems unwarranted. Compositorial error is possible.

2.4.91/910 executed] F; headed POPE. Cairncross emends, but hexameters are frequent enough in Shakespeare's verse.

2.4.117 wiped] F1 (whipt). *OED* records the F1 spelling in the 15th c.; F2 modernizes (as here).

2.4.132/951 gentles] This edition (*conj.* McKerrow); gentle F1; gentle sir F2; gentleman SISSON; gentlemen CAIRNCROSS (anon. *conj.*)

2.5.3/956 rack] F (Wrack). See *OED sb*.³

2.5.6-7/959-60 Argue ... Mortimer, | *Nestor*-like ... Care.] This edition (*conj.* McKerrow); *Neftor*-like ... Care, | Argue ... Mortimer. F. Mortimer is more plausibly compared to Nestor than are his 'Locks' or 'death'.

2.5.11/964 like to] F; look like VAUGHAN (*conj.*); are like CAIRNCROSS (*conj.*)

2.5.19/972 vnto his] F1; his F2-4; to his ROWE. F2's error may arise from a botched attempt to make the emendation Rowe succeeded in completing; the metrically irregular repetition of 'vnto' is certainly suspicious.

2.5.34/987 is he] F; is CAIRNCROSS

2.5.44 dis-ease] F (Diſeaſe)

2.5.71/1024 K.] F2 (King); *not in* F1. Omission would be particularly easy if the word were abbreviated (as sometimes elsewhere).

2.5.75/1028 the third] F2; third F1. *The* is an easy word to omit in any circumstances; but eyeskip could have contributed here.

2.5.76/1029 the King] This edition; hee F; Bolingbroke POPE; he, Bolingbroke CAPELL. Pope and Capell recognized that F is not only unmetrical but—more important—incomprehensible: 'hee' clearly refers to someone other than 'Edward' (2.5.76/1029) or 'Clarence' (2.5.75/1028) or 'my Mother' (2.5.74/1027), or Richard (2.5.71/1024), but who is not clear. Pope identified him—as have most commentators—with Henry IV, mentioned at 2.5.63/1016; but the name 'Bolingbroke' has not yet occurred, which would rule out Pope's emendation, even if the implausibility of the alleged error did not. Besides, since Bolingbroke was long dead, the present verb 'doth' (2.5.77/1030) would be inappropriate. The person who 'doth bring his Pedigree' from John of Gaunt is not the dead Henry IV but the living Henry VI, who could be readily enough identified simply as 'the King'. But although these words would make immediate sense of the passage, and would have been acceptable politically at the time of the play's composition (when England had no 'King'), by 1622 'the King' would dangerously suggest James I rather than Henry VI, and could have been deliberately altered by someone in Jaggard's shop in order to forestall objection. Alternatively, manuscript 'the K.' could have produced F's reading, if for any reason 'K.' were obscured.

2.5.84/1037 Cambridge, then,] CAIRNCROSS; ~, ~, F

2.5.108/1061 passage] F; passing CAIRNCROSS

2.5.113/1066 be all] F; befall THEOBALD. Shakespeare has 'fair befall' five times, all in early plays (*Shrew*, *Richard III*, *Richard II*, *LLL*); but Shakespeare probably did not write this scene.

2.5.129/1082 myn ill] CAIRNCROSS; my will F; my ill THEOBALD

3.1.0.2-5/1082.2-4 *Winchester; ... white Roses*] This edition; *Winchefter, Warwick, Somerfet, Suffolk, Richard Plantagenet* F. Although the dialogue of this scene does not mention the roses, in 2.4/Sc. 12 the lords promised to wear them 'for euer', and they clearly do so again in 3.4/Sc. 17 and 4.1/Sc. 22.

3.1.46/1127 Protector] F; Lord Protector KEIGHTLEY (W. S. Walker)

3.1.52/1134 GLOSTER] HANMER; *Warw⟨icke⟩*. F

3.1.53/1135 WARWICKE] HANMER; *not in* F; *Som⟨erset⟩*. THEOBALD. Hanmer agrees with F in assigning the following words to Warwick, but simply deprives him of the preceding three ('Roame thither then'). See previous note.

3.1.54/1136 SOMERSET] F (*Som.*); *War⟨wick⟩*. THEOBALD

3.1.54/1136 soe] SISSON (McKerrow); ſee F

3.1.55/1137 Me thinkes] F; *Som⟨erset⟩*. Methinks THEOBALD

3.1.64/1146 entertalke] HART. The compositor in F probably intended to set two words, but the spacing between 'r' and 't' is minimal.

1 HENRY VI

3.1.64 intertalk] F (enter talke). For the compound—not in *OED*—see Golding's Ovid, ii. 201.
3.1.83 pebble] F (peeble)
3.1.85/1165 Pate] F; pates POPE
3.1.90.1/1170.1 *The skirmish ceases*] This edition; *not in* F
3.1.115/1195 Yeeld my Lord Protector] F; My Lord Protector, yield POPE
3.1.145/1225 kinde] F; and kind COLLIER 2
3.1.167/1247 alone] F2; all alone F1
3.1.172/1252 humble seruice] F; faithful service POPE. Although F's repetition of the adjective is suspicious, without a confident identification of the authorship of this scene no restoration can be attempted.
3.1.175 gird] F (gyrt)
3.1.190.1/1270.1 *Senet.*] This edition; *Senet. Flourish.* F1; *Flourish* F2. Since 'Senet' was a set of notes played by a trumpet or cornetts, this looks like a duplicated direction. Dekker's *Satiromastix* has 'Trumpets sound a florish, and then a sennate' (F4; 3.1.266.2), which shows that a distinction could if necessary be made. But any such distinction seems pointless here, or at 3.8.27.1/1538.1.
3.1.203/1283 should loose] F2; loofe F1. Alternatively, one might conjecture 'loose it'.
3.2.13 Qui] F (Che)
3.2.13 la pauure gens] F (la pouure gens); pauvre gens ROWE. Sanders's note supports this modernization; it is clearly preferable to Rowe's emendation.
3.3.0.2/1301.1 *Alanson, Reignier*] CAMBRIDGE; *Alanfon* F. CAPELL instead altered the speech-prefix at 3.3.6/1307, assigning the speech to Alençon. René may well be a late addition to the scene, intended to replace Alençon. (See Introduction.)
3.3.0.2/1301.1 *and French Souldiers*] CAPELL; *not in* F
3.5.0.5/1324.3-4 *Alanson, and Reignier*] COLLIER; *and Reigneir* F; *and Alanson* HANMER
3.5.30/1354 Away Captaines] F; Captains, away ROWE
3.5.32 Goodbye] F (God b'uy)
3.5.32/1356 but to tell you] F; to tell you but CAIRNCROSS
3.5.63/1387 Sir *Iohn*] F; John CAIRNCROSS
3.5.73/1397 glad] F; fled VAUGHAN (*conj.*)
3.7.36.1/1456.1 *Enter Burgonie*] CAIRNCROSS; *not in* F; *Enter the Duke of Burgundy and forces* CAPELL (after 'French March', four lines previously)
3.7.46/1466 Foe.] POPE; ~, F
3.7.48/1468 Eyes,] F2; ~. F1
3.8.0.1/1511.1 *Flourish.*] This edition; *not in* F. Such sound effects are virtually obligatory for such a formal royal entrance.
3.8.0.3-6/1511.2-4 *Exeter . . . red Roses*] This edition; *Yorke, Suffolke, Somerfet, Warwicke, Exeter* F
3.8.13/1524 Lord] F; *not in* CAPELL
3.8.27.1/1538.1 *Senet.*] This edition; *Senet. Flourish.* F1; *not in* F2. See 3.1.190.1/1270.1.
4.1.0.1/1556.1 *Flourish.*] This edition; *not in* F. See following note.
4.1.0.1/1556.1 *Enter*] F (c.w.); *Actus Quartus. Scena Prima.* | *Enter* F (text)
4.1.0.4-6/1556.2-4 *Exeter . . . Paris*] This edition; *Yorke, Suffolke, Somer-|fet, Warwicke, Talbot. and Gouernor Exeter.* F. As usual, the direction does not mention the roses, which are certainly worn here. '*Exeter*' looks like an (unintentionally ambiguous) addition to the original direction.
4.1.8.1/1564.1 *Enter Falstaffe*] F. CAPELL added '*Exeunt Gov. and Train. King comes from his Throne*', and the first part of this direction has been generally accepted. However, this produces an awkward silence and exit: Falstaff's interruption of the ceremony would be much more dramatic.
4.1.14 thee] F (the)
4.1.19/1575 Patay] MALONE (Capell); *Poictiers* F. F is probably an authorial error, since it would be an unlikely misreading of 'Patay'. The author of 4.1/Sc. 22 probably did not write 1.1.105-47/105-47.
4.1.48/1604 my] F2; *not in* F1. 'My Lord Protector' occurs four times in this play, and ten times elsewhere in the canon.

4.1.54/1610 Pretend] F; Portend ROWE 3
4.1.163/1719 these] F; the CAIRNCROSS
4.1.173.1/1729.1 *Flourish*] THEOBALD. F places the word after '*Exeunt.*' on a new type line immediately before '*Manet*'. The Folio misplacement presumably results from some sort of late addition or additions, perhaps by someone going through the foul papers, or by a Folio proof-corrector. But the eight-line dialogue between York and Warwick, and the stage direction which precedes it (4.1.174-81/1730-7), might be a late addition; if so, whoever added it might simply have forgotten to delete '*Flourish*' at 4.1.181.1/1737.1, where it had originally been appropriate, but no longer was so.
4.1.180/1736 I wist] CAPELL; I wifh F; I wis THEOBALD. An easy ligature error (fh *for* ft). Compare *Antony* 1.3.11/265.
4.1.191/1747 that] F; sees CAIRNCROSS; at VAUGHAN (*conj.*)
4.2.3/1753 Captaine] This edition; Captaines F. Editors since MALONE alter the preceding entrance direction to include '*others*'; but these serve no function, and it seems more likely that F1's '*Captaines call*' results from metathesis for '*Captaine calls*'. See next note.
4.2.3/1753 calls] F2; call F1
4.2.15/1765 GENERALL] THEOBALD; *Cap.* F. See 4.2.3/1753. 'Captain', the more inclusive noun, could cover the same rank as 'General'; probably Shakespeare's own inconsistency (as often in foul papers).
4.2.29/1779 vyre] This edition; ryue F. Few editors have been satisfied by F. But neither 'driue' (JOHNSON *conj.*) nor 'ayme' (MCKERROW *conj.*) is idiomatic; 'roue' (WILSON, *conj.* Hart) assumes a most implausible misreading, and in any case refers to firing at a fixed target, which hardly seems appropriate. McKerrow also conjectured 'tyre', but admitted that it was 'a much less likely' misreading; the required sense is rare, and first recorded in Middleton's share of *Timon* (3.7.4/1226). Although Vaughan's 'rain' is superficially attractive, the conjectured misreading (ain/yu) is not easy, and the 'y' in this case is not likely to be a compositorial sophistication of copy 'i': Compositor B elsewhere set 'riu-' 65 times, and 'ryu-' never. None of the available alternatives is satisfactory. The conjecture 'vyre' assumes two easy minim misreadings, or metathesis. *OED* records a verb *vire*, meaning 'whirl or throw', in transitive and intransitive uses (1375-1586); *Artillerie* could of course mean 'missiles, shot' (*sb.* 3). Alternatively, *OED* records 'vire' as a Southern dialect variant of 'fire': compare *Titus* 4.2.107/1634 (figure/vigour) and *Antony* 2.7.112/1245 (fats/vats).
4.2.29 fire] See previous note.
4.2.34 due] F (dew). *OED* and editors interpret as a rare obsolete variant of *dow* (= *endue, endow*); but 'give or recognize as your due' seems more likely in context, and *OED* records an impersonal use of the verb in 1603 in a related sense (*v.*²).
4.2.43.1/1793.1 *Exit one or more*] This edition; *not in* F
4.2.50/1800 mad, and] F4; ~ : And F1
4.3.5/1811 Talbot:] F2; ~ˏ F1
4.3.5/1811 along,] F2; ~. F1
4.3.8/1814 Burdeaux] F. CAIRNCROSS (McKerrow) adds an '*Exit*', but since York and his army must exit at 4.3.53/1859, the messenger could go with them.
4.3.53/1859 *Exit*] F2; *not in* F1. Some recent editors revert to F1, arguing that Lucy remains on stage. But failure to mark exits followed soon by re-entrance is common in Shakespeare; Lucy, if on stage, is left awkwardly standing through 4.4.1-9/1860-8, when he should be urgently seeking aid for Talbot.
4.4.9.1/1868.1 *Enter Lucie*] CAPELL; *not in* F. See preceding note.
4.4.16/1875 legions] ROWE; *Regions* F. Shakespeare's lower-case 'l' could sometimes be misread as a minim: compare *Macbeth* 1.2.13/24, *Richard III* 1.1.134/134, *Othello* 5.1.1/2767. Compositor B added large numbers of emphasis capitals to his copy in the Histories.
4.4.19/1878 vnaduantagd] This edition; in aduantage F. Contorted glosses cannot conceal the fact that F here asserts that Talbot is 'in aduantage'; even if he were (he is not), Lucy in pleading for aid would hardly make such a statement. The proposed un/in

and e/d misreadings would be easy in Shakespeare's hand, and made easier by the rarity of the compound.

4.4.26/1885 and] F2; *not in* F1

4.4.27/1886 *Reignard*] F; Reignier ROWE. Compare *Duke of York* 5.7.38/2896 ('*Reynard*'). This is the only appearance of the character's name in Shakespeare's scenes, and F is unlikely to be a misreading.

4.4.31/1890 horse] HANMER (Theobald); hoaſt F. An easy misreading.

4.4.41/1900 ayde] F; side CAIRNCROSS. Cairncross's conjecture is lent plausibility by the earlier occurrence of 'ayde' four times on this Folio page (4.3.44, 4.4.11, 23, 29/1850, 1870, 1882, 1888), which could have encouraged compositorial substitution here.

4.5.13/1918 And shall] F (*text*); Shall F (*c.w.*)

4.5.39/1944 shamd] HUDSON (W. S. Walker); ſhame F

4.6.0.3/1960.4 *The English driue off the French*] This edition; *not in* F. Compare 1.7.0.2/526.2.

4.7.32.1/2049.1 *Alarum . . . bodyes*] CAPELL; *not in* F

4.7.50.1/2067.1 *with a French Herald*] CAPELL; *not in* F. This character's presence depends upon acceptance or rejection of Pope's emendation of the following line. If Lucy enters unattended, his entrance should be preceded by a 'Parley' trumpet call (as it might in any case). Capell also called for attendants, but Lucy and the Herald could carry off the bodies.

4.7.51/2068 Herald] F; *not in* POPE. Like Pope, Cairncross omits this word on grounds, relining the speech accordingly (. . . know | Who . . .); he conjectures that a theatrical adapter, wishing to eliminate Lucy as a role, substituted 'Herald' above the original speech-prefix, and that Compositor B misinterpreted this as an addition to the dialogue. But changing 'Lucy' to 'Herald' does not save a speaking part, or solve any casting problems. On the other hand, an original 'Herald' might have been later altered to 'Lucy', identifying him with the character in 4.3-4.4/Sc. 24-5. This would better explain the alleged error in this line (with 'Lu' to the left of 'Herald'). Since Lucy was a Stratford figure not named in the chronicles, his presence in 4.3-4.4/Sc. 24-5 presumably derives from Shakespeare; if, as seems possible, the end of this scene represents a revision of an original separate scene not by Shakespeare, Lucy's presence here might well be a late addition. If 'Herald' is omitted, Lucy addresses his speech to the French nobles. See Introduction.

4.7.63 Wexford] F (*Waſhford*)

4.7.64 Goodrich] F (*Goodrig*)

4.7.66/2083 Lord *Cromwell . . .* Lord *Furniuall*] F; Cromwell . . . Furnival CAIRNCROSS (Capell)

4.7.70 *Maréchal*] F (*Marſhall*). The word was sometimes trisyllabic in English usage (see *OED* and *1 Henry IV* 4.4.2/2458); here at *History of Lear* 17.9/2211 it is a French title with a French syllabification, and modernization seems logical.

4.7.89/2106 haue them] THEOBALD ('em); haue him F. See 4.7.94/2111. Perhaps evidence of imperfect revision of the scene.

4.7.94/2111 with them] F2; with him F1

4.7.94.1/2111.1 *Exeunt . . . bodyes*] This edition (after CAPELL); *not in* F

5.1.0.1/2113.1 SENNET.] F. The unique use of italic capitals here, and the word's unusual separation on a line of its own, both suggest that it was distinct from the rest of the stage directions in Compositor B's copy. Compare 3.1.109.1/1270.1 and 3.8.27.1/1538.1, both set by Compositor A ('*Senet*'), where the word seems for other reasons to be a subsequent addition to the direction.

5.1.0.2/2113.2 *and others*] CAPELL; *not in* F. See 5.1.25/2138.

5.1.2 Armagnac] F (*Arminack*)

5.1.17 Armagnac] F (*Arminacke*)

5.1.27.1-2/2140.1 *in Cardinals habite*] CAPELL; *not in* F. In the text as it stands, Winchester must be dressed as a Cardinal in this scene. See Introduction.

5.1.49/2162 wherein ship'd] F1; where inshipp'd F4

5.1.59/2172 nor] This edition; neither F. Grammatically, Elizabethan English permitted either 'neither . . . nor' or 'nor . . . nor'; this meant that a poet could choose, for the first term, either a one or a two syllable word, of identical meaning. *Neither* is used, in this position, 47 times in the Shakespeare canon when a two-syllable word is clearly required. It occurs only three times when a single syllable is required, all in the Folio, and all set by a single compositor (B): here, *Shrew* 4.3.93/1972, and *Duke of York* 1.1.200/200. It is therefore highly probable that these three anomalies result from Compositor B's unconscious modernizing, and that the metrically correct form should be restored in all three lines.

5.2.17-18/2192-3 PUCELL Now . . . feare. | Of] This edition (*conj*. Sanders); Now . . . feare. | *Pucel.* Of F. Sanders himself adopts an alternative emendation, removing Burgundy's speech-prefix from before 5.2.16/2191 and placing it (rather than *Pucel*) before 5.2.17/2192. George Walton Williams ably defends the alternative adopted here (*SSu* 36, p. 183).

5.3.0.1/2196.1 *le Pucell*] ROWE (*la*); *de Pucell* F. See note to 1.3.82.1/280.1. But this passage was set by Compositor B, and apparently written by a different playwright.

5.3.8/2204 speede and quicke] DYCE; ſpeedy and quicke F; speedy quick POPE. Misreading (e/y) assisted by assimilation to 5.3.5/2201.

5.3.11/2207 Regions] F; legions SINGER (Warburton)

5.4.15/2240 comest] ROWE; comſt F. F's line is so crowded that it omits the final stop. For the rhythm of the line compare 3.8.44/1555, probably by the same author, where *miscreant* is disyllabic.

5.5.4/2244 And . . . side. | I . . . peace,] CAPELL; I . . . peace, | And . . . ſide. F

5.5.12/2252 his] This edition (*conj*. McKerrow); her F. 'Suffolk would perhaps be more likely to compare himself to a male swan than to a female one—and both defend their young' (McKerrow). See 'his' in 5.5.13/2253 (at the top of l6ᵛ, which B set before l6, of which 5.5.12/2252 is the last line: two Folio pages thus intervened between B's setting of the two lines).

5.5.13-16/2253-6 Keeping . . . Oh stay:] F (*text*); Oh ſtay: F (*c.w.*). See 5.5.16/2256.

5.5.13/2253 his] F1; hir F2

5.5.18/2258 streame] SINGER 2 (Collier MS); ſtreames F

5.5.24/2264 heere to heere] This edition (*conj*. McKerrow); heere F. None of the other conjectures to fill out this line ('here thy prisoner', 'prisoner here', 'here alone', 'here in place', 'present here') explains the alleged error or contributes to the line's meaning; McKerrow explains the error, and creates a neat balancing of 'tongue' (Suffolk) and 'hear' (Margaret). Early texts do not always distinguish the spelling of adverb and verb.

5.5.27/2267 makes the senses rough] F; mates the senses vouch MCKERROW (*conj*.). Many conjectures have been made, few plausible. Editors who retain F usually gloss *rough* as 'dull', but love or beauty does not normally dull the senses; rather, they intensify or confuse them. 'Agitated' (*adj*. 4a, b) seems a better gloss. McKerrow's 'vouch' (independently conjectured by Bullen) would be the first occurrence of a rare word, which seems out of key with the style of the passage and not over-plausible palaeographically. But 'mates' (= amazes) is very attractive: perhaps we should read 'mates the senses rough' (G.T.) or 'mates the senses tough' (S.W.W.).

5.5.39/2279 I were best to] F; 'Twere best to POPE; I were best CAPELL

5.5.41 random] F (randon)

5.5.64/2304 Lady] F; Lady, sweet Lady LETTSOM (*conj*.)

5.5.84.1/2324.1 *Enter . . . Trumpets*] This edition (after CAPELL); *not in* F

5.5.92/2332 Assent] This edition; Conſent F. Cairncross conjectured that the line was 'probably corrupt'; the repetition of 'consent' is both pointless and suspicious. 'Consent' would be an easy compositorial substitution for 'Assent', even without the danger of assimilation here. Since 'give consent' occurs at 5.5.92/2332 and 5.7.23, 25/2589, 2591 (probably written by the same author, but set later by the compositor), it seems probable that the first occurrence of 'consent' is the error.

1 HENRY VI

Shakespeare never uses the verb, and the noun appears only in *All Is True*, but the word was common, and specifically occurs 'in the formal phrase *assent and consent*' (*sb.* 5b, 1574+).

5.5.110/2350 Countrys] CAPELL; Country F; county MALONE. Capell follows Hall's plural and spelling.
5.5.131/2371 Madam] F; Maid CAIRNCROSS
5.5.135/2375 modestlie] F2; modeftie F1
5.5.148/2388 Mad] F; And CAPELL; 'Mid WILSON (Collier); Maid MCKERROW (Perring, in Cambridge). 'Maid-naturall . . . means of course "simple as a maiden"' (McKerrow). Compare 'maid-pale peace' (*Richard II* 3.3.97/1614). But the compound is strained, and uncharacteristic of the language of Act 5. F can be defended as 'passing all rational bounds . . . extravagant . . . wild' (*OED*, a. 7), in opposition to 'Art'. Of emendations, 'Mid' is attractive, and not disabled by the fact that it does not appear elsewhere in the Shakespeare canon.
5.6.1.1/2392.1 Enter Pucell, guarded] This edition; not in F (which includes 'Pucell' in the opening stage direction). CAPELL and subsequent editors bring the Shepherd on here, with Joan; but it seems more appropriate that they meet on stage.
5.6.10 an't] F (and)
5.6.37/2428 one,] MARSHALL (Malone); me, F
5.6.49/2440 No, misconceyued,] F4; ~∧~, F1
5.6.49/2440 Arce] ROWE; Aire F. See note to 2.2.20/697.
5.6.68/2459 ingling] This edition (*conj.* McKerrow); iugling F. *OED* does not record a sexual sense for F's word, and none of the alleged parallels—*2 Henry IV* 2.4.128/1162, *Troilus* 2.3.70/1231, 5.2.25/2851—requires it. It has been suspected elsewhere only because of this passage. The sexual meaning of *ingle* is well established in the 1590s, and F could result from the simplest of errors.
5.6.70/2461 we will] F2; we'll F1. Compositor B commits similar errors (when working from known copy) at *1 Henry IV* 1.3.254/571, *Much Ado* 1.1.49/49, 1.1.88/88, etc. (See Werstine.) In this case 'we'll' would be an especially easy substitution, after 'Well'. Alternatively, one might conjecture 'Well well' at the beginning of the line (J.J.).
5.6.74 Machiavel] F (Macheuile)
5.6.91.1/2482.1 Winchester] F (Cardinall). F also has 'Car.' in the speech-prefix at 5.6.94/2485. See Introduction.
5.6.101/2492 some matter] F; the same CAIRNCROSS
5.6.114/2505 seuere] F; several CAIRNCROSS (Vaughan)
5.6.121/2512 poyson'd] F; prison'd THEOBALD
5.7.35/2601 therefore] F. Perhaps 'therefor 't'; for contraction of 'it' before 'may' compare *Winter's Tale* 1.2.116/163, *Pilgrim* 14.9, 10, etc. 'It' would be 'that contract' (5.7.28/2594), which editors in any case assume is the implicit subject of the verb.
5.7.39/2605 Lord] F1; good Lord F2
5.7.44 Armagnac] F (Arminacke)
5.7.60/2626 Y^t] CAIRNCROSS; not in F; It ROWE; Which WILSON (C. B. Young). The choice between *Which* and *That* is arbitrary; but the latter is frequently enough omitted elsewhere, while the canon affords no clear instances of omission of *which*.
5.7.64/2630 bringeth] F; ybringeth This edition *conj.* No parallels have been offered for a pronunciation of *contrary* as 'conterary', and *OED* records no such spellings.
5.7.72/2638 Will answer our] F; Answer our POPE; Will answer HUDSON (Steevens)
5.7.82/2648 loue] F2; Ioue F1
5.7.101.1/2667.1 with Exeter] This edition; not in F. Editors since CAPELL add this to the direction at 5.7.103/2669, but King Henry has specifically asked someone to 'conduct' him, and so his exit is more likely than Gloucester's to be accompanied. This staging would leave Gloucester and Somerset—two key antagonists in *The First Part of the Contention*—as the last two characters on stage.

INCIDENTALS

61 Paris,] ~∧ 80 Armes;] ~∧ 96 crowned] crown'd 361 contriud'st] contriued'ft 398 cry.] ~: 444 ransomed] ranfom'd 688 happend] happened 806 gatherd] gathered 879 meditating,] ~, 918 ripend] ripened 964 witherd] withered 1157 What] *King.* What 1209 Winchester] Winchefter 1398 recouerd] recouered 1541 Yorke:] ~■ 1582 there] thete 1643 complain?] ~, 1667 braine-sicke] braine-|ficke 1668 slight] flight 1731 Orator.] ~.) 1788 witherd] withered 1814 Burdeaux.] ~, 1855 losse,] ~: 1921 Talbots] Taibots 1953 seuerd] feuered 1978 encountered] encountred 2040 fauourd] fauoured 2166 deliuerd] deliuered 2191 there.] ~: 2209 silence] filenee 2225 droopeth] droopeth 2232 be.] ~: 2240 stake.] ~∧ 2302 in] iu 2363 newes,] ~. 2385 lurke.] ~, 2386 praise,] ~. 2401 so:] ~∧ 2449 torture] tortute 2449 shortened] fhortned 2451 discouer] difcouet 2452 warranteth] wartanteth 2628 wedlocke] wedloeke

FOLIO STAGE DIRECTIONS

1.1.0.1-5/0.1-0.5 *Dead March. | Enter the Funerall of King Henry the Fift, attended on by | the Duke of Bedford, Regent of France; the Duke | of Gloster, Protector; the Duke of Exeter Wer-|wicke, the Bishop of Winchester, and | the Duke of Somerset.*
1.1.56/56.1 *Enter a Messenger.*
1.1.88.1/88.1 *Enter to them another Messenger.*
1.1.95/95 *Exit.*
1.1.102.1/102.1 *Enter another Messenger.*
1.1.166/166 *Exit Bedford.*
1.1.169/169 *Exit Gloster.*
1.1.172/172 *Exit.*
1.1.177/177 *Exit.*
1.2.0.1/177.1 *Sound a Flourish.*
1.2.0.1-3/177.1-2 *Enter Charles, Alanson, and Reigneir, marching | with Drum and Souldiers.*
1.2.21/198 *Exeunt.*
1.3.0.1-2/198.1-2 *Here Alarum, they are beaten back by the | English, with great losse.*
1.3.0.2-3/198.2-3 *Enter Charles, Alanson, and Reigneir.*
1.3.24.1/222.1 *Enter the Bastard of Orleance.*
1.3.39/237 *Exit Bastard*
1.3.42.1-2/240.1 *Enter Ioane Puzel.*
1.3.49.1/247.1 *Reigntir, Alanson stand apart*
1.3.82.1/280.1 *Here they fight, and Ioane de Puzel overcomes.*
1.3.129/327 *Exeunt.*
1.4.0.1/327.1 *Enter Gloster, with his Seruing-men.*
1.4.14.1/341.1 *Glosters men rush at the Tower Gates, and Wooduile | the Lieutenant speakes within.*
1.4.28.1-2/355.1-2 *Enter to the Protector at the Tower Gates, Winchester | and his men in Tawney Coates.*
1.4.55.1-3/382.1-3 *Here Glosters men beat out the Cardinalls men, | and enter in the hurly-burly the Maior | of London, and his Officers.*
1.4.68.1/395.1 *Here they skirmish againe.*
1.4.85.1/413.1 *Exeunt.*
1.4.89/416 *Exeunt.*
1.5.0.1/416.1 *Enter the Master Gunner of Orleance, and | his Boy.*
1.5.20.1/436.1 *Exit.* (after 1.5.19/435)
1.5.21.1/437.1 *Exit.*

1 HENRY VI

1.6.0.1-2/437.2-3   Enter Salisbury and Talbot on the Turrets, | with others.
1.6.34.1/471.1   Enter the Boy with a Linstock.
1.6.47.1-2/484.1-2   Here they shot, and | Salisbury falls downe.
1.6.75.1/512.1   Here an Alarum, and it Thunders and Lightens.
1.6.77.1/514.1   Enter a Messenger.
1.6.79.1/518.1   Here Salisbury lifteth himselfe vp, and groanes.
1.6.89.1/526.1   Alarum. Exeunt.
1.7.0.1-4/526.2-5   Here an Alarum againe, and Talbot pursueth the Dolphin, | and driueth him: Then enter Ioane de Puzel, | driuing Englishmen before her. | Then enter Talbot.
1.7.3.1/529.1   Enter Puzel.
1.7.8.1/534.1   Here they fight.
1.7.12.1/538.1   They fight againe.
1.7.14.1-2/540.1-2   A short Alarum: then enter the Towne | with Souldiers.
1.7.18.1/544.1   Exit.
1.7.26.1/552.1   A short Alarum.
1.7.32.1/558.1   Alarum. Here another Skirmish.
1.7.39.1/565.1   Exit Talbot.
1.7.39.1-1.8.0.1/565.1-2   Alarum, Retreat, Flourish.
1.8.0.1-3/565.2-4   Enter on the Walls, Puzel, Dolphin, Reigneir, | Alanson, and Souldiers.
1.8.31/596   Flourish. Exeunt.
2.1.0.1-2/596.1-2   Enter a Sergeant of a Band, with two Sentinels.
2.1.7.1-3/603.1-3   Enter Talbot, Bedford, and Burgundy, with scaling | Ladders: Their Drummes beating a | Dead March.
2.1.39.1/635.1   Cry, S. George, A Talbot.
2.1.39.2-5/634.2-5   The French leape ore the walles in their shirts. Enter | seuerall wayes, Bastard, Alanson, Reignier, | halfe ready, and halfe vnready.
2.1.49.1/644.1   Enter Charles and Ioane.
2.1.78.1, 2.1.79.1/673.1-3   Exeunt. | Alarum. Enter a Souldier, crying, a Talbot, a Talbot: | they flye, leauing their Clothes behind.
2.1.83/677.1   Exit.
2.2.0.1-2/677.2   Enter Talbot, Bedford, Burgundie.
2.2.3.1/680.1   Retreat.
2.2.33.1/710.1   Enter a Messenger.
2.2.59.1/736.1   Whispers. (after 'minde')
2.2.60.1/737   Exeunt.
2.3.0.1/737.1   Enter Countesse.
2.3.3.1/740   Exit.
2.3.10.1/747.1   Enter Messenger and Talbot.
2.3.31.1/768.1   Enter Porter with Keyes.
2.3.60.1-2/797.1-2   Winds his Horne, Drummes strike vp, a Peale | of Ordenance: Enter Souldiors.
2.3.82/819   Exeunt.
2.4.0.1-3/819.1-3   Enter Richard Plantagenet, Warwick, Somerset, | Poole, and others.
2.4.113/932   Exit.
2.4.114.1/933   Exit.
2.4.134.1/953.1   Exeunt.
2.5.0.1-2/953.2-3   Enter Mortimer, brought in a Chayre, | and Iaylors.
2.5.32.1/985.1   Enter Richard.
2.5.114/1067   Dyes.
2.5.121.1/1074.1   Exit.
2.5.129/1082   Exit.
3.1.0.1-6/1082.1-5   Flourish. Enter King, Exeter, Gloster, Winchester, Warwick, | Somerset, Suffolk, Richard Plantagenet. Gloster offers | to put vp a Bill: Winchester snatches it, teares it.
3.1.74.1/1156.1   A noyse within, Downe with the | Tawny-Coats.
3.1.77.1/1158.1   A noyse againe, Stones, Stones.
3.1.78.1/1158.2   Enter Maior.
3.1.88.1/1168.1   Enter in skirmish with bloody Pates.
3.1.94.1/1174.1   Skirmish againe.
3.1.106.1/1186.1   Begin againe.
3.1.151/1232   Exeunt.
3.1.190.1/1270.1   Senet. Flourish. Exeunt.
3.1.190.1/1270.1   Manet Exeter.
3.1.205/1285   Exit.

3.2.0.1-2/1285.1-2   Enter Pucell disguis'd, with foure Souldiors with | Sacks vpon their backs.
3.2.12.1/1297.1   Knock.
3.2.16.1/1301.1   Exeunt.
3.3.0.1-3/1301.2   Enter Charles, Bastard, Alanson.
3.3.8.1-2/1309.1-2   Enter Pucell on the top, thrusting out a | Torch burning.
3.3.18.1/1319.1   Alarum.
3.4.0.1/1319.2   An Alarum. Talbot in an Excursion.
3.4.5/1324   Exit.
3.5.0.1-6/1324.1-4   An Alarum: Excursions. Bedford brought | in sicke in a Chayre. | Enter Talbot and Burgonie without: within, Pucell, | Charles, Bastard, and Reignier on the Walls.
3.5.19.1/1343.1   They whisper together in counsell.
3.5.33/1357   Exeunt from the Walls.
3.5.62.1/1386.1   Exit.
3.5.62.2-3/1386.2-3   An Alarum: Excursions. Enter Sir Iohn | Falstaffe, and a Captaine.
3.5.67/1391   Exit.
3.5.68/1392   Exit.
3.5.68.1/1392.1-2   Retreat. Excursions. Pucell, Alanson, and | Charles flye.
3.5.73.1/1397.1   Bedford dyes, and is carryed in by two in his Chaire.
3.6.0.1-2/1397.2-3   An Alarum. Enter Talbot, Burgonie, and | the rest.
3.6.23/1420   Exeunt.
3.7.0.1-2/1420.1   Enter Charles, Bastard, Alanson, Pucell.
3.7.28.1/1448.1   Drumme sounds a farre off.
3.7.30.1/1450.1   Here sound an English March.
3.7.32.1/1452.1   French March.
3.7.35.1/1455.1   Trumpets sound a Parley.
3.7.91/1511   Exeunt.
3.8.0.1-7/1511.1-5   Enter the King, Gloucester, Winchester, Yorke, Suffolke, | Somerset, Warwicke, Exeter: To them, with | his Souldiors, Talbot.
3.8.27.1/1538.1   Senet. Flourish. Exeunt. | Manet Vernon and Basset.
3.8.37.1/1548.1   Strikes him.
3.8.45/1556   Exeunt.
4.1.0.1-6/1556.1-4   Enter King, Glocester, Winchester, Yorke, Suffolke, Somer-|set, Warwicke, Talbot. and Gouernor Exeter.
4.1.8.1/1564.1   Enter Falstaffe.
4.1.77.1-2/1633.1-2   Enter Vernon and Bassit.
4.1.173.1-2/1729.1-2   Exeunt. Manet Yorke, Warwick, Exeter, Vernon.
4.1.181.1/1737.1   Exeunt. | Flourish. Manet Exeter.
4.1.194/1750   Exit.
4.2.0.1-2/1750.1-2   Enter Talbot with Trumpe and Drumme, | before Burdeaux.
4.2.2.1/1752.1   Sounds.
4.2.2.1-2/1752.1-2   Enter Generall aloft.
4.2.38.1/1788.1   Drum a farre off.
4.2.41/1791   Exit
4.3.0.1-3/1806.1-2   Enter a Messenger that meets Yorke. Enter Yorke | with Trumpet, and many Soldiers.
4.3.16.1/1822.1   Enter another Messenger.
4.3.53/1859   Exit
4.4.0.1/1859.1   Enter Somerset with his Armie.
4.4.46.1/1905.1   Exeunt.
4.5.0.1 /1905.2   Enter Talbot and his Sonne.
4.5.55/1960.1   Exit.
4.6.0.1-3/1960.1-4   Alarum: Excursions, wherein Talbots Sonne | is hemm'd about, and Talbot | rescues him.
4.6.57/2017   Exit.
4.7.0.1-2/2017.1-2   Alarum. Excursions. Enter old | Talbot led.
4.7.16.1-2/2033.1-2   Enter with Iohn Talbot, borne.
4.7.32.1/2049.1   Dyes
4.7.32.2-4/2049.2-3   Enter Charles, Alanson, Burgundie, Bastard, | and Pucell.
4.7.50.1/2067.1   Enter Lucie.
4.7.96/2113   Exit.
5.1.0.1-2/2113.1-2   SENNET. | Enter King, Glocester, and Exeter.

1 HENRY VI

5.1.27.1-2/2140.1-2 Enter Winchester, and three Ambassadors.
5.1.50.1-2/2163.1-2 Exeunt.
5.1.55, 62/2167, 2175 Exeunt (after 5.1.62/2175)
5.2.0.1-3/2175.1-2 Enter Charles, Burgundy, Alanson, Bastard, | Reignier, and Ione.
5.2.7.1/2182.1 Enter Scout.
5.2.21-5.3.0.1/2196-2196.1 Exeunt. Alarum. Excursions.
5.3.0.1/2196.1 Enter Ione de Pucell.
5.3.4.1/2200.1 Thunder.
5.3.7.1/2203.1 Enter Fiends.
5.3.12.1/2208.1 They walke, and speake not.
5.3.17.1/2213.1 They hang their heads.
5.3.19.1/2215.1 They shake their heads.
5.3.23.1/2219.1 They depart.
5.3.29/2225 Exit.
5.4.0.1-2/2225.1-2 Excursions. Burgundie and Yorke fight hand to | hand. French flye.
5.4.15.1/2240.1 Exeunt.
5.5.0.1-2/2241.2 Alarum. Enter Suffolke with Margaret | in his hand.
5.5.1.1/2241.1 Gazes on her.
5.5.15.1/2255.1 She is going
5.5.86.1-2/2326.1 Sound. Enter Reignier on the Walles.
5.5.101.1/2341.2 Trumpets sound. Enter Reignier.
5.5.130.1/2370.1 Shee is going.
5.5.140.1/2380.1 Kisse her.
5.5.151.1/2391.1 Exit
5.6.0.1-2, 5.6.1.1/2391.2, 2392.1 Enter Yorke, Warwicke, Shepheard, Pucell. (before 5.6.1/2392)
5.6.33/2424 Exit.
5.6.91.1/2482.1 Exit. | Enter Cardinall.
5.6.115.1-2/2506.1 Enter Charles, Alanson, Bastard, Reignier.
5.6.175/2566 Exeunt
5.7.0.1-2/2506.2-3 Enter Suffolke in conference with the King, | Glocester, and Exeter.
5.7.101.1/2667.1 Exit.
5.7.102/2668.1 Exit Glocester.
5.7.108/2674 Exit

RICHARD III

THE play was entered in the Stationers' Register on 20 October 1597:

Andrewe Wife / Entred for his copie vnder thande of
  m^r Barlowe, and m^r warden
  Man./ The tragedie of kinge
  Richard the Third wth the
  death of the duke of Clarence

The title-page of the first edition (Q1), dated 1597 (*BEPD* 142), declares that it was 'Printed by Valentine Sims, for Andrew Wise'. In fact Simmes printed only the first seven sheets; signatures H–M, in a different type, are apparently the work of Peter Short. Jackson identified two compositors in Short's section, but his conclusions have been destabilized by the more extensive researches of Zimmerman: she points to a number of features which suggest either a single compositor, or a pattern of compositor distribution incompatible with Jackson's. Jackson identified only one compositor in Simmes's section; Jowett and Taylor ('With New Additions') note that the distribution of O/Oh spellings suggests two. None of these compositor attributions seems secure enough to warrant tabulation, or editorial confidence. Collations by Greg (1959) and Smidt (1969) have turned up few press variants.

The quarto was reprinted in 1598 (Q2), 1602 (Q3), 1605 (Q4), 1612 (Q5), 1622 (Q6), 1629 (Q7), and 1634 (Q8). Q2 contains two lines which apparently result from a press variant in Q1, not present in any of the four extant copies (1.1.102-3/102-3); otherwise the derivative quartos contain no readings which can lay claim to any authority independent of the extant copies of Q1 itself. Nevertheless, the derivative quartos are of considerable importance in establishing Shakespeare's intentions. The text printed in the First Folio (F) clearly derives, in certain respects, from an independent manuscript, which differed from Q in hundreds of readings; just as clearly, it also derives from one or more of the late derivative quartos. Like Folio *King Lear* and *Troilus and Cressida*, Folio *Richard III* was apparently set from quarto copy, heavily annotated by reference to an authoritative manuscript.

In 1864 the Cambridge editors judged that 'The respective origin and authority of the first Quarto and first Folio texts of *Richard III* is perhaps the most difficult question which presents itself to an editor of Shakespeare'. The question in fact consists of several different questions, each complex, and all complexly interrelated.

The first question is the nature of the manuscript which lies behind Q1. In 1936 Patrick provided the first detailed and comprehensive argument that Q was a 'bad' quarto, based upon a memorial reconstruction of the play as performed; Greg (1938) proposed that the reconstruction was made communally by the company itself, to replace a missing promptbook; Taylor has offered a conjectural reconstruction of the circumstances which might have led to this unusual procedure. Smidt, who initially attacked Patrick's hypothesis (1964), subsequently endorsed the view that memory played a key part in the formation of Q's text (1970). At present, Patrick's hypothesis holds the field, and has held it, virtually uncontested, for half a century. Nevertheless, Quarto *Richard III* has often been paired with Quarto *King Lear* as a 'doubtful' text, and the recent rehabilitation of *Lear* necessarily reopens the question of *Richard III*. In particular, the example of *Lear* raises again the possibility, extensively debated by earlier editors, that Quarto *Richard III* might represent an authorial first draft, rather than a memorial reconstruction.

Despite a sympathetic re-examination of the differences between the two texts of *Richard III*, it seems to us unlikely that any large proportion of them results from authorial revision. The variants do not cluster or coalesce into patterns which imply any discernible strategy of revision; instead, the degree of similarity between the two texts drastically declines in the speeches of Clarence's two murderers, or anonymous messengers, or (to a lesser extent) Buckingham. Such patterns of variation are most easily explained by a method of transmission dependent upon the memories of individual actors—especially during a provincial tour, where the hired men who normally played certain less important roles might not be available. Taylor shows that the Quarto can, because of other variants, be played by a smaller cast with less equipment than the Folio. Substantial Quarto variants which cannot be explained by such expedients make the play more effective theatrically than F. Q is shorter than F, and most of the material present only in F consists of static poetic elaboration which slows up the dramatic pace. We find it easier to believe that Shakespeare on reflection intelligently cut such elaborations than that he so unintelligently padded out a play already taxingly long. By contrast, the only major passage unique to Q, the so-called 'clock' dialogue (4.2.102-18/ 2424-42), is a dramatic gem, which could easily result from an inspired afterthought; it is difficult to believe that anyone would have deliberately singled it out as the only passage in the play which should be cut. In such respects Q, rather than F, looks like a version of the play which has weathered performance: Q offers a more 'experienced' text, one which has both suffered and benefited from direct contact with the theatre. On the basis of such variants one naturally hypothesizes that Q represents a later stage of the text than F, and this conclusion, based on examination of the larger features of both texts, is occasionally reinforced by verbal variants. Thus the Folio contains the line, 'Of you Lord *Wooduill*, and Lord *Scales* of you' (after 2.1.67/1108): but Woodville and Scales were different titles for the same person, a person already addressed in the previous line by another of his titles ('*Riuers*'). The Folio stage direction, likewise, calls for the entrance of both '*Riuers*' and '*Wooduill*' (2.1.0.2-4/1041.2-

3). This error has been plausibly traced to an ambiguous passage in Holinshed. The Quarto does not contain the offending line, or the duplication in its entrance direction; one is tempted to say that Q deliberately removed both, for it seems all but certain that F's error originated in Shakespeare's foul papers, and that Q here represents a 'corrected' state of the text. Furthermore, correction of the error requires further acquaintance with the chronicles: even the most 'alert bookkeeper' could hardly be expected to check all the relevant genealogies. Likewise, at 2.4.1-2/1355-6 F has Richard's party proceed from Stony Stratford to Northampton on their way up to London; this makes sense only by reference to the chronicles, in which Richard deliberately backtracks. Q, by contrast, reverses the names, thereby making immediate geographical sense of the speech. The variant need not have originated with Shakespeare, but again there seems little doubt that Q is later. In general, F in its verbal variants is closer than Q to the play's acknowledged sources.

If Shakespeare extensively revised *Richard III*, then Q apparently represents the later text. This supposition obviously contrasts with the other revised plays (*Lear*, *Hamlet*, etc.), where in each case the text printed later represents the later version; it instead corresponds to the situation in *Henry V* and *Romeo*, where the text first printed appears to be a memorially reconstructed account of the play in performance. As a class, the heavily revised plays all date from after *1 Henry IV* (1596), when Shakespeare was securely established as the leading dramatist of the capital's leading company; *Richard III*, by contrast, was written early in the 1590s, at an early stage in Shakespeare's career, in a period of great uncertainty and flux in the fortunes of the London companies. The luxury of extensive literary revision seems more likely in the later period, and the nature of the revising in these later plays gives us a model by which to judge arguments for revision in *Richard III*. No one has been tempted to see Q as, in the great mass of its verbal variants, a Shakespearian revision of F; instead, in bulk the Folio readings are more compact, more metrical, more meaningful, more crafted than their Q counterparts. If verbal revision accounts for these variants, then F must be the revision. But this conclusion contradicts the abundant evidence that Q is the later version. Moreover, it collapses the explanation of Q as a memorially contaminated text, and so forces us to regard its special character as that of a foul-paper text. But just as comparison of *Richard III* with Shakespeare's revised plays undermines confidence in the hypothesis of extensive revision, so does comparison of Q with Shakespeare's foul paper texts. The quartos of *Titus*, *Love's Labour's Lost*, *Dream*, and *Romeo* (Q2), or the Folio text of *Errors*—all early plays, all probably set from foul papers—supply nothing parallel to the metrical sloppiness of Q *Richard III*; indeed, as has often been demonstrated, Shakespeare is far more respectful of metrical regularity in his early than his later work. Nor does Q *Lear* provide a parallel for Q *Richard III*, for in *Lear* the problem is lineation, not metre. Faulty lineation can be reasonably attributed to special factors in a particular printing shop; wholesale metrical corruption cannot be, especially when a text was set in two different shops by at least two (and probably more) different compositors.

Q *Richard III* thus contains a few features manifestly later than their counterparts in F; but for the overwhelming bulk of verbal variants F reproduces a more satisfactory text. Q cannot be, in its entirety, a revision of F, and yet it seems equally clear that F cannot be, in its entirety, a revision of Q. The mix is exactly what we find in the other memorial texts. If we compare memorial texts as a class with authorially variant plays as a class, Q *Richard III* clearly belongs to the former. But Q is, undoubtedly, unusually accurate as memorial texts go; hence the hypothesis of communal reconstruction. This hypothesis satisfactorily accounts for Q *Richard III*, and has been perceived to do so, in a way that such theories have never satisfactorily explained Q *Lear*, or either substantive text of *Troilus*, *Othello*, or *Hamlet*.

The hypothesis that Q derives from a memorial reconstruction obviously entails certain consequences for our view of the origins of F. The more immediate question is whether the two Folio compositors (A and B) worked from an annotated exemplar of Q3, or of Q6, or from a manuscript deriving from either. Two passages (3.1.0.1-149.1, 5.5.4-end/1426.1-1575.1, 3095-end) clearly derive from Q3, with almost no alteration. But for the rest of the text, although the substantive links between F and derivative quartos make it clear that the latter influenced the former, substantive evidence in itself cannot determine whether Q3 or Q6 was used, and some scholars have supported the hypothesis that some sort of transcript intervened between the quartos and F. The matter has been debated inconclusively for a century, despite notable contributions by Walton (1955, 1971) and Bowers. Taylor, in the most extensive study to date, argues that the incidentals evidence points to the direct use of both Q3 and Q6, in an alternating pattern based on quarto and folio pagebreaks, and on the need to interleave major insertions from the manuscript.

1.1.0.1-1.2.154/0.1-316	Q3
1.2.155-212/317-74	Q6
1.2.212.1-1.3.6/412.1-418	Q3
1.3.7-1.3.126/419-538	Q6
1.3.127-1.3.254/539-666	Q3
1.3.255-1.3.272/667-84	Q6
1.3.273-1.3.311/685-723	?
1.3.311-1.4.11/724-76	Q3
1.4.14-1.4.78/779-843	Q6
1.4.79-1.4.222/844-985	Q3
1.4.213-1.4.250/976-1013	Q6
1.4.251-1.4.270/1014-1033	Q3
1.4.271-2.1.135/1034-1176	Q6
2.1.136-2.2.33.1/1177-1206.1	Q3
2.2.134-2.3.42/1207-1349	Q6
2.3.43-3.1.139/1350-1565	Q3
3.1.140-3.1.166/1566-1592	Q6
3.1.167-3.2.4/1593-1627	Q3
3.2.5-3.2.43/1628-1666	Q3?
3.2.44-3.2.80/1667-1703	Q3
3.2.81-3.2.117/1704-1740	Q3?
3.2.118-3.4.85/1741-1850	Q3
3.4.86-3.4.107/1851-1872	Q3?
3.5.0.1-3.5.57/1872.1-1929	Q6?
3.5.58-3.5.97/1930-1969	Q6
3.5.98-3.6.10-11/1970-1986-7	Q6
3.6.12-397.19/1988-2009	Q3?
3.7.19-3.7.60/2009-2050	Q6
3.7.61-3.7.113/2051-2103	Q3

3.7.114–3.7.143/2104–2133	Q6
3.7.144–4.1.0.2/2134–2227.4	Q6
4.1.7–4.4.55/2234–2561	Q3
4.4.56–4.4.210/2562–2715	Q6
4.4.210–4.4.221/2716–2726	Q3
4.4.222–4.4.273/2727–2778	Q6
4.4.274–4.4.304/2779–2809	Q3
4.4.305–4.4.403/2810–2908	Q6
4.4.404–4.4.456/2909–2961	Q3
4.4.457–4.4.463/2962–2968	Q6?
4.4.464–5.1.23/2969–3017	Q6
5.1.24–5.3.16/3018–3063	Q3
5.3.17–5.4.20/3064–3085	Q6
5.4.25–5.8.41.1/3090–3450.1	Q3

Taylor's hypothesis has formed the basis for our edition.

The Folio text therefore represents a synthesis of two elements of drastically different authority: a printed base, consisting of derivative reprints of a memorially reconstructed quarto, and an unknown manuscript of high authority. In general terms, the authority of the manuscript can be inferred from the Shakespearian superiority of most Folio variants, but its exact character has remained a puzzle, partly because the manuscript's features can only be discerned through the screen of Q3, Q6, the unknown annotator, and two veteran Folio compositors. It was at one time believed that F's direct use of Q3 in two places arose because a manuscript had been patched with some leaves from Q3, and the prompt-book seemed the most likely manuscript to have received such extraordinary attention. Taylor's account of the incidentals evidence makes this hypothesis unnecessary, and also implies that the manuscript was badly defective in the middle and at the end. Such conclusions do not favour the supposition that the manuscript was the prompt-book of a popular play. Moreover, as noted above, F seems a text closer to the author's original composition than Q, which by contrast shows clear signs of theatrical provenance. One might therefore suspect (with Walker) that the manuscript authority for F was Shakespeare's own foul papers. But F is relatively regular in its speech-prefixes and thorough in its stage directions, far more so than the recognized foul-paper texts. It also, apparently, contained a number of misreadings: 1.1.134/134 'play' (for Q 'prey'), 2.1.57/1098 'vnwillingly' (for Q 'vnwittingly'), etc. As in Folio *Troilus and Cressida*, it is difficult to explain such errors except on the assumption that the manuscript itself clearly called for the wrong word. The rather 'literary', gestural character of some Folio stage directions—'*She lookes scornfully at him*', '*Speakes to himselfe*'—also suggest a transcript designed for a patron: Shakespeare's foul-paper texts contain few such directions. It thus seems probable that the manuscript was a transcript, presumably though not certainly scribal, of Shakespeare's foul papers.

The respective origin and authority of the first Quarto and first Folio texts of *Richard III* might therefore be visualized in the stemma which follows. The complexity of this hypothesis explains the difficulty encountered by eighteenth- and nineteenth-century editors, trying to select readings by the light of nature and little else. At the same time, this complexity necessitates a correspondingly complex editorial procedure.

In the first place, it will be seen that the incidentals of F have almost no authority. They derive from the incidentals of a memorially transmitted text, itself sophisticated by two to five intervening reprints, and by the preferences of two experienced and interfering Folio compositors. This textual base has been sporadically corrected, in respect to substantive readings, by reference to a manuscript; but the manuscript itself appears to have been a transcript, is of unknown date, and influences F only through the mediation of an unknown annotator (as well as the compositors). The spelling, punctuation, italicization, and capitalization of either text of *Richard III* thus have even less claim than usual to any Shakespearian authority. Nevertheless, the incidentals of Q1 are at least not derived from any earlier edition, and they accord with normal practice in the decade of the play's composition; those of F are, by contrast, both derivative and anachronistic. Consequently, we have adopted Q1 as copy-text for incidentals, departing from it only (*a*) where a substantive variant in F has been adopted, or (*b*) F restores a Q1 reading which has been corrupted in its Q3 or Q6 copy. Only in such cases can F's incidentals lay any claim to possible manuscript authority, and in such cases we have assumed that the annotator would have made the minimal alteration necessary in order to correct the quarto text. (These procedures are justified, and discussed in greater detail, in Taylor's 'Copy-Text and Collation'.)

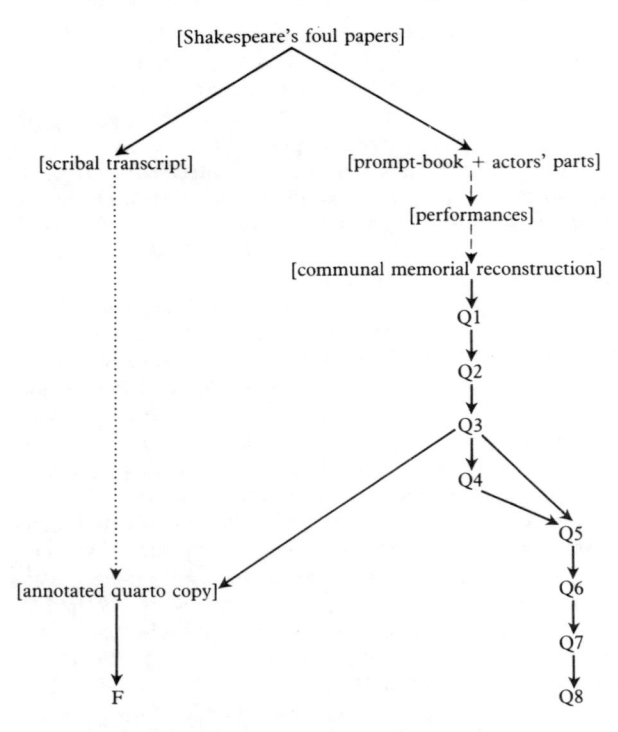

F must obviously be the control-text—as it has been for all editions of the play. But the nature of F's transmission makes a confident reliance upon all its readings impossible. Errors in the derivative quartos which have been passively reproduced in F need to be corrected by reference to Q1; Q1 can also be used to correct apparent misreadings in F (1.1.134/134, etc.), or errors apparently resulting from ambiguous marking up of quarto copy (1.2.189/351, etc). F omits all four examples of 'zounds' in Q (1.4.122/886, 1.4.142/905, 3.7.209/2199, 5.5.162/3252), as well as a Q reference to 'Christs deare bloud shed for our grieuous sinnes' (1.4.185/948); other

Folio texts demonstrate that the editors were particularly sensitive to such allusions. (See Taylor, 'Zounds'.) Deliberate expurgation seems almost certain here, but the rest of the text seems not to have suffered from censorship ('God' occurs 105 times). Studies by Werstine and Taylor of the compositors' work elsewhere demonstrate that a reasonable scattering of compositorial error must be expected.

Discriminating use of Q1 to correct error and sophistication in F is clearly necessary, and recent editors, inhibited by the fear of 'bad' quartos, have made less use of Q1 than the facts require. But Q1 can only be used to correct errors which originate either in the later quartos, or in F itself; another important source of error in F cannot be corrected by reference to Q1, because Q1 is itself the source of error. F derives from Q1, and Q1 is a memorially reconstructed text; *Richard III* is therefore, like *Pericles*, a play for which we are dependent upon a text in some ways fundamentally unreliable. Unlike *Pericles*, of course, most of *Richard III* has been corrected by reference to a more reliable document. Nevertheless, that correction was demonstrably sporadic, because it missed a number of inherited Q3 and Q6 errors; it must also have missed errors inherited directly from Q1, and the analysis of the annotator's efficiency here and elsewhere suggests that the number of such oversights may be substantial. Moreover, for two passages (3.1.0.1-148/1426.1-1574, 5.5.4-end/3095-end) the Folio effected little or no correction of dialogue, either because of a physical defect in the manuscript or a spiritual defect in the annotator. Surprisingly, these two passages have been emended less than any others in the play; they have been ignored even by editors like Wilson, who did attempt to correct joint QF error elsewhere. The conjectural emendation of such errors by Wilson and Walker has fallen into some disrepute, partly because they exercise it on Folio texts which we now believe were not set from Quarto copy (*2 Henry IV*, *Hamlet*, and *Othello*), and on texts where the Quarto is not as corrupt as they believed (*Lear*; and all of the above). But for *Richard III* F's derivation from a seriously inadequate quarto can hardly be doubted. Moreover, Walker's attention to metrical regularity and rhetorical pattern as a basis for such emendation is clearly more appropriate to *Richard III* than to later texts like *Othello* and *Troilus*. Finally, the bulk of the Folio text is evidently reliable, and this serves as a useful control by which to test suspected passages. No one contends that two passages in *Richard III* deliberately revert to the Quarto's less polished style. We have therefore been particularly attentive to possible memorial error in the two uncorrected areas, and readier than some editors to emend suspected QF errors elsewhere.

All these editorial procedures involve the emendation of F in an effort to bring the 1623 printed text closer to Shakespeare's foul papers, by eliminating scribal and compositorial error, editorial interference, passive retention of Quarto-copy error, and the cumulative seventeenth-century sophistication of sixteenth-century incidentals. If these procedures are successful, the resulting reconstructed foul-paper version should be comparable to an edited text of Quarto *Titus Andronicus* or Folio *Henry V*. But even after we have reached this stage, a major editorial problem remains—as it remains in *Titus Andronicus* and *Henry V*. In both these plays, as in *Richard III*, the foul-paper version is supplemented by another text of much less authority, which none the less contains a number of variants which almost certainly reflect contemporary theatrical practice. As noted above, Q1 contains apparent revisions of dialogue at 2.1.67/1108 and 2.4.1-2/1355-6; it adds a brilliant passage in 4.2/Sc. 17; its substitutions of Brakenbury for the Keeper in 1.4/Sc. 4, of Dorset for the messenger in 2.4/Sc. 8, of Catesby for Ratcliffe and Lovell in 3.4/Sc. 12 and 3.5/Sc. 13, and of Catesby for Surrey in 5.3/Sc. 11 are all dramatic improvements which cannot be due either to limitations of casting or (especially in a communal reconstruction by Shakespeare's own company) to memorial error. In all such cases an editor must choose between a text which clearly represents Shakespeare's first intention and another which apparently represents an alteration made by the time the play was performed; as elsewhere in this edition, it has seemed to us desirable to offer readers the text in its fully realized theatrical embodiment, and we have therefore accepted such Q variants. They are marked in the Textual Notes by an asterisk.

Major passages present in F but not Q pose an even more complicated problem. Editors who routinely conflate other two-text plays have routinely conflated *Richard III* too, dismissing Q's 'misguided' cuts as theatrical in origin. For the memorially reconstructed texts, like *Henry V*, we have recorded some particularly interesting major omissions without feeling able to act upon them; but the other such quartos are heavily abridged, and for the most part poorly reported, two facts which make it impossible to be sure whether all such passages were omitted in performance, and whether all such cuts represent normal London practice. Such objections can hardly be made to the cuts in Q *Richard III*: the text is so well reported that its memorial origins have sometimes been doubted, it is longer than any Shakespeare play but *Hamlet*, and the major omissions would only reduce its playing time by five to ten minutes. Major Quarto omissions thus cannot be credibly dismissed as accidents, either of memory or venue, nor do most seem to result from limitations of cast. Consequently, they stand on an editorial par with major omissions in Folio *Hamlet*, *Troilus*, and *Lear*, and we have respected them as such. As elsewhere, such passages are printed as an appendix to the text.

The play contains a handful of difficulties of a more ordinary kind. Q is undivided; F supplies a division into five acts. F also produces correct scene divisions through 3.4/Sc.12; it omits divisions for 3.5/Sc. 13, 3.6/Sc. 14, 3.7/Sc. 15, and 4.3/Sc. 18, consequently misnumbering 4.4/Sc. 19 and 4.5/Sc. 20; nor does it provide any scene divisions after 5.2/Sc. 22 (Richmond's arrival with his army). The second half of the compositors' copy is clearly less regular than the first in this matter, though whether through negligence in the manuscript or by the annotator cannot be determined. Modern editors mark only three additional scenes in Act 5 (5.3/Sc. 23, 5.4/Sc. 24 and 5.5/Sc. 25), because the entire sequence from the end of 5.2/Sc. 22 till the end of the play clearly takes place at Bosworth, with one or two tents on the stage continuously until the actual battle. (Editors in fact do not call for the tent's removal at all.) But several changes of time occur during this sequence, and the stage is several times cleared of actors, and we have accordingly applied the same principle here as elsewhere. Our scenes 5.7/Sc. 27 and 5.8/Sc. 28 correspond to the traditional 5.4 and 5.5; the traditional 5.3 we divide into 5.3/Sc. 23, 5.4/Sc. 24, 5.5/Sc. 25, and 5.6/Sc. 26.

In speech-prefixes Q identifies the protagonist as 'Gloucester' (variously spelled) until he is crowned, when he becomes 'King'; in Folio prefixes he is 'Richard' throughout. (This variation resembles that between Q and F *Richard II*.) Since both texts are probably at some remove from autograph, we have kept Q's theatrically valuable distinction between Richard's early and late appearances, but retained F's unifying Christian name: 'RICHARD GLOCESTER' (as at 1.3.12/424) and 'KING RICHARD'. Likewise, QF 'Richmond' becomes in our speech-prefixes 'HENRY EARL OF RICHMOND', so that in the final scene he can speak, after being crowned, as 'KING HENRY'. An even more serious problem is created by Lord Stanley, Earl of Derby, where both Q and F are inconsistent. We identify the character as 'Stanley' in speech-prefixes and stage directions; where control-text directions call him 'Derby', this title has been retained ('Lord Stanley Earl of Derby', etc.). We have recorded cases where Q or F identifies him, in prefixes, as 'Derby'.

F is the control-text for substantive readings, and the Textual Notes record all substantive departures from F; they also discuss a number of particularly attractive Q readings. In two passages (3.1.0–148/1426.1–1574, 5.5.4–end/3095-end), F declines to the status of a mere reprint of Q3, with little or no consultation of manuscript; for these passages the textual notes therefore record all substantive departures from Q1, and all textual variants between Q1, Q3, and F. For the remainder of the text, 'Rejected Quarto Variants' are listed separately, as are 'Q1 Readings Restored by F'. These two lists between them will enable a reader to reconstruct all departures from the incidentals in the dialogue of Q1 caused by the acceptance of F's superior authority for substantives; these lists therefore serve the dual purpose of a historical collation and a record of emended incidentals. The normal record of 'Emendations of Incidentals' lists, as elsewhere, only such changes as would seem required even if Q1 were our only text. We also provide a list of 'Semi-Substantive Metrical Markings', which records variants in elision which affect the modern-spelling edition: neither Q nor F has any reliable authority in such matters, but we have in the modern-spelling text adopted metrical elisions or expansions from either, where they seem useful to modern readers as a clue to scansion. Because our modernized text spells the elided form of the past participle (-ed) in the same way that early texts normally indicate the unelided form, we have, for ease in interpreting this list, supplied an accent (-èd) for the relevant readings. All such accents are editorial. A full record of the original 'Stage Directions' in both texts is provided, and the collations therefore only record controversial departures from F.

R. B. McKerrow's work on *Richard III* had reached an advanced stage; references in our Textual Notes are to his galley proofs.

G.T./(S.W.W.)

WORKS CITED

Bowers, Fredson, 'The Copy for Folio *Richard III*', *SQ* 10 (1959), 541–4
Daniel, P. A., Introduction to Griggs's Facsimile (1884)
Furness, Horace Howard, Jr., ed., *The Tragedy of Richard the Third* (1908)
Greg, W. W., *The Library*, IV, 19 (1938), 118–20 (review of Patrick)
—— ed., *Richard the Third 1597*, Shakespeare Quarto Facsimiles No. 12 (1959)
Hammond, Antony, ed., *King Richard III*, Arden (1981)
Honigmann, E. A. J., 'On the Indifferent and One-Way Variants in Shakespeare', *The Library*, V, 22 (1967), 189–204
—— ed., *King Richard the Third*, New Penguin (1968)
—— 'The Text of *Richard III*', *Theatre Research*, 7 (1965), 48–55
Jackson, MacD. P., 'Two Shakespeare Quartos: *Richard III* (1597) and *I Henry IV* (1598)', *SB* 35 (1982), 173–91
Koppel, Richard, *Textkritische Studien über Shakespeares Richard III. und King Lear* (1877)
More, Sir Thomas, *The History of King Richard the Third*, ed. Richard S. Sylvester (1963)
Patrick, David L., *The Textual History of 'Richard III'* (1936)
Smidt, Kristian, *Iniurious Impostors and 'Richard III'* (1964)
—— ed., *The Tragedy of King Richard the Third: Parallel Texts of the First Quarto and the First Folio with Variants of the Early Quartos* (1969)
—— *Memorial Transmission and Quarto Copy in 'Richard III': A Reassessment* (1970)
Spedding, James, 'On the Quarto and Folio of *Richard III*', Shakespeare Society Transactions (1875–6)
Taylor, Gary, 'Copy-Text and Collation (with special reference to *Richard III*)', *The Library*, VI, 3 (1981), 33–42
—— '*Richard III*: The Nature and Preparation of the Folio Text (forthcoming)
Thompson, A. N., ed., *The Tragedy of King Richard the Third*, Arden (1907)
Walker, Alice, *Textual Problems of the First Folio* (1953)
Walton, J. K., *The Copy for the Folio Text of 'Richard III'* (1955)
—— *The Quarto Copy for the First Folio of Shakespeare* (1971)
Wilson, John Dover, ed., *Richard III*, New (1954)
Zimmerman, Susan, 'The Uses of Headlines: Peter Short's Shakespearian Quartos *I Henry IV* and *Richard III*', *The Library*, VI, 7 (1985), 218–55

TEXTUAL NOTES

Title *The Tragedy of King Richard the Third*] THE TRAGEDY OF | King Richard the third. | Containing, | His treacherous Plots againſt his brother Clarence: | the pittiefull murther of his iunocent nephewes: | his tyrannicall vſurpation: with the whole courſe | of his deteſted life, and moſt deſerued death. Q (*title-page*); *The Tragedy of Richard the third* Q (*running title*); The tragedie of kinge Richard the Third with the death of the duke of Clarence S.R.; The Tragedy of Richard the Third: | with the Landing of Earle Richmond, and the | Battell at Boſworth Field. F (*head title*); *The Life and Death of Richard the Third*. F (*running titles, table of contents*). The omission of '*King*' from F's head title may be accidental, since the line is tightly justified; but the variation between head title and running title is more substantial than in any other Folio text.

1.1.26/26   spie] Q; ſee F. Q's is the rarer reading. See Taylor, 'Praestat'.
1.1.32/32   inductions] Q3–8, F; induċtious Q1
1.1.40/40   murtherer] Q3–8, F; murtherers Q1
1.1.49/49   Belike] POPE; O belike QF. '"O" is almost certainly an actor's interpolation retained through negligence in F. It interferes both with the metre and the sense' (McKerrow).
1.1.52/52   for] Q; but F. F's anticipation of 'but' in 1.1.53/53 could be compositorial or scribal.
1.1.65/65   tempts] F; tempers Q1; temps Q3; tempts Q6. As Q3

was F's copy here, it is difficult to believe that the compositor would have *first* chosen one correction of an ambiguous misprint, and *then* invented a word ('harsh') to correct the resulting metrical deficiency. If he noticed and wanted to correct the metrical deficiency, he could hardly fail to relate it to the misprint he had just noticed and corrected, especially as that correction involved a choice between one or two syllables.

1.1.65/65   harsh] F; *not in* Q. See preceding note.
1.1.67/67   Woodeuile] CAPELL; Wooduile Q; *Woodeulle* F
1.1.73   Mrs] QF (Miſtreſſe). Elizabethan *Mistress* could be used of a married or unmarried woman, and so has not normally been modernized; but here 'Mrs' usefully informs modern readers and spectators of Shore's marital status (which was well known to Elizabethan audiences).
1.1.74/74   ye] Q; you F. F's 'you' could easily be a compositorial substitution. See *Dream* 5.1.274/1975, *Henry V* 2.2.174/781, etc.
1.1.75/75   for his] F2; for her F1; to her for his Q
1.1.84/84   I beseech] QF; Beseech DYCE. Shakespeare uses *Beseech* without a subject only once before 1600 (in *Romeo*); three other lines in this play have an extra initial syllable (3.2.3, 3.4.56, 3.7.81/1626, 1821, 2071).
1.1.87/87   your] F; his Q. Q contains a potentially ludicrous ambiguity.
1.1.88   An't] F1 (and). See *Henry V* 4.7.156/2570.
1.1.92/92   iealous] Q; iealious F. Some editors take F's spelling to indicate trisyllabic pronunciation; but B often uses the spelling elsewhere, where metre requires a disyllable; and feminine tetrameters occur elsewhere.
1.1.96/96   kin] MARSHALL; kindred QF. Elsewhere *kin* and *kindred* are consistently used as purely metrical alternatives (Sipe). For the alleged memorial error, compare 3.7.202/2192 (Q kin/F Kindred).
1.1.102–3/102–3   BRAKENBURY ... me?] Q2–8 (*Bro.*), F (*Bra.*); *not in* Q1. These two lines presumably derive from a press variant in Q1, not found in any extant copy. Compare Quarto *History of Lear* 20.186/2515.
1.1.104/104   I] Q; I do F. See next note.
1.1.104/104   do withal] This edition; withal QF. Q's 'I beseech' is here acceptable as an extra initial syllable, since it links with the preceding (short) line to form a line-divided foot; whereas 'and withal' is markedly awkward. Compositor B could have misinterpreted the annotator's intentions on where to make the insertion.
1.1.106/106   CLARENCE We] F, Q (text); We Q (c.w.)
1.1.113/113   deerer] This edition; deeper QF; nearer WILSON. The pointless QF repetition strongly suggests assimilation; but Wilson's 'nearer', as the far commoner idiom, seems relatively unlikely to have been memorially displaced by the unusual 'deeper'. But 'deerer' would have been more likely to lead to assimilation to 'deeper', and so to have been overlooked by the Folio collator. The adverbial use of *deerer* is common; for the sense compare 'How dearly would it touch thee to the quick' (*Errors* 2.2.133/511). *Deep* and *dearer* are juxtaposed elsewhere (*Richard II* 1.3.150/429).
1.1.116/116   or] Q; or elſe F. F is either unmetrical, or produces an uncharacteristic stress on 'for', when the stress should fall naturally on the (ambiguous) 'lie'. Stressing 'for' also destroys the symmetry of 'lí-ver-yóu' / 'lié-for-yóu'. After 'or', F's 'else' could easily result from scribal or compositorial interpolation.
1.1.125/125   the] Q1; this Q3–8, F
1.1.134/134   prey] Q; play F
*1.1.139/139   Paul] Q; Iohn F. Shakespeare may have originally thought of John because his emblem was an eagle (1.1.133/133). But hereafter Richard swears consistently by Paul, and the theatrical decision to bring this first instance into line with the others makes good dramatic sense.
1.1.146/146   haste] COLLIER 2; horſe QF. 'Collier's reading is plausible both because "haste" might easily have been misread as "horse" and because the adverbial use of "post haste" was usual

whereas "with post horse", though its meaning is clear enough, was not' (McKerrow).
1.2.15/177   Cursed . . . hence:] WILSON (Walker); F *places after* 1.2.16/178; *not in* Q
1.2.19/181   Wolues, to] F; adders Q; vrchines MCKERROW (*conj.*)
1.2.27/189   death] QF; life WILSON (Blackstone). This seems to be contradicted at 4.1.75–6/2302–3 ('More miserable made by the Life of thee, | Then thou hast made me by my deare Lordes death'); Wilson therefore not only emended this line, but sought an explicit contrast in the next by reading 'As I am by my young Lord's death, and thee'. This introduces the notion of death, but only by presuming three separate oversights by the collator (the interpolated 'made', the omitted 'death', and the omitted possessive), in a line where he made two corrections; it also leaves 'and thee' even more anomalous, as a parallel to 'Lord's death'. Editors have thus not followed Wilson in this more radical rewriting. But unless 1.2.28/190 is drastically altered, 'death' too must be allowed to stand. Discrepancies of this kind are common enough in Shakespeare; the form of the curse, in each case, fits Anne's situation at the moment, and an audience will not remember the exact wording.
1.2.38/200   HALBERD] HAMMOND; Gent⟨leman⟩. QF. Although Shakespeare may have written 'Gentleman' or its equivalent, Hammond's alteration makes clear that one of the halberdiers (rather than those carrying the coffin) confronts Richard.
1.2.39/201   stand] Q; Stand'ſt F
1.2.50/212   &] QF; *not in* POPE
1.2.56/218   Ope] This edition; Open QF. All Shakespeare's (and Marlowe's) other uses of *congealed* or *congealèd* are accented on the second syllable; neither Cercignani nor Dobson provides any evidence for an alternative pronunciation. *OED*'s only examples are this line itself and the (much later) *Comus* 448: 'Wherewith she freez'd her foes to congeal'd stone'. But Milton often ended lines with two unstressed syllables followed by two stresses: compare, in the immediate vicinity, 'Dian her dread bow' (440), 'adoration, and blanck awe' (451), 'to the soul's essence' (461). Q's accentuation here is thus extremely suspect, and easily rectified by the emendation of 'Open' to 'Ope' (a variant Shakespeare consistently uses for metrical purposes).
1.2.60/222   deed] Q; Deeds F
1.2.61/223   supernaturall] This edition; moſt vnnaturall QF. QF's phrase simply repeats the idea of 'vnnaturall' at 1.2.60/222; it also offers a relatively common word in place of (conjecturally) a relatively uncommon one. Anne means that Richard's brutish evil has provoked supernatural intervention (as will again happen at Bosworth). 'Supernaturall' also illuminates the biblical allusion in 'deluge', and provides an appropriate transition to 'Oh God . . .'.
1.2.70/232   no] Q; nor F
1.2.73   truth] Q1 (troth), Q2–8, F (truth)
1.2.78   diffused] QF (defuſed)
1.2.78/240   infection] QF. McKerrow notes: If we take 'infection' in its usual sense of 'corruption', 'disease', it gives a poor antithesis and little sense, and it is tempting to suppose that we have here the negative 'in-' prefixed, for the nonce, to the stem of 'perfection', thus meaning 'imperfection' (cf. Lat. *infectus*, 'unfinished').
1.2.78/240   a] Q; *not in* F
1.2.80/242   t'accuse] RIVERSIDE (Spedding); to curſe QF
1.2.92/254   hand] Q; hands F
1.2.101/263   yea] Q1; yea Q3–8, F; ye—yea HONIGMANN (Ritson). Q1's 'yea' is an acceptable period spelling of *ye*. There are five clear tetrameters elsewhere in the text (and many in other texts), so Honigmann's emendation seems unwarranted.
1.2.101   ye] Q1 (yea)
1.2.120/282   of that accurſt effect] WILSON (Walker); and moſt accurſt effect QF; and most accursed th'effect HANMER. Riverside glosses *effect* as 'effector', but there are no parallels, and *effector* itself is not cited till 1601. The QF reading thus makes no real sense. Recent editors have not followed Wilson, perhaps because the annotator corrects a word earlier on this line; but annotator eyeskip from 'the cause' (1.2.120/282) to 'the cause' (1.2.121/

283) would be easy enough. Edward's alternative conjecture ('of that most cursed effect') seems unlikely since Shakespeare consistently uses *cursed* (disyllabic) in this sense and *curst* (monosyllabic) for the sense 'shrewish'.

1.2.126/288   rend] Q; rent F

1.2.127/289   sweet] Q; y^t F. F could result from contamination from the preceding line—or even from deliberate compositorial substitution in a cramped line. *Sweet beauty* occurs in Sonnets 106 and 127, and *Shrew* 1.1.165/439; only the last of these could possibly have contaminated an actor's memory, and (Q) contamination from *Shrew* seems less probable than (F) contamination from the adjacent line.

1.2.154/316   drops:] Q. F here adds 12 lines, reproduced among Additional Passages. See Introduction.

1.2.154/316   Shamd] Q, F (*text*); For F (*c.w.*). F's catchword would be correct had Folio q6^r ended two lines earlier.

1.2.172/334   *He rises*] HAMMOND (*at end of line*); *not in* QF

1.2.183/345   man was] Q3–8, F; was man Q1. Though F's reading could be merely derivative, it offers the more metrical and the more unusual word order.

1.2.189/351   RICHARD GLOCESTER] Q (*Glo.*); *not in* F. F indents the line to the point where speech-prefixes are normally set.

1.2.190/352   LADY ANNE... giue.] Q; *not in* F

1.2.200/362   House] F; place Q. Hall has 'place'; Holinshed omits the noun, which may account for F (Smidt, *Memorial Transmission*, p. 39). Q could arise from memorial confusion with 1.3.34/355.

1.2.213/375   RICHARD... corse.] Q; *not in* F

1.2.213/375   Sirs] Q; *not in* HANMER

1.2.213/375   GENTLEMAN] F; Ser⟨uant⟩. Q

1.2.214/376   black Friers] This edition (*conj.* F. P. Barnard, in Furness); white Friers QF. Shakespeare's sources agree in sending the body to Blackfriars, from where it was transported by water to Chertsey; there is no discernible motive for the change, which would be an easy memorial error.

1.2.221/383   my] F; her Q. Hammond defends Q on the grounds that 'Richard does *not* hate these people'; but see 1.1.31, 1.3.300, 1.4.227, 3.4.52, 4.1.85/31, 712, 990, 1817, 2312. Q could easily arise from assimilation to the two pronouns in the preceding lines.

1.2.223/385   w^{t}all] Q3–8, F (withall); at all Q1

1.2.238   denier] F (denier). Italicization as a foreign word seems desirable not only to forestall ambiguity but as a guide to the actor's pronunciation.

1.3.1/413   theres no doubt] QF; no doubt This edition *conj.* Of 34 other uses of *no doubt* in the Shakespeare canon only *More* II.D.163/162 is parallel ('And thers no doubt, but mercy may be found'). QF's 'theres' produces a relatively awkward phrase and a hexameter.

1.3.5/417   with] Q2–8, F; *not in* Q1

1.3.6/418   If... me.] Q (... of me). F gives the line twice (spanning a page-break).

*1.3.7/419   RYUERS] Q; If he were dead, what would betide on me | Gray. F (*text*); Gray. F (*c.w.*). F's catchword does not anticipate its repetition of the last line on the following page. Its speech-prefix might easily arise from assimilation; even if correct, F might represent an earlier version with the Q revision bringing Rivers more fully into the conversation. See 1.3.30, 54/442, 466.

1.3.11/423   Ah] F; Oh Q. Honigmann ('One Way Variants') notes that F changes Q 'O(h)' to 'Ah' eleven times in *Richard III*. But the changes are probably authoritative: as he notes, generally the Folio prefers 'Oh', and the highest frequencies of 'Ah' are all in early plays: *Duke of York* (29), *Contention* (20), Folio *Richard III* (17), *Romeo* (16), *Titus* (14). No other text has more than ten.

1.3.17/429   come] Q1; comes Q3–8, F

1.3.17/429   Lords] Q; Lord F

1.3.30/442   RYUERS] Q; Qu⟨eene⟩. F

1.3.33/445   With] Q1; What Q3–8, F. Q1's word, besides being intelligible, produces a more unusual construction, with ellipsis of '(Are you come) with...'; F merely repeats the commoner derivative reading of its copy.

1.3.43/455   are they] Q; is it F. With F's reading the QF 'them' in the next line is noticeably awkward (and not easily emended). It seems possible that the change here is Compositor B's, and meant to secure agreement with 'complaines'; compare F's sophistication at 1.3.17/429.

1.3.43/455   complaine] Q8; complaines Q1–7, F. See preceding note.

1.3.54/466   RYUERS] Q; Grey. F

1.3.54/466   whom] Q1; home Q6; who F. F's reading could result either from line justification, or miscorrection of its Q6 copy.

1.3.58/470   Grace] F; perſon Q. Q might be right, given that 'Grace' occurs at the end of 1.3.54/466 and 1.3.55/467.

1.3.68–9/480–1   that... it] POPE; that thereby he may gather | The ground of your ill will and to remoue it Q1–6 [Q6 grounds]; that he may learne the ground F. Pope's reconstruction uses no word not in Q1, and is the best we are likely to get; but F's text is most easily explained by assuming that the annotator had crossed out Q6's last eight words entirely and then, perhaps because momentarily distracted, forgotten to replace them with the manuscript alternative.

1.3.98/510   I] F; yea Q. Honigmann ('One Way Variants') pointed to Folio variants in *1 Henry IV*, *2 Henry IV*, and *Richard III* as evidence of a Folio editor's distaste for *yea*. But Shakespeare himself overwhelmingly preferred *I* (Ay) to *Yea*, in both good quarto and Folio texts: discounting *Richard III* entirely, the ratio is 768 *ay*/200 *yea*. Even more strikingly, this overall preference is only violated in six individual texts: *All Is True* and *Kinsmen* (collaborations with Fletcher), *Richard II*, *2 Henry IV*, and *Much Ado* (all set by Simmes, mostly by his Compositor A), and *1 Henry IV* (which there are other reasons for regarding as a scribal text). Moreover, even though the frequency of *Yea* is already anomalous in Q1 *Richard II*, Q2 *Richard II* (also set by Simmes) increases it further, substituting 'Yea' for one of only three remaining uses of 'I' (3.2.138/1441). In the three Simmes texts overall, the proportion is 6 *ay*/60 *yea* (or, using Q2 *Richard II*, 5/61). And of all the bad quartos, only that set by Simmes makes much use of *yea* (*Hamlet* Q1 = 6; all other bad quartos = 2). The anomaly in relation to *yea* thus resides not in F, but in early quartos printed by Simmes. If we exclude the Simmes texts, and the two collaborations, Shakespeare's preference outside *Richard III* is 748 *ay*/123 *yea*; so Folio *Richard III* (26/2) is clearly unexceptionable. Instead, Q *Richard III*—most of which was set by Simmes—is anomalous, and on the eight occasions when F substitutes 'I' for 'Yea', F probably restores Shakespeare's own preference.

1.3.114/526   Tell... said,] Q; *not in* F

1.3.118/530   remember] Q; do remember F. Compositor B may be stretching his copy; he mislines repeatedly hereabouts to waste space near the end of a cast-off Folio page (r1).

1.3.153/565   may you] Q; you may F. Q's is the less usual word order.

1.3.155   Ah] This edition; A QF; Ay HAMMOND. As Margaret says she is 'altogether joyless' in the next line, it would be preposterous for her to claim here that she 'enjoys a little joy'. Neither 'as' nor 'and' nor 'ay' (spelled 'I') is a satisfactory emendation, and 'Ah', which makes sense, is merely an alternative interpretation of the texts' ambiguous 'A'.

1.3.160/572   of] Q; off F

*1.3.166/578   go:] Q. F adds three lines, reproduced among Additional Passages. Smidt (*Impostors*, p. 107) and Malone note that, since she is allowed to return, it would be better if Margaret's banishment were not mentioned at all; it seems likely that the lame explanation was deliberately dropped. Compare *Tragedy of Lear*'s omission of *History*'s Sc. 17.

1.3.197/609   my] Q; our F. Q better echoes 'thy' in 1.3.196/608; F could be a scribal or compositorial error.

1.3.203   'stalled] QF (ſtald, ſtall'd)

1.3.214–15/626–7   If... Exceeding] F, Q (*text*); Excee- Q (*c.w.*)

1.3.257/669   blasts] Q2–8, F; blaſt Q1

1.3.270/682   was] Q; is F

1.3.271/683 RICHARD GLOCESTER] WILSON (Walker); Buck⟨ingham⟩. QF. Q's ascription could be defended if Margaret turned to the others again at 1.3.273/685 (Honigmann), but 1.3.273/684 seems clearly linked to what follows (charity . : . uncharitably, shame . . . shamefully), the call for 'charity' is typical of Richard, and assigning Buckingham this line diminishes the force of his later intervention and Margaret's response to it. Hammond suggests that Margaret does not attend to the speaker of this line, but only to its content; such a defence contends that the attribution is inept, and resorts to a wrenching of dramatic logic which editors regularly damn when perpetrated in the theatre. The F annotator, especially if he had glanced first at Q6, could easily here misread 'Ric.' as 'Buc'.

1.3.289/701 rãckle] rankle Q2-8, F; rackle Q1

1.3.290/702 nought] COLLIER 2; not QF. An easy aural error. Although Marshall cites two parallels for 'haue to do' (*Measure* 1.1.63/63, *Contention* 5.3.56/3092), there are none for 'haue not to do'; 'haue nought to do' recurs at 1.1.98/98, *Venus* 638 ('hath nought to do with such foule fiends') and *Lucrece* 1092 ('For day hath nought to do what's done by night').

1.3.302/714 HASTINGS] Q; Buc⟨kingham⟩. F

1.3.302 on] F (an), Q (on). According to *OED*, the recognized spelling 'an' for the preposition is without etymological or other significance.

1.3.307/719 QUEENE ELIZABETH] Q (Qu.); Mar⟨garet⟩. F; Haſt⟨ings⟩. Q6

1.3.311/723 as for] QF; for POPE

*1.3.319/731 you my gracious Lo:] ALEXANDER; you my noble Lo: Q1; you my noble Lord Q3; yours my gracious Lord F. Though F's 'Lord' for the ambiguous Q1 'Lo:' could be attributed to the influence of Q3, the change to 'yours' is difficult to dismiss; one must assume that F preserves the reading of its manuscript, based (like the opening stage direction) on confusion about the number of her kinsmen present with the Queen. Q must represent the necessary theatrical correction.

1.3.319 lords] Q (Lo:). See preceding note.

1.3.325/737 whom] Q; who F

1.3.330/742 withall whet me] QF; withall they whet me KEIGHTLEY; whet me withall This edition conj.

1.3.340, 348/752, 760 A MURTHERER] Q (Execu.), F (Vil.); 1. Murtherer POPE (subs.)

1.3.353/765 MURTHERERS] HAMMOND; Vil. F. F's abbreviation is ambiguous, and Hammond's a reasonable interpretation of it. (Editors usually specify 'First Murderer'.)

*1.4.0.2/765.3 Brakenbury] Q (Brokenbury); and Keeper F

*1.4.1/766 BRAKENBURY] Q (Brok.; throughout); Keep⟨er⟩. F (until 1.4.71/836). F's pointless and undramatic division of the scene between the Keeper and Brakenbury could have resulted from inconsistent speech-prefixes in Shakespeare's foul papers; even if Q were a revision, it seems clearly preferable.

1.4.13/778 there] Q6, F (There); thence Q1. As F was here set from Q3, its agreement with Q6 must be coincidence.

1.4.19/784 sought] POPE; thought QF. Pope's reading makes much better sense (expressing action rather than intention), the aural-memorial error could easily have been made in Q1, 'thought' echoes 'Me thought' (1.4.18/783), and the collator was clearly being inattentive in this passage—he missed three derivative readings in 1.4.22/787 and 1.4.23/788.

1.4.22/787 waters] Q1; water Q6, F

1.4.22-3/787-8 my . . . my] Q1; mine . . . mine Q2-8, F

1.4.25/790 Ten] Q; A F. F's reading could easily result from dittography; some rhetorical progression seems desirable.

1.4.26/791 ouches] This edition (conj. McKerrow); anchors QF; ingots WILSON (Kinnear). 'Anchors' is anomalous in the context, and in Q1 could easily be a misreading of 'ouches'; the word would then have been even easier for the F annotator to misinterpret, glancing from Q6 to his manuscript (in what was clearly an inattentive period). J. C. Maxwell's parallel with *The Faerie Queene* (quoted in Wilson) is especially striking: 'All the huge threasure, which the sea below | Had in his greedie gulfe deuoured deepe, | And him enriched through the ouerthrow |

And wreckes of many wretches . . . there heaped was . . . Gold, amber, yuorie, perles, owches, rings' (III. iv. 22-3).

1.4.29/794 those] Q; the F

1.4.32/797 Which] Q; That F

1.4.39/804 find] F; ſeeke Q1; keepe Q3-8. F's 'find' might be a compositorial correction of the clearly erroneous 'keepe'; Q1's 'seeke' seems more appropriate.

1.4.50/815 cried] Q; ſpake F

1.4.58/823 me thoughts] Q1; me thought Q3-8, F

*1.4.66/831 Brakenbury] Q (Brokenbury); Keeper, Keeper, F. See 1.4.1/766.

*1.4.68/833 me.] Q. F adds four lines, reproduced among Additional Passages. See Introduction.

1.4.69/834 Keeper, I pray thee] This edition; I pray thee gentle keeper Q; Keeper, I prythee F

*1.4.72/837 Sorrow] Q; *Enter Brakenbury the Lieutenant*. | Bra⟨kenbury⟩. Sorrow F. See 1.4.1/766.

1.4.72/837 breakes] Q2-8, F; breake Q

1.4.82/847 2 MURTHERER] F; Execu⟨tioner⟩. Q; First Murd⟨erer⟩. MALONE

1.4.91/856 of] Q; from F. Shakespeare uses 'guiltless of' in *Hamlet*, *Lear*, and *Kinsmen*; 'guiltless from' never occurs elsewhere, and the last example in *OED* dates from 1378.

1.4.92.1/857.1 *He throwes down the keies*] This edition; *not in* QF. F's *and there* (for Q's *here are*) strongly suggests that Brakenbury does not actually hand them the keys; and we would hardly expect them to be lying on the floor or on a table. Wilson's conjecture, that he wants to avoid personal contact with the murderers, seems the most dramatic explanation of F's phrasing.

1.4.97/862 I] Q1; we Q3-8, F

1.4.114/878 pray thee] Q; prythee F

1.4.122/886 Zounds] Q; Come F

1.4.135 shamefaced] ſhamefac'd F; ſhamefaſt Q. As *shamefaced* was originally merely an etymological misinterpretation of *shamefast*, with no difference in sense, F's form may represent no more than a Jaggard sophistication, the more so in that in Shakespeare's only other use of the word, *Duke of York* 4.10.20/2391, F also has *shame-fac'd* for the quartos' *shamefast*. But, in any case, the word should be modernized to *shamefaced*.

1.4.140/903 trust to] Q2-8, F; truſt to | To Q1

1.4.142/905 Zounds] Q; *not in* F

1.4.151/914 on] F; ouer Q; o'er This edition conj. Compare *Titus* 3.1.0.3/1016.3 ('on' for 'ou^r').

1.4.157/920 2 MURTHERER] F (2); *not in* Q. Q subsequently reverses the order of the two murderers from 1.4.158-65/921-8.

1.4.163/926 1] Q6, F; 2 Q1

1.4.181-2/944-5 death? . . . law] F2; death, . . . law? Q, F1

1.4.184/947 to haue redemption] Q; for any goodneſſe F

1.4.185/948 By . . . sinnes] Q; *not in* F. This and the preceding variant seem clearly due to censorship in F.

1.4.202/965 Vnripst] Q1-6, F; Vnripſt Q7

1.4.202 Unripped'st] F (Vnripſt)

1.4.208/971 ye] Q; you F. Compare *Dream* 5.1.279/1980, *1 Henry IV* 2.2.86/796, and *Henry V* 2.2.174/781 (all involving Compositor B).

1.4.217 struck] ſtrucke F; ſtroke Q1; ſtrooke Q2-8. The repeated variation of this word throughout the derivative quartos and in F, as well as B's treatment of it in other Folio reprints, confirms that no more than a spelling variant is involved.

1.4.232/995 And . . . other,] Q; *not in* F

1.4.234/997 of] Q1; on Q6, F

1.4.237/1000 As] POPE; Right as QF. F's addition of 'Come' later in this line is almost certainly authoritative: interpolation is the rarest form of error in B's work, and usually confined to pronouns, articles, and copula and auxiliary verbs. The Folio addition produces an acceptable feminine caesura. But if we retain QF's 'Right', then the line has another licence (extra initial syllable), created by exactly the sort of superfluous interjection which memorial transmission is most likely to introduce; moreover, the line has *two* such interjections. Since one of these

('Come') is almost certainly genuine, it seems likely that the other ('Right') is not.

1.4.238/1001 that sends] F; hath sent Q1; that sent Q2-8

1.4.244/1007 Make] Q2-8, F; Makes Q1

1.4.258-62/1021-5 Which... distresse—] KNIGHT (Johnson); after 1.4.251/1014, F (~.); not in Q. TYRWHITT places 'Which... life?' after 1.4.253/1016, and 'As... distress' after 1.4.256/1019. WILSON places as F, but adds 'Even so I beg.' between 'life' and 'as'. The need to crowd this insertion into the upper right-hand margin of the Q3 page which served as F's copy here makes inadvertent misplacement especially probable. Tyrwhitt's arrangement involves an inexplicable change from *thou* to *you* in mid-sentence, and presupposes *two* mispositionings. Wilson's (based on J. C. Maxwell's conjecture) leaves the F order intact, with its interruption of the *relent* word-play and the 'if you were in my position' argument; nor is Wilson's explanation of the error plausible, since if the eye skipped from 'beg' to 'beg', the second clause would have been omitted, not the first. The interrupted sentence and broken line of F and Knight are much more attractive dramatically. Clarence turns to the second murderer immediately after the harsh reply of the first (1.4.252/1015), and the idea of flattery (1.4.255/1018) leads naturally to the subject of princes (1.4.257/1020, and the insertion).

1.4.264/1027 serue] Q; do F. If Compositor B had retained 'serue', he could not have fitted even the truncated stage direction '*Stabs him.*' into the line, which in turn would have thrown him off a whole line at the bottom of this crowded column.

1.4.268/1031 guilty murder done] Q; murther F. As at 1.4.264/1027 above, B could not have retained the full Q line without pushing the following entrance direction on to a separate line which, because of casting-off difficulties, he apparently did not have to spare. See also lineation notes, 1.4.269-70/1032-3.

1.4.270/1033 heauen] Q6, F (Heauen); heauens Q1

2.1.0.3-4/1041.3 *and Grey*] CAPELL; *Woduill* F; *&c* Q. See 2.1.67, 68/1108, 1109.

2.1.5/1046 in] Q; to F; at CAPELL

2.1.5/1046 to] Q1b, Q3-8, F; from Q1a

*2.1.7/1048 Hastings and Riuers] ROWE; *Dorset* and *Riuers* F; Riuers and Hastings Q. McKerrow notes that F's error 'is inexplicable unless it has derived from the MS', and compares Shakespeare's confusion over 'Nell' in *Contention* 3.2.26/1590.

2.1.19/1060 your] Q; you F. Although *son* can mean 'stepson', F's line is ambiguous, where Q's is not; and clarity of relationships is theatrically essential in this play, with its multiplicity of familial and political loyalties.

2.1.33/1074 but] QF; nor This edition *conj*. Wilson defends the confusion of syntax as typical, but Buckingham's speeches are not well reported, and F could be merely repeating a memorial error. Riverside's suggestion that the ambiguity may be intended as ironic seems clearly contradicted by Buckingham's reminiscence in 5.1/Sc. 21.

*2.1.50/1091 Brother] Q; Gloster F. Q underscores the relationships in a theatrically helpful way; see 2.1.19/1060.

2.1.57/1098 vnwittingly] Q; vnwillingly F

2.1.59/1100 By] Q; To F

2.1.66 lodged] Q (logde)

*2.1.67/1108 Of you... of you] Q; Of you and you, Lord *Riuers* and of *Dorset* F. There is nothing wrong with F as it stands, but Q's variant seems related to the alteration in the next line. (See following note.) Having discovered that Rivers, Woodville, and Scales were one man, Shakespeare seems to have mentioned Grey here, to add to the numbers in the Queen's diminished retinue. Grey is also associated with Rivers in death, historically and in the play (3.3/Sc. 11). Moreover, substitution of Grey for Dorset necessitated rewriting the line, since a lord may be 'of Dorset' (F) but not 'of Grey'; and the revised line takes exactly the same form as the omitted line following.

*2.1.68/1109 me,] Q; me: | Of you Lord *Woduill*, and Lord *Scales* of you, F. Rivers, Woodville, and Scales are names for the same man; the mistake is clearly Shakespeare's, based on an ambiguous sentence in Hall, but the revision also seems authoritative. In any case, the line probably belongs after 2.1.67/1108.

2.1.70/1111 English man] Q; Englishmen F, Q7-8. There may be some point in *man*, given Richard's rivalry with the Queen; Q7-8 confirm that the F reading need have no authority.

2.1.82/1123 RYUERS] Q; *King* F. With Q a communal reconstruction, there is little reason to suspect that the reporters all misremembered who spoke this line; while 'Riu'. might easily be misread, at some stage in F's transmission, as 'Kin.'

2.1.85/1126 one] Q; man F. F may be an authorial or scribal anticipation of 2.1.88/1129; its sexual distinction is inept.

2.1.89/1130 winged] Q2-8, F; wingled Q1; winglet This edition *conj*. OED's first citation of *winglet* is from Florio's *Talare* (1611): 'certain shoes with winglets as Mercury is feigned to wear on his feet'.

2.1.90 bore] F (bare), Q. The variants are not substantive. See *Contention* 4.9.77/2809.

2.1.93/1134 but] Q; and F. F could easily have arisen from assimilation to the preceding line.

2.1.93/1134 bloud] Q2-8, F; blond Q1

2.1.97/1138 pray thee] Q; prethee F

2.1.105/1146 slew] Q; kill'd F. The repetition of Derby's 'slew' (2.1.101/1142) seems deliberate and desirable; 'kill'd' could be an inferior authorial alternative, or a scribal or compositorial substitution.

2.1.108/1149 at] Q; and F

2.1.120/1161 pluckt] Q2-8, F; puckt Q1

2.1.131/1172 once] Q; onee F

2.1.136/1177 fruits] F; fruit Q. Shakespeare never uses the singular in this sense, but uses the plural seven times, including the almost identical 'This is the fruites of whoring' (*Othello* 5.1.118/2884).

2.2.1/1184 BOY] Q (*throughout*); Edw⟨ard⟩. F (*only here*). The Folio annotator presumably altered only the first prefix, intending all the others to be similarly corrected by the compositor, who misunderstood the annotator's direction. The Folio manuscript therefore presumably identified the boy as 'Edward' throughout; but this is potentially confusing, his sister ('Margaret') is never named, to name both of them would be even more confusing, and Q's prefix seems more helpful. (The boy's name is not mentioned in the dialogue, so F's use of it must derive from Holinshed, and hence from Shakespeare.)

2.2.3/1186 you] Q; *not in* F

2.2.13/1196 this] Q; it F. F's 'it' could be a scribal or compositorial (or authorial) anticipation of 'it' in the next line; 'this' is more emphatic, and more easily takes the required metrical stress.

2.2.24/1207 cheeke] Q2-Q5, F1; cheekes Q6; checke Q

2.2.25/1208 on my] Q2-6, F; in my Q1

2.2.26/1209 his] Q; a F. Perhaps F's alteration is misplaced and belongs in the preceding line: 'Bad me rely on him as on [a] father, | And he would loue me dearely as his child.' F is certainly feeble as it stands.

2.2.27/1210 shapes] Q; shape F

2.2.28 visor] Q (visard), F (Visor). The variants are not substantive: compare *vile/vild*. F modernizes, as do we.

*2.2.33.1/1216.1 ears] Q; ears, | *Riuers & Dorset after her* F. Q's omission of Dorset and Rivers from this scene (for which see also 2.2.88, 2.2.110/1271, 1293) does not result from difficulties of casting, and has much to recommend it, dramatically. See Introduction.

2.2.39/1222 marke] WILSON (Maxwell); make QF. The same error occurs at *Henry V* 2.2.136/743.

2.2.47/1230 I] Q; *not in* F

2.2.68/1251 their] QF; your This edition *conj*.

2.2.83/1266 weepe] Q; weepes F

2.2.84-5/1267-8 and... weep] Q; *not in* F

*2.2.88/1271 lamentation.] F (Lamentation.); lamentations. Q. F adds 12 lines, reproduced among Additional Passages. See Introduction.

2.2.88.1-110/1271.1-1293 Enter... King.] F is copy-text for this passage.

2.2.105/1288 hartes] Q (hearts); hates F. Either the compositor or scribe could easily misread 'hartes' as 'hates'.

2.2.106 splinted] Q1, F (splinterd); splinted Q2–8

*2.2.110/1293 King.] Q. F adds 18 lines, reproduced among Additional Passages. See Introduction.

*2.2.112/1295 Ludlow] Q; London F. F's error here and below may derive from the fact that Richard was historically in the north at the time of Edward's death; and it may be related to the apparent confusion about whether 2.4/Sc. 8 takes place in London or York.

2.2.114/1297 waighty] Q; not in F. F's line is metrically acceptable whether or not 'busines' is considered trisyllabic; but Q's is more regular, the additional word seems apt in context, Richard is the most reliable of the reporters, and the Folio omission could easily be a scribal or compositorial error.

2.2.115/1298 QUEENE . . . YORKE] STAUNTON (subs.); not in F; Anſ. Q. Q presumably gives a misreading of Amb⟨o⟩.

2.2.115/1298 With . . . hearts.] Q; not in F

2.2.117/1300 Gods sake] Q; God ſake F

2.2.124/1307 Ludlow] Q; London F. See 2.2.112/1295.

2.3.3/1310 Heare] F; 1 ⟨Cittizen⟩ Heare Q. This variant throws off Q's speech-prefixes for the First and Second Citizens until restored at 2.3.10/1317.

2.3.13/1320 Which] F; That Q. Q creates a simple (and Shakespearian) confusion of two constructions: 'In him there is a hope of government' and 'In him there is a hope that . . . govern well'. However, the second construction runs into difficulties with 'No doubt' (2.3.15/1322). F also creates a confusion of two constructions, with hope meaning 'potential' (OED, sb.¹ 4): the council and Prince Edward himself will govern well both Edward's potential for government and 'the government'. The second construction, 'govern the government', is arguably tautological but not untypical. This scene in Q is not very well reported, and there seems no reason to reject F—and even less reason to suppose, with Johnson and Malone, that both texts have here omitted a line.

2.3.22/1329 1 CITTIZEN] F (1.); 2 ⟨Cittizen⟩ Q. This throws off Q's attributions for 2.3.31/1338 and 2.3.38/1345.

2.3.31/1338 will be] F; ſhalbe Q. Hall and Holinshed have 'should . . . be' (Smidt, Memorial Transmission, p. 40).

2.3.35/1342 make] Q; makes F

2.3.43/1350 Ensuing] Q, F (c.w.); Purſuing F (text)

*2.4.0.1/1354.1 Cardinall] Q; Arch-biſhop F. Hall and Holinshed, both of which Shakespeare clearly consulted elsewhere in the play, disagree over whether the same man was involved in the events of this and the following scene. As F's independent authority ceases at the beginning of 3.1/Sc. 9, we cannot even be certain that Shakespeare ever envisaged two characters; for if 'Cardinall' were corrected to 'Arch-bishop' here, and not in 3.1/Sc. 9 (because of a gap in the manuscript), the Folio would appear to call for two characters, when in fact only two names for the same character are at issue. But even if the Folio manuscript did envisage two, the Quarto change cannot be attributed to casting difficulties, and in view of its dramatic effectiveness and thematic relevance is most likely authoritative.

*2.4.1/1355 CARDINALL] Q (throughout scene); Arch⟨bishop⟩. F (throughout scene)

2.4.1/1355 heare] Q1; heard Q3–6, F

*2.4.1/1355 them] This edition; not in QF. This insertion of the redundant ethical dative (for which see Abbott §220, OED them, 1b) is the most unobtrusive way of rectifying the metre while retaining Q's geographical transposition. (See next note.) Neither Capell's 'rested' here nor Pope's wholesale rewriting of the line—'I heard they lay the last night at Northampton'—is at all plausible; but such metrical deficiencies are common in the reporting of Q1, and almost anyone who could have transposed the locations would have been capable of making a metrical adjustment at the same time. F of course could not have corrected the proposed omission because its text differed. Alternatively, one might accept Capell's 'rested' here, and emend 'rest' to 'lay' in the next line, assuming that the reviser simply transposed the two available verbs.

*2.4.1–2/1355–6 Northhampton. | At Stonistratford] Q; Stony Stratford, | And at Northampton F. See Introduction. As Thompson pointed out, though the F order is historically correct, it would be extremely odd for the Cardinal to report the retrograde movement, without knowing its causes, and yet not remark on its peculiarity. Although historically the events dramatized in this scene took place in London, while the next scene requires that young York's sanctuary be close at hand, the presence here of the Duchess of York, young York, and—in F—the Archbishop of York, might naturally have led Shakespeare initially to imagine the scene taking place in York, in which case the F order makes dramatic sense as it stands.

2.4.9/1363 young] Q; good F. F's repetition is awkward and could easily result from compositorial or scribal anticipation.

2.4.12/1366 Nunckle] This edition; Nnckle Q1; Vnkle Q2–8, F

2.4.13/1367 groce] This edition; great QF; ill WILSON (Maxwell). As Maxwell says, great is a reporter's antithesis to small; the rhetorical pattern should be chiastic; and the emendation is supported by Tilley (W238). But gross serves these features as well as ill, and has the additional advantages of preserving the alliterative pattern, and making both the memorial substitution (great/gross) and the Folio annotator's oversight ('groce' misread 'grete' under the influence of context) easier to explain.

2.4.21/1375 CARDINALL Why] Q; Yor⟨ke⟩. And F. Q's speech-prefix is usually accepted, and F's could arise from confusion in a scene where three Yorks are present; but Q's attribution, and the surprised 'Why', also prepare for the Cardinal's innocence in 3.1./Sc. 9. See also 2.4.36/1390.

2.4.22/1376 yet] Q2–8, F; yer Q1

2.4.26, 31/1380, 1385 pray thee] Q; prythee F

*2.4.36/1390 CARDINALL] Q; Dut⟨chesse of Yorke⟩. F. See 2.4.21/1375.

*2.4.37/1391 Dorset] Q; a Meſſenger F. This variant cannot be due to casting difficulties in Q, for anonymous messengers place no restrictions on doubling possibilities, while named recurring characters do. Moreover, although the speeches were clearly written for a messenger, they are not really incongruous in Dorset's mouth, as some editors suggest: the Queen does not greet her son because she is immediately swept up in the anxiety generated by his bad news, and as all the characters exeunt together at scene's end, the dramatic impression is that Dorset goes into sanctuary with her. (See also 3.1.0.3–4/1426.3–4.) Moreover, as Dorset is the only surviving male representative of the Queen's faction, and will later be dispatched to join Richmond, it seems dramatically valuable to bring him on here, the more so when Q omits his appearance in 2.2/Sc. 6.

*2.4.37/1391 your sonne, Lo: Dorset] This edition (conj. Vaughan); a Meſſenger F; your ſonne, Lo: M. Dorſet Q. Q's 'M.' (for 'Marques') is an easy contamination from the following line.

*2.4.38/1392 Lo: Marques] Q; not in F

*2.4.38/1392 DORSET] Q (throughout scene); Meſ⟨ſenger⟩. F (throughout scene)

2.4.40/1394 then] Q; not in F

2.4.42/1396 And with them,] This edition; With them, Sir Q; and with them, | Sir F. There is no reason to suspect F's addition (especially as it makes the postponement of 'prisoners' easier, syntactically); but by itself it produces an unmetrical line, which the omission of Q's 'Sir' would rectify. Q adds such titles repeatedly.

*2.4.48/1402 our] Q; my F. Q seems more appropriate in reply to her son Dorset.

2.4.50/1404 iet] Q. F's 'Tutt' is merely a common phonetic variant of Q.

2.4.64/1418 death] Q; earth F. If the 'd' of 'death' had been accidentally omitted, a proof corrector would perhaps have been more likely to connect 'eath' to 'earth' than to 'death' (McKerrow).

3.1.0.1/1426.1] Beginning with this stage direction (or just after it) the Folio loses its independent authority until circa 3.1.148/

1574. Q is the control-text in this interim; because F provides no correction, the text is exceptionally corrupt. See Introduction.

3.1.0.2-3/1426.2-3 *Lord Cardinall, with others*] F; *Cardinall, &c.* Q

3.1.0.3-4/1426.3-4 *Lord . . . Darby*] This edition (*conj*. Proudfoot); *not in* QF. In the exit direction at 3.1.149.1-2/1575.1-2 Q1-3 call for 'Dorſ.'; F has 'and Dorſet'. Hanmer specifically excluded Dorset and added the Archbishop (whom he substituted for the Cardinal throughout this scene); most editors avoid the problem by a vague call for others at the beginning and end of the scene, avoiding any specific mention of Dorset. 'Dar.' would easily be misread 'Dor.'

3.1.9/1435 Nor] Q; No F

3.1.14/1440 hearts] QF; deeds This edition *conj*.

3.1.22/1448 hastes] This edition; comes QF. Both the triple repetition of 'come' in the next three lines (particularly 'comes not . . . come, or no') and the flatness of the Q reading encourage conjecture. 'Hastes', besides punning on the name and picking up the accusation in 'slug' (and preparing for 'sweating'), also more readily takes the required metrical stress ('hástes not') than does 'comes'.

3.1.24/1450 In happie time] This edition; And in good time QF. Buckingham says 'And in good time | Here comes' at 2.1.45-6/1086-7 and 'Now in good time here comes' at 3.1.95/1521; 'And in good time here . . . comes' also occurs at 4.1.12/2239, and again at 3.4.21/1786 as an error for F's 'In happie time, here comes'. Memorial confusion would be very easy, especially as three of these occur in Buckingham's speeches, and a fourth when he is present. The phrases at 2.1.45-6/1086-7 and 4.1.12/2239 are confirmed by F; that at 3.4.21/1786 is a Quarto error. This leaves 3.1.24/1450 and 3.1.95/1521, both in a passage where we must rely entirely on Q, and the repetition within so brief a passage strengthens the probability of error in one or the other. 'Now in good time' (3.1.95/1521) appears nowhere else in the play, and is an appropriate reaction to the reappearance of Hastings and the Cardinal, only 34 lines after their exit. By contrast, 'And in good time' (3.1.24/1450) appears twice elsewhere, once in Buckingham's part, and seems particularly inappropriate here. The Prince has been complaining about how tardy Hastings has been; Hastings has *not* arrived 'in good time'. The phrase here is thus almost certainly corrupt. At 3.4.21/1786 the phrase is an error for 'In happie time', which occurs elsewhere at *Shrew* Ind.88/88 ('you are come . . .') *Romeo* 3.5.111/2045, *Caesar* 2.2.60/955 ('you are come. . .'), *Hamlet* Add. Pass. P.10/10 ('comming . . .'), *All's Well* 5.1.6/2429 and *Othello* 3.1.29/1417 (both immediately following an entrance). We accept 'In happie time' as the most economical Shakespearian alternative to Q; 'Vpon his cue' (as at 3.4.26/1791 and *Henry V* 3.6.122-3/1518-19) would be more expressive but less safe.

3.1.29/1455 haue] Q1, F; *not in* Q3, Q5-8

3.1.31/1457 Fie] QF; Why This edition *conj*. 'Fie, what' occurs only nine lines before; astonishment seems more appropriate to Buckingham's persona here.

3.1.33/1459 to send] Q1-2, Q4, Q6-8, F; theſend Q3

3.1.38/1464 the] Q1-2, Q4-8, F; to Q3

3.1.39/1465 Anone expect him] This edition; Anone expect him here QF; Expect him here WILSON (Steevens). The time seems much more important than the place.

3.1.40/1466 in heauen] Q1; *not in* Q3-8, F

3.1.41/1467 sacred] This edition; holy QF. Hall and Holinshed both have 'sacred priuilege' in this speech. *Holy* is weaker, less specific, and commoner than *sacred* (in Shakespeare, 208 to 56); it occurs 21 times elsewhere in *Richard III*, and could easily be a memorial substitution.

3.1.42/1468 blessed] QF; *not in* Pope

3.1.43/1469 deepe] Q1; great Q3-8, F

3.1.46/1472 not] This edition; but QF. Q's line makes sense as it stands, but so far as Buckingham (rather than the audience) is concerned, it makes the wrong sense, for it charges the Cardinal to be more *gross* (an appeal hardly likely to appeal to a righteous man) when in fact Buckingham's subsequent arguments urge a more *refined* and subtle understanding of the true nature of sanctuary. The many attempts by 18th- and 19th-c. editors to rectify this difficulty by emending 'grossenes' or 'age' are entirely unsatisfactory; but the difficulty does exist, and is easily rectified by this change. Buckingham, moreover, is the least reliable of the reporters. (See the next five notes.)

3.1.46/1472 age.] This edition (*conj*. Heath) ; ~, QF

3.1.52/1478 And therefore] Q, F1; Therefore F2. Q1's reading is decisively supported by the chronicles: '*and therefore* as for the conclusion of my mynde' (Buckingham); 'he can here haue no priuilege whiche can haue neither will too aske it, nor yet malice or offence to nede it. *And therefore* they recon no priuilege broken' (the Cardinal, trying to persuade the Queen to release her son); 'But my sonne can deserue no sanctuary, you saye, *and therefore* he cannot haue it' (the Queen replying). In all three instances Holinshed and Hall substantively agree. The metrical awkwardness of QF must therefore be rectified by other means; since 'And therefore' and 'can not haue it' are both endorsed by the sources, the problem must lie in the prepositional phrase ('in mine opinion')—a filler, readily vulnerable to memorial substitution, and not endorsed by the chronicles. Near the beginning of the equivalent speech in Hall (and Holinshed), Buckingham says, 'And therfore I ensure you faithfully, for my mynde' and here says 'as for the conclusion of my mynde'. The element common to both asseverations is 'mind', for which the reporter could easily have substituted 'opinion'. Shakespeare uses the idiom 'in my mind' in this sense 7 times, mostly in pre-1600 plays. 'Mind' in place of 'opinion' leaves the line a syllable short, but in the chronicle on both occasions the pronoun 'he' is included before 'can'.

3.1.52/1478 my minde, he] This edition; mine opinion, QF. See preceding note. Alternatively, one might substitute 'in my iudgement', for which Q substitutes 'in mine opinion' at 3.4.43/1808.

3.1.53/1479 longs] This edition; is QF. York clearly *is* in the sanctuary; Buckingham's entire argument is over whether he belongs there.

3.1.54/1480 You . . . charter] This edition; You breake no priuiledge nor charter there QF. Q's terminal repetition of 'there' is feeble and unnecessary. Without it, however, the line is a foot short, and since no other word seems appropriate at the end of the line, the only alternative to the solution here adopted would be an adjective before 'priviledge' or (less plausibly) 'charter'. But such an adjective—holy, blessed, sacred—would add nothing to the argument, and in fact emphasize a property Buckingham wishes to obscure. 'Thereby', on the other hand, contributes to the structure of the argument, picks up (without merely repeating) 'then', 'thence', and 'there', and explains the memorial error.

3.1.59/1485 I come] This edition; I go QF. 'I go' is an odd response to the question 'Are you coming with me?'; elsewhere in Shakespeare it is always used by a character who is going off *alone*, or at least not in the company of the person he addresses. See, for instance, 3.5.99, 3.7.52, 4.4.359, 4.4.383, 5.5.9/1971, 2042, 2864, 2888, 3100. The last of these ('I goe, my Lord') is spoken by Norfolk, whose part could be doubled with Hastings's. QF seem clearly wrong, and the simplest metrical solution would be 'I come my Lord'.

3.1.60.1/1486.1 *Exeunt Cardinall & Hastings*] F (*and*); *not in* Q1; *Exit Car. & Haſt.* Q3-8. Q3-8, F all place after 3.1.59/1485.

3.1.63/1489 seemes] Q1; thinkſt Q3-8, F. Q1's 'it seemes best' is unparalleled in the canon, and could easily be a memorial error for 'seemeth best' (as at *Contention* 3.1.195/1376); *seemeth* occurs 10 times in Shakespeare's early work.

3.1.65/1491 shall repose] Q; should repose This edition *conj*.

3.1.74/1500 liege.] This edition; Lo: QF. Buckingham uses the phrase 'my gracious lord' at 3.1.70/1496 and 3.1.90/1516, and it occurs six times elsewhere in this play; the jingle (Upon recórd, my gracious lórd) makes it almost certainly corrupt here. The simplest change would be 'my gratious liege' (as at *K. John* 1.1.95/95 and *Duke of York* 2.2.9/800) or 'most gratious liege' (as at 5.3.4/3051, *not in* Q). Either is demonstrably Shake-

RICHARD III

spearian, and removes a lame repetition and an awkward jingle which are almost certainly not.

3.1.78/1504 all-] Q1; *not in* Q2-8, F

3.1.85/1511 t'enrich] This edition; enrich QF. Q's reading produces a unique and difficult use of *what* to mean 'that with which', a difficult use of *with* (which must be understood with *enrich*, despite its position), a redundant auxiliary (*did enrich* rather than *enriched*), and a defective rhetorical pattern (A verb B, B verb infinitive A). The emendation removes the first difficulty entirely, makes *did* an independent verb, and thereby makes 3.1.85/1511 and 3.1.86/1512 more exactly parallel. 'With' remains slightly odd, but as the result of a much more characteristic confusion of constructions: (1) 'he was a famous man: to enrich his wit with what his valour did . . .'; (2) 'with what his valour did . . . to make his valour live'. Even this grammatical ambiguity could be clarified, and the whole statement made yet more compact, by emending 'His wit' in 3.1.86/1512 to 'Which wit'; but, although two emendations are not implausible in a memorial text like this, it seems wisest to make do with one.

3.1.87/1513 made] HANMER; makes QF. Although Caesar *lives* 'in fame' with a continuous present verb, death *made* its assault on him at a particular past time: it did at that time kill him, but could not conquer him.

3.1.87/1513 this] Q1; his Q2-8, F

3.1.88/1514 yet] CAPELL; now QF. Capell's word, describing a continued persistence over the many intervening centuries, is much more apt than Q's, which would need an intensive ('euen now') to make its point.

3.1.90/1516 good] CAPELL; gratious QF

3.1.96/1522 louing] Q1; Noble Q3-8, F

3.1.97/1523 dread] Q1; deare Q3-8, F

3.1.101/1527 noble Cosen] This edition; Cofen noble QF. The epithet not only comes more naturally here (compare 'louing brother' above), but in this position provides a better parallel for York's pert reply ('gentle vncle').

3.1.102/1528 Vnckle, well] This edition; Vnckle QF. Without some addition, York does not answer Richard's question: none of Shakespeare's other uses of this formula (or the related *how doth* . . .) suggests that *I thank you* would in itself be a sufficient answer. Moreover, it is his 'faring well' that prompts York's remembrance of the jibe about his growth. The emendation leaves the line a syllable long; but an extra stressed syllable after the caesura occurs elsewhere at 2.2.93/1276 (set from manuscript); hence there seems no need to omit the boy's natural 'O' of recollection. However, such an interjection could easily be an actor's interpolation.

3.1.107/1533 He . . . you then] This edition; Then he . . . you QF. Q1's order gives a most anomalous sequence of stresses in the last half of the line: either 'be*hold*ing to *you* than I' (with no possibility of a caesura to make the extra syllable acceptable, and an unnatural emphasis on *you*) or 'be*hold*ing to you than I' (which requires a feminine caesura after the fourth foot—almost impossible at this period of Shakespeare's versification). The transposition gives either a perfectly regular line (if we presume elision of *he* is as often elsewhere required by Q1) or one with the common licence of an extra initial stress. Not only are memorial transpositions of such conjunctions common in Q1; they are most likely to be moved in Q1 from the middle to the beginning of the line.

3.1.109/1535 as] COLLIER MS; as in QF. Q's phrasing (which could easily arise from dittography) implies that Richard is not his kinsman; metrically the line scans with or without the second 'in' (due to the syllabic ambiguity of 'power'). Symmetry with 3.1.108/1534 also argues for Collier's emendation.

3.1.110/1536 render] This edition; giue QF; then give HANMER; give to KEIGHTLEY (*conj.*). Elsewhere in the line KEIGHTLEY added 'gentle Uncle', THEOBALD, 'this *your* dagger'. All such conjectures rectify the metre by adding words superfluous to the sense; all assume normal transmission rather than memorial error. *Render*—which means both 'give' and 'yield, legally surrender'—adds to the meaning and completes the metre; 'giue' could easily have been substituted as the more common word, used several times in the following lines.

3.1.111/1537 with all] Q3-8, F; withall Q1

3.1.113-14/1539-40 giue, | It being but] This edition; giue, | And being but Q, F1; giue't, | Being LETTSOM (*conj.* in Dyce 2); giue, | And being F2; give, | And but ANON. (*conj.* in Cambridge). The hexameter in 3.1.114/1540 could be accepted; more important is the awkward syntax. Lettsom's solution, however, though adopted in part by Wilson, requires two emendations but destroys the parallel terminations of the two lines. Omission of 'but' removes what seems a necessary emphasis; omission of 'being' requires a difficult ellipsis: 'and (a beggar) (of) but a toy . . .'. There thus seems no possibility of shortening the hexameter; the syntax is more simply resolved by the single emendation offered here.

3.1.120/1546 heauy] Q1; weightie Q2-7, F

3.1.121/1547 I'd] HANMER; I QF. Honigmann's defence of Q—'I value it lightly'—destroys the motive for Richard's next line (and York's original request): if he doesn't value it, why did he ask for it, and why does Richard proceed to say 'what, you insist on having it?'

3.1.123/1549 as] Q1; as as Q3; as, as, F

3.1.132/1558 sharpe prodigal] This edition; fharpe prouided Q; sharp-provided THEOBALD; sharply pointed COLLIER MS. Singer objected that Q 'could never be a misprint for' Collier's reading: but it could be a memorial substitution. However, 'sharply pointed' is merely a roundabout way of saying 'sharp', which hardly improves Q. No parallels have been offered for Q, or for Theobald's interpretation of it: 'supplied with sharpness' is, again, merely 'sharp'. For our emendation compare 'prodigall wittes' (*LLL* 5.2.64/1814). Shakespeare twice describes *tongues* as prodigal (*Richard II* 1.3.245/524, *Hamlet* 1.3.116-17/529-30); the word could mean both 'abundant' and 'wasteful'; and, as it was most often associated with the parable of the Prodigal Son, it is appropriately applied to young York.

3.1.132-3/1558-9 reasons: . . . Vnckle,] F; ~ , . . . ~ : Q1; ~ , . . . ~ , Q3

3.1.133/1559 giues] Q1, Q4, F; giue Q3, Q5-7; showes This edition *conj.* Q's idiom appears nowhere else in Shakespeare, nor have parallels been offered from other authors. Shakespeare often uses *show* of emotions or attitudes, and see *Hamlet* 3.2.22-3/1749-50 ('shew . . . scorne her own Image').

3.1.136/1562 My . . . along] QF. None of the many attempts to pad out this line carries any conviction.

3.1.141/1567 needes] Q1; *not in* Q2-8, F

3.1.143/1569 there] This edition; *not in* QF. The sequence of stresses in Q is highly irregular, the most natural enunciation of the line requiring an extra initial stress followed by a reversed foot. The addition not only seems contextually valuable in itself, but regularizes the metre, and allows a proper emphasis on *you*.

3.1.148/1574 and] F; *not in* Q; so WILSON (Maxwell). F's authority resumes, sporadically, here or in the next stage direction; it resumes in full at 3.1.166/1592. From here on, however, it is again treated as the control-text. Thus, given F's probable authority here, it is unsafe to reject 'and', the more so as Maxwell's 'so' implies a more extra-dramatic species of utterance.

3.1.149/1575 we] This edition; I QF. If we accept F's conjunction (see preceding note), the QF pronoun here is anomalous: we should expect: 'come, brother, and let us go to the Tower'. Moreover, the fate of both boys is sealed by this exit; the plural pronoun seems more appropriate.

3.1.153/1579 parlous] Q7, F4; perillous Q1-6, F1. RIVERSIDE draws attention to Richard's use of the 'stronger' full form; but F here, dependent on a defective manuscript, merely repeats Q. The word must in any case scan disyllabically. McKerrow, who emended, noted that *perilous* is not recorded in the sense 'clever, shrewd, mischievous' (*parlous, a.* 2), which seems relevant here. For the alleged error compare 2.4.35/1389 (Q perilous; F parlous).

3.1.156/1582 hither] QF; *not in* POPE. The word may indeed be memorial, but a hexameter is not itself sufficient grounds for emendation, and the word seems valuable as a indication of Catesby's likely physical distance from the others.

3.1.161/1587 Lo: William] POPE; William Lo: QF

3.1.166/1592 will not] F (Will); what will Q. F regains its full authority at this line.

3.1.169/1595 farre] F; a farre Q. Q (unmetrically) agrees with the sources, but this seems coincidental.

*3.1.170/1596 purpose,] Q. For F see Additional Passages. As Koppel pointed out, Catesby delivers no such message, and in the next scene Hastings clearly already knows all about the council. The two lines are a false start typical of Shakespeare's foul papers, and cleared up in the theatrical text behind Q.

3.1.174/1600 y^r] Q (your); the F. F might easily result from misreading (y^r as y^e). Compare Henry V 4.3.119/2268 and All's Well 4.3.245/2182.

3.1.185-6/1611-12 RICHARD GLOCESTER. . . Lord.] QF. Q repeats these lines verbatim (substituting Tirrel for Catesby and Ye for You) at 4.2.84-5/2407-8; F retains them here and omits them there; DANIEL conjectures they should be omitted here and retained at 4.2.84-5/2407-8. F's retention here could result from oversight, though its alteration of the Q3 speech-prefix from 'Glo.' to 'Rich.' suggests otherwise; but there seems no ground for doubting that F's omission in 4.2/Sc. 17 was anything but deliberate. Hence, it would appear that the manuscript contained the lines here but not there; Q's repetition would then simply be a memorial error. However, the lines are unmistakably more appropriate in 4.2/Sc. 17 than here: for Catesby does not see Hastings until early the next morning, and need not report back to Crosby House, since Buckingham meets him at Hastings's. Moreover, as we have already seen another Folio false start earlier in this scene, involving a similar discrepancy about the timing of Catesby's visit to Hastings (3.1.170/1596), the appearance of these lines in F need not surprise us unduly: they could represent a false start, with the same lines used again later on a more appropriate occasion; F would then have preserved an abandoned intention, and Q the final text. Unfortunately, were this true we would expect either (a) the lines not to occur here in Q, or (b) the lines to occur in the Folio in 4.2/Sc. 17. The first case would arise if a false start had been properly omitted from the final acting text; the second could occur if Shakespeare used the lines twice in his foul papers, the repetition being inadvertently preserved in the prompt-book. Either of these situations would be plausible enough; the facts of the text preclude either. As it is, we are forced to suppose that Q not only gives us the lines in their (eventual) proper place, but also accidentally interpolates them at the very point where they first occurred as a manuscript false start; either that, or a wholly unauthorized memorial transcription across several scenes simply happened to produce a much more satisfactory dramatic arrangement—one which not only better fits the evident sequence of events, but which makes much greater use of Richard's concern for promptness, by associating it with the murder of the children ('Foes to my rest, and my sweet sleepes disturbers') before he sleeps. In 3.1/Sc. 9, the question of his sleeping has no significance beyond its denotation of a point in time; in 4.2/Sc. 17, it seems strikingly pertinent and suggestive in itself.

Richard speaks the first line on both occasions; Buckingham is present for the first and enters immediately after the second (which provides his entrance cue). Memorial association is certainly possible, then; though the presence of both actors does nothing to tell us in which direction the transposition went. However, such major transpositions are rare in this report; Richard is the best of the reporters; and both occurrences of the lines are intimately bound up with exits and/or an entrance. All these factors make accident an implausible explanation, as does the dramatic appropriateness of the second, and apparently unauthorized, occurrence.

Finally, the second occurrence does seem to be at least verbally contaminated by the first, for we (twice) is more appropriate here, referring to Buckingham and Richard, than in 4.2/Sc. 17, where Richard nowhere else uses the royal plural to Tyrrel.

In conclusion: the presence of these lines in 3.1/Sc. 9 appears to represent a false start (like that at 3.1.170/1596) which, (unlike the latter) survived into the prompt-book, and from there through the actors' memories into Q. Their presence in 4.2/Sc. 17 seems to represent deliberate addition, though—hardly surprisingly—with some verbal contamination of the pronoun, as a result of the same actor having spoken an almost identical line earlier in the play. Editorially, then, one can hardly omit the lines from 3.1/Sc. 9, though directors would be justified in doing so (as some have done); and whether an editor retains them in 4.2/Sc. 17 depends upon one's willingness to attribute their striking appropriateness there to chance.

3.1.187/1613 House] F; place Q. See 1.2.200/362.

3.1.188/1614 My] POPE; Now my QF

3.2.1/1624 from Lo:] POPE; from the Lo: QF

3.2.3/1626 my Lord Stanely] F (Stanley); thy Mafter Q. Hall and Holinshed, later in this episode, have 'my lorde thy maister'; but aside from the difference in context, both Q and F are in some respects closer to the sources than the other; nor is this surprising, given Q's frequent variants in such forms of address.

3.2.8/1631 boare] Q6-8, F (Bore); beare Q1

3.2.17/1640 counsels] Q; Councell F

3.2.71/1694 morrow: good] QF; morrow, and good POPE

3.2.74/1697 you doe] Q; not in F. Q's resulting hexameter is metrically acceptable, though Wilson may be right in omitting 'My Lo:'.

3.2.82/1705 the] QF; their This edition conj.

3.2.85/1708 the day is spent.] F; not in Q. Given the ambiguity of 'spent' Q's omission might well be deliberate.

3.2.87/1710 talkt] Q1; talke Q3-8, F

*3.2.90.1/1713.1 Hastings] Q (Haftin.); not in F

*3.2.91/1714 follow presently] Q; talke with this good fellow F. Q is preferred only because it may relate to the 'Hastings' variant: if the pursuivant is an uncanny 'summoner from a higher authority', then it is at least possible that no one else sees him.

3.2.91.1/1714.1 Exit . . . Catesby] Q3-8, F; not in Q1

*3.2.92/1715 Well met Hastings,] Q; How now, Sirrha? F

*3.2.95/1718 I met thee] Q; thou met'ft me F. Q is here closer to Hall.

*3.2.102/1725 Hastings] Q; fellow F

*3.2.103/1726 God saue your Lordship] Q; I thanke your Honor F. Q's line is pointedly more appropriate.

*3.2.107.1/1730.1 He whispers in his eare.] Q; Prieft. Ile wait vpon your Lordfhip. F. Maxwell's conjecture that the Folio line, which occurs again at 3.2.118/1741, represents an erroneous duplicate insertion by the annotator, is made even more implausible by the fact that it is here given a different speech-prefix. But Q seems to have deliberately replaced F's ineffectual half-line with a whispered conference, which Buckingham then plausibly misinterprets as confession.

HAMMOND adds 'Exit Priest' here; but McKerrow notes 'Neither Q nor F provides the Priest with a separate exit and as there might be a sinister touch of irony in his attaching himself to Hastings it is perhaps best to suppose that he remained on the stage until the end of the scene.'

3.3.7/1748 RATCLIFFE . . . out.] F. Q puts this line at 3.3.22/1763, in place of 'Make hafte, the houre of death is expiate' (F). F's repetition of Ratcliffe's sentiment might have been thought slightly ridiculous; but the Q omission could easily be inadvertent.

3.3.7/1748 liues] Q3-8, F; linea Q1; lines Q2

*3.3.14/1755 heads . . . heads,| When fhee exclaim'd on Haftings, you, and I, F. Less important than the fact that Margaret cursed Dorset, not Grey, is the contrast between this speech and the next: Grey remarks on the present fulfilment of part of Margaret's curse, Rivers responds by praying that the rest of it will also be fulfilled. Q's omission of this line, which spoils the effect by mentioning Hastings, thus seems deliberate and defensible.

3.3.16-17/1757-8 Hastings . . . Richard] Q; Richard . . . Haftings F. Q's, the order in which they die, seems preferable.

*3.4.0.3/1765.2 Catesby] This edition (after Q); Ratcliffe, Louell F. Catesby must be included among 'the lords' called for in Q's entrance direction, for he replaces F's Ratcliffe and Lovell at the end of the scene. The Q change cannot be due to casting difficulties and has numerous dramatic advantages (not least its elimination of Ratcliffe's magical journey from Pomfret to London in the time it takes Hastings and Buckingham to walk to the Tower). The objection that Catesby 'is supposed to be at the other council' (Wilson) unnecessarily assumes that the two councils are simultaneous, and that no one present at the first is present at the second.

3.4.4/1769 that] Q; the F. The demonstrative seems much more appropriate; F's reading could have easily arisen by scribal or compositorial contamination from the preceding line.

3.4.4/1769 solemn] This edition; royall QF. The repetition of this adjective is suspicious. See Hall's account of this episode, where the counsel engages in much communing 'for the honourable solemnitee of the coronacion, of the whiche the tyme appointed aproched so nere' (repeated verbatim by Holinshed). Compare *Richard II* 4.1.309-10/2141-2, 'on wednesday next, we solemnly set downe Our Coronation'; Shakespeare often uses the adjective of ceremonial occasions.

3.4.6/1771 BISHOP OF ELY] F (Ely.); Ryu⟨ers⟩. Q1; Bi∫h⟨op⟩. Q3-8. The Q1 compositor could easily misread 'By' as 'Ry', and then misexpand; he had already set three prefixes for Rivers earlier on this same page. The change of prefix in F confirms that its endorsement of Q3's guess reflects consultation of copy.

3.4.9/1774 me thinks] Q; we thinke F. Though F's reading almost certainly derives from the manuscript, 'we thinke' would be an easy scribal error for 'me thinks', which seems more appropriate.

3.4.10/1775 harts] QF; minds This edition *conj*. 'Minds' would be a more appropriate response, and 'hearts' could easily be an anticipation of 3.4.53/1818 ('For by his face straight shall you know his heart').

3.4.18 lords] F; Lo: Q

3.4.22 lords] F; L. Q

3.4.26/1791 not you] Q; you not F. Q's is the more unusual word order.

3.4.32/1797 your] QF; the This edition *conj*. This conjecture would allow elision of 'in the', thereby making elision of 'strawberries' unnecessary. See 3.1.174/1600.

3.4.39/1804 worshipfull] Q; wor∫hipfully F. F would be an easy error, which disrupts the metre.

3.4.41/1806 goe with] F; follow Q. Q's variant may be related to its (apparently) keeping Buckingham on stage.

3.4.41.1/1806.1 *Exeunt Richard ⌈and Buckingham⌉*] POPE; *Exeunt.* F; *Ex. Gl.* Q. Q also omits Buckingham from Richard's re-entry at 3.4.58.1/1823.1. Either this is deliberate (perhaps to suggest that Richard surprises even Buckingham with the speed of his next action), or Q—uncharacteristically—neglects to mention who accompanies the main figure (in which case Catesby might enter at 3.4.58.1/1823.1, if it was felt he should be at 'the other council'; see note on 3.4.0.3/1765.2 above).

3.4.55/1820 likelihood] Q; liuelyhood F

3.4.56/1821 he is] QF; is he This edition *conj*.

3.4.58/1823 STANLEY I ... not.] This edition; *Dar.* I pray God he be not, I ∫ay Q; *not in* F. The 'I say'—which could easily be a memorial interpolation—is awkward and redundant, and as emended the line forms a disguised amphibious section with 'I pray you all'.

3.4.58.1/1823.1 *and Buckingham*] F; *not in* Q. See 3.4.41.1/1806.1.

3.4.65/1830 whatsoeuer] Q; who∫oe're F. More, Hall, and Holinshed agree with Q.

3.4.68/1833 See] Q; Looke F. More and Holinshed support Q. (Hall phrases differently.)

3.4.78/1843 Some see it done] Q; *Louell and Ratcliffe*, looke that it be done F. See 3.4.0.3/1765.2.

*3.4.79.1/1844.1 *Catesby*] Q; *Louell and Ratcliffe* F

3.4.82/1847 raise] Q (race); row∫e F. F's variant is presumably based on a misreading of 'raise' as 'rouse'; but 'rouse' most probably stood in the manuscript, as the collator would be unlikely to commit the error himself, with the right word in front of him in Q3.

3.4.83/1848 But] Q; And F. F's repetition could easily result from anticipation.

*3.4.94/1859 CATESBY] Q; *Ra⟨tcliffe⟩*. F

3.4.98/1863 th'aire] Q7; aire Q1-6, F. The QF reading would require the sense 'who builds his hope in air, out of your good looks'. But this seems the wrong emphasis, for it implies that there are many other ways of building hopes in the air; while Q7's emendation specifically associates the insubstantiality with the 'good looks'.

*3.4.102/1867 CATESBY] This edition; *Lou⟨ell⟩. F ; not in* Q

3.4.102-5/1867-70 Come, come ... vpon.] F (*Richard*); *not in* Q. We have retained these lines; but the omission is probably deliberate. Both of F's speeches for Hastings's guardians begin 'Come, come, dispatch', and Q sensibly omits the second of these. The three lines of Hastings's speech may have been omitted from Q because of censorship: this prophecy would be directed to the audience, after all.

3.5.4/1876 wert] Q; were F. As Wilson notes, Shakespeare nowhere else uses F's form of the subjunctive.

3.5.6/1878 Tremble ... Straw:] This edition (*after* CAPELL); *after* 3.5.7/1879 F; *not in* Q. As Capell remarked 'deepe suspition' is the natural corollary of 'Speake, and looke backe, and prie on euery side'; these actions instead express guilt and fear, which is (like 'ghastly lookes' and 'inforced smiles') a different aspect of the deep tragedian.

3.5.8/1880 suspition:] POPE; ~, QF

3.5.11/1883 At any time] F; *not in* Q. The omission is conceivably deliberate, as (in conjunction with the changes in the following lines) it produces a regular pentameter between 3.5.11 and 12/1883 and 1884.

*3.5.11.1/1883.1 *Maior*] Q; *Maior, and Catesby* F

*3.5.12/1884 RICHARD GLOCESTER ... Maior] Q; But what, is Catesby gone? | *Rich.* He is, and ∫ee he brings the Maior along F. This is clearly related to the substitution, here and in 3.4./Sc. 12, of Catesby for Lovell and Ratcliffe.

*3.5.13/1885 Let ... him.] Q; *not in* F. The addition (accepted by most earlier editors) seems dramatically valuable, in making clear to the audience the confusion orchestrated for the Mayor's benefit. There is no particular reason to suspect that the actor of Buckingham inserted it.

3.5.14, 16/1886, 1888 *calling as to one within*] This edition; *not in* QF

3.5.15-17/1887-9 Harke ... sent.] F. Q's arrangement—3.5.17, 3.5.16, 3.5.15/1889, 1888, 1887—is probably due to the difficulty of remembering the order of lines which, in the theatre, overlap and interrupt one another.

3.5.16/1888 Catesby] QF. This vocative does not, as editors seem to suppose, contradict Q's substitution of Catesby for Lovell and Ratcliffe; for the 'Catesby' Richard calls to 'ouerlooke the wals' can be as imaginary as the unnamed figure he calls to 'Looke to the drawbridge'.

3.5.19/1891 innocence] Q1; innocencie Q2-8, F

*3.5.19.1/1891.1 *Catesby*] Q; *Louell and Ratcliffe,* F

*3.5.20/1892 O ... Catesby] Q; Be patient, they are friends: *Ratcliffe, and Louell* F

*3.5.21/1893 CATESBY] Q; *Louell*. F

3.5.25/1897 earth,] F (Earth,); ~_∧_ Q (*and editors*). F's addition of a comma in the middle of this phrase seems too unusual to be simply dismissed as compositorial, particularly as it gives a more emphatic sense to 'a christian'.

3.5.25/1897 christian,] F (Chri∫tian.); chri∫tian, | Looke ye my Lo: Maior. Q. The Q addition could refer to the actual head.

3.5.31 attainture] attainder QF. From *OED attainder, attaindure,* and *attainture* it is clear that no real distinction was made between the two words; moreover, we are here dependent for the actual spelling upon the aurally transmitted text of Q1. The context clearly requires the *taint* of suspicion, rather than the consequence of legal condemnation.

3.5.32/1904 The] This edition; Well, well, he was the QF. Part-lines in mid-speech are extremely rare in this play and Shakespeare's other early work. Wilson, following Pope, omitted 'That euer liu'd' as a memorial interpolation, but 'Well, well, he was' is more obviously redundant: Buckingham may be holding the head, and in any case there could be no confusion over whom he means. For the ellipsis, see, for instance, *Tempest* 4.1.188/1644 (of Caliban, talked about but not present): 'PROSPERO A Deuill, a borne-Deuill, on whose nature . . .'.

*3.5.48/1920   I] Q; *Buck*. I F. Q's continuation of the lines to the Mayor is hard to dismiss as accidental; the access of sycophancy is entirely appropriate, even comic.

*3.5.50/1922   RICHARD GLOCESTER] Q4 (*Glo.*); *Clo.* Q3; *Dut*⟨*chesse*⟩. Q1; *not in* F. F continues the speech to Buckingham. But Q changes one of the first person references to another (royal) plural, and (since it has replaced Lovell and Ratcliffe with Catesby) its reference to the 'haste of these our friends' can only refer to Catesby *and* Buckingham. These related changes of wording and antecedent suggest that the Q attribution is as deliberate as it is appropriate; moreover, the actor playing Richard is the most reliable of the reporters. As for Q1's error '*Dut*.', it is (as Q3's guess suggests) more probably a misreading of '*Gloc*.' than of '*Buc*.' F's own reading might result from confusion of '*Buc*.' and '*Ric*.'

3.5.54/1926   we] Q; I F

3.5.54/1926   heare] WILSON (Keightley); heard QF

3.5.56/1928   treason] Q; Treaſons F. Hall and Holinshed three times in this context use the singular (Smidt, *Memorial Transmission*, p. 40). An easy compositorial or scribal error.

3.5.60/1932   word] Q; words F

3.5.64/1936   cauſe] Q1; eaſe Q6; caſe Q7–8, F. F was here set from Q6.

3.5.72/1944   meetest vantage] F; meeteſt aduantage Q1; meeteſt aduantage Q6. Though Q6 was copy here, Compositor A is unlikely to have changed 'aduantage' to 'vantage' on his own initiative, especially as he could correct the metre (if he wanted to) simply by eliding 'meetest'—a kind of change he made scores of times throughout the text.

3.5.74/1946   Cittizen] QF; merchant This edition *conj*. 'Cittizen' is extra-metrical, and occurs 10 lines before; 'merchant' is how Hall describes the man; and the annotator, glancing from his Q6 word to his manuscript, might easily accept 'marchant' as 'citiſen(e)'.

3.5.81/1953   raging] F; ranging POPE; luſtfull Q

3.5.82/1954   listed] Q; luſted F

*3.5.101/1973   Now] Q. For F see Additional Passages. F's three additional lines could easily have been rewritten to accommodate the disappearance of Lovell and Ratcliffe ('Go Catesby . . . And then to Friar . . .'); their omission therefore seems deliberate—and desirable, for they are wholly superfluous.

3.5.101/1973   in] Q; goe F. Compositor A had set F's word three times in the last five lines; both the lameness of the repetition, and the ease of error by association, argue for Q.

3.5.103/1975   notice] Q; order F. Presumably F arose by attraction from 3.5.101/1973.

3.5.103/1975   maner] Q3–4, F (manner); maner of Q1–2, Q5–6. F was probably set from Q6 here.

3.6.9/1985   liberty] QF; large This edition *conj*.

3.6.13/1989   naught] Q1; nought Q3–F

3.7.7/1997   insatiate] Q; vnſatiate F. Shakespeare nowhere else uses *vnsatiate*; he uses *insatiate* (which also agrees with his sources) three times elsewhere; and F's reading could easily result from a minim misreading.

3.7.11/2001   resemblance] F; dissemblance This edition *conj*. Although *OED* gives the sense 'The external appearance, or characteristic features peculiar to an individual . . .' (*resemblance*, sb.¹ 2) with a first citation in 1390, with the exception of this passage all the examples listed before 1636 have a context which permits a reflective sense, rather than the absolute 'semblance' which seems required here.

3.7.14/2004   face] This edition; forme QF. As Richard is prominently deformed, *form* is ludicrously inappropriate; in the chronicles, it is Richard's *face* which is compared to his father's; and the annotator, glancing from the quarto line to the manuscript, could easily accept 'face' as 'forme' (*a* being often misread as *o* + minim). The emendation has the further merit of turning a defect into a dramatic advantage: for by specifying *face*, Buckingham encourages an audience to remember that in other respects Richard is obviously *not* the 'right idea of [his] father'.

3.7.20/2010   mine] Q1; my Q3–8, F

3.7.25   statuas] QF (ſtatues)

3.7.30/2020   spoke] QF; so spoke This edition *conj*. The accentuation of the QF line is peculiar: contrast 'For I was spoke to, with Sir Henry Guilford' (*All Is True* 1.3.66/539) and 'It would be spoke to' (*Hamlet* 1.1.43/43). An easier conjecture would be 'be bespoke to' (in the vague contemporary sense 'be spoken to'), but this seems an unfortunate collocation.

3.7.33/2023   spoke] F; ſpake Q1; ſpeake Q6. Shakespeare used *spoke* three times as often as *spake*. If F were a conjectural emendation of Q6's obvious error, one would expect a return to Q1 (which involves only the omission of an 'e').

3.7.35/2025   At] F; At the Q. Ath This edition *conj*. Hall has 'at the', Holinshed 'in the'.

3.7.37/2027   And . . . few.] F; *not in* Q. The disparity between 3.7.36/2026 and 3.7.38/2028 is funnier without this line.

3.7.40/2030   wisedomes] Q; wiſdome Q3–7, F

3.7.43–4/2033–4   BUCKINGHAM No . . . Lo: | RICHARD GLOCESTER] Q (*Buc*. . . . *Glo*.); *not in* F

3.7.45/2035   BUCKINGHAM] Q3–8, F; *Glo*. Q1

3.7.49/2039   build] Q; make F. Hammond ably defends Q, which plays on both senses of 'ground'. F could be a scribal or compositorial substitution, or an authorial variant improved between the foul papers and the prompt-book.

3.7.50/2040   request] Q; requeſts F. Hall and Holinshed have the singular three times in this episode, the plural never. See 3.7.101/2091.

3.7.52/2042   I goe, and if you] F (∼ : ∼); Feare not me, if thou canſt Q. 'If thou canst' makes a much better parallel to 'As I can' in 3.7.53/2043, while 'Feare not me' is more pointed than the purely denotative 'I goe'. We therefore prefer Q; but its authority must remain dubious, as F's reading cannot be explained as a scribal or compositorial error. Moreover, F switches unaccountably from *you* in 3.7.52/2042 to *thee* in 3.7.53/2043. Abbott §234, which justifies such switches, cites only this passage, *Richard III* 1.4.256–8/1019–21—where he accepts Tyrwhitt's questionable transposition—and *Pericles* 2.1.197–8/ 2215–16, where the text is unreliable (see note). The change in *Caesar* 5.1.73–6/2170–3 comes between sentences.

3.7.53/2043   thee] QF; them This edition *conj*. See preceding note.

3.7.54/2044   weele] Q; we F

3.7.58/2048   Now] F; Here coms his ſeruant: how now Q; *not in* POPE. Wilson plausibly conjectures that the collator's deletion line should have gone one word further. Only here and at 3.7.83/2073 is *Catesby* required to be trisyllabic.

3.7.72   lolling] QF (lulling)

3.7.72/2062   day bed] Q; Loue-Bed F. F's reading is redundant; 'day bed' is both more pointed, given the Elizabethan attitude towards daytime sexual activity, and more Shakespearian (see *Twelfth Night* 2.5.46/1031).

2080   perfit] F; perfect Q. As Folio Compositor A seems to have preferred *perfect*, F's form might have some authority.

3.7.94.1/2084.1   a lofte] Q2–F; *a lofte* Q1

3.7.94.1/2084.1   two bishops] QF. Honigmann takes this as a manuscript false start, and hence as evidence of Q access to foul papers, because Richard has in 3.5/Sc. 13 sent for two friars to perform this function. But Q excises the lines sending for the friars; so there is no need to presume any extra-theatrical knowledge.

3.7.101/2091   request] Q; requeſts F. See 3.7.50/2040.

3.7.125/2115   hir] Q1 (her); his Q3–8, F

3.7.126/2116   Hir] Q (Her); His F. Having read Q3–6 'his' in 3.7.125/2115, the annotator would be likely to misinterpret manuscript 'hir' as 'his', here and in 3.7.127/2117. Alternatively, the manuscript itself might have contained the error.

3.7.127/2117   Hir] POPE; His F

3.7.143/2133   condition:] Q. F adds 10 lines; see Additional Passages.

RICHARD III

3.7.160/2150 no doubt vs] Q; (no doubt) vs F1; vs (no doubt) F2

3.7.203 equally] QF (egallie)

3.7.209/2199 zounds ile] Q; we will F

3.7.209/2200 RICHARD GLOCESTER O ... Buckingham.] Q (Glo.); not in F

3.7.210.1/2200.1 Exeunt] F (after 3.7.209/2199); not in Q. As F omits 3.7.210/2200, it is impossible to tell whether its direction should precede or follow Richard's line; but Buckingham is clearly not yet off stage when it is spoken.

3.7.210.1/2200.1 and some others] This edition; not in QF

*3.7.212/2202 ANOTHER] Q (Ano.); not in F. This change is clearly deliberate, and dramatically apt.

3.7.214/2204 Exit one or more] This edition; not in QF; Exit Catesby THEOBALD

3.7.214/2204 stone] POPE; ſtones QF

3.7.215/2205 intreates] Q; entreaties F. Q's is the rarer reading: see Taylor, 'Praestat'.

3.7.230/2220 kind] This edition; not in Q1; King Q3–8, F. Q1 is unmetrical, while the unauthoritative Q3 reading is awkwardly redundant (as are none of Shakespeare's other uses of the formula). Richard is repeatedly called kind; the word would be especially ironic and appropriate here, where Richard's 'kind' acquiescence in their appeals requires an unnatural deposition of his nephews; and the word is graphically close enough to the Q3 guess to make oversight highly plausible.

3.7.231/2221 ALL BUT RICHARD] F (All.); Mayor. Q. Q's prefix may indicate that the citizens are as unenthusiastic here as they were earlier.

3.7.237/2227 coosine] Q; Couſins F

4.1.0.2–4/2227.4–6 at one doore ... at another doore] Q; not in F. F also changes the grouping of the names, placing them in order of rank; but Q's is clearly the required arrangement.

4.1.0.3/2227.5 with Clarence daughter] THEOBALD; not in QF. See next note.

4.1.2–7/2229–34 Led ... awaie] F; Qu. Siſter well met, whether awaie ſo faſt Q. We have retained F because the absence of lines from Q may be due to the unavailability of a fifth boy actor. But Clarence's daughter serves no significant dramatic purpose, and is ignored for the remainder of the scene: the cut may therefore be authorial.

4.1.4/2231 Prince] F; princes THEOBALD

4.1.11.1/2238.1 Brakenbury] CAPELL; not in QF

4.1.15/2242 BRAKENBURY] CAPELL (throughout scene); Lieu⟨tenant⟩. QF (throughout scene)

4.1.28/2255 one] F; an Q. These are confusible in Shakespeare's hand; so Q could be right.

4.1.34/2261 swoone] F; found Q. As Compositor A nowhere else uses this form, the change presumably reflects the manuscript.

4.1.46/2273 counted Englands] This edition; Englands counted QF. This is the only occurrence of this word in this sense (OED, ppl. a.); nor are there any relevant examples of the verb count used absolutely as 'esteem, value'. One could either transpose, presuming an error by the Q compositor overlooked (like 3 derivative transpositions) by the annotator; or emend 'counted' to 'crowned', words graphically so similar that the annotator could easily have misread the one under the influence of the other. But the latter leaves Q's unusual reading unexplained, and both Queen Margaret and Queen Elizabeth are more concerned with the regard implied by counted Queen than with the redundant adjective crowned. (Counted is also more appropriate as a reflection of Margaret's attitude: for to her Elizabeth never has been Queen, though commonly regarded as such.)

4.1.54/2281 hatcht] Q2–8, F; hatch Q1

4.1.57/2284 in] Q; with F. 'In all vnwillingnes' better balances 'in all haſt'.

4.1.74/2301 so madde,] Q1; ſo badde, Q3–8; ſo mad, F; so, made FERRERS (conj. in Cambridge). One's confidence in Ferrers's emendation is much reduced by the fact that F here apparently corrected its quarto copy by reference to manuscript; to emend one must therefore presume independent corruption in both texts. See next note.

4.1.75/2302 made] This edition; not in QF. This emendation supplies the verb which 'by' (4.1.75/2302), the parallel with 'made' (4.1.76/2303), and 1.2.26/188 all seem to require, on the assumption that the Folio annotator or compositor overlooked a Q error. It therefore seems more probable than Ferrers's emendation of 4.1.74/2301, while producing a characteristic word-play on mad and made. (The line is metrical if, as elsewhere, 'by the' is elided to one syllable.)

4.1.80/2307 mine] Q6, F; my Q1. F was here set from Q3.

4.1.89/2316 DORSET] F, Q1; Qu⟨een⟩. Q2–8. Though editors often adopt or defend Q2, the agreement of Q1 and F can hardly be dismissed here, the more so as it seems a deliberate attempt to bring Dorset into the scene, for the Duchess of York's summing up. Dorset takes leave of glory because he only acquired it through his mother, who now has none, and whom he is about to leave.

4.1.91.1/2318.1 Exit Dorset] This edition; not in QF. Q provides no exits for this scene; F adds a final speech by Elizabeth, which requires all the characters to remain on stage to the end of the scene, when they 'Exeunt'. In Q's arrangement it seems preferable for them to exit individually.

4.1.92/2319 tend] F; garde Q. But guard seems a better parallel to guide. Perhaps an authorial variant.

4.1.92.1/2319.1 Exeunt ... daughter] This edition; not in QF

4.1.93.1/2320 Exit Elizabeth] This edition; not in QF

4.1.96 racked] QF (wrackt). Most editors have followed Hanmer's interpretation as 'wrecked', but the spelling might equally stand for 'racked' which gives better sense (McKerrow).

4.1.96/2323 teene.] Q. F here adds seven lines; see Additional Passages.

4.1.96.1/2323.1 Exit] This edition; not in Q

4.2.0.1/2323.2 Sound] F (c.w.); Scena Secunda. | Sound F (text)

4.2.0.2–3/2323.3 with other Nobles] Q; Ratcliffe, Louel F

4.2.3.1/2326.1 a Sennet] This edition; not in QF

4.2.3.1–2/2326.1 Here ... throne] Q; not in F

4.2.14/2337 liege] Q; Lord F. Though Q is generally unreliable with respect to such formulae, here F's repetition of lord could plausibly result from contamination by the end of 4.2.12/2335; most earlier editors accepted liege.

4.2.20/2343 immediately] This edition (conj. Wilson); ſuddenlie QF. Maxwell remarked that the repetition of 'suddenlie' was suspicious, while Wilson noticed the Q substitution of 'immediately' in 4.2.27/2350 (for F 'presently'). It is also noteworthy that immediately occurs nowhere in F—which means that its presence in Q at 4.2.27/2350 cannot result from contamination with any other passage—and that the word is strongly associated with this period of Shakespeare's vocabulary: of 20 occurrences, only two post-date 1600, while 9 occur in Errors, Titus, Contention, LLL, Dream, and Romeo. And elision of here it presents no difficulties. (Alternatively, one might read 'presently performed'.)

4.2.21/2344 saist thou now] F (ſay'ſt); ſaiſt thou Q1–5; ſaieſt thou Q6. Since F was here set from Q3, its addition of 'now' might conceivably be metrical botching, based on Q3's monosyllabic representation of 'saist'.

4.2.47/2370 How now] QF. If a metrical emendation were made, omission of these two words (common to both texts) would be more acceptable than Wilson's omission of 'what's the newes', which F deliberately creates from Q1's 'what neewes with you'. Wilson's emendation is only acceptable if we presume that 'Lord Stanley' and 'what's the newes' were alternatives in the foul papers, one replacing the other; the scribe of the F manuscript kept both, while the Q tradition omitted the first.

*4.2.50/2373 those partes beyond the seas] Q; the parts F. Q's additional phrase creates an unassimilated part-line; but several such already exist in this scene. There is no reason to doubt that F represents a genuine Shakespearian text; but Q clarifies an important narrative point which F leaves cryptic.

4.2.55/2378 borne] Q; poore F. The point of Richard's dynastic plot is to find someone of low birth on whom to dispose of the possible rival heir; 'poore' simply repeats the sense of 'mean'. Q's reading is further supported by Holinshed, who says that Richard planned

243

4.2.72/2395 but I] QF; I SPEDDING (*conj.*)
4.2.73/2396 there] Q; then F
4.2.81/2404 Tis] Q; There is F. Q seems much more idiomatically dismissive and shocking, and is metrically acceptable.
4.2.81/2404 it is] Q3–F; is it Q1, Q6. Though Q3 was F's copy here, the following line seems to require a statement, not a question.
*4.2.84–5/2407–8 ⌈KING RICHARD⌉ Shal . . . lord.] Q (*King*); *not in* F. Q's addition seems integrally related to the 'clock-passage' below (4.2.102–18/2424–42). Richard here asks to hear of the princes' deaths 'ere I sleep'; later, he twice asks what time it is; on being told, 'Vpon the stroke of ten', he says 'let it strike', which has a sinister meaning entirely lost on Buckingham; Buckingham's obtuseness leads to Richard's outburst. This passage, by explicitly raising the prospect of a quick execution of the princes, helps to explain Richard's preoccupation with the time and with striking; moreover, after Anne's description of his sleepless nights, 'ere we sleep' is particularly ironic. (See note to 3.1.185/1511.)
4.2.90/2413 to] Q; vnto Q is unidiomatic and unmetrical. As *unto* for *to* is a common enough compositorial or scribal substitution, Wilson's solution—omitting QF 'Well' and accepting F's 'vnto'—seems relatively implausible.
4.2.101/2424 perhaps,] Q; *not in* F
*4.2.101–19/2424–42 BUCKINGHAM . . . to day.] Q (*Buck.*); *not in* F
4.2.104/2427 My] Q; My soueraigne This edition *conj.*
4.2.113/2436 But] POPE; Wel, but Q. 'Wel' is extrametrical here, and the kind of word easily interpolated by actors or reporters; it is repeated more metrically and aptly in Richard's next line.
*4.2.120/2443 Whie . . . no?] Q; May it pleafe you to refolue me in my fuit. F. The variant here seems related to the preceding passage: F's mild reiteration—a call for attention, for some decision, instead of ramblings about prophecies and threats to Stanley—makes good sense in the F context, but seems inappropriate after the peremptory question and insults of Q. The exasperation of 'Why then' is more appropriate to the latter; 'resolue me' takes on a quite different implication ('if I'm annoying you, let it strike indeed, give me a decision'), while 'whether you wil' (eventually) specifically replies to 'I am not in the giuing vaine *to day*'.
4.2.121/2444 Thou] F; Tut, tut, thou Q. Q's addition may be 'actor's gag'; but if so it suggests what a good actor Burbage was.
4.3.1–2/2449–50 act . . . deed] F (*Act*); deed . . . act Q. Such transpositions in Q are usually of no authority; but Q does produce a more striking alliterative pattern (deed is done, arch act).
4.3.4/2452 whom] Q, F2; who F1
4.3.5/2453 ruthles] Q1; ruthfull Q3–8, F. Q1 reads 'ruthles peece of'; F transposes the adjective (as here).
4.3.8/2456 two] Q; to F
4.3.10 one] Q1 (on); Q3–8, F (one)
4.3.13/2461 And] F; Which Q1; When Q6. F has sometimes been rejected as an unauthorized correction of Q6's obviously incorrect reading; but F was here set from Q3.
4.3.15/2463 once] Q, F4; one F1
4.3.25/2473 gaue] Q3–8, F; giue Q1
4.3.31/2479 KING RICHARD] Q3–8 (*King.*), F (*Rich.*); *Tir.* Q1
4.3.31/2479 at] Q; and F
2487 godnight] Q1; good night Q3–8, F. Q's form is perfectly acceptable: it occurs three times in *Blurt Master Constable*, while related forms (God morrow) occur often. As the difference here is only semi-substantive, F's manuscript may have had 'good'; but F could also arise from mere oversight.
4.3.40 Breton] QF (*Brittaine*)
4.3.42/2490 ore] Q; on F. F makes sense; but it could also easily result from a scribal misreading of 'ore' as Shakespeare's 'one' spelling of *on*. Q's reading seems much more pointed: Richmond disdainfully 'looks over' the crown, examines it, like a potential purchaser (*OED*, v. 41), and also proudly 'looks down on it', 'considers himself above it' (Schmidt, comparing 'Let Anthony looke ouer Cæsars head', *Antony* 2.2.5/579).
4.3.43.1/2491.1 Ratcliffe] F; Catesby Q. The change is not attributable to casting requirements, and can hardly have resulted from error in a communal memorial reconstruction (in which Richard, Catesby, and Ratcliffe all clearly participated). But Q's variant could have resulted from the misreading of a manuscript abbreviation '*rat*' as '*cat*'. As there is no dramatic reason for changing one to the other here, this seems the most reasonable explanation for the variant. If the misinterpreted abbreviation stood in the foul papers, either text could be in error; but given the plethora of abbreviations in Q, it seems more probable that the mistake was made by the Q compositors. Ratcliffe's presence here is especially advantageous in the Q arrangement, where he has not appeared since 3.3./Sc. 11.
4.3.45/2493 Good newes or bad] Q; Good or bad newes F
*4.3.46/2494 Ely] Q; Mourton F. In following the sources F obscures the fact that 'Mourton' is the Bishop of Ely, whom we have seen in 3.4/Sc. 12; the change is a dramatic improvement, which itself requires knowledge of the chronicles. See 4.4.398/2903.
4.3.53/2501 leades] Q; leds F
4.3.55/2503 an] This edition (*conj.* Theobald); and QF. The line could conceivably be addressed to Ratcliffe, as Riverside's gloss seems to suppose ('note Richard's next equation of himself with Jove'); but this is ridiculously excessive, while the rhyme argues for a more sententious and patterned utterance. But given the text as it stands, the antecedent for 'Ioues Mercurie' must be 'expedition'—though the latter can certainly be Richard's 'wing', how can his own speed, and more particularly his own wing, be his messenger and herald? The line further requires us to understand 'and [therefore] herald'; and though this construction is not impossible, it—and the incongruous but unavoidable suggestion that 'Jove is Mercury and herald for a king'—does nothing to increase one's confidence in the line. Theobald conjectured, as a solution to all these difficulties, 'Jove's Mercurie's an herald', but the first emendation is ugly and unnecessary, and the verb can be supplied by the preceding 'be': 'expedition be my wing, and Mercury [be] my herald'. This then leads to a command to Ratcliffe. *And* in error for *an* also occurs at *Two Gentlemen* 4.1.47/1537, *Much Ado* 2.3.25/849, *All's Well* 2.2.58/829, *Hamlet* Add. Pass. E.2/2, *Timon* 3.6.17/1124 (perhaps by Middleton), and *Henry V* 4.6.8/2382 (Folio version).
4.4.10/2515 vnblowne] Q; vnblowed F. Since Compositor B set 'blow'd' once elsewhere (*Othello* 3.3.186/1634), F's variant has been regarded as non-substantive.
*4.4.17–19/2522–4 DUTCHESSE OF YORKE . . . dead?] F (*Edward Plantagenet*); *after* 4.4.34/2539 Q (*subs.*). The traditional F arrangement has been accepted, as it is certainly what Shakespeare originally wrote, while Q's transposition could be a memorial error. But York's announcement that her tongue is 'still and mute' might come more appropriately as her *final* utterance before Margaret's intervention; in which case Q's omission of 4.4.20–21/2525–6 would be deliberate.
4.4.30/2535 innocents] Q; innocent F
4.4.30.1/2535.1 ⌈They⌉ sit] This edition; *not in* F. Editors since Capell have the Duchess sit here and the Queen follow at 4.4.34.1/2539.1. But speaking in favour of this new arrangement are: the ambiguity of reference in the preceding speech; the fact that 'rest them here' would naturally imply that the Queen was sitting; the fact that the following speech provides no obvious cue for sitting down; and the objection that two shattered women (one eighty years old) might more naturally *help* each other to sit. And theatrically, if Elizabeth sits at 4.4.34.1/2539.1, her action is immediately upstaged by Margaret's coming forward at 4.4.34.2/2539.2.
4.4.36 seniory] Q (*fignorie*), F (*figneurie*)
4.4.39/2544 Tell . . . mine,] Q; *not in* F
4.4.41/2546 Husband] Q; Richard Q; Harry CAMBRIDGE
4.4.44/2549 Richard] QF; husband This edition *conj.*
4.4.45/2550 holpst] Q3–8, F2; hopft Q1; hop'ft F1
4.4.52–3/2557–8 That . . . earth,] F; *not in* Q; *lines transposed* CAPELL
4.4.56 charnel] QF (*carnal*). Not previously modernized. *OED* cites this passage under *carnal*, with the sense 'Carnivorous; *fig.* bloody, murderous' (*a.* 6). But this is its only citation, and none

of the other uses of the word leads naturally to this literal or figurative sense. On the other hand, *carnal* and *charnel* both derive from the Latin *carnāl-is*; *carnary* is a 16th-c. form for 'charnel house', and *charnel* as an adjective dates from the 15th c. At least one other *OED* citation seems relevant: Sir Thomas Browne's 'Carnal Interrment or burying' (1658, *OED*, *a*.¹), where both 'interment of a body' and 'interment in a charnel' seem pertinent. And for the related *carnage*, *charnage* clearly existed as a dialect form. A unique, strained, and figurative sense 'carnivorous' thus seems less likely than a confusion of the doublets *carnal* and *charnel*, the more so in that the latter has clear associations with 'pew-fellow', 'Preys on the issue of his mother's body', and 'That dog ... Thy womb let loose to chase us to our graves'. Moreover, even if *charnel* were not a legitimate modernization, it would remain an easy emendation, with Q deriving from aural and/or memorial error, and F from oversight (the difference between the two words consisting only of a single medial letter).

4.4.59/2564 wife] Q2–8, F; wifes Q1
4.4.64/2569 Thy] Q; The F
4.4.64 quite] Q6; quitte Q1; quit F
4.4.73/2578 hand at hand] Q2–6, F; hand at handes Q1
4.4.77/2582 plead] DANIEL; pray QF. For the rhyme see Cercignani, p. 78.
4.4.93/2598 are] Q1; be Q3–8, F
4.4.100/2605 For Queene ... care,] Q; *after* 4.4.101/2606, F
4.4.107/2612 wert] Q1; art Q3–6; waſt F
4.4.111/2616 halfe my burthened yoke] QF; yet but halfe my yoke This edition *conj*. The annotator is clearly being inattentive here: he retains Q6 errors at 4.4.93, 4.4.112/2598, 2616, and (two in) 4.4.118/2623. The ineffective repetition of 'burden(ed)'— which occurs yet again at 4.4.168/2673—is suspicious, and the difficulty of the sequence of thought makes it more so. Lines 4.4.109–10/2614–15 must mean 'You usurped my great position; aren't you also making an unjustified claim to my magnitude of suffering?' This fits in well with the competition in grief throughout the scene. Then, in 4.4.111–12/2616–17, Margaret agrees to *give* her what she's laying claim to: 'you can have not only my position, but my grief' or 'you can have not only as much grief as me, but enough for both of us'. Either interpretation of the 'halfe' and 'all' makes good sense. The difficulty is in 4.4.111/2616, the transition between these two ideas, which also contains one of the two uses of *burden*. 'Now thy proud necke' seems perfect, contrasting present and past, with 'proud' related to the usurpation of Margaret's place. But in the second half of the line 'burthened' adds little or nothing, while we would expect a greater emphasis on (only) 'halfe', and something to link the past and present of 4.4.109–11/2614–16 more explicitly to the future of 4.4.112–13/2617–18 (in which Elizabeth will bear not merely half but all the burden). The conjecture emphasizes the pivotal contrast between 'halfe' and 'all', makes clear the transition between 4.4.109–110/2614–15 and 112–13/2617–18, and removes the redundant and suspicious 'burthened'. One must presume that the collator missed this line entirely; but in this passage that does not seem improbable.
4.4.112/2617 wearie] Q1; wearied Q6–8, F
4.4.118/2623 nights ... daies] Q1; night ... day Q3–8, F
4.4.127/2632 Client] Q1; Clients Q4, Q7–8, F
4.4.128/2633 recorders] This edition (*conj*. Wilson); ſucceeders QF. Walker pointed out that a parallel seems wanted for 'atturnies' and 'Orators'; both images personify words as the (legal) representatives who speak for the properly mute 'calamitie'. Moreover, as Vaughan long ago objected, 'succeeders' does not itself make legal sense: 'the person who dies is never bequeathed, and the possession which is bequeathed is not what dies' (iii. 115). Even if we interpret the line to mean that, because the joys have died intestate, they leave nothing but words of complaint behind, the words would properly be the *inheritance*, not the *inheritor*. Words can merely record the fact that joys have been abruptly cut off. 'Recorders' (as a wind instrument) also lends a particular aptness to 'Aerie'. 'Succeeders' would be an easy aural-memorial error, in the context of 'intestate' and 'Aerie' (suggesting *heir*); it occurs elsewhere in *Richard III* (5.8.30/3439); and with the exception of the initial letter it would look very similar to 'recorders'—especially to an inattentive collator, glancing from Q6 to the manuscript.
4.4.128/2633 intestate] Q; inteſtine F
4.4.128/2633 ioies] QF; iarres MCKERROW (*conj*.)
4.4.141/2646 Where] Q; Where't F
4.4.175/2680 in] Q; with F. However we interpret the crux in 4.4.176/2681, the Duchess is called *out of* Richard's company, not *with*; 'Humphrey Hower' or 'Hewer' thus graced the Duchess *in* Richard's company (i.e. while he was present) but did not grace her *with* his company (i.e. did not provide her with that company). F's reading is the kind of memorial error either a scribe or compositor is capable of, under the influence of context; most earlier editors adopted Q.
4.4.176/2681 Hewer] This edition; *Hower* F; houre Q. The QF 'hour' has never been explained; 'Hewer' makes good sense both as the name of a servant and as a jingle on 'houre', and also explains the uncharacteristic spelling, capitalization, and italicization of F's text. The presumed e/o error is unusually easy in context. See Taylor, '*Humfrey Hower*', *SQ* 33 (1982), 95–7.
4.4.180/2685 pray thee] This edition; prythee F; *not in* Q. F was set by Compositor B, who has as usual imposed his preference.
4.4.188/2693 heauy] Q; greeuous F. F's adjective could be a compositorial or scribal substitution, since 'griefe' appears only two lines above. 'Heauy' seems more appropriate to 'take with' and 'tire', and has a range of other relevant meanings: violent, serious, profound, sad, oppressive.
2705 moe] Q1; more Q2–8, F
4.4.216/2721 births] Q; Birth F
*4.4.221/2726 life.] Q. F adds 14 lines: see Additional Passages.
4.4.225/2730 or] Q1–5; and Q6, F
4.4.243/2748 yᵗ] This edition; it QF. In QF there is no ambiguity in the Queen's reply to prompt Richard's question; as emended the line is not only more emphatic, but also ambiguous (since it could be an incomplete sentence). See an identical error at *Othello* 3.3.445/1892 (Q and F).
4.4.254/2759 would I] Q1; I would Q3–8, F
4.4.260/2765 sometimes] Q1; ſometime Q3–6, F
4.4.270/2775 is] Q; *not in* F
*4.4.273/2778 this.] Q. F here adds 55 lines: see Additional Passages.
4.4.286/2791 loue] Q; low F
4.4.295/2800 KING RICHARD ... past.] Q1's *arrangement*; *not in* Q2–8; *after* 4.4.296/2801, F
4.4.296/2801 QUEENE ELIZABETH] Q1 (*Qu.*); *not in* Q3–8, F
4.4.297/2802 KING RICHARD] Q (*King*); *not in* F
4.4.300/2805 holie] Q; Lordly F. As Smidt observes, Q's word better fits 'Saint' George and the preceding 'prophand' (*Impostors*, p. 92); Hammond accepts Q. F's alteration is presumably deliberate, but could easily have been misplaced for the adjective in the same penultimate position in the line below.
4.4.301/2806 Lordlie] This edition; knightlie QF. See previous note. Since Richard is king, it seems odd to emphasize the lesser 'knightlie' rank, and Q's word could easily have been substituted because of the common association of *knight* with *garter*. The progression holy–lordly–kingly makes better sense than F's lordly–knightly–kingly.
4.4.307/2812 yᵗ] Q (that); it F
4.4.308/2813 God ... Gods] Q; Heauen ... Heauens F
4.4.323/2828 in] Q1; with Q5–8, F. Q6 was copy here.
4.4.327/2832 orepast] Q; repaſt F
4.4.342/2847 by] Q2–8, F; *not in* Q1
*4.4.343/2848 good] Q; deare F. Q seems a clear improvement, since 'good-mother' meant 'mother-in-law' (*OED*; 1536+); compare 'good-mother' in *Hamlet* 3.2.105/1832 and 'good brother' in *Antony* 2.7.116/1249.
4.4.348/2853 pieuish, fond] Q; peeuiſh found F
4.4.354/2859 I burie] F, Q3; I buried Q1; Ile burie Q4–8; Ide burie This edition *conj*. As Q6 served as copy here, F's agreement with Q1 cannot be dismissed as an oversight; but a marginal in-

struction for *de* or *d* might have been misinterpreted as 'delete'. But since F is intelligible, and independently supported by Q1, it seems safer to retain it.

4.4.356/2861   recomfiture] Q; recomforture F. F's reading may represent no more than a normalized spelling. Either is a nonce usage; *comfiture* exists in a sense ('preserving, as with spices') appropriate to the preceding lines, whereas 'comforture' is a spelling of *comforter*. *OED* lists other cases of word-play on *comfit* and *comfort*.

4.4.362.1/2867.1   *Enter Ratcliffe*] Q; F *places after* 4.4.363/2868. There seems no need to add the traditional direction for Catesby here, as he could easily have come on with the '*Traine*' at 4.4.135.1/2640.1.

4.4.374–5/2879–80   CATESBY ... hither,] F; *not in* Q. This line and a half has little to recommend it, especially as it necessitates emendation in 4.4.375/2880 and produces an awkward repetition ('come hither', 'comst thither'); but Q's more economical arrangement could easily result from memorial compression.

4.4.375/2880   Ratcliffe] ROWE; *Catesby* F

4.4.379/2884   to him] F; him Q3–8; them Q1

4.4.391/2896   mile] Q; miles F. Elsewhere without authority F substitutes plurals like this for the older collective singular, which predominates in the good quartos.

4.4.395   renegade] QF (runnagate). *Runnagate* is a development of the original *renegat* based on a false etymology; the original form was then reintroduced as a continental borrowing, eventually replacing *runnagate*. *Renegatte* appears in 1598, *renegade* in 1599, *renegant* in 1549, *renegate* in 1375 (later coexisting with *runnagate*, and never fully replaced by it). The coexistence of all these forms, without distinction of meaning, strongly argues that no particular significance attaches to the *runnagate* spelling here, which would distinguish it from modern *renegade*. (In *Twelfth Night* 3.2.66/1414, however, *renegado* is clearly meant to be exotic, that form having only been introduced two years before.)

*4.4.398/2903   Elie] Q; *Morton* F. See 4.3.46/2494.

4.4.421/2926   I, I] Q; I F. F's line is tightly justified, so much so that its speech-prefix is not indented the normal amount.

4.4.428/2933.1   *Exit Stanley*] Q3–5 (*Exit. Dar.*), Q6 (*Exit.*)F; *not in* Q1

4.4.431   Courtenay] QF (Courtney)

4.4.434   Guildfords] QF (Guilfords)

4.4.438/2943   ye] F, Q6; you Q1–5. Q3 copy here.

4.4.441/2946   floud ... water] Q; Floods ... Waters F. Q agrees with Holinshed.

*4.4.445/2950   Ratcliffe ... gaue him] Q; There is my Purse, to cure that Blow of thine F. Q seems a deliberate change of stage business, and can hardly be blamed on a lack of properties here. But since Richard is apparently in armour, it would not be surprising if he had no purse at hand. The Q switch from Messenger to Ratcliffe to Messenger again also seems entirely appropriate to Richard's nervous style here.

4.4.452   Breton] QF (Brittaine)

4.4.453/2958   Dorsetshire] Q6, F; Dorſhire Q1. Q3 copy here.

4.4.458   Bretagne] QF (Brittaine)

4.4.465/2970   tidings,] Q1; newes, Q6; Newes, but F

4.5.2/2976   this] Q; the F

*4.5.5/2979   aide] Q; ayde. | So get thee gone: commend me to thy Lord F. See notes to 4.5.16–18/2990–2.

4.5.8/2982   men] QF; gentlemen This edition *conj*.

4.5.10/2984   Talbot,] QF; Talbot, and POPE

4.5.12/2986   ap] Q6, F; vp Q1. Q6 copy here; but 'ap' in the sources.

*4.5.16/2990   commend me to him] Q; I kiſſe his hand F. F also uses Q's phrase in its additional line after 4.5.5/2979 (which seems to have been conflated with this one, as a consequence of Q's transposition of 4.5.17–18/2991–2).

*4.5.17–18/2991–2   Tell ... daughter,] Q's *arrangement*; F *places after* 4.5.5/2979. Aside from the fact that Q's rearrangement, if accidental, would represent a most uncharacteristic error, it has the advantages of giving the scene's most important news a more emphatic position, of removing the double dispatch and commendations (4.5.5, 16/2979+, 2990), and of creating in Stanley's last speech a marked contrast between Elizabeth's news and '*my* mind'. F combines the bad news of withheld aid and the good news of Elizabeth's consent in the first speech, without ever relating them, and leaving the scene to tail off with a list of uninteresting names; Q gives the bad news, followed by a query, followed by the climactic good news. Capell, Malone, Steevens, and Cambridge all preferred Q.

*4.5.17/2991   Tell him] Q; Withall ſay, that F. The variant here seems related to Q's transposition.

5.2.8/3031   spoils] CAPELL; ſpoild QF. Under the influence of printed copy it would have been easy to misread a terminal 's' as terminal 't'.

5.2.11/3034   Lies] Q; Is F. F offers a less specific, commoner word, which does not develop the swine image.

5.2.11/3034   centry] F (Centry); center Q. F's spelling cannot be attributed to Compositor B, and—given the '-er' spelling of Q's suffix—is unlikely as an error. Though the primary meaning is clearly 'centre', *OED* can give no explanation for the origin of the '-ry' termination, and it seems here a deliberate portmanteau effect, relating *center* to *sentry* (*OED*, sb.¹ 1, 'a military watch-tower' i.e. a sentry-box, a place of surveillance and defence) and *sanctuary* ('sentry', sb.²). Both these latter senses could be spelled 'centry'; the first is clearly appropriate to Richard's military posture, and the second intensifies the sense of outrage, the bloody boar treating a holy place as his sty.

5.2.12/3035   Neare] Q; Ne're F

5.2.17/3040   swordes] Q; men F

5.2.24/3047   makes] Q6, F; make Q1. Q3 copy here.

5.3.0.2–3/3047.3   *Catesbie, with others*] Q; *and the Earle of Surrey* F. Q's substitution of Catesby for Surrey (who appears and speaks only here) makes excellent sense dramatically, and cannot be attributed to limitations of cast. Likewise its specification of '*others*' to attend on Richard.

5.3.1.1/3048.1   *Soldiers begin to pitch ⌈a tent⌉*] This edition; *not in* QF. Albert Weiner argues persuasively that only one tent is needed (*SQ* 13 (1962), 258–60).

5.3.2/3049   Whie, how now Catesbie] Q; My Lord of Surrey F

5.3.2/3049   sad] Q2–8, F; bad Q1

5.3.3/3050   CATESBY] Q (*Cat*,); *Sur*. F

5.3.10/3057   vtmost] Q1b, F; greateſt Q1a, Q2–8

5.3.18.1/3065.1   *at one door*] HAMMOND; *not in* QF

5.4/Sc. 24] THEOBALD; *not in* QF. The multiple staging and the issue of whether the action requires one tent or two does not essentially affect the problem of scene division here. There is clearly an imagined interval of time between the preceding '*Exeunt*' and this entrance, for Richard could not ' suruey ... the ground' if the sun had already 'made a golden set'; there is also clearly an imagined change of place. There are further unequivocal changes of the imagined locale at 5.5/Sc. 25 and 5.6/Sc. 26. The Ghosts can bridge the two locales because they are supernatural; they could also appear on the upper stage, which would make their ability to see both camps immediately intelligible, theatrically.

5.4.0.1/3065.2   *at an other door*] HAMMOND; *not in* QF

*5.4.0.2–3/3065.3   Oxford] F. Capell added Herbert, whose presence is required by F's added lines after 5.4.4/3069 (here omitted). Herbert is a dramatic nonentity who takes no further part in the action, and Q in not specifying which 'Lordes' attend on Richmond leaves open the possibility that Dorset replaced Herbert throughout. Moreover, since we must have Dorset—see next note—it seems desirable to limit the number of characters who must enter the tent at scene's end.

5.4.0.3/3065.3   Dorset] F. Q does not specify 'the Lordes' which it requires here. Hammond follows Capell in omitting Dorset, claiming that the name is 'a copyist's error for Herbert'. Since the Folio copyist had encountered 'Herbert' twice in the last hundred lines, once in the prefix 'Her.', this error seems most unlikely, even if the palaeographical confusion were easier than it is. Although Hall specifically says that Dorset was not at Bosworth, having been left behind in France as a hostage, Shakespeare tells us he is in England 'in armes' against Richard (4.4.450/2955), and he would sense the valuable dramatic function of linking Richmond to Elizabeth's family and the first half of this play. Q's apparent omission of his lines could be due to limitations of cast, and since F repeats Q for most of Act 5, Dorset might perhaps have played a larger part than we can now recover.

5.4.0.3/3065.3 &c.] Q; not in F

*5.4.4/3069 standerd,] Q. F places 5.4.21-4/3096-9 here, and adds 'My Lord of Oxford, you Sir *William Brandon*, | And your Sir *Walter Herbert* ſtay with me.' F's two additional lines could be kept; but they read awkwardly without the transposed four, and—given the general quality of Richmond's reporting—seem to have been deliberately omitted from Q.

*5.4.21-4/3086-9 Giue . . . Power,] Q; after 5.4.4/3069, F. This transposition cannot be plausibly explained as a memorial error, and is dramatically advantageous.

5.5.0.1/3091.2 A Table brought in] This edition; not in QF

5.5.0.3/3091.3 &c.] Q1; not in Q3-8, F

5.5.3/3094] Q1 is the control-text for the remainder of the play, though a handful of Folio variants are considered or adopted, as derived from the damaged final leaves of the manuscript. The following collations presume that later quartos follow earlier ones, and that F agrees with Q3, unless otherwise stated.

5.5.3/3094 giue . . . paper] QF; not in POPE

5.5.7/3098 Good] Q; My Lord of This edition conj.

5.5.8/3099 centinells] F (Centinels); centinell Q

5.5.10/3101 KING RICHARD Stur] F, Q (text); Sturr Q (c.w.)

5.5.11/3102 Catesby] Q; Ratcliffe F

5.5.11/3102 CATESBY] POPE; Rat. QF

5.5.15/3106 Exit Catesby] CAMBRIDGE; not in QF

5.5.18/3109 heauy.] F; ~, Q

5.5.19/3110 Ratcliffe] Q6, F (italic); Ratliffe Q1. There is no substantive authority for this alteration to the name hereafter; it has been made on the assumption that F's use of 'Ratcliffe' consistently elsewhere reflects a manuscript preference.

5.5.21/3112 thou] Q; not in F

5.5.25/3116 some] This edition; a boule of QF. It is the repetition of *a bowl of wine* which arouses suspicions, so that attempts to repair the metre by emending elsewhere—reading 'I'm' for 'So I am' (POPE) or omitting 'giue me' (WILSON)—have little to recommend them. Calls for 'some wine' occur at *Much Ado* 3.5.50/1634, *2 Henry IV* 5.3.25/2945, *Caesar* 2.2.126/1021, *Macbeth* 3.4.87/1111 ('Giue me some Wine'), *Othello* 2.3.62, 68, 90/1068, 1074, 1096, *Antony* 2.7.29, 3.11.72, and 4.16.4/1161, 1772, and 2530 ('Giue me some wine').

5.5.29/3120 Leaue me. Bid my guard watch,] This edition; Bid my guard watch, leaue me. QF. A reversed final foot is exceptionally improbable at this stage of Shakespeare's career. Moreover, the command 'leaue me' naturally follows the answer to his enquiry after ink and paper (all that he needs before they go) and naturally precedes the command to his watch (which Ratcliffe can only execute by leaving).

5.5.30-1/3121-2 About . . . tent | Ratcliffe and] This edition; Ratliffe, about . . . tent | And QF. In Q 5.5.30/3121 is a foot long, and 5.5.31/3122 a foot short; both defects are remedied by the transposition of a vocative from the beginning to the end of a phrase—one of the commonest types of memorial error.

5.5.31.1/3122.1 &c.] This edition; not in QF. The attendants called for at the beginning of this scene must either exit, or stand guard over Richard during the remainder of the scene (as Hammond suggests). But this latter arrangement is more likely if—as in Hammond—two tents are on stage. The attendants might leave with Norfolk, Catesby, or after 5.5.18/3109.

5.5.31.1-2/3122.1-2 Richard writes, and later sleepes] This edition; not in QF. Richard clearly must sleep, though editors neglect to specify when it happens. Unlike Richmond, he does not signal an immediate intention to sleep, and his repeated calls for ink and paper suggest that he intends to draw the 'plan of battle' which he later describes (5.6.21-30/3336-45); he does so in isolation, in contrast to Richmond. Given the formality of the sequence, Richard may not fall asleep until Richmond does.

5.5.32/3123 sit] Q2; ſet Q1

5.5.35/3126 louing] Q1; noble Q3

5.5.43/3134 mortal sharing] This edition; mortal ſtaring Q. Steevens hyphenated Q and interpreted it as 'staring or glaring fatally (upon its victims)'. But the context requires war as an *arbitrator*; the terror of its visage to all and sundry is not only irrelevant but detrimental. The idea of war's grim appearance is a commonplace (*Richard III* 1.1.9/9, *K. John* 3.1.30/979, *1 Henry IV* 4.1.115/2239, etc.), as is the fatal stare of the basilisk; so that a reporter could easily have substituted it, by a simple aural error, for the more appropriate but unusual *sharing*. Alternatively, Q's reading could result from simple compositorial substitution of the ligature ſt for the ligature ſh. *Sharing* has two common obsolete senses: 'to divide or apportion in shares between two or more recipients' (*OED*, v.² 1) and 'to shear, cleave, cut into parts' (v.¹). Thus war is not only the arbitrator who assigns *mortals* their lot or share, but also a *fatal* arbitrator, one who cuts men down (as in the images elsewhere of 'sharpe' or 'trenching' war 'like an ill sheathed knife') with 'the Sheeres of destiny' (*K. John* 4.2.91/1712).

5.5.45/3136 deceiue the time] QF. McKerrow thought this phrase probably corrupt; we do not.

5.5.53/3144 sundried] Q3; ſundried Q1

5.5.57/3148 thoughts] Q1; noiſe F; joys MUSGROVE (conj. in Walton, 1955). McKerrow notes that F might be modernized to 'noyes' (= annoyances), which makes some sense but still seems decidedly inferior to Q.

5.5.67/3157 the] Q1; thy Q3-5, F

5.5.70.1/3161.1 young] Q1; not in Q3

5.5.70.1/3161.1 Edward] This edition; *Edward, ſonne Harry the ſixt*, Q1; *Edward, ſonne to Henry the ſixt* Q2

5.5.70.1/3161.1 aboue] This edition; *to Ri.* Q1 (at end of direction); not in Q3-8, F. The ghosts could enter from one side door (near Richard) and cross to exit at the other (near Richmond); but aside from the fact that such prosaic entrances would be most atypical of supernatural figures, such an arrangement draws direct attention to the incongruities of distance. They could also enter from a trapdoor between the two figures, though this might suggest that they all (including the innocent princes and 'holy Harry') come from hell, and would create problems with exits if one ghost were going back down the trap while another was rising. Entry above would be natural for supernatural figures; would put them in a theatrically commanding position, reflecting their power as the spokesmen of God and destiny; and would allow them to address both sleepers as well as the audience, without difficulty. Q1's 'to Ri.' may be a duplicated direction of address, like others in the scene, or an indication that, in the provincial performance for which Q was presumably reconstructed, a suitable upper stage was not available.

5.5.72/3163 to morrow, | Prince . . . sixt.] This edition; to morrow. Q. Q identifies Edward on his entrance as '*young Prince Edward, ſonne Harry the ſixt*'. (See note above.) As Edward is the one ghost we have not seen in this play this identification would be much more helpful in the dialogue than in a stage direction—especially as he is also the *first* ghost. Substitution in stage directions of material that belongs in dialogue occurs in other memorial texts. Compare 5.5.85/3176 and 5.5.93/3184, where 'Let me sit heauie on thy soule to morrow' is likewise followed by an identifying phrase in apposition. *Henry* is a trisyllable at 2.3.16/1323 and elsewhere.

5.5.79/3170 deadlie] Q1; not in Q2

5.5.84/3175 Comforts] This edition; Doth comfort QF. In restoring the metrical sequence of the first half of this line it seems better to omit the superfluous auxiliary 'Doth' than the pertinent pronoun 'thy'.

5.5.84/3175 thy sleepe liue] Q; ſleepe: Liue F; sleepe, liue thou This edition conj.

5.5.85/3176 sit] Q2; ſet Q1

5.5.85/3176 on] Q5; in Q1

5.5.93/3184 RIUERS] Q3; *King* Q1

5.5.93/3184 on] Q5; in Q1

5.5.97/3188 pointles] COLLIER 2; not in QF. As several critics have observed, some epithet is needed to correspond to 'edgeles' in

5.5.117/3208, and *pointless* occurs in this sense in Hall (*OED pointless*, 1). Defences of the appropriateness of a four-foot line here are slightly absurd, given that we are entirely dependent on a text known to be severely corrupt, in a scene heavily dependent on formality and repetition.

5.5.99/3190   Wil] Q2; Wel Q1

5.5.99.2-107/3190.2-3198   *Enter ... florish*] Q1; *after* 5.5.112/3203, Q3. The transposition in Q3 of the princes' entry, to follow Hastings, raises two problems. First, the Q3 order appears to be correct; but Q3 is apparently without independent authority, and the change is of a kind unlikely to be made by a printer, for the advantages of the Q3 order are only apparent to a reader well acquainted with the whole play. If the Q3 alteration had no such advantages, we could safely dismiss it as an accident, perhaps the result of an eyeskip independently corrected; if Q3 had some claim to authority we could accept its arrangement, explaining Q1's 'mistake' as best we could. We can see no way of attributing Q1's arrangement to casting difficulties, nor does it have any obvious dramatic advantages; however, the slight deviation from chronological order is in itself well within the range of Shakespeare's practice, which characteristically disregards such pedantic niceties. The Q1 order *could* result from simple memorial error; but such an error, involving the entrances of three actors who were apparently involved in the reconstruction, is most unlikely. It thus seems to us (*a*) that there is nothing intrinsically un-Shakespearian about the Q1 order (*b*) that Q1's order cannot be convincingly explained as the result of mechanical constraints or collective memorial error, and (*c*) that Q3's arrangement, however tidy, is without discernible authority. There are at least four explanations of how the variant could have arisen in Q3: (1) a miscorrected eyeskip, (2) deliberate but unauthorized editorial sophistication, (3) the use, as copy for Q3, of a copy of Q2 used as the prompt-book for a production of the play, (4) access to an authoritative manuscript which was completely ignored throughout the rest of the text. Any of the first three options seems considerably more plausible than the fourth.

5.5.100/3191   GHOSTS] F; *Ghoft.* Q1; *Gho.* Q3-8
5.5.101/3192   lead] Q1; laid Q2
5.5.103/3194   soules bid] Q; foule bids F
5.5.104/3195   Richmond, sleepe,] F; ~, ~, Q
5.5.110/3201   Hastings then] This edition; Haftings, QF; Hastings, and POPE; Hastings. So COLLIER 2. Pope's and Collier's emendations are mere connectives, and Collier's disturbs the simplicity of the 'dispaire and die' refrain; 'then' has at least the merits of alliteration and a pointed temporal reference, in a sequence obsessed with past, present, and future.

5.5.130/3221   fals] Q; fall F
5.5.130.1/3221.1   vp] Q1; *not in* Q3
5.5.130.1/3221.1   a] Q1; his F, Q8
5.5.134/3225   now] Q1; not Q2
5.5.137/3228   am] Q2; and Q1
5.5.139/3230   reason:] F; ~, Q
5.5.140/3231   My selfe] CAPELL; What my felfe Q
5.5.141/3232   Alacke] Q; *not in* POPE. This could have been interpolated by anticipation of 'alas' in 5.5.143/3234; McKerrow omitted it.
5.5.150/3241   periurie] Q1; *not in* Q3
5.5.153/3244   to the] Q1; all to the Q3-8; all to'th' F
5.5.155/3246   will] Q1; fhall Q3
5.5.156/3247   Nay] F; And Q
5.5.158/3249   had] Q1, F; *not in* Q2-8
5.5.159/3250   Came] Q1, F; Came all Q3-8
5.5.162/3253   Zoundes, who is] Q; Who's F
5.5.163/3254   My] Q7; Ratcliffe, my Q1
5.5.166-8/3257-9   KING RICHARD ... Lord.] Q; *not in* F
5.5.166/3257   dreame,] Q. VAUGHAN transposes 5.5.158-61/3249-52 to follow 5.5.166/3257.
5.5.167/3258   all our friendes proue] WILSON; our friendes proue all QF
5.5.168/3259   Ratcliffe] POPE; O Ratcliffe QF
5.5.176/3267   see] Q1; heare Q3

5.5.176.1/3267.1   *Richard & Ratliffe*] F; *not in* Q
5.5.176.2-3/3267.2   *sitting in his Tent*] F; *not in* Q
5.5.177/3268   LORDS] Q3-8; *Lo.* Q1; *Richm.* F
5.5.180/3271   ⌈A LORD⌉ How ... Lord?] Q. This might be omitted (This edition *conj.*).
5.5.180/3271   A LORD] Q (*Lo.*); Lords. F. The opening line, 'Good morrow', can easily be spoken collectively, and it might in fact be odd for only one lord to greet Richmond in this way. But this line and 5.5.189/3280 are more naturally spoken by a single individual.
5.5.186/3277   soule] Q; Heart F
5.5.189/3280   A LORD] Q (*Lo.*); Lords. F4. See 5.5.180/3271.
5.5.191/3282   Much that I could saie] This edition; More than I haue said Q. Wilson suspects that something has been omitted before this speech; but Q's words need only mean—and must mean, if they are right—'More than I have already said before'. However, both the awkward metre (with its unparalleled stress on 'haue') and the misleading expression of this idea suggest memorial corruption; so does the dramatically awkward fact that Richmond goes on to say, at great length, 'more than [he has] said'. All these difficulties are overcome by reading 'Much that I could saie'. Confusions involving tenses, auxiliaries, and *much*, *more*, or *most* are of course common in memorial texts; specifically, Q's phrase might have been influenced by 'looke what I haue said' (1.3.114/526; spoken in a scene where the Richmond actor was almost certainly present, in some other role) and 'What shal I saie more then I haue inferd?' (5.6.44/3359, the corresponding point in Richard's oration; but there appropriate, as here not).
5.5.193/3284   to] QF; vs This edition *conj.* Although *OED* does record a few instances of *forbid* without the personal object, followed by an infinitive (*v.* 1d(*b*)), the construction occurs nowhere else in Shakespeare.
5.5.193/3284   on] POPE; vpon QF
5.5.196/3287   forces] This edition; faces QF. The common idiom 'before [one's] face' has apparently misled the reporter or compositor.
5.5.199/3290   friends] This edition; gentlemen QF. Richmond addresses his listeners as 'felowes and frends' in the sources—not as 'gentlemen', which is extrametrical, and easily picked up memorially from earlier speeches.
5.5.204/3295   foile] Q1; foile Q3
5.5.209/3300   sweate] Q1; fweare Q3
5.5.212/3303   foyzon] This edition; fat QF; foes WALKER (*conj.*). The parallelism of the preceding and following clauses makes 'fat' innately suspicious, but 'foes' does not make good sense, or explain what would be a most peculiar memorial error. But 'foison' produces the right word-play with 'foes', and a word for which 'fat' would be a natural memorial substitution (rendered easier by the common phrase 'fat of the land'). The change in the tense of the following verb, metrically required by this emendation, merely brings it into parallel with the preceding 'You sleepe'.
5.5.212/3303   paies] This edition; fhall paie QF. Though a feminine caesura is possible, tense errors are common, and would be especially likely after 'fat' had disrupted the metre. It thus seems more likely that the metre should be regular, and 'paies' parallel to 'You sleepe' (5.5.210/3301) and 'quits' (5.5.216/3307)—the more so in that the 'countries foyzon' would be supporting them not simply in the future, but now, in the course of the campaign itself.
5.5.219-20/3310-11   this ... my] This edition; my ... this QF. His body is not yet a cold corpse. Likewise, the bold attempt is not simply his but (implicitly) the whole army's, and indeed 'For me' specifically isolates how *he* will respond to the failure of their *common* venture. In 5.5.221/3312 he does speak of 'my attempt', but there he is saying that they will all profit from his personal success, while here he tells how he alone would respond to their common failure. *Thrive* thus means both 'succeed' and 'live': 'I will die if we fail, and if I live (and, therefore, succeed), what I gain you shall all share'.
5.5.221/3312   to] This edition; the QF. Abbott §417 gives parallels

for Q's redundant noun clause, but in this case the unnaturalness of expression is compounded by syntactical repetition ('the gaine of... The least of') and a redundant pronoun ('his' for 'a'). Here too our only text is known to be unreliable. The emendation clarifies not only the syntax of 5.5.221-2/3312-13 but also the contrast between 5.5.219-20/3310-11 and 5.5.221-2/3312-13: instead of graciously offering them a part of the spoils they will help to win, Richmond promises them all a part of what he personally wins.

5.5.223/3314   bold, and] STAUNTON; boldlie, and QF; boldly, POPE
5.5.224.1/3315.1-2   Exeunt... trumpets] not in QF
5.6/Sc. 26] This edition (after POPE); not in QF. The stage is cleared and the place changes. Moreover, from this point on two tents become an inconvenience, especially in the alarums and excursions which precede 5.8/Sc. 28. Richmond's tent could be dismantled during the preceding scene; or, if there were only one, it could now serve as Richard's, and be dismantled during this scene.
5.6.0.2/3315.3   Catesby] F; not in Q
5.6.5.1/3320.1   Clocke strikes] F; The clocke striketh Q
5.6.12/3327   not] Q2; nor Q1
5.6.15-16/3330-1   me,... Richmond?] F; ~ ?... ~, Q
5.6.23/3338   out all] Q1; not in Q2
5.6.25/3340   placed strongly] This edition; ſhall be placed QF. The repetition of 'shall be' (three times in four lines, and again in 5.6.30/3345) is suspicious, especially here where a subordinate clause would be more natural and less intrusive. Q moreover gives no idea of why Richard puts the archers there. Holinshed here has: 'in the fore Frount he placed the archers like a strong fortified trench or bulworke'. For strongly see OED, 1b ('So as to resist attack or displacement, firmly, solidly, securely').
5.6.27/3342   this] Q1; the Q3
5.6.27/3342   multitude] This edition; foote and horſe QF. The repetition is suspicious, the more so because Q omits the chronicles' explanation of the tactical manœuvre: to make his army look, at a distance, even more overwhelmingly superior than it was, and so dishearten Richmond's soldiers. 'Multitude' is from the chronicles' account here. QF also, wrongly, implies that one general is in charge of infantry and the other of cavalry.
5.6.28/3343   ourself] POPE; not in QF. The metrical emendation is supported by Holinshed ('After this long vantgard folowed King Richard him self...'), and clarifies the tactical issue, which is the leadership of the two parts of the army, and more specifically Richard's own position—for it was generally known that the death of Richard himself decided the battle. Other metrical emendations of the line—follow 'them' or 'then' or 'an' or 'after'—are entirely superfluous.
5.6.29/3344   both sides] This edition; either ſide QF. Holinshed has 'hauyng horsmen for wynges on both the sides of his battail'. Q would be an easy memorial error; Pope's alternative emendation ('which' for 'whose puissance') is much less plausible, especially as puissance appears nowhere else in this play, and is a relatively rare word.
5.6.31/3346   boote,] Q3; bootes, Q1
5.6.32/3347   NORFFOLKE A good] F, Q (text); A good Q (c.w.)
5.6.33/3348   paper] POPE; not in QF. Q's preceding stage direction, typically, has given the information which should be communicated by the dialogue.
5.6.34   Jockie] QF (Iocky)
5.6.34/3349   to] CAPELL (based on Hall and Holinshed); ſo QF
5.6.37/3352   each] POPE; euery QF
5.6.37/3352   vnto] Q; to F
5.6.39/3354   Conscience is but] Q1; Conſcience is Q3; For Conſcience is F
5.6.43.1/3358   His... army] Q; not in F
5.6.47   Bretons] QF (Brittains)
5.6.49/3364   ventures] CAPELL; aduentures QF. These two interchangeable words are elsewhere always used to fit the metre, and the presumed memorial substitution is easy.
5.6.50/3365   to you] Q1; you to Q2
5.6.52/3367   distraine] WARBURTON; reſtraine QF

5.6.54   Bretagne] QF (Brittaine)
5.6.54/3369   mothers] QF; brother's HAMMOND. Q's reading is based on a misprint in Holinshed; historically, Richmond's patron was the Duke of Burgundy. But this 'brother' has no existence in the play, while Richard's mother has quite clearly turned against him: Holinshed's misprint seems to have contributed to Shakespeare's conception of the play, and so we retain it.
5.6.55/3370   milkesope] Q6, F (Milke-ſop); milkeſopt Q1
5.6.65/3380   in] Q1; on Q3
5.6.67/3382   Drum afarre off] F; not in Q
5.6.68/3383   Fight] Q1; Right Q3-7, F
5.6.68/3383   bold] Q1; boldly Q2
5.6.71.1/3386.1   Enter a Messenger] F; not in Q
5.6.73/3388   My lord] QF; My gracious lord This edition conj. Vocatives are the least reliable feature of Q.
5.6.74/3389   yong] This edition; his ſonne QF. '[His] son George' has already occurred three times, each in reference to the loss of his head; so that memorial contamination is unusually probable. Of several conjectures (off with his George's, off with George's, off with son George's, off with his son's) only this one seems plausible: young George occurs twice elsewhere, and tender George once.
5.6.81/3396   helmes] Q1; helpes Q3, Q5-7, F
5.6.81/3396   Exeunt] Q1; not in Q3
5.7.1, 6/3397, 3402   calling] This edition; not in QF
5.7.2/3398   To a soldier] This edition; not in QF. Most editors either bring on Norfolk or leave the action here unexplained. There is no difficulty in presuming Norfolk's presence, for he could have come on stage during the excursions; the difficulty is his exit, which all editors but Hammond leave unmentioned. It is inept that Norfolk does not reply at all, and once Richard enters, neither he nor Catesby pays the all-important Norfolk any attention. Norfolk could exit to Richard's rescue just before Richard enters from another door (Hammond's solution), but this seems comic. Norfolk could leave silently, his desertion unremarked by Catesby; but aside from its dramatic ineptness, this departs from Shakespeare's sources, where Norfolk remains conspicuously loyal, dying in Richard's cause. In some productions Norfolk dies in this scene; but if he were already dying Catesby could hardly expect much help from him, and if he were fighting during the scene, and mortally wounded at the end, there would hardly be leisure for Catesby's narrative. Moreover, since F does add 'Alarums.' after Catesby's speech, if Norfolk did exit or die at that point, we might expect F to record the fact. Given these difficulties about what to do with Norfolk once he is on, and the fact that neither text calls for his presence at all, it seems most probable that Norfolk is to be imagined somewhere off stage: Catesby is searching for him. But 5.7.2-5/3398-401 can hardly be shouted across a battlefield; unless Catesby speaks them directly to the audience, he must have an on-stage listener. For this purpose any of Richard's followers will do, and some could still be on stage, from the preceding excursions.
5.7.3/3399   an] Q1-7, F; and Q8
5.7.6.1/3402.1   Alarums.] F; not in Q
5.7.13/3409   Exeunt] THEOBALD; not in QF
5.8.0.3/3409.2-3   Exit Richmond.] HAMMOND; not in QF. Richmond can hardly enter in the next stage direction unless he exits here. Because Shakespeare makes Richard's death the result of a single combat with Richmond, the whole army is not present, and hence has—at the most prosaic level—to be told that Richard is dead. Moreover, Shakespeare does not dramatize Richmond's victory as a fluke resulting from Richard's death in combat, but as a divinely ordained victory against superior odds; therefore he does not imply that the fighting immediately stops with Richard's death. Richmond's exit here solves the problem, first pointed out by Dyce, of Stanley's entry with the crown; for either Richmond could drag off the body, or Stanley could pick it up as he enters and moves towards Richmond.
5.8.0.3-4/3409.3   Retrait and Flourish] F (Retreat,); then retrait being ſounded Q
5.8.0.5/3409.4   diuers] F; not in Q

5.8.0.5-6/3409.5 &c.] Q1; not in Q3
5.8.3/3412 bearing the crowne] This edition. QF include this phrase in the entrance direction above, implying that Stanley enters with the crown; this position leaves the staging ambiguous.
5.8.4/3413 this ... roialtie] Q1; this ... roialties Q2-8; thefe ... Royalties F
5.8.7/3416 enioy it,] Q1; not in Q3
5.8.7.1/3416.1 He sets the crowne on Henries head] CAPELL (subs.); not in Q
5.8.8-9/3417-18 KING ... But] F, Q (text); But Q (c.w.)
5.8.9/3418 yong George Stanley, is he] This edition; is yong George Stanley Q. The metre clearly calls for emendation, but all of the many conjectures add something extraneous or intrusive: first, is (POPE) now, is (DYCE 2) pray, is (KEIGHTLEY) is your son George (CAPELL) is thy young George (WILSON) is the young George (MARSHALL). The solution adopted here has at least the merit of a more dramatic rhythm and syntax, and the negative advantage of not adding unwarranted modifiers to an urgent question.
5.8.11/3420 if it please you] Q; if you pleafe F
5.8.11/3420 now] Q; not in F
5.8.13/3422 STANLEY] F (Der.); not in Q
5.8.13-14/3422-3 Robert Brakenbury,| Water Lord Ferrers] This edition; Water Lord Ferris, fir | Robert Brookenbury Q. Memorial transpositions are easiest in lists of this kind, and Shakespeare normally versifies such casualty lists. Brakenbury is not called sir at this point in the chronicles.
5.8.14 Walter] Q1 (Water), Q6-8, F
5.8.14/3422 Ferrers] CAPELL (based on Holinshed); Ferris QF
5.8.15/3424 becomes] ROWE; become QF
5.8.27/3436 that] JOHNSON; this Q
5.8.28/3437 Vnited] This edition; Deuided Q. No one has explained what Q's line could mean, and the point is surely that the dire division is the only thing they have had in common. The proposed memorial error (substitution of an antonym) would be especially easy after 'deuided' in 5.8.27/3436.

5.8.28/3437 deuision,] JOHNSON; ~. QF
5.8.32/3441 their] Q1; thy Q3-7, F
5.8.32/3441 his] WILSON (Maxwell); thy QF
5.8.36/3445 bloudy] Q. This epithet is suspicious, given 'streames of bloud' in 5.8.37/3446; but no alternative is compelling.
5.8.37/3446 forth] This edition; in Q. The image in Q, of England standing in a stream weeping, seems uncharacteristically grotesque here. Shakespeare often associates blood, wounds, and weeping—'purple tears that his wound wept' (Venus 1054), 'my heart wept blood' (Winter's Tale 5.2.88/2775-6), 'will you have them weep our horses' blood' (Henry V 4.2.12/2098)—and weep forth occurs at Winter's Tale 4.4.548-9/2155-6. The image of England weeping and bleeding seems more compact and characteristic; it also provides a better parallel for 5.8.36/3445 (the traitor pulling something back, England gushing something forth: see 2.2.68/1251, 'All springs reduce their currents to mine eies').
5.8.41.1/3450.1 Flourish.] This edition; not in QF. Q does not provide a final exit at all, so its omission of what seems a necessary final flourish is not surprising. F's 'Exeunt' is probably compositorial, and in any case is cramped on to the final line of text, with no room for a music cue.

Additional Passages

A.2 No, when] F; not͵ when POPE. A plausible emendation: see Furness.
D.4 pay] POPE; repay F
G.2 Penker] CAPELL; Peuker F
I.7 Sorrowe] ROWE; Sorrowes F
K.11 Mine] F; More VAUGHAN
K.36 Lone] THEOBALD; Loue F. An exceptionally easy misreading.
K.37 Of ten times] THEOBALD; Often-times F

REJECTED QUARTO VARIANTS

1.1.13/13 lute] (Lute); loue
1.1.42/42 day] dayes
1.1.50/50 should be] fhalbe
1.1.61/61 Hath] Haue
1.1.71/71 secure] is fecurde
1.1.83/83 our] this
1.1.84/84 BRAKENBURY] F (Bra.) throughout; Bro⟨kenbury⟩. Q throughout
1.1.88/88 Brakenbury] (italic); Brokenbury Q (throughout)
1.1.101/101 to] he
1.1.106/106 CLARENCE We] We Q1 (c.w.)
1.1.133/133 Eagles] Eagle
1.1.139/139 that] this
1.1.143/143 Where] What
1.2.1/163 load] lo Q1; Lord Q3-6
1.2.11/173 hand] hands
1.2.11/173 wounds] holes
1.2.12/174 these] thofe
1.2.14/176 O cursed] Curft
1.2.14/176 holes] fatall holes
1.2.16/178 Cursed] Curft be
1.2.19/181 Wolues, to] adders
1.2.24-5/186-7 view,| And ... vnhappineffe.] view.
1.2.27-8/189-90 More ... Then] As ... As
1.2.28/190 young] poore
1.2.31/193 this] the
1.2.36/198 Villaines] Villaine
1.2.76/238 Crimes] euils
1.2.79/241 Of] For
1.2.86/248 shalt] fhouldft
1.2.88/250 That] Which

1.2.89/251 Then say] Why then
1.2.89/251 were not slaine] are not dead
1.2.94/256 murd'rous] bloudy Q1; bloodly Q3-6
1.2.98/260 That] Which
1.2.100/262 That] Which
1.2.100/262 dream'st] dreamt
1.2.105/267 better] fitter
1.2.116/278 something] fomewhat
1.2.120/282 was't] art
1.2.122/284 that] which
1.2.124/286 liue] reft
1.2.127/289 not] neuer
1.2.128/290 it] them
1.2.137/299 kill'd] flew
1.2.141/303 He] Go to, he
1.2.141/303 thee] you
1.2.148/310 mine] my
1.2.154/316 aspects] (Afpects); afpect
1.2.156/318 smoothing] foothing
1.2.156/318 word] words
1.2.159/321 lip ... it was] lips ... they were
1.2.163/325 brest] bofome
1.2.167/329 for I did kill King Henrie] (For); twas I that kild your husband
1.2.169/331 stabb'd yong Edward,] kild King Henry:
1.2.172/334 thy] the
1.2.175/337 That] Tufh that
1.2.177/339 This] That
1.2.186/348 shalt thou] fhall you
1.2.191/353 my] this
1.2.194/356 Seruant] fuppliant

RICHARD III

1.2.198/360	may] would
1.2.198/360	you] thee
1.2.199/361	most] more
1.2.200/362	House] place
1.2.223/385	no Friends] nothing
1.2.233/395	abase] debaſe
1.2.237/399	halts] halt
1.2.237/399	mishapen] vnſhapen
1.2.243/405	a] ſome
1.3.5/417	eyes] words
1.3.6/418	on] of
1.3.8/420	harmes] harme
1.3.21/433	praier] (prayer); praiers
1.3.27/439	on] in
1.3.32/444	Are come] Came
1.3.36/448	I Madame] (Madam); Madame we did
1.3.37-8/449-50	Betweene . . . betweene] Betwixt . . . betwixt
1.3.41/453	height] higheſt
1.3.47/459	looke] ſpeake
1.3.53/465	With] By
1.3.63/475	on] of
1.3.66/478	That] Which
1.3.66/478	action] actions
1.3.67/479	Children] kindred
1.3.67/479	brothers] (Brothers); brother
1.3.77/489	I] we
1.3.80/492	while] whilſt
1.3.80/492	great] many faire
1.3.90/502	meane] cauſe
1.3.92/504	Lord, for—] Lord.
1.3.97/509	desert] deſerts
1.3.101/513	and] not in Q
1.3.106/518	Of] With
1.3.106/518	that oft I] I often
1.3.109/521	so baited] thus taunted
1.3.109/521	stormed] baited
1.3.111/523	him] thee
1.3.115/527	auouch't] auouch
1.3.116/528	I dare . . . Towre.] not in Q
1.3.119/531	killd'st] ſleweſt
1.3.121/533	I] yea
1.3.125/537	spent] ſpilt
1.3.126/538	I] Yea
1.3.131/543	you] yours
1.3.132/544	this] now
1.3.136/548	I] Yea
1.3.143/555	this] the
1.3.147/559	Soueraigne] lawfull
1.3.150/562	thereof] of it
1.3.161/573	am] being
1.3.163/575	Ah] O
1.3.169/581	This] The
1.3.173/585	scornes] ſcorne
1.3.191/603	Should] Could
1.3.194/606	Though] If
1.3.196-7/608-9	that . . . that] which . . . which
1.3.201/613	death] loſſe
1.3.210/622	his] your
1.3.223/635	while] whileſt
1.3.228/640	heauy mothers] (heauie Mothers); mothers heauy
1.3.230/642	detested—] deteſted, &c.
1.3.233/645	I . . . mercy then] (mercie); Then I . . . mercy
1.3.233/645	did thinke] had thought
1.3.243/655	day] time
1.3.244/656	this] that
1.3.260/672	touches] toucheth
1.3.261/673	I] Yea
1.3.271/683	Peace, peace] Haue done
1.3.274/686	my hopes by you] my hopes (by you) F; by you my hopes Q
1.3.276/688	that] my
1.3.277/689	done, haue done] done
1.3.278/690	Ile] I will
1.3.280/692	Noble] Princely
1.3.285/697	I will not thinke] Ile not beleeue
1.3.287/699	take heede] beware
1.3.289/701	to the] thee to
1.3.300/712	to] of
1.3.301/713	yours] your Q1; you Q3-8
1.3.305/715	muse why] wonder
1.3.306/718	to her] not in Q
1.3.308/720	Yet] But
1.3.308/720	her] this
1.3.313/725	thereof] of it
1.3.320/732	I . . . mee] we . . . vs
1.3.321/733	We wait vpon] Madame we will attend
1.3.322/734	begin] began
1.3.325/737	cast] laid
1.3.327/739	Darby, Hastings] (Derby, Haſtings); Haſtings, Darby
1.3.328/740	tell them 'tis] ſay it is
1.3.330/742	it] me
1.3.331/743	Dorset] (italic); Vaughan
1.3.335/747	odde old] old odde
1.3.335/747	forth] out
1.3.339/751	thing] deede
1.3.342/754	Well] It was well
1.3.348/760	Tut, tut,] Tuſh feare not,
1.3.350/762	go] come
1.3.351/763	fall] drop
1.3.352-3/764-5	straight . . . Lord] not in Q
1.4.3/768	fearefull dreames, of vgly sights] (Dreames); vgly ſights, of gaſtly dreames
1.4.8/773	my Lord, I pray you tel me] I long to heare you tell it
1.4.9/774	that . . . Tower] not in Q
1.4.10/775	And] I
1.4.10/775	to crosse to] for
1.4.14/779	heauy] fearefull
1.4.18/783	falling] ſtumbling
1.4.21/786	O] Lord,
1.4.23/788	sights of vgly death] vgly ſights of death
1.4.24/789	Me thoughts] Me thought
1.4.28/793	All . . . Sea,] not in Q
1.4.35/800	these] the
1.4.36-7/801-2	and . . . Ghost:] not in Q
1.4.37/802	but] for
1.4.38/803	Stop'd] Kept
1.4.41/806	Who] Which
1.4.42/807	in] with
1.4.43/808	No,] O
1.4.45/810	I] Who
1.4.46/811	sowre] grim
1.4.53/818	with] in
1.4.54/819	shriek'd] ſquakt Q1; ſqueakt Q2-8
1.4.57/822	vnto torment] (Torment); to your torments
1.4.59/824	me] me about
1.4.63/828	my] the
1.4.64/829	marueile] (maruell); marueile my
1.4.65/830	I] I promiſe you, I
1.4.65/830	(me thinkes)] not in Q
1.4.66/831	Ah] O
1.4.66/831	these] thoſe
1.4.67/832	That] Which
1.4.67/832	giue] beare
1.4.69/834	sit] ſtay
1.4.69/834	a-while] not in Q
1.4.76/841	imaginations] (Imaginations); imagination
1.4.78/843	betweene] betwixt
1.4.78/843	name] (Name); names
1.4.80-1/845-6	1. MURTHERER Ho, who's heere? | BRAKENBURY] not in Q
1.4.81/846	What would'st thou Fellow] In Gods name what are you

1.4.81/846	cam'st thou] (camm'ft); came you	1.4.198/961	sacrament] (Sacrament); holy facrament
1.4.84/849	What] Yea, are you	1.4.203/966	was't] wert
1.4.85/850	1 MURTHERER 'Tis better (Sir) then to be tedious] (1. 'Tis); 2 *Exe.* O fir, it is better to be briefe then tedious	1.4.205/968	such] fo
		1.4.208/971	He] Why firs, he
1.4.86/851	Let him see] Shew him	1.4.209/972	that] this
1.4.86/851	and] *not in* Q	1.4.210/973	auenged] reuenged
1.4.92/857	There . . . keies] (afleepe . . . Keyes); Here are the keies, there fits the Duke a fleepe	1.4.210/973	the] this
		1.4.211/974	O . . . publiquely,] *not in* Q
1.4.93/858	the King, and fignifie to him] his Maiefty, and certifie his Grace	1.4.213/976	or] nor
		1.4.219/982	our Duty] the diuell
1.4.94/859	to you my charge] my charge to you	1.4.219/982	faults] (Faults); fault
1.4.95/860	You may sir, 'tis] Doe fo, it is	1.4.220/983	Prouoke] Haue brought
1.4.96/860-1	Far you well.] *not in* Q	1.4.220/983	slaughter] murder
1.4.98/863	hee'l] then he will	1.4.221/984	If you do] Oh if you
1.4.100/865	Why] When he wakes, | Why foole	1.4.223/986	are] be
1.4.100/865	vntill] till	1.4.225/988	shall] will
1.4.101/865	great] *not in* Q	1.4.229/992	1 MURTHERER] (1); *Am.*
1.4.102/867	hee'l] he will	1.4.235/998	1 MURTHERER] (1); *Am.*
1.4.107/871	warrant] F (Warrant); warrant for it	1.4.237/1000	come] (Come,); *not in* Q
1.4.108/872	the] *not in* Q	1.4.237/1000	you deceiue your] thou deceiu'ft thy
1.4.109/873	me] vs	1.4.238/1001	to destroy you heere] hither now to flaughter thee
1.4.110-11/874-5	1 MURDERER I . . . liue.] *not in* Q	1.4.239-40/1002-3	he bewept my Fortune, | And] when I parted with him, | He
1.4.112/876	Ile] *not in* Q		
1.4.112/876	and] *not in* Q	1.4.242/1005	I] 2
1.4.114/878	Nay,] *not in* Q	1.4.242/1005	when] now
1.4.114/878	little] while	1.4.242/1005	you] thee
1.4.115/878-9	this passionate humor of mine] my holy humor	1.4.243/1006	earths] worlds
1.4.115/879	it was] twas	1.4.244/1007	2] I
1.4.116/880	tels] would tel	1.4.245/1008	Haue you . . . your soules] Haft thou . . . thy foule
1.4.118/882	Some] Faith fome	1.4.247/1010	are you . . . your . . . soules] art thou . . . thy . . . foule
1.4.120/884	deede's] F (deed's); deede is		
1.4.124/887	Where's] Where is	1.4.248/1011	you will] thou wilt
1.4.125/888	O, in] In	1.4.249/1012	O] Ah
1.4.126/889	When] So when	1.4.249/1012	they] he
1.4.128/891	'Tis no matter, let] Let	1.4.250/1013	the] this
1.4.130/893	What] How	1.4.252/1015	Relent? no] Relent
1.4.131/894	with it] with it, it is a dangerous thing	1.4.255/1018	thine] thy
1.4.132-3/895-6	A man . . . A man] he . . . He	1.4.263/1026	2 MURTHERER . . . Lord.] *not in* Q
1.4.134/897	'Tis] It is	1.4.264/1027	Take that, and that] I thus, and thus
1.4.136/899	a man] one	1.4.264/1027	all] *not in* Q
1.4.137/900	(by chance)] *not in* Q	1.4.265/1028	drowne] chop
1.4.138/902	Townes] all | Townes	1.4.265/1028	you] thee
1.4.141/904	liue] F, Q2; to liue	1.4.265/1028	within] in the next roome
1.4.142/905	'tis] ('Tis); it is	1.4.266/1029	dispatcht] performd
1.4.145/908	but] *not in* Q	1.4.267/1030	hands] hand
1.4.147/910	I] Tut, I	1.4.269/1032	How now?] *not in* Q
1.4.147/910	fram'd] in fraud	1.4.269/1032	what mean'st thou that thou help'st me not?] Why doeft thou not helpe me,
1.4.148/911	me] me, | I warrant thee		
1.4.149/912	man] fellow	1.4.270/1033	you haue beene] thou art
1.4.149/912	thy] his	1.4.275/1038	Well, Ile go hide the] Now muft I hide his
1.4.150/913	fall to worke] to this geere	1.4.276/1039	Till that] Vntill
1.4.152/915	then] then we wil	1.4.276/1039	giue] take
1.4.152/915	throw . . . into] chop . . . in	1.4.277/1040	will] muft
1.4.154/917	and] *not in* Q	1.4.278/1041	then] here
1.4.156/919	Soft he wakes.] Harke he ftirs,	2.1.1/1042	Why so] So
1.4.157/920	Strike] fhall I ftrike	2.1.1/1042	haue I] I haue
1.4.158/921	wee'l] firft lets	2.1.5/1046	more] now
1.4.167/930	Your . . . pale?] *not in* Q	2.1.6/1047	made] fet
1.4.168/931	Who sent you hither? Wherefore do you come] Tell me who are you, wherefore come you hither	2.1.9/1050	soule] heart
		2.1.18/1059	is] are
1.4.169/932	2 MURTHERER] Am⟨bo⟩.	2.1.18/1059	from] in
1.4.169/932	I, I] I	2.1.23/1064	There] Here
1.4.176/939	drawne] cald	2.1.25/1066	KING . . . Marquesse.] (Dorfet . . . Haftings); *not in* Q
1.4.176/939	among] from out	2.1.27/1068	inuiolable] vnuiolable
1.4.178/941	is . . . doth] are . . . doe	2.1.28/1069	I] I my Lord
1.4.189/952	our] the	2.1.33/1074	Vpon your Grace] On you or yours
1.4.190/953	Vassailes] (Vaffals); Vaffaile	2.1.39/1080	heauen] God
1.4.191/954	table] (Table); tables	2.1.40/1081	loue] zeale
1.4.192/955	will you] F (Will); and wilt thou	2.1.44/1085	blessed] perfect
1.4.194/957	hand] hands	2.1.46/1087	Sir Richard Ratcliffe, and the Duke] (*Richard Ratcliffe*); the noble Duke
1.4.196/959	hurle] throw		

2.1.53/1094 Lord] liege
2.1.54/1095 Among] Amongſt
2.1.76/1117 Lord] liege
2.1.76/1117 Highneſſe] Maieſty
2.1.79/1120 so flowted] thus ſcorned
2.1.80/1121 gentle] noble
2.1.85/1126 the] this
2.1.88/1129 man] ſoule
2.1.98/1139 heare me] grant
2.1.99/1140 say] ſpeake
2.1.99/1140 requests] demaundſt
2.1.104/1145 that tongue] the ſame
2.1.106/1147 bitter] cruell
2.1.107/1148 wrath] rage
2.1.108/1149 bid] bad
2.1.109/1150 Who spoke] Who ſpake
2.1.109/1150 spoke of] of
2.1.112/1153 at] by
2.1.117/1158 his] his owne
2.1.117/1158 did giue] gaue
2.1.131/1172 begge] pleade
2.1.135/1176 Ah] oh
2.1.140/1181 Come Lords will you go] But come lets in
2.1.142/1183 BUCKINGHAM . . . Grace.] not in Q
2.2.1/1184 Good Granam tell vs] (Grandam) ; Tell me good Granam
2.2.3/1186 DAUGHTER] Boy.
2.2.3/1186 weepe so oft] wring your hands
2.2.5/1188 BOY] Gerl.
2.2.6/1189 Orphanes, wretches] (Orphans, Wretches); wretches, Orphanes
2.2.7/1190 were] be
2.2.8/1191 both] much
2.2.11/1194 sorrow] labour
2.2.11/1194 waile] weepe for
2.2.12/1195 you conclude my Granam] you conclude, (my Grandam) F ; Granam you conclude that Q
2.2.13/1196 mine] my
2.2.15/1198 earnest] daily
2.2.16/1199 DAUGHTER And so will I.] not in Q
2.2.21/1204 to it] not in Q
2.2.23/1206 my Vnckle] he
2.2.24/1207 And pittied me] And hugd me in his arme
2.2.25/1208 Bad] And bad
2.2.27/1210 Ah] Oh
2.2.28/1211 deepe vice] foule guile
2.2.29/1212 I] Yea
2.2.34/1217 Ah] Oh Q1 ; Wh Q3
2.2.40/1223 thy] your
2.2.41/1224 when] now
2.2.41/1224 gone] witherd
2.2.42/1225 that want their sap] the ſap being gone
2.2.46/1229 nere-changing night] perpetuall reſt
2.2.50/1233 with] by
2.2.54/1237 That] Which
2.2.56/1239 left] left thee
2.2.57/1240 Husband] children
2.2.58/1241 hands] limmes
2.2.59/1242 Clarence and Edward] (Clarence, and Edward) ; Edward and Clarence
2.2.60/1243 Thine,] Then,
2.2.60/1243 moane] griefe Q1 ; ſelfe Q6
2.2.60/1243 a] not in Q
2.2.61/1244 woes] plaints
2.2.62/1245 Ah] Good
2.2.63/1246 kindred] (Kindred) ; kindreds
2.2.64/1247 DAUGHTER] Gerl.
2.2.65/1248 widdow-dolour] widdowes dolours
2.2.67/1250 complaints] laments
2.2.69/1252 moone] (Moone) ; moane
2.2.71/1254 Ah] Oh
2.2.71/1254 deere] eire Q1 ; heire Q3-8

2.2.72, 75, 78/1255, 1258, 1261 CHILDREN] Ambo.
2.2.72/1255 Ah] Oh
2.2.78/1261 Were] Was
2.2.78-9/1261-2 so deere a . . . so deere a] a dearer . . a dearer
2.2.80/1263 Greefes] mores
2.2.81/1264 is] are
2.2.82/1265 an] not in Q
2.2.89/1272 Sister] Madame
2.2.91/1274 helpe our] cure their
2.2.95/1278 breast] minde
2.2.98/1281 That is] Thats
2.2.99/1282 that] why
2.2.101/1284 heauie mutuall] mutuall heauy
2.2.109/1292 fet] fetcht
2.2.113/1296 Sister] mother
2.2.117/1300 at home] behinde
2.2.120/1303 Prince] King
2.2.123/1306 as] like
2.3.1/1308 Good morrow Neighbour] Neighbour well met
2.3.3/1310 Yes] I
2.3.4/1311 Ill] Bad
2.3.5/1312 giddy] troublous Q1 ; troubleſome Q2-6
2.3.6/1313 Neighbours, God speed] Good morrow neighbours
2.3.6-7/1313-14 I CITTIZEN . . . sir. | 3 CITTIZEN] not in Q
2.3.7/1314 the] this
2.3.8/1315 I sir, it is too true, God helpe the while] It doth
2.3.16/1323 Henry] (italic) ; Harry
2.3.17/1324 in] at
2.3.18/1325 no, no, good friends, God wot] (No, no . . .) ; no good my friend not ſo
2.3.22/1329 Why so] So
2.3.22/1329 his] the
2.3.23-4/1330-1 his . . . his] the . . . the
2.3.25/1332 emulation, who shall now] emulation now, who ſhall
2.3.28/1335 Sons, and Brothers, haut] (haught) ; kindred hauty
2.3.31/1338 will be] ſhalbe
2.3.32/1339 are seen] appeare
2.3.33/1340 then] the
2.3.38/1345 hearts] ſoules
2.3.38/1345 feare] bread Q1 ; dread Q3-8
2.3.39/1346 You] Yee
2.3.39/1346 reason (almost)] almoſt reaſon
2.3.40/1347 dread] feare
2.3.41/1348 dayes] times
2.3.43/1350 danger] dangers
2.3.44/1351 water] (Water) ; waters
2.3.46/1353 Marry we were] We are
2.3.46/1353 Iustices] Iuſtice
2.4.2/1356 they do rest] will they be
2.4.7/1361 Ha's] Hath
2.4.13/1367 do] not in Q
2.4.20/1374 his rule were true] this were a true rule
2.4.21/1375 so] Madame, ſo
2.4.21/1375 is, my gracious Madam] is
2.4.22/1376 he is] ſo too
2.4.25/1379 To touch his growth, neerer then he toucht mine] That ſhould haue neerer toucht his growth then he did mine
2.4.26/1380 yong] prety
2.4.31/1385 this] ſo
2.4.33/1387 wast] wert
2.4.35/1389 parlous] perilous
2.4.39/1393 report] vnfolde
2.4.39/1393 doth] fares
2.4.46/1400 the] theſe
2.4.47/1401 Lord] Lady
2.4.48/1402 ruine] downfall
2.4.51/1405 awlesse] (aweleſſe) ; lawleſſe
2.4.52/1406 Blood] death
2.4.61/1415 Brother to Brother] not in Q
2.4.62/1416 to] againſt
2.4.66/1420 Madam, farwell.] not in Q

2.4.66/1420	Stay, I will go] Ile go along	3.2.112/1735	The] Thofe
2.4.72/1426	Go] Come	3.2.113/1736	toward] to
3.1.169/1595	farre] a farre	3.2.113/1736	tower] (Tower); tower my Lord
3.1.170/1596	doth stand] ftands	3.2.114/1737	my Lord,] not in Q
3.1.170/1596	to] Vnto	3.2.114/1737	can] fhall
3.1.171/1597	If thou do'st finde him tractable to vs] if he be willing	3.2.114/1737	there] not in Q
3.1.172/1598	tell] fhew	3.2.116/1739	Nay] Tis
3.1.181/1607	Lord] friend	3.2.118/1741	will you] fhall we
3.1.183/1609	goe] not in Q	3.2.118/1741	go] (goe); go along
3.1.184/1610	can] may	3.2.118/1741	HASTINGS . . . Lordship.] not in Q
3.1.187/1613	House] place	3.3.1/1742	RYVERS] (Riuers.); Ratl. Come bring foorth the prifoners. | Ryu.
3.1.189/1615	Lo:] (Lord); William Lo:		
3.1.190/1616	head, something] (Head: | Something); Head man, fomewhat	3.3.1/1742	Ratcliffe] (italic); Ratliffe
		3.3.4/1745	blesse] keepe
3.1.190/1616	determine] doe	3.3.6/1747	VAUGHAN . . . heereafter.] (Vaugh.); not in Q
3.1.192/1618	all] not in Q	3.3.12/1753	seate] (Seat); foule
3.1.193/1619	was] ftood	3.3.13/1754	to thee] thee vp
3.1.194/1620	hand] hands	3.3.13/1754	bloud] (blood); blouds
3.1.195/1621	kindnes] (kindneffe); willingnes	3.3.13/1754	bloud] (blood); blouds
3.2.1/1624	My Lord,] What ho	3.3.18/1759	praier] (prayer); praieis
3.2.1/1624	knockes] knockes at the dore	3.3.19/1760	sonnes] (Sonnes); fonne
3.2.1/1624	One] A meffenger	3.3.22/1763	Make . . . expiate] Come come difpatch, the limit of your linea is out
3.2.2/1625	What is't] Whats		
3.2.3/1626	my Lord Stanley] (Stanley); thy Mafter	3.3.23/1764	here] all
3.2.4/1627	appeares] fhould feeme	3.3.23/1764	imbrace.] (embrace); ~‸
3.2.5/1628	selfe] Lordfhip	3.3.24/1765	Farewell] And take our leaue
3.2.6/1629	What] And	3.3.24/1765	againe] not in Q
3.2.7/1630	Then certifies your Lordship, that this Night,] And then he fends you word.	3.4.1/1766	Now Noble Peeres] My Lords at once
		3.4.3/1768	speake] fay
3.2.8/1631	the] to night the	3.4.3/1768	the] this
3.2.8/1631	rased off] rafte	3.4.4/1769	Is] Are
3.2.9/1632	kept] held	3.4.4/1769	ready] fitting
3.2.13/1636	you will presently] prefently you will	3.4.6/1771	iudge] gueffe
3.2.14/1637	with him toward] into	3.4.6/1771	day] time
3.2.19/1642	good friend] feruant	3.4.9/1774	Your Grace] Why you my Lo:
3.2.22/1645	without] wanting	3.4.10/1775	We] Who I my Lo? we
3.2.23/1646	simple] fond	3.4.10/1775	for] but for
3.2.25/1648	pursues] purfues vs Q1; purfue vs Q3-8	3.4.12/1777	Or] nor
3.2.31/1654	Ile goe, my Lord, and] My gratious Lo: Ile;	3.4.12/1777	I] I no more
3.2.36/1659	will] it will Q1; twill Q3-8	3.4.12/1777	my Lord,] not in Q
3.2.41/1664	Before Ile] Ere I will	3.4.17/1782	gracious] Graces
3.2.43/1666	I, on] Vpon	3.4.18/1783	Honorable] noble
3.2.43/1666	life,] life my Lo:	3.4.21/1786	In happie] Now in good
3.2.49/1672	my aduersaries] mine enemies	3.4.23/1788	trust] hope
3.2.55/1678	which] who	3.4.24/1789	designe] defignes
3.2.57/1680	Well Catesby, ere] I tell thee Catesby. Cat. What my Lord? | Haft. Ere	3.4.27/1792	had] had now
		3.4.31/1796	My] Haft. I thanke your Grace. | Glo. My
3.2.57/1680	older] elder	3.4.31/1796	Elie, when] (Ely); Elie, Bifh. My Lo: | Glo. When
3.2.63/1686	that] who	3.4.34/1799	Mary and will, my Lord, with all my heart] I go my Lord
3.2.69/1692	Come on, come on,] What my Lo:		
3.2.75/1698	dayes] life	3.4.35/1800	of] not in Q
3.2.76/1699	so . . . as] more . . . then	3.4.38/1803	That] As
3.2.80/1703	were] was	3.4.39/1804	Child] fonne
3.2.83/1706	stab] fcab	3.4.41/1806	your selfe a while,] you hence my Lo:
3.2.85/1708	What,] But come my Lo:	3.4.43/1808	my judgement] mine opinion
3.2.85/1708	toward] to	3.4.46/1811	the Duke of Gloster] (protector)
3.2.86/1709	Come, come, haue with you: Wot you what, my Lord] I go: but ftay, heare you not the newes	3.4.48/1813	this morning] to day
		3.4.50/1815	that he bids] he doth bid
3.2.87/1710	To day] This day	3.4.50/1815	such] fuch a
3.2.87/1710	the Lords] thofe men	3.4.52/1817	Can] That can
3.2.91/1714	on] you	3.4.57/1822	were he] if he were
3.2.93/1716	your Lordship please] it pleafe your Lo: Q1; it pleafe your good Lordfhip Q3-8	3.4.57/1822	had] would haue
		3.4.59/1824	tell me what] what doe
3.2.94/1717	man] fellow	3.4.64/1829	Princely] hold
3.2.102/1725	there, drinke that for me] hold fpend thou that	3.4.67/1832	their euill] this ill
3.2.104-5/1727-8	PRIEST . . . heart] (Iohn); Haft. What Sir John, you are wel met	3.4.70/1835	And this is] This is that
		3.4.73/1838	deed] thing
3.2.106/1729	in your debt] beholding to you	3.4.73/1838	Noble] gratious
3.2.106/1729	last] laft daies	3.4.75/1840	Talkst thou to] (Talk'ft); Telft thou Q1
3.2.108/1731	What . . . priest, Lo: Chamberlaine] (Prieft, Lord); How now Lo: Chamberlaine, what . . . prieft	3.4.76/1841	I sweare] not in Q
		3.4.77/1842	dine] dine to day I fweare,

3.4.79/1844	rise] come		3.6.11/1987	cannot see] fees not
3.4.82/1847	our helmes] (helmes); his helme		3.6.12/1988	whoe] (who); whoes
3.4.83/1848	did scorne it, and disdaine] difdaind it, and did fcorne		3.6.12/1988	bold] blinde
3.4.85/1850	started] ftartled		3.6.14/1990	ill] bad
3.4.87/1852	need] want		3.7.1/1991	how now] my Lord
3.4.89/1854	too] twere		3.7.3/1993	say] and fpeake
3.4.89/1854	triumphing, how] ~∧ at		3.7.5-6/1995-6	his ... France,] (Lucy); not in Q
3.4.89/1854	enemies∧] (Enemies); ~ :		3.7.7/1997	desire] defires
3.4.90/1855	To day] How they		3.7.8/1998	And ... Wiues,] not in Q
3.4.94/1859	Come, come, dispatch,] Difpatch my Lo:		3.7.11/2001	And ... Duke.] not in Q
3.4.96/1861	grace] ftate		3.7.18/2008	your] the
3.4.96/1861	mortall] worldly		3.7.20/2010	toward] to an Q1; to Q3, Q6
3.4.97/1862	God] heauen		3.7.23/2013	And] A and
3.4.98/1863	hope] hopes		3.7.24/2014	they ... word,] not in Q
3.4.98/1863	good] faire		3.7.26/2016	Starde] (Star'd); Gazde
3.4.107/1872	who] that		3.7.29/2019	vsed] wont
3.5.3/1875	againe beginne.] (begin); beginne againe		3.7.35/2025	At] At the
3.5.5/1877	Tut] Tut feare not me.		3.7.38/2028	gentle] louing
3.5.15/1887	BUCKINGHAM ... drumme.] (Hearke ... Drumme); after 3.5.16/1888 Q		3.7.39/2029	chearefull] louing
			3.7.41/2031	euen here] fo
3.5.15/1887	a] I heare a		3.7.45/2035	intend] and intend
3.5.16/1888	RICHARD GLOCESTER ... wals.] (Catesby, o're-looke ... Walls); after 3.5.17/1889 Q		3.7.46/2036	you spoke with, but by] fpoken withall, but with
			3.7.48/2038	betweene] betwixt
3.5.17/1889	Lord Maior, the] The		3.7.50/2040	And be] Be Q
3.5.17/1889	sent] fent for you		3.7.51/2041	still answer nay, and] fay no, but
3.5.19/1891	and guard] not in Q		3.7.55/2045	Go, go] You fhal fee what I can do, get you
3.5.24/1896	Creature] man		3.7.55/2045	leads, the Lord Maior knocks] (Leads); leads
3.5.25/1897	the] this		3.7.56/2046	Welcome, my L.] (Lord); Now my L. Maior
3.5.31/1903	liu'd] laid		3.7.58/2048	your Lord to my request?] he.
3.5.33/1905	imagine] haue imagined		3.7.59/2049	He ... grace, my Noble Lord,] (entreat ... Grace); My Lord, he ... grace∧
3.5.34/1906	that] not in Q			
3.5.35/1907	it, that∧ the] it∧ you ? The		3.7.63/2053	suites] fuite
3.5.36/1908	This day had] Had this day		3.7.65/2055	the gracious Duke] thy Lord againe
3.5.38/1910	Had he done] What, had he		3.7.66/2056	Aldermen] Cittizens
3.5.41/1913	in] to		3.7.67/2057	in matter] and matters
3.5.46/1918	your good Graces] you my good Lords		3.7.70/2060	signifie so much vnto him straight] tell him what you fay my Lord
3.5.51/1923	end] death			
3.5.52/1924	louing] longing		3.7.78/2068	vertuous] gracious
3.5.53/1925	Something] Somewhat		3.7.79/2069	his Grace] himfelfe
3.5.53/1925	meanings] meaning		3.7.79/2069	thereof] thereon
3.5.61/1933	and] or		3.7.80/2070	not] neuer
3.5.62/1934	doe not doubt] doubt you not		3.7.81/2071	defend] forbid
3.5.63/1935	our] your		3.7.82/2072	here Catesby comes again	Now] (Catesby); how now
3.5.66/1938	censures of the carping world] (Cenfures ... World); carping cenfures of the world			
			3.7.83/2073	his Grace] your Lord
3.5.67/1939	Which] But		3.7.84/2074	He] My Lo. he
3.5.67/1939	intent] intents		3.7.85/2075	come to] fpeake with
3.5.68/1940	you heare] not in Q		3.7.87/2077	He feares, my Lord,] My Lord, he feares∧
3.5.69/1941	good] not in Q		3.7.90/2080	we] I
3.5.69/1941	Maior, we bid farwell] adue		3.7.90/2080	to him in ... loue] in ... loue to him
3.5.70/1942	Goe after] After Q		3.7.93/2083	much] hard
3.5.80/1952	stretcht vnto] ftretched to		3.7.95/2085	his Grace] he
3.5.82/1954	a] his		3.7.95/2085	tween] (tweene); between
3.5.85/1957	insatiate] vnfatiate		3.7.98-9/2088-9	And ... man.] not in Q
3.5.87/1959	true] iuft		3.7.101/2091	eare] eares
3.5.91/1963	Yet] But		3.7.105/2095	I do beseech your Grace to] (doe); I rather do befeech you
3.5.92/1964	Because, my Lord, you know∧] Becaufe∧ you know, my Lord,			
			3.7.107/2097	Deferr'd] Neglect
3.5.93/1965	Doubt] Feare		3.7.112/2102	eie] (eye); eies
3.5.95/1967	selfe: and so my Lord adue] (fo, my Lord,); felfe Q. See 3.5.101/1972.		3.7.114/2104	might] not in Q
			3.7.115/2105	On] At
3.5.99/1971	I goe, and towards] About		3.7.115/2105	your] that
3.5.100/1972	for ... affords] (Newes ... Guild-Hall affoords); to heare	What news Guildhall affordeth, and fo my Lord farewell		3.7.117/2107	Know then] Then know
			3.7.120/2110	Your State ... Birth,] not in Q
			3.7.123/2113	Whiles] Whilft
3.5.104/1976	Haue any tyme] (time); At any tyme haue		3.7.125/2115	The] This
3.6.1/1977	Here] This		3.7.127/2117	Royall ... Plants,] not in Q
3.6.3/1979	to day] this day		3.7.129/2119	darke ... deepe] blind ... darke
3.6.5/1981	haue] not in Q		3.7.131-2/2121-2	charge ... Land] foueraingtie thereof
3.6.6/1982	sent] brought		3.7.140/2130	Cause] fuite
3.6.8/1984	Hastings liued] (Haftings liu'd); liued Lord Haftings		3.7.141/2131	cannot tell, if] know not whether
3.6.10/1986	Whoe is] (Who); Why whoes Q1; Why who Q3-7		3.7.148/2138	the ... of] my ... by

RICHARD III

3.7.151/2141	That I would] As I had
3.7.155/2145	thank'd there is] (thank'd,); thanked there's
3.7.156/2146	were there need] if need were
3.7.161/2151	that] what
3.7.169/2159	was he] he was
3.7.170/2160	his] that
3.7.173/2163	off] by
3.7.174/2164	to] of
3.7.174/2164	Sonnes] children
3.7.177/2167	wanton] luſtfull
3.7.178/2168	his degree] al his thoughts
3.7.181/2171	call] terme
3.7.188/2178	forth] out
3.7.188/2178	Noble Anceſtrie] royall ſtocke
3.7.189/2179	times] time
3.7.192/2182	BUCKINGHAM . . . loue.] *not in* Q
3.7.194/2184	this care] (Care); theſe cares
3.7.195/2185	Maieſtie] dignitie
3.7.202/2192	kindred] (Kindred); kin
3.7.211/2201	him] them
3.7.211/2201	sweet Prince,] my lord, and
3.7.212/2202	If you denie them,] Doe, good my lord, leaſt
3.7.212/2202	will] do
3.7.213/2203	Will] Would
3.7.213/2203	cares] (Cares); care
3.7.214/2204	Call] Well, call
3.7.217/2207	sage] you ſage
3.7.221/2211	foule-fac't] (foule.fac'd); foule-fac't Q1; ſo foule fac't Q3-8
3.7.225/2215	doth knowe] (know); he knowes
3.7.226/2216	of this] thereof
3.7.229/2219	Royall] kingly
3.7.230/2220	worthie] royall
3.7.232/2222	may] will
3.7.233/2223	please, for] will, ſince
3.7.235/2225	And . . . leaue] *not in* Q
3.7.236/2226	Worke] taske
3.7.237/2227	my] good
4.1.1/2228	OF YORKE] (*Yorke.*); *not in* Q
4.1.7/2234	Sister,] (~ :); Siſter well met,
4.1.7/2234	awaie] (away); awaie ſo faſt
4.1.8/2235	LADY ANNE] (*Anne.*); *Duch.* Q1; *Duch. Glo.* Q3-8
4.1.10/2237	gentle] tender
4.1.14/2241	doth] fares
4.1.14/2241	Prince, and my young Sonne of *Yorke*?] Prince? (*Yorke*);
4.1.15/2242	Right wel] (well); Wel
4.1.15/2242	deare] *not in* Q
4.1.15/2242	Madam:] (Madame); Madam, and in health, but
4.1.15/2242	patience] leaue
4.1.16/2243	them] him
4.1.17/2244	strictlie] (ſtrictlie); ſtraightlie
4.1.18/2245	King?] King? whie,
4.1.18/2245	I] I crie you mercie, I
4.1.20/2247	betweene] betwixt
4.1.21/2248	shall barre] ſhould keepe
4.1.24/2251	bring me to their sights] feare not thou
4.1.26/2253	No, Madame . . . so] I doe beſeech your graces all to pardon me
4.1.27/2254	and therefore pardon me] I may not doe it
4.1.31/2258	straight] go with me
4.1.33/2260	Ah] O
4.1.33/2260	asunder] in ſunder
4.1.36/2263	LADY ANNE . . . newes.] *not in* Q
4.1.37/2264	Be of good cheare:] Madam, haue comfort,
4.1.37/2264	Mother,] *not in* Q
4.1.38/2265	gone] hence
4.1.39/2266	dogges] dogge
4.1.39/2266	thy] O
4.1.48/2275	howres] time
4.1.50/2277	In your behalfe, to] To and welcome you
4.1.50/2277	way,] (~ :); way,
4.1.56/2283	come,] *not in* Q
4.1.58/2285	O] I
4.1.60/2287	braines] (Braines); braine
4.1.61/2288	Venome] poyſon
4.1.63/2290	Goe, goe,] Alas,
4.1.65/2292	why?] *not in* Q
4.1.69/2296	deare] dead
4.1.75/2302	More] As
4.1.75/2302	Life] death
4.1.76/2303	Then] As
4.1.78/2305	With in so small a time] Euen in ſo ſhort a ſpace
4.1.81/2308	hitherto] euer ſince
4.1.81/2308	held] kept
4.1.81/2308	mine] my
4.1.81/2308	rest] ſleepe
4.1.83/2310	Did I enioy] Haue I enioyed
4.1.84/2311	with . . . awak'd] (timorous Dreames); haue bene waked by his timerous dreames
4.1.87/2314	Poore heart adieu] Alas poore ſoule
4.1.87/2314	complaining] complaints
4.1.88/2315	with] from
4.1.90/2317	that] thou
4.1.93/2320	and] *not in* Q
4.2.2-3/2325-6	BUCKINGHAM My . . . KING RICHARD] (*Buck. . . . Rich.*); *not in* Q
4.2.6/2329	Glories] honours
4.2.8/2331	let them] may they
4.2.9/2332	Ah] O
4.2.11/2334	speake] ſay
4.2.12/2335	louing Lord] gracious ſoueraigne
4.2.18/2341	wast] wert
4.2.23/2346	freezes] freezeth
4.2.25/2348	little breath, some] (litle); breath, ſome little
4.2.25/2348	deare] my
4.2.26/2349	in this] herein
4.2.27/2350	you herein presently] your grace immediatlie
4.2.28/2351	gnawes his] bites the
4.2.32-3/2355-6	High . . . circumspect. ǀ Boy.] Boy, high . . . circumſpect.
4.2.34, 37, 41/2357, 2360, 2364	PAGE] *Boy.*
4.2.36/2359	will] would
4.2.37/2360	I] My lord, I
4.2.38/2361	spirit] mind
4.2.42/2365	I partly know the man:] *not in* Q
4.2.42/2365	Boy] preſentlie
4.2.44/2367	counsells] (counſailes); counſell
4.2.46/2369	Well, be it so.] *not in* Q
4.2.47/2370	Lord Stanley,] (*Stanley*); *not in* Q
4.2.47/2370	what's the neewes] (newes); what neewes with you
4.2.48/2371	Know my louing] My
4.2.49/2372	The Marques Dorset as I heare] (Marqueſſe *Dorſet*); I heare the Marques Dorſet
4.2.52/2375	Come hither] *not in* Q
4.2.52/2375	Rumor] (rumor); *Cat.* My Lord. ǀ *King.* Rumor
4.2.53/2376	very grieuous sicke] ſicke and like to die
4.2.59/2382	Queene] wife
4.2.70/2393	Lord.] ſoueraigne.
4.2.72/2395	Please you] I my Lord
4.2.74/2397	disturbers] diſturbs
4.2.79/2402	Hearke, come] Come
4.2.80/2403	this] that
4.2.82/2405	for it] too
4.2.83/2406	I will dispatch it straight] Tis done my gracious lord
4.2.87/2410	request] demand
4.2.88/2411	rest] paſſe
4.2.89/2412	the] that
4.2.90/2413	sonne] (Sonne); ſonnes
4.2.91/2414	the] your
4.2.94/2417	Which you haue] The which you
4.2.94/2417	shall] ſhould

RICHARD III

4.2.97/2420 request] demand
4.2.98/2421 I doe remember me] As I remember
4.2.122/2445 And . . . deepe] Is it euen so, rewardst he my true
4.2.123/2446 such] such deepe
4.3.6/2454 Albeit] Although
4.3.7/2455 Melted] Melting
4.3.7/2455 milde] kind Q1; not in Q6
4.3.8/2456 storie] (Story); stories
4.3.9/2457 O] Lo
4.3.9/2457 the] those Q1; these Q6
4.3.9/2457 gentle] tender
4.3.11/2459 alablaster innocent] (Alablaster); innocent alablaster
4.3.17/2465 When] Whilst
4.3.19/2467 she] he
4.3.20/2468 Hence] Thus
4.3.22/2470 beare] bring
4.3.23/2471 health] haile
4.3.23/2471 Lord] leige
4.3.27/2475 done] done my Lord
4.3.30/2478 where (to say the truth)] how or in what place
4.3.32/2480 When] And
4.3.35/2483 then] soone
4.3.35-6/2483-4 TIRREL I . . . KING RICHARD] (Tir. . . . Rich.); not in Q
4.3.39/2487 this] the
4.3.43/2491 go I] I go
4.3.44, 46/2492, 2494 RATCLIFFE] Cat⟨esby⟩.
4.3.50/2498 Strength] armie
4.3.51/2499 learn'd] heard
4.3.56/2504 Go] Come
4.4.4/2509 enemies] aduersaries
4.4.9/2514 poore] young
4.4.18/2523 still and mute] mute and dumbe
4.4.20-1/2525-6 QUEENE MARGARET . . . debt.] (Plantagenet . . . Plantagenet . . . Edward . . . Edward); not in Q
4.4.26/2531 Dead life, blind sight,] Blind sight, dead life,
4.4.28/2533 Breefe . . . dayes,] not in Q
4.4.31/2536 Ah] O
4.4.31/2536 assoone] aswel
4.4.34/2539 Ah] O
4.4.34/2539 wee] I
4.4.37/2542 greefes] woes
4.4.50/2555 bloud] (blood); blouds
4.4.63/2568 kill'd] stabd
4.4.66/2571 Matcht] Match
4.4.67/2572 stab'd] kild
4.4.68/2573 franticke] tragicke
4.4.76/2581 from hence] away
4.4.78/2583 and] to
4.4.87/2592 faire] sweete
4.4.88/2593 what thou wast,] which thou wert‸
4.4.88-90/2593-5 a garish . . . shot, | A signe . . . a breath, a bubble,] F's arrangement; a breath, a bubble, | A signe . . . a garish . . . shot, Q
4.4.93/2598 two Sonnes] children
4.4.94/2599 and kneeles, and sayes] to thee, and cries
4.4.102, 104/2607, 2609 she . . . she] one . . . one
4.4.103/2608 For . . . one:] not in Q
4.4.104/2609 For . . . none,] after 4.4.102/2607 Q
4.4.105/2610 whirl'd] F; whe'eld Q1; wheel'd Q2-8
4.4.112/2617 head] necke
4.4.115/2620 shall] will
4.4.120/2625 sweeter] fairer
4.4.127/2632 their] your
4.4.130/2635 will] do
4.4.131/2636 nothing els] not at al
4.4.134/2639 that] which
4.4.135/2640 The Trumpet sounds] I heare his drum
4.4.136/2641 me in] not in Q
4.4.137/2642 O] A
4.4.141/2646 branded] grauen
4.4.143/2648 poore] two

4.4.147-8/2652-3 Where . . . Hastings?] (kinde); where is kind Hastings, Riuers, Vaughan, Gray?
4.4.159/2664 That] Which
4.4.160/2665 DUTCHESSE . . . heare.] (Dut. . . . Rich.); not in Q
4.4.161/2666 words] speach
4.4.164/2669 torment, and in] anguish, paine and
4.4.172/2677 slye, and bloudie] (bloody); bloudie, trecherous
4.4.173/2678 More . . . hatred:] not in Q
4.4.178/2683 eye] sight
4.4.179/2684 you Madam] your grace
4.4.180/2685 Strike . . . speake.] not in Q
4.4.181-3/2686-8 You . . . So.] (shall); Du. O heare me speake for I shal neuer see thee more. | King. Come, Come, you art too bitter.
4.4.187/2692 more behold] looke vpon
4.4.199/2704 talke] speake
4.4.201/2706 slaughter] murther
4.4.210/2715 of] from
4.4.212/2717 a . . . Princesse] of . . . bloud
4.4.214/2719 safest onlie] (onely); onlie safest
4.4.217/2722 ill] bad
4.2.222-3/2727-8 enterprize . . . warres] dangerous attempt of hostile armes
4.4.225/2730 by me were harm'd] were by me wrongd
4.4.228/2733 gentle] mightie
4.4.230/2735 Vnto] No to
4.4.230/2735 Fortune] honor
4.4.232/2737 sorrowe] (sorrow); sorrowes
4.4.235/2740 I and] yea and
4.4.241/2746 date] doe
4.4.250/2755 do intend] meane
4.4.251/2756 Well] Saie
4.4.252/2757 else should bee] should be else Q1; shhould else Q2-8
4.4.253/2758 Euen so] I euen I
4.4.253/2758 how] (How); what
4.4.253/2758 it] it Maddame
4.4.255/2760 being] that are
4.4.259/2764 wil she] (will); she wil
4.4.261-2/2766-7 steept . . . bloud, | A handkercher,] (blood . . . hand-kercheefe); a handkercher‸ steept . . . bloud
4.4.262-3/2767-8 which . . . body,] not in Q
4.4.264/2769 wipe] drie
4.4.264/2769 withall] therewith
4.4.265/2770 moue] force
4.4.266/2771 Letter] storie
4.4.266/2771 deeds] acts
4.4.268/2773 I] yea
4.4.270/2775 You] Come, come, you
4.4.270/2775 Madam] not in Q
4.4.276/2781 Tell her,] Saie that
4.4.276/2781 that] which
4.4.279/2784 vaile] waile
4.4.282/2787 in force] inforce
4.4.284-5/2789-90 As . . . As] So . . . So
4.4.290/2795 plainly to her] in plaine termes
4.4.290/2795 tell] tell her
4.4.292/2797 Your] Madame your
4.4.294/2799 graues] graue
4.4.299/2804 I sweare] I sweare by nothing
4.4.300-2/2805-7 Thy . . . Thy . . . Thy] The . . . The . . . The
4.4.302/2807 Glory] dignitie
4.4.303/2808 would'st] wilt
4.4.305/2810 Then . . . misus'd] F's arrangement; after 4.4.376/2812 Q
4.4.305/2810 is selfe misus'd] (selfe.misvs'd); thy selfe misuseft
4.4.309/2814 didst feare] (didd'st); hadst feard
4.4.309/2814 with] by
4.4.310/2815 my husband] my brother Q1-Q6a; thy brother Q6b-Q8
4.4.311/2816 Thou had'st not] Had not bene
4.4.311/2816 brothers died] (Brothers); brother slaine

257

RICHARD III

4.4.313/2818	head] brow
4.4.316/2821	Bed-fellowes] plaie-fellowes
4.4.317/2822	the] a
4.4.318/2823	What . . . now.] *not in* Q
4.4.318/2823	The] By the
4.4.319/2824	the] *not in* Q
4.4.321/2826	time⌃ past wrongd by the,] (paſt, wrong'd by thee.); time, by the paſt wrongd,
4.4.322/2827	Fathers] parents
4.4.325/2830	barren] withered
4.4.327/2832	times ill-vs'd] time miſuſed
4.4.329/2834	Affayres⌃] attempt,
4.4.331/2836	Heauen . . . houres:] *not in* Q
4.4.334/2839	proceeding] proceedings
4.4.334/2839	deere] pure
4.4.338-9/2843-4	my ſelfe⌃ . . . the land] (my ſelfe, and thee; . . . Land); this land and me, | To thee her ſelfe
4.4.340/2845	Death,] Sad⌃
4.4.346/2851	my] by
4.4.350/2855	you] thee
4.4.353/2858	Yet] But
4.4.355/2860	will] ſhall
4.4.360/2865	And . . . mind] *not in* Q
4.4.361/2866	and so] *not in* Q
4.4.363/2868	How now, what newes?] *not in* Q
4.4.364/2869	Most mightie] My gracious
4.4.365/2870	our shores] (Shores); the ſhore
4.4.373/2878	good] *not in* Q
4.4.373/2878	Catesby, flie] (flye); Flie
4.4.375/2880	post] (poſte): poſt thou
4.4.376/2881	thither] there
4.4.377/2882	stay'ſt . . . here] ſtandſt . . . ſtill
4.4.378/2883	Liege, tell me your Highneſſe pleaſure] Soueraigne, let me know your minde
4.4.381/2886	that] *not in* Q
4.4.382/2887	suddenlie] (ſuddenly); preſentlie
4.4.383/2888	CATESBY I goe. *Exit*] (*Cat.*); *not in* Q
4.4.384/2889	may it please you, shall I] is it your highnes pleaſure, I ſhall
4.4.387/2892	changd.] (chang'd:); changd ſir, my minde is changd.
4.4.387/2892	Stanley] (*Stanley*); How now
4.4.388/2893	STANLEY] F (*throughout scene*); *Dar.* Q (*throughout scene*)
4.4.388/2893	Liege] Lord
4.4.389/2894	well may be reported] it may well be told
4.4.391/2896	need'ſt] doeſt
4.4.392/2897	the neerest] a neerer
4.4.397/2902	Well] Well ſir, as you gueſſe
4.4.399/2904	here] there
4.4.404/2909	makes] doeth
4.4.404/2909	seas] (Seas); ſea
4.4.409/2914	my good Lord] mightie liege
4.4.411/2916	be] are
4.4.415/2920	me] Richard
4.4.417/2922	King] ſoueraigne
4.4.418/2923	Pleaseth] Pleaſe it
4.4.422/2927	But Ile . . . thee] I will . . . you Sir
4.4.425/2930	Go then, and] (Goe); Well, go
4.4.425/2930	but⌃] but heare you,
4.4.426/2931	heart] faith
4.4.431/2936	Edward] (*Edward*); William
4.4.432/2937	elder brother] (Brother); brother there
4.4.434/2939	In Kent, my Liege,] My Liege, in Kent⌃
4.4.436/2941	the Rebels] their aide
4.4.436/2941	and] and ſtill
4.4.436/2941	growes strong] increaſeth
4.4.437/2942	great] the Duke of
4.4.439/2944	There, take thou that⌃ till] (that,); Take that vntill
4.4.439/2944	bring] bring me
4.4.440-1/2945-6	The . . . | Is,] (Is,); Your grace miſtakes, the newes I bring is good, | My newes is⌃
4.4.442/2947	Buckinghams] (*Buckinghams*); The Duke of Buckinghams
4.4.443/2948	wandred away alone] fled
4.4.444/2949	I] O I
4.4.444/2949	thee] you
4.4.444/2949	mercie] mercie, I did miſtake
4.4.446/2951	proclaym'd,] giuen out,
4.4.447/2952	Reward to] Rewardes for
4.4.447/2952	the Traytor in] in Buckingham
4.4.448/2953	lord] (Lord); liege
4.4.450/2955	in Yorkeshire are] are vp
4.4.451/2956	But] Yet
4.4.451/2956	Highneſſe] grace
4.4.452/2957	by Tempest] *not in* Q
4.4.454/2959	Vnto the shore,] *not in* Q
4.4.454/2959	those . . . Banks] them . . . ſhore
4.4.458/2963	his course againe] away
4.4.463/2968	That is] Thats
4.5.2/2976	deadlie] (deadly); bloudie
4.5.5/2979	holdes off] (holds); with holdes
4.5.12/2986	And] *not in* Q
4.5.13/2987	And] With
4.5.13/2987	other] moe
4.5.13/2987	great name] noble fame
4.5.14/2988	doe they] (do); they doe
4.5.14/2988	power] courſe
4.5.16/2990	Well hye thee to] Retourne vnto
4.5.19/2993	My] Theſe
4.5.19/2993	letter] (Letter); letters
5.1.2/2996	good] *not in* Q
5.1.2, 11/2996, 3005	SHERIFFE] (*Sher.*); *Rat.*
5.1.3/2997	Gray & Riuers,] (*Gray & Riuers,*); Riuers, Gray,
5.1.10/3004	fellowe] (Fellow); fellowes
5.1.11/3005	is] is my Lord
5.1.13/3007	which] that
5.1.15/3009	and] or
5.1.17/3011	whom most I trusted] I truſted moſt
5.1.20/3014	which] that
5.1.24/3018	in] on
5.1.24/3018	bosomes] boſome
5.1.25/3019	Thus] Now
5.1.25/3019	falles heauy on] is fallen vpon
5.1.25/3019	necke] head
5.1.28/3022	leade me Officers] ſirs, conuey me
5.2.17/3040	OXFORD] 1 *Lo.*
5.2.18/3041	this] that
5.2.18/3041	guiltie] (guilty); bloudie
5.2.19/3042	HERBERT] 2 *Lo.*
5.2.19/3042	turne] flie
5.2.20/3043	BLUNT] 3 *Lo.*
5.2.20/3043	what] who
5.2.21/3044	deerest] greateſt
5.2.21/3044	flye] ſhrinke
5.3.1/3048	tent] (Tent); tentes
5.3.2/3049	look you] (looke); lookſt thou
5.3.4/3051	My Lord of] *not in* Q
5.3.4/3051	Norffolke] (Norffolke); Norffolke, come hether
5.3.4-5/3051-2	NORFFOLKE . . . KING RICHARD] *not in* Q
5.3.6/3053	louing] gracious
5.3.7/3054	tent] (Tent); tent there
5.3.9/3056	Traitors] foe
5.3.10/3057	power] number
5.3.11/3058	battalia] (Battalia); battalion
5.3.13/3060	Faction] partie
5.3.14/3061	the] my
5.3.14/3061	tent] (Tent); tent there
5.3.14/3061	Come Noble] valiant
5.3.15/3062	ground] field
5.3.17/3064	lacke] want
5.4.3/3068	token] ſignall
5.4.4/3069	Sir] Where is Sir

5.4.4/3069 you] he
5.4.5/3070 keepes] keepe
5.4.9/3074 Captain‸ do for me] (Captaine) do for me F; Blunt‸ before thou goeſt
5.4.10/3075 do you] doeſt thou
5.4.16/3081 Sweet . . . with] (*Blunt,*); Good captaine Blunt beare my good night to
5.4.17/3082 Note] ſcrowle
5.4.19/3084 And . . . to night,] *not in* Q

5.4.20/3085 Good night good Captaine] Farewell good
5.4.20/3085 Come Gentlemen,] *not in* Q
5.4.24/3089 Power] ſtrength
5.4.25/3090 Let] Come, let
5.4.26/3091 my] our
5.4.26/3091 Dew] aire
5.5.1/3092 is't] is
5.5.2/3093 It's] It is ſixe of clocke, full
5.5.2/3093 my Lord, it's nine a clocke] *not in* Q

QI READINGS RESTORED BY F

21 scarſe] F; ſcarce Q1; *not in* Q3-8
51 whats] Q1; what is Q3-8; what's F
255 Margaret] Q1; Margret Q3-6; *Margaret* F
258 brothers] Q1; brother Q3-8; Brothers F
277 keene] F; keen Q1; kind Q3-8
317 friend] Q1-5; friends Qb; Friend F
371 Barkley] Q1; Bartley Q3; Bartly Q6; *Barkley* F
437 do] F; doe Q1: *not in* Q3-8
446 speaks] F; ſpeakes Q1; ſpeaketh Q3
466 all] Q1, F; *not in* Q6
615 rights] Q1, F; glorie Q2-6; Rights F
656 poiſenous] Q1, F; poiſoned Q2-8; poyſonous F
735 miſchiefes] Q1; miſchiefe Q3-8; Miſcheefes F
781 pact] Q1; paſt Q2-8; pac'd F
797 woo'd] F; woed Q1; wade Q6
819 Dabled] Q1; Dadled Q6; Dabbel'd F
839 titles] Q1; tiles Q6; Titles F
855 hereby] Q1; thereby Q3-8; heereby F
896 ſweare] Q1; ſteale Q3-8; Sweare F
900 purſſe] (Purſſe); purſe Q1; piece Q3-8
986 meede] Q1; need Q3-6; meed F
1052 truly] F; truely Q1; *not in* Q3-8
1219 ſoule] Q1; ſelfe Q6; Soule F
1382 olde] Q1; hold Q3; old F
1384 byting] biting Q1; pretie Q2-8
1387 His Nurſe?] F; His nurſe: Q1; *not in* Q2-8
1661 How] F; Howe Q1; Who Q3-6
1808 ſudden] Q1; ſodaine Q1; ſodain Q2-8
1822 lookes] Q1; face Q2-8; Lookes F
1937 wiſh'd] F; wiſht Q1; wiſh Q6
1964 mother] Q1; brother Q6; Mother F1
2168 Seduc'd] F; Seduc‸t Q1; Seduc't Q2; Seduce Q6

2278 ta'ne] F; tane Q1; taken Q2-8
2304 ere] F; eare Q1; euen Q2-8
2332 do I] Q1-2, F; I do Q3-8; doe I F
2357 My] Q1-2, F; *not in* Q3-8
2389 will] Q1, F; *not in* Q2-8
2460 were] Q1, F; like Q3-8
2468 both . . . Remorſe,] F, Q1 (conſcience . . . remorſe); *not in* Q3-8
2493 comſt] Q1; comeſt Q3-8; com'ſt F
2502 wing] Q1, F; wings Q3-8
2503 Ioues] Q1, F; Ioue Q3, Q5; *Ioue* Q6-8
2530 *Harry*] Q1, F; *Mary* Q3-8
2551 and] Q1, F; till Q2-8
2565 thine] Q1, F; thee Q2-8
2575 ſmothred] Q1; ſmoothered Q6; ſmother'd F
2586 bunch] Q1, F; hunch Q2-8
2639 ſweet] Q1, F; ſweete Q2-5
2676 Thy . . . venturous] F, Q1 (manhood . . . bold,); *not in* Q3-8
2683 diſgracious] Q1, F; gratious Q3-7
2729 I] Q1, F; *not in* Q6
2751 ſoules loue] Q1, F; ſoule Q6
2751 thou loue] Q1, F; thou Q2-5
2788 her ſweet life] Q1, F; that title Q3-8
2801 I till hart ſtrings] Q1, F (I, . . . heart-ſtrings); *not in* Q3-8
2812 life] Q1, F; ſelfe Q3-8
2860 they] Q1, F; there Q3-8
2991-2 the . . . daughter] F (*Elizabeth*), *after* 2979; the Queene hath hartelie conſented, | He ſhall eſpouſe Elizabeth her daughter Q (*at this point*)
3018 owne] Q1, F; *not in* Q3-8
3066 ſet] F; ſete Q1; ſeate Q2-5; ſeat Q6
3078 lies] Q1, F; lieth Q4, Q6-8

SEMI-SUBSTANTIVE METRICAL MARKINGS

1.1.7 alarums] Q2-8, F; alarmes Q1
1.1.44 Tend'ring] F: tendering Q
1.1.45 to the] Q; to'th F
1.1.50 chriſtened] Q2-5, F; chriſtenèd Q1
1.1.109 whatſoe'er] F; whatſoeuer Q1
1.1.141 conſumed] F; conſumèd Q
1.2.4 Th'untimely] F; The vntimely Q
1.2.10 ſlaughtered] Q3, F; ſlaughterèd Q1
1.2.56 congealèd] congeald QF
1.2.62 mad'ſt] F; madeſt Q
1.2.64 heav'n] F; heauen Q
1.2.64 murd'rer] F (murth'rer); murtherer Q
1.2.78 diffuſed] F; defuſed Q
1.2.86 excuſed] Q; excuſèd F
1.2.97 ſland'rous] F; ſlaunderous Q
1.2.103 damnèd] Q3-8, F; damnd Q1
1.2.131 o'erſhade] F; ouerſhade Q
1.2.133 revenged] F; reuengèd Q
1.2.202 monaſt'ry] F; monaſtery Q
1.2.241 marv'lous] F; merueilous Q

1.3.2 accuſtomed] F; accuſtomèd Q
1.3.56 injured] F; iniurèd Q
1.3.78 impriſoned] F; impriſonèd Q
1.3.109 ſcorned] F; ſcornèd Q
1.3.134 murd'rous] F (murth'rous); murtherous Q
1.3.177 fall'n] F (falne); fallen Q
1.3.181 e'er] F; euer Q
1.3.205 lengthened] F; lengthenèd Q
1.3.238 breathed] F; breathèd Q
1.3.278 I'll] F (Ile); I will Q
1.3.331 revenged] F; reuengèd Q
1.4.16 befall'n] F(befalne); befallen Q
1.4.33 ſcattered] F; ſcatterèd Q
1.4.39 wand'ring] F; wandering Q
1.4.40 ſmothered] F; ſmotherèd Q
1.4.235 leſſoned] Q; leſſonèd F
1.4.271 ſaved] F; ſauèd Q
2.2.69 wat'ry] Q; waterie F
2.2.74, 75 he's] F; he is Q1; is he Q6
2.2.124 we'll] F; we will Q

RICHARD III

2.4.15 flow'rs] F(Flowres); flowers Q	4.1.17 charged] F; chargèd Q
3.1.8 dived] F; diuèd Q	4.2.86 considered] F; confiderèd Q
3.1.51 claimed] F; claimèd Q	4.2.93 Th'] F; The Q
3.1.51 deserved] F; deferuèd Q	4.2.120 whe'er] whether Q; *not in* F
3.1.56 ne'er] F; neuer Q	4.3.19 e'er] F; euer Q
3.1.57 o'errule] F; ouerrule Q	4.4.39 o'er] ouer Q; *not in* F
3.1.160, 166 think'st] F; thinkeft Q	4.4.69 Th'] F; The Q
3.2.10 determined] F; determinèd Q	4.4.72 reserved] F; referuèd Q
3.2.11 th'other] F; the other Q	4.4.86 heaved] F; heauèd Q
3.2.23 he's] F; he is Q	4.4.95 flattered] flatterèd QF
3.2.24 mock'ry] F; mockery Q	4.4.111 burdened] F (burthen'd); burthenèd Q
3.2.34 tott'ring] F; tottering Q	4.4.170 desp'rate] F; defperate Q
3.2.58 on't] F; on it Q	4.4.172 confirmed] F; confirmèd Q
3.2.68 deserved] F; deferuèd Q	4.4.227 discovered] Q; difcouerèd F
3.2.76 'tis] F; it is Q	4.4.228, 313 Th'] F; The Q
3.2.82 o'ercast] F; ouercaft Q	4.4.319 wrongèd] F; wrongd Q
3.2.90 let us] Q; let's F	4.4.327 Misused . . . used] F; Mifufed . . . vfed Q
3.2.100 e'er] F; euer Q	4.4.421 wouldst]F; wouldeft Q
3.4.20 he'll] F; he will Q	5.1.21 turned] F; turnèd Q
3.4.51 there's] F; there is Q	5.3.8 all's] F; all is Q
3.4.65 th'offenders] F; the offenders Q	5.5.2 It's] F; It is Q
3.4.65 whatsoe'er] whatfoeuer Q; whofoe'er F	5.5.42 th'] F; the Q
3.4.69 withered] F; witherèd Q	5.5.65 Th'] F; The Q
3.5.16 o'erlook] F; ouerlooke Q	5.5.76 butchered] Q3, F; Butcherèd Q1
3.5.45 deserved] F; deferuèd Q	5.5.100 smothered] Q3; fmotherèd Q1
3.5.50 determined] F; determinèd Q	5.5.150 high'st] F; higheft Q
3.5.58 haply] F; happily Q	5.5.151 dir'st] F; dyreft Q
3.5.66 T'avoid] F; To auoyde Q	5.5.167 thinkest] thinkft QF
3.5.91 'twere] F; it were Q	5.5.203 slaughtered] F; flaughterèd Q
3.6.3 o'er] F; ouer Q	5.6.4 smiled] F; fmilèd Q
3.6.9 unexamined] F; vnexaminèd Q	5.6.22 orderèd] Q; ordred F
3.7.7 Th'] F; the Q	5.6.42 to't] F; to it Q
3.7.110 ungoverned] F; vngouernèd Q	5.6.62 conquered] conquerèd QF
3.7.186 proffered] F; profferèd Q	5.8.25 slaughtered] Q; flaughterèd F
3.7.204, 219 whe'er] F (where); whether Q	

INCIDENTALS

11 aduersaries,] ~.   29 daies,] ~.   32 laid,] ~ₐ   44 ap-pointed] Q1b (ap-|pointed; ap-|po nted Q1a   106 obey.] ~,   114 well.] ~ :   122 Hastings] haftings   123 Lord.] ~ :   143 he,] ~ₐ   150 liue:] ~,   158 intent,] ~.   177 Cursed] Cnrfed F   227 quicke,] ~.   236 angry.] ~,   415 it,,ill,] ~, ~ₐ   417 eyes.] ~ₐ F; words, Q   434 Darby, notwithstanding,] ~ₐ ~,   486 Gloster,] F; Gl.   533 King,] ~.   606 not,] ~,   625 the?] ~ₐ   625 me.] ~ₐ   626 If] Q (*text*); Excee- Q (*c.w.*)   659 mine.] ~,   673 more,] ~.   734 braule.] ~ₐ   759 May,] ~,   773 dreame,] ~,   773 me.] ~ₐ F   778 hatches:] ~ₐ   780 Lancaster,] ~ :   782 hatches,] ~ :   799 such] fueh   809 soule.] ~,   815 periury,] ~.   837 howers,] ~ₐ   883 within] with|(in Q (*a turnover*)   892 entertaine it.] ~,   1024 life?] ~, F   1058 Hastings] haftings   1087 Duke.] ~,   1279 Loue,] Q; ~ₐ F   1290 cherisht,] ~. F; ~, Q   1297 busines.] ~,   1316 world.] ~,   1332 neerest,] ~ :   1350 see,] ~.   1384 | beene] heene   1411 tost,] ~ :   1413 broiles,] ~,   1414 ouerblowne, themselues,] ~, ~,   1415 Brother,] ~ ; F   1695 roode,] ~.   1717 now,] ~.   1721 selfe)] ~.)   1752 Richard] Richatd   1774 mind.] ~,   1836 Shore,] ~.   1879 side,] ~ :   2010 ende,] ~.   2043 selfe,] ~ ?   2170 got,] ~.   2224 grace,] ~.   2228 heere?] ~,   2228 Plantagenet,] ~ ?   2249 Fathers,] ~,   2272 And] (indented, as though for a speech-prefix)   2278 delaie.] ~ :   2286 that] thar   2297 Richards] Richatds   2319 Go] F, Q (*text*); Goe Q (*c.w.*)   2324 Buckingham.] ~,   2479 Tirrel] Tirre!   2481 good,] ~.   2546 Richard kild] Ricard ~   2592 onelie,] ~.   2668 haftie?] ~ₐ   2675 furious,] ~.   2690 Eare] Eeare   2699 victorie] victoric   2706 slaughter,] ~.   2731 the] rhe   2732 good.] ~,   2738 honor,] ~ ?   2745 the] thc   2759 you,] ~.   2763 harts:] ~ₐ   2797 quicke.] ~,   2807 disgrac't] difgrac't   2876 Norffolke.] Norff.   2889 Salisbury.] ~,   3020 quoth] quorh   3020 sorrow,] ~.   3129 that:] ~ₐ   3137 doubtful] doubful   3185 die.] ~,   3203 Englands] Engiands   3206 perturbations] preturbations   3220 Richmonds] Richmons   3274 departure] depature   3288 Richard,except,] ~, ~,   3299 in] ln   3319 purpose.] ~,   3325 bodie,] ~.   3326 Ratcliffe.] Rat.   3344 maine] matne   3356 conscience, swords,] ~ₐ ~,   3381-2 wiues, . . . daughters?] ~ ? . . . ~,   3388 come.] ~,   3413 roialtie,] ~.

QUARTO STAGE DIRECTIONS

1.1.0.1/0.1 *Enter Richard Duke of Glocester solus.*	1.1.144/144 *Exit Hast.*
1.1.40.1-2/40.1 *Enter Clarence with	a gard of men.* (opposite 'soule' and 'comes', 1.1.41/41; see lineation notes)	1.1.162.1/162.1 *Exit.*
1.1.117.1-2/117.1-2 *Exit Clar.*	1.2.0.1-3/162.2-4 *Enter Lady Anne with the hearse of Harry the 6.*
1.1.122.1/122.1 *Enter Lord Hastings.*	1.2.32.1/194.1 *Enter Glocester.*
	1.2.144/306 *Shee spitteth at him.* (after 'he')

RICHARD III

1.2.170.1/332.1	*Here she lets fall	the sword.* (opposite 1.2.170-1/332-3)
1.2.212.1/374.1	*Exit.*
1.2.214.1/376.1	*Exeunt. manet Gl.* (after 1.2.215/377)
1.2.250/412	*Exit.*
1.3.0.1-2/412.1-2	*Enter Queene, Lord Riuers, Gray.*
1.3.16.1-2/428.1	*(Enter Buck. Darby*
1.3.41.1/453.1	*Enter Glocester.*
1.3.109.1/521.1	*Enter Qu.	Margaret.* (opposite 1.3.109-110/521-2)
1.3.301/713	*Exit.*
1.3.321.1/733.1	*Exeunt man. Ri.*
1.3.336.1/748.1	*Enter Executioners.* (after 1.3.337/749)
1.3.353.1-2/765.1-2	*Exeunt.*
1.4.0.1-2/765.3	*Enter Clarence, Brokenbury.*
1.4.79.1/844.1	*The murtherers enter.*
1.4.87.1/852.1	*He readeth it.*
1.4.264/1027	*He stabs him.* (after 'serue')
1.4.273/1036	*Exit.*
1.4.278/1041	*Exeunt.*
2.1.0.1-4/1041.1-3	*Enter King, Queene, Hastings, Ryuers, Dorcet, &c.*
2.1.44.1-2/1085.1	*Enter Glocest.*
2.1.95.1/1136.1	*Enter Darby.*
2.1.135.1/1176	*(Exit.* (turned up)
2.1.142/1183	*Exeunt.* (after 2.1.141/1182; see textual notes)
2.2.0.1-2/1183.1-2	*Enter Dutches of Yorke, with Clarence Children.*
2.2.33.1/1216.1	*Enter the	Quee.* (opposite 2.2.33-4/1216-17)
2.2.88.1-3/1271.1-2	*Enter Glocest.	with others.* (opposite 2.2.88-9/1271-2)
2.2.115.1/1298.1	*Exeunt man, Glo. Buck.*
2.3.0.1-2/1307.1-2	*Enter two Cittizens.*
2.3.5.1/1312.1	*Ent. ano-|ther Citt.* (opposite 2.3.5-6/1312-13)
2.3.47/1354	*Exeunt.*
2.4.0.1-2/1354.1-2	*Enter Cardinall, Dutches of Yorke, Quee. young Yorke.*
2.4.37/1391	*Enter Dorset.*
2.4.72/1426	*Exeunt.*
3.1.0.1-4/1426.1-4	*The Trumpets sound. Enter young Prince, the Dukes of Glo-|cester, and Buckingham, Cardinall, &c.*
3.1.16.1/1442.1	*Enter Lord Maior.* (after 3.1.17/1443)
3.1.23.1/1449.1	*(Enter L. Hast.*
3.1.94.1-2/1520.1	*Enter young Yorke, Hastings, Cardinall.*
3.1.149.1-2/1575.1-2	*Exeunt Prin. Yor. Hast. Dors. manet. Rich. Buck.*
3.1.197/1623	*Exeunt.*
3.2.0.1/1623.1	*Enter a Messenger to Lo: Hastings.*
3.2.1.1/1624.1	*Enter L. Hast·*
3.2.31.1/1654.1	*Enter	(Cates.* (opposite 3.2.31-2/1654-5)
3.2.68.1/1691.1	*Enter Lord Stanley.*
3.2.90.1/1713.1	*Enter Hastin.	(a Purssuant.* (opposite 3.2.90-1/1713-14)
3.2.102.1/1725.1	*He giues	(him his purse.* (opposite 3.2.102-3/1725-6)
3.2.103.1/1726.1	*(Enter a priest.* (after 'Hast. What Sir John, you are wel met', which follows 3.2.103/1726)
3.2.107.1/1730.1	*He whis-|(pers in his eare.*
3.2.107.2/1730.2	*Enter Buckingham.*
3.2.118.1/1741.1	*Exeunt.*
3.3.0.1-3/1741.2-4	*Enter Sir Rickard Ratliffe, with the Lo: Riuers,	Gray, and Vaughan, prisoners.*
3.3.24/1765	*Exeunt.*
3.4.0.1-3/1765.1-3	*Enter the Lords to Councell.*
3.4.20.1/1785.1	*(Ent. Glo.* (turned down below 3.4.21/1786)
3.4.41.1/1806.1	*Ex. Gl.*
3.4.45.1/1810.1	*Enter B.	of Ely.* (opposite 3.4.44-5/1809-10)
3.4.58.1/1823.1	*Enter Glocester.*
3.4.79.1/1844.1	*Exeunt. manet	Cat. with Ha.* (opposite 3.4.79-80/1844-5)
3.4.107/1872	*Exeunt.*
3.5.0.1-3/1872.1-2	*Enter Duke of Glocester and Buckingham in armour.*
3.5.11.1/1883.1	*Enter Maior.*
3.5.19.1/1891.1	*Enter Catesby	with Hast. head.* (opposite 3.5.19-20/1891-2)
3.5.69.1/1941.1	*Exit Maior.* (after 3.5.70/1942)
3.5.100/1972.1	*Exit Buc.* (after 3.5.101/1973)
3.5.104/1976	*Exit.*
3.6.0.1/1976.1	*Enter a Scriuener with a paper in his hand.*
3.6.14/1990	*Exit*
3.7.0.1-2/1990.1	*Enter Glocester at one doore, Buckingham at another.*
3.7.55.1/2045.1	*Exit.*
3.7.57.1/2047.1	*Enter Catesby.*
3.7.70/2060	*Exit.*
3.7.82.1/2072.1	*Enter Cates.* (after 'Catesby', 3.7.83/2073)
3.7.91.1/2081.1	*Exit Catesby.*
3.7.94.1-2/2084.1-2	*Enter Rich. with two bishops a loste.*
3.7.237.1-2/2227.1-2	*Exeunt.*
4.1.0.1-4/2227.3-6	*Enter Quee. mother, Duchesse of Yorke, Marques Dorset, at	one doore, Duchesse of Glocest. at another doore.*
4.1.11.1/2238.1	*Enter	Lieutenant.* (opposite 4.1.11-12/2238-9)
4.1.27.1/2254.2	*Enter L. Stanlie.*
4.2.0.1-3/2323.2-4	*The Trumpets sound, Enter Richard crownd, Bucking-|ham, Catesby with other Nobles.*
4.2.3.1-2/2326.1	*Here he ascendeth	the throne.* (opposite 4.2.3-4/2326-7)
4.2.27/2350	*Exit.*
4.2.46.1/2369.1	*Enter Darby.*
4.2.67.1/2390.1	*Enter Tirrel.*
4.2.80.1/2403.1	*he wispers in his eare.*
4.2.84.1/2407.1	*Enter Buc.*
4.2.121.1/2444.1	*Exit.*
4.2.125.1/2448.1	*Exit.*
4.3.0.1/2448.2	*Enter Sir Francis Tirrell.*
4.3.22.1/2470.1	*Enter Ki. Richard.*
4.3.35/2483	*Exit Tirrel.* (after 4.3.34/2482)
4.3.43.1/2491.1	*Enter Catesby.*
4.3.57.1/2505.1	*Exeunt.*
4.4.0.1/2505.2	*Enter Queene Margaret sola.*
4.4.7.1/2512.1	*Enter the Qu. and the Dutchesse of Yorke.* (after 4.4.8/2513)
4.4.125.1/2630.1	*Exit Mar.* (after 4.4.126/2631)
4.4.136.1-2/2640.1-2	*Enter K. Richard marching with Drummes	and Trumpets.*
4.4.151.1/2656.1	*The trumpets*
4.4.196.1/2701.1	*Exit.*
4.4.361.1/2866.1	*Exit.*
4.4.362.1/2867.1	*Enter Rat.*
4.4.387/2892	*Enter Darbie.* (after 'you')
4.4.428.1/2933.2	*Enter a Messenger.*
4.4.433.1/2938.1	*Enter another Messenger.*
4.4.436.1/2941.1	*Enter another Messenger.*
4.4.438.1/2943.1	*He striketh him.* (after 4.4.437/2942)
4.4.448.1/2953.1	*Enter another Messenger.*
4.4.461.1/2966.1	*Enter Catesbie.*
4.4.469.1/2974.1	*Exeunt.*
4.5.0.1-2/2974.2-3	*Entee Darbie, Sir Christopher.*
4.5.20/2994	*Exeunt.*
5.1.0.1-2/2994.1-2	*Enter Buckingham to execution.*
5.2.0.1-3/3023.2-3	*Enter Richmond with drums and trumpets.*
5.2.24.1/3047.1	*Exit.*
5.3.0.1-3/3047.2-3	*Enter King Richard, Norffolke, Ratcliffe,	Catesbie, with others.*
5.3.18.1/3065.1	*Exeunt.*
5.4.0.1-3/3065.2-3	*Enter Richmond with the Lordes, &c.*
5.5.0.1-3/3091.2-3	*Enter king Richard, Norff. Ratcliffe	Catesbie, &c.*
5.5.31.1/3122.1	*Exit. Ratliffe*
5.5.31.3-4/3122.3-4	*Enter Darby to Richmond in his tent.*
5.5.60.1/3151.1	*Exunt.*

RICHARD III

5.5.70.1/3161.1 *Enter the ghost of young Prince Edward, sonne* | *Harry the sixt, to Ri.*
5.5.71/3162 *to Ri.*
5.5.75/3166 *To Rich.*
5.5.77.1/3168.1 *Enter the ghost of Henry the sixt.*
5.5.78/3169 *to Ri.*
5.5.82/3173 *To Rich.*
5.5.84.1/3175.1 *Enter the Goast of Clarence.*
5.5.90/3181 *To Rich.*
5.5.92.2-3/3183.1 *Enter the ghosts of Riuers, Gray, Vaughan.*
5.5.98/3189 *to Ri.*
5.5.99.2/3190.2 *Enter the ghosts of the two yong Princes.*
5.5.100/3191 *to Ri.*
5.5.104/3195 *To Rich.*
5.5.107.2/3198.2 *Enter the ghost of Hastings.*
5.5.111/3202 *To Rich.*
5.5.112.2/3203.2 *Enter the ghost of Lady Anne his wife.*
5.5.118/3209.1 *To Rich.*
5.5.120.1/3211.1 *Enter the Goast of Buckingham.*
5.5.127/3218 *To Rich.*
5.5.130.1/3221.1 *Richard starteth vp out of a dreame.*
5.5.160.1/3251.1 *Enter Ratcliffe.*
5.5.176.1/3267.1 *Exeunt.*
5.5.176.2-3/3267.2 *Enter the Lordes to Richmond.*
5.5.190.1/3281.1 *His oration to his souldiers.*
5.6.0.1-2/3315.3 *Enter King Richard, Rat. &c.*
5.6.5.1/3320.1 *The clocke striketh.* (after 'there', 5.6.6/3321)
5.6.17.1/3332.1 *Enter Norffolke.*
5.6.32.1/3347.1 *he sheweth him* | *a paper.* (opposite 5.6.32-3/3347-8)
5.6.43.1/3358.1 *His Oration to his army.*
5.6.81/3396 *Exeunt.*
5.7.0.1/3396.1 *Alarum, excursions, Enter Catesby.*
5.7.6.1/3402.1 *Enter Richard.*
5.8.0.1-6/3409.1-5 *Alarum, Enter Richard and Richmond, they fight,* | *Richard is slain* | *then retrait being sounded. Enter Richmond, Darby, bearing the* | *crowne, with other Lords, &c.*

FOLIO STAGE DIRECTIONS

1.1.0.1/0.1 *Enter Richard Duke of Gloster, solus.*
1.1.40.1-2/40.1 *Enter Clarence, and Brakenbury, guarded.* (after 1.1.41/41)
1.1.117.1-2/117.1-2 *Exit Clar.*
1.1.122.1/122.1 *Enter Lord Hastings.*
1.1.144/144 *Exit Hastings.*
1.1.162.1/162.1 *Exit*
1.2.0.1-3/162.2-4 *Enter the Coarse of Henrie the sixt with Halberds to guard it,* | *Lady Anne being the Mourner.*
1.2.32.1/194.1 *Enter Richard Duke of Gloster.*
1.2.144/306 *Spits at him.*
1.2.158.1/320.1 *She lookes scornfully at him.*
1.2.166.1-2/328.1-2 *He layes his brest open, she offers at with his sword.*
1.2.170.1/332.1 *She fals the Sword.*
1.2.212.1/374.1 *Exit two with Anne.*
1.2.214.1/376.1 *Exit Coarse*
1.2.250/412 *exit.*
1.3.0.1-2/412.1-2 *Enter the Queene Mother, Lord Riuers,* | *and Lord Gray.*
1.3.16.1-2/428.1 *Enter Buckingham and Derby.*
1.3.41.1/453.1 *Enter Richard.*
1.3.109.1/521.1 *Enter old Queene Margaret.* (after 1.3.110/522)
1.3.301/713 *Exit.*
1.3.316/728 *Speakes to himselfe.* (after 'aduisde')
1.3.317.1/729.1 *Enter Catesby.*
1.3.321.1/733.1 *Exeunt all but Gloster.*
1.3.336.1/748.1 *Enter two murtherers.*
1.4.0.1-2/765.3 *Enter Clarence and Keeper.* (Fb; not in Fa)
1.4.0.1-2/765.3 *Enter Brakenbury the Lieutenant.* (after 1.4.71/836; see Textual Notes)
1.4.79.1/844.1 *Enter two Murtherers.*
1.4.87.1/852.1 *Reads*
1.4.96/861 *Exit.* (after 1.4.94/859)
1.4.264/1027 *Stabs him.* (after 'serue' (F 'do'))
1.4.265.1/1028.1 *Exit.*
1.4.268.1/1031.1 *Enter 1.Murtherer*
1.4.273/1036 *Exit.*
1.4.278/1041 *Exit*
2.1.0.1-4/1041.1-3 *Flourish.* | *Enter the King sicke, the Queene, Lord Marquesse* | *Dorset, Riuers, Hastings, Catesby,* | *Buckingham, Wooduill.*
2.1.40.1/1081.1 *Embrace*
2.1.44.1-2/1085.1 *Enter Ratcliffe, and Gloster.* (after 2.1.46/1087)
2.1.80.1/1121.1 *They* | *all start.* (opposite 2.1.80-1/1121-2)
2.1.95.1/1136.1 *Enter Earle of Derby.*
2.1.135.1/1176 *Exeunt some with K. & Queen.*
2.1.142/1183 *exeunt.*
2.2.0.1-2/1183.1-2 *Enter the old Dutchesse of Yorke, with the two* | *children of Clarence.*
2.2.33.1/1216.1 *Enter the Queene with her haire about her ears,* | *Riuers & Dorset after her.*
2.2.88.1-3/1271.1-2 *Enter Richard, Buckingham, Derbie, Ha-|stings, and Ratcliffe.* (after Additional Passage D)
2.2.115.1/1298.1 *Exeunt.* | *Manet Buckingham, and Richard.* (after 'With all our hearts'; see Textual Notes)
2.2.124.1/1307.1 *Exeunt*
2.3.0.1-2/1307.2-3 *Enter one Citizen at one doore, and another at* | *the other.*
2.3.5.1/1312.1 *Enter another Citizen.*
2.3.47/1354 *Exeunt.*
2.4.0.1-2/1354.1-2 *Enter Arch-bishop, yong Yorke, the Queene,* | *and the Dutchesse.*
2.4.37/1391 *Enter a Messenger.*
2.4.72/1426 *Exeunt*
3.1.0.1-4/1426.1-4 *The Trumpets sound.* | *Enter yong Prince, the Dukes of Glocester, and Buckingham,* | *Lord Cardinall, with others.*
3.1.16.1/1442.1 *Enter Lord Maior.* (after 3.1.17/1443)
3.1.23.1/1449.1 *Enter Lord Hastings.*
3.1.60.1/1486.1 *Exit Cardinall and Hastings.* (after 3.1.59/1485)
3.1.94.1-2/1520.1 *Enter young Yorke, Hastings, and Cardinall.*
3.1.149.1-2/1575.1-2 *A Senet. Exeunt Prince, Yorke, Hastings, and Dorset.* | *Manet Richard, Buckingham, and Catesby.*
3.1.187.1/1613.1 *Exit Catesby.*
3.1.197/1623 *Exeunt.*
3.2.0.1/1623.1 *Enter a Messenger to the Doore of Hastings.*
3.2.1.1/1624.1 *Enter Lord Hastings.* (after 3.2.2/1625)
3.2.31/1654 *Exit.*
3.2.31.1/1654.1 *Enter Catesby.*
3.2.68.1/1691.1 *Enter Lord Stanley.*
3.2.90.1/1713.1 *Enter a Pursuiuant.*
3.2.91.1/1714.1 *Exit Lord Stanley, and Catesby.*
3.2.102.1/1725.1 *Throwes him his Purse.*
3.2.103/1726 *Exit Pursuiuant.*
3.2.103.1/1726.1 *Enter a Priest.*
3.2.107.2/1730.2 *Enter Buckingham.* (after 'Lordship'; see Textual Notes)
3.2.118.1/1741.1 *Exeunt.*
3.3.0.1-3/1741.2-4 *Enter Sir Richard Ratcliffe, with Halberds, carrying* | *the Nobles to death at Pomfret.*
3.3.24/1765 *Exeunt.*
3.4.0.1-3/1765.1-3 *Enter Buckingham, Darby, Hastings, Bishop of Ely,* | *Norfolke, Ratcliffe, Louell, with others,* | *at a Table.*
3.4.20.1/1785.1 *Enter Gloucester.*

RICHARD III

3.4.34/1799.1 *Exit Bishop.*
3.4.41.1/1806.1 *Exeunt.*
3.4.45.1/1810.1 *Enter the Bishop of Ely.*
3.4.58.1/1823.1 *Enter Richard, and Buckingham.*
3.4.79.1/1844.1 *Exeunt.* (after 3.4.78/1843)
3.4.79.1/1844.1 *Manet Louell and Ratcliffe, with the | Lord Hastings.*
3.4.107/1872 *Exeunt.*
3.5.0.1-3/1872.1-2 *Enter Richard, and Buckingham, in rotten Armour, | maruellous ill-fauoured.*
3.5.11.1/1883.1 *Enter the Maior, and Catesby.* (after 3.5.12/1884; see Textual Notes)
3.5.19.1/1891.1 *Enter Louell and Ratcliffe, with Hastings Head.*
3.5.69.1/1941.1 *Exit Maior.*
3.5.100/1972.1 *Exit Buckingham.*
3.5.104/1976 *Exeunt.*
3.6.0.1/1976.1 *Enter a Scriuener.*
3.6.14/1990 *Exit.*
3.7.0.1-2/1990.1 *Enter Richard and Buckingham at seuerall Doores.*
3.7.55.2/2045.2 *Enter the Maior, and Citizens.*
3.7.57.1/2047.1 *Enter Catesby.*
3.7.70/2060 *Exit.*
3.7.82.1/2072.1 *Enter Catesby.*
3.7.91.1/2081.1 *Exit.*
3.7.94.1/2084.1 *Enter Richard aloft, betweene two Bishops.*
3.7.210.1/2200.1 *Exeunt.* (after 'Buckingham'; see Textual Notes)
3.7.216.1/2206.1 *Enter Buckingham, and the rest.*
3.7.237.1-2/2227.1-2 *Exeunt.*
4.1.0.1-4/2227.3-6 *Enter the Queene, Anne Duchesse of Gloucester, the | Duchesse of Yorke, and Marquesse Dorset.*
4.1.11.1/2238.1 *Enter the Lieutenant.*
4.1.27/2254.1 *Exit Lieutenant.*
4.1.27.1/2254.2 *Enter Stanley.*
4.1.91.1, 4.1.92.1, 4.1.93.1, 4.1.96.1/2318.1, 2319.1, 2320.1, 2323.1 *Exeunt.* (after 4.1.96/2323)
4.2.0.1-3/2323.2-4 *Sound a Sennet. Enter Richard in pompe, Buck-|ingham, Catesby, Ratcliffe, Louel.*
4.2.3.1-2/2326.1 *Sound.*
4.2.27/2350 *Exit Buck.*
4.2.42.1/2365.1 *Exit.*
4.2.46.1/2369.1 *Enter Stanley.*
4.2.67.1/2390.1 *Enter Tyrrel.*
4.2.80.1/2403.1 *Whispers.*
4.2.84.1/2407.1 *Enter Buckingham.* (after 'Exit'; see next and Textual Notes)
4.2.85/2408 *Exit.* (after 4.2.83/2406)
4.2.121.1/2444.1 *Exit.*
4.2.125.1/2448.1 *Exit.*
4.3.0.1/2448.2 *Enter Tyrrel.*
4.3.22.1/2470.1 *Enter Richard.*
4.3.43.1/2491.1 *Enter Ratcliffe.*
4.3.57.1/2505.1 *Exeunt.*
4.4.0.1/2505.2 *Enter old Queene Margaret.*
4.4.7.1/2512.1 *Enter Dutchesse and Queene.* (after 4.4.8/2513)
4.4.125.1/2630.1 *Exit Margaret.*
4.4.135.1-2/2640.1-2 *Enter King Richard, and his Traine.*
4.4.151.1/2656.1 *Flourish. Alarums.*
4.4.196.1/2701.1 *Exit.*
4.4.361.1/2866.1 *Exit Q.* (after 4.4.360/2865)
4.4.362.1/2867.1 *Enter Ratcliffe.* (after 4.4.363/2868)
4.4.383/2888 *Exit.*
4.4.387/2892 *Enter Lord Stanley.*
4.4.428/2933.1 *Exit Stanley.*
4.4.428.1/2933.2 *Enter a Messenger.*
4.4.433.1/2938.1 *Enter another Messenger.*
4.4.436.1/2941.1 *Enter another Messenger.*

4.4.438.1/2943.1 *He striketh him.*
4.4.448.1/2953.1 *Enter another Messenger.*
4.4.461.1/2966.1 *Enter Catesby.*
4.4.469.1/2974.1 *Florish. Exeunt*
4.5.0.1-2/2974.2-3 *Enter Derby, and Sir Christopher.*
4.5.20/2994 *Exeunt*
5.1.0.1-2/2994.1-2 *Enter Buckingham with Halberds, led | to Execution.*
5.1.29.1/3023.1 *Exeunt Buckingham with Officers.*
5.2.0.1-3/3023.2-3 *Enter Richmond, Oxford, Blunt, Herbert, and | others, with drum and colours.*
5.2.24.1/3047.1 *Exeunt Omnes.*
5.3.0.1-3/3047.2-3 *Enter King Richard in Armes, with Norfolke, Ratcliffe, | and the Earle of Surrey.*
5.3.18.1/3065.1 *Exeunt*
5.4.0.1-3/3065.2-3 *Enter Richmond, Sir William Brandon, Ox-|ford, and Dorset.*
5.4.26.1/3091.1 *They withdraw into the Tent.*
5.5.0.1-3/3091.2-3 *Enter Richard, Ratcliffe, Norfolke, & Catesby.*
5.5.11/3102 *Exit*
5.5.31.1/3122.1 *Exit Ratclif.*
5.5.31.3-4/3122.3-4 *Enter Derby to Richmond in his Tent.*
5.5.60.1/3151.1 *Exeunt. Manet Richmond.*
5.5.70/3161 *Sleeps.*
5.5.70.1/3161.1 *Enter the Ghost of Prince Edward, Sonne to | Henry the sixt.*
5.5.75/3166 *to Richm.*
5.5.77.1/3168.1 *Enter the Ghost of Henry the sixt.*
5.5.82/3173 *To Richm.*
5.5.84.1/3175.1 *Enter the Ghost of Clarence.*
5.5.90/3181 *To Richm.* (omitting speech-prefix)
5.5.92.2-3/3183.1 *Enter the Ghosts of Riuers, Gray, and Vaughan.*
5.5.97/3189 *to Richm.*
5.5.99.2/3190.2 *Enter the Ghosts of the two yong Princes.* (see Textual Notes for F's transposition, from Q3, of 5.5.99.2-107/3190.2-3198)
5.5.104/3195 *to Richm.*
5.5.107.2/3198.2 *Enter the Ghost of Lord Hastings.*
5.5.111/3202 *to Rich.*
5.5.112.2/3203.2 *Enter the Ghost of Anne, his Wife.*
5.5.113/3204 *to Rich.*
5.5.118/3209.1 *to Richm.*
5.5.120.1/3211.1 *Enter the Ghost of Buckingham.*
5.5.121/3212 *to Rich.*
5.5.127/3218 *to Richm.*
5.5.130.1/3221.1 *Richard starts out of his dreame.*
5.5.160.1/3251.1 *Enter Ratcliffe.*
5.5.176.1/3267.1 *Exeunt Richard & Ratliffe,*
5.5.176.2-3/3267.2 *Enter the Lords to Richmond sitting | in his Tent.*
5.5.190.1/3281.1 *His Oration to his Souldiers.*
5.6.0.1-2/3315.3 *Enter King Richard, Ratcliffe, and Catesby.*
5.6.5.1/3320.1 *Clocke strikes.* (after 'there', 5.6.6/3321)
5.6.17.1/3332.1 *Enter Norfolke.*
5.6.67/3382 *Drum afarre off*
5.6.71.1/3386.1 *Enter a Messenger.*
5.7.0.1/3396.1 *Alarum, excursions. Enter Catesby.*
5.7.6.1/3402.1 *Alarums. | Enter Richard.*
5.8.0.1-3/3409.1-2 *Alarum, Enter Richard and Richmond, they fight, Richard | is slaine.*
5.8.0.3-6/3409.3-5 *Retreat, and Flourish. Enter Richmond, Derby bearing the | Crowne, with diuers other Lords.*
5.8.41.1/3450.1 *Exeunt*

Additional Passages

G.3.1 *Exit.*

VENUS AND ADONIS

The first known edition (Q1; STC 22354), printed by Shakespeare's fellow townsman Richard Field in 1593, survives in only one copy. It had been entered in the Stationers' Register on 18 April:

Richard Feild / Entred for his copie Vnder thandẹ
  of the Archbiſſhop of Cant
  and mr warden Stirrop, a booke
  intuled Venus and Adonis.
Aſſigned our to
Mr Harriſon ſenr
25 Iunij 1594

It was sold by John Harrison, and a note by the entry records 'Assigned our to | Mr Harrison senr | 25 Iunij 1594'. It was frequently reprinted. We record the only two substantive variants (ll. 56, 123), other than obvious errors, in Q2 (1594); both occur in the inner forme of Sheet B, and could be Q1 press variants passed on to Q2. The poem is well printed, probably from Shakespeare's manuscript. Notes to the modern-spelling text are indicated by '(M)'.

S.W.W./(G.T.)

WORK CITED
Maxwell, J. C., ed., *The Poems*, New (1966)

TEXTUAL NOTES

8 (M) fields'] Q (fields)
56 feathers] Q1; feather Q2
123 are] Q1; be Q2
193 shines but] Q; *altered to* ſhineth *but by hand in the unique copy*
198 earthly] Q1; this earthly Q8. The unique copy of Q1 has 'this' added by hand.
208 Speake,] Q7; ~∧ Q1
466 losse] HUDSON 2 (W. S. Walker); loue Q. Maxwell emends, conjecturing that Q's 'loue' was 'presumably caught from l. 464'. Other editors tend to retain Q while admitting that emendation is 'tempting' (Riverside). Without it, Q's 'bankrout' is pointless.
621 fret,] Q5; ~∧ Q1
654 aire] Q; earth This edition *conj*. A puff of air can extinguish a flame; otherwise air feeds rather than abates fire. An unconscious substitution is possible.

680 (M) overshoot] Q (ouer-ſhut). A few editors, including Riverside (glossing 'conclude') follow Q, but that gives poor sense; *OED* records 'overshoot' frequently from the 14th c., gives 'overshut' only as a variant of it, and records 'shut' as a 16th- and 17th-c. spelling of 'shoot'.
745 not] Q. Editors do not comment, but an intensifier (e.g. 'e'en') seems required; perhaps Shakespeare's logical error.
748 th'impartiall] Q2; the th'impartiall Q1
754 sons] Q2; ſuns Q1
832 deeply] Q; doubly WHITE (W. S. Walker)
873 (M) twine] Q (twin'd; *possibly past tense*)
1013 stories,] MALONE (Theobald); ~, Q
1031 as] Q3; are Q1
1054 was] Q7; had Q1

INCIDENTALS

111 obayed,] ~.   147 disheueld] diſheueled   185 Sowring] So wring   235 Within] Q1 *c.w.*, Q2; Witin Q1 *text*   256 from] ftom   290 proportiond] proportioned   301 and] aud   372 thee.] ~∧   393 But] Bnt   406 thee.] ~∧   432 woūding.] ~∧   476 fingers,] ~.   638 naught] nanght   678 hoūds.] ~∧   834 so.] ~,   876 brake.] ~,   1068 troubled.] ~∧

THE RAPE OF LUCRECE

The poem was well printed, probably from Shakespeare's manuscript, by Richard Field in 1594 (STC 22345). The Stationers' Register for 9 May reads: 'Mʳ Harriſon Senʳ Entred for his copie Vnder thand of Mʳ | Cawood Warden, a booke intituled | the Ravyſhement of Lucrece'. John Harrison is named as publisher on the title-page. The Argument may not be by Shakespeare. Though the title-page calls the poem *Lucrece*, the head title and running titles are 'The Rape of Lucrece', which probably stood in the manuscript. Proof-corrections noted by Rollins (New Variorum) in sheets B and I, and on K1 (24, 31, 50, 125, 126, 1182, 1335, 1350) are recorded below; we cannot tell whether Shakespeare made them; at 1350, it is unclear which is the corrected state. Quotation marks set off some of the more aphoristic lines; we reproduce these in the old-spelling text only.

S.W.W./(G.T.)

WORKS CITED

Gildon, Charles, ed., *Poems* (1710)
Maxwell, J. C., ed., *The Poems*, New (1966)

TEXTUAL NOTES

Title *The Rape of Lucrece*] Q (*head title, running titles: all capitals*); LVCRECE. Q (*title-page*); a book intituled the Rauyshment of Lucrece S.R.
24 mornings] Qb; morning Qa
31 Appologie] Qa; Apologies Qb. See Maxwell, 148.
50 Colatium . . . ariued] Qa; Colatia . . . arriued Qb. The correct form is 'Collatia', as the press-corrector may have known; or Shakespeare may have been inconsistent.
56 (M) or] Q (ore); *sometimes interpreted* o'er
57–8 entituled, . . . doues,] GILDON; ~, . . . ~, Q
125 himselfe betakes] Qa; themſelues betake Qb
126 wakes] Qa; wake Qb
347 (M) hour—] Q (howre.)
352 resolution] Q; dauntless resolution CAPELL (*conj.*); constant resolution G.T. *conj.* Either 'résolútion' rhymes with 'ábsolútion' or a foot is missing; 'constant resolution' appears at *Henry V* 2.4.35/891.
425 (M) Slaked] Q (Slakt)
550 blows] MALONE; blow Q
650 soueraigne, . . . hast,] MALONE; ~, . . . ~, Q
755 (M) in] Q; = e'en G.T. *conj.*
800 the] Q (*most copies*); ˏhe Q (*Elizabethan Club, Yale copy*)
950 (M) oak's] Q (oakes)
950 blemish] This edition (G.T.); cheriſh Q; perish JOHNSON. Like many editors since Warburton, Maxwell 'can scarcely believe the text is sound, as one would expect some action hostile to springs to balance "To dry . . . sap"'. Maxwell nevertheless follows Q, supposing that Shakespeare 'rather carelessly slipped in an example of the more beneficent side of Time's activity . . .'. The rhetoric of the stanza is against Q, and editors might have been readier to emend if they had thought of a more plausible substitute. Neither 'perish' nor 'blemish' is a likely source of graphical error, but 'blemish' makes good sense, is used by Shakespeare, and might be misread as 'cherish' in a blotted or smudged manuscript.
1182 by] Qb; for Qa
1229 inforst,] Q4; ~, Q1
1236 (M) drops'] Q (drops)
1258 (M) full-filled] Q (fulfild)
1263 insue,] Q3; ~. Q1
1316 stain's] This edition (G.T.); ſtain'd Q. Q makes it seem that Lucrece's excuse for what has happened is itself defiled, whereas she means 'coloured with blood the excuse for her stain, her dishonour'.
1335 blast] Qb; blaſts Qa
1350 this patterne of the] Q (*some copies*); the patterne of this Q (*other copies*)
1475 Thine] COLLIER; Thy Q. 'Thy eye' (1475) at the beginning of the line clearly corresponds with 'thine eye' (1476) at the end of the line, and error in 1475 would be particularly easy after the compositor had set 'Thy heat' at the beginning of 1473. (This is the only example in *Lucrece* of *thy* or *my* before the vowel-sound *eye-*.)
1544 armed, to] COLLIER; armed to Q; armed; so MALONE. Some editors take 'beguild' as a variant of 'beguile'. Collier's reading provides the right parallelism between 'too beguiled' and 'yet defiled'; *beguiled* means 'concealed or disguised by guile' (*OED*).
1546 vice: . . . cherish,] Q5; ~, . . . ~: Q1
1662 wreathed] DYCE 2 (W. S. Walker); wretched Q
1680 on] Q1; one Q3
1713 in it] MALONE (Capell MS); it in Q
1832 abhominations,] Q3; ~. Q1

INCIDENTALS

1 besiegd] besieged   74 kild,] ~.   111 heaud-vp] heaued-vp   129 resoluing,] ~. Q   130 abstaining.] ~, Q
163 sleepe] ſleeep   188 slaughtred] ſlaughtered   355 dissolution] diſſolution   440 scale,] ~.   482 conquerd] conquered
515 slay,] ~.   877 traytors] rraytors   883 mak'st] makeſt   884 blowst] bloweſt   922 inclination,] ~.   1122 feathred] feathered   1134 skill.] ~,   1247 smoothnesse,] ~;   1249 remaine,] Q3; ~. Q1   1254 withred] withered
1486 sounds,] ~;(?)   1498 borrow.] ~,   1537 tooke.] ~,   1707 poyson'd] poyſoned   1761 bare-bon'd] bare bon'd(?)

THE COMEDY OF ERRORS

The First Folio is the first and only authoritative edition (F); the play was entered in the Stationers' Register along with the other titles original to F. *The Comedy of Errors* there appears after four plays apparently set from transcripts by Ralph Crane, and before four plays set from earlier quarto editions. *The Comedy of Errors*, however, cannot derive from either kind of copy, and was probably set from an authorial manuscript of some kind.

Certainly, stage directions and speech-prefixes—as Chambers (*Shakespeare*, i. 306-7), Greg (*Folio*, 200-2), and McKerrow all demonstrated—betray features which are more likely to have originated with the author than anyone else. No fewer than three distinct characters (among them Egeon) are referred to as '*Marchant*', '*Mer.*', or '*Mar.*' in the speech-prefixes. On his first entrance Antipholus of Syracuse is cited as '*Antipholis Erotes*', a designation resulting at 2.2.14/392 in the prefix '*E. Ant.*', although elsewhere '*E.*' is used as the abbreviation for '*Ephesian*' in headings for Antipholus, Dromio, and Merchant of Ephesus. Other stage directions offer information of no apparent stage utility. Thus, there is an entry at 4.4.40.1-2/1230.1-2 for '*a Schoole-master, call'd Pinch*', although his occupation nowhere receives mention in the dialogue. The direction '*Enter Adriana, wife to Antipholis Sereptus*' (2.1.0.1-2/263.1-2) provides information about her status that the book-keeper could very well manage without; yet one can readily see the playwright setting it down. The direction at 5.1.332.1/1681.1, '*All gather to see them*', following the appearance of the Abbess with Antipholus and Dromio of Syracuse, suggests an authorial solicitude for the impact of a dramatic entry upon the assembled cast.

Other examples of such inconsistencies and superfluities have been noted by recent editors, and form the basis of the orthodox view that the directions and prefixes are authorial: a scribe (or even an author) preparing a fair copy would probably have regularized many of these features. But Paul Werstine has pointed out that such authorial papers might themselves be used as a playbook. He shows that the extent of such inconsistencies has been exaggerated, that some may be compositorial in origin, and that similar 'deficiencies' can be found in extant prompt-books. Nevertheless, there are difficulties with this alternative hypothesis: Werstine is perhaps prone to lay too much blame upon the compositors, and to assume whenever compositorial error is possible it is also probable. He supposes that the players' official 'book' was supplied to the printers—which, though not impossible, would certainly be unusual. He claims that 'the book could be sacrificed in the printing of the Folio with no loss to the company. Should they have wanted to perform the play again, their playbook was available in print'—but the text in print did not contain the Revels' Office licence, which was the playbook's chief value to the company. Werstine objects that transcripts were expensive; but at least five Folio comedies are acknowledged to have been set from transcripts, and early in his career Shakespeare himself might well have been expected to supply the company with a fair copy of his work (which could then be marked up as a prompt-book). More seriously, Werstine finds no evidence in the text of use in the theatre: actors' names, duplicated directions, isolated extra-syntactical calls for essential properties, warning directions. He in fact goes out of his way convincingly to discredit the few pieces of such evidence hitherto advanced by editors. We are thus left with a text which shows much evidence of authorial practice, but no evidence of theatrical use, and little concern for theatrical convenience. The orthodox view—that the play was set from foul papers—is thus probably correct.

The Folio's act divisions are difficult to attribute to undivided foul-paper copy: even if we reject Baldwin's learned defence of their academic respectability, no one would deny that the divisions are structurally intelligent, and seem beyond the normal capacity or brief of a printer. They might reflect Shakespeare's expectation of an Inns of Court performance; since such private performances would almost certainly employ intervals between the acts, and since that performance might have been the play's première and was certainly its earliest recorded performance, the presence of act divisions in (apparently) the foul papers has persuaded us to retain them as a genuine reflection of performances. (See Taylor's 'The Structure of Performance'.) Moreover, the superfluous '*Exeunt omnes*' at 4.4.147.1/1337.1 seems to us more likely to result from marginal annotation of a manuscript (Greg's conjecture) than from an unparalleled and remarkably stupid interpolation by the compositor (Foakes's alternative). It seems likely that a few annotations related (indeterminably) to performance had been made, at some stage, on the author's draft.

One peculiarity of the text of *Errors* is its use of location directions ('*Enter . . . from the Courtizans*', etc.); editors plausibly interpret these as evidence that three 'houses' (the Phoenix, Porcupine, and Priory) were indicated by signs at the back of the stage. Such conventionalized arcade settings were apparently used in academic and Court performances. The Folio does not provide such location directions consistently; we have supplied them, in square brackets, whenever it is clear that characters enter from or exit into one of the three locations.

McKerrow's work on this play had reached an advanced stage; after his death, Alice Walker made extensive notes of her own, indicating her agreements and disagreements with his decisions. In addition to these sources, we have been able to draw upon a draft text and commentary prepared by S. Schoenbaum in 1978.

G.T./(S.W.W.)

THE COMEDY OF ERRORS

WORKS CITED

Baldwin, T. W., *On the Compositional Genetics of 'The Comedy of Errors'* (1965)

Cuningham, Henry, ed., *The Comedy of Errors*, Arden (1907; rev. 1926)

Foakes, R. A., ed., *The Comedy of Errors*, Arden (1962)

Tannenbaum, S. A., 'Notes on *The Comedy of Errors*', *Shakespeare Jahrbuch*, 68 (1932), 117-18

Wells, Stanley, ed., *The Comedy of Errors*, New Penguin (1972)

Werstine, Paul, 'Editorial Sauciness: The Case of *Comedy of Errors*', Shakespeare Association of America seminar paper, 1985; revised as '"Foul Papers" and "Prompt-books": Printer's Copy for Shakespeare's *Comedy of Errors*', forthcoming in *SB*

Wilson, John Dover, ed., *The Comedy of Errors*, New (1922)

TEXTUAL NOTES

1.1.17/17 seene at] POPE; ſeene at any F

1.1.22/22 ransome] F2; to ∼ F1

1.1.38/38 me happy] This edition (*conj.* Shilletto, *N&Q*, 22 February 1873, p. 152); me F1; me too F2

1.1.41, 1.1.62, 1.2.1, 4.1.85, 4.1.94, 5.1.357, 5.1.361/41, 62, 159, 1001, 1010, 1706, 1710 Epidamnum] POPE; *Epidamium* F. This error occurs in the work of two compositors (B and C).

1.1.42/42 the] THEOBALD; he F

1.1.54/54 meane born] This edition; meane F1; poor meane F2; meaner DELIUS 2 (W. S. Walker). See Taylor, 'Metrifying'.

1.1.93/93 *Epidarus*] F; *Epidamnus* THEOBALD (*conj.*)

1.1.102/102 vpon] POPE; vp F1; up upon F2

1.1.116/116 barke] F2; backe F1

1.1.123/123 thee] F2; they F1

1.1.143-4/143-4 Which ... disanull, | Against ... dignity,] THEOBALD; Againſt ... dignity, | Which ... diſanull, F

1.1.151/151 helth] WILSON; helpe F; life ROWE; pelf CUNINGHAM

1.2.0.1/158.1 *from the Bay*] This edition; *not in* F. Compare 4.1.84.1/1000.1.

158.1 *Eraticus*] This edition (*conj.* Steevens); *Erotes* F; *Eratus* TANNENBAUM (*conj.*). For a (strained) defence of F, see Baldwin, pp. 104-5. '*Eratus*' would be an easier emendation, if it could mean 'wandering'; but if Shakespeare intended that meaning, his Latin must have been 'small' indeed.

1.2.0.2/158.2 *a Marchant ⌈of Ephesus⌉*] This edition; *a Marchant* F; *First Merchant* DYCE. This merchant, who knows Antipholus, should probably be distinguished from the one who enters the action at 4.1.0.1/916.1 (who knows neither Antipholus). In speech-prefixes at 1.2.24/182 and 1.2.32/190 he is '*E. Mar.*', which distinguishes him from the merchants later in the play; though the '*E.*' might stand for Ephesus or Epidamnum, everywhere else it is used for the former, which has therefore been preferred.

1.2.4/162 ariuall] F2; a riuall F1

1.2.40/198 (vnhappie)] F2; (vnhappie a) F1; (unhappy), ah, RIVERSIDE (McKerrow)

1.2.66/224 clocke] POPE; cooke F

1.2.102/260 liberties] HANMER; liberties F. 'As the author has been enumerating not acts but persons', Hanmer's emendation 'seems right' (Johnson).

2.1.0.1/263.1 *from the Phœnix*] This edition; *not in* F. All such directions in the text are editorial.

263.2 *Sureptus*] This edition (*conj.* Tannenbaum); *Sereptus* F

2.1.8/271 M^{rs}] This edition (S.W.W.); Maſter F. Influenced by the reading in the previous line, the compositor may have misexpanded an abbreviated form in his copy.

2.1.12/275 ill] F2; thus F1. McKerrow conjectures that manuscript 'yl' may have been misread 'y^s'.

2.1.60/323 thousand] F2; hundred F1

2.1.63/326 come home] THEOBALD 2; come F

2.1.67/330 thy mistresse not] This edition (*conj.* Seymour); not thy miſtreſſe F. Foakes defends F on the grounds that 'the force of the passage lies in the echoing "mistress" at the end of each phrase'; but in the preceding line 'mistresse' is followed by 'sir', and so there can be no obstacle to its being followed here by 'not'. F offers the more common (but less metrical) word order.

2.1.78/341 beating,] WELLS; ∼ : F

2.1.106 o'] F (a)

2.1.109/372 hir] This edition; his F. Without clear contextual guidance as to gender, the compositor may have misread 'hir' in his copy.

2.1.110-11/373-4 will,_∧_ | Weare gold,] THEOBALD; will, | Where gold,_∧_ F

2.1.111/374 and yet] This edition; and F. For a discussion of the complex crux in 2.1.109-11/372-4, see Taylor, 'The Comedy of Errors: A Textual and Sexual Crux' (forthcoming).

378.2 *Erraticus*] This edition (*conj.* Steevens); *Errotis* F. See the note to 158.1.

2.2.12/390 didst] F2; did didſt F1

2.2.81/459 men] POPE 2; them F

2.2.99/477 tyring] POPE; trying F

2.2.148/526 then] F; thou WALKER (*conj.*)

2.2.149/527 vnstain'd] HANMER (Theobald); diſtain'd F. Some editors retain F, glossing as 'unstained'; but the usual sense of *distained* in Shakespeare is the opposite: 'defiled', 'sullied'.

2.2.178/556 stronger] F4; ſtranger F1

2.2.189/567 ofred] CAPELL; free'd F1; sured WALKER (*conj.*)

2.2.193/571 Oafes] THEOBALD; Owles F. There is no need to suppose a missing word: tetrameters are common.

2.2.197/575 Drone] THEOBALD; *Dromio* F; drumble RIVERSIDE

2.2.198/576 not I] THEOBALD; I not F

3.1.31.1/631.1 *Enter ... Phœnix*] This edition; *not in* F. F provides entrance directions for Nell and Adriana, though they are also clearly 'within' the house; however the scene was staged, Dromio of Syracuse was probably as visible to an audience as the two women.

3.1.32/632 *within the Phœnix*] This edition; *not in* F; *within* ROWE. The scene can be staged in several ways; this formulation—used here throughout the scene—makes the situation clear for a reader, without prescribing a particular staging.

3.1.47/647 pate] This edition; face F; office FOAKES. Dromio's 'face' is not the target of his master's and mistress's anger, which is instead repeatedly aimed at his 'pate' (1.2.65/223; 1.2.82/240; 2.1.77/340; 2.2.221/599; 3.1.75/675). The conjectured c/t misreading is common; for p/f compare *Hamlet* 5.2.9/3276. The error might also have been assisted here by assimilation to 'place' at the end of 3.1.46/649.

3.1.47/647 an ame] WILSON; a name F

3.1.47.1/647.1, etc. *Nell*] This edition; *Luce* F. Of the two names given the character, 'Nell' (3.2.111/836) is inextricably bound up with the dialogue, as 'Luce' (throughout the scene) is not.

3.1.53-5/653-5 well. |⌈...⌉| EPHESIAN ANTIPHOLUS] This edition (Malone); ∼. | *Anti.* F. Rather than mark a lacuna, editors normally follow THEOBALD in emending 'hope' in 3.1.55/655 to 'trow'. More probably a line of doggerel rhyming with 'hope' has been omitted. We conjecture '*E. Dro.* Thou wouldst answer well to hanging, if I had a rope'. Compare *All's Well* 2.2.51-2/822-3 ('you would answere very well to a whipping'), spoken by a woman to a servant/clown.

3.1.76/676 you sir] F2; your ſir F1

3.1.90/690 this:] ROWE; ∼_∧_ F

3.1.90/690 her wisedome] ROWE; your wiſedome F

3.1.92/692 her] ROWE; your F

3.1.107/707 once] F2; *not in* F1

3.1.117 Porcupine] F (*Porpentine*). Similarly throughout.

3.1.124/724 *Exit Goldsmith*] This edition; *not in* F

3.1.124.1-2/724.1-2 Dromio . . . Porpentine] This edition; not in F. Dromio could exit earlier, but it seems desirable to indicate that the characters exit in three different directions.
3.2.1/725 LUCIANA] ROWE; *Iulia.* F
3.2.4/728 building] THEOBALD; buildings F
3.2.4/728 ruinous] CAPELL (Theobald); ruinate F
3.2.16/740 attaint] ROWE; attaine F
3.2.20/744 deeds is] F1; deeds are F2; deed is WALKER (conj.)
3.2.21/745 but] THEOBALD; not F
3.2.26/750 wife] F2; wiſe F1
3.2.46/770 sisters] F2; ſiſter F1
3.2.49/773 bed] F2; bud F1
3.2.49/773 them] CAPELL (Edwards); thee F
3.2.57/781 wher] ROWE 2; when F
3.2.66/790 am] F; mean POPE; aim CAPELL
3.2.104/829 for why?] F; forwhy$_\wedge$ WALKER (conj.)
3.2.111/836 &] THEOBALD (Thirlby); is F
3.2.124/849 her hand] This edition (conj. Walker); the hand F. Compare 'her buttockes', 'her forhead', 'her chin', 'her breth'. The compositor 'erroneously repeated the earlier "the" in the' speech (Walker).
4.1.17/933 her] ROWE; their F
4.1.87/1003 she] CAPELL; ſir ſhe F
4.1.98 ropës] F (ropes)
4.2.5/1034 case,] F4 (subs.); ~ ? F1
4.2.6/1035 Of,] F2; Oh, F1; On$_\wedge$ MCKERROW (conj.)
4.2.30/1059 How?] This edition (conj. McKerrow); ~ $_\wedge$ F. So understood, Luciana's question means 'What's the matter? Hast thou . . .'—Dromio, of course, answering as if the question had been asked as to the *manner* in which he lost his breath (McKerrow).
4.2.35/1064 Fairie] F; Fury POPE 2 (Theobald)
1067 lands] Fb; lans Fa
4.2.38 launds] Fb (lands)
4.2.47-8/1076-7 at, | That] F2; at. | Thus F. Both Folios place Luciana's exit between the two lines, which no doubt facilitated the misinterpretation.

4.2.60/1089 a be] STAUNTON; I be F
4.3.13/1107 redemption from] This edition; not in F; rid of THEOBALD. As Wilson noted, 'got rid of' is a later idiom. But Walker noted that 'One would expect a punning allusion to "redemption" (cf. [4.2.46/1075]) as a link between the gold for which he has been sent and the following "old Adam".'
4.3.27 Moorish] F (Moris). OED lists under 'Morris', but the etymology is 'moorish', and that form coexisted with 'morris'; 'Moorish' is clearly more helpful for a modern reader.
4.3.60/1154 you do] F2; do F1
4.3.61/1155 and] WHITE (Ritson); or F
4.3.65/1159 thou] F4; then F1
4.4.43/1233 to prophesie] DYCE; the propheſie F
4.4.81/1271 shame] F. 'All editors retain this, which however does not give very good sense. A misprinted "hame" (for "harme") might easily be miscorrected into "shame"' (McKerrow).
4.4.105/1295 those] ROWE; theſe F
4.4.114/1304 his] WELLS (Tannenbaum); this F
5.1.46/1395 much much] F2; much F1
5.1.49/1398 at] F2; of F1. The 'of' could have been caught from its identical position in the line above (Walker).
5.1.67/1416 glanced] F; glanc'd at POPE
5.1.119 point's] F (points). 'No one seems to have noticed that a dial does not point at anything, for the word definitely meant the flat plate of the sundial. Probably modern spelling should be "dial point's at", taking *point* to be the pointed shadow on the dial' (McKerrow).
5.1.122/1471 death] F3; depth F1
5.1.169/1518 MESSENGER] F2; not in F1
5.1.322/1671 bay] ROWE; boy F
5.1.348-53/1697-1702 DUKE Why . . . together.] F; *placed after* 5.1.363/1712 CAPELL
5.1.351/1700 his] COLLIER; her F
5.1.405/1754 nere] DYCE; are F
5.1.408/1757 ioy] RANN; go F
5.1.409/1758 Festiuitie] DYCE (Johnson); Natiuitie F; felicity HANMER

INCIDENTALS

130 labourd] laboured   291 sway.] ~$_\wedge$ 353 wit?] ~,   381 out.] ~$_\wedge$ 382 report,] ~.   854 chalkie] chalkle
952 Good] Cood   1037 spight.] ~$_\wedge$ 1134 Delay] Fb; delay Fa   1167 cherrie-stone] cherrie-|ſtone   1270 contraries] crontraries   1280 did.] ~:   1291 both.] ~$_\wedge$ 1298 him.] ~$_\wedge$ 1300 me?] ~,   1300 Iailor thou,] ~ ?
1380 stand.] ~:   1443 forth.] ~$_\wedge$ 1478 death.] ~$_\wedge$ 1549 dishonord] diſhonored   1658 extremity] e$_\wedge$tremity
1716 Lord.] ~$_\wedge$ 1761 imbarkt?] ~$_\wedge$ 1768 wife.] ~,

FOLIO STAGE DIRECTIONS

1.1.0.1-2/0.1-2 *Enter the Duke of Ephesus, with the Merchant of Siracusa, | Iaylor, and other attendants.*
1.1.158/158 *Exeunt.*
1.2.0.1-2/158.1-3 *Enter Antipholis Erotes, a Marchant, and Dromio.*
1.2.18/176.1 *Exit Dromio.*
1.2.32/190 *Exeunt.*
1.2.40.1/198.1 *Enter Dromio of Ephesus.*
1.2.94/252.1 *Exeunt Dromio Ep.*
1.2.105/263 *Exit.*
2.1.0.1-2/263.1-2 *Enter Adriana, wife to Antipholis Sereptus, with | Luciana her Sister.*
2.1.42.1/305.1 *Enter Dromio Eph.*
2.1.115.1/378.1 *Exit.*
2.2.0.1/378.2 *Enter Antipholis Errotis.*
2.2.6.1/384.1 *Enter Dromio Siracusia.*
2.2.23.1/401.1 *Beats Dro.*
2.2.111.1/489.1 *Enter Adriana and Luciana.* (after 2.2.112/490)
3.1.0.1-2/600.2-3 *Enter Antipholus of Ephesus, his man Dromio, Angelo the | Goldsmith, and Balthaser the Merchant.*

3.1.47.1/647.1 *Enter Luce.*
3.1.61.1/661.1 *Enter Adriana.*
3.1.124.1-2/724.1-2 *Exeunt.*
3.2.0.1-2/724.3-4 *Enter Iuliana, with Antipholus of Siracusia.*
3.2.70.1/794.1 *Exit.*
3.2.70.2/794.2 *Enter Dromio, Siracusia.*
3.2.161.1/886.1 *Exit*
3.2.170.1/895.1 *Enter Angelo with the Chaine.*
3.2.184/909 *Exit.*
3.2.191/916 *Exit.*
4.1.0.1-2/916.1 *Enter a Merchant, Goldsmith, and an Officer.*
4.1.13.1-2/929.1-2 *Enter Antipholus Ephes. Dromio from the Courtizans.*
4.1.21/937.1 *Exit Dromio*
4.1.84.1/1000.1 *Enter Dromio Sira. from the Bay.*
4.1.108.1/1024.1 *Exeunt*
4.1.113/1029 *Exit*
4.2.0.1/1029.1 *Enter Adriana and Luciana.*
4.2.28.1/1057.1 *Enter S. Dromio.*

THE COMEDY OF ERRORS

4.2.47/1076 Exit Luciana. (after 'at')
4.2.61.1/1090.1 Enter Luciana.
4.2.65.1/1094.1 Exit.
4.3.0.1/1094.2 Enter Antipholus Siracusia. (Fb reads Siracuſia; Fa Siracuſian)
4.3.11.1/1105.1 Enter Dromio. Sir.
4.3.44.1/1138.1 Enter a Curtizan.
4.3.80.1-2/1174.1 Exit.
4.4.0.1/1190.1 Enter Antipholus Ephes. with a Iailor.
4.4.7.1/1197.1 Enter Dromio Eph. with a ropes end.
4.4.40.1-2/1230.1-2 Enter Adriana, Luciana, Courtizan, and a Schoole-|master, call'd Pinch.
4.4.45.1/1235.1 Beats Dro.
4.4.106.2/1296.2-3 Enter three or foure, and offer to binde him: | Hee striues.
4.4.131.1-4/1321.1-3 Exeunt. Manet Offic. Adri. Luci. Courtizan
4.4.144.1-2/1334.1-2 Enter Antipholus Siracusia with his Rapier drawne, | and Dromio Sirac.
4.4.147.1/1337.1 Runne all out. (after 'bound againe')
4.4.147.1-2/1337.1-2 Exeunt omnes, as fast as may be, frighted.
4.4.159/1349 Exeunt

5.1.0.1/1349.1 Enter the Merchant and the Goldsmith.
5.1.9.1-2/1358.1-2 Enter Antipholus and Dromio againe.
5.1.32.1-2/1381.1-2 They draw. Enter Adriana, Luciana, Courtezan, & others.
5.1.37.1-2/1386.1-2 Exeunt to the Priorie.
5.1.37.3/1386.3 Enter Ladie Abbesse.
5.1.130.1-3/1479.1-3 Enter the Duke of Ephesus, and the Merchant of Siracuse | bare head, with the Headsman, & other | Officers.
5.1.168.1/1517.1 Enter a Messenger.
5.1.184.1/1533.1 Cry within.
5.1.186.1-2/1535.1-2 Enter Antipholus, and E. Dromio of Ephesus. (after 5.1.190/1539)
5.1.282.1/1631.1 Exit one to the Abbesse.
5.1.331.1-3/1680.1-3 Enter the Abbesse with Antipholus Siracusa, | and Dromio Sir.
5.1.332.1/1681.1 All gather to see them.
5.1.410.1-2/1759.1-2 Exeunt omnes. Manet the two Dromio's and | two Brothers.
5.1.416.1/1765.1 Exit
5.1.430/1778 Exeunt.

LOVE'S LABOUR'S LOST

The first surviving edition is the quarto of 1598 (*BEPD* 150), printed by W[illiam] W[hite] for Cuthbert Burby, and described on the title-page as 'A | PLEASANT | Conceited Comedie | CALLED, | Loues labors loſt. | As it was preſented before her Highnes | this laſt Chriſtmas. | Newly corrected and augmented | *By W. Shakeſpere.*' There is no Stationers' Register entry. Burby was to publish the good quarto of *Romeo and Juliet* the following year. This claims to be *Newly corrected, augmented, and amended;* the resemblance in wording has led to the conjecture that the quarto of *Love's Labour's Lost*, like Q2 of *Romeo and Juliet*, had been preceded by a bad quarto, now lost. This is possible, but it seems to us more likely that the title-page claim is a publisher's exaggeration, and that Q is a straight reprint of an earlier quarto which has not survived; for Burby's quarto gives every sign of having been printed, whether directly or at one remove, from foul papers. Speech-prefixes are highly irregular, some demonstrably wrong; directions are often inadequate; above all, the text incorporates both unrevised and revised versions of at least two passages which must derive from the author's papers. (And there are other passages which we may feel Shakespeare *should* have revised, e.g. 5.2.747-69/2500-22, with their tangled syntax.)

Price identified four compositors at work in Q; Werstine (1978), in an article published almost simultaneously, found only two; the two reconstructions almost never overlap. Werstine's analysis, making extensive use of evidence from other books printed by White, is perhaps the more likely to be correct, but in the circumstances allocation of pages to workmen is even more than usually arbitrary. More significant than the exact attribution of pages is Werstine's more recent demonstration (1984) that the pattern of spellings in Q strongly resembles that in White's reprints, as opposed to his texts printed from manuscript copy. This evidence, among much else, undermines Draudt's attempt to argue that 'Printer's Copy for the Quarto of *Love's Labour's Lost* (1598)' was a combination of foul papers and a heavily annotated exemplar of an earlier, lost 'bad quarto'. Draudt simply assumes that there was only one compositor (p. 121); he explains as the result of 'a change of copy' inconsistencies in speech-prefixes and character names of a kind which occur often in texts apparently printed from foul papers; he makes no allowance for the possibility that Shakespeare's ideas about the names and roles of characters might be least secure at the beginning of the play, but become more so in the course of composition. Draudt takes the 'absence of gross errors' in sheets A-C (1.1.1-3.1.100/1-833) as evidence of tidier copy (p. 123); the following collations reveal no such disparity between the first sheets and the remainder of the play. Similarly, the distribution of variants in character names does not fit the pattern he conjectures: he admits that it does not work at all for Biron, Longueville, Dumaine, Boyet, or Costard, whereas for the variants Princess/Queen, Armado/Braggart, and Boy/Page there are in each case one or more exceptions, and for Jaquenetta the single exception occurs in the later 'foul paper' area of Q. Draudt also relies on Price's conjectures about the varying speed of presswork; such conjectures are, as D. F. McKenzie had demonstrated a decade before, highly unreliable. Finally, Draudt leans heavily upon the allegedly parallel cases of *Romeo and Juliet* Q2 and *Hamlet* Q2. He insists on the similarity of *Romeo*'s title-page, while ignoring cases like *Richard III* Q3, where the title-page's 'Newly augmented' is demonstrably misleading. He conjectures that Burby secured his copyright for Q by previous publication of a lost 'bad' quarto, though he might just as easily have done so by previous publication of a lost 'good' quarto. He takes the occurrence of part-roman stage directions on sheets A-D of Q as evidence of bad quarto influence, noting that such mixed directions also occur in the 'bad' quarto of *Hamlet* (p. 122); but they also occur in the 'good' quarto of *A Midsummer Night's Dream*; moreover, they do *not* occur in Q2 of *Hamlet*, and hence there is in this respect no parallel at all between Q *Love's Labour's Lost* and Q2 *Hamlet*. Both Q2 *Romeo* and Q *Love's Labour's Lost* contain 'duplicated passages' (p. 124); but these occur in *Romeo* in a part of the text apparently set from foul papers, and hence support the hypothesis that Q *Love's Labour's Lost* was set from foul-paper rather than bad quarto copy. Although the use as copy of a mixture of bad quarto and foul papers cannot be disproven, it remains to be proven, and all evidence so far produced is compatible with the simpler hypothesis that Q is a straight reprint of a lost 'good' quarto, itself set directly from Shakespeare's foul papers.

Burby's claim to be presenting an 'augmented' text has been upheld by Lever's belief that in the final songs Shakespeare drew on Gerard's *Herbal*, published in 1597; but this claim is denied—correctly, we think—by Kerrigan ('Shakespearean Revision'). Nor can we easily credit the claim that Burby's text is in any sense 'corrected'; the quarto abounds in gross errors. Punctuation appears to be largely compositorial. Press variants were first collated by Werstine's 'Variants'. Versions of 4.2.106-19/1184-97, 4.3.57-70/1300-13, and 4.3.99-118/1342-61 appeared in *The Passionate Pilgrim* (1599); the last of these extracts also appeared in *England's Helicon* (1600).

The Folio text (F) is a reprint of Q from a copy which had, we believe, been somewhat cursorily corrected from a playhouse manuscript (see Wells, 'The Copy'). Certainly, not all of the variation between Q and F can be attributed to the Folio compositors (B, C, and D). Draudt argues that these variants originate with some sort of unauthorized 'editor'; it seems to us more likely that they result, as Folio variants in *The Merchant of Venice* and *A Midsummer Night's Dream* and *Much Ado About Nothing* demonstrably do, from sporadic consultation of a playhouse manuscript. Though generally inferior even to Q, F yields a few valuable readings, and suggests that, as we should expect, the text as acted had undergone some revision. It is also at least theoretically possible, if the lost Quarto was a 'good' one, that F was set from it, rather than the 1598 text we know.

The most difficult editorial problems centre on Sc. 3/2.1, where there is an apparent confusion between Katherine and Rosaline. Wilson's solution (indebted to Capell and H. B. Charlton) requires so much effort to understand that a reader who masters it is predisposed to reward himself with belief. It requires the supposition that Shakespeare intended the ladies to be masked. We prefer the solution offered by John Kerrigan ('Shakespeare at Work'), which does away with the masking theory and attributes the source of the confusion to vacillation on Shakespeare's part about the ladies' names. Kerrigan supposes that, in his first draft, Shakespeare wrote the duologue between Biron and Katherine (114-27/591-604), intending Katherine to be the name of Biron's mistress, but did not write the interchange between Biron and Rosaline printed later in the scene (180-93/656-70). Revising, he decided to substitute for the duologue that he had already written a different one, in which he used the name Rosaline, by this time established in his mind as the name of Biron's beloved; but he wrote it on a separate sheet of paper which was misplaced in the printing. We accept the notion as to the source of the confusion, but are somewhat sceptical that the 'misplaced' passage should fit as well as it does where it was, supposedly by accident, printed. We need postulate no substantive revision if we suppose simply that, in writing the lines as they stand in Q, Shakespeare paired Biron with Katherine and at a later stage, having decided on a change of name, altered the prefix correctly at 180-93/656-70, but failed to make the necessary changes elsewhere. (G.T. adds the possibility that in the prefixes at 181-92/658-69 'Ros.' is an expansion of a misreading of 'Ka.' as 'Ro.', perhaps influenced by the mistaken supposition that the speaker is the 'Rosalin' of 195/672.) Alternatively, the second duologue may be a later addition, composed to give greater prominence to Biron and Rosaline after Shakespeare had made his final decision about her name. This would entail a change of intention about the lords: Shakespeare may have originally intended them to remain on stage after Navarre's *Exit*. (sic), but then have imagined all but Biron leaving with Navarre; it would have been easy enough both for him to add 'Enter Dumaine' (193.1/671.1) and 'Enter Berowne' (208.1/685.1), and to forget to add an entry for Longueville (196.1/673.1). No certainty is possible; but this hypothesis permits us to print both exchanges as part of the text, while leaving it open to a director to make any adjustments that he may feel to be appropriate.

Another problem, more easily solved than explained, relates to the frequent confusion in 4.2's speech-prefixes between Holofernes and Nathaniel (see notes to 66/1145 ff.). When these characters first appear, they are named 'Holofernes, the *Pedant* and *Nathaniel*' in the direction (4.2.0.1-2/1081.1-2); the first prefix for Holofernes is '*Ped.*'; Nathaniel is '*Nat.*', then '*Curat Nath.*', after which personal names only are used up to 120/1198, though evident confusion has begun at 66/1145. A clue that this confusion derives from the author is found at 135/1214, when, in dialogue, 'Sir' (appropriate to the curate, Nathaniel) is used along with 'Holofernes'. An effort to avoid this confusion, G.T. suggests, would explain the reversion to the generic *Pedant* at 120/1198 and for most of the rest of the scene. Moreover, in the transition, as it were, between the use of personal and generic prefixes, redundant prefixes occur twice, where what should be one speech is divided between '*Nath.*' and '*Ped.*' (120-1/1198-9, 130-5/1208-14). This suggests a marginal note changing the attribution from the more potentially confusing personal to the simpler generic names; it also, in the mistaken identification of Nathaniel with the Pedant, perpetuates the confusion evidenced in 'Sir Holofernes' at 135/1214. After this scene, Shakespeare kept himself straight by using only generic names as prefixes for Holofernes and Nathaniel.

It has long been recognized that Q includes two unrevised passages in 4.3/Sc. 7. We print them as Additional Passages, along with another first suggested as a draft in the Riverside edition.

Love's Labour's Lost includes numerous scraps of Latin, printed with many errors in Q. It is impossible to determine with absolute confidence which errors should be attributed to the compositor, which to Shakespeare, and which to his characters. We have corrected the errors except where they seem crass enough to be interpreted as comic blunders on the part of the speaker; Dr J. W. Binns, of the University of York, has offered generous and valuable advice. In Q, the play is undivided; the Folio marks act divisions; scene divisions are editorial.

S.W.W./(G.T.)

WORKS CITED

David, Richard, ed., *Love's Labour's Lost*, Arden (1951)
Draudt, Manfred, 'Printer's Copy for the Quarto of *Love's Labour's Lost* (1598)', *The Library*, VI, 3 (1981), 119-31
—— 'The "Rosaline-Katherine Tangle" in *Love's Labour's Lost*', *The Library*, VI, 4 (1982), 381-96
Furness, H. H., ed., *Love's Labour's Lost*, New Variorum (1904)
Hart, H. C., ed., *Love's Labour's Lost*, Arden (1906)
Kerrigan, John, ed., *Love's Labour's Lost*, New Penguin (1982)
—— 'Shakespeare at Work: the Katherine-Rosaline Tangle in *Love's Labour's Lost*', *RES*, NS 33 (1982), 129-36
—— '*Love's Labour's Lost* and Shakespearean Revision', *SQ* 33 (1982), 337-9
Lever, J. W., 'Three Notes on Shakespeare's Plants', *RES*, NS 3 (1952), 117-29
McKenzie, D. F., 'Printers of the Mind: Some Notes on Bibliographical Theories and Printing-House Practices', *SB* 22 (1969), 1-75
Price, George R., 'The Printing of *Love's Labour's Lost* (1598)', *PBSA* 72 (1978), 405-34
Ridley, M. R., ed., *Love's Labour's Lost*, New Temple (1934)
Wells, Stanley, 'The Copy for the Folio Text of *Love's Labour's Lost*', *RES*, NS 33 (1982), 137-47
Werstine, Paul, 'Editorial Uses of Compositor Study', *AEB* 2 (1978), 153-65
—— 'Variants in the First Quarto of *Love's Labour's Lost*', *SSt* 12 (1979), 35-47; supplemented in *PBSA* 73 (1979), 493-4
—— 'The Editorial Usefulness of Printing House and Compositor Studies', in *Play-Texts in Old Spelling: Papers from the Glendon Conference*, ed. G. B. Shand and Raymond C. Shady (1984), 35-64
Wilson, John Dover, ed., *Love's Labour's Lost*, New (1923; rev. 1962)

TEXTUAL NOTES

Title *Loues labors lost*] A PLEASANT Conceited Comedie CALLED, Loues labors loſt. Q (*title-page*); *A pleasant conceited Comedie: called Loues Labor's loſt* Q (*running titles*); Loues Labour's loſt. F (*head title; running titles*); Loues Labour loſt. F (*table of contents*). There is no head title for Q, or S.R. entry; Meres calls the play '*Loue labors lost*'. Usually modernized to *Love's Labour's Lost*, though *Love's Labours Lost* is an alternative interpretation of Q's title-page.

1.1.0.1 *Biron*] Q's 'Berowne' is a transliteration of the French name; cf. Nashe, *Christ's Tears Over Jerusalem*, Epistle to 1594 edn.: 'if of beere he talkes, then straight he mocks the Countie Berowne in France' (ii. 182). Shakespeare rhymes the name with 'moon' (4.3.230/1472). See also *Re-Editing*, p. 25.

1.1.0.2 *Longueville*] Q's 'Longauill' (also 'Longauil' and 'Longauile') is a transliteration of the French name.

1.1.0.2 *Dumaine*] a transliteration, with some corruption, of the name of the Duc de Mayenne; scansion and rhyme require two syllables.

1.1.24/24 three] F; thee Q
1.1.31/31 pompe] F; pome Q
1.1.62/62 feast] THEOBALD; faſt Q
1.1.104/104 any] Q; an POPE
1.1.114/114 sworne] Q. Editors often adopt F2's 'swore' for the rhyme; but Shakespeare nowhere else uses 'swore' as a past participle. See also Furness's long note drawing attention to the rhyme 'o'er' and 'sworn', 1.1.293, 295/291, 293.

1.1.127/127 BEROWNE] THEOBALD; *continued to Longueville*, Q (with 'Ber.' before 1.1.131/132)
1.1.127/127 gentiletie] Q (gentletie). Wilson thinks this is Shakespeare's spelling; but four syllables are needed.
1.1.130/130 can possible] Q; can possibly POPE; ſhall poſſibly F. See *OED possible*, C.
1.1.185, 1.2.10, 11, 16 Señor] Q spells 'Signeor' except at 1.1.185/199 ('Signeour'). See *Re-Editing*, 27–8.
1.1.193/194 laughing] CAPELL; hearing Q
1.1.214/214 simplicitie] F; ſinplicitie Q. Q's reading is defended by some as a joke.
1.1.227–52/227–53] Q prints the King's speech continuously, with Costard's interruptions bracketed.
1.1.242/242 Minow] Q; minion SISSON (Johnson). See Sisson, *New Readings*.
1.2.244/243 mee?] F; ~. Q
1.1.252/251 with with] THEOBALD (*subs.*); Which with Q. 'Which' makes no sense in the context; in secretary hand, spelt 'w^th' and 'w^ch' (as by Hand D), the words would be easily confused.
1.1.283/281 KING] F (*Fer.*); Ber. Q
1.1.292/290 be your keeper] Q; your keeper be G.T. *conj*. An easy transposition; but the King has been speaking prose.

1.2.0.1 *Mote*] Editors retain Q's *Moth*, a regular spelling of 'mote'; 'the copious allusions to the small stature of the page unmistakably point to this meaning'; though this is 'generally accepted, as explanatory and glossarial notes in several editions suggest, the necessary consequence, that the name should be modernized along with the common noun, has not yet been effected by a single editor—despite the widespread conviction that the traditional form no longer conveys the original Elizabethan sense' (Schäfer, 13). See also Kerrigan, 'Shakespearean Revision', and his edition, which spells 'Mote'.

1.2.8 juvenal] *etymologically distinct from* 'juvenile'
1.2.14 epitheton] Q (apethaton)
1.2.96/398 blushing] F2; bluſh-in Q. Riverside follows Q, without comment; 'are' might be a plural by attraction; even so, the absence of an article supports 'blushing'. It is, perhaps, conceivable that 'blush-' represents an assimilated form of 'blushes'.
1.2.137/440 DULL] THEOBALD; Clo. Q
1.2.154 Master] F; M. Q never spells out this word with a personal name; Costard refers to 'Monsier *Berowne*' 4.1.53/984, and perhaps should use the French word here. Nathaniel has 'Maister Person', 4.2.82/1160.

2.1.13/490 PRINCESSE] Q more frequently calls her 'Queene' in prefixes; this seems to be Shakespeare's imprecise use; we standardize until after she is addressed as a queen (5.2.719/2471).
2.1.21/498] F's redundant prefix 'Prin.' may reflect a cut in performance of the scene's previous lines. See Wells, 'The Copy'.
2.1.32/509 Importunes] F; Importuous Q
2.1.34/511 visagd] F; viſage Q
2.1.39/516 L. *Longauill*] CAPELL; *Longauill* Q. Supported, though not absolutely demanded, by metre, 'L⟨ord⟩.' is a likely courtesy, easily omitted as it duplicates the prefix. Curiously, the accident recurs in David's collations.
2.1.40/517 MARIA] ROWE; 1.*Lady*. Q
2.1.41 Périgord] Q (*Perigort*). 'Perigort' is 'probably derived from the Province of Perigord in S.W. France' (Sugden).
2.1.42 Fauconbridge] *also at* 2.1.205 *and Henry V* 3.5.44
2.1.44/521 partes] F; peerelſſe Q (doubtless a misprint for 'peerelesse' or 'peerlesse', itself possibly a misreading and respelling of 'pertes' (Wilson) or misexpansion of 'ptes'). The Folio reading may reflect annotated copy, or may be a guess (it is not certainly correct). As 'peerless' is appropriate to the context, it is also possible that the compositor, misled by the words' similar openings, accidentally omitted 'parts', and that the annotator, seeing it inserted, mistook it for a substitution. This assumes a hexameter. Proudfoot conjectures 'peerless parts'.
2.1.45/522 Well fitted in artes] Q; In arts well fitted G.T. *conj*.
2.1.53/530 MARIA] ROWE; *Lad*. Q; *Lad*.1. F
2.1.56/533 KATHERINE] ROWE; 2 *Lad*. Q
2.1.61 Alençon's] Q (*Alanſoes*). At 2.1.195/672 Q has 'Alanson'; Wilson is followed by some editors in preferring 'this Anglicized form', but it is merely a phonetic variant.
2.1.64/541 ROSALINE] F; 3 *Lad*. Q
2.1.88/565 vnpeepled] F (vnpeopled); vnpeeled Q. See Wilson.
2.1.100/577 it, will,] CAPELL (*subs.*); it will, Q
2.1.115–26/592–603 ROSALINE] F; *Kath*⟨*erine*⟩. Q
2.1.130/607 of] F; of, of Q
2.1.144 On] Q (One)
2.1.190, 5.2.277 Non point] Q (*No poynt*). See *Re-Editing*, 26.
2.1.195/672 Katherin] SINGER (Capell); *Rosalin* Q
2.1.196.1/673.1 *Enter Longauill*] F2; *not in* Q
2.1.210/687 Rosalin] SINGER; Katherin Q
2.1.221–4, 224/698–701 KATHERINE] Q (*La*. ... *La*. ... *La*.)
2.1.252/729 made] Q; made me G.T. *conj*.
2.1.254–8/731–5 ROSALINE ... MARIA ... KATHERINE ... MARIA ... KATHERINE] *Lad*. ... *Lad*.2 ... *Lad*.3 ... *Lad*. ... *Lad*. Q; *Lad*. *Ro*. ... *Lad*. *Ma*. ... *Lad*.2 ... *La*.1 ... *Lad*.2. F. Our ascriptions are based on F, assuming that its First and Second Ladies here correspond with those at 2.1.40/517, and 2.1.56/533.

3.1.13/748 throate, as if] THEOBALD; throate, if Q
3.1.14/749 singing loue,] THEOBALD; ~ₐ Q
3.1.14/749 through the nose] F2; through: noſe Q
3.1.17/752 thinbellie] F; thinbellies Q
3.1.23/757–8 note: do you note? men, that] MALONE (*subs.*); note: do you note men that Q. We interpret 'make men who are most given to these, men of note: do you observe what I say?—men' (i.e. not unmanly). But the passage may be corrupt.
3.1.26/760 pennie] HANMER (Theobald); penne Q
3.1.64 voluble] Q (volable). Some editors retain Q's spelling, glossing as 'quick-witted' (Wilson) or as 'a coinage ... to express Moth's quickness of movement' (David). But the word is not in *OED*, *voluble* is used elsewhere of Mote (2.1.76/553), and 'volable' may be a quasi-phonetic spelling, a misreading, or a foul-case error.
3.1.70.1/803–4 salue in the male] MALONE (*after* Johnson; the F2); ſalue, in thee male Q
3.1.140, 143, 145, 147, 151, 153, 169/872, 875, 877, 879, 883, 885, 900] In Q, each line starts with 'O'; the second 'O' is omitted in F. Cambridge omitted them all, on the grounds that they represent a misreading of '*Bero*.'; the prefix to each

272

line here is regularly 'Ber.', whereas 'Bero.' occurs frequently elsewhere. Hart defended 'O' as an affectation of Biron's.
3.1.165   guerdon] Q (gardon). Q spells 'gardon' as if to distinguish Costard's pronunciation from Biron's. But this was an accepted pronunciation, and as the word seems unfamiliar to Costard, he must copy what he hears.
3.1.175/906   Iunior] HART; Iunios Q
3.1.184/915   What? I] Q; What I? I MALONE
3.1.185/916   Clocke] F2; Cloake Q
3.1.199/930   shue, grone] Q; sue and groan F2, etc. But the line is in any case irregularly stressed, and to introduce syllabic regularity seems pointless.
4.1.3/934   BOYET] F (Boy.); Forr. Q. Forr. is possibly based on a misreading of Lor⟨d⟩.
4.1.50/981   fit] Qb; fir Qa
4.1.62/993   beautifull] Q; more beautiful TYRWHITT
4.1.65/996   sets] Qa; ſet Qb
4.1.65/997   penurious] WILSON; pernicious Q
4.1.66/998   was] Qb; is was Qa
4.1.69/1000   See] Q; saw F2. 'See' is an archaic past tense, used e.g. by Shallow, 2 Henry IV (Q1), 3.2.28/1551.
4.1.70/1001   see] Q; saw ROWE
4.1.74/1006   Kinges] Q2; King Q1
4.1.106/1038   Exit attended] F (Exeunt.)
4.1.107   suitor] An interpretation of Q's 'shooter'. Riverside regards 'shooter' as the primary sense, because Boyet already knows who the suitor is; but that need not stop him from teasingly asking.
4.1.129/1061   did hit it] F4; did hit Qb; hid hit Qa
4.1.135/1067   pin] F2; is in Q
4.1.143-8/1075-80   Editors have suspected that the lines were misplaced. David, following Dyce and Staunton, asks what Armado and Mote are 'doing in this scene'. But if we interpret Q's 'ath toothen side' as 'on the other hand' (see OED side, IV, 17b) the difficulty disappears. See Re-Editing, 54-5.
4.1.143/1075   ath toother] KEIGHTLEY (o'th't'other); ath toothen Q; to th'one WILSON. Cf. Troilus (Q1), 3151: 'Ath' tother side'.
4.1.145/1077   Absence of a rhyme to 'sweare' suggests loss of a line; the compositor of Q was crowding his page.
4.1.147/1079   a] F2; not in Q
4.1.147.1/1079.1   Shoot within] as here, CAPELL; after 4.1.148/1080, Q (in roman)
4.1.147.1   Shout] Q's 'Shoot' is a spelling variant, though it could conceivably mean 'a noise of shooting'.
4.2.3/1083   sanguis] Q (in roman); sanguine (written sanguĩe) GREG (conj. in Wilson)
4.2.5/1085   Celo] Q; caelum DYCE
4.2.12, 20   a 'auld grey doe'] This edition; a haud credo Q. We follow A. L. Rowse's interpretation (TLS, 18 July 1952), spelling according to the sense in which Dull uses the words.
4.2.29/1108   of] TYRWHITT; not in Q
4.2.36/1115   Dictynna . . . Dictynna] ROWE; Dictiſima . . . dictiſima Q. We assume misreading, though Holofernes could be in error.
4.2.38/1116   dictima] Q; Dictinna F2. Most editors emend, but the variation in Q suggests at least that Dull differs from Holofernes.
4.2.49/1127   twas] Qb; was Qa
4.2.50/1128   PEDANT Sir] Q ('Holo. Sir' text); Sir Q (c.w.)
4.2.52/1130   call I] CAMBRIDGE; cald Q; I have called ROWE
4.2.61/1139   o sore ell:] CAPELL (O sore L!); o ſorell: Q; o' sorel! JOHNSON; one sorel. CAMBRIDGE; O-sorel! DAVID. We interpret 'O harsh l', i.e. harsh in that it makes 50 'sores' (punningly).
4.2.66-105/1144-82   PEDANT] ROWE; Nath. Q
4.2.70/1148   pia mater] ROWE; prima-|ter Q
4.2.71-2/1149-50   in whom] F; whom Q
4.2.73, 103/1151, 1180   NATHANIEL] ROWE; Holo. Q
4.2.77/1155   ingenious] CAPELL; ingenous Q
4.2.79/1157   sapit] Q2; ſapis Q
4.2.82/1160   Pers on] HALLIWELL (pierce-one); Perſon Q
4.2.84/1162   liklest] Q; likeſt F; likeliest WILSON. We assume idiosyncratic spelling, cf. 'maidenlest' (History of Lear 424), and perhaps 'buſie left' (Folio Tempest 1111).
4.2.86/1164   Of] Q. Q is explained away by Cambridge as a remnant of 'Holof.' used as a speech-prefix. R. David points out that the prefix does not occur thus, and explains 'Of' as 'a sort of savouring of the expression'. Keightley read 'Oh'. We interpret 'Of' as Latin de, as used in the title of an epigram.
4.2.92-3/1170-1   Facile . . . ruminat] Q. The errors are here interpreted as part of the characterization. J. W. Binns writes: 'The Variorum points out that "Facile precor" is not impossible Latin ("Easily I pray"). I don't think I have seen it remarked that pecas, as pronounced, whether to an audience or compositor, would be the same as peccas meaning "you are sinning" or "you are getting it wrong". One could then get a meaning from the quarto reading: "Easily, I pray, since you are getting everything wrong under the cool shade, [it] or [there] ruminates". If this is meant as a joke, it would be funnier to take pecas as I have suggested rather than as a simple error for pecus. In Mantuan, Fauste is the name of a person. But as an adverb it means "happily", "fortunately", and is not too far removed from "facile" ("easily, compliantly, readily"), which in the adjectival form facilis also means "fortunate". Facile therefore seems to me to be a clever variation on Fauste.'
4.2.96-7/1174-5   Venichia, Venichia, | Que non te vide, que non te perrechia.] vemchie, vencha, que non te vnde, que non te perreche. Q. We attempt to reconstruct a quasi-phonetic spelling which may lie behind Q.
4.2.103/1180   NATHANIEL] ROWE 2; continued to Nathaniel (for Holofernes), Q
4.2.119/1196   singeth] This edition (Proudfoot); ſinges Q. Q is metrically irregular, which is not Holofernes's criticism. Presumably Nathaniel should make errors of pronunciation justifying the criticism.
4.2.120/1197   apostraphus] HART (conj. OED); apoſtraphas Q
4.2.121/1198   canzonet] THEOBALD; cangenct Q
4.2.121/1198   Here] continued to Holofernes, THEOBALD; given to Nathaniel, Q
4.2.125/1202   inuention?] THEOBALD; in-|uention‸ Q
4.2.127-8   domicella—virgin] Q (Damoſella virgin). See Re-Editing, 53.
4.2.129/1206   sir] This edition; ſir from one mounſier Berowne, one of the ſtrange Queenes Lordes Q. Jaquenetta has just said that the letter was given to her by Costard and written by Armado. She has no means of knowing that Biron wrote it, and he is not a foreign lord. None of the suggested emendations is plausible; editors admit bewilderment. Presumably a muddle of Shakespeare's, or the remnant of a changed intention.
4.2.130/1207   PEDANT] THEOBALD; Nath. Q
4.2.133/1210   writing] ROWE; written Q
4.2.135/1213   Sir] continued to Holofernes, THEOBALD; assigned to Ped⟨ant⟩. Q. See note to 4.2.130/1207 above.
4.2.135/1213   Nathaniel] CAPELL; Holofernes Q
4.2.155/1233   ben] ROWE 2; bien Q. But a mixture of French and Italian (in either affectation or error) may be intended.
4.3.12, 14   melancholy] Q (mallicholie, recorded by OED as an indifferent variant)
4.3.36/1278   wilt] F; will Q
4.3.46/1288   KING] ROWE 2; Long⟨auill⟩. Q
4.3.56/1298   Slop] THEOBALD; Shop Q. Wilson retains 'shop', glossing 'the organ of generation' and citing OED, sb. 3c; but OED's gloss is 'A place where something is produced or elaborated, or where some operation is performed. Often said of the heart, liver, or other internal bodily organs.' It cites the phrase 'shops of generation' (1688), but this does not justify Wilson's interpretation of 'shop' alone, nor is this supported by other Shakespearian usage. Wilson has been followed by later editors, sometimes glossing 'codpiece'.
4.3.72/1314   ydolatarie] F; ydotarie Q
4.3.84/1326   heires] Q; hair WILSON (Capell). Abbott, 334.
4.3.91/1333   I] JOHNSON; not in Q
4.3.104/1346   can] Q; gan Passionate Pilgrim, England's Helicon
4.3.106/1348   Wisht] Passionate Pilgrim, F2; Wiſh Q
4.3.108/1350   Ayre] Q; Ah! JOHNSON (conj).

4.3.110/1352 thorne] *England's Helicon*; throne Q
4.3.115/1357 great] COLLIER MS; *not in* Q; ev'n ROWE 2. A metrical emendation. The commonest Shakespearian epithet for Jove is 'great'.
4.3.120/1362 true loues] ROWE; trueloues Q
4.3.140/1382 One] Q; One that G.T. *conj.*
4.3.144/1386 Fayth so] GLOBE (W. S. Walker); Fayth Q; Our faith This edition *conj.* (Cambridge's belief that a word cannot have been omitted because 'Faith' is the catchword does not hold if Q is, as it may be, a reprint.)
4.3.153/1395 coaches] ROWE 2; couches Q
4.3.153/1395 coaches. In your teares,] HANMER; couches in your teares. Q
4.3.174/1416 to . . . by] CAPELL; by . . . to Q. Some editors (e.g. David, Riverside) follow Q, but it is hard to see how Biron is betrayed *to* the other men.
4.3.178/1420 like you] DYCE (W. S. Walker); like Q. See Sisson, *New Readings*.
4.3.180/1422 Ione] Qb; Loue Qa
4.3.181 pruning] Synonymous with 'preening', but the words appear to have been distinct.
4.3.196/1438 Where hadst thou it?] Q repeats the speech-prefix (after the stage direction).
4.3.206/1448 ene] DYCE 2 (even); and Q. We presume a misreading.
4.3.246/1488 word] Q. All editors adopt Theobald's 'wood' (the reading also of Rowe's first edition, perhaps unintentionally). See *Re-Editing*, 44.
4.3.253/1495 Stile] This edition (*conj.* Shapiro, N&Q, NS 2 (1955), 287–8); Schoole Q. Unless one believes in 'The School of Night' as a secret society, 'school' seems improbable; some recent editors defend it (e.g. Sisson, 'night is the scholar or pupil of blackness, darkness', *New Readings*, i. 115), but we find this strained, and Shapiro's conjecture provides a good alternative, in that 'style' (if spelt 'Stile', easily misread as 'Scole', then respelt by the compositor) is a good parallel with 'badge' and 'hue'.
4.3.257/1499 and] F4; *not in* Q
4.3.281/1523 Nothing] F2; O nothing Q
4.3.287/1529 O] Q; *omitted*, CAMBRIDGE
4.3.293/1535] At this point Q prints the lines given as Additional Passage A. Capell seems to have been the first to note the problem.
4.3.335/1577 authours] CAPELL; authour Q
4.3.337/1579 Let] F2; Lets Q
4.3.343/1585 standards] Q's 'ſtandars' may be a legitimate spelling; *OED* records 'stander' for 'standard'—and a bawdy pun is likely.
4.3.359 *Allons, Allons!*] THEOBALD; Alone alone Q (*treated here as a phonetic spelling, cf.* 5.1.145/1747)
5.1.20/1624 *sine* b] RIDLEY; fine Q. Q has been defended, but Schmidt cites only one instance in Shakespeare of 'fine' as an adverb (in *Cymbeline*), and two of 'finer'.
5.1.25/1629 *insanire*] SINGER 2; in-|famie Q. Usually emended to 'insanie' (*conj.* Warburton), recorded only once elsewhere; Collier 2 read 'insania', followed by Wilson. The infinitive fits better with 'to make frantic, lunatic', and may as easily lie behind Q's misreading.
5.1.27/1631 bone] THEOBALD; bene Q
5.1.28/1632 Bone?] THEOBALD; Bome Q
5.1.28/1632 Boon for boon] CAMBRIDGE (bon, fort bon); boon for boon Q
5.1.31/1635 *gaudio*] gaudeo F2. See Binns, 126.
5.1.33/1637 Quare] F2; Quari Q
5.1.47/1796 *pueritia*] F2; puericia Q (*the medieval spelling*)
5.1.55/1659 waue] F; wane Q
5.1.55 *Mediterraneum*] Q (meditaranium). The Latin form (which Hart finds in Greene's *Menaphon*, 1587) seems appropriate to Holofernes; the English 'Mediterranean' is first recorded in 1594.
5.1.65/1667 *circum circa*] THEOBALD; vnū cita Q; manu cita DAVID
5.1.76 *preambulate*] Editors usually treat as English, but *OED* does not record till 1609, and Latin is more appropriate here.
5.1.88/1690 choise] F3; choſe Q
5.1.94 important] COLLIER (Capell); important Q; importunate F

5.1.99 mustachio] (F); muſtachie Q. Q's spelling suggests a pronunciation closer to the Spanish (and so more appropriate to Armado) than to the French 'moustache', taken over into English.
5.1.112/1715 Nathaniel] CAPELL; Holofernes Q
5.1.114/1717 rendred] F; rended Q
5.1.114/1717 assistance] HANMER; asſiſtants Q
5.1.120-1/1723-4 my selfe, *Iudas Machabeus*, and this gallant Gentleman, *Hector*] This edition (Proudfoot); my ſelfe, and this gallant Gentle-|man *Iudas Machabeus* Q. Rowe omitted 'my selfe'; David suggested that the passage is 'an unrevised draft, with no part as yet assigned to Holofernes'. Proudfoot writes: 'Misplacing of (*a*) "and this gallant Gentleman" or (*b*) "*Iudas Machabeus*" and consequential omission of "*Hector*" would yield: "*Iosua*, your selfe, my selfe, *Iudas Machabeus*, and this gallant Gentleman, *Hector*; this swaine, . . .". If either (*a*) or (*b*) were marginal, or interlined, misplacing could easily have ensued.'
5.1.140/1742 fadge not] Q. In *Re-Editing* (49–50) I proposed 'fadge now', taking 'Antique' to mean the show that is being planned, while admitting the 'alternative possibility' that Armado 'means that if the proposed pageant fails, they will have something, "an Antique" (perhaps the dialogue of the Owl and the Cuckoo which ends the play)'. R. J. C. Watt, of the University of Dundee writes: 'I want to take up your challenge on p. 50 and try to persuade you of the rightness of Armado's *fadge not*. I am sure that your own "alternative possibility" is the right one and that Armado means "Even if this fails, we'll have a show".

'Armado is not looking forward with exultation to success; he is irritated that Holofernes has commandeered the project which the King had entrusted to *him*. See how abruptly Holofernes had done so at 5.1.111/1714. Antagonism between the two runs through Act V. Armado's remarks leading up to *fadge not* are critical ("Pardon, sir; error") and sceptical ("For the rest of the Worthies?") about Holofernes's proposals. Armado's irritation persists beyond this scene, surfacing again in the pageant itself with his complaints about the schoolmaster's vanity (5.2.526-7/2276-7).

'This brings us to "Shall I tell you a thing?" Because it is spoken too soon after Holofernes's self-important "Shall I have audience?", it must be a retort. Armado must stress the personal pronoun—"Shall *I* tell you a thing?"—both because it's a retort and because it conveys the exasperation of one who is being crowded out of a discussion of his own project.

'Armado, then, is still keen on an "antic", but not on *this* antic, which he thinks is no good.' I accept this.
5.1.145 Allons] ROWE (after Q, Alone)
5.2.3-4/1753-4 as here, Q; *transposed* HUDSON (W. S. Walker)
5.2.17/1767 bin a] F; bin Q
5.2.43 ho!] (HANMER); How? Q
5.2.46/1796 ieſt, I beshrew] This edition; ieſt, and I beſhrow Q; jest, and beshrew CAPELL
5.2.53, 57/1803, 7 MARIA] F (*Mar.*); Marg. Q
5.2.53/1803 these Pearls] F; theſe Pearle Q. Possibly 'these' should read 'this'.
5.2.65/1815 hests] DYCE (Knight); deuice Q. A rhyme is called for, and easily provided; 'deuice' may represent Shakespeare's first thought.
5.2.67/1817 persuaunt-like] This edition; perttaunt like Q. See *Re-Editing*, 34–5.
5.2.74/1824 wantonnesse] F2; wantons be Q
5.2.80/1830 stabde] F; ſtable Q
5.2.83/1833 Peace.] THEOBALD (*subs.*); Peace, Q
5.2.89/1839 Siccamore] F; Siccamone Q
5.2.93/1843 companions, warely,] F (*subs.*); companions warely, Q
5.2.96/1846 they] F; thy Q
5.2.121/1871] Absence of a rhyme for 'guess', and of a referent for 'thus', suggests that a line has dropped out. Furness records a suggestion by Tiessen, of 1878: 'Hats furr'd, bootes piked, in long and motley dress'. G.T. proposes: 'In sheepskins, masks, furred hats, beards, boots, quaint dress'; 'masks' gives point to the Princess's 'For Ladies we will euery one be maſkt'

(5.2.128/1878), and all the items of clothing are mentioned in 16th-c. dramatic portrayals of Russians.

5.2.123/1873   parlee] Q; parle CAPELL
5.2.124/1874   Loue-suit] DYCE (Collier); Loue-feat Q
5.2.130/1880   Q follows this with the two lines given as Additional Passage B, which Riverside conjectures to be an unrevised version of 5.2.131-2/1881-2.
5.2.133/1883   too] F; two Q
5.2.140/1890   Their] Q (text); The Q (c.w.)
5.2.147/1897   hir] F2; his Q
5.2.151/1901   nere] F2; ere Q
5.2.158/1908   BEROWNE] Q; Boyet THEOBALD. Many editors accept Theobald's emendation, as 'it is Boyet "that put Armado's page out of his part"' (337/2086) (Wilson). But this could refer to 5.2.170-1/1920-1; and the deflationary tone suits Biron.
5.2.162/1912   euer] F; euen Q
5.2.211/1961   yet:] HANMER (subs.); yet, Q
5.2.215/1965] Absence of a rhyme for 'man' along with confusion in speech-prefixes suggests that a line has dropped out (see Wilson); it may have had something to do with the *man in the moon*.
5.2.217/1967   ROSALINE] THEOBALD; *before previous line*, Q
5.2.242-55/1992-2005   KATHERINE] ROWE; *Maria* Q
5.2.259/2009   sence, so sensible,] POPE; sence so sensible, Q
5.2.264.1/2014.1] Many editors follow Capell in moving the *Exeunt* to the following line: but that is spoken by the Princess *in propria persona* and so, surely, to the men's backs.
5.2.264.2/2014.2   *The Ladies vnmaske*] David suggests '"The ladies dismask" might be inserted' at 5.2.297/2046; but his note seems not to distinguish between *favours* and *masks*. It would be natural for the ladies to 'dismask' as soon as the men depart; Boyet suggests that they *change Fauours* (5.2.293/2042)—i.e. each resume wearing her own suitor's favour—so that confusion will no longer be possible.
5.2.273/2023   Ah, they] This edition; They Q; O they F2. We presume confusion with the last letter of 'Rosa.'
5.2.277   *Non point*] Q (No poynt)
5.2.310/2059   run] F4; runs Q
5.2.310/2059   ouer] STEEVENS; ore Q
5.2.342   Construe] Confture Q. *OED*'s main entry is for 'construe'; Q's spelling, not recorded, seems possible, so we retain it as an old spelling, modernizing to 'construe' (instead of normalizing to the obsolete 'conster') as this is metrically acceptable.
5.2.375/2124   foolish.] ROWE (subs.); ∼, Q
5.2.408/2157   affectation] ROWE; affection Q. Q is retained by some modern editors, but the error is a simple one and the emendation justifiable by rhyme, metre, and sense.
5.2.415/2164   begin: Wench] DAVID; begin Wench Q; begin, wench THEOBALD
5.2.446/2195   ey-sight, and] Q. If, as Keightley conjectured, a line rhyming with 'me' was omitted, it may have been due to eyeskip from 'eyesight' to 'and', omitting the end of one verse line and the beginning of another. But the sense is satisfactory, and this may be a simple irregularity.
5.2.464/2213   sanie] F (subs.); faine Q
5.2.466/2215   smyles,] F; ∼, Q
5.2.483/2232   manage] THEOBALD (subs.); nuage Q; manager F
5.2.483   manège] See *As You Like It* 1.1.11.
5.2.501/2250   they] F; thy Q
5.2.514/2263   least] F; beft Q
5.2.517   There] Q (Their), CAPELL. A spelling variant which has the force of an emendation.
5.2.543   leopard's] libbards Q (an indifferent variant)
5.2.554/2304   PRINCESSE] F2; *Lady.* Q. Shakespeare may for once have used '*Lady*' as a prefix for the Princess; or possibly Costard should kneel to the wrong lady.
5.2.563/2313   this] F; his Q. Capell retains Q, interpreting 'smells "No" in his, . . .'.
5.2.595   proved] F (prou'd); proud Q

5.2.640/2392   gilt] F; gift Q
5.2.658.1/2410.1   *Berowne steps foorth*] Q's direction, omitted by Rowe and many later editors, restored by Wilson with the note: 'Berowne's exit is not only natural but even necessary as a preliminary to Costard's sudden intervention.' This supposes (*a*) that '*steps foorth*' means 'leaves the stage'—'comes forward' is more probable: cf. 4.3.149/1391; (*b*) that Costard has left the stage at 5.2.582/2333, though there the Princess says merely 'Stand aside'; (*c*) that Costard's 'intervention' is unprompted by the dialogue: see the following note. Moreover, Q marks no re-entry for either Biron or Costard. T. W. Craik (*N&Q* 20 (1973), 133) interprets '*Berowne*' as a misreading of '*Clowne*'. We interpret the direction as an instruction to Biron, checked by the Princess, to attempt to stop Armado from continuing.
5.2.665/2417   The partie is gone.] *spoken by Armado*, POPE; *centred and italicized*, Q. Theobald gave to Costard; but, interpreted as alluding to Hector's being dead, the words fit with 5.2.654/2406; and they serve to prompt Costard's interruption (see David's note). They seem to belong to Armado himself, not to the role he is playing, and are most easily interpreted as a defensive response to yet another interruption by one of the lords—a more irritated version of 5.2.654/2406. For this reason, we postulate a lost speech. (G.T.'s conjecture 'As Hannibal surmounted elephants' is in keeping with the spirit of the scene.)
5.2.683/2435   on stir] ROWE; or ftir Q
5.2.706/2458   MOTH] Q's prefix, 'Boy.', could refer to Boyet, but Mote seems more likely to know what is said.
5.2.720/2472   QUEENE] Q frequently uses this prefix for the Princess earlier. Editors regularize to 'Princess' throughout; but the phrase 'your Maiestie' suggests that Shakespeare thought of her as succeeding to her father's throne; her alternative designation as Queen, common in Q, also suggests that Shakespeare thought of her in these terms.
5.2.726-9/2478-81   spirites. | If . . . breath, your . . . it.] ROWE; fpirites, | If . . . breath (your . . . it.) Q
5.2.730/2482   nimble] THEOBALD; humble Q. David supports Q, interpreting 'complimentary, civil'; but the misreading is easy, and in all nine cases where Shakespeare uses 'humble' preceded by the indefinite article, the form is 'an', not—as here—'a'.
5.2.741   jostle] Q (iuftle). An indifferent variant.
5.2.745/2497   double] Q; dull COLLIER 2
5.2.756/2508   straing] CAPELL; ftraying Q
5.2.763/2515   them] POPE; *not in* Q
5.2.767/2519   both,] F; ∼, Q
5.2.771/2523   the] F; *not in* Q. Omission seems likely; in place of F's 'the', an adjective such as 'sweet' or 'fair' is possible.
5.2.775/2527   in] HANMER; *not in* Q; are F
5.2.800/2552   instance] Q. Editors adopt F's 'instant'; but this seems to be a predating of *OED*'s *instance*, II.4, 'An instant, a moment', first recorded in 1631.
5.2.809/2561   hermite] WILSON (Pollard); herrite Q; euer F
5.2.809/2561]   Both Q and F include the six lines printed as Additional Passage C. Theobald regarded them as 'the author's draught', noting that both Thirlby and Warburton thought they 'should be expunged'.
5.2.811/2563   A wife?] *continued to Dumaine*, DYCE; *part of Katherine's next line*, Q
5.2.879/2631   Ver begin] *as part of Armado's speech*, F; *separated from the previous words by a space, and preceded by* 'B.', Q
5.2.880/2632   SPRING] *not in* Q
5.2.881, 882/2634-5   *as here*, THEOBALD; *in reverse order*, Q
5.2.902/2654   foull] F; full Q
5.2.914/2666   ARMADO] F (*Brag.*); *not in* Q
5.2.915/2667   You that way, we this way.] F; *not in* Q
5.2.915.1/2667.1   *Exeunt omnes, seuerally*] *Exeunt omnes.* F; *not in* Q

Additional Passages

A.10   poysons vp] Q. An unusual expression. Theobald's 'prisons up' is plausible (see Wilson's note); but *up* frequently serves 'merely to emphasize the import of the verb' (*OED, adv.*¹, 18);

and Shakespeare nowhere else uses *prison* as a verb. G.T. conjectures 'freezes' spelt 'freyses', citing *K. John* 3.4.150/1455, 'freeze vp their zeale', and *Romeo* 4.3.16/2365, 'freezes vp the heate of life'.

C.2 ranke] ROWE; rackt Q

REJECTED FOLIO VARIANTS

1.1.27/27 bancrout quite] bankerout
1.1.72/72 but] and
1.1.109/109 Clymbe . . . the gate] That were to clymbe ore the houſe to vnlocke the gate
1.1.130/130 can possible] ſhall poſſibly
1.1.151/152 speake] breake
1.1.156/157 other] others
1.1.182/183 Farborough] Tharborough
1.1.263/262 keepe] keeper
1.1.302/300 till] vntill
1.2.40/341 fitteth] fits
1.2.48/349 do call] call
1.2.50-1/351 heere is] here's
1.2.51/352 yele] you'll
1.2.88/390 maculate] immaculate
1.2.121/424 suffer him to] let him
1.2.122/425 a'] hee
1.2.124/427 well.] well. *Exit.*
1.2.132/435 that] what
1.2.155/456 too silent] ſilent
1.2.165/466 was *Sampson*] *Sampſon* was
2.1.60/537 he] ſhe
2.1.65/542 if] as
2.1.80/557 A LORD] (*Lord.*); *Ma.*
2.1.130/607 the one] th'one
2.1.142/619 repaide] repaie
2.1.143/620 A] An
2.1.167/644 I will] would I
2.1.171/648 within] in
2.1.174/651 faire] farther
2.1.176/653 shall we] we ſhall
2.1.180/657 my none] my owne
2.1.184/661 foole] ſoule
2.1.203/680 on] a
2.1.213/690 O you] You
2.1.219/696 KATHERINE] (*Lady Ka.*); *La. Ma.*
2.1.219/696 BOYET] (*Bo.*); continued to *La. Ma.*
2.1.234/711 did] doe
2.1.244/721 where] whence
2.1.245/722 you to] out to
3.1.0.1/735.2 *Song.* (added after the direction)
3.1.7/743 Maister, will] Will
3.1.11/746 your] the
3.1.12/747 eylids] eie
3.1.56/789 The] Thy
3.1.81-9/814-22 *not in* F
3.1.129/862 honour] honours
3.1.138/870 then] then a
4.1.6/937 Ore] On
4.1.14/945 againe] then again
4.1.126/1058 And I] I
4.1.132/1064 a'the] a th
4.1.143/1075 toother] to the
4.2.4/1084 the] a
4.2.34/1113 tel me] tell

4.2.84/1162 liklest] likeſt
4.2.99/1177 not . . . not] not
4.2.140/1218 royall hand] hand
4.2.152/1230 before] being
4.3.82/1324 in] of
4.3.100/1343 euer] euery
4.3.166/1408 to tune] tuning
4.3.192/1434 twas] it was
4.3.214/1456 shew] will ſhew
4.3.216/1458 were] are
4.3.291/1533 gainst] againſt
4.3.337/1579 Let vs] (Lets vs); Let's
5.2.7/1758 a] on
5.2.11/1761 yeere] yeeres
5.2.45/1795 *not in* F
5.2.55/1805 not wish] wiſh
5.3.133/1883 you] your
5.2.138/1888 mockerie] mocking
5.2.148/1898 speakers] keepers
5.2.184/1934 her] you
5.2.208/1958 do but vouchsafe] vouchſafe but
5.2.220/1970 we] you
5.2.224/1974 you your] your
5.2.240/1990 that] you that
5.2.313/2062 thither] *not in* F
5.2.316/2065 peckes] pickes
5.2.317/2066 God] Ioue
5.2.324/2073 A] He
5.2.335/2084 due] dutie
5.2.351/2100 mens] men
5.2.369/2118 *Russian*] Ruſsia
5.2.390/2139 were] are
5.2.434/2183 not you] you not
5.2.483/2232 manage] (nuage); manager
5.2.524/2274 A] He
5.2.524/2274 God his] God's
5.2.525/2275 That is] That's
5.2.529/2279 *Exit*] *not in* F
5.2.540/2290 picke] pricke
5.2.540/2290 in his] in's
5.2.574/2325 a feard] affraid
5.2.578/2329 fayth] inſooth
5.2.633/2385 *Hectors*] *Hector*
5.2.655-6/2407-8 When . . . man] *not in* F
5.2.689/2441 bepray] pray
5.2.708/2460 a weares] hee weares
5.2.723/2475 intreat] entreats
5.2.731/2483 too] ſo
5.2.746/2498 eare] ears
5.2.775/2527 this in] (this); theſe are
5.2.791/2543 the] their
5.2.809/2561 hermite] (herrite); euer
5.2.827/2579 thy] my
5.2.871/2623 yeere] yeares

INCIDENTALS

5 buy,] ~ :   10 desires,] ~ .   24 resolud] F; reſolued Q   29 delyghts,] ~ :   30 slaues.] ~ ,   43 day,] ~ :
57 common] cammon   63 fine,] ~ .   117 strictst] ſtricteſt   130 publique] publibue   133 Embassie] Embaſſaie

166 inchaunting] inchannting 171 Knight͜] ~: 188 Contempts] Contempls 193 patience.] ~͜ 215 flesh.] ~͜
216 welkĩs] welkis 258 *Officer*] Gfficer 269 worst] woſt 291 deliured] (F1); deliuered 299 prosperitie] proſperie
300 affliccĩõ] afflicciõ 403 owe.] ~͜ 427 woman] womand 479 Cõsider] Coſider 517 Maddame:] ~͜
519 solemnized͜] ~. 527 cut, ... wils͜] ~͜ ... ~, 538 *Alansões*] *Alanſoes* 548 ieſt,] ~. 551 tales,] ~.
617 friendship] faiendſhip 619 demaund] pemaund 638 speciall] ſpciall 646 may͜] ~, 650 hart͜] ~. 705 lyes)]
~͜ 706 eyes͜] ~. 731 speakst] ſpeakeſt 791 *Minnime*] (roman) 804 plaine] pline 831 flat] Q, F (*set as if a catchword*) 865 oũce] ouce 869 remuneration] remuration 902 Critick] Crietick 980 Mistres] Miſtrs 1001 ouercame,] couercame, 1051 *Fraunce*] *Frannce* 1052 touching] touchiug 1069 bowle.] ~͜ 1083 *sanguis*] (*roman*) 1101 *bis coctus*] (*roman*) 1109 indiscreet] indiſtreell 1130 Deare͜] ~: 1181 stanze] ſtauze 1186 bowed.] ~͜ 1187 eyes͜] ~͜ 1199 elegancie,] *c.w.*; ~, 1203 *Imitarie*] *imitarie* 1205 virgin] (*italic*) 1219 forgiue] forgine 1249 do,] ~͜ 1268 smot͜] ~. 1299 heauenly] heanenly 1309 vapour-vow:] ~͜ 1313 deitie,] ~. 1321 transformd] transformed 1339 Ode] Odo 1345 Veluet͜] ~, 1361 plaine͜] ~. 1399 ashamd] a ſhamed 1423 mee:] ~͜
1462 *Inde*͜] ~. 1464 blind͜] ~. 1520 lyes͜] ~ ? 1553 sound͜] ~. 1557 daintie͜] ~, 1560 Subtil] Subtit
1585 standards] ſtandars 1600 be fitted] befitted 1603 forsworne] forſorne 1625 d e t] det 1629 *intelligis*] *inteligis*
1634 *Videsne*] *Vides ne* 1645 *honorificabilitudinitatibus*] (*roman*) 1678 Arts-man] (*italic*) 1706 secrecie] ſecretie 1772 Youle] Yole 1802 compyld] compyled 1820 hatcht͜] ~. 1841 purposd] purpoſed 1848 embassage.] ~͜ 1870 apparild] appariled 1878 Ladies͜] ~; 1884 deceyud] (F1) deceyued 1891 withall͜] ~. 1924 strangers] ſtranges
1938 measurd] meaſured 1955 remooud] remooued 1965 to it.] ~, 1972 this measure,] this meaſue ͜ 1976 cannot] cennot 1987 greeuest] greeueſt 2016 wonderd] wondered 2027 seruant͜] ~, 2047 vailing] varling 2055 pende,] ~. 2058 hand.] ~, 2062 thither?] ~, 2078 hushering,] ~. 2081 one,] ~. 2084 honie-tongd] honie-tonged
2087 thou͜] ~ ? 2091 speaches] ſpaches 2125 With] Wtih 2234 partest] partſt 2297 It *is great sir*] (*all in italic*)
2302] (*italic except* 'Pompey') 2315 *liud*] liued 2319 Conquerour] Conqueronr 2340] (*italic*) 2343] (*italic*)
2352 Elder] Flder 2396 Peace] (*italic*) 2401 *I am that Flower*.] (*roman*) 2405 Hector's] Heċtor's 2412] (*italic*)
2417] (*italic*) 2456 haue] hane 2463 interrupptst] interrnppteſt 2475 intreat͜] ~: 2490 Loue͜] ~, 2500 time,]
~. 2502 deformd] deformed 2504 seemd] ſeemed 2506 vaine,] ~. 2507 like the eye,] ~. 2513 grauities,]
~. 2536 therefore] rherefore 2557 intitled] intiled 2561 then, my hart͜] then my hart, 2584 estates] eſtetes
2585 wit:] wi: 2631 The other] th'other

Additional Passages

A.2 Booke,] ~. A.18 womãs] womas

QUARTO STAGE DIRECTIONS

1.1.0.1-2/0.1-2 Enter Ferdinand K. of Nauar, Berowne, | Longauill, and Dumaine.
1.1.178.1-2/179.1-2 *Enter a Constable with Costard with a letter.*
1.1.303/301 *Exeunt.*
1.2.0.1/301.1 *Enter Armado and Moth his page.*
1.2.119.1-2/422.1-2 *Enter Clowne, Constable, and Wench.*
1.2.137.1/440.1 *Exeunt.*
1.2.158/459 *Exit.*
1.2.176/477 *Exit.*
2.1.0.1-2/477.1-3 *Enter the Princesse of Fraunce, with three | attending Ladies and three Lordes.*
2.1.36/513 *Exit Boy.* (F; after 2.1.35/512, Q)
2.1.80/557 *Enter Boyet.*
2.1.88.1/565.1 *Enter Nauar, Longauill, Dumaine, & Berowne.*
2.1.178.1/655.1 *Exit.*
2.1.193/670 *Exit.*
2.1.193.1/670.1 *Enter Dumaine.*
2.1.196/673 *Exit.*
2.1.208/685 *Exit Longauil.*
2.1.208.1/685.1 *Enter Berowne.*
2.1.214/691.1 *Exit Bero.*
2.1.259.1/735.1 *Exeunt omnes.*
3.1.0.1/735.2 *Enter Braggart and his Boy.*
3.1.67.1/800.1 *Enter Page and Clowne.*
3.1.131/864 *Exit.*
3.1.139.1/871.1 *Enter Berowne.*
3.1.168/899.1 *Exit.*
4.1.0.1-3/931.1-3 *Enter the Princesse, a Forrester, her Ladyes, | and her Lordes.*
4.1.40/971.1 *Enter Clowne.*
4.1.60/991 *Boyet | reedes.* (left of 'By' and 'true', 4.1.60-1/991-2)
4.1.127/1059 *Exit·* (F; after 4.1.125/1057 Q)
4.1.138.1, 147.1, 148/1070.1, 1079.1, 1080 *Exeunt. Shoot within.* (after 4.1.148/1080)

4.2.0.1-2/1080.1-2 Enter *Dull, Holofernes, the* Pedant *and* Nathaniel.
4.2.80.1/1158.1 *Enter Iaquenetta and the Clowne.*
4.2.144/1222 *Exit.*
4.2.163/1241 *Exeunt.*
4.3.0.1/1241.1 *Enter Berowne with a paper in his hand, alone.*
4.3.19.1/1261.1 *He standes a side. The King entreth.*
4.3.41.1/1283.1 *Enter Longauill. The King steps a side.*
4.3.56.1/1298.1 *He reades the Sonnet.*
4.3.73.1/1315.1 *Enter Dumaine.*
4.3.98.1/1340.1 *Dumaine reades his Sonnet.*
4.3.186.1-2/1428.1-2 *Enter Iaquenetta and Clowne.* (F; after 'King', 4.3.187/1429 Q)
4.3.193.1/1435.1 *He reades the letter.*
5.1.0.1-2/1604.1-2 *Enter the Pedant, the Curat, and Dull.*
5.1.15.1/1619.1 *Draw-out his Table-booke.*
5.1.29.1-2/1633.1-2 *Enter Bragart, Boy.*
5.1.148.1/1750.1 *Exeunt.*
5.2.0.1-2/1750.2-3 *Enter the Ladyes.*
5.2.78.1/1828.1 *Enter Boyet.*
5.2.155.1/1905.1 *Sound Trom.*
5.2.156.2-4/1906.2-4 *Enter Black-moores with musicke, the Boy with a | speach, and the rest of the Lordes disguysed.*
5.2.159.1/1909.1 *The Ladyes turne their backes to him.* (after 5.2.160/1910)
5.2.264.1/2014.1 *Exe.*
5.2.310.1/2059.1 *Exeunt.*
5.2.310.2-3/2059.2-3 *Enter the King and the rest.*
5.2.315/2064 *Exit.*
5.2.337.1/2086.1 *Enter the Ladies.*
5.2.484.1/2233.1 *Enter Clowne.*
5.2.508.1/2257.1 (*Exit.* (turned up)
5.2.519.1/2268.1 *Enter Bragart.*
5.2.529/2279 *Exit.*
5.2.541.1/2291.1 *Enter Pompey.*
5.2.558.2/2308.2 *Enter Curate for Alexander.*

5.2.575.1/2326.1 Exit Curat. (after 5.2.581/2332)
5.2.582.1-2/2333.1-2 *Enter Pedant for Iudas, and the Boy for Hercules.*
5.2.589.1/2340.1 Exit Boy.
5.2.625.1/2377.1 *Eeter Braggart.*
5.2.658.1/2410.1 *Berowne steps foorth.*

5.2.709.1/2461.1 Enter a Messenger Mounsier Marcade.
5.2.718.1/2470.1 Exeunt Worthys
5.2.865.1/2617.1 Enter Braggart.
5.2.877/2629 Enter all.
5.2.880/2632 The Song.

A MIDSUMMER NIGHT'S DREAM

The play was entered in the Stationers' Register on 8 October 1600:

Tho. Fyſſher   Entred for his copie vnder the
handẹ of mr Rodes / and the
Wardens. A booke called
A mydſõmer nightẹ dreame

An edition (Q1) 'for *Thomas Fisher*' duly appeared, dated 1600 (*BEPD* 170), probably printed by Richard Bradock. A second edition (Q2) claims on its title-page to be 'Printed by James Roberts, 1600', but is in fact one of the falsely dated quartos printed in 1619 (see General Introduction). Q2 is evidently an unauthoritative reprint, which occasionally corrects Q1 errors conjecturally but more often introduces new errors of its own. The text in the Folio (F) was set from a copy of Q2, and retains many of its errors and abnormalities. However, unlike the compositor(s) of Q2 the compositors of F clearly had access to a manuscript, for F introduces a number of variants, particularly in stage directions, which can only have come from such a source. Like *Much Ado*, *Love's Labour's Lost*, and *Merchant* (printed before and after it), Folio *Dream* appears to have been set from quarto copy, annotated sporadically by reference to a manuscript.

It is now generally agreed that Q1 was set from autograph foul papers. Errors and inconsistencies in stage directions combine with inconsistent designation of characters and a large number of 'Shakespearian' spellings: these are analysed in detail by Greg (*Folio*) and Brooks. Nothing in the text points to a specifically theatrical manuscript; nor are there any reliable indications of even desultory annotation by a bookkeeper. Brooks agrees with Turner, that the text seems to have been set by only one compositor. However, in the absence of investigations of other Bradock publications little can be said about the printing, and Turner's conclusions about the order of setting have been seriously undermined by Blayney (pp. 92-3). No one has undertaken a collation of press variants in the eight extant copies of Q; we have discovered one such variant ourselves (2.2.49/672) but have not attempted a systematic collation. The forme in question (inner C) apparently contains no other variants, though some such variants may have been lost, due to damage to the only extant copy with the corrected state.

Wilson believed that, for *Dream* as other plays, the underlying manuscript represents a text which evolved over the course of several years, an early original being overwritten and adapted by later wholesale revision. Although this elaborate hypothesis has been dismantled and discarded by subsequent scholarship, there has been almost universal acceptance of Wilson's claim that the extensive and unusual mislineation at the beginning of Act 5 results from confusion created by Shakespeare's own marginal additions to the original dialogue (5.1.1-84/1701-84). Turner, who considered possible bibliographical explanations for all the mislineation in Q, confirmed that these passages very probably reflect confusion in the copy. Full details of this and other mislineation are as usual recorded among 'Emendations to Lineation', but for convenience we include, as an appendix, a conjectural reconstruction of the passage as originally written.

It is generally recognized that the source for many of F's substantive variants from Q must have been a prompt-book. The specification '*Tawyer with a Trumpet before them*' (5.1.125.1/1825.1) presumably refers to William Tawyer, described in a 1625 burial register as 'Mr Heminges man' and named among 'Musitions and other necessary attendantes' of the King's Men in a 1624 exemption order (Bentley, *Jacobean and Caroline Stage*, ii. 590). The fact that—outside F itself—we possess no record of Tawyer earlier than 1624 suggests that this stage direction originated in a relatively late revival. The play apparently continued to be popular long after its first performances (*c.*1594-6): there was a court performance on New Year's night, 1604, and Edward Sharpham's allusion to Thisbe's death in *The Fleire* (*c.*1606) presumes an audience's familiarity with performances of Shakespeare's play. The omission of 5.1.314-15/2015-16 is almost certainly a consequence of the 1606 Acte to Restraine Abuses, and on the evidence of other Folio texts is more likely to have originated in the theatre than in the printing house (see Taylor, 'Zounds Revisited'). The Folio act divisions also point to later performances. The King's Men appear not to have made use of such intervals before about 1609. (See Taylor, 'The Structure of Performance'.) The divisions can in this case hardly originate in the printing house, for they are supplemented by the direction '*They sleepe all the Act*' (after 3.3.48/1441.1), where '*Act*' has the technical theatrical meaning 'interval between the acts'.

Though editors have agreed that a prompt-book influenced F, they have differed on how much authority to accord its variants. The act divisions almost certainly reflect the imposition of a later convention of performance, and as they twice interrupt otherwise continuous scenes we have agreed with other editors in treating them as a misrepresentation of Shakespeare's structural intentions. Moreover, annotation of the compositors' Q2 copy seems to have been confined—as usual in the Comedies—almost entirely to stage directions and speech-prefixes: all but a handful of verbal variants can be accounted for by the normal frequencies and types of Folio compositor error. All such verbal variants originating in F are relegated to a separate list of 'Rejected Folio Variants' (except, of course, for the few we have accepted, or discuss in the textual notes).

The remaining Folio variants—those involving speech-prefixes and stage directions—must be treated with more respect. Some of these clearly originate in the prompt-book; others are clearly necessary; others involve the alteration of

Q readings which seem acceptable to a casual or even an alert reader, and which therefore can hardly have originated in the whims of an unassisted printing-house 'editor'. Without strong evidence to the contrary, one must therefore assume that the prompt-book is the authority for all added or substantially altered Folio directions and speech-prefixes. Some of these variants might derive from late revivals, over which Shakespeare had no control; but none certainly do, and only the act divisions and Tawyer's name can be confidently associated with performances later than those in the mid 1590s. Although each direction has been considered on its merits, we have found no reason to doubt that the bulk of the Folio directions represent the play as originally and authoritatively staged. Those directions which clearly envisage a different staging from that implied by Q seem to us to be dramatic improvements for which Shakespeare was probably responsible.

Removing the Folio's intrusive divisions for Acts 3 and 4 significantly affects the traditional scene divisions. Scene 4 continues from 650 to 1020 (= traditional 2.2 + 3.1/623.2-981). The traditional 3.2/Sc. 5 should be broken into two scenes: the stage is apparently cleared at 3.2.413/1394, when Robin and Demetrius leave before Lysander re-enters. Although the action of Robin's abuse of the men clearly continues, the cleared stage can suggest a gap in time and place, which usefully contributes to the ease with which an audience accepts the subsequent wearied surrender of Lysander and Demetrius. We therefore end Scene 5 at 3.2.413/1390. Scene 6 then covers 3.3.14/1391 to 4.1.215/1657 (= end of traditional 3.2, and 4.1). Scene 6 corresponds to the traditional 4.2. We agree with editors before Dyce in marking a new scene after the *Exeunt* at 5.1.363/2064: the traditional 5.1 thus becomes 5.1/Sc. 8 and 5.2/Sc. 9.

G.T./(J.J.)

WORKS CITED

Brooks, Harold F., ed., *A Midsummer Night's Dream*, Arden (1979)
Cuningham, Henry, ed., *A Midsummer Night's Dream*, Arden (1905, rev. 1930)
Furness, H. H., ed., *A Midsummer Night's Dream*, New Variorum (1895)
Gould, George, *Corrigenda and Explanations of the Text of Shakspere: A New Issue* (1884)
Hodgdon, Barbara, 'Gaining a Father: the Role of Egeus in the Quarto and the Folio', *RES*, NS 37 (1986), 534–42
Nicholson, B., 'Shakspeariana', *N&Q* (16 January 1864), 49–50
Turner, Robert K., Jr., 'Printing Methods and Textual Problems in *A Midsummer Night's Dream*, Q1', *SB* 15 (1962), 33–55
Wells, Stanley, ed., *A Midsummer Night's Dream*, New Penguin (1967)
Wilson, John Dover, ed., *A Midsummer Night's Dream*, New (1940)

TEXTUAL NOTES

Title *A Midsommer nights dreame*] Q1 (*title-page (roman), head title (roman)*); A mydſōmer nightę dreame S.R.; A Midſommer nightes dreame Q1 (*running titles*)
1.1.4/4   wanes] Q2, F; waues Q1
1.1.10/10   New] ROWE; Now QF
1.1.19.1/19.1   *Lysander*] F; Lyſander *and Helena*, Q1; *Lyſander, Helena*, Q2
1.1.24/24   Stand forth *Demetrius.*] ROWE. QF italicize and centre on a separate line. Though QF has been defended as a stage direction (E. A. J. Honigmann, 'Re-enter the Stage Direction', *SSu* 29 (1976), 117–26, p. 124), it produces either two incomplete lines or (if rearranged) a defective caesura; Shakespeare's other texts provide no parallel for such directions; and the compositor usually uses roman for names in stage directions. Compare '*Thysby* stand forth' (3.1.75/862). See next note.
1.1.26/26   Stand forth *Lisander.*] ROWE. QF italicize and centre on a separate line. See preceding note.
1.1.27/27   This] F2; This man Q, F1
1.1.127.2/127.2   *Manet Lysander and Hermia*] F; *not in* Q
1.1.136/136   lowe] THEOBALD; loue QF
1.1.139/139   merit] This edition; elſe, it QF. See next note. The emendation is defended by Gary Taylor in *N&Q* 226 (1981), 333.
1.1.139/139   friends] Q; merit F
1.1.154   due] Q1 (dewe), Q2-F (due)
1.1.159–60/159–60   And . . . sonne: | From . . . leagues:] JOHNSON; From . . . leagues? | And . . . sonne: Q, F (*subs.*). These are the last two lines on a Q1 page (A4), and so in bibliographical context correspond to two lines apparently transposed in Quarto *Lear*. (See note to *History of Lear* 7.367–8/1375–6.)
1.1.187/187   Your words I] Q, F1; Your words Ide F2; Yours would I HANMER. Hanmer's emendation is simply a development of the sense imposed by F2; F2's emendation itself derives from Q2's repunctuation of the end of the line. (See next note.)
1.1.187/187   *Hermia*, ere I goe,] Q1; *Hermia*, ~ ~, Q2, F. Q1's punctuation leaves the division of sentences ambiguous. If we assume that 'ere I go' belongs to the following rather than the preceding sentence, then 'Your words I catch' makes the same sort of sense as 'Sicknesse is catching': a statement of fact, followed by a wish, the two linked by a pun on 'catch'.
1.1.191/191   ild] HANMER; ile QF
1.1.200/200   *Helen*, is no fault] This edition; *Helena*, is no fault Q1; *Helena* is none Q2, F. Q2's reading can have no authority, unless it derives from an unrecorded Q1 press variant, a possibility made most unlikely by the fact that Q1 is difficult to explain as an error for Q2. But Q1 is metrically irregular, and Shakespeare elsewhere varies the name for metrical purposes. Until later on this Q1 page (B1: 1.1.208/208), the character has been consistently called 'Helena', and the short form is not used again until D1 (2.2.150/773); consequently, whether setting was seriatim or by formes the compositor who set this line would not yet have encountered the truncated name. Compositorial error thus seems more likely than deliberate metrical irregularity.
1.1.212/212   slights] This edition; flights QF. The general 'tricks' seem more appropriate to this sententious aside than the specific 'flights'; 'slights' was a recognized spelling of *sleights*; misreading or ligature confusion would easily account for Q1's reading.
1.1.216/216   swete] THEOBALD; ſweld QF
1.1.219/219   stranger companies] THEOBALD; ſtrange companions QF
1.2.23/274   stones] This edition (*conj.* Collier MS); ſtormes QF. An easy minim misreading. Compare *Caesar* 3.2.221–5/1607–11: 'But were I *Brutus*, | And *Brutus Antony*, there were an Antony | . . . should moue | The stones of Rome . . .' As a claim for histrionic prowess in a 'condoling' role, to be able to move even stones seems more extravagantly relevant than an (unidiomatic) claim to 'move storms'. For spectators who knew the story of Pyramus, 'mooue stones' would be unintentionally comic.
1.2.24/275   rest, yet,] THEOBALD; ~ ~, QF
1.2.73/324   ALL THE REST] *All.* Q
2.1.7/362   Moones] STEEVENS; Moons QF (*tightly justified lines*). For Shakespeare's use of the archaic disyllabic genitive, see Cercignani, p. 287.
2.1.20   wroth] QF (wrath)

A MIDSUMMER NIGHT'S DREAM

2.1.22, 65 stol'n] F (ſtolne)
2.1.35 villag'ry] Q1 (Villageree), Q2–F (Villagree). Only three syllables seem intended.
2.1.58/413 make roome] POPE; roome QF; room now DYCE; roomer NICHOLSON (*conj.*). The line is metrically irregular, and Shakespeare nowhere else treats *room* as disyllabic. Moreover, although Shakespeare uses the imperative ('Room!') on three occasions, elsewhere it always occurs at the beginning of a sentence rather than inside it. This objection applies to Dyce's conjecture as well as QF; Shakespeare offers no parallels for such a conjunction of *room* and *now*, nor does *now* supply a better explanation of the conjectural omission than does Pope's 'make'. Shakespeare uses the phrase *make room* three times elsewhere (*K. John* 1.1.255/255, *Merchant* 4.1.15/1824, *Much Ado* 2.1.76–7/482–3); the first of these occupies exactly the same point in a verse line. Alternatively, one might conjecture 'give room', as at *Romeo* 1.5.26/600 and *All's Well* 1.2.67/295, or 'room ho', as at *Caesar* 3.4.16/2354. For apparent accidental omission of *make* compare *2 Henry IV* 2.1.126/735 (F); for *give*, Q2 *Hamlet* 4.6.31/2802. Nicholson's 'roomer' does not occur elsewhere in Shakespeare, is only recorded as the comparative of an adverb, and does not have the meaning he alleges (*OED* room, adv. 3).
2.1.61/416 Fairies] THEOBALD; Fairy QF
2.1.69/424 steppe] Q1; ſteepe Q2, F
2.1.78/433 *Perigouna*] WHITE (after THEOBALD); Perigenia QF
2.1.79/434 *Ægles*] CHAMBERS (after ROWE); Eagles QF
2.1.85 margin] QF (margent)
2.1.97 murrain] QF (murrion)
2.1.101/456 cheere] HANMER (Theobald); heere QF
2.1.109/464 thinne] HALLIWELL (Tyrwhitt); chinne QF
2.1.111 mock'ry] F (mockry)
2.1.158/513 the] F; *not in* Q
2.1.183 off] Q1 (of)
2.1.190/545 slay ... slayeth] THEOBALD (Thirlby); ſtay ... ſtayeth QF
2.1.194 thee] Q1 (the)
2.1.201/556 nor] F; not Q
2.1.206 lose] Q1 (looſe)
2.1.244.1/599.1 *Exit ... him*] ROWE (*subs.*); *not in* Q1; *Exit.* Q2, F
2.1.254/609 these] QF; those This edition *conj.* As Oberon is holding a flower, QF's word is potentially misleading.
2.1.268.1/623 *Exeunt*] Q; *Exit.* F. F's variant could be deliberate, and its repetition of Q's later '*Enter Oberon*' (2.2.32.2/655.2) inadvertent, as happens elsewhere. If so, Oberon could immediately make clear theatrically his invisibility to or concealment from Titania and her train when they enter, thus obviating the need to explain how he gets past the sentinel.
2.2.9/632 I. FAIRY] CAPELL; *not in* QF
2.2.13, 24/636, 647 CHORUS] CAPELL; *not in* QF
2.2.20, 31/643, 654 I. FAIRY ... 2. FAIRY] Q. F reverses these numerals. This might be a compositorial error, but the change may be deliberate. If in the prompt-book the song were not broken down into sections, but simply attributed to the Fairies collectively, then the exit line which follows might reasonably be attributed to '1. Fairy' (the first to be given a speaking part, and here acting as leader). If the annotator as a result changed the attribution of 2.2.31/654, but left 2.2.20/643 standing, this would produce two consecutive attributions to the same character, and a compositor might alter 2.2.20/643 on his own initiative to remove the anomaly.
2.2.25–30/648–53 Sing ... with lullaby.] &c. QF (after melody,)
2.2.30.1/653.1 *Titania sleepes*] *Shee ſleepes* F (after 2.2.32/655); *not in* Q
2.2.31–2/654–5 Hence ... Centinell] *indented as part of the song*, Q1; *indented and italicized as part of the song*, Q2, F
2.2.44–5/667–8 comfort ... Be it] Q2, F; comfor ... Bet it Q1. It is possible the two errors are related (Brooks), though neither line shows any sign of looseness, and the affected words are not adjacent. Wilson thinks 'Bet' the contracted form for 'Be it', with the 'it' unintentionally duplicated. Certainly the metre suggests that construction is intended, whether or not orthographically indicated.
2.2.49/672 good] Q2, F; god Q1. This line is press-variant in Q (see incidentals), but in the Bodleian copy—the only copy extant which has the corrected state—the first half of the line is missing, because of a large tear which begins here.
2.2.53/676 is] Q2, F; it Q1
2.2.71.1/694.1 *They sleepe*] F; *not in* Q
2.2.93/716 *Exit Demetrius*] F; *not in* Q
2.2.110/733 shewes] Q; her ſhewes F; shows her BOSWELL (Malone)
2.2.111/734 thy heart] QF; my heart DYCE (W. S. Walker)
2.2.155 ate] QF (eate)
3.1.46/832 SNOUT] CAMBRIDGE; Sn. Q, F1; Snug. F2
3.1.49.1/835.1 *Enter Robin the Pucke, inuisible*] F (*Enter Pucke*); *not in* Q. F here adds '*Enter Pucke.*' but also retains the Q direction '*Enter Robin*' at 3.1.70.1/857.1, immediately before he speaks. '*Pucke*' and '*Robin*' are of course the same character, and Greg cites this duplicated direction as clear evidence of 'the clumsiness' of the Folio editor. Every editor since Rowe has ignored the added F direction, and at an elementary level the Folio text is self-evidently either incomplete or contradictory: either one entrance direction is wrong, or—if both are correct—an intervening exit direction is missing.

The latter alternative seems relatively unlikely, because inept: Robin would enter silently, then quickly exit for no apparent reason, and very shortly afterwards re-enter, again for no obvious reason. Therefore, one entrance direction is probably wrong, and originally Shakespeare must have intended Robin to enter at the later point (3.1.70.1/857.1). Editors who wish to present the text as it stood in Shakespeare's pre-theatrical manuscript may reasonably prefer Q's text, but any editor committed to entertain possible authorial revision must consider F's alternative. The addition of '*Enter Pucke*' at 3.1.49.1/835.1 must be deliberate, and must reflect consultation of the manuscript: the alteration may have gone wrong, but no one will claim that the variant results from mere compositorial error in reprinting unaltered Q2 copy. But though F's addition at 3.1.49.1/835.1 must be deliberate, in one way or another, F's retention at 3.1.70.1/857.1 ('*Enter Robin*') could easily be inadvertent, since F here merely reproduces its Q2 copy, a retention readily explained by passive error on the part of either the annotator or compositor.

An editor must therefore weigh the claims of two alternatives: either Robin should in fact enter at 3.1.49.1/835.1, or the Folio text reflects a manuscript alteration which has somehow gone wrong. Editors have merely posited that the Folio direction at 3.1.49.1/835.1 results from gross 'incompetence'—indeed, unparalleled incompetence, for which no explanation is provided. A man collating Q2 against a manuscript, and occasionally adding and altering stage directions, has no conceivable reason to duplicate a stage direction already present in Q2, or gratuitously to place that direction 24 lines too early, in a context which provides neither any incentive for such an interpolation nor any possibility of confusion with the direction's proper location. Wilson suggested that the addition resulted from a prompter's warning, of a kind found in some later prompt-books; Greg objected, 'why an isolated example?' But this is not an insuperable objection, and in other cases such duplication may have been avoided because the annotator was intelligent enough to realize that, for instance, '*Enter Lysander: and Hermia*' (2.2.40.1/663.1) anticipated another '*Enter Lisander and Hermia*' four lines below. Here, he might have been misled by the change of nomenclature ('Robin' to 'Pucke'). On this assumption the annotator's behaviour at least makes sense, and Q's reading can be retained. But it also remains possible that Robin *did* enter at 3.1.49.1/835.1. After all, a puck is by nature mischievous and unpredictable. The Folio entrance is immediately preceded by Bottom's call for 'A Calender, a Calender: looke in the Almanack: finde out Moone-shine, finde out Moone-shine' (3.1.48–9/834–5). Robin's appearance at this point would, to the audience, guarantee comic mischief, even before he spoke. By the very next speech Quince seems somehow to have acquired an almanac—

he replies, 'Yes: it doth shine that night'—and in performance the production and consultation of the book is almost inevitably the occasion of some sort of comic business. Can Robin's entrance at this very moment, between the question and its answer, be entirely coincidental? This is precisely the kind of change which might arise in rehearsal: with the need to produce a prop, a clear opportunity for clowning, and a mischievous puck standing by for his entrance, the suggestion might naturally arise that the puck somehow comically supply the book, or contribute to the associated comic business. Robin's silent presence throughout the following dialogue also creates dramatic opportunities. Theatrically, F's early entrance has everything to recommend it.

3.1.64/850 and] DYCE (Collier MS); or QF

3.1.70/857 cue.] This edition; cue. | *Enter Robin.* QF. See note to 3.1.49.1/835.1

3.1.76/863 of] QF; have COLLIER 2; ha' WILSON. Compare *History of Lear* 24.301/3084, where 'of' is substituted in error for 'haue'. To produce consistent sense, one must either emend 'of' here or 'hath' in 3.1.79/866, but an audience is most unlikely to notice the inconsistency of syntax.

3.1.77/864 Odours, odours] F; Odours, odorous Q; Odorous, odorous CUNINGHAM (Collier); 'Odious'—odorous ALEXANDER

3.1.78/865 Odours] F; Odorous BROOKS (Jenkins)

3.1.79/865 hath] QF; that ROWE 1; doth ROWE 3. See note to 3.1.76/863.

3.1.82/869 ROBIN] F (*Puck.*); Quin. Q. F also adds 'Pir.' to the '*Exit.*' in the preceding line.

3.1.82/869 *Exit*] CAPELL: *not* in QF. See 3.2.13-19/994-1000.

3.1.89/876 brisly] This edition; brisky QF. Thisbe's other commendations of Pyramus are absurd, but a young man would naturally be 'brisk'. On the other hand, for Elizabethan writers the hallmark of a juvenile was his lack of a beard, so *bristly*—a word Shakespeare uses in *Venus* and the *Sonnets*—would be suitably incongruous. By contrast, 'brisky' is recorded nowhere else. The proposed misreading would be easy; for the spelling see *OED*.

3.1.89 juvenile] Q (Iuuenall). The *-al* spelling is early (twice in Shakespeare and once in 1607), superseded by the *-ile* alternative (1625+). Here there seems no reason *not* to modernize.

3.1.97.1/883.1 *Enter ⌐Robin, leading⌐*] This edition (after CAPELL); *not* in QF

3.1.97.1/883.1 *Bottom . . . head*] THEOBALD; *not* in Q. See note to 3.1.106.1/893.2.

3.1.100/887 *The Clownes all Exit*] F; *not* in Q

3.1.101/888 about] QF; 'bout DYCE 2 (W. S. Walker)

3.1.106/893.2 *Enter . . . head*] This edition (after F: '*Piramus with*'); *not* in Q, ROWE. See note to 3.1.97.1/883.1.

3.1.142/930 owne] Q2, F; owe Q1. Riverside, the first edition to have noted Q1's reading, retains it, presumably on the strength of *OED*'s recognition of the form (*a.γ*). But this would not only be an exceptionally late occurrence of the form (13th–16th c.), but the only one in the Shakespeare canon, which has 'owne' over 800 times. Simple compositorial error seems almost certain.

3.1.154/942 *Pease-blossome . . . Mustard-seede*?] Q1; ~. Q2; *not* in F. See note to 3.1.154.1-2/942.1-2.

3.1.154 Mote] QF (*Moth*). Since we learn nothing of this character, it is hard to judge which meaning was uppermost in Shakespeare's mind; but his two clear references to the insect (*Merchant* 2.9.78/1135, *Othello* 1.3.256/542) are both derogatory, and he refers to 'mote(s)' much more frequently.

3.1.154.1-2/942.1-2 *Enter foure . . . Mustard-seede*] *Enter foure Fairyes* Q; *Enter Peaſe-bloſſome, Cobweb, Moth, Muſtard-|ſeede, and foure Fairies* F. The Folio compositor apparently misinterpreted the preceding line of dialogue as part of this stage direction.

3.1.155/943 A FAIRY . . . ANOTHER . . . ANOTHER . . . ANOTHER . . . ⌐ALL FOUR⌐] This edition; *Fairies.* Q1; *Fai.* Q2, F. ROWE first divided the speech among the four fairies; CAPELL first assigned 'Where shall we goe?' to '*All.*' (though in a sense this merely reverts, for the end of the line, to Q1's prefix). WHITE identified the order of speakers with the order of names in Titania's summons; STEEVENS-REED 2 (Farmer) omitted the third 'and I' and gave 'where shall we goe?' to the fourth fairy.

3.1.158 apricots] QF (Apricocks).

3.1.167/955 A FAIRY] This edition; *1. Fai.* QF; *Peaseblossom* DYCE

3.1.167-8/955-6 mortall. | ⌐ANOTHER⌐ Haile.] CAPELL (mortal! 2. hail!); mortall, haile. QF; mortall! | *Cob.* Hail! DYCE

3.1.169-70/957-8 ANOTHER . . . ANOTHER] This edition; *2. Fai. . . . 3. Fai.* QF; *3 . . . 4* CAPELL: *Moth . . . Mus.* DYCE

3.1.180/975 you of] DYCE; you Q, F1; your F3

3.1.193/981 loue's] POPE; louers QF

3.2.0.1/981.1 *solus*] F; *and Robin goodfellow* Q

3.2.3.1/984.1 *Enter Robin goodfellow the Pucke*] F (*Enter Pucke*); *not* in Q. See preceding note.

3.2.6/987 loue.] ROWE; ~, QF

3.2.7/988 bower,] Q2; ~. Q1

3.2.15/996 brake:] ROWE; ~, QF

3.2.16/997 take,] Q2; ~: Q1

3.2.19/1000 Mimmick] F; Minnick Q1; Minnock Q2

3.2.25/1006 our stampe] QF; a stump JOHNSON (Theobald). Robin says that later 'senselesse things *begin* to doe them wrong' (3.2.28/1009; our italics), which makes *stump* unlikely here.

3.2.80/1061 so] POPE; *not* in QF

3.2.85/1066 sleepe] ROWE; flippe QF

3.2.101/1082 *Exit*] Q2, F; *not* in Q1

3.2.121.1/1102.2 *Helena, Lysander following her*] This edition; *Lyſander, and Helena* QF. See 2.1.187.1/542.1.

3.2.137/1118 HELENA] This edition; *not* in QF. W. S. Walker conjectured that a line might have been omitted; Furness justified the absence of a rhyme by 'The new turn given to the dramatic action'. But the other awakenings in the play justify no such procedure, and it would be more natural for Helena's voice to waken Demetrius, as it woke Lysander earlier. Prompt-books since 1755 have occasionally added material here, or deleted Lysander's line. It would be natural, given the tit for tat of the repartee, for Helena to name Demetrius in her retort; some allusion to vision—wishing not to see Lysander?—would neatly prompt Demetrius' waking speech; Shakespeare elsewhere rhymes 'you' with 'view'. It seems almost certain that neither Helena nor Lysander notices Demetrius on the ground; that would duplicate the effect of the earlier scene, and in any case seems ruled out by Oberon's prediction that 'The noyse, they make, | Will cause *Demetrius* to awake'. One might also expect Helena's line to be in some way ironic, in relation to what immediately follows it, or what the audience knows as she speaks it. But confident restoration is beyond an editor's scope.

3.2.138/1119 awaking] F ('*Awa.*' *at end of preceding line*); *not* in Q

3.2.151/1132 soules] QF; flouts HANMER; scoffs JOHNSON (*conj.*); scorns JOHNSON (*conj.*); ieeres This edition *conj.*

3.2.165 here] Q1 (heare), Q2 (heere), F (here)

3.2.202/1183 is all quite forgot] This edition; is all forgot QF. The metrical irregularity has prompted many conjectures. Additions of 'this' and 'then' have little to recommend them; 'it' (Spedding *conj.*) could easily have been omitted, but the Shakespeare canon offers no parallels for the resulting phrase. Malone ('is all now') and Reed ('now is all') agreed to add 'now', though to different effect; the word is relevant, and Shakespeare juxtaposes 'now' and 'forget' at *Duke of York* 4.8.45/2297. But Shakespeare modifies the verb *forget* ten times with the adjective *quite*, and if metrical emendation is to be attempted 'quite' is easily the most Shakespearian restoration possible.

3.2.214/1195 like] THEOBALD; life QF

3.2.216 rend] QF (rent)

3.2.221/1202 passionate] F; *not* in Q

3.2.238/1219 I,] Q2, F; ~⌐ Q1

3.2.251/1232 praiers] THEOBALD; praiſe QF. 'Pleas' is a possible alternative to Theobald's solution.

3.2.258/1239 No, no, Sir] F; No, no Q. See next note.

3.2.258/1239 yeeld:] This edition; heele⌐ Q1; hee'l⌐ Q2; *not* in F. See Gary Taylor, 'A Crux in *A Midsummer Night's Dream*', *N&Q* 230 (1985), 47-9.

3.2.261 off] Q1 (of)

A MIDSUMMER NIGHT'S DREAM

3.2.280/1261 doubt] POPE; of doubt QF
3.2.300/1281 gentlemen] Q2, F; gentleman Q1
3.2.327/1308 but] Q2, F; hut Q1
3.2.330 *minimus*] QF. Johnson's was the first edition not to italicize this word: this is its first occurrence in English literature, it exactly reproduces the Latin form, and was almost certainly perceived as Latin.
3.2.339.1/1320.1 *Exit Lysander and Demetrius*] F; *Exit.* Q2; *not in* Q1
3.2.345/1326 HERMIA . . . say.] *not in* F. See next note.
3.2.345/1326 *Exit*] CAPELL; *Exeunt.* Q; *not in* F. White defended F's omission: the line is pretty feeble, and a silent exit chasing Helena would be as or more effective. The added stage direction in the following line makes it reasonably clear that a manuscript was consulted hereabouts.
3.2.345.1/1326.1 *Oberon and Robin come forward*] WELLS (subs.); *Enter Oberon and Pucke* F; *not in* Q. A parallel for F's odd direction occurs in Dekker's *If This Be Not a Good Play, the Devil is in it*, where the Quarto has 'Enter King as a Frier' at 5.2.19, though the King speaks an aside at 5.2.10 and hears at least some of the dialogue before his Quarto entrance. In *Dream*, no editor has taken F's direction literally. Oberon and Robin do not appear earlier on N6 or N6ᵛ, set by Folio Compositor D, and N5ᵛ (on which they last appear) was set by C; the Folio direction might be compositorial in origin, or—more probably—an ambiguous 'Oberon and Pucke' in the margin (of the manuscript or Q2) might have been misunderstood as a direction for entrance. Compare 3.3.8.1/1402.2, below (on the same Folio page).
3.2.375/1355 imploy] Q1, F4; apply Q2; imply F1. F1 almost certainly represents a bungled correction of Q2.
3.2.385/1366 gone,] ALEXANDER; ~ : Q
3.2.386/1367 vpon:] ALEXANDER; ~, Q
3.2.387/1368 exild] ALEXANDER (Thirlby); exile Q; dxile F. Another bungled correction.
3.2.389/1370 OBERON] QF. THIRLBY conjectured that Oberon's speech should have begun two lines earlier (3.2.387/1368).
3.2.405/1384, etc. *shifting places*] This edition; F *places after* 3.3.4/1398; *not in* Q. Brooks dismisses F's addition as an editorial insertion, prompted by 'shifting euery place' (3.3.11/1405). But although the verbal form of the direction has undoubtedly been based on the dialogue phrase, this similarity by no means accounts for F's addition. Neither the annotator nor the compositor would have reached 3.3.11/1405 yet, and no one has even pretended to give an explanation for someone in the printing house going back eight lines in order to add a nonsensical stage direction echoing (or, more properly, anticipating) a dialogue phrase. Nothing in the context of 3.3.4/1398 elicits such editorial interference; the stage direction in fact occurs in the middle of the only speech in this sequence where 'shifting places' is senseless, because only one actor is on stage, engaged in a reflective decision-making soliloquy. Editors regularly dismiss Folio additions like '*lye down*' (3.3.6/1400) because the action they describe is implicit in and so prompted by the dialogue; but, by the same token, bewildering additions like this one have a strong presumption to authority.

Wilson also dismissed this Folio addition, but before doing so he provided the best explanation of its presence and meaning: 'The stage-business [in Robin's game of blind-man's buff with Lysander and Demetrius], involving as it did the entry and re-entry of both men, one after the other, to say nothing of still more complicated movements on the part of Puck, would need careful and probably frequent rehearsal. What more natural than that the stage-manager should make a special note in the margin of this critical passage in the prompt-book . . . ?' (pp. 156-7). Wilson spoils this reasonable suggestion by linking it with his hypothesis that the prompt-book was itself a marked-up exemplar of Q1, later collated by Jaggard with an exemplar of Q2. But the implausibility of Wilson's textual hypothesis in no way impairs the plausibility of his explanation of this particular crux. Moreover, two details strongly support Wilson's explanation. One is the fact that the added direction occurs approximately in the middle of the Robin-Demetrius-Lysander sequence; another is the difficulty of indicating the appropriate stage business in any other way. A marginal direction '*shifting places*', with a vertical line or bracket indicating that it applies to a range of the preceding and following dialogue, is the most economical and intelligible way to explain the staging of this sequence. The Folio has reproduced the position of the added words, in so far as it places them opposite a certain line of the text; but the need to fit that direction into a tight column made it impossible to use the brackets, vertical lines, or even the marginal white space which would make the direction intelligible. (Similar constraints of format affect any modern edition, and we have therefore resorted to repeating the direction opposite all of the speeches to which it most probably applies.)

3.2.404/1386 *Exit Lysander*] THEOBALD; *not in* QF; *Lysander wanders about, following the voice* BEVINGTON. Bevington claims it is 'not clearly necessary' for Lysander to exit; but since Robin apparently proceeds to mimic Lysander's voice, it would be particularly confusing if he remained on stage, 'following' Robin's changed voice and not responding to Demetrius' real one. Contemporary prompt-books often fail to mark exits and rapid re-entrances like this.
3.2.407/1388 Speake: in some bush?] CAPELL; ~ ₐ ~ . QF
3.2.413/1394 *Exeūt*] Q; *Exit.* F. The longer Q word would not have fitted F's column.
3.3.0.1/1394.1 *Enter Lysander*] THEOBALD; *not in* QF. See note at 3.2.404/1386.
3.3.6/1400 He lyes down] lye down. F (*at end of line*); *not in* Q
3.3.8.1/1402.2 *Enter*] F; *not in* Q
3.3.14/1408 shalt] Q2, F; ſhat Q1
3.3.26.1/1420.1 *Enter Hermia*] This edition; *not in* Q1; *after* 3.3.28/1422 Q2, F; *after* 3.3.29/1423 ROWE
3.3.37/1431 to] ROWE; *not in* QF
3.3.39/1433 thou] QF. The metre could be made more regular by reading 'then thou' (assuming haplography) or 'thou now' (assuming simple omission); but 3.3.36/1430 has an identical syllabic pattern.
3.3.48/1441.1 *Exit*] ROWE; *not in* Q; *They ſleepe all the Act.* F. See Introduction.
4.1.0.1/1441.2 *Faieries*] This edition; *Faieries: and | the king behind them.* QF. See note at 4.1.44.2/1485.2.
4.1.16/1457.1 *Exit Cobweb*] This edition; *not in* QF. Bottom dismisses Cobweb here, and one would expect him to depart on his mission; QF elsewhere omit many necessary exits. The action here has been obscured by the crux at 4.1.23/1464 (see note).
4.1.20 courtesy] Q1 (curtſie), Q2, F (courteſie). The 'primary' sense is indeterminable, and as a modernization *courtesy* has at least the merit of being similarly unspecific.
4.1.22 Cavaliery] QF (Caualery). The QF spelling is normal for the period, except in its odd -y suffix.
4.1.23/1464 *Pease-blossom*] RANN; *Cobwebbe* QF. Editors claim that Q's alliteration looks deliberate, but it might equally well explain a compositorial error—as might the fact that Cobweb's name had been set three times since Peaseblossom was mentioned.
4.1.24 marvellous] Q1 (maruailes), Q2 (maruailous), F (maruellous)
4.1.29.1/1470.1 *Rurall Muſicke*] *Muſicke Tongs, Rurall Muſicke.* F; *not in* Q. Capell, typically, claimed that 'This scenical direction is certainly an interpolation of the players, as no such direction appears in either [Quarto], and Titania's reply is a clear exclusion of it'. But the absence of the direction from Q proves nothing about its legitimacy, and Titania's reply need not be interpreted as 'a clear exclusion' of Bottom's request. Although a prolonged musical interlude seems unlikely, background music is entirely possible. Moreover, the odd duplication in F's direction increases the probability that the action was always intended. It is difficult to explain why the book-keeper should add '*Rurall Muſicke*' and then duplicate his own addition with the further addition '*Muſicke Tongs*'. But if the vague '*Rurall Muſicke*' stood in the fair copy, a book-keeper might well add the marginal specification, '*Muſicke Tongs*'. The fair copy could, of course, have been autograph, and if so '*Rurall Muſicke*' is Shakespeare's own descriptive direction.

A MIDSUMMER NIGHT'S DREAM

4.1.35/1476 thee of] This edition; thee QF; thee thence HANMER; for thee COLLIER (*conj.*). Most editors have agreed that a syllable is missing, and Hanmer's emendation was once widely accepted. But Shakespeare never used the locution 'fetch thence', though he used the verb frequently, with a variety of adverbs; moreover, 'thence' is a relatively long word, not often omitted. Shakespeare's practice elsewhere suggests that the missing word is either 'straight', 'in', 'off', or 'downe'. 'In' would not take the necessary stress, 'downe' seems unfortunate (because the squirrel's hoard is often on the ground), and 'straight' is a longish word not elsewhere omitted. 'Off', by contrast, is a short word omitted elsewhere (for instance Q3 *1 Henry IV* 1.2.163/267); three times in *Dream*, and a number of times in other foul-paper texts, the word is spelled 'of', and 'of' is omitted even more frequently than 'off'. Moreover, 'fetch off' had the idiomatic sense 'bring out of a difficulty, deliver, rescue' (*OED*, v. 16a); Shakespeare elsewhere uses it twice of Paroles' attempt to recover his drum. Since Titania specifies that a 'venturous Fairy' must undertake this mission, 'fetch off' seems especially appropriate.

4.1.36 peas] QF (pease)

4.1.40/1481 al waies] THEOBALD; alwaies QF

4.1.44.2/1485.2 *and Oberon, meeting*] This edition; *and Oberon* F; *not in* Q. Shakespeare originally intended Oberon to enter with Titania and the fairies (4.1.0.1-3/1441.2-4); but he made no dramatic use of Oberon's presence during the subsequent fifty lines, and his Folio entrance here creates no dramatic problems. Obviously, the added Folio entrance at 4.1.44.2/1485.2 conflicts with the retained Folio direction at 4.1.0.1-3/1441.2-4, but the failure to modify Q2's earlier direction is entirely characteristic of the Folio, which passively retains many Q2 readings it should have altered. There thus seems little reason to doubt that, of the Folio's two entrances for Oberon here, the second is deliberate and the first accidental. Nor does there seem any valid reason for rejecting the Folio reading, which presumably derives from the prompt-book. Oberon has encountered Titania only twice before: once when she is with her train, once when she is alone and asleep. The second encounter exactly duplicates this one: there, after she dismisses her train and falls asleep he enters to apply the magic juice to her eyes; here (according to the Folio), after she dismisses her train and falls asleep he enters and removes the spell by applying a different potion. If this structural parallel had occurred in Q, it would probably have been acclaimed as a stroke of dramatic genius. The Folio arrangement also has a practical advantage: an audience need not worry about why the other fairies fail to see Oberon.

4.1.54 flow'rets] QF (flouriets). 'Florets' would be equally acceptable. QF's anomalous 'i' may be an error.

4.1.72 o'er] QF (or). Theobald first proposed this interpretation, which is usually regarded as an emendation. But see *Kinsmen* 1.4.45/524, and the many examples of 'on' as an error for 'or' (meaning 'o'er').

4.1.81/1522 these, fiue,] THEOBALD (Thirlby); thefe, fine, QF

4.1.82.1/1523.1 *Still Musick*] THEOBALD; *Muſick ſtill*. F; *not in* Q. See Brooks's note, and *As You Like It* 5.4.105.1/2602.1.

4.1.84/1525 *The Musick changes*] This edition (*after* WILSON); *not in* QF

4.1.95/1536 nightes] This edition; nights Q1; the nights Q2, F. See 2.1.7/362.

4.1.101.2/1542.2 *Sleepers Lye still*] F (*after* 4.1.100/1541); *not in* QF. A necessary instruction in the theatre (but not for a printing-house editor), since the next winding of horns (4.1.137.2/1578.2) will wake them.

4.1.101.3/1542.3 *Winde hornes*] F (*Winde Hornes.*); *Winde horne* Q1; *Winde hornes*. Q2. Both quartos place the direction after 'traine.'

4.1.101.3-4/1542.3-4 *Egeus, Hippolita*] F; *not in* Q

4.1.104 vanguard] QF (vaward)

4.1.112/1553 Beare] QF; boar HANMER (Theobald)

4.1.116/1557 Seemd] F2; Seeme Q, F1

4.1.127/1568 this is] Q2, F; this Q1

4.1.137.2/1578.2 *Shoute ... vp*] This edition; *Shoute within: they all ſtart vp. Winde hornes.* Q; *Hornes and they wake.* | *Shout within, they all ſtart vp.* F. F's addition clearly duplicates part of what it retains from Q2, since the lovers can hardly 'start vp' unless 'they wake'. Moreover, this combination of retained and added directions gives the impression that the horns precede the shout; Q1's direction, by contrast, suggests that the waking precedes the horns. F independently confirms what may be suggested by Q: that '*Winde hornes*' was added separately from (and after?) the rest of the direction. Theseus's speech specifies what logic would infer, that the *shoute* ('Goe, bid') precedes the *hornes*, which 'wake' the lovers. As here transposed, '*Winde hornes*' can be both a playhouse direction and the context of the off-stage shout.

4.1.171/1612 see Hermia] QF; saw Hermia STEEVENS 2; did see Hermia ROWE 1; Hermia saw ROWE 3. See the note to *LLL* 4.1.69/1000.

4.1.172/1613 But,] Q2, F; ~, Q1. This emendation seems necessary if we are to interpret 'But like' as 'Only as'. This in turn allows us to retain QF's 'But' in the next line.

4.1.172/1613 in sicknesse] STEEVENS-REED 2 (anonymously conjectured in *The Student*, Oxford, 1760); a ſickneſſe QF. Furness defends QF ('I see no nonsense in claiming that a man loathes a sickness. We all do'), but this defence requires emendation of 'But' in the next line and destroys the contrast between the two lines. Capell, followed by Kittredge and others, glosses 'sicknesse' as 'a sick thing or one sick'. Although Shakespeare does elsewhere use abstract for concrete in this way, there are no parallels—in Shakespeare or other writers—for this concrete use of *sickness*, which would be especially unfortunate here, because of the very ambiguity noted by Furness. And if Shakespeare meant what Capell meant, why did he not write 'sickman' instead of 'sicknesse'? Corruption thus seems probable. Steevens's emendation is supported by the apparent ease with which Shakespeare's 'a' could be misread as two or more minims. But 'a sickman' is also attractive, since Shakespeare elsewhere treated the compound as one word (see *Coriolanus* 1.1.176/174 and *OED*).

4.1.173/1614 But] QF; Yet HANMER; Now CUNINGHAM (Furness)

4.1.185.1-2/1626.1-2 *Exit ... traine*] F (*Exit Duke and Lords.*); *not in* Q1; *Exit.* Q2

4.1.190/1631 found] Q2, F; fonnd Q1

4.1.191/1632 It] F; Are you ſure | That we are awake? It Q. F's omission is of a kind very difficult to attribute to compositorial error. Q's additional sentence—doubly anomalous metrically, and superfluous—is not nonsensical, and hence an unlikely target for alleged 'editorial' tampering. F's omission therefore presumably derives from the prompt-book. That prompt-book may have been an autograph fair copy; even if it were not, we have no reason to suspect that the phrase would be particularly objectionable to actors: even editors who attribute major cuts in other Folio plays to the actors have not claimed that this cut was made 'to shorten the play'. Shakespeare is the man most likely to have cut these words, and probably intended to do so even in the foul papers: the sentence bears all the hallmarks of a first shot abandoned *currente calamo*.

4.1.197/1638 let vs] Q2, F; lets Q1

4.1.197.1/1638.1 *Exeunt Louers*] F (*Exit Louers.*); *Exit.* Q2; *not in* Q1

4.1.197.2/1638.2 *Bottom wakes*] F; *not in* Q

4.1.204/1645 t'expound] RIVERSIDE; expound Q1; to expound Q2, F

4.1.207/1648 a patcht foole] F; patcht a foole Q

4.1.211 ballad] QF (Ballet)

4.1.214/1655 a Play] QF; our play W. S. WALKER (*conj.*)

4.1.215/1657 at her] QF; after THEOBALD

4.1.215/1657 *Exit*] Q2, F; *not in* Q1

4.2.0.1/1657.1 *Flute*] ROWE 3; *Flute, Thisby* QF

4.2.0.1/1657.1 *Snout, and Starueling*] F; *and the rabble* Q

4.2.3/1660 STARUELING] F; *Flut.* Q

4.2.27/1686 no] F; *not* Q. F seems idiomatically right; Wilson, the first editor to revert to Q, offered no parallels.

4.2.40.1/1700 *Exeunt*] F; *not in* Q

5.1.0.1/1700.1 Egeus] F; *not in* Q. There can be no doubt that this addition and the related changes to speech-prefixes come from the prompt-book. For a defence of the critical merits of the change, see Hodgdon. Assertions that it was made for reasons of doubling are unfounded and implausible.

5.1.0.1/1700.1 his Lords] F; Philoſtrate Q. His = Theseus'; for the form of the direction see 4.1.101.4/1542.4

5.1.34/1734 o^r] F (our); Or Q. Q misinterprets the abbreviation, and in mislining the passage capitalizes the word as the beginning of a verse line.

5.1.35/1735 Egeus] F; Philoſtrate Q. Perhaps 5.1.35/1735 should have been deleted, when the name was altered here and elsewhere.

5.1.38, 42, 61, 72, 106/1738, 1742, 1761, 1772, 1806 EGEUS] F (Ege.); Philoſtrate Q (5.1.38/1738; *variously abbreviated thereafter*)

5.1.44/1744 LYSANDER] F; *The.* Q

5.1.46, 50, 54, 58/1746, 1750, 1754, 1758 THESEUS] F; *not in* Q

5.1.48, 52, 56/1748, 1752, 1756 LYSANDER] F; *not in* Q

5.1.59/1759 strange blacke] CAPELL (Upton); ſtrange QF. QF's reading has been interpreted as '[equally] prodigious snow', but why should their play be compared to snow? The allegedly 'unjustifiable' expectation of an oxymoron is itself created by the passage, with its rapid succession of tedious/brief, tragical/mirth, merry/tragical, tedious/brief, hot/ice, concord/discord. The manner is entirely characteristic of Shakespeare's early verse. Moreover, snow is particularly liable to prompt Shakespeare to such contrasts: witness 'kindle fire with snow' (*Two Gentlemen* 2.7.19/948), 'a Snow in Mayes new fangled showes' (*LLL* 1.1.106/106), 'amity . . . Tweene snow and fire' (*Merchant* 3.2.30–1/1310–11), 'wallow naked in December snow | By thinking on fantasticke sommers heate' (*Richard II* 1.3.261–2/540–1); 'cold Snow melts with the Sunnes hot Beames' (*Contention* 3.1.223/1404), merciful 'as snow in haruest' (*Richard III* 1.4.237/1000), 'In winter with warme teares Ile melt the snow' (*Titus* 3.1.20/1036), 'Whiter then new snow on a Rauens backe' (*Romeo* 3.2.19/1601), 'high *Taurus* snow . . . turns to a crowe' (*Dream* 3.2.142–3/1123–4), 'draweth frō my snowhite pen the ebon coloured Incke' (*LLL* 1.1.237–8/237), and 'a snowie Doue trooping with Crowes' (*Romeo* 1.5.47/621). All of these examples are from the same period as *Dream*, and they reinforce in the strongest possible way the contextual expectation of an oxymoron here. So too does the metrical deficiency of the passage as it stands. Shakespeare elsewhere uses *wondrous* 35 times in verse; it is always disyllabic.

If, as seems almost certain, the line is corrupt, then either a word has been omitted after 'strange' or 'strange' is an error for some other word (or both). Most of the conjectures which litter the collations of Furness assume that 'strange' is wrong. But the phrase *wondrous strange* occurs twice elsewhere in Shakespeare (*Duke of York* 2.1.33/615, *Hamlet* 1.5.166/783; see also 'wondrous single', *Coriolanus* 2.1.36/790). Moreover, most of the conjectural alternatives are unusual adjectives: scorching, seething, scalding, flaming, fiery, sooty, sable, swarthy. The commonplace adjective 'hot' for 'ice' gives us no particular reason to expect a vividly particular attribute for snow here; nor would we expect an adjective which emphasizes heat, because then *hot ice* and [X] *snow* would become mere repetitions. Those conjectures which emphasize some other conventional attribute of snow are much more attractive contextually, but are all less attractive palaeographically.

Conjectural misreadings have accumulated because editors prefer in general to emend something present than to supply something absent. But Q clearly omits several words elsewhere, and the parallels for *wondrous strange* make omission likelier than coincidentally Shakespearian substitution. Shakespeare's other snow conceits suggest that a contrast of colour is most likely; to the examples already cited may be added 'Lawne as white as driuen snow, | Cypresse blacke . . .' (*Winter's Tale* 4.4.219–20/1825–6) and 'Black *Macbeth* | Will seeme as pure as Snow' (*Macbeth* 4.3.53–4/1600–1). Both parallels support Upton's conjecture 'wondrous strange [black] snow'. Shakespeare uses *black* 177 times, often in such contrasts or oxymorons. The only other appropriate monosyllable is *jet* (conj. Perring), which Shakespeare uses only six times, and only once in contrast (to ivory). *Black* therefore seems far and away the most probable and Shakespearian solution. In *Dream*, as elsewhere in Shakespeare, it is usually spelled 'blacke', and the omission might have occurred through haplography (stran*ge* *blacke* snow)—or, of course, by simple inadvertence.

5.1.76/1776 EGEUS] This edition; *Phi.* QF. Although Philostrate might be included among the 'Lords' who enter with Theseus at the beginning of the scene, it seems absurd for him to intervene in this fashion, especially as his mere presence draws unnecessary and undesirable attention to the fact that Egeus has taken over his role as Master of the Revels. If Philostrate never appears, an audience is unlikely to be troubled by this minute discrepancy between the first and last scenes of the play; if he appears, and more particularly if he speaks this speech, the inconsistency cannot go unnoticed. Almost certainly F has simply failed to alter one of its copy prefixes.

5.1.84.1/1784.1 Exit Egeus] This edition; *not in* QF; *Exit Philostrate* POPE

5.1.91/1791 duty cannot doe,] QF; (willing) duty cannot do, THEOBALD; duty cannot do, yet would, COLERIDGE (conj. in Cambridge); duty would, but cannot do, F. A. MARSHALL (conj., recorded by Halliwell)

5.1.105.1/1805.1 Enter Egeus] This edition; *not in* QF; *Enter Philostrate* CAPELL

5.1.107.1/1807.1 Florish Trumpets.] F (*Flor. Trum.*); *not in* Q. The plural was probably intended: see note to *Hamlet* 3.2.129.1/1857.1

5.1.107.1/1807.1 Quince as] F (subs.: *placing 'Quince.' to the right of the entrance direction*); *not in* Q

5.1.125.1/1825.1 Enter ⌈with a Trumpet before them⌉] ALEXANDER; *Tawyer with a Trumpet before them.| Enter* F; *Enter* Q. See Introduction.

5.1.139–40/1839–40 night, | Did] QF. The formal ineptitude probably results from textual corruption, but may be deliberately comic; no one has ventured to invent a line to rhyme with *name*.

5.1.150.1/1850.1 Exit . . . Wall] F (*Exit all but Wall.*); *Exit* Lyon, Thysby, *and* Moonſhine QF (*after* 5.1.153/1853)

5.1.155/1855 Snowt] F; *Flute* Q

5.1.166.1/1866.1 Enter . . . Pyramus] *Enter Pyramus* F (*after* 5.1.167/1867); *not in* Q

5.1.190/1890 vp in thee] F; now againe Q. Though Q cannot be right, it is not likely to be a misreading of the words in F. Shakespeare's other rhymes with *me*, or uses of *lime* or *hair* or *stones* offer no help; given the pun on stones, it might be relevant that *knit* can mean 'to geld (a ram)' (*OED*, v. 1c). Perhaps *againe* is a misreading of a word ending -nie, -mie, or -rie.

5.1.93/1893 loue, thou art,] HANMER; ~ ∧ ~ , QF

5.1.195 Lemander] QF (*Limander*)

5.1.197, 198 Shaphalus] QF (*Shafalus*)

5.1.204/1904 Exit] F (*Exit Clow.*); *not in* Q. F's 'Clow.' presumably stands for all three actors, even though Bottom and Flute almost certainly begin their exit before Snout.

5.1.205–8/1905–8 Now . . . warning] This passage contains three cruxes in quick succession, and even after the most venturous emendation it remains feeble: in performance it is often—and perhaps wisely—omitted altogether. One expects a joke about the wall moving. Instead, two proverbs are hinted at, neither very cogently: 'walls have ears', and 'Love your neighbour, but keep your hedge', and various related aphorisms about the wisdom of fences. The three cruxes are discussed separately, but in fact a truly convincing solution to any one of them might illuminate the others.

5.1.205/1905 wall] COLLIER; Moon Q; morall F; Mural POPE 2; mure all THEOBALD; mure BROOKS. Neither Q nor F can in itself be right, nor is either easily understood as an error for the other. Pope's 'murall' is last recorded in this sense in the mid sixteenth century, and seems pointlessly archaic here. 'Mure' is much more acceptable, but Theobald's 'all' is hopeless padding and

Brooks's 'mure' not easily misread as 'Moon'. Collier's conjecture has been accepted simply because (*a*) it makes sense (*b*) it explains F's error as a bungled correction (*c*) F's variant almost certainly comes from the prompt-book. Q's error need not be a simple misreading.

5.1.205/1905 downe] F; vſed Q; rased BROOKS. Brooks's conjecture makes the same sense as F, but by conjecture rather than authority; although either 'mure' or 'rased' might be acceptable, in combination they sound pointlessly affected.

5.1.208/1908 heare] QF; leave GOULD (*conj.*). Gould's conjecture makes some sense, and is palaeographically attractive. Editors defend Q by reference to the proverbial 'walls have ears'; but no reference has been made to Wall *hearing* the lovers' conversation, and the word seems a feeble anticipation of the verb in the next line. Q seems unlikely to be right, but a convincing emendation depends upon the sense of Theseus' preceding speech, of which no one can be confident.

5.1.216/1916 beasts_∧ in,] ROWE 3; ~, ~_∧ QF

5.1.259.1/1960.1 *Lyon roares, Thisby droppes her mantle and runs off*] *The Lion roares, Thisby runs off* F; *not in* Q

5.1.269/1970 gleames] STAUNTON (Knight); beames Q, F1; streams F2

5.1.306/2007 prooue] Q2, F; yet prooue Q1

5.1.307/2008 before_∧] ROWE; ~ ? QF

5.1.309.1/2010.1 *Enter . . . Thisby*] F (*Enter Thisby*: after 5.1.308/2009); *not in* Q. F for no apparent reason divides Theseus' speech into verse, breaking the line after 'starre-light': perhaps an annotator's mark, indicating where to place the stage direction, was misinterpreted as a line-break.

5.1.313 mote] QF (moth)

5.1.314 warrant] Q (warnd)

5.1.325/2026 lippes] QF; brows THEOBALD

5.1.345/2046 BOTTOM] F; *Lyon*. Q. F's reading could not have been supplied without reference to a manuscript, for there is nothing self-evidently wrong with Q: though everyone prefers F, surely no one would adopt it if the emendation were merely conjectural.

5.1.347 bergamask] QF (Bergomaske)

5.1.355.1/2056.1 *Bottom and Flute*] This edition; *not in* QF. Most editors since Rowe have all the clowns dance, but Bottom specifies two, and only two are on the stage—himself and Flute.

5.2.1/2065 Lyon] ROWE; Lyons QF

5.2.2/2066 behoules] THEOBALD (Warburton); beholds QF. The neologism 'behoules' could easily have been misread as the common 'behoulds'; for the spellings see *OED*.

5.2.13 we] Q1 (wee). Modern 'wee' might be intended; but *OED*'s only Shakespearian example (*Merry Wives* 1.4.20/420) is dubious, and the metrical pattern discourages any special emphasis on the adjective here. Q uses this spelling for the pronoun 26 times elsewhere.

5.2.30.1/2094.1 *The Song.*] F; *not in* Q. F centres and italicizes the following speech, omitting the prefix for Oberon. The change may result from a misunderstood annotation: if '*The Song*' were added by the annotator from the prompt-book, then it might have been misunderstood by the printer as a heading for the following lines. It seems relatively unlikely that Shakespeare intended F's arrangement (see Brooks). However, it might represent a modification in a posthumous revival, at a time when the original song had been lost or forgotten.

5.2.31/2095 OBERON] *not in* F. See preceding note.

5.2.49–50/2113–14 And . . . rest.] STAUNTON (Singer); Euer . . . reft, | And . . . bleft. QF

REJECTED FOLIO VARIANTS

1.1.131/131 my] mine
1.1.132/132 Eigh me:] *not in* F
1.1.132/132 I could euer] euer I could
1.1.140/140 eyes] eie
1.1.143/143 momentany] momentarie
1.1.160/160 remote] remou'd
1.1.163/163 Can not] Cannot
1.1.167/167 to a] for a
1.1.182/182 your] you
1.1.225/225 dote] dotes
1.1.229/229 doe] doth
1.1.239/239 is so oft] is oft Q2; is often F1; often is F2
1.1.244/244 this] Q1, F; his Q2
1.1.248/248 this] his
1.2.9/260 to] on to
1.2.20/271 gallant] gallantly
1.2.60/312 here] there
1.2.62/313–14 if it bee] if] be
1.2.64/315 *extempore*] extemporie
1.2.74/325 if] if that
1.2.77/329 you,] *not in* F
1.2.88/339 colour] colour'd
2.1.65/420 hast] waſt
2.1.77/432 not thou] thou not
2.1.80/435 *Antiopa*] Atiopa
2.1.91/446 pelting] petty
2.1.136/491 doe I] I doe
2.1.177/532 when] whence Q2
2.1.191/546 vnto] into
2.1.210/565 vſe] doe
2.1.243/598 Ile] I
2.2.14/637 our] your
2.2.54/677 wee can] can you
2.2.55/678 interchained] interchanged
2.2.146/769 they] that

3.1.27/812 your ſelfe] your ſelues
3.1.41/827 them] him
3.1.81/868 *Exit*] Exit. Pir.
3.1.101/888 ROBIN] Q (*Rob.*); *Puk*. F
3.1.121/909 with little] and little
3.1.180/968 you of] of you
3.1.182/970 *Muſtardſeede.*] Muſtard-ſeede. | *Peaſ. Peaſe-bloſſome*.
3.2.5/986 haunted] gaunted
3.2.58/1039 murtherd] murdered Q2; murderer F
3.2.60/1041 looke] looks
3.2.69/1050 haue] a
3.2.99/1080 doe] doth
3.2.123/1104 come] comes
3.2.146/1127 all are] are all
3.2.152/1133 were] are
3.2.183/1164 thy] that
3.2.211/1192 an] a
3.2.321/1302 HELENA] *Her*.
3.2.336/1317 aby] abide
3.2.347/1328 wilfully] willingly
3.2.380/1361 nights ſwift] night ſwift Q2; night-ſwift F
3.3.23/1417 ſometimes] ſometime
4.1.27/1468 ſome] Q1, F; ſome ſome Q2
4.1.70/1511 as] thou as
4.1.79/1520 this] his
4.1.92/1533 Fairy] Faire
4.1.124/1565 hollowd] hallowed
4.1.177/1618 more will here] will heare more Q2; ſhall heare more F
4.1.202/1643 haue had] had
4.2.28/1687 right] *not in* F
5.1.16/1716 ayery] airy Q2; aire F
5.1.144/1844 trusty] *not in* F
5.1.172/1872 ô ſweete, ô] thou ſweet and
5.1.183/1883 enter now] enter

286

5.1.196/1896   I, like *Helen*] like *Helen*
5.1.221/1921   as] one
5.1.224/1924   on] of
5.1.240/1941   doe] doth
5.1.270/1971   take . . . Thisby] taſte . . . Thisbies
5.1.279/1980   ye] you

5.1.314-15/2015-16   he . . . bleſſe vs] *not in* F
5.1.352/2053   hangd] hung
5.2.3/2067   Whilſt] Whileſt
5.2.52/2116.1   *Exeunt. Manet Robin*] *Exeunt.* Q; *not in* F
Epi.4/2120   these] this Q2

INCIDENTALS

35 vnhardned] vnhardened (Huntington); ~, Q1 (*Bodleian*), Q2, F   57 looke.] ~,   152 patience] patienee   163 lou'ſt] F; loueſt Q   189 melody.] Q1   194 HERMIA I] Q (*text*); I Q (*c.w.*)   245 diſſolu'd] Q2; diſſolued Q1   277 split:] ~, QF   292 FLUTE] Fla.   397 speak'ſt] Q2; ſpeakeſt Q1   405 witherd] withered QF   477 mee.] ~,   508 certaine] cettaine   672 deere,] Q (*Bodleian*); ~, Q (*all other copies*)   694 HERMIA With] Q (*text*); With Q (*c.w.*)   714 thus.] ~,   778 thought] thoughr   792 bully,] Q2; ~, Q1   855 your] yonr   871 QUINCE I] Q (*text*); I Q (*c.w.*)   881 and,] ~,   919 enamourd] enamoured QF   1033 From] Frow   1039 murtherd] murthered   1065 growe,] ~.   1141 derision.] ~,   1221 sweete] ſweeete   1261 Therefore] Thefore   1376 notwithstanding] notwiſtanding   1455 much] mueh (?)   1471 desir'ſt] deſireſt   1585 enmitie.] ~,   1612 betroth'd] Q2; betrothed Q1   1774 toyld] toyled QF   1774 vnbreathd] vnbreathed QF   1829 *Thisby*] *Thſby*   1890 haire] hayire

QUARTO STAGE DIRECTIONS

1.1.0.1-2/0.1   *Enter* Theseus, Hippolita, *with others.*
1.1.19.1-2/19.1-2   *Enter* Egeus *and his daughter* Hermia, *and* Lysander | *and* Helena, *and* Demetrius.
1.1.127.1/127.1   *Exeunt.*
1.1.179.1/179.1   *Enter* Helena.
1.1.224/224   *Exit* Hermia.
1.1.225/225   *Exit* Lysander.
1.1.251/251   *Exit.*
1.2.0.1-4/251.1-4   *Enter* Quince, *the Carpenter; and* Snugge, *the Ioyner; and* Bottom, *the Weauer; and* Flute, *the Bellowes mender; &* | Snout, *the Tinker; and* Starueling *the Tayler.*
1.2.104/355   *Exeunt.*
2.1.0.1-2/355.1-2   *Enter a* Fairie *at one doore, and* Robin goodfellow | *at another. Enter the King of Fairies, at one doore, with his traine;* | *and the Queene, at another, with hers.*
2.1.145.1/500.1   *Exeunt.*
2.1.187.1/542.1   *Enter* Demetrius, Helena *following him:*
2.1.246.1/601.1   *Enter* Pucke. (after 2.1.247/602)
2.1.268.1/623.1   *Exeunt.*
2.2.0.1/623.2   *Enter* Tytania *Queene of Fairies, with her traine.*
2.2.8.1/631.1   *Fairies sing.*
2.2.32.2/655.2   *Enter* Oberon.
2.2.40.1/663.1   *Enter* Lysander: *and* Hermia.
2.2.71.2/694.2   *Enter* Pucke.
2.2.89/712   *Exit.*
2.2.89.1/712.1   *Enter* Demetrius *and* Helena *running.*
2.2.140/763   *Exit.*
2.2.150/773   *Exit.*
2.2.160/785   *Exit.*
3.1.0.1-2/785.1-2   *Enter the Clownes.*
3.1.49.1/835.1   *Enter* Robin. (after 3.1.70/857)
3.1.81/868   *Exit.* (after 3.1.70/857)
3.1.106/893.1   *Exit.*
3.1.108.1/895.1   *Enter* Snowte.
3.1.112.1/899   *Enter* Quince.
3.1.113.1/900.1   (*Exit.* (turned up on to same type line as '*Enter* Quince')
3.1.154.1-2/942.1-2   *Enter foure Fairyes.*
3.1.193/981   *Exit.*

3.2.0.1/981.1   *Enter King of* Fairies, *and* Robin goodfellow.
3.2.40.1/1021.1   *Enter* Demetrius *and* Hermia.
3.2.81/1062   *Exit.*
3.2.87.1/1068.1   *Ly doune.*
3.2.109.1/1090.1   *Enter* Puck.
3.2.121.2/1102.2   *Enter* Lysander, *and* Helena.
3.2.176.1/1157.1   *Enter* Hermia.
3.2.345/1326   *Exeunt.*
3.2.401.1/1382.1   *Enter* Lysander.
3.2.405/1386   *Enter* Demetrius.
3.2.413/1394   *Exeūt.*
3.3.8.1/1402.2   Robin, *and* Demetrius.
3.3.18.1/1412.1   *Enter* Helena.
3.3.24.1/1418.1   *Sleepe.*
4.1.0.1-3/1441.2-4   *Enter Queene of* Faieries, *and* Clowne, *and* Faieries: *and* | *the king behinde them.*
4.1.44.2/1485.2   *Enter* Robin goodfellow.
4.1.101.1-2/1542.1-2   *Exeunt.*
4.1.101.2-3/1542.3-4   *Enter* Theseus *and all his traine. Winde horne.*
4.1.137.2/1578.2   *Shoute within: they all start vp. Winde hornes.*
4.2.0.1/1657.1   *Enter* Quince, Flute, Thisby *and the rabble.*
4.2.14.1/1671.1   *Enter* Snug, *the Ioyner.*
4.2.22.1/1681.1   *Enter* Bottom.
5.1.0.1-2/1700.1   *Enter* Theseus, Hyppolita, *and* Philostrate.
5.1.27.1-2/1727.1   *Enter Louers;* Lysander, Demetrius, Hermia *and* | Helena.
5.1.107.1/1807.1   *Enter the Prologue.*
5.1.125.1-3/1825.1-4   *Enter* Pyramus, *and* Thisby, *and* Wall, *and* Moone-|shine, *and* Lyon.
5.1.150.1/1850.1   *Exit* Lyon, Thysby, *and* Mooneshine. (after 5.1.153/1853)
5.1.185.1/1885.1   *Enter* Thisby. (after 5.1.186/1886)
5.1.216.1/1916.1-2   *Enter* Lyon, *and* Moone-shine.
5.1.257.1/1958.1   *Enter* Thisby.
5.1.265.1/1966.1   *Enter* Pyramus. (after 5.1.266/1967)
5.1.363/2064   *Exeunt.*
5.2.0.1/2064.1   *Enter* Pucke.
5.2.20.1-2/2084.1-2   *Enter King and Queene of Fairies, with all their traine.*

ROMEO AND JULIET

Romeo and Juliet (BEPD 143) evidently escaped licensing in the Stationers' Register prior to the first published edition (Q1), dated 1597. The title-page identifies neither author nor publisher, but names the printer as John Danter; it states that the play 'hath been often (with great applause) plaid publiquely, by the right Honourable the L. of *Hunsdon* his Seruants'—so referring to Shakespeare's company as it was known between July 1596 and March 1597. Hoppe (*The Bad Quarto*) established that Danter printed only Sheets A–D. The remainder, E–K, set from a fount of smaller type, was the work of another printer whom Hoppe suggested and Henning confirmed to be Edward Allde. From Sheet G onwards, Allde introduced printers' ornaments between scenes and at other convenient points, evidently to fill up the expected number of sheets for his portion. Lavin proposed that the copy (at least for A–D) was cast off in advance so that the two printers could work concurrently; he argued that, although the title-page dates the play slightly later, *Romeo* was probably printed by March 1596/7, before the beginning of old-style 1597. Haggard examined type-recurrence to show that Q1 was set by formes.

Even though Q1 names no publisher, was not licensed, and, as will be seen, was based on a pirated text, Hoppe believed that it was not published surreptitiously. Danter was probably recognized as holding *de facto* copyright. Cuthbert Burby, for whom the 1599 edition of *Romeo* (Q2) was printed, retained the title until its transfer in 1607; on account of Burby's associations with Danter, Hoppe concluded that Burby acted as bookseller also for Q1, and perhaps virtually as publisher.

The title-page of Q2 states that it was 'Printed by Thomas Creede, for Cuthbert Burby'. According to Cantrell and Williams, two compositors set the text; Compositor A set all but K3ᵛ (4.4.127.2-168/2533.1-2572) and L3-M1 (5.3.87-252/2777-2942), the responsibility of B. Q2 claims on the title-page to be '*Newly corrected, augmented, and amended*'; it certainly provides a substantially varying, fuller, and more authoritative text, such as could only be produced from a manuscript independent of the copy for Q1.

'Permissive' stage directions, erratically varying speech-prefix forms (in particular for Capulet's wife), and repeated indications of *currente calamo* false starts all indicate that this manuscript was Shakespeare's rough draft. Though highly authoritative, the resultant text has two serious limitations. First, the foul papers repeatedly proved difficult for the Q2 compositors; the text they set is riddled with misinterpretations of the copy and confusions preserved from it. Secondly, Q1 certainly influenced Q2, and indeed a section of Q2 is agreed to have no authority independent of Q1.

Q1 influence on Q2 is damaging, as Q1 is not a reliable text. Hoppe convincingly showed that Q1 was set from a manuscript originally compiled by actors, identifying them as probably those who played Romeo and Paris. He suggested that they were disaffected players leaving Shakespeare's company to join the reconstituted Pembroke's Men early in 1597. Some 'un-Shakespearian' verse in Q1 was presumably supplied to complete the text where the report was deficient: a completely rewritten version of 2.5/Sc. 11 and, most notably amongst shorter passages, an alternative five lines at 3.2.57-60/1639-42. Hoppe rejected his own suggestion that the versifier was the playwright Henry Chettle, Danter's ex-partner as stationer and his continuing associate. Sidney Thomas subsequently argued that Chettle was well placed to contribute to the text underlying Q1, and that spelling and parallels of vocabulary and imagery are consistent with Chettle's authorship of the 'un-Shakespearian' material ('Henry Chettle and the First Quarto'). Chettle may have been responsible for the more informative and picturesque of Q1's stage directions, whose details are not dissimilar to those of his own *Hoffman*.

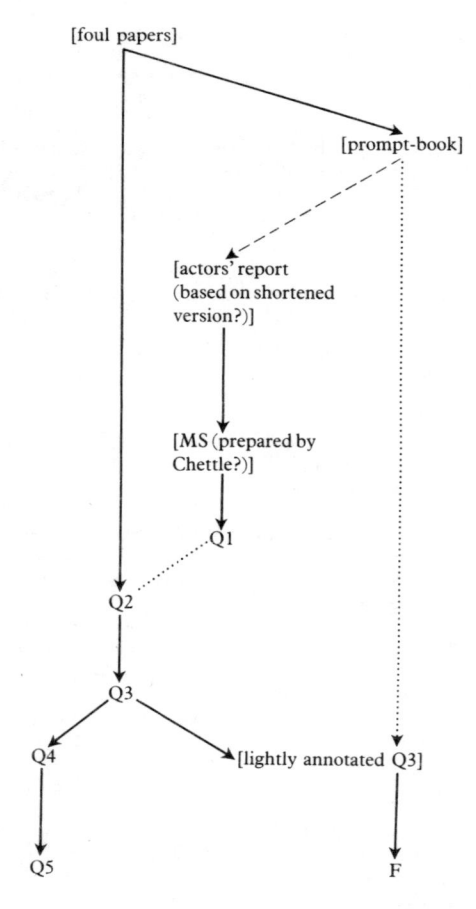

Some of the material not in Q1 might have been cut

deliberately, and some of the most significant staging variations reduce the number of actors' parts. If the actors and versifier were preparing a text for performance by the new Pembroke's Men, they could have originated such changes; but it is equally or more likely that the actors reproduced a version which had been adapted by Shakespeare's company for provincial performance. The copy for Q1 may not have been a theatrical manuscript but one prepared specifically for publication.

An anomaly of Q1 is that the Nurse's speeches in 1.3/Sc. 3 and 1.5/Sc. 5—that is, the scenes where she appears in the portion of the text set in Danter's shop—are in italic type. Greg (*Problem*, p. 62) proposed that the actor playing the Nurse may have supplied an independent manuscript of his own part written out from memory in Italian script. If Greg is right, the Nurse's speeches in the sheets Danter set, though derived independently of the rest of Q1, have the same memorial quality. However, the Servingman's speech 1.3.102-5/454-7 is also set in italic in Q1, suggesting that the speeches affected were in a distinct hand in the copy manuscript itself.

All editors agree with Gericke that the end of 1.2/Sc. 2 and the beginning of 1.3/Sc. 3 were set in Q2 directly from Q1. Presumably, a leaf of Shakespeare's manuscript was missing. Within the boundaries of this section, which may be defined as 1.2.52-1.3.36/301-88, Q1 is in this edition the copy-text, as Q2 has the status of a reprint. Q2 here has virtually no substantive variants and many striking agreements of incidentals. The layout and typography are clearly influenced by Q1; most notably, it takes over Q1's curious use of italic type for the Nurse's speeches (a habit perpetuated beyond the narrowly defined limit of direct Q1 copy to the end of Q2's sheet B at 1.3.83/435).

Whereas the influence of Q1 hereabouts establishes beyond doubt the presence of a copy in the Q2 printing house, the situation in 1.2-3/Sc. 2-3 is of no help in solving the wider problem of defining the influence of Q1 on Q2 elsewhere. The perpetuation in Q2 of a unique and localized feature in Q1 need not imply that Q1 supplied primary copy (annotated from the foul-paper manuscript) for Q2. There would remain a coincidence of italic speeches in Q1 and absence in Q2 of material from the manuscript, no matter what the relationship between the quartos. Further, the areas of the texts affected are far from identical. In Q1 the Nurse's speeches are italic in two scenes, but in Q2, in just one. Within 1.3/Sc. 3 we can only be confident that 31 type lines in Q2 were set directly from Q1: considerably less than the similarly derived section of 1.2 where there is no shared typographical anomaly.

In a limited number of cases (2.1.0.1/731.1, where Romeo enters '*alone*' in both texts; 2.3.92.1/1154.1, '*Enter Nurse and her man*' in both texts; 3.1.131.1/1517.1, '*Fight, Tibalt falles*' Q1, '*They fight. Tibalt falles.*' Q2; and perhaps less distinctly elsewhere) Q1's stage directions evidently affect those in Q2. Q1 again influenced Q2 at 2.1.13/744 ('Abraham: Cupid'—see note), where they share anomalous punctuation and a probable verbal error. As with the stage directions, italics make the words especially noticeable on a casual glance at the page in Q1. It is inconclusive that occasionally the two texts have runs of a few lines without substantive variants. A more interesting case of Q1 affecting Q2 is discussed in the note to 3.5.31/1965; here, as in 1.2-3/Sc. 2-3, but on a more limited scale, the manuscript may have been deficient.

By examining incidentals, in particular shared 'emphasis' capitals, Wilson ('The New Way') establishes, with varying degrees of certainty, a number of other passages where Q1 influenced Q2, but his evidence falls short of affirming his hypothesis (first put forward by Hjort) that Q2 was set from an annotated copy of Q1. In their edition, Wilson-Duthie cite 1.4.56-92/514-50, 2.1.83-4/814-15, and 2.1.232/963 as particular problems of the text best explained in terms of such copy; as our textual notes to these passages show, the difficulties are equally or better interpreted as arising from features of Shakespeare's manuscript itself. Hosley ('Quarto Copy') elaborated on Thomas's earlier objections ('The Bibliographical Links') to the practicability of printing from a copy which would largely consist of inserts. He also drew attention to erroneous Q2 readings, often to be found close to lines influenced by Q1, such as indicate not annotation but the use of manuscript copy. Cantrell and Williams similarly found indications of manuscript copy in compositorial departures from preferred speech-prefix forms.

Most critics now agree that for the most part Q2 was set directly from Shakespeare's papers. The precise extent of Q1's influence on Q2 cannot be measured. There may be particular lines outside the recognized passage in 1.2-3/Sc. 2-3 where Q1 provides the only authority for Q2; such a situation must, however, be unusual, and in those places where Q1 does strongly influence Q2 it seems probable that the manuscript was at least glanced at wherever it was extant.

On 22 January 1607 the title for *Romeo* was transferred in the Stationers' Register with 15 other books, 3 of them Shakespeare plays, from Burby to Nicholas Ling; later in the same year (19 November) Ling transferred the title to John Smethwick. Q2 provided copy for the subsequent edition of 1609 (Q3), from which were printed another quarto (Q4) and the First Folio text (F; see Reid, 'Quarto Copy'), both in 1623. The use of Q3 as copy for F might suggest that at the time of printing Q4 was not yet available.

F used to be regarded as an entirely unauthoritative reprint; this view does not now seem tenable. Whilst accepting that few plays in the First Folio received less editorial supervision than *Romeo and Juliet*, Reid argues that the printers' copy was lightly annotated by someone familiar with the play on stage or with reference to a theatrical manuscript. The latter would be more consistent with the usual treatment of printed copy for Folio plays. Annotations were probably almost entirely confined to details of stage directions and speech-prefixes.

In this edition, all rejected readings originating in F are collated in a list after the Textual Notes. Q1 is only recorded where it offers readings which might be corrections or authorial revisions of Q2. Recent editors have recognized the varying reliability of Q2 on account of the fluctuating and perhaps sometimes undetectable influence of Q1, and have accepted that Q1's stage directions provide important information as to how the play was performed. This edition allows for the potential presence in the Q1 text of Shakespeare, as possible reviser of details of the final theatrical text, but recognizes the presence of another hand, probably that of Chettle, contributing material which might be difficult to distinguish from the authorial. We accept that a small number of reliable emendations may have been introduced in F (see notes to 1.5.0.1/573.2 and 1.5.13/587).

After an initial 'Actus Primus. Scœna Prima.' F is undivided. Rowe first indicated act and scene divisions. His apportioning of acts, though now generally followed and accepted in this edition, was challenged by Theobald and Capell. Theobald delayed the opening of Act 2 until after the Chorus; more radically, Capell began Act 2 at 1.4/Sc. 4, Act 3 at 2.3/Sc. 9, and Act 4 at 3.5/Sc. 16. This edition rejects the editorial scene division initiated by Rowe at 2.1.42.1/773.1, where the location is unchanged and the action continues. Line references to the traditional 2.2 may be found in 2.1 in the modern-spelling format by adding 42. Subsequent scene numbers in Act 2 are one lower than has been usual.

This edition benefits from consultation of McKerrow's unpublished papers for the Oxford Shakespeare, as will be evident from the Textual Notes.

J.J./(S.W.W.)

WORKS CITED

Cantrell, P. L., and George Walton Williams, 'The Printing of the Second Quarto of *Romeo and Juliet* (1599)', *SB* 9 (1957), 107-28

Crow, John, 'Editing and Emending', in *Essays and Studies* (1955), 1-20

Daniel, P. A., ed., *Romeo and Juliet* (1875)

Dowden, E., ed., *Romeo and Juliet*, Arden (1900)

Duthie, G. I., 'The Text of Shakespeare's *Romeo and Juliet*', *SB* 4 (1953), 11-33

Evans, G. Blakemore, ed., *Romeo and Juliet*, New Cambridge (1984)

Gaines, Barry, 'Another Example of Dialect from the Nurse In *Romeo and Juliet*', *SQ* 32 (1981), 96-7

Gericke, Robert, '*Romeo and Juliet* nach Shakespeares Manuskript', *Shakespeare Jahrbuch*, 14 (1879), 207-73

Gibbons, Brian, ed., *Romeo and Juliet*, Arden (1980)

Greg, W. W., 'Principles of Emendation in Shakespeare', in *Aspects of Shakespeare*, ed. J. W. Mackail (1933), 128-201

Haggard, Frank E., 'Type-Recurrence Evidence and the Printing of *Romeo and Juliet* Q1 (1597)', *PBSA* 71 (1977), 66-73

Halstead, William P., *Shakespeare as Spoken: A Collation of 5000 Acting Editions and Promptbooks of Shakespeare*, 12 vols. (1977-80), vol. ix

Hankins, John E., ed., *Romeo and Juliet*, Pelican (1969)

Harrison, G. B., ed., *The Most Excellent and Lamentable Tragedy of Romeo and Juliet*, Penguin (1959)

Henning, Standish, 'The Printer of *Romeo and Juliet*, Q1', *PBSA* 60 (1966), 363-4

Hjort, Greta, 'The Good and Bad Quartos of *Romeo and Juliet* and *Love's Labour's Lost*', *MLR* 21 (1926), 140-6

Holmer, Joan Ozark, '"Runawayes Eyes": A Fugitive Meaning', *SQ* 33 (1982), 97-9

Hoppe, Harry R., ed., *Romeo and Juliet* (1943)

—— *The Bad Quarto of 'Romeo and Juliet': A Bibliographical and Textual Study* (1948)

—— 'The Corrupting Influence of the Bad Quarto on the Received Text of *Romeo and Juliet*', *SQ* 4 (1953), 11-33

Hosley, Richard, ed., *Romeo and Juliet*, Yale (1954)

—— 'Quarto Copy for Q2 *Romeo and Juliet*', *SB* 9 (1957), 129-41

Lavin, J. A., 'John Danter's Ornamental Stock', *SB* 23 (1970), 29-34

Lower, Charles B., '*Romeo and Juliet*, IV.v: A Stage Direction and Purposeful Comedy', *SSt* 8 (1975), 177-94

Melchiori, G., 'Peter, Balthasar, and Shakespeare's Art of Doubling', *MLR* 78 (1983), 777-92

Reid, S. W., 'The Editing of Folio *Romeo and Juliet*', *SB* 35 (1982), 43-66

—— 'Quarto Copy for Folio *Romeo and Juliet*', *The Library*, VI, 5 (1983), 118-25

Thomas, Sidney, 'The Bibliographical Links between the First Two Quartos of *Romeo and Juliet*', *RES* 25 (1949), 110-14

—— 'Henry Chettle and the First Quarto of *Romeo and Juliet*', *RES*, NS 1 (1950), 8-16

—— 'The Queen Mab Speech in *Romeo and Juliet*', *SSu* 25 (1972), 73-80

Smallwood, R. L., '*Romeo and Juliet* V.iii. 107-8', *SQ* 26 (1975), 298-9

Wells, S. W., 'The Bettering of Burby' (review of *Romeo and Juliet*, edited by Brian Gibbons), *TLS*, 20 June 1980, p. 710

Williams, George Walton, 'A New Line of Dialogue in *Romeo and Juliet*', *SQ* 11 (1960), 84-7

—— ed., *The Most Excellent and Lamentable Tragedie of Romeo and Juliet* (1964)

Wilson, John Dover, 'The New Way with Shakespeare's Texts, II: Recent Work on the Text of *Romeo and Juliet*', *SSu* 8 (1955), 81-99

—— and George Ian Duthie, eds., *Romeo and Juliet*, New (1955)

TEXTUAL NOTES

Title *The . . . Iuliet*] Q2 (*title-page and head title above* 1.1/Sc. 1); *The moſt lamentable Tragedie of Romeo and Iuliet*. Q2 (*running title*); AN | EXCELLENT | conceited Tragedie | OF | Romeo and Iuliet Q1 (*title-page*); The moſt excellent Tragedie of | Romeo and Iuliet. Q1 (*head title above* 1.1/Sc. 1; *similarly running title, sigs.* A4ᵛ-D); *The excellent Tragedie of Romeo and Iuliet.* Q1 (*running title, sigs.* E-K); THE TRAGEDY OF | ROMEO AND IVLIET F (*head title; similarly running title*)

Pro.0.1-14/0.1-14 *Prologue . . . mend.*] Q; *not in* F. The omission is probably accidental, a consequence of the layout of F's quarto copy, which had the Prologue set on A2 with the verso blank, and the head title and play beginning on A3. If the play was cast off from the head title, most of a quire would have been set before the compositor turned to the opening of the play.

Pro.1-14/1-14 *Two . . . mend.*] Q2. Q1's 12-line version has a number of variants. These probably arise from misrecollection and consequent reconstruction.

1.1.21/35 ciuil] Q2; cruel Q4

1.1.26/40 in] Q1; *not in* Q2. Q2 is not impossible, as *it* could be equivalent to *its*. But omission of *in* would be an easy error after *it*, and the previous line supports the Q1 reading.

1.1.30.1 *Abraham*] Q (*Abram*). Similarly throughout. As equivalent to *auburn* and in the expression *Abraham-men/Abram-men*, OED lists the forms under the same entries.

1.1.30.1-2/44.1-2 *of the Mountagues*] Q1; *not in* Q2

1.1.31/45 of the] Q2; two of the Q1. Q2 is grammatically acceptable (see Williams's note) and the harder reading; Q1 anticipates 'two Seruingmen of the Mountagues' in the stage direction that in Q2 follows.

1.1.37/51 side] Q1; ſides Q2

1.1.41/55 disgrace] Q2, Q1; a diſgrace Q3

1.1.45/59 of] Q2; on Q1

1.1.60.1-77.2/74.1-91.2 *They draw . . . factions*] They draw, *to them enters* Tybalt, *they fight, to them the Prince, old* Mountague, *and his wife, old* Capulet *and his wife, and other Citizens and part them*. Q1 (*with no dialogue*)

1.1.69.1/83.1 *They fight*] Q1 (*see previous note*), F (*Fight.*); *not in* Q2

1.1.69.1-2/83.1-2 *Citizens ⌜of the Watch⌝*] Q (*Citizens*). Here and in

3.1/Sc. 12 presumably the same body as the final scene's Watchmen.

1.1.70/84 CITIZENS OF THE WATCH] Offi⟨cer(s)⟩. Q2

1.1.73/87 CAPULETS WIFE] Q2 (*Wife.*). The usual prefix in modern texts, 'Lady Capulet', is an editorial construct appearing nowhere in Q2; it is by no means certain that the Capulets and Montagues belong to the nobility. Q2 variously identifies the character as (Capulet's) Wife, (Juliet's) Mother, or Lady (of the House). The commonest speech-prefix designation is '*La⟨dy⟩.*', which is ambiguous and in every case but one comes after a more specific entry direction establishing her as Capulet's Wife or, less frequently, (Juliet's) Mother. Other prefixes are '*Ca. Wi.*', '*Capu. Wi.*', '*M.*', '*Mo.*', '*Wi.*', and '*Wife.*'.

1.1.101/115 MOUNTAGUE] Q2 (*Mounta.*); M⟨ountagues⟩: *wife.* Q1

1.1.117/131 driue] Q2; drew Q1; draue Q3. Q2 could be an error for *draue* or *droue*, but see Wilson-Duthie for other (though non-Shakespearian) examples of Q2's past tense.

1.1.119/133 this Citie] Q2; the Citties Q1; the City THEOBALD; this city's WILSON-DUTHIE

1.1.144/158 his] Q3; is Q2

1.1.150/164 sunne] POPE (Theobald); fame Q2

1.1.174/188 create] Q1; created Q2

1.1.176/190 welseeĩg] Q4 (welfeeming); welfeeĩg Q2; beft feeming Q1. For the tilde error, see note to 2.1.107/838.

1.1.186 to too] Q (too too)

1.1.187/201 made] Q2; raifde Q1

1.1.189/202 louers] POPE; louing Q2; a louers Q1

1.1.194/208 ROMEO Tut] Q2 (*text*), Q1; But Q2 (*c.w.*); Rom⟨eo⟩. But F3

1.1.194/208 lost] Q; left DANIEL (Allen)

1.1.199/213 Bid a . . . make] Q1; A . . . makes Q2

1.1.208/222 vnharmd] Q1 (vnharm'd); vncharmd Q2

1.1.212/226 rich, in bewtie,] Q1; ~, in ~, Q2

1.1.215/229 makes] Q4; make Q2

1.1.230/244 The] Q2 (*text and corrected c.w.*); (Ie Q2 (*uncorrected c.w.*). The uncorrected catchword is inexplicable unless a misreading of 'ye'.

1.2.0.1/249.1-2 and ⌈Peter,⌉ a Seruingman] This edition; *and the Clowne* Q2; *not in* Q1; *and a Servant* ROWE. Q1 supplies '*Enter Seruingman.*' after 1.2.31/280. Peter is not mentioned by name in Q until 2.3.96/1158. As Shakespeare identified the Servingman of 1.2/Sc. 2 as the company's clown and Peter as Will Kemp (at 4.4.127.2/2533.1: see stage direction list), one can be fairly confident that the anonymous figure of 1.2/Sc. 2 was named Peter as Shakespeare proceeded in writing the play. The present editorial change has been anticipated in several theatrical productions (see Halstead). For a different interpretation, see Melchiori, who recognizes that the Servingman would be played by the same actor as Peter, but regards them as separate characters. It is difficult to see any meaningful purpose in such a distinction.

The Capulet servingmen of 1.5/Sc. 5 and 4.4/Sc. 20 might have doubled with Samson and Gregory, but are representative figures without sustained identity; for instance the Montagues' Abram could also easily play a Capulet servingman later in the play.

1.2.13/262 made:] WILLIAMS (*following* Q1, maried:); made: | Earth hath fwallowed all my hopes but fhe, | Shees the hopefull Lady of my earth: Q2. Williams rejects these lines as two authorial attempts which were both abandoned.

1.2.16/265 agreed] Q2; agree Q3

1.2.26/275 limping] Q2; lumping Q1. Q1 is possible; it gives an unusual reading, and would lead to a simple error. Q2's 'limping' is desirable to explain why April treads 'on the heele' of winter.

1.2.27/276 femelle] Q1 (female); fennell Q2. Williams defends Q2, giving evidence that fennel was emblematic of flattery; but (*a*) the sense remains incommunicable, and (*b*) fennel is not usually regarded as a spring bud. Nevertheless, the plant reference in 'buds' would encourage an error naming a plant. 'Femelle' (a common spelling) would give a simple misreading of minims.

1.2.30/279 Which one more] Q2; Such amongft Q1; On which more CAPELL

1.2.30 on] Q2 (one)

1.2.34/283 there] Q2; here Q1

1.2.36/285 PETER] This edition; Seru⟨ingman⟩. Q. Similarly throughout scene. See note to 1.2.0.1/249.1-2.

1.2.36/285 written, here:] Q1 (~, ~, *and adding* 'and yet I knowe not who are written here'); written. Here, Q2

1.2.45 One] Q2 (On)

1.2.65/314 Countie Anfelme] Q; Countie Anselmo DYCE (Capell); *The Countie* Anselme WILLIAMS. Wilson-Duthie find *Anselme* in Bandello and Painter. Normal Italian pronunciation would be as three syllables.

1.2.66/315 Vitruuio] F3; Vtruuio Q

1.2.70/319 and Liuia] Q1; Liuia Q2. Q1 has a page-break after '*and*'; the Q2 compositor was here setting from Q1 (see Introduction).

1.2.75-6/324-5 Whether . . . to] THEOBALD (Warburton); Whether to supper? | Ser⟨uingman⟩: To Q; Whither? | Ser⟨vant⟩. To CAPELL. Williams (who follows Capell) rightly suggests an error of reporting. 'To supper' remains a plausible contribution to the dialogue if given to Peter.

1.2.79/328 thee] Q1; you Q2

1.2.83/332 *Exit*] F; *not in* Q

1.2.91/340 fires] POPE; fire Q

1.3.4/356 Where is] This edition; Wher's Q. Q1 provides the only authority for the quarto reading.

1.3.34/386 with] Q1 (with); with the Q2. Modernized 'wi'th''.

1.3.37/389 yeares] Q2 (*yeares*); yeare Q1. The variant occurs at the probable boundary of the passage in Q2 where Q1 served as a sole copy (see Introduction). Q1 is more idiomatic; but Q2 probably has manuscript authority, as is testified by the variants immediately following and the recurrence of this variant at 1.3.48/400.

1.3.38/390 she could] Q2 (*fhe could*); could Iuliet Q1

1.3.38/390 byth] Q2 (*byth*); by the Q1

1.3.39/391 run and] Q2 (*run and*); *not in* Q1

1.3.48/400 yeares] Q2 (*yeares*); yeare Q1. See note to 1.3.37/389.

1.3.49/401 Iule] Q2 (Iule); Iuliet Q1; Iulet F. Q1 has Iuliet throughout the speech; F has 'Iul(i)et' here only.

1.3.68/420 honore] Q1 (honor); houre Q2. Possibly an example of tilde error, but 'no' could be misread 'w'.

1.3.69/421 honore] Q1 (honor); houre Q2

1.3.73/425 mothers. By my count,] F; ~, by my ~. Q2

1.3.93/445 manies] Q2; many Q5

1.3.97/449 bigger: women] F; ~, ~ Q2

1.3.101/453 it] Q1; *not in* Q2

1.3.101.1/453.1 Peter] This edition; Seruing⟨man⟩. Q2; Clowne Q1. Similarly the prefix at 1.3.102/454 Compare note to 1.2.0.1/249.1-2.

1.3.106/458 *Exit* ⌈*Peter*⌉] F ('*Exit.*', *after* 1.3.105/457); *not in* Q

1.4.0.1-3/459.1-3 *Enter . . . torches*] Enter Maskers with Romeo and a Page. Q1

1.4.0.2-3/459.2-3 *bearing . . . torches*] torchbearers Q2; *Torchbearers, and drums* THEOBALD. Q2 is sometimes taken to indicate that the torchbearers and drummer(s) are additional to the 5 or 6 masquers. 1.4-5/Sc. 4-5 are excessive in their demands for extras. Their requirement for speaking parts for 9-10 men (depending on the number of servingmen at the beginning of 1.5/Sc. 5) and 3 boys corresponds closely enough to the usual maximum number of speaking parts in any sequence of action in Shakespeare's plays to suggest that he was not oblivious to the limitations of staging. We observe Shakespeare's unusually extravagant demands for extras, but interpret them conservatively. See note to 1.4.115.1/573.1.

1.4.6-8/465-7 Crowkeeper, . . . entrance.] Q1 (crow-keeper: . . .); Crowkeeper. Q2. Editors agree that Q2 omits two lines; these constitute a self-contained unit such as could have been a marginal addition or a later revision.

1.4.23/482 MERCUTIO] Q4; Horatio. Q2

1.4.30/489 for a visor] Q; for a visage G.T. *conj.*

1.4.31 quote] Q2 (cote). This and Q1's 'coate' were common spellings.
1.4.31/490 deformitie] Q1; deformities Q2. The singular gives a rhyme. Shakespeare nowhere else uses the plural.
1.4.34/493 betake] Q2, F; betakes Q3
1.4.39/498 dun] Q3; dum Q2; done Q1, F. Copy 'dun' gives the easiest explanation of Q2. Q3 restores what Shakespeare probably wrote. The senses 'done' and 'dun' are simultaneous in Romeo's speech; as 'dun' must be read in Mercutio's reply, we prefer to give Romeo 'done' in the modernized text, to emphasize the word-play.
1.4.41-2/500-1 mire, | Of] Q1; ~, | Or Q2; ~. | Or F. Q2 may have a bungled proof correction: see following note.
1.4.42/501 saue your reuerence] F; saue you reuerence Q2; this surreuerence Q1
1.4.45 MERCUTIO] From this point to the end of the scene, the line numbering in the first and second printing of our modern-spelling edition is one too many. We follow the uncorrected form.
1.4.46/504 like lights] JOHNSON; lights lights Q2; like Lampes Q1; light lights DANIEL (Nicholson); light lamps GREG (conj.). Q2's error probably depends on its second 'lights' standing in the copy. Nicholson's conjecture supposes a rather easier error in Q2 than Johnson's reading, but posits error in both words in Q1. By Johnson's reading, both texts have plausible errors. It explains Mercutio's 'good meaning' better, clarifying the distinction between literal and figurative. It also avoids awkward repetition: Shakespeare never elsewhere speaks of lighting lights, let alone in a line where 'lights' is already repeated.
1.4.48/506 fiue] MALONE (Wilbraham); fine Q2; right Q1
1.4.55/513 BENUOLIO ... she?] Q1; not in Q2. See note to 1.4.56-92/514-50. Keightley accepted Q1's line, as did Daniel, who attributed it to Romeo. The conclusion to the Queen Mab speech, 'This is she' (which editors often interpret as an interrupted utterance) makes better sense if the speech is a reply to the Q1 question. Q1 rarely expands on Q2, especially in the first half of the play; in view of Q2's overt space-saving (see following notes), Q1's additional and theatrically attractive line is probably authoritative. It would be surprising if the space-saving expedient of setting verse as prose in the Queen Mab speech was in itself exactly sufficient to accommodate the text to be set; we suppose the compositor was also forced to omit a line (though it is also possible that the line was added as a revision).
1.4.56/514 MERCUTIO] KEIGHTLEY; not in Q
1.4.56-92/514-50 She ... bodes] The Queen Mab speech presents a series of textual difficulties whose editorial treatment is closely involved with the question of the copy for Q2.

Q2 omits 1.4.69-71/527-9 and prints 'She ... bodes' as prose; 'bodes' ends a page (C2), and the remainder of the speech on its verso is set as normal verse. Q1 prints all as verse; much of the text is relatively close to Q2, but Q1 omits 'Her Charriot ... Coachmakers:' (1.4.69-71/527-9) and originates a re-arrangement followed in this edition at 1.4.74-8/532-6. Q2's prose to its page-break, combined with an absence of other signs of space shortage in sheet C, least of all on C2ᵛ, suggests either that C2ᵛ had already been set in type (i.e. setting was by formes, outer first, or the prose section was reset), or that the compositor was working rigorously to a casting-off mark. Whether in casting off or in a first setting, a certain amount of material, about a dozen lines, was not allowed for. The division by pages between prose and verse makes implausible Thomas's proposal ('The Queen Mab Speech') that the text of this speech, exceptionally, was set from a memorially derived manuscript in prose. Wilson-Duthie claim that 'if one corrects Mer.'s verse in Q1 so as to bring it into accordance with Q2, it becomes clear that the Q2 compositor, baffled by the problem of lineation, would almost inevitably decide that the easiest and quickest solution was to set up the bulk of the speech as prose'. But (a) in such copy the end of the speech, which the compositor set as verse, would be particularly heavily annotated; (b) in the speech as a whole there is no more variation between Q1 and Q2 than there is in many other places; (c) apart from the three lines not in Q1, the print in Q1 would remain a good guide to lineation no matter how heavy the annotation.

Wilson-Duthie needed to explain the prose setting in terms of confusion over lineation, not the discrepancy in length between prose and verse settings, because the difference between the number of lines in Q1 and Q2 is inadequate to make up that discrepancy. If there was confusion as to the length of the speech, the original estimate must have been based on a manuscript in which the potential for miscalculation was much larger than Q1 copy would permit. Such confusion could result from a single error if lines were added on an insert slip.

Arguing against manuscript copy, Wilson-Duthie state that the passages most to be suspected as additions in such a manuscript are 'Sometime ... Benefice.' (1.4.78-82/536-40), and 'Her waggō ... maid.' (1.4.61-8/519-26) or 'Her Charriot ... Coachmakers:' (1.4.69-71/527-9); these add up, taking the more favourable option, to one line more (13) than the space saved by prose setting (12). The length of the text from 'O then I see Queene Mab hath bin with you' to 'bodes' in our edition is the same as in Wilson-Duthie's, the addition of Benvolio's question (see note) balancing the omission after 1.4.74/532. But we posit an original of 13 lines more than the prose setting, as the line we believe to have been later revised out would still have stood in the manuscript. In other words, we propose the foul papers had one line more than Q2: Benvolio's 'Queen Mab whats she?' from Q1. In so far as Wilson-Duthie raise a real objection, Q1's extra line answers it.

But it is not necessary to accept as the only possible additions the passages which Wilson-Duthie identify. Certainly, the 'Courtiers knees ... Courtiers nose' duplication might indicate expansion hereabouts, but the length of any added passage is indeterminable. The verse preceding 'Her Charriot' could, like almost any section of the speech, contain an addition, but of anything from ten lines down to one. It is not essential to assume that the earlier part of the speech was supplemented at all; for instance 'Sometime she driueth ... bodes' (1.4.83-92/541-50), perhaps complemented with 'Through louers brains ... strait' (1.4.73-4/531-2) could constitute an alternative insert.

Finally, the compositor's problem was not necessarily confined to the one speech. Another part of the scene may have been expanded in the foul papers, causing an error in casting off; the one place with sustained verse-speech would have offered a unique opportunity to save space by setting prose. It is even possible that the Servingmen's dialogue beginning 1.5/Sc. 5 (13 type lines) was not reckoned in the original casting (see note to 1.4.115.1/573.1).

1.4.61-8, 69-71/519-26, 527-9 Her wagō ... maid, Her Charriot ... Coachmakers] Q2; Her Charriot ... Coachmakers not in Q1; passages transposed, DANIEL (Lettsom). Lettsom thought it 'preposterous' that Mercutio should 'speak of the parts of a chariot ... before mentioning the chariot itself'. But the hazel-nut constitutes only a part of the chariot as a whole, the coachwork. The passage does not give a descriptive synthesis of its catalogue of parts. Mention of the part which actually holds Queen Mab is deferred temporarily, as description of the occupant herself is deferred indefinitely. Nevertheless, the catalogue is drawn together, at its conclusion in Q2, by the suggestion that squirrel and old grub assemble the coach. 'Time out of mind, the Fairies Coatchmakers' signifies an overall and traditional responsibility, and leads easily to the summary 'and in this state': the coach-makers are the accepted guarantors of Queen Mab's style and stateliness. In contrast, the transposed text gives the awkward transition:

> Not half so big as a round little worme,
> Prickt from the lazie finger of a [maid].
> And in this state she gallops night by night,

This transposition, first made by Daniel and followed by most recent editors, should be rejected. Q1's omission therefore does not influence the Q2 text. On the other hand, Q2's position for the lines not in Q1 is more conducive to memorial error in Q1 than the greater prominence they have in the editorially emended text, where they initiate the description of Queen Mab's carriage.

1.4.58/516 Alderman] Q2; Burgomaſter Q1
1.4.59/517 ottamie] Q; atamies Q3, F. Q1's 'Atomi' agrees with Q2's correct Latin plural, from which *atomy*, as a singular noun, derives. For the 'o' spelling, compare Q2's 'obsoluer' and 'absolu'd' (3.3.50/1775 and 3.5.233/2167).
1.4.60/518 Athwart] Q1; Ouer Q2. Possibly an authorial revision: Q1 gives the rarer word (7 to 152 instances in Shakespeare) and the more radical variant on repeated *ore*.
1.4.63-5/521-3 Her ... bone] This edition (*conj.* Duthie); her traces of the ſmalleſt ſpider web, her collors of the moonſhines watry beames, her whip of Crickets bone Q2; The traces are the Moone-ſhine watrie beames, | The collers crickets bones Q1. Duthie observed that 'It is difficult to visualize moonbeams as collars round the necks of tiny coach-horses, but the framework of the common spider's-web might suggest the shape of a horse's collar'. Q2 would give an unusual error, but it is possible that Shakespeare, whilst hastily writing down a passage of lines already more or less formed in his mind, should make a *currente calamo* and uncorrected error of transposition. The simplest correction might be to transpose 'traces' and 'collors', but Q1, which supports the emendation of 1.4.63/521, agrees with Q2's order of these nouns.
1.4.65 film] Q2 (Philome)
1.4.68/526 Prickt] Q2 (prickt); Pickt Q1
1.4.68/526 maid] Q1; man Q2
1.4.74/532 Ore] Q1 (O're); On Q2
1.4.74/532 strait,] This edition (*following* Q1's *omission of* Q2's *next verse line*); ſtrait, ore Lawyers fingers who ſtrait dreame on fees, Q2. For 'Courtiers nose' (1.4.78/536) Q1 reads 'Lawers lap'. 'Lap' is unlikely to be right, as it destroys the connection between the part of the body and the dream sensation ('smelling'), but Thomas points out that Seymour's conjectured emendation 'lip' overcomes this problem. Q1's reading effectively deals with Q2's repetition of 'Courtiers' from 1.4.74/532 ('Courtiers knees ... Courtiers nose'), and in so doing it names a figure who can equally or more intelligibly be thought of as 'smelling out a sute'. Having substituted 'Lawers' for the second 'Courtiers', it omits 'ore Lawyers fingers who strait dreame on fees,' which in Q2 follows 1.4.74/532, and so avoids repetition of 'Lawers'. The emendation also avoids repeating 'nose' ('mens noses ... Courtiers nose ... Persons nose') but this gain is partly offset by 'Ladies lips ... Lawers lip'. Unlike Q1's arbitrary omission of 1.4.69-71/527-9, these variants seem deliberately and desirably to supply the finishing touches which the text in Q2 seems to require, and in this edition are regarded as authorial improvements.
1.4.77/535 breaths] Q1 (breathes); breath Q2
1.4.78/536 Lawyers] Q1 (Lawers); Courtiers Q2
1.4.78/536 lip] This edition (*conj.* Seymour); noſe Q2; lap Q1
1.4.79/537 dreames] Q2, Q1, F; dreame Q3
1.4.81/539 as a] Q2; that Q1; as G.T. *conj.*
1.4.82/540 dreames he] Q1 (dreames he); he dreams Q2
1.4.85/543 spanish blades] Q2; countermines Q1
1.4.91/549 Elflocks] Q1 (Elfelocks); Elklocks Q2
1.4.92/550 vntangled] Q; entangled F3
1.4.104/562 face] Q1; ſide Q2; ſute MCKERROW MS (*conj.*)
1.4.114/572 Direct] Q2; Directs Q1
1.4.114/572 saile] Q1; ſute Q2. Williams objects to the terminology of Q1's continued nautical metaphor, but *sail* is here probably not the canvas but 'An act of sailing; a voyage or excursion in a sailing vessel' (OED sb.² 1). OED's first illustration is from *Othello* 5.2.275/3172, where the word is again a metaphor for the mortal life of the hero of a love-tragedy: 'heere is my butt | And verie Sea-marke of my vtmost Saile'. *Romeo* becomes the earliest known instance of the sense.
1.4.115.1/573.1 exeunt] THEOBALD; *not in* Q2. The absence of any direction here in Q1 is of no significance, as it omits the following episode and leads straight on to 1.5.15.2/580.2. Q2's erroneous 'Enter Romeo' after 'Napkins' might be a false start, or evidence that Shakespeare provided the dialogue as a later addition, whereby he originally intended the Servingmen (instead of the masquers?) to pass over the stage without dialogue; for which compare *Macbeth*, beginning of 1.7/Sc. 7. 'Enter Romeo' may therefore testify that an exit before the Servingman's entry was intended. If the Servingmen's dialogue was indeed an afterthought, its absence in Q1 may show that it remained expendable when actors were in short supply (compare note to 1.5.13/587). At 1.5.15.2-6/589.2-6 the formula 'Enter x to y' leaves it unclear whether the masquers enter or are already on stage, but the only other use of this formula in *Romeo*, at 5.2.0.1/2661.1, is clearly an example of entry from separate doors. It is doubtful that Shakespeare would have intended a large party of revellers with torches to remain on stage during the Servingmen's dialogue. A practical advantage of an exit is that nameless and masked revellers in 1.4/Sc. 4 could become the practically anonymous invited guests of 1.6/Sc. 6. The saving of parts would be twofold, as most masquers and male guests would require partners with whom to dance.

1.5.0.1/573.2 *Peter and other Seruingmen*] This edition; *Seruingmen* Q2. For the identification of the chief Servingman as Peter, see note to 1.2.0.1/249.1-2. The same role of authority is suggested at 1.3.102-5/454-7. Q2 maintains a distinction between 'Ser.' (= Peter) and the other Servingmen specified only by numerals.

After *Napkins*, Q2 has, on a new type line, 'Enter Romeo.' (see previous note). F alters to '*Enter Seruant.*' This might be guesswork, but happens to conform with the distinction in speech-prefixes between 'Ser.' and the perfunctory numbers, and the corresponding distinction in roles between the chief Servingman and the others. The change might derive from a manuscript (or an annotator recalling performance) if in performance F's '*Seruant*', this edition's Peter, entered separately from the other Servingmen—which would be an attractive staging. Whatever the source of Q2's error, any entry annotated in the Folio compositor's copy would appear to be equivalent to the printed entry. Other possible indications of a consulted manuscript include F's omission of '*their*' before '*Napkins*' and the prefix alteration discussed in the note to 1.5.13/587.
1.5.8 marzipan] Q2 (March-pane)
1.5.13/587 1.] F (~ˌ); 3. Q2. See note to 1.5.0.1/573.2 for other possible indications of annotation from a manuscript underlying F. F's anomalous omission of a stop after '1', if not a coincidence, could have arisen from the compositor's diversion to an annotation. The altered numeral is unlikely to be an accident, and is readily explained as a theatrical alteration. The sequence 1.4-6/Sc. 4-6 would put severe casting demands on an Elizabethan company; a reduction in the number of Servingmen would save a part. There is a strikingly similar reduction from three to two Grooms in Folio *2 Henry IV* at the beginning of 5.5/Sc. 17.
1.5.14/588 longest] This edition; longer Q2. Other examples of the proverb quoted in ODEP have *longest*, which seems required grammatically. *Longer* probably anticipates *liuer*.
1.5.15.1/589.1 *They ... chaires*] *Exeunt.* Q2. Servingmen are required in the following episode. Though there is a notional change of location here, it is doubtful if the stage is cleared. The Servingmen are themselves instrumental in indicating a change of location if they bring properties on stage.
1.5.15.2-6/589.2-6 *Enter ... Mercutio*] *Enter old* Capulet *with the Ladies.* Q1 (*omitting the episode with the Servingmen*). See note to 1.4.115.1/573.1. The Musicians might either appear on the stage or play from the music room behind the upper acting area.
1.5.17/591 walke] Q2; haue Q1
1.5.17/591 a bout] POPE; about Q
1.5.18/592 Ah ha] Q1 (ah ha); Ah Q2
1.5.38/612 sir] Q2; far Q1. Q1 might be right, but Q1's *By Ladie sir* at 1.5.33/607 may, as a misplaced recollection, support Q2.
1.5.39/613 CAPULET] Q2 (1. *Capu.*), Q1 (*Cap:*); 3. *Cap.* F. As F is followed in this edition at 1.5.13/587, the present rejected Folio reading demands comment. Possible explanations of F as error are: (*a*) contamination from 'thirty' (the previous word); (*b*)

misunderstood copy annotation. This could have occurred if Q1 is right in reading 'three' for Q2's '2.' in 1.5.40/614.

1.5.40/614 2. yeares ago.] Q2; three yeares agoe, | Good youths I faith. Oh youth's a iolly thing. Q1

1.5.47/621 showes a snowie Doue] Q2; Shines a ſnow-white Swan Q1. Probably a reporter's recollection of 1.2.88–9/337–8 and 1.2.100/349.

1.5.48/622 yonder] Q2; this faire Q1

1.5.93/667 gentler] This edition (Dowden); gentle Q. Commentators have been hard pressed to explain the quartos' reading; Jenkins (in ʼnew Arden), Wells, and Evans all accept that Dowden's suggested emendation is attractive. Given that Q2 and Q1 both have numerous errors and that the loss of the comparative '-r' is an easy mistake, the common reading could be a coincidence. Alternatively a glance at Q1 may have corrupted the Q2 compositor's reading of the copy manuscript. Some editors have preferred to emend 'sin' (see following note) but the coincidental error becomes harder to explain, and the emended reading is less convincing.

1.5.93/667 sin] Q; fine THEOBALD (Warburton); pain WILSON-DUTHIE. See previous note.

1.5.94/668 readie] Q1 (ready), Monckton Milnes MS; did readie Q2. The manuscript, which we have not been able to consult, is described in the Sotheby Catalogue, 22 July 1980, Lot 585. It contains two extracts from Romeo, totalling 12 lines, and is said to be likely to derive from another manuscript rather than a printed text.

1.5.121.1/695.1 They . . . eare] Q1; not in Q2

1.5.126.1–3/700.1–3 Exeunt . . . leaue] Exeunt. Q1; not in Q2

1.5.131/705 here] Q2; there Q1

1.5.141/715 tis . . . tis] Q2; this . . . that Q1; this . . . this F. Williams defends Q2 as dialectal.

2.0.0.1–14/717.1–31 Enter Chorus . . . sweete. Exit] Q2 (but without 'Enter' and 'Exit'); scene not in Q1

2.0.4/721 matcht] Q3; match Q2

2.1.3/734 Romeo, Romeo] Q2; Romeo Q1. Q1 gives a pentameter with Q2's 'He is wise'.

2.1.6–7/737–8 ⌈MERCUTIO⌉ Nay . . . Romeo] Q1 (reading Call, nay for Q2 Nay); Nay . . . Mer⟨cutio⟩. Romeo Q2. Q2 sets 'Nay . . . too.' as a separate line.

2.1.7/738 louer] Q2; liuer Q1

2.1.9/(M) one] Q2 (on), Q1

2.1.10/741 pronounce‸] Q1 (Pronounce); prouaunt, Q2

2.1.10/741 doue] Q1; day Q2

2.1.12/743 heir] Q1; her Q2

2.1.13/744 Adam‸ Cupid:] STEEVENS 2 (Upton); Abraham: ~‸ Q2, Q1; Abraham‸ ~ Q4, F. The punctuation unequivocally shows that Q1 influenced Q2. If this is true of the punctuation, it may equally be true of the preceding word. Names are particularly likely to be checked in a printed text available for consultation, but Q1's italics makes the two names and the intervening colon obvious at a casual glance. As the punctuation error passed from Q1 to Q2, the preceding word in Q1 must have been looked at by the Q2 compositor. Q2 is thus insecure: the immediate source of the reading may be Q1, and if it is an error, there is no need to explain it as a misreading. It seems unlikely that Abraham Cupid would be understood as 'Abraham-man Cupid' (Knight) or that 'old as Abraham' was a recognized proverb (Hoppe). Abraham as 'auburn' is possible, if somewhat pointless, but (a) the word is identified neither as a colour nor as applicable to the hair only and so inevitably looks like a forename; (b) if the word is adjectival, the italic setting in Q2 highlights the influence of Q1. Adam is used similarly in Much Ado 1.1.242/245 (though the context makes the allusion to Adam Bell less obvious there than here). Q1 therefore probably has a memorial error which slipped into Q2. Five other substantive emendations of Q2 required in 2.1.1–13/732–44 suggest difficult manuscript copy.

2.1.13/744 trim] Q1; true Q2. Q1 preserves the word in the ballad Mercutio quotes (which Shakespeare seems to have known well), and so is evidently right.

2.1.38/769 open ars and] WILSON-DUTHIE; open, or Q2; open Et cætera Q1; open-arse or HOSLEY

2.1.42.1/773.1 Exit . . . Mercutio] Q4, F (Exeunt.); Exit. Q2

2.1.50/781 sicke] Q2; pale Q1

2.1.58/789 do] Q1; to Q2

2.1.62/793 eye] Q2; eyes Q1

2.1.73/804 passing] Q1 (pacing); puffing Q2. See Wilson-Duthie. Some editors retain Q2, but OED suggests that period uses of puff indicate a vigorous action. OED gives pace as a 16th-c. spelling of pass.

2.1.83–4/814–5 nor any . . . name.] MALONE; ô be ſome other name, | Belonging to a man. Q2; nor any other part. Q1. Williams and Gibbons defend Malone's reading. Q1 simply omits a verse line, as elsewhere. Its unique 'nor any other part' is especially significant as it makes sense of material in Q2 which it does not itself print. Q2's deficiency and mislocation have no obvious cause. Perhaps Shakespeare added, as a single marginal annotation split into its part-lines, 'nor any other parte | belonging to a man'. The first part-line might be unnoticed by the compositor, or illegible, or at a cursory glance assumed to be a repetition of 'nor arme nor face' (only nor/other would look distinctly different). If the Q2 compositor thought he needed to incorporate just the part-line 'belonging to a man', its mislocation is easy to understand: (a) it would be simpler to treat it as a discrete unit which did not split a verse line, (b) Q2 makes better sense than the part-line in the correct position with 'nor other parte' omitted ('. . . Nor arme nor face belonging to a man').

Alice Walker conjectured a more radical restoration: that 'ô be some other name' should precede 'Whats Mountague'. She supposes that the Q2 compositor ran on two separate marginal annotations in his Q1 copy, substituting them for 'nor any other parte'. The present explanation is analogous to Walker's but does not depend on the hypothesis of Q1 copy for Q2.

2.1.85/816 Whats‸ in a name?] Q1; Whats‸ in a name‸ Q2; What? in a names‸ F. F must be a blundered correction.

2.1.86/817 word] Q2; name Q1. Many editors follow Q1, but there is no adequate reason to suspect that Q2 is corrupt. The error is probably one of memorial substitution in Q1 under the influence of repeated 'name'. Even if the variant arises through misreading, corruption from 'word' to 'name' is, in the context, more likely than the reverse.

2.1.87/818 were] Q1; wene Q2

2.1.101/832 vttering] Q2; vtterance Q1

2.1.103/834 maide] Q2; Saint Q1

2.1.107/838 kiſmen] Q1 (kinſmen); kiſmen Q2. A tilde error that affects the same word at 2.3.6/1065, 3.1.145/1531, 3.1.148/1534, and 3.1.175/1561. Similar omissions account for Q2 error at 1.1.176/190, 2.3.27/1087, 3.3.15/1740, 3.5.225/2159, and perhaps 3.3.143/1868 and 5.3.159/2849. Tildes are also omitted in Q LLL, a play written in the same period; this text, like Romeo, was set from Shakespeare's papers, but by different printers.

2.1.125/856 waſht] Q1; waſheth Q2

2.1.134/865 false: . . . periuries‸] Q1; ~‸ . . . ~. Q2

2.1.141/872 hauior] Q1 (hauiour); behauior Q2

2.1.143/874 more conning] Q1 (more cunning); coying Q2; more coying Q4; more coyning F2; the coyning WILLIAMS. Evans follows Q4, but, for an emended reading, the idiom is very strained. Williams postulates copy 'coÿing'; 'conning' misread 'coining' would scarcely be a harder error, and allows Q1's 'more' to stand in a reading more convincing than F2's. Compare 'cunning to be strange' with Miranda's dismissal of 'bashful cunning' (Tempest 3.1.81/1177). See also Gibbons's note.

2.1.146/877 truloue] Q2; true loues Q1, F

2.1.149/880 vow] Q2; ſweare Q1

2.1.152/883 circld] Q1 (circled); circle Q2

2.1.155/886 gracious] Q2; glorious Q1. Q1's reading is probably a recollection of 2.1.69/800.

2.1.177.1/908.1 Nurse calls within] F ('Cals within.' 1 line later); not in Q

2.1.188 rite] Q2 (right)

2.1.190 lord] Q2 (L.), Q1, F
2.1.190-1/921-2 world . . . Madam.] CAPELL (*following* F: world. | *Within*: Madam.); world. Madam. Q2. Q2 prints 'Madam.' here and at 2.1.194/925 spaced right of Juliet's speech; F similarly prints '*Within*: Madam.' justified right in both lines.
2.1.193-5/924-6/ thee . . . come)] CAPELL (*following* F: theee *Within*: Madam. | (By and by I come)); thee (by and by I come) Madam. Q2
2.1.196/927 strife] Q2 (ſtrife); sute Q4. Wilson–Duthie follow Q4, which gives the same word as the corresponding passage in Shakespeare's source Brooke. *OED* describes the required sense of *strife* as 'rare', and cites examples before 1623 only from Shakespeare. Though Shakespearian, *strife* might have appeared corrupt; the context might have suggested Q4's 'correction'. There is not likely to be significance in Q4 agreeing with Brooke.
2.1.199/930 *Exit*] F; *not in* Q
2.1.205/936 hoarse] Q; husht DANIEL
2.1.207/938 mine,] Q1; *not in* Q2; Fame DANIEL
2.1.208/939 Romeos name. Romeo?] Q1 (*as 2 lines*: name.|); Romeo. Q2; Romeo's name CAMBRIDGE. Williams plausibly conjectures a damaged manuscript to explain Q2's omissions at the end of this and the previous line. He considers '*Romeo?*' an actor's interpolation, but Romeo's response suggests that Q1 is right. There is no valid objection to Q1 at a point where, through Q2's agreed omission, Q1 supplies the only text of any authority.
2.1.212/943 My Niesse] WILSON–DUTHIE; My Neece Q2; Madame Q1; My Deere Q4
2.1.223/954 That] Q2; Who Q1
2.1.223/954 his] Q2; her Q1. Williams defends Q2.
2.1.225/956 silke] Q1; ſilken Q2. *Silk* and *silken* are here semantically indifferent but metrically distinct. Compare 2.1.141/872.
2.1.229-32/960-3 Parting . . . ⌈ROMEO⌉ Sleep . . . Would] Q1; Parting . . . Iu⟨liet⟩. Sleep . . . Ro⟨meo⟩. Would Q2; Ro⟨meo⟩. Parting . . . Iu⟨liet⟩. Sleepe . . . Rom⟨eo⟩. Would Q3, F; Romeo. Parting . . . Juliet. Sleep . . . Would HOSLEY (*attributing the lines following* Would . . . rest *to Romeo*). Most editors follow Q1, an arrangement persuasively endorsed by Williams.
2.1.232/963 rest.] Q1. Q2 continues:

> The grey eyde morne ſmiles on the frowning night,
> Checkring the Eaſterne Clouds with ſtreaks of light
> And darkneſſe fleckted like a drunkard reeles,
> From forth daies pathway, made by *Tytans* wheeles.

These lines in Q2 are a variant version of the Friar's speech beginning 2.2/Sc. 8 as printed in both Q2 and Q1. Editors must choose between Q2's two arrangements: many follow F2 rather than Q1 and attribute the lines to Romeo.

Wilson–Duthie and Hosley interpret Q1's attribution of the lines to the Friar as an error passed on to Q2, whereby the correct version from the manuscript (the lines as attributed to Romeo, 'Version A') was annotated in the Q1 copy as a replacement; the annotated lines were printed in Q2 before the version taken from Q1 itself ('Version B') so as to give a duplication. Even if the hypothesis of annotated quarto copy were accepted, it is difficult to see why the reporter of Q1 should have made the initial and fundamental mistake of attributing lines he evidently remembered quite well to the wrong speaker in the wrong scene. Furthermore, Q2's Version B does not look like a simple reprint of Q1 (see following notes), as it must be if the annotator simply intended the lines to be deleted.

Williams and Gibbons, though unsympathetic to Wilson–Duthie's textual hypothesis, also followed Version A. Williams suggests that Shakespeare first gave the lines to the Friar, but later decided to transfer them to Romeo; accordingly a slightly altered version of the lines was annotated in the manuscript for addition to Romeo's speech, to become Version A in Q2. A serious problem is that further elaboration is necessary to explain why Q1 gives what Williams believes to be Shakespeare's abandoned first intention. Williams posits that a theatre scribe, like the Q2 compositor, misunderstood Shakespeare's papers: seeing a duplication, he removed the annotated Version A and preserved Shakespeare's first intention. But even Shakespeare did not transcribe his own papers, and if a scribe made the same error as the Q2 compositor, why should the error have been accepted in performance? Williams comments, 'If Shakespeare was aware of the error, he probably shrugged it off as too trivial to be bothered about'. Yet the envisaged authorial revision is perhaps the most drastic alteration Shakespeare made to the text; it alters both sides of the scene-break so radically that it is difficult to accept that Shakespeare would shrug off its loss.

Williams's hypothesis runs into difficulties because it argues for the reverse of what the textual evidence implies. In this edition, Q1 is taken as decisive testimony that the final assignation was to the Friar and that Version B is Shakespeare's revision. There is nothing in Q2 to suggest that it does not reflect the arrangement indicated in the manuscript, apart from any mark it may have had for deletion; present editorial treatment would allow of in-text or marginal duplication in Shakespeare's manuscript.

Wilson–Duthie put forward literary arguments for preferring Version A; even if these established a definitely 'better' text (which they do not), they would be of doubtful value for determining the order in which Shakespeare composed the passages. The closer echo of Golding in Version A actually suggests that it is the earlier: a text is more likely to evolve away from a source than towards it. Similarly, Wilson–Duthie's belief that the lines are more in keeping with Romeo's diction might indicate that they were *originally* written for him. Doubtless the reattribution could be defended in either direction on literary grounds. The insecurity of such arguments is highlighted by Evans's belief (New Cambridge) that Version A represents a false start for 2.2/Sc. 8, abandoned so that Shakespeare could add 2.1.233-4/964-5, and hence that Shakespeare never assigned the lines to Romeo. This hypothesis assumes that Shakespeare would rewrite four lines in order to insert two at the end of a previous scene, and involves unnecessary complications over the layout of the manuscript. Nevertheless it points to the same editorial policy as is followed in this edition: that Version A is omitted and the attribution of Version B to the Friar at the beginning of the new scene is retained.

2.1.233/964 siers close] WILSON–DUTHIE (Delius); Friers cloſe Q2; fathers Q1
2.2.0.1/965.1 *Frier Lawrence*] Frier Q2; Frier Francis Q1
2.2.2/967 Checkring] Q1, Q2 (*Version* A); Checking Q2 (*Version* B). The agreement of Version A (which may have been more legible than Version B in the copy for Q2) with Q1 (which is textually closer to Version B) suggests that 'Checking' is an error.
2.2.3/968 fleckeld darknesse] Q2 (*Version* B); flecked darkenes Q1; darkneſſe fleckted Q2 (*Version* A)
2.2.4/969 path, and *Titans* fierie] Q1; path, and *Titans* burning Q2 (*Version* B); pathway, made by *Tytans* Q2 (*Version* A). Version B could give either an awkward junction between added passage and original text, later revised as in Q1, or a compositorial anticipation of the following line.
2.2.6/971 day] Q2; world Q1
2.2.16/981 Plants, hearbes] Q2; hearbes, plants Q1.
2.2.18/983 to] Q; to't HANMER
2.2.22/987 sometimes] Q1; ſometime Q2
2.2.22.1/987.1 *Enter Romeo*] Q; *after* 2.2.30/995 POPE
2.2.26/991 slaies] Q1 (ſlaies), F (ſlayes); ſtaies Q2
2.2.27/992 Kings] Q2; foes Q1
2.2.55/1020 and] Q; reſt F. F's more unusual reading is difficult to explain if it has no authority. If it derives from a manuscript (or late performance) one must further suppose either that Shakespeare made at least minor revisions after the play reached the state represented in Q1, or that Q1 influenced Q2. Q1's unadopted 'my sonne' immediately before does not encourage the second hypothesis. F is rejected because there is not a class of comparable verbal variants where F possibly improves on common quarto readings. Perhaps the line-endings 'drift' and 'shrift' indirectly contaminated F.
2.2.72/1037 it] Q2; loue Q1. Q1 might preserve an authorial improvement.

2.2.74/1039 yet ring] Q4; yet ringing Q2; ring yet Q1
2.3.1/1060 Where] Q2, Why, where CAPELL (*following* Q1: Why whats become of *Romeo*?). Q2 sets 2.3.1-2, 4-5/1060-1, 1063-4 as prose. 'Why' is not necessary to the verse arrangement, as an omitted first syllable is an acceptable metrical licence. If, however, Shakespeare was originally undecided as to whether Mercutio should speak prose or verse here, he might have added 'Why' in a manuscript later than the copy for Q2. For 'Why' in 2.3.4/1063 Q1 has 'Ah'.
2.3.6-8/1065-7 BENUOLIO *Tibalt* . . . MERCUTIO A] Q2; Mer⟨cutio⟩: *Tybalt* . . . *Some* Q1
2.3.6/1065 kīsman] Q1 (kinfman); kifman Q2
2.3.13/1072 runne] Q2; fhot Q1
2.3.17/1076 BENUOLIO] Q1, F; Ro⟨meo⟩. Q2
2.3.19/1078 he fights] Q2; Catfo, he fightes Q1. 'Catso' puns on both 'cats' and 'pricksong'. *OED* records no instance before 1602.
2.3.20/1079-80 he rests] Q2; refts me Q1
2.3.21/1080 minum rests] Q2; minum reft Q1; minum F
2.3.24 hai] Q (Hay)
2.3.27/1087 phantacīes] WILLIAMS (Crow); phantacies Q2; fan-|tafticoes Q1. See note to 2.1.107/838.
2.3.31/1091 pardon mees] Q1 (pardonmees), F (pardon-mee's); pardons mees Q2
2.3.37/1097 was] Q2; was but Q1. See following note.
2.3.38/1098 wench, marrie] Q2; drudg, yet Q1. Q2's type line 'flowed . . . marrie' is widely spaced and could easily accommodate a three-letter word. As the compositor could have set 'she' after 'marrie', proof or press correction must be suspected. The compositor may have removed instead of correcting an error for 'yet', or 'but' earlier in the line.
2.3.63/1124-5 wits faints] Q2; wits faile Q1; wits faint Q5; wit faints F2
2.3.64 Switch . . . switch] Q (Swits . . . fwits)
2.3.92.1/1154.1 *Enter* . . . *man*] F; *after* 'geare' *in* Q. Some editors consider *Heeres goodly geare* a comment on Mercutio's jesting. There is probably no significance in Q2's positioning of the direction, which, like its wording, probably derives straight from Q1.
2.3.94-5/1156-7 [BENUOLIO] A . . . MERCUTIO *Two*] This edition (Williams); A . . . Mer⟨cutio⟩. *Two* Q2; Mer⟨cutio⟩. A . . . Ben⟨uolio⟩: *Two* Q1. Williams points out that the speech Q2 gives to Mercutio is more in character for him than Benvolio. The reporter of Q1 could easily have switched speech assignations, but presumably only if, as is attractive from a dramatic point of view, a new speaker spoke 'A sayle, a sayle'. Q1 therefore gives limited support to Williams's conjecture, which departs from Q2 less radically than Q1 itself.
2.3.107/1169 for] Q1; *not in* Q2. Compare 2.3.109/1171. In Q2 'Ro⟨meo⟩. . . . mar.' is a tightly justified line in a passage with other indications that the compositor was saving space; 'for' may have been omitted deliberately. Q1 avoids Q2's awkward 'God hath made, himself', in which the dislocated emphatic pronoun might be confused as a reflexive.
2.3.124.1/1187.1 *He* . . . *sings*] Q1; *not in* Q2
2.3.135/1198 *Exeunt* . . . *Benuolio*] Q1 (*Exeunt Benuolio, Mercutio.*), F (*Exit. Mercutio, Benuolio.*); *Exeunt.* Q2
2.3.144 skeans-mates] Q (fkaines mates)
2.3.144-5/1208 *to Peter*] Q1 (*She turnes to Peter her man.*); *not in* Q2
2.3.149/1212 if] Q2; you know my toole is as foone out as anothers if Q1
2.3.151/1214 part] Q2; member Q1
2.3.187/1250 I warrant] F2; Warrant Q2
2.3.188-98/1251-61 Well . . . letter] *prose in* Q2. The boundary between verse and prose in the Nurse's speeches is sometimes unclear. Capell's arrangement has not proved popular, but gives a verse passage in which most lines are regular or accountable in terms of acceptable metrical licences. The speech is not in Q1.
2.3.193/1256 I] Q; I do CAPELL
2.3.200 Ah,] Q2 (A∧)
2.3.200/1263 dogs,] Q3; dog, Q2

2.3.205 Ay,] Q2 (I∧)
2.3.207/1270 *giuing Peter her fan*] *not in* Q. See following note.
2.3.207/1270 *Before* and *apace*] Q2; take my fanne, and goe before Q1. Q1 probably is verbally unauthoritative, but must reflect comic stage business.
2.3.207.1-2/1270.1-2 *Exit* . . . *doore*] *Exit.* Q2; *Ex. omnes.* Q1; *Exit Nurfe and Peter.* F
2.4.5/1275 glides] Q2; glide F4
2.4.11/1281 three] Q3; there Q2
2.4.14-15/1284-5 loue, | And] Q4, F; ∼ . | M. And Q2. Q2's 'M.' is indented as a speech-prefix.
2.4.26/1296 iaunce] Q2; iaunt Q1. Gaines effectively establishes the noun *jaunce* as a dialect word.
2.4.26/1296 haue I] Q2; haue I had Q1; had I DANIEL (*conj.*)
2.4.50 ah,] Q2 (a∧)
2.4.55 and] Q2 (an)
2.4.68 hie] Q2 (high)
2.4.77-2.5.37/1347-85 Go . . . one.] Q2. Q1 has an almost completely different and 'un-Shakespearian' text, evidently written to supply a deficiency in the underlying manuscript. See Introduction.
2.5.15.1/1363.1 *somewhat* . . . *Romeo*] Q1; *not in* Q2
2.5.27/1375 musicks] Q4, F (mufickes); muficke Q2
2.5.34/1382 sum of halfe my] Q2; sums of half my JOHNSON; half my sum of CAPELL; half of half my This edition *conj.* Q2 retained in modern spelling as 'sum up sum' gives an awkward, tautological, and unsatisfactory reading. Q4 and F modernize 'sum vp some'; the result may be defended as an expressive illogicality appropriate to Juliet (the half is conceivable, but the part less than it remains too large to be defined), and a word-play typical of *Romeo*. If Q2 is corrupt, Capell's reading would presumably suggest misplacement of words inserted in the manuscript, which in turn assumes an original four-foot line. Alternatively, 'sum vp sum of halfe' could quite easily be compositorial corruption of 'sum vp halfe of halfe'.
2.5.37/1385 *Exeunt*] Q1 (*Exeunt omnes.*); *not in* Q2
3.1.0.1/1385.1 *Enter* . . . *men*] Q2; *Enter Benuolio, Mercutio.* Q1. Here and at 3.1.33.1/1418.1 Q1 may reflect reporting of a production with a reduced cast.
3.1.2/1387 Capels are] Q1; Capels Q2; Capulets Q4, F
3.1.8/1394 him] Q2; it Q1
3.1.28 ribbon] Q2 (ri-|band)
3.1.33.1/1418.1 *Enter* . . . *others*] Q2; *Enter Tybalt.* Q1 (*after* 3.1.34/1419)
3.1.34/1419 the *Capulets*] Q2; a *Capolet* Q1
3.1.59/1444 loue] Q2; hate Q1
3.1.67/1452 iniurd] F (iniur'd); iniuried Q2; iniured Q1. Shakespeare is unlikely to have introduced a semantically undistinguished but metrically distinguished form where this creates a metrical irregularity.
3.1.73 stoccado] Q2 (ftucatho), Q1 (ftockado)
3.1.74/1459 come, will you walke] HANMER; will you walke Q2; come back, come back Q1. Q2 is metrically deficient and of uncertain significance (especially if Tybalt is, as Q1 suggests, making to leave). 'Come', as well as restoring the metre, makes it clear that Mercutio is, in effect, offering a challenge. 'Come' is doubly evidenced in Q1, which could readily result from a half-recollection of the emended text but bears little relation to Q2.
3.1.88.2, 3.1.89.1/1474.2-3, 1475.1 *Tybalt* . . . *in, Exeunt* . . . *followers*] *Tibalt vnder Romeos arme thrufts Mercutio, in and flyes.* Q1; *Away Tybalt.* Q2; *Exit Tybalt.* F. See following note.
3.1.89/1475 [PETRUCHIO] *Away Tybalt.*] WILLIAMS (Greg); *Away Tybalt.* Q2 (*as stage direction*). Williams defends the emendation in 'A New Line of Dialogue'. Petruccio is otherwise a ghost; Shakespeare may have left a perfunctory prefix or none at all. The line was probably added marginally; this would explain both the misinterpretation as a stage direction, and the interruption of Q2's otherwise regular metre. Compare 5.3.71/2761.
3.1.91/1477 both your] DYCE; both Q2; your Q1; both the F
3.1.92-108/1478-94 What . . . houses.] Q2. Q1 has transpositions

and new material:

> *Rom:* What art thou hurt man, the wound is not deepe.
> *Mer:* Noe not ſo deepe as a Well, not ſo wide as a barne doore, but it will ſerue I warrant. What meant you to come betweene vs? I was hurt vnder your arme.
> *Rom:* I did all for the beſt.
> *Mer:* A poxe of your houſes, I am fairely dreſt. Sirra goe fetch me a Surgeon.
> *Boy:* I goe my Lord.
> *Mer:* I am pepperd for this world, I am ſped yfaith, he hath made wormes meate of me, & ye aske for me to morrow you ſhall finde me a graue-man. A poxe of your houſes, I ſhall be fairely mounted vpon foure mens ſhoulders: For your houſe of the *Mountegues* and the *Capolets*: and then ſome peaſantly rogue, ſome Sexton, ſome baſe ſlaue ſhall write my Epitaph, that *Tybalt* came and broke the Princes Lawes, and *Mercutio* was ſlaine for the firſt and ſecond cauſe. Wher's the Surgeon?
> *Boy:* Hee's come ſir.
> *Mer:* Now heele keepe a mumbling in my guts on the other ſide, come *Benuolio*, lend me thy hand: a poxe of your houſes.

Q1's additions may be an interpolation, presumably by the dramatist-editor of the reported text most plausibly identified as Chettle. It certainly seems too extensive and literary for an actor's insertion. The other possibility is that Shakespeare himself added the material. The following parallels are at least suggestive:

1. *The epitaph*. In *LLL* 4.2.50–1/1128–9 Holofernes composes a rhymed 'extemporal epitaph'. See also *Richard II* 3.3.167–8/1684–5, *Hamlet* 3.2.124–9/1852–7, *Timon* 5.5.71–8/2290–7, and *Pericles* 18.31–7/1756–62. For the idiom 'write my Epitaph', compare *Merchant* 4.1.117/1926 and *Timon* 5.2.70/2151.

2. 'Broke the Princes Lawes'. In *Richard II* 2.3.167–8/1232–3 'breake our countries lawes' ends a line in a couplet rhymed with 'pawse'. The *laws/cause* rhyme occurs in Sonnet 49.13–14.

3. *Pun on 'mount'*. Compare *Henry V* 2.4.57/913.

4. *Pun on 'Capulet'*. Compare *Hamlet* 3.2.100–102/1826–9 (*Capitol/capital*; also on the name *Brutus* with *brute*).

5. *Satirical attitude to sexton*. Compare *K. John* 3.1.250/1199.

Most idioms in the Q1 passage can be paralleled in Shakespeare. The most notable exception is *peasantly*, not elsewhere in Shakespeare; *OED* cites only one example before 1598. But 'some peasantly ſlaue … some base rogue' echoes 'O, what a rogue and peasant slave am I' (*Hamlet* 2.2.551/1481), apart from the dubious 'the sovereign power' Hoppe's only example of a reporter's supposed borrowing from *Hamlet*, a sequence of events most implausible for Shakespeare's play).

In itself, *mumbling* might be an anticipation of 3.5.173/2107, but this gives no hint of Mercutio's striking image of the surgeon mumbling in his guts (compare Flamineo's 'There's a plumber laying pipes in my guts', *White Devil* 5.6.145).

These considerations point towards Shakespeare's authorship, though not conclusively. If so, Q1 represents either a radically reorganized passage, in which the original material was fragmented, or a badly reported version of the revised text, in which the reporter introduced transpositions and omitted material. The major omission in Q1, 'sounds … arithmatick' (1.3.100–2/1486–8), coincides with its major interpolation, suggesting the first alternative (whereby a lesser amount of bad reporting is not, of course, precluded). An editor accepting Shakespeare's authorship of the Q1 passage might take Q1 as control-text here, whilst recognizing, as always, that Q2 gives a more authoritative reading where the phrasing is equivalent, and that the more minor omissions could be due to bad reporting.

3.1.100   Zounds] Q2 (ſounds)
3.1.108/1494   ſoundly, to,] F3; ~, ~, Q2
3.1.110/1496   this] Q2, Q1; his Q3
3.1.113/1499   Cozen] Q2; kinſman Q1
3.1.120.1/1506.1   *Enter Tybalt*] Q1, F; *not in* Q2
3.1.122/1508   He gad] This edition; He gan Q2; A liue Q1; Alive POPE; Again CAPELL; He gone HARRISON; He gay HOPPE; He yare WILLIAMS. Pope's correction of Q1 gives an adequate reading, but leaves Q2 unexplained. Capell's 'Again' to 'He gan' is not a likely one-stage error. 'Gone' does not fit the situation of Tybalt returning. Williams rightly objects to 'gay' as referring only to clothing in Shakespeare, but his 'yare' inevitably suggests preparedness for an act rather than the sprightliness after it; 'yare in triumph' is an odd idiom. Q2 might be explained as a dialectal infinitive of *go* or an error for 'gon', a form of the infinitive still current in the 17th c., but it is hard to see why either should appear uniquely here. *Gad*, though a common verb in the period, is unusual in Shakespeare; significantly, the only other occurrence is in *Romeo* itself (4.2.16/2318). One must suppose that the compositor made the misreading, fairly easy in Shakespeare's hand, 'gad'/'gane'. The word effectively suggests Tybalt's enjoyment of both life and freedom from restraint or punishment, as well as in indicating his carefree insolence. The phrase is an indignant exclamatory question: 'what, *he* gad in triumph?'

3.1.124/1510   eid] Q1 (eyed); end Q2; and Q3
3.1.129/1515   Either] Q2; Or Q1
3.1.136.1/1522.1   *Exit Romeo*] Q2; *Exeunt* Q1
3.1.140.1–2/1526.1–2   *Enter … all*] Q2; *Enter Prince, Capolets wife.* Q1
3.1.142/1528   all,] Q1, F; ~ : Q2
3.1.145, 3.1.148/1531, 1534   kiſman] Q1 (kinſman); kisman Q2
3.1.147/1533   O Cozen,] Q2; *not in* CAPELL
3.1.150/1536   fray] Q1, F; bloudie fray Q2. The readings of Q1 and F cannot readily be ascribed to coincidence. Repetitions of 'bloud' in the previous speech suggest that Shakespeare might himself have deleted 'bloudie', either unclearly in the foul papers or at a later date.
3.1.153–74/1539–60   and … die] Q2. Q1 gives a comparable account, but in lines with only occasional phrases in common with Q2.
3.1.156/1542   take] Q2; make CAPELL (*conj.*)
3.1.165/1551   agent] This edition (McKerrow MS); aged Q2; agill Q1. McKerrow commented, 'I accept [*agill*] from Q1 as possible, but the use is somewhat strange and "agile" does not occur elsewhere in Shakespeare. It is, I think, probably wrong, and suspect that the word should be "agent", i.e. *doing* something as opposed to talking, or possibly as a Latinism = effective'. The emendation emphasizes the common origin of words and action in thought, itself proverbially swift. For the arm as agent, compare *Two Gentlemen* 1.3.46/333, 'Here is her hand, the agent of her heart'. *OED* does not record *agent* as an adjective before 1620, but describes the noun (from 1579) as 'the *adj*. used *absol*'. If Shakespeare never used *agile*, Chettle (see Introduction) did so (*Hoffman*, MSR, 2001: 'noe woodnimphes here | Seeke with their agill steps to outstrip the Roe'; note spelling).
3.1.175/1561   kiſman] Q3 (kinſman); kisman Q2
3.1.183/1569   MOUNTAGUE] Q4; Capu⟨let⟩. Q2; La⟨dy⟩. Mont⟨ague⟩. THEOBALD
3.1.187/1573   hates] Q1; hearts Q2. Notwithstanding the reverse error in Q1 at 3.2.73/1655, *hates* would be especially prone to misreading as *hartes* in Shakespeare's handwriting. Q2 gives a dubiously intelligible reading: *OED* does not support *proceeding* as 'events arising from', the nearest sense being the evidently rare 'egress'. 'Your hearts proceeding' is neutral or even extenuating; the rest of the speech, like 'hates', is unequivocally condemnatory.
3.1.191/1577   I] Q1; It Q2
3.1.196.1/1582.1   *Exeunt with the body*] *Exit.* Q2; *Exeunt omnes.* Q1; *Exeunt.* F
3.2.1/1583   IULIET] Q1, F; *not in* Q2
3.2.6/1588   runnawayes] Q2; th' Run-away's THEOBALD (Warburton); runnaway KITTREDGE (Blackstone, in Steevens-Reed). A notorious crux, variously emended; but Q2's 'runnawayes' is unlikely to be seriously corrupt. The verbal similarities with *Merchant* 2.6.47/905 ('close night doth play the runaway', preceded by 'loue is blinde and louers cannot see', 2.6.36/894) strongly confirm that Q2 has the right word. Holmer dem-

onstrated that *runaway* could mean 'fugitive' or 'vagabond' and convincingly defended Q2. Terminal '-s' error remains possible, especially as the letters '-yes' are repeated in 'eyes'.

3.2.9/1591 By] Q4; And by Q2. Perhaps a false start in Shakespeare's manuscript. Sisson defends Q2.

3.2.15/1597 grown] ROWE; grow Q2. Many recent editors follow Q2, but the presumed ellipsis, 'Think' for 'and think', is clumsy. A misreading would be easy.

3.2.19/1601 on] F2; vpon Q2. Q2 may give a dittography from 3.2.18/1600, or a remnant of a first version of the line in which 'new' was not present.

3.2.21/1603 I] Q2; hee Q4. Wilson and most earlier editors adopt Q4; recent editors, perhaps more willing to allow Juliet sexual ecstasy, retain Q2. The objection that 'Rom⟨eo⟩ must die before he can be cut up into little stars' (Wilson) may be refuted: Juliet here sees Romeo almost as a supernatural spirit; he will act upon her and cause her to 'die'. The vivid alternation from *Romeo* to *I* may be compared with the unexpected change from active to passive in 3.2.26-7/1608-9.

3.2.31.1-2/1613.1-2 wringing . . . lap] Q1; *with cords* Q2
3.2.37 Ah, welladay] Q2 (A weraday)
3.2.42/1624 it ˏ] Q2; ~? CAPELL
3.2.45-6 'Ay' . . . 'I'] Q2 (I . . . I)
3.2.47/1629 darting] Q3; arting Q2
3.2.48 'Ay'] Q2 (I)
3.2.49 shut] Q2 (ſhot). Hankins follows Hoppe in accepting 'shot', giving a detailed note. No emendation is involved in reading 'shut'.

3.2.51/1633 Briefe ˏ sounds ˏ] F4; ~, ~, Q2. McKerrow (MS) pointed out that the compositor evidently understood 'sounds' as the expletive *zounds*.

3.2.51/1633 of] F; *not in* Q2; or COLLIER MS. Alternative metrical emendations would be 'determine me my' (McKerrow *conj.*) or 'determining'.

3.2.56 swoonèd] Q2 (founded)
3.2.60 one heavy bier] Q2 (on heauie beare)
3.2.72-4/1654-6 ⌈NURSE⌉ It . . . ⌈IULIET⌉ O . . . Did] *speech-prefixes as* Q1; It . . . Nur⟨se⟩. O . . . Iu⟨liet⟩. Did Q2
3.2.76/1658 Douefeatherd] THEOBALD; Rauenous douefeatherd Q2. Editors agree that Q2 preserves a rejected first thought.
3.2.79/1661 damned] Q4; dimme Q2
3.2.86/1668 Theres] Q2; There is Q1
3.2.87/1669 disemblers all] This edition (G.T.); all diſſemblers Q2. The transposition solves the only difficulty in Q2, which can be explained as compositorial error influenced by 'All periurde' etc. Editors usually follow Capell in retaining Q2's wording but reline to divide after 'trust' and 'periurde', a change which does not solve the metrical irregularity. In Q2 'Theres no trust' is amphibious with 'In such a gorgious Pallace'; emended 3.2.87/1669 is a regular hexameter. Capell's relineation is not sufficiently justified.

Some editors have identified 'all nought' as a problem: that it should follow 'men' and end a verse line (DANIEL, *conj.* Fleay), or, preserving Q2's lineation, that it should be removed entirely (HOSLEY). Fleay produced a regular pentameter by reading 'All perjured, all dissemblers, all forsworn', but Q1's retention of 'periurde, all forsworne' argues against this; similarly, Q1's preservation of four qualifiers gainsays Hosley.

If Shakespeare wrote the line as in Q2 he may have been prompted later to revise it. Q1 has 'All false, all faithles, periurde, all forſworne', which suggests a transposition of part-lines, though its substitutions do not look like convincing examples of authorial improvement. One might posit 'All naught, dissemblers, periurde, all forsworne', but even if Q2 were not correctable assuming simple error, an editor would hesitate to adopt a reading so conjectural.

3.2.128 corpse] Q2 (courſe)
3.3.0.1, 3.3.3.1/1725.2, 1728.1 *Enter Frier Lawrence . . . Enter Romeo*] Q1 (*Enter Frier. . . . Enter Romeo.*); *Enter Frier and* Romeo. Q2 (*at beginning of scene*)
3.3.10/1735 vanisht] Q; 'banished' DOWDEN (*conj.*)
3.3.15/1740 Hēce] Q1 (Hence); Here Q2. The same emendation is made at 3.5.225/2159. See note to 2.1.107/838.
3.3.19/1744 banisht] Q1; blaniſht Q2
3.3.26/1751 rusht] Q; brush'd COLLIER MS
3.3.40-3/1765-8 But . . . death?] GLOBE; Q2 *has*:

[1] This may flyes do, when I from this muſt flie,
[2] And ſayeſt thou yet, that exile is not death?
[3] But *Romeo* may not, he is baniſhed.
[4] Flies may do this, but I from this muſt flie:
[5] They are freemen, but I am baniſhed.

Q1 prints ll. 3 and 4; F prints ll. 1-3. F's editing looks improvised, as l. 3 does not follow from l. 2. Unless Q2 was set from Q1, the lines they share must have stood in the text as eventually determined. The crux clearly arises from a false start; l. 1 was evidently replaced by l. 4 and so can be abandoned. The outstanding editorial problems are: (*a*) should l. 2 (evidently a sequel to l. 1, so part of the first version) have been cancelled or placed after l. 5? (*b*) do ll. 3 and 5 constitute a secondary duplication? These problems may be considered in turn.

(*a*) Line 2 is not duplicated by other material. It provides a strong transition from the conceit of flies to the passage beginning at 3.3.44/1769, and indeed logically initiates that passage. Its position may be explained if ll. 3-5 were added in the margin of the manuscript and so misplaced in Q2.

(*b*) Of ll. 3 and 5, the former is easily the likelier to have been superseded if one replaced the other, as: (*i*) it comes first and so is likely to have been written first; (*ii*) it repeats 'But *Romeo* may not' from 3.3.33/1758, where l. 5 introduces a new idea. But l. 3 is in Q1, so (assuming manuscript copy for Q2) certainly was not omitted. Both lines should therefore be preserved, even though Q1 omits l. 5 (with ll. 1-2 and 3.3.38-9/1763-4.

This edition therefore follows a common editorial arrangement accepted by Riverside, Williams, and Gibbons. The commonest alternative is to print ll. 3, 1 (in some editions, including Cambridge, reading 'but' for 'when'), 5, and 2. This arrangement, initiated by the Cambridge editors, is untenable unless Q2 was set from an annotated copy of Q1. Even then, Q2 would, on the basis of the Cambridge text, be difficult to explain.

1775 obſoluer] Q2. This peculiar spelling (compare 'ottamie', 517) recurs at 2167.
3.3.52/1777 Thou] Q1; Then Q2
3.3.61//1786 men] Q1; man Q2
3.3.73.1/1798.1 *Knocking within*] *They knocke.* Q2; *Knocke* F3.
3.3.75.1/1800.1 *Still knocke within*] *Slud knock.* Q2; *Knocke.* F. McKerrow (MS) and Jenkins (in new Arden) independently suggested that 'Slud' is a corruption of 'Still'. As an alternative, if Friar Laurence may be permitted the word (compare 'Gods will'), 'Slid' might have been annotated for insertion before 'Run'. Q1 cannot arbitrate, as it omits 'Run . . . by and by'.
3.3.82/1807 Where is] Q1; Wheres Q2
3.3.85-6/1810-11 O . . . euen] Q; Fri⟨ar⟩. O . . . Nurse. Even STEEVENS 2 (Farmer)
3.3.91/1816 *rising*] Q1 (*He rises.*); *not in* Q2
3.3.92/1817 Spakst] Spakeſt Q. Q1 may have influenced Q2's ametrical form, as the line stands prominently at the top of a page in Q1.
3.3.107/1832 He . . . away] Q1; *not in* Q2. Gibbons rejects this direction, but the Nurse's restraint of Romeo would give point to the Friar's accusation that his behaviour is *womanish*: the direction is consistent with other comic undercutting of Romeo's exaggerated conduct. In 1.1/Sc. 1 Montague's wife restrains her husband to comparable effect.
3.3.109/1834 denote] Q1; deuote Q2
3.3.112/1837 And] Q2; Or Q1
3.3.116/1841 that . . . liues] F4; that in thy life lies Q2; too, that liues in thee Q1
3.3.137/1862 happie] Q2; happy too Q1
3.3.140/1865 light] Q2; lights Q1
3.3.142/1867 mishaued] Q2; misbehaude Q1; miſhaped F. See Williams. Q2, as against Q1, is probably right, though the

accentuation is odd. Shakespeare nowhere else used either *mishaved* or *misbehaved*.

3.3.142/1867 sullen] Q; a sullen F2
3.3.143/1868 pouts vpō] Q4 (powts vpon); puts vp Q2; frownſt vpon Q1; putteſt vp F
3.3.161.1/1886.1 Nurse ... againe] Q1 (... goe ...); not in Q2
3.3.162/1887 sir,] Q2; is, Q1
3.3.164/1889 Exit Nurse] Q1; not in Q2
3.3.167/1892 disguisd] Q3; diſguiſe Q2
3.3.172/1897 calls] Q2; cryes Q1
3.4.11.1/1910.1 Paris ... againe] Q1 (... goe ... Capolet calles ...); not in Q2
3.4.13/1912 be] Q1; me Q1
3.4.16/1915 here, of] Q2; with Q1; there of KEIGHTLEY; yeere of WILSON. Wilson attractively suggests a spelling of *ear* conducive to misreading, but 'her ere' in the previous line might also have been influential if Q2 is corrupt. Compare *Antony* 3.6.58-9/1533-4: 'acquainted | My greeued eare withall'.
3.4.23/1922 Weel,] Q1 (Wee'le,); Well, Q2. Perhaps a simple misreading, but *Will* immediately above may have influenced Q2.
3.4.34/1933 Afore] Q; 'Fore THEOBALD
3.4.34/1933 very] Q2; 'very very Q1; not in F. Q2 divides 3.4.34-5/1933-4 after 'by and by'; Q1 divides after 'late'.
3.5.0.1/1934.3 aloft] Q2; at the window Q1
3.5.13/1947 Sun exhald] HOSLEY; Sun exhale Q2; Sunne exhales Q1; ſen exhales ANON. (*conj.* in Cambridge)
3.5.19/1953 the] Q1; the the Q2
3.5.31/1965 changd] ROWE 3; change Q. The Q2 compositor is recognized to have been making particular use of Q1 hereabouts; the only variants, incidental or substantive, in 3.5.27-31/1961-5 are (Q1 as lemma):

3.5.28/1962 Discords,] ~,
3.5.30/1964 this] ſhe

From the second of these it appears that Q2 may not be entirely dependent on Q1. Nevertheless, variants are of less certain status than elsewhere in the play, both here and in the lines continuing to the entry. This direction, not itself in Q1 and initiating some lines not in Q1, is also suspicious:

Enter Madame and Nurſe.
Nur. Madam.
Iu. Nurſe.

Madame is a unique spelling in Q2; more pertinently, (*a*) it is scarcely credible that Shakespeare would at this stage in the play have named Juliet '*Madame*', and (*b*) Juliet does not enter here. The direction looks as if it may have been improvised in the printing house owing to deficient copy.

3.5.36.1/1970.1 Enter Nurse ⌜hastily⌝] Q1 (... haſftely); Enter Madame and Nurſe. Q2. For Q2, see note to 3.5.31/1965. Q1 transposes material, delaying the Nurse's intervention until just before Capulet's wife enters.
3.5.42.1/1976.1 He ... goes downe] He goeth downe. Q1; not in Q2
3.5.43/1977 my] Q1; ay Q2; ah F2. Q2's 'ay', as distinct from the usual 'I', is found nowhere else in Shakespeare, and is very rare in the period (Evans discovered the only known instance in *Mucedorus* (1598)). Q1 has 'my Lord, my Loue, my Frend', thus repeating thrice a word which could be misread as Q2's highly anomalous 'ay'. This edition follows Hosley in emending 'ay' whilst rejecting the Q1 line as a whole.
3.5.54/1988 JULIET] Q2 (c.w.), Q1; Ro⟨meo⟩. Q2 (text)
3.5.55/1989 thee, now] POPE (similarly Q1, ~, ~,); ~, ~, Q2
3.5.64/1998 her ... wife] Mother Q2; Iuliets Mother, Nurſe Q1. See following note.
3.5.67.1/2001.1 She ... below] She goeth downe from the window. Q1; not in Q2. Q1 has no dialogue between the Nurse's warning at 3.5.39-40/1973-4 and the present direction, so '*She*' might apply to either the Nurse or Juliet; Q1 follows, after a spacing ornament, with:

Enter Iuliets Mother, Nurſe.
Moth: Where are you Daughter?
Nur: What Ladie, Lambe, what Iuliet?

Iul: How now, who calls?
Nur: It is your Mother.
Moth: Why how now Iuliet?

Despite Q1's complications, it may safely be inferred that the episode that follows takes place with Juliet on the main stage, as Q2 in itself most plausibly requires. Q2 provides no dialogue to occupy the moments of Juliet's descent; the staging may not have been fully envisaged when Shakespeare first drafted the passage. Williams suggests that Q1's use of material from the opening of 1.3/Sc. 3 was a theatrical expedient, but this assumes that Shakespeare did not himself supply some lines for the promptbook and that Q1 does not introduce a reporter's recollection of the theatrically similar earlier episode.

3.5.82/2016 him] Q4; not in Q2
3.5.106/2040 I] Q4; not in Q2
3.5.123-4/2057-8 these ... CAPULETS WIFE Here] Q2. Collier, in his second edition, gave the last part-line of Juliet's speech to her mother; McKerrow (MS) thought he might have been right.
3.5.123.1/2057.1 and Nurse] Q2; not in Q1. For Q1, see notes to 3.5.64/1998 and 3.5.67.1/2001.1.
3.5.126/2060 earth] Q2; Ayre Q4. Gibbons compares *Lucrece* 1226.
3.5.130-1/2064-5 showring? ... body, ... counteſaits, a] Punctuation as Q1 (subs.); ~, ... ~? ... ~. A Q2
3.5.139/2073 giues] Q3; giue Q2
3.5.149/2083 chopt] Q2; chop Q1
3.5.151/2085 proud? ... you,] Q4; ~, ... ~? Q2
3.5.156/2090 Out] Q2 (text), Q1; You Q2 (c.w.). The catchword anticipates 3.5.157/2091.
3.5.158/2092 kneeling] Q1 (*She kneeles downe.*); not in Q2
3.5.167/2101 curse] Q2; croſſe Q1
3.5.172/2106 ⌜CAPULET⌝ O] Q1 (Cap: Oh); Father, ô Q2. See also following note. McKerrow (MS) plausibly suggests that Capulet's speech was a marginal addition.
3.5.173/2107 ⌜NURSE⌝ May] Q4; May Q2
3.5.175/2109 CAPULETS WIFE] Q2 (Wi.), Q1 (Mo:), F (La.)
3.5.176-7/2110-11 worke, play, | Alone in companie] HOPPE; houre, tide, time, worke, play | Alone in companie Q2 (*dividing before* Day); early, late, at home, abroad, | Alone, in company, waking or ſleeping Q1 (*dividing before* Day). Hoppe restores the text that Shakespeare probably first wrote, which, as relined, gives a pentameter. 'Houre, tide, time' look like tentative suggestions for forming compounds with 'day' and/or 'night'. Q1 shows that this idea was not followed up. But its excess of oppositions, as compared with Q2, may indicate that Shakespeare decided to expand the line differently. The resultant text cannot be restored with any confidence. 'Early, late' is suspect, as it occurs earlier in the scene ('downe so late or vp so early', 3.5.66/2000). 'At home, abroad' and 'waking or sleeping' are both Shakespearian oppositions, but 'waking or sleeping' seems misplaced. If Shakespeare expanded to give a full line beginning 'Day', one might conjecture 'Day, night, waking or sleeping, at home, abroad | Alone in companie'.
3.5.180/2114 lind] CHAMBERS; liand Q2; trainde Q1; limb'd HOSLEY. Crow suggested that Q2 gives a spelling variant of *liened*, but there is no such adjective in *OED*, which cites only one instance of *lien* (sb.¹ 2) before 1741. Furthermore, the sense of *lien* does not fit the context. Either *lined* or *limbed* would serve better, though Shakespeare elsewhere uses neither word to mean 'descended'. 'Liand' might easily be misread 'limd' in Shakespeare's handwriting; the reverse error is not so expected, but 'limd' would have a small advantage over 'lind' as the source of a hypothetical misreading. But Q2's unusual form might arise from misinterpretation of an unusual spelling—or preserve such a spelling in its own right. *Lined* as 'covered on the inside', hence, 'supplied with riches' or 'endowed with qualities' interestingly anticipates 3.5.181/2115, giving a compelling link in imagery between lining and stuffing (for *Timon* 4.1.14/1350 Schmidt glosses *lined* as 'stuffed, padded'). Such a reading of 'nobly lind' might be considered cryptic if it were not helpfully glossed in the following line. 'Lind' also has a sexual equivocation (compare *As You Like It* 3.2.103-4/1247-8), as do 'Stuft' and 'parts'. 'Lineally

descended' might be admitted as a secondary sense for *lined*, adding to the complexity of association entirely absent from *limbed*.

3.5.225/2159 hĕce] HANMER; here Q2
3.5.226/2160 Speakst thou] Q2; Speakſt thou this Q1; Speakeſt thou Q3
2167 obsolu'd] Q2. See note to 1775.
3.5.235/2169 *watching her go*] Q1 (*She lookes after Nurſe.*); *not in* Q2
3.5.235/2169 wicked] Q2; curſed Q1
4.1.10/2186 do] Q2; doth Q1, Q3
4.1.16.1/2192.1 *Iuliet*] Q2; *Paris* Q1
4.1.43.1/2219.1 *Exit*] Q2; *Exit Paris.* Q1, F
4.1.45/2221 cure] Q1; care Q2. The text is emended in the same way at 4.4.92/2499.
4.1.72/2248 slay] Q1 (ſlay); ſtay Q2
4.1.81/2257 hide] Q2; ſhut Q1. Q2's repetition with 4.1.85/2261 is the kind of feature Shakespeare might revise.
4.1.83/2259 chaples] Q1; chapels Q2
4.1.85/2261 Tombe] WILLIAMS (Malone; *similarly* Q1); *not in* Q2; ſhroud Q4; graue F. Q1 conflates lines to give, 'Or lay me in tombe with one new dead'. McKerrow (MS) also proposed to follow Malone's suggestion. See Williams.
4.1.92/2268 the] Q2; thy Q1, Q3
4.1.94/2270 distilling] Q2; diſtilled Q1
4.1.98/2274 breath] Q1; breaſt Q2
4.1.100/2276 wany] HOPPE (Kellner); many Q2; paly Q4; mealy F2. The misreading probably influenced Q2's punctuation ('fade').
4.1.110/2286 In] Q3; Is Q2
4.1.110/2286 Beere,] HANMER; Beere,| Be borne to buriall in thy kindreds graue: Q2. Q2 is agreed to preserve a first version replaced by 4.1.111-12/2287-8.
4.1.111/2287 shalt] Q3; ſhall Q2
4.1.115 and] Q2 (an)
4.1.116/2292 waking] Q3; walking Q2
4.2.0.1-2/2302.2 ⌈*two*⌉ *Seruing men*] *Seruing men, two or three* Q2; *Seruingman* Q1. The dialogue seems to limit Shakespeare's permissive direction. There are two clear exit points for (single) Servingmen; by 4.2.44/2346 none remains on stage. A third Servingman would enter and exit spuriously.
4.2.9/2311 *Exit Seruingman*] Q1; *not in* Q2
4.2.14/2316 ſelfewilld harlottry] Q1 (ſelfewild harlotrie); ſelfewield harlottry Q2 (*most copies*); ſelfewieldhar lottry Q2 (*other copies*). Compare 'wield' with 'liand' at 3.5.180/2114, where again the form is so unusual as to suggest that it might derive from the copy, not from misreading.
4.2.21/2323 kneeling] Q1 ('She kneeles downe.' *after Juliet's speech*); *not in* Q2
4.2.26/2328 becoming] ROWE; becomd Q2; becomed F. Q2 is metrically anomalous and gives a word otherwise unrecorded (*OED*). The error is unexpected, but 'bounds' immediately below might contaminate 'becoming'.
4.2.37.1/2339.1 *Iuliet and Nurse*] Q1 (*Nurſe and Iuliet*), F; *not in* Q2
4.2.41/2343 vp her] Q2; her up HUDSON (Lettsom). Compare 4.2.45/2347 (which F emends).
4.2.47.1/2349.1 *Exeunt* ⌈*seuerally*⌉] *Exit.* Q2; *Exeunt.* Q1; *Exeunt Father and Mother* F
4.3.13.1/2362.1 *Exeunt . . . Nurse*] Q2 has '*Exeunt.*'; Q1 provides separate exits, the Nurse leaving after 4.3.5/2354.
4.3.39 this] Q2. Possibly a spelling of *these*, as Q3 reads.
4.3.48/2398 O] Q2; Or Q4
4.3.48/2398 wake] Q4; walke Q2
4.3.57/2407 *Romeo, Romeo, Romeo . . . thee*] Q2; *Romeo I come, this doe I drinke to thee* Q1. Editors are divided as to whether emendation is needed. Williams follows Nicholson's conjecture that the third *Romeo* is an error of dittography. 'Heeres drinke' might alternatively be a false start for 'I drinke to thee'. Wilson implausibly explains Q2 as a corruption of Q1. Nor can Q1 be regarded as revision, for the speech as a whole is a shortened and reconstructed verse paraphrase, making use of many ideas and phrases in Q2, but with few accurately reproduced lines. As the present line in Q2 contains an accumulation of metrical licences rather than actual corruption, and as these licences can be explained in terms of Juliet's frenzied state of mind, Q2 has been retained.

4.3.57.1-2/2407.1-2 *She . . . curtaines*] *She fals vpon her bed within the Curtaines.* Q1; *not in* Q2
4.4.0.1/2407.4 *with hearbes*] Q1 (*with hearbs*); *not in* Q2
4.4.13/2420 *three . . . Baskets*] *three or foure with ſpits and logs, and Baskets* Q2; *Seruingman with Logs & Coales* Q1
4.4.20/2427 faithe] Q4 (faith); father Q2
4.4.42 welladay] Q2 (wereaday)
4.4.43.1/2450.1 *Enter Capulets wife*] Q1, F (*Enter Mother.*); *not in* Q2
4.4.60/2467 FRIER] Q2; Par⟨is⟩: Q1
4.4.60/2470 see] F2 (*similarly* Q1); *not in* Q2. Q1 has: 'Deflowerd by him, see, where she lyes'.
4.4.67/2474 all:] Q4 (∼;); ∼ ⌃ Q2
4.4.67.1-2/2474.1-2 *Paris . . . together:*] Q1 (*All at once cry out and wring their hands.*); *not in* Q2. See Lower, who convincingly argues that the four lamenters speak together. Some directors have followed Lower's acceptance of the Q1 direction, but this is the first edition to do so. In view of Q2's arrangement (see note to 4.4.70-3/2477-80) it seems doubtful whether Shakespeare envisaged simultaneous delivery when he wrote the foul papers; Q1's stage direction presumably arises from a revised treatment of the lines.

Q1 begins with two lines spoken by all four lamenters:

All cry: And all our ioy, and all our hope is dead,
Dead, loſt, vndone, abſented, wholy fled.

Q1's rewritten speeches of lamentation suggest that the reporter was able to make little of the performed confusions. The two-line speech is not plausible as an authorial addition, especially as Shakespeare nowhere else uses *absented*.

4.4.68/2475 long] Q1; loue Q2
4.4.70-3/2477-80 Beguild . . . death] This edition (Lower). These lines, prefixed 'Par⟨is⟩.' follow the Nurse's speech below in Q2. Paris's two speeches in Q2 when combined form a six-line unit which, if Q1's '*All at once cry out*' is accepted, is spoken simultaneously with the six-line speeches of the other grievers.
4.4.82/2489 behold] Q3; bedold Q2; bedole EVANS (*conj.*)
4.4.92/2499 cure] THEOBALD; care Q2
4.4.108/2515 All in] ROWE; And in Q2; In all Q1
4.4.109/2516 fond] F2; ſome Q2
4.4.122.1-2/2529.1-2 *They . . . Musitions*] *Exeunt manet.* Q2; *They all but the Nurſe goe foorth, caſting Roſemary on* | *her and ſhutting the Curtens.* | *Enter Muſitions.* Q1; *Exeunt.* F
4.4.123-71/2530-75 ⌈1.⌉ MUSITION . . . dinner] For the Musician identified as the first, Q2 has prefixes '*Musi⟨tion⟩.*' (1), *Fid⟨ler⟩*. (2), and '*Min.*' or '*Minſt⟨rel⟩*. (6); these speeches are all attributed to '*Mu⟨sition⟩.*' (as distinct from '2. M.', etc.) in F and, where they exist, to '*1.*' in Q1. If it were not for the testimony of Q1 and F, the Fiddler might possibly be identified with one of the other musicians (a problematic alternative to the emendations discussed in the note to 4.5.156/2561).
4.4.127/2533 ⌈1.⌉ MUSITION] Q1 (*1.*); *Fid⟨ler⟩*. Q2
4.4.127/2533 by my] Q1; my my Q2
4.4.127.1/2533 *Exit Nurse*] Q1 (*one line earlier*); *Exit omnes.* Q2; *not in* F. The following episode could have been added as an afterthought in Shakespeare's manuscript.
4.4.127.2/2533.1 *Peter*] Q4, F; *Will Kemp* Q2; *Seruingman* Q1
4.4.130/2536 ⌈1.⌉ MUSITION] F (*Mu.*); *Fidler.* Q2
4.4.132/2538 full of woe:] Q4; full: Q2. Q4 completes the song-title.
4.4.134/2540 ⌈1. MUSITION⌉] Q1 (*1.*), F (*Mu.*); *Minſtrels.* Q2
4.4.149/2554 ⌈PETER⌉ Then . . . I] Q4; Then . . . *Peter.* I Q2. In Q2 *Then . . . wit* is set on a separate type line (see lineation note). It may have been a late addition to the copy.
4.4.152/2557 griefe] Q1; griefes Q2. See following note. If 'And . . . oppresse' is accepted from Q1 on the basis of its occurrence in the poem Peter quotes, 'griefe' should also be accepted, on the basis that it too is common to Q1 and Edwardes's poem.
4.4.153/2558 And . . . oppresse,] Q1; *not in* Q2. Peter quotes

Richard Edwardes's poem 'In commendation of Musicke', which begins: 'Where griping grief ye hart would wound, (and dolful domps ye mind oppresse) | There musick with her siluer sound . . .'. Most recent editors adopt Q2's omitted line from Q1. Q2 and Q1 agree, against Edwardes, in reading *When, doth*, and *Then*.

4.4.156/2561   Mathew Minikine] This edition; Simon Catling Q2; Simon ſound Pot Q1. Q1 gives no name for the third Musician; 'Mathew minikine' is the name it substitutes for Q2's 'Hugh Rebick'. Shakespeare may have reflected that 'Catling' is correctly a small lute-string, whereas the first Musician is a fiddler (see note to 4.4.124-71/2530-75)—as perhaps are they all. Staging the play would bring such details to the fore. Q1's substitution of Simon Soundpo(s)t is unconvincing in a (Q2) line in which 'siluer sound' is repeated, and probably appears in that line as a result of memorial confusion; it leaves a Musician unnamed and suggests no reason beyond memorial error for the disappearance of 'Hugh Rebick'. In its meaning, *minikin* is equivalent to *catling*, but also applies to the small string of a viol, an instrument whose player is a fiddler. Shakespeare elsewhere uses *minikin* in *History of Lear* 13.39/1855. There too it is alliterated ('minikin mouth') and alludes, as probably in *Romeo*, to the pitch and tone of a human voice. The *Lear* parallel makes it highly probable that Shakespeare revised the name.

As 'Simon' survives in Q1, Shakespeare must, if he introduced Mathew Minikin, have made a second adjustment, the substitution at 4.4.162/2566 of the newly redundant 'Simon' for 'Iames' in order to give a second alliterative name.

4.4.159, 162/2563, 2566   Prates] Q2; Pret(t)ie Q1
4.4.159/2563   Hugh Rebick] Q2; Mathew minikine Q1. See note to 4.4.153/2558.
4.4.162/2566   Simon] Q1 (*as name paired with sound* Po(s)t); Iames Q2. See note to 4.4.153/2558.
5.1.1/2576   truth] Q2; Eye Q1
5.1.3   lord] Q2 (L.), Q1
5.1.11.1/2586.1   booted] Q1; *not in* Q2
5.1.15/2590   fares my *Iuliet*] Q1; doth my Lady *Iuliet* Q2; doth my *Iuliet* POPE. Q2 evidently duplicates from the line above, but it is not agreed how extensively it does so. Williams follows Pope's reading, arguing that it depends on less error in Q2. However, Pope also assumes corruption in Q1, from a repeated reading to a varied one, and from one of the commonest verbs to a more specific one (in Shakespeare, over 1,070 *doth* to 32 *fares*). The varied and strengthened verb in Q1 is consistent with the varied and particularized noun (*Lady* to '*Iuliet*'). Q2 is likely to have a more radical error than Williams allows.
2599   in] Q2. For 'e'en'; probably a Shakespearian spelling.
5.1.24/2599   defie] Q1 (defie); denie Q2. Williams defends Q1.
5.1.24/2599   you] Q2; my Q1
5.1.33.1/2608.1   Exit Balthazer] Q1 (Exit Balthazar.); Exit. Q2 (*after* 'Lord', 5.1.32/2607); Exit. Man. F (*as* Q2)
5.1.56/2632   Enter Apothecarie] Q1, F; *not in* Q2
5.1.70/2645   starueth] Q2; stareth ROWE. *Stareth* is also the (un-authoritative) reading in Otway's 1679 adaptation of *Romeo* called *Caius Marius*. Malone pointed out that Q1's 'And starued Famine dwelleth in thy cheekes' supports Q2.
5.1.76/2651   pay] Q1; pray Q2. Editors generally follow Q1, but McKerrow (MS) considered Q2 defensible.
5.1.84.1-86/2659.1-2661   Exit Apothecarie . . . Exit] A minor clarification of Q2 and Q1's '*Exeunt.*' at the scene-end.
5.2.0.1/2661.1   Enter Frier Iohn] Q1; Enter Frier Iohn *to Frier Lawrence.* Q2. Q1 has no entry for Friar Laurence.
5.3.0.1-2/2690.2-3   with . . . Torch] *not in* Q2; *with flowers and ſweete Water* Q1
5.3.3/2693   yeug tree] Q1 (Ew-tree); young tree Q2. Williams's construction of copy-spelling 'yeug' (cf. *OED*'s 'yeugh') is probably justified as the error recurs at 5.3.137/2827.
5.3.4/2694   thy] Q2; thine Q1
5.3.12/2702   strewing flowers] Q1 (*Paris ſtrewes the Tomb with flowers.*); *not in* Q2
5.3.20(M)   rite] Q2 (right)

5.3.20.1/2710.1   Balthazer] Q1 (*Balthaſar*); Peter Q2. In Q2 Balthazar is named once in dialogue, at 5.1.12/2587, and in his final speech-prefix '*Balth.*' at 5.3.271/2961. The confusion with Peter continues in the prefixes for 5.3.40/2730 and 5.3.43/2733.
5.3.20.1-2/2710.1-2   with . . . Iron] Q1 (*with a torch, a | a mattocke, and a crow of yron*); *not in* Q2
5.3.22/   that] Q2, F; this Q1 the Q3
5.3.25/2715   light:] Q3; ~, Q2
5.3.40, 43/2730, 2733   BALTHAZER] Q1 (*Balt:*); Pet⟨er⟩. Q2
5.3.44.2/2734.1-2   Romeo . . . Tombe] *not in* Q2; *Romeo opens the tombe.* Q1. For '*begins to*' compare 5.3.73/2763. There is no indication that Romeo sees Juliet before 5.3.84/2774. The most attractive staging is that Romeo first prises open doors, then after killing Paris draws back curtains behind them—the same curtains which earlier enclosed Juliet's bed.
5.3.62/2752   Put] Q2; Heape Q1
5.3.68/2758   conniuration] CAPELL; commiration Q2; coniurations Q1; commiſſeration Q3; commination WILLIAMS (Mommsen). See new Arden note.
5.3.70.1/2760.1   They fight] Q1; *not in* Q2 (*but see following note*)
5.3.71/2761   PAGE] Q1 (*Boy:*), Q4; *not in* Q2; Pet⟨er⟩. F. The one-line speech is in Qq2-3 set as a stage direction in centred italics. Greg (*Problem*, p. 61, n.2) suggests a marginal insertion in the copy—as, evidently, at 3.1.89/1475.
5.3.102-3/2792-3   Shall I beleeue | That] THEOBALD; I will beleeue, | Shall I beleeue that Q2; O I beleeue that Q1. *I will beleeue* is evidently a false start in Shakespeare's manuscript.
5.3.107/2797   pallat] Q2; pallace Q3. Hosley and Smallwood defend Q2.
5.3.108/2798   Depart againe] Q4. Q2 has:

> Depart againe, come lye thou in my arme,
> Heer's to thy health, where ere thou tumbleſt in.
> O true Appothecarie!
> Thy drugs are quicke. Thus with a kiſſe I die.
> Depart againe . . .

In its admittedly condensed version of 5.3.108-20/2798-2810 Q1 gives no indication of the extra passage in Q2, which, as comparison with the following lines shows, is clearly a rejected first draft.
5.3.120.1/2810-1   He . . . dies] *not in* Q2; Falls. Q1
5.3.120.2/2810.2-3   Crowe, and Spade] Q2; *not in* Q1
5.3.136/2826   vnthriftie] Q2; vnluckie Q3. Q2's usage is uncommon but acceptable. Q3 might be dismissed entirely if Q1 did not substitute 'vnluckie' for 'an vnkind' at 5.3.145/2835: as McKerrow (MS) pointed out, this might suggest that the word occurred somewhere in the passage.
5.3.137/2827   yeug] POPE (*following* Q1 *at* 5.3.3/2693); yong Q2
5.3.139.1/2829.1   He . . . weapons] Q1 (*Fryer ſtoops . . . blood . .*); *not in* Q2
5.3.146.1/2836.1   Iuliet . . . rises] Q1 (*Iuliet riſes.*); *not in* Q2
5.3.159/2849   Come go] Q1; come, come Q1. As a possible error, 'go' could be explained as anticipating 'go(od)' and/or 'Go' beginning the next line. Copy 'cō' would facilitate error, especially if the tilde was unclear or absent, as evidently elsewhere. But Q2's idiom is acceptable.
5.3.163/2853   drunke] Q2; drinke Q1, Q3. Q1 uniquely has 'leaue' for 'left'.
5.3.167/2857   CHIEF WATCHMAN] Watch. Q2. Similarly at 5.3.171/2861 and 5.3.194/2884; also 5.3.198/2888 ('*Wat.*'). Evidently the same speaker is '*Chief. watch.*' at 5.3.182/2872 and '*Chiefwatch.*' at 5.3.186/2876. Q1 refers to him as '*Cap.*' or '*Capt.*' (for '*Captaine*'). F varies '*Watch.*' with '*Con⟨stable⟩.*' at 5.3.182/2872 and 5.3.186/2876.
5.3.169/2859   rust] Q2 (ruſt); Reft Q1. Williams and Gibbons defend Q2.
5.3.169.1/2859.1   She . . . dies] *not in* Q2; *She ſtabs herſelfe and falles.* Q1; *Kils herſelfe.* F
5.3.169.2/2859.2   Enter Page and Watch] Q1 gives '*Enter watch.*' before the Watchman's first speech and again after an ornament

following 'She stabs herselfe and falles.'; Q2 has its one direction, 'Enter Boy and Watch.' in the former position. This partial coincidence is not especially notable, as characters speaking within were often thought of as having entered the stage area.

5.3.170/2860 PAGE] Q4, F (*Boy.*); Watch boy. Q2
5.3.180.1/2870.1 ⌈*Watchmen*⌉ *with*] *not in* Q2; *one with* Q1
5.3.181/2871 ⌈2.⌉ WATCHMAN] ROWE (*similarly* Q1); Watch⟨*man*⟩. Q2. Q1 identifies as '*1.*', as distinct from the Captain, but gives the same prefix to the Watchman accompanying the Friar. The editorial numbering is implied in Q2's sequence of prefixes for 5.3.181–3/2871–3: 'Watch.', Chief. watch.', '3. Watch.'
5.3.186/2876 too] F; too too Q2
5.3.186.1/2876.1 *with others*] Q1; *not in* Q
5.3.188.1/2878.1 *Enter . . . wife*] Q2 has 'Enter Capels.' here and '*Enter Capulet and his wife.*' after 5.3.200/2890, a duplication not in Q1, which omits the dialogue between the Prince and the Chief Watchman. Q4 and F emend as in this edition. Evans adds '*Capulet and Lady Capulet enter the tomb.*' after 5.3.200/2890 and interprets the second entry as a return from the tomb. Alternatively, 5.3.188.1–200/2878.1–2896 might be a late addition in the manuscript; if so, it constitutes a highly effective elaboration of the passage's urgency and confusion.

5.3.189/2879 is so shrikd] DANIEL (Cambridge); is ſo ſhrike Q2; they ſo ſhriek Q3
5.3.193/2883 our] CAPELL (Johnson); your Q2
5.3.198/2888 slaughterd] Q4, F; Slaughter Q2
5.3.208/2898 more early] Q1; now earling Q2. Q2's 'now' seems pointless, and could be a misreading of 'more'. Romeo is not only earlier down than Montague is up; he is also more emphatically and irreversibly down.
5.3.210/2900 Griefe . . . breath.] Q2; And yong *Benuolio* is deceaſed too: Q1
5.3.231/2921 that] Q4; thats Q2
5.3.246/2936 as] Q2; at KEIGHTLEY
5.3.257/2947 awakening] Q2; awaking Q3
5.3.273/2963 place, to . . . monument.] F; ~. To . . . ~ˌ Q2
5.3.274/2964 Letter he] Q; Letter G.T. *conj.*
5.3.280/2970 PAGE] Q (*Boy.*), F
5.3.298/2988 raise] Q4, F; raie Q2; erect Q1. Hosley defends *raie* as meaning 'array'. This seems unlikely, and conflicts with Q1's synonym for *raise*.
5.3.302/2992 *Romeos by his Ladies*] Q2; R*omeo by his Lady* Q1, F
5.3.309.1/2999.1 *Exeunt*] F (*Exeunt omnes.*); *not in* Q

REJECTED FOLIO VARIANTS

1.1.1/15 on] Q2; of Q1; A
1.1.3/17 and] Q2; If Q1, F
1.1.4/18 of] Q2; of the Q1; o'th
1.1.14/28 Tis true] Q2; Thats true Q1; True
1.1.22/36 I will] Q2; & Q1; and
1.1.31/45 house of] Q2; houſe of the
1.1.51/65 But if] Q2; If
1.1.57/71 sir] Q2; *not in* F
1.1.67/81 drawne] Q2; draw
1.1.69.2/83.2 *or partysons*] Q2; *not in* F
1.1.77/91 MOUNTAGUES WIFE] Q2 (M.*Wife.*2.), F (2.*Wife.*)
1.1.77/91 one] Q2; a
1.1.86/100 brawles] Q; Broyles
1.1.143/157 other] Q2; others
1.1.210/224 bide] Q2; bid
1.1.211/225 ope] Q; open
1.1.215/229 waste:] Q2; waſt?
1.2.40/289 here] Q2; *not in* F
1.2.64/313 daughters] Q; daughter
1.2.101/350 shall scant shewˌ] Q (ſhall ſcant ſhewˌ); ſhall ſcant ſhell, Fa ſhew ſcant ſhell, Fb
1.3.37/389 a leuen] Q; a eleuen
1.3.49/401 Iule] Q2 (Iule); Iuliet Q1; *Iulet*
1.3.67/419 dispositions] Q2; diſpoſition
1.4.20/479 so] Q2; to
1.4.41/500 mireˌ] Q; ~.
1.4.45/503 in] Q; I
1.4.57/515 an] Q; *not in* F
1.4.64/522 spider] Q2; Spiders
1.4.74+1/532+1 dreame] Q2; dreamt (*see textual note*)
1.4.80/538 a] Q; *not in* F
1.4.87/545 eare] Q; eares
1.5.0.2/573.3 *Napkins*] Q2; *their napkins*
1.5.3/576 all] Q2; *not in* F
1.5.8/581 loues] Q; loueſt
1.5.25.1–2/599.1–2 *the . . . gentlewomen*] *they* Q2; *the*
1.5.26/600 hall, a hall] Q2; Hall, Hall
1.5.39/613 CAPULET] Q2 (1. *Cap.*), Q1 (*Cap*:); 3 *Cap.*
1.5.52/626 For I nere] Q2; I neuer Q1; For I neuer
1.5.68/642 this] Q; the
1.5.79/653 my] Q; the
1.5.91/665 bittrest] Q2; bitter Q1, F
1.5.94/668 two] Q; to
1.5.134/708 wedding] Q; wedded

1.5.141/715 learnt] Q; learne
2.1.10/741 Crie] Q; Cry me F
2.1.16/747 and] Q; *not in* F
2.1.25/756 there] Q; *not in* F
2.1.89/820 tytle: *Romeo*ˌ] ~, ~ˌ Q2; ~ˌ ~ˌ Q1; ~ˌ ~,
2.1.132/863 me] Q; *not in* F
2.1.135/866 laughes] Q2; ſmiles Q1; laught
2.1.146/877 trulove] Q2; true loues Q1, F
2.1.149/880 blessed] Q; *not in* F
2.1.202/933 toward] Q; towards
2.1.222/953 farther] Q2; further Q1, F
2.2.55/1020 and] Q; reſt
2.2.92/1057 housholds] Q; houſhould
2.3.21/1080 minum rests] Q2; minum reſt Q1; minum
2.3.27/1087 by Iesu] Q; Ieſu
2.3.47/1107 good] Q2; *not in* F
2.3.60/1120 soly] Q; ſole-|
2.3.76/1138 in to] Q; into
2.3.80/1142 a broad] Q; abroad
2.3.85/1147 hide] Q; hid
2.3.91/1153 for] Q; or
2.3.109/1171 well] Q; *not in* F
2.3.161/1224 ROMEO] Q; Nur⟨ſe⟩.
2.3.176/1239 good] Q2; thou Q1; thou good
2.3.187/1250 mans] Q2; man
2.3.192/1255 see a] Q2; a ſee
2.3.207.1–2/1270.1–2 *Exit . . . doore*] *Exit.* Q2; *Ex. omnes.* Q1; *Exit Nurſe and Peter.*
2.4.11/1281 Is] Q2; I
2.4.4/1274 heraulds] Q; Herauld
2.4.40/1310 leg] Q; legs
2.4.44/1314 as gentle] Q2; gentle F
2.4.46/1316 this] Q2; this this
2.4.50/1320 a my] Q2; o my
2.4.52/1322 iaunsing] Q2; iaunting Q4, F
2.4.53/1323 not] Q2; ſo
2.5.8/1356 inough,] Q2; ~.
2.5.23/1371 is] Q2; in Q4, F
2.5.24/1372 ROMEO] Q2; Fri⟨*er*⟩.
2.5.33/1381 such] Q2; ſuch ſuch
3.1.48/1433 zounds] Q2; Come
3.1.68/1453 loue] Q; lou'd F
3.1.87/1473 Forbid this] Q2; Forbid Q3; Forbidden
3.1.91/1477 your] Q1; *not in* Q2; the

ROMEO AND JULIET

3.1.100/1486 sounds] Q2; What
3.1.122/1508 *Mercutio*] Q2; *Mercutio's*
3.1.140/1526 name] Q2; names
3.1.157/1543 *Tybalt*] Q2; *Tybalts*
3.1.192/1578 out] Q2; our
3.1.196/1582 but] Q2; not
3.2.37/1619 hees dead, hees dead, hees dead] Q2; hee's dead, hee's dead
3.2.95/1677 at] Q2; *not in* F
3.2.106/1688 *Tybalts*] Q2; *Tibalt*
3.2.121/1703 with] Q2; which
3.3.40-3/1765-8 But . . . death] *See textual note*
3.3.48/1773 Howling] Q; Howlings
3.3.52/1777 a little speake] Q2; but speake a word Q1; speake
3.3.63/1788 dispute] Q; dispaire
3.3.65/1790 I, *Iuliet* thy] Q; *Iuliet* my
3.3.73.1/1798.1 *Knocking within*] *Nurse knockes.* Q1; *They knocke.* Q2; *Knocke.*
3.3.75.1/1800.1 *Still knocke within*] *Slud knock.* Q2; *Knocke.*
3.3.92/1817 Spakst] Q; Speak'st
3.3.97/1822 canceld] Q; conceal'd
3.3.102/1827 deadly] Q; dead
3.3.138/1863 becomes] Q2; became
3.3.139/1864 turnes] Q2; turne Q3; turn'd
3.3.140/1865 of blessings] Q2, Q1; of blessing Q3; or blessing
3.3.142/1867 mishaued] Q2; misbehaued Q1; mishaped
3.3.143/1868 pouts vpõ] Q4 (powts vpon); puts vp Q2; frownst vpon Q1; puttest vp
3.3.158/1883 all the] Q2; all this Q1; all
3.4.34/1933 very] Q2; very, very Q1; *not in* F
3.5.21/1955 the] Q; *not in* F
3.5.35/1969 light it] Q; itli ght
3.5.53/1987 our times] Q2; the time Q1; our time
3.5.65/1999 It is] Q; Is it
3.5.111/2045 that] Q; this
3.5.115/2049 there] Q2; *not in* F
3.5.119/2053 wooe] Q2; woe
3.5.135/2069 thy] Q2; the
3.5.147/2081 hate] Q; haue
3.5.151/2085 And . . . you,] Q2; *not in* F
3.5.171/2105 gossips] Q; gossip
3.5.174/2108 bowle] Q; bowles
3.5.176/2110 night,] night, houre, tide Q2; night, houre, ride
3.5.192/2126 starue] Q; straue
3.5.209/2143 Alack] Q2; Hlacke
3.5.212-13/2146-7 Faith . . . nothing] *1 line* Q2; is|
3.5.236/2170 Is it] Q; It is
3.5.242/2176 *Exit*] Q; *Exeunt.*
4.1.34/2210 my] Q; thy
4.1.40/2216 we] Q; you
4.1.43.1/2219.1 *Exit*] Q2; *Exit Paris.* Q1, F
4.1.47/2223 straines] Q2; streames
4.1.54/2230 with this] Q2; with' his
4.1.56/2232 *Romeos*] Q2; *Romeo*
4.1.75/2251 from] Q; fro
4.1.101/2277 shuts] Q2; shut
4.1.115-16/2291-2 an . . . waking,] Q2 (. . . walking); *not in* F
4.1.121/2297 feare] Q2; care
4.2.26/2328 becoming] becomd Q2; becomed
4.2.36/2338 there is] Q2; there's
4.2.45/2347 vp him] Q2; him vp
4.3.16/2365 life] Q2; fire
4.3.56/2406 a] Q2; my
4.4.13/2420 is] Q2; haue you Q1; *not in* F
4.4.109/2516 vs all] Q2; all vs
4.4.127.1/2533 *Exit Nurse*] Q1; *Exit omnes.* Q2; *not in* F
4.4.132-3/2538-9 O play . . . comfort me.] Q2; *not in* F
5.1.4/2579 this . . . vnaccustomd] Q2; thisan . . . vccustom'd
5.1.19/2594 liues] Q2; liue
5.1.32/2607 No matter] Q2; Mo matter
5.1.33.1/2608.1 *Balthazer*] Q1 (*Balthazar*); *not in* Q2; *Man*
5.1.38/2613 a] Q2; he Q1; *not in* F
5.1.80/2655 There is] Q2; There's
5.2.1.1/2662.1 *Lawrence*] Q2; *Frier Lawrence*
5.3.1/2691 aloofe] Q2; aloft
5.3.19/2709 way] Q2; was Q1; wayes
5.3.34/2724 farther] Q2; further
5.3.60/2750 these] Q2; those
5.3.71/2761 PAGE] Q1 (*Boy:*), Q4; *not in* Q2; *Pet⟨er⟩.*
5.3.94/2784 art] Q2; are
5.3.100/2790 thine] Q2; thy
5.3.135/2825 feare] Q2; feares
5.3.148/2838 where is] Q2; where's
5.3.160/2850 not away] Q2; notuaway
5.3.161/2851 loues] Q2; lo:es
5.3.163/2853 left] Q2; left
5.3.169/2860 This is] Q2; Tis is Q3; 'Tis in
5.3.182/2872 CHIEF WATCHMAN] Q2 (*Chief. watch.*); *Con⟨stable⟩.*
5.3.186/2876 CHIEF WATCHMAN] Q2 (*Chiefwatch.*); *Con⟨stable⟩.*
5.3.188/2878 morning] Q2; mornings Q4, F
5.3.192/2882 our] Q2; out
5.3.213/2903 is in] Q; in is
5.3.271/2961 BALTHAZER] Q (*Balth.*); *Boy.*

INCIDENTALS

97 hands₍ₐ₎] ~,   98 mistempred] mistempered   103 *Veronas*] *Neronas*   132 Sycamour] Syramour   141 shunnd] shunned   248 forget.] ~,   306 read?] ~, Q1   353 daughter:] ~, Q1   354-6 Now . . . *Iuliet*] Italic for roman and roman for italic in Q1 and Q2, similarly for all the Nurse's speeches to 432.   355 come,] ~., Q1   361 again,] ~, Q1   363 knowest] knowest Q1   372 she, . . . soules,] ~, . . . ~, Q1   376 shee, marie] ~, ~ Q1   381 Doue-house] ~-|~ Q1   387 Doue-house,] ~, Q1   410 commst] commest   444 the faire₍ₐ₎] ~ ~,   486 loue:] ~,   489 A . . . I] indented   505 iudgement] indgement   512 you.] ~: (*see textual note to* 513)   531 loue,] ~,   547 And] & (*see lineation note*)   570 forfeit] forfeit   584 boy] Q2 (*text*); Boy Q2 (*c.w.*)   592 mistresses] mistesses   599 gentlemen:] ~,   715 tis.] ~, (*some copies*)   722 belou'd] beloued   738 passion,] ~,   757 coniurd] coniured   820 tytle:] ~,   832 tongues] tongus   835 camst] camest   868 thinkst] thinkest   889 sweare: . . . thee,] ~, . . . ~:   923 meanst] meanest   927 griefe.] ~,   963 rest.] ~,   978 many,] ~,   998 distemperd] distempered   1016 wounded, both,] ~, ~,   1026-7 marriage: . . . vow,] ~,, . . . ~:   1032 young] yonng   1038 sighes, . . . cleares,] ~, . . . ~,   1050 now,] ~. (*at foot of page*)   1158 Peter.] ~:   1235 shrieud] shrieued   1263 name, . . . the,] ~, . . . ~,   1268 times.] ~,   1272 promisd] promised   1291 lookst] lookest   1293 shamst] shamest   1347 Go,] ~,   1429 consortst] consortest   1453 thou] thon   1453-4 deuise, . . . loue:] ~: . . . ~,   1503 gallant] gallanr   1512 gaust] gauest   1520 amazd] amazed   1524 murtherer] mutherer   1540 displeasure:] ~,   1589 vnseene.] ~,   1626 rord] rored   1732 companie.] ~?   1748 smilst] smilest   1793 mightst thou speake] mightst ~ ~   1817 Spakst] Spakest   1820 remoud] remoued   1843 raylst] raylest   1846 shamst] shamest   1860 dead,] ~.   1959 talke,] ~,   1977 so?] ~, (*see also textual note*)   1991 lookst] lookest   2016 pardon] padon   2072 deliured] deliuered   2105 Prudence, smatter,] ~, ~,   2106 treason. . . . Godigeden.] ~, . . . ~,   2188 teares,] ~.   2226 hearst] hearest   2231 heart, and *Romeos*,] ~, . . . and ~,   2231-2 hands: . . . seald,] ~, . . . ~:   2252 darst] darest   2275 fade,] ~:   2286 vncoured] vncouered   2297 feare.] ~,

ROMEO AND JULIET

2427 Thou] Twou 2471 deflowered] deflowred 2499-2500 not, ... confusions,] ~, ... ~, 2607 matter,] ~,
2623 scattred] scattered 2644 fearst] feareſt 2698 hearst] heareſt 2702 strew.] ~, 2716 hearst] heareſt
2731 friendship] friendſhid 2797 night,] ~. 2841 noyse.] ~, 2894 missheathed] misſheathd 2915 impeach] i peach
(*some copies*) 2997 pardond] pardoned

QUARTO STAGE DIRECTIONS

Pro.0.1/0.1 The Prologue.
1.1.0.1-2/14.2-3 *Enter Sampson and Gregorie, with Swords and Bucklers, of the | house of* Capulet.
1.1.30.1-2/44.1-2 *Enter two other seruing men.* (after 1.1.31/45)
1.1.54.1/68.1 *Enter Benuolio.*
1.1.60.1/74.1 *They fight.*
1.1.62.1/76.1 *Enter Tibalt.*
1.1.69.1-2/83.1-2 *Enter three of foure Citizens with Clubs or partysons.*
1.1.71.1/85.1 *Enter old* Capulet *in his gowne, and his wife.*
1.1.73.1-2/87.1-2 *Enter old* Mountague *and his wife.* (after 1.1.75/89)
1.1.77.3/91.3 *Enter Prince Eskales, with his traine.*
1.1.100.1-2/114.1-2 *Exeunt.*
1.1.152.1/166.1 *Enter Romeo.*
1.1.156.1/170.1 *Exeunt.*
1.1.235/249 *Exeunt.*
1.2.0.1/249.1-2 *Enter Capulet, Countie Paris, and the Clowne.*
1.2.35.1/284.1 *Exit.*
1.2.42.1/291.1 *Enter Benuolio, and Romeo.* (after 1.2.43/292)
1.2.63.1/312.1 (Q1) *He reads the Letter.*
1.3.0.1/352.1 (Q1) *Enter Capulets wife and Nurse.*
1.3.4.1/356.1 (Q1) *Enter Iuliet.*
1.3.101.1/453.1 *Enter Seruing.*
1.3.107/459 *Exeunt.*
1.4.0.1-3/459.1-3 *Enter Romeo, Mercutio, Benuolio, with fiue or sixe other | Maskers, torchbearers.*
1.4.115.1-1.5.0.1-2/573.1-3 *They march about the Stage, and Seruingmen come forth with | Napkins. | Enter Romeo.*
1.5.15.1/589.1 *Exeunt.*
1.5.15.2-6/589.2-6 *Enter all the guests and gentlewomen to the | Maskers.*
1.5.25.1-2/599.1-2 *Musick playes and they dance.*
1.5.91/665 *Exit.*
1.5.143/717 *Exeunt.*
2.0.0.1/717.1 *Chorus.*
2.1.0.1/731.1 *Enter Romeo alone.*
2.1.2.2/733.2 *Enter Benuolio with Mercutio.*
2.1.42.1/773.1 *Exit.*
2.1.202.2/933.2 *Enter Iuliet againe.*
2.1.234/965 *Exit.*
2.2.0.1/965.1 *Enter Frier alone with a basket.*
2.2.22.1/987.1 *Enter Romeo.*
2.2.94/1059 *Exeunt.*
2.3.0.1/1059.1 *Bnter Benuolio and Mercutio.*
2.3.33.1/1093.1 *Enter Romeo.*
2.3.92.1/1154.1 *Enter Nurse and her man.* (after 2.3.93/1155)
2.3.135/1198 *Exeunt.*
2.3.207.1-2/1270.1-2 *Exit.*
2.4.0.1/1270.3 *Enter Iuliet.*
2.4.17.1/1287.1 *Enter Nurse.*
2.4.78.1/1348.1 *Exeunt.*
2.5.0.1/1348.2 *Enter Frier and Romeo.*
2.5.15.1/1363.1 *Enter Iuliet.*
3.1.0.1/1385 *Enter Mercutio, Benuolio, and men.*
3.1.33.1/1418.1 *Enter Tybalt, Petruchio, and others.*
3.1.54.1/1439.1 *Enter Romeo.*
3.1.108.1/1494.1 *Exit.*
3.1.115.1/1501.1 *Enter Benuolio.*
3.1.131.1/1517.1 *They Fight. Tibalt falles.*
3.1.136.1/1522.1 *Exit Romeo.*
3.1.136.2/1522.2 *Enter Citizens.*
3.1.140.1-2/1526.1-2 *Enter Prince, olde* Mountague, Capulet, | *their wiues and all.*
3.1.196.1/1582.1 *Exit.*
3.2.0.1/1582.2 *Enter Iuliet alone.*
3.2.31/1613 *Enter Nurse with cords.* (after 'my Nurse')
3.2.143.1/1725.1 *Exit.*
3.3.0.1, 3.3.3.1/1725.2, 1728.1 *Enter Frier and* Romeo. (at 3.3.0.1/1725.1)
3.3.70.1/1795.1 *Enter Nurse, and knocke.*
3.3.73.1/1798.1 *They knocke.*
3.3.75.1/1800.1 *Slud knock.*
3.3.78/1802 *Knocke.* (after 'come, I come')
3.3.80.1/1805.1 *Enter Nurse.* (after 3.3.78/1803)
3.3.174/1899 *Exeunt.*
3.4.0.1/1899.1 *Enter old Capulet, his wife and* Paris.
3.4.35.1-2/1934.1-2 *Exeunt.*
3.5.0.1/1934.3-4 *Enter Romeo and Iuliet aloft.*
3.5.36.1/1970.1 *Enter Madame and Nurse.*
3.5.59/1993 *Exit.*
3.5.64/1998 *Enter Mother.*
3.5.123.1/2057.1 *Enter Capulet and Nurse.* (after 3.5.125/2059)
3.5.195/2129 *Exit.*
3.5.203/2137 *Exit.*
3.5.242/2176 *Exit.*
4.1.0.1/2176.1 *Enter Frier and Countie* Paris.
4.1.16.1/2192.1 *Enter Iuliet.* (after 4.1.17/2193)
4.1.43.1/2219.1 *Exit.*
4.1.126/2302 (*Exit.*
4.2.0.1-2/2302.1-2 *Enter Father Capulet, Mother, Nurse, and | Seruing men, two or three.*
4.2.14.1/2316.1 *Enter Iuliet.*
4.2.37.1/2339.1 *Exeunt.*
4.2.47.1/2349.1 *Exit.*
4.3.0.1/2349.2 *Enter Iuliet and Nurse.*
4.3.5.1/2354.1 *Enter Mother.*
4.3.13.1/2362.1 *Exeunt.*
4.4.0.1/2407.1-4 *Enter Lady of the house and Nurse.*
4.4.2.1/2409.1 *Enter old* Capulet.
4.4.12.1/2419.1 *Exit Lady and Nurse.*
4.4.13/2420 *Enter three or foure with spits and logs, | and Baskets.* (after 'there')
4.4.22/2429 *Play Musicke.* (after 4.4.20/2427)
4.4.23.1/2430.1 *Enter Nurse.*
4.4.48.1/2455.1 *Enter Father.*
4.4.59.1/2466.1-2 *Enter Frier and the Countie.*
4.4.122.2/2529.2 *Exeunt manet.*
4.4.127.1/2533 *Exit omnes.*
4.4.127.2/2533.1 *Enter Will Kemp.*
4.4.171/2572 *Exit.*
4.4.162/2575 *Exit.*
5.1.0.1/2575.1 *Enter Romeo.*
5.1.11.1/2586.1 *Enter Romeos man.*
5.1.33.1/2608.1 *Exit.* (after 'Lord', 5.1.32/2607)
5.1.84, 86/2659, 2661 *Exeunt.* (after 5.1.86/2661)
5.2.0.1/2661.1 *Enter Frier Iohn to Frier* Lawrence.
5.2.1.1/2662.1 *Enter Lawrence.*
5.2.22/2683 *Exit.*
5.2.29/2690.1 *Exit.*
5.3.0.1-2/2690.1-2 *Enter Paris and his Page.*
5.3.17.1/2707.1 *Whistle Boy.*
5.3.20.1-2/2710.1-2 *Enter Romeo and Peter.* (after 5.3.21/2711)
5.3.120.2/2810.2-3 *Entrer Frier with Lanthorne, Crowe, | and Spade.*
5.3.159/2849 *Exit.*

304

5.3.169.2/2859.2	*Enter Boy and Watch.* (after 'warme', 5.3.167/2857)
5.3.180.1/2870.1	*Enter Romeos man.*
5.3.182.1/2872.1	*Enter Frier, and another Watchman.*
5.3.186.1/2876.1	*Enter the Prince.*
5.3.188.1/2878.1	*Enter Capels.*
5.3.188.1/2878.1	*Enter Capulet and his wife.* (after 5.3.200/2890)
5.3.206.1/2896.1	*Enter Mountague.*

RICHARD II

Richard II (*BEPD* 141) was entered in the Stationers' Register by Andrew Wise on 29 August 1597:

    Andrew Wife./. Entred for his Copie by appoyntm ^t
                from Mr Warden Mañ / The
                Tragedye of Richard the Seconde

The first Quarto (Q1) appeared in the same year, printed for Wise by Valentine Simmes, with a title-page advertising a text '*As it hath beene publikely acted by the right Honourable the Lorde Chamberlaine his Seruants*'. Further quartos, Q2 and Q3, appeared in 1598, with title-pages naming Shakespeare as author. The play was transferred from Wise to Matthew Law on 25 June 1603; Law published quartos in 1608 (Q4) and 1615 (Q5). Each quarto after Q1 was a reprint of its immediate predecessor, but Q4 introduced for the first time a text of the 'abdication episode' (4.1.145–308/1977–2140). In some copies of Q4 a reset title-page accordingly advertised '... With new additions of the Parlia-|ment Sceane, and the depofing | of King Richard, | As it hath been lately acted by the Kinges | Maiefties feruantes, at the Globe'. Hasker demonstrated that the First Folio text (F) was set primarily from a copy of Q3. A further quarto, Q6, was printed from F in 1634.

The stage directions in Q1 are authorial in character, and the text is thought to derive directly from Shakespeare's foul papers or from a non-theatrical transcript of them. The relative absence of the inconsistencies, confusions, and Shakespearian spellings associated with foul-paper texts leads to the suspicion that a transcript intervened. However, the only convincing evidence for such a transcript is the preference for the spelling 'Oh' where Shakespeare preferred 'O'. It remains possible — perhaps even most probable — that Q was set from well-ordered authorial papers. Hinman pointed to features of the text indicating that the copy for Q was cast off by formes; he also identified the stints of two compositors who set the play: Simmes's Compositors A and S. Press corrections have been found in five formes; these were listed by Hinman. There are several indications that the copy was consulted during press correction: most remarkably, two full lines of text were restored at 2.1.187/801 and 2.2.33/949.

The printer's copy for F was evidently annotated with reference to a prompt-book. Some critics believe that the prompt-book was a marked-up copy of Q1, but it was more probably a manuscript. In F, new directions are introduced, and extant ones reworked to make them more specific, more accurate, and occasionally more concise. F is a valuable source of information for details of the play's staging. Most of its directions are wholly or partly assimilated into the directions in this edition, though preference is given to the wording of Q1 directions where they give equivalent information. Other changes in F include the emendation of about half of the corrupt or unauthoritative readings of Q3, a version of the abdication episode (not in Q3) which is independent of the Q4–5 text, expurgation of some of Q's profanity, and omission of a number of lines and passages printed in Qq1–5. Except in the first scene, F alters all quarto prefixes denoting Richard or Bolingbroke as King, probably on prompt-book authority. F also introduces act and scene divisions; these are followed in this edition except where F fails to introduce a necessary scene division at 5.3–4/Sc. 16–17 (see note to 5.4.0.1/2518.3). Here Capell is followed as the first editor using the Folio system of scene divisions to introduce a new scene.

The Folio text has been examined in some detail by Jowett and Taylor in 'The Folio Text of *Richard II*', which underlies the editorial policy of this edition and provides discussion of individual Folio readings. Jowett and Taylor gather the various evidence for and against reference to the prompt-book, and thereby build up a picture of how effectively and where the quarto copy was annotated. They show that there was considerable fluctuation in the annotators' efficiency. It is not adequate to follow Greg in judging the annotation as 'superficial'. Some areas of the text were carefully collated. Almost all the Folio readings accepted by recent editors occur in these well-annotated areas. The annotator was most effective in the first 900 lines, subsequent isolated pockets which include substantial parts of 3.2/Sc. 10, and large sections of the fifth act (Sc. 14–18). In such passages F is a more reliable source of authoritative readings than has been realized.

Craven has shown that Simmes's Compositor A, who set most of Q, was prone to particular types of error which are usually hard to detect: trivial substitutions, omissions, and transpositions. Such errors are sometimes correctable through reference to F. But a number of Q/F variants which typically give radically different readings of a noun, verb, or adjective are not readily explained as corruption by Simmes's Compositor A or at any other stage of textual transmission. Contrary to Pollard, it is difficult to see why actors should have introduced such changes; Ure's additional provision of a corrupting annotator working on the Folio copy is no more persuasive in explaining these variants. Much more plausible is the Riverside's suggestion that they represent 'possible Shakespearean second thoughts' (p. 838). They can be seen to alter the text for reasons which would only appeal to the author.

On the basis of these considerations, over forty Folio readings have been admitted in this edition which are rejected in the Arden, New Penguin, and Riverside editions. Most of these readings can be associated with nearby independent evidence of prompt-book consultation.

There is one passage in F where significant Q1/F agreements or authoritative F variants should not occur. Hasker had interpreted a series of Q5/F correspondences in Act 5 as indicating that missing final leaves in the Q3 copy for F had been replaced by leaves from a copy of Q5. In fact the Q5-influenced passage is restricted to 52 Folio lines (5.5.70–118/

2599-2647). Conjecturally, the deficiency in the manuscript prompt-book arose when a single leaf was lost, and this was repaired with a transcript from Q5; Q5 readings in F would thus have been annotated on to the Q3 copy from the repaired prompt-book. The nature of the variants in the passage supports the view that they have no independent authority.

F's omissions of material not in the quartos consist of four single lines and five passages of between 4 and 26 lines each. The single-line omissions could arise from scribal or compositorial oversight, though 3.2.45/1348 and perhaps also 3.2.178/1481 might have been deliberately deleted in the prompt-book. The remaining passages are almost certainly prompt-book deletions. Most plausibly Shakespeare himself was responsible. Even if he did not personally mark them, they can be taken to have his active or tacit assent. The longer passages are not printed in our text, but are appended as additional passages. As one cannot be sure that any of the individual lines omitted in F were intended for deletion, they have been retained.

The most significant single difference between Q1 and F is the latter's inclusion of the abdication episode. It is widely accepted that the episode was censored; most probably a passage was disallowed for stage performance. The usual assumption is that the extant episode was simply omitted during the period of Queen Elizabeth's reign and subsequently reinstated. An alternative sequence of events would be that the Master of the Revels ordered a rewriting of an even more controversial original version. Despite the probability that the Quarto text introduces a short 'bridge' phrase after its cut ('Let it be so, and loe', 4.1.309/2141), other variants in this and the following line probably originate in the prompt-book; the degree of variation here is more marked than elsewhere. Q's 'proclaime' for 'set downe' and 'be ready all' for 'prepare your selues', and also F's provision at the beginning of the scene of a herald who is not required in the extant text, may be relics of a lost first version. In either situation the actors themselves, the Bishop of London as licenser, or the printers or publishers may have cut the original version of the abdication scene from the papers which served as copy for Q1.

A comparison of the text for the abdication episode in Q4 and F demonstrates the superiority of the latter text, which is used as control text for the episode in this edition. Q4 is extensively mislined, especially towards the end of the passage, and has a series of omitted part-lines which cannot be explained as deliberate cuts or an early version. These features suggest a reported text. Folio Compositor A, who set the passage in F, shows no influence of Q4 or Q5 in his departures from habitual spellings, and the Q4 text is unlikely to have influenced F. Where variant readings occur, F usually has the preferred reading, though Q4 does seem to preserve a few authoritative readings where F is corrupt. The complex relationship between the quartos, inferred manuscripts, and F may be summarized in the stemma which follows.

Despite the particular uses of F, Q1 remains the control text throughout, except for the abdication episode. A number of metrical contractions in F, mostly obvious elisions, have been rejected. As Q was probably set from Shakespeare's papers, the expanded forms probably derive from his hand; there is no reason to suppose he would have regarded the readings as errors. Exceptions to the convention of reserving '-ed' for syllabic verb endings are emended, as the large majority of these exceptions may be attributed to Compositor A. Rejected readings originating in F and Folio restorations of Q1 readings from corrupt printed copy are recorded in lists appended to the Textual Notes.

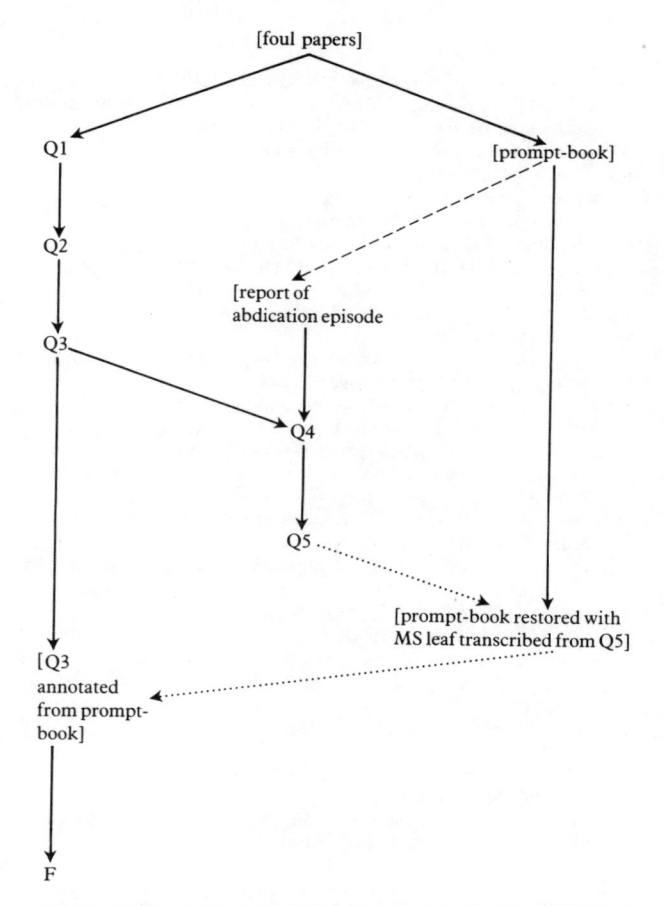

J.J./(S.W.W.)

WORKS CITED

Black, M. W., ed., *The Life and Death of King Richard the Second*, New Variorum (1955)
—— ed., *The Tragedy of King Richard the Second*, Pelican (1957)
Craven, Alan E., 'Simmes' Compositor A and Five Shakespeare Quartos', *SB* 26 (1973), 37-60
—— 'The Reliability of Simmes's Compositor A', *SB* 32 (1979), 186-92
Gurr, Andrew, ed., *King Richard II*, New Cambridge (1984)
Hasker, Richard, 'The Copy for the First Folio *Richard II*', *SB* 5 (1952-3), 58-68
Hinman, Charlton, ed., '*Richard II*': *The Quarto of 1597*, Oxford Shakespeare Quarto Facsimile (1966)
John, Ivor B., ed., *The Tragedy of King Richard II*, Arden (1912)
Jowett, John, and Gary Taylor, 'Sprinklings of Authority: The Folio Text of *Richard II*', *SB* 38 (1985), 151-200
Muir, Kenneth, ed., *The Tragedy of King Richard the Second*, Signet (1963)
Pollard, A. W., ed., '*King Richard II*': *A New Quarto* (1916)
Ure, Peter, ed., *King Richard II*, Arden (1956)
Wells, Stanley, ed., *King Richard the Second*, New Penguin (1969)

TEXTUAL NOTES

Title *The Tragedie of King Richard the second*] Q (*title-page and running title*); The Tragedie of Richard the Second S.R.; The life and death of King Richard | the Second. F (*head title*); The life and death of Richard the second. F (*running title*)

1.1.2 bond] Q (bande)
1.1.15/15 presence,] POPE; ~ˌ QF
1.1.20/20 Manie] QF; May many POPE
1.1.22 others'] Q (others). Usually interpreted 'other's'.
1.1.53 hushed] Q (huiſht). Alternatively modernized 'whisht'.
1.1.56/56 returndˌ] F; ~, Q
1.1.66/66 Where euer] QF; Where never POPE
1.1.118/118 by my] F; by Q
1.1.139/139 But] Qb, F; Ah but Qa. Qa probably gives regularized dittography of 'A' just above.
1.1.152/152 gentlemen] F (Gentlemen); gentleman Q
1.1.157/157 time] F; month Q. See Jowett and Taylor, pp. 191–2.
1.1.162/162 Harry, when?] POPE (*following Q2 and F's punctuation, but omitting 'obedience bids'*); Harry? whenˌ obedience bids, Q1. H. F. Brooks, in Ure's Arden edition, plausibly conjectured that the copy had 'When . . . againe' as one line; that the compositor began following copy, then, realizing the need to divide, set the verse-line 'Obedience . . . againe' without cancelling his first 'obedience bids'.
1.1.178/178 Reputation,] Q2, F; ~ˌ Q1
1.1.186/186 downe] F; vp Q. This variant is probably connected with a change of staging (Wells). 'Throw vp' suggests a command to surrender the gage to Richard, who would probably be on a raised throne.
1.1.189–90/189–90 height, . . . Dastard?] Qb, *similarly* F; ~ ? . . . ~, Qa
1.1.192/192 parle] F; parlee Q. The forms might have been regarded as indifferent variants.
1.1.195.1/195.1 *Exit Gaunt*] F; *not in* Q. F must preserve either a prompt-book annotation or a foul-paper direction omitted in Q.
1.1.205/205 *Exeunt*] F; *Exit.* Q
1.2.0.1/205.1 *Iohn . . . the*] Q; *Gaunt, and* F
1.2.1/206 Glocesters] F (Glouſters); Woodſtockes Q. Q's only reference to Gloucester as Woodstock; evidently a foul-paper irregularity emended in the prompt-book.
1.2.40/245 heauen] QF; God POPE. In the following line, 'his' may refer back to 1.2.37/242 or be the neuter possessive equivalent to *its*.
1.2.42/247 alas] Qb, F; *not in* Qa
1.2.44/249 farewell olde Gaunt] QF; farewel, old *Gaunt* farewel POPE
1.2.48/253 butcher] Qb, F; butchers Qa
1.2.58/263 it] Q2, F; is Q1
1.2.59/264 emptieˌ] Qb, F; emptines, Qa
1.2.70/275 heare] Qb, F; cheere Qa
1.3.0.1/279.1–2 *Lord . . . Aumerle*] *Lord Marſhall and the Duke Aumerle* Q; *Marſhall, and Aumerle* F
1.3.6.1/285.1 *The . . . with*] Q; *Flouriſh.* | *Enter King,* F
1.3.6.2–3/285.2 *Gaunt . . . nobles*] *his nobles* Q; *Gaunt, Buſhy, Bagot, Greene, & others* F
1.3.6.3–4/285.3–4 *When . . . defendant*] Q (*reading 'the' for 'Mowbray'*); *Then Mowbray in Ar-|mor* F
1.3.6.4–5/285.4 *and Herald*] F (*and Harrold*); *not in* Q
1.3.15 thee] Q (the). A spelling found repeatedly in Q, and not subsequently recorded except in cases of ambiguity.
1.3.25.2/304.2 *The trumpets sound*] Q; *Tucket* F
1.3.25.2–3 *Bullingbrooke . . . armour*] Q (*omitting 'Bullingbrooke'*); *Hereford* F
1.3.25.3/304.3 *and Herald*] F (*and Harold*); *not in* Q
1.3.26/305 aske] QF; demand of MARSHALL (Ritson)
1.3.31–2/310–11 hither, . . . lists?] Q4, F; ~ ? . . . ~, Q1
1.3.33/312 comest] Q5; comes Q1; com'ſt F
1.3.43 daring-hardy] Q (~, ~). The comma is equivalent to a hyphen, as elsewhere in Q.
1.3.44, 46, 99 Marshal] Q (Martiall)

1.3.55/334 iust] F; right Q. Shakespeare may have emended to avoid the rhyme with 'fight'; 'fight' is a rhyme-word again 5 lines later.
1.3.58 thee] Q (the)
1.3.84/363 innocence] QF; innocency CAPELL. An easy error, but *innocence* can be disyllabic, giving a four-foot line.
1.3.108/387 his God] Qb, F; God Qa
1.3.117.1/396.1 *A . . . sounded*] F (*A charge ſounded*); *not in* Q
1.3.122.1–4/401.1–4 *A . . . Mowbray*] *A long Flouriſh.* F; *not in* Q
1.3.127/406 ciuill] Qb, F; cruell Qa
1.3.127/406 swords] F; ſword Q
1.3.127–8/406–7 swords, | Which] F. Q has an additional passage omitted in F. See Introduction.
1.3.130/409 wrathfull yron] Qb, F; harſh reſounding Qa
1.3.166/445 then] F; *not in* Q. If the F reading were guesswork, McKerrow's conjectures 'a' or 'to' before 'speechlesse' would be convincing alternatives. But F appears to have been well annotated against the prompt-book in this area of the text.
1.3.174/453 you owe] F; y'owe Q
1.3.186 far] Q (fare). Sometimes understood as modern-spelling *fare*.
1.3.215/494 night] Q4, F; nightes Q1
1.3.220/499 sudden] F; ſullen Q. Both readings may be authorial. John claimed that 'there is hardly any doubt that "sullen" is preferable to "sudden" here'. Yet a cause of grief, which is what 'sorrowe' means here, can only with difficulty be understood as 'sullen', and 'sudden' is clearly more appropriate to Richard's banishment of Bolingbroke as a cause of Gaunt's sorrow. The only other occurrence of the adjective *sullen* in *Richard II* is just 34 lines below; F's omission of four lines (see following note) brings the two 'sullen's closer together. The proximity suggests both an authorial origin for 'sullen' and another possible motive for changing it. For 'sudden sorrowe', compare *2 Henry IV* 4.1.309/2157.
1.3.231–2/510–11 father: | Alas] F. Q has an additional passage omitted in F. See Introduction.
1.3.238.1–2/516.1–2 ⌈*Flourish*⌉ . . . *Bullingbrooke*] *Exit.* | *Flouriſh.* F; *not in* Qa; *Exit.* Qb
1.3.251 travel] Q (trauaile)
1.3.256–7/535–6 returne. | BULLINGBROOKE] F. Q has an additional passage omitted in F. See Introduction.
1.3.272/551.1 *Exeunt*] Q; *not in* F
1.4.0.1/551.1 *the . . . another*] *King, Aumerle, Greene, and Bagot* F; *the King with Buſhie, &c at one dore, and the* | *Lord Aumarle at another* Q. Q's entry for '*Bushie, &c*' is inconsistent with that at 1.4.51.1/602.1 Both the sequence of writing and the indications that the later direction was altered in the copy for Q (see note) suggest that the opening direction represents Shakespeare's first thoughts. See also note to 1.4.22/573.
1.4.7/558 grew] F; blew Q. Probably an authorial change; see Jowett and Taylor, pp. 189–90.
1.4.19/570 Coosen, Coosin] F (Coſin (Coſin)); Coofensˌ Cooſin Q
1.4.21–2/572–3 friends. . . . Bushie,] Q1; ~, . . . ~ : F. The changed punctuation in F probably resulted from compositorial misunderstanding, encouraged by the annotations and the copy comma after 'Bushie'.
1.4.22/573 Bushie, Bagot heere and Greene] Q6; Bushie, Q1; Buſhy: heere *Bagot* and *Greene* F. The Q/F variant relates to the conflict in staging between Q's directions for 1.4.0.1/551.2 and 1.4.51.1/602.1. Editors have been troubled to explain why Q has a satisfactory but probably shortened line whereas F preserves the wording appropriate to Shakespeare's first thoughts as expressed in the scene's opening direction. (F's punctuation probably results from the break between printed copy and annotation.) The simplest of the many possible explanations would be that F preserves the words Shakespeare originally wrote: that the inconsistency stood uncorrected in the prompt-book. The somewhat crude deletion in Q1 would accordingly have been made in the printing house (the error was similarly spotted by the printer of Q6, working from F). Interference at this stage

might explain why the text was brought into line with the direction at 1.4.51.1/602.1 whilst the even more obviously needed correction of the opening direction was not effected. As 1.4.22/573 and 1.4.51.1/602.1 are on adjoining pages in the same forme (C2ᵛ and C3) a compositor or (more likely) proof-corrector might easily notice the inconsistency and so make a simple deletion; the opening direction, however, appears on the opposite forme (C2). In such circumstances neither text would give an authoritative reading which fits the staging as finally determined, and Q1 would have no more authority for its correction than Q6 for its. On account of dramatic sense, economy of alteration, and metrical regularity, Q6 provides the reading most likely to have been adopted in performance.

1.4.26/577 What] Qb, F; With Qa

1.4.27-9/578-80 smiles, . . . him.] F (*after* Q3, ∼, . . . ∼,); ∼. . . . ∼, Q1

1.4.46/597 hand:] F; ∼ˬ Q

1.4.51.1-1.4.52/602.1-603 *Enter . . . newes?*] F (*. . . Bushy . . .*); *Enter Bushie with newes.* Q. Wilson and others have convincingly explained this variant as a misunderstanding of a squeezed revision in the Q1 copy; 'with' would be the compositor's interpretation of 'wᵗ'.

1.4.58/609 in his] F; in the Q1; into the Q2. An unauthoritative metrical emendation of Q2-3 would almost certainly simply have restored Q1's reading. The change of two distinct words suggests that accidental substitution in F is unlikely. Prompt-book authority is indicated.

1.4.63/614 late.] F; late, | Amen (*indented*) Q; late! | *All.* Amen. STAUNTON. Q omits a speech-prefix before 'Amen', but this does not adequately explain why F omits the speech. As preceding notes show, the manuscript was evidently well consulted around here when the copy was prepared for F; it should also be noted that 'God' in 1.4.63/614 was changed to 'heauen' and '*Exeunt*' on the same print line as 'Amen' in Q became '*Exit*'. 'Amen' was probably omitted in the prompt-book.

2.1.0.1/614.2 *Iohn of*] Q; *not in* F

2.1.0.2/614.2 *carried in a chaire*] WILSON; *not in* QF. Q adds '*&c.*' after 'Yorke', which some editors take to include Northumberland. This is unlikely as F neither names him nor preserves Q's '*&c.*'—which probably simply indicates attendants bearing the chair.

2.1.0.2/614.3 *the . . . Yorke*] Q; *Yorke* F

2.1.18/632 whose . . . feard] This edition; whofe tafte the wife are found Q1; whofe ftate the wife are found Q2; his ftate: then are found F1; whose taste the wise are fond CAMBRIDGE (Collier). Editors have variously emended the line; in Q1 only the last word is suspect (F's correction must be unauthoritative). The Cambridge emendation has won a surprising degree of acceptance considering that by a straightforward reading 'fond' is almost opposite to the sense required. Ideally 'loath' or 'ware' would be most appropriate, but it is difficult to see how either could be corrupted to 'found'. 'Feard' would be sufficiently graphically similar to 'found' to encourage contamination from the following line-end. The wise may usually be expected to take a more stoical attitude to flattery, but here it is specifically called 'venome'; moreover, the sense may merely be 'wary'.

2.1.48/662 as a] Q4, F; as Q1

2.1.68.1/682.1 and] Q; *not in* F

2.1.68.1-3/682.1-2 [*Aumerle,*] . . . *Willoughby*] F (. . . *Bushy . . . Ros . . .*); *&c.* Q

2.1.70/684 raignde] SINGER 2 (Blackstone/Ritson); ragde QF; rangde MCKERROW MS (*conj.*). See Gurr's note.

2.1.102/716 incaged] F; inraged Q

2.1.113/727 now,] THEOBALD (*and manuscript correction in* Q, *Devonshire copy*); now not, Q; and F

2.1.115-16/729-30 And | KING RICHARD And thou a] F; And thou | *King.* A Q. F is unlikely to have been changed without prompt-book authority. The decision to abandon the awkward transferred pronoun was probably Shakespeare's.

2.1.125/739 brother] Q2; brothers Q1, F. Surprisingly F restores the apparently correct 'brother' in the Q3 copy to the Q1 reading.

Unless this is a coincidence, it would appear that Q1 and F perpetuate an error deriving from Shakespeare's papers.

2.1.147.1/761.1 *Enter Northumberland*] F; *not in* Q

2.1.157/771 kernes] Qb, F; kerne Qa

2.1.162/776 coine] Qb, F; coines Qa

2.1.169/783 my] Qb, F; his Qa

2.1.178/792 the] F; a Q

2.1.187/801 KING RICHARD . . . my] Qb, F; My Qa. There may have been some difficulty in the manuscript. See also lineation notes.

2.1.201/815 say] Qb, F; lay Qa

2.1.224.1/838.1 *Flourish*] F; *not in* Q

2.1.224.1-3/838.1-3 *Exeunt . . . doore*] *Exeunt King and Queene* Q; *not in* F

2.1.224.3-4/838.3-4 *Willoughby, and Rosse*] F (*. . . & Rossᶴ*); *not in* Q

2.1.233/847 that thou wouldst] KEIGHTLEY; thou wouldft Q; thou'dft F. An easy error in Q. F emends perhaps with an eye as much to squeezing the type line as to metrical emendation: 'the Duke' becomes 'th'Du.'

2.1.240 more] Q (mo)

2.1.255/869 his] F; his noble Q. Folio Compositor B rarely made accidental omissions either of medial words or in verse (Werstine, p. 271); here he probably acted with authority.

2.1.258/872 Kings growen] Q3, F; King growen Q1; King grows MCKERROW MS (*conj.*). F is set from well annotated copy hereabouts, and lends some support to Q3.

2.1.278/892 Port le] F (Port *le*); *le* Port Q. Q gives Holinshed's form; F establishes the more usual form, presumably as a result of revision.

2.1.278 Blanc] Q (Blan)

2.1.279/893 Brittaine] Q1, F; Brittanie Q2

2.1.281/895 Thomas . . . Arundell,] RIVERSIDE; *not in* QF; The son of Richard Earl of Arundel MALONE. The context clearly indicates a missing line. This omission was probably due to censorship: a later Thomas, son of Philip Howard, Earl of Arundel, was held in enmity by Queen Elizabeth. Riverside's version of the missing line (anticipated by Hudson except for his reading 'his son' for 'son') not only names Thomas, so giving a line more likely to have been censored, but is also closer to Holinshed than is Malone.

2.1.282/896 Exeter,] F; ∼ˬ Q

2.1.284/898 Thomas Ramston] MUIR; Iohn Ramfton QF. 'Thomas' is historically correct, and is the name given by Holinshed; the metre suggests that Shakespeare also intended it. Abbreviations *Tho* and *Iho* were confusable; hence the same error (for the same character) in *Henry V* 4.1.94/1874. But 'Iohn' could alternatively anticipate 'Sir Iohn Norbery'.

2.1.286/900 Coint] F (*Quoint*); Coines Q

2.2.0.1/916.1 Bagot] Q; and Bagot F

2.2.11/927 me, . . . soule ˬ] F; ∼ˬ . . . ∼, Q

2.2.12/928 At . . . with] This edition; At . . . at Qa; With . . . at Qb, F. The line as in Qb gives a difficult sense, which the emendation largely resolves. To tremble *with* suggests the inward emotion (fear, grief) rather than the external cause. Rowe's awkward emendation 'trembles ˬ at,' suggests unease about 'With nothing trembles'. No editor appears to have taken Qa into account. Whereas 'wᵗ' for *with* could be misread 'at', such an error is less likely at the beginning of a line and more likely after a preceding 'at'. If copy 'At . . . wᵗ' gave Qa's 'At . . . at', the corrector could have easily marked the wrong 'at' for alteration. Some corroboration for the emendation is found in 2.2.13/929 where 'with' is the preposition used in qualification of the second part of 2.2.12/928.

2.2.16/932 eye] F; eyes Q

2.2.19/935 Shew] Qb, F; Shews Qa

2.2.31/947 As thought,] This edition; As thoughtˬ Q1; As though Q2, F. Editors follow Q2, taking the parenthesis to begin after *As*. This gives a more difficult reading than Q1 with its punctuation emended as in this edition. The conceit in Q1 is intelligible if 'on thinking . . . thinke' is established as the parenthesis, leaving the first 'thought' as subject of 'Makes'.

2.2.31/947 on thinking] QF; in thinking CAPELL. Q's repeated 'on' is more suspect than its repeated 'thought'. The first 'on' makes the sense more difficult, but the repetition may be part of the line's poetic patterning. In 2.2.78/994 Qa comparably reads 'in the earth', following 'in heauen', which would be similarly defensible were not the press corrections evidently authoritative.

2.2.33-4/949-50 BUSHIE ... QUEENE] Qb, F; *prefixes and intervening speech not in Qa*

2.2.40.1/956.1 *Enter Greene*] F; *not in Q*

2.2.54/970 lords] Qb, F; lord Qa

2.2.54 Beaumont] Q (Beaumond)

2.2.58/974 whereupon] QF; whereon POPE

2.2.59/975 broke] Q2, F; broken Q1

2.2.71 bonds] Q (bands)

2.2.72.1/988.1 *Enter ... gorget*]] *Enter Yorke* F; *not in Q*

2.2.76/992 speake] QF; *not in* POPE

2.2.78/994 on] Qb, F; in Qa. Compare note to 'on thinking', 2.2.31/947.

2.2.81 lose] Q (loofe)

2.2.85.1/100.1 *Enter a Seruingman*] *Enter a feruant.* F; *not in Q*

2.2.88/1004 they are colde] QF; cold POPE

2.2.91/1007 send me] QF; send POPE; to send me HUDSON (*conj.*). See following note.

2.2.110/1026 Thus disorderly thrust] QF; Disorderly thus thrust POPE; Thus thrust disorderly STEEVENS. This passage contains a concentration of metrical licences reflecting York's agitation. In other contexts the line might be emended; here one cannot be confident that the irregularity was not deliberate.

2.2.114/1030 Is] QF; He is CAPELL

2.2.119/1035 Castle] F; *not in Q*. Q is unlikely to have an accidental omission; F's addition must be deliberate. Berkeley is nowhere else described as a castle in *Richard II*, but in *1 Henry IV* 1.3.246/563 Northumberland locates the events of *Richard II* 2.3/Sc. 7 as 'At Barkly castle'. The variant therefore inferrably arises from authorial alteration from an earlier to a later preference. The printer's copy for F was not well annotated hereabouts, but an additional word at a line-end would be a particularly prominent variant. Editors usually give 'but . . . vneuen' (2.2.120-1/1036-7) as a verse line. Q is difficult to explain except as reflecting manuscript layout, and the annotator introducing 'Castle' made no adjustments to lineation (unless they were ignored). Lineation in this edition is based on the assumption that Shakespeare would run on a part verse line with the following line, and that the verse is otherwise as Shakespeare intended.

2.2.122.1-2/1038.1-2 *Exeunt ... Green*] Q (*Exeunt Duke, Qu man. Bufh. Green.*); *Exit* F

2.2.138/1054 Will the hatefull commoners] This edition (G.T.); Will the hatefull commons QF; The hateful commons will POPE. There is no grammatical basis for a caesura after 'commons', so the line is quite clearly metrically anomalous. The misreading supposed here (or even omission of a word such as 'now' after 'commons') is more likely than Pope's transposition. 'Commons' could be contamination from the the same word 9 lines above.

2.2.145/1061 GREENE] QF; BAG⟨OT⟩. CAPELL

2.2.148-9/1064-5 ⌈BAGOT⌉ Farewell ... BUSHIE Well] WHITE; Farewell ... Bush⟨ie⟩ Well Q; Bush⟨y⟩. Farewell ... Well F. Black and Wells follow White in emending. The arrangement is more dramatically attractive: Bagot repeatedly insists on parting where the others are inclined to delay the moment. F's speech-prefixes are generally reliable, and a misunderstood copy annotation would be an obvious cause for this exception. If the collator noticed a discrepancy while annotating the exit direction (*not in Q*) on to the copy, he may simply have written 'Ba.' before 2.2.148/1064. This would easily be misunderstood by the compositor as 'Bu.', an instruction to emend the text as set in F.

2.2.149.1-2/1065.1-2 *Exeunt ... doore*] This edition; *not in Q*; *Exit.* F; *Exeunt.* ROWE

2.3.0.1/1065.3 *Bullingbrooke ... Hereford,*] *Hereford,* Q; *the Duke of Hereford, and* F

2.3.9 Cotswold] Q (Cotfhall)

2.3.20/1085 Harry] Q; H. F

2.3.30 lordship] Q (Lo:), F

2.3.36/1101 Hereford,] Q3; Herefords Q1

2.3.56.1/1121.1 *Enter ... Willoughby*] F; *not in Q*

2.3.67/1132 *Enter Barkly*] F ('*Enter Barkely*', *after* 'here'); *not in Q*

2.3.80.1/1145.1 *Enter Yorke*] F; *not in Q*

2.3.91/1156 then more] Q1; more than Q2, F

2.3.98/1163 the] F; *not in Q*

2.3.122/1187 in] Q1; of Q2, F

2.3.124/1189 kinsman] F (Kinfman); coufin Q. This line is separated from one of the areas showing repeated signs of annotation in Folio copy by F's perpetuation of Q2's 'of' at 2.3.122/1187 (see Jowett and Taylor, Table 2, p. 176, where 2.3.122/1187 is TLN 1234). Q2 may actually be right, but if it is not, the corrector's eye would easily skip the error, especially if it had spotted a variant as prominent as cousin/kinsman at a line-ending just below. The change may have been authorial: 'cousin' had already been used just two lines previously and the repetition could have been seen as clumsy or confusing. But if the variant is explained by compositorial substitution, Simmes's Compositor A is much more likely to have erred than Folio Compositor A.

2.3.157/1222 to] Q2, F; vnto Q1

2.4.0.1/235.2 *erle ... captaine*] Q; *Salisbury, and a Captaine* F

2.4.1, 7/1236, 1242 WELCH CAPTAINE] *Welch.* Q; *Capt.* F

3.1.0.1/1259.1 *Bullingbrooke ... Hereford*] *Duke of Hereford* Q; *Bullingbrooke* F

3.1.0.2/1259.3 *Rosse, Percie, Willoughby*] F; *not in Q*

3.1.1.1/1260.1 *Enter*] *not in Q* (*see stage direction list*); *with* F (*continuing opening entry*)

3.1.32/1291 England] F; England, Lords farewell Q. This would be a remarkable omission for the usually careful Folio Compositor A. As an authorial revision, the omitted words would remove the 'farewell/hell' rhyme, perhaps thought a jingle.

3.1.42/1301 Lords] QF; my lords POPE

3.1.43 Glyndŵr] Q (Glendor). See note to *1 Henry IV* 1.1.40/40.

3.2.0.1/1303.1 *Flourish ... colours*] *Drums: Flourifh, and Colours. | Enter* F; *not in Q*

3.2.0.1/1303.1-2 *the King*] Q; *Richard* F

3.2.0.1/1303.2 *and* ⌈*souldiers*⌉] F (*and Souldiers*); *&c.* Q

3.2.1/1304 Hertlowghly] This edition (*after an Evesham monk's life of Richard II*, 'Hertlowli'); Barkloughly QF. Shakespeare's erroneous form derives from Holinshed, who has *Barclowlie* and *Barclowly*. This is evidently an error for *Hertlowli* or *Hertlow*, the form given for the place in the life of Richard II by a monk of Evesham; the place in question is Harlech.

3.2.1 Harlechly] Modernized from 'Hertloughly' (see previous note).

3.2.2/1305 my] QF; my good POPE

3.2.3/1306 your late] QF; your POPE; late STEEVENS

3.2.28-9/1331-2 all. | AUMERLE] F. Q has an additional passage omitted in F. See Introduction.

3.2.31/1334 friends] F; power Q. See Jowett and Taylor, p. 118.

3.2.34/1337 that] QF; and HANMER

3.2.36/1339 bloudy] Q2, F; bouldy Q1; boldly HUDSON (Collier). Whether Q2 or Collier gives the better reading is debatable, but there are two reasons for following Q2. First, Q1 invariably spells 'boldly' and 'bloudy' (or 'bloudie'). These forms favour a compositorial mis-setting of the latter. Second, the Folio copy was annotated from the prompt-book around here. In particular Q3 'his' is corrected to 'this' in the following line. This is not an obvious change to make without authority. The annotator would be at least as likely to note a 'bloudy/boldly' variant between quarto copy and manuscript had there been one. F's retention of the copy reading gives the Q2 reading potential authority.

3.2.51/1354 from] F; off from Q

3.2.80/1383 sluggard] F; coward Q. For F here and in 3.2.81, 98, 174, and 199/1384, 1401, 1477, 1502, see Jowett and Taylor, p. 187-9.

3.2.81/1384 forty] F (fortie); twenty Q

3.2.82/1385 name,] F (Name:); ~⌃ Q

3.2.86 *Scrope*] Q (*Scroope*). Similarly at 3.2.188 and 190, and 3.3.27.

3.2.98/1401 losse,] F (Loſſe,); and Q.

3.2.114-15/1417-18 bils, ... seate,] Q1; ~, ... ~, Q2, F

3.2.130/1433 offence] F (Offence); *not in* Q. The expanded wording is associated with relineation in 3.2.129-30/1432-3. F's version is not 'pitifully weak' (Pollard), but probably represents Shakespeare's second thoughts. See Jowett and Taylor, pp. 170-1.

3.2.166 through] Q (thorough)

3.2.174/1477 waile theyr present woes] F (... their ...); fit and waile theyr woes Q. Shakespeare probably originated the F reading to avoid the close similarity between his original line and *Duke of York* 5.4.1/2594.

3.2.175/1478 waile] QF; woe This edition *conj.* Both Black and Wells comment on the awkwardness of this line. The difficulty lies in construing 'to waile' as 'towards wailing'. 'Woe' presents no such problem. 'Waile theyr woes' in the previous line in Q would encourage confusion (as would 'wayes' itself). 'Woe' would give a rhyme with 'foe' and reinforce the verbal echoing which is already a feature of the speech. Emendation would be more plausible, however, if F did not show evidence of manuscript consultation in the previous line.

3.2.179/1482 come,] QF; ~, CAPELL

3.2.199/1502 faction] F (Faction); partie Q.

3.2.214.1/1517.1 *Exeunt*] F; *not in* Q

3.3.0.3/1517.2 *with drumme and colours*] F (*with Drum and Colours*); *not in* Q

3.3.0.3/1517.3 souldiers] *Attendants* F; *not in* Q

3.3.13/1530 with you] F; *not in* Q. Editors generally follow F. But Q makes sense, and as the Q compositor went to the trouble of making a turn-down to set 'with him' (3.3.12/1529) as a line-ending, its lineation must be presumed to reflect copy. F's inserted words and changed lineation may derive from authorial revision. The less likely alternative is that the Q compositor deliberately omitted words in 'with you' to accommodate his turn-down.

3.3.30/1547 Lord] F; Lords Q

3.3.35/1552 Vpon] F (vpon); on both Q. Q's lineation is permissible. F extensively relines hereabouts (see lineation notes), but so unsuccessfully that Compositor B must have made the lineation changes on his own initiative. He would be prompted to do so by the expansion, from 'H. Bull.' to 'Henry Bullingbrooke', which would have rendered the copy run-on part-line too wide for the Folio measure. The inconvenient expanded form probably derives from the prompt-book. Combined with the consideration that it would be unusual for a substitution to replace one word with two or vice versa, this points to 'Vpon' as an authoritative reading. 'Vpon' would usually be accounted the weaker reading, because it is less specific. There is, however, a possible motive for authorial revision. The lines in F admit only one logical intepretation, but 'on both his knees' may have seemed comically ambiguous in relation to 'doth kisse'.

3.3.58-9/1575-6 raigne, | My waters] F (raine | My Waters); ~. | My water's Q. The line-break is also a page-break between formes (G4-G4ᵛ) in Q.

3.3.58 rain] Q (raigne)

3.3.60.4-7/1577.4-7 *The ... Salisbury*] *The tumpets sound, Richard appeareth on the walls.* Q; *Parle without, and anſwere within: then a Flouriſh. | Enter on the Walls, Richard, Carlile, Aumerle, Scroop, | Salisbury.* F

3.3.74 An] Q (And)

3.3.90/1607 is] F; ſtandes Q. This line was set by Folio Compositor A, who is unlikely to have introduced such a substitution. The effect of removing the 'standes/hand' jingle suggests authorial revision. In both respects, compare 3.1.32/1291.

3.3.99 pastures'] Q (paſtors)

3.3.118/1635 a prince and] SISSON; princeſſe Q1; a Prince Q3; a Prince, is F. F appears improvised, and Sisson plausibly argues that 'prince &' in the manuscript would give an easier misreading as well as less awkward sense.

3.3.126/1643 We] Q4, F; *King* We Q1. There may have been a cancelled line or lines following 3.3.125/1642, in which Northumberland replied to Richard.

3.3.126/1643 selfe] F; selfes Q

3.3.167/1684 there] QF; here VAUGHAN (*conj.*). Q's 'therein laide; there lies' looks suspiciously dittographical. 'There' begins Richard's 'epitaph'. 'Here lies' would be the more usual opening, and would so clarify the sense.

3.3.170/1687 mocke] F (mock); laugh Q. Possible authorial revision. The connotations of *mock* are more exact and appropriate.

3.3.176 you. May ... down?] QF (~, may ... ~.). Alternatively punctuated as Q.

3.3.186.1/1703 *He kneeles downe*] Q (*he* ...); *not in* F

3.3.207.1/1724.1 [*Flourish.*] *Exeunt*] F; *not in* Q

3.4.0.1/1724.2 *with ... Ladies*] *with her attendants* Q; *and two Ladies* F

3.4.6/1730 [2.] LADY] WELLS; *Lady* QF. QF have undifferentiated '*Lady*' and '*Man.*' (F '*Ser.*') throughout the scene.

3.4.11/1735 ioy] ROWE 3; griefe QF

3.4.24.1/1748.1 *a ... men*] *Gardeners* Q; *a Gardiner, and two Seruants* F

3.4.27 pins] Q (pines)

3.4.29/1753 change:] F; ~, Q

3.4.30/1754 yong] Q1; yon Q2, F (yond)

3.4.30 apricots] Q (Aphricokes)

3.4.35/1759 too] F; two Q

3.4.58/1782 garden. We] CAPELL; garden, Q1; garden, Q3, F

3.4.68/1792 then] POPE; *not in* QF

3.4.81/1805 Camst] Q2, F; Canſt Q1

3.4.81/1805 this] Q1; theſe Q2, F. Q1 may give an old spelling of *these*, but compare 'this newes'.

3.4.108/1832 *Exeunt*] Q; *Exit.* F

4.1.0.1-5/1832.1-3 *Enter ... Westminster*] *Enter Bullingbrooke with the Lords to parliament.* Q; *Enter as to the Parliament, Bullingbrooke, Aumerle, Nor-|thumberland, Percie, Fitz-Water, Surrey, Carlile, Abbot | of Weſtminſter. Herauld, Officers, and Bagot.* F

4.1.1/1833 *Enter ... officers*] *Enter Bagot.* Q; *not in* F (*see previous note*)

4.1.14/1846 that you had rather] QF; you rather had POPE

4.1.21/1853 him] Q3, F; them Q1; my Q2

4.1.42 Fitzwalter] Q (Fitzwaters), F (*Fitzwater*). Similarly at 5.6.12.1. *Fitzwaters* was probably Shakespeare's form, though Q, like F, has *Fitzwater* at 4.1.51.

4.1.48 An] Q (And)

4.1.50-1/1882-3 foe. | SURRY]. F. Q has an additional passage omitted in F. See Introduction.

4.1.53/1885 Tis] Q; My Lord, | 'Tis F. F relines 4.1.51-5/1883-7: 'Fitzwater| time| talke| Lord| then| true| by heauen|'. This procedure is inexplicable except as space-wasting, which is especially plausible as the compositor—probably Compositor B—was nearing the end of column b on d1ᵛ. 'My Lord' is therefore evidently an interpolation to waste a type line. Compositor B has been detected behaving similarly in *Richard III*, *Contention*, *Hamlet*, *King Lear*, and, most spectacularly, *2 Henry IV*. The casting-off error created only a local difficulty. It probably related to the passage in Q immediately before 4.1.51/1883 which F omits. As precisely 3 lines are wasted, it is likely that only the unnamed lord's speech was discounted in casting off (see Additional Passages), and that no allowance was made for omitting Aumerle's three-line retort.

4.1.53/1885 true,] Q2, F; ~, Q1

4.1.67/1899 my] Q3, F; *not in* Q1; the Q2

4.1.92/1924 Bishop of Carleil] This edition; B. Q1. Editors usually follow Q3 and F, expanding only to 'Bishop'. The full name gives a regular pentameter, and takes advantage of the only opportunity to name the character.

4.1.103/1935 of ... fourth] F (of that Name the Fourth); fourth of that name Q. See Jowett and Taylor, p. 190, and Gurr's note.

4.1.136/1968 you] Q2, F; yon Q1

4.1.136/1968 reare] F; raiſe Q. F corrects Q3's 'against his' to 'against this', pointing independently to consultation of manuscript. 'Reare' could be Shakespeare's revision or 'raise' a compositorial substitution (Q giving the commoner idiom).

4.1.139/1971 Preuent] POPE; Preuent it QF
4.1.145-308/1977-2140 May . . . fall.] F (*and similarly* Q4); *not in* Q1. See Introduction.
4.1.145/1977 Commons] F; common Q4
4.1.146/1978 BULLINGBROOKE] F; *not in* Q4
4.1.149/1981 here] F; are here Q4
4.1.152/1984 look'd] F; looke Q4
4.1.156/1988 Knee] F; limbes Q4. Q4 has the less usual and conceivably the authoritative reading here.
4.1.171/2003 Henry] F; Harry Q4
4.1.172/2004 Giue . . . Cousin,] F; *not in* Q4. This is the only substantial omission in Q4's text of the abdication episode before 4.1.266/2098, and Q4 may reflect an alternative staging whereby Richard enters bearing the crown and sceptre himself.
4.1.173/2005 Here Cousin, on] Q4, F; On JOHNSON
4.1.173/2005 Hand,] F; hand, and Q4
4.1.173/2005 thine] F; yours Q4. Richard again uses the familiar second person to address Bolingbroke at 4.1.289-91/2121-3.
4.1.179/2011 Griefes] F; griefe Q4
4.1.200/2032 dutious Oathes] F; duties rites Q4
4.1.205/2037 are made] F; that sweare Q4
4.1.210/2042 Henry] F; Harry Q4
4.1.219/2051 follyes? . . . Northumberland,] F; Folly, . . . ~ ? Q4
4.1.227/2059 all] F; *not in* Q4
4.1.227/2059 vpon] Q4; vpon me F. Q4 is distinctive and acceptable. It is rather more plausible that the Folio compositor should have supplied 'me' perhaps under the influence of 'my' immediately below, than that the last word of the line should have been omitted in Q4.
4.1.231/2063 deliuer'd] Q5, F; deliuer Q4
4.1.241/2073 and] Q4; a F
4.1.245/2077 Nor] Q4; No, nor F
4.1.254 An] F (And)
4.1.254/2086 word] F; name Q4. An open-ended variant: a substitution or misreading in either text.
4.1.260 torment'st] Q4, F (*both* 'torments'). See Abbott 340.
4.1.266/2098 that] F; the Q4
4.1.266/2098 and . . . reade.] F; *not in* Q4
4.1.271/2103 Thou . . . me.] F; *not in* Q4
4.1.271/2103 this Face] F; this Q4. Q4 is probably influenced by 4.1.273/2105 (or Marlowe).
4.1.274-5/2106-7 like . . . which] F; *not in* Q4
4.1.276/2108 That] F; And Q4
4.1.279/2111 an] F; a Q4
4.1.286/2118 manner] F; manners Q4. 'These' apparently agrees with 'laments'. Q4 is often followed, but the more authoritative text gives a clear case of a harder reading which remains within the bounds of acceptability.
4.1.286/2118 laments] Q4, F; lament CAPELL
4.1.287/2119 shadowes, . . . vnseene, Griefe,] F; ~, . . . ~, | ~, Q4
4.1.289/2121 There . . . substance:] F; *not in* Q4
4.1.290/2122 For . . . bountie,] F; *not in* Q4
4.1.294/2126 Shall . . . it?] F; *not in* Q4
4.1.295/2127 Cousin?] F; Coose, why: Q4
4.1.301/2133 haue] F; haue it Q4
4.1.303/2135 Then] F; Why then Q4
4.1.309-10/2141-2 On . . . your selues] Q4, F; Let it be so, and loe on wednesday next, | We solemnly proclaime our Coronation, | Lords be ready all Q1. Q4's concurrence with F testifies that F has prompt-book authority. 'Let it be so, and loe' therefore appears to be an addition made to bridge the gap left by the deleted scene, or a remnant of an earlier version of the episode excised in Q. The other variants have more likely alterations made in the prompt-book. See Introduction, and Jowett and Taylor, pp. 194-8.
4.1.310.1-2/2142.1 Exeunt . . . Aumerle] Q (subs.); Exeunt. F
4.1.322/2154 I will] MALONE; Ile QF. See lineation note.
5.1.0.1/2155.1 with her Ladies] with her attendants Q; and Ladies F

5.1.6.1/2161.1 and guard] F (*and* Guard); *not in* Q
5.1.25/2180 stricken] F; throwne Q. See Ure's note. Q and F obscure the metre further by mislining ('plot|').
5.1.32/2187 the] Q1; thy Q2
5.1.35/2190 RICHARD] F (*Rich.*); *King.* Q. Richard retains the prefix *King* in Q for the rest of 5.1/Sc. 18 (but not at 5.1.16/2171 nor in 5.5/Sc. 18).
5.1.41 thee] Q (the)
5.1.44/2199 fall] F; tale Q. In F Richard equates his story to the 'falls of princes' genre (Jowett and Taylor, p. 189).
5.1.62/2217 He] QF; And he ROWE; He then MCKERROW MS (*conj.*)
5.1.66/2221 friends] F; men Q. Q can misleadingly suggest that the 'loue of wicked men' is for someone else, not each other.
5.1.78/2233 Queene] F; wife Q. See Jowett and Taylor, p. 191.
5.1.80 Hallowmas] Q (Hollowmas)
5.1.84/2239 NORTHUMBERLAND] F (*North.*); *King* Q. If Q is not corrupt, as some editors have believed, the variant probably results from authorial revision. There is evidence for similar revision, introducing a third character into a dialogue for two by changing a prefix, elsewhere in Shakespeare. But 5.1.83/2238 is obviously addressed to Northumberland, and 5.1.84/2239 is a fitting reply for him to make. In this context of alternating prefixes, '*King*' could have been read in from above or below: compare 5.3.109/2483.
5.2.0.1/2257.4 Duke . . . Dutchesse] Q; Yorke, and his Duchesse F
5.2.11 thee,] Q (the‸), F (thee‸). The definite article occasionally prefixes a title (*the* Douglas, *the* Talbot), but this does not seem appropriate here.
5.2.17/2274 the,] F (thee,); ~‸ Q
5.2.40.1/2297.1 Enter Aumerle] F; *not in* Q
5.2.41/2298 my] QF; our CRAVEN (*conj.*)
5.2.52/2309 hold . . . triumphs] F (Hold those Iusts & Triumphs); do these iusts & triumphs hold Q. Shakespeare evidently revised this line (Jowett and Taylor, p. 190). F's 'those', however, is probably an error.
5.2.55/2312 preuent it] CAPELL; preuent QF; prevent me ROWE
5.2.71.1/2328.1 He . . . reades it] Q; Snatches it F
5.2.78/2335 by my life, my] POPE; by my life, by my Q1; my life, my Q2, F. Typical Simmes's Compositor A error.
5.2.82/2339 sonne] F (Sonne); Aumerle Q
5.2.85.1/2342.1 His . . . bootes] Q; Enter Seruant with Boots. F (*after* 5.2.84/2341)
5.2.108-9/2365-6 a . . . any] Qb, F; any . . . a Qa
5.2.116 And] Q (An). Similarly at 5.3.66.
5.2.117.1/2374.1 Exeunt [seuerally]] Exit F; *not in* Q
5.3.0.1-2/2374.2-3 Enter . . . nobles] Enter the King with his nobles. Q; Enter Bullingbrooke, Percie, and other Lords. F
5.3.1/2375 tell] F; tell me Q
5.3.10/2384 Which] F; While POPE. Compare *Henry V* 3.2.49/1120 and Taylor's note to 3.2.46 in his Oxford edition (1982).
5.3.14/2388 these] F; those Q
5.3.20-3/2394-7 As . . . heere] Some editors reline and emend: 'But yet| hope| forth|' (Ure); 'both| hope in him| forth|' (Gurr).
5.3.21/2395 dayes] F; yeares Q. The two most plausible explanations of this variant are: (*a*) the Q1 compositor introduced a substitution contaminated by 'heere' at the end of the following line; (*b*) Shakespeare originally wrote 'yeeres', but emended in the prompt-book to avoid the jingle with 'heere'.
5.3.22/2396 amazed] Q; *not in* F
5.3.30/2404 the] DYCE 2 (Lettsom); my QF
5.3.35/2409 I may] Q2, F; May Q1
5.3.37/2411 The . . . crieth] Q; Yorke within. F
5.3.41 foolhardy] Q (foole, hardie). An example of a comma used for modern hyphen.
5.3.43.1-2/2417.1 Enter Yorke] F; *not in* Q
5.3.55/2429 lest] This edition (Craven); left thy QF. Craven's conjecture improves both metre and sense. The line could have been contaminated by 'thee' in the next line, directly below 'thy'.
5.3.72/2446 within] F ('Dutchesse within' on type line above speech-prefix); *not in* Q
5.3.73/2447 voicd] Q3, F; voice Q1

5.3.80.1/2454.1   Enter . . . Yorke] F (Enter Dutcheſſe.); not in Q
5.3.91/2465   kneele] F; walke Q
5.3.100/2474   mouth] Q2, F; month Q1 (turned letter)
5.3.104/2478   shall] F; ſtill Q. Q is perhaps contaminated by 'till', and makes doubtful sense.
5.3.108/2482   haue] QF; crave WALKER (conj.)
5.3.109/2483   KING HENRY] Q2, F; yorke Q1
5.3.111   An] Q (And)
5.3.117   Pardonnez-moi] Q (Pardonne moy)
5.3.124/2498   thy] Qb, F; this Qa
5.3.133-4/2507-8   I . . . heart] Q; with all my heart | I pardon him POPE. The verse line's internal rhyme may be a transition from couplets to blank verse.
5.3.142/2516   so] This edition (Craven); not in Q1, F; too Q6
5.4.0.1/2518.3   Enter] F; Manet Q. F's failure to mark a scene-break is evidently influenced by the staging envisaged in Q: see Jowett and Taylor, pp. 179-80.
5.4.0.1/2518.3   sir . . . men] sir Pierce Exton, &c. Q; Exton and Seruants F
5.4.3, 6/2521, 2524   1. . . . . 2.] This edition; not in QF
5.4.3, 6/2521, 2524   MAN] Q; Ser. F
5.4.3/2521   Those] F; Theſe Q
5.4.11/2529   Exeunt] F (Exit.); not in Q
2529.1   alone] Q; not in F
5.5.13-14/2542-3   faith . . . faith] F (Faith . . . Faith); word . . . word Q. F's reading is probably an authorial revision to avoid the repeat of 5.3.120/2493.
5.5.17/2546   small needles] Q; Needles F. Q3-5 also read 'small poſterne', which F corrects to 'poſterne'. Presumably a copy annotation was over-interpreted.
5.5.20   through] Q (thorow), F
5.5.22/2551   pride.] F; ~, Q
5.5.27/2556   set] Q1; ſit Q3, F
5.5.33/2562   treason makes] F (Treaſon makes); treaſons make Q. It is appropriate for treason to be personified (or even dramatically characterized), as is penury.
5.5.41/2570   The muſike plaies Q (after 'heare'); Muſick F (after 5.5.38/2567). F's positioning is anticipatory, as often in prompt-books.
5.5.55/2584   sounds that telle] POPE; ſound that telles QF. Q's particularly violent lack of concord probably results from metathesis. The passage in F was set without reference to an independent manuscript (see Introduction), and so cannot offer potential authoritative correction.
5.5.56/2585   that] F; which Q. 'Which' probably anticipates the same word in the following line, and creates a confused succession of dependent clauses.
5.5.58/2587   houres, and times] F (Houres, and Times); times, and houres Q. Ure and others, through following Q, recognize F's word order as more logical; in F the sense is also reinforced by pararhyme: 'teares/houres'; 'grones/times'.

5.5.65/2594   a ſigne] Q2, F; aſigne Q1
5.5.66.1/2595.1   of the stable] Q; not in F
5.5.69/2598   hither] QF; in hither KEIGHTLEY
5.5.94/2623   Spurre, galld] F (Spur-gall'd); Spurrde, galld Q. Q's apparent misreading was probably facilitated by the copy use of a comma as a hyphen, a feature preserved elsewhere in Q. The correction cannot have independent authority if this part of the text was annotated against a page of prompt-book manuscript deriving from Q5 (see Introduction), but would have been quite obvious to scribe, annotator, or compositor.
5.5.94.1/2623.1   keeper . . . meate] one to Richard with meate Q; Keeper with a Diſh F
5.5.97.1/2626   Exit] F; Exit Groome. Q
5.5.104.1/2633.1   Exton . . . in] The murderers ruſh in. Q; Enter Exton and Seruants. F
5.5.106/2635   thy owne] Q1, F; thine owne Q5
5.5.107.1/2636.1   Here] Q; not in F
5.5.118.1-3/2647.1-3   Exeunt . . . doore]] F (Exit.); not in Q
5.6.0.1-2   ⌈Flouriſh.⌉ . . . attendants]] Enter Bullingbrooke with the duke of Yorke. Q; Flouriſh. Enter Bullinbrooke, Yorke, with | other Lords & attendants. F
5.6.8/2655   Salisbury, Spencer, Blunt] F (Salsbury, Spencer, Blunt); Oxford, Salisbury, Blunt Q1; Oxford, Salisbury, Q2. Q1's authorial error was evidently corrected in the prompt-book.
5.6.11-12/2658-9   KING . . . gaines.] Q, Fb; not in Fa
5.6.12.1/2659.1   Lord] Q
5.6.17/2664   not] Q2, F; nor Q1
5.6.18/2665.1   Harry . . . guarded] H Percie Q; Percy and Carlile F
5.6.29.1/2676.1   the] Q; a F
5.6.43/2690   through the] F; through Q; thorough CAMBRIDGE
5.6.52.1   Exeunt ⌈with the coffin⌉] Exeunt. F; not in Q

Additional Passages

A.5   Drawes] Qb; Draw Qa
A.5   sleepe,] Qa; sleepe, Qb
B.1   had't] Q; had it THEOBALD
B.3   sought] Qb; ought Qa
C.2   remember] This edition (G.T.); remember me Q; remind me GURR. *Remind* is not recorded before 1645. For the idiom, compare *Tempest* 1.2.409/475, 'The Ditty do's remember my drown'd father'.
D.2   heauen] Q; if heaven POPE
D.4 (M)   ſuccour] Q (fuccors). Q gives the old singular (see *OED*): the one instance in the canon where the 's' form quite clearly is singular, though *Contention* 3.1.285/1466 could be similarly interpreted.
E.3   may] CAPELL; it may Q
E.4   ſunne to ſunne] CAPELL; ſinne to ſinne Q

REJECTED FOLIO VARIANTS

1.1.57/57   doubled] doubly
1.1.73/73   haue] hath
1.1.77/77   spoke . . . worse] ſpoke, or thou canſt Q2; ſpoke, or what thou canſt Q3; ſpoken, or thou canſt F
1.1.116/116   nay, my] nay our
1.1.137/137   did I] I did
1.1.187/187   God] heauen
1.1.187/187   deepe] foule
1.1.191/191   my] mine
1.2.37/242   Gods . . . Gods] Heauens . . . heauens
1.2.42/247   complaine] complaint
1.2.43/248   God] heauen
1.2.43/248   and] to
1.2.47/252   set] ſit
1.2.65/270   ah] Oh

1.3.14/293   and thy] and thine
1.3.17/296   come] comes
1.3.18/297   God] heauen
1.3.20/299   and my] and his
1.3.28/307   plated] placed
1.3.29/308   formally] formerly Q5, F
1.3.37/316   Gods] heauens
1.3.39/318   he is] he's
1.3.69/348   earthly] earthy
1.3.71/350   vigour] rigor
1.3.76/355   furbish] furniſh
1.3.78/357   God] Heauen
1.3.82/361   aduerse] amaz'd
1.3.85/364   God] heauen
1.3.86/365   King] Kings

RICHARD II

1.3.101/380	God]	heauen
1.3.174/453	God]	heauen
1.3.177/456	God]	heauen
1.3.179, 180/458, 459	neuer]	euer
1.3.180/459	nor]	or
1.3.182/461	neuer]	euer
1.3.191/470	the]	this
1.3.197/476	God]	heauen
1.3.265/544	neuer]	euer
1.3.270/549	that]	which
1.4.14/565	words]	word
1.4.27/578	smiles]	ſoules
1.4.53/604	grieuous]	verie
1.4.58/609	God]	heauen
2.1.12/626	at]	is
2.1.27/641	Then]	That
2.1.52/666	famous by]	famous for
2.1.109/723	wert]	were
2.1.110/724	this]	his
2.1.113/727	now,]	now not, Q1; and F
2.1.119/733	chasing]	Q (chafing); chafing F
2.1.128/742	Hast thou]	Thou haſt
2.1.160-1/774-5	charge, . . . assistance,]	~, . . . ~,
2.1.164/778	ah]	Oh
2.1.183/797	kinred]	kindreds
2.1.203/817	the]	his
2.1.227/841	reuenewes]	reuennew
2.1.233/847	thou wouldst]	thou'dſt
2.1.239/853	God]	heauen
2.1.252/866	a]	o'
2.1.284/898	Ramston]	*Rainſton*
2.2.3/919	life-harming]	Q1; half-harming Q3; ſelfe-harming F
2.2.25/941	more]	more's
2.2.27/943	weepes]	weepe
2.2.41/957	God]	Heauen
2.2.52/968	Ah]	O
2.2.72/988	Hope lingers]	hopes linger
2.2.76/992	Gods]	heauens
2.2.77/993	Should . . . thoughts,]	*not in* F
2.2.98/1014	God]	Heau'n
2.2.99/1015	Comes]	Come
2.2.100/1016	God]	heauen
2.2.103/1019	no]	two Q2; *not in* F
2.2.108/1024	go muster]	muſter
2.2.123/1039	go for]	go to
2.2.126/1042	vnpossible]	impoſsible
2.2.129/1045	that is]	that's
2.2.134/1050	euer haue beene]	haue beene euer
2.3.6/1071	your]	our
2.3.29/1094	last we]	we last
2.3.35/1100	directions]	direction
2.3.86/1151	no vnckle]	*not in* F
2.3.89/1154	those]	theſe
2.3.133/1198	I]	*not in* F
2.3.144/1209	wrong]	Wrongs
3.1.37/1296	Gods]	Heauens
3.2.20/1323	pray thee]	prethee
3.2.39/1342	light]	Lightning
3.2.45/1348	Whilst . . . Antipodes,]	*not in* F
3.2.56/1359	God]	Heauen
3.2.68/1371	Ouerthrowes]	Orethrowes
3.2.108/1411	beards]	Beares
3.2.111-15/1414-18	In . . . rebell]	. . . Armes: . . . Crowne, . . . Eugh: . . . State, . . . Bills: . . . Seat, (*following* Q3 *for* 'Bills: . . . Seat,')
3.2.135/1438	wound]	hand
3.2.151/1454	Gods]	Heauens
3.2.178/1481	And . . . selfe:]	*not in* F
3.2.207/1510	them]	'em
3.3.17/1534	ouer our heads]	Q1; ouer your heads Q3; ore your head F
3.3.58/1575	whilst]	while
3.3.65/1582	tracke]	tract
3.3.92/1609	open]	ope
3.3.145/1662	a]	o'
3.3.198/1715	you deserue]	you deseru'd
3.3.200/1717	handes]	Hand
3.4.25/1749	come]	commeth Q2; comes F
3.4.28/1752	They will]	They'le
3.4.59/1783	Do]	And
3.4.67/1791	of]	and
3.4.70/1794	doubt]	doubted
3.4.91/1815	you will]	you'l
3.4.101/1825	these]	this
3.4.102/1826	Pray God]	I would
4.1.8/1840	once it hath]	it hath once
4.1.12/1844	mine]	my
4.1.32/1864	simpathie]	ſympathize
4.1.37/1869	it, twenty times,]	it, ~ ~,
4.1.53/1885	Tis]	My Lord, | 'Tis
4.1.80/1912	he is]	hee's
4.1.82/1914	neuer]	ne're
4.1.105/1937	God]	Heauen
4.1.120/1952	forfend]	forbid
4.1.124/1956	God]	Heauen
5.1.32/2187	correction, mildly,]	~, ~,
5.1.71/2226	you]	ye
5.2.18/2275	the one]	one
5.2.22/2279	Alac]	Alas
5.2.28/2285	gentle]	*not in* F
5.2.58/2315	see]	ſees
5.2.73/2330	What is]	What's
5.2.74/2331	who is]	who's
5.2.75/2332	God]	Heauen
5.2.76/2333	is it]	is't
5.2.78/2335	mine]	my
5.2.103/2360	wouldst]	wouldeſt
5.2.109/2366	or]	nor
5.3.4/2378	God]	heauen
5.3.9/2383	beate . . . rob]	rob . . . beate
5.3.36/2410	be]	me
5.3.48/2422	treason]	reaſon
5.3.61/2435	held]	Q1; hald Q3; had F
5.3.72/2446	Gods]	heauens
5.3.74/2448	thy]	thine
5.3.80/2454	she is]	she's
5.3.83/2457	rest rest]	reſt reſts
5.3.97/2471	Ill . . . grace.]	*not in* F
5.3.108/2482	prayer]	prayers
5.3.110/2484	Say]	But
5.3.129/2503	God]	heauen
5.3.135/2509	and]	*not in* F.
5.3.144/2518	God]	heauen
5.4.7/2525	wishtly]	wiftly
5.5.5/2534	hammer it]	hammer't
5.5.29/2558	misfortunes]	misfortune
5.5.38/2567	be]	am
5.5.46/2575	checke]	heare
5.5.83/2612	he]	he had
5.6.47/2694	what]	that
5.6.51/2698	mournings]	mourning

Q1 READINGS RESTORED IN F

Q1–F reading as lemma, followed by derivative Quarto reading and origin.

1.1.24/24   an] in Q3
1.1.60/60   and I] and Q2
1.1.146/146   my] the Q2
1.1.189/189   beggar-feare] begger-face Q2
1.1.198/198   liues] life Q2
1.2.35/240   thine] thy Q2
1.3.72/351   at] a Q3
1.3.86/365   liues] lies Q3
1.3.117/396   forward] forth Q2
1.3.135/414   fields] field Q2
1.3.140/419   to] vnto Q2
1.3.181/460   lowring] louing Q3
1.3.226/505   vpon] with Q2
1.3.230/509   vrgde] vrge Q2
1.4.10/561   our] your Q2
1.4.21/572   come] comes Q2
2.1.10/624   haue] hath Q3
2.1.12/626   close] glose Q2
2.1.53/667   for] in Q2
2.1.87/701   I] O Q2
2.1.106/720   thy reach] they reach Q3
2.1.128/742   out and] and Q2
2.1.147/761   and all] and Q2
2.1.172/786   noble] the noble Q2
2.1.211/825   landes] land Q3
2.1.244/858   gainst] againſt Q2
2.1.246/860   Gainst] Againſt Q2
2.1.253/867   NORTHUMBERLAND] Q1 (North.); Willo. Q2
2.1.272/886   spie] eſpie Q2
2.1.279/893   Brittaine] Brittanie Q2
2.1.293/907   our] our Countries Q2
2.1.295/909   Broking] broken Q3
2.2.16/932   eye] eyes Q2
2.3.3/1068   here in] in Q2
2.3.101/1166   thousand] thouſands Q2
2.3.111/1176   thy] my Q2
2.3.116/1181   for] or Q3
2.3.117/1182   then my] then Q2

3.1.7/1266   deaths] death Q2
3.1.18/1277   you] they Q2
3.2.37/1340   this] his Q2
3.2.49/1352   tremble] trembled Q2
3.2.112/1415   bowes] browes Q3
3.2.113/1416   ewe] wo Q3
3.2.131/1434   loue] loue's Q3
3.2.134/1437   heads] head Q2
3.3.21/1538   royally is] is royally Q2
3.3.145/1662   of] of a Q2
3.3.165/1682   As] And Q2
3.3.203/1720   be my] be Q2
3.4.43/1767   as in] in Q2
3.4.56/1780   is it] it is Q2
3.4.108/1832   In the] In Q2
4.1.40   liue] liue I Q2
4.1.73/1905   at] of Q2
4.1.89/1921   that] a Q2
4.1.106/1938   may I] I may Q2
4.1.108/1940   that] *not in* Q2
4.1.113/1945   here] not here Q2
4.1.136/1968   against this] againſt his Q3
5.1.35/2190   but beasts] but beaſt Q3
5.1.46/2201   simpathize] ſimpathie Q2
5.1.72/2227   twixt] betwixt Q2
5.1.74/2229   twixt] betwixt Q2
5.1.87/2242   thou for] for Q2
5.1.95/2250   dumbly] doubly Q2
5.2.2/2259   of] *not in* Q2
5.2.89/2346   thou not] not thou Q2
5.2.109/2366   like to] like Q2
5.3.16/2390   vnto] to Q2
5.3.17/2391   commonst] commoneſt Q2
5.3.21/2395   sparkes] ſparkles Q2
5.3.100/2474   come] do come Q2
5.5.14/2543   the] thy Q2
5.5.17/2546   posterne] ſmall poſterne Q3
5.5.32/2561   King] king Q2; a King Q3
5.5.36/2565   kingd] king Q2; a king Q3
5.5.46/2575   in a] in Q2
5.5.50/2579   me his] his Q2

INCIDENTALS

1 honourd] honoured   56 returnd,] ~,   10 death,] ~. [?]   102 traitour] taitour   129 debt,] ~.   133 slewe] Q (*text*); flew Q (*c.w.*)   152 ruld] ruled   178 Reputation,] ~,   228 fashiond] faſhioned   229 liu'st] lieuſt   240 What] Q (*text*); what Q (*c.w.*)   248 defence.] ~,   253 breſt] Qa; breaſt Qb   291 comst] comſt   440 portculist] Qa; portcullift Qb   446 breath.] ~,   473 euer] euet (?)   494 extinct] extint   495 inch] intch   522 returnst] returneſt   563 word,...craft,] ~,...~,   574 Obserud] Obſerued   614 late.] ~,   623 listned] liſtened   699 No,] ~,   704 flattrest] flattereſt   732 Darst] Dareſt   749 withred] withered   760 his,] ~,   787 first.] ~,   793 frownd] frowned   803 pardond] pardoned   836 lou'd] loued   844 disburdned] diſburdened   869 atchiude] atchiued   877 kinsman,] ~,   889 Northumberland,] ~,   901 furnisht] furniſhed   940 (thrice,gracious] ,~ (~   959 hopst] hopeſt   977 Bullingbrook.] ~,   982 ioynde.] ~,   1051 Bristow] Briſt.   1089 learnt] learned   1165 men,] ~.   1209 wrong,] ~,   1252 assurd] aſſured   1269 disfigurd] disfigured   1288 deliured] deliuered   1325 Throwe] Q (*text*); Throw Q (*c.w.*)   1331 all.] ~,   1362 Welcome] *King* Welcome   1458 poisond] poiſoned   1459 muthred] murthered   1531 length.] ~ :   1538 Lord,] ~. (*at foot of page*)   1551 Bullingbroke] Bull.   1557 restord] reſtored   1560 slaughtred] ſlaughtered   1561 Bullingbroke] Bulling.   1568 tottred] tottered   1578 See] *Bull.* See   1658 Bullingbroke,] ~,   1708 vnpleasd] vnpleaſed   1724 Lord.] ~ :   1746 weepe...good.] ~ ;...?   1771 disordord] diſordered   1773 hath] htah   1773 suffred...disordred] ſuffered...diſordered   1778 Greene.] ~,   1785 selfe:] ~,   1797 speaking:] ~,   1809 weyde.] ~,   1884 ,Aumerle,] (~)   1903 banisht] baniſhed   1954 deed.] ~,   2021 stay.] ~ : F   2158 whose] wohſe   2169 lodgd] lodged   2182 weakened] weakned   2217 knowst] knoweſt   2262 misgouernd] miſgouerned   2281 well-gract] well-graced   2314 writing.] ~,   2329 Treason] *Yorke* Treaſon   2329 slaue.] ~,   2361 thy] rhy   2374 pardond] pardoned   2407 ere] cre   2414 feare.] ~,   2421 writing] writtng   2444 life,] ~,   2544 And] & (*see lineation note*)   2554 last,] ~,   2575 disordred] diſordered   2580 iarre,] ~,   2598 comst] comſt   2618 proud] prond   2641 die.] ~,   2649 consumd] conſumed   2664 Fitzwaters] Fitz.

Additional Passages

A.3 riuall-hating] Qb; ~,~ Qa   A.5 sleepe,] Qa; ~, Qb   B.3 partiall] Qa; partial Qb   D.4 profred] profered

RICHARD II

QUARTO STAGE DIRECTIONS

1.1.0.1-2/0.1-2   ENTER KING RICHARD, IOHN | OF GAVNT, WITH OTHER | Nobles and attendants.
1.1.19.1-2/19.1   Enter Bullingbrooke and Mowbray.
1.1.205/205   Exit.
1.2.0.1-2/205.1   Enter Iohn of Gaunt with the Duchesse of Glocester.
1.2.74.1/279.1   Exeunt.
1.3.0.1-2/279.2-3   Enter Lord Marshall and the Duke Aumerle.
1.3.6.1-5/285.1-4   The trumpets sound and the King enters with his nobles; when | they are set, enter the Duke of Norfolke in armes defendant.
1.3.25.2-3/304.2-3   The trumpets sound. Enter Duke of Hereford | appellant in armour.
1.3.200/479   Exit.
1.3.237.1-2/516.1-2   Exit. (Qb; not in Qa)
1.3.272/551.1   Exeunt.
1.4.0.1-2/551.2-3   Enter the King with Bushie, &c at one dore, and the | Lord Aumarle at another.
1.4.51.1/602.1   Enter Bushie with newes.
1.4.63.1/614.1   Exeunt.
2.1.0.1-2/614.2-3   Enter Iohn of Gaunt sicke, with the duke of Yorke, &c.
2.1.68.1-3/682.1-2   Enter king and Queene, &c. (after 2.1.70/684)
2.1.139.1/753.1   Exit.
2.1.215/829   Exit.
2.1.224.1-4/838.1-4   Exeunt King and Queene: Manet North.
2.1.302/916   Exeunt.
2.2.0.1/916.1   Enter the Queene, Bushie, Bagot.
2.2.122.1-2/1038.1-2   Exeunt Duke, Qu. man. Bush. Green.
2.3.0.1-2/1065.3-4   Enter Hereford, Northumberland.
2.3.20/1085   Enter Harry Persie. (after 'here')
2.3.170.1/1235.1   Exeunt.
2.4.0.1/1235.2   Enter erle of Salisbury and a Welch captaine.
3.1.0.1-3, 3.1.1/1259.1-2, 1260.1   Enter Duke of Hereford, Yorke, Northumberland, | Bushie and Greene prisoners. (at 3.1.0.1-3/1259.1-2)
3.1.44/1303   Exeunt.
3.2.0.1-3/1303.1-2   Enter the King Aumerle, Carleil, &c.
3.2.58.1/1361.1   Enter Salisb.
3.2.86/1389   Enter Scroope. (after 'here')

3.3.0.1-3/1517.2-3   Enter Bull. Yorke, North.
3.3.19/1536   Enter Percie. (after 'here')
3.3.60.4-8/1577.4-7   The trumpets sound, Richard appeareth on the walls.
3.3.186.1/1703.1   (he kneeles downe.
3.4.0.1/1724.2   Enter the Queene with her attendants
3.4.24.1/1748.1   Enter Gardeners.
3.4.102.1/1826.1   Exit
3.4.108/1832   Exeunt.
4.1.0.1-5/1832.1-3   Enter Bullingbrooke with the Lords to parliament.
4.1.1/1833   Enter Bagot.
4.1.97.1/1929.1   Enter Yorke.
4.1.310.1/2142.1   Exeunt.
4.1.310.1-2/2142.1   Manent West. Caleil, Aumerle.
4.1.323/2155   Exeunt.
5.1.0.1/2155.1   Enter the Queene with her attendants.
5.1.6.1/2161.1   (Enter Ric.
5.1.50.1/2205.1   Enter Northum.
5.1.102.1-3/2257.1-3   Exeunt.
5.2.0.1/2257.4   Enter Duke of Yorke and the Dutchesse.
5.2.71.1/2328.1   He pluckes it out of his bosome and reades it.
5.2.85.1/2342.1   His man enters with his bootes.
5.2.110.1/2367.1   Exit.
5.3.0.1-2/2374.2-3   Enter the King with his nobles.
5.3.22/2396   Enter Aumerle amazed. (after 'heere')
5.3.37/2411   The Duke of Yorke knokes at the doore and crieth.
5.3.144.1-2, 5.4.0.1/2518.1-3   Exeunt. Manet sir Pierce Exton, &c.
5.5.0.1/2529.1   Enter Richard alone.
5.5.41/2570   the musike plaies (after 'heare')
5.5.66.1/2595.1   Enter a groome of the stable.
5.5.94.1/2623.1   Enter one to Richard with meate.
5.5.97.1/2626   Exit Groome.
5.5.104.1/2633.1   The murderers rush in.
5.5.107.1/2636.1   Here Exton strikes him downe.
5.6.0.1-2/2647.4-5   Enter Bullingbrooke with the duke of Yorke.
5.6.4.1/2651.1   Enter Northumberland.
5.6.12.1/2659.1   Enter Lord Fitzwaters.
5.6.18.1-2/2665.1   Enter H. Percie.
5.6.29.1/2676.1   Enter Exton with the coffin.

FOLIO STAGE DIRECTIONS: THE ABDICATION EPISODE

4.1.148/1980   Exit.
4.1.152.1-2/1984.1-2   Enter Richard and Yorke.

4.1.265.1/2097.1   Enter one with a Glasse.

KING JOHN

SHAKESPEARE'S *King John* (*BEPD* 398), first printed in the 1623 First Folio (F), is closely related to a two-part play published in 1591, *The Troublesome Reign of John King of England* (*BEPD* 101-2). The existence of an earlier printed text of a similar play probably explains why *King John* was not entered in the Stationers' Register. Despite *Troublesome Reign*'s greater length, the two plays show considerable similarities in structure, though their language has only isolated points of similarity. One play is evidently the principal source for the other. In his Arden edition, Honigmann developed Alexander's challenge to the conventional view that *Troublesome Reign* was the earlier play. He has been answered effectively by Ribner and Smallwood, but has more recently, in *Shakespeare's Impact on his Contemporaries*, advanced further arguments attempting to show that *King John* was written before *Troublesome Reign*. There remain substantial objections to Honigmann's interpretation.

F supplies the only authoritative text, set by Compositors B and C. The nature of the copy is disputed. Stage directions such as '*Enter before Angiers . . .*' (2.1.0.1/276.1), '*. . . to the gates*' (2.1.299.5/575.5-6), and '*. . . on the walles*' (4.3.0.1/1891.2) suggest events as imagined by the playwright. There are few if any signs of theatrical annotation, though Greg thought '*Iohn brought in*' (5.7.27.1/2482.1) a possible example (*Problem*, p. 143 n.). The text is, however, exceptionally clean for foul-paper copy, especially in the later scenes, and the provision of act divisions would be unusual for a Folio play printed from such copy.

In the same note, Greg records Walker's view that Acts 1 to 3 (Sc. 1-6) may have been set from foul papers and Acts 4 and 5 (Sc. 7-16) from a prompt-book. Greg found this unlikely. Whilst rejecting Walker's hypothesis, Jowett and Taylor show that between 4.2.171/1792 and 4.2.217/1838 there is a strongly marked change in the preferred spelling of the exclamation *o(h)*, from 'o' to 'oh'. This idiosyncrasy can be attributed neither to the compositors nor to Shakespeare (who preferred the short spelling), and so indicates a change in the copy—most logically, a change of scribes in a transcript intervening between the foul papers and F.

The removal of profanity that has evidently taken place, though sometimes attributed to a printing-house editor, was more probably conducted by the scribes. Whereas both scribes intervened in this way, the second (Y) achieved a consistency unmatched by the first (X) (Taylor, 'Zounds'). The purging of the text would indicate that the manuscript was compiled after the Act to Restrain Abuses of 1606. Similarly, the presence of act divisions points to the manuscript's preparation or use after the King's Men began to observe act intervals around 1609. Both features suggest that the transcript was made with future theatrical use in mind. As in other respects there are signs that the manuscript was not annotated for prompt use—for example, the text is deficient in directions for music—it remains unlikely that it had served as a prompt-book before 1623. A projected revival may have been abandoned; alternatively, the scribes may have been commissioned to supply clean copy for Jaggard which could be used in the theatre subsequently.

F must therefore be considered as a text set from a late scribal transcript. Non-authorial revision is at least a possibility, though in fact no textual feature of F is helpfully reinterpreted on such a hypothesis. Scribal sophistication and error might occur at any point in the text. Scribe Y was probably a successful sophisticator: almost all the supposed foul-paper features belong to the portion of the text ascribed to X.

In the case of the speech-prefixes for 2.1.1-2/277-8 (see notes) and 2.1.150/426, X may have faithfully reflected difficulties in the copy, or may himself have contributed to the textual problems. Whichever explanation is right, similar circumstances may have led to the surprising speech-prefix identification of the Citizen of Angers as Hubert at 2.1.325/601 and thereafter.

Wilson first suggested that the Citizen and Hubert were the same character; Honigmann elaborates on the hypothesis and acts upon it in his text. Wilson pointed out that Shakespeare portrays Hubert as evidently of low birth, a departure from the aristocrat of his sources. This view has been challenged by Jones, who also contrasts the Bastard's opinion of the Citizen in 2.1/Sc. 2 and Hubert later in the play. The transition from a French citizen—unnamed in the dialogue, without personal ties with any other character and conspicuously neutral in his political affiliation—to the trusted confidant of King John remains abrupt, unexplained, and bewildering. If Shakespeare initiated a conflation of characters, he did not see it through to completion. The name Hubert may not be introduced until the middle of 2.1/Sc. 2 because Shakespeare (or someone else) had the play's casting requirements in mind. In the passage where the first prefix for Hubert occurs the two Heralds add to the English and French parties and the Citizen on the walls, giving the largest commitment of speaking parts anywhere in the play. Admittedly it is difficult to believe that the manuscript was annotated to indicate doubling as opposed to conflation: (*a*) one would expect either consistent alteration or just a single annotation (though the scribe might conceivably later have extended single annotation to subsequent prefixes); (*b*) such annotation would be expected when the *second* character first appears; and (*c*) there is no exceptional problem solved by this particular doubling. However, anyone looking at the point of greatest pressure on the cast might have decided that, for economy of casting and perhaps other reasons, it would be attractive to conflate parts, and so made provisional notes in the manuscript. Whatever the circumstances, the most important point for an editor is that any attempt to conflate characters seems incomplete in the extant text. If the scribes were working from Shakespeare's foul papers, additional material may have been supplied in a collateral prompt-book. As the editor cannot provide such material, the best option is to revert to Shakespeare's original conception, evidently prompted by *Troublesome Reign*, and retain the separate identities of the Citizen and Hubert.

The Folio act and scene divisions present some problems. F's duplicated '*Actus Quartus*' is readily explicable: the second is an error for '*Actus Quintus*'. F omits a scene-break at 3.2–3.3/Sc. 4–5; this may arise because '*Exit*' was misinterpreted as applying only to the Bastard. Editors since Capell have made the necessary correction. More puzzling are F's act and scene headings '*Scæna Secunda.*' (2.1/Sc. 2 in this edition), '*Actus Secundus*' (2.2/Sc. 3) and '*Actus Tertius, Scæna prima.*' (3.1/949.2). F's second act is a mere 76 lines long, and its third act almost certainly begins without there being a scene-break in the accepted sense of a cleared stage. The marking in the transcript of the controversial act division must have been intended to create a theatrical break where the original text provided continuous action. Similar mid-scene act-breaks introduced in theatrical manuscripts underlie the divisions indicated in Folio *Dream*, *Titus*, and *Measure*.

The short act preceding '*Actus Tertius, Scæna prima.*' is usually explained as printing-house error: an annotation for the second scene of Act 2 misinterpreted as the beginning of '*Actus Secundus*'. If so, the mistake was rectified by altering the heading (not set in type until after '*Actus Secundus*') which originally began the second act, to '*Scæna Secunda.*' The first error would have led to the sequence 1.1, 2.1, 2.1; the final arrangement gave 1.1, 1.2, 2.1.

This whole procedure is especially odd as the two headings were set by different compositors, one working forwards through the text, the other backwards. It is therefore possible that F preserves a change of intention in the marking of act and scene divisions that is connected with the unusual location of the beginning of 3.1. Acts 1 and 2 could have been marked on the usual assumption that scenes were not being divided to create act-breaks. The subsequent introduction of an act-break in the middle of what otherwise would have been 2.1 would so create a highly distorted division of material in the first two acts, a deficiency that was not subsequently set right.

In the original-spelling text of this edition, no scene-break is marked where F begins the third act as the action without act-breaks is continuous. The modern-spelling text observes F's act-break as an accurate indication of how the play would later have been staged when revived with act intervals. As its positioning is clearly incompatible with F's break beginning the second act, the editorial rearrangement initiated by Rowe in 1714 has been followed.

King John was the test case in Gary Taylor's 'Metrifying Shakespeare', which illustrated that there was little metrical corruption but identified where such corruption does occur. There are in general relatively few verbal errors in F, but this edition goes further than any previous edition in restoring the profane use of 'God' where F inferably substitutes 'heauen'.

J.J./(G.T.)

WORKS CITED

Alexander, Peter, *Shakespeare's 'Henry VI' and 'Richard III'* (1929)
—— *Shakespeare's Life and Art* (1939)
Furness, Horace Howard, ed., *King John*, New Variorum (1919)
Hinman, Charlton, 'Shakespearian Textual Studies: Seven More Years', in Clifford Leech and J. M. R. Margeson, eds., *Shakespeare 1971* (1972), 37–49
Honigmann, E. A. J., ed., *King John*, Arden (1954)
—— *Shakespeare's Impact on his Contemporaries* (1982)
John, Ivor B., ed., *King John*, Arden (1907)
Jones, Emrys, *The Origins of Shakespeare* (1977)
Jowett, John, and Gary Taylor, 'With New Additions', Appendix I, 'Oh and O'
Ribner, Irving, ed., *King John*, Pelican (1962)
Smallwood, R. L., ed., *King John*, New Penguin (1974)

TEXTUAL NOTES

Title *The life and death of King Iohn*] F (*head title and running title*)
1.1.0.1/0.1 *Florish.*] This edition (G.T.); *not in* F. F is deficient in directions for music, etc. In this edition these have been supplied on the basis of Shakespeare's theatrical practice elsewhere.
1.1.0.3/0.2 *them*] HONIGMANN; *the* F
1.1.11/11 To] F; Of JOHN (*conj.*)
1.1.11 Poitou] F (*Poyctiers*). Forms ending in *-ers* are consistently used by Shakespeare, and also by Holinshed and others, to denote the province. Modern usage distinguishes the province from the town. As the word is disyllabic in Shakespeare, 'Poyctiers' can be modernized without difficulty.
1.1.18/18 with-held,] F. Elsewhere F ends a speech with a comma only twice: once where *Exeunt* immediately follows (2.1.299/575) and once where the speech is interrupted (3.1.127/1076). Here there are no extenuating circumstances for an error, and an interrupted speech would be dramatically attractive.
1.1.20/20 for controlement] F; for control VAUGHAN (*conj.*)
1.1.25/25 report,] F; ~ˌ CAPELL
1.1.38 fearful-bloody] F (~ˌ~)
1.1.43.1/43.1 *who whispers to Essex*] CAPELL (*subs.*); *not in* F. This action is intrinsically probable, and finds support in *Troublesome Reign*'s similar direction.

1.1.49/49 expeditious] F1; expeditions F2
1.1.49 Falconbridge] F (*Faulconbridge*). Similarly throughout. Compare note to Taylor's Oxford *Henry V* 3.5.44; in *K. John* the name is English and fictitious. 'Faulcon' is the most common spelling for *falcon* in Shakespeare.
1.1.79/79 selfe.] ROWE; ~ˌ F
1.1.92/92 father?] F1; ~, F2
1.1.134/134 ratherˌ be:] This edition (*conj.* Vaughan); ratherˌ beˌ F; rather,—beˌ CAPELL
1.1.147/147 It] F1; I F2
1.1.161/161 arise] STEEVENS; rife F. The metre shows an irregularity not usually acceptable in *K. John*. The formality of action and the rhymed couplet emphasize the need to emend, especially as *rise/arise* are merely metrical variants; 'arise' in 1.1.162/162 suggests a parallelism.
1.1.188/188 'Tis too] F2; 'Tis two F1
1.1.208/208 smacke] THEOBALD; ſmoake F. The word needs to be the same as 'smacke' in 1.1.209/209 to make the latter intelligible. As *smoke* could mean 'suspect' (transitive) it was occasionally possible for the two words to overlap in meaning (see Honigmann), but this seems unlikely here.
1.1.209-12/209-12 am I:... no,... motion:] SMALLWOOD (*subs.*); ~ˌ... ~:... ~ˌ F

1.1.227 unreverent] F (vnreuerend)
1.1.231 Philipˏ Sparrow] F (~, sparrów). Most editors follow Warburton or Steevens in interpreting F's comma after 'Philip' as an exclamation or question mark. This fragments a set expression. F's comma might indicate a momentary pause, but is more likely to be equivalent to a hyphen: compare 'mercy, lacking' (4.1.120/1608).
1.1.231 James!] F (~,). The exclamation is often understood to end at 'sparrow', with 'James' initiating the following sentence.
1.1.236/236 doeˏ] F; ~ — HONIGMANN. Smallwood seems right (also as against Pope and subsequent editors, who read 'get me?' in 1.1.237/237) to read 'Could [he] get me' as a conditional clause continuing 'Sir Robert could doe well'.
1.1.236/236 marrie] Honigmann follows F4 in introducing a comma after 'marry' and reads 'marry' as a verb ('Sir Robert could . . . marry').
1.1.237/237 Could a] This edition (conj. Maxwell); Could F; Could he POPE. F makes little sense and is metrically defective. The clipped form 'a' would be more easily dropped than Pope's 'he' (the traditional emendation) and is an idiom used elsewhere in *K. John* by no other character but the Bastard. After this reading had been independently adopted in this edition, it was discovered that Maxwell conjectured 'a' in a marginal annotation to his copy of the New (Cambridge) edition.
1.1.237/237 me,] F2; ~ˏ F1
1.1.247 Robert,] F (~ˏ)
1.1.256/256 to my] F; to thy HUDSON 2 (Staunton). See following note.
1.1.257/257 Thou] F4; That F1. Emendation of 'my' (1.1.269/269) to 'thy' gives a plausible alternative reading, but F's 'my' is supported by the Bastard's following speech, where he seeks to allay his mother's feelings of guilt. The other alternative of an interjectory 'Heaven!' (1.1.256/256), whereby 'lay not . . .' is addressed to the Bastard, creates the practical difficulty for the actor of invoking then immediately disinvoking heaven. Copy 'yᵘ' could easily be misread 'yᵗ'.
2.1.0.1 Angers] F (Angiers). Similarly throughout.
2.1.0.4 *the Duke of Austria*] F (*Auſtria*). Editors usually entitle him Archduke, but he is elsewhere in F *Duke*. *Archduke* was probably unknown to Shakespeare, and not used by the historical character.
2.1.1, 18/277, 294 KING PHILIP] DYCE 2; Lewis F. Honigmann explains in detail how repeated use of 'King' as a speech-prefix for King Philip might have caused speech-prefix error in the opening of 2.1/Sc. 2 and at 2.1.146-8/425-7 (though Shakespeare seems to have distinguished Philip as 'Fran⟨ce⟩.' or 'Fra⟨nce⟩.' after King John's entry at 2.1.83/359). Honigmann conjectures the following arrangement in the copy:

Lewis. Before Angiers well met braue Austria.
King. Arthur that great fore-runner of thy bloud,
                                                      (2.1.1-2/277-8)

King. Lewis, determine what we shall doe strait.
Lew. Women & fooles, breake off your conference.
King. King Iohn, this is the very summe of all:
                                                   (2.1.149-51/425-7)

This hypothesis supposes (a) that the usual practice of maintaining separate columns for speech-prefixes and dialogue was not observed; (b) that the same confusion between prefixes and dialogue occurred in two separate places, in each case affecting the same prefix but manifesting itself as two quite different errors; (c) that in both cases there was an obscure or missing full stop after the prefix; (d) that someone would object to 'King Arthur' (which, at a superficial reading, might easily refer to the legendary figure); (e) that the more obvious and correct explanation for the presumed 'King. King' at 2.1.151/427 was not perceived. It is likelier that there has been a straightforward confusion as to the name of the French king. This would be despite the correct '*Philip King of France*' in the opening direction. Authorial inconsistency might provide the best explanation. Holinshed

himself, in Shakespeare's secondary source, made the same mistake when describing the betrothal of the Dauphin and Blanche. Moreover, inconsistency could reflect a contemplated departure from the sources, to avoid giving the same name to the major fictional character as to the French king. But it is alternatively possible that the scribe was confused, and undertook some misconceived correction. In the opening direction '*Lewis*' immediately follows '*King of France*', and the comma after it suggests that he is not the same figure as '*Dauphin*'. In this edition, the more elaborate emendations effected by Honigmann have not been accepted.
2.1.2/278 Arthur] F; K⟨ing⟩. Phi⟨lip⟩. Arthur HONIGMANN
2.1.18 A] F. Alternatively 'Ah', as Fleay conjectured.
2.1.37/313 worke,] F4; ~ˏ F1
2.1.63/339 Ate] ROWE; Ace F
2.1.106/382 this] F; his RANN (Mason)
2.1.106/382 Geffreyes: . . . God,] ROWE; ~ˏ . . . ~ : F
2.1.113/389 breast] F2; beaft F1
2.1.119/395 Excuse,] F; ~ ; MALONE. Neither punctuation has a clear advantage.
2.1.127/403 Iohn, in manners,] CAPELL (Roderick); ~ , in ~ˏ F
2.1.144 shows] F (ſhooes)
2.1.149/425 King *Philip*] THEOBALD; King *Lewis* F; Phi⟨lip⟩. Lewis CAPELL. See note to 2.1.1/277.
2.1.150/426 KING PHILIP] THEOBALD; Lew⟨is⟩. F
2.1.151/427 King] F; K⟨ing⟩ Phi⟨lip⟩. King HONIGMANN
2.1.152/428 Aniowe] THEOBALD; Angiers F. Here and at 2.1.488/764 Shakespeare appears to confuse the province and the besieged town. Elsewhere he maintains a distinction, as do Holinshed and *Troublesome Reign*.
2.1.169/445 Drawe] CAPELL; Drawes F
2.1.187/463 plague: . . . sinneˏ . . . iniury,] CAMBRIDGE (Roby); ~ˏ . . . ~ : . . . ~ˏ F
2.1.200.1/476.1 *a Citizen*] F; *certain Citizens* CAPELL; HONIGMANN (Wilson) reads HUBERT. See Introduction.
2.1.201/477 CITIZEN] F; Hub⟨ert⟩. HONIGMANN (Wilson). Similarly at 2.1.267, 270, and 281/543, 546, and 557. See Introduction.
2.1.214/490 French,] ROWE; ~ . F
2.1.215/491 Confront your] ROWE; Comfort yours F. Honigmann reads 'Comforts your', interpreting ironically. 'Yours' is probably a mental-aural anticipation of 'Cities'.
2.1.232/508 in, your] CAPELL; ~ . Your F
2.1.259 roundure] F (rounder). Compare 'venter' for *venture*, etc.
2.1.287 chevaliers] F (Cheualiers). Not modernized to 'cavaliers' as the term probably characterizes the speaker as French.
2.1.289/565 on's] F; on his POPE
2.1.299.5/575.5 *Trumpet*] This edition (G.T.); *Trumpets* F. Compare 2.1.311.2/587.2 where there is only one '*Trumpet*' in F. Much of the dramatic effect of this scene depends upon symmetry. F's plural could be the compositor's anticipation of 'gates' or an authorial error echoing 'Enter the Kings Herolds with Trumpets . . .' (i.e. the English and French Heralds each with his trumpeter[s]) in *Troublesome Reign*.
2.1.325/601 CITIZEN] ROWE; Hubert. F. Apart from 2.1.368/644 (see note), the Citizen's subsequent speech-prefixes (2.1.363/639, 2.1.417/693, 2.1.424/700, 2.1.481/757) are similarly 'Hub⟨ert⟩.' in F. See Introduction.
2.1.327/603 your] F2; yonr F1. F2's emendation is likelier than the alternative 'yond'.
2.1.335/611 ronne] F2 (runne); rome F1. Compare 5.4.56/2383. 'Rome' (roam) lacks the connotations of rapid and powerful forward motion that seem to be required here.
2.1.362 who's] F (whoſe)
2.1.368/644 CITIZEN] ROWE; Fra⟨nce⟩. F; Hub⟨ert⟩. HONIGMANN (Wilson). See note to 2.1.325/601. Copy 'Hu' or 'hu' could be misread 'ffra' or 'Fra'.
2.1.371/647 Kingd] TYRWHITT; Kings F. Editors are divided over Tyrwhitt's emendation; however, no reading of F can avoid the contradiction 'Kings of our feare, vntill our feares . . . | Be . . . depos'd'. The usual editorial commas around 'resolu'd' identify it as an adjectival past participle, which could be 'being dissolved'

or 'having been made resolute'. Whether turned to fortitude or to nothing, the fears then need no purging or deposing, and 2.1.372/648 is pre-empted. However, if 'resolu'd' is verbal, 'resolu'd', 'purg'd', and 'depos'd' become three equivalent expressions.

2.1.425/701 neece] SINGER 2; neere F. The equivalent line in *Troublesome Reign* (II. 2.1.423) confirms Singer's reading.

2.1.435/711 compleat o,] HANMER; compleat of, F; completed SISSON. No satisfactory parallels have been found for *compleat of*. Honigmann suggests that the interjection 'O' could be spelt 'of', but it is more likely that the scribe or compositor interpreted 'o' as 'o'' (or saw 'o, as 'o'') and regularized to 'of'.

2.1.436 nothing—. . . . want—] F (~, . . . ~,). Warburton first indicated definite parenthesis by introducing brackets. Smallwood rather unconvincingly glosses 'nothing which could really be called a lack'.

2.1.463/739 Cannon,] CAPELL; ~ˌ F

2.1.488/764 Aniow] POPE 2; Angiers F. See 2.1.152/428 above.

2.1.489/765 side] F2; fide F1

2.1.501 sun] F (sonne). Shakespeare did not always distinguish the primary sense in word-play.

2.1.524/800 shall] STEEVENS–REED; still F; will POPE. A substitution influenced by the previous line and the general similarity of *shall* and *still*. The compositor may have been working from a scribal transcript with italic 'h'.

2.1.536/812 assur'd] F (assur'd); affied HUDSON 2

2.1.540 rites] F (rights)

2.1.572 lose] F (loose)

2.2.69 and] Cambridge interprets as 'an't', which gives a good reading, whereby Constance desires the proud kind of grief which will make her stoop. With 'and', 'griefe' is an absolute with which Constance identifies her own 'sorrowes' because it will necessarily make her stoop.

3.1.33–4 heavens, . . . Kings! . . . cries,] This is Capell's interpretation of F's 3 commas, and the usual one. An alternative, less close to the sequence of ideas, would be ~ ! . . . ~ˌ . . . ~.

3.1.34/983 God] This edition (G.T.); heauens F. The metaphor of 'heavens' as a 'husband' is odd; but in the imagery of Christianity Christ is the 'husband' of the Church, and also specifically the 'husband' of a woman entering a nunnery. The contrast with 'vngodly' (3.1.35/984) suggests that the vocative might be 'God', but almost equally attractive would be 'Lord': the collocation *lord . . . husband* occurs 10 times elsewhere.

3.1.36/985 daie] THEOBALD; daies F. F echoes the plural 'houres' directly above.

3.1.36 sun set] F (Sun-set). 'Set' anticipates 'Set armèd discord'.

3.1.62/1011 God] This edition (G.T.); heauen F. Shakespeare 4 times identifies kings as divine 'deputies', always of a personalized deity rather than abstract heaven (*Contention* 3.2.289–90/1851–2, *Richard II* 1.2.37–8, 3.2.53, 4.1.116–17/242–3, 1356, 1948–9).

3.1.74/1023 task] THEOBALD; taft F; tax ROWE 3

3.1.81/1030 God] HONIGMANN (Collier); heauen F

3.1.111/1060 right,] ROWE 3; ~. F

3.1.122/1071 yt] SMALLWOOD (Maxwell); that F. 'Yt' restores the usual idiom; the compositor probably understood 'yt' as 'yt'.

3.1.162/1111 God] This edition (G.T.); Heauen F. *God knows* appears 28 times in Shakespeare; *heaven knows* appears, in uncensored plays, only in Q *Othello* (1622), which is anomalous in most other respects, and has probably suffered some expurgation.

3.1.185/1134 crased] This edition; cased F; chased POPE; chafed THEOBALD; caged COLLIER 3. Of the proposed readings, 'crased' would be most easily misread as 'cased'.

3.1.197/1146 Is not] F; Is't not JOHNSON; Is most HANMER; Is yet WARBURTON. Pandolf gives a paradox which he expounds through his definition of 'truth' in the next two lines.

3.1.206–13 But . . . swear;] These lines have been variously punctuated; this edition substantially follows F. The syntax inevitably gives a convoluted and obscure meaning.

3.1.208/1157 troth] This edition; truth F. As is demonstrated by 2.1.501/777, Shakespeare does not appear to have been clinical in distinguishing the spelling-form of the primary sense of a word in passages of word-play. Emendation is needed here because, despite Pandolf's sophistic ambiguity, there is a distinction between John's pledge (which is far from the *truth*) and the truth itself. *Troth/truth* is therefore probably a verbal quibble in itself, underlined by the rhyme/pararhyme with 'oath'.

3.1.210/1159 swearst] This edition; sweares F. Second person singular ending in '-s' is usually found in Shakespeare only after '-t' (e.g. *splits*). Honigmann suggests a third person singular, but this gives a particularly difficult reading.

3.1.224/1173 Wilt] CAPELL; Wil't F. The colloquial use of *be* ('be silent, shut up') recognized by Capell and Furness, is not in *OED* or *EDD*, but is analogous with Shakespearian *Let be* and dialectal *I'll be as I am* (where *be* means 'abide'). *Will it not be* was a fairly common Elizabethan phrase (Dent, B112.2), but seems to have little sense and less dramatic function here.

3.1.263–4/1212–13 lies . . . liues] F; lives . . . lives CAPELL; lies . . . li'es FLEAY

3.1.269/1218 The blood] F; The best HUDSON 2 (W. S. Walker)

3.2.0.1 Alarum] F (Alarums). Shakespeare made no distinction between the singular and plural. Regularization avoids the suggestion of a quantitative difference.

3.3.2/1234 So] F; More HUDSON (Lettsom); And SISSON

3.3.8–10/1240–2 Of . . . libertie:] This edition (G.T.); Of hoording Abbots: imprisoned angells | Set at libertie: the fat ribs of peace | Must by the hungry now be fed vpon: F. 'Imprisoned . . . libertie' is taken to be a marginal addition to the foul papers which was misplaced in the transcript. See Taylor, 'Metrifying'.

3.3.26/1258 tune] F; time POPE

3.3.39/1271 race] F; ear DYCE; face SISSON (Bulloch)

3.3.52/1284 broadeid] POPE; brooded F. F is sometimes, implausibly, defended as meaning 'vigilant (as a brooding hen)'.

3.4.12/1317 cause] F; course HANMER

3.4.27/1332 forth from] F. 'From forth' (Collier MS), the more usual word order, would remove a minor metrical irregularity.

3.4.44/1349 art not] F4; art F1

3.4.48/1353 God] This edition (G.T.); heauen F. (*I*) *would to God* appears 13 times in uncensored texts; *I would to heaven* never.

3.4.64/1369 friends] ROWE 3; fiends F

3.4.110 world's] F (words). A spelling variant.

3.4.133/1438 an] F; one COLLIER (conj.). *One* might have been written 'on' (evidently a Shakespearian spelling), giving a simple misreading.

3.4.149/1454 soe vilely] This edition (G.T.); so euilly F. Cercignani explains 'euilly' as probably representing the variant *eelly*, but the only other example he cites is from a part of *Timon* now attributed to Middleton. There are no other instances of *evilly* in the canon; the present line is particularly suspect as a unique usage combined with a metrical anomaly. *Vilely* strengthens the interpretation of 'borne' as *born*, giving a telling reading in a play concerned with legitimacy, one in which Hubert is later repeatedly insulted as a 'villaine' for the act in question, and in which the act itself is called 'vilde' at 3.4.138/1443 and 4.2.242/1863.

3.4.149 born] F (borne). See previous note.

3.4.182/1487 make] CAPELL; makes F. F probably anticipates 'strange'.

3.4.182/1487 strange] F1; strong F2

4.1.7/1495 scruples,] F4; ~ˌ F1

4.1.18/1506 be as] F; be POPE

4.1.23/1511 God] This edition (G.T.); heauen. See note to 3.4.48/1353.

4.1.42 handkerchief] F (hand-kercher)

4.1.50 lain] F (lyen)

4.1.55/1543 heauen] F. F is here confirmed by Shakespeare's practice elsewhere: he writes of heaven 'pleas'd' 6 times in uncensored texts; of God, never.

4.1.63/1551 his] CAPELL; this F

4.1.77/1565 Gods] This edition (G.T.); heauen F. Shakespeare uses *for God(s) sake* 24 times; the only example of *for heaven(s) sake* in an uncensored text is at *Othello* 5.1.51/2817.

4.1.80 wince] F (winch)
4.1.81 angerly] F. See note to *Two Gentlemen* 1.2.62/209.
4.1.91 mote] F (moth)
4.1.91, 131/1579, 1619 God] This edition (G.T.); heauen F. *Othello* provides the only examples of *O heauen* in an uncensored text; *O God* is frequent.
4.1.114/1602 eyes] STEEVENS; eye F
4.1.119/1607 extends] F; extend POPE
4.1.120 mercy-lacking] F (~, ~)
4.2.1/1622 againe crown'd] F3; againſt crown'd F1
4.2.10/1631 guard] F; gaud G.T. *conj.*
4.2.28/1649 do better] F; better do STAUNTON (*conj.*)
4.2.31/1652 worser] SMALLWOOD (Maxwell); worſe F. Alternatively, one might emend the metre with 'the excuse'.
4.2.42/1663 when] TYRWHITT; then F; the ROWE 3
4.2.56-7/1677-8 then . . . should] F; shou'd . . . then POPE. As an error, F could be explained as miscorrected 'should . . . should'.
4.2.73/1694 Dos] F4 (Does); Do F1
4.2.117/1738 eare] DYCE 2; care F. The reading of the damaged and badly printed first letter has been widely disputed. Other occurrences of this type in F establish it as 'c', but in several instances it is used as 'e' (Hinman, i. 430; c24). The reading therefore remains open to doubt. Whereas 'care' is applicable in a general way, 'eare' has an exact and enriching sense, as is shown by the Messenger's all-too-literal reply.
4.2.191 grip] F (gripe)
4.3.16 Who's] F (Whoſe). 'Whose' is the only spelling of *who's* in *K. John* (also at 2.1.362/638 and 5.6.1/2411). All three instances were set by Compositor B. Previous editors, retaining F's 'Is' at 4.3.17/1908 (see note), read the possessive.
4.3.16/1907 with me] F; missive COLLIER (*conj.*); warrant WILSON (*conj.*); notice SISSON. *Private* is nowhere recorded in the sense necessary for F's reading ('private communication'). Wilson posited a two-stage error beginning with an abbreviated 'warrant' ('wnt' to 'with' to 'with me'). To the conjectured misreadings may be added 'wisper', but none is entirely convincing. Any emendation of 'with me' to a noun also leaves a confused antecedent to 'generall', which most logically should refer to 'the Dolphines loue'. See following note.
4.3.17/1908 Tis] This edition; Is F. A simple error or—more likely—a scribal (or compositorial) 'correction', assuming 'Whose' as the relative pronoun. Compare the more problematic emendations of 'with me' offered in the previous note.
4.3.33/1924 man] F2; mans F1; manners HONIGMANN
4.3.41/1932 you haue] F1; haue you F3. F3 may be a correct emendation; if so, the 'you' ending the preceding phrase would have facilitated the F1 compositor's transposition. But although F3 gives a slightly more natural sense, there is nothing demonstrably wrong with F1's reading.
4.3.89/1980 life] F; self DYCE; name G.T. *conj.*
4.3.147 scramble] F (ſcamble). See note to Taylor's Oxford *Henry V* 1.1.4.
4.3.156 cincture] F (center)
5.1.3 Pope,] F (~ ₐ)
5.1.7/2058 'fore] F; for MASON (*conj.*)
5.1.24.1/2075.1 Exeunt . . . Iohn] CAPELL (*subs.*); *Exit.* F. Most editors follow F, implying that attendants remain on stage. A cleared stage emphasizes John's weakness and vulnerability, especially in the short soliloquy that thereby follows. The conversation with the Bastard is most effective as a private dialogue.
5.1.54 glisten] F (gliſter). *Glisten* and *glister* both derive from Middle English *glise*, and are identical in meaning; *glister* is now obsolete except as an archaism or in possible dialect usage. Shakespeare invariably uses *glister* where we would say *glisten*; the modernization therefore does not obscure any Shakespearian nuance.
5.2.10/2140 an vn-urged] DAWSON; an vn-urg'd F; unurg'd POPE
5.2.26/2156 Was] F1; Were F2. F1 gives a possibly acceptable form, or a grammatical licence influenced by 'Isle'.
5.2.36/2166 Gripple] STEEVENS; cripple F. Capital C/G confusion would come easily to a compositor unfamiliar with *Gripple*.
5.2.36 gripple] *OED* describes *gripple* as an alteration of *grapple*; its suggestion that the word was influenced by *grip* is sufficiently plausible to warrant retaining it.
5.2.43/2173 thou] F4; *not in* F1
5.2.59/2189 warm of] F; of warm CAMBRIDGE (Heath)
5.2.83/2213 warres] F; war POPE
5.2.104/2234 bankd] F; hailed JOHN (*conj.*); bail'd This edition *conj.* Steevens pointed out that in *Troublesome Reign* 'these salutations were given to the Dauphin as he *sailed along the banks* of the river'; *OED* accepts *bank* here as 'To coast, to skirt'. Honigmann understands a card-playing term, but cites no convincing example of such a verb. 'Hail'd' might anticipate the townspeople's cry of greeting. 'Bail'd' supposes less radical error; it might mean 'liberated' or 'secured, guaranteed, protected'.
5.2.108/2238 no, on] F; on POPE
5.2.133 unhaired] F4; (vn-heard)
5.2.135 these pigmy] F (this Pigmy)
5.2.145/2275 his] ROWE; this F
5.3.8, 16/2318, 2326 Swinshed] HALLIWELL; Swinſted F. Shakespeare followed *Troublesome Reign* in mistaking Swineshead for nearby Swinstead, where there is no abbey. Holinshed correctly refers to 'Swineshead'.
5.4.17 more] F (moe)
5.4.32 daybreak] F (day breake)
5.4.34/2361 Cresset] This edition (*conj.* Cambridge); Creſt F. Figurative applications of *crest* are contrived, especially in the context of smoke and fire imagery. The emendation gives an apposite sense, and is supported by the only other instance of *cresset* in Shakespeare: in *1 Henry IV* 3.1.14/1493, the 'cressets' are also described as 'burning', and are likewise a metaphor for heavenly bodies.
5.5.3/2391 measurd] POPE; meaſure F
5.5.7 tatt'ring] F's 'tott'ring' is a spelling variant, and the change to 'tatt'ring' a modernization which establishes the primary sense in this context (though the connotations of *tott'ring* are also present).
5.5.7/2395 clearly] F; cleanly CAMBRIDGE (*conj.*)
5.6.1-3/2411-13 Whose . . . thee?] Some editors redistribute these lines between the speakers, believing that the two questions in Hubert's speech of 5.6.3-5/2413-15 cannot be said by the same speaker. However, the second question is more plausible as a reaction to 'Whether doest thou go?' than to 'What's that to thee?' Hubert has not asked an unanswered question, unless 'What's that to thee?' is such, but (a) 'A Friend' is an evasive answer, and (b) Hubert has rapidly lost the initiative in the questioning. An error in the prefixes could only plausibly be explained if a scribe supplied prefixes after writing dialogue, and did so working up from the foot of the page.
5.6.4 Why,] F. Alternatively, the exclamation followed by a comma.
5.6.13/2423 eieles] THEOBALD; endles F. The objection to 'endles' is not just that it has no positive value in its context, but that it gives a misleading characterization of night in a compact and cryptic line. The defence of 'endless night' as a 'common cliché' (Honigmann) can work the other way: the scribe or compositor could easily misread it from a less familiar expression.
5.6.38/2448 heauen] F; God G.T. *conj.* Shakespeare never elsewhere describes the heavens as 'mighty', but uses the adjective of 'God(s)' 6 times. However, it is heaven that threatens *indignation* in *Richard III* 1.3.214-18/626-30.
5.7.16/2471 inuinsible] SMALLWOOD (Steevens); inuiſible F; insensible HANMER; invisited COLLIER (*conj.*); invasible WILSON (*conj.*); unusable SISSON. The reverse error occurs in Q and F *2 Henry IV* 3.2.308/1833. The paradox of the conquered body as 'inuinsible' (i.e. incapable of further defeat) is a natural development from the paradox of 5.7.13-14/2468-9.
5.7.17/2472 minde] ROWE 3; winde F
5.7.21/2476 Signet] ROWE 3 (*subs.*); Symet F
5.7.42 strait] F (ſtraight)
5.7.58/2513 module] F. *Model* and *module*, though etymologically distinct and with different ranges of meaning, were in many senses confused to the extent that they could sometimes be considered spelling variants. Here *model* gives the better sense in

KING JOHN

modern usage. But Shakespeare seems, arbitrarily, to have attached the sense 'delusive image' to *module*, which has therefore been retained.
5.7.60/2515 God] WORDSWORTH; heauen F
5.7.88/2543 our own] WORDSWORTH (Collier); our F. A possible alternative to F's metrically corrupt line is Dyce's 'sinewèd', but Folio *K. John* is unusually regular in marking syllabic *-ed*.

5.7.97/2552 Princes] F; nobles ELZE (*conj.*)
5.7.108/2563 kinde of] This edition (G.T.); kinde F. Most editors make the metrical emendation '... giue you thankes', but 'kinde of soule' improves the sense by removing Henry's apparent tone of complacent self-gratulation. Compare *Troilus* 3.2.144/1719: 'I haue a kind of selfe ...'.

INCIDENTALS

61 certaine] cerraine   123 kept] Fa; ~. Fb   182 A] Baſt. A   362 heauen,] ~.   408 father.] ~,   453 eld'ſt] eldeſt   528 th'inuolnerable] th'involuerable   543 ſubiects:] ~,   575 right.] ~,   580 ſcattred] ſcattered   582 diſcolourd] diſcoloured   582 earth] earrh   603 your] yonr   657 mount,] ~.   678 Towne] Townc   730 from] ftom   745 match,] ~,   748 vnsur'd] vnſur,d   764 Toraine,] ~.   809 daughter] daughtet   810 hands.] ~,   826 turn'd] turn,d   938 Enuenom] Euvenom   1008 limbs.] ~,   1018 Archbishop] Arſhbiſhop   1082 That's] That,s   1118 our] onr   1177 slaughtred] ſlaughtered   1242 Imprison'd] impriſoned (*see textual note*)   1308 ſcattred] ſcattered   1401 Remembers] Remembets   1512 Hubert.] ~:   1521 Arthur] Arthnr   1665 reform'd,] ~.   1681 exercise?] ~,   1874 hand,] ~.   1920 greefes] greefcs   2034-5 vp? ... Royaltie,] ~, ... ~?   2183 with] wirh   2205 foſtred] foſtered   2275 Englishman:] ~.   2304 Legate] Lcgate   2310 doubt.] ~,   2319 the] rhe   2329 French.] ~,   2429 Breefe] Brcefe   2520 eare.] ~,   2531 againe,] ~.   2565 time,] ~:

FOLIO STAGE DIRECTIONS

1.1.0.1-3/0.1-2 *Enter King Iohn, Queene Elinor, Pembroke, Essex, and Sa-|lisbury, with the Chattylion of France.*
1.1.30.1/30.1 *Exit Chat. and Pem.*
1.1.43.1/43.1 *Enter a Sheriffe.*
1.1.49/49 *Enter Robert Faulconbridge, and Philip.* (after 'you')
1.1.181.1/181.1 *Exeunt all but bastard.*
1.1.216.1/216.1 *Enter Lady Faulconbridge and Iames Gurney.* (after 1.1.221/221)
1.1.232.1/232.1 *Exit Iames.*
1.1.276.1/276 *Exeunt.*
2.1.1-5/276.1-4 *Enter before Angiers, Philip King of France, Lewis, Daul-|phin, Austria, Constance, Arthur.*
2.1.49.1/325.1 *Enter Chattilion.*
2.1.75.1/351.1 *Drum beats.* (after 2.1.77/353)
2.1.83.1-3/359.1-2 *Enter K. of England, Bastard, Queene, Blanch, Pembroke, | and others.*
2.1.200.1/476.1 *Trumpet sounds. | Enter a Citizen vpon the walles.*
2.1.299.1-3/575.1-3 *Exeunt*
2.1.299.4-5/575.4-6 *Heere after excursions, Enter the Herald of France | with Trumpets to the gates.*
2.1.311.1-2/587.1-2 *Enter English Herald with Trumpet.*
2.1.333.1-4/609.1-3 *Enter the two Kings with their powers, | at seuerall doores.*
2.1.504.1/780.1 *Whispers with Blanch.*
2.1.561.1/837.1 *Exeunt.*
2.1.599/875 *Exit.*
2.2.0.1-2/875.1 *Enter Constance, Arthur, and Salisbury.*
3.1.0.1-4/949.2-4 *Enter King Iohn, France, Dolphin, Blanch, Elianor, Philip, | Austria, Constance.*
3.1.60.1/1009.1 *Enter Pandulph.*
3.1.273.1/1222.1 *Exeunt.*
3.2.0.1-2/1222.2-3 *Allarums, Excursions: Enter Bastard with Austria's | head.*
3.2.4.1-2/1225.1 *Enter Iohn, Arthur, Hubert.* (after 3.2.3/1224)
3.2.10.1-2/1232.1-2 *Exit.*
3.3.0.1-3/1232.3-4 *Alarums, excursions, Retreat. Enter Iohn, Eleanor, Arthur | Bastard, Hubert, Lords.*
3.3.73.1-2/1305.1-2 *Exeunt.*
3.4.0.1-2/1305.3 *Enter France, Dolphin, Pandulpho, Attendants.*
3.4.16.1-2/1321.1-2 *Enter Constance.*
3.4.105/1410 *Exit.*
3.4.106.1/1411.1 *Exit.*
3.4.183/1488 *Exeunt.*
4.1.0.1-2/1488.1-2 *Enter Hubert and Executioners.*

4.1.8.1/1496.1 *Enter Arthur.*
4.1.133/1621 *Exeunt*
4.2.0.1-3/1621.1-2 *Enter Iohn, Pembroke, Salisbury, and other Lordes.*
4.2.66.1/1687.1 *Enter Hubert.*
4.2.102.1/1723.1 *Exeunt*
4.2.105.1/1726.1 *Enter Mes.* (after 4.2.103/1724)
4.2.131/1752 *Enter Bastard and Peter of Pomfret.*
4.2.176/1797 *Exit*
4.2.182.1/1803.1 *Enter Hubert.*
4.2.270.1/1891.1 *Exeunt.*
4.3.0.1-2/1891.2 *Enter Arthur on the walles.*
4.3.10.1/1901.1 *Dies*
4.3.10.2-3/1901.2 *Enter Pembroke, Salisbury, & Bigot.*
4.3.20.1/1911.1 *Enter Bastard.*
4.3.73.1/1964.1 *Enter Hubert.*
4.3.115.1/2006.1 *Ex. Lords.*
4.3.160.1/2051.1 *Exit.*
5.1.0.1-2/2051.2 *Enter King Iohn and Pandolph, attendants.*
5.1.24.1/2075.1 *Exit.*
5.1.29.1/2080.1 *Enter Bastard.*
5.1.79/2130 *Exeunt.*
5.2.1-3/2130.2-3 *Enter (in Armes) Dolphin, Salisbury, Meloone, Pem-|broke, Bigot, Souldiers.*
5.2.64.1/2194.1 *Enter Pandulpho.* (after 5.2.63/2193)
5.2.117.1/2247.1 *Enter Bastard.*
5.2.180.1-2/2310.1-3 *Exeunt.*
5.3.0.1-2/2310.4-5 *Alarums. Enter Iohn and Hubert.*
5.3.4.1/2314.1 *Enter a Messenger.*
5.3.17/2327 *Exeunt.*
5.4.0.1-2/2327.1 *Enter Salisbury, Pembroke, and Bigot.*
5.4.6.1/2333.1 *Enter Meloon wounded.*
5.4.61/2388 *Exeunt*
5.5.0.1-2/2388.1 *Enter Dolphin, and his Traine.*
5.5.8.1/2396.1 *Enter a Messenger.*
5.5.22/2410 *Exeunt*
5.6.0.1-2/2410.1-2 *Enter Bastard and Hubert, seuerally.*
5.6.45/2455 *Exeunt*
5.7.0.1-2/2455.1 *Enter Prince Henry, Salisburie, and Bigot.*
5.7.5.1/2460.1 *Enter Pembroke.*
5.7.27.1/2482.1 *Iohn brought in.*
5.7.48.1/2503.1 *Enter Bastard.*
5.7.118.1/2573.1 *Exeunt.*

THE MERCHANT OF VENICE

The first known reference to *The Merchant of Venice* (BEPD 172) occurs in the Stationers' Register for 22 July 1598:

Iames Robertes. / Entred for his copie vnder the hande
        of bothe the wardens, a booke
        of the Marchaunt of Venyce
        or otherwiſe called the Iewe
        of Venyce / Provided that
        yt bee not prynted by the ſaid Iames
        Roberte or anye other whatſoeuer
        wthout lycence firſt had from the
        Right honorable the lord Chamberlen

A further entry was made on 28 October 1600:

Tho. haies   Entred for his copie vnder the
                hande of the Wardens & by
                Conſent of m^r Roberte A
                Booke called the booke of the
                m chant of Venyce

Two quarto editions survive; the title-page of each dates it 1600. One was 'Printed by *I. R.* for Thomas Heys' (Q1); the other, its title-page claims, 'by *I. Roberts*' (Q2). Q2, thought until the twentieth century to be the earlier (and thus, as in the old Cambridge, frequently designated 'Q1'), is now known to be one of the falsely dated texts printed by the Jaggards for Thomas Pavier in 1619 (see the General Introduction). A third edition was included in the First Folio (F).

It seems certain that both Q2 and F were printed from copies of Q1: Q2 from a copy which contained the corrected state of G4^v; F from a copy with the uncorrected state. Q2 (like the other Pavier reprints) was extensively edited, though there is no reason to suppose its variants derive from any authoritative source. In the preparation of F, some theatrical manuscript appears to have been consulted: besides correcting some of Q1's more obvious errors, F adds a number of stage directions, chiefly music cues. It is unlikely, however, that consultation of this theatrical document went far, if at all, beyond the retrieval of stage directions: too many of Q1's flaws are preserved to warrant a hypothesis of a more thorough overhaul. For the same reason it is most unlikely that the copy of Q1 used in the preparation of F had itself been used in the theatre. However, isolated further consultation remains a possibility: the few instances of censorship evident in F (see Rejected Folio Variants 1.2.74/260, 1.2.107/293, and 5.1.157/2439) could derive from occasional reference to the theatrical document (which, had it been censored at all, would probably have been more thorough in its expurgation of the deity than is F); on the other hand, and perhaps more probably, these few alterations may reflect the efforts of the Folio editor to clean up the text. We provide a list of 'Rejected Folio Variants' which includes all substantive F variations from Q1 not adopted in our text.

With the possible exception of F's stage directions, then, Q1 is our only authority for *The Merchant of Venice*, and it is upon this edition that our text is based.

Nineteen copies of Q1 are known; one came to light only in the 1970s (see Gabler). Brown examined the six copies in England, but found no variants other than that on G inner (G4^r; 4.1.72-3/1881-2), which had long been known. He reports, however, that McManaway observed in the Huntington copy a variant state of K inner (K2^r; 5.1.300/2582). In both cases the earlier state appears to be the result of the compositor's error, and the later genuinely correct.

Though it is now generally agreed that the manuscript behind Q1 was very close to Shakespeare's own, its precise character remains uncertain: in all probability it was either a reasonably fair copy in Shakespeare's own hand, or a very accurate transcript of such a document.

Q1 appears to have been set by two compositors. The one whom Brown calls 'X' probably set sheets C, E, G, I, and K; the other, 'Y', probably set sheet A from its first page of text (2^r), and the whole of sheets B, D, F, and H. In other words,

1.1.0.1–2.1.17/0.1–514	was probably set by	Y
2.1.18–2.5.3/515–805		X
2.5.4–2.9.27/806–1084		Y
2.9.28–3.2.102/1085–1382		X
3.2.103–3.4.18/1383–1658		Y
3.4.19–4.1.140/1659–1949		X
4.1.141–423/1950–2232		Y
4.1.424–5.1.307/2233–2589		X

In eight scenes of the play Venetian gentlemen with maddeningly similar names appear. For the first five of these scenes (1.1/Sc. 1, 2.4/Sc. 7, 2.6/Sc. 9, 2.8/Sc. 11, and 3.1/Sc. 13) they are identified, but never in the dialogue, and so never to the audience, as 'Salerino' ('Salaryno', 'Salarino', 'Salari.', 'Saleri.', 'Salar.', 'Sala.', 'Sal.') and 'Solanio' ('Salanio', 'Solan.', 'Sola.', 'Sol.'). In 3.2/Sc. 14 a gentleman messenger whose four speech-prefixes are 'Sal.' is identified once in a stage direction and is addressed five times in the dialogue as 'Salerio'. Solanio reappears, all editors agree, in 3.3/Sc. 15, but two of the three references to him in this scene—none of which is in the dialogue—are in error ('Salerio' 3.3.0.1/1604.1, 'Sal.' 3.3.24/1628; only 'Sol.' 3.3.18/1622 is right). Salerio returns in 4.1/Sc. 18: though omitted from the scene's opening entry direction, both of his speeches are prefixed with the unabbreviated 'Salerio' (4.1.14/1823, 4.1.106/1915). Various solutions to this rather tedious problem have been proposed: we accept Wilson's, which maintains that Salerino and Salerio comprise a single character. Only when Shakespeare had occasion to identify this character to the audience, in the dialogue of 3.2/Sc. 14, does he appear to have decided on the name 'Salerio' (see Okamoto). We take this to represent the author's final wish on a matter of probably small concern to him, and view the seven surviving references to 'Salerino' in one or the other of its unabbreviated spellings in the earlier part of the play as a negligent oversight: the twenty-five other, abbreviated, references to the character in that earlier part of the play may as easily be read as abbreviations for 'Salerio' as for 'Salerino', and so would not have required alteration. We silently normalize all Salerino speech-prefixes to 'Salerio'. In stage directions, where we permit a wider range of spellings, we have altered 'Salarino', when that form occurs, to 'Salario'.

Two particularly striking peculiarities of Q1, both related to its printing, require comment. The first is the frequent use of lower-case letters initially in verse lines. These, which occur only sporadically in sheets A–C, but are numerous from D on, are usually explained as the result of a shortage of capitals in the printing house. We accept this explanation, and silently normalize them.

The other peculiarity is the superfluity of question marks. These too are usually explained as the result of a shortage of type. Since, however, they occur only on sheets G, I, and K, all identified as the work of one compositor, they may result from either a personal quirk or, as is more likely since they do not occur in sheets C and E (also set by him), from a shortage of stops and commas in his case only. These we selectively emend, noting our alterations among the incidentals.

Our subtitle, *'or otherwise called the Iew of Venyce'*, derives from the original Stationers' Register entry. This may merely reflect a popular alternative title for *The Merchant of Venice* (as *Beatrice and Benedick* seems to have been for *Much Ado*). But the *Merchant* entry appears to have been a staying entry, to prevent publication. If so, it must derive from the theatre, not from a bookseller, suggesting that members of Shakespeare's company regarded *The Jew of Venice* as an acceptable alternative title. *The Death of Robert Earl of Huntingdon* (BEPD 180) affords a parallel for the 'otherwise called' formula.

Q1 is undivided. Act divisions were first introduced by F and scene divisions by Rowe: these traditional act-scene divisions we follow.

No work by McKerrow on *The Merchant of Venice* survives. Alice Walker's edition of the play for the Oxford Shakespeare had reached an advanced state, however, and upon this typescript we have occasionally drawn.

W.L.M./(S.W.W.)

WORKS CITED

Brown, John Russell, 'The Compositors of *Hamlet* Q2 and *The Merchant of Venice*', SB 7 (1955), 17-40
—— ed., *The Merchant of Venice*, Arden (1955)
Clark, W. G., and William Aldis Wright, eds., *The Merchant of Venice*, Clarendon (1905)
Gabler, Hans Walter, '*Merchant of Venice* Preserved', N&Q, NS 25 (1978), 128-9
Kyd, Thomas, *The Spanish Tragedy*, edited by Philip Edwards, Revels (1959)
Noble, Richmond, *Shakespeare's Use of Song* (1923)
Okamoto, Yasumasa, '"The Three Sallies" Reconsidered: A Case Study in Shakespeare's Use of Proper Names', *Shakespeare Studies* [Tokyo], 15 (1976-7), 57-75
Wilson, John Dover, ed., *The Merchant of Venice*, New (1926)

TEXTUAL NOTES

Title The . . . Venyce] This edition (*after Q half-title and S.R. entry*); The comicall Hiftory of the Mer-|chant of Venice. Q (*half-title, sig. A2ʳ, and running title subs.*); The moft excellent | Hiftorie of the Merchant | of Venice. | With the extreame crueltie of *Shylocke* the Iewe | towards the fayd Merchant, in cutting a iuft pound | of his flefh: and the obtayning of *Portia* | by the choyfe of three | chefts. | *As it hath beene diuers times acted by the Lord | Chamberlaine his Seruants*. | Written by William Shakefpeare. Q (*title-page*); The Merchant of Venice F

1.1.19 Peering] Q (Piring)
1.1.27/27 Andrew decks] DELIUS (~, ~); ~ docks Q, F; ~ dock'd ROWE; Andrew's decks COLLIER (*conj.*). 'Rowe's emendation seems suspiciously like a mere makeshift. The verb "dock" is not elsewhere used by Shakespeare and was not, in any case, a common Elizabethan word. It suggests moreover a safer harbourage than that implied by the context. As the ship seems to be envisaged as completely overset, "decks" is in many ways more satisfactory than the usual emendation' (Walker).
1.1.113/113 Yet is] This edition (S.W.W.); It is Q, F; Is ROWE. The compositor may have misread a hastily written 'yet' as 'yt'.
1.2.46 An] Q (&)
1.2.58/243 Trassell] Q, F; Tassell F3; throstle POPE. 'It is doubtful whether Q1's spelling with "T" for "Th" should be allowed to stand. Neither *O.E.D.* nor *E.D.D.* quotes a parallel spelling and perhaps therefore we should read "Thrassell". Unfortunately the word does not occur sufficiently frequently to enable one to determine whether Q1's reading is certainly an error and it has been allowed to stand chiefly because it passed muster in both Q2 and F1. A printer's transposition in F2 to "Tarssell" led to "Tassell" in F3-Rowe' (Walker). 'Thrassell' is not recorded by *OED* before 1661.
1.2.86 An] Q (and)
1.2.120/306 foure] Q, F. The women have discussed six. This may be an authorial error, or it may be evidence of revision. Both positions have been defended.
1.3.23/339 water theeues, and land theeues, I meane Pyrats] Q, F; land-thieves and water-thieves I mean pirates SINGER (Eccles). Wilson adopts the transposition, but in view of the chiasmus at 3.1.58-9/1215-16 ('warmed and cooled by the same Winter and Sommer') there seems little need. Besides, Shylock may be punning here not only on 'rat', and thus 'pirate', but also on 'pier'—'I mean "pier-rats" '—who would be 'land-thieves', yet ones who plundered ships.
1.3.31/348 aside] WILSON; *not in* Q, F. Wilson observes that it would be most unlike Shylock to reveal his hate openly at this point: after all, he accepts an invitation to dinner later on (2.5/Sc. 8).
1.3.83 peeled] Q (pyld), F (pil'd)
1.3.59/376 ANTHONIO *Shylocke*] Q ('*An. Shylocke*' text); *Shylocke* Q (c.w.)
1.3.101/418 goodly] Q, F; godly ROWE
1.3.110/427 cut-throate,] HUDSON; ~ₐ Q, F
1.3.111 spit] Q, F (spet). Q's form relates to the verb *spete*, obsolete by the 16th c. *OED* records *spet* as an alternative spelling of both *spit* and *spat*: given that *call* in the previous line is in present tense, we modernize to *spit*.
1.3.124 spat] Q, F (spet). See the preceding note. Here, given the sense and that both *spurned* and *called* (1.3.125, 126/442, 443) are in the past tense, we modernize *spet* to *spat*.
1.3.125/442 day,] F (~;); ~ₐ Q
1.3.125/442 time,] F; ~, Q
1.3.152 the Jew] Q. Capell suggests as an alternative modernization 'thee, Jew'.

2.1.0.1/497.1 *Flourish Cornets*] F (*Flo. ~*); not in Q. F centres the direction on a separate line, after '*traine*'.
2.1.26 Suleiman] Q (Solyman)
2.1.28 heart] Q (hart), F
2.1.31 the lady] Q, F; POPE modernizes to 'thee, lady'. Walker observes: 'Editors from F2-Rowe apparently took "the" as the definite article: F2 generally distinguished between "the" and "thee"'. Michael J. Warren ('A Note on *The Merchant of Venice*, II.i.31', *SQ* 32 (1981), 104–5) suggests that Morocco, who uses 'the lady' several times in 2.7/Sc. 10, may address only the first few lines of this speech directly to Portia; the rest of the speech (from 'By this Symitare', 2.1.24/521) may be, as are many of his speeches in the later scene, a publicly addressed declamation.
2.1.35/532 rage] Q, F; page POPE 2 (Theobald, *Shakespeare Restored*); wag WILSON; rogue SISSON; rag GALLOWAY (conj., in *N&Q* 201 (1956), 330–1)
2.1.46.1/543.1 *Flourish Cornets*] F ('*Cornets*', after 2.1.45/542); not in Q
2.2.3–8/546–51 Iobbo] Q2 (Gobbo); Iobbe Q1, F. Probably a compositor's misreading.
2.2.9 Via] Q (*fia*)
2.2.90/634 hase] Q (haſe). Presumably 'has'. 'The spelling is curious in a printed book of this date but the final "e" was clearly deliberate (as the use of long s shows) and it seems therefore best to leave it as it may represent a MS. spelling' (Walker).
2.2.93/637 last] Q2; loſt Q1, F
2.2.170/714 a sute] Q2, F; ſute Q1. The phrase *I have a suit* is used twice elsewhere in the canon (*Contention* 4.7.3/2458, *Othello* 3.3.81/1529); variants of the phrase are used twice elsewhere ('had a suite', *2 Henry IV* 5.1.64/2756; 'hath a suite', *Caesar* 2.4.44/1083); nowhere else is anything like *I have suit* used. The error, dropping the 'a', would be an easy one.
2.4.5/768 as] F4; vs Q, F. While QF may be right—the phrase *spoke us* meaning, as Capell commented, *bespoke us*—as here seems the more idiomatic reading. Shakespeare nowhere else uses *spoke us* in Capell's sense, and an a/u misreading, especially in Shakespeare's hand, would have been easy.
2.4.8 o'clock] Q (of clocke)
2.4.9/772 *with a Letter*] F; not in Q
2.4.14 Love-news] Q1 (Loue, newes); ~ˏ~ Q2, F. Q1's comma seems to function as a hyphen. See the note to 2.9.100/1157.
2.4.21/784 Goe.] THEOBALD (~. —); ~ˏ Q, F
2.5.28/830 there] Q; their F
2.5.42 Jewës] Q (Iewes), F. Often modernized to 'Jewess''. However, *Jew* is common gender in Shakespeare; the expression *a Jew's eye* was proverbial for something of great value (Tilley J 53); and the disyllabic pronunciation of the possessive required here is paralleled in *The Travels of the Three English Brothers* (1607): 'Of a *Iewes* feaſt, is a Chriſtians heart:' (F1ᵛ, 6); 'A Chriſtians torture, is a *Iewes* bliſſe,' (F1ᵛ, 27).
2.6.14/872 younker] ROWE; younger Q, F (yonger). Q may be right: *younger* was fairly commonly used substantively in the sense of 'young person' and, as Wilson observes, receives some support from the allusion in 2.6.16, 19/874, 877 to 'the strumpet wind', possibly a reference 'to the harlots with whom the "younger", or Prodigal, wasted his substance'. But, juxtaposed as it is with *prodigal* (2.6.17/875), Q's *younger* seems feebly repetitious.

Q cannot be explained simply as a compositorial misreading of manuscript 'younker', however: all recorded forms of *younker* (from the Dutch or German *jonker* or *junker* = young nobleman) include a 'k', and 'g' for 'k' is a virtually impossible misreading. If Shakespeare had meant *younker* we must suppose he would have written it with a 'k' (as he appears to have in *Duke of Yorke* 2.1.24/606, 'Yonker', a foul papers text). But while Q cannot be a misreading of MS 'younker', it may well represent a compositorial simplification, the substitution of a more familiar word for an unfamiliar one. This is what we suppose—that Shakespeare wrote *younker* for which the compositor substituted the feebler, but more familiar, 'younger'.
2.6.19.1/877.1 *with a torch*] This edition; not in Q. We presume Lorenzo gives this to Jessica on her entrance 'below'

(2.6.57.1/915.1); alternatively, she, and not Lorenzo, may enter '*with a torch*'.
2.6.24/882 therein] This edition (G.T.); then Q. Our emendation, meaning 'in that affair', 'in that circumstance' (*adv.* 2), improves the line's metre and is paralleled elsewhere in Shakespeare's works.
2.6.25 Ho] Q (Howe), F (Hoa). See 5.1.109.
2.6.51 gentile] Q (gentle), F
2.6.58/916 gentlemen] Q2, F; gentleman Q1
2.7.12 withal] Q (withall); *possibly* with all
2.7.18/943 threatens,] ROWE (~.); ~ˏ Q, F
2.7.69/994 tombes] CAPELL (Johnson); timber Q, F. *Timber* can be used as a plural noun (*sb.*¹ 6), but a monosyllable is, metrically, to be preferred. In support of Johnson's conjecture Malone cited Sonnet 101, line 11, 'gilded tombe', and Wilson compared Matthew 23: 27 (Bishops'): 'for ye are lyke vnto paynted ſepulchres [Geneva: whited *or, painted*) tombes], which indeede appear beautiful outward: but are within ful of dead (*mens*) bones, and of all filthyneſſe'. Brown observes that *gilded* and *painted* are linked in *Richard II* 1.1.179/179: 'Men are but guilded loame, or painted clay.' To misread '*tombes*' as '*timber*' would be easy.
2.7.77.1/1002.1 *Flourish Cornets*] F; not in Q. 'F1 (followed by F2–4) has the stage direction "*Flo. Cornets*" after the entry of Salarino and [Solanio] in the next scene where there can be no doubt that a Flourish is misplaced... Capell removed it to the beginning of this scene and Dyce adopted it here as well where, perhaps, it ought to have been printed in F1' (Walker).
2.8.12/1016 SOLANIO I] Q ('*Sol. I*' text); I (c.w.)
2.8.39/1043 Sluber] Q2, F (Slubber); ſlumber Q1
2.8.42/1046 minde of loue] Q, F. Walker, finding the repetition of the phrase 'of loue' at the end of line 2.8.44/1048 awkward, noted Heath's suggestion that on its first occurrence, here, it means *please, I beseech you*. *OED* (*love, sb.* 7b), however, does not support this suggestion. Most editors print as in Q, and gloss 'minde of loue' as 'loving mind': with this interpretation we concur.
2.9.47/1104 chaft] Q; chaffe F. *OED* does not record 'chaft' as a variant spelling of the noun *chaff*. Walker observes that the Q spelling is probably not a compositorial error for 'chaff' since it requires the two typepieces 'f' and 't' rather than the single 'ff' ligature. Nor is it very likely the result of a foul-case error for 'chafe', another unrecorded form, which requires the implausible e/t error. Probably the terminal 't' is correct: see Cercignani, p. 315.
2.9.48/1105 varnist] Q; varniſht F. Q's form, probably deliberate since the ſt ligature was used, appears to have been acceptable: *OED* records (*varnished, ppl. a.* 1) another occurrence in 1599. Shakespeare uses the word only twice elsewhere; in both cases it is spelt 'varniſht'.
2.9.100/1157 Bassanio, Lord loue] ROWE; ~ˏ ~, ~ Q. Cupid ('Lord loue') is mentioned in the previous line. In defence of Q, however, Brown observes 'It is just possible that Q's "Bassanio Lord" stands for Lord Bassanio, and that Nerissa, apostrophizing, says that he may love if he wishes, because it is clear, from her eagerness, that Portia would reciprocate'. It may be, however, that Q's comma here functions as a hyphen, as in 2.4.14/777.
3.1.19/1177 my] Q, F; thy THEOBALD
3.1.20.1/1177.1 *Enter Shylocke*] Shylock may begin to enter even earlier, immediately after 3.1.18/1175.
3.1.69/1226 MAN] ROWE (*subs.*); not in Q, F
3.1.71.1/1229.1 *Enter Tuball*] Q, F. 'The duplication of this entry after [3.1.73.1/1231.2] in Q1 may be due to a prompter's having moved back the belated entry at [3.1.73.1/1231.2] without marking the latter for deletion' (Walker).
3.1.99/1258 heard] NEILSON-HILL (Kellner); heere Q, F (here); where? ROWE. It would have been easy for the compositor to mistake a terminal manuscript 'd' for 'e': this may in turn have led him to see a medial 'a' as an 'e', or to alter, deliberately, medial 'ea' to 'ee'. *OED* does not record the form 'heerd', though,

of course, it remains possible that this was what stood in the manuscript.

3.1.106/1265 sweare,] Q (*the comma is uncertain*); ~ₐ F
3.2.19/1299 Puts] Q, F; Put F2. See Abbott, 333.
3.2.22 piece] Q (peize)
3.2.61/1341 liue.] JOHNSON; ~ₐ Q, F
3.2.62.1/1342.1 *Here Musicke.*] F; *not in* Q. Portia's frequent calls for music in the preceding speech may be in reference to an unaccompanied song, but this is unlikely.
3.2.63, 67/1343, 1347 ONE FROM PORTIAS TRAYNE] This edition; *not in* Q, F. Editors have not usually assigned prefixes to the two stanzas of this song. Capell is here an exception: to line 3.2.63/1343 he prefixed '1. V.' and to line 3.2.67/1347 '2. V.', presumably meaning to indicate the two voices.
3.2.66/1346 ALL] WILSON (Lawrence); *not in* Q, F. Q prints '*Replie, replie*' on the same line as '*How . . . nourished?*' This suggested to W. J. Lawrence that the phrase was a refrain, to be sung by 'All'. Lawrence's suggestion first appeared in Noble (p. 49).
3.2.67/1347 eyes] F; eye Q. The first stanza establishes a three-rhyme pattern, which F, but not Q, follows in the second stanza.
3.2.71/1351 *Ile begin it*] JOHNSON (subs.); *in roman, as if not part of the song* Q, F. Johnson was the first to include this in the song.
3.2.81 vice] Q (voyce). See Brown's note to this line and Cercignani, p. 245.
3.2.93/1373 makes] F; maketh Q; make POPE
3.2.101/1381 Therefore thou] Q2; Therefore then thou Q1, F. Shakespeare nowhere else uses *therefore then*. Probably, as Wilson observes (in his note to 3.2.101), the 'misprint ["then"] and the correction ["thou"] have been left side by side'.
3.2.106/1386 palenes] Q, F; plainness THEOBALD. Greg suggested to Wilson that manuscript '"plaines" was accidentally misprinted "paliness" and was then wrongly corrected' (Wilson's note to 3.2.106). Brown, however, defends 'palenes', and concludes with Malone's suggestion that the 'Thy' earlier in this line should be stressed.
3.2.110 shudd'ring] Q (ſhyddring), F (ſhuddring)
3.2.112 rain] Q (raine), F; *possibly* rein COLLIER 2 (Johnson)
3.2.139/1419 A] Q; Baſſ. A F. The Q word begins a new page (F1ᵛ); the catchword on the previous page is '*Baſſ.*'
3.2.199/1479 I lou'd, . . . intermission,] THEOBALD (subs.); ~ₐ . . . ~, Q, F. 'Q's pointing is defensible if *intermission* can mean relief, pastime; then [the next line] would mean "my lot is the same as yours"' (Brown).
3.2.204 roof] Q (rough), F
3.2.235/1515 indicating] This edition; *not in* Q. See the note to *Contention* 1.3.184.1/550.1.
3.2.283 Cush] Q (Chus). Cush was the son of Ham (Genesis 10: 6).
3.2.300/1580 thorough] STEEVENS 2; through Q, F
3.3.0.1/1604.1 *Salanio*] F (*Solanio*); *Salerio* Q. The Q error may have resulted from the compositor erroneously expanding a manuscript abbreviation (either a careless 'Sal', which is what we assume, or 'Sol' which, in Shakespeare's hand, could easily be mistaken for 'Sal').
3.4.23/1663 heere other things.] THEOBALD subs. (Thirlby); heere other things, Q; here other things, F3
3.4.23 hear] Q (heere), F. See the previous note.
3.4.49/1689 Padua] THEOBALD; Mantua Q, F. QF probably represents Shakespeare's error: elsewhere in the play (4.1.108, 118, 5.1.268/1917, 1927, 2550) Bellario is placed in Padua. Civil Law was studied in the University of Padua.
3.4.50/1690 cosins hands] Q2; coſin hand Q1; coſins hand F. Shakespeare uses the forms '*into somebody's hand*' and '*into somebody's hands*' interchangeably. The errors presumed by Q2 (a dropped terminal 's') and F (transposition) are equally plausible. Once elsewhere in this play (3.4.24/1664) Shakespeare uses the formula, and there he employs *hands*. This tilts us in favour of Q2 here.
3.4.53/1693 Traiect] ROWE; Tranect Q, F. The proposed misreading, 'an' for manuscript 'ai', would be very easy: Shakespeare's spurred 'a' could well be mistaken for 'a-minim', which in turn,

when followed by the single minim of an 'i', could be read 'a-minim-minim' or 'an'.

3.4.82/1722 my] F; my my Q
3.5.20 e'en] Q (in)
3.5.26/1750 comes.] Q2, F; come? Q
3.5.72/1796 merrit it] POPE (subs.); meane it, Q1, F; winne it G. JOICEY conj. in *N&Q*, 8th series, 2 (1892), 445. The error probably resulted from misreading; 'merrit' occurs twice elsewhere in *Merchant* (2.9.38, 42/1095, 1099).
3.5.79/1803 for a] F; for Q
4.1.0.2/1809.2 *Salerio*] CAPELL (SALERINO, Solanio, *and Others*); *not in* Q, F
4.1.29/1838 his] Q2, F; this Q1
4.1.29/1838 state] Q2, F; ſtates Q1. The easy misreading would have been suggested by the previous one (see the preceding note).
4.1.30/1839 flint] Q2; flints Q1, F
4.1.49/1858 vrine.] CAPELL (Thirlby); ~ₐ Q, F
4.1.49/1858 affection,] CAPELL (Thirlby); ~. Q, F
4.1.50/1859 Mʳˢ] This edition; Maiſters Q, F; Mistress CAPELL (Thirlby); Master JOHNSON (Thirlby)
4.1.50 Mistress] See the previous note.
4.1.55/1864 woollen] Q, F. Various emendations have been proposed, a number of which—including Capell's conjecture 'wauling' and Cartwright's 'wailing'—seek to change the reference from the bagpipe's appearance to its sound. But 'woollen' makes perfectly good sense, and to emend here would come closer to improving than to restoring Shakespeare.
4.1.72/1881 You may as] Q1b, Q2; *not in* Q1a; Or euen as F
4.1.72/1881 Woolfe,] Q1a, Q2, F; Woolfeₐ Q1b
4.1.73/1882 Why he hath made] Q1b, Q2; *not in* Q1a, F
4.1.73/1882 bleate] F; bleake Q. Shakespeare uses the form 'bleak(e)' seven times, always, except here, to mean modern *bleak*; he uses 'bleat(e)' three times, always to mean modern *bleat*. It seems more probable that Q 'bleake' is here an error for 'bleate' than that it equals the dialectal word *blake* (= *bleat*).
4.1.74/1883 Pines] F; of Pines Q
4.1.99/1908 tis] Q2, F; as Q1; is CAPELL. 'The letters *ti* might conceivably be misread as an open *a* with an initial overhead stroke' (Wilson's note to 4.1.100).
4.1.119/1928 both,] Q2 (~,); ~? Q1; ~. F
4.1.121/1930 forfait] ROWE 3; forfaiture Q, F
4.1.122 sole . . . soul] HANMER (F: 'ſoale . . . ſoule'); ſoule . . . ſoule Q
4.1.127/1936 inexorable] F3; inexecrable Q, F. No meaningful parallel for Q is known. The form has been found in three other texts: the 1592 quarto of Kyd's *Spanish Tragedy* (3.12.46), which Philip Edwards, the play's Revels editor, believes to be a misprint for *inexplicable*; Constable's *Diana* (1594), where it is generally thought to be a misprint for *inexorable*; and *Grim the Collier of Croydon* (c.1600, pub. 1662; BEPD 826), where it appears to be a malapropism for *inexorable* (see Ralph Leavis, '"Inexecrable": A Fourth Occurrence?', *N&Q*, NS 29 (1982), 129).
4.1.149/1958 Your] Q, F; Cle⟨rk⟩. [*reads.*] *Your* CAPELL. There is no reason to suppose a clerk reads the letter: the repeated speech-prefix (4.1.164/1973) is not unusual in Q following read matter (see, for example, the incidentals emendations to 999, 1129, and the textual note to 3.2.139/1419).
4.1.227/2036 No] Q2, F; Not Q1
4.1.253 I] Q, F; Ay, BROWN (*conj.*)
4.1.359 formerly] Q (formorly), F; formally HANMER
4.1.393/2202 not] Q2; not to Q, F
4.1.395/2204 GRATIANO] Q2, F; Shy⟨locke⟩. Q1
4.1.420/2229 as] Q, F; as a Q2.
4.1.423/2232 *to Anthonio*] CAMBRIDGE; *not in* Q, F. It may be, however, that Portia speaks to Bassanio throughout, and that, as Wilson observed, 'The gloves are asked for in order that the ring may be exposed to view.' But 'It seems natural that as Antonio had been requested to "gratify" his deliverer [4.1.403/2212], Portia should take something from him as well as from Bassanio, whose obligation was less . . . The emphatic

THE MERCHANT OF VENICE

"you," closing line [4.1.424/2233], seems also to bear out our interpretation' (Clark and Wright).
4.2.0.1/2263.1 *Portia and*] F; *not in* Q
4.2.19.1/2282.1 *Exeunt*] F; *not in* Q
5.1.41/2323 *M. Lorenzo sola*] Q2; & *M. Lorenzo sola* Q, F; *and M. Lorenza, sola* F2; *and Mrs. Lorenza, sola* F3
5.1.48-9/2330-1 morning. | LORENZO Sweete soule, let's] STEEVENS-REED; morning sweete soule. | *Loren⟨zo⟩*. Let's Q, F. Rowe is the first to assign the epithet to Lorenzo, but he emends 'soule' to 'Love'.
5.1.51/2333 *Stephano*] Q2; *Stephen* Q1, F. Wilson (in his note to 5.1.52) suggests that Q1 may represent a compositor's expansion of 'Steph.' in his copy.
5.1.65/2347 it in] Q1; in it Q2, F
5.1.87/2369 *Erebus*] F (*Erobus*); *Terebus* Q
5.1.109 ho] Q (how). See 2.6.25.
5.1.109/2391 *Musicke ceases*] F; *not in* Q. F places the direction after 'awak'd', line 5.1.110/2392.
5.1.121.1/2403.1 *A Tucket sounds*] F; *not in* Q
5.1.152/2434 it] Q2, F; *not in* Q1
5.1.179/2461 *to Portia*] This edition; *not in* Q. This speech may be addressed to Nerissa.
5.1.233/2515 my bedfellow] Q2, F; mine bedfellow Q1. Though Q1 may be correct, Q2, F seems the superior reading. 'Mine' could have been caught from the previous line.
5.1.300/2582 intergotory] Qb, F (intergatory); intergory Qa

REJECTED FOLIO VARIANTS

1.1.87/87 tis] it is
1.1.93/93 sir Oracle] sir an Oracle
1.1.115/115 are as] are
1.1.155/155 me now] *not in* F
1.2.7/192 meane] smal
1.2.16/201 then to] then
1.2.20/206 reasoning] reason
1.2.21/206 the fashion] fashion
1.2.22-3/208 who . . . who] whom . . . whom
1.2.24/210 is it] it is
1.2.42/227 afeard] afraid
1.2.49/234 rather] rather to
1.2.62/247 shall] should
1.2.74/260 Scottish] other
1.2.107/293 pray God graunt] wish
1.2.119/305 How nowe, what newes] *not in* F
1.3.48/365 well-wone] well-worne
1.3.63/380 ye] he
1.3.121/438 can] should
1.3.132/449 for] of
1.3.135/452 penaltie] penalties
1.3.150/467 bodie] bodie it
1.3.177/494 The] This
1.3.178/495 termes] teames
2.1.30/527 a] he
2.2.26/569 but] *not in* F
2.2.52/595 sir] *not in* F
2.2.175/719 faults,] ~ ;
2.2.176/720 thou art] they are
2.3.9/751 in] *not in* F
2.3.13/755 somthing] somewhat
2.4.11/774 it shal seeme] shall it seeme
2.5.1/803 shalt] shall
2.5.46/848 and] but
2.6.2/860 make] make a
2.6.6/864 seale] steale
2.6.44/902 are you] you are
2.7.4/929 This] The
2.7.5/930 many] *not in* F
2.7.41/966 vastie] vaste
2.8.6/1010 came] comes
2.9.7/1064 you] thou
2.9.45/1102 peasantry] pleasantry
3.1.6/1163 gossip] gossips
3.1.28/1185 fledge] fledg'd
3.1.34/1191 my blood] bloud
3.1.54/1211 his] the
3.1.85/1243 whats] how much is
3.2.17/1297 if] of
3.2.33/1313 doe] doth
3.2.61/1341 much much] much
3.2.149/1429 me] my
3.2.158/1438 something] nothing
3.2.159/1439 vnlessond . . . vnpractized] vnlessoned . . . vnpractiz'd
3.2.171/1451 Lords] Lord
3.2.196/1476 haue] gaue
3.2.209/1489 is, so] is so, so
3.2.215.1-2/1495.1-2 *a messenger from Venice*] *not in* F
3.2.317/1597 but see] see
3.3.2/1606 lent] lends
3.5.5/1730 a] of
3.5.30/1754 there's] there is
3.5.73/1797 In] Is
4.1.21/1830 exacts] exact'st
4.1.42/1851 aunswerd] answered
4.1.64/1873 answers] answer
4.1.76/1885 fretten] fretted
4.1.78/1887 what's] what
4.1.141/1950 curelesse] endlesse
4.1.143/1952 to] in
4.1.166/1975 come] Came
4.1.201/2010 Court] course
4.1.221/2030 I doe] do I
4.1.224/2033 offred] offered
4.1.255/2064 doe] should
4.1.256/2065 Is it so] It is not
4.2.260/2069 You] Come
4.1.275/2084 but] not
4.1.287/2096 who] whom
4.1.305/2114 Take then] Then take
4.1.324/2133 be it but] be it
4.1.331/2140 you] thee
4.1.341/2150 so taken] taken so
4.1.395/2204 shalt thou] thou shalt
4.1.398/2207 home with me] with me home
4.1.448/2257 gainst] against
5.1.34/2316 is] it
5.1.37/2319 vs] vs vs
5.1.51/2333 I] *not in* F
5.1.62/2344 eyde] eyed
5.1.82/2364 the time] time
5.1.153/2435 your] the
5.1.157/2439 no Gods my Iudge] but wel I know
5.1.209/2491 my honour] mine honor
5.1.220/2502 For] And
5.1.233/2515 that] the
5.1.249/2531 his] thy
5.1.258/2540 me] *not in* F
5.1.272/2554 euen but] but eu'n
5.1.303/2585 bed,] ~ ,

INCIDENTALS

57 Here] *Sola.* Here 112 tõgue] togue 564 who (God)] ~ ~ 585 mee] Q (*text*); me Q (*c.w.*) 618 murder] muder 668 catercosins.] ~, 691 Sonne.] ~‸ 759 ashamde] aſhamed 768 Torch-bearers.] ~, 801 peruſe] pervſe 860 Desir'd] defired 999 Cold] *Mor.* Cold 1042 aunswerd] aunſwered 1120 iudgement] iudement 1129 Still] *Arrag.* Still 1348 *dies*‸] ~ : 1349 lies:] ~‸ 1354 ornament.] ~, 1460 multitude,] ~. 1492 honord] honored 1660 soule,] ~ ; 1661 cruelty;] ~, 1671 Monastery] Monaſtry 1752 corners.] ~ ? 1761 *Launcelet.*] ~ ? 1768 dinner.] ~ ? 1769 stomacks.] ~ ? 1771 dinner.] ~ ? 1797 heauen.] ~ ? 1804 that.] ~ ? 1805 dinner.] ~ ? 1806 stomack.] ~ ? 1809 it.] ~ ? 1810 grace.] ~ ? 1826 leadst] leadeſt 1842 Iewe.] ~ ? 1847 freedome.] ~ ? 1850 that.] ~ ? 1855 pigge.] ~ ? 1856 Cat,] ~ ? 1862 pigge,] ~ ? 1863 Cat,] ~ ? 1870 him.] ~ ? 1872 cruelty.] ~ ? 1873 answers.] ~ ? 1876 first.] ~ ? 1888 hart.] ~ ? 1891 will.] ~ ? 1892 sixe.] ~ ? 1895 bond.] ~ ? 1915 day.] ~ ? 1917 Padua.] ~ ? 1918 letters.] ~ ? 1918 Messenger.] ~ ? 1919 *Anthonio.*] ~ ? 1921 blood.] ~ ? 1926 Epitaph.] ~ ? 1928 grace.] ~ ? 1930 there.] ~ ? 1973 You] Duke. You 2048 Bond.] ~, 2155 prou'd] proued 2166 contriud] contriued 2235 this.] ~ ? 2237 this.] ~ ? 2239 it.] ~ ? 2243 me.] ~ ? 2267 *Lorenzo.*] ~ ? 2282 you] yov 2300 lou'd] loued 2308 friend.] ~ ? 2338 eares.] ~‸ 2362 floods,] ~. 2364 nature.] ~, 2366 moud] moued 2374 candle.] ~ ? 2380 house.] ~ ? 2382 day.] ~ ? 2383 Madam.] ~ ? 2388 Renne.] ~ ? 2395 voyce.] ~ ? 2395 home.] ~ ? 2400 comming.] ~ ? 2473 ring.] ~ ? 2474 mine.] ~ ? 2480 displeasure.] ~ ? 2490 ring.] ~ ? 2504 Doctor.] ~ ?

QUARTO STAGE DIRECTIONS

1.1.0.1/0.1 Enter *Anthonio, Salaryno,* and *Salanio.*
1.1.56.1/56.1 Enter *Bassanio, Lorenso,* and *Gratiano.*
1.1.68.1/68.1 *Exeunt Salarino, and Solanio.*
1.1.112.1/112.1 *Exeunt.*
1.1.185.1/185.1 *Exeunt.*
1.2.0.1/185.2 Enter *Portia* with her wayting woman *Nerrissa.*
1.2.118.1/304.1 Enter a Seruingman. (after 1.2.119/305)
1.2.131/317 *Exeunt*
1.3.0.1/317.1 Enter *Bassanio* with *Shylocke* the Iew.
1.3.35.1/352.1 Enter *Anthonio.* (after 1.3.37/354)
1.3.176/493 *Exit.* (after 'you')
1.3.180/497 *Exeunt.*
2.1.0.1-4/497.1-3 Enter *Morochus* a tawnie Moore all in white, and three | or foure followers accordingly, with *Portia,* | *Nerrissa,* and their traine.
2.1.46.1/543.1 *Exeunt.*
2.2.0.1/543.2 *Enter the Clowne alone.*
2.2.29.1/572.1 Enter old Gobbo with a basket.
2.2.105.1/649.1 Enter Bassanio *with a follower or two.* (after 2.2.107/651)
2.2.162/706.1 *Exit Clowne.*
2.2.167.1/711.1 *Enter Gratiano.*
2.2.168/712.1 *Exit Leonardo.* (after 2.2.167/711)
2.2.198/742.1 *Exeunt.*
2.3.0.1/742.2 *Enter Iessica and the Clowne.*
2.3.21/763 *Exit.*
2.4.0.1/763.1 *Enter Gratiano, Lorenso, Salaryno, and Salanio.*
2.4.9/772 *Enter Launcelet.* (after 'newes')
2.4.21/784 *Exit Clowne.* (after 2.4.23/786)
2.4.27/790 *Exit.*
2.4.39/802 *Exeunt.*
2.5.0.1-2/802.1-2 *Enter Iewe and his man that was the Clowne.*
2.5.9.1/811.1 *Enter Iessica.*
2.5.54.1/856.1 *Exit.*
2.5.56.1/858.1 *Exit.*
2.6.0.1/858.2 *Enter the maskers, Gratiano and Salerino.*
2.6.19.1/877.1 *Enter Lorenzo.*
2.6.25.1/883.1 *Iessica aboue.*
2.6.57.1/915.1 *Enter Iessica.*
2.6.59.1/917.1 *Exit.*
2.6.59.2/917.2 *Enter Anthonio.*
2.6.67/925 *Exeunt.*
2.7.0.1-2/925.1-2 Enter *Portia* with *Morrocho* and both | theyr traines.
2.7.77.1/1002.1 *Exit.*
2.7.79.1/1004.1 *Exeunt.*
2.8.0.1/1004.2 *Enter Salarino and Solanio.*
2.8.53/1057 *Exeunt.*
2.9.0.1/1057.1 *Enter Nerrissa* and a Seruiture.
2.9.3.2-3/1060.2-3 Enter *Arrogon,* his trayne, and *Portia.*

2.9.83.2/1140.2 *Enter Messenger.*
2.9.100/1157 *Exeunt.*
3.1.0.1/1157.1 *Solanio and Salarino.*
3.1.20.1/1177.1 Enter *Shylocke.* (after 3.1.22/1179)
3.1.68.1/1225.1 Enter a man from Anthonio.
3.1.71.1/1229.1 *Enter Tuball.*
3.1.73.1/1231.1-2 *Exeunt Gentlemen.*
[3.1.73.2/1231.3] *Enter Tuball.* (duplicating 3.1.71.1/1229.1)
3.1.121/1280 *Exeunt.*
3.2.0.1-2/1280.1-2 Enter *Bassanio, Portia, Gratiano,* and all | their traynes.
3.2.62.1-2/1342.1-2 *A Song the whilst Bassanio comments on the caskets | to himselfe.*
3.2.215.1-2/1495.1-2 Enter *Lorenzo, Iessica,* and *Salerio* a messenger | from Venice. (after 3.2.217/1497)
3.2.234.1/1514.1 open the letter.
3.2.324/1604 *Exeunt.*
3.3.0.1-2/1604.1-2 Enter the *Iew,* and *Salerio,* and *Anthonio,* | and the Iaylor.
3.3.17/1621 *Exit Iew.*
3.3.36/1640 *Exeunt.*
3.4.0.1-2/1640.1-2 Enter *Portia, Nerrissa, Lorenzo, Iessica,* and a | man of *Portias.*
3.4.44.1/1684.1 *Exeunt.*
3.4.85/1725 *Exeunt.*
3.5.0.1/1725.1 *Enter Clowne and Iessica.*
3.5.24.1/1748.1 *Enter Lorenzo.*
3.5.59/1783 *Exit Clowne.*
3.5.85/1809 *Exeunt.*
4.1.0.1-2/1809.1-2 Enter the Duke, the *Magnificoes, Anthonio, Bassanio,* | and *Gratiano.*
4.1.14.1/1823.1 *Enter Shylocke.*
4.1.117.1/1926.1 *Enter Nerrissa.*
4.1.163.1/1972.1 Enter *Portia* for *Balthazer.*
4.1.397.1/2206.1 *Exit.*
4.1.404.1/2213.1 Exit Duke and his traine.
4.1.445.1/2254.1 *Exeunt.*
4.1.451.1/2260.1 *Exit Gratiano.*
4.1.454/2263 *Exeunt.*
4.2.0.1/2263.1 *Enter Nerrissa.*
4.2.4.1/2267.1 *Enter Gratiano.*
5.1.0.1/2282.2 *Enter Lorenzo and Iessica.*
5.1.24.1/2306.1 *Enter a Messenger.*
5.1.38.1/2320.1 *Enter Clowne.*
5.1.68.1/2350.1 play Musique.
5.1.88.1/2370.1 *Enter Portia and Nerrissa.*
5.1.126.1-2/2408.1-2 Enter *Bassanio, Anthonio, Gratiano,* and their | followers.
5.1.307/2589 *Exeunt.*

1 HENRY IV

1 Henry IV (BEPD 145) was entered in the Stationers' Register on 25 February 1598:

Andrew Wyſe /. Entred for his Copie vnder thandͤ of Mʳ Dix: and Mʳ Warden Man a booke intituled The hiſtorye of Henry the iiijᵗʰ wᵗʰ his battaile at Shrewſburye againſt Henry Hottſpurre of the Northe wᵗʰ the conceipted mirthe of Sʳ Iohn Falſtoff

Of the earliest quarto, only a fragment of a single copy (Folger) is known to be extant. It consists of Sheet C, and supplies copy for 1.3.199-2.3.19/516-818 in this edition. The quarto has hitherto been known as Q0; it is here referred to as Q1, with the result that later quartos are numbered one higher than has been customary. Q1 probably appeared in Wise's shop shortly after the S.R. entry, for a second edition, Q2, was brought out before the end of (old style) 1598. Q2, which supplies the most authoritative text for all of the play except 1.3.199-2.3.19/516-818, was printed for Wise by Peter Short; it appears to be a fairly accurate reprint of Q1 (which had been set from the same fount), but has been cast off anew to save space and notably omits 'fat' at 2.3.19/818. Jackson ('Two Shakespeare Quartos') identified two compositors, but Zimmerman has since argued that a single compositor worked on the entire quarto, probably setting at least part of it by formes. Greg and Hinman record three minor press variants.

Later derivative quartos are: Q3 (1599), Q4 (1604), Q5 (1608), Q6 (1613), Q7 (1622), and Q8 (1632). Qq4-7 were published by Matthew Law, to whom the title was transferred on 25 June 1603. Q6 provided the printers with copy for the First Folio text (F). Sir Edward Dering's early seventeenth-century manuscript adaptation of the two parts of *Henry IV*, based mostly on *1 Henry IV*, appears to have no independent authority.

It has sometimes been thought that Q1 was set from Shakespeare's papers. The stage directions are authorial in character, and it is not plausible that the manuscript served as a prompt-book. But the following evidence builds up to a positive indication of scribal copy:

1. Q consistently departs from Shakespeare's preference *between* in favour of *betwixt* (Jackson, 'Two Shakespeare Quartos').

2. Up to 1600 Shakespeare evidently favoured *pray thee*; in Q *1 Henry IV*, *prithee* predominates overwhelmingly (Jackson, 'The Manuscript Copy').

3. According to Waller, outside the Fletcherian scenes of *All Is True* and *Two Noble Kinsmen*, there is a higher incidence of *ye* and *y'* than in any other play in the canon. *1 Henry IV* has 29; other relatively higher-counting plays, all collaborative and/or early, are *1 Henry VI* (23), *Titus* (21), *Contention* (20). These contrast with plays of the same period set from foul papers: *2 Henry IV* (5), *Henry V* (2).

4. Outside the Fletcher collaborations and three plays printed by Simmes, the most authoritative texts of Shakespeare's plays prefer *I* (*ay*) to *yea* by 775 to 125 (see note to *Richard III* 1.3.98/510). In *1 Henry IV* the preference is markedly reversed: the eight instances of *I* to 21 of *yea* give a ratio which varies from the normal distribution by a factor of over 16.

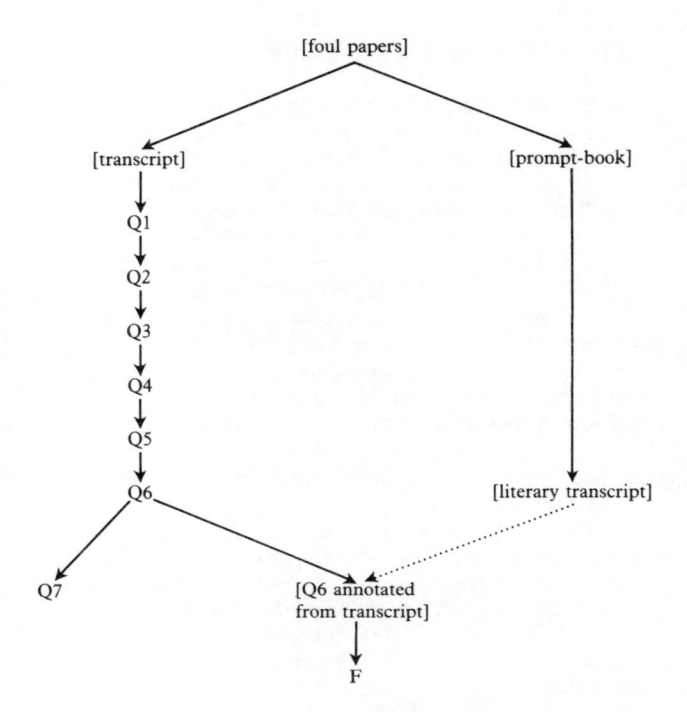

5. There are eight examples of the *-eth* inflexion of verbs in the stage directions of *1 Henry IV*; in the remaining substantive texts of the canon there are only another 16. Three of those other examples occur in Act 1 of *1 Henry VI* (probably written by Thomas Nashe); another four examples occur in *All Is True*, where they may be due to collaboration with Fletcher. No other play has more than two examples. The quarto of *1 Henry IV* thus strikingly departs from a consistent pattern in all other Shakespeare texts.

6. The quarto is also unusual in its treatment of entrance or exit directions which contain two or more names. On ten occasions it does not join these names together with 'and' or 'with', as is normal in other authoritative texts. In fact, there are more such directions without a conjunction (10) than with 'and' (9). No other good quarto is comparable:

	with *and*	without *and*
Titus	23	0
Romeo (Q2)	28	0
Richard II	8	4
LLL	14	1
2 Henry IV	25	5
Dream	18	0

Merchant	23	0
Much Ado	23	2
Hamlet (Q2)	32	2
Lear	30	0
Troilus	15	5
Othello	35	0
Kinsmen	25	5

For both total figures and relative proportions, *1 Henry IV* is anomalous.

7. Q is also unusual in using the plural '*manent*' when more than one character remains on stage (5.1.120.1/2616): the rest of the canon boasts only two parallels (*Much Ado* 1.1.153.1/153.1, *Richard II* 4.1.310.1/2142.1).

8. '*Earle of Westmerland*' occurs four times in the stage directions of Q (1.1.0.2/0.1–2, 5.1.0.2/2496.3, 5.4.0.3/2797.2–3, 5.5.0.2–3/2959.3–4); the only other reference to the character in directions is '*Lord of Westmerland*' at 4.2.48.1/2309.1. Even there, '*Lord*' could be an error for '*Earl*'; but the important point is that the character's rank is specified all five times. '*Westmerland*' occurs another thirteen times in stage directions in the substantive texts of *2 Henry IV*, *Henry V*, and *Duke of York*; on each occasion the name alone appears without title or rank. Scholars agree that both Quarto *2 Henry IV* and Folio *Henry V* were set from Shakespeare's own foul papers.

9. The contracted *prithee* is unusual not only for its predominance over *pray thee*, but also in its spelling. The only spelling in Q1 is 'preethe' (three times); the same spelling occurs sixteen times in Q2, the only other being 'prethe' (four times). 'Preethe' occurs elsewhere only twice in the entire canon (*Shrew* 5.1.54/2314, 'Pree the'; Quarto *Lear* 1.4.130/624; both in prose). If the spelling is compositorial, the same compositor must have set Sheet C of Q1 and all of Q2; an indication that it is not a compositorial preference comes at 2.1.34/647, where Q1 'preethe' is set 'prethe' in Q2. 'Preethe' does not occur in Q *Richard III*, which was set from the same fount as Q1 and Q2 *1 Henry IV*.

10. At 2.5.538/1464 and 2.5.543/1469 (see textual notes) two consecutive speech-prefixes are evidently omitted; the resulting text is self-consistent. The error is most plausibly partly or wholly scribal.

11. As Walker pointed out, Q is sparse in its use of contracted forms; expansions are more likely to be scribal than compositorial.

12. The text is tidier, and the speech-prefixes more regular, than is usual in a foul-paper text.

13. The play as a whole has undergone an almost systematic revision of certain characters' names. It is plausible that the copy for Q1 was prepared in order to demonstrate that these name-changes had been made, and the general success in introducing them systematically would have been difficult to achieve by marking all the required alterations (some 330) in Shakespeare's papers.

The most important revision of names is known to have taken place after the play reached the stage, and the others probably belong to the same time. As is well documented, the character subsequently known as Sir John Falstaff was originally a scurrilous portrayal of Sir John Oldcastle, a historical figure of Henry IV's reign who was often regarded as a proto-Protestant martyr. As a result of 'offence beinge worthily taken by Personages descended from his title' (by whom are implied members of the Cobham family) the name Oldcastle was emended to Falstaff (or as Q has it, 'Falstalffe'). Subsequent plays featuring the character, including *2 Henry IV*, perpetuate the name Falstaff, and in the Epilogue to *2 Henry IV* Shakespeare announced that Falstaff should not be taken as a portrayal of Oldcastle. In *1 Henry IV* itself the name Oldcastle has been completely replaced and the title-page of Q prominently advertises '*the humorous conceits of Sir | Iohn Falstalffe*'. There are no signs that the text has been altered in other ways as a result of this change; indeed at 1.2.41–2/148 there remains a glance at 'my old lad of the castle'. The details of the historical evidence for Oldcastle in *1 Henry IV* and its implications for the editor of the play are discussed by Taylor in 'The Fortunes of Oldcastle' and 'Richard James'. Both 'Olde-castle' and 'Falstalffe' are authoritative readings which belong to the text as finished and performed. If substituting 'Falstaff' was an inspired response to pressure from the Cobhams, it nevertheless of necessity eliminated an important dimension of the character as first and freely conceived: a scurrilously satirical representation of a revered historical figure. More incidentally, it introduces a metrical irregularity in verse, and, as in 'old lad of the castle', destroys some arch word-play on 'old', one of the character's distinctive attributes, and 'Olde-castle', his name.

Though Shakespeare may have been reconciled to the new name when he characterized Falstaff in later plays, it made its entry into *1 Henry IV* as a response to unsolicited censorship. The major disadvantage in restoring the original, as we restore 'God' where censorship law demanded its alteration to 'heauen', is that it makes manifest an inconsistency between the first performed version of *1 Henry IV* and the remaining Falstaff plays. However, there is no evidence that even the two parts of *Henry IV* were performed in sequence. The theatrical unit was the individual play, as consequently was the textual unit in lost manuscripts and extant printed books. In Shakespeare's lifetime the two *Henry IV* plays were published only separately, in different years, in quartos printed in different shops, from different kinds of manuscript, and sold by different stationers. *1 Henry IV* may and indeed should be edited according to its own criteria.

Restoration of 'Oldcastle' highlights the differences in character between the figure represented in *1 Henry IV* and Falstaff in *2 Henry IV*. But, as with other name-changes (Philip Falconbridge to Sir Richard Plantagenet in *King John*, a woman's assumption of her husband's surname, etc.), the old and new names designate the same individual. A measure of this continuity can be maintained in an edited Complete Works by taking 'SIR IOHN' as the standard speech-prefix and, where they do not already appear, inserting the same words before the names 'Oldcastle' and 'Falstaff' in stage directions. For those wishing, for example, to perform the *Henry IV* plays in sequence, the substitution of 'Falstaff' for 'Oldcastle' is relatively simple. However, one cannot continue to print 'Falstaff' in edited texts and expect readers optionally to read in an alternative which has been thoroughly alienated from its context. The editorial restoration of 'Oldcastle' is the first stage in a process which will restore its familiarity in a play where it, in precedence to 'Falstaff', belongs.

External documentation reveals nothing of other revised names in *1 Henry IV*. It is from an anomalous reference in Q to 'Falstalffe, Haruey, Rossill, and Gadshil' at 1.2.160/263–

4 and from three speech-prefixes for 'Ross.' at 2.5.175/1105, 2.5.177/1107, and 2.5.181/1111 that we learn that Peto and Bardolph (Q 'Bardoll') originally had other names. Harvey and Russell, unlike Oldcastle, are not found in Shakespeare's sources for *1 Henry IV*, though a Sir John Russell (see Introduction to *2 Henry IV* and note to 2.2.0.1/804.3) is mentioned elsewhere in Holinshed. Shakespeare's contemporaries would, however, have recognized Harvey as the name of the Earl of Southampton's stepfather, and Russell as the family name of the Earls of Bedford. A deceased Sir John Russell had been husband to the self-styled Dowager Lady Russell who in November 1596 campaigned against the Lord Chamberlain's Men's proposal to move to the Blackfriars and establish a new theatre there. These names, if not included in the reformation of the play on account of the objection to Oldcastle, might therefore have caused offence in their own right.

The changes discussed so far were evidently imposed on the text after the play reached the stage. A potential complication to restoring the original names is that at 2.2.47.1-50/757.1-760 and in QF speech-prefix variants at 2.5.174-81/1104-11 there are independent signs of confusion between Russell/Bardolph and Gadshill (see textual notes). However, in 'The Thieves in *1 Henry IV*' Jowett argues that these features reflect changes of authorial intention in the foul papers, and so are separable from the later systematic revision of names. Shakespeare's original names Oldcastle, Russell, and Harvey can be restored without creating new inconsistencies. Ours is the first edition to do so.

The often-alleged substitution of Peto for Poins at the end of 2.5/Sc. 8 and 3.3/Sc. 11 is unlikely to have occurred. Most recently, Fredson Bowers has argued that the supposed anomaly arises from annotations indicating doubling of parts—a somewhat implausible hypothesis if, as most critics agree, the manuscript underlying Q was not theatrical in nature. There are two generally accepted reasons why Poins should be substituted: that Poins is earlier Hal's confidant, and should continue to be so, and that at 3.3.199/2115 there is a metrical irregularity unless 'Peto' (or 'Rossill') is emended to 'Poins'. Neither is convincing.

Russell says so little before the closing episode of 2.5/Sc. 8 that no violence is done upon his characterization by Hal's confidence in him. As Falstaff says in Q 'bid my Lieutenant Peto meet me' (4.2.9/2270), we must reckon with Russell/ Peto as a military leader whether or not he is admitted into the Prince's presence at the ends of 2.5/Sc. 8 and 3.3/Sc. 11. Q to this extent supports its own readings in the passages where they are contested. Russell/Peto's emergence from the tavern twilight should not be judged by standards of naturalism especially inappropriate to minor characters. As with Poins, his association with Hal leads to his disappearance from the play: as the action moves to the battlefield, Oldcastle is increasingly isolated.

The argument from the metre of 3.3.199/2115 collapses when the line is put in context. In 3.3.198-202/2114-18, not one line is metrically regular. Pope and other editors regarded the passage as prose, and perhaps rightly. In this edition, the verse arrangement is retained; even so, emendation of the offending name on metrical grounds is by no means justifiable.

The First Folio text was not a simple reprint of Q6. Changes to stage directions and speech-prefixes and the introduction of act and scene divisions are the most obvious indications that the copy had been annotated. Many oaths are softened or completely removed. The expurgator was alert to less obvious forms of profanity such as biblical allusions; the compositors are particularly unlikely to have been responsible. Walker attributed the prevalence of minor variants in F to the careless work of Compositor B, who set over half the text. However, her concentration on this single text led her to overestimate B's capacity for error. Werstine has shown that B set an uncharacteristic number of variants in his stints on *1 Henry IV*, and that the compositor's alleged carelessness cannot account for them all. It may be inferred that readings were annotated in the printer's copy. If there is rather less variation in the stints of B's workmate Compositor A/J, this is probably because, as evidently elsewhere (for example in *LLL* and *Richard II*), the first and last parts of the text, set by Compositor B, were more efficiently annotated.

Annotations might derive from a manuscript, as Wilson believed, or, as Greg maintained (*Folio*, 264-5), have no other authority than the 'improvements' which a printing-house editor thought desirable. It is scarcely conceivable that Shakespeare intended many of its variants. But Reid persuasively argues that at least some of the annotation derived from a manuscript, one which showed certain 'literary' characteristics. Reid believes that collation must have been careful in order to be worthwhile, but the example of other Folio plays, notably *Richard II* (the play preceding *1 Henry IV*), suggests that it was not necessarily or even normally so thorough; the extent of compositorial error accumulated from Q3 to Q6 but not corrected in F indicates that the manuscript of *1 Henry IV* was consulted much less effectively even than that of *Richard II* (though some of F's restorations of Q1/Q2 readings are almost equally persuasive evidence that at these points the manuscript *was* consulted). Reid envisaged a manuscript similar to the copy for Folio *Twelfth Night*, and attributed features inconsistent with this picture to a second stage of annotation made without reference to the manuscript. If instead F provides glimpses of a text similar to that which is seen extensively in Folio *2 Henry IV*, an idiosyncratically literary manuscript which may itself have derived from the prompt-book, an unaided printing-house editor becomes unnecessary to the textual hypothesis: all variants likely to be annotations can be explained as annotations from such a manuscript, and most miscorrections of copy error can be attributed to Compositor B. It may be conjectured that a single scribe prepared literary transcripts of the two *Henry IV* plays.

Two particular Folio variants need to be considered if this conclusion is to be sustained. They are interdependent, deliberate, physically separate, and wrong: a combination of characteristics which suggest an editor's unaided work. F omits Poins's entry at 1.2.105.1/209.1 and instead adds his name to the characters to enter at the beginning of the scene. It has been suspected that the annotator was trying to make sense of '*Poynes*' at the beginning of 1.2.106/210 which was italicized and inset in Q6 and so was indistinguishable from a speech-prefix. By any such account, a manuscript cannot have been consulted for this alteration—and stage directions are the most likely area of the text to have been collated with the manuscript. But an annotator unfamiliar with the play on stage is unlikely to have noticed a problem in the first place, and it is even more unlikely that an annotator familiar with the play on stage would emend at such obvious variance with the required staging. The emendation does not even adequately solve the supposedly perceived problem. F's transferred entry is best explained as a feature of a literary manuscript. Folio *2 Henry IV* shows a similar tendency wrongly to introduce characters at the beginning of a scene; one need only suppose that a similar phenomenon occurred here.

A manuscript such as that envisaged to lie behind F would contain many readings resulting from scribal sophistication. Folio *1 Henry IV* has always been recognized as the source for a few unobvious but convincing corrections of Q. It might also incorporate revisions in the scribe's copy made by Shakespeare himself. Application of similar criteria to those used for evaluating variants in *2 Henry IV* indeed identifies a small number of Folio variants most satisfactorily attributed to authorial revision. It is of considerable significance that these readings cluster together; they fall within 1.2.165–79/268–80, 1.3.25–133/342–50, and 1.3.209–10/536–7 (see textual notes). Other, rejected, Folio readings which deserve consideration include those of 1.3.231/548, 2.4.86/906 (omission of 'all things'), 2.5.10–11/944, 2.5.51/985, 2.5.59/993, and 5.4.160/2957 (introduction of 'again').

F's colloquial contractions probably correct scribal expansions underlying Q, and in this edition have been adopted. Again significantly, most of them are concentrated in 1.3/Sc. 3 and 1.4/Sc. 4: another indication that this part of the copy for F was relatively well annotated.

F's act and scene divisions are generally followed in this edition. Additional scene-breaks have been supplied in two places, initiating the traditional 5.3/Sc. 18 and this edition's Sc. 6/2.3. Editors have not identified a scene-break in the latter because the action is virtually continuous, but Q indicates that the stage is cleared. It is unlikely that '*Enter*' here indicates that characters who have remained in view come forward: (*a*) '*Enter*' rarely has such a sense; (*b*) the Prince and Poins would have to put on their disguises on stage whilst the main stage business continued; (*c*) they would then come forward merely to retire again. Though the staging is fluid, the cleared stage emphasizes a change in location between the thieves' exeunt and entry. F's failure to provide a scene-break is a consequence of the missing '*Exeunt*' in the quarto copy (and hence F itself)—as happens again at the scene-break first made by Capell beginning 5.3/Sc. 18.

J.J./(S.W.W.)

WORKS CITED

Bevington, David, ed., *Henry IV, Part 1*, Oxford (1987)
Bowers, Fredson, 'Establishing Shakespeare's Text: Poins and Peto in *1 Henry IV*', *SB* 34 (1981), 189–98
Davison, P. H., ed., *Henry IV, Part 1*, New Penguin (1968)
Greg, W. W., and Charlton Hinman, eds., *Henry the Fourth, Part 1: 1598*, Oxford Shakespeare Quarto Facsimile (1966)
Hemingway, S. B., ed., *The First Part of King Henry IV*, New Variorum (1936)
Humphreys, A. R., ed., *The First Part of King Henry IV*, Arden (1960)
Jackson, MacD. P., 'Two Shakespeare Quartos: *Richard III* (1597) and *1 Henry IV* (1598)', *SB* 35 (1982), 173–91
—— 'The Manuscript Copy for the Quarto (1598) of Shakespeare's *1 Henry IV*', *N&Q*, NS 33 (1986), 353–4
Johnson, T., publisher, *The Works of Mr. William Shakespear* (1710)
Jowett, John, 'The Thieves in *1 Henry IV*', *RES*, NS 38 (1987), 325–33
—— 'The Transformation of Hal', *N&Q*, NS 34 (1987), 208–10
Mahood, M., *Shakespeare's Wordplay* (1957)
Reid, S. W., 'The Folio *1 Henry IV* and its Copy' (forthcoming)
Taylor, Gary, 'The Fortunes of Oldcastle', *SSu* 38 (1985), 85–100
—— 'William Shakespeare, Richard James, and the House of Cobham', *RES*, NS 38 (1987), 334–54
Walker, Alice, 'The Folio Text of *1 Henry IV*', *SB* 6 (1954), 45–59
Waller, Frederick O., 'The Use of Linguistic Criteria in Determining the Copy and Dates for Shakespeare's Plays', in Waldo F. McNeir and Thelma N. Greenfield, eds., *Pacific Coast Studies in Shakespeare* (1966), 1–19
West, Gilian, '"Titan," "Onyers," and Other Difficulties in the Text of *1 Henry IV*', *SQ* 34 (1983), 330–3
Williams, G. W., and G. B. Evans, eds., '*The History of King Henry the Fourth*' as Revised by Sir Edward Dering, Bart. (1973)
Wilson, John Dover, ed., *The First Part of the History of Henry IV*, New (1949)
Zimmerman, Susan, 'The Uses of Headlines: Peter Short's Shakespearian Quartos *1 Henry IV* and *Richard III*', *The Library*, VI, 7 (1985), 218–55

TEXTUAL NOTES

Title *The Hystorie of Henry the fourth*] Q1 (*running title*); THE | HISTORY OF | HENRIE THE | FOVRTH; | With the battell at Shrewsburie, | *betweene the King and Lord* | Henry Percy, ſurnamed | Henrie Hotſpur of | the North. | *With the humorous conceits of Sir* | Iohn Falſtalffe. Q2 (*title-page*); THE HISTORIE OF | Henry the fourth. Q2 (*head title*); The Firſt Part of Henry the Fourth, | with the Life and Death of HENRY | Sirnamed HOT-SPVRRE. F (*head title*); *The Firſt Part of King Henry the Fourth*. F (*running title and table of contents*). The Q2 running title is '*The Hiſtorie of Henrie the fourth*.', varied '. . . Hiſtorie. . .', '. . . hiſtory . . .', and '. . . Henry . . .'. Faulty imposition gives transposed headlines in the facing pages of inner forme D. The S.R. entry is as the Q2 title-page, but with '*betweene . . . surnamed*' shortened to 'against', and 'conceipted mirthe' for '*humorous conceits*'. 'Conceipted mirthe' could have appeared on the Q1 title-page.

1.1.0.2/0.2 *other* ⌈*lords*⌉] Editors usually follow the Dering MS in including Sir Walter Blunt, but it is theatrically awkward for him to stand around until announced as 'new lighted from his horse' (1.1.63/63)—after which he still remains silent. *Here* at 1.1.62/62 can mean merely 'here at court'.

1.1.39/39 Herfordshire] Q2 (Herdforſhire), Q7, F (Herefordſhire), Q8. Q2's anomalous form is probably a compositorial error. Although 'e' could easily be misread 'd', the absence of 'd' after '. . . for' suggests that the compositor accidentally set 'd' after the first 'r' rather than the second.

1.1.40 Glyndŵr] Q (Glendower). Similarly throughout. *Glendower* is a rough transliteration of the Welsh vowels, and hence a spelling variant. It is misleading in that the pronunciation is always disyllabic and sometimes stressed on the first syllable. *Glendower* has been an established anglicization, but historians now usually accept the correct Welsh form.

1.1.55 Holmedon] Q. The modern form *Humbleton* suggests three syllables. Compare *Pomfret* for Pontefract.

1.1.62/62 a deere] Q5b, F; deere Q2

1.1.69/69 bloud did] Q6, F; ∼. Did Q2

1.1.71/71 the Earle] POPE; Earle QF

1.1.73 Moray] Q (Murrey)

1.1.75–6/75–76 not? | WESTMERLAND In faith it is a] POPE; not? In faith it is. | Weſt⟨merland⟩. A QF. It is sometimes pointed out that Q's space after 'not' would accommodate a missing prefix. However, the copy for Q would be unlikely to have a new speech beginning on the same line as the end of the previous one, and the mechanics of the error are difficult to explain in terms of an omitted prefix. More plausibly, 'In faith it is' was inserted in a manuscript.

1.1.93/93 vse‸ he keepes,] Q4, F; ∼, he ∼‸ Q2

1.2.0.1/107.3 *and Sir Iohn Olde-castle*] This edition (G.T.; *following early allusions*); *and Sir Iohn Falſtaffe* Q; *Sir Iohn Fal-|ſtaffe and Pointz* F. Falstaff is found in Q and F for Oldecastle throughout (see Introduction); the usual form in Q is 'Falstalffe'. The spelling 'Olde-castle' is taken from the name's one occurrence in Shakespeare: *2 Henry IV* Epi. 30/3226–7. For F's relocation from 105.1/209.1 of Poins's entry, see Introduction.

1.2.16/123 a king] Q2; king Q3, F

1.2.33/140 proofe‸ now. A] ROWE; ∼. Now‸ a QF

1.2.79/184 similes] Q6; ſmiles Q2, F

1.2.80/185 sweet] Q3, F; ſweer Q2

1.2.105.1/209.1 *Enter Poines* Q; *not in* F

1.2.106/210 Poynes:] THEOBALD; ∼‸ Q2; *Poines.* Q5, Q6, F (*as speech-prefix*). See Introduction.

1.2.112–13/217–8 Iohn, Sacke and Sugar Iacke?] This edition (Mahood); Iohn Sacke, and Sugar Iacke? Q2; Iohn *Sacke* and *Sugar*, Iacke Q6; Iohn Sacke and Sugar: Iacke? F; John Sack-and-Sugar? Jack! ROWE. Most editions follow Rowe, though Humphreys and others have refined this reading by adding a dash after 'Sack' derived from Q2's comma. The apparent virtue of the dash is its conservatism, but Q2 needs emending in any case; all editors follow the unauthoritative isolation of 'Iacke'. Q2's comma after 'Iohn' might be the equivalent to the inception of a hyphenated phrase (as perhaps is the comma after 'foot' in 'came in, foot, and hand' at 2.5.221/1148). The alternative to Rowe adopted in this edition not only gives a crisper phrasing, but is more pointed in that, as Mahood remarked, *jack* can mean 'leather drinking-vessel, tankard'.

1.2.126 visors] Q (vizards). Similarly at 1.2.176 and 2.2.52. See note to *Richard III* 2.2.28.

1.2.160/263–4 Haruey, Rossill, and Gadshil] QF; Harvay *Peto* and Bardolff DERING MS; *Bardolph, Peto,* and *Gads-hill* THEOBALD. See Introduction.

1.2.160 Russell] Q (Roſsill)

1.2.165/268 But how] F; How Q. See notes to 1.2.172/274 and 1.2.179/280. The 'Yea'/'I' variant at 1.2.172/274 points to consultation of a manuscript behind F; the two separate but linked variants at 1.2.165/286 and 1.2.179/280 suggest the same. Whereas 'Yea' at 1.2.172/274 is probably a quarto error, the transposition of 'But' across 14 lines has the character of an authorial revision, especially as it avoids Q's repeated 'Yea, but' (or Shakespeare's original repetition of 'I, but') in the Prince's consecutive replies at 1.2.172/274 and 1.2.179/280. These variants occur just over sixty lines before the most radically reworked passage in F, which is itself associated with other changes in 1.3/Sc. 3 (see notes to 1.3.26/343, etc.).

1.2.172/274 I] F; Yea Q. For Shakespeare's overwhelming preference for 'I', see Introduction and note to *Richard III* 1.3.98/510. The variant is best explained as an authoritative correction from manuscript in F of a scribal or printing-house corruption in Q. The omitted 'Yea' at 1.2.179/280 might be a misinterpreted annotation to the same effect ('I' interpreted as a slash), but more plausibly relates to the variant at 1.2.165/268.

1.2.179/281 But] F; Yea, but Q. See notes to 1.2.165/268 and 1.2.172/274.

1.2.187/289 liues] Q2; lyes Q3, F

1.2.192–214/295–317 I . . . wil.] A manuscript version of the speech (BL Egerton MS 2446, fol. 13, dated 14 April 1628) shares the error 'soile' (1.2.212/315) with Qq5–6 and F, and so is evidently transcribed from one of these texts.

317.2 blunt] Q2. A feature of Q is its occasional use of lower-case initial letters for proper names. These probably preserve details of an underlying manuscript, and so are retained. An exception is made of repeated 'iacke' (see Incidentals), where Q evidently deploys lower-case because of shortage of the upper-case letter.

1.3.12 too] Q (to)

1.3.25/342 was] Q2; is Q2; he Q6. See following note.

1.3.26/343 Who either through enuie] F (. . . enuy); Either enuie therefore Q. This passage (1.3.25–7/342–4) is the first of a series of readings in 1.3, all set by Compositor B on Folio page e1, in which F differs from Q in a way not accountable as error (Werstine, 'Folio Compositors', p. 266). Nor are F's changes well explained as a result of damage in the printed copy, unless that damage was made good by reference to the manuscript: if 'enuy therefore' was legible in the Q6 copy, an unauthorized correction would have to be both deliberately wrong and less obvious than the required reading, whereas if 'enuy' was missing, a corrector would have to be gifted with considerable luck to guess it. Here, and at 1.3.65, 126, 131, and 133/382, 443, 448, and 450, the Folio readings are taken as deliberate authorial changes incorporated from the manuscript.

'Through' might be emended 'thorough', but 'enuie' can be accented on the second syllable.

1.3.27/344 Was] F; Is Q. See previous note.

1.3.52/369 or] F; or he Q

1.3.65/382 Made me to answer] F; I anſwered Q. F's reading almost certainly derives from the consulted manuscript, and can only be explained as an authorial alteration. Further evidence of annotation from an authoritative source comes 2 lines earlier, where Q6's apparently satisfactory 'haue been himselfe' is corrected to the Q2 reading 'himselfe haue beene'. The Folio text varies more markedly from the phrasing at 1.3.51/368; as with its rewording at 1.3.26/343, the tone becomes more defiant and accusatory.

1.3.83/400 the] Q3, F; that Q2

1.3.115 Owain] Q (Owen). Similarly throughout.

1.3.122/439 youle] F (you'll); you wil Q

1.3.126/443 Although it be with] F; Albeit I make a Q. See note to 1.3.26/343.

1.3.131/448 In his behalfe] F; Yea on his part Q. See note to 1.3.26/343. At 1.3.127.1/444.1 F successfully reintroduces an entry missing in Q6, correctly identifying the character where the context does not establish his name. Again an authoritative annotation is suggested.

1.3.133/450 downfall] F; down-trod Q. The variant is of the type associated with minor authorial adjustments as seen in *Richard II* and elsewhere. It is especially likely to derive from the manuscript as other readings in this passage, one just two lines above, also appear to do so. F gives an acceptable but unusual past-participle form, one that Shakespeare used elsewhere, for this very word, at *Macbeth* 4.3.4/1551.

1.3.192–3/509–10 swim. . . . West,] Q3 (∼, . . . ∼,) F (∼ : . . . ∼,); ∼, . . . ∼. Q2

1.3.199/516 HOTSPUR] Q6, F; *no speech-prefix in* Q1

1.3.209–10/526–7 a while . . . me.] F; a while. Q. F's part-line is not convincingly explained except as an authorial addition incorporated from a manuscript. Compare similar part-lines in Folio *2 Henry IV*.

1.3.237/554 whipt] Q2, F; whip Q1

1.3.240/557 de'ye] F; do you Q

1.3.241/558 vpon't] F; vpon it Q

1.3.253/570 to't] F (too't); to it Q

1.3.254/571 Weele] F (Wee'l); We wil Q

1.3.260/577 granted. . . . You my Lord,] THEOBALD (Thirlby); ∼‸ you my ∼. QF

1.3.264/581 ist] F (is't); is it Q

1.3.265 Bristol] Q (Briſtow)

1.3.265 Scrope] Q (Scroop). Q similarly has 'Scroope' at 4.4.3/2459 and 5.5.38/2997.

1.3.271/588 well] Q; wond'rous well F. F's addition may not derive from a manuscript. The line is set in F two lines from the foot of column b of e1ᵛ, with a line-break introduced after 'I smell it'. Compositor B, who set the page, was evidently accustomed to adding a word or words to his copy in order to facilitate or disguise space-wasting. The verse-line without 'wond'rous' would easily fit the Folio measure; with it, a line-break becomes necessary.

1.3.276 well aimed] Q (~, ~). The comma is equivalent to a hyphen.
1.3.287/604 course.] ROWE; ~ˬ QF
1.3.289 Lord] Q (Lo:)
1.3.292/609 our] Q2, F; out Q1
2.1.1/614 Ant] F (an't); An it Q
2.1.24 races] Q (razes)
2.1.40/652-3 quoth a] F (quoth-a); quoth he Q
2.1.55 Weald] Q (wild)
677 Saine] Q. Possibly a misprint, but *OED* records early forms without 't', including the 16th-c. spelling 'sayn'.
2.1.68/681 hees] F (hee's); he is Q
2.1.73/686 foot landrakers] Q4, F; footland rakers Q1
2.1.76/689 Oiezres] This edition; Oneyres QF; owners HANMER; mynheers CAPELL; ones,—yes COLLIER (*conj.*); O-yeas DAVISON. Humphreys comments, 'What is wanted . . . is something facetiously grandiloquent, recognizable as a title, yet far-fetched'. Malone's conjecture 'onyers', from *O.Ni*, *oni*, which Humphreys follows, is unintelligible; it is a particularly unlikely construct as the first known example of *O.Ni* is 1644, and its meaning is there explained. Davison's reading is attractive as far as it goes, but does not give a title and necessitates an unlikely conjectural spelling ('Owyres'). 'Oiez' is a recognized spelling variant, and the addition of the suffix '-res' gives both a closer analogy with 'Burgomasters' and a more directly applicable sense. The result is a nonce-word, but in context a recognizable one, with a combination of letters that could easily have confused a compositor. See also note to 'min-heires' at *Merry Wives* 2.1.206/765.
2.1.86 recipe] Q (receyte)
2.1.97/710 Exeunt] F; *not in* Q.
2.2.0.1/710.1 Haruey, ⌈Rossill⌉] This edition; *and Peto, &c.* Q; *and Peto* F; *not in* CAPELL; BARDOLPH *and* PETO, *at some distance* MALONE
2.2.1.1/711.1 Exeunt . . . doore] This edition; *not in* QF
2.2.4/714 Exit Poynes] This edition; *not in* QF; *They retire.* DYCE
2.2.10/720 Exit] This edition; *not in* QF; *Retires.* DYCE
2.2.17 two-and-twenty] Q (xxii:), F
2.2.21/732 Rossill, Haruey] This edition; Bardoll, Peto Q; *Bardolph, Peto* F. Similarly throughout, in text, stage directions, and speech-prefixes, except at 1.2.160/263; see Introduction and Jowett, 'The Thieves in *1 Henry IV*'.
2.2.27/738 vpon't] F; vpon it Q
2.2.28.1-2/739.1-2 Enter . . . Rossill] This edition; *not in* QF. Dyce has the Prince come forward at 2.2.31/742, and his three companions at 2.2.50/760 (after 'voice').
2.2.31/742 PRINCE Peace] Q (*text*), F; Peace Q (*c.w.*)
2.2.40 Prince, Hal] Q (~, ~). This is the only example of *Prince* collocated with *Hal(l)* in the play (and at *2 Henry IV* 5.5.41/3129 'King Hall' is a comic construction). Q's comma may indicate two distinct vocatives.
2.2.47.1/757.1 Gadshill] QF; Gadshill *and* Bardolph ROWE; GADSHILL; BARDOLPH, *and* PETO, *with him* CAPELL. Editors' introduction of Bardolph (i.e. Russell) here makes little theatrical sense and is an expedient designed to make sense of the text in Q at 2.2.50-1/760 (see note).
2.2.47.1/757.1 vizarded] This edition; *not in* QF
2.2.50-2/760-2 Gadshill, what newes. | ⌈GADSHILL⌉] This edition; Bardoll, what newes. | Bar⟨doll⟩. QF; Bard⟨olph⟩. What newes? | Gads⟨hill⟩. STEEVENS (Johnson). Editors who follow Q, as is usual, emend the stage directions so that Bardolph (i.e. Russell) enters with Gadshill at 2.2.47.1/757.1. But both on its own terms and in relation to the textual problem of 2.5.174-81/1104-11, Q is best explained here as reflecting foul-paper confusion between Russell/Bardolph and Gadshill. See Jowett, 'The Thieves in *1 Henry IV*'.
2.2.57.1/767.1 They . . . vizardes] This edition; *not in* QF
2.2.73.1/783.1 Exeunt . . . Poynes] MALONE; *not in* QF
2.2.75.2/785.2 amongst . . . Carriers] This edition; *not in* QF
2.2.76, 84/786, 794 ⌈1⌉ TRAUAILER] MALONE; *unnumbered in* QF
2.2.78/788 their] This edition; our QF. The Travellers surely dismount when descending the hill to assist the horses. Corruption could easily arise, either accidentally or deliberately, after 'our horses' and 'weele walke a foote a while'.
2.2.80/790 ⌈2⌉ TRAUAILLER] DYCE 2; *unnumbered in* QF; Trav⟨ellers⟩. MALONE
2.3.13/812 al] Q1; *not in* Q3, F
2.4.4/822 respect] Q7, F; the reſpect Q2. Q2 gives an idiom unexampled in Shakespeare and an awkward repetition of 'the'; it also misquotes the letter.
2.4.48 thee] Q (the)
2.4.54/874 ransomd] DYCE 2 (Capell); ranſome QF
2.4.62/882 hest] QF; heft WEST (*conj.*). An attractive emendation. *OED*'s one instance of *heft* meaning 'A heave, a strain; a heaving effort' (*sb.* 4) is from Shakespeare (*Winter's Tale* 2.1.47/559). Typographical error is not possible, as 'ſt' is a ligature and 'ft' separate typepieces, but Q could arise from simple misreading.
2.4.69/889 a Roane] Q4, F; Roane Q2
2.4.84/904 to] This edition; vnto QF. The speech is prose in Q; 'vnto' is set at the end of a line and may have been expanded to aid justification, but is an easy substitution.
2.4.89 maumets] Q (mammets)
2.5.8 christen] Q. In this context semantically indifferent with 'Christian' (the form in Q6), but unique as an adjective in Shakespeare and probably here an imitation of the Puritan-influenced idiom of a citizen.
2.5.32/966 president] F; preſent Q
2.5.35/969 POINES] Q5, F; Prin⟨ce⟩. Q2
2.5.65 o'] Q (a). Similarly at 5.1.136.
2.5.120/1051 Titan,] POPE; ~ˬ QF; Butter, THEOBALD. Theobald's emendation has rightly been thought to weaken the sense (see Humphreys) and is an awkward substitution. If Q is seriously wrong, perhaps 'pittifull harted Titan' is a wrongly-placed addition which should appear after 'see Titan'.
2.5.121 sun's] Q (sonnes)
2.5.126/1056 Exit Frances] This edition; *not in* QF. Editors usually leave Francis on stage until 2.5.486/1414, but an exit here allows the part to end as it began, with comic business, instead of trailing into a ghost.
2.5.168.1/1098.1 He . . . sword] This edition; *not in* QF
2.5.174/1104 PRINCE] F; Gad⟨shill⟩. Q
2.5.175, 177, 181/1105, 1107, 1111 GADSHILL] F; Roſſ⟨ill⟩. Q. Wilson argued that Gadshill cannot be intended to speak 2.5.174/1104 (see previous note), and that the prefix in Q was probably an addition to the copy manuscript designed to replace 'Ross.'. The Folio emendation is surely good evidence of annotation from a manuscript, though F is followed even by editors who deny the text such authority. The probable reason why the speeches were originally given to Russell but were transferred to Gadshill, not Bardolph, is that Shakespeare originally intended a single character, but decided, perhaps whilst writing the later part of 2.4, that Gadshill and Russell should be distinct (see Jowett, 'The Thieves in *1 Henry IV*').
2.5.196.1/1125.1 He . . . fight] This edition; *not in* QF
2.5.205.1/1133.1 He . . . buckler] This edition; *not in* QF
2.5.248/1176 elfskin] Q4, F; elfſkin Q2
2.5.252/1180 to't] F; to it Q
2.5.327/1255 Exit] This edition; *not in* QF. An exit is required before 2.5.486.2/1414.2, where Russell re-enters; editors usually supply it immediately before this point. It is doubtful whether Shakespeare would have envisaged such a staging without supplying either intervening dialogue (such as we find if the Hostess exits at 2.5.486.1/1414.1, to re-enter at 2.5.490.1/1418.1) or stage directions as elsewhere in *1 Henry IV* for distinctive aspects of staging. Russell's 'Choler' gives a good natural cue for his—but not the Hostess's—exit.
2.5.333 talon] Q (talent)
2.5.343/1271 O.] QF (~ˬ), DERING MS (Owen). Sir John's 'Owen, Owen, the same' is much more intelligible if Poins actually said 'Owen' himself. It is only necessary to suppose that Shakespeare used the initial 'O' as an abbreviation. Hand D in *More* did not habitually place a full stop after such initials, so the text is

1 HENRY IV

scarcely corrupt; however, such pointing would usually have been introduced in Q1 or Q2.

2.5.343   Owain] Q (O). See previous note.

2.5.368–372   But . . . afraid] Q has question marks after 'afeared', 'again', and 'afraid'. 'Thou being heir-apparent' could be interpreted as belonging to the first question. The modernized punctuation substantively follows F.

2.5.383   joint-stool] Q (ioynd stoole)

2.5.396   Father] Q (father), F. Taken to be God the Father, but alternatively Sir John as Henry the father.

2.5.397/1324   tristfull] DERING MS, ROWE; truſtfull QF

2.5.405/1332   yet] Q4, F; ſo Q2

2.5.458   reverend] Q (reuerent)

2.5.478/1405   leane] Q3, F; lane Q2

2.5.486.1/1414.1   *Exit hostesse*] This edition; *not in* QF; *Exeunt Hostess, FRANCIS, and BARDOLPH* MALONE. Sisson would have the Hostess conveyed off stage at 2.5.401/1328, but her appreciative comment at 2.5.399–400/1326–7 does not sound like someone taking leave of Sir John's performance. See notes to 2.5.126/1056 and 2.5.327/1255.

2.5.498/1425   made] Q, F1; mad F3. F3 may give a modernization: 'made' appears as a spelling of *mad* in *2 Henry IV* 2.1.106/714 and Sonnet 129.9. This makes the crux more finely balanced (compare Humphreys's note), but though not necessarily a more conservative reading, 'made' gives better sense.

2.2.508/1434   *Exeunt . . . Gadshill*] *Exit* F; *not in* Q

2.5.508/1434   Poines] See note to 2.5.533/1459 etc.

2.5.529, 530   Good . . . good] Q (God . . . god)

2.5.533, 536, 553/1459, 1462, 1479   HARUEY] This edition; *Pet⟨o⟩.* Q; *Poins.* DERING MS, STEEVENS (Johnson). Similarly 'Haruey' at 2.5.542/1478. It has often been thought that Poins, not Harvey/Peto, should remain on stage after 2.5.508/1434 and at the end of 3.3. See Introduction.

2.5.538/1464   HARUEY] This edition; *Peto.* F; *not in* Q

2.5.543/1469   PRINCE] F; *not in* Q

3.1.4.1/1483.1   *Mortimer . . . sit*] BEVINGTON (subs.); *not in* QF

3.1.7/1486   *Hotspur sits*] This edition; *not in* QF

3.1.48/1527   *standing*] This edition; *not in* QF

3.1.48/1527   speaketh] This edition; ſpeakes QF. POPE and others have preferred the metrical expansion 'there is', but the resultant metre remains awkward.

3.1.67/1546   heres] F (heere's); here is Q

3.1.97/1576   cantle] F; ſcantle Q

3.1.126   metre] Q (miter)

3.1.129   on] Q (an)

3.1.152/1631   the least] CAPELL; leaſt QF

3.1.182   nobleman] Q (noble man)

3.1.187.1–2/1666.1–2   *Mortimers . . . Welsh*] This edition; *not in* QF

3.1.197/1676   thou downe powrest] KEIGHTLEY (Seymour); thou powreſt downe Q; thou powr'ſt down F; down thou pourest SEYMOUR (conj.). Other metrical emendations are 'down too' (CAPELL) and 'two swelling' (POPE); neither is convincing, and both depend on the secondary emendation of 'powrest'. Seymour's suggested 'down thou pourest' is attractive, but depends on transposition of 'down' across two words. His alternative adopted by Keightley assumes a transposition of single words, one which would be encouraged by the original's unusual word order.

3.1.207.1/1686.1   *sits . . . and*] This edition; *not in* QF

3.1.228/1707   hees] F (hee's); he is Q

3.1.259/1739   hot,] Q5 (Hot,), F; Hot. Q2

3.2.59   won] Q (wan)

3.2.84/1825   gorgde] Q3, F; gordge Q2

3.2.96   then] Q (than)

3.2.112   swaddling-clothes] Q (ſwathling cloaths)

3.2.156/1897   intemperature] F; intemperance Q. Wilson defended F as the better reading.

3.2.157   bonds] Q (bands)

3.3.0.1–2/1921.1–2   *with . . . waist*] WILSON (subs.); *not in* QF

3.3.34/1955   thats] Q4; that Q2

3.3.56/1976   tith] THEOBALD; tight QF. Sisson conjectures copy spelling 'tihte' for *tithe*, but it is not necessary to suppose a manuscript transposition of 'th': *OED* gives 'tite' as an erroneous 17th-c. spelling of *tight*.

3.3.73   four-and-twenty] Q (xxiiii.), F

3.3.85.6/2004–5   *raising his trunchion*] This edition; *not in* QF

3.3.87.1/2006.1   *and Haruey*] See note to 3.3.199/2115.

3.3.118   no thing] Q (nothing)

3.3.134   owed] Q (ought)

3.3.173   guests] Q (gheſſe)

3.3.178   beef] Q (beoffe)

3.3.191   two-and-twenty] Q (xxii.), F

3.3.199/2115   Haruey] This edition; Peto QF; Poins DERING MS, STEEVENS (Johnson). The character who must enter with the Prince is only identified in this reading. See Introduction and note to 2.5.533/1459.

3.3.202   o'clock] Q (of clocke)

3.3.206/2124   *Exit*] CAPELL; *not in* Q2; *Exeunt.* Q3; *Exeunt omnes.* F. Q's omitted exit and entry directions give the appearance of continuous action. F's expanded wording might indicate that the reading was checked in the manuscript. At first glance, '*Exeunt*' is exactly what is needed, but F's direction may be prompter's shorthand for staggered exits. If an annotation came (indirectly) from a prompt-book in late use, it would be important for that manuscript clearly to indicate a cleared stage before the act-break.

4.1.0.1–2/2124.1   *Enter . . . Douglas*] Q3, F (. . . *Harrie Hotſpur . . . and Dowglas*); *not in* Q2. Q2 never refers to *Harry Hotspur*.

4.1.12.1/2136.1   *a Messenger*] F; *one* Q

4.1.18   jostling] Q (iuſtling)

4.1.20/2144   my lord] CAPELL; my mind Q2; his mind Q4, F

4.1.31/2155   sicknesse staies him,] This edition; ſickneſſe, QF; sickness holds him; CAPELL. Rowe and many subsequent editors consider that Hotspur runs on to the next part of the letter without completing his sentence, and supply a dash for Q's comma after 'sicknesse'. It is more likely that words are missing and need to be supplied. For another lacuna that may be related, see note to 4.1.98–100/2222–4.

4.1.50   sole] Q (ſoule). Q's spelling is applicable to either *sole* or *soul*, and gives no indication of the primary sense. *Soul* is taken as subordinate because it is (*a*) less consistent with 'bottom' and 'list', (*b*) abstract, (*c*) an indirect application of the word (*OED*'s first illustration of figurativè sense 7).

4.1.55/2179   is] F; tis Q

4.1.98   ostriches] Q (Eſtridges). An *Estridge* is alternatively a goshawk, but few critics support such an interpretation here.

4.1.98–100/2222–4   that with the wind | ⌈. . .⌉ | Baiting] This edition (conj. Malone); that with the wind | Baited QF; that wing the Wind, | Baited ROWE; and with the wind | Baiting HANMER. The passage has troubled editors, though recent texts follow Q—perhaps because emendation of no individual word leads to a convincing text. Q is best explained as having a missing line followed by a corruption of 'Baiting'. See Jowett, 'The Transformation of Hal'.

4.1.106   cuishes] Q (cuſhes)

4.1.109/2233   dropt] Q3, F; drop Q2

4.1.117/2241   altar] Q5, F; altars Q2

4.1.124   corpse] Q (coarſe)

4.1.127/2251   cannot] Q6b, F; can Q2

4.1.127   this] Q. Possibly an old spelling of *these*, but if so it is odd to find it in a context where the singular is acceptable.

4.1.128/2252   yet] Q6, F; it Q2

4.1.135   merrily] Q (merely). Similarly at 5.2.12/2648.

4.2.3   Coldfield] Q (cop-|hill)

4.2.16   yeomen's] Q (Yeomans)

4.2.24   ensigns] Q (Ancients)

4.2.31   feazed ensign] Q (fazd ancient)

4.2.34   tattered] Q (tottered)

4.2.57/2318   all] QF; at This edition conj. Q gives an odd reading. 'At' could easily be misread 'al', especially as 'all' occurs just four words earlier.

4.3.23/2364 horse] Q5, F; horſes Q2
4.3.26/2367 the halfe] STEEVENS; the halfe of QF; half of POPE
4.3.30/2371 our] Q2, F. Q7's 'ours' is an inflexional modernization: 'our' is acceptable as an absolute possessive, and is found again at 5.4.156/2953.
4.3.65/2406 innocencie] QF; innocence POPE
4.3.74/2415 heires, as Pages, followed] F4 (subs.); ~, as Pagesfollowed Qa; ~, as Pages, followed Qb, F1
4.3.84/2425 Countreys] Q6b, F; Countrey Q2
4.3.115.1/2456.1 Exeunt] F; no stage direction in Q
4.4.0.1 Michael] Q (Mighell). Similarly throughout.
4.4.30 more] Q (mo)
4.4.35/2491 not,] Q3, F; ~, Q2
5.1.2/2498 bulky] Q2; busky Q3, F
5.1.42, 58 Doncaster] Q (Dancaſter)
5.1.83/2579 our] F; your Q. There is no self-evident error in Q, but on closer examination F has the more plausible reading. Some or all of the following variants may attest to occasional manuscript consultation behind F hereabouts:
    4.4.16/2472 what with] Qq2-3, F; what Qq 4-6
    5.1.5/2501 by his] Qq2-3, F; by the Q4; by Qq 5-6
    5.1.40/2536 outdare] Q2, F; outdate Qq 3-6
    5.1.73/2569 Proclaimd] Q2, F; Proclaimed Qq 3-6
    5.1.90/2586 actiue, valiant] Qq 2-3, F; actiue, more valiant Qq 4-6
    5.1.100/2596 in a] Q2, F; in Qq 3-6
5.1.84/2580 this] QF; this dire G.T. *conj.* 'Dearely' may be trisyllabic (Cercignani, pp. 355-6), though the Shakespeare canon offers no parallel for such a pronunciation.
5.1.131/2627 then?] Q3, F; ~, Q2
5.1.138/2633 wil it] Q3, F; wil Q2
5.2.3/2639 vndone] Q6, F; vnder one Q2
5.2.8/2644 Supposition] QF; Suspicion ROWE
5.2.10/2646 nere] F (ne're); neuer Q
5.2.70/2706 On] QF; Upon POPE
5.2.88.1/2724.1 Messenger] F; not in Q
5.2.92-3/2728-9 draw I | a sword, whose] Q (*dividing after* sword); I draw a Sword, | Whoſe worthy F. The variants are of very doubtful provenance. 'I draw' gives a firmer line-end than 'draw I', but the interpolation of 'worthy' establishes a regular pentameter of 'Whose . . . staine' based on the QF line-break after 'sword'. Compositor B is known to make occasional metrical interpolations, and Shakespeare never describes a sword or 'temper' as 'worthy'. The transposition could be an error, though conceivably in Q rather than F.
5.2.94-5/2730-1 withall, . . . day.] Q3, F ~. . . . ~, Q2
5.3.1/2737 in the] T. JOHNSON; in QF
5.3.22/2758 A foole,] CAPELL; Ah foole, QF
5.3.29.1/2765.1 Exeunt] F; no exit direction in Q
5.3.36 ragamuffins] Q (rag of Muffins)
5.3.40 stand'st] Q (stands)
5.3.41 noble man] Q. Usually modernized 'nobleman'.
5.3.43/2779 as yet ar] DYCE 2; are yet Q; are F. Q collapses into prose in a line whose subject matter continues in the heroic vein. The resemblance of 'as' and 'ar' would make scribal error easy. F's reading may be a further mistake, but as Compositor B squeezed 'What . . . sword' on to one type line and F also omits 'I', 'yet' may have been deliberately omitted.
5.3.48/2784 He is] QF; He's sure VAUGHAN (*conj.*)
5.3.51 gett'st] Q (gets)
5.3.61/2797 Exit] F; not in Q
5.3.61/2797 with Blunts body] This edition; not in QF
5.4.23.1/2820.1 Enter Douglas] F; not in Q
5.4.57 Sir] Q (S.), F
5.4.57/2854 Exit] F; Exit Ki⟨ng⟩: Q
5.4.67/2864 Nor] F; Now Q
5.4.75.1/2872.1 who] F; he Q
5.4.91 thee] Q (the)
5.4.97 rites] Q (rights)
5.4.108, 110 Embowelled] Q (Inboweld). Similarly 'inbowel', 5.4.110.
5.4.127.2/2924.2 Prince, Iohn,] Q3 (~, and Iohn); ~, | Iohn Q2
5.4.147/2945 take't on] F; take it vpon Q
5.4.151/2948 ere] F (e're); euer Q
5.4.156/2953 The Trumpet] QF. Their Trumpet G.T. *conj.*
5.4.156/2953 our] Q2; ours Q3, F. See note to 4.3.30/2371.
5.5.15.1/2974.1 Exeunt . . . garded] F (*Exit Worceſter and Vernon.*); not in Q
5.5.37/2996 bend,] Q5, F; ~, Q2

REJECTED FOLIO VARIANTS

Readings not accepted in this edition which originate in F

1.1.28/28 now is twelue month] Q2; is twelue month Q4; is a tweluemonth F
1.1.42/42 A] And a
1.1.64/64 Staind] Strain'd
1.1.66/66 welcom] welcomes
1.1.103/103 so] and ſo
1.2.0.1/107.3 prince] Henry Prince
1.2.4/111 after noone] in the afternoone
1.2.20/127 by my troth] not in F
1.2.39/146 By the Lord thou] Thou F
1.2.41/148 the . . . Hibla] is the hony
1.2.56/162 it not] it
1.2.63/169 by the Lord] not in F
1.2.73/178 Zbloud] not in F
1.2.82/187 to God] not in F
1.2.88-9/193-4 wisedome . . . and] not in F
1.2.93/198 am I] I am
1.2.95-6/200-1 by the Lord] not in F
1.2.100/204 Zounds where] Where F
1.2.105.1/209.1 Enter Poines] not in F
1.2.106/211 match] Watch
1.2.121/226 bin] not in F
1.2.128/232 night] not in F
1.2.136/240 by my faith] not in F
1.2.144/247 By the lord, ile] Ile F
1.2.150/253 God giue thee] maiſt thou haue
1.2.151/254 him] he
1.2.214/317 Exit] not in F
1.3.0.2/317.2 with] and
1.3.20.1/337.1 Exit Worcester] not in F
1.3.22/339 name] not in F
1.3.41/358 bore] bare
1.3.45/362 termes] tearme
1.3.59/376 This] That
1.3.70/387 What ere Lord] Q2; What e're Q3; What euer F
1.3.76/393 he] not in F
1.3.107/424 bare] baſe
1.3.111/428 not him] him not
1.3.120/437 you] ye
1.3.129/446 Zounds] Yes
1.3.134/451 in the] Q2; in'the Q6; i'th F
1.3.143/460 not he] he not
1.3.157/474 starue] ſtaru'd
1.3.160/477 weare] were
1.3.183/500 to you] Q2; you Q6; vnto you F
1.3.213/530 God] heauen
1.3.231/548 him poisond] Q (him poiſoned); poyſon'd him F
1.3.234/551 waspe-stung] Q1; waſpe-tongue Q3; Waſpe-tongu'd F
1.3.245/562 Zbloud, when] When F
1.3.247/564 candy] caudie

1 HENRY IV

1.3.252/569 I] for I
1.3.254/571 Ifaith] infooth
1.3.271/588 well] wond'rous well
1.3.296.1/613.1 Exeunt] exit
2.1.6/619 poore] the poore
2.1.9/622 that] this
2.1.11/623 Ostler] the Oſtler
2.1.14/627 bee] Q1; to be Q6; is F
2.1.16/629 by the Maſſe] not in F
2.1.17/630 christen] in Chriſtendome
2.1.26/639 Gods bodie, the] The F
2.1.36/649 by God ſoft] ſoft I praye ye
2.1.37/650 I fayth] not in F
2.1.63/676 pray thee] prythee
2.1.79/692 (zoundes)] not in F
2.1.79/693 to] vnto
2.1.80/693 pray] to pray
2.1.88/701 by my faith] not in F
2.1.88/701 thinke] thinke rather
2.1.89/702 Ferneſeed] the Fernſeed
2.1.92/705 purchaſe] purpoſe
2.1.96/709 my] the
2.2.0.1/710.1 Haruey, ⌜Rossill⌝ and Peto, &c. Q; and Peto F
2.2.11/721 theeues] Theefe
2.2.12/722 the] that
2.2.22/732 ile robbe] I rob
2.2.23/733 drinke] to drinke
2.2.29/740 vpon] light vpon
2.2.29/740 all, giue mee] all. Giue
2.2.35/746 zbloud] not in F
2.2.59/769 Poynes] not in F
2.2.61/771 How many be there] Q1; How many be they Q3; But how many be they Q4; But how many be F
2.2.63/773 Zounds will] Will F
2.2.67/777 Well, we] Q1; Well, weele Q4; Wee'l F
2.2.75.2/785.2 the] not in F
2.2.80/790 Ieſus] Ieſu
2.2.86/796 are yee] are you
2.3.5.2/804.2-3 sir . . . Gadshill] the theeues Q; Theeues F
2.3.11.2-3/810.2-3 and . . . too,] not in F
2.4.16/836 by the Lord] I proteſt
2.4.16/836 a good] as good a
2.4.21/841 Zoundes and] By this hand, if
2.4.32/852 skim] skim'd
2.4.33/854 forward] forwards
2.4.66/886 ago] agone
2.4.78/898 In faith] In ſooth
2.4.85/905 In faith] Indeede
2.4.86/906 And if] if
2.4.86/906 all things] not in F
2.4.93/913 you . . . you] ye . . . ye
2.4.96/916 you speake] thou ſpeak'ſt
2.4.103/923 you] thee
2.4.104/924 farther] further
2.4.109/929 far wil] Q2; farewill Q6; farre wilt F
2.5.7/941 all] not in F
2.5.8/942 christen] not in F
2.5.9/943 ſaluation] confidence
2.5.10-11/944 and tel] telling
2.5.12-3/946-7 (by . . . me)] not in F
2.5.16/950 they] then they
2.5.51/985 Anon] Anon, anon
2.5.59/993 Lord] Lord ſir
2.5.78/1011 thou not] thou
2.5.87.1/1018.1 Enter Poines] after 2.5.86/1017
2.5.117/1048 and foote them] not in F
2.5.126/1056 lime in it] in't (Fa); lime (Fb)
2.5.133/1063 psalmes, or any thing] all manner of ſongs
2.5.144/1073 Zoundes ye fat] Ye fatch
2.5.144-5/1074 by the Lord] not in F
2.5.190/1120 God] Heauen

2.5.240/1167 Zoundes, and I were] No: were I
2.5.248/1176 Zbloud] Away
2.5.261/1188 here] not in F
2.5.263/1191 run] ranne
2.5.270/1198 By the Lord,] not in F
2.5.271/1199 you] ye
2.5.278/1206 by the Lord,] not in F
2.5.281/1209 titles of good] good Titles of
2.5.287/1215 O Iesu, my] My F
2.5.301/1229 birlady] not in F
2.5.306/1234 Faith tell] Tell F
2.5.374/1302 ifaith] not in F
2.5.394/1321 O Iesu,] not in F
2.5.399/1326 Iesu] rare
2.5.448/1375 Zbloud] Yfaith
2.5.449/1376 I faith] not in F
2.5.475/1402 God] Heauen
2.5.487/1415 most] moſt moſt
2.5.491/1419 Iesu] not in F
3.1.9/1488 cheeke lookes] cheekes looke
3.1.30/1509 topples] Q2; toples Q6; tombles F
3.1.127/1606 cansticke] Candleſtick
3.1.168/1647 come] doe
3.1.197/1676 powrest] powr'ſt
3.1.243/1723 Hart, you] You F
3.2.4/1745 God] Heauen
3.2.29/1770 God] Heauen
3.2.59/1800 wan] wonne
3.2.130/1871 God] Heauen
3.2.153/1894 God] Heauen
3.2.154/1895 he be pleaſd I shall performe] I performe, and doe ſuruiue
3.3.23/1944 my] thy
3.3.34/1955 thats Gods Angell] Q4; that Gods Angell Q2; not in F
3.3.46/1968 God] Heauen
3.3.48/1969 Zbloud,] not in F
3.3.49/1970 Godamercy, so] So F
3.3.61/1981 Gods light] not in F
3.3.69/1989 they] and they
3.3.73/1992 pound] pounds
3.3.83/2002 O Iesu,] not in F
3.3.86/2005 Zbloud and] and if
3.3.87.2/2006.2 vpon] on
3.3.88/2007 ifaith] not in F
3.3.92/2011 doth] Q2; dow Q6; does F
3.3.115/2034 thing] nothing
3.3.117, 118/2036, 2037 God] heauen
3.3.129/2047 an] not in F
3.3.147/2065 prince] a Prince
3.3.151/2070 and] if
3.3.152/2070 I pray God] let
3.3.172/2090 cherish] and cheriſh
3.3.190/2107 of the age] not in F
4.1.6/2130 God] heauen
4.1.12.1/2136.1 with letters] not in F
4.1.13/2137 thou] not in F
4.1.17/2141 Zounds, how,] How?
4.1.17/2141 sicke] ſicke now
4.1.85/2209 tearme] Q2; deame Q6; Dreame F
4.1.137.1/2261.1 Exeunt] Exeunt Omnes.
4.2.9/2270 at] the
4.2.31/2293 fazd] Q2; faczde Q6; fac'd F
4.2.32/2294 as] that
4.2.57/2318 night] to Night
4.3.34/2375 God] Heauen
4.3.115/2456 And] And't
4.3.115/2456 God] Heauen
5.1.25/2521 I] I do
5.1.71/2567 your] not in F
5.1.72/2568 articulate] articulated
5.1.120.1/2616.1 manent] Manet

1 HENRY IV

5.1.126/2622 God] heauen
5.1.130/2626 yea,] not in F
5.1.137/2633 tis] Is it
5.2.3/2639 are we] we are
5.2.29/2665 newes] newe
5.2.92/2728 draw I] I draw
5.2.93/2729 whose] Whose worthy
5.3.0.1/2736.2 enters] entereth
5.3.0.2/2736.3 to] vnto
5.3.11/2747 a yeelder thou proud] Q2; to yeeld, thou proud Q6; to yeeld, thou haughty F
5.3.13/2749 Lord] Lords
5.3.13.1/2749.1 They . . . enter] Fight, Blunt is flaine, then enters
5.3.15/2751 triumpht vpon] Q2; triumpht ouer Q4; triumphed o're F
5.3.29.2/2765.2 Enter] and enter
5.3.34/2770 God] heauen
5.3.37/2773 they are] they
5.3.41/2777 lies] likes
5.3.43/2779 as yet are] are yet Q; are F
5.3.43/2779 I] not in F
5.3.50/2786 before God] not in F
5.3.54.1/2790.1 it . . . be] out
5.3.55.1/2791.1 He . . . bottle] Throwes it

5.4.5/2802 your] you
5.4.10/2807 God] heauen
5.4.15/2812 Gods] heauens
5.4.16/2813 God] heauen
5.4.33/2830 and] fo
5.4.37.1/2834.1-2 of Wales] not in F
5.4.38/2835 thy] they
5.4.50/2847 God] heauen
5.4.68/2865 God] heauen
5.4.73.1/2870.1 They fight] Fight
5.4.83/2880 earthy and] Q2; earth and Q3; earth and the F
5.4.86/2883 Fare thee wel] Farewell
5.4.100.1/2897.1 He . . . ground] not in F
5.4.112/2909 Zbloud twas] 'Twas F
5.4.120/2917 Zounds] not in F
5.4.122/2919 by my faith] not in F
5.4.127/2924 with] not in F
5.4.127.1/2924.1 He takes vp] Takes
5.4.149/2946 zounds] not in F
5.4.160/2957 God] heauen
5.4.160/2957 great] great again
5.5.2/2961 not we] we not
5.5.14/2973 the] not in F

INCIDENTALS

52 Hotspur] Hotfpur   117 taffata,] ~;   258 Eastcheap.] ~,   333 peremptorie] percmptorie   342 deliured] deliuered   363 questiond] queftioned   373 soueraignst] foueraigneft   386 considred] confidered   428 slandred] flandered   532 You,] ~,   548 poisond] poifoned   559 kept,] ~,   588 well.] ~,   690 in,] ~,   714 close.] ~:   733-4 true-man] true-|man   741 hangd.] ~:   812 scattred] fcattered   868 murmur,] ~,   871 sallies, and retyres,] ~, and ~,   877 sleepe] fleeepe   1003 not-pated] not-|pated   1089 morning.] ~,   1141, 1183, 1196, 1227 Iacke] iacke   1230 lions, to,] Qb; ~, ~, Qa   1257, 1259 Iacke] iacke   1346 Harrie, now,] Qb; ~, ~, Qa   1352 corpulent,] ~,   1368 Hare.] ~,   1373 My] Mv   1383 dropsies,] ~,   1438 Now] Pr⟨ince⟩. Now   1462 What] Pr⟨ince⟩. What   1495 Shakd] Shaked   1512 In] Jn   1524 sonne,] Qb; ~? Qa   1532 them?] ~,   1582 wind?] ~,   1617 night.] ~,   1619 your,] ~,   1665 schoold,] ~,   1724 comfit-makers] comfit-|makers   1727 giu'st] giueft   1819 gaze,] ~.   1830 desird] defired   1851 capitall,] ~. (at foot of page)   1856 Enlarged] Enlargd   1864 nearst] neareft   2015, 2019 Iacke] iacke   2033 womanhood] womandood   2084 Iacke] iacke   2094 court,] ~,   2101 thing.] ~,   2123 world,] ~,   2129 world.] ~,   2231 feathred] feathered   2285 now] Q (text); nowe Q (c.w.)   2310, 2322 Iacke] iacke   2326 inough] inongh   2330 bare,] ~,   2727 talking,] ~,   2752 won, here,] ~, ~,   2798 bleedst] bleedeft   2832 bearst] beareft   2844 redeemd] redeemed   2883 hart,] ~,   2953 The] Pr⟨ince⟩. The

QUARTO STAGE DIRECTIONS

1.3.296.1-2.3.19/613-818 from Q1; others from Q2

1.1.0.1-2/0.1-2 Enter the King, Lord Iohn of Lancaster, Earle of | Westmerland, with others.
1.1.107.1/107.1 Exeunt.
1.2.0.1/107.3 Enter prince of Wales, and Sir Iohn Falstaffe.
1.2.105.1/209.1 Enter Poines.
1.2.191/294 Exit Poines.
1.2.214/317 Exit.
1.3.0.1-3/317.1-2 Enter the King, Northumberland, Worcester, Hotspur, | sir Walter blunt, with others.
1.3.20.1/337.1 Exit. Wor.
1.3.122.1/439.1 Exit King
1.3.127.1/444.1 Enter Wor. (after 'vncle', 1.3.128/445)
1.3.296.1/613.1 Exeunt.
2.1.0.1/613.3 Enter a Carrier with a lanterne in his hand.
2.1.7.1/620.1 Enter another Carier.
2.1.31.1/644.1 Enter Gadshill:
2.1.47.1, 2.1.46/660.1, 659 Enter Chamberlaine,   Exeunt.
2.2.0.1/710.1 Enter Prince, Poynes, and Peto &c.
2.2.4.1/714.1 Enter Falstalffe.
2.2.28.1/739.1 They whistle,
2.2.47.1/757.1 Enter Gadshill.
2.2.75.2/785.2 Enter the trauailers,

2.2.89.1-2/799.1-2 Here they rob them and bind them. Exeunt.
2.3.0.1/799.3 Enter the Prince and Poynes.
2.3.5.2-3/804.2-3 Enter the theeues againe.
2.3.9.1-2, 2.3.11.1-3/808.1-2, 810.1-4 As they are sharing the prince & Poins | set vpon them, they all runne away, and | Falstalffe after a blow or two runs away | too, leauing the bootie behind them. (opposite 2.3.10-11/809-10)
2.3.19/818 Exeunt.
2.4.0.1/818.1 Enter Hotspur solus reading a letter.
2.4.34.1/854.1 Enter his Lady.
2.4.114/934 Exeunt
2.5.0.1, 2.5.2.1/934.1, 936.1 Enter Prince and Poines. (at 2.5.0.1/934.1)
2.5.35.1/969.1 Enter Drawer.
2.5.79.1-3/1011.1-3 Here they both cal him, the Drawer stands amazed not knowing | which way to go. Enter Vintner.
2.5.87.1/1018.1 Enter Poines.
2.5.112.1/1043.1 Enter Falstaffe.
2.5.118.1/1049.1 he drinketh.
2.5.155.1/1085.1 He drinketh.
2.5.286.1/1214.1 Enter hostesse
2.5.300/1228 Exit.
2.5.328.1/1256.1 Enter Falstalffe. (after 2.5.327/1255)

1 HENRY IV

2.5.486.2/1414.2   *Enter Bardoll running.*
2.5.490.1/1418.1   *Enter the hostesse.*
2.5.511.2/1437.1   *Enter Sheriffe and the Carrier.*
2.5.531.1/1457.1   *Exit*
2.5.535.1-2/1461.1-2   *He searcheth his pocket, and findeth certaine papers.*
2.5.553.1/1479.1   *Exeunt*
3.1.0.1-2/1479.2-3   *Enter Hotspur, Worcester, Lord Mortimer, | Owen Glendower.*
3.1.142/1621   *Exit*
3.1.186.1-2/1665.1-2   *Enter Glendower with the Ladies.* (after 3.1.187/1666)
3.1.193.1-2/1672.1-2   *Glendower speakes to her in Welsh, and she answeres | him in the same.*
3.1.195.1/1674.1   *The Ladie speakes in Welsh.*
3.1.199.1/1678.1   *The Ladie againe in welsh.*
3.1.207.1-2/1686.1-2   *The Ladie speakes againe in Welsh.*
3.1.225.2/1704.2   *The musicke playes.*
3.1.240.1/1720.1   *Here the Ladie sings a welsh song.*
3.1.257.1/1737.1   *Exit.*
3.1.261.1/1741.1   *Exeunt.*
3.2.0.1/1741.2   *Enter the King, Prince of Wales, and others.*
3.2.3.1/1744.1   *Exennt Lords.*
3.2.161.1/1902.1   *Enter Blunt.* (after 3.2.162/1903)
3.2.180/1921   *Exeunt.*
3.3.0.1/1921.1-2   *Enter Falstalffe and Bardol.*
3.3.50.1/1970.1   *Enter host.*
3.3.87.1-3/2006.1-3   *Enter the prince marching, and Falstalffe meetes him | playing vpon his trunchion like a fife.*
3.3.175/2093   *Exit Hostesse*
4.1.12.1/2136.1   *Enter one with letters.* (after 'him')
4.1.85.1/2209.1   *Enter sir Ri: Vernon.*
4.1.137.1/2261.1   *Exeunt*
4.2.0.1/2261.2   *Enter Falstalffe, Bardoll.*
4.2.11/2272   *Exit*
4.2.48.1/2309.1   *Enter the Prince, Lord of Westmerland.*
4.2.75/2336   *Exit.*
4.2.78.1, 4.2.81/2338.1, 2341   *Exeunt.* (after 4.2.81/2341)
4.3.0.1-2/2341.1   *Enter Hotspur, Worcester, Doug: Vernon.*
4.3.31.1-2/2372.1-2   *The trumpet sounds a parley. Enter sir Walter Blunt.*
4.4.0.1/2456.3   *Enter Archbishop of Yorke, sir Mighell.*
4.4.40.1/2496.1   *Exeunt*
5.1.0.1-3/2496.2-4   *Enter the King, Prince of Wales, Lord Iohn of Lancaster, Earle of | Westmerland, sir Walter Blunt, Falstalffe.*
5.1.8.1-2/2504.1-2   *The trumpet sounds. Enter Worcester*
5.1.114.1/2610.1   *Exit Worcester.*
5.1.120.1/2616.1   *Exeunt: manent | Prince, Falst.* (opposite 5.1.120-1/2616-17)
5.1.140.1/2636   *Exit.*
5.2.0.1/2636.1   *Enter Worcester, sir Richard Vernon.*
5.2.26.1/2662.1   *Enter Percy.* (after 5.2.25/2661)
5.2.33/2669   *Exit. Dou.*
5.2.40.1/2676.1   *Enter Douglas.*
5.2.78.1/2714.1   *Enter a Messenger.*
5.2.88.1/2724.1   *Enter another.*
5.2.100.1, 5.3.0.1-4/2736.1-4   *Here they embrace, the trumpets sound, the king enters with his | power, alarme to the battel, then enter Douglas, and sir Wal-|ter Blunt.*
5.3.13.1/2749.1   *They fight, Douglas kils Blunt, then enter Hotspur.*
5.3.29.2/2765.2   *Alarme, Enter Falstalffe solus.*
5.3.38.1/2774.1   *Enter the Prince.* (after 5.3.39/2775)
5.3.54.1-2/2790.1-2   *The Prince drawes it out, and finds it to be a bottle of Sacke.*
5.3.55.1/2791.1   *He throwes the bottle at him. Exit.*
5.4.0.1-3/2797.1-3   *Alarme, excursions. Enter the King, the Prince, Lord Iohn | of Lancaster, Earle of Westmerland.*
5.4.23/2820   *Exit.*
5.4.37.1-2/2834.1-2   *They fight, the king being in danger, Enter Prince of Wales.*
5.4.42.1/2839.1   *They fight, Douglas flieth.*
5.4.57/2854   *Exit Ki:*
5.4.57.1/2854.1   *Enter Hotspur.*
5.4.73.1-2/2870.1-2   *They fight: Enter Falstalffe.*
5.4.75.1-3/2872.1-3   *Enter Douglas, he fighteth with Falstalffe, he fals | down as if he were dead, the Prince | killeth Percy.*
5.4.100.1/2897.1   *He spieth Falstalffe on the ground.*
5.4.109/2906   *Exit.*
5.4.109.1/2906.1   *Falstalffe riseth vp.*
5.4.127.1-2/2924.1-2   *He takes vp Hotspur on his backe. Enter Prince | Iohn of Lancaster.*
5.4.155.1/2952.1   *A retraite is sounded.*
5.4.158.1/2955.1   *Exeunt.*
5.4.162.1/2959.1   *Exit.*
5.5.0.1-4/2959.2-5   *The Trumpets sound. Enter the King, Prince of Wales, Lord | Iohn of Lancaster, Earle of Westmerland, with Worcester, | and Vernon prisoners.*
5.5.45.1/3004.1   *Exeunt*

THE MERRY WIVES OF WINDSOR

The earliest text of *Merry Wives* (*BEPD* 187) is the First Quarto of 1602. This was printed 'for Arthur Iohnson' by Thomas Creede, following an entry in the Stationers' Register dated 16 January 1602:

Io. Buſby.   Entred for his copie vnder the hand of Mr Seton / A booke called · An excellent & pleaſant conceited cõmedie of Sr Io Faulſtof and the merry Wyves of Windeſor

There immediately follows another entry, in a second hand, transferring the title to Johnson; Sir John's surname is here given as 'Faulſtafe'. The transfer has been taken as evidence that Busby was reluctant to be directly responsible for publishing a manuscript of surreptitious origin. This assumption has convincingly been disputed by Gerald D. Johnson, who shows that double entries were common for titles in which Busby had an interest, and that they probably indicate a joint venture with the second publisher.

Q was reprinted in 1619 (Q2). In 1623 a considerably fuller text appeared in the First Folio (F); a quarto of 1630 (Q3) reprints F. As is usual, this edition takes F as its control text.

Merry Wives, set by Compositors B and C, with some help from D, is the third of the opening four comedies in F, a group for which the copy was evidently transcripts prepared by Ralph Crane (see General Introduction). Crane was responsible for incidental features such as the widespread and distinctive use of parentheses, hyphens, and, to a lesser extent, apostrophes. He must also have introduced F's 'massed' entries: stage directions at the beginning of each scene listing all the characters who appear in that scene. These replace all other stage directions except the usual '*Exeunt*' or '*Exit*' at the end of a scene and two mid-scene directions in 5.5: '*Enter Fairies*' (5.5.35.1-5/2531.1-4) and '*The Song*' (5.5.91.1-2/2587.1-2). Crane may also have numbered F's scene divisions, which are followed in this edition.

Crane's sophistications make it difficult to establish the nature of his copy. It seems that most profanity has been removed or toned down in the Folio text. F is so clean of profanity that Crane cannot, to judge by his limited interferences in other texts, have been solely responsible: he was probably working from a manuscript which was itself expurgated. A prompt-book used after the 1606 Act disallowing profanity in the theatre might have been treated in this way (see Taylor, 'Zounds'). F's regular act divisions (followed in this edition) also suggest late theatrical copy underlying Crane's transcript, though one cannot rule out the possibility that Crane introduced them. The absence of serious staging problems may reflect a theatrical manuscript in which such problems had been resolved, though again any such conclusion must be tentative. One peculiarity, the reappearance of Pistol disguised as Hobgoblin in the final scene, is inter-

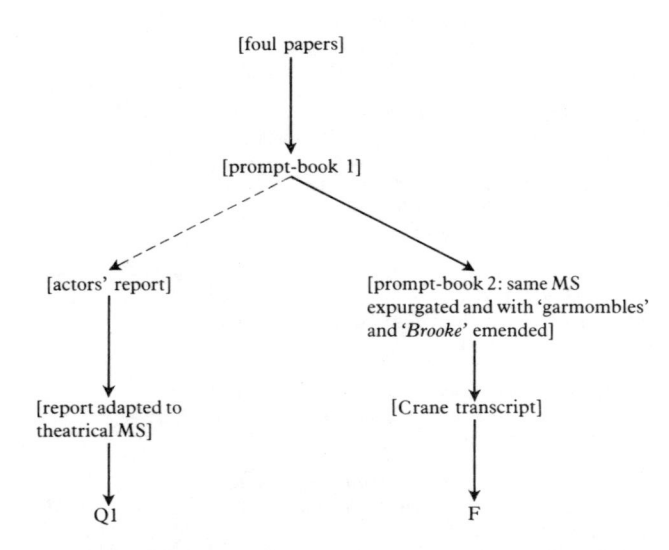

```
            [foul papers]
                 |
                 v
          [prompt-book 1]
           /            \
          /              \
[actors' report]    [prompt-book 2: same MS
                     expurgated and with 'garmombles'
                     and 'Brooke' emended]
      |                   |
      v                   v
[report adapted to   [Crane transcript]
 theatrical MS]           |
      |                   v
      v                   F
     Q1
```

preted in this edition as a consequence of doubling parts (see note to 5.5.40/2536); here at least a prompt-book feature may have survived into F.

Some controversy surrounds the status of the Quarto text (for a summary, see Roberts). The early view that it is a first draft is not now accepted. In their editions, Hart and Greg identified Q as a text based on memorial transmission. Greg pinpointed the actor who played the Host as the principal compiler of the report; he also recognized that the text has been subjected to theatrical adaptation and abridgement. Bracy, denying the memorial stage of transmission, believed that all features of the manuscript from which Q was set can be attributed to adaptation. Yet Bracy does not demolish Hart and Greg's considerable evidence for memorial error; nor does he adequately account for Greg's telling observation that the text is fuller, closer to F, and less prone to error in episodes where the Host is present, in particular in his own lines.

Major signs of adaptation are as follows. Apart from a recollection of 5.1.2/2426 in the beginning of Q's version of 5.5/Sc. 23, the first four scenes of Act 5 are omitted entirely. 3.4/Sc. 11 and 3.5/Sc. 12 are transposed in Q. Its omission of the following scene, F's 4.1/Sc. 13 (William's Latin lesson) and its rearrangement of dialogue elsewhere so as to avoid having Robin speak can be seen as associated changes which save two speaking parts, both for boy actors. Where F calls the inner room of Caius' house the 'Closset', Q consistently refers to the 'Counting-house'. This repeated variant in 1.4/Sc. 4 is probably connected with Caius' opening line in Q's version of 2.3/Sc. 7: '*Iohn Rugbie* goe looke met your eies ore de stall'. The location of 2.3/Sc. 7 has evidently been moved to Caius' house, so making more of the innovation of representing this house as a quacksalver's shop or stall.

Q could conceivably be, as Greg originally believed, based on a report of an adapted version. But in *Folio*, p. 334, Greg revised his earlier opinion, declaring that deliberate abridgement took place when the report was compiled, in order to provide a new theatrical manuscript. This might have been used in provincial performances. The nature of the text indeed suggests that steps have been taken to turn a grossly inadequate report into a roughly intelligible and coherent text. Where there were lapses in the report, new material was evidently supplied, with the result that passages owing nothing to Shakespeare can make better sense than badly remembered passages which preserve a mangled caricature of the original. If the rewriting was subsequent to a surreptitious report, the new material could have had nothing to do with Shakespeare.

Q's patchwork of varyingly reported and new material gives way in the final scene to a completely rewritten text with only fleeting phrases in common with F. Unlike F, Q makes no allusions to the Order of the Garter. Such material would have quickly lost the topicality it had in the recorded court performance of 1597 for which the play was probably commissioned, and might have meant little to a provincial audience. But the scene cannot have been rewritten just in order to make limited cuts. Long's alternative hypothesis, that Q represents an earlier Shakespearian version played before Queen Elizabeth, and F a later revised text as played before King James, does not seem tenable, if only because the most distinctly 'occasional' material linking the text with court performance in 1597 has then to be seen as a Jacobean addition. As with the bad reporting of the final scenes of other reported texts (notably Q *Henry V*), the reporter behind Q presumably failed to reproduce any semblance of the original. In *Merry Wives* a new scene would therefore have been put together, based on the events, but few of the words, of Shakespeare's version.

Q is agreed to be based on a stage version; it is therefore of significance to the textual history of F that both texts have an almost unintelligible subplot whose deficiencies cannot be attributed to incomplete foul papers. Despite Green's plea to the contrary, the episode concerning the theft of the Host's horses was probably censored. Any cuts due to censorship must have been imposed before the texts diverged. Q accordingly must be based on a textual antecedent of F. If there were any differences between F and Q which arose through authorial revision, F should incorporate Shakespeare's later improvements. But identifiable signs of revision in F are limited and arise from particular historical exigencies. Its expurgation of profanity has already been mentioned. The profane reading can often be restored by reference to Q, though some careful editorial judgements are required: Q may itself alter the oath involved or (particularly in badly reported passages) introduce new oaths on its own account. *God* (or *God's*) only occurs 4 times in F; in the *Henry IV* plays it appears 113 times. On the evidence of Q, of Shakespeare's practice elsewhere, and of patterns of expurgation elsewhere, we have gone further than previous editors in attempting to restore profanity, but even so *God* is used sparingly in our text for a play in which Sir John appears; our text remains at the low end of the spectrum of profanity compared with Shakespeare's unexpurgated non-classical plays.

Two apparent satirical allusions to individuals have also disappeared in F. In view of the Cobhams' objection to Oldcastle in *1 Henry IV* (see Introduction), Ford's disguise as 'Brooke' in Q inevitably suggests a glance at the influential Brooke (Cobham) family; F systematically reads '*Broome*'. The pun on *brook* as 'stream' at 2.2.146-7/930-1 confirms Q's name as the original reading. Editors who restore '*Brooke*' do not usually accept Q's 'cosen garmombles' ('Cozen-Iermans' in F) at 4.5.72/2322. Here Q probably makes a joking allusion to the German prince Count Mömplegard, one which is unlikely to have been added after 1597. As Green realized, it was evidently an actor who recalled the satirical thrusts which survive in Q, so it may be inferred that they were not censored before the play reached the stage. Green argued that '*Brooke*' was restored by an actor who remembered earlier performances. But the mere use of the name Brooke may have been insufficient pretext for Cobham to intervene when the play was originally performed in 1597, especially as he was then still, unlike Ford, unmarried. The name could have been censored at a later date. Shakespeare (or his company) may have wished to remove 'garmombles', perhaps never censored, because it had lost topicality and become meaningless.

If F was set from a transcript of the prompt-book and Q from a text adapted *after* a report had been prepared, Q is of particularly limited value, even compared with other bad quarto texts. In several instances it has been alleged that F omits lines which Q preserves. Errors of eyeskip or omitted verse lines may occur in any text, but there is no reason why F *Merry Wives* should be more deficient than other texts. We supply lines from Q at 1.3.20, 2.2.2, 3.1.97, and 4.4.42/323, 786, 1276, and 2201. The third of these is an incontrovertible omission which can be restored from Q with confidence; the fourth is in a passage which is almost certainly deficient in F but where the line in Q may be no more than the best approximation available to the words Shakespeare wrote.

Like any text which has been transcribed (probably more than once) and subsequently set in print, F has acquired some unintended corruptions. Occasionally F can be corrected with a reading from Q, though it is more usual to find that the passage in Q is insufficiently reliable. Q's stage directions are useful in the absence of mid-scene directions in F, but need not always be followed as they were in some cases supplied with a different staging in mind. A further use of Q lies in its capacity to confirm Folio readings: the very divergence between the texts gives a particular authority to their shared readings. As a source of alternative readings to F, Q must be treated with circumspection.

In this edition, rejected Quarto readings are only recorded where they offer likely alternatives to F in the light of the present account of the text, or where the reading requires discussion for other reasons. Q's profanity is regularly recorded except in the most widely divergent passages. On account of the nature of the Quarto text and its importance for restoring profanity, an unusual number of recorded readings from Q require discussion. For this reason, a separate list of rejected Quarto readings has not been compiled: such readings are included in the textual notes. Q's stage directions are uniquely important for a bad quarto; a list of them is therefore provided.

We have benefited from the comments of T. W. Craik, editor of the forthcoming Oxford edition of *Merry Wives*.

J.J./(G.T.)

WORKS CITED

Bowers, Fredson, ed., *The Merry Wives of Windsor*, Pelican (1963)
Bracy, William, *'The Merry Wives of Windsor': The History of Transmission of Shakespeare's Text* (1952)
Green, William, *Shakespeare's 'Merry Wives of Windsor'* (1962)
Greg, W. W., ed., *The Merry Wives of Windsor, 1602* (1910)
Hart, H. C., ed., *The Merry Wives of Windsor* (1904)
Hibbard, G. R., ed., *The Merry Wives of Windsor*, New Penguin (1973)
Johnson, Gerald D., 'John Busby and the Stationers' Trade, 1590-1612', *The Library*, VI, 7 (1985), 1-15
Lambrechts, Guy, 'Proposed New Readings in Shakespeare: The Comedies', in *Hommage à Shakespeare: Bulletin de la Faculté des Lettres de Strasbourg* (1965)
Long, John H., 'Another Masque for *The Merry Wives*', *SQ* 3 (1952), 39-43
Oliver, H. J., ed., *The Merry Wives of Windsor*, Arden (1971)
Proudfoot, Richard, 'The Year's Contributions to Shakespearian Study: 3. Textual Studies', *SSu* 25 (1972), 193-200
Roberts, J. A., '*Merry Wives* Q and F: The Vagaries of Progress', *SSt* 8 (1975), 143-75
Wilson, John Dover, ed., *The Merry Wives of Windsor*, New (1921)

TEXTUAL NOTES

Title *The Merry Wiues of Windsor*] F; A | Moſt pleaſaunt and | excellent conceited Co-|medie, of Syr *Iohn Falſtaffe*, and the | merrie Wiues of *Windſor*. | Entermixed with ſundrie | variable and pleaſing humors of Syr *Hugh* | the Welch Knight, Iuſtice *Shallow*, and his | wife Couſin M. *Slender*. With the ſwaggering vaine of Auncient *Piſtoll*, and Corporall *Nym*. Q (*title-page*); A pleaſant conceited Co-|medie, of Syr *Iohn Falſtaffe*, and the | merry Wiues of *Windſor*. Q (*head title*); *A pleaſant Comedie, of the merry Wiues of Windſor* Q (*running title*); An excellent & pleaſant conceited cōmedie of Sᵣ Io Faulſtof and the merry Wyves of Windeſor S.R. (*entry*). Note the prominence of Sir John Falstaff in Q.

1.1.7/7   Rato-lorum] F (Rato lorum); Rotulorum Q3
1.1.16/16   Coad] This edition; Coat F. This is the logical extension of the emendation in 1.1.20/20: it is widely agreed that the humour depends on Evans mispronouncing 'coat' with a '-d' sound, though Johnson's conjecture 'is not an old coat' produces a reading that does not depend on such word-play. Shakespeare may not have indicated the Welsh pronunciation, in which case the text need only have been corrupted at 1.1.20/20. But conscious scribal regularization is also possible.
1.1.20/20   Code] WILSON; Coate F. See Wilson and previous note.
1.1.21-2/21-2   There might be a lacuna here.
1.1.23/23   marring] F1; marrying F2
1.1.25   py'r Lady] F (per-lady)
1.1.30   compromises] F (compremiſes)
1.1.35   'visaments] F (viza-ments). Evans is attempting 'visements', a recorded aphetic form of *advisements*; *z* was a common variant for *s* in these words, and the only peculiarity of Evans's pronunciation is the intrusive sounding of a medial *a*.
1.1.38/38   sword] F; swort HIBBARD. There is no equivalent speech in Q. A pun on *sort* would give better sense to Evans's odd comment. *Sort* meaning 'destiny' is last recorded in *OED* in 1581, but the equivalent verb meaning 'come to a conclusion' was common. In *Troilus* 1.3.369/804 Shakespeare used *sort* to mean 'lot'. *OED* gives only one, Middle-English, precedent, but for Shakespeare the noun was probably a deverbal coinage. Similarly, perhaps, in *Merry Wives*. The swort/sort pun would be difficult if *sword* was always pronounced with a clear 'w', but the context in *Troilus* suggests that the unusual noun is used for the sake of similar word-play: 'make a lottry | And by deuice let blockish *Aiax* draw | The sort to fight with *Hector*'.
1.1.41/41   Geo.] THEOBALD (George); Thomas F. The error in F may be an unresolved authorial inconsistency, but 'Geo.' in Shakespeare's handwriting could perhaps be misread 'Tho.'
1.1.44   woman?] F (~.)
1.1.45, 1.1.132, 4.4.79   fery] F (ferry). F's doubled consonant might be due to line-justification, to copy-spelling, or to compositorial association with *ferry* rather than *very*; but no characterizing pronunciation seems intended. The shorter spelling occurs at 1.1.234, 3.1.48, and 3.3.162.
1.1.53/53   SLENDER] F (Slen.); Shal⟨low⟩. CAPELL. See Oliver's note.
1.1.56/56   SHALLOW] CAPELL; Slen⟨der⟩. F
1.1.60   Master] F ('Mʳ'). Similarly expanded throughout.
1.1.83   Cotswold] F (Cotſall)

1.1.98   Master] F (M). 'M' in dialogue is similarly interpreted throughout, unless separately noted. In speech-prefixes, Compositor C sets '*M*.' for 'Master' on the first folio page; elsewhere, Compositor B reserves it for 'Mistress'. See note to 4.4.25/2184.
1.1.110   Council] F (Councell)
1.1.111   counsell] F (coun-|cell)
1.1.117-18/116-17   *Bardolf, Nym*, and *Pistoll*] F; *Piſtoll and Nym.* They carried mee to the Tauerne and made mee drunke, and afterward picked my pocket Q. Editors have sometimes incorporated Q's added material, but it is less than necessary, and it is far from clear how such an omission would occur in F.
1.1.121   Mephistopheles] F (*Mephoſtophilus*)
1.1.130/129   Garter] Q3; Gater F
1.1.144   Ed] F (Yead)
1.1.152   advised] F (auis'd)
1.1.172-3/171-2   Nay . . . within] F; No more now, | I thinke it be almoſt dinner time, | For my wife is come to meet vs Q. Q's alternative is 'theatrical' in that it allows Anne to remain on stage as the adaptation requires: after 1.1.180/179 Q has '*Exit all, but Slender and mistresse Anne*.' and leads straight on to its own version of the dialogue following 1.1.245/243.
1.1.219   positable] F (poſſitable)
1.1.231/231   contempt] THEOBALD; content F. It is not necessary to conjecture a misreading of unrecorded 'contemt'; the text could be corrupted from 'contempt' to 'content' through the familiarity of the proverb.
1.1.234   faul'] F (fall)
1.1.287/284   Mistris] F; Nay be God miſteris Q. In Q the line is part of Slender's last speech in the scene, and the conclusion is different: Anne, not Slender, backs down to avoid being troublesome.
1.2.3/293   o'man] Q (woman); Nurſe F. Even in the speech of Evans, 'dry-Nurse' is an implausible alternative to, or even clarification of, 'Nurse'. The catalogue of terms, each followed by 'or his', would encourage scribal or compositorial eyeskip, or momentary confusion. The original might conjecturally have been a third term: 'maide' could facilitate confusion with 'dry-Nurse' on account of the graphical similarity to 'nurse'. But there are insufficient grounds for rejecting Q in favour of such a reading.
1.3.9   kaiser] F (Keiſer)
1.3.9   pheezer] F (Pheazar). The Host clearly means *vizier*, but what he actually says is the comically inappropriate *pheezer*.
1.3.14/317   lime] Q (lyme); liue F
1.3.19/322   hungarian] F; gongarian Q
1.3.20/323   His minde is not heroick:] Q (. . . heroick.); *not in* F. Q itself omits 'He was gotten in drink'. Nim's separate observations in Q and F are complementary; in particular, it is difficult to see a conceited humour in F alone. F's phrase is memorable, and is unlikely to have been misrecalled as the phrase in Q. Furthermore, Q is itself distinctive and witty. It is possible that Shakespeare originally wrote 'His minde is not heroick' and only later added 'He was gotten in drink'. Crane, or an earlier scribe, might have interpreted the addition as a substitution. Alternatively F suffers from omission through eyeskip ('drinck . . . heroick'). Q's omission is not in itself exceptional. For another instance where Q and F

have distinct alternatives which evidently require conflation, see 2.2.2-5/786-9.

1.3.25/328 minutes] F; minim's COLLIER 2 (Bennet-Langton). Q agrees with F; the emendation is otherwise attractive.

1.3.29/332 There is no remedy] F; Well, afore God Q.

1.3.44/347 studied her well] Q; ſtudied her will F. F's repeated 'will' is pointless, and suggests an error. POPE's repeated 'well' is little better. COLLIER retained the first 'will' and emended the second to 'well', but this almost loses sight of the quibble on *will* as 'testament', and disagrees with Q.

1.3.48/351 he] F; She Q

1.3.48/351 a legion] ROWE 3; a legend F; legians Q

1.3.77/380 oth'] F2; ith' F1

1.3.78/381 humor] Q; honor F

382 Page] F. Perhaps an error for the character, but compare '*Tapster*' at 318.

1.3.85/388 Stars] COLLIER 2 (Collier MS); Star F; Fairies Q. Q gives an unlikely memorial corruption. If it arises from a misreading, its plural substantiates Collier's emendation of F—though Greg believed that the reporter mistook Welkin for the name of a witch or spirit.

1.3.87, 92/390, 395 Ford] F; Page Q. Wilson, following Q, nevertheless recognized that it is Ford who will be possessed with yellowness. As Oliver observed, Shakespeare evidently changed his mind about which character visits which husband (or committed an oversight). Emendation probably departs from what Shakespeare wrote (F is difficult to explain in terms of errors of transmission) and creates a new inconsistency.

1.3.88/391 Page] F; Ford Q. See previous note.

1.3.94/397 this] POPE; the F. F's peculiar construction is not typical of Nim's speech. Wilson, following a conjecture by Jackson, emended 'mine' to 'mind', retaining 'the'. The resulting expression remains unconvincing in its idiom.

1.4.20/420 wey-face] CAPELL; wee-face F. In the following phrase Q describes Slender's beard as 'whay coloured', an unlikely substitution for 'yellow' unless influenced by 'wey' in the misrecalled text. Shakespeare almost certainly never used the adjective *wee* (but see note to *Dream* 5.2.13), and the word may have been unknown to him. 'Whay-face', on the other hand, occurs in *Macbeth* 5.3.19/1914.

1.4.34/434 We … shent] F; Ieſhu bleſſe me, we are all vndone Q (after 1.4.64/465)

1.4.35/435 for Gods sake] Q (For …); not in F

1.4.42/442 vn boyteere] ROWE; vnboiteene F; Une boitine CRAIG; une boite en HART; une boite, une PROUDFOOT (conj.). For the problems and methods of editing French passages in Shakespeare, see Taylor's note to the Oxford *Henry V* 3.4. Inconsistencies of number and gender are preserved in our old-spelling text but corrected in modernization.

1.4.42 vert] F (verd)

1.4.47/448 ma] ROWE; mai F1; F gives a common misreading of Shakespeare's *a*, and is probably not a legitimate spelling.

1.4.47 fort] F (for)

1.4.47/448 chaude] ROWE; ehando F

1.4.47 m'en] F (man)

1.4.47/448 vai] ROWE; voi F; vais voir OLIVER

1.4.48 la Cour] F (le Court)

1.4.48/449 Court,] ROWE; ~ ∧ F

1.4.48/449 affaire] ROWE; affaires F

1.4.50 Mets-le] F (mette le). Alternatively, '*Mettez-le*'.

1.4.50/451 a] This edition; au F. F is clearly incorrect, and may result from a misreading of Shakespeare's characteristic 'a' (as with '*mai*' 3 lines above).

1.4.50/451 ma] F (mon)

1.4.50/451 pochet] This edition; pocket F. F sets the English word as if it were French, and needs emending either typographically or substantively. F's italicization might derive from copy, though: Crane's usual handwriting was itself interspersed with italic 'h'. The letter in the compositor's copy might therefore have borne a sufficient resemblance to 'k' to induce the compositor to set the familiar English word. The only defence of F's English word

in a French sentence is that it is introduced as a comic mistranslation: Caius probably means his doctor's case. But it is implausible for Caius to translate the sentence's most difficult word alone, and the effect of comic failure to understand can be achieved without this device.

1.4.54/455 and] Q3; aad F

1.4.58 qu'ai-j'] F (que ay ie)

1.4.63-4/464-5 O … Closset] F; O Ieſhu vat be here, a deuella, a deuella Q

1.4.64 larron] F (La-roone)

1.4.82/484 ballee] THEOBALD; ballow F. Modernized *baile*.

1.4.88/489 your] CAPELL; yoe your F1; for your F2. F1's 'yoe' is extremely suspicious. It gives a difficult and implausible reading. As a spelling of *you* it is found nowhere else in Shakespeare, and is not in *OED*. Furthermore, although the type line ending 'your' is regularly spaced, the lines immediately above and below are abnormally squeezed:

> ly moued, you ſhould haue heard him ſo loud, and ſo melancholly: but notwithſtanding man, Ile doe yoe your Maſter what good I can: and the very yea, & the no is, y̅

There is no logic to this squeezing if it occurred during composition. The upper line is the less suspect, but abandons C's usually generous spacing around punctuation in order to fit just the first two letters of 'melancholly'. Towards the end of the lower line, which is also closely spaced around its punctuation, C set an ampersand; he ended the line with the contraction 'ye'. With its sequence of short words, no line could be easier to justify. 'The', or even 'is', could have been set on the following line. The irregular setting suggests that the type has been adjusted after composition. The type line with 'yoe' in it may have originally begun with 'melancholly' and ended with a hyphen after the 's' or 't' of 'Master', the text reading, 'doe yoe Master'. Hence 'yoe' would be an error for 'your', influenced by 'doe' (C's less usual spelling). The corrector would demand correction of 'yoe' to 'your', but the compositor, misunderstanding the corrector's mark, would, by this hypothesis, insert 'your' whilst leaving 'yoe' standing. To accommodate the new word, he would take back the first letters of 'melancholly' and take over the letters of 'Master' preceding the line break (replacing 'ſ' and 't' with a ligature). In the lower line he would first create space at the right hand end, then move along the standing type, then insert the letters for 'Master'. There is probable evidence of such a procedure: 'Master' is slightly inset from the margin, suggesting that a thin quad was inserted to make the line tight.

Such an explanation is conjectural, but takes account of all the observed facts. Without it, it is not apparent why 'yoe' should be both an anomalous form and a superfluous word. But whatever its origin, 'yoe' fairly clearly should not have been set.

1.4.90-100/490-500 I may … Page] F. In a roughly equivalent passage located before Caius enters, Q has Quickly say 'For I tell you friend, he puts all his priuities in me'.

1.4.96 advised] F (a-uis'd)

1.4.111 matter-a] F (mattr'a). Lambrechts interprets 'a ver' as 'he were'.

1.4.114 Jarteer] F (Iarteer). Might alternatively be modernized to *Yarteer* (depending on whether 'I' is for 'J' or 'I'). Compare note to 4.5.72/2322.

1.4.122-3/522-3 An— | *Exeunt Caius and Rugby* | ass] This edition (G.T. *and* Craik); An-fooles F. The double function of *An* as name and article is completely spoiled by the following noun beginning with a consonant: as an article, *An* is puzzling if not incommunicable. The ass's head is particularly appropriate to *Merry Wives* as it anticipates Falstaff's antlers or deer's head in Act 5. 'A fool's head of your own' and 'An ass-head of your own' were parallel proverbial phrases, so substitution would be particularly easy (compare note to 1.1.231/231). Shakespeare concretizes the ass-head in *Dream*, but nowhere else alludes to the fool's head version of the proverb.

1.4.134/534 In truth Sir, and] F. In F 'and' is superfluous, though it might reflect Quickly's garrulous speech. The word might easily have been interpolated in anticipation of the following phrases beginning 'and'. Alternatively, if 'In truth' replaces an earlier profanity, it could have been preceded by a reply to Fenton such as 'Well', which would have been accidentally deleted with the profanity or subsequently overlooked.

1.4.153/553 I will] HANMER; wee will F. Confusion of singular and plural pronouns is not typical of Mistress Quickly's verbal mistakes, but is a common error of transmission. F gives a particularly easy error in view of (*a*) the following word 'will'; (*b*) 'we' in the next line; (*c*) the preponderance of words beginning 'w' (7 in 3 lines).

2.1.1/561 haue I] Q3; haue F

2.1.5/565 precisian] F; physician COLLIER 2 (Johnson)

2.1.22-3/582 ith Deuills] F3; with | The Deuills F1; a Gods Q. Though swearing by the Devil's opposite, Q gives some evidence that an oath was intended. F1's reading probably arises from a dittography: 'ith | The'. This could have stood in Crane's transcript (F's lineation, which takes prose as verse, almost certainly reflects the layout of the copy), or could have been first set by the compositor and later unauthoritatively 'corrected'.

2.1.28/587-8 O God that I knew how to] Q; how shall I F

2.1.31, 33/590, 592 by my faith] This edition (G.T.); trust me F. This passage is not in Q. *Trust me* is a weak asseveration often substituted for expurgated oaths, but rarely used by Shakespeare in reliable texts. See Taylor, 'Zounds'.

2.1.55/614 praisd] THEOBALD; praife F (c.w. to D4 and text)

2.1.59/618 place] F; pace RANN (Mason)

2.1.60/619 150 Psalms] This edition; hundred Pfalms F; hundredth Psalm ROWE. Hart noted that, of all the psalms, the hundredth would be particularly inappropriate here, for it is a psalm of praise and joy. It is also particularly short (5 verses), where F alludes to their length by compounding them. Rowe's emendation assumes an easy error if Shakespeare used *hundred* as an ordinal, but it is far from clear that he did so: *OED* gives only one example of the form after 1413, and even this may be an archaism. But F's 'the hundred Psalms' relates to no fixed group and amounts to only two-thirds of the total number, 150. If Shakespeare wrote '150', the middle numeral might easily be misread (the date below Munday's signature on the manuscript of *John a Kent* has been interpreted by modern scholars as 1590, 1595, or 1596). Or Shakespeare may have written 'cl', and the 'l' been subsequently overlooked. Though the Folio sometimes demonstrably expands to full words, both arabic and roman numerals are found in printed texts of Shakespeare's plays. One need only assume a single numeral error.

2.1.84/643 straine] F; stain POPE

2.1.98 goodman] F (Good | man)

2.1.129/689 adieu] F; And theres the humor of it Q

2.1.136 Cathayan] F (*Cataian*)

2.1.149/708 Looke who comes yonder] F; God saue me, fee who yonder is Q. In Q, the line anticipates Mistress Quickly's entry. The line in the equivalent position is 'See where our husbands are'.

2.1.158/717 with you] F; for you G.T. *conj*. Compare *Caesar* 2.2.121/1016.

2.1.171/730 I marry do's he] F; perhaps | He hath spoke merrily, as the fashion of fat men | Are Q (*location approximate*). Greg thought Q's words had 'a genuine ring'.

2.1.179/738 ranting] F; ramping Q. F has the more unusual word: the first instance of *ranting* in *OED*.

2.1.182/741 God blesse you Bully-Rooke, God blesse you] This edition; How now Bully Rooke F; God bleffe you my bully rookes, God bleffe you Q. As the Host is the speaker, Q should be particularly reliable.

2.1.183/742 Gentleman.] HANMER (*after* Q); ~∧ F. In F, the word ends a type line.

2.1.199/758 guest-Caualeiro] KITTREDGE; gueft-Caualeire F. In *Dream* 4.1.22/1463 Shakespeare uses 'Caualery' as synonymous with *cavaliero*, but his only use of 'Caualier' is to mean a sprightly knight in the field, not an urban gallant. The Host elsewhere uses the '-o' form three times, two of them in the present passage (2.1.184/743, 2.1.188/747; 2.3.67/1156). The present exception is probably due to a simple *o/e* misreading.

2.1.200/759 FORD] Q; Shal⟨low⟩. F. F extends the sequence of prefixes in which Shallow alternates with the Host—an easy error in working from a manuscript in which the speech-prefixes were in a separate column from the speeches themselves. As Crane usually did not arrange prefixes in a separate column, the error is probably scribal, not compositorial.

2.1.202/761 Brooke] Q (Rrooke); Broome F. Elsewhere Q has 'Brooke'; F has 'Broome' throughout. See Introduction.

2.1.206/765 min-heires] HANMER (Theobald); An-heires F; on here COLLIER (Theobald); Ameers WILSON (Hart). This crux is particularly difficult as it is often thought to be linked to a similar crux in *1 Henry IV* 2.1.76/689, where in a comparable though not wholly equivalent context Q1 reads 'Oneyres'. It is unsatisfactory to suppose that both forms represent a single word which is now lost. Capell was admirably consistent in emending both words in the same way, but it is grossly improbable that his 'mynheers' should be corrupted by different agencies in such a broadly similar way (in one instance by plausible misreading and the other not) on the only two occasions Shakespeare used the word. Similar objections apply to other words, and no other proposed emendation is as satisfactory for both contexts. It is more likely that the two forms represent corruptions of distinct words. If the problems are considered separately, different solutions are suggested; for example, an '-ers' type of termination is appropriate to *1 Henry IV*, where '-heires' in *Merry Wives* invites interpretation as Dutch or German for 'gentlemen'. Copy 'min' would easily be read as 'ann'. The emendation anticipates 'mine Host' in Shallow's reply.

2.1.217 than] F (then)

2.2.2-5/786-9 I will retort ... open] This edition (G.T.); Why then the world's mine Oyfter, which I, with fword will open F; *I will retort the fum in equipage* Q. Q's line is thoroughly typical of Pistol, and has often been thought genuine. It is not adequately explained as memorial recollection of *Henry V* 2.1.49/534, as that line offers no parallel for the distinctive use of *equipage*—a word found nowhere else in Shakespeare's plays, but once in the Sonnets (32.12). Both *retort* and *equipage* are typical of Shakespeare's comic use of military jargon. Wilson and Bowers conflated: WILSON supplied Q's line before Sir John's opening speech; BOWERS added it after 'open'. These reconstructions, especially Wilson's, do not suggest ready explanations as to how the line came to be omitted in F. (Q's omission requires no special explanation as it is a typical result of reporting.) If F omits a second speech in which Sir John says 'Not a penny', the Folio reading would easily result from eyeskip.

2.2.9/793 Coach-fellow] F; couch-fellow THEOBALD

2.2.19/803 throng] F; thong POPE. Shakespeare only used *thong* once, and then as a part of a horse's bridle.

2.2.23 Ay, ay, I] F (I, I, I)

2.2.24/808 God] Q; heauen F. Compare 1.1.33/33 and 1.1.34/34. Shakespeare offers no parallels for 'the feare of heauen'.

2.2.26/810 you, you Rogue will] HIBBARD; you Rogue, will F; you Rogue, will you This edition *conj*. Mid-sentence vocative *rogue* without the second person pronoun is unexampled in Shakespeare. Sir John's 'you Rogue' particularly strongly suggests a vocative with attached pronoun, but 'you' in F must serve as subject of 'will en-sconce'. Q gives a reasonably good report up to 'lurch', then continues 'And yet you stand vpon your honor, you rogue. You, you.' This recapitulates the beginning of the speech, but may have been encouraged by vocative 'you Rogue' in the original. Hibbard's emendation addresses a genuine difficulty in F. Scribe or compositor would easily reduce 'yet you, you' to 'yet, you'. Arguably the interrogative would be more appropriate to the context. This too could be corrupted by simple error, though the error Hibbard assumes is an even easier one.

2.2.30/814 relent] F; recant Q. In defence of Q, compare Shakespeare's one other use of *recant*, *Merchant* 4.1.388/2197: 'I doe recant' (though the verb is there transitive). Shakespeare nowhere else has *I do relent* (though *relent* is always intransitive).

2.2.30/814 wouldst] Q; would F. The irregular reading was probably produced by contamination from 'would' immediately below in the following text line.

2.2.52/836 God-blesse] Q (~ₐ); heauen-bleſſe F. Q and F's 'his Seruants' (2.2.53/837) continues Q's reading.

2.2.66 rustling] F (ruſhling)

2.2.105/889 Blessing] F; Gods blessing This edition *conj.* Compare Quickly's 'Gods blessing of your good heart' in Q *2 Henry IV* 2.4.307/1336, similarly altered to ' 'Blessing on your good heart' in F. Shakespeare's only use of *blessing on your/his heart* without *God* in an unexpurgated text is in verse (*Richard II* 5.5.64/2593) and may have been determined by metre.

2.2.108/892 O God no, sir] Q (. . . no, . . .); *not in* F

2.2.131/915 Puncke] F; pink WARBURTON

2.2.147/931 ore'flowes] F; o'erflow with POPE. Pope's 'with' is unnecessary, but his omission of F's terminal '-s' is plausible.

2.2.148 Aha] F (ah ha)

2.2.149/933 encompass'd you] F; caught you a the hip Q. Q has colloquial vigour, is an idiom used by Shakespeare, and is comically appropriate. It could represent an authorial reading, but is a common expression and may equally be seen as a substitution for F's more sophisticated witticism, which the reporter may have forgotten.

2.2.150/934 God blesse] This edition; 'Bleſſe F; God ſaue Q. The apostrophe is characteristic of Crane, and may here indicate that he saw a deleted profanity in his copy.

2.2.168/952-3 halfe, or all] COLLIER 2 (Collier MS); all, or halfe F

2.2.170/954 I know . . . may] F; O Lord, I would I could tell how to Q

2.2.199/983 Iewell. That] THEOBALD; ~, that F

2.2.223.1/1008.1 He offers money] This edition; *not in* QF. Falstaff may actually accept the money here, depending on whether *make bold with* at 2.2.242/1028 means 'presume to take' or 'presume to use freely'.

2.2.225/1010 exchange] Q3; enchange F. F is contaminated by the previous word, 'in'.

2.2.233/1019 soule] F; suit COLLIER 2 (Collier MS)

2.2.243.1/1029.1 He takes the money] This edition; *not in* QF

2.2.253/1039 spokes-mate] Q (~ₐ ~); aſſi-|ſtant F. Q has a strong claim to be authorial on the basis of the word's appropriateness and rarity. *OED* cites one instance before Shakespeare wrote *Merry Wives*, in Stanyhurst's *Aeneis* (1582), which Shakespeare might have read. The only other quotation is 1640, where the word is associated with 'pander'. F's 'assistant' may be a substitution, perhaps influenced by the somewhat similar appearance of 'appointment'.

2.2.288/1074 Wittoll, Cuckold] F; wittold, godeſo Q. Q transposed this passage into Ford's speech beginning 3.5.128/1843. Q's profanity is nowhere found in a reliable Shakespeare text.

2.2.297/1083 God] Q; Heauen F. In similar expressions, Shakespeare invokes praise of God, the gods, the Lord, and Jupiter, but not heaven.

2.2.301/1087-8 Gods my life] Q; fie, fie, fie F. Shakespeare elsewhere uses the profanity in *Much Ado* 4.2.68/2047 and *Dream* 4.1.201/1642.

2.3.17/1105 God blesse] Q; 'Bleſſe F. Q makes the Host the third character to greet Caius, and attributes Shallow's greeting to Page, but the wording is sufficiently accurate to testify for the profanity.

2.3.18/1106 God saue] Q; 'Saue F. See previous note.

2.3.20/1108 'Giue] F; God giue This edition *conj.* This speech is not in Q.

2.3.23/1112 thee passe,] FQ; thy passe, CRAIK (*conj.*)

2.3.24 punto] F (punĉto)

2.3.27 Galen] F (Galien)

2.3.52/1140 word] Q; *not in* F. Hanmer interpreted 'a' as *ah*, but Q (in a passage quite well reported) would be most unlikely to render the same word as an article if it were the interjection. F's omission was no doubt encouraged by the similarity of 'word'

and the beginning of 'Mounseur' (presumably with lower-case initial).

2.3.52 Monsieur] F (Mounſeur)

2.3.73/1162 PAGE, SHALLOW, *and* SLENDER] MALONE; *All.* F

2.3.80/1169 Cride-game] FQ; Cry aim WARBURTON

2.3.84/1173 patiences] Q (patinces); patients F

3.1.5 Petty] F (pittie)

3.1.11/1189 Ieshu plesse me] Q (Ieſhu ples mee); 'Pleſſe my ſoule F; Jeshu pless my soul RIVERSIDE. *My soul* does not occur elsewhere in Shakespeare as the object of *bless*.

3.1.29/1207 God] This edition (G.T.); Heauen F. Shakespeare nowhere outside *Merry Wives* uses the expression *Heaven prosper*, but has *God prosper* in *2 Henry IV* 3.2.289/1813 and *Gods prosper* in *Lear*: *History* 14.90/2013 and 20.29-30/2357-8, *Tragedy* 3.7.90/1993 and 4.5.29-30/2236-7.

3.1.33/1211 gowne] F; cowne Q. The mispronunciation suggested by Q gives an obscenity (*coun*, 'cunt'). However, the same quibble is possible with *gown* itself—given an appropriate context. The reporter may have been recalling and misplacing a quibble from 4.2.63/1997, where a joke is more likely.

3.1.39/1217 God saue] Q; 'Saue F

3.1.40/1218 God plesse] Q; 'Pleſſe F

3.1.59 pottage] F (porredge). *OED* describes *porridge* as an 'altered form' of *pottage*; its first recorded use is *c.*1532. In Shakespeare's time both had the single meaning 'thick soup'. Porridge/porredge is probably an indifferent spelling variant of *pottage*. In Shakespeare's works *pottage* is found only once (*Lear*: *History* 11.49/1672, *Tragedy* 3.4.52/1700), but *porridge* nine times, so there is no reason to consider Evans's 'porredge' a form deliberately altered for comic effect. Modern editions printing 'porridge' suggest a confusion that could not originally have existed.

3.1.71/1250 question: let] F; ~ . | Shal⟨low⟩. Let Q. The prefix in Q is one of a series of evidently linked and deliberate changes. Shallow takes a role parallel to the Host's: before the Host's speech he says 'Keep them aſunder, take away their weapons'. Page's assistant in doing so must be Slender, who has no other role in the scene in Q.

3.1.75/1254 patience:] JOHNSON; ~ₐ F

3.1.81/1260 By Ieshu] Q; *not in* F

3.1.81/1260 Vrinal] F; vrinalls Q

3.1.83/1262 Diable] F; O Ieſhu Q. F's oath (which occurs elsewhere in Caius' speeches at 1.4.63/464) seems too unusual and characteristic to be a substitution. Q simply echoes 'By Ieshu' three lines above.

3.1.86/1265 As . . . you] F; So kad vdge me Q. F's reading again seems too characteristic to result from simple expurgation (and would itself have been objectionable to some Christians).

1270 excellant] F (excellant). F's anomalous spelling probably phonetically represents the French word.

3.1.93 Machiavel] F (Machiuell)

3.1.97/1276 Giue . . . (Tereſtiall) so:] Q (Giue . . .ₐ tereſtiall, | So,); *not in* F

3.1.103/1282 Lads] Q (lads); Lad F

3.1.104/1283 Afore God] Q; Truſt me F. See Taylor, 'Zounds'.

3.2.26/1320 Has] F; Hath COLLIER MS. *Hath* is Shakespeare's preferred form in reliable texts.

3.2.45/1339 By my faith] Q; Trust me F. See note to 2.1.31, 2.1.33/590, 592.

3.2.55/1349 Mʳ] F; ſonne Q. Slender might not be presumptuous enough to address Page as 'Father' if he could not expect recognition as potential son. Compare Page's *sonne Slender* at 3.4.74/1680 and 5.2.2./2455. 'Mʳ' could be read in from immediately below, but more plausibly 'sonne' results from memorial error.

3.3.3/1381 Robert] BOWERS; Robin F

3.3.13 Datchet] F (Dotchet)

3.3.38 pumpkin] F (Pumpion)

3.3.45/1423 Ile . . . Lord] F; By the Lord Q; Ile ſpeake it before the beſt Lord G.T. *conj.* If profanity has been expurgated, F's entire phrase seems too elaborate to be a substitution for an original simple 'By the Lord'. The simple addition of 'best' before 'Lord' could turn a religious statement into a social one. However, F is entirely in keeping with the social comedy of *Merry Wives*: Sir John projects himself as a man of the court, here as elsewhere.

3.3.52/1430   Tyre-valiant] F; tire vellet Q; tire-volant STEEVENS (*conj.*); Tyre-gallant G.T. *conj.* 'Vellet' is an old spelling of *velvet*. *Gallant* has the right associations with both showy dress and ships, but can scarcely have been corrupted in both texts to words beginning with 'v'.

3.3.56/1434   By the Lord] Q; *not in* F. Sir John uses Q's phrase six times in *1 Henry IV* and twice in *2 Henry IV*—but never, according to F, in *Merry Wives*.

3.3.60/1438   with Nature] This edition (G.T.); not Nature F; Nature CRAIK (*conj.*). ALEXANDER emended the punctuation alone but left a contrived reading which is difficult to convey: 'what thou wert, if Fortune thy foe were, not Nature, thy friend'. 'With' resolves the difficulty. The substitution is not arbitrary: a word graphically similar to the first syllable of the following word replaces a word graphically similar to the previous word, 'were'. Craik similarly sees anticipation of 'Nature' in 'not', but suggests dittography rather than substitution.

3.3.64/1442   thee, ther's] Q (~ | Ther's); ~. Ther's F
3.3.71   Mistress] F (M.)
3.3.74   kiln] F (kill) .
3.3.117/1493   For shame] F; Gode body Q. Q is not sufficiently well reported hereabouts to warrant adoption of an asseveration Shakespeare elsewhere used once (*1 Henry IV* 2.1.26/639).
3.3.141/1518   Look] F; Lord G.T. *conj.*
3.3.147/1524   IOHN] OLIVER; Ser⟨uant(s)⟩. F
3.3.157/1534   vncope] Wilson; vncape F; uncase SISSON; escape HIBBARD. F can scarcely be right: Shakespeare never used *cape* to mean 'cloak', and *OED* suggests that there was no such sense at the time except in the set expression *Spanish cape*. 'Vncape' begins with a run of minims, but no emendation has been found which is based on misreading of minims. Hand D in *More* wrote 'p' both with and without a fore-limb, so an 'op'/'ap' misreading could be even easier than 'o'/'a'. Wilson understood *uncope* to mean 'unmuzzle', but this is a puzzling nonce-word, especially as Shakespeare never used *cope* in the appropriate sense. However, 'cope' is also a spelling of *coop*, a verb Shakespeare did use in the general sense 'to confine (persons) within small space . . . to cage, cabin', and in his own extension of this sense (*K. John* 2.1.25/301), 'to enclose for protection or defence' (*OED*). 'Vncope' as *uncoop* is immediately intelligible as an intransitive verb, for it is parallel and almost synonymous with 'vnkennell', which has an explicit direct object.

3.3.162/1539   This is] F; By Ieshu these are Q. Here and at 3.3.200/1575 'By Ieshu' seems to have been introduced in Q in a mechanical way at the beginning of Evans's speeches. Such characterization by verbal tag is typical of a reporter's work, though the repeated use of the expression is evidence that it was used in some instances in the original text (see 3.1.1, 3.1.81, 4.2.180/1189, 1260, 2116).

3.3.171/1548   what] HARNESS; who F. Strictly speaking, as Oliver pointed out, Ford asked neither who nor what was in the basket. Whereas 'Whether beare you this?' may imply a query as to the purpose of the basket, and therefore suspicion as to its contents, Ford cannot be understood to demand the identity of someone he suspects to be in the basket.

3.3.183/1560   foolish] F2; foolishion F1
3.3.193   Ay, I] F (I, I)
3.3.194/1571   me] This edition (Capell); you F. Q does not preserve the line. In F the contrast between 'you' and 'your thoughts' is strained, especially as Ford has been acting extravagantly and in full accordance with his suspicions. Capell's conjecture is more trenchant as well as more intelligible, particularly in the force it lends to Ford's 'Amen'. In context the error would be an easy one.

3.3.199   Ay, Ay, I] F (I, I: I)
3.3.200/1575   If] F; By Ieshu if Q. See note to 3.3.162/1539.

3.3.201-2/1576-7   heauen . . . iudgement] F; *I am an arrant Iew: Now God plesse me* Q
3.3.217   heartily] F (hartly)
3.3.226   Master] F (M.)
3.3.226.1/1601.1   Exeunt . . . Caius] HIBBARD; *not in* QF; *Ford and Page go forth . . .* WILSON Wilson supplies an exit for Mistress Ford and Mistress Page at 3.3.217/1592, which is plausible. Other editions, for example new Arden and Riverside, less plausibly have Ford and Page leave at 3.3.226.1/1601.1 and their wives remain on stage until the scene ends.

3.3.230/1605-6   A . . . mockeries] F; *By so kad vdgme, M. Fordes is* | *Not in his right wittes* Q. Q uses the oath twice elsewhere (3.1.86/1265 and 4.4.78/2238), but only here could it be justified as an attractive reading. One might suspect that, as with 'By Ieshu', the repetition of the oath as a characteristic of Evans's speech indicates that it was used somewhere in the original text. But whereas Shakespeare, on the evidence of other plays, used *Jesu* as a way of characterizing the speech of Welsh characters, he did not use *So God judge me* under any circumstances.

3.4.12/1618   FENTON] Q3; *not in* F. F indents the line, so that 'No' is immediately below the prefix 'An.', but fails to supply a prefix.
3.4.12/1618   heauen] F; God G.T. *conj. God speed* is the usual expression.
3.4.21/1627   then: Harke] THEOBALD; ~, harke F
3.4.37   Mistress] F (M.)
3.4.45/1651   by God] Q (be God); *not in* F
3.4.55/1661   Odd's-hart-lings] F; Godefo Q. F is also profane and more unusual than Q (which, though common enough elsewhere, never occurs in a reliable Shakespeare text).
3.4.56/1662   God] Q; Heauen F
3.4.57/1663   God] This edition; Heauen F. Q omits the phrase. Consistency with 'God/Heauen' in the previous line seems desirable.
3.4.66/1672   Fenton] Q3; Fenter F1
3.4.88/1694   selfe,] F; ~ ; WARBURTON
3.4.96/1702   and] F; or HANMER. Mistress Quickly misquotes the proverbial 'a fool or a physician'. The misuse of a set expression gives some point to a misreading that would otherwise be merely confusing.

3.5.8/1723   'Sblood the] Q (Sblood, the); The F. Q's oath is one of the most objectionable in the period, and (along with 'swounds) was singled out for particular expurgation in the Folio.
3.5.8/1723   slighted] Q; slided Q. Q's facile sense and unusual past-tense form suggest it is a corruption, though F's 'slighted' requires a pun on, or at least an echo of, *slided* (as well as *sleight*, 'deceive, trick').
3.5.10/1725   blinde bitches] FQ; bitch's blind THEOBALD. F may be understood as '(a litter of) blind bitch's puppies', or as a transferred epithet.
3.5.16/1732   By the Lord] Q; I should haue beene F. See note to 3.3.56/1434.
3.5.18   Mistress] F (M.)
1744   Pullet-Spersme] F. The unusual form 'spersme' looks like a confusion on the analogy of 'spasme'.
3.5.33   Mistress] F (M.)
3.5.36/1751   Alas . . . good-heart] F; O Lord sir Q. Q's common and summary profanity begins a badly reported passage. *Alas the day* also occurs at 4.2.62/1996, where Q part-verifies F with 'Alas'.
3.5.56/1771   By the Masse] Q; Oh F
3.5.56/1771   he] Q; be F
3.5.57/1772   God blesse] This edition; God saue Q; Blesse F
3.5.63/1778   sped] F; how sped Q
3.5.77/1792   God] Q; good lucke F
3.5.79/1794   by] Q; in F. F could easily have been influenced by 'intelligence' and 'inuention'.
3.5.82/1797   By the Lord] Q; Yes F. See 3.3.56/1434. Something stronger than a lame 'Yes' is highly desirable.
3.5.88/1802   what] F; by the Lord for your sake Q. Q conflates material around 'sufferd' at 3.5.89/1803 and 'suffered' at 3.5.100/1814; it is not well reported. The reporter seems to have seized on 'by the Lord' as a typical oath for Sir John, with

the result that it occurs three times in a single speech. We accept only the first as authoritative.

3.5.108/1822 it] F; by the Lord it Q. See previous note.

3.5.112/1826 serge] F; forge CAPELL (*conj.*). Forges are associated with heat, not cooling.

3.5.112 surge] F (ſerge)

4.1.1 Mistress] F (M.)

4.1.12/1867 'Blessing] F; Gods blessing This edition *conj*. See notes to 2.2.105/889 and 2.2.150/934.

4.1.55/1911 *Genitiuo*] DOUAI MS, SINGER; *Genitiue* F

4.1.56 Jenny's] F (Ginyes)

4.1.60–1 hick ... hack ... whorum] F (*hic* ... *hac* ... *horum*)

4.1.63/1919 Lunatics] CAPELL; Lunaties F

4.1.71/1927 que] F; *quæ* POPE. Evans has difficulty with the Latin vowel in the following line, and above at 4.1.38/1894 ('*hag*' for '*hæc*').

4.1.72/1928 Ques] F; *quæs* POPE

4.2.5 accoutrement] F (accuſtrement)

4.2.18/1953 lines] F; vaine Q; lunes THEOBALD

4.2.23/1958 this his] F; this COLLIER (*conj.*). F's 'his' is redundant, and could have been interpolated by a scribe or compositor under the influence of 'this', 'dis-', and/or 'he is'.

4.2.50/1985 Birding-peeces. | ⌈MISTRIS PAGE⌉ Creepe] DYCE (Malone); ~-~: creepe F.

4.2.51 kiln-hole] F (kill-hole)

4.2.59/1994 PAGE] MALONE; Ford. F1. F1 has two consecutive speeches attributed to Mistress Ford. F2 unconvincingly solves the problem by omitting the prefix at 4.2.61/1996. Wilson follows F1, but agrees with a private conjecture by Greg that there is a missing prefix for Mistress Page before 'vnlesse'. Simple substitution would be the easier error. Malone's emendation is supported by Q: '*Fal.* Why then Ile goe out of doores. | *Mi. Pa.* Then your vndone, your but a dead man'. F's equivalent to the speech Q gives Mistress Page ('If ... *Iohn*') is particularly appropriate to her, for it is she who has entered from outside with news of Ford's supposed ambushing brothers.

4.2.65/2000 Good hearts] F; For Gods ſake Q. There are parallels for F at 4.5.117/2367 and *The Tempest* 1.1.25/26–7. If Q preserves the original text, which is possible, Shakespeare himself is likely to have emended the profanity.

4.2.67/2002 The fat woman] F; *Gillian* Q. Q feeds in the name of the well-known scurrilous comic figure here and at 4.2.157/2094; F at 4.2.169/2105 refers to her as 'mother *Prat*'.

4.2.67–8 Brentford] F (Brain-|ford). Similarly throughout.

4.2.90/2025 direct] Q3; direct direct F

4.2.91/2027 straight.] F. Q adds: '*Fal*⟨*staffe*⟩. Come for Gods ſake, any thing.' This is dramatically effective, and loss of such a line from F could, in particular, follow from deletion of profanity. However, Q's line is a mixture of phrases from preceding lines in Q—'Come goe with me', 'for Gods sake', and 'any extremitie'—and so may be a reconstruction.

4.2.93/2029 him] F2; *not in* F1

4.2.93/2029 Exit Mistris Ford] CAPELL (after 4.2.91/2027); *not in* QF. Mistress Ford exits in order to fetch the servants, who otherwise appear without explanation. Compare 3.3/Sc. 10, where they have to be elaborately summoned from off stage, even though they are part of a preconcerted plan. Moreover, Mistress Page's couplets look like a scene-ending address to the audience; it would be surprising if anyone else were on stage. Their purpose is to cover the time between Mistress Ford's exit and her entrance with the servants. The staging would have the effect of clearing the stage and so creating a scene-break, were it not for the stage-property of the buck-basket, which is probably on stage already and so establishes continuity of time and place.

4.2.97.1/2033.1 Mist. Ford with] CAPELL; *not in* FQ

4.2.101, 103/2037, 2039 IOHN] OLIVER; I Ser⟨uant⟩. F

4.2.102/2038 ROBERT] OLIVER; 2 Ser⟨uant⟩. F

4.2.103/2039 as lief] F2; lief as F1

4.2.106/2042 villains] COLLIER 2 (Collier MS); villaine F

4.2.108/2043 ging] F2; gin F1

4.2.108 gang] F2 (ging)

4.2.115/2052 this is] Q3; thi is F1

4.2.121/2058 God be] This edition; Gods my Q; Heauen be F

4.2.132/2069 PAGE] This edition (Lambrechts); *M. Ford*. F. F could result from two-stage error: (*a*) confusion with the prefixes above or below, giving '*Ford*.', (*b*) the obvious correction to the obvious error of three successive prefixes for Ford.

4.2.152/2089.1 Exeunt ... basket] OLIVER; *not in* FQ

4.2.157/2094 Aunt] F; *Ant*, *Gilliā* Q. See note to 4.2.67/2002.

4.2.168/2104 not strike] Q3; ſtrike F

4.2.173 runnion] F. The word occurs elsewhere only in *Macbeth* 1.3.5/83, and there has the form 'ronyon', which must therefore be regarded as an alternative modern spelling.

4.2.180/2116 Ieshu] Q; yea, and no F. *OED* describes F's phrase as 'a formula of asseveration in the form of, and substituted for, an oath', and cites no examples before Shakespeare. It is closest in sound to *By Jesu*. As Shakespeare associates the expression with the mealy-mouthed, not the Welsh, one would expect *Jeshu* here. If *Jeshu* is right, the substitution of a Shakespearian idiom in F is most straightforwardly explained if Shakespeare made the alteration, though as Shallow uses the expression at 1.1.80/79 this conclusion is not inevitable.

4.2.182/2118 his] F; her Q. F's 'his' could be an easy error for 'hir', but may quite plausibly be intended as what we might now call a comic Freudian slip.

4.2.188/2124 By my troth] Q; Trust me F. See note to 2.1.31, 33/590, 592

4.2.210/2146 it, then ‸] F; it‸ then, HANMER

4.3.1/2148 Germanes desire] CAPELL; Germane deſires F

4.3.7/2154 them] Q; him F

4.3.9/2156 house] Q; houſes F. F may be contaminated by 'horses' on the line above.

4.4.6/2165 Cold] ROWE; gold F. An easy misreading of capital letters; compare 'cripple' for 'Gripple' in *K. John* 5.2.36/2166.

4.4.25/2184 MISTRIS] F (M.). Apart from here and at 5.5.211/2707, 'M.' occurs in speech-prefixes either when the wife or husband is not on stage, or as 'Mistress' when the husband has an immediately adjacent speech.

4.4.27/2186 Herne] F; *Horne* Q. Similarly throughout. Greg believed that the name should be '*Horne*', as in Q.

4.4.31/2190 trees] HANMER; tree F. The loss of the plural form would be encouraged by the singular 'Oake' in the previous line.

4.4.32/2191 makes] F2; make F1

4.4.42/2201 Disguis'd ... head] Q (Diſguiſed like *Horne*, with huge horns on his head,); *not in* F. There is limited word-for-word correspondence between Q and F hereabouts. But, considered independently of Q, F appears to have omitted a line explaining the plot, whose contents are represented very plausibly by the line at the equivalent point in Q.

4.4.44/2203 shape. When] CAPELL; ~, when F.

4.4.49 oafs] F (Ouphes)

4.4.60/2219 ⌈MISTRIS⌉ FORD] ROWE; Ford. F. Shakespeare or Crane may have written ambiguous 'M.'.

4.4.69/2228 That will be excellent] F; So kad vdge me the deuiſes is excellent Q (*as first line of Evans's preceding speech*)

4.4.69 vizors] F (vizards)

4.4.72/2231 tire] THEOBALD (*after* Q); time F. Q has: '*Mis. For.* But who will buy the silkes to tyre the boyes? | *Pa.* That will I do, and in a robe of white | Ile cloath my daughter ...'. 'Silke' and 'tyre' are in the same line in Q, and the sequence 'That will I ... and in ...' leads to a reference to a robe. Similarly, in lines influenced by the present speech, Q1 has Mistress Page say 'And in that Maske, Ile make the Doctor steale my daughter *An*': 'Maske', like 'robe', is a plausible substitution for 'tire', but not for 'time'.

4.4.81/2240 quickly] F; *Quickly* THEOBALD. Except in stage directions, Quickly is always given the title Mistress or, once, 'nursh-a'.

4.5.41/2290 SIMPLE] ROWE; Fal ⟨ſtaffe⟩. F

4.5.51/2300 Sir‸ tike,] REED; Sir: like, F; tike, Q; sir Tike; like STEEVENS (Farmer). 'Tike' is an unlikely memorial substitution for 'like'. Misreading is possible in either direction, though *like* is by far the commoner word and therefore the more likely to be corrupt. Pistol uses *tike* as an insult in *Henry V* 2.1.29/514.

4.5.54/2303 art] Q; are F

4.5.59.1/2308.1 muddie] This edition; not in FQ. It would be odd if Bardolph were not muddy. Benvolio, Frederick, and Martino appear muddy in the episode of *Doctor Faustus* to which Bardolph alludes at 4.5.65/2314-15.

4.5.60/2309 O Lord] Q; Out alas F

4.5.71/2321 three] F; three forts of Q. Q may recall an authorial original (compare following note). *Sort* is used oddly, though the phrase may be Evans's way of saying 'a sort (i.e. disreputable band) of three'. But there has been some rewriting of this passage in Q, presumably after the report was made: for instance, the entries of Evans and Caius are transposed, both Caius and Evans have lines gloating on their revenge, and Evans's farewell is 'grate why', which has been interpreted as a rendering of Welsh *cadw chwi*, 'God bless you'.

4.5.72/2322 Cozen-Garmombles] Q; Cozen-Iermans F. *Garmombles* was a word used by Nashe, but Q contains an almost inescapable allusion to Count Mömplegard (see Introduction). Such a joke must have belonged to early performances. If Shakespeare himself voluntarily made the deletion, he was reacting to the lost topicality of the allusion, not seeking to improve the play in the normal sense. But anyone may have substituted 'Iermans' for 'Garmombles', having recognized that the characters are the 'Germane-diuels' of 4.5.65/2314, the 'Germanes' of 4.5.67/2317. The present line is the only time *Germany* or *German(s)* is spelt with 'I' except for Caius' comic pronounciation indicated by 'Iamanie' (4.5.81/2331; cf. 'Iarteer' for *Garter*). Late annotation by Shakespeare or someone else could possibly be indicated.

2323 Readins] F; similarly Q (Readings). Q and probably F give regular old spellings of Reading (Old English *Readingas*; Domesday Book *Reddinges*).

4.5.73 Colnbrook] F (Cole-Brooke)

4.5.96/2346 enough] F; inough to say my prayers Q

4.5.103/2353 O Lord sir, and] Q; And F. Compare the Hostess's 'O Lord I' in *2 Henry IV* 2.1.7/617.

4.5.109-10/2360 Braineford. But] THEOBALD; ~, but F

4.5.117/2367 here is] F. It is difficult to know how much licence to allow the speech of some characters in *Merry Wives* before corruption is suspected. In this instance, 'here is' could be a dittography of the same words in the line above. One might conjecture 'there is' or 'here'.

4.6.16-17/2386-7 fat ... Scene] F; Wherein fat Falftaffe had a mightie fcare Q

4.6.26/2396 euer] POPE; euen F. Q has 'still against that match'. Oliver claims that this could recall either reading, but it surely points more strongly to Pope's emendation, which makes better sense and assumes a very easy misreading.

4.6.38/2408 denote] CAPELL; deuote F

4.6.39 visorèd] F (vizarded)

5.1.22 Goliath] F (Goliah). F gives a common old spelling (described as incorrect by *OED*).

5.2.2/2455 light] F; lights CRAIK (*conj.*). Compare note to 5.2.11/2464.

5.2.2-3/2455-6 my daughter.] F2; my, F1

5.2.10 struck] F (ftrooke)

5.2.11/2464 Lights] This edition; Light F. F would give the commonest of errors in a text with several stages of transmission. 'Lights' is less ambiguous and more accurate than 'Light'. The plural is also suggested by its rhyme with 'Spirits' (compare 'euill' and 'deuill' in the same speech).

5.2.12/2465 God] This edition (G.T.); Heauen F. See note to 3.1.29/1207.

5.3.12/2479 Hugh] CAPELL; Herne F; *Evans* THEOBALD; *not in* HART

5.4.0.1/2491.1 disguis'd as a Satyr] DYCE; not in FQ. Capell describes all who enter as 'vizarded, and disguis'd for Fairies'. Dyce introduced consistency with Q's direction at 5.5.35.1-5/2531.1-4. Oliver has insufficient confidence in Q to specify the disguise, but there are no good grounds for doubting it: a satyr makes an effective grotesque pair with a hobgoblin.

5.5.1 struck] F (ftroke)

5.5.11 foul fault] F (fowle-|fault)

5.5.28.1/2524.1 A noise within] BOWERS; *There is a noife of hornes* Q; *not in* F. At 4.4.51/2210 Mistress Page plans for the fairies to have rattles in their hands, presumably to make a supernatural-sounding noise. The sound of hunting-horns is fitting in its way, but not particularly appropriate to Sir John's reaction to the noise or to the tone of the fairies' entry. Q may represent an alternative staging introduced when the scene was rewritten, or simply anticipate the '*noyse of hunting*' in the direction following 5.5.101.5/2597.5.

5.5.30/2526 God] Q; Heauen F

5.5.41, 5.5.82, 5.5.87/2537, 2578, 2583 HOB-GOBLYN] This edition (*following* WILSON (Harness): *Puck*.); Pift⟨oll⟩, F; *Sir Hu*⟨*gh*⟩. Q. Q simplifies the staging, but F clearly requires a speaker other than Evans (see 5.5.87/2583). It is scarcely credible that Pistol should, without explanation or comment, appear in disguise after an absence of over 1,600 lines. The best explanation, one rejected by Oliver, is that the prefix indicates the actor who played Pistol, and not the character. In F's massed entry for the scene, Pistol's name comes last: contrary to Crane's habit of listing groups of characters in order of appearance, it follows '*Slender, Fenton, Caius*' who only enter later. Crane would have made up his massed directions by collating a scene's directions in his copy. Pistol inferably did not appear in the normal course of these. Crane probably added the name later when he found it as a speech-prefix or an annotation.

5.5.48 Bead] F (Bede), Q (Pead)

5.5.56 oafs] F (Ouphes)

5.5.67/2563 More] F2; Mote F1

5.5.69 em'rald tufts] F (Emrold-tuffes)

5.5.80/2576 God] Q; Heauens F. G.T. conjectures 'now' after 'me'. If this conjecture is right, disyllabic 'Heauens' is required. But Q's 'God blesse me from that wealch Fairie' concurs with F in denying such a reading. Shakespeare used the expression *God defend* someone many times and *Heavens defend* never. The plural is not, however, the usual or most obvious emendation of *God*, and, as Shakespeare uses *Heavens* in analogous phrases, he may have been responsible for making the alteration when profanity was removed.

5.5.116/2612 meat] WILSON; meete F. Wilson pointed out that 'meat' was a recognized spelling of *mate*, and that *meet* and *mate* were therefore confusible.

5.5.118.1/2614.1 He ... hornes] Falftaffe pulles of his bucks head Q (*following fairies' exeunt*, 5.5.101.6-7/2597.6). Q's stage directions may indicate a different property from the pair of horns to which the text refers, and may reflect more general non-Shakespearian changes in the last scene. It seems theatrically pointless for Sir John to take off the horns immediately before he is mocked on account of them.

5.5.120/2616 By the Lord] Q; not in F. See note to 3.3.56/1434.

5.5.150/2646 FORD] F; MISTRIS FORD This edition *conj*.

5.5.193/2689 white] ROWE 3; greene F. Here and at 5.5.197/2693 and 5.5.203/2699 F is puzzlingly at variance with the text earlier: one would expect inconsistencies of staging to have been corrected. Q has its own scheme, evidently reflecting an alternative staging, whereby Caius takes a fairy in red; Slender, green; and Fenton takes Anne dressed in white.

5.5.197/2693 greene] ROWE 3; white F

5.5.201 un garçon] F (oon Garfoon)

5.5.201 un paysan] F (oon pefant)

5.5.203/2699 greene] POPE; white F

5.5.211/2707 MISTRIS] F (M.). See note to 4.4.25/2184.

5.5.235/2731 so (Sir Iohn:)] F; ~:— Sir John, THEOBALD

THE MERRY WIVES OF WINDSOR

INCIDENTALS

1-2 Star-Chamber] ~-|~ F; ſtar-cham-|ber Q   7 Rato-lorum] Rato lorum   47-8 deaths-bed] ~-|~   92 betweene] be tweene
168 vertuous] vertuons   233 discretion-answere] diſcetion-anſwere   375 humor-Letter] ~-|~   384 And] & (*see Lineation Notes*)   411 breede-bate] ~-|~   440 adown'a,] ~.   443-4 greene-a-Box] ~-|~-~   451 quickly] (*italic*)   465 La-roone] (*roman*)   540 Fenton] Feuton   558 him] hiim   594 beleeue] beleeee   615 wel-behaued] ~-|~   747 Bully-Rooke] ~-|~   806 honor] hononor   809 shuffle] ſhufflle   812 bold-beating-oathes] ~-|~-~   1025 too-too] ~-|~
1078 Welsh-man] ~-|~   1120 (Boy.)] (~ˬ)   1122 no-come] ~-|~   1123 Doctor) he] Doćto)rhe   1138-9 Church-man] ~-|~   1141 Mocke-water] ~-|~   1194 Riuers] Ruiers   1242 acquainted] acquaiuted   1385 briefe.] ~,   1402 vs?] ~ˬ   1445 likeˬ] ~.   1507 Falstaffe] Faiſtaffe   1571 thoghts.] ~ˬ   1597 so?] ~:   1599 Companie.] ~ˬ
1600 make-a-the-turd] ~-~-theturd   1604 with all] withall   1635 you.] ~ˬ   1676 Fenton,] ~.   1781 Cornuto Curnuto   1825 Dutch-dish] ~-|~   1827 Horse-shoo] ~-|~   1847-8 Buck-baskets] ~-|~   1851-2 Pepper-Boxe] ~-|~   1856 horne-mad] ~-|~   1893 hic,] ~ˬ (?)   1903 O, Vocatiuo, O] O, ~, O   1919 O'man] F (*text*); 'Oman F (*c.w.*)   2007 Mistris] Miſtriis   2032 oftenˬ] ~,   2200 vs,] ~.   2367 good-hearts] ~-|~   2419 in] Fb; id Fa
2477 heart-breake] ~-|~   2697 oon Garsoon . . . oon pesant] (*roman*)   2705 pardon.] ~ˬ   2733 Ford.] ~:

QUARTO STAGE DIRECTIONS

1.1.0.1-2/0.1 *Enter Iustice* Shallow, *Syr* Hugh, *Maister* Page, | *and* Slender.
1.1.100.1/99.1 *Enter Syr* Iohn Falstaffe, Pistoll, Bardolfe, | *and* Nim.
1.1.171.1, 174.1-2/170.1, 173.1-2 *Enter Mistresse* Foord, *Mistresse* Page, *and her* | *daughter* Anne.
1.1.177.1/176.1 *Syr* Iohn *kisses her.*
1.1.180.1/179.1 *Exit all, but* Slender *and* | *mistresse* Anne.
1.1.279.1/277.1 *Enter Maister* Page.
1.1.293.1/290.1 *Exit omnes.*
1.2.0.1/290.2 *Enter sir* Hugh *and* Simple, *from dinner.*
1.2.13/303 *Exit omnes.*
1.3.0.1-2, 1.3.1.1/303.1-2, 304.1 *Enter sir* Iohn Falstaffes *Host of the Garter,* | Nym, Bardolfe, Pistoll, *and the boy.*
1.3.14/317.1 *Exit Host.*
1.3.18.1/321.1 *Exit* Bardolfe.
1.3.79.1/382.1 *Exit* Falstaffe, | *and the Boy.*
1.3.97/400 *Exit omnes.*
1.4.0.1/400.1 *Enter Mistresse* Quickly, *and* Simple.
1.4.36.1/436.1 *He steps into the Counting-house.*
1.4.40.1/440.1 *And she opens the doore.*
1.4.52.1/453.1 *Enter* Iohn.
1.4.84.1/485.1 *The Doctor writes.*
1.4.122.1/522.1 *Exit Doctor.* (after 1.4.121/521)
1.4.160/560 *Exit omnes.*
2.1.0.1/560.1 *Enter Mistresse* Page, *reading of* | *a Letter.*
2.1.30.1/589.1 *Enter Mistresse* Foord.
2.1.96.1-2/656.1-2 *Enter* Ford, Page, Pistoll *and* Nym.
2.1.120/680 *Exit* Pistoll.
2.1.129.1/689.1 *Exit* Nym.
2.1.148.1/707.1 *Enter Mistresse* Quickly. (equivalent position)
2.1.158.1-2/717.1-2 *Exit Mistresse* Ford, *Mis.* Page, *and* Quickly. (equivalent position)
2.1.178.1, 183.1/737.1, 742.1 *Enter Host and* Shallow.
2.1.192.1/751.1 Ford *and the Host talkes.* (omitting the Host's speech)
2.1.218/777 *Exit Host and* Shallow. (equivalent position)
2.1.225/784 *Exit omnes.*
2.2.0.1/784.1 *Enter Syr* Iohn, *and* Pistoll.
2.2.32.1/816.1 *Enter Mistresse* Quickly.
2.2.129.1/913 *Exit Mistresse* Quickly. (after a farewell following Falstaff's speech)
2.2.139.1/923.1 *Enter* Bardolfe.
2.2.149.1-2/933.1 *Enter* Foord *disguised like* Brooke.
2.2.276/1062 *Exit* Falstaffe.
2.2.302/1088 *Exit* Ford.
2.3.0.1/1088.1 *Enter the Doctor and his man.*
2.3.16.2-3/1104.2 *Enter* Shallow, Page, *my Host, and* Slender. (equivalent position)
2.3.73.1/1162.1 *Exit all but the Host and Doctor.*
2.3.89/1178 *Exit omnes.*
3.1.0.1-2/1178.1-2 *Enter Syr* Hugh *and* Simple.

3.1.34.2-3/1212.2 *Enter* Page, shallow, *and* Slender.
3.1.67.1-2, 68.1/1246.1, 1247.1 *Enter Doctor and the Host, they* | *offer to fight.*
3.1.103/1282 *Exit Host.*
3.1.115.1/1294.1 (*Exit omnes*
3.2.8.1/1302.1 *Enter M.* Foord. (previous dialogue omitted)
3.2.43.1-3/1337.1-2 *Enter* Shallow, Page, host, Slender, Doctor, | *and sir* Hugh. (equivalent position)
3.2.77.1/1370.1 *Exit* Shallow *and* Slender,
3.2.80/1373 *Exit host.*
3.2.85/1378 *Exit omnes.*
3.3.0.1, 3.3.4.1/1378.1, 1382.1 *Enter Mistresse* Ford, *with two of her men, and* | *a great buck busket.*
3.3.17.1/1395.1 *Exit seruant* (equivalent position)
3.3.38.1/1416.1 *Enter Sir* Iohn.
3.3.86.1/1463.1 Falstaffe *stands behind the aras.* (2 lines after Mistress Page enters)
3.3.86.2/1463.2 *Enter Mistresse* Page. (equivalent position)
3.3.132/1509 (*A side.* (refers to following line)
3.3.133.1-3.3.142.2.3/1510.1-1519.2 *Sir* Iohn *goes into the basket, they put cloathes ouer him,* | *the two men carries it away:* Foord *meetes it, and all* | *the rest,* Page, Doctor, Priest, Slender, Shallow. (without intervening dialogue)
3.3.166/1543 *Exit omnes.*
3.3.188.1/1565.1 *Enter all.* (equivalent position)
3.3.226.1, 3.3.230.1/1601.1, 1606 *Exit omnes:*
3.4.0.1/1606.1 *Enter M.* Fenton, Page, *and mistresse* | Quickly. (3.4 transposed with 3.5)
3.4.21.1-2, 63.1/1627, 1669.1 *Enter M.* Page *his wife, M.* Shallow, *and* Slender. (transposing dialogue of 3.4.22-64/1628-70)
(*they whisper.*) (referring to Page and Slender, six lines after Page's entry)
3.4.75.1, 3.4.94.1/1681.1, 1700.1 *Exit* Page *and his wife.* (staging reorganized)
3.4.75.1, 3.4.94.1/1681.1, 1700.1 *Exit omnes but* Quickly. (before Quickly's speech)
3.4.100.1/1706.1 (*Exit Fen.* (after 3.4.99/1705, in a passage preceding 3.4.76-94/1682-1700)
3.4.109/1715 *Exit.*
3.5.0.1/1715.1 *Enter Sir* Iohn Falstaffe. (3.5 transposed with 3.4)
3.5.23.1/1738.1 *Enter Mistresse* Quickly. (equivalent position)
3.5.53/1768 *Exit mistresse* Quickly.
3.5.55.1/1770.1 *Enter* Brooke. (after 3.5.56/1771)
3.5.127.1/1843 *Exit* Falstaffe.
3.5.140/1856 *Exit omnes.*
4.2.0.1/1935 *Enter Syr* Iohn.
4.2.0.1, 4.2.97.1/1935.1, 2033.1 *Enter misteris* Ford *and her two men.* (beginning scene with dialogue of 4.2.98/2034 ff.)
4.2.9.1/1944.1 *He steps behind the arras.*
4.2.9.2/1944.2 *Enter mistresse* Page. (2 lines before next direction)

349

THE MERRY WIVES OF WINDSOR

4.2.75, 97/2010, 2033 *Exit Mis. Page, & Sir Iohn.* (equivalent position; following passages omitted)
4.2.103.1-3/2039.1-2 *Enter M. Ford, Page, Priest, Shallow, the two men | carries the basket, and Ford meets it.*
4.2.166.1-2, 4.2.171.1, 4.2.174/2102.1-2, 2107.1, 2110 *Enter Falstaffe disguised like an old woman, and mi-|steris Page with him, Ford beats him, and hee | runnes away.*
4.2.187/2123 *Exit omnes.*
4.2.211/2147 *Exit both.*
4.3.0.1/2147.1 *Enter Host and Bardolfe.*
4.3.11/2158 *Exit omnes.*
4.4.0.1-2/2158.1-2 *Enter Ford, Page, their wiues, Shallow, and Slen-|der. Syr Hu.*
4.4.80, 4.4.81.1, 4.4.88.1/2239, 2240.1, 2247.1 *Exit omnes.*
4.5.0.1/2247.2 *Enter Host and Simple.*
4.5.21.1/2269.1 *Enter Sir Iohn.* (after 4.5.23/2271)
4.5.59.1/2308.1 *Enter Bardolfe.*
4.5.67.1/2317.1 *Enter Sir Hugh.*
4.5.76.1/2326.1 *Exit.*
4.5.76.2/2326.2 *Enter Doctor.* (transposing Evans's and Caius' entries)
4.5.83/2333 *Exit.*
4.5.86.1/2336.1 *Exit.*
4.5.96.1/2346.1 *Enter Mistresse Quickly.* (after 4.5.97/2347)
4.5.120/2370 *Exit omnes.*
4.6.0.1/2370.1 *Enter Host and Fenton.*
4.6.54.1/2424.1 *Exit omnes.*
5.5.0.1-2/2493.1-2 *Enter sir Iohn with a Bucks head vpon him.*
5.5.14.1/2510.1 *Enter mistris Page, and mistris Ford.* (after Falstaff's speech)
5.5.28.1, 5.5.32.1-2, 5.5.35.1-5/2524.1, 2528.1, 2531.1-4 *There is a noise of hornes, the two women run away. | Enter sir Hugh like a Satyre, and boyes drest like Fayries, | mistresse Quickly, like the Queene of Fayries: they | sing a song about him, and afterward speake.* (after 5.5.29/2525; without intervening dialogue)
5.5.87.1/2583.1 *They put the Tapers to his fingers, and he starts.*
5.5.91.1-2, 5.5.101.1-9, 5.5.118.1/2587.1-2, 2597.1-8, 2614.1 *Here they pinch him, and sing about him, & the Doc-|tor comes one way & steales away a boy in red. And | Slender another away he takes a boy in greene: And | Fenton steales misteris Anne, being in white. And | a noyse of hunting is made within: and all the Fai-|ries runne away. Falstaffe pulles of his bucks head, | and rises vp. And enters M. Page, M. Ford, and | their wiues, M. Shallow, Sir Hugh.* (after 5.5.91/2524; omitting words of song)
5.5.173.1/2669.1 *Enter Slender.* (omitting the line spoken by Slender)
5.5.199.1/2695.1 *Enter the Doctor.* (transposing the entries of Slender and Caius)
5.5.206.1/2702.1 *Enter Fenton and Anne.* (equivalent position)
5.5.237/2733 *Exit omnes.*

FOLIO STAGE DIRECTIONS

1.1.1-2/0.1 *Enter Iustice* Shallow, Slender, *Sir* Hugh Euans, *Master | Page, Falstoffe, Bardolph, Nym, Pistoll, Anne Page, | Mistresse Ford, Mistresse Page, Simple.*
1.1.293.1/290.1 *Exeunt.*
1.2.0.1/290.2 *Enter Euans, and Simple.*
1.2.13/303 *Exeunt.*
1.3.0.1-2/303.1-2 *Enter Falstaffe, Host, Bardolfe, Nym, Pistoll, Page.*
1.3.97/400 *Exeunt.*
1.4.0.1/400.1 *Enter Mistris Quickly, Simple, Iohn Rugby, Doctor, | Caius, Fenton.*
1.4.160/560 *Exit.*
2.1.0.1/560.1 *Enter Mistris Page, Mistris Ford, Master Page, Master | Ford, Pistoll, Nim, Quickly, Host, Shallow.*
2.1.225/784 *Exeunt.*
2.2.0.1/784.1 *Enter Falstaffe, Pistoll, Robin, Quickly, Bardolffe, | Ford.*
2.2.302/1088 *Exit.*
2.3.0.1/1088.1 *Enter Caius, Rugby, Page, Shallow, Slender, Host.*
2.3.89/1178 *Exeunt.*
3.1.0.1-2/1178.1-2 *Enter Euans, Simple, Page, Shallow, Slender, Host, Caius, | Rugby.*
3.2.0.1/1294.2 *Mist. Page, Robin, Ford, Page, Shallow, Slender, Host, | Euans, Caius.*
3.2.85/1378 *Exeunt*
3.3.0.1/1378.1 *Enter M. Ford, M. Page, Seruants, Robin, Falstaffe, | Ford, Page, Caius, Euans.*
3.3.230.1/1606 *Exeunt.*
3.4.0.1/1606.1 *Enter Fenton, Anne, Page, Shallow, Slender, | Quickly, Page, Mist. Page.*
3.4.109/1715 *Exeunt*
3.5.0.1/1715.1 *Enter Falstaffe, Bardolfe, Quickly, Ford.*
3.5.140/1856 *Exeunt.*
4.1.0.1-2/1856.1 *Enter Mistris Page, Quickly, William, Euans.*
4.1.80/1935 *Exeunt.*
4.2.0.1/1935.1 *Enter Falstoffe, Mist. Ford, Mist. Page, Seruants, Ford, | Page, Caius, Euans, Shallow.*
4.2.211/2147 *Exeunt*
4.3.0.1/2147.1 *Enter Host and Bardolfe.*
4.3.11/2158 *Exeunt*
4.4.0.1-2/2158.1-2 *Enter Page, Ford, Mistris Page, Mistris | Ford, and Euans.*
4.5.0.1/2247.2 *Enter Host, Simple, Falstaffe, Bardolfe, Euans, | Caius, Quickly.*
4.5.120/2370 *Exeunt.*
4.6.0.1/2370.1 *Enter Fenton, Host.*
4.6.54.1/2424.1 *Exeunt*
5.1.0.1/2424.2 *Enter Falstoffe, Quickly, and Ford.*
5.1.29.1/2453 *Exennt.*
5.2.0.1-2/2453.1 *Enter Page, Shallow, Slender.*
5.2.14/2467 *Exeunt.*
5.3.0.1-2/2467.1 *Enter Mist. Page, Mist. Ford, Caius.*
5.3.24/2491 *Exeunt*
5.4.0.1-3/2491.1-2 *Enter Euans and Fairies.*
5.4.4/2495 *Exeunt*
5.5.0.1-2/2495.1 *Enter Falstoffe, Mistris Page, Mistris Ford, Euans, | Anne Page, Fairies, Page, Ford, Quickly, | Slender, Fenton, Caius, Pistoll.*
5.5.35.1-5/2531.1-4 *Enter Fairies.*
5.5.91.1-2/2587.1-2 *The Song.*
5.5.237/2733 *Exeunt*

2 HENRY IV

2 Henry IV (BEPD 167) was entered in the Stationers' Register with *Much Ado About Nothing* on 23 August 1600:

Andrewe Wyſe
Willm̃ Aſpley   Entred for their copies vnder the handẹ of the wardens. Twoo bookẹ. the one called: Muche a doo about nothinge. Thother the ſecond pte of the Hiſtory of Kinge Henry the iiijth wth the humo^{rs} of Sr Iohn Fallſtaff: Wrytten by m^r Shakeſpere

The play was printed for Wise and Aspley within a few months by Valentine Simmes (who also printed *Much Ado*); the title-page of the Quarto (Q) bears the date 1600. Q appeared in two issues; in the second (QB), E3–4 were replaced by a new sheet of four leaves; hence E1 and 2 are pages retained from the original sheet E, and E3–6 (E3, 4, and 5 numbered) make up the new sheet. The second issue adds an entire scene, 3.1/Sc. 8; to accommodate it, 2.4.345–392.1/1373–1420.1 and 3.2.0.1–102/1523.1–1626 (ending at 'yong') were reset with the new scene inserted between them. Ferguson has shown that Simmes's Compositor A set all of the first issue (QA) and the new sheet of QB.

The play as a whole is not known to have been reprinted before it appeared in the 1623 Folio in a substantially different text (F); this was set by Compositor B assisted by the compositor identified as 'A' or 'J'.

Q is a good example of a text printed directly from the author's papers. Speech-prefix forms vary considerably; for instance Doll Tearsheet is given as '*Tere.*', '*Doll*', '*Dorothy*', '*Dol*', '*Teresh.*', and '*Doro.*' in 2.4/Sc. 7, and then, as she is dragged to prison in 5.4/Sc. 16, '*Whoore*'. Within the speeches themselves are a number of errors or anomalies which probably result from marginal insertions or interlineations; see, for example, notes to 1.2.47/300, 1.3.79/580, 4.1.30/1877, and 5.5.23–4/3111–12. Stage directions also show idiosyncrasies of the author at work. Fauconbridge (1.3.0.2/501.2), Kent (4.3.0.2/2324.2), and possibly Will (after 2.4.16/1057) are named in single directions but are then forgotten. Q's '*Blunt*', who enters in 3.1/Sc. 8 and 5.2/Sc. 14, is without dramatic function in those scenes, but is addressed as on stage in 4.2/Sc. 11. The text also preserves recollections of the names Shakespeare originally gave to Falstaff and Bardolph when writing *1 Henry IV*: the prefix '*Old.*' for Falstaff at 1.2.122/374 probably stands for Oldcastle (a conceivable alternative is 'Old man'); '*sir John Russel*' who enters '*with other*' at the beginning of 2.2/Sc. 5 gives evidence of Bardolph's original identity, complete with social rank and forename. The interpretation of this direction would be doubtful if taken in isolation from the name changes in *1 Henry IV*; Q supplies an entry specifically for '*Bardolfe and boy*' later in the scene at 2.2.61.1/865.1. The opening direction indicates not only a lapse to an earlier name but also a change of intention: Shakespeare probably had not conceived of the dialogue between the Prince and Poins when he wrote the direction. In 5.2/Sc. 14 the King's three younger sons similarly enter twice without any possibility of there being an intervening exit.

The most remarkable evidence for Shakespeare reworking his material before it was transcribed into fair copy probably lies in the bibliographical fact of the two issues of Q. The inserted scene 3.1/Sc. 8 stands apart in that no other part of the play depends on it or assumes its existence. In 'The Three Texts of *2 Henry IV*', Jowett and Taylor argue that the most reasonable explanation for the exclusion of this self-contained material from QA is that the scene, originally written on a separate manuscript leaf, contained material that was intended for insertion at an intermediate point in another leaf; in other words, that Shakespeare added the scene after writing the play (or at least that part of the play where the scene appears); see Illustration 22 above.

Jowett and Taylor go on to examine passages present in F but not Q, and which have usually been regarded as cuts in Q. Two of them (1.1.188–208/228–48 and 4.1.55–79/1902–26) are indeed evidently cuts of censorable material which damage the text through their excision. These could have been censored by the Bishop of London, who was the licensing authority for printed books, or prudently omitted by the printers themselves. The remaining passages (1.1.165–78/205–18, 1.3.21–4/522–5, 1.3.36–55/537–56, 1.3.85–108/586–609, 2.3.23–45/996–1018, and 4.1.101–37/1948–85) are more convincingly explained as additions made in the Folio text. Their subject-matter is related, and is in turn connected with the material of 3.1/Sc. 8. Shakespeare seems to have begun to expand the historical matter of the play, and in particular the links with the events he had dramatized in *Richard II* and *1 Henry IV*, whilst still working on the foul papers. He evidently continued this process of expansion and consolidation, perhaps shortly afterwards when preparing or by adding to the fair copy which was to serve as the prompt-book, a direct or indirect transcript of which must accordingly have eventually served as the printer's copy for F. This would happen with least complication if Shakespeare himself provided the fair copy, though we cannot be sure that he actually did so.

Q is subject to the kind of errors that Craven discovered plaguing the work of Simmes's Compositor A. In other respects it is a highly authoritative text. Unfortunately, the manuscript from which it was set was not only pre-theatrical but also, to a serious extent, unfinished—to a greater degree in QA than in QB. Most readers will expect a text which is as close as possible to the play as it stood when finished and performed. However, the text that reaches us in F is far from a reliable reproduction of the prompt-book. The corruption of the text took place in three particular and identifiable stages: excision of profanity, sophistication by a scribe preparing the transcript which intervened between the fair copy and F, and an extraordinary degree of deliberate compositorial intervention by Compositor B. To these conscious interventions one must add the mistakes which may accrue at any stage of transmission.

F shows two particular characteristics of a prompt-book in use after 1610. Profanity would probably be removed from any prompt-book in use after the passing of the 1606 Act outlawing its use in the theatre. In some instances the alteration to the text was more subtle than a simple deletion or a mechanical substitution such as *heauen* for *God*. Most strikingly, at 2.3.17/990 Q's 'the God of heauen brighten it' becomes in F 'may heauenly glory brighten it', which can be regarded as an improvement. Shakespeare himself may have had a hand in adjusting the text to the requirements of the Act. The Folio text is supplied with act divisions; these too might derive from the theatre, though they would not have been introduced until *c.*1608–9.

This prompt-book must have been copied by a scribe who both obscured some of its theatrical features and interfered with its language to give it a more formal or 'literary' character. The excessive use of round brackets and some stage directions which have been interpreted as inclining to the 'massed' direction in F have led to speculation that the scribe was Ralph Crane (see General Introduction). F also provides a full-page table of 'THE ACTORS NAMES' listing every speaking part, similar to those found appended to some plays transcribed by Crane. However, round brackets are characteristic of Jacobean scribes other than Crane; the frequency of other classes of punctuation is not consistent with Crane; the anomalous entries are not truly 'massed'; the list of characters, whatever its origin, may not have been an integral part of the copy manuscript, but have been added to F simply in order to take up a spare page (see below, and compare Introduction to *Timon of Athens*).

Nor would Crane be expected to treat his text in the cavalier manner of the scribe behind F, who must be responsible for literally hundreds of minor variants. In F, contractions are expanded, colloquialisms and solecisms are formalized, and irregular aspects of syntax are regularized. Though even here F might occasionally preserve the correct text or incorporate an authorial refinement, in general these sophistications undoubtedly originate with the scribe.

The same scribe could have supplied F's scene divisions and undertaken some tidying up of stage directions. He presumably omitted 'theatrical' directions such as entries for mutes or calls for off-stage sound. Most puzzling of F's stage directions are those where a character or characters are named at the beginning of a scene but only enter later. In 3.2/Sc. 9, as Prosser convincingly argues, the recruits should enter mid-scene, but are given their only entry in the opening direction. Jowett, in 'Cuts and Casting', has explained this direction and those beginning 4.1/Sc. 10 and 5.3/Sc. 15 (where characters are prematurely named who later have a second entry where they actually should appear) as a consequence of the text's theatrical origin. In each of the three directions, casting difficulties would demand that an actor or actors leaving the stage at or near the end of the previous scene must re-enter in another role in the course of the scene that the entry direction begins. The directions could thus arise from prompt notes intended to ensure that the actors were ready to appear in their second parts. In 3.2/Sc. 9 the scribe might have noticed the duplication of a series of remarkably named characters and so, having already written out one entry for them at the head of the scene, eliminated the direction where they should actually enter.

In her analysis of F, Prosser amplified the role of the scribe to a figure who altered the text in ways quite outside the credible bounds of scribal sophistication. Her premiss that the transcript was 'based solely on QA and Shakespeare's foul papers' (p. 17) is highly problematic, and is entirely incompatible with the present textual hypothesis. As the scribe's copy evidently contained major authorial additions, it may also have included less obvious verbal alterations that Shakespeare himself introduced. For each variant thought to underlie the printing of F, the competing claims of author and scribe must be considered and evaluated. Jowett argues that verbal deletions connected with the staging (as in the opening lines of 2.4/Sc. 7 and 5.5/Sc. 17) or potentially arising from recognized developments in Shakespeare's composition of the play (as after 2.4.51/1090, 2.4.132/1166, and at 2.4.143–4/1177, and in the closing lines of the same scene) suggest the author's hand.

A further and substantially independent consideration is whether, and if so, how, Q also influenced the Folio text. Shaaber and Taylor ('Zounds') argue convincingly that F cannot have been set directly from a marked-up copy of Q. Q nevertheless seems to have exerted some influence. As is generally recognized, Q and F share a limited number of common errors. The most interesting of these is 'rage' (4.1.34/1881), where most editors recognize that the emendation 'rags' gives a much better reading. Further, at 2.2.61.1/865.1 Q's identification of Sir John's page as '*Bardolfes boy*' (presumably a misreading or misinterpretation of '*Bardolfe, boy*') looks as if it has influenced F's '*and Bardolph and his Boy*'. Finally, about two-thirds of Q's round brackets are replicated in F. As F uses round brackets freely, a proportion of the shared brackets may be due to coincidence, but, given the unpredictable positions in which many of them are found, it is hardly possible that all may be explained in this way. Nor does it seem plausible that the shared brackets derive independently from Shakespeare's papers. In the reset passages of Q's signature E, the compositor retained three sets of brackets and introduced a further four sets; he is therefore likely to have originated most of those in Q as a whole. Some of these must themselves have influenced F.

Two of the above considerations offer an insight into the nature of Q's influence on F. If, as appears to be so, the Folio compositors were working from a transcript heavily marked with brackets, it seems unlikely that both of them would import more brackets from Q. The anomalous '*Enter Bardolph and his Boy.*' occurs again in F at 3.2.51.1/1575.1. This is the only other occasion when F uses Q's preferred '*Boy*' as against '*Page*' (inferably the prompt-book designation), but here cannot derive directly from Q as Q reads '*Enter Bardolfe, and one with him.*' Although Compositor A/J might hypothetically have conflated a manuscript and Quarto stage direction at 2.2.61.1/865.1, it is unlikely that he would recall this detail and, without any prompting, repeat the error several Folio pages later. As elsewhere in F, the misleading interference with stage directions may be attributed to the scribe, here acting on the prompting of Q earlier in the text.

Most QF agreements treated as error in this edition occur in a section of less than 300 lines (considerably less in Q's unexpanded text) between 3.2.308/1833 and 4.1.245/2093. Within this passage, errors are paired at 4.1.34-6/1881-3 and 4.1.173-8/2021-6. For whatever reasons (perhaps connected with the particular attention required in order to follow Q in a section where F has additional pasages, or because the top or bottom of successive manuscript leaves gave difficult copy) Q seems to have influenced the scribe to the extent that occasional Quarto errors were preferred in this section. Similarly, if F's stage direction at 2.2.61.1/865.1 betrays Quarto influence, it may not be coincidental that Q and F share an error 44 lines later in a passage where there are indications of other possible Quarto influence on F (see notes to 2.2.108/911, etc.). Apart from the immediate editorial significance of such groupings, it should be noted that (*a*) the two areas of particular Quarto influence were set by different Folio compositors; (*b*) Compositor A/J broke off work on *2 Henry IV* between setting 3.2.308/1833 and beginning to work on the section containing QF shared errors in Act 4. Both observations tend to confirm that Quarto influence was already incorporated in the copy for F. We follow Humphreys in believing that the scribe had a manuscript and a copy of Q available:

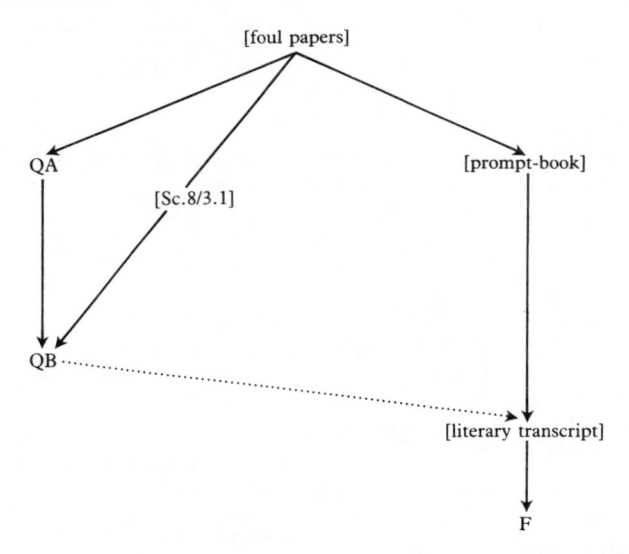

```
              [foul papers]
             /     |      \
            /      |       \
           /       |        \
         QA    [Sc.8/3.1]  [prompt-book]
          |        |          |
          |        |          |
          ↓        ↓          |
         QB ·················→|
                              ↓
                     [literary transcript]
                              |
                              ↓
                              F
```

The scribe's task was clearly to transcribe the manuscript, and he must have used Q only as a secondary document at which he occasionally glanced. A few QF readings can be identified as errors without positing mere coincidence.

In view of Werstine's work, we can no longer accept Walker's view of Compositor B as a source of numerous and unprovoked corruptions. Prosser, in the most persuasive part of her study, postulates that this compositor interfered with the text in response to specific and unusual circumstances. *2 Henry IV* was printed on Folio pages f6ᵛ and all of quires g and gg; the latter is an irregular quire introduced as an addition to the original casting plan, betraying a miscalculation over the space needed for the Histories up to but not including *Henry V* (which had already been printed). Prosser describes how faulty casting off created successively two contrasting problems for Compositor B. Although Prosser is probably wrong in envisaging a second casting off after work had begun on the play, she successfully demonstrates the unique casting-off difficulties in *2 Henry IV* and masses a wealth of detail to show its consequences. In working back from the middle of quire g to g1, Compositor B had to take extraordinary measures to save space; when composing the central portion of gg, which has four more pages than a regular quire, he faced exactly the opposite problem and had large amounts of space to waste. Prosser explains this turn-round in the compositor's fortunes, and demonstrates the consequences of both situations. Compositor B was constrained in quire g to omit odd words to save type lines, and occasionally to make larger cuts. In gg, he actually added words and phrases in order to push the print on to new type lines. Unlike the scribal intervention, which shows itself as a continuum of particular kinds of variant throughout the text, the compositor's deliberate changes to the text fall into two areas respectively of contraction and expansion, both of which contrast in the nature of their variants with sections of the text where there was neither a shortage nor a superfluity of space.

This edition aims to reproduce the substantive features of the stage version of the text underlying F. Though the large majority of variants from Q must be rejected as corruptions in F, there are grounds for accepting more Folio readings than have generally been admitted, on the basis of either corruption in Q or authorial alterations subsequent to the foul papers. Readings likely to be authorial variants (marked with an asterisk in the Textual Notes) include a number of deletions in F (see, in particular, notes to 2.2.22/826, 2.4.51/1090, 2.4.392/1420, 3.1.52/1472, and 3.2.309/1833), as well as some added part-lines (see note to 4.1.30/1877). The more substantial deletions are appended to our text as Additional Passages.

Q serves as the copy-text for incidentals. Where material in QA was reset in QB, QA provides the more authoritative text. The Textual Notes and list of Incidentals provide a record of known press corrections in Q; the Textual Notes record substantive variants between QA and QB. Variants in the different states of Q derive from the collation undertaken by Berger and Williams. There are no known press variants in F.

F's names are followed where they result from revision or correction (F 'Basingstoke', Q 'Billingsgate'), or where Q evidently introduces error (F 'Sure-card', Q 'Soccard'), but not where F merely sophisticates. We retain the wording of Q's stage directions where adequate, but incorporate Folio directions which reflect changed staging. F's presumably theatrical act divisions are observed. Its scene divisions form the basis of scene division in this edition, except for the editorial scene-break introduced at 4.1-2/Sc. 10-11. F's scene numbers but not its divisions differ in Act 1 as F counts the Induction as the first scene. The traditional editorial scene-breaks after 4.1.226/2074 and 4.3.132/2457 are not required, as the stage is not cleared, and have been abandoned in favour of F's continuous action.

J.J./(S.W.W.)

WORKS CITED

Berger, Thomas L., and George Walton Williams, 'Notes on Shakespeare's *2 Henry IV*', *AEB* 3 (1979), 240-53
—— 'Variants in the Quarto of Shakespeare's *2 Henry IV*', *The Library*, VI, 3 (1981), 109-18
Betterton, Thomas, *The Sequel of Henry the Fourth*, adaptation (1721)
Cowl, R. P., ed., *The Second Part of Henry the Fourth*, Arden (1923)
Craven, Alan, 'Simmes' Compositor A and Five Shakespeare Quartos', *SB* 26 (1973), 37-60
—— 'The Reliability of Simmes's Compositor A', *SB* 32 (1979), 186-9
Davison, P. H., ed., *The Second Part of King Henry the Fourth*, New Penguin (1977)
Ferguson, W. C., 'The Compositors of *Henry IV Part 2*, *Much Ado about Nothing*, *The Shoemakers' Holiday*, and *The First Part of the Contention*', *SB* 13 (1960), 19-29
Hart, Alfred, *Shakespeare and the Homilies* (1934)
Humphreys, A. R., ed., *The Second Part of King Henry IV*, Arden (1966)
Jowett, John, 'Cuts and Casting: Author and Book-keeper in the Folio Text of *2 Henry IV*' (forthcoming)
—— and Gary Taylor, 'The Three Texts of *2 Henry IV*', *SB* 40 (1987), 31-50
Maxwell, J. C., '*2 Henry IV*, II.iv.91 ff.', *MLR* 42 (1947), 485
Melchiori, Giorgio, 'Sir John Umfrevile in *Henry IV*, Part 2, I.i. 161-79', *Real*, 2 (1984), 199-209
Pollard, A. W., 'Variant Settings in *II Henry IV*', *TLS*, 21 October 1920, p. 680
Prosser, Eleanor, *Shakespeare's Anonymous Editors: Scribe and Compositor in the Folio Text of '2 Henry IV'* (1981)
Shaaber, M. A., ed., *The Second Part of Henry the Fourth*, New Variorum (1940)
Wilson, John Dover, ed., *The Second Part of the History of Henry IV*, New (1946)

TEXTUAL NOTES

Title   The second part of Henry the fourth] Q (*head title* (... fourth,), *adding* 'continuing to his death, and coro-|nation of Henry the | fift.'; *running title*); THE | Second part of Henrie | the fourth, continuing to his death, | *and coronation of Henrie* | the fift. | With the humours of fir Iohn Fal-|ftaffe, *and fwaggering* | Pistoll. Q (*title-page*); the fecond pte of the History of Kinge Henry the iiijth wth the humo^{rs} of Sr Iohn Fallstaffe S.R.; The Second Part of Henry the Fourth, | Containing his Death: and the Coronation | of King Henry the Fift. F (*head title*). *The fecond Part of King Henry the Fourth*. F (*running title*)

Induction] F; *heading not in* Q
Ind.6/6   tongues] Q; Tongue F
Ind.8/8   men] Q; them F
Ind.13/13   Whiles] Q; Whil'ſt F
Ind.13/13   griefes] F; griefe Q. Q levels the idiom. Terminal 's' is more easily lost than acquired (though both errors are common).
Ind.16/16   Iealousies,] Q; ~, F. Q indicates in its punctuation and selective capitalization a personified Jealousy's conjectures.
Ind.21   anatomize] Q (anothomize)
Ind.27   rebels'] Q (rebels). Alternatively 'rebel's'.
Ind.34/34   that] Q; the F
Ind.35/35   hold] THEOBALD; hole QF
Ind.36/36   Where] F; When Q
1.1.1/41   aboue] WILSON; *not in* QF. Shaaber suggests the use of a third door, but (*a*) it is uncertain that Shakespeare's theatre was so equipped (*b*) Wilson's staging is more theatrically effective. The only consideration against the upper acting space is that it does not seem to be used elsewhere in the play.
1.1.13/53   God] Q; heauen F
1.1.28/68   who] Q; whom F
1.1.33/73   with] Q; frō F. Compare previous line.
1.1.34/74   Lord Bardolfe] This edition (Capell); ſir Iohn Vmfreuile QF. Most critics agree that Lord Bardolph and 'sir Iohn Vmfreuile' are the same person (though Melchiori argues that 'Vmfreuile' is a separate figure who never appears on stage). Shakespeare evidently renamed the character. The name here was not altered in the foul papers or, to judge by F, the manuscripts behind F. We cannot know whether the change required to make the line consistent with the rest of the text was made in performance. Nevertheless, there is no sufficient reason for perpetuating an error of oversight which causes confusion if not unintelligibility.
   The emended text gives a four-foot line and an awkward repetition of *lord*. There are a number of ways of avoiding these features which are consistent with Shakespeare's usage; for example, 'the noble Bardolfe' or 'My lord, tis true Lord Bardolfe'.
1.1.36/76   hard] Q; head F
*1.1.41/81   ill] F; bad Q. Q may be contaminated by the previous word, 'had', but authorial alteration to avoid 'had bad' is possible.
1.1.44/84   forward] Q; forwards F. 'Forwards' occurs elsewhere in Shakespeare only in Sonnet 60.4 and Folio *1 Henry IV* 2.4.35/854. For the latter, compare note to 1.2.207/458.
1.1.44/84   armed] Q; able F. F's 'his able heeles' is contaminated by 'his able Horse' in the line above.
1.1.55/95   should the] F; ſhould that Q. Q's 'that gentleman that' looks like an error of anticipation.
1.1.59/99   Spoke] Q; Speake F
1.1.59/99   a venter] Q; aduenture F. *OED* describes Q's form as improper; all the more reason to regard F as a sophistication.
1.1.62/102   whereon] Q; when F
1.1.79/119   my] Q; mine F. Abbott notes that '*Mine* is almost always found before "eye", "ear", &c. where no emphasis is intended' (237). F nevertheless looks like a sophistication: Q's 'my' probably arises from Shakespeare following the form he had used in the previous line.
1.1.83/123   dead.] F; ~? Q
1.1.88/128   an] Q; thy F
*1.1.96/136   say so] F; *not in* Q. The first of a number of variants where F completes part-lines in Q. See note to 4.1.30/1878.
*1.1.103/143   knolling] F; tolling Q. Shaaber compared F's 'culling' for Q's 'toling' at 4.3.204/2529, in a passage fairly clearly revised by Shakespeare.
1.1.106/146   God] Q; heauen F
1.1.109/149   Harry] Q; Henrie F
1.1.126/166   To] F (Too); So Q. Q's 'So' probably anticipates 'soon'.
1.1.137/177   these] Q. F's 'this' is a possible spelling variant.
1.1.155/195   this] Q; the F. F is suspect, as it could well be contaminated by 'the', just above and also before a noun beginning in *w*.
1.1.161/201   LORD BARDOLFE] F; *Vmfr*⟨*euile*⟩. This ſtrained paſſion doth you wrong my lord. | *Bard*⟨*olfe*⟩. Q; *L. Bardolph*. This ... lord. | *Morton*. WILSON; MELCHIORI *conjectures*: MORTON. This ... lord. | LORD BARDOLPH. The foul papers must have been particularly confused here: '*Vmfr*.' is, as appears from 1.1.30-6/70-6 (see note to 1.1.34/74), the same character as Lord Bardolph, who in Q has the line following the one given '*Vmfr*.' (which indeed seems to require another speaker). Wilson and Melchiori both dismiss F. Wilson assumes that the Q compositor, faced with a corrected prefix for '*Vmfr*.', set the original and its correction by relocating the beginning of Morton's speech; Melchiori suggests multiple stages of annotation underlying Q.
   The simplest explanation of Q is that 'Sweet ... honor,' was a marginal addition intended to replace 'This ... lord.'. The survival of the anomalous prefix '*Vmfr*.' would be explained by the survival of the line itself: prefix '*Bard*.', which in Q duplicates it, would have been intended to supersede it. Q's comma after 'honor', for what it is worth, may have arisen because the compositor did not immediately realize that the insertion was followed

by a new speech, or may reflect a pen-stroke marking the end of the insertion.

This hypothesis may be constructed from Q alone. However, it is confirmed by F, which produces exactly the text Shakespeare would accordingly have intended.

1.1.162/202   MOURTON] QF. See previous note. WILSON advances the prefix to 1.1.161/201; MELCHIORI conjectures that it should be delayed to 1.1.165/205.

1.1.163/203   Leane on your] F (Leane-on ~); Leaue on you Q

1.1.163-4/203-4   ore, . . . passion,] F; ~, . . . ~, Q

1.1.165-78/205-18   You . . . be?] F; not in Q. See Introduction.

1.1.177/217   doth] This edition; hath F1. F2's unauthoritative emendation 'brought' for 'bring' gives equally good sense, but the assumed error is not a common one. In contrast, 'what doth'/'what hath' is a very easy error, especially after 'What hath' in the previous line.

1.1.177/217   bring] F1; brought F2. See previous note.

1.1.181/221   was] F; twas Q. F demands the less usual sense of if ('whether'). Q may anticipate 'ten' or be a substitution typical of Simmes's Compositor A.

1.1.182/222   ventur'd, . . . proposde,] QF; ~, . . . ~, CAPELL

1.1.187/227   dare] Q; do F

1.1.188-208/228-48   The . . . him.] F; not in Q. See Introduction.

1.1.200-1/240-1   Religion: . . . Thoughts,] ROWE; ~, . . . ~ : F

1.1.214/254   and] Q; nor F

1.2.0.1/254.1   Page] In Q the term is used here, in the prefix to 1.2.3/257, and in the entry following 5.5.4/3092; elsewhere he is 'boy' or 'Boy'. F overwhelmingly prefers the more specific 'Page', which is likely to be the form adopted in the prompt-book.

1.2.5   more] Q (moe)

1.2.7/261   clay man] POPE; clay-man QF. Probably foolishly compounded by the Q compositor, influenced by the context. The scribe preparing the copy for F may have glanced at Q and found some apparent logic in its hyphen.

*1.2.8/262   tends] F; intends Q. The variant is clearly linked to that at 1.2.17/271. *Tends* and *set* are Shakespeare's usual words. There are possible motives for authorial revision: 'intends' tangles with 'inuent' and 'inuented' and 'in-set' amounts to a tautology with 'in', which follows.

1.2.11/265   orewhelmd] F (o'rewhelm'd); ouerwhelmd Q. F is especially plausible as it usually gives the less informal reading.

1.2.14/268   iudgement. Thou] F; ~, thou Q

1.2.16/270   heels.] F; ~, Q

1.2.17/271   set] F (fette); in-fet Q. See note to 1.2.8/262.

1.2.20/274   fledge] Q; fledg'd F. F, being less idiomatic, is probably a scribal variant.

1.2.21/275   off] Q; on F. F might be sophistication or error ('one on'). The similar variant at 1.2.243/494 suggests the former.

1.2.22/276   & yet] Q; yet F

1.2.23/277   God] Q; Heauen F

1.2.23/277   tis] Q; it is F

1.2.26/280   heele] Q; he will F

1.2.28/282   hees] Q; he is F

1.2.29   Dumbleton] Q (Dommelton), F (Dombledon)

*1.2.30/284   sloppes] F (Slops); my floppes Q. Q might be unrevised or contain a compositorial error prompted by 'my short cloake'. F is more idiomatic.

1.2.34/288   pray God] Q; may F

*1.2.35/289   rascally,] F (~-); rafcall: Q. Q's colon may be the compositor's attempt to understand his copy. The problem with this variant is its relation, if any, to that at 1.2.37/291 where, conversely, a '-y' is lost from a qualifier in F. In the present instance F gives the more usual idiom, though Q is also possible; at 1.2.37/291 Q is usually not accepted. Shaaber speculates that both '-y's are intrusions, but this is unlikely in two opposing but closely located variants, especially as 'smoothy' is difficult to account for by the common processes of error. The double variant is difficult to explain in terms of textual transmission, though a misinterpreted proof correction in Q is just possible; the alternative is to suppose authorial changes.

*1.2.37/291   smooth-pates] F; fmoothy-pates Q. See previous note.

1.2.41   lief] Q (liue), F (liefe)

1.2.42/296   a] Q; hee F

1.2.43-4/297-8   am a] Q; am F

1.2.47/300   it,] F; ~ : wheres Bardolf, Q. Q's 'wheres Bardolf' is clearly misplaced (see following note). The error may arise from ambiguously placed words in the foul papers. As 'wheres Bardolf' cannot itself have been an afterthought, '& yet . . . light him' might be an authorial addition made in the margin of the foul papers.

1.2.48/302   him: wheres Bardolf.] F (~. Where's *Bardolfe?*); him. Q. See previous note.

1.2.49/303   in] Q; into F. Q is idiomatic. F may sophisticate, or anticipate 'to' after 'Smithfield'.

1.2.52/306   and] Q; If F. A recurring variant: F has *if* for Q *and* 25 times.

1.2.52/306   but a] Q; a F

1.2.74/326   begging] Q; beg F. The three print-lines of Sir John's speech at the foot of column b of g1ᵛ show repeated signs of cramming in order to accommodate the cast-off copy. Compositor B probably reduced the participle to save space.

1.2.76/328   want] F; need Q. Substitution of synonyms and near-synonyms is characteristic of Simmes's Compositor A. The words are too closely equivalent particularly to suggest authorial alteration, though this too is possible.

1.2.89/341   me, so,] F (~ ~?); ~, ~, Q

1.2.95/347   God] Q; *not in* F

1.2.96/348   of] Q; of the F. The variant may be connected with F's omission of 'God'.

1.2.99/351   haue] Q; hath F

1.2.99/351   age] F; an ague Q. Wilson suggested that Q arises from press (or proof) correction—presumably a guessed correction of 'an age'. Q's omitted space between 'ague' and 'in' supports this hypothesis.

1.2.100/352   time in you] Q; time F. F's omission saves a type line at the end of the speech. The Folio page (g2) is crowded, and Compositor B repeatedly shortened his text.

1.2.103/355   for] Q; *not in* F

1.2.105/357   And] Q; If it F

1.2.111/363   God] Q; heauen F

1.2.111/363   pray you] Q; pray F. In F the omission occurs in conjunction with a turn-up. See note to 1.2.114/366.

*1.2.113/365   is . . . it] F (~ (as I take it)); as I take it? is Q

1.2.114/366   and't . . . of] Q; a F. Evidently deliberate omission in F (though Prosser, pp. 81-2, attributes the omission of 'kind of' to the scribe).

1.2.114/366   in] Q; of F. The variant could be connected with the preceding omission, as 'of' appears before 'sleeping' Q, but not in F: either Compositor B substituting under the influence of the words he had deliberately omitted, or F preserving the remnant of a scribal dittography ('of sleeping of').

1.2.122/374   SIR IOHN] Q (*Old.*), F (*Fal.*). See Introduction.

1.2.127/378   doe become] Q; be F. An ampersand and a missing full-stop after 'Physitian' are signs of space-saving in F.

1.2.139/391   himselfe] Q; him F. In F, the speech fits on a crowded type line; there is no space above or below for a turnover. The variant saves beginning a new type line for 'lesse.'

1.2.141/393   are] Q; is F. F's reading facilitates the omission of 'is' before 'great'.

1.2.142/393   is] Q; *not in* F. F's line is again crowded, and the omission saves a type line.

1.2.144/396   greater] QF; great BETTERTON

1.2.144   waist] QF (waste)

1.2.144/396   slenderer] F; flender Q

1.2.151/403   th'vnquiet] Q; the vnquiet F

1.2.156/407   smell] Q; to fmell F

1.2.161/412   in] Q; on F

1.2.165/416   ill] Q; euill F. Consistency with 1.2.166/417 is presumably required. It might be conjectured that Shakespeare intended to change both readings to 'euill', except that 'ill' seems necessary in 1.2.166/417 to give the sense 'faulty, flawed', as applied to clipped coins. A scribe may have substituted (de-

355

liberately or unconsciously) his preferred form of a familiar phrase.
1.2.170/421 times] Q; *not in* F
1.2.171 bearherd] Q (Berod), F (Beare-heard)
1.2.171/422 &] Q; and hath F. The fussy tinkering with the grammar is probably scribal.
1.2.173/424 this] F; his Q
1.2.174/424 thē are] F (them) ∼); the one Q
1.2.176/426 doe] Q; *not in* F
1.2.177 vanguard] Q (vaward)
1.2.184/435 your chinne double,] Q; *not in* F
1.2.186/437 yet] Q; *not in* F. The circumstances again resemble 1.2.139/391, though, as the preceding word is also of three letters and begins with 'y', accidental omission is possible.
1.2.187-8/438-9 about... afternoone,] Q; *not in* F. On account of Compositor B's tendency to make omissions in this part of the text, Q has been retained, but it should be noted that a type line probably was not saved by the present omission, and that there are no later attempts to prevent 'Silke, and olde Sacke' from running on to a new type line.
1.2.190/442 further] Q; farther F
1.2.194/445 him:] F (∼.); ∼‸ Q
1.2.194/445 th'yere] F (th'eare); the yeere Q. Q's spelling 'yeere' (ear) is unusual: *OED* only gives 'yere'. The five-letter spelling and expanded colloquial 'th'' help justification (in particular, avoid splitting 'Prince'). Such expedients are legitimate compared with Folio Compositor B's gross interference in F.
1.2.199/451 God] Q: heauen F
1.2.201/452 God] Q; Heauen F
*1.2.203-4/454 and prince Harry] F (and Prince Har-|ry); *not in* Q
1.2.207/458 Yea] Q; Yes F. Almost half of Q's instances of *yea* are changed in F to 'yes' or 'I'. The alteration is probably a scribal habit, one which is also reflected in Folio *1 Henry IV* and *Richard III*.
1.2.209/460-1 by the Lord] Q; if F
1.2.211/463 & it] Q; if it F
*1.2.212/463] my bottle, would] F (∼ Bottle, ∼); a bottle. I would Q. Q's punctuation is clearly wrong; the verbal variants are not so obvious. F is preferred because (a) 'my', being the more specific word, is not a likely corruption of 'a'; (b) Compositor B does not gain space by omitting 'I'; (c) the scribe behind F would typically prefer a formal, expanded reading such as 'I would'; (d) the variants are evidently linked: F gives a possessive to 'bottle' but avoids excessive self-emphasis by dropping 'I'. In particular, (d) suggests that Shakespeare tinkered with the text here.
1.2.215-21/466-72 but... motion] Q; *not in* F. Cowl and Chambers believed that the passage was censored, but Prosser (p. 84) argued persuasively that Compositor B took a drastic measure to end the Folio page (g2) at the casting-off point. The cut is 10 lines from the end of the page; g2ᵛ was already set in type. Compositor B's previous space-saving attempts on the page had proved insufficient. A large single cut was the only solution, but would have been impractical in the short speeches following 1.2.221/472.
1.2.222/473 God] Q; heauen F
1.2.230/481 a] Q; he F
1.2.243/494 of] Q; on F. See note to 1.2.21/275.
1.2.244/495 *exit page*] *not in* QF
1.2.246/497 the other] Q; th'other F
1.2.247/497 Tis] Q; It is F
1.2.250/501 *exit*] *not in* Q; *Exeunt.* F
1.3.1/502 cauſe] Q; cauſes F
1.3.1/502 knowne] Q; kno F. F gives a recognized though unusual spelling of *know*, one of several indications of space-saving in the type line (despite a space set between 'Means' and the following colon). If 'known' had been set, the line would not have fitted the measure—though it might just have done so if the scribe or compositor had not introduced the almost certain error 'causes'. It remains uncertain that Compositor B introduced the reading deliberately. Perhaps his desire for a short word was conducive to a misreading of minims.

1.3.18/519 Yea] Q; I F
*1.3.21-4/522-5 Till... admitted.] F; *not in* Q. See Introduction.
1.3.26/527 caſe] F; cauſe Q. Probably an 'a'/'au' misreading in Q.
*1.3.28/529 on] F; and Q. Humphreys defends Q, but 'and' might be a misreading of copy-spelling 'one'. Alternatively, F's 'on' and 'with' in 1.3.29/530 may result from Shakespeare adjusting the text. The variants certainly seem to be related, in that they affect the same point in two parallel and adjacent lines. The second could, if an authorial change, be a consequence of the first: the effect is to avoid 'on... | ... in', which might make the parallel structure of the lines look mechanical.
*1.3.29/530 with] F; in Q. See previous note.
1.3.36-55/537-56 Yes... else,] F; *not in* Q. See Introduction.
1.3.36-7 war—... action,... foot—] F (∼,... ∼ : ∼,). F's punctuation is a justifiable way of representing the sense. Attempts to preserve a heavy stop after 'action' have often been associated with emendation of the wording: 'in this' for 'if this' (Johnson's conjecture; first adopted by STEEVENS), or 'Impede' (POPE) or 'Induc'd' (conjectured by Henley) for 'Indeed'. It is doubtful that the passage needs emending, though Malone believed that a line was lost.
1.3.58 one] Q (on)
1.3.58/559 an] Q; a F
1.3.66/567 a] F; ſo, Q; so a KITTREDGE (Collier). Q is puzzling, notwithstanding Abbott's examples of omitted articles (83-4). Perhaps the compositor, anticipating the next line, set 'to'. Q's 'so' would then be a press-corrector's guess. Alternatively the compositor may have failed to observe a *currente calamo* correction in Shakespeare's papers.
1.3.71/572 Are] F; And Q
1.3.78/579 not] F; not to Q
1.3.79/580 He... Welch] F (He leaues his backe vnarm'd, the French, and Welch); French and Welch he leaues his back vnarmde, they Q; To *French,* and *Welsh,* he leaves his back unarm'd, | They CAPELL. Q sets as prose, which, as Shaaber points out, signals difficult copy. Shaaber convincingly suggests that 'the French and Welch' were added to the copy as an interlineation or marginal addition, though 'the' might not have been included if the first three letters of 'they' were supposed to stand for it.
1.3.84/585 substituted] QF; substitute RIDLEY
1.3.84/585 gainst] F ('gainſt); againſt Q
*1.3.85-108/586-609 ARCHBISHOP... worst".] F; *not in* Q. See Introduction.
*1.3.109/610 MOWBRAY] F; *Biſh⟨op⟩*. Q An adjustment in connection with F's inserted passage.
2.1.0.2 *Fang*] Q (*Phang*), F
2.1.4/614 iſt] Q; Is it F
2.1.5/614-15 wil a] Q; Will he F
2.1.5/615 too't] Q; to it F
2.1.7/617 O Lord] Q; I F
2.1.10/620 Yea] Q; I F
2.1.12/622 for] Q; *not in* F. The Folio page, g3, is again cramped; Snare's speech is squeezed onto a single type line which could not have been turned over at the end, and which shows repeated signs of space-saving.
2.1.15-16/625 most... a] Q; and that moſt beaſtly: he F. A verbal adjustment to remove profanity, followed by scribal sophistication.
2.1.16/626 does] Q; doth F
2.1.21/631 And I] Q; If I F
2.1.21/631 and a] Q; if he F
2.1.22/632 vice] F (Vice); view Q
2.1.23/633 by] Q; with F. 'With' would easily be substituted under the influence of 'within' in the previous speech.
2.1.24/633 you] Q; *not in* F
2.1.24/633 hees] Q; he is F
2.1.26/636 a] Q; he F
2.1.26/636 continuantly] F; continually Q. Compare 2.1.102/709, where it is F that evens Mistress Quickly's irregularity.
2.1.28 Lombard] Q (Lumbert), F

2 HENRY IV

2.1.29/639   pray you] Q; pra'ye F. F's variant enables Compositor B to squeeze 'since' on to the type line.
2.1.32/642   one] QF; Lone THEOBALD
2.1.34-5   fobbed] Q (fubd)
2.1.35/644   and fubd off, from] Q; from F. Easy error or obvious space-saving in F.
2.1.39/649   knaue] Q; not in F.
*2.1.45/655   Sir Iohn,] F (~ Iohn,); not in Q.
2.1.45/655   mistris‸ quickly] Qb (~ Quickly), F (Miſt. *Quickly*); ~, ~ Qa. The compositorial misunderstanding in Qa must arise from use of minuscule initial 'q' in the copy.
2.1.50/658-9   thee in the channel] Q; thee there F. F's omission saves a type line by the end of the speech. Compositor B may have imagined a more direct advantage. As he ended a sentence (. . . 'there.') at the end of the type line, and as the speech continues 'Wilt thou?', he may have thought for a moment that the sentence ended the speech.
2.1.52/661   a] Q; O F
2.1.53/662   a] Q; O F
2.1.57/665   PHANG] F; Offic⟨er⟩. Q
2.1.58-9/666-7   or . . . ta] Q; Thou wilt not? thou wilt not? F. The scribe evidently realized that a simple regularization of 'not' to 'wilt not' would give a ridiculous reading, and rationalized accordingly.
2.1.59   wot'a] Q (wot ta)
2.1.61/669   PAGE] Q (*Boy*), F I; *Fal⟨ſtaffe⟩*. F3
2.1.62/670   tickle] Q; tucke F. *Tuck* could mean 'rebuke', but is not found elsewhere in Shakespeare. F probably results from misreading.
2.1.62.1/670.1   and his men] Q; not in F. See note to 4.2.0.1-2/2197.1-2.
2.1.63/671   What is] Q; What's F. Q gives a pentameter (compare 2.1.66-9/674-7).
2.1.69/677   thou] Q; not in F. F's variant is probably scribal. The line is at the foot of a column in F, but Compositor B would not have needed to omit 'thou'.
*2.1.75/682-3   al, all] F (all: all); al Q. F is distinctive and deliberate, and emphasizes the pun on 'some'. An accidental omission would be far easier than a duplication, but Shakespeare might have added the second 'all'.
2.1.78/686   a] Q; o' F
*2.1.81/689   fie, what] F (Fy, what); what Q
2.1.82/689   man] Q; a man F
2.1.90/698   vpon] Q; on F
2.1.91/699   Wheeson] Q; Whitſon F. Q probably gives a dialectal form.
2.1.92/700   liking his father] Q; lik'ning him F. The variant in the verb form is a modernization: *OED* does not record the required sense of *like* (v.² 1b) after 1622. Such a change could be more or less unconscious, and is probably scribal. F's 'him' gives a different sense from 'his father'. Compositor B may have altered the text, though the line is only the fifth of a 19-line speech.
2.1.100-1/708   thou not] Q; not thou F
2.1.102/709   so familiarity] Q; familiar F. Possible scribal normalization or compositorial shortening to accommodate 'poore' to the measure.
2.1.106   mad] Q (made), F
2.1.116/724-5   you haue . . . to me] Q; I know you ha' F. Compositor B avoids the easy setting whereby 'you haue' would end a type line, squeezing on the first three letters of 'practis'd'.
2.1.117-18/726-7   and . . . person.] Q; not in F. As in g2, the compositor evidently made particularly severe cuts as he approached the end of the page.
2.1.119/728   Yea in truth] Q; Yes in troth F. Q's 'truth' becomes 'troth' in F four times.
2.1.120/729   Pray thee] Q; Prethee F
2.1.122/730   with] Q; not in F. F's omission saves a type line.
2.1.126/735   make] Q; not in F
2.1.127/736   my humble] Q; your humble F
2.1.129/737   do] Q; not in F
2.1.132/741   th'effect] Q; the effect F

2.1.136/745   Harry] Q; *Henrie* F
2.1.139/748   Faith] Q; Nay F
2.1.145/754   SIR IOHN . . . for] This type line begins g3ᵛ in F; in the pages that follow the compositors did not face the severe space-saving problems presented in g3-1ᵛ.
2.1.148/757   hangers] Q; hangings F. Q is unusual but acceptable.
2.1.149/758   tapestries] F (Tapiſtries); tapeſtrie Q
2.1.149   ten pound] Q (x. £), F (tenne pound)
2.1.150/758-9   and twere] Q; if it were F
2.1.150/759   theres] Q; there is F
2.1.152/760   the] Q; thy F
2.1.153/761-2   dost not know me,] Q; not in F. The omission can be explained as accidental: an eyeskip from 'with me' to 'know me'. However, two such errors are unlikely to have occurred in a single line, least of all at the same stage of transmission. The reduction of Q's 'come, come' to F's 'come' must be considered as a separate problem (see following note).
*2.1.153/762   come] F; come, come Q. See previous note. In contrast, the present variant is likely to be deliberate, especially as F similarly (but more unequivocally) reduces Q's 'come, come, come' to 'Come' at 5.1.47/2739. Such alterations are scarcely within the scope of scribal sophistication as it would usually be understood: it affects substantive content, not incidentals or other niceties of presentation. The similarity between the two variants suggests authorial responsibility. Another omission in F involves the loss of repeated *come(s)*, and is even more clearly authorial (see note to 2.4.392/1420). See also note to 5.1.9/2700-1.
2.1.155/763   Pray thee] Q; Prethee F
2.1.156/764   ifaith I am] Q; I F
2.1.156-7/764   so God saue me] Q; in good earneſt F
2.1.160/768   though] Q; although F
2.1.168/776   better] Q; bitter F
*2.1.169/777   good] F; not in Q. Q may arise from anticipation of 2.1.171/779 or 2.1.172/780, but Shakespeare could have added 'good' at a later stage in order to vary the repeated 'my lord' and add to Sir John's obsequiousness. F also adds 'good' at 2.2.86, 92, 2.4.294-5 and 3.2.193/889, 895, 1323, and 1718: a recurring variant suggesting authorial changes (though 2.4.294-5/1323 may be a special case).
2.1.170/778   to night] Q; laſt night F. F sophisticates.
2.1.171/779   Basingstoke] F; Billingſgate Q
2.1.188/796   Counties] Q; Countries F
2.2.0.1/804.3   and Poynes] *Poynes, ſir Iohn Ruſſel, with other* Q; *Pointz, Bardolfe, and Page* F. Anticipates the entry at 2.2.61.1/865.1. F's interpretation of Q thus seems correct, but the variant remains problematic: either the scribe was influenced by Q and mistakenly incorporated the characters whilst correctly identifying them (which seems unlikely), or the prompt-book retained the corrected but redundant names.
2.2.1/805   Before God] Q; Truſt me F
2.2.2/806   Ist] Q; Is it F
2.2.4/808   Faith it does] Q; It doth F
2.2.10/814   by my] Q; in F
2.2.15/819   hast, viz] F (haſt? (Viz.)); ~‸ with Q
2.2.15   videlicet] F (Viz.)
2.2.16/820   ones] F; once Q. An easy confusion not only because of the words' similar sound: 'ones' was a recognized spelling of *once*.
2.2.18/822   another] Q; one other F
2.2.20/824   keepest] Q; kept'ſt F
2.2.21/825   thy] F; the Q
*2.2.22/826   made a shift to] F; not in Q. See following note.
*2.2.22/826   holland.] F; holland: and God knows whether thoſe that bal out the ruines of thy linnen ſhal inherite thy kingdom: but the Midwiues ſay, the children are not in the fault where-|vpon the world increases, and kinreds are mightily ſtrengthened. Q. The omission in F is not adequately explained as censorship (official or otherwise) on account of profanity. If the passage was emended to remove profanity in the usual way, 'God' would become 'heauen' or 'who', and 'inherite his kingdom' might become 'be saued'. Like F's omissions at 3.1.52/1472 and

3.2.309/1833, the lines occur in a long speech and are essentially digressive. Poins's rebuke applies more fittingly to the quips on 'low Countries' and 'holland' than the pseudo-puritan moralizing that in Q follows (though the omission loses a possible quibble in 'labored'). In Q, the Prince's speech ends on a relatively serious note ('inherit his kingdom', etc.) that leads into the subject of his father's sickness; in F, the entirely superficial tone is maintained until Poins reminds the Prince of his father. The Folio addition of 'made a shift to' (see previous note) is undoubtedly designed to sharpen the speech's new ending; the two slighter changes in Poins's reply may be attributed to the same stage of authorial alteration.

*2.2.25/829   lying] F; being Q
*2.2.25/830   yours] F; yours at this time Q
2.2.28/832   faith] Q; not in F
2.2.32/836   youle] F (you'l); you will Q. In Q, 'you' ends a type line. The compositor may have expanded to help justification.
2.2.33/837   Mary] Q; Why F
2.2.38/842   By this hand, thou] Q; Thou F
2.2.55   engrafted] Q (engraffed). Compare 5.3.3.
2.2.57/861   By this light] Q; Nay F
2.2.57/861   spoke on] Q; ſpoken of F
2.2.62/866   by the masse] Q; Looke, looke F
2.2.63/867   a] Q; he F
2.2.64/868   looke] Q; ſee F. F's variant must be a consequence of emending 'by the masse' to 'Looke, looke'. The changes hint at authorial responsibility for dealing with the profanity.
2.2.66/870   God saue] Q; Saue F
2.2.68/872   vertuous] Q; pernitious F. Q clearly has the word required. F is not plausible as a scribal improvement. There is no clear motive for the change. Even if a scribe arbitrarily decided that a derogatory adjective must come before 'asse', he could have produced a closer antonym such as *unvirtuous*, *virtueless*, or *villainous*. F's 'pernitious' might arise from a misinterpretation of copy in which the first syllable was illegible through blotting or overwriting, but as a 'v' with an initial long upstroke might resemble a 'p', a misreading or a substitution influenced by graphical form and context is possible.
2.2.70/874   ist] Q; Is it F
2.2.72/876   A calls me enow] Q; He call'd me euen now F
2.2.72   e'en now] Q (enow)
*2.2.75/879   red peticote] This edition (Monro); peticote Q; new Petticoat F; new red petticoat COLLIER (conj.). 'New' is pointless, and would easily be misread from 'red'. If the word was added to a scribe's copy as an interlineation, it may have been particularly difficult to read. Such a situation would also explain its absence in Q, whether the word was interlined in or, more straightforwardly, absent from the printer's copy.
2.2.75/879-80   and so] Q; & F. *So* seems idiomatically right, and could easily be omitted. It probably did not appear in the Folio compositor's copy, for it would have helped him justify if he could have ended the line 'and so' instead of '& pee-'.
2.2.77/881   Has] Q; Hath F
2.2.79/882   rabbet] F (Rabbet); rabble Q
2.2.82/885   Althea] F; Althear Q. Q gives a typical misreading of Shakespeare's 'a'.
2.2.85/888   tis] Q; it is F
*2.2.86/889   good] F; *not in* Q. It is scarcely credible that 'good' here and at 2.2.92/895 can have been twice interpolated or omitted by accident, especially as the variant occurs elsewhere, and one would not expect a scribe repeatedly to interfere with the text in this way. The changes were probably made by Shakespeare. See note to 2.1.169/777 for other instances.
2.2.89/892   And] Q; If F
2.2.89/892   hangd] Q; be hang'd F
*2.2.90/893   be wrongd] F (~ wrong'd); haue wrong Q. Shakespeare may have opted in favour of a 'hangd'/'wrongd' chime.
*2.2.92/895   my good] F; my Q. See note to 2.2.86/889.
2.2.101/904   how] Q; *not in* F. F's reading would be possible if Sisson's distribution of speech-prefixes were accepted (see following note), but F agrees with Q's prefixes. 'How' is a simple omission before 'he', especially over a type line-break.
2.2.102/905-6   POYNES Iohn ... euery] QF; John ... *Poins*. Every SISSON
2.2.102/905   Iohn] Q; Sir John CAPELL (conj.)
2.2.103/906   has] Q; hath F
2.2.105/909   theres] Q; there is F
2.2.107/910   conceiue:] F1 (~ ?), F4; ~ˏ Q
2.2.108/911   borowers] THEOBALD (Warburton); borowed QF. See notes to 2.2.102/905-6, 2.2.115/919, and 2.2.117/921 for other possible, if individually doubtful, indications of local Quarto influence on F.
2.2.109/913   or] Q; but F. F probably anticipates 'but' in the next line.
2.2.110/914   the] Q; to the F. F probably again anticipates.
2.2.115/919   Romanes] QF; Roman WARBURTON
2.2.116/920   Sure he] F; He sure Q. *Sure he* is a Shakespearian idiom; *he sure* is not (except, once, as a result of inversion 'is he sure bound', *Titus* 5.2.164/2261). The transposition was probably made by Simmes's Compositor A, who was prone to such errors.
2.2.117, 126/921, 930   I commend mee ... My] *no speech-prefixes* F; I commend mee ... *Poynes* My Q; P⟨rince⟩. *Henry*. I commend me ... *Poins*. My THEOBALD. Q may reflect an original intention for the Prince to read this part of the letter (or an indecision), but F's arrangement, self-consistent and dramatically plausible, need not be rejected.
2.2.124/928   familiars] F; family Q
2.2.124/928   sisters] Q; Sifter F
2.2.126/930   Ile] Q; I will F
2.2.131/935   God send the wench] Q; May the Wench haue F
2.2.136/940   Yea] Q; Yes F
2.2.153/957   come to] Q; in F. F is rejected as an authorial change as it creates an ambiguity: *yet* as 'already' or 'still'.
2.2.157/961   you] Q; ye F
2.2.158/962   rode] QF. A cryptic reading. Were it not for the QF agreement, one might posit 'common rode'.
2.2.163/968   letherne] Q; Leather F
2.2.164/969   like] F; as Q. The variant would be a typical substitution by Simmes's Compositor A.
2.2.165/970   declension] F; defcenſion Q. F is supported by (*a*) similar usages elsewhere in Shakespeare, as against no instances of *declension*, (*b*) the quibble it gives on *case*. Shakespeare elsewhere uses *declension* and *case* in the grammatical sense only in *Merry Wives*, which he wrote at about the same time as *2 Henry IV*.
2.2.166/971   prince] F (Prince); pince Q
2.2.167/972   euery] F; enery Q
2.3.1/974   pray thee] Q; prethee F
2.3.2/975   euen] Q; an euen F
2.3.9/982   Gods] Q; heauens F
2.3.10/983   that] Q; when F
2.3.11/984   endeerd] F (endear'd); endeere Q
2.3.12/985   hearts deere] Q; heart-deere F
2.3.17/990   the God of heauen] Q; may heauenly glory F. F's emendation of profanity may be held to improve the line, and was probably effected by Shakespeare—though only under pressure of emending profanity generally.
*2.3.23-45/996-1018   He ... Graue.] F; *not in* Q. See Introduction.
2.3.32/1005   wondrousˏ him!] ROWE; ~ ! ~, F
*2.4.1, 10/1042, 1051   1 DRAWER] F; Fran⟨cis⟩. Q. See note to 2.4.13/1054.
2.4.1/1042   the diuel] Q; *not in* F
2.4.4/1045   2 DRAWER] Q (*Draw.*), F
2.4.4/1045   Mas] Q; *not in* F
2.4.12/1053   heare] Q; haue F
2.4.12.1-3/1053.1-3   *exit ... Enter 2 Drawer*] *not in* QF. See following note. The staging may appear to be unusual, but incidental comings and goings of functionaries tend to pass unmarked in texts of the period. Compare 2.4.372.1/1401.1, where Bardolph inferably re-enters after an exit occupying five words.

*2.4.13/1054 2 DRAWER] F; Dra⟨wer⟩. Diſpatch, the roome where they ſupt is too hot, theile come in ſtraight. | *Francis* Q; *no prefix before* 'Dispatch' POPE; 3 Draw⟨er⟩. Dispatch . . . *Francis* ALEXANDER (Ridley). Up to this point Q's Francis is the First Drawer in F. Hereafter Francis becomes the Second Drawer. This change is clearly deliberate, and follows from the omission of Q's speech. Q probably gives an accurate account of the confused state of Shakespeare's foul papers, and F of the way these papers were brought to order in the prompt-book. The correspondence between Q and F in indicating no more than two Drawers with strictly alternating speeches suggests that even if Shakespeare half-intended a third drawer when he wrote the foul papers (as is suggested by the irrelevantly located '*Enter Will.*' after 2.4.16/1057), such a plan cannot have been realized in the prompt-book. F solves most of the problems inherent in Q's confused text. Prosser's contention that the scribe himself restructured the episode (pp. 42–5) is intrinsically implausible in terms of the role it attributes to the scribe, and moves into difficulties if the scribe was not working from the foul papers. F is the less busy text; it gives clearer emphasis to the news about the Prince and Master Poins.

Q calls for Francis and another Drawer, F for a First and Second Drawer. In the play in performance, there would be no way of telling which, if either, of the Drawers was Francis. There would be little purpose in following F's redistribution of speeches but retaining Q's name for one of the Drawers, as F reconstructs any identity 'Francis' may have had: he would retain only two of his four speeches.

There is a connection between the Folio variants here and at the end of the similar sub-scene opening 5.5/Sc. 17 (see note to 5.5.4–4.1/3092–3092.1). Again the directing intelligence is authorial in kind. However, considerations of casting must influence the changes at the beginning of 5.5/Sc. 17, whereas there would have been no particular casting difficulties at the beginning of 2.4/Sc. 7. See Jowett, 'Cuts and Casting'.

2.4.17/1058 1 DRAWER] F; Dra⟨wer⟩. Q; 3 Draw⟨er⟩. ALEXANDER
2.4.17/1058 By the mas] Q; Then F
2.4.17/1058 old] Qb; oll Qa. It is conceivable that 'oll' represents a dialectal pronunciation, but 'd' could easily be misread 'l' in Shakespeare's hand, and 'vtis' may not have encouraged the compositor to seek intelligibility.
*2.4.19/1060 2 DRAWER] F; *Francis* Q
2.4.19.1/1060 exeunt] Q (exit.), F (*Exit.*) '*Exit*' for '*exeunt*' is scarcely an error in Elizabethan play texts. Rowe's '*Exeunt*' has not found favour with recent editors, though Prosser noted that it allowed Sir John to bellow 'empty the iourdan' to off-stage attendants. The staging does not demand a scene-break: compare note to 5.5.4–4.1/3092–3092.1.
2.4.20/1061 Yfaith] Q; *not in* F
2.4.23–4/1064 in good truth law] Q; *not in* F
2.4.24/1065 yfaith] Q; *not in* F
2.4.26/1067 we] F (wee); one Q. Probably a compositorial error in Q.
2.4.29/1069 thats] Q; that was F
2.4.31/1070 loe] Q; Looke F
2.4.35/1074 good faith] Q; good-footh F
2.4.36/1075 and] Q; if F
2.4.38/1077 A pox damne you, you] Q; You F
2.4.42/1080 them, I] F; I Q
2.4.43/1082 cooke help to] Q; Cooke F. See following note.
2.4.43–4/1082–3 you helpe to] QF; you This edition *conj*. F's omission of the first 'help to' looks deliberate but weakens the sense. However, the sense would be strengthened if the phrase was omitted on both occasions. Shakespeare may have made two deletions, but marked the second one ineffectively.
2.4.45/1084 you:] F; ~, Q
2.4.46/1086 Yea Iesu] This edition (*conj*. Ridley); Yea ioy Q; I marry F. The variant hints at a profanity underlying both texts. 'Iesu' makes much better sense than 'ioy'. See also Ridley.
*2.4.51/1090 brauely.] F; brauely. | *Doll* Hang your ſelfe, you muddie Cunger, hang your ſelfe. Q. The first of three omissions in F (also after 2.4.132/1166, and 2.4.143–4/1177) which are most convincingly explained as deliberate cuts made by Shakespeare when reviewing the episode leading up to the sudden inception of Pistol's rant. See Jowett, 'Cuts and Casting'.
2.4.52/1091 By my troth] Q; Why F
2.4.54/1093 ygood truth] Q; in good troth F
2.4.66 Enſign] Q (Antient). Similarly elsewhere.
2.4.66/1103 pistol's] Q; Piſtoll is F
2.4.72/1107–8 no by my faith] Q; *not in* F
2.4.72/1108 among] Q; amongſt F
2.4.78/1114 ye] Q; you F
2.4.81/1117 nere] Q; neuer F
*2.4.81/1117 your] F; & your Q
2.4.82/1118 swaggrer] QF; swagger a HUMPHREYS (Maxwell). QF makes good sense; we take *ensign-swaggerer* as a compound, but alternatively the Hostess understands *ancient* (see note to 2.4.66) as 'inveterate'.
2.4.83/1119 debuty tother] Q; Duputie, the other F
2.4.84/1120 twas] Q; it was F
2.4.84/1120 wedsday] Q; Wedneſday F
2.4.84–5/1120 I good faith] Q; *not in* F
2.4.87/1123 saide he] Q; ſayth hee F
2.4.88/1124 a] Q; hee F
2.4.95/1130 yfaith] Q; hee F
2.4.96/1132 heele] Q; hee will F
2.4.101/1137 by my troth] Q; *not in* F
2.4.105/1140 and twere] Q; if it were F
2.4.106.1/1141.1 Bardolfe, page] and Bardolfes boy Q; and Bardolph and his Boy F. Q presumably derives from a misunderstanding of the foul papers. F must result from the scribe consulting Q and adjusting any stage directions accordingly. Further adjustment, without consultation of Q, must have occurred in 3.2.51.1/1575.1, where F again has 'Bardolph and his Boy'. The scribe presumably recalled the present direction and interpolated 'his' (perhaps also changing F's usual '*Page*' to '*Boy*'). None of this reflects an intention to make changes to the substantive content of the stage directions.
2.4.107/1142 God saue] Q; 'Saue F
2.4.113/1147 proofe, sir,] F (~ (~)); ~ : ~, Q
2.4.113/1147 shall not] Q; ſhall F
2.4.116/1149 bullets, Ile] Q; Bullets: I will F
2.4.126/1160 and] Q; if F
2.4.126.1/1160.1 *She brandishes a knife*] *not in* QF. See following note.
2.4.128.1/1162.1 *Pistol drawes his sword*] *not in* QF. Doll's sarcastic 'Since when' is evidently a reaction to Pistol asserting himself as a soldier. As Doll has just threatened to stab him, the text indicates that the quarrel is already threatening to degenerate into a brawl with weapons. Editors usually accept that 'Hiren' at 2.4.156/1190 is in part a reference to Pistol's sword, and often indicate as much in a stage direction; clearly the sword is drawn before 2.4.180/1213. The present stage of the quarrel provides the most effective context.
2.4.129/1163 Gods light] Q; what F
2.4.131/1165 God . . . but] Q; *not in* F
*2.4.132/1166 this.] F; this. | *ſir Iohn* No more Piſtol, I would not haue you go off here, diſcharge your ſelfe of our company, Piſtoll. Q. See note to 2.4.51/1090.
2.4.137/1170 and] Q; If F
2.4.143/1176 Gods light] Q; *not in* F
*2.4.143–4/1177 captaine odious,] F; as odious as the word occupy, which was an excellent good worde before it was il ſorted, Q. See note to 2.4.51/1090.
2.4.144/1178 too't] Q; to it F
2.4.148/1182 of] Q; on F
2.4.151/1185 by this hâd] Q; *not in* F. An oath, albeit a mild one.
2.4.152/1186 th'infernal] Q; the Infernall F
2.4.153/1187 Where] F; with Q
2.4.155/1189 fates:] F (Fates:); faters, Q. Q would constitute Shakespeare's only use of *faitor*. As Pistol threatens to murder

2.4.157/1191 tis] Q; it is F
2.4.158/1192 yfaith] Q; *not in* F
2.4.162/1196 mile] Q; miles F
2.4.163/1197 Cæsars] Q; Cæfar F
2.4.164 Trojan] Q (troian), F (Troian)
2.4.171/1204 Die men] F; Men Q
2.4.171/1204 dogges,] F (Dogges;); ∼∧ Q
2.4.173/1206 A] Q; On F
2.4.175/1208 for Gods sake] Q; I pray F
2.4.177/1210 giues] Q; giue me F
2.4.178/1211 contento] Q; contente F. As Pistol's allusive phrases are generally inaccurate and uneven, Q is probably right. F would be typical enough of the underlying scribe's tidying.
2.4.181/1214 no things] Q; no-|thing F
2.4.185/1218 For Gods sake thrust] Q; Thruft F
2.4.190/1223 and a] Q; if hee F
2.4.190–1/1223-4 a shall] Q; hee fhall F
2.4.196 Untwine] Q (vntwinde)
2.4.197/1230 goodly] Q; good F
2.4.199/1232 pray thee ... pray thee] Q; prethee ... prethee F
2.4.204/1236 afore] Q; before F
2.4.208/1240 pray thee] Q; prethee F
2.4.208/1240 rascal's] Q; Rascall F
2.4.211/1243 a made] Q; hee made F
2.4.213/1244 a] Q; of F
2.4.214/1245 Yea] Q; Yes F
2.4.215/1246 i'th] Q; in the F
2.4.217 Ah,] Q (A∧). Similarly 2.4.219 and 222.
2.4.219/1250 yfaith] Q; *not in* F
2.4.223/1253 A] F; Ah Q
2.4.225/1255 and ... and] Q; if ... if F
2.4.231/1261 Yfaith and] Q; And F
2.4.233-4/1263 a ... a] Q; on ... on F
2.4.233, 234 o'] Q (a). Similarly elsewhere.
2.4.238/1267 humour's] Q; humor is F
2.4.239-40/1268-9 a would ... a would] Q; hee would ... hee would F
2.4.240/1269 a chipt] Q; haue chipp'd F
2.4.240 ha'] Q (a)
2.4.241/1270 has] Q; hath F
2.4.242/1271 wit's] Q; Wit is F
2.4.243/1272 theres] Q; there is F
2.4.245/1274 does] Q; doth F
2.4.246-7/1276 a plaies] Q; hee playes F
2.4.250/1280 boote] F (Boot); bootes Q. F is more intelligible, as 'boote' may be generic or specific (anticipating 'Legge'). Q probably results from terminal 'e'/'s' misreading.
2.4.253/1282 a has] Q; hee hath F
2.4.255/1285 a] Q; an F
2.4.256/1285 the scales] F; fcales Q
2.4.259/1289 Lets] Q; Let vs F
2.4.260/1290 where] Q; if F
2.4.260 whe'er] Q (where)
2.4.266/1296 th'Almanacke] Q; the Almanack F
2.4.268/1298 masters,] F; mafter, Q
2.4.271/1301 By my troth] Q; Nay truely F
2.4.276/1305 wilt] Q; wilt thou F
2.4.277/1306 a thursday] Q; on Thurfday F
2.4.277/1306 shalt] Q; thou fhalt F
2.4.279/1308 weele] Q; wee will F
2.4.279/1308 thou't] Q; Thou wilt F
2.4.281/1310 By my troth thou't] Q; Thou wilt F
2.4.282/1310 and] Q; if F
2.4.283/1312 a'th] Q; the F
2.4.294-5/1323 grace: by my troth] Q; good Grace: F. F's 'good' probably substitutes for the effufiveness lost with the deletion of the oath. The change may be authorial.
2.4.295/1324 now the Lord] Q; Now Heauen F
2.4.296/1325 O Iesu] Q; what F

2.4.305/1334 now] Q; euen now F. The use of unqualified *now* to mean 'just now' may be distinct to Shakespeare: *OED* gives no instances in the period, but Schmidt cites *Coriolanus* 1.9.79/706. Q is almost certainly what Shakespeare originally wrote; F's regularization of a distinct idiom is characteristic of the scribe who prepared the printer's copy.
2.4.307/1336 Gods blessing of] Q; 'Bleffing on F
2.4.310/1339 Yea] Q; Yes F
2.4.317/1346 a] Q; on F
2.4.319/1348 bread-chipper] Q; Bread-chopper F
2.4.322/1351 i'th] Q; in the F
*2.4.324/1353 him] F; thee Q. Humphreys compares 2.1.76-8/684-6 for the mid-sentence change of addressee. That example is closer to the Folio version: in both the change is only made after a close which Humphreys represents with a colon. Shakespeare perhaps found the Folio version more theatrically workable.
2.4.327/1356 faith] Q; *not in* F
2.4.332/1360 thy] Q; the F
*2.4.340/1368 outbids] F; blinds Q; behind WILSON (*conj.*); bloats WALKER (*conj.*); attends HUMPHREYS; binds DAVISON; brands BERGER *and* WILLIAMS (*conj.*). Whether or not Q is correct (it evidently is not), the variant is hard to explain except as involving authorial revision. The principal question for an editor accepting Folio additions and revisions is whether F's reading is corrupt. The idea of the devil outbidding the good angel is perfectly appropriate. The problem lies in 'him too': 'him' must refer to the angel, not the Page, whereas 'too' requires 'him' to be the Page. Strictly speaking, the revision was not properly assimilated into its context—a situation which can easily arise when a single key word is altered. However, it is doubtful if any difficulty would have been noticed in theatrical performance.
2.4.342/1370 shees] Q; fhee is F
2.4.343/1371 th'other] Q; the other F
2.4.350/1378 whats] Q; What is F
2.4.356/1385 too'th] Q; to the F
2.4.366/1395 south,] QB, F; ∼. QA
2.4.388.1/1416.1 *Enter Bardolfe*] *not in* QF. Editors usually leave Bardolph either at the door (which amounts to an entry) or within.
2.4.391.1/1419.1 *exit*] *not in* QF. See following note.
*2.4.392/1420 good Doll.] F (∼ Doll.); good Doll, come, fhee comes blubberd, yea? wil you come Doll? Q. If, as Wilson believed, Bardolph should speak 'come' and 'yea ... Doll', one would expect the difficulty to have been resolved, not obliterated in F. Wilson explains Q as arising from cramped copy at the foot of a manuscript page. Jowett and Taylor argue against this view. Even less plausible is Dyce's interpretation of 'She comes blubberd' as a stage direction. The only real difficulty in Q is the change in verb from 'runne' to 'come' before the change in address from Doll to Bardolph; especially in context, the first 'come' could easily be a misreading of 'runne'.

F just might result from eyeskip, but the last line of a scene would be especially prominent and so resistant to such error. The line is a plausible target for authorial intervention, for its deletion alters the staging of the scene-end. In Q, Bardolph waits for Doll, assuming he is on stage, and the Hostess evidently leaves with them. In F the pace is faster; Bardolph probably leaves immediately after his last speech, the Hostess urges Doll to follow, but presumably herself leaves in another direction. Another possible and related motive for the change might be the interpolation of 3.1/Sc. 8 after the foul papers were originally written. In the original text without 3.1/Sc. 8, the repetitions of 'come' at the end of 2.4/Sc. 7 and the beginning of 3.2/Sc. 9 provide continuity. The repeated 'runne', on the other hand, provides a better anticipation of the beginning of 3.1/Sc. 8 ('Go ... make good speed'). As with deletions earlier in the scene, this deletion may have arisen from Shakespeare reviewing the original text just before the point where he had introduced changes.
3.1.0.1-103/1420.2-1523] QB; *not in* QA. See Introduction.
3.1.14/1434 sound] Q; founds F. The first of a series of terminal 's' variants in 3.1/Sc. 8; others are at 3.1.24, 35, 54, 76, and

80/1444, 1455, 1474, 1496, and 500. In most cases there are slender grounds for preferring one reading over another, though F's 'Clamours' must be wrong. 'Two yeere' (3.1.54/1474) is the more idiomatic reading, with Folio sophistication as at 2.4.162/1196 and 3.2.207/1732; 'letter' is plausibly inconsistent with 'letters' in 3.1.2/1422; 'sound' and 'clamour' occur in a context of plural mid-line nouns in previous lines. In the first four readings F can thus be readily explained as sophistication or error. In the last two, F gives the more expected idiom. Q's 'natures' (3.1.76/1496), however, emphasizes the distinct identities of 'times', which are treated as discrete organisms which, though now 'deceast', 'come to life' from 'seedes'. This argument in favour of Q's 'natures' must equally support F's 'beginnings'. Further, Shakespeare nowhere else uses *beginning* with a plural pronoun; his one other instance of *beginnings* (*Henry V* 2.2.184/791, 'our beginnings') is with a plural pronoun and in a play written soon after *2 Henry IV*. Q gives an unlikely and awkward reading which need not be accepted. It seems that the clustering of terminal 's' variants is on the whole a consequence of scribal sophistication, but that in one instance, the last, F corrects an error in Q.

3.1.18/1438 maste] F (Maſt); maſſe Q.
3.1.22/1442 billowes] F (Billowes); pillowes Q
3.1.24/1444 deaffing clamour] Q; deaff'ning Clamors F
3.1.26/1446 thy] F; them Q
3.1.27/1447 seaboy] F (Sea-Boy); ſeaſon Q. Ridley read 'sea's son', which, though a contrived resolution of the variants, hints at the subconscious word-play which probably led to Q's substitution.
3.1.31.1/1451.1 *Enter Warwike and Surry*] F; *Enter Warwike, Surry and sir Iohn Blunt.* Q. Shakespeare evidently changed his mind about having Blunt in this scene, though he was still evidently thinking of three lords when he specified 'all' at 3.1.34/1454. The direction in F is consistent with the scene's opening line.
3.1.35/1455 letter] Q; Letters F. See note to 3.1.14/1434.
3.1.44/1464 God] Q; Heauen F
*3.1.52/1472 liquors!] F liquors!, | The happieſt youth viewing his progreſſe through, | What perills paſt, what croſſes to enſue? | Would ſhut the booke and ſit him downe and die: | Q. F's omission of these despairing lines has usually been blamed on the religious susceptibilities of the Master of the Revels or the scribe who prepared the copy. Neither explanation is satisfactory. The passage is outside the usual parameters of state censorship. The scribe is a relatively unknown quantity, but in all other cases expurgation is best explained in terms of the single and inevitable process of theatrical censorship: there is no reason to suppose that the scribe was sensitive to religious matters, let alone to the point of imposing censorship on his own account. A similar theory has been put forward for F's omitted lines at 2.2.22/826 (see note), but if one reconstructs that passage as it would have appeared after routine expurgation of profanity in the theatre, which would have been necessary in a prompt-book used after 1606, little is left for conscientious objection to seize on. In contrast, the cut can readily be seen as a coherent authorial deletion. Like those following 2.2.22/826, 2.4.143-4/1177, and 3.2.309/1833, the omitted lines can be seen as digressive. The Folio text flows directly from 'Chances mocks | And Changes' to the example of Richard and Northumberland; the Quarto passage develops logically out of the matter that precedes, but moves to a point of disengagement from life which contrasts with the vigorous imagery before and the intense interest in human affairs after. Johnson noted 'some difficulty' in 'What perills past, what crosses to ensue': 'it seems to make *past perils* equally terrible with *ensuing crosses*'. If the future is akin to the past, which has made the youth happy, he is unlikely to resolve to die. Johnson's objection highlights the way the passage F omits slides uncertainly from the dynamism of contrast to the stasis of despair. It is easier to see Shakespeare raising such objections to himself than it is to see a censor deleting the lines.
3.1.54/1474 yeare] Q; yeeres F
3.1.67/1487 God] Q; Heauen F
3.1.76/1496 natures] Q; nature F

3.1.79/1499 who] Q; which F
3.1.80/1500 beginnings] F; beginning Q
3.1.92/1512 voice,] F (subs.); ~, Q
3.1.94/1514 soule] Q; Life F. F softens the oath from the immortal to the mortal. The variant recurs at 4.1.286/2134.
3.2.0.1/1523.1 *Enter ... Silens*] Q; *Enter Shallow and Silence: with Mouldie, Shadow, Wart, Feeble, Bull-calfe.* F. Q supplies no entry for the recruits. Prosser argues a convincing case against F's staging, and supports (though for different reasons) Davison's provision of entries for the recruits as they are summoned later in the scene, as followed in this edition. However, neither Davison nor Prosser adequately explains F. Prosser believes that the scribe expanded the opening entry, so giving evidence of his lack of theatrical sense. This implies that the scribe's copy provided no entries for the recruits, a deficiency not to be expected in a prompt-book.

There are two instances later in the play (at the beginning of 4.1/Sc. 10 and 5.3/Sc. 15) of characters being named in F in the opening directions when they do not enter until later in the scene; in both these intances F provides second entries at the appropriate point. These two 'massed' but duplicated entries cannot be explained in terms of the scribe making good the deficiencies in his copy. All three directions may, however, arise through the scribe's misinterpretation of annotations made in the prompt-book (see Introduction). In the case of 4.1/Sc. 10 and 5.3/Sc. 15, the scribe copying the prompt-book might not have noticed the resulting duplications. In 3.2/Sc. 9 the succession of individual entries of characters with distinctive names, and who are nowhere else mentioned, could scarcely have escaped his attention. If he had already written out the opening direction, his obvious course would be to omit the later entries.

For further details, see Jowett, 'Cuts and Casting'.
3.2.1/1524 on, giue] QA, F; on ſir, giue QB. In duplicated passages, QB seems to be an unauthoritative and perhaps hastily composed reprint.
1527 SCILENS] The 'Sc' spelling, which also appears in the Hand D addition to *Sir Thomas More*, is almost certainly Shakespeare's. Q shows a slight preference for the 'S' only form. Exceptionally, our standardized speech-prefix spelling is that of the minority form: it is distinctly Shakespearian and may have been used more widely in the compositor's copy.
3.2.8/1531 no] Q; nay F
3.2.8/1531 sir,] Qa, F; ~ : QB
3.2.12/1535 A] Q; Hee F
3.2.12/1535 a] Q; of F
3.2.16/1539 By the masse] Q; *not in* F
3.2.19/1542 Barnes] Q; *Bare* F
3.2.21/1544 a] Q; of F
3.2.22/1545 bona robas] F (*Bona-Roba's*); bona robes Q
3.2.26/1549 This sir John, coosin] QA, F; Cooſin, this ſir Iohn QB
3.2.28/1551 ,sir Iohn,] QA, F; (~ ~) QB
3.2.28/1551 see] Q; ſaw F
3.2.29/1552 a was] Q; hee was F
3.2.32/1555 Iesu, Iesu] Q; Oh F
3.2.33/1556 my] Q; mine F
3.2.36/1560 (as the Psalmist saith)] Q; *not in* F
3.2.37/1561 Stamford] F (Stamford); Samforth Q. Q begins with a literal error and ends with a spelling variant.
3.2.38/1562 By my troth] Q; Truly Couſin F
3.2.42/1566 Iesu, Iesu, dead! a] Q; Dead? See, ſee: hee F
3.2.43/1567 a shot] Q; hee ſhot F
3.2.43/1567 a Gaunt] Q; of Gaunt F
3.2.44/1568 a] Q; hee F
3.2.45/1569 ith] Q; in the F
3.2.46/1570 a fourteene] Q; at foureteene F
3.2.51.1/1575.1 page] one with him Q; *his Boy* F. See Introduction. The scribe who probably introduced '*his Boy*' evidently departed from both his manuscript copy and Q, recalling Q at 2.4.106.1/1141.1 (see note). He is most likely to have done so if the manuscript specifically required the Boy or Page. The original

'one' may in the prompt-book have been identified with the Boy because of shortage of men actors in this scene.

3.2.54/1578 SHALLOW] F; *Bardolfe* QAa; *not in* QAb, QB. This is the only known press-correction in QA of material later reset in QB. Berger and Williams demonstrate which text is corrected, arguing that QAb gives an unauthoritative miscorrection of self-evident error.

3.2.58/1582 good] QA, F; *not in* QB. The cluster of variants on 'good' (here, 3.2.73/1597, and 3.2.81/1605) is difficult to attribute to a single cause.

3.2.60/1585 by heauen,] Q; *not in* F
3.2.65/1589 accommodated] F; accommodate Q
3.2.67/1591 infaith] Q; *not in* F
3.2.69/1593 euer were] Q; euery where F
3.2.72/1596 Pardon] QA, F; Pardon me QB. See following note.
3.2.73/1597 this] QA, F; this good QB. In setting the expansion to Sheet E, Simmes's Compositor A had to stretch his copy. The present speech, on E6ᵛ, is generously spaced, and forces 'thing.' at the end of it onto a fresh type line. QB's addition of 'me' and 'good' may therefore be compositorial insertions to waste space. If such behaviour recalls that of Folio Compositor B, the reason lies in the comparable but exceptional difficulties they faced. On the other hand the variant could be merely an error of contamination in QB, similar to the interpolation in the compositor's original setting of 3.2.81/1605.

3.2.75-6/1599-1600 by heauen,] Q; *not in* F
3.2.78/1602 a may be] Q; he F
3.2.81/1605 your] Q; your good Q. Probably a compositorial anticipation.
3.2.82/1606 by my troth] Q; Truft me F
3.2.82/1606 like] Q; looke F. F evens out the distinctive idiom. For Q, see *OED like*, v.¹ 4.
3.2.85/1609 Surcard] F (*Sure-card*); Soccard Q
3.2.92/1616 dozen] Q; dozen of F
3.2.96/1620 let me see, so] QA, F; fo QB. The omission in QB has no effect on the number of type lines, and is almost certainly a simple error.

*3.2.97/1621 so, yea] This edition; fo (fo, fo) yea Q; yea F. Despite the occasionally idiosyncratic use of round brackets in Q (as in other texts of the period), it is odd that words thus marked off in Q should be omitted in F. Q may reflect a provisional or definite deletion of the final 'so, so'. F could easily omit a third 'so' by mistake. For a contrasting modification of a similar line, whereby elements unaffected here are omitted ('let me see', 'yea mary'), see note to 5.1.9/2700-1. This link between variants is particularly suggestive; the more widespread tendency to reduce Shallow's repetitions is also most convincingly ascribed to Shakespeare (though error would be easy enough in an individual case such as 3.2.213/1738).

3.2.98/1622 do͜ ... do͜] QB, F; ~, ... ~, QA
3.2.99.1/1623.1 Enter Mouldy]; *not in* Q; as part of opening direction for 3.2./Sc. 9 in F. Similarly with the entries of the other recruits. See note to 3.2.0.1/1523.1.
3.2.100/1624 and't] QA; and it QB; if it F
3.2.104/1628 and't] Q; if it F
3.2.106/1630 yfaith] Q; *not in* F
3.2.107/1631 infaith] Q; *not in* F
3.2.109/1633 SIR IOHN Pricke him.] F; *Iohn prickes him*. Q (indented from right-hand margin on same type line as 'well said'). Cowl noted that the Quarto compositor's interpretation of the speech as a stage direction may be 'in consequence of some disarrangement in the MS'. '*Iohn*' is nowhere found as a speech-prefix in this part of the text and is never found alone in stage directions. Either the prefix or the whole speech (with prefix) may have been altered, so giving either a prefix running into speech or a cramped marginal addition. But as the speech is short and intrinsic to the dialogue, it is possible that the compositor at first omitted the line, and that Q gives a (conveniently) misinterpreted proof correction.

3.2.110/1634 and] Q; if F
3.2.120/1644 th'other] Q; the other F
3.2.120/1644 see,] F (~:); ~͜ Q

1644-6 Shadow. | SIR] A mechanical error affects the line numbering across this and a number of subsequent page-breaks in the first impression of our original-spelling edition, to which the *Companion* is keyed.

3.2.121/1646 Yea] Q; I F
3.2.129/1654 not] F; much Q
3.2.133/1658 fill] Q; to fill F
3.2.140/1666 him] Q; him downe F. F wastes space (see Introduction) by setting between one-third and half a line of quads after 'downe', and placing 'Sir *Iohn*?' on a line of its own. 'Downe' is likely to be an interpolation to avoid even more quads.
3.2.141/1667 for his] F; for Q
3.2.148/1674 SHALLOW] QF; *Fal⟨staff⟩*. THEOBALD. Sir John's joke at the expense of Shallow as well as Feeble (3.2.151-2/1677-8) has more point if Shallow has just tried his hand at interviewing the recruit.
3.2.152/1677-8 hee'd a] Q; he would haue F
3.2.166/1691 sir] Q; *not in* F. F may omit as a consequence of the similarity between ['fuf]fice' and 'fire'—or, to infer a possible Shakespearian spelling influencing a scribe working from Shakespeare's holograph, ['fuf]fic' and 'fir'.
3.2.168/1693 next] Q; the next F. Prosser (pp. 110-11) explains the expansion as compositorial. Compositor B stretched his copy so as to end a type line after 'who is', and Prosser suggests that he would have added 'the' to avoid setting 'next' on a type line by itself. Yet eight lines above he set 'low' of 'Shal-|low' alone on a type line. Prosser may nevertheless be right, but the variant is within the range of possible interference by the sophisticating scribe.

3.2.169/1694 o'th] Q; of the F
3.2.170/1695 lets] Q; let vs F
3.2.172/1697 Fore God] Q; Truft me F
3.2.172/1697 pricke] Q; pricke me F. Another possible example of F compensating for the loss of profanity: the ethic dative (not a form likely to be introduced by a scribe) gives added emphasis to the verb.
3.2.174/1699 Lord] Q; *not in* F
3.2.175/1700 th'art F; thou art] Q
3.2.176/1701 Lord] Q; *not in* F
3.2.179/1703 caught] F; cought Q. *OED* gives 'cought' as a 15th-c. spelling of the past tense of *catch*, but Q is probably contaminated by 'cough'.
3.2.185/1710 There] F; Here Q
3.2.189/1714 by my] Q; in good F
*3.2.193-4/1718-19 good ... that] F (... Mafter *Shallow*: No ...); mafter *Shallow* Q. Prosser (p. 108) convincingly argues that the speech has been set in F so that it runs on to a second type line. The full prefix '*Falstaffe*.' and the unabbreviated 'Master' in themselves demonstrate Compositor B's concern to stretch copy. Prosser admits that the line in F 'does sound like Falstaff' and 'is appealing'. The interpolation of *good* is not elsewhere in F associated with compositorial expansion (see note to 2.1.169/677), and Prosser gives no comparable examples of B adding a repeated phrase at the end of a speech. The Folio version of the speech would present an unusually good opportunity for stretching to two type lines by 'legitimate' means on account of its length, and occurs at a position (near the foot of gg1) where the need for such expansion would be especially clear. The 'legitimate' expansion is therefore to be expected whether or not new material was added, and is indeed little more than routine in this part of *2 Henry IV*. Its bearing on the compositor's copy is not decisive. F expresses Sir John's reluctance to accept the passage of time much more forcefully than does Q; the variant is most persuasively attributed to authorial revision.

3.2.195/1720 twas] Q; it was F
3.2.201/1726 By the masse] Q; *not in* F
3.2.201/1726 too'th] Q; to the F
3.2.206/1731 Clem. inn] This edition; Clements inne Qc, F; Clemham Qa, Qb. One of several press variants in the second stage of correcting Sheet F (inner) which suggest reference to

copy. See also 3.2.227/1752, 3.2.309/1833, 4.1.12/1859, and 4.1.30/1877.

3.2.207/1732   yeare] Q; yeeres F

*3.2.213/1738   in] F; that we haue, in Q. A marginal variant. See notes to 3.2.97/1621 and 5.1.9/2700-1.

3.2.214   Hem, boys] Q (Hemboies), F (Hem-boyes)

3.2.215/1740   Iesus] Q; Oh F

3.2.218/1743   heres] Q; heere is F

3.2.220   lief] Q (liue)

3.2.227/1751   old] Qc, F; *not in* Qa, Qb. The expanded text was accommodated by reducing 'master' to 'M.'

3.2.228/1752   has] Q; hath F

3.2.232/1756   By my troth] Q; *not in* F

3.2.233/1757   God] Q; *not in* F

3.2.233/1757   ile nere] Q; I will neuer F

3.2.233-4/1757-8   and't ... and't] Q; if it ... if it F

3.2.234/1758   man's] Q; man is F

3.2.235/1759   serue's] Q; ſerue his F

3.2.237/1761   th'art] Q; thou art F

3.2.238/1762   Faith ile] Q; Nay, I will F

3.2.257/1781   heres] Q; Where's F. F is probably influenced by the 'w' ending 'Shallow', and/or anticipates 'Wart'.

3.2.258/1782   a shall] Q; hee ſhall F

3.2.269/1792-3   thas, thas, thas] Q; thus, thus, thus F

3.2.272   chapped] Q (chopt).

3.2.273/1797   yfaith] Q; *not in* F

3.2.273/1797   th'art] Q; thou art F

3.2.274/1798   theres] Q; there is F

3.2.278-82/1802-6   and a ... a ... a ... a ... a ... a come] Q; and hee ... hee ... hee ... hee ... hee ... he come F

3.2.282/1806   nere] Q; neuer F

3.2.284   will] Q (wooll), F

3.2.284-5/1808-9   God keep you] Q; Farewell F

3.2.289/1813   the Lord bleſſe you, God] Q; Heauen bleſſe you, and F

3.2.290/1814   God] Q; and F

3.2.290/1814   peace:] F (~.); ~ˏ Q

3.2.290/1814   as you] F; at your Q. F clarifies.

3.2.290-1/1814-15   my houſe F; our houſe] Q

3.2.292/1816   ye] Q; you F

3.2.293/1817   Fore God] Q; I F

3.2.293/1817   you would] Q; you would, Maſter *Shallow* F. F's addition balances the omitted profanity.

3.2.294/1818   God keep you] Q; Fare you well F

3.2.296/1820   On] F; Shal⟨low⟩. On Q. As Shaaber suggested, the Q compositor may have misinterpreted '*exit Shal.*' in his copy. This would be especially likely if '*Shal*' was added to the copy as an afterthought. Sir John would appear to exit then continue speaking if the original manuscript layout resembled Q without the '*Shal.*' prefix.

3.2.298/1822   Lord, Lord,] Q; *not in* F

3.2.302/1826   Turne-bull] Q; Turnball F

3.2.305/1829   a was] Q; hee was F

3.2.307/1831   a was] Q; Hee was F

3.2.308/1833   inuiſible] ROWE; inuincible QF. See note to 4.1.34/1881.

3.2.308/1833   a] Q; Hee F

3.2.309/1833   genius] Qc, F; gemies Qa, Qb.

*3.2.309/1833   famine,] This edition; famine, yet lecherous as a monkie, & the whores cald him mandrake, a came ouer in the rereward of the faſhion, and ſung thoſe tunes to the ouer-ſchutcht huſwiues, that he heard the Car-men whiſtle, and ſware they were his fancies or his good-nights, Q; Famine: hee came euer in the rere-ward of the Faſhion: F. Though the second of F's cuts, if in isolation, could result from a large eyeskip, the two together are virtually inexplicable except as authoritative. They cancel the diversion from Shallow's thinness to his lechery, lines which might be regarded as inconsistent with Sir John's assertion earlier in the speech that Shallow's youth was not in fact wild. However, F's two cuts leave 'hee came euer in the rere-ward of the Faſhion:' an irrelevant obtrusion in the satire on Shallow's thinness. It seems that the scribe misunderstood the extent of marks for cancellation in his copy.

3.2.310-11, 314/1835, 1839   a Gaunt] Q; of Gaunt F

3.2.312/1836   a nere] Q; hee neuer F

3.2.315/1840   trust] F (truſs'd); thruſt Q. F has the rarer and more specific word. It gives point to 'and all his aparell', as *truss* can be specifically 'To pack up one's clothes' (*OED*, *v.* 3), or to gird up a garment. This is the only use of *truss* ascribable to Shakespeare.

3.2.316/1840   eele-skin] Qb, Qc, F; eele-ſhin Qa

3.2.317/1842   has] Q; hath F

3.2.318/1842   ile] Q; I will F

3.2.318/1842   be] Qb, Qc, F; he Qa

3.2.319/1843   t'shal] Q; it ſhall F

3.2.319/1844   ile] Q; I will F

3.2.322/1846   him: let] Qa, Qb; ~, till Qc

4.1.0.1-3/1847.1-2   *Enter ... Gaultree*] Q names [Lord] '*Bardolfe*' after Mowbray; Shakespeare subsequently consigns him to Scotland with Northumberland, and F omits the name here. See note to 3.2.0.1/1523.1 for F's inclusion of Westmorland in this entry.

*4.1.0.2/1847.2   *Colleuile*] F; *not in* Q. See Taylor, 'Zounds'. Coleville, like Westmorland, might have been added in the prompt-book as an annotation; the order in which the scribe put them when transcribing the prompt-book ('*Westmerland, Coleuile*') would be arbitrary. In this edition, Coleville is taken to be the captain who leaves at 4.1.297.1/2145.1.

4.1.0.3   *Gaultres*] Q (*Gaultree*). Similarly at 4.1.2/1850.

4.1.12/1859   could] Qc, F; would Qa, Qb

4.1.30/1877   Then my L.] Qc, F; *not in* Qa, Qb. These words were almost certainly added as an afterthought in the foul papers; it is otherwise unlikely that they would have been omitted in Qa. The Qa/Qb variant is identical in kind with Q/F variants where F supplies a part-line which makes up a regular pentameter; Q neatly illustrates the authorial origin of such part-lines in F by showing Shakespeare evidently making a similar alteration before the text was transcribed for the prompt-book.

The compositor fitted the added words on the same type line as the next verse line by taking up space to the right of the line, shortening prefix '*West.*' to '*We.*', and shortening 'doe' to 'do'.

4.1.34/1881   rags] SINGER 2 (Walker); rage QF. Even the minority of recent editors who retain 'rage' (for example, Davison) recognize the superiority of the emended reading. In 4.1.1-53/1849-1900 there are no verbal variants between Q and F, and 'appeard' at 4.1.36/1883 is evidently a second instance of shared error. Quarto influence on F is here almost certain, though its extent and the point at which it occurred are less clear. The absence of scribal variants does not necessarily indicate that the compositor consulted Q: the passage presents no profanity, no contractions which could be expanded without damage to metre, no grammatical irregularities, and only one form the scribe sometimes disfavoured ('and't'). The moved stage direction '*Enter Westmerland*' probably indicates a feature of the manuscript, especially as F advances the entry to the position expected in a prompt-book. If the scribe preparing the copy for F had access to a copy of Q, the manuscript from which the scribe was working may have been difficult to read or deficient here. Consultation of Q may have been confined to three lines; the shared round brackets around 'in these great affaires' reflect a more general and casual Quarto influence (see Introduction), and other shared incidentals of punctuation in 'ouer-liue' (4.1.15/1863), 'him', (Qc, 4.1.17/1865), and 'peace'. (4.1.46/1894; see note on Incidentals), though suggestive, are not conclusive.

Another QF shared error occurs 55 type lines in Q before 'rage', at 3.2.308/1833. In a theatrical manuscript, this would occupy a few lines less, as the prose ending 3.2/Sc. 9 would have a wider margin than the Quarto column. The gap between the errors suggests that the top or bottom of a manuscript leaf may have been damaged on both sides. The undamaged part of the leaf presumably supplied the scribe's copy for the intervening lines. However, the inference of a damaged manuscript affecting the scribe's procedure at two points is by no means certain. In Q, 'inuincible' at 3.2.308/1833 is particularly prominent, being the first word on a page. If the scribe noticed the word, he may not even have realized that the word in his copy manuscript, with its succession of minims, was any different. See also notes to 4.1.173/2021 and 4.1.178/2026.

4.1.36/1883 appeard] POPE; appeare QF. See previous note.
4.1.45/1892 figure] Qc, F; figures Qa, Qb
4.1.54/1901 end:... diseasde,] F; ~ₐ ... ~ : Q
4.1.55-79/1902-26 And ... wrong.] F; *not in* Q
4.1.71/1918 our most] F; careless HUMPHREYS (*conj.*)
4.1.71/1918 shore] WILSON (Vaughan); there F; sphere HANMER; flow SISSON
4.1.80/1927 daies] F (dayes); daie's Q
4.1.92-3/1939-40 diuine. ... common wealth] Qb, F; diuine, | And confecrate commotions bitter edge. | *Biſhop* My brother Generall, the common wealth | To brother borne an houſhold cruelty, Qa. Shaaber convincingly argued that Qa preserves lines Shakespeare intended to be deleted.
*4.1.101-37/1948-85 O ... King.] F; *not in* Q. The speech-prefix 'West.' is set before 4.1.138/1986 in Q. See Introduction.
4.1.106/1953 Either] F; Or POPE. F's reading may be a scribal sophistication.
4.1.110/1958 Fathers] F; father HANMER. Franz describes the genitive in apposition to 'Norfolkes' as 'exceptional' (3rd edn., 1924, para. 684a).
4.1.114/1962 force] THEOBALD; forc'd F
4.1.137/1985 indeed] THEOBALD (Thirlby); and did F; and eyed CAMBRIDGE (*conj.*)
4.1.167-8/2015-16 grieuances. ... redrest,] F; ~, ... ~. Q
4.1.173/2021 to our] F; our Q
4.1.173/2021 confinde] CAPELL; confinde QF; confirm'd HANMER. Most recent editors follow QF, understanding that 4.1.173/2021 is taken with the preceding lines. Humphreys objects to the unintelligibility of this arrangement, and takes 4.1.173/2021 as leading in to 4.1.174-5/2022-3. This creates a new difficulty with the sense of 'To vs and [to] our purposes'. Emendation of 'confinde' allows three parallel clauses, 'Each seuerall article ... redrest', 'All members ... Acquitted', and 'present execution ... [confinde]'; in the last, 'vs' relates back to 'members', and 'our purposes' to 'Each seuerall article'. Misreading of 'confinde', would be easy, especially as the following lines might suggest 'confinde'. All editors since Theobald emend QF 'At' to 'And' at 4.1.178/2026 (see note); this is not only a harder error graphically but also one which creates a self-evidently unacceptable line. Q almost certainly influenced F directly or indirectly here, and may have done so two lines earlier.

Consign occurs five times elsewhere in Shakespeare of which one is in *2 Henry IV* ('consigning', 5.2.142/2916). In *Henry V*, 'Demands' and 'a hard Condition' are consigned to (5.2.90/2945 and 288/3156). The intransitive usage is distinct to Shakespeare.

4.1.178/2026 And] THEOBALD (Thirlby); At QF. Here similar circumstances arise to those discussed towards the end of the note on 4.1.34/1881: another shared QF error 47 lines later (4.1.245/2093), might suggest that the beginning or end of a manuscript leaf was damaged. Again there are reasons for doubting the inference: both lines have emended profanity, which may be taken to derive from the scribe's copy, on the same line as the shared error. All one can say with conviction is that the scribe or compositor deliberately or unconsciously absorbed a number of readings from Q whilst preparing the end of 3.2/Sc. 9 and the first 250 lines of 4.1/Sc. 10. See also notes to 4.1.173/2021 and 4.1.183/2031.

4.1.178/2026 God] Q; Heauen F
4.1.183/2031 not, that,] F2; ~, ~ₐ Q, F1
4.1.187/2035 Yea] Q; I F
4.1.225/2073 Gods] Q; heauen's F
4.1.225/2073 set] Q; *not in* F. Perhaps deleted to allow a disyllabic 'heauen's'.
4.1.226.2-3/2074.2-3 with ... wine] *and his armie* Q; *not in* F. Q is misleading, at least to modern readers and perhaps absolutely, as the meeting takes place between the armies; F is unreliable, as it evidently omits mutes elsewhere (in particular, '*the rest*' at 4.2.22.1-2/2220.1-2). There may be a discrepancy between the required action and Q's stage direction reflecting Shakespeare's confusion about how to marry Holinshed's two accounts of the episode with the increased prominence Shakespeare gave to Prince John's complicity. Q need not be interpreted literally, and may preserve abandoned authorial first thoughts. See note to 4.1.323.1/2171.1.

4.1.234/2082 Than] F (Then); That Q
4.1.234/2082 man] F; man talking Q
4.1.243/2091 God] Q; Heauen F
4.1.245/2093 th'imagind] ROWE 3; th'imagine QF. See note to 'And', 4.1.178/2026.
4.1.245/2093 God himselfe] Q; Heauen it felfe F
4.1.250 Employ] Q (*c.w. and text*) (Imply), F. Q's duplication of 'Imply' confirms it as the copy form. Editors have treated it as an error, but in the period *imply* and *employ* had overlapping meanings on account of their common derivation.
4.1.251-2/2099-100 name, ... dishonorable:] F (~, ... ~ ?); ~ : ... ~ₐ Q
4.1.252/2100 tane] Q; taken F
4.1.253/2101 God] Q; Heauen F
4.1.254/2102 his] Q; Heauens F
4.1.264 Hydra son] Q (~, ~), F (~-~). Q's comma is equivalent to a hyphen.
4.1.274/2122 this] F; his Q
4.1.286/2134 soule] Q; Life F. See note to 3.1.94/1514.
4.1.286 shall.] Q (~,)
4.1.292-3/2140-1 redresses. | ⌈PRINCE JOHN⌉ I] F; ~, | I Q. The quarto compositor may have originally omitted the prefix '*Prince*' at 4.1.293/2141 then misinterpreted a corrector's instruction to insert it, instead replacing 'Hast⟨ings⟩.' two lines below with '*Prince*'.
4.1.295/2143 HASTINGS] F; *Prince* Q. See previous note.
4.1.297.1/2145.1 *exit* ⌈*Colleuile*⌉] See note to 4.1.0.2/1847.2.
4.1.323.1/2171.1 *with Captaines*] *not in* QF. The introduction of strong military support here, instead of at Prince John's entry, is desirable because: (*a*) it explains how Prince John is supposed to know that the army has not dispersed; (*b*) it reinforces Westmorland's role in arresting the rebels; (*c*) it gives ironic significance to Westmorland's departure to dismiss the army; (*d*) by allowing Prince John to enter without strong support, it makes him appear deceptively vulnerable, in keeping with his peaceful overtures.
*4.1.327/2175 Our ... disperst,] F (... difpers'd:); My lord, our army is difperft already, Q.
4.1.328/2176 take their courses] Q; tooke their courfe F
4.1.330/2178 toward] Q; towards F
*4.1.343/2191 rebellion,ₐ ... yours:] F (Rebellion, and fuch Acts as yours:]; rebellion: Q
4.1.347/2195 God] Q; Heauen F
4.1.347/2195 hath] Q; haue F
4.1.348 these] Q (this), F. 'This' in the copy for Q would induce the error 'traitour'.
4.1.348/2196 traitours] F; traitour Q
4.2.0.1-2/2197.1-2 *Alarum ... Colleuile*] *Alarum Enter Falſtaffe excurſions* Q; *Enter Falſtaffe and Colleuile*. F. Q's '*Alarum*' could have been omitted by the scribe preparing the copy for F along with other directions for sound effects. F's omission of '*excursions*' is of uncertain origin. It may result from a revised staging, but it is here understood to have been omitted with '*Alarum*' by the scribe. Q similarly omits both Q's sound effect '*Retraite*' and '*the rest*' at 4.2.22.1-2/2220.1-2. There at least F is deficient: 4.3.24/2222 appears to be addressed to a band of followers, and later in the scene (4.2.73/2270) Prince John addresses 'my lords'. (F also, like Q, omits Blunt who is addressed and leaves at 4.2.72/2269.) The scribe probably eliminated stage-business generally, including mute characters, to suppress the theatrical origin of his text. Probably the Lord Chief Justice's men in 2.1/Sc. 4, and perhaps Prince John's '*armie*' in 4.1/Sc. 10, disappear from F by the same process.
4.2.2/2199 I pray] F; *not in* Q
4.2.6-7/2203-4 shalbe still] Q; fhall ftill be F

4.2.22.1-2/2220.1-2 Enter ... souldiers] Q (Enter Iohn Weſtmerland, and the rest.); Enter Prince Iohn, and Weſtmerland. F. See note to 4.2.0.1-2/2197.1-2.
4.2.24/2222 further] Q; farther F
4.2.24.1/2222 Retraite] Q (on the same type line and to the right of the entry); not in F.
*4.2.40/2238 Rome] F; Rome, there coſin Q (c.w. their); Rome there, Cæsar THEOBALD; Rome, their Cæsar SISSON; Rome, three words HUMPHREYS. Q must be corrupt; 'Cæsar' might plausibly be misread 'Cousin'. F's omission is presumably unconnected with Q's corruption, and may be attributed to Shakespeare.
4.2.44-8/2241-5 I know ... foote] These lines approximate to verse, though, unlike 4.2.66-8/2263-5, the distinctive Folio variant (its omission of 'else') does not seem designed to improve the metre.
4.2.46/2243 by the Lord Q; I ſweare F
4.2.47/2244 else] Q; not in F. See note to 4.3.44-8/2241-5. A deletion could have been made in connection with the emendation of profanity in the same clause.
4.2.48/2245 on't] Q; of it F
*4.2.67/2264 gau'st] F; gaueſt Q. See following note.
*4.2.67/2264 away] F; away gratis Q. Q and F print 4.2.66-8/2264-6 as prose, but the elision and two omissions in F are evidently designed to establish the lines as verse (as also in 4.2.78-80/2275-7). F's failure to reline as verse shows that the alteration was not connected with the text's presentation on the page.
*4.2.68/2265 Haue] F; Now, haue Q. See previous note.
*4.2.80/2277 pray] F; not in Q. As in 4.2.66-8/2263-5, F's variant establishes the passage as verse.
4.2.83/2280 but] F; not in Q
4.2.87/2284 none] Q; any F
*4.2.104/2301 illuminateth] F; illumineth Q. Shakespeare's two other usages of illumine are in early works, Two Gentlemen and Venus; illuminate occurs in Caesar, a play a little later than 2 Henry IV. The variant is therefore well explained as authorial.
4.2.108/2307 his] F; this Q. Q probably anticipates 'this valour' or echoes the end of the previous word, 'with'.
4.2.119/2316-17 humane principle] Q; Principle F
4.3.1/2325 God] Q; Heauen F
4.3.32/2356 melting] F; meeting Q
4.3.33/2357 he is] Q; hee's F
4.3.39/2363 line] F (Line); time Q
*4.3.52/2376 accompanied, canst thou tell that?] F (accompanyed? Canſt ...); accompanied? Q. Compare 4.3.15/2339. Canst thou tell can mean 'do you know' or 'are you prepared to say'.
4.3.72/2396 further] Q; farther F
4.3.77/2401 other] Q; others F
4.3.94/2419 heauen] F; heauens Q
4.4.103/2428 full,] F; ~. Q
*4.3.104/2429 write ... letters] F (write ... Letters); wet ... termes Q. The corrected variants have the hallmark of authorial revision. For 'wet'/'write', compare 'blinds'/'outbids' at 2.4.340/1368. 'Wet' has caused difficulty; though the interpretation is not usual, it perhaps makes best sense as a variant of whet. Q nevertheless puzzles because (a) 'whet' is difficult to convey orally in the present context; (b) 'words' and 'terms' are here practically synonymous. Q cannot be explained as a corruption of F's reading, but it is easy to see why Shakespeare might have revised his first thoughts. Humphreys considered F a little glib, but it merely replaces an obscure reading with a clear one.
4.3.117/2442 out,] Q; ~: F
*4.3.120/2445 and will breake out] F; not in Q
*4.3.132/2457 chamber: softly pray] F (Chamber: ſoftly 'pray); chamber. Q
4.3.144/2469 altred] Qb, F; uttred Qa
4.3.156/2481 night! Sleepe ... now,] CAPELL; ~, ſleepe ... ~! Q; ~: ſleepe ... ~, F. Capell's was the first edition to indicate that 'O ... night' is not a vocative of 'sleepe'.
4.3.162/2487 scaldst] QF; scalds THEOBALD
4.3.165/2490 moue:] F (~.); ~, Q

4.3.174/2499 where] Q; heere F
4.3.175/2500 God; Q; Heauen F
*4.3.180/2505 how fares your grace?] F; not in Q
*4.3.184/2509 him.] F; him: he is not here. Q
4.3.198/2523 sleepe] Q; ſleepes F
*4.3.204/2529 Culing] F (culling); toling Q. Cowl is probably right in explaining this and the following added part-line in F as authorial revisions.
*4.3.204-5/2529-30 The vertuous sweetes, | Our] F (... Sweetes, our); Our Q. See previous note. The Folio version prompts relineation from 4.3.198/2523 (see lineation note), which reduces the number of part-lines in the speech from four to two.
4.3.205/2530 thighs] F (Thighes); thigh Q; thighs are POPE; thighs all HANMER
4.3.210/2535 haue] RIDLEY; hands Q; hath F. Ridley's reading would facilitate the error in Q; F gives a typical scribal sophistication.
4.3.221/2546 thought:] F; ~, Q
4.3.223/2548 mine] Q; my F
4.3.224/2549 my] Q; mine F
4.3.236/2561 Whom] Q; Which F. Q seems admissible. For the variant, compare 3.1.79/1500.
4.3.240/2565 thine] Q; thy F
4.3.248/2573 Harry] Q; Henry F
4.3.252/2577 scumme:] F; ~, Q
4.3.253/2578 will] Q; ſwill F. F anticipates 'ſweare', under the influence of the context ('scumme', etc.).
4.3.261/2586 on] Q; in F
4.3.268/2593 moist] Q; moſt F
*4.3.276/2601 true and inward] F (true, ...); inward true and Q. If the variant reflects an error of transposition, either text could be corrupt. However, such a transposition would be of an unusual kind, and authorial revision is more likely. The motive might have been to bring 'inward' into clearer apposition with 'exterior'.
4.3.277-8/2602-3 bending.... me:] F; ~, ... ~. Q
4.3.278/2603 God] Q; Heauen F
4.3.286/2611 this] Q; the F
4.3.289/2614 worst of] F; worſe then Q. Shaaber finds Q without sense but difficult to account for as an error; it is, however, the sort of substitution to be found elsewhere in the work of Simmes's Compositor A.
4.3.290/2615 fine, in karrat is] F (... Charract, ...); fine, in karrat Q
4.3.293/2618 thy] Q; the F
*4.3.293/2618 my] F; my moſt Q. Q is more readily explained as error, as 'most' could be a dittography from the line above. The line might alternatively have been revised: Shakespeare may have felt that most was overused in these two lines.
4.3.303, 307/2628, 2632 God] Q; heauen F
*4.3.306/2631 O my sonne,] F (O my Sonne!); not in Q. Perhaps a revision prompted by Holinshed's 'Well, faire sonne' at this point.
4.3.307/2632 put it] F; put Q
4.3.308/2633 win] Q; ioyne F. Almost certainly a misreading in F.
4.3.312/2637 God] Q; Heauen F
4.3.333/2658 all thy] QF; all my RANN (Tyrwhitt)
4.3.347/2672 God] Q; heauen F
*4.3.349/2674 My gracious liege,] F; not in Q
4.3.364/2687 God] Q; heauen F
*5.1.1/2693 pie,] F; pie ſir, Q. 'Sir' is probably deleted because from 5.1.7/2699 it is much repeated as a characteristic of Davy's diction. Compare the variant at 5.1.19/2711, which gives the word greater emphasis in F by bringing it to the beginning of one of his speeches.
*5.1.8/2700 Dauy, Dauy, Dauy] F; Dauy, Dauy, Dauy, Dauy Q. See following note.
*5.1.9/2700-1 see, William] F (ſee: William); ſee, Dauy, let me ſee, yea mary William Q. 'Mary' is emended as a profanity only once in F, and is retained 15 times. 'Yea mary' is typical as a garrulity of Shallow's; it therefore has common ground with the repeated phrase 'let me see'. Whereas an author would be aware of this particular aspect of 'yea mary', a scribe would be oblivious or

365

indifferent to it. The most plausible explanation for F's cut is a single one: minor authorial revision. Further modifications of Shallow's repetitiveness occur at 3.2.97/1621 and 5.1.47/2739 (see notes). Oddly 3.2.97/1621 has 'yea mary' immediately after F's omission, and repeated 'let me see' before it. The reason is probably that Shakespeare modified two lines with similar structure: repetitions, indicating indecision, followed by 'yea mary'. Modification of two such similar but physically remote lines is particularly suggestive of authorial alteration, especially as the way they are modified makes them less similar.

5.1.12 headland] Q (hade land), F (head-land)
*5.1.19/2711 Sir] F; Now ſir Q. 'Now' would not be prone to accidental omission, and its removal is not the kind of change associated with the scribe. As a revision, the deletion would avoid repeating from 5.1.15/2707 and would alter the tone of Davy's interruption.
5.1.21/2713 lost] Q; loſt the other day F. Prosser convincingly argues that F's addition pushes 'Fayre' on to a new type line, and was probably introduced to do so (p. 98). Other Folio additions which have the same effect are also similar in substance: 'lately' (5.4.6/3065) and 'now' (5.4.9/3067).
5.1.21/2713 Hinckly] F (Hinckley); Hunkly Q. Q gives an implausible variant, but 'inc' would easily be misread.
5.1.22/2714 A] Q; He F
5.1.24/2716 tinie] Q; tine F. See note to adjective tine in OED.
5.1.26/2718 Yea] Q; Yes F
5.1.29/2721 back-bitten] Q; bitten F. F almost loses the word-play on 'back'.
5.1.30 marvellous] Q (maruailes), F. Wilson takes Q's form to be Shakespearian.
5.1.33/2725 a'th] Q; of the F
5.1.34/2726 is] Q; are F
5.1.37/2729 God] Q; heauen F
5.1.40/2732 this] Q; theſe F. A possible spelling variant.
5.1.41/2733 and] Q; and if F
5.1.42/2734 litle] Q; but a very litle F. Prosser explains how the two additions in Davy's speech enable the compositor to set the last syllable of 'Counte-|nanc'd' on a new type line (p. 98). The spelling 'litle' is probably Shakespeare's; its survival in F is especially surprising in view of the compositor's efforts to stretch copy.
5.1.44/2736 you] Q; your Worſhip F. See previous note.
5.1.45/2737 to, I say,] F (too, | I ſay); ~ˏ ~ ~, Q
*5.1.47/2739 come,] F (Come,); come, come, come Q. See note to 2.1.153/762.
5.1.50/2742 all] F; not in Q
5.1.59/2751 him Q]; of him F. F's idiom is not Shakespearean.
5.1.73/2765 a] Q; he F
5.1.73/2766 without] Q; with F. F probably anticipates 'Lye (with . . .)'.
5.2.0.1-2/2772.2-3 Enter . . . doore]] F (Enter the Earle of Warwicke, and the Lord Chiefe Iuſtice.); Enter Warwike, duke Humphrey, L. chiefe Iuſtice, Thomas Clarence, Prince, Iohn, Weſtmerland. Qa; . . . Prince, Iohn . . . Qb. Shakespeare evidently did not anticipate the opening dialogue when writing the direction in Q.
5.2.16/2790 he] Q; him F
5.2.19/2793 O God] Q; Alas F
5.2.21/2795 GLOUCESTER and CLARENCE] Q (Prin. ambo), F (Glou. Cla.)
5.2.36/2810 th'impartiall] Q; th'Imperiall F
5.2.38-9/2812-13 remission. . . . me,] F; ~ , . . . ~. Q
5.2.39/2813 truth] Q; Troth F
5.2.43/2817 God] Q; heauen F
5.2.46/2820 mixe] F; mixt Q
5.2.50/2824 by my faith] Q; to ſpeake truth F
5.2.59/2833 Yet] Q; But F
5.2.62/2836 PRINCE . . . CLARENCE] Q (Bro.), F (Iohn, &c.)
*5.2.62/2836 other] F; otherwiſe Q
5.2.96/2870 your] Q; you F
5.2.109/2883 not] Q; no F
5.2.111/2885 Iustice: you . . . me,] F (~. You . . . me:); ~ˏ . . . ~: Q

5.2.139/2913 you] Qb, F; your Qa
5.2.142/2916 God] Q; heauen F
5.2.144/2918 God] Q; Heauen F
5.3.0.2/2918.2 Dauy] Q; not in F. The scribe copying the prompt-book probably saw two entries for Davy with no intervening exit; he may accordingly have deleted Davy from the opening entry, then, realizing that Davy must be on stage from the beginning, decided to delete the second entry instead. If the reinstatement of the initial entry was not clearly indicated, the compositor would consequently give Davy no entry at all (Jowett, 'Cuts and Casting').
5.3.0.3/2918.3 page] Q; Page, and Piſtoll F. F's duplication of the entry at 5.3.83.1/3003.1 probably derives from a prompt note supplied because of casting difficulties. Pistol was evidently played by the same actor as Warwick (see note to 5.5.40.1-3/3128.1-2), who is on stage until the end of 5.2/Sc. 14. See also note to 3.2.0.1/1523.1.
5.3.1/2919 my] Q; mine F
5.3.3/2921 mine] Q; my F
5.3.3 grafting] Q (graffing)
5.3.5/2923 Fore God you] Q; You F
*5.3.5-6/2923-4 here a . . . and a] F (heere . . .); here . . . and Q
5.3.13/2932 by the mas] Q ; not in F
5.3.18/2938 God] Q; heauen F
*5.3.25/2945 Good master Bardolfe:] F (~ M. ~); Giue maſter ~ˏ Q. As error, the variant (in either direction) is more complex than misreading of literals. Both Q and F give good sense; Q's is the more straightforward text, but there is theatrical point to F as a deliberate alteration.
5.3.30/2950 must] Q; not in F
5.3.35/2955 wags] Q; wagge F. Q's striking lack of concord probably reflects Silence's drunkenness.
5.3.41.1/2961.1 Enter Dauy] Q; not in F. See note to 5.3.0.2/2918.2.
5.3.42/2962 Theres] Q; There is F
5.3.48 thee,] QF (theˏ)
5.3.51/2971 And] Q; If F
5.3.52/2972 a'th] Q; of the F
5.3.55/2975 too'th] Q; to the F
5.3.58/2978 tiny] Q; tyne F
5.3.60 cavalieros] Q (cabileros)
5.3.62/2982 And] Q; If F
5.3.63/2983 By the mas youle] Q; You'l F
5.3.65/2985 Yea] Q; Yes F
5.3.66/2986 By Gods liggens] Q; not in F
5.3.67/2987 that,] F (~.); ~ˏ Q
5.3.67/2987 a] Q; He F
5.3.68/2988 tis] This edition; a tis Q; he is F. Recent editors follow Wilson in emending the punctuation so that 'a' completes the phrase 'a will not out'. The idiom remains strained; we posit, with support from F, a false start in the copy for Q, or a backward eyeskip from 'out' to 'that' by the compositor.
5.3.72/2992 looke,] Q; ~ , F
5.3.81/3001 And't] Q; If it F
5.3.85/3005 God saue you] Q; 'ſaue you ſir F
5.3.87/3007 no man] Q; none F
5.3.87-8/3007-8 good: sweete Knight,] Q; ~ , ~ ~ : F
5.3.89/3009 this] Q; the F
5.3.90/3010 Birlady] Q; Indeed F
5.3.90/3010 a] Q; he F
5.3.93/3012 in thy] F; ith thy Q; i'thy NEILSON
5.3.95/3014 And] Q (and); not in F. F's omission would be induced by the '-nd' ending of two consecutive words in a passage Q and F print as prose.
5.3.98/3017 pray thee] Q; prethee F
5.3.103/3022 Couetua] Q; Couitha F
5.3.111/3030 theres] Q; there is F
5.3.112/3031 or] Q; or to F
5.3.126/3045 Knighthood] F; Knight Q
5.3.136/3055 blessed] Q; Happie F. A change which avoids the mild profanity of a biblical echo.

5.3.136/3055   that] Q; which F
5.3.137/3056   to] Q; vnto F
5.3.140/3059   these] Q; thoſe F
*5.4.0.1/3059.1-2   Beadles ... Tere-sheet] Sincklo and three or foure officers Q; Hosteſſe Quickly, Dol Teare-ſheete, and Beadles F. 'Sincklo' was the name of an actor who must have been particularly thin. The direction in F was probably rewritten by Shakespeare; otherwise: (a) the Hostess is unlikely to have been named 'Quickly'; (b) Dol might have been called 'Whoore', as she is in Q's speech-prefixes, or, if the prefixes were already revised, 'Dol' with no surname; (c) officers would have been retained as an adequate generic description, especially as neither the text nor even F's speech-prefixes mention beadles. In other words, the information in F's direction is more exact than the circumstances require or the following text warrants.
5.4.1-2/3060   to God that] Q; not in F
5.4.5/3064   cheere] Q; cheere enough F. Prosser explains F's two expansions in this speech and the one in 5.4.9/3067 as deliberate compositorial insertions to waste space (p. 101).
5.4.6/3065   two] Q; two (lately) F. See previous note.
5.4.9/3066   and] Q; if F
5.4.9/3067   I] Q; I now F. See note to 5.4.5/3064.
5.4.9/3067   wert] Q; had'ſt F
5.4.11/3069   the Lord] Q; not in F
5.4.12/3069   he] F (hee); I Q. Q may anticipate 'I pray' in the next line.
5.4.13/3070-1   pray God ... miscarry] Q; would ... might miſcarry F
5.4.17/3075   amongst] Q; among F
5.4.18/3076   you what, you] Q; thee what, thou F
5.4.20/3077   blewbottle] Q; blew-|Bottel'd F
5.4.23/3081   God] Q; not in F
5.4.23/3081   orecom] F (o'recome); ouercom Q
5.4.27/3084   I] Q; Yes F
5.4.27   Ay,] Q (I∧)
5.4.29/3086   Atomy] Q; Anatomy F. Though 'atomy' became an established usage that was not merely jocular, OED gives no illustrations of the form before the present one: the Hostess presumably does make a humorous error.
5.5.0.1/3088.1   two ... rushes] ſtrewers of ruſhes Q; two Groomes F
5.5.3/3091   ⌈1⌉ GROOME] F; 3 Q. See 'Cuts and Casting'.
5.5.3/3091   Twill] Q; It will F
5.5.3/3091   a] Q; of the F
*5.5.4-4.1/3092-3092.1   coronation. Exeunt | Enter] F; coronation, diſpatch, diſpatch. | Trumpets ſound, and the King, and his traine paſſe ouer the ſtage: after them enter Q. The Groom's last speech in Q seems contradictory, in that it first argues that there is plenty of time and then urges haste. A change of speaker might have been intended, but the deletion of the words in F suggests another explanation. F also deletes Q's procession over the stage before the entry of Sir John and his companions. Q's 'dispatch, dispatch' is probably a reaction to the third and final trumpet call. As this is postponed until 5.5.39/3128.1 in the revised staging, Q's words become superfluous.

The change in staging itself simplifies the action, reserving the processional entry for the moment immediately before the rejection of Sir John. It also economizes on actors, eight of whom would be unavailable to join the procession—or twelve if one includes Doll, the Hostess, and the minimum of two Beadles (see note to 5.4.0.1/3059.1-2), who leave the stage just four lines before the procession enters. The Folio text looks less theatrical, but is not: it allows for a grander procession at a more apposite moment.

In F, the stage is cleared of actors, but the rushes remain on stage and indicate continuity of time and place. As in As You Like It 3.2.10-10.1/1155-1155.1, where the letters hung on the trees perform a similar function, there is no requirement for a scene-break. See also 2.4.19.1-2/1060.1-2 above, where editors usually keep a Drawer on stage, but where the set table has the function of the rushes here. In view of the structural similarity between the opening of 2.4/Sc. 7 and 5.5/Sc. 17, it may be no accident that in both cases the Folio deletion of speech is connected with the staging and involves the word dispatch. Similarly with the staging itself: in 2.4/Sc. 7 F stabilizes the number of Drawers as two; here F reduces the number of Grooms from three to two.

*5.5.5/3093   Robert] F; not in Q. Prosser's account of F as compositorial space-wastage (pp. 101-2) is not convincing, especially as the previous line in which Shallow is named Robert, 5.3.118/3041, is (in F) 63 lines earlier, and is unlikely to have appeared on the same manuscript page.
5.5.6/3095   a] Q; he F
5.5.9/3097   God bleſſe] Q; Bleſſe F
5.5.13/3101   tis] Q; it is F
5.5.13/3101   no] Q, Fb; bo Fa
5.5.15/3103   SHALLOW] F; Piſt⟨ol⟩. Q. See note to 5.5.17 and 19/3105 and 3107.
5.5.16/3105   of] Q; in F
5.5.17, 19/3105, 3107   PISTOL] QF; 'Shal⟨low⟩.' BETTERTON. Editors are divided on whether to follow F's prefixes for 5.5.15, 17, and 19/3103, 3105, and 3107, or to attribute all three speeches to Shallow, but seem agreed that the Folio prefix for 5.5.15/3103 is not an error.

Q's missing speech-prefix at 5.5.24/3113 may be explained as a result of an inserted passage in the foul papers. If 'But' in 5.5.24/3112 was interlined, the insertion might consist of 5.5.15-23/3103-11. An insertion might be cramped and especially prone to obscure or omitted speech-prefixes. If prefixes for 5.5.15, 17, and 19/3103, 3105, and 3107 were unintelligible, the compositor would understandably continue the alternation of speeches between Sir John and Pistol. The anomalies of 5.5.15-24/3103-12 therefore might plausibly have a single origin. An alternative explanation of the speech-prefix variants at 5.5.17/3105 and 19/3107 would be that Q gives Shakespeare's first intention.

In either case, the simplest inference would be that F is correct. To explain F as error, further elaboration is needed: most plausibly, a single annotation in the prompt-book designed to transfer three speeches to Shallow might have been misinterpreted by the scribe (compare 1 Henry IV 2.2.47.1-52/757.1-62 and 2.5.174-81/1104-11), and/or Q itself might have influenced him. In relation to the hypothesis that Q results from misinterpretation of the manuscript, the first of these possibilities is incompatible, and the second requires still further elaboration to account for the scribe's reliance on Q just at the point where it was corrupt. The case for a misinterpreted revision is also problematic: F can only be considered wrong on the assumption that Shakespeare must have given speeches of inane repetition to Shallow, whereas the hypothesis of revision relies on him having first given them to Pistol.

Though the assignment of 5.5.17 and 19/3105 and 3107 to Shallow is attractive, it is by no means certain that F is wrong: the grounds for departing from both substantive texts are not adequate and any account of how they originated is altogether too tentative.

5.5.23/3111   most] F; beſt Q
5.5.23-4/3111-12   certain. | ⌈SIR IOHN⌉ But] F (certaine ...); certaine: but Q. The most straightforward explanation of Q's error would be that Shallow's speech was inserted as an afterthought and no second prefix for Sir John was provided.
*5.5.26/3114   affaires] F (affayres); affaires elſe Q. The variant could be a dittography in Q; if it is a deliberate change it would be more characteristic of an author than a scribe.
5.5.28/3116   absque] F2; obsque Q, F1. See Binns. A Latin phrase is especially likely to have been checked in Q when the copy for F was prepared.
5.5.28/3116   all] F; not in Q
5.5.38/3126   truth] Q; troth F
5.5.40.1-3/3128.1-2   prince ... others] and his traine Q; Brothers, Lord Chiefe Iuſtice F. As F is specific about the named characters in the King's train, it is to be noted that Warwick is absent. The

reason is almost certainly that the actor playing Warwick also played Pistol.
5.5.41/3129 God saue] Q; Saue F
5.5.43/3131 God saue] Q; 'Saue F
5.5.48/3136 becomes] Q; become F. F omits terminal 's' here and at 5.5.67, 69, and 78/3155, 3157, and 3167. This cluster recalls similar variants in 3.1/Sc. 8 (see note to 3.1.14/1435). As there, F probably sophisticates.
5.5.51/3139 awake] F; awakt Q
5.5.55 fool-born] Q (~-borne). Either 'born' or 'borne' is possible.
5.5.57/3145 God] Q; heauen F
5.5.67/3155 euills] Q; euill F.
5.5.69/3157 strengths] Q; ſtrength F
*5.5.71/3159 our] F; my Q
5.5.73/3162 Yea] Q; I F
5.5.78/3167 aduauncements] Q; aduance-|ment F.
5.5.80/3169 cannot] Q; cannot well F. Prosser explains this and the following Folio insertion as compositorial space wastage (p. 103).
5.5.80/3169 giue] Q; ſhould giue F. See previous note.
5.5.85/3175 I feare that] F (I ~, that); that I feare Q. F more effectively anticipates the reply 'Feare no colours'.

5.5.94/3184 tormenta . . . contenta] Q; tormento, ſpera contento F
5.5.105/3195 heard] Q; heare F
Epi.10/3207 did meane] F (did meane); meant Q
Epi.15/3212 infinitely.] F (infinitely.); infinitely: and ſo I kneele downe before you; but indeed, to pray for the Queene. Q. See note to Epi. 32-3/3229-30.
Epi.20/3217 woulde] Q; will F
Epi.23/3220 before] F (before); not in Q
Epi.29/3226 a] Q; he F
Epi.30/3227 died a] F (died a); died Q
Epi.32-3/3229-30 and . . . Queene] F (in italics); after 'infinitely' (Epi.15/3212) Q. The Epilogue was evidently written in two stages, the first part originally ending with the words that in F close the second part. Q has the full text, but its failure to relocate the lines which should end the play betrays the stages of composition.
Epi.32/3229 kneele] F; I kneele Q

Additional Passages

A.3 fault,] POPE; ~ˌ Q
B.2 a] Q; hee F
B.2 euer] F; ouer Q

INCIDENTALS

137 tongue] tongne   184 Weakned] F; Weakened Q   201 honor.] ~,   220 venturd] F; ventured Q   227 truth,] ~.
357 lordship] lorſhip   375 listning,] ~ˌ (with inked vertical bar)   521 far,] ~.   528 lin'd] F; lined Q   607 againe] agine F
753 chambers.] ~-   875 pottle-pots] ~-|~   933 me, thus,] ~, ~.   972 euery] enery   1093 rewmatique] rew | matique
1135 Cheter] Chetcr   1201 captane] Qa; captaine Qb   1213 hart, lie] Qb; hartlie Qa   1228 grieuous] grieuons   1241 valiaunt] vliaunt   1267 Sirra] Sirr a   1348 bread-chipper] ~-|~   1422 Warwicke] War   1436 leauſt] F leaueſt Q   1513 feard] feared   1520 vnſeaſond] F; vnſeaſoned Q   1611 commission] QB; commſſion QA   1620 see, let me see, so] ~ˌ let me see, ſo (with inked vertical bar)   1621 Mouldy,] ~ˌ (with inked vertical bar)   1625 limbde,] QB; ~, QA   1684 mouse,] Qb, Qc; ~ˌ Qa
1706 Come,... goe] Qa; ~,..., go Qb, Qc   1714 dinner,] Qa; ~ : Qb, Qc   1726 could] conld   1733-4 that, that] Qa; ~, ~ Qb, Qc   1734-5 Iohn,... well] Qa; ~,... wel Qb, Qc   1738 haue, in] Qb, Qc; ~ˌ ~ Qa   1751 master] Qa, Qb; M. Qc (see textual note)   1758 destiny] deſtny   1771 Shadow] Sadow   1864 him,] Qa, Qb; ~, Qc   1878 doe] Qa, Qb; do Qc (see textual note)
1882 countenaunſt] Qb, Qc; counteenaunſt Qa   1893 peace:] ~.   1935 denied?] ~ˌ   2111 shoud] F; ſhoued Q   2214 thought] Qb; thoght Qa   2215 schoole of tongs] Qa; ſchool of tongues Qb   2236 enemy:] ~,:   2239 curtesie] Qb; cnrteſie Qa   2282 loue me . . . cãnot] Qb loueme . . . canot Qa   2357 notwithstanding,] ~ˌ   2394 needfull] needfnll   2426 large.] ~,
2435 And] Aud   2469 it.] ~,   2569 compound] compouud   2621 murdred] F; murdered Q   2644 earth:] ~,
2650 answered] F; anſwerd Q   2655 the] the' (?)   3128 roard] F; roared Q   3229 night:] ~. (see textual note)

Additional Passages

A.3 whereupon] where-|vpon

QUARTO STAGE DIRECTIONS

Ind.0.1/0.1 *Enter Rumour painted full of Tongues.*
Ind.40/40 *exit Rumours.*
1.1.0.1/40.1 *Enter the Lord Bardolfe at one doore.*
1.1.6/46 *Enter the Earle Northumberland.*
1.1.27.1/67.1 *enter | Trauers.* (opposite 1.1.25-6/65-6)
1.1.59/99 *enter Mor-|ton.* (opposite 1.1.59-60/99-100)
1.1.214/254 *exeunt.*
1.2.0.1-2/254.1-2 *Enter sir Iohn alone, with his page bearing his sword | and buckler.*
1.2.53.1/307.1 *Enter Lord chiefe Iustice.*
1.3.0.1-2/501.1-2 *Enter th'Archbishop, Thomas Mowbray (Earle Marshall) the | Lord Hastings, Fauconbridge, and Bardolfe.*
1.3.110.1/611.1 *ex.*
2.1.0.1-3/611.2-3 *Enter Hostesse of the Tauerne, and an Officer or two.*
2.1.38.1/648.1 *Enter sir Iohn, and Bardolfe, and the boy.* (after 2.1.42/652)
2.1.62.1/670.1 *Enter Lord chiefe iustice and his men.*
2.1.134.2/743.2 *enter a messenger.* (after 2.1.135/744)
2.1.167.1-2/775.1 *exit hostesse and sergeant.* (after 2.1.164/772)
2.2.0.1/804.3 *Enter the Prince, Poynes, sir Iohn Russel, with other.*

2.2.61.1/865.1 *Enter Bardolfe and boy.* (after 2.2.62/866)
2.2.168.1/973.1 *exeunt.*
2.3.0.1-2/973.2-3 *Enter Northumberland his wife, and the wife to Harry Percie.*
2.3.68/1041 *exeunt.*
2.4.0.1-3/1041.1-3 *Enter a Drawer or two.*
[2.4.16/1057] *Enter Will.* (after 'word')
2.4.19.1/1060 *exit*
2.4.19.2/1060.1-2 *Enter mistris Quickly, and Doll Tere-sheet.*
2.4.30.1/1069.1 *enter sir Iohn.* (after 2.4.31/1070)
2.4.65.1/1102.1 *Enter drawer.*
2.4.106.1/1141.1 *Enter antient Pistol, and Bardolfes boy.*
2.4.226.1/1256.1 *enter musicke.* (after 2.4.227/1257)
2.4.235.1/1264.1 *Enter Prince and Poynes.*
2.4.354.1/1383.1 *Peyto knockes at doore.*
2.4.369.1/1398.1 *exeunt Prince and Poynes.*
2.4.385.1/1413.1 *exit.* (QB; not in QA)
2.4.392.1-2/1420.1 *exeunt*
3.1.0.1/1420.2 *Enter the King in his night-gowne | alone.* (QB)
3.1.31.1/1451.1 *Enter Warwike, Surry and sir Iohn | Blunt.* (QB)
3.1.103/1523 *exeunt* (QB)

2 HENRY IV

3.2.0.1/1523.1 *Enter Iustice Shallow, and Iustice | Silens.*
3.2.51.1/1575.1 *Enter Bardolfe, and one with him.* (after 3.2.53/1577)
3.2.79.1/1603.1 *Enter Falstaffe.* (QA; *Enter sir Iohn Falstaffe.* QB)
3.2.216.1/1741.1 *exeunt.*
3.2.238.1/1762.1 *Enter Falstaffe and the Iustices.*
3.2.323/1847 *exit*
4.1.0.1-3/1847.1-2 *Enter the Archbishop, Mowbray, Bardolfe, Hastings, within | the forrest of Gaultree.*
4.1.18/1865 *Enter messenger*
4.1.24.1/1871.1 *Enter Westmerland* (after 4.1.25/1873)
4.1.180.1/2028.1 *Exit Westmerland* (after 'decide it')
4.1.221.1/2069.1 *Enter Westmerland.* (after 4.1.222/2070)
4.1.226.2-3/2074.2-3 *Enter Prince Iohn and his armie.* (after 4.1.224/2072)
4.1.312.1/2160.1 *shout.*
4.1.323.1/2171.1 *enter Westmerland.* (after 4.1.322/2170)
4.1.327/2175 *enter Hastings*
4.2.0.1-2/2197.1-2 *Alarum Enter Falstaffe excursions*
4.2.22.1-2, 24.1/2220.1-2, 2222 *Enter Iohn Westmerland, and the rest. Retraite* (after 4.2.23/2221)
4.2.68/2265 *enter Westmerland.*
4.2.121.1/2318.1 *Enter Bardolfe.* (after 4.2.122/2319)
4.3.0.1-3/2324.2-4 *Enter the King, Warwike, Kent, Thomas duke of Clarence, | Humphrey of Gloucester.*
4.3.80/2404 *Enter Westmerland.* (after 'Westmerland')
4.3.93/2418 *enter Harcor.* (after 'newes')
4.3.139/2464 *Enter Harry*
4.3.178/2503 *exit.*
4.3.179/2504 *Enter Warwicke, Gloucester, Clarence.* (after 4.3.178/2503)
4.3.208.1/2533.1 *Enter Warwicke* (after 4.3.210/2535)
4.3.217.1/2542.1 *Enter Harry* (after 4.3.216/2541)
4.3.219/2544 *exeunt.*
4.3.353.1-2/2678.1-2 *enter Lancaster.*
5.1.0.1-2/2692.2-3 *Enter Shallow, | Falstaffe, and Bardolfe* (opposite 4.3.368-9/2691-2)
5.2.0.1-2/2772.2-3 *Enter Warwike, duke Humphrey, L. chiefe Iustice, Thomas | Clarence, Prince Iohn, Westmerland.* (Qb; . . . *Prince, Iohn*ₐ . . . Qa)
5.2.13.1-2/2787.1-2 *Enter Iohn, Thomas, and Humphrey.*
5.2.41.1/2815.1 *Enter the Prince | and Blunt* (opposite 5.2.41-2/2815-16)
5.2.144/2918 *exit.*
5.3.0.1-3/2918.1-3 *Enter sir Iohn, Shallow, Scilens, Dauy, Bardolfe, page.*
5.3.41.1/2961.1 *Enter Dauy.*
5.3.71.1/2991.1 *One knockes at doore.* (after 5.3.69/2989)
5.3.83.1/3003.1 *enter Pistol.* (after 5.3.82/3002)
5.3.140/3059 *exit.*
5.4.0.1-2/3059.1-2 *Enter Sincklo and three or foure officers.*
5.5.0.1/3088.1 *Enter strewers of rushes.*
5.5.4.1-2/3092.1-2 *Trumpets sound, and the King, and his traine passe ouer the | stage: after them enter Falstaffe, Shallow, Pistol, | Bardolfe, and the Boy.*
5.5.40.1-3/3128.1-2 *Enter the King and his traine.*
5.5.88.1-2/3178.1-2 *Enter Iustice | and prince Iohn* (opposite 5.5.87-8/3177-8)
5.5.94.1-2/3184.1 *exeunt.* (after 5.5.93/3183)

FOLIO STAGE DIRECTIONS

Ind.0.1/0.1 *Enter Rumour.*
Ind.40/40 *Exit.*
1.1.0.1, 1.1.1/40.1, 41 *Enter Lord Bardolfe, and the Porter.* (at 1.1.0.1/40.1)
1.1.6/46 *Enter Northumberland.*
1.1.27.1/67.1 *Enter Trauers.* (after 1.1.29/69)
1.1.59/99 *Enter Morton.* (after 'Newes')
1.1.214/254 *Exeunt.*
1.2.0.1-2/254.1-2 *Enter Falstaffe, and Page.*
1.2.53.1/307.1 *Enter Chiefe Iustice, and Seruant.*
1.2.250/501 *Exeunt*
1.3.0.1-2/501.1-2 *Enter Archbishop, Hastings, Mowbray, and | Lord Bardolfe.*
2.1.0.1-3/611.2-3 *Enter Hostesse, with two Officers, Fang, and Snare.*
2.1.38.1/648.1 *Enter Falstaffe and Bardolfe.*
2.1.62.1/670.1 *Enter. Ch. Iustice.*
2.1.134.2/743.2 *Enter M. Gower*
2.1.198.1-2/804.1-2 *Exeunt*
2.2.0.1/804.3 *Enter Prince Henry, Pointz, Bardolfe, | and Page.*
2.2.61.1/865.1 *Enter Bardolfe.*
2.2.168.1/973.1 *Exeunt*
2.3.0.1-2/973.2-3 *Enter Northumberland, his Ladie, and Harrie | Percies Ladie.*
2.3.68/1041 *Exeunt.*
2.4.0.1-3/1041.1-2 *Enter two Drawers.*
2.4.19.1/1060 *Exit.*
2.4.19.2/1060.1-2 *Enter Hostesse, and Dol.*
2.4.30.1/1069.1 *Enter Falstaffe.* (after 'Iohn')
2.4.65.1/1102.1 *Enter Drawer.*
2.4.106.1/1141.1 *Enter Pistol, and Bardolph and his Boy.*
2.4.226.1/1256.1 *Enter Musique.*
2.4.235.1/1264.1 *Enter the Prince and Poines disguis'd.*
2.4.356.1/1385.1 *Enter Peto.*
2.4.369.1/1398.1 *Exit.*
2.4.385.1/1413.1 *Exit.*
2.4.392.1-2/1420.1 *Exeunt.*
3.1.0.1/1420.2 *Enter the King, with a Page.*
3.1.3.1/1423.1 *Exit.*
3.1.31.1/1451.1 *Enter Warwicke and Surrey.*
3.1.103/1523 *Exeunt.*
3.2.0.1/1523.1 *Enter Shallow and Silence: with Mouldie, Shadow, | Wart, Feeble, Bull-calfe.*
3.2.51.1/1575.1 *Enter Bardolph and his Boy.*
3.2.79.1/1603.1 *Enter Falstaffe.*
3.2.295.1/1819 *Exit.* (after 3.2.294/1818)
3.2.323/1847 *Exeunt.*
4.1.0.1-3/1847.1-2 *Enter the Arch-bishop, Mowbray, Hastings, | Westmerland, Coleuile.*
4.1.18/1865 *Enter a Messenger.*
4.1.24.1/1871.1 *Enter Westmerland.*
4.1.221.1/2069.1 *Enter Westmerland.* (after 4.1.22/2070)
4.1.226.2-3/2074.2-3 *Enter Prince Iohn.*
4.1.297.1/2145.1 *Exit.*
4.1.318.1/2166.1 *Exit.* (after 4.1.320/2168)
4.1.322.1/2170.1 *Exit.*
4.1.323.1/2171.1 *Enter Westmerland.*
4.1.327/2175 *Enter Hastings.*
4.1.349/2197 *Exeunt.*
4.2.0.1-2/2197.1-2 *Enter Falstaffe and Colleuile.*
4.2.22.1-2/2220.1-2 *Enter Prince Iohn, and Westmerland.* (after 4.2.23/2221)
4.2.68/2265 *Enter Westmerland.*
4.2.72.1/2269.1 *Exit with Colleuile.*
4.2.82.1/2279.1 *Exit.*
4.2.121.1/2318.1 *Enter Bardolph.*
4.2.127.1/2324.1 *Exeunt.*
4.3.0.1-3/2324.2-4 *Enter King, Warwicke, Clarence, Gloucester.*
4.3.80/2404 *Enter Westmerland.*
4.3.93/2418 *Enter Harcourt.*
4.3.139/2464 *Enter Prince Henry.*

369

4.3.178/2503 Exit.
4.3.179/2504 Enter Warwicke, Gloucester, Clarence. (after 'Exit', 4.3.178/2503)
4.3.208.1/2533.1 Enter Warwicke.
4.3.217.1/2542.1 Enter Prince Henry.
4.3.219/2544 Exit.
4.3.353.1-2/2678.1-2 Enter Lord Iohn of Lancaster, | and Warwicke.
4.3.369.1/2692.1 Exeunt.
5.1.0.1-2/2692.2-3 Enter Shallow, Silence, Falstaffe, Bardolfe, | Page, and Dauie.
5.1.79.1/2772.1 Exeunt
5.2.0.1-2/2772.2-3 Enter the Earle of Warwicke, and the Lord | Chiefe Iustice.
5.2.13.1-2/2787.1-2 Enter Iohn of Lancaster, Gloucester, | and Clarence.
5.2.41.1/2815.1 Enter Prince Henrie. (after 5.2.42/2816)
5.2.144/2918 Exeunt.

5.3.0.1-3/2918.1-3 Enter Falstaffe, Shallow, Silence, Bardolfe, | Page, and Pistoll.
5.3.83.1/3003.1 Enter Pistoll.
5.3.140/3059 Exeunt
5.4.0.1-2/3059.1-2 Enter Hostesse Quickly, Dol Teare-sheete, | and Beadles.
5.4.31/3088 Exeunt.
5.5.0.1/3088.1 Enter two Groomes.
5.5.4/3092 Exit Groo.
5.5.4.1-2/3092.1-2 Enter Falstaffe, Shallow, Pistoll, Bardolfe, and Page.
5.5.40.1-3/3128.1-2 The Trumpets sound. Enter King Henrie the | Fift, Brothers, Lord Chiefe | Iustice.
5.5.71/3159 Exit King.
5.5.94.1-2/3184.1 Exit. Manet Lancaster and Chiefe Iustice.
5.5.107/3197 Exeunt

MUCH ADO ABOUT NOTHING

Much Ado About Nothing is first mentioned in a Stationers' Register entry of 4 August [1600]:

As yo^w like yt. .	/ A booke	
Henry the Fift. .	/ A booke	
Euery man in his Humo^r.	/ A booke	to be ſtaied
The cõmedie of muche A doo about nothinge.	/ A booke	

The meaning of this 'staying entry' has been much disputed: the most recent thorough consideration of the problem, by Knowles (pp. 353–64), suggests that the entry was only an attempt by the Chamberlain's Men to ensure that they were paid for any such plays printed. *Much Ado* was entered for publication in the normal manner, along with *2 Henry IV*, on 23 August 1600. (See *2 Henry IV*.) The first and only quarto (Q) appeared in the same year, printed by Valentine Simmes for Andrew Wise and William Aspley (*BEPD* 168); standing type from the title-page to *2 Henry IV* was reused. The text appears to have been set throughout by Simmes's Compositor A, whose work has been extensively studied by Ferguson and Craven (see *Richard II*). According to Hinman (pp. xiii–xv), the pattern of recurring type suggests that setting was seriatim; John Hazel Smith pointed out that the change in headlines beginning with sheet H (5.1.6/2070) suggests some interruption or disruption of printing.

There is general agreement that Q was set from Shakespeare's foul papers. Speech-prefixes are inconsistent, and in 4.2/Sc. 13 preserve the names of actors whom Shakespeare had in mind as he wrote: the prefixes for Dogberry include [Will] Kemp, and for Verges, [Richard] Cowley. Other evidence of foul papers includes 'ghost' characters (e.g. Leonato's wife, Innogen, mentioned in the opening directions of Acts 1 and 2, but who says nothing and is never addressed or referred to), failure to indicate entries and exits, and loose ends in the dialogue. The effect of such characteristics on editorial practice is discussed by Wells.

The play was reprinted in the First Folio from a copy of Q that had been lightly annotated as the result of a cursory comparison with the prompt-book. There are about 140 changes, most of them clearly accidental, though some obvious errors are corrected. The only ones that appear to have any authority are in stage directions, and seem to reflect the practice of Shakespeare's company. For instance, the direction for the entrance of the revellers (2.1.77.1/483.1) adds '*Maskers with a drum*', and at 2.3.35.2/859.2 the phrase '*and Iacke Wilson*'—the name of a musician of the King's Men—is substituted for '*Musicke*'. In Q, the text is undivided: F introduced the act divisions. (Scene divisions derive from the eighteenth-century editors.)

Q, then, is the only text with real authority, though F is occasionally of use to an editor. Q contains at least twelve exceptions to the practice of indicating sounded or unsounded -ed endings by spelling. This high proportion is probably due to Compositor A (see *Richard II*), so regularity has been imposed on our original-spelling text. Press variants are taken from the list in the Oxford Quarto Facsimile, supplemented by Paul Werstine's 'The Bodmer Copy of Shakespeare's *Much Ado About Nothing* Q1', *N&Q*, NS 30 (1983), 123–4.

S.W.W./(G.T.)

WORKS CITED

Hinman, Charlton, ed., *Much Ado About Nothing*, Shakespeare Quarto Facsimiles, 15 (1971)
Knowles, Richard, ed., *As You Like It*, New Variorum (1977)
Smith, John Hazel, 'The Composition of the Quarto of *Much Ado About Nothing*', *SB* 16 (1963), 10–26
Wells, Stanley, 'Editorial Treatment of Foul-Paper Texts: *Much Ado About Nothing* as Test Case', *RES*, NS 31 (1980), 1–16
Wilson, John Dover, ed., *Much Ado About Nothing*, New (1923, 1953)

TEXTUAL NOTES

Title *Much adoe about Nothing*] Q, F (*title-page, running titles*); Much adoe about | Nothing Q (*head title*); Much adoo about Nothing. F (*table of contents*); The cõmedie of muche | A doo about nothinge S.R. (4 August); Muche a Doo about nothinge S.R. (23 August)

1.1.1, 9/1, 9 Pedro] ROWE; Peter Q. All later references to the character are as 'Pedro'.

1.1.34/34 Benedicke] The usual form is Benedict, which occurs in Q only at 1.1.84/84. There is 'some evidence for an English form *Benedick*, derived directly from the Latin, e.g. the surnames *Benedick*, *Bendixson*, and Shakespeare's Benedick . . .' (E. G. Withycombe, *Oxford Dictionary of English Christian Names*, 1945; 3rd edn. 1977).

1.1.40 bird-bolt] Q (Burbolt)

1.1.140/140 all, Leonato. Signior] COLLIER 3; all: Leonato, ſignior Q

1.1.148/148 brother,] COLLIER (*subs*.); ~ : Q

1.1.189 i'faith,] The alternative punctuation, 'i'faith;' (originating with Capell) which turns 'Wear the print of it' into a main clause, is equally possible.

1.2.6/318 euent] F2; euents Q

1.3.4/340 it] THEOBALD; *not in* Q

1.3.45/382 brothers] F; bothers Q

1.3.50 on] Q (one), F

2.1.0.2/406.2–3] Q provides no entry for Margaret and Ursula in this scene. Their presence is not required till 2.1.77.1/483.1, but as they are members of Leonato's household, it seems better for them to enter here than with the masquers. Q's 'kinsman' in this direction is a ghost.

2.1.35 bearherd] Q's 'Berrord', implying colloquial pronunciation, is sometimes expanded to 'bear-ward', but *OED* prefers 'bearherd' as this is the full form found elsewhere in Shakespeare.

2.1.42/448 Peter for] This edition; ~ : ~ Q. See *Re-Editing*, 36-7.

2.1.77.1-3/483.1-3] Q's direction provides no entrance for Borachio; its last words ('*or dumb Iohn*') may possibly conceal a reference to him. Q does not direct that any of those entering be masked. F adds '*Maskers with a drum.*'

2.1.78/484 a bout] WILSON; about Q

2.1.90, 2.1.93, 2.1.95/496, 499, 501 BALTHASAR] THEOBALD; *Bene.* Q

2.1.140.1/547.1] F replaces Q's '*Dance*' with '*Musicke for the dance.*' The direction for music is repositioned here to provide a cue for 'wee must follow the leaders'.

2.1.178, 2.1.332, 4.1.316 County] This common form of 'Count' is 'apparently an adoption of AF. *counte*, or OF and IE. *conte*, with unusual retention of final vowel, confused in form with COUNTY¹' (*OED*). Shakespeare uses both forms; this one may be felt to add a little local colour.

2.1.183 drover] Most modern editors retain Q's 'Drouier', but this is an indifferent variant.

2.1.197.1/605.1] Q is obviously wrong in directing Don John, Borachio, and Conrad to enter here. F reads '*Enter the Prince.*' Some editors follow Q in bringing on Leonato and Hero, but they have nothing to say, and as F probably reflects the practice of Shakespeare's company, it seems better to follow its rearrangement, bringing Leonato and Hero on at 2.1.244.1-2/654.1-2.

2.1.244.1-2/654.1-2] See 2.1.197.1/605.1. F reads '*Enter Claudio and Beatrice, Leonato, Hero.*'

2.3.1.1/825.1 *Enter Boy*] Q gives him no entry, and marks his exit at the end of 2.3.5/829, perhaps so as not to interrupt Benedick's long speech with a direction; but Benedick's remark can be addressed to the retreating boy, or even to no one in particular, as if he were puzzling over the boy's statement. In spite of Benedick's request, the boy does not return.

2.3.24/849 made an] F; made and Q

2.3.35.2/859.2] Q's '*Musicke*' seems merely an anticipation of Balthasar's entry, though some editors call for '*Music within*' here. F substitutes '*and Iacke Wilson*' for '*Musicke*', omitting the later entry for Balthasar; no doubt this represents theatre practice; Wilson was presumably a singing actor.

2.3.41/865 hid-foxe] WARBURTON; kid-foxe Q. 'Kid-fox' is unknown (a young fox is a cub); and Benedick is not particularly young. Capell supported the emendation with 'Hide Fox, and all after' (*Hamlet* 4.2.29-30/2474-5); we may add 'Ile warrant wee'le vnkennell the Fox' (Ford seeking Falstaff, *Merry Wives* 3.3.155-6/1532-3). Hulme (247-8) suggests that 'kid' may mean 'discovered' (from the verb *kithe*), which is possible, though Benedick does not know that he is discovered.

2.3.61/885 BALTHASAR] CAPELL; *not in* QF

2.3.133/958 vs of] F; of vs Q

2.3.163, 5.1.78 doffed . . . doff] Editors, following Q, usually spell 'daffed', 'daff', but this is an indifferent variant; both 'daff' and 'doff' occur in early texts of Shakespeare.

3.1.111/1188 one . . . wil] Qa; on . . . will Qb

3.2.26/1219 can] POPE; cannot Q. This is almost certainly a correction of Shakespeare's own logical error.

3.2.50/1243 DON PEDRO] F; *Bene.* Q

3.2.54-5/1247-8 now crept into a lute-string, and now gouernd by stops] Q; new-governed DYCE (W. S. Walker); new-crept WILSON (Boas). See *Re-Editing*, 44-5.

3.2.87-8/1280-1 brother, I . . . heart,] Qa; brother (I . . . heart) Qb

3.2.88/1281 holpe] Qb; hope Qa

3.2.93/1286 of] Qb; *not in* Qa

3.2.102/1295 me] Qb; ~, Qa

3.2.104/1297 her then,] HANMER; her, then Q

3.2.114/1307 her, to morrow,] CAPELL (*subs.*); her to morrow Q

3.3.8 desertless] Many editors follow Q's spelling, 'desartlesse', in the second vowel; but this is a normal spelling, not a Dogberryism.

3.3.10, 16/1327, 1333 WATCH 2 . . . WATCH 1] *Watch* 1 . . . *Watch* 2 Q. The leader of the watch becomes *Watch* 1 in Q at 3.3.85/1403, so it seems best to give him this prefix here.

3.3.13/1330 name,] Qa; ~ : Qb

3.3.24 vagrom] Q. *OED* first records here, as an 'Illiterate alteration of VAGRANT'; it seems to be a deliberate Dogberryism rather than an indifferent spelling variant.

3.3.36, 43, 47, 52, 64, 103, 121, 168 A WATCHMAN] In Q, each speaker is designated merely '*Watch*'. Editors usually divide the speeches between the two who have spoken so far, but Shakespeare obviously thought of the watch as a group of at least three men (cf. 3.3.10/1327), possibly four or five. A director is free to distribute the speeches among them.

3.3.85, 93/1403, 1411 WATCH 1] Q assigns these speeches merely to *Watch*, but they come best from the leader.

3.3.123/1442 I] Qb; *not in* Qa

3.3.157, 159, 162, 165/1476, 1478, 1481, 1484] Q assigns alternately to '*Watch* 1' and '*Watch* 2'. The first speech comes appropriately from the leader, previously called '*Watch* 2'. Wilson says that the third 'should surely go to Seacoal, who had first identified *this vile thief*'. This is based on his unwarranted assumption that only two watchmen speak; nevertheless, it is not unreasonable to follow Q in allocating the third speech to the speaker of the first.

3.3.167-8/1486-7 CONRADE Masters, | WATCH Neuer speake] THEOBALD (*subs.*); *Conr. Mafters, neuer fpeake* Q. See Stanley Wells, 'A Crux in *Much Ado About Nothing* III. iii. 152-63', *SQ* 31 (1980), 85-6.

3.4.1/1493 Good] Qb; God Qa

3.4.17/1509 in] F; it Q

3.4.23/1515 HERO God] Q, F (*text*); *Bero.* God F (*c.w.*)

3.5.9 off] STEEVENS-REED (Capell); of Q

3.5.23/1608 and 'twere] F; and't twere Q

3.5.32/1617 talking. As] CAPELL (*subs.*); talking as Q

3.5.37/1622 troth he is, as] Qb; troth, he is as Qa

4.1.158-60/1803-5 fortune, | [. . .] | By] This edition; fortune, by Q. Q sets the opening lines of the Friar's speech in cramped prose, possibly as the result of faulty casting-off of copy; as Cambridge notes, 'Some words were probably lost in the operation . . .'.

4.1.204/1849 princes left for dead,] THEOBALD; princeſſe (left for dead,) Q. The Q reading is possible; Hero is not literally a princess, but the Countess Olivia is twice addressed so (*Twelfth Night* 3.1.96/1281 and 5.1.296/2395), and Count Claudio is included among the 'princes' (4.1.187/1832). So 'princess' could be a courtesy title, or an inconsistency. But Theobald's emendation clarifies the line of thought: because the princes left Hero apparently dead, they may easily be led to believe that she *is* dead.

4.1.317 Comfit] Most editors retain Q's 'Comfect', but this is an indifferent variant of 'comfit'.

4.2.1/1981 DOGBERRY] Q (*Keeper*)

4.2.2, 5/1982, 1985 VERGES] Q (*Cowley*)

4.2.4/1984 DOGBERRY] Q (*Andrew*)

4.2.9, 25, 30, 34, 39, 42, 48, 54, 68, 72/1989, 2005, 2010, 2014, 2019, 2022, 2027, 2033, 2047, 2051 DOGBERRY] Q (*Kemp*)

4.2.12, 15/1992, 1995 DOGBERRY] Q (*Ke.*)

4.2.18/1998 DOGBERRY] Q (*Kem.*)

4.2.49/2028 VERGES] Q (*Conſt.*)

4.2.49/2028 mass] Q. F's 'th'masse' is plausible.

4.2.65/2044 DOGBERRY] Q (*Conſtable*)

4.2.66-7/2045-6 VERGES Let them be in the hands | CONRADE Of Coxcombe] WARBURTON, etc.; *Couley* Let them be in the hands of Coxcombe. Q. Warburton first divided into two speeches, reading 'in hand'; he follows F in giving the first speech to the Sexton; Theobald had given the whole passage to Conrad. Many other emendations have been suggested; the second speech could be spoken by Borachio.

4.2.70/2048-9 them. Thou] F3 (*subs.*); them, thou Q

5.1.16/2080 Bid sorrow wagge,] CAPELL; And forrow, wagge, Q
5.1.38 pish] Q (puſh). An indifferent variant.
5.1.97/2161 an] ROWE; *not in* Q. A metrical emendation; 'an' could have been omitted by haplography or eyeskip (an/ou).
5.1.116/2180 likt] Q; like F2
5.1.188/2253 Lacke-beard there,] F; Lacke-beard, there Q
5.2.44/2434 came for] ROWE 2; came Q
5.2.56/2447 maintaine] CAPELL; maintaind Q
5.2.78/2469 self. So] ROWE; ſelf ſo Q
5.2.85.1/2476.1 *Enter Vrsula*] Q; F brings her on after 5.2.83/2474.
5.2.94/2485 exeunt] F (*Exeunt.*); exit. Q
5.3.3-10/2488-95 Done . . . dumb] These lines follow the Lord's, with no distinct speech-prefix, in Q, and are headed '*Epitaph.*' The following line ('Now musick sound . . .') is ascribed to Claudio in Q, and the song has no prefix other than '*Song*'.
5.3.10/2495 dumb] F; dead Q
5.3.22/2507 CLAUDIO] ROWE; *Lo*. Q. Q's reading may be simply a variant prefix for Claudio, though it is just possible that an attendant lord is acting as his spokesman.
5.3.32 speed 's] Q (ſpeeds)
5.4.33.1/2551.1-2 *with attendants*] F, *for* Q's '*and two or three other.*'
5.4.54/2572 ANTHONIO] THEOBALD; *Leo*. Q. See 5.4.14-17/2532-5; but the mistake may be Shakespeare's.
5.4.97/2615 BENEDICKE] THEOBALD (Thirlby); *Leon*. Q

REJECTED FOLIO VARIANTS

1.1.49/49 he is] he's
1.1.85/85 a] he
1.1.88/88 You will neuer] You'l ne're
1.1.91/91 are you] you are
1.1.101/101 sir] *not in* F
1.1.134/134 yours] your
1.1.140/140 That] This
1.1.168/168 thinkest] think'ſt
1.1.213/215 spoke] ſpeake
1.1.292-3/293-4 and . . . her] *not in* F
1.1.295/296 you do] doe you
1.2.4/316 strange] *not in* F
1.2.8/321 mine] my
1.2.9/321 much] *not in* F
1.3.6/342 brings] bringeth
1.3.8/344 at least] yet
1.3.22/358 true] *not in* F
1.3.36/373 make] will make
1.3.57/393 me] *not in* F
1.3.67/404 a] of
2.1.15/421 a] he
2.1.28/434 on] vpon
2.1.48/454 father] *not in* F
2.1.56/461 an] *not in* F
2.1.71/478 sincke] ſinkes
2.1.88/494 Ioue] Loue
2.1.130/537 pleases] pleaſeth
2.1.178/585 county] Count
2.1.202/610 thinke I] thinke,
2.1.206/614 vp] *not in* F
2.1.228/637 iester, that] Ieſter, and that
2.1.233/642 as her] as
2.1.257/667 my] this
2.1.261/671 his] a
2.1.276/686 that] a
2.1.296/706 her] my
2.1.311/721 a] of
2.1.338/748 my] *not in* F
2.2.29/803 don] on
2.2.32/806 loue] a loue
2.2.43/817 truth] truths
2.2.49/822 you] thou
2.3.32/856 I] *not in* F
2.3.45-6/869-70 excellencie | To] excellency, | To ſlander Muſicke any more then once. | *Prince.* It is the witneſſe ſtill of excellencie, | To
2.3.71/895 was] were
2.3.165/991 a] he
2.3.177/1003 Before] 'Fore
2.3.180/1006 CLAUDIO] *Leon*.
2.3.184/1010 most] *not in* F
2.3.191/1017 seeke] ſee
2.3.199/1025 so] to haue ſo
2.3.212/1038 their] the
3.1.0.1/1077.1 *Gentlewomen*] *Gentlemen*
3.1.58/1135 sheele] ſhe
3.1.79/1156 then] to
3.1.104/1181 limd] (limed); tane
3.1.106/1183 traps.] traps. *Exit.*
3.2.31-4/1225-7 or . . . dublet] *not in* F
3.2.26/1229 it] it to
3.2.57/1250 conclude, conclude] conclude,
3.2.119/1312 midnight] night
3.2.124/1317 sequele.] ſequele. *Exit.*
3.3.34/1351 to talke] talke
3.3.41/1358 those] them
3.3.76/1394 statutes] Statues
3.3.122/1441 yeere] yeares
3.3.134/1453 and I] and
3.3.146/1465 they] thy
3.4.43/1536 see] looke
3.5.23/1608 pound] times
3.5.30/1615 ha] haue
3.5.86/1640 examination] examine
3.5.61/1645 Iaile.] Iaile. *Exeunt.*
4.1.20/1665 not . . . do] *not in* F
4.1.77/1722 so] *not in* F
4.1.88/1733 are you] you are
4.1.96/1741 spoke] ſpoken
4.1.127/1772 rereward] reward
4.1.134/1779 smirched] ſmeered
4.1.153/1798 two] *not in* F
4.1.163/1808 beate] beare
4.1.276/1921 sweare] ſweare by it
4.1.292/1937 it] *not in* F
4.1.317/1962 Counte Comfect] Comfect
4.2.332/1977 so I] ſo
4.2.17-20/1997-2000 CONRADE . . . villaines] *not in* F
4.2.49/2028 mass] th'maſſe
4.2.63/2042 Leonatoes] *Leonato*
5.1.6/2070 comforter] comfort
5.1.7/2071 doe] doth
5.1.63/2127 mine] my
5.1.108-10.1/2172-4.1 you . . . *Antonio*] you. | *Leo.* No come brother, away, I wil be heard. *Exeunt amb.* | *Bro.* And ſhal, or ſome of vs wil ſmart for it. *Enter Ben.* Q; you. | *Enter Benedicke.* | *Leo.* No come brother, away, I will be heard. | *Exeunt ambo.* | *Bro.* And ſhall, or ſome of vs will ſmart for it. F
5.1.157/2223 said she] ſaies ſhe
5.1.250.1/2316.1 *Enter . . . Sexton*] *Enter Leonato, his brother, and the Sexton.* Q; *Enter Leonato.* F
5.1.317.1/2384.1 *Exeunt . . . Verges*] *not in* Q; *Exeunt after following line*, F
5.2.32/2422 names] name
5.2.37/2427 rime . . . rime] time . . . time

MUCH ADO ABOUT NOTHING

5.2.39/2429 nor] for
5.2.71/2462 monument] monuments
5.2.71/2462 bell rings] Bels ring
5.4.7/2525 sorts] fort

5.4.33/2551 Heere . . . Claudio] *not in* F
5.4.80/2598 that] *not in* F
5.4.81/2599 that] *not in* F
5.4.106/2624 what] *not in* F

INCIDENTALS

156 her.] ~,   335 skill] shill   373 only.] ~,   706 heart.] ~ₐ   1028 expectation.] ~ₐ   1061 Against] Aganſt   1077 picture.] ~,   1085 ripend] ripened   1137 featured,] ~.   1181 limd] limed   1270 of,] Qa; ~, Qb   1286 for . . . of,] Qa; (for . . . of) Qb   1307 congregationₐ] Qa; ~, Qb   1330 name,] Qa; ~: Qb   1438 deformed] Qb; deſermed Qa   1441 yeere a . . . down] Qa; yeere, a . . . downe Qb   1468 oths,] ~.   1619 see,] Qa; ~: Qb   1622 troth he is, as] Qb; troth, he is as Qa   1741 namd] named   1759 Benedickeₐ Frier] Qa; ~, ~ Qb   1764 vp.] Qa; ~? Qb   1769 eies,] Qa; ~: Qb   1773 Grieud] Grieued   1779 mird] mired   1782 lou'd] loued   1784 mine,] ~:   1785 her:] ~,   1790 attird] attired   1793 Ladyₐ] Qa; ~, Qb   1794 truly not,] truly, not   1799 lou'd] loued   1871 Th'Idæa] Th Idæa   2048-9 them. Thou] them, thou   2149 gentleman, I] gentleman I,   2151 lou'd] loued   2173 No. Come] No come   2177 Lord.] ~:   2201 subiect.] ~ₐ   2213 sweete] Q (*c.w.*); ſweeete (*text*)   2352 disposeₐ] ~,   2358 Hyrd] Hyred   2488 slanderous] ſlauderous   2579 lou'd] loued   2580 certainer,] Qa; ~. Qb   2594 deceiu'd] deceiued   2606 Fashiond] Faſhioned

QUARTO STAGE DIRECTIONS

1.1.0.1-2/0.1-2   *Enter Leonato gouernour of Messina, Innogen his wife, Hero | his daughter, and Beatrice his neece, with a | messenger.*
1.1.90.1-2/90.1-2   *Enter don Pedro, Claudio, Benedicke, Balthasar | and John the bastard.*
1.1.153.1/153.1   *Exeunt. Manent Benedicke & Claudio.*
1.1.191.1/192.1   *Enter don Pedro, Iohn the bastard.*
1.1.272/273   *exit*
1.1.311/312   *exeunt.*
1.2.0.1-2/312.1-2   *Enter Leonato and an old man brother to Leonato*
1.2.24.1/336   *exeunt.*
1.3.0.1-2/336.1-2   *Enter sir Iohn the bastard, and Conrade his companion.*
1.3.37.1/374.1   *Enter Borachio.* (after 1.3.38/375)
1.3.69/406   *exit.*
2.1.0.1-2/406.1-3   *Enter Leonato, his brother, his wife, Hero his daughter, and | Beatrice his neece, and a kinsman.*
2.1.77.1-3/483.1.-3   *Enter prince, Pedro, Claudio, and Benedicke, and Balthaser, | or dumb Iohn.*
2.1.144.1-2/551.1-2   *Dance exeunt*
2.1.161.1/568.1   *exeunt: manet Clau.*
2.1.172.1/579.1   *Enter Bene-|dicke*
2.1.189/597   *exit*
2.1.197.1/605.1   *Enter the Prince, Hero, Leonato, Iohn and Borachio, | and Conrade.*
2.1.244.1-2/654.1-2   *Enter Claudio and Beatrice.*
2.1.257/667   *exit.*
2.1.319/729   *exit Beatrice.*
2.1.362.1/773   *exit.*
2.2.0.1./773.1   *Enter Iohn and Borachio.*
2.2.51.1/824.1   *exit.*
2.3.0.1./824.2   *Enter Benedicke alone.*
2.3.7/831   *exit.* (after 2.3.5/829)
2.3.35.2/859.2   *Enter prince, Leonato, Claudio, Musicke.*
2.3.41.1/865.1   *Enter Balthaser with musicke.*
2.3.61/884.1   *The Song.*
2.3.89/913   *Exit Balthaser.*
2.3.232.1/1058.1   *Enter Beatrice.*
2.3.244/1070   *exit.*
2.3.251/1077   *exit.*
3.1.0.1-2/1077.1-2   *Enter Hero and two Gentlewomen, Margaret, and Vrsley.*
3.1.23/1100   *Enter Beatrice.* (after 3.1.25/1102)
3.1.116/1193   *exit.*
3.2.0.1-2/1193.1-2   *Enter Prince, Claudio, Benedicke, and Leonato.*

3.2.71.1./1264.1   *Enter Iohn the Bastard.*
3.3.0.1-2/1317.1-2   *Enter Dogbery and his compartner with the Watch.*
3.3.91.1/1409.1   *exeunt.*
3.3.91.2/1409.2   *Enter Borachio and Conrade.*
3.3.173/1492   *exeunt.*
3.4.0.1./1492.1   *Enter Hero, and Margaret, and Vrsula.*
3.4.35.1/1528.1   *Enter Beatrice.*
3.4.88.1/1581.1   *Enter Vrsula.*
3.5.0.1-2/1585.2-3   *Enter Leonato, and the Constable, and the Headborough.*
3.5.53.1/1637.1   (*exit* after 3.5.49/1633; intended to refer to Leonato's subsequent line)
4.1.0.1-3/1645.1-3   *Enter Prince, Bastard, Leonato, Frier, Claudio, Bene-|dicke, Hero, and Beatrice.*
4.1.257.1/1902.1   *exit.*
4.2.0.1-3/1980.2-4   *Enter the Constables, Borachio, and the Towne clearke | in gownes.*
4.2.84.1/2064   *exit.*
5.1.0.1/2064.1   *Enter Leonato and his brother.*
5.1.44.1/2108.1   *Enter Prince and Claudio.*
5.1.110.1/2174.1   *Exeunt amb.*
5.1.110.2/2174.2   *Enter Ben.*
5.1.196.1-2/2261.1-2   *Enter Constables, Conrade, and Borachio.*
5.1.250.1/2316.1   *Enter Leonato, his brother, and the Sexton.*
5.1.322.1/2389.1   *exeunt*
5.2.0.1/2389.2   *Enter Benedicke and Margaret.*
5.2.23/2413   *Exit Margarite.*
5.2.39.1/2429.1   *Enter Beatrice.* (F; after 5.2.40/2430, Q)
5.2.85.1/2476.1   *Enter Vrsula.*
5.2.94/2485   *exit.*
5.3.0.1-2/2485.1-2   *Enter Claudio, Prince, and three or foure with tapers.*
5.3.3/2487.1   *Epitaph.*
5.3.11.1/2496.1   *Song*
5.3.33.1/2518.1   *exeunt.*
5.4.0.1-2/2518.2-3   *Enter Leonato, Benedick, Margaret Vrsula, old man, Frier, Hero.*
5.4.12.1/2530.1   *Exeunt Ladies.* (after 5.4.16/2534)
5.4.33.1/2551.1-2   *Enter Prince, and Claudio, and two or three other.*
5.4.51.1-2/2569.1-2   *Enter brother, Hero, Beatrice, Margaret, Ursula.*
5.4.123.1/2640.1   *Enter Messenger.*
5.4.127.1/2645.1   *dance.*

HENRY V

Henry V is included in a Stationers' Register entry of 4 August [1600], in a list of plays 'to be staied': for this memorandum, see *Much Ado About Nothing*. It was entered again on 14 August 1600, when its copyright was transferred to Thomas Pavier:

Thomas Entred for his Copyes by direction
Pavyer of Mr White warden vnder his
 hand wrytinge ·· These Copyes
 followinge beinge thinges formerlye
 printed & sett over to the sayd Thomas
 Pavyer ·· viz.

 The Pathway to knowlege
 The historye of Henrye the vth wth
 the battell of Agencourt

The text 'formerlye printed' was probably the quarto (Q1) with the title 'THE CRONICLE | Hiftory of Henry the fift, | With his battell fought at *Agin Court* in | *France*. Togither with *Auntient* | *Piftoll*', printed in 1600 by Thomas Creede for Thomas Millington and John Busby (*BEPD* 165). The single press variant discovered in Q1 by Berger is of no editorial significance. Berger concludes that the text was set throughout by Creede's Compositor A. (See *Romeo and Juliet*.) This text was reprinted for Pavier in 1602 (Q2) and 1619 (Q3); both were printed from Q1, and the latter (falsely dated '1608') was one of the Pavier Quartos. (See General Introduction.) A substantially different text was printed in the First Folio (F).

The nature and relationship of Q and F is discussed at length in Taylor's 'Three Studies in the Text of *Henry V*' (1979) and also in his edition of the play (1982). Our text essentially reproduces Taylor's. Readings are discussed only when the text departs from the OET edition.

F, the fuller and more important text, derives throughout from foul papers, as is evident from the stage directions. As in all such cases, a scribal transcript of foul papers cannot be ruled out, but seems improbable, particularly as there is a significant number of 'Shakespearian' spellings, while the misreadings suggest a hand similar in all respects to what we can infer of Shakespeare's own. Q appears to be the memorial reconstruction of an abridged text; the two reporters took the parts of Exeter and Gower, with Gower doubling a mute in 1.2/Sc. 2, Cambridge in 2.2/Sc. 5, and (probably) Bourbon in 2.4/Sc. 7, and 4.5/Sc. 21. Scenes for which the reporters were on stage are the most reliable in Q1; scenes in which both were present are especially so. The text behind Q had apparently been adapted for performance by a smaller cast, and those of its alterations which might result from limitations of cast have been regarded as without authority. However, a number of its major variants are either indifferent in terms of casting, or even seriously complicate casting problems. The

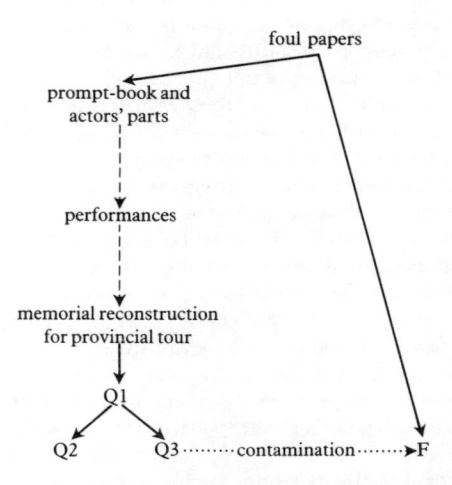

```
                              foul papers
                             ↙         ↘
        prompt-book and
        actors' parts
              ↓
        performances
              ↓
        memorial reconstruction
        for provincial tour
              ↓
             Q1
           ↙    ↘
         Q2      Q3 ········ contamination ········▶ F
```

most important of these are Q's substitution of Clarence for Bedford, of Warwick for Westmorland (in 4.3/Sc. 19, and perhaps elsewhere), of Bourbon for Britain (3.5/Sc. 13), and of Bourbon for the Dauphin (3.7/Sc. 15, 4.2/Sc. 18, 4.5/Sc. 21); all have been adopted in this text. So have a greater number of verbal variants from Q than is usual; this eclecticism is justified in 'Three Studies'. Q is exceptionally 'naïve' as memorial reconstructions go, in that little or no attempt seems to have been made to supplement or sophisticate the text when memory failed. Most of the readings adopted from Q appear to be simply corrections of F errors, but in a few cases Q's reading must represent deliberate revision. The few such verbal revisions cluster in the best-reported scenes; presumably there were more in other scenes, but the quality of the reporting precludes their recovery.

Q readings which involve profanity represent a particularly difficult problem, in that differences between Q and F in this respect could result from sporadic censorship in F or sporadic actors' interpolations in Q. But of the seventeen profanities present in Q but not F, only six seem editorially defensible, and this edition adopts only three: 'gads lugges' at 2.1.28/514 ('my hand', F), 'Godes plud' at 3.2.21/1091 (not in F), and 'By Iesu' at 5.1.38/2806 ('I say', F). We have also adopted Q at 4.8.10/2605, where F seems to have softened Q. The three other profanities which have serious claim to inclusion—at 4.1.77/1857, 4.1.196/1977, and 4.7.1/2414—have been recorded in the separate list of rejected Q variants. This list includes only those readings which, though finally rejected from this edition, seem nevertheless to have serious merits, which other editors might regard as sufficient to justify emendation of F.

Q3 creates special problems. A full collation of Q3 variants will be provided by Thomas L. Berger in the New Variorum edition, in progress; we have undertaken a similar collation ourselves, but do not print it here because it would have to be keyed to the Quarto text. Such collation establishes that *Henry V*, like most and perhaps all of the Pavier collection, was 'edited' before it reached the compositors. (Two compositors have been identified by Andrews (1977); one closely resembles Folio Compositor B.) This 'editing' did not involve access to any additional authoritative documents: with the exception of 'Crispianus' (4.7.89/2502), not a single Q3 variant required access to any special knowledge not inferable from the text of Q1, and 'Crispianus' only required a knowledge of contemporary saints' days. (See note.) Scores of examples of grotesque nonsense are left uncorrected, because correction would have required consultation of another manuscript, or of Shakespeare's chronicle sources. The editing of Q3 *Henry V* therefore most closely resembles that of F2. (See General Introduction.) The editor has provided a few extra necessary directions; conjecturally emended obvious Q1 errors; sporadically improved Q1's verse, when it can be readily adjusted to metrical normality. Many of these editorial adjustments are, on the evidence of F, mistakes: F either supports Q1 or shows that it should have been emended in a different way. In addition, Q3 extensively rearranges Q1's verse lines. (Q1 sets the entire play as verse.) These rearrangements are presumably compositorial in origin, and can almost all be explained by two causes: tight Q1 lines would not fit the Q3 measure, and on some pages the Q3 compositor was clearly stretching his text in order to fit it into cast-off pages. The second cause is important, because it also explains Q3's additions to the text. For most of the play Q3 variants are all readily explicable as editorial improvements or compositorial errors, but five pages (F2^v, F3, F4^v, G1, G2^v), in the inner formes of two adjacent sheets, all set by compositor 'B', contain a dozen added words and phrases. In each case, the additions coexist with clear evidence of space-wasting (space added around stage directions, relineation of text and stage directions), and presumably arose from a desire to make the rearranged short verse appear less flagrantly improbable. (See General Introduction.)

Cairncross (1956) proposed that the Folio text had been set up from extensively annotated quarto copy, making use of both Q2 and Q3. Walter, in an appendix to his revised edition (1960), and Taylor ('Three Studies') showed that there was no evidence for the use of Q2, a conclusion which in itself seriously weakened Cairncross's theory. Taylor, more extensively, showed that the cited correspondences between Q3 and F were not sufficient to demonstrate the use of printed copy, which in this instance would have needed to be annotated to an extraordinary and impracticable degree. However, this conclusion needs to be modified in the light of three weaknesses in Taylor's argument. Like all previous investigators, Taylor confined himself to evaluating the hypothesis that a quarto was actually marked up and used as printer's copy. It is equally possible that Q3, which had been printed by Jaggard in 1619, was simply available in the shop in 1622 and that it was sporadically consulted by the Folio compositors. In coping with foul authorial papers twenty years old, a printed crib, however inadequate, may have been thought desirable and found useful. Although the procedure creates nightmares for an editor, there can be little doubt that such sporadic consultation of an earlier 'bad' edition affected parts of Q2 *Romeo*, Q2 *Hamlet*, Folio *Contention*, and Folio *Duke of York*. (See the Introductions to those plays.) The issue of Q3 influence therefore cannot be decided on the basis of the traditional simple dichotomy between (*a*) use of annotated quarto copy and (*b*) no contamination by Q3 at all; we must also consider (*c*) the possibility of compositorial consultation. Moreover, it is now clear that 'editorial' use of the Pavier quartos in the preparation of F was greater than anyone realized in 1979: the relevant Pavier quarto was used as copy for *Dream* and *Lear* and consulted for both *Contention* and *Duke of York*. In terms of the larger pattern of Folio copy, it therefore seems likely that Jaggard would have made some subsidiary use of Q3 in setting *Henry V*. Finally, Taylor unwisely assumed that Cairncross and Evans (1974) had between them provided a comprehensive list of correspondences between Q3 and F; subsequent collation has revealed a number of additional links.

All substantive Q3/F correspondences are listed and discussed in the Textual Notes. These correspondences can be usefully divided into distinct categories. Many result from (1) simple Q3 corrections of Q1 errors. Given the number of Q3 'corrections' which do not correspond with F, the number of such emendations endorsed by F is not surprising. Equally unremarkable are (2) cases where a Q3 sophistication happens to coincide with Shakespeare's own strong preference, demonstrable in early quartos as well as other Folio texts (3.2.45/1115, 3.6.112/1507, etc.). Whatever the number of examples in these two categories, they can prove nothing about Q3 influence on F. The crucial variants are those where (3) a sophistication or error in Q3 is reproduced in F. The Q1 reading may be supported by Shakespeare's sources (2.2.174/781), a strong parallel in another Shakespeare play (2.3.38/836), Shakespeare's invariable practice elsewhere (4.3.125/2274), or metre (2.4.75/931, 2.4.124/980). In each of these key examples the strength of the case for the Q1 reading has been overlooked by previous investigators, including Cairncross himself. None of these readings is, in F, blatantly nonsensical, nor should we expect them to be, for the entire purpose of a printed crib would be to help the compositors make better sense of their difficult manuscript copy; but cumulatively these examples are, we have come reluctantly to believe, compelling. Moreover, they are supplemented by (4) cases where F agrees with Q1-3, apparently in error. Taylor (1982), working on the assumption that Q and F were entirely independent, was nevertheless forced to concede three such cases (1.2.74/307, 3.3.8/1133-4, 4.3.118/2267); twice elsewhere he recorded early emendations which he regarded as improvements, and only refused to adopt these because he believed the F reading was independently supported by Q (4.3.59/2208, 5.1.77-8/2847-8). These examples support those in category (3) not only by their number but by their clustering: three such suspicious readings occur between 4.3.59/2208 and 4.3.125/2274, and four more between 2.2.174/781 and 2.4.124/980. In the light of such correspondences, one must view with considerable scepticism cases where (5) Q3 and F agree in a dubious sophistication or modernization of Q1 (2.2.96/703, 2.2.97/704, 4.8.72/2667, 5.1.14/2781). Each of these coincidences might result from 'the independent operation of the same agency' (Taylor, 'Three Studies'), a sophisticating compositor in Jaggard's shop; but it does seem remarkably unfortunate that such sporadic sophisticating tendencies seized upon exactly the same words in these two texts, while leaving other examples untouched. Such correspondences tend to corroborate suspicions of Q3 influence, though in themselves they could not demonstrate it.

This text therefore departs from the Oxford edition in its acceptance of the probability of sporadic contamination of F by Q3. In about a dozen places we have accordingly emended the text. However, it remains clear that consultation of Q3 was sporadic and that Q3 did not actually serve as printer's copy; we have therefore been cautious in departing from F.

Q has no act or scene divisions. F does not demarcate scenes, and its act-division is imperfect: Acts 1 and 5 are correctly indicated, but there is no division before the second speech of the Chorus (2.0/Sc. 3), where Johnson and all subsequent editors have marked the beginning of Act 2. As a result of this oversight, the Folio marks Acts 3 and 4 as 2 and 3, and begins its Act 4 after 4.6/Sc. 22, a clearly impossible arrangement. This edition departs from the traditional editorial scene-numbering in three respects. The appearances of the Chorus are in the modern-spelling edition numbered 2.0, 3.0, etc., being thus counted as separate scenes without throwing off the numeration of the rest of each act. After the Boy's soliloquy at Harfleur, the stage is cleared and so we mark a new scene (3.3/Sc. 11); before Henry's entrance to the gates of Harfleur, the stage is not cleared, and so we do not mark a new scene division, instead continuing with 3.3/Sc. 11.

This play raises particularly difficult problems of modernization, because of the passages of French, the profusion of French names, and the possible dialect significance of unusual spellings in the speech of Scots, Irish, and Welsh characters.

G.T./(S.W.W.)

WORKS CITED

Andrews, John F., 'The Pavier Quartos of 1619—Evidence for the Compositors' (unpublished Ph.D. thesis, Vanderbilt University, 1971)
Berger, Thomas L., 'The Printing of *Henry V*, Q1', *The Library*, VI, 1 (1979), 114-25
Cairncross, Andrew S., 'Quarto Copy for Folio *Henry V*', SB 8 (1956), 67-93
Dorius, R. J., ed., *Henry V*, Yale (1955)
Evans, H. A., ed., *Henry V*, Arden (1903)
Fletcher, Ronald S. W., ed., *Henry V*, New Clarendon (1941)
Harbage, Alfred, ed., *Henry V*, in *Works*, Pelican (1969)
Humphreys, A. R., ed., *Henry V*, New Penguin (1968)
Jackson, MacDonald P., *SSu 37* (1984), p.203
Kittredge, G. L., ed., *Henry V* (1943)
Moore Smith, G. C., ed., *Henry V*, Warwick (1893)
—— ed., *Henry V*, Oxford (1982)
Walter, J. H., ed., *Henry V*, Arden (1955)
Wilson, John Dover, ed., *King Henry V*, New (1947; rev. 1955)
Wright, W. A., ed., *Henry V*, Clarendon (1882)

TEXTUAL NOTES

Title *The Life of Henry the Fifth*] F (*head title and running titles*); *The Life of King Henry the Fift* F (*table of contents*); THE CRONICLE Hiſtory of Henry the fift Q
Pro.17 account] F (*Accompt*)
1.1.4 scrambling] F (ſcambling)
1.2.0.2/133.1 Clarence] Q; Bedford, Clarence F
1.2.1/134 KING HARRY] F (*King.*). 'Harry' is the form overwhelmingly preferred (24 occurrences); 'Henry', outside the title, is used only twice (5.2.0.1, 5.2.238/2855.1, 3096).
1.2.33/166 BISHOP OF CANTERBURY] F; Biſh⟨op⟩. Q3; *not in* Q1. An obvious correction.
1.2.38/171 succedant] F2; ſuccedaul F1
1.2.40 gloss] QF (gloze)
1.2.45, 52, 63 Saale] F (Sala)
1.2.45 Elbe] F (Elue); *Elme* Q
1.2.50/183 ther] Q (there); then F
1.2.52 Elbe] F (Elue)
1.2.72/205 fine] Q; find F
1.2.74/207 Heire] Q (heire); th'Heire F
1.2.74/207 Lingard] SISSON (Wilson); *Lingare* F; *Inger* Q. F's misreading may have been influenced by Q.
1.2.77/210 Ninth] POPE; Tenth F
1.2.82/215 Ermengard] SISSON (Wilson); *Ermengare* F
1.2.90-1/223-4 day, | Howbeit,] Q; ~. ~, F
1.2.99/232 sonne] Q; man F
1.2.113/246 another] Q3, F; an other Q1. Q3 consistently treats this as one word, but this preference coincides with Shakespeare's: the dramatic good quartos have 96 examples, to only 10 of *an other*. There are additional examples at 2.1.8, 3.6.157, and 5.1.59/493, 1553, and 2827.
1.2.115/248 those] TAYLOR; theſe F
1.2.125/258 cause; and means, and might,] THEOBALD; ~, ~, ~; F
1.2.131/264 Blood] F3; Bloods F1
1.2.138 raid] F (roade)

1.2.147/280 vnmaskt his power] Q; went with his forces F
1.2.147/280 vnto] TAYLOR; into F; for Q
1.2.154/287 the brute thereof] BOSWELL; the brute hereof Q; th'ill neighbourhood F
1.2.163/296 y^{or}] Q (your); their F; her CAPELL (Johnson)
1.2.166/299 A LORD] Q (Lord.); Biſh⟨op of⟩. Ely. F; Westmorland CAPELL
1.2.182/315 Congreeing] F; Congrueth Q; Congruing POPE
1.2.183/316 True:] Q; *not in* F
1.2.197/330 Maiestie] Q; Maieſties F
1.2.199/332 lading] Q; kneading F
1.2.208/341 Flye] Q; Come F
1.2.212/345 End] Q; And F
1.2.213/346 defect] Q; defeat F
1.2.221, etc. Dauphin] QF (Dolphin)
1.2.276/409 haue I] TAYLOR; haue we Q1; we haue Q3; I haue F. Taylor defended the emendation without reference to Q3, which demonstrates the ease of compositorial transposition in this context.
1.2.284/417 from] Q; with F
1.2.287/420 I] Q; And F
1.2.310.1-2.0.0.1/443.1-2 Flourish. Exeunt | Enter] DYCE; *Exeunt. | Flouriſh. Enter* F
2.0.20/463 But see, thy fault,ˌ France hath in thee found out,] F; But see,ˌ thy fault! *France . . . out*ˌ CAPELL
2.0.24 Scrope] F (*Scroope*)
2.0.32/475 perforce] TAYLOR; *not in* F
2.1.2/487 Good morrow] Q3, F; Godmorrow Q1. Q1's form only appears once in a good quarto (*Troilus* 5.1.68/2800) and once in a reliable Folio text (*Henry V* 4.1.3/1783); two other examples occur in texts set from scribal copy (*1 Henry IV* 2.5.530/1456) or in a passage doubtfully Shakespearian (*1 Henry VI* 3.5.1/1325). Against these must be set dozens of examples in good quartos alone. Q3's consistent alteration of 'Godmorrow' to 'Good morrow', which might independently have affected this and

2.1.3 Ensign] F (Ancient)
2.1.22/507 mare] Q; name F
2.1.25/510 Godmorrow ancient *Pistoll.*] Q; *not in* F
2.1.28/513 NYM] Q; *not in* F
2.1.29 tick] F (Tyke)
2.1.29/514 gads lugges] Q; this hand F
2.1.32/517 Gentlewomen] F, Q3; honeſt ~ Q1. Q1's additional word may be defended as characteristic of Quickly's generally repetitive style, but the repetition here seems of little use; moreover, a compositor sporadically consulting Q3 may substitute and add words from the printed text, but seems less likely to omit manuscript words just because they were omitted from Q3: Q3 influence is more probably active than passive.
2.1.34.1/519.1 *Nym drawes his sword*] *not in* QF
2.1.36/521 adultery] Q3, F; adultry Q1
2.1.36.1/521.1 *Pistoll drawes his sword*] *not in* QF
2.1.45 marvellous] F (meruailous)
2.1.47 pardie] F (perdy)
2.1.58-60/543-5 O . . . exhale] Q3, F; Q1 treats as verse, but divides after 'might' and 'groaning'. Except for Pistol's final couplet (5.1.84-5/2854-5), this is the only one of his speeches set as verse in F; here, as in 5.1, the Q3/F lineation is correct, but it may be suggestive that F aligns as verse at all.
2.1.60 ex-hale] F (*not hyphenated*)
2.1.60.1/545.1 *Pistoll and Nym drawe*] Q (They ~); *not in* F
2.1.61.1/546.1 *He drawes*] *not in* QF
2.1.64.1/549.1 *They sheath their swords*] *not in* QF
2.1.70/555 thee defie] Q; defie thee F
2.1.77/562 enough.] Q (inough); enough to, F; enough, too. RIVERSIDE
2.1.77.1/562.1 *running*] TAYLOR; *not in* QF
2.1.79/564 you] HANMER; your F
2.1.85/570 *with Boy*] CAPELL; *not in* F
2.1.95/580 *drawing his sword*] *not in* QF
2.1.97.1/582.1 *He sheaths his sword*] *not in* QF
2.1.98/583 Corporall] F3; Coporall F1
2.1.101/586 NYM I . . . shillings?] TAYLOR; *Nim.* I . . . ſhillings I woon of you at beating? Q; *not in* F
2.1.111/596 that's] F2; that F1
2.1.111.1/596.1 *Nim and Bardolph sheathe their swords.*] *not in* QF
2.1.112/597 come of] F1; came of Q, F2
2.1.113 Ah] F (A)
2.1.115/600 *Exit*] TAYLOR; *not in* F
2.1.122.1/607.1 *Exeunt omnes*] Q; *not in* F
2.2.0.1/607.2 *Gloucester*] Q; *Bedford* F
2.2.0.2/607.2 *Westmerland*] F; *not in* Q; *Warwick* TAYLOR (*conj.*)
2.2.1/608 GLOUCESTER] Q (*throughout scene*); Bed⟨ford⟩. F (*throughout scene*)
2.2.26/633 a] F; one TAYLOR (*conj.*)
2.2.35/642 yʳ] Q (their); the F
2.2.52/659 'gainst] Q3 (gainſt), F; againſt. Q1. Metrically required.
2.2.72/679 haue] F1-3; hath Q, F4
2.2.84/691 him] Q, F2; *not in* F1
2.2.85/692 vilde] F; *not in* Q
2.2.95, 96/702, 703 a] Q1; haue Q3, F. This contraction only appears in the Folio once (where it follows Quarto copy). It appears 7 times in good quartos: 4 are altered to 'haue' in F, 1 to 'ha'.
2.2.96/703 vse:] Q; ~? F
2.2.101/708 one] WILSON 1955 (Maxwell); and F; from Q
2.2.104/711 a] F2; an F1
2.2.105 whoop] F (hoope)
2.2.111/718 And] F; All HANMER
2.2.113/720 being] F; are TAYLOR (*conj.*)
2.2.115/722 thee, bad] F; ~, ~ POPE
2.2.118 demon] F (Dæmon)
2.2.125/732 seeme] F; or seem POPE
2.2.136/743 marke] THEOBALD; make F
2.2.136/743 the] POPE; thee F

2.2.136 endowed] F (indued)
2.2.137/744 suspition. I . . . thee,] POPE; ſuſpition, I . . . thee. F
2.2.144/751 Henry] Q; *Thomas* F
2.2.145/751 Masham] Q; *Marſham* F
2.2.155/762 heartily in sufferance] TAYLOR; in ſufferance heartily F1; I in sufferance heartily F2
2.2.162 'quit] QF (quit)
2.2.164/771 and fixt] Q; *not in* F
2.2.173/780 haue] Q1; *not in* F1; three F2
2.2.174/781 ye] Q1; you Q3, F. The only occurrence of *ye* in Q1, and agreeing with Holinshed (which Shakespeare follows closely here). Compositor B is only known to have altered 'ye' to 'you' once elsewhere in the Folio (*Dream* 5.1.279/1980), so Q3 contamination is perhaps more likely than coincidental sophistication.
2.2.190.1/797.1 *Exit omnes*] Q; *not in* F
2.3.16/814 babeld] THEOBALD; Table F
2.3.22/819 on] Q3, F; at Q1. Q1 seems wrong, and Q3's correction is not beyond the wit of an early editor or compositor.
2.3.24/821 vppard, and vpard] WILSON; vp-peer'd, and vpward F; vpward, and vpward Q
2.3.30/827 and said] Q3 (& ſed), F; and he ſed Q1. Q1's reading could easily have arisen from contamination by 2.3.38/836. Elsewhere in the canon, Shakespeare used *and* [*he/she/it*] *said* only twice: *Tempest* 1.2.57/123 (verse), *Henry V* 3.7.104/1677. By contrast, *and said*, with a third person singular pronoun implied, occurs 12 times. Verse examples may have been influenced by metrical considerations, but even if we restrict ourselves to prose *and said* is clearly preferred (6 to 2). Moreover, only one of the parallels uses the same first verb: 'So he doth you, my lord, and said' (*1 Henry IV* 3.3.133/2051, spoken by Quickly). On balance, therefore, the odds favour the Q3/F reading, and the coincidence might arise from (*a*) F following the authoritative manuscript reading, (*b*) Q1 corrupting it memorially, from the influence of 2.3.38/836, and (*c*) Q3 shortening the Q1 line, in order to fit it into a smaller measure.
2.3.39/837 hellfire] Q1; hell Q3; Hell F. Shakespeare's only other use of *hell-fire* is at *1 Henry IV* 3.3.30/1951, where Sir John uses it as a metaphor for Rossill's [= Bardolph's] nose. Since Q1 is remarkably free of memorial contamination by other plays, this parallel is more likely to be the result of the author's than the reporters' association.
2.3.46/844 word] Q1; world F, Q2. Although sense can be made of F, all editors have preferred Q1, which is probably correct. (See Jackson.) A single such correspondence between Q2 and F does not establish any direct bibliographical relationship between them.
2.3.48/846 Dogge, my Ducke.] Q (dog, my deare.); ~ : My Ducke, F
2.3.57 housewifery] F (Huſwiferie)
2.4.0.3/856.2 *Burbon*] Q; *Britaine* F
2.4.4/860 Burbon] Q; Britaine F
2.4.32/888 great State] F; regard Q. We revert here to F, in response to Jackson's demonstration (see note to 2.3.46/844) that Q's context here seems influenced by memories of 1.1.23-8/57-62.
2.4.33/889 aged] Q; Noble F
2.4.57/913 Mountant] TAYLOR; Mountaine F; mounting THEOBALD
2.4.59/915 Heroicall] F; heroic ROWE
2.4.75/931 attended] CAPELL; *not in* QF
2.4.75, 116/931, 971 England] Q1; of England Q3, F. The fact that F agrees with Q3 twice makes this reading doubly suspicious. In 5.2 '*brother* [*England, France*]' occurs 3 times, always metrically; elsewhere in the history plays, '*brother* [*title*]' occurs 26 times, metrically, and '*brother of* [*title*]' 4 times metrically. The only 3 possible exceptions to this practice are all in Act 4 of *Duke of York* (of which Shakespeare's authorship has been doubted: see Introduction): 4.1.9, 4.4.14, and 4.6.16/1855, 2062, and 2136. In the context of the canon as a whole, it is now clear—as it was not in 1979—that both lines are genuinely anomalous, metrically.
2.4.102/958 And] F; He ROWE; A TAYLOR (*conj.*)

HENRY V

2.4.106/962 Turnes he] Q; Turning F
2.4.106-7/962-3 the Widdowes . . . Blood] QF (subs.); the dead men's blood, the widows' tears, | The orphans' cries JOHNSON (conj.)
2.4.107/963 pining] Q; priuy F; privèd WALTER
2.4.112 too] Q (too), F (to)
2.4.117/973 defiance,] QF; ~ ; CAPELL
2.4.117/973 contempt;] TAYLOR; ~ , QF
2.4.123/979 for] Q; of F
2.4.132 Louvre] QF (Louer)
2.4.140/996 rising] CAPELL; not in F
2.4.146.1-3.0.0.1/1002.1-2 Flourish. Exeunt | Enter] DYCE; Exeunt. | Flourish. Enter F
3.0.4/1006 Douer] F; Hampton THEOBALD
3.0.6/1008 fanning] ROWE; fayning F
3.0.17 Harfleur] F (Harflew)
3.1.0.1-20/1037.1-2 Alarum . . . Ladders] TAYLOR; Enter the King, Exeter, Bedford, and Gloucester | Alarum: Scaling Ladders at Harflew F
3.1.7/1044 coniure] WALTER; commune F; summon ROWE
3.1.17/1054 noblest] F2; Noblish F1; noble MALONE
3.1.24/1061 mē] F4; me F1
3.1.32/1069 Straÿing] ROWE; Straying F
3.2.9, 14, 18/1079, 1083.1, 1087.1 sings] not in QF
3.2.21/1091 Godes plud] Q; not in F
3.2.21/1091 breaches] Q; breach F
3.2.27.2/1097.1 Fluellen . . . Nym] TAYLOR; not in QF
3.2.28/1098 runs] RANN (Capell); wins F
3.2.28.1/1098 Exit all but ⌈the Boy⌉] CAPELL; Exit F
3.2.36-7/1107 whole Weapons] F; Weapons whole TAYLOR (conj.)
3.2.45/1115 halfepence] Q3, F; hapence Q1. Q1's form never appears elsewhere in Shakespeare; Q3/F's occurs 10 times (6 in good quartos, once in *More*). Thus, Q3's preference coincidentally agrees with Shakespeare's.
3.2.46 Calais] F (Callice)
3.2.49 handkerchiefs] F (Hand-kerchers)
3.3.0.1-2/1125.1 and Fluellen, meeting] not in QF
3.3.8/1133 himselfe, foure yard vnder,] TAYLOR; ~ ∧ ~ ∧ QF. Possible Q3 contamination.
3.3.8/1134 Cheshu] F; Iefus Q1; Iefhu Q3. Taylor (1982) remarked that F's '*sh* for *s*' is anomalous, and that the 'Ch' form may be meant to recall the Welsh obsession with cheese; the anomaly would be removed and the pun clarified by reverting to Q1's form of the second syllable. In the Q paraphrase of 3.6.12/1405, Q1's 'Iefus' again becomes 'Iefhu' in Q3; The phrase does not appear in F. See also 4.7.109/2522.
3.3.16 has] F (ha's)
3.3.18 Roman] (not italicized in F)
3.3.23 anciant] F (aunchiant)
3.3.29 Good e'en] F (Godden)
3.3.31 pioneers] F (Pioners)
3.3.33 trumpet] F (Trompet)
3.3.39 vouchsafe] F (voutfafe)
3.3.46 captains] F (Captens)
3.3.47 quite] F (quit)
3.3.52 An] F (and)
3.3.52 besieched] F (befeech'd)
3.3.53/1179 nothing,] F; ~ ; CAPELL
3.3.58 these] F (theife)
3.3.59 slumber] F (flomber)
3.3.60/1186 ay∧ ow Got a] TAYLOR (T. W. Craik); ay, or goe to F
3.3.61 suirely] F (fuerly)
3.3.61 brief] F (breff)
3.3.62/1188 heard] F; hear CAMBRIDGE (Walker)
3.3.63 twae] F (tway)
3.3.65 nation—] POPE; ~ . F
3.3.67 bastard] F (Bafterd)
3.3.67/1194 Rascall?] ROWE; ~ . F; ~ — WRIGHT
3.3.83/1211 Exit] F; not in Q; Exeunt ROWE
3.3.80.1/1211.1 Flourish.] CAPELL; not in F; alarum Q (at end of direction)

3.3.115/1243 headdy] F2; headly F1
3.3.118/1246 Defile] ROWE 1714; Defire F
3.3.126.1/1254.1 on the Wall] CAPELL (at 3.3.83.1/1211.1); not in QF
3.3.130/1258 dread] Q; great F
3.3.134/1262 Exit Gouernour] HUMPHREYS; not in F
3.3.137/1265 all. For vs, deare Vnckle,] POPE; all∧ for vs, ~ . F
3.3.141.1/1269.1 The Gates are opened] not in F
3.4.1/1270 bien parlas] F1; parlois bien F2; parte fort bon Q
3.4.1 parles] F (parlas), Q (parte)
3.4.3/1272 Vn] ROWE; En F
3.4.4/1273 ie apprene] F2; ie apprend F1
3.4.5/1274 parler] F2; parlen F1
3.4.5/1274 Coment] F2; Comient F1; Coman Q
3.4.7/1276 E] (continued to Catherine) THEOBALD; *Alice.* E F
3.4.8/1277 ALICE] THEOBALD; *Kat⟨herine⟩*. F
3.4.8/1277 le oublie∧ le] F2; ~ , e F1
3.4.8/1277 doyts, mays∧] CAPELL; doyt∧ ~ , F1
3.4.9/1278 souendray] F2; fouemeray F1
3.4.9/1278 sont] CAPELL; ont F
3.4.10/1279 oui] ROWE; ou F
3.4.11/1280 KATHERINE] THEOBALD; *Alice.* F
3.4.11/1280 de Fingres] CAPELL; le Fingres F
3.4.12/1281 escholier. l'ay] THEOBALD; ~ | *Kath⟨erine⟩*. *l'ay* F
3.4.13 les] (F2); F1 (le)
3.4.14 Les] (F2); F1 (Le)
3.4.14/1283 nous] CAMBRIDGE; not in F
3.4.14 nails] F (Nayles)
3.4.19, 43, 54/1288, 1295, 1322 Arma] Q (arma); Arme F
3.4.20/1289 le] F2; de F1; de Q
3.4.22/1291 repiticiō] F2; repiticio F1
3.4.38/1307 N'aue vos y] F1; N'auez vous pas F2; N'avez-vous RIVERSIDE
3.4.40/1308 Non e] TAYLOR; Nome∧ F1; Nomme, F2-4; Non, ROWE
3.4.41 mailès] F (Maylees)
3.4.44/1312 Sauf] ROWE; Sans F
3.4.44/1312 honeur] F2; honeus F1
3.4.45/1313 dy] F2; de F1
3.4.46/1314 les pieds] F2; les pied F1; le pied DYCE
3.4.46/1314 le] Q (roman); de F
3.4.46/1314 robe] Q (roman); roba F
3.4.47/1315 De Foot] Q (de foote); Le Foot F
3.4.47/1315 de] CAPELL; le QF
3.4.47, 48, 52, 55/1315, 1316, 1320, 1323 Coune] Q (con); Count F
3.4.48/1316 De Foot, & de] CAPELL; Le Foot, & le FQ
3.4.48/1316 ils] WILSON; il F1; ce F2
3.4.52/1320 de Foot & de] CAPELL; le Foot & le F
3.4.53/1320 neant moÿs] F2; neant moys F1
3.4.55/1322 Foot, de] Q (subs.), F3; Foot, le F1
3.4.57.1/1325.1 Exeunt] Q; Exit F
3.5.0.2/1325.3 Burbon] Q; not in F; Duke of Britain ROWE
3.5.10/1335 BURBON] Q; *Brit⟨ain⟩*. F
3.5.11/1336 de] F2; du F1; deu Q; Dieu WILSON (Greg)
3.5.26/1351 Poore may we] KEIGHTLEY; Poore we F1; Poore we may F2; Lest poor we HUMPHREYS
3.5.32/1357 BURBON] THEOBALD; *Brit⟨ain⟩*. F; speech not in Q
3.5.32-3 'To . . . corantos'] STEEVENS (subs.); quotation marks not in F
3.5.40 Delabret] F (Delabreth)
3.5.42 Burgundy] F (Burgonie)
3.5.43/1368 Vaudemont] F2; Vandemont F1
3.5.44 Beaumont] F (Beumont)
3.5.44 Fauconbridge] F (Faulconbridge); Fauconberg CAPELL
3.5.45/1370 Foys] CAPELL; Loys F
3.5.45/1370 Lestrake] WILSON; Leftrale F. (Holinshed's spelling.)
3.5.45 Lestrelles] F (Leftrale). (The modern form of the name.)
3.5.45/1370 Bouicqualt] THEOBALD; Bouicquall F
3.5.45/1370 Charolayes] CAPELL; Charaloyes F
3.5.46/1371 Knigts] POPE 2 (Theobald); Kings F
3.5.54, 64 Rouen] F (Roan)

3.5.60   fore] F (for). Compare *All's Well* 4.4.3 and *Kinsmen* 1.4.49.
3.6.25/1419   Of] Q; and of F
3.6.29/1423   hir] Q (her); his F
3.6.36/1430   an] Q3, F; and Q1. Obvious correction.
3.6.54/1449   executions] Q; execu-|tion F
3.6.55   *fico*] F (*Figo*), Q (figa)
3.6.59-61/1454-6   PISTOLL I . . . thunder?] Q; *Exit.* F (*after* l. 58)
3.6.62/1457   is this . . . of?] Q; this is an arrant counterfeit Rafcall, F
3.6.90/1485   com'st] TAYLOR; cam'ſt F; come Q
3.6.100/1495   reasonnable] F; very reaſonably Q; very reasonable POPE
3.6.100/1495   part, I] F; parts, like you now, | I Q1; parts, | I Q3. Q3's omission might be accidental (across the line-break), or deliberate (because Q1 as it stands is nonsense, probably an error for 'loke you now', 'i' and 'o' being adjacent in the type case). But Q1 adds catch-phrases like this sporadically to Fluellen's speeches, and Q3's compositorial error probably simply undid a Q1 memorial error.
3.6.103   bubuncles] F (bubukles)
3.6.104   o'] F (a)
3.6.109/1504   here] Q; *not in* F
3.6.112/1507   vpbrayded] Q3, F; abraided Q1. Q3 coincidentally alters to Shakespeare's own preference ('Three Studies', 49).
3.6.113/1508   Lenitie] Q (lenitie); Leuitie F
3.6.158/1554   There's] Q3 (there's), F; there is Q1. Metrically required.
3.6.172/1568   to morrow, bid] QF; ~. Bid JACKSON (*conj. in N&Q*, NS 13 (1966), 133-4)
3.7.0.2/1568.2   Burbon] Q; Dolphin F
3.7.7/1575   BURBON Q (*throughout scene*); Dolph⟨in⟩. F (*throughout scene*)
3.7.12/1580   pasteres] F2; poſtures F1
3.7.13/1581   ah ha] TAYLOR; ch'ha F; *Ça, ha* THEOBALD; ha, ha CAPELL
3.7.14   hares] F (hayres)
3.7.14/1582   *che a*] CAPELL; ches F; chez THEOBALD
3.7.20/1588   heat, of] Q3 (heate), F; heate, a Q1. Shakespeare often uses the abbreviation *a* or *o'* for *of*, but *a' the* or *o' the* is comparatively rare. In this case parallelism also supports Q3/F.
3.7.61/1632   had a] Q3, F; had had a Q1. Obvious correction.
3.7.45   *Me*] (*not italicized in* F)
3.7.45   prescribed] F (preſcript)
3.7.58   lief] F (liue)
3.7.63/1634   vomissement] F3; vemiſſement F1
3.7.64/1634   et] ROWE; eſt F
3.7.64/1635   truye] ROWE; leuye F
3.7.88/1660   Duke of *Burbon*] Q; Dolphin F
4.0.16/1743   name.] STEEVENS 2 (Tyrwhitt); nam'd, F
4.0.20   cripple] F (creeple)
4.0.26   lank lean] F (*hyphenated*)
4.0.27/1754   Presented] F; Presenteth HANMER
4.0.46/1773   define,] F2; ~. F1
4.0.47/1774   Night.] ROWE; ~, F
4.1.0.1-2/1780.2   then ⌈Clarence⌉] TAYLOR; Glouceſter F
4.1.3   Good] F (God)
4.1.3/1783   Clarence] TAYLOR; Bedford F
4.1.35.2/1815.2   to him] Q; *not in* F
4.1.36/1816   vous] F; ve Q; va ROWE
4.1.45   heart-of-gold] F (*not hyphenated in* QF)
4.1.50-1   *le roi . . . Leroi*] F (*le Roy . . . Le Roy*)
4.1.66/1846   fewer] F; lewer Q1; lower Q3
4.1.94/1874   Tho.] THEOBALD; Iohn F
4.1.97   wrecked] F (wrackt)
4.1.104   human] F (humane)
4.1.120/1900   alone] COLLIER; ~ : F
4.1.125/1905   minds.] ROWE; ~, F
4.1.149/1930   Seruant] Q3 (ſeruant), F; ſeruants Q1. Obvious correction.
4.1.156/1937   deaths] Q; death F
4.1.157/1937   propose] TAYLOR; purpoſe F; craue Q

4.1.178   mote] F (Moth)
4.1.185/1966   BATES] Q (3. *Lord.*); Will⟨iams⟩. F
4.1.186/1967   ₍ I doe] Q (*subs.*); *Bates.* I doe F.
4.1.210/1991   Heere's] Q3 (Here's), F; Here is Q. The Folio compositor was deliberately wasting space in this line, because 'thine' would not fit at the end and could not be divided; he would have had every incentive to keep the expanded form 'Heere is' if it had stood in the manuscript. Q3 repeatedly contracts such words.
4.1.221   enough] F (enow)
4.1.226/2007   *Exit Souldiers*] Q's placement; *Exit Souldiers* F (*at* 4.1.221/2002)
4.1.228   care-full] F (*not hyphenated*)
4.1.233/2014   What,] KNIGHT; ~ ? F
4.1.242/2023   adoration] F2; Odoration F1
4.1.272/2053   *Hiperiō* F ; *Hiperio* F1
4.1.288/2069   or] MOORE SMITH; of F; if STEEVENS 2 (Tyrwhitt)
4.1.288   ere] MOORE SMITH (or)
4.1.288/2069   numbers,] POPE; ~ : F
4.1.295/2076   haue I] Q; I haue F
4.1.301/2082   ill] TAYLOR; all F
4.1.305/2086   friends] Q; friend F
4.2.0.1/2086.2   Burbon] TAYLOR; Dolphin F
4.2.0.2/2086.2   and Ramburs] TAYLOR; Ramburs, and Beaumont F; *Rambures, and others* CAPELL
4.2.1/2087   Armour, vp,] F2; ~, ~, F1
4.2.2/2088   BURBON] TAYLOR (*throughout scene*); Dolph⟨in⟩. F (*throughout scene*)
4.2.2/2088   *Monte*] F; *Montez à* STEEVENS (Capell)
4.2.2   *Varlet, lacquais*] F (Verlot Lacquay); varlot lackey RIVERSIDE
4.2.4/2090   *Via,*] F; ~ ! THEOBALD
4.2.4   *eaux*] F (ewes)
4.2.4/2090   *terre*] F; *la terre* ROWE
4.2.5/2091   *plus?*] CAPELL; puis, F
4.2.5/2091   *feu*] F; *le feu* ROWE
4.2.6/2092   *Cieu*] MUNRO (Wilson); Cein F; *Ciel* THEOBALD
4.2.11/2097   dout] ROWE; doubt F; doube TAYLOR (*conj.*)
4.2.16   yon] F (yond)
4.2.18   shells] F (ſhales)
4.2.25/2111   gainst] F2; againſt F1
4.2.25/2111   exceptions] F1; exception F3
4.2.35/2121   Sonnance] JOHNSON; Sonuance F
4.2.39   Yon] F (Yond)
4.2.43   bankrupt] F (banqu'rout)
4.2.46/2132   hands] TAYLOR (*conj.* Capell); hand F
4.2.47/2133   drooping] F2; dropping F1
4.2.48   pale dead] F (*hyphenated*)
4.2.49/2135   pald] HUDSON; pale F
4.2.50   chewed] F (chaw'd)
4.2.52/2138   them, all,] TAYLOR; ~, ~, F; ~, ~, ROWE
4.2.60/2146   Guidon.] RANN; Guard: on, F
4.3.0.1/2149.2   Clarence] Q; Bedford F
4.3.0.2/2149.3   Warwick] TAYLOR; Weſtmerland F
4.3.0.3/2149.3   the] TAYLOR; his F
4.3.2/2151   CLARENCE] TAYLOR; Bedf⟨ord⟩. F
4.3.3/2152   WARWICK] Q (*throughout scene*); Weſt⟨merland⟩. F (*throughout scene*)
4.3.4/2153   There's] Q3, F; There is Q1. Metrically necessary.
4.3.6   b'wi'] F (buy)
4.3.8/2157   Clarence] Q; Bedford F
4.3.11, 15/2160, 2164   CLARENCE] TAYLOR; Bedf⟨ord⟩. F; *speeches not in* Q
4.3.13-14/2162-3   And . . . valour] Q's arrangement; F places between 11 and 12
4.3.19/2168   Warwick] Q; Weſtmerland F
4.3.26   ernes] F (yernes)
4.3.34/2183   presently] Q; Weſtmerland F
4.3.44/2193   t'old] TAYLOR; (*conj.* Keightley); old F
4.3.48/2197   And . . . day:] Q; *not in* F
4.3.49/2198   yet] F; yea MALONE (*conj.*)
4.3.59/2208   remembered] ROWE; remembred QF. Although QF is possible metrically, Rowe is certainly better. Shakespeare treats

the word as four syllables at the end of a line at Sonnet 74.12, and given its importance to this speech such emphasis seems appropriate.

4.3.65-6/2214-15 they were not here; | And hold their Manhoods cheape] F; And hold their manhood cheape Q1; They were not there Q3. Q3's 'there' seems inferior to F's 'here', though the correction is perhaps within the reach of a compositor. Taylor ('Three Studies') grouped this with other Q3 interpolations, as of no significance; but unlike the other words and phrases added by Q3 this cannot be motivated by a desire to stretch cast-off copy (see Introduction); moreover, it (*a*) replaces a phrase in Q1, and (*b*) fits a metrical pattern discernible in F but not in the quartos. So we conjecture that the Q1/Q3 variant results from a bungled press correction in Q1, with the added phrase accidentally replacing the half-line it was intended to supplement. For comparable part-lines apparently added as press corrections which survive only in a reprint, compare *Richard III* 1.1.102-3/102-3 and *History of Lear* 20.186/2515. Only five copies of this portion of Q1 survive, so a lost press variant is not improbable.

4.3.106/2255 grasing] F2; crasing Q, F1. See *OED v.*² for the sense ricochet. F is clearly susceptible to Q contamination in this vicinity, and Q could be an easy aural or memorial substitution.

4.3.118/2267 as] TAYLOR; or QF; for HANMER. Taylor (1982) defended this emendation, assuming that the QF errors were independent; this is still possible, but the nearby contamination from Q3 suggests that F may follow Q3 here.

4.3.119/2268 yʳ] Q (your); the F

4.3.125/2274 'em] ROWE; am Q1; Vm Q3, F. As a contraction of *them* Q1's 'am' never appears in the canon, and this Folio line is the only occurrence of 'vm', against 170 examples of *em*, in the entire Folio. *Vm* only appears elsewhere 3 times (*History of Lear* 7.284, 24.25/1292, 2808).

4.3.129/2278 come] TAYLOR (*conj.* Cambridge); come againe F

4.3.131 vanguard] F (Vaward)

4.4.2-11/2284-93 FRENCH SOULDIER ... Ransome.] F (French.); not in Q

4.4.4/2286 Quallitie?] F4 (Quality₍); Qualtitie F1

4.4.4/2286 calino] MALONE; calmie F

4.4.12/2294 miserecorde] F2; miferecordie F1

4.4.12/2294 pitiez] F2 (pitie), Q (petie); pitez F1

4.4.12-13 moi ... 'Moy'] F (moy ... Moy)

4.4.14/2296 Or] HANMER (Theobald); for F

4.4.26 Master] Q; M. F

4.4.27 Master] CAPELL; M. F

4.4.34 à cette heure] F (afture)

4.4.35/2317 gorge] Q3 (roman), F; gage Q1. Obvious correction.

4.4.36-7 oui ... foi, | Peasant,] F (Owy, cuppele gorge permafoy₍ pefant,)

4.4.49/2331 prisonier] F2; prifonner F1

4.4.49/2331 neant-moins] F2; neant-mons F1

4.4.49/2331 luy ci] TAYLOR (Avern-Carr); layt a F1; lui F2; l'avez MALONE

4.4.50/2332 promete] F2; promets F1; promis MALONE

4.4.52/2334 Ie] F2; Ie F1

4.4.53/2335 remerciens] F2; remercious F1

4.4.53-4/2336 le ai tombe] SISSON; le intombe F1; ie ne tombe F2; je tombe RIVERSIDE

4.4.54/2336 mains,] F2; main. F1

4.4.54/2336 comme] TAYLOR (*conj.* Capell); not in F

4.4.54/2336 pense] F2; peufe F1

4.4.55 treis] F (tres)

4.4.55 distingué] F (diftinie)

4.4.63/2345 Suiue] ROWE; Saaue F1; Suave F4

4.5/Sc. 21] In the Folio both the Dauphin and Bourbon appear in this scene; consequently this is the only scene in which the substitution of Bourbon for the Dauphin at Agincourt involves more than the alteration of speech-prefixes. For the Folio version of the scene see Additional Passages. The differences between Q and F are discussed in 'Three Studies', 104-5.

4.5.0.2/2355.1 Burbon] TAYLOR; (*after Q's 'Enter the foure French lords'*); Burbon, Dolphin F

4.5.2/2357 signeur] F2; figueur F1

4.5.2/2357 perdu ... perdu] ROWE; perdia ... perdie F

4.5.3/2358 BURBON] Q; Dol⟨phin⟩. F

4.5.3/2358 Mor du] Q; Mor Dieu F

4.5.4/2359 Reproach] F; Reproach, reproach CAPELL

4.5.6/2361 away.] Since the actor of Gower, one of the reporters, probably doubled as Bourbon in this scene, Q's omission of 4 lines found in F at this point (including a speech by Bourbon and one by the Dauphin, whom Bourbon replaces) presumably represents the text as performed rather than memorial error. See Additional Passages.

4.5.7/2362 ORLEANCE] F; Con⟨ftable⟩. Q

4.5.7/2362 enow] Q3, F; inough Q1. Grammatical correction.

4.5.7-10/2362-5 We are ... Order] Q's *arrangement*; F *places after* 4.5.17/2372.

4.5.10/2365 Order] Q; Order now F

4.5.12/2367 home] Q; hence F

4.5.13/2368 leno] Q; Pander F

4.5.14/2369 by a slaue] Q; a bafe flaue F

4.5.15/2370 contaminated] F; contamuracke Q; contaminate CAPELL

4.5.19/2374.1 Exit omnes] Q; Exit. F

4.6.2/2376 all's] Q3 (als), F; all is Q1. Metrically required.

4.6.14-15/2388-9 face, | And] Q; face. | He F

4.6.15/2389 deare] Q; my F

4.6.22 grip] F (gripe)

4.6.30/2404 had not] Q3, F; not Q1. Obvious correction.

4.6.34/2408 mistfull] THEOBALD (Warburton); mixtfull F. See Jackson. 'Mistful' is not elsewhere recorded before the 19th c., and the unfamiliarity of the word—combined with aural similarity, and the influence of 'compound'—could have caused the Folio substitution.

4.6.37.1/2411.1 The souldiours ... Prisoners] TAYLOR; not in QF

4.6.39/2413 PISTOLL Couple gorge.] Q (Pift.); not in F

4.6.39/2413 Exit omnes] Q; Exit F

4.7.5/2418 there's] Q3, F; there is Q1.

4.7.11/2424 Monmouth. Captaine Gower,] Q (Monmorth. | Captain ~); ~, ~ : F

4.7.15/2428 not] Q3, F; nat Q1. Q1 might be intended as dialect, but 'a' and 'o' are adjacent in the typecase. It seems unwise to distract here from the more important mispronunciation 'pig' (= big = great).

4.7.21 e'en Macedon] F (in *Macedon*); Macedon indeed Q

4.7.23, 110/2436,2524 World] TAYLOR; Orld F; worell Q

4.7.29/2442 alike as] F; fo like, as Q; as like as ROWE

4.7.41/2454 made an end] Q; made F

4.7.52.2-3/2465.2 ⌈Orleance,⌉ and other] TAYLOR; with F

4.7.55 yon] F (yond)

4.7.73/2486 our] TAYLOR; with F; the CAPELL; their MALONE

4.7.78 Jerk] F (Yerke)

4.7.89/2502 Crispian] This edition; Cryfpin Q1; Crifpianus Q3; Crifpianus F. Q1's reading is unmetrical and nonsensical. Taylor ('Three Studies', pp. 50-2) established that 'Crispianus' was a common form of the second brother's name and that Q3 could have been a deliberate correction based on knowledge of the popular saints' story. However, although other forms—Crispinian, Crispinianus—would not fit the metre and so can be dismissed, 'Crispian' would be as acceptable as 'Crispianus'. Indeed, anyone who recognized Q1's error and knew the story would have only two metrical options: 'Crispian' and 'Crispianus'. Neither form appears elsewhere in Q, so the corrector would have to act on his own knowledge or preference. He might have been influenced by Q1's 'Crispines' (4.3.46/2195) and 'Cryspines' (4.3.48/2197), both of which might have suggested the Latin suffix; moreover, the last recorded use of 'Crispian', outside the play, dates from 1577, whereas 'Crispianus' occurred in popular works in the first quarter of the 17th c. Either factor might explain Q3's choice of 'Crispianus', or it may simply have been random. But this may well have been the wrong choice. 'Crispianus' appears nowhere else in Shakespeare's play; 'Crispian' is used 4 times, once in the collocation '*Crispine*

Crispian' (4.3.57/2206). Moreover, Q1's text—which is identical to F's for this speech, barring the final word—is difficult to explain as a compositorial error for 'Crispianus', and equally difficult to explain as a deliberate repetition. But Q1's 'Cryspin' would become 'Cryspian' by the addition of a single type, which a compositor might easily have omitted inadvertently. 'Crispian' therefore better accounts for Q1's error and better accords with Shakespeare's usage elsewhere; it would also have been, c.1622, the more unusual reading. Q3 contamination seems likely. (F was here set by Compositor B, who may also have set this portion of Q3.)

4.7.108/2521   Countryman] Q; Countrymen F
4.7.109/2522   Ieshu] F; Iefus Q1; Iefu Q3. F is suspicious: it agrees with Q3 in the termination, and adopts the anomalous medial 'sh', which Q3 elsewhere imposed (perhaps under the influence of Q1 *Merry Wives*, reprinted as part of the Pavier collection). Compositor B, who elsewhere 'improved' dialect speech, may be responsible for the 'sh' here.
4.7.112/2525   God] Q; Good F
4.7.115/2529   *Exit . . . herald*] CRAIG-BEVINGTON; *Exit Heralds* Q; *not in* F
4.7.123/2537   a liue] CAPELL; aliue F
4.7.127/2541   a liud] TAYLOR; aliue F
4.7.132   gentleman] F (Ientleman)
4.7.135   Beelzebub] F (Belzebub)
4.7.152/2566   were] Q3, F; was Q1. Grammatical correction.
4.7.153/2567   from his] F; off from his Q1; from's Q3. Shakespeare elsewhere has *off from* in prose only once (*Merry Wives* 4.5.63/2312); even in verse, where the redundancy serves a metrical purpose, it occurs only 6 times.
4.7.153/2567-8   any man] F; any do Q1; any Q3. Q3's omission was made for metrical reasons (the Quartos set the speech as verse). But in F's context, adaptation of Q1's variants here and above would produce three end-stopped tetrameters in a row—which seems undesirable in prose.
4.7.156   an] F (and)
4.7.157   does] F (doo's)
4.7.161   An't] F (and)
4.7.161/2575-6   that I would see] TAYLOR; that I might fee F; I would but fee him Q; that I might see it CAPELL
4.7.163   an't] F (and)
4.8.7/2602   the] Q3, F; the the Q1
4.8.10/2605   Gods plud, and his] This edition; 'Sblud F; Gode plut, and his Q1; Gods ~ Q2? Q3. 'God's wounds' and 'God's blood' were the two most objectionable oaths of the period, almost always altered in Folio texts (see Taylor, 'Zounds'); here, 'Sblud might represent a softening of the fuller, more explicit Q1 form. Q1, moreover, makes an unusual, witty, and blasphemous comparison between Christ's blood (which has been spilt) and Williams's (which Fluellen intends to spill). Such creative profanity is uncharacteristic of reporters, and so more probably authorial. Since 'and his' only makes sense in contrast to 'Gods', reducing the profanity would also entail omitting the other two words. Compare *Richard III* 3.7.209-10/2199-2200.
4.8.10   any's] F (anyes)
4.8.20/2620   what is] Q1; What's Q3; what's F. Parallels for both forms of the phrase abound. Even if Q3 did not contaminate F here, Compositor B made similar contractions elsewhere, and here might be particularly tempted to repeat the phrase at 4.8.20/2615. The Q1 reading in F's context usefully distinguishes the King's tone from Warwick's, and makes his speech metrical (as usually elsewhere).
4.8.42/2637   thou] Q3, F; thou thou Q1
4.8.44   An't] F (And)
4.8.52/2647   but as] Q3, F; as Q1. Q1 is possible, but less emphatic, and Shakespeare uses 'but as' in this sense over 30 times elsewhere.
4.8.72/2667   shilling] Q1; filling Q3, F. Q1 has 'shilling' 3 times—here, in place of 'twelve-pence' at 4.8.64/2659, and in place of 'groat' at 5.1.55/2823; in each case Q3 alters to 'filling'. The same compositor probably set both texts here (B), and the dialect spelling is unlikely to be authoritative, whether or not Q3 contaminated F.

4.8.77, 96   Jean] F (Iohn)
4.8.77/2672   Bouchiqualt] THEOBALD; Bouchiquald F
4.8.92   Delabret] F (Delabreth)
4.8.94/2689   Rambures] F; Ranbieres Q1; Rambieres Q3. A coincidental part-correction in Q3. F is confirmed by Holinshed; Q3 cannot result from access to authority, because it leaves the rest of the names in this speech in the mess Q1 made of them.
4.8.95   Great-Master] F (*not hyphenated*)
4.8.95   Guiscard] F (Guichard)
4.8.98   Edouard] F (Edward)
4.8.100/2695   Vaudemont] F2; Vandemont F1
4.8.100/2695   Lestrake] WILSON; Leftrale F. See note to 3.5.45/1370.
4.8.100   Lestrelles] F (Leftrale)
4.8.104/2699   Kyghley] TAYLOR; Ketly F; Kikely WILSON. See Tanselle.
4.8.110-11/2705-6   losse, . . . th'other?] POPE; loffe? . . . th'other, F
4.8.113/2708   we] F2; me F1
4.8.117   an't] F (and)
4.8.121/2716   in] Q; *not in* F
4.8.126   more-happy] F (*not hyphenated*)
5.0.7/2728   there seene] F1; And there being seene F2
5.0.0.10   Pales-in] F (*not hyphenated*)
5.0.10/2731   Maids] TAYLOR; *not in* F1; with F2
5.0.17/2738   Where, . . . him,] POPE; Where, . . . him, F
5.0.29/2750   hy louing] TAYLOR; by louing F; loving ROWE
5.0.39-40/2760-1] *Lacuna marked by this edition*; But these now | We pass in silence over CAPELL. F clearly seems to have omitted a line or more here, perhaps 'and the death | O'th' Dolphin, leape we ouer'.
5.1.5   scald] F (fcauld)
5.1.9   salt] F (fault)
5.1.14/2781   a] Q1; he Q3; hee F. Even if Q3 did not contaminate F here, Q1's colloquialism might have been sophisticated. Compositor A could not get 'cock' on to this line, and so needed to stretch his copy; atypically, he spelled both 'heere' and 'hee', and may have used the full form here for reasons of justification.
5.1.18, 30   Trojan] F (Troian)
5.1.24/2791   appetites] Q3, F; appetite Q1. Q3 also altered Q1 'stomacke' (= F 'affections') to a plural, bringing both words into agreement with the plural 'disgestions' (QF). It is possible that F also sophisticated both terms for similar reasons: Fluellen does mix singulars and plurals in lists at 4.1.73-4/1853-4 and 5.1.43-4/2811-12. But most of Fluellen's lists, in both texts, use plurals consistently, and it seems more likely that Q3 here fortuitously emended to a correct reading.
5.1.25   digestions] F (difgeftions)
5.1.25   does] F (doo's)
5.1.30/2797   thou shalt] Q3, F; thou fhall Q1
5.1.32/2799   in the meane time] F; meane time Q1; But in the meane time Q3. Q3's expansion is part of a more general effort to extend its copy for this page (F4ᵛ), which includes wasting space around stage directions, adding a stage direction, relining the text, and adding 7 words to the dialogue in the bottom half of the page. In this case part of the expansion coincides with Shakespeare's own preference: *mean time* is elsewhere entirely restricted to verse, whereas *in the mean time* occurs 7 times in prose (*Much Ado*, *Dream*, *Hamlet*, *All's Well*, *Kinsmen*). The dissimilarity of contexts in Q and F also makes contamination unlikely.
5.1.38/2806   By Iesu] Q; I fay F
5.1.39/2807-8   and foure nights] Q; *not in* F. The absence of these words from F would be easier to explain if Q had memorially transposed them: if 'foure nights and foure dayes' stood in the manuscript, simple eyeskip could have produced F's 'foure dayes'.
5.1.45.1/2813.1   *Fluellen threatens him*] TAYLOR; *not in* F
5.1.50/2818   do] F. Wordsworth's emendation 'do it' is unnecessary: 'much good do you' occurs, in the speech of ordinary

characters, in Middleton's *No Wit, No Help* 2.1.171, 313, and Middleton and Rowley's *Wit at Several Weapons* 5.1.
5.1.55/2823 hold you] F; *not in* Q1; Looke you now Q3; For Q3's expansion compare 5.1.30/2797. On this page (G1), Q3 wastes space in and around stage directions, mislines, and adds 8 words to the dialogue. This addition is a mere catch-phrase; F's is less predictable and more appropriate, and unlikely to be influenced by Q3's.
5.1.61/2830 I will] Q3, F; ile Q1
5.1.63 b'wi'] F (bu'y), Q (bwy)
5.1.67 begun] F (began)
5.1.76 hussy] F (huſwife)
5.1.77/2847 *Nell*] CAPELL; *Doll* F, Q. Given the evidence of Q3 contamination elsewhere, Q's reading no longer provides secure evidence that the error 'survived into the play as performed' (Taylor, 1982); the earlier association of Doll with 'spital' (2.1.71-4/556-9) might have caused a reporter (rather than the author) to confuse the names.
5.1.78/2848 a malady] F; malady POPE
5.1.85/2855 swere] Q; ſwore F
5.2.0.2/2855.1 *Clarence*] TAYLOR; *Bedford* F
5.2.12/2867 England] F2; Ireland F1. In support of Walter's conjecture that the manuscript read 'Ingland' it may be noted that the spelling occurs in Hand D's addition to *More* (ll. 73, 129).
5.2.42 even-plashed] F (euen pleach'd)
5.2.45 fumitory] F (Femetary)
5.2.50/2905 Sythe, all,] ROWE 3; Sythe, withall, F; scythe, withal, RIVERSIDE. See Jackson. If Shakespeare spelled the first word 'cyth' (see *OED*), it might have been misread 'wyth' and modernized to 'with' (J.J.); Compositor A may have looked at the same word twice, or Shakespeare might inadvertently have written 'cyth' twice.
5.2.54 An all] F (And all); And as CAPELL
5.2.55/2910 wildnesse,] CAPELL; ~. F
5.2.61 diffused] F (defus'd)
5.2.77/2932 curset orie] WILSON; curſelarie F; curſenary Q1; curſorary Q3
5.2.93 Haply] F (Happily)
5.2.108 *Pardonnez*] F (*Pardonne*)
5.2.108/2963 vat] ROWE; wat F

5.2.120/2975 tongeus] F1; tongues F2
5.2.121/2975 is de Princesse] F; is de princess say KEIGHTLEY
5.2.169 *ennemi*] F (*ennemie*)
5.2.171/3027 it is] F, Q3; tis Q1. Parallelism (is it . . . it is) supports Q3/F.
5.2.177/3033 vat] ROWE; wat F
5.2.178/3034 tell thee] Q3, F; tell it thee Q1. For Q1 compare 'tell it him' (*2 Henry IV* 4.3.143/2468) and 'tell it you' (*Romeo* 5.1.21/2596); but the idiom is rare in Shakespeare, and apparently only used for metrical reasons.
5.2.181/3037 suis le possesseur] TAYLOR (*conj.* Fuzier); sur le poſ-|ſeſſion F
5.2.187 parlez] F (parleis)
5.2.188/3045 melieur] ROWE; melieus F1
5.2.202 scrambling] F (skambling)
5.2.215 chère et divine] F (cher & deuin)
5.2.216, 263 majesté] F (Maieſtee). F's spellings are unique in the canon, and so presumably intended to imitate a non-English pronunciation.
5.2.245/3103 de Roy mon pere] F; the King my father Q1; de King my father Q3. Surely coincidental.
5.2.252/3110 abbaisse] F; abaissiez CAMBRIDGE
5.2.252/3110 grandeur] F2; grandeus F1
5.2.253/3111 de vostre Seigneurie] CAMBRIDGE; noſtre Seigneur F
5.2.253/3111 indigne] POPE; indignie F
5.2.254 treis] F (tres)
5.2.260 façon] F (faſhon)
5.2.261/3119 vat] ROWE; wat F
5.2.261/3119 baisse] THEOBALD; buiſſe F
5.2.263/3121 entende] TAYLOR; entendre F. Sidney Fisher points out (privately) that Catherine would not use the infinitive; the error could easily arise from compositorial assimilation to the following 'bettre'.
5.2.267 curtsy] F (curſie)
5.2.312/3172 yᵗ] TAYLOR; *not in* F
5.2.319/3179 neuer] ROWE; *not in* F
5.2.327/3187 WARWICK] TAYLOR; Weſt⟨morland⟩. F
5.2.328/3188 so] TAYLOR; *not in* F1; then F2
5.2.351/3211 ALL] CAPELL; *Lords.* F
5.2.360/3220 Paction] THEOBALD; Pation F

REJECTED QUARTO VARIANTS

THE CRONICLE History of Henry the fift Q
1.2.34/167 your selues, your liues] F; your liues, your faith Q
1.2.44/177 is] F; lyes Q
1.2.161/294 whom] F; Whom like a caytiffe Q
1.2.208/341 wayes] F; seuerall wayes Q
1.2.233/366 waxen] F; paper Q
1.2.243/376 is] F; are Q
1.2.254/387 spirit] F; ſtudy Q
1.2.296/429 weepe,] F; ~, Q
2.1.16-17/501-2 It . . . wrong] F; Yfaith miſtresse quickly did thee great wrong Q
2.1.30/515 terme] F; title Q
2.1.35/520 Lady] F; Lord heeres Corporall *Nims* Q
2.1.69/554 *Couple a gorge*] F; Couple gorge Q
2.1.80/565 face] F; noſe Q
2.1.107/592 profits] F; profit Q
2.1.114/599 quotidian Tertian] F; taſhan contigian Q
2.2.11/618 treachery.] F; trechery. | *Exe*⟨*ter*⟩. O the Lord of *Maſsham*. Q
2.2.29/636 True: those] F; Euen thoſe Q
2.2.52/659 this] F; the Q
2.3.15/812 end] F; ends Q
2.3.24/821 knees] F; knees, and they were as cold as any ſtone Q
2.3.57/855 close . . . command] F; faſt thy buggle boe Q
2.4.4/860 the] F; you Q

2.4.23/879 And] F; But Q
2.4.32/888 Embassie] F; Embaſſage Q
2.4.131/987 the] F; thoſe Q
2.4.137/993 masters] muſters
3.2.22/1092 Cullions.] F; raſcals, will you not vp to the breaches? Q
3.3.92/1220 lye] F; be Q
3.3.128/1256 Succours] F; ſuccour Q
3.3.129/1257 yet not] F; not yet Q
3.6.10/1403 World] F; worell Q
3.6.19/1413 Here is] F; Do you not know him, here comes Q
3.6.29, 30/1423, 1424 blinde . . . blinde] F; Plind . . . plind Q
3.6.35/1429 makes] F; is make Q
3.6.43/1438 little] F; pettie Q
3.6.52/1447 my Brother] F; my owne brother Q
3.6.69/1464 Warres,] F; wars Onely Q
3.6.71/1466 perfect] F (perfit), Q (perfect)
3.6.78/1473 Sute] F; ſhout Q
3.7.59/1630 his] F; her Q
3.7.104/1677 hee sayd] F; said Q
3.7.116/1690 Pox] F; Iogge Q
3.7.123/1696 Tents] F; Tent Q
4.1.44/1824 Then . . . King.] F; O then . . . King? Q
4.1.77/1857 If] F; Godes ſollud if Q
4.1.196/1977 You] F; Mas youle Q

HENRY V

4.3.10/2159 And my kind Kinsman] F; My Lord of *Warwicke* Q
4.3.12/2161 EXETER] F (*Exe.*); *Clar⟨ence⟩*. Q
4.3.52/2201 his mouth] F; their mouthes Q
4.4.27/2309 firke . . . ferret] F; ferit . . . ferke Q
4.5.7/2362 ORLÉANCE] F (*Orl.*); *Con⟨stable⟩*. Q
4.5.17/2372 liues] F; liues | Vnto thefe Englifh, or elfe die with fame Q
4.7.1/2414 Kill] F; Godes plud kil Q
4.7.6/2419 ha'] F; haue Q
4.7.43/2456 kild] F; is kill Q
4.7.45/2458 turn'd] F; is turne Q
4.7.66/2479 How now] F; Gods will Q
4.7.138/2552 blacke] F; too blacke Q
4.8.56/2651 made] F; had made Q
5.1.81/2851 Ile] F; will I Q
5.2.83-5/2938-40 Vnckle . . . *Huntington*] F; Lords Q

INCIDENTALS

219 So that,] ~, ~ˌ F   301 begin.] begia   307 then] theu   373 meaning] meauing   418 husbands] hnŝbands   471 dye,] ~. F   582 course.] ~ˌ   608 traitors.] ~ˌ   651 much] mueh   671 Knight,] ~ : F   703 vse:] ~ ?   744 suspition.] ~, F   744 thee,] ~. F   769 sentence.] ~ˌ F   848 Yoke-fellowes] ~-|~   849 Horse-Leeches] ~-|~   1277 *doyts, mays*] ~ˌ ~, F   1292 *maues*ˌ] ~,   1828 heart-string] ~-|~   2087 Armour, vp] ~ˌ ~, F   2121 Sonnance] Sonuance F   2126 Ill-fauor'dly] Ill-fauoredly F   2160 thee.] ~ :   2161 to day:] ~.   2197 Crispines] Q (*roman*)   2336 *mains*,] ~.   2377 Maiesty.] ~ˌ   2416 offert;] ~ˌ   2425 what] What   2429 great] grear   2435 porne] F (*text*); ~. F (*c.w.*)   2477 Liege.] ~ˌ   2554 law.] ~ˌ   2557 So,] ~, F   2738 Where,] ~, F   2781 Turky-cock] ~-|~   2582-3 Turky-cocks] ~-|~   2995 spoken,] ~.   3111-12 seruiteur. Excuse moy,] ~ˌ excufe moy.

FOLIO STAGE DIRECTIONS

Pro.0.1/0.1 Enter Prologue.
Pro.35/34 Exit.
1.1.0.1/34.1 Enter the two Bishops of Canterbury and Ely.
1.1.99/133 Exeunt.
1.2.0.1-3/133.1-2 Enter the King, Humfrey, Bedford, Clarence, | Warwick, Westmerland, and Exeter.
1.2.6.1-2/139.1 Enter two Bishops.
1.2.233.1/366.1 Enter Ambassadors of France.
1.2.297.1/430.1 Exeunt Ambassadors.
1.2.310/443.1 Exeunt.
2.0.0.1/443.2 Flourish. Enter Chorus.
2.0.4.2/485 Exit
2.1.0.1/485.1 Enter Corporall Nym, and Lieutenant Bardolfe.
2.1.24.1/509.1 Enter Pistoll, & Quickly.
2.1.77.1/562.1 Enter the Boy.
2.1.85/570 Exit
2.1.94.1/579.1 Draw
2.1.111.2/596.2 Enter Hostesse.
2.2.0.1-2/607.2 Enter Exeter, Bedford, & Westmerland.
2.2.11.1-2/618.1-2 Sound Trumpets. | Enter the King, Scroope, Cambridge, and Gray.
2.2.178.1/785.1 Exit.
2.2.190.1/797.1 Flourish.
2.3.0.1-2/797.2-3 Enter Pistoll, Nim, Bardolph, Boy, and Hostesse.
2.3.58/856 Exeunt
2.4.0.1/856.1 Flourish.
2.4.0.1-3/856.1-2 Enter the French King, the Dolphin, the Dukes | of Berry and Britaine.
2.4.64.1/920.1 Enter a Messenger.
2.4.75/931 Enter Exeter.
2.4.140.1/996.1 Flourish.
2.4.146.1/1002.1 Exeunt.
2.4.146.1-3.0.0.1/1002.1-2 Flourish. Enter Chorus.
3.0.33.1/1035.1 Alarum, and Chambers goe off.
3.0.35/1037 Exit.
3.1.0.1-2/1037.1-2 Enter the King, Exeter, Bedford, and Gloucester. | Alarum: Scaling Ladders at Harflew.
3.1.34.1/1071.1 Alarum, and Chambers goe off.
3.2.0.1/1071.2 Enter Nim, Bardolph, Pistoll, and Boy.
3.2.20.1/1090.1 Enter Fluellen.
3.2.28.1/1098 Exit.
3.2.54/1125 Exit.
3.3.0.1-2/1125.1 Enter Gower.
3.3.18.1/1144.1 Enter Makmorrice, and Captaine Iamy.
3.3.78.1/1206.1 A Parley.
3.3.83/1211 Exit.
3.3.83.1-2/1211.1-2 Enter the King and all his Traine before the Gates.
3.3.126.1/1254.1 Enter Gouernour.
3.3.141.1-2/1269.1-2 Flourish, and enter the Towne.
3.4.0.1-2/1269.3-4 Enter Katherine and an old Gentlewoman.
3.4.57.1/1325.1 Exit.
3.5.0.1-3/1325.2-3 Enter the King of France, the Dolphin, the | Constable of France, and others.
3.5.68.1/1393.1 Exeunt.
3.6.0.1/1393.2-3 Enter Captaines, English and Welch, Gower | and Fluellen.
3.6.18.1/1412.1 Enter Pistoll.
3.6.59.1/1454.1 Exit. (after 3.6.57/1452; see textual notes)
3.6.88.1-2/1483.1-2 Drum and Colours. Enter the King and his | poore Souldiers.
3.6.114.1/1510.1 Tucket. Enter Mountioy.
3.6.172/1568 Exeunt.
3.7.0.1-2/158.1-2 Enter the Constable of France, the Lord Ramburs, | Orleance, Dolphin, with others.
3.7.87/1659 Exit.
3.7.121.1/1694.1 Enter a Messenger.
3.7.153/1727 Exeunt.
4.0.0.1/1727.1 Chorus.
4.0.53/1780.1 Exit.
4.1.0.1-2/1780.2 Enter the King, Bedford, and Gloucester.
4.1.12.1/1792.1 Enter Erpingham.
4.1.35.1/1815.1 Exeunt. (after 4.1.34/1814)
4.1.35.2/1815.2 Enter Pistoll.
4.1.64.1/1844.1 Exit. (after 4.1.63/1843)
4.1.64.2-3/1844.2-3 Manet King.
4.1.64.2/1844.2 Enter Fluellen and Gower.
4.1.82.1/1862.1 Exit.
4.1.84.1-2/1864.1-2 Enter three Souldiers, Iohn Bates, Alexander Court, | and Michael Williams.
4.1.226/2007 Exit Souldiers. (after 4.1.221/2002)
4.1.281.1/2062.1 Enter Erpingham.
4.1.285/2066 Exit.
4.1.302.1/2083.1 Enter Gloucester.
4.1.305.1/2086.1 Exeunt.
4.2.0.1-2/2086.2 Enter the Dolphin, Orleance, Ramburs, and | Beaumont.
4.2.6.1/2092.1 Enter Constable.
4.2.13.1/2099.1 Enter Messenger.
4.2.37.1/2123.1 Enter Graundpree.
4.2.63/2149.1 Exeunt.

HENRY V

4.3.0.1-3/2149.2-3 *Enter Gloucester, Bedford, Exeter, Erpingham | with all his Hoast: Salisbury, and | Westmerland.*
4.3.16/2165 *Enter the King.*
4.3.67.1/2216.1 *Enter Salisbury.*
4.3.78.1/2227.1 *Tucket. Enter Montioy.*
4.3.129.1/2277 *Exit.* (after 4.3.128/2276)
4.3.129.2/2279.1 *Enter Yorke.*
4.3.133/2282 *Exeunt.*
4.4.0.1/2282.1 *Alarum. Excursions. | Enter Pistoll, French Souldier, Boy.*
4.4.73/2355 *Exit.*
4.5.0.1-2/2355.1 *Enter Constable, Orleance, Burbon, Dolphin, | and Ramburs.*
4.5.5.1/2360.1 *A short Alarum.*
4.5.19/2374.1 *Exit.*
4.6.0.1-2/2374.2-3 *Alarum. Enter the King and his trayne, | with Prisoners.*
4.6.34.1/2408.1 *Alarum*
4.6.39/2413 *Exit* (after 4.6.38/2412; see textual notes)
4.7.0.1/2413.1 *Enter Fluellen and Gower.*
4.7.52.1-3/2465.1-3 *Alarum. Enter King Harry and Burbon | with prisoners. Flourish.*
4.7.63.1/2476.1 *Enter Montioy.*
4.7.113/2527 *Enter Williams.*
4.7.149/2563 *Exit.*
4.7.166/2581 *Exit.*
4.7.180/2595 *Exeunt.*
4.8.0.1/2595.1 *Enter Gower and Williams.*
4.8.1.1/2596.1 *Enter Fluellen.*
4.8.9.1/2604.1 *Strikes him.*
4.8.19.1-2/2614.1 *Enter Warwick and Gloucester.*
4.8.23.1/2618.1 *Enter King and Exeter.* (after 4.8.24/2619)
4.8.72.1/2667.1 *Enter Herauld.*
4.8.126.1/2721.1 *Exeunt.*
5.0.0.1/2721.2 *Enter Chorus.*
5.0.46.1/2767.1 *Exit.*
5.1.0.1/2767.2-3 *Enter Fluellen and Gower.*
5.1.13.1/2780.1 *Enter Pistoll.*
5.1.28/2795 *Strikes him.*
5.1.64/2833 *Exit*
5.1.75.1/2845 *Exit*
5.1.85/2855 *Exit.*
5.2.0.1-5/2855.1-4 *Enter at one doore, King Henry, Exeter, Bedford, Warwicke, | and other Lords. At another, Queene Isabel, | the King, the Duke of Bourgougne, and | other French.*
5.2.98/2953 *Exeunt omnes. | Manet King and Katherine.*
5.2.278.1-2/3137.1-2 *Enter the French Power, and the English | Lords.*
5.2.353.1/3213.1 *Flourish.*
5.2.369.1/3229.1 *Senet. Exeunt.*
Epi.0.1/3229.2 *Enter Chorus.*

JULIUS CAESAR

Julius Caesar (BEPD 403) was one of the sixteen plays entered in the Stationers' Register by Edward Blount and Isaac Jaggard on 8 November 1623. The First Folio is the only authoritative text. The play was exceptionally well printed; it has mostly regular speech-prefixes, and was provided with act divisions. Work on the text began with two compositors, A and B, but the former gave up his regular stints after setting three pages. Four pages show press variants; these are mostly minor, but on one page (ll5) a handful of substantive corrections were made. The alteration of '*Loud Alarums*' at 5.5.23.1/2393.1, which appears satisfactory, to '*Low Alarums*' strongly suggests that here at least the copy was consulted, and this is probably true of other corrections on the page.

In a number of places F prints divided verse lines which have sometimes been thought to preserve an expressive authorial feature of the printer's copy. In his edition, Maurice Charney usually preserves the Folio arrangement. However, most split verse lines can be explained as necessary breaks where a line would not fit the Folio measure, compositorial space-wasting to follow the requirements of casting off, or relineation influenced by syntax characteristic of Compositor A. In this edition the same criteria for lineation have been followed as in other plays.

The copy for F must have been well ordered and legible, and did not give rise to the features associated with foul papers. Though directions such as '*Enter Cæsar and his Traine.*' (1.2.178.1/253.1), '*Enter Brutus in his Orchard.*' (2.1.0.1/562.1) and '*Enter Brutus and goes into the Pulpit.*' (3.2.0.1/1387.2) are probably Shakespeare's words, they could easily have survived in a prompt-book. The prevalence of directions calling for music and other sound effects and for specific properties, actions, and staging arrangements suggests theatrical annotation. In the penultimate line of 2.1/Sc. 4 F calls for '*Thunder*'. This is the only such effect in the scene, but 2.2./Sc. 5 opens with '*Thunder & Lightning.*' The first direction looks like an addition supplied by a later hand. This may provide the key to interpreting '*March.*' at 5.1.20/2117. Elsewhere, '*Low March within.*' (4.2.24.1/1763.1) clearly requires a sound effect, a marching drumbeat. '*March.*' at 5.1.20/2117 is immediately followed on the next line with '*Drum. Enter Brutus, Cassius, & their Army.*' Thus '*March.*' is probably an annotation anticipating '*Drum.*', as in the extant prompt-book for *Two Noble Ladies* (MSR, ll. 1662–4), where an annotator has marked 'Low March. | w^{thin}' opposite the scribe's 'A drum far off'.

A further sign of theatrical annotation lies in the preparation of the text for doubling at least one actor's part. As Wilson first suggested and Fredson Bowers ('The Copy for Shakespeare's *Julius Caesar*') affirmed, it appears that Ligarius had to be played by the same (lean) actor as Cassius. As a result, Ligarius has disappeared from the group of conspirators in the assassination scene (3.1/Sc. 8). In 2.2/Sc. 5, a scene in which Ligarius does appear, Cassius is in F conspicuously absent from the group of conspirators who meet Caesar (it was Cassius who earlier suggested that all the conspirators, including himself, should be present). Though Publius is last named in the entry direction, this previously unknown character is the first to greet Caesar. Publius has evidently been introduced as a substitute for Cassius. The editorial implications are not straightforward. F presumably has the merit of representing the play as performed. Nevertheless, F's disposition of characters seems particularly awkward and improvised. If the copy for F was either a late prompt-book or a transcript of one, as the presence of act divisions might suggest, the doubling of Cassius and Ligarius could belong to a revival staged when the original actors were no longer available. Even if the doubling dates back to earliest performances, it is likely that the company's composition was not as Shakespeare had envisaged: under normal circumstances, he would have known the principal actors at his disposal. An editor might feel justified in retaining F, but, as Bowers argued, the alternative should be considered. Cassius easily and convincingly replaces Publius in 2.2/Sc. 5; Ligarius presents a greater problem, as any lines he spoke in 3.1/Sc. 8, or any lines spoken to him, are lost. In this edition both characters have been restored. No attempt has been made to fabricate dialogue for Ligarius, or to indicate lacunae where dialogue may have existed.

Although F is on the whole well furnished with stage directions, there are deficiencies. Bowers ('The Copy for Shakespeare's *Julius Caesar*') drew attention to the absent exit for senators and plebeians in 3.1/Sc. 8. A number of difficulties are concentrated in 4.2/Sc. 12. As Wilson noted, the scene's first entry direction causes confusion. In F it reads '*Drum. Enter Brutus, Lucillius, and the Army. Titinius and Pindarus meete them.*' Here the characters are almost certainly wrongly grouped, and the direction is inconsistent with the action that follows. Wilson suggested that Lucillius leads Brutus' army on stage, meeting Brutus who emerges from his tent. But it is implausible that Brutus' 'Army' should have visited Cassius, and unconvincing that Brutus should give the order to stand to an approaching army. Wilson presupposed a static scene location which, as 3.1/Sc. 8 demonstrates, is not a necessary convention in the Elizabethan theatre. (There are no indications that an actual structure representing Brutus' tent is erected on the stage, as there are in *Richard III*.) The most plausible arrangement is that Lucillius, Titinius (see textual note), and Pindarus meet Brutus and the army; Lucillius has visited Cassius as Brutus' representative, and Titinius and Pindarus return with him, representing Cassius. The scene specifically becomes Brutus' tent only when the army leaves the stage. At the scene's opening, Lucius must be amongst the army, but as a boy is unlikely to pass on the order to stand, the stage direction and prefix cannot be resolved by assuming that scribe or compositor took Lucius to be Lucillius.

Inferably F preserves a grouping that Shakespeare made before he had fully realized how the action of the scene would progress. In the lines that follow Lucillius has two mutually incompatible roles, the main one being to report from Cassius' camp, and the secondary one, though the first to be established, to pass on the order to stand in Brutus' army. Lucillius' 'Giue the word ho, and Stand' immediately after Brutus' 'Stand ho' is consistent with the role implied by F's stage direction. Shakespeare let the only named soldier in Brutus' army pass on the order to stand. Either the arrangement was not altered, or a subsequent annotation was disregarded at a later stage of transmission. This edition emends the anomaly by attributing the order to an unnamed soldier.

From their initial sketching in 4.2/Sc. 12, the roles of Pindarus and Titinius develop in ways that differ from first suggestions. Pindarus in 4.2/Sc. 12 is a responsible and well-respected officer, while the silent Titinius is appointed to guard Brutus' tent with the serving-boy Lucius. Later, Titinius is entrusted to a dangerous and responsible task, and is described by Cassius as 'my best Friend', whilst Pindarus emerges as a bondman who is addressed as 'Sirrah'. The Parthian Pindarus somewhat ignominiously runs away after killing Cassius, whereas Titinius plays 'a Roman part' when he finds Cassius dead and kills himself. These later actions are largely determined by Shakespeare's source material; but in the earlier scene, where North's Plutarch gives no mention of these characters, Shakespeare was evidently uncertain as to their proper roles.

This interpretation justifies the text in F at 4.2.52-4/1789-91, where editors commonly switch the names and subsequent roles of Lucillius and Lucius, mainly on the grounds of social propriety. The supposed transposition in F is not as simple as usually considered. But if Titinius starts as a vaguely defined low-ranking character, there is no objection to Lucius guarding the tent with him.

A further characteristic of the text in 4.2/Sc. 12 is a supposed revision. Brents Stirling has claimed that variant speech-prefixes for Cassius are indications of revised passages in the copy manuscript. It has long been suspected that one of the two passages concerned with Portia's death (4.2.198-211/1935-48 and 4.2.235-46/1972-83) must be a revision, the original passage remaining accidentally uncancelled. This theory was first put forward to account for Brutus' allegedly peculiar behaviour whereby in the second passage he seems ignorant of Portia's death after himself telling Cassius of it in the first. The variants '*Caf.*' and '*Caff.*' in place of the usual '*Caffi.*' appeared to confirm 4.2.198-211/1935-48 as a later addition in the copy. The area of variant speech-prefixes implied a revision beginning at the Poet's entry (4.2.179.1/1916.1) and including 4.2.220/1957 (though necessarily excluding Titinius and Messala's entry and Brutus' intervening speech, these being structurally necessary to the original scene). Stirling claimed that similar speech-prefix variation for Cassius in 2.1/Sc. 4 indicates a complete revision of that scene, the extant version being a conflation of two earlier scenes.

However, Jowett demonstrates that the mechanics of typesetting account for the variant prefixes. The usual form '*Caffi.*' was abandoned when Compositor B had no '*ffi*' ligatures available, or when Compositor A, setting part of 2.1, had an inadequate supply. Confirmation is given by the occurrences of '*fsi*' as separate letters; these coincide with the variant speech-prefixes. The accepted view of revision in Act 4 can only be based on an impression of inconsistency in the representation of Brutus' character. Clayton amongst others has argued for the dramatic coherence of F. As the Folio text is defensible, there are no adequate grounds for assuming that revision took place. There is even less basis for believing that 2.1/Sc. 4 was revised.

Demonstration of revision was central to Bowers's hypothesis for the printer's copy. It illustrated use of an 'intermediate transcript', a fair copy of the author's draft made as a working document for preparing the text for the theatre, and the copy for the annotated prompt-book itself. The supposed revision and the annotated stage directions allegedly show this process. Once it is recognized that revision cannot be assumed, the only remaining reason for postulating an intermediate transcript is the inadequacy of some stage directions for theatrical use. But in surviving prompt-books some essential directions were omitted and some problems of staging were left unresolved. Given that the printer's copy was clean and legible, a manuscript considered to have inadequate stage directions could simply have had directions added, so saving the otherwise unnecessary labour of producing a new transcript. The printer's copy may reasonably be assumed to have been the prompt-book itself, or a transcript of it.

Occasional Italianate name-endings replacing the more usual -*us* forms (see textual note to 1.2.5/80), and the forms '*Varrus*' and '*Claudio*' varying historical Varro and Claudius, do not derive from North and are probably Shakespearian, as also is '*Mur(r)ellus*', F's consistent variation of North's '*Marullus*'. In this edition, instead of using North's variably accurate forms as a flexible yardstick to establish 'standard' forms, the variants are retained. F's '*Calphurnia*' remains in the old-spelling text, but is treated as an indifferent but misleading variant in the modernized text, where *Calpurnia* is read. Apart from these proper names, characteristic Shakespearian spellings have not been noted in F.

A final feature of F is its omission of the end of the line recorded and ridiculed by Jonson, '[Know Caesar doth not wrong] but with just cause' (3.1.47/1134). Jonson mocks this apparent self-contradiction in *Discoveries* and the Prologue to *The Staple of News* (1625), testifying not only that Shakespeare actually wrote the missing four words, but also, presumably, that he did not blot them out. The joke's continuing currency after the publication of F may suggest that the full line was still spoken in stage productions. It appears either that Shakespeare added the words after the copy for F had been prepared (which seems unlikely), or that they were omitted or deliberately deleted from the text in the printing house, or that Shakespeare or his successors in the theatre themselves latterly deleted the line. This edition departs from usual editorial procedure by including the missing words recorded by Jonson, though the words 'Caesar thou dost me wrong', attributed in *Discoveries* to Metellus, are excluded as they may simply gloss Metellus' earlier speech.

In this edition, the editorial scene-break after 4.2.54/1791, generally recognized as an error but retained, has been abandoned. Line references to 4.3/Sc. 13 may be found in 4.2/Sc. 12 in this edition by adding 52 to the traditional line number.

In other respects the scene divisions are the usual ones, as established by the eighteenth-century editors; the act divisions are those of F.

A number of unauthoritative quartos were published in the late seventeenth century, some undated. One of the undated quartos, known as Q5, might be early eighteenth-century, and indeed may have appeared after Rowe's edition of 1709.

J.J./(S.W.W.)

WORKS CITED

Bowers, Fredson, 'The Copy for Shakespeare's *Julius Caesar*', *South Atlantic Bulletin*, 43 (1978), 23–36
—— 'Establishing Shakespeare's Text: Poins and Peto in *1 Henry IV*', *SB* 34 (1981), 189–98
Charney, Maurice, ed., *The Tragedy of Julius Caesar* (1969)
Clayton, Thomas, 'Shall Brutus Never Taste of Portia's Death But Once?', *SEL* 23 (1983), 237–55
Craik, G. L., *The Language of Shakespeare: Illustrated in a Philological Commentary on his 'Julius Caesar'* (1857)
D., J., *N&Q* (6 October 1877), p. 263
Dorsch, T. S., ed., *Julius Caesar*, Arden (1955)
Herr, J. G., *Scattered Notes on the Text of Shakespeare* (1879)
Humphreys, Arthur, ed., *Julius Caesar*, Oxford (1984)
Jowett, John, 'Ligature Shortage and Speech-prefix Variation in *Julius Caesar*', *The Library*, VI, 6 (1984), 244–53
MacMillan, Michael, ed., *The Tragedy of Julius Caesar*, Arden (1902)
Sanders, Norman, ed., *Julius Caesar*, New Penguin (1967)
Stirling, Brents, '*Julius Caesar* in Revision', *SQ* 13 (1962), 188–205
Wilson, John Dover, ed., *Julius Caesar*, New (1949)

TEXTUAL NOTES

Title *The Tragedie of Iulius Cæsar*] F (*head title*) (THE TRAGEDIE OF | IVLIVS CÆSAR), F (*running title*); *Iulius Cæsar* S.R.
1.1.18/18 mean'st] F; meanest DORSCH. Dorsch seems right in regarding 1.1.18–19/18–19 as a verse line, but the emendation is not necessary. F gives a five-foot line with extra stressed initial syllable and feminine ending. The former is an acceptable licence, especially where the previous line ends in an unstressed syllable (giving here, in effect, a prose-verse bridge). 'Meanst' is more abrupt and dramatically appropriate.
1.1.23/23 withal,] F; with all. CAPELL
1.1.37/37 Pompey? ... oft,] ROWE 3; ~, ... ~? F
1.1.61 whe'er] F (where)
1.2.0.4/75.4 after ... Flauius] The tribunes have no role in the scene, and were omitted by some earlier editors. Wilson believed they provided a 'background of contempt', and their silence may indicate their impotence (they are later, ambiguously, described as having been 'put to silence'—1.2.286/362). Their re-entry where F and all editors supply a scene-break is not a problem: '*after them*' indicates the main ceremonial entry as intervening dramatic action.
1.2.5/80 Antonio's] F; Antonius POPE. 'Antonio' occurs at 1.2.6/81, 1.2.8/83, 1.2.191/266, and 1.3.37/435, and 'Octauio's' at 3.1.278.1/1365.1 and 5.2.4/2227. Shakespeare may sometimes, though not in all cases, have introduced the '-o' form for the sake of a euphonious genitive. The emendation *Antony('s)* is made in most editions. As a regularization, this represses Shakespeare's variety of form and probably misrepresents Elizabethan attitudes to classical subject matter. Two other possible explanations should be discounted. First, that a quirk of penmanship led to misreading. This would be unlikely to apply to both the medial *o* of the genitives and the terminal *o* of other cases. Second, '*us*' ligature shortage. In at least some examples there was demonstrably no such problem. And the '-o' forms would be a desperate expedient (especially for the genitives, where three characters would stand for the ligature) when separate '*us*' can be set up, as in other names they often demonstrably were in cases of ligature shortage.
1.2.11–12/86–7 remember; ... this,] ROWE; ~, ... ~; F
1.2.74/149 Laughter] F; laugher ROWE
1.2.104/179 Saide Cæsar] This edition (G.T.); *Cæsar* faide F. In F the reversed first and second foot gives a double metrical anomaly. Either scribe or compositor could have transposed, especially as F's word-order is the more common one.
1.2.114 Ay] F (I). The pronoun is often read.
1.2.129 Alas] Often understood as Cassius' own ironic comment.
1.2.140/215 were] This edition; are F. *OED* gives *at sometime* as meaning 'At one time; in former times, formerly'. This set expression is more fitting than *at some time* (vaguely 'at a certain time'). Cassius' theme is that men have lost the independence they once had. *OED*'s last instance of *at sometime* is 1579. This is near enough the date of *Caesar* to suggest that it could have been still current. But it may have been unfamiliar by 1623; this would facilitate corruption from 'were' to 'are'.
1.2.156/231 Walles] ROWE; Walkes F. Copy 'le' could easily be misread 'k' by scribe or compositor (and the spelling subsequently normalized). A sympathetic gloss on *wide walks* such as 'extensive strolling-places', when put in context, only shows up the improbability of this being the correct reading.
1.2.167/242 not (so with] THEOBALD; not fo (with F
1.2.245 chapped] F (chopt)
1.2.248 swooned] F (fwoonded)
1.2.251 swoon] F (fwound)
1.2.254/330 like,] ROWE; ~, F
1.2.301 digest] F (difgeft)
1.3.28 Hooting] F (Howting)
1.3.30 'These ... natural'] F has no quotation marks. Editors usually take the line to be a single quotation.
1.3.128/526 In Fauors] Q1691; Is Fauors F; Is feav'rous ROWE/Q5; is favour'd CAPELL
2.1.15/577 him,] ROWE (*subs.*); ~, F
2.1.40/602 Ides] THEOBALD; firſt F
2.1.67/629 of] F2; of a F1
2.1.83/645 putte,] DYCE 2 (Coleridge); path, F1; path, F2. Kittredge supplies a unique parallel for *path* used intransitively: 'Their pleasant course straung traces hath, | On tops of trees that groundles path' (1578). But this example is a piece of conceited language where the use of *path* seems to be deliberately exceptional in order to draw attention to the paradox expressed. Here, on the other hand, the oddness of 'path' detracts from the clause, already subordinate, which holds the main content ('thy natiue semblance on'). Sisson describes 'putt'/'path' as 'a misreading for which there is a very probable pattern of writing'; this is certainly true of 'u'/'a', but less certainly of 'tt'/'th'. More likely is 'tte'/'tth', 'patth' being an attested 16th-c. spelling.
2.1.96/658 Cinna, this] CAPELL; this, Cinna F. The emendation makes a verse line of F's line of prose in a verse passage.
2.1.121 women,] F (~.). F punctuates similarly at 2.1.135 and 4.1.37.
2.1.135 oath;] F (~.)
2.1.212 eighth] F (eight)
2.1.236 You've] F (Y'haue)
2.1.245 wafture] F (wafter). Probably a Shakespearian coinage: see *OED*.
2.1.254 you,] F. Alternatively modernized with a comma, giving vocative 'Brutus'; similarly with 'gentle', 2.1.278/840.
2.1.266/828 his] F2; hit F1
2.1.279/841 the] F2; tho F1
2.1.308/870 that] F; there that POPE; that that CAPELL
2.1.312/874 LIGARIUS] F (Cai⟨us⟩.). Similarly throughout scene.

2.1.333/895] To the right of 'on' F has the stage direction *'Thunder.'* See Wilson, Sisson, and Introduction.

2.2.19/914 fight] F; fought WHITE

2.2.23/918 do] F1; did F2

2.2.46/941 are] CAPELL (Thirlby); heare F; were THEOBALD. Sisson's defence of 'were' deserves consideration, but presupposes that 'weare' was an acceptable past-tense spelling (*OED* only gives it for the subjunctive). Dorsch posits 'hear' as 'are styled, are reputed'; this is not convincing. Brooks, in Dorsch's edition, conjectured intermediate stages of error: 'He are' (scribe), then 'We He are' (correcting annotator), hence 'We he are' (compositor, before correction). Such a process would have been easier if the first letter of the line was not capitalized in the manuscript. Alternatively, 'we are' may have just looked sufficiently similar to 'heare' to induce a single-stage error involving an element of dittography.

2.2.81/976 Of] HANMER; And F. An easy error in the context of repeated 'and', one beginning the line directly above. The repetitions in F are themselves suspicious; the present 'And' considerably weakens the sense.

2.2.107.1-2/1002.1-2 ⌈*Cassius,*⌉ *Brutus . . . and Cynna*] This edition; *Brutus . . . Cynna, and Publius* F. See Introduction.

2.2.108, 109/1003, 1004 *Cassius*] This edition; *Publius* F

2.2.109/1004 CASSIUS] This edition; *Pub⟨lius⟩.* F

2.2.126/1021 me,] In some copies of F followed by full stop or irregular inking.

2.4.30-1 lady. If . . . me,] F (∼, if . . . ∼:)

2.4.33 harms] F (harme's)

3.1.0.1-5/1087.2-6 *Enter . . . Senators*] For the editorial grouping of characters, see *Re-Editing,* p. 73.

3.1.0.4/1087.5 *Ligarius*] This edition; *not in* F. See Introduction.

3.1.39/1126 lawe] MALONE (Johnson); lane F

3.1.47/1134 but with iust cause:] This edition (*following* Ben Jonson, '*Discoveries*'); *not in* F. See Introduction. F's line-break is after 'cause'.

3.1.102/1190 CASKA] F (*Cask.*); *Cass⟨ius⟩.* POPE

3.1.114/1202 States] F2; State F1

3.1.116/1204 lyes] F2; lye F1

3.1.175/1263 unstrunge] This edition; in ſtrength F; no strength CAPELL; unfraught ANON. (*conj. in* Cambridge). Editors' attempts to make sense of F's perverse reading have not been notably successful. Humphreys records the conjectures 'unstrengthened' and—the basis for the present reading—'unstringed'. Though the latter is found in *Richard II* 1.3.156/435 (probably for the sake of its extra syllable), the only form of the verb *string* in Shakespeare is *strung*; 'vnstrunge' might fairly easily be read 'in strengt'. Humphreys considers the unstringing of arms 'a forced metaphor', but the sense of *string* 'to make tense, brace, give vigour or tone to (the nerves, sinews, the mind, its ideas or impressions, etc.)' (*OED, v.* 3) was already established in the language, and Shakespeare repeatedly used the noun *string* to mean 'fibre, nerve, tendon'. There is no difficulty if 'Armes' takes the primary sense of the limbs (as suggested by 'receiue you in'), not armour and weapons. 'Vnstrunge' will inevitably suggest the more literal meaning of relaxing a bow (an arm of the other kind) or a musical instrument. The latter is the sense in *Two Gentlemen* 3.2.77/1470, but with a glance at *OED*'s sense 3: 'For *Orpheus* Lute, was strung with Poets sinewes'. The lute's ability to 'soften steel' (3.2.78/1471) may be compared with the 'leaden points' of the conspirators' swords and the inferably soft 'temper' of their hearts.

3.1.175/1263 malice] F; welcome COLLIER MS (*conj.*); amity HUDSON (Singer). Wilson found 'amitie' 'graphically easy'.

3.1.200/1288 Coarse?] ROWE; ∼, F

3.1.200 corpse] F (Coarſe)

3.1.209 heart] F (Hart)

3.1.210 strucken] F (ſtroken)

3.1.237 utter?] F (∼.)

3.1.261/1348 hand] F; hands WHITE (Becket)

3.1.265/1352 limbes] F; Loins COLLIER MS (*conj.*)

3.1.278.1/1365.1 *Octauio's*] F; *Octavius'* POPE. See note to 1.2.5/80.

3.1.286/1372 for] F2; from F1

3.1.288/1374 Began] F; Begin HANMER

3.1.294/1381 corpse] F (courſe)

3.2.1/1388 ALL THE PLEBEIANS] F (*Ple.*). The absence of a distinguishing number suggests that all the plebeians speak, as does the plural pronoun.

3.2.40.1/1427.1 *others*] Antony's revised plan was for Octavius' servant to help bear the body and witness the following episode (3.1.293-300/1380-7). The action reverts to Antony's first idea (3.1.289-93/1376-80): evidently the same servant returns from Octavius at 3.2.254/1640.

3.2.50/1437, etc. 4.] HUMPHREYS; 2 F. The Second Plebeian is amongst those who leave to hear Cassius speak.

3.2.51/1438, etc. 5.] HUMPHREYS; 4 F. See previous note.

3.2.73/1459 ALL THE PLEBEIANS] F (*All.*); SANDERS *attributes to* SECOND PLEBEIAN

3.2.105/1491 art] F2; are F1

3.2.111/1497 hee not] DYCE 2 (Craik); hee F; he, my CAPELL. The sense seems to require the negative, and the emendation remedies a defective caesura, a relatively rare licence in this play. 'Has . . . place' is the last line on a page in F, and 'his place.' is printed as a turn-up. Shortage of space may have led Compositor B deliberately to omit 'not', perhaps believing that the sense was unaffected.

3.2.113/1499 Mark'd] F (*text*); Marke F (*c.w.*)

3.2.199-200/1585-6 reueng'd. | ⌈ALL THE PLEBEIANS⌉ Reuenge] GLOBE; reueng'd: Reuenge | F

3.2.216/1602 wit] F2; writ F1

3.3.2/1652 vnlucky] WARBURTON; vnluckily F. F combines a difficulty of sense with a metrical anomaly.

4.1.37 imitations,] F (∼.)

4.1.44/1732 meanies] This edition (*conj.* J.D.); meanes F. There is no difficulty in the sense of F: for *make* as 'to raise, to gather, to assemble, to bring together', see examples cited by Schmidt, *Make,* 5. The line is, however, violently ametrical. It may be remedied by assuming eyeskip omission after *meanes* ('. . . and our means'—*conj.* WILSON) or 'our' ('. . . Sinewes, our'— G.T. *conj.*), or an omitted line-end ('stretch'd to the utmost'—MALONE; 'our best meanes stretcht out'—F2). These radical and variably plausible departures from F leave (except for F2) two adjacent stressed syllables in 'meanes stretcht'. J.D.'s conjecture, which many editors do not even record, supplies an appropriate word used twice elsewhere by Shakespeare, posits no greater error than an omitted 'i' after the minims of 'n', and establishes an internally regular four-foot line.

4.2.0.1-2/1739.1-2 *Drum . . . them*] See Introduction.

4.2.0.2/1739.2 *Titinius*] Wilson pointed out that Titinius might more plausibly enter with Cassius at 4.2.30/1769, and emended accordingly. Although a prompt-book stage direction might be inaccurate about the grouping of characters who enter, one would not expect Titinius' entry to be marked in the wrong position to this extent, especially as '*Cassius and his Powers*' enter at the correct point. An ignored or misplaced annotation seems unlikely, but cannot be ruled out. But there is nothing actually wrong with Titinius entering at the beginning of the scene, especially if Shakespeare thought of him as a minor character who need not be implicated in the dialogue (see Introduction). F's entry is therefore retained.

4.2.2/1741 SOULDIER] This edition; *Lucil⟨lius⟩.* F. See Introduction.

4.2.7/1746 change] F; charge WARBURTON

4.2.7/1746 Officers] F; offices JOHNSON (*conj.*). The parallel in diction and ideas in *Henry V* 5.2.358/3218 lends Johnson's conjecture support, but *All's Well* 3.5.17/1509 ('a filthy Officer he is in those suggestions') equally supports F.

4.2.13-14/1752-3 Lucillius: . . . you,] ROWE (*subs.*); ∼, . . . ∼: F

4.2.34-6/1773-5 1. SOULDIER . . . 2. SOULDIER . . . 3. SOULDIER] CAPELL; *not in* F

4.2.52, 54/1789, 1791 Lucillius . . . Let *Lucius*] F; Lucius . . . Lucilius WHITE; Lucius . . . Let Lucilius COLLIER 3. See Introduction.

4.2.81/1818 bay] F1; baite F2

4.2.82/1819 baye] THEOBALD; baite F. See Wilson's note. Terminal

JULIUS CAESAR

'e' could be easily misread 't', as perhaps at 3.1.175/1263. 'Baye' takes up 'bay the Moone', and has the senses, both Shakespearian, 'howl at' and 'hold at bay'; it anticipates 'hedge me in', whereas *bait* suggests 'allure out'.

4.2.101/1838   stand] F; staie G.T. *conj.* Usually *stand* and *crouch* are antithetical, and the line remains paradoxical however *stand* is glossed. The conjecture therefore would give an easy misreading: *stay* would have the sense 'wait upon'. Alternatively, 'and' might have been intended to be 'or'.

4.2.142   friend's] F (Friends)

4.2.165/1902   Humour] F; honour CRAIK (*conj.*)

4.2.172/1909   temper'd too.] F2; remper'd too.s F1. The redundant terminal 's' is a turned letter.

4.2.206/1943   Impatienc] This edition (Capell); Impatient F. See Wilson's note. Capell's explanation that Shakespeare deliberately introduced a nonsensical reading to avoid a collision of sound with 'absence' is not convincing, and MacMillan failed to produce a true parallel for the licence of grammar he envisages.

4.2.209   distraught] F (diſtract). *Distraught* is historically a modification of *distract* and has taken on its meanings, *distract* becoming archaic. Instances in Shakespeare suggest no semantic distinction: the forms seem to be indifferent variants.

4.2.225   tenor] F (Tenure)

4.2.233/1970   I *Cicero*] CAPELL; *Cicero* F. The defective caesura is a rare licence in *Julius Caesar*. The compositor might easily drop the single letter, especially immediately before another capital.

4.2.234/1971   proscription.] F3; ∼∧ F1

4.2.264   off,] F (∼.)

4.2.271/2008   to] F2; ro F1

4.2.303/2040   will] F2; will it F1

5.1.20.1-3/2117.1-3   *Drum ... within.* As suggested in the Introduction, F's '*March*' is probably an annotator's duplication of '*Drum*'. Nevertheless, both the on-stage and entering armies march—both, presumably, to drums.

5.1.42/2139   teethe] F3; teethes F1

5.1.55/2152   Swords] This edition (*conj.* Herr); Sword F. Plural swords are logically required for plural traitors; they also more meaningfully recall the multiple attack of Caesar's assassins.

5.1.71/2168   as] F; at KEIGHTLEY

5.1.79/2176   Ensigns] HUMPHREYS (Lettsom); Enſigne F

5.1.88/2185   giue] POPE; giue vp F. Trisyllabic feet are often suspect in Shakespeare, and this is the only example in *Caesar*. The familiarity of the expression would facilitate memorial substitution by the compositor.

5.1.95/2192   rest] ROWE; rests F

5.2.4/2227   Octauio's] F; Octavius' POPE. See note to 1.2.5/80.

5.3.96   whe'er] F (where). Also at 5.4.30.

5.3.96/2325   haue not] Fb; haue Fa. See Introduction for Fb's probable authority.

5.3.100/2329   mo] Fb; no Fa

5.3.100   more] Fb (mo)

5.3.103/2332   *Thasos*] THEOBALD; *Tharſus* F. Shakespeare's 'a' was easily misread 'ar'.

5.4.7/2345   LUCILLIUS] MACMILLAN; *not in* F; Bru⟨tus⟩. ROWE. F indents 'And' as for a speech-prefix.

5.4.12, 15/2350, 53   ⌜1.⌝ SOULDIER] F (Sold⟨ier⟩.)

5.4.17/2355   thee] POPE; thee F

5.5.23.1/2393.1   Low] Fb; Loud Fa. See Introduction.

5.5.33/2403   thee, to, *Strato.*] THEOBALD; ∼, ∼∧ ∼, F

5.5.76/2446   With all] F3; Withall F1

INCIDENTALS

30 Holyday] Holy-|day	53 your] Fb; yonr Fa (*location uncertain*; see Hinman)	96 March.] ∼∧	99 againe.] ∼ : (?)
770 flattred] flattered	815 Condition] Condltion	816 Brutus] Brntus	926 Princes.] ∼∧	1278 Trebonius.] ∼,
1358 quartred] quartered	1388 satisfied.] ∼,	1397 rendered] rendred	1422 Brutus] Btutus	1586 Reuenge,] ∼∧ F
1650 moud] moued	1689 prickt.] ∼∧	1741 Stand] Fb; Srand Fa	1899 loud'st] loued'ſt	1900 loud'st] loued'ſt
1963 Addition?] ∼.	2057 slumber] ſlumbler	2084 *Lucius*] Lucus	2127 words:] ∼∧	2300 thou *Pindarus*?] Fb; ∼ ∼. Fa
2342 *Marcus*] Fb; *Marcns* Fa	2357 hee] Fb; kee Fa	2448 ordred] ordered		

FOLIO STAGE DIRECTIONS

1.1.0.1-2/0.1-2   *Enter Flauius, Murellus, and certaine Commoners* \| *ouer the Stage.*

1.1.60.1/60.1   *Exeunt all the Commoners.*

1.1.75/75   *Exeunt*

1.2.0.1-4/75.1-4   *Enter Cæsar, Antony for the Course, Calphurnia, Portia, De-\|cius, Cicero, Brutus, Cassius, Caska, a Soothsayer: af-\|ter them Murellus and Flauius.*

1.2.26.1/101.1   *Sennet. Exeunt. Manet Brut. & Cass.*

1.2.80.1/155.1   *Flourish, and Shout.*

1.2.133/208   *Shout. Flourish.*

1.2.178.1/253.1   *Enter Cæsar and his Traine.*

1.2.215.1-2/290.1   *Sennit.* \| *Exeunt Cæsar and his Traine.*

1.2.294/370   *Exit.*

1.2.307/383.1   *Exit Brutus.*

1.2.322/398   *Exit.*

1.3.0.1-2/398.1-2   *Thunder, and Lightning. Enter Caska,* \| *and Cicero.*

1.3.40/438   *Exit Cicero.*

1.3.40.1/438.1   *Enter Cassius.*

1.3.99/497   *Thunder still.*

1.3.129.1/527.1   *Enter Cinna.*

1.3.152/550   *Exit Cinna.*

1.3.164/562   *Exeunt.*

2.1.0.1/562.1   *Enter Brutus in his Orchard.*

2.1.5.1/567.1   *Enter Lucius.*

2.1.9/571   *Exit.*

2.1.34.1/596.1   *Enter Lucius.*

2.1.38.1/600.1   *Giues him the Letter.*

2.1.43/605   *Exit.*

2.1.45.1/607.1   *Opens the Letter, and reades.*

2.1.58.1/620.1   *Enter Lucius.*

2.1.59.1/621.1   *Knocke within.*

2.1.69.1/631.1   *Enter Lucius.*

2.1.85.1-2/647.1-2   *Enter the Conspirators, Cassius, Caska, Decius,* \| *Cinna, Metellus, and Trebonius.*

2.1.99.1/661.1   *They whisper.*

2.1.191.1/753.1   *Clocke strikes.*

2.1.227.1/789.1   *Exeunt.* \| *Manet Brutus.*

2.1.232/794   *Enter Portia.*

2.1.302.1/864.1   *Knocke.*

2.1.308/870   *Exit Portia.*

2.1.308.1-2/870.1-2   *Enter Lucius and Ligarius.* (after 'with hast')

2.1.333/895   *Thunder* \| *Exeunt* (opposite 'on' and 'then')

2.2.0.1-2/895.1-2   *Thunder & Lightning.* \| *Enter Iulius Cæsar in his Night-gowne.*

2.2.3.1/898.1   *Enter a Seruant.*

2.2.7/902   *Exit*

2.2.7.1/902.1   *Enter Calphurnia.*

2.2.37/932   *Enter a Seruant.*

2.2.56.1/951.1   *Enter Decius.*

2.2.107.1-2/1002.1-2   *Enter Brutus, Ligarius, Metellus, Caska, Trebo-\|nius, Cynna, and Publius.*

JULIUS CAESAR

2.2.115I/1010.1 *Enter Antony.*
2.2.129/1024 *Exeunt*
2.3.0.1/1024.1 *Enter Artemidorus.*
2.3.16/1039 *Exit.*
1.4.0.1/1039.1 *Enter Portia and Lucius.*
2.4.21.1/1060.1 *Enter the Soothsayer.*
2.4.40/1079 *Exit*
2.4.48.1/1087.1 *Exeunt*
3.1.0.1–5/1087.2–6 *Flourish. | Enter Caesar, Brutus, Cassius, Caska, Decius, Metellus, Tre-|bonius, Cynna, Antony, Lepidus, Artimedorus, Pub-|lius, and the Soothsayer.*
3.1.76/1163 *They stab Cæsar.*
3.1.76.1/1163.1 *Dyes*
3.1.95.1/1183.1 *Enter Trebonius.*
3.1.122.1/1210.1 *Enter a Seruant.*
3.1.143/1231 *Exit Seruant.*
3.1.147.1/1235.1 *Enter Antony.*
3.1.256.1/1344.1 *Exeunt. | Manet Antony.*
3.1.248.1/1365.1 *Enter Octauio's Seruant.*
3.1.300/1387 *Exeunt*
3.2.0.1/1387.1 *Enter Brutus and goes into the Pulpit, and Cassi-|us, with the Plebeians.*
3.2.40.1–2/1427.1–2 *Enter Mark Antony, with Cæsars body.*
3.2.62/1448 *Exit*
3.2.252.1/1638 *Exit Plebeians.*
3.2.254/1640 *Enter Seruant.* (after 'Fellow?')
3.2.264.1/1650 *Exeunt*
3.3.0.1, 3.3.4.1/1650.1, 1654.1 *Enter Cinna the Poet, and after him the Plebeians.* (before 3.3.1/1651)
3.3.38.1/1688.1 *Exeunt all the Plebeians.*
4.1.0.1/1688.2 *Enter Antony, Octauius, and Lepidus.*
4.1.11/1699 *Exit Lepidus*
4.1.51/1739 *Exeunt*
4.2.0.1–2/1739 *Drum. Enter Brutus, Lucillius, and the Army. Titinius | and Pindarus meete them.*
4.2.24.1/1763.1 *Low March within.*
4.2.30/1769 *Enter Cassius and his Powers.*
4.2.54.1–3/1791.1–3 *Exeunt | Manet Brutus and Cassius.*
4.2.179.1/1916.1 *Enter a Poet.*
4.2.192.1/1929.1 *Exit Poet*
4.2.211.1/1948.1 *Enter Boy with Wine, and Tapers.*
4.2.213.1/1950.1 *Drinkes*
4.2.216.2/1953.2 *Enter Titinius and Messala.*
4.2.285/2022 *Enter Lucius.* (after 4.2.284/2021)
4.2.290/2027 *Enter Lucius with the Gowne.*
4.2.292.1/2029.1 *Exeunt.*
4.2.298/2035 *Enter Varrus and Claudio.*
4.2.319.1/2056.1 *Musicke, and a Song.*
4.2.327.1/2064.1 *Enter the Ghost of Cæsar.*
4.2.369.1–2/2097.1–2 *Exeunt*
5.1.0.1/2097.3 *Enter Octauius, Antony, and their Army.*
5.1.12/2109 *Enter a Messenger.*
5.1.20.1–5/2117.1–5 *March. | Drum. Enter Brutus, Cassius, & their Army.*
5.1.66.1/2163.1 *Exit Octauius, Antony, and Army*
5.1.69.1, 70/2166.1, 2167 *Lucillius and Messala stand forth.* (after 'you', 5.1.69/2166)
5.1.126.1/2223 *Exeunt.*
5.2.0.1/2223.1 *Alarum. Enter Brutus and Messala.*
5.2.2.1/2225.1 *Lowd Alarum.*
5.2.6.1/2229.1 *Exeunt*
5.3.0.1–2/2229.2–3 *Alarums. Enter Cassius and Titinius.*
5.3.8.1/2237.1 *Enter Pindarus.*
5.3.19/2248 *Exit.*
5.3.32/2261.1 *Showt.*
5.3.35.1/2264.1 *Enter Pindarus.*
5.3.49.1–2/2276.1–2 *Enter Titinius and Messala.*
5.3.89.1/2318.1 *Dies*
5.3.89.2–3/2318.2–3 *Alarum. Enter Brutus, Messala, yong Cato, | Strato, Volumnius, and Lucillius.*
5.3.95/2324 *Low Alarums*
5.3.109.1/2338.1 *Exeunt.*
5.4.0.1–2/2338.2–3 *Alarum. Enter Brutus, Messala, Cato, Lucillius, | and Flauius.*
5.4.6.1/2344.1 *Enter Souldiers, and fight.*
5.4.16.1/2354.1 *Enter Antony.* (after 5.4.15/2353)
5.4.32.1–3/2370.1–3 *Exeunt.*
5.5.0.1–2/2370.4–5 *Enter Brutus, Dardanius, Clitus, Strato, | and Volumnius.*
5.5.23.1/2393.1 *Low Alarums.* (Loud Alarums. Qa; Low Alarums Qb)
5.5.29.1/2399.1 *Alarum still.*
5.5.42.1/2412.1 *Alarum. Cry within, Flye, flye, flye.*
5.5.51/2421 *Dyes.*
5.5.51.1–2/2421.1–2 *Alarum. Retreat. Enter Antony, Octauius, Messala, | Lucillius, and the Army.*
5.5.80.1/2450.1 *Exeunt omnes.*

AS YOU LIKE IT

As You Like It was first printed in the First Folio, set by Compositors B, C, and D. It had been entered in the Stationers' Register on 4 August 1600 (see Introduction to *Much Ado About Nothing*, p. 371), but no edition followed. It is also included in the entry of 8 November 1623 for the Folio (see pp. 32, 34). The general assumption has been that F was set from a prompt-book or a transcript of it. Knowles challenges this, arguing for 'some kind of transcript from foul papers, perhaps embodying some annotation by the prompter' (p. 334). However, it seems to us relatively unlikely that the copy was specifically an 'intermediate transcript', midway between foul papers and prompt-book. Knowles here relies heavily upon Bowers's conclusions about *Julius Caesar*, which we do not accept. Another supposed parallel, *1 Henry IV*, is exceptional, because of the influence of political censorship. (See the Introductions to both plays, above.) Knowles also assumes that pre-Restoration prompt-books were more regular and comprehensive than the extant manuscripts give us any reason to suppose. If the prompt-book were based on an autograph fair copy, it might preserve certain 'Shakespearian' features. Finally, Knowles concedes that F's scene divisions tell against the theory of an 'intermediate' transcript, since these would serve no purpose in such a manuscript, and are unlikely to have originated in the printing house. Consequently, an intermediate transcript seems no more likely than foul papers, and we can at present do no more than acknowledge that the copy was either the prompt-book or a literary transcript, either from the prompt-book itself or the foul papers.

The text is generally clean, though corruption may be suspected at a number of points. Its division into acts and scenes is satisfactory, except that as Orlando's appearance at the beginning of 3.2 is self-contained, it might well be regarded as a separate scene; but the action is continuous.

'What shall he haue that kild the Deare?' (4.2.10-19/2078-87) appeared as a round for four voices in John Hilton's *Catch that Catch Can* (1652), and an alternative text of 'It was a louer and his lasse' (5.3.15-38/2465-88) is found in Thomas Morley's *First Book of Airs* (1600). They are collated below.

A problem arises over the expansion of 'M^r'. Wherever the full form of the prefix occurs, it is *Monsieur* (not 'Master'). The abbreviation is used for Corin speaking of Touchstone (3.2.11/1156) and Ganymede (3.2.84/1228), and for Touchstone speaking of Jaques (3.3.66/1634) and Oliver Martext (3.3.88/1656). Traditionally, it has regularly been expanded to 'Master'. We adopt *Monsieur* in the third instance, as this form is regularly used to or of Jaques. 'Master' seems marginally more appropriate to the context at 3.2.84/1228, and is also adopted in the other two instances, though with no certainty that it is right.

S.W.W./(G.T.)

WORKS CITED

Knowles, Richard, ed., *As You Like It*, New Variorum (1977)
Latham, Agnes, ed., *As You Like It*, Arden (1975)
Maxwell, J. C., *RES* 27 (1976), 343-5 (review of Latham)
Oliver, H. J., ed., *As You Like It*, New Penguin (1968)
Wilson, John Dover, ed., *As You Like It*, New (1926)

TEXTUAL NOTES

Title *As you Like it*] F (*head title, running titles, table of contents*); As yo^w like yt S.R. (1600); As you like it S.R. (1623)

1.1.11 manège] F (mannage). Editors spell 'manage'; but *OED* gives this as '*Obs. exc. arch.* (Now usually MANÈGE.)'.

1.1.53, 55 villein . . . villeins] F (villaine . . . villaines). 'Villain', usually adopted, obscures the word-play.

1.1.54 Bois] F (Boys). Recent editors retain F, and actors usually pronounce accordingly; but Shakespeare clearly intended the name to be French.

1.1.83 Denis] F (Dennis). For no obvious reason, editors retain F; 'Denis' is the standard modern spelling.

1.1.104/105 shee] F3; hee F1

1.1.109, etc. Ardenne] F (*Arden*). Editors spell 'Arden'. Lodge has Arden as the French place-name. Other recorded spellings in English writers are 'Ardenia', 'Ardenna', and 'Ardeyn'. Though there is a forest of Arden in Warwickshire, and though Shakespeare's mother's name was 'Arden', other French names in *As You Like It*, and the reference in this very scene to 'Robin Hood of England', show that he refers to the French forest, even if in Anglicized spelling and with an expectation that the English pronunciation would be adopted.

1.1.153/155 OLIUER] *not in* F

1.2.3/168 I] ROWE 3; *not in* F

1.2.41.1/206.1, etc. Touchstone the Clowne] THEOBALD 2 (*subs.*); Clowne F

1.2.51/216 and] MALONE; *not in* F. Sometimes F2's equally acceptable emendation of 'perceiveth' to 'perceiving' is followed.

1.2.79/244 CELIA] THEOBALD; Ros⟨alind⟩. F. F's attribution has been defended, but a sudden shift of attention by Touchstone from Celia, who has asked the question, to Rosalind seems unlikely; and Touchstone has no obvious motive to be satirical about Rosalind's father, who in any case is in no position to whip him.

1.2.79-80/244 him. Enough,] HANMER; him enough; F

1.2.87/252 le] F2; the F1

1.2.232/397 loue,] loue; F

1.2.233/398 The line is metrically anomalous. Perhaps we should read 'exceeded here', making a regular hexameter (G.T.).

1.2.262/427 shorter] ROWE 3; taller F

1.2.279, 1.3.0.1, 1.3.1, 89, 95, 2.4.0.1/444, 444.1, 445, 533, 539, 747.1 Rosalind] Rosaline F. F's spelling occurs only in the work of Compositor D, 'who always uses this spelling, perhaps because he had set the name in *LLL* [TLN] 932, 1030, 1089, and 1297 a short time before his stint in *AYLI*' (Knowles, 326).

1.3.56/500 likelihood] F2; likelihoods F1
1.3.95/539 *Rosalind, lacks thou then*] This edition (G.T.); *Rosaline lacks then* F. F's apparent shift from the third to the second person is awkward. Theobald's emendation of 'thee' in the following line to 'me' has been adopted by some editors. The present reading assumes that 'lacks' is a shortened form of 'lackest' and that 'thou' has been omitted. An acceptable alternative is 'lack'st thou . . .', which makes the sentence a statement, not a question.
1.3.118/562 will.] This edition; will, F. Most editions either follow F, which suggests that Rosalind's 'outside' will somehow be 'in (her) heart', or punctuate 'and—in my heart | Lie there what hidden woman's fear there will—', which seems unnecessarily complicated.
1.3.128 essayed] F (aſſaid)
1.3.136/580 we in] F2; in we F1. F1 is defended by some editors, and may be correct: the column was set by Compositor D, who rarely transposes; but 'go in' sounds too limiting; the emphasis is rather on 'goe . . . to libertie . . .'.
2.1.26 Jaques] Fully modernized, 'Jaques' would be 'Jacques'; but the pronunciation is sometimes disyllabic (2.1.26, 54, 5.4.192/607, 635, 2689), and the modern French pronunciation would obscure the pun on 'jakes'.
2.1.49/630 much] F2; muſt F1
2.1.56/637 should] This edition (*conj.* Proudfoot); doe F. F's reading, accepted by editors, seems the reverse of the required sense.
2.1.59/640 the] F2; *not in* F1
2.1.62/643 to kill] F; kill CAPELL (*a metrical regularization; repetition of 'to' is redundant and could be accidental*)
2.3.16/686 ORLANDO] F2; *not in* F1
2.3.30/700 ORLANDO] F2; Ad⟨am⟩. F1
2.3.74/742 seauenteene] ROWE; ſeauentie F
2.4.1/748 wearie] THEOBALD; merry F
2.4.41/788 thy] they F
2.4.41/788 wound] F2; would F1
2.4.46/793 batlet] F2; batler F1. 'Batlet' is recorded as a dialect word in Yorkshire and Warwickshire, whereas 'batler' is not found elsewhere; the misreading is easy.
2.4.47 chapped] F (chopt). Editors spell 'chopped' but the spellings were used indifferently, and 'chapped' is the modern form.
2.4.68/816 you] F2; your F1
2.4.73 travel] (F3); trauaile F1
2.4.82, etc. cot] F (Coate). Editors usually spell 'cote', but '*Cote* in this sense having become obs., or merely dial., about 1625, *cot* has been revived as a poetical and literary term' (*OED Cot, sb.*¹).
2.5.1/848 AMYENS] F has the heading 'Song', and no prefix; Capell first attributed the song to Amiens.
2.5.35/882 ALL] F has no prefix, but the heading '*Song*' and the phrase '*Altogether heere.*' Possibly Amiens should sing the first four lines, joined by the others for the last two.
2.5.40-2/887-9 *see . . . Weather*] *ſee. &c.* F
2.5.46/893 IAQUES] F2; Amy⟨ens⟩. F1
2.7.55/978 aught but] This edition (G.T.); *not in* F. Theobald's emendation, 'Not to seem', has been generally accepted; but omission at the start of a line is less likely than within it, the repetition of 'Not . . . not' is awkward, and 'Doth' in 2.7.54/977 is also an auxiliary. *Aught but* is common in Shakespeare. See Taylor, 'Inventing'.
2.7.87/1010 comes] F2; come F1
2.7.175/1098 AMYENS] There is no prefix in F, but the heading 'Song.'
2.7.183/1106 *Then*] ROWE; The F
2.7.191-4/1114-17 *sing . . . iolly*] ſing, &c. F
2.7.202/1125 master] F2 (*subs.*); maſters F1
3.2.29/1173 complaine] F; complaine of want G.T. *conj.*
3.2.115 graft] F (graffe). Editors read 'graff', but this is '*arch.*; in ordinary use superseded by GRAFT' (*OED, v.*¹).
3.2.122/1266 a] ROWE; *not in* F
3.2.122/1266 *bee?*] ROWE; bee, F

3.2.142/1286 *hir*] ROWE; *his* F
3.2.155 How now, back, friends.] Not an emendation, but an interpretation; F reads 'How now backe friends:'; some editors interpret 'How now? Back-friends!'
3.2.232/1376 such] F2; *not in* F1. Sometimes 'forth' is emended to 'such', with no addition; but this page was set by Compositor B, who was liable to omit words. Shakespeare's only other use of 'drop forth' appears to be in this play, at 4.3.35/2122.
3.2.239/1383 thy] ROWE; the F. Some modern editors do not emend.
3.2.351/1496 deifying] F2; defying F1
3.2.359/1504 are] F2; art F1
3.3.18/1584 it] COLLIER (Mason); *not in* F
3.3.50-1/1617-18 so. Poore men alone?] THEOBALD; ſo poore men alone: F
3.3.86/1654 CLOWNE] F2 (*Clo.*); Ol⟨iuer⟩. F1
3.4.27/1693 a] F2; *not in* F1. Oliver does not emend; but this was set by Compositor C, especially liable to omit.
3.4.39 puny] F (puiſny). Most editors spell as F; Wilson spells 'puisne'. *OED* cites this use under *puisne, a.* 3, 'Small, insignificant, petty; now spelt PUNY. *Obs.*'
3.5.28/1749 deere] F; my dear HANMER (Taylor)
3.5.45/1766 my] F1; mine F2. A plausible change: Compositor C, when setting from printed copy, 3 times changed copy *mine* to *my*. *My* or *thy* is particularly unusual before the vowel (*eye-*).
3.5.129/1850 I] This edition (*conj.* Maxwell); *not in* F1. F2 reads 'I have'; Maxwell's suggestion is preferable both metrically and on the grounds that omission is more likely within a line than initially.
4.1.1/1862 be] F2; *not in* F1
4.1.17/1879 my] F2; by F1. Variorum 1821 omits 'in', reading 'which my often . . .', which is also plausible.
4.1.57 beholden] F (beholding)
4.1.72 warr'nt] F (warne). Cambridge records this as an anonymous conjectured emendation. Knowles cites *OED warn, v.*³, '*Obs. rare*', 'To protect, to defend', but this is last recorded in 1449. Wilson argues that 'warne' is a misreading of 'warnd', a dialectal pronunciation—as is 'warn'—of 'warrant'.
4.1.147 hyena] F (Hyen). The disyllabic form is not otherwise recorded later than the 14th c. Shakespeare does not use the word elsewhere. This could be an error.
4.1.200/2060 it] F2; in F1
4.2.2/2070 A LORD] MALONE; Lord. F
4.2.7/2075 ANOTHER LORD] MALONE; Lord. F
4.2.10/2078 LORDS] *not in* F, which has the heading 'Muſicke, Song.'
4.2.12-13/2080-1 *Then . . . burthen*] *not in* HILTON
4.2.14/2082 thou] you HILTON
4.2.14/2082 *the*] a HILTON
4.2.15/2083 wast] was HILTON
4.2.16/2084 wore] bore HILTON
4.2.17/2085 bore] wore HILTON
4.3.41, 45/2128, 2132 F prints 'Read.' at the beginning of each line.
4.3.79/2166 bottom.] CAPELL (∼;); ∼ₐ F
4.3.98, 5.2.26 handkerchief] F (handkercher). F's spelling is common in Shakespeare; *OED* says it was 'common in literary use in the 16-17 c., and remained the current spoken form for some time after handkerchief was commonly written'. So it may be regarded as an indifferent variant.
4.3.104/2191 it selfe.] THEOBALD; it felfeₐ F
4.3.106/2193 antiquitie,] RANN; ∼ : F
4.3.143/2230 I'] F1 (I); In F2 (*and most editors*)
4.3.156/2243 his] F2; this F1
5.2.4 persevere] F (perſeuer). F's spelling indicates the normal pronunciation. *Persevere* 'became universal by *c.*1680' (*OED*).
5.2.7/2339 her] ROWE; *not in* F
5.2.31/2363 ouercame] F2; ouercome F1
5.2.93/2426 obedience] COWDEN CLARKE (Malone); obſeruance F
5.2.109/2442-3 I satisfie] DYCE 2 (Douce); I ſatisfi'd F. Parallelism seems to require 'satisfie', and 'satisfi'd' incongruously suggests

AS YOU LIKE IT

that her marriage to Orlando will be proof of a prehistory of promiscuity. The proposed misreading would be very easy.

5.3.15/2465   BOTH PAGES] *not in* F, which has the heading 'Song.'
5.3.17/2467   *feild*] fields MORLEY
5.3.18/2468   *In*] KNIGHT; *In the* F. 'In springtime' is the reading of the song as printed in Morley's *First Book of Airs* (1600) and in the other stanzas in F.
5.3.18/2468   *ring*] RANN; *rang* F. Knowles cites 'Advocates' MS' as first source of emendation.
5.3.23/2473   *folks*] fooles MORLEY
5.3.33-8/2483-8   JOHNSON; *after* 5.3.20/2470, F. This is also Morley's arrangement.
5.4.3/2499   do not] F; not G.T. *conj.*
5.4.21/2517   your] ROWE 3; you your F

5.4.79/2576   to the] F2; to F1
5.4.112/2609   *hir*] F3; *his* F1. In the next line, *his* is often emended to 'her'; this may well be right, but Rosalind's next line, 'To you I giue myselfe, for I am yours', may support F1's reading.
5.4.146/2643   daughter; welcome] HANMER; daughter welcome, F
5.4.149, 181/2646, 2678   IAQUES DE BOYS] ROWE 1; 2. *Bro.* F
5.4.162/2659   them] ROWE; him F
5.4.195/2692   so] This edition (*conj.* Maxwell); *not in* F. Most editors follow F2 in emending to 'We will'. A few recent editors (e.g. Riverside, Oliver) do not emend, but regularity of metre seems more desirable in a final couplet than elsewhere, and Maxwell's suggestion also improves the balance of the couplet.
5.4.196/2693   trust they'l end,] POPE; truft, they'l end,ˏ F

INCIDENTALS

414 ouerthrowne.] ~ˏ   525 lips.] ~ˏ   743 more.] ~ˏ   1100 ingratitude.] ~ˏ   1217 good:] ~ˏ   1411 rings?] ~ˏ   1672 colour.] ~:   1722 Phebe.] ~ˏ   2229 place,] ~.   2470 spring.] ~.   2492 You] you   2529 Magitian,] ~.   2608 hether,] ~.   2666 were] wete   2681 bequeath:] ~ˏ

FOLIO STAGE DIRECTIONS

1.1.0.1/0.1   *Enter Orlando and Adam.*
1.1.23.1/24.1   *Enter Oliuer.*
1.1.80.1/81.1   *Ex. Orl. Ad.*
1.1.83.1/84.1   *Enter Dennis.*
1.1.90.1/91.1   *Enter Charles.*
1.1.153/155   *Exit.* (after 1.1.152/154)
1.1.163/165   *Exit.*
1.2.0.1/165.1   *Enter Rosalind, and Cellia.*
1.2.41.1/206.1   *Enter Clowne.*
1.2.87.1/252.1   *Enter le Beau.*
1.2.138.1-2/303.1-2   *Flourish. Enter Duke, Lords, Orlando, Charles, | and Attendants.*
1.2.201.1/366.1   *Wrastle.*
1.2.204.1/369.1   *Shout.*
1.2.219.1-2/384.1-2   *Exit Duke.*
1.2.246.1/411.1   *Exit.*
1.2.248.1/413.1   *Enter Le Beu.*
1.2.279/444   *Exit*
1.3.0.1/444.1   *Enter Celia and Rosaline.*
1.3.34.1/478.1   *Enter Duke with Lords.*
1.3.88.1/532.1   *Exit Duke, &c.*
1.3.137.1/581   *Exeunt.*
2.1.0.1-2/581.1-2   *Enter Duke Senior: Amyens, and two or three Lords | like Forresters.*
2.1.68.1/649.1   *Exeunt.*
2.2.0.1/649.2   *Enter Duke, with Lords.*
2.2.21/670   *Exeunt.*
2.3.0.1/670.1   *Enter Orlando and Adam.*
2.3.77/747   *Exeunt.*
2.4.0.1-3/747.1-3   *Enter Rosaline for Ganimed, Celia for Aliena, and | Clowne, alias Touchstone.*
2.4.16.1/763.1   *Enter Corin and Siluius.*
2.4.40/787   *Exit.*
2.4.99/847   *Exeunt.*
2.5.0.1-2/847.1-2   *Enter, Amyens, Iaques, & others.*
2.5.1/847.3   *Song.*
2.5.35/881.1   *Song. Altogether heere.*
2.5.59.1/906.1   *Exeunt*
2.6.0.1/906.2   *Enter Orlando, & Adam.*
2.6.17/923.1   *Exeunt*
2.7.0.1/923.2   *Enter Duke Sen. & Lord, like Out-lawes.*
2.7.7.1/930.1   *Enter Iaques.*
2.7.87.1/1010.1   *Enter Orlando.*
2.7.166.1/1089.1   *Enter Orlando with Adam.*
2.7.175/1097.1   *Song.*

2.7.204/1127   *Exeunt.*
3.1.0.1/1127.1   *Enter Duke, Lords, & Oliuer.*
3.1.18/1145   *Exeunt*
3.2.1/1145.1   *Enter Orlando.*
3.2.10/1155   *Exit*
3.2.10.1/1155.1   *Enter Corin & Clowne.*
3.2.85.1/1229.1   *Enter Rosalind.*
3.2.120.1/1264.1   *Enter Celia with a writing.*
3.2.159/1303   *Exit.*
3.2.245.1/1389.1   *Enter Orlando & Iaques.*
3.2.419/1566   *Exeunt.*
3.3.0.1/1566.1-2   *Enter Clowne, Audrey, & Iaques.*
3.3.57.1/1624.1   *Enter Sir Oliuer Mar-text.*
3.3.98/1666   *Exeunt*
3.4.0.1/1666.1   *Enter Rosalind & Celia.*
3.4.41.1/1708.1   *Enter Corin.*
3.4.54/1721   *Exeunt.*
3.5.0.1/1721.1   *Enter Siluius and Phebe.*
3.5.7.1-2/1728.1-2   *Enter Rosalind, Celia, and Corin.*
3.5.81/1802.1   *Exit.*
3.5.140/1861   *Exeunt.*
4.1.0.1-2/1861.1-2   *Enter Rosalind, and Celia, and Iaques.*
4.1.24.1/1885.1   *Enter Orlando.*
4.1.190/2050   *Exit.*
4.1.208/2068   *Exeunt.*
4.2.0.1/2068.1   *Enter Iaques and Lords, Forresters.*
4.2.10/2077.1   *Musicke, Song.*
4.2.19/2087   *Exeunt.*
4.3.0.1/2087.1   *Enter Rosalind and Celia.*
4.3.5.1/2092.1   *Enter Siluius.* (after 4.3.3/2090)
4.3.41/2128   *Read.*
4.3.45/2132   *Read.*
4.3.75/2162.1   *Exit. Sil.*
4.3.75.1/2162.2   *Enter Oliuer.*
4.3.183/2270.1   *Exeunt.*
5.1.0.1/2270.2   *Enter Clowne and Awdrie.*
5.1.9.1/2279.1   *Enter William.*
5.1.58/2328   *Exit*
5.1.58.1/2328.1   *Enter Corin.*
5.1.62/2332   *Exeunt*
5.2.0.1/2332.1   *Enter Orlando & Oliuer.*
5.2.12.1/2344.1   *Enter Rosalind.*
5.2.70.1/2403.1   *Enter Siluius & Phebe.*
5.2.118/2451   *Exeunt.*
5.3.0.1/2451.1   *Enter Clowne and Audrey.*

394

5.3.5.1/2456.1   Enter two Pages.
5.3.15/2464.1   Song.
5.3.46/2496   Exeunt.
5.4.0.1-2/2496.1-2   Enter Duke Senior, Amyens, Iaques, Orlan-|do, Oliuer, Celia.
5.4.4.1-2/2500.1   Enter Rosalinde, Siluius, & Phebe.
5.4.25.1/2521.1   Exit Ros. and Celia.
5.4.34.1/2530.1   Enter Clowne and Audrey. (after 5.4.33/2529)
5.4.105.1/2602.1   Still Musicke. (after 5.4.105.2/2602.2)
5.4.105.1-2/2602.1-2   Enter Hymen, Rosalind, and Celia.
5.4.138.1/2635.1   Song.
5.4.148.1/2645.1   Enter Second Brother.
5.4.194/2691   Exit.
5.4.196.1/2693.1   Exit
Epi.21.1/2714.1   Exit.

HAMLET

Hamlet was first entered in the Stationers' Register on 26 July 1602.

Iames Roberte   Entred for his Copie vnder the hande
of mr Paſſeild & mr waterſon warden
A booke called the Revenge of Hamlett
Prince Denmarke as yt was
latelie Acted by the Lo: Chamberleyn
his ſervante

The first known edition (Q1) is a quarto dated 1603 (*BEPD* 197a); the title-page, which alludes to Shakespeare's company as 'his Highnesse seruants', must have been printed after 19 May, when the Chamberlain's Men became the King's Men. This edition was 'printed for N.L. [Nicholas Ling] and Iohn Trundell' by Valentine Simmes (Pollard, pp. 73-4). Roberts, who entered the play in 1602, neither published nor printed the edition of 1603; the relationship of the Stationers' Register entry to the first edition has therefore been a matter of conjecture and dispute. Pollard in 1909 suggested that Roberts's entry was made on behalf of the company, in order to block publication by anyone else (pp. 63-75); Chambers in 1930 thought that Roberts (a printer) wanted to stake a claim in the play, which he could then sell or trade to a stationer (*Shakespeare*, i. 146). Johnson, in 1985, in the context of a full study of Ling's career, shows that he habitually benefited 'from other stationers who located copy and brought it to him for help in publishing the editions. Or, similarly, he bought or assumed copyrights that had been entered by and in some cases published by other stationers' (p. 203). For this reason, Johnson conjectures that Trundle provided the copy for Q1, and that Ling had reached a private arrangement with Roberts (his favourite printer). Technically Q1 is 'pirated' in that those who published it did so despite its entry to another man. Whether the irregularity of its publication reflects irregularity in the acquisition of printer's copy cannot be confidently asserted. According to Greg's count, the Q1 text is 2,200 type lines long (*Folio*, 52); according to universal consensus, its text is—with a handful of exceptions—verbally inferior to either of the other substantive editions.

A second edition (Q2; *BEPD* 197b) was 'Printed by I.R. [= James Roberts] for N.L. [= Nicholas Ling]'; three copies (all in the United States) are dated 1604 on the title-page; four (all in Europe) are dated 1605. Other press variants were identified by Wilson (*MSH*) and Hinman (1964). Brown identified two compositors, 'X' and 'Y', who apparently set Q1 of *The Merchant of Venice* and Q2 of *Titus Andronicus* (both printed by Roberts in 1600).

X: 1.1.0.1-1.5.184/0.1-801
2.2.162b-2.2.578/1091b-1508
3.3.21-3.4.185a/2137-2399a (with Add. Pass. H)
4.5.88-4.5.120/2644-2676
4.7.85-4.7.108/2889-2912
5.1.281-5.2.357.2/3251-3625.2

Y: 1.5.185-2.2.162a/802-1091a
2.2.579-3.3.20/1509-2136
3.4.185b-4.5.87/2399b-2643
4.5.121-4.7.84/2677-2888
4.7.109-5.1.280/2913-3250

The identification of compositorial stints in Q2 *Hamlet* seems reasonably secure; the relationship between these two compositors and those in *Merchant* Q1 is, necessarily, less certain, but nevertheless plausible.

In addition to a manuscript, the compositors of Q2 made use of an exemplar of Q1. The contamination of Q2 by Q1 was first demonstrated by Greg (*Folio*, 331-2), on the basis of anomalies of typography and layout, and has been accepted by all subsequent investigators. This dependence is most obvious in the play's first five scenes; thereafter the evidence of contamination becomes sporadic and difficult to assess. It is generally agreed, however, given the clear dependence at the beginning of the play, that an exemplar of Q1 was available to the compositors, and hence liable to be consulted on occasion, potentially to the detriment of the text.

Nevertheless, such contamination can only affect those areas of Q2 which correspond to Q1 closely enough to make Q1 of use to a compositor trying to decipher a manuscript. The title-page of Q2 advertises itself as 'Newly imprinted and enlarged to almost as much againe as it was, according to the true and perfect Coppie'. Whether or not 'true and perfect', the printer's copy was undoubtedly 'enlarged', since in Q2 the text stretches to 3,800 type lines—literally 'almost as much againe as it was' in Q1.

Q2 was reprinted in 1611 (Q3: *BEPD* 197c); that reprint was itself reprinted in an undated quarto (Q4: *BEPD* 197d), probably of 1622 (Jenkins, 1982, pp. 17-18). Q4 was reprinted in 1637 (Q5: *BEPD* 197g). After the Restoration the play appeared in a succession of so-called 'Players' Quartos', claiming to represent the play 'As it is now Acted' (1676, 1683, 1695, 1703). None of these editions has any authority. The first three reprints (Q3, Q4, and Q5) were all published by John Smethwick, to whom Ling's copyright was transferred in the Stationers' Register on 19 November 1607.

Smethwick was a member of the syndicate which, in 1623, published the First Folio (F1), which contains a third substantive text of the play, materially different from Q2 or any of its descendants. F1 was set by three compositors—B, E, and I—whose stints have been identified by Hinman (1963) and Taylor (1981). E was responsible for only two pages: the great bulk was set by B.

Although its major additions and numerous variants make it clear that F derives in some way from a manuscript, its bibliographical relationship with Q2 has been disputed.

Walker (1951) argued that F was set from a heavily annotated exemplar of Q2; this view was challenged by Jenkins (1955) and Walton (1971), but remained widely influential. Taylor (1983) demonstrated through an analysis of punctuation that E's pages could not have been set from Q2; a further study of spelling and punctuation ruled out the use of Q2 by either B or E (Taylor, 1985). Hibbard (1987) independently showed that the 'common errors and unusual spellings' offered as evidence of F's dependence upon Q2 are less reliable than had been supposed. The cumulative weight of evidence now makes it demonstrable that Q2 did not serve as printer's copy for F.

Nevertheless, the elimination of Q2 as actual printer's copy by no means rules out the occasional consultation of a quarto by the Folio compositors (as Q1 was consulted by the compositors of Q2). Just as Q2 and Q1 are linked by the common publisher Ling, so Q3-4 and F are linked by the common publisher Smethwick. This parallel has been obscured by the concentration upon Q2, which itself arose from Walker's recurrent obsession with the direct use of quartos as Folio printer's copy. If any quarto were to serve as copy for F, it had to be Q2: where Q2 and F agree in peculiarities of spelling or punctuation, these forms are anomalous or old-fashioned, and hence taken as reliable evidence of related transmission; where Q3-4 and F agree in incidentals (against Q2), such agreements will almost invariably involve a more 'modern' form, which can be dismissed as independent sophistications. The very nature of the evidence being examined favoured Q2. But since we are no longer dealing with the possibility of direct use as printer's copy—for the data which eliminated Q2 also eliminate its early reprints—the whole issue of which quarto might have influenced F needs to be reconsidered. The spelling and punctuation of F will have derived primarily from its own manuscript copy; although some influence from the incidentals of a consulted quarto is possible, any such influence should be sporadic, and hence the greater similarity of F to the incidentals of one quarto or another in selected lines or passages hardly constitutes reliable evidence. For the great majority of the 'unusual' incidentals linking Q2 and F, Q2-4 are identical; moreover, if—as all recent investigators agree—the manuscript used as copy for F derived from that used for Q2, certain similarities linking Q2 to F might result from common manuscript origin, so that the divergence of Q3-4 need be of no significance in evaluating their claims to have influenced F.

If an exemplar of Q2, Q3, or Q4 was occasionally consulted by the Folio compositors, it would have been consulted not for spelling, punctuation, or capitalizations—matters over which compositors exercised their own authority—but for clarification of substantive readings. Persuasive evidence of such consultation can therefore only come from Folio agreement with a quarto in readings which appear to be errors. Such errors might be of two kinds: (a) errors originating in Q2, and (b) errors originating in derivative reprints.

Most editors agree that Q2-4 and F agree in error at TLN 111, 400, 539, 736, 1880, 3114, and 3530; two other likely candidates are 1624 and 3067, though in each case we believe emendation unnecessary. All of these readings except 1624 are shared by Q3-4; consequently, all support the hypothesis of quarto contamination, and only one (1624) discriminates between Q2-4.

F also shares a number of readings which first appear in Q3. Some are obvious and necessary corrections; Q3's agreement with F is recorded in our collations, but is of no significance in determining possible influence. More serious is the Q3-4/F agreement in a definite error at 509, combined with another eleven agreements in indifferent variants (778, 994, 1039, 1619, 2439, 2836, 2901, 3160, 3176, 3306, and 3588). The number of these is in itself suspicious: of pre-1623 quartos which he believed did not serve as Folio copy, Walton found a greater number of agreements only in *Lear* Q2 (whose influence upon F has since been massively documented). Noticeably, the one Q3-4/F agreement in error comes, like over half of the suspected Q2-4/F shared errors, in Act 1; suspected shared errors occur in the vicinity of Q3-4/F agreements in indifferent variants at 3114-76 (three) and 3530-88 (two). A mere 898 Folio lines (out of 3906) thus account for eleven of the twenty suspicious substantive links between F and Q3.

Q4 takes over all these Q3 variants which agree with F, and adds two others: an error at 2270, and an indifferent variant (3507) which is close to two other suspect readings (3530, 3588).

Such agreements between Q3-4 and F are, in our experience, enough to induce some anxiety in an editor. Moreover, the circumstantial evidence for contamination of F by one of these quartos increases this anxiety. We have no reason to believe that Smethwick in 1623 possessed a copy of Q2, but he certainly possessed copies of either Q4 (assuming it was indeed printed in 1622) or Q3. Smethwick's 1637 quarto edition (Q5) was demonstrably influenced by the Folio text, as Walton established. For every other play in which Smethwick or Jaggard had a previous interest, the Folio text was in some way influenced by an exemplar of a quarto— usually a late one.

Although contamination of F by occasional consultation of Q3 or Q4 is in the nature of the case not provable, it seems to us probable. We have, however, not taken this possibility as a licence for frequent rejection of readings shared by Q2 and F. It has meant, in practice, the retention of a few indifferent Q2 readings where we would otherwise (as a matter of policy) have adopted F, if F had not been anticipated by Q3-4; it has meant the emendation of half a dozen readings, common to Q2-4 and F, which previous editors have usually emended anyway. In only one case (539) has it led to emendation of a line substantially identical in all three substantive editions: this occurs in the part of Q2 most highly dependent upon Q1, and the part of F where consultation of a quarto seems to have been most frequent.

In practice, the demonstrable contamination of Q2 by Q1 has more general and more serious editorial consequences than the possible contamination of F by consultation of Q3 or Q4. Moreover, although such contamination means that in a few cases the agreement of Q2 and F may conceal error, an editor's main problem is to decide what to do when Q2 and F differ, as they often do. Editorial judgement on these variants will depend upon (and contribute to) an editorial hypothesis about the nature of the manuscripts which lie behind Q1, Q2, and F; but the foregoing summary of the bibliographical relationship between the early editions nevertheless establishes an important distinction. Where Q1 and Q2 agree against F, it is difficult to evaluate that agreement, because it may result from (a) contamination of Q2 by Q1, or (b) error in F. But where Q1 and F agree against Q2, that agreement cannot result from the contamination of one printed edition by another, because the printed text of F bears no relationship to the printed text of Q1 (except, possibly, where both agree with Q2-4). The manuscript behind Q1 may be related to the manuscript behind F; but there can be no direct contamination of F by Q1 itself.

It is now generally agreed that the copy for Q1 was a memorial reconstruction of the play as it was, in the words of the title-page, 'diuerse times acted by his Highnesse seruants in the Cittie of London: as also in the two Vniuersities of Cambridge and Oxford, and elsewhere'. The evidence for this conclusion is discussed in detail by Duthie, Jenkins (1982), and Hibbard (1987). Gray first identified the reporter as the actor who played Marcellus; he probably doubled Voltemand and Lucianus. This entire hypothesis has been challenged by Weiner and, more recently, Urkowitz. Urkowitz's argument in particular hinges upon a wholesale rejection of the possibility of memorially reconstructed texts; we believe that the existence of such a category of texts can be demonstrated (see General Introduction); discussion of *Hamlet* Q1 may therefore reasonably be confined to a consideration of whether it belongs to that category. The extreme variability in its verbal quality makes it difficult to assign convincingly to any period of Shakespeare's—or any author's—career. In places it bears every hallmark of Shakespeare's mature manner; other passages could only be attributed to Shakespeare at all if they were written earlier than any of his acknowledged work. Moreover, these disparities coincide, not with any discernible structural or artistic pattern, but with the presence or absence of certain minor characters, which could have been played by a single hired man. In terms of artistic homogeneity Q1 *Hamlet* is less plausible as a coherent alternative authorial text than the first editions of *Shrew*, *Contention*, *Richard Duke of York*, or *Richard III*: we also believe that those editions have a memorial origin, but Shakespeare's earlier style is less drastically incompatible with memorial pastiche, so the verbal texture of these editions is not so evidently incongruous as the dialogue of Q1 *Hamlet*. Moreover, for *Hamlet* we possess a third substantive text. If we possessed only Q1 and Q2, or Q1 and F, one could at least construct an argument which saw Q1 as the precursor of a superior version, postulating a simple vector of development: 'Q1⇨Q2' (or 'Q1⇨F'). Everyone agrees that, if Q1 were an authorial text, it would have to be much earlier than the text represented by Q2 or F; everyone also agrees that F represents a later development of the text than Q2. The vector of authorial revision should therefore be: 'Q1⇨Q2⇨F'. But in every significant structural respect Q1 is closer to F than to Q2; even at the level of verbal detail, the occasional agreements of Q1 with Q2 against F are all attributable to Q1's bibliographical contamination of Q2, or to simple compositorial error in F, or to expurgation of profanity in F. If Q1 were an authorial text, it would have to be (impossibly) both earlier than Q2 and later than F. This configuration of incompatibly early and late features characterizes all the apparently memorial texts.

Recognition of the character of Q1 has been unnecessarily complicated by knowledge of two lost texts dramatizing the Hamlet story. One is *Der Bestrafte Brudermord*, first published in full in 1781 from a manuscript now lost, and since then often translated into English (*Fratricide Punished*). This text undoubtedly derives from theatrical performance in Germany in the early seventeenth century, presumably—initially—by English actors on tour. Jenkins (1982) and Hibbard (1987), who discuss this version in detail, show that it agrees with the Q1 text in numerous features, and reasonably conclude that it derives literally from the printed text of Q1, used as a prompt-book by the touring Englishmen. It therefore has no independent authority as a text representing professional performance in London.

Far more important in the history of textual criticism of *Hamlet* is a lost English play of the 1580s. The most substantial reference to it is by Thomas Lodge, who in his *Wits Miserie*, of 1596, alludes to 'the Visard of ye ghost which cried so miserably at ye Theator like an oister wife, Hamlet, reuenge'. This and other allusions (Jenkins, 1982, 82-4) demonstrate the existence and familiarity of an English play on the Hamlet story—a play which anticipated the one we know in certain of its departures from the narrative sources. On 9 June 1594, Henslowe recorded takings of eight shillings 'at Hamlet'; the play is traditionally known as the 'ur-*Hamlet*'. Its authorship is unknown; it is usually conjecturally attributed to either Thomas Kyd or William Shakespeare. But no clear external evidence exists for either attribution, and we cannot put much faith in internal evidence drawn from a lost text. Nevertheless, it would be convenient if the 'lost' play were by Shakespeare, and its text preserved in Q1. To this hypothesis there are two serious documentary objections (quite apart from the arguments already advanced for Q1's memorial character). The only words which we possess of the lost play ('Hamlet, revenge') do not appear in Q1; nor does a *Hamlet* appear in Meres's 1598 list, despite the fact that the earliest apparent allusion to it is in 1589, and it apparently achieved some notoriety. So we agree with other modern editors in seeing no reason to identify Shakespeare as the author and Q1 as the authentic text of the earlier play. Nevertheless, it seems to us impossible to argue, as recent editors have done, that the lost play can have had no influence at all upon Q1. The possibility of such influence obviously exists, and it could only be comprehensively evaluated if we possessed a text of the lost play. Editors have been drawn to dismiss this possibility out of a laudable scepticism about attempts to reconstruct the lost play on the evidence of Q1, and a not so laudable preference for tidiness. Where Q1 most drastically departs from Q2 and F, the possibility of contamination by memories of the earlier play cannot be proven, but it cannot be dismissed either. Certainly, it is intriguing that the part of Gertrude in Q1 contains (*a*) the most drastic departure from Q2 and F, (*b*) the only feature in which Q1 agrees with earlier narrative accounts, against Q2 and F, and (*c*) several striking verbal parallels with *The Spanish Tragedy*, not present in Q2 or F. The part of Gertrude in performances of the lost play would have been taken by a boy actor; a boy actor of the late 1580s or early 1590s could well be a hired man in 1600-3, playing parts like Marcellus and Voltemand. Such hypotheses cannot be proved, but they do demonstrate that a simple mechanism of contamination exists, and that as a consequence it would be dangerous to place much faith in those features of Q1 which differ significantly from both Q2 and F.

Wilson established that Q2 was set from Shakespeare's foul papers (*MSH*); Jenkins (1982) and Hibbard (1987) reconsider and confirm the hypothesis, in detail. Wilson's hypothesis of a single incompetent and hurried compositor has, however, been overturned by the work of Bowers (1955), Brown, and Cantrell and Williams; though both compositors made mistakes, they cannot be blamed for more than a fraction of the variation between Q2 and F. Edwards believes that the compositors' copy was badly worn in places; but the only 'evidence' for this hypothesis is the existence of a number of lines where (*a*) he prefers the Folio reading, and (*b*) the Q2 variant cannot be explained as a normal compositorial misreading or substitution. Since in each case the Q2 reading is perfectly defensible as Shakespeare's, and has been preferred by some editors, such variants are better explained as examples of authorial revision. Other texts were set from foul papers considerably older than those of *Hamlet*, without showing signs of serious deterioration. Nor is there any plausible pattern to the alleged deterioration. Edwards's hypothesis is an *ad hoc* conjecture with the sole purpose of staving off the possibility of authorial verbal revision.

Another anomalous feature of Q2's copy, according to editors from Wilson to Jenkins, is that it had been marked up by someone other than the author, who called for a number of cuts. Cuts might, of course, be marked in foul papers, and there may be an example in Addition I, where a deletion marker might explain the loss of a half-line from both Q2 and F. But such cuts are most likely to have been made by the same person responsible for the rest of the foul papers (the author), and it is implausible to suppose that a book-keeper called in the foul papers for the omission of passages which nevertheless appear in subsequent manuscripts (and hence in F). Hibbard effectively disposes of the argument that extended passages present in F but not Q2 were present in the foul papers. The hypothesis of cuts, like that of a defective manuscript, is simply an editorial expedient designed to rule out the possibility of major authorial revisions—in this case, late additions, not composed until after completion of the foul papers.

If we evaluate Q2 on its own terms, simply as a document, without attempting to explain its verbal divergencies from F, then it appears to have been set from ordinary foul papers, supplemented in the printer's shop by consultation of Q1. Likewise, if we evaluate F on its own terms, simply as a document, then it appears to have been set from a transcript.

A number of features point to a scribal, rather than holograph, transcript. The predominance of the spelling 'oh' departs from Shakespeare's own preference (Jowett and Taylor), and can hardly be attributed to the compositors (Taylor, 1985). The number of obvious errors in Compositor B's stints, and their kind, far exceeds what we would expect from his work throughout the rest of the Folio (Taylor, 'Compositor B'). Patterns of mislineation also suggest that F was set from scribal copy (Werstine, 'Line Division', 96–7). The heavy punctuation in Compositor E's stints, which probably reflects the punctuation of the manuscript with unusual fidelity, does not resemble anything in *Sir Thomas More* or the good quartos apparently set from holograph (Taylor, 1983). A few verbal sophistications in F, not attributable to the compositors, also point to scribal interference (1.2.135/291, 1.2.185–6/341–2, 1.5.35/652)—though the extent of such sophistication has been exaggerated (see notes to 1.2.248/404, 1.3.49/462, etc.). In several places F betrays signs of sporadic expurgation;

although the Folio compositors might have intervened independently to remove particularly offensive oaths ('swounds, 'sblood), they cannot be responsible for all the altered profanity (Taylor, 'Zounds'). Nor can the compositors, or Folio editors, be held accountable for the provision of sensible act and scene references for the first six scenes (1.1–2.2). The provision of scene divisions, especially, points to a literary manuscript (Taylor, 'Act Intervals'). Since the first six scenes also account for almost all the deliberate expurgation of profanity in F, one must suspect that the printer's copy for those scenes differed in some way from the printer's copy for the remainder of the play: either the copy was prepared by two different scribes (as in *King John*), or a single scribe was working from two different kinds of manuscript (as in *Cymbeline*?). The matter requires—and deserves—further investigation.

To summarize: the manuscript authority for Q2 was Shakespeare's own foul papers, and the manuscript authority for F was a late and apparently literary scribal transcript. On this basis one can immediately conclude that Q2 is more likely to preserve Shakespeare's own incidentals, and accordingly we have adopted Q2 as the copy-text for incidentals.

In evaluating substantive variants, however, a great deal depends upon an editor's hypothesis about the character and sources of the manuscript that served as Folio copy. Previous editors have noted that F's treatment of stage directions and speech-prefixes is more thorough and consistent than Q2's. Although these features still fall short of modern theatrical standards, they fall well within the range expected of a Renaissance prompt-book, despite the repeated protestations of editors that the Folio manuscript 'could not' have served as the official prompt-book of the King's Men. However, F does not name any actors, or contain any duplicated warning directions, or conspicuously call for necessary properties. The absence of such features is far more important than the mere presence of a few inconsistencies. The manuscript might well have derived from a prompt-book, but it need not have, and it gives no clear signals of actually having been one.

The evidence usually cited as proof of F's theatrical derivation is, for the most part, unreliable. On occasion, the Folio calls for one or two fewer attendants than Q2; Wilson and others saw such changes as evidence of a prompter's concern for theatrical economy. However, these changes in no way affect the casting pattern for the play as a whole; they save no actors, and consequently cannot be confidently attributed to a theatrical functionary. They might just as easily derive from an author's concern for dramatic economy. Wilson also noted that Folio variants occasionally seem to echo or anticipate passages elsewhere in the play; he attributed such repetition to the memory of a prompter exceptionally familiar with the play, who let his memory interfere with his responsibilities as a scribe. But the person most likely to have held so much of the play's language in mental suspension is Shakespeare, not the book-keeper; Shakespeare, unlike the book-keeper, had no responsibility to copy faithfully what was in front of him, and might well have echoed himself in this way (consciously or not) when making a fair copy. Jenkins stigmatized a number of passages present only in F as 'actors' interpolations' (1960); but he offered, and still offers (1982), no plausible mechanism to account for the preservation of such interpolations in the manuscript. In every case, in labelling such passages as 'interpolations' an editor simply expresses his personal distaste for them; no attempt is made to demonstrate that they are 'un-Shakespearian'; other critics have often applauded the same passages, and other canonical works provided parallels for many of them (*Division*, 406-9). Finally, although one or two variants have occasionally been attributed to censorship by the Master of the Revels, none of the proposed examples seems to us—or to most recent critics—at all persuasive.

Noticeably, all the foregoing arguments attempt to prove that F derives from a theatrical manuscript by condemning certain Folio variants as unauthorized theatrical debasements of Shakespeare's intentions. They are not objective descriptions of a text, but elements of an editorial polemic.

The best evidence that F represents a more theatrical text than Q2 is its repeated agreement with Q1 against Q2, in matters of verbal and theatrical substance. These shared readings are bibliographically independent, for the printed text of Q1 could hardly have contaminated the printed text of F directly. If Q1 and F are related, they must be related because the manuscripts behind them in some way shared a common origin, an origin which post-dates the foul papers which lie behind Q2. If we accept the argument that Q1 derives from a memorial reconstruction, then Q1 itself stands outside the normal processes of textual transmission, and can only be related to F through the medium of theatrical performance. If Q1 reflects performances in or before 1603, then F can only be related to Q1 if it, too, in some way reflects early performances. But since no one supposes that F is a memorial reconstruction, F can only reflect such performances if it in some way derives from a theatrical manuscript which post-dates the foul papers and pre-dates 1604. F might not be that manuscript itself; it might only be a copy of it; but in either event F, whether at one or more removes, reflects a theatrical manuscript of 1600-3.

This conclusion will in itself account for much of the variation between Q2 and F. If we temporarily ignore all theories which attempt to discredit one document or another, then the facts at our disposal indicate that one text descends from authorial foul papers, and the other text descends from an early theatrical manuscript. That early theatrical manuscript might easily have been a prompt-book, created by annotating a fair copy of the foul papers. Normally, the first transcript of the foul papers served as a prompt-book; we should resist editorial efforts to multiply unnecessary entities. What matters, editorially, is the space between (*a*) the foul papers, and (*b*) the first theatrically motivated transcript of it. Some editors—Jenkins and Edwards, conspicuously—regard that interval as the threshold of debasement: what happens before belongs to Shakespeare, what happens afterwards belongs to someone else. We do not share their view. Instead, we regard that interval as a natural episode of authorial refinement, drawing upon the author's own second thoughts and upon the author's responses to any advice he may receive from his talented and trusted professional colleagues. These differences in interpretation result from irreconcilably opposed ideologies of literary production.

It can hardly be denied that some major substantive changes took place between (*a*) and (*b*): the prompt-book was not simply a more legible and tidy copy of the foul papers. Q2 contains numerous extended passages not present in F (see Additional Passages); F contains several such passages not present in Q2. These differences cannot be explained by the normal operation of compositorial error, and must reflect features of the underlying manuscripts. Edwards argues, in our view persuasively, that a coherent literary strategy unites some of the Folio's cuts to some of the Folio's additions: by cutting some things, and adding others, the Folio has been made into a slightly different work of art. Such arguments could be taken farther than Edwards cares to take them. For instance, the Folio omits Additional Passage P, in which 'a Lord' enters bringing a message to Hamlet from the King and Queen. It has usually been suggested that this cut reflects a penny-pinching prompter's desire to reduce the number of minor parts; but since this character appears nowhere else, and since he appears in the middle of a scene in which only two other characters are present, his role could be doubled by any hired man without in any way increasing the number of actors required or the expense of mounting a production. The only dramatic purpose served by this character's appearance—otherwise he does nothing but tell us what we already know, and forewarn us of what we already expect—is the message he brings from Gertrude to Hamlet: 'The Queene desires you to vse some gentle entertainment to *Laertes*, before you fall to play'—to which Hamlet replies, 'Shee well instructs me'. Thus, in Q2 Gertrude tells Hamlet to attempt a reconciliation with Laertes, just before Hamlet attempts such a reconciliation. In F, where this passage does not appear, Gertrude is in no way responsible for prompting this change in Hamlet's behaviour. Instead, as part of an extended passage present only in F, earlier in this very scene, Hamlet says 'But I am very sorry good *Horatio*, | That to *Laertes* I forgot my selfe; | For by the image of my Cause, I see | The Portraiture of his; Ile court his fauours:' (5.2.76-9/3343-6). In F Hamlet himself decides, without the need of any prompting from Gertrude or anyone else, to seek a reconciliation with Laertes—and does so by explicitly making, for himself and the audience, a comparison between his situation and Laertes'. Q2 and F thus give us two entirely different motivations for the crucial change in Hamlet's behaviour to Laertes. The traditional conflated text, in sorry contrast, instead combines these two explanations, without comment, making the anonymous lord's entrance and his message a wholly superfluous intrusion upon the dramatic progress of the play's final scene. Since it can hardly be doubted that Shakespeare wrote the extended Folio passage which provides one motive for Hamlet, and since the addition of that passage seems clearly related to the omission of the Q2 passage which provides an alternative motive, it seems obvious that Shakespeare himself was responsible for at least one Folio cut. If he was responsible for one cut, he could be responsible for others.

Edwards, who surprisingly does not see the relationship between these variants, argues that Shakespeare was responsible for almost all of the cuts. But Edwards wishes to avoid the obvious conclusion that such cuts and additions belong to the creative interval between the foul papers and the first theatrical transcript; he instead supposes that all these genuine authorial changes were present in the foul papers. In order to permit this hypothesis he has to conjecture that the Q2 compositors ignored instructions to delete a number of passages present in the printed text of Q2 (but deleted from F), and that they also failed to include a number of passages allegedly present in the original foul papers (and actually present in F). There is, of course, no evidence for either supposition, and considerable implausibility in their union.

Why should an editor wish to propose an intrinsically implausible hypothesis for which there is no evidence? Because it allows the editor to isolate the author's own creative processes in a single manuscript, and to isolate the debasement of those intentions in other manuscripts with which the author had no connection. For in the normal course of events we should expect such deletions and additions, not indicated or present in Q2, to have taken place in another manuscript, and the only such manuscript available is the theatrical transcript which must have intervened between the foul papers and F. And if one admits the presence of a revising author in that theatrical transcript, a revising author co-operating with his professional colleagues, then one inevitably raises the possibility that such a revising author was responsible, actively or acquiescently, for all the substantial changes made in that manuscript. By postulating that the two phases of alteration (authorial revision, theatrical adaptation) took place in two separate manuscripts, Edwards provides an apparently 'physical' basis for the distinction between them. But this distinction is, in practice, illusory and arbitrary. Our only evidence for either phase of alteration is F; Edwards arbitrarily decides that certain of the variants in F result from authorial revision (in the foul papers) and that others result from non-authorial debasement (in the theatrical transcript). The only basis for the distinction between these two putative origins—and the only evidence for the existence of these two phases—is that Edwards approves of some variants and disapproves of others.

In dealing with major additions or deletions it has usually been recognized that the variants must be, however unauthoritative, for the most part deliberate: they are not easily attributable to scribal or compositorial error. Individual verbal variants, by contrast, may result from mere error. Edwards conjectures that Shakespeare's revisions consisted entirely of adding and cutting major blocks of material, without any accompanying minor verbal variation. This postulate seems to us intrinsically implausible: that is not usually how creative artists work. Moreover, in this instance—as in every other in the Shakespeare canon—major additions and omissions coexist with massive verbal variation: the constant correlation of the two types of variant suggests that both have a single cause. Moreover, although there can be no doubt that the compositors of both texts and the scribe behind F made mistakes, one must postulate an exceptional and extraordinary amount of incompetence in order to explain all the minor verbal variation. Finally, in some cases both variants are so unusual, so apt, or so Shakespearian, that editors have reached no consensus about which is authoritative, or how to explain the alleged error which accounts for its alternative. Thus, it seems to us intrinsically probable that Shakespeare was responsible for much of the verbal variation between Q2 and F.

Editors reject this conclusion because it is often impossible to provide obvious or compelling reasons for the verbal revision. Major additions or omissions demonstrably change the shape or meaning of a scene, a character, or a whole play; they can be defended as conscious artistic choices. Minor changes of wording seldom have such major consequences or causes, and hence are harder for an editor to justify. This explains why an editor like Edwards can defend most major variants while categorically denying the possibility of any minor ones. But the different problems created for editors by these two types of variant should not obscure the fact that, for authors, they are part of a creative continuum; it does not make sense to argue, on principle, that Shakespeare could be responsible for one but not the other. Edwards's untenable division of variants contributes to, or results from, his untenable division of manuscripts. Since he believes that Shakespeare's own engagement with the text began and ended in the foul papers, Edwards cannot allow Shakespeare to have prepared a fair copy; if Shakespeare did not prepare a fair copy, Shakespeare would have had no opportunity to make minor verbal revisions; hence, all the verbal variants between Q2 and F must result from error in one text or the other. Once you accept the premiss, certain editorial consequences inevitably follow, and appear to be grounded upon a logical and principled adherence to a given 'bibliographical' situation; but the premiss is itself arbitrary and implausible, and it inevitably leads to arbitrary choices between variants. Shakespeare could, for all we know, himself have prepared the fair copy which, appropriately annotated, served as the company's official prompt-book—and the assumption that he did so will explain the coexistence, in any derivative of that prompt-book, of major cuts, major additions, and numerous verbal variants. We see no reason to suppose multiple causes for this complex, when a single cause will serve.

This edition therefore operates on the assumption that Shakespeare prepared a fair copy of the foul papers, that in making that fair copy he revised the text in a number of ways, and that F derives, at one or possibly more removes, from that fair copy. This textual situation might be visualized in terms of the following stemma:

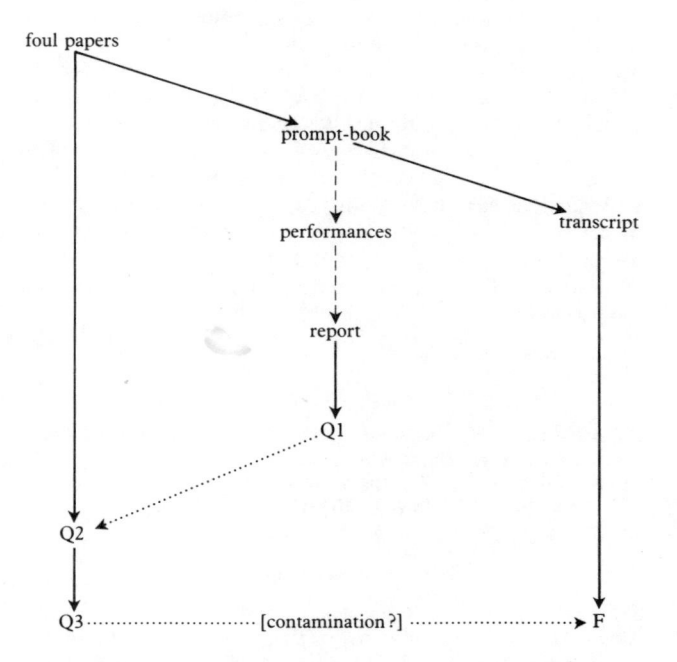

```
foul papers
    |
    |─────────────────────┐
    |                     |
    |              prompt-book
    |                     |
    |                     |──────────┐
    |              performances      |
    |                     |          |
    |                     |          |
    |                  report        |
    |                     |          |
    |                     ↓          |
    |                    Q1          |
    |                   ↙            |
    ↓                               transcript
   Q2                                 |
    |                                 |
    ↓                                 ↓
   Q3 ·········· [contamination?] ·········· F
```

Of all the two-text plays, *Hamlet* comes closest to *Lear* in the scale and complexity of the textual variation apparently resulting from authorial revision. *Lear* has, in recent years, monopolized most of the energies of textual critics, and consequently the character and purposes of the revision there are better understood; but we are confident that an equally thorough survey of *Hamlet* will be equally fruitful. Edwards's textual hypothesis, however unsatisfactory, at least represents an advance over previous studies in recognizing the artistic logic behind several major Folio variants, and in accepting that only Shakespeare could have been responsible for that revision; Edwards's failure results from an impossible effort to compromise between two irreconcilable positions.

Since we believe that Shakespeare revised the play after completing the foul papers, and that the fruits of that revision survive in F, we have adopted F as the control-text for substantive variants. We therefore accept F's substantive variants unless we believe that they result from compositorial error in F itself, or from scribal error in the manuscript which served as printer's copy for F. Extended passages present in Q2 but not F are reproduced among Additional Passages. The Textual Notes record all departures from F (or from Q2, in the case of Additional Passages). Rejected Quarto Variants are recorded in a separate list. Q1 readings are recorded, in either list, only when Q1's testimony may be pertinent to the authority of either Q2 or F. Variants which, in our judgement, probably result from authorial revision are asterisked.

The quartos contain no act or scene divisions; F marks act and scene divisions up to and including 2.2; all other divisions are editorial. The division for Act 4 derives from the 1676 Quarto, presumably reflecting Restoration theatrical practice (and possibly Caroline theatrical practice); it occurs in the middle of a scene, and hence no scene division is marked in the old-spelling edition. In the modern-spelling edition we have preserved the traditional act-scene division (which has no authority) simply for convenience, and because no alternative act division would have any greater authority, since Shakespeare apparently wrote the play without theatrical intervals in mind.

In editing this play we have worked particularly closely with G. R. Hibbard. Although his Oxford Shakespeare edition of *Hamlet* was not published until after the Oxford Complete Works, it was completed before our edition, and we have drawn extensively upon it. His Textual Introduction and commentary discuss at greater length certain matters treated summarily here. In turn, we have here considered Edwards's textual hypothesis at some length partly because it appeared too late to be discussed by Hibbard.

G.T./(S.W.W.)

WORKS CITED

Bailey, Samuel, *On the Received Text of Shakespeare's Dramatic Writings and its Improvement*, 2 vols. (1862-6)
Bowers, Fredson, 'The Printing of *Hamlet* Q2', *SB* 7 (1955), 41-50; 'addendum', *SB* 8 (1956), 267-9
—— 'The Textual Relation of Q2 to Q1 *Hamlet* (I)', *SB* 8 (1956), 39-66
Brown, John Russell, 'The Compositors of *Hamlet* Q2 and *The Merchant of Venice*', *SB* 7 (1955), 17-40
Cantrell, Paul L., and George Walton Williams, 'Roberts' Compositors in *Titus Andronicus* Q2', *SB* 8 (1956), 27-38
Chambers, E. K., ed., *Hamlet*, Warwick (1894)
Clark, W. G., and W. A. Wright, eds., *Hamlet*, Clarendon (1872)
Dowden, Edward, ed., *Hamlet*, Arden (1899)
Duthie, George Ian, *The 'Bad' Quarto of 'Hamlet'* (1941)
Edwards, Philip, ed., *Hamlet Prince of Denmark*, New Cambridge (1985)
Furness, H. H., ed., *Hamlet*, 2 vols., New Variorum (1877)
Gray, H. D., 'The First Quarto *Hamlet*', *MLR* 10 (1915), 171-80
Hibbard, G. R., 'Common Errors and Unusual Spellings in *Hamlet* Q2 and F', *RES*, NS 37 (1986), 55-61
—— ed., *Hamlet*, Oxford Shakespeare (1987)
Hinman, Charlton, note to second impression (1964) of *Hamlet: Second Quarto 1604-5*, ed. W. W. Greg, Shakespeare Quarto Facsimile 4
Hudson 1879: *Hamlet*, ed. Henry N. Hudson, Annotated English Classics series (1879)
Jenkins, Harold, 'The Relation between the Second Quarto and the Folio Text of *Hamlet*', *SB* 7 (1955), 69-83
—— 'Playhouse Interpolations in the Folio Text of *Hamlet*', *SB* 13 (1960), 31-47
—— ed., *Hamlet*, Arden (1982)
Jennens, Charles, ed., *Hamlet* (1773)
Jervis, Swynfen, *Proposed Emendations of the Text of Shakespeare's Plays* (1860)
Johnson, Gerald D., 'Nicholas Ling, Publisher 1580-1607', *SB* 38 (1985), 203-14
Marshall, Frank, *A Study of Hamlet* (1875)
Nosworthy, J. M., *Shakespeare's Occasional Plays* (1965)
Parrott, T. M., and Craig, Hardin, eds., *The Tragedy of Hamlet* (1938)
Pollard, A. W., *Shakespeare Folios and Quartos: A Study of the Bibliography of Shakespeare's Plays* (1909)
Spencer, T. J. B., ed., *Hamlet*, New Penguin (1980)
Taylor, Gary, 'The Shrinking Compositor A of the Shakespeare First Folio', *SB* 34 (1981), 96-117
—— 'The Folio Copy for *Hamlet*, *King Lear*, and *Othello*', *SQ* 34 (1983), 44-61
—— 'Folio Compositors and Folio Copy: *King Lear* in its Context', *PBSA* 79 (1985), 17-74
—— 'The Sins of Compositor B' (seminar paper, Shakespeare Association of America, 1982; forthcoming)
Tschischwitz, Benno, ed., *Shakspere's Hamlet, Prince of Denmark* (1869)
Urkowitz, Steven, '"Well-sayd olde Mole": Burying Three *Hamlets* in Modern Editions', in *Shakespeare Study Today* (1986), 37-70
Walker, Alice, 'The Textual Problem of *Hamlet*: A Reconsideration', *RES* 2 (1951), 328-38
—— *Textual Problems of the First Folio* (1953), 121-37
Walton, J. K., *The Quarto Copy for the First Folio of Shakespeare* (1971)
Weiner, Albert, ed., *Hamlet: The First Quarto 1603* (1962)
Werstine, Paul, 'Line Division in Shakespeare's Dramatic Verse: An Editorial Problem', *AEB* 8 (1984), 73-125
Wilson, John Dover, *The Manuscript of Shakespeare's 'Hamlet' and the Problems of its Transmission*, 2 vols. (1934; rev. edn. 1963)
—— ed., *Hamlet*, New Shakespeare (1934; rev. 1954)

TEXTUAL NOTES

Title *The Tragedie of Hamlet Prince of Denmarke*] Q2 (*head title, running titles*), F (*head title*), Q1 (*running titles*); THE Tragicall Hiftorie of HAMLET, *Prince of Denmarke* Q2 (*title-page*); *The Tragedie of Hamlet* F (*running titles, table of contents*); THE Tragicall Hiftorie of HAMLET *Prince of Denmarke* Q1 (*title-page, head title*)

1.1.24-5/24-5 along, | With vs$_\Lambda$] Q2; $\sim_\Lambda \sim$; F; along$_\Lambda$ with vs$_\Lambda$ | Q1
1.1.60/60 he] Q1-2; *not in* F
1.1.62 sledded] F; Q1-4 (fleaded)
1.1.62 Polacks] F (Pollax); Q1-2 (pollax)

1.1.86/86   heraldy] Q2; Heraldrie F, Q1, Q3. A mere spelling variant.
1.1.93/93   desseignd] F2; deſſeigne Q2; deſeigne Q3; deſigne F1
1.1.131/131   morne] Q2; day F; morning Q1
1.1.139/139   say] Q1-2; ſayes F
1.1.144/144   takes] Q1-2; talkes F
1.1.155/155   Lets] Q1-2; Let F
1.2.8/164   sometime] Q2; ſometimes F
1.2.21   Co-leaguèd] Q2 (Coleagued), F (Colleagued). The primary sense 'in league with' and the obsolete inflection both discourage modernization to 'Colleaguèd (with)', which to a modern reader inevitably suggests 'having become a colleague of'.
1.2.24   bonds] F; Q2 (bands)
1.2.34/190   Valtemand] Q2; Voltemand F (also at 204); Voltimar Q1. It seems relatively unlikely that there is any significance to the difference in spelling between Q2 and F; Q2 is preferred as closer to authorial incidentals.
1.2.35/191   bearers] Q1-2; bearing F. Easily assimilated to *greeting*.
1.2.38   dilated] F; Q2 (delated). For Q2's spelling see OED. Shakespeare may have intended a pun on the verb *delate* ('transmit, convey').
1.2.58-60/214-16   wroung . . . consent] Q2; *not in* F. See Hibbard.
1.2.67/223   sonne] Q2; Sun F. A mere spelling variant: both senses are clearly present.
1.2.77   good-mother] F (good Mother). See OED for the common use of this compound to mean 'mother-in-law', 'step-mother'. This bitter sense seems Hamlet's primary meaning here, as also at 3.2.105/1832 and 3.4.27/2241; he uses the collocation more often than any other character in the canon.
270   retrogard] Q2-4; retrograd Q5; retrograde F1, F4; retrogarde F2-3. OED regards the Q2 spelling as dubious; F2 either made the same mistake as Q2 (transposition of types) or used the same acceptable form. In an old-spelling edition the agreement of Q2 (1604), F2 (1632), and another book cited by OED (1509) seems sufficient to legitimize the form.
1.2.119/275   pray thee] Q2; prythee F. A mere spelling variant, in which F has a consistent tendency to prefer 'prythee'. See *Richard III* 1.4.69/834.
1.2.128.1/284.1   Florish] Q2; *not in* F, Q1
1.2.132   canon] QF (cannon)
1.2.134/290   Seeme] Q2; Seemes F
1.2.135/291   ah] Q2; Oh F. The same variant occurs at 2.2.226, 504, 3.2.279, and 5.2.20/1157, 1434, 2008 and 3287; 'ah' only occurs once in F, in the phrase 'ah ha' at 1.5.152/769. Such consistency looks like a scribal habit in dealing with the palaeographically ambiguous 'a/o' by which Shakespeare indicated an exclamation; among his plays a comparable dearth of 'ah' can be found only in the texts of *Tempest, Measure, Winter's Tale* (all from Crane copy), *Macbeth, Caesar* (both from scribal copy), and—alone from apparently autograph copy—*Merchant*. We have therefore retained Q2.
1.2.141/297   beteeme] Q2; beteene F
1.2.150/306   God] Q1-2; Heauen F
1.2.165/321   Marcellus.] Q2; F (*text*) indents, like a speech-prefix; F (c.w.) is 'Mar-'
1.2.167/323   Wittenberg] Q2; Wittemberge F
1.2.176/332   prethee] Q2, Q1 (pre thee); pray thee F
1.2.185/341   a] Q2; he F, Q1
1.2.186/342   A] Q2; He F, Q1
1.2.195/351   Gods] Q1-2; Heauens F. 'God' seems more appropriate to 'loue'; but Shakespeare never uses Q's or F's phrase elsewhere.
1.2.204/360   distil'd] Q1-2; beſtil'd F
1.2.205/361   gelly‸ with the act of feare‸] This edition; ~‸ ~, F; ~, ~‸ Q2; ~. ~‸ Q1
1.2.209/365   Where as] Q1, Q5; Whereas Q2, F
1.2.236   hundred] Q2 (hundreth), F
1.2.237/393   BOTH SOULDIERS] Q2 (Both.); *All.* F; Mar⟨cellus⟩. Q1. Shakespeare is often vague or misleading about 'All' directions; F probably reflects an indifferent authorial variant.
1.2.239   grizzly] F (griſly)
1.2.242/398   walke] Q1-2; wake F

*1.2.248/404   what soeuer] Q1, F, Q3 (*as one word*); what ſomeuer Q2. F has been described as a sophistication or modernization, but it occurs 19 times elsewhere; there are only two Shakespearian parallels for Q2.
1.2.251   eleven] Q2 (a leauen), F
1.3.1   inbarqued] Q1 (inbarkt), Q2 (inbarckt), F (imbark't). For the word see OED (*inbark*, 1612). F's variant may result from a simple minim error, or deliberate modernization, or a minim error assisted by the relative unfamiliarity of the quarto form. Elsewhere the Folio and Shakespearian texts strongly prefer 'em-' as a spelling of the common verb, the only possibly authorial exception being *Errors* 5.1.412/1761 (imbarkt).
*1.3.3/416   conuoy] F (Conuoy); conuay Q2. Q2 could be a legitimate spelling of *convey* (see OED, v.), which was current as a noun (though not used elsewhere by Shakespeare).
1.3.5/418   fauour] Q2; fauours F. F is possible, but 'it' (1.3.6/419) favours Q2.
1.3.8/421   Forward] Q2, F3; Froward F1
1.3.9/422   perfume and] Q2; *not in* F
1.3.10/423   so?] ROWE; ~. Q2, F
1.3.16/429   will] Q2; feare F
*1.3.21/434   sanity and] HANMER (Theobald); ſanctity and F; ſafty and Q2; safety and the WARBURTON. Warburton's emendation is needed to make Q2's reading metrical; Theobald's, to make F sensible. There is no reason to assume that one reading lies behind both texts.
1.3.21/434   whole] Q2, F2; weole F1
1.3.40/453   their] Q2; the F
1.3.46/459   watchman] Q2; watchmen F, Q3
*1.3.49/462   Whilst] F; Whiles Q2. Wilson, among instances of F's tendency 'to modernize certain words', claims that 'F1 generally prints "whilst" and Q2 "whiles"' (*MSH*, 243). Jenkins repeats this claim (201). In fact both texts—and Shakespeare generally—prefer 'while' (17 times in common); they also agree on 'whilst' 3 times. F only differs from Q2 4 other times in respect to the form of this word (1.5.96, 2.2.107, 3.4.139, 5.2.348/713, 1035, 2353, 3616); no pattern of sophistication is discernible. 'Whiles' is the form Shakespeare uses least often throughout the canon (including the good quartos).
1.3.57/470   thee] Q1-2; you F. F could have been contaminated by the first half of the line; it seems more appropriate for the shift to *thee* to coincide with the change of subject.
1.3.65/478   new hatcht] Q2; vnhatch't F; new Q1
1.3.74/487   al] This edition (*conj.* A. R. Cripps); a Q1-4, F. See *TLS* (8 Jan. 1938), 28; also K. A. Rockwell, *N&Q* 202 (1957), 84. Q1 has 'generall' for Q2/F 'generous' later in the line, which may represent a misplaced aural memory. The Q2 or F compositor might have been confused by what looked like 'or of almost' or 'ar of almost', hence resorting to consultation of an earlier print. And compare 4.7.108/2912: 'Most generous, and free from all contriuing'.
1.3.74/487   chiefe] Q1-2, F (cheff); choice COLLIER 2. See Jenkins, who notes that Q1's anticipation of the word strongly supports its authenticity; nor should such a common word as *choice* have caused such consternation.
1.3.109/522   Roning] COLLIER 2; Roaming F; Wrong Q2; Wronging POPE; Wringing THEOBALD (Warburton)
*1.3.114/527   all the] F; almoſt all the holy Q2. F produces a part-line, so that Polonius interrupts her rhythm (as he does her previous speech); 'holy' is arguably redundant in conjunction with 'heauen'. Either Folio omission might be accidental, but their conjunction makes the variation more likely to be deliberate.
1.3.117/530   Lends] Q1-2; Giues F
1.3.120/533   from] Q2; For F. The same error occurs at Folio *Coriolanus* 3.3.114/2043 and *Caesar* 3.1.286/1373.
1.3.125   tether] Q2 (tider), F (tether)
1.3.128/541   die] Q2; eye F
1.3.129/542   imploratators] This edition; imploratotors Q2; implorators F, Q4. Editors reject Q2, but in any event the word occurs nowhere else, and one can hardly be dogmatic about its form: Q2 might result from dittography, or F from haplography

HAMLET

(or contamination from Q4). Metrically, Q2 is preferable, producing a hexameter rather than an anomalous anapaest. For the superfluous *at* suffix compare *visitate, invocate, consolate, illuminate, ruinate*, etc.

1.3.130/543 bauds] POPE 2 (Theobald); bonds Q2–4, F
1.4.1 shrewdly] Q2 (fhroudly), F
1.4.1/550 it is] Q2; is it F
1.4.7.1–2/556.1 A . . . of] Q2; *not in* F; Sound Trumpets Q1. Some stage direction is clearly missing here in F: if it had stood in the manuscript after 1.4.7/556, it might have been omitted because it falls between Folio pages (1.4.7/556 on nn6ᵛ, 1.4.8/557 on Oo1) or because of crowding on Oo1: there is no room for it on the type line of 1.4.8/557 or 1.4.9/558, and the whole page is crowded, with no type lines wasted and several saved by unusual expedients, probably because of inaccurate casting off. Whether F intended the same action as Q2 can only be conjectured: the dialogue itself only explicitly requires 'kettle Drum and Trumpet'.
1.4.10/559 wassell] Q1–2; waffels F
1.4.23/572 intents] Q1–2; euents F
1.4.26/575 ô] Q2, Q1 (O); Oh, oh F
1.4.34 glimpses] Q1–2 (glimfes), F
1.4.37/586 the,] Q1–2; thee; F
600 somnet] Q2; Sonnet F. Editors since Rowe emend to 'summit'; but the recurrence of Q2's form at 3.3.18/2134 and at *History of Lear* 20.57/2385—the word's only occurrences in the canon—confirms it as a Shakespearian spelling.
1.4.51 cliff] Q2 (cleefe), F (Cliffe)
1.4.53/602 assume] Q1–2; affumes F
1.4.57 off] Q2 (of), F
1.4.59 artere] Q2 (arture), F (Artire). For the form see *OED*. Q1's 'Artiue' is presumably a simple compositorial misreading of a similar spelling. A disyllable is metrically required.
1.5.1/618 Whether] Q1–2; Where F. F's variant might be due to the crowding of this line of type.
1.5.19 on] Q2–F (an), Q1
1.5.20 porcupine] QF (Porpentine)
1.5.22/639 list *Hamlet* list, ô list] lift *Hamlet*, oh lift F; lift, lift, ô lift Q2; Hamlet Q1. Q1 confirms F's vocative; but F's omission of Q2's second 'list' may well be accidental, since as it stands F's line is metrically anomalous, while hexameters (as produced by conflation of Q2 and F) are common.
1.5.24/641 God] Q1–2; Heauen F. 'O God' occurs at *Duke of York* 2.5.21, 61/1058, 1098, *Richard III* 1.2.62, 2.1.132/224, 1173, Add. Pass. C.1, *Romeo* 2.4.18, 3.5.204/1288, 2138, and *Much Ado* 2.3.104/929: eight examples, all from plays written before 1606. 'O heauen' occurs five times elsewhere, but four of these occasions are in late or expurgated texts (*Two Gentlemen* 5.4.36, 59, 109/2066, 2089, 2139; *Kinsmen* 3.6.156/1661); the single exception is *Othello* 1.1.171/172, where both Q and F seem likely to have suffered expurgation. Even if the example from *Othello* is genuine, the clear preponderance of Shakespeare parallels favours 'God' here.
1.5.29/646 with] F1, Q1; I with Q2, F2. Editors universally reject F, but ellipsis of the nominative is common (see Abbott, 399, 401) and the agreement of Q1 and F hard to dismiss. Moreover, Q1 and F also agree on 'know it' earlier in the line, where Q2 has 'know't'; Q2's variants in combination produce a normal line, as do those of Q1 and F, but conflation produces a line less regular than any substantive text.
1.5.33/650 rots] F; rootes Q1–2. Jenkins and Hibbard defend Q; Edwards supports F; obviously, either reading is defensible. To us the only advantage of 'rootes' is that it may suggest 'making oneself even harder to move'—but plants can't move anyway. The verb *to root* instead suggests to us growth and active expansion (as at *Henry V* 5.2.46/2901, cited by Jenkins). F's variant adds a suitably opprobrious verb as the moral centre of the sentence: to forget, to be a useless weed, to fatten oneself in ease, is to *rot*. See also 'rotten weed' in the '*Spes Altera*' version of Sonnet 2.
1.5.35/652 Tis] Q1–2; It's F. The Shakespeare canon contains 1,526 occurrences of *tis*, to only 35 of *it's*; of those 35, one is in a non-Shakespearian portion of a collaborative play (*1 Henry VI* 5.6.82/2473) and 4 derive from memorially reconstructed texts (*Richard III* 5.5.2/3093 (2); *Pericles* 6.10, 16.36/711, 1560), while another 4 are textually variant (*Othello* 2.3.98, 4.3.52/1104, 2714; *Troilus* 4.2.54/2220; *Tragedy of Lear* 2.1.89/973; also *Tragedy of Lear* 1.4.199/704, where Riverside and Spevack reject F's 'It's'). Of the 26 which remain, only 3 occur in good quartos (*Troilus* 1.2.207, 266/352, 409, *Hamlet* 3.4.68/2282); another 7 occur in Folio texts of doubtful copy (*Coriolanus* and *Antony*); all the remainder come in texts set from scribal copy. Probability therefore strongly favours the assumption that F is a scribal or compositorial sophistication of the form in the quartos.
1.5.43/660 witt] POPE; wits Q2–4, F; will Q1
1.5.43/660 with trayterous gifts,] Q2; hath Traitorous guifts. F; with gifts, Q1
1.5.45/662 to his] Q1–2, F3; to to this F1; to this F2
1.5.49/666 hand in hand, euen] HIBBARD; ~, ~ Q2, F. See *Cymbeline* 1.4.68–9/334–5 ('a kind of hand in hand comparison') where the copy apparently did not indicate the compound by hyphenation.
1.5.55 angel] Q2 (Angle), Q1 (angle), F (Angell)
1.5.58 scent] QF (fent)
1.5.67 alleys] QF (allies)
1.5.69 eager] F (Aygre), Q1–2
1.5.71/688 barckt] Q1–2; bak'd F
1.5.75/692 of Queene] Q1–2; and Queene F
*1.5.84/701 howsoeuer] F, Q1; howfomeuer Q2. F has been dismissed as a sophistication or modernization, but variants of *howsoever* occur 15 times elsewhere, while there are only two parallels for Q2's form—one at *Merchant* 3.5.84/1808, set by the same printer.
1.5.93/710 hold, hold] Q2; hold F, Q3
*1.5.107–8/724–5 My tables, | My tables] This edition; My Tables, my Tables F; My tables Q1–2. Q1's agreement with Q2 is, as often, ambiguous; F's repetition creates no problem if the extrametrical 'My tables' is treated, for lineation purposes, as a separate part-line (which, as often elsewhere, was not separated in the manuscript). F elsewhere increases Hamlet's characteristic repetition: see 1.5.104/721, etc.
1.5.114/731 within] F; *not in* Q1–2. Q1 agrees with F in placing the speech before Horatio and Marcellus enter (rather than after, as in Q2), which implies that the speech is spoken within.
1.5.117/734 HAMLET] Q2 (Ham.); Mar⟨cellus⟩. F
1.5.120/737 i'st] Q1–2; ift F
1.5.137 whirling] Q1 (wherling), Q2 (whurling), F (hurling). *OED* notes the early confusion of *whirl* and *hurl* under both words.
1.5.140/757 Horatio] Q1–2; my Lord F
1.5.153/770 on] F (one), Q2
1.5.158/775 our] Q1–2; for F
1.5.164/781 earth] Q1–2; ground F. F's synonym could have been substituted under the influence of 1.5.158/775.
*1.5.171/788 so ere] F, Q1; fo mere Q2. Jenkins dismisses F as a modernization, but Q2's form only appears once elsewhere (*Hamlet* 3.2.387/2115); for F's there are 11 parallels. See also notes to 1.2.248/404 and 1.5.84/701. For analogous words also—whenceso(m)ever, whenso(m)ever, whereso(m)ever, whoso(m)ever—the Shakespeare canon consistently prefers the '-ever' forms (21 to 2).
1.5.175/792 this, head shake] Q1–2; thus, ~ F; thus, head shaked HIBBARD
1.5.178/795 they] Q1–2; there F
1.5.179/796 out) to note,] STEEVENS–REED 2 (Malone); ~, ~) Q2; ~, ~, F, Q1
2.1.1/809 this] Q1–2; his F
2.1.3 marv'lous] F (maruels), Q2 (meruiles)
2.1.4/812 to] Q2; you F
2.1.4/812 inquire] Q2; inquiry F. Either word could be a simple misreading of the other; we prefer Q2 on the principle of *praestat insolitior lectio*.
2.1.14/822 As] Q2; And F

2.1.40   sullies] Q2 (fallies), F (fulleyes)
*2.1.47/855   and the addition] F (Addition); or the addistion Q2. Q2 is unlikely to be a simple error for F: neither misreading, nor confusion of the t/ſt types, is probable. If the original reading were 'addiction', Q2's error—confusion of ct/ſt ligatures—would be easy to understand; Shakespeare uses addiction in the sense 'inclination' at Henry V 1.1.55/89 and Othello 2.2.6/999.
2.1.49/857   a this, a doos,] Q2; he this? | He does: F
2.1.50/858   By the masse] Q2; not in F
2.1.58/866   a] Q2; he F
2.1.60   sale] F (faile), Q2 (fale)
2.1.62/870   carpe] Q2; Cape F
2.1.69   b'wi'] QF (buy)
2.1.69/877   buy ye] Q2; ~ you F
2.1.69/877   far ye] Q2; ~ you F
2.1.77/885   i'th name of God] Q2; in the name of Heauen F. Oaths by God's name appear 22 times elsewhere in the canon; there is no parallel for F's reading.
2.1.80   stockings] Q2 (ſtockins), F
2.1.92/900   a] Q2; he F
2.1.98/906   shoulder] Q1-2; ſhoulders Q3-5, F1-4, ROWE. Not having found any parallels for F's idiom, we have excluded it, but its acceptance in 17th-c. texts suggests that the idiom may have been current.
2.1.102/910   Come,] Q2; not in F
2.1.113   quoted] Q2 (coted), F. See Modernizing, p. 11.
2.1.113/921   fear'd] Q2; feare F
2.1.115/923   By heauen] Q1-2; It ſeemes F
2.2.0.1/928.1   Florish.] Q2; not in F, Q1
2.2.10/938   deeme] F; dreame Q2. F's reading cannot result from the simple compositorial omission of 'r': Compositor B always spells 'dream-' (106 times), never 'dreem-'. In fact, the spelling 'dreem-' never occurs in the Shakespeare canon.
2.2.13   vouchsafe] Q2 (voutſafe), F
2.2.17/945   Whether . . . thus] Q2; not in F
2.2.20/948   is] Q2; are Q3, F. Even if F were not influenced by Q3-4, it might independently have sophisticated the grammar.
2.2.29/957   But we] Q1-2; We]; Which we This edition conj. It is difficult to explain why F should have omitted 'but' here.
2.2.31/959   seruice] Q2; Seruices F
2.2.39/967   I] Q2; not in F
2.2.43/971   Assure you] F; I aſſure Q1-2. F is not only the rarer but the more metrical reading; Q1 could result from the simplest of memorial substitutions; its text here ('I assure your grace') does not deserve enough confidence to warrant alteration of F.
2.2.45/973   and] Q1-2; one F. An easy misreading.
2.2.48/976   it hath] Q2; I haue F; it had Q1. Assimilation to the second half of the line.
2.2.52/980   fruite] Q2; Newes F. Assimilation to the first half of the line.
2.2.58/986   my] Q2; not in F. A tight line in F, which can be turned neither up nor down, in a crowded column of a cast-off page (oo2ᵛ): the omission, which produces a less metrical line, may well be compositorial.
2.2.59/987   Voltemand] Q2; Voltumand F
2.2.99/1027   tis tis] Q2; it is F
2.2.112/1041-2   heare: these] JENKINS; heare: thus Q2; heare, theſe F
2.2.126/1055   solicitings] Q2; ſoliciting F
2.2.150/1079   wherein] Q2; whereon F
2.2.162/1091   dooes] Q2; ha's F
2.2.168/1097   But] Q2; And F
2.2.180/1109   tenne] Q1-2; two F
2.2.183/1112   good] F, Q2; God HANMER (Warburton). Compare 'a great eating country' (More II.D.7)
2.2.189/1118   a sayd] Q2; he ~ F
2.2.190/1119   a is] Q2; he ~ F
2.2.197/1126   reade] Q1-2; meane F. Contamination from the first half of the line.
2.2.201/1130   lacke] Q2; locke F. Simple misreading.
2.2.202/1131   most] Q2; not in F; pittifull Q1

2.2.214/1145   My Lord, I will take] Q1-2; My Honourable Lord, I will moſt humbly | Take F. As Jenkins suggests, these Folio variants—on the penultimate line of oo3, where 15 lines have been mis-set as verse in order to stretch badly cast-off copy—are probably compositorial padding. Compare Contention 4.7.141/2600, Timon 5.1.3-38/1968-2005, Tragedy of Lear 4.5.158-9/2365-6, and Richard III 1.4.264-70/1027-33, where in similar circumstances Compositor B is guilty of similar sophistications.
*2.2.217-18/1148-9   except my life, my life, my life] This edition; except my life, my life F; except my life, except my life, except my life Q2. Almost no one has found F's reading convincing, yet it is difficult to explain as a mere error for Q2's. But F could easily result from simple eyeskip if Shakespeare in revising intended a triple repetition not of the whole prepositional phrase, but only of 'my life'.
2.2.221/1152   the] Q2; my F. Probable contamination from 'my Lord' in 2.2.219/1150.
2.2.226/1157   A] Q2; Oh F. See 1.2.135/291.
2.2.280/1210   of] Q1-2; not in F
2.2.292   off] Q2 (of), F
2.2.295/1225   discouery, and] Q2; ~ˬ of F
2.2.296/1226   Queene,] Q2; ~ : F
2.2.298/1228   heauily] Q2; heauenly F
*2.2.301/1231   orehanging] F (ore-hanging); orehanging firmament Q2. For 'orehanging' as a substantive see OED (1548+); the alternative formation 'overhang' is not recorded until the 19th c. The roof of the stage could be described as an 'orehanging', but not as a 'firmament'; F's variant here helps sustain the theatrical punning in this passage.
2.2.314/1244   then, when] Q1-2; when F
2.2.325/1255   tickled] F, Q1; tickle CLARENDON (Staunton)
2.2.342/1272   be-ratle] F2; be-ratled F1
2.2.349/1279   like most will] WILSON; like moſt F; most like POPE
2.2.366/1296   s'bloud] Q2; not in F. See second note to 3.2.357/2085.
2.2.385   Haply] Q2, F (Happily)
2.2.392/1322   was] Q1-2; not in F
2.2.396/1326   came] Q2; can F
2.2.400/1330   indeuidible] Q2; indiuible F. (Haplography.)
2.2.400/1331   Sceneca] Q2; Seneca F. Given Shakespeare's peculiar use of sc- in words like silence, Q2's spelling cannot confidently be corrected; Shakespeare is as likely as the compositor here to have been influenced by association with 'scena'; he may even have regarded the spelling as a private pun.
2.2.401/1332   light,] F; ~ˬ Q2
2.2.402/1332   liberty,] JOHNSON (subs.); ~ : Q2; ~ . F
2.2.421/1352   pious chanson] Q2; Pons Chanſon F; godly Ballet Q1
2.2.425/1356   valanct] Q2; vallanced Q1; valiant F
2.2.435/1365   good] Q1-2; not in F
2.2.438   caviare] Q1-2 (cauiary), F (Cauiarie)
2.2.440/1370   iudgements] Q1-2; iudgement F
2.2.446-7/1376-7   as wholesome as sweete, & . . . fine] Q2; as wholeſome as ſweete Q1; not in F
2.2.447/1377   One] Q2; One cheefe F; a Q1. F's interpolation might result from a scribal eyeskip, inadequately corrected.
2.2.458   heraldry] Q2 (heraldy), F, Q1
2.2.459/1389   totall] Q1-2; to take F
2.2.467/1397   so proceede you] Q2; not in F; ſo goe on Q1
2.2.471   antique] Q2, F (anticke). No doubt punning on 'antic'.
2.2.476/1406   Then senselesse Illium,] F; not in Q2. Q1 omits the remainder of the speech; Jenkins thinks Q2's omission of these three words is due to Q1's cut being marked in Q2's copy, with the Q2 compositor mistakenly taking the beginning of the intended cut as a deletion of this phrase. But it seems impossible that Polonius was ever meant to say 'This is too long' after a mere six lines of verse; Hamlet (whom he has just praised) spoke fifteen, without complaint. The omission could be due to simple eyeskip, from 'senselesse' to 'seeming'; eyeskip would be even easier if Q2's manuscript read 'senselesse Illium'. Alternatively, the foul papers may have had an entire verse line here, ac-

cidentally omitted: the preceding lines can be divided into six regular lines, instead of five lines with two part-lines (Greeks| arm| command| drives| wide| falls|—as, substantively, in Q1). Although even an editor committed to Q2 must accept F's version of the missing phrase, in considering explanations for Q2's apparent lacuna one cannot simply assume that Q2's manuscript had the same reading as F's.

2.2.481   reverend] Q2 (reuerent), F
2.2.490/1420   A rowsed] Q2, F (A ro wſed); Aroused COLLIER
2.2.492/1422   Armor] Q2; Armours F
2.2.501/1431   to the] Q1–2; to'th F
2.2.504–5/1434–5   mobled] Q1–2; inobled F
2.2.506/1436   Mobled] Q1; Inobled F; not in Q2
2.2.507/1437   flames] Q2; flame F
2.2.511   alarm] F, Q1 (Alarum), Q2
2.2.521   whe'er] Q2 (where), F (whether); if Q1
2.2.522/1452   prethee] Q2; Pray you F
2.2.528/1458   liue] Q1–2; liued F
2.2.531/1461   much] Q2; not in F; farre Q1
2.2.536/1466   Exit Polonius] F (Exit Polon.), Q1 (exit.). Q2 instead has 'Exeunt Pol. and Players' after 2.2.548/1478; but the independent agreement of Q1 and F can hardly be ignored as a reflection of theatrical practice.
2.2.540, 544/1470, 1474   PLAYERS] Q1; Play. F; Play. Q2. Q2 uses the same ambiguous prefix for all the Player speeches in this scene, and so might intend all to be spoken by one actor. F elsewhere has '1. Play.', and this clearly distinguishes these two speeches from their predecessors; in this it agrees with Q1, which—in addition to specifying 'players' here—has Hamlet say 'Come hither maisters' at the equivalent of 2.2.537/1467.
2.2.541   ha't] Q2 (hate), F
2.2.547   till] Q2 (tell), F. The same spelling occurs at 4.5.158/2714 and 5.1.296/3267. See also 'well' (3671). These spellings occur, apparently, in the work of both Q2 compositors.
2.2.550   b'wi'] F, Q2 (buy)
2.2.555/1485   wand] Q2; warm'd F
2.2.557   and] Q2 (an), F
2.2.577/1507   s'wounds] Q2; Why F; Sure Q1. See second note to 3.2.357/2085.
2.2.580/1510   a] Q1–2; haue Q3, F. Even if F were not influenced by Q3–4 here, it regularly sophisticates 'a' to 'haue': see note to *Henry V* 2.2.95, 96/702, 703.
2.2.581/1511   offall, bloody, baudy] Q2; Offall, bloudy: a Bawdy F
2.2.584/1514   Why,] Q2; Who? F. F might be defended as a contemporary spelling of *whoa* (see OED), with the query understood as an exclamation mark: Hamlet calls his rhetoric to a halt.
*2.2.585/1515   the deere murthered] F (Deere); a deere murthered Q2; my deare father Q1; a deare father murthered Q3. As Wilson recognized, 'since "father" is in any case clearly understood [the reporter who prepared the text of Q1] may have supplied the word himself' (MSH, p. 301). Q2 and F not only offer the *difficilior lectio*; they agree on the absence of 'father' and on the trisyllabic spelling 'murthered'. Moreover, Q1's reading—'I the sonne of my deare father'—makes explicit the redundance of 'father' in any version of the line. Shakespeare elsewhere regularly puns on deer/dear, and frequently associates 'deer' with death. (Edwards also retains F here.)
2.2.598/1528   a] Q2; he F
3.1.1   And] Q2 (An), F
3.1.32/1568   heere] Q2; there F
3.1.45/1581   please you] Q2; pleaſe ye F. The last word in a line which in F fills the column measure.
3.1.50/1586   sugar] Q2; ſurge F. F could result from simple compositorial transposition of the spelling 'sugre'. Compositor B is particularly prone to such literal errors.
3.1.51/1587   too true] Q2; true F
3.1.57.1/1593.1   Exeunt King and Polonius] CAPELL; Exeunt. F; not in Q2. Neither text mentions an arras in this scene, as Hamlet 3.4.7.1/2221.1 and K. John 4.1.2/1490 do; moreover, unlike those two scenes, this one contains an entrance direction for the characters who have been hiding (Q2 and F) and an exeunt direction when they hide (F).
3.1.73/1609   Th'] Q2; The F
3.1.73/1609   proude] Q2; poore F
3.1.76/1612   th'] Q2; the F
3.1.89/1625   awry] Q2; away F. Q2's is the rarer reading; F, an easy misreading.
3.1.99/1635   you know] Q1–2; I know F
3.1.101/1637   their perfume lost,] Q4 (subs.); ~, Q2; then perfume left: F
3.1.112/1648   with] Q1–2; your F
3.1.135/1671   no where] Q1–2; no way F
3.1.140/1676   go] F (Go); not in Q2. 'To a Nunnery goe' occurs seven times in Q1; three times in F; only twice in Q2. Q1's excessive repetition thus tends to support F's variant here.
3.1.145/1681   paintings too] Q1; paintings Q2; pratlings too F
3.1.146/1682   hath] Q1–2; has F
3.1.146/1682   face] Q1–2; pace F. For p/f misreadings compare the press variant 'pall/fall' at 5.2.9/3276 (Q2 'pall' uncorr.; Q2 'fall' corr.)
3.1.146/1682   selfes] Q1–2; ſelfe F
3.1.158/1694   And] Q2; Haue F
3.2.5/1732   with] Q1–2; not in F
3.2.7/1734   your] Q2; not in F
3.2.9/1736   heare] Q1–2; ſee F
3.2.10   tatters] Q1–2 (totters), F
3.2.10   split] Q2 (ſpleet), F, Q1
3.2.13/1740   would] Q1–2; could F
3.2.19/1746   ore-steppe] Q2; ore-ſtop F
3.2.32/1759   nor no man] HIBBARD; nor | man Q2; or Norman F; Nor Turke Q1
3.2.54/1781   HAMLET Nay] F, Q2 (c.w.); Nay Q2 (text)
3.2.58/1785   tongue, licke] Q2; ~, like F
3.2.60   feigning] F (faining)
3.2.61/1788   her] Q2; my F
3.2.77/1804   thy] Q2; my F
3.2.82/1809   stithy] Q2; Stythe F. F means the same thing (see OED stith); but metrically a disyllable is preferable, and e/y misreading would be easy.
3.2.82/1809   heedfull] Q2, F4; needfull F1–3
3.2.86/1813   a] Q2; he F
3.2.94/1821   mine now, my Lord, you] JOHNSON; mine now, my Lord. | You Q2; mine. Now, my Lord, you F; My Lord, you Q1
3.2.127   by'r Lady] F (byrlady), Q2 (ber Lady)
3.2.127/1855   a must] Q2; he muſt F
3.2.127–8/1855–6   a suffer] Q2; he ſuffer F
3.2.129.1–2/1857.1–2   Hoboyes play. The dumbe show enters. Enter] F; The Trumpets ſounds. Dumbe ſhow followes. Enter Q2 (text); Enter Q2 (c.w.)
3.2.131   malhecho] Q2 (Mallico), F (Malicho), Q1 (Mallico)
3.2.134/1862   this fellow] Q1–2; theſe Fellowes F
3.2.136/1864   a] Q2; he Q1; they F
3.2.145   posy] F, Q1 (Poeſie), Q2 (poſie)
3.2.157   former] Q2; forme F
3.2.165/1893   their] Q2; my F
3.2.167/1895   kind,] Q2; ~. F
3.2.187/1915   eyther] Q2; other F
3.2.188/1916   ennactures] Q2; ennactors F
3.2.190/1918   Greefe ioyes] F; Greefe ioy Q2. Although Q2 is clearly in error, its copy might have had 'Greefes ioy, ioy griefes', which would create a rhetorically neater line.
3.2.190   grieves] Q2 (griefes), F
3.2.195/1923   fauourite] Q2; fauourites F
3.2.207/1935   me giue] Q2; giue me F
3.2.231   wince] Q2, F (winch), Q1
3.2.231   unwrung] Q2 (vnwrong), F (vnrung), Q3
3.2.233/1961   as good as a] Q1–2; a good F
3.2.237/1965   mine] Q2; my F. F's variant may be due to justification.
3.2.239   mis-take] Q2, F (miſtake); muſt take Q1
3.2.239/1968   your] Q1–2; not in F

3.2.246 ban] Q2, F, Q1 (bane)
3.2.249/1978 A] Q2; He F, Q1
3.2.259/1988 stricken] Q2 (ſtrooken), F (ſtrucken), Q1
3.2.272 pajock] Q2 (paiock), F1 (Paiocke), F2 (Pajocke); Paicock Q1676; Pecock Q1695; peacock POPE
*3.2.278.1/2007.1 *Enter Rosencrans and Guyldensterne*] F places the direction here; Q1 also places it before Hamlet's rhyme at 3.2.280-1/2009-10, and this agreement must reflect stage practice. (In Q2 it immediately precedes Guildenstern's speech below.) In F, their entrance prompts Hamlet's request for recorders.
3.2.279/2008 Ah ha,] Q2; Oh, ha? F
3.2.281 pardie] Q1-2 (perdy), F (perdie)
3.2.310/2039 as you] Q2; you F
3.2.314 struck] Q2 (ſtrooke), F (ſtroke)
3.2.346/2074 fingers] Q2; finger F
3.2.357/2085 it speak,] Q2; it. F. Perhaps accidentally related to the next variant.
3.2.357/2085 s'bloud] Q2; Why F; Zownds Q1. F's substitution probably originated in the printing house: see Taylor, 'Zounds'.
3.2.357/2085 I] Q1-2; that I F. Given the other disturbances to this line of type (see two preceding notes), F's additional word might be a compositorial expedient to avoid resetting the whole paragraph.
3.2.364/2092 yonder] Q1-2; that F
3.2.365/2093 of] Q1-2; like F
3.2.366/2094 masse] Q2, F4; Miſſe F1. F1 is no more than a variant spelling or form: see *OED*, sb.¹. Censorship need not be presumed.
3.2.366/2094 and tis,] Q2; and it's, F; T'is Q1. See 1.5.35/652.
3.2.371/2099 HAMLET Then] F, Q2 (c.w.); Then Q2 (text)
*3.2.374-6/2102-4 POLONIUS . . . friends:] F (Friends); Leaue me friends. | I will, ſay ſo. By and by is eaſily ſaid, Q2. Though the Q2 compositor might theoretically be responsible for two successive omitted prefixes, and though the foul papers may not have marked Polonius's exit, the transposition of 'Leaue me friends' and the strange lineation of the whole passage suggest that the foul papers were confusing here. Perhaps 3.2.371-5/2099-2103 (Then . . . said) were a marginal addition in the foul papers.
3.2.388/2116 *Exit*] Q1-2; *not in* F, Q4
3.3.14/2130 weale] Q2; ſpirit F
3.3.15 cease] Q2 (ceſſe), F
3.3.18 summit] Q2 (ſomnet), F (Somnet), ROWE. See 600.
3.2.72.1/2188.1 *Hee kneeles*] Q1 (hee); *not in* Q2, F
3.3.73/2189 a] Q2; he F
3.3.74/2190 a] Q2; he F
3.3.77/2193 sole] Q2; foule F. F might be a variant spelling, but *OED* last records it as such in the 15th c.
3.3.80/2196 A] Q2; He F, Q1
3.3.81/2197 flush] Q2; freſh F
3.3.88 hint] QF (hent)
3.4.1/2215 A] Q2; He F
3.4.4/2218 silence] Q2, F; ſhrowde Q1; 'sconce HANMER
3.4.7.1/2221.1 *Polonius hides behind the Arras*] exit Cor⟨ambis⟩. Q1 (*after Polonius's speech*); *not in* Q2, F
3.4.12/2226 a wicked] Q2; an idle F
*3.4.16/2230 But would you were not so, you] This edition; But would you were not ſo. You F; And would it were not ſo, you Q2; And (would it were not so) you POPE
3.4.31/2245 better] Q2; Betters F
3.4.36 brassed] Q2 (braſd), F (braz'd)
3.4.41 off] Q2 (of), F
3.4.43/2257 sets] Q2; makes F
3.4.54/2268 this] Q2; his F, Q3
3.4.64/2278 brother] Q2; breath F
3.4.78/2292 And] Q2; As F
3.4.80 grainèd] F. Q2's 'greeued' probably results from minim misreading of 'greined', a variant spelling of F's word (see *OED*).
3.4.93.1/2307.1 *in his night gowne*] Q1; *not in* Q2, F
3.4.108/2322 you doe] Q2; you F; thus you Q1

3.4.109/2323 th'incorporall] Q2; their corporall F
3.4.112/2326 haire] Q2; hairs ROWE
3.4.113 on] Q2, F (an)
3.4.122/2336 whom] Q2, F2; who F1
3.4.142 o'er] F (or)
3.4.143/2357 rancker] Q2; ranke F
3.4.144/2358 these] F (this), Q2
3.4.166/2380 blowt] Q2; blunt F
3.4.166 bloat] Q2 (blowt)
3.4.172 mad] Q2; made F
3.4.191/2405 *Exit Hamlet tugging in Polonius*] F (subs.); *Exit lugging in Polonius* JENKINS; *Exit*. Q2; *Exit Hamlet with the dead body.* Q1. See next note.
4.1.0.1/2405.1 *Enter King*] F; *Eenter King, and Queene, with Roſencraus and Guyldenſterne*. Q2; *Enter the King and Lordes*. Q1. For the act-break, see Introduction. Despite Jenkins, there is nothing wrong with Q2's direction: immediate re-entry is acceptable, so long as the character enters with a new group. Q2 also has '*Exit*' for '*Exeunt*' elsewhere. The agreement of F and Q1 in specifying that only Hamlet exits, and in omitting Gertrude from the following entrance direction, thus apparently results from a deliberate change of staging.

The treatment of Rosencrantz and Guildenstern is more problematic. In Q2 they enter (4.1.0.1/2405.1), are dismissed (4.1.4/2409), are called back (4.1.32/2436), are dismissed again (4.1.36.1/2441.1), and enter again (after 4.2.3/2448). F simplifies this sequence by deleting the first two actions. F's change must be deliberate, for it involves two separated but related omissions (4.1.0.1/2405.1 and 4.1.4/2409). Q1 also simplifies the Q2 sequence, by omitting its second and third elements. But Q1 seems farther than F from Q2, for F and Q2 agree in keeping the Queen's narrative to Claudius (4.1.6-31/2411-36) confidential. Moreover, in Q2 (where the lords are present) the locale has, by a clearing of the stage, shifted from Gertrude's closet, so that the lords' entrance does not seem inappropriate; F's change of staging keeps the scene in Gertrude's closet, and only allows the lords to enter when summoned. Q1 seems, by comparison with F, less concerned with the locale. Q1 might represent a further deliberate modification of staging; but it might also result from memorial compression.

4.1.1./2406 matter] Q2; matters F
4.1.1/2406 sighes, these profound heaues,] Q2; ~. ~, F. See lineation note.
4.1.6/2411 sea] Q1-2; Seas F
4.1.11/2416 O] Q2; On F
4.1.21/2426 let] Q2; let's F. Though no editor since Pope has accepted it, F might be defended as a typical shift of construction.
4.1.26/2431 a] Q2; He F
4.1.34/2439 mothers closet] Q2; Mother Cloſſets F. Metathesis (Compositor B).
4.2.16-17/2461-2 like an ape an apple] PARROTT-CRAIG (Farmer); like an Ape F; like an apple Q2; as an Ape doth nuttes Q1
4.3.7/2482 neuer] Q2; neerer F
4.3.20/2495 a] Q2; he F
4.3.21/2496 politique] Q1-2; *not in* F
4.3.23/2498 our selues] Q2; our ſelfe F
4.3.24-5/2500 seruice, two dishes but to one table,] Q2; ſeruice, to diſhes, ~, F; ſeruices, two diſhes, to one meſſe: Q1
4.3.26-8/2502-5 KING Alas . . . that worme.] Q2; *not in* F; Looke you, a man may fiſh with that worme | That hath eaten of a King, | And a Beggar eate that fiſh, | Which that worme hath caught. Q1
4.3.38/2515 A will] Q2; He will F; hee'le Q1
4.3.44/2521 is] Q2; at F
4.3.50/2527 thē] Q2; him F
4.3.59.1/2536.1 *Exit. ⌜Guyldensterne⌝*] This edition; *not in* Q2, F
4.5.12/2568 might] Q2; would F
*4.5.14/2570 QUEENE] F (Qu.); Hora⟨tio⟩. Q2. Editors who follow Q2 here usually insert a speech-prefix for Gertrude before 4.5.16/2572 ('Let her come in').

4.5.16.1/2572.1 *Horatio withdraws, to admit Ophelia*] HIBBARD; *not in* F, Q2
4.5.20.1/2576.1-2 *her haire downe, with a Lute*] Q1 (*playing on a Lute, and her haire downe finging*); *not in* Q2; F. Q1 specifies a conventional—and Shakespearian—detail associated with the theatrical representation of female madness; the lute is unlikely to have been added in a provincial tour, or by a reporter, and so presumably reflects normal theatrical practice.
4.5.23/2579 OPHELIA (*sings*)] Q2 (ſhee ſings. | *Oph.*). F omits the direction but italicizes Ophelia's songs.
4.5.41 God'ield] Q2, F (God dil'd), Q1 (God yeeld)
4.5.51 clothes] Q2 (cloſe), F, Q1
4.5.55 Ophelia—] JENKINS; ~. Q2, F
4.5.66/2622 thus] Q2; this F
4.5.76/2632 sorrowes come] Q2; ſorrowes comes F
4.5.77/2633 battalians] Q2; Battaliaes F. See *Richard III* 5.3.11/3058, where Compositor B sets the same form for copy 'battalion'.
4.5.87/2643 Feeds] Q2; Keepes F
4.5.87/2643 this] Q2; his F
4.5.90/2646 Wherein] Q2; Where in F
4.5.95/2651 is] Q2; are F, Q3. See note to 2.2.20/948.
4.5.98 impetuous] Q2 (impitious), F (impittious)
4.5.109.1/2665.1 *Laertes ⌈with his followers at the doore⌉*] THEOBALD; *Laertes with others* Q2 (*after* 4.5.108/2664); *Laertes* F (*after* 4.5.108/2664). F's following dialogue makes it clear that he is accompanied, although the 'others' may not get past the threshold of the stage doors.
4.5.116/2672 thats calme] Q2; that calmes F. Metathesis (Compositor B).
4.5.118/2674 browe] F (brow), Q2; brows Q1676
4.5.126/2682 Where is] Q2; Where's F
4.5.140/2696 i'st] Q2; if F
4.5.141 sweepstake] Q2 (ſoopſtake), F (Soop-ſtake), Q1 (Swoop-ſtake-like)
4.5.146/2702 Pelican] Q2; Politician F
4.5.150/2706 sencibly] Q2; ſencible Q3; ſenſible F
4.5.152.1-154.1/2708.1-2710.1 *A noyse ... Ophelia*] SPENCER; *A noyſe within.* | *Enter Laertes.* | *Laer⟨tes⟩.* Let her come in. | How now, what noyſe is that?* Q2; *A noiſe within. Let her come in.* | *Enter Ophelia.*| *Laer⟨tes⟩.* How now? what noiſe is that? F; *A noise within.* [*Ophelia is heard singing.*] | Let her come in. | *Laer⟨tes⟩.* How now, what noise is that? | *Enter* OPHELIA. JENKINS
4.5.154.1/2710.1 *as before*] Q1; *not in* Q2, F
4.5.167/2723 rain'd] Q2; raines F
4.5.168/2724 fare you well my Doue.] F italicizes as part of the song; Q2 prints this line (like the song) in roman, apparently as verse; CAPELL first clearly separated it.
4.5.176/2732 Pancies] Q2, F2; panſey Q1; Paconcies F1
4.5.184/2739 a made] Q2; he made F
4.5.188-9/2743-4 a ... a] Q2; he ... he F, Q1
4.5.197/2752 God a mercy] Q1-2; Gramercy F
4.5.198.1/2753.1 *Exeunt Ophelia and Queene*] This edition (*conj.* J. P. Kemble); *not in* Q2; *Exeunt Ophelia* F; *exit Ofelia.* Q1. Edwards notes that Kemble's direction became customary in the theatre. It seems relatively unlikely that Claudius intends Gertrude to hear his subsequent speeches to Laertes, with their clearly implied allusions to revenge upon Hamlet; Gertrude next enters to report on Ophelia; and the emendation explains F's anomalous verb.
4.5.199/2754 ô God] Q2; you Gods F
4.5.200 commune] F (common), Q2
4.5.212 trophy] Q2 (trophe), F
4.5.213 rite] Q2 (right), F
4.5.215/2770 call't] Q2; call F
4.6.5.1/2777.1 Saylers] Q2; Saylor F. The other references in this scene are consistently plural; F's variant is of no significance to the play's casting pattern, and could result from the easiest of scribal or compositorial slips.
4.6.8/2780 A] Q2; Hee F
4.6.8 an't] Q2 (and), F (and't)
4.6.9/2781 Embassador] Q2; Ambaſſadours F
4.6.12/2784 HORATIO Q2 (*Hor.*); *not in* F

4.6.23/2796 thine] Q2; *your* F
4.7.11/2815 tha'r] Q2; they are F
*4.7.14/2818 coniunctiue] F; concliue Q2. It is hard to see Q2 as a misreading of F, especially because Q2 produces an apparent disyllable, which agrees with Q2's 'She is' earlier in the line. The obvious alternative, which combines elements of F and Q2, is 'coniunct' (*History of Lear* 22.14/2713); but the proposed misreading is not easy. The alternative 'conioyne' is not recorded elsewhere, but would be a typically Shakespearian formation from adjective 'conioined'. Even better, both palaeographically and as sense, would be a neologism 'contrine', produced by adding the prefix *con* to the technical astrological term *trine*: like 'conjunctiue', this would contribute to the subsequent astrological imagery, in terms of the 'trine' of Gertrude, 'heart', and 'soul'.
4.7.21/2825 Guilts] HIBBARD; Giues Q2; Gyues F; crimes ELZE (*conj.*)
4.7.21/2825 graces] F (Graces), Q2; graues ELZE (*conj.*; = greaves)
4.7.24/2828 aym'd] Q2; arm'd F
*4.7.27/2831 Who has] JOHNSON; Who was F; Whoſe worth Q2; Who once QUINCY (MS, cited in Furness)
4.7.49/2853 abuse, and] Q2; abuſe? Or F
4.7.56/2860 diddest thou] F; didſt thou Q2; he dies Q1; diest thou WILSON 2 (Marshall)
4.7.67/2871 since] Q2; hence F
4.7.70/2874 can] Q2; ran F
4.7.78/2882 Lamord] Q2; Lamound F
4.7.80/2884 the] Q2; our F
4.7.80/2884 made] Q2; mad F (*a possible spelling variant*)
*4.7.85/2889 you;] Q2; ~ₐ F. Q2 follows this with two lines not present in F: see Additional Passages.
4.7.85/2889 sirₐ this] Q2; Sir. This F. See preceding note. F's mispunctuation of this line is worth recording only because the error apparently post-dates the Folio cut.
4.7.89/2893 What] Q2; Why F
*4.7.98/2902 your fathers sonne in deede] F4 (*subs.*); your Fathers ſonne indeed F1; indeede your fathers ſonne Q2; in deed your father's son MALONE
4.7.111/2915 passe] F; pace Q2. According to *OED* 'passe' was an acceptable spelling of *pace*, but not vice versa; hence F appears to be a correction, rather than a mere modernization.
4.7.112 Requite] F (Requit), Q2
4.7.115/2919 that but dippe] Q2; I but dipt F; if I but dipt This edition *conj.*
4.7.123/2927 shape, if this should fayle,ₐ] ROWE; ~ₐ ~, Q2; ~, ~; F
4.7.128/2932 cunnings] Q2; commings F. For F's misreading compare *All's Well* 5.3.219/2737, *Troilus* 3.2.129/1704.
4.7.129 ha't] Q2 (hate), F
4.7.130/2934 that] Q2; the F
*4.7.134/2938 how now sweet Queene.] F2 (*subs.*); how ſweet Queene. F1; How now Gertred, Q1; but ſtay, what noyſe? Q2
4.7.136/2940 they] Q2; they'l F
4.7.140/2944 Therewith] Q2; There with F, Q3
4.7.140/2944 make] Q2; Hauing made Q1; come F
4.7.144 crownet] Q2 (cronet), F (Coronet)
4.7.153/2957 theyr] Q1-2; her F
4.7.154/2958 lay] Q2; buy F
4.7.156/2960 Alas, then,ₐ is she drownd.] HIBBARD; Alas, then, is ſhe drown'd? F; Alas then is ſhe drownd. Q3; Alas, then,ₐ ſhe is drownd. Q2; So, ſhe is drownde: Q1. Q1 may have contaminated Q2; or Q3, F; or neither, either.
4.7.164 douts] F (doubts). See note on Additional Passage B.21.
5.1.4, 22 coroner] Q2, F (Crowner)
5.1.9/2980 se offendêdo] F (*Se offendendo*); ſo offended Q2; *so offendendo* HIBBARD
5.1.12/2982 to act] Q2; an Act F
5.1.14 Goodman] Q2 (good man), F
5.1.23 on't] Q2 (an't), F
5.1.25/2995 a] Q2; of F
5.1.29/3000 Christen] Q2; Chriſti-|an F
5.1.33/3004 A] Q2; He F

HAMLET

5.1.55.1/3026.1 *Enter . . . a farre off*] F; *Enter Hamlet and Horatio* Q2 (after 5.1.64/3035), Q1 (after 5.1.60/3031)

*5.1.60/3031 stoope] Q1 (ſtope), F (ſtoupe); ſoope Q2. Wilson explained Q2's reading as the result of an 'omitted letter' (*MSH*, 118); but if the compositor had intended to set F's word he would have used the ligature 'ſt', rather than two distinct types. Q2 is a recognized spelling of the noun *sup*, meaning 'A small quantity of liquid such as can be taken into the mouth at one time; a mouthful; a sip' (*OED*, sb.¹, quotations 1570+).

5.1.64/3035 there a was nothing a] Q2; *there was nothing* F
5.1.65/3036 a] Q2; he F
5.1.70/3041 daintier] F; dintier Q2. Although *OED* gives no parallels, Q2 may be an acceptable spelling of the alternative '-ei-' pronunciation (Dobson, §226).
5.1.74.1/3045.1 *He throwes vp a skull*] *he throwes vp a ſhouel.* Q1; *not in* Q2, F
5.1.76/3047 twere] Q2; it | were F. Q2's 'twere' would not have fitted at the end of the Folio line 5.1.76/3047, and Compositor E would have been hard put to stretch out the line with enough extra spaces if he had carried 'twere' entirely over on to 5.1.77/3048.
5.1.77/3048 this] Q2; It F. Again, the end of a justified prose line in F: 'this' would not fit, it would be awkward to space out the line, and 'it' occurs in the same position in the line above.
5.1.79/3050 would] Q2; could F
5.1.84/3055 a] Q2; he F, Q1
5.1.87 chapless] Q2 (Choples), F (Chapleſſe)
5.1.88/3059 and] Q2; if F
5.1.96/3067 of] Q1, Q2, F2; of of F1
5.1.108/3079 th'inheritor] Q2; the Inheritor F. F may again be due to justification problems.
5.1.112 calf-skins] Q2 (Calues-skinnes), Q3, F (Calue-skinnes)
5.1.115/3086 sirra] Q2; Sir F
5.1.117/3088 (*Sings*)] *not in* Q2; *not in* F (which italicizes following words)
5.1.135 these] Q1-2 (this), F
5.1.137/3108 heele] Q1-2; heeles F. Compositor E is especially prone to errors involving omission or addition of terminal 's'.
5.1.137/3108 the Courtier] Q1-2; our Courtier F
5.1.147-8/3118-19 a . . . a . . . a] Q2; he . . . hee . . . he F
5.1.148/3119 tis] Q2; it's F. See 1.5.35/652.
5.1.150/3121 him there, there] Q2; him, there F
5.1.157/3128 Sexten] Q2; ſixeteene F
5.1.160/3131 a . . . a] Q2; he . . . he F, Q1
5.1.162/3133 a] Q2; he F, Q1
5.1.166/3137 a will] Q2; he will F
5.1.175-6/3146-7 this same skull sir] Q2; This ſame Scull Sir, this ſame Scull ſir F. Compositor E, who set this Folio page, was guilty of pointless dittography ten times in plays set from known copy (Werstine, *Division*, 300); and compare 5.1.96/3067 ('of of'). Although deliberate repetition is possible, F's reading would be more attractive without the repeated 'sir'.
5.1.182/3153 now how] Q1-2; how F
5.1.187/3158 not] Q2; No F
5.1.187/3159 grinning] Q2; Ieering F
5.1.196 Pah] F (puh), Q2
5.1.200/3171 a] Q2; he F
5.1.208/3179 Imperiall] F; Imperious Q1-2. See Nosworthy, 136-7, and 'Th'Imperiall *Cæsar*' (*Cymbeline* 5.6.476/3281).
5.1.212.3/3183.2 *a Priest*] Q1; *not in* Q2, F. Q1 and F agree in identifying the character in speech-prefixes as a '*Priest*'.
5.1.214 rites] Fa (rights), Q2, Fb (rites)
5.1.216/3187 of] Q2; *not in* F
5.1.221 warrantise] F (warrantis)
5.1.224/3195 prayers] Q2; praier F. See first note to 5.1.137/3108.
5.1.243/3213 treble woe] Q2; terrible woer F. Compositor E's error here would make more sense if his copy read 'woes'.
5.1.247.1/3217.1 *Leaps in the graue*] F; *Leartes leapes into the graue* Q1; *not in* Q2
5.1.250/3220 To'retop] Q2; To o'retop F, Q1
5.1.251/3221 griefe] Q2; griefes F. See first note to 5.1.137/3108.

5.1.253/3223 Coniures] Q2; Coniure F. See first note to 5.1.137/3108.
5.1.255.1/3225.1 *Hamlet leapes in after Leartes*] Q1 (in the right margin); *not in* Q2, F. Q1's direction is confirmed by the *Elegy on Burbage* ('Oft haue I seen him leap into the graue').
5.1.259/3229 For] Q1-2; Sir F
5.1.263/3233 ALL ⌜THE LORDS⌝ Gentlemen.] Q2 (*All.*); *not in* F
5.1.263/3233 HORATIO Q2 (*Hora.*); *Gen.* F. F's prefix (for '*Gentlemen*'?) is presumably, though not simply, related to the preceding omission.
5.1.272/3242 S'wounds] Q2; Come F. See second note to 3.2.357/2085.
5.1.272 thou'lt] Q2 (th'owt), Q1 (thou wilt), F (thou'lt). It seems worth preserving the colloquialism taken up in the following lines.
5.1.273/3243 woo't fast,] Q2; *not in* F; wilt faſt, Q1
5.1.285/3255 cuplets] Q2; Cuplet F
5.1.292/3262 your] Q2; you F
5.2.7/3274 praysd] Q2; praiſe F
5.2.8/3275 sometime] Q2; ſometimes F, Q4
5.2.9/3276 pall] F (paule), Q2a; fall Q2b; fail POPE
5.2.21/3288 reasons] Q2; reaſon F
5.2.26 struck] Q2 (ſtrooke), F (ſtrucke)
5.2.30/3297 villainies] CAPELL; villaines Q2, F
5.2.31 Ere] Q2 (Or), F
5.2.38/3305 Th'] Q2; The F
5.2.38/3305 effect] Q2; effects F
5.2.41/3308 like] Q2; as F
5.2.49/3316 ordinant] Q2; ordinate F
5.2.52/3319 the forme of th'] Q2; forme of the F. F is metrically anomalous, and the omission/expansion of *the* in adjacent prepositional phrases might result from miscorrection (an error particularly probable in Compositor E's stints).
5.2.55/3322 sequent] Q2; ſement F
5.2.59/3326 defeat] Q2; debate F
5.2.74/3341 *interim's*] F; *interim is* HANMER
5.2.79/3346 court] ROWE; count F
5.2.89 chuff] Q2 (chough), F (Chowgh)
5.2.89/3356 say] Q2; ſaw F
5.2.93/3361 sir] Q2; *not in* F
5.2.103/3371 a] Q2; he F
5.2.106/3374 Nay good my Lord] Q2; Nay, in good faith, F
5.2.112/3380 King sir] Q2; ſir King F
5.2.112/3380 hath wagerd] Q2; ha's wag'd F; hath layd a wager Q1
5.2.115/3383 hanger] Q2; Hangers F. See Jenkins.
5.2.124/3392 bet] Q2; but F
*5.2.125/3393 impon'd as] F; all Q2; all 'impawned' as WILSON; all impon'd, as KITTREDGE. Perhaps Q2 should have read 'all what you call it'.
5.2.126/3394 layd sir,] Q2; laid, F
5.2.128/3396 ont] This edition; one F; layd on Q2. The voluminous unresolved debate about the terms of this wager has assumed that F is a mere error: omission of 'layd' combined with the misreading (or eccentric spelling) 'one' for 'on'. The alleged (double) error is not in itself very probable; it also, suspiciously, involves the repetition of 'layd', a key source of commentators' difficulty.

As Jenkins says, 'a moment's thought will show that if you bet on a man's not exceeding his opponent by three hits, you cannot lay *on* but are laying *against* his making twelve for nine. Hence there is something to be said for the view that *he* now refers to Laertes' (pp. 561-2). If we remove the repetition of 'layd', this identification of he with 'Laertes' is even easier. Laertes 'hath', according to the terms of the wager ('ont') a dozen passes ('twelue') in which to score nine hits ('for nine'). The language is elliptical, as betting jargon often is, but it at least does not produce contradictory nonsense (as does Q2). As Dr Johnson realized, 'In a dozen passes one must exceed the other more or less than three hits', and in fact Laertes could win the wager with eight hits instead of nine; but Shakespeare was always susceptible to simple mathematical confusions of this kind ('twelve' minus 'three' equals 'nine'), and audiences for the same reason unthinkingly accept them.

5.2.128/3396 nine] Q2; mine F. An easy minim error. (See preceding note.)
5.2.128/3396 it] Q2; that F. (Presumably 'yt' interpreted as 'yᵗ'.)
5.2.137/3405 purpose,] THEOBALD; ~ ; Q2, F
5.2.137/3405 and] Q2; if F
5.2.143/3411 *Exit Ostricke*] Q1 ('*exit*' opposite 5.2.142/3410); *not in* Q2, F
5.2.144/3412 hee] *not in* Q2; A RIVERSIDE (Parrott–Craig)
5.2.145/3413 turne] Q2; tongue F
5.2.148/3416 A] Q2; He F
5.2.148/3416 a] Q2; hee F
5.2.149/3417 has] Q2; had F
5.2.149/3417 many] Q2; mine F
*5.2.153/3421 fand] HANMER (Warburton); fond F; prophane Q2; profound TSCHISCHWITZ (Bailey)
5.2.154/3422 triall] Q2; tryalls F. See 5.1.137/3108.
5.2.158/3426 all] F, Q1; ill all's Q2. F makes sense as an incomplete foreboding sentence. (In both texts Hamlet clearly interrupts his own train of thought.)
5.2.163/3431 it] Q2; *not in* F
*5.2.169/3437 ha's ought of what he leaues] F; of ought he leaues, knowes Q2; owes aught of what he leaves HANMER; knows aught of what he leaves JOHNSON; knows of ought he leaues SPENCER; of aught he leaves knows aught JENKINS. Hanmer and Johnson emend F; Spencer and Jenkins, Q2.
5.2.190/3458 brother] Q1–2; Mother F
5.2.196/3464 vngord] Q2; vngorg'd F
5.2.203 off] Q2 (of), F
5.2.222/3490 trumpet speake] Q2; Trumpets ſpeake F. Since Q2 and F agree on singular 'trumpet' in 5.2.223/3491, the plural here is probably an error, aided by assimilation to the following 's-'; but in subsequent stage directions both Q2 (twice) and F (once) call for plural '*Trumpets*'.
5.2.224/3492 heauen] Q2, F; heauens Q3
5.2.225/3493 *Trumpets the while he drinkes*] This edition; *Trumpets* | *the while* Q2 (opposite 5.2.225–6/3493–4); *not in* F
5.2.228/3496 my Lord] Q2; on ſir F
5.2.236/3504 set it] Q1–2; ſet F
5.2.237/3505 *They play againe*] Q1; *not in* Q2, F
5.2.241/3509 Heere *Hamlet* take my] Q1–2; Heere's a F
5.2.244.1/3512.1 *Shee drinkes*] Q1; *not in* Q2, F. In Q1 this direction occurs on a line of its own between the Queen's 'Here *Hamlet*, thy mother drinkes to thee' (= 5.2.242/3510) and the King's '*Do not drinke Gertred: O t'is the poyſned cup!*' (= 5.2.243, 245/3511, 3513).
5.2.255/3523 *Laertes wounds . . . Laertes*] *In ſcuffling they change Rapiers.* F; *They catch one anothers Rapiers, and both are wounded. Leartes falles downe*, Q1; *not in* Q2
5.2.256/3524 *The Queene falles downe*] Q1 (*continuing direction at* 5.2.255/3523); *not in* Q2, F
5.2.259/3527 mine owne] Q2; mine F
5.2.263/3531 *She dies*] Q1 ('*and dies*', *continuing direction at* 5.2.255/3523); *not in* Q2, F
5.2.264 Ho!] Q2 (how₄), F (How?), Q1 (ho,)
5.2.264/3532 *Exit Ostricke*] *not in* F, Q2, Q1
5.2.275/3543 ALL THE COURTIERS] Q2, F (*All.*)
5.2.277 Here] Q2 (Heare), F (Heere)
5.2.278 off] Q2 (of), F
5.2.283/3551 *Dyes*] F; *Leartes dies.* Q1; *not in* Q2
5.2.291/3559 cause a right] Q2; cauſes right F
5.2.295/3563 hate] Q2; haue't F
5.2.296/3574 god] Q2; good F; fie Q1. Many early editors accepted F, but Q1 supports Q2's exclamation, and good/God errors occur elsewhere, even without intervention by the censor (as at *Henry V* 4.7.113/2527).
5.2.297/3565 shall liue!] F; ſhall I leaue Q2; wouldſt thou leaue Q1; I leaue HIBBARD
5.2.303/3571 th'embassadors] Q2, F; the ambaſſaders POPE. Most editors follow Pope, but a line with an extra initial stressed syllable is as acceptable as an hexameter, especially when it forms part of a line-divided foot (as here).
5.2.309/3577 th'occurrants] Q2; the occurrents F
5.2.312/3580 cracks] Q2; cracke F
5.2.314.1/3582.1 *Embassadors*] Q1–2; *Ambaſſador* F. F's singular here could result from the simplest of compositorial or scribal errors; the single ambassadorial speech repeatedly uses the plural (in all three texts).
5.2.314.2/3582.2 *with Drumme, Colours, and Attendants*] F; *with his traine* Q1; *not in* Q2
5.2.318/3586 This] Q2; His F
5.2.320/3588 shot] F (ſhoote), Q2
5.2.339/3607 th'inuenters] Q2; the Inuentors F
5.2.343 rights] F (Rites), Q1–2
5.2.344/3612 now] Q1–2; are F
5.2.345/3613 also] Q1–2; always F

Additional Passages

A.8 tenantlesse] Q4; tennatleſſe Q2
A.10 At] HIBBARD; As Q2; *lacuna marked before* 'As' JENNENS
A.14 feard] PARROTT–CRAIG (Collier); feare Q2; fearce Q3
A.18 Climature] WHITE (Dyce); Climatures Q2
B.1 (M) revel] Q2 (reueale), Q3
B.11 the] POPE; their Q2
B.20 euile] KEIGHTLEY (Jervis); eale Q2; ill JENNENS; e'il KITTREDGE; ev'l RIVERSIDE
B.21 ouer] This edition (*conj.* Jackson); of a Q2; oft HEATH (*conj.*); often STEEVENS–REED 2; of 'em HUDSON 1879. No one has offered a convincing defence of Q2, or a convincing explanation of the apparent error as palaeographical. As an aural-cum-memorial compositorial error, *ouer* is no less implausible than *often* (the usual editorial option). According to Jürgen Schäfer's *Documentation in the OED: Shakespeare and Nashe as Test Cases* (1980), Shakespeare was responsible for the first recorded use of 33 compounds based on *over-* (24 of them verbs). *Over* intensifies the sense; *often* weakens it. See next note.
B.21 doube] This edition (*conj.* K. Elze, *Athenaum*, 11 Aug. 1866, p. 186); doubt Q2; dout MALONE. See note to *Henry V* 4.2.11/2097. The only evidence for 'doubt' as a spelling of *dout* is Folio *Hamlet* 4.7.164/2698, which was not set from autograph copy. In order to defend *dout* here Jenkins (echoing Dowden) must give it an otherwise unattested sense—'efface, render invisible'—whereas its normal meaning is clearly 'utterly extinguish' (a light, or fire); which does not seem appropriate to the sense or the image. The emendation adopted here instead supposes the easy misreading of terminal 'e' as 't' (compare 3.2.296/2025 (about/aboue) and 3.2.300 (stare/start)). The verb is often used to mean 'cover with some sticky or greasy substance' (v. 2), 'soil' (v. 4), 'paint coarsely and inartistically' (v. 5), 'cover with a spacious exterior' (v. 7). This verb is therefore appropriate to the image of a 'noble substance' (something substantial and fine, *covered* with something thin and crude); it carries on the language of 'Soyle', 'ore-grow'th', 'complextion', 'ore-leauens', and 'stamp'.
B.21 (M) overdaub] This edition (*conj.* Neil in Cambridge). See preceding notes.
E.2 An] THEOBALD; And Q2
E.2 cheere] Q2; chair STEEVENS (*conj.*)
G.1–2 eate₄ | Of habits deuillish] This edition; eate₄ | Of habits deuill Q2; eat₄ | Of habit's devil ROWE; eat, | Of habits evil THEOBALD (Thirlby); eat₄ | Of habits, devil, JOHNSON; eat, | Oft habits' devil STAUNTON; eat₄ | Of habits vile HIBBARD. Theobald and Hibbard make sense of the passage by emending away what seems its characteristic and meaningful distinction between *devil* and *angel*. Our emendation retains the contrast, presupposing simple eyeskip (deuil*lish is*). Shakespeare's other uses of *devilish* are all treated, metrically, as disyllabic, producing here an acceptable extra unstressed syllable before the caesura.
G.5 refraine to night] F; to refraine night Q2
G.9 either in] This edition; either Q2; Maister Q3; either curb

MALONE; either shame HUDSON 1879; either house CHAMBERS (Bailey *and* Forsyth); either lodge JENKINS (Clarendon). This conjecture produces the same sense as 'house' or 'lodge' (for which see Jenkins); but interpolates a word much easier for a compositor to omit. For *in* as a verb, meaning 'take in, bring in, gather in', see *OED*, and *All's Well* 1.3.45/349 (in a context of adultery, as here).

H.6 (M) and't] Q 1676; an't Q2
I.1 so] CAPELL; *not in* Q2, F; For THEOBALD
I.1 enuious] JENKINS; *not in* Q2, F; haply THEOBALD
I.1 slaunder] THEOBALD; *not in* Q2, F; rumour THEOBALD (*conj. in S.R.*); Malice CAMBRIDGE (*conj.*); Envy CAMBRIDGE (*conj.*); calumny STAUNTON (*conj.*); suspicion TSCHISCHWITZ. J. E. Hankins—in *Backgrounds of Shakespeare's Thought* (1978), 20-3—points to parallels between this passage and the description of the House of *Fama* in Ovid's *Metamorphoses*, xii. 39-63; these support Theobald's conjecture 'Rumour'. But the Shakespearian parallels cited by Jenkins strongly favour 'slander'.

J.16-18 HAMLET Two . . . straw, | This] Q2; Two . . . straw.| HAMLET This HIBBARD (anon. *conj.*)
J.17 now] HIBBARD; *not* Q2
L.1 thescrimures] WHITE; the Scrimures Q2
L.1 (M) Th'escrimers] See preceding note.
N.2 gentleman] Q4; gentlemen Q2
N.4 feelingly] Q3; ſellingly Q2a; fellingly Q2b
N.8 dosie] Q2a; dazzie Q2b; dizzie Q3
N.8 (M) dizzy] Q2a (dofie). See *OED* ('dozy'), previous note, and *MSH*, 132.
N.9 yaw] Q2a; raw Q2b
N.20 too't] Q2a; doo't Q2b
N.20 rarely] THEOBALD; really Q2. The only other occurrence of Q2's word in the canon is *Kinsmen* 2.1.6/551, and is in any case not comparable.
N.34 his] Q5; this Q2

REJECTED QUARTO VARIANTS

*1.1.11/11 stand, who's] F (Stand:) ftand ho, who is
1.1.13/13 souldier] F (Soldier), Q1 (fouldier); fouldiers
1.1.14/14 ha's] hath Q1-2
1.1.19/19 MARCELLUS] F (*Mar.*); Hora⟨tio⟩. Q1-2
1.1.30/30 two nights haue] F (Nights); haue two nights Q1-2
*1.1.41/41 it not] F, Q1; a not
1.1.42/42 horrowes] Q2, F (harrowes); horrors Q1
*1.1.43/43 Question] F, Q1; Speake to
1.1.60/60 th'] F; the Q1-2
1.1.64/64 iust] iump Q1-2
*1.1.67/67 my] F, Q1; mine
1.1.72/72 why] F, Q1; with
1.1.72/72 cast] F (Caft); coft Q1-2
1.1.87/87 those] F, Q1; thefe
1.1.88/88 on] F; of Q1-2
1.1.90/90 returnd] F (return'd); returne
*1.1.92/92 cou'nant] F (Cou'nant); comart
1.1.97/97 landlesse] F (Landleffe; laweleffe Q1-2
*1.1.100/100 And] As
*1.1.102/102 compulsatiue] F (Compulfatiue); compulfatory
*1.1.106/106 land.] For Q2 see Additional Passages.
*1.1.119/119 you] F, Q1; your
*1.1.121/121 at] *not in* Q2
*1.1.141/141 The] F, Q1; This
1.1.142/142 can] dare Q1-2
*1.1.142/142 walke] F, Q1; fturre
1.1.145/145 the] that Q1-2
*1.1.148/148 Easterne] Eaftward
*1.1.156/156 conueniently] F, Q1; conuenient
*1.2.9/165 of] to
*1.2.11/167 one . . . one] an . . . a
*1.2.21/177 the] this
*1.2.40/196 VALTEMAND] F (*Volt.*); Cor⟨nelius⟩. Vo⟨ltemand⟩. Q2; *Gent.* Q1
*1.2.50/206 Dread my] My dread Q2; My gratious Q1
*1.2.55/211 towards] toward
*1.2.58/214 He] F, Q1, Q3; *not in* Q2; A PARROTT-CRAIG
1.2.67/223 so] fo much
*1.2.67/223 i'th'] in the
*1.2.68/224 nightly] nighted
*1.2.77/233 good] coold
*1.2.82/238 shewes] chapes Q2; fhapes Q3
1.2.83/239 denote] deuote
*1.2.85/241 passeth] paffes
*1.2.96/252 a] or
*1.2.112/268 towards] toward
*1.2.127/283 heauens] F (Heauens); heauen
1.2.129/285 solid] fallied Q1-2 (i.e. 'sullied')

1.2.132/288 sealfe,] F (Selfe-); feale,
*1.2.132/288 ô God, ô God] F (O . . . O); ô God, God
1.2.133/289 weary] wary
*1.2.135/291 fie, fie] fie
*1.2.137/293 to this] thus
*1.2.143/299 would] F, Q1; fhould
*1.2.149/305 euen she] *not in* Q2
*1.2.151/307 mine] F, Q1; my
*1.2.155/311 of] in
*1.2.169/325 haue] heare
*1.2.170/326 mine] my
*1.2.174/330 to drinke deepe] F, Q1; for to drinke
1.2.177/333 see] F, Q1; *not in* Q2
1.2.182/338 Ere] F, Q1; Or
*1.2.182/338 I had euer] F; euer I had Q1-2;
1.2.184/340 Oh where] Where Q1-2
1.2.198/354 wast] Q2, F; vaft Q1
1.2.200/356 Arm'd at all poynts, exactly,] F (points); Armed at poynt, exactly, Q2; Armed to poynt, exactly, Q1
1.2.200/356 *Cap a Pe*] Capapea Q1-2
*1.2.213/369 watcht] F, Q1, Q3; watch
1.2.224/380 indeede] F, Q1 (indeed); *not in* Q2
1.2.225, 226, 227/381, 382, 383 BOTH SOULDIERS] F (*Both.*); *All.* Q1-2
1.2.235/391 very like,] Q1; F (∼ :); *not in* Q2
1.2.239/395 grisly] grifsl'd Q2; grifleld Q1
1.2.241/397 Ile] I will Q1-2
*1.2.242/398 warrant you] warn't
1.2.247/403 treble] tenible Q1, tenable Q2
*1.2.248/404 what soeuer] F; Q1, what fomeuer. See text notes.
1.2.250/406 ye] you Q1-2
1.2.253/409 loue] loues, your loues Q1; loues Q2
*1.2.256/412 foule] F, Q1; fonde Q2; foule Q3
1.3.3/416 conuoy, is assistant,] F (Conuoy, ∼ ;); conuay, in afsiftant,
*1.3.12/425 bulke] F (Bulke); bulkes
*1.3.12/425 his] this
*1.3.18/431 For . . . Birth:] *not in* Q2
*1.3.21/434 the] this
*1.3.26/439 peculiar Sect and force] particuler act and place
*1.3.34/447 within] you in
1.3.45/458 th'] the
1.3.48/461 steepe] F, Q2b; ftep Q2a
*1.3.49/462 Whilst] Whiles
1.3.49/462 like] *not in* Q2
*1.3.59/472 See] Looke
1.3.62/475 The] Those Q1-2
*1.3.63/476 to] F, Q1; vnto Q2

HAMLET

*1.3.65/478 comrade] F (Comrade); courage Q1-2; comrague *conj.* Cyril Brett (*N&Q* (28 May 1904), 425-6)
*1.3.68/481 thine] thy
1.3.74/487 Ar] F, Q1 (Are), Q3; Or Q2
*1.3.74/487 generous,] F; ~, Q2; generall, Q1
1.3.75/488 bee] F (be); boy
1.3.76/489 lone] loue
*1.3.77/490 duls the] dulleth Q2; dulleth th' PARROTT-CRAIG (*conj.*)
*1.3.83/496 inuites] inuefts
*1.3.105/518 Ile] I will
*1.3.106/519 his] thefe
1.3.115/528 springes] F, Q1 (Springes); springs Q2
*1.3.120/533 Daughter] *not in* Q2
*1.3.121/534 somewhat] something
*1.3.123/536 parley] parle
*1.3.128/541 the] that
1.3.131/544 beguile] beguide
1.4.2/551 a] Q1 (An); *not in* Q2
*1.4.6/555 then it] it then
*1.4.16/565 And] F, Q1; But Q2
*1.4.18/567 obseruance.] For Q2 see Additional Passages.
1.4.30/579 enurn'd] interr'd Q1-2
1.4.42/591 wafts] waues Q1-2
*1.4.44/593 will I] F, Q1; I will
1.4.50/599 my Lord] F, Q1, Q2b; my Q2a
1.4.52/601 beetles] bettles Q2; beckles Q1
*1.4.55/604 it?] F; ~, Q2. See Additional Passages.
*1.4.56/605 wafts] waues
*1.4.57/606 hand] hands
1.4.64/613 imagination] F, Q1; imagion
1.5.18/635 knotty] knotted Q1-2
*1.5.20/637 fretfull] F, Q1; fearefull
*1.5.22/639 *Hamlet*] F, Q2; *not in* Q2
1.5.29/646 Hast, hast] F: Hafte Q1; Haft Q2
*1.5.29/646 know it] F, Q1; know't
*1.5.29/646 with] F, Q1; I with
1.5.35/652 mine] my Q1-2
1.5.41/658 mine] my Q1-2
1.5.47/664 a] *not in* Q2
1.5.55/672 lust] F, Q1 (Luft); but
1.5.56/673 sate] fate Q1; fort Q2
*1.5.58/675 mornings] Q1, F (Mornings); morning
1.5.59/676 mine] my Q1-2
*1.5.60/677 in] F, Q1; of
1.5.62/679 Hebonon] Hebona Q1-2
1.5.63/680 mine] my Q1-2
1.5.64/681 leaperous] leaprous Q1-2
1.5.68/685 posset] posseffe
1.5.77/694 vnanneld] F (vnnaneld); vnanueld
1.5.79/696 With all] F, Q1; Withall
*1.5.84/701 howsoeuer] F, Q1; howfomeuer
1.5.84/701 pursuest] purfues
*1.5.91/708 Adiew, adiew, *Hamlet*] F (Adue, adue); Hamlet adue, adue, adue Q1; Adiew, adiew, adiew Q2
1.5.95/712 stiffely] fwiftly
*1.5.96/713 while] whiles
*1.5.104/721 yes, yes] F, Q1; yes
1.5.110/727 I'm] I am Q1-2
1.5.114/731 HORATIO & MARCELLUS] Hor⟨atio⟩. Q1; Hora⟨tio⟩. Q2
1.5.116/733 Heauen] Heauens Q1-2
*1.5.118/735 HORATIO] F, Q1; *Mar⟨cellus⟩.*
*1.5.119/736 HAMLET] F, Q2; *Mar⟨cellus⟩.* Q1
*1.5.119/736 bird] and
*1.5.123/740 you'll] F, Q1; you will
*1.5.126/743 my Lord] F, Q1; *not in* Q2
1.5.127/744 nere] neuer Q1-2
1.5.130/747 i'th'] in the Q1-2
*1.5.133/750 desires] F, Q1; defire Q2
1.5.134/751 ha's] hath Q1-2
1.5.134/751 desire] Q2, F; defires Q1
1.5.135/752 mine] my Q1-2

*1.5.136/753 Looke you, Ile] looke you ... ile Q1; I will Q2
1.5.138/755 I'm] I am Q1-2
1.5.152/769 Ah ha] Ha, ha Q1-2
*1.5.161-2/778-9 Neuer ... heard, | Sweare by my sword.] F (heard: ... Sword), Q1 (*subs.*); Sweare by my fword, | Neuer ... heard. Q2
*1.5.163/780 Sweare] F, Q1; Sweare by his fword
1.5.169/786 our] your Q1-2
*1.5.171/788 so ere] F, Q1; fo mere
1.5.174/791 time] times Q1-2
1.5.177/794 well] well, well Q1-2
*1.5.180-1/797-8 not to doe, | So ... you: sweare.] F, Q1 (*subs.*); doe fweare, | So ... you. Q2. See lineation notes.
1.5.184/801 With all] Withall Q2; In all Q1
2.1.29/837 no, as] F; not a whit, no not a whit ... As Q1; as Q2
*2.1.39/847 warrant] wit
*2.1.41/849 i'th'] with
*2.1.47/855 and] or
*2.1.47/855 addition] F (Addition); addiftion
*2.1.52-3/860-1 consequence: at friend, | Or so, and Gentleman] confequence Q1-2
*2.1.55/863 closes with you] clofeth with him Q1; clofes Q2
*2.1.56/864 tother] F, Q1; th'other
*2.1.57/865 and such] or fuch
2.1.58/866 gaming, there, ortooke] F (o'retooke); gaming, there, or tooke
*2.1.62/870 takes] take
*2.1.76/884 Alas my Lord] O my Lord, my Lord
*2.1.78/886 Chamber] cloffet
*2.1.96/904 That] As
*2.1.100/908 help] F, Q1; helps
*2.1.106/914 passion] pafsions
*2.1.112/920 speed] heede
*2.1.120/928 loue.] loue, | Come.
2.2.0.2/928.1, etc. Rosencrans] F (Rofincrance); Rofencraus Q2
*2.2.5/933 I] *not in* Q2
*2.2.6/934 Since not] Sith nor
*2.2.10/938 deeme] dreame
*2.2.12/940 since] fith
*2.2.12/940 humour] hauior
*2.2.16/944 occasions] F (Occafions); occafion
2.2.33, 34/961, 962 Rosencrans] F (Rofincrance); Rofencraus
*2.2.36/964 ye] you
*2.2.37/965 the] thefe
*2.2.43/971 Assure you my] I affure my Q2; I affure your Q1
*2.2.50/978 I doe] F (do); doe I
*2.2.54/982 sweet Queene, that] deere Gertrard
*2.2.57/985 o're-hastie] F (o're-hafty); haftie
*2.2.73/1001 three] F, Q1; threefcore
*2.2.78/1006 his] this
*2.2.86/1014 very] F, Q1; *not in* Q2
*2.2.91/1019 since] *not in* Q2
*2.2.98/1026 he is] hee's
*2.2.107/1035 whil'st] while
2.2.111-12/1040-1 that's ... heare:] F; Q2 *prints in italic*
*2.2.113/1042 these.] thefe &c.
*2.2.125/1054 shew'd] fhowne
2.2.126/1055 aboue] about
*2.2.137/1066 winking] working
*2.2.142/1071 precepts] F (Precepts); prefcripts
2.2.143/1072 his] F, Q3; her
*2.2.146/1075 repulsed] repell'd
2.2.148/1077 watch] Q3, F (Watch); wath
2.2.149/1078 to a] to
*2.2.151/1080 waile] mourne
2.2.152/1081 'tis] *not in* Q2
*2.2.153/1082 likely] like
*2.2.154/1083 I'de] I would
*2.2.175/1104 Excellent, excellent] Excellent
*2.2.175/1104 y'are] F, Q1; you are
*2.2.186/1115 not as] as

*2.2.190/1119 farre gone, farre gone] farre gone
*2.2.197/1126 you] F, Q1; that you Q2
*2.2.198/1127 slaue] rogue
*2.2.200/1129 or] &
2.2.204/1133 you your selfe] your selfe Q1-2
*2.2.204-5/1134 should be] shalbe Q1; shall growe Q2
2.2.209/1140 Indeede] By the masse Q1
2.2.209/1140 that is out o'th'] that's out of the Q1-2
2.2.211/1142 sanity] F (Sanitie); sanctity
2.2.213-14/1144-5 sodainely . . . him, and] not in Q2
*2.2.216/1147 Sir] F, Q1; not in Q2
*2.2.217/1148 more] F, Q1; not more Q2
*2.2.223/1154 Mine] My
2.2.225/1156 exlent] F (excellent); extent Q2
*2.2.226/1157 ye] you
*2.2.229/1159 ouer] euer
2.2.230/1160 cap] F (Cap); lap
*2.2.234/1164 fauor] F (fauour); fauors
*2.2.237/1167 what's the] F (What's); What
*2.2.238/1168 that the] the
*2.2.241-70/1171-1200 Let me . . . attended;] F; not in Q1-2
*2.2.273/1203 euen] euer
*2.2.276/1206 deale] come, deale
*2.2.279/1209 Why any] Any
*2.2.287/1217 could] can
*2.2.298/1228 exercise] exercises
*2.2.301/1231 orehanging] (ore-hanging); ~ firmament
*2.2.302-3/1233 appeares no other thing] appeareth nothing
*2.2.303/1233 then] but
*2.2.304/1234 What a] What
*2.2.305/1235 faculty] faculties
*2.2.309-10/1240 no, nor] F, Q1; nor Q2
*2.2.310/1240 woman] F (Woman), Q1, Q3; women
*2.2.314/1244 you] F, Q1; yee
*2.2.321/1251 of] F, Q1; on
*2.2.324-5/1254-5 the Clowne . . . sere] F; The clowne shall make them laugh | That are tickled in the lungs Q1; not in Q2
2.2.326/1256 blank] F, Q3 (blanke); black
*2.2.328/1258 take] take such
*2.2.336/1266 they are] are they
*2.2.337-62/1267-92 HAMLET How . . . load too.] not in Q2
2.2.337/1267 rusty] restie Q1
*2.2.363/1293 strange] very strange
*2.2.363/1293 mine] my
*2.2.364/1294 mowes] mops and moes Q1; mouths Q2
*2.2.365/1295 fortie] (forty); fortie, fifty
2.2.365/1295 an] a Q1-2
*2.2.371/1301 come] come then
*2.2.372/1302 the] this
2.2.373/1303 lest] let
2.2.373/1303 my] F, Q3; me
*2.2.374/1304 outward] outwards
*2.2.384/1314 swathing] swadling Q1-2
*2.2.385/1315 he's] he is
*2.2.388/1318 for a] a Q1-2
*2.2.389/1319 so] F, Q1; then
*2.2.395/1325 mine] my
*2.2.398/1328 Pastoricall] Pastorall
*2.2.399-400/1329-30 Tragicall-Historicall: Tragicall-Comicall-Historicall-Pastorall:] Comicall historicall, Pastorall, Tragedy historicall: Q1; not in Q2
2.2.422/1353 abridgments come] F (Abridgements); abridgment comes Q1-2
*2.2.423/1354 Y'are] Ham⟨let⟩. You are
*2.2.424/1355 my] F, Q1; not in Q2
*2.2.425/1355 thy] F (Thy), Q1; why thy
*2.2.427/1358 byr lady] F (Byrlady), Q1 (burlady); by lady
*2.2.428/1358 nerer] F (neerer); nerer to
*2.2.431/1362 french] F, Q1 (French); friendly
2.2.432/1362 Faukners] F (Faulconers), Q1 (Falconers); Fankners
2.2.435/1365, etc. 1. PLAYER] Players Q1; Player. Q2

*2.2.443/1373 was] F, Q1; were
*2.2.445/1375 affectation] affection
*2.2.447/1377 in it] F, Q1; in't
2.2.448/1378 tale] F (Tale), Q1; talke
*2.2.449/1379 where] F, Q1; when
*2.2.456/1386 the] F, Q1; th'
2.2.458/1388 dismall, head to foote,] F (~ : Head ~); ~, ~, Q1; ~ˏ ~, Q2
*2.2.462/1392 damned] a damned
*2.2.463/1393 vilde] Lords
*2.2.463/1393 murthers] F (Murthers); murther
2.2.470, 504, 507/1400, 1434, 1437 1. PLAYER] Play. Q1-2
*2.2.473/1403 match] matcht
2.2.476/1406 Then senselesse Illium,] not in Q2
*2.2.477/1407 his] this
2.2.483/1413 And like] Like
*2.2.492/1422 Mars his] F (Mars); Marses
*2.2.497/1427 fallies] F (Fallies); follies
*2.2.504/1434 O who] F, Q1; a woe
*2.2.506/1436 good: Mobled Queene is good] F, Q1; good Q2. See text notes.
2.2.511/1441 th'] the Q1-2
*2.2.516/1446 husbands] F (Husbands), Q1, Q3; husband
*2.2.524/1454 rest] rest of this
*2.2.525/1455 ye] you
*2.2.526/1456 Abstracts] F, Q1; abstract
*2.2.531/1461 bodykins] bodkin
*2.2.532/1462 should] F, Q1; shall
*2.2.541/1471 for a] F, Q1; for
*2.2.542/1472 dosen ˏ or] F, Q1; dosen lines, or
*2.2.543/1473 ye] you
*2.2.550/1480 ye] to you
*2.2.554/1484 whole] owne
*2.2.555/1485 his] the
*2.2.556/1486 in's] in his
*2.2.560/1490 to Hecuba] F, Q1; to her
2.2.562/1492 the Cue] that
*2.2.567/1497 faculty] faculties
2.2.575/1505 by'th'] by the
*2.2.583/1513 Oh Vengeance!] not in Q1-2
*2.2.584/1514 I sure,] why sure Q1; not in Q2
*2.2.585/1515 the] a
*2.2.589/1519 scullyon] F (Scullion); scalion Q1; stallyon Q2
*2.2.589/1519 braine] F (Braine), Q1; braines Q2b; braues Q2a
*2.2.590/1520 I] F, Q1; hum, I
*2.2.598/1528 but] doe
*2.2.600/1530 be the] be a
*3.1.1/1537 circumstance] conference
*3.1.20/1556 about] heere about
*3.1.27-8/1563-4 on] To] into
3.1.30/1566 too] two
*3.1.34/1570 selfe (lawful espials)] selfe, Q2
*3.1.35/1571 Will] Wee'le
*3.1.48/1584 lonelines] F (lonelinesse); lowlines
*3.1.57/1593 let's] not in Q2
*3.1.74/1610 despriz'd] F (dispriz'd); despiz'd
*3.1.78/1614 these] not in Q2
*3.1.85/1621 of vs all] F, Q1; not in Q2
3.1.87/1623 sicklied] sickled
*3.1.88/1624 pith] pitch
*3.1.94/1630 well, well, well] well
*3.1.98/1634 No, no] No, not I
*3.1.101/1637 the] these
3.1.109/1645 your honestie] F (Honesty); you
3.1.120/1656 enoculat] F (innocculate); euocutat
3.1.123/1659 to] not in Q2
*3.1.130-1/1666-7 heauen and earth] F (Heauen . . . Earth), Q1; earth and heauen
*3.1.131/1667 all] F, Q1; not in Q2
*3.1.140/1676 go,] F (Go); not in Q2
*3.1.144/1680 O heauenly] Heauenly

*3.1.145/1681   too] F, Q1; not in Q2
*3.1.147/1683   gig, you amble] F (gidge); fig, and you amble Q1; gig, & amble
*3.1.147/1683   lispe,] lift,
*3.1.147-8/1683-4   and nickname] and you nickname Q1; you nickname Q2
*3.1.149/1685   your ignorance] F (Ignorance), Q1; ignorance
*3.1.150/1686   more marriages] F (Marriages), Q1; mo marriage
*3.1.155/1691   expectansie] expectation
*3.1.159/1695   musick] F (Muficke); mufickt
3.1.160/1696   that] what
*3.1.161/1697   tune] time
*3.1.162/1698   feature] F (Feature); ftature
3.1.164/1700   see.] F, Q2a; fee. exit Q1, Q2b
*3.1.170/1706   to] for to
*3.1.180/1716   this] his
*3.1.186/1722   griefes] F (Greefes); griefe
3.1.191/1727   vnwatcht] F (vnwatch'd); vnmatcht
*3.2.3/1730   your] F, Q1; our
*3.2.4/1731   had spoke] fpoke
*3.2.6/1733   the] not in Q2
*3.2.20/1747   ouer-doone] F (ouer-done); ore-doone
*3.2.23/1750   owne feature] F (Feature); feature
*3.2.25/1752   make] makes
*3.2.27/1754   the which] which
3.2.29/1756   praife] F (praife); prayfd
*3.2.31/1758   the] th'
*3.2.37/1764   vs, Sir] vs
*3.2.45/1772   it.] Q2, F; it. | And then you haue fome agen, that keepes one fute | Of ieafts, as a man is knowne by one fute of | Apparell, and Gentlemen quotes his ieafts downe | In their tables, before they come to the play, as thus: | Cannot you ftay till I eate my porrige? and, you owe me | A quarters wages: and, my coate wants a cullifon: | And, your beere is fowre: and, blabbering with his lips, | And thus keeping in his cinkapafe of ieafts, | When, God knows, the warme Clowne cannot make a ieft | Vnleffe by chance, as the blinde man catcheth a hare: | Maifters tell him of it. | players We will my Lord. | Ham. Well, Q1
*3.2.50/1777   ROSENCRANS and GUYLDENSTERNE] F (Both); Ros.
*3.2.50/1777   We will] I
3.2.54/1781   HAMLET] F; Q2 (c.w.); not in Q2 (text)
*3.2.60/1787   faining] fauning
*3.2.62-3/1789-90   distinguish, her election, | Hath] ~, ~, | S'hath
*3.2.66/1793   Hath] Haft
*3.2.67/1794   comingled] F (co-); comedled
*3.2.78/1805   mine] my
*3.2.85/1812   To] In
3.2.87/1814   detecting] detected
*3.2.96/1823   I did] did I
3.2.98/1825   And what] What Q1-2
*3.2.104/1831   good] deere
*3.2.109-10/1836-7   HAMLET I meane . . . Lord.] HAMLET Vpon your lap, Q1; not in Q2
*3.2.131/1859   this is] F, Q1; this
*3.2.131/1859   miching] F (Miching), Q1 (myching); munching Q2
*3.2.131/1859   that] F, Q1; it
3.2.135/1863   counsell] F, Q1; not in Q2
*3.2.137/1865   you'l] F, Q1; you will
3.2.149/1877   orbed] F (Orbed); orb'd the
3.2.157/1885   your] F, Q3; our
*3.2.160/1888   For] F; For women feare too much, euen as they loue, | And
*3.2.160/1888   holds] hold
*3.2.161/1889   In] Eyther none, in
3.2.162/1890   loue] Lord
*3.2.163/1891   so.] For Q2 see Additional Passages.
*3.2.172/1900   Wormwood,] F; O wormewood, Q1; That's Q2
*3.2.173/1901   PLAYER QUEENE] F (Bapt.); not in Q2 (which places Hamlet's preceding interruption in the margin)
*3.2.181/1909   like] the

*3.2.190/1918   ioyes] ioy
*3.2.208/1936   night,] For Q2 see Additional Passages.
*3.2.212/1940   once] F, Q1; once I be
*3.2.212/1940   be] F, Q1, Q4; be a
3.2.213/1941   HAMLET If . . . now.] F, Q1; Q2 places in the right margin opposite 3.2.211-12/1939-40
*3.2.219/1947   protests] F, Q1; doth proteft
3.2.226/1954   how?] ~, Q1-2
*3.2.229/1957   o'] F; A Q1; of Q2
*3.2.240/1969   pox,] F (Pox); a poxe, Q1; not in Q2
3.2.244/1973   Confiderat] F, Q1 (Confederate); Confiderat
3.2.246/1975   infected] F, Q1, Q3; inuected
3.2.248/1977   vsurpe] vfurps Q1-2
3.2.249/1978   for's] for his Q1-2
*3.2.250/1979   writ in] written in very
*3.2.254/1983   HAMLET What . . . fire.] F, Q1; not in Q2
*3.2.258/1987   COURTIERS] F (All.); Pol⟨onius⟩.
*3.2.262/1991   So] Thus Q1-2
*3.2.264/1993   two] not in Q2
*3.2.266/1995   sir] not in Q2
*3.2.290/2019   rather] not in Q2
*3.2.292/2021   his] the
*3.2.293/2022   farre] not in Q2
3.2.296/2025   start] ftare
*3.2.305/2034   of my] of
*3.2.307/2036   GUYLDENSTERNE] F (Guild.); Rof⟨encraus⟩.
*3.2.309/2038   answers] anfwere
*3.2.315/2043   astonish] ftonifh
*3.2.317/2045   admiration] admiration, impart
*3.2.323/2051   So I] And
*3.2.325/2053   freely] furely
*3.2.325/2053   of] vpon
*3.2.330/2058   I] I fir
*3.2.332/2060   Recorder] Recorders
*3.2.332/2060   see] fee one
*3.2.345/2073   'Tis] It is
3.2.346/2074   thumbe] the vmber
*3.2.347/2075   excellent] eloquent
*3.2.355/2083   the top of] not in Q2
*3.2.359/2087   can fret me, you] can frett mee, yet you Q1; fret me not, you Q2
*3.2.371/2099   HAMLET] F, Q1, Q2 (c.w.); not in Q2 (text)
*3.2.371/2099   will I] i'le Q1; I will Q2
3.2.378/2106   breaths] breakes
*3.2.380/2108   bitter busines as the] F (bufineffe); bufines as the bitter
*3.2.385/2113   daggers] F (Daggers), Q1; dagger
*3.3.6/2122   dangerous] neer's Q2; near us Q1676
*3.3.7/2123   Lunacies] F; browes Q2; lunes THEOBALD; braues PARROTT-CRAIG (Wilson)
*3.3.17/2133   it is] F (It); or it is Q2; O, 'tis WILSON
3.3.22/2138   ruine] F (Ruine); raine
3.3.23/2139   with] not in Q2
*3.3.25/2141   vpon] about
*3.3.26/2142   ROSENCRANS and GUYLDENSTERNE] F (Both.); Ro⟨sencraus⟩.
3.3.50/2166   pardond] F (pardon'd); pardon
3.3.58/2174   shoue] fhowe
*3.3.73/2189   it, pat,] it, but,
*3.3.73/2189   praying] a praying
3.3.75/2191   reuendgd] F (reueng'd), Q1; reuendge
*3.3.79/2195   Oh] Why
*3.3.79/2195   hyre and Sallery] F; bafe and filly Q2; a benefit Q1
*3.3.81/2197   With all] Withall
*3.3.91/2207   gaming,] F; game, Q1; game, a Q2
3.4.4/2218   e'ene] euen
*3.4.5/2219   with him] not in Q2
*3.4.6/2220   HAMLET (within) Mother, mother, mother.] Ham⟨let⟩. Mother, mother. Q1; not in Q2
3.4.7/2224   warnt] F (warrant); wait
3.4.20/2234   inmost] moft

HAMLET

*3.4.22/2236	Helpe helpe] F (~, ~,); Helpe Q1–2		*4.5.56/2612	la?] not in Q2
*3.4.22/2236	helpe, helpe, helpe] F; helpe Q2; Helpe for the Queene Q1		*4.5.64/2620	So] F, Q1; (He anfers.) So
*3.4.29/2243	'twas] it was		*4.5.68/2624	should] would
*3.4.37/2251	is] be		*4.5.75/2631	death] death, and now behold
*3.4.47/2261	doth] dooes		4.5.80/2636	their] not in Q2
*3.4.48/2262	Yea] F; Ore Q2; And WILSON		*4.5.91/2647	persons] perfon
*3.4.49/2263	tristfull] heated		*4.5.94/2650	QUEENE ... this?] How now, what noyfe is that? Q1 (continuing the King's speech); not in Q2
3.4.52/2266	HAMLET] F; before 3.4.51/2265, Q2		*4.5.95/2651	Where] Attend, where
*3.4.56/2270	or] and		*4.5.104/2660	They] The
3.4.58/2272	heauen-kissing] heaue, a kifsing		*4.5.110/2666	the King] this King
3.4.70/2284]	For Q2 see Additional Passage F.		*4.5.136/2692	world] worlds
3.4.71/2285]	For Q2 see Additional Passage F.		*4.5.140/2696	Fathers death] Father
*3.4.78/2292	panders] pardons		*4.5.151/2707	pearce] F (pierce); peare
*3.4.79/2293	mine eyes into my very] my very eyes into my		*4.5.157/2713	by] with
3.4.80/2294	greined] F (grained); greeued		*4.5.158/2714	turnes] turne
*3.4.81/2295	not leaue] leaue there		*4.5.161/2717	an old] F, Q1; a poore
*3.4.85/2299	mine] my		*4.5.162-4/2718-20	Nature ... loues.] not in Q2
3.4.87/2301	tyth] F (tythe); kyth		*4.5.166/2722	Hey ... hey nony:] F (italic); not in Q2
*3.4.95/2309	you] your		*4.5.167/2723	on] F (italic); in
*3.4.130/2344	Extafie?] not in Q2		*4.5.171/2727	sing] sing a
3.4.134/2348	I] not in Q2		*4.5.176/2732	loue] F, Q1; you loue
*3.4.136/2350	a] that		*4.5.181/2736	Herbe-Grace] F; herbe of Grace Q2; hearb a grace Q1
*3.4.139/2253	Whil'st] Whiles		*4.5.181/2736	Oh] not in Q1–2
3.4.142/2356	or] on		*4.5.181/2736	must] F, Q1; may
*3.4.149/2363	leue] F (liue); leaue		4.5.186/2741	Thought] F, Q2; Thoughts Q1
*3.4.150/2364	mine] my		*4.5.186/2741	affliction] F (Affliction); afflictions Q1–2
*3.4.151/2365	not,] For Q2 see Additional Passages.		*4.5.193/2748	as white] F (italic), Q1; was as white
3.4.152/2366	Refraine to night] to refraine night		*4.5.194/2749	All] F (italic), Q1; not in Q2
*3.4.154/2368	abstinence,] For Q2 see Additional Passages.		*4.5.198/2753	Christian] Chriftians Q2; chriften Q1
*3.4.163/2377	Thus] This		*4.5.198/2753	I pray God.] F, Q1; not in Q2
*3.4.163/2377	behind.] F (behinde); behind. | One word more good Lady.		*4.5.198/2753	buy ye] buy you Q2; be with you Q1
3.4.170/2384	rauell] rouell		4.5.199/2754	see] F; not in Q2
*3.4.185/2399	HAMLET This] For Q2 see Additional Passages.		*4.5.211/2766	buriall] funerall
3.4.189/2403	foolish] F, Q1; moft foolifh		*4.6.2/2774	SERVANT] Gent.
*4.1.4/2409	Ah my good] Beftow this place on vs a little while.| Ah mine owne		*4.6.2/2774	Saylors] Sea-faring men
*4.1.9/2414	He whyps his Rapier out, and] F (whips); Whyps out his Rapier, Q2; [Hamlet ...] whips me | Out his rapier, and Q1		*4.6.9/2781	comes] came
*4.1.10/2415	his] F, Q1; this		*4.6.21/2793	good] F (italic); not in Q2
*4.1.38/2443	To] And		*4.6.22/2795	hast] F (italic); fpeede
*4.1.39/2444	doone,] For Q2 see Additional Passages.		4.6.25/2797	bore] F (italic); bord
*4.2.1-3/2446-8	stowd. | ROSENCRANS and GUYLDENSTERNE (within) Hamlet, Lord Hamlet. | HAMLET What] F (ftowed. | Gentlemen within ... Ham.); ftowd, but foft, what Q2		4.6.29/2801	He] So
4.2.5/2450	Compounded] F, Q3; Compound		4.6.31/2802	giue you] you Q2; make you Q3
*4.2.29-30/2474-5	him, hide Fox, and all after] him		*4.7.6/2810	proceeded] proceede
*4.3.16/2491	Guildensterne?] not in Q2		*4.7.7/2811	crimefull] criminall
*4.3.16/2491	my] the		*4.7.8/2812	safetie,] F (Safety); fafetie, greatnes,
4.3.29/2506	KING] F, Q1; King. King		*4.7.11/2815	And] But
*4.3.35/2512	indeed if] F (~,~); if indeed		*4.7.14/2818	She's] She is
*4.3.35/2512	this] within this		*4.7.14/2818	coniunctiue] concliue
*4.3.38/2515	ye] you Q1–2		4.7.20/2824	Would] Worke
*4.3.39/2516	of thine,] not in Q2		*4.7.22/2826	loude a wind] F (loud a Winde); loued Arm'd
*4.3.42/2519	With fierie Quicknesse] not in Q2		*4.7.24/2828	And] But
*4.3.54/2531	and so] F, Q1; fo		*4.7.24/2828	had] haue
*4.3.66/2543	coniuring] congruing		*4.7.36/2840	How now? What Newes?] not in Q2
4.3.70/2547	were] will		*4.7.36/2840	Letters ... Hamlet.] not in Q2
4.3.70/2547	begun] begin		*4.7.37/2841	This] Thefe
4.4.3/2550	Claimes] Craues Q1–2		*4.7.40/2844	them] them| Of him that brought them
*4.4.9/2556	safely] foftly		*4.7.44/2848	your] F (italic); you
*4.4.9/2556	Exeunt marching] For Q2 see Additional Passages.		*4.7.45/2849	th'occasions] F (th'Occafions); the occafion
*4.5.1, 4/2557, 2560	HORATIO] F (Hor.); Gent⟨leman⟩.		*4.7.46/2850	and more strange] F (italic); not in Q2
*4.5.9/2565	ayme] yawne		*4.7.47/2851	Hamlet.] F (roman); not in Q2
*4.5.32/2588	stone.] F, Q1; ftone.| O ho.		*4.7.52/2856	aduise] deuife
*4.5.37/2593	Larded] F, Q1; Larded all		*4.7.53/2857	I'm] I am
4.5.38/2594	graue] F, Q1; ground		4.7.55/2859	shall] F, Q1; not in Q2
*4.5.40/2596	ye] you Q1–2		4.7.59/2863	If so you'l] I my Lord, fo you will
*4.5.41/2597	God] F, Q1; good		4.7.61/2865	checking] the King
*4.5.45/2601	Pray you] Pray		*4.7.67/2871	Some] For Q2 see Additional Passages.
			*4.7.69/2873	I'ue] I haue
			*4.7.71/2875	into] vnto
			*4.7.74/2878	past] topt
			4.7.74/2878	my] me

415

*4.7.83/2887	especially] especiall	*5.1.205/3176	into] to
4.7.85/2889	you;] For Q2 see Additional Passages.	*5.1.211/3182	winters] waters
*4.7.88/2892	him] you	*5.1.212/3183	soft, aside] soft₍ₐ₎ awhile Q2; Stand by a while Q1
*4.7.96/2900	it,] For Q2 see Additional Passages.	*5.1.213/3184	that] this
*4.7.107/2911	on] ore	*5.1.220/3191, etc.	PRIEST] F, Q1; Doct⟨or⟩.
4.7.111/2915	passe] pace	*5.1.221/3192	warrantis] F1; warrantie Q2, F2
*4.7.113/2917	that] not in Q2; the Q3	*5.1.223/3194	haue] been
*4.7.127/2931	should] did	*5.1.225/3196	Shardes,] not in Q2
*4.7.131/2935	prepard] F (prepar'd); prefard	*5.1.226/3197	Rites] Crants
*4.7.138/2942	aslant a] ascaunt the	*5.1.232/3203	sage] a
*4.7.139/2943	hore] horry	*5.1.243/3213	t'haue] haue
*4.7.143/2947	cold] cull-cold	*5.1.244/3214	trebble] double
*4.7.146/2950	the] her	*5.1.259/3229	and] not in Q2
*4.7.149/2953	tunes] F, Q1; laudes	*5.1.260/3230	something in me] F, Q1; in me something
*4.7.163/2967	of] a	*5.1.261/3231	wisenesse] F (wisensse); wisedome Q1-2
*4.7.164/2968	doubts] drownes	*5.1.261/3231	away] F (Away); hold off Q1-2
*5.1.1/2972	that] when she	5.1.275/3245	doost thou come] F (Dost); doost come Q2; Com'st thou Q1
*5.1.3/2974	is, and] is,		
*5.1.12/2983	and to] to	*5.1.282/3252	KING] F, Q1; Quee⟨ne⟩.
5.1.12/2983	performe; argall,] ∼, or all;	5.1.283/3253	thus] this
*5.1.34-7/3005-8	OTHER Why . . . Armes?] not in Q2 (which leaues a gap at the end of the line between 'Armes' in 5.1.33/3004 and 'Ile' in 5.1.37/3008)	*5.1.291/3261	you] thee
		5.1.296/3266	shortly] thirtie Q2a; thereby Q2b
		*5.2.1/3268	let me] shall you
*5.1.43/3014	Frame] not in Q2	5.2.5/3272	me thought] my thought
*5.1.59/3030	that] not in Q1-2	5.2.6/3273	bilbos] F (Bilboes), Q3 (bilbo's); bilbo
5.1.59/3030	lasts] Q2, F; last Q1	*5.2.9/3276	deare] deepe
*5.1.60/3031	to Yaughan,] in, and₍ₐ₎	*5.2.9/3276	teach] learne
*5.1.65/3036	busines, that] F (businesse); busines?	*5.2.18/3285	vnseale] vnfold
*5.1.66/3037	at] in	*5.2.20/3287	Oh] A Q2 (interpreted as 'Ah' WILSON)
*5.1.72/3043	caught] F (italic); clawed	*5.2.28/3295	me] now
*5.1.73/3044	intill] F (italic); into	*5.2.41/3308	should] might
*5.1.76/3047	th'] the	5.2.44/3311	like, assis] F (Assis); like, as sir
*5.1.78/3049	ore-Offices] F (o're₍ₐ₎); now ore-reaches	*5.2.45/3312	know] knowing
*5.1.82/3053	good lord] F (Lord); sweet lord	*5.2.47/3314	the] those
*5.1.84/3055	ment] F, Q1 (meant), Q3; went	5.2.53/3320	Subscribd] F (Subscrib'd); Subcribe Q2; Subcrib'd Q3
5.1.87/3058	masserd] F (Mazard), Q3 (mazer); massene	*5.2.58/3325	Why . . . imployment] not in Q2
*5.1.90/3061	'em] them	*5.2.60/3327	Doth] Dooes
*5.1.95/3066	might] may	*5.2.64/3331	thinkst] thinke
*5.1.96/3067	quiddits] F (Quiddits); quiddities	*5.2.68/3335	conscience,] ∼ ?
*5.1.96/3067	quillets] F (Quillets), Q1; quillites Q2; quillities Q3	*5.2.69-81/3336-48	To . . . heere?] F; Q1 (subs.); not in Q2
*5.1.98/3069	rude] madde	5.2.83/3350	humbly] F, Q3; humble
*5.1.103-4/3074-5	recoueries, is . . . of his recoueries,] F (Recoueries: Is . . . Recoueries); recoueries,	*5.2.91/3358	friendshippe] F (friendship); Lordshippe
		5.2.93/3361	with all] F, Q3; withall
*5.1.105/3076	will his] will	*5.2.94/3362	put] not in Q2
*5.1.106/3077	double ones too] doubles	*5.2.95/3363	'tis] it is
*5.1.108/3079	hardly] scarcely	*5.2.99/3367	Me] F (Mee), Q1; But yet me
*5.1.113/3084	that] F, Q1; which	5.2.99/3367	soultry] F, Q3; fully
5.1.117/3088	O] F (italic); or	5.2.99/3367	for] or
*5.1.117-18/3088-9	made, . . .	For . . . meete.] F (italic); made	For such a ghest most meet. Q1; made.	*5.2.102/3370	but] not in Q2
		*5.2.106/3374	mine] my
*5.1.120/3091	it is] tis	*5.2.107/3375	sir] For Q2 see Additional Passages.
*5.1.121/3092	and] not in Q2	*5.2.108/3376	at his weapon] not in Q2. See Additional Passages.
*5.1.122/3093	'tis] it is	*5.2.113/3381	impon'd] has impaund
*5.1.135/3106	taken] tooke	*5.2.115/3383	or] and
*5.1.138/3109	a] F, Q3; not in Q2	*5.1.118/3386	carriages?] For Q2 see Additional Passages.
*5.1.140/3111	all] not in Q2	5.2.119/3387	carriages] F (Carriages); carriage
*5.1.141/3112	o'recame] ouercame	*5.2.121/3389	cannon] F (Cannon); a cannon Q2; the canon Q1
*5.1.144/3115	the] that	5.2.121-2/3390	might be] be might Q2a; be might Q2b
*5.1.145/3116	was mad] is mad	*5.2.127/3395	you] your selfe
*5.1.160/3131	Ifayth] F (Ifaith), Q1 (I faith); Fayth	*5.2.135/3403	'tis] it	is
*5.1.161/3132	now adaies] not in Q1-2	*5.2.138/3406	Ile] I will
*5.1.168/3139	now: this Scul, has laine in the] now hath lyen you i'th	*5.2.139/3407	redeliuer] deliuer Q2. (In place of 5.2.139-42/3407-10 Q1 has 'I shall deliuer your most sweet answer'.)
*5.1.169/3139-40	three & twenty] 23. Q2; this dozen Q1	*5.2.139/3407	ee'n] not in Q2
*5.1.176/3147	was] was sir Q2; was one Q1	*5.2.143/3411	Yours, yours;] Yours₍ₐ₎
*5.1.179/3150	Let me see.] I prethee let me see it, Q1; not in Q2	5.2.144/3412	hee] not in Q2
*5.1.181/3152	borne] bore	*5.2.148/3416	Complie] sir Q2a; so sir Q2b
*5.1.183/3154	my] in my	*5.2.149/3417	Beauy] breede
*5.1.183/3154	is] it is	*5.2.151/3419	outward] out of an
*5.1.188/3160	Chamber] F, Q1; table	5.2.152/3419	yisty] F (yesty); histy
*5.1.203/3174-5	it; as thus.] as thus₍ₐ₎ Q1; it. Q2	5.2.153/3421	wennowed] F (winnowed); trennowed

*5.2.154/3422 out.] For Q2 see Additional Passages.
*5.2.155/3423 this wager] not in Q2
*5.2.158/3426 but] not in Q2
5.2.161-2/3430 gaingiuing] F (gain-giuing); gamgiuing
*5.2.165/3433 there's a] F, Q1; there is
*5.2.166/3434 now] F, Q1; not in Q2
*5.2.170/3438 betimes] betimes, let be
*5.2.172/3440 I'ue] I haue
*5.2.176/3444 sore] a fore
*5.2.186/3454 Sir, in this Audience,] not in Q2
*5.2.189/3457 mine] F, Q1; my Q2
5.2.196/3464 keepe] not in Q2
5.2.196/3464 till] all
*5.2.198/3466 do] not in Q2
*5.2.200/3468 foiles: Come on] F (Foyles); foiles
*5.2.208/3476 hath] has
5.2.210/3478 better'd] better
5.2.219/3487 Vniõ] F (vnion); Vnice Q2a; Onixe Q2b
*5.2.239/3507 A touch . . . confesse] I doé confeſt Q2; I, I grant, a tuch, a tuch Q1
*5.2.250/3518 'tis almost gainst] it is almoſt againſt Q2; it goes almoſt againſt Q1
*5.2.251/3519 but] doe but
*5.2.253/3521 affear'd] ſure
*5.2.257/3525 is't] is it
*5.2.266/3534 Hamlet, Hamlet,] F (~. ~,); Hamlet,
*5.2.268/3536 houre of] houres
*5.2.269/3537 thy] F, Q1; my
*5.2.277/3545 murdrous] not in Q2
5.2.278/3546 thy Vnion] F, Q1; the Onixe
5.2.279/3547 King Dyes] The king dies. Q1; not in Q2
*5.2.297/3565 shall liue] wouldſt thou leaue Q1; ſhall I leaue Q2; I leave HIBBARD
*5.2.316/3584 ye] you
5.2.318/3586 proud] imperious Q1; prou'd Q2
5.2.333/3601 to th'] F, Q3; to
*5.2.337/3605 forc'd] for no
5.2.346/3614 on] no
*5.2.348/3616 whiles] while
*5.2.352/3620 royally] royall Q1-2
*5.2.353/3621 rights] F (rites); right
*5.2.355/3623 body] F, Q1; bodies

INCIDENTALS

3 King.] ~,   4 houre.] ~,   12 Dane.] ~,   18 Marcellus.] ~,   53 you,ont] ~ -~   106 Romeage] Q2a; Romadge Q2b   119 death,] ~.   268 you:] ~, Q2; ~. F   282 tell,] ~.   365 deliuer'd] F; deliuered   397 to night;] to nigh,   463 treads,] ~.   483 by] Q2a; buy Q2b   511 truth.] ~,   558 rowse,] ~.   571 hell,] ~.   611 heau'n] heauen Q1-2; Heau'n F   694 vnanneld] vnanueld Q2; vnnaneld F   743 heau'n,] heauen, Q1; heauen. Q2; Heau'n, F   884 affrighted.] ~,   940 nabor'd] F (subs.); nabored   957 obey,] ~.   1009 consider'd] F; confidered   1033 thus.] ~,   1049-52 O deere . . . him] roman   1049 Ophelia] italic   1053 Hamlet] italic   1054 This] Pol. This   1157 Guyldensterne] Guylderſterne   1236 moouing,] F (subs.); ~, Q2   1236 admirable?] F; ~, Q2   1237 Angell?] F; ~, Q2   1255 sere,] Q1 (subs.); ~ : F   1362 en to't] ento't   1438 rheume] rehume   1549 with] wirh   1728 pronounc'd] pronoun'd   1822 say.] ~,   1824 Actor.] ~,   1900 wormwood.] ~,   2019 choller.] ~,   2101 by.] ~,   2150 bed,] ~.   2185 ingag'd] F; ingaged   2264 act.] ~,   2265 Index.] ~,   2365 Assume] Aſſune   2383 fingers,] ~.   2486 How] King. How   2511 there] thrre   2699 enemies.] ~,   2777 greeted,] ~.   2802 Come] Hor. Come   2838 lou'd] Q3, F; loued   2844 receiu'd] F; receiued   2852 What] King. What   3041 sence.] ~,   3174 modesty] modeſty (?)   3216 Depriu'd] F; Depriued   3231 hand.] ~,   3237 lou'd] F; loued   3246 graue?] ~,   3325 imployment.] ~, F   3354 him, he] him, | He   3381 against] againſt   3447 wrong'd] F; wronged   3559 liu'ſt] F; lieuſt   3599 arriu'd] arriued Q2, F   3620 proou'd] F, Q1 (subs.); prooued

Additional Passages

B.2 taxde] taxed   K.10 riband] ribaud   M.9 thrifts] thirfts

QUARTO STAGE DIRECTIONS

1.1.0.1/0.1 *Enter Barnardo, and Francisco, two Centinels.*
1.1.10.1/10.1 *Enter Horatio, and Marcellus.*
1.1.14/14.1 *Exit Fran.*
1.1.37.1/37.1 *Enter Ghost.*
1.1.49/49 *Exit Ghost.*
1.1.106.1/106.1 *Enter Ghost.*
1.1.108.1/108.1 *It spreads | his armes.*
1.1.119.1/119.1 *The cocke | crowes.*
1.1.156/156 *Exeunt.*
1.2.0.1-4/156.1-4 *Florish. Enter Claudius, King of Denmarke, Gertrad the Queene, | Counsaile: as Polonius, and his Sonne Laertes, | Hamlet, Cum Alijs.*
1.2.128.1/284.1 *Florish. Exeunt all, | but Hamlet.*
1.2.159.1/315.1 *Enter Horatio, Marcellus, and Bernardo.*
1.2.253.1/409.1 *Exeunt.*
1.2.257.1/413.1 *Exit.*
1.3.0.1/413.2 *Enter Laertes, and Ophelia his Sister.*
1.3.51.1/464.1 *Enter Polonius.*
1.3.87/500 *Exit Laertes.*
1.3.136/549 *Exeunt.*
1.4.0.1/549.1 *Enter Hamlet, Horatio and Marcellus.*
1.4.7.1-2/556.1-2 *A florish of trumpets | and 2. peeces goes of.*
1.4.18.1/567.1 *Enter Ghost.*
1.4.38.1/587.1 *Beckins.*
1.4.63.1/612.1 *Exit Ghost and Hamlet.*
1.4.68/617 *Exeunt.*
1.5.0.1/617.1 *Enter Ghost, and Hamlet.*
1.5.114.1/731.1 *Enter Horatio, and Marcellus.*
1.5.151/768 *Ghost cries vnder the Stage.*
1.5.191/808 *Exeunt.*
2.1.0.1/808.1 *Enter old Polonius, with his man or two.*
2.1.74.1/882.1 *Enter Ophelia.*
2.1.75/883 *Exit Rey.*
2.1.120/928 *Exeunt.*
2.2.0.1-2/928.1-2 *Florish. Enter King and Queene, Rosencraus and | Guyldensterne.*
2.2.39.1/967.1 *Exeunt Ros. and Guyld.*
2.2.39.2/967.3 *Enter Polonius.*
2.2.58/986 *Enter Embassadors.*
2.2.85.1/1013.1 *Exeunt Embassadors.*
2.2.109.1/1037.1 *Letter. (after 2.2.116/1035)*
2.2.168.1/1097.1 *Enter Hamlet.*

HAMLET

2.2.171.1/1100.1 Exit King and Queene.
2.2.220.1/1151.1 Enter Guyldersterne, and Rosencraus.
2.2.368.1/1298.1 A Florish.
2.2.380.1/1310.1 Enter Polonius.
2.2.422.1/1353.1 Enter the Players.
2.2.546/1476 Exeunt Pol. and Players.
2.2.550/1480 Exeunt.
2.2.606/1536 Exit.
3.1.0.1-2/1536.1-2 Enter King, Queene, Polonius, Ophelia, Rosencraus, Guyl-|densterne, Lords.
3.1.29.1/1565.1 Exeunt Ros. & Guyl.
3.1.57.2/1593.2 Enter Hamlet.
3.1.152/1688 Exit.
3.1.164/1700 Exit.
3.1.164.1/1700.1 Enter King and Polonius.
3.1.191.1/1727 Exeunt.
3.2.0.1/1727.1 Enter Hamlet, and three of the Players.
3.2.45.1/1772.1 Enter Polonius, Guyldensterne, & Rosencraus.
3.2.50.1/1777.1 Exeunt they two.
3.2.51/1778 Enter Horatio.
3.2.89/1816 Enter Trumpets and Kettle Drummes, King, Queene, | Polonius, Ophelia.
3.2.129.1-14/1857.1-15 The Trumpets sounds. Dumbe show followes. | Enter a King and a Queene, the Queene embracing him, and he her, he | takes her vp, and declines his head vpon her necke, he lyes him downe vp-|pon a bancke of flowers, she seeing him asleepe, leaues him: anon come in an | other man, takes off his crowne, kisses it, pours poyson in the sleepers eares, | and leaues him: the Queene returnes, finds the King dead, makes passionate | action, the poysner with some three or foure come in againe, seeme to con-|dole with her, the dead body is carried away, the poysner wooes the Queene | with gifts, shee seemes harsh awhile, but in the end accepts loue.
3.2.133.1/1861.1 Enter Prologue. (after 3.2.134/1862)
3.2.147.1/1875.1 Enter King and Queene.
3.2.217.1/1945.1 Exeunt.
3.2.231.1/1959.1 Enter Lucianus.
3.2.258.1/1987.1 Exeunt all but Ham. & Horatio.
3.2.278.1/2007.1 Enter Rosencraus and Guyldensterne.
3.2.331.1/2059.1 Enter the Players with Recorders.
3.2.360.1/2088.1 Enter Polonius.
3.2.388/2116 Exit.
3.3.0.1/2116.1 Enter King, Rosencraus, and Guyldensterne.
3.3.26.1/2142.1 Exeunt Gent.
3.3.26.2/2142.2 Enter Polonius.
3.3.35.1/2151.1 Exit.
3.3.72.2/2188.2 Enter Hamlet.
3.3.96/2212 Exit.
3.3.98/2214 Exit.
3.4.0.1/2214.1 Enter Gertrard and Polonius.
3.4.7.2/2221.2 Enter Hamlet.
3.4.93.1/2307.1 Enter Ghost.
3.4.127.1/2341.1 Exit Ghost.
3.4.191/2405 Exit.
4.1.0.1/2405.1 Enter King, and Queene, with Rosencraus | and Guyldensterne.
4.1.34.1/2436.1 Enter Ros. & Guild.
4.1.40/2445 Exeunt.

4.2.0.1/2445.1 Enter Hamlet, Rosencraus, and others.
4.2.30/2475 Exeunt.
4.3.0.1/2475.1 Enter King, and two or three.
4.3.11/2486 Enter Rosencraus and all the rest.
4.3.16.1/2491.1 They enter.
4.3.55/2532 Exit.
4.3.70/2547 Exit.
4.4.0.1/2547.1 Enter Fortinbrasse with his Army ouer the stage.
4.5.0.1/2556.1 Enter Horatio, Gertrard, and a Gentleman.
4.5.20.1/2576.1 Enter Ophelia.
4.5.23/2579 shee sings.
4.5.29/2585 Song.
4.5.35.1/2591.1 Enter King.
4.5.37/2593 Song.
4.5.47/2603 Song.
4.5.94/2650 A noise within.
4.5.95.1/2651.1 Enter a Messenger.
4.5.107.1/2663.1 A noise within.
4.5.109.1/2665.1 Enter Laertes with others.
4.5.152.1/2708.1 A noyse within.
4.5.154.1/2710.1 Enter Ophelia.
4.5.165/2721 Song.
4.5.188/2743 Song.
4.5.217/2772 Exeunt.
4.6.0.1/2772.1 Enter Horatio and others.
4.6.5.1/2777.1 Enter Saylers.
4.6.33/2804 Exeunt.
4.7.0.1/2804.1 Enter King and Laertes.
4.7.35.1/2839.1 Enter a Messenger with Letters.
4.7.134/2938 Enter Queene.
4.7.164/2968 Exit.
4.7.167/2971 Exeunt.
5.1.0.1/2971.1 Enter two Clownes.
5.1.55.1/3026.1 Enter Hamlet and Horatio.
5.1.61/3032 Song.
5.1.71/3042 Song.
5.1.91/3062 Song.
5.1.212/3183 Enter K. Q. | Laertes and | the corse.
5.1.290/3260.1 Exit Hamlet | and Horatio.
5.1.297/3267 Exeunt.
5.2.0.1/3267.1 Enter Hamlet and Horatio.
5.2.82.1/3348.1 Enter a Courtier.
5.2.170.1-4/3438.1-4 A table prepard, Trumpets, Drums and officers with Cushions, | King, Queene, and all the state, Foiles, daggers, | and Laertes.
5.2.225/3493 Trumpets | the while.
5.2.235/3503 Drum, trumpets and shot. | Florish, a peece goes off.
5.2.301/3569 A march a | farre off.
5.2.301.1/3569.1 Enter Osrick.
5.2.314.1/3582.1 Enter Fortenbrasse, with the Embassadors.
5.2.357.1/3625.1 Exeunt.

Additional Passages

J.1.1 Enter Hamlet, Rosencraus, &c.
J.57 Exit.
P.0.1 Enter a Lord.

FOLIO STAGE DIRECTIONS

1.1.0.1/0.1 Enter Barnardo and Francisco two Centinels.
1.1.10.1/10.1 Enter Horatio and Marcellus.
1.1.14/14.1 Exit Fran.
1.1.37.1/37.1 Enter the Ghost.
1.1.49/49 Exit the Ghost.
1.1.106.1/106.1 Enter Ghost againe.
1.1.122/122.1 Exit Ghost.
1.1.156/156 Exeunt
1.2.0.1-4/156.1-4 Enter Claudius King of Denmarke, Gertrude the Queene, | Hamlet, Polonius, Laertes, and his Sister O-|phelia, Lords Attendant.
1.2.25.1/181.1 Enter Voltemand and Cornelius.
1.2.41.1/197.1 Exit Voltemand and Cornelius.
1.2.128.1/284.1 Exeunt
1.2.128.1/284.1 Manet Hamlet.
1.2.159.1/315.1 Enter Horatio, Barnard, and Marcellus.
1.2.253.1/409.1 Exeunt.
1.2.257.1/413.1 Exit.

HAMLET

1.3.0.1/413.2 Enter Laertes and Ophelia.
1.3.51.1/464.1 Enter Polonius.
1.3.87/500 Exit Laer.
1.3.136/549 Exeunt.
1.4.0.1/549.1 Enter Hamlet, Horatio, Marcellus.
1.4.18.1/567.1 Enter Ghost.
1.4.38.1/587.1 Ghost beckens Hamlet.
1.4.63.1/612.1 Exeunt Ghost & Hamlet.
1.4.68/617 Exeunt.
1.5.0.1/617.1 Enter Ghost and Hamlet.
1.5.91/708 Exit.
1.5.114.1/731.1 Enter Horatio and Marcellus.
1.5.151/768 Ghost cries vnder the Stage.
1.5.191/808 Exeunt.
2.1.0.1/808.1 Enter Polonius, and Reynoldo.
2.1.74.1/882.1 Enter Ophelia.
2.1.75/883 Exit.
2.1.120/928 Exeunt.
2.2.0.1-3/928.1-2 Enter King, Queene, Rosincrane, and Guilden-|sterne Cumalijs.
2.2.39.1/967.1 Exit.
2.2.39.2/967.3 Enter Polonius.
2.2.58/986 Enter Polonius, Voltumand, and Cornelius.
2.2.85.1/1013.1 Exit Ambass.
2.2.109.1/1037.1 The Letter.
2.2.168.1/1097.1 Enter Hamlet reading on a Booke.
2.2.171.1/1100.1 Exit King & Queen.
2.2.220.1/1151.1 Enter Rosincran and Guildensterne.
2.2.368.1/1298.1 Flourish for the Players.
2.2.380.1/1310.1 Enter Polonius.
2.2.422.1/1353.1 Enter foure or fiue Players.
2.2.536/1466 Exit Polon.
2.2.550/1480 Exeunt. | Manet Hamlet.
2.2.606/1536 Exit
3.1.0.1-2/1536.1-2 Enter King, Queene, Polonius, Ophelia, Ro-|sincrance, Guildenstern, and Lords.
3.1.29.1/1565.1 Exeunt.
3.1.57.1/1593.1 Exeunt.
3.1.57.2/1593.2 Enter Hamlet.
3.1.152/1688 Exit Hamlet.
3.1.164.1/1700.1 Enter King, and Polonius.
3.1.191.1/1727 Exeunt.
3.2.0.1/1727.1 Enter Hamlet, and two or three of the Players.
3.2.45/1772 Exit Players.
3.2.45.1/1772.1 Enter Polonius, Rosincrance, and Guildensterne.
3.2.49/1776 Exit Polonius.
3.2.50.1/1777.1 Exeunt.
3.2.51/1778 Enter Horatio.
3.2.89/1816 Enter King, Queene, Polonius, Ophelia, Rosincrance, | Guildensterne, and other Lords attendant with | his Guard carrying Torches. Danish | March. Sound a Flourish.
3.2.129.1/1857.1 Hoboyes play. The dumbe shew enters.
3.2.129.1-14/1857.2-15 Enter a King and Queene, very louingly; the Queene embra-|cing him. She kneeles, and makes shew of Protestation vnto | him. He takes her vp, and declines his head vpon her neck. | Layes him downe vpon a Banke of Flowers. She seeing him | a-sleepe, leaues him. Anon comes in a Fellow, takes off his | Crowne, kisses it, and powres poyson in the Kings eares, and | Exits. The Queene returnes, findes the King dead, and | makes passionate Action. The Poysoner, with some two or | three Mutes comes in againe, seeming to lament with her. | The dead body is carried away: The Poysoner Wooes the | Queene with Gifts, she seems loath and vnwilling awhile, | but in the end, accepts his loue.   Exeunt
3.2.133.1/1861.1 Enter Prologue.
3.2.147.1/1875.1 Enter King and his Queene.
3.2.217.1/1945.1 Sleepes
3.2.217.1/1945.1 Exit
3.2.231.1/1959.1 Enter Lucianus.
3.2.248.1/1977.1 Powres the poyson in his eares.
3.2.258.1/1987.1 Exeunt
3.2.258.1/1987.1 Manet Hamlet & Horatio.

3.2.278.1/2007.1 Enter Rosincrance and Guildensterne.
3.2.331.1/2059.1 Enter one with a Recorder.
3.2.360.1/2088.1 Enter Polonius.
3.2.375/2103 Exit.
3.3.0.1/2116.1 Enter King, Rosincrance, and Guildensterne.
3.3.26.1/2142.1 Exeunt Gent.
3.3.26.2/2142.2 Enter Polonius.
3.3.72.2/2188.2 Enter Hamlet.
3.3.96/2212 Exit.
3.3.98/2214 Exit.
3.4.0.1/2214.1 Enter Queene and Polonius.
3.4.7.2/2221.1 Enter Hamlet.
3.4.24/2238 Killes Polonius.
3.4.93.1/2307.1 Enter Ghost.
3.4.127.1/2341.1 Exit.
3.4.191/2405 Exit Hamlet tugging in Polonius.
4.1.0.1/2405.1 Enter King.
4.1.31.1/2436.1 Enter Ros. & Guild.
4.1.36.1/2441.1 Exit Gent.
4.1.40/2445 Exeunt.
4.2.0.1/2445.1 Enter Hamlet.
4.2.3/2448 Enter Ros. and Guildensterne.
4.2.30/2475 Exeunt
4.3.0.1/2475.1 Enter King.
4.3.11/2486 Enter Rosincrane.
4.3.16.1/2491.1 Enter Hamlet and Guildensterne.
4.3.55/2532 Exit
4.3.70/2547 Exit
4.4.0.1/2547.1 Enter Fortinbras with an Armie.
4.4.9/2556 Exit.
4.5.0.1/2556.1 Enter Queene and Horatio.
4.5.20.1/2576 Enter Ophelia distracted.
4.5.35.1/2591.1 Enter King.
4.5.72/2628 Exit.
4.5.94/2650 A Noise within.
4.5.95.1/2651.1 Enter a Messenger.
4.5.107.1/2663.1 Noise within. Enter Laertes.
4.5.152.1/2708.1 A noise within. Let her come in.
4.5.154.1/2710.1 Enter Ophelia.
4.5.198.1/2753.1 Exeunt Ophelia
4.5.217/2772 Exeunt
4.6.0.1/2772.1 Enter Horatio, with an Attendant.
4.6.5.1/2777.1 Enter Saylor.
4.6.12/2784 Reads the Letter.
4.6.33/2804 Exit.
4.7.0.1/2804.1 Enter King and Laertes.
4.7.35.1/2839.1 Enter a Messenger.
4.7.41.1/2845.1 Exit Messenger
4.7.134/2938 Enter Queene.
4.7.164/2968 Exit.
4.7.167/2971 Exeunt.
5.1.0.1/2971.1 Enter two Clownes.
5.1.55.1/3026.1 Enter Hamlet and Horatio a farre off.
5.1.60.2/3031.2 Sings.
5.1.71/3042 Clowne sings.
5.1.91/3062 Clowne sings.
5.1.212/3183 Enter King, Queene, Laertes, and a Coffin, | with Lords attendant.
5.1.246.1/3217.1 Leaps in the graue.
5.1.289/3260.1 Exit.
5.1.296/3267 Exeunt.
5.2.0.1/3267.1 Enter Hamlet and Horatio.
5.2.81.1/3348.1 Enter young Osricke.
5.2.170.1-4/3438.1-4 Enter King, Queene, Laertes and Lords, with other Atten-|dants with Foyles, and Gauntlets, a Table and | Flagons of Wine on it.
5.2.213.1/3481.1 Prepare to play.
5.2.228.1/3496.1 They play.
5.2.235/3503 Trumpets sound, and shot goes off.
5.2.254/3522 Play.
5.2.255/3523 In scuffling they change Rapiers.

HAMLET

5.2.274.1/3542.1 *Hurts the King.*
5.2.279/3547 *King Dyes.*
5.2.283/3551 *Dyes.*
5.2.301/3569 *March afarre off, and shout within.*
5.2.301.1/3569.1 *Enter Osricke.*

5.2.311/3579 *Dyes*
5.2.314.1-2/3582.1-2 *Enter Fortinbras and English Ambassador, with Drumme, | Colours, and Attendants.*
5.2.357.1-2/3625.1-2 *Exeunt Marching: after the which, a Peale of | Ordenance are shot off.*

TWELFTH NIGHT

Twelfth Night first appeared in print in the Folio of 1623 (F). The text, set throughout by Compositor B, is generally clean, apart from some obvious errors (at e.g. 1.3.95, 1.3.97, 1.3.130, 2.5.112, 2.5.140/196, 198, 231, 1098, 1125, etc.). Wilson, Greg, and others supposed it to derive from a prompt-book, but Turner has convincingly argued that it 'was printed from a scribal copy'. The marking of the ends of Acts 1, 2, and 4 ('Finis Actus Primus', etc.) is virtually conclusive evidence for some sort of literary transcript, rather than foul papers or prompt-book; as always, however, what the scribe was himself copying is harder to determine. Turner and Lothian-Craik (who summarize and develop Turner's arguments) believe that the scribe copied Shakespeare's working papers, but this conclusion is based almost entirely upon questionable assumptions about the comprehensive regularity of early prompt-books, combined with an unreasonable expectation that someone preparing a 'literary' transcript of the prompt-book would preserve theatrical annotations such as the names of particular actors, marginal notes about props, or added early 'warning' directions. In the circumstances it seems to us impossible to be confident about the scribe's own copy.

Hinman has shown that there was apparently some delay in securing the copy for *Twelfth Night* and *The Winter's Tale*, since setting skipped from *All's Well* to *King John* and part of *Richard II* before returning to complete the Comedies. The *Winter's Tale* was apparently set from a Crane transcript, and one which shows strong signs of being later than the other four he prepared for the Folio; it seems possible that the copy for *Twelfth Night* was also specially prepared for the Folio, though evidently by a different (and unidentified) scribe. The Folio texts which it most resembles are those of *As You Like It* and *Julius Caesar*.

Wilson is among those who believe that the text shows signs of revision subsequent to performance; Lothian and Craik summarize the evidence and find it unconvincing (pp. xxii-xxiii). We concur with their conclusion (p. xxv) that 'nothing was added with the exception of what may be called editorial decoration'—an allusion to the 'Finis Actus Primus', etc., and to the division into acts and scenes, which is accepted by editors. If the scribe's copy was a prompt-book, the act divisions may have later theatrical authority.

S.W.W./(G.T.)

WORKS CITED

Adams, Barry B., 'Orsino and the Spirit of Love', *SQ* 29 (1978), 52-9
Donno, E. S., ed., *Twelfth Night*, New Cambridge (1985)
Lothian, J. M., and T. W. Craik, eds., *Twelfth Night*, Arden (1975)
Turner, Robert K., 'The Text of *Twelfth Night*', *SQ* 26 (1975), 128-38
Wilson, John Dover, ed., *Twelfth Night*, New (1930, 2nd edn. 1949)

TEXTUAL NOTES

1.1.1, etc./1 ORSINO] F (*Duke.*). F's prefix is consistent, but in dialogue Orsino is 'Duke' only four times (1.2.22/62, 1.2.42/82, 1.2.51/91, 1.4.1/239), 'Count' thirteen times. Probably, as Turner suggests, Shakespeare's conception may have changed during composition; the scribe may have imposed consistency.
1.1.5/5 sound] F; south POPE
1.1.10/10 capacitie,] ROWE; ~, F
1.1.11/11 Sea, nought] ROWE 2; Sea. Nought F. F is painstakingly defended by Barry B. Adams, but the hiatus in both sound and sense seems unacceptable. For love's large capacity, compare 2.4.99-100/960-1
1.1.25 years' heat] (HARNESS); yeares heate F; years hence ROWE
1.1.37/37 supply'd,] ROWE; ~, F
1.2.14/54 Arion] POPE; Orion F
1.2.36-7/76-7 sight | And company] F; company | And sight HANMER
1.2.48/88 pray thee] This edition (G.T.); prethee F. Compositor B regularly imposed his preferred form 'prethee', a sophistication that would obscure the symmetry of 'pray thee'/'pay thee'.
1.3.49/150 SIR ANDREW] F2; *Ma.* F1
1.3.52 Mary Accost] (ROWE); *Mary,* accoft F
1.3.95/196 curle by] THEOBALD; coole my F
1.3.97/198 me] F2; we F1
1.3.97 does't] F (doft)
1.3.99 housewife] F (hufwife)

1.3.125 cinquepace] F (Sinke-a-pace). F's spelling may be intended to point the pun, but *cinquepace* is the primary sense, and *OED* records *sinkapace* in Harington (1596) with no pun.
1.3.130/231 diuers] This edition; dam'd F; dunne COLLIER; flame ROWE. See *Re-Editing*, 33-4.
1.3.134/235 That's] F3; That F1
1.4.28/266 Nuntio's] F. The genitive case is illogical but not, perhaps, un-Shakespearian. Nevertheless he may have written 'Nuntius' (*OED*, 1605) or 'Nuncius' (*OED*, 1613-16).
1.5.28.2/309.1 *and Attendants*] THEOBALD; *not in* F. Their presence is required by 1.5.35/317 and 1.5.68/349. No provision is made for their departure.
1.5.110/392 for, heere he comes:] CAMBRIDGE (*subs.*); for, heere he comes. F
1.5.142 He's] F (Ha's)
1.5.154/436 in] F; e'en CAPELL (*after* F)
1.5.160.1/443.1 *Viola*] F2; *Violenta* F1
1.5.168 'countable] comptible F. *OED* lists as a spelling of 'countable', 'often aphetic for "accountable"'.
1.5.174/457 I] F (*c.w.*); *not in text*
1.5.191/475 not mad] F; mad RANN (Mason); but mend COLLIER (Staunton). Craik follows Rann. We take Olivia to mean 'if you have any sense, go; if (also) you have anything reasonable to say [cf. *OED reason, sb.*¹ 18b], say it quickly (before going)'.
1.5.197/481 tell me your minde] F; *assigned to Olivia*, WARBURTON. Sisson (*New Readings*) effectively defends F.

1.5.212 lady—] THEOBALD (Ladie. F)
1.5.244/528 With . . . teares] A four-foot line, but not 'metrically defective' (Lothian-Craik): cf. e.g. 1.2.19/59, 3.1.109/1294, 3.4.10/1486, 4.1.25/1891, 4.3.28/2093, 5.1.380/2479.
1.5.291 County's] CAPELL after F (Countes)
2.2.12/643 the] F; no DYCE (Malone). Lothian-Craik ably defend F.
2.2.20/651 straight] This edition (G.R.P.); not in F1; sure F2. See Re-Editing, 50-1. F1 might be defended as a four-foot line with an extra initial unstressed syllable (not uncommon in this play).
2.2.31/662 our] F2; O F1
2.2.32/663 made of,] RANN (Thirlby, Tyrwhitt independently); made, if F
2.3.9/681 liues] F; life ROWE
2.3.33/706 giue a—] F2; giue a‸ F1 (at end of justified line; omission is possible)
2.3.72 Cathayan] Catayan F (usually spelt 'Cataian'; indifferent variants)
2.3.95 an] F (and)
2.3.113/786 mouth, too] F; LOTHIAN-CRAIK adds 'Exit'. Feste seems to be absent by 2.4.167-8/842, but Shakespeare makes no obvious provision for his departure.
2.3.130/802 a nayword] ROWE after F (an ayword). Riverside follows F, noting that 'Shakespeare seems to have been the first to use the phrase and its etymology is doubtful.' But 'nayword', unlike 'ay-word', is authenticated elsewhere; Shakespeare uses it twice in Merry Wives (meaning 'password'); and to the ear the forms are indistinguishable.
2.4.33/893 worne] F; won HANMER. See Lothian-Craik.
2.4.49 I prithee, sing] F (interpreted as 'Ay, prithee sing', THEOBALD)
2.4.50/910 The song | CLOWNE] not in F
2.4.52/912 Fye . . . fie] F; Fly . . . fly ROWE
2.4.87/948 I] HANMER; It F
2.4.98/959 suffer] F; suffers ROWE
2.5.32, 36/1017, 1021 SIR TOBY] F (To.); Fabian WILSON
2.5.47 sleeping—] F (fleeping.)
2.5.58-9/1043-4 my—some] COLLIER; my fome F
2.5.81/1067 FABIAN F (Fa.); DONNO (Wilson) reads SIR TOBY
2.5.82/1068 SIR TOBY] F (To.); DONNO (Wilson) reads FABIAN
2.5.112/1098 staniel] HANMER; ftallion F
2.5.117-18 portend? . . . me.] F (portend, . . . me?)
2.5.127/1112 sequell. That] ROWE; fequell that F
2.5.140/1125 borne] ROWE; become F
2.5.140/1125 atcheeue] F2; atcheeues F1
2.5.154/1138 vnhappy. Daylight] CAPELL; vnhappy daylight F
2.5.171/1155 deere] F2; deero F1 (interpreted by Daniel and Dyce as 'dear, O': easy foul-case error)
3.1.8/1193 King] F2; Kings F1
3.1.63/1248 And] F; Not RANN (Johnson)
3.1.67/1252 wisemen] CAPELL (Theobald 2); wifemens F
3.1.111 here] F (heare)
3.1.123 grece] grize F. Editors either retain F or alter to 'grise'; OED lists as 'grece'.
3.2.7/1354 thee the] F2; the F1
3.2.46/1393 downe, go about it] F; down. Go, about it CAPELL
3.2.50/1397 the] F; thy HANMER (Thirlby)
3.2.63/1411 nine] THEOBALD; mine F
3.3.15/1443 euer oft] F; ever thanks; and oft THEOBALD; ever. Oft STEEVENS. A four-stress line is allowable, and 'ever oft' a conceivable variant of the idiomatic 'ever and oft'.
3.3.36/1464 latched] KEIGHTLEY (Hunter); lapfed F. Editors and OED strain to justify F, but this looks like one of Compositor B's substitutions.

3.4.23/1499 OLIUIA] F2; Mal. F1. Lothian-Craik ably support the emendation, but doubt remains as F1 could most easily be explained as an error for Mar⟨ia⟩.
3.4.69/1545 tang] CAPELL; langer with F
3.4.87/1563 How . . . man] F; spoken by Sir Toby WILSON
3.4.156-7 sense (aside)—less] F's 'fence-leffe' appears to use the hyphen to signal the aside.
3.4.159 me'—] F (me.)
3.4.168/1643 If] To. If F
3.4.170/1645 You] F2; Yon F1
3.4.198/1674 out] THEOBALD; on't F. To Craik's support for Theobald we may add that Compositor B has a tendency to introduce redundant apostrophes.
3.4.202/1678 goes] F; Go MALONE
3.4.202/1678 greefes] F; grief ROWE
3.4.221/1697 sir, . . . sure,] THEOBALD (subs.); fir‸ . . . fure, F
3.4.240 competent] F (computent). H. M. Hulme (Explorations, p. 165) attempts to defend F as an independent word, but OED records 'computent' as a spelling of competent, and the sense seems adequate.
3.4.265/1742 The Folio direction clears the stage, but the action is evidently continuous, so a new scene is not marked. Fabian and Viola are visible to Sir Toby (3.4.273-4/1750-1), and directors often keep them on stage.
3.4.267 virago] F (firago)
3.4.278 Capulet] (DYCE, after F's Capilet)
4.1.25/1891 and there, and there,] F; and there, and there, and there, CAPELL
4.2.5/1936 in] F2; in in F1
4.2.6/1936 such] F (c.w.); in fuch (text). (The text repeats 'in' from the previous page.)
4.2.71/2002 to the] ROWE; the F; t'the RIVERSIDE
4.2.71/2002 To Maria] DONNO; not in F
4.2.86 Master] F (M.). At 2.3.129/801 Maria speaks of 'Monsieur Malvolio', which might be preferred here.
5.1.6.1/2106.1 Curio is a mere supernumerary, and may be a 'ghost'.
5.1.57 freight] F (fraught: from parallel roots, identical in meaning)
5.1.67 dear] F. Though the meaning is close to 'dire', the words are distinct.
5.1.75 wreck] F (wracke). Lothian-Craik spell 'wrack' to show that the modern "wreck" is not synonymous, as it is at [5.1.264/2363]', where they alter the identical form to 'wreck'; but 'wreck' conveys the required sense (cf. COD, 2, 'greatly damaged or disabled . . . person').
5.1.112/2212 hath] CAPELL; haue F
5.1.173 He's] F (H'as)
5.1.194 he's] F (has)
5.1.198 passy-measures pavan] F (paffy meafures panyn). The dance name from Italian 'passe-, passa-mezzo' occurs in various forms; Sir Toby may be struggling to pronounce it. But 'pavyn' is an indifferent variant of 'pavan' (or 'pavane').
5.1.198/2297 pauyn] F2; panyn F1
5.1.203/2302 helpe,] MALONE (subs.); ~‸ F
5.1.283 He's] F (has)
5.1.399 had] F. Lothian-Craik suggest "had' (for 'I had'), but this may be too limiting in lines which include much generalization, and at a point when Feste begins to speak as an actor rather than as a fictional character.
5.1.402/2501 With] F2; not in F1

INCIDENTALS

53 strong] fttong	78 deliuerd] deliuered	117 woer.] ~‸	135 moreouer] moreour	151 acquaintance.] ~‸
192 fencing,] ~‸	196 will] wlll	197 nature.] ~‸	204 Count] Connt	205 her.] ~,	208 swear't] swear‸t
252 the] rhe	260 returne.] ~,	302 points.] ~‸	369 guiltlesse] guitleffe	530 him.] ~‸	604 Heauens] Heanens
771, 773, 775, 776] (roman, except for 'Toby')	943 her‸] ~ :	1072 her] het	1086 alter'd] alter‸d	1123-38 In . . .

TWELFTH NIGHT

vnhappy] (roman)   1133 thee] thce   1137 fingers.] ~∧   1138 the] tht   1192 Church.] ~∧   1194 Church] Chureh   1279 seruice.] ~■   1320 me?] ~:   1328 beautifull,] ~?   1348 longer.] ~:   1380 him,] ~∧   1436 trauell] rrauell   1449 night.] ~∧   1458 Th'offence] Th∧offence   1491 merry] metry   1529 let] ler   1535 looked] look∧d   1576 heart.] ~∧   1591 sathan.] ~∧   1628 Law.] ~∧   1645 for't] fot't   1743 hee's] hee∧s   1797 Orsino.] ~∧   1845 true] ttue   1862 sword.] ~∧   1929 me.] ~∧   2051 brains.] ~∧   2053 gone] goue   2069 Anthonio] Authonio   2214 him.] ~∧   2276 home] homc   2279 incardinate] incardinatc   2369 from] ftom   2469 Lord] Lotd

FOLIO STAGE DIRECTIONS

1.1.0.1–2/0.1–2 Enter Orsino Duke of Illyria, Curio, and other | Lords.
1.1.22/22 Enter Valentine. (after 'her')
1.1.40.1/40.1 Exeunt
1.2.0.1/40.2 Enter Viola, a Captaine, and Saylors.
1.2.60/100 Exeunt
1.3.0.1/100.1 Enter Sir Toby, and Maria.
1.3.40.1/142.1 Enter Sir Andrew.
1.3.77/178 Exit Maria
1.3.137/238 Exeunt
1.4.0.1–2/238.1–2 Enter Valentine, and Viola in mans attire.
1.4.8.1/246.1 Enter Duke, Curio, and Attendants.
1.4.42/280 Exeunt.
1.5.0.1/280.1 Enter Maria, and Clowne.
1.5.28.2/309.1 Enter Lady Oliuia, with Maluolio.
1.5.94.1/376.1 Enter Maria.
1.5.105/387 Exit Maluo.
1.5.110.1/392.1 Enter Sir Toby.
1.5.124/407 Exit
1.5.133.1/416.1 Enter Maluolio.
1.5.158/441 Exit.
1.5.158.1/441.1 Enter Maria.
1.5.160.1/443.1 Enter Violenta.
1.5.278/562 Exit
1.5.289/573 Enter Maluolio.
1.5.297/581 Exit.
2.1.0.1/585.2 Enter Antonio & Sebastian.
2.1.38.1/626.1 Exit
2.1.43/631 Exit.
2.2.0.1–2/631.1–2 Enter Viola and Maluolio, at seuerall doores.
2.2.16/647 Exit.
2.3.0.1/672.1 Enter Sir Toby, and Sir Andrew.
2.3.13.1/686.1 Enter Clowne.
2.3.38/711 Clowne sings.
2.3.68.1/741.1 Catch sung
2.3.68.2/741.2 Enter Maria.
2.3.82.1/754.1 Enter Maluolio.
2.3.120/792 Exit
2.3.170/844 Exit
2.3.185.1/859.1 Exeunt
2.4.0.1/859.2 Enter Duke, Viola, Curio, and others.
2.4.13.1/873.2 Musicke playes.
2.4.40.1/900.1 Enter Curio & Clowne.
2.4.49.1/909.1 Musicke.
2.4.50/909.2 The Song.
2.4.77/938 Exit
2.4.124.1/985.1 exeunt
2.5.0.1/985.2 Enter Sir Toby, Sir Andrew, and Fabian.
2.5.11.1/996.1 Enter Maria.
2.5.21/1006 Exit
2.5.21.1/1006.1 Enter Maluolio.
2.5.172.1/1156.1 Exit
2.5.178.1/1162.1 Enter Maria.
2.5.201/1185.1 Exeunt.
3.1.0.1–2/1185.2–3 Enter Viola and Clowne.
3.1.58/1243 exit

3.1.67.1/1252.1 Enter Sir Toby and Andrew.
3.1.82.1/1267.1 Enter Oliuia, and Gentlewoman. (after 'preuented', 3.1.83/1268)
3.1.128.1/1313.1 Clocke strikes.
3.1.162.1/1347.1 Exeunt
3.2.0.1/1347.2 Enter Sir Toby, Sir Andrew, and Fabian.
3.2.50.1/1397.1 Exit Sir Andrew.
3.2.62.1/1410.1 Enter Maria.
3.2.80/1428.1 Exeunt Omnes.
3.3.0.1/1428.2 Enter Sebastian and Anthonio.
3.3.48.1/1476.1 Exeunt.
3.4.0.1/1476.2 Enter Oliuia and Maria.
3.4.15.1–2/1491.1–2 Enter Maluolio. (after 'hither', 3.4.14/1490)
3.4.54.1/1530.1 Enter Seruant.
3.4.62/1538 exit
3.4.82.1/1558.1 Enter Toby, Fabian, and Maria.
3.4.123/1599 Exit
3.4.139.1/1615.1 Enter Sir Andrew.
3.4.180/1655 Exit
3.4.192.1/1668.1 Enter Oliuia and Viola.
3.4.212.1/1688.1 Enter Toby and Fabian.
3.4.251/1728 Exit Toby.
3.4.265/1742.1 Exeunt.
3.4.265.1/1742.2 Enter Toby and Andrew.
3.4.281.1/1758.1 Enter Fabian and Viola.
3.4.301.1/1778.1 Enter Antonio.
3.4.310.1/1787.1 Enter Officers.
3.4.364/1842 Exit
3.4.384.1/1865.1 Exit
4.1.0.1/1865.2 Enter Sebastian and Clowne.
4.1.22.1/1888.1 Enter Andrew, Toby, and Fabian.
4.1.43.2/1909.2 Enter Oliuia.
4.1.64/1930 Exeunt
4.2.0.1–2/1930.1–2 Enter Maria and Clowne.
4.2.11.1/1941.1 Enter Toby.
4.2.20.1/1950.1 Maluolio within.
4.2.72/2003 Exit
4.2.134/2065 Exit
4.3.0.1/2065.1 Enter Sebastian.
4.3.21.1/2086.1 Enter Oliuia, and Priest.
4.3.35/2130 Exeunt.
5.1.0.1/2100.1 Enter Clowne and Fabian.
5.1.6.1/2106.1 Enter Duke, Viola, Curio, and Lords.
5.1.45/2145 Exit
5.1.45.1/2145.1 Enter Anthonio and Officers.
5.1.93.1/2193.1 Enter Oliuia and attendants.
5.1.148/2248 Enter Priest.
5.1.169.1/2269.1 Enter Sir Andrew.
5.1.187.1/2286.1 Enter Toby and Clowne.
5.1.205.2/2304.2 Enter Sebastian.
5.1.278.1/2377.1 Enter Clowne with a Letter, and Fabian.
5.1.323.1/2422.1 Enter Maluolio.
5.1.384.1/2483.1 Exeunt
5.1.385/2483.2 Clowne sings.

TROILUS AND CRESSIDA

The play was entered in the Stationers' Register on 7 February 1603:

Mr Roberte.   Entred for his copie in full Court holden this day · to print when he hath gotten sufficient aucthority for yt. The booke of Troilus and Cresseda as yt is acted by my lo: Chamblens Men

Possibly Roberts never obtained sufficient authority. In any case, he appears not to have published the play, which was entered again on 28 January 1609:

Ri. Bonion / Henry Walleys   Entred for their Copy vnder thande of Mr Segar deputy to Sr George Bucke & m.^r ward Lownes a booke called, The history of Troylus & Cresssida

A quarto (Q), printed for the publishers by George Eld, appeared in 1609 (*BEPD* 279). This edition is found in two distinct states. In one (Qa), the title is given as 'THE | Historie of Troylus and Cresseida. | *As it was acted by the Kings Maiesties | seruants at the Globe*'; in the other (Qb), it is 'THE | Famous Historie of | Troylus *and* Cresseid. | *Excellently expressing the beginning* | of their loues, with the conceited wooing | of *Pandarus* Prince of *Licia*', and an epistle has been added (headed 'A neuer writer, to an euer reader. Newes.'). This altered title-page and added epistle were apparently printed at the same time as the final half-sheet of the play's text. (See Williams, 'The "Second Issue"'.) As the epistle explicitly reinforces the omission of Qa's reference to performance, it seems clear that, between the initiation and the completion of printing, the publishers came to believe that the play had never been performed. The accuracy of this belief is a matter of dispute. Baldwin believed that the epistle was written in late 1602 or early 1603, in anticipation of the publication alluded to in the first Stationers' Register entry (Variorum, pp. 350–61); Taylor has provided additional arguments for this conclusion ('Bibliography, Performance, and Interpretation', pp. 118–20). This hypothesis assumes that *Troilus and Cressida* was indeed 'a new play' (as the epistle calls it) in January 1603, and is hence inextricably bound up with the dating of its composition (see 'Canon and Chronology'). Honigmann has urged that the play dates from the first half of 1601, that the epistle should be trusted, that the play had by 1609 never been publicly acted, and that it remained unacted because of fears that it might be interpreted as a political allegory on the Earl of Essex ('Date and Revision'). Honigmann's conjecture about the date and censorship of the play is more persuasive than any yet available; he may also be right about a 'private' performance at Cambridge, though the 'evidence' for this is as tenuous as that associating the play with the Inns of Court. (See text note at Add. Pass. B.21.) The epistle is printed among commendatory Poems and Prefaces.

Williams's doctoral dissertation identified two compositors in Q (Eld A and Eld B), on the basis of spelling habits and of A's tendency to set colons for full stops: his conclusions are summarized and evaluated in Walker's edition (pp. 129–31), and reinforced by Jackson's study of Shakespeare's *Sonnets*. (Eld also printed the *Sonnets*, and Jackson identifies the same two workmen in that text.) Palmer has since shown that sheet F was printed by a third workman (pp. 304–6). The conjectural stints are as follows:

Eld A: 1.1.1–1.2.281/0.1–425
       1.3.293–2.2.102/728–1051
       2.3.204–3.1.100/1365–1521
       3.3.51–4.1.45 (wherefore)/1834–2130
       4.4.4–4.7.20/2281–2576,
       4.7.174–5.2.124/2730–2950
       5.2.163–98/2989–3024
       5.4.23 (Now the sleeue,)-end/3166–end

Eld B: 1.2.282–1.3.292/426–727
       2.2.103–2.3.203/1052–1364
       4.1.45 (I fear)–4.4.3/2130–2280
       4.7.21–173/2577–2729
       5.2.125–62/2951–88
       5.3.0–5.4.23 (Trojan)/3025–3166

Eld C: 3.1.101–3.3.50/1522–1833

A and B differed markedly in their treatment of punctuation, especially colons and question marks; A was apparently more prone to omissions of single words and (in *Sonnets*, at least) 'memorial' substitution, while B was especially prone to misreading. Such associations increase confidence in certain traditional emendations, while decreasing confidence in the authority of Q's incidentals.

Hillebrand collated fourteen of the fifteen extant copies of Q (Variorum, p. 323). He does not identify which copy he failed to collate, but in his list of variants specifically refers to all copies but those at Eton, the Folger Library, and the Victoria and Albert Museum (two copies, one defective): he assigns sigla to all but the defective Victoria and Albert copy, which may have been the copy he omitted. Hillebrand misrepresented the press variant at 1658/3.2.82, recording only the change of spelling (thene/then), and not Qa's duplication of the word itself. Palmer, moreover, identified two more variants in a copy which Hillebrand did collate (Malone's). Palmer also suggested that 'the acquisition of fresh copy' may account for certain peculiarities in the printing of Sheet F (pp. 304–5). Sheet F was printed with a new skeleton by a new compositor, and underwent much more stop-press correction than any other sheet (14 of 19 recorded variants). These facts may

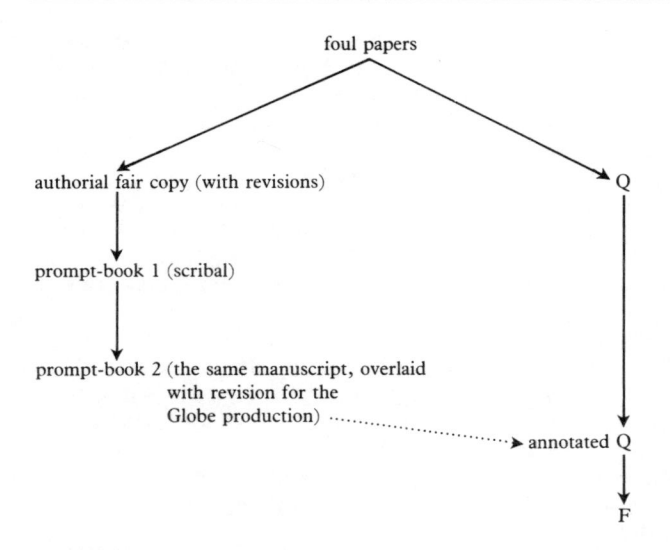

```
                    foul papers
                   /          \
                  /            \
                 ↓              \
      authorial fair copy        \
         (with revisions)         ↓
                │                 Q
                ↓                 │
      prompt-book 1 (scribal)     │
                │                 │
                ↓                 │
      prompt-book 2 (the same manuscript, overlaid
           with revision for the
           Globe production) ·········→ annotated Q
                                        │
                                        ↓
                                        F
```

well be interrelated, but they bear no obvious or discernible relation to Palmer's conjecture that 3.2.59-95/1635-71 was a later insert in the copy. This is, indeed, approximately the length of a quarto page (35 lines of type, as opposed to a norm of 38); but one would not expect material accidentally overlooked or added later to bear any relation to the length of printed pages, rather than manuscript ones. (Compare Q *2 Henry IV*, where the added passage is the approximate length of two manuscript pages.) Palmer relies on the unreliable evidence of type-shortages as his only grounds for the conjecture that F1ᵛ-F4ᵛ were not set until sheets G and H were also in type. Only a much more thorough analysis of Eld's work on this and other quartos would justify any conjecture about the causes for the peculiarities of this sheet, and any such explanation would seem unlikely to bear much editorial fruit.

It has been widely assumed, since Chambers first suggested it (*Shakespeare*, i. 438-9), that the copy for Q was a transcript of Shakespeare's foul papers. However, this hypothesis depends less upon the evidence of Q itself than upon certain assumptions about F, and it will be most convenient to consider the copy for both texts simultaneously.

The play was originally intended to stand, in the Folio, after *Romeo and Juliet*; in one copy of the Folio *Troilus* begins on the verso of a leaf which contains on its recto the end of *Romeo*. (These pages are reproduced in Hinman's facsimile, pp. 916-19.) Hinman's analysis of the sequence of printing makes it reasonably certain that four pages of *Troilus* were at this time set into type and printed. One of these (*gg3ᵛ) is the cancelled title-page, preserved in a single copy of F (Folger 71): another (*gg5) does not survive, but was probably printed along with its forme-mate page in *Romeo*, gg2ᵛ (*Printing and Proof-Reading*, ii. 231-64). Two others—numbered '79' and '80'—were used in the eventual setting of the play, where they are placed (as they must have been originally) immediately after the title-page. *Titus* and *Romeo*, the two preceding Folio plays, were set from quarto copy, only minimally amended, and the three pages of pre-cancellation *Troilus* which survive make it quite clear that the original intention was to produce a simple reprint of the extant Quarto. Since a text of the play was obviously available to Jaggard, and since the play's eventual inclusion testifies to Shakespeare's authorship, it is generally assumed that the initial setting of *Troilus* was abandoned because of difficulties over copyright. The play was eventually included in the Folio only at the last moment: the Catalogue does not name it, and Hinman established that its text was set after the Preliminaries, as the very last job in the volume. It was placed, unpaginated, after *All Is True* (the last of the Histories) and before *Coriolanus* (originally intended as the first of the Tragedies). The added Prologue in fact occurs before the title-page, on a page of its own; the title-page was reset, from *gg3ᵛ; gg4 and gg4ᵛ were inserted; the remainder of the play was freshly set, with a different running title (omitting the original '*The Tragedie of*'). The last change may well be fortuitous: the running title for *Timon of Athens* also omits this formula. For a purchaser of the completed volume, the 'Tragedies' section began, albeit untidily, with 'THE TRAGEDIE OF | Troylus and Cressida'.

Between the abandoned original setting and the eventual completed one, Jaggard had evidently acquired a manuscript, or access to one: the new prologue suggests as much, and the impression is confirmed by the hundreds of substantive variants between Q and F in the newly set pages, beginning with ¶1 (Greg, 'The Printing'). Jaggard thus clearly possessed both a copy of Q, as is evident from the original setting, and a manuscript, as is evident from the textual variation in the eventual setting; Williams demonstrated, on the basis of bibliographical links between Q and F, that the Folio compositors worked, beginning with ¶1, from a copy of Q annotated by reference to a manuscript ('Shakespeare's *Troilus and Cressida*'). The incidentals of F are thus without authority, since F is in this respect derivative, merely offering Q's spelling and punctuation as sophisticated by Jaggard's compositors. In these circumstances, Q must be treated as the copy-text for incidentals. (See Taylor, 'Copy-Text and Collation'.)

The relationship between the manuscript behind Q and that consulted for F has been disputed. In 1930 Chambers proposed, on the basis of a critical interpretation of two passages (4.5.98-9/2535-6, 5.3.116-18/3140-2), and in the context of doubts that Shakespeare was responsible for the Epilogue, that F was set from Shakespeare's foul papers; since the copy for Q could hardly have served as a prompt-book, Q must therefore have been set from a scribal transcript of the same foul papers. This hypothesis held the field for half a century. However, Taylor has challenged Chambers's interpretation of the two passages, arguing that they provide dubious evidence of the relationship between Q and F, and the more objective evidence—of stage directions, and of apparent misreadings transferred from the manuscript on to the printer's Quarto copy—strongly suggests that the manuscript Jaggard consulted was a scribal transcript, probably prepared for theatrical use. By contrast, all the objective evidence (wholesale absence of necessary stage directions, presence of vague or authorial directions, confusion in the ascription of speeches, Shakespearian mislineation, Shakespearian marginal insertions, Shakespearian spellings, Shakespearian misreadings, Shakespearian punctuation) points to the use of foul papers as copy for Q.

Honigmann ('Date and Revision') reiterates earlier arguments that certain Folio variants look like abandoned first thoughts; but we find these examples as ambiguous and unreliable as ever. On the basis of them he proposes that Q was prepared from an authorial fair copy, containing careful verbal revisions, intended for a private patron; but Q is, by every objective criterion, drastically different from other fair copy texts, including those presumably prepared by Shakespeare himself (*Venus* and *Lucrece*). Nor can the *Sonnets* represent a comparable transcript for the same patron (p. 54), for they contain a recurring misreading unique in the canon (see Introduction). Honigmann further proposes that F was set from a scribal transcript, prepared for theatrical use, of the unrevised foul papers; but, as usual, this theory of F entirely depends upon the (untenable) theory for Q—and he must in any case concede that for certain variants the Folio provides later authorial variants than Q. We see no reason to abandon the simpler hypothesis that authorial revisions are contained, as usual, in the later theatrical text (F). We have therefore acted upon the hypothesis that Q was set directly from foul papers, and F from an exemplar of Q annotated by reference to a prompt-book.

Authorial revision has often been suspected as the source of many of the variants in *Troilus*, and Honigmann devoted a chapter to it in his important reconsideration of *The Stability of Shakespeare's Text*. Walker, who consistently denied the possibility of revision anywhere in the canon, in *Troilus* attempted to explain the variants as corruptions introduced by three intermediaries: Eld's compositors, Jaggard's compositors, and the literary scribe who prepared Eld's copy. We now know considerably more about two of these agents, and have ceased to believe in the third. Comparison with the *Sonnets*, or with Eld's many other Jacobean play quartos, does not encourage the supposition that Q has suffered massive corruption in the printing house; Werstine's extensive studies of the work of Jaggard's compositors B and E, who set much of the Folio text, has demonstrated that they can reasonably be held accountable for only a tiny proportion of the variants. The other Jaggard compositor who worked on *Troilus* has been identified as 'H', a workman not present anywhere else in the Folio; but the kinds and quantities of variant in his stints do not differ noticeably from those elsewhere. Much of the variation between the printed texts must therefore reflect variation in the underlying manuscripts. Since one of the manuscripts was apparently autograph, and the other a prompt-book, most of the verbal variants between them are presumably authorial; since the prompt-book must be the later of such two manuscripts, it presumably contains Shakespeare's revised text. We have therefore adopted F as our control-text, preferring its substantive readings unless they seem demonstrably wrong or unlikely.

'Rejected Quarto Variants' are listed separately; this list includes a few variants also separately discussed in the Textual Notes, in order to provide a comprehensive account of rejected Quarto dialogue alternatives. Variants which seem to us most probably to result from authorial revision are asterisked, enabling students who wish to do so to reconstruct an edited text of the Quarto version of the play, and to study the presumably authorial variants in bulk. Stage directions from both texts are listed below.

Neither text contains act or scene divisions. The traditional act division was introduced by Rowe. We follow Pope in marking a new scene at the entrance of Menelaus, Paris, and Thersites (5.8/Sc. 24); Dyce and subsequent editors ignored the cleared stage here, consequently misnumbering 5.9/Sc. 25 and 5.10/Sc. 26 as 5.8 and 5.9. We also follow Q and F in marking a general *Exeunt* at 4.2.76, and hence in marking a new scene (4.3/Sc. 12) with the subsequent entrance of Pandarus and Cressida. This throws off the traditional scene-numbering for the remainder of the Act. Furthermore, in the middle of 4.6/Sc. 15 (= traditional 4.5) the stage is again apparently cleared, and consequently we begin a new scene after 4.6.119.

G.T./(S.W.W.)

WORKS CITED

Deighton, K., ed., *Troilus and Cressida*, Arden (1906)
Greg, W. W., 'The Printing of Shakespeare's *Troilus and Cressida* in the First Folio', *SB* 3 (1951), 273–82; repr. in *Collected Papers*, 392–401
Hillebrand, H. N., and T. W. Baldwin, eds., *Troilus and Cressida*, New Variorum (1953)
Honigmann, E. A. J., *The Stability of Shakespeare's Text* (1965)
—— 'The Date and Revision of Troilus and Cressida', in *Textual Criticism and Literary Interpretation*, ed. Jerome McGann (1985), 38–54
Jackson, MacD. P., 'Punctuation and the Compositors of Shakespeare's *Sonnets*, 1609', *The Library*, V, 30 (1975), 2–24
Muir, Kenneth, 'A Note on the Text of *Troilus and Cressida*', *The Library*, VI, 1 (1979), 168
—— ed., *Troilus and Cressida*, Oxford (1982)
Nosworthy, J. M., *Shakespeare's Occasional Plays* (1965)
Palmer, Kenneth, ed., *Troilus and Cressida*, Arden (1982)
Seltzer, Daniel, ed., *The History of Troilus and Cressida*, Signet (1963)
Taylor, Gary, 'Copy-Text and Collation (with special reference to *Richard III*)', *The Library*, VI, 3 (1981), 33–42
—— '*Troilus and Cressida*: Bibliography, Performance, and Interpretation', *SSt* 15 (1982), 99–136
Upton, John, *Critical Observations on Shakespeare* (1746)
Walker, Alice, ed., *Troilus and Cressida*, New (1957)
Williams, Philip, 'The 1609 Quarto of *Troilus and Cressida* and its Relation to the Folio Text of 1623', unpublished Ph.D. thesis (University of Virginia, 1949)
—— 'The "Second Issue" of Shakespeare's *Troilus and Cressida*, 1609', *SB* 2 (1949), 25–33
—— 'Shakespeare's *Troilus and Cressida*: The Relationship of Quarto and Folio', *SB* 3 (1951), 131–43

TEXTUAL NOTES

Title *Troylus and Cressida*] F (*most running titles*); The booke of Troilus and Cresseda S.R. (1603); THE hiſtory of Troylus and Creſſida S.R. (1609); The Hiſtorie of Troylus and Creſſeida. Qa (*title-page*); THE Famous Hiſtorie of Troylus and Creſſeid. Qb (*title-page*); The hiſtory of *Troylus* and *Creſſeida*. Q (*head-title; running titles, all italic*); THE TRAGEDIE OF Troylus and Creſsida. F (*title-page; initial running titles, all italic*). Given the disagreement between the primary sources—including Q's preface—it seems best to leave the question of genre in abeyance in the title (as in the earliest document).

Pro.1–31] *not in* Q. The addition of this Prologue may be related to the altered ending.

Pro.12/12 *Barkes*] F2; *Barke* F1. Though all editors follow F2, given the marked poetic diction of the speech F1 seems just possible as a collective singular.

Pro.12 barques] F2 (Barkes)

Pro.13 freightage] F (*frautage*)
Pro.17/17 Antenorides] THEOBALD; Antenonidus F
Pro.18 full-filling] F (*fulfilling*)
Pro.19/19 *Sparre*] THEOBALD (*Sperre*); *Stirre* F. Shakespeare's 'a' is more likely than his 'e' to be misread as a minim. For the sense and spelling, see *OED spar, v.*¹.
Pro.25/25 conditions] F; condition WALKER
1.1.0.1–1.2.231/31.1–375 Enter ... and how he] F in these pages simply reprints Q, with a few errors; therefore its readings and press variants are here treated as without substantive authority.
1.1.17/50 must] Q; muſt needes F
1.1.25/55 heating] Q, Fa; heating of Fb. Most editors accept Fb's addition, but it is unnecessary and without authority.
1.1.26/56 yea] Q; you F. Q's spelling, found elsewhere (*OED*), is repeated at 1.2.46/192; F is a sophistication.
1.1.26/56 chance] Q; chance to F
1.1.31/61 when she] ROWE; then ſhe Q
1.1.31/61 is she] ROWE 2; ſhe is Q
1.1.37/67 a sconce] This edition (*conj.* W. C. Hazlitt); a ſcorne Q; a storm ROWE. Despite many objections to Rowe's emendation, it continues to be accepted because *ascorn* (meaning 'scornfully') is only recorded elsewhere once, in 1485, and does not make exceptionally good sense. But *askance* ('obliquely, askew') does, and this spelling of the word (attested by *OED*) also occurs at *Shrew* 1126 (a sconce); 'rn' for 'nc' would be an easy minim misreading.
76 *Cassandræs*] Q. For this unusual form of the possessive compare *Othello* 2.1.81/763: *Deſdemonaes*.
1.1.53/83 heart,] F; ~ : Q
1.1.54/84 voice;] THEOBALD; ~, Q
1.1.55/85 discourse͵] MALONE; ~ : Q. All three punctuation changes attempt to clarify the objects of the two verbs ('Powrest', 'Handlest'); some editors place a heavier stop after 'haire' or 'gate' (1.1.54/84), making 'Handlest' refer backward rather than forward; some follow 'discourse' with a dash or opening parenthesis.
1.1.71/101 on of you] F; of you Q
1.1.75/105 not kin] Fb; kin Q, Fa
1.1.77/107 care I] F; I Q
1.1.101/131 recides] F; reides Q
1.2.0.1/146.1 aboue] This edition; *not in* Q. Pandarus later says 'shall we stand vp here and see them as they passe' (1.2.173–4/319–20); the review parade of Trojan warriors is most easily staged with Pandarus and Cressida on the upper stage.
1.2.17/163 they] F; the Q
1.2.22/168 farced] WALKER (Theobald); fauced Q
1.2.30/176 man] Q; strange man This edition *conj*. Cressida's preceding and following speeches in this scene scan as verse.
1.2.36.1/182.1 *Enter Pandarus*] DYCE; *not in* Q; *at* 193 F. F has no authority; if Pandarus is to enter above (see 1.2.0.1/116.1), he cannot appear until just before the remark he is meant to hear.
1.2.46/192 yea] Q, F1; ye F2; you THEOBALD. See 1.1.26/56.
1.2.48/194 vp?] Editors since F2 have silently altered the question mark here to a full stop, but surely Cressida is being facetious: *gone* can mean 'pregnant' and *vp* 'erect'.
1.2.68/214 iust͵] ROWE; ~, Q
1.2.82/228 will] Q; wit ROWE. Editors have generally accepted Rowe's emendation because it makes more obvious sense as a point of praise. But *will* can be used positively or neutrally as 'resolution' and 'faculty of mind which governs choice', while at the same time allowing several relevant but unintended senses: 'carnal appetite', 'penis', and 'obstinacy'.
1.2.112/258 lifte] F (lift); lifte Q
1.2.125/272 the] F2; thee Q, F1
1.2.143/290 pot] F; por Q
1.2.143/290 or] This edition; *not in* Q. The progress of the dialogue seems to presume that Hecuba's eyes ran over like an overheated pot, and that Cassandra did not laugh so violently ('there was a more moderate fire ...'); the following question therefore seems to require a disjunctive here.
1.2.187/333 a man] F; man Q

1.2.188/334 iudgements] Q; iudgement F
1.2.200/346 mans] F; man Q. Q might be defended by interpreting 'heart good' as a compound: there are no parallels, but Shakespeare has 24 other 'heart' compounds.
1.2.210/355 hurt home] Q; home hurt ROWE
1.2.220.1/364.1 *A Shout*] MUIR; *not in* Q
1.2.231/375 lookes, and how] At this point F regains its independent authority and becomes the control-text. Acceptance of subsequent F readings will therefore normally be recorded only in the historical collation (list of rejected Q readings).
1.2.236/380 an eye] Q; money F. F's weaker word could easily arise from misreading.
1.2.237/381 comes] Q; come F. Here and in all subsequent indifferent variants involving terminal 's' Q has been preferred, because its one stage of transmission offers less opportunity for this very common type of error than do F's three stages.
1.2.251/395 season] Q; ſeaſons F
1.2.253/397 pie] For confirmation of a suspected sexual innuendo here compare Henry Porter's *Two Angry Women of Abington*: 'Nimble as a Doe.—Backt [i.e. baked] in a Pie.—Of ye.—Good meate ye know.' (MSR, ll. 2607–9) and Beaumont and Fletcher's *Love's Pilgrimage*, 'I have a cold pie for ye' (2.2.30). In both cases the context is unmistakably bawdy, and suggests that 'pie' = female sexual organ (perhaps because a slice of pie resembles the triangle of female pubic hair?) conceived as a 'meat pie', 'cold pie', etc.
1.2.253/397 date is] Q, F4; dates F1–3
1.2.257/401 wiles] QF; will JOHNSON (*conj.*)
1.2.259/403 lie, at] Q, F2; lye at, at F
1.2.270/414 house] F; house there he vnarmes him: Q. 'The [Q] statement really adds nothing ... If an explanation is needed for Troilus' being at Pandarus' house, it is not provided by the equally unexplained statement that he is unarming there' (Hillebrand).
1.2.277.1/421.1 *Exeunt Pandarus* ⌈*and Alexander*⌉] This edition; *Exit Pand*⟨*arus*⟩. F; *not in* Q. Capell added an exit for Alexander after Cressida's speech, but it seems likelier that this was intended as a soliloquy. There is no obvious cue for an earlier exit, and Shakespeare probably forgot about Alexander after 1.2.52/198 ('So he saies here'); perhaps a cue was provided in the prompt-book by some rewriting in the earlier portion of the scene, where F merely reprints Q (without access to the prompt-book).
1.2.285 price] Q; prize F. The QF spellings were interchangeable; F's has now become figurative, where Q's emphasizes the commercial image.
1.2.290/434 Then] Q; That F. F4 reverses the order of 1.2.288–9/ 432–3, which makes good sense in itself and also makes sense of F's 'That' here; Rowe to Warburton, who unknowingly accepted the F4 variant, also accepted F's 'That'; Johnson was the first to reject F4's order, and the first to accept Q's 'Then'. One could accept 'That' by presuming that F failed to alter Q's order in the preceding couplet.
1.2.290/434 contents] F (Contents); content Q. Though either text is acceptable, Q is susceptible to the aural misinterpretation 'my heart is content', and may have been deliberately altered to remove the ambiguity.
1.3.1 jaundice] QF (Iaundies)
1.3.7/442 Infects] Q; Infect F. Many editors follow F and emend QF 'diuerts' to ROWE's 'divest'. Either form would be acceptable Elizabethan usage. Though F might have overlooked the Q error in the second word, it seems less likely that Q made the same error twice in the line than that F made it once.
1.3.18/453 shames] Q; ſhame F
1.3.50/485 flee] CAPELL; fled QF
1.3.53/488 Retorts] HUDSON (Dyce); Retires QF; Rechides STAUNTON (Lettsom). If a compositor correctly read *chid*⟨*ing*⟩ in the next word but one, he seems unlikely to have misread ⟨*re*⟩*chides* as *retires* here.
1.3.58/493 th'] Q; the F
1.3.62/497 euerye hand] This edition; and the hand QF; all the hands DEIGHTON (Orger). Deighton's reading presupposes

unrelated error in two separated words; although our solution may seem more drastic, palaeographically it is easier.

1.3.66/501   On] Q; In F
1.3.74/509   his] QF; her F4
1.3.83   masque] QF (maske). Interpreting *mask* as 'vizard' makes the word merely redundant; understood as *masque*, it contributes an image of social and musical order in key with the remainder of the speech, and giving a concrete occasion for action in which *th'vnworthiest* might *shew as fairly*.
1.3.84/519] This edition. Keightley first conjectured that a line is lost between 1.3.83 and 85/518 and 520, and some contrast with 'th'vnworthiest' seems required. Hillebrand glosses *Degree* (1.3.82/517) as 'high degree', thereby providing the required contrast; but *OED* gives no parallel for this gloss, which would be particularly unfortunate here, in the first occurrence of a word so crucial to the following argument.
1.3.87/522   Infixture] This edition; In fifture Q; Infifture F. Delius conjectured 'In fixture'; the preposition does not seem appropriate (as it would govern all the succeeding nouns), but 'Infixture' is an attractive compound: see *OED* for *fixture* (a word rare outside Shakespeare at this period), *infix* (*All's Well* 5.3.48/2566, *K. John* 2.2.503/779), and *infixion*. However interpreted, Shakespeare must have invented a compound here. F offers a compound formed upon *insist*, which Shakespeare only uses elsewhere in the inappropriate modern sense ('assert or maintain persistently': *Caesar* 2.1.244/806, *Coriolanus* 3.3.17/1946). Two meanings have been elicited from *insisture*: (*a*) 'steady continuance' (*b*) the moment of apparent stasis, when a planet, as viewed from earth, seems to pause before reversing its former motion (Baldwin). The second meaning is implausible not primarily because of its arcane technicality (Walker), but because there is no obvious correspondence between the astronomical figure and the image of society which Ulysses is proposing. The first gloss—'steady continuance of motion' (Palmer)—is based upon *OED insist, v.* 2. This interpretation is much more plausible and intelligible, but strains the sense of a word relatively unusual to begin with, and creates problems for the image—because the great astronomical problem posed by the Ptolemaic system was why the movement of the planets was so erratic, stopping and starting, slowing down and speeding up. *Insisture* hardly seems the right word. By contrast, 'infixture' adds to the astronomical and social conceit a term of stability: the earth was the 'fixed' centre of the universe, the 'fixed' stars maintained their place in the firmament, and even the planets were believed to be 'fixed' in their moving Ptolemaic spheres. Ulysses later complains that the failure to observe degree leads to the loss of 'fixure' in society (1.3.101/536). 'Infixture' seems more appropriate and more Shakespearian than 'Insisture', and could easily result from Q's misreading of a nonce word; F's 'correction' might be compositorial, and even if it results from consultation of copy the annotator's reading of the manuscript would have been heavily influenced by Q's interpretation.
1.3.91/527   ill Aspects of Planets euill] F; influence of euill Planets Q. Though both variants are probably authorial, F's 'Planets euill' is the rarer word order, so Q's could easily result from normal compositorial error.
1.3.101   fixture] QF (fixure) See note to *Winter's Tale* 5.3.67/2929.
1.3.106/541   primogenitie] Q; primogenitiue F; primogeniture ROWE
1.3.117   resides] QF (recides). Though the QF spelling can clearly mean 'resides' (as at 1.1.101/131 and 3.2.144/1719), Dobrée argues that it must here derive more directly from the Latin *recadere*, and mean 'falls down', because justice does not merely 'come between' right and wrong, but is on the side of right. But Dobrée's sense is not paralleled in English before 1628, and would probably be indistinguishable aurally. Justice comes between opposing contenders, both of whom claim to be right (though one is wrong). The line is parenthetical: the jar of right and wrong is *endless*, but justice does not always 'fall down'.
1.3.118/553   their] Q; her F
1.3.127/562   it is] Q; is it F
1.3.137/572   liues] F; ftands Q. Though almost all editors since Capell have preferred Q, F is not easily explicable as an error and picks up the imagery of *feuer* (1.3.133, 135, 139/568, 570, 574), *sick* (1.3.132, 139/567, 574), *sicknesse* (1.3.140/575), and *sinnews* (1.3.136/571): Troy lives and is well because they are weak and sickly.
1.3.156   scaffoldage] QF (fcaffollage, Scaffolage). Q's intrusive 'o' is presumably a literal error, but otherwise the QF form is well attested (see *OED scaffold, scaffoldage, scaffolding*).
1.3.159   a-mending] QF (a mending). One might interpret QF as 'amending', but in the sense 'repair' (*amend, v.* 5) this is now archaic.
1.3.161/596   seeme] Q; feemes F
1.3.177/612   all] QF; elce This edition *conj.* For the 'elce' spelling (which could more easily be misread *all*) see *Troilus* 1.3.327/762. If not supplied by emendation 'else' or 'otherwise' must be inferred.
1.3.188   self-willed] F (felfe-will'd), Q (felfe-wild). Q is a possible substantive variant, but seems likelier to be a mere spelling variant (omission of the apostrophe being common in Shakespearian foul-paper texts). Compare *1 Henry IV* 3.1.194/1673 (selfe wild) and *Sonnet* 6.13 (selfe-wild).
1.3.189/624   place] QF; pace POPE
1.3.190/625   and] F; *not in* Q. Almost all editors prefer Q, but feminine caesurae abound in this and Shakespeare's other plays, so there seems little reason to regard F as an error, rather than as authorial second thought or a correction of Q.
1.3.202/637   calls] Q; call F
1.3.207/642   swinge] Q; fwing F. Possibly a mere spelling variant; the connotations of *swinge* seem more appropriate to *rudeness*.
1.3.209/644   finesse] Q; fineneffe F. This too may be a mere Q spelling variant (compare the spellings 'playnes', 'prophaness'); or a Folio sophistication based on a scribal or compositorial assumption that it was one. But *finesse* seems more apt to Ulysses' argument and *OED* (*sb.* 4) quotes Daniel (1615) showing that *finesse* could then take the required accentuation (*finesses* rhyming with *businesses*). The Variorum does not record Q's variant.
1.3.213.1/648.1   *and a trumpeter*] SISSON; *not in* QF. Aeneas addresses a trumpeter at 1.3.253/688, says that he 'bring[s] a trumpet to awake' Agamemnon's ear (1.3.248/683), and that Hector told him to 'take a Trumpet' (1.3.260/695). But F's stage direction at 1.3.256.1/691.1 calls for *Trumpets*, and F here does not mention a trumpeter though adding the entrance for Aeneas. Thus there might be more than one trumpeter, on or off stage.
1.3.221/656   heart] This edition; head QF. The repetition of *head*(s) seems pointlessly awkward, leading MUIR (following Kinnear) to read 'host' for 'heads' in 1.3.220/655; Palmer, more plausibly, emends to 'lords'. But contamination from a following line is less likely than from a preceding one. Ulysses calls Agamemnon 'Heart of our numbers' earlier (1.3.55/490), and *heart* sustains the physical imagery (ears, arm, heads, heart, eyes).
1.3.226/661   on] F; bid Q. Though all editors since Pope have preferred Q, F makes good sense, and is hard to account for as an error.
1.3.233/668   vnarm'd] QF; vnmou'd This edition *conj.* This epithet seems pointless as a term of praise, and made superfluous as a qualifier ('*when* they are unarmed') by the next line. As the word consists almost entirely of minims, misreading would be particularly easy.
1.3.236/671   great] Q; *not in* F. Most editors follow F, on metrical grounds; but it is difficult to account for Q's word as an interpolation, and easy enough to regard F's omission as accidental. See next note.
1.3.236/671   accorn] This edition; accord QF. Editors interpret 'Ioue's accord' as a parenthetic 'God willing'; but aside from the lack of parallels, this leaves *great* unaccounted for, and creates the impression that the Trojans *lack* heart. Moreover, as Aeneas 'corrects' his boastfulness in 1.3.237/672, we would expect him to be at his *most* boastful here, rather than diminishing the force of his retraction by anticipating it. Finally, 'God willing' or its equivalent would be more appropriate to a claim about their

success, than to one about their high spirits. *Accorn* presumes an easy misreading (compare 3.1.244/1405, Q error 'boord' for 'boorn'), also attributable to assimilation to *swords* earlier in the line. The acorn is the seed of great Jove's tree, the oak (see *As You Like It* 3.2.230-2/1374-6), and full of heart because, proverbially, the little acorn grows into the great oak. *Heart* = the meat of an acorn or nut (*OED*, 18; see also *heart of oak*, *OED*, 19b). The emendation also restores metrical regularity.

1.3.240/675   that the] Q; that he F

1.3.241/676   repining the] This edition; the repining QF. QF is metrically anomalous, and F2's omission of 'But' (accepted by every editor up to Capell) has no plausibility. But Q could have transposed these two words, especially as it substitutes the more common order; as transposed, *repining* can be interpreted either as a present participle or adverbially, while *the enemy* is easily elided (compare 1.3.203/638 and 3.2.27/1603).

1.3.260/695   restie] Q; rufty F. Q seems more appropriate to what Hector says in 2.2 and to Aeneas' role here (the challenger not wishing to suggest deficiency, but restlessness). F could easily be a scribal error.

1.3.262/697   among] Q; among'ft F. Shakespeare prefers *among* (94 to 40) and *among'st* could result from assimilation to *fair'st*.

1.3.264/699   feares] QF; flies This edition *conj*. 'Flies' better balances 'seeks', and avoids the awkward anticipation of 'feare' in 1.3.265/700.

1.3.290/725   mould] F; hofte Q. Q has been so widely preferred that some defence of F seems necessary. 'Grecian mould' plays upon several senses of the noun: 'character' (*sb.*³ 9), 'model, exemplar' (*sb.*³ 5: the Greeks as a famous model of valour), 'land, region' (*sb.*¹ 6), and 'earth, regarded as the material of the human body' (*sb.*¹ 4). The last two senses would have been old-fashioned, and so help characterize Nestor; the second is pertinent to one of the play's chief preoccupations; the fourth (earth) contrasts with the 'spark of fire' in the next line. Finally, Nestor puns, unintentionally, on the sense 'fungus', a suggestion encouraged by the contextual emphasis on age, and contributing to the play's celebrated emphasis on (tempting or repulsive) food. Q's 'hoste' is, by contrast, acceptable but tame.

1.3.294/729   vambrace] Q; Vantbrace F. The difference is not substantive, and both forms are equally obsolete.

1.3.298/733   proue] Q; pawne F. F's reading was perhaps prompted by the association of 'three drops of blood' with the pawnbroker's sign (Nosworthy, p. 64); but the association could also account for a scribal misreading. Nestor might pawn his blood, but he surely does not intend to pawn his truth.

733   troth] Q; truth F. Mere spelling variant.

756   weare] Q; were F. Mere spelling variant: 'weare' occurs in Sonnets 98, 127, 140 (also printed by Eld).

1.3.337   indices] QF (indexes). The alternative modern form better indicates the required accentuation.

1.3.344/779   ˏAs twere, from forth vs all,ˏ] This edition; (As twere, from forth vs all) Q; ˏ As 'twere, from forth vs all: F

1.3.346/781   from hence receiues] F (receyues); receiues from hence Q. Walker claims that 'transposition is commoner in F', but no evidence exists to support such a claim, and F (being the more unusual order) is less likely to result from inadvertence.

1.3.348/783   in] F1; *not in* F2. Though all editors but Malone follow F2, F1 makes sense if *in* is interpreted *e'en* (as Alice Walker interpreted it in the next line). For parallels to F1's metre here, see 4.7.159/2715 ('Beate lowd the Taborins, let the Trumpets blowe'), 5.2.154/2980 ('Admits no orifex for a point as subtle'), 5.3.87/3111 ('How poore *Andromache* shrils her dolours foorth'), etc.

1.3.348   e'en] F (in)

1.3.380/815   Now *Vlisses*] QF; Ulysses, | Now STEEVENS; Now, | Ulysses KITTREDGE. Kittredge recognized that 'Now' is simply an extra initial syllable preceding a hexameter; but there is no need to place such extra initial monosyllables on a separate line. If desired, regularity would be best restored by the omission of 'Now', as an uncancelled first shot.

2.1.6/825   then] Q; *not in* F

2.1.14/833   thou] Q; you F

2.1.14/833   vnsifted] This edition; vnfalted Q; whinid'ft F; vinew'dest KNIGHT (*after* UPTON); vnwhimd'st This edition *conj*. Editors regularly adopt Upton's suggestion that F's reading derives from *vinew*, 'mouldy'. But there are no parallels for this word spelt *vh*; nor is *vh* common in other words, as *wh* is; nor can the *h* be easily interpreted as a compositorial preference, for the compositor has set a non-word. Besides, how does *beating* rectify 'mouldiness'? The common emendation therefore seems unacceptable palaeographically and as sense in its context. Since F was set from Q, the annotator must have seen and identified in his manuscript a word that was clearly *not* Q's 'vnsalted'; then Compositor B must have misread and/or misinterpreted the marginal corrction. *OED* cites *whim* as a variant of *wim* = 'to winnow'; *whimdest* could easily be misread *whinid(e)st*; and if the annotator only intended to strike out part of Q's word, but accidentally cancelled it all (or if the compositor so interpreted his intentions), manuscript 'vnwhimdest' ('most unwinnowed') could have resulted in F's 'whinid'st'. This, by a different route, would give the same meaning as THEOBALD's 'unwinnowd'st'; however, it presumes so much corruption that it can inspire little confidence. Q's 'vnsalted' is unsatisfactory because leaven is not normally salted anyway; nor, despite alleged biblical echoes, does *vnsalted leauen* easily convey the idea that Thersites is like salt that has lost its savour, or like corruptible matter not seasoned by God's grace. But *vnsalted* could easily be a misreading of *vnsifted*, thereby giving the same meaning as Theobald's 'unwinnowd'st', an adjective related to bread-making, and an image which leads into *beating* (the flailing which precedes winnowing, as part of the sifting process).

2.1.19/838   a thy] F3 (o' thy); ath thy QF (*subs.*)

2.1.21/840   Todes stoole] F; Tode-ftoole Q. Though all editors seem to prefer Q, most not even recording F, F is not only sensible, and much more insulting, but also the rarer reading: F might easily have been corrupted into commonplace Q, but it is more difficult to imagine Q rarified into F. The absence of Q's hyphen confirms that F's change is deliberate.

2.1.28   foot. An] RIVERSIDE (anon. *conj.*); foot, and QF

2.1.30/849   Greece.] F; Greece, when thou art forth in the incurfions thou ftrikeft as flow as another. Q. 'This sentence is so irrelevant to the preceding words of Thersites and so below his usual level of expression that one can only believe it was deliberately cut' (Hillebrand).

2.1.43-4/862-3   AIAX ... THERSITES] QF. WALKER (followed by subsequent editors) omits both prefixes, arguing that all of this belongs to Thersites. But this presupposes two interpolated prefixes in Q, overlooked by F in a passage where F was clearly attending to speech-prefixes; neither hypothesis is credible. The inferred allusion to Ajax's name does not seem sufficient reason to attribute 'Thou stool for a witch' to Thersites, the more so as Ajax has already (2.1.21/840) called him a 'Todes stoole'.

2.1.45/864   in thy skull] This edition; *not in* QF. Capell suggested adding 'in thy head' after 'braine'; but Shakespeare twice elsewhere refers to brains in 'skulls' (*Tempest* 5.1.59-60/1778-9, *Twelfth Night* 1.5.109/391-2), but never locates them in 'heads'. Capell's location of the insert leaves it unexplained; we have placed it between the end of one prose line ('hast') and the beginning of the next ('no'), an interval where omissions are common.

2.1.46   asnico] QF (*Afinico*). Editors usually modernize to *OED*'s 'Asinego'. But this is the word's first occurrence, and the spelling and italicization both suggest that Shakespeare intended to reproduce the Spanish 'asnico'.

866   thrash] Q; threfh F. Spelling variants only.

2.1.57/875   yee thus] Q; you this F. F's variants could easily be a sophistication and a misreading, though they could conceivably be indifferent authorial variants.

2.1.64/882   I do so] F; fo I do Q. Q repeats the word order of 2.1.62/880, and may be contaminated by it.

2.1.82/900   needle] For evidence that—like 'eye'—this word contains a sexual innuendo, see *Henry V* 2.1.33/518; Middleton and Rowley (?), *The Spanish Gypsy*, 2.1.186-8, 'O that I were your needle's eye! | How through your linen would I fly'; Beaumont and Fletcher, *Love's Cure*, 1.2.17, 'a better needle'; *Two Angry Women*, 2517-19; etc. In all these examples the context is unmistakably sexual.

2.1.92/910 bad the] Q; bad thee F

2.1.102/920 and] Q; if F. Folio texts elsewhere sophisticate *and* to *if*.

2.1.102/920 a knocke] KITTREDGE (Cambridge); he knocke F; knocke Q. See next note; Folio texts elsewhere sophisticate *a* to *he*.

2.1.102/921 a were] Q; he were F

2.1.106/924 your] THEOBALD; their QF

2.1.108/926 war] F (warre); wars Q. Thersites is presumably punning on *ware* = 'field-produce, crops' (*sb.*³ 3c), which could be spelt 'war' or 'warre'. This pun favours F's singular, since *ware* apparently does not occur in the plural in this sense.

2.1.110/928 to—] QF; to! CAPELL

2.1.112/930 wit] CAPELL; *not in* QF

2.1.114/932 peace] Q; *not in* F. F's omission might be authorial.

2.1.115/933 brach] ROWE; brooch QF

2.1.118/936 Clatpoles] Q; Clotpoles F. Q's italics suggest that the compositor may have mistaken the word (here in its first recorded occurrence) for another classical name. But why 'hang'd like clatpoles'? *Pole* could mean 'tradesman's sign' (*sb.*¹ 2b), and *clod* = 'blockhead' (*sb.* 5; *clot, sb.* 4): 'hung up as the trademarks of stupidity'?

2.2.0.1/949.2 Senet.] This edition; *not in* Q. It would be most unusual for an official (and royal) entrance like this not to be preceded by a trumpet call; a sennet is particularly associated by Shakespeare with royal entrances, and matches the entrance for the parallel Greek council scene (1.3/Sc. 3).

952 domage] Q; damage F. (Mere spelling variants.)

2.2.9/958 toucheth] Q; touches F

2.2.18 tithe-soul] WILSON; *not hyphenated in* QF. Compare 'tithe-pig'. Alternatively, one might emend to 'tithed', as at *Timon* 5.5.31/2250.

2.2.26/975 father] F; fathers Q. F's singular seems decidedly more apt; Riverside was the first edition to accept Q (interpreting *father's*).

2.2.34/983 reason] Q; reaſons F. F could easily result from contamination from 'reasons' two lines above.

2.2.37/986 reason] QF; reaſons ROWE 3

2.2.44-5/993-4 And . . . reason,] Q; *lines transposed* F

2.2.47/996 hare] Q; hard F

2.2.49/998 Make] Q; Makes F

2.2.55/1004 madde] Q; made F

2.2.70/1019 sure] This edition (*conj.* Schmidt, in *Lexicon*); fiue Q; fame F. In 'Bibliography, Performance, and Interpretation' G.T. conjectured 'sine', but Schmidt's conjecture (independently made by J. H. Walter, in Palmer's edition) offers a word (and a spelling) Shakespeare used elsewhere (as at 5.1.73/2805), one which could just as easily be misread *siue* or *same*, and which has a more obvious relevance to discarded food and the adjective *vnrespective*. (Also, because *sewer* and *shore* were apparently homonyms, the word could have been suggested by the earlier maritime imagery.)

2.2.70 sewer] For 'sure' as a spelling of modern *sewer*, see OED, 5.1.73/2805, and *Pericles* 19.200/1971.

2.2.89/1038 neuer fortune] Q; Fortune neuer F. Q's rarer order is less likely to result from inadvertence.

2.2.93/1042 But] QF; Base HANMER. *A thing so stolne* refers to the manner of the theft, described in the preceding line, rather than to the object itself (which would require *the thing so stolne*); the thieves are therefore unworthy of such fear (i.e. such fear is beneath them), as witnessed by the nobility of their previous conduct ('That in their country did them that disgrace . . .'). Hanmer's 'Base', though palaeographically and rhetorically attractive, cannot be right because 2.2.93/1042 is an oblique assertion of the Trojans' innate nobility, not their baseness.

2.2.103/1052 old] F; elders Q; eld COLLIER (Theobald). If 'eld' stood in his manuscript, the Folio annotator need only have struck through Q's last three letters; if F is an error, it must have stood in the prompt-book, and 'eld' (accepted by almost all editors) must have been Shakespeare's own revision of Q 'elders'. But F is acceptable as it stands, meaning either 'old age' (*OED, sb.*² 3, citing this passage) or 'old people' (*OED, adj.* 1) or 'an old person' (*OED, sb.*¹ 1, last citation 1532).

2.2.103-209/1052-1158 old . . . shrike] As Muir first noted, between these two variants F shows no signs of access to manuscript copy; Q therefore again becomes the control-text for this passage (equivalent to two manuscript pages). See notes on 2.2.119/1068, 2.2.143/1092, and 2.2.163/1112.

2.2.104/1053 canst] Q; can F

2.2.105/1054 clamours] Q; clamour F

2.2.110 Ah . . . ah] QF (a . . . a). This spelling is well attested in (Q2) Shakespeare; for the idiom, compare 'a woe' at Q2 *Hamlet* 2.2.504/1434. One might also punctuate 'Cry, Trojans, cry "Ah, Helen!" and "ah, woe!"'

2.2.119/1068 the] MUIR (th'); *not in* QF

2.2.143/1092 but these] QF; these but This edition *conj*.

2.2.163/1112 But] THEOBALD; And QF. Without a disjunction we must interpret *glozd, but superficially* as 'expounded [the subject], but [only] superficially', an awkward and unparalleled gloss. Agreement of Q and F is worthless here, and *but/and* substitutions occur elsewhere. (See for instance *Richard III* 2.1.93/1134 where Q1-6 and all editors read *But* for F *And*.)

2.2.177/1126 partiall] QF. For examples of trisyllabic *partial* (which makes emendation unnecessary here), compare Day's *Parliament of Bees*, Chap. 5, Massinger's *Bashful Lover* 5.3.24, Massinger and Field's *Fatal Dowry* 5.2.54, etc.

2.2.184/1133 nations] Q; Nation F

2.2.209/1158 shrike] Q; ſtrike F

2.3.6/1167 Ile see] QF; I see WALKER (*conj*)

2.3.12/1173 yee] Q; thou F. F's reading, rejected by all editors since Capell, seems based on a misunderstanding of the syntax; it is most probably compositorial.

2.3.14/1174 armd] QF; aim'd HUDSON (Dyce)

2.3.16/1177 their] Q; the F. Q has been accepted by virtually every editor since Malone.

2.3.18/1179 Neopolitan] Q; *not in* F

2.3.19/1180 dependant] F; depending Q. F's variant here (accepted by all editors until Seltzer) is more difficult than the preceding to account for as a compositorial error, and the resumption of reference to manuscript is confirmed by F's *Enter Patroclus* two lines below. F therefore now clearly regains its status as the control-text.

2.3.21.1/1182.1 at the doore to the Tent] This edition; *not in* QF. Recent editors have had Patroclus speak from within, despite F's direction; but it seems likelier that he simply appeared briefly in a doorway.

2.3.23/1184 Exit] This edition; *not in* QF. Prompt-books are casual about recording exits-and-quick-re-entries, and Patroclus seems to hear only the end of Thersites' next speech. He need do no more than turn back to face into the tent.

2.3.24/1185 could a] Q; could haue F

2.3.32.1/1193.1 Enter Patroclus] WALKER (anon. *conj.*); *not in* QF

2.3.34/1195 prayer] Q; a prayer F

2.3.36/1197 PATROCLUS Amen.] Q; *not in* F

2.3.46/1207 Thersites] Q; thy ſelfe F

2.3.54-9/1215-20 PATROCLUS . . . Patroclus is a foole.] F; *not in* Q. The absence of these lines from Q almost certainly results from eyeskip.

2.3.66/1227 the] QF; thy ROWE 2

2.3.66/1227 Creator] F; Prouer Q. Q is nonsense as it stands. Baldwin's gloss ('anyone who thinks it necessary to prove') is not supported by *OED*; nor is Mason's ('ask that question of yourself, who prove that you are'), since *OED* does not record the sense 'demonstrator, one who shows something to be true' until 1738. *Prouer* could mean 'an offender who confesses and turns state's evidence against his accomplices' (*OED*, II. 2), which would fit Thersites himself; but this would require us to assume that in Q (not F) 'Make that demand of the Prouer' should have been assigned to Achilles. Alternatively, one might emend to 'Provider'; but *OED* does not record that as a title for the deity until 1678.

2.3.67.1–2/1228.1–2 Enter . . . Calcas] Q's *position*; *after* 2.3.65/ 1226 F; *after* 2.3.74/1235 DYCE. As Ulysses later says 'We saw him at the opening of his tent' (2.3.83/1244), the entrance could occur where Q puts it. F on the other hand looks like a slightly anticipatory prompt-book instruction.

2.3.67.1–2/1228.2 & Calcas] QF; *not in* CAPELL

2.3.71/1232 whore, and a Cuckold] Q; Cuckold and a Whore F. The choice being entirely indifferent, F's longer stemma of transmission suggests that its reading is more likely to be accidental.

2.3.72/1233 emulous,] Q; emulations, F1; emulatious, F3

2.3.78/1239 facd] This edition; fate Q; fent F; shent THEOBALD; fobbed SISSON. Hulme (followed by Palmer) defended Q as meaning 'ignore, set aside' (p. 260); but the parallels are late, Scottish, and take different objects. Sisson rightly objects that Theobald's emendation, which the Variorum regarded as unchallengeable, is implausible as an emendation of Q or F; but Q and F would be easier misreadings of 'facd' than of 'fobd', and the sense— 'braved, bullied, behaved with effrontery toward'—seems more appropriate than 'put off'.

2.3.80/1241 so] Q; of F; of't This edition *conj.*

2.3.80/1241 least] Q; fo F

2.3.82/1243 so say] F; fay fo Q. Though editors prefer Q, F's rarer order produces a normal hexameter, rather than Q's much less acceptable rhythmical licence (assuming that *say* would normally be stressed).

2.3.86/1247 you will] Q; will F

2.3.87/1248 'tis] Q; it is F

2.3.105/1266 his legs] Q; His legge F

2.3.105/1266 flexure] Q; flight F

2.3.117/1278 on] Q; of F

2.3.117/1278 beheld] QF; upheld MASON (*conj.*)

2.3.119/1280 Yea, and] F; Yea Q. Most editors prefer Q, presumably for metrical reasons, but lines with an extra initial syllable occur elsewhere (1.3.225/660, 2.3.235/1396, 3.3.137/ 1920, 4.1.36/2121, etc.) and it is difficult to explain F's addition as an error (unless it was meant to replace 'Yea').

2.3.119/1280 vnholsome] Q; vnholdfome F

2.3.121/1282 come] Q; came F

2.3.125/1286 tend] Q; tends F

2.3.129–30/1290–1 His pettish . . . action] F (*subs.*); His courfe, and time, his ebbs and flowes, and if | The paffage, and whole ftreame of his commencement Q. Q's 'and if' (2.3.129/1290) and 'his' (2.3.130/1291) are probably simple errors for F's 'as if' and 'this', and Walker conjectures 'commencement' for 'commencement'; but otherwise the variants clearly represent deliberate revision.

2.3.129/1290 lunes] HANMER; lines F; time Q. F could mean 'course of action or conduct' (*OED*, sb.² 27), but this less specific sense seems weaker than the easy emendation 'lunes', which leads naturally into the following tidal imagery.

2.3.129/1290 his] F; and Q. Walker prefers Q, rejecting F as 'possibly due to repetition'; but this could also be said of Q, and since Shakespeare clearly revised the remainder of the lines, 'his' could be his too.

2.3.135/1296 Bring] Q, Fb; ₐring Fa

2.3.139/1300 second] Q, Fb; fecond Fa

2.3.166/1327 the] F; th' Q. Though F might be an error, it could be a deliberate change, to remove the jingle 'share th'ayre'.

2.3.170/1331 worth] Q; wroth F

2.3.174/1335 himfelfe] Q; it felfe F

1339 lead] Q; led F. Mere spelling variants (*OED*).

2.3.216–19/1378–80 AIAX . . . VLISSES . . . warme] This edition. Q assigns all this to Ajax; F divides the speeches as here, but in the opposite order (giving the first to Ulysses); RIVERSIDE assigns all to Ulysses; THEOBALD kept F's prefixes, but began Nestor's speech five words earlier (thereby assigning him 'he's not yet through warme'). 'A would have ten shares' (= he wants it all) could apply equally to Achilles or Ajax; neither Q nor F has any intrinsic superiority. The remainder, however, seems much more apt in reference to Ajax's tractability (leading naturally into Nestor's following advice and Ulysses' subsequent speech) than as a comment by Ajax on how he will manhandle Achilles; it therefore seems to belong to Ulysses, to whom neither text gives it. But Riverside's solution presumes an inexplicable substitution in Q followed by a correction in F which inexplicably resulted in the cancelled prefix being moved five words forward: the alternative adopted here presumes only an omitted prefix in Q (as at 1.2.142, 2.1.39/289, 859) and a marginal correction in F's copy accidentally transposed by the compositor. If the corrected copy had

Vllis.   Aiax.   A would have ten shares. ₐ I

the compositor could easily have put the first prefix first, and the second second, rather than vice versa as the annotator had intended.

2.3.220 Farce] QF (force)

2.2.225/1386 do's] Q; doth F

2.3.229/1390 valiant—] Q; ~. F. Q's dash seems unlikely to be accidental, while F's punctuation is generally without authority. Here the juxtaposition 'as valiant—A hoarson dog' may be intentionally comic.

2.3.230/1391 thus with vs] F; with vs thus Q. F's, the rarer order, diminishes the jingle 'vs thus'.

1399 gat] Q; got F. An indifferent variant; like F, we modernize to 'got'.

2.3.237/1398 Fam'd] Q; Fame F

2.3.238/1399 beyond all erudition] F; all thy erudition Q. Q's variants are difficult to explain unless Q has omitted a *be* (Thrice fam'd beyond be all thy erudition); Q would then represent an earlier alternative.

2.3.239/1400 thine] Q; thy F

2.3.245/1406 Thy] F. Q's 'This' is an acceptable spelling of *These*: see 3.1.148/1569.

2.3.252/1413 VLISSES] F; Neft⟨or⟩. Q. Almost all editors prefer Q, which probably represents Shakespeare's original intention; but it is Ulysses by whom Ajax is *ruld*, and who praises him like a father.

2.3.254/1415 great] Q; *not in* F

2.3.256/1417 to day to Troy] This edition; to Troy QF; to Troy to-day HUDSON 2 (Lettsom). Lettsom's addition produces metrical regularity and the expected contrast with *tomorrow*; transposing it makes a rhetorically and syntactically stronger line, with the presumed error more easily explained by eyeskip (*to day to Troy*).

2.3.261/1422 faile] Q; may faile F

2.3.261/1422 hulkes] Q; bulkes F

3.1.6/1428 notable] Q; noble F. Q is not only the less common word, but less easy to explain as an error.

3.1.17/1439 titles] Q; title F

3.1.28/1450 thou] Q; thou art F

3.1.32/1454 visible] HANMER; inuifible QF; indivisible WALKER (Daniel); invincible BECKET (*conj.*)

3.1.35/1457 not you] Q; you not F

3.1.38/1460 Cressid] Q; Creffida F. F could have arisen from contamination by 3.1.34/1456.

3.1.42.1/1463.1 Hellen] Q; Helena F

3.1.42.1/1463.1 attended ⌈by musicians⌉] This edition; *not in* QF. THEOBALD added attendants, apparently implied by 'al this faire company' (3.1.43–4/1464–5); since the musicians are required later, and have been with Paris and Helen earlier off stage, they seem the likeliest candidates. Could F's anomalous '*Helena*' be related to its omission of the necessary '*attendants*' (the annotator starting to write the word, or 'and', then breaking off, and the compositor taking 'a-' as a suffix)? Helen of Troy is never called 'Helena' in Shakespeare (but see Puttenham's *Arte of English Poesie*, Ff2 (p. 257), G3ᵛ (p. 47)).

3.1.52/1473 Nel, he] F; *Nel.* he Q; *Hel*⟨en⟩. He ALEXANDER. Helen is never elsewhere given the prefix *Nel*, though Paris once addresses her by that nickname (3.1.134/1555); Q is more likely to have made a common ,/. error than to have failed to capitalize the first word of a speech; and though F's punctuation is probably compositorial, Alexander's emendation presumes that the annotator overlooked the correct speech-prefix, in copy which was presumably much more regular than Q in the form and layout of such prefixes. F makes entirely acceptable dramatic sense.

3.1.54.1/1475.1 *She ticles him*] This edition; *not in* QF. This seems necessary to explain *in fits* (3.1.56/1477), and is supported by Pandarus' earlier account of Helen tickling Troilus (1.2.132/ 279), his use of *ticles* in the song he eventually sings (3.1.116/1537), and Helen's touching him later in the scene (3.1.103-5/1524-6).

3.1.56/1478 will,] This edition; *well*, QF. Walker suspected corruption: *well* is odd as a part-repetition of *well said*, or as an adverb modifying *you say so*, or as an interjection, and though *fits* (= 'strains of music') is obviously appropriate to the context, the exact point remains obscure; one would expect some more intelligible play on the sense 'spasms'. *Will*, often elsewhere confused with *well*, would have two meanings directly related to the pun on *fits*: 'do you insist on' (saying so while laughing) and 'will you in future' (say as much in a song).

3.1.70 Ay, faith] QF (I faith). As the same Q compositor twice elsewhere sets *yfaith*, it seems best to interpret the 'I' here as the usual form for modern *ay*. See 3.1.124/1545.

3.1.81/1502 sweet] Q; sweere F 3.1.124

3.1.84/1505 Ile lay my life] Q; *not in* F. F is conceivably deliberate ('You mustn't know *where* he sups—with Cressida', i.e. you know who, but mustn't know where) but more probably accidental.

3.1.84, 86, 89/1505, 1507, 1510 dispēser] This edition; diſpoſer QF. As Muir remarks, 'no one . . . has given a convincing explanation of the word in this context'. Emendation to 'dispenser' assumes an easy e/o misreading, combined with an overlooked (or absent) tilde. Unlike *dispose*, *dispense* has a whole range of meanings relevant to this context. Most immediately, *dispense* could mean 'give a dispensation, exemption, indulgence, or pardon' (*v.* 4, 5, 6, 9, 10, 15) and 'to set aside the obligation, observance, or practice of (any duty, etc.)' (*v.* 12). Cressida thus provides Troilus with his 'dispensation', his 'excuse', not to attend dinner at the palace. A *dispense* was also 'a place where provisions are kept; a storeroom, pantry, or cellar' (*sb.*¹ 3; 1622) and a *dispenser* 'a steward' (2a)—which has a witty pertinence to the issue of 'where [Troilus] sups', and with whom. Pandarus' reply, 'your poor dispēsers sick', plays on two meanings of *dispense*: 'the act of spending; money to spend' (*sb.*¹ 1), and 'to make up (medicine) according to a prescribed formula' (*v.* 3). The first sense has a witty pertinence to *poore*; the second, to *sick*. Moreover, the notion of Cressida as a dispenser of medicine has an obvious relevance to the larger pattern of imagery, in which Troilus' love is treated as a disease which Cressida could cure— an ironic image, given the diseased fate which awaits Cressida herself. Likewise, the recurrent characterization of love in terms of wealth gives *dispense* in the sense 'expenditure' a larger appropriateness than anyone in this scene realizes—and 'poore dispēser' is an ironic foretaste of Cressida's eventual impoverished destiny. One might expect an epithet three times emphatically applied to Cressida to have such larger pertinences to her role, and *dispēser* fulfils this expectation in other senses too. Aside from a 'dispenser of cures', she is, notoriously, one who 'sets aside the binding force of an oath or obligation' (*dispense, v.* 11); she is also, of course, 'one who dispenses . . . bestows' (*dispenser*, 1)— bestowing her favours, and her scarf, on first Troilus and then Diomedes. Finally, *dispense* can mean 'a state of uncertainty; an undetermined condition; suspense' (*sb.*²)—and, as she makes clear in her first soliloquy (1.2.278-91/422-35), Cressida believes that she must keep her lover in exactly this condition, in order to sustain her power over him. In all these senses, Cressida is, as Shakespeare portrayed her, an archetypical 'dispenser'.

3.1.87/1508 makes] Q; make F

1525 haste] Q; haſt F. *OED* records 'haste' as a spelling of *hast* for the 15th–16th c.; it is therefore clearly acceptable in a manuscript of 1602-3, and a print of 1609.

3.1.104.1/1525.1 *She strokes his fore-head*] This edition; *not in* QF

3.1.110/1531 PANDARUS In . . . so. | *Loue*] Fb; In . . . ſo. | Pan⟨darus⟩. *Loue* Fa; Pand⟨arus⟩: *Loue* Q (omitting In . . . so.). F's uncorrected version, giving the added words as a continuation of Paris' speech, presumably arose from the ambiguous placement of the marginal addition on the compositor's copy of Q.

3.1.111/1532 still loue still more] Q; ſtill more F

3.1.117, 119/1538, 1540 oh oh] POPE; *oh ho* QF. *OED* confirms Pope's belief (supported by almost all editors) that *oh ho* would not be used for the sound of groaning apparently required here, in contrast to *ha ho he*. In Chettle's *Tragedy of Hoffman* (1631), *ho* is likewise press-corrected to *oh* (MSR, l. 1380).

3.1.121, 122/1542, 1543 Oh o] POPE; *O ho* QF. See preceding note.

3.1.122-3/1543-4 ha— | hey ho] REED (Ritson); *ha----hey ho* QF. QF treat '*hey ho*' as part of the song; Palmer defends this. But though *hey ho* is common enough as a musical refrain, there is no evidence for its being a sound 'suggestive of sexual enjoyment', nor does it (as a sigh would) add anything to the song's meaning or tone. Moreover, as a sigh *hey ho* ironically suggests the musical sense *not used*, whereas as a common refrain it cannot incorporate the alternative rejected sense.

3.1.124/1545 I faith] Q; yfaith F. F probably represents a compositorial normalization, based on a misinterpretation of Q. (See note to 3.1.70.) Editors silently accept F.

3.1.130.1/1551.1 *Alarum*] This edition; *not in* QF. Some off-stage sound-effect seems likely, as a cue for Pandarus' abrupt change of subject. See 3.1.144.1/1565.1 and 1.1.88.1/118.1.

1569 this] Q; theſe F. Editors accept F as an emendation, but F merely modernizes a legitimate Early Modern English form (*OED these*, form γ; see also ε). See also notes to 2.3.245/1406, 5.1.12/2745 and 5.3.107/3131.

3.1.155/1576 PARIS] Q; *not in* F. F is possible, and may be related to the thee/her variant, but the line seems more convincing as his response to her preceding speech than as a sudden eruption of affection from her. F could well be an error; Q certainly represents Shakespeare's intention at some point.

3.1.155/1576 Sweet, aboue thought,] F4; ∼, ∼, Q, F1; ∼, ∼, POPE

3.2.0.1/1576.2 *Troylus Man*] QF. Probably the same character identified as '*Boy*' at 1.2.267.1/411.1.

3.2.12/1588 Pandar] Q; Pandarus F. The connotations of the shortened form seem deliberate here: compare *Ado* 1.1.235-7/239-40 ('hang me vp at the doore of a brothel house for the signe of blinde Cupid')—which lends an additional significance to 'painted' wings.

3.2.19/1595 pallats taste] QF; pallat tastes HANMER. Not only might *pallats* be used figuratively here for 'senses', but it could literally mean both their palates, and might even play on the sense (used in Chaucer, and current long after Shakespeare) 'small bed' (*pallet sb.*²).

3.2.20/1596 repured] Q; reputed F

3.2.22/1598 tun'd] Q; and F

3.2.30/1606 spirite] Q; ſprite F. Shakespeare's eight uses of *sprite* are all rhyme words in pre-1600 works.

3.2.32/1608 as short] Q; ſo ſhort F

3.2.44 thills] Q (filles), F (fils). *OED* lists *fill* (*sb.*²) as merely an obsolete variant of *thill*, which is still current.

3.2.65/1641 feares] F3; teares QF

3.2.66 cherubims] QF (Cherubins)

3.2.68/1644 safer] Q; ſafe F

3.2.73/1649 Nor] Q; Not F

3.2.78 monstruosity] QF. A distinct form, derived from French *monstruosité* rather than Latin *monstrōsitās*.

3.2.89/1665 crowne yt] F (it); louer part Q; cover it PALMER (Delius). Q's 'part' presumably derives from misreading 'y' as 'p'; for *yt* = 'it' see *Merchant* 2.4.34/797 (Q1). Delius's conjecture may well recover the original Q reading, revised in F.

3.2.115/1690 glance, that euer;] F2; ∼, ∼, Qb, F1; ∼ : ∼, Qa

3.2.117/1692 till now not] Q; not till now F. Q's order puts the stress on *till*, and F shows little evidence of dialogue corrections in this area.

3.2.119/1694   grone] Q; grow F
3.2.129/1704   Conning] POPE; Comming QF
3.2.129/1704   in my] This edition; from my QF. 'From' is acceptable in Q, but the two Folio changes in 3.2.130/1705 make it impossible there. For *in [my] weaknesse* see *Richard II* 3.2.177/1480 and *Troilus* 1.3.137/572.
3.2.146-7/1721-2   foole. Where is my wit? | I] F; foole. I Q
3.2.148/1723   speake so] Q; ſpeakes ſo F
3.2.156/1731   flames] QF; flame WALKER (Tannenbaum)
3.2.170/1745   trueth] Q; truths F
3.2.172/1747   Wants] Q, F1; Wont F2
3.2.188/1763   wind or] Q; as Winde, as F
3.2.189/1764   or] Q; as F
3.2.196/1771   paine] Q; paines F
3.2.204/1779   with a bed,] HANMER; *not in* QF
3.2.205.1/1781.1   *Exeunt Troylus and Cressid*] CAPELL; *Exeunt* Q; *not in* F
3.2.207/1783   Pander] Q; and Pander F
3.3.1-94/1784-1877   Now .. reflection] Though the Folio variants in 3.3.1/1784 and 3.3.3/1786 have been given the benefit of the doubt, F shows no clear evidence of manuscript authority until *shining* (3.3.95/1878) which, despite Muir, is difficult to credit as a compositorial substitution. Q thus becomes the control-text in the interim.
3.3.1/1784   you] F; *not in* Q
3.3.3/1786   your] F; *not in* Q
3.3.4/1787   come] F4; loue Q, F1
3.3.5/1788   profession] This edition; poſſeſſion QF. This easy emendation produces a much stronger and more appropriate sense — 'religious vow on entering an order' (*OED*, 1) and 'a particular religious order' (*OED*, 2) — which does not merely anticipate 'poſſeſt conueniences' two lines below. *Possession* also presupposes an unusual usage, and many editors emend to Capell's 'possessions'.
3.3.29   off] F, Q (of)
3.3.34/1817   bring word If] QF; bear word that MUIR. QF makes reasonable sense: 'bring back word whether Hector is willing to have his challenge taken up tomorrow' (i.e. does his intention still hold, and is tomorrow an acceptable day).
3.3.37.1/1820.1   *Enter*] F; *not in* Q
3.3.37.1/1820.1   in] F; stand in Q. The change in the form of this stage direction could be compositorial or editorial, but it strongly suggests prompt-book practice; instead of his manuscript being actually defective, the annotator may here merely have skimped his work, by checking only stage directions and leaving the dialogue uncollated.
3.3.39/1822   passe] Q; to paſſe F
3.3.59/1842   *Exeunt Agamemnon and Nestor*] CAPELL; *not in* QF
3.3.60/1843   *Exit*] CAPELL; *not in* QF
3.3.63/1846   *Exit*] CAPELL; *Exeunt* QF. The QF staging (with the generals passing by Achilles individually, but leaving the stage collectively) is possible; but given the insecurity of F's authority here, and the fact that *Exeunt* itself might cover a series of rapid individual exits, Capell's interpretation of the action seems more plausible.
3.3.67/1850   vse] DYCE 2 (W. S. Walker); vſ'd QF
3.3.75/1858   honour for] Q; honour'd for F
3.3.80/1863   Doth one] QF; Do th'one ANON. (*conj. in* Cambridge)
3.3.85/1868   not worth in me] QF; in me not worth ROWE
3.3.95/1878   shining] F; ayming Q. It is difficult to explain this variant as compositorial; yet of the next 6 Folio variants, 4 are clear errors, and the other 2 (at 3.3.97/1880 and 3.3.111/1893) indifferent, and plausible as unauthorized substitutions. Moreover, F retains one clear Q error (3.3.105/1888). However, the shared error is one that could easily have been overlooked, while the mere number of Folio dialogue variants (7 in 21 lines, opposed to only 2 in the preceding 91) argues for a return of manuscript authority. F therefore regains its status as control-text, though (as elsewhere) some of the variants it retrieved from the manuscript were themselves errors.
3.3.97/1880   giuers] Q; giuer F

3.3.100-1/1883-4   To ... behold it selfe] Q; *not in* F. Eyeskip.
3.3.105/1888   mirrord] HUDSON (F2 *manuscript correction*); married QF
3.3.107/1890   at] Q; it at F
3.3.110/1893   man] Q; may F
3.3.111/1894   be] Q; is F. F's commoner syntax could easily result from scribal or compositorial contamination from 'is' in 3.3.110/1893.
3.3.115/1898   th'are] Q; they are F
3.3.120-2/1903-5   The vnknowne ... are] F's *lineation*; is there| not what| there are| Q. F's relineation hardly seems worth the trouble; perhaps 'heauens what a man is there?' was intended for cancellation, as an unnecessary and hypermetrical anticipation of 'Nature what things there are' and 'O heauens what some men do' (3.3.127/1910). 'A very horse' would follow naturally in apposition to 'Ajax'; it seems rather odd in answer to 'what a man is there?'
3.3.132/1915   fasting] Q; feaſting F
1918   one] Q; on F. F is the mere normalization of a Shakespearian spelling.
3.3.142/1925   ingratitudes] QF; ingratitude HANMER
1932   on] Q; one F. F merely normalizes an unusual Shakespearian spelling.
3.3.156/1939   abiect, reere] HANMER; abiect, neere F
3.3.162/1945   welcome] POPE; the welcome QF
3.3.163/1946   farewell] Q; farewels F
3.3.172/1955   giue] THEOBALD (Thirlby); goe QF
3.3.177/1960   sooner] Q; begin to F. F has been contaminated by 3.3.176/1959.
3.3.178/1961   not stirs] F; ſtirs not Q. F's, the rarer order, is also more metrical.
3.3.178/1961   once] Q; out F. F could easily result from misreading.
3.3.184   drove] QF (draue)
3.3.192/1975   ought] This edition; thought QF. In QF this phrase and the next simply duplicate one another, by means of a pointless repetition of 'thought(s)'. The proposed error could be due to anticipation and/or dittography ('with ⟨th⟩ought').
3.3.193/1976   infant] This edition (*conj*. Malone); *not in* QF. Malone's addition clarifies the image and rectifies the metre; the repeated and unconvincing attempts to emend 'cradles' instead only testify to the editorial preference for palaeographical reconstruction. Compare 'beget | A generation of still-breeding thoughts' (*Richard II* 5.5.8/2537), 'Fancie dies | In the cradle where it lies' (*Merchant* 3.2.68-9/1348-9), 'My thoughts were like vnbridled children grone' (*Troilus* 3.2.119/1694) and 'infants empty of all thought' (*Troilus* 4.2.6/2172).
3.3.203/1986   his Iland] ROWE 3; her Iland F; our Ilands Q. F's *her* could be dismissed as an anticipation if it were not related to the singular/plural variant; F's singular could be dismissed if it were not related to the pronoun; but it is hard to believe that the two 'errors' were independently made. Rowe's emendation makes good sense of F, while presuming an easy his/hir misreading.
3.3.218/2001   ayre] Q; ayrie ayre F. F's reading probably results from simple dittography (ayre/ayre) subsequently sophisticated into sense.
3.3.237/2020   as] This edition; *not in* QF. Why should Ajax actually go up and down asking either for himself or for a privy? Thersites later claims that Ajax is raving, but what is surely needed is an action arrogant but comprehensible, which Thersites makes sound ridiculous. The emendation, presuming eyeskip or haplography (as asking), explains what Ajax is actually doing (stalking up and down), while applying to it an absurd metaphor (like a man asking for someone), made more absurd by the supposed object of his search (himself — or a privy). It also explains how Ajax can rave 'in saying nothing' (3.3.242/2025): according to QF he *is* saying something for he is *asking for himselfe*; the emendation restores him to mute pomposity.
3.3.244/2027   a] Q; he F
3.3.248/2031   this] Q; his F
3.3.261/2045   his presence] Q; hit preſence F (*turned* 't')
3.3.262/2046   make] Q; make his F

3.3.267/2051 magnanimous] Q; magnanimious F. *OED* records *magnanimious* as a mere spelling variant: it is used by Shakespeare only here and at *All's Well* 3.6.67/1662 (both prose), while characters like Falstaff, Fluellen, and Armado used *magnanimous*; so no especially pompous form seems intended.

3.3.289/2072 yee] Q; you F

3.3.293/2076 am ferd] This edition; am ſure QF; fear DANIEL (*conj.*). 'I am sure' is nonsense immediately after 'I know not'; Shakespeare uses *I am afeard* several times elsewhere, and *feard* (in various spellings) could take the same sense as *afeard* (*OED feared, ppl. a.* 2, 3). The relatively unusual form *feard* for *afeard* would make the misreading easier.

4.1.0.3/2085.3-4 with torches] QF; *and others, with torches* CAPELL (*subs.*). QF *torches* can here mean 'torchbearers'. *OED* does not list this sense, but compare Folio *Othello* 1.2.28/214 (*Enter Cassio, with Torches*), and *Macbeth* 2.1.0.1-2/478.1 (*Enter Banquo, and Fleance, with a Torch before him*).

4.1.9/2094 speech: wherein,] Q; ~, within; F

4.1.10/2095 in] F; *not in* Q. Most editors prefer Q, presumably as the 'stronger' phrase; but F makes sense, produces a common hexameter where Q has a most unusual caesura (unless *Diomed* is elided), and is relatively unlikely as an interpolation prompted by 'within' in the preceding line. As for Q's aesthetic merits, F is even stronger if *in* is interpreted *e'en*, as elsewhere.

4.1.10 e'en] F (in). See above.

*4.1.17/2102 But] F; Lul'd Q. Q's nonsense is unlikely as a misreading of *But*, but could easily result from *Loke* (as at Q 5.9.5/3284, and *LLL* Q 5.2.251/2001), with *look when* taking the common sense 'whenever'. F thus presumably represents an authorial revision (though possibly a compositorial sophistication).

4.1.17/2102 meete] Q; meetes F

4.1.21/2106 back-ward:] THEOBALD; ~, QF

4.1.21/2106 gentlenesse,] THEOBALD; ~ : QF

4.1.33/2118 despightfull'ſt] F (deſpightfull'ſt); deſpightfull Q. Though editors prefer Q, F's double superlative is well paralleled elsewhere (Abbott, 11).

4.1.37/2122 twas] Q; it was F

4.1.45/2130 whereofore] Q; whereof F; thereof CAPELL (*conj.*)

4.1.67/2152 nor leſſe] Q; no leſſe F

4.1.68/2153 as he] QF; as thee PALMER. Though 'thee' is attractive and palaeographically straightforward, Diomed addresses Paris as *you*, not *thee*.

4.1.80/2165 but] WHITE (Jackson); not QF. Despite elaborate defences of the QF reading, as Paris does *not* praise Helen, unemended the line appears to say that he means to sell her. Paris like Diomed will 'hold this vertue well' by, like a tradesman, not engaging in praise or blame unless prompted by economic motives; so, as he doesn't intend to sell Helen, he won't bother to praise her. Palmer's alternative double emendation—of 'what wee' to 'that not'—less plausibly produces the same sense.

4.2.4/2170 lull] HUDSON 1881 (Lettsom); kill QF; still JACKSON (*conj.*). It is hard to believe that *kill* is 'a pretty daintiness for "subdue", "overpower"' (Deighton). 'Lull' anticipates the following imagery and could easily be misread 'kill'. Jackson's conjecture, presuming case-error, would equally well account for Q's reading but makes the Folio annotator's failure to spot it less plausible.

4.2.6/2172 As to] This edition (*conj.* Keightley); As QF. Keightley's obvious addition seems required by the sense; the QF reading has presumably been preferred for metrical reasons. But the emendation is metrically acceptable, presuming a line-divided foot, like those which occur at least four times elsewhere in this text (3.3.142, 4.1.36, 4.2.29, 5.3.13/1924, 2120, 2194, 3036). The apparent errors at 4.1.80/2165 and 4.2.4/2170 do not inspire much confidence in the Folio annotator's attentiveness hereabouts.

4.2.12/2178 ioyes] Q; eyes F

4.2.20.1/2186.1 *She veils her selfe*] This edition; *not in* QF. There must be some reason that Pandarus pretends not to recognize her later (4.2.26-7/2192-3). She presumably veils herself out of embarrassment, in anticipation of his mockery. Pandarus thus pretends not to know her not only because she is veiled, but because the veiling implies maidenly modesty—something no longer appropriate for his cousin Cressid.

4.2.26/2192 heere] Q; Heare F

4.2.34 Ah] QF (a)

4.2.34 capocchia] QF (*chipochia*)

4.2.44.1/2210.1 *Exeunt Troylus and Cressida*] CAPELL; *Exeunt* QF. As F must be presumed to have overlooked a necessary entrance below (4.2.46.1/2212.1, *Enter Aeneas*) and in fact shows no signs of manuscript copy between 4.2.22/2188 and 4.2.60.1/2226.1, it is equally possible that Pandarus should leave when Cressida first tells him to (4.2.38/2204), then re-enter just after she and Troilus exit here; in which case QF's scene-clearing *Exeunt* would be correct, and a new scene should be marked here.

4.2.54/2220 its] Q; tis F. Q's is decidedly the rarer reading, and F shows little sign of manuscript influence on its dialogue hereabouts.

4.2.57 Whoa] QF's 'Who' is a recognized variant spelling (*OED*).

4.2.58/2224 you are] Q; y'are F. Few have been tempted by F's jingling *ere y'are ware*, which could easily be a compositorial or scribal error.

4.2.60/2226 *Exit Pandarus*] This edition; *not in* QF. Pandarus' exit is necessary to explain F's explicit instruction for his entry at 4.3.0.1/2242.1; it is also the natural interpretation of the action.

4.2.68/2234 Diomedes] Q; Diomeds F

4.2.69/2235 so concluded] Q; concluded ſo F

4.2.75/2241 secrecies] SINGER 2 (Steevens); ſecrets QF. Though *secrets* has been defended as trisyllabic, there are no Shakespearian parallels. *Secrecies* could mean 'secrets' (*OED*, 3, citing 1598 'nature it selfe with all her secrecies'), the word is used elsewhere in this sense by Shakespeare, and the proposed misreading (*secrettes* for *secrecies*) would be relatively easy for both the Q compositor and the F annotator (or prompt-book scribe). Both *secrecy* and *nature*, moreover, could mean 'pudend': see *OED secrecy*, 3b, and *nature, sb.* 8. For the former the first quotation is *c.*1675; but compare 'secret things', 'secret parts', 'secrets', and 'secretly open' elsewhere in Shakespeare.

4.3/Sc. 12] This edition. F's stage directions require a scene-break; see Introduction and next note.

4.3.0.1/2243.1 *Enter Pandarus and Cressida*] F; *not in* Q (which has 'Enter Creſſ⟨ida⟩' at 4.3.4/2246). The minor Folio variant on the exact position of Cressida's entry is indifferent; but F's addition of an entrance for Pandarus seems impossible to explain as an error and makes sense both of the preceding action and of the QF *Exeunt* at 4.2.76/2242. Q's omission of the entrance is of little significance, since it omits many necessary entrances.

4.3.5/2247 ah] Q; ha F

4.3.11/2253 Pray thee] Q; Pry thee F. The variant is not substantive.

4.3.27/2269 force] Q; orce F

4.3.28/2270 extreamitie] F (extremitie); extreames Q. Editors prefer Q, presumably on metrical grounds; but hexameters are common enough, and *extremity* is equally if not more appropriate: it can mean 'the utmost penalty' (*OED*, 3b), as well as the range of senses in common with *extreme*.

4.3.31/2273 Ile] Q; I will F

4.4.3/2280 vs] POPE; *not in* QF. There is only one parallel defective caesura in this play (1.3.314/749), and there are no parallels for 'comes upon' without an object.

4.4.9/2286 owne] Q; *not in* F

4.5.4/2293 violenteth] Q; no leſſe F

4.5.9/2298 droſſe] Q; croſſe F

4.5.10.1/2299.1 *Enter Troylus*] Q; *after* 4.5.9/2298 F. F's variant seems due to spacing considerations.

4.5.11 Ah] QF (a)

4.5.11/2300 ducks] Q; ducke F

4.5.14/2303 you] This edition; *not in* QF. Neither Shakespeare in his many other uses of the verb *embrace* nor *OED* gives any parallels for the QF reading: all other absolute uses of *embrace* are reflexive. Pandarus elsewhere addresses both Troilus and Cressida as 'you' (rather than 'thee'). *You* is omitted at least four times elsewhere: *Errors* 4.3.60/1154, *LLL* 4.3.178/1420 (QF), *Shrew* 2.1.79/887, and *Richard III* 2.2.3/1186 (F).

4.5.23/2312 strain'd] Q; ſtrange F

4.5.36/2325 embrasures] QF. Walker claims that this 'could only suggest "windows" to an Elizabethan audience', but in fact the *OED*'s first example of that sense in English is from 1702.

4.5.40/2329 breuity] Q, F (breuitie); breuite This edition *conj*. The QF reading is metrically anomalous; the 16th-c. form *breuite* could easily be misread as the more common *brevity*; and *brevite* also profits from the associations of the verb *brevit* ('to ransack, forage').

4.5.40/2329 one,] Q; our, F

4.5.47/2336 Distasted] Q; Diſtaſting F

4.5.47.1/2336.1 *Enter Æneas*] F (*Æneus*); *not in* Q. No more than an appearance in a doorway is required; F's addition can hardly be accidental, whereas its failure to omit Q's following '*within*' (see next note) could well be inadvertent, or indicative of theatrical uncertainty about this species of half-entrance.

4.5.48/2337 ÆNEAS] This edition; *Æneus within* QF. See preceding note.

4.5.53.1/2342.1 *Exit with Æneas*] This edition; *not in* QF; *Exit Pandarus* THEOBALD

4.5.56/2345 When] Q; *Troy⟨lus⟩. When* F

4.5.77/2366 guifts] THEOBALD 2; guift F

4.5.77/2366 nature, flowing,] HANMER; *not in* Q; nature, | Flawing, F1; nature, | Flowing, F2. Staunton, followed by many modern editors, regarded F1's intended 'flowing' as a replacement for Q's 'swelling', which the compositor instead misinterpreted as an addition.

4.5.79/2368 nouelty] Q; nouelties F

4.5.82/2371 a feard] Q; affraid F. F makes the same change at *LLL* 5.2.574/2325, where it is clearly without authority.

4.5.99/2388 at the doore] This edition; *within* QF. That Paris actually appears is suggested not only by the Folio exit at 4.5.101/2390 but also by the way that Troilus addresses him in the following speech. The QF direction could easily be an acceptable theatrical shorthand for this kind of ambivalent 'entrance'.

4.5.100.1/2389.1 *Exit Paris*] This edition; *Exit* F (*after* 4.5.101/2390); *not in* Q. It seems impossible to explain away F's direction as an error, or an exit for Cressida; but it could be a slightly misplaced exit for Paris, presuming that he appears briefly in the doorway. (See note to 4.5.47.1/2336.1.)

4.5.119/2408 vsage] Q; viſage F

4.5.122/2411 zeale] WARBURTON (Theobald); ſeale QF

4.5.122/2411 thee] Q; *not in* F

4.5.123/2412 In] Q; I F

4.5.132/2421 you] Q; my F

4.5.144/2433 DEIPHOBUS] MALONE (Ritson); *Dio*. F

4.5.148/2437 *Exeunt*] ROWE; *after* 4.5.143/2432 QF

4.6.0.1-64/2437.1-2501 *Enter ... game.*] F in this passage shows no sign of manuscript influence, and repeats several suspicious or erroneous Q readings; it is therefore here regarded as a mere reprint.

4.6.0.2/2437.2 *a trumpet*] This edition; *not in* QF

4.6.0.2/2437.2 *&c*] THEOBALD; *Calcas. &c.* QF

4.6.2/2439 time, with starting courage.] THEOBALD; ∼. With starting courage, QF

4.6.14/2451 yond] Q; yong F

4.6.17.1/2453.1 *Enter ... Cressida*] THEOBALD; *not in* QF; *after* 4.6.13/2450 F2

4.6.30/2467 And parted ... argument.] Q; *not in* F

4.6.38/2475 MENELAUS] WHITE (Tyrwhitt); *Patr⟨oclus⟩*. QF. The apparent absence of manuscript authority for F here makes this emendation even more attractive.

4.6.44/2481 not] F; nor Q

4.6.49/2486 too] WALKER (Ritson); then QF; two PALMER (Johnson); then, too KINNEAR (*conj*.)

4.6.54.1/2491.1 *They talke apart*] This edition; *not in* QF. Editors since Rowe have the two go off here, but this leaves the Folio *Exeunt* at 4.6.64.1/2501.1 inexplicable; the arrangement offered here makes equally good dramatic sense.

4.6.56/2493 Ther's] Q; Ther's a F

4.6.60 accosting] QF (a coaſting). As *OED* records 'acoast' and 'accoast' as contemporary variant spellings of *accost*, and as initial *a* was separated off in other compounds, there seems no reason to regard the QF form as erroneous; Theobald's popular conjecture 'accosting' is in fact only a modernization.

2498 vnclapse] Q; vnclaſpe F. Q's variant, treated by editors as a literal error, is recorded by *OED* as a variant spelling (current 15th-17th c.).

4.6.62/2499 ticklish] Q; tickling F

4.6.64.1/2501.1 *Exeunt Diomed and Cressid*] This edition; *Exennt* F; *not in* Q. See note to 4.6.54.1/2491.1. F here regains its access to manuscript authority, and hence its status as control text.

4.6.64.2/2501.2 *Flowrish*] Both Q and F have one flourish at this point, Q at the head of its entrance direction, F at the end of its; most editors since Theobald substitute two flourishes, one here and one at the head of the editorial entrance direction (transposed one or two lines below).

4.6.67/2504 *comming forward*] CAPELL (*Aeneas preceding*); *not in* QF. The staging envisioned seems to be like that in *2 Henry IV* 4.1/Sc. 10, with the two armies on opposite sides of the stage, and Aeneas going between them.

4.6.71/2508 they] Q; *not in* F

4.6.75/2512 ACHILLES] POPE (*after* Dryden); *Aga⟨memnon⟩*. QF. Walker and some recent editors retain the first four words for Agamemnon, but it seems less likely that both Q and F would overlook (instead of misread) a speech-prefix, and the reason offered ('the generosity of the first half line seems more appropriate to Agamemnon') based upon a dubious interpretation.

4.6.94/2531 breath] Q; breach F

4.6.94/2531 *Exeunt Aiax, Diomed, Hector, and Æneas*] This edition; *not in* QF; *Ajax and* Hector *enter the Lists, Æneas and* Diomed *marshalling*: Greeks *range themselves on one Side, and* Trojans *upon the other, without*. CAPELL (*after* 4.6.95/2532). Capell's arrangement, followed by all editors (usually reduced to 'Ajax and Hector enter the lists'), puts the lists on stage; the remainder of the scene (see following notes) clearly suggests they are off stage, as in *Richard II* (1.3/Sc. 3). It also seems preferable to mark the direction here, with the remaining line and a half addressed to Ulysses: this allows an interval which makes 'They are oppos'd already' more credible.

4.6.99/2536 They call him *Troylus*;] F; *not in* Q. Though editors reject this part-line (repeated below at 4.6.111/2548), it is hard to explain as an error, and probably represents a deliberate addition, intended to identify which of the Trojans Ulysses is talking about. It is possible that F should have omitted 4.6.111-12/2548-49 when it added this.

4.6.119/2556 *Exeunt*] This edition; *not in* QF. The Folio entrance below for '*Agamemnon and the rest*' (see note to 4.7.42.1/2598.1) requires them to exit at some point after this line, and the following dialogue seems to presume their absence. (Both Q and F frequently omit exit directions.) The only motive for an exit is an excited move closer to the lists, which must therefore be presumed to be off stage (see note to 4.6.94.1/2531.1). The exeunt could be naturally managed in stages, a few characters at a time crowding forward and off during lines 4.6.117-19/2554-6.

4.7/Sc. 16] The exeunt and entrance apparently required at this point result in a clearing of the stage and a change of location (though little or no time has elapsed) and so represent a proper scene-break. See Introduction.

4.7.0.1-2/2556.1-2 *Enter ... interposing*] This edition; *not in* QF. Hector and Ajax must enter fighting, in order to explain their movement from off to on stage (within imaginary lists).

4.7.0.2/2556.2 *trumpets cease*] This edition. Both Q and F place *trumpets | cease* in the right-hand margin, *trumpets* to the right of 4.6.119/2556, *cease* to the right of Diomedes' speech. CAPELL placed *interposing* to the right of Diomedes' speech and *Trumpets cease* to the right of Aeneas'; modern editors generally place *Trumpets cease* immediately after 4.6.119/2556. It seems likeliest that the ambiguous QF marginal position indicates that the trumpets cease between Agamemnon's speech and Diomedes'; but it would be most natural for the trumpets to bridge the proposed scene-break, stopping only when Diomedes and Aeneas signal or move to stop the fighting.

4.7.12/2568 on] QF; in This edition *conj.* Compare *Cymbeline* 3.3.93/1448, 'The Princely blood flowes in his Cheeke'.

4.7.28/2584 could] Q; could'ſt F

4.7.41/2597 *Exit Æneas*] This edition; *not in* QF. Aeneas is sent to fetch the others who (according to our proposed reconstruction, and as the instruction itself implies) are off stage.

4.7.42.1/2598.1 *Enter Agamemnon and the rest*] F; *not in* Q. Though editors commonly ignore it, or interpret *Enter* as 'come forward', this entrance direction is very difficult to explain away. The editorial unwillingness to accept it derives from the 18th-c. assumption that the lists are on stage throughout. See preceding notes.

4.7.59.1/2615.1 *and Troylus*] This edition; *not in* QF. Editors do not specify that the Greek generals each embrace Hector, as implied by the text; but here 'brace of brothers' indicates that Menelaus embraces Hector and either Paris or Troilus. As Paris seems an unlikely candidate (as well as a minor character), Troilus was probably intended.

4.7.72/2628 th'] Q; thy F. Q is 'probably intended to represent an elided form of *thy*' (Riverside; see also Cercignani, p. 290), and if so the difference between Q and F is not substantive but accidental, with Q likelier to preserve Shakespeare's form of the word.

4.7.77/2633 hem'd] F; ſhrupd Q; shrapd SISSON. Sisson's emendation, based on the dialect word *shrape* (= 'catch or trap'), makes good sense of Q; but it does not follow that F is 'patently editorial'—it could easily, like many other variants, represent authorial revision.

4.7.119/2675 pray thee] Q; prythee F. See 5.2.41/2867.

4.7.147/2703 haue] Q; *not in* F

4.7.168/2724 you] Q; thee F

5.1.5/2738 botch] THEOBALD; batch QF

5.1.12 these] Q (this), F (theſe). See note to 1569.

5.1.26/2758 cur, no] Q; Curre F

2760 sacenet] Q; Sarcenet F. As *OED* records another 16th-c. spelling without the r (sesynet), Q's spelling seems acceptable, and F's variant therefore non-substantive.

5.1.57 mule] F; Q (Moyle)

5.1.57 fitchew] F; Q (Fichooke)

5.1.59/2792 *Menelaus! I*] This edition; ~ₐ ~ Q; ~, ~ F

5.1.62/2795 sprites] Q; ſpirits F

5.1.65/2797 light] F; lights Q. F's singular may here reflect stage practice.

2802 God night] Q; goodnight F. F is merely a normalization.

5.1.71/2803 Lord *Menelaus*] QF; *Menelaus* CAPELL. The metre of the QF line is uniquely anomalous in this play, and 'Lord' could represent contamination from the preceding line or an abandoned first thought.

5.1.73 sewer] QF (ſure)

5.1.89/2821 it, that] This edition; it, that it F; it, it Q. F makes poor sense (astronomers predict it, and predict that it is prodigious), and only Knight has accepted it; but 'that' could easily have been added when it should instead have been substituted for the second 'it'.

5.2.2, 5/2829, 2831 at the doore] This edition; *not in* QF; *within* HANMER

5.2.3/2830 your] Q; you F

5.2.8.2/2834.2 *Enter Thersites, vnseene*] This edition; *not in* QF; *after* 5.2.5.1/2831.1 ROWE. For Thersites to enter at some point after Troilus and Ulysses seems both more realistic (he left Achilles' tent some time after them) and more dramatic (two distinct surreptitious entrances being better than one, and easier to manage theatrically). The pause provided by Cressida's whispering provides just the sort of dramatic interval earlier provided by Diomedes' waiting for her entrance.

5.2.11/2837 sing] Q; finde F. For the obscene pun on 'sing' (= masturbate), compare Fletcher's *Valentinian* 4.3.34, 'singing whores'; Middleton's *Your Five Gallants*, 'They're natural at prick-song' (2.1.45), etc.

5.2.12/2838 Cliff] Q; life F. For the obscene pun on 'cliff' (= vulva) compare Dekker's *Noble Spanish Soldier* 4.2.14, *More Dissemblers Besides Women*, 5.1 (F1ᵛ), 'Do you know but one Cliff?', etc.

5.2.14/2840 CRESSIDA] F2; Cal⟨chas⟩. QF

5.2.23/2849 forsworne.] Q; a forſworne.—F

5.2.28/2854 do] Q; doe not F

5.2.41/2867 prethee] Q; pray thee F

5.2.42/2868 all hells] Q; hell F

5.2.59/2885 la] THEOBALD; lo QF

5.2.74/2900 ha't] Q; haue't F

5.2.85–6/2911–12 DIOMED As . . . CRESSID Nay . . .ₐ He] This edition (*conj.* Theobald); ₐ As . . . Dio⟨medes⟩: Nay . . . Creſ⟨sida⟩: He QF. In his edition Theobald, followed by all editors, adopted Thirlby's alternative conjecture and simply omitted both prefixes. But Q is most unlikely to have interpolated two prefixes out of the blue, and F unlikely to have overlooked such a double error. On the other hand the F annotator could have overlooked a compositor's misplacement of the prefixes by one line, a much more plausible double error in Q.

5.2.86/2912 doth take] Q; rakes F

5.2.92/2918 on's] Q; one F

5.2.105/2931 TROYLUS] HANMER; Ther⟨sites⟩: QF

5.2.105/2931 you] Q; me F

5.2.116/2942 said] Q; ſay F. F could easily arise from the misreading 'saie'.

5.2.124/2950 th'attest] Q (*upside-down apostrophe*); that teſt F

5.2.138/2964 a] Q; he F

5.2.142/2968 be sanctimonies] Q; are ſanctimonie F

5.2.147/2973 By-fould] Q; By foule F

5.2.164/2990 in be] This edition; be QF; be but DYCE 2 (W. S. Walker). QF is clearly anomalous metrically, but Walker's conjecture strongly suggests the common sense 'only', instead of the required 'even' (*OED, conj.* 6b, but never in Shakespeare outside its dubious use in 'but now'). By contrast *e'en* is appropriately ambiguous, meaning either 'worthy Troilus himself' or 'be even half attached'. If spelled 'in', the word might have been deliberately omitted by the Q compositor, as apparent nonsense.

5.2.170/2996 as I] F2; I Q, F1

5.2.170/2996 Cressid] Q; Creſſida F

5.2.176/3002 sunne] Q; Fenne F

5.3.4/3028 in] Q; gone F

5.3.5/3039 all] Q; *not in* F

5.3.20/3044 lawfull,] MALONE (Tyrwhitt); ~ : F

5.3.21/3045 giue much, to vse] MALONE (Tyrwhitt); count giue much to as F. Tyrwhitt's emendation presumes that 'count' is an inadequately deleted first thought, or an interpolation picked up from two lines above. None of the scores of other conjectures carries any conviction.

5.3.30/3054 aside] This edition; *not in* QF. Hector would almost certainly have prevented this, if he had heard it.

5.3.47/3071 Mother] Q; Mothers F

5.3.75 sire] QF (ſir). The stronger senses of 'royal person' and 'father' seem uppermost here. For the interchangeability of the two forms in early usage see *OED*.

5.3.85/3109 do] Q; doth F

5.3.87/3111 shrils] Q; shrileth This edition *conj.* QF is metrically anomalous; hexameters, by contrast, are plentiful. The clearly erroneous Folio 'doth' (for 'do') two lines above might be a correction gone astray.

5.3.87/3111 dolours] Q; dolour F

5.3.92/3116 yet] Q; yes F

5.3.94/3118 exclaime] QF; exclaims WALKER (Tannenbaum)

5.3.104 phthisic] QF (tiſick). Though editors retain 'tisick' as a 'dialectal' form, it was not dialectal but commonplace in Shakespeare's time, and is still pronounced as QF spelt it.

5.3.107/3131 athis] ROWE (o' these); ath's Q; o'th' F1; o'th' F3. Dyce and some others retain QF, presumably as an unrecorded colloquial form, glossing 'of these'; but *oth's dayes* is surely unpronounceable as well as unexampled. For the conjectured spelling 'this', see 3.1.148/1569.

5.3.107/3131 o' these] See preceding note.

5.3.116–18/3140–2 PANDARUS ... name.] F; *not in* Q. Both Q and F have these lines at Add. Pass. B.1–3 (with verbal variants in Pandarus' speech); but this position seems to represent Shakespeare's final intention. See Introduction.

5.3.117/3141 broker,] QF (*at* Add. Pass. B.1–3); brother͜, F1 (*here*); brother, F2 (*at* Add. Pass. B.2); brothel͜, F3 (*at* Add. Pass. B.2)

5.4.9/3152 stale] Q; ſtole F

5.4.11/3153 proou'd not] WALKER; not proou'd QF

5.4.15/3158 began] QF; begin ROWE

5.4.23.1/3166.1 *Exit Diomed* ⌈*driuing in*⌉ *Troylus*] This edition; *not in* QF. Both Thersites' 'now the sleeue, now the sleeue' and the following scene suggest that Diomedes should have the advantage here. Fighting exits, in theatres which use doors rather than open 'wings', are difficult to manage unless one combatant is clearly driving the other off.

5.4.23.2/3166.2 *behind*] This edition; *not in* QF. Thersites clearly does not see Hector arrive; just as clearly Hector, with his 'vice of mercy', does not take advantage of Thersites' vulnerability.

5.4.29.1/3172.1 *Exit Hector*] This edition; *not in* QF; *after* 5.4.28/3171 ROWE

5.5.0.1/3176.2 *Seruants*] F; *Seruant* Q. Though editors adopt Q, F's extra servant(s) may remain on stage, to be sent off at 5.5.17–18/3193–4 ('Go beare ... And bid'). Walker instead brings on extra Greeks with Nestor. (See 5.5.16.1/3192.1.)

5.5.6/3182 Polidamas] Q; *Polidamus* F

5.5.7/3183 Margareton] This edition; *Margarelon* QF. So the name is spelled in all the known sources: Q's 'l' would be an easy misreading in an unfamiliar name, which the F collator would be correspondingly most likely to miss.

3187 *Epistropus*] QF; *Epistrophus* STEEVENS. Although editors follow Steevens's return to the spelling of the sources, an *h* is relatively unlikely to be overlooked or misread by both the Q compositor and the F annotator, and the p/ph spelling variant (common enough in other words) could well be Shakespeare's; *Cedius*, *Margareton*, and *Thoas* (see preceding and following notes) are, by contrast, very easy misreadings.

5.5.11/3187 *Cedius*] CAPELL; *Cedus* QF

5.5.12/3188 *Thoas*] POPE; *Thous* QF

5.5.17/3193 Go] Q; Coe F

5.5.18.1/3194.1 *with the body*] This edition; *not in* QF. Nestor's first words most naturally imply that the body has been brought on stage; unless he enters with others he must therefore carry or drag it on himself. As someone must then carry it off again, Walker (who has Agamemnon exit after his speech) brings on 'other Greeks' here. But Agamemnon, according to both texts, is still on stage, his exit having been interrupted by Nestor's dramatic entry; and Diomedes' *Servants* are still present to carry off the body (see note to 5.5.0.1/3176.2).

5.5.22 schools] QF (ſculls)

5.5.24/3200 strawy] Q; ſtraying F

5.5.47/3223 braue] This edition; *not in* QF. This addition restores the metre of a clearly anomalous line, and also—unlike other proposed emendations ('shew me', 'now shew', 'and shew')—permits the normal accentuation of *queller*. *Braue* provides a suitably angry and sarcastic word, which could have been omitted by eyeskip.

5.6.7/3232 the] CAPELL; thy QF

5.6.11.1/3236.1 *Fight*] This edition; *not in* QF. See next note.

5.6.12.1/3237.1 *Exit Troylus* ⌈*driuing Diomed and Aiax in*⌉] This edition; *Exit Troylus* F (*after* 5.6.11/3236); *not in* Q; *Exeunt fighting* ROWE (*after* 5.6.11/3236). See note to 5.4.23.1/3166.1 Hector's comment, and the fact that he does not go to his brother's aid, indicate that Troilus is winning. The form of the F direction is also suggestive. Hector clearly enters before the others are off stage.

5.6.12.2/3237.2 *behind*] This edition; *not in* QF. Achilles could not easily enter from the same door through which Troilus and the others exeunt fighting, and so presumably enters from a direction Hector is not facing. Whether Achilles takes advantage of his position is ambiguous, but 'ha' might represent an attempt at a surprise stroke from behind.

5.6.13/3238 ha] Q; *not in* F

5.6.13.1/3238.1 *Achilles is bested*] This edition; *not in* QF. In Caxton he is wounded; *dropping his sword* was Capell's suggestion; Walker suggests 'he may be merely out of breath'. Nothing in the dialogue supports or precludes any of these alternatives; which one an editor adopts crucially affects the interpretation of Achilles, of Hector, of the subsequent murder of Hector, and of the tone of this little sequence (and thus the ending of the play) as a whole.

5.7.6/3262 armes] Q; arme F

5.8/Sc. 24] CAPELL; *not in* QF. Dyce was the first editor to mark no scene-break here, and has been followed on the authority of the Cambridge edition; but the stage is cleared, and there is no evident continuity between Achilles' last and Thersites' first line.

5.8.0.1/3265.1 *then*] CAPELL (*subs.*); *not in* QF (*Enter Therſi:Mene: Paris*). Whether we see them fighting before Thersites intervenes to 'interpret' them for us makes some difference to the tone of the scene.

5.8.3/3267 horn'd] ALEXANDER (Kellner); hen'd QF

5.8.3/3267 spartan] Q; ſparrow F

5.8.4.1/3268 *Exit Menelaus* ⌈*driuing in*⌉ *Paris*] This edition; *Exit Paris and Menelus* QF. See notes to 5.4.23.1/3166.1 and 5.6.12.1/3237.1. Thersites' comment ('the bull has the game, ware hornes') makes it clear Menelaus has the upper hand.

5.8.4.2/3268.1 *behind*] This edition; *not in* QF

5.8.8–9/3272 am bastard] Q; am a Baſtard F

5.8.14/3278 *Exit*] CAPELL; *not in* QF

5.8.15/3279 *Exit*] Q; *Exeunt* F

5.9.0.1–2/3279.1–2 ⌈*dragging*⌉ *the one in sumptuous armour*] This edition; *not in* QF. He clearly enters with the body; it would be most convenient (and ironic) if he dragged it.

5.9.1.1/3280 *taking off the helmet*] This edition; *not in* QF. Hector's first line—'Most putrified core so faire without'—suggests that his victim is discovered to be diseased (perhaps disfigured by syphilis?). The body could hardly have 'putrified' within minutes of being killed, and the within/without antithesis has an obvious thematic pertinence.

5.9.7/3286 darkning] Q; darking F

5.9.10.1/3289.1 ⌈*The Myrmidons*⌉ *kill Hector*] This edition; *not in* QF. The usual editorial directions—'Hector falls', 'They fall upon Hector and kill him'—leave it silently ambiguous whether Achilles participates; this locution draws attention to the theatrical option.

5.9.13/3292 and] Q; *not in* F

5.9.15/3294 retire] Q; retreat F

5.9.15.1/3294.1 *Another Retreat*] This edition; *not in* QF. The dialogue clearly requires two distinguishable signals. F's substitution of 'retreat' for Q 'retire' in the dialogue here (and 'sounds' for 'sound'?) might have resulted from a misunderstood annotation, intended to supply a second direction.

5.9.16/3295 sound] Q; ſounds F

5.9.20/3299 baite] Q; bed F

5.10.1/3302 *within*] Q; *not in* F

5.10.2/3303 slaine,] F; ~͜ Q

5.10.8/3309 his] QF; this LETTSOM (*conj.*)

5.11.2.1/3312.1 *Enter Troylus*] F; *after preceding line* Q. See next note.

5.11.3/3313 TROYLUS] F; *before preceding line* Q. F's movement of the speech-prefix one line down (and related movement of the entrance direction) seems to be a deliberate alteration of the original intent, in Q, to give 5.11.2/3312 to Troilus. The difference is one of dramatic import and characterization: F's simpler statement makes the announcement less rhetorical and more devastated.

5.11.7/3317 smite] HANMER; ſmile QF

5.11.12/3322 feare͜] Q; ~, F

5.11.17/3327 their] Q; there F

5.11.20/3330 Coold] POPE; Could Q; Coole F

437

5.11.21-2/3331-2 But march away, | *Hector* is dead:] F; *not in* Q. Nosworthy conjectures that the words not in Q were a later addition, designed to create a closing couplet, and that the remainder of the scene was omitted in the Folio version. See Introduction.

3334 pitch] Q. F's 'pight' is a mere spelling variant, and Q is likelier to reflect Shakespeare's own form.

5.11.31.1/3341.1 *Exeunt, marching*] This edition; *not in* QF. For the QF ending, see Additional Passages. That ending cannot have coexisted with the three lines from it which F adds at the end of 5.3/Sc. 19; therefore the Q ending, with Pandarus' epilogue, must presumably have been marked for omission in the promptbook, with the Folio collator (or compositor) overlooking or ignoring the signal to delete.

Additional Passages

B.2 *Strikes him*] ROWE; *not in* QF. This blow is presumably the 'goodly medicine for my aking bones' Pandarus refers to (B.4). See 5.3.108/3132.

B.2 ignomy, and] F; ignomyny, Q

B.3.1 *Exeunt all but Pandarus*] Q; *Exeunt* F

B.21 Some two monthes hence] QF. The hypothesis that *Troilus* was written for, or performed at, the Inns of Court is heavily dependent upon this line—the natural 'here' where someone might make a will, it is alleged. But of course not every dying man was expected to drag himself to the Inns of Court in order to make a will. The more natural interpretation of 'here' is 'the stage': why should Pandarus make his will on stage 'some two monthes hence'? Because he expects to die, on stage, some two months later. In other words, rather than alluding to an extra-theatrical visit to the Inns of Court by the actor/character, the epilogue—more normally—may be promising the reappearance of the character in a sequel. Nosworthy proposed that Shakespeare changed his mind, during the course of composition, about the scope and nature of the play (as he allegedly did in *1 Henry IV*); Honigmann (1985) has supported this conjecture, urging that Shakespeare was tentatively planning, or had already begun, a sequel. Pandarus' intrusion at the end of the play therefore need not be explained as an anomalous extra-theatrical address to a specific audience for a single performance, but as a more normal epilogue: alluding to the (notorious) presence of bawds and whores in public playhouses on the South Bank (hence 'Winchester'), and promising a sequel. 'Some two monthes hence' is, on the evidence of Henslowe's records, not at all unreasonable as an interval between the première of a play and the première of its sequel. In this case (as in many others) the hoped-for sequel apparently never materialized.

There has always been something unsatisfactory about the hypothesis that *Troilus* was written specifically for an Inns of Court audience: the only Shakespeare plays known to have been performed at such a venue (*Errors, Twelfth Night*) show no signs of being tailored for such an audience; entertainments at the Inns of Court generally reveal no predilection for arcane learning or exotic subject matter; the Troy story had recently been dramatized at a rival public playhouse. If we abandon the Inns of Court conjecture, then Palmer's dating of the play on the basis of the 'two monthes' allusion also collapses. The Epilogue remains unique, and in character, but its uniqueness results from the modification of a recognizable convention.

B.25 *Exit*] ROWE 3; *Exeunt* F; *not in* Q

REJECTED QUARTO VARIANTS

Pro.1-31/1-31] *not in* Q
1.2.232/376 ne're] neuer
1.2.239/383 i'th'] in the
1.2.243/387 among] amongſt
1.2.250-1/394-5 so forth] ſuch like
1.2.254/398 another] a
1.2.254/398 one] a man
1.2.263/407 too] two
1.2.270/414 house.] houſe there he vnarmes him:
1.2.274/418 Ile be] I wilbe
1.2.290/434 contents] (Contents); content
1.3.1/436 the] theſe
1.3.1/436 on] ore
1.3.12/447 euery] euer
1.3.18/453 thinke] call
1.3.26/461 lowd] broad
1.3.30/465 thy] the
1.3.30/465 godly] god like
1.3.35/470 pacient] (patient); ancient
1.3.54/489 nerue] (Nerue); nerues
1.3.55/490 spirit] ſpright
1.3.60/495 thy] the
1.3.66/501 the heauens ride) knit all Greekes] F (Heauens); heauen rides) knit all the Greekiſh
1.3.69-74/504-9 AGAMEMNON Speak ... VLYSSES] *not in* Q
1.3.74/509 basis] baſes
1.3.92/527 ill Aspects] influence
1.3.92/527 Planets euill] euill Planets
1.3.102/537 to] of
1.3.110/545 meets] melts
1.3.119/554 includes] include
1.3.128/563 in] with
1.3.137/572 liues] ſtands
1.3.149/584 aukward] ſillie
1.3.159/594 vnsquard] ('d); vnſquare
1.3.164/599 iust] right

1.3.190/625 and] *not in* Q
1.3.195/630 and discredit͵] our ~͵
1.3.218/653 eares] eyes
1.3.226/661 on] bid
1.3.244/679 affaire] (affayre); affaires
1.3.247/682 whisper] whiſper with
1.3.249/684 sence] ſeat
1.3.249/684 the] that
1.3.253/688 lowd] (loud); alowd
1.3.259/694 this] his
1.3.264/699 That seeks] (ſeekes); And feeds
1.3.273/708 compasse] couple
1.3.286/721 or meanes] a meanes
1.3.287/722 Ile be] I am
1.3.290/725 mould] hoſte
1.3.291/726 One] A
1.3.291/726 on] (one); no
1.3.294/729 this] my
1.3.294/729 braune] (brawne); braunes
1.3.295/730 wil] *not in* Q
1.3.299/734 forbid] for-fend
1.3.299/734 youth] men
1.3.300-1/735-6 Amen. | AGAMEMNON Faire] (*Aga.*); Amen: faire
1.3.302/737 first] ſir
1.3.309/744 This 'tis:] *not in* Q
1.3.318/753 The] True the
1.3.318/753 euen] *not in* Q
1.3.327/762 Yes] Why
1.3.328/763 his honour] (Honor); thoſe honours
1.3.330/765 this] the
1.3.334/769 wilde] vilde
1.3.346/781 from hence receiues] (receyues); receiues from hence
1.3.346/781 the] a
1.3.348-50/783-5 Which ... Limbes.] *not in* Q
1.3.352/787 shew our foulest] F (fowlest); Firſt ſhew foule Q
1.3.354/789 yet to shew] ſhall exceed

TROILUS AND CRESSIDA

1.3.355/790	Shall shew the better] By shewing the worse first
1.3.361/796	weare] share
1.3.363/798	we] it
1.3.366/801	did] do
1.3.370/805	as the worthier] for the better
1.3.381/816	of it] thereof
1.3.384/819	tarre] arre
1.3.384/819	their] a
2.1.8/827	there] *not in* Q
2.1.17/836	oration] (Oration); oration without booke
2.1.18/837	a] *not in* Q
2.1.21/840	Todes stoole] F (Toads); Tode-stoole Q
2.1.26/845	a] *not in* Q
2.1.30/849	Greece] Greece, when thou art forth in the incursions thou strikest as slow as another
2.1.38-9/857-8	AIAX Coblofe. ǀ THERSITES Hee] F (*subs.*); *Aiax Coblofe,* ǀ Hee
2.1.41/860	AIAX] *not in* Q
2.1.42/861	THERSITES] *not in* Q
2.1.46/865	thou] (Thou); you
2.1.64/882	I do so] so I do
2.1.72/890	I] It
2.1.76/894	Ile] I
2.1.89/907	for a] the
2.1.102/920	out] at
2.1.106/924	on their toes] *not in* Q
2.1.108/926	war] F (warre); wars
2.1.123/941	fift] first
2.2.13/963	Surety] Surely
2.2.26/975	father] (Father); fathers
2.2.32/981	at] of
2.2.35/984	tells] (tels); tell
2.2.46/995	Lets] (Let's); Sets
2.2.51/1000	holding] keeping
2.2.57/1006	inclineable,] attributiue;
2.2.63/1012	shores] shore
2.2.66/1015	chose] choose
2.2.69/1018	spoild] (spoyl'd); soild
2.2.73/1022	of] with
2.2.78/1027	stale] pale
2.2.85/1034	he] be
2.2.85/1034	Noble] worthy
2.2.103/1052	old] elders
2.3.19/1180	dependant] depending
2.3.25/1186	wouldst] (would'st); couldst
2.3.30/1192	art] art not
2.3.49/1210	maist] must
2.3.54-9/1215-20	PATROCLUS ... *Patroclus is a foole.*] *not in* Q
2.3.62-3/1223-4	*of Agamemnon*] *not in* Q
2.3.66/1227	to] ()
2.3.66/1227	Creator] Prouer
2.3.68/1229	*Patroclus*] Come *Patroclus*
2.3.73-4/1234-5	Now ... all.] *not in* Q
2.3.79/1240	appertainments] appertainings
2.3.82/1243	so say] say so
2.3.87/1248	the] a
2.3.88/1249	A word my Lord.] *not in* Q
2.3.98/1259	counsell that] composure
2.3.119/1280	and] *not in* Q
2.3.129/1290	pettish] course, and
2.3.129/1290	ebbs, his] (ebs); ~ˬ and
2.3.129/1290	as] and
2.3.130/1291	carriage of this action] streame of his commencement
2.3.140/1301	enter you. ǀ *Exit Ulisses*] entertaine.
2.3.151/1312	it] pride
2.3.152/1313	*Aiax*] *not in* Q
2.3.157/1318	hate the] do ~
2.3.159/1320	Yet] And yet
2.3.174/1335	gainst] downe
2.3.185/1346	do] (doe); doth
2.3.189/1350	Must] Shall
2.3.191/1352	titled] liked
2.3.198/1360	this] his
2.3.200/1362	pash] push
2.3.201/1363	a] he
2.3.209/1370	let] tell
2.3.209/1370	humors] (humours); humorous
2.3.212/1373	a] of
2.3.220/1381	praises] praiers
2.3.220/1381	poure in, his] (in:); poure, his
2.3.224/1385	You] Qb, F; Yon Qa
2.3.230/1391	thus with vs] with vs thus
2.3.238/1399	beyond, beyond all] beyondˬ all thy
2.3.244/1405	boorn,] (bourne); boord:
2.3.245/1406	Thy] This
2.3.252/1413	VLISSES] F (*Vlif.*); *Nest.*
2.3.259/1420	cull] call
3.1.1/1423	not you] you not
3.1.3/1425	SERUANT] F (*throughout scene*); *Man.* Q (*throughout scene*)
3.1.25/1447	meane friend.] meane:
3.1.31/1453	who's] who is
3.1.37/1459	that] *not in* Q
3.1.86/1510	poore] *not in* Q
3.1.94/1515	horrible] horribly
3.1.103/1524	lord] (Lord); lad
3.1.109/1530	loue, loue] Qb, F; loue, lone Qa
3.1.114/1535	shaft confounds] (Shaft); shafts confound
3.1.145/221566	from] from the
3.1.155/1576	thee] her
3.2.3/1579	he] *not in* Q
3.2.8/1584	Like] Like to
3.2.10/1586	those] these
3.2.36/1612	vnawares] Fb; vnwares Q, Fa
3.2.60/1636	*Cressida*] F *Cressed* Q
3.2.77/1654	This is] This
3.2.82/1658	thene] thene ǀ then Qa; then Qb, F
3.2.89/1665	crowne yt no perfection] (it:); louer part no affection
3.2.92/1668	to faire] Qb, F; to to faire Qa
3.2.107/1682	are] bee
3.2.130/1705	soule] very foule
3.2.130/1705	from me] *not in* Q
3.2.146-7/1721-2	Where ... what.] F; I would be gone: ǀ Where is my wit? I know not what I speake, Q
3.2.156/1731	aye] age
3.2.176/1751	Yet] *not in* Q
3.2.181/1756	and] or
3.3.1/1784	you] *not in* Q
3.3.3/1786	your] *not in* Q
3.3.95/1878	shining] ayming
3.3.114/1897	th'applause,] the applause.
3.3.120/1903	The] Th'
3.3.123/1906	abiect] obiect
3.3.136/1919	shrinking] shriking
3.3.152/1935	hedge] turne
3.3.154/1937	hindmost] him, most
3.3.155-7/1938-40	Or ... on:] *not in* Q
3.3.158/1941	paste] (past); passe
3.3.163/1946	O] *not in* Q
3.3.178/1961	Than] (Then); That
3.3.178/1961	not stirs] stirs not
3.3.190/1973	graine of Plutoes gold] thing
3.3.191/1974	th'] the
3.3.191/1974	deepes] depth
3.3.217/2000	a] *not in* Q
3.3.226/2009	we] they
3.3.258/2042	to him] *not in* Q
3.3.265/2049	most] *not in* Q
3.3.269/2053	Grecian] *not in* Q
3.3.269/2053	&c.] *not in* Q
3.3.285/2068	a] of the
3.3.291/2074	he's] *not in* Q
3.3.291/2074	a] of

439

3.3.296/2079   carry] beare
4.1.5/2090   you] your
4.1.10/2095   in] *not in* Q
4.1.17/2102   But] Lul'd
4.1.33/2118   deſpightfull'ſt] (deſpightful'ſt); deſpightfull
4.1.38/2123   *Calcha's*] *Calcho's*
4.1.41/2126   doe thinke] beleeue
4.1.54/2139   in the] in
4.1.55/2140   merits] deſerues
4.1.55/2140   moſt] beſt
4.1.58/2143   ſoylure] ſoyle
4.1.68/2153   which] the
4.1.78/2163   you] they
4.2.15/2181   hidiouſly] tediouſly
4.2.66/2232   vs] him
4.2.66/2232   for him] *not in* Q
4.2.75/2241   nature] neighbor *Pandar*
4.3.14-15/2256-7   knees, I beseech you] knees,
4.3.28/2270   extreamitie] (extremitie); extreames
4.4.2/2279   Of] For
4.5.6/2295   affection] affections
4.5.49-50/2338-9   ſo | Cries, come,ᴧ | Cries,ᴧ ſo
4.5.53/2342   the root] my throate
4.5.57/2346   my] *not in* Q
4.5.63/2352   there's] there is
4.5.77/2366   Their . . . nature] *not in* Q
4.5.79/2368   person] portion
4.5.122/2411   towards] to
4.5.136/2425   Ile] I
4.5.142/2431   in] to
4.5.144-8/2433-7   DEIPHOBUS . . . Chiualrie.] *not in* Q
4.6.44/2481   not] nor
4.6.67/2504   you] the
4.6.75/2513   diſpriſing] miſpriſing
4.6.96/2533   ULISSES] F (*Vlis.*), *indented as a speech-prefix*; *Vlisses*: Q (*not indented*)
4.6.96-7/2533-4   They are oppos'd already | AGAMEMNON] (*Aga.*); *not in* Q
4.6.99/2536   They call him *Troylus*;] *not in* Q
4.6.101/2538   Speaking in] Speaking
4.7.16/2572   Of our ranke feud] *not in* Q
4.7.17/2573   drop] day
4.7.45/2601   mine] my
4.7.47/2603   of] all
4.7.49-54/2605-10   But . . . integritie,] *not in* Q
4.7.62/2618   that I] thy
4.7.62/2618   th'] the
4.7.62/2618   oath] earth
4.7.71/2627   And ſeene thee ſcorning] Deſpiſing many
4.7.74/2630   vnto] to ſome
4.7.77/2633   hem'd] ſhrupd
4.7.83/2639   let] O let
4.7.90/2646   As . . . courtesie] *not in* Q
4.7.136/2692   the] an
4.7.139/2695   ſtithied] (ſtythied); ſtichied
4.7.156/2712   you] we
4.7.158-9/2714-15   him. | Beate lowd the Taborins] himᴧ | To taſte your bounties
4.7.165/2721   on heauen nor on] (heauen,); vpon the heauen nor
4.7.171/2727   As] But
4.7.176/2732   belou'd, she lou'd] beloued,ᴧ my Lord
5.1.4/2737   core] curre
5.1.14/2746   boy] box
5.1.15/2747   thought] ſaid
5.1.18/2750   guts] the guts
5.1.18/2750   Catarres,] *not in* Q
5.1.19/2751   i'th'] in the
5.1.19-20/2752   and the like] *For Q see Additional Passages.*
5.1.23/2755   mean'ſt] meanes
5.1.28/2760   ſleide] (Sleyd); ſleiue
5.1.35/2767   in to] into
5.1.51/2783   br] (Brother); be
5.1.53/2785   hanging] *not in* Q
5.1.53/2785   brs] (Brothers); bare
5.1.54/2787   farced] (forced); faced
5.1.56/2789   he is] (hee); her's
5.1.57/2789   dog] (Dogge); day
5.1.60/2793   me not] me
5.1.65/2797   light] lights
5.1.74/2806   at once] *not in* Q
5.1.94/2826   his] *not in* Q
5.2.16/2843   should] ſhall
5.2.33/2859   one] a
5.2.35/2861   you] *not in* Q
5.2.39/2865   Nay] Now
5.2.40/2866   diſtraction] diſtruction
5.2.45/2871   Why how now] How now my
5.2.48/2874   adew] *not in* Q
5.2.56/2882   theſe] *not in* Q
5.2.58/2884   But] *not in* Q
5.2.63/2889   ſweete] my
5.2.70-1/2896-7   I . . . CRESSID] F (*Cres.*); *not in* Q
5.2.89/2915   CRESSID] *not in* Q (*which indents the line, as though for a speech-prefix*)
5.2.94/2920   By] And by
5.2.120/2946   Coact] (coact); Court
5.2.125/2951   had deceptious] were deceptions
5.2.137/2962   ſoile] (ſoyle); ſpoile
5.2.145/2971   is] was
5.2.146/2972   thy ſelfe] it ſelfe
5.2.155/2981   *Ariachne's*] F (*Ariachnes*); *Ariathna's* Qa; *Ariachna's* Qb
5.2.160/2986   fiue] finde
5.2.163/2989   bound] giuen
5.2.172/2998   in] on
5.3.14/3038   CASSANDRA] (*Caſſ.*); *Creſ.*
5.3.20-3/3044-7   To . . . CASSANDRA] *not in* Q
5.3.60/3084   But by my ruine.] *not in* Q
5.3.88/3112   diſtraction] deſtruction
5.3.96/3120   of] worth
5.3.116-18/3140-2   PANDARUS . . . name.] *not in* Q (*see text notes*)
5.3.117/3141   ignomie and] ignomyny (*at* Add. Pass. B.2)
5.4.3/3145   yong] *not in* Q
5.4.24/3167   thou Greeke] Greeke
5.5.5/3181   SERUANT] *Man.*
5.5.22/3198   ſcaled] ſcaling
5.5.25/3201   the] a
5.5.35/3211   loſt] loft
5.5.41/3217   luck] luſt
5.6.26/3251   thou] I
5.9.3/3282   good] my
5.9.11/3290   thou, now] F (:); thou next, come
5.9.15/3294   part] prat
5.9.16/3295   Troyan trumpets] (Troian Trumpets); Troyans trumpet
5.10.1/3302   shout] *not in* Q
5.10.1/3302   that] this
5.10.5/3306   a man as good] as good a man
5.11.4/3313   TROYLUS] *before* 5.11.3/3312
5.11.16/3326   ſcrich-oule] (ſcreechoule); ſcrich-ould
5.11.21-2/3331-2   it ſelfe. But march away, | *Hector* is dead:] it ſelfe,
5.11.23/3333   vile] proud

Additional Passages

B.5/5   world, world, world] world, world
B.8/8   deſir'd] lou'd
B.18/19   your] my
B.19/20   hold-dore] hold-ore

INCIDENTALS

43 infancy.] ~ :   61 comes:] ~ ₐ   81 madde ₐ] ~ :   82 loue:] ~ ?   88 sence ₐ] ~ :   99 *Pandarus*,] ~ .   120 *Hellen*] *Helleu*   128 *Daphnes*] *Daphues*   189 Illium] Illum   205 two.] ~ :   209 him.] ~ :   210 *Troylus*.] ~ :   212 *Hector*.] ~ ,   226 come] eome   240 *Paris*.] ~ ,   257 will he] ~ hc   261 came] eame   267 valiantly] valianty   275 egge.] ~ :   292 this] rhis (?)   338 nod?] ~ :   339 see.] ~ ,   349 off.] ~ :   366 priest.] ~ ;   378 choice] choiee   384 *Troylus*, nere looke,] ~ , ~ , (*text*); ~ , ~ ₐ (*c.w.*)   390 well.] ~ :   397 out.] ~ :   399 lie.] ~ :   410 watching.] ~ :   411 another.] ~ :   416 Neice.] ~ :   417 vncle:] ~ :   418 by.] ~ :   419 vncle.] ~ :   420 *Troylus*.] ~ :   427 "Things] ,, ~   429 "Men] ,, ~   440 reard,] ~ .   462 winnows] winnowss   495 reuerend (for] ~) ~   591 scaffollage] fcoaffollage   647 sonnes.] ~ ,   664 god ₐ] F (God); ~ ,   729 wither'd] F; withered   733 bloud.] ~ ,   756 braine ₐ] ~ ,   781 conqu'ring] F; conquering   782 selues,] ~ .   807 fall ₐ] ~ ,   846 itch.] ~ :   859 bisket.] ~ ,   862 witch.] ~ :   871 dog.] ~ :   908 *Thersites*] *Thefites*   920 brains] beains   952 *Hellen*,] ~ , (953 (As] ₐ ~   954 consum'd ₐ] ~ :   965 worst:] ~ ₐ   974 King ₐ] ~ :   976 summe.] ~ .   979 dyminutiue] dyminutue   982 them;] ~ ₐ   982 father ₐ] ~ ;   1008 merit.] ~ ,   1019 vnrespectiue] vnrefpectue   1023 truce] ttuce   1045 cry.] ~ :   1046 voice.] ~ ,   1048 *Cassandra*] *Crffandra*   1057 Illion] I lion   1090 pursuite.] ~ ,   1128 each] eaeh   1164 worthy] worrhy   1251 him.] ~ ,   1258 their] theit   1274 wingd] winged QF   1287 Disguise ₐ] ~ .   1294 him:] ~ .   1322 none,] ~ .   1360 applause.] ~ ,   1362 goe.] ~ ,   1460 *Paris*] *Pa is*   1468 words.] ~ :   1473 harmony.] ~ :   1474 no.] ~ :   1475 sir.] ~ :   1477 fits.] ~ :   1481 certainely.] ~ :   1483 mary] Q (*c.w.*); marry F, Q (*text*)   1485 Lord.] ~ ,   1496 super, you] ~ . You   1498 Queene, my] Queenem, y   1513 Queene.] ~ :   1520 twaine] tawine   1524 now:] ~ ₐ   1533 bow,] ~ .   1544 ho.] *ho*, 1550 deedes ₐ] Qa; ~ , Qb   1644 Blinde] Q ('blinde' *c.w.*); Blind Q (*text*)   1686 loue'd] F (lou'd); loued Q   1692 much,] Qb; ~ ; Qa   1694 vnbridled] vnbrideled QF   1703 scylence] Qa; fylence Qb   1712 *Cressid*.] ~ :   1723 wisely.] ~ ,   1725 confession,] ~ .   1728 might,] ~ ₐ   1728 aboue.] ~ ,   1729 woman,] ~ .   1731 loue,] ~ .   1732 youth,] ~ .   1747 simeles, truth] fimele's ₐ truth   1747 iteration:] ~ .   1748 moone:] ~ .   1751 truth,] ~ .   1752 authentique] authentique   1754 nombers.] ~ ,   1758 vp,] ~ .   1770 another:] ~ ₐ   1797 benefit,] ~ .   1799 behalfe.] ~ :   1804 *Cressed*] Qb; Creffed Qa   1804 exchange,] ~ .   1805 deni'd ₐ] Qa; ~ , Qb   1816 fairly] farrly Qa; farely Qb   1818 answer'd] F; anfwered Q   1826 vnplausiue] vnpaulfiue   1831 pride ₐ] Qa; ~ : Qb   1831 knees ₐ] ~ ,   1842 Lord.] ~ :   1842 day.] ~ :   1844 Cuckould] Cnckould   1845 Ha.] ~ :   1851 aultars.] ~ :   1905 what.] ~ ₐ   1951 calumniating] calumniati g   1964 tent,] ~ .   1972 prouidence] prouidencc   2006 necessary,] ~ .   2053 armie,] ~ .   2115 to morrow.] ~ —   2208 deceiu'd] F; deceiued Q   2210 here.] ~ ,   2219 me.] ~ :   2221 sworne:] ~ ₐ   2249 sweete] fweeet   2322 taking: iussles roughly by,] ~ , ~ :   2328 selues:] ~ ;   2332 heauen,] ~ .   2341 teares?] ~ ₐ   2356 expos'd] expof d   2431 field.] ~ , (?)   2471 *Patroclus*] *Patrolus*   2497 comes,] ~ .   2515 nothing.] ~ :   2516 *Achilles*] *Achillei*   2556 dispos'd] difpo'd   2575 drain'd] drained QF   2619 *quondam*] *quandom*   2675 thee.] ~ ,   2678 lim.] ~ ,   2695 helme.] ~ .   2736 hight.] ~ ₐ   2740 worshippers,] ~ .   2742 Troy.] ~ ,   2745 tricks.] ~ ,   2747 varlot.] ~ ,   2761 tossell] toflell   2764 PATROCLUS] ('*Pat*.') F, Q (*text*); Tat. Q (*c.w.*)   2784 shooing-horne] Qb; fhooing-horue Qa   2791 rowe,] ~ .   2798 whit.] ~ :   2809 *Nestor*] *Nector*   2840 yes.] ~ :   2847 then.] ~ ,   2851 open.] ~ ,   2871 wither'd] withered QF   2888 patience.] ~ :   2891 patience.] ~ :   2898 againe.] ~ :   2921 will] wlll   2930 doe] doc   2940 "Mindes] ,, ~   2948 heart,] ~ .   2987 loue,] ~ .   2988 reliques,] ~ .   3017 gates.] ~ ₐ   3031 brother] brothet   3032 intent] intenr   3053 mean'st] F; meaneft Q   3065 sword,] ~ .   3122 beleeue,] ~ .   3127 read.] ~ ,   3141 lacky] Q ; lackie F. (*For placing, see Textual Notes*.)   3145 *Diomede*,] ~ .   3162 after.] ~ ,   3181 Lord.] ~ :   3183 *Margareton*,] ~ .   3184 prisoner,] ~ .   3190 bruisd] bruifed QF   3210 him,] ~ .   3309 befriended,] ~ .   3312 night.] ~ ,   3338 still,] ~ .

QUARTO STAGE DIRECTIONS

1.1.0.1/31.1   *Enter* Pandarus *and* Troylus.
1.1.88/118   *Exit*.
1.1.88.1/118.1   *Sound alarum*.
1.1.104.1/134.1   *Alarum Enter Æneas*.
1.1.112.1/142.1   *Alarum*.
1.1.166/146   *Exeunt*.
1.2.0.1/146.1   *Enter* Cressid *and her man*.
1.2.172.1/318.1   *Sound a retreate*. (after 1.2.170/316)
1.2.180.1/326.1   *Enter Æneas*.
1.2.184.1/330.1   *Enter* Antenor. (after 1.2.185/331)
1.2.194.1/340.1   *Enter* Hector.
1.2.205.1/350.1   *Enter* Paris.
1.2.213.1/358.1   *Enter* Helenus: (after 1.2.214/359)
1.2.222.1/366.1   *Enter* Troylus. (after 1.2.223/367)
1.2.267.1/411.1   *Enter Boy*:
1.2.291/435   *Exit*.
1.3.0.1-2/435.1   *Enter* Agamemnon. Nestor, Vlisses, Diomedes, | Menelaus *with others*.
1.3.256.1/691.1   *Sound | trumpet*. (opposite 1.3.256-7/691-2)
1.3.384.1/819.1   *Exeunt*.
2.1.0.1/819.2   *Enter* Aiax *and* Thersites.
2.1.120/938   *Exit*.
2.2.0.1-2/949.2-3   *Enter* Priam, Hector, Troylus, Paris *and* Helenus.
2.2.99.1-2/1048.1-2   *Enter* Cassandra *rauing*. (after 2.2.95/1044)
2.2.111/1060   *Exit*.
2.2.212/1161   *Exeunt*.

2.3.0.1/1161.1   *Enter* Thersites *solus*.
2.3.36.1/1197.1   *Enter* Achilles.
2.3.67.1-2/1228.1-2   *Enter* Agam: Vliss: Nestor, Diomed, Aiax & Calcas. (turned 'e' in 'Nestor')
2.3.156.1/1317.1   *Enter* Vlisses.
2.3.261/1422   (*Exeunt*. after '*Enter* Pandarus.')
3.1.0.1-2/1422.1-2   *Enter* Pandarus.
3.1.42.1/1463.1   *Enter* Paris *and* Hellen.
3.1.144.1/1565.1   *Sound a retreat?*
3.1.155.1/1576.1   *Exeunt*.
3.2.0.1-2/1576.2-3   *Enter*. Pandarus Troylus, *man*.
3.2.37.1/1613.1   *Enter pandar and* Cressid.
3.2.205.1/1781.1   *Exeunt*.
3.2.207/1783   *Exit*.
3.3.0.1-2/1783.1-2   *Enter* Vlisses, Diomed, Nestor, Agamem, Chalcas.
3.3.37.1/1820   *Exit*,
3.3.37.1/1820.1   Achilles *and* Patro *stand in their tent*.
3.3.59, 60, 63/1842, 1843, 1846   *Exeunt*. (after 3.3.63/1846)
3.3.232.1/2015.1   *Enter* Thersites. (after 3.3.234/2017)
4.1.0.1-3/2085.2-4   *Enter at one doore* Æneas, *at another* Paris, Deiphobus, | Autemor, Diomed *the Grecian with torches*.
4.1.81, 4.2.0.1/2166, 2166.1   *Exeunt*. *Enter* Troylus *and* Cresseida.
4.2.37.1/2203.1   *One knocks*. (after 4.2.38/2204)
4.2.42.1/2208   *Knock*. (after 4.2.43/2209)
4.2.44.1/2210.1   *Exeunt*.
4.2.76/2242   *Exeunt*.

4.3.0.1/2242.1   *Enter Cress.* (before 4.3.4/2246)
4.4.0.1-2/2277.2-3   *Enter Paris, Troyl. Æneas; Deiphob, Anth. Diomedes.* (*Æneas;* Qa; ~, Qb)
4.4.12/2289   *Exeunt.*
4.5.0.1/2289.1   *Enter Pandarus and Cresseida.*
4.5.10.1/2299.1   *Enter Troylus.*
[4.5.48/2337]   *within.* (after speech-prefix)
4.5.98/2387   *within.*
4.5.99/2388   *within.*
4.5.148/2437   *Exeu.* (after 4.5.143/2432, where scene ends)
4.6.0.1-2/2437.1-2   *Enter Aiax armed, Achilles, Patroclus, Agam. | Menelaus, Vlisses, Nester, Calcas. &c.*
4.6.64.2, 65.1-2/2501.2, 2502.1-2   *Flowrish enter all of Troy.* (after 4.6.64/2501)
4.6.115.1/2552.1   *Alarum.*
4.7.0.2./2556.2   *trumpets | ccase.* (opposite 'Aiax and 'more', 4.6.119-4.7.1a/2556-7a)
4.7.160.1/2716.1   *Exeunt.*
4.7.177/2733   *Exeunt.*
5.1.0.1/2733.1   *Enter Achilles and Patroclus.*
5.1.4/2737   *Enter Thersites.*
5.1.63.1-2/2795.1-2   *Enter Agam: Vlisses, Nest: and Diomed with lights.*
5.1.76.1/2808.1   *Exeunt Agam: Menelaus.*
5.1.84.1-3/2816.1-3   *Exeunt.*
5.1.95/2827   *Enter Diomed.*
5.2.7/2833   *Enter Cressid.*
5.2.61/2887   *Exit.*
5.2.65.1/2891.1   *Enter Cress.*
5.2.114/2940   *Exit.*
5.2.184.1/3010.1   *Enter Eneas.*
5.2.191.1/3017.1   *Exeunt Troyl. Eeneas and Vlisses.*
5.2.198/3024   *Exit.*
5.3.0.1/3025.1   *Enter Hector and Andromache.*
5.3.7/3031   *Enter Cassandra.*
5.3.28.1/3052.1   *Enter Troylus.*
5.3.30/3054   *Exit Cassan.*
5.3.60.1/3084.1   *Enter Priam and Cassandra.*
5.3.81.1/3105.1   *Exit Androm.*
5.3.97.1/3121.1   *Alarum.*
5.3.99.1/3123.1   *Enter Pandar.*
5.3.118.1/3142.1   *Exeunt.*

5.4.0.1/3143.2   *Enter Thersites: excursions.*
5.4.23.2/3166.2   *Enter Hector.*
5.4.33/3176.1   *Exit.*
5.5.0.1/3176.2   *Enter Diomed and Seruant.*
5.5.5.1/3181.1   *Enter Agamem.* (after 'proofe')
5.5.16.1/3192.1   *Enter Nestor.*
5.5.29.1/3205.1   *Enter Vlisses.*
5.5.42.1/3218.1   *Enter Aiax.*
5.5.43/3219.1   *Exit.*
5.5.44/3220.1   *Exit.* (after 5.5.45/3221)
5.5.45.1/3221.1   *Enter Achilles.*
5.5.49.1/3225.1   *Exit.*
5.6.0.1/3225.2   *Enter Aiax.*
5.6.1.1/3226.1   *Enter Diom.*
5.6.5.1/3230.1   *Enter Troylus.*
5.6.12.2/3237.2   *Enter Achil:*
5.6.19/3244   *Exit.*
5.6.21/3246   *Enter Troyl:* (after 'thee')
5.6.26/3251   *Exit.*
5.6.26.1/3251.1   *Enter one in armour.*
5.6.31/3256   *Exit.*
5.7.0.1/3256.1   *Enter Achilles with Myrmidons.*
5.7.8/3264   *Exit.*
5.8.0.1/3264.1   *Enter Thersi: Mene: Paris.*
5.8.4.1/3268   *Exit Paris and Menelus.*
5.8.4.2/3268.1   *Enter Bastard.*
5.8.15/3279   *Exit.*
5.9.0.1-2/3279.1-2   *Enter Hector.*
5.9.4.2-3/3283.2-3   *Enter Achilles and Myrmidons.*
5.9.14.1/3293.1   *Retreat:*
5.9.22.1/3301.1   *Exeunt:*
5.10.0.1-3/3301.2-4   *Enter Agam: Aiax, Mene: Nestor, Diom: | and the rest marching.*
5.10.2/3303   *within.*
5.10.9.1/3310.1   *Exeunt.*
5.11.0.1/3310.2   *Enter Æneas, Paris, Antenor, Diephobus.*
5.11.2.1/3312.1   *Enter Troylus.* (after 5.11.1/3311)

Additional Passages

B.0.1   *Enter Pandarus.*
B.3.1   *Exeunt all but Pandarus.*

FOLIO STAGE DIRECTIONS

1.1.0.1/31.1   *Enter Pandarus and Troylus.*
1.1.88/118   *Exit Pand.*
1.1.88.1/118.1   *Sound Alarum.*
1.1.104.1/134.1   *Alarum. Enter Æneas.*
1.1.112.1/142.1   *Alarum.*
1.1.116/146   *Exeunt.*
1.2.0.1/146.1   *Enter Cressid and her man.*
1.2.36.1/182.1   *Enter Pandarus.* (after 1.2.34/180)
1.2.172.1/318.1   *Sound a retreate.* (after 1.2.170/316)
1.2.180.1/326.1   *Enter Æneas.*
1.2.184.1/330.1   *Enter Antenor.* (after 1.2.185/331)
1.2.194.1/340.1   *Enter Hector.*
1.2.205.1/350.1   *Enter Paris.*
1.2.213.1/358.1   *Enter Hellenus.* (after 1.2.214/359)
1.2.222.1/366.1   *Enter Trylus.* (after 1.2.223/367)
1.2.236.1/380.1   *Enter common Souldiers.*
1.2.267.1/411.1   *Enter Boy.* (after 1.2.266/410)
1.2.277.1/421.1   *Exit Pand.*
1.2.291/435   *Exit.*
1.3.0.1-2/435.1-2   *Senet. Enter Agamemnon, Nestor, Vlysses, Diome-|des, Menelaus, with others.*
1.3.212/647   *Tucket*
1.3.213.1/648.1   *Enter Æneas.*
1.3.256.1/691.1   *The Trumpets sound*

1.3.306.1/741.1   *Exeunt. | Manet Vlysses, and Nestor.*
1.3.384/819.1   *Exeunt*
2.1.0.1/819.2   *Enter Aiax, and Thersites.*
2.1.11.1/830.1   *Strikes him.*
2.1.56.1/874.1   *Enter Achilles, and Patroclus.*
2.1.120/938   *Exit.*
2.1.131/949.1   *Exit.*
2.2.0.1-2/949.2-3   *Enter Priam, Hector, Troylus, Paris and Helenus.*
2.2.99.1-2/1048.1-2   *Enter Cassandra with her haire about | her eares.* (after 2.2.95/1044)
2.2.111/1060   *Exit.*
2.2.212/1161   *Exeunt.*
2.3.0.1/1161.1   *Enter Thersites solus.*
2.3.21.1/1182.1   *Enter Patroclus.*
2.3.36.1/1197.1   *Enter Achilles.*
2.3.67.1-2/1228.1-2   *Enter Agamemnon, Vlisses, Nestor, Diomedes, | Aiax, and Chalcas.*
2.3.69/1230   *Exit.*
2.3.101.1/1262.1   *Enter Patroclus.*
2.3.140.1/1301.1   *Exit Vlisses.*
2.3.156.1/1317.1   *Enter Vlysses.*
2.3.261, 3.1.0.1/1422, 1422.1   *Exeunt. Musicke sounds within.*
3.1.0.1-2/1422.1-2   *Enter Pandarus and a Seruant.*
3.1.42.1/1463.1   *Enter Paris and Helena.*

TROILUS AND CRESSIDA

3.1.144.1/1565.1 Sound a retreat.
3.1.155.1/1576.1 Exeunt.
3.2.0.1-2/1576.2-3 Enter Pandarus and Troylus 'Man.
3.2.2.1/1579.1 Enter Troylus.
3.2.15.1/1591.1 Exit Pandarus.
3.2.27.1/1603.1 Enter Pandarus.
3.2.32/1608.1 Exit Pand.
3.2.37.1/1613.1 Enter Pandarus and Cressida.
3.2.96.1/1672.1 Enter Pandarus.
3.2.205.1, 207/1781.1, 1783 Exeunt. (after 3.2.207/1783)
3.3.0.1-2/1783.1-2 Enter Vlysses, Diomedes, Nestor, Agamemnon, | Menelaus and Chalcas. Florish.
3.3.37/1820 Exit.
3.3.37.1/1820.1 Enter Achilles and Patroclus in their Tent.
3.3.59, 60, 63/1842, 1843, 1846 Exeunt. (after 3.3.63/1846)
3.3.232.1/2015.1 Enter Thersi.
4.1.0.1-3/2085.2-4 Enter at one doore Æneas with a Torch, at another | Paris, Diephœbus, Anthenor, Diomed the | Grecian, with Torches.
4.1.52/2137 Exit Æneas
4.1.81/2166 Exeunt.
4.2.0.1/2166.1 Enter Troylus and Cressida.
4.2.24.1/2190.1 Enter Pandarus. (after 4.2.22/2188)
4.2.37.1/2203.1 One knocks. (after 4.2.36/2202)
4.2.42.1/2208.1 Knocke. (after 4.2.43/2209)
4.2.44.1/2210.1 Exeunt
4.2.60.1/2226.1 Enter Troylus.
4.2.76/2242 Exennt.
4.3.0.1/2242.1 Enter Pandarus and Cressid.
4.3.35.1/2277.1 Exeunt.
4.4.0.1-2/2277.2-3 Enter Paris, Troylus, Æneas, Deiphebus, An-|thenor and Diomedes.
4.4.12/2289 Exeunt.
4.5.0.1/2289.1 Enter Pandarus and Cressid.
4.5.10.1/2399.1 Enter Troylus. (after 4.5.9/2298)
4.5.47.1/2336.1 Enter Æneus.
[4.5.48/2337] within. (after speech-prefix)
4.5.98/2387 within.
4.5.99/2388 within.
4.5.100.1/2389.1 Exit. (after 4.5.101/2390)
4.5.106.1-2/2395.1-2 Enter the Greekes.
4.5.139.2/2428.2 Sound Trumpet.
4.5.148/2437 Exeunt. (after 4.5.143/2432)
4.6.0.1-2/2437.1-2 Enter Aiax armed, Achilles, Patroclus, Agamemnon, | Menelaus, Vlisses, Nestor, Calcas, &c.
4.6.64.1/2501.1 Exennt.
4.6.64.2, 65.1-2/2501.2, 2502.1-2 Enter all of Troy, Hector, Paris, Æneas, Helenus | and Attendants. Florish. (after 4.6.65/2502)
4.6.115.1/2552.1 Alarum.
4.7.0.2/2556.2 trūpets | cease. (opposite 'Aiax' and 'more' 4.6.119-4.7.1a/2556-7a)
4.7.42.1-3/2598.1-2 Enter Agamemnon and the rest.
4.7.160.1/2716.1 Exeunt
4.7.177/2733 Exeunt.
5.1.0.1/2733.1 Enter Achilles, and Patroclus.
5.1.4/2737 Enter Thersites.
5.1.44/2776 Exit.
5.1.63.1-2/2795.1-2 Enter Hector, Aiax, Agamemnon, Vlysses, Ne-|stor, Diomed, with Lights.
5.1.66/2798 Enter Achilles.
5.1.84.1-3/2816.1-3 Exeunt.
5.1.95/2827 Exeunt
5.2.0.1/2827.1 Enter Diomed.

5.2.5.1/2831.1 Enter Troylus and Vlisses.
5.2.7/2833 Enter Cressid. (after 5.2.6/2832)
5.2.61/2887 Exit.
5.2.65.1/2891.1 Enter Cressid.
5.2.108.1/2934.1 Exit. (after 'then')
5.2.114/2940 Exit.
5.2.184.1/3010.1 Enter Æneas.
5.2.191.1/3017.1 Exeunt Troylus, Æneas, and Vlisses.
5.3.0.1/3024.1 Enter Hecter and Andromache.
5.3.7/3031 Enter Cassandra.
5.3.28.1/3052.1 Enter Troylus.
5.3.30/2054 Exit Cassandra.
5.3.60.1/3084.1 Enter Priam and Cassandra.
5.3.81.1/3105.1 Exit Andromache.
5.3.93/3117 Exit.
5.3.97.1/3121.1 Alarum.
5.3.99.1/3123.1 Enter Pandar.
5.3.118.1, 5.4.0.1/3142.1, 3142.2 A Larum. Exeunt.
5.4.0.1/3142.2 Enter Thersites in excursion.
5.4.16.1/3159.1 Enter Diomed and Troylus.
5.4.23.2/3166.2 Enter Hector.
5.4.33/3176.1 Exit.
5.5.0.1/3176.2 Enter Diomed and Seruants.
5.5.5.1/3181.1 Enter Agamemnon.
5.5.16.1/3192.1 Enter Nestor.
5.5.29.1/3205.1 Enter Vlisses.
5.5.42.1/3218.1 Enter Aiax.
5.5.43/3219 Exit.
5.5.44/3220.1 Exit. (after 5.5.45/3221)
5.5.45.1/3221.1 Enter Achilles.
5.5.49.1/3225.1 Exit.
5.6.0.1/3225.2 Enter Aiax.
5.6.1.1/3226.1 Enter Diomed.
5.6.5.1/3230.1 Enter Troylus.
5.6.11.2/3236.2 Enter Hector.
5.6.12.1/3237.1 Exit Troylus. (after 5.6.11/3236; before 'Enter Hector')
5.6.12.2/3237.2 Euter Achilles.
5.6.19/3244 Exit.
5.6.21/3246 Enter Troylus. (after 'Brother')
5.6.26/3251 Exit.
5.6.26.1/3251.1 Enter one in Armour.
5.6.31/3256 Exit.
5.7.0.1/3256.1 Enter Achilles with Myrmidons.
5.7.8/3264 Exit.
5.8.0.1/3264.1 Enter Thersites, Menelaus, and Paris.
5.8.4.1/3268 Exit Paris and Menelaus.
5.8.4.2/3268.1 Enter Bastard.
5.8.14, 15/3278, 3279 Exeunt. (after 5.8.15/3279)
5.9.0.1-2/3279.1-2 Enter Hector.
5.9.4.2-3/3283.2-3 Enter Achilles and his Myrmidons.
5.9.14.1/3293.1 Retreat.
5.9.22.1/3301.1 Exeunt.
5.10.0.1-2/3301.2-4 Sound Retreat. Shout. | Enter Agamemnon, Aiax, Menelaus, Nestor, | Diomed, and the rest marching.
5.10.9.1/3310.1 Exeunt.
5.1.0.1/3310.2 Enter Æneas, Paris, Anthenor and Deiphœbus.
5.11.2.1/3312.1 Enter Troylus.

Additional Passages

B.0.1 Enter Pandarus.
B.3.1 Exeunt.
B.25 Exeunt.

SONNETS
AND 'A LOVER'S COMPLAINT'

The Sonnets were entered in the Stationers' Register on 20 May 1609:

Tho. Thorpe Entrd for his copie vnder the handẹ of m^r Wilſon & m^r Lownes Warden a Booke called Shakeſpeares ſonnettẹ

The volume (Q; STC 22353) was printed for Thomas Thorpe by George Eld in the same year. H. E. Rollins, who collated all thirteen extant copies of Q (*Variorum*, ii. 5), discovered press variants in outer C, outer D, inner and outer F, outer H, and inner I. A few further non-substantive variants have been noted in the title-page by Randall McLeod ('A Technique of Headline Analysis'), who has also privately communicated another incidental variant in outer D (49.3). MacDonald P. Jackson has shown that Q was probably set by two compositors who punctuated 'in very different ways', so the punctuation cannot be regarded as Shakespeare's. There are also some fourteen instances of the misprint 'their' for 'thy', occurring in the work of both compositors. No other generally accepted occurrence of this misprint is found in the entire corpus of Shakespeare's works, and there is only one agreed instance of the reverse error (Q3 *Richard III* 5.5.32/3123, where it is a printer's error, not a misreading). This strongly suggests that the printer's manuscript was a transcript not in Shakespeare's hand. In spite of a few cruxes, the Sonnets are not badly printed. There is no evidence that Shakespeare had anything to do with their publication; on the other hand, as Katherine Duncan-Jones has shown, Thorpe was a reputable publisher, and there is nothing intrinsically irregular about his publication. His quarto was reprinted in 1640 by John Benson, who published a pirated volume called *Poems: Written by W. Shakespeare, Gent.* which includes most of the sonnets along with *A Lover's Complaint*, *The Phoenix and Turtle*, *The Passionate Pilgrim*, and poems by other authors including Milton, Jonson, and Herrick. The sonnets are reordered, some are run together, they are given titles, and some have verbal changes designed to make them refer to a woman instead of a man. None of the many subsequent, more serious attempts to reorder the sonnets has won general assent.

A number of individual sonnets survive in seventeenth-century manuscripts: a full list is given in Peter Beal's *Index of British Literary Manuscripts*. None of these manuscripts is itself earlier than *c*.1620; however, Francis Meres in 1598 mentioned Shakespeare's 'sugred Sonnets among his priuate friends', which means that some, at least, of the poems were circulating in manuscript a decade before they reached print. It is thus possible that the extant manuscripts derive from such manuscripts. Since Q itself seems to have been set from a transcript, the printed text is at least two removes from Shakespeare's originals; some of the extant manuscripts might be only one remove from autograph. The manuscripts therefore deserve more meticulous study than they have received: this edition is the first to be based upon a collation of all the known manuscripts. One manuscript (Folger MS V.a.148) contains an anthology which runs together the texts of several sonnets, in whole or part; this manuscript demonstrably derives from the 1640 edition, and its variants are not collated below. The remaining manuscripts fall into two groups. In some the variants are—like those in the Folger manuscript—few, trivial, and/or clearly wrong (see notes to Sonnets 32 and 71); these manuscripts can be linked to printed sources. For other sonnets (2, 8, 106, 128) the variants are more numerous, and dependence upon printed sources is either impossible or, at least, indeterminable. For Sonnets 2 and 106, in particular, the variants are so substantial that they amount in effect to a different version of the poem. It seems most unlikely that such extensive variation results from mere scribal ineptitude, particularly as the manuscript readings are characteristic both of Shakespeare's early style and of the themes and imagery of the relevant sonnets themselves. A full account of the manuscripts of Sonnet 2, with a defence of the authenticity of the variants, is given by Gary Taylor. We print, among Additional Passages, texts of '*Spes Altera*' (in parallel with Sonnet 2) and 'On His Mistris Beauty' (in parallel with 106). Versions of 138 and 144 had appeared in *The Passionate Pilgrim* (1599?); we also print these in parallel to the Quarto version.

In 'A Lover's Complaint' there are 'about as many errors as one would expect to find in the same number of lines of a reasonably good dramatic text' (Maxwell), and the punctuation is often misleading. The poem was probably printed from the same transcript as the Sonnets. Notes to the modern-spelling text of both the Sonnets and the complaint are indicated by '(M)'.

S.W.W./(G.T.)

WORKS CITED

Manuscripts

B1   British Library Add. MS 10309, fol. 143 (*c*.1630; Margaret Bellasys)
B2   British Library Add. MS 21433, fol. 114^v (*c*.1630; Inns of Court)
B3   British Library Add. MS 25303, fol. 119^v (*c*.1620s-30s; Inns of Court)
B4   British Library Add. MS 30982, fol. 18 (*c*.1631-3; Daniel Leare)
B5   British Library, Sloane MS 1792, fol. 45 (early 1630s; 'I. A.' of Christ Church)
F2   Folger Shakespeare Library, MS V.a.170, pp. 163-4 (*c*.1625-35)
F3   Folger Shakespeare Library, MS V.a.345, pp. 145 (*c*.1630)

N University of Nottingham, Portland MS Pw V 37, p. 69 (c.1630)
R Rosenbach Museum and Library, MS 1083/17, fols. 132ᵛ-133 (c. 1638-42; Horatio Carey)
W Westminster Abbey, MS 41, fol. 49 (1619-30s; George Morley)
Y Yale University, Osborn Collection, b. 205, fol. 54ᵛ (1625-35)

Books and Articles

Benson, John, comp., *Poems* (1640)
Booth, S., ed., *Sonnets* (1977)
Brooke, T., ed., *Sonnets* (1936)
Butler, Samuel, ed., *Sonnets* (1899)
Duncan-Jones, K., 'Was the 1609 *Shake-speares Sonnets* really Unauthorized?', *RES*, NS 34 (1983), 151-71
Gildon, Charles, ed., *Works*, vol. vii (1710), vol. x (1728)
Housman, R. F., ed., *A Collection of English Sonnets* [1835]
Ingram, W. G., and Theodore Redpath, ed., *Sonnets* (1964, rev. 1978)
Jackson, MacDonald P., 'Punctuation and the Compositors of Shakespeare's *Sonnets*, 1609', *The Library*, V, 30 (1975), 2-23
Lintott, Bernard, ed., *Poems*, 2 vols. [1709, 1711]
McLeod, Randall, 'A Technique of Headline Analysis, with Application to *Shakespeare's Sonnets*, 1609', *SB* 32 (1979), 197-210
—— 'Unemending Shakespeare's Sonnet 111', *SEL* 21 (1981), 75-96
Maxwell, J. C., ed., *Poems*, New (1966)
Palgrave, F. T., ed., *Songs and Sonnets* (1865)
Partridge, A. C., *A Substantive Grammar of Shakespeare's Nondramatic Texts* (1976)
Pooler, C. K., ed., *Sonnets*, Arden (1918, rev. 1931, 1943)
Rollins, H. E., ed., *Sonnets*, New Variorum (1944)
Sewell, G., ed., *Works*, vol. vii (1725)
Seymour-Smith, M., ed., *Sonnets* (1963)
Taylor, Gary, 'Some Manuscripts of Shakespeare's Sonnets', *The Bulletin of the John Rylands Library*, 68 (1985), 210-46
Wells, Stanley, 'New Readings in Shakespeare's Sonnets', in *Elizabethan and Modern Studies*, ed. J. P. Vander Motten (1985)
Wyndham, G., ed., *Poems* (1898)

TEXTUAL NOTES

1] number not in Q
2] For another version of this sonnet, present in eleven manuscripts, see Additional Passages. Another manuscript—St John's, Cambridge, MS S. 23 (James 416), fols. 38ʳ-38ᵛ (c.1630s-40s)—closely resembles the Quarto text. The sonnet is entitled, and attributed to 'W. Shakspere'. The spelling of the name is possibly significant. (See Taylor.)
2.4 totter'd] Q; tatter'd MS
2.9 deseru'd] Q; deferues MS
2.10 answere this faire] Q; fay that this faire MS. This variant is intriguing, in that it appears to stand half-way between Q and 'Spes Altera'. See Additional Passages.
2.11 my old] Q; thy old MS. See notes to 'Spes Altera', in Additional Passages.
2.11 excuse,] MS; ~ ₐ Q. The punctuation seems desirable, to indicate the switch from direct address.
5.14 (M) Lose] Q (Leefe). Q's form is cognate with 'lose', which superseded it; 'leese' occurs nowhere else in Shakespeare.
8] Also extant in BL Add. MS 15226, fol. 4ᵛ (c.1630), with the title 'In laudem musice et opprobrium contemptori[s] eiusdem'. Most of the poems in the relevant section of this manuscript have Latin titles; this descriptive title is therefore of uncertain authority.
8.2 Sweets] Q; Sweete MS. The manuscript reading, if correct, must be a vocative (as Malone and many editors interpret the parallel 'Musick to heare' in the preceding line). The vocative use is common in Shakespeare (see Schmidt), who also juxtaposes the plural and singular—as here in the manuscript line—at *Hamlet* 5.1.239/3210, 'Sweets to the sweet'.
8.6 thine] Q; thy MS
8.8 the parts that] Q; a parte, wᶜʰ MS. The MS variant was defended by Pooler.
8.10 in] Q; on MS
8.11 sier, and child] Q; Childe, and Syer MS
8.12 Who] Q; wᶜʰ MS
8.12 one pleasing note do] Q; this single note dothe MS. (Possibly an authorial variant.)
8.14 wilt] Q; shalt MS
11.11 Looke ₐ] Q; ~, CAPELL
11.11 the] Q; thee SEWELL 1
12.4 ensiluer'd ore] This edition; or siluer'd ore Q; all silver'd o'er MALONE; are silver'd o'er GILDON; o'er silver'd all CAMBRIDGE 2 (Nicholson). See Wells, 'New Readings . . .'.
13.7 Your] BENSON; You Q
13.13 (M) love,] Q (~ₐ)
17.14 twise, in it ₐ] CAPELL; twife in it, Q
19.5 fleet'st] Q; fleets DYCE 2
19.14 euer liue] Q; liue euer NICHOLSON (*conj.* in Cambridge). Q's inverted foot adds emphasis.
20.7 (M) hues] Q (Hews)
23.14 with . . . wit] wit . . . wiht Q
24.1 steeld] Q; stelled CAPELL. See Ingram and Redpath.
24.13 art,] GILDON; ~ ₐ Q
25.9 might] CAPELL; worth Q; fight MALONE (Theobald)
25.11 quite] Q; worth WHITE (Theobald)
26.12 thy] CAPELL; their Q
27.10 thy] CAPELL; their Q
28.5 ethers] Q; others BENSON. OED records Q's spelling from the 13th to the 16th c.
28.12 (M) gild'st] Q (guil'ſt). Q may be a phonetic spelling.
28.12 the eauen] LINTOTT: th'eauen Q
28.14 strength] CAPELL; length Q
31.8 thee] GILDON; there Q
31.9 Thou Q (*text*); To (*c.w.*)
32] Also extant in Folger MS V.a.162, fol. 26 (mid 17th c.) entitled 'a Sonnet'; but both MS variants appear to be errors. See also Sonnet 71.
32.8 hight] Q; high MS
32.11 birth] Q; loue MS
33] Also extant in Folger MS V.a.148, Pt. 1, fol. 23 (c.1660).
33.11 alack] Q; alas MS
34.12 crosse] CAPELL; loſſe Q
34.13 (M) sheds] Q (ſheeds)
35.8 thy . . . thy] CAPELL; their . . . their Q; thy . . . their WYNDHAM
37.7 thy] CAPELL; their Q
39.12 doth] MALONE; doſt Q
40.7 this selfe] Q; thyself GILDON. See Ingram and Redpath.
41.8 he] Q; she MALONE. The emendation, often adopted, may be right; but ll. 1-4 and 10-11 imply that the friend is open to temptation, and Q may be consciously witty in suggesting that the woman's wooing fires the man.
41.12 (M) troth] Q (truth)
43.11 thy] MALONE (Capell); their Q
44.12 attend ₐ] LINTOTT; ~, Q
44.13 naught] GILDON; naughts Q
45.5 For] Q; So INGRAM AND REDPATH. 'For' is acceptable since ll. 4-14 explain the coming and going mentioned in l. 4.
45.11 assured ₐ] BENSON; ~, Q
45.12 thy] GILDON; their Q
46.0-1 46 | Mine] Q (*text*); Mine (*c.w.*)
46.3, 8, 13, 14 thy] CAPELL; their Q
46.9 (M) 'cide] Q (ſide)
47.10 art] CAPELL; are Q. Q is possible, but the misreading is easy.
47.11 noe] CAPELL; nor Q; not BENSON
50.6 (M) dully] Q (duly)
51.10 (M) perfect'st] Q (perfects)

51.11   raign] This edition (G.T.); naigh Q; weigh G. C. M. SMITH (Bray). See Wells, 'New Readings . . .'.
54.14 (M)   fade] Q (vade)
54.14   by] Q; my CAPELL
55.1   monuments,] MALONE; monument, Q
56.13   Or] CAPELL; As Q; Else PALGRAVE. Sisson (*New Readings*) defends Q, but a word marking the alternative nature of the images seems called for. If initial words were not capitalized in the MS, misreading is possible.
58.7   patience, tame,] GILDON; ~ ∧ ~ , Q
61.8 (M)   tenor] Q (tenure)
62.7   for] Q; so HUDSON 2 (Lettsom)
62.10 (M)   chapped] Q (chopt)
63.5 (M)   travelled] Q (trauaild)
65.12   of] MALONE; or Q
67.6   seëing] CAPELL; feeing Q. See Ingram and Redpath.
68]   Also extant in Folger MS V.a.148, Pt. I, fol. 22ᵛ (c.1660).
69.3   due] GILDON 2; end Q
69.5   Thy] MALONE (Capell); Their Q
69.14   soyle] BENSON; folye Q
70.0-1   70 | That] Q (*text*); That (*c.w.*)
70.1   are] Q; art BENSON
70.6   Thy] CAPELL; Their Q
71]   Also extant in Folger MS V.a.162, fol. 12ᵛ (mid 17th c.), entitled 'A fonnet'. This manuscript duplicates Q's parentheses in ll. 9 and 10, and is probably derivative.
71.2   surly sullen] Q; sullen surly MS
71.8   you] Q; me MS
72.6   To doe more for me] Q; To doe for me more G.T. *conj.*
73.4   ru'ind] BENSON; rn'wd Q
76.7   tel] CAPELL; fel Q
77.10   blācks] CAPELL (Theobald); blacks Q
82.0-1   82 | I grant] Q ('I Grant' *text*); I grant (*c.w.*)
82.8   these] This edition; the Q. The emendation strengthens both sense and metre.
85.3   Reserue thy] BUTLER; Referue their Q. The phrase has been much emended (see Rollins and Booth). 'Reserve, which commonly meant "preserve" (as in 32.7) does not appear to need the editorial repairs suggested for it, but *their* may well be another instance of one of the commonest printer's error [sic] in Q, "their" for "thy" . . . "Reserve thy character" makes better sense than [Q]' (Booth, who nevertheless retains Q). 'Character' as 'personal appearance' is first but undisputably recorded in *Twelfth Night* (1.2.47/87).
86.13 (M)   filled] Q (fild)
89.3   Speake] Q (*text*); The Qa (*c.w.*)
89.11   profane] Qb (prophane); proface Qa
90.11   shall] BENSON; ftall Q
91.9   better] BENSON; bitter Q
95.12   turnes] Q; turn SEWELL
99.4   dwells,] GILDON; ~ ? Q
99.9   One] SEWELL; Our Q
99.13 (M)   ate] Q (eate)
100.14   preuenst] Q; prevent'st GILDON. Gildon's is an acceptable modernization, but Q is presumably from 'prevene', common from the 15th to the early 18th centuries (not noted by New Variorum, etc.).
102.8   hir] R. F. HOUSMAN; his Q. Booth defends Q, but 'her' in ll. 10 and 13 is against it, and the misreading is easy.
106]   Also extant in two manuscripts. See Additional Passages.
106.0-1   106 | When] Q ('106 | WHen' *text*); When (*c.w.*)
106.8   Eu'n] MS (Pierpont Morgan); Euen Q
106.12   skill] MSS; ftill Q
108.3   now] Q; new MALONE
111.1   with] GILDON; wifh Q. Gildon's emendation, first abandoned by Seymour-Smith, was strongly attacked by Randall McLeod ('Unemending Shakespeare's Sonnet 111'). He demonstrates that Q's ligature cannot be a simple setting error; but misreading is not impossible, nor is accidental substitution. Stephen Booth (3rd printing, 1980) was persuaded by McLeod, but we find it very difficult to see why the poet should ask the recipient to tell fortune to chide him while going on to say that he is already fortune's victim.
112.14   y'are dead] Q; are dead CAPELL. Malone (2) interpreted 'y'are' as 'they are', supposing misunderstanding of 'y' meaning 'th' for 'y' as an abbreviation of 'ye'; 'th'are' occurs elsewhere in Shakespeare. Capell avoids the redundancy but leaves no explanation for the error. The interpretation 'ye are' has been defended, implausibly: it makes sense within the couplet, but not in relation to the earlier part of the sonnet: the friend's supposed death would give the poet no excuse for ignoring the opinions of others.
113.6   latch] CAPELL; lack Q
113.10   sweet-fauor] Q; sweet favour'd DELIUS (*conj.*). A. C. Partridge (*A Substantive Grammar of Shakespeare's Nondramatic Texts* (Charlottesville, Virginia, 1976)) classifies with three other instances in the Sonnets of hyphenated adjective + noun; but possibly the past participial ending in 'deformedft' is proleptically understood here.
113.13   more, repleat,] GILDON; ~ ∧ ~ , Q
113.14   makes mine eye] CAPELL; maketh mine Q. Perhaps 'eye' was accidentally omitted, and 'makes' expanded to fill the line.
116]   Manuscript versions of this sonnet are discussed by John P. Cutts in 'Two Seventeenth-Century Versions of Shakespeare's Sonnet 116', *SSt* 10 (1977), 9–16; see also W. M. Evans, 'Lawes' Version of Shakespeare's Sonnet CXVI', *PMLA* 51 (1936), 120-2.
116]   119 Q (all copies except Bodley–Caldecott)
117.10   surmise accumilate] MALONE; ~ , ~ Q
118.10   were, not,] GILDON; ~ , ~ ∧ Q
121.11   beuel,] GILDON 1; ~ ∧ Q
125.6-7   rent, . . . sweet,] CAPELL; ~ ∧ . . . ~ ; Q
126.2 (M)   sickle-hour] Q (fickle, hower)
126.8   mynuits] MALONE (Capell); mynuit Q
126.12   After this line Q prints parentheses for each line of an imagined couplet.
127.9   Misterfse] Q. *OED* records related spellings.
127.10   brow] INGRAM AND REDPATH; eyes Q; brows BROOKE (Staunton); hairs CAPELL
128]   Also extant in Bodleian MS Rawl. poet. 152, fol. 34 (c.1625-1640s), which may represent an earlier draft of the poem. The manuscript was first noticed by R. H. A. Robbins in *N&Q* 212 (1967), 137–8; but his transcription is inaccurate, and he is unnecessarily dismissive of the variants.
128.1   my musike] Q; deere deerest MS. Both texts depend upon repetition here—'musick musick' (Q), 'deere deerest' (MS), though Q better introduces the poem's theme. For Shakespearian word-play involving repetitions of 'deer' in various inflections, compare *Errors* 3.2.62/786, *1 Henry IV* 5.4.106-7/2903-4, *Dream* 3.1.79/866, and *Romeo* 3.2.66/1648.
128.2   motion] Q; mocions MS. Probably an error in the MS, though its grammar is acceptable.
128.3   swayst,] CAPELL; ~ , Q; swaies, MS (*error*)
128.5   Do] Q; o how MS. MS is unmetrical, but the error seems unlikely to derive from simple corruption of 'Do'; either 'o' or 'how' could be correct, and the other word an unconscious interpolation.
128.5   Iackes] Q; kies MS. Most editors here understand Q's reading as an authorial error for 'keys' (see Rollins), although Q has been defended as technically precise (Gene M. Moore, *N&Q* 230 (1985), 31–2). This defence, however, presumes a context in which the virginals are being tuned, but not played; it would be natural if 'keys' were Shakespeare's thought, and later altered for the sake of a pun on 'jacks'. See l. 13.
128.5   leape] Q; leapes MS (*error*)
128.7   reape] Q; reped MS (*error*)
128.8   woods] Q; wood MS (*error*)
128.9   tikled] Q; tuched MS. Either word might be a misreading of the other (ticled/tuched); Q's is the more unusual, and the more complex, but MS is acceptable as an unrevised reading: Shakespeare describes kisses as the 'touching' of lips at *Venus* 115, *Othello* 4.3.37/2699, and *Pericles* 22.64/2330. Moreover,

'tickled' is disyllabic, whereas 'tuched' could be a monosyllable, thus rendering it compatible with the MS variants elsewhere in this line.

128.9 they] Q; the fain MS. Presumably the MS is an error for 'they fain'.

128.11 thy] GILDON; their Q; youre MS. This variant must be related to those in l. 14. As noted in the Introduction, Q is particularly prone to errors of 'their' for 'thy'; 'they' is used elsewhere in this sonnet, in both texts; and Robbins notes that the poet never elsewhere addresses the Dark Lady as 'you'. However, the Quarto's apparent consistency in the matter might be the result of revision, when the sonnets were put together in a sequence (see Taylor, 'Some Manuscripts'), and the manuscript here switches from 'thee' in the quatrain to 'you' in the sestet, which might be deliberate.

128.13 sausie Iackes] Q; then those keyes MS. See the related variant at l. 5.

128.14 thy fingers] BENSON; their fingers Q; youre fingers MS. See l. 11.

128.14 thy lips] Q; youre lipes MS. See l. 11.

129.9 (M) Mad] Q (Made)

129.10 quest, to haue,] CAPELL; ~, ~, Q

129.11 (M) proved] Q (proud)

129.11 a] MALONE; and Q

131.9 sweare,] MALONE; ~, Q

131.14 (M) slander,] Q (slaunder,)

131.14 (M) think,] Q (~,)

132.2 torment] Q; torments BENSON. Abbott, 349.

132.6 the East] GILDON 2; th'Eaſt Q

132.9 (M) mourning] Q (morning)

135.1, 2, 11, 12, 14 (M) Will] Q (Will)

135.13 (M) no vnkinde no] Q (no vnkinde, no). Variously interpreted (e.g. '"No," unkind, no' (Ingram and Redpath)) and emended, but 'unkind' as a noun seems likely (Brook, p. 84).

136.2, 5, 14 (M) Will] Q (Will)

136.6 (M) Ay] Q (I)

137.11 not,] SEWELL 1: ~, Q

138] For an alternative version see Additional Passages.

138.12 to haue] *Passionate Pilgrim*; t'haue Q

140.13 belyde] BENSON; be lyde Q

142.0–1 142 | Loue] Q ('142 | LOue' text); Loue Q (c.w.)

143.13 (M) Will] Q (Will)

144] For an alternative version see Additional Passages.

144.6 side] *Passionate Pilgrim*; fight Q

144.9 (M) fiend] Q (finde)

146.2 ⌜   ⌝] GLOBE; My finfull earth Q. A notorious crux; see Wells, 'New Readings . . .'.

148.8 mens: no,] Q; men's, no. DYCE 2 (Lettsom)

153.8 strang] Q; strong TUCKER (Tyler). To other arguments defending Q as 'strange' (see Booth) may be added the gloss 'foreign': venereal diseases were associated with foreigners.

153.14 eyes] BENSON; eye Q

A LOVER'S COMPLAINT

7 (M) sorrow's] Q (ſorrowes,)

37 (M) beaded] Q (bedded). Cercignani, p. 169.

41 (M) monarch's] Q (Monarches)

51 ganne] MALONE; gaue Q

61 fastly] Q (faſtly); softly MAXWELL *conj.* (faftly)

102 May] Q; March This edition *conj.* The inversion is odd, and though Shakespeare associates May with winds in Sonnet 18 (l. 3), the month more traditionally associated with *winds* that are unruly is March (*Winter's Tale* 4.4.120/1725).

112 (M) manège] Q (mannad'g)

118 Came] SEWELL; Can Q

123–4 sleep: . . . weepe,] SEWELL; ſleep, . . . weepe: Q

131 Consents] MALONE; Conſent's Q

139 labour] This edition (*conj.* Wyndham); labouring Q. Maxwell remarks that this 'would certainly regularize the construction', and the error would be easy.

161 wils] MAXWELL; wits Q

182 woo] CAPELL MS; vovv Q

198 (M) pallid] Q (palyd; *sometimes interpreted as* 'paled', *which properly means* 'having grown pale')

204 (M) hair] Q (heir)

208 th'annexations] This edition (G.T.); th'annexions Q; the annexions CAPELL MS. Editors follow Capell; both 'annexion' and 'annexation' are first recorded in 1611 except for this instance; *OED*'s first other example of 'annexion' in this sense is from 1641.

228 (M) Hallowed] Q (Hollowed). Cercignani, p. 98.

229 (M) me, your minister for you,] This edition; me, your ~, Q; me, your minister, ~, COLLIER; me your minister, for you, STEEVENS. Maxwell (following Pooler) remarks that '"for you" is obscure, since the similes were not offered for her service'; taken as an intensifier for *minister* (i.e. 'on your behalf') it makes sense.

229 your] Q; their G.T. *conj.*

233 A] DYCE 2 (Malone); Or Q

241 Playing] This edition (*conj.* Capell); Playing Q; Paling MALONE. Q has been (weakly) defended, but the repetition is implausible, and 'Playing' seems right in 242. 'Paling' does not give strong sense. As Maxwell says, 'Planing' gives an appropriate metaphor: 'smoothing the place (in a pillow) which has not in fact had any impression made on it'. I differ from Maxwell in supposing that the metaphor is of a heart rather than a pillow: cf. Sonnet 24, 1–2: 'Mine eye hath play'd the painter and hath steeld, | Thy beauties forme in table of my heart.'

251 emur'd] GILDON; enur'd Q. For the spelling, see *LLL* Q1, 3.1.854, 4.3.304/854, 1546 (Maxwell).

252 (M) now, to tempt, all,] GILDON; now to tempt all Q; now, to tempt all, MALONE

252 procurd] BENSON; procure Q

260 Nunne] CAPELL MS; Sunne Q

261 (M) ay] Q (I)

270 kindred,] BENSON; ~, Q

293 O] GILDON; Or Q

Additional Passages

Spes Altera] For this text see Taylor, 'Some Manuscripts'. For manuscript identifications, see Works Cited. Copy-text is W; the collations given to the right of the bracket record the reading of all manuscripts which do not agree with the reading in the lemma.

Spes Altera] B1, B2, B3; Spes Altera A song F3; To one y^t would dye a Mayd B4, B5, F2, W, Y; A Lover to his Mistres N; The Benefitt of Mariage. R

1 forty] threſcore B1; 40 B4 (?)

1 winters] yeares R

2 trench] drench R

2 feild] cheeke B2, B3

3 youthes] youth B5, F3

3 faire] fairer R

3 Liu'rie] B1; liuery W, B2, B3, B4, B5, F2, F3, N; feild R

3 accounted] accompted B3; eſteemed N

4 like] like like B5

4 weeds] cloaths F2

5 beeing askt] if we Aſk B2; if wee ask B3; aſkt R

5 lyes] lye W (cropped)

6 Where] Where's B1, B2, B3, F3, N, R

7 these] thoſe Y; *not in* B4

7 hollow suncken] hollow-ſunken B1

8 eaten] beaten F2

8 prayse] prayſl W (cropped); prayes B4; pleasure B5

9 O] *not in* B5

9 how] whow B4

9 much] far Y; *not in* B5

9 bewtyes] bewtious Y

10 pretty] little B2, B3

11 Saues] Saud Y

11 my] mine N

11 account] accompt B3

11 makes my old] makes me old B4; makes no old F2; yeilds mee an N; makes the old R; make no old Y

SONNETS AND 'A LOVER'S COMPLAINT'

13   new borne] made younge B2, B3
14   feelst] felſt B2, B3, B4
14.1 W.S.] N (*opposite title*)
On His Mistris Beauty] This sonnet survives in two manuscripts: Pierpont Morgan MA 1057, p. 96 (*c*.1630s), hereafter 'M', and Rosenbach MS 1083/16, p. 256 (*c*.1630), hereafter 'RO'. Rollins printed an inaccurate transcript of M. Where the manuscripts differ, we have generally—as with '*Spes Altera*'—preferred the variant endorsed by Q; this principle arbitrates between all but three of the variants, and in ll. 10 and 11 the corrupt reading is obvious. In l. 8 we have preferred M's metrical elision. Because M more often agrees with Q against R, we have chosen it as copy-text. However, it seems unlikely that RO derives from M, as it three times agrees with Q against M; one of these agreements results from correction of an obvious error, but the other two are indifferent variants.

2   diſcriptions] RO (deſcriptions); diſcription M
3   rime] RO; mine M (*but with 'rime' written in the margin as a correction*)
6   hand] RO; hands M
6   of eye] M; or eye RO
8   Ev'n] M; Euen RO
9   their] M; theſe RO
10 these] RO; thoſe M
11 saw] M; ſay RO
11 diuininge] M; deceiuing RO
12 your] Q; thy M, Ro. None of the other sonnets—with the dubious exception of the MS of 128—mixes 'you' and 'thee' forms.
13 wee]; me RO
13 present] M; pleaſant RO
14 tongues] M; tongue RO

INCIDENTALS

2.14 could.] ~,   5.7 gon,] ~.   5.8 where.] ~,   6.4 beauties] beautits   8.14 thee,] MS; ~ˏQ   9.10 it.] ~ˏ   10.2 vnprouident.] ~ˏ   16.14 skill.] ~,   18.14 thee.] ~,   19.3 iawes] yawes   19.13 Time,] ~ˏ   22.3 forrowes] forrwes   24.12 thee.] ~ˏ   26.11 totter'd] tottered Q   26.14 me.] ~ˏ   27.6 thee,] Qb; ~ ; Qa (BL–Bright)   28.5 enimies] enimes   28.14 stronger.] ~ˏ   31.10 trophies] tropheis   33.14 staineth] ſtainteh   35.14 me.] ~,   38.12 Eternall] Q (*text*); Eternall (*c.w.*)   39.7 giue,] ~ :   43.14 me.] ~,   47.10 selfe] Qb; ſeife Qa (Rosenbach)   51.3 should] ſhoulld   55.7 burne,] ~ :   55.9 enmity] emnity   56.11 see,] ~ :   56.14 rare.] ~ :   57.9 ieallous] iealious (?)   60.5 light,] ~.   60.6 Crawles] Q (*text*); Crawls (*c.w.*)   62.11 read.] ~ˏ   62.14 daies.] ~,   68.7 second life] ſcond life   70.8 vnstained] vnſtayined   70.12 inlarg'd] inlarged   73.1 yeare] yeeare   74.12 remembered] remembred   75.14 away.] ~,   76.4 strange?] Q (*question mark not visible in Folger-Locker copy*)   76.8 proceed?] Q   76.14 told.] ~,   79.14 pay.] ~,   85.6 vnletter'd] vnlettered   88.1 dispoſde] diſpode   91.13 take,] ~,   96.11 mightst] mighſt   97.10 vn-father'd] vn-fathered   102.1 seeming,] ~ˏ   104.12 deceau'd] deceued   108.14 dead.] ~,   117.12 waken'd] wakened   117.14 loue.] ~ˏ   120.4 hammer'd] hammered   120.8 suffer'd] suffered   122.1 Thy] TThy   124.2 vnfather'd] vnfathered   125.7 forgoing] Forgoing   126.7 skill,] ~.   129.9 in pursuit] In ~   136.7 prooue,] ~.(?)   136.14 lou'st] loueſt   138.14 flatterd] flattered   143.2 fether'd] fethered   150.6 deeds,] Qb; ~ ; Qa (Trinity)   151.7 may,] may,

A LOVER'S COMPLAINT

18 seasond] ſeaſoned   28 commixt] commxit   44 perus'd] peruſˏd (?)   78 attended] atttended   142 of] ol   177 maid,] ~ˏ (?)   192 th'] th,   242 vnconstrained] vnconſtraind

VARIOUS POEMS

No collected edition of Shakespeare's non-dramatic works appeared in his lifetime; nor did any such authoritative collection appear posthumously. The edition of Shakespeare's *Poems* published by John Benson (1640: STC 22344) is clearly derivative and unreliable, depending wholly upon available printed sources which it debases and rearranges. Subsequent seventeenth-century collections of poems spuriously attributed to Shakespeare, and works ambiguously attributed to 'W.S.', are discussed elsewhere in this volume, in the section on 'Canon and Chronology'.

The canon of Shakespeare's miscellaneous verse must therefore be based upon two kinds of sources: early editions which attribute to him individual poems (*Passionate Pilgrim*, 'The Phoenix and Turtle'), and manuscript attributions, mostly occurring in miscellanies compiled between 1625 and 1650. Unlike Donne or Ralegh, Shakespeare is not often mentioned in such manuscripts; the few ascriptions which do occur are not contradicted by other, more reliable sources; most of the poems involved can be linked to Shakespeare's personal acquaintances (often by means of biographical connections which are unlikely to have been widely known in the mid-seventeenth century). Individual items are separately discussed below, but as a class these manuscript attributions seem to deserve more respect than they have hitherto been accorded. The printed attributions, by contrast, probably deserve less respect, since publishers had an obvious motive for misattribution, while the compilers of private miscellanies did not.

Because of the biographical interest of some of the miscellaneous manuscript poems, they have most often been discussed by biographers, not textual critics. Rowe began this tradition, discussing the Combe epitaph in the 'Life'; Steevens, Malone, and Boswell appended further examples of such occasional verse to their reprinting of Rowe's biography, and the most detailed twentieth-century discussions are those of Chambers, Schoenbaum, and Honigmann. Only Adams has considered a group of these poems from a textual rather than a biographical perspective. Chambers noted in 1930 that there was 'no complete collection' of such attributions, and he did not attempt to supply one; subsequent scholars have added to his list piecemeal, but no complete collection has until now been attempted.

We have not included items based on sources which cannot now be traced. Steevens, for instance, in 1778 (i. 204-5) transcribed a note allegedly transcribed by William Oldys (1696-1761) from 'Poetical Characteristicks, 8 vo. MS. vol. I. some time in the Harleian Library; which volume was returned to its owner'; this note recorded 'Verses by Ben Jonson and Shakespeare occasioned by the motto to the Globe Theatre.—*Totus mundus agit histrionem*':

> *Jonson.*
> If, but *stage actors*, all the world displays,
> Where shall we find *spectators* of their plays?
> *Shakespeare.*
> Little, or much, of what we see, we do;
> We're all both *actors* and *spectators* too.

Both the Oldys manuscript and its source are lost; we do possess a marginal note by Oldys in a printed volume, but it does not attribute the verses and offers a different text of them (Chambers, *Shakespeare*, ii. 274-82). In the circumstances one cannot responsibly afford the attribution much credit. Equally suspect is a ballad stanza satirizing one 'Lucy', reported by Steevens (vol. i, part 2, p. 223) from Oldys on the testimony of 'a very aged gentleman living in the neighbourhood of Stratford', who repeated it from memory; Capell (*Notes*, ii. 75) identified Steevens's source for the stanza as Mr Thomas Jones (died 1703?). Malone printed the entire ballad (Boswell, ii. Appendix). Malone also printed, from a lost manuscript of 1727-30, a report of an incident *c.*1690, in which Professor Joshua Barnes transcribed another ballad on Lucy which he had heard in Stratford (vol. i, part 1, 107; Chambers, *Shakespeare*, i. 20, ii. 257). Schoenbaum (pp. 79-87) sceptically discusses the whole Lucy episode. Even less reliable is Francis Peck's 1740 printing of an epitaph on Tom Combe (reproduced in Schoenbaum, 186).

Chambers noted a number of items discussed in miscellaneous nineteenth-century sources (*Shakespeare*, i. 550). Two of these reported by Halliwell (*Marriage*, 93) are in fact only attributed in the manuscript to 'W.S.'; both (Crum A 130, F 100) were written by William Strode (1602-45). Another piece ('From the fair Lavinian shore') was reported by Thoms (pp. 49-50), who claimed that the poem was attributed to Shakespeare in John Playford's *Musical Companion* (1673: Wing P2490). Though one stanza of the poem is printed there (p. 115), the words are not attributed. The stanza, and its music, had been printed earlier in John Wilson's *Cheerfull Ayres or Ballads* (1660: Wing W2908), p. 3; five stanzas of the same poem appeared in the anonymous *Prince D'Amour* (1660: Wing R2189), pp. 177-8, three stanzas in Edward Phillips, *Mysteries of Love and Eloquence* (1658: Wing P2066), p. 70, and three stanzas were printed as Song 159 in the anonymous *New Academy of Complements* (1669: Wing N529); none of these sources attributes the piece. A single stanza also appears, unattributed, in an autograph Playford manuscript of several Wilson songs (Folger MS V.a.411, fol. 9). Crum records two manuscript copies in the Bodleian (F 767); each is of the same single stanza with music, and each is headed 'Glee a 4 Voc.' followed on the same line by 'Dr Wilson'. The attribution to Wilson is undoubtedly intended to refer to the musical setting; Crum assigns the poem to 'Robert Davenant'. Robert was the elder brother of Sir

William Davenant, and a fellow of St John's College, Oxford, preferred to the parsonage of West Kington, Wiltshire (see *DNB* for Sir William D'Avenant); we know of no other poems ascribed to him, nor of the basis for Crum's attribution. A seventeenth-century tradition, reported by Aubrey, recounts that Shakespeare often stopped at the house of William and Robert's parents, and that William was suspected of being Shakespeare's bastard son (Chambers, *Shakespeare*, ii. 254).

These circumstances are worth reporting only because Thoms refers to another source for the attribution to Shakespeare: a manuscript miscellany compiled before 1631 by 'Richard Jackson' (now Edinburgh University Library MS H-P, Coll. 401). Since the printed attribution appears to be a ghost, Shakespeare's claim rests entirely upon this manuscript. Here, though, the ascription of 'From the fair Lavinian shore' to Shakespeare appears to be based on a misunderstanding. Folio 60ᵛ of the manuscript is headed, in the top margin, 'shakespeares rime he made at the myter in fleete streete'. There then follow, in what appears to be another hand, 27 lines of verse, the first 7 of which burlesque 'From the fair Lavinian shore'. After these 27 lines, at the bottom of the page, occurs the following garbled version of lines 29-32 of Jonson's 'Inviting a Friend to Supper' (*Works*, viii. 65) written in what seems to be the same hand as the heading, and marginally identified, also in the same hand, as 'shake|speare | rime':

> Giue me a cup of rich canarie wine
> wch yet's the myters (thē he drinkes, after sayes/
> but now is mine
> of wch had Horace & Anacrᵉᵒⁿ tasted
> their liues as well as lines till now had lasted.

The heading thus appears to refer not to the burlesque of 'From the fair Lavinian shore', but (incorrectly) to these four lines. Since John Payne Collier was the first to draw attention to this manuscript (*History*, iii. 275-6), the heading, the marginal note, and the four lines themselves may all be forgeries. The entire manuscript—which we traced only shortly before this volume went to press—deserves further investigation.

In 1836, Collier printed the texts of two other poems. One, attributed to 'W.S.' and dated 1606, was allegedly found in a seventeenth-century English manuscript miscellany in the Hamburg City Library; Collier says its existence was communicated to him by 'the late English Professor at the University of Heidelberg' (*New Particulars*, p. 66). It consists of three six-line stanzas, and begins 'My thoughts are wing'd with hopes, my hopes with love: | Mount, Love, unto the Moone in clearest night'. Even if this manuscript is genuine, the 'W.S.' ascription is ambiguous (see 'Canon and Chronology'); and Collier failed to note that the song was printed in Dowland's *First Book of Songs or Airs* (1597: STC 7091). Less ambiguous are the initials 'W.Sh.' which Collier reports appended to a 62-line court entertainment, which begins 'As this ys endelesse, endelesse be your ioye; | Valew the wish and not the wishers toye' (*New Particulars*, pp. 64-6). Chambers does not mention either item in his catalogue of known or suspected Collier forgeries (*Shakespeare*, ii. 384-93); we have not attempted to trace either manuscript.

For the manuscript poems printed in this edition we have checked, personally or at second hand, the first-line indexes for the Bodleian, Folger, Rosenbach, Yale, Harvard, Huntington, and British Libraries; there might, of course, be other copies in the many manuscripts in other collections. (Beal's invaluable *Index* unfortunately does not list manuscripts of Shakespeare's miscellaneous poems: he confines himself to the printed canon, and does not treat the poems in *The Passionate Pilgrim* which are not independently attributed to Shakespeare elsewhere.) We hope that increased familiarity with these neglected poems will alert other scholars to their presence, attributed or unattributed, in other sources.

In preparing this edition Stanley Wells has taken primary responsibility for *The Passionate Pilgrim* and 'The Phoenix and Turtle', and Gary Taylor for the remainder. Notes to the modern-spelling text are indicated by '(M)'.

G.T., S.W.W./(W.L.M., G.T., S.W.W.)

WORKS CITED

Adams, J. Q., 'Shakespeare as a Writer of Epitaphs', in *The Manly Anniversary Studies in Language and Literature* (1923), 78-89
—— ed., *The Passionate Pilgrim* (1939)
Collier, John Payne, *The History of English Dramatic Poetry, and Annals of the Stage to the Restoration*, 3 vols. (1831)
—— *New Particulars Regarding the Works of Shakespeare* (1836)
Crum, Margaret, *First-Line Index of English Poetry 1500-1800 in Manuscripts of the Bodleian Library Oxford*, 2 vols. (1969)
Halliwell, J. O., ed., *The Marriage of Wit and Wisdom* (1846)
Honigmann, E. A. J., *Shakespeare: the 'lost years'* (1985)
Schoenbaum, S., *William Shakespeare: A Documentary Life* (1975)
Strode, William, *Poetical Works*, ed. Bertram Dobell (1907)
Thoms, William J., *Anecdotes and Traditions* (1839)

A SONG

This untitled poem survives in at least two seventeenth-century manuscript miscellanies. The first, Bodleian Rawlinson poet. MS 160, is one of a number of manuscripts amassed by Richard Rawlinson (1689-1755) and donated to the Bodleian in 1756; the presence of this poem, attributed to William Shakespeare, was noted in Bodleian catalogues compiled by Falconer Madan (1895) and Margaret Crum (1969). Malone is the earliest Shakespeare scholar known to have seen the manuscript; he referred to the Elias James epitaph (see below) and to Basse's Epitaph on Shakespeare (see Commendatory Poems and Prefaces). Malone's interest in the two other items was biographical, and his failure to mention 'Shall I die' is, in context, not surprising. Nevertheless, Malone was remiss either in not examining the entirety of the miscellany, or in failing to report this item— for whether or not he credited its authenticity himself, his own opinion did not entitle him to suppress an early attribution. However, like subsequent scholars Malone made no attempt at a systematic survey of manuscript attributions. This fault was perpetuated by Chambers, who (like Malone) personally examined the manuscript, transcribing the Elias James epitaph, noting two poems which help to date the miscellany, and (mis)reporting its version of the Basse epitaph. An unknown number of modern scholars also examined the manuscript, without reporting the Shakespeare attribution; we know of at least four, and Foster[1] claims to know of fourteen. The failure of modern scholars to report the item almost certainly results from an assumption that, appearing as it does in a well-known and catalogued manuscript in a major library, its existence had already been made known, and its attribution discredited, long before; only a historian of Shakespearian attribution was likely to be aware of the total editorial silence on this item. Even scholars convinced that the attribution was erroneous would almost certainly have reported it, if aware that previous editors had overlooked it. The Bodleian text was first published (*New York Times* and London *Sunday Times*, 24 November 1985), and its attribution first discussed, by Taylor[1]. The poem's publication precipitated a flurry of critical and scholarly comment, much of it conducted in newspapers and periodicals. In this Introduction and the following textual notes we do not attempt to reproduce all the commentary (already voluminous) on the subject of the poem and its authenticity; Taylor[4] provides a history and bibliography of the first months of the controversy.

Publication of the Bodleian text led to the discovery, by Dr Stephen Parks, of another text in the Beinecke Library at Yale (*New York Times*, 25 December 1985). Osborn b.197 is a manuscript miscellany compiled by Tobias Alston; its text of the poem (pp. 135-6) differs from the Bodleian text (fols. 108-9) in a number of readings, and does not attribute the poem.

Most attention has been devoted to the question of the authenticity of the Bodleian attribution. Taylor[1] defended the general reliability of the miscellany's attributions; his account was challenged in details by Robbins, Beal, and Foster[1]; Taylor[3] responded to these comments and attempted to substantiate the manuscript's credentials in more detail. Four of its 54 other attributions are questionable; but in three of these four cases the mistake (assuming it is one) is widespread in texts of the period. The Shakespeare attribution cannot be due to such causes; nor is the poem plausibly attributable to William Strode (1602-45), whose initials might have been misinterpreted as Shakespeare's. Attribution of the poem to Shakespeare rests not only upon the general accuracy of the miscellany, but also upon the general reliability of manuscript attributions to Shakespeare, and the fact that the miscellany contains another poem—the Elias James epitaph—also plausibly attributed to Shakespeare.

Taylor[1] also considered a variety of internal evidence which supported the external evidence of the Bodleian attribution. One element of this evidence was a comprehensive list of verbal parallels between the poem and the Shakespeare canon, including necessarily a good many commonplace ideas and images. Criticism of Taylor's internal evidence has hitherto been largely confined to selective quotation of and commentary upon the more commonplace or trivial items on this list. Taylor[3] reported the results of a comparison of the original list with the available concordances to nine other major poets of the period; even after the parallels duplicated in other writers have been eliminated, twenty-two remain—some, in our opinion, striking. These verbal parallels are supported by the evidence of rhymes, by the proportion of *hapax legomena*, by the chronological clustering of 'rare' words; all these features, like the verbal parallels, confirm each other in associating the poem with Shakespeare's work in the early to mid 1590s.

Further internal evidence has been provided by other scholars. The closest parallel for the poem's stanza structure—as noted first by Harriett Hawkins (privately), then by Robbins—is with *Dream* 3.3.36-46/1430-40. The beginning of Robin Goodfellow's charm, like the first six lines of each stanza in the poem, has the following rhyme-scheme: aa|bb|c|dd|ee|c (where the vertical rules indicate line-breaks). In each case, the short lines with internal rhymes consist of only two metrical feet, composed of two or three syllables; the third and sixth lines consist of trochees. (A poem ('Obsequies') attributed to 'W.S.' and included by Bernard Dobell in his edition of Strode has a related though not identical rhyme scheme and uses short, irregular lines; Dobell regards its attribution to Strode as doubtful.) Bradley Efron and Ronald Thisted, applying a statistical test they developed in 1976 based upon a profile of Shakespeare's vocabulary, confirmed that the relation between the distribution of frequencies of words in the poem matched that of the Shakespeare canon almost perfectly (see Kolata).

For the most part, objections to this cumulative external and internal evidence have been based upon personal judgements of the quality of the poem. Such criticisms have been considered in detail in Taylor[2] and Taylor[3]; they are intrinsically, and in practice, unreliable. More specific negative evidence—chiefly accumulated by Pendleton—is considered in detail below. It may safely be said that the internal and external evidence for the authenticity of 'Shall I die' has been considered in greater detail than the evidence for any other single short poem printed in this or any other edition of Shakespeare's works, with the possible exception of 'A Lover's Complaint'. Although, like any other attribution, it might be discredited in future by the discovery of new evidence, until such time it seems to us to deserve a place in a collected edition.

The relationship of the Bodleian (B) and Yale (Y) manuscripts is of most importance in establishing the poem's text (not its authenticity). Taylor[3] noted that the two miscellanies as a whole are clearly related to one another, on the basis of the number of items they have in common. Taylor is at work upon an annotated catalogue of the contents of both manuscripts, relating the contents of each to one another and to manuscripts in other major, catalogued collections; this should eventually provide a basis for further investigation of the practices and sources of both compilers. It can, however, already be noted that B and Y share two variants in Basse's Epitaph on Shakespeare which do not appear in any of the other manuscript and printed texts we have collated (see Commendatory Poems). On the evidence of the datable poems they contain, B seems to have been compiled in 1637, Y in 1639.

Other things being equal, the relative dating of the manuscripts would lead an editor to choose B as copy-text. Taylor[3] gave, within the limits of space available, a summary assessment of the textual variants; as promised, the variants are discussed in greater detail here. Foster[2] challenged the choice of B as copy-text; his interpretations of individual variants are recorded and considered below. It will be seen that we find his criteria for preferring variants inconsistent and implausible. Foster[2] also alleged that Y's lineation more accurately reflects the source manuscript from which both B and Y derive, at whatever remove. Y treats each stanza as consisting of only four (long) lines; B by contrast generally divides each stanza into ten (mostly short) lines. (For exact details see the Lineation Notes.) Foster[2] argued that B's use of initial majuscules is haphazard, and that its distribution of such majuscules is best explained on the assumption that its copy had them only at the beginning of the four 'long' lines indicated by Y. But in any arrangement of the poem, we would expect the first word of a stanza or a sentence to begin with a majuscule; certain other words—like 'I'—are also consistently capitalized. Once we eliminate such cases, the differences between B and Y are more striking than the similarities. Y's arrangement might be due to a simple desire to save space—it is, in general, a more cramped manuscript than B—or it might reflect a musical text, in which the words of one or two stanzas were written underneath the appropriate line of music, and the other stanzas crowded together below. Whatever the choice of copy-text, we do not think many editors or readers will be tempted by Y's arrangement, since B's work more helpfully makes visible the stanza's formal structure.

The choice of copy-text is in this instance a matter of convenience rather than substance. It does not affect the validity of the attribution, since there can be no suspicion that B derives directly from Y; on the evidence of the shared errors at lines 68 and 82, both derive at whatever remove from a scribal transcript of the author's poem (whoever the author might be). In only the most utterly indifferent of the variants might our choice have been different had we selected Y as copy-text. But we remain of the opinion that B is the more reliable, and the one closer to an authorial source.

The other editorial problem raised by a work of this nature is the criteria for emendation. In evaluating metrical variants between B and Y, or those affecting rhymes, the internal evidence of other lines and stanzas will suffice. Taylor[1] has been criticized, particularly by Robbins and Foster, for the modernization at line 5 and the emendation at line 68, on the grounds that both are designed to lend artificial support to the attribution of the poem to Shakespeare. A text which makes sense is more likely to have been written by Shakespeare than one which does not; but any editor of the poem will recognize that, whoever wrote it, when it left the author's hands it probably made sense, and that the sense could easily have been corrupted in several places by the exigencies of transmission in Caroline manuscript miscellanies. In emending the text where it seems to us manifestly corrupt we have, where relevant, drawn attention to parallels between the emended phrase and the canon to which this poem is, on other grounds, attributed; but this process is no more circular than all textual emendation.

In contrast to other items in the *Complete Works*, this poem has not previously been edited; editorial history persuades us that future editors will improve upon our own preliminary efforts, and the following textual notes are therefore offered with particular diffidence.

WORKS CITED

Beal, Peter, correspondence in *TLS*, 3 January 1986, p. 13 and 24 January 1986, p. 88

Burgess, Anthony, 'Is it really Shakespeare?', *New York Times Book Review*, 22 December 1985, p. 3

Efron, Bradley, and Ronald Thisted, 'Estimating the number of unseen species: How many words did Shakespeare know?', *Biometrika*, 63 (1976), 435

Foster[1]: Donald Foster, correspondence in *TLS*, 24 January 1986, pp. 87-8

Foster[2]: Donald Foster, correspondence in *TLS*, 7 March 1986, p. 247

Giroux, Robert, correspondence in *New York Times Book Review*, 19 January 1986, p. 24

Kolata, Gina, 'Shakespeare's New Poem: An Ode to Statistics', *Science* (24 January 1986), 335-6 (reporting on research by Efron and Thisted); also 'So bethumped with words', *Science 86*, 7 (May 1986), 65-6

Pendleton, Thomas, correspondence in *New York Times Book Review*, 19 January 1986, p. 24

Robbins, Robin, *TLS*, 20 December 1985, pp. 1449-50 (response to Taylor[1])

Sheen, Erica and Jeremy Maule, correspondence in *TLS*, 17 January 1986, p. 61

Taylor[1]: Gary Taylor, *New York Times Book Review*, 15 December 1985, pp. 11-14; *TLS*, 20 December 1985, pp. 1447-8 (substantively the same article)

Taylor[2]: Gary Taylor, *New York Times Book Review*, 22 December 1985, p. 3 (reply to Burgess)

Taylor[3]: Gary Taylor, *TLS*, 31 January 1986, pp. 123-4 (summary and evaluation of previous comment)

Taylor[4]: Gary Taylor, 'Scholarship and the Media: The Case of "Shall I Die?"' (forthcoming)

NOTES

Title A Song] This edition; *not in* B, Y. For the poem's genre, see Burgess, Taylor[2], Sheen and Maule, Beal, and Taylor[3]. This title does not, of course, commit one to the view that the lyric was written for music, though that is a possibility.

4 tend] B, Y. The first publication of the poem (*New York Times*, 24 November 1985) read 'fend'; although this typographical error was corrected by an editorial errata note the next day, subsequent mass media quotations almost inevitably reproduced the error. Both manuscripts undoubtedly read 'tend', the aphetic form of *attend*, meaning 'wait upon' (passive) in contrast to 'send' (active).

5 (M) sue] B (ſhewe), Y (ſhew). The initial *New York Times* publication modernized B to 'show'; Taylor[1] accepted Stanley Wells's subsequent conjecture that 'shew' was an unusual spelling of *sue*, by analogy with the unique spelling 'shue' in the first quarto of *LLL* at 3.1.199/930 (which all editions since 1631 have accepted as a spelling of the word *sue*). Whether we regard 'sue' as a modernization or an emendation, it seems necessary here, and those who object to it have not explained what sense they make of 'show'. 'Shall I appear'—the only sense which can be extracted from the absolute intransitive use of the verb—does not seem pertinent. In terms of the rhyme, either word is acceptable: see Dobson, ii. §244, and *Shrew* 4.1.196-7/1756-7 (where 'shew' meaning *show* rhymes with 'shrew'). Whether we regard 'sue' as an emendation or modernization, the Shakespearian form in *LLL* is pertinent in explaining either the spelling or the error (based upon misinterpretation of the unusual spelling). Foster[2] accuses Taylor of 'concealing the emendation', but Taylor[1] drew public attention to it, on the occasion when it was first made; Foster also accuses Taylor of claiming that 'shew' was an Elizabethan, or Shakespearian, spelling of *sue*, whereas Taylor[1] made these claims of only the 'sh-' form. But the 'sh-' form is the only peculiarity of the spelling; *sue* is indifferently spelled, throughout the period, with '-ew' or '-ue' to represent the vowel sound.

10 ioÿing] Y (Ioyninge); Ioying B. Although Taylor[3] and Foster[2] agree in rejecting Y's variant, in the senses 'physically coupling' and 'marrying' it adds more to the passage than B's 'Ioying': 'ioying neuer' simply repeats the idea in 'mourn' and 'despair', whereas 'Ioyninge neuer' contains a commitment to be satisfied with no other liaison—either you, or no one. Errors involving the authorial omission of a tilde, or the compositorial failure to spot it, are very common in the period (and in Shakespeare's canon).

11 vent my lust] Pendleton alleges that this must mean 'express my love', and that Shakespeare never uses the word *lust* elsewhere simply as a synonym of *love*. But it is impossible to assert that *lust* here must mean 'love' alone, rather than 'desire' or 'carnal appetite'—especially given the double meaning of *vent* as 'utter'

and 'discharge, emit', which in conjunction with *lust* in its explicitly sexual sense creates a double entendre entirely characteristic of the style of the poem (and of Shakespeare).

12 explaine, inward] Philip Brockbank remarks (*privately*) that the wit of the contrasted prefixes seems typically Shakespearian. There are in the canon 33 examples of 'in-' and 'ex-' prefixes in the same line, including 'inward . . . exprest' (*Lucrece* 91) and 'inwards . . . extreames' (*2 Henry IV* 4.2.103-4/2301).

13 by my] B, Y; by *conj*. MacD. P. Jackson (*privately*). See line 16. Jackson would retain B's 'breeding'.

13 conceaving] This edition; breeding B; bred Y. Taylor[2] noted that the failure of lines 13 and 16 to rhyme in B was probably due to error, especially as B here repeats the word used in the identical position of the previous stanza. In this period (and in Shakespeare) *breeding* and *conceiving* were used synonymously, and Shakespeare uses *conceive* with the preposition *by* elsewhere (*Henry V* 5.2.51/2906, etc); scribal synonym substitution would be particularly easy here, under the influence of the preceding stanza. The emendation restores not only the rhyme but the syllabic correspondence between the third and sixth lines of this stanza. By contrast, Y's variants produce a rhythmical pattern found nowhere else in the poem: an ionic (two unstressed followed by two stressed syllables) instead of the trochaic sequence found in the third and sixth lines of every other stanza. Moreover, it is difficult to see how B's reading could derive from Y's, which is perfectly sensible, rhymes, does not have the '-ing' terminations, and does not call for editorial intervention. On the other hand, Y's text could easily derive from B's, the failure of B to rhyme leading to sophistication of the final word of both lines: 'breeding' shortened to the past tense 'bred', 'deceiving' shortened to 'dead'. B's 'deceaving' leads into 'suspicious doubt' in a way that 'dead' does not at all; and B's anacoluthon is much more likely to be sophisticated into Y's grammatical tidiness than Y to be sophisticated into B.

16 all my hopes] B, Y; hope's *conj*. MacD. P. Jackson (*privately*). See line 13. Jackson would retain B's 'deceaving'; he notes that 'The emendation regularizes the lines' otherwise hopelessly anomalous metre and obviates the need for a dash indicating a break in the syntax'; he proposes that 'all my' was caught from the line above. But this still leaves the shared reading in line 13 unexplained; coincidental double error in both texts seems to us less likely than the supposition that B is correct except for a single substitution in line 13.

16 deceaving] B; dead Y. See preceding note.

17 Suspitious doubt, oh] B; O sufpitious doubt, Y. Foster[2] also prefers B.

19 Fie] Y; Fly B. Taylor[1], working from the Harvard concordance (based upon the 1974 Riverside edition), cited two parallels for the B reading from *Twelfth Night* 2.4.52/912; but J. M. Lothian and T. W. Craik in their new Arden edition of *Twelfth Night* (1975) successfully defended the Folio reading 'Fie away, fie away' (accepted also by this edition). Thus, Y is defensible and idiomatic; but it also provides what is undoubtedly the rarer reading (Taylor[3] found no parallels in any of the concorded canons).

21 accuse] B; excufe Y. Foster[2] regards Y's reading as an indifferent variant, but it still seems to us nonsense to say that it is an abuse to excuse her.

25-6 Ioy or annoy | or affliction] Pendleton comments: 'The syntax is odd here, for the speaker foresees not three but only two possibilities: good fortune ("joy") or misfortune (in the form of either "annoyance" or "affliction"). The correlatives "or . . . or"—the Elizabethan equivalents of our "either . . . or"—thus connect two components that, taken together, comprise a single alternative within a larger "either . . . or" situation. By my count, Shakespeare uses the "or . . . or" correlatives 47 times but never in this strange syntactical manner.' Compare 'Neuer harm, | Nor spell, nor charm' (*Dream* 2.2.16-17/639-40), which is exactly parallel, except that it uses the negative form of the correlative pair ('nor . . . nor' instead of 'or . . . or'); as in the poem, the nouns contrasted by this construction—*spell* and *charm*—are to all intents and purposes synonymous. (This parallel should perhaps be added to the list of striking verbal correspondences between the poem and the Shakespeare canon; noticeably, it comes from the same period as most of the others.) *OED* notes this use of *or* to 'connect two words denoting the same thing' (*conj.*[2] 6); Schmidt gives a number of Shakespearian examples.

27 I will] B; ile Y. An indifferent variant, since Y produces a rhythm paralleled in stanzas 8 and 9. We have preferred B only because its rhythm is commoner in the poem.

28 pleasure] B; pleafures Y. Indifferent, though the singular is more usual in this idiom.

29 wil] Y; wit B. Already conjecturally emended, independently of Y, by Taylor[1]. G. Blakemore Evans (*privately*) notes a parallel for the B reading at *Romeo* 2.3.58/1118—'sure wit'—but in context B seems nonsensical.

29 seeme] B, Y; seeke G.T. *conj*. *Not seek to* occurs at *Two Gentlemen* 2.7.21/950, *K. John* 4.2.133/1754, and *As You Like It* 1.3.101/545; 'not seeme to' only at *Coriolanus* 5.1.8/2733. See also *K. John* 2.1.133/409, where 'would blot' means 'wishes to blot'. (The jingle 'not blot' occurs at *Lucrece* 1322.)

29 blot‸] ~ . B; ~ , Y

30 doth] B; to doe Y. Foster[2] regards Y as an indifferent variant, but the metre is unparalleled in the final line of any other stanza, and we cannot see that it makes acceptable sense: B means 'wronging him [who] doth her duty' (which would indeed blot someone's reputation), whereas Y means 'wronging him [in order?] to do her [self?] duty'. Alternatively, one might take 'for . . . him' as a parenthesis, so that 'to doe her duty' carries on from 'I will bear her pleasure with patience'; but quite apart from the strain on the syntax, this leaves the referent for 'him' unexplained.

30.1 4] Y; *not in* B. The beginning of the fourth stanza falls at the top of fol. 108ᵛ in B.

31 it] B; I Y. Foster[2] agrees that B is preferable, though he denies that Y is nonsensical; we can discern no sense in 'I did seem . . . I did walk'.

34 I did walke, I did talke] Giroux objects to this singsong doublet; but compare 'talke with you, walke with you' (*Merchant* 1.3.33-4/350-1).

38 pleasure] Y; our pleafure B. Y's reading was independently conjectured, on metrical grounds, by Mrs E. E. Duncan-Jones (*privately*).

41 did find] B; it fine Y. Y's reading does not agree with the past tenses of the preceding or following lines; nor does it rhyme. The reading could easily have arisen from misreading of 'find' as 'fine', followed by sophistication of the preceding word.

44 shooke] B, Y. Pendleton objects that Shakespeare only uses this verb of 'a rough action'; but compare for instance *History of Lear* Sc. 17.30/2232, 'there she shooke | The holy water from her heauenly eyes' (of Cordelia's tears), which seems no more violent than the shaking of hair by the breeze. One must also make some allowance for the fact, here as elsewhere, that the severity of the rhyme scheme may have led to some wrenching of the poet's normal idioms (whoever the author).

49 You] Y; Then B; Them TAYLOR[1]. Y's reading might be a conjectural sophistication of the nonsense of B; 'Them' is grammatically acceptable (as at *K. John* 4.2.50/1671) and more easily explains the error. But it seems safer to accept the reading of a manuscript here. See Taylor[3] for an appreciation of the contribution to the sense provided by Y's address to the readers of the poem.

50 force] B; forces Y. Foster[2] calls Y's reading 'clearly preferable', but it produces a rhythm found in the final line of no other stanza, by means of a plural which adds nothing to the sense (if anything detracting from it), and could easily have arisen from contamination by 'beawties'.

52 neat] This edition; next B, Y. The passage as it stands in the manuscripts seemed to us corrupt from the moment we attempted to modernize the punctuation. Pendleton rightly objects that 'without wrinkles' is an absurd modifier for 'eyebrows'—which

is how 'browes' must be glossed in the unemended text. However, this absurd interpretation of 'browes' depends entirely upon the word 'next' in line 52, which is intrinsically suspicious, repeating as it does a word in the previous line. If the author had written 'neat', the adjective could easily have been corrupted to 'next' under the influence of context. With 'neat', the passage can be construed in two different ways: either her 'forehead . . . doth lie', and 'Her faire browes' are a separate item in the catalogue of her attractions; or 'neat' begins a new sentence, in which 'browes' are essentially synonymous with 'forehead'. The ambiguity of the syntax allows 'those' (line 54) to be understood as alluding to either brows or eyebrows. *Neat* is a common adjective of praise in this period, being variously glossed as 'delicate, pretty' (Schmidt), 'clean; elegant, fine; nicely made or proportioned' (*OED*, a. 1, 5, 7b, 12); 'handsome, splendid, fine' (Massinger, *Plays and Poems*, ed. Philip Edwards and Colin Gibson, 5 vols. (1976), v. 319); it can also be used adjectivally. There may also be a pun on the sense 'tidy', in relation to 'without wrinkles': at *Henry V* 5.2.228-9/3086-7 ('Old Age, that ill layer vp of Beautie, can doe no more spoyle vpon my Face') and *2 Henry IV* 5.1.76-7/2769-70 ('you shall see him laugh til his face be like a wet cloake ill laide vp') Shakespeare metaphorically envisages a wrinkled face as the consequence of a piece of clothing having been untidily stored.

55 win] B; winns Y. B is grammatically more regular, but Y is possible; Foster[2] agrees in preferring B, but the variants are indifferent.

57-8 In her cheekes . . . beawties banner] W. L. Godshalk (*TLS*, 7 March 1986, p. 247) cites parallels from Surrey and Wyatt (deriving from Petrarch) for the conceit of 'the facial banner'. But none of these includes the specific locution 'in her cheeks' or specifically identifies the banner as 'beauty's'—the two features which link this passage strongly with *Romeo* 5.3.94-5/2784-5. Taylor[3] did not find these elements in any of the concorded canons.

61 Thin] B; Then Y. Pendleton objects that in Shakespeare's usage *thin* 'never characterizes that which is desirable'—though he gives an example of a positive sense himself from *Hamlet* 1.5.70/687. Foster[2] defends Y, on the grounds that 'thin' is not an adjective one usually finds in commendation of Elizabethan lips; on similar grounds Mrs E. E. Duncan-Jones had independently conjectured 'Twin' (*privately*). But the Yale manuscript itself contains another poem which, among the 'thirty things' for which Helen of Troy 'was admird', mentions her 'thinne' lips (p. 121); nor do 'fat' lips seem a desirable alternative. Shakespeare's other allusions to lips do not make clear any preference on the matter; moreover, *thin* is clearly related to *fed* and *sweets*, later in the sentence. (This might explain the error, but such associative links between words are characteristic of Shakespeare, even when the exact correspondences between the related images cannot be logically worked out.) Foster interprets 'Then' as a sequential adverb, citing the two examples of *next* in the previous stanza; but the first is indicative of place, not sequence (meaning 'next to'); so, if it is not emended (see note to line 52) is the second; nor are the intervening items (eyes, cheeks) introduced by such an adverb; nor is *then* used in a similar fashion elsewhere in the poem. Although Taylor[3] was mistaken in describing Y's reading as nonsense, it still seems to us to produce poor sense. Either reading could easily be an error for the other, or 'Twin', which produces a finer image than either: Shakespeare describes lips as 'twyning Cherries' which 'shall their sweetnes fall | Vpon thy tastefull lips' at *Kinsmen* 1.1.177-8/209-10.

68 their culd] This edition; thats cald B; thats calld Y; the world TAYLOR[1] (Wells). Wells's conjecture provides a common catchphrase ('all the world'), for a passage where both manuscripts offer nonsense. The emendation adopted here assumes a much easier misreading of the second word, involving misinterpretation of one letter instead of three; for the error, compare *Troilus* 2.3.259/1420, where all editors follow F in reading 'cull' in place of the nonsensical reading 'call' of Q (set from Shakespeare's foul papers); Shakespeare's open spurred 'a' makes misreading as 'u' particularly easy and common. The spelling 'culd' for the past participle is consistently used in the Shakespeare good quartos (*LLL* 4.3.232/1474, 5.1.88/1690, *Titus* 4.1.44/1443, *Romeo* 4.3.7/2356). For the first word, while it is true that 'ye' can easily be misread 'y^t', the terminal 's' in 'thats' is difficult to explain by such a process; by contrast, terminal 's' can easily be misread as 'r'. On purely mechanical grounds, then, 'their culd' provides a more plausible emendation of the manuscript reading; moreover, the relatively unusual word 'culd' is more likely to stimulate scribal misunderstanding than the common phrase 'all the world'. For the image, compare *LLL* 4.3.232-3/1474-5: 'Of all complexions the culd soueraigntie | Do meete as at a faire in her faire cheeke'. (None of the other concorded canons examined in Taylor[3] contains any comparable parallel.)

70 admiracions] B (admiracons); admiration Y. B's simple literal error was not recorded in earlier collations because it is not substantive; Y's singular is clearly an error, on the evidence of the rhyme with 'commendations'; it is probably not even intentional, because the 'n' occurs at the very edge of the page. Giroux (in ignorance of Y's reading) calls the plural 'a solecism' and opines that the 'singular would obviously be better', taking the need for the plural for the sake of the rhyme as evidence of a sloppiness uncharacteristic of Shakespeare. It seems to us, instead, that one of the most characteristic merits of Shakespeare's style, remarked upon by many critics, is his ability to turn abstract nouns into concrete ones, just as the author of this poem does by turning *admiration* into 'individual acts of admiration, hence *admirations*'. The 'solecism' could easily have been avoided by use of the singular in line 68.

71-3 Pretty . . . asunder] Foster[2] claims that these lines refer to 'the woman's breasts, largely exposed by a plunging neckline (as was the fashion among gentlewomen from about 1612 to 1640)'. Although the fashion for baring the breasts completely is a Jacobean development, it is clear that this passage does not refer to totally exposed breasts, but only to the exposed cleavage—the 'bare' or 'bar' which 'parts those plots which besots'. The fashion for plunging necklines developed much earlier than 1612. As Lacey Baldwin Smith notes, 'The Elizabethan compromise was to open the ruff in front, expose the neck and breasts, and offset the ruff with stiff gauze butterfly wings at the back of the head. A similar compromise was achieved by retaining the complete ruff but lowering the cut of the bodice and covering the upper chest and shoulders with a partlet . . . often of a highly transparent material' ('Style is the Man: Manners, Dress, and Decorum', in *William Shakespeare: His World, His Work, His Influence*, ed. John F. Andrews, 3 vols. (1985), i. 211). Numerous examples can be seen in the art of the period, as for instance in Roy Strong's *Tudor and Jacobean Portraits*, 2 vols. (1969); see also Janet Arnold, *Patterns of Fashion: The cut and construction of clothes for men and women c.1560-1620* (1985). Taylor[1] agrees with Foster[2] that the main reference is to the woman's breasts; Foster[2] objects to Taylor's suggestion that there may be a subsidiary reference to her thighs. As this is the only reference to any part of the body lower than the neck, it seems to us difficult to rule out a variety of erotic senses, especially given the vagueness of 'plots'.

71 Pretty] Y (Pritty): A pretty B. Y is metrically preferable, and B could result from the easiest of interpolations.

71 bare] Pendleton comments that *bare* is 'almost always a deprecatory word' which 'never carries the sense of sexual enticement or attraction it has here'. But Shakespeare's only use of *bare* as a substantive (as here), at *Lover's Complaint* 95, occurs in a description by a frustrated lover of the beloved's irresistible attractions.

72 which] B; witte Y. Foster[2] agrees that Y is nonsensical.

73 asunder] B; funder Y. Foster[2] denies that Y is 'nonsensical' (Taylor[3]); but *sunder* is last recorded by *OED* as an adverb with the sense 'apart, asunder' in 1539. Y's reading is also, as Foster acknowledges, metrically anomalous.

74 It is] B; is it Y. Foster² regards Y as an indifferent variant, but a question seems to us difficult to justify here.
75 soe rare] B; so | so rare Y. Y's duplication is undoubtedly accidental, resulting from its run-over of the line.
77 (M) mis-shape] B (miſhap), Y (miſhappe). For the sense and spelling see *OED*. Taylor¹ and other printings have retained the B spelling, interpreting it as *mishap*, in the sense 'unlucky accident'; but this seems less appropriate than 'misshapen feature'. There may well be a pun on 'accident' (with the idea that substance only declines from 'Nature's perfection' through accident), but the primary meaning seems to be 'mis-shape'. The word does not appear elsewhere in the Shakespeare canon; seven of his eight uses of the adjective occur in early works, from *Duke of York* to *Romeo*.
82 from] TAYLOR¹; For B, Y. For the error compare Folio *Hamlet* 1.3.120/533.
83 plenty] Y (plentye); in plenty B. Y's reading produces syllabic correspondence in the third and sixth lines of this, as of other stanzas.

UPON A PAIR OF GLOVES

This poem is found on p. 177 of a manuscript miscellany, now in the possession of the Shakespeare Birthplace Trust Records Office (MS ER.93), compiled by Sir Francis Fane (1611-80). It was first described in print by E. M. Martin—in 'Shakespeare in a Seventeenth Century Manuscript', *The English Review*, 51 (1930), 484-9—and has been further discussed by E. I. Fripp, *Shakespeare: Man and Artist*, 2 vols. (1938), 401-2, and Mark Eccles, *Shakespeare in Warwickshire* (1961), 57-8. Alexander Aspinall was a Stratford schoolmaster from 1582 to 1624. The pun on 'will' would be characteristic of Shakespeare; previous commentators seem not to have noticed the striking parallel at *Pericles* Sc. 14.17/1373: 'Yet my good will is great, though the gift small'. The poem is followed on the same manuscript page by a transcription of 'Shaxpers Epitaft' (from the gravestone) and the final couplet of the Combe epitaph. The purpose of the peculiar spelling and spacing of the word(s) before 'Asbenall' is obscure: though perhaps merely an error for 'Alisander', it may conceal some private joke, and we have preserved it in the hope that some better explanation might be forthcoming.

THE PASSIONATE PILGRIM

The first, octavo edition (O1; STC 22341.5), printed probably in 1599, survives only partially, in two sheets bound with two of the second edition (O2; STC 22342), which is dated 1599. The fragmentary O1 was first identified in 1939; it contains poems 1-5 and 16-18. O2 is control-text for the remaining poems. The third edition (O3; STC 22343), of 1612, is based on O2, but adds poems by Thomas Heywood. The standard bibliographical study is in J. Q. Adams's facsimile edition, which records press variants in O2.

The present edition includes poems 1 and 2, variants of Sonnets 138 and 144, because they may preserve genuine Shakespearian variants; they are printed among 'Additional Passages', after the Sonnets. We omit poems 3, 5, and 16, extracts from *Love's Labour's Lost*, which had already appeared in print; we also omit poems 8 and 20, which had appeared in Richard Barnfield's *Poems in Divers Humours* (1598: STC 1488), 11 (from Bartholomew Griffin's *Fidessa More Chaste than Kind* (1596: STC 12367)), and 19, a version of three of the six stanzas of Christopher Marlowe's 'Come live with me and be my love' along with the last stanza of the reply attributed to Sir Walter Ralegh, which were to appear in *England's Helicon* (1600: STC 3191).

Four additional stanzas of poem 12 appear in the 1628 edition of Thomas Deloney's *Garland of Good Will* (STC 6553.5), sigs. G4-G5ᵛ, the earliest known surviving edition of a work to which Nashe had referred in 1596. Not all the poems in *Garland* are by Deloney. Poem 17 appeared, without ascription, in Thomas Weelkes's *Madrigals* (1597: STC 25204).

Some of the poems in our edition are found in manuscript collections now in the Folger Library: 4 is in both MS V.a.339 (Fo2), fol. 203 and MS V.b.43 (Fo3), fol. 22; 7 is in Fo2, fol. 203ᵛ; 18 is in MS V.a.89 (Fo1), p. 25 and in Fo2, fol. 191ᵛ. They are partially collated by Rollins; the variants collated below are based on a fresh consultation of the manuscripts.

For ease of reference we have retained the traditional numbering of the eleven poems we print here. Shakespeare's authorship of these poems is, however, very doubtful: the publisher had an obvious commercial motive for false ascription, and the reliability of the ascriptions which can be tested does not inspire confidence.

WORKS CITED

Adams, J. Q., ed., *The Passionate Pilgrim* (1939)
Prince, F. T., ed., *Poems*, Arden (1960)
Rollins, H. E., ed., *Poems*, New Variorum (1938)

NOTES

4.1 Sweet] O1; ffaire Fo3
4.4 could] O1; can Fo3
4.5 eare] Fo2; eares O1
4.8 soft] sought Fo2
4.10 refusde] O1; did ſcorne Fo3
4.10 her] O2; his O1
4.11, 12 touch . . . smile . . . least] O1; take . . . bluſht . . . ſmild Fo3
4.13 queen] O1; *not in* Fo3
4.14 rose] O1; bluſht Fo3
4.14 ah] O1; ô Fo3
6.12 this] O1; the Fo2
6.14 Oh] O1; ah Fo2
7.11 mids] O1; midſt O3, Fo2
9.2] *Lacuna first noted by* MALONE
10.1, 2 (M) faded] O2 (vaded)
10.8, 9 (M) left'st] O2 (leftts)
12.12 (M) stay'st] O2 (ſtaies)
13.2, 6, 8 (M) fadeth . . . faded . . . faded] O2 (vadeth . . . vaded . . . vaded)
14.17 Philomela sings] PRINCE (Cambridge); Philomela fits and fings O2
14.19 (M) dite] O2 (ditte)
14.20 daylight] This edition (anon. *conj.* in Cambridge); *not in* O2
14.24 (M) sighed] O2 (ſight)
14.27 a moone] MALONE 2 (Steevens); an houre O2
17.3 (M) faith's] O1 (Faithes)
17.4 (M) Heart's] O1 (harts)
17.6 wot),] *Weelkes's Madrigals*; ~)ₐ O1
17.16 (M) freighted] O1 (fraughted)
17.27 Heard] This edition; Heards O1
17.27 stands] O1; ſtand *Weelkes's Madrigals, England's Helicon*

17.28 backe] *Weelkes's Madrigals*; blacke O1
17.33 lasse] *Weelkes's Madrigals*; loue O1
17.34 mone] *England's Helicon*; woe O1
18.12 sale] O2; sell MALONE (Steevens)
18.45 be] Fo2; by O1

POEM 18: AN ALTERNATIVE VERSION

Poem 18 is found in two Folger manuscripts, Fo1 and Fo2 (see above). Both represent a version of the poem clearly deriving from an alternative textual tradition to that behind the version printed in *The Passionate Pilgrim*, and the differences between these two versions of the poem show every sign of authorial variation. Since, however, Shakespeare may not have written the poem, the interest of the variants is limited.

The text which follows is edited from Fo2 (fol. 191ᵛ), a commonplace book compiled by two anonymous owners between about 1630 and 1650. J. P. Collier later added 83 ballads on blank leaves of the manuscript (see Giles E. Dawson, 'John Payne Collier's Great Forgery', *SB* 24 (1971), 1-26); Collier was not responsible for any of the *Passionate Pilgrim* texts in the miscellany, but he almost certainly interpolated the attributions to 'W.S.' which were added, in another ink and hand, at the bottom of this and the other poems from *The Passionate Pilgrim*. (The miscellany also contains, on fols. 205ᵛ-207ᵛ, unattributed extracts from *Richard II*.) In spite of the miscellany's late date, it seems to represent a text of poem 18 closer to the author's original than that in Fo1, also a miscellany, though one which appears to have been compiled much earlier, c.1585-1600. Fo2 also contains texts of poems 6, 4, 9, 7, and 1 (fols. 203-203ᵛ), which are grouped together but which show little variation from *The Passionate Pilgrim*. Beneath the poem we record variants (and readings accepted) from Fo1.

when yᵗ thine eye hath chofe yᵉ Dame
& ftald yᵉ Deere yᵗ yᵘ wouldst strike
let reafon rule thinges worthy blame
as well as partiall fancie like
5   afke counfell of some other head:
neither vnwife nor yet vnwed:/

And when yᵘ comeft thy tale to tell
whet not thy tongue wᵗʰ filed talke
least she fome fubtle practice fmell
10 a cripple foone can fpie a halt
but plainely faye yᵘ lovest her well:
& set thy body foorth to sell.

vnto her will frame all thy waies
spare not to spend & chiefely there
15 where thy expence may sound thy praife
& still be ringinge in her eare
yᵉ strongest towres fort or towne,
yᵉ goulden bullet beateth downe/

Serue always wᵗʰ affured trust
20 & in thy suite be ever true
vntill thy lady pue vniust
preffe never thou to change for newe
when time doth ferue thee be not slack
to pffer though shee put it back

25 What if shee frowne wᵗʰ forowes be bent
her cloudie lookes will calme at night
when yᵗ phaps shee will repent
yᵗ so diffembled her delight
& thrice defire it ere be day,
30 yᵗ wᵗʰ fuch scorne she put away./

What if she striue to trie thy strength
& ban & braule & fwere thee nay
her feeble force will yeeld at length

& craught will caufe her thus to say
35 had women bene as stronge as men,
by cock you had not had it then/

Thinke women seeke to match wᵗʰ men
to liue in finne & not to faint
here is no heaven be holy then
40 till time shall thee wᵗʰ age attaint
were kiffinge all yᵉ Ioyes in bed:
one woman would another wed/

A thoufand wiles in wantons lurkes
diffembled wᵗʰ an outward shew
45 the tricks & toyes the meane to worke
yᵉ cock yᵗ treads them doth not know
hast yᵘ not heard it saide full ofte:
a womans nay doth stand for nought/

ho now enough & more I feare
50 for if my mʳˢ hard this songe
she would not stick to warme my eare
to teach my tongue to be so longe
yet would shee smile here be it sayde
to heere her feacrets thus bewrayde./

2   wouldst] wouldeft
4   partiall fancie] fancye parcyall
5   afke] take
6   vnwed] vnwayde
10 fpie] Fynde
10 a halt] one haulte
11 faye] Fo1; *not in* Fo2
12 body] pson
13 vnto] And to
13 waies] Fo1; way Fo2
15 expence] expences
16 & still be ringinge in] (in in); by ringinge allwayes in
17 towres fort] caftell tower
18 beateth] hathe beat
20 ever] humble
21 vntill] vnleffe
22 preffe] feeke
22 for newe] anewe
23 thee be] then be
25 if shee frowne wᵗʰ forowes] thoughe her frowninge browes
26 calme] cleare
26 at] ere
27 when yᵗ phaps shee will] And fhe perhappes will fone
28 so] fhe
29 thrice] twice
29 it ere] ere it
31 if] thought (*altered to* thoughe)
31 thy] her
32 ban] chide
32 fwere] faye
34 will caufe] hathe taught
36 by cock] in faythe
36 not had] not got
37 women seeke] (wome); woemen loue
38 to liue in finne & not to faint] and not to liue foe like a fainte
39 be] they
40 till time shall thee wᵗʰ age] beginne when age dothe them
43 A thousand wiles in wantons lurkes] The wyles and guyles that in them lurkes
45 the meane to worke] (he); & meanes to woorke
46 doth] fhall
47 hast yᵘ] have yoʷ
47 it] that
49 ho now] Nowe hoe
49 & more] too muche
50 if my mʳˢ hard] if my ladye heare

51 would] will
51 warme] ringe
53 ſmile] bluſhe

Note: In the manuscript of Fo2, stanzas are not separated, and the closing couplet of each stanza (except the fourth and last) is run on as one line.

THE PHOENIX AND TURTLE

The poem first appeared in 1601, untitled and ascribed to 'William Shake-speare', among poems appended to Robert Chester's *Loves Martyr: or Rosalins Complaint. Allegorically shadowing the truth of Loue, in the constant Fate of the Phoenix and Turtle* (STC 5119; sigs. Z3ᵛ-Z4ᵛ). The appended poems are called 'DIVERS | Poeticall Essaies on the former Sub-|iect; viz. the Turtle and Phoenix. | Done by the best and chiefest of our | moderne writers, with their names sub-|scribed to their particular workes: neuer before extant'. The poem was also included in Benson's unauthorized 1640 edition of Shakespeare's *Poems* (see the section on 'Canon and Chronology').

NOTES

Title] See above.
44 compounded,] GILDON 2; ~.
58 rest.] Q; ~, MALONE

VERSES UPON THE STANLEY TOMB AT TONG

These verses are preserved in at least four seventeenth-century manuscripts: University of Nottingham, Portland MS Pw.V.37, p. 12 (N), Folger MS V.a.103, Pt. I, fol. 8 (Fo), Bodleian MS Rawlinson poet. 117, fol. 269ᵛ (B), and an autograph manuscript of Sir William Dugdale's, appended to his *Visitation of Shropshire* in 1664, now at the College of Arms, MS C.35, fol. 20 (D). N and Fo are in the same hand, and are plausibly dated *c*.1630; both attribute the poem to Shakespeare, as does Dugdale. B does not attribute the verses or identify for whom they are written; but textually it is clearly corrupt and derivative. It omits two lines altogether (lines 5-6), transposes two others (lines 11-12 follow line 4), contains another seven substantive variants not supported by the other texts, and conflates all the verses as a single poem, beginning 'Not monumentall stones'. For purposes of ascription and text, B is useless.

The words of the verses themselves are virtually identical in N, Fo, and D; but their title, subject, and arrangement present serious editorial problems. D (first printed by Malone, vol. i, part 1, 130; see also vol. i, part 2, 284-5) appends the verses to a description of the monument at Tong; he does not give them a title, or identify for whom they were written, but he does set them out in the order adopted here ('Aske . . . Not monumental stone . . .'), and does indicate their position on the monument. N and Fo, which in this respect constitute one witness, set them out in the opposite order, identifying what they treat as the first poem (lines 7-12) as 'An Epitaph on Sʳ Edward Standly Ingrauen on his Toombe in Tong Church', and entitling what they treat as a second poem (lines 1-6) 'On Sʳ Thomas Standley'. This version was first printed by Halliwell (1853: i. 162), from Fo, and has dominated subsequent discussion of the verses, by Chambers (*Shakespeare*, i. 551-4) and Honigmann (*Shakespeare*, pp. 77-83). But the treatment of the verses as two separate epitaphs could easily arise from their ambiguous placement on the tomb; are two matching sets of verses at opposite ends of a tomb two poems, or the two stanzas of one poem? 'Aske who lies here' certainly looks like the beginning of an epitaph, and line 7 follows naturally from line 6. The verses thus may have originally constituted a single epitaph, which was later construed as two, perhaps because by the time the tomb was erected there were two Stanleys to whom it might apply. Given the uncertainty about the date of the tomb, the uncertainty about which Stanley is being honoured, and the differences between the manuscripts, it seems best to preserve as much ambiguity as possible, editorially. We have therefore modified the manuscript title from N and Fo, preserving the reference to the Stanley tomb at Tong (on which D agrees), but omitting the specific allusions to Edward and Thomas; we have taken the architectural headings from D, in the order in which he gives them, thus preserving the architectural ambiguity about whether one poem or two is intended.

Stylistically, there is no reason to deny Shakespeare's authorship of the verses; his early connections with the Stanley family are demonstrable, but unlikely to have been widely known in 1630 or 1664. Chambers alleges that Dugdale may have taken his attribution from the early miscellany, but it is intrinsically more probable, in context, that it derives from his visit to the church, and hence presumably represents independent testimony to Shakespeare's authorship. Chambers, from the other inscriptions on the tomb, dates it *c*.1600-3; the verses may be earlier or later, depending upon their subject, but in our ordering of the poems we have accepted this conjectural date.

The inscriptions still survive on the tomb; they are reproduced in the General Introduction, and serve as copy-text. The manuscripts have no textual authority, though they do correct one obvious literal (line 6, 'MONYENTAL' on the tomb).

NOTES

3 STONY] earthlye B
3 IS] his B
7 STONE] ſtones Fo, B
7, 8 OVR] thy B
9 MEMORY] monument B
10 AND] or B
11 WHEN ALL TO TYMES] And when to tyme B

ON BEN JONSON

This epitaph is preserved in at least four seventeenth-century manuscripts: Bodleian MS Ashmole 38, p. 181 (B), Folger MS V.a.180, fol. 79ᵛ (Fo1), Folger MS V.a.275, fol. 177 (Fo2), and twice, with minor variants, in Archbishop Thomas Plume's MS 25 in Maldon, Essex (P1: fol. 77; P2: fol. 51). Of these, B (compiled by Nicholas Burgh *c*.1650) and P (*c*.1657) attribute it to Shakespeare; we have adopted B as copy-text. In P1, Jonson 'made of himſ⟨elf⟩' the first two lines; 'ſhakſpr̃ tk. ye pen fr̃ him & made ys'. But in P what Shakespeare made was a new beginning to the epitaph ('Here lies Benjamin—wth short hair up. his Chin—'), followed by lines 3-4 as reproduced by the other manuscripts.

B and P1 are reproduced photographically in Schoenbaum, 206; P1 and P2 are transcribed, with other Plume anecdotes, in Jonson, *Works*, i. 184-8. For a defence of its authenticity see Adams, 'Epitaphs'.

NOTES

Title On Ben Johnson] Ben: Johnsons F01 (*in a series of epitaphs*); A Epitaph on Ben Johnson F02
0.1-3 Mr Ben . . . his Epitaph] B; *not in* F01, F02. For P see head-note.
1 lies Ben] B, F01, P; lieth F02
2 That] B, F02; Who F01, P
2 was once] B, F01, P1; once was F02, P2
2.1 he giues . . . wrighte] B; *not in* F01, F02
3 Who while hee liu'de] B; In his life F01; while he liued F02; who wl he lived P
4 being dead is] B; hee's dead, F01; hee is dead is worth F02; he's bd is P1; he is bd is P2. Chambers (*Shakespeare*, ii. 247) transcribes P's 'bd' as 'buried'.

AN EPITAPH ON ELIAS JAMES

This poem is known to exist in two texts. The first occurs in a manuscript miscellany of c.1637 (Bodleian MS Rawlinson poet. 160, fol. 41), which also contains a text of 'A Song' (see above). This manuscript entitles the poem 'An Epitaph' and attributes it to 'Wm: Shakeſpeare'. This text has been known to scholars since Malone first drew attention to it. The other text was first noticed in 1986, as a result of the interest generated by the attribution to Shakespeare of 'A Song'. Hilton Kelliher, in a letter to the *London Review of Books* (22 May 1986), p. 4, noted that the poem was included in the 1633 edition of John Stow's *Survey of London* (STC 23345), prepared by Anthony Munday, H. Dyson, and others; it appears there among a collection of additional 'Monumentall Inscriptions', where it is said to have stood in 'Andrew Wardrope' (i.e. the church of Saint Andrew by the Wardrobe), 'In the South Ile, at the lower end of the Church' (p. 825; sig. Aaaa3). Leslie Hotson, in *Shakespeare's Sonnets Dated* (1949), pp. 111-40, 207-17, had shown that Shakespeare would have been acquainted with Elias James, a brewer with premises close to the theatre; but Hotson could not prove that the James whom Shakespeare knew was the James for whom this epitaph was written. Kelliher, having identified the site of the tomb on which the epitaph was originally written, traced James to a burial register entry (dated 24 September 1610) in the parish of St Andrews: 'Elias James Brewer who gave 10 pounds to the poore of this parishe'. As Kelliher notes, this reference clearly establishes that the brewer Shakespeare knew was indeed the subject of the epitaph, and that he 'died a godly life'. The tomb is no longer extant, having failed to survive the Fire of London and the subsequent restoration by Wren; the 1633 transcript therefore represents our only evidence of the wording of the inscription. We have therefore chosen the 1633 text (S) as copy-text, since it is earlier than the manuscript (B) and claims to have been copied directly from the tomb. As Kelliher notes, however, the use of italics for 'Helias Iames' and the division of the lines (pleased| yet| nature| debt| reposes| died| strongly| verified| death| tell| life|) both clearly derive from the edition itself, not the tomb, and so have been ignored. The inscription was probably carved throughout in capitals if, as claimed, it once appeared on a tomb, but we have not attempted to restore these.

The first printings of the Oxford edition wrongly state that James died in 1620.

NOTES

3 reposeth] B; repoſes S. B's form appears at *Richard II* 2.4.6/1241; S is unparalleled in the canon. More generally, the -eth termination, being obsolescent in the 1630s, is more likely to have been altered than imposed by a copyist.
4 strongly in him] S; in him ſtrongly B
5 a] S; the B. Compare 'a known truth' (*All's Well* 2.5.29/1224); there is no Shakespearian parallel for B's alternative.

AN EXTEMPORARY EPITAPH ON JOHN COMBE, A NOTED USURER

Versions of this epitaph are widespread. Full accounts are given by Chambers (*Shakespeare*, ii. 138-41) and Schoenbaum (pp. 184-6), though the latter does not mention the Dobyns or Fane manuscripts. We have adopted as copy-text Folger MS V.a.147, fol. 72 (F01) transcribed in 1673 by 'I Robert Dobyns being at Stratford upon Avon & visiting the Church there'. Dobyns, who also transcribed the epitaph on Shakespeare's tomb, noted that the Combe epitaph was 'vpon ye Monument of a noted usurer', and that 'Since my being at Stratford the heirs of Mr Combe have caused these verses to be razed so yt now they are not legible'. They probably were originally carved throughout in capitals, but we have not attempted to restore these.

The verses were first printed in the form that we give them, and associated with Combe (died 1614), in an addition (L2v) to Richard Brathwait's *Remains after Death* (1618: STC 3582), as reissued with P. Hannay's *A Happy Husband* (1619: STC 12747). This text (BR) does not attribute the verses. In 1634 a Lieutenant Hammond noted, after a visit to Stratford, that 'Mr Wm Shakespeere' had written 'some witty, & facetious verses' upon 'Mr Combe'; but he did not record them (British Library, MS Lansdowne 213, fol. 332v). In Bodleian MS Ashmole 38, p. 180 (B1), Nicholas Burgh (c.1650) quoted the last line and a half ('Who . . . Combe'), under the title 'On John Combe, A Couetous rich man Mr Wm Shak-spear wright this att his request while hee was yett liueing for his Epitaph'. In 1681 John Aubrey, in Bodleian MS Aubrey 6, fol. 109 (B2), also records the lines as 'this extemporary Epitaph' by Shakespeare upon Combe; Rowe repeats the story (vol. i, p. xxxvi). The epitaph is also transcribed, as by Shakespeare upon Combe, in Folger MS V.a.345, p. 232 (F03); an unattributed text is in Folger MS V.a.180, fol. 79v (F02), compiled by Sir Francis Fane c.1655-6, and on p. 177 of another Fane manuscript (see above, 'Upon a Pair of Gloves'). The collations record all variants in these texts.

The poem could have been attributed to Shakespeare simply because he was the most famous citizen (and the only poet) of Stratford, where Combe lived and died. The joke in the first couplet became a favourite epitaph for usurers, as Chambers shows, beginning in 1608 with 'Ten in the hundred lies under this stone, | And a hundred to ten to the deuil he's gone.' The Combe epitaph, allegedly written during his lifetime, could of course be earlier than 1608; or its author could have adapted as the opening for a Stratford epitaph a witticism he had heard in London. The pun on 'engraued' in line 1 seems Shakespearian, and does not occur in alternative versions of the epitaph, which usually rhyme on 'stone' and 'gone'.

NOTES

1-2 Tenn . . . saued] *not in* B1, FANE, Fo2; Ten in the Hundred the Devill allowes | But Combe will have twelve he swears & vowes: B2; Ten in' th hundred by ye lawes you may haue | But Twenty in' th hundred the diuel doth craue' Fo3
1 here lyes] This edition; here lyeth Fo1; lies here ROWE; must lie BR
1 engraued] Fo1, ROWE; in his graue BR
2 A] Fo1; 'Tis ROWE; but BR
2 his soule is not saued] Fo1 (*subs.*), ROWE; whether God will him have? BR
2 not] now Fo1
3 If . . . lyes] Hay hay sayth Tom toule who is FANE, Fo2
3 anny one] Fo1, B2; any Man ROWE; any Fo3
3 lyes] B1, B2, Fo3, ROWE; lyeth Fo1, Fo2
4 Oh ho] Fo1 ROWE; Ho ho FANE Fo2; Oh Br; hough B1; Hoh! B2; Bau wough Fo3
4 tis my] FANE, Fo1, Fo3, B2, ROWE; my BR; t'is my sonn Fo2, B1

ANOTHER EPITAPH ON JOHN COMBE

The only source for this epitaph is Bodleian manuscript Ashmole 38, p. 180, in which it immediately follows the other Combe epitaph, and is attributed at the end 'W. Shak.'. Combe did leave a generous bequest to the poor (Public Record Office, Prob. 11/126; formerly P.C.C. 118 Wood), and a bequest to Shakespeare. Unlike the other epitaph, this one is not common, nor ever associated with anyone else, and it fits well the pattern of amicable relations between Shakespeare and the Combe family.

NOTES

Title] *not in* MS
0.1 W. Shak.] hee MS

UPON THE KING

This poem is printed beneath the engraving of King James I on the frontispiece of the edition of his *Works* (1616: STC 14344), edited by James Mountague (or Montagu), Bishop of Winchester. The twinned engraving and poem reappeared in the 1620 edition (STC 14345), and in the Latin edition (1619: STC 14346). The poem is also found beneath another engraving of James, and one of Charles I, and it seems clear from various states of the engraving that the engraving and poem were sold separately as a broadsheet (Hind, pp. 57-8, 259-60, 287; Plates 28, 154, 174). None of these printed sources attributes the poem, or gives it a title. Of the several manuscript texts from the period in the Bodleian, British Library, and Folger, most do not attribute it; but Folger V.a.160 (*c*.1633-4, according to Beal) and V.a.262 (*c*.1650) entitle it, respectively, 'Shakespeare on the King' (p. 2, second series) and 'Shakespeare Upon the King' (p. 131). The attribution was first drawn to scholarly attention in Boswell's edition (i. 481), probably reporting Malone's discovery, though it is unclear whose opinions the edition is quoting. Boswell's source was clearly V.a.262.

Bodleian MS Ashmole 38 entitles the poem 'Certayne verfes wrighten by m^r Robert Barker | His ma^{tis} Printer vnder his ma^{tis} picture' and concludes it 'finis R B' (p. 39). This clearly refers to the 1616 edition, printed by Barker, and hence 'wrighten' is ambiguous: it may mean 'composed' or only 'engraued'.

It would not have been unusual for Shakespeare to compose, as many of his contemporaries did, such a poem in praise of the monarch; it might have been written especially for the *Works*, or written for some other occasion and subsequently used for the *Works*. Shakespeare was the chief dramatist of the only theatrical company patronized by King James himself, and in the absence of a poet laureate might have served such a function. Stylistically the poem gives little evidence of authorship, being, as it is, so constrained by the conventions of its genre. We note below a few verbal parallels, which seem not to have been recorded hitherto.

We adopt the 1616 *Works* as copy-text, and do not record variants in the manuscripts; whoever the author, the 1616 text is authoritative.

WORK CITED

Hind, Arthur M., *Engraving in England in the Sixteenth and Seventeenth Centuries: Part 2, The Reign of James I* (1955)

NOTES

1 Crounes . . . compasse] Compare *Richard II* 2.1.100-1/714-15 ('thy Crowne, | Whose compasse'), *Henry V* 4.1.291/2072 ('compassing the Crowne').
2 Triumphes . . . tombes] See *Venus* 1013-14 ('tombes . . . triumphs'); *triumph(s)* are also associated with death or funerals at *Romeo* 2.5.10/1358, *Titus* 1.1.176/176, and *Caesar* 3.1.150/1238.
3 Of . . . none] Compare Sonnet 74.7 ('The earth can haue but earth').
3 partaker] Compare *Winter's Tale* 2.1.43/555 ('partake . . . knowledge').
4 knowledge] For the association of knowledge and sovereignty see *History of Lear* Sc. 4.227/721 (a scene full of topical analogies to King James). Shakespeare often associates knowledge with the divine aspect of humanity: see *LLL* 1.1.113/113, *As You Like It* 3.3.7-8/1573-4, *Contention* 4.7.73/2530, *All's Well* 1.1.28-29/29-30 ('If knowledge could be set vp against mortallitie').

EPITAPH ON HIMSELF

These words are carved on the slab covering the poet's grave in Stratford. Schoenbaum (250-1, 262) notes three late seventeenth-century manuscript attributions of the epitaph to Shakespeare, and he reproduces two of these documents. Antedating all three is Folger MS V.a.180, fol. 79ᵛ, compiled by Sir Francis Fane *c.*1655–6, which quotes among a number of other epitaphs (including those on Jonson and Combe elsewhere attributed to Shakespeare) the last two lines of this one, and describes it as 'Shakespeares on himselfe'. Also probably antedating Schoenbaum's earliest noted attribution of the poem to Shakespeare is Folger MS V.a.232, a compilation begun in 1669 by Henry Newcombe, which claims that the epitaph was placed on Shakespeare's tomb 'by his own appointm̃' (p. 63).

SIR THOMAS MORE

'THE Booke of Sir Thomas Moore' survives only in manuscript (British Library Harleian MS 7368). The manuscript contains material written in a number of different hands, most of them clearly identifiable as those of theatrical professionals of the late sixteenth and early seventeenth centuries. The chief editorial problems raised by the play concern its date and authorship; these are discussed in 'Canon and Chronology'. The two passages attributed to Shakespeare occur on folios 8, 8^v, 9, and 9^v (Addition II.D) and on fol. 11*^{b} (Addition III). The first passage is written in Hand D (believed to be Shakespeare), with later alterations by Hand C (a theatrical scribe). The second passage is written in Hand C, probably copying the work of Hand D.

Because these passages survive in a theatrical manuscript, they confront editors with problems not elsewhere encountered in Shakespeare's dramatic works. Hand D's handwriting is not particularly legible; it has been further obscured by the author's (and scribe's) additions, deletions, and revisions. Fol. 8 was badly obscured by a misguided Victorian attempt to preserve the manuscript by pasting thick tracing paper over some of the pages. The tracing paper was eventually removed from the verso, though much damage had already been done; it remains on the recto, which is as a result in several places simply impossible to decipher with confidence. Fol. 9 is the most legible. Such difficulties do not seriously endanger the verbal substance of Addition II.D, but they do cause uncertainty about some of its incidentals—and those incidentals are of unusual importance, seeing that they may be the only truly Shakespearian incidentals we possess. (They have been usefully concorded by Clayton.)

The very authority of the details of presentation of the manuscript creates an editorial problem. Unlike Shakespeare's other dramatic work, his contribution to *Sir Thomas More* has not been pre-processed by a Renaissance printer, and hence preserves conventions which do not normally survive into print. For instance, although there can be no doubt that Hand D abbreviated certain speech-prefixes, there can be equally little doubt that most of the abbreviated speech-prefixes in printed texts also derive from the author; in accordance with our editorial policy throughout the Complete Works, we have for the convenience of readers consistently expanded and normalized such prefixes in both the original- and the modern-spelling editions. Likewise, where Hand D changed his mind in the course of writing, we have accepted his revised intentions; we do not preserve, in the reading text, intentions which he had abandoned. Nevertheless, it seemed desirable, within the context of the Oxford edition, to provide scholars with a diplomatic transcript of the allegedly holograph pages, and we accordingly print such a transcript below. In addition, the recto of fol. 9 is reproduced in the General Introduction (Illustration 4); fol. 8 is so difficult to decipher that a photograph is of little use, and the verso of fol. 9 contains only three or four letters. (All four pages are reproduced in Schoenbaum, 112-15; many other reproductions have been printed.)

The diplomatic transcript follows the conventions (but not all of the readings) of Greg^2. The notes record differences of interpretation and apparent slips of the pen—the most common being an inexactness about the precise number of minim strokes in certain letters or combinations of letters. In re-examining the manuscript we have been guided by the advice of G. R. Proudfoot, and by 'Peter Blayney's numerous new readings and unpublished notes' (referred to by Melchiori, p. 101). It has been alleged that the spacing of words in D's addition is irregular: Pollard, followed by Urkowitz (p. 132), claimed that spaces occur anomalously in the middle of words, and Melchiori claims that Hand D shares with Shakespeare a habit of 'marking the end of a sentence in the middle of a line simply by leaving a wider space between its last word and the first word of the next sentence' (p. 104). We had intended to attempt a precise record of such anomalies, but after a renewed investigation of the manuscript neither we nor Proudfoot can see any evidence for such claims. As in all handwriting, the size of the gaps between letters and words varies, in ways which resist consistent transcription into print; but we cannot discern any significance in the fluctuations of spacing. If sometimes Shakespeare leaves slightly more space between a word which ends one sentence and that which begins another, that fact probably reflects no more than a pause in composition; it seems unlikely to represent a conscious strategy of 'punctuation'.

The nature of Hand D's contribution also creates editorial problems. Hand D wrote only a small part of a long text composed by several other playwrights; more important, his share apparently constitutes a late addition. We have no reason to believe, and many reasons to doubt, that Hand D helped to plan the play as a whole, in either its original or its adapted state; in fact, his contribution differs from all the others in the degree to which it ignores or contradicts the intentions of the larger work. In these circumstances, we have chosen to include only the additions attributable to Hand D, extracting them from the play, and treating them almost as though they were fragments of a lost work. The play of *Sir Thomas More*, like many other plays of the period, deserves to be read and appreciated in its own right; but we believe that most readers of Shakespeare's works are chiefly interested in the small portion of the play which Shakespeare apparently wrote.

The decision to present Hand D's contribution in isolation from the play as a whole has consequences, not always appreciated, for the editing of Addition II.D itself. As Melchiori forcefully argued, a number of Hand C's changes to the text result from his desire to make D's work more compatible with the surrounding play. If readers are interested primarily in Hand D's work, they should be able to read that work in the final form which Hand D gave to it, before it had been massaged by Hand C. In our edited text, therefore, we have accepted all Hand D's own revisions to the text, but have ignored Hand C's.

This procedure in some ways represents a departure from our practice elsewhere in the Complete Works, where we have generally regarded the more 'theatrical' text as a better embodiment of Shakespeare's final intentions. We have made an exception in this case in part because of the exceptional way in which we treat *Sir Thomas More* itself: the fragments we include cannot, in themselves, be appreciated as a 'play', but only as parcels of dramatic literature. But Hand D's involvement with this text also seems to us uncharacteristic of the involvement one would expect from Shakespeare in the production of his own plays. *Sir Thomas More* cannot have been considered, by anyone, as Shakespeare's property; it might even have been produced, in the end, by another company; the requirements of the play as a whole obviously and naturally took precedence over Hand D's minor contribution, apparently written with only a rather slapdash and casual interest in the thrust and detail of the work as a whole. In this instance Hand D's intentions had to bow to the needs of the play; but in Shakespeare's own plays, the intentions of the author and the needs of the play naturally coincided. For these reasons a procedure which seems to us reasonable elsewhere is better abandoned here.

G.T./(S.W.W.)

WORKS CITED

Clayton, Thomas, *The 'Shakespearean' Addition to The Booke of Sir Thomas Moore*, Shakespeare Studies Monographs, 1 (1969)
Dyce, Alexander, ed., *More: A Play; Now First Printed* (1844)
Evans, G. B., ed., *The Riverside Shakespeare* (1974)
Greg[1]: W. W. Greg, ed., *Sir Thomas More*, MSR (1911)
Greg[2]: W. W. Greg, 'Special Transcript of the Three Pages', in *Shakespeare's Hand in the Play of 'Sir Thomas More'*, ed. A. W. Pollard (1923)
Melchiori, Giorgio, 'Hand D in *Sir Thomas More*: An Essay in Misinterpretation', *SSu* 38 (1985), 101-14
Pollard, A. W., 'Shakespeare's Text', in *A Companion to Shakespeare Studies*, ed. Harley Granville-Barker and G. B. Harrison (1934)
Schoenbaum, S., *William Shakespeare: Records and Images* (1981)
Tannenbaum, Samuel A., 'Shakspere's Unquestioned Autographs and the Additions to *More*', *Studies in Philology*, 22 (1925), 133-60
Thompson, E. Maunde, *Shakespeare's Handwriting* (1916)
Urkowitz, Steven, *Shakespeare's Revision of 'King Lear'* (1980)

TEXTUAL NOTES

II.D.0.1 Lincoln] JENKINS; Enter Lincoln MS (Hand C). Hand D in writing the passage seems to have imagined that these characters were on stage already; he does not provide an entrance for them, and C obviously, at least in part, misinterpreted D's intention. Although in an edition of the whole play an entrance has to be provided somewhere, in isolation the fragment does not require one.

II.D.0.1 betts] JENKINS; Clown. Georg betts williamson MS (Hand C). Shakespeare does not provide a role for the clown or Williamson, or distinguish the two Bettes characters.

II.D.0.1 Sherwin] JENKINS; not in MS. See l. 35 below.

II.D.0.1–0.2 and prentisses armed;] JENKINS (subs.); others MS (Hand C)

II.D.0.2-3 Moor, the other sherif, Palmer, Cholmeley,] This edition (conj. Melchiori); not in MS (Hand C). Editors usually call for these characters to enter at l. 32.

II.D.0.3 stand aloof] This edition; not in MS. Melchiori has this second set of characters enter at another door, but it is not clear whether Hand D wanted them to 'enter' at all (see above); the scene as he apparently envisaged it only requires that they be somehow separated from the other group until l. 22, when the Sergeant intervenes.

II.D.29/29 now prentisses symple] This edition (conj. Melchiori); now prenty prentiſſes ſymple MS. Melchiori's explanation, that 'prenty' is 'a cue-word representing the beginning of the original speech' (p. 103), seems to us implausible; but it could be an unintended duplication, abandoned in mid-word but not cancelled.

II.D.35/35 SHERWIN] This edition; Sher MS (D); Williamson MS (C)

II.D.43/43 SOME] This edition (conj. Melchiori); all MS

II.D.44/44 OTHERS] This edition (conj. Melchiori); all MS (D; *deleted by* C)

II.D.55/55 SOME] This edition; all MS

II.D.56/56 OTHERS] This edition; all MS

II.D.91/91 ordere] GREG[1], BLAYNEY; orderd THOMPSON, GREG[2] ('doubtful'), EVANS

II.D.155-6/154-5 ONE] This edition; *All*. DYCE; all MS (opposite l. 154/153)

III.18/III.18 stings] This edition; ſtate MS. Scribe C's 'state' simply repeats the idea of 'natures' in the preceding line; serpents have sharp teeth, fangs, or stings, but it is clumsy to speak of their 'sharp state'; nor does 'state' contrast readily with the specific 'skinns' earlier in the line. For 'sharp stings' compare *As You Like It* 2.7.189/1112, *All's Well* 3.4.18/1468, *Winter's Tale* 2.3.87/869. Misreading of Shakespeare's spurred 'a' as 'in' and terminal 'e' as terminal 's' would be easy enough; t/g confusion is less normal, but the misreading could have been encouraged by misinterpretation of the sense, under the influence of 'natures'.

INCIDENTALS

Line references and lemmas refer to the transcript printed below.

3 Beeff] The first 'e' has been altered from some other letter.
5 Linco] 'in' has two minims only, but the first is dotted.
10 william] 'm' has two minims only.
10 trash,:] THOMPSON, GREG[2], EVANS; ~; GREG[1]
12 dung] 'un' has five minims.
17 ſeriant] The initial letter, though undoubtedly prominent, is probably minuscule (THOMPSON) rather than majuscule (GREG[1]); the letter form is Italian.
19 ſhowe] 'w' blotted, possibly altered.
22 how ſay yo[u] now prenty] Later addition.
22 prenty] 'n' has one minim only.
30 williamſon] Beginning of C's addition, written on top of D's 'Sher'.
30, 32 Shrewſbury] GREG[2], EVANS; Shrowſbury GREG[1], THOMPSON. Either interpretation is possible.
37 Wiſdome] GREG[1], EVANS; wiſdome THOMPSON, GREG[2]
38 all no . . . ſhr] Later addition; deletion of prefix apparently C's.

38 Shrewſbury] GREG, EVANS; Shrowſbury THOMPSON. Either interpretation is possible.
43 yeoman] 'o' altered, probably by Ċ, from some other letter.
45] This line and the rule above it were added later.
59 watchins] 'c' altered, apparently from the beginning of 'h'.
70 D] Crossed out by both D and C.
71 handycraftes] 'The termination *es* is probably intended, but the *e* is malformed' (Thompson), being represented only by a small blot (Greg²).
72 noyce] 'y' altered from 'w'.
80 gott·,·] GREG² (notes); ~ ; THOMPSON, BALD, GREG² (text); ~, GREG¹; ~ ;· EVANS
85 hand] A very small dot after this word; some stop possibly intended.
89 Bett͟e] Deleted by the same hand and ink as those in which the following prefix is written.
90 moor] First attributed to Hand D by TANNENBAUM, accepted by Greg (*Library*, IV, 9 (1928), 202-11), EVANS; attributed to Hand C by GREG¹, THOMPSON, GREG². The letter forms differ from those used by D elsewhere, but the ink appears to be his.
93 your] GREG², EVANS; yoʳ GREG¹, THOMPSON, BALD
101 and] 'n' has three minims.
103 &] Written on top of 'his', not above the line.
107 are‸] What GREG, THOMPSON, and EVANS record as a stop or raised stop appears to be merely the end of the flourish.
110 and your] 'A word was interlined for insertion between these two words, but it appears to have been wiped out while the ink was still wet' (THOMPSON). THOMPSON conjectured 'bend'; GREG², 'hye'; EVANS, 'hyde'; BLAYNEY, 'thoſe'; PROUDFOOT, 'ffye' (independently of Greg). The conjectures of Greg, Evans, and Proudfoot are much more plausible as interpretations of what is visible; Proudfoot's, unlike Greg's, makes sense as a replacement

for 'and'. Although Evans claims that 'hyde' makes sense in context, the description of kneeling as a process of 'hiding your knees' seems strained.
112-14 is . . . by obedienc] Deletions by Hand C, unless otherwise noted.
113 ryot,] BALD; ~ ; GREG¹, THOMPSON, GREG², EVANS
113 why] MELCHIORI alleges that this was deleted by Hand D independently of its deletion by Hand C; but we can see no evidence of any deletion mark other than C's. Metrically, the revised line is entirely acceptable with the interjection, which produces only a (common) extra unstressed syllable before the caesura.
113 warrs] Deleted by Hand D.
117 founde] 'un' has three minims only.
118 ther] 'r' altered from 'ir'.
122 alas alas] Deleted by Hand C.
125 .] GREG² thought that the indentation of 'as' occurred in order to avoid a 'small hole in the paper'; BLAYNEY identifies a smudged-out 'c'. We are not sure of Blayney's identification of the letter involved, but a smudged-out letter does seem likely.
127 flanders] 'r' is malformed
130 ſtraingers·,] This edition; ~. GREG¹; ~, THOMPSON, GREG², BALD; ~ ; EVANS
131 barbarous] Second 'r' altered from 'b'.
140 montaniſh] 'n' has three minims.
141 vs] Deleted by Hand C.
146 maieſtrat] BLAYNEY notes that the terminal 'e' recorded by previous transcribers is not fully formed, though perhaps intended.
147 found] 'un' has only three minims.
147 yt] GREG²; yᵗ BLAYNEY

TRANSCRIPT OF ADDITION II.D

Enter Lincoln. Doll. Clown. Georg betts   williamſon others
And A ſergaunt at armes

FOLIO 8ᵃ

Lincolne	Peace heare me, he that will not ſee [a red] hearing at a harry grote, butter at a levenpence a pou[nde, meale at] nyne ſhilling͟e a Buſhell and Beeff at fower nob[les a ſtone, lyſ]t to me	
~~other~~ Geo bett	yt will Come to that paſſe yf ſtrain[gers be ſu]fferd mark him	
Linco	our Countrie is a great eating Country, argo they eate more in our Countrey then they do in their owne	5
~~other~~ betts clow	by a half penny loff a day troy waight	
Linc	they bring in ſtraing rootes, which is meerly to the vndoing of poor prentizes, for what͟e ~~a watrie~~ a ſorry pſnyp to a good hart	
~~oth~~ william	traſh traſh,: they breed ſore eyes and tis enough to infect the Cytty wᵗ the palſey	10
Lin	nay yt has infected yt wᵗ the palſey, for theiſe baſterd͟e of dung as you knowe they growe in Dvng haue infected vs, and yt is our	

SIR THOMAS MORE

	infeccion will make the Cytty ſhake which ptly Coms through the eating of pſnyps	15
~~o~~ Clown · betts Enter	trewe and pumpions togeather	
ſeriant	what ſay y[ou] to t[he] mercy of the king do you refuſe yt	
Lin	you w[oo]ld haue [.s] vppon thipp woold you no marry do we not, we accept of the kinge mercy but wee will ſhowe no mercy vppõ the ſtraingers	20
ſeriaunt	you ar the ſimpleſt thinge that eu' ſtood in ſuch a queſtion	
Lin	now prenty how ſay you prentiſſes ſymple downe wth him	
all	prentiſſes ſymple prentiſſes ſymple X Enter the L maier Surrey Shrewſbury	25
~~Sher~~ Maior	hold in the kinge name hold	
Surrey	frende maſters Countrymen	
mayer	peace how peace I ~~ſh~~ Charg you keep the peace	
Shro·	my maſters Countrymen	
~~Sher~~ williamson	The noble Earle of Shrewſbury lette hear him	30
Ge bette	weele heare the Earle of Surrey	
Linc	the earle of Shrewſbury	
bette	weele heare both	
all	both both both both	
Linc	Peace I ſay peace ar you men of Wiſdome ~~ar~~ or what ar you	35
Surr	~~But~~ what you will haue them but not men of Wiſdome	
all	weele not heare my L of Surrey, ~~all~~ no no no no no Shrewſbury ſhr	
moor	whiles they ar ore the banck of their obedyenc thus will they bere downe all thinge	40
Linc	Shreiff moor ſpeakes ſhall we heare ſhreef moor ſpeake	
Doll	Lette heare him a keepes a plentyfull ſhrevaltry, and a made my Brother Arther watchin[s] Seriant Safes yeoman lete heare ſhreeve moore	

all	Shreiue moor moor more Shreue moore	45

FOLIO 8ᵇ

moor	[ev]en by the rule yoᵘ haue among yoʳ fealues Comand ftill audience	
all	[S]urrey Sury	
all	moor moor	
Lincolne bett<i>e</i>	peace peace fcilens peace	50
moor	Yoᵘ that haue voyce and Credyt wᵗ the ~~mv~~ nvmber Comaund them to a ftilnes	
Lincolne	a plaigue on them they will not hold their peace the deule Cannot rule them	
moor	Then what a rough and ryotous charge haue yoᵘ to Leade thofe that the deule Cannot rule good mafters heare me fpeake	55
Doll	I byth mas will we moor thart a good howfkeeper and I thanck thy good worfhip for my Brother Arthur watchins	
all	peace peace	60
moor	look what yoᵘ do offend yoᵘ Cry vppõ that is the peace; not [on] of yoᵘ heare prefent had there fuch fellowes lyvd when yoᵘ wer babes that coold haue topt the p[ea]ce, as nowe yoᵘ woold the peace wherin yoᵘ haue till nowe growne vp had bin tane from yoᵘ, and the bloody tymes coold not haue brought yoᵘ to ~~theife~~ the ftate of men alas poor thing<i>e</i> what is yt yoᵘ haue gott although we graunt yoᵘ geat the thing yoᵘ feeke	65
~~D~~ Bett	marry the removing of the ftraingers wᶜʰ cannot choofe but much ~~helpe~~ advauntage the poor handycraftes of the Cytty	70
moor	graunt them remoued and graunt that this yoʳ ~~y~~ noyce hath Chidd downe all the matie of Ingland ymagin that yoᵘ fee the wretched ftraingers wᵗ their babyes at their back<i>e</i>, ~~and~~ their poor lugage plodding tooth port<i>e</i> and coft<i>e</i> for tranfportacion and that yoᵘ fytt as king<i>e</i> in your defyres aucthoryty quyte fylenct by yoʳ braule and yoᵘ in ruff of yoʳ ~~yo~~ opynions clothd what had yoᵘ gott ·,· Ile tell yoᵘ, yoᵘ had taught how infolenc and ftrong hand fhoold prevayle how orderd fhoold be quelld, and by this patterne not on of yoᵘ fhoold lyve an aged man for other ruffians as their fancies wrought	75 80

	wth sealf same hand sealf reasons and sealf right	85
	woold shark on yo{u} and men lyke ravenous fishes	
	woold feed on on another X	
	2	
Doll	before god that͜e as trewe as the gospell	
	2	
~~Bette~~ lincoln	nay this a sound fellowe I tell yo{u} lets mark him	
	2	
moor	Let me sett vp before yor thoughts good freind͜e	90
	on suppofytion, which if yo{u} will marke	
	yo{u} shall pceaue howe horrible a shape	
	your ynnovation beres, first tis a sinn	
	which oft thappostle did forwarne vs of vrging obedienc to aucthory[ty]	
	and twere ~~in~~ no error yf I told yo{u} all yo{u} wer in armes gainst [g	95

FOLIO 9{a}

all	marry god forbid that	
	2	
moo	nay certainly yo{u} ar	
	for to the king god hath his offyc lent	
	of dread of Iustyce, power and Comaund	
	hath bid him rule, and willd yo{u} to obay	100
	and to add ampler matĩe to this	
	he ~~god~~ hath not ~~le~~ only lent the king his figure	
	&	
	his throne ~~his~~ sword, but gyven him his owne name	
	calls him a god on earth, what do yo{u} then	
	rysing gainst him that god himsealf enstalls	105
	but ryse gainst god, what do yo{u} to yor sowles	
	in doing this o desperat ~~ar~~ as you are	
	wash your foule mynds wt teares and those same hand͜e	
	that yo{u} lyke rebells lyft against the peace	
	[ ]	
	lift vp for peace, and your vnreuerent knees	110
	~~that~~ make them your feet to kneele to be forgyven	
	~~is safer warrs, then euer yo{u} can make~~	
	~~in in to yor obedienc~~ ·	
	~~whose difcipline is ryot, why euen yor warrs hurly~~	
	tell me but this	
	~~cannot pceed but by obedienc~~ what rebell captaine	
	n	
	as mutyes ar incident, by his name	115
	can still the rout who will obay ~~th~~ a traytor	
	or howe can well that pclamation sounde	
	when ther is no adicion but a rebell	
	to quallyfy a rebell, youle put downe straingers	
	kill them cutt their throts possesse their howses	120
	and leade the matie of lawe in liom	
	~~alas alas~~	
	to slipp him lyke a hound; ~~fayeng~~ say nowe the king	
	as he is clement,. yf thoffendor moorne	
	shoold so much com to short of your great trespas	
	[.]as but to banysh yo{u}, whether woold yo{u} go· X	125

	what Country by the nature of yor error X	
	fhoold gyve you harber go yo^u to ffraunc or flanders	
	to any Iarman pvince, ~~to~~ fpane or portigall	
	nay any where ~~why yo^u~~ that not adheres to Ingland	
	why yo^u muft need̨e be ftraingers·, woold yo^u be pleafd	130
	to find a nation of fuch barbarous temper	
	that breaking out in hiddious violence	
	woold not afoord yo^u, an abode on earth	
	whett their detefted knyves againft yor throtes	
	fpurne yo^u lyke dogge, and lyke as yf that god	135
	owed not nor made not yo^u, nor that the elament̨e	
	yor	
	wer not all appropriat to ~~their~~ Comforte·	
	but Charterd vnto them, what would yo^u thinck	
	to be thus vfd, this is the ftraingers cafe X	
all	and this your montanifh inhumanyty	140

    2

fayth a faies trewe letts ~~vs~~ do as we may be doon by

    2

~~all~~ **Linco**   weele be ruld by yo^u mafter moor yf youle ftand our
                freind to p̨cure our p̨don

    2

moor   Submyt yo^u to theife noble gentlemen
           entreate their mediation to the kinge   145
           gyve vp yor fealf to forme obay the maieftrat
           and thers no doubt, but mercy may be found   yf yo^u fo feek [yt]

                                            FOLIO 9^b

all

MEASURE FOR MEASURE

Measure for Measure was one of sixteen of Shakespeare's plays entered in the Stationers' Register by Edward Blount and Isaac Jaggard on 8 November 1623. The First Folio (F), in which *Measure* was set by Compositors B, C, and D, gives the only authoritative text for almost all the play. *Measure* is the fourth of the four comedies opening the volume, a group of plays evidently set from transcripts prepared by Ralph Crane, whose characteristics are noted in the General Introduction. There is no attempt to introduce massed stage directions. Crane may have compiled the list of 'The names of all the Actors' appended to the text; it is only mentioned here that the Duke has a name, Vincentio.

The Folio text, as would be expected, betrays few indications of the nature of Crane's copy. Recent editors have often considered that such signs as survive point to foul papers. There is, however, nothing in *Measure* that is inconsistent with prompt-book copy, and the most reliable evidence indicates that Crane did work from such a manuscript. Crane fairly reliably followed copy for his spelling of *o/oh*, as did the Folio compositors who set *Measure*. Shakespeare strongly favoured the short spelling; *Measure* strongly favours the long. The preference apparently indicates that Crane was working from some sort of transcript. After 1.4.5/322 we read in a centred direction '*Lucio within.*', and similarly after 4.3.102/2032 '*Isabella within.*' These directions look as if they derive (indirectly) from prompt annotations. Similarly, in F '*Enter Isabella.*' is placed immediately before she speaks within at 3.1.44/1150; prompt annotation is suggested. Although Crane sometimes interfered with profanity, the systematic omission of profanity in *Measure* can scarcely be attributed to him; nor would it stem from Shakespeare's hand in a play written before the 1606 Act against profanity. The absence of profanity is entirely consistent with a prompt-book prepared or reformed after 1606. Similarly, act divisions would probably not be a feature of Shakespeare's foul papers for *Measure* (or the original prompt-book), whereas act intervals would be usual in later theatrical performance.

The song beginning Act 4, the only one in the play, also appears in *Rollo, Duke of Normandy* (1616-19; also known as *The Bloody Brother*) by Fletcher and others; it there has a second stanza. Boswell suggested that the song was added to *Measure* in the printing house. O'Connor and Walker urged that the song and the Duke's dialogue with Mariana were a theatrical interpolation, a theory recently developed by Jowett and Taylor, who argue in 'With New Additions' that an adapter introduced into *Measure* a stanza from a popular song in a popular play—*Rollo*—some years after Shakespeare's death.

When the text is reconstructed by removing the interpolated song and the concomitant dialogue after it, the Folio scenes headed '*Actus Tertius. Scena Prima.*' and '*Actus Quartus. Scæna Prima.*' become continuous action: the Duke does not leave the stage. If the act-break results from non-authorial adaptation, a nearby problem in the Folio text can be explained. F's short soliloquy 'O Place and greatnes' (4.1.58/1705) has long been recognized as far too short for it to be plausible that Isabella meanwhile explains her predicament to Mariana and persuades her to act as her substitute in her assignation with Angelo; the soliloquy is also confusingly irrelevant to its context. It appears to belong, as Warburton and others noted, in the Folio's previous scene. Jowett and Taylor argue that the adapter transposed this soliloquy with the longer and more appropriate soliloquy beginning 'He who the sword of Heauen will beare' (3.1.517/1625), which in F closes the third act. By so doing, he created a theatrically convincing lead into the new act-break, to which the shorter soliloquy was less well suited.

If theatrical adaptation took place around the Folio act break beginning the fourth act, it almost certainly also accounts for a long-suspected duplication in 1.2/Sc. 2. In F the news of Claudio's imprisonment is given twice: first with Mistress Overdone as announcer, and then with Pompey advising a now ignorant Overdone (for the second, see Additional Passage A.2-9, ending 'him'). Jowett and Taylor develop the view that the first of these episodes, and therefore the entire passage with Lucio and the anonymous two gentlemen in which it inseparably appears (1.2.0-82/83.2-163), is an addition designed to replace F's opening dialogue between Pompey and Overdone. The episode apparently added shows several characteristics which suggest that Shakespeare did not write it, and many characteristics suggesting the hand of the dramatist who is most likely to have done so: Thomas Middleton. The text Crane transcribed therefore seems to have been a prompt-book in use after Shakespeare's death which incorporated theatrical adaptation by Middleton (probably assisted by a second person who made the alterations enabling the act-break between Acts 3 and 4). Middleton would have supplied the substantial passage of dialogue beginning 1.2/Sc. 2; Crane transcribed both this and the short passage it was designed to replace.

Another suspect feature of the text that can be explained as a result of adaptation is the presence of a silent Juliet in the altered 1.2./Sc. 2. Where the Provost and Claudio first enter, Middleton probably provided the entry for her in the direction we print at 1.2.105.1-2/185.1-2, and a re-entry for the two gentlemen; he is probably also responsible for her presence, again silent, in the final scene from 5.1.476.2/2640.2.

Jowett and Taylor suggest that the inclusion of the Justice in the stage direction at 2.1.0.1/406.3 and the dialogue he has with Escalus at 2.1.264-75/672-83 might result from adaptation; and that, although Lucio probably always had a role in 2.2/Sc. 6, Middleton may have added to it. But these are doubtful cases, and the absence of signs of adaptation elsewhere suggests that the rest of *Measure* is by Shakespeare, and is unaltered.

If the text was indeed adapted after Shakespeare's death, F represents neither Shakespeare's version nor, on account of its preservation of Shakespeare's original in 1.2/Sc. 2, the adapted version. An editor accepting the hypothesis might remove Middleton's alterations to 1.2/Sc. 2, cut out the song and following dialogue in 4.1/Sc. 10, transpose the Duke's soliloquies to their original order, and delete Juliet's entry at 5.1.476.2/2640.2. These changes would restore the text as Shakespeare conjecturally first wrote it. There is a need for such a text, but it may be premature to provide it in the present edition. The hypothesis on which it depends is untested by scholarly opinion at large, and its consequences for a restored text are radical. Furthermore, as suggested above, the distinction between adapted and original material is not unequivocally clear: the restored text might well be contaminated with remnants of the revision (and/or possibly exclude Shakespearian material if lines of doubtful origin were excised). In order that the reader may examine the postulated original text and study the nature of the adaptations in 1.2/Sc. 2 and 3.1-4.1/Sc. 9-10, we supply additional passages showing 1.2.0.1-1.2.116/83.2-196 and 3.1.515-4.1.26/1623-1712 as Shakespeare probably wrote them. All the changes made in order to reconstruct these passages are original to this edition.

Our text of the play as a whole is that of the adapted version presumably acted by the King's Men just a year or two before work began on printing from Crane's transcript. The only way in which this substantially differs from the Folio text is that we omit seven lines written by Shakespeare but evidently intended to be omitted in the adaptation. The decision to omit these lines is the minimum consequence of our textual hypothesis; however, the same decision could be made independently of that hypothesis, as it depends only on recognition of a duplication, not on the identification of two hands.

Measure is a particularly clear example of act divisions in F having theatrical origins independent of the text as first written. As the adapted version is the basis for the present text, these divisions are observed in the original-spelling and modern-spelling formats alike. F has scene divisions which are for the most part reliable. Editors since Capell have divided Act 3 into two scenes, beginning 3.2 at 3.1.270.1/1377.1; this edition reverts to F, which indicates continuous action. Traditional line-references to 3.2 may be located in 3.1/Sc. 9 by adding 270. We follow editors since Rowe in removing the scene-break of F's 'Scena Tertia' (1.2.105/185) and in renumbering the following scenes in Act 1.

The one part of the play where F is not the sole authority is the song. This is extant not only in the authoritative 1639 and 1640 Quartos of *Rollo* and a corrupt text in the 1640 edition of Shakespeare's *Poems*, but also in a number of manuscripts. F is distinct from all but one derivative manuscript in supplying only one stanza; it also differs in its indication of repeated phrases and its reading 'but' in l. 6 where all non-derivative texts have 'though'. At least one manuscript is highly authoritative: a song-book originally belonging to the composer who set the song to music, John Wilson. A full collation and analysis of variants is given by Jowett and Taylor in their Appendix 3. F's repeated phrases may reflect performance; 'but' is likely to be a simple error, and in this edition is emended. Other substantive manuscript variants in the first stanza are recorded in textual notes. The variant reading is attributed to the text representing what is judged to be the earliest version with that reading. Most manuscripts are evidently derivative from the text as preserved in Wilson's song-book.

J.J./(S.W.W.)

WORKS CITED

Becket, Andrew, *Shakespeare's Himself Again*, 2 vols. (1815)
Davenant, William, *The Law against Lovers* (adaptation of *Measure*), in *Works* (1673)
Eccles, Mark, ed., *Measure for Measure*, New Variorum (1980)
Hunter, G. K., 'Six Notes on *Measure for Measure*', SQ 15 (1964), 167-72
Kellner, Leon, *Erläuterungen und Textverbesserungen zu vierzehn Dramen Shakespeares* (1931)
Lambrechts, Guy, 'Proposed New Readings in Shakespeare: the Comedies (I)', *Hommage à Shakespeare: Bulletin de la Faculté des Lettres de Strasbourg*, 43 (1965), 945-58
Lever, J. W., ed., *Measure for Measure*, Arden (1965)
Melchiori, Giorgio, 'Hand D in *Sir Thomas More*: An Essay in Misinterpretation', *SSu* 38 (1985), 101-14
Noble, Richmond, *Shakespeare's Biblical Knowledge and Use of the Book of Common Prayer* (1935)
Nosworthy, J. M., ed., *Measure for Measure*, New Penguin (1969)
O'Connor, Frank, *The Road to Stratford* (1948)
Orger, J. G., *Critical Notes on Shakespeare's Comedies* (1890)
Ridley, M. R., ed., *Measure for Measure* (1935)
Taylor, Gary, '*Measure for Measure*, IV.ii.41-46', SQ 29 (1978), 419-21
Walker, Alice, 'The Text of *Measure for Measure*', RES, NS 34 (1983), 1-20
Watt, R. J. C., 'Three Cruces in *Measure for Measure*', RES, NS 38 (1987), 227-33
Wilson, John Dover, ed., with A. Quiller-Couch, *Measure for Measure*, New (1928)

TEXTUAL NOTES

Title *Measure, for Measure*] F (head title) (MEASVRE, | For Meafure.); ~ ˏ for Meafure F (running title), S.R.
1.1.8/8 But this] This edition; But that F; Put that ROWE. This edition follows Sisson in regarding 'to . . . able' as an imperative phrase. Sisson gives two glosses (*New Readings*, i. 74); the first appears to ignore 'But that', and the second unconvincingly relates it to Angelo's 'Science'. To this extent he has resolved the generally recognized difficulty. If Shakespeare wrote 'But this', the phrase would lend emphasis to the Duke's following words; the rest makes good sense as Sisson perceived it. The emendation obviates both the conjectures of Hanmer and others that a phrase or line is missing, and Johnson's double conjecture 'sufficiencies your worth is abled'.

The combination of metrical licences would be less irregular if Shakespeare had conceived of (though presumably not written) 'But this' as a separate short verse line. Alternatively, the words might have belonged to the previous line; the space right of 'remaines' is insufficient to set them, so compositorial relineation may be suspected.

1.1.48 metal] F (mettle). Similarly 2.4.48.

1.1.51/51 leauen'd] NOSWORTHY (Dent); a leauen'd F
1.2.4/87 Heauen...its] F. Genitive *its* was not used by Shakespeare in 1603-4, but was used by Middleton after 1619 (Jowett and Taylor). If an adapter's hand were not present in this passage (see Introduction), 'its' would be good evidence of emended profanity ('God...his').
1.2.18 wast] F (was't)
1.2.33-4 piled...pilled] F (pil'd...pil'd)
1.2.42.1 *Mistress Overdone*] F (*Bawde*). In F's stage directions and speech-prefixes Mistress Overdone is always referred to as Bawd and Pompey as Clown. Some non-authorial regularization may have taken place.
1.2.48 dolours] F (Dollours)
1.2.61 pray thee] F (pray'thee)
1.2.67/148 head] F; Head is ROWE; head's CAPELL
1.2.71 Julietta] F (*Iulietta*). Alternatively modernized to the Italian *Giulietta*, but 'Iuliet' cannot be similarly treated.
1.2.83 *Pompey*] F (*Clowne*). See note to 1.2.42.1.
1.2.83-4/164-5 you. | CLOWNE] This edition. F adds a passage which the preceding dialogue evidently replaces. See Introduction and Additional Passage A.
1.2.107.1/187.1 *Exeunt Bawd and Clowne*] ROWE; *Exeunt. | Scena Tertia.* F. In F the entry of the Provost etc. follows the scene-break, which was presumably introduced because the stage was apparently clear. Crane may have been faced with an entry trailing down several lines of the margin in the prompt-book—especially likely if the direction was expanded when the text was adapted (see Introduction).
1.2.114/194 bonds] SISSON; words F. Lever retains 'words' and adds a full stop after 'waight'; Wilson suspected missing material after 'waight' (a theory one might accept without believing, as he implies, that 1.2.114-5/194-5 originally were spoken by Juliet). The misreading 'bonds'/'words' is plausible; 'bonds' greatly clarifies the sense.
1.2.117/197 Liberty.] F2 (subs.); ~ˌ F1
1.2.126/206 morality] ROWE (Davenant); mortality F. No recognized sense of *mortality* fits. *Morality* is 'moral lesson' (the experience of imprisonment), 'moral instruction' (Claudio's words as a prisoner), and 'moral allegory' (the exemplary display of Claudio).
1.2.138/219 propogation] F; procuration COLLIER 2 (Jackson *and* MS note in Folger copy 21 of F2 *dated before* 1733); prorogation SISSON (Malone). F gives a difficult sense, though one which is both possible and thematically relevant. The emendations do not suggest particularly plausible misreadings, and the very difficulty argues here against substitution.
1.2.144 Unhapp'ly] F (Vnhappely)
1.2.156/237 foureteene] RANN (Theobald); nineteene F. The inconsistency with 1.3.21/284 in F is scarcely likely to be deliberate, as it is pointless. In view of the graphical similarity of the numbers, in arabic or, more particularly, roman numerals, it is probable that the error is a misreading rather than an authorial inconsistency. Elsewhere Shakespeare used *nineteen* only twice—and one of these (*Antony* 3.7.58/1631) is straight from Plutarch. Fourteen is of some significance as the age of sexual maturity in Shakespeare.
1.2.164 prithee] F (pre'thee). Similarly 1.3.45.
1.2.171/252 prone] F; pow'r *or* prompt JOHNSON (*conj.*); proue BECKET (*conj.*); grace SISSON; pure SISSON (*conj. in New Readings*). Only Sisson has had the confidence to emend here. His 'grace' is palaeographically attractive, but such an obvious word is unlikely to have been misread as the more unusual 'prone'.
1.2.172/253 moue] F; moues ROWE (Davenant). Probably not the 'subjunctive used indefinitely after the relative' (Abbott, 367), but 'due to the influence of the two precedent adjectives' (Lever). Compare 3.1.127-9/1232-4.
1.2.176/257 thy] This edition (*conj.* Lever); the F. In F, 'the like' is unrelated to any object of comparison; indeed the logical but unintended sense would be the like of Isabella ('she'). Lever points out that 'thy like' rhetorically balances 'thy life'. Corruption would be facilitated by the commonness of *the like* as a set expression.
1.3.0.1/263.3 Frier] This edition (*conj.* Lever); Frier Thomas F. In later scenes the Friar is called Peter. It is difficult to imagine that Shakespeare intended two friars, especially as the lengthy intervening action and the friar's habit would blur any individuality they might have. 'Thomas' is probably an authorial inconsistency perpetuated in the prompt-book. One cannot say whether the name would have been ignored or acted upon in the theatre. For the reasons already suggested, one would expect the former; if a single actor doubled the parts the question would be academic.
1.3.10/273 a witlesse] WILSON (Nicholson); witleffe F1; and witlesse F2; with witless CAMBRIDGE (*conj.*). Defective caesura and sense strongly suggest a missing word in F1. 'With' and 'a' are both plausible; 'a' is particularly easy to omit, whilst 'with' might induce eyeskip to 'witlesse'.
1.3.20/283 weedes] F; Steeds THEOBALD; wills BULLEN (Thirlby); jades LEVER (Orger). G. K. Hunter has pointed out that *weeds* is associated with *curb* in *Hamlet* 3.4.142-6/2356-60 and *2 Henry IV* 4.3.54-62/2378-86 (also *headstrong*: 'his head-strong riot hath no curbe'), and *weed* with *unbitted* in *Othello* 1.3.322-31/608-17. The line remains a strikingly mixed metaphor. Nevertheless, *bit* may have a secondary sense 'cutting blade', *curb* is commonly used figuratively, and *headstrong* may suggest 'growing strongly in the head' (though this sense is not in *OED*); such secondary senses appropriately hint at decapitation. The complex and rich associations suggest Shakespeare's hand. The emendations are all palaeographically attractive, and, as with 'prone' (1.2.171/252), the combination of contextual unexpectedness and suggestive meaning argues against corruption.
1.3.27/290 More mock'd becomes] This edition; More mock'd F; become more markt DAVENANT (*conj.*, *reading* 'Till it in time' *for* 'in time the rod'); Becomes more mock'd POPE. The sense is defective in F, and 'becomes' is usually considered to have been omitted. The error is much more likely to have taken place in the middle of the line than at its beginning.
1.3.42/305 fight] F; sight POPE
1.3.43/306 T'alow in] This edition; To do in F; So do in THEOBALD; To do it HANMER; To do me HALLIWELL; To die in STAUNTON (*conj.*). The context seems to require a verb which will convincingly take 'my nature' as its object. 'Do' scarcely suffices. 'To doe' might be read for copy 't'alow', 'to'low, or 'to alow'. *Allow in* is 'allow to be in', hence 'expose to', and is so consistent with the imagery of a battle.
1.4.5/322 Sisterhood] F2; Sifterftood F1
1.4.51/368 and] F; in KEIGHTLEY
1.4.53/370 giuing-out] F; givings out ROWE. F's 'were' is probably subjunctive (cf. Abbott, 368).
1.4.60/377 fast.] F2; ~ˌ F1
1.4.78/395 makes] F; make ROWE 3
2.1.12/418 your] ROWE (Davenant); our F
2.1.21-3/427-9 What...on theeues? what's...ceizes] This edition; what's...ceizes; What...on theeues F. Lever argues that 'what's...ceizes' is likely to be an added afterthought. It does not seem necessary to follow him in conjecturing that the line-break was intended to be after 'made', and that 'That' is a non-Shakespearian sophistication. Although the metre is irregular in the two lines containing 'what's...ceizes' in F (the licences are the same as in this edition), it is the difficulty of sense which gives the strongest indication that something is wrong. If 'what's...ceizes' is omitted, the text not only is left with a regular pentameter ('Guiltier...Lawes'), but also fluently moves from the first sentence concerned with the thief on the jury to the second. 'What's...ceizes' gives a very appropriate lead-in to the jewel image; this otherwise appears after a sudden transition of both idea and image, with the referent of 'Iewell' deduced only with difficulty. Its positioning is therefore problematic for both the thief image, which is interrupted, and the jewel image, which is detached. Lever was probably right in

regarding the sentence as an afterthought, but missed the most pressing reason for regarding it as such: that it was evidently misplaced when incorporated with the text.

2.1.21/427 What] F; who WILSON

2.1.21/427 Lawe] ROWE (Davenant); Lawes F. The emendation is not merely grammatical, though F's grammatical licence is particularly violent. F invites the misinterpretation 'What do the laws that thieves pass on thieves know?' Such an interpretation probably encouraged the error in the first place. But 'that . . . theeues' must, unless one accepts Wilson's emendation of 'What' (see previous note), be the complement of 'knowes'. The required sense is much more intelligible if Angelo is talking about the law in general, not specific laws.

2.1.34/440 execute] This edition; executed F. F's extra syllable would be acceptable at a caesura, but is most suspect here. Though Shakespeare did not elsewhere use *execute* as a past participle, Abbott gives other examples of the construction (342); at 2.2.158/841 'dedicate' is a similar participle.

2.1.38 Some . . . fall] F (*in italic*). F marks a *sentencia*.

2.1.39/445 from brakes of vice] STEEVENS 2; from brakes of Ice F; through Brakes of Vice ROWE; from brakes of justice CAPELL; from brakes of ice COLLIER (Steevens). Interpretations of F as it stands are strained (see both rejected and accepted readings in Lever's note). 'Vice' would easily be corrupted to 'Ice' through momentary memorial error: a scribe or compositor confusing readings when the sounds of the words 'of vice' were in his mind. As the 'Devil's brake' (i.e. snare) may have been familiar from miracle plays (see New Variorum note), the idea of 'snares of vice' could have been readily intelligible.

2.1.121 All Hallow Eve] F (Allhallond-Eue). Quoted in *OED* under *All hallow eve* (*All-hallow*, 4).

2.1.123/529 lower] F; lowe ECCLES (*conj.*).

2.1.220 spay] F (splay). *OED* describes *splay* as an 'Alteration of SPAY'.

2.2.25/708 God saue] CAMBRIDGE (Thirlby) 'Saue F. Here and at 2.2.167/850 the valediction *Save* is marked with an apostrophe in F, suggesting that it has been shortened to remove profanity. In both instances the metre is also defective.

2.2.60/743 it] F1; it backe F2; it in WILSON. F gives an acceptable four-foot line if 'call it' is elided. Editors (most of whom emend) have not noticed that *call again* could mean 'revoke' (*call*, v. 24.b). The present instance post-dates *OED*'s last illustration (1587).

2.2.75/758 that were] F; that are WARBURTON. Warburton accused F of 'false divinity', perhaps rightly.

2.2.98/781 raw] This edition; now F; new POPE; now born KEIGHTLEY. F gives a particularly difficult reading ('Either now [hatched and born] or . . . in progress to be hatched and born') and, as Lever points out, is awkwardly repeated in 2.2.100/783. Pope's 'new' remains elliptical and gives another repetition which is not so much 'well balanced' (Lever) as, once again, awkward. As an error, 'now' could easily have been influenced by 'now' in the same position in 2.2.100/783 (or even by 'note' in the same position in 2.2.96/779), but could be a simple misreading. The sense 'raw' gives is now obsolete but exactly right: 'unripe, immature' (*OED*, *a*. 4). Shakespeare uses *raw* in this way, and again figuratively, in *Richard II* 2.3.41-3/1106-8: 'I tender you my seruice, | Such as it is, being tender, raw, and young, | Which elder daies shal ripen'.

2.2.101/784 yeer] HANMER (Thirlby); here F; where MALONE (Tyrwhitt). See Wilson's note. 'Yeer' is a spelling of *ere*.

2.2.119 Split'st] F (Splits)

2.2.129/812 our selfe] F; yourself THEOBALD (Warburton)

2.2.136 advised] F (auis'd)

2.2.153 shekels] F (Sickles). *Sickle* derives from Hebrew *sheqel* via late Latin *siclus*. The consistent use of 'sicle' and 'sycle' in the Coverdale Bible where other versions have 'shekel' shows these forms to be, in Elizabethan English, indifferent variants on *shekel*. *OED*'s distinct usages, both unique, occur in the early 18th c., when 'sicle' as a spelling variant had become obsolete.

2.2.154/837 rate are] F; rate is HANMER; rates are JOHNSON

2.2.165/848 prayer is crossd] This edition (G.T.); prayers croffe F; prayer's cross'd LEVER (Kellner). Lever noted that ' "Cross" in this sense was only used transitively (*O.E.D. v.* 14)', and the various glosses that have been put forward testify to the difficulty in F. Though Lever's emendation is orthographically straightforward, the resultant reading is awkward to communicate in speech, particularly as the redundancy of the contraction (*prayer* can be monosyllabic) encourages the listener to assume the plural. The contraction may have stood in Crane's transcript, but is unlikely to be authorial.

2.2.167/850 God saue] HUDSON 2 (Thirlby); 'Saue F. See note to 2.2.25/708.

2.3.11/886 flawes] F; flames WARBURTON (Davenant)

2.3.35/910 heauen . . . it] F; God . . . him This edition *conj.*

2.3.42/917 Lawe] HANMER (Thirlby); Loue F. See Mason's note (quoted by Wilson and in New Variorum).

2.4.4/923 God] NOSWORTHY (Thirlby); heauen F. Noble defends the emendation, citing biblical parallels. Lever compares James I's *Basilicon Doron* (1599): 'Keepe God more sparingly in your mouth, but aboundantly in your harte'. *Measure* alludes elsewhere to this work.

2.4.9/928 seard] HANMER; feard F; sere HUDSON 2 (Heath); frayed (*spelt* fraid) SISSON (Kellner). Johnson supported F, but it is unlikely to be correct. It is not plausible that a written 'good thing' should be 'feard', and even less that 'feard' is compatible with 'tedious'. Recent editors have usually preferred to emend two literals and read 'sere', presumably concurring in Heath's judgement that 'Sear'd . . . signifies *scorched*, not *old*'. *OED* in fact defines neither *sere* nor *seared* as 'old'. The only sense of *seared* in Shakespeare's time was 'Dried up, parched, withered' (*OED*)—exactly the same as etymologically related *sere*. Either word might imply age. There is no objection to the simpler emendation.

2.4.12/931 in] This edition (Walker); for F. See Walker, p. 12.

2.4.16/935 horne] F; horns WALKER (*conj.*). Walker's reading plausibly removes the ambiguity of antecedent to ' 'Tis', which in our text must refer to 'good Angell' (see following note). If 'not' were emended to 'yet', ' 'Tis' must refer to singular 'horne'.

2.4.17/936 now the] This edition (Wilson); not the F; yet the JOHNSON (*conj.*). F lends itself to no convincing gloss, and editors' attempts to explain 2.4.16-7/935-6 are contorted and contradictory. Whereas compression of thought is intrinsic to the lines, a particular difficulty lies in F's negative 'not'. The conjectures 'now' and 'yet' give contrasting interpretations, either of which is acceptable. 'Now', however, gives the easier misreading or substitution.

2.4.45/964 Gods] NOSWORTHY; heauens F. Again F's inferable emendation of profanity obscures both the sense and a biblical allusion (Genesis 1: 27).

2.4.48/967 moalds] This edition (*conj.* Malone); meanes F; mints WILSON (Steevens). Lever glosses *means* as 'instruments', citing *OED mean, sb.*² 9 (actually 10). But it is quite clear that 'instrument' in *OED*'s definition is intended abstractly ('. . . agency . . .'); *means* cannot really suggest minting or procreation. 'Mints' is an inexact term for the coinage metaphor: in Shakespeare's use elsewhere it signifies 'the place where money is coined' (Schmidt), which does not supply the expected image of the mould itself, and even *OED sb.*¹ 2.b, 'a set of machines for coining', is scarcely right. 'Mints' also abandons *mettle* as 'spirit', which requires a word which can imply 'womb' independently of the coin image. 'Moalds' fulfils both functions of the required word. Apart from the 'l'/'n' literals it gives an easy misreading.

2.4.53/972 or] ROWE (Davenant); and F

2.4.58/977 then for] F; than ROWE 3

2.4.65 soul,] F (~.). Some editors increase the weight of F's pointing so that the following line is not dependent on the present one.

2.4.75/994 craftily] ROWE (Davenant); crafty F

2.4.76/995 me be] F2; be F1

2.4.80/999 en-shield] F; enshell'd KEIGHTLEY (Thirlby); enshielded KITTREDGE; enceil'd LEVER. The emendations are all concerned to give a regular past-participle form, but see 2.1.34/440 and note.

2.4.89-90/1008-9 other) ... question,] This edition (*conj.* Watt); ~,... ~) F. A difficult passage which Watt clarifies by suggesting a misplaced parenthesis. KEIGHTLEY followed an anonymous conjecture in Singer in emending 'losse' to 'loose'.

2.4.94/1013 all-binding-Law] JOHNSON (Thirlby); all-building-Law F; all-bridling law BULLEN. See Lever.

2.4.103/1022 longing haue] F; longing I've ROWE; longing I have CAPELL; long I have HUDSON

2.4.105/1024 Then] F (*text*); That F (*c.w.*)

2.4.112/1031 Ignominie] F2 (Ignominy); Ignomie F1. Shakespeare is unlikely to have preferred the ametrical form.

2.4.123 federy] F (fedarie). Often modernized 'feodary', following F2; but this suggests 'feudatory', which, as *OED* points out, does not give a likely sense.

2.4.124/1043 thy] F; this HARNESS (Malone)

2.4.143/1062 for it] ROWE 3 (Davenant); for't F

2.4.185 More] F ("More). F marks the line as a *sententia*.

3.1.4 I've] F (I'haue)

3.1.20 exist'st] F (exifts)

3.1.29/1135 sire,] ROWE (Cotgrave, *English Treasury of Wit and Language* (1655)); fire,ᴀ F1; sire? F4

3.1.31 serpigo] F (Sapego)

3.1.38/1144 in] POPE; yet in F. F is evidently contaminated by 'Yet in' on the line below; it gives an awkward repetition, especially in view of 'yet' in 3.1.40/1146.

3.1.51/1157 me ... them] MALONE (Steevens 2); them ... me F. Early editors, from F2 onwards, radically and variously rephrased the line.

3.1.67/1173 Though] ROWE 3; Through F

3.1.89/1195 ennew] KEIGHTLEY; emmew F

3.1.92/1198 precize,] KNIGHT (Tieck); prenzie, F1; Princely,ᴀ F2; priestly,ᴀ HANMER (Warburton). See Lever's note. The spelling adopted in this edition gives a relatively easy misreading. It is, however, difficult to understand why the same error should have been perpetrated twice (here and three lines below). One possibility is that the compositor only misread once, but that a corrector ambiguously instructed that the readings should be brought into conformity. At 1.3.50/314 'precise' occurs not only as a description of Angelo, but also four words before 'guard' (compare 3.1.95/1201).

3.1.94 damnedest] F (damneft)

3.1.95/1201 precize] KNIGHT (Tieck); prenzie F1; Princely F2; priestly HANMER (Warburton); precious NOSWORTHY. See note to 3.1.92/1198.

3.1.121/1227 delated] HANMER; delighted F. Lever follows F, but finds it problematic and recognizes Hanmer's reading as more fitting to the context. The spelling 'delated' for *dilated* is recorded in *OED*, occurs in Q2 *Hamlet* 1.2.38/193, and could easily be confused with 'delited'. For the sense ('expansive, having full scope'), in opposition to confinement, see *Troilus* 2.3.245/1406. For the imagery, see *Hamlet* 1.1.135-6/135-6: 'The extrauagant and erring spirit hies | To his confine'. Compare also Isabella's lines to Claudio above: 'perpetuall durance, a restraint | Though all the worlds vastiditie you had | To a determin'd scope' (3.1.66-8/1172-4). Isabella here describes prison; Claudio's hell is 'To be imprison'd' (though, paradoxically, 'in the viewlesse windes'). The theme of liberty and restraint is, of course, persistent in *Measure*.

3.1.127/1233 thought,] CAPELL; ~, F; thoughts THEOBALD. Crane or the compositor probably took 'that ... thought' as a parenthesis, as did some of Shakespeare's early editors.

3.1.130/1236 penury] F2; periury F1

3.1.170/1277 falsifie] HANMER (Thirlby); fatisfie F; fortify LAMBRECHTS (*conj.*). F's 'satisfie' is normally retained by modern editors, but makes little sense with 'resolution' as object. Corruption could have been subconsciously influenced by 'satisfaction' 11 lines above, but misreading of 'falsifie' or 'fortifie' would be easy enough; both make good sense. *Falsify* is more complex and apt. It can mean both 'prove false to' and 'produce a counterfeit of', the latter hinting at a further image of false coinage. Whether or not coinage is implied, *falsify* contributes to the theme of being and seeming. In context it is especially relevant as the Duke is himself giving Claudio a false sense of the imminence of his death. Shakespeare elsewhere uses *falsify* only once (*1 Henry IV* 1.2.208/311); significantly it is associated with *hopes*: 'falsifie mens hopes'.

3.1.191 him.] F (~ :)

3.1.200/1307 aduisings; ... good,] POPE; ~, ... ~; F

3.1.216/1323 to her] F1; to her by F2 by her KELLNER (*conj.*). 'To' has the force 'even to the point of' or 'according to'. Acceptance of F involves rejecting Dyce's interpretation of 'Shee' as emphatic object of 'have married'.

3.1.249-50/1356-7 time ... place] F; place ... time LEVER (Ridley). Either place or time might 'answere to conuenience'; time 'may haue all shadow, and silence in it' if the dead of night is stipulated. Ridley's transposition does not depend on an easy error in F.

3.1.255/1362 heare] LEVER; heere F. *OED* does not record 'heere' as a spelling of *hear* after the 15th c.; F probably gives an error rather than an old spelling. However, as 'heare' was a recognized 17th-c. spelling of *here*, error would be easy—especially in view of possible contamination from 'heereafter'. The same error evidently occurs at 5.1.32/2197.

An alternative possibility is that 'heere' preserves a word, or part of a word ('heerin', 'heereby') which 'by this' replaces.

3.1.268/1375 be quickly] F. A past participle may be missing (S.W.W.).

3.1.270-270.1/1377-1377.1 *Exit | Enter*] F. Editors usually follow Capell in beginning a new scene, but the Duke remains on stage.

3.1.277/1385 Law;] F; ~,ᴀ CAPELL (Thirlby). 'Gowne' has often been understood as the object of 'allow'd'.

3.1.278/1386 furd] F; facd G.T. *conj.*

3.1.278/1386 one] RANN (Thirlby) (on); and F

3.1.293/1401 eate, array] THEOBALD (Bishop); ~,ᴀ away F

3.1.107/1415 Free from] F2; From F1. Sense, metre, and syntactical balance point to F2's emendation. Both Shakespeare and Crane would be likely to write the first letter of a verse line in minuscule.

3.1.307/1415 or] BULLEN (Johnson); as F. The line probably needs this second emendation to establish that faults should only wishedly be free from 'seeming'; F suggests that they actually are so.

3.1.314/1422 extracting] F; extracting it ROWE 3

3.1.341-2/1448-9 bondage: If ... patiently, why] THEOBALD; ~,ᴀ if ... ~ : Why F

3.1.375/1482 is a] F; has no HANMER (Thirlby)

3.1.375/1483 vngeneratiue] THEOBALD; generatiue F. Perhaps an error provoked by the last syllable of 'motion'. In F, 'motion' ends a type line, as does 'con-' of 'congeal'd' immediately above it. The compositor, confusing these type-line endings, may have thought he had already set the 'vn-' prefix. But compare 3.1.483/1592. A deliberate miscorrection is possible, especially as *OED* cites no instance of *ungenerative* before Theobald's emendation. Shakespeare coined many new words by adding prefixes, and is more likely than Theobald to have originated this word.

3.1.426/1534 againe.] JOHNSON; ~ ? F

3.1.440/1548 not] HANMER; now F.

3.1.447.1/1555.1 *Enter ... Bawd*] F. Editors usually follow THEOBALD 2 in adding officers to the entry, and providing an exit for Overdone guarded by them after 'words', 3.1.465/1573. See Jowett and Taylor.

3.1.482/1590 it] F3; as it F1

3.1.483/1592 inconstant] HUDSON 2 (Staunton); constant F. F might give a 'correction' by a thoroughly confused scribe.

3.1.517-38/1624-46 He ... contracting] F. See Introduction. The transposition of soliloquies in Additional Passage B was first proposed by Kellner.

3.1.530/1638 Make my] This edition (Walker); Making F; Make a ALEXANDER

3.1.531/1639 strings] Fb; ftings Fa

4.1.0.1/1646.1 *Mariana [discouer'd]*] *Enter Mariana* F. The scene evidently begins with a static tableau. See Jowett and Taylor.

1646.2-1647 *Song | BOY*] Song. F (*in position of speech-prefix*)

4.1.0.1 boy] Song. F

4.1.2/1648 were] F; are BODLEIAN MS RAWL. POET. 65, fol. 26ᵛ, FOLGER MS 452.4, fol. 20. The song as it appears in texts of *Rollo* and in other 17th-c. texts is fully collated and discussed in Jowett and Taylor.

4.1.3/1649 the] like *Rollo* Q1639, Q1640. The manuscript texts agree with F.

4.1.3/1649 of] F; the BODLEIAN MS ENG. POET. f.27, pp. 66–7

4.1.5–6/1651–2 bring againe, bring againe . . . seal'd in vaine, seal'd in vaine.] F. No other 17th-c. texts of the song indicate the repeats except F2–3 (both repeats) and F4 (first repeat only). The repetitions are probably a feature particular to the song as sung in the revival of *Measure*, perhaps as an alternative to the repetition of the last two lines in their entirety indicated in Wilson's setting of the two-stanza text.

4.1.6/1652 though] BODLEIAN MS MUS. b.1, fol. 19ᵛ; but F. See Introduction. The MS is John Wilson's song-book.

4.1.6/1652 vaine.] F. The second stanza, in the authoritative text of Wilson's song-book, reads:

> Hide o hide those hills of snow
> that thy froazen bosom beares
> on whose topps the Pinkes yᵗ grow
> are yet of those yᵗ Aprill weares
> But first sett my poore heart free
> bound in those Icye chaines by thee

4.1.29 plankèd] F (planched)

4.1.34/1681 Vpon . . . night] See lineation note. Shakespeare may have added this line as an afterthought, so splitting 'There haue I made my promise, to call upon him'. Lever suggests that 'Vpon . . . night' was mislocated by a scribe, but Melchiori (pp. 104–6) adduces a similar line-splitting interlineation in Hand D's addition to *Sir Thomas More* (l. 126). Relocation could scarcely be said to improve the passage.

4.1.53/1700 and so] LEVER; and F; and I POPE; and oft DYCE 2. The line is justified in F; the following long line makes a turn-down impracticable, and as 4.1.53/1700 heads a column, a turn-up would be out of the question. The compositor may have been induced to omit a word.

4.1.58–63/1705–10 Oh . . . fancies] F. See Introduction. Warburton conjectured that the soliloquy should follow 3.1.447/1555.

4.1.60/1707 their . . . Quest] This edition; theſe . . . Queſt F1; these . . . Quests F2; their . . . Quests HANMER. Editors before Alexander accepted that F1 was corrupt. In view of the sentence-structure and the usually adjectival function of 'contrarious', it is only with difficulty that 'Quest' can be understood as a verb (as it is nowhere else in Shakespeare), especially as 'these false' is left without an antecedent to be qualified. F2 plausibly makes a noun of 'Quest(s)' by introducing concord with 'these'. However, as Crane's usual spelling was 'theis', the emendation 'their' achieves the same result without postulating a harder error. 'These . . . Quests' reads well if one follows Warburton's proposed relocation of the soliloquy to after 3.1.447/1555, whereby it could refer to the likes of Lucio. But Warburton is unlikely to be right, and so offers no support to the emendation. 'Their' refers back to the false eyes and so makes the speech self-contained. It is more appropriate whether the speech is located as in F or in place of 'He who the sword of Heauen will beare' (3.1.517–38/1624–46), the position Shakespeare evidently intended for it (see Introduction).

4.1.74/1721 Tilthes] THEOBALD; Tithes F

4.2.41–2/1761–2 Theefe. | CLOWNE If] F; thief, Clown: If THEOBALD; thief. | If CAPELL (Heath). See Taylor's note on this passage.

4.2.56 yare] F (y'are)

4.2.65 travailer's] F (Trauellers)

4.2.90/1810 vnlisting] WHITE (Mason); unfifting F1; inlisting F4; unresisting ROWE; unshifting CAPELL; resisting COLLIER 2. Mason's conjecture depends on a single literals error which can be explained as simple misreading or as compositorial anticipation of the following ligature.

4.2.102–3/1822–3 This . . . DUKE] RANN (Thirlby); *Duke.* This . . . Pro⟨uost⟩. F

4.2.102/1822 Lords.] Lords₍ F. A misunderstood abbreviation for 'lordships', as ROWE 3 and subsequent editors emend.

4.2.122/1842 ⌜PROUOST⌝ . . . *Letter*)] ROWE; *The Letter.* F (centred above on a separate type line)

4.2.202/1922 writ] F; here writ HANMER; right COLLIER 2 (conj.)

4.3.14 Drop-hair] F (*Drop-heire*). 'Heire' is an established old spelling of *hair*, which is almost certainly the dominant sense.

4.3.15/1945 Forthright] WARBURTON; *Forthlight* F

4.3.25/1955 friends] F1; friend F3

4.3.56/1986 I sweare] F; By the Lord This edition conj. 'I sweare' would be a typical substitution for a profane oath such as might be expected of Barnardine. See Introduction.

4.3.68/1998 Ragozine . . . Pirate] The name and occupation may have been changed in the course of revision; see Jowett and Taylor.

4.3.68 Ragusine] F (*Ragozine*). Similarly at 4.3.73 and 5.1.532. For the apparent etymology, see Lever.

4.3.86/2016 yonder] ROWE 3; yond F; th' under HANMER

4.3.89/2019 Angelo] F; Varrius NOSWORTHY (Wilson). The inconsistency between the contents of this letter and the eventual meeting-place with Angelo is best explained as a deliberate contradiction, as is apparent from the bewilderment of Escalus and Angelo over the Duke's conflicting letters in 4.4./Sc. 13.

4.3.96 well-balanced] F (weale-ballanc'd)

4.3.125 convent] F (Couent)

4.3.129/2059 can₍] F; ~, ROWE. Lever defends F.

4.4.5/2108 redeliuer] CAPELL (Thirlby); re-|liuer F1; deliuer F2. *OED* only records *reliver* elsewhere in two 15th-c. legal documents. The line-break would be conducive towards the compositor omitting 'de' after setting 're'.

4.4.13/2116 proclaim'd:] CAPELL; ~₍ F. Shakespeare probably punctuated lightly and allowed the verse line to stand as a unit of sense. In transmission, the speech became arranged as prose.

4.4.24/2127 dares her no] F; warns her not HARNESS (conj.); says her no KEIGHTLEY; dares her not COLLIER 4 (Steevens); dare she not ORGER (conj.); cries her no G.T. conj. The sense of 'dares' is difficult to pinpoint if the phrase is taken at face value, though it is quite clear what Angelo means. The simplest explanation is that the negative has a transferred position: reason *un*dares Isabella *to do so*.

4.4.25/2128 of a] F; a THEOBALD; so DYCE (Lettsom); a so HENLEY

4.4.25 off] F (of)

4.5.6/2142 Flauio's] RIVERSIDE (Theobald); *Flauia's* F; *Flavius's* ROWE. For Shakespeare's practice of varying Italianate '-o' and Latinate '-us' name endings, see note to *Julius Caesar* 1.2.5/80.

4.5.8/2144 Valentīus] CAPELL (Thirlby); *Valencius* F. F's '*Valencius*' is both metrically awkward and an improbable name.

5.1.0.3/2165.3 Officers] not in F. Perhaps understood to be included amongst 'Citizens'. Most editors are prompted by 5.1.250–1/2415–16 to add the Provost to the opening entry, but Lever pointed out that this is unnecessary.

5.1.13/2178 me your] F3; we your F1; we our LEVER

5.1.32/2197 me, heare] CHAMBERS (Keightley); me, heere F. Compare 3.1.255/1362.

5.1.86/2251 i'the] F; in the POPE

5.1.124/2289 and] F; in This edition conj.

5.1.167/2332 her face] F2; your face F1

5.1.238/2403 euen to] CAPELL; to F; unto POPE. F is metrically defective. Capell's intensifier is marginally preferable to Pope's semantically indifferent reading; *unto* occurs nowhere else in *Measure*, and eyeskip from the end of 'them' to the end of 'euen' would be easy.

5.1.242/2407 against] F1; gainst F2

5.1.291 fore] F (for). Editors usually retain 'for'.

5.1.308–9/2472–3 you . . . his] F; him . . . his WHITE 2 (Blackstone); you . . . this HANMER; you . . . your JOHNSON

5.1.372 wast] F (was't)

5.1.372 e'er] F (ere)

5.1.408 measure still for measure] F (*Meaſure* still for *Meaſure*). F's emphasis on the allusion to the play's title was probably

introduced by Crane. 'Cities Institutions' (1.1.10/11) is similarly emphasized with italics in F.
5.1.415-6 husband. . . . honour] F (~, . . . ~,)
5.1.420/2584 confiscation] F2; confutation F1
5.1.476.2/2640.2 *and Iulietta*] F. See Introduction.
5.1.508/2672 If any woman] F; If any woman's HANMER (Thirlby); Is any woman CAMBRIDGE. See Lever's note.
5.1.538/2702 thats] F2; that F1

Additional Passages

B.8 well met.] This edition; well met, and well come. F. 'Well come' is omitted because metrically redundant in the reconstructed text, and because the play on 'well met . . . well come' is closely paralleled in Middleton (see Jowett and Taylor).

INCIDENTALS

35 touch'd] tonch'd   105 proportion,] ~.   165 You] you (*see Additional Passage A*)   176-7 Common-wealth] ~-|~   260 ticke-tacke] ~-|~   472 Sir:] ~?   677 remedie.] ~:   724 Actor.] ~:   743 this,] ~‸   775 slept:] ~‸   782 hatch'd] hatc'hd   884 needfull.] ~‸   1016 supposd] suppoſed   1077 report] reporr   1166 twaine.] ~:   1258 Mercy] F (*text*); Mercie F (*c.w.*)   1438 goe,] ~‸   1502-3 with-drawing] ~-|~   1509 fellow.] ~‸   1539 Tunne-dish] Fb; Tunner-dish Fa (*reported by Tannenbaum; unconfirmed*)   1542-3 house-eeues] ~-|~   1602 merrie] merrrie   1648-50 That . . . Lights] that . . . lights   1703 haste,] ~‸   1753 I,] F (*c.w.*); ~‸ F (*text*)   1940-41 Peach-colour'd] ~-|~   1942-3 Deepe-vow] ~-|~   2018 Angelo.] ~‸   2026 forme,] ~.   2168 your] yonr   2184 time.] ~‸   2221 caracts] Fb; characts Fa (*reported by Hart and Wilson; unconfirmed*)   2252 proceed.] ~,   2281 ripned] ripened   2296 this'] this 'a   2378 Enough] Enoug   2382 promised] promis'd   2390 affiancd] affianced   2439 shee] F (*c.w.*); She F (*text*)   2488 bald-pate] ~-|~   2569 tongue:] ~.   2607 gouernd] gouerned   2614 subiects,] ~‸   2660 yours.] ~‸

FOLIO STAGE DIRECTIONS

1.1.0.1/0.1   *Duke, Escalus, Lords.*
1.1.24/24   *Enter Angelo.*
1.1.75/75   *Exit.* (after 1.1.74/74)
1.1.83.1/83.1   *Exeunt.*
1.2.0.1/83.2   *Enter Lucio, and two other Gentlemen.*
1.2.42.1/125.1   *Enter Bawde.*
1.2.79.1/160.1   *Exit.*
1.2.82.1/163.1   *Enter Clowne.* (after 1.2.83/164)
1.2.105.1-2/185.1-2   *Enter Prouost, Claudio, Iuliet, Officers, Lucio, & 2. Gent.* (after 'Exeunt.', 1.2.107.1/187.1, and 'Scena Tertia.')
1.2.107.1/187.1   *Exeunt.*
1.2.182.1-2/263.1-2   *Exeunt.*
1.3.0.1/263.3   *Enter Duke and Frier Thomas.*
1.3.54.1/317.1   *Exit.*
1.4.0.1/317.2   *Enter Isabell and Francisca a Nun.*
1.4.6/323   *Lucio within.* (on line before speech-prefix '*Luc.*')
1.4.89.1-2/406.1-2   *Exeunt.*
2.1.0.1/406.3   *Enter Angelo, Escalus, and seruants, Iustice.*
2.1.32.1/438.1   *Enter Prouost.* (after 2.1.31/437)
2.1.40.1/446.1   *Enter Elbow, Froth, Clowne, Officers.*
2.1.133.1/539.1   *Exit.* (after 2.1.132/538)
2.1.245/653   *Exit.*
2.1.275/683   *Exeunt.*
2.2.0.1/683.1   *Enter Prouost, Seruant.*
2.2.6/689   *Enter Angelo.*
2.2.25/708   *Enter Lucio and Isabella.*
2.2.192.1/875.1   *Exit.*
2.3.0.1-2/875.2-3   *Enter Duke and Prouost.*
2.3.9.1/884.1   *Enter Iuliet.*
2.3.41/916   *Exit.*
2.3.44/919   *Exeunt.*
2.4.0.1/919.1   *Enter Angelo.*
2.4.17/936   *Enter Seruant.* (after 'there')
2.4.30/949   *Enter Isabella.* (after 'Maid')
2.4.170.1/1089.1   *Exit*
2.4.187/1106   *Exit.*
3.1.0.1-2/1106.1   *Enter Duke, Claudio, and Prouost.*
3.1.47.1/1153.1   *Enter Isabella.* (after 3.1.43/1149)
3.1.181/1288   *Exit.*
3.1.270/1377   *Exit.*
3.1.270/1377   *Enter Elbow, Clowne, Officers.*
3.1.308.1/1416.1   *Enter Lucio.* (after 3.1.307/1415)
3.1.443/1551   *Exit.*
3.1.447.1/1555.1   *Enter Escalus, Prouost, and Bawd.* (after 3.1.448/1556)
3.1.538/1646   *Exit*
4.1.0.1/1646.1-2   *Enter Mariana, and Boy singing. | Song.*
4.1.1/1646.2   *Song.*
4.1.6.1/1652.1   *Enter Duke.*
4.1.20.1/1666.1   *Enter Isabell.*
4.1.24/1671   *Exit.*
4.1.49.1/1696.1   *Enter Mariana.* (after 4.1.48/1695)
4.1.57.1/1704.1   *Exit.*
4.1.63/1710   *Enter Mariana and Isabella.* (after 'agreed')
4.1.74/1721.1   *Exeunt.*
4.2.0.1/1721.2   *Enter Prouost and Clowne.*
4.2.18.1/1738.1   *Enter Abhorson.*
4.2.29/1749   *Exit.*
4.2.45.1/1765.1   *Enter Prouost.*
4.2.58.1/1778.1   *Exit* (after 4.2.57/1777)
4.2.60.1/1780.1   *Enter Claudio.*
4.2.70/1790   *Enter Duke.* (after 'Father')
4.2.101.1/1821.1   *Enter a Messenger.*
4.2.122/1842   *The Letter.*
4.2.209/1930   *Exit.*
4.3.0.1/1930.1   *Enter Clowne.*
4.3.18.1/1948.1   *Enter Abhorson.*
4.3.23/1953   *Barnardine within.* (on line before speech-prefix '*Bar.*')
4.3.35.1/1965.1   *Enter Barnardine.* (after 4.3.33/1963)
4.3.44.1/1974.1   *Enter Duke.*
4.3.60.1/1990.1   *Exit*
4.3.62.2/1992.2   *Enter Prouost.* (after '*Exit*', 4.3.60.1/1990.1)
4.3.88.1/2018.1   *Exit.* (after 4.3.87/2017)
4.3.97.1/2027.1   *Enter Prouost.*
4.3.102/2032   *Exit*
4.3.103/2033   *Isabell within.* (on line before speech-prefix '*Isa.*')
4.3.108.1/2038.1   *Enter Isabella.* (after 'expected')
4.3.145.1/2075   *Enter Lucio.* (after 'heere')
4.3.172/2103   *Exeunt*
4.4.0.1/2103.1   *Enter Angelo & Escalus.*
4.4.18/2121   *Exit.* (after 4.4.17/2120)
4.4.33.1/2136.1   *Exit.*
4.5.0.1/2136.2   *Enter Duke and Frier Peter.*
4.5.10.1/2146.2   *Enter Varrius.*
4.5.13/2149   *Exeunt.*
4.6.0.1/2149.1   *Enter Isabella and Mariana.*
4.6.8.1/2158.1   *Enter Peter.*
4.6.16/2165   *Exeunt.*
5.1.0.1-3/2165.1-3   *Enter Duke, Varrius, Lords, Angelo, Esculus, Lucio, | Citizens at seuerall doores.*

5.1.18.2/2183.2 Enter Peter and Isabella.
5.1.166/2331 Enter Mariana. (after 'Witnes Frier')
5.1.257.1/2422.1 Exit. (after 'Slanderers')
5.1.277.1, 279.1-2/2442.1, 2444.1 Enter Duke, Prouost, Isabella. (after 5.1.275/2440)
5.1.376.1-2/2540.1 Exit.
5.1.396.1/2560.1 Enter Angelo, Maria, Peter, Prouost. (after 'Brother')
5.1.476.1-2/2640.1-2 Enter Barnardine and Prouost, Claudio, Iulietta.

[Printed after the play]

The Scene Vienna.
The names of all the Actors.
Vincentio: the Duke.
Angelo, the Deputie.
Escalus, an ancient Lord.
Claudio, a yong Gentleman.
Lucio, a fantastique.
2. Other like Gentlemen.
Prouost.
Thomas. ⎫ *2. Friers.*
Peter.   ⎭
Elbow, a simple Constable.
Froth, a foolish Gentleman.
Clowne.
Abhorson, an Executioner.
Barnardine, a dissolute prisoner.
Isabella, sister to Claudio.
Mariana, betrothed to Angelo.
Iuliet, beloued of Claudio.
Francisca, a Nun.
Mistris Ouer-don, a Bawd.

OTHELLO

Othello was first printed in 1622 (Q1, *BEPD* 379) by Nicholas Okes. Honigmann (*Stability*) argued that three compositors worked on it, but Millard T. Jones (in an unpublished University of Kansas Ph.D. thesis of 1974) more convincingly found only one, a conclusion independently supported by T. L. Berger (unpublished seminar paper, S.A.A., 1982). Q had been entered in the Stationers' Register on 6 October 1621:

> Tho: Walkley   Entred for his copie vnder the handes of Sr George Buck, and Mr Swinhowe warden, The Tragedie of Othello the moore of Venice

Walkley's short Epistle is printed on p. lii. A different text appeared in the 1623 Folio. F has about 160 lines not present in Q1, and there are over one thousand verbal variants as well as many differences in spelling and punctuation. Over fifty oaths in Q1 are not found in F, doubtless as a result of the Profanity Act of 1606.

The long-held belief that both Q1 and F derived from a single original (Chambers, *Shakespeare*, i. 459) was difficult to reconcile with the many substantive differences, and gave rise to complicated theories of memorial contamination and editorial interference (see e.g. Greg, *Problem*, 357-74). Q1 was generally held to represent a text shortened in the theatre. Greg, noting the equally Shakespearian quality of the alternative versions of certain passages, postulated original foul papers containing many *currente calamo* revisions, perhaps even 'alterations made by the author or with his authority after his draft had been officially copied' (*Folio*, 368-9). Ridley thought that 'in F we have probably a good deal of Shakespeare's second thoughts, but also, almost certainly, a good deal of divergence from the original for which he was not responsible' (p. xliii). Consequently he based his edition, exceptionally, on Q1. More recently the hypothesis (Honigmann, *Stability*, 'Revised Plays'; Coghill) that Q represents an unrevised, F an authorially revised text has done away with the need to suppose that Q must derive from a prompt-book representing a shortened version of the original play or that its dialogue was influenced by memories of performance. At the same time it does not preclude the possibility that Q1 represents a prompt-book of the unrevised version.

As the nature of the copy for Q and F, and the relationship between the two editions, are crucial to an editor's treatment of the play, we give our views below.

Q1

Q1's stage directions are generally authorial in style (Greg, *Folio*, 360). Some of their authorial features might have survived into a prompt-book; so might their failure to mark Othello's re-entrance (after an unmarked exit at 1.2.49/235) at 1.2.52.1-2/239.1-2; but an incorrect entry for Desdemona (1.3.46.1-2/332.1-2) tells against prompt-book copy, as do certain other features discussed below.

If Q1 is not from a prompt-book it must be either from the author's papers (foul or fair) or a scribal transcript. The speech-prefixes are remarkably uniform (Greg, *Folio*, 361), lacking the inconsistencies found in such 'good' quartos as *Much Ado*, *Romeo*, and *Love's Labour's Lost*. This might suggest no more than Shakespeare's own fair copy.

Some features point to a scribal transcript:

(a) The text is unique among Shakespeare quartos in its division into acts. (There is no marker at the beginning of the play or of Act 3.) This division might have been introduced in the printing house. But absence of a heading for Act 3 slightly favours the hypothesis that the divisions were in the copy (on the grounds that the omission of markers from the original copy is marginally more likely to go uncorrected than the omission of markers provided in the printing house). It is also relevant that the act divisions coincide with those in F, which appears to be independently derived. Act divisions appear not to have been observed in the public theatres till about 1609 (but might possibly have been observed in court or university performances before then). It is possible to suppose that a scribe copying foul papers marked divisions where he remembered them occurring in performance.

(b) Some of Q1's directions suggest a scribe being helpful to a reader rather than a compositor simply trying to follow copy: for instance, in 'Enter a 2. Messenger' (1.3.33.1/319.1) and 'Enter a third Gentleman' (2.1.19.1/701.1), the use of the indefinite article in such a direction with either '2' or '3' or 'Second' or 'Third' is paralleled in the Shakespeare canon only at *Timon* 1.2.185/472 (ascribed to Middleton: 'Enter a third seruant'), and *All Is True* 4.1.56/2009.3 (ascribed to Fletcher: 'Enter a third Gentleman'). Nor does it recur in the Folio text of *Othello*.

(c) At 5.2.262/3159 is the direction 'Gra. *within.*' followed by the prefix 'Gra.' on the next line. A stage direction of this kind occurs only five times elsewhere in the canon, at *Measure* 1.4.6, 4.3.23, 108/323, 1953, and 2038, *Twelfth Night* 4.2.20.1/1950.1, and Folio *Richard II* 5.3.72/2446. None of these is believed to be a foul-papers text.

(d) Two related peculiarities of the Quarto text both suggest scribal interference (as Greg suggests, *Folio*, 360). At 2.1.52/734 it reads:

> *Enter a Messenger.*
> Mess. A saile, a saile, a saile.
> Cas. What noyse?
> Mess. The Towne is empty, on the brow o'th sea, otand [*sic*] ranckes of people, and they cry a sayle.

In the Folio, this reads:

> *Within.* A Saile, a Saile, a Saile.

Cassio What noise?
Gent. The Towne is empty; on the brow o'th'Sea
Stand rankes of People, and they cry, a Saile.

The dialogue is identical in both; Folio's direction for the cry to be '*Within*' makes perfect sense, whereas Q1 is nonsensical in bringing a messenger on stage before Cassio asks 'What noyse?' There is, then, no reason to suspect revision in F. Nor is the error likely to derive from a prompt-book: as Greg remarks, 'The book-keeper would hardly have introduced an imaginary character' (*Folio*, 360). More probably Q1 represents an attempt to make sense of a manuscript reading which failed to indicate the source of 'A saile . . .'. Though such interpretative alteration might not be beyond the wit of a compositor, it is beyond his normal brief. (The passage, incidentally, remains awkward in F as it is not clear how the '*Gent.*' knows what is happening.)

Similarly, at 1.3.12/298 Q1 reads:

Enter a Messenger.
One within. What ho, what ho, what ho?
Sailor. A messenger from the Galley.
Du⟨ke⟩. Now, the businesse?
Sailor. The *Turkish* preparation makes for *Rhodes*,
So was I bid report here, to the state.

At F1, the equivalent passage is:

Saylor within. What hoa, what hoa, what hoa.
Enter Saylor.
Officer. A Messenger from the Gallies.
Duke. Now? What's the businesse?
Sailor. The Turkish Preparation makes for Rhodes,
So was I bid report here to the State,
By Signior *Angelo*.

The dialogue is similar though not identical. Folio makes perfect dramatic sense (it has brought '*Officers*' on at the beginning of the scene). Q1 is muddled. Greg says 'The Sailor who enters at 1.iii.13 (rather than 12) is called a "Messenger" because he is so described in the text, though the prefix "Sailor" remains at l. 14 and has apparently been erroneously substituted for "Officer" (as in F) at l. 13.' In fact Q1 has not so far introduced either officers or sailors in this scene (though an officer appears in a speech-prefix at 1.3.34/319). We may conjecture that the line 'A messenger from the Galley' was unattributed in Shakespeare's papers, and that a scribe gave it, illogically, to '*Sailor*' simply because the next speech but one was ascribed to a sailor.

The evidence suggests, then, that Q1 was printed from a scribal transcript of Shakespeare's foul papers. An attempt to date such a transcript must be highly speculative. If it was made for presentation, it was presumably copied before the text was revised. If the act divisions were part of the original transcript, this might suggest that revision occurred in 1609 or later, but we cannot discount the possibility that act divisions were used before 1609 for special performances, and it is just such performances that might have encouraged the preparation of a presentation copy. In any case, divisions might have been marked on a presentation copy without being observed in performance. The unexpurgated nature of Q1 does not in itself affect the dating as there would have been no need to remove profanities from a literary transcript.

Walkley, the publisher of Q1, printed four King's Men's plays besides *Othello* between 1619 and 1625. All seem to have been from private transcripts: *A King and No King* (1619) has an epistle implying that the copy came from Sir Henry Neville, the publisher's dedicatee; it and the other three plays (*The Maid's Tragedy* (1625), *Philaster* (1622), and *Thierry and Theodoret* (1621)) all contain profanities, and all, according to the latest scholarly investigations, were printed from transcripts.

The Folio

Alice Walker contended that the copy for F was a heavily annotated copy of Q1; this hypothesis was the general consensus for some thirty years. But it seems to us to have been decisively disproved by the work of J. K. Walton (on substantive readings), G. Taylor (on punctuation and spelling), and MacD. P. Jackson (on misreadings in F). We therefore assume that F was set from an independent manuscript.

If Q1 derives from foul papers, F1 cannot have done. So it must derive from a transcript. As we accept that it represents a revised text, there must have existed a transcript by Shakespeare himself (unless we suppose that he wrote the revisions on a scribally prepared prompt-book: but they are too numerous and, many of them, too trivial for this to be credible). There are several reasons for believing that another hand intervened.

(*a*) The F stage directions are more businesslike, less authorial, and less full than Q's. They are not strongly theatrical: for example, they omit '*A shot*' (2.1.56.1/738.1), '*Trumpets within*' (2.1.180.1/861.1), '*A bell rung*' (2.3.153.1/1159.1), '*A Trumpet*' (4.1.207.1/2335.1), along with a number of directions for necessary action. Particularly striking is the total absence from F of music cues. (Admittedly, *Othello* calls for fewer flourishes and the like than plays about royalty; but trumpets are unequivocally required at the points mentioned in Q1, as are the 'Instruments' mentioned at 4.2.174/2585 (where Rowe added a direction for them).)

(*b*) The punctuation is considerably heavier than we should expect from a foul-papers text (and than that of Q1); in particular, there is an exceptional proportion of parentheses. This heavy punctuation cannot be wholly or even primarily compositorial, since the text was set in part by Compositor E, who recorded copy punctuation with unusual conservatism.

(*c*) F spells out in full a number of words and expressions which are colloquially abbreviated in Q1, at the expense of metre in 3.4.187/2116. Comparison with the work of both Folio compositors elsewhere demonstrates that few if any of these expressions can be compositorial in origin.

(*d*) F has a strong preference (117:34) for 'Oh' over 'O', which appears to have been Shakespeare's preferred spelling. Both compositors almost invariably reproduced the copy spellings of this exclamation.

Summary

Our textual hypothesis is as follows:

Q1 represents a scribal copy of foul papers.

F represents a scribal copy of Shakespeare's own revised manuscript of the play.

F therefore brings us closer to Shakespeare's final text than Q1.

Q1's scribe obliterated fewer authorial characteristics than F's.

It is therefore reasonable to take Q1 as the basic copy-text, to graft on to it passages found only in F, and to observe Shakespeare's substitutions and alterations at other points. This procedure has the disadvantage of producing a text with mixed characteristics in its incidentals, but this would be true of any critical edition of *Othello*, since the use of F as copy-text would involve the restoration of Q1's profanities and colloquialisms. Since Q1's incidentals are so much closer to those of foul-papers texts than are F's, it seems proper to adopt in *Othello* the same procedures we have applied to *Richard III*, *Hamlet*, and *Troilus*.

We nevertheless follow F in all readings which make acceptable sense, whether or not we prefer them to Q1's, unless we suspect them of corruption, and except in stage directions, which may have been tampered with by the scribe.

We collate all substantive and semi-substantive variants in F that we do not adopt (e.g. expurgations, etc.), and its substantive press variants; other press variants are recorded in Hinman, i. 312–16.

Sophistications pose a special problem. Both texts display evidence of scribal sophistication, especially in the use of abbreviated and unabbreviated forms. In Q1, 'em' occurs frequently for 'them'; in F, not at all; in the canon as a whole it is found mostly in late plays, especially *All Is True*, *Two Noble Kinsmen*, and *Timon*—all collaborative—but also in *Coriolanus* (15 times) and *Tempest* (17 times). We follow Q. Somewhat similarly, Q often uses 'ha' for 'haue'; F, never. Again, we follow Q. Where F uses 'if' for Q's 'an', we follow Q. More complex is the variation between 'has' and 'hath'. F has 'hath' for Q1's 'has' in 22 places; this suggests a degree of sophistication, but Q1's 'hath/has' ratio (38:35) also misrepresents the Shakespearian norm (Honigmann, 'One-way Variants', 200). As there is no satisfactory way of determining which particular usages in either text may be Shakespearian, and as overall F corresponds more closely to the norm, we follow F. Another set of variants (strongly supporting the view that Q1 derives from a transcript) relates to 'i'the' and 'ith''. Q1 has six instances of 'i'the', a form which elsewhere occurs only three times in all the copy-texts for the Shakespeare canon. Here too we follow F. In spite of efforts to identify and correct the sophistications mentioned here, and others, many more must remain.

In the Textual Notes that follow, Qa refers to the uncorrected, Qb to the corrected first state of sheets in Q1; Qc to the uncorrected, Qd to the corrected second state. There are three states of correction in F: a, b, and c.

The belief that F represents a revised text entails the corollary that Q1 has its own integrity and, therefore, independent interest. We lack the space to print an edited text of Q1, but in the Notes, and the list of rejected Quarto readings, we place an asterisk before those readings most likely to have been affected by revision.

S.W.W./(G.T.)

WORKS CITED

Coghill, Nevill, *Shakespeare's Professional Skills* (1964)
Furness, H. H., ed., *Othello*, New Variorum (1886)
Honigmann, E. A. J., *The Stability of Shakespeare's Text* (1965)
—— 'On the Indifferent and One-Way Variants in Shakespeare', *The Library*, V, 22 (1967), 189–204
—— 'Shakespeare's Revised Plays: *King Lear* and *Othello*', *The Library*, VI, 4 (1982), 142–73
Jackson, MacD. P., 'Printer's Copy for the First Folio Text of *Othello*: The Evidence of Misreadings', forthcoming in *The Library*
Muir, Kenneth, 'The Text of *Othello*', SSt 1 (1965), 227–39
—— ed., *Othello*, New Penguin (1968)
Ridley, M. R., ed., *Othello*, Arden (1958)
Ross, Lawrence J., ed., *Othello*, Bobbs-Merrill (1974)
Sanders, N. J., ed., *Othello*, New Cambridge (1984)
Taylor, Gary, 'The Folio Copy for *Hamlet*, *King Lear*, and *Othello*', SQ 34 (1983), 44–61
—— 'Folio Compositors and Folio Copy: *King Lear* and its Context', PBSA 79 (1985), 17–74
Upton, John, *Critical Observations on Shakespeare* (1746)
Walker, Alice, ed., *Othello*, New (1957)
Walton, J. K., *The Quarto Copy for the First Folio of Shakespeare* (1971)

TEXTUAL NOTES

Title *The Tragedy of* Othello *the Moore | of Venice*] Q (*Tragœdy*, title-page); THE TRAGEDIE OF | Othello, the Moore of Venice. F, S.R.
1.1.1/1 Tush] Q; *not in* F. Not a profanity, but perhaps omitted in parallel with Iago's 'S' blood' (1.1.4/4).
1.1.4/4 S'blood] Q; *not in* F
1.1.24/24 toged] Q; Tongued F
1.1.24 togaed] Editors usually spell 'togèd'; *OED* distinguishes *toge* (from the French) from *toga*, but this is the first recorded use of the adjectival participle, and in speech the forms are indistinguishable.
1.1.28/28 other] Q; others F
1.1.32/32 God] Q; *not in* F
1.1.53/53 'em] Q; them F
1.1.66/66 full] Q; fall F
1.1.66/66 thicklips] Q; Thick-lips F
1.1.79/79 theeues, theeues, theeues] Q; Theeues, Theeues F
1.1.86/86 Zounds sir] Q; Sir F
1.1.101/101 brauery] Q; knauerie F. Though F could be an authorial substitution, its weakening of the sense along with the graphic resemblance justifies the general preference for Q (the rarer reading).

1.1.110/110 Zouns] Q; *not in* F
1.1.118/119 now] Q; *not in* F
1.1.153/154 stands] QF; stand POPE
*1.1.174/175 maidhood] F (Maidhood); manhood Q. Q might alternatively be emended to 'womanhood' (G.T.).
1.1.184/185 night] Q; might F. An easy misreading; see Sanders.
1.2.34/220 Duke] Q; Dukes F
1.2.46/232 sent] Q; hath ſent F
1.2.55/241 comes another] Q; come sanother Fb; come another Fa
1.2.59/245 *Roderigo*, Come] Q; *Rodorigo*, come Fa; *Rodorigoc*? Cme Fb
1.2.60/246 em] Q; them F
1.2.69/255 darlings] Q; Dearelings F
1.2.88/274 I] Q; *not in* F
1.3.1/287 There is] Q; There's F
1.3.1/287 these] Q; this F (*a possible spelling variant*)
*1.3.6/292 the ayme] F; they aym'd Q. Q may be an error for 'they ayme', meaning 'they conjecture'; F is acceptable as 'conjecture' (*OED*, *sb.* 1).
1.3.43/329 beleeue] QF; relieve WALKER (Capell)
1.3.46.1/332.1 *Cassio*] QF. Capell omitted him, and is followed by Cambridge and some modern editors (Walker, Alexander, Sisson,

Muir), presumably as a 'ghost'. Other editors (e.g. Kittredge, Ridley) bring him on here but provide no distinct exit for him, though he must leave before the scene's final conversation between Iago and Roderigo followed by Iago's soliloquy. Concurrence of Q and F as well as the fact that he had been sent to fetch Othello suggests that he should be silently present during the first part of the scene; we take him off with the Duke (1.3.293.1-2/579.1-2).

1.3.53/339   nor] Q; hor F
*1.3.55/341   hold on] F; any hold of Q. Q's additional word is not needed for either sense or metre (the line is either a pentameter or a hexameter; the previous line is a hexameter).
1.3.58/344   it is] QF; yet is WALKER
*1.3.59/345   SENATORS] F (Sen.); All. Q. F's prefix could indicate only one senator (as it more clearly does at 1.3.110/396).
1.3.64/350   Saunce] Qb; Since Qa; Sans F
1.3.73/359   SENATORS] CAPELL; All. QF. Cf. 1.3.59/345.
1.3.90/376   tale] Q; u Tale F
1.3.99/385   maimd] Q; main'd F (a spelling variant)
1.3.106/392   vpon] Q; vp on F
1.3.106/392   DUKE] Q (Du.); not in F (which however splits the verse line)
1.3.107/393   ouert] Q; ouer F
1.3.110/396   A SENATOR] F (Sen.); 1 Sena. Q. See 1.3.59/345.
1.3.122/408   till] Q; tell F (a spelling variant)
1.3.129/415   battailes] Q; Battaile F
1.3.129/415   fortunes] Q; Fortune F
1.3.139/425   Antrees] Q; Antars F. First recorded use; next in Keats. We regard Q and F as spelling variants.
1.3.140/426   and hils, whose heads] Q; Hills, whofe head F
1.3.142/428   other] Q; others F
1.3.143/429   Anthropophagie] Q; Antropophague F
1.3.144/430   Doe grow] Q; Grew F. If, in an earlier stage of transmission, 'Doe' had been accidentally omitted, 'grow' could have been misread as 'grew'.
1.3.146/432   thence] Q; hence F
1.3.154/440   intentiuely] Q; inftinctiuely F. F is hard to justify, and probably a corruption.
*1.3.158/444   kisses] F; fighes Q. Muir regards F as 'obviously impossible', but it is difficult to explain as an error. Desdemona may be thought of as impulsively affectionate.
1.3.188/474   bu'y] Q; be with you F
1.3.197/483   em] Q; them F
1.3.200/486   Into your fauour] Q; not in F. Probably an accidental omission.
1.3.218/504   pierced] QF; piecèd THEOBALD (Warburton). See Sanders.
1.3.218/504   eare] Q; eares F. Typical Compositor E error.
1.3.229/515   Cooch] Q; Coach F
1.3.248/534   I did] Q; I F
1.3.264/550   me] CAPELL (Upton); my QF. A much disputed passage. Agreement of Q and F argues against error, but the unusual syntax may have misled both scribes into the same easy misreading.
1.3.270/556   instruments] Q; Inftrument F. F may be right, but the metaphor introduced by 'seele' is better sustained by the plural, and Compositor E is notoriously susceptible to errors involving addition or omission of terminal 's'.
1.3.278/564   DESDEMONA .... This night] Q; not in F. Accidental omission as a result of eyeskip seems likely.
1.3.291/577   A SENATOR] F (Sen.); 1 Sena. Q
1.3.300/586   the] Q; the the F
1.3.311/597   ha] Q; haue F
1.3.322/608   Time] QF; tine WALKER. See Ross.
1.3.326/612   beame] THEOBALD; braine F; ballance Q
1.3.330-1/616-17   our vnbitted] Q; or vnbitted F
1.3.350/637   error] Q; errors F
1.3.355/641   a super subtle] Q; fuper-fubtle F
*1.3.357/643   pox a] Q; pox of F
1.3.377/663   a] Q; not in F
1.3.380/666   He ha's] F2; She ha's F1; Ha's Q
1.3.395/681   ha't] Q; haue't F
2.1.0.1-2/682.2-3   MONTANO] F (throughout). Q spells Montanio seven times, Montano three. The '-io' form may attempt to represent Italian pronunciation as in 'Montagna'; the name Montano occurs in at least six other plays of the period, Montanio not at all.
2.1.0.1-2/682.2-3   Enter .... Gentlemen] Perhaps one or both of the Gentlemen should be on the upper level. This would explain Montano's opening question and add vividness to 2.1.11-17/693-9 (which would become a direct reaction to the spectacle); see also note to 2.1.52/734.
2.1.7/689   ha] Q; hath F
2.1.13   mane] Q (mayne), F (Maine)
2.1.27   Veronessa] Q; Verenneffa F
2.1.34/716   prayes] Q; praye, F. F's spacing suggests that the 's' was set but did not ink.
2.1.41/723   3 GENTLEMAN] Q (3 Gent.); Gent. F
2.1.43/725   arriuance] Q; Arriuancie F. This is the first recorded occurrence of either spelling; the few other instances are as Q.
2.1.44/726   this] Q; the F
2.1.52/734   VOYCES (within)] F (Within, as prefix); Enter a Meffenger | Meff. Q. Q is obviously wrong. Perhaps it merely implies that a messenger should call 'A saile ... in' before entering (Walker). But 2.1.54-5/736-7 are tenuous as a message, and a messenger's entry would indicate that something had happened without off-stage cries. Perhaps 2.1.52/734 and 2.1.54/736 were unattributed in the MS and the Q scribe invented the messenger and his entry. F makes sense if we assume that the Gent. of 2.1.54/736 is one of those already on stage, perhaps on an upper level, and that he has only to look off stage to see that 'The towne is empty ...'.
*2.1.54/736   A GENTLEMAN] F (Gent.); Meff. Q
*2.1.57/739   A GENTLEMAN] F (Gent.); 2 Gen. Q
*2.1.60/742   A GENTLEMAN] F (Gent.); 2 Gent. Q
2.1.66   engineer] F (Ingeniuer): OED does not record F's spelling, but it is close to the French ingénieur which OED offers as the origin of the English word.
*2.1.67/749   GENTLEMAN] F (Gent.); 2 Gent. Q
2.1.83/765   And bring all Cypresse comfort,—] Q; not in F
2.1.89/771   me] Q; not in F
2.1.95/777   VOYCES (within)] A saile, a saile] F (Within., A Saile, a Saile., after harke, A faile.); Q ([within.] A faile, a faile, after company ?, 2.1.92/774)
*2.1.97/779   A GENTLEMAN] F (Gent.); 2 Gent. Q
*2.1.97/779   their] Q; this F
2.1.108/790   ha] Q; haue F
2.1.111/793   ha] Q; haue F
2.1.115   hussies] QF (houfwiues, Hufwiues)
2.1.123   essay] QF (affay)
2.1.177/859   an] Q; and F
2.1.215/896   hither] Q; thither F. Roderigo must be addressed; F could easily arise from scribal or compositorial misunderstanding.
*2.1.219/900   must] F; will Q
2.1.228/909   againe] Q; a game F
2.1.229/910-11   appetite, Louelines] THEOBALD; appetite. Loue lines Q; appetite. Louelineffe F
2.1.243/924   has] Q; he's F
2.1.261/943   mutualities] Q; mutabilities F
2.1.302/984   trace] F; crufh Q. Most editors reject both readings; Steevens's 'trash', once customary, is 'inappropriate to Roderigo' (Muir) and 'the reverse of Shakespearian in style' (Walker); Walker reads 'leash' as it 'suggests holding in with a view to slipping, thus looking forward to "putting on"'. This may lie behind Q, but F's 'trace' seems acceptable as 'pursue, dog' (OED, 5): so Halliwell, paraphrasing 'whose steps I carefully watch in order to quicken his pace' (Furness).
2.1.305/987   ranke] Q; right F. F's weak reading is probably an accidental substitution.
*2.2.6/999   addiction] Q2; minde Q1; addition F
2.2.10/1004   Heauen blesse] Q; Bleffe F
2.3.35/1041   ha] Q; haue F
2.3.56/1062   to put] Q; put to F
2.3.60/1066   God] Q; heauen F
2.3.69/1075   God] Q; Heauen F
2.3.74/1080   English man] Q; Englifhmen F

OTHELLO

2.3.89/1095 Then] Q; And F
2.3.91/1097 Fore God] Q; Why F
2.3.95/1101 God's] Q; heau'ns F
2.3.103/1109 ha] Q; haue F
2.3.104/1110 God forgiue] Q; Forgiue F
*2.3.109/1115 GENTLEMEN] F (Gent.); All. Q
2.3.132 engraffed] QF (ingraft)
2.3.137/1143 voyces...helpe] Q (Helpe, helpe, within.); not in F
2.3.139/1145 Zouns, you] Q; You F
2.3.151/1157 godswill] Q; Alas F
2.3.152/1158 sir,] Q; not in F
2.3.155/1161 godswill] Q; Fie, fie F
2.3.155/1161 hold] Q; not in F
2.3.157/1163 Zouns,] Q; not in F
2.3.160/1166 place of sence] QF; sense of place HANMER. Schmidt lists as a 'peculiar passage'; editors often emend. But Q and F support each other, and common error seems most unlikely. 'Place' may mean 'stance', 'attitude', 'mental position' (cf. All's Well, 'that same knaue that leades him to those places' (3.5.85/1577), and Arden note), giving the meaning 'forgotten every position of common sense and respect'. Riverside glosses 'i.e. the ordinary decencies'.
2.3.161/1167 hold, hold] Q; hold F
2.3.183/1189 be] Q; to be F
2.3.200 Essays] QF (Assayes, Assaies).
2.3.200/1206 Zouns, if I] Q; If I once F
2.3.211/1217 leagu'd] POPE; league QF.
2.3.214/1220 ha] Q; haue F
2.3.226/1232 the] Q; then F
2.3.246/1252 now] Q; not in F
2.3.255/1261 God] Q; Heauen F
2.3.256/1262 ha] Q; haue F
2.3.257/1263 ha] Q; haue F
2.3.260/1266 thought] Q; had thought F
2.3.283/1289 O God] Q; Oh F
2.3.307/1314 I'le] Q; I F
2.3.310/1317 denotement] Q2; deuotement QF. An easy misreading, especially after 'deuoted'; and 'denotement' would be a first occurrence.
2.3.323/1332 here] Q; not in F
2.3.334/1343 wer't] Q (Wer't); were F
2.3.356/1365 ha] Q; haue F
2.3.360/1369 ha] Q; haue F
2.3.365/1374 hast] Q; hath F
2.3.368/1377 bi'the masse] Q; Introth F
2.3.375/1384 awhile] QF (a while); the while THEOBALD. Often emended, but Q and F agree, and the phrase could mean 'draw the Moor apart for a while'.
3.1.3/1390 ha] Q; haue F
3.1.8-9 tail...tale] Q (tayle...tayle), F (tale...tale)
3.1.18/1405 ha] Q; haue F
3.1.21/1408 my] Q; me, mine F; mine THEOBALD
3.1.25/1412 Generals wife] Q (Cenerals wife); Generall F. F looks like a compound error: accidental omission of 'wife' at one stage leading to deliberate alteration of 'Generals' at another.
3.1.29/1417 CASSIO Doe good my friend:] Q; not in F
3.1.30/1418 ha] Q; haue F
3.1.31/1419 ha] Q; haue F
3.1.48/1436 To take the saf'st occasion by the front] Q (safest); not in F. F probably results from eyeskip on the word 'To'.
3.3.16/1464 circumstance] Q; Circumstances F. Shakespeare's usage elsewhere supports Q.
3.3.53/1501 Yes faith] Q; I sooth F
3.3.61/1509 or] Q; on F
3.3.75/1523 Birlady] Q; Trust me F
3.3.96/1544 you] Q; he F
3.3.110/1558 By heauen] Q; Alas, F
3.3.116/1564 In] Q; Of F
3.3.136/1584 to me] Qb, F; tome (Qa)
3.3.140/1588 that all slaues are free to,] Q; that: All Slaues are free: F
3.3.144/1592 But some] Q; Wherein F

3.3.152/1600 oft] Q; of F
3.3.153/1601 Shapes] QF; Shape KNIGHT
3.3.153/1601 that your wisedome then] WALKER; I intreate you then Q1; that your wisedome F; that your wisedome yet Q2. Walker's reading suggests a simpler explanation of F's error than Q2's, accepted by most editors.
*3.3.159/1607 What dost thou meane?] F; Zouns. Q. F is not a direct substitution for Q's oath; Shakespeare is holding back Othello's anguish.
3.3.166/1614 By heauen] Q; not in F
*3.3.174/1622 fondly] KNIGHT; strongly Q; soundly F. Knight emends F's reading; Q is probably an authorial alternative.
3.3.179/1627 God] Q; Heauen F
3.3.184/1632 once] Q; not in F
3.3.189/1637 well] Q; not in F
3.3.206/1654 God] Q; Heauen F
*3.3.208/1656 keepe't] Q2 (after F, 'kept'); keepe Q
3.3.214 see] QF (seale, seele)
3.3.219/1667 Ifaith] Q; Trust me F
3.3.221/1669 my] Q; your F
3.3.250/1698 To] Qc, F; Iag. To Qd. Obviously a bungled attempt to supply the missing speech-prefix from 3.3.249/1697.
3.3.253/1701 hold] Q; not in F
3.3.261.1/1709.1 Exit.] F, Qa; not in Qb
3.3.263/1711 qualities] Q; Quantities F
3.3.267 Haply] Q (Happily); F
3.3.276/1724 keepe] Qb; leepe Qa
3.3.277/1725 of] Q; to F
3.3.282/1730 O then heauen mocks] Q; Heauen mock'd F. F's short line could be deliberate; the change of tense seems wrong.
3.3.289/1737 Faith] Q; Why F
3.3.300/1748 ha] Q; haue F
3.3.316/1764 faith] Q; but F
3.3.319/1767 with it] Q; with't F. F's variant may be due to justification of a crowded line in a crowded column.
3.3.343/1790 of] Q; in F
3.3.358/1805 and] Qb, F; aud Qa
3.3.364/1811 taking...throat] See A. C. Sprague, Shakespeare and the Actors (1944), 197-200.
3.3.364/1811 thou] Qc, F; you Qd
3.3.380/1827 buy you] Qb, F; buy, you Qa
3.3.380/1827 mine] F, Qd; thine Qc
3.3.391/1838 My] F; Her Q2 (and many editors). The emendation is purely interpretative.
3.3.396/1843 sir,] Q; not in F
3.3.400/1847 superuisor] Q; super-vision F
3.3.413/1860 ha't] Q; haue't F
3.3.428/1875 laie] ROWE; then layed Q; laid F; then lay POPE. See 3.3.429/1876.
3.3.428/1875 ore] F; ouer Q. F's variant relates to its omission of 'then', earlier in the line; the two variants in concert produce a hexameter, in place of Q's fourteener. See lineation notes.
*3.3.429/1876 sigh....kisse...cry] F; sigh'd...kissed...Cried Q. Editors prefer Q, but F is explicable as a revision of tenses.
3.3.434/1881 IAGO] Q (Iag.); prefixed to 3.3.435/1882 (Iago.) F. Error would be easy, and it would be an odd interruption of Othello's mounting conviction for him to call the adultery a doubt immediately after referring to it as a conclusion.
3.3.445/1892 yt] MALONE; it QF. Given the spate of 'it' in this context, misinterpretation of 'yt' would have been exceptionally easy.
*3.3.455/1902 mind] F (minde); mind perhaps Q
3.3.458/1905 knows] WHITE (Southern); keepes F; feels Q2. Accidental substitution seems likely (though Sisson, supposing addition, reads 'Never retiring ebbs'). Q2 'has custom in its favour' but '"knows"...is attractive' (Walker).
3.3.463/1910 he kneeles] Q (after 3.3.454/1901); not in F. Q's direction, though placed after a speech of Iago, must refer to Othello, and seems to imply that he should kneel to say 'O blood...'. F's version suggests that he should kneel later.
3.4.31 where] Q (were), F

3.4.55/1984	faith] Q; indeed F	
3.4.61/1990	Or] Q (c.w.); Intirely to her loue: But if ſhe loft it, | Or (text). (The text repeats at the top of l1 the last line of H4ᵛ.)	
3.4.75/2004	Ifaith] Q; Indeed? F	
3.4.77/2006	God] Q; Heauen F	
3.4.77/2006	seene it.] Q; seene't F (a crowded line)	
3.4.81/2010	Heauen bleſſe] Q; Bleſſe F	
3.4.86/2015	sir] Q; not in F	
3.4.91-2/2020-1	DESDEMONA I pray talke me . . . handkercher.] Q (Deſ. . . . Oth.); not in F (easy eyeskip)	
3.4.96/2025	Ifaith] Q; Infooth, F	
3.4.97/2026	Zouns] Q; Away F	
3.4.100/2029	the] Qd, F; this Qc	
3.4.168/2097	Ifaith] Q; Indeed F	
3.4.184/2113	by my faith] Q; in good troth F	
4.1.28/2155	Conuinced] Qd, F; Coniured Qc	
4.1.32/2159	Faith] Q; Why, F	
4.1.35/2162	Zouns,] Q; not in F	
4.1.50/2177	No, forbeare,] Q; not in F. The words are not absolutely essential, but metre suggests that their omission was accidental.	
4.1.52/2179	he] Qd, F; he he Qc	
4.1.64/2191	Good] Qd, F; God Qc	
4.1.76/2203	vnſuting] Qd; vnfitting Qc; refulting F. F's reading seems inexplicable. Qd is preferred to Qc as there seems no reason for the change other than consciousness of error.	
4.1.78/2205	scuse] Q; ſcuſes F	
4.1.93	hussy] QF (huſwife)	
*4.1.94/2221	cloath] F (Cloath); cloathes Q. The singular could mean 'clothing' (OED cloth, sb. II).	
*4.1.97/2224	restraine] F; refraine Q. F is justified by OED 7a.	
4.1.100/2227	conster] Q; conſerue F; construe ROWE. Rowe no doubt reflects F's manuscript copy; since 'conſtrue' requires a ligature, the compositor (E) must have misread manuscript 't' as 'e'. But Rowe's emendation is only a variant form of Q.	
4.1.102/2229	now] Q; not in F	
4.1.106/2233	power] Q; dowre F (where 'd' is probably a turned 'p')	
4.1.110/2237	a woman] Q; woman F	
4.1.111/2238	ifaith] Q; indeed F	
4.1.122/2249	Faith] Q; Why F	
4.1.125/2252	Ha] Q; Haue F	
4.1.129/2256	beckons] Q; becomes F	
4.1.131/2258	the sea] Q; the the Sea- Fa; the Sea- Fb	
*4.1.132-3/2260	and fals me] F (falls); by this hand ſhe fals Q. Possibly an expurgation, but F has the phrase at 4.1.171/2298 and Shakespeare may have preferred not to use it till then, where it carries heavy irony.	
4.1.148/2275	whole] Q; not in F. Probable eyeskip.	
4.1.156/2283	An . . . an] Q; If . . . if F. A recurrent Folio sophistication.	
4.1.159/2286	Faith] Q; not in F	
4.1.161/2288	Faith] Q; Yes F	
4.1.171-3/2298-2300	IAGO . . . whore.] F; not in Q. That Q's omission of this speech is an error is clear from the catchword, 'Iag.', on K1.	
4.1.183/2310	So] Q; ſo Fb; ſo Fa	
*4.1.210/2338	this,] F3; ~, F1; not in Q	
4.1.212/2340	God saue the] Q; Saue you F	
4.1.232/2360	the letter] Q; thle etter Fa; thLetter Fb	
4.1.235/2363	By my troth] Q; Truſt me F	
4.1.248/2376	an] Q; not in F	
4.1.281/2408	denote] Q; deonte Fa; deuote Fb	
4.2.5/2416	'em] Q; them F	
4.2.16/2427	ha] Q; haue F	
4.2.24/2435	ha] Q; haue F	
4.2.32/2443	nay] Q; May F	
4.2.33/2444	knees] Q; knee F. F is a justified line, set by Compositor E.	
4.2.34-5/2445-6	words, | But not the words] Q; word. F	
4.2.46	haply] F (happely), Q	
4.2.49/2460	God] This edition (G.T); heauen Q; Heauen F. F's reading could result from deliberate expurgation, and it alters the following line to match. But in Q 'he' strongly suggests that the word here should be 'God'. Occasional substitutions of this kind occur in otherwise unexpurgated texts; within the 13 preceding lines, Q's compositor (or scribe) had already copied 'heauen' three times (4.2.38/2449, 4.2.40/2451, 4.2.41/2452).	
4.2.50/2461	he] Q; they F. See preceding note.	
*4.2.57/2468	and mouing] F; vnmouing Q. Even editors (e.g. Ross) who believe F to incorporate revisions regard F as 'a sophistication to remove the apparent illogicality of the Q reading' (Muir, SSt), But Schmidt (under 'and'), glossing 'slowly mouing', offers several parallels (to which may be added Lear: History 15.71/2099; Tragedy 4.1.67/2066, 'a Cliffe, whose high and bending head' (F)) where 'and' has almost the force of 'yet'.	
4.2.66/2477	I here] QF (heere); Ay, there THEOBALD.	
4.2.66	Ay] QF (I)	
4.2.71/2482	ne're] Q; neuer F	
4.2.97/2508	ha] Q; haue F	
4.2.105/2516	ha] Q; haue F	
4.2.116/2527	ha] Q; haue F	
4.2.120/2531	hearts] Q, Fb; heart Fa	
4.2.145/2556	heauen] Q; Heauens F. A Compositor E page.	
4.2.152/2563	O God] ALEXANDER; O Good Q; Alas F. The change in F is consonant with profanity in Q, where the capital also suggests that 'God' stood in the ms.	
4.2.159/2570	them, in] Q2; them: or F; them on ROWE	
4.2.171/2582	And he does chide with you.] Q; not in F. Accidental omission seems likely.	
4.2.180/2591	dafts] F. Q's 'dofftſt' is probably an indifferent pronunciation variant.	
4.2.187/2598	Faith] Q; not in F	
4.2.187-8/2598-9	I haue heard too much, for your words, and] Q; I haue heard too much: and your words and Fb; And hell gnaw his bones, Fa. See Walton, 215-27.	
4.2.193/2604	em] Q; them F	
4.2.229/2640	takes] Q; taketh F. F's inflection is rare in Shakespeare's later work, and helps to fill a justified line.	
4.2.233/2644	of] Q; not in F	
4.3.12/2674	He] Q; And F. Accidental anticipation in F seems more likely than revision.	
4.3.20/2682	in them] Q; not in F.	
4.3.22/2684	faith] Q; Father F	
4.3.23/2685	thee] Q; not in F	
4.3.37/2699	nether] Fb; neither Fa	
4.3.38/2700	Soule ſat] Fb; Sonle ſet Fa	
4.3.38/2700	sighing] Q2; ſining Fa; finging Fb	
4.3.74/2736	vds pitty] Q; why F	
4.3.103/2765	God] Q; Heauen F	
5.1.1/2767	Bulke] Q; Barke F	
5.1.22/2788	heare] Q; heard F	
5.1.34	dear] QF (deare, deere)	
5.1.36/2802	Forth] Q; For F	
5.1.51	heaven's] F (heauen), Q (heauens)	
5.1.62/2828	em] Q; them F	
5.1.91/2857	O heauen] Q; yes, 'tis F	
5.1.106/2872	out] Q; not in F	
5.1.109/2875	an] Q; if F. Compare 4.1.156/2283	
5.1.116/2882	dead] Q; quite dead F. See Walker. Ross's 'quite.' is ingenious, but not paralleled elsewhere in Shakespeare.	
5.1.125/2891	fough] Q; not in F	
5.2.37/2934	so] Q; not in F	
5.2.62/2959	Then Lord] Q; O Heauen F	
5.2.74/2971	vsde the] F (vſ'd thee); ----vds death Q; —ud's death!—us'd thee ALEXANDER. See Ridley, who points out that Q could easily have arisen from misreading of the spellings adopted here.	
5.2.82/2979	'em] Q; them F	
5.2.88/2985	an] Q; if F	
5.2.93/2990	DESDEMONA O Lord, Lord, Lord.] Q (Deſ.); not in F	
5.2.96/2993	that am] Fb, Q; am that Fa	
5.2.106/3003	ha] Q; haue F	

5.2.110/3007	Should] Q; Did F. Knight and Riverside follow F, but its meaning is unclear.	5.2.260	ice-brook's] Q (Ifebrookes) F (Ice brookes). See Ridley.
5.2.127/3024	O Lord,] Q; Alas! F	5.2.295/3192	liue] Qd F; loue Qc
5.2.136/3033	heard] Q; heare F	5.2.356/3253	Indian] Q; Iudean F. This notorious crux is well discussed by Richard Levin (SQ 33 (1982), 60–7); the discussion is continued in G. Walton Williams's review article in SS 36 (1983), 193-4. Levin does not allow for the possibility that F is a revision of Q, but it seems unlikely that if Shakespeare had wished to effect so crucial a change, he would have altered none of the surrounding text, if only to regularize the metre.
5.2.166/3063	worst] Q; wotſt F		
5.2.224/3121	God, O heauenly God.] Q; Heauen! oh heauenly Powres! F		
5.2.225/3122	Zouns] Q; Come F		
5.2.227/3124	em] Q; them F		
5.2.247/3144	here] Q; *not in* F		

REJECTED QUARTO VARIANTS

*1.1.2/2	thou] you		1.2.17/203	Will] Weele
*1.1.2/2	hast] has		*1.2.20/206	Which when I know,] *not in* Q
*1.1.4/4	you'l] you will		*1.2.22/208	Seige] height
*1.1.10/10	Off-capt] Oft capt		*1.2.28/214	yond] yonder
*1.1.14/14	warre:] (~,) warre:| And in conclufion,		*1.2.29/215	Those] Thefe
1.1.16/16	chose] chofen		*1.2.32/218	is it they?] (Is); it is they.
1.1.26/26	th'election] the election		1.2.35/221	you] your
*1.1.29/29	Christen'd] Chriftian. For 'christened' as 'converted to Christianity', see *OED*.		*1.2.38/224	What is] What's
			*1.2.41/227	sequent] frequent
*1.1.29/29	be be-leed] be led		1.2.46/232	about] aboue
1.1.30/30	Creditor. This Counter-caster,] Creditor, this Counter-cafter:		*1.2.48/234	I will but] Ile
			*1.2.54/240	Haue with you.] Ha, with who?
*1.1.32/32	Morships] (Moorefhips); Worfhips		*1.2.65/251	things] thing
*1.1.34/34	Why] But		*1.2.66/252	(If . . . bound)] *not in* Q
*1.1.36/36	And not by] Not by the		*1.2.70/256	t'incurre] (encurre); to incurre
1.1.37/37	th'] the		*1.2.73-8/259-64	Iudge me . . . thee,] *not in* Q
*1.1.38/38	affin'd] (Affin'd); affign'd		1.2.79/265	For] Such
*1.1.43/43	all be] be all		*1.2.85/271	whether] (Whether); where
*1.1.54/54	these] (Thefe); Thofe		*1.2.86/272	To] And
1.1.61/61	doth] does		*1.2.92/278	bring] beare
*1.1.65/65	Dawes] Doues		1.3.4/290	hundred forty] (Hundred fortie); hundred and forty
1.1.67/67	carry't] carry'et		*1.3.10/296	in] to
*1.1.69/69	streets] (Streets); ftreete		*1.3.11/297	Article] Articles
*1.1.72/72	chances] changes		*1.3.12/298	SAILOR (*within*)] (*Saylor within.*); *One within,*
1.1.72/72	on't] out		*1.3.13/299	OFFICER] (*Officer.*); *Sailor*
1.1.80/80	your Daughter] (daughter); you Daughter		*1.3.13/299	Gallies] Galley
*1.1.85/85	your doores lockt] (Doores lock'd); all doore lockts		*1.3.13/299	Now? What's] Now,
			*1.3.16/302	By Signior *Angelo*.] *not in* Q
*1.1.86/86	y'are] you are		*1.3.25-31/311-17	For that it stands . . . profitlesse] *not in* Q
*1.1.88/88	now, now] now		*1.3.32/318	Nay,] And,
*1.1.96/96	worser] (worffer); worfe		1.3.36/322	them with] with
*1.1.105/105	spirits] fpirit		*1.3.37/323	I SENATOR . . . guesse?] (*Sen.*); *not in* Q
*1.1.105/105	their] them		*1.3.38/324	MESSENGER] (*Meff.*); *not in* Q
1.1.112/112	seruice, and] feruice, Q		1.3.38/324	re-stem] refterine; refterne Q2
*1.1.117/118	comes] come		*1.3.40/326	toward] towards
*1.1.123-39/124-40	If't be your pleasure . . . your selfe] *not in* Q		*1.3.44/330	he] here
			*1.3.46/332	to] (To); wifh
*1.1.142/143	thus deluding you] this delufion		1.3.51/337	lack't] lacke
*1.1.147/148	place] pace		1.3.55/341	griefe] griefes
*1.1.148/149	producted] produc'd		*1.3.63/349	(Being not . . . sense,)] *not in* Q
1.1.150/151	How] Qa, F; Now Qb		1.3.69/355	your] its
*1.1.154/155	none] not		*1.3.69/355	yea,] *not in* Q
*1.1.156/157	hell paines] (hell apines); hells paines		*1.3.82/368	soft] fet
1.1.160/161	Sagitary] Sagittar		*1.3.87/373	feates] F (Feats); feate
*1.1.167/168	she deceiues] (deceaues); thou deceiueft		*1.3.87/373	broyles] (Broiles); broyle
*1.1.168/169	moe] more		*1.3.93/379	proceeding I am] proceedings am I
*1.1.176/177	Yes sir: I haue indeed] (Sir); I haue fir;		1.3.94-5/380-1	bold:	Of spirit,] (Spirit); bold of fpirit,
*1.1.177/178	would] that		*1.3.100/386	could] would
1.1.178/179	you] yon		*1.3.106/392	vouch] youth
*1.1.182/183	you] *not in* Q		*1.3.107/393	wider] certaine
*1.1.182/183	on] me on		*1.3.108/394	Then these] Thefe are
*1.1.185/186	I will] Ile		*1.3.109/395	seeming, do] feemings, you
*1.2.2/188	stuffe o'th'] ftuft of		*1.3.115/401	Sagitary] Sagittar
*1.2.4/190	Sometime] Sometimes		*1.3.118/404	The Trust . . . of you,] *not in* Q
1.2.5/191	t'haue] to haue		*1.3.122/408	truely] faithfull
*1.2.10/196	pray you] pray		*1.3.123/409	I do confesse . . . blood,] *not in* Q
*1.2.11/197	Be assur'd] For be fure		1.3.133/419	spoke] fpake
*1.2.15/201	or] and			
*1.2.16/202	The] That			

OTHELLO

*1.3.134/420 accidents by] (Accidents); accident of
*1.3.137/423 slauery, of] (flauery. Of); flauery, and
*1.3.138/424 portance in] with it all
*1.3.138/424 trauellours] (Trauellours); trauells
*1.3.141/427 my processe] (Proceffe); the proceffe
*1.3.144/430 these things] (Thefe); this
*1.3.147/433 Which] And
*1.3.153/439 parcells] (parcels); parcell
*1.3.156/442 distressefull] diftreffed
*1.3.159/445 in faith] Ifaith
1.3.165/451 hent] (hint); heate
*1.3.176/462 on my head] lite on me
*1.3.183/469 the Lord of] Lord of all my
1.3.188/474 ha] Q; haue F
*1.3.193/479 Which . . . heart] not in Q
*1.3.204/490 new] more
*1.3.219/505 I humbly beseech you proceed to th' affaires of state] (Affaires of State); Befeech you now, to the affaires of the ftate
*1.3.220/506 a most] moft
*1.3.223-4/509-10 more soueraigne] fo-|ueraigne
*1.3.228/514 graue] (Graue); great
*1.3.232/518 do] would
*1.3.236/522 reference] reuerence
*1.3.237/523 With] Which
*1.3.239/525 Why at her Fathers?] If you pleafe, bee't at her fathers. Most editors accept Q, but F (interpreted as an exclamation) makes dramatic sense and is metrically acceptable (Othello's speech ending with a trimeter).
*1.3.240/526 I will] Ile
*1.3.242/528 Nor would I] Nor I, I would not
*1.3.245/531 your prosperous] a gracious
*1.3.247/533 T'assist] And if
*1.3.247/533 you *Desdemona*] ----fpeake
*1.3.249/535 storme] fcorne
*1.3.251/537 very quality] vtmoft pleafure
*1.3.257/543 why] which
*1.3.260-1/546-7 Let her haue your voyce. | Vouch with me Heauen,] (voice); Your voyces Lords: befeech you let her will, | Haue a free way. F is evidently revised. The short line is abrupt; conceivably a vocative, if not 'Your voyces Lords', was accidentally omitted.
*1.3.265/551 to] of
*1.3.267/553 great] good
*1.3.268/554 When] For
*1.3.269/555 Of] And
*1.3.269/555 seele] foyles
*1.3.270/556 offic'd] actiue
*1.3.274/560 Estimation] reputation
*1.3.276/562 her] not in Q
*1.3.276/562 th'affaire cries] (Affaire); the affaires cry
1.3.277/563 answer it . . . away to night.] anfwer, you muft hence to night,
*1.3.279/565 nine] ten
1.3.279/565 i'th'] i'the
*1.3.282/568 And] With
*1.3.282/568 and] or
*1.3.283/569 import] concerne
*1.3.283/569 So please] Pleafe
*1.3.292/578 if thou hast eyes] (eies); haue a quicke eye
*1.3.293/579 and may] may doe
*1.3.297/583 them] her
*1.3.299/585 matter] matters
*1.3.303/589 think'st] thinkeft
*1.3.306/592 If] Well, if
*1.3.306/592 after] after it
*1.3.308/594 is torment] is a torment
*1.3.309/595 haue we] we haue
*1.3.311/597 Oh villanous:] not in Q
*1.3.312/598 betwixt] betweene
1.3.313/599 man] a man
*1.3.320/606 are our] are

*1.3.336/622 haue profest] profeffe
*1.3.339/625 thou the] thefe
1.3.341-2/627-8 be long, that *Desdemona* should] (long,); that *Defdemona* fhould long
*1.3.342/628 to] vnto
*1.3.343/629 he his] he
*1.3.344/630 in her] not in Q
*1.3.348/635 bitter as] acerbe as the
*1.3.349/635-6 She must change for youth: when] When
*1.3.351/637 choyce. Therefore] (choice); choyce; fhee muft haue change, fhee muft. Therefore
1.3.357/644 drowning thy selfe] drowning
*1.3.357-8/644 it is] tis
*1.3.361-2/647-8 hopes . . . issue] hopes
*1.3.364/650 re-tell] tell
1.3.365/651 hath] has
*1.3.366/652 coniunctiue] communicatiue
*1.3.368/654 me] and me
*1.3.374/660 Ile sell all my Land. *Exit*] what fay you? | *Iag.* No more of drowning, doe you heare? | *Rod.* I am chang'd. *Exit Roderigo.* | *Iag.* Goe to, farewell, put money enough in your purfe:
*1.3.381/667 But] Yet
*1.3.385/671 his] this
*1.3.385/671 plume] make
*1.3.386/672 In] A
*1.3.386/672 how, let's] (How? Let's); how, ---let me
*1.3.387/673 eares] eare
1.3.389/675 hath] has
*1.3.391/677 is of] not in Q
*1.3.391/677 nature] (Nature); nature too
*1.3.392/678 seeme] feemes
2.1.3./685 heauen] F (Heauen); hauen
2.1.5/687 hath spoke] does fpeake
*2.1.8/690 mountaines melt on them] (Mountaines); the huge mountaine mes lt [sic] [pied]
*2.1.11/693 foaming] (Foaming); banning
*2.1.12/694 chidden] chiding
*2.1.15/697 euer fixed] (euer-fixed); euer fired
*2.1.19/701 to] they
*2.1.20/702 Laddes: our] Lords, your
*2.1.21/703 *Turkes*] (Turkes); *Turke*
2.1.22/704 A noble] (Noble); Another
*2.1.24/706 their] the
*2.1.29/711 on Shore] afhore
*2.1.35/717 Heauens] Heauen
*2.1.40-1/722-3 Euen till . . . regard] not in Q
*2.1.44/726 you,] to
*2.1.44/726 warlike] worthy
2.1.45/727 Oh] and
*2.1.46/728 the] their
*2.1.56/738 gouernor] (Gouernor); guernement Q1; gouernement Q2
*2.1.57/739 their] the
*2.1.58/740 friends] (Friends); friend
2.1.64/746 quirkes of] not in Q
*2.1.65/747 th'essentiall] the effentiall
2.1.66/748 tyre the Ingeniuer. | *Enter Gentleman* | How now, who has put in?] (ha's); beare all excellency: --- now, who has put in? | *Enter 2. Gentleman.*
*2.1.68/750 CASSIO] not in Q
*2.1.68/750 Ha's] He has
2.1.69/751 hy] (high); by Q
*2.1.71/753 ensteep'd, to enclog] (enclogge); enfcerped; to clog
*2.1.73/755 mortall] common
*2.1.75/757 spake] fpoke
*2.1.81/763 Make loues quicke pants in] And fwiftly come to
*2.1.84/766 on shore] afhore
*2.1.85/767 You] Ye
*2.1.98/780 See for the Newes] So fpeakes this voyce
2.1.103/785 Sir,] For,
*2.1.104/786 oft bestowes] has beftowed

483

*2.1.105/787	You would] You'd		*2.2.7/1000	Nuptiall] Nuptialls
*2.1.107/789	Infaith] I know		*2.2.9/1002	of Feasting] *not in* Q
*2.1.108/790	it still, when I ha leaue] it, I; for when I ha lift		2.2.10/1003	haue] hath
2.1.112/794	of doore] adores		*2.3.2/1007	that] the
2.1.116/798	DESDEMONA] (*Def.*); *not in* Q (*which however indents the line*)		*2.3.4/1009	direction] directed
			*2.3.6/1011	to't] to it
*2.1.120/802	write] thou write		*2.3.10/1015	That] The
*2.1.130/812	braines] (Braines); braine		*2.3.10/1015	'tweene] twixt
*2.1.133/815	vseth] vsing		*2.3.14/1018	o'th'clock] aclock
*2.1.136/818	fit] hit		*2.3.18/1023	She's] She is
*2.1.139/821	an haire] (heire); a haire (*a common spelling*)		*2.3.20/1025	shes] ſhe is
*2.1.140/822	fond] *not in* Q		*2.3.22/1027	to] of
2.1.141/823	i'th'] i'the		*2.3.24/1029	is it not] (Is); tis
*2.1.146/828	thou praisest] that praiſes		*2.3.25/1030	She] It
*2.1.149/831	merrit] (merit); merrits		*2.3.29/1034	of] of the
2.1.160/842	See ... behind:] (*ital.*); *not in* Q		*2.3.37/1043	infortunate] vnfortunate
*2.1.161/843	wightes] (*ital.*); wight		2.3.48/1054	hath] has
*2.1.171-2/853-4	with as ... will I ensnare ... Fly] (With); as ... will enſnare ... Flee		*2.3.48/1054	out] outward
			*2.3.51/1057	else] lads
*2.1.173/854-5	giue thee in thine owne courtship] (Courtſhip); catch you in your owne courteſies		*2.3.52/1058	honours] (Honours); honour
			*2.3.55/1061	they] the
*2.1.177/859	very] (Very); *not in* Q		*2.3.56/1062	Am I] I am
*2.1.179/860	to your] at your		*2.3.64/1070	*clinke*] clinke, clinke
*2.1.186/867	calmes] (Calmes); calmeneſſe		*2.3.66/1072	O, mans] (Oh); a
*2.1.196/877	powers] (Powers); power		*2.3.74/1080	exquisite] expert
*2.1.199/880	discords] diſcord		*2.3.80/1086	I'le] I will
*2.1.204/885	does my] (do's); doe our		*2.3.82/1088	*and*] *not in* Q
*2.1.204/885	this] the		2.3.84/1090	them] 'em
*2.1.219/900	must] will		*2.3.89/1095	thy] thine
2.1.219-20/900-1	thee this: *Desdemona*] thee, this *Deſdemona*		2.3.94/1100	to be] *not in* Q
*2.1.224-5/905-6	to ... prating] (To); and will ſhe ... pra-ting		*2.3.96/1102	must] that muſt
			*2.3.96-7/1102-3	saued, and there be soules must not be saued] ſaued
*2.1.225/906	thy] the			
*2.1.226/907	it] ſo		*2.3.98/1104	It's] It is
*2.1.229/910	to giue] giue		*2.3.101/1107	too] *not in* Q
*2.1.234/916	in] to		*2.3.107/1113	left] left hand
*2.1.237/918	eminent] eminently		*2.3.108/1114	I speake] ſpeake
*2.1.239/920	further] farder		*2.3.110/1116	Why very] Very
2.1.240/921	humaine] (Humaine); hand-		*2.3.110/1116	thinke then] thinke
*2.1.240/922	compasse] compaſſing		*2.3.112/1118	To th'] To the
*2.1.241-2/922-3	most hidden loose affection? Why none, why none: A slipper, and subtle] (Affection); hidden affect-|ions: A ſubtle ſlippery		*2.3.114/1120	He's] He is
			*2.3.118/1124	puts] put
			*2.3.121/1127	euermore his] euermore the
*2.1.242/924	finder] finder out		*2.3.123/1129	It were] Twere
*2.1.243/924	occasion] occaſions		*2.3.126/1132	Prizes] Praiſes
*2.1.244-5/925-6	aduantages, though true aduantage neuer present it selfe. A diuelish knaue] (Aduantages ... Aduantage); the true aduantages neuer preſent themſelues		*2.3.126/1132	vertue] vertues
			2.3.127/1133	lookes] looke
			*2.3.134/1140	Not] Nor
			*2.3.141/1147	I'le] (Ile); but I'le
2.1.248/930	hath] has		*2.3.142/1148	Twiggen-] wicker
*2.1.253/935	Blest pudding.] (Bleſs'd); *not in* Q		*2.3.145/1151	Nay, good] Good
*2.1.254-5/936-7	Didst not marke that?] *not in* Q		*2.3.145/1151	I pray you sir] (Sir); pray ſir
*2.1.256/938	that I did:] *not in* Q		*2.3.148/1154	you're] you are
*2.1.257/939	obscure] *not in* Q		2.3.152/1158	*Montano*] Montanio
*2.1.260/942	Villanous thoughts *Roderigo*, when] (Rodorigo); When		*2.3.154/1160	that which] that that
			*2.3.156/1162	You'le be asham'd] You will be ſham'd
2.1.261/943	hard at] hand at		2.3.157/1163	th'] the
*2.1.262/944	Master, and] *not in* Q		*2.3.157/1163	He dies.] *not in* Q
*2.1.262/944	th'] the		2.3.159/1165	Hold, hoa:] Hold, hold
*2.1.263/945	Pish.] *not in* Q		2.3.162/1168	ariseth] ariſes
*2.1.264/946	the] your		2.3.164/1170	hath] has
*2.1.268/950	course] cauſe		*2.3.166/1172	for] forth
*2.1.271/953	he's] he is		*2.3.169/1175	what is] (What); what's
*2.1.272/954	may strike] with his Trunchen may ſtrike		*2.3.174/1180	for] to
*2.1.274/956-7	taste againe] truſt again't		*2.3.176/1182	breastes] breaſt
*2.1.278/960	the] *not in* Q		*2.3.180/1186	Those] Theſe
*2.1.280/962	you] I		*2.3.181/1187	comes] came
*2.1.288/970	louing, noble] (Noble); noble, louing		*2.3.181/1187	are] were
*2.1.294/976	lustie] luſtfull		*2.3.186/1192	mouthes] men
*2.1.297/979	or] nor		*2.3.189/1195	to it] to't
*2.1.298/980	euen'd] (eeuen'd); euen		*2.3.195/1201	sometimes] ſometime
2.2.1/994	HERALD] (Herald.); *not in* Q			
*2.2.3/997	euery] that euery			
*2.2.4-5/998	to make] make			

2.3.199/1205	collied] coold	*3.3.62/1510	on Wensday] or Wensday
*2.3.208/1214	quarrel] (Quarrell); quarrels	*3.3.64/1512	Infaith] Ifaith
*2.3.210/1216	began't] began	*3.3.66/1514	example] examples
2.3.211/1217	partially] partiality	*3.3.68/1516	T'incurre] (T'encurre); To incurre
*2.3.214/1220	cut] out	*3.3.70/1518	would] could
*2.3.217/1223	This] Thus	*3.3.71/1519	mam'ring] muttering
*2.3.228/1234	oath] oaths	*3.3.83/1531	difficult waight] difficulty
*2.3.229/1235	say] see	*3.3.89/1537	be] be it
*2.3.233/1239	cannot I] can I not	*3.3.99/1547	thought] (Thought); thoughts
*2.3.245/1251	(Deere?)] not in Q	*3.3.102/1550	oft] often
2.3.256/1262	reputation, Oh] (Reputation:) not in Q	*3.3.104/1552	I indeed] Indeed
*2.3.257/1263	of] sir of	*3.3.110/1558	thou ecchos't] he ecchoes
*2.3.261/1267	sence] offence	*3.3.111/1559	thy] his
*2.3.266/1272	more] not in Q	*3.3.112/1560	dost] didst
*2.3.272/1278	slight] light	*3.3.113/1561	euen] but
*2.3.272/1278	and so] and	3.3.119/1567	conceite] (Conceite); counsell
*2.3.273-5/1279-81	Drunke?...shadow] not in Q	*3.3.123/1571	thou'rt] thou art
*2.3.285-6/1292	pleasance, Reuell] (reuell); Reuell, pleasure	*3.3.124/1572	giu'st them] giue em
*2.3.293/1300	&] not in Q	3.3.125/1573	fright] affright
*2.3.294/1301	befalne] so befalne	*3.3.128/1576	They're] They are
*2.3.298/1305	them] em	*3.3.128/1576	dilations] denotements,
*2.3.300/1307	Oh strange!] not in Q	*3.3.130/1578	be sworne] presume
*2.3.300/1307	inordinate] vnordinate	*3.3.131/1579	what] that
*2.3.300/1308	ingredient] (Ingredient); ingredience	*3.3.136/1584	as to] to
*2.3.306-7/1313-14	a time man] some time Q	*3.3.137/1585	thy] the
2.3.309/1316	hath] has	*3.3.137/1585	thoughts] thought
*2.3.311-12/1318-19	her helpe] her, shee'll helpe	*3.3.138/1586	words] word
*2.3.312/1319	of so] so	*3.3.143/1591	that] a
*2.3.313/1320	shee] (she); that shee	*3.3.145/1593	Sessions] Session
*2.3.315/1322	broken ioynt] braule	*3.3.154/1602	conceits] coniects
*2.3.318/1325	it was] twas	*3.3.155/1603	Would] You'd
*2.3.321/1329-30	I will] will I	*3.3.156/1604	his] my
*2.3.331/1340	Th'] The	*3.3.158/1606	and] or
*2.3.342/1351	the] their	*3.3.160/1608	woman] woman's
*2.3.344/1353	whiles] while	*3.3.161/1609	their] our
2.3.345/1354	fortune] (Fortune); fortunes	*3.3.166/1614	thoughts] (Thoughts); thought
*2.3.353/1362	them] em	*3.3.169/1617	OTHELLO Ha?] not in Q
*2.3.357/1366	And] not in Q	*3.3.169/1617	my Lord, of] not in Q
*2.3.358-9/1367-8	and so, with...a little more wit, returne againe] (And...Wit); as that comes to, and...with that wit returne	*3.3.171/1619	The] That
		3.3.186/1634	blow'd] F; blowne Q. See Taylor, Henry V (1982), note to 3.3.34.
2.3.364/1373	hath] has	*3.3.197/1645	this] it
*2.3.367/1376	Yet] But	*3.3.202/1650	eies] (eyes); eie
*2.3.372/1381	Two] Some	3.3.207/1655	not] not in Q
*3.1.3/1390	in] at	*3.3.208/1656	leaue't] leaue
*3.1.4/1391	i'th'] i'the	3.3.221/1669	y'are] you are
3.1.5/1392 (and throughout)	MUSITIAN] (Mus.); Boy	*3.3.228/1676	Which] As
*3.1.6/1393	pray you,] pray, cald	*3.3.228/1676	aim'd not] (aym'd); aime not at
*3.1.12-13/1400	for loues sake] of all loues	*3.3.228/1676	worthy] trusty
*3.1.19/1406	vp] not in Q	3.3.229/1677	y'are] you are
*3.1.20/1407	into ayre,] not in Q	*3.3.237/1685	Foh, one] Fie we
*3.1.38/1426	for't] for it	*3.3.238/1686	disproportions] disproportion
*3.1.41/1429	sure] soone	*3.3.243/1691	farewell:] not in Q
*3.1.52/1440	Desdemon] Desdemona	3.3.249/1697	IAGO] (Iago.); not in Q
*3.1.54/1442	CASSIO I am much bound to you.] not in Q	*3.3.250/1698	farther] further
*3.2.2/1444	Senate] State	*3.3.251/1699	Although 'tis] Tho it be
*3.2.6/1448	We'll] (Well); We	3.3.255/1703	his] her
*3.3.3/1451	warrant] know	*3.3.264/1712	dealings] dealing
*3.3.4/1452	cause] case	*3.3.270/1718	vale] valt
*3.3.10/1458	I know't] O sir	*3.3.275/1723	of] in
3.3.12/1460	strangenesse] strangest	*3.3.276/1724	the] a
*3.3.14/1462	That] The	*3.3.289/1729	Looke where she] Desdemona
*3.3.28/1476	thy cause away] thee cause: away	*3.3.281/1731	beleeue't] beleeue it
*3.3.31/1479	purposes] purpose	*3.3.284/1732	Ilanders] (Islanders); Ilander
*3.3.38/1486	steale] sneake	3.3.287/1735	do you speake so faintly] is your speech so faint
*3.3.39/1487	your] you	*3.3.290/1738	it hard] your head
*3.3.54/1502	hath] has	3.3.291/1739	well] well againe
*3.3.54/1502	griefe] (greefe); griefes	*3.3.301/1749	he will] hee'll
*3.3.55/1503	To] I	3.3.303/1751	nothing, but to please] nothing know, but for
*3.3.56/1504	Desdemon] Desdemona	*3.3.306/1754	You haue a] A
*3.3.62/1510	noone] morne	*3.3.308/1756	wife] thing

*3.3.315/1763	stolne] ſtole		*3.4.62/1991	loathed] lothely
3.3.317/1765	th'] the		*3.4.64/1993	wiu'd] (Wiu'd); wiue
*3.3.318/1766	'tis] it is		*3.4.67/1996	loose't] looſe
*3.3.320/1768	what is] what's		*3.4.71/2000	course] (courſe,); make
*3.3.322/1770	Giu't mee] (me); Giue mee't		*3.4.74/2003	which] with
*3.3.324/1772	acknowne] you knowne		*3.4.75/2004	Conseru'd] Conſerues
*3.3.329/1777	The Moore ... poyson:] not in Q		*3.4.79/2008	rash] raſhly
*3.3.332/1780	act,] (acte); art,		*3.4.80/2009	is't out] is it out
3.3.333/1781	mines] (Mines); mindes		3.4.80/2009	o'th'] o' the
*3.3.338/1785	to me?] (mee); to me, to me?		*3.4.84/2013	How?] Ha
*3.3.342/1789	know't] know		*3.4.85/2014	see't] ſee it
*3.3.345/1792	fed well,] not in Q		*3.4.88/2017	Pray you] I pray
*3.3.354/1801	troopes] (Troopes); troope		*3.4.89/2018	the] that
3.3.357/1804	th'] the		*3.4.100/2029	of it] not in Q
*3.3.360/1807	you] ye		*3.4.105/2034	doe't] (doo't); doe it
*3.3.360/1807	rude] wide		*3.4.111/2040	Office] duty
3.3.361/1808	Th'] The		*3.4.114/2043	nor my] neither
*3.3.361/1808	dread clamours] (Clamours); great clamor		3.4.119/2048	shut] ſhoote
*3.3.366/1813	mine] mans		*3.4.135/2064	is he] can he be
*3.3.378/1825	forgiue] defend		*3.4.143/2072	their]the
*3.3.381/1828	lou'st] lieueſt		*3.4.145/2074	a] that
3.3.381/1828	thine] F, Qd: mine Qc		*3.4.147/2076	obseruancie] obſeruances
*3.3.385/1832	sith] ſince		3.4.158/2087	they're] they are
*3.3.388-95/1835-42	OTHELLO By the World ... satisfied.] not in Q		*3.4.158/2087	it is] (It); tis
*3.3.398/1845	and I] F; I Q; and POPE		*3.4.160/2089	the] that
*3.3.403/1850	them ... them] em ... em		*3.4.167/2096	is't] is it
*3.3.404/1851	do] did		*3.4.173/2102	Oh] No
*3.3.413/1860	might] may		*3.4.174/2103	leaden] laden
*3.3.414/1861	shee's] (she's); that ſhee's		*3.4.175/2104	continuate] conuenient
*3.3.416/1863	in] into		3.4.180/2109	Well, well.] not in Q
3.3.424/1871	wary] merry		*3.4.185/2114	neither] ſweete
*3.3.426/1873	oh,] out,		*3.4.187/2116	I would] I'de
*3.3.426/1873	then] and then		*3.4.192-3/2121-2	BIANCA Why ... you not.] not in Q
3.3.433/1880	denoted] deuoted		4.1.3, 5/2130, 2132	in bed] abed
*3.3.437/1884	yet be] but be		*4.1.9/2136	If] So
*3.3.444/1891	If it] If't		*4.1.21/2148	infectious] infected
3.3.449/1896	true] time		*4.1.27/2154	Or] Or by the
*3.3.451/1898	the hollow hell] thy hollow Cell		4.1.33/2160	What? What?] But what?
*3.3.454/1901	Yet] Pray		4.1.36/2163	handkercher, Confessions, hankercher] (Handkerchiefe: Confeſſions: Handkerchiefe); handkerchers, Confeſſion, hankerchers
*3.3.455/1902	blood, blood, blood] blood, Iago, blood			
3.3.456-63/1903-10	Neuer, Iago ... Heauen,] Neuer:		*4.1.36-42/2163-9	To confeſſe ... O diuell.] (Hand-kerchiefe) F; not in Q
*3.3.469/1916	execution] excellency			
*3.3.469/1916	hands] hand		*4.1.43/2170	on, my medicine workes] (My Medicine); on my medicine, worke
*3.3.471/1918	in me] not in Q			
*3.3.472/1919	businesse] worke ſo		*4.1.58/2185	you not, by] you? no by
*3.3.477/1924	at your] as you		*4.1.59/2186	fortune] (Fortune); fortunes
*3.3.478/1925	dam her, dam her] (damne her, damne her); dam her		*4.1.63/2190	it] not in Q
			*4.1.67/2194	lye] lyes
*3.4.1/1930	where] where the		*4.1.70/2197	Cowch] Coach
3.4.5/1934	CLOWNE] (Clo.); not in Q (but speech indented)		*4.1.75/2202	here, o're-whelmed] (heere); here ere while, mad
*3.4.5/1934	He's] He is		4.1.79/2206	Bad] Bid
*3.4.5/1934	me] one		4.1.79/2206	returne] retire
*3.4.5/1935	'tis] is		*4.1.80/2207	Do but] but
*3.4.8-10/1936-9	CLOWNE To tell ... of this?] (Clo ... Deſ.); not in Q		*4.1.81/2208	Fleeres] geeres Qc; Ieeres Qd
			4.1.85/2212	hath] has
*3.4.12/1941	here, or he lies] (heere); not in Q		*4.1.87/2214	y'are] you are
*3.4.13/1942	mine owne] my		*4.1.101/2228	behauiours] behauiour
*3.4.19/1948	on] in		4.1.114/2241	or] F (o're); on Q
*3.4.21/1950	mans Wit] a man		*4.1.114/2241	well said,] not in Q
*3.4.22/1951	I will] I'le		*4.1.117/2244	ye] you
*3.4.22/1951	it] of it		*4.1.118/2245	marry. What? A customer;] marry her? I
*3.4.23/1952	the] that		*4.1.121/2248	they] not in Q
3.4.25/1954	haue lost] looſe		*4.1.122/2249	that you] you ſhall
3.4.32/1961	til] (till); Tis Qa; Let Qb		*4.1.125/2252	you scor'd me? Well.] (ſcoar'd); you ſtor'd me well
*3.4.33/1962	is't] is it		*4.1.131/2258	the other] tother
*3.4.37/1966	hath] yet has		*4.1.132/2259	the] this
3.4.39/1968	Hot,] Not,		*4.1.136/2264	shakes] hales
*3.4.40/1969	prayer] (Prayer); praying		*4.1.139/2266	oh,] not in Q
*3.4.48/1977	now] come,		*4.1.140/2267	throw it] throw't
*3.4.51/1980	sorry] ſullen		*4.1.143/2270	CASSIO Tis] (Caſ. 'Tis); tis
3.4.60/1989	Intirely ... lost it] repeated at head of next page in Q, but with catchword for 3.4.61/1990			

OTHELLO

*4.1.149/2276 know not] not know
*4.1.151/2278 your] the
*4.1.159/2286 in the streets] i'the ftreete
4.1.171-3/2298-2300 Iago. Yours ... whore] not in Q (which however has 'Iag.' as catchword)
*4.1.176/2303 that] not in Q
*4.1.177/2304 I,] And
4.1.180/2306 hath] has
*4.1.188/2315 Oh, a thousand, a thousand] A thoufand thoufand
*4.1.191/2318 Nay] I
*4.1.191-2/2318-19 Iago, oh Iago, the pitty of it Iago] (Iago: oh); Iago, the pitty
*4.1.193/2320 are] be
*4.1.194/2321 touch] touches
*4.1.209/2337 I warrant something] Something
4.1.209/2337 Venice] (Venice); Venice fure
4.1.210/2338 comes] Come
*4.1.210/2338 Duke] Duke, and
*4.1.211/2338 wife's] wife is
*4.1.214/2342 the] not in Q
*4.1.228/2356 'twixt my] betweene thy
*4.1.230/2358 T'attone, them] Fb (quad showing before 'them'); T'attone, them Fa; To attone them Q
*4.1.239/2367 Why,] How
*4.1.245/2373 womans] womens
*4.1.260/2387 home] here
*4.1.267/2394 Is this the nature] (Nature); This the noble nature
*4.1.273/2400 what] as
*4.1.278/2405 his] this
*4.2.3/2414 Yes,] Yes, and
*4.2.8/2419 o'th'] o'the
*4.2.10/2421 her gloues, her mask] (Gloues ... Mask); her mask, her gloues
*4.2.17/2428 heauen] (Heauen); heauens
*4.2.19/2430 their Wiues] her Sex
*4.2.25/2436 you] not in Q
*4.2.33/2444 doth] does
*4.2.43/2454 Ah] O
*4.2.43/2454 Desdemon] Defdemona
*4.2.45/2456 motiue of these] occafion of thofe
4.2.48-9/2459-60 lost ... lost] left ... left
*4.2.49/2460 I] Why I
4.2.50/2461 rain'd] ram'd
*4.2.51/2462 kind] kindes
*4.2.53/2464 vtmost] not in Q
*4.2.54/2465 place] part
*4.2.56/2467 The] A
*4.2.57/2468 finger] fingers
*4.2.57/2468 at—] (at.); at -- oh, oh,
*4.2.65/2476 thou] thy
*4.2.68/2479 as summer] (as Sommer Fb; as a Sommer Fa); as fummers
*4.2.69/2480 thou] thou blacke
*4.2.70/2481 Who ... faire,] why ... faire?
*4.2.70/2481 and] Thou
*4.2.74/2485 vpon] on
*4.2.75-8/2486-9 Committed? ... deedes. What commited?] not in Q
*4.2.81/2492 hollow] hallow
*4.2.82/2493 committed?] (commited); committed, impudent ftrumpet.
*4.2.87/2498 other] hated
*4.2.91/2502 forgiue vs] forgiuenefle Q
*4.2.92/2503 then] not in Q
*4.2.96/2507 gate of] gates in
*4.2.96/2507 you, you: I you] (You,); I, you, you, you
*4.2.104/2515 DESDEMONA. Who is ... Lady.] not in Q
*4.2.106/2517 answeres] anfwer
*4.2.108/2519 my] our
*4.2.109/2520 Here's] (Heere's); Here is
*4.2.110/2521 very meete] very well

4.2.112/2523 small'st] F; fmalleft
*4.2.112/2523 least misvse] Fc; mife vfe Fa; mfvfe Fb; greateft abufe Q
*4.2.117/2528 to] at
*4.2.120/2531 That] As
*4.2.120/2531 beare it] beare
*4.2.123/2534 said] fayes
4.2.129/2540 Hath] Has
*4.2.130/2541 and her friends] (And); all her friends
*4.2.132/2543 for't] for it
*4.2.134/2545 I will] I'le
*4.2.142/2553 forme] (Forme); for me
*4.2.143/2554 most villanous] outragious
*4.2.147/2558 rascalls] (Rafcalls); rafcall
*4.2.148/2559 th'West] the Weft
*4.2.148/2559 dore] (doore); dores
*4.2.149/2560 them] him
*4.2.155-68/2566-79 Here I kneele ... make me.] (Heere); not in Q
*4.2.173/2584 It is] Tis
4.2.173/2584 warrant] warrant you
4.2.174/2585 summon] fummon you
*4.2.175/2586 The . . . the meate.] (Venice); And the great Meffengers of Venice ftay,
*4.2.182/2592 me now,] me, thou
*4.2.182/2592 keep'st] keepeft
*4.2.188/2599 performances] (Performances); performance
*4.2.190/2601 With naught but truth:] not in Q
*4.2.191/2602 my meanes] meanes
*4.2.192/2603 deliuer] deliuer to
4.2.193/2604 hath] has
*4.2.194/2605 expectations] expectation
*4.2.195/2606 acquaintance] acquittance
*4.2.196/2607 well] good
*4.2.197-8/2608 nor tis] it is
*4.2.198/2609 nay I think it is] (Nay); by this hand, I fay tis very. F may be a conscious expurgation.
*4.2.201/2612 I tell you, 'tis] I fay it is
*4.2.203/2614 I will] I'le
*4.2.207/2618 and said] and I haue faid
*4.2.210/2621 instant] time
*4.2.212/2623 exception] conception
*4.2.213/2624 affaire] (Affaire); affaires
*4.2.217/2628 in] within
*4.2.220/2631 enioy] enioyeft
*4.2.223/2634 what is it? Is] is
*4.2.225/2636 commission] (Commiffion); command
*4.2.237/2648 I: if] I, and if
*4.2.237/2648 a right] right
*4.2.238/2649 harlotry] (Harlotry); harlot
*4.3.2/2663 'twill] it fhall
4.3.7/2668 on th'] o' the
*4.3.8/2669 dismisse] difpatch
*4.3.8/2669 looke't] (look't); looke it
*4.3.13/2675 bid] bad
*4.3.19/2681 checks, his] checks and
*4.3.21/2683 those] thefe
*4.3.24/2686 these] thofe
4.3.27/2689 had] has
*4.3.30-51/2692-2713 I haue much ... not next.] Brabarie ... Æmi ... Def. ... Æmil. ... Def. ... Æmil. ... Def.); not in Q
*4.3.51/2713 who is't] who's
*4.3.52/2714 It's] It is
*4.3.53-5/2715-17 DESDEMONA I call'd ... mo men.] (Def.); not in Q
*4.3.56/2718 So] Def. Now
4.3.57/2719 Doth] does
*4.3.58-61/2720-3 DESDEMONA I haue heard ... question.] (Æmilia); not in Q
*4.3.64/2727 doe't] (doo't); doe it
*4.3.65/2727 i'th'] in the
*4.3.66/2728 Would'ft] Would
*4.3.66/2728 deed] thing

*4.3.67/2729	world's] world is	*5.2.15/2912	thee] it
*4.3.69/2731	Introth] Good troth	*5.2.16/2913	Oh] A
*4.3.70/2732	Introth] By my troth	5.2.16/2913	dost] doth
*4.3.71/2733	done] done it	*5.2.17/2914	to] her selfe to
*4.3.72/2734	nor for measures] or for mea-|sures	*5.2.17/2914	sword. One more, one more] (Sword); sword once more
*4.3.73/2735	Petticotes] (Petticoats); or Petticotes	*5.2.19/2916	one] (One); once Q
*4.3.73/2735	petty] such	*5.2.19/2916	that's] this
*4.3.74/2736	all] not in Q	*5.2.22/2919	where] when
*4.3.76/2738	for't] for it	5.2.22/2919	doth] does
*4.3.79/2741	i'th'] i'the	*5.2.26/2923	Desdemon] Desdemona
*4.3.84/2746	To'th'vantage] to the Vantage	*5.2.31/2928	Alacke] Alas
*4.3.85-102/2747-64	But I do thinke . . . instruct vs so.] not in Q	*5.2.34/2931	heauens] (Heauens); heauen
*4.3.103/2765	vses] vsage	*5.2.39/2936	you're] you are
*5.1.4/2770	on] of	*5.2.44/2941	I, and] And
*5.1.7/2773	stand] sword	*5.2.48/2945	I hope, I hope,] I hope,
5.1.8/2774	deed] dead	*5.2.57/2954	Presently] Yes, presently
5.1.9/2775	hath] has	*5.2.60/2957	conception] (Conception); conceit
*5.1.11/2777	quat] (Quat); gnat	*5.2.67/2964	in's] in his
5.1.12/2778	angry: now,] F (~. Now); ~,~:	5.2.68/2965	my] thy
*5.1.14/2780	gaine] game	*5.2.69/2966	makes] makest
*5.1.16/2782	Of] For	*5.2.73/2970	Let] And let
5.1.19/2785	hath] has	5.3.73/2970	hath] has
*5.1.21/2787	much] not in Q	*5.2.80/2977	Oh, my feare interprets] My feare interprets then
5.1.22/2788	die, but] (dye, But); die, be't	*5.2.84/2981	Out] O
*5.1.24/2790	mine] my	*5.2.90/2987	OTHELLO Being . . . pawse.] not in Q
*5.1.25/2791	know'st] think'st	*5.2.92/2989	It is] Tis
5.1.27/2793	maimd] (maym'd); maind	*5.2.95/2992	noise] voyce
*5.1.27/2793	helpe] (Helpe); light	*5.2.99/2996	I would] I'de
*5.1.30/2796	It is] Harke tis	*5.2.102/2999	high] here
*5.1.35/2801	vnblest fate hies] (Fate highes); fate hies apace	*5.2.104/3001	best to do] the best
*5.1.39/2805	voice] (voyce); cry	*5.2.106/3003	wife: what wife?] wife, my wife;
*5.1.43/2809	grone, 'tis] (groane, Tis); grones, it is a	5.2.109/3006	th'] the
*5.1.48/2814	light] (Light); lights	*5.2.111/3008	That] not in Q
*5.1.50/2816	We] I	*5.2.111/3008	Oh] not in Q
*5.1.50/2816	Doe] (Do); Did	*5.2.119/3016	neerer] neere the
*5.1.51/2817	heauen] heauens	5.2.121/3018	hath] has
*5.1.57/2823	me,] (mee); my,	*5.2.129/3026	that was] it is
5.1.58/2824	that] the	5.2.132/3029	hath] has
*5.1.61/2827	there] here	*5.2.137/3034	the] a
*5.1.64/2830	dog.] (Dogge); dog, -- o, o, o.	*5.2.143/3040	art] as
*5.1.65/2831	men i'th'] him i'the	*5.2.150/3047	had] nay, had
*5.1.65/2831	these] those	*5.2.154/3051	on her] not in Q
*5.1.72/2838	is't] is it	*5.2.157/3054	itterance, woman,] (Woman?); iteration? woman,
*5.1.78/2844	my sweete *Cassio*, O] (My sweet *Cassio*: Oh); O my sweete	*5.2.158-61/3055-8	EMILLIA Oh Mistris . . . honest *Iago*.] (*Æmil*. . . . *Oth*.); not in Q
*5.1.80/2846	haue thus] thus haue	*5.2.169/3066	that] the
*5.1.83-4/2849-50	IAGO Lend me . . . hence] not in Q	*5.2.172/3069	known] know
*5.1.87/2853	be a party in this Iniurie] beare a part in this	*5.2.173/3070	hoa,] O
*5.1.88/2854	Come, come;] not in Q	5.2.174/3071	hath] has
*5.1.95/2861	your] you	*5.2.177/3074	murders] (Murthers); murder
*5.1.100/2866	He, he] He	*5.2.178/3075	GRATIANO] (*Gra*.); *All*.
*5.1.100/2866	the] a	*5.2.181/3078	thou'rt] thou art
*5.1.104/2870	between] betwixt	*5.2.192-200/3089-97	My . . . O villany! villany!] not in Q
*5.1.107/2873	Gentlemen] Gentlewoman	*5.2.210/3107	horrible] terrible
*5.1.108/2874	gastnesse] ieastures	*5.2.211/3108	Desdemon] Desdemona
*5.1.109/2875	stare] stirre	5.2.213/3110	in twaine] atwane
*5.1.109/2875	heare] haue	*5.2.216/3113	reprobance] (Reprobance); reprobation
*5.1.113/2879	Alas what is the matter? What is] 'Las what's the matter? what's	*5.2.221/3118	that] the
5.1.114/2880	hath] has	*5.2.225-6/3122-3	out, 'twill out: I peace? | No, I will speake as liberall as the North] out, 'twill: I hold my peace sir, no, | I'le be in speaking, liberall as the ayre
*5.1.118/2884	fruites] (fruits); fruite	*5.2.232/3129	of] on
*5.1.118/2884	prythe] (Prythe); pray	*5.2.236/3133	steale't] steale it
*5.1.123/2889	Oh fie] Fie, fie	*5.2.238/3135	giue] gaue
5.1.129/2895	hath] has	*5.2.241/3138	wife] woman
*5.1.130/2896	on, afore] on, I pray	5.2.243/3140	hath] has
5.1.131/2897	makes] markes	5.2.246/3143	you this] your
*5.2.10/2907	thy light] (Light); thine	*5.2.253-5/3150-2	What did . . . Willough.] not in Q
*5.2.11/2908	cunning'st] cunning	*5.2.258/3155	alas] I die
*5.2.13/2910	re-Lume] returne	*5.2.260/3157	was] is
*5.2.13/2910	thy rose] the rose		
*5.2.15/2912	needes must] (needs); must needes		

OTHELLO

*5.2.264/3161 with] to
5.2.271/3168 your] you
*5.2.273-9/3170-6 Be not affraid . . . ill-Starr'd wench,] *not in* Q
*5.2.283/3180 cursed,] *not in* Q
*5.2.284/3181 ye] you
*5.2.288/3185 *Desdemon!* dead *Desdemon*] *Defdemona, Defdemoua* [sic]
*5.2.288/3185 O, o] (Oh, oh); O, o, o
*5.2.289/3186 vnfortunate] infortunate
*5.2.290/3187 that] this
*5.2.293/3190 that] *not in* Q
*5.2.294/3191 Wrench] Wring
*5.2.297/3194 was] wert
*5.2.298/3195 cursed] damned
*5.2.299/3196 shall] fhould
*5.2.301/3198 I did] did I
*5.2.305/3202 neuer gaue] did neuer giue
*5.2.306/3203 your] you
*5.2.307/3204 I pray] pray
5.2.324/3221 t'haue] to haue
*5.2.325/3222 interim] nicke
*5.2.327/3224 thou] the
*5.2.328/3225 that] a
*5.2.330/3227 but] *not in* Q
*5.2.346/3243 bring] bring him
*5.2.347/3244 before you goe] *not in* Q
*5.2.351/3248 me, as I am] them as they are
*5.2.360/3257 medicinable] (Medicinable); medicinall
*5.2.367/3264 that is] that's
*5.2.373/3270 loading] (Loading); lodging
*5.2.377/3274 on] to

INCIDENTALS

44 marke,] F; ~.   48 nought] noughe   63 externe,] ~.   78 ho.] ~,   124 If't] If,t   160 him,] F; ~:
165 bitternesse:] F(~.); ~,   173 Fathers, from hence,] ~, ~,   188 Conscience,] ~.   189 murther] murrher   203 cable.]
~,   206 that] That   207 promulgate] provulgate   216 in.] ~:   224 you.] ~:   228 anothers] anothets
238 married.] ~,   266 warrant;] ~?   301 state,] ~.   310 it,] ~.   322 fleete.] ~,   337 night.] ~,   363 approou'd]
F; approoued   413 lou'd] F; loued   414 question] F; queftioned   428 eate,] F; ~;   443 suffer'd] F; fuffered   443 done,]
F; ~,   449 lou'd] F; loued   452 past,] ~.   453 them] rhem   481 soule,] ~.   523 accomodation,] ~?   537 Euen]
Fuen   595 prescription, to dye,] F; prefcription, to dye,   689 sea,] ~.   712 *Cypres*.] ~,   721 *Othello*,] ~.   725 arriuance.]
~,   737 Stand] otand   749 Generall.] ~,   752 gutter'd] F; guttered   758 *Iago*,] ~.   763 armes,] ~.   764 spirits,]
~.   772 arriu'd] F; arriued   775 the sea] Q; Sea F   857 kist] rift   868 waken'd] F; wakened   875 Fate.] ~,
896 Harbour] Habour   973 peraduenture,] ~.   1020 *Desdemona*,] ~.   1029 loue?] ~.   1056 watch.] watch,
1074 boyes.] ~,   1088 *King* . . . *peere*] (*all but* 'Stephen' *roman*)   1129 were] wete   1143 Helpe, helpe] (*italics*)   1258 strife.]
~,   1343 Moore,] ~.   1349 course.] ~,   1379 billited] bill,ted   1398 maisters] Q (*text*); ~, Q (*c.w.*)   1403 say] faay
1427 honest] ~:   1436 saf'st] safeft   1558 me,] ~.   1572 weigh'st] F; weigheft   1578 honest.] ~,   1596 think'st] F;
thinkeft   1596 mak'st] F; makeft   1607 thoughts.] ~,   1616 custody.] ~:   1628 iealousie] ~,   1685 such, a will,] F;
~, ~,   1691 repent.] ~:   1711 learn'd] F; learned   1717 Chamberers] F, Qd; Chamlerers Qc   1733 presence.] ~,
1779 distast,] ~.   1795 know't] know'r   1809 Occupation's] Qb, F; Oceupation's Qa   1854 this,] ~.   1858 circumstances]
circumftanees   1880 conclusion.] ~,   1882 proofes,] ~.   1923 aliue.] ~.   1970 castigation,] Qb; ~, Qa
1981 handkercher.] ~,   1988 Twould] Qa; T'would Qb   2014 see't.] ~,   2069 *Cipres*] Qc; *Cypres* Qd   2078 vnhandsome,]
Qc; ~, Qd   2079 vnkindnesse] Qc; vnkindenffe Qd   2085 answer'd] F; anfwered   2113 *Bianca*.] ~,   2121 pray] ptay F
2135 heauen.] F; ~:   2152 say, . . . abroad,] Qc; ~ (. . . ~) Qd   2154 voluntary] voluntaty   2162 that's] Qa; thar's Qc
2167 Instruction] Iuftruction F   2185 thou] Qd; thon Qc   2208 gibes] Qc; Iibes Qd   2216 cunning] Qd; cunuing Qc
2251 else.] ~,   2269 comes.] ~,   2284 not, come] Fb, Qc; not, come Fa   2295 *Iago*.] F; ~,   2299 him, and,] Fb; him, and,
Fa   2327 night.] F; ~,   2404 blood,] ~.   2433 much:] ~.   2485 What,] F; ~,   2668 instant. I] inftant,
2668-9 return'd forthwith] return'd, forthwith   2684 one:] F; ~,   2703 Willough.] Wtllough.   2705, 2716 *Sing Willough,
Willough, Willough.*] *Sing Willough, &c.*   2707 *Willough,*] *Willough, &c.*   2713 Harke] --harke,   2715 then] Fb; theu Fa
2804 murder.] ~,   2814 weapons.] ~,   2924 Lord.] ~:   2947 will, so] F; will, fo   2948 gau'st] gaueft   2965 periur'd]
F; periured   2971 That] Thar   2981 weep'st] F; weepeft   2997 Yes,— . . . . by:—] Yes,, . . . by:,   3023, 3032 murder'd]
murdered   3089 murther'd] murthered   3126 wise,] ~.   3144 recouer'd] F; recouered   3184 liquid] Qd; liquit Qc
3189 fable,] ~,

QUARTO STAGE DIRECTIONS

1.1.0.1/0.1 Enter *Iago* and *Roderigo*.
1.1.81.1-2/81.1-2 *Brabantio at a window.*
1.1.161.1/162 *Exit.*
1.1.161.1-2/162.1-2 Enter *Barbantio in his night gowne, and seruants | with Torches.*
1.1.185/186 *Exeunt.*
1.2.0.1/186.1 Enter *Othello, Iago, and attendants with Torches.*
1.2.28/214 Enter *Cassio with lights, Officers, | and torches.* (opposite 'worth' and 'yond' (Q 'yonder'); see lineation note)
1.2.52.1-2/238.1-2 Enters *Brabantio, Roderigo, and others with lights | and weapons.*
1.2.100.1/286.1 *Exeunt.*
1.3.0.1-2/286.2-3 Enter *Duke and Senators, set at a Table with lights | and Attendants.*
1.3.12.1/298.1 Enter *a Messenger.* (after 'sense')
1.3.33.1/319.1 Enter *a 2. Messenger.*
1.3.46.1-2/332.1-2 Enter *Brabantio, Othello, Roderigo, Iago, Cassio, | Desdemona, and Officers.*
1.3.121.1/407.1 *Exit two or three.* (after 1.3.120/406)
1.3.168.1/454.1 Enter *Desdemona, Iago, and the rest.* (after 1.3.169/455)
1.3.293.1-2/579.1-2 *Exeunt.*
1.3.300.1/586.1 *Exit Moore and Desdemona.* (after 1.3.301/587)
1.3.374/660.1 *Exit Roderigo.* (equivalent position; see Rejected Quarto Variants)
1.3.396.1/682.1 *Exit.*
2.1.0.1-2/682.2-3 Enter *Montanio, Gouernor of Cypres, with | two other Gentlemen.*
2.1.19.1/701.1 Enter *a third Gentleman.*
2.1.43.1/725.1 Enter *Cassio.*
[2.1.52/734] Enter *a Messenger.* (after 'cure')
2.1.56.1/738.1 *A shot.* (after 'least', 2.1.58/740)
2.1.60/742 *Exit.*
2.1.66/748 Enter *2. Gentleman.* (after 'in')
2.1.83/765 Enter *Desdemona, Iago, Emillia, and Roderigo.* (after 2.1.81/765)

OTHELLO

2.1.95/777 [*within.*] *A saile, a saile.* (after 2.1.92/774)
2.1.180.1, 182.1/861.1, 863.1 *Trumpets within.* | *Enter* Othello, *and Attendants.* (after 'Trumpet', 2.1.181/862)
2.1.199/880 *they kisse.* (at end of line)
2.1.213.1-2/894.1-2 *Exit.*
2.1.284/966 *Exit.*
2.1.311/993 *Exit.*
2.2.0.1/993.1 *Enter a Gentleman reading a Proclamation.*
2.3.0.1/1005.1 *Enter* Othello, Cassio, *and* Desdemona.
2.3.11.1/1016.1 *Exit* Othello *and* Desdemona.
2.3.11.2/1016.2 *Enter* Iago.
2.3.43/1049 *Exit.*
2.3.57/1063 *Enter* Montanio, Cassio, | *and others.* (opposite 'Isle' and 'come'; see lineation note)
2.3.112.1/1118.1 *Ex.*
2.3.127.1/1133.1 *Enter* Roderigo. (after 2.3.128/1134)
2.3.129/1135 *Exit Rod.*
2.3.137/1143 *Helpe, helpe, within.* (after 2.3.135/1141)
2.3.138.1/1144.1 *Enter* Cassio, *driuing in* Roderigo.
2.3.149.1/1155.1 *they fight.*
2.3.153.1/1159.1 *A bell rung:* (after 2.3.150/1156)
2.3.156/1162 *Enter* Othello, *and Gentlemen with weapons.*
2.3.242.1/1248.1 *Enter* Desdemona, | *with others.* (opposite 2.3.242-3/1248-9)
2.3.252.1/1258.1 *Exit Moore, Desdemona, and attendants.* (after 2.3.253/1259)
2.3.326/1335 *Exit.*
2.3.353/1362 *Enter* Roderigo.
2.3.372, 378/1381, 1387 *Exeunt.* (after 2.3.378/1387)
3.1.0.1, 3.1.2.1/1387.1, 1389.1 *Enter* Cassio, *with Musitians and the Clowne.* (at 3.1.0.1/1387.1)
3.1.29/1417 *Enter* Iago. (after 3.1.28/1416)
3.1.38.1/1426.1 *Exit.* (after 'free')
3.1.39.1/1427.1 *Enter* Emilla.
3.1.54.1/1442.1 *Exeunt.*
3.2.0.1/1442.2 *Enter* Othello, Iago, *and other Gentlemen.*
3.2.6/1448 *Exeunt.*
3.3.0.1/1448.1 *Enter* Desdemona, Cassio *and* Emillia.
3.3.28/1476 *Enter* Othello, Iago, *and Gentlemen.*
3.3.32/1480 *Exit Cassio.*
3.3.90.1/1538.1 *Exit Desd. and Em.*
3.3.261.1/1709.1 *Exit* (Qb; not in Qa)
3.3.281/1729 *Enter* Desdemona *and* Emillia. (after 'beleeue't', 3.3.283/1731)
3.3.293.1/1741.1 *Ex. Oth. and* | *Desd.* (opposite 3.3.294-5/1742-3)
3.3.303.1/1751.1 *Enter* Iago. (after 3.3.302/1750)
3.3.324.1/1772.1 *Exit Em.* (after 3.3.325/1773)
3.3.333/1781 *Ent. Othello.* (after 3.3.332/1780)
3.3.463/1910 *he kneeles.* (after 3.3.454/1901)
3.3.465.1/1912.1 *Iago kneeles:* (after 3.3.467/1914)
3.3.482/1929 *Exeunt.*
3.4.0.1/1929.1 *Enter* Desdemonia Emilla *and the Clowne.*
3.4.22/1951 *Exit.*
3.4.31/1960 *Enter* Othello.
3.4.97/2026 *Exit.*
3.4.104/2033 *Enter* Iago *and* Cassio. (after 3.4.100/2029)
3.4.165.1/2094.1 *Exeunt Desd.* | *and* Emillia. (opposite 3.4.163-4/2092-3)
3.4.165.2/2094.2 *Enter* Bianca. (after 3.4.165/2094)
3.4.198/2127 *Exeunt.*
4.1.0.1/2127.1 *Enter* Iago *and* Othello.
4.1.42.1/2168.1 *He fals downe.*
4.1.46/2173 *Enter* Cassio. (after 'now *Cassio*')
4.1.98/2225 *Ent. Cassio:* (after 4.1.96/2223)
4.1.141.1/2268.1 *Enter* Bianca.
4.1.157.1/2284 *Exit.*
4.1.165/2292 *Exit Cassio.*
4.1.207.1, 209.1/2335.1, 2337.1 *A Trumpet.* | *Enter* Lodouico, Desdemona, *and Attendants.* (after 4.1.206/2334)
4.1.265.1/2392.1 *Exit.* (Qa; not in Qc)
4.1.284/2411 *Exeunt.*
4.2.0.1/2411.1 *Enter* Othello *and* Emillia.
4.2.20.1/2431.1 *Exit* Emillia. (after 'slander')
4.2.24.1/2435.1 *Enter* Desdemona *and* Emillia.
4.2.32.1/2443 *Exit Em.*
4.2.96/2507 *Enter* Emillia. (after 4.2.89/2500)
4.2.98/2509.1 *Exit.*
4.2.109.1/2520.1 *Exit.*
4.2.112.1/2523.1 *Enter* Iago. | *and* Emillia. (opposite 'Madam' and 'you', 4.2.113/2524; see lineation note)
4.2.176.1/2587.1 *Exit women.*
4.2.176.2/2587.2 *Enter* Roderigo. (after 4.2.177/2588)
4.2.249/2661 *Ex. Iag. and Rod.*
4.3.0.1-2/2661.1-2 *Enter* Othello, Desdemona, Lodouico, Emillia, | *and Attendants.* (after 4.2.247/2659)
4.3.9.1/2671.1 *Exeunt.* (after 4.3.8/2670)
4.3.104/2766 *Exeunt.*
5.1.0.1/2766.1 *Enter* Iago *and* Roderigo,
5.1.22.1/2788.1 *Ent. Cas.*
5.1.27.1/2793.1 *Enter* Othello.
5.1.37.1/2803.1 *Ex.*
5.1.37.2/2803.2 *Enter* Lodouico *and* Gratiano.
5.1.46.1/2812.1 *Enter* Iago *with a light.*
5.1.75.1/2841.1 *Enter* Bianca.
5.1.112.1/2878.1 *Enter Em.*
5.1.131/2897 *Exeunt.*
5.2.0.1-2/2897.1-2 *Enter* Othello *with a light.*
5.2.19.1/2916.1 *He* | *kisses her.* (opposite 5.2.19-20/2916-17)
5.2.92.1/2989.1 *he stifles her.*
5.2.93.1/2990.1 *Emillia calls within.*
5.2.114/3011 *Ent. Emil.*
5.2.134/3031 *she dies.*
5.2.174.1/3071.1 *Enter* Montano, Gratiano, Iago, *and others.*
5.2.205/3102 *Oth. fals on the bed.*
5.2.242.1-2/3139.1-2 *The Moore runnes at* Iago. Iago *kils his wife.* (after 'wife' (Q 'woman'), 5.2.241/3138)
5.2.244/3141 *Exit* Iago.
5.2.250/3147 *Exit Mont. and Gratiano.*
5.2.258/3155 *she dies.*
5.2.262/3159 *Gra. within.*
5.2.288.1-2/3185.1-2 *Enter* Lodouico, Montano, Iago, *and Officers,* | Cassio *in a Chaire.*
5.2.365.1/3262.1 *He stabs himselfe.*
5.2.369.1/3266.1 *He dies.*
5.2.381.1/3278.1 *Exeunt omnes.*

FOLIO STAGE DIRECTIONS

1.1.0.1/0.1 *Enter* Rodorigo, *and* Iago.
1.1.146/147 *Exit.*
1.1.161/162 *Exit.*
1.1.161.1-2/162.1-2 *Enter* Brabantio, *with Seruants and Torches.*
1.1.185/186 *Exeunt.*
1.2.0.1/186.1 *Enter* Othello, Iago, Attendants, *with Torches.*
1.2.28/214 *Enter* Cassio, *with Torches.* (after 'yond')
1.2.52.1-2/238.1-2 *Enter* Brabantio, Rodorigo, *with Officers, and Torches.* (after 1.2.55/241)
1.2.100.1/286.1 *Exeunt*
1.3.0.1-2/286.2-3 *Enter* Duke, Senators, *and Officers.*
1.3.12.1/298.1 *Enter Saylor.*
1.3.33.1/319.1 *Enter a Messenger.*
1.3.46.1-2/332.1-2 *Enter* Brabantio, Othello, Cassio, Iago, Rodorigo, | *and Officers.* (after 1.3.47/333)

OTHELLO

1.3.168.1/454.1 Enter Desdemona, Iago, Attendants. (after 1.3.169/455)
1.3.293.1-2/579.1-2 Exit.
1.3.300.1/586.1 Exit.
1.3.374/660.1 Exit.
2.1.0.1-2/682.2-3 Enter Montano, and two Gentlemen.
2.1.19.1/701.1 Enter a Gentleman.
2.1.43.1/725.1 Enter Cassio.
2.1.60/742 Exit.
2.1.66/748 Enter Gentleman.
2.1.83/765 Enter Desdemona, Iago, Rodorigo, and Æmilia.
2.1.182.1/863.1 Enter Othello, and Attendants.
2.1.213.1-2/894.1-2 Exit Othello and Desdemona.
2.1.284/966 Exit.
2.1.311/993 Exit.
2.2.0.1/993.1 Enter Othello's, Herald with a Proclamation.
2.2.11/1005 Exit.
2.3.0.1/1005.1 Enter Othello, Desdemona, Cassio, and Attendants.
2.3.11.1/1016.1 Exit.
2.3.11.2/1016.2 Enter Iago.
2.3.43/1049 Exit.
2.3.57/1063 Enter Cassio, Montano, and Gentlemen. (after 'come')
2.3.111/1117 Exit.
2.3.127.1/1133.1 Enter Rodorigo.
2.3.138.1/1144.1 Enter Cassio pursuing Rodorigo.
2.3.156/1162 Enter Othello, and Attendants.
2.3.242.1/1248.1 Enter Desdemona attended.
2.3.252.1/1258.1 Exit.
2.3.326/1335 Exit Cassio.
2.3.353/1362 Enter Rodorigo. (after 'now Roderigo')
2.3.372/1381 Exit Rodorigo.
2.3.378/1387 Exit.
3.1.0.1/1387.1 Enter Cassio, Musitians, and Clowne.
3.1.20/1407 Exit Mu.
3.1.29/1417 Exit Clo.
3.1.29/1417 Enter Iago.
3.1.38.1/1426.1 Exit (after 'free')
3.1.39.1/1427.1 Enter Æmilia.
3.2.0.1/1442.2 Enter Othello, Iago, and Gentlemen.
3.2.6/1448 Exeunt
3.3.0.1/1448.1 Enter Desdemona, Cassio, and Æmilia.
3.3.28/1476 Enter Othello, and Iago.
3.3.32/1480 Exit Cassio.
3.3.90.1/1538.1 Exit.
3.3.261.1/1709.1 Exit.
3.3.281/1729 Enter Desdemona and Æmilia. (after 'comes')
3.3.293.1/1741.1 Exit. (after 3.3.292/1740)
3.3.303.1/1751.1 Enter Iago.
3.3.324.1/1772.1 Exit Æmil.
3.3.333/1781 Enter Othello. (after 'so')
3.3.482/1929 Exeunt.
3.4.0.1/1929.1 Enter Desdemona, Æmilia, and Clown.
3.4.22/1951 Exit Clo.
3.4.31/1960 Enter Othello. (after 'comes')
3.4.97/2026 Exit Othello.
3.4.104/2033 Enter Iago, and Cassio.
3.4.138/2067 Exit (after 3.4.137/2066)
3.4.165.1/2094.1 Exit (after 3.4.164/2093)
3.4.165.2/2094.2 Enter Bianca.
3.4.198/2127 Exeunt omnes.
4.1.0.1/2127.1 Enter Othello, and Iago.
4.1.42.1/2168.1 Falls in a Traunce.
4.1.46/2173 Enter Cassio.
4.1.98/2225 Enter Cassio. (after 'comes')
4.1.141.1/2268.1 Enter Bianca. (after 4.1.142/2269)
4.1.157.1/2284 Exit
4.1.209.1/2337.1 Enter Lodouico, Desdemona, and Attendants. (after 4.1.206/2334)
4.1.265.1/2392.1 Exit.
4.1.284/2411 Exeunt.
4.2.0.1/2411.1 Enter Othello and Æmilia.
4.2.20.1/2431.1 Exit Æmilia.
4.2.24.1/2435.1 Enter Desdemona, and Æmilia.
4.2.32.1/2443 Exit Æmi.
4.2.96/2507 Enter Æmilia. (after 4.2.94/2505)
4.2.98/2509.1 Exit.
4.2.109.1/2520.1 Exit.
4.2.112.1/2523.1 Enter Iago, and Æmilia.
4.2.176.1/2587.1 Exeunt Desdemona and Æmilia.
4.2.176.2/2587.2 Enter Rodorigo.
4.2.249/2661 Exeunt.
4.3.0.1-2/2661.2-3 Enter Othello, Lodouico, Desdemona, Æmilia, | and Atendants.
4.3.9.1/2671.1 Exit. (after 4.3.8/2670)
4.3.104/2766 Exeunt
5.1.0.1/2766.1 Enter Iago, and Rodorigo.
5.1.22.1/2788.1 Enter Cassio.
5.1.27.1/2793.1 Enter Othello.
5.1.37.1/2803.1 Exit Othello.
5.1.37.2/2803.1 Enter Lodouico and Gratiano.
5.1.46.1/2812.1 Enter Iago.
5.1.75.1/2841.1 Enter Bianca.
5.1.131/2897 Exeunt
5.2.0.1-2/2897.1-2 Enter Othello, and Desdemona in her bed.
5.2.92.1/2989.1 Smothers her.
5.2.93.1/2990.1 Æmilia at the doore.
5.2.114/3011 Enter Æmilia. (after 'now')
5.2.174.1/3071.1 Enter Montano, Gratiano, and Iago.
5.2.250/3147 Exit.
5.2.288.1-2/3185.1-2 Enter Lodouico, Cassio, Montano, and Iago, | with Officers.
5.2.369.1/3266.1 Dyes
5.2.381.1/3278.1 Exeunt.

[Printed after the play]

    The Names of the Actors.

Othello, *the Moore.*
Brabantio, *Father to Desdemona.*
Cassio, *an Honourable Lieutenant.*
Iago, *a Villaine.*
Rodorigo, *a gull'd Gentleman.*
Duke of Venice.
Senators.
Montano, *Gouernour of Cyprus.*
Gentlemen of Cyprus.
Lodouico, *and* Gratiano, *two Noble Venetians.*
Saylors.
Clowne.
Desdemona, *Wife to Othello.*
Æmilia, *Wife to Iago.*
Bianca, *a Curtezan.*

ALL'S WELL THAT ENDS WELL

The only substantive text is that printed in the First Folio (F), entered in the Stationers' Register with the other 'new' titles in the collection (see pp. 32, 34). Compositor B was responsible for the bulk of it, and two pages (2.1.6/565–2.2.38/809) were set by C. Only two pages (1.3.17/321–2.1.5/564) were set by the more reliable Compositor D, whose errors are generally less frequent and easier to correct.

The Folio compositors were almost certainly setting from Shakespeare's own foul papers. The influence of foul papers has long been recognized in the variant speech-prefixes, ghost characters (Violenta in 3.5/Sc. 13; but see also the Citizens in that scene, and the head-notes to 4.3/Sc. 18 and 5.3/Sc. 23), and literary stage directions: '*Enter the King with diuers yong Lords, taking leaue for the Florentine warre*' (2.1.0.1–3/559.2–4), '*She addresses her to a Lord*' (2.3.77/915), '*Parrolles and Lafew stay behind, commenting of this wedding*' (2.3.184.1–2/1022.1–2), '*Enter Count Rossillion and the Frenchmen, as at first*' (3.6.0.1/1594.2–3), '*Enter one of the Frenchmen, with fiue or sixe other souldiers in ambush*' (4.1.0.1–2/1762.1–2). In 5.3/Sc. 23 Paroles is given two different entrances, the first (at 5.3.159/2677) obviously incorrect. Of course, these anomalies might have been preserved in a transcript of foul papers, but both general and particular considerations argue against such an intermediate manuscript here. It could have served no known purpose, and has left no traces of its presence. More particularly, the spelling and punctuation of the Folio text argue for direct use of Shakespearian foul copy. Although investigators have remarked on the paucity of Shakespearian spellings, this is hardly surprising in a play set almost wholly by Compositor B. A few such spellings do nevertheless appear: 'on' for *one* (2.5.28/1223, and probably 1.1.145/147), 'in' for *e'en* (3.2.18/1327 and perhaps 4.2.40/1899), ''ton tooth' for *t'one to th'* (1.3.173/477), 'Angles' for *angels* (3.2.128/1436, as also Q2 *Hamlet* 1.5.55/672 and *The Two Noble Kinsmen* 1.1.16/49). But the most convincing evidence against a transcript is F's punctuation, which suggests that the compositors were working from a virtually unpunctuated manuscript—like the Hand D portions of *Sir Thomas More*. Absence of punctuation where the sense requires it, insertion of punctuation where the sense forbids it, misplacement of punctuation so that individual clauses are attached to the wrong sentence—these failures are amply documented in the following textual notes and the list of emended incidentals. A more particular peculiarity of punctuation, which occurs elsewhere in Shakespearian autograph texts, also appears: the use of commas as hyphens ('jarring, concord . . . discord, dulcet' 1.1.168/171; cf. *Merchant* 2.4.14/777). The unusually high number of errors and cruces in the text also suggests difficult ('foul') copy.

These foul papers may, however, have been annotated by a book-keeper. As W. J. Lawrence pointed out in *Shakespeare's Workshop* (1928; pp. 48–74), *All's Well* is the only public theatre play written before 1609 which calls in its stage directions for cornetts, an instrument before then very strongly associated with the boys' companies. The instruments are not used for any particular or unusual dramatic purpose, and seem much more typical of the practice of the King's Men after 1609 than before. The layout of the directions may also be suggestive of a book-keeper: '*Flourish Cornets.*' at 1.2.0.1/228.1 occupies a separate line, and at 2.1.0.1/559.2 '*Flourish Cornets.*' occurs incongruously at the end of a long direction. We would not expect the Folio's division into five acts to have stood in foul papers, and yet it is much more sensible than the editorial divisions found in *Shrew* and *Henry V*, and might well reflect late theatrical practice (see Taylor, 'Act Intervals'). Such indications of theatrical annotation are most easily explained by the conjecture that the original prompt-book for *All's Well* was lost (as happened to *Winter's Tale* and Fletcher's *Bonduca*, for instance), and that prior to the preparation of a new prompt-book for a revival the foul papers were read and sporadically annotated by the book-keeper (as happened to Fletcher's *The Mad Lover*). Greg suggests that 'Some long dashes in the printed text and some broken lines suggest cuts or alterations, and in occasional inconsequences and contradictions and in imperfectly assimilated chunks of prose it is easy to find evidence of botching' (*Folio*, p. 353). We see little justification for such pessimism, as the annotator's interference with the text (if any) must, on the evidence of its inadequate stage directions, have been minimal.

Chambers (*Shakespeare*, i. 450) believed that the annotator was responsible for the occasionally redundant identification of the two French lords, as 'E.' and 'G.' as well as '1.' and '2.'; Hunter (pp. xv–xvii) has cast doubt on these conjectures, but the King's Men did include a Gough (active c.1592–1621) and Ecclestone (1610–11, 1614–23) during the period when a revival might have been contemplated. Whoever is responsible, the brothers Dumaine cause a notorious textual problem, though its extent has perhaps been exaggerated. If we assume that the First Lord = G, and Second = E (as in their first two scenes), only three difficulties arise. The first, and least troubling, is that at 4.1.1/1763. F's speech-prefix is '*1. Lord E.*'; but, as the association of E and G with first and second has not been used in the immediately preceding scenes, Shakespeare might well at this point not have remembered precisely which was which; he (or an annotator, or Compositor B) might also have been influenced by the immediately preceding direction, '*Enter one of the Frenchmen*'. In any case, there is no doubt that E is here required, and the error has no other textual consequences. The second problem occurs at the end of 3.6/Sc. 14, where between 3.6.109/1705 and 3.6.118/1714 the identifications of E and G are reversed, G rather than E leaving the stage. F's speech-prefixes have been defended by Fredson Bowers, on the basis of a contradiction first noticed by Dover Wilson: in 4.3/Sc. 18, it is E who tells G about Bertram's nocturnal appointment with Diana, whereas in the traditional emended text of 3.6/Sc. 14 G had accompanied Bertram to Diana's house. An editor here has his choice of contradictions. If he retains F, after Captain E announces 'I must go . . .', Bertram—instead of replying—turns to Captain G and tells him 'Your brother, he shall go along with me', at which point Captain G departs. But Bertram intends to 'go along' to Diana's, whereas E's intention was to go to set the trap for Paroles, as we see him doing in the next scene but one. F thus produces a very awkward ending to 3.6/Sc. 14; it gives G nothing to do, while requiring E to be in two places at once—leaving with Bertram for Diana's at the end of 3.6/Sc. 14, and capturing Paroles in 4.1/Sc. 16, though Bertram does not reach Diana's until 4.2/Sc. 17. The awkwardness of this arrangement, in performance, can hardly be overlooked. On the other hand, the traditional emendation makes the sequence of scenes 3.6/Sc. 14 to 4.2/Sc. 17 perfectly clear; but 4.3/Sc. 18 potentially contradicts the ending of 3.6/Sc. 14. But this contradiction is only potential and implicit; if an audience paused to puzzle out probabilities, it might realize that G is likelier than E to know about Bertram's rendezvous. But we did not actually see G in 4.2/Sc. 17, nor was he referred to, and *a priori* there is nothing disconcerting or improbable about E's knowing in this instance what G does not. In short, the contradiction created by emending 3.6/Sc. 14 is one entirely typical of Shakespeare, invisible to the audience and never even noticed until 1929; the contradictions created by retaining F are dramatically awkward and impossible to conceal; they were emended by Shakespeare's first editor, Rowe. Moreover, to explain F Bowers ('Shakespeare at Work') must postulate 'clumsy revision', whereas to justify emending it we need only presuppose a moment of inattention or distraction—during composition itself, or afterwards, when inserting speech-prefixes—in which Shakespeare (or the annotator) momentarily reversed the identities. It thus seems to us that the traditional solution is correct, and that it requires us to suppose no textual disturbance or confusion beyond the three prefixes in the ten affected lines.

The third problem also involves an apparent contradiction in 4.3/Sc. 18, where G takes charge of the interrogation of Paroles, when we would have expected E—who captured him in 4.1/Sc. 16, and conducted his interrogation there—to perform this function. But the extent of the confusion here has been exaggerated, for in fact it affects only two lines (4.3.122/2060 and 4.3.129/2077), where one of the brothers speaks gibberish. 4.3.129/2077 has the prefix *Cap.*; whether E or G was intended is of course impossible to tell, though all editors concur in giving the line to G. They do so, presumably, because F assigns 4.3.122/2060 to G. The contradiction thus rests entirely upon the speech-prefix for this line. But all editors already agree that F here contains an error of attribution, for the words 'hush, hush', which F puts at the end of Bertram's preceding speech (4.3.121/2059), should be assigned to one of the brothers. If confusion of prefixes has undoubtedly occurred, and if a serious contradiction in the dramatic action rests entirely upon the authority of F's prefix here, then it seems reasonable to posit the same source for both problems: namely, that the prefix *Cap. G.* belongs where editors have put it (before 'Hush, hush'), and that the following speech should be assigned to *Cap. E.* Either emendation presupposes that F has omitted a speech-prefix before 'hush hush', and misplaced that prefix after 'hush hush'; the traditional emendation assumes that the space after 'hush hush' was empty, whereas ours assumes that it was occupied. A similar error occurs in *1 Henry VI*, where F's *Warw.* in 3.1.52/1134 has been moved, by all editors since Hanmer, to 3.1.53/1135, and replaced in 3.1.52/1134 by *Glou.* In *1 Henry VI*, as (we suggest) in *All's Well*, an adjoining speech-prefix has been misplaced, and in the process ousted another. Moreover, even if this emendation were not justified bibliographically, it would represent the most economical solution to a confusion in foul papers which would have had to be rectified in performance.

One other, trivial, problem is what to call these two characters. The usual 'First Lord' and 'Second Lord' is ambiguous (another First and Second Lord appear in 2.3/Sc. 6) and ignores the surname Shakespeare eventually gives them, thereby obscuring their family relationship and (for a reader, at least) their significant individuality. They might be called 'E. Dumaine' and 'G. Dumaine', but this, besides seeming odd, would probably misrepresent Shakespeare's intentions; we have therefore consistently distinguished them as First Lord Dumaine and Second Lord Dumaine.

Our text contains an unusually high number of emendations and original readings. This is largely a consequence of the recognized inadequacy of the text, which the Cambridge editors of 1863 singled out as the worst-printed play in the First Folio (vol. i, p. xxvii); an inadequacy which we can now probably attribute to the presence of Compositors B and C, to the foulness of the manuscript, and to the fact that up to this point the Folio compositors had been setting mainly (or entirely) from printed or scribal copy, and were here in their first encounter with really foul autograph, in a text verbally far more complex and difficult than the early *Comedy of Errors* and *Taming of the Shrew*.

Act divisions reproduce those in F; scene divisions are editorial and traditional. F contains much variety and inconsistency in speech-prefixes; these have been analysed by Bowers ('Foul Papers'), who shows that for the most part they must reflect copy. The variation is best studied in facsimiles, in conjunction with compositorial attribution and order of setting; our collations do not record such inconsistencies, unless there is genuine confusion about the character intended. However, where the prefixes in a scene 'characterize' a figure (*Old* Countess, *Captain* E, etc.), the relevant detail has where possible been incorporated into the character's entrance direction for that scene.

G.T./(S.W.W.)

WORKS CITED

Bowers, Fredson, 'Foul Papers, Compositor B, and the Speech-Prefixes of *All's Well That Ends Well*', SB 32 (1979), 60–81
——— 'Shakespeare at Work: The Foul Papers of *All's Well That Ends Well*', in *English Renaissance Studies: Presented to Dame Helen Gardner*, ed. John Carey (1980), 56–73
Brigstocke, W. D., ed., *All's Well That Ends Well*, Arden (1904)
Everett, Barbara, ed., *All's Well That Ends Well*, New Penguin (1970)
Hunter, G. K., ed., *All's Well That Ends Well*, Arden (1959; rev. 1962)

Lambrechts, Guy, 'Proposed New Readings in Shakespeare, The Comedies', *Hommage à Shakespeare: Bulletin de la Faculté des Lettres de Strasbourg* (May-June 1965), 167

Walker, Alice, 'Six Notes on *All's Well That Ends Well*', *SQ* 33 (1982), 339-42

Wilson, John Dover, ed., *All's Well That Ends Well*, New (1929; rev. 1952)

TEXTUAL NOTES

Title *All's Well*ˏ *that Ends Well*] F (*some running titles*); ALL'S Well, that Ends Well. F (*head title, some running titles*); All is well, that Ends well F (*table of contents*); All's wellˏ that ends well S.R.

1.1.0.2/0.2 *Hellen*] This edition; *Helena* F. The trisyllabic form occurs only 3 other times (1.1.49/50, 2.4.0.1/1137.2, 2.5.53.1/1248.1), only the first of these in dialogue. The disyllabic form occurs 25 times. It thus seems probable that Shakespeare, initially inconsistent, eventually abandoned the trisyllabic form; so an editor forced to choose one name or the other should adopt Shakespeare's own preference, *Hellen*.

1.1.18/19 honestie;] ROWE; ~ˏ F

1.1.25 Gérard] The French name; editors follow F in not using an accent.

1.1.25 de Narbonne] F (de Narbon). 'Of Narbonne', a French town near Roussillon; editors retain F.

1.1.38/39 promises;] ROWE 3; ~ˏ F. F's punctuation hardly has sufficient authority to justify the contortions here required to make sense of it. See Taylor, '*Praestat*'.

1.1.49/50 *Hellen*] This edition; *Helena* F. See note to 1.1.0.2/0.2.

1.1.50/51 haue—] F; have it. WARBURTON; have. STEEVENS. See Taylor, '*Praestat*'.

1.1.54/55 not] THEOBALD; *not in* F. See Taylor, *Praestat*.

1.1.67/68 Farwell.] CAPELL; ~ˏ F

1.1.97.1 *Paroles*] F (*Parrolles*, elsewhere *Parolles*). Shakespeare clearly intended the French word, and there is no justification for disguising it.

1.1.114-15/115-16 valiantˏ in the defence,] REED; ~, ~ˏ F. Hunter, followed by recent editors, argues that the emendation contradicts 'the presupposition of the sentence following, i.e. is *not* valiant in the defence'. But it is because virginity is 'valiant in the defence' that it *wishes* to make resistance, and enquires after a stratagem which will compensate for its recognized weakness. The Folio punctuation is not only awkward, but could imply that virginity would *not* be weak 'in the offence'.

1.1.127/128 got] F2; goe F1

1.1.145/147 t'on] RIVERSIDE; ten F

1.1.155 wear] F (were)

1.1.161/164 virginityˏ yet:] F; virginity; yet,ˏ at the court This edition *conj*.

1.1.183/186 Exit] THEOBALD; *not in* F

1.2.0.2-3/228.2-3 the two ... Attendants] This edition; *and diuers Attendants* F. For the two lords, see the Textual Introduction. How many others (if any) were envisaged is unclear.

228.2 Dumaine] This word occurs 4 times in F: 3 times it is spelt with the terminal '-e'; only once, at 2225, is it spelt 'Dumain', and there the truncated spelling is almost certainly the consequence of justification.

1.2.1 Sienese] F (Senoys). The *i* in the stem can be elided, without harm to the metre, and *-ese*, which occurs in Gascoigne's *Supposes* (1566) 1.2 ('Scenese' throughout), is the only modern termination. The degeneration of the diphthong into *ē* is, in any case, common.

1.2.18/246 Rosillion] F2; *Roſignoll* F1

1.2.52/280 him:] F2; ~ˏ F1

1.2.56/284 This] F; Thus POPE. Compare a similar error in Q2 *Hamlet* 5.1.283/3253.

1.2.76.1/304.1 [Flourish.] Exeunt] This edition (*after* ROWE); Exit | *Flouriſh*. F. For similar ambiguous placement of a *Flourish* direction, see *Henry V* 1.2.310.1/443.1 and 2.4.146.1/1002.1.

1.3.0.2/304.2 behind] This edition; *not in* F

1.3.42/346 Madam—] ALEXANDER; ~ˏ F

1.3.52 Chairbonne] F (*Charbon*)

1.3.52/356 Poyson] CAMBRIDGE; *Poyſam* F

1.3.58/362 A Prophet? I] This edition; A Prophet,ˏ I F; A prophet I, CAPELL. F's 'I' is of course ambiguous, and the compositor's copy presumably virtually unpunctuated. Lavatch comically takes 'foule mouth'd and calumnious knaue' as a synonym for *prophet*.

1.3.58 Ay] F (I). See preceding note.

1.3.59.1/364 sings] This edition; *not in* F

1.3.69/373 sings] WILSON; *not in* F

1.3.72-3/376-7 stood, | With that she sighed as she stood,] ſtood, *bis* | F. F's '*bis*' after 1.3.72/376 calls for the line's repetition.

1.3.84/388 ere] COLLIER 1; ore F; *or* CAPELL; one COLLIER 2. Capell's reading has the same sense as Collier 1, but *or* meaning 'before' is not normally spelt 'ore'.

1.3.111/415 Dian no] CRAIG; Diana no THEOBALD; *not in* F. In this play Shakespeare distinguished between 'Diana' the character and 'Dian' the goddess; he also prefers 'Dian' elsewhere.

1.3.167/471 lonelinesse] THEOBALD; *loueline∫∫e* F

1.3.173/477 tooth other] F2; tooth to th'other F1

1.3.198/502 intenable] SISSON; intemible F

1.3.212/516 to finde not] This edition (*conj.* Walker); not to finde F. For post-position of 'not' with this verb, compare *LLL* 4.2.120/1197 and *Cymbeline* 3.5.158/1815 ('And finde not her, whom thou pursuest'). The compositor might easily transpose the word by placing after the wrong one of two adjacent verbs (seek ... find).

2.1.3/562 gaineˏ all,] JOHNSON; ~, ~ˏ F

2.1.15-16/574-5 it: when ... shrinkes,] POPE; ~, ~ : F

2.1.23/582.1 *Some Lords stand aside with the King*] This edition (*after* CAPELL); *not in* F; *Exit.* POPE. Pope's arrangement supposes that '*the King*' has been omitted from the entrance direction at 2.1.59.1/618.1; it would entail beginning a new scene there. Editors are usually vague or silent about the eventual departure of the silent lords and attendants; we have marked it at 2.1.98.1/657.1. Shakespeare may have forgotten about them.

2.1.42/601 with his sicatrice,] THEOBALD; his ficatrice, with F

2.1.48/607 Stay,] F1; ~ : F2. Bertram, a young ward, can hardly be thought of as *supporting* the King; so if F1 is retained *stay* must mean 'wait for'. Paroles's next speech then directly relates to this reply, as it persuades Bertram not to stay but instead follow the lords off stage. F2's punctuation either results in an interpretation—'(I will) stay, (because of) the King'—which contradicts his previous promise and eventual conduct, or creates an awkward blocking problem, with the King apparently moving or turning round here—'Stay: the King'—and yet not re-entering the scene effectively until 2.1.61/620. F1's punctuation, minimal though its authority is, thus seems preferable to F2's.

2.1.55-6/614-15 after ... farewell] F. One does not normally answer an injunction ('After them ... take') with a conjunction ('And I will do so'). Bertram's speech would make better sense as a reply to 'such are to be followed'; not only does this produce much better logic and grammar ('it is a general rule that such persons should be followed—and I will follow them'), but it also turns a colourless exit line into a meaningful and dramatic one (though the devil lead the measure, Bertram will follow). Paroles's injunction might have been a marginal insertion which belonged at the end of Paroles's *next* speech, but which Compositor C (easily enough) misinterpreted and misplaced. That C was not at his most attentive here is suggested by the errors at 2.1.42/601, 2.1.61/620, and 2.1.62/621.

2.1.61/620 fee] THEOBALD; ſee F. F is idiomatically awkward, dramatically flat, and irrelevant to what follows and precedes;

the proposed error is exceptionally easy. See also the following note.

2.1.62/621 bought] THEOBALD; brought F. Editors interpret 'brought his pardon' as 'brought (news that will ensure) his pardon'. The proposed ellipsis is difficult; it does not relate to the King's preceding line (whether emended or not); it contradicts Lafeu's entrance line (which asked for pardon for the very tidings which he is now claiming will themselves ensure his pardon); and it anticipates the exciting good news which is then disregarded until 2.1.67/626. For all these reasons, and because 'Then' and 'stands' (and the word-play throughout this passage) strongly encourage the expectation of some witty rejoinder to the King's reply, F seems wrong and Theobald right. The conjectured memorial-cum-aural-cum-graphic substitution is typical of Compositor C; for an identical error, see Q8 of *Richard III* (1.2.249/411). Either *fee* = 'pay', with the King tossing Lafeu some money which Lafeu then returns, or *fee* = 'charge, exact a fee from' (not recorded in *OED*, but see *fee*, *sb.*² 7; and the general phenomenon is of course common), with Lafeu paying the King, and then interpreting it as a 'bribe' (*fee*, *sb.*² 10c, v.¹ 3b).

2.1.92.1/651.1 disguised] This edition; *not in* F. Editors have taken Lafeu's recognition of Helen at 2.3.45/883 ('PARROLLES . . . is not this *Helen*? | LAFEW Fore God I thinke so') as ironically understated, or imagined him musing there on the King's recovery (and thus not hearing, or disregarding, Paroles's question). Both interpretations seem strained and undramatic, and the obvious implication of the line is that he did not recognize Helen earlier—which means she must have been somehow disguised. This fits well not only with her immediate purpose (to gain access to the King, and temporarily conceal her identity from those who know her humble origins or might guess her intended choice of husband), but also with her later actions. See 2.1.96/655 ('A Traitor you doe looke like') and *Caesar* 2.1.73-8/635-40: '. . . their Hats are pluckt about their Eares, | And halfe their Faces buried in their Cloakes, | That by no meanes I may discouer them | By any marke of fauour . . . O Conspiracie, | Sham'st thou to shew thy dang'rous Brow by Night . . .'

2.1.108/667 two, more deare:] STEEVENS 2; ~ : ~ₐ F
2.1.138 flow'n] F (flowne). The apostrophe is adopted to differentiate this, the obsolete strong past participle of *flow*, from the modern past participle of *fly*.
2.1.139/698 dried.] This edition; ~ₐ F. See the next note. The punctuation is, again, presumably compositorial; see similar errors at 2.1.15-16, 108/574-5, 667, etc.
2.1.140-1/699-700 denied, . . .]] This edition; ~ . F. That—as Johnson conjectured—a line has been omitted here seems certain from the lack of a rhyme for 'there', in the midst of a passage of 40 consecutive couplets, and by the difficulty of relating 2.1.140/699 to the preceding clause. This edition conjectures 'By th' least haue they been compass'd to appear'. See Taylor, 'Inventing'.
2.1.144/703 ffitts] COLLIER (Theobald); ſhifts F
2.1.155/714 Imposture] CAPELL; impoſtrue F. Capell's emendation, which presupposes an easy misreading or compositorial transposition of types, produces an acceptable period spelling of *impostor* (see *OED*), which we (following F3 and editors) modernize.
2.1.162/721 coacher] HUNTER (anon. *conj.*); torcher F
2.1.164/723 her] F; his ROWE
2.1.171/730 shame;] THEOBALD; ~ₐ F
2.1.172/731 ballads,] This edition; ~ : F; ~ₐ THEOBALD. So punctuated, Helen's speech begins with three phrases, each of three words, then follows with three more phrases, each with a past participle in apposition to the other two ('Traduc'd . . . Seard . . . extended'). Rhetorically, this is much more powerful, and more immediately coherent, than either the Folio or the usual editorial alternatives (which usually entail a heavier stop after 'otherwise' in 2.1.173/732).
2.1.173/732 nay] SINGER 2 (Malone); ne F. Dramatically and rhetorically, Helen surely wants her willingness to die after torture to be the climax of this speech, and it is to this offer alone that the King responds (2.1.179/738 ff.); F's 'ne', producing the sense 'nor is this the worst' (what Everett, while retaining it, calls 'an almost impossible phrase'), may do credit to the value Helen puts on her modesty, but it deflates her (and Shakespeare's) climax. By contrast, 'nay, worse of worst' indicates the climax and allows of much more forcible delivery; it gives due weight to the shame of the preceding lines (which is 'the worst'), and to the climactic offer of torture and death (which are the worser part of the worst). F's reading could be an aural error: see *LLL* 5.1.23/1627 ('neigh' abbreviated 'ne'), and 5.1.25/1629 (Latin *ne*), which suggest how a compositor might inadvertently have set 'ne' when carrying the sound of 'nay' in his head. Alternatively, if *nay* were spelt 'na' (*OED*), it might have been misread or misinterpreted.

2.1.175/734 speak,] This edition; ~ₐ F. The line fills F's column, leaving no room for punctuation. One can say 'speak a sound', but not 'speak his sound within an organ'. The next line construes easily in apposition.
2.1.181/740 all] F; health and all BRIGSTOCKE (*conj.*). Of the several attempts to supply the missing foot (honour, virtue), Brigstocke's is the only attractive conjecture; but the metrical deficiency may be deliberate, in such a list.
2.1.192/751 heauen] THEOBALD (Thirlby); helpe F
2.2.5/774 To] F; But to THEOBALD. F's text is acceptable if Lavatch pauses after 'but'.
2.2.17/787 quatch-buttock] F. To the myriad of conjectures the unknown 'quatch' has spawned we might add 'quaich', a 17th-century Scottish word (= a shallow drinking cup), also recorded in the *EDD*. If, as we believe, *All's Well* is Jacobean, the word's use here is not impossible.
2.2.21 taffeta] F (taffety)
2.2.29/799 beyond] This edition; below F. Although no one comments upon this speech, 'below' seems wrong in contrast to 'beneath': the Constable, and anything 'beneath' him, would by definition also be 'below' the Duke. For *beyond* in contrast to *beneath* compare *Cymbeline* 4.1.10-11/1936-7. The proposed error is part graphical, part memorial (contamination from 'beneath').
2.2.38-39/809 I pray you] F3; La⟨dy⟩. I pray you F. The Countess is consistently identified as 'Lady' in the speech-prefixes of this scene. If a short speech by the clown has been omitted, its content is irrecoverable, and its omission has not disturbed the dialogue.
2.2.58/829 An end sir, to] ROWE 3; And end sir, to F1; And end; sir, to F3
2.3.27 dolphin] F (Dolphin). The pun, and the apparent primacy of the 'dolphin' sense, preclude the usual modernization to *Dauphin*.
2.3.30 facinorous] F (facinerious). Given Heywood's *facinorious* (*OED*), F's spelling cannot be regarded as a comic blunder by Paroles, and neither the *er/or* variant, nor the optional *-i-*, justifies regarding it as a distinct or semantically significant 'form'.
2.3.37/875 made] F. One must understand an ellipsis 'made (of it; i.e. of the miracle)'. *OED* gives no examples of such an ellipsis (*use*, *sb.* 1c); nor does Abbott. Of the 21 occasions when Shakespeare employs the *make use* idiom, this is the only one not followed by the required prepositional phrase. It thus seems possible that 'of't' or 'of it' has been omitted.
2.3.42 Lustig] F (Luſtique). F's spelling, and the several parallels listed in *OED*, are clearly attempts to reproduce the Dutch pronunciation.
2.3.45 vinaigre] F (vinager). There is no reason to suppose that the spelling differences are significant; Paroles, who is French, cannot be supposed to be mispronouncing his native tongue.
2.3.63/901 these] This edition; thoſe F. Compare 'this youthfull parcell' (2.3.53/891) and 'these boyes' (2.3.61/899, 2.3.94/932). The error is exceptionally easy and occurs often.
2.3.66/904 ALL BUT HELLEN] This edition; *All*. F. F might mean 'All' of the '3 or 4' Lords she addresses, or the whole Court (with or without the King); as often, the prefix is unspecific.
2.3.71/909 choose; but be refused,] RANN; ~ , ~ ; F
2.3.77/915 *She addresses her to a Lord*] WILSON; *after* 2.3.63/901, F
2.3.80 ambs-ace] F (Ameſ-ace)

2.3.95/933 her] F2; heere F1
2.3.97/935 HELLEN] F3; *La.* F1
2.3.126 when] THEOBALD (Thirlby); whence F
2.3.130/968 name;] CAPELL (*after* F4); ~ ? F1. Some editors claim that the Folio question mark is used here loosely for rhetorical emphasis, but they cite no parallels, and it seems likelier that F's punctuation is based on a compositorial misinterpretation ('Is good without a name? Vilenesse is so').
2.3.131/969 it is] F2; is is F1
2.3.138/976 words˄ a slaue,] F2; ~, ~˄ F1
2.3.139/977 graue˄] STEEVENS; ~ : F
2.3.141 dammed] F (damn'd). The Folio spelling is ambiguous: compare *OED* dam, v.¹ and Q2 *1 Henry IV* 3.1.98/1577 ('Ile haue the currant in this place damnd vp'). To speak of 'damned oblivion' as a tomb surely introduces an unintended ambiguity here; whereas the image of 'dust and dammed oblivion' is both appropriate and characteristic.
2.3.141/979 Tombe˄] THEOBALD; ~. F
2.3.147/985 selfe; if ... choose—] This edition; felfe, if ... choofe. F. Commentators interpret the Folio as meaning either 'you as a ward have no right to choose at all' (in which case Bertram is wronging *the King* not himself), or 'if you choose for yourself, you could only choose worse' (which would seem to require 'Thou'dst wrong') or 'you wrong yourself by having to *strive* at all, when offered such a wife' (which is difficult to communicate, and makes *to choose* redundant). The speech would be clearer and more dramatic if a curt and emphatic 'Thou wrong'st thyself' were followed by a new beginning, 'If thou should'st strive to choose' (either conciliatory or aggressive), which is then interrupted by the hitherto silent Helen.
2.3.169/1007 eies:] ROWE (*subs.*); ~, F
2.3.171/1009 it,] ROWE (*subs.*); ~ : F
2.3.289/1129 detested] ROWE (detefted); detected F
2.3.290 capriccio] F (Caprichio). Although there are uses of *caprichious* antedating this by a few years, this is a first occurrence, and the word remained an affectation into the next decade; thus it seems best to italicize it, as a foreign word.
2.4.15/1152 fortunes] CAPELL (Heath); fortune F
2.4.25 title] F. Hunter's conjecture 'tittle' represents an alternative modernization, not an emendation, as *OED* makes clear; but although *tittle* is surely being played on, *title* seems the primary sense.
2.4.34/1172 PARROLLES In my selfe, knaue.] This edition; *not in* F; *Parolles.* In myself. WILSON (Nicholson). Even without the repeated speech-prefix *Clo⟨wne⟩.*, an omission would be almost certain; the repetition makes it virtually incontestable. See Taylor, 'Inventing'.
2.4.55/1193 you, ⌜*Exit Parrolles at one doore*⌝ | come] This edition (*after* Theobald); you˄ come F (with *Exit Par.* after 2.4.54/1192)
2.5.15-17 sir ... Sir! ... 'Sir' ... 'Sir' 's] This edition (*after* Theobald and Hunter); fir ... Sir? ... fir ... firs F. Lafeu's first 'sir' could be innocent, or a barbed repetition of Paroles's vocative. If it is innocent, Paroles's following 'Sir' could be a genuine question, rather than an indignant exclamation. But the repeated insistence on the word makes innocence unlikely, while a genuine question would be difficult to construe (as Lafeu clearly does) as the fictional tailor's name. Given this deliberate misinterpretation it seems best to capitalize Lafeu's next 'sir', treating it as a proper name rather than a vocative. The last 'sir', however, could be another barbed vocative or the proper name again (in apposition to 'he').
2.5.26/1221 End] COLLIER; And F
2.5.47/1242 wit] This edition (*conj.* Singer); *not in* F. Editors interpret F as 'have (deserved) or intend to deserve'. This is an awkward ellipsis involving a retrospective past tense inferred from the infinitive, while ignoring an alternative construction ('have to deserve'). *Have or will* is a natural disjunctive (which F2 adopts, by omitting *to*); so is *have this or that*; so is *have or will to have*. But F's awkward construction produces none of these. *Wit or will* (which Shakespeare contrasts at *Two Gentlemen* 2.6.12/898, *LLL* 2.1.49/526, *Twelfth Night* 1.5.29/310, and *Lucrece* 1299) means 'capacity or desire', and produces a much more damning indictment than 'past performance and future intention'. Alternatively, *or wit* (which Wilson mistakenly attributes to Singer) would provide a neat explanation for the error (eyeskip); but *wit* produces a more economical phrase.
2.5.50/1245 not] SINGER 2; *not in* F. See Taylor, 'Inventing', note 4.
2.5.53.1/1248.1 attended] This edition; *not in* F. This addition is necessary if F's attribution of 2.5.88/1283 is to be retained.
2.5.63/1260 you] F; it This edition *conj.* The repetition of 'intreate you' is suspicious in itself, and throws the emphasis on the verb—'more than ask why I *entreat* (instead of commanding)'—rather than the thing entreated. Emending to 'it' would improve the meaning and explain the error, the repetition of 'intreat' leading to mistaken repetition of 'you'.
2.5.88/1283 Where ... farewell] F; *Ber⟨tram⟩*. Where are my other men, Monsieur?—farewell THEOBALD 2. See 2.5.53.1/1248.1.
2.5.88.1/1283.1 *Exit Hellen* ⌜*with attendants at one doore*⌝] This edition; *Exit* F
3.1.6/1292 opposer] F; opposer's HANMER
3.1.17/1303 nation] ROWE; nature F. Modern editors retain F, glossing 'temperament, disposition'. But why should this be specified? Does the speaker mean to say that *only* those who are young *and* of his disposition will come? F thus implies that *only* those who are of that disposition 'surfet on their ease'. Rowe's emendation not only makes better sense, but is more likely in the context (the conduct of the French nation, in regard to this war) and assumes an easy misreading, here assisted by assimilation (*yonger*, *sure*, *pleasure*).
3.1.23/1309 to the] F2; to'th the F1
3.1.30 heard] F (hard)
3.2.9/1318 sold] F3; hold F1
3.2.13/1322 Lings] F1; ling F2
3.2.19/1328 COUNTESSE (*reads a Letter*)] ROWE; *A Letter.* F. Perhaps the absence of a prefix here is related to the Clown's unexplained exit: F might have omitted a short line, such as 'Get you gone sirra', prefixed by '*Lad.*' (the usual speech-prefix form in this scene). The compositor's eye could have skipped from marginal '*Lad.*' to marginal '*Let⟨ter⟩*'.
3.2.43/1351 heard] HANMER; heare F
3.2.56.1/1364.1 ⌜*She*⌝ *reads alowd*] CAPELL; *not in* F. As Helen says 'Look on' the letter, rather than 'List to', one would expect the Countess, instead of Helen, to read it. Compare 3.4.3-18/1453-68, where no speech-prefix is given to indicate that the Steward reads the letter, and none to indicate that the Countess resumes after he has finished; and 5.3.141/2659, where the Gentleman brings the letter, which editors usually have the King read, though F does not indicate a change of speaker. This edition therefore conjectures 'COUNTESSE (*reads the Letter*)' here, and 'HELLEN This ...' at 3.2.61/1369.
3.2.65/1373 engrossest˄] F4; ~, F1
3.2.112/1420 cleue] This edition; moue F; wound COLLIER 2. F's 'moue' does not make much sense, whether or not we emend 'peering': what is the contrast between *mouing* and *not touching*, or the relation between *moue* and *pierce*? Where is the sense of danger in *mouing*? There might be a contrast between *moue* and *still*, but this would require emending the hyphen in 'still-peering' to a comma, and in any case what is such a contrast doing here? But given the emendation to 'peecing' (which is justified independently; see next note), 'moue' is especially difficult, not relating satisfactorily to 'peecing' itself (how does moving necessitate piecing?) or to the implied victims of the analogy (who are not moved but killed or wounded). All the parallels cited by editors for the idea of a self-repairing invulnerability use much more explicit verbs: 'it *parteth* the air' (Wisdom of Solomon, 5: 12); 'To cut through ayre, and leaue no print behind you' (Jonson, *Catiline*, 3.522); 'to his blanck, | Transports ... And hit the woundlesse ayre' (*Hamlet* Add. Pass. I.3-5); 'with bemockt-at-Stabs | Kill the still closing waters' (*Tempest* 3.3.63-4/1410-11); see also Fletcher and Massinger's *Sea Voyage* (1622): 'cleave the Ayre' (Beaumont and Fletcher's *Comedies and Tragedies*

(1647: Wing 1581), sig. Aaaaa3ᵛ, column 1, line 31). The emendation 'cleue' is graphically plausible, being easily misread as 'moue'. Several of Shakespeare's other uses of *cleave* have strong associations with this passage (*LLL* 4.1.135/1067, *Antony* 3.4.31/1446, 4.15.39/2387, *Venus* 942).

3.2.112/1420 still-peecing] STEEVENS 2 (anon. conj.); ſtill-peering F. Sisson claims that the gloss of *piecing* as 'piecing itself together again' is purely *ad hoc*, but *OED* records it in 1622, and the reflexive sense is a natural development. The 'jingle' of *piercingly-piecing*, which Sisson derides, seems to us markedly Shakespearian. All the proposed glosses on 'peering' are relevant only tangentially if at all, and/or involve strained and elliptical interpretations.

3.4.4/1454 STEWARD] CAPELL; *not in* F (which has '*Letter*.')
3.4.9/1459 hie;] F3; ~, F1
3.4.10/1460 peace,] F3; ~. F1
3.4.18/1468 COUNTESSE] CAPELL; *not in* F
3.4.19 Reynaldo] There seems no reason to retain F's Rynaldo, instead of the normal modern form.
3.4.27/1477 whom] F; which HANMER
3.5.5/1497 greatest] ROWE; great'ſt F. In order to stretch cast-off copy Compositor B arranged 3.5.1-15/1493-1507 as bogus verse. Shakespeare's other uses of the elided form all occur in verse, and the elision here seems to be part of B's 'authentication' of his verse arrangement.
3.5.11/1503 the] F1; *not in* F4. See previous note. The article, which contributes to an apparent iambic rhythm, might be an interpolation: the closest parallel to the line is *Richard III* 4.4.232/2737, 'Flatter my sorrowe with report of it', where the article is absent.
3.5.15/1507 a Gentleman] F. See previous notes. These words are superfluous, and could have been interpolated by Compositor B in order to drive 'His companion' on to a separate type line of 'verse'. Shakespeare does not elsewhere juxtapose *gentleman* and *companion*. The words could have been suggested to B from 3.5.56/1549 (on X2, which B set just before X1ᵛ).
3.5.19/1511 their] This edition; theſe F1; the F3. As F3 indicates, F1 is not idiomatic, since there is no apparent referent for 'these' except the preceding items, whereas 'and' leads us to expect an addition to the list. Manuscript 'their' could easily be misread as 'theis', a common manuscript spelling almost invariably normalized by compositors to 'these'.
3.5.33/1525 you] F2; *not in* F1. Riverside's defence of F1, by analogy with *art bound*, does not alter the fact that there are no parallels for this use of *are bound* (assimilation being in any case far easier with *art*). F sets as prose, and the conjectured omission occurs—as often—between the end of one line and the beginning of the next.
3.5.66/1558 warᵗ] GLOBE; write F
3.5.85/1577 those places] This edition; theſe places F. Attempts to emend 'places' (to 'paces', 'pranks', or 'passes') have produced nothing satisfactory or plausible; 'those' would presuppose a much easier error, and make 'places' itself much more intelligible: either demonstrative could imply 'the places we were talking about', but 'those' is less ambiguous, and more amenable to a derogatory or insinuating pronunciation. Since neither Helen nor the audience has heard them talking about the said places, 'those' would be more intelligible to both.
3.6.27 laager] F (Leager). The proper modern spelling of the now quite common English derivative of the Dutch *leger*; the word is intended as military jargon.
3.6.28 adversary's] F (aduerſaries). F's spelling is ambiguous, and with the article the singular seems more appropriate than 'adversaries' (which would usually require 'our'). Redundant possessives are of course common.
3.6.37/1631 his] ROWE; this F
3.6.38/1633 oure] THEOBALD; ours F. 'Oure' would have been an acceptable spelling of modern *ore*.
3.6.99 embosked] F (imboſt). According to *OED* the two forms are etymologically identical and interchangeable, and the more technical and rarer modern word here seems desirable in order to discourage the irrelevant senses of modern *emboss*. Alternatively, one might spell 'ambushed', which derives from the same French root, and which continued to be spelt 'em-' into the 17th c.

3.6.109/1705 ⌈2.⌉ LORD DUMAINE] ROWE; *Cap.G.* F (= First Lord). See Introduction.
3.6.113, 118/1708, 1714 ⌈1.⌉ LORD DUMAINE] ROWE; *Cap.E.* F (= Second Lord). See Introduction.
3.7.19/1733 Resolud] COLLIER; Reſolue F
3.7.21 important] F. Shakespeare does not seem to have regarded this as an elided form of *importunate*, but as a separate adjective formation.
3.7.34/1748 after] F1; after this F2; afterwards COLLIER (*conj*).
3.7.46/1760 wicked act] WARBURTON; lawfull act F. Modern editors accept Malone's explanation, that Helen's act is as lawful as her intention; but though this is obviously what the line has to mean if F is retained, three *lawfuls* in a row (with a fourth only eight lines before) are difficult to accept, especially when a contrast seems not only rhetorically desirable, but equal or better sense: for Helen admits to its being 'a sinfull fact' in the very next line, and though her intention is undoubtedly lawful, in the pursuit of it she not only deceives her husband, and bribes an innocent girl to commit perjury on her behalf, but also makes a man fornicate with a woman he does not intend to, and to do so lustfully (lust being considered as sinful with your wife as with another woman). Helen's act, though lawful in a legalistic sense, is wicked in other senses: the last line thus applies to both herself and Bertram in *both* its clauses. Meaning and rhetoric thus argue strongly for the emendation, as does the ease of dittography in these circumstances. Given the desirability of rhetorical symmetry, and the probability of a memorial error, Warburton's 'wicked' is markedly preferable to 'lawless' or 'unlawful'.
4.1.0.1/1762.1 2. Lord Dumaine] CAMBRIDGE; *one of the Frenchmen* F. See Introduction.
4.1.1/1763 ⌈2.⌉ LORD DUMAINE] 1.*Lord E.* F. See Introduction.
4.1.17-18/1779-80 fancie: not . . . another,] NEILSON (Perring); ~ , ~ : F
4.1.23.1/1785.1 *Clocke strikes*] This edition; *not in* F. Compare *Twelfth Night* 3.1.128.1/1313.1, *Richard III* 5.6.5.1/3320.1, *Caesar* 2.1.191.1/753.1, *Cymbeline* 2.2.50-1/847.1.
4.1.42/1804 Mute] HANMER (Warburton); Mule F. Despite Sisson's claim that it was proverbial, I can find no evidence of a traditional association of mules with muteness, and Hunter's claim that Shakespeare associates *mules* and *silence* at *Coriolanus* 2.1.242-3/999-1000 ('that to's power he would | Haue made them Mules, silenc'd their Pleaders') is somewhat misleading, as the point of *mules* seems differently explicated by the following lines ('holding them | In humane Action, and Capacitie | Of no more Soule nor fitnesse for the World, | Then Cammels in the Warre, who haue their Prouand | Onely for bearing Burthens, and sore blowes | For sinking vnder them'). A reference to Balaam's ass (who is in any case not elsewhere called a mule) is implausible as an emendation and impossible as an allusion. There is thus no convincing explanation for 'Mule' either by itself or in relation to the conventional Turkish name Bajazet; 'Mute' (an easy emendation, graphically) provides both, as well as the direct parallel from *Henry V*: 'Like Turkish mute, shall haue a tongue-lesse mouth' (1.2.232/365). Hunter's objection to this parallel, that the mute *has* no tongue, is surely the point: either Paroles will get a tongue from someone without one (i.e. get no tongue), or buy one from someone who has a tongue to sell (i.e. because it has been cut out).
4.1.66/1828 ⌈SOULDIERS⌉ (*seuerally*)] This edition; *All.* F
4.1.70 Moscows] F (*Muskos*). '*Muskos* Regiment' presumably means 'regiment of Muscovites' or 'Muskovite regiment'. In either case, it represents a recognizable nonce-formation, based upon the contemporary forms *Muscovy*, *Muscovite*, *Muscovian* (which were also sometimes spelt 'Mos-'). A similar nonce-formation on the stem *Moscow* is needed to convey the intended sense to a modern reader or listener.
4.1.73/1835 Italian, or French] F; French or Italian DYCE (*conj*.)

4.1.90/1852   art] F3; are F1
4.2.27/1886   Ioues] F; God's GLOBE (Cambridge); Love's WHITE (Johnson). *Jove* arises naturally from association with Diana's own name, and the incongruity is probably deliberate in a scene largely concerned with false oaths; Jove in one sense clearly can serve as a synonym for 'the supreme deity', but in another sense he is not God, so that an oath by his attributes both is and is not valid. As for the emendation 'Love's', it is contradicted by 'him' in 4.2.30/1889, and more generally (as Hunter shows) by the course of the argument, and parallels in other plays. *All's Well* shows no evidence of conscious expurgation (see Taylor, 'Zounds'), and Shakespeare uses 'Ioue' in similar contexts elsewhere.
4.2.40/1899   toyes in such a surance] This edition; rope's in fuch a fcarre F. One of the most notorious cruces in the canon; no emendation has won widespread acceptance. This conjecture satisfies all the complicated requirements of the sense, and is well supported by parallel passages. See Gary Taylor, 'Textual Double Knots: make rope's in such a scarre' (forthcoming in *Susquehanna University Studies*).
4.2.40   e'en] F (in). See previous note.
4.2.70/1929   Exit Bertram] This edition; *not in* F1; *Ex.* F2 (*after* 4.2.68/1927)
4.2.76/1935   I] F1; I'le F3
4.3.0.1-2/1937.1-2   *and some two or three Souldiours*] F. These have nothing to do or say, and as the opening dialogue is most appropriately a confidential one, they might reasonably be regarded as ghost characters.
4.3.26/1964-1   Nobility, . . . streame,] THEOBALD; ∼, . . . ∼, F
4.3.51/1988   is] F; was This edition *conj*. This kind of memorial substitution is characteristic of Compositor B. Alternatively, 'pretence is' might be a rationalization of 'pretences'.
4.3.82/2019   commendations] F; commendation ROWE 3
4.3.85/2022   1. LORD DUMAINE] F3 (*Cap. G.*); Ber⟨tram⟩. F
4.3.89/2026   a peece;] ALEXANDER; ∼, F
4.3.93/2030   affected] F1; effected F3. Though all editors make the emendation, without comment, and though *OED* supports a clear spelling distinction between the two words, I can find no parallels in *OED* or Shakespeare for a direct object like *needs* for the verb *effect*. One effects an intention, or a purpose, or even an emotion ('effect your rage'); a king can 'effect your suits'; but nowhere is a *need* effected. If F1 read 'effect', we could probably accept it as a figurative use; but F3's emendation *creates* an odd construction, to replace a construction only marginally (if at all) more unusual. For *affect* can mean 'seek the attainment of' (*OED*, v.¹ 1), which could take *need* as a figurative object—as could the sense 'fancy, like, or love' (*OED*, v.¹ 2), which would fit Bertram's actions equally well. Moreover, *affect* also means 'taint, infect' (*OED*, v.² 1), which reinforces earlier and later images of Bertram's diseased lust.
4.3.102   model] F (module). *Module* is obsolete in this sense.
4.3.121/2059   1. LORD DUMAINE] HANMER; *not in* F. See 4.3.122/2060.
4.3.122/2060   ⌈2.⌉ LORD DUMAINE] This edition (= *Cap. E.*); Cap⟨tain⟩. G. F. See Introduction.
4.3.123/2061   *Porto tartarossa*] This edition. F prints as one word, but division makes the 'meaning' (= bring the tortures of hell) clearer.
4.3.129/2067   ⌈2.⌉ LORD DUMAINE] THEOBALD 2 (= *Cap* E.); Cap⟨tain⟩. F; FIRST LORD (= *Captain G*) ROWE
4.3.142/2080   1. LORD DUMAINE] This edition (*conj.* Ritson); *not in* F. Most editors follow Capell in transposing F's speech-prefix for Bertram, so that he speaks these four words as well as those which follow; but given some confusion in the prefixes hereabouts, it seems more dramatic to have two comments rather than one, and to leave Bertram's evaluative judgement in a speech of its own.
4.3.149/2087   2. LORD DUMAINE] F. There seems no reason to re-assign this (as some editors have suggested) to Bertram, who would hardly speak so of his own judgement; the speech is *aimed at* Bertram.
4.3.165/2102   dye] DYCE 2 (W. S. Walker); liue F; liue but HANMER.

Several editors retain F, explaining 'live only this present hour'; but dramatically this is incommunicable. Either omission of 'but' or memorial substitution of a word by its opposite is equally possible; 'dye' seems slightly more pointed.
4.3.168/2105   *Guilliam*] This edition (*conj.* Wilson); *Guiltian* F. F's name is nonsense, and a very easy misreading of *Guilliam*. Hunter suggests that Shakespeare invented strange names to suggest an international force, but 'Guillaume' does this as well as (or better than) *Guiltian*.
4.3.168-70   Gratii . . . Bentii] These (F's spellings) might stand for the Florentine family names *Grazzi* and *Benci*.
4.3.169/2106   Chitopher] F; Christopher WILSON (*conj.*)
4.3.191   sheriff's] F (Shrieues)
4.3.201/2138   Lordship] POPE; Lord F
4.3.213/2150   it be] F; y^t be This edition *conj.*
4.3.245/2182   y^e] F3; your F1
4.3.261-2/2198-9   bed-cloathes: but they about him] This edition (*conj.* W. Watkiss Lloyd, *N&Q* (1 March 1890), p. 164); bed-cloathes about him: but they F. In F 'about him' is redundant, and fudges the comic punch (which is clearly on 'bed-cloathes'), while 'they' is ambiguous and unprepared for. Lloyd's transposition simultaneously solves both problems. The error could have arisen from a marginal insertion, or memorial transposition.
4.3.268/2206   him, for me,] ALEXANDER; ∼ ∧ ∼, F
4.3.281/2220   Cardecue] F2; Cardceue F1
4.3.281   *quart d'écu*] F (Cardceue). Shakespeare's spelling (as emended) is a phonetic rendering of the French, as confirmed by 'kar-de-kew' in Eliot's *Ortho-epia Gallica* (1593: STC 7574), p. 58. This passage may antedate *OED*'s first citation (1605), and there is no evidence that *cardecue* had taken on any independent existence as an English word.
4.3.282-4/2221-3   and cut . . . and a . . . perpetually] F. Cowden Clarke conjectured that 'assume' or 'ensure' had been omitted between 'and' and 'a'; alternatively, the order of the two clauses might be reversed (due to the ambiguous placement of an addition).
4.4.3   fore] F (for)
4.4.9   Marseilles] F (*Marcellæ*; also *Marcellus*, at 4.5.80/2397)
4.4.16/2297   you] F4; your F1
4.4.31/2312   y^t] This edition; the F. Everett's interpretation of the 'word' as 'yet' makes excellent and subtle sense of this difficult passage, for which no other satisfactory meaning has been found; but the interpretation is difficult to communicate without a more specific clue to the antecedent. The proposed error is an easy one, even without the probability of anticipation, as here.
4.5.4/2321   else] This edition; *not in* F. The sentence is incomplete in F, for the conditional expressed by 'had been' has no corresponding condition attached to it. 'Else' completes the sense by a minimal alteration.
4.5.7   humble-bee] 'Bumble-bee' is the more common modern form, but it seems undesirable to alter a spelling which is essentially onomatopoeic.
4.5.8/2325   a] This edition; I F; he HANMER (Theobald). F leaves 'him' ambiguous, and implies the irrelevant suggestion that the Countess introduced her son to Paroles.
4.5.18/2335   grasse] This edition (*conj.* Hook, *SQ* 2 (1951), 387-8); hearbes F. F's antithesis between 'herbs' and 'nose-herbs' is feeble and obscure; Wilson's conjecture, 'knot-herbs', is not a known locution, and would be aurally indistinguishable from F. By introducing 'grass' in Lafeu's speech, this emendation lets us keep 'grace' in Lavatch's, which all editors emend to *grass*. ('Grace' is nowhere else in Shakespeare or *OED* used as a spelling of *grass*.)
4.5.39/2356   name] ROWE; maine F
4.5.40/2356   fisnamie] WILSON; fifnomie F
4.5.40   phys'namy] The old spelling ('fisnamie') represents the contracted form of the modern 'physiognomy'. A pun on 'name' is clearly intended.
4.5.49/2366   since] HANMER; fure F; for CAPELL. An easy minim misreading. Lavatch begins the speech explaining why he ap-

proves of the devil, but ends avoiding his court; 'but' is the pivot of the argument, and one expects the clause it introduces to explain the shift. F's 'sure' serves no purpose, for if anything it implies that something in the preceding sentence contradicts the idea of the devil as 'Prince of the world'—whereas 'ever' to keep 'a good fire' is a sign of wealth and status.

4.5.49/2366-7   the Nobilitie] This edition (Collier MS); his ∼ F. The same error occurs at *Merchant* 3.1.54/1211, *Richard II* 1.4.58/609, 2.1.203/817, *1 Henry IV* 5.1.53/2549 (Q5), and *Romeo* 5.3.267/2957 (Q3). In this case the substitution may have been deliberate voluntary censorship, either by the printer or by an annotator of the foul papers.

5.1.6/2429   Enter a gentle Astringer] F. See Dessen, 132–5.

5.2.1   Master] F (M^r). The abbreviation could represent *Monsieur* or *Master*; the latter seems marginally more appropriate for Lavatch, though *Monsieur* might be dramatically effective as exaggerated deference.

5.2.4/2468   mood] F. Theobald emended this to 'moat'; while rejecting this, all editors seem to assume that a pun on 'moat' (used as fishponds and sewage dumps) or 'mute' (bird droppings) is necessary to make sense of what follows. But such a pun is difficult to extract from the word itself; if the sense were necessary, emendation would seem justified. But in fact Lavatch needs no cue for such scatological abuse, beyond 'smell somewhat strong' and Paroles's appearance—which is surely meant to contrast strikingly with his earlier extravagance.

5.2.23/2487   ingenious] F. Defences of F's reading as ironic, or as a nonce in-genious (stupid), or as 'conscious' (of his own contemptibility) are not very convincing; nor is Brigstocke's conjecture 'ingenerous'. 'High-born' (*OED*, 5, 1638) might make sense, if we interpret '(but now) decayed'. This edition conjectures 'disingenious' (*OED*, from 1646) or 'indigenious' (punning on 'indigent').

5.2.24/2488   similes] THEOBALD; ſmiles F. See the identical error at *1 Henry IV* 1.2.79/184.

5.2.32/2496   vnder her] F2; vnder F1

5.2.40/2504   one] F3; *not in* F1. Modern editors put 'word' in quotation marks without adding 'one', but this still leaves the joke oblique and misses the mocking echo of 'one single word' (5.2.35–6/2499–500).

5.3.0.2/2518.1   Lafew] This edition; *La few, the two French Lords* F. The lords are probably ghost characters here: they have nothing to say or do, and their mute presence is awkward, during the disentanglement of events to which they were material witnesses.

5.3.27/2545   ATTENDANT] This edition; Gent⟨leman⟩. F

5.3.31.1-2/2549.1-2   with . . . kneeles] This edition; *not in* F. For the patch see 4.5.93–7/2411–15, and Dessen, 136–8.

5.3.51/2569   Stain'd] This edition (*conj.* Lambrechts); Scorn'd F. 'Scorn'd' does not really fit with 'warpt', 'extended', 'contracted'; 'stain'd' would, and would also relate directly to the object of this verb ('a faire colour'). The easy misreading would have been made even easier by contamination from 'scornfull' two lines above.

5.3.59/2577   carried,] ROWE; ∼ˌ F

5.3.60/2578   grace] This edition (*conj.* Lambrechts); great F. F's word occurs in the same position two lines above, where it is clearly appropriate; the repetition is itself suspicious, and the sense dubious—for the sender of the pardon is in this case Bertram, whom the King would hardly call 'great'. For *grace* meaning 'pardon', see *OED*, sb. 15; for comparable compounds, sb. 21 ('grace-giver', etc). Shakespeare inverts many such compounds; he elsewhere associates *grace* and *sour* (*Richard II* 3.4.106/1830), and has another King ask 'did not we send grace?' (*1 Henry IV* 5.5.2/2961, where—as here—the grace so sent does no good). The compositor probably substituted a commonplace word, suggested by the context, for Shakespeare's unusual compound.

5.3.60/2578   sender,] THEOBALD; ∼, F

5.3.72/2590   COUNTESSE] THEOBALD; *not in* F

5.3.97/2615   ingag'd] F; ungag'd THEOBALD

5.3.102/2620   Plutus] ROWE 3; *Platus* F

5.3.115/2633   coniecturall] F2; connecturall F

5.3.141/2659   KING] ROWE; *not in* F

5.3.157/2675   since,] STEEVENS 2 (Tyrwhitt); ſir, F; sith, DYCE

5.3.185/2703   them: fairer,] HANMER (Theobald); ∼, ∼ : F

5.3.198   hit] F. Some editors modernize to 'it', but 'she has hit the mark' seems the more dramatic interpretation.

5.3.199/2717   Iemme;] This edition; ∼, F. Either the punctuation here must be emended, or 'it' altered to 'yet' in 5.3.201/2719.

5.3.219/2737   infnite conning] SINGER 2; infuite comming F. For *cunning* spelt 'conning', see *OED*.

5.3.221/2739   my] This edition (*conj.* W. S. Walker); any F. An easy misreading; the conjecture produces better metre and alliteration. Compare *History of Lear* 4.253/747.

5.3.248   gentleman] F (Gent.). *OED* records probable examples of the colloquially shortened form 'Gent' from 1564, but it only occurs twice in dialogue in Shakespeare, both set by Compositor B in prose in a tightly justified line. See *Winter's Tale* 4.4.308/1915.

5.3.315/2833   are] ROWE; is F. The error is conceivably Shakespeare's, stemming from a momentary confusion about whether the challenge was in Helen's letter or the Countess's; the *&c.* suggests that Shakespeare perhaps meant to check the original wording. The error could easily be Compositor B's, but even if it is authorial, it needs to be corrected.

Epi.4/2858   strift] F1; strife F2. F1's reading could be an error for 'strife'; but *strift* is a legitimate form surviving well into the 19th c., and bearing the same relationship to *strife* as *drift* to *drive* or *thrift* to *thrive*, and differing from those words only in that it has been superseded in modern usage by the alternative substantive form. So it seems right to retain 'strift' in old spelling (while remarking that it appears not to occur elsewhere in Shakespeare) but to use the alternative form in a modern-spelling text.

INCIDENTALS

87 me.] ∼,   116 war-like] ∼-|∼   271 And] Aud   310 when of] whenof   323 I] w   375 done, fond,] ∼, ∼,   430 rightlie] righlie   430 belong:] ∼,   451 distempred] distempered   451 wet,] ∼?   456 honord] honored   483 forsweare't:] ∼,   489 disclose,] ∼:   502 Siue,] ∼.   596 And] &   597 Farwell] Farewll   699 th'] the   719 great'st] greateſt   836 legges] legegs   858 indeede;] ∼,   873-4 great trancendence] grear ∼   896 Mistris,] ∼;   961 dislik'st,] ∼)   962 daughter)] ∼,   1030 succeeding.] ∼,   1134 hard:] ∼,   1145 things.] ∼, ∼,   1334 *Your vnfortunate sonne,*] (not a separate line in F, but separated from the end of the letter by a 3 cm. gap)   1394 Which] whlch   1457 haue] hane   1481 worth] worrh   1574 Gentleman?] ∼,   1579 Iacke-an-apes] Iacke,an-apes   1592 me,] ∼.   1623 present] preſcnt   1655 recouered;] ∼,   1769 Captaine] Captaiue   1865 monument.] ∼,   1885 me,] ∼.   1958 rebellon!] ∼,   1973 measure] meaſurc   2039 ha's] ha s   2058 me.] ∼:   2079 will.] ∼:   2212 *Mile-end*] ∼-|∼   2232 out-runnes] ∼-|∼   2323 aduanc'd] aduanc d   2387 home,] ∼.   2401 It] Ir   2512 office] offiee   2514 comming,] ∼,   2584 done,] don,e   2591 meete,] ∼.   2615 ingag'd,] ∼.   2632 falsely,] ∼:   2634 out;] ∼,   2635 thou] rhou   2641 taxe] taze   2647 wrap'd] wrap d   2671 discou'rie;] ∼,   2728 sickens,] ∼:   2728 truth:] ∼,   2802 him.] ∼,   2852 Resoluedly] Reſolduedly

ALL'S WELL THAT ENDS WELL

FOLIO STAGE DIRECTIONS

1.1.0.1-3/0.1-2 *Eneer yong Bertram Count of Rossillion, his Mother, and | Helena, Lord Lafew, all in blacke.*
1.1.97.1/98.1 *Enter Parrolles.*
1.1.182.1/185.1 *Enter Page.*
1.1.225/228 *Exit*
1.2.0.1-3/228.1-3 *Flourish Cornets. | Enter the King of France with Letters, and | diuers Attendants.*
1.2.17.1/245.1 *Enter Bertram, Lafew, and Parolles.*
1.2.76.1/304.1 *Exit | Flourish.*
1.3.0.1-2/304.2 *Enter Countesse, Steward, and Clowne.*
1.3.94/398.1 *Exit.*
1.3.123.1/427.1 *Exit Steward.*
1.3.123.2/427.2 *Enter Hellen.*
1.3.255/559.1 *Exeunt.*
2.1.0.1-4/559.2-5 *Enter the King with diuers yong Lords, taking leaue for | the Florentine warre: Count, Rosse, and | Parrolles. Florish Cornets.*
2.1.59/618 *Exeunt.*
2.1.59.1/618.1 *Enter Lafew.*
2.1.92.1/651.1 *Enter Hellen.*
2.1.98.1/657.1 *Exit.*
2.1.210.1/769.1 *Florish. Exit.*
2.2.0.1/769.2 *Enter Countesse and Clowne.*
2.2.66/837 *Exeunt*
2.3.0.1/837.1-2 *Enter Count, Lafew, and Parolles.*
2.3.39.1/877.1 *Enter King, Hellen, and attendants.*
2.3.52.1/890.1 *Enter 3 or 4 Lords.*
2.3.77/915 *She addresses her to a Lord.* (after 2.3.63/901)
2.3.184.1/1022.1 *Exeunt*
2.3.184.1-2/1022.1-2 *Parolles and Lafew stay behind, commen-|ting of this wedding.*
2.3.232/1072 *Exit.*
2.3.239.1/1079.1 *Enter Lafew.*
2.3.261.1/1101.1 *Exit*
2.3.263.1/1103.1 *Enter Count Rossillion.* (after 2.3.261/1101)
2.3.297.1/1137.1 *Exit*
2.4.0.1/1137.2 *Enter Helena and Clowne.*
2.4.12.1/1149.1 *Enter Parrolles.*
2.4.55/1193 *Exit Par.* (after 2.4.54/1192)
2.4.56/1194 *Exit*
2.5.0.1/1194.1 *Enter Lafew and Bertram.*
2.5.13.1/1208.1 *Enter Parrolles.*
2.5.53.1/1248.1 *Enter Helena.*
3.1.88.1/1283.1 *Exit*
3.1.0.1-3/1286.2-3 *Flourish. Enter the Duke of Floreuce, the two Frenchmen, | with a troope of Souldiers.*
3.1.23/1309 *Flourish.*
3.2.0.1/1309.1 *Enter Countesse and Clowne.*
3.2.18/1327 *exit*
3.2.19/1328 *A Letter.*
3.2.32.1/1340.1 *Enter Clowne.*
3.2.44.1-2/1352.1-2 *Enter Hellen and two Gentlemen.*
3.2.100/1408 *Exit.*
3.2.131/1439 *Exit.*
3.3.0.1-3/1439.1-3 *Flourish. Enter the Duke of Florence, Rossillion, | drum and trumpets, soldiers, Parrolles.*
3.3.11/1450 *Exeunt omnes*
3.4.0.1/1450.1 *Enter Countesse & Steward.*
3.4.4/1454 *Letter.*
3.4.42/1492.1 *Exeunt*
3.5.0.1/1492.2 *A Tucket afarre off. | Enter old Widdow of Florence, her daughter, Violenta | and Mariana, with other | Citizens.*
3.5.29.1/1521.1 *Enter Hellen.*
3.5.37/1529 *A march afarre.*
3.5.75.1/1567.1 *Drumme and Colours. | Enter Count Rossillion, Parrolles, and the whole Armie.*
3.5.93.1/1586.1 *Exit.*
3.5.102.1/1595.1 *Exeunt.*
3.6.0.1/1595.2-3 *Enter Count Rossillion and the Frenchmen, | as at first.*
3.6.41.1/1635.1 *Enter Parrolles.*
3.6.84/1679 *Exit*
3.6.118.1/1714.1 *Exeunt*
3.7.0.1/1714.2 *Enter Hellen, and Widdow.*
4.1.0.1-2/1762.1-2 *Enter one of the Frenchmen, with fiue or sixe other | souldiers in ambush.*
4.1.23.1/1785.1 *Enter Parrolles.*
4.1.63.1/1826.1 *Alarum within.*
4.1.90.1-2/1852.1 *Exit*
4.1.90.3/1852.2 *A short Alarum within.*
4.1.96.1/1859.1 *Exit*
4.2.0.1/1859.2 *Enter Bertram, and the Maide called | Diana.*
4.2.78/1937 *Exit*
4.3.0.1-2/1937.1-2 *Enter the two French Captaines, and some two or three | Souldiours.*
4.3.77.1/2014.1 *Enter a Messenger.*
4.3.84.1/2021.1 *Enter Count Rossillion.*
4.3.118.1-2/2056.1-2 *Enter Parrolles with his Interpreter.*
4.3.324.1/2263.1 *Exeunt.*
4.3.331/2270 *Exit*
4.3.342/2281 *Exit.*
4.4.0.1/2281.1 *Enter Hellen, Widdow, and Diana.*
4.4.36/2317 *Exeunt*
4.5.0.1/2317.1 *Enter Clowne, old Lady, and Lafew.*
4.5.62/2379 *exit*
4.5.92.1/2410.1 *Enter Clowne.*
4.5.105/2423 *Exeunt*
5.1.0.1-2/2423.1-2 *Enter Hellen, Widdow, and Diana, with | two Attendants.*
5.1.6.1/2429 *Enter a gentle Astringer.* (after 'time')
5.2.0.1/2464.1 *Enter Clowne and Parrolles.*
5.2.18.1/2482.1 *Enter Lafew.*
5.3.0.1-2/2518.1-2 *Flourish. Enter King, old Lady, Lafew, the two French | Lords, with attendants.*
5.3.31.1/2549.1 *Enter Count Bertram.*
5.3.128.1/2646.1 *Enter a Gentleman.*
5.3.141/2659 *A Letter.*
5.3.156.1/2674.1 *Enter Bertram.* (after 5.3.152/2672)
5.3.159/2677 *Enter Widdow, Diana, and Parrolles.* (after 'that')
5.3.234.1/2752.1 *Enter Parrolles.*
5.3.306/2824 *Enter Hellen and Widdow.*
5.3.335.1/2854.1 *Flourish.*
Epi.6.1/2860.1 *Exeunt omn.*

TIMON OF ATHENS

Timon of Athens (*BEPD* 402) was one of the plays first entered in the Stationers' Register on 8 November 1623. The entry anticipates publication in the First Folio (F), which provides the only authoritative text. Compositor B set all but one page of the play (Gg3^v: Compositor E). *Timon* is found between *Romeo* and *Caesar*, a position which Hinman shows was first assigned to *Troilus*. Owing to delays in securing copyright for *Troilus*, printing of that play was postponed; in the mean time, work continued on the plays that were to follow. When *Timon* was substituted, the surrounding text had already been printed. Two quires had been allotted to *Troilus* and the last page of *Romeo* (Gg1), which was set with *Timon*. Despite compositorial space-wasting, the replacing play proved too short to fill the second quire. The verso of the quire's last leaf is blank; the recto is supplied with a generously spaced list of characters which was almost certainly included, and probably compiled, specifically to occupy the page.

Hinman's analysis shows that if *Troilus* had not been delayed, *Timon* would have been printed later in F or not at all. *Timon* is the only play in the Tragedies section whose title does not name it as a tragedy. It may also be unique amongst the tragedies in being set from foul papers. Furthermore, the play is usually regarded as of doubtful status—an abandoned, revised, or collaborate text. If so, it is especially plausible that *Timon* was not amongst the plays originally planned to appear in F.

F certainly provides a text with some notable inconsistencies and some verse passages of fragmented style and licentious metre. The text's peculiarities go beyond those associated with other Shakespeare plays set from foul papers. Lake, Jackson, and Holdsworth, developing a suggestion first made independently by Sykes and Wells, have shown, we believe conclusively, that parts of *Timon* were written by Thomas Middleton. Middleton's hand gives the play its irregularity of style. In the most detailed and comprehensive study, Holdsworth identifies the following as by Middleton (queries mark doubtful attributions): 1.1.276-86/277-87(??), all of 1.2/Sc.2, 2.2.0.1-2.2.44/573.2-617(?), all of 3.1-6/Sc. 5-10, most of 3.7/Sc. 11 (3.7.0.1-3.7.36/1222.1-1257(?) and from 3.7.104.1/1326.1 to the end), 4.2.0.1-29.1/1377.1-1406.1(??), 4.2.30-51/1407-28, and the end of 4.3/Sc. 14 (from 4.3.459.1/1887.1); his hand is probably also to be found in parts of 2.2/Sc. 4 after 2.2.115/688.

Change of author probably determined that the interview between Flavius and Ventidius arranged at the end of 2.2/Sc. 4 never materializes. The episode with the Poet and Painter anticipated at 4.3.353/1781 is probably delayed in order to incorporate a contribution from Middleton at an appropriate point (see note to 5.1.0.1-114.1/1965.3-2081.2). A scene even more poorly assimilated into the play is 3.5/Sc. 9, where Alcibiades is banished after pleading mercy for an unidentified friend. It is not in itself unusual to begin the active participation of a major character or initiate a new plot development a little over halfway through a play. Vagueness as to the events surrounding the friend's crime is intrinsic to the scene; for the play as a whole, these events do not matter. Though the quality of the writing has been criticized, much of the difficulty lies in the scene's intrusion in a long and otherwise continuous sequence concerned solely with Timon's desertion by his friends. The scene might attractively be relocated after Timon's self-banishment; the reference to Alcibiades' banishment at 3.7.53-5/1275-7 indicates that that event was expected to come earlier, but the passage in which this reference is made might be Shakespeare's only contribution to the entire sequence from before the banishment to Timon's departure from Athens, in which case the possibility of confusion between authors remains.

The classical measure of a talent is used in *Timon* to quantify loans and debts. Wide fluctuation in the number of talents cited in different parts of the play can be explained in terms of joint authorship: Shakespeare and Middleton had different ideas as to the measure's value. In 1.1/Sc. 1 Shakespeare, evidently aware that a talent was a considerable sum, specifies five or three of them; Middleton in 3.1-4/Scs. 5-8 uses higher figures, and shows uncertainty what to cite as an appropriate number. After first mentioning 'fifty', he three times gives a vague 'so many' (see note to 3.2.12/877), then at 3.2.39/904 'fifty fiue hundred'; at 3.4.91/1085 the sum is again 'fifty'. The fluctuation in 2.2/Sc. 4 from fifty (2.2.189/762) to a thousand (2.2.195/768) to five (2.2.222 and 225/795 and 798) possibly indicates a change in authorship from Middleton to Shakespeare after 2.2.195/768.

Joint authorship might affect the roles of the lords identified in the stage directions and speech-prefixes for 3.1-3/Sc. 5-7 (though not in dialogue when they are on stage) as Lucullus, Lucius, and Sempronius. These figures should presumably be amongst the anonymous lords at least of 3.7/Sc. 7, and might even take the main speaking roles. Elsewhere, a single speech-prefix at 1.2.127/414 ambiguously identifies a '*Luc.*' in that scene (see note). The three lords are named in the opening direction for 3.7/Sc. 11 in this edition, but no attempt has been made to equate them individually with the lords identified by number in the Folio's speech-prefixes.

Timon is only distinct from most other foul-paper texts in that it is of joint authorship. The characteristics of the underlying manuscript are those of a collaborative rough draft in which each author's contributions were in his own hand. The task of imposing overall consistency and coherence was not taken as far as it might have been in a prompt-book. In this, *Timon* resembles *1 Henry VI*, another collaborative play set in F from foul papers. The theory that *Timon* was abandoned unperformed is mere speculation, especially as *1 Henry VI* clearly did reach the stage.

The language of the play is often contorted in the parts Shakespeare wrote and, to a student of Shakespeare, unfamiliar in the parts he did not. As might be expected in a foul-paper text, a number of cruxes remain which evidently arise from difficult copy. These include misreadings and, if the interpretations offered in this edition are right, a mislocation (4.3.9-13/1437-41) and a duplication (following 5.4.2/ 2213).

F's absence of act and scene divisions (apart from the notional 'Actus Primus, Scœna Prima.' that opens the play) is also predictable in a play printed from a pre-theatrical manuscript, though act divisions would have no place in a manuscript prepared before Shakespeare's company began to perform at the Blackfriars. The editorial identification of acts and scenes initiated by Capell is for the most part followed in this edition. Capell begins Act 5 at an awkward point, but one difficult to improve upon. If a break is accepted here, as it has been in this edition, a scene-break is also required where we follow Capell in beginning 5.2/Sc. 16, though usual editorial procedure has been to maintain continuity. We also establish a scene-break at the beginning of 3.5/Sc. 9. Unlike the breaks before 5.1/Sc. 15 and 5.2/Sc. 16, the cleared stage may here indicate a change in location, to another room in Timon's house.

J.J./(S.W.W.)

WORKS CITED

Arrowsmith, W. R., 'A Few Supplemental Notes on Some Passages in Middleton's "Plays"', *N&Q*, 2nd Series, 1 (1856), 85-6
Bailey, Samuel, *On the Received Text of Shakespeare's Dramatic Writings and Its Improvement*, 2 vols. (1862-6)
Becket, Andrew, *Shakespeare's Himself Again*, 2 vols. (1815)
Bulloch, John, *Studies on the Text of Shakespeare. With Numerous Emendations* (1878)
Hibbard, G. R., ed., *Timon of Athens* (1970)
Holdsworth, R. V., *Middleton and Shakespeare: The Case for Middleton's Hand in 'Timon of Athens'* (forthcoming)
Jackson, MacD. P., *Studies in Attribution: Middleton and Shakespeare* (1979)
Jackson, Zachary, *Shakespeare's Genius Justified* (1811)
Lake, David J., *The Canon of Thomas Middleton's Plays: Internal Evidence for the Major Problems of Authorship* (1975)
Oliver, H. J., ed., *Timon of Athens*, Arden (1963)
Seymour, F. H., *Remarks Critical, Conjectural, and Exploratory, upon the Plays of Shakespeare*, 2 vols. (1805)
Shadwell, T., *The History of Timon of Athens*, adaptation (1678)
Sykes, H. Dugdale, *Sidelights on Elizabethan Drama* (1924), 1-48
Wells, William, '*Timon of Athens*', *N&Q* 215 (1970), 266-9
Wilson, F. P., 'Shakespeare and the Diction of Common Life', *Proceedings of the British Academy*, 27 (1941), 167-97, pp. 179-80
Wilson, John Dover, and J. C. Maxwell, eds., *Timon of Athens*, New (1957)

TEXTUAL NOTES

Title *The Life of Timon of Athens*] F (head title) (THE LIFE OF TYMON | OF ATHENS.); *Timon of Athens*. F (table of contents, running title), S.R. For the spelling of *Timon*, see third paragraph of note to 5.4.2/2213. *Timon* is the only play in the Tragedies section of F not described as a tragedy (see Introduction); the title clearly has not been regularized, and was probably influenced by the model of the major source, North's translation of Plutarch's *Lives*.

1.1.0.3/0.3 *and Mercer*] F. Some editors delete. Sisson notes possible confusion due to an abbreviation for 'Merchant', but this does not adequately explain why the compositor added a fictitious Mercer after correctly identifying the Merchant. If 1.1.7-8/7-8 suggests one artisan with the Jeweller, 1.1.6/6 suggests more. This edition supplies an exit for the Mercer on the analogy of the Senators' passage over the stage; the Mercer exists to make a visual impression. But an authorial change of intention is also possible.

1.1.4/4 strange] F; so strange ROWE
1.1.9/9 MERCHANT] F (*Mer.*) Similarly elsewhere in the scene. The same prefix could stand for the Mercer.
1.1.21/21 Goume, which ouses] JOHNSON; Gowne, which vfes F. *OED* records 'goume' as a 16th-c. spelling of *gum*.
1.1.25/25 chafes] THEOBALD; chafes F
1.1.40/40 man] THEOBALD; men F. See Sisson in defence of F and Hibbard in reply, both here and at 1.1.47/47.
1.1.47/47 tax] ALEXANDER (Staunton); wax F; verse COLLIER 2 (Collier MS); man KINNEAR (*conj.*)
1.1.56/56 seruice] POPE; feruices F
1.1.73/73 scope.] THEOBALD; ~_∧_ F
1.1.88/88 hands] F2; hand F1
1.1.88/88 fal] SISSON; fit F; slip ROWE; sink DELIUS (*conj.*)
1.1.132/132 be *Timon*] F. Suspect; a word or phrase may be missing, or a word corrupted to '*Timon*'.
179, 183 *Apermantus*] Middleton is not thought to have written this part of the scene, but the spelling is evidently his preferred form.
1.1.181/181 Wee will] STEEVENS 2; Wee'l F. Perhaps influenced by 'Hee'l' directly below in F. POPE emended to 'bear it', which posits a harder error but avoids the unwanted idiom 'bear with . . . '.
1.1.215/216 cost] F3; caft F1
1.1.216/217 APEMANTUS] *Ape.* F (*some copies*); *pe.* F (*others*)
1.1.237/238 augury but] This edition; angry wit F; aug'ry wit BECKET (*conj.*); angry wit but HOLDSWORTH (*conj.*). Few editors are convinced by F's reading. There are two difficulties: (*a*) 'angry' is difficult to explain as a qualifier of 'wit' (*b*) the expression seems to say the opposite of what is required (i.e. that I had not the wit *not* to be a lord). Holdsworth's conjecture is the most effective answer to the second objection. 'Augury' could be misread 'angery', a current spelling of *angry*, especially as the compositor may have been influenced by the association of 'anger' and 'lords' at 1.1.208-10/208-10; this error would in turn facilitate the misreading, itself easy, of 'but' as the noun 'wit'. In *Two Gentlemen* 4.4.66-7/1814-15, 'good bringing vp, fortune, and truth' can be recognised through 'Augury'. The idea of circumstance interfering with what is supposedly preordained is taken up in Apemantus' next speech (1.1.240/241).
1.1.251/252 so, their;] CAPELL; ~ ; ~_∧_ F. F's spelling of *there* and arrangement as prose are conducive to misinterpretation ('their Aches').
1.1.253/254 mongst] CAPELL; amongeft F. F sets the speech as prose, with 'amongest' ending a type line. The unusual 'e' as well as the 'a' may have been introduced to aid justification.
1.1.259.2/260.2 two Lords] F; Lucius and Lucullus ROWE. Similarly for their speech-prefixes.
1.1.261/262 1. LORD] 1 F. Similarly formatted to end of scene for both lords. F usually sets a full stop after a qualifying number, but not where the numeral stands alone.
1.1.276/277 Come] F2; Comes F1
1.1.277/278 taste] F2; rafte F1
1.1.283/284 of] F; or JOHNSON (*conj.*)
1.1.286/287 1. LORD] CAPELL; *not in* F
1.2.0.3/287.4 Senators] States F
1.2.0.3-4/287.4 the Athenian Lords] ROWE included amongst them Lucius, Lucullus, and Sempronius. If 1.2.181-9/468-76 did not

suggest that the first two at least are absent, it might be desirable to include these lords in 1.2, though there would be no basis for deciding which, if any, of the speaking parts should be attributed to them. But see note to 1.2.127/414.

1.2.1-2/288-9 Most . . . peace] F. F's line division is probably compositorial (see lineation notes). Editors often divide after 'Gods'. 'To' is probably necessary grammatically, but may be elided with the next syllable. The present line division prevents 'my' from being extrametrical.

1.2.20/307 1. LORD] F; Luc⟨ius⟩. ROWE. Similarly throughout scene. See note to 1.2.127/414.

1.2.25 Ye'ue] F (ye'haue)

1.2.28/315 yond] F; yonder POPE. With 'angrie' trisyllabic ('anger-y') as at 3.6.57/1164, Pope's emendation gives a regular pentameter.

1.2.28/315 euer] ROWE; verie F

1.2.37-8/324-5 for . . . nere] F; 'fore . . . e'er WARBURTON

1.2.41/328 too] F; to't HUDSON (Warburton)

1.2.48/335 proued. If] ROWE; ~, if F

1.2.53/340 2. LORD] F; Lucull⟨us⟩. ROWE. Similarly throughout scene.

1.2.57/344 sinner] F; fire COLLIER 2 (Collier MS); liar KEIGHTLEY; sigher BULLOCH (conj.)

1.2.80/367 thou] POPE 2; then thou F. See lineation notes. The context would encourage error.

1.2.88/375 thousands, did] THEOBALD; ~ ? Did F

1.2.95/382 'em;] ~ ? F. Staunton pointed out that 'if we . . . of 'em' and 'should we . . . for 'em' might be alternatives, one of which should have been cancelled. Wilson thought the question mark in F supported this suggestion.

1.2.102/389 ioyes,] F (~,); joy, ROWE. F seems to fall between two readings; emendation of the incidental assumes least error.

1.2.103-4/390-1 me thinks: . . . Faults,] ROWE; ~ ~, . . . ~. F

1.2.110.1/397.1 Sound Tucket within] In F a duplicating entry for the masquers follows (see stage direction list). The second entry for them is itself anticipatory.

1.2.120/407 best] F; blest CAPELL (conj.)

1.2.122 Th'ear,] F (There,). F's ambiguous form combines an unmarked elision with a recognized spelling of ear.

1.2.123/410 smell, all] STEEVENS-REED 2; all F; Smell THEOBALD (Warburton). Most editors emend. Oliver follows F, but notes indications that type may have dropped out and been reset: a possible source of corruption, though 'smell, all' would invite eyeskip. F sets to 'bosome' as prose and 'There . . . rise' as a verse-line; the emendation gives two pentameters.

1.2.127/414 1. LORD] CAPELL; Luc. F. Rowe identifies 'Luc.' as Lucius, giving the Second Lord the contrasting prefix 'Lucull.' (see notes to 1.2.20 and 53/307 and 340). Oliver expands the present prefix to 'Lucullus'. As 1.2.181-9/468-76 suggest that neither lord is present in this scene, the text is inconsistent unless 'Luc.' is emended to anonymity, in keeping with the rest of the scene. The identification of him as the First Lord is, of course, as arbitrary as deciding between Lucius and Lucullus.

1.2.128 Hey-day] F (Hoyday)

1.2.148/435 LADY] STEEVENS (Johnson); Lord. F

1.2.151/438 'tends] This edition; attends F

1.2.165.1-2/452.1-2 Enter . . . exits] not in F. Either authorial oversight led to a misplaced entry at 1.2.175.1/462.2, or Flavius enters twice.

1.2.169/456 accept] F2; accept it F1

1.2.244/532 paper] F; proper THEOBALD 2 (Warburton)

2.1.9 straight,] F (~,)

2.1.13/552 sound] F; found HANMER. 2.1.12-13/551-2 ('It cannot . . . safety') follow naturally from the sea imagery of 2.1.3-4/542-3 ('Still . . . waste'). The intervening lines might be an insertion.

2.1.33/572 Take] DYCE; I go fir? | Take F. F can only be defended (whether understood as 'I go, sir' or 'Ay, go, sir') as facetious humour at the expense of Caphis in an otherwise serious scene. If correct, the Senator's 'I go . . . with you' would be a single verse-line; F's split is readily explained as a consequence of dittography.

2.1.34/573 in, Count] THEOBALD (in compt); ~. Come F. Most recent editors follow F, but explanations of 'haue the dates in' are strained. Most logically it would mean 'haue the dates put in', but bonds would already have dates. Sisson objects to the emendation that compt 'seems impossible as a misreading of Come', but this is not true of the now standard spelling 'Count'. The sense of the emendation is 'take the dates into account'; the line might ironically anticipate or be recalled in 'Takes no accompt | How things go from him' (2.2.3-4/576-7).

2.2.4/577 resumes] ROWE; refume F

2.2.9.1/582.1 and Seruants of] not in F

2.2.11-12/584-5 VARROES SERUANT . . . ISIDORES SERUANT] Var. . . . Ifid. F. Similarly throughout scene.

2.2.37/610 broken] HANMER; debt, broken F; debt, of broken POPE; date-broke STEEVENS-REED 2; date-broken MALONE. Wilson-Maxwell identified F as an undeleted false start. 'Debt' was probably abandoned as the next line was conceived.

2.2.60/633 ALL SERUANTS] F (Al.). Similarly 'All.' at 2.2.62, 66, 91, 95, and 116/635, 639, 663, 667, and 689.

2.2.71, 99/644, 671 Mistris] THEOBALD; Mafters F. Probably an expansion of the abbreviation 'M.' or 'Ms.'

2.2.76/649 PAGE] F (Boy.)

2.2.91/663 I,] CAPELL; ~, F

2.2.121/694 meruell,] F; ~; ROWE

2.2.125/698 proposd] F2; propofe F1

2.2.132/705 sumd] This edition (S.W.W.); found F1; found F2. Editors usually follow F2. Wilson-Maxwell commented, 'The correction is certain', but had to add, 'though no recognized sense of "find" exactly fits'. With 'sound' the image might be the same as at 2.1.13/552, where many recent editors accept F. Both speeches have imagery of moving water for Timon's perilous finances (see 2.2.138-9/711-12). But a metaphor of sounding the depth of water is difficult to accept here because (a) the context obstructs such a reading—unlike 'sound' in 2.1.13/552, the other references to water do not come before this 'sound'; (b) 'sound' gives an irregular sequence of tense, or the inflexional licence discussed in Abbott, 341-2. Neither F1 nor F2 is satisfactory. Misreading of 'sumd' would be scarcely harder than of 'found'.

2.2.140/713 (too . . . time] F; yet now's too late a time HANMER; yet now's a time too late HUDSON (Collier MS)

2.2.152/725 or] F; of HIBBARD (Cambridge)

2.2.163/736 Timons] F; Lord Timon's ALEXANDER (Steevens)

2.2.182/755 Flaminius] ROWE; Flaui⟨us⟩. F

2.2.183/756 ALL SERUANTS] F (Ser.)

2.2.185/758 to day] F; but today G.T. conj. The rest of this episode, and Timon's speeches elsewhere in 2.2, are in verse. The present speech, set as prose in F, is versifiable, except for the irregularity of the present line. Metrical emendation might be justified in a Shakespeare passage, but verse and prose are often confusingly intermingled in Middleton's writing.

2.2.201/774 Treasure] F2; Treature F1

2.2.203/776 not,] F; not—but, HANMER; not, what— DYCE 2

2.2.217 ingenuously] F (Ingeniously). For the lack of distinction, see OED ingenious, a. II, ingeniously, adv. 2, and ingenuous, a. 6.

3.1.0.2/802.3 Lucullus, . . . Master,] ~, . . . ~, F

3.1.55/858 Slaue] F; slander DYCE (conj.)

3.1.56/859 this Hower,] POPE; his Honor, F; his humour COLLIER MS (conj.); dishonour KEIGHTLEY. See Wilson-Maxwell.

3.1.60/863 Nature] F; nurture HANMER

3.2.3/868 1. STRANGER] 1 F. Similarly formatted throughout scene, and for the Second and Third Strangers.

3.2.12/877 so many] F; fifty THEOBALD. We follow F here, and also for its two other instances of 'so many' (3.2.24 and 37/889 and 902) and its inflated 'fifty fiue hundred' at 3.2.39/904. Emendation of 'so many' would be based on the words being provisional fillers for an as yet undecided figure; if 'fifty fiue hundred' compounds a first and second authorial reading, which we do not accept (see note), it would represent further evidence

503

of Middleton's confusion as to the value of a talent (see Introduction). It seems doubtful, however, whether Middleton, if undecided, would actually repeatedly write 'so many' rather than leaving a gap or inserting a provisional number. It is even more doubtful that 'so many' should be emended in one or two endings but not the other(s): the words are unlikely to be intended both as fixed parts of the text and provisional fillers in the same episode. A conjectural solution which would allow 'fifty fiue hundred' to stand whilst according consistent treatment to each 'so many', would be to emend all three to 'fifty fiue'. We instead assume humour of evasiveness and innuendo, leading to the grotesque overstatement of 'fifty fiue hundred'.

3.2.23/888 not mistooke] This edition (Johnson); mi-|ſtooke F. F has not been convincingly glossed; 'mistooke him, and' is difficult to see as an ironic aside or a conspiratorial confession to the audience. An omission would be easy after the monosyllables 'his: yet had hee'.

3.2.24/889 so many] F. See note to 3.2.12/877.

3.2.28, 38, 61/893, 903, 926 LUCIUS] F2 (*Luci.*); *Lucil⟨ius⟩*. F1

3.2.35 He's] F (Has). Similarly at 3.3.13, 3.6.66, 4.3.452, and 4.3.471.

3.2.37/902 so many] F; fifty ROWE. See note to 3.2.12/877.

3.2.39/904 fifty fiue hundred] F; 500 COLLIER MS (*conj.*). 'F's "fifty fiue hundred" is supported by Middleton's notable fondness for the number fifty-five; cf. *Your Five Gallants* A2 (1.1.12), "fiftie five shillings"; *Black Book* (Bullen, VIII, 20); *Women Beware Women* 1.3.94; *Revenger's Tragedy* 4.2.55; and in *Old Law* 1.1.269, "fifty-five" is juxtaposed with "so many".' (R. V. Holdsworth, privately.) If 'fiue' adds to 'fifty', 'hundred' cannot be an alternative reading unless F's error is compounded by loss of the article 'a' or 'one'. Lucius presumably misunderstands, or pretends to do so; Servilius would otherwise be unlikely to reply as he does. Servilius may give Lucius a note, which he misreads.

3.2.48/913 before ... and vndo] F; before, and ... undo Z. JACKSON (*conj.*)

3.2.48/913 before] HANMER; before for a F. Wilson-Maxwell suggested a dittography.

3.2.48/913 . part] F; dirt THEOBALD; profit HEATH (*conj.*); park JOHNSON (*conj.*).

3.2.50/915 do] ; do't CAPELL

3.2.50/915 I I] COLLIER 2 (Collier MS); I F

3.2.66/931 spirit] THEOBALD; ſport F

3.3.4/957 these] F; three ROWE; these three POPE

3.3.5/958 Owes] F1; Owe F2

3.3.12/965 Thriue] F; Thrice WILSON-MAXWELL (Johnson). The emendation, which is more comprehensible than F's awkward reading, might allude to St Peter's denials of Christ. But 'Thriue' seems necessary to the image of physicians, who, like Timon's creditors, live well on their clients' debilities: the emendation fails to put physicians in a bad light.

3.3.21/974 I 'mong'st Lords] DELIUS; 'mong'ſt Lords F; 'mong'st Lords I F2

3.3.23 He'd] F (Had)

3.3.31/984 striues] F; strives not HANMER

3.4.0.2/994.2 Seruants of] not in F. Compare 2.2.9.1/582.1. Editors usually minimize the number of anonymous servants who are called by their masters' names. Caphis is the only servant of Timon's flatterers who certainly has an individual name; Isidore, Varro and Lucius all certainly lend their names to their servants. The other servants in 3.4./Sc. 8 have names used in dialogue as if indifferent in kind from 'Varro' and 'Lucius'; Caphis is not so treated because he is not mentioned by name in the scene where he mixes with 'Varro' and 'Isidore'.

3.4.1/995 ⌜1.⌝ VARROES SERUANT] *Var⟨roes⟩. man.* F. The Servants' subsequent prefixes give their masters' names only. See previous note.

3.4.5.1/999.1 a Seruant of] not in F. See note to 3.4.0.2/994.1.

3.4.16/1010 recouerable: I feare,] JOHNSON; ~, I ~ : F

3.4.27/1021 And] F; 'Tis WILSON-MAXWELL (*conj.*)

3.4.41/1035 that, | he knowes ⌞ you] F, ~ ; he ~ . You HIBBARD

3.4.45/1039 2. VARROES SERUANT] 2. *Varro.* F; 1. *Var⟨ro's⟩. Serv⟨ant⟩.* MALONE; Both *Var⟨ro's⟩. Serv⟨ants⟩.* DYCE

3.4.46/1040 Friend] F; friends DYCE

3.4.59/1053 If] F4; If't F1

3.4.78/1072 an answer] ROWE; anſwer F

3.4.86/1080 HORTENSIUS SERUANT] CAPELL (HOR⟨TENSIUS⟩.); 1. *Var⟨ro⟩.* F

3.4.86/1080 ⌜1. and⌝ 2. VARROES SERUANTS] MALONE; 2. *Var⟨ro⟩.* F

3.5.8/1101 Sempronius: Al luxors,] This edition (Fleay); ~ ⌞ Vllorxa: F1; *Sempronius*: F2; Sempronius; Ventidius, WHITE. Editors usually follow F3's resigned deletion, which Sisson rather ingeniously defends. Fleay's conjecture may have been tendentious, as he thought Tourneur wrote *Revenger's Tragedy* and revised *Timon*. Emendations cannot vindicate authorship attributions, but reliable authorship attributions can illuminate textual problems. According to *OED*, luxor is unexampled outside Middleton's work, but occurs three times in it (*Black Book* D3, *Father Hubbard's Tale* E2b, *Revenger's Tragedy* 1.1.9—for the authorship of which, see Jackson). A compositor unfamiliar with 'luxors' might be excused for trying to construct a latinate name from his copy.

3.5.11/1104 There is] CAPELL: There's F

3.6.1/1108 Lords] DYCE 2; Lord F

3.6.1/1108 too't] F; to it ROWE

3.6.4 'im] F ('em)

3.6.4.1/1111.1 Enter ... Attendants] Most editors retain F's entry at the beginning of the scene (see stage direction list). F's formula '*meeting them*' implies a separate entry, and so, we believe, a delayed one. Thus in the scene's first two speeches the senate is in private debate; the following two speeches are of greeting.

3.6.14/1121 his] F; this HANMER (Warburton)

3.6.14/1121 Fate] F; fault POPE; fact HANMER. 'Fate' is here understood as in *Pericles* 21.62/2080, as a spelling of *feat*, used in the neutral sense, 'action, deed' (*OED, sb.* 1) or the negative 'evil deed, crime' (*sb.* 4; last recorded 1599). This seems to be the primary sense, though 'fate' is also possible, and might, through word-play or an association of ideas, give a simultaneous secondary meaning. In *Yorkshire Tragedy*, MSR, 654-6 'The Scithians in their marble hearted fates' are responsible for 'deeds' that are 'acted' in 'their relentlesse natures', suggesting that Middleton elsewhere might have associated *feat* and *fate* in the single word, with the primary emphasis again on *feat*. (For the authorship of *Yorkshire Tragedy*, see, in particular, MacD. P. Jackson.)

3.6.16-17/1123-4 Nor ... fault)] F. ROWE transposed lines, retaining F's 'And' in 3.6.17/1124. F's parentheses around 'And ... fault' make it appear plausible that 3.6.17/1124 is a marginal insert, but (*a*) parentheses also appear in 3.6.13 and 14/1120 and 1121; (*b*) Johnson's emendation (see following note) gives better sense.

3.6.17/1124 An] JOHNSON; And F

3.6.21/1128 vnnoted] F; innated BECKET (*conj.*); unwonted ANON. (*conj. in Cambridge*). F might be variously emended ('vnrated', 'vnmoued', 'vnmated', etc.). 'Vnnoted', though an odd word for describing 'passion', gives an acceptable 'Paradox', and is as convincing as any emendation.

3.6.22/1129 behaue his] ROWE; behooue his F; behave in's HANMER

3.6.32/1139 Out-sides] F. The sense 'outer garments' is not recorded in *OED* before 1614.

3.6.49-50/1156-7 Lyon, ... Iudge,] ROWE; ~ ? ... ~ ? F

3.6.49/1156 fellon] JOHNSON; fellow F

3.6.61/1168 Why I] F2; Why F1; I POPE

3.6.65/1172 em] F2; him F1. The same contraction may have appeared in the copy for *them* as for *him*, as evidently in 3.6.4/1111.

3.6.80/1187 Honour] F1; Honours F2

3.6.81/1188 returnes] F; return DYCE 2

3.6.95/1202 in few] F; few in RANN (Johnson)

3.6.100/1207 not ... your] CAPELL; not ... our F; but ... your THEOBALD (*conj.*); now ... your WARBURTON. An easy pronoun error after 'our waightier Iudgement'. Theobald and Warburton assumed that a swollen spirit would be an angry one, but it

3.6.114/1221 most] F; worst HIBBARD
3.7.0.2/1222.2 *Lucullus, Lucius, Sempronius*] SISSON (*also including* Ventidius); *not in* F. Sisson identifies the First, Second, Third, and Fourth Lords as Lucullus, Lucius, Sempronius, and Ventidius respectively: a plausible but arbitrary arrangement.
3.7.1/1223 1. LORD] F (1). Similarly formatted throughout the scene for all the Lords.
3.7.19/1241 heares] F1; heare F3; here's F4
3.7.34/1257 o'th'] F; as o' the ROWE
3.7.40.1/1262.1 *A Table and stooles*] *The Banket* F. F has no direction at 3.7.47.1/1269.1.
3.7.54/1276 1. *and* 2. LORDS] F (*Both.*)
3.7.79/1301 Foes] WARBURTON; Fees F
3.7.80/1302 tagge] COLLIER 2 (anon. *conj.* in Rann); legge F; lag ROWE. Wilson-Maxwell compare *Coriolanus* 3.1.247/1692.
3.7.84.2/1306.2 *and stones*] *not in* F. Presumably part of Timon's 'Physicke' (3.7.99/1321), as suggested by 3.7.114/1336, and as in the academic play *Timon* (which probably influenced the writing of this scene), MSR, 2065-8, where Timon throws at his guests stones painted as artichokes.
3.7.90/1312 with your] WARBURTON; you with F
3.7.90/1312 Flatterie] DYCE 2 (W. S. Walker); Flatteries F
3.7.95/1317 Fooles] F; tools THEOBALD (*conj.*)
3.7.97/1319 Maladie] F; maladies HANMER
3.7.104/1326 *Exit*] F. There is no scene-break here, as the stage is not cleared of properties, nor, perhaps, of servants.
3.7.106/1328 the] F2; rhe F1
3.7.108/1330 humors] F1; humor F3
3.7.111-12/1333-4 ⌜3.⌝ LORD ... ⌜2.⌝ LORD] CAPELL; 2. ... 3. F
4.1.6/1342 steeds. To ... Filthes,] POPE 2 (Theobald; *similarily* Shadwell); ~, to ... ~. F
4.1.8-9/1344-5 fast; ... backe,] THEOBALD (anon.; *similarly* Shadwell); ~ˬ ... ~ ; F
4.1.13/1349 Sonne] F2; Some F1
4.1.21/1357 let] HANMER (*similarly* Shadwell); yet F. Johnson sees a contrast between the dissolution of 'confounding contraries' and Timon's desire to perpetuate the 'confusion' that brings about such dissolution; this seems strained.
4.2.10/1387 to] F; from HANMER
4.2.33/1410 or to] F; or so STAUNTON (White); as to G.T. *conj.* See Abbott, 350.
4.2.35/1412 compounds] F; comprehends COLLIER 2 (W. S. Walker). Walker posits a fairly easy error, but the emendation is unnecessary except to establish a rhyme.
4.2.36/1413 varnisht] F; vanish'd POPE; banish'd SINGER (*conj.*)
4.2.41/1418 do's] F4 (does); do F1
4.3.9-10, 11-13/1437-8, 1439-41 It ... leane: | Raise ... Honor.] This edition; Raiſe ... Honor. | It ... leaue: F. Attempts to emend 'Brothers' seem misguided: Timon is again talking about two men of different fates but identical origin (see Oliver). But 'Brothers' cannot refer to the born senator and beggar, whose origins are opposed. Either Shakespeare mixes the otherwise distinct images in reverting to the brothers, or lines are transposed. In F, the two lines 'It ... leane' interrupt the new concern about how society regards those with reversed fortunes. As placed in this edition, they develop the previous sentence's discourse on *nature* as 'innate attributes' (implied original similarity), 'kindred' (brothers), and 'natural existence' (feeding on pasture). The lines' combined inappropriateness to their context and appropriateness to another suggest that they should be relocated. Material was probably added marginally in the copy and misplaced by the compositor. The marginal addition could have been the longer 'Raise ... Honor' rather than 'It ... leane'. Both have errors which might testify to difficult copy (see following notes and incidentals), and either would introduce a second part-line.
4.3.9/1437 Brothers] F; wether's THEOBALD (Warburton); rother's COLLIER (Singer 2). See previous note.
4.3.10/1438 leane] F3; leaue F1

4.3.11/1439 demit] This edition (Staunton); deny't F; denude THEOBALD; deject HUDSON (Arrowsmith); deknight ANON. (*conj.* in Cambridge). Oliver's search for an implied antecedent of (*i*)*t* is not convincing. Wilson-Maxwell rightly object to F's failure in antithesis. They follow Arrowsmith, arguing that 'deiect' would easily be misread 'deniet'; however 'demit' or 'demitt' would more readily give the same error, especially as *demit* unlike *deject* might have been unfamiliar to the compositor. Arrowsmith finds parallels to the opposition of *raise* and *deject* in Middleton; this is suggestive, but *raise* is an unremarkable antonym to either word, and the passage is not attributed to Middleton. However, one cannot rule out Middleton adding 'Raise ... Honor' to a passage in Shakespeare's hand. *Demit* (OED, v.¹) or *dimit* appears to have become fairly common during the 17th c. OED's first example is 1556; its first illustration of the relevant sense ('humble, abase') is 1611, a few years after *Timon*.
4.3.12/1440 Senator] ROWE; Senators F
4.3.15/1443 say] F2; fay F1
4.3.16 grece] F (grize)
4.3.18/1446 All's obliquie] F; all's obloquy ROWE; all is oblique POPE
4.3.23 fang] F (phang)
4.3.27/1455 idle] F; idol COLLIER 2 (Collier MS)
4.3.31/1459 why this? what this] Wilson-Maxwell suggest that the line's first 'why this' may be a false start.
4.3.39/1467 wapper'd] SINGER 2 (Malone); wappen'd F. Compare *unwappered* in *Kinsmen* 5.6.10/2659.
4.3.41/1469 at, this] ROWE; ~. This F
4.3.43 puts] F (puttes). F may give a form of the second person singular (Abbott, 340), but a relative with an antecedent in the second person can take a verb in the third (Abbott, 247). Compare 4.1.2/1338, where the verb stem does not end in 't', and so the third person is indicated, and 5.2.16/2097.
4.3.74-5/1502-3 promise ... not performe] HIBBARD; not promiſe ... performe F. Hibbard convincingly defends the emendation, though it is doubtful if, as he claims, it turns the passage to verse (F sets 'Promise me ... none' as a verse line). F's illogical reading is best explained as an uncorrected authorial lapse.
4.3.88/1516 Tubfast] THEOBALD (Warburton); Fubfaſt F
4.3.117/1545 Barres] STEEVENS (Johnson); Barne F; bared HIBBARD
4.3.122/1550 thy] POPE; the F
4.3.123/1551 Obiects] F; abjects COLLIER 2 (Farmer)
4.3.133/1561 PHRYNIA *and* TIMANDRA] F (*Both.*). Similarly at 4.3.149/1577 and 4.3.167/1595.
4.3.135/1563 Wholsōnes] This edition (G.T.); Whores F; whore POPE; whole THEOBALD (Warburton). F is difficult to interpret; the usual glosses are contrived and contradictory. Add the imperfect repetition 'make a Whore ... make Whores' and the plural-to-singular of 'Whores, a Bawd', and the passage is highly suspect. It is also weak in that it fails to establish an example, in Timon's misanthropic vein, of nature turned to vice, to contrast with that of gold's reformative power—a weakness shared by Warburton's conjecture. If gold makes something a bawd, the noun should probably be a model of virtue or a virtue itself. Elsewhere Shakespeare describes several abstract conditions corrupted to bawd: mercy (*Measure* 3.1.152/1258), majesty ('made his Maiestie the bawd', *K. John* 2.2.59/934), virtue (*Richard II* 5.3.65/2439), reason (*Venus and Adonis* 792), and reputation ('mak'st faire reputation but a bawd', *Lucrece* 623); in *Hamlet* 3.4.78/2292, 'reason panders [F; pardons Q2] will'. An error solely of contamination is possible, but is less likely than contamination prompted by the form in the manuscript, especially as F's suspect word ('Whores') is not identical to that inferably contaminating it ('Whore'). There does not seem to be a word for an appropriate virtue which is monosyllabic and whose form would be conducive to contamination. 'Wholesomeness' answers all the criteria except that of length; it extends the line to an unexceptionable hexameter. The compositor may have substituted 'Whores' under the influence of context, parallel syntax, and similarity of sound and spelling at the beginning of

the words. We offer a spelling in which the graphical similarity at the end of the words might have further encouraged the error, especially if the copy was difficult, as it seems to have been elsewhere in 4.3/Sc. 14. Indeed an alternative explanation of F would be that if the copy omitted a tilde (compare note to *Romeo* 2.1.107/838), the compositor may have set nonsense, in which case F's reading could be a corrector's guess.

Shakespeare does not elsewhere use *wholesomeness*, but has *wholesome* (36), *unwholesome* (10), and *wholesom'st* (1). *Wholesomeness* embraces both the physical and the moral. As a property of a human body, it contrasts appropriately with the diseases Timon attributes to prostitution. It also has some relevance as an attribute of food, sexuality and eating being repeatedly emphasized aspects of financial and physical consumption.

4.3.135/1563   a Bawd] F; abhorr'd COLLIER 2 (Collier MS)
4.3.144/1572   paine sick] This edition (Becket); paines fix F. F's 'six months' is arbitrary and practically meaningless. *Pain-sick* adds to the eight compounds listed by Spevack with *sick* as the second element.
4.3.156/1584   scolds] ROWE; fcold'ſt F
4.3.186/1614   thy] POPE (*similarly* Shadwell)
4.3.186/1614   do] F; do's ROWE (*similarly* Shadwell); doth CAPELL. Many editors accept that the root hates humanity; the sense is surely that humanity despises the root. *Who* for *whom* is common enough (Abbott, 274).
4.3.194/1622   Marrowes,] F; marrowy, WHITE (Dyce)
4.3.194/1622   Vines] F; veins WARBURTON
4.3.196   unctuous] F (Vnctious)
4.3.205/1633   fortune] ROWE (*similarly* Shadwell), SOUTHERN MS (*in copy of* F4); future F. Oliver follows F, but *OED* does not record *future* in the sense 'prospective condition' (*sb.* 3b) before 1858.
4.3.209/1637   Woods] F; weeds THEOBALD (Warburton)
4.3.216/1644   bad] F1; bid F2
4.3.224/1652   mosst] HANMER; moyſt F. Sisson, F. P. Wilson, and Hibbard defend F; Maxwell-Wilson support Hanmer. The emendation is encouraged by the context of the sentence (its emphasis on age—moistness in a plant would be associated with vigour and youth); defenders of F refer to the wider context of the surrounding passage. Compositor B may have consciously altered or unconsciously substituted for a word he did not recognize.
4.3.226/1654   when] F; where WHITE (*similarly* Shadwell)
4.3.244/1672   Out-liues,] ROWE; ~ : F
4.3.252/1680   claspt: . . . Dogge.] F; ~ . . . . ~ , HIBBARD
4.3.255   drudges] F (drugges). F's spelling does not necessarily indicate a monosyllable.
4.3.256/1684   command] ROWE; command'ſt F
4.3.272/1700   ragge] F; rogue COLLIER 2 (Johnson). Sisson defends F.
4.3.286/1714   my] ROWE (*similarly* Shadwell); thy F
4.3.306, 309, 311   medlar . . . medlar . . . meddlers] F (medler . . . Medler . . . Medlers)
4.3.365-6/1793-4   name thee. . . . beate thee,] THEOBALD; name ~ , . . . beate ~ ; F
4.3.366/1794   Ide] HANMER; lle F
4.3.385/1813   Sonne and ſire] ROWE; Sunne and fire F
4.3.397   to . . . to] F (too . . . too)
4.3.400/1828   APPEMANTUS Mo] F; Mo HANMER
4.3.400/1828   them] ROWE; then F
4.3.401/1829   1. THEEFE] F (1). Similarly formatted for all the thieves throughout the scene.
4.3.411/1839   OTHER THEEUES] F (*All.*)
4.3.414/1842   ALL THEEUES] F (*All.*). Similarly at 4.3.416 and 417/1844 and 1845.
4.3.416/1844   too] F; two COLLIER 2 (Collier MS)
4.3.421   hips] F (Heps)
4.3.435/1863   Take] F; takes HANMER
4.3.436/1864   Villanie] ROWE; villaine F
4.3.436/1864   protest] F; profeſe G.T. *conj.*
4.3.436-7/1864-5   doo't, . . . Workemen.] POPE ~ . . . . ~ , F

4.3.446/1874   Ha's] F; Have POPE. The apostrophe probably derives from copy, and tells against compositorial substitution.
4.3.450/1878   steale no] COLLIER 2 ſteale F; steal not ROWE. Wilson-Maxwell defend F, glossing 'if you steal less because of this, may gold destroy you whatever happens'. But 'howsoere' suggests 'whether you do or not': it is very doubtful whether F will sustain Wilson-Maxwell's interpretation.
4.3.455/1883   vs,] ROWE; ~ , F
4.3.458/1886   Athens, there] F; ~ . | 2. *Thief.* There WARBURTON
4.3.472/1900   vnto] F; to POPE
4.3.476/1904   grant'st, th'art] STEEVENS-REED 2; grunt'ſt, th'art a F; grantest th'art a POPE
4.3.476/1904   man,] F2; ~ . F1
4.3.479/1907   I,] F; ~ ; STEEVENS 2. DELIUS first identified F's 'I' as the affirmative *ay*.
4.3.493/1921   milde] HANMER; wilde F
4.3.510/1938   A] POPE; If not a F; is't not a ROWE
4.3.521/1949   exchange] F; exchange it HANMER; exchange't CAPELL
4.3.526/1954   Ha's] F; Have POPE; Ha' ANON. (*conj.* in Cambridge). See note to 4.3.446/1874, where the following would make 'Ha' impossible.
5.1.0.1-114.1/1965.3-2081.2   Enter . . . Caue] This episode is anticipated at 4.3.353/1781 as if it will immediately follow; there may have been a change of intention as to the sequence of episodes. But the Poet and Painter episode cannot have been written to precede the appearance of the thieves: (*a*) an episode is required between the Steward's exit and the end of Sc. 14 (Act 4) and his return with the Senators at 5.2.0.1/2081.3; (*b*) 5.1.6-8/1971-2 refer back to the thieves episode. Conjecturally it was not established where Middleton's contribution of the Steward episode that in F concludes 4.3/Sc. 14 should be placed until after 4.3.353/1781 was written; when it became apparent that it should conclude Sc. 14 (Act 4), it was decided to defer the Poet and Painter episode so that it could separate the Steward's appearances.
5.1.5/1970   Phrinia] ROWE 3; Phrinica F
5.1.6/1971   Timandra] F2; Timandylo F1
5.1.39/2006   Nay . . . him.] F. Conjecturally the Painter should speak this line. If the dialogue continues from before Timon's aside, a change of speaker would be expected; the following two lines look like a response to the suggestion to seek Timon. HANMER answered the first objection to F by transposing the prefixes to 5.1.39 and 42/2006 and 2009. But 'blacke-corner'd' is likely to be an image of a painting.
5.1.43/2010   blacke-corner'd] F; black-cover'd COLLIER 2 (anon. *conj.* in Steevens)
5.1.51/2018   worship] ROWE; worſhipt F
5.1.65/2032   go, naked,] THEOBALD; ~ , | Naked, F
5.1.69/2036   men] F2; man F1
5.1.106/2074   apart] F3; a part F1
5.2.1/2082   is in] F3; is F1
5.2.11/2092   chance] F3; chanc'd F1
5.2.18/2099   Cantherizing] F1; Catherizing (*for* cauterizing) F2. Probably an authorial confusion between 'cauterizing' and 'cantherides'.
5.2.30/2111   Which] F; And HANMER; But CAPELL; Where KINNEAR (*conj.*)
5.2.32/2113   sence] ROWE; ſince F
5.2.33/2114   fail] CAPELL; fall F; fault HANMER
5.2.67   reverend'st] F (reuerends). F's spelling seems determined by the same principle of euphony which leads to '-s' terminations for second-person singular '-st' after stems ending in 't'.
5.2.78/2159   it] F (*some copies*); t F (*others*)
5.2.105/2186   foure] F; sour ROWE. Usually emended; Wilson-Maxwell defend F.
5.3.1, 13/2195, 2207   ⌈3.⌉ SENATOR] SISSON; 1 F
5.3.5/2199   ⌈4.⌉ SENATOR] SISSON; 2 F
5.3.8/2202   made] F; had HANMER
5.3.14/2208   ⌈1.⌉ SENATOR] SISSON; 3 F
5.4.2/2213   this?] This edition; this? | *Tymon* is dead, who hath

out-ftretcht his fpan, | Some Beaft reade this; There do's not liue a Man. F. These lines are the first of Timon's epitaphs in F. The Soldier's claim to be unable to read the tomb is usually explained in terms of there being two epitaphs on it, the present one in the vernacular and the one read by Alcibiades at 5.5.71-8/2290-7 in a classical tongue. In the absence of other indications, this *ad hoc* rationalization is unconvincing. F looks like an authorial fresh start or rewriting. If the epitaph is deleted, the scene makes complete sense and the play's conclusion is more effective. Perhaps the end of the play was first sketched out with the discovery of the epitaph entirely separate from the siege of Athens; it would then have been decided to delay the reading of the epitaph, to substitute the epitaphs from North's Plutarch (the source of 5.5.71-8/2290-7), and to introduce the device of the wax tablet to bridge the locations.

The arrangement of 5.5/Sc. 19 supports this hypothesis: the lines dealing with the epitaph (5.5.65.2-86/2284.2-2305) make up a detachable episode inserted awkwardly into the closing scene, leaving the Senators' descent and the opening of the gates inconclusively separate from the reading of Timon's epitaph. Originally the text might have read 'Descend, and keepe your word[s], | And I will vse the Oliue, with my Sword', so giving a rhymed couplet before 'each . . . Leach'. The descent would then be part of a final ceremonial exeunt.

Timon is nowhere else in the text spelt with a 'y', though it is so spelt in the head-title and three times in the list of characters; it is nevertheless not credible that the two lines were inserted in the printing house, and it is difficult to see what significance, if any, the anomaly may have.

5.5.24/2243 greefe] F; griefs THEOBALD
5.5.28/2247 ˌShame (that they wantedˌ cunning) in excesseˌ] THEOBALD (subs.); (Shameˌ that they wanted, cunningˌ in exceſſe) F1; ˌShame (that they wantedˌ cunningˌ in excess) F2. JOHNSON, following F1's medial punctuation, reads 'coming' for 'cunning'. Oliver follows F2; Hibbard convincingly defends Theobald's reading.
5.5.37/2256 Reuenges] STEEVENS 2; Reuenge F
5.5.55/2274 Desend] F2; Defend F1
5.5.62/2281 remedied to] F1; remedied by F2; render'd to DYCE (Chedworth); remanded to HIBBARD. Many editors follow Dyce, though Schmidt defended F. *Remedy* is disyllabic elsewhere in Shakespeare, so F is not ametrical. The sense is clear if 'But' is understood as compressed 'but it' and 'to' takes its common sense 'according to'.
5.5.65.1/2284.1 Trumpets . . . walles.] not in F. CAPELL first indicated that the Senators descend. No previous editor has supplied trumpets, but (*a*) trumpets would be usual to mark a ceremonial restoration of peace; (*b*) trumpets are used earlier in the scene; (*c*) a musical flourish would give the Senators time to descend (and cover any noise the actors made in doing so). For the absence of a stage direction in F, see note to 5.4.2/2213.
5.5.65.2-66/2284.2-85 Souldier . . . SOULDIER] *a Meſſenger* | *Meſ.* F
5.5.75-8/2294-7 Heere . . . gate.] Runs together two epitaphs from North's Plutarch, the first ('*Heere lies . . . left*') supposedly written by Timon himself, the second ('*Heere lye . . . gate*') attributed by Plutarch to the poet Callimachus. For '*Caitifs*' (5.5.74/2293) North has 'wretches'.

INCIDENTALS

108 enfranchizd] enfranchized   169 suffred] suffered   194 Timon.] ~ˌ   199 likest] lik'ſt   227 feign'd] fegin'd
259 depart] depatt   288 honourd] honoured   308 Hang'd] Handg'd   358 Apermantus.] ~ˌ   359 Captaineˌ] ~, (see lineation note)   413 welcome] wecome   586 it.] ~,   636 and] &   712 loued] lou'd   766 health,] ~;
813 bountifull] bouutifull   849 liud] liued   914 Seruilius,] ~.   995 Hortensius.] ~.   1108 voyce,] ~.   1221 'Tis] ˌTis   1273 it.] ~ˌ   1282 toward.] ~ˌ   1328 the] rhe   1437 Lards,] ~.   1441 Who] who (see textual note)
1470 damned] damn'd   1533 Conquered] Conquer'd   1558 giu'st] gieuſt   1658 Trunkes,] ~, (?)   1715 thine.] ~ˌ
1727 mind.] ~ˌ   1815 lou'd] loued   2018 aye,] ~:   2242 their] rheir   2250 death,] ~;   2293 You,] you,

FOLIO STAGE DIRECTIONS

1.1.0.1-3/0.1-3 *Enter Poet, Painter, Ieweller, Merchant, and Mercer,* | *at seuerall doores.*
1.1.38.1/38.1 *Enter certaine Senators.*
1.1.95.1-4/95.1-4 *Trumpets sound.* | *Enter Lord Timon, addressing himselfe curteously* | *to euery Sutor.*
1.1.111/111 *Exit.*
1.1.111.1/111.1 *Enter an old Athenian.*
1.1.155.1/155.1 *Exit*
1.1.179/179 *Enter Apermantus.* (after 1.1.177/177)
1.1.242.1/243.1 *Trumpet sounds. Enter a Messenger.*
1.1.249.1/250.1 *Enter Alcibiades with the rest.*
1.1.259.1/260.1 *Exeunt.*
1.1.259.2/260.2 *Enter two Lords.*
1.1.286/287 *Exeunt.*
1.2.0.1/287.1 *Hoboyes Playing lowd Musicke.*
1.2.0.1-6/287.1-6 *A great Banquet seru'd in: and then, Enter Lord Timon, the* | *States, the Athenian Lords, Ventigius which Timon re-*|*deem'd from prison. Then comes dropping after all Ape-*|*mantus discontentedly like himselfe.*
1.2.60.1/347.1 *Apermantus Grace.*
1.2.110.1, 127.1-2/397.1, 414.1-2 *Sound Tucket. Enter the Maskers of Amazons, With* | *Lutes in their hands, daunting and playing.* (after 1.2.110/397)
1.2.111.1/398.1 *Enter Seruant.* (after 1.2.112/399)
1.2.118.1, 127.1-2/405.1, 414.1-2 *Enter Cupid with the Maske of Ladies.* (after 1.2.118/405)
1.2.141.1-4/428.1-4 *The Lords rise from Table, with much adoring of Timon, and* | *to shew their loues, each single out an Amazon, and all* | *Dance, men with women, a loftie straine or two to the* | *Hoboyes, and cease.*
1.2.153/440 *Exeunt.*
1.2.162/449 *Exit.*
1.2.172.2/459.2 *Enter a Seruant.*
1.2.175.1/462.1 *Enter Flauius.*
1.2.180.1/467.1 *Enter another Seruant.*
1.2.185/472 *Enter a third Seruant.*
1.2.205/492 *Exit*
1.2.232.1/519.1 *Exeunt Lords*
1.2.248/536 *Exit*
1.2.251/539 *Exit*
2.1.0.1/539.1 *Enter a Senator.*
2.1.14/553 *Enter Caphis.*
2.1.34.1/573.1 *Exeunt*
2.2.0.1/573.2 *Enter Steward, with many billes in his hand.*
2.2.9.1-2/582.1-2 *Enter Caphis, Isidore, and Varro.*
2.2.13.1-2/586.1-2 *Enter Timon, and his Traine.*
2.2.44.1/617.1 *Exit.*
2.2.44.2/617.2 *Enter Apemantus and Foole.*
2.2.70.1/643.1 *Enter Page.*
2.2.85/657 *Exit*
2.2.115.1/688.1 *Enter Timon and Steward.* (after 2.2.116/689)

2.2.120.1/693.1   *Exeunt.*
2.2.182.1/755.1   *Enter three Seruants.*
2.2.229.1/802.1   *Exeunt*
3.1.0.1-3/802.2-4   *Flaminius waiting to speake with a Lord from his Master, | enters a seruant to him.*
3.1.3.1/805.1   *Enter Lucullus.*
3.1.28.1/831.1   *Enter Seruant with Wine.*
3.1.49/852   *Exit L.*
3.1.62/865   *Exit.*
3.2.0.1/865.1   *Enter Lucius, with three strangers.*
3.2.24.1/889.1   *Enter Seruilius.*
3.2.61/926   *Exit Seruil.* (after 3.2.60/925)
3.2.63/928   *Exit.*
3.2.88/953   *Exeunt.*
3.3.0.1-2/953.1-2   *Enter a third seruant with Sempronius, another | of Timons Friends.*
3.3.26/979.1   *Exit*
3.3.41.1/994.1   *Exit*
3.4.0.1-4/994.2-4   *Enter Varro's man, meeting others. All Timons Creditors to | wait for his comming out. Then enter Lucius | and Hortensius.*
3.4.5.1/999.1   *Enter Philotus.*
3.4.35/1029   *Enter Flaminius.*
3.4.41.1/1035.1   *Enter Steward in a Cloake, muffled.*
3.4.66.1/1060.1   *Enter Seruilius.*
3.4.79.1/1073.1   *Enter Timon in a rage.*
3.4.96/1090   *Exit Timon.*
3.4.99.1/1093.1   *Exeunt.*
3.5.0.1/1093.2   *Enter Timon.*
3.5.14.1/1107.1   *Exeunt*
3.6.0.1, 4.1/1107.2, 1111.1   *Enter three Senators at one doore, Alcibiades meeting them, | with Attendants.* (at 3.6.0.1/1107.2)
3.6.101/1208   *Exeunt.*
3.6.115/1222   *Exit.*
3.7.0.1-3/1222.1-3   *Enter diuers Friends at seuerall doores.*
3.7.24.1/1246.1   *Enter Timon and Attendants.* (after 3.7.25/1247)
3.7.40.1/1262.1   *The Banket brought in.*
3.7.104/1326   *Exit*
3.7.104.1/1326.1   *Enter the Senators, with other Lords.*
3.7.114.1/1336.1   *Exeunt the Senators.*
4.1.0.1/1336.2   *Enter Timon.*
4.1.41/1377   *Exit.*
4.2.0.1/1377.1   *Enter Steward with two or three Seruants.*
4.2.15/1392   *Enter other Seruants.* (after 'Fellowes')
4.2.29.1/1406.1   *Embrace and part seuerall wayes.*
4.2.51/1428   *Exit.*
4.3.0.1/1428.1   *Enter Timon in the woods.*
4.3.45/1473   *March afarre off.*
4.3.48/1476   *Enter Alcibiades with Drumme and Fife in warlike manner, | and Phrynia and Timandra.*
4.3.176.1/1604.1   *Exeunt.*
4.3.197.1/1625.1   *Enter Apemantus.*
4.3.399.1/1827.1   *Enter the Bandetti.* (after 'Exit Apeman.', 4.3.400.1/1828.1)
4.3.400.1/1828.1   *Exit Apeman.*

4.3.459.1/1887   *Exit Theeues.*
4.3.459.2/1887.1   *Enter the Steward to Timon.*
4.3.537.1/1965.1-2   *Exit*
5.1.0.1/1965.3   *Enter Poet, and Painter.*
5.1.22.1/1989.1   *Enter Timon from his Caue.* (after 5.1.29/1995)
5.1.114/2081.1-2   *Exeunt*
5.2.0.1/2081.3   *Enter Steward, and two Senators.*
5.2.15.1/2096.1   *Enter Timon out of his Caue.*
5.2.108.1/2189.1   *Exit Timon.*
5.2.113/2194   *Exeunt.*
5.3.0.1/2194.1   *Enter two other Senators, with a Messenger.*
5.3.13/2207   *Enter the other Senators.*
5.3.17/2211   *Exeunt*
5.4.0.1/2211.1   *Enter a Souldier in the Woods, seeking Timon.*
5.4.8/2219   *Exit.*
5.5.0.1-2/2219.1-2   *Trumpets sound. Enter Alcibiades with his Powers | before Athens.*
5.5.2.1/2221.1   *Sounds a Parly. | The Senators appeare vpon the wals.*
5.5.65.2/2284.2   *Enter a Messenger.*
5.5.70.1/2289.1   *Alcibiades reades the Epitaph.*
5.5.90.1/2309.1   *Exeunt.*

[Printed after the play]

THE
ACTORS
NAMES.

TYMON *of Athens.*
Lucius, And
Lucullus, two Flattering Lords.
Appemantus, a Churlish Philosopher.
Sempronius another flattering Lord.
Alcibiades, an Athenian Captaine.
Poet.
Painter.
Ieweller.
Merchant.
Certaine Senatours.
Certaine Maskers.
Certaine Theeues.
Flaminius, one of Tymons Seruants.
Seruilius, another.
Caphis.
Varro.
Philo. } *Seuerall Seruants to Vsurers.*
Titus.
Lucius.
Hortensis
Ventigius. one of Tymons false Friends.
Cupid.
Sempronius.
With diuers other Seruants,
And Attendants.

KING LEAR

King Lear exists in two substantially different editions. The first is a quarto (Q1), whose title-page identifies it as 'Printed for *Nathaniel Butter*, and are to be sold at his shop in *Pauls* Church-yard at the signe of the Pide Bull neere St. *Austins* Gate. 1608' (*BEPD* 265). This quarto was printed by Nicholas Okes; it had been entered in the Stationers' Register on 26 November 1607:

Na. Butter	Entred for their copie vnder thande of
Io. Buſby	Sr Geo. Buck knight & Thwardens
	A booke called. Mr Willm Shakeſpeare
	his hiſtorye of Kinge Lear as yt was
	played before the Kinge maieſtie at
	Whitehall vppon St Stephans night
	at Xp̄īm̄s Laſt by his maties ſervante
	playinge vſually at the globe on the
	Bankſyde

A second quarto edition (Q2) reads simply 'Printed for *Nathaniel Butter*. 1608'. The priority of Q1 was not established until 1866; between 1908 and 1910 Greg, Pollard, and others demonstrated that Q2 was one of a group of plays printed in 1619 by William Jaggard for Thomas Pavier. (See General Introduction.) Though Q2 played an important part in the history of the text's transmission, it reprints Q1 with no apparent access to independent manuscript authority. A third quarto (Q3) appeared in 1655.

King Lear was also included among the Tragedies in the First Folio; that text (F) was reprinted in the derivative folios of 1632, 1663, and 1685, and in Rowe's three editions (1709-14). The Folio text contains about 100 lines not printed in Q; it does not contain about 300 lines (including one whole scene) which are present in Q; it also differs from Q in hundreds of substantive readings, and divides the play into acts and scenes.

In 1723 Pope became the first editor to incorporate readings from Q into the text of F; in 1733 Theobald carried the process further, producing an edition based upon full-scale conflation of the two early sources. No eighteenth-century editor provided a sound hypothesis which would justify such massive emendation of the Folio (or the Quarto), but Theobald's procedure has been followed in all subsequent editions. In the twentieth century editors have most often described Q as a reported text, and F as an abridged theatrical adaptation; but no such hypothesis has succeeded in satisfying, in all of its features, even the adherents of conflation, let alone those who oppose it.

Although earlier scholars sometimes raised the possibility that F represents a revision of the original play (represented by Q), until recently that hypothesis had not been seriously or systematically explored. In 1931 Madeleine Doran (*The Text of 'King Lear'*) argued that Q was set from Shakespeare's foul papers, and hence that many verbal variants between the texts were authorial (although in 1941, reviewing Greg, she retracted some of her earlier conclusions). In 1976 Michael Warren's 'Quarto and Folio *King Lear* and the Interpretation of Albany and Edgar' reopened the issue, claiming that the two texts presented these two characters in significantly different ways; since 1976, studies by Urkowitz, Stone, Taylor ('The War in *King Lear*', *SSu 33* (1980), 27-34), Blayney (*The Texts of 'King Lear'*), Honigmann, and other scholars have argued at great length the case for the artistic integrity and independence of the two early versions.

The hypothesis that we possess, in Q and F, Shakespeare's original version and Shakespeare's revision of *King Lear* necessitates a radical departure from traditional editorial practice; but traditional editorial practice itself represents a radical departure from the early texts. Because the editorial tradition has never been justified by a coherent or credible textual hypothesis, a conservative editor would have to reject it, even if the possibility of revision did not exist. On the other hand, even those editors who accept the essential independence of the two texts might only reprint one: either the original (Q), or the revision (F). For other plays which we believe Shakespeare to have revised, we have attempted to provide edited texts which, so far as possible, represent the text as it stood after Shakespeare revised it, and a similar procedure might have been adopted here. But scholars have generally agreed that the variants in *Lear* represent a special case: attempts to dismiss Q as a 'bad quarto' derive in part from the perception that it differs from F in ways not paralleled by other collateral texts (like the good quartos of *Hamlet*, *Troilus*, and *Othello*), and scholars who have supported the hypothesis of revision have generally spoken of Q and F as different 'versions' of the play. Moreover, the Folio revision probably took place several years after the original composition. These considerations, combined with the play's importance, make it desirable to prepare edited texts of both early 'versions'.

The following Textual Notes to the two versions do not attempt to discuss or justify every variant between them. *Division* contains a useful 'Index of Passages Discussed' (pp. 471-82) keyed to the analysis of such variants in *Division* itself and in four major discussions which preceded it (Stone, Taylor 'War', Urkowitz, Warren); Blayney's volume contains its own index. Since 1982 the discussion of variants, increasingly in critical studies chiefly devoted to other matters, has proliferated; the paperback reprint of *Division* (1986) contains a bibliography of such studies up to the end of 1985 (p. x)—to which should be added the chapter on *King Lear* in Gary Taylor's *Moment by Moment by Shakespeare* (1985).

G.T./(S.W.W.)

THE HISTORY OF KING LEAR
(BASED ON THE QUARTO OF 1608)

BLAYNEY demonstrates that Q1 was probably printed in December and January of 1607-8; it was set seriatim by two compositors (Okes's B and C): C set Sc. 17.0–Sc. 18.30/2203-88; Sc. 20.95-205/2424-2533; Sc. 20.264–Sc. 21.55/2590-2659; and Sc. 24.118/2901 (after 'summons') to the end. B set the remainder of the play. *Lear* was apparently the first play Okes had printed, and it would have made heavy demands on his limited supply of type: type-shortage probably accounts, in part, for some of the text's deficiencies, particularly the peculiarity of the punctuation and lineation. Even after every allowance has been made for the possibility that Quarto variants may be authorial alternatives rather than errors, Q1 remains exceptionally unreliable in its distinctions between prose and verse, and in its arrangement of verse. Shortages in the type case, unfamiliarity with this kind of material, compositorial error, ambiguity and alteration in the manuscript can probably account for all such errors of lineation, though it may be difficult to differentiate between these causes in any particular instance.

The twelve extant copies of Q1 contain an exceptional number of press variants: full lists and discussions of these can be found in Greg (1940) and Blayney (1982). From these variants, and from the many evident errors in Q, it is apparent that the handwriting of the printer's copy was not easily legible, and that the manuscript was particularly subject to kinds of misreading associated with the 'Hand D' addition to *Sir Thomas More* and with the quartos apparently set from Shakespeare's foul papers. In the frequent inadequacy of its stage directions and the inconsistency of its designation of characters the manuscript also resembles an author's draft rather than a scribal fair copy or a prompt-book. Such evidence suggests that Q was set from foul papers, and that it may in fact reproduce certain features of such manuscripts more faithfully than any other Shakespeare quarto. Such 'bibliographical' evidence tends to confirm the literary arguments, advanced by a number of recent critics, that the Quarto represents a legitimate early version of the play. But, as noted in the preface to *Division*, 'any comprehensive defence of the Quarto's authority would have to provide . . . a detailed critical consideration of many individual variants' (p. vii). The following Textual Notes attempt to provide the beginnings of such a defence. The preparation and explanation of a text of the Quarto itself constitutes an important part of the case for the existence and integrity of the two versions.

Unlike the Folio, Q contains many readings which are obviously nonsensical or inadequate, and the chief problem for an editor is the extent to which it should be corrected by reference to F. Naturally, we have retained Q wherever we could make defensible sense of it; but having decided in any specific case that Q is probably corrupt, one must still decide whether to accept F's reading, or to adopt an editorial conjecture. Acceptance of F is always easier, and in one respect safer: if an editor accepts that F represents Shakespeare's own revision, then the F reading in such cases is presumably Shakespearian, even if Shakespeare did not intend it to stand in Q. However, the entire purpose of editing Q and F separately is to preserve the separate integrity of each, and such a purpose is not well served by importing revised readings into an unrevised fabric. Moreover, one chief weakness of the policy of wholesale conflation was its inability to provide plausible explanations for the great bulk of variation between the two texts; a coherent editorial alternative cannot reasonably resort to dozens of emendations which leave the apparent corruption in Q wholly unexplained. We have therefore attempted, as far as possible, to emend Q—where emendation seems desirable—as though F did not exist, seeking in every case the most plausible explanation of the apparent error, and the most economical restoration of sense.

In a very real sense, the Quarto version of the play has never been edited: Rowe did not know of Q's existence, and editors from Pope onwards have simply used Q to supplement F. Blayney's unpublished 'reference text' of Q (1979) was the first critical edition of Q itself; we are, as the notes reveal, often indebted to that edition, and grateful for Dr Blayney's generosity in allowing us access to his text before its publication.

Q does not contain act or scene divisions, and like most of Shakespeare's other plays it was written for continuous performance. Since Q stands outside the eighteenth-century editorial tradition, no convention of act-scene reference to this text has been established; nor does it seem desirable that any such misleading convention should now be imposed upon it. We have therefore simply numbered the scenes continuously, without interpolating act divisions. The Folio divisions belong to the revision, and cannot be retrospectively imposed on a different structure. The scene divisions themselves create no problem, except at the point where Kent falls asleep in the stocks (7.167/1174). In both Q and F, Kent remains on stage—asleep—during Edgar's soliloquy, waking up shortly after Edgar exits and Lear enters. The stage is not cleared; F marks no scene division before Edgar's entrance or after his exit; both texts envisage the same sequence of action, and F's division of scenes is elsewhere complete. Eighteenth-century editors were nevertheless troubled by the apparent reappearance of the fugitive Edgar before Gloucester's residence, and by the apparent compression of time; Steevens therefore made Edgar's soliloquy a new scene, followed by yet another scene in which Lear and his party discover Kent in the stocks. This arrangement, followed by all subsequent editors, makes unwarranted assumptions about consistency

THE HISTORY OF KING LEAR

of time and place in the pre-Restoration theatre, and we have here followed both early texts in regarding as one uninterrupted scene the action from Kent and Oswald's entrance to the exeunt of Cornwall, Regan, Gonoril, Oswald, and Gloucester.

In the notes that follow, BL2 refers to an annotated copy of Q in the British Library: shelfmark C.34.k.17.

G.T./(S.W.W.)

WORKS CITED

Blayney, Peter W. M., *The Texts of King Lear and Their Origins*, vol. i, *Nicholas Okes and the First Quarto* (1982)
—— ed., *King Lear*, unpublished edition of Q (see Introduction)
Craig, W. J., ed., *King Lear*, Arden (1901)
Doran, Madeleine, *The Text of 'King Lear'* (1931)
—— review of Greg, *The Variants*, RES 17 (1941)
Duthie, G. I., ed., *Shakespeare's 'King Lear': A Critical Edition* (1949)
Furness, H. H., ed., *King Lear*, New Variorum (1880)
Greg, W. W., *The Variants in the First Quarto of 'King Lear': A Bibliographical and Critical Inquiry* (1940)
Harsnet, Samuel, *A Declaration of Egregious Popish Impostures* (1603); extracts reprinted in Bullough (vii. 414-20)
Honigmann, E. A. J., 'Shakespeare's Revised Plays: *King Lear* and *Othello*', *The Library*, VI, 4 (1982), 142-73
Jennens, Charles, ed., *King Lear* (1770)
Muir, Kenneth, ed., *King Lear*, Arden (1952)
Ridley, M. R., ed., *King Lear*, New Temple (1935)
Schmidt, A., ed., *King Lear* (Berlin, 1879)
Stone, P. W. K., *The Textual History of 'King Lear'* (1980)
Tate, Nahum, *The History of King Lear* (1681), repr. in Christopher Spencer, ed., *Five Restoration Adaptations of Shakespeare* (1965)
Taylor, Gary, 'Four New Readings in *King Lear*', N&Q, NS 29 (1982), 121-3
Urkowitz, Steven, *Shakespeare's Revision of King Lear* (1980)
Warren, Michael, 'Quarto and Folio *King Lear* and the Interpretation of Albany and Edgar' in *Shakespeare, Pattern of Excelling Nature*, ed. David Bevington and Jay L. Halio (1978)
Wright, W. A., ed., *King Lear*, Clarendon (1881)

TEXTUAL NOTES

Title The Historie of King Lear] Q (running title); M. William Shak-fpeare | HIS | Hiftorie, of King Lear. Q (head title), S.R.; M. William Shak-fpeare: | HIS | True Chronicle Hiftorie of the life and | death of King LEAR and his three | Daughters. | With the vnfortunate life of Edgar, fonne | and heire to the Earle of Glofter, and his | fullen and affumed humor of | TOM of Bedlam: Q (title-page). For the Stationers' Register see the Introduction.
2, 34.2, 119 Cornwell] Q. Shakespeare had an uncle by marriage called Cornwell: see Mark Eccles, *Shakespeare in Warwickshire* (1961).
1.36/36 Exit] F; not in Q; Exeunt Gloucester and Edmund CAPELL
1.40 off] Q (of)
1.54/54 as] F; a Q
1.103/103 misteries] F2; miftreffe Q; miferies F1
1.103/103 night] F; might Q. Q could be defended—'the mysteries and the might of Hecate'—but the construction would be awkward; the proposed easy misreading produces more natural syntax and a more explicit contrast with 'the sun'. The substantive 'might' occurs often in Shakespeare's early work, but only once after *Othello*.
1.112/112 bee as] Q. See Cercignani (p. 291) on the elision.
1.120/120 dowers] F; dower Q
1.131 crownet] QF (coronet)
1.138/138 mad] Q2, F; man Q1
1.166/166 next] BLAYNEY; tenth QF
1.211/211 your] F; you Q
1.218/218 acknow] This edition; may know Q; make knowne F. Compare *Othello* 3.3.324/1772, where Q has 'you knowne' for F 'acknowne'. Unless Cordelia awkwardly switches from France to Lear in mid-sentence, Q must be emended.
1.222/222 the] HANMER; for QF. The syntax requires a noun clause, not a prepositional phrase, and QF's 'for' could easily arise from contamination.
1.233/233 a] F; and Q. For confusion of *a* and *and* see *All Is True* 2.4.171/1243, Sonnet 129.11, and *Winter's Tale* 1.2.106/153.
1.247/247 my] F; thy Q
1.257/257 Flourish.] F; not in Q. (The usual accompaniment of a royal exit, often absent in foul papers.)
1.258/258 Ye] ROWE 2; The QF. Rowe's emendation is almost certainly no more than an alternative interpretation of an ambiguous manuscript 'ye/yᵉ'.
1.269/269 At Fortunes armes] QF; at Fortunes armes STONE (conj., p. 193); as Fortunes almes CAPELL. In *Othello* Cassio proposes to set himself 'in some other course, | To fortunes almes' (3.4.119-20/2048-9), and though Stone believes the *Othello* passage should also be emended, as the object of a disgraced man's quest 'Fortune's charity' makes immediately recognizable and idiomatic sense. The same cannot be said of Regan's use of the phrase here: but Stone's 'at Fortune's arms' (meaning 'from Fortune's arms') seems equally unidiomatic. Capell's 'as' also presupposes an easy error, but is aurally unfortunate (as fortunes alms). It would be surprising if a compositorial misreading in Quarto *Lear* produced an unusual phrase Shakespeare had used the year before in *Othello*, while the *Othello* passage itself suggests that Shakespeare could here have imagined 'Fortunes almes' as 'the place where Fortune dispenses petty charity'.
1.270/270 the worst] This edition; the worth Q; the want F; the words STONE (conj., p. 192). It seems unlikely that Regan is being, as Blayney suggests, 'simply ironic' ('you are well worth the dowry you have forfeited'), or that she means 'you are well worth the valuation (i.e. 'Nothing') that you have asked for'. Both interpretations seem difficult to communicate, in a way that F's 'the deprivation that you have sought' is not. It is possible that F here restores the reading of Q's own copy, but Q's error of assimilation—if it is one—would be much easier to explain if the manuscript read 'worth the worst that you have wanted'. *The worst* is an important concept in the play; Cordelia has, in Regan's view, asked for (*wanted*) 'the worst', and deserves (*well are worth*) what she has got; in fact, she deserves even worse than she has received, and so is *worth* any *worst* which she still lacks (*haue wanted*). Certainly, however we construe it, to say that Cordelia is 'worth the wanted worst' is intelligibly venomous in a way that 'worth the wanted worth' is not.
2.3/301 Stand in] QF. Stone conjectures *Stand on* = 'value, set store by' (p. 192); but Wright (see Furness) cited Psalms 38, 'And I truly am set in the plague' (Prayer Book).
2.4/302 curiositie] QF; courtesy THEOBALD
2.13/311 dull eyed] BLAYNEY (Stone); dull lyed Q
2.14/312 creating] F; creating of Q. Q presumably interpolated the grammatically expected preposition. (Blayney notes at least five instances of interpolated *of* in Okes's setting of Shirley's *Relation of his Travels*.)
2.15/313 thē] F; the Q
2.20/318 tooth'] QF; top the CAPELL. For a defence of QF see Thomas Clayton, 'Disemending *King Lear* in Favour of Shakespeare', N&Q 229 (1984), 207-8; see also Malcolm Pittock, '"Top the Legitimate"?', in the same issue, pp. 208-10. There may also be a pun on *tooth* (= bite, *OED* v. 3, 1579+).
2.36/333 BASTARD] Qb (*Ba.*); not in Qa
2.77 ay] Q (I)
2.111/408 honesty] F; honeft Q
2.118/415 spirically] F (Sphericall); fpirituall Q. Q's error is much

511

more understandable if the copy had the obsolete 'spir' spelling of the noun *sphere* (for which see *OED*). This form might also have permitted a pun on *spiracle*, meaning 'breathe, spirit' (particularly, 'spirit' as 'breath of God'), for which see *OED* (*spiracle, sb.*¹ 1).

2.127 maidenliest] Q (maidenleſt). Compare Dekker and Middleton's *1 Honest Whore* 5.1.48 ('stormest' for *stormiest*), *Cymbeline* 4.2.207/2158 ('easilest' for *easiliest*), and *Tempest* 3.1.15/1111 ('busielest' for *busiest*).

2.129/426 ons Q out] This edition; out Q; Pat F. Duthie suggests that the Q compositor misread 'my cu' as 'myne'; Blayney, that he was simply bewildered by 'my Q', and gave up. It seems to us more likely that *mine* itself is right, contrasting *my cue* (in the sense 'the role I must play': see *OED, sb.*² 4) with Edgar's *cue* (the name 'Edgar', which cues his entrance). This contrast in the two senses of *cue* corresponds to the contrast between the two 'parts': Edgar 'old Comedy', Edmund 'villanous melancholy'. It therefore seems probable that 'mine' is right, and that an earlier use of 'cue' has been accidentally omitted. Eyeskip from 'ons' to 'out' would be easy enough. Compare *Richard III* 3.4.26/1791 ('Had you not come vpon your kew . . .').

2.130 sigh] Q (sithe)

2.131/428 them] Q; *Tom* F. Stone would emend Q; he suggests that the name was spelled 'Thom' in Q's copy (p. 178).

2.165/463 I doe] QF; I, I doe This edition *conj.*

4.0.1/495.2 *disguised*] ROWE; *not in* QF. Since the disguise-name 'Caius' is not mentioned until the end of the play, the formula 'Kent as Caius' would seem inappropriate here.

4.2 diffuse] QF (defuſe)

4.39–41 me. . . . dinner.] JENNENS; ~ . . . ~, QF

4.46.1/540.1 *Exeunt seruant ⌈and Kent⌉*] This edition; *not in* QF; *Exit a Knight* DYCE. If Kent is to speak 4.48/543 he must exit at some point. Blayney has him leave after 'What say's the fellow there', with 'call the clat-pole backe' addressed to a Gentleman, and referring to Kent, rather than Oswald.

4.46.1/541.1 *Enter Kent ⌈and seruant⌉*] This edition; *not in* QF. Blayney staggers the entrances.

4.68/562 this foole] Q; my Foole F

4.69 these] QF (this)

4.74.1/568.1 *crossing the stage*] This edition; *not in* QF

4.89/583 if you haue] BLAYNEY; you haue Q

4.104/598 my] This edition; any Q; all my F. See 4.253/747.

4.105 off] QF (of)

4.108/602 Ladie the brach] STEEVENS; Ladie oth'e brach Q; theLady Brach F

4.110/604 gall] F; gull Q

4.149/643 ladies] Qb; lodes Qa

4.173/667 learne to] Qb; learne Qa

4.186/680 now,] Qb; thou, Qa

4.202/696 it] F; *not in* Q

4.222/716 notion, weakens] F; ~, weaknes Q

4.223/717 lethergied] F; lethergie Q. Q sets this speech as prose. If Blayney's lineation (treating 'Weakens, or his discernings are lethergied' as one line) is correct, then 'lethergic' (accented on the second syllable) would be metrically preferable—and arguably an easier explanation for Q's error.

4.233/727 Vnderstand] Q; To vnderstand F. Shakespeare uses line-divided feet often in this period.

4.239/733 more like to] This edition; more like Q; it more like F, BL2. Some addition is required metrically. Though words like *it* and *to* are often omitted, there is here no particular reason why *it* should have been, whereas *to* could easily have been omitted (*a*) by assimilation to 'like a' earlier in Q's line, or (*b*) because *like* and *like to* are synonymous. The more convoluted construction—'Inne, [which] epicurisme . . .'—also seems appropriate to Gonoril.

4.239/733 tauerne, or] tauerne, or Q; Tauerne, or a F. Though Q could easily have omitted an *a*, the line is metrically acceptable if a caesura is understood after 'tauerne'.

4.247.1/741.1 *Exit one or more*] BLAYNEY [*Exeunt some*]; *not in* QF

4.253/747 will that wee—prepare my] This edition; will that wee, prepare any Q; will, speake Sir? Prepare my F

4.253.1/747.1 *Exit one or more*] This edition; *not in* QF

4.256–7/750–1 list: | My traine, are] F; liſt, my traine, and Q. The manuscript probably contained no punctuation after 'list', thereby facilitating Q's misunderstanding; the colon has been provided here purely to aid comprehension.

4.276 thwart] Q (thourt)

4.276/770 disnatur'd] F; disuetur'd Q

4.278/772 cadent] F; accent Q. Though both Stone and Blayney disparage Folio 'cadent', it makes perfectly acceptable sense, especially in a culture where Latin was widely taught and known. Blayney provides an earlier English example of the Scots word *eident* (or *ident*) at *John of Bordeaux* 1026 (MSR); however, this word seems unlikely to have been spelled with an initial 'a' here (as Blayney conjectures)—an unattested spelling which would have made it indistinguishable from the incongruous *aydant* (as at 18.18/2276). Stone's suggestion that the compositor 'accidentally omitted the s' of *accenst* is impossible, since the ſt ligature would have been required if the compositor intended to set 'accenſt'. *Ardent*, still widespread in the literal sense 'fiery, burning', would seem a more plausible emendation than either of these; but we cannot claim that it is more likely than F's 'cadent' to have stood behind Q's 'accent' (though it does suppose only two misread letters, rather than three).

4.281/775 That she may feele,] Q1; *not in* Q2, F. This repetition could be mere compositorial dittography, but iterative incoherence is characteristic of *Lear*.

4.283.1/777.1 *Exeunt Lear, ⌈Kent, Foole and seruants⌉*] This edition; *not in* Q; *Exit.* F; *Exit Lear, Kent, and Foole* BLAYNEY. Blayney follows Duthie in calling for the rest of Lear's train to exit at 4.266/760, but a struggle of exits seems unlikely, and the departure Lear calls for there might well be interrupted by Albany's following speech. The exit here, by contrast, clearly takes place, and Q's repetition of 'Goe, goe, my people?' might well suggest resumption of the exit earlier interrupted.

4.293/787 And should make the, worst blasts] This edition; ſhould make the ∧ worſt blaſts Q; Should make thee∧ worth them. | Blaſtes F; Should make the worſe: blafts BLAYNEY. Q's 'the' is easily understood as F's 'thee', but *worst* for *worth* is not an intrinsically easy error, especially when compounded by apparent omission of *them*. F seems unlikely to preserve Q's original reading. Though palaeographically easy, Blayney's 'worse' strains both sense and metre. The conjecture adopted here presumes that Lear breaks off before finishing his sentence, *thee* distracting his attention from his own tears back to Gonoril, whom he then curses. So emended, in Q Lear presumably intends to say that his tears *should* make Gonoril repentant, or ashamed; precisely because they do *not*, he curses her. In F, Lear not only, more self-controlled, finishes his sentence; he makes the very different statement that his tears shame him by assigning to Gonoril a value she does not deserve. He then curses her because she has made *him* weep shamefully, rather than (as here) because she does not weep herself.

Stone (p. 216) defends Q, arguing (as here) that Lear breaks off in mid-sentence ('should make the worst—blasts and fogs vpon the,'), but this seems clumsy as well as unmetrical.

4.293, 295 thee] Q (the,) F

4.293/787 the,] This edition; the∧ Q; thee: | Th' F. Q's copy might well have read 'the, the' (as Blayney supposes).

4.294/788 Vntented] Qb (vntented); vntender Qa. Stone defends Qa, suggesting that the press-corrector 'may have been unfamiliar with' *vntender*, and noting that the word's first recorded occurrence is in *Lear*. But since that is at 1.99/99, both the compositor and the proof-corrector would already have encountered it; moreover, since *untenderly* dates from the 15th c., the negative adjective could hardly have caused much confusion in 1607. Stone objects that 'a wound may be untented . . . but it is hardly possible to speak of an untented *wounding*' (p. 216); but *OED* notes two earlier examples of *wounding* (vbl. sb. 2) as a mere synonym of *wound*.

4.295/789 Pearce] Qb (pierce); peruse Qa. 'Pearst', *Dream* 3.2.59/1040 (Q), and *Titus* 4.4.31/1850 (Q) ('pearst')—seems more likely to lie behind Q's misreading 'peruse'. ('Pearce' spellings are also common in Shakespeare.)

4.295/789 about the,] F (~.); ~, Q
4.297/791 cast Q] F; you caſt Q
4.310/804 with the:] F; with, Q
4.324/818 And after] Qa (&); & haſten Qb. Q's press-correction is palaeographically unlikely, and leaves the line a syllable short (see next note); moreover, Gonoril follows Oswald (Sc. 7), and so contradicts herself if she here calls for his quick return (though the inconsistency could result from Shakespeare's own change of plan).
4.324/818 retinue] This edition; returne QF. See Taylor, 'Four New Readings'. For the accentuation compare Massinger's *City Madam* 3.3.47. G. W. Williams (*SSu* 36 (1983), pp. 192-3) objects (*a*) that as emended the line could only mean 'follow your followers' and (*b*) that a retinue would be inappropriate for a steward. But *after* meaning 'afterwards' is well attested; for similar constructions, see especially 'Read o're this, | And after this' (*All Is True* 3.2.202-3/1695-6; also *Timon* 4.3.105-6/1532-3 and *Coriolanus* 2.2.52/1075). There thus seems no reason why 'Get you gon, | And after your retinue' could not mean 'Go you now, and your retinue (go) afterwards, follow you'. This assumes that 'get you gone' means 'depart for Regan's castle'; alternatively, it could mean 'leave my presence', in which case 'after your retinue' would mean 'go get, seek, look for the retinue to attend you'. Elliptical uses of *after* without a verb are common; see for instance, 'hide Fox, and all after' (*Hamlet* 4.2.29-30/2474-5; also *Coriolanus* 1.3.64/378). However we interpret Gonoril's command, either construction of *after* seems idiomatic. As for Oswald's having a 'retinue', Q introduces him as 'Gentleman' (Sc. 3), and a steward could be a man of very high rank (see *OED*). The social incongruity, if any, was probably less obvious to a Jacobean than to a modern audience. Even if the impropriety were glaring, Shakespeare might have intended an ironic contrast between Gonoril's provision of a 'retinue' for her steward, while dismissing and finally proposing to abolish the 'retinue' of her father, the King.
4.325/819 milkie] Qb; mildie Qa
4.327/821 ataxt] DUTHIE (Greg); alapt Qa; attaskt Qb; at task F
4.327/821 for want] Qb; want Qa; for harmless want BLAYNEY (*conj.*). If 'pardon y'are' is understood (as here) to form a line-divided foot, there is no metrical deficiency to call for emendation. Blayney conjectures that an omitted adjective was not restored because it would not fit into the Q line, but 'harmles', 'hurtles', 'silly', and similar antonyms to *harmfull* could have been accommodated with no (or minimal) alteration to the rest of the line.
4.328/822 praisd] F; praiſe Q
5.8/834 were] Q2; where Q1
5.19/845 stands] Q2; ſtande Q1
5.46-7/872-3 I would not be mad ... I would not be mad] Q; not mad ... I would not be mad BLAYNEY. After 'let me not be mad', Q's further repetition of 'I would not be mad' seems feeble (as well as unmetrical), and one naturally suspects that one phrase has been contaminated the other. Blayney follows F in abbreviating the first occurrence of the phrase, postulating 'a kind of eyeskip', but it seems inherently likelier that the second phrase should be contaminated by a memory of the line before. This would be especially easy—and maybe even deliberate—if the manuscript had 'I not mad' ('I' = *ay*, as usual in Shakespeare texts). This produces a metrically acceptable hexameter. Compare *Coriolanus* 2.3.67, 'Ay, not mine own desires'. However, we retain Q, because it does make sense, and Lear speaks rhythmical prose or broken verse elsewhere in this scene.
6.1.0.1/877.2 Curan] QF. This should perhaps be modernized to 'Currant', of which it is an alternative early form.
6.9/886 Not, I,] Q; Not, I, F. For Q's idiom Blayney—who adopts F, as do all other editors—cites Fletcher's *The Little French Lawyer* 2.3 (*Comedies and Tragedies*, 1647, sig. I1ᵛ). See also Sharpham's *Cupid's Whirligig*, I2ᵛ ('did you not perceiue it?—Not, I protest'), Fletcher and Massinger's *Sea Voyage* 2.2 (p. 23), and Middleton's *Your Five Gallants* ('And this is all now, i'faith.—Not; I durſt go further'); the anonymous *Charlemagne*, l. 214 (MSR), 'thou onlye art happynes.—Not great lord'; and Day's *Humour out of Breath*, 4.3 (p. 316), 'how now, gallant, not gone yet?—Not, I thank you, lady'.

6.15.1/892.1 Enter Edgar at a window aboue] This edition; *Enter Edgar* Q1 (*in the left margin, before 'it selfe', the first word of a line set as prose*); *Enter Edgar* Q2 (*after 'Which' in* 6.18/895, *before the prose line in which 'Brother, a word' occurs*); *Enter Edgar* F (*before 'Brother, a word'*). Q2 and F place the direction in the most obvious place for it, but Q1's 'more difficult' position is hard to account for as a compositorial error. In 1.2/Sc. 2 there is a similar gap between Edgar's visual entrance and his entry to the dialogue, and in 2.4/Sc. 7 there is a similar juxtaposition of Edgar with a silent on-stage figure (Kent). Q1's direction, as interpreted here, places Edgar's entrance just before Edmund begins to talk of him; in turn, Edmund's first subsequent line ('My father hath set gard to take my brother') explains to an audience why Edgar is peering nervously from an upstairs window. See also note to 6.19.1/896.1
6.18/895 breefnes wit and] This edition; breefnes and Q. It seems unlikely that F ('Which I muſt act, Briefeneſſe, and Fortune worke') restores the reading of Q's copy; resort to F here assumes that 'acte' was (implausibly) misread as 'aſke', and 'I' independently omitted. 'Which must aske breefnes' itself makes good sense. But 'and fortune help' (despite Stone, p. 216) does not; 'and fortune's help' would, but produces equally poor metre. We suspect a noun has been omitted before 'and'. Either 'wit and fortune' (as at *As You Like It* 1.2.97/262) or 'time and Fortune' (as at *Timon* 3.6.10/1117) is possible; but the 'time and Fortune' parallel is in a scene probably written by Middleton. Shakespeare elsewhere writes of '*times* helpe' (*Lucrece* 983), but also of 'his quicke wit, and his queasie stomacke' (*Ado* 2.1.383/769—in a speech plotting to deceive someone 'of a noble strain . . . and confirmde honesty'). The evidence of Shakespeare's usage elsewhere thus marginally favours *wit*. More important, in Edmund's last scene he had decided to 'haue lands by *wit*' (2.170/468), and he seems likelier here to ask for chance and cleverness to help him perform the business 'which must aske breefnes', than to call on 'time' to help him be brief. *Wit* also fits into a chain of verbal images in these three lines: *question*, *ask*, *briefness* (= brevity, concision), *word*, and *say*. Finally, *wit* is the shorter word (which may itself explain its omission) and one misreadable as *and* (in which case the compositor might have deliberately 'corrected' what he read as 'and and fortune helpe').
6.19.1/896.1 Edgar climbes downe] This edition; *not in* QF. That Edgar *is* 'above' seems evident from Edmund's call to him to 'discend'; but no time is allotted (as usually happens) for Edgar to descend by the tiring-house steps. If Shakespeare had wanted the usual staging, he could easily have provided it by having Edmund call Edgar ('Brother, a word, discend brother I say') before addressing the audience for three lines ('My father ... fortune helpe'). It thus appears that Shakespeare deliberately forwent the usual technical expedient, and this implies that he did not want the usual staging. It would be natural—and dramatically effective—for Edgar in these circumstances simply to climb over the upper stage railing and jump or climb down to the main stage, with or without Edmund's help.
6.27/904 you] BLAYNEY; your Q; your ſelfe F
6.29/906 cunning] F; crauing Q
6.36/913 ho, helpe?] This edition (*conj.* Stone); no, helpe? Q1; no, helpe? Q2, F. Stone's conjecture is supported by the fact that 'n' and 'h' are adjacent in the type case, and by the absence of parallels for 'no helpe?' Compare 'What how helpe' (*Hamlet* 3.4.23/2236); *ho* is juxtaposed with *help* 13 times elsewhere in the canon. Those who retain Q1's 'no' must emend its comma; the agreement of Q2 and F is meaningless, given Q2's demonstrable influence on F.
6.36/913 and others] BLAYNEY; *not in* Q; *and Seruants with Torches* F. F's direction probably represents the original intention, but

513

neither the identity of the others, nor their props, are specified by the dialogue, and Urkowitz (p. 27) argues that they never appear on stage at all.

6.47/924 fine] F; a fine Q

6.51 lanced] Q (lancht). *OED* records this form under the verb *launch*; but the forms seem to have been interchangeable, and for a modern reader *lance* is immediately intelligible, and *launch* misleading.

6.54 ghasted] QF (gafted). The obsolete verb *gast* is now only current in the form *aghast*.

6.54.5/931-2 Or . . . I know not] This edition; *not in* QF. It seems likely that Q has accidentally omitted a verse line, and that F has rewritten the passage accordingly. One would expect another *or* after 'Or whether' (6.55/932); Duthie defends the irregularity as indicative of 'Edmund's perturbation', but this difficulty is itself the only syntactical evidence of any such 'perturbation'; Edmund's speech elsewhere in this scene is markedly complex and controlled. It is also difficult to believe that Q's 'but', in 6.56/933, could be an error for F's 'Full' (or 'ful'); 'but', if correct, must be contradicting a previous statement, but no such statement is available as Q stands. 'Or whether gasted by the noyse I made' thus leads us to expect a corresponding completion in the immediately following line, while 'But sodainly I fled' implies an antecedent in the immediately preceding line; both existing lines point to a lacuna between them. For the common idiom 'I know not, but' see for instance *Tragedy of Lear* 1.4.55, 2.2.455/559, 1469. Though the beginning and end of the missing line can be inferred with some confidence, its middle is beyond recovery.

6.58/935 And found, dispatch] Q1. Blayney interprets 'And' as 'if', follows Q2 and F in placing a stronger stop after 'found', and assumes that 'dispatch' is addressed to attendants who exeunt at the end of the speech. Stone would emend 'found' to 'found' (p. 178).

6.65 pitched] QF (pight)

6.70/947 no, what] F; no. what Q1; nowhat STONE (*conj.*, p. 187). The meaning 'nothing' offered by Stone (last recorded in 1530) is difficult to make sense of here.

6.78.1/955.1 *Trumpets within*] ROWE; *not in* Q; *Tucket within* F (after 'it' 6.77/954)

6.83/960 haue] Q; haue due F. Q's metre is acceptable if 'kingdome | May' is understood as a line-divided foot.

6.89/966 dost] Q, F1; does F2

6.95/972 tende] THEOBALD; tends Q; tended F

6.100/977 the spoyle and waſt] BLAYNEY; theſ e— and waſt Qa, Q2; the waſt and ſpoyle Qb; th'expence and waſt F. Any explanation of this variant must assume that Qb inadvertently transposed the two nouns, in correcting the first. Maxwell's conjecture ('the fee', in Muir) and Malone's ('the use') fail to explain Qa's dash (probably an indication that the compositor could not decipher several letters which followed) and assume that the proof-reader simply guessed; Greg's 'the spence' introduces a word for which there are no Shakespearian parallels, and which does not discernibly improve or alter the meaning. Stone's 'the seise' (= the possession) provides a weaker meaning through the agency of a form only recorded once elsewhere (*OED*). It seems best to assume that the press-corrector properly deciphered Shakespeare's manuscript, and that F represents a deliberate rewriting. See F.

6.100/977 his] Qb; this his Qa

6.119/996 This] This edition (*conj.* Stone); Thus QF. It is much easier to suppose that 'This' was misread 'Thus' than that F's 'threadding' was taken for Q's 'threatning'. And although Regan has no reason to claim that she was 'threatning' the night, it does suit her purposes to claim that she has sought out Gloucester *despite* the unseasonable threatening weather.

6.120/997 poyse] Qb; priſe Qa, Q2, F. See *Division*, 362-3.

6.123/1000 deferences] Qb (diferences); defences Qa. The uncorrected reading suggests that the manuscript used the 'de' spelling (see *OED*); the modern word 'deference' is first recorded in 1647, so no ambiguity would have arisen.

6.123/1000 lest] Qb; beſt Qa, Q2, F

6.123 least] Q (left)

6.124/1001 home] Qb, F; hand Qa, Q2

7.1/1008 deuen] Qa, euen Qb, Q2; dawning F. Stone (p. 194) defends Qa as a variant spelling, on the analogy of 'good-den'. Greg (*Variants*, p. 158) suggested that Qa was an error for 'dauen', an unrecorded spelling of 'dauing' or 'dawin' (= dawn). Greg contends that the time is 'not evening but early morning before sunrise'; but the only evidence for this assertion is F's own reading in this line, and Stone's interpretation seems likelier as an explanation of Qa. Blayney also accepts Qa.

7.1 Good even] Q (Good deuen)

7.40.2/1047.2 ⌈then⌉ *Gloster* ⌈then⌉] This edition; *Glofter* Q

7.62 Z] QF (Zedd)

7.67/1074 haue you] RIDLEY; you haue Q

7.73/1080 intrencht] This edition (*conj.* Stone); intrench Q; intrince F

7.73/1080 vnloose:] F; inlooſe, Q

7.75/1082 fier] F; ſtir Q

7.78/1085 doges] F; dayes Q

7.80 Smile] QF (Smoile)

7.82/1089 Camulot.] F; Camulet., Q1; Camulet. Q2

7.90/1097 Than] Q2, F; That Q1

7.93/1100 ruffines] F (roughnes); ruffines Q. The use of an fi ligature implies that the compositor deliberately set 'ruffines', but he nevertheless probably misread the manuscript. *Ruffines* is not recorded elsewhere, and though it could be a neologism based on *ruffy* (= 'a devil or fiend'; related to *ruffin* = 'ruffian'), Shakespeare never uses this root word, 'devilishness' seems less appropriate than 'roughness', and *ruffines* is metrically anomalous. Though 'rough' is the normal spelling in Shakespeare texts, this might reflect printing-house normalization; 'ruff(e)' is attested by *OED*, and occurs at *History of Lear* 11.2/1625 (Q), *Errors* 4.2.35/1064, and *Contention* 3.2.175/1739 (the two Folio occurrences representing departures from compositorial preference, and hence presumably reflecting copy). The word might have been spelled 'ruffenes' here, but minim misreading (or miswriting) seems likelier than e/i confusion.

7.95/1102 He muſt be plaine] Q; An honeſt mind and plaine F; Honeſt he muſt be, plaine This edition *conj.* Blayney accepts F. Q is comparatively flat, a foot short, and quite possibly contaminated by the following phrase ('he muſt ſpeake truth'); but it seems implausible to suppose that 'an' and 'mind' have been omitted, 'honeſt' misread 'he muſt', and 'be' substituted for 'and'. On the other hand, 'Honest he must be, plaine' could easily have been corrupted, either by the compositor correcting what he assumed was an unintended repetition in his copy ('he muſt he muſt'), or by simple eyeskip.

7.104/1111 flickering] POPE; flitkering Q; flicking F

7.105/1112 dialect] F; dialogue Q. On the analogy of 'auricular' (2.92/388), the manuscript might have spelled 'dialegte', though this is nowhere else recorded.

7.106/1113 I know] QF; know S.W.W. *conj.*

7.115-16/1122-3 man, that, | That] Q1; man, that, | That Q2; Man, | That F; man, | That' FURNESS. Furness assumes that in F 'it' has been absorbed into the final 't' of 'that'. One might conjecture that Q's 'That' should have been 'It' (*yt* misread as *yt*, or contaminated by the preceding word).

7.118/1125 flechment] F; flechuent Q

7.121/1128 anſient] F; auſrent Qa; miſcreant Qb

7.127/1134 Stoking] F; Stobing Qa; Stopping Qb

7.127/1134 Fetch forth the stockes] QF. Blayney adds '*Exeunt some*'.

7.131.1/138.1 *Stockes brought out*] F; *not in* Q. Dyce and other editors place this direction after Cornwall's next speech.

7.133/1140 speakes] Q2, F; ſpeake Q1. Either 'speakes' or 'spake' would plausibly rectify Q1's error.

7.137/1144 contemned] BLAYNEY; contaned Qa; temneſt Qb; contemneſt'st CAPELL

7.150/1157 out] Q2, F; ont Q1

7.154/1161 say] Qa; ſaw Qb, Q2, F

7.159/1166   myrackles] F; my rackles Qa; my wracke Qb
7.161/1168   now] This edition; not Qa; moſt Qb, Q2, F. See Taylor, 'Four New Readings'.
7.163/1170   For] ROWE; From QF. This whole passage—'and shall find time | From this enormious state, seeking to giue | Losses yʳ remedies'—is one of the most difficult cruxes in the canon. It seems more likely that the implicit subject of the clause is 'Who' (i.e. Cordelia), rather than 'I'; not only is 'Who' nearer, but we are expecting news of what Cordelia will do, and in the stocks Kent seems unlikely to 'find time' to improve the situation. Moreover, if the conjecture 'now' is accepted in 7.161/1168, then 'shall find time' here explicitly contrasts with it, suggesting that both refer to the same agent. In itself, then, 'and shall find time' would create no difficulties of syntax or sense, and consequently there is little to be gained from Jennens's suggestion that 'and . . . remedies' is part of the letter which Kent reads aloud. The difficulty is not external (to relate these two lines to their context) but internal (to make sense of these words as a sequence of thought, whether in or out of quotation marks). Nor can we easily assume that Kent reads two isolated phrases, out of context, from the letter. This would be an extraordinary procedure anyway, and naturalistic explanations ('the light is bad', 'he's falling asleep') only indicate the state of desperation to which critics have been driven. Of the two phrases into which the passage might reasonably be divided, 'seeking to giue losses yʳ remedies' makes obvious self-contained sense, relevant either to Kent himself now or Cordelia in prospect. Kent might be congratulating or commiserating with himself, but in the circumstances we expect news of Cordelia. The problem with the passage thus resides wholly in the first phrase, 'and shall find time | From this enormious state', which if it were read from the letter would seem to be a complete unit—unless we are to imagine Kent reading three unrelated snippets from a letter, the first and third of which just happen to sound like continuations of his own previous sentence. The crux lies very clearly in the second phrase, 'From this enormious state'—or rather in the relationship between this phrase and its surroundings. We expect Cordelia to 'find time' *for* something, or *to do* something; hence Rowe's emendation 'and shall find time | *For* this enormious state'. Certainly, 'enormious state' is so apt and unusual a collocation that it seems unlikely to be compositorial rather than Shakespearian; the corruption must lie elsewhere. Blayney alters 'this' to 'hir'; the conjecture is palaeographically plausible, but we have no reason to believe that Cordelia's state (i.e. France) is an enormity, and the emendation does little to solve the other problems of meaning in the passage. Since 'this . . . state' (i.e. Britain) is indeed 'enormous', we are not inclined to emend 'this', either. Hence, 'and shall find time' and 'this . . . remedies' both seem to make good contextual sense; only 'From' is both a source of fundamental difficulty and an easy source of error. E. Sullivan's defence of 'From' (*TLS*, 20 Dec. 1923) as 'away from' is ably confuted by Muir; one might add that it leaves 'and shall find time' unresolved. 'From' could easily be an error for 'Form' (Cuningham; see Muir), 'Frame', or 'For' (Rowe). The two verbs require 'time' to be understood as their subject; this creates an implausibly passive construction, with Cordelia watching Time take care of the difficulties. 'For', by contrast, leaves Cordelia at the centre of attention, produces an intelligible idiom, and presupposes an easy error (which recurs at *Coriolanus* 3.3.114/2043 and *Caesar* 3.1.286/1372). This is, moreover, just the kind of error which occurs frequently in this passage in Q, and which is most likely to escape press-correction (in Q, with several substantive corrections in this speech) or annotation (in F). More dramatic solutions—such as the assumption that a line has dropped out—seem unlikely, given the extensive press-correction here, at least some of it clearly by reference to copy. We have therefore reverted to Rowe's simple emendation, which seems most likely to represent Shakespeare's intentions.
7.164/1171   yʳ] Qb (their); and Qa. For the inferred manuscript form, see Greg, *Variants*, p. 160.
7.164/1171   ouerwatcht] Q2, F; ouerwatch Q1

7.165/1172   Take] Qb; Late Qa
7.167/1174   He sleepes. | *Enter Edgar*] Following Steevens, editors mark a new scene (2.3) here, and another at 7.187-187.1/1194-1194.1. But the stage is never cleared in this sequence, and (since changes of locale are not the primary determinant of a new 'scene') there seems no reason to depart from F.
7.167/1174   heard] F; heare Q
7.171/1178   Dos] F; Doſt Q. Either 'Doth' or 'Doe' is also possible.
7.176/1183   elfe] F; elſe Q
7.181/1188   and] Qb; *not in* Qa
7.182/1189   Pins] Qb; Pies Qa
7.183/1190   from] Qb; frame Qa
7.183/1190   fermes] F; ſeruice Q. For the inferred spelling see *OED*.
7.186/1193   Tuelygod] Qa; Turlygod Qb, Q2, F; tirlery-gaud STONE (conj., p. 195). 'Trumpery' does not seem very appropriate as a disdainful epithet for a naked beggar—quite apart from the fact that Stone's emendation is implausible and its result unparalleled. But no parallels have been found for Shakespeare's word either, and since F merely repeats Q2 which repeats Qb, the Q1 compositor and proof-corrector themselves provide our only evidence for Shakespeare's word. The corrector either (*a*) recognized the word, or (*b*) consulted the copy in an attempt to decipher it better; in either case, his reading would be preferable to Qa. However, it is possible that (*a*) the corrector himself misread the manuscript, or (*b*) the compositor bungled the intended correction. Any choice between these explanations must be based on a conjecture about Shakespeare's meaning. 'Tuel' could be an obsolete spelling of *tewel*, *towel*, *twelve*, or *twill*; of these only the second seems appropriate, since it could mean 'a cloth used as a part of dress' (sb. 2b) or one used 'for covering the altar' (sb. 2a). This might refer to the beggar's loincloth, with its ecclesiastical sense punningly relevant to *god*. *Tewly*—meaning 'weak, sickly'—would also have been appropriate, and was sometimes spelled 'tuely'. As 'towelly-god' or 'sickly, weak god', Qa is defensible.

Qb's 'Turly' is less easily defined. As a Scots adjective it is recorded from 1742, meaning 'full of twirls or whirls' (*OED tirlie*); this might be thought relevant to the 'dance' or a mad beggar, but the connection is rather strained. There is also a single occurrence in the Coventry Corpus Christi plays (*c*.1500), defined by *OED* as 'jinking or whisking about . . . with the accompaniment of rhythmical meaningless words'; however, all other examples are trisyllabic (see *OED terlerie*, *tirlerie*, *turlerie*), and the insistence on jollity in all *OED*'s examples hardly seems appropriate to Tom. The available senses for *turly* are thus unattractive. *Turl* could mean 'pull or strip off (the clothes from a person . . .)' (*tirl*, *v*.² 1); or 'to twirl' (*tirl*, *v*.³ 1), or 'to make a rattling noise' (*tirl*, *v*.³ 3). Unfortunately, the first and most appropriate of these senses is Scottish and Northern dialectal. Moreover, although the substantive *towel* could have been given a *y* suffix, this seems most unlikely to have happened with any verb *tirl*. Qb can only be defended as a colloquial corruption whose etymology and meaning are irrecoverable; Qa, on the other hand, makes something like sense as it stands.

However, it seems relatively unlikely that Qb's 'r' should have gone anywhere else in the line. Neither *gord* (= false dice), nor *grod* (= grown) is attractive; nor does *god* seem suspicious: it has an obvious pertinence to the beggar's cry, and suggests the numinous awe accorded the naked, half-human outcast by most cultures. Poor Tom is, after all, mistaken for 'a spirit' on his first appearance. If the 'r' is to be inserted anywhere, it does seem to belong to the first half of the word. *Trely* and *Turely* and *Tuery* produce nonsense. *Truelygod* is a conceivable but not a compelling compound. 'Truel' could also be a spelling of *trull* (prostitute), *trowel*, or *troll*; of these only *troll*—which could mean 'to ramble, to walk about or to and fro' (*v*. 1), or 'to sing in the manner of a round or catch' (*v*. 10)—seems relevant. *Trolly* is also used in various compounds expressing contempt (see *OED trolly-lolly*). If Qb's 'r' belongs anywhere, it seems more appropriate before than after 'u'.

Qa's *Tuelygod* is more intelligible than Qb's *Turlygod*; but Qb is undoubtedly a deliberate alteration, which may reflect consultation of copy. On the other hand, the press-corrector might have misread (as *r*) a letter the compositor got right (as *e*); or he might have intended only to change the spelling (to *Tuilygod*), with his correction misinterpreted by the compositor (marginal *i* misread as *r*). In the absence of exact parallels, any choice between Qb and Qa will be somewhat arbitrary; we have preferred Qa as the earlier and more intelligible reading.

7.187-187.1/1194-1194.1 *Exit. | Enter*] Steevens marks a new scene (2.4) here.

7.188/1195 home] F; hence Q. Compare *Henry V* 4.5.12/2367.

7.190/1197 purpose] Q; purpoſe in them F. F might be right, but feminine tetrameters are metrically acceptable, the sense does not require emendation, and no cause for accidental omission is evident. F's addition also necessitates the (otherwise unnecessary) emendation of 'his' to 'this'.

7.193 cruel] F; Q (crewell)

7.194/1201 heedes] F; heeles Q

7.205/1213 propose] This edition; purpoſe Q; impoſe F. For similar errors see Folio *Much Ado* 3.1.12/1089 and (conjecturally) Folio *Henry V* 4.1.157/1937. None of Shakespeare's other 172 uses of *purpose* has the accentuation Q requires, and 'intend' in any case seems inappropriate. The proposed error could easily result from misreading or substitution; the Q compositor had set the word twice already in the last 100 lines; and *propose* is not only metrically regular but better sense ('display', 'propose for acceptance'). F's 'impose' also makes sense, but seems less likely to lie behind Q's error.

7.214/1222 meinie] F; men Q. Q makes sense and, though irregular, could be paralleled metrically; but the presence of *meiny* in related contexts in Harsnet, the ease of misreading the rare 'meinie' for commonplace 'menne', and the metrical irregularity combine to support the emendation.

7.221/1229 Hauing] QF; I, hauing This edition *conj*. The conjectural addition would improve the syntax and produce a line-divided foot.

7.226/1234 Historica] F4; Hiſtorica QF

7.251 pardie] Q (perdy)

7.255/1263 Inſolēce] BLAYNEY; Iuſtice Q; fetches F. Stone (p. 49) conjectures 'Iuſles' (= jostles, justles), but *OED* gives no parallels for the sense Stone gives the word; Shakespeare does not elsewhere use the noun (first recorded in 1607). Insolence makes better sense and is no more difficult palaeographically.

7.264/1272 fatᵣ] Qb (father); fate, Qa. For the inferred manuscript form, see Greg, *Variants*, p. 161.

7.265/1273 his] Qb; the Qa

7.265/1273 commands] Qb; come and Qa

7.265/1273 tends] Qa; her Qb; their ALEXANDER

7.266/1274 Fierie? the] BLAYNEY; The fierie Qa; Fierie Qb; Fiery? The fiery F. (The question mark may not have been in Q's copy.)

7.267/1275 No] Qb; Mo Qa

7.270/1278 cōmands] Q2; Cōmand Q1

7.287.2/1295.1-2 *and others*] BLAYNEY; *not in* Q; *Seruants* F

7.289.1/1297.1 *Kent here set at liberty*] F; *not in* Q

7.293/1301 deuorſe] Qb (diuorſe); deuoſe Qa

7.293/1301 scrine,] This edition; fruit, Qa; tombe, Qb. See Taylor,'Four New Readings'.

7.299/1307 deplored] BLAYNEY (Stone); deptoued Qa; depriued Qb; deprau'd F

7.300/1308 you] F; *not in* Q

7.305/1313 in] F; on Q

7.323/1331 LEAR] Q2; *not in* Q1 (which does indent the line as though it were the beginning of a speech)

7.329/1337 Thy] F; The Q

7.340/1348 *Trumpets within*] ROWE; *not in* Q; *Tucket within* F (*one line earlier*)

7.344.1/1352.1 *He strikes the Steward*] This edition; *not in* QF. It is possible that 'Who struck my seruant' refers to Oswald's earlier encounter with Kent, but if we did not possess F it seems likely that editors would have added a blow here.

7.348/1356 your] F; you Q

7.367-8/1375-6 To be ... Ayre] THEOBALD. In Q and F the lines appear in the opposite order ('To be ... owle' after 'To wage ... Ayre'); see Blayney's explanation of the presumed error (i. 215).

7.372/1380 beg] Q2, F; bag Q1

7.380/1388 that lies within] Q; that's in F. Hexameters are common enough in Shakespeare, but the phrase which creates this one seems exceptionally feeble. Perhaps 'within' was a *currente calamo* replacement for 'that lies'.

7.381 boil] QF (bile)

7.423/1431 need] F; deed Q

7.426/1434 life is] F; life as Q1; life's as Q2. Q2's reading, adopted by some editors, is equally plausible. No other examples of is/as error are found in Shakespeare.

7.434/1442 so] F; to Q

7.435/1443 tamely] F; lamely Q

7.442.1/1450.1 *Storme within*] This edition; *not in* Q. F has '*Storme and Tempest*' at the end of its verse line (after 'weeping'). Q gives no directions at all for the storm, but some stage effect seems likely before Cornwall's 'twill be a storme' (7.446/1454), and this seems as good a place as any.

7.444/1452 into] F; in Q. Both idiom and metre seem to require this change; for the same error see *2 Henry IV* 1.2.49/303 (Q in, F into).

7.444/1452 flawes] F; flowes Q

7.445.1/1453.1 *Gloster*] Q2 (*Gloceſter*); *Leiſter* Q1

7.448/1456 blame,] HANMER; ~ QF

8.0.1/1474.1 *Storme.*] F (*Storme ſtill*); *not in* Q

8.0.1-2/1474.1 *1. Gentleman*] This edition; *a Gentleman* Q. This gentleman reappears in 4.3/Sc. 17, 4.6/Sc. 20, and 4.7/Sc. 21, associated with Kent and Cordelia; he should be distinguished from the messenger figure (associated with Regan and Gonoril) who appears in 4.2/Sc. 16 and 5.3/Sc. 24. (Throughout the play, numerals added to the speech-prefix GENTLEMAN are editorial.)

8.9/1483 outstorme] MUIR (Steevens); outſcorne Q

8.20-1 Cornwall; | But true it is.] BLAYNEY; ~ ~, Q1; ~. ~, Q2

8.36/1510 am] F; *not in* Q

8.45/1519 In which indeuor Ile this way, you that] This edition; Ile this way, you that Q; in which your pain | That way, Ile this F; for whom Ile seeke | This way, you that BLAYNEY (*conj.*). Q can only be defended by interpreting 'Ile this way, you that' as parenthetically (and unmetrically) interrupting Kent's sentence; F suggests that Shakespeare would have found such an interpretation as impossibly strained as we do. F also suggests the gist of what Q appears to omit; but (although Blayney in some despair accepts it) F can hardly represent what stood in Q's copy. The conjecture 'In which indeuor' gives much the same sense as F, without requiring any emendation of Q's intact 'Ile this way, you that'. It also helps to clarify the lineation of the passage. Q, presumably following its manuscript, prints the Gentleman's preceding speech as one line, though it naturally divides (as does the following first line of Kent's speech) into two part-lines. On the evidence of his practice elsewhere Shakespeare would probably have written the half-line plus whole line at the beginning of Kent's speech on one manuscript line. The probable manuscript lineation could be reconstructed thus (using diagonal slashes to indicate intended verſification breaks):

    I will goe seeke the King.
Gent. giue me your hand, / haue you no more to say?
Kent. few words but to effect / more than all yet: that when we haue found the King /
  [ ] Ile this way, you that, /
  he that first lights on him, hollow the other./

This would give five complete verse lines at the end of the scene, rather than (as in F) four complete lines bracketed by two unassociated part-lines. If this was the intended lineation—and it is not only neater, but also explains Q's mislineation of the first line and a half of Kent's speech—then what we need to fill Q's lacuna is the five-syllable beginning of a verse line (= In which indeuor).

Q's error can be variously explained. Blayney observes that

Q's erroneous catchword suggests that, as originally set up, F3ᵛ included one line of text which for some reason was later shifted (in whole or in part) to the top of F4. Blayney deduces, reasonably, that a line of text on F3ᵛ had been accidentally omitted, and that an attempt to rectify this error in foul proofs necessitated moving one line forward to F4. Since any such attempt at correction was, manifestly, imperfectly carried out (the catchword not being changed), it is equally possible that only one half of the intended restoration was completed. Alternatively, the compositor may simply have omitted a half-line accidentally, his eye skipping from 'in' to 'ile', or his memory dropping a simple phrase (as happened at 20.156/2485 and 24.164/2947; see also Blayney, i. 572, 614, 628, for examples from other Okes books).

8.46–9.0.1/1520–1520.2   on . . . Enter] Q ('On him, hollow the other. *Exeunt.* | *Enter*' text); *Enter* (c.w.)
9.0.1/1520.2   *Storme.*] F (*Storme ſtill*); *not in* Q
9.2/1522   caterackes] F; caterickes Q
9.2/1522   Hiricanos] F; Hircanios Q
9.8   germens] QF (Germains)
9.8   spoil] QF (spill). *OED* notes that in this sense (= 'destroy, ruin') '*spoil* has taken the place of the earlier *spill*'.
9.16/1536   taxe] F; taske Q. See Q's press-correction at 4.327/821, where *attaskt* was substituted for what seems to have been copy *ataxt*.
9.35/1555   but] Qb; hut Qa
9.37.1/1557.1   *He sits*] This edition; *not in* QF. It seems unlikely that Lear speaks his first two speeches sitting down; the reference to *patience* would be a natural cue for such action (compare 'She sate like Patience on a Monument', *Twelfth Night* 2.4.114/975).
9.44/1564   wanderers] F; wanderer Q
9.54/1574   simular man] Q; Simular F. Because *simular* could be used as adjective or noun, either text makes sense; metrical emendation seems unwarranted, because *simular* is also treated as a disyllable at *Cymbeline* 5.6.201/3007.
9.54   simular] This might be modernized to *similar* which is first recorded in 1611, and Shakespeare (*Lear* and *Cymbeline*) is the last *OED* citation of *simular* till Cowper and other Romantic Shakespeare-influenced uses.
9.58/1578   concealed centers] Q; concealing Continents F. Blayney adopts F on metrical grounds, conjecturing that the compositor could not make out the second word and deliberately altered the first to accord with his own guess. But Q makes sense, and the metre is acceptable if we divide the speech's last three lines as Q rather than F does.
9.60/1580   then] F; their Q
9.66/1586   you] F; me Q
9.72/1592   your] F; you Q
9.75   tiny] Q (tine). See *Twelfth Night* 5.1.385/2484.
10.3/1602   tooke] Q2, F; tooke me Q1
10.25/1623   The] F; the |
11.0.1/1623.1   *Storme.*] CAPELL; *not in* Q; *Storme ſtill* F (*after* 'indure', *line* 11.3/1626)
11.2/1625   The] Qb (the); the | the Qa. Q sets this speech as prose.
11.4/1627   here] F; *not in* Q
11.6/1629   contentious] F; crulentious Qa; tempeſtious Qb
11.10/1633   roring] Qb, F; raging Qa, Q2
11.12/1635   this] Qb; the Qa, Q2, F
11.14/1637   beates] Qb, F; beares Qa, Q2
11.18/1641   In such a night as this!] Q; in ſuch a night, | To ſhut me out? Poure on, I will endure: | In ſuch a night as this? F. Blayney cites this as an example of variants in which 'it is reasonably evident' that Q is wrong, and indeed eyeskip is an obvious possibility here. But Honigmann (pp. 169–70) shows that Shakespearian interpolations often end with echoes of the point at which they began; moreover, the first 'in such a night' occurs at the end of a verse line, the second at the beginning, which reduces (while not eliminating) the probability of eyeskip. Q of course makes sense as it stands. Metrically, the last four lines of the speech require relineation, but in a text so badly aligned as Q this hardly justifies suspicion of corruption; nor does the fact that Q leaves the passage with one unassimilated part-line in mid-speech (a licence which occurs elsewhere). The metrical irregularity *might* result from textual error; equally, though, it *might* have stimulated textual revision. Since our own examination of F's textual history gives us no reason to believe that Shakespeare, when revising, had ready access to his own original manuscript, it seems to us more likely that F is an authorial expansion, than the restoration of words originally included in Shakespeare's foul papers.

11.22   own] Q (one)
11.24.1/1647.1   *Exit Foole*] BLAYNEY; *not in* Q. F adds two lines here; the Foole exits during them. Q gives no clear signal for the exit; it might come after 'Prethe goe in thy selfe' (11.22/1645) or at the end of Lear's speech.
11.37/1660   A spirit,] Q; A ſpirite, a ſpirite, F. Blayney adopts F, assuming that the Foole (uncharacteristically) should speak an iambic pentameter here.
11.39.1/1662.1   *Enter . . . begger*] THEOBALD; *not in* Q. F calls for Edgar to enter with the Fool, at 11.33.1/1656.1.
11.46/1669   fire] Q. Stone's conjecture 'firth' (p. 180) is attractive, but see *Dream* 2.1.5/360, where the spirit wanders 'Thorough flood, thorough fire'.
11.52/1676   starre-blasting] F; ſtarre-bluſting Q
11.54–5/1678   there, and] Q2; there, and | and Q1
11.56/1679   has his] F2; his Q; Ha's F1. F1's error seems more likely to arise from miscorrection of Q copy than from entirely independent error.
11.72/1695   word] POPE; words Q
11.90/1713   no nonny] F; no on ny Q. Blayney reports that 'in some copies there are traces between "no" and "on" which could be the remains of a badly damaged "n"'.
11.90/1713   Dolphin] QF. This might be modernized to 'Dauphin', of which it would be a common spelling; but the animal seems more relevant here than the title. Only the King of France could call the Dauphin 'my boy'. (But see textual notes to *Tragedy*.)
11.90/1713   cease,] Q2; caeſe, Q1; Seſey: F. Blayney argues convincingly that nonsense is unlikely here. (See textual notes to *Tragedy*, also.)
11.99/1722   lendings] Qb; leadings Qa
11.99/1722   on bee true.] Qa; on, Qb; vn-|button heere. F. Qb cannot represent the manuscript reading, and since it appears to result from failure to complete a directed alteration, there is some temptation to adopt F. However, (*a*) there is no indication that 'heere' stood in Q's copy; (*b*) if 'vnbutton' were the intended correction, then 'on' should also have been deleted; (*c*) the uncorrected reading makes local and contextual sense. Even if the press-corrector did consult the manuscript, and deciphered it more successfully than the compositor had, we have no way of knowing what he found there, and 'vnbutton heere' would hardly recommend itself as a palaeographically plausible conjecture, if it did not stand in F. At *Hamlet* 1.3.75/488 Q2 has 'boy' for F 'be'; the reverse error might have occurred here ('boie ⇨ bee' or 'boy ⇨ bee'), especially since the Fool (whom Lear often calls 'boy') speaks immediately afterwards. At *Romeo* 2.1.13/744 Q2 has 'true' for the 'trim' of Q1, accepted by almost all modern editors, and *trim* would have several appropriate senses here. It could be understood adverbially (= 'trimly, neatly, sprucely', as at *Romeo* 2.1.13/744, *OED adv.* 1, 2; as Schmidt says, most of Shakespeare's uses of adverb and adjective are ironic, as *trim* would be here), or as a substantive exclamation, in apposition to the clothes Lear is removing (= 'ornaments? decoration?'), or even as an imperative (= 'trim me of these superfluities, deck me out by undressing me'). Even if we assume that Qa's 'bee true' was a simple misreading, possible emendations are many—and the error may not have been entirely palaeographical.
11.102/1725   ons] F; in Q
11.103.1/1726.1   *with a ⌈torch⌉*] F; *not in* Q. Shakespeare might have written 'lanterne' (or 'lanthorne') as he does in *Romeo* (Q2) and *1 Henry IV* (Q1), but *torch* occurs more frequently and could be used of a lamp (*OED*, *sb.* 1).

11.104/1727 fliberdegibet] F; Sriberdegibit Qa; fliberdegibek Qb
11.105/1728 giues] Qb; gins Qa
11.106/1729 & the] Qb; the Qa
11.106/1729 pin, squenies] DUTHIE (Greg); pin-|queues Qa; pin, | ſquemes Qb; Pin, ſquints F
11.106/1729 hare] Qb; harte Qa
11.109/1732 Swithune] This edition (*after* TATE); ſwithald Q; *Swithold* F. This name has provoked much commentary but little scholarship. Theobald noted the only parallel yet discovered, 'Sweete S. *Withold* of thy lenitie, defend vs from extremities' (*Troublesome Reign*, 1184). On the basis of this he emended F to 'S. *Withold*'. This is a reasonable and attractive emendation, only weakened by the fact that nothing whatever is known of this figure invoked by the friar in *Troublesome Reign*. Tyrwhitt suggested that 'Withold' was a corruption of 'Vitalis', and this has since been repeated as though it were a fact, but no evidence has ever been offered for this rather unlikely derivation, and Tyrwhitt himself conceded that nothing in the life of Vitalis (an unremarkable Bolognese martyr of the third century) suggested any link with Shakespeare's rhyme. Wright asserted that Vitalis 'was apparently involved in cases of nightmare or incubus', but the only evidence for this is *Lear* itself. W. J. Craig repeated Wright's assertion and added (again without evidence) that 'Swithold' itself was 'probably a corruption of Saint Vitalis'; Duthie repeats this, adding that the corruption was 'current' and citing Craig as evidence, and on this basis retains F. But although 'Vitalis' might conceivably (though improbably) have been corrupted in pronunciation to 'Withold', it is impossible to believe that the written abbreviation 'S.' for 'Saint' led to the fusion of 'Saint Vitalis' into 'Swithold'.

An altogether likelier identification was provided by, of all people, Nahum Tate, who in his adaptation altered the name to 'Swithin'. Swithun (also spelled 'Swithin') was a popular early English saint, famous for healing, and prominently associated with rain; his appropriateness in Edgar's rhyme is obvious. Warburton quoted a similar charm addressed to 'Saint George', and Swithun shares with Saint George the key elements of popularity and the historical environment of early Christian Britain. Moreover, Swithun could be alluded to (and in this case would have to be) without explicitly *calling* him 'Saint', an anachronism which cannot be avoided if we accept Theobald's interpretation ('S. Withold'). Finally, 'ſwithune' could have been misread as Q's 'ſwithald', a/u and l/minim misreadings being common enough in Shakespeare texts. Greg (*Aspects*, p. 166) thought that F's change to 'Swithold' was 'probably accidental' and pointed out that it created a not-necessarily-desirable anticipation of the syllable 'old' at the end of the line; in fact, the compositor might have accidentally set 'Swithold' under the influence of 'old'. It might also have occurred accidentally through association of Q's peculiar word with the 'Saint Withold' alluded to in *Troublesome Reign*. F's reading could thus easily derive from Q's, without deliberate alteration by the annotator. F capitalizes the word simply because it begins a verse line, and italicizes it because it is clearly in context a name; both modifications would normally have been the compositor's responsibility, and need not have required an annotator's attention.

One hesitates to emend Shakespeare on the guidance of Tate, since it is always possible that Tate merely simplified Shakespeare. However, 'ſwithald' can only be defended as a completely fictitious name, whereas everything else in Poor Tom's patter has a referent. The Q compositor at this point clearly had no idea what he was setting ('swithald footed thrice the old a nellthu night more'), and it is hardly surprising that he should fail to recognize the name. And if one must emend, 'Swithun' seems a more appropriate name, and a more plausible emendation, than 'S. Withold'.
11.109 wold] QF (old)
11.110/1733 A] Qa (a); he Qb. (Q aligns as prose.)
11.110/1733 mett the] met the Qb; nellthu Qa
11.110/1733 mare] Qb; more Qa
11.110 foal] QF (fold). See textual notes to F.

11.111/1734 her, a light] F; her, O light Q
11.113/1736 arint . . . arint] Q; aroynt . . . aroynt F. Blayney adopts F's spelling, but Hulme has found 'bid me arent the wich' in a Stratford court record (p. 17), so there seems no reason to emend Q's spelling in favour of that preserved in two late transcripts (F *Lear* and F *Macbeth*, 1.3.5/83).
11.113/1736 witch] Qb; with Qa
11.118/1741 tode pole] tod pole Qb, F; tode pold Qa, Q2. Though the correction of 'pold' to 'pole' is necessary, the word's first element was often spelled in the same ways as 'toad' (which is what it means), and hence need not be corrected to 'tod' (for which *OED* offers no parallels). The corrector presumably wanted the modern form 'tad', but only half of his alteration was carried out.
11.118/1741 wall-neut] Qb (newt), F (Neut); wall-wort Qa, Q2
11.128/1751 smolking] This edition; ſnulbug Q; *Smulkin* F; *Smulking* BLAYNEY. Blayney seems right in arguing that the final 'g' was probably in Q's copy, but if one accepts that Shakespeare was thinking of Harsnet's devil 'Smolkin' (the only reason for emending Q at all), then one might as well emend the first vowel to 'o'. F's spelling could be the result of incomplete correction, or might have been influenced by unconscious association with the noun *smulkin* (*OED*, 1571-1617).
11.132/1754 mahu] F; ma hu Q. Harsnet has 'Maho'.
11.148/1770 him] Q; him once more F
1783-4 him, | I wil keep stil,] F; him, ~, Q
11.167/1789 towre] F; towne Q
12.12/1803 were not] F; were Q
13.5/1821 deserne] This edition (*conj.* Stone); deſerue Q; reward F. Compare 16.51/2157.
13.5.1/1821.1 *Exit Gloster*] CAPELL; *not in* Q; *after* 13.3/1819 *in* F (*Exit*)
13.6/1822 Fratereto] F; Fretereto Q. Harsnet spells the name with an 'a', and 'little brother' seems more pertinent to Edgar and the play than 'little corrosive' (*OED fretter, sb.*¹).
13.12 hissing] Q1 (hiſzing), Q2 (hissing), F (hizzing). Q1's spelling could be due to a ligature shortage.
13.15/1831 health] Q; heels SINGER 2 (Warburton)
13.17/1833 Iusticer] THEOBALD; Iuſtice Q. See 13.51/1867 and the press-variant at 16.78/2174.
13.19-20/1835-6 wantst thou eyes, at trol madam,] This edition; wanſt thou eyes, at | tral madam, Q1; wantſt thou eies at tri-|all madam, Q2. See *Division*, 486-8.
13.21/1837 boorne] CAPELL; broome Q
13.21 burn] CAPELL (boorne)
13.30 cushions] Q (cuſhings)
13.31/1847 the] POPE; their Q. Wright first suggested that 'their evidence' means 'the evidence against them'; Furness endorsed this, and all subsequent editors merely repeat it. But no one has provided parallels for the alleged idiom; *OED* shows that use of the possessive, or of constructions with *of* or *from*, indicate the source of testimony, not its object; *the* and *their* are often confused by scribes and compositors in this period, and in this case 'their' could easily result from contamination by the preceding phrase.
13.32, 33, 34/1848, 1849, 1850 *To Edgar . . . To Foole . . . to Kent*] CAPELL; *not in* Q
13.32 robed] Q (robbed)
13.34/1850 ot'h] Q; of the HANMER. The line is tightly justified in Q, with no possibility of turning up or down.
13.43/1859 she] Q2, BL2; *not in* Q1
13.47 join-stool] Q (ioyne ſtoole)
13.49 on] Q (an)
13.62/1877 mungril,] ROWE; ~, QF
13.62-3/1877-8 grim, | Hoūd] F; grim-hoūd Q (*setting the speech as prose*)
13.63/1878 him] Q; Hym F; lym HANMER. Blayney convincingly discredits Hanmer's emendation (usually accepted).
13.88/1903 take vp take vp] F; Take vp to keepe Qa; Take vp the King Qb. F seems much likelier than Qb to be misread as 'to keepe'.
14.6/1929 reuenges] F; reuenge Q

14.8/1931 festinat] F2; feſtuant Q; feſtiuate F1. Stone (p. 182) conjectures 'feſtinant' (after BL2 'feſtiuant'), saying this is 'no more or less of a coinage than *festinate*'. But Shakespeare used 'festinately' at *LLL* 3.1.5/741, *festinate* as a verb occurs in Nashe's *Have With You to Saffron Walden* (3.91.8), and *festination* dates from 1540, whereas *festinance* and *festinancy*, cited by Stone, are first recorded in 1730 and 1660. The F2 reading (which F1 was clearly aiming at) presumes that the Q1 compositor saw one minim too many, where Stone presumes that he saw one too few; palaeographically there is nothing to choose between them.

14.9/1932 posts] F; poſt Q. Omission of the 's' would be particularly easy for a compositor carrying 'posts shall' in his head, and it seems odd for Cornwall to imply that they have only one messenger, who will be kept busy going back and forth.

14.15/1938 questants] This edition; queſtrits Q; queſtriſts F. See *Division*, 488.

14.23/1946 we] Q; well we F. Though Q could easily have omitted 'well' by eyeskip (as Blayney suggests), metrical emendation is unnecessary, since a defective initial foot is acceptable, especially (as here) where it could form a part of a line-divided foot (before us, | Though *we* may . . .).

14.56/1979 anoynted] Qb (annoynted), F; aurynted Qa

14.57/1980 as] F; of Qa; on Qb

14.57/1980 bowd] BLAYNEY (Greg); lou'd Qa; lowd Qb

14.58/1981 boyd] F; layd Qa; bod Qb

14.59/1982 stelled] Qb, F; ſteeled Qa, Q2

14.60/1983 holpt] Q; holpe F. Blayney suspects that Q may be an eccentric Shakespearian portmanteau of *holpe* and *helpt*; but the form also occurs in Dekker and Middleton's *1 Honest Whore* 1.5.193 ('holp't').

14.61/1984 hould] F; heard Q

14.63/1986 cruels ile subscribe] This edition (*conj.* Stone); cruels elſe ſubſcrib'd Q; Cruels elſe ſubſcribe F; cruel ſelfe ſubſcrib'd BLAYNEY. Defences of either text as it stands require strained and unparalleled paraphrases of *subscribe(d)* as 'yield to compassion on occasion' or 'yield to feelings of compassion under strong provocation' or 'set aside, leave out of consideration'. Either 'ſubſcrib'd' or 'ſubſcribe' could be an error for the other, but the real problem seems to lie elsewhere. Stone's conjecture was based on the assumption that Q's 'elſe' was a phonetic error, though he admits that 'it is odd to find a comparatively elaborate word such as "else" emerging from [phonetic] confusion' (p. 197). But misreading of terminal 's' as 'e' is common, and though i/e misreadings are not, under the influence of the preceding word (ending '-els') a compositor might have misread 'ile' as 'els'. Stone assumes that the entire phrase belongs to the following sentence ('All cruel people or creatures I am, if necessary, willing to countenance, but come what may I shall see the winged vengeance . . .'). However, the *else* which Stone has removed seems necessary to his interpretation ('I shall countenance all *other* cruel creatures, but . . .'), and the resulting gloss is as strained as those it replaces. The phrase makes better sense as a continuation of Regan's hypothetical speech to her porter: 'Good porter, turn the key; all cruel creatures I will countenance, accept' or 'Good porter, turn the key; all cruel actions I surrender, give up, renounce'. The very ambiguity of the phrase then becomes an asset, and the verb *subscribe* can take its usual senses, without resort to involutions of paraphrase.

14.71/1994 you] Q2, F; *not in* Q1

14.75/1998 to Cornwall] This edition; *not in* QF. Furness suggested the rest of the line should be spoken by Cornwall; Kittredge (following Craig) assigned it to Regan.

14.80/2003 Regan stabs him again] This edition; *not in* QF

14.81.1/2004.1 He . . . eye] This edition; *Treads out the other Eye* ROWE; *Dashing Gloster's other Eye to the Ground* CAPELL

14.84/2007 enkindle] F; vnbridle Q. See *Division*, p. 456.

14.85 quite] Q (quit)

14.95/2018 Exit one or more with Gloster] BLAYNEY (*Exit a ſeruant . . .*); *not in* Q; *Exit with Glouſter* F (*after* 'Douer', 14.92/2015)

14.95/2018 and the body] This edition; *not in* QF

14.97/2020 2] CAPELL; *not in* Q

14.98, 104/2021, 2027 3] CAPELL; 2 Q

14.101/2024 2] CAPELL; 1 Q

14.102/2025 rogish] Qa; *not in* Qb. For a conjectural explanation of Qb's omission (not entirely convincing), see Blayney, i. 249-50.

15.2/2030 flattered, to be worst,] POPE (*subs.*); ~ˬ ~ , Q

15.4/2032 esperance] F; experience Q. Duthie conjectures that Q's copy may have had 'eſperence', but this spelling is not recorded; it seems likelier that the compositor misinterpreted his copy as 'experiance' (which is recorded) and normalized the spelling.

15.7/2035 partie,eyd] Qb (parti,eyd); poorlie, leed Qa; poorelie,ˬ led Q2, F. F was clearly influenced, at some stage in its transmission, by the uncorrected state of inner H, so its concurrence with Qa need have no authority. Qb offers the *difficilior lectio*, and must result from consultation of copy. Qa's 'poorlie, leed' could have arisen from misreading of 'partie, eyd' as 'porlie, led', followed by dittography of 'e' in the second word. Commas as hyphens occur elsewhere in Shakespearian foul-paper texts. For the presumed copy spelling, see *LLL* 2724 (partie coted).

15.8/2036 hate] QF; hold A. WALKER (*conj.*; see Muir)

15.9/2037 Edgar stands aside] This edition; *not in* QF. Clearly the Old Man does not see Edgar until 15.22/2050; whether Edgar hears the intervening dialogue may be debated.

15.15/2043 sir,] Q; sir, but This edition *conj.*

15.35/2063 to] F; are toth' Q. Q is unmetrical and, in supplying an article before *wanton boys*, unidiomatic: compare *All Is True* 3.2.360/1853 ('like little wanton Boyes') and *Kinsmen* 5.2.18/2302 ('like wanton Boyes'). Compositorial assimilation to the second half of the line would be easy.

15.36/2064 kill] F; bitt Q

15.37/2065 that must play foole] F; that muſt play the | foole Q; must play the fool POPE

15.38/2066 He comes forward] This edition; *not in* QF. See 15.9/2037.

15.41/2069 hence] F; here Q

15.55 thee] Q (the)

15.57/2085 as . . . lust,] HUDSON (W. S. Walker); Of luſt, as *Obidicut*, Q

15.57/2086 Hobbididence] Q; Hoberdidance MUIR; *Hobbididdance* CAPELL. Muir emends to Harsnet's form, but leaves Q '*Obidicut*' (Harsnet 'Hoberdicut'). If one modified name is here acceptable, both surely are, and the proposed er/i misreading is not likely. Capell's emendation of the suffix only (-ence/-ance) is more attractive.

15.59/2087 fliberdigebit] POPE (*Flibbertigibbet*); *Stiberdigebit* Q. The error suggests that the initial capital is compositorial in origin. See next notes.

15.59/2087 moking,] DUTHIE (1961); Mobing, Q (*arranging as verse*); mopping THEOBALD

15.59/2087 mowing] THEOBALD; *Mohing* Q; mouthing BLAYNEY (*conj.*). This error suggests that the initial capitals and italics in the preceding names are all compositorial.

15.68/2096 vndoe] F; vnder Q

15.72/2100 sawcely] This edition; firmely Q; fearfully F. See *Division*, 457.

16.10/2116 defie] This edition (*conj.* Stone); deſire Q; diſlike F. Substitution of antonyms is a rare compositorial error, and 'desire' is not the most obvious antonym to 'dislike'. This usage of *defy* (= reject, disdain, regard with contempt or defiance) is well-attested and Shakespearian.

16.12/2118 cowish] QF; curriſh BLAYNEY. 'Quarrelsome, malicious' seems less apt a description of 'milk-livered' Albany than 'cowish' (which is also the rarer word).

16.12/2118 terrer] Qb, F; curre Qa, Q2; tenor STONE (*conj.*). Stone objects that *terror* 'seems too strong a word'; but Gonoril is not given to understatement. Shakespeare never elsewhere uses *tenor* in the sense required here ('typical procedure', 'character, nature'), though these meanings were available (*OED*, *sb.*¹ 2b, 3b); palaeographically, Qb's 'terrer' is an easier emendation of

16.15/2121 *Edmund*] Q2, F; *Edgar* Q1
16.21/2127 comand] command Qb, F; coward Qa, Q2
16.26/2132 *Exit Bastard*] ROWE; not in Q; *Exit* F (*after preceding line*)
16.27/2133 a] Qb; not in Qa
16.28/2134 My foote vſurps my body] Qa; A foole vſurps my bed Qb; My Foole vſurpes my body F. Thomas Clayton has defended Qa by reference to two commonplaces of Renaissance thought: the husband as his wife's 'head', and the notion of a 'body politic': Albany, who should be Gonoril's head, is no more than a foot, and usurps a place of which he is unworthy ('Old Light on the Text of *King Lear*', *Modern Philology*, 78 (1981), 347-67). One might add that the line has an ironic secondary meaning of which Gonoril is unaware: in its slang sexual sense *foot* (= French *foutre*, 'to fuck') suggests that Gonoril has allowed her sexual organs to dominate her body entirely (and unnaturally). The press-corrector, not understanding the line, made what sense of it he could. Qb seems unlikely to have stood in the copy: the compositor would have had to misread 'foole' as 'foote' (easy), substitute 'My' for 'A' by contamination from 'my' later in the line (possible) and misread '-ed' as '-ody' (unlikely). Even if these errors were individually more plausible than they are, collectively they impose some strain on the imagination.
16.29/2135 whiſtling] Qb; whiftle Qa
16.32/2138 it] Qa; ith Qb; its Q3. Qb is probably a miscorrection, and the corrector might have intended Q3's 'its' (though 'h' and 's' are not normally confused). But even if we could be sure of this intention, it might be a printer's modernization, not a reflection of Shakespeare's manuscript.
16.44/2150 benifacted] This edition; benifliƈted Qa; benifited Qb. See Taylor, 'Four New Readings'.
16.46/2152 this] Qb; the Qa. Greg suggests 'that the corrector wrote "thes" (for *these*) and that "this" is a misprint' (*Variants*, p. 173). But the corrector need only have added 's' to Qa; the preceding 'e' need not have been touched, by corrector or compositor. The corrector may have added 'is', intending 'theis', but misunderstood by the compositor; but the spelling 'theis' never occurs elsewhere in Q, and would seem rather extravagant in so tight a line. Since 'this' is a recorded 15th-17th-c. spelling of 'these', probably used elsewhere by Shakespeare (see below), it seems safest to accept Qb as a restoration of the manuscript. The Qa reading could result from compositorial substitution, or an unfulfilled intention to set 'thes'.
16.46 these] Qb (this)
16.48/2154 Humanity] Qb; Humanly Qa
16.51/2157 deſerning] F; deſeruing Q
16.55/2161 noyſles] Qb (noyſeles); noyſtles Qa. Greg (*Variants*, p. 174) is right in saying that 'confusion of "ft" and "ſe" is very easy in many secretary hands', but since Qa uses an ft ligature, 'noyſtles' cannot be a typographical error for 'noyſeles'. It could, however, be a foul-case error for 'noyſles'; the press-corrector, when correcting the error, also called for a change in the spelling.
16.56/2162 flaxen begin threats] This edition; thy flayer begin threats Qa; thy ſtate begins thereat Qb; thy state begins to threat JENNENS; thy ſlyre biggin threats STONE (*conj*.). For a full discussion see *Division*, 488. For the derisive use of *biggin*, compare 'a filthy, course biggin' (worn by an old usurer) in Nashe's *Pierce Penilesse*, A3ᵛ (McKerrow, i. 162), and—even more relevant—'take my helmet: giue your mistris my night-cap. Are my Antlers swolne so big, that my biggen pinches my browes' (Dekker and Webster, *Westward Ho*, 2.1.14-15). At *Satiromastix* 5.2.238—a 'Biggin' instead of a crown for Horace—the object is clearly derisory, as it is again in Massinger's references to a man forced to wear 'an ould womans biggen for a night cap' (*The Picture*, 4.2.127), and to a soldier forced to transform 'my hat to double clouts and biggins' (*Unnatural Combat* 4.2.127). See also *Volpone* 5.9.5, and Herford and Simpson's note (ix. 731). For *flaxen* see Dekker's *Blurt Master Constable* (ed. Berger), 2.2.121-2, 'Flaxen hayr'd men are such pulers, and such pidlers, and such Chicken-heartes'.

16.56 biggin] Qa (begin). See *OED*.
16.59/2165 ſhewes] Qb; ſeemes Qa. Stone suggests that the manuscript spelling was 'sewes' (p. 184); but the Qa error could easily result from compositorial substitution rather than misreading. All other occurrences of the word in Shakespeare texts are spelt sh-.
16.64/2170 dislocate] Q3; difſecate Q1
16.67/2173 mew] Qb; now Qa
16.69/2175, etc. 2. GENTLEMAN] This edition; *Gen*. Q. See note at 8.0.1-2/1474.1.
16.75/2181 and amongst them] QF. Hanmer and Capell suspected corruption, and others have remarked on the failure to mention Regan. But see *Much Ado* 5.1.187/2252, 'you haue among you, kild a sweet and innocent lady', and *2 Henry IV* 5.4.16-17/3074-5, 'the man is dead that you and Pistoll beat amongst you'. These parallels suggest the gloss 'between them' (i.e. Cornwall and Regan together), though as it stands the referent for *them* depends less on grammar than on an audience's knowledge. Conceivably something has dropped out, but the agreement of Q and F, and their metrical regularity, argue against this.
16.78/2184 You] Qb (you); your Qa
16.78/2184 Iustisers] Qb; Iuſtices Qa, Q2, F
17.9/2211 Marshall] Q; Mareschal POPE. Though Pope's emendation is out of favour, Q could easily have omitted a single *e*, or have adopted its own preferred spelling of a word in what the compositor regarded as prose. OED notes that *mereshall* and *marishal* were both correct spellings in the period; the latter at least (like *marischal* and *meriscall*) strongly suggests trisyllabic punctuation.
17.9 Maréchal] Q (Marſhall). See preceding note, and *1 Henry VI* 4.7.70/2087.
17.12/2214 sir] THEOBALD; ſay Q
17.17/2219 ſtroue] BL2, POPE; ſtreme Q
17.21/2223 seemd] POPE; ſeeme Q
17.29/2231 night,] Q1; ~? Q2. See next note.
17.30/2232 Let pietie not be beleeft] This edition; Let pitie not be beleeft Q1; Let pity ne'er believe it POPE. Q2's 'beleeu'd' is merely a modernized spelling of Q1's 'beleeft'. As Blayney points out, Pope's 'believe it', followed by Jennens and others (without emending 'not'), is unlikely, since the verbal form 'beleef'- is not recorded except in the spelling of the past participle. Stone (p. 184) conjectures 'beleft', the past tense of *beleave* = 'abandon'; but Shakespeare never uses the word, and *OED*'s last accurate example occurs in 1557. (The example quoted from Thomas May's 1631 translation of Lucan's *Pharsalia*—'Wondering at fortune's turns, and scarce is he | Beleft, relating his own misery'—in context clearly means 'believed', and so belongs—where it is in fact also found—among examples of the past participle of *believe*: *OED*, v. 5).

Blayney also demonstrates that Q1's line is accidentally indented—presumably because of the loss of a type (visible or invisible) somewhere in the line. However, his own conjecture—'Left pitie not be beleeft,'—does not account for, and cannot be explained by, the apparent accident, since (as he says) 'an ink-ball cannot pull the "l" from an "ft" ligature'. Nor is the proposed error easy to explain on other grounds; though he offers two other quarto errors as parallels ('not' at uncorrected 7.149/1156, and 'queſtrits' at 14.15/1938), in both cases we disagree with his diagnosis of the error involved (see above). Although the emendation makes communicable sense of the line, it requires the Gentleman to supply a debatable motive for Cordelia's action, and to shift out of reported speech without any transition (such as is supplied, later in the line, by 'there'). It also leaves the line metrically anomalous.

Our own conjecture—'pietie' for 'pitie'—explains/is explained by Q's missing type; even without this anomaly, a missing type, or misreading of 'pietie' as 'pitie', would easily account for the proposed error. The emendation also produces metrical regularity in the first half of the line and (like Pope's) assumes a strong caesura, which makes the extra stressed syllable 'there' more acceptable. *Piety* also provides a sense as good as, and arguably better than, *pity*. Lear could have been *pitied* by anyone; but Cordelia's insistence on 'father . . . sisters, sisters . . . sisters . . . father, sisters' indicates that what most disturbs and dismays her is the violation of familial decorum. *Piety* could itself mean 'pity' (*OED*, *sb.* 1, last example 1606); but it had the more usual sense 'faithfulness to the duties naturally owed to parents and relations, superiors . . . affectionate loyalty and respect, esp. to parents' (*OED*, *sb.* 3).

Blayney objects that 'let pity not be believed' is a sentiment hardly appropriate to Cordelia, and the same objection could be made to our own emendation. But this objection loses its force if we accept Q1's punctuation of the preceding line, understanding 'What, not to let piety be heeded, even in the storm, the night?' (Alternatively, 'do not believe that filial piety exists [if this is true]'.)

As elsewhere in this scene, Quarto Compositor C apparently omits a strong stop required in mid-line; this presumably reflects the manuscript. In the modern-spelling edition we have added the query only for intelligibility's sake.

17.30 believed] Q (beleeft)

17.32/2234 maystered] This edition (*conj.* Stone); moyftened her Q. Q is defensible, if we understand 'clamour' vaguely as 'grief'; but *clamour* elsewhere always suggests noise of some sort, here particularly the outcries of grief. It seems odd to say that 'exclamations of grief moistened' anything (it grotesquely suggests spitting), especially when the most natural interpretation of the Gentleman's speech is that he describes a sequence of events: cries, then 'there she shooke', 'then away she started'. The outcries can hardly have moistened Cordelia, if they precede rather than coexist with the action described in this sentence. Moreover, though one might accept without cavil 'grief moistened her cheeks', the idea that 'grief moistened her' conjures up an unfortunately ridiculous image. Q is also metrically irregular, and though an extra stressed syllable after the caesura has to be accepted above, the occurrence of the same unusual licence twice within three lines is highly irregular.

Most modern editors follow Capell in omitting 'her' and understanding 'She first raised a clamour and then moistened the clamour—i.e. her outcry . . . was succeeded by tears' (Duthie, p. 409). This interpretation has the further advantage of suggesting the common Shakespearian image of tears as 'raindrops' which 'lay the wind' of sighs, or exclamations of grief; it also makes the line metrical. The compositor's alleged interpolation of 'her' has been explained as a contamination from the preceding line, or an unconscious (or deliberate) provision of a direct object for 'moystened'. It might also result from misreading: 'her' and 'then' are readily confused, and 'her, then' could result from a conflation of two guesses (one the proof-corrector's, perhaps) as to the interpretation of one word in the copy.

We might therefore conclude, with most editors, that (*a*) 'her' should probably be omitted, and (*b*) 'clamour' is a direct object, and refers to Cordelia's earlier outcries. But the line still creates problems: it assumes that Cordelia first cried out, then wept, then left. But the two preceding speeches have already described for us, at length, Cordelia weeping; it seems absurd to suggest that she only now wept, and thus quelled her outcries with tears. Since the Gentleman goes on to describe her leaving the room, in order 'To deale with griefe alone', it seems more natural to suppose that she here *stops* weeping, as she *stops* crying out. The difficulty of interpretation here is created by the ambiguity of 'shooke . . . from her . . . eyes': this could mean that she sprinkled tears from her eyes; or that she brusquely dislodged or removed or cast out the tears from them. Cordelia's tears are elsewhere described as guests 'in' her eyes, which 'parted' from them and 'trild' down her cheeks, as 'patience' strove with her sorrow; the motion suggested by 'shooke . . . from' seems to us more appropriate to the energetic effort (by shaking her head, or wiping her eyes) to stop her tears—followed by her equally energetic departure, and the resolution to 'deale with' her grief 'alone'.

We have therefore accepted Stone's palaeographically plausible conjecture 'mayftered' for 'moyftened'. Shakespeare uses the verb a number of times: see especially 'euery one can master a griefe, but he that has it' (*Much Ado* 3.2.26–7/1219–20).

18.2/2260 ract] This edition; vent Q; vext F. Q is unlikely as an error for F; for 'ract' see *Division*, 458.

18.3 fumitor] Q (femiter)

18.4/2262 bur-docks] HANMER; hor-docks Q; Hardokes F. A botanical and hence textual crux. Q and F probably represent the same word; authorial revision seems unlikely. Collier's interpretation of Q as 'hoar-docks', i.e. white docks, is seconded by Mats Rydén (*Shakespearean Plant Names: Identifications and Interpretations* (1978), 55–7); but this would have to be 'a word invented by Shakespeare', which seems unlikely in a list which must be immediately intelligible to an audience, and convey all the appropriate associations at once. Nor is 'hor' paralleled as a spelling of *hoar* (though it looks acceptable enough). Collier's interpretation therefore seems unlikely. R. Prior (*Popular Names of British Plants* (1879), p. 102) suggested that *Hardock* was simply another name for 'burdock'; Skeat rightly dismissed this as 'a wild guess' for which there is no evidence (Introduction to Fitzherbert's *Book of Husbandry* (1882), p. xxx). Drayton in the Eighth Eglog of *Idea The Shepheards Garland* (1593) mentions a plant 'Harlocke'; Drayton came from Warwickshire, and did not alter the word in the revised editions of 1606 and 1619. But his word keeps very different company from Shakespeare's, being mentioned along with 'sweete Cetywall, | The hony-suckle . . . The Lilly and the Lady-smocke', and collected by a maiden in May 'to deck her summer hall'. Wright found the names 'hardhake' and 'yardehok' in herbals, and thinks either could easily have been corrupted to the form(s) in *Lear*; but if the medial aspirate disappeared from either, its second syllable would be indistinguishable from the common (but here allegedly inappropriate) plant name 'dock'. Moreover, Q—which is closer to Shakespeare in its incidentals—by its hyphen identifies the word's second element as 'docks'. Skeat noted 'haudoddes' in Fitzherbert's 1534 herbal, but this seems palaeographically unlikely as the word beneath either Q or F.

Most modern editors retain F, modernizing to 'hardocks'; but 'dokes' is not recorded as a spelling of the common 'docks', and is probably a compositorial (or scribal) error. If Compositor B were working from manuscript, F's agreement with Q's error would be difficult to explain, for this is a species of error which Shakespeare *should* have corrected when transcribing Q1, and independent coincidental misreading by Q and F compositors seems unlikely. However, if B made use of annotated Q2 copy, the annotator might well have been puzzled by Q2's 'hor-docks', checked it against the manuscript, and corrected or miscorrected the Q2 word. Either the annotator, under Q2's influence, may have partly misinterpreted the manuscript, or the compositor (under the same influence) may have misinterpreted the correction. In any event, the use of annotated copy makes the variant form in F easier to understand.

The texts as they stand can only be interpreted as the name(s) of a plant otherwise never referred to in this way, about which in consequence nothing is known; the nature of the passage makes this seem unlikely. Hanmer's 'burdock', by contrast, would be immediately intelligible and entirely appropriate (see *OED*, and Frank McCombie, 'Garlands in *Hamlet* and *King Lear*', *N&Q* 226 (1981), 133); it could, moreover, very easily have been misread 'hor-dockes' or 'Hardo[c]kes'. We have therefore adopted it, as did most 18th- and 19th-c. editors.

18.6/2264 the centuries] This edition; a centurie is Q; A Centery F; Centuries BLAYNEY. Blayney plausibly suggests that Q's 'centurie is' results from a misreading of 'centuries'. None the less, it seems unlikely that the compositor interpolated 'a' (apart from the fact that this produces a less metrical line than Q). But substitution of *a* for *the*, and vice versa, is common.

18.6/2264 send] F; fent Q

18.8/2266 *Exit one or more*] *not in* QF. Since Cordelia later says

'seeke, seeke, for him' (18.19/2277), it is possible that no one leaves yet.
18.28/2286   insight] Q2 (infite), F; in fight Q1.
19.4/2292   L.] Lord F; Lady Q. F seems right; Q's error probably arose from abbreviation in the manuscript.
19.11/2299   edmund] F; and now Q. Blayney interprets Q's 'and now' as a continuation of 19.9/2297, enclosing 'It was . . . vs' in parentheses. Neither the construction nor the ambiguity is attractive, and 'mund' could have been misread 'nowe.'
19.15/2303   after] This edition; after him Q; after him, Madam, F. The compositor could easily have interpolated an object after 'after': the result is unmetrical in an otherwise metrical scene, and F's addition was probably intended as a replacement.
19.15/2303   letters Madam.] BLAYNEY; letters, Q1; Letters. Q2, F. All Oswald's other speeches in this scene address Regan as 'Madam' or 'Lady', and the omitted punctuation is also suspicious (Blayney). F adds the word earlier in the line.
19.27   I, madam?] F; Q (I Madam.)
20.0.1/2328.2   with a staff] This edition; not in QF. See below, second note to 20.233/2561.
20.2/2330   vp it now] F; it vpnow Q. Q's order is idiomatically possible (see Furness) but unmetrical; Blayney notes that Q's spacing error suggests that 'vp' was omitted in foul proofs, and then inserted in the wrong place.
20.39/2367   snuff] Q2; fnurff Q1
20.40/2368   blesse him] F; bleffe Q
20.42/2370   may] Q2, F; my Q1
20.53/2381   alenth] This edition (conj. Stone); at each QF. Stone's conjecture is better than Jervis's 'at length' (Proposed Emendations, 1860), a phrase which Shakespeare always elsewhere uses (12 times) to mean 'eventually'. Moreover, one need not suppose a 'complex error', as Stone does (p. 202), since 'lenth' is a well-attested spelling of length (OED); aural transmission need not be postulated. No one has provided any parallels for the alleged idiom in QF, which could easily arise from misreading.
20.57/2385   somnet] F; fommons Q; somnets STONE (conj., p. 185)
20.65/2393   how now,] This edition; how, Q; How is't? F. There is no reason 'is't' should have been omitted here; 'now', on the other hand, is a word frequently omitted in any event, and especially liable to homoeoteleuton here. (Compare Hamlet 5.1.182/3153, where F has 'how' for Q2 'now how'.) The emendation produces better metre and sense.
20.68/2396   begger] Q2, F; bagger Q1. Q1's error perhaps results from metathesis (though 'begger' is the usual spelling in this text).
20.78/2406   often would it] Q1; often 't would F. If the line were metrically regular in Q's copy, the compositor might have transposed 'would' and 'it' (assuming the elision was not indicated in the manuscript), or he might have substituted 'often' for copy 'oft' (as in Folio Dream 1.1.239/239).
20.80   Bear] Q1 (Bare,), F; Bare, Q2. OED records the 'bare' spelling from 14th-18th c.
20.81   ne'er] Q (neare)
20.91   Ha!] Q (hagh). See OED.
20.98/2427   saide,] BLAYNEY; ~, Q1; ~ : Q2, F. Blayney also accepts F's added 'that' after 'thing', but his chief reason for believing that the word stood in Q's copy is metrical, and the speech seems prose to us.
20.98, 102   to] Q1 (toe), Q2 (too)
20.103/2432   ague-proofe] F; argue-proofe Q
20.105/2434   euery] Q2, F; euer Q1
20.108/2437   die] Q1; dye F. Metrically F's reading is preferable, and Q's error would be easy to account for; but metrical emendation of Lear's uncertain verse seems unsafe here.
20.110/2439   Dos] F (Do's); doe Q
20.116/2445   dos] F (do's); do Q
20.117/2446   To] F; not in Q
20.118/2447   The] F; to Q
20.130/2459   Shall] F; fhould Q
20.134   of't] Q (oft)
20.151   An] Q (And)

20.151/2480   cur,] Q1; ~ ? Q2; ~ : F
20.152-3/2481-2   dogges, obade] F; dogge, fo bade Q. See Blayney's palaeographical explanation of Q's reading, and Urkowitz's challenge to the assumption that it represents an aural error (pp. 132-3).
20.156/2485   Thy bloud as] This edition; thy bloud Q; thou F. The only objection to Q's phrase is metrical irregularity; F (though—like Q—setting the speech as prose) rectifies the metre. But it seems relatively unlikely that the Q compositor set 'thy bloud' for copy 'thou'. In the printed text of Q, 'thy bloudy' (20.154/2483) appears above and immediately to the left of 'thy bloud'; but if the manuscript was correctly aligned as verse, the two phrases should not have been juxtaposed. Moreover, the alleged contamination was only partial. It produces a sensible line, one which contrasts 'bloudy' (= violent) with 'thy bloud' (= 'your emotions', especially 'your sexual impulses'). This antithesis seems too pertinent to have resulted from an inherently unlikely error. Metrical acceptability can be achieved by less drastic means. As, like other short words, is often omitted: see LLL 3.1.13/748 (Q), Merchant 1.1.115/115 (F), Troilus 5.2.170/2996, Romeo 2.4.44/1314 (F), Hamlet 3.2.310/2039 (F), and Othello 3.3.136/1584 (Q). Shakespeare sometimes uses it without an expressed correlative (see Schmidt, i. 55); here, the implicit comparison could be either 'as hotly lusts as hers does' or 'as hotly lusts to use her as to whip her'. The resulting line is a regular hexameter, of which Q Lear contains dozens of examples.
20.158   tattered] Q (tottered)
20.161/2490   no teares now] This edition (conj. Blayney); no now Q; Now, now, now, now. F. Q and F print this speech as prose; modern editors follow Rowe in arranging it as verse. Blayney marks a lacuna, chiefly on metrical grounds. F's reading is metrically acceptable (regular except for a feminine caesura), but seems unlikely to lie behind Q: Q might easily have omitted one 'now', but it would be extravagant to conjecture that it omitted two, and at the same time set 'no' for the first 'now'. But though F may not restore the reading of Q's manuscript, we may give some weight to the facts (a) that F expands the phrase so that metrically it completes 20.161/2490, and cannot be the beginning of 20.162/2491, and (b) that F emends Q's sense as well as its metre. 'Now' is susceptible to idiomatic iteration, with various meanings: compare Thersites' 'Now the pledge, now, now, now' (Troilus 5.2.66/2892), or the Jailer's Daughter's 'Now, now, it beates upon it; now, now, now' (Kinsmen 3.4.7/1326; usually attributed to Fletcher, but containing several Lear echoes), or Fabian's 'Oh peace, peace, peace, now, now' (Twelfth Night 2.5.55/1040). Whether or not it relates to anything happening on stage, F's reading is intelligible and self-contained, as an exclamation, in a way Q's words (for which we have found no Shakespearian parallel) are not. Q's 'no now' is, in itself, meaningless, and the context gives no clue to any accompanying set of actions which might give it meaning. This is not the way Lear's mad speeches are written; elsewhere they give clear instructions to the actor on the sequence of Lear's thoughts and actions.

Blayney is thus probably correct in suspecting a lacuna. He considers three categories of solution to the crux. 'A verb such as "see" or "know" may have been lost from before Q's comma'; but any such addition would add nothing to the meaning of the preceding phrase, and leave 'no not' itself equally obscure (unless independently emended). 'Secondly, there may have been two words in copy where Q has only "no".' But none of his specific suggestions contributes anything to the context; all but 'now, now' leave the phrase obscure, and it (removing 'no' altogether) requires a double emendation. 'Thirdly, and to me most attractively, the copy may have had a phrase telling Gloster not to weep—"no grief now", "no tears now", "weep not now"—and thus preparing the ground for the beginning of Lear's next speech.' 'Weep not now' requires a double emendation, but the other two are equally plausible, and provide better sense than Q or the other alternatives; and of the two, 'tears' is distinctly preferable. It has a direct and specific physical relation to 'eyes', which are the subject of Lear's preceding sentence (and of much of the surrounding dialogue); it is itself an important, recurring word in *Lear* (4.278, 292, 13.55, 17.13, 19, 18.18, 27, 21.45, and 68/772, 786, 1871, 2215, 2221, 2276, 2285, 2650 and 2673); Lear on his next two appearances tells someone not to weep (21.68, 24.23-5/2673, 2806-8); and a similar injunction occurs at *Pericles* 13.39/1354 ('O no teares *Lycherida*, no teares'). *Grief* by contrast is abstract; is less frequent and less important in *Lear*; and is not used by Shakespeare in any similar imperative.

20.173/2502 shooe] F; ſhoot Q

20.174/2503 felt] F; fell Q

20.176/2505, etc. ⌜1.⌝ GENTLEMAN] This edition; Gent. QF. See 8.0.1-2/1474.1

20.177/2506 deere‸] Q1; deere Daughter— F. Blayney plausibly suggests that in Q 'daughter' should have been turned up or down, and so may have been omitted accidentally; but Q is acceptable as an interrupted sentence (as F must be, in any case).

20.184/2513 a man a man] F; a man Q

20.186/2515 ⌜1.⌝ GENTLEMAN Good Sir.] Q2 (*Gent.*); not in Q1. See *Division*, 363-4.

20.194/2523 speaking] This edition; ſpeaking of QF. For *speak* meaning 'tell, describe, express', see Schmidt and *OED*. The unmetrical 'of' thus adds nothing to the sense, and would be an easy compositorial interpolation in the circumstances.

20.199/2528 ought] Q; ought (Sir) F

20.204-5/2532-3 Neere . . . thoughts] As Stone remarks this speech 'is easily the most complex and baffling textual difficulty in the play' (p. 210). It is usually assumed that Q commits six errors in the space of 13 words; but F is not itself easy to understand, and some of the alleged errors in Q are difficult to explain. We have therefore discussed them all individually, at the same time relating proposed problems or solutions to the difficulties elsewhere.

20.204/2532 speedy foot] F; ſpeed fort Q1; ſpeed for't Q2. Q2 makes the only available sense out of Q1 as it stands; but, besides being unmetrical, the phrase 'on speed' has no Shakespearian parallels, and the 'it' no discernible meaning. There are several o/r misreadings in Q, and since Compositor C apparently preferred the spelling 'ſpeed' (see 20.198/2527 above) he might well have normalized what he saw as 'ſpeede'—either by overlooking a penultimate 'i', or misreading '-y' as '-e'. Compare *All's Well* 3.4.37/1487 ('will ſpeede her foote'), and *Cymbeline* 3.4.79/1541 ('foot' in error for 'for't').

In isolation 'ſpeeded' would be an easier emendation of Q1's 'ſpeed' (assuming simple haplography rather than misreading followed by normalization). But Shakespeare never elsewhere uses this past participle adjectivally, and *OED* records no parallels; moreover, if Compositor C realized that this word was 'speeded' (but simply mis-set it), then he would have been much less likely to misinterpret 'foot' as the nonsensical 'fort'.

20.204/2532 foot‸ the maine, deſcryers] This edition; fort‸ the maine‸ deſcryes, Q1; for't, the maine‸ deſcries, Q2; foot: the maine‸ deſcry‸ F. Q1's punctuation is almost certainly wrong: as often elsewhere, Compositor C has simply placed a comma at the end of the line, and no punctuation elsewhere, even though the sense-break occurs somewhere in the middle. Unless 'Standſt' in the next line is drastically emended, some subject for it is required here. So F is probably right in removing Q1's comma, and interpreting the last word of the line as a noun. This leaves two problems: what noun does Q's 'deſcryes' represent, and where should the new sentence begin?

F follows Q2 in breaking the line *before* 'the maine'; this gives a rather difficult modifier to what is (in F) a neologism (the use of *descry* as a noun). If the break were placed *after* 'the maine', the Gentleman could be understood to say 'the main part [of "the other army"] is near and on speedy foot': for the use of *main* adjectivally of a part of an army compare 'our main battle's front' (*Duke of York* 1.1.8/8) and 'the main battle' (*Richard III* 5.6.29/3344). In fact, a common gloss of the phrase as punctuated in F—'sight of the main part of the army is hourly expected' (Duthie)—assumes this interpretation of 'the maine',

so the only question is whether this sense fits more easily with the first or second part of the Gentleman's speech. Since the Gentleman knows where the other army is, and that it is travelling swiftly, it seems rather odd to suggest that the 'main part' of that army has not yet been sighted. One might gloss 'main' less specifically as 'principal', and further assume that 'the principal sighting' occurs when both armies come in full sight of one another; this seems the best sense that can be made of F, but it would not be an easy expression, even if the use of *descry* as a noun were not so unusual (the only other example *OED* lists is in Speed's 1611 *Chronicle of Great Britain*). Finally, for what it is worth, Shakespeare juxtaposes *the main* and *descry* in *Othello* (a play usually assumed to have been written not long before Quarto *Lear*, with which it has numerous verbal links); there, as proposed here, *the main* belongs to the preceding phrase: 'I cannot, twixt the heauen and *the main*, | *Descry* a sail'.

We have discussed the problem of punctuation first because it directly affects our approach to Q's 'deſcryes'. This word seems, on the face of it, unlikely to be correct. The use of a plural would make the neologism even more difficult to understand here; if we accept Q2-F's punctuation, 'the principal sightings' would have to mean 'the appearance of each army in full view of one another', which seems impossibly strained. If Q's plural is to be retained, we must apparently break the Gentleman's first sentence *after* 'main': in this case, Q might mean 'sightings (of the other army) occur hourly'. Whether the remainder of the sentence will bear this meaning remains to be seen; but if we do punctuate after rather than before 'the maine', F's singular noun has little attraction: after saying that the enemy's main army is near and approaching swiftly, the Gentleman would hardly continue 'sighting of it is hourly expected' (it must have been sighted already, in order for him to have such information), or 'sighting of it occurs hourly' (which says the same thing as Q, but uses a singular to *mean* a plural, where Q simply uses the plural).

If we accept the proposed repunctuation, F's reading loses its plausibility but Q's still faces two difficulties. First (as discussed below) Q's impossible 'Standſt' is most easily explicable if the copy had 'Stands'; however, as Blayney notes, the third person plural in *-s* is common in Shakespeare. But 'deſcryes | Stands' is still difficult: the unusual usage combined with a plural and an ambiguous verb form obscures the sense 'sightings occur'. In Speed ('Without danger of descry') and F ('the main descry') the syntax and the singular form make it clear enough that *descry* must be understood as a noun; 'descryes stands' is, by comparison, unnecessarily confusing.

We have here adopted the conjecture 'deſcryers' for Q's 'deſcryes'. *OED* records this word from 1599; because it existed already, and because agent-nouns formed by adding *-er* to a verb are in any case readily intelligible, *descryers* creates no difficulties of communication, and moreover has the advantage of transforming the abstract 'sightings' into the particular 'those who espy, scouts, spies'. As an emendation it also makes Q1's error easier to understand: rather than adding *-es* to a word for no particular reason, it assumes that Compositor C simply failed to set the intended *r*, or misread the unusual word as a familiar verb. (He clearly had no idea what the passage meant.)

This emendation has two further advantages. If we break the Gentleman's speech *after* 'the maine', then we would expect the second half of it to offer some contrast: *descryers* does just that. 'The main part (of their army) is nearby and rapidly approaching; (their) scouts and spies (already) demand our hourly attention'. The Gentleman's specification of 'the main' in F's punctuation is less apt, because 'the main' part of the army is what he and Edgar have all along been talking about. *Descryers* thus helps to explain the relationship between the two halves of the Gentleman's speech, and it also makes that speech serve a valuable function in the plot. For the next thing that happens in the scene, after the Gentleman's departure, is the entrance of a *descryer* from the enemy: Oswald.

20.205/2533 Stands] F; Standſt Q. Q's inflection must be wrong; even if a question were possible here, the Gentleman elsewhere addresses Edgar as 'you' (20.198/2527). The error is probably due to aural assimilation (*stands*[*t*] *on*); as such, it is easier to understand if the manuscript's word ended in 's'.

The only other explanation for Q's error is that 'ſt' should have been the beginning of the line's second word, rather than the end of its first; but this would require the further assumption that *on* or *on the* was a misreading for something else, and no attractive conjecture presents itself.

20.205/2533 on] QF. This preposition, apparently never questioned, creates much of the difficulty in understanding the whole sentence. *OED* gives no particular sense of the phrase *stand on* which seems appropriate to the usual glosses. It can mean 'insist on' (see Schmidt 7e(1), with many examples), but if we accept F's punctuation of the preceding line, 'the principal sighting' (which has not yet occurred) can hardly 'insist on the hourly thought(s)' except in a very strained sense. This gives us further reason for doubting that F's singular should be adopted here. Likewise, the obscurity of Q1's 'deſcryes' would be compounded by the need to interpret 'insist on' figuratively. But scouts and spies (their own, and the enemy's) *could* literally as well as figuratively 'insist on' hourly attention. Q's preposition here thus makes better sense with the emendation *descryers* than it does with either Q's 'descryes' or F's 'descry'.

Schmidt himself (accepting F's authority unquestionably in *Lear*) glosses 'stands on' as 'is on' (7e(6)). But in two of his other examples of this sense the meaning is clearly 'insist on' (*2 Henry IV* 4.1.163/2011, *Henry V* 3.6.75/1470; see Taylor's note on the latter, in the Oxford Shakespeare edition). The third (*Pericles* 16.32/1556-7: 'the sore tearmes we stand vpon with the gods') occurs in a text of dubious authority, and—like the two other examples—involves standing on *terms* or *conditions*. The *Lear* example bears no similarity to any of these, and Schmidt's paraphrase ('is to be expected every hour') reveals the extent to which he has been forced to recast the entire sentence.

If we read *descryers* in the previous line, *on* here can be understood with the verb *stand*; if we do not read *descryers*, then *on* must be related primarily to *thought(s)*. But 'on the thought(s)' is not a very natural locution, and Shakespeare elsewhere never uses the preposition *on* before *thought(s)*, except after the verb *tend* and *think*, where the preposition is idiomatically associated with the preceding verb rather than the following object. It is much more normal (there are dozens of Shakespearian examples) to speak of something being 'in the thought(s)'. In particular, compare *2 Henry IV* 5.2.31/2805 ('You stand in coldest expectation'), *Lear* 15.4/2032 ('stands still in esperance') and 18.23-4/2281-2 ('our preparation stands in expectation of them'). All three of these examples say what the Folio text is widely assumed to mean, and they express this meaning through the phrase 'stand in [expectation]'. We suspect that the Folio readings elsewhere in this speech only make sense if we emend 'on' to 'in' here, and interpret 'the hourly thought' to mean 'what is hourly expected'. (This meaning is noticeably easier to extract from F's singular *thought* than Q's plural.) Substitution of *on* for *in* is an easy enough error for scribes or compositors to commit; in this case the Folio error might have been carried over from Q2 copy (where, of course, it is *not* an error, only becoming one in F's altered phrase). We therefore emend the Folio text here, but not the Quarto.

20.205/2533 thoughts] Q; thought F. For Q's plural after the article compare *All's Well* 4.4.23/2304 ('When sawcie truſting of the cosin'd thoughts') and *Titus* 4.1.84/1483 ('To stir a mutinie in the mildest thoughts').

20.217/2545 bounty] Qb, Q2, F; bornet Qa
20.217/2545 the benizon] Qb, Q2, F; beniz Qa
20.218/2546 send thee,] BLAYNEY; ſaue thee. Qa; *not in* Qb, Q2, F
20.218/2546 boot, to boot.] Qb, Q2; *not in* Qa; boot, and boot. F
20.219/2547 first] Qb, Q2, F; *not in* Qa
20.231/2559 vortnight] Qb, Q2, F; fortnight Qa
20.233/2561 costerd] Qb, Q2, F; coſter Qa
20.233/2561 battone] BLAYNEY (Furnivall); bat-|tero Qa; bat Qb, Q2; Ballow F

20.262/2589 venter] RIDLEY; Venter Q1; *not in* Q2, F
21.0.1/2605.2 *Soft muſicke.*] DYCE (Capell); *not in* Q. There is no other natural point at which to introduce the music, before 21.23/2628 ('louder the muſicke there'); editions of the conflated text usually introduce it after Lear's entrance (as marked by F) and the Doctor's speech (only in Q), but such placings seem unnecessarily arbitrary.

21.0.1-2/2605.2 *and Kent disguised*] BLAYNEY; *Kent and Doctor* Q; *Kent, and Gentleman* Fb; *Kent, Doctor, and Gentleman* CRAIG. Unless the Quarto compositor accidentally omitted 'Gentleman' from this stage direction, it must be assumed that Shakespeare had not fully worked out the detail of the scene when he wrote this direction. If the Doctor does enter here, he must stand apart silent while Kent and Cordelia converse, ignoring him; it seems more likely that Cordelia would turn to him as soon as he entered. Q's entrance direction thus looks like an authorial anticipation of the format of a scene, rather than a precise instruction for the character to enter now.

21.8/2613 me] Q; *not in* F
21.11.1/2616.1 *Enter Doctor and 1. Gentleman*] BLAYNEY; *not in* QF. See note to 21.0.1-2/2605.2
21.19-21/2624-6 1. GENTLEMAN ... DOCTOR] CAPELL; *Doct. ... Gent.* Q
21.23.1/2628.1 *Lear is [discouered] asleepe*] This edition; *not in* Q. Alexander and Sisson have the Doctor draw the curtains; this is possible, but seems unnecessarily explicit. F has Lear carried on in a chair, but since the chair could be brought to Cordelia, such a mode of entry seems incompatible with 'Please you draw neere' (which F omits).

21.33/2638 Perdu] THEOBALD; *Per du* Q
21.34/2639 iniurors] CAPELL; iniurious Q; Enemies F. Q's word, besides being dubiously metrical, adds nothing to the following line ('Though he had bit me'); F substitutes a metrical word which *does* add something, which transforms the possessive *mine* into its opposite ('Mine Enemies'), and increases the contrast with Lear: '*mine enemy*'s dogge' vs. '*their father*'. But, though F's word confirms one's conviction that Q is inadequate, F's 'Enemies' is unlikely to be what stood in Q's copy: elsewhere in Shakespeare F's word is spelled 'enn-' only once (*Henry V* 5.2.169/3025, where it probably represents the French word); it is never spelled 'eni-' or 'enni-'; nor could *enemy* be spelled with an initial *i*, or *injurious* with an initial *e*. Capell's emendation, by contrast, assumes only that the Q compositor saw (or Shakespeare wrote) one minim stroke too many in the initial succession of minims (*iniur*), and misread *r* as *u* (another easy minim error). And as Blayney notes, Capell's emendation also seems more appropriate (in Q, at least): it emphasizes the injury done to Cordelia herself, rather than presupposing a state of mutual hostility.

Editors of conflated texts have rejected Capell's emendation because F makes straightforward sense, whereas 'iniuror' requires emendation of what has been regarded as an inferior text. But for an editor of Q, 'iniurors' is unmistakably more attractive than 'Enemies'. Its only drawback is that it leaves the line metrically unsatisfactory: F by contrast (assuming the common elision 'en'my') would produce an acceptable tetrameter. But though tetrameters are acceptable, there are hundreds of pentameters for every tetrameter, and one should not accept an otherwise implausible emendation simply because it produces a marginally less irregular line. In F, moreover, which abridges this speech, 'Mine Enemies dogge' is an isolated part-line: F is therefore poor evidence of whether we should expect two syllables or four between Q's 'mine' and Q's 'dogge', because in either event F would have been left with an equally acceptable half-line. Therefore, whoever emended Q's 'iniurious' to F's 'Enemies' appears to have been dissatisfied with Q's sense, but was not attempting to restore Q's metre. Capell's 'iniurors' is the most plausible emendation of Q's 'iniurious', and if we want to restore the metre we must emend the line elsewhere.

21.34/2639 mean'st] This edition; *not in* Q. Metrically, the line's last foot is defective, and one would expect a monosyllabic adjective modifying 'dogge'. (See the preceding note. For misreading accompanied by omission elsewhere in Q see the press variants at 4.327/821, 11.99/1722, and 20.217/2545.) Moreover, one would expect that adjective to intensify the contrast between Cordelia and her sisters. They reject *their own*, she accepts someone else's (someone, in fact, she has reason to hate); they reject *their benefactor*, she accepts someone who has harmed her; they reject *a human being* (father), she accepts an animal (dog). The number of Shakespearian monosyllabic adjectives, reasonably applied to dogs, which extend these contrasts is limited. Shakespeare elsewhere speaks of 'vilde . . . Dogges' (*Cymbeline* 5.6.253/3059) and of 'Low-crooked-curtsies, and base Spaniell fawning' (*Caesar* 3.1.43/1130): these suggest that Shakespeare—like others—naturally thought of dogs in terms of lowness, baseness, and vileness. This range of adjectives provides an obvious and relevant contrast between the 'low, base, vile' dog which Cordelia accepts and the King her sisters reject. And since a king is the highest of mortals, and since Cordelia's contrast depends upon a series of superlatives ('the greatest cases of dislike to be overcome by pity': Verplanck), one would expect the dog not simply to be base or vile, but basest or vilest. Of the available superlatives, *basest* is ruled out metrically, and *lowest* seems unlikely as a modifier of *dogge*; this leaves *vil'st* and *mean'st*. Shakespeare only used *vilest* once elsewhere (*1 Henry IV* 5.4.90/2887), disyllabically; but he used the adjective *mean(e)st* 12 times, once of an animal (*Pericles* 19.125/1896, 'the meanest byrd'—in contrast to a princess), and also treats the adjective (twice) or verb (9 times) as a monosyllable (mean'st). Moreover, *meanest* has just been used in contrast to *king*: 'A sight most pitifull in the meanest wretch, | Past speaking in a King' (20.193-4/2522-3).

21.46/2651 know] Q1; know ye Q2; do you know F. Q1 makes sense and is metrically acceptable, either forming a feminine tetrameter with 4.7.46/2738, or a hexameter with 4.7.48/2740.

22.3/2702 abdication] Qa; alteration Qb. See *Division*, 459.

22.28/2727 Yet] BLAYNEY; Not Q

22.28 bold's] Q (bolds). Previous editors here interpret Q as 'emboldens'; this modernization is Blayney's.

22.32/2731 pore] This edition (*conj*. Collier); dore Q; deare MALONE (*conj.*). Collier's conjecture has perhaps been unfairly dismissed, because based on the belief that Q2 (reading 'doore') was the first edition. But *OED* records 'pore' as a 17th-c. spelling, and 'dore' could thus easily result from an accidentally turned 'p'. Malone's conjecture (which Muir defends) presumes the manuscript spelling 'dere' but Gonoril's dismissive attitude is unlikely to describe these 'domestic . . . particulars' as *dear*. Shakespeare uses *poor* in combinations of two or more adjectives before a noun dozens of times; he is also remarkably fond of alliterative combinations of *poor* with another word ('Poore pelting', 7.184/1191, etc. He describes a house as 'poor' at *Romeo* 1.2.22/271, *As You Like It* 5.4.60/2557, *Winter's Tale* 5.3.6/2868, and *Cymbeline* 3.6.56/1853—so the collocation of *domestic* and *poor* would be natural enough. See also 'poore Mechanicke Porters' (*Henry V* 1.2.200/333), which combines alliteration on *poor* with two adjectives, one ending in *-ic*. The conjectured error could have been encouraged by alliteration: the error made the middle word alliterate with the preceding, rather than the following, word.

22.36/2735 Exit with his powers] This edition; *not in* QF. If Edmund were intending to exit with Albany, there would be no need to promise that he will attend him at his tent; the line seems to mean 'I'll be with you immediately', just before an exit. This would make visually clear Regan's following exchange with Gonoril: Regan wants her sister to come along with her and Albany so that she isn't given the chance to follow Edmund.

22.55.1/2754.1 *He offers Albany a paper*] This edition; *not in* QF. Whether Albany takes the paper immediately, or at all, is debatable.

22.56/2755 Here] F; Hard Q. Alternatively, there might be a line missing after 'forces'.

22.59/2758 sisters] Q2, F; sifter Q1

22.60/2759 stung] F; sting Q

23.0.2/2772.2 led by] This edition; *not in* Q

24.24/2807 goodier] This edition; good Q; good yeares F; gore crows STONE (*conj.*). See *Division*, 489.

24.28/2811 One] Q (text); And (*c.w.*)

24.38.2/2821.2 another Captaine,] This edition; *not in* QF. The captain and a trumpeter are the only specific individuals later called for by the scene (except for the Herald, who at this point is presumably off stage—see note to 24.105.2/2888.2). However, both of these figures *could* come on with the Herald himself; all the first part of the scene requires is one or more attendants to exit with Regan. It would also be logical to suppose that this original body of attendants provided the one or more who later follow Gonoril out (one of whom, presumably, returns as a 'Gentleman'). But it would be natural for Albany's entourage to include a Captain, and less logical to assume that he enters as an appendage to a herald.

24.42/2825 then] Q; them F

24.45/2828 send] Qb, Q2, F; faue Qa

24.46/2829 and appointed guard,] Qb, Q2; *not in* Qa, F

24.48/2831 comen] Qb (common); coren Qa

24.48/2831 bossom] Qa; boffome Qb

24.48/2831 on] F; of Q

24.54/2837 Wee] Qb (wee); mee Qa

24.56/2839 sharpnes] Qb; fharpes Qa

24.79/2862 BASTARD . . . good] Q; Reg⟨an⟩. . . . thine F. In itself a drum can 'prove' neither that Edmund's title is 'good', nor that Regan's is Edmund's; but 'let the drum strike' is here probably a challenge to battle, seen as the ultimate test of legitimacy of power. Edmund's assumption here (in Q) that he still has an army is later punctured by Albany (24.102-4/2885-7). Jackson (*SSu 37* (1984), p. 210) conjectures that Q's 'good' is right, but that its attribution is wrong; but in Q Regan's last three speeches are all concerned with her sickness (a pattern F disrupts). And why need Regan prove that her *own* title is good?

24.83 bar] QF (bare). See *OED*.

24.85 banns] QF (banes)

24.105.2/2888.2 Enter a Herald and a trumpet] This edition; *not in* Q; *Enter a Herald* HANMER. The trumpeter might enter as a part of Albany's entourage (see note to 24.38.2/2821.2), but he would be a natural attendant for a herald.

24.108/2891 2. CAPTAINE] This edition; Cap. Q

24.108.1, 114/2891.1, 2897 Trumpet sounds] *not in* Q (*which leaves a $\frac{5}{8}$ inch space between* 'Sound?' *and* 'Againe?')

24.119/2902 tooth,] THEOBALD; ~. Q1; ~ : Q2, F

24.120 ere] Q (are). See *OED*. The same modernization was made in BL2.

24.129/2912 fortune] F; fortun'd Q

24.132/2915 Confpirante] F; Confpicuate Q; Conspirate CAPELL

24.136/2919 ar] F; As Q1 (*as first word of a verse line*); Is Q2. Stone independently conjectures 'is', which is grammatically possible. But Q2 is without authority, there are no certain as/is errors elsewhere in the canon, and Q1 'are' is unanimously emended to Q3 'as' at *Venus* 1031.

24.140/2923 tong] F; being Q. Q's 'being' essentially repeats 'outside' (24.139/2922), and is aurally awkward in this line; *say* and *breathes* strongly suggest that F is right. On the misreading see Duthie, p. 423.

24.141/2924 My] This edition (*conj*. BL2); By Q. See Stone, pp. 69-70. For the error compare *As You Like It* 4.1.17/1879, *Twelfth Night* 1.3.95/196, *Richard III* 4.4.346/2851, and *Romeo* 4.5.127/2533.

24.143/2926 hated ly] F; hatedly Q

24.143/2926 oreturne] This edition; oreturnd Q; ore-whelme F; returnd BLAYNEY. See *Division*, 460. Stone's unmetrical conjecture 'returnd to' is unnecessary, as Blayney notes; see Abbott, 198. But Abbott's examples all involve much easier constructions than that proposed here. Both Stone and Blayney assume that *With* is here instrumental ('by means of'), a sense they find unsatisfactory; but it could as easily be associative ('at the same time'). F, and the simplest emendation of Q, both have Edmund declare that he intends to overwhelm or overturn both the lie and Edgar himself. Stone and Blayney, as alternatives, offer a more difficult misreading in Q and a more difficult construction in the emended sentence.

24.146.1/2929.1 *Flourish.*] This edition; *not in* Q; *Alarums.* F (*after the following speech*). F is unusual; only a flourish can be inferred from Q.

24.146.1/2929.1 *Bastard is vanquisht*] This edition; *not in* QF; *Edmund falls* HANMER. Editors follow Hanmer, but this is unnecessarily and perhaps misleadingly specific.

24.147/2930 ALL] BLAYNEY (Van Dam); *Alb.* QF

24.164/2947 ignobly] This edition (*conj.* Blayney); *not in* Q. Of Blayney's two other conjectures, 'vnnobly' is not used elsewhere by Shakespeare (nor recorded before 1618) and 'vnkindly' elsewhere in Shakespeare takes only its modern sense, rather than 'contrary to the law of kind, of family relationship' (which would seem better here). Shakespeare used *ignobly* 4 times elsewhere, including once in *History of Lear* (14.33/1956); it is used in explicit contrast to *noble* at *1·Henry VI* 2.5.35/988 (possibly not by Shakespeare). Therefore, if a word has been omitted, it is most probably 'ignobly'; this not only fills out the metre, but provides what seems a desirable contrast with 'noble' (24.161/2944) and 'no lesse in bloud' (24.163/2946).

24.166/2949 vices,] F; vertues, Q. We accept F's emendation on the assumption that Q could represent a compositorial antonym substitution. But this is a relatively rare species of error, and Q's manuscript may have read 'actions'. Q's 'vertues' would be a plausible misreading, and *actions* could take the relevant secondary senses 'sexual activity' (as at *Pericles* 16.8/1532) and 'lawsuit' (by association with *iust* and *scourge*).

24.182/2965 with] Q; we F. Many earlier editors retained Q, adopting Jennens's 'we'd' for 'would' later in the line; *we'd* occurs in *All's Well*, and even 'we would' would be metrically acceptable, and presumes an easy error in Q. But Q is probably intelligible as it stands.

24.196 smilingly] Q (ſmillingly). *OED* records 'smill' as a 17th-c. spelling of *smile*.

24.203/2986 To amplifie, too much,] This edition; to amplifie, too much, Q. This passage has given commentators great difficulty, partly because of the ambiguity of 'but another'. However, there is no reason why Edgar should be discussing the prospect of *amplifying* (sorrow, or a tale) 'too much'; *to amplifie* itself implies enlarging upon something. Likewise, the construction as it stands leaves 'would make' without an object. Both these difficulties are resolved by assuming that 'too much' belongs with what follows rather than what precedes. Edgar is then saying: 'This would have seemed the conclusion; but to amplify another (sorrow, or tale of sorrow) would turn what-is-already-too-much into much more (than too-much), and top extremity'. Compare 'More then a little, is by much too much' (*1 Henry IV* 3.2.70/1814). The Q compositor, dealing with virtually unpunctuated copy, has as elsewhere simply put a comma at the end of what he set and/or saw as the end of a verse line.

24.205/2988 there in] Q; there THEOBALD
24.210/2993 him] THEOBALD; me Q
24.247.1/3030.1 *Exit 2. Captaine*] This edition; *not in* QF; *Exit Edgar* MALONE. Schmidt suggested 'Exit a Captain' and Theobald 'Exit a Messenger'; the solution adopted here essentially follows these, but specifies the one captain known to be on stage. The only character other than Lear who later shows knowledge of what went on off stage is the '*Cap.*' who speaks at 24.271/3054; this cannot be Edmund's Captain (presumably the 'slaue that was a hanging thee'), and one would expect the person dispatched to save Lear to be the one who re-enters with him and reports on off-stage events. Edgar *could* exit with this Captain, but there is no need for him to do so, and he reacts to Lear's entrance—just as Albany and Kent do. Moreover, one does not want Lear's most important entrance to be cluttered with attendants: one is necessary, but two (including a major character) would be superfluous and unfortunate. Finally, this reconstruction of Q's staging, which seems the most economical on Q's own terms, produces essentially the same arrangement as F (except that F replaces the Second Captain with a Gentleman). Conformity of Q and F cannot be assumed, but where it results from the simplest interpretation of both texts it cannot be lightly dismissed.

24.252.3/3035.2-3 *followed by 2. Captaine*] This edition; *not in* QF. See note to 24.247.1/3030.1.

24.257/3040 *He lays her downe*] This edition; *not in* QF
24.265/3048 you] Q2, F; your Q1
24.271/3054 [2.] CAPTAINE] This edition; *Cap.* Q
24.279/3062 you] F; *not in* Q
24.283/3066 from your first] F; from your life Q. Q can only be defended by interpreting it as 'from the beginning of your period of difference and decay'; this seems very strained. However, 'life' is not the easiest misreading of 'firſt' (though rſt/ife would be plausible enough), and the error might be in Q's preposition: perhaps 'from' was substituted for 'in' (as at *Richard III* 2.1.18/1059) or 'through'.

24.286/3069 foredoone] F; foredoome Q1; fore-doom'd Q2
24.290/3073 [3.] CAPTAINE] This edition; *Capt.* Q
24.292/3075 great] F; *not in* Q. The metre suggests that a monosyllable has dropped out here, and F's solution echoes the Homilies: 'Some worldly witted men think it a *great decaye* to the quiete and prudent gouernynge of their commonwealthes to geue eare to the simple and playne rules . . . of our Sauiour' (II.x.Pt.i). But there is no particular reason why 'great' should have dropped out of Q here, and as an alternative one might suggest 'darke'. This would better explain Q's error (mind- or eyeskip: darke decay) and fit the context (see 24.285/3068); Shakespeare often contrasts *comfort* with *dark*: see *Richard III* 5.5.33/3124, *Titus* 2.2.9-10/636-7, *Dream* 2.2.44/667, 3.3.19-20/1413-14, and *History of Lear* 14.83/2006. *Dark* also seems more appropriate to Q's final moments.

24.296/3079 honors] Q2, F; honor Q1
24.301/3084 haue] Q2, F; of Q1
24.310/3093 *Lear dies*] This edition; *not in* Q

INCIDENTALS

60 Albanies] Q2; Albaines Q1   65 heart,] ~,   72 And] & Q (*mid-line*)   135 shaft.] ~,   145 low,] Q2; ~, Q1   285 slenderly,] Q (ſlen-|derly, *text*). The word is split between two pages: the catchword, 'derly', is followed by a full stop.   324 none.] ~:   328 Lord.] ~,   329 then] Qb; rhen Qa   329 terrible] Q2; terribe Q1   360 respect,] Q2; ~, Q1   425 bastardy;] Q2; ~, Q1   475 vs,] ~,   476 hunting,] ~,   541 whers] Q (*text*); wher's (*c.w.*)   758 Lear,] ~. Q1   791 And] & Q (*as prose*)   826 euent.] ~, Q1   930 quarrels] Q2; ~, Q1   993 You,] you,   1001 seuerall] Qa; ſeueral Qb   1021 suyted] Qb (ſhewted); ſnyted Qa   1022 wosted stocken] Qa; worſted-stocken Qb   1028 clamarous] Qa; clamorous Qb   1046 strike.] Qa; ~? Qb   1091 more,] Q2; ~, Q1   1109 aspect,] F; ~. Q   1132 respect] Qb; reſpcċt Qa   1135 set] Qa; ſit Qb   1143 correction,] Qb; ~, Qa   1144 basest] Qb; beleſt Qa   1168 beene] Qa; bin Qb   1178 scape,] ~,   1207 daughter] Q2; daugter Q1   1207 say.] ~,   1229 wit,] Q2; ~, Q1   1236 within.] ~, Q1   1269 why] Q (*text*); Why (*c.w.*)   1272 speake] Qa; ſpeak Qb   1273 seruise] Qa; ſeruice Qb   1285 practise,] ~,   1291 Coknay] Qb; Cokney Qb   1292 past] Qa; pâſt Qb   1352 her,] Qa; her, Qb   1353 varlot] Qa; varlet Qb   1357 Alow] Qa (alow); allow Qb   1460 purpos'd] Q2; puspos'd Q1   1474 Reg.] ~, Q1   1487 furre] Qb; ſurre Qa   1511 outwall] Qa; out-wall Qb   1523 drencht,] Q2; ~, Q1   1530 holly] Qa; holy Qb   1564 Gallow,] ~, Q   1592 can,] Q2; ~, Q1   1593 Poore,]

THE HISTORY OF KING LEAR

F; ~, Q   1600 this,] Q2; ~, Q1   1611 home,] ~, Q1   1620 Instătly] inſtăly   1637 their,] Fb; ~, Q, Fa   1697 cold.] Q2; ~, Q1   1705 paramord] F; paromord Q   1707 greedines,] ~,,   1709 ruslings] Q2; ruſlngs Q1   1717 more,] ~ 1720 sophisticated] Q2; ſo phiſticated.Q1   1732 old,] Qa; ~, Qb   1829 backe.] ~,   1841 fiend] Q2; ſiend Q1   1849 And] & Q1 (*as prose*)   1889 garments,] ~, Q   1893 so.] ~,   1899 And] & Q (*in mid-line*)   1904 me,] Qb; ~, Qa 1912 suffers, suffers,] ~, ~, Q   1919 bewray] ~, Q   1925 letter,] Q2; ~, Q1   1928 company.] Qb. This word is a turnover in Q, on the second line of H1; Qa has the same turnover (without the full stop) on the last line of G4ᵛ.   1944 farewell,] ~. Q   2006 *Edmund*] Edmuud   2022 And] & Q (*as prose*)   2053 not,] Q2; ~. Q1   2086 of dumbnes] Q2; oſ dumbnes Q1 2090 plagues,] Q2; ~. Q1   2127 this,] Qb; ~, Qa   2132 deere] Qa; deer Qb   2147 lick,] ~.   2154 selfe] Qa; ſelf Qb   2158-9 know'st, | Fools do] know'ſt, foolsdo Qb; know'ſt, fools, do Qa   2163 Whil's] Qa; Whil'ſt Qb   2166 horid] Qa; horrid Qb   2220 goodliest,] Q2; ~, Q1   2220 seene,] ~,   2221 teares,] ~,   2222 way,] ~, Q   2223 know,] Q2; ~, Q1   2224 thence,] Q2; ~, Q1   2225 dropt,] ~,   2225 briefe,] ~,   2232 shooke,] Q2; ~, Q1   2237 beget,] Q2; ~, Q1   2246 turnd her,] Q2; ~, Q1   2247 rights,] Q2; ~, Q1   2249 mind,] Q2; ~, Q1   2254 cause,] Q2; ~, Q1   2264 sustayning,] F; ~, Q   2271 repose,] ~,   2272 him,] Q2; ~, Q1   2273 power,] Q2; ~, Q1   2276 be aydant] Q2; beaydant Q1   2276 remediat,] Q2; ~, Q1   2278 life,] ~.   2320 more,] ~,   2384 no?] Q2; no l Q1 2389 depriu'd,] Q2; ~, Q1   2405 Enough] Q (*text*); Inough (*c.w.*)   2407 place.] Q2; ~, Q1   2468 eyes.] ~, 2502 stratagem] Q ('ſtra-|tagem' *text*). The word is split between two pages: the catchword is 'gem'.   2539 Well,] Q2; ~, 2545 heauen,] Qa; ~, Qb   2560 out,] Qa; ~, Qb   2569 out,] Qa; ~, Qb   2570 British] Qa; Brittiſh Qb   2575 you, down] Qa; ~, ~ Qb   2576 of,] Qa; ~, Qb   2580 minds,] Qa; ~, Qb   2586 gayle] Qa; iayle Qb   2590 O] *Edg.* O Q 2591 life,] ~.   2622 proceed,] Q2; ~, Q1   2623 arayd?] Q2; ~, Q1   2625 him.] Q2; ~, Q1   2628 there.] Q2; ~, Q1   2632 Kind] Klnd Q1   2632 Princesse.] ~, Q1   2633 flakes,] Q2; ~, Q1   2638 *Perdu*,] ~, Q1 2641 father] father Q1   2685 setling.] ~ : Q1   2702 he's] Qa; hee's Qb   2704 miscaried.] ~, Q1 2705 Madam.] Q2; ~, Q1   2720 and] Qb; nd Qa   2754 vew] Qa; view Qb   2755 guesse] Q2, F; queſſe Q1 2766 countenance] Q2; countenadce Q1   2781 indure,] F; ~, Q   2823 well,] Qa; ~, Qb   2830 more,] Qa; ~, Qb 2836 time,] ~, Q   2905 *Gloster.*] ~, Q   2906 sword,] Q2; ~. Q1   2913 traytor,] ~. Q   2921 liest.] Q2; ~, Q1 2921 should] Q2; ſholud Q1   2925 head,] F; ~. Q   2930 him.] ~,   2933 beguild.] ~,   2954 prophecie,] Q2; ~, Q1   2966 once,] ~.   2969 rings,] ~,   2981 say.] ~,   2984 this.] F; ~, Q1   2996 life,] Q2; ~, Q1 2997 twice,] ~, Q   2997 sounded,] Q2; ~. Q1   2999 disguise] diguiſe Q1   3024 briefe,] ~, Q   3024 writ,] F; ~, Q   3061 *Caius.*] ~, Q1   3092 wracke,] Q2, F; ~, Q1

QUARTO STAGE DIRECTIONS

1.0.1/0.1   *Enter Kent, Gloster, and Bastard.*
1.33.1/33.1   *Sound a Sennet,*
1.34.1-3/34.1-3   *Enter one bearing a Coronet, then Lear, then the | Dukes of Albany, and Cornwell, next Gonorill, Regan, Cor-|delia, with followers.*
1.177.1-2/177.1   *Enter France and Burgundie with Gloster.*
1.257/257   *Exit Lear and Burgundie.*
1.273.1/273.1   *Exit France & Cord.*
1.297.1/298.1   *Exeunt.*
2.0.1/298.2   *Enter Bastard Solus.*
2.21.1/319.1   *Enter Gloster.*
2.44.1/341.1   *A Letter.*
2.128.1/425.1   *Enter Edgar* (printed in the margin before '*Edgar*', 2.128/425)
2.165/463   *Exit Fdgar.*
2.171/469   *Exit.*
3.0.1/469.1   *Enter Gonorill and Gentleman.*
3.26.1/495.1   *Exit.*
4.0.1/495.2   *Enter Kent.*
4.6.1/501.1   *Enter Lear.*
4.42.1/537.1   *Enter Steward.* (after 4.43/538)
4.90.1/584.1   *Enter Foole.* (after 4.91/585)
4.181.1/675.1   *Enter Gonorill.* (after 4.182/676)
4.251.1/745.1   *Enter Duke.*
4.332/826   *Exeunt*
5.0.1-2/826.1   *Enter Lear.*
5.7/833   *Exit*
5.49/875   *Exit.*
5.51.1/877.1   *Exit*
6.0.1/877.2   *Enter Bast. and Curan meeting.*
6.15.1/892.1   *Enter Edgar* (printed in the margin)
6.36/913   *Enter Glost.*
6.85.1/962.1   *Enter the Duke of Cornwall.*
6.130/1007   (*Exeunt* (after 6.128/1005)
7.0.1-2/1007.1-2   *Enter Kent, and Steward.*
7.40.1-3/1047.1-3   *Enter Edmund with his rapier drawne, Gloster the Duke | and Dutchesse.*
7.167/1174   *sleepes.*

7.167/1174   *Enter Edgar.*
7.187/1194   *Exit*
7.187.1/1194.1   *Enter King.*
7.253.1/1261.1   *Enter Lear and Gloster.*
7.287.1-2/1295.1-2   *Enter Duke and Regan.*
7.340.1/1348.1   *Enter Steward.*
7.345.1/1353.1   *Enter Gon.*
7.445.1-2/1453.1   *Exeunt Lear, Leister, Kent, and Foole.*
7.453/1461   *Enter Glo* (in the margin after 7.452/1460)
7.466.1/1474   *Exeūt*
8.0.1-2/1474.1-2   *Enter Kent and a Gentleman at seuerall doores.*
8.46.1/1520.1   *Exeunt.*
9.0.1/1520.2   *Enter Lear and Foole.*
9.37.1/1557.1   *Enter Kent.*
10.0.1-2/1599.1   *Enter Gloster and the Bastard with lights.*
10.20/1618   *Exit.*
10.25/1623   *Exit.*
11.0.1-2/1623.1   *Enter Lear, Kent, and foole.*
11.103.1/1726.1   *Enter Gloster.*
12.0.1/1791.1   *Enter Cornewell and Bastard.*
12.25/1816   *Exit.*
13.0.1-3/1816.1-2   *Enter Gloster and Lear, Kent, Foole, and Tom.*
13.78.1/1893.1   *Enter Gloster.*
13.94.1/1909.1   *Exit.*
14.0.1-2/1923.1-2   *Enter Cornwall, and Regan, and Gonorill, and Bastard.*
14.11.1/1934.1   *Enter Steward.* (after 14.12/1935)
14.21/1944   *Exit Gon. and Bast.* (after 14.20/1943)
14.26.1-2/1949.1   *Enter Gloster brought in by two or three,*
14.77.1/2000.1   *draw and fight.* (after 14.76/1999)
14.78.1/2001.1   *Shee takes a sword and runs at him behind.*
14.96.1/2019.1   *Exit.*
14.105.1/2028.1   *Exit.*
15.0.1/2028.2   *Enter Edgar.*
15.6.1/2034.1   *Enter Glost. led by an old man.* (after 'age', 15.9/2037)
16.0.1/2106.1   *Enter Gonorill and Bastard.*
16.2/2108   *Enter Steward.* (after 'maister')
16.28.1/2134.1   *Exit Stew.*

16.67.1/2173.1   Enter a Gentleman. (after 16.68/2174)
16.86/2192   Exit.
16.96/2202   Exit.
17.0.1-2/2202.1   Enter Kent and a Gentleman.
17.56-18.0.1/2258-2258.1   Enter Cordelia, Doctor and others. Exit
18.21/2279   Enter messenger.
18.30/2288   Exit.
19.0.1/2288.1   Enter Regan and Steward.
19.40.1/2328.1   Exit.
20.0.1-2/2328.2-3   Enter Gloster and Edmund.
20.34.1/2362.1   He kneeles.
20.41.1/2369.1   He fals. (after 'well', 20.41/2369)
20.80/2408   Enter Lear mad. (after 20.82/2410)
20.175.1/2504.1   Enter three Gentlemen.
20.192.1/2521.1   Exit King running.
20.207.1/2535.1   Exit.
20.218/2546   Enter Steward.
20.235.1/2563.1   they fight.
20.242.1/2570.1   He dies.
20.253.1/2581.1   A letter.
20.277/2603   A drum a farre off.
20.279.1/2605.1   Exit.
21.0.1-2/2605.2   Enter Cordelia, Kent and Doctor.
21.84/2689   Exeunt. Manet Kent and Gent.
21.94/2699   Exit.

22.0.1/2699.1   Enter Edmund, Regan, and their powers.
22.19.1/2718.1   Enter Albany and Gonorill with troupes.
22.39.1/2738.1   Enter Edgar
22.41/2740   Exeunt. (after 'word', 22.41/2740)
22.54/2753   Exit. (after 22.52/2751)
22.54.1/2753.1   Enter Edmund.
22.58/2757   Exit
22.73/2772   Exit
23.0.1-4/2772.1-4   Alarum. Enter the powers of France ouer the stage, Cordelia with | her father in her hand.
23.0.1-4/2772.1-4   Enter Edgar and Gloster.
23.4/2776   Exit.
23.4.1/2776.1   Alarum and retreat.
24.0.1-2/2783.1-2   Enter Edmund, with Lear and Cordelia prisoners.
24.38.1-2/2821.1-2   Enter Duke, the two Ladies, and others.
24.114.1-2/2897.1-2   Enter Edgar at the third sound, a trumpet before him.
24.156.1/2939.1   Exit. Gonorill.
24.218/3001   Enter one with a bloudie knife,
24.227/3010   Enter Kent (after 24.228/3011)
24.233.1/3016.1   The bodies of Gonorill and | Regan are brought in. (opposite 24.234-5/3017-18)
24.252.2/3035.2   Enter Lear with Cordelia in his armes.
24.289.1/3072.1   Enter | Captaine.

THE TRAGEDY OF KING LEAR
(BASED ON THE FOLIO OF 1623)

HINMAN demonstrated that Folio *Lear* was set by Compositors B and E; Howard-Hill (*A Reassessment*) has since shown that E set rather more of the play than Hinman thought. Werstine ('Folio Editors'), on the basis of a thorough survey of the work of both compositors elsewhere in the Folio, analysed the kinds and quantities of error we should expect in their stints here. The editorial usefulness of compositor study has probably been demonstrated more effectively in Folio *Lear* than in any other play.

Identification of the compositors has been crucial in determining the nature of the printer's copy. Greg's examination of press variants in Q1, by demonstrating a clear link between F and printing-house errors in different exemplars of Q, made it clear that F in some way derives from Q. Greg, committed to the view that Q represented a debased text, could only explain such derivation by assuming that Q served as printer's copy for F, and he identified two key variants (at 1.4.322/828 and 5.3.45/2685) which suggest the use of Q1 rather than Q2. The assumption that Q1 served as printer's copy for F, which governed the editing of *Lear* for four decades, was thus based entirely on evidence of textual derivation (transmission of readings) rather than bibliographical dependence. This unexamined assumption depended upon the belief that Q and F were both defective reproductions of a single lost archetype, and collapsed with it. Stone, Taylor ('Folio Compositors'), and Howard-Hill ('The Problem') have demonstrated clear links in punctuation, spelling, and substantive variants between Q2 and Compositor E's stints. Such links are less remarkable in B's stints, and Stone proposed that B worked directly from manuscript. But the difference seems more likely to reflect E's exceptional conservatism in retaining features of his copy, than any difference in the copy itself. Taylor's more thorough study of B's stints suggests that the number of links in spelling and punctuation between F and Q2 is, in terms of B's practice elsewhere, what we should expect if Q2 were his copy. The proposed allocation of different kinds of copy to the two compositors would be an exceptional procedure which creates more problems than it solves, and it seems reasonable to assume that, here as elsewhere, both men worked from the same materials.

The compositors' Q2 copy must have been annotated by reference to an independent manuscript. Yet this manuscript itself apparently derived from Q1: F repeats press-variant errors present in Q1 but not Q2 (1.4.320/826, 1.4.322/828, 5.3.45/2685). It thus seems probable that the revision began initially on a copy of Q1, and this conclusion is compatible with the evidence of sources, style, vocabulary, act divisions, and topical allusions (including possible censorship), which all suggest that the revision took place several years after the original composition (see Taylor, 'The Date and Authorship' and 'Act Intervals').

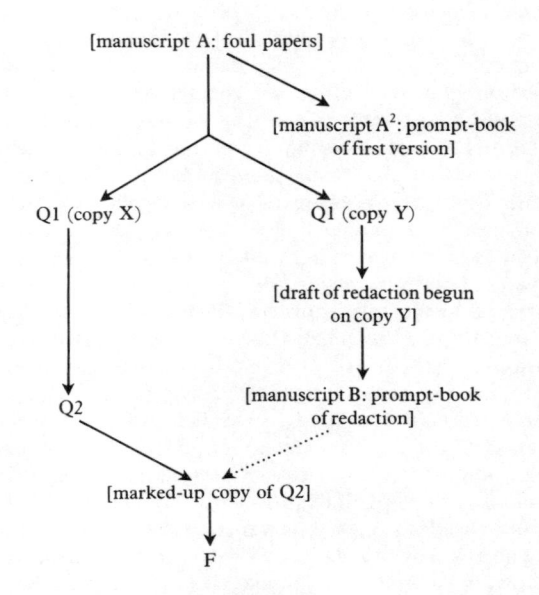

```
[manuscript A: foul papers]
         │
         ├──────────────┐
         │              ▼
         │       [manuscript A²: prompt-book
         │        of first version]
         ▼              │
    Q1 (copy X)    Q1 (copy Y)
         │              │
         │              ▼
         │       [draft of redaction begun
         │        on copy Y]
         ▼              │
         Q2             ▼
         │       [manuscript B: prompt-book
         │        of redaction]
         ▼              ┊
    [marked-up copy of Q2]
              │
              ▼
              F
```

Howard-Hill (1985) has challenged F's alleged dependence upon Q1. If Q1 influenced F, then it did so indirectly, because the document immediately behind F is — as everyone now agrees — either Q2 or a manuscript. The key piece of evidence for Q1 influence (though not the only one) is the phrase 'and appointed guard' (5.3.45/2685), omitted from F and from the uncorrected state of Q1. We assume that Shakespeare, working from an exemplar of Q1, simply failed to rectify this omission, because Q1 makes sense without it; Howard-Hill offers alternative explanations (p. 172). All of these alternatives, however — including his ingenious suggestions about manuscript insertion — postulate coincidental omission of the same phrase by widely separated agents of transmission. Such a coincidence seems to us, as it did to Greg, unlikely, though we cannot claim that such coincidences are 'necessarily' impossible. Textual critics always deal in relative probabilities, and in constructing our own stemma for *King Lear* we committed ourselves to the assumption that coincidental omissions of a complete, identical phrase should not occur in two unrelated documents fifteen years apart. If we accept that assumption — as did Greg and all subsequent editors, none of them committed to the hypothesis of authorial revision — then Q1 must have influenced F, and can hardly have done so unless it influenced the manuscript which was the source for

F's variants. If we reject that assumption, and allow improbable coincidence to play such a large part in textual transmission, then it is hard to see how textual hypotheses can be constructed at all.

The complicated derivation of F creates several complex editorial problems. The Quarto has a simple derivation (printed directly from foul papers) but contains much evident error, error which apparently results from misreading of a difficult authorial manuscript: emendation is therefore obviously necessary and difficult, but rewarding. The Folio by contrast offers a clean and intelligible text, with a complicated history of derivation and sophistication: emendation is easy, but not obviously necessary, and not at all rewarding.

Because F was (we believe) set from Q2 copy, it would have been possible to treat it in the way we have treated *Troilus*, *Othello*, and *Hamlet*: accepting Q1 as copy-text for incidentals, but inserting into that tissue of incidentals actual substantive variants from the control-text F. Such a policy would have the advantage of emphasizing F's very limited authority for incidentals: F's spelling and punctuation are almost wholly the result of normal compositorial sophistication of Q2's own (derivative) incidentals. However, Q's incidentals are already recoverable from the edited Quarto version (and its textual apparatus); Q1's erratic incidentals, particularly its punctuation, have in any case to be often emended by reference to Q2 or F; and the two texts in parallel serve as a useful illustration of the dramatic extent to which Folio incidentals reflect late printing-house rather than early authorial practice. Finally, Howard-Hill continues to argue (1985) that an intermediate transcript intervened between Q2 and F. Werstine has provided yet further evidence for F's dependence upon Q2, in its treatment of lineation (1984, p. 121); nevertheless, logically, no amount of correspondence between the substantives and incidentals of Q2 and those of F can *prove* that F was set from Q2, rather than from a remarkably faithful transcription of Q2. In discounting such a transcription one is arguing from economy of hypothesis—but the real world is not always economical. Moreover, while no amount of correspondence can prove direct dependence, significant departures from correspondence might disprove it, and hence it is always possible that a future investigator will discover some important disparity between Q2 and F, hitherto overlooked, which would definitively establish the presence of an intervening transcript. Hence, although at this time Howard-Hill's hypothesis of an intervening transcript seems to us unnecessary, it cannot be disproven, and might yet be proven, and the uncertainty it generates increases the desirability of preserving the Folio incidentals.

We have therefore treated F as both copy-text and control-text for the Folio version. However, in order to allow readers to reconstruct all F readings which may result from consultation of manuscript, we provide a complete collation of Q2 variants. The list includes Q2 departures from Q1, as well as a record of unauthoritative Q1 press variants reproduced in Q2. Any Q2 departures from Q1 which recur in F are recorded in the Textual Notes; nonsensical literal errors in Q2 are excluded.

F divides the play into acts and scenes. We have accepted F's division of Act 2 into only two scenes rather than four: see the Introduction to Q. F mistakenly numbers 4.6 as 'Scæna Septima'. Because Shakespeare seems to have revised the play at a time when intervals had become normal theatrical practice, act-breaks are here given the same prominence reserved for the late plays. In purely chronological terms F *Lear* should probably be placed between *The Winter's Tale* and *Cymbeline*, but it has seemed preferable to juxtapose the two versions of the play.

It is necessarily difficult to determine much about the nature of the manuscript consulted in annotating the compositors' Q2 copy. A number of apparent misreadings, apparently transferred from the manuscript on to Q2, suggest that it may have been a scribal, not an autograph, transcript—though the paucity of such errors, in contrast for instance with Folio *Troilus*, is within the range of an author copying his own work. The apparent efficiency of the manuscript in identifying characters and supplying businesslike stage directions suggests that it may have been the promptbook, a supposition which would also explain why the publishers went to the trouble of annotating Q2 rather than printing directly from a clean manuscript. However, in the absence of actors' names, duplicated directions, or warnings for the use of properties, confidence about the use of a prompt-book, or a transcript of one, is unattainable.

However, a number of details of the stage directions of F suggest that the manuscript consulted by the printers was scribal. Storms occur often enough in Shakespeare's plays, but they are usually cued by directions for 'lightning' (nine times) and/or 'thunder' (twenty-one times), in a variety of texts set from both scribal and autograph copy; only Folio *Lear* uses the stage direction 'Tempest' (2.2.457.1/1471.1) or 'Storme' (2.2.457.1/1471.1, 3.1.0.1/1495.2, etc.). Folio *Lear* also calls for characters to enter '*seuerally*' three times (2.1.0.1/884.1, 2.2.0.1/1013.1, 3.1.0.1-2/1495.2-3). This formula occurs only another three times in the entire canon—*Shrew* 4.1.164.1/1724.1, *K. John* 5.6.0.1-2/2410.1-2, and *Kinsmen* 1.5.16.1/544—and of these parallels that in *K. John* occurs in a scribal text, while those in both *Shrew* and *Kinsmen* might be scribal. By contrast, characters are directed to enter '*at seueral doores*' or '*seueral ways*' thirteen times, in texts of varied provenance; and the formula 'at one doore . . . at another' also occurs frequently. Although not so unmistakably anomalous as '*Tempest*' and '*Storme*', the Folio's '*seuerally*' is relatively unlikely to be Shakespeare's own formula. The word '*here*', in the stage direction at 2.2.299.1/1313.1, is also extremely rare in autograph texts (see Taylor, 'Shakespeare and Others'). Although Shakespeare might conceivably have phrased stage directions in a 'literary' transcript differently from in his foul papers, it would be simpler to assume that such uncharacteristic locutions testify to the presence of a scribe—a scribe perhaps more interested in the convenience of readers than in preparing a text for use in the theatre. (For comparable anomalies see *The Tempest*.)

The use of variant forms of the word *does* may also be revealing. In the acknowledged good quartos, the form 'does' occurs 42 times, the form 'do's' only 5 times. Only in *Troilus* does 'do's' predominate (4 occurrences, to only 1 'does'). In *Kinsmen* 'does' predominates in Shakespeare's stints, 'do's' occurs consistently in Fletcher's. The same pattern can be observed in the Folio, where 'does' predominates, with the following exceptions:

	does	*do's*
Tempest	1	13
Measure	2	7
Merry Wives	2	16
Winter's Tale	0	23
Cymbeline	2	6
As You Like It	0	1
Contention	0	1
Macbeth	8	16
Lear	1	14
Othello	0	15

In *As You Like It* and *Contention* the number of occurrences is too small to warrant confident conclusions—although *As You Like It* is generally regarded as a scribal text, and the line in *Contention* occurs in a scene which may not be by Shakespeare. But in eight plays the anomaly cannot be easily dismissed, and in all eight cases it probably derives from scribal interference. Five of the undoubtedly anomalous plays were probably set from Ralph Crane transcripts; in the six Folio texts probably set from Crane transcripts, 'do's' predominates over 'does' by 65 to 8. All editors agree that *Macbeth* and *Othello* were set from scribal copy, although the identity of the scribe has not been determined. If we disregard the Crane plays, *Macbeth*, and *Othello*, the remaining Folio plays set from manuscript copy contain 118 occurrences of 'does' to only 39 of 'do's'. These proportions are not so striking as those in the good quartos, probably because more of the Folio texts were set from scribal copy; but they still demonstrate a strong preference for 'does', a preference which is presumably Shakespeare's own. The overwhelming predominance of 'do's' in Folio *Lear* therefore suggests scribal interference.

The preference for 'do's' cannot, in *Lear* or in most other Folio plays, be attributed to the compositors. Compositor B in the Folio as a whole prefers 'does'; in his stints 'do's' only predominates when he is working on one of the plays (listed above) which have a strong preference for that form, a preference extending through the work of more than one compositor and hence presumably reflecting the manuscript copy. Compositor E preferred 'does' in *Antony* and *Hamlet*, where it predominates overall, and 'do's' in *Othello* and *Cymbeline*, where it predominates, thus suggesting that in this—as in so many other respects—he accurately reproduced the incidentals of his copy. In eight cases in Folio *Lear* Compositor B set 'do's' when the quartos had nothing, or some other word; in two cases Compositor E set 'do's' in a similar situation. Thus, ten of the Folio's fourteen uses of 'do's' apparently reflect either the preference of the manuscript, or of the annotator who transferred readings from the manuscript on to an exemplar of Q2; yet another 'do's' could come from quarto copy. These examples thus do not help us to establish the nature of the copy the compositors used, but they do confirm that the use of 'do's' almost certainly reflects the preferences of someone other than the compositors or Shakespeare himself.

However, at TLN 2411 Compositor B set 'do's' where the quartos read 'does'; at TLN 163, 2762, and 2976 Compositor E set 'do's' where the quartos read 'does'. In these four cases the anomalous form cannot be due to the activities of an annotator, transferring readings from a manuscript on to Q2, for such an annotator would have no reason to interfere with Q2 at all: the variant is not substantive. Either these four examples must be attributed to the four compositors, imposing a preference (which we have little reason to suppose), or they reflect a scribal preference in the manuscript itself—in which case the compositors were working from a transcript, as Howard-Hill conjectures, and not from Q2 itself.

The use of apostrophes in the word *has* also lends some support to Howard-Hill's interpretation. The usefulness of 'h'as' as a clue to scribal interference is discussed in the Introduction to *All Is True*. Here, we may note that both Compositor B's uses of the apostrophied form in *Lear*, and three of Compositor E's, occur in substantive variants, and hence might be due to an annotator; but Compositor E also set 'ha's' once (1.5.28/861) where the quartos have 'has'. On the evidence of Compositor E's work elsewhere, the departure from Q is unlikely to reflect a preference of his own—though single anomalies of this kind can never be ruled out.

Five apostrophes hardly constitute decisive evidence of the existence of an intervening transcript, but they do at least hint at that conclusion. The survey of these forms also isolates another un-Shakespearian feature of the incidentals of F, and tends to cast doubt on the hypothesis that the manuscript authority for F was holograph. But if what lies behind F is a transcript, merging features of Q2 and of some other (manuscript) source, then it becomes even more difficult than before to characterize the manuscript which, at one remove, provided the authority for Folio variants. The features of the Folio which suggest scribal interference could originate in the intervening Q2-based transcription; the manuscript which the scribe was copying might have been authorial, might have been a prompt-book, or might have been neither. In short, if Howard-Hill is right about printer's copy for the Folio, then we find ourselves in a situation very similar to that prevailing in the Crane texts, where the presence of an interfering scribe for the most part successfully obscures the kind of copy the scribe was himself copying. Certainly, no 'bibliographical' evidence exists which allows us to determine the provenance and authority of the underlying manuscript; everything depends, in such situations, upon an analysis of the variants themselves. All in all, although in the last five years an extraordinary amount of new data has been brought to bear on the problem of the printer's copy for F, a confident solution still eludes us. However, for an editor of the Folio version an exact definition of the copy, though desirable, matters rather less than the knowledge that it was heavily influenced by Q2, either directly or at one remove, and that its incidentals have little authority.

Our account of Folio press variants has been informed by the work of Michael Warren, in his forthcoming *The Complete King Lear*; Warren, working with Blayney, at a number of points revises Hinman's interpretation of the evidence. As in *The History of King Lear*, we have been given access to Blayney's edited text of the Quarto version, which has occasionally affected our interpretation of Folio variants; specific debts are recorded among the Textual Notes. When emending F by importing into it a variant from Q, we have noted whether such emendations were made in the later folios or by Rowe. These later editions have no independent authority, but they were prepared without access to Q, and hence indicate that the Folio text seemed objectionable on its own terms to some early readers.

In the Textual Notes, 'see Q' indicates a reference to the corresponding passage in *The History of King Lear* and its notes.

G.T./(S.W.W.)

WORKS CITED

Blayney, Peter W. M., *The Texts of King Lear and Their Origins*, vol. i, *Nicholas Okes and the First Quarto* (1982)
—— ed., *King Lear*, unpublished edition of Q (see Introduction)
Duthie, G. I., ed., *Shakespeare's 'King Lear': A Critical Edition* (1949)
—— and John Dover Wilson, eds., *King Lear*, New (1960; cited as Duthie-Wilson)
Furness, H. H., ed., *King Lear*, New Variorum (1880)
Greg, W. W., *The Variants in the First Quarto of 'King Lear': A Bibliographical and Critical Inquiry* (1940)
Halio, J. L., ed., *King Lear*, Fountainwell (1973)
Howard-Hill, T. H., *A Reassessment of Compositors B and E in the First Folio Tragedies* (1977), summarized with additions in 'New Light on Compositor E of the Shakespeare First Folio', *The Library*, VI, 2 (1980), 156-78
—— 'The Problem of Manuscript Copy for Folio *King Lear*', *The Library*, VI, 4 (1982), 1-24
—— 'The Challenge of *King Lear*' (review of *Division*), *The Library*, VII, 2 (1985), 161-79
Hunter, G. K., ed., *King Lear*, New Penguin (1972)
Jennens, Charles, ed., *King Lear* (1770)
Muir, Kenneth, ed., *King Lear*, Arden (1952)
Ridley, M. R., ed., *King Lear*, New Temple (1935)
Schmidt, A., ed., *King Lear* (Berlin, 1879)
Stone, P. W. K., *The Textual History of 'King Lear'* (1980)
Tate, Nahum, *The History of King Lear*, adaptation (1681)
Taylor, Gary, 'The War in *King Lear*', *SSu 33* (1980), 27-34
—— 'Four New Readings in *King Lear*', *N&Q*, NS 29 (1982), 121-3
—— 'The Date and Authorship of the Folio Version', in *The Division of the Kingdoms* (1983), 351-468
—— '*Troilus and Cressida*: Bibliography, Performance, and Interpretation', *SSt 16* (1983), 99-136
—— 'Folio Compositors and Folio Copy: *King Lear* and its Context', *PBSA 79* (1985), 17-74
—— 'Textual Double Knots: make rope's in such a scarre', forthcoming in *Susquehanna University Studies*
Werstine, Paul, 'Folio Editors, Folio Compositors, and the Folio Text of *King Lear*', in *The Division of the Kingdoms*, ed. G. Taylor and M. Warren (1983)

TEXTUAL NOTES

1.1.55/56 words] Q; word F. F's line is cramped, and *OED*'s only parallel—in Jonson's *Poetaster*, 3.5.25—is an error, since 'words' occurs in all early texts and is required by the rhyme.

1.1.74/75 possesses] Q (poſſeſſes); profeſſes F

1.1.100 Haply] F (Happily)

1.1.110/111 miseries] F2; miſeries F1; miſtreſſe Q. F1's reading cannot have resulted from typographical error, since F2 (as Q) requires an ſt ligature.

1.1.139 crownet] F (Coronet)

1.1.155/156 a] Q, F2; *not in* F1

1.1.156/157 nere feard] RIVERSIDE (Furness); nere feare F; nor feare Q

1.1.161/162 ALBANY *and* ⌜CORDELIA⌝] HALIO; Alb. Cor. F; Alb. Corn. ROWE. F is ambiguous, but on bibliographical grounds 'Cor'. is likelier to be Cordelia; for these and other arguments, see *Division*, 143-51.

1.1.169/170 sentence] Q, Fa, F2; ſentences Fb. F's press-correction seems clearly both wrong and deliberate: see Hinman, i. 304-6. Although error in the copy cannot be ruled out, it is equally possible that a proper correction has been misplaced. Terminal 's' could sensibly have been added to 'power', or 'potencie' (1.1.171/172): but the first of these is contextually unattractive, the second rather distant from the miscorrection.

1.1.175/176 seuenth] COLLIER 2; tenth F. F's change of 'Four' and 'fift' to 'Fiue' and 'sixt' seems designed to lead up to 'seuenth' here (which cannot, for that very reason, have been Q's copy reading). Q's evident error 'tenth' probably suggested, by rhyme, the authorial correction/revision 'seuenth' (or *se'nth*, as it would have been pronounced), and the two earlier words were adjusted accordingly. F, set from Q2 copy, might easily have failed to transfer the manuscript correction.

1.1.179/180 sith thus] F; ſince thus Q1; ſince Q2. F's line is crowded, '*sith thus*' is not very felicitous, and the need to insert '*thus*' immediately after might have given Compositor E the hint (consciously or not) to alter '*since*' to '*sith*'. All but one of Shakespeare's 21 other uses of 'sith' occur in plays written by 1604.

1.1.187/188 CORDELIA] Cor. F; Gloſt. Q1; Glo. Q2. See note to 1.1.161/162.

1.1.215/216 best] Q; *not in* F. (A metrical emendation.)

1.1.215/216 deer'st] This edition; deereſt QF. F reproduces Q, which is unreliable for such terminations (and in any case aligns differently); in this case assimilation to 'best' is also probable. Shakespeare uses 'dear'st' seven times elsewhere (all in late plays).

1.1.225/226 well] Q; will F. No modern editor accepts F; for the alleged error compare *1 Henry IV* 2.4.107/927 (Q1 'will', Q4 'well'). Compositor C is guilty of a similar error at *Titus* 1.1.366/366 ('tell' for copy 'till'). See 1.4.1/504.

1.1.230/231 the] HANMER; for QF. See Q.

1.1.267/268 Ye] ROWE; The QF. See Q.

1.1.281/282 couert] RANN (Mason); couers QF. F appears to retain accidentally a Q reading which had been revised. In the altered context of F's version of the rest of the line, Q's verb is awkward, and although time proverbially 'discloses all' (Tilley T 333), and 'tries all' (T 336), and 'tries truth' (T 338), the image of time covering faults is not only eccentric but dramatically irrelevant. The t/s misreading, easy enough intrinsically, would be especially likely for the Folio annotator, who would have had Q's 'couers' in front of him.

1.2.1/309 EDMOND] Baſt. F. At the beginning of the play, and again later in this scene (1.2.155/465, 1.2.161/471, 1.2.167/477), F uses '*Edm.*' prefixes; throughout Act 1 it uses the spelling '*Edmond*', which it also substitutes for *Bastard* in the play's first stage direction. All these facts suggest that the manuscript had 'Edmond' in directions and prefixes; that an attempt was initially made to impose this preference in F; but that in the end inertia led to retention of most of Q2's '*Bastard*' directions and speech prefixes. We have, consequently, imposed '*Edmond*' consistently in prefixes (as a reflection of the manuscript), though by our normal numerical criteria '*Bastard*' would have been preferred. Quarto '*Bastard*' is changed to '*Edmond*' or '*Edmund*' in Folio stage directions three times, and returned three times; in speech-prefixes, the same change is made six times. With one exception (2.2.41.1/1054.1), all Folio uses of '*Bastard*' in directions and prefixes could derive from Q copy.

1.2.4/312 curiosity] QF; curtesy THEOBALD

1.2.21/329 to'th'] QF; top th' CAPELL. See Q.

1.2.128/437 Fut,] Q; *not in* F. F's omission is almost certainly due to censorship: see *Division*, 77-8, 109-10.

1.2.132/441 sith] Q1; ſigh Q2; ſighe F (*in a justified prose line*)

1.2.167/477 *Exit Edgar*] Q1; *after* 1.2.166/476 Q2; *Exit*. F (*after* 1.2.166/476)

THE TRAGEDY OF KING LEAR

1.3.18-19/501-2 so, | Ile] F. Werstine notes that, working from Q2 copy, it would have been easy to eyeskip from 'I' to 'Ile', thereby omitting Q's 'I would breed from hence occasions, and I shall, that I may speake' ('Folio Editors', 284). However, F's omission accords well enough with other changes in Goneril's character here, and—combined with F's omission of 'very'—produces equally acceptable verse.

1.4.1/504 well] Q, F2; will F1. See 1.1.225/226.
1.4.2 diffuse] QF (defuse)
1.4.22/525 thar't] Q1; thou art Q2, F
1.4.31/534 canst] Q1; canſt thou Q2, F
1.4.44/547 You you] F; you Q. F's repetition might easily result from dittography.
1.4.49/553 Daughter] Q, F3; Daughters F1. A typical Compositor E error.
1.4.54/558 A] Q1; He Q2, F
1.4.70 these] QF (this)
1.4.98/602 ones] Q2, F; on's Q1. Since Shakespeare evidently often spelled *one* as 'on', Q1's 'on's' probably means 'one's' (as in Q2 and F) rather than 'on his' (which seems less idiomatic).
1.4.108 off] QF (of)
1.4.111/616 the Lady Brach] F; Ladie oth'e brach Q. Q seems an error (see note), but could have been corrected simply by striking out 'o'. F looks instead like a deliberate revision, perhaps prompted by Q's error: instead of 'a bitch named Lady' (Q, as emended), it offers 'a lady named Bitch'.
1.4.135/640 know] Q1; thou know Q2, F
1.4.143/648 Crowne] Q, F2; Crownes F1. See 1.4.49/553.
1.4.144/649 at'h] Q1; on thy Q2, F
1.4.159/664 Fooles] Q, F3; Foole F1. See 1.4.49/553.
1.4.160/665 Pry'the] Q, F3; Pry'thy F1
1.4.180/685 nor crum] Q, F2; not crum F1
1.4.186/691 riots. Sir,] CAPELL; ~,) ~, Q1; ~, Q2; ~, ~. F
1.4.199/704 it's] F1: it Q, F2. Possibly another example of Compositor E's weakness for terminal 's'.
1.4.236.1/741.1 *Exit one or more*] This edition; *not in* QF
1.4.266-7/771-2 That she may feele, | That she may feele,] Q1 (*setting as prose*); That she may feele, Q2 (*prose*), F (*verse*). See Q.
1.4.269.1/774.1 *Exit Lear, ⌜Kent, and Attendants⌝*] This edition; *Exit.* F; *not in* Q. See Q. Since F calls for Lear's re-entrance alone, the Fool presumably remains on stage while the others leave (as he does again below). Editors retain F, and so must interpret 'Away, away' either as an address to Fool (who must then deliberately ignore it), or as an exclamation directed at Lear himself, alone (a usage for which there are no parallels in Shakespeare).
1.4.271/776 more of it] F1; of it F2; the cause Q. Few editors before Schmidt (who obsessively favoured F) accepted F's reading, which is metrically awkward; but no emendation, or explanation of the suspected error, suggests itself.
1.4.291/795 *Exit*] Q2, F; *not in* Q1. Either this [Folio] '*Exit*' or that at 1.4.269.1/774.1 must be inadequate, since Lear's train (including Kent) must at some point leave the stage. Naturally some suspicion attaches to 1.4.291/795, which may suffer from Q2's influence; most editors since Rowe get the train off at this point. But Lear last addresses his train at 1.4.269.1/774 ('Away, away'), no one refers to them after that line, and it would seem most natural for them to leave then. See note at 1.4.269.1/774.1. Compositor B substituted '*Exit.*' for copy '*Exeunt.*' at *Merchant* 1.1.112.1/112.1 (and similar errors occur often in plays set from manuscript).
1.4.319/825 hasten] Qb, F; after Qa, Q2. Qb's variant seems unauthoritative (see Q), but F's revision was clearly based on it: see Taylor, 'Date and Authorship', 358-9.
1.4.320/826 milky] Qb, F; mildie Qa, Q2
1.4.322/828 You] F2; Your F1
1.4.322/828 attaskt] Qb; at task F; alapt Qa, Q2; ataxt DUTHIE (Greg). Qb's form presumably stood in the manuscript, which means that Shakespeare at least passively accepted it.
1.5.0.1/833.1 *First Gentleman*] This edition; *Gentleman* F. It seems almost certain that the Folio version intends the same gentleman to appear here, in 2.2, 3.1, 4.3, 4.5, and 4.6. So interpreted, the Gentleman becomes an important minor role, linking the two halves of the play, Lear and Kent and Cordelia; his use in 4.6, particularly, becomes much more comprehensible, dramatically. See also note to 3.1.0.2/1495.2-3. (All identifications of 'Gentleman' as 'First' in directions and speech-prefixes hereafter are editorial.)
1.5.1/834 *To Gentleman, giuing him a Letter*] JENNENS; *not in* QF. See *Division*, 445, n. 115.
1.5.2/835 *Exit Gentleman*] This edition; *not in* QF
1.5.3/836 *to Kent, giuing him a Letter*] JENNENS; *not in* QF
1.5.24/857 a may] Q1; he may Q2, F
2.1.0.1/884.1 *Curan*] QF. See Q.
2.1.2/886 you] Q, F2; your F1
2.1.15.1/898.1 *Enter . . . aboue*] This edition. See Q.
2.1.19.1/903.1 *Edgar climbes downe*] This edition; *not in* QF. See Q.
2.1.36/920 ho, helpe?] This edition (*conj.* Stone). See Q.
2.1.36/920 where's] Q2, F; where is Q1. F is more consistent than Q1 in marking such metrical elisions, and would probably have read 'where's' even if Q2 hadn't.
2.1.39/923 stand's] Q1; ſtand his Q2; ſtand F. See Taylor, 'Folio Compositors', 27.
2.1.44/928 But] QF (*text*); Gainſt Fa (*c.w.*)
2.1.53/937 right] Q2, F; rights Q1. Though Q's plural is possible (and has hence been retained there), F's reading is preferred by all editors, and may well represent a correction (anticipated by Q2).
2.1.54 ghasted] QF (gaſted)
2.1.57/941 found,] Q1; ~ ; Q2, F
2.1.69/953 I should] Q, ROWE; ſhould I F
2.1.70/954 I,] Q; *not in* F. This may be a simple compositorial omission; but it might be an incomplete correction, 'I' being struck out for replacement by 'yea'. For *yea, though* see *Lucrece* 204, *Much Ado* 2.3.141/967, *Othello* 1.3.69/355, *Cymbeline* 5.6.100/2905; there are no Shakespearian parallels for *I, though*. Here 'I' (ay) is potentially confusing, and I doubt that editors would have conjectured it without Q: Rowe solved the metrical difficulty by emending to 'although'.
2.1.77/961 said he?] F; I neuer got him, Q. Duthie defends conflation on the grounds that F's 'said he?' was an addition misinterpreted as a replacement. But the result is an irregular fourteen-syllable line, and F can be interpreted as a genuine question rather than a mere indignant exclamation—a question which shows Gloucester on the brink of a thought which would destroy Edmond. Cornwall's tucket, however, interrupts that development, and turns his thoughts back into the subject of his previous speech.
2.1.78/962 why] Q, ROWE; wher F
2.1.86/970 strange newes] Q, ROWE; ſtrangeneſſe F
2.1.94/978 tend] THEOBALD; tends Q; tended F. See Q.
2.1.99/983 th'expence,] F; thſe— Qa, Q2; the waſt Qb. See Q.
2.1.99/983 spoyle] Qb; waſt Qa, Q2, F. See preceding note. It seems likely that the Qa/Q2 variant should have been corrected, to bring it into conformity with Qb (which was in the copy of Q on which the revision was initiated). It alliterates and contrasts better with F's 'expence'.
2.1.119/1003 poyse] Qb; priſe Qa; prize Q2, F
2.1.122/1006 lest] Qb; beſt Qa, Q2, F
2.1.122/1006 thought it] Q, F2; though it F1; thought SCHMIDT
2.2.1/1014 dawning] F; deuen Qa; euen Qb, Q2. If Qa were an error, F might result from revision on a copy which contained it; but see Q.
2.2.4/1017 I'th'] Fb; It'h Q1; In the Q2; I 'th' Fa
1027 suited] F; ſnyted Qa; ſhewted Qb, Q2. Unless E (uncharacteristically) altered the spelling on his own initiative, F's reading appears to show the influence of the form present in Qa (and Shakespeare's original foul papers).
1028 woosted-stocking] F; woſted ſtocken Qa; worſted-ſtocken Qb, Q2. E retains his Q2 copy's hyphen, but reverts (possibly via the manuscript) to the Qa form of the first word.
2.2.21/1034 clamourous] Q, F3; clamours F1

533

2.2.41.1/1054.1 *then*] This edition; *not in* QF
2.2.64/1077 you'l] Q1; you will Q2, F
1087 holly] Fa; holy Fb. Though ambiguous, Fa's spelling could take the same meaning as Fb's in 17th-c. usage.
2.2.75/1088 to] Q; t' F. The metrically desirable elision of the preposition 'to' to 't'' later in the line seems to have led the compositor or scribe to anticipate the same elision here; though Riverside accepts it, *t*' for the adverb—never normal—would here make the nonce word *intrince* unintelligible.
2.2.78/1091 Reneag] Q; Reuenge F
2.2.79/1092 gall] F1; gale Q, F2. Since 'varry' has no nautical or meteorological associations outside this passsage, the fact that Q's 'gale' fits so well with 'halcyon' should not tell decisively against F1's 'gall', which might mean 'a state of mental soreness or irritation' (*sb.*² 2; 1591+). However, F2's independent emendation does support Q.
2.2.83/1096 and] Q1; if Q2, F
2.2.98/1111 tak't] Q1; take it, Q2, F. (An unnecessary metrical correction, which sacrifices an apt colloquialism.)
2.2.106/1119 flickring] POPE; flicking F; flitkering Q
2.2.120/1133 dread] Q; dead F1
2.2.123/1136 ancient] F; auſrent Qa; miſcreant Qb, Q2. Whether or not Qb is correct, if it had stood in Shakespeare's exemplar of Q1 he might have let it stand, whereas Qa would demand correction, and could have suggested F.
2.2.127/1140 respect] Q; reſpects F. A typical Compositor E error, in a line already full of sibilants; it weakens the parallelism with singular 'malice', and few early editors accepted it.
2.2.129/1142 Stocking] F; Stobing Qa; Stopping Qb, Q2. See preceding note.
2.2.139.1/1152.1 *They put Kent in the Stocks*] This edition; *not in* QF
2.2.141/1154 Gentlemen] Q1; gentleman Q2, F (Gentleman)
2.2.142/1155 good] Q1; *not in* Q2, F
2.2.142.1/1155.1 *Exeunt. Manet Glouster and Kent*] DYCE; *not in* Q1; *Exit.* Q2, F
2.2.143/1156 Dukes] Q, F2; Duke F1. See 1.4.49/553
2.2.150/1163 to] Q1; too Q2, F
2.2.151/1164 say] Qa; ſaw Qb, Q2, F. See Q.
2.2.158/1171 now] This edition; not Qa; moſt Qb, Q2, F. See Q.
2.2.160/1173 For] ROWE; From QF. See Q.
2.2.167/180 vnsuall] Q1, F3; vnuſall Q2, F1. The Q2/F spelling is not recorded elsewhere, and looks like a simple literal error which Compositor E mechanically repeated.
2.2.181/1194 Sheep-Coates] Q, ROWE; Sheeps-Coates F. See 1.4.49/553. F's form is unparalleled.
2.2.182/1195 Sometime] Q; Sometimes F. See 1.1.49/553, and Werstine, 'Folio Editors', 285.
2.2.183/1196 *Tuelygod*] Qa; *Turlygod* Qb, Q2, F. See Q.
2.2.186/1199 Messenger] Q, F3; Meſſengers F1. See 1.4.49/553.
2.2.192/1205 mans] Q; man F1; man is F2. See 1.4.49/553.
2.2.207/1221 painting] F1; panting Q, F2. Though universally rejected, F1's reading makes pertinent and characteristic sense: see *OED*, *v.*¹ 2b ('to depict or describe in words; to set forth as in a picture'), 3c ('To adorn or variegate with or as with colours; to deck, beautify, decorate, ornament'), 6 ('To talk speciously . . . To flatter or deceive with specious words'). The use with *forth* was current from 1558 to 1649 (*v.*¹ 10), meaning 'To express or display by painting . . . to depict as in a painting or vivid description'. Though 'halfe breathlesse' naturally suggests 'panting', this fact could itself account for F2's (or Q's) error for F1's more unusual—and more pertinently abusive—verb. Moreover, F1's word—with its strong suggestions of cosmetics—naturally anticipates the 'arrant whore' of F's added speech at 2.7.221-30/1236-44.
2.2.210/1224 whose] Q; thoſe F. An easy substitution for Compositor E.
2.2.222/1236 wild] F2; wil'd F1. An apostrophe error characteristic of Compositor E: see 2.2.480/1494.
2.2.232/1246 Histerica] F4; Hiſterica Q, F1
2.2.237/1251 the] Q, F2; the the F1

2.2.248/1262 giues] Q, Fb; giue Fa. See 1.4.49/553.
2.2.249/1263 haue] Q, F2; hause F1. Hunter emends F to 'ha'' here, conjecturing that two marginal corrections have been unintelligently conflated: 'ha' (for Q 'haue') and 'vse' (for Q 'follow'). Although this conjecture is attractive, it leaves unexplained F's use of terminal 's' for medial 'ſ'. It seems more likely that the intrusive 's' has slipped from the end of F's 'giues' in the line above—which in F's uncorrected state is 'giue'.
2.2.253/1267 begin] Q1; begins Q2, F
2.2.262/1276 fetches,] Fb; ∼ₐ Fa; Iuſtice, Q. See Taylor, 'Folio Compositors', 27.
2.2.274/1288 commands, tends,] F; come and tends, Qa; commands her, Qb, Q2
2.2.276/1290 Fiery? The fiery] F; The fierie Qa; Fierie Qb, Q2; Fierie? *the* BLAYNEY. Blayney suggests that F's reading results from a botched attempt to make the correction he conjectures (which we have adopted for Q); but there seems little reason to impugn F's effective and metrical reading. One could as easily conjecture that Qb's 'Fierie' was meant as an addition to, rather than a replacement for, Qa's 'The fierie'.
2.2.301/1315 you] Q, F2; your F1
2.2.303/1317 Mothers] Q, F2; Mother F1
2.2.303/1317 scrine] This edition; fruite Qa; tombe Qb, Q2, F. See Taylor, 'Four New Readings'.
2.2.305/1319 *Exit Kent*] RIVERSIDE (Ringler); *not in* QF
2.2.341/1355 blister] F; blaſt her pride Q; blister pride SCHMIDT; blister her pride MUIR. Recent editors retain F, glossing the preceding *fall* as 'strike'. This seems unlikely: there are no Shakespearian parallels, and the only *OED* support is 'To bring or throw to the ground; to overthrow' (*v*. 51; first example 1629). Hunter glosses 'to fall on her', but of course the object is precisely what is apparently missing. Almost certainly *fall* means 'to drop from a high or relatively high position . . . [used] of what comes or seems to come from the atmosphere' (1.d). The whole clause presumably depends on *drawn*: the *fogs* are *drawn* from the *sun* in order that they may be dropped, and used to cause blisters. So understood, the passage does not require emendation.
2.2.344 tender-hafted] F (tender-hefted). The 'heft' spelling is well-attested for *haft*; *OED* and most editors so understand the word here. 'Heaved by tenderness' seems a grotesque alternative.
2.2.355.1/1369.1 *Enter Steward*] Q; *after* 'Stockes' F; *after* 'heere' at 2.2.357/1371 DYCE. RIVERSIDE reverts to F, but Oswald's entry virtually answers Cornwall's question.
2.2.359/1373 sickly] F3; fickly F1; fickle Q. Q's *fickle* is a pertinent dig at Goneril's inconstancy (and hence undercuts Oswald's 'pride' in her favour); but it might suggest or provoke some sympathy for Oswald's predicament. Moreover, 'diseased grace' is a possible oxymoron (he calls her 'a disease' at 2.2.395/1409, for instance), and *sickly* could also mean 'Causing sickness or ill-health' (usually of a climate), in a way which goes with 'Diuels in'. Moroever, fi/ſi typographical confusion is exceptionally easy, while e/y error here presupposes error in the manuscript, combined with complete inattention by the annotator.
2.2.359/1373 a] Q1; he Q2, F
2.2.382-3/1396-7 To be . . . ayre] THEOBALD; *in reverse order* QF. See Q.
2.2.385/1399 hot-bloodied] Fb; hot-blooded Fa. Hinman regarded Fb as a 'quite unsatisfactory' reading which could only be accounted for 'as a mistake on the part of the printer' (i. 309-10), but it is the form used in *OED*'s only early citation of the compound (*Merry Wives* 5.2.2/2497).
2.2.459/1473 mad] Q, Fb; mads Fa
2.2.462/1476 blame,] HANMER; ∼ₐ QF
2.2.478/1492 to] Q1; too Q2, F
2.2.480/1494 wild] Q, F3; wil'd F1. See 2.2.222/1236.
3.1.0.2/1495.2-3 [*First*] *Gentleman*] This edition; *a Gentleman* QF. In Q, no 'Gentleman' has yet appeared: 1.5 calls for a servant and 2.2 for a knight. So in Q the article makes sense; here in F, it seems to imply a new character. Elsewhere F calls for 'Gentleman' only, reserving '*a Gentleman*' for the character, clearly different, who appears in 5.3 (5.3.196.1/2830.1). F therefore probably

retains the article here inadvertently, from its Q2 copy: the manuscript probably read '*Gentleman*' (its normal manner of identifying the character which this edition calls 'First Gentleman').

3.2.3/1531   drownd] Q; drown F
3.2.50   pother] F (pudder), Q. See *OED*.
3.2.83/1611   When Nobles are their Taylors Tutors] F. No one seems to have doubted this line, but it might make better sense if 'Nobles' and 'Taylors' were transposed. It is natural, in the morality of Shakespeare's age and the practice of all ages, for those of high rank to teach, to serve as models for, those of low rank; contemporary satirists complained about the aristocracy reversing this natural order. See for instance *The Second Maiden's Tragedy* (King's Men, 1611), where the righteous Govianus scornfully addresses two anonymous (and despicable) 'Nobles': 'Do but entertain | A tailor for your tutor, to expound | All the hard stuff to you, by what name and title | Soever they be called' (1.1.93-6). Later in the same play a 'painter' who deals in cosmetics is described (5.1.36-7) as 'a court schoolmaster... A ladies' forenoon tutor'. (Both passages were censored.) Transposition of the two names here would make the satirical point clearer.
3.2.85-6/1613-14   Then ... confusion] DUTHIE-WILSON (1960); *after* 3.2.92/1620 F (*as 1 verse line*). Most previous editors followed Warburton in transposing 3.2.93-4/1621-2 instead. The error must have been due to confusion in the manuscript, or in the annotator's marking up of Q2: it can hardly be simple compositorial error, and in any case bridges the page-break between rr2ᵛ (Compositor B) and rr3 (Compositor E, and set before rr2ᵛ).
3.3.17/1641   for't] Q1; for it Q2, F
3.4.10/1658   thy] Q, F2; they F1
3.4.10/1658   roaring] F, Qb; raging Qa, Q2.
3.4.12/1660   this] Qb; the Qa, Q2, F
3.4.26/1674   *Kneeling*] This edition; *not in* QF. This direction is suggested by F's description of the following speech as a prayer.
3.4.31   looped] F (lop'd)
3.4.36.1-2/1684.1-2   *Enter Foole ⌈and Edgar as a Bedlam Beggar in the Houell⌉*] This edition; *Enter Edgar, and Foole*. F; *not in* Q. Although Edgar clearly does not 'Come forth' until Kent orders him to do so at 3.4.43/1691, he might reasonably appear at a window, or in the doorway, to speak his enigmatic entrance line, before disappearing back into the hovel. Compare the staging of prison scenes, and the general phenomenon of characters on the edge of the playing space (discussed in Taylor, '*Troilus and Cressida*: Bibliography, Performance, and Interpretation', 11-17).
3.4.43/1691   *Edgar comes forth*] This edition; *not in* QF; *Enter* Edgar, *disguis'd like a Madman*. THEOBALD
3.4.44/1692   thorough] Q1; through Q2, F
3.4.45/1693   cold] Q; *not in* F. F's omission of 'cold' twice within seven words is suspicious. It seems likely that only one of the adjectives should have gone, but that the instruction to omit one led to unconscious omission of the other; Compositor E was particularly prone to omission between lines of prose (as here). The preceding phrase makes sense enough without 'cold', but 'cold' here seems essential to provide a contrast with 'warm'. Finally, the fact that a similar injunction occurs in *The Taming of the Shrew*—'go by S. Ieronomie, goe to thy cold bed, and warme thee' (Ind.7-8/7-8)—makes it likely that an allusion to some lost play or poem is intended, a probability which reinforces the authority of Q's adjective here. That Edgar himself says 'cold windes' later in this scene (3.4.92/1743) does not offer the same confirmation of the adjective in the previous phrase; in fact, the repetition may have motivated F's change.
3.4.46/1694   two] Q; *not in* F. Since Lear's preceding and his following speeches are verse, prose seems unlikely here, and F as it stands can hardly be construed as verse.
3.4.49/1697   led through] Q, F2; led though F1
3.4.50/1698   Foord] Q; Sword F. 'Sword' is a period spelling of *sward* ('grassy turf', 'earth's surface covered with herbage', or—

rarely—'surface of the water')—but this hardly seems obstacle enough to qualify for inclusion in Edgar's list. F is not an easy compositorial error for Q. Of alternatives, *fiord* is not recorded till 1674 (of Scandinavia), and would in any case not explain F's error, since it would require only changing one letter ('foord' to 'fiord'). Collier's attractive 'swamp' is first recorded in 1624, as a North American import. The anonymous conjecture 'flood' is also attractive, and has none of the compelling disadvantages of other conjectures; but it presupposes that F's misreading stood in the manuscript itself; and if the error originates in the manuscript, 'foord' might have caused it as easily as—or more easily than—'flood'. Resort to Q seems the safest option.
3.4.54, 55   Bless] F (Blisse)
3.4.72/1721   alow: alow, loo, loo] F; a lo lo lo Q. *OED* understands *alow* as a variant of *halloo*, but finds no other examples of the form; '*Alow!*' would mean 'Below decks' (*alow*, 3), which seems no more irrelevant than 'Fathom and half'. Likewise, though Q's repeated *lo* might be an alternative spelling of *loo*, no parallels have been recorded; it might be a refrain from the same ballad as the rest of the line, or simply a repeated imperative *Lo!* (Look, look, look!). It seems unsafe to assume that Q and F mean the same thing, or that either clearly enough 'means' anything specific enough to allow for confident modernization.
3.4.85/1735   deeply] Q2; deeply Q1; deerely F
3.4.92-3/1743-4   Sayes suum, mun, nonny] F; hay no on ny Q. Q is easily emended to 'hay no nony', a nonsense-refrain associated with sexual euphemism. (See Q.) F, by contrast, must in its entirety represent a deliberate change which makes (to us) no recognizable sense at all. Syntactically, 'suum, mun, nonny' is what the 'winde ... Sayes', so Knight's suggestion that Edgar in some way imitates the sound of the wind can hardly be resisted. *OED* records a verb *sum*, meaning 'to hum softly' (*c.*1440); Shakespeare is unlikely to have known this but it demonstrates a similar onomatopoeic effect. By contrast, 'nonny' would certainly have been for Jacobean audiences a recognizable word, and one which was almost certainly produced deliberately by a correction of Q; 'suum', too, is close to Latin *sum* (I am), which a large proportion of Shakespeare's audience would know, and which would create a teasing possibility of meaning. Both 'suum' and 'nonny' are thus probably an accurate reflection of the manuscript: nonsensical in an onomatopoeic, teasing, recognizable way. But 'mun' might be corrupt: apparent nonsense is easy enough to misread, Shakespeare's minims gave most printers difficulty, and 'mum' would be an attractive alternative.
3.4.93   Dauphin] F (Dolphin). See next note.
3.4.93/1744   sesey] This edition; *Sefey* F1; *Seffey* F2; caefe Q1; ceafe Q2. F's capital, combined with italics, suggests that Compositor B thought he was setting a proper name; no such name is known, and the construction does not encourage that interpretation, and it therefore seems legitimate to emend to lower case. What the word means remains obscure, though an imperative or interjection seems called for. Malone and subsequent editors interpret as 'sessa', which occurs at *Shrew* Ind.5/5; but we can hardly be confident that the same word is intended, given the disparity of form (*Shrew* 'Seffa', *Tragedy of Lear* 3.4.93/1744 'Sefey', 3.6.32/1879 'fefe'). The *Shrew* context provides no association with dogs, as *Lear* 3.6.32/1879 does; 'trot' at 3.4.94/1744 could be used of other quadrupeds besides horses (*OED*), so dogs might be relevant here too. The hunting cry 'sa sa' may be pertinent; so may the interjection *sess*, which *OED* records in 1608 (in the form 'Ses, ses') as 'a call to a dog when giving it food'. No one has provided parallels for 'Dolphin' as the name of a dog or horse; or for 'my boy' as a contemporary idiom for addressing an animal. Since Q1 probably means 'cease' (see Q), it seems significant that F here could so easily represent French *cessez* (as Johnson, and possibly F2, understood it). F's odd use of italics would be explained by the switch to a foreign language, which might have been prompted by the preceding 'Dolphin' (in its meaning 'Dauphin', intended here or not). The syntax of the whole clause suggests an address to one party

('Dolphin') concerning another ('him'); the second party is to be allowed to 'trot by', and it would be natural enough to interpret the imperative to the first party as an instruction to refrain from interfering. 'Cease' (barking, or interfering) thus makes more obvious sense than 'sa! sa!' (an incitement to pursuit and capture). Johnson's interpretation thus seems markedly preferable to any other.

3.4.93   *cessez*] F (*Sesey*). See preceding note.
3.4.102-3/1752-3   Come, vnbutton heere.] F; come on be true. Qa, Q2; come on, Qb
3.4.108/1758   fiend] Q; *not in* F. An easy eyeskip.
3.4.109/1759   till the] Q; at F. See Duthie, 178-9.
3.4.110/1760   and the Pin, squints] F; & the pin, fquemes Qb; the pin-|queues Qa; the pinqueuer Q2; squenies DUTHIE (Greg). Q2 would certainly have driven the annotator to check his manuscript, and if he (or the scribe who prepared the manuscript) did not know what 'squenies' meant, it is unlikely he would have 'sophisticated' it to a use of 'squints' not elsewhere recorded till 1637. Anyone intent upon clarifying and simplifying the language here would presumably have altered to 'makes the eye squint', or something similar; F's apparent stretching of usage seems more characteristic of an author (and Shakespeare in particular).
3.4.113/1763   *Swithune*] This edition (*after* TATE); *Swithold* F; fwithald Q. See Q.
3.4.113   wold] QF (old)
3.4.114/1764   A] Qa; he Qb, F
3.4.114/1764   nine fold] Q; nine-fold F. Although *OED* follows Capell in identifying F's 'nine-fold' as nine attendants or retainers, it provides no other examples beyond an imitation of this passage by Sir Walter Scott. Tyrwhitt's suggestion that *fold* is an alternative form of *foal*, influenced by the rhyme, is supported by examples of excrescent final *d* elsewhere in Shakespeare (Cercignani, 318); alternatively, *fold* might refer to coils in a serpent's body (*sb.*³ 1e), appropriate enough for a devil. Neither interpretation permits F's hyphen, probably based on compositorial misunderstanding.
3.4.114   foal] QF (fold). See preceding note.
3.4.122/1772   Tod-pole] F, Qb (tod pole); tode pold Qa; toade pold Q2
3.4.127/1777   had] Q; *not in* F
3.4.132/1782   Smulkin] F; fnulbug Q. See Q.
3.4.157/1807   a] Q1; he Q2, F
3.4.163/1813   in't] Q1; into th' Q2, F
3.5.25/1847   deerer] Q; deere F
3.6.26/1873   Mongrill,] ROWE; ~, QF
3.6.27/1874   Hym] F. See Q.
3.6.28/1875   Bobtaile] Q; Or Bobtaile F
3.6.28/1875   tike] Q, F4; tight F1. F1 makes sense if 'Bobtaile' is understood as a substantive (see *OED*, C. 1, 2), and 'tight' as 'skilful, alert, lively' (*a.* 3) or 'steadfast, constant' (*a.* 5). However, as an approving adjective 'tight' seems less characteristic of Tom's rhyme than the opprobrious 'tike'. Q's word could easily have been misread 'tite', and then normalized, by the manuscript scribe or Jaggard's annotator—especially since it makes good local sense.
3.6.28/1875   Trondle] Q1 (trūdle), Q2 (trundle); Troudle F. F seems unlikely to result from misreading, since 'Troudle' is not a word; compositorial inadvertence seems likelier. Although Compositor B could have omitted the 'n' accidentally, *OED* does not record 'troundle' as a variant spelling; it does record 'trondle' as a 17th-c. spelling, and so foul-case error, or a turned 'n', probably accounts for F's form.
3.6.32/1879   Do, de, de, de: sese] F; loudla doodla Q. See 3.4.93/1744. Since Q's variant seems to be nonsense, F's need be nothing else, although the motives for exchanging one bit of nonsense for another remain obscure. Since Compositor B set 3.6.32/1879 before 3.4.93/1744, one might have expected him to repeat 'Sesey' here, if that were in his copy; his failure to do so perhaps suggests that different 'words' are intended. By itself the letter combination 'sese' here might be a spelling of *cease*, *cess*, *see*, *seize*, *sess*, or *siser*; but these words are either irrelevant or historically unlikely. 'Cease' (or some variant) makes sense at 3.4.93/1744, but not here, where Tom has driven the dogs away. It thus seems probable that 'sese' is either nonsense, or an interjection of unknown meaning, unrelated to '*Sesey*'. Likewise, there seems no reason to repunctuate the preceding syllables as 'Do de, de, de' (or the run of similar syllables at 3.4.55/1703-4).
3.6.36/1883   makes] Q; make F. Schmidt defends F, citing Abbott, 367 ('Subjunctive used indefinitely after the relative'). But of only four examples Abbott cites in Shakespeare, one is misquoted (*Lucrece* 1344 reads 'bosomes lie', making the false concord explicable by association), and two involve the idiom 'as please (object)'. This leaves only *Measure* 1.2.172/253 and this passage (not cited by Abbott), both in texts which owe their authority to a scribal transcript, and in one of which a collateral substantive text supplies the normal alternative. Moreover, the passage in *Measure* may well be due to a false plural 'prone and speechless dialect'. Given the ease with which compositors or scribes can omit terminal 's', and Shakespeare's overwhelming preference for the indicative in such circumstances, error seems probable here.
3.6.36/1883   hard-hearts] F. Editors follow Q, removing the hyphen, but the compound was current as a verb and an adjective (*OED*), and on the analogy of *hard-head*(s) could easily have been understood as a substantive ('persons with hard hearts').
3.6.43.1/1890.1   *Enter Gloster*] Q; *after* 3.6.39/1886 F. See *Division*, 117.
3.6.53/1900   Take vp, take vp] F; Take vp to keepe Qa, Q2; Take vp the King Qb. See Introduction.
3.6.55.1/1902.1   *Kent ... armes*] This edition; *not in* F. See *Division*, 101.
3.7.0.1/1902.2   *Regan,*] Q2, F; *and Regan, and* Q1
3.7.8/1910   festinate] F2; feftiuate F1; feftuant Q. See Q.
3.7.21/1924   *Exeunt Gonerill and Edmond*] Q (*Exit Gon. and Bast.*); *Exit* F. F's variant probably arose from shortage of space: Q's direction was simply shortened to '*Exit*', which is wrong (since it only applies to 'Gonerill').
3.7.63/1966   Cruels ile subscribe:] This edition (*conj.* Stone); cruels elfe fubfcrib'd, Q; Cruels elfe fubfcribe: F. See Q.
3.7.75/1978   *To Cornwall*] This edition; *not in* QF. See Q.
3.7.80/1983   *Regan stabs him againe*] This edition ; *not in* QF.
3.7.81.1/1984.1   *He ... eye*] This edition ; *not in* QF. See Q.
3.7.96.1/1999.1   *with the body*] This edition ; *not in* QF.
4.1.2/2001   flatter'd:] POPE; ~, Q; ~, F
4.1.2/2001   worst,] Q; ~ : F
4.1.10/2009   partie-eyd] Qb (parti,eyd); poorlie, leed Qa; poorely led Q2, F. See Q. Though the number of Qa readings from inner H which occur in the Folio makes it highly probable that Shakespeare worked from an exemplar of Q1 which contained the uncorrected state of that forme, *some* of the Qa readings may occur in F because of a failure to correct Q2 (which derives from Q2 here); even if we knew which readings came from the manuscript, they would have only a passive authority. We have therefore emended all such readings: see 4.2.30/2103, 4.2.36/2109, 4.2.47/2120.
4.1.11/2010   hate] QF; hold. WALKER (*conj.*)
4.1.12/2011   *Edgar stands aside*] This edition; *not in* QF. See Q.
4.1.32/2031   A] Q1; He Q2, F
4.1.40/2039   *He comes forward*] This edition; *not in* QF. See Q.
4.1.42/2041   Get thee away] F; Then prethee get thee gon Q. Werstine ('Folio Editors', 283) thinks this may be an instance of Compositor B omitting the beginning of a line ('Then prethee'); but conflation produces an unmetrical line, unless we also adopt Q's 'gon'. It seems excessive to attribute three variants in five words to the compositor. F's tetrameter is acceptable, especially as 'I, my lord' may be regarded as an amphibious section.
4.2.0.1-2/2073.2-3   *at one doore ... at another*] This edition; *not in* QF. If Oswald enters now (rather than during Goneril's speech, as in Q), it is presumably from another direction.
4.2.17/2090   names] F; armes Q. Though modern editors normally

adopt Q, there seems insufficient reason to abandon F here. In Q *armes* = 'weapons'; at *Winter's Tale* 1.2.37/84 a distaff is a woman's weapon, and *Cymbeline* 5.5.33-4/2539-40 speaks of nobleness 'which could have turn'd | A Diſtaffe, to a Lance'. These parallels establish the probable authenticity of Q's reading, which has forced most conflating editors to adopt it; but the authenticity of Q's variant need not impugn F's. Shakespeare might have altered Q because the corporal sense of 'armes' was ludicrously encouraged by 'hands'; and he would have been especially alert to any such pun, having used it several times elsewhere (*John* 4.3.47/1938, *Shrew* 2.1.221/1029, *Hamlet* 5.1.33/3004, *Troilus* 1.3.273/708). As 'names [of husband and wife], reputations, authorities', F of course makes sense; see also *Measure* 1.4.46/363 ('change their names'), where as here *change* = 'exchange'; *husbandry* occurs two lines before.

4.2.29/2102 My Foole vsurpes my body] F; My foote vſurpes my body Qa; My foote vſurpes my head Q2; A foole vſurps my bed Qb. See Q. Q2 (head) must in this case have been corrected by reference to the manuscript, which contained the same reading as Qa (body); unless F's 'Foole' is a compositorial error—which seems too much of a coincidence—Q2's 'foote' (Qa) must also have been deliberately altered. Although 'My' may be a retained Q2 error, in this case it seems best to treat F's entire sentence as a unit, and hence to retain it as an accurate reflection of Shakespeare's revised text.

4.2.29.1/2102.1 *Enter Albany*] F. Editors follow Q in having Oswald exit after his speech; this is, however, not strictly necessary, and his presence increases the indecorum of the quarrel, and (perhaps) confirms his inseparability from his mistress.

4.2.30/2103 whistling] Qb; whiſtle Qa, Q2, F. See 4.1.10/2009.

4.2.36/2109 shewes] Qb; seemes Qa, Q2, F. See note to 4.1.10/2009.

4.2.43/2116 thereat-enrag'd] Q, F2; threat-enrag'd F1. F1 could as easily result from Compositor B omitting a single type as from misreading of, or in, the manuscript. F1 is not impossible, but Q provides more metrical and apter sense.

4.2.44/2117 and among'st them] QF. See Q.

4.2.47/2120 Iusticers] Qb; Iuſtices Qa, Q2, F. See 4.1.10/2009.

4.2.55.1/2128.1 *Exit with Oswald*] This edition; *not in* F; *Exit*. Q. If Oswald does not leave earlier (see 4.2.29.1/2102.1), and if Goneril exits here, then Oswald must go with her. However, the absence of an exit direction in F may be correct: her presence, and her reaction to the Messenger's next revelation, could be dramatically effective.

4.3.3/2141 Femitar] Q; Fenitar F. See 'Folio Compositors', 20.

4.3.4/2142 Burdockes] HANMER; Hardokes F; hor-docks Q. See Q.

4.3.8/2146 *Exit one or more*] See Q.

4.3.18/2156 Good mans] Q, F3; Goodmans F1

4.3.18/2156 distres] Q; deſires F. Werstine notes that F's reading is unlikely to result from substitution by Compositor B ('Folio Editors', 286), and Stone calls F 'not altogether impossible' (222). But no editor since Rowe has accepted F, which could be due to a misreading in the manuscript. Alternatively, a simple ligature error (producing 'difires' in place of 'diftres') might have been miscorrected in foul proofs.

4.4.6/2173 Letters] Q1; letter Q2; Letter F

4.4.15/2182 after, Madam] This edition; after him, Madam F; after him, Q. A metrical emendation. 'Madam' could have been intended by the annotator to replace rather than (as the compositor misunderstood) to follow Q's him. See Q.

4.4.39/2206 him] Q, F2; *not in* F1

4.5.7/2214 speak'st] Q2; ſpeakeſt Q1

4.5.17/2224 walke] Q, ROWE; walk'd F

4.5.22/2229 heard, so high.] F; heard, its so hie, Q1; heard: it is so hie, Q2

4.5.53/2260 alenth] This edition (*conj.* Stone); at each QF. See Q.

4.5.66/2273 strangenesse.] Q2 (~:); ~, F; ~, Q1

4.5.67/2274 Cliffe,] Q2; ~. F; ~, Q1

4.5.69/2276 me thoughts] Q1; me thought, Q2, F

4.5.71/2278 enraged] F; enridgd Q. Editors prefer Q, but Shakespeare describes the sea as enraged 11 times elsewhere; he also associates fiends with rage at *Richard III* 1.4.218/981 and *Lear* 3.4.123/1773. Shakespeare could easily be as responsible for F's adjective as Q's.

4.5.83/2290 crying] F; coining Q. F's variant may have been prompted by censorship: see Taylor, 'Date and Authorship', 483.

4.5.92 Whew!] F (Hewgh). *OED* lists no other examples of this word under F's spelling; 'heugh' is not recorded until 1852, and seems clearly derived from Shakespeare's use here. *OED* defines it as 'an imitation of the sound of whistling' and cross-refers to *Whew*—an interjection current then as now, which gives the appropriate range of meanings in a form intelligible to modern readers.

4.5.99/2306 said,] BLAYNEY; ~, Q1; ~: Q2, F. See Q.

4.5.122/2329 Tha're] Q1; they are Q2, F

4.5.160/2367 Through] Q; Tho-|rough F. F's unmetrical substitution straddles a page-break in a passage set as justified prose; 'Through' could not be split, and Compositor B almost certainly added the 'o' for reasons of page make-up.

4.5.161/2368 Plate sinne] THEOBALD 2; Place finnes F

4.5.183.1/2390.1 ⌈*2 Gentlemen*⌉] This edition; *a Gentleman* F; *three Gentlemen* Q. See *Division*, 447.

4.5.184/2391 him. Sir,] ROWE; him, firs, Q1; him, firs. Q2 (*omitting remainder of speech*); him, Sir. F

4.5.201/2408 speaking] This edition; ſpeaking of QF. See Q.

4.5.207-8/2414-15 heares that, | That] Q; heres, | That Q2; heares that, which F. See Taylor, 'Folio Compositors', 27.

4.5.212/2419 in] This edition; on QF. See Q.

4.5.225/2432 To boot, and boot] F; to ſaue thee Qa; to boot, to boot Qb. By combining Qa and Qb one may conjecture (as Blayney does) that Shakespeare originally wrote 'to send thee boot, to boot' (an emendation we have accepted in the Quarto version). But the two documents which contributed to Jaggard's copy for F did *not* combine Qa and Qb. Q2 derives from Qb here, and so has 'to boot, to boot'; Compositor B might have emended this, on his own initiative, as nonsense. If so, however, the annotator must have left it uncorrected, which means that two errors (of oversight, then sophistication) must be presumed. One would not expect the manuscript to have reproduced Q2 here, because—on the evidence of 5.3.45/2685—it apparently derived from an exemplar of Q1 in which the outer forme of sheet K was uncorrected. This means that Shakespeare, in revising the play, would have confronted 'to ſaue thee' in his copy of Q1. One might well expect him to regard this as unsatisfactory; it is less easy to know what he would have done with it. However, it seem unlikely that he would have, coincidently, altered it to Qb's 'to boot, to boot'; hence, the manuscript almost certainly differed from Q2. F also differs from Q2. It would therefore seem most economical to suppose that F differs from Q2 *because* the manuscript did, and that F's variant results from consultation of the manuscript rather than oversight compounded by compositorial sophistication. This requires us to assume that Shakespeare, when he came to this point in Q1, discarded the Qa 'to ſaue thee' as nonsense, did not remember (or care to preserve) exactly what he originally wrote, but did remember and restore the word-play on 'boot'. A similar combination of partial recall combined with partial revision must be assumed often elsewhere, and seems acceptable here. We have therefore retained F. However, the annotator or the compositor might have substituted 'and' for the wrong 'to': 'And boot to boot' would be more intelligible.

4.5.225/2432 happie;] Q2; ~, F. See Taylor, 'Folio Compositors', 68-9.

4.5.231/2438 Durst] Q1; darſt Q2, Dar'ſt F

4.5.234/2441 'cagion] Q; 'caſion F. F could easily result from substitution of the common for the unusual form.

4.5.236/2443 voke] Q1; volke Q2, F. (Probably an unintentional normalization.)

4.5.237/2444 swaggerd] Q1; zwaggar'd Q2, zwaggerd F. Here and elsewhere Q2 (and hence F) elaborate the indications of dialect in Edgar's speech, in a manner typical of Jaggard's shop. (See for instance Q3 of *Henry V*.)

4.5.238/2445 so] Q1; zo Q2, F

4.5.240/2447 ice] F; ile Q. Stone calls F's form 'a Northernism', an error resulting from misreading of manuscript; but see Kökeritz, 39, 279-80.

4.5.240/2447 Batton] BLAYNEY (Furness); bat-|tero Qa; bat Qb, Q2; Ballow F. F's word, for which there are no parallels, looks like a misreading of the same word behind Qa's 'battero'.

4.5.241/2448 ile] Q1; chill Q2, F. Q1 might, alternatively, be emended to 'ice', as at 4.5.240/2447.

4.5.243/2450 Sir] Q1; zir Q2, Zir F

4.5.256/2463 sorrow] Q1; sorry Q2, F

4.5.258/2465 manners:] F; ~, Q

4.5.258/2465 not.] POPE; ~, Q1, F; ~, Q2. Stone (272) regards F's mispunctuation as clear evidence of derivation from Q1, via the manuscript. This assumes serious misunderstanding in the manuscript, and conflicts with the clear evidence of Q2 influence on this Folio column. It seems more likely—as Rowe and Johnson assumed—that 'Leaue' governs 'manners' as well as 'waxe' (intelligibly enough), and that Compositor B inadvertently omitted a stronger stop after 'not'. Whether this interpretation of the sense derives from manuscript cannot be determined, but since Q1 is ambiguous, we have no other evidence of Shakespeare's preference here.

4.5.269/2475 and for you her owne for] Q1 (roman); not in Q2, F

4.5.269/2475 venter.] RIDLEY; Venter, Q1; not in Q2, F

4.6.0.1/2492.2 4.6] This edition; Scæna Septima F. See Taylor, 'Date and Authorship', 417-18.

4.6.0.2/2492.1 and] Q, Fb; not in Fa. See Taylor, 'Folio Compositors', 27-8.

4.6.20.1/2512.1 Enter ... Seruants] F (subs.); not in Q. See Taylor, 'Date and Authorship', 411-14. Richard Knowles ('The Case for Two Lears', SQ 36 (1985), 115-20) reports Blayney's conjecture that F's staging reflects a provincial tour. But (a) there is no evidence that the play was toured; (b) even if it were, the play requires musicians elsewhere, and musicians regularly toured; (c) different venues would allow or require different stagings, and one could not expect the company to enforce one option in all locales; (d) even if the staging were changed on tour, such changes should not have affected the prompt-book, or been passed on to a literary transcript.

4.6.22/2514 not of] Q, F3; of F1. F1 might be defended: the Gentleman wanting Cordelia's help in case Lear were not temperate. However, this seems unlikely, especially when compounded with metrical irregularity.

2515 restauratian] F; reſtoratiō Q1; Reſtoration Q2. Editors—and Howard-Hill ('The Problem', 10)—comment on the peculiarity of F's spelling, which is not recorded in OED; but it recurs in Dekker's Whore of Babylon, 3.2.142; Compositor E set the word nowhere else, and this might be his preferred spelling.

4.6.29/2521 warring] Q; iarring F. Q seems much more appropriate here, and Compositor E could have substituted 'iarring' from above (where it would have been written in the margin of his Q2 copy).

4.6.51/2543 your hands] Q; yours hand Fa; your hand Fb. Fa looks like compositorial metathesis, followed by (in Fb) correction without reference to copy.

4.6.52/2544 mocke] Q1; mocke me Q2, F

5.1.3/2572 abdication] Qa; alteration Qb, Q2, F

5.1.14/2583 me] Q; not in F

5.1.29/2598 Exeunt both the Armies] FURNESS; ~ F (at 5.1.27/2596); Exeunt. Q1 (after 'word'); Exit. Q2 (at 5.1.27/2596). F corrects Q2's wording but retains its misplacement.

5.1.36/2605 loue] Q; loues F. See 1.4.49/553.

5.1.42.1/2611.1 He ... paper] This edition; not in QF. See Q.

5.3.13/2653 ˏpoore Roguesˏ] Q, F2; (~) F1

5.3.24/2664 goodyeare] This edition; good Q; good yeares F. See Division, 488-9. See also John Day's Isle of Gulls, 'What a gudyere aile you mother' (H2ᵛ).

5.3.25/2665.1 Exeunt. Manet Edmond and the Captaine] BLAYNEY (after Theobald); not in Q1; Exit Q2, F

5.3.37.2/2677.1-2 with Drumme and Trumpet] This edition; not in F. See Taylor, 'The War', 33.

5.3.45/2685 and appointed guard,] Qb, Q2; not in Qa, F. F returns not only (presumably via the manuscript) to Qa's text, but also to its lineation. Q2 divides into two lines (as here), whereas Q1a and F both set 'To send ... retention' as one line. (Qb has an even longer line, with a turnover.) Since the annotator need not have altered Q2's lineation when he excised the three words, and since Compositor E is apparently never guilty of such gratuitous relineation (and was wasting space elsewhere on this page), the manuscript must have followed Q's arrangement.

5.3.76/2716 attaint] Q; arreſt F

5.3.77/2717 Sister] Q, ROWE; Siſters F. See 1.4.49/553.

5.3.91/2731 he is] Q, F2; hes F1

5.3.112/2752 lost:] THEOBALD; ~, QF

5.3.113/2753 tooth,] THEOBALD; ~. Q1; ~ : Q2, F

5.3.120/2760 Behold it is the priuiledge] Q; Behold it is my priuiledge, | The priuiledge F. Duthie plausibly suggested that F's redundant and unmetrical reading resulted from an erroneous first start, 'my priuiledge' not being properly cancelled before the correct reading 'the priuiledge' (1949, p. 422). But if the error were compositorial, as he suggested, it seems unlikely that the first line would have been finished (filled in with blank spaces) and a new line begun with the currente calamo correction; moreover, since the page was set by Compositor E, it was probably proof-read more carefully than usual, and—though errors do slip through—something so blatant as this shouldn't have. If the proposed duplication occurred in the manuscript, however, the annotator might well have transferred it to the printer's copy, since it makes acceptable sense. Compositor E would then have split the line because it would not fit his column.

5.3.120/2760 Honour] This edition; Honours F; tongue Q. No one seems to have questioned F's plural, but all the other nouns in the four following lines are singular, as is Q's variant here; Compositor E is notoriously apt to add terminal 's'; and 'integrity or good name or high rank' (singular) seems more appropriate here than 'honours won, marks of esteem earned' (plural).

5.3.123/2763 Despight] Q; Deſpiſe F. F can hardly result from misreading of Q, or typographical error; even in manuscript, 'ſ' and 't' are not easily confused; F's error presumably results from substitution. Always elsewhere E spelled 'despight' (as in Q), not 'despite' (as presumed by Duthie, in explanation of F's error).

5.3.134/2774 ˏsome say,ˏ] Q; (~) F

5.3.135/2775 well demand,] This edition (Hudson); well delay, F; claim, delay, ECCLES (conj. in Furness). As Eccles asked, 'how can he be said to "disdain and spurn" that which, without delay, he determines to undertake?' Moreover, with 'delay', the whole clause added by F ('What ... delay') can only refer to the combat, which hardly seems appropriate to what precedes or follows. Goneril later claims that Edmond is 'By th' law of Armes ... not bound to answer | An vnknowne opposite' (5.3.143-4/2783-4); she says nothing about a right to 'delay', instead stressing—as do the preceding lines here—Edgar's refusal to give his name. Edgar's identity is, of course, the crucial dramatic fact here, and 'demand' is a good technical verb in a trial by combat (as at Richard II 1.3.7/286). Emendation to 'demand' thus makes the meaning of the added line, and its relation to the context, much clearer. The misreading could have been made by (a) the scribe who prepared the manuscript, (b) the annotator who transferred the line to the margin of Q2, or (c) Compositor E. But the error would hardly have been possible unless 'demād' or 'demand' were misread 'delaie', and given E's conservatism it was probably the scribe or annotator who normalized the latter to 'delay'. For l/minim misreadings, see Taylor, 'Textual Double Knots', note 20.

5.3.137/2777 those] Q1; theſe F. Q2 omits the whole line, which therefore must have been reintroduced by the annotator. Q1's 'those' seems much more appropriate, and F could result from an easy and common misreading by scribe, annotator, or compositor.

5.3.141.1/2781.1 Alarums. Fight] ROWE; Alarums. Fights F (after

5.3.142/2782); *not in* Q. The second plural probably results from assimilation or Compositor E's fondness for terminal 's'; the misplacement from the direction's ambiguous marginal status in the manuscript or the annotated quarto.

5.3.141.1/2781.1 *Edmond is vanquished*] This edition; *not in* QF. See Q.

5.3.142/2782 ALL] BLAYNEY (Van Dam); *Alb.* QF

5.3.143/2783 Armes] Q; Warre F. 'What governs trial by combat is the law of arms, and even if a 'law of Warre' were supposed to exist it would be irrelevant' (Blayney).

5.3.146/2786 stople] Q1; ftop Q2, F

5.3.150-1/2790-1 Most monstrous! | O,] F; Moft monftrous, Q1; Monfter, Q2. In Q the whole speech is addressed to Gonoril; in F the question is directed at Edmond. Q2's error would have made it easier for the annotator to supply the first three words in the margin, rather than attempt so complicated a correction of Q2; we therefore take F's punctuation as authoritative, linking 'O' to the following question rather than (as in Globe and other editions) the preceding exclamation. This relates F's added interjection to its change of addressee. See also lineation notes.

5.3.225/2865 the Captaine,] Q1; *not in* Q2, F

5.3.226.1/2866.1 [*Exit Gentleman*]] This edition; *not in* QF. Most editors follow Q in attributing this line to Albany, and thus send off Edgar; Theobald had a 'Messenger', Schmidt a 'Captain', exit. Since F requires a '*Gent⟨leman⟩.*' to enter with or soon after Lear, it seems sensible to have him exit here. The use of the same Gentleman for both functions has, in any case, an ironic appropriateness. See Q.

5.3.231.3/2871.2-3 *followed by the Gentleman*] This edition; *not in* QF. See above.

5.3.232/2872 Howle, howle, howle, howle] Q; Howle, howle, howle F. See *Division*, 285.

5.3.232/2872 you] Q, F3; your F1

5.3.236/2876 *He lays her downe*] This edition; *not in* QF

5.3.252/2892 them] Q; him F. Compositor E commits the same error at *Titus* 2.3.257/910.

5.3.256/2896 This] SCHMIDT (W. S. Walker); this is F. Compare *Cymbeline* 5.5.64/2570. Compositor E interpolated 'is' at *Troilus* 1.2.113/259.

5.3.265/2905 You'r] Q1; You are Q2, F2; Your are F

5.3.268/2908 thinke I] Q1; I thinke Q2, F

5.3.285/2925 *To Kent*] This edition; *not in* QF. See *Division*, 71.

REJECTED SECOND QUARTO VARIANTS

1.1.171/172 made] make
1.1.182/183 hast] hath
1.1.188/189 of] or
1.1.222/223 plant] plaint
1.1.299/301 starts] ftars
1.2.15/323 a] *not in* Q2
1.2.68/374 It is his.] F; ~? Q1; Is it his? Q2
1.2.84/390 fhold] fhal
1.3.0.1/483.1 and] and a
1.4.64/568 wrong'd] is wrong'd
1.4.69/573 intoo't] F; into't Q1; into it Q2
1.4.101/605 on's] of his
1.4.107/611-12 Coxcombes] F: coxcombs Q1; coxcombe Q2
1.4.129/634 for't] for it
1.4.143/648 i'th'] in the
1.4.162/667 And] If
1.4.174/679 now thou] Qb, F; thou, thou Qa, Q2
1.4.218/723 should] you fhould
1.4.219/724 a] one
1.4.230/735 Which] ; that Q1; and Q2
1.4.235/740 repents] F; repent's Q1; repent's vs Q2
1.4.241/746 lyest.] F; lift, Q1; leffer, Q2
1.4.280/785 vntented] Qb, F; vntender Qa, Q2
1.4.281/786 Pierce] Qb, F; peruse Qa, Q2
1.4.322/828 attaskt] Qb; at task F; alapt Qa, Q2
1.4.327/833 *Exeunt*] *Exit.*
1.5.16/849 she's] fhe is
1.5.23/856 fide 's] F; fide's Q1; fide his Q2
1.5.31/864 to his] vnto his
2.1.0.1/884.1 *seuerally*] F; *meeting* Q1; *meetes him* Q2
2.1.10-12/894-6 CURAN Haue ... word.] *not in* Q2
2.1.26/910 'gainst] F; gainft Q1; againft Q2
2.1.122/1006 differences] F, Qb (diferences); defences Qa, Q2
2.1.123/1007 home] Qb, F; hand Qa, Q2
2.1.129/1013 *Exeunt*] Q F; *Exit.* Q2 (*after* 1071, 'vfe')
2.2.89/1102 do's] F; does Q1; doth Q2
2.2.111/1124 too't] to it
2.2.123/1136 reuerent] vnreuerent
2.2.134/1147 selfe] *not in* Q2
2.2.135/1148 of] off
2.2.156/1169 miracles] F; my rackles Qa; my wracke Qb, Q2
2.2.184.1/1197.1 *Foole, and Gentleman*] *and a Knight* Q2; *not in* Q1
2.2.191-2/1204-5 by'th' ... by'th' ... by'th'] by the ... by the ... by the
2.2.193/1206 then] hen

2.2.198/1212 do't] do it
2.2.199/1213 do't] do it
2.2.238/1252 And] If
2.2.294/1308 'em ... 'em] vm ... vm Q1; them vp ... vm Q2
2.2.333/1347 blacke] blacke
2.2.334/1347 strooke] ftroke
2.2.354/1368 to'th'] to the
2.2.372/1386 Sir] *not in* Q2
2.2.406/1420 Sir] *not in* Q2
2.2.441/1455 life is] F; life as Q1; life's as Q2
2.2.449/1463 so] Q1; too Q2
2.2.458/1472 hundred] *not in* Q2
2.2.459/1473 Or] *not in* Q2
2.2.481/1495.1 *Exeunt*] *Exeunt omnes*
3.1.25/1520 feare] doubt
3.2.2/1530 Cataracts] caterickes Q1; carterickes Q2
3.2.6/1534 Sindge] finge Q1; fing Q2
3.2.36.1/1564.1 *Enter Kent*] *after* 'patience' Q1; *after* 'nothing' Q2
3.2.50/1578 pudder] Thundring
3.3.22/1646 me] to me
3.4.6/1654 contentious] F; crulentious Qa, Q2; tempeftious Qb
3.4.9/1657 Thou'dst] thou wouldft
3.4.14/1662 beates] F, Qb; beares Qa, Q2
3.4.16/1664 too't] to it
3.4.41/1689 name's] name is
3.4.74/1724 o'th'] at'h Q1; of the Q2
3.4.99/1749 on's] ons Q1; ones Q2
3.4.108/1758 Flibbertigibbet] F; *fliberdegibek* Qb; *Sriberdegibit* Qa; *Sirberdegibit* Q2
3.4.109/1759 giues] Qb, F; gins Qa, Q2
3.4.110/1761 Hare-lippe] F, Qb (hare lip); harte lip Qa, hart lip Q2
3.4.114/1764 A met the Night-Mare] Qb (he), F (He); a nellthu night more Qa; anel-|thu night Moore Q2
3.4.117/1767 Witch] Qb, F; with Qa, Q2
3.4.122/1772 wall-Neut] Qb (wall newt), F; wall-wort Qa, Q2
3.4.123/1773 furie] fruite
3.4.159/1809 true] truth
3.4.160/1810 hath] has
3.5.10/1832 of] off
3.6.0.1-2/1847.1 *Kent disguised, and Gloucester*] *Glofter and Lear, Kent, Foole, and Tom* Q1; *Glocefter, Lear, Kent, Foole, and Tom* Q2
3.6.9/1856 be] may be
3.6.38/1885 garments] garment
3.6.42/1889 i'th'] in the
3.6.48/1895 in't] in it

3.7.44/1947 late] lately
3.7.45/1948 You haue] haue you
3.7.56/1959 Annointed] F, Qb (annoynted); aurynted Qa, Q2
3.7.58/1961 buoy'd] F, Qb (bod); layd Qa, laid Q2
3.7.59/1962 Stelled] F, Qb; steeled Qa, Q2
4.1.44/2043 toward] to Q2. (Further evidence that this form 'toward' derives from the Folio's manuscript: see *Division*, 276.)
4.1.63/2062 do's] doth
4.1.72/2071 I shall] shall I
4.2.12/2085 terror] F, Qb (terrer); curre Qa, Q2
4.2.21/2094 command] Qb, F; coward Qa, Q2
4.2.24/2097 fare thee well] far you well Q1; faryewell Q2
4.2.28/2101 thee a] Qb, F: thee Qa, Q2
4.2.29.1/2102.1 Enter Albany] *not in* Q1; Enter the Duke of Albeney Q2 (after Goneril's next speech)
4.3.8/2146 wisedome] wisedome do
4.3.19/2158 Enter a] Enter F; Enter a Q2
4.4.3/2170 Sister is] sister's
4.4.8/2175 on] on a
4.4.14/2181 o'th'] of the
4.5.17/2224 beach] beake
4.5.21/2228 Pebble chafes] peebles chafe
4.5.26/2233 th'] the
4.5.34/2241 Is] tis
4.5.45/2252 had thought] thought had
4.5.78/2285 'twould] would it Q1; would he Q2
4.5.99/2306 euery thing] all
4.5.116/2323 lacke] want
4.5.135/2342 of it] oft Q1; on't Q2
4.5.142/2349 no] *not in* Q2
4.5.182/2389 Son in Lawes] sonnes in law
4.5.185/2392 Your ... Daughter] *not in* Q2
4.5.188/2395 shall haue] shall haue a
4.5.193/2400 water-pots.] F; waterpots, I and laying Autums | dust. | *Lear.* Q1; water-pottles, I and laying Au-|tumnes dust. *Gent.* Good Sir. | *Lear.*
4.5.198/2405 and] if
4.5.207/2414 euery one] euery ones
4.5.214/2421 Her] His
4.5.268/2474 *affectionate*] your ~ Q1; & your ~ Q2
4.5.278/2484 thy] his
4.6.11/2503 be't] be it
4.6.11/2503 good] *not in* Q2
4.6.16/2508 That] *not in* Q2
4.6.21/2513 Be] (Before the speech Q1 has the prefix '*Gent.*', Q2 the prefix '*Kent*'.)
4.6.41/2533 do you know me] know me Q1; know ye me Q2
4.6.42/2534 where] when
4.6.56/2548 in my perfect] perfect in my
4.6.61/2553 not] no
5.1.3/2572 he's] he is
5.1.8/2577 but then] then
5.1.9/2578 In] I, Q1; ~, Q2
5.1.28/2597 man] one
5.1.41/2610 o're-looke] looke ore
5.1.57/2626 intends] entends Q1; extends Q2
5.1.12/2652 and sing] *not in* Q2
5.3.19/2659 by th'] by the
5.3.37.1/2677.1 Albany] Duke Q1, the Duke Q2
5.3.38/2678 shew'd] shewne
5.3.47/2687 bosome] blossomes
5.3.51/2691 at] at a
5.3.79/2719 this] her
5.3.114/2754 Yet am I Noble] *not in* Q2
5.3.115/2755 Which] What
5.3.121/2761 my] *not in* Q2
5.3.125/2765 to thy] to the
5.3.130/2770 are] Is
5.3.143/2783 answer] offer
5.3.150/2790 for't] for it
5.3.163/2803 thee he] he thee
5.3.170/2810 know't] know it
5.3.194/2834 be] be any
5.3.196/2836 Hearing of this.] *not in* Q2
5.3.202/2842 confesses] has confest
5.3.207/2847 vs] *not in* Q2
5.3.211/2851 thing] things
5.3.220/2860 in it) to'th'] into ~ the
5.3.230/2870 That ... selfe] *not in* Q2
5.3.234/2874 she's] O, she is
5.3.237/2877 or] and
5.3.238/2878 Why then she] she then
5.3.241/2881 which] that
5.3.244/2884 you Murderors,] your murderous~ Q1; you murdrous~ Q2
5.3.246/2886 Ha:] *not in* Q2
5.3.251/2891 haue] ha
5.3.251/2891 with my good] that with my
5.3.254/2894 not] none
5.3.267/2907 fore-done] fore-doom'd
5.3.285/2925 you vndo] vndo
5.3.289/2929 hates him] hates him much
5.3.296/2936 gor'd] good

INCIDENTALS

95 mend] Fa: Mend Fb   95 speech a] Q, Fb; speec ah Fa   147 wouldst] F4; wouldest F1   160 LEAR] Kear.   161 KENT] Lent.   161 swear'st] swear.st   179 reuok'd] ~,   189 Burgundie] Bugundie   224 Maiesty,] Q; ~. F   229 dishonour'd] Q1; dishonoured Q2, F   235 t'haue] t~haue F (*with an apostrophe floating after* had'st *in the line above, at different heights in different copies of F*)   271 nam'd] named QF   318 Bastardie] Barstadie F   325 Fathers] Farhers F   421 Villain,] F (*partially inked space sometimes mistaken for comma*)   429 predominance,] ~.   434 Starre.] ~,   457 all.]~,   549 Clot-pole] ~-|~   691 endured] Q; endur'd   758 mou'd] moued   829 prais'd] prai'sd   892 eare-kissing] (*Some copies show nothing in the space between* 'r' *and the hyphen, but others have faint inking which suggests the* 'e' *present in Q.*)   969 came] Q, Fb; csme Fa   979 bad.] Q, Fb; ~, Fa   988 your] yout   1027 three-suited, hundred] three-suited-hundred   1059 that strikes] Fb (strikes); that; s strikes Fa   1109 Nature] Q, Fb; Narure Fa   1138 King,] ~.   1143 sit till] Q, Fb; si ttill Fa   1152 restrain'd] restrained QF   1175 heauie] heanie   1176 shamefull] shamefnll   1202 thy] ahy   1203 Garters,] ~∧   1212 Iuno] Iuuo   1248 With] Wirh   1262 counsell,] Fa; ~∧ Fb   1276 fetches,] Fb; ~∧ Fa; Iustice, Q   1329 restrain'd] restrained   1416 when] Q, Fb; wheu Fa   1454 then Nature] Q, Fb; then Nattue Fa   1462 Daughters] Q, Fb; Daughte s Fa   1470 Ile,] Q, Fb; ~, Fa   1475 and's] an'ds   1655 skin: so,] F *press-correction* (*Huntington copy*); skin.so∧ Fa; skinso: Fb   1662 there,] Fb; ~∧ Q, Fa   1669 lies, let] Fb; lie slet Fa   1703 Traitor] Q, Fb; T aitor Fa   1725 commit not∧] Q; ~, F   1739 nor] Nor   1766 troth∧ plight] Q; troth-plight F   1792 ventur'd] ventured F   1880 dry.] Q, Fb, Q; hin Fa   1904 him] Fb, Q; hin Fa (*reported*). (Fa *is in fact either a defective m or one not inking properly.*)   1916 hence.] ~,   1919 Lords∧] Q; ~, F   2057 heauens] heau'ns   2107 eye∧ discerning] Q1; ~-~ F   2143 Darnell∧] Q, F *c.w.*: ~,   2168 Madam.] Q; ~, F   2188 much,] Q; ~∧ F   2264 Bourne,] Q; ~∧ F   2270 Tyrants] Tyranrs   2281 preseru'd] preserued QF   2295 Crow-keeper] Q; ~-|~ F   2470 done,] Q1; ~: Q2, ~. F   2475 *Seruant*,] ~.   2477 indistinguish'd] Q1, F4; vndistinguisht Q2; indinguish'd F   2479 in the] in rhe   2573 selfe-reprouing] Q2; selfereprouing F

THE TRAGEDY OF KING LEAR

2590 particular] Q, F2; particurlar F1   2609 fare thee well] farethee well *to preceding blank line*)   2723 arm'd] armed   2723 Trumpet] Trmpet   2665 'em] e'm   2678 straine,] Q; ~‸ F (*comma shifted to preceding blank line*)   2740 Trumpet] Trumper   2747 Againe] *Her.* Againe   2748 Againe] *Her.* Againe   2766 illustrious] Q, F2; illuſtirous F1   2779 scarsely] Q2; ſcarely F   2846 tremble,] Q; ~. F   2908 dead.] Q; ~‸ F   2926 this?] Fb; ~, Fa

FOLIO STAGE DIRECTIONS

1.1.0.1-2/0.1   *Enter Kent, Gloucester, and Edmond.*
1.1.32.1, 33.1-2/33.1, 34.1-2   *Sennet. Enter King Lear, Cornwall, Albany, Gonerill, Re-|gan, Cordelia, and attendants.*
1.1.35/36   *Exit.*
1.1.186/188   *Exit.*
1.1.186.1-2/188.1-2   *Flourish. Enter Gloster with France, and Bur-|gundy, Attendants.*
1.1.266/267   *Flourish. Exeunt.*
1.1.282.1/283.1   *Exit France and Cor.*
1.1.306/308.1   *Exeunt.*
1.2.0.1/308.2   *Enter Bastard.*
1.2.22.1-2/330.1   *Enter Gloucester.*
1.2.47/354   *Glou. reads.*
1.2.115/423   *Exit*
1.2.130.1/439.1   *Enter Edgar.*
1.2.167/477   *Exit.*
1.2.173/483   *Exit.*
1.3.0.1/483.1   *Enter Gonerill, and Steward.*
1.3.20/503   *Exeunt.*
1.4.0.1/503.1   *Enter Kent.*
1.4.7.1-2/510.1-2   *Hornes within. Enter Lear and Attendants.*
1.4.43.1/546.1   *Enter Steward.*
1.4.45/548   *Exit.*
1.4.75.1/579.1   *Enter Steward.*
1.4.92.1/596.1   *Enter Foole.*
1.4.169.1/674.1   *Enter Gonerill.*
1.4.235/740   *Enter Albany.*
1.4.269.1/774.1   *Exit.*
1.4.273.1/778.1   *Enter Lear.*
1.4.290/795   *Exit*
1.4.300/806   *Exit*
1.4.312/818   *Enter Steward.*
1.4.327/833   *Exeunt*
1.5.0.1-2/833.1   *Enter Lear, Kent, Gentleman, and Foole.*
1.5.8/841   *Exit.*
1.5.50.1/884   *Exeunt.*
2.1.0.1/884.1   *Enter Bastard, and Curan, seuerally.*
2.1.13.1/897.1   *Exit.*
2.1.15.1/898.1   *Enter Edgar.*
2.1.32.1/916   *Exit Edgar.*
2.1.36/920   *Enter Gloster, and Seruants with Torches.*
2.1.77.1/961.1   *Tucket within.*
2.1.84.1/968.1   *Enter Cornewall, Regan, and Attendants.*
2.1.129/1013   *Exeunt. Flourish.*
2.2.0.1-2/1013.1   *Enter Kent, and Steward seuerally.*
2.2.41.1-3/1054.1-2   *Enter Bastard, Cornewall, Regan, Gloster, Seruants.*
2.2.133.1/1146.1   *Stocks brought out.*
2.2.142.1/1155.1   *Exit.*
2.2.150/1163   *Exit.*
2.2.164/1177   *Enter Edgar.*
2.2.184/1197   *Exit.*
2.2.184.1/1197.1   *Enter Lear, Foole, and Gentleman.*
2.2.234.1/1248.1   *Exit.*
2.2.260.1/1274.1   *Enter Lear, and Gloster:*
2.2.291.1/1305.1   *Exit.*
2.2.297.1-2/1311.1   *Enter Cornewall, Regan, Gloster, Seruants.*
2.2.299.1/1313.1   *Kent here set at liberty.*
2.2.355/1369   *Tucket within.*
2.2.355.1/1369.1   *Enter Steward.*
2.2.360.1/1374.1   *Enter Gonerill.*
2.2.457.1/1471.1   *Storme and Tempest.*
2.2.459.1/1473.1   *Exeunt.*
2.2.467/1481   *Enter Gloster.*
2.2.481/1495.1   *Exeunt.*
3.1.0.1-2/1495.2-3   *Storme still. Enter Kent, and a Gentleman, seuerally.*
3.1.33/1528   *Exeunt.*
3.2.0.1/1528.1   *Storme still. Enter Lear, and Foole.*
3.2.36.1/1564.1   *Enter Kent.*
3.2.78.1/1606.1   *Exit.*
3.2.96/1624   *Exit.*
3.3.0.1/1624.1   *Enter Gloster, and Edmund.*
3.3.19/1643   *Exit.*
3.3.24/1648   *Exit.*
3.4.0.1/1648.1   *Enter Lear, Kent, and Foole.*
3.4.3/1651   *Storme still*
3.4.27.1/1675.1   *Exit.*
3.4.36.1-2/1684.1-2   *Enter Edgar, and Foole.*
3.4.58.1/1707.1   *Storme still.*
3.4.94.1/1744.1   *Storme still.*
3.4.103.1/1753.1   *Enter Gloucester, with a Torch.*
3.4.152.1/1802.1   *Storm still*
3.4.172/1822   *Exeunt*
3.5.0.1/1822.1   *Enter Cornwall, and Edmund.*
3.5.25/1847   *Exeunt.*
3.6.0.1-2/1847.1   *Enter Kent, and Gloucester.*
3.6.5.1/1852.1   *Exit*
3.6.5.2-3/1852.2   *Enter Lear, Edgar, and Foole.*
3.6.43.1/1890.1   *Enter Gloster.*
3.6.55.1/1902.1   *Exeunt*
3.7.0.1-2/1902.1-2   *Enter Cornwall, Regan, Gonerill, Bastard, | and Seruants.*
3.7.11.1/1914.1   *Enter Steward.*
3.7.21/1924   *Exit*
3.7.26/1939   *Enter Gloucester, and Seruants.*
3.7.78.1/1981.1   *Killes him.*
3.7.92/1995   *Exit with Glouster.*
3.7.96.1/1999.1   *Exeunt,*
4.1.0.1/1999.2   *Enter Edgar.*
4.1.9/2008   *Enter Glouster, and an Oldman.*
4.1.51/2050   *Exit*
4.1.74.1/2073.1   *Exeunt.*
4.2.0.1-2/2073.2-3   *Enter Gonerill, Bastard, and Steward.*
4.2.26/2099   *Exit.*
4.2.29.1/2102.1   *Enter Albany.*
4.2.37.1/2110.1   *Enter a Messenger.*
4.2.65/2138   *Exeunt.*
4.3.0.1-2/2138.1-2   *Enter with Drum and Colours, Cordelia, Gentlemen, | and Souldiours.*
4.3.20/2158   *Enter Messenger.*
4.3.29/2167   *Exeunt.*
4.4.0.1/2167.1   *Enter Regan, and Steward.*
4.4.40.1/2207.1   *Exeunt*
4.5.0.1-2/2207.2-3   *Enter Gloucester, and Edgar.*
4.5.80/2287   *Enter Lear.*
4.5.183.1/2390.1   *Enter a Gentleman.*
4.5.199.1/2406.1   *Exit.*
4.5.214.1/2421.1   *Exit.*
4.5.225/2432   *Enter Steward.*
4.5.260.1/2467.1   *Reads the Letter.*
4.5.282.1/2488.1   *Drum afarre off.*
4.5.286.1/2492.1   *Exeunt.*
4.6.0.1-2/2492.2-3   *Enter Cordelia, Kent, and Gentleman.*
4.6.20.1/2512.1   *Enter Lear in a chaire carried by Seruants*
4.6.77/2569   *Exeunt*

5.1.0.1-2/2569.1-2 Enter with Drumme and Colours, Edmund, Regan. | Gentlemen, and Souldiers.
5.1.15.1-2/2584.1-2 Enter with Drum and Colours, Albany, Gonerill, Soldiers.
5.1.27.1/2596.1 Enter Edgar.
5.1.29/2598 Exeunt both the Armies.
5.1.41/2610 Exit.
5.1.41.1/2610.1 Enter Edmund.
5.1.45/2614 Exit.
5.1.60/2629 Exit.
5.2.0.1-4/2629.1-4 Alarum within. Enter with Drumme and Colours, Lear, | Cordelia, and Souldiers, ouer the Stage, and Exeunt. | Enter Edgar, and Gloster.
5.2.4.1/2633.1 Exit.
5.2.4.2/2633.2 Alarum and Retreat within. | Enter Edgar.
5.2.11.1/2640.1 Exeunt.
5.3.0.1-3/2640.1-2 Enter in conquest with Drum and Colours, Edmund, Lear, | and Cordelia, as prisoners, Souldiers, Captaine.
5.3.25/2665.1 Exit.
5.3.37/2677 Exit Captaine.

5.3.37.1-2/2677.1-2 Flourish. Enter Albany, Gonerill, Regan, Soldiers.
5.3.95.1/2735.1 Enter a Herald.
5.3.101.1/2741.1 A Trumpet sounds.
5.3.102/2742 Herald reads.
5.3.106.1/2746.1 1· Trumpet
5.3.107.1/2747.1 2 Trumpet.
5.3.108.1/2748.1 3 Trumpet.
5.3.108.2/2748.2 Trumpet answers within.
5.3.108.2/2748.2 Enter Edgar armed.
5.3.141.1/2781.1 Alarums. Fights.
5.3.150/2790 Exit.
5.3.196.1/2836.1 Enter a Gentleman.
5.3.204.1/2844.1 Enter Kent.
5.3.205.1/2845.1 Gonerill and Regans bodies brought out.
5.3.231.2-3/2871.2-3 Enter Lear with Cordelia in his armes.
5.3.270/2910 Enter a Messenger.
5.3.287/2927 He dies.
5.3.302.1/2942.1 Exeunt with a dead March.

MACBETH

'*Mackbeth*' (BEPD 404) is among the plays listed in the Stationers' Register general entry for the Folio on 8 November 1623, and was first printed in that volume, where it was set by Compositors A and B. Their copy is fairly generally agreed to have been a prompt-book (Greg, *Folio*, 392-5). Various features of the play suggest that it has been shortened (ibid., 389-90) and, even more strongly, that it contains material not by Shakespeare. Suspicion centres on the two songs referred to in F only by their opening phrases ('*Come away, come away, &c.*', '*Blacke Spirits, &c.*'), and spreads to the rest of 3.5/Sc. 16, to Hecate's lines introducing 'Blacke Spirits', and to part, at least, of Hecate's speech introducing the dance at 4.1.141/1432, because of their stylistic divergence from the remainder of the play. Songs with the same opening phrases are found in Thomas Middleton's play *The Witch*, which survives only in a manuscript transcribed by Ralph Crane, and is of uncertain date (though recent studies converge in suggesting composition *c*.1613). Middleton's epistle tells us that his play was 'ignorantly-ill-fated'; it had been 'Acted by his Maties Seruants at the Black-friers'. It seems likely that two of its songs were used in a revision of *Macbeth*, probably for court performance, at some time after Shakespeare had ceased to be active with the King's Men; and it is quite possible that Middleton was responsible for whatever alterations and additions were made to the play. (See 'Canon and Chronology'.)

It is clear that, in our present state of knowledge, we cannot hope to recover the text as originally performed. Editors have been content to follow the Folio in giving merely the cue-lines for the songs. But the songs are extant, and there is at least presumptive evidence that they were sung in full in pre-Restoration performances of *Macbeth*. This evidence lies in the fact that when William Davenant came to revise the play for performances at Dorset Gardens in 1672-3, he included songs from *The Witch* even though he is highly unlikely to have known Middleton's play. As the Malone Society editor remarks, 'It seems more likely that the Duke of York's men were in possession of some stage-copy of *Macbeth* than that they derived these lines from a manuscript of *The Witch*: Davenant had received proprietary rights in *Macbeth* and other Shakespearian plays in December 1660' (pp. x-xi). This presumptive chain of transmission justifies J. M. Nosworthy's claim (acted on for the first time in our edition) that 'There is every reason why the two songs should be incorporated in the main text since they were clearly an integral part of the play in its later form, and since songs, whether or not Shakespeare wrote them, are normally set out in full in both quartos and Folio' (p. 53).

Although Davenant's use of the songs warrants the assumption that they had been given in full in performances of *Macbeth* by Shakespeare's company, Davenant's extensive alterations to the text of the play must raise the suspicion that divergences between his text of the songs and *The Witch* result from adaptation made by him rather than by Middleton (or whoever else had adapted the play for the King's Men). So we base our text of the songs on *The Witch*, collating them with the versions printed in 1674 in Davenant's adaptation. The first of the songs had appeared in 1673 in a text of the play based on the Folio; presumably the publishers acquired a text of the song from the theatre. This version is substantially the same as that printed in 1674 except for the allocation of lines. The Yale manuscript of Davenant's version offers no significant differences in wording.

An early account of a performance of *Macbeth* is found in the astrologer Simon Forman's manuscript 'Booke of Plaies' (Bodleian Library, Ashmole MS 208, fols. 200-13), describing plays he had seen. Forman saw *Macbeth* on Saturday, 20 April 1611 (wrongly dated '1610'). His account confirms that the Folio text represents accurately in most respects the play as acted in Shakespeare's lifetime; but in its omissions, and variations from F, it also gives some possible clues to the nature of the adaptation which the play apparently underwent after Shakespeare's death. For instance, despite Forman's interest in the supernatural, he does not mention Hecate, or the cauldron scene; he also describes the weird sisters as 'Nimphes', who are encountered in a wood (rather than upon the heath). The text we print is based on E. K. Chambers's slightly edited transcript (*Shakespeare*, ii. 337-8).

In Mackbeth at the Glob, 161⌈1⌉, the 20 of Aprill Saturday, ther was to be obserued, firste, howe Mackbeth and Bancko, 2 noble men of Scotland, Ridinge thorowe a wod, ther stode before them 3 women feiries or Nimphes, And saluted Mackbeth, sayinge, 3 tyms vnto him, haille Mackbeth, king of Codon; for thou shalt be a kinge, but shalt beget No kinges, &c. Then said Bancko, What all to Mackbeth And nothing to me. Yes, said the nimphes, haille to thee Bancko, thou shalt beget kinges, yet be no kinge. And so they departed & cam to the Courte of Scotland to Dunkin king of Scotes, and yt was in the dais of Edward the Confessor. And Dunkin bad them both kindly wellcome, And made Mackbeth forth with Prince of Northumberland, and sent him hom to his own castell, and appointed Mackbeth to prouid for him, for he would sup with him the next dai at night, & did soe. And Mackebeth contriued to kill Dunkin, & thorowe the persuasion of his wife did that night Murder the kinge in his own Castell, beinge his guest. And ther were many prodigies seen that night & the dai before. And when Mack Beth had murdred the kinge, the blod on his handes could not be washed of by Any meanes, nor from his wiues handes, which handled the bloddi daggers in hiding them, By which means they became both moch amazed & Affronted. The murder being knowen, Dunkins 2 sonns fled, the on to England, the ⌈other to⌉ Walles, to saue them selues, they being fled, they were supposed guilty of the murder of their father, which was nothinge so. Then was Mackbeth crowned kinge, and then he for feare of Banko, his old companion, that he should beget kinges but be no kinge him selfe, he contriued the death of Banko, and caused him to be Murdred on the way as he Rode. The next night, beinge at supper with his noble men whom he had bid to a feaste to the which also Banco should haue com, he began to speake of Noble Banco, and to wish that he wer ther. And as he thus did, standing vp to drincke a Carouse to him, the ghoste of Banco came and sate down in his cheier behind him. And he turninge About to sit down Again sawe the goste of Banco, which fronted him so, that he fell into a great passion of fear and fury, Vtterynge many wordes about his murder, by which, when they hard that Banco was Murdred they Suspected Mackbet.

Then MackDove fled to England to the kinges sonn, And soe they Raised an Army, And cam into Scotland, and at Dunston Anyse overthrue Mackbet. In the meantyme whille Macdouee was in England, Mackbet slewe Mackdoues wife & children, and after in the battelle Mackdoue slewe Mackbet.

Obserue Also howe Mackbetes quen did Rise in the night in her slepe, & walke and talked and confessed all, & the docter noted her wordes.

F's act and scene division has been generally accepted except in the final stretch of action, from 5.6/Sc. 26. F divides this into two scenes, the second beginning at 5.7.0.1/2041.2, and some later editors have added breaks at 5.10.0.1/2071.2 and 5.11.0.1/2105.4 (so Wilson, Muir, etc.). Hunter prints from 5.6/Sc. 26 as a single scene; but Pope's break after Macbeth's death seems right, less for considerations of place (Muir) than because a time interval may be presumed.

S.W.W./(G.T.)

WORKS CITED

Chambers, E. K., ed., *Macbeth*, Red Letter (n.d.)
Davenant, William, adapter, *Macbeth* (1674)
—— ed. Christopher Spencer, *Davenant's 'Macbeth' from the Yale Manuscript* (1961)
Ellis, Havelock, ed., *The Witch*, in vol. ii of Thomas Middleton, Mermaid, 2 vols. (1887–90)
Foakes, R. A., ed., *Macbeth*, Bobbs-Merrill (1968)
Furness, H. H., ed., *Macbeth*, New Variorum (1874)
Hunter, A. (Harry Rowe), ed., *Macbeth*, 2nd edition (1799)
Hunter, G. K., ed., *Macbeth*, New Penguin (1967)
Middleton, Thomas, *The Witch*, MSR, ed. W. W. Greg and F. P. Wilson (1950, for 1948)
Muir, Kenneth, ed., *Macbeth*, Arden (1951, etc.)
Nosworthy, J. M., *Shakespeare's Occasional Plays* (1965)
Shakespeare, William, *Macbeth* (1673)
Wilson, John Dover, ed., *Macbeth*, New (1947, revised 1951)

TEXTUAL NOTES

1.1.1/1   againe?] F; ~ˌ HANMER
1.1.5/5   the set] F; set POPE
1.1.9–10/9–10   2. WITCH *Padock* calls. | 3. WITCH Anon. | ALL Faire] SINGER 2 (Hunter); *All. Padock calls*ˌ anon: faire F; *2 Witch. Padock* calls—anon! | *All.* Fair POPE
1.2.0.3/11.3   Captaine] F; Sergeant. GLOBE. Malcolm calls him 'Serieant' (to avoid a jingle with 'Captiuitie'?); 'rank and function were not so clearly distinguished in the Scottish Army List for 1605' (Sisson, *New Readings*).
1.2.13   galloglasses] *after* F (Gallowgroſſes). F, apparently an error for 'Gallowglasses', is usually modernized to 'gallowglasses'. See OED.
1.2.14/25   Quarry] F; quarrel HANMER. Holinshed's use in the corresponding passage of the phrase 'rebellious quarell' means, says Muir, that Hanmer's emendation 'may be regarded as certain'. But 'his damned Quarry' makes perfect sense as 'its [i.e. Fortune's] condemned victim': i.e. fortune shone temporarily upon him. Shakespeare may diverge slightly as well as wholly from Holinshed.
1.2.26/37   breake] POPE; *not in* F1; breaking F2
1.2.31, 49, 1.3.93   Norwegian] F (Norweyan)
1.2.32/43   furbusht] F. Rowe's 'furbisht', treated by editors as an emendation, modernizes a normal spelling.
1.2.46/57   haste] F2; a haſte F1. The indefinite article with 'haste' is rare in Shakespeare, and 'a' is the word most frequently interpolated.
1.2.56   point, rebellious,] F; pointˌ rebellious, THEOBALD
1.2.59   Norways'] F (Norwayes)
1.2.61   Colum's] F (Colmes). Two syllables are needed; the island's present name is Inchcolm. 'Saint *Colme*' is Columba, shortened to either Columb or Colum; St Columb is a Cornish place-name.
1.3.30   weird] F (weyward)
1.3.37/115   Foris] POPE; Soris F
1.3.89   rebels'] F (Rebels)
1.3.94/172   make,] ROWE; ~ˌ F
1.3.95/173   haile] ROWE; Tale F
1.3.96/174   Came] ROWE; Can F
1.3.117/195   Cawdor to me] F; Cawdor me G.T. *conj.*
1.4.1/235   Are] F2; Or F1
1.5.22   'Thus . . . do'] For the quotation marks (*not in* F), see Muir.
1.5.28/321   Metaphysicall] F; metaphysic POPE. 'Metaphysic' was a regular adjective.

1.5.29, 30, 33, 37/322, 323, 326, 330   Seruant] CAPELL (*Attendant*); Messenger F
1.5.62/355   time,] THEOBALD; ~. F
1.5.64/357   the innocent] ROWE; th'innocent F
1.6.0.1/365.1   Hoboyes, and Torches] F. Wilson omits, as torches are 'most inappropriate to one of the few sunlit scenes'. The direction may be an accidental anticipation of that at 1.7.0.1/396.1, but the scene is not necessarily 'sunlit'.
1.6.4/369   Marlet] ROWE (martlet); Barlet F. 'Marlet' is an obsolete form of 'martlet'.
370   Mansonry] F; masonry POPE 2. This is OED's only occurrence before a 19th c. imitation; 'manson' is recorded as a 15th c. spelling of *mansion*.
1.6.5   mansionry] F (Manſonry)
1.6.6/371   Iutty] STEEVENS-REED 2; ~ˌ F
1.6.9/374   most] ROWE; muſt F
1.6.26   count] F (compt). An indifferent variant.
1.7.5/401   all, heere] ROWE; all. Heere F
1.7.6   shoal] F (Schoole). Theobald's reading 'shoal', strictly a modernization, has the force of an emendation.
1.7.22/418   Cherubin] F; cherubins MUIR (Cuningham). Though Shakespeare always uses 'cherubins' elsewhere, he may have been temporarily aware of the plural sense.
1.7.28/424   th'other.] F; th' other— ROWE
1.7.47/443   do] ROWE; no F
1.7.59   fail!] F (faile?)
1.7.68/464   lyes] F1; lie F2
2.1.0.1/478.2   Torch] F. '"Torch" implies a torch-bearer' (Wilson); 'Fleance probably acts as torch-bearer' (Muir). The direction at 2.1.9/487, '*a Seruant with a Torch*', surely implies that the servant carries the torch. However, as Banquo unloads sword and armour on to Fleance, a separate torch-bearer would be convenient.
2.1.55/533   strides] POPE; ſides F
2.1.56/534   sure] CAPELL (Pope); ſowre F. Shakespeare may have spelt 'sewre': see Wilson, *Manuscript of Shakespeare's 'Hamlet'*, 2 vols. (1963), 116.
2.1.57/535   way they] ROWE; they may F
2.2.8/550   Enter Macbeth [*aboue*] . . . Exit] CHAMBERS; *Enter Macbeth* F; *Mac.* [*Within*] STEEVENS. Chambers's suggestion seems the best way of accounting for F's entry direction; a brief appearance would make clear that it is Macbeth who speaks, and would ironically exploit the 'darkness' of the scene.

2.2.13/555   Enter ... below] CAMBRIDGE (*but following* STEEVENS *at* 2.2.8/550); *not in* F. See preceding note.
2.2.33–4   'Sleep ... sleep'] *as quotation* JOHNSON; *quotation extending to* Feast (2.2.38/580) HANMER
2.2.35   sleave] F (Sleeue)
602   incarnardine] F's spelling, though 'erroneous' (*OED*), may have stood in the manuscript.
2.3.5/619   time] F; time-server WILSON; time-pleaser KRABBE (*conj.* in *N&Q*, 218 (1972), 141–2); farmer FOAKES. F's phrase, meaning 'well-timed', is acceptable.
2.3.42.1/656.1   Exit Porter] This edition; *not in* F. He might leave later.
2.3.58/672   time. The] F; time, the KNIGHT
2.3.80/694   horror.] THEOBALD; horror. Ring the Bell. F. See Sisson, *New Readings*.
2.3.89.1/703.1   Enter ... Rosse] F. Capell omitted Ross, perhaps rightly; Macbeth and Lennox had exited together, whereas Ross appears as from nowhere. But a 'ghost' seems unlikely in a prompt-book: Ross might attend Lady Macbeth on her exit, or leave at 2.3.133.1/747.1.
2.3.111/725   Out-ran] JOHNSON; Out-run F. *OED* does not record 'run' as a past tense; misreading would be easy.
2.4.38/797   Well,] THEOBALD; ~∧ F
3.1.2, 3.4.132, 4.1.152   weird] F (weyard)
3.1.23/824   talke] MALONE; take F; take't KEIGHTLEY (Warburton). Some editors let F pass without comment; Wilson glosses 'tomorrow will serve'. But Malone's emendation makes excellent sense, and the error is easy; the reverse error occurs at *Hamlet* 1.1.144/144 (talkes F, takes Q2 and editors) and *Henry V* 2.1.50/535 (talke Q, take F and editors).
3.1.46/847   word with you:] F; word: STEEVENS–REED 2
3.1.71/872   Seedes] F; seed POPE. Though F seems unidiomatic, it is logically acceptable.
3.1.76/877   MURTHERERS] F (*Murth.*); 1 Mur. STEEVENS–REED 2. F uses '*Murth.*', unnumbered, three times in this scene, and each time it would be appropriate for both to speak. See also 3.1.116/917 and 3.1.140/941.
3.1.77   speeches?] F (~ :), ROWE; ~ ?— MUIR
3.1.80/881   selfe.] F; ~ ? MUIR
3.1.107/908   heart,] POPE; ~ ; F
3.1.113/914   wearie] F; weary'd CAPELL
3.1.116, 140/917, 941   MURTHERERS] DYCE, *after* F (*Murth.*). See note to 3.1.76/877.
3.1.131/932   perfect Spy] F. Much discussed. Johnson thought 'Spy' referred to the Second Murderer. Wilson postulated that 'a line or two, making the reference clear, has been cut' after the previous line. Proposed emendations of 'Spy' are unconvincing. Possibly 'perfect' should read 'perfect'st'. The best explanations of 'Spy' relate it to the sense of 'advance guard': Schmidt glosses 'i.e. that which will precede the time of the deed, and indicate that it is at hand'.
3.2.15/959   scorch'd] F; scotch'd THEOBALD
3.2.51/995   pale] F; paled HUDSON (Staunton)
3.3.7/1008   and] F2; end F1
3.4.0.3/1024.4   Lady sits] This edition; *not in* F
3.4.77/1101   time] WHITE; times F
3.4.88/1112   of] ROWE; o' F
3.4.104/1128   I inhabit then] F1. Often doubted, but no suggested emendation (see Furness) is convincing. Henley suggested that 'inhabit' expresses 'continuance in a given situation', comparing Milton, *Paradise Lost* vii. 162.
3.4.134/1158   worst:] JOHNSON; ~ , F
3.4.143/1167   in deed] THEOBALD; indeed F
3.5.34/1201   SPIRITS ... within] This edition; *Muſicke and a Song* F. We interpret F's direction as a call for an anticipation of the opening lines of the song found in *The Witch*; there they are given only once, but Davenant has '*Heccate, Heccate, Heccate! Oh come away*' in this position, and a cue for Hecate's lines; this seems needed. Many editors of *Macbeth*, printing only the cue line of the song, follow Capell in supposing that all of it should be sung at this point; but this is not suggested by F's directions, is not what Davenant prints, and is not consonant with the action required by the song.
3.5.37.1/1204.1   The Song] MIDDLETON (*Song ... in y*e *aire.*)
3.5.38/1205   SPIRITS ⌈*within*⌉] This edition; *Sing within.* F, 1673. *Song ... in y*e *aire* MIDDLETON. F follows its direction with '*Come away, come away, &c.*'. In Middleton the recurring direction '*in y*e *aire*' may mean simply that the singers are heard but not seen, though some kind of descent is required by the later direction '*A Spirit like a Cat descends*'. F's direction clearly implies that the singers should be off stage, initially at least; Hecate's 'my little spirit see | Sits in a Foggy cloud' permits but does not require the use of a machine. Davenant has *Machine descends* after 'stays for me', but even in his version the song is '*within*' and nothing suggests that all the singers were on the machine. Wilson directs '*A cloud descends*' but, not printing the song, makes no provision for the entrance or exit of its singers.
3.5.38–9/1205–6   Come ... away.] MIDDLETON; Come away Heccate, Heccate! Oh come away: DAVENANT.
3.5.40/1207   I come, I come, I come, I come] MIDDLETON; I come, I come. DAVENANT.
3.5.43/1210   SPIRITS ⌈*within*⌉] This edition; *in y*e *aire*. MIDDLETON (*bracketed beside* 3.5.44–5/1211–12); 2. DAVENANT
3.5.43/1210   ANOTHER SPIRIT ⌈*within*⌉ Heere.] This edition; heere∧ WITCH; 3. Here, DAVENANT
3.5.44/1211   OTHER SPIRITS ⌈*within*⌉] This edition; *in y*e *aire* MIDDLETON (*bracketed beside* 3.5.44–5/1211–12)
3.5.44/1211   And Hoppo too, and Hellwaine too] MIDDLETON (*no clear prefix*); 3. Here, and *Hopper* too, and *Helway* too. DAVENANT
3.5.45/1212   We ... we lack but] MIDDLETON (*no clear prefix*); 1. We want but you, we want but DAVENANT
3.5.47/1214   then] MIDDLETON; the DAVENANT
3.5.47/1214   mount.] MIDDLETON; mount, | I will but &c. DAVENANT
3.5.47.1/1214.1   Spirits appear aboue] This edition (*after* MIDDLETON, which has '*aboue*' bracketed right of 3.5.48–50/1215–17)
3.5.47.1/1214.1   A Spirit like a Cat descends] MIDDLETON (*bracketed left of* 3.5.49–50/1216–17); *placed here* ELLIS; *not in* DAVENANT. This placing gives time for the descent; Witch marks the spirit's arrival at ground level.
3.5.48/1215   SPIRITS ⌈*aboue*⌉] This edition; *aboue* MIDDLETON (*bracketed right of* 3.5.48–50/1215–17 (. . . so long)); 1. DAVENANT
3.5.48/1215   Ther's one comes downe] MIDDLETON; Here comes down one DAVENANT
3.5.48–9/1215–6   dues | A kisse] due, a Kiss DAVENANT
3.5.50/1217   long I muse, I muse] MIDDLETON (*long*|); long, I muse DAVENANT
3.5.52/1219   HECAT] MIDDLETON; 2. DAVENANT
3.5.52/1219   what newes: what newes?] MIDDLETON; What News? DAVENANT
3.5.53/1220   SPIRIT LIKE A CAT] ELLIS; *not in* MIDDLETON, DAVENANT
3.5.53/1220   still to] MIDDLETON; fair for DAVENANT
3.5.54/1221   Refuse: Refuse] MIDDLETON; refuse DAVENANT
3.5.55/1222   HECAT] MIDDLETON; *not in* DAVENANT
3.5.55/1222   Flight.] At this point in *The Witch* Hecate's son, Firestone, says 'hark, hark, the Catt sings a braue *Treble* in her owne language'. This is not part of the song, and seems irrelevant to *Macbeth*, though it might indicate a vocal flourish. Davenant omits.
3.5.55.1/1222.1   She ... sings] ELLIS (subs.), *after* MIDDLETON, which has the speech-prefix '*Hec. going vp*' before the next line
3.5.56/1223   goe] MIDDLETON; go, and DAVENANT
3.5.58/1225   SPIRITS *and* HECAT] This edition; *not in* MIDDLETON; 3. DAVENANT
3.5.58/1225   pleasure 'tis] MIDDLETON; pleasure's this DAVENANT
3.5.59/1226   ride in the] MIDDLETON; sail i'th' DAVENANT
3.5.60/1227   When] MIDDLETON; While DAVENANT
3.5.61/1228   And ... toy, and] MIDDLETON; To Sing, to Toy, to Dance and DAVENANT
3.5.63/1230   Seas] MIDDLETON; Hills DAVENANT
3.5.63/1230   and misty] DAVENANT; *our Mistris* MIDDLETON
3.5.64/1231   Steeples] 1673 *and* DAVENANT; Steepe MIDDLETON

3.5.67/1234 no yelps] MIDDLETON; nor Yelps DAVENANT
3.5.68/1235 not] MIDDLETON; nor DAVENANT
3.5.69/1236 Or . . . throat] MIDDLETON; Nor . . . Throats DAVENANT
3.5.70/1237 SPIRITS ⌈aboue⌉] This edition; *not in* MIDDLETON (*which has* 'aboue' *to the right of the first phrase of the repeated lines*).
3.5.70-3/1237-40 No . . . reache] MIDDLETON (*No Ring of Bells &c.*); *not repeated* DAVENANT
3.5.73.1-2/1240.1-2 Exeunt . . . Hecat] This edition. F provides no separate exit for Hecate, though she must go before the Witches speak their last line.
3.6.4/1245 was] F. Lettsom conjectured 'is', but see *OED* dead, 1d: '*to be dead* was anciently used in the sense . . . "put to death, be killed"'.
3.6.14/1255 I, and] F; ay, POPE
3.6.24/1265 Sonne] THEOBALD; Sonnes F
3.6.38/1279 their] F; the HANMER. Editors usually emend to provide an antecedent to 'he' (Macbeth) in 3.6.40/1281. Some corruption (perhaps by omission) probably explains the anomaly; but it is not likely to be in this line.
4.1.10, 20/1301, 1311 double, toile] F; double, toil STEEVENS
4.1.23 Witches'] F (Witches)
4.1.38.1/1329.1 Enter . . . Witches] F; *Enter Hecate* RITSON
4.1.43.1/1334.1 The Song] F calls for '*Muficke and a Song. Blacke Spirits, &c.*' 'Musicke' presumably refers to an instrumental accompaniment.
4.1.44/1335 HECAT] DAVENANT; *not in* MIDDLETON. In *The Witch*, Hecate introduces the song with 'stir: stir about: whilst I begin the *Charme*'. The direction reads '*A Charme Song: about a Vessell.*'
4.1.46/1337 4. WITCH] This edition; *not in* MIDDLETON
4.1.47/1338 Fire-drake . . . Luckey] *continued to* 1. ⟨Witch⟩ DAVENANT; 2: YALE MS
4.1.48/1339 Liard] ELLIS; Liand MIDDLETON; Lyer DAVENANT. 'Liard' is the reading in Middleton's source, Scot's *Discovery of Witchcraft*.
4.1.48/1339 Liard . . . in] *continued to* 1. ⟨Witch⟩ DAVENANT; Hec⟨at⟩. YALE MS
4.1.49/1340 ALL] DAVENANT (*Chor.*); *not in* MIDDLETON
4.1.49/1340 Round . . . about, about] MIDDLETON; A round, a round, about, about, DAVENANT
4.1.51/1342 4. WITCH] This edition; 1. *witch* MIDDLETON
4.1.52/1343 Put . . . that.] MIDDLETON; O put in that, put in that DAVENANT
4.1.53, 56/1344, 1347 5. WITCH] This edition; 2. MIDDLETON
4.1.53/1344 Libbards Bane] MIDDLETON; Lizards brain DAVENANT
4.1.54/1345 a graine.] DAVENANT; *againe*, MIDDLETON. *Witch* makes sense, but the oddity of a grain of brain suggests that Davenant, altering 'Libbards Bane', may have the correct reading here.
4.1.55/1346 4. WITCH] This edition; 1. MIDDLETON
4.1.55/1346 The . . . the] MIDDLETON; Here's . . . here's DAVENANT
4.1.56/1347 Those . . . madder] MIDDLETON; That will make the Charm grow madder. DAVENANT. In *Witch*, an allusion to the dramatic situation; the line may have been altered in the King's Men's performances; but the allusion to a 'red-haired wench' (4.1.58/1349), also more meaningful in *The Witch* than in *Macbeth*, is retained by Davenant, though with an indefinite article.
4.1.57/1348 in: ther's all, and rid] MIDDLETON; in all thefe, 'twill raife DAVENANT
4.1.58/1349 A WITCH] This edition; Fire⟨stone⟩. MIDDLETON
4.1.58/1349 a] DAVENANT; *the* MIDDLETON. The unspecific article is more suited to *Macbeth*.
4.1.59/1350 ALL *Round*] MIDDLETON (*all Round*)
4.1.59-60/1350-1 Round . . . keepe-out] MIDDLETON (*Round: around: around &c.:*); Around, around, &c. DAVENANT
4.1.75/1366 Germaines] POPE; Germaine F
4.1.75 all together] F (altogether)
4.1.85 power—] ROWE, *after* F (~.)
4.1.99/1390 assurance,] POPE; ~: F
4.1.109/1400 Dunsinane] ROWE; Dunfinane F
4.1.113/1404 Rebellious dead] F; Rebellious head THEOBALD (Warburton); Rebellion's head HANMER (Theobald). See Sisson, *New Readings*.

4.1.114/1405 on's high place] This edition; our high plac'd F. Muir discusses the oddity of this line and suggests that Macbeth might have been disguised (but the witches obviously know who he is) or that the lines may be spoken by a witch (but their tone seems wrong). Our emendation supposes easy misreading; 'on's' occurs at 5.1.61/1850.
4.1.127.1-2/1418.1-2 A shew . . . and Banquo] THEOBALD (*subs*.); *A fhew of eight Kings, and Banquo laft, with a glaffe in his hand.* F
4.1.135 eighth] F (eight). See *OED*.
4.1 139 blood-baltered] F (Blood-bolter'd). See *OED*.
4.1.141/1432 HECAT] This edition (Cambridge). As the witches' leader, Hecate is the natural speaker.
4.1.167/1458 th'edge] F; the edge ROWE 3
4.2.22/1485 none] WILSON (Cambridge); moue F
4.2.70-1/1531-2 ones. | . . . thus, me thinkes] F2; ones, | . . . thus, Me thinkes F
4.2.84/1545 shagge-hear'd] SINGER 2 (Steevens); shagge-ear'd F. See Wilson.
4.3.4/1551 downfall] F; down-faln WARBURTON. *OED* records 'fall' as a form of the past participle.
4.3.15/1562 discerne] F; deserve THEOBALD. See Sisson, *New Readings*.
4.3.15/1562 wisedome] F. See Abbott, 403.
4.3.29/1576 I pray] F; pray W. S. WALKER *conj.*
4.3.35 affeered] F (affear'd)
4.3.60/1607 Sodaine] F; Sullen G.T. (*conj.*). Compositor B's preferred spelling for 'sudden' is 'sodaine'; 'sudden' could be a misreading of 'sullen'.
4.3.73/1620 cold. The] F; cold, the THEOBALD. Still often but unnecessarily emended.
4.3.108/1655 accust] F1; accurst F2; accused WILSON. *OED* does not record 'cuss' meaning 'curse' in the period, but F1 is probably a rendering of the pronunciation noted by Cercignani, 358.
4.3.134/1681 thy] F2; they F1
4.3.155/1702 with] Fb; my with Fa
4.3.161/1708 not] F2; nor F1
4.3.237/1784 tune] ROWE 2; time F. F might be defended as 'rhythm' (*OED*, 12a), but the misreading is easy.
5.1.24/1814 sense are] F; sense is ROWE; sense' are DYCE (W. S. Walker). As Dyce implies, the word was used as a plural: Franz, 189, citing *Othello* 4.3.93/2755.
5.1.35/1825 feare,] THEOBALD; feare? F
5.3.5/1901 Consequences] F; consequence SINGER. Muir and others emend, but with no help to metre: a hexameter.
5.3.21 Seyton!—] F (~,)
5.3.22 say!—This] F (say, this)
5.3.24/1920 way] May STEEVENS 2 (Johnson)
5.3.38/1934 Give me mine Armor:] Wilson directs '*Seton goes to fetch it*', and at 5.3.48/1944 '*Seton returns with armour and an armourer, who presently begins to equip Macbeth*'. Shakespeare may not have worked out the detailed business of arming Macbeth.
5.3.41/1937 Cure her] F2; Cure F1
5.3.46/1942 fraught] This edition (?; *anon. conj. in* Furness); ftufft F. Much discussed. Malone defended F's 'stufft . . . stuffe' as a characteristic repetition, but this one seems less purposeful than those he cites. A partial parallel is provided by *Othello*, 'swell bosome with thy fraught', 3.3.458/1900. Some editors alter 'stuffe' to, e.g., 'grief' (COLLIER MS); the most attractive emendation of 'stuffed' other than 'fraught' is 'charged' (*conj.* Wilson).
5.3.57/1953 Cyme] F1; senna F4 (Cæny, F2). As 'Cyme' is a botanical term, emendation seems hazardous. *OED* first records in 1725, but it has been traced back to 1634 (see Muir), in Holland's *Pliny*, where it is used of the tops of colewort, said to be purgative. As Muir says, properly it 'is the top of any plant, not specifically of the Colewort', but Cercignani remarks that in *Macbeth* it need not represent the hypermetrical *senna* but 'may well stand for *cyme* (Fr *cyme*) in the sense of "tops and tendrils of the colewort"'.
5.4.0.1-3/1960.1-3] Almost all editors follow Malone in adding

Lennox and Ross. An exception is Wilson, who notes that they 'have nothing to say'. Foakes argues that 'Lennox (present in [5.2/Sc. 22]) and Ross (who clearly fights in Malcolm's army, see [5.8/Sc. 28]) should appear here', but the Folio suggests that in some performances, at least, they did not.

5.4.11/1971 gone] CAPELL; giuen F. F is sometimes defended, but the repetition is suspicious.

5.5.37/2018 shall] F1; shalt F2. See OED, 2β.

5.5.40/2021 pall] A. HUNTER (Johnson); pull F. OED, citing F's 'pull' as its first example in this sense before 1780, defines 'to rein in (one's horse)'. But this implies deliberate action; 'pall' makes better sense, and the misreading is easy.

5.7.14.1/2055.1 with the Body] This edition; not in F. Editors make no provision for removal; but old Siward does not notice a body on his entry, and at 5.11.10/2115 Ross says that the boy is 'brought off the field'.

5.10.34.2–3/2105.2-3 Enter . . . body] F reads: 'Exeunt fighting. Alarums. | Enter fighting, and Macbeth slaine'. Earlier editors followed Pope in omitting 'Enter . . . slaine'. Wilson's restoration of this entry is accepted by later editors. There is no reason why Macbeth should not be killed on stage, nor is it necessary to speculate that the duel should end 'on the inner stage, before which the traverse would be drawn to conceal the dead body of Macb.' (Wilson).

5.11.25/2130 ALL BUT MALCOLME] F (All.)

INCIDENTALS

24 Gallowglasses] Gallowgroſſes 363 further.] ~, (?) 370 lou'd] loued 406 Inuenter.] ~, 530 Offerings] Offrings 1032 thanks.] ~ₐ 1140 worse.] ~ₐ 1206 away.] ~ₐ MIDDLETON 1210 Puckle?] ~ₐ MIDDLETON 1213 count.] ~ₐ MIDDLETON 1217 muse, I muse,] ~, ~. MIDDLETON 1218 the] MIDDLETON; th' DAVENANT 1219 come?] ~ MIDDLETONₐ 1221 Refuse.] ~ : MIDDLETON 1233, 1237 sounds,] ~ MIDDLETONₐ 1273 aboue,] ~) 1296 throw.] ~ₐ 1337 in.] ~ MIDDLETONₐ 1339 in.] ~ MIDDLETONₐ 1344 Bane.] ~ₐ MIDDLETON 1346 Adder.] ~ₐ MIDDLETON 1348 all,] ~. MIDDLETON 1380 thanks,] ~ₐ 1505 with all] withall 1625 ill-compos'd] ill-compos,d 4.3.174/1721 Relation,] ~ ; 4.3.180/1727 'em.] ~ₐ 4.3.235/1782 selfe,] ~ₐ 5.3.54/1950 pristine] priſtiue 5.5.36/2017 false] fhlſe 5.8.6/2061 vnbattred] vnbattered 5.10.8/2079 labour.] ~, (?)

FOLIO STAGE DIRECTIONS

1.1.0.1/0.1 Thunder and Lightning. Enter three Witches.
1.1.11/11 Exeunt.
1.2.0.1-3/11.1-2 Alarum within. Enter King Malcome, Donal-|baine, Lenox, with attendants, meeting | a bleeding Captaine.
1.2.44.2/55.2 Enter Rosse and Angus.
1.2.67.1/78.1 Exeunt.
1.3.0.1/78.2 Thunder. Enter the three Witches.
1.3.27.1/105.1 Drum within.
1.3.35.1/113.1 Enter Macbeth and Banquo.
1.3.76.1/154.1 Witches vanish.
1.3.86.1/164.1 Enter Rosse and Angus.
1.3.156/234 Exeunt.
1.4.0.1-2/234.1-2 Flourish. Enter King, Lenox, Malcolme, | Donalbaine, and Attendants.
1.4.14/248 Enter Macbeth, Banquo, Rosse, and Angus.
1.4.55/288 Exit.
1.4.60/293 Flourish. Exeunt.
1.5.0.1/293.1 Enter Macbeths Wife alone with a Letter.
1.5.29/322 Enter Messenger.
1.5.37/330 Exit Messenger.
1.5.53/346 Enter Macbeth.
1.5.72/365 Exeunt.
1.6.1-3/365.1-3 Hoboyes, and Torches. Enter King, Malcolme, | Donalbaine, Banquo, Lenox, Macduff, | Rosse, Angus, and Attendants.
1.6.10/375 Enter Lady.
1.6.31/396 Exeunt
1.7.1-3/396.1-3 Ho-boyes. Torches. | Enter a Sewer, and diuers Seruants with Dishes and Seruice | ouer the Stage. Then enter Macbeth.
1.7.28/424 Enter Lady.
1.7.82.1/478.1 Exeunt.
2.1.0.1/478.2 Enter Banquo, and Fleance, with a Torch | before him.
2.1.9/487 Enter Macbeth, and a Seruant with a Torch.
2.1.30.1/508.1 Exit Banquo.
2.1.32/510 Exit.
2.1.61.1/539.1 A Bell rings.
2.1.64/542 Exit.
2.2.0.1/542.1 Enter Lady.
2.2.8/550 Enter Macbeth.
2.2.55/597 Exit.
2.2.55/597 Knocke within.
2.2.61.1/603.1 Enter Lady.
2.2.63/605 Knocke.
2.2.67/609 Knocke.
2.2.71.1/613.1 Knocke. (after 'deed')
2.2.72/614 Exeunt.
2.3.0.1/614.1 Enter a Porter. | Knocking within.
2.3.2.1/616.1 Knock.
2.3.6.1/620.1 Knock.
2.3.11.1/625.1 Knock.
2.3.14.1/628.1 Knock.
2.3.18.1/632.1 Knock.
2.3.20.1/634.1 Enter Macduff, and Lenox.
2.3.41.1/655.1 Enter Macbeth. (after 2.3.40/654)
2.3.51/665 Exit Macduffe.
2.3.62/676 Enter Macduff.
2.3.73/687 Exeunt Macbeth and Lenox. (after 'awake, awake')
2.3.80/694 Bell rings. Enter Lady.
2.3.85/699 Enter Banquo.
2.3.89.1/703.1 Enter Macbeth, Lenox, and Rosse.
2.3.95.1/709.1 Enter Malcolme and Donalbaine.
2.3.133.1/747.1 Exeunt.
2.3.145.1/759.1 Exeunt.
2.4.0.1/759.2 Enter Rosse, with an Old man.
2.4.20/779 Enter Macduffe.
2.4.42.1/801.1 Exeunt omnes
3.1.0.1/801.2 Enter Banquo.
3.1.10.1-2/811.1-2 Senit sounded. Enter Macbeth as King, Lady Lenox, | Rosse, Lords, and Attendants.
3.1.41/842 Exit Banquo.
3.1.45.1/846.1 Exeunt Lords.
3.1.49/850 Exit Seruant.
3.1.73.1/874.1 Enter Seruant, and two Murtherers.
3.1.74/875 Exit Seruant.
3.1.141.1, 143/942.1, 944 Exeunt. (after 3.1.143/944)
3.2.0.1/944.1 Enter Macbeths Lady, and a Seruant.
3.2.5/949 Exit.
3.2.9.1/953.1 Enter Macbeth.
3.2.57/1001 Exeunt.
3.3.0.1/1001.1 Enter three Murtherers.
3.3.14/1015 Enter Banquo and Fleans, with a Torch.
3.3.23.1/1024.1 Exeunt.

MACBETH

3.4.0.1-3/1024.2-3 Banquet prepar'd. Enter Macbeth, Lady, Rosse, Lenox, | Lords, and Attendants.
3.4.7.1/1031.1 Enter first Murtherer.
3.4.31/1055 Exit Murderer.
3.4.36/1060 Enter the Ghost of Banquo, and sits in Macbeths place.
3.4.87.1/1111.1 Enter Ghost.
3.4.120.1/1144.1 Exit Lords.
3.4.143/1167 Exeunt.
3.5.0.1/1167.1 Thunder. Enter the three Witches, meeting | Hecat.
3.5.34/1201 Musicke, and a Song.
3.5.37.1/1204.1 Sing within. Come away, come away, &c.
3.5.74.1/1241.1 Exeunt.
3.6.0.1/1241.2 Enter Lenox, and another Lord.
3.6.50.1/1291.1 Exeunt
4.1.0.1/1291.2 Thunder. Enter the three Witches.
4.1.38.1/1329.1 Enter Hecat, and the other three Witches.
4.1.43.1/1334.1 Musicke and a Song. Blacke Spirits, &c.
4.1.63.1/1354.1 Enter Macbeth.
4.1.84.1/1375.1 Thunder. | 1. Apparation, an Armed Head.
4.1.88.1/1379.1 He Descends.
4.1.92.1/1383.1 Thunder. | 2 Apparition, a Bloody Childe.
4.1.97.1/1388.1 Descends.
4.1.102.1-2/1393.1-2 Thunder | 3 Apparation, a Childe Crowned, with a Tree in his hand.
4.1.110/1401 Descend.
4.1.121.1/1412.1 Hoboyes (after 4.1.122/1413)
4.1.127.1-2/1418.1-2 A shew of eight Kings, and Banquo last, with a glasse | in his hand.
4.1.148.1/1439.1 Musicke. | The Witches Dance, and vanish.
4.1.151/1442 Enter Lenox.
4.1.172/1463 Exeunt
4.2.0.1/1463.1 Enter Macduffes Wife, her Son, and Rosse.
4.2.30/1493 Exit Rosse.
4.2.65.1/1526.1 Enter a Messenger.
4.2.74/1535 Exit Messenger
4.2.80/1541 Enter Murtherers. (after 'faces')
4.2.86.1-2/1547.1-2 Exit crying Murther.
4.3.0.1/1547.3 Enter Malcolme and Macduffe.
4.3.140.1/1687.1 Enter a Doctor.
4.3.146.1/1693.1 Exit. (after 'amend')
4.3.160/1707 Enter Rosse.
4.3.242/1789 Exeunt

5.1.0.1-2/1789.1-2 Enter a Doctor of Physicke, and a Wayting | Gentlewoman.
5.1.17.1/1807.1 Enter Lady, with a Taper.
5.1.65.1/1854 Exit Lady.
5.1.76.1/1865.1 Exeunt.
5.2.0.1-2/1865.2-3 Drum and Colours. Enter Menteth, Cathnes, | Angus, Lenox, Soldiers.
5.2.31.1/1896.1 Exeunt marching.
5.3.0.1-2/1896.2-3 Enter Macbeth, Doctor, and Attendants.
5.3.10.1/1906.1 Enter Seruant.
5.3.31/1927 Enter Seyton.
5.3.64/1960 Exeunt
5.4.0.1-3/1960.1-3 Drum and Colours. Enter Malcolme, Seyward, Macduffe, | Seywards Sonne, Menteth, Cathnes, Angus, | and Soldiers Marching.
5.4.21/1981.1 Exeunt marching
5.5.0.1-2/1981.2-3 Enter Macbeth, Seyton, & Souldiers, with | Drum and Colours.
5.5.7/1988 A Cry within of Women. (after 'noyse')
5.5.27/2008 Enter a Messenger.
5.5.50/2031.1 Exeunt
5.6.0.1-2/2031.2-3 Drumme and Colours. | Enter Malcolme, Seyward, Macduffe, and their Army, | with Boughes.
5.6.10.1/2041.1 Exeunt | Alarums continued.
5.7.0.1/2041.2 Enter Macbeth.
5.7.4.1/2045.1 Enter young Seyward.
5.7.12/2053 Fight, and young Seyward slaine.
5.7.14.1/2055.1 Exit.
5.8.0.1/2055.2 Alarums. Enter Macduffe.
5.8.10/2065 Exit. Alarums.
5.9.0.1/2065.1 Enter Malcolme and Seyward.
5.9.6.1/2071.1 Exeunt. Alarum
5.10.0.1/2071.2 Enter Macbeth.
5.10.3/2074 Enter Macduffe.
5.10.8/2079 Fight: Alarum
5.10.34.1/2105.1 Exeunt fighting. Alarums.
5.10.34.2/2105.2 Enter Fighting, and Macbeth slaine.
5.11.1-2/2105.4-6 Retreat, and Flourish. Enter with Drumme and Colours, | Malcolm, Seyward, Rosse, Thanes, & Soldiers.
5.11.19.1/2124.1 Enter Macduffe, with Macbeths head.
5.11.25.1/2130.1 Flourish.
5.11.41.1/2146.1 Flourish. Exeunt Omnes.

ANTONY AND CLEOPATRA

Antony and Cleopatra was entered in the Stationers' Register on 20 May 1608:

Edw. Blunt Entred alſo for his copie by
the lyke Aucthoritie. A booke
Called. Anthony & Cleopatra

(This follows the entry of *Pericles* authorized by Sir George Buc and 'Master Warden Seton'.) But the play was first printed in the First Folio, by Compositors B and E; this provides the only authoritative text (F). Proof corrections are exceptionally numerous. At 2084/4.3.10 we note a previously unrecorded, incidental variant. Hinman notes no variants in the forme in which it occurs; it may result simply from an accident of the press.

The manuscript appears to have been in a more finished condition than most of Shakespeare's foul papers, but shows no signs of originating in a prompt-book. Ghost characters and directions for entry of characters who play no part in the subsequent action are found in the opening directions for 2.6/Sc. 11, 3.2/Sc. 24, 4.2/Sc. 27, 4.6/Sc. 31, and 5.2/Sc. 43. Certain anomalies are probably authorial (e.g. the direction '*Enter Alexas from Caesar*' (1.5.34/479) when he actually comes from Antony, and the prefixes '*Alex⟨as⟩*' at 4.4.24/2118 where '*Capt⟨aine⟩*' is needed, '*Eros*' at 4.5.1, 3, 7/2133, 2135, 2139 where '*Soul⟨dier⟩*' is needed, and '*Dol⟨abella⟩*' at 5.1.28, 31/2607, 2610 where '*Agrippa*' is needed). Stage directions are sometimes inadequate, notoriously so in the scenes located in Cleopatra's 'monument' (4.16/Sc. 41, 5.2/Sc. 43), though Hinman has shown that at a point (5.2.34/2690) where Greg (*Folio*, 400) supposed that Shakespeare left a blank because he 'had not made up his mind respecting the mechanics of the action' the deficiency is almost certainly the responsibility of the compositor and the result of faulty casting off of copy. Wilson's conjectures that the text includes passages meant for cancellation were refuted by David Galloway (see note to 4.16.12-13/2499-2500). Most editors assume that the Folio text was printed either from Shakespeare's papers in a late stage of composition or from his own fair copy (in so far as there is a distinction); however, the predominance of the longer 'oh' spelling violates Shakespeare's apparent preference, and may point to some sort of transcript of foul papers. (See John Jowett and Gary Taylor, 'With New Additions'.) The Folio text is undivided; to the standard division we add a scene reference at 4.7.4/2192, so 4.7.4 onwards becomes 4.8/Sc. 33 in our edition, and 4.8-15 become 4.9-16/Sc. 34-41.

Treatment of proper names causes problems; when F's spelling suggests compositorial misreading of a spelling intended to represent the historical name we emend (e.g. at 3.6.75/1550 we read 'Licaonia' (F2) for F1's 'Licoania' and at 3.7.21/1594 'Brundisium' (F2) for F1's 'Brandisium'), but when F's spelling suggests that Shakespeare has varied the name found in his sources, we follow F (e.g. 'Thidias' for North's 'Thyreus' (3.12.31/1805, etc.; see also e.g. note to 3.7.20/1593)).

S.W.W./(G.T.)

WORKS CITED

Deighton, K., *The Old Dramatists* (1896)
Furness, H. H., ed., *Antony and Cleopatra*, New Variorum (1907)
Harrison, G. B., ed., *Antony and Cleopatra*, Penguin (1937)
Jones, Emrys, ed., *Antony and Cleopatra*, New Penguin (1977)
Ridley, M. R., ed., *Antony and Cleopatra*, Arden (1954)

TEXTUAL NOTES

Title *The Tragedie of Anthonie, and Cleopatra*] F (*head title*); *The Tragedie of Anthony, and Cleopatra* F (*running title*); *Anthony and Cleopater.* F (*table of contents*); *Anthony & Cleopatra* S.R.

1.1.11   in] F; e'en *This edition conj.*
1.1.43/43   Why,] F; ~, RIDLEY
1.1.49/49   now] F; new WARBURTON
1.1.52/52   how] RIDLEY; who F1; whose F2. Most editors follow F2, but transposition of letters seems as likely as verbal substitution, and 'how' makes easier sense.
1.1.57.2/57.2   *and, by another doore, the Messenger*] *This edition*; *not in* F; *followed by the Messenger* RIVERSIDE
1.2.0.1-2/64.1-2   *Enter ... attendants*] *This edition*; *Enter Enobarbus, Lamprius, a Southſayer, Rannius, Lucillius, Charmian, Iras, Mardian the Eunuch, and Alexas* F. Rannius and Lucillius are ghost characters; so is Lamprius, unless he is the Soothsayer. Shakespeare may have wished to dress the stage, but as these three have no identity elsewhere, their names are irrelevant. Mardian too says nothing in this scene, but later achieves the identity denied to the others. Ridley interestingly suggests that Enobarbus, the Soothsayer, and two or three other Romans should enter by one door and, simultaneously, Cleopatra's women, Mardian, and Alexas by another. Capell is followed by some later editors in bringing on Enobarbus at 1.2.11/74; and the Soothsayer might enter at 1.2.6/70 (*conj.* RIDLEY).
1.2.5/69   charge] THEOBALD (Warburton, *and* Southern MS, *cited in* Cambridge); change F. See Sisson, *New Readings*; the same error has been thought to occur at *Caesar* 4.2.7/1746.
1.2.12.1/76.1   *Enter ... exeunt*] *This edition*; *not in* F. Presumably Enobarbus' order should be obeyed: see e.g. 1.2.40-1/104-5.
1.2.34/98   fertill] THEOBALD (Warburton); fore-tell F
1.2.56-7/121-2   Alexas, come] THEOBALD; *Alexas. Come* F (*on a fresh line, as a new speech*)
1.2.72.1/137.1   *Enter Cleopatra*] *as here* F; *after next line* CAPELL
1.2.74/139   Saw you,] F2; Saue you, F1
1.2.79/144   Alexas] F2; Alexias F1
1.2.80.1/145.1   *with a Messenger*] F; *and Attendants* ROWE

1.2.86/151 warre, from Italy,] HANMER; ∼ˬ ∼, F
1.2.87/152 worst] F; worse HANMER
1.2.90/155 done. With me 'tis] WILSON (E. G. Spencer-Churchill); done, with me. 'Tis F
1.2.104/169 windes] F; minds HANMER (Warburton). See Sisson, *New Readings*.
1.2.106.1/171.1 *Enter another Messenger*] F; *omitted by* ROWE
1.2.107 ho] F (how)
1.2.108/173 2. MESSENGER] This edition; 1. Meſ. F; 1 A⟨ttendant⟩. CAPELL. For this passage, see *Re-Editing*, 37–41.
1.2.108/173 ANTHONY] This edition; *not in* F
1.2.109/174 2. MESSENGER] This edition; 2. Meſ. F; 2. A⟨ttendant⟩. CAPELL; *Attend*. ROWE
1.2.109.1/174.1 *Exit 2. Messenger*] This edition; *not in* F
1.2.112/177 3. MESSENGER] This edition; 3. Meſ. F
1.2.124.1/189.1 *Enter Enobarbus*] *as here* DYCE; *after* 'hatch' F
1.2.130/195 occasion] ROWE; an occaſion F
1.2.156-8/221-3 shewes ... new] The sense is difficult, but no satisfactory emendation has been suggested.
1.2.172/237 leue] POPE; loue F
1.2.177/242 Hath] F2; Haue F1
1.2.186 hair] F (heire)
1.2.188/253 place is vnder vs, requires,] F2; places vnder vs, require,ˬ F1; places under us require, RIDLEY
1.3.11/265 Iwis] WILSON (anon. conj. in Cambridge); I wiſh F
1.3.20/274 What ... woman you] F; what ... woman? You ROWE
1.3.72 well;] F (∼ˬ)
1.3.74/328 giue true euidence] F (*sometimes questioned*)
1.3.80/334 blood:] ROWE; ∼ˬ F
1.3.82/336 my] F2; *not in* F1
1.3.104/358 goes] F1; goest F2. See Brook p. 122.
1.4.3/363 Our] SINGER; One F
1.4.8/368 vouchsafd] JOHNSON; vouchſafe F
1.4.9/369 the] F3; th' F1
1.4.9/369 abstracte] F2; abſtracts F1
1.4.40/400 *Exit*] This edition; *not in* F
1.4.44/404 dear'd] THEOBALD (Warburton); fear'd F; lov'd COLLIER 2.
1.4.46/406 lackying] THEOBALD (anon., MS); lacking F
1.4.47/407 *Enter ... Messenger*] CAPELL; *not in* F. See Ridley. Other messengers enter unannounced, and speak without preliminaries at 1.1.17.1, 4.6.6/17.1, 2155.
1.4.55/415 *Exit*] This edition; *not in* F.
1.4.56/416 Wassailes] POPE; Vaſſailes F
1.4.57/417 Was] F; Wast STEEVENS 2; wert F2
1.4.57/417 Modena] JOHNSON (*after* North); *Medena* F.
1.4.58 Hirtius] F (*Hirſius*)
1.4.58/418 Pansa] F2; Pauſa F1
1.4.66/426 brows'd] F1; browsedst F2
1.4.76/436 we] F2; me F1
1.4.76 council] ROWE *after* F (counſell)
1.4.85/445 knew] F; know DYCE 2 (W. S. Walker)
1.5.3/448 Mandragora] JOHNSON; *Mandragoru* F
1.5.5/450 time,] ROWE; ∼ : F
1.5.23/468 Arme] F; Acme This edition *conj*. F is dubious (Ridley) and would be a very easy misreading of 'acme', especially as that was still felt to be a Greek word (*OED*, recording from 1570); it does not occur elsewhere in Shakespeare.
1.5.34/479 *Enter Alexas*] ROWE; *Enter Alexas from Cæsar.* F
1.5.47/492 Arme-iaunct] This edition; Arme-gaunt F. None of the many proposed solutions to this crux (see Ridley, Appendix A) has commanded general assent; Sisson (followed by Riverside) defends F, unconvincingly. Shakespeare uses 'jaunce' at *Richard II* 5.5.94/2623: 'Spurrde, galld, and tirde by iauncing Bullingbrooke' (Q1) and *Romeo* 2.4.26/1296: 'what a iaunce haue I?' and 2.5.52/1322: 'catch my death with iaunſing vp and downe' (Q2). *OED*, defining '?To make (a horse) prance up and down', records no other instances before 1792. The sense is good, implying that the horse that Antony 'soberly' mounted was exhausted by being ridden by one in armour or by its own armour (cf. *OED jaunt, v.* I. i). The unfamiliarity of the word would make it susceptible to misreading; it might even have been spelt with initial 'g' (cf. Palsgrove, cited by *OED*: 'And you gaunce your horse up and downe thus upon the stones, he wyll be naught within a whyle ...').

1.5.49/494 dumbd] THEOBALD; dumbe F
1.5.60/505 man] F2; mans F1
2.1.2, 5, 16, 18, 38/524, 527, 538, 540, 560 MENECRATES ... MENECRATES ... MENAS ... MENAS ... MENAS] MALONE; *Mene.* throughout in F. 2.1.42/564 shows that Menas must speak 2.1.38/560. Johnson gave all the speeches to him. Sisson (*New Readings*) discerns 'a difference in character, the first two speeches being of a philosophic turn of thought, the rest those of a man concerned with facts and soldiering'. Conceivably Menas' entry should be delayed till 2.1.16/538. Menecrates appears in no other scene.
2.1.21 waned] F (wand). Steevens-Reed 2 (Percy) read 'wan'd', not distinguishing between 'waned' and 'wanned'; a case can be made for both, as well as for 'want' (Z. Jackson) and 'wan' (spelt 'wane').
2.1.23/545 Libertine, in a field of Feasts,] This edition (G.T.); Libertine in a field of Feaſts, F
2.1.38 ne'er] F (neere)
2.1.41/563 war'd] F2; wan'd F1
2.1.43/565 may giue way to greater] F; to greater may giue way G.T. *conj*.
2.1.44/566 all,] ROWE; ∼ : F
2.2.7/581 Anthonio's] F; Antonius' STEEVENS 2
2.2.27.1/601.1 *Anthony and Cæsar embrace*] This edition (Nicholson); *Takes him by the hand* SINGER 2
2.2.27.1/601.1 *Flourish*] F; *omitted by* HANMER. Some modern editors also omit, but the direction seems unlikely to be accidental and probably implies a formal salute.
2.2.48/622 Theame] F; then (thenne) DEIGHTON
2.2.49/623 yᵉ] HANMER; your F. Hanmer's 'the', not usually adopted, is more idiomatic and easily justified assuming misreading of 'ye' as 'yt'.
2.2.57/631 you haue] F; you've not ROWE; you'd have SISSON
2.2.59/633 defects of iudgement to me] F; to me defects of judgement CAPELL.
2.2.74/648 must,] THEOBALD; ∼ˬ F
2.2.79/653 admitted, then:] F; admitted: then,ˬ ROWE
2.2.96/670 knowledge:] ROWE ; ∼, F
2.2.103/677 Noble] F1; nobly F2
2.2.107/681 spoken] F; spoke G.T. *conj*.
2.2.112/686 Souldier onely,] THEOBALD; Souldier, only,ˬ F
2.2.120-1/695-6 staunch, ... world,] ROWE (*subs*.); ∼ˬ ... ∼ : F
2.2.126/701 not so] ROWE; not, ſay F
2.2.127/702 reproofe] HANMER (Warburton); proofe F
2.2.153/728 hand.] THEOBALD; ∼ˬ F
2.2.168/743 Mount-Mesena] F; Mount-Misenum ROWE. Shakespeare follows Plutarch.
2.2.168-9/743-4 strength | By land? | CAESAR] F; strength. *Caesar* By land HANMER. Ridley supports Hanmer, but the error is not easily explained, and no change is needed.
2.2.194 Cydnus] F (Sidnis)
2.2.201/776 Loue-sicke with them. The] POPE; Loue-ſicke. | With them F
2.2.211 glow] F (gloue)
2.2.213/788 Gentlewomen] F2; Gentlewoman F1
2.2.233 eat] F's 'eate' might be interpreted as 'ate'.
2.2.239/814 breathlesse powre breath forth] F; breathless, power breathe forth POPE
2.2.239 breathless, pour breath] This edition (*conj*. Daniel), *after* F
2.3.4/830 Good ... sir] F1; *spoken by Octavia* F2
2.3.12/838 Gone thither] This edition (G.T.); Thither F; hither HUDSON (Mason). Both sense and metre call for emendation; omission would be particularly liable to occur at the line division.
2.3.14/840 To Egypt againe] F; againe to Egypt CAPELL
2.3.20/846 a feard] COLLIER 2 (Thirlby); a feare F
2.3.22/848 thee: no more but,] THEOBALD; thee,ˬ no more but: F
2.3.28/854 away] POPE; alway F

2.4.6/872   at the] F2; at F1
2.4.9/875   MECENAS and AGRIPPA] F (*Both.*)
2.5.2/878   CHARMIAN, IRAS and ALEXAS] F ('*Omnes.*')
2.5.10-11/886-7   to'th'Riuer. There . . . off,] F4; to'th'Riuer there . . . off. F1
2.5.12/888   find] THEOBALD; fine F
2.5.26/902   Anth*ony*o's] F; Antonius DELIUS
2.5.28/904   him, there] POPE; him. There F
2.5.37/913   face. If] ROWE; face if F.
2.5.43/919   is] CAPELL (Tyrwhitt); 'tis F
2.5.52/928   But] F2; Bur F1
2.5.54/930   the] F; thy HANMER
2.5.81.1/957.1   *Exit Charmian*] DYCE; *not in* F
2.5.84/960   *with Charmian*] DYCE; *not in* F
2.5.104/980   act] This edition (*conj.* Case); art F. Cambridge records 15 different attempts to emend; modern editors strain to justify F. Our emendation supposes a very easy misreading: the Messenger does not *act*, or commit, the offence that he knows of. See *Re-Editing*, 38-9.
2.6.0.1/996.2   *Pompey and Menas*] as here ROWE; F lists Pompey after Agrippa
2.6.16/1012   the] F2; *not in* F1
2.6.19/1015   is] F2; his F1
2.6.39/1035   CAESAR, ANTHONY and LEPIDUS] CAPELL; *Omnes.* F
2.6.43/1039   telling, you] THEOBALD; telling. You F
2.6.53/1049   There is] ROWE; ther's F. F's form (which occurs within a line) could easily be due to line-justification.
2.6.67/1063   meanings] MALONE (Heath); meaning F
2.6.71/1067   o'] COLLIER MS; *not in* F; of F3
2.6.78/1074   ha' prais'd ye] F; have prais'd you CAPELL
2.6.83/1079   CAESAR, ANTHONY and LEPIDUS] CAPELL; *All.* F1
2.7.1-14/1133-46   I SERUANT] F (1)
2.7.1/1133   be man] F. A suspect reading, as it does not lead into what follows; one might expect e.g. 'lie, man' or (by a less explicable error) 'be unmanned'.
2.7.4-11/1136-43   2. SERUANT] F ('2')
2.7.16.3/1148.3   *and a Boy*] JONES; *not in* F
2.7.29.1/1161.1   *Anthony, Pompey and Lepidus sit*] This edition (*They sit* COLLIER MS); *not in* F. It seems from 2.7.39/1172 and 2.7.53/1186 that the wine is slow to come.
2.7.39.1/1172.1   *Menas whispers in Pompey's Eare*] This edition (*after* F, '*Whispers in's Eare.*', placed at end of line after 'anon'). Editors usually take F's direction to refer to 'Forbeare me till anon', but if that were so it would apply equally to the previous 3 speeches; and it would be odd for such a direction to be used of words to be heard by the audience. More probably Shakespeare meant it to indicate that Menas continues to whisper to Pompey until the latter's outburst at 2.7.52/1185.
2.7.88/1221   part then is] ROWE; part, then he is F
2.7.95/1228   grow] F1; grows F2. See Ridley.
2.7.108/1241   beate] F1; bear THEOBALD
2.7.110/1243   BOY] COLLIER MS; *not in* F
2.7.112   vats] F (Fattes)
2.7.116   good-brother] F (Good Brother). See Gerald A. Smith, '"Good Brother" in *King Lear* and *Antony and Cleopatra*', *SQ* 25 (1974), 284.
2.7.117/1250   of:] ROWE 2; of, F
2.7.121   Splits] F (Spleet's)
2.7.121/1254   speakes: the] Fa; speakest: he Fb
2.7.125/1258   Fathers] F2; Father F1
2.7.127/1260   *Menas.* MENAS Ile] This edition (*conj.* Ridley). *Menas:* Ile F. See Ridley.
2.7.129/1262   heare] Fb; heare a Fa
2.7.129/1262   a loud] ROWE 3; aloud F
2.7.131/1264   saies a] F; Sessa RIDLEY (*conj.*)
3.1.5, 27, 34/1269, 1291, 1298   SILLIUS] *Romaine.* F
3.1.14/1278   to] Fa; too Fb
3.1.37/1301   there] Fb; their Fa
3.2.3/1304   are] Fb; art Fa
3.2.10/1311   AGRIPPA] ROWE; *Ant.* F
3.2.11/1312   Spake] F1; Speake F3

3.2.16/1317   Figures] HANMER; Figure F
3.2.20/1321   *trumpet within*] CAPELL; *not in* F; *after* 'so' RIDLEY
3.2.26   bond] F (Band)
3.2.31/1332   for] F; sir G.T. *conj.* Capell emended to 'for far', which does not solve the metrical problem. 'Sir' gives a stress after the caesura, with a short pause after it, making a metrically acceptable reversed foot of 'better'.
3.2.49/1350   at] F2; at the F1.
3.2.49/1350   full of] Fa; of full Fb
3.2.52/1354   that, . . . Horse,] Fa; that, . . . Horse, Fb
3.2.59/1361   weept] THEOBALD; weepe F
3.3.17   gait? Remember] F (gate, remember)
3.3.18   looked'st] POPE's *interpretation of* F's look'ft
3.4.5/1420   me;] ROWE; me, F
3.4.8/1423   them, most narrow measure lent me.] ROWE; then most narrow meafure:lent me, F
3.4.9/1424   took't] THEOBALD (Thirlby); look't F
3.4.24/1439   yours] F2; your F1
3.4.30/1445   Your] F2; You F1
3.4.38/1453   ha's] F2; he's F1
3.5.12/1465   world] HANMER; would F
3.5.12/1465   hast] HANMER; hadft F
3.5.12/1465   chaps,] THEOBALD; ~, F
3.5.12   chops] F (chaps)
3.5.14/1467   one the] CAPELL (Johnson); *not in* F
3.6.5/1480   the] F; their COLLIER MS.
3.6.13/1488   he ther] JOHNSON; hither F
3.6.13/1488   Kings of Kings] ROWE; King of Kings F
3.6.19/1494   reported,] F2; ~, F1
3.6.21/1496   knowes] F1; know F3
3.6.29/1504   being, that,] ROWE; being, that, F
3.6.61/1536   obstruct] THEOBALD (Warburton); abftract F
3.6.72/1547   Mauchus] F. As Sisson notes, a possible spelling of Plutarch's 'Malchus' (THEOBALD), which also occurs in the New Testament; though also possibly a misprint for North's 'Manchus'.
3.6.74/1549   Comagene] ROWE; Comageat F
3.6.74/1549   *Polemon*] THEOBALD (*after* North); *Polemen* F
3.6.75/1550   Licaonia] F2; Licoania F1
3.6.81/1556   negligent danger] F; danger negligent G.T. *conj.*
3.6.88/1563   their] THEOBALD; his F
3.7.4/1577   it is] F2; it it F1
3.7.5/1578   Is't not, denounc'd] ROWE; If not, denounc'd F
3.7.20/1593   *Camidius*] F also spells '*Camidias*'; we regard the as/us distinction as a mere spelling variant (though it could result from misreading), retaining both forms in the old spelling but standardizing the speech-prefix (and modern-spelling text) to '*Camidius*'. North has '*Canidius*'.
3.7.21/1594   Brundisium] F2; Brandufium F1
3.7.23/1596   Torine] F2; Troine F1
3.7.51/1624   Actium] POPE; Action F
3.7.56/1629   impossible;] POPE; ~, F
3.7.69   leader's led] F (Leaders leade)
3.7.72/1645   CAMIDIUS] POPE; *Ven.* F
3.7.78   Taurus] F (*Towrus*)
3.7.78/1651   Well I] ROWE 3; Well, I F
3.7.80/1653   in] ROWE; with F
3.7.80   throws] F (throwes). Some editors follow Theobald's 'throes'.
3.10.4/1668   Scarrus] He may be the 'Soldiour' of 3.7; see J. Leeds Barroll, 'Scarrus and the Scarred Soldier', *Huntington Library Quarterly*, 22 (1958), 31-9.
3.10.10/1674   riband red] This edition (*conj.* Thiselton); ribaudred F. Furness rejects Thiselton's conjecture and arguments in favour of F interpreted as 'ribauldried'. But that is unparalleled. The u/n misreading is easy (see, for example, the incidentals note to *Hamlet* Add. Pass. K.10 which records the misreading in Q2 of 'ribaud' for 'riband') and the image of Cleopatra decked in red ribbons like a horse (for which see Ridley's note) or a whore is especially striking alongside that of the fatal, red death-tokens of the plague.
3.10.14/1678   Iune] F2; Inne F1

3.10.17   luffed] F (looft)
3.10.27/1691   he] F2; his F1
3.10.36/1700   *Exeunt seuerally*] Camidius might leave at 3.10.34/1698 (so Capell).
3.11.6/1706   ATTENDANTS] F (*Omnes.*)
3.11.19/1719   that] CAPELL; them F
3.11.28.1/1728.1   *Sits downe*] COLLIER 2; *not in* F. Not usually adopted but desirable in view of Antony's next words.
3.11.47   seize] F (ceafe). The words were interchangeable.
3.11.58/1758   towe] ROWE; ftowe F
3.11.59/1759   Thy] THEOBALD 2; The F
3.12.0.1/1774.2   *Thidias*] F; *Thyreus* THEOBALD. F's form (also 'Thidius') suggests deliberate variation from North.
3.12.0.1/1774.2   *Dollabella*] F2; *Dollobello* F1
3.12.13/1787   Lessens] F2; Leffons F1. Sisson defends F, but its meaning would be difficult to convey.
3.12.29/1803   As . . . inuention,ₐ] HANMER; From . . . inuention, F. Modern editors follow F, but it offers strained sense, and 'From' could be accidentally repeated from 3.12.27/1801.
3.12.31/1805   *Thidias*] F; *Thyreus* THEOBALD
3.13.9-10/1819-20   oppos'd, . . . question? 'Twas] F; ~ . . . ~, 'twas This edition *conj.*
3.13.10/1820   mooted] This edition (Johnson); meered F. F is without parallel, though editors adopt, with doubt as to meaning. Though 'mooted' is not recorded adjectively till 1650, the verb was well established and gives excellent sense.
3.13.25/1835   Caparisons] POPE; Comparifons F
3.13.33/1843   alike. That] ROWE; alike, that F
3.13.54/1864   *Cæsar*] F2; *Cæfars* F1
3.13.55/1865   embrac'd] HUDSON (Capell); embrace F
3.13.74/1884   this in] F; this; in THEOBALD (Warburton)
3.13.74/1884   deputation] THEOBALD (Warburton); difputation F
3.13.76-7/1886-7   kneele | Till] JONES (Muir); kneele. | Tell him, F
3.13.93/1903   *Enter Seruants*] THEOBALD; *Enter a Seruant* F. The change is justified by 'fellows' (3.13.99/1909) and '*Exeunt seruants with Thideus*' (3.13.104.1/1914). Possibly the MS had e.g. '*Enter Seru.*'
3.13.103/1913   this] POPE; the F
3.13.113/1923   eyes:] WARBURTON; ~ₐ F
3.13.139/1949   whipt for] THEOBALD; whipt. For F
3.13.149   abyss] F (Abifme). See Sonnet 112.9.
3.13.154.1/1964.1   *Seruant with*] This edition; *not in* F. It seems unlikely that the Servant who brought Thidias in should remain.
3.13.165   Caesarion] F (*Cæfarian*)
3.13.165/1975   smite] ROWE; fmile F
3.13.168/1978   discandying] THEOBALD (Thirlby); difcandering F
3.13.171   sits] F (fets)
3.13.201/2011   on] ROWE; in F
4.1.3/2016   Combat,] ROWE; ~. F
4.2.0.2/2029.3   *Alexas*] F; *omitted by* CAPELL.
4.2.1/2030   *Domitius*] ROWE; *Domitian* F
4.2.10/2039   *Enter Seruitors*] ROWE; *Enter 3 or 4 Seruitors*. F. Most modern editors follow F, but the dialogue calls for at least 6.
4.2.19/2048   SERUITORS] MALONE (*Serv.*); *Omnes*. F.
4.2.38   fall. My] ROWE (*after* F: 'Fall (my')
4.3/Sc. 28]   Editors have variously altered the numbering of the Soldiers who speak. We alter only 4.3.7/2081, to make it clear that one of the second party addresses one of the first. Possibly Shakespeare did not allocate numbers to the speakers.
4.3.7/2081   3. SOULDIOUR] CAPELL; 1 F
4.3.7   an] F (and)
4.4.3/2097   thine] F; mine HANMER
4.4.5-6/2099-100   too, | What's this for? | ANTHONY] MALONE (Capell); too, Anthony. | What's this for? [*all spoken by Cleopatra*] F
4.4.13   doff't] F (daft)
4.4.24/2118   CAPTAINE] ROWE; *Alex*. F
4.4.25/2119   SOULDIERS] F (*All*.)
4.4.32/2126   thee,ₐ] ROWE; ~. F
4.5.1/2133   SOULDIER] THEOBALD (Thirlby); *Eros*. F
4.5.3, 7/2135, 2139   SOULDIER] CAPELL; *Eros*. F

4.5.17/2149   Dispatch.] STEEVENS; ~ₐ F
4.6.0.2/2149.2   *and Dolabella*] F; *omitted by* CAPELL (*adding* 'and Others')
4.6.8   van] F (Vant)
4.6.10.1-2/2159.1-2   *Exeunt . . . another*] This edition; *Exeunt*. F; *Exeunt Caesar, and Train* CAPELL.
4.6.12/2161   disswade] F; perswade ROWE
4.6.15/2164   *Camidius*] F2; *Camindius* F1
4.6.19/2168   more] F2; mote F1
4.6.36/2185   doo't, I feele.] ROWE; doo't. I feeleₐ F
4.7.0.1-2/2188.1-2   *Alarum. Enter Agrippa ⌈with Drummes and Trumpets⌉*] This edition; *Alarum, Drummes and Trumpets*. | *Enter Agrippa*. F. Editors since Capell bring on soldiers with Agrippa. As an *Alarum* was normally sounded by drums and trumpets, the direction is repetitive unless we take *Drummes and Trumpets* to refer to musicians who appear on stage. 'Retire' (4.7.1/2189) could be an instruction to sound a retreat.
4.8/Sc. 33]   This edition. Editors run on with 4.7/Sc. 32, but the stage is cleared.
4.8.10   hares, behind] F (Hares,ₐ behinde)
4.9.0.1-2/2204.3   *Drummes and trumpets*] WILSON; *not in* F
4.9.2/2206   gests] THEOBALD (Warburton); guefts F
4.9.2/2206   *Exit a Soldier*] This edition; *not in* F. Antony's commands are likely to be obeyed, and a summons to Cleopatra motivates her entrance (4.9.11/2215).
4.9.18/2222   My] F2; Mine F1
4.13.4/2293   Augures] POPE; Auguries F; Augurers CAPELL. F's form (followed by Riverside) is unsupported by *OED* as 'augurer'.
4.13.21/2310   spannell'd] HANMER (spaniel'd); pannelled F. *OED* records 'spannel' as a dialect spelling.
4.13.37/2326   Dolts] F; doits WARBURTON (Thirlby)
4.14.1/2339   hee's] F1; he is F2
4.14.10/2348   death. To] POPE; death to F
4.15.4/2352   tower'd] ROWE; toward F
4.15.10/2358   distaines] This edition; diflimes F; dislimn's ROWE. Though 'dislimns'—'fades away', and perhaps 'loses its limbs' like a body on a *rack*—is a possible Shakespearian coinage, the word is not recorded before Rowe, or again till 1826, when De Quincey describes it as 'a Shakespearian word'; 'dislimb' dates from 1662. 'Distaines' makes equally good sense (*OED*'s definitions include 'deprive of . . . colour, brightness . . .', 'to dim'), is genuinely Shakespearian (cf. e.g. *Lucrece* 786), and might easily give rise to F's reading.
4.15.14   knave.] ROWE (*after* F, 'Knaue),ₐ')
4.15.19/2367   *Caesar*] ROWE; *Cæfars* F
4.15.38/2386   The] F; This JOHNSON (*conj*.)
4.15.93.1/2441.1   *Eros stabs*] This edition; *Killes* F. Most editors move the direction to the end of Eros' speech, but F's placing suggests that those words follow his action.
4.15.104/2452   *and Decretas*] ROWE; *not in* F
4.15.107,132/2455, 2480   ALL THE GUARDS] F (*All*.)
4.15.110/2458   DECRETAS] F2; *Dercetus*. F1
4.15.122/2470   sent word] POPE; fent you word F. Modern editors revert to F, but the metre is improbable and contamination easy.
4.15.138.1/2486.1   *and Eros*] This edition. Shakespeare makes no special provision for the removal of Eros' body and editors have not marked it, but he must be either carried off or concealed by the drawing of a curtain.
4.16.0.1/2486.2   *and her Maides*] F; *omitted* ROWE. Possibly '*with Charmian & Iras*' merely duplicates this.
4.16.6/2492   *Enter Diomed,⌈below⌉*] COLLIER: *Enter Diomed* F. Collier's direction is not as certain as subsequent acceptance of it suggests. Realistically, Diomed is unlikely to gain admission to the monument; yet his instruction to Cleopatra 'Looke out o'th other side your Monument' may suggest that he enters behind her, '*aloft*'. If Diomed were '*aloft*', Cleopatra would probably call for his help; but he could depart after giving his message.
4.16.12-13/2499-2500   Help . . . hither] F; *intended for omission* WILSON (*conj.*). See David Galloway, *N&Q* 203 (1958), 330-5.
4.16.39/2525   when] F; where POPE
4.16.42/2528   ALL THE LOOKERS-ON] F (*All*.)

4.16.43/2529 I . . . Egypt, dying] F; *intended for omission* WILSON (*conj*.). See note to 4.16.12-13/2499-2500.
4.16.46 hussy] F (Huſwife)
4.16.56/2542 liu'd₍ₐ₎ the] THEOBALD; liued. The F
4.16.75 e'en] F (in)
4.16.77 chores] F (chares)
4.16.89/2575 do it] POPE; doo't F
5.1.0.1-2/2579.2-3 Enter . . . Proculeius] *as here* RIVERSIDE. For F, see s.d. list. Attendants may also be present.
5.1.0.2/2579.3 Mecenas] THEOBALD (Thirlby); *Menas* F
5.1.2/2581 but] HANMER; *not in* F
5.1.15/2594 reaued] *This edition* (G.T.); round F. F is metrically deficient and weak in sense. Steevens conjectured 'ruin'd', Johnson a lost line. The verbs *reave* and *rive* were confused (*reave, v.²*); 'reaued' seems more likely to have given rise to 'round' than 'riued'. The sense would thus be 'burst' with secondary 'bereft'. There is a close parallel in *Caesar*: 'I have seene Tempests, when the scolding Winds | Haue riu'd the knotty Oakes . . .' (1.3.5-6/403-4), in a passage which also offers lions in the streets. The idea of a split world is recurrent in *Antony*, e.g. 'As if the world should cleaue, and that slaine men | Should soader up the Rift' (3.4.31-2/1446-7).
5.1.18/2597 yᵗ] POPE; the F
5.1.26/2605 sad₍ₐ₎] F; ~, HANMER
5.1.27/2606 a] F2; *not in* F1
5.1.28, 31/2607, 2610 AGRIPPA] THEOBALD; *Dola⟨bella⟩*. F. Presumably Shakespeare's error.
5.1.36 lance] F (launch)
5.1.39/2618 looke] F; look'd HANMER
5.1.52/2631 Egyptian, yet the] WILSON (Lloyd); Egyptian yet the, F. Often debated; in this interpretation the messenger does not reply to Caesar's question but goes straight into his message; 'poore' seems suited to Cleopatra in view of 'Confin'd in all she has'.
5.1.53/2632 all she has,] ROWE; all, ſhe has₍ₐ₎ F
5.1.54/2633 desires,] ROWE 2; deſires, F
5.1.59/2638 liue] ROWE (Southern MS); leaue F
5.1.70/2649 ALL BUT CÆSAR] F (*All*.)
5.2.0.1/2656.1 *and Mardian*] F; *omitted by* CAPELL.
5.2.7/2663 dung] F; dug THEOBALD (Warburton)
5.2.8.1/2664.1 *Enter Proculeius*] F; *Enter Proculeius, and Gallus, below* HANMER; *Enter, to the gates of the Monument,* PROCULEIUS, GALLUS, *and Soldiers* MALONE (Capell). See Ridley, Appendix 4, 234-5.
5.2.34.1/2690.1 *Enter . . . behind*] HARRISON (*subs*.); *not in* F. Hinman (ii. 508-9) shows that absence of a direction in F is almost certainly the result of faulty casting off of copy. Though it is now clear that Gallus need not be involved in the capture (as he is in Plutarch), he has been instructed to 'go . . . along' after Proculeius, and may have been named in the lost direction.
5.2.35/2691 PROCULEIUS] F; *Gal⟨lus⟩*. MALONE. Editors have usually followed Malone because of F's repeated speech-prefix, but Hinman's demonstration that a direction was probably omitted (see previous note) removes the need to question F's ascription.
5.2.80/2736 O] THEOBALD; *not in* F
5.2.86/2742 Automne 'twas] THEOBALD (Theobald *and* Thirlby); *Anthony it was* F
5.2.95/2748 or] F3; nor F1
5.2.103/2759 smites] CAPELL; ſuites F
5.2.136.1/2792.1 *Enter Seleucus*] *not in* F. Most editors, following Capell, bring him on at 5.2.108.1-2/2764.1-2, with Caesar and his train; but, as Ridley asks, 'what is he doing there?' Riverside attempts to palliate the improbability by printing here '*Seleucus following*'. Wilson writes that he 'belongs . . . to the Monument . . . and naturally *comes forward* when called at [5.2.136/2792]', but marks no entrance for him. Entrance immediately following Cleopatra's question may seem too pat; yet he can hardly be present from the beginning of the scene. A director might well have him slip on in advance of his cue, whether or not at Caesar's entrance.
5.2.153/2809 Soule-lesse₍ₐ₎] POPE; ~, F
5.2.174/2830 merits in our name,] JOHNSON; merits, in our name₍ₐ₎ F
5.2.204/2860 shall] F1; shalt F2
5.2.212/2868 Ballad] F2; Ballads F1
5.2.219/2875 my] F2; mine F1
5.2.224/2880 Cidnus] ROWE; Cidrus F
5.2.274.1/2930.1 *Exit leauing the basket*] *This edition*; *not in* F. See *Re-Editing*, 77.
5.2.308/2964 vilde] CAPELL; wilde F. F is defensible ('desert', 'savage'), but 'vile world' occurs at *Contention* 5.3.403/3076 and Sonnet 71.4, is paralleled by e.g. *Macbeth* 3.1.110/911 and *1 Henry IV* 5.4.90/2887, and fits the *contemptus mundi* tone of Cleopatra's end.
5.2.312/2968 awry] ROWE 2; away F
5.2.313/2969 play—] F; ~. CAPELL. Often emended, but F's direction also suggests interruption.
5.2.319.1/2975.1 *Exit a Guardsman*] *This edition*; *not in* F. He might re-enter with Dolabella.
5.2.336-7/2992-3 Diadem₍ₐ₎ . . . Mistris;] POPE; ~; . . . ~₍ₐ₎ F
5.2.360.1-2/3016.1-2 *on her bed*] *This edition*; *not in* F. See 5.2.350/3006, which presumably implies that Cleopatra should be on the bed as it is removed.

INCIDENTALS

15 reckon'd.] ~₍ₐ₎   93 prou'd] proued   98 And] & (*in prose*)   170 awhile] awhlle   180 me.] ~₍ₐ₎   227 and] aud   279 first] fitſt   297 Seruicies] Seruicles (*see* OED)   408 Menecrates] Menacrates   483 Queene] Qu ene   515 againe,] ~ :   521 Hee₍ₐ₎ F (c.w.); he. (*text*)   573 hands.] ~₍ₐ₎   649 it.] Fb; it? Fa   669 poyson'd] poyſoned   703 deseru'd] deſerued   782 Venus] Venns   790 Helme,] ~.   829 prayers] ptayers   842 side.] ~₍ₐ₎   846 a feard, . . . o're-powr'd:] ~ : . . . ~,   1001 consider'd] conſidered   1023 Fathers] Fatherrs   1026 present) . . . take,] preſent₍ₐ₎ . . . take)   1029 imbrac'd.] ~₍ₐ₎   1045 heere.] ~,   1048 gain'd] gained   1050 Fortune] Fotune   1054 composition] compoſion   1055 vs.] ~,   1133 o'their] o'th'their   1136 Coulord] Conlord   1141 greater] greatet   1173 What] Whar   1192 off them,] ~, ~   1264 Hoa,] Fa; ~, Fb   1269 Ventidius] Fb; *Ventidus* Fa   1338 serue] ſeure Fa   1342 farethee] Fa; fare thee Fb   1349 tongue] tougue   1359 yeare indeed . . . troubled . . . rume] Fa; yearindeed . . . trobled . . . rheume Fb   1372 pleas'd] Fb; plaes'd Fa   1381 speake,] Fb; ~₍ₐ₎ Fa   1384 dwarfish,] ~₍ₐ₎. A redundant comma appears 2 lines below.   1488 proclaim'd] proclaimed   1512 like.] ~₍ₐ₎   1608 Muliters] Militers   1870 deserud] deſerued   2084 List, list] (*Chatsworth copy in Lee facsimile*); ~₍ₐ₎ ~ (*Norton facsimile, etc.*)   2101 this.] ~,   2140 Hee] F (c.w.); He (*text*)   2160 Iewry] Iewrÿ   2206 And] & (*within the line*)   2292 'tis] 'ris   2458 fly.] ~₍ₐ₎   2498 Antony.] ~₍ₐ₎ (*at end of line*)   2542 liud] liued   2639 vngentle.] ~,   2672 Queene] Queece   2682 dependäcie] dependacie   2697 languish?] ~,   2712 Egypt,] ~.   2769 obey.] ~,   2800 known.] ~₍ₐ₎   2846 thee] th₍ₐ₎e   2975 sent] ~₍ₐ₎   3016 Solemnity] Solmemnity

ANTONY AND CLEOPATRA

FOLIO STAGE DIRECTIONS

1.1.0.1/0.1 Enter Demetrius and Philo.
1.1.10/9 Flourish. Enter Anthony, Cleopatra, her Ladies, the | Traine, with Eunuchs fanning her.
1.1.17.1/17.1 Enter a Messenger.
1.1.57.1-2/57.1-2 Exeunt with the Traine.
1.1.64/64 Exeunt
1.2.0.1-2/64.1-2 Enter Enobarbus, Lamprius, a Southsayer, Rannius, Lucilli-|us, Charmian, Iras, Mardian the Eunuch, | and Alexas.
1.2.72.1/137.1 Enter Cleopatra.
1.2.80.1/145.1 Enter Anthony, with a Messenger.
1.2.81.1/146.1 Exeunt.
1.2.106/171 Exit Messenger.
1.2.106.2/171.1 Enter another Messenger.
1.2.111/176 Enter another Messenger with a Letter.
1.2.124.1/189.1 Enter Enobarbus. (after 'hatch')
1.3.0.1/254.1 Enter Cleopatra, Charmian, Alexas, and Iras.
1.3.12.1/266.1 Enter Anthony.
1.3.106/360 Exeunt.
1.4.0.1-2/360.1-2 Enter Octauius reading a Letter, Lepidus, | and their Traine.
1.4.33/393 Enter a Messenger.
1.4.85/445 Exeunt
1.5.0.1/445.1 Enter Cleopatra, Charmian, Iras, & Mardian.
1.5.34/479 Enter Alexas from Cæsar.
1.5.77/522 Exeunt
2.1.0.1-2/522.1-2 Enter Pompey, Menecrates, and Menas, in | warlike manner.
2.1.27/549 Enter Varrius.
2.1.52/574 Exeunt.
2.2.0.1/574.1 Enter Enobarbus and Lepidus.
2.2.14/588 Enter Anthony and Ventidius.
2.2.14.1/588.1 Enter Cæsar, Mecenas, and Agrippa.
2.2.27.1/601.1 Flourish.
2.2.177.1-2/752.1-2 Flourish. Exit omnes. | Manet Enobarbus, Agrippa, Mecenas.
2.2.251.1/826.1 Exeunt
2.3.0.1/826.2 Enter Anthony, Cæsar, Octauia betweene them.
2.3.9/835 Exit.
2.3.9.1/835.1 Enter Soothsaier.
2.3.29.1/855.1 Exit.
2.3.38/864 Enter Ventigius. (after 'lies')
2.3.40/866 Exeunt
2.4.0.1/866.1 Enter Lepidus, Mecenas, and Agrippa.
2.4.10.1-2/876.1-2 Exeunt.
2.5.0.1/876.3 Enter Cleopater, Charmian, Iras, and Alexas.
2.5.2.1/878.1 Enter Mardian the Eunuch.
2.5.23/899 Enter a Messenger. (after 'Italie')
2.5.61.1/937.1 Strikes him downe.
2.5.62.1/938.1 Strikes him.
2.5.64.1/940.1 She hales him vp and downe.
2.5.73/949 Draw a knife.
2.5.74/950 Exit.
2.5.84/960 Enter the Messenger againe. (after 'cause')
2.5.120.1/996.1 Exeunt.
2.6.0.1-4/996.2-5 Flourish. Enter Pompey, at one doore with Drum and Trum-|pet: at another Cæsar, Lepidus, Anthony, Enobarbus, Me-|cenas, Agrippa, Menas with Souldiers Marching.
2.6.83.1/1079.1 Exeunt. Manet Enob. & Menas
2.6.136/1132 Exeunt.
2.7.0.1-2/1132.1-2 Musicke playes. | Enter two or three Seruants with a Banket.
2.7.16.1-3/1148.1-3 A Sennet sounded. | Enter Cæsar, Anthony, Pompey, Lepidus, Agrippa, Mecenas, | Enobarbus, Menes, with other Captaines.
2.7.39.1/1172.1 Whispers in's Eare. (after 2.7.38/1171)
2.7.109.1/1240.1-2 Musicke Playes. Enobarbus places them hand in hand.
2.7.110/1240.3 The Song.
2.7.130.1/1263.1 Sound a Flourish with Drummes.
2.7.131.1/1264.1 Exeunt.
3.1.0.1-3/1264.2-4 Enter Ventidius as it were in triumph, the dead body of Paco-|rus borne before him.
3.1.37.1/1301.1 Exeunt.
3.2.0.1/1301.2 Enter Agrippa at one doore, Enobarbus at another.
3.2.22.1/1323.1 Enter Cæsar, Anthony, Lepidus, and Octauia.
3.2.67/1368 Kisses Octauia.
3.2.67.1-3/1368.1-3 Trumpets sound. Exeunt.
3.3.0.1/1368.4 Enter Cleopatra, Charmian, Iras, and Alexas.
3.3.2/1370 Enter the Messenger as before. (after 'Sir')
3.3.47/1415 Exeunt.
3.4.0.1/1415.1 Enter Anthony and Octauia.
3.4.38/1453 Exeunt.
3.5.0.1/1453.1-2 Enter Enobarbus, and Eros.
3.5.22/1475 Exeunt.
3.6.0.1/1475.1 Enter Agrippa, Mecenas, and Cæsar.
3.6.38.1/1513 Enter Octauia with her Traine.
3.6.98/1573.1 Exeunt
3.7.0.1/1573.2 Enter Cleopatra, and Enobarbus.
3.7.19/1592 Enter Anthony and Camidias.
3.7.53/1626 Enter a Messenger.
3.7.60/1633 Enter a Soldiour.
3.7.66.1/1639.1 exit Ant. Cleo. & Enob.
3.7.78.1/1651.1 Enter a Messenger.
3.7.81/1654 exeunt
3.8.0.1/1654.1 Enter Cæsar with his Army, marching.
3.8.6.1-2/1660.1-2 exit.
3.9.0.1/1660.3 Enter Anthony, and Enobarbus.
3.9.4/1664 exit.
3.10.1-5/1664.1-5 Camidius Marcheth with his Land Army one way ouer the | stage, and Towrus the Lieutenant of Cæsar the other way: | After their going in, is heard the noise of a Sea-fight. | Alarum. Enter Enobarbus and Scarus.
3.10.4/1668 Enter Scarrus.
3.10.23.1/1687.1 Enter Camidius.
3.11.0.1/1700.1 Enter Anthony with Attendants.
3.11.24.2/1724.2 Sits downe
3.11.24.3/1724.3 Enter Cleopatra led by Charmian and Eros.
3.11.74.1/1774.1 Exeunt
3.12.0.1-2/1774.2-3 Enter Cæsar, Agrippa, and Dollabello, with others.
3.12.6/1780 Enter Ambassador from Anthony.
3.12.36.1-2/1810.1-2 exeunt.
3.13.0.1/1810.3 Enter Cleopatra, Enobarbus, Charmian, & Iras.
3.13.12.1/1822.1 Enter the Ambassador, with Anthony.
3.13.36/1846 Enter a Seruant. (after 'yet')
3.13.45/1855 Enter Thidias.
3.13.65/1875 Exit Enob.
3.13.85/1895 Enter Anthony and Enobarbus.
3.13.93/1903 Enter a Seruant.
3.13.104.1/1914 Exeunt with Thidius.
3.13.132/1942 Enter a Seruant with Thidias. (after 'whipt')
3.13.154.1/1964.1 Exit Thid.
3.13.196.1/2006.1 Exeunt.
3.13.203/2013 Exeunt.
4.1.0.1-2/2013.1-2 Enter Cæsar, Agrippa, & Mecenas with his Army, | Cæsar reading a Letter.
4.1.16.1/2019.1 Exeunt
4.2.0.1-2/2019.2-3 Enter Anthony, Cleopatra, Enobarbus, Charmian, | Iras, Alexas, with others.
4.2.10/2039 Enter 3 or 4 Seruitors. (after 4.2.9/2038)
4.2.45/2074 Exeunt.
4.3.0.1/2074.1 Enter a Company of Soldiours.
4.3.6/2080 They meete other Soldiers.
4.3.7/2081 They place themselues in euery corner of the Stage.
4.3.10/2084 Musicke of the Hoboyes is vnder the Stage.
4.3.16/2090 Speak together. (after 4.3.15/2089)
4.3.20.1/2094.1 Exeunt.
4.4.0.1-2/2094.2-3 Enter Anthony and Cleopatra, with others.

ANTONY AND CLEOPATRA

4.4.2.1/2096.1 Enter Eros.
4.4.18/2112 Enter an Armed Soldier.
4.4.23.1/2117.1 Showt.
4.4.23.1-2/2117.1-2 Trumpets Flourish. | Enter Captaines, and Souldiers.
4.4.34.1/2128.1 Exeunt.
4.4.38/2132 Exeunt
4.5.0.1-2/2132.1-2 Trumpets sound. Enter Anthony, and Eros.
4.5.17/2149 Exit
4.6.0.1-2/2149.1-2 Flourish. Enter Agrippa, Cæsar, with Enobarbus, | and Dollabella.
4.6.6/2155 Enter a Messenger.
4.6.10.1-2/2159.1-2 Exeunt.
4.6.19/2168 Enter a Soldier of Cæsars.
4.6.29/2178 Exit
4.6.39/2188 Exit.
4.7.0.1-2/2188.1-2 Alarum, Drummes and Trumpets. | Enter Agrippa.
4.7.3/2191 Exit.
4.8.0.1/2191.1-2 Alarums. | Enter Anthony, and Scarrus wounded.
4.8.5/2196 Far off. (after 'heads', 4.8.3/2194)
4.8.7.1/2198.1 Enter Eros.
4.8.13.1/2204.1 Exeunt
4.9.0.1-2/2204.2-3 Alarum. Enter Anthony againe in a March. | Scarrus, with others.
4.9.11/2215 Enter Cleopatra.
4.9.39/2243 Exeunt.
4.10.0.1/2243.1-2 Enter a Centerie, and his Company, Enobarbus followes.
4.10.29/2272 Drummes afarre off.
4.10.33.1/2276.1 exeunt
4.11.0.1/2276.2 Enter Anthony and Scarrus, with their Army.
4.11.9/2285 exeunt
4.12.0.1/2285.1 Enter Cæsar, and his Army.
4.12.4/2289 exeunt.
4.13.0.1/2289.1-2 Alarum afarre off, as at a Sea-fight. | Enter Anthony, and Scarrus.
4.13.3/2292 exit.
4.13.9/2298 Enter Anthony.
4.13.30/2319 Enter Cleopatra.
4.13.39/2328 exit Cleopatra.
4.13.49/2338 exit.
4.14.0.1/2338.1 Enter Cleopatra, Charmian, Iras, Mardian.
4.14.10/2348.1 Exeunt.
4.15.0.1/2348.2 Enter Anthony, and Eros.
4.15.22/2370 Enter Mardian.

4.15.37/2385 exit Mardian.
4.15.43.1/2391.1 exit Eros
4.15.54.1/2402.1 Enter Eros.
4.15.103/2451 Killes himselfe.
4.15.104/2452 Enter a Guard.
4.15.109/2456 exeunt
4.15.112/2460 Enter Diomedes.
4.15.128.1/2476.1 Enter 4. or 5. of the Guard of Anthony.
4.15.138.1/2486.1 Exit bearing Anthony
4.16.0.1-2/2486.2-3 Enter Cleopatra, and her Maides aloft, with | Charmian & Iras.
4.16.6/2492 Enter Diomed.
4.16.9.1/2495 Enter Anthony, and the Guard.
4.16.38.1/2524.1 They heaue Anthony aloft to Cleopatra.
4.16.93.1/2579.1 Exeunt, bearing of Anthonies body.
5.1.0.1-2/2579.2-3 Enter Cæsar, Agrippa, Dollabella, Menas, with | his Counsell of Warre.
5.1.3.1/2582.2 Enter Decretas with the sword of Anthony.
5.1.48.1/2627.1 Enter an Aegyptian. (after 'sayes', 5.1.51/2630)
5.1.60/2639 Exit.
5.1.68.1/2647.1 Exit Proculeius.
5.1.77/2656 Exeunt.
5.2.0.1/2656.1 Enter Cleopatra, Charmian, Iras, and Mardian.
5.2.8.1/2664.1 Enter Proculeius.
5.2.63/2719 Enter Dolabella.
5.2.69.1/2725.1 Exit Proculeius (after 'him')
5.2.108.1-2/2764.1-3 Flourish. | Enter Proculeius, Cæsar, Gallus, Mecenas, | and others of his Traine.
5.2.110/2766 Cleo. kneeles.
5.2.186.1/2842.1 Flourish. | Exeunt Cæsar, and his Traine.
5.2.192.1/2848.1 Enter Dolabella.
5.2.193/2849 Exit (after 'thankes', 5.1.203/2859)
5.2.222/2878 Enter Charmian.
5.2.228.2/2884.2 A noise within.
5.2.229/2885 Enter a Guardsman.
5.2.232/2888 Exit Guardsman.
5.2.237/2893 Enter Guardsman, and Clowne.
5.2.238/2894 Exit Guardsman.
5.2.274.1/2931 Exit
5.2.308/2964 Dyes.
5.2.313.1/2969.1 Enter the Guard rustling in, and Dolabella.
5.2.323/2979 Charmian dyes.
5.2.323.1/2979.1 Enter Dolabella.
5.2.327.1/2983.1 Enter Cæsar and all his Traine, marching. (after 'hinder')
5.2.360.1-2/3016.1-2 Exeunt omnes

PERICLES

Pericles was entered in the Stationers' Register on 20 May 1608:

Edw Blount.   Entred for his copie vnder thande of Sr Geo. Buck knight & Mr Warden Seton A booke called. The booke of Pericles prynce of Tyre

The phrasing of this entry suggests that the manuscript submitted was the official company book. The original 'R' presumably indicates receipt of the fee; its deletion may imply cancellation of the entry. Certainly, Blount never published any extant edition of *Pericles* (or of *Antony*, entered at the same time). The first edition (*BEPD* 284a) was a quarto, dated 1609, published by Henry Gosson, who published a second edition (284b) the same year, using the same setting of type for the title-page. In Q1 sheets A, C–E differ in their running titles from B, F–I; there are also differences in type-face. Greg identified the printer of A, C–E as William White; Blayney identified the other printer as Thomas Creede. Edwards (1952) identified one compositor (x) in White's sheets and two (y, z) in Creede's. These divisions were confirmed, with one slight modification, by Hoeniger (1963). MacDonald P. Jackson has further corroborated them, noting that Compositor x used a measure about three millimetres wider than that employed by the other two compositors, who can be readily distinguished by their spacing practices: z usually (82%) spaced commas in short lines, y usually did not (23%). The spacing evidence confirms Hoeniger's reassignment of F3 and F4^v from z to y (or an additional compositor). The division by pages is indicated in the diplomatic edition. In our reconstructed text, it is as follows:

x: Sc. 1, 1–201/1–201
    Sc. 5, 16.1–Sc. 15.4/506.1–1377

y: Sc. 1, 202–Sc.2, 129.1/202–342.1
    Sc. 15.5–143/1378–1516 ('haue')
    Sc. 16, 49–Sc. 18, 22/1573–1747
    Sc. 21, 25 ('HELICANUS')–Sc. 22, 29/2043 ('HELICANUS')–2295

z: Sc. 3, 1–Sc. 5, 16/343–506
    Sc. 15, 144–Sc. 16, 48/1516 ('her')–1572
    Sc. 18, 22.2–Sc. 21, 25 ('him?')/1747.2–2043 ('him?')
    Sc. 22, 30–end/2296–end.

Editorially, the most important difference between these compositors is their treatment of line division—though even this has perhaps been exaggerated (see Taylor, 'Transmission').

The division of work between shops, and between compositors y and z, is peculiar. It has been widely assumed that sheet B was originally set by White, and that the extant sheet represents a resetting by Creede. Musgrove's alternative assumption, that work on sheet B was delayed as the printer awaited additional copy, is implausible. But it is not obvious why sheet B should have needed resetting in its entirety, or why if such resetting were necessary it should be given to the second printer. According to Hoeniger, Compositor x set by formes (p. xxvii); but y and z each set batches of four or more consecutive pages, involving both inner and outer formes. Creede's copy may therefore only have been cast off by half-sheets, and inaccurate casting off seems to have affected the text only on G2^v, where at the end of a stint Compositor y mislined the text in order to stretch it (17.46–18.22/1719–47).

The few press variants in the nine extant copies of Q, which were collated by Hoeniger, do not suggest any consultation of copy. However, Hoeniger is unjustified in taking this lamentable but ordinary procedure as evidence of particularly 'hasty and careless printing' (p. xxxviii). Nor is shared printing in any way irregular, being a common commercial activity in this period (Blayney). Although an ordinary number of errors in Q is no doubt due to misreading and other compositorial mistakes, such sources can only account for a small proportion of the evident corruption. The division of work on Q between (certainly) two printers and (probably) three compositors provides the strongest possible evidence that the deficiencies of the text—present in the work of both printers—originate in the manuscript copy, not in the process of printing.

Q's deficiencies are of several interlocking kinds. First, there is massive mislineation and confusion of prose and verse, which in this instance cannot be reasonably attributed to the printer(s): by contrast with Quarto *Lear* (set by one printer who had never before attempted a play, and whose later play quartos often contain significant quantities of similar mislineation), Quarto *Pericles* was set by two experienced printers. Such mislineation suggests that we may be dealing with a reported text, and this supposition is reinforced by many other features. Metrically, Q as it stands—even allowing for normal compositorial error—can hardly belong to any period of Shakespeare's career; it shows the same kind of rhythmical disorganization evident in memorial texts. It also often repeats itself verbally, in ways which suggest that one correct use of a phrase, idiom, or image has contaminated another passage. (Many such repetitions are identified in the following notes.)

Lineation, metre, and verbal repetition can be, to a large degree, objectively described, and related to a Shakespearian norm. In all such features Q can be unpolemically described as 'significantly abnormal', and because of its printing history that abnormality can be confidently located in the printers' copy itself. In trying to account for these anomalies in the manuscript one enters, inevitably, the realm of speculation. In particular, one can only 'explain' a Quarto anomaly by (*a*) conjecturing how the text can be emended, to restore a

'Shakespearian' verbal pattern, and then (*b*) offering a mechanism by which the 'correct' editorial conjecture could be 'corrupted' into the Quarto 'error'. This mechanism operates in all emendations, and hence to some degree in all editing. But the process becomes particularly obvious, and unusually important, in a case like *Pericles*, where the layer of corruption has seemed, to almost all readers, extraordinarily deep and broad. Hence, the 'evidence' which we offer for the hypothesis that Q is a reported text resides, to a large extent, in the following textual notes: the emendations we have adopted, the attendant explanations given for Q readings which seem to us corrupt.

What has seemed to most readers the most obvious characteristic of Q—the gross unevenness in dramatic quality and verbal style—is, unfortunately, not quantifiable; nor, however, can it be ignored. Most earlier scholars assumed that these discrepancies arose from collaborative authorship; Edwards (1952) tried instead to attribute them entirely to the method by which the text was transmitted, alleging that there were two reporters with very different methods of reporting. Taylor, drawing upon the criticisms of other scholars, has argued that Edwards's hypothesis is in practice self-contradictory, unsubstantiated, unparalleled, and unlikely. He proposes instead that, like other memorial texts, Q was reported by one or more actors: the boy who played Lychorida and Marina (probably also doubling a mute page in Sc. 6 and a mute lady in Sc. 7), and probably also a hired man, doubling a number of small parts (including, perhaps, a fisherman and the Pander). Taylor also proposes that the reporters had acquired, presumably surreptitiously, a copy of Gower's part, perhaps because the Gower-actor was the master of the Marina-boy. Taylor's reconstruction is, necessarily, conjectural, but it does account for many features of Q, and at the least seems a better working hypothesis than others so far offered.

The exact mechanism of reporting offered by Taylor is less important than the challenge to Edwards's hypothesis, with its attempt to 'save' the entirety of the play for Shakespeare. Bibliographical conjecture based on internal evidence is no more 'objective' or 'scientific' than a conjectural attribution based on internal evidence. We believe that no textual theory can make it credible that Shakespeare wrote the bulk of the first nine scenes, and that a variety of evidence points to George Wilkins as his probable collaborator. (See 'Canon and Chronology'.)

Wilkins's part-authorship of the original play lends even greater significance to a novella he published in 1608: 'The Painfull Aduentures of Pericles Prince of Tyre. Being The true History of the Play of *Pericles*, as it was lately presented by the worthy and ancient Poet Iohn Gower' (*STC* 25638.5). This pamphlet, not discovered until 1839, was unavailable to the play's earliest editors; of the two extant copies, only one (at Zurich) contains the dedication signed by Wilkins. The pamphlet openly professes to be based on the play, and this claim is substantiated by many details in which *Painfull Aduentures* (hereafter '*P.A.*') agrees with Q against all other versions of the story. Hence, *P.A.* is, and admits to being—what Q also apparently represents—a 'reported text' of the play.

Like any reported text, *P.A.* is of variable accuracy and value. Wilkins clearly drew, not only upon the play (which he advertises), but also upon Twine's *The Pattern of Painfull Aduentures*, which in places he plagiarizes word for word (without acknowledgement). The author(s) of the play also used Twine, but far less slavishly: Gower is their main source. When *P.A.* reproduces Twine verbatim we can give it little credence as a report of the play. Editorially, the most significant features of *P.A.* are, accordingly, those which diverge from Twine. Bullough provides edited texts of both Twine and *P.A.* (and the play's other primary source, Gower's *Confessio Amantis*); for ease of reference all our quotations of these documents refer to page-numbers in Bullough's edition, though we have in fact checked these against the British Library copies. (*P.A.* is printed in black-letter type, with roman used for emphasis; in our text and notes we have translated black-letter into roman type, with italic for emphasis.)

Ideally, any student of the text of *Pericles* would wish to have parallel diplomatic editions of *P.A.*, Twine (as a control on *P.A.*), and Q. Practically, an editor's collations must take Q as copy-text, and record *P.A.* only selectively. But such procedural difficulties should not continue to obscure the fact that *P.A.* is a 'substantive' text of *Pericles*: a 'reported' text (like Q), one cast in the mode of a prose narrative (unlike Q), one contaminated by Twine (unlike Q), but a substantive text nevertheless. In some places Q and *P.A.* strikingly confirm each other's testimony; in others, they are so close verbally that it is impossible to judge, when they differ, which is more probably correct; in others, Q has been regularly emended to coincide with *P.A.* (sometimes by editors unaware of *P.A.*'s existence). If Q were itself better than it is, *P.A.* might be of little editorial significance; but given the generally acknowledged inadequacy of Q, *P.A.* becomes enormously important. Two reports are obviously better than one.

Moreover, although in its plagiarism of Twine and its narrative format *P.A.* is obviously inferior to Q as an editorial document, in one crucial respect it is superior: the author of *P.A.* is the man most likely to have been Shakespeare's collaborator in writing the play. Scholars have in the past been puzzled by Wilkins's apparent reliance on memory, in compiling *P.A.*: if he were part-author, why did he not have a text of the play, which he would copy as mechanically as he did Twine? But the part-author of a Jacobean collaborative play need never have possessed a personal copy of the whole manuscript. Moreover, once the play was purchased by a theatrical company they became sole owners, and the playwright(s) could only acquire copies by the grace of the company. *Pericles* was obviously a popular play, and the King's Men would have every incentive to prevent the early circulation of loose copies. Moreover, for a collaborative play Wilkins may not even have possessed, afterwards, his own foul papers. A fair copy would need to be made for use by the company; Shakespeare, as the senior collaborator, may have made this copy himself (thus enabling him to smooth any joins between the two shares, or to revise his partner's work as he saw fit), or he may have arranged for a fair copy to be made by a scribe employed by the company. In either eventuality Wilkins's foul papers would have passed out of his hands well before the play was performed; the fair copy would be made for the company, and Wilkins himself would have no right or opportunity to ask for the foul papers to be returned. Thus, in the natural course of events Wilkins might have found himself, in 1608, without a written text even of his own portion of the play. Moreover, the company may have had good reason to ensure, in Wilkins's case, that the playwright retained no copy. As Prior has demonstrated, the documentary records of Wilkins's life leave us in little doubt that he was an unscrupulous petty criminal whose literary and theatrical career abruptly terminated in 1608. More particularly, Wilkins's earlier play for the King's Men, *The Miseries of Enforced Marriage*, was, despite its evident popularity, published in 1607, apparently from authorial foul papers, with an apparently authorial epigraph on the title-page. *The Trauailes of the three English Brothers*, of which he was part-author, was also published in 1607, with an epistle signed by the three authors (*BEPD* 248). Both plays, which draw upon topical material, must have been fairly new at the time of their publication. Wilkins's other major publication is a translation of 'The Historie of Iustine' (1606: *STC* 24293), which for the most part plagiarizes an earlier translation as unabashedly as *P.A.* in places plagiarizes Twine. All these publications would have given the King's Men cause to be cautious in their dealings with Wilkins, in relation to copyright in his plays. *P.A.* confirms the same pattern of activity: the pamphlet was clearly designed to cash in on the theatrical success of *Pericles*. The 1608 Stationers' Register entry, if it is a 'blocking entry', is easily reconciled with the assumption that the company suspected that Wilkins would try to publish the play without their consent. Finally, it may not be entirely coincidental that after 1608—despite the popularity of *Miseries* and *Pericles*—the King's Men and the other London companies had no further dealings with Wilkins.

Whatever the precise history of his relationship with the King's Men, there is nothing intrinsically implausible in the twin assumptions that (*a*) Wilkins wished to exploit financially the success of a play he had already sold to the King's Men, and (*b*) Wilkins no longer had a manuscript of the play. In these circumstances he would be forced to rely upon his memory, supplemented by lazy plagiarism of Twine. He would obviously know the parts of the play he had written himself much better than he knew Shakespeare's share; verbal resemblances between *P.A.* and Q are sporadic and casual in the second half of the play, but much more sustained and detailed in the first half. We have accordingly made much more editorial use of *P.A.* in what we believe to be Wilkins's share of the play (Sc. 1-9). We have also drawn upon *P.A.* for the forms of characters' names, since *P.A.* derives directly from one of the authors, whereas Q is based at least in part upon memory, aural transmission, and subsequent transcription by a third party.

The relative merits of specific variants between Q and *P.A.* are discussed in the following textual notes, but two structural differences—both involving the presence in *P.A.* of material absent from Q—require more extended comment. At 9.24/980 in Q King Simonides compliments Pericles on his 'sweete Musicke this last night', but in Q Pericles has been offered no opportunity to perform this music. A playwright might perhaps use such a reference as a *substitute* for the performance itself (in order to indicate Pericles' musical skills without having to display them), but Simonides' words are more plausibly interpreted as referring to an episode shown on stage. In Chapter 6 of *P.A.* Wilkins devotes a page to describing such an episode.

Throughout the portions of his novel corresponding to the play's first nine scenes, Wilkins adheres almost exactly to Q's plot, recalling the play's cues for entries and switching the focus of his narrative in accord with the play's scene divisions. Parts of Wilkins's opening chapter paraphrase, plagiarize, or expand Twine's novel, as introduction to Pericles' encounter with the incestuous Antiochus and his daughter. Twine is also used to fill out the story of Pericles' relief of Tharsus, and Chapter 4 of *P.A.* begins with some invented material, followed by some borrowing from Twine, to spin out Gower's lines about the storm which introduce the shipwrecked Pericles in Sc. 5. Otherwise Wilkins does not deviate in any significant degree from the play as Q presents it. It would be uncharacteristic of Wilkins's method in recounting the material covered by the play's first nine scenes to invent an episode as substantial as that in which Pericles sings and plays an instrument.

In both the play's sources, Gower's poem and Twine's prose fiction, Pericles displays his skill in playing the harp and singing at the banquet, after Thaisa has played and sung to him in order to cheer him up. But Q replaces this particular musical interlude with dancing—an improvement from the dramatic point of view, since it avoids any suggestion of Pericles' showing off by outperforming Thaisa as a musician and allows instead for the spectacle of a wordless ritual of courtship. (*P.A.* gives the dancing far less space than the singing, alluding only to 'much time being spent in dancing and other reuels'.)

Thus both the play's sources substantiate *P.A.*'s independent testimony that *Pericles* included a musical episode not present in Q, and modern productions usually essay to supply this deficiency. A song attractively contributes to the theatrical quality of the play (and particularly the play's first half). Thematically, it contributes to the larger structure of the play, naturally taking its place alongside Thaisa's reawakening to music, Marina's profession as music teacher, the song sung to Pericles, the music of the spheres, and the characteristic Shakespearian opposition of music and tempest. Moreover, such a scene could have given the King's Men no difficulty in practice, for their *Volpone* (1606) also includes a virtuoso set-piece, involving a solo song by the protagonist, who accompanies himself on an instrument. Finally, Q as a report is void of sound effects, so its omission of the song itself is not surprising; if (as *P.A.* indicates) the scene in question only involved Pericles himself, and a brief initial appearance by one or more attendants, then the reporter(s) would not have been present, and could not report it. Our reconstruction—on the basis of *P.A.*—of this short scene (Sc. 8a) is discussed in the textual notes. This reconstruction is necessarily conjectural in detail; but we are confident that such a scene existed.

The other passage for which *P.A.* contains material not present in Q is the play's most famous crux: the encounter between Lysimachus and Marina in the brothel (Sc. 19). In *P.A.*, in converting Lysimachus Marina speaks at much greater length than in Q; moreover, Lysimachus afterwards confesses that he had originally come to the brothel with wicked intentions, whereas in Q he claims instead to have had 'no ill meaning'. Taylor ('Transmission') argued that no mechanism of textual transmission could account for Q having accidentally omitted the material present in *P.A.*, and that Q as it stood was theatrically intelligible. These propositions still seem to us correct. But Jackson still felt very strongly that the *P.A.* outline of the scene was preferable. Moreover, in spring 1986 a production of *Pericles* at the Shakespeare Festival (Stratford, Ontario) made use of proofs of our reconstructed text of the play; but they balked at our refusal to expand or alter Q's text of that encounter. In this reaction they simply confirmed a long-standing tradition in the modern theatre, which has usually resorted to the addition of some cobbled rendering of *P.A.* We were thus confronted with an apparently irresolvable impasse between (*a*) the widespread theatrical and critical conviction that *P.A.* better represents Shakespeare's intentions, and (*b*) the implausibility of any hypothesis which would explain Q's accidental omission and alteration of this material.

Taylor now proposes that this enigma can be readily resolved as the result of censorship. In *P.A.* Lysimachus—variously described as the 'ruler', 'Gouernour', and 'regent' of Mytilene—visits a brothel as a regular customer; he tells Marina not to worry, because his authority can turn a blind eye on her prostitution; on the other hand, if she displeases him he can punish her. Marina's initial response dwells almost entirely upon Lysimachus's 'abuse' of his 'authority' and 'Iustice'. During the Jacobean period the Master of the Revels was particularly sensitive to allusions to the promiscuity of courtiers: passages containing such material were censored in *The Second Maiden's Tragedy*, *The Honest Man's Fortune*, *Eastward Ho*, *Cynthia's Revels* (and possibly *Kinsmen*: see Introduction, below). *P.A.*'s account is extremely objectionable, politically; Q's is entirely innocuous. We therefore believe that Q represents, with reasonable accuracy, the censored text of the play, as actually performed (and hence as familiar to the reporter); but that *P.A.* gives us, in essence, the more dangerous and more dramatic original. We have therefore attempted a scholarly reconstruction of the censored material, in so far as it can be recovered from *P.A.*; the textual notes discuss in detail the difficulties posed by any such reconstruction. As Taylor observed ('Transmission'), verbally the quality of the added material has clearly suffered from its transmission through the filter of Wilkins's (relative) mediocrity; but when relieved of some of his wordiness, and the mannerisms of his prose, the passages are, we believe, not noticeably incongruous in their dramatic context.

Early editors of *Pericles*, understanding little or nothing about its transmission, but able to see for themselves that it was grossly corrupt, emended Q freely; recent editors, knowing far more, do far less. The most influential contribution to the editing of *Pericles* in this century has been Fredson Bowers's Introduction to his text of Webster and Dekker's *Sir Thomas Wyatt*, in Dekker's *Dramatic Works* (i. 402-4). Bowers there asserts that 'The most that can ordinarily be expected of the editor of a "bad" quarto is that he attempt chiefly to emend errors which there is some reason to assign to the compositor and thus to recover what is often the equal impurity of the underlying printer's copy'; as a result, 'Paradoxically ... the editorial principles adopted for this play are more conservative than those for Dekker's "good" texts'. Both Maxwell and Hoeniger quote Bowers approvingly, and other editors follow in practice the same principles.

Whether or not these principles are correct for *Sir Thomas Wyatt*, they seem to us obtuse and unhelpful for *Pericles*. They lead to a situation in which the 'worst' text is edited as though it were the 'best'. In this climate of opinion, the editor, intent upon preserving his own integrity and protecting himself from the criticism of his scholarly peers, 'Did nothing'. However fallible, an editor (or editors collectively), studying intensively Q, *P.A.*, the play's sources, the verbal and theatrical style of the dramatist(s) in their uncorrupted work, and the nature of memorial corruption in other texts, is in a far better position than the ordinary reader or actor to attempt to reconstruct something closer than Q to an authentic text of the play. In the case of *Sir Thomas Wyatt*, an editor's failure to accept this obligation is relatively unimportant, because the play itself is unimportant: little read, never revived, never a masterpiece. But *Pericles* is a masterpiece, widely read and revived increasingly often. Moreover, more materials survive for such a reconstruction of *Pericles*. We possess not one report but two, the second by (we believe) one of the original collaborators; for the other and more important collaborator (Shakespeare) we possess texts, concordances, and centuries of scholarship which have contributed to our understanding of the nature and idiosyncrasy of his verbal style. In the preparation of this edition we have also been able to make use of computer-generated concordances of both *P.A.* and *Miseries*, Wilkins's only uncontested non-collaborative works. We have therefore attempted to reconstruct a text of *Pericles* closer to its state when it left the hands of its author(s). For those who wish to study the unedited primary document, we have also provided, in the original-spelling edition, a truly conservative text, in the form of a diplomatic reprint of Q.

Q was reprinted in 1609 (Q2), 1611 (Q3), 1619 (Q4), 1630 (Q5), and 1635 (Q6). Each of these reprints was printed from its immediate predecessor, though Q6 made some use of Q4 as well as Q5. Q4 itself was—like other texts in the Pavier collection—clearly 'edited', by someone without access to any authoritative document but with a desire to make some sense of nonsense. (See General Introduction, pp. 34-6.) The play was included in a group of seven apocryphal plays added to the second issue of F3 (1664), which supplied inept act divisions and an unreliable list of dramatis personae. From F3 the play passed to F4 and Rowe. Pope excluded it, with the other apocryphal plays, and it consequently dropped out of the main lines of the editorial tradition until 1780, when Malone edited it in his *Supplement to the Edition of Shakespeare's Plays Published in 1778* (1780); Steevens then edited it for STEEVENS-REED (1785), and Malone included it in his own edition of the *Plays and Poems* (1790). For the purposes of *Pericles* these three editions—undoubtedly the most important in the play's editorial history—will be identified as 'MALONE', 'STEEVENS', and 'MALONE 2'. Thereafter the play becomes a regular part of the editorial tradition, and editions are identified by their usual sigla.

Q is not divided into acts or scenes. The play is irregularly divided into sections by the appearances of Gower (Sc. 1, 5, 10, 15, 18, 20, 22). F3 marked act divisions (to coincide with Gower's appearances) at Sc. 5 and 18; Malone, at Sc. 5, 10, 15, and 20. Any arrangement requires that some of Gower's appearances mark the beginning of a new act, while others do not; the use of the chorus figure therefore cannot be compared to *Henry V*. Moreover, in some cases (Sc. 1, 5, 15, 22) Gower's speeches overlap with the following scene, so that his exit does not coincide with a clearing of the stage. The traditional division thus misrepresents the original structure of performance so drastically that it cannot be redeemed; since our reconstructed text cannot easily be compared with earlier editions anyway, convenience of reference is not a significant issue. We have therefore given the play continuous scene references in both the original- and modern-spelling editions.

Because of the special circumstances of the text, and the pervasive interrelationship of various kinds of corruption, it has seemed desirable to abandon our usual analytic division of the textual apparatus, and to include modernizations (signalled by modern-spelling reference only), emendations of substantives, incidentals (I), lineation (L), and notes on stage directions in a single list. We also provide fuller information than usual on the editions and scholars responsible for changes of lineation, incidentals, and directions, so that readers may form a clearer idea of the collaborative, cumulative character of the restoration of *Pericles*.

The collations also depart from normal practice in recognizing that our text is the result of a close collaboration between Gary Taylor and MacDonald P. Jackson (editor of the forthcoming Oxford Shakespeare edition); 'This edition' thus indicates that an emendation has been jointly conceived; if one editor or the other is responsible for a conjecture which both have subsequently endorsed, his initials are appended. It will be observed that, in general, the joint emendations usually concern stage directions or cases of resort to *P.A.* The editors are also jointly responsible for the policy of indicating elisions orthographically in verse. Since Q is so unreliable in the texture of its incidentals, we have emended its orthography in order to indicate elisions which are (a) apparently required by the verse, and (b) indicated orthographically, at least occasionally, in authoritative Shakespearian texts. The editors are responsible for all such incidental emendations recorded below which are not attributed to some other source.

G.T./M.J.

WORKS CITED

Blayney, Peter W. M., *The Texts of 'King Lear' and Their Origins* (1982)
Brooks, see Hoeniger
Deighton, K., ed., *Pericles*, Arden (1907)
Edwards, Philip, 'An Approach to the Problem of *Pericles*', SSu 5 (1952), 25-49
—— ed., *Pericles Prince of Tyre*, New Penguin (1976)
Hoeniger, F. D., ed., *Pericles*, Arden (1963); with numerous conjectures by Harold F. Brooks
Lillo, George, *Marina* (1738): an adaptation, which anticipates some editorial emendations
McManaway, James G., ed., *Pericles Prince of Tyre*, Pelican (1961)
Maxwell, J. C., ed., *Pericles*, New (1956); with conjectures by John Dover Wilson
Miseries: George Wilkins, *The Miseries of Enforced Marriage*, ed. Glenn H. Blayney, MSR (1964)
Mommsen, T., ed., *The Painfull Adventures of Pericles* (1857)
Musgrove, S., 'The First Quarto of *Pericles* Reconsidered', SQ 29 (1978), 389-406
Prior, Roger, 'The Life of George Wilkins', SSu 25 (1972), 137-52
—— 'George Wilkins and the Young Heir', SSu 29 (1976), 33-9
Ridley, M. R., ed., *Pericles*, New Temple (1935)
Round, P. Z., ed., *Pericles*, in MARSHALL, vol. viii (1890)
Schanzer, Ernest, ed., *Pericles*, Signet (1965); also contributed conjectures to Hoeniger's edition
Taylor, Gary, 'The Transmission of *Pericles*', PBSA 80 (1986)
Tiessen, E., 'Beiträge zur Feststellung und Erklärung des Shakespeare-Textes', *Englische Studien*, 3 (1880), 15-42
Tonson, Jacob (publisher), *Pericles Prince of Tyre* (1734)
Theobald, Lewis: unpublished marginalia in copies of Q4 (Folger) and Q6 (University of Pennsylvania)
Trent, W. P., 'Some Textual Notes on *Pericles*', in *Shakespeare Studies*, ed. B. Matthews and A. H. Thorndike (1916)

TEXTUAL NOTES

THE NAMES ... chastitie.] *P.A.*; not in Q. The characters are listed by order of appearance; we have followed the same principle in our additions, for speaking characters.

PERSONAGES] *Perſonages mentioned P.A.*

Thalyart] The '-t' spelling is preferred consistently by the sources and *P.A.*, and on the name's only occurrence in Gower's speeches. *P.A.* also prefers '-y' (7 to 2), and as the name only occurs in Wilkins's share we have adopted Wilkins's apparent preference.

Helycanus] *Helycamus P.A. P.A.* consistently prefers 'Hel' (27 times), and 'Hel' also occurs four times in Gower's speeches (5.17, 10.27, 18.13, 22.114/507, 1096, 1738, 2380). We have thus adopted 'Hel-', though Q overall prefers 'Hell-' (44 to 6). Both *P.A.* and Q mix their spellings of the second syllable—*P.A.* preferring 'y', Q preferring 'i'; we have left these as they stand in Q, adopting the numerically favoured 'i' (also endorsed by Gower's *Confessio*) in speech-prefixes.

Eschines] So *P.A.* consistently (twice); *Escanes* in Q (5 times), or *Escenes* (18.15/1740). In Wilkins's share of the play, we have followed his preferred form.

Dyonysa] We have used this form in speech-prefixes, which is consistently preferred in *P.A.* (28 occurrences); for the same reason we have adopted it in the text, in Wilkins's share of the play. However, we have retained '*Dioniza*' in the text of Shakespeare's share, because it is used three times in later Choruses; Shakespeare's spelling may have differed from Wilkins's.

Symonides] Consistently preferred in *P.A.* (23 times); 7 times in Q (twice in Gower's speeches), to only 4 of 'Sim-'.

Thaysa] So the name is consistently spelled in *P.A.* (31 occurrences), and once in Q (3. Ch.)—the only occurrence of the name in Gower's speeches.

Lichorida] *P.A.* spells 'Licor-' once, 'Lycor' 14 times. But this character does not appear at all in Wilkins's portion of the play, and hence *P.A.*'s testimony is of dubious value. 'Lichorida' occurs only three times in Q, but two are the only occurrences of the name in Choruses; this form has therefore been preferred in prefixes over Q's more common 'Lychorida'.

Cerimon] Preferred consistently in *P.A.* (11 times), and by Q (8, to 7 'Cery-'), including the name's only occurrence in Gower's speeches (22.116/2384).

Phylemon his seruant] not in *P.A.* The name only occurs in Q.

Boult, a] *P.A.* The name does not appear in *P.A.*

Lysimachus] Strongly preferred by both *P.A.* and Q.

Title Pericles Prynce of Tyre] S.R.; THE LATE, | And much admired Play, | Called | Pericles, Prince | of Tyre. | With the true Relation of the whole Hiſtorie, | aduentures, and fortunes of the ſaid Prince: | As alſo, | The no leſſe ſtrange, and worthy accidents, | in the Birth and Life, of his Daughter | MARIANA. Q (*title-page*); The Play of Pericles | Prince of Tyre. &c. Q (*head title*). As the Stationers' Register entry refers to 'The booke', we have followed its incidentals.

Sc. 1] F3 (*Actus Primus. Scena Prima.*). Editors since Malone regard Gower's speech as a Prologue, with the first scene proper beginning with the entrance of Antiochus and his court. But the heads remain on stage across this alleged scene-break; nor do

PERICLES

Gower's other appearances encourage Malone's separation of them from the rest of the dramatic action. See Introduction.

1.6/6 Holyales] MALONE (Theobald); Holydayes Q; Whitson-ales MAXWELL (*conj.*). Q does not rhyme, and Theobald's is the minimal emendation. But *OED* under Whitsun cites 'This is a Tale | Would befit a Whitson-ale' (1614). Shakespeare at *Henry V* 2.4.25/881 and *Winter's Tale* 4.4.134/1739 associates Whitsun with related performances (pastoral and morris dancing).

1.11/11 these] Q2; thoſe Q1
1.17 This'] Q (This)
17 (I) then;] MARSHALL; ~ˌ Q
1.18/18 Buylt vp ... for] Q; builded ... as TWINE
1.21/21 Pheere] MALONE (Theobald); Peere Q. Hoeniger and subsequent editors have reverted to Q, on the evidence of *OED sb.* 3, glossing as 'companion, mate'. But the only example of the word meaning 'mate, wife' is from c.1330; the few other examples all mean 'companion', and there are no examples of the idiom 'take a [wife]', which the sense requires here. The alternative, *fere*, was itself an old-fashioned, but intelligible, word.
24 (I) heau'n] heauen
1.27/27 Bad child,] Q. Wilson conjectured that these words are the only remnant of a lost couplet about the daughter, parallel to what follows on the father.
1.29/29 By] MALONE; But Q. Editors who retain Q have to assume that 'by' is understood, though not spoken.
1.30/30 Was] Q; Made MAXWELL. See *P.A.*, 'The custome of sinne made it accompted no sinne' (497). But Maxwell's emendation produces a bewildering dislocation of word order, especially confusing with the disyllabic past participle form 'account'.
1.30 account'] Q (account'd)
38 (I) tould, not,] Q2, Q1 (MS); ~, ~, Q1
1.39/39 a wight] F3; of wight Q1; of weight Q6; of might STEEVENS (*conj.*).
1.39.1/39.1 *A row of heads is reueuealed*] This edition; *not in* Q. Most editors assume that the heads are visible from the beginning of the scene, but they might then distract from the spectacular effect of Gower's entrance; they could just as easily—and perhaps more effectively—be revealed here.
41 (I) th'] the
41-2 (I) eye, | I giue, my cause,] MALONE; ~, ~ˌ ~, Q. Recent editors have reverted to Q for 42, but nevertheless emend the punctuation of 41, and assume a difficult ellipsis.
1.42.1/42.1 *Sennet.*] This edition; *not in* Q. Ceremonial royal entries are almost inevitably accompanied by some sort of fanfare, and sennets are often specified. Q contains few directions for sounds.
1.42.2/42.2 *Lords ... ornaments*] This edition; *not in* Q. From *P.A.* 498.
1.45-7/45-7 (L) I ... enterprise] MALONE; emboldned| hazard| Q
1.48/48 Musicke! | *Musicke sounds* | Bring] HOENIGER; Muſickeˌ bring Q; ˌBring MALONE
1.50/50 Fit for th'] This edition (*conj.* Elze); For Q; For the MALONE; Fit for ANON. (*conj.* in Cambridge)
50 eu'n] euen
52 (I) gaue, ... presence;] SCHANZER; gaue; ... preſence, Q
1.54/54 In ... perfections to knit] This edition (G.T.); To knit in ... perfections Q; Their best perfections in her to knit STEEVENS (*conj.*). Steevens's desire to restore the rhyme seems justified, but he unnecessarily transposed 'in her' as well.
55 (I) apparel'd] Q4; appareled Q1
57 (I) eu'ry] euery
1.60 razed] Q (racte)
65 (I) the] Q3; th' Q1
1.67/67 boundlesse] ROWE; bondleſſe Q
71 (I) dang'rous] dangerous
1.71.1/71.1 *He ... heads*] This edition; *not in* Q
1.72.1/72.1 *He ... daughter*] This edition; *not in* Q
1.73/73 Heau'n like face] This edition; face like Heauen. Transposition produces a rhetorically attractive parallelism with the preceding line.
1.79/79 semblants] This edition (G.T.); ſemblance Q. See *OED.* A concrete plural seems required to match 'Princes', 'tongues', 'Martyrs', and 'cheekes'; Q would be an easy aural error.
1.79/79 bloodlesse] This edition; pale Q. The reporter substitutes a synonym which weakens the horror and rhetoric of the description. For *pale* and *bloodless* as synonyms, see *Contention* 3.2.162/1726, *Troilus* 1.3.134/569, *Titus* 3.1.256/1272. It is as unnatural for a *semblance* to be *bloodless* as for a *tongue* to be *speechless*.
1.83/83 From] MALONE; For Q. Recent editors cite *OED for, prep.* 23 c, d; but no one has found a parallel for the idiom *desist for*.
88 (I) remembred] Q2; remembered Q1
91 (I) Heau'n] Heauen
94 (I) eu'ry] euery
1.98/98 blow (*Antiochus*)] Q; blow. | Ant⟨iochus⟩. MALONE. In Q there is a page-break between 1.98/98 and 1.99/99.
1.99/99 ANTIOCHUS] ALEXANDER, Q (MS); *not in* Q. See preceding note.
1.99.1/99.1 *He ... Riddle*] HOENIGER; *not in* Q. From *P.A.* 498.
1.101/101 thou] Q; so This edition *conj.*
1.102, 103 'sayed] Q (ſayd)
1.106.1/106 ⌈*He takes vp and reads*⌉ *aloude*] This edition; *not in* Q. From *P.A.* 498.
1.108/108 which] Q; that *P.A.* (498)
1.110/110 in] Q; from *P.A.* (498)
1.113/113 this] *P.A.* (498); they Q
1.115.1/115.1 *Aside*] This edition; *not in* Q. CAMBRIDGE adds this direction at the beginning of the line, but the first five words can be public.
116 (I) heau'n] heauen
1.118.1/118.1 *He ... daughter*] This edition; *not in* Q; *Takes hold of the hand of the Princess.* MALONE; *Aside to the Princess* RIVERSIDE. Malone's direction is contradicted by 1.130/130.
124 (I) Y'are] You are
126 (I) Heau'n] Heauen
132 (I) dang'rous] dangerous
1.139/139 like] This edition; is like Q
142 (I) cleare,] STEEVENS (Mason); ~; Q
143 (I) them;] STEEVENS (Mason); ~, Q
144 (I) heau'n] heauen
1.152/152 ha's] This edition; he ha's Q. Q's 'he' produces a superfluous stress after the caesura, and could easily result from anticipation of 1.186/186; without it the syntax is ambiguous, suggesting—in an elision typical of Wilkins—'thy head (which) has found ...'.
1.154/154 our] F3; your Q
1.156/156 cansell] F3; counſell Q
156 of] Q, Malone; off F3
1.163/163 your worth and our degree] This edition (G.T.); our honour and your worth Q; our honour, your degree STEEVENS (*conj.*)
1.163.1/163.1 *Flourish.*] This edition; *not in* Q. See 1.42.1/42.1.
1.163.1/163.1 *Exeunt*] MALONE; *not in* Q
1.170/170 you'r] F3; you Q
1.171/171 vncomely] MAXWELL (Delius); vntimely Q. See *P.A.*, 500.
179 shew] Q; shun MALONE. See next note.
1.179 'schew] Q (ſhew), THEOBALD. Hoeniger defends Q with parallels from *Patient Grissil* 1.1.44-5 and Dekker and Wilkins's *Jests to Make You Merry* (Grosart, ii. 333); he conjectures that the form is etymologically related to modern *shy*, but an aphetic form of *eschew* seems preferable as a modernization.
1.185.1/185.1 *Enter*] HOENIGER begins a new scene here (1.1b), but the heads are probably still on stage: see 1.213.1/213.1.
1.186-9/186-9 (L) He ... manner] This edition; meaning| head| infamie| sinne| Q
1.186/186 the which] This edition (G.T.); which Q. This metrical emendation produces an idiom characteristic of Wilkins and the first half of *Pericles*.
1.192, 193, 196, 212/192, 193, 196, 212 Thaliart] This edition; Thaliard Q. See 'THE NAMES ...'. Aural confusion of d/t would be easy.

1.194-5/194-5 (L) And...faythfulnes] This edition (G.T.); actions| Q
1.194/194 And to your secrecie] This edition (G.T.); And Q. See next note. Q offers a more commonplace construction (nominative-predicate-direct object-indirect object) which produces two metrically irregular lines.
1.195/195 actions; for] This edition (G.T.); actions, | To your secrecie; and for Q. See preceding note.
1.196-7/196-7 (L) Behold, . . . gold] This edition (G.T.); *Thaliard*| Q. The rhyme seems deliberate.
1.202-3/202-3 (L) Enough . . . haste] MALONE; *prose* Q
1.202.1/202.1 *Enter a Messenger*] DYCE; Q places before Antiochus' speech.
1.202.1/202.1 *hastily*] *P.A.* 500; *not in* Q
1.204/204 Your Maiestie] This edition (G.T.); My Lord Q. Titles and vocatives are the least reliable feature of memorial texts, and Q here repeats 1.201/201, unmetrically. See 1.209/209.
1.204/204 *Exit*] MALONE; *not in* Q
1.205-9/205-9 (L) As . . . dead] This edition; *prose* Q; thou| shot| mark| return| MALONE
1.205/205 after; like] This edition (G.T.); after, and like Q
1.208/208 it be to say] This edition (G.T.); thou fay Q
1.209/209 Your Maiestie,] This edition (G.T.); *not in* Q. Even in Q Antiochus' command echoes the messenger's report, with the rhyming substitution of 'dead' for 'fled'; it seems desirable both that the repetition be more emphatic (by including the vocative) and that it constitute a full verse line. See 1.204/204.
1.210/210 If] This edition (G.T.); My Lord, if Q. A superfluous commonplace extrametrical vocative, in a speech which already has one.
1.210-11/210-11 (L) If . . . highnesse] STEEVENS (*subs.*); *prose* Q
1.210/210 in] This edition (G.T.); within Q
1.211/211 farewell] This edition (G.T.); fo farewell to Q
1.212/212 ANTIOCHUS] Q4, Q1 (MS); *not in* Q1
1.212/212 *Exit Thalyart*] DYCE; *not in* Q
1.213.1/213 *Exit.*] Q2; *not in* Q1
1.213.1/213.1 *The heads are concealed*] This edition; *not in* Q. The presence of the heads could usefully serve as a 'location' marker for Antioch.
Sc. 2] MALONE; *not in* Q
2.0.1/213.2 *distempered*] This edition; *not in* Q. From *P.A.* 501 ('his Princes distemperature').
2.1/214 *Exeunt Lords*] ALEXANDER; *not in* Q. For attendants who enter only to be dismissed, compare *1 Henry IV* 3.2.0.1-3.1/1741.2-44.1, *Much Ado* 2.3.1.1-2.3.7/825.1-831, etc.

Edwards, who suspects that the order of events has been garbled in this scene, considers ludicrous the 'filing in' and out and in again of the lords. But the two or three lords that we might expect the company to have provided would scarcely constitute a 'file' and there is no need for a procession here. The point of their brief initial appearance is to show that Pericles is back in Tyre and to establish his insistence on being alone. The comparative regularity of the verse in this scene suggests that it is rather well reported. Pericles' long soliloquy, however inert poetically, is metrically flawless. It is unlikely that a reporter capable of rendering it so well would be wildly confused about the scene's development. The long account that Pericles gives Helicanus of his experience in Antioch is also perfectly coherent.

2.3/216 Be my] DYCE; By me Q
218 (I) should] Q2; ftould Q1
2.7/220 fearde's] DYCE 2 (W. S. Walker); fearde is Q
2.10/223 cares] This edition (G.T.); the Q. Something seems needed to balance 'pleasures' in the preceding line. See following note.
2.10/223 authors] This edition (G.T.); others Q. For the meaning see *OED* 1c ('He who gives rise to or causes an action, event, circumstance, state, or condition of things'), 2 ('One who begets; a "father"'), and compare two passages by Wilkins: 'I did beget thee for my comforter, | And not to be the Author of my care' (*Miseries* 887-8); 'for you, to be author of my more misfortune' (*P.A.* 535). In *Miseries*, as here, there is a pun on 'parent'; in both, as here, the 'author' causes distress. (These are the only two uses of the word in *Miseries* and *P.A.*) There is also, here, a play on the sense 'writer' (*OED* 3), contrasting with 'Art'. An easy aural or graphical error.
229 (I) me;] Q4; ~∧ Q1
2.18/231 hee's] Q; he COLLIER (Steevens)
2.20/233 honour him] ROWE; honour Q
2.25/238 thostint] MALONE (Tyrwhitt); the ftint Q
2.30/243 am] MALONE (Farmer); once Q; care SISSON
2.33.1/246.1 among them olde Helicanus] DYCE (*subs.*); *not in* Q. For the adjective see *P.A.* 501.
2.35/248 And . . . comfortable] This edition (M.J.); *prose* Q
2.35/248 mind peacefull] This edition (M.J.); mind till you returne to vs | peacefull Q. Q here anticipates Pericles' injunction to lords to 'returne to vs' (2.55/268). Omission of the phrase from line 2.35/248, where it is metrically superfluous, eliminates the Second Lord's 'clairvoyance' (Edwards) over the secret journey that Pericles presently decides upon in the company of Helicanus alone.
2.37-42/250-5 You . . . contradict it.] This edition (G.T.); *not in* Q. From *P.A.*, where Helicanus 'not sparingly towld' Pericles 'he did not wel so to abuse himselfe, to waste his body there with pyning sorrow, vpon whose safety depended the liues and prosperity of a whole kingdome, that it was ill in him to doe it, and no lesse in his counsell to suffer him, without contradicting it' (501). Although Edwards's suspicions of wholesale corruption in this scene seem unjustified (see notes above), two difficulties do exist: it is not clear why Helicanus accuses the lords of flattery, or clear what in the king's conduct he criticizes. Insertion here of these lines from *P.A.* solves both problems: explicitly criticizing Pericles' melancholy, and claiming that it is 'ill' of his council to let it go unrebuked. This comment on the nobles' failure to comment on Pericles' behaviour then leads naturally into the tirade against flattery.
2.41-2/254-5 Tis . . . contradict it] Bullough conjectures 'If ill in you to do't, 'twere ill in me | To suffer you without reproving it'. The second line follows *P.A.* closely, only substituting 'reproving' for 'contradicting'; we have preserved *P.A.*'s verb, instead altering the preposition for the metre's sake. *Reproofe* occurs below (2.47/260).
257 (I) flattrie] flatterie
258 (I) flattred] flattered
2.46-7/259-60 (L) To . . . order] Q4; stronger| Q1
2.46/259 winde] EDWARDS (Steevens); fparke Q; blast COLLIER (Mason); breath MALONE; spur SISSON
2.49/262 a] MALONE; *not in* Q
2.50.1/263.1 *He kneeles*] This edition; *not in* Q; *Kneeling* MALONE 2 (at 2.63/276); *Kneeling* COLLIER 2 (after 2.52/265)
264 (I) pardon] Q2; paadon Q1
2.55/268 *Exeunt Lords*] MALONE 2; *not in* Q
2.55/268 Hellicane] This edition (*conj.* Musgrove); Hellicans Q1; Hellicanus Q2
2.55-6/268-9 (L) And . . . lookes] MALONE; haft| Q
269 (I) mooued] MALONE; Mooude Q
2.59/272 browes] This edition (G.T.); face Q. The emendation postulates an easy memorial substitution, and produces a 'rhyme' typical of the first half of the play.
273 (I) heau'n] heauen
2.60-1/273-4 (L) How . . . nourishment] MALONE; heauen| Q
2.62/275 (L) Thou . . . thee] Q; *2 lines* MALONE: power|. The usual editorial rearrangement has little to recommend it; hexameters are common.
275 (I) pow'r] power
2.63/276 (L) I . . . blowe] This edition (G.T.); *2 lines* Q: my felfe|. The full hexameter would not have fitted Q's measure.
2.63/276 you but] Q4; but you Q1
2.64/277 *lifting him vp*] This edition (*P.A.* 501); *not in* Q
2.64/277 (L) Rise . . . flatterer] Q; *2 lines* STEEVENS: rise,|
2.65/278 for it] Q4; fort Q1
2.65/278 the heau'ns] This edition (G.T.); heauē Q1; heauen Q2; high heaven STEEVENS. Compare 'and Heauen forfend' (*P.A.* 1785); 'the heauens' occurs 6 times in *P.A.*

2.68/281 makst] MALONE; makes Q. The single parallel which Hoeniger offers for Q's ungrammatical construction (*Othello* 5.2.68-9/2965-6) is variant: the Quarto has the grammatical form.

2.69-70/282-3 (L) To . . . your selfe] KNIGHT; *prose* Q

2.70/283 you] STEEVENS; you your felfe Q

2.75/288 Where as] Q2; Whereas Q1

2.78/291 As children are heau'ns blessings, to parents obiects,] This edition (G.T.); *not in* Q; For royal progeny are general blessings STEEVENS (*conj.*); Worthy to heir my throne; for kingly boys W. S. WALKER (*conj.*). It seems clear that a line has been omitted, and that at the least a lacuna should be marked. In a reconstructed text it seems proper for editors to venture to fill the lacuna. One expects, from the context, a sententia; given the style of these scenes a sententia is likely to be expressed in rhyme, so that the missing line probably rhymed with 'subiects'; the only likely rhyme word is *obiects*—meaning 'any thing regarded with love . . . inspiring sympathy' (Schmidt) or 'Something which on being seen excites a particular emotion, as admiration' etc. (*OED*, sb. 3b). *Issue* are most likely to be described as the 'obiects' of their parents (as in *Lear*: History 1.1.205/205, Tragedy 1.1.213/214). As for the beginning of the line, one expects a causative conjunction to link the rhyming sententia with the preceding statement; 'As' seems preferable to 'For', because its graphic similarity to 'Are' at the beginning of the next line might explain the Quarto's omission (by eyeskip). After the conjunction one expects a synonym for 'issue' which can govern 'Are': babes, children, offspring, progeny. Walker's conjecture 'boys' seems unhappy, given the play's exclusive preoccupation with female children. Moreover, both Walker and Steevens assume that the missing line refers exclusively to *royal* children, but there is little to be said about such children which is not already expressed by the following line, and for the purposes of a gnomic generalization it would be best to begin with a reflection upon *all* children, before proceeding to the specific category of royal ones. The most obvious and appropriate generalization in this context is, as Steevens recognized, the proverbial 'bairns are blessings' (as at *All's Well* 1.3.25-6/329-30). Compare Wilkins's *Miseries* 2674-5: 'Heauen . . . bleste you with children, | And at heauens blessings, all good men reioyce'. This parallel suggests that the first half of the line identifies children as 'blessings' or 'heauens blessings'; if the second half ends with the word 'obiects', then the line has to have a divided structure (like the following line). The following line contrasts 'Princes' with 'subiects', and a similar contrast between 'heauens' and some human figure(s) seems probable here. But 'and parents obiects' would be unfortunately ambiguous, suggesting that *parents* (symmetrically to 'children') are themselves *obiects*; the use of 'to' solves this problem, and creates a parallel with the rhyming clause 'ioies *to* subiects'. The resulting line remains, of course, highly speculative; but it makes sense of the text in a manner characteristic of these scenes, of Wilkins, and of the period. It also contributes—as any solution to the crux must—to the play's preoccupation with the relationship of parents and children.

2.84/299 seemes] Q1; feeme Q2

2.86/299 of] This edition (anon. conj. in Cambridge); of a Q

2.88/301 me] ROWE; *not in* Q

2.89/302 feares] F4; feare Q

2.91/304 dout, as] MALONE; doo't, as Q; doubt it, as STEEVENS; doubt, as 'tis MAXWELL

2.91/304 doubt no] This edition (*conj.* Brooks); no Q

2.94/307 To . . . ope] Q. One suspects that this line should end with 'bed', for rhyme's sake; but if so the corruption is drastic.

2.100/313 reprou'dst] Q; reprovest MALONE

2.105/318 griue] Q5; griue for Q1

319 (I) giu'n] giuen

2.110-15/323-8 (L) Will . . . be] ROWE; *prose* Q

2.113/326 Or] STEEVENS; Or till the Q. Superfluous extrametrical contamination from the previous line.

2.117/330 in my absence wrong thy liberties] This edition (G.T.); wrong my liberties in my abfence Q. The editorial transposition (to restore the metre) presumes a reporter's transposition. Emendation to 'thy' (conjectured by Collier) makes the sense much clearer, and leads more naturally into Helicanus's answering 'Wee'. The pronoun substitution could easily arise from reporter or compositor error.

2.120 Tarsus] Q (*Tharfus*)

2.126/339 sure cracke] F3; cracke Q; cracke them MAXWELL. F3's metrical emendation is more meaningful than Maxwell's, and alliterates characteristically with 'shuns'.

2.127/340 we'll] MALONE; will Q. It is unnecessary to suppose that a line has been lost after 2.126/339: Wilkins is demonstrably fond of placing a single unrhymed line between couplets.

2.129.1/342.1 Exeunt] ROWE; *Exit.* Q

Sc. 3] MALONE; *not in* Q

3.0.1, 32/342.1, 374 Thaliart] This edition; *Thaliard* Q. See note to 1.192/192.

3.1-10/343-52 (L) So . . . of *Tyre*] Q paragraphs the prose, starting a new (indented) line with 'So', 'Well', 'Now', and 'Husht'.

3.2-3/344-5 and am . . . but if I doe it] This edition (G.T.); *not in* Q. Maxwell convincingly conjectured that 'the reporter has dropped one horn of the dilemma'; but the error could be compositorial, resulting from simple eyeskip from one 'if I doe it' to another. Maxwell's conjecture was 'if I *kill him* and am caught, I am *likely* to be hanged *here, and* if I doe' (our italics). Since 'kill' has already been mentioned, Q's 'doe it' seems acceptable; repetition of 'doe' both improves the symmetry and increases the probability of haplography. 'Like'—which has the same meaning as 'likely'—is both more colloquial and better balances monosyllabic 'sure'. 'Here' is acceptable but flat and repetitious; 'abroad' better balances 'home', and contains an appropriate pun ('out of doors' and 'in a foreign country'). Finally, 'but' seems more appropriate to introduce the antithetical clause than 'and'.

3.11-14/353-6 (L) You . . . trauaile] ROWE; *prose* Q (first line divided after '*Tyre*')

3.12/354 question] MAXWELL; queftion mee Q

3.13/355 seald] ROWE; fea-|led Q

3.15, 19, 26/357, 361, 368 aside] MALONE; *not in* Q

3.16-19/358-61 (L) If . . . at Antioch] ROWE; *prose* Q

359 (I) ₐWhy (as] F3; (∼ₐ ∼ Q

359 (I) vnlicensde] vnlicenfed

361 (I) Antioch,] Q4; ∼. Q1

3.20-5/362-7 (L) Royall . . . death] ROWE; *prose* Q

3.22/364 lest that hee] STEEVENS; left hee Q1; left that Q4. Hoeniger's suggestion that 'doubting' is trisyllabic is wholly unsubstantiated. Q4 presumably intended Steevens's correction.

366 (I) Ship-mans] ∼-|∼

3.26-30/368-72 (L) Well . . . Tyre] MALONE; *prose* Q

3.28/370 Kings ears it] WHITE (Dyce); Kings feas Q; King it sure STEEVENS (Percy). As emended by Dyce, 'it' could have been omitted easily, because it falls between two Q prose lines.

3.29/371 on the Seas] STEEVENS (Malone *and* Percy); at the Sea Q; at the seas COLLIER 2

372 Comming forward] This edition (G.T.); *not in* Q

3.31/373 Lord *Thaliart* am I, of *Antioch*.] This edition (G.T.); *not in* Q. It is suspicious that Helicanus knows who Thaliart is without an introduction; suspicion is compounded by Q's omission of the speech-prefix (see next note). Eyeskip, or reporter omission, would have been easy.

3.32/374 HELICANUS] Q4; *not in* Q1; All. (*MS correction in Bodleian* Q1). The prefix is missing both from the text and the catchword.

3.32/374 of *Antioch*] This edition (G.T.); from *Antiochus* Q. Q's repetition—'from *Antiochus* . . . welcome | From him . . . come'—is suspicious, and a reporter could easily have confused an initial indication of place (of Antioch) with a subsequent indication of person (from Antiochus).

3.33-7/375-9 (L) From . . . came] ROWE; *prose* Q

3.33/375 King *Antiochus*] This edition (G.T.); him Q. See preceding notes. Unemended, the speech must begin with a four-syllable part-line, which is rare. 'King *Antiochus*' balances 'princely *Pericles*'.

3.36/378 Lord's] This edition (G.T.); Lord has Q
3.36/378 betoke] Q2 (betooke); betake Q1; betaken EDWARDS
3.37/379 Now my] EDWARDS; now Q1; my Q4
3.38-41/380-83 (L) Wee . . . Tyre] ROWE; *prose* Q
3.38/380 enquire] This edition (*conj.* W. S. Walker); defire Q; inquire of HUDSON 2
3.41/383 *Exeunt*] Q2; *Exit.* Q1
Sc. 4] MALONE; *not in* Q
388 (I) aspire,] Q4; ~ ? Q1
390 (I) ene] euen
4.8/391 they're] ROWE; they are Q
4.8/391 midges] This edition (G.T.); mifchiefs Q. Most editors have felt that Q's word is corrupt, conjecturing 'mistful' (STEEVENS), 'mistie' (SINGER 2), 'misery's' (W. S. WALKER), 'weakness'' (KINNEAR). Although *mischief* in the sense 'misfortune' is well attested (*sb.* 1), it is not clear why their griefs should be 'but' felt or seen with the eyes of misfortune (one would expect the victim's eyes to exaggerate the magnitude of the misfortune), or how the line contrasts with groves which grow higher by being topped. *Midges*, by contrast, are a suitable image of smallness; their attacks are 'felt'; they are naturally associated with 'Groues'. A 'midge's eyes' are small, and hence suggest diminutive grief; but midges can also 'rise' (like groves) and multiply (if 'topped', or sexually mounted). Q's 'mischiefs' could be an aural error.
4.13/396 our sorrowes dictate] This edition (G.T.); and forrowes Q; and sorrows cease not SCHANZER; and sorrows force us EDWARDS. This couplet is obelized as hopelessly corrupt by both Maxwell and Hoeniger. The emendation of 'and' to 'our' presupposes an easy misreading, and allows 'sorrowes' to control 'toungs'—or vice versa, depending upon one's interpretation of the syntax. Of proposals for the missing verb, 'dictate' seems superior to 'force' or 'cease', because of its double meaning: 'command' but also 'read aloud'.
4.13/396 to] Q1; doe Q2; too MALONE
396 (I) deepe,] MALONE; ~ : Q
4.14/397 to] Q1; do MALONE 1; too MALONE 2
397 (I) weepe,] Q3; ~. Q1
4.15-17/398-400 (L) Till . . . comfort them] COLLIER; proclaime| while| awake| Q
4.15/398 loungs] STEEVENS; toungs Q
398 (I) fetch] feteh
399 (I) heau'n] heauen
4.17/400 helpes] MALONE; helpers Q
401 (I) seu'rall] feuerall
4.20/403 As you thinke] This edition (M.J.); Ile doe my Q. Q has Dionyza ludicrously respond to Cleon's rhetoric as though it were a literal request. The reporter must have misunderstood. Presumably the author intended Dionyza simply to acquiesce in her husband's desire to orate.
4.22/405 or] This edition (G.T.); on Q. Q is unidiomatic; no parallels have been offered, and misreading would be easy.
4.22 o'er] See above.
406 (I) eu'n] euen
4.23/406 the] Q3; her Q1
407 (I) tow'rs] towers
4.26/409 ietted and] Q; jetted all DYCE; jetted so G.T. *conj.* Q's reflexive use of 'adorn'de' is unparalleled.
416 (I) heau'n] heauen
4.34/417 Those] DYCE 2; Thefe Q
4.36/419 they] Q2; thy Q1
4.39/422 two sumers] *P.A.* (502); too fauers Q
4.47/430 weeping] This edition (G.T.); *not in* Q. From *P.A.* 503: 'heere standes one weeping, and there lies another dying'. Q is pointless: it means no more than 'lords and ladies stand around weeping'. *P.A.*'s contrasts make much better sense of 'stands', and of Q's opposition between 'here' and 'there', 'lord' and 'lady'.
4.47/430 there lies] This edition (M.J.); and there Q. See above.
4.47/430 dying] This edition (G.T.); weeping Q. See above.
4.54/437 heede] COLLIER 2; heare Q
4.55.1/438.1 ⌜*fainting*⌝ *Lord of Tharsus* ⌜*slowly*⌝] This edition; *Lord* Q. *P.A.* 503: 'a fainting messenger came slowly into them'.

4.57-8/440-1 (L) Here . . . t'expect] This edition (G.T.); *prose* Q; Here| haste| MALONE
4.57/440 thou] Q4; thee Q1
4.57/440 bringst,] This edition (G.T.); ~ ∧ Q. The change of punctuation makes it clear that 'in hast' modifies 'speake' rather than 'bringst': 'speak in haste, though you move slowly'.
4.58/441 t'expect] This edition; to expect Q
4.59-60/442-3 (L) Wee . . . hitherward] Q4; *prose* Q1
4.59/442 shore] Q; coastes *P.A.* (503)
4.61/444 thought] Q; fear'd M.J. *conj.* Alternatively, the whole part-line might be omitted.
446 succeede] fucccede
4.64/447 neighbour] This edition; neighbouring Q. From *P.A.* 503, 'some neighbour nation (taking aduantage of their present mishap)'. Q repeats 465.
4.66/449 Hath] ROWE 3; That Q
4.66/449 these] MALONE (Steevens); the Q
4.68/451 mē] MALONE (men); mee Q; we STEEVENS (*conj.*)
4.70-2/453-5 (L) That's . . . foes] MALONE; *1 line of verse ending* 'feare' *followed by prose* Q
4.72/455 not] This edition (G.T.); not as Q. An easy memorial repetition, superfluous and extrametrical.
4.73/456 hims] MALONE; himnes Q
4.75/458 and what they can,] Q; *not in* STEEVENS. One sympathizes with the desire to reduce the wordiness of this speech, but 'will' and 'can' do convey a pertinent contrast. See 485.
4.76-8/459-61 (L) What . . . heere] MALONE; *1 line ending* 'lowest', *followed by prose* Q
459 (I) feare?] Q4 (~,); leaue ∧ Q1
4.77/460 Our graues] This edition (G.T.); our grounds Q1; the ground's Q4; On ground's MAXWELL. Editors cite Tilley G 464, 'He that lies upon the ground can fall no lower'. But this leaves 'halfeway there' nonsensical or flat, and the proverb may itself explain the memorial or compositorial error. If—as most editors agree—the line is corrupt, Q1's 'grounds' is as likely a candidate as its 'our' (which is demonstrably pertinent to their collective state). A grave is naturally described as 'low'—see for instance *K. John* 2.1.164/440, *Timon* 5.5.84/2303—and the idea of being halfway in the grave is related to the proverb 'One foot in the grave' (*ODEP*, p. 396). Finally, in a passage of *P.A.* not taken from Twine, Wilkins refers to music which could 'haue drawne backe an eare, *halfe way within the graue*' (513, our italics). In *P.A.*'s account of this episode, Cleon ends his address to the messenger by imploring their enemies at least to 'affoord them buriall' (503). The proposed error—graues/grounds—involves an easy misreading.
460 (I) lowest,] Q4; ~ ? Q1
461 (I) Gen'rall] Generall
4.79/462 (L) To . . . comes] ROWE; *prose* Q
4.79/462 comes?] This edition; comes, and what he craues? Q. 'What he craues' simply repeats 'for what he comes', and repeats a phrase elsewhere ('what they craue', 7.46/809). Without it Cleon's question is syntactically balanced (for what he comes . . . whence he comes) and metrically regular.
4.80/463 *Exit*] MALONE 2; *not in* Q
4.82.1/465.1 *the Lord again, conducting*] HOENIGER (*subs.*); *not in* Q. From *P.A.* 503.
4.87-8/470-1 Since entering your vnshut gates haue witness'd | The widow'd] This edition (G.T.); And feene the Q. Pericles cannot have seen 'as farre as *Tyre*' the streets of Tharsus: rather, he heard of their misery before coming, and since coming has seen it for himself. See *P.A.*: Pericles 'no sooner entred into their vnshut gates, but his princely eies were partaking witnesses of their widowed desolation' (503).
4.89/472 hearts] HUDSON 2 (W. S. Walker); teares Q. The corruption may lie deeper: G.T. *conj.* 'to your sorrows to add feares'.
4.92/475 fraught] This edition (G.T.); ftuft Q. Q repeats 4.66/449; *P.A.* has 'those his shippes which their fears might cause them to think were fraughted with their destruction, were intreasured with corne' (503).
4.93/476 importing] DYCE; expecting Q

478 (I) hunger staru'd] Q4; ~-~ Q1
4.96/479 *falling on their knees and weeping*] This edition; *not in* Q. From *P.A.*: 'not hauing strength enough to giue a showte for ioy, gazing on him, and heauen, fell on their knees, and wept' (504).
4.96/479 (L) The ... you] This edition (G.T.); *2 lines* Q: protect you|
4.97-9/480-2 (L) Arise ... men] ROWE; *2 lines* Q: reuerence|
4.99/482 me, my] This edition (G.T.); our selfe, our Q. Q is extrametrical. See *P.A.*: 'to giue me safe harborage, and hospitalitie for my shippes and men' (504).
4.102/484 thought] Q; aught MALONE
486 (I) heau'n] heauen
4.105 ne'er] Q (neare)
Sc. 5] This edition; *not in* Q; *Actus Secundus*. F3; Act II Scene I ROWE
5.4/494 Proue] STEEVENS; That Will proue Q. Q seems wrong not only metrically, but in its shift of tense.
5.11/501 Tharsis] This edition (*conj.* Musgrove); Tharſtill Q1; Tharſus Q4
5.12/502 speken] WHITE; ſpoken Q
5.14/504 His Statue build] This edition (G.T.); Build his Statue Q. This seems the simplest of many conjectures seeking to remedy the metre of this line; it presumes transposition of unusual word order.
5.16.6/506.6 with their traines] MALONE 2 (*subs.*); *not in* Q
5.17/507 Helican] Q3 (Hellican); Helicon Q1. Malone's 'Helicane' is a mere modernization; Q3's form appears in Gower (582).
5.19/509 for that] This edition (*conj.* Proudfoot); for though Q; for thy SINGER 2
5.22/512 Sent word] This edition (G.T.); Sau'd one Q; Sends word STEEVENS (Theobald)
5.24/514 hid] Qa; had Qb
5.24/514 intent] Qb; in Tent Qa
5.24/514 murdren] This edition (*conj.* Maxwell); murdred Qa; murder Qb
5.25/515 Tharsis] Q1; Tharſus F3
5.27/517 dëing] This edition (G.T.); doing Q; knowing MALONE (Steevens). An easy misreading. *Deem* was often spelt 'deme' (*OED*).
5.36 aught] Q (ought)
5.38.1/528.1 *Enter Pericles wette*] This edition; *after* 5.40/530 Q. The misplacement of this direction could be due to the two different kinds of transmission (manuscript for Gower's speech; reported for the scene). See Introduction.
5.38.1/528.1 *and halfe naked*] This edition; *not in* Q. In Twine Pericles is 'cast vp now naked' (434); in Gower, 'All naked' (643). Complete nudity is unlikely on the Jacobean stage, but shipwrecked characters are elsewhere described as '*wet*' and '*halfe naked*' (Heywood, *The Foure Prentices of London*, ii. 176-7); in modern productions, too, Pericles usually enters with little on. This 'nakedness' agrees well with the action at 5.119-21/609-11, and seems emblematically significant, in contrast to his princely apparel in the preceding scenes.
5.40/530 *Exit*] MALONE; *not in* Q
5.40.1/530.1 *Thunder and lightning*] This edition; *not in* Q
5.41/531 PERICLES] Editors since Malone mark the beginning of a new scene, but Gower's 'heere he comes' makes it probable that the action is continuous.
5.45/535 Seas] Q; sea ROWE 3
5.46/536 my] Q; me MALONE
5.51.1/541.1 *He sits.*] This edition; *not in* Q. It seems most unlikely that the exhausted shipwrecked Pericles 'stands' aside during the following sequence; it would be awkward for an actor to speak his asides lying down, and in any case such a staging would anticipate the climactic collapse at 5.118.1/608.1. Sitting—like that of Constance, or Lear, in their distress—thus seems likely. In Twine 'when he had recouered to land, wearie as he was, he stoode vpon the shoare, and looked vpon the ... sea, saying ...' (434); the source thus suggests that his opening speech is spoken standing up.

5.51.2/541.2 two] This edition; *three* Q. The third probably lags behind the others; see following notes.
5.51.2/541.2 poore] This edition; *not in* Q. See *P.A.*, 'these poore countrey people' (506), 'the poore Fisherman' (507), 'the poore Fishermen' (508), and Twine, 'a poore fisherman' (435).
5.52/542 MAISTER] This edition; 1. Q. See *P.A.*, 'the maister Fisherman' (507), and 5.56, 59/546, 549, etc.
5.52, 53, 55/542, 543, 545 *calling*] This edition; *not in* Q. The second fisherman would hardly address orders to his master, and so presumably speaks to the third (5.53-4/543-4); at 5.56/546 the third answers 'Maister', apparently in response to 5.55/545, with 'I say' and the correspondence of 'pelch' and 'Patch-breech', seems clearly addressed to the same figure as 5.52/542.
5.52/542 What, ho,] MALONE; What, to, Q; What's, to, TRENT (*conj.* in Hoeniger)
5.52 Pilch] Q (pelch)
5.55.1-3/545.1-3 *Enter ... beholde*] This edition; *not in* Q. The description—'rough ... beholde'—comes from Twine (p. 434), which seems clearly to have influenced the conception of this character (compare 'pelch', 'Patch-breech'). For the timing of his entrance see preceding notes.
5.55.3-4/545.3-4 *he ... repaire*] This edition; *not in* Q. See *P.A.*, where the fishermen 'were come out of their homely cottages to dry and repaire their nettes, who being busied about their work ... passed away their labour with discourse to this purpose, in comparing the Sea to Brokers and Vsurers ... Againe comparing our rich men to Whales ...' (506). The detail of the nets does not come from Twine or other sources, so *P.A.* either invents it or takes it from the play; but it is superfluous to the narrative, and serves a clear purpose in performance, giving the fishermen something to do during their conversation. It also agrees with 5.53-4/543-4: since the Second Fisherman himself exits to draw a net out of the sea at 5.136-136.1/627-627.1, he is presumably not here asking for nets to be pulled in, but brought out. Compare the sewing women in *Coriolanus* 1.3/Sc. 4.
5.57-75/547-65 (L) Looke ... all] MALONE; *verse* Q: now| wanion| men| now| heare| them| our selues| much| tumbled| flesh| washt| Sea| a-land| little ones| fitly| tumbles| him| mouthfull| land| swallow'd|
5.58/548 fetch'th] Q1; fetch thee Q4
5.72/563 deuowres] F4; deuowre Q
5.74/564 they] Q; they've MALONE; they ha' MAXWELL (Cambridge)
5.77-8/567-8 (L) But ... belfrie] MALONE; *verse* Q: Sexton|
5.80/570 3. FISHER-MAN] Q4; 1. Q (*c.w. and text*)
5.80-5/570-5 (L) Because ... minde] MALONE; *verse* Q: too| belly| Belles| left| againe|
575 (I) minde,] Q4; ~. Q1
5.87-8/577-8 (L) We ... honey] MALONE; *verse* Q; Drones|
5.89 finny] Q (fenny)
580 (I) th'] the
5.93/583 *Comming forward*] This edition; *not in* Q
5.94-6/584-6 (L) Honest ... after it] MALONE; *verse* Q: you|
584 (I) Honest,] Q2; ~, Q1
5.95/585 scracht] SINGER 2; ſearch Q; scratch it MALONE (Steevens)
5.95 and] Perhaps 'an' meaning 'if'.
5.98-9/588-9 (L) What ... way] MALONE; *verse* Q; Sea|
5.104-6/594-6 (L) No ... working] MALONE; *verse* Q: begge| Greece|
5.116/606 craue] This edition (G.T.); aske Q. See 5.128-9/619-20.
5.118/608 pray] Q4; pray you Q1
5.118.1/608.1 *He fals downe*] This edition; *not in* Q. In Twine he 'fell down prostrate' at the fisherman's feet (434); *P.A.* describes 'the chiefe of these Fishermen ... lifting [Pericles] vp from the ground' (507).
5.119 quoth-a] Q (ke-tha)
5.119 an] Q (and)
5.120/610 to ... ground] This edition; *not in* Q. See note to 5.118.1/608.1.
5.123/613 halidays] MALONE; all day Q
614 more, or] MALONE (Farmer); ~ ; ~ Q
5.123 moreo'er] See preceding note.

5.129-30/620-1 (L) But . . . whipping] MALONE; *verse* Q: craue|
5.130   an] Q (and)
5.131/622 all your] Q4; you Q1; your Q4
5.134-6/625-7 Beadle. | MAISTER Thine office sirrah, | 2. FISHER-MAN Is to] This edition (G.T.); Beadle; but Maister, Ile goe Q. Q's transition to the exit of the two fishermen is abrupt and transparent; but *P.A.* has 'the maister Fisherman commaunding his seruants to goe dragge vp some other nettes' at this point (p. 507). Taylor ('Transmission') conjectured that one of the fishermen here doubled one of the bawds later; if so, this passage could be contaminated by recollection of Boult's 'but Ile go searche the market' (16.23/1548). The Master addresses the other fishermen as 'thou' elsewhere. See next note.
5.136/627 other Nets, Ile goe] This edition (G.T.); Net Q. See preceding note.
5.136.1/627.1 *Exit with 3. Fisher-man*] MALONE (*subs.*); *not in* Q
5.138/629 *seating himselfe by Pericles*] This edition; *not in* Q. From *P.A.* 507.
5.141-2/632-3 (L) Why . . . Simonides] MALONE; *verse* Q: Pentapoles|
5.141/632 is] Q2; I Q1
5.144/635 I sir, and he deserues so to be cal'd] Q; Yea, and rightly so called sir *P.A.* (507)
5.144-5/635-6 (L) I . . . gouernement] *verse* Q: cal'd|
5.146-8/637-9 He . . . shore] Q; *prose* MALONE. It seems unlikely that Pericles collapses into prose in only this and the next speech, while maintaining metrical speech throughout the rest of the scene.
5.146-7/637-8 from his subiects | He gaines] STEEVENS; he gaines from | His subiects Q. An easy memorial transposition; Q substitutes the commoner word order.
5.148/639 shore] Q; place *P.A.* (507)
5.149-52/640-3 (L) Mary . . . partes of] MALONE; *verse* Q: you| birth-day|
5.149/640 some halfe] *P.A.* (507); halfe Q
5.150/641 faire Daughter] Q; princely daughter named *Thaysa P.A.* (507)
5.151/642 and] Q; in the honour of which *P.A.* (507)
5.151/642 Princes] Q; many ~ *P.A.* (507)
5.152/643 for] Q; in hope to gaine *P.A.* (507)
5.153-4/645-6 (L) Were . . . there] This edition (G.T.); desires| Q; *prose* MALONE
5.153/645 Were but] *P.A.* (507); Were Q; Did but STEEVENS
5.153/645 aunswerable | To] *P.A.* (507); equall to Q; equal STEEVENS. Q substitutes the less apt, more general, commoner word (*answerable* occurs only 3 times in Shakespeare; *equal*, 57 times). This emendation and the preceding produce acceptable verse for Pericles, in what would otherwise be anomalous prose.
5.156/648 get himselfe] This edition (G.T.); get Q. *Get* presumably means (*a*) acquire (*b*) conceive, beget. 'Himselfe' is in any case implied, but the sense of the passage is obscure unless the word is explicitly spoken (witness the confusion of editors). It contrasts with (*a*) the man's wife (*b*) the customer to whom he sells her, who 'gets' children on her, and by whom the husband 'gets' wealth.
5.156/648-9 for with] This edition (G.T.); for Q. Hoeniger cites numerous parallels for the underlying satiric sense of the sexual innuendo in this passage. But 'deal' by itself cannot mean 'trade'; another preposition is required. 'Deal for with' means both 'acquire in exchange for (his wife's soul, which he surrenders by prostituting her)', and 'negotiate about with (his wife's conscience, which may resist his desire to prostitute her)'.
5.158-62/650-4 (L) Helpe . . . Armour] MALONE; *verse* Q: Net| out|
5.160.1/652.1 *Before helpe comes, vp comes their prize*] This edition; *not in* Q. See *P.A.*: 'before helpe came, vp came the Fish expected, but prooued indeede to be a rusty armour' (508).
5.163/655 pray] Qb; pary Qa
5.164/656 yet] Qa; yet Qb. The Qa spelling is acceptable, though rare and obsolescent (*OED*).
5.164/656 thy] DELIUS (Theobald); *not in* Q. Confirmed by *P.A.*, 'all her crosses' (508).
657 (I) giu'st] giueſt

5.165/657 losses] This edition (*conj.* Elze); felfe Q. See *P.A.*: 'so accompting all his other losses nothing' (508). *P.A.* in the same passage has 'repayre his fortunes', but 'Fortune . . . repayre my fortunes' seems awkward, and *P.A.*'s alternative provides a rhyme.
658 (I) owne,] Q5; ~ˏ Q1
660 (I) eu'n] euen
663 (I) sau'd] faued
663 (I) it : in like necessitie,] MALONE (Theobald); ~ˏ ~ : Q
5.172/664 forfend,] This edition (G.T.); protectˏ Q. Shakespeare uses this verb 10 times, always in prayers to God(s). Here it improves the metre, disentangles the syntax, and jingles characteristically with 'defend'. See next note.
5.172/664 theˏ same may] This edition (G.T.); thee, Fame may Q; theeˏ from, 't may MALONE; theeˏ from! may't STAUNTON. Q is nonsensical and its mispunctuation seemingly a consequence of its misreading. Malone's emendation of 'Fame' leaves 'may' without a subject, requiring further emendation or the assumption of a difficult ellipsis. The new emendation assumes misreading of 'fame' as 'fame', followed by misinterpretation of the ambiguous spelling 'the'. See preceding note.
5.174/666 spares] Q; spare MALONE
5.175/667 haue] Q1; hath Q2; they've MALONE
667 (I) giu'n't] giuen't
5.177/669 in's] Q4; in his Q1
673 (I) lou'd] loued
675 (I) Sou'raignes] Soueraignes
5.184/676 with't] STEEVENS; with it Q
5.185/677 fortunes] STEEVENS (Mason); fortune's Q
5.188/680 lernd] This edition; borne Q. See *P.A.*: 'telling them, that with it hee would shew the vertue hee had learned in Armes' (508).
5.189 d'ye] Qa (di'e), Qb (do'e)
5.195/687 this] This edition (G.T.); them Q; it MALONE
5.197/689 I'm] This edition; I am Q
5.198/690 rapture] ROWE 3; rupture Q. Confirmed by *P.A.* (508).
5.201/693 delightsome] This edition (G.T.); delight Q; delightfull F3, Q1 (MS). An adjective is evidently required, but 'delightfull' is a mere commonplace guess; 'delightsome', with the same meaning, was in current literary use, and alliterates typically.
5.203-4/695-6 (L) Onely . . . Bases] MALONE; *1 line* Q. A line-divided foot.
5.203/695 friends] DYCE; friend Q
5.205-7/697-9 (L) Wee'le . . . my selfe] MALONE; *verse* Q: haue| paire|
5.208/700 equale] MAXWELL (Staunton); a Goale Q; egal BULLEN (*conj.*)
5.209.1/701.1 *Exeunt with Nets and Armour*] This edition; *not in* Q; *Exeunt.* ROWE
Sc. 6] This edition; *not in* Q; [ACT II.] SCENE II. MALONE
6.0.1/701.2 *Sennet.*] This edition; *not in* Q. See 1.39.1/42.1.
6.0.1-2/701.2-3 *with Lords in attendaunce*] This edition; *with attendaunce* Q; *Lords, and Attendants* MALONE
6.0.2/701.3 *and sit on 2. thrones*] This edition; *not in* Q. See 6.6/707, and *P.A.*, 'They thus seated' (508).
6.2-3/703-4 (L) They . . . them selues] This edition; *2 lines* Q: comming|
6.2/703 They] This edition; They are my Leidge, and Q
6.4/705 daughter] MALONE; daughter heere Q
6.7/708 *Exit one*] MALONE (*Exit a Lord*); *not in* Q
6.8/709 my] STEEVENS; my royall Q. Probably contamination from 6.24/725 (where the phrase is metrical). Such vocatives are the least reliable feature of reported texts.
712 (I) Heau'n] Heauen
6.13/714 Renowne] MALONE; Renownes Q. The emendation seems worth making for the sake of symmetry, and because terminal 's' errors are so common (even in texts normally transmitted).
6.14/715 office] This edition (*conj.* Steevens); honour Q
6.16.1/717.1 *Flourish.*] This edition; *not in* Q. It would be odd for such entrances *not* to be accompanied by fanfares, as they regularly were in English royal entertainments.

6.16.1/717.1 *richly armed*] This edition; *not in* Q. From *P.A.* (508).
6.16.2–3/717.2–3 *and ... Thaysa*] MALONE (*subs.*); *not in* Q. From *P.A.* (508–9); we follow its wording more closely than Malone and other editors. Malone also initiated the convention of only specifying the action for the first knight, and leaving it implicit for the others; but the formulaic repetition of the direction mirrors the artificiality of the ceremony.
6.21.1/722.1 *She ... King*] HOENIGER (*subs.*); *not in* Q. See *P.A.* (509); again we follow Wilkins more closely, and repeat the direction for the other knights.
6.23.1–2/723.1–2 *He ... Knight*] HOENIGER (*subs.*); *not in* Q. Hoeniger has the shield returned 'through' Thaisa; this is possible but not necessary.
6.26/727 *An Armed*] This edition (G.T.); Is an Armed Q; Is an arm'd ROWE
727 (I) conquer'd] F3; conquered Q
6.27/728 *thus*] This edition; thus in Spaniſh Q. The phrase 'in Spanish' does not occur in *P.A.* (509), and probably expresses no more than the reporter's own confusion, as the motto can hardly be turned into Spanish. See next notes.
6.27 *Piùe*] Q, *P.A.* (Pue), HOENIGER; *Piu* MALONE; *Mas* MALONE (*conj.*)
6.27/728 *Per ... per*] Q; *Por ... por* ROWE 3
6.27/728 *dolceza*] HOENIGER (Hertzberg *conj.* in Maxwell); doleera Q; dolcera *P.A.* (509); dulçura MALONE
6.27 *che*] Q (kee), *P.A.* (qui), HERTZBERG (*conj.* in Maxwell); *chi* ROWE 3; *que* MALONE
6.27 *forza*] Q (forſa), *P.A.* (sforſa), ROWE 3; *fuerça* MALONE; *fuerza* DYCE
6.28/729 *You ... force.*] This edition; *not in* Q. From *P.A.*: 'more by lenitie than by force' (509). The ceremonial character of the occasion strongly endorses *P.A.*'s provision of a comment from the King on all six imprese. The gloss in *P.A.* can be made metrical by omission of its second 'by'. Simonides' comments, in both Q and *P.A.*, often relate the motto directly to the knight or Thaisa; here, alternatively, one might conjecture 'You conquer' (though that seems an unfortunate repetition of 6.26/727).
6.29/730 what's] Q4; with Q1; who MAXWELL
6.29–31/730–2 (L) The third ... *apex*] STEEVENS; deuice| Q1
731 (I) Chiualry] Q2; Chiually Q1
6.31/732 *pompæ*] *P.A.* (509); Pompey Q
6.32–3/733–4 *Desire ... enterprise.*] This edition; *not in* Q. See note to 6.28/729. The gloss in *P.A.*—'the desire of renowne drew him to this enterprise' (509)—is correct in substance, but must be modified to produce verse, and can hardly be squeezed into a single line. Any conjecture must be built upon the two metrical phrases 'desire of renowne' and 'him to this enterprise'. The only other element absolutely required, and provided by *P.A.*, is a verb linking the two phrases; but the verb alone can hardly consume the extra syllables required to produce two verse lines. The present conjecture takes account of (*a*) the rhyme in Simonides' next gloss, and in his speeches generally (*b*) the recurrence of 'which' and 'the which' constructions in this sequence, and generally in Sc. 1–9. For 'deuise' see *OED*, *v.* 5d ('represent by art').
6.34/735 *A Knight of Athens, bearing*] This edition; *not in* Q. The formal nature of the scene suggests that *P.A.* is right to identify all the knights; identification of some but not others is theatrically awkward. In *P.A.* this emblem is borne by a man 'of *Athens*' (509). His rank is not specified, and Wilkins describes all the tilters as 'Princes' (508); but Q's stage direction identifies him as a knight, which therefore seems the safest specification. Addition of an identity for the fourth knight also rectifies the metre here.
6.37/738 this] This edition (*conj.* Maxwell); his Q; her w. s. WALKER (*conj.*)
6.37/738 &] Q: at MAXWELL
6.39/740 *And who the fift?*] This edition; *not in* Q. See note to 6.34/735. This is the only knight whose identification is not in Q prompted by some such question from Simonides. If the Fifth Knight is to be identified—see next note—then a short question is needed to fill out the verse line.
6.39–40/740–1 *a Prince of Corinth, | Presents*] This edition; *not in* Q. See *P.A.*, 'a Prince of *Corinth*' (509). Though in *P.A.* he is the second knight, bearing the third knight's device, Corinth is the only location specified in *P.A.* which remains for Q's fifth knight. Moreover, Corinth had a reputation for wealth (see Stubbes), so the gold of the emblem is unusually appropriate.
6.43/744 *So ... into*] This edition; *not in* Q. From *P.A.* 509 (... looked ...).
6.43.3–6/744.3–6 *Pericles ... Thaysa*] MALONE (*subs.*); *not in* Q. We follow *P.A.*'s wording (509).
6.44–5/745–6 (L) And ... deliuereth] STEEVENS; which| Q; what's| himself| DYCE
6.45/746 deliuereth] This edition (*conj.* Maxwell); deliuered Q
6.47/748 wither'd] ROWE; withered Q
6.49/750 Frō] This edition (M.J.); A pretty morrall frō Q. A suspicious repetition of 5.76/567.
6.54/755 T'] This edition; To Q
6.56/757 Vnto] This edition; To Q
6.56/757 furnisht] Q; furnished MALONE
6.60/761 for] SCHANZER (anon. *conj.*); by Q
6.60.1/761.1 *Cornets*] This edition; *not in* Q. Cornetts are used to indicate the beginning and progress of an off-stage tilt in *Kinsmen* 5.3, the closest Shakespearian parallel for the action here.
6.61–2/762–3 (L) But ... Gallerie] MALONE; comming| Q
6.62/763 *Exeunt*] ROWE; *not in* Q
6.62.1/763.1 *Cornets and*] This edition; *not in* Q. See 6.60.1/761.1.
6.62.1/763.1 *within*] DYCE; *not in* Q
Sc. 7] This edition; *not in* Q; [ACT II.] SCENE III. MALONE
7.0.1/763.3 *A stately banquet is brought in.*] MALONE (*A Banquet prepared*); *not in* Q. See *P.A.*: 'Pericles as chiefe ... with all the other Princes, were by the Kings Marshall conducted into the Presence, where *Symonides* and his daughter *Thaysa*, with a most stately banquet stayed to giue them a thankefull intertainment' (509).
7.0.2/763.4 *Thaysa,*] MALONE; *not in* Q
7.0.2/763.4 *and their traine*] This edition; *not in* Q; *Lords* MALONE; *Lords, Ladies* KITTREDGE. In fact such supernumeraries are not required by the dialogue, though the occasion seems to call for a full stage. But 'traine' is conveniently ambiguous about whether any women are present, besides Thaisa.
7.0.2–3/763.4–5 *at one doore ⌈, and⌉ at another doore*] This edition; *not in* Q
7.0.3/763.5 *a Marshall*] CRAIG; *not in* Q. See *P.A.* (quoted above).
7.0.3–4/763.5–6 *conducting Pericles and the other*] This edition; and Q
7.1/764 *(to the Knights)*] This edition; Knights, Q. Q's word is extrametrical and superfluous: bad quartos often translate stage action into dialogue.
7.2/765 To] F4; I Q
7.7/770 You're] This edition; You are Q
7.7/770 Princes, and] Q; *not in* STEEVENS
7.11/774 yours] Q4; your Q1
7.13/776 Artists] STEEVENS (Malone); an Artiſt Q. The plural is not only more metrical, but better agrees with 'some' and 'others'.
7.15/778 You are] This edition; And you are Q1; And you Q4; And you're MALONE
7.17 Marshal] Q (Martiall)
7.23/786 Haue] Q1; That Q4
7.24/787 Enuied] SISSON (Trent); Enuies Q1; Enuie Q4. The manuscript fragment with several quotations from *Pericles* recorded by Beal (British Library, Add. MS 41063, fol. 87) agrees with Q4 in this and the preceding variant; which suggests it is both late and derivative.
7.24/787 shall] Q1; do Q4
7.25.1–2/788.1–2 *Pericles ... Thaysa.*] This edition; *not in* Q. From *P.A.* (510).
7.25.2–3/788.2–3 *The guests ... nothing*] This edition; *not in* Q. From Twine (436); Gower makes the same point, in different words (734–7).
7.26, 28, 35, 36/789, 791, 798, 799 *Aside*] CAMBRIDGE; *not in* Q
7.26/789 thoughts] Q. This is not an obvious attribute for Jove, and suspiciously anticipates 7.27/790; nor does it provide either a parallel for Thaisa's oath or an attribute especially appropriate to

the character (as hers is). Jove is described as 'the king of gods' at *Troilus* 2.3.11/1171.

7.27/790 distast] This edition (*conj.* Collier); refift Q. Q must take an unparalleled, awkward sense, and could easily arise from memorial or compositorial error.

7.27/790 but] HUDSON 2 (Mason); not Q. Though retained by some editors, Q would have to mean 'not thinking of him makes me lose my appetite', and hence 'thinking about him gives me an appetite'. But this is contradicted not only by Thaisa's next speech, but by *P.A.*: 'they could not spare so much time to satisfie themselues with the delicacie of their viands, for talking of his prayses' (510), in which thinking of Pericles is incompatible with eating.

7.29/792 (I am amaz'd)] This edition (G.T.); *not in* Q. The eate/meat rhyme, and the metre of this speech, strongly suggest that 4 syllables are missing, which would parallel Simonides' '(I wonder)', and correspond to *P.A.*'s 'as it were by some diuine operation, both King and daughter, at one instant were so strucke in loue' (510). It also seems dramatically appropriate that Thaisa herself should express some astonishment at so sudden an infatuation.

7.29-31/792-4 (L) all ... gallant gentleman] STEEVENS; vnsauoury| Q

7.31/794 To the King] HOENIGER; *not in* Q

7.31-2/794-5 Sure ... countrie Gentleman] Q. The two short repetitive lines are suspect; but the parallelism may be deliberate, and no expansion is attractive.

7.31-2/795-6 (L) Hee's ... more] BOSWELL; *1 line* Q

7.33-4/796-7 (L) then ... passe] MALONE; Staffe| Q

7.34/797 broke] This edition; broken Q. The use of *broke* or *broken* is elsewhere in the Shakespeare canon based entirely on metrical considerations (the lone exception being Q *Richard II* 2.2.59/975, where F emends to 'broke', restoring the metre). Even though this scene was probably not written by Shakespeare, the Shakespeare canon provides a large sample, which suggests that contemporary poets would have regarded the two forms as semantically indifferent, with the choice between them governed by metrical considerations.

7.36/799 Yon] Q2; You Q1

7.37/800 me] Q4; *not in* Q1

7.37/800 what] EDWARDS; that Q

7.42/805 sonnes] MALONE; fonne Q

7.42/805 a] STEEVENS; like a Q

7.42/805 night] Q. Edwards alleges that 'The eclipsed sun is properly a glow-worm *in the day*, temporarily extinguished or invisible' (p. 36), and hence that the rhyme has been invented by the reporter, and the image muddled. But Pericles is now in the 'night' of his fortune, bereft both of his sun-like father and of his glorious inheritance; even in the night, the glow-worm's light is insignificant compared to the sun's: a light so dim that it can only be seen when no other light competes with it.

7.48, 51/811, 814 THE OTHER KNIGHTS] This edition; Knights. Q. It seems unlikely that Pericles joins in any of this cheerful communal dialogue; the sources, and *P.A.*, stress his noticeable sorrow here, and Simonides remarks on it immediately after this exchange.

7.49/812 stor'd] MALONE; ftur'd Q

7.50/813 you do] Q4; do you Q1

7.50/813 full] This edition (G.T.); fill Q. Q can only be an imperative verb, which requires the entire line to be interpreted as a self-sufficient parenthesis in the middle of Simonides' sentence. With 'full', the first two lines of the speech are a conceit: the cup is full to the brim, as you are full of love, and for a lover the natural 'brim' is his mistress's lip, the consummation to which he aspires. For a related metaphor, see 'Steep'd me in pouerty, to the very lips' (*Othello* 4.2.52/2463).

7.56-8/819-21 (L) O ... them] This edition; Daughter| aboue| Q; daughter| above| comes| MALONE

821 (l) eu'ry] euery

7.59/822 so doing] This edition (G.T.); doing fo Q. Compare 'not so doing' at *Coriolanus* 3.2.26/1809 (the only other instance in the canon of these three words in juxtaposition).

7.59/822 like] This edition (G.T.); like to Q

7.61/824 entertaine] DYCE 2 (W. S. Walker); entraunce Q1; enterance Q4

7.62/825 beare] This edition (*conj.* Wilson); fay wee drinke Q. Hoeniger claims that *P.A.* 'gives as much support for *drink* as for *bear*'. But it is already clear from Q that Simonides drinks (7.51/814); in *P.A.*, 'calling for a boule of wine, hee dranke to him, and so much further honoured him, that he made his daughter rise from her seate to beare it to him' (510). Simonides could himself tell Pericles, across the table, that he drinks to him; he has, in fact, already made such an announcement to all the knights. Both the dramatic sequence and the evidence of *P.A.* thus support Wilson's conjecture; without it, 'my profer' (862) makes little or no sense; and Thaisa clearly does take the bowl to Pericles (7.73/836), though in the text of Q she has not been told to do so.

7.69/832 Furthermore] HOENIGER; And furthermore Q; And further MALONE

7.69/832 know] MALONE; know of him Q

7.70.1/833.1 *Thaysa ... Pericles*] This edition; *not in* Q

7.71-2/834-5 you, | Wishing] This edition; you. | *Peri.* I thanke him. | *Tha.* Wifhing Q. Pericles' short speech interrupts Thaisa's sentence, is not integrated into the metrical structure, and looks like an anticipation of his next speech.

7.73.1/836.1 *He pledges the King*] This edition; *not in* Q

7.79/842 vnconstant] This edition; *not in* Q; and vnconftant *P.A.* (510). *P.A.* reproduces this speech almost verbatim, except as noted below. It is suspicious that *P.A.* so readily produces an extra iambic pentameter line, and the two key words it adds—*unconstant* and *unfortunately*—occur nowhere else in the play, and so cannot have originated in a misplaced memory of some other phrase.

7.79-80/842-3 bereft | Vnfortunately both] This edition; reft Q; moft vnfortunately bereft both *P.A.* (510)

844 (l) And] Q2; and Q1

7.81/844 driuen] Q; throwen *P.A.* (510)

7.81.1/844.1 *Thaysa ... King*] This edition; *not in* Q

7.83-4/846-7 (L) A ... seas] This edition; *1 line* Q; Tyre| COLLIER

7.83/846 (seeking aduentures) | Was] This edition; *not in* Q. Q's speech is metrically defective, does not contain a verb, and omits any equivalent of Pericles' 7.77-8/840-1; all three deficiencies are rectified by a concise paraphrase of 7.78-9/841-2 (Who ... aduentures ... Was).

7.84/847 solely] This edition (G.T.); onely Q; newly ELZE (*conj.*). Q, if correct, must take an unparalleled meaning, and could easily result from aural or synonym substitution for *solely*, which can mean both 'singly, alone' and 'only, merely'. Under the former sense *OED* cites Wilkins's translation of *The Historie of Justine* (Llij).

7.86/849 mis-haps] This edition; misfortune Q. From *P.A.* (see next note). Q's repetition is suspicious. *Mishap(s)* was normally strongly accented on the second syllable.

7.87.1-96/851.1-859 *The King ... KING*] This edition (G.T.); *not in* Q. From *P.A.*: 'Which mis-haps of his the king vnderstanding of, hee was strucke with present pitty to him, and rising from his state, he came foorthwith and imbraced him, bade him be cheered, and tolde him, that whatsoeuer misfortune had impayred him of, Fortune, by his helpe, could repayre to him, for both himselfe and Countrey should be his friendes, and presently calling for a goodly milke white Steede, and a payre of golden spurres, them first hee bestowed vppon him, telling him, they were the prises due to his merite, and ordained for that dayes enterprise: which kingly curtesie *Pericles* as thankefully accepting. Much time beeing spent in daunting and other reuells,' (510). This passage does not derive from Twine, and the reporter's memory might easily skip from one of Simonides' efforts to brighten the atmosphere (the gifts) to another (the dance).

861 (l) E'un] Euen

7.99/862 Your limbs will] This edition (G.T.); Will Q; Will very F2;

PERICLES

Your steps will well ANON. (*conj.* in Cambridge). Q2's syntax and metre are both defective; 'steps' are not normally 'in armour', but 'limbs' are both armoured and used in the dance. The use of 'limbs' would also prepare for the pun on 'armes' below.

7.102.1/865.1 *The Knights*] MALONE; *They* Q

7.104/867 Come] This edition (*conj.* Elze); Come ſir Q. Q is extrametrical; see next note.

7.105/868 sir,] This edition (*conj.* Brooks); *not in* Q. See previous note. Memorial misplacement of vocatives is common.

7.105/868 that] This edition (G.T.); *not in* Q

868 yᵉ] This edition (G.T.); you Q. See 'their' and 'those' below.

7.110.1/873.1 *They*] Q; *The Knights and Ladies* MALONE. See S. H. Long, 'Laying the Ghosts in *Pericles*', *SQ* 7 (1956), 39–42, for an argument that only Pericles and Thaisa dance. It seems best to preserve the ambiguity of Q.

7.112/875 Lights, pages, to] This edition (G.T.); Pages and lights, to Q; Pages and lights, STEEVENS. Steevens's alternative metrical emendation preserves the presence of pages on stage; if ladies are, as seems probable, also present, the number of boy actors required seems excessive.

7.113–14/876–7 (L) These ... owne] MALONE; Lodgings| Q

876 (I) seu'rall] ſeuerall

877 (I) giu'n] giuen

7.114/877 should] MAXWELL (Wilson); *not in* Q; to F3; shall WILSON (*conj.*). Hoeniger retains Q text and lineation, claiming that 'the intention may well have been to elide *we have*'; but such an elision does not solve the rhythmical problem in the second half of 7.114/877, or the syllabic deficiency of 7.113/876. See *P.A.*: 'giuing order, that *Pericles* Chamber should be next his owne' (510–11).

7.116/879 KING] Q3; *not in* Q1

882 (I) best.] Q2; ~: Q1

7.119.1/882.1 *Exeunt*] MALONE; *not in* Q

7.119.1/882.1 ſeuerally] This edition; *not in* Q. See 7.113/876.

Sc. 8] This edition; *not in* Q; [ACT II.] SCENE IV. MALONE

8.0.1 *Aeschines*] Q (*Eſcanes*), *Eſchines P.A.* (512). See 'THE NAMES ...' and Jackson, *N&Q* 220 (1975), 173–4.

884 (I) liu'd] liued Q

8.3–6/885–8 (L) For ... glory] MALONE; minding| that| heynous| pride| Q

885 (I) minding‸] Q4; ~, Q1

8.4/886 hold] This edition (G.T.); with-hold Q. Q says the same thing, extrametrically.

8.7–9/889–91 (L) When ... him] MALONE 2; in| daughter| Q; chariot| him| DYCE

8.9/891 him, both apparell'd all in Iewells] This edition (G.T.); him Q. The added words are from *P.A.* (511) (apparrelled).

8.10–11/892–3 (L) A ... ſtounke] MALONE; ſhriueld| Q

8.11/893 Their] STEEVENS; thoſe Q. From *P.A.* (511).

893 (I) ene] euen

8.13/895 hands] This edition (G.T.); hand Q. The plural seems required to balance 'eyes', as well as being the natural complement to 'their'; *P.A.* 511 has 'eyes' and 'hands'.

8.14–16/896–8 (L) And ... reward] MALONE; great| ſhaft| Q

8.14/896 iustice] Q; just STEEVENS. An extra syllable at a caesura is not unusual, and *P.A.* has 'Iustice' twice in this passage (511).

898 (I) heau'ns] heauens

8.16.1/899.1 three] MALONE; two or three Q

8.16.1/899.1 and stand aside] This edition; *not in* Q

905 (I) welcome,] Q2; ~‸ Q1

8.26/908 (L) Your ... loue] ROWE; *2 lines* Q: what|

8.26/908 your] Q; the STEEVENS. Steevens may be right, but Q's construction—'your prince, [which] you love'—seems typical of the style of this part of the play.

8.29/911 step] This edition (G.T.); breath Q. Q could arise from aural or memorial error: a step proves life as easily as breath, and more naturally relates to 'ground'.

912 (I) resolude] reſolued

8.31/913 giue's] Q1; gives Q5

8.32/914 leaue] Q; leaves MALONE

8.33/915 death in deeds‸] This edition (*conj.* Brooks); death indeed, Q; death's indeed‸ MALONE. Brooks's solution is less ambiguous than Malone's, and better explains the error.

8.34/916 this: Kingdomes] MAXWELL; this‸ Kingdome is Q

8.36/918 vtter] This edition (G.T.); *not in* Q. The only other proposed solution to Q's metrical deficiency is STEEVENS's drastic 'will soon to ruin fall'. The phrase 'vtter ruine(s)' is found in *P.A.* (533) and in *Duke of York* 1.1.254/255.

8.38/920 vnto as] This edition (G.T.); vnto our Q; vnto—our ALEXANDER. An easy misreading or substitution, which makes sense of Q's tortured syntax.

8.39/921 kneeling] This edition; *not in* Q. Some such referent seems desirable for Q's 'thus'.

8.40/922 By] ALEXANDER (Theobald); Try Q; For SINGER 2 (Dyce)

8.40/922 cause,] SINGER 2 (Dyce); ~; Q

8.41.1/923.1 *The Lords rise*] This edition; *not in* Q

8.44/926 But ... loue,] This edition (G.T.); *after* 8.48/930 Q. As the line stands in Q the transition it effects is meaningless, since the nobles can only search for Pericles if they have first conceded a delay; nor does 'this loue' have any clear referent. As conjecturally transposed, 'this loue' picks up 'If that you loue Prince *Pericles*' only three lines before, and the line is a pivot between Helicanus' outright rejection of their suffrages and his compromise proposal of a postponement (during which Pericles will be actively sought).

8.45/927 longer then, let me] This edition (G.T.); longer, let me Q; longer, let me then STEEVENS. The word, added to repair the metre, makes better sense in the altered context (see preceding note): 'then' follows naturally from 'if'.

8.46/928 Further to beare] EDWARDS (Hoeniger); To forbeare Q; To further bear BAILEY (*conj.* in Cambridge)

8.49/931 seeke] This edition (G.T.); ſearch Q. Q probably anticipates the word in 8.50/932.

8.49/931 your noble Prince] This edition (G.T.); like nobles Q; like noblemen STEEVENS; your noble king ANON. (*conj.* in Cambridge). Q makes poor metre and poor sense, as there is no contrast between 'nobles' (or 'noblemen') and 'noble subiects'. The anonymous conjecture seems right, metrically providing the right contrast; but Pericles is usually identified as 'Prince', not 'King', in both Q and *P.A.*

8.51/933 returne] Q. One expects a rhyme here, or at 8.47–8/929–30; one 'returne' or the other is probably an error.

8.55/937 vs] GLOBE; *not in* Q; it MALONE (Steevens); so COLLIER (*conj.*). Perhaps the entire line should be omitted, on the assumption that—having misplaced 8.56–7/938–9—the reporter found it necessary to invent a paraphrased conclusion to this speech.

8.56–7/938–9 If in the ... there.] This edition (G.T.); *after* 8.29/911 Q (~,). This couplet seems misplaced. Without it, 8.30–2/912–14 create none of the problems which have bedevilled commentators; nor do the Lords anticipate the advice which Helicanus eventually gives them (that they seek out Pericles for themselves). Instead, the scene follows the same natural progress as *P.A.* (512): the lords ask Helicanus to prove that Pericles is dead or to become King himself; he tries to dissuade them, but in the end only gains a postponement, in which he urges them to try to trace Pericles. A reporter could easily have misplaced the lines, the opposition between 'liues' and 'dead' (8.30–1/912–13) recalling the similar opposition here.

8.56/938 liue] Q; trauaile G.T. *conj.* Q bathetically repeats the verb of 8.28/910 and 8.30/912; both senses of 'trauaile' contrast with 'rest' (8.57/939), and better suit 'seeke'. See *P.A.*: 'since he only knew their Prince was gone to trauell, and that, that trauell was vndertaken for their good' (512). If 8.58/940 is a reporter's gabble, then 'trauels' there may represent a memory of the verb in this line.

8.59/941.1 *Exeunt*] ROWE; *not in* Q1; *Exit.* Q4

Sc. 8a] This edition (G.T.); *not in* Q. See Introduction. This short scene is editorially reconstructed from *P.A.*: 'whereas all the other Princes vppon their comming to their lodgings betooke themselues to their pillowes, and to the nourishment of a quiet sleepe, he of the Gentlemen that attended him, (for it is to be noted, that vpon the grace that the king had bestowed on him, there was of his Officers toward him no attendance wanting) hee desired that hee might be left priuate, onely that for his instant solace they would pleasure him with some delightfull Instrument, with which, and his former practise hee intended to passe away the tediousnesse of the night insteade of more fitting slumbers.

His wil was presently obeyed in all things since their master had commaunded he should be disobeyed in nothing: the Instrument is brought him, and as hee had formely wished, the Chamber is disfurnished of any other company but himselfe' (512–13). Bullough provides an alternative reconstruction (551–2), which verbally departs from *P.A.* more extensively than we do.

8a.0.1/941.2 *Gentlemen*] *P.A.* Q at the end of Sc. 7 calls for 'pages', which are an alternative possibility here.

8a.0.1/941.2 *with lights*] This edition; *not in P.A.* These properties usefully establish the continuity with the end of Sc. 7, and immediately establish the setting.

8a.1/942 1. GENTLEMAN . . . sir] *P.A.* has nothing exactly corresponding to such an announcement, but the narrative takes up when Pericles arrives at 'his lodging' (512), and some such declaration seems desirable from an audience's point of view. Pericles' speech—indirectly reported in *P.A.* (513)—is most naturally versified by beginning with a part-line.

8a.6/947 1. GENTLEMAN Presently.] It seems relatively unlikely that one of the gentlemen would exit without a word; 'presently' occurs in *P.A.* in the sentence which corresponds to the next line.

8a.8.1/949.1 *a stringed Instrument*] *P.A.* refers to the 'fingering' of the instrument, and Pericles sings while he plays (513); in Twine it is a harp (438).

8a.9/950 I thanke you.] There is nothing comparable in *P.A.* or Bullough's reconstruction, but it would be jarringly untypical of Pericles not to express thanks (as he does seven times elsewhere in 1.1–7.52/1–815).

8a.9–10/950–1 Now . . . sleepe.] Used in *P.A.* of the other knights (513); Bullough has the curt command, 'Now leave me'. Some formula of dismissal is needed; Pericles is characteristically courteous; and the lines emphasize, by contrast, his own inability to sleep (the same purpose they serve in *P.A.*).

8a.10.2/951.2 *Pericles playes, and singes*] *P.A.* describes this musical interlude verbally: 'hee beganne to compell such heauenly voyces from the sencelesse workemanship, as if *Apollo* himselfe had now beene fingering on it, and as if the whole Sinode of the gods, had placed their deities round about him of purpose, to haue beene delighted with his skill, and to haue giuen prayses to the excellencie of his art, nor was this sound only the rauisher of al hearers, but from his owne cleere breast hee sent such cheerefull notes, which by him were made vp so answerable to the others sound, that they seemed one onely consort of musike, and had so much delicacie, and out of discordes making vp so excellent a coniunction, that they had had power to haue drawne backe an eare, halfe way within the graue to haue listned vnto it, for thus much by our story we are certaine of, that the good *Symonides* (being by the height of night, and the former dayes exercise, in the ripenesse of his contentfull sleepe) hee reioyced to be awakend by it, and not accompting it a disease that troubled him in the hearing, but a pleasure wherewith hee still wished to be delighted. In briefe, hee was so satisfied to heare him thus expresse his excellence, that hee accompted his Court happy to entertaine so worthy a guest, and himselfe more happy in his acquaintance' (513). Bullough accordingly has Simonides 'In the next room' awake and listen, then speak in soliloquy a versified version of this description. But *P.A.* does not attribute the words to Simonides; they are most naturally explained as an attempt to compensate (descriptively) for the narrative's inability to reproduce the 'ravishing' theatrical effect of the song. Simonides can hardly be describing the qualities of Pericles' voice while Pericles is simultaneously singing. Bullough's reconstruction also requires simultaneous staging. Simonides would have to appear in his nightgown, and he can hardly remain in his nightgown in Sc. 9. Q marks the beginning of Sc. 9 as a new scene; in Bullough it is a continuation of this scene—which creates further problems. It thus seems reasonable to assume that in performance the song made its own effect, without the need for compliments from Simonides.

8a.11–13/952–4 Day . . . on.] From *P.A.*: 'But day that hath still that soueraigntie to drawe backe the empire of the night, though a while shee in darkenesse vsurpe, brought the morning on' (513). Bullough attributes these words to Simonides (see previous note). Pericles needs to be given a reason for ceasing, and the audience needs to know that he has stayed awake the entire night.

8a.14–15/955–6 I . . . me.] From *P.A.*: 'euen in the instant came in *Pericles*, to giue his Grace that salutation which the morning required of him' (514). In *P.A.* this occurs on the occasion of Pericles' entrance in Sc. 9, but the motive is best explained here, since it gives Pericles a reason to leave his lodging/the stage.

Sc. 9] This edition; *not in* Q; [ACT II.] SCENE V. MALONE

9.0.2/956.2 *entering at another doore*] MALONE; *not in* Q

9.4–5/960–1 (L) A . . . get] This edition (G.T.); knowne| Q; herself| means| MALONE; life| known| STEEVENS

9.5/961 none can] This edition (G.T.); by no meanes can I Q. Q's prepositional phrase is repeated, more appropriately, at 9.7/963; here it is unmetrical, and throws off the lineation of the speech.

9.6/962 haue] MAXWELL (W. S. Walker); get Q. 'Have access' is the normal idiom in both Shakespeare (seven times) and Wilkins (*P.A.* 534; 537, 'haue accesse to her').

9.7–8/963–4 it is impossible, | She . . . Chamber:] This edition (G.T.); ſhe hath ſo ſttrictly | Tyed . . . Chamber, that t'is impoſſible: Q. Q creates insoluble metrical and lineation problems as it stands, easily resolved by transposition of the floating phrase 't'is impossible', which allows 'She . . . Chamber' to stand as an integral verse line. Q's 'that' belongs to its postposition of the phrase.

965 (I) liu'rie] liuerie

9.12/968 Loth] Q; Though ~ STEEVENS; Right ~ ANON. (*conj. in* Cambridge)

9.12.1/968.1 *Exeunt Knightes*] DYCE; *not in* Q1; *Exit.* Q2

9.13–14/969–70 So . . . Knight] This edition; *3 lines* Q: dispatcht | heere | ; *3 lines* MALONE: So | letter |

9.15/971 light.] This edition (G.T.); light. | T'is well Miſtris, your choyce agrees with mine: Q. Every element of the omitted line is repeated elsewhere: 'I like that well' (9.16/972), 'I do commend your choyce' (9.18/974). See subsequent notes.

9.18/974 Mistris t'is well,] This edition (G.T.); Well, Q. See preceding note. This comment is much more appropriate here, where its ambiguity—it is well (absolutely), it is well for you that my choice agrees with yours—responds to the impertinence of her 'absolute' behaviour. In Q 'Well' is a pointless extrametrical repetition contributing to an unassimilated mid-speech part-line. We have supposed that 'Mistris t'is well' was misplaced by the reporter, who also (unmetrically) transposed the vocative. (STEEVENS first adopted our word order, leaving the phrase following 9.15/971.)

9.18–20/974–6 (L) I . . . dissemble that] STEEVENS; longer| comes| Q

9.18/974 your] This edition (G.T.); her Q. See note to 9.15/971 (Q), where it follows 'T'is well Mistris'.

9.20–1/976–7 that | In shew, I haue determin'd on in heart] This edition (G.T.); it Q. From *P.A.*: 'in the instant came in *Pericles* . . . when the king intending to dissemble that in shew, which hee had determined on in heart' (514).

979 (I) much,] ~ : Q1

9.24–5/980–1 night: my eares, | I do protest,] STEEVENS; night: | I do proteſt, my eares Q; night: I do | Protest, my ears MALONE. Malone saves Q's (unreliable) word order by means of an (intolerable) line-break.

9.29/985 my good] Q; good my G.T. *conj.*

9.30/986 (L) Let . . . daughter] This edition (G.T.); *2 lines* Q: thing|

9.30/986 thinke you of my Daughter] This edition (G.T.); do you thinke of my Daughter, ſir Q; do you think, sir, of | My daughter STEEVENS

9.31/987 And] This edition (G.T.); And fhe is Q1; And fhees Q2
9.33/989 My Daughter sir,] MALONE; Sir, my Daughter Q
9.34/990 So well indeed] This edition (G.T.); I fo well Q
9.37.1/993.1 He . . . reads] This edition; not in Q
9.39.1/995.1 He . . . feete] This edition; not in Q; Kneels HOENIGER (Schanzer). From P.A. (515).
998 (I) aymde] Q4; aymed Q1
9.43/999 her.] This edition; her. | king. Thou haft bewitcht my daughter, | And thou art a villaine. | Peri. By the Gods I haue not; Q. Simonides' charge is repeated by P.A. (515), with greater verbal and dramatic authority, at 9.47-50/1003-6 (see following notes). 'By the Gods' recurs at 9.53/1009. Q's lines scan awkwardly, however arranged, and look like a paraphrased misplacement. In P.A. the equivalent of 9.41-3/997-9 and 9.44-6/1000-2 is a single speech.
9.44-6/1000-2 (L) Neuer . . . displeasure] ROWE; thought| actions| loue| Q
9.47/1003 Thou lyest like a Traytor] This edition; Traytor, thou lyeft Q. From P.A.: the King 'tolde him, that like a traitour, hee lyed. Traytour, quoth Pericles? I, traytour, quoth the king,' (515).
9.47-50/1003-6 traytor, | That . . . Childe.] EDWARDS; traytor. Q. From P.A. (515); we depart from P.A. (and Edwards) only in reading 'With' for 'with the'.
9.51/1007 rising] This edition; not in Q. See 9.39.1/995.1.
9.51-2/1007-8 Who cals me Traytor, vnlesse it be the King, | Eu'n in his bosome] This edition (G.T.); Euen in his throate, vnleffe it be the King, | That cals me Traytor Q. The transposition of the opening phrases of these two lines yields a much more intelligible and speakable sense, while according also with P.A.: Pericles 'boldely replyed, That were it any in his Court, except himselfe, durst call him traytor, euen in his bosome he would write the lie' (515).
9.52/1008 will write] This edition (P.A. 515); returne Q. A much more vivid expression: 'bosome' corresponds with 'will write', as Q's commonplace 'throate' does with 'returne'.
9.54/1010 bloud] This edition; thoughts Q. From P.A.: 'his bloud was yet vntainted' (515).
9.56/1012 in search of Honour] This edition (P.A. 515); for Honours caufe Q. Q echoes 8.40/922.
9.57/1013 your] HUDSON (W. S. Walker); her Q. From P.A.: 'he came into his Court in search of honour, and not to be a rebell to his State' (515).
9.60-2/1016-18 I . . . witnesse] This edition; No? heere comes my Daughter, fhe can witneffe it Q. Malone noted Q's echo of Othello 1.3.169/455, 'Here comes the Lady, let her witnesse it'; Maxwell and others note that memories of Othello have probably influenced the reporter here. The line in Othello is the cue for the entrance of Desdemona, who (like Marina) would have been played by the company's principal boy; if Marina were the reporter of Q, the chances of contamination are obvious. We have therefore adopted P.A.'s account: the King 'answered, he should prooue it otherwise, since by his daughters hand, it there was euident, both his practise and her consent therein' (515).
9.64-5/1020-1 By what you hope of heauen, or desire | By your best wishes heere i'th' worlde fulfill'd,] This edition; not in Q. From P.A.: Pericles upon Thaisa's entrance 'demaunded of her by the hope she had of heauen, or the desire she had to haue her best wishes fulfilled heere in the worlde' (516).
9.68/1024 made] This edition (G.T.); that made Q. Omission of the relative (which restores the metre) is characteristic of the style of Scenes 1-9.
9.69-70/1025-6 (L) Why . . . glad] MALONE; offence| Q
9.71/1027 How minion] This edition (P.A. 516); Yea Miftris Q. A much more vivid phrase; Q echoes 9.18/974.
9.72/1028 Aside] Q (in margin opposite 9.97/1051)
9.72-96/1028-52 on't, (to Thaysa) is . . . onely childe] This edition; on't with all my heart, Q. We follow P.A. (516) in expanding this dialogue: 'How minion, quoth her Father (taking her off at the very word, who dare be displeased withall?) Is this a fit match for you? a stragling Theseus borne we knowe not where, one that hath neither bloud nor merite for thee to hope for, or himselfe to challenge euen the least allowaunce of thy perfections, when she humbling her princely knees before her Father, besought him to consider, that suppose his birth were base (when his life shewed him not to be so) yet hee had vertue, which is the very ground of all nobilitie, enough to make him noble: she intreated him to remember that she was in loue, the power of which loue was not to be confined by the power of his will. And my most royall Father, quoth shee, what with my penne I haue in secret written vnto you, with my tongue now I openly confirme, which is, that I haue no life but in his loue, neither any being but in the enioying of his worth. But daughter (quoth Symonides) equalles to equalls, good to good is ioyned, this not being so, the bauine of your minde in rashnesse kindled, must againe be quenched, or purchase our displeasure. And for you sir (speaking to prince Pericles) first learne to know, I banish you my Court, and yet scorning that our kingly inragement should stoope so lowe, for that your ambition sir, Ile haue your life. Be constant, quoth Thaysa, for euerie droppe of blood hee sheades of yours, he shall draw another from his onely childe.' Bullough also reconstructs this passage but is less conservative in retaining P.A.'s wording.
9.73/1029 A . . . where] EDWARDS, saying this line 'proclaims its genuineness and is altogether too good to lose', inserts it nonsensically after 9.105/1058.
9.97/1053 yea] This edition (G.T.); not in Q. See 9.71/1027. Q is metrically deficient.
9.98/1054 you, not,] This edition (G.T.); ~, ~, Q1; ~; ~, Q4. The line is probably deliberately ambiguous; there seems little necessity to emphasize one meaning at the expense of the other.
9.100/1056 aside] Q (in the margin opposite 9.101/1057)
9.102.1, 103.1/1058.1, 1059.1 He catches . . . hand] This edition; not in Q. From P.A.: the King 'catching them both rashly by the handes, as if hee meant strait to haue inforced them to imprisonment, he clapt them hand in hand, while they as louingly ioyned lip to lip' (516).
9.103-5/1059-61 (L) Therefore . . . wife] This edition (conj. Elze); frame| heare you| make you| Q
9.105/1061 I shall] This edition (G.T.); Ile Q; I will STEEVENS
9.105/1061 He claps . . . together] This edition; not in Q. See note to 9.102.1/1058.1.
9.106-9/1062-5 (L) Nay . . . pleas'd] MALONE; hands| ioynd| griefe| Q
9.106.1/1062.1 Pericles . . . kisse] This edition; not in Q. See note to 9.102.1/1058.1.
9.107.1/1063.1 He parts them] This edition; not in Q
9.108/1064 your further] This edition (G.T.); further Q; a further MALONE. Malone merely patches the metrical deficiency; but 'your' makes better sense, and a better rhetorical contrast.
9.108/1064 you] This edition; you both Q. Q is extrametrical, and suspiciously anticipates 9.111/1067.
1065 (I) pleas'd] pleafed
1066 (I) Eu'n] Euen
9.113/1069 Then] MALONE; And then Q
Sc. 10] This edition; ACT III. MALONE
10.2/1071 about the house] MALONE; about the houfe Q
10.6/1075 fore] STEEVENS (Malone); from Q
10.7/1076 Crickets] ROWE 3; Cricket Q
10.7/1076 sing at] Q; at MAXWELL (Collier)
1076 (I) th'] the
10.8/1077 As] MALONE (Steevens); Are Q; Aye DYCE; E'er SINGER 2 (Dyce); All DELIUS; Sing MAXWELL
10.10/1079 Where by] Q2; Whereby Q1
10.13 eche] Q (each). Properly modern 'eke', but the older consonant is preserved for the rhyme.
10.14/1083 dumbe] Q; dark MAXWELL (Daniel)
10.14.1/1083.1 Dumbe shew.] Q5; not in Q1
10.14.3/1083.3 comes [hastily] in to them] This edition; meetes Q. From P.A.: 'came hastily in to them' (517).
10.14.8-10/1083.8-10 with . . . an other] MALONE (subs.); not in Q
10.17/1086 Coignes] ROWE 3; Crignes Q
10.21 stead] Q (fteed)
1090 (I) quest:] ROWE 3; ~, Q

1090 (I)   *Tyre*₍ₐ₎] ROWE 3; ~ : Q
10.29/1098   mutanie] Q; mutine STAUNTON. *P.A.* confirms Q (518); for the elision compare *Coriolanus* 3.1.129/1574.
10.29/1098   mutanie₍ₐ₎ there, hee] STEEVENS; mutanie, hee there₍ₐ₎ Q. Q's word order, though kept by modern editors, is awkward metrically and grammatically.
10.29/1098   appease] STEEVENS; oppreſſe Q. *P.A.* confirms (518).
1103 (I)   *Pentapolis*] Q6; *Penlapolis* Q1
1104 (I)   *Irauyshed*] MALONE (Steevens); *Iranyſhed* Q
1110 I)   crosse?] ~₍ₐ₎
10.46/1115   fortunes mood₍ₐ₎] MALONE (Theobald); fortune mou'd, Q
1125 (I)   conuay,] MALONE; ~ ; Q
1126 (I)   not₍ₐ₎] MALONE; ~ ? Q
1126 (I)   told;] MALONE; ~ , Q
1127 (I)   hold₍ₐ₎] MALONE; ~ : Q
10.60/1129   sea] ROWE 3; ſeas Q
10.60/1129   *Pericles*] Q; prince STEEVENS
10.60/1129   specke] This edition (G.T.); ſpeake Q. The obsolete inflection seems desirable, for the sake of a rhyme; Q's compositor could easily have normalized, consciously or not, the eccentric form.
10.60/1129   *Exit*] Q5; *not in* Q
Sc. 11] This edition; *not in* Q; [ACT III.] SCENE I. MALONE. There is no indication of overlap between Gower's speech and Pericles'.
11.0.1/1129.1   *Thunder and Lightning*] This edition; *not in* Q
11.1/1130   The] Q; Thou ROWE. For *the* with a vocative see Franz §261 and *1 Henry IV* 1.2.156/259. Q's 'The' might alternatively represent a misinterpretation of ambiguous manuscript yᵉ/ye; Shakespeare often uses 'ye gods' as a vocative, and at *Troilus* 2.3.10-12/1171-3 switches from addressing one god as 'thou' to addressing another as 'ye'.
1131 (I)   heau'n] heauen
1132 (I)   Brasse,] MALONE; ~ ; Q
11.4/1133   call'd] Q; recall'd DYCE 2
1133 (I)   deepe;] MALONE; ~ , Q
1135 (I)   sulph'rous] ſulphirous
11.7/1136   thou] MALONE; then Q
11.7/1136   stormest₍ₐ₎] DYCE; ſtorme₍ₐ₎ Q; storm, MALONE. Malone's emendation seems the more conservative, but entails a substantive emendation of punctuation (with 'venomously' modifying 11.8/1137); Dyce's presumes only the omission of a single type (an ſt ligature).
11.8   spit] Q (ſpeat); split HOENIGER (*conj.*)
1139 (I)   Vnheard.] MALONE; ~₍ₐ₎ Q
11.11   patroness] Q (patronesse)
11.11/1140   mydwife] MALONE (Steevens); my wife Q
11.14.1/1143.1   *with an Infant*] STEEVENS; *not in* Q
11.16-18/1147-9 (L)   Who...Queene] MALONE; *2 lines* Q; doe|
11.26-7/1155-6 (L)   Patience...charge] This edition; *1 line* Q
1156 (I)   Ene] Euen
11.27.1/1156.1   *She...Infant.*] This edition; *not in* Q
11.27.1-2/1156.1-2   *Pericles...weepes*] This edition; *not in* Q. See *P.A.*: 'We must intreate you to temperance sir...as you respect your owne safety, or the prosperitie of that prety Babe in your armes. At the naming of which word Babe, *Pericles* looking mournfully vpon it, shooke his head, and wept' (520). In *P.A.* the Master is speaking, but 11.27/1156 is the only comparable moment in Q.
1157 (I)   blust'rous] bluſterous
1160 (I)   e'er] euer Q
1162 (I)   Heau'n] Heauen
1163 (I)   th'] the
11.34/1163   Poore inch of Nature,] HOENIGER (Collier); *not in* Q. From *P.A.* (519).
1164 (I)   Eu'n] Euen
11.36/1165   partage] This edition (*conj.* Edwards); portage Q. Q has never been satisfactorily explained, and has two specific meanings ('porthole', 'mariner's part-cargo') which would be suggested by the context but are confusingly irrelevant. These senses themselves could, on the other hand, help to account for Q's error, which is anyway an easy one (aurally or palaeographically).

Partage was current in the sense 'the share apportioned to one' (*OED sb.* 2, 1436+).
11.37.1/1166.1   ⌈*the Maister*⌉ *and a Sayler*] This edition; *two Saylers* Q. In *P.A.* only 'the Maister' appears (520); this may be implied by Q's '*1. Sayl⟨er⟩.*' in speech-prefixes. One would not expect anyone less than the ship's master to convey such demands to a prince.
11.38, 43, 47, 51/1167, 1172, 1176, 1180   MAISTER] This edition; *1. Sayl⟨er⟩.* Q (variously abbreviated). See preceding note.
11.40/1169   its worst] This edition (G.T.); the worst Q. For the idiom see *Othello* 5.2.166/3063, *Coriolanus* 5.2.105/2904-5, *Macbeth* 3.2.26/970 ('Treason ha's done his worst'), *Sonnets* 19.13, 92.1. Q could arise from assimilation to the second half of the line.
11.43/1172   calling] This edition; *not in* Q
1172 (I)   Slake] Qa; Slacke Qb
11.43-4/1172-3 (L)   Slake...selfe] F4; *verse* Q: wilt thou|
11.43   Slack] Qa (slake), Qb
11.43   bow-lines] Q (bolins)
11.45, 69/1174, 1198   SAYLER] This edition; *2. Sayl⟨er⟩.* Q (variously abbreviated). See note at 11.38/1167.
11.45-6/1174-5 (L)   But...not] This edition; *verse* Q: billow|
11.45   an] Q (and)
11.47-9/1176-8 (L)   Sir...dead] This edition; *verse* Q: hie| Ship|
11.50/1179   but] This edition; *not in* Q. Compare *P.A.*: 'the Prince seeking againe to perswade them, tolde them, that it was but the fondnes of their superstition to thinke so' (520). Whether or not the sailors were intended to speak verse in this passage, Pericles clearly should, and the addition strengthens both sense and metre.
11.51-3/1180-2 (L)   Pardon...'er] This edition; *verse* Q: obserued|
1181 (I)   obserued,] Q4; ~ . Q1
11.52/1181   custome] SINGER (Boswell); eaſterne Q
11.53/1182   'er] Q1; her Q4
11.53/1182   for...straight.] MALONE; ~ : Q (after 'meet;', 11.54/1183)
11.54.1-2/1183.1-2   *She...bed.*] EDWARDS (*subs.*); *not in* Q
11.54.2/1183.2   *Pericles...Infant*] This edition; *not in* Q. It is awkward for Pericles to hold the baby during his emotional speech, and he apparently no longer has it at 11.66-7/1195-6.
11.59/1188   the oaze] STEEVENS; oare Q. Edwards objects that this traditional emendation is 'almost certainly wrong'; the parallel at *Tempest* 3.3.100/1447—'my Sonne ith Ooze is bedded'—he dismisses because the passage describes a *corpse* lying *in the mud* while this one concerns a *coffin* being cast to lie *with simple shells*. The alleged contrast between corpse and (be-corpsed) coffin seems irrelevant; moreover, Shakespeare elsewhere associates 'the Owse and bottome of the Sea' (*Henry V* 1.2.164/297) with sunken treasure, comparable to the rich chest in which Thaisa is buried. As Shakespeare nowhere else alludes to sea-shells we can hardly legislate on whether he would have found the association with 'ooze' incongruous; he seems elsewhere to have treated 'ooze' as a synonym for 'sea-bottom' (*Cymbeline* 4.2.206/2157). Compare *Richard III* 1.4.16-41/781-798, which imagines corpses and treasure scattered on the 'slimy bottome'. The r/z misreading is easy, and omission of 'the' could be due to reporter or compositor.
11.61/1190   And] STEEVENS; The Q
11.61/1190   aye] STEEVENS (Malone); ayre Q; e'er GLOBE. Compare *Troilus* 3.2.156/173: 'To feed for aye her lampe and flames of loue'. Shakespeare elsewhere has no compounds with either *e'er* or *aye* (though several with *ever*).
11.64/1193   Paper] Q2; Taper Q1
11.66/1195   Coffer] MALONE; Coffin Q
11.68.1/1197.1   *Exit Lichorida*] MALONE 2; *not in* Q
11.69-70/1198-9 (L)   Sir...ready] MALONE; *verse* Q: hatches|
11.72, 74/1201, 1203   MAISTER] This edition; 2. Q; EDWARDS *reads* FIRST SAILOR. We follow Edwards in interpreting the prefix as an error, but identify the 'First' sailor as 'Maister' throughout. See note to 11.37.1/1166.1.
11.73/1202   from] MAXWELL (Collier); for Q

11.74/1203 breake of] Q. Omission of these words would make the metre more regular; however, Shakespeare nowhere uses *By day* to mean 'by dawn', and does use *breake of day* elsewhere. 'Day breake' (*OED*, 1530+) would be even more attractive metrically, though again Shakespeare does not use it. See next note.

11.74/1203 Make] This edition; O make Q. There is little need for exclamatory passion in issuing instructions for a ship's course; the line has too many syllables, and reporters often add interjections.

11.78.1-3/1207.1-3 *Exit ... curtaines*] This edition; *Exit*. Q; *Exeunt* ROWE. Pericles must depart separately from the sailors, and Thaisa's body must be concealed at some point in the scene. After the Sailor's speech at 11.69-70/1198-9, it would be natural and theatrically effective for him to exit through the trapdoor.

Sc. 12] This edition; *not in* Q; [ACT III.] SCENE II. MALONE

12.0.1/1207.4 poore man and a] HOENIGER (subs.); *not in* Q. The omission might have been compositorial. In *P.A.* Cerimon is 'this morning in conference with some that came to him both for helpe and for themselues, and reliefe for others; and some that were relating the crueltie of the last nights tempest' (521).

12.2/1209 those] SCHANZER; thefe Q

12.2.1/1209.1 *Exit Phylemon*] HOENIGER; *not in* Q

12.4/1211 seen] This edition (G.T.); been in Q. Of the three close parallels for this speech cited by Malone and subsequent editors, two use the verb 'seen' (*Macbeth* 2.4.1-4/760-3, *Caesar* 1.3.5-10/403-8), the other 'heard' (*History of Lear* 9.48/1568). The substitution also improves the metre.

12.5 ne'er] Q (neare)

12.7/1214 in] This edition (M.J.); to Q. Cerimon, versed in nature's cures (12.35/1242), knows that none can be effective in this case. Possible anticipation of 'to' in the next line. Q makes a general statement about the human condition ('nature'); but Cerimon is diagnosing a particular patient, and asserting that only supernatural aid could help him now—a mere physician is helpless.

12.8/1215 to poore man] HOENIGER (Brooks); *not in* Q; To Philemon MALONE

12.8/1215 to th'] This edition; to the Q

12.9/1216 *Exeunt ... seruant*] HOENIGER; *not in* Q

12.9/1216 morrow] Q; morrow, sir STEEVENS

12.10/1217 Lordship.] ~, Q

12.10-11/1217-18 (L) Gentlemen ... early] STEEVENS; *1 line* Q

12.11-12/1218-19 (L) Sir ... sea] STEEVENS; *1 line* Q

12.14-16/1221-3 (L) The ... house] MALONE; *2 lines* Q: topple|

12.18/1225 our] The speech might be better without this word; it could then be relined, dividing after 'cause', and leaving Cerimon's words at 12.18/1225 as an unassimilated short line.

12.19-20/1226-7 lordship should, | Hauing ... you, at] This edition (G.T.); Lordſhip, | Hauing ... you, ſhould at Q. In Q 12.19/1226 is metrically defective and 12.20/1227 overloaded; editors move 'Hauing' to the end of 12.19/1226 (MALONE), but the resulting line-break is odd and pointless, and it seems more likely that the reporter transposed the auxiliary verb.

12.20/1227 this hower] This edition (M.J.); thefe early howers Q. Neither 'these early hours' nor 'this early hour' occurs elsewhere in Shakespeare; 'at this hour' is frequent, and creates a regular pentameter; Q's 'early' repeats 'so early' in 12.11, 17/1218, 1224.

12.22/1229 to] This edition (G.T.); ſhould Q. Q may have substituted the more common reading under the influence of the preceding sentence; 'be' can more easily take the required metrical stress, if preceded by 'to'.

1230 (I) compell'd] compelled

12.23-38/1230-45 (L) I ... Bagges] MALONE; Cunning| Riches| expend| former| god| Physicke| Authorities| famyliar| dwels| the | cures | delight | or | Q

12.23/1230 held] MALONE; hold Q. Hoeniger doubts the emendation, but compare 'My life I neuer held' (*History of Lear* 1.147/147), 'I haue euer held' (*Antony* 2.7.56/1189).

12.26/1233 dispend] This edition (G.T.); expend Q. Previous editors have noted that 'dispend', in *P.A.*'s parallel to this passage (521),

may be the correct word: although Shakespeare uses *expend* three times elsewhere, none of the parallels involves material possessions; 'dispend' alliterates with 'darken', and is the rarer word. The fact that Shakespeare does not use it elsewhere is irrelevant: all his good texts contain a high proportion of unique usages.

12.33/1240 dwels] Q; dwell F4

12.34/1241 so] This edition (G.T.); *not in* Q; I MALONE. Malone's emendation adds nothing but metrical padding, since the pronoun is in any case implicit. 'So' alliterates, clarifies the logical transition, and reduces the sense that Cerimon is boasting, or telling his listeners what they already know.

12.35/1242 doth giue] Q; gives MALONE (Theobald). Shakespeare's late works contain many hexameters, and Q allows a greater emphasis on 'me'.

12.36/1243 and cause] This edition (G.T.); in courſe Q. Editors suspect 'serious corruption' in this line, but Shakespeare uses 'true delight(s)' at *Dream* 3.3.40/1434 and *As You Like It* 5.4.196/2693; 'a more content' recurs at *Kinsmen* 2.2.100/699 (Fletcher?), and there are four other examples of 'a more [noun]', including 'a more delight' (*Venus* 78). The line's apparent lameness is isolated in the linking phrase 'in course of', which manages to be both unidiosyncratic and superfluous. Q's 'in course' could be a corruption—by mishearing or misreading or both—of 'and cause', meaning 'and [more] cause'. Alternatively, one might emend to 'more cause'.

1244 (I) tott'ring] This edition; tottering Q. Elided thus on all four of its other occurrences in Shakespeare.

12.38/1245 pleasure] Q; pleaſure STEEVENS

12.39/1246 glad] This edition (G.T.); pleaſe Q. Steevens's emendation of the preceding line eliminates a striking image; it is much more likely that the verb in this line has been contaminated by a memory of the earlier phrase.

12.39-45/1246-52 (L) Your honour ... neuer] This edition (*conj.* W. S. Walker); *Ephesus*| themselues| restored| payne| *Cerimon*| Q. Editors follow Malone, who kept Q's lineation, only moving 'pour'd foorth' back to the end of 12.39/1246. In a normal text this more conservative policy would make sense, but here—as the previous speech demonstrates—mislineation is endemic.

1247 (I) pour'd] MALONE; Poured Q

1249 (I) restor'd] reſtored

12.42/1249 alone] This edition (G.T.); *not in* Q. Compare *K. John* 1.1.210/210 'And not alone in habit and deuice ... But'. Editors agree that this is what Q must mean, but do not explain how it could communicate this meaning as it stands.

12.43/1250 personall] Q. Always treated by Shakespeare as disyllabic.

1250 (I) ene] euen

12.45/1252 neuer—] MALONE; ~. Q; ~ raze. DYCE. The omission can hardly be due to the reporter, since the drift of the sentence is so obvious that anyone could supply the conclusion. Hoeniger blamed the error on a compositor, but accidental omission of the final word of a speech, followed by a full stop, is unusual. The obviousness of the missing conclusion makes its omission dramatic and intelligible, while filling the lacuna produces an undramatic resounding triteness.

12.45.1/1252.1 *Phylemon and one or two*] This edition (G.T.); *two or three* Q. Q correctly identifies Philemon in the stage direction at 12.1/1208 because he is called in the same line; but as Q stands the identification is pointless. In Twine Cerimon's assistant plays a crucial role; and *P.A.* also emphasizes 'a seruant of his' (522).

12.46/1253 etc. PHYLEMON] This edition (G.T.); Seru⟨ant⟩. Q (variously abbreviated). See preceding note.

12.48-50/1255-7 (L) Sir ... wracke] STEEVENS; shore| Q; Sir| shore| MALONE. Lines 12.46-7/1253-4 are amphibious, belonging with both 12.45/1253 and 'Sir, euen now'.

12.49/1256 The sea tost vp] This edition (G.T.); did the ſea toſſe vp Q; did the sea toss MALONE. Compare 'tost it vpon our shore' (see first reference to 12.54/1261), probably a memorial repetition of this line. As alternative formations of the past tense, 'tossed' and 'did toss' are easily confusible memorially; Shakespeare never uses 'did toss' but has 'toss'd' 7 times.

12.50/1257 Set't] Q. For the contraction compare *Let't* (5 times in Shakespeare).

12.51-2/1258-9 (L) What . . . heauie] MALONE; *1 line* Q

12.52-3/1259-60 did . . . sir,] This edition (G.T.). Q places this question and answer after 'bitum'd' at 12.58/1265; Maxwell notes that Cerimon's 'pointless question smacks of the reporter', and Hoeniger conjectured that it belonged after 'wracke', 12.50/1257: 'Cerimon is then directly answering the servant's statement'. But Cerimon's incredulity is most naturally prompted by his recognition of the chest's weight. This recognition is followed in Q by the command 'Wrench it open' (12.54/1261), a command pointlessly repeated at 12.58/1265—a repetition most easily explained by the reporter's misplacement of Cerimon's question and the servant's answer. Moreover, 'cast it up' seems at first an innocent synonym for 'tost vp' (12.49/1256), but through the ambiguity of 'cast' naturally initiates the vomiting imagery of 12.55-6/1262-3.

12.53-4/1260-1 (L) I . . . eager] This edition (*conj.* Brooks); *1 line* Q

12.54/1261 Or a more eager] This edition (G.T.); as toſt it vpon ſhore Q. Q lamely repeats 12.49/1256. In *P.A.* the chest is cast on shore 'by a more eager billow' (521). The image is striking, and 'eager' here contributes to the developing imagery of sickness: compare Sonnet 118, *Richard II* 2.1.37/651, *Hamlet* 1.5.69/686, and *All Is True*, 4.2.24/2096, where Shakespeare associates eagerness—which can mean 'bitterness'—with sickness or indigestion.

12.54/1261 CERIMON] This edition (G.T.); *not in* Q; but see second note to 12.58/1265.

12.54.1/1261.1 The . . . worke] This edition (*conj.* Brooks); *not in* Q

12.56-7/1263-4 (L) T'is . . . vs] This edition; *1 line* Q

12.56/1263 by] This edition (*conj.* Hoeniger); *not in* Q

12.56/1263 queasie] This edition (*conj.* Hoeniger); *not in* Q. Hoeniger shows that the verbal associations of this word elsewhere in Shakespeare strongly resemble this passage.

12.58/1265 bittum'd] MALONE; bottomed Q

12.58/1265 They force the lid] This edition (G.T.); *not in* Q. Cerimon's preceding words indicate a particular attention to the manner in which the chest has been sealed; his next words suggest that the odours inside have been released.

12.58-9/1265-6 (L) soft . . . sense] This edition (*conj.* Hoeniger); *1 line* Q

12.58/1265 soft] This edition (*conj.* Hoeniger); Cer⟨imon⟩. Wrench it open ſoft Q. See note to 12.52-3/1259-60.

12.60.1/1267.1 They . . . off] This edition; *not in* Q

12.62-3/1269-70 (L) Shrowded . . . Spices] This edition (*conj.* Hoeniger); prose Q

12.62/1269 and crownd,] This edition (G.T.); *not in* Q. In *P.A.* Cerimon finds her 'so crowned, so royally apparelled, so intreasured as before' (522). The added detail completes the verse line, and allows 'balm'd . . . Spices' to be preserved as a verse line. (Steevens and most editors break it after 'entreasur'd'.)

1270 (I) Balm'd] Q4; balmed Q1

1270 (I) entreasur'd] STEEVENS; entreaſured Q

12.64-5/1271-2 (L) A . . . Characters] STEEVENS; *prose continued* Q; me| MALONE; Apollo| HOENIGER (*conj.*)

1271 (I) to!] MALONE; ~∧ Q

12.64.1/1271.1 He . . . Chiſt] This edition; *not in* Q

12.65/1272 i'th'] This edition; in the Q. The elision is required however we divide the lines.

1279 (I) Besides,] Q4; ~, Q1

1281 (I) liu'ſt] lieuſt Q1

12.75/1282 euen] Q4; euer Q1

12.76-83/1283-90 (L) Nay . . . dead] MALONE; looks| sea| Closet| yet| spirits| Q

12.77/1284 looke] Q. Maxwell calls the repetition 'scarcely Shakespearian', and conjectures 'see'. But compare *Troilus* 1.2.197/343, 'looke how hee lookes', and *Hamlet* 3.2.120-1/1848-9, 'looke you how cheerefully my mother lookes'.

1284 (I) looks.] ~∧

12.77/1284 rash] This edition (*conj.* Malone); rough Q. See *P.A.*, 'condemning them for rashnesse' (523).

12.78/1285 a Fire] Q; fire STEEVENS. An extra stressed syllable after a caesura is common enough in Shakespeare's late plays.

12.79/1286 all my] Q; all the STEEVENS

12.79.1/1286.1 *Exit Phylemon*] This edition (G.T.); *not in* Q; *Exit a servant* DYCE

12.81/1288 And . . . againe] Q. For the rhythm compare *Lucrece* 1475 ('Thy eye kindled the fire that burneth here'), where 'kindled' forms a reversed foot in mid-line (as here).

12.82-4/1289-91 I . . . recouer'd] Q (*subs.*). Edwards replaces these words with a passage from *P.A.*: 'I haue read of some Egyptians, who after foure houres death, (if man may call it so) haue raised impouerished bodies, like to this, vnto their former health' (522). If the patient is Egyptian, the doctor might be assumed to be; there is little to choose between Q and *P.A.* Given 12.92/1299 ('fiue'), Q's '9' seems more likely than *P.A.*'s 'foure'. *P.A.*'s 'some Egyptians' seems less apt than Q's 'an Egiptian' (which occurs also at *Othello* 3.4.56/1985). *Appliance* is a word Shakespeare uses elsewhere in medical contexts; 'like to' is characteristic of Wilkins. (M.J.)

12.82/1289 haue heard] MALONE (Steevens); heard Q; haue read *P.A.* (522)

12.83/1290 9. howers] This edition (G.T.); that had 9. howers lien Q

12.84/1291 applyaunces] DYCE; applyaunce Q

1291 (I) recouer'd] SINGER; recouered Q. Both the syllabic '-ed', and the rhyme it creates, are uncharacteristic of Shakespeare's late style.

12.84.1/1291.1 *Phylemon*] This edition (G.T.); *one* Q

12.85-6/1292-3 (L) Well . . . haue] Q4; and| Q1

12.85/1292 Well sayd, well sayd] Q. This repetition occurs at *Othello* 4.1.114/2241.

12.86/1293 still] MAXWELL (Delius); rough Q

12.87-9/1294-6 (L) Cause . . . Gentlemen] This edition (G.T.); you| blocke| ayre| Q

12.87/1294 *Musick*] HOENIGER; *not in* Q

12.87 vial] Q (Violl). Both from Gower and *P.A.* have Cerimon pour a 'liquor' in Thaisa's mouth. Hoeniger, who interprets this word as a reference to a viol, dismisses this coincidence, claiming that Wilkins here consulted Gower; but this is the sole instance of the alleged influence. Wilkins, as co-author of the play, would certainly have read Gower, but in *P.A.* he was lazily plagiarizing Twine, and there is no reason to believe that he dipped into Gower for this simple detail. Moreover, if fire, warm clothes, and music are sufficient to revive Thaisa, why does Cerimon call for 'all my Boxes in my Closet' (12.79/1286)? And what is in those boxes, if not medicines?

12.90-3/1297-1300 (L) This . . . againe] STEEVENS; liue| her| howers| Q

1297 (I) awakes;] STEEVENS; ~∧ Q

12.90-1/1297-8 warmth | Breaths] STEEVENS; warmth breath Q1; warm breath Q2

1300(I) flow'r] flower

12.93-5/1300-2 (L) The . . . euer] MALONE; *2 lines* Q: wonder|

12.94/1301 set] MALONE; ſets Q

12.95-7/1302-4 (L) She . . . lost] MALONE; *2 lines* Q: ey-lids|

1303 (I) heau'nly] heauenly

12.99-102/1306-9 (L) The . . . bee] MALONE; *3 lines* Q: appeare| weepe|

1308 (I) weepe,] Q4; ~. Q1

12.102-3/1309-10 (L) O . . . this] MALONE; Lord| Q

12.104/1311 (L) Is . . . rare] *1 type line* Q

12.104-8/1311-15 (L) Hush . . . vs] MALONE; hands| linnen| relapse| Q

12.104/1311 gentle] STEEVENS; my gentle Q

Sc. 13] This edition; *not in* Q; *Actus Tertius.* F3; [ACT III.] SCENE III. MALONE

13.0.1/1315.2 at Tharsus] Q4; Atharſus Q1

13.0.2/1315.3 and . . . Babe] MALONE (*subs.*); *not in* Q

13.1-3/1316-18 (L) Most . . . peace] MALONE; *prose* Q
13.3-5/1318-20 (L) you . . . you] MALONE; *2 verse lines* Q: thankfulnesse|
13.5-7/1320-2 (L) Your . . . vs] MAXWELL (W. S. Walker); mortally| Q
13.5/1320 strokes] ROUND; ſhakes Q; shafts STEEVENS
13.6/1321 hurt] STEEVENS; hant Q
13.7/1322 woundingly] DEIGHTON (Schmidt *and* Kinnear); wondringly Q
13.7-9/1322-4 (L) O . . . her] ROWE; *prose* Q; Queen| pleas'd| hither| F4
13.8/1323 you'd] ROWE; you had Q
13.9/1324 T'haue] This edition; to haue Q
13.9-11/1324-6 (L) We . . . end] STEEVENS; vs| in| Q
1325 (I) pow'rs] powers
13.10/1325 should] This edition (M.J.); Could Q
13.13/1328 nam'd so] named ſo Q; so nam'd G.T. *conj.*
13.14/1329 and leaue] STEEVENS; leauing Q. Q is metrically and syntactically awkward, and anticipates 'beseeching' in the next line.
13.15-17/1330-2 (L) The . . . borne] STEEVENS; *2 lines* Q: her|
13.17-25/1332-40 (L) Feare . . . generation] MALONE; Grace| which| child| vile| relieu'd| that| it| Q
1334 (I) pray'rs] prayers
13.25/1340 th'] This edition; the Q
13.25-29/1340-4 (L) I . . . remayne] MALONE; goodnes| maried| honour| Q
1343 honour,] MALONE; ~, Q. In the original-spelling edition, by removing this comma we leave the syntactical relationship of 'all' ambiguous; in the modern-spelling text, we accept Malone's view that it modifies 'we'.
13.29/1344 Vnsisserd] STEEVENS; vnſiſterd Q. See *P.A.* 'his head should grow vncisserd' (524).
13.29 hair] Q (heyre), STEEVENS
13.30/1345 show ill] SINGER 2 (Theobald); ſhew will Q
13.32/1347 DYONYSA I] Q ('*Dion.* I' *text*); *Cler.* I (*c.w.*)
13.32-7/1347-52 (L) I . . . heauen] MALONE; *prose* Q
13.35/1350 CLEON] Q4; *Cler.* Q
13.36/1351 th' masted] This edition (G.T.); the mask'd Q; the vast HUDSON 2 (Dyce); the moist W. S. WALKER (*conj.*); the mighty KINNEAR (*conj.*); the calmest ELZE (*conj.*). Editors gloss Q as 'deceivingly calm'. Aside from the difficulty of communicating this alleged sense, what would its dramatic function be? Cleon wishes Pericles 'The gentlest winds of heauen', and he has no reason to hint darkly that the sea is less friendly than it seems; nor does any such foreboding serve a dramatic purpose—for Pericles' voyage from Tharsus is, atypically, uneventful. Q's reading therefore seems to us corrupt; but previous conjectures seem feeble. *OED*'s first citation of *masted* in this sense (*ppl. a.*¹) dates from 1627, but Shakespeare uses the noun 11 times, and the neologism would be typical of his style. For the resulting image of Neptune, compare *Antony* 4.15.58-9/2406-7 ('and o're greene Neptunes backe | With Ships, made Cities'). The 'masts' lead naturally by association to 'winds'. The conjectured error could be aural or palaeographical.
13.38-9/1353-4 (L) I . . . teares] MALONE 2; *prose* Q; embrace| O, no tears| tears| MALONE I
1353 (I) deer'st] deereſt
13.40-1/1355-6 (L) Looke . . . Lord] MALONE; *prose* Q
13.41/1356 Exeunt] ROWE; *not in* Q
Sc. 14] This edition; *not in* Q; [ACT III.] SCENE IV. MALONE
14.2-3/1358-9 (L) Lay . . . Characters] MALONE; command| Q
14.2/1358 are al] This edition (G.T.); are Q; are now MALONE. Q's line is a syllable short, and the line-break lame. Shakespeare never uses 'now' in conjunction with the noun or verb 'command', but does so use 'all' 10 times. Alternatively, Q's 'are' might be an error for 'attend'. Compare 'attends your Ladiships command' (*Two Gentlemen* 4.3.5/1706) and 'attend his maiesties command' (*All's Well* 1.1.4/4). The compositor might have misread 'al' as a nonsensical duplication of 'at'.
14.4-10/1360-66 (L) It . . . ioy] ROWE; *prose* Q

1361 (I) eu'n] euen
14.5/1361 eaning] F3; learning Q; yielding MASON (*conj.*); yeaning WHITE (Mason); bearing RIDLEY (*conj.*)
1362 (I) deliuerd] deliue-|red
14.6/1362 th'] This edition; the Q
1365 (I) liu'rie] liuerie
14.11/1367 CLEON] Q6; *Cler.* Q1
14.13/1369 till . . . expire you may abide,] HUDSON 2 (Fleay); you may abide till . . . expire, Q
14.16/1372 THAYSA] Q4; *Thin.* Q1
14.17.1/1373.1 Exeunt] ROWE; *Exit.* Q
Sc. 15] This edition; *not in* Q; ACT IV. MALONE
15.4/1377 ther's] Q; there MALONE
15.8/1381 Musick,] TONSON; Muſicks, Q. Q is defensible, but the emendation (independently adopted by Malone) seems preferable.
15.10/1383 hir] STEEVENS; hſe Q
15.10/1383 the hart] STEEVENS; the art Q; th' heart RIVERSIDE
1384 (I) gen'rall] generall
15.14/1387 Seeks] ROWE; Seeke Q
1388 (I) kind:] MAXWELL (Dyce); ~, Q
15.15/1388 our *Cleon* has] This edition (G.T.); our *Cleon* hath Q; hath our Cleon MALONE (Steevens); *Cleon* doth own DANIEL (*conj.* in Cambridge). As Maxwell notes, Steevens's emendation requires an unparalleled accentuation of the name. Compositorial or memorial substitution of 'hath' for 'has' is common, and Shakespeare increasingly used 'has' in his later work. See next note.
15.16/1389 full growne lasse] This edition (G.T.); full growne wench Q; wench full grown MALONE (Steevens). Shakespeare elsewhere rhymes on both *lass* and *has*, but never on *grown*. Moreover, *lass* is strongly associated with Shakespeare's late work: 8 of 11 uses post-date 1605. 'Wench' would be an easy substitution.
1390 (I) Ene] Euen
15.17/1390 ripe] Q2; right Q1
15.17/1390 right] COLLIER; ſight Q; fight MALONE (Theobald)
15.21/1394 they] Q; she MALONE
1396 (I) neele] MAXWELL; needle Q; neeld MALONE. See 20.5/1999.
1398 (I) it,] Q2; ~, Q1
15.26/1399 bird] MALONE (Theobald); bed Q
1402 (I) *Dian,* still,] MALONE; ~, ~, Q
15.32/1405 With Doue] MUNRO; The Doue Q; With the dove STEEVENS (Mason)
15.32/1405 might] STEEVENS (Mason); might with Q. See previous note.
15.38/1411 murder] This edition (*conj.* W. S. Walker); murderer Q. Compare 'the present death of *Hamlet*' (*Hamlet* 4.3.67/2544), etc.
15.42.1/1415.1 A tombe is reuealed] This edition; *not in* Q. Lychorida's 'graue' or 'tombe' is clearly required later (15.66, 68/1439, 1441), and is prominent in *P.A.*'s account of this scene (527-9). Gower's line is a natural cue for its discovery, and visually relates this chorus to the next.
1417 (I) wrath,] F3; ~. Q1
1418 (I) th'] This edition; the Q
15.47/1420 carrie] STEEVENS; carried Q
15.48 on] Q1 (one), Q2
15.50.1/1423.1 Enter . . . Leonine] This edition; *after* 15.52/1425 Q. Compare 5.38.1/528.1
15.52/1425 Exit] Q. Editors since MALONE mark a scene-break, beginning 'ACT IV SCENE I'; but see note to 15.421/1415.1 and 15.50.1/1423.1.
15.53-8/1426-31 (L) Thy . . . which] ROWE; *prose* Q
15.55/1428 i'th'] This edition; in the Q
15.57-8/1430-1 or . . . Vnflame] This edition; in flaming, thy loue boſome, enflame Q; thy love inflame SISSON. A major crux; many other emendations were proposed by earlier editors. Essentially one must choose between emending the words Q offers, or excising some of those words as duplications. Sisson, the most persuasive advocate of excision, proposed that the copy was 'foul papers . . . with corrections *currente calamo*'; Hoeniger, rejecting his textual hypothesis, rejected his emendation too. But a reporter

is just as capable as an author of 'corrections *currente calamo*' (Maxwell). Nevertheless, one would expect 'loue' to be the first shot, not 'bosome' (as Sisson assumed). But 'bosome' is always disyllabic in Shakespeare. Although 'bosome' might itself be a memorial substitution for 'breast', the need for further emendation to support it weakens one's confidence in Sisson's solution. Equally disconcerting, Shakespeare often juxtaposed the words in Q: 'pitty, loue, nor feare' (*Duke of York* 5.6.68/2832), 'flames of loue' (*Troilus* 3.2.156/1731), 'conscience is borne of loue' (Sonnet 151.2), 'and sway in loue . . . haue enflamde desire in my breast' (*Pericles* 1.62-3/62-3); *love* and *bosom* are juxtaposed at *Two Gentlemen* 3.1.249/1268, *Measure* 1.3.3/268, *LLL* 4.3.134/1376, *Merchant* 3.4.17/1657, Sonnet 9.13; Shakespeare imagines conscience as a deity 'in my bosome' (*Tempest* 2.1.283/856) and writes of 'the bosome of my Conscience' (*All Is True* 2.4.179/1251). Such evidence strongly suggests that both 'loue' and 'bosome' belong in this context, and hence that Sisson's policy of excision is wrong. See following notes.

15.57/1430 or] DEIGHTON; in Q

15.57/1430 fanning,] This edition (G.T.); flaming, Q. Q's repetition of 'in flaming' and 'enflame' is deeply suspicious; nor is it easy to see how two objects—one 'cold' and the other 'flaming'—could be yoked in having a single effect upon Leonine's bosom. If 'flame' is right below, it is presumably wrong here. Shakespeare often associates the verb *fan* with cold or cooling: 'fan'd snow' (*Winter's Tale* 4.4.362/1969), 'fanne our people cold' (*Macbeth* 1.2.50/61), 'the Fan | To coole a Gypsies Lust' (*Antony* 1.1.9-10/9-10), 'turne the Sunne to yce, with fanning in his face' (*Henry V* 4.1.199/1980-1); the verb figuratively suggests loss of courage or resolution in *Macbeth* and in 'fan you into dispaire' (*Coriolanus* 3.3.131/2060). Compare also 'the loue I beare him, | Made me to fan you thus' (*Cymbeline* 1.6.177-8/699-700). These parallels cluster remarkably in Shakespeare's late work. The unusual nature of the image, and anticipation of the verb in the next line, easily explain the reporter's error.

15.57/1430 loue thy] SINGER (anon. *conj.*); thy loue Q. Also adopted by Deighton, and those who accept his other emendations.

1430 (I) bosome,] ~,

15.58/1431 Vnflame] This edition (G.T.); enflame Q; Enslave DEIGHTON. Deighton objects that it is hard 'to understand how "*cold* conscience" can "inflame"'. But 'Enslave' and 'nicely' are an odd combination, and 'Enslave' is not suggested or supported by the other imagery of this speech. *Enslave* is first recorded by *OED* in 1643; *vnflame* in 1635; Shakespeare was a great coiner of words, often by means of *en-* or *un-* prefixes, and on such grounds 'vnflame' is as plausible as 'enslaue'—and involves a simpler misreading (of one letter, instead of three). *OED*'s first citation is close to this passage: 'Where neither . . . doubt afflicts, nor baser fear | Unflames your courage in pursuit' (Francis Quarles, *Emblems*, III. Pro. 22). Finally, Shakespeare elsewhere juxtaposes *bosom* and *breast* with images of figurative heat (*K. John* 5.7.30/2485, *Titus* 3.1.212/1228, *Duke of York* 2.1.83/665, *2 Henry IV* 1.3.13/514), and cold (*Romeo* 1.4.102/560, *Contention* 5.2.35-6/3071-2, *Richard II* 1.2.34/239, *Complaint* 259, 292); there are no such collocations with *slave(s)*.

15.59-60/1432-3 (L) Ene . . . purpose] MALONE; prose Q

1432 (I) Ene] Euen

15.60-1/1433-4 (L) I . . . creature] EDWARDS; *I line* Q

15.61-2/1434-5 But . . . her] Q. *P.A.* suggests that something may be missing here: 'he resolued her in blunt wordes, that he was come to kill her, that hee was hired vnto it by Dyonysa her foster mother, that she was too good for men, and therefore he would send her to the gods, that if she would pray, pray, for hee had sworne to kill her' (528-9). The beginning and end of this passage—which is not based on Twine—clearly and closely correspond to 15.116-122/1489-95, and the middle echoes 15.60-2/1433-5 (the link being mention of Dionyza). G.T. conjectures 'But yet she is a goodly creature.— I, | Too good for men : the fitter then the Gods should haue her'.

15.62/1435 The fitter then] Q; 'Tis then the fitter that M.J. *conj.*

15.62-3/1435-6 her. | Here] Q; her. Here | STEEVENS. A line-divided foot. See note to 15.63/1436, 'weeping'.

15.62.1-2/1435.1-2 Enter . . . flowers] MALONE; *after* 15.64/1437 Q

15.62.1/1435.1 to the tombe] This edition; *not in* Q

15.63/1436 weeping] This edition (*conj.* Mason); weeping for Q. Q's superfluous preposition—Shakespeare often uses the verb transitively—creates an hexameter, thus contributing to the irregularity of an implausibly irregular passage.

15.63/1436 nurses] STEEVENS (Percy); Miſtreſſe Q. If 'nurſes' were misread 'miſtres' it could be normalized to 'Miſtreſſe'. Alternatively, the error might be memorial: perhaps 'fostress'?

15.65-72/1438-45 (L) No . . . friends] ROWE; prose Q

15.66/1439 graue] F3; greene Q. Editors traditionally cite Lord Chalfont's gloss 'the green turf with which the grave of Lychorida was covered' (cited by Malone). But Chalfont cited only a single parallel—'My ashes cold shall be buried on this greene, | Enioy that good this bodie nere possest' (Fairfax's 1600 translation of *Godfrey of Bulloigne*, vii. 314-15). The Fairfax context makes the use of 'greene' unexceptional and intelligible, as the *Pericles* context does not. In this context a compositor could easily misinterpret 'graue' as 'grene'. Shakespeare often speaks of *strewing*—especially of flowers—upon graves: *Romeo* 5.3.17, 280/2707, 2970; *Hamlet* 5.1.243/3213, *Cymbeline* 4.2.286, 392/2237, 2343.

1439 (I) Flow'rs] Flowers

15.68/1441 tombe] This edition (G.T.); graue Q. Shakespeare does not elsewhere use *graue* to refer to the structure erected on top of the burial pit (as the context here requires); nor does he use *hang* in such conjunction with *grave*. But 'hang . . . vpon (her/the) tomb' occurs twice in *Much Ado* (5.1.276, 5.3.9/2342, 2494); in *P.A.* Leonine 'attends for [Marina] at *Lychoridaes* Toombe' (528); *P.A.* also speaks of her 'monument' (526) and 'sepulchre' (527), but never of her 'graue'. Memorial substitution thus seems probable. (If F3 is correct in 15.66/1439, the repetition of 'graue' is also suspicious.)

15.71/1444 but] This edition (G.T.); *not in* Q1; like Q4; as MAXWELL (Cambridge)

15.71/1444 ceaselesse] This edition (G.T.); laſting Q; blasting MALONE (*conj.*); lashing CRAIG (*conj.*). Both earlier conjectures are feeble because they lose the image of 'storme perpetuall' (*Winter's Tale* 3.2.212/1223) by presuming mere compositorial error. But 'the repetition smacks of the reporter' (Hoeniger), and 'doth last' in 15.69/1442 is confirmed by the parallel at *Cymbeline* 4.2.219-20/2170-1 ('Flowers | Whil'st Sommer lasts'). Q's adjective here is thus probably memorial, and 'lasting' has been substituted for some two-syllable synonym. Of the available Shakespearian alternatives *endless* is more frequent (12 occurrences) but also commonplace, and requires emendation of 'a' to 'an'; *ceaseless*—as at *Lucrece* 967—is a much rarer word (see *OED*), and thus more prone to memorial substitution. *P.A.* twice juxtaposes *cease* and *tempest* (521, 522).

15.73/1446 How . . . alone?] Q. See *Macbeth* 3.2.10/954: 'How now, my Lord, why doe you keepe alone'. Hoeniger thinks that '*Macbeth* was in Shakespeare's mind all through this scene', but the words are spoken by Lady Macbeth—who, like Marina, would have been played by the company's leading boy (the reporter?).

15.73/1446 why doe] Q1; doe G.T. *conj.*

15.73/1446 doe yow keep] Q1; doe you weepe Q2; de'ye weepe Q4; keep you HUDSON 2

15.74/1447 is] Q; *Philoten*'s M.J. *conj.*

15.76/1449 Haue you] Q1; You haue Q4; Have you not MALONE (*conj.*)

15.76-7/1449-50 fauour | Is changd] SCHANZER; fauours | Changd Q; favour's chang'd MALONE; favour's Changèd CAMBRIDGE

15.78/1451 Giue me your flowers come,] This edition (G.T.); Come giue me your flowers Q; Come, come, give me your wreath of flowers MALONE. The line's metrical irregularity is easily rectified by transposition of the interjection, which a reporter could easily misplace.

15.78/1451 ore] This edition (Theobald); ere Q; on HUDSON 2.

Lexically the difference between *on* and *o'er* is insignificant here, and Theobald's conjecture presupposes less corruption.

15.78/1451   margent] HUDSON (Theobald: 'margin'); marre it Q

15.79/1452   is percing] This edition (G.T.); is quicke Q; 's quick MALONE; quicker ANON. (*conj.* in Cambridge). The earlier conjectures record an unease with Q's metre in this line, but the real impetus for emendation comes from the following line. See next notes. Shakespeare uses *piercing* 13 times, including *All's Well* 3.2.112-13/1420-21 ('aire | That sings with piercing').

15.80-1/1453-4 (L)   And... her] This edition (G.T.); stomacke| Q; Come| STEEVENS

15.80/1453   And quicke,] This edition (G.T.); And it perces, Q; Piercing, STEEVENS. Although the air might be piercing, and might sharpen the appetite, it does not 'pierce the stomach'. Q's line is also, for Shakespeare, metrically impossible. The reporter might easily transpose the two attributes, resulting in metrical confusion in two adjacent lines. (See note to 15.79/1452.)

15.80/1453   it sharpes] This edition (G.T.); and ſharpens Q; and sharpens well STEEVENS; and sharps W. S. WALKER (*conj.*); and will sharp HUDSON 2. The other conjectures rectify the metre by superfluous alterations of the sense. This form of the verb was common; it does not occur elsewhere in Shakespeare, but he only used the alternative 4 times (3 in verse, where metre required it). The reporter could easily have misplaced the pronoun, attaching it to the wrong verb in the line (see previous note); in the previous phrase it is redundant, but here it makes the sense easier to communicate.

15.80/1453   come] Q. This might be memorial filler, but feminine caesuras are common enough.

15.81/1454   th'] This edition (G.T.); the Q

15.81-2/1454-5 (L)   No... seruāt] ROWE; *1 line* Q

15.82-92/1455-65 (L)   Come... old] ROWE; *prose* Q

1457 (I)   eu'ry] euery

15.90/1463   resume] MAXWELL (Wilson); reſerue Q

15.92-3/1465-6 (L)   Care... alone] ROWE; *prose* Q1; *separate line* Q4

15.93-4/1466-7 (L)   Well... it] ROWE; *1 line* Q

15.94/1467   truly] This edition (G.T.); yet Q. Q is unmetrical, and redundant. For 'but truly' compare *Much Ado* 3.5.19/1604, *Hamlet* 2.1.87/895, *Antony* 5.2.270/2926, and *Merry Wives* 4.1.4-5/1859-61 ('But truely... Mistris *Ford* desires you to come').

15.95/1468   Nay] This edition (G.T.); Come, come Q. Dionyza has already used the same interjection four times in her last two speeches—including a 'Come, come' at the beginning of her last speech. *Nay* was idiomatically used 'not simply to deny or refuse, but to reprove, to correct, or to amplify what has been said before' (Schmidt); here it contributes to a line-divided foot.

15.95-7/1468-70 (L)   I... sed] This edition (G.T.); *prose* Q1; you| least| Q4

1470 (I)   warnt] warrant

15.98-100/1471-3 (L)   Ile... of you] ROWE; *prose* Q

15.99/1472   Pray you] MALONE; pray | Q. The omission might be compositorial, as 'you' would fall between prose lines in Q—a frequent occasion for omission.

15.100.1/1473   *Exit Dioniza*] MALONE; *not in* Q

15.103/1476 (L)   My... feare] ROWE; *prose* Q (but 'Is' is capitalized in mid-line after a comma)

1476 (I)   nurse] Q2; nutſe Q1

15.103/1476   ses] Q; said MALONE

15.104-5/1477-8 (L)   But... ropes] ROWE; *prose* Q; galling| Hands ROWE; galling| MALONE

15.104/1477   Mariners] This edition (M.J.); Saylers Q. An easy unmetrical memorial substitution.

15.105/1478   with] MALONE; *not in* Q

15.105/1478   ropes] Q; the ropes ROWE

15.106-7/1479-80 (L)   And... decke] MALONE; *prose* Q; Mast| ROWE

1479 (I)   endur'd] ROWE; endured Q

15.109-13/1482-6 (L)   When... skip] ROWE; *prose* Q

15.111/1484   Once] This edition (G.T.); and Q. MALONE conjectured that a line was missing ('O'er the good ship the foaming billow breaks, | And...'); STEEVENS transposed 15.111-5/1484-8 to follow 15.107/1480. Sense is more easily restored by assuming a simple misreading, and interpreting 'washes off' as intransitive (*v.* 15d).

15.114-5/1487-8 (L)   From... confusion] MALONE; *prose* Q; Stern| calls| ROWE

15.114/1487   stemme] MALONE; ſterne Q

15.116/1489   prayers] Q; prayers speedily STEEVENS

15.118-9/1491-2 (L)   If... tedious] ROWE; *prose* Q

15.120/1493   The] This edition (G.T.); for the Q. Q's conjunction is superfluous and extrametrical: reporters often make implicit connectives explicit.

15.120-1/1493-4 (L)   The... haste] MALONE; *prose* Q; Ear| ROWE

15.121/1494   Why would you] This edition (G.T.); Why, will you Q1; Why, will you Q2. As Q2 makes clear, Q1's syntax idiomatically suggests that 'Why' is a mere interjection; 'would' better fits the question, and better parallels 15.122/1495.

15.122-9/1495-1502 (L)   Why... offended] MALONE; *prose* Q; can| hurt her| word| Creature| Mouse| Worm once| ROWE

1495 (I)   kild? | Now,] MALONE; kild, now? Q

15.128/1501   I] Q; Nor MAXWELL (Daniel). Maxwell accuses Q of 'mincing fatuousness'; but that is a fault no emendation can alleviate. 'Nor' produces an image of Marina killing mice, hurting flies, and treading on worms—in each case 'against her will'—and weeping every time. It seems better to take 15.127/1500 as a general confession of innocence, followed by an admission of a single transgression, modified by extenuating circumstances (once... against my will... wept).

15.128/1501   once on a worme] This edition (G.T.); vpon a worme Q1; vpon a worme once Q4. Q4's clarification is not strictly necessary, but does seem an improvement.

15.129/1502   for it] Q4; fort Q1

15.130-1/1503-4 (L)   Wherein... danger] ROWE; *prose* Q; or| STEEVENS; death| life| BROOKS (*conj.*)

15.130/1503   anie profit] Q; profit STEEVENS

15.131/1504   danger] STEEVENS; any danger Q. An easy memorial interpolation, under the influence of the preceding line.

15.131-2/1504-5 (L)   My... doo't] ROWE; *prose* Q

15.133-9/1506-12 (L)   You... weaker] ROWE; *prose* Q

1507 (I)   fauour'd] ROWE; fauoured Q

1511 (I)   life, Come,] Q2; lifeCome, Q1

15.139/1512   *drawing out his sword*] This edition; *not in* Q; *He seizes her* GLOBE. From *P.A.* 529.

15.139-40/1512-13 (L)   I... dispatch] MALONE; *1 line* Q

15.140.1/1513.1   *running*] This edition; *not in* Q. From *P.A.* 529.

15.141.1/1514.1   *Leonine runs away*] MALONE; *not in* Q

15.141.1/1514.1   *and hides behind the tombe*] This edition; *not in* Q. From Twine, which serves as the blueprint for the action here: 'he ran away as fast as he could, and hid himselfe behind the sepulchre' (454). See 15.42.1/1415.1.

15.144.1/1517   *Pirats, ⌜carrying Marina⌝*] This edition; *not in* Q; *Pirates with Marina* MALONE. In Twine 'the Pyrats... caried her away to their ships' (454); in *P.A.*, 'carried her to their shippes' (529).

15.144.2/1517.1   *Leonine ⌜steales backe⌝*] This edition; *Enter Leonine* Q. From *P.A.*: 'hauing fledde some distance from them, and obseruing them not to pursue, he secretly stole backe' (529); *not in* Twine. MALONE initiated a new scene here (4.2), but even if Leonine fully exits at 15.141.1/1514.1 the tomb presumably remains on stage, and there is no lapse of time.

15.145-50/1518-23 (L)   These... remaine] ROWE; *prose* Q

15.146   An] Q (and). Understanding this word as the beginning of a conditional clause removes a bathetic declaration of the obvious (M.J.).

15.147/1520   shee'le] MALONE; ſhee will Q

15.151.1/1524.1   *The tombe is concealed*] This edition; *not in* Q

Sc. 16]   This edition; *not in* Q; [ACT IV.] SCENE III. MALONE; [ACT IV.] SCENE II. DYCE

16.0.1/1524.2   *A brothel signe.*] This edition; *not in* Q; Mytilene. A Room in a Brothel. MALONE; *Mytilene. In front of a Brothel.*

HOENIGER (Brooks). Brooks seems right about the location, which could easily have been signalled to a Jacobean audience by one of the signs familiarly used for brothels.

16.0.1-2/1524.2-3 the Pander . . . Boult] This edition; *the three Bawdes* Q; *Pander, Boult and Bawd* F3

16.4/1528 lose] This edition (G.T.); loſt Q. An easy misreading. Alternatively, one might read 'this last mart'.

16.4/1528 too much] Q2; too much much Q1; much ANON. (*conj.* in Cambridge)

16.5/1529 wenchlesse] This edition (*conj.* Maxwell); too wenchleſſe Q. An easy contamination from the preceding phrase.

16.6/1530 out] Q; short G.T. *conj.*

16.8/1532 they with] Q; with MALONE

16.10-11/1534-5 what ere wee pay for them] Q. Compare 'at what rate soeuer' (*P.A.* 531).

16.19/1543 they're too] MALONE; ther's two Q. An easy aural error.

16.34/1558 sorts] Q; trades MALONE

16.36/1560 mystery] This edition; trade Q. There is no discernible difference in meaning, connotation, or respectability between *profession* and *trade* (see *OED*); if anything, the former was more prestigious. Shakespeare elsewhere uses *mystery* ironically of a bawd's occupation (*Othello* 4.2.32/2443) and a hangman's (*Measure* 4.2.27-39/1747-59); like *profession* and *calling*—but unlike *trade*—the word also has religious connotations, which suit the context. Many professions were not *mysteries* ('recognized guilds'); moreover, however secretive prostitution might be it was never 'an enigma' or 'a closely guarded secret'. A reporter might easily have substituted the common synonym 'trade', which lacks all these particular pertinences.

16.36/1560 It's] Q; crying hem is G.T. *conj.* Compare *Othello* 4.2.31/2442.

16.38/1562 to the Pirats] This edition; *not in* Q; *To Marina* MALONE

1562 (I) wayes‸ my maisters‚] Q1; ~ . ~ , MALONE

16.40/1564 A PIRAT] ROWE; *Sayler.* Q; *Pirate* MALONE

16.49/1573 BOULT I] Q; . *Pirate. I* LILLO (Malone); *Boult. It* DYCE. See Hoeniger's defence of Q.

16.49/1573 hundred Sestercies] This edition; thouſand peeces Q. See *P.A.*, 'a hundred Sestercies of golde' (531), and Twine, 'an hundred sestercies of gold' (456). A reporter might easily have substituted Q's less specific phrase; there seems little reason for Shakespeare to abandon his source in such a detail.

16.53.1/1577.1 *Exeunt Pander and Pirats*] MALONE; *not in* Q

16.61/1585 (L) Alacke . . . slow] ROWE; *prose* Q. This line is metrically anomalous, but no solution is compelling. Perhaps 'so slacke-slow', on the analogy of compounds like 'willful-slow' (Sonnet 51.13).

16.62-4/1586-8 (L) He . . . mother] MALONE 2; *prose* Q; pirates| over-board| MALONE 1

16.63/1587 had but] MALONE; had not Q; Had ROWE 3

16.64/1588 To] MALONE; for to Q

16.71-2/1595-6 (L) The . . . die] MALONE 2; *prose* Q; I| MALONE 1

16.72/1596 like] Q4; *not in* Q1

1597 (I) pleasure] Q2; peaſure Q1

16.81/1606 not a] Q; no G.T. *conj.*

16.87-8/1612-13 must stir] Q4; ſtir Q1

16.88/1613 vp:] This edition (*conj.* Hoeniger); vp: *Boults returnd.* Q. Memorial texts often enough substitute dialogue for action, and vice versa.

16.88.1/1613.1 *Enter Boult*] Q4; *not in* Q1

16.96/1621 watred, as] This edition (G.T.); watred, and Q1; ſo watred, that Q4; water'd‸ and HOENIGER. Hoeniger plausibly contends that the sense required to link the two clauses is 'as if'; but there is no evidence that *and* can take such a sense, while *as* frequently does. An easy memorial substitution.

16.102/1627 Verolles] MALONE (Veroles); *Verollus* Q

16.108/1633 of] EDWARDS (W. S. Walker); in Q

16.110/1636 all] This edition (G.T.); *not in* Q

16.114/1640 to despise] MALONE; ‸ deſpiſe Q

1642 (I) Louers, seldome‚] MALONE; ~ ‸ ~ , Q

16.122/1648 BAWD] F3; *Mari.* Q (text and c.w.)

16.129/1655 (L) Who . . . it] MALONE; *a separate line* Q

16.132/1658 *giuing him money*] This edition; *not in* Q

16.136-7/1662-3 reapst . . . setting forth] This edition (M.J.); haſt . . . report Q. There is no parallel in Shakespeare for 'hast' a harvest, and 'report' suspiciously repeats the previous sentence. Shakespeare often collocates reap and harvest (*As You Like It* 3.5.104/1825, *Contention* 3.1.381/1562, *Richard III* 2.2.104/1287, Sonnet 128.7); 'setting forth' can mean 'to recommend, praise' (used of a woman's beauty at *Lucrece* 32), and *set* can mean 'plant' (*Winter's Tale* 4.4.100/1705, etc.). Memorial error assisted by aural similarity.

16.140.1/1667 *Exit*] This edition; *not in* Q. If Boult is being paid and sent into town, he should not enter the house with the women.

16.146/1673 with me] This edition (G.T.); with vs Q. See 16.140.1/1667; the plural could have been picked up, by compositor or reporter, from the preceding line. Alternatively one might omit the phrase altogether.

16.146/1673 *Exeunt.*] F3; *Exit.* Q

16.146/1673 *The signe is remoued*] This edition; *not in* Q. See note to 16.0.1/1524.2.

Sc. 17] This edition; *not in* Q; [ACT IV.] SCENE IV. MALONE; [ACT IV.] SCENE III. DYCE

17.0.1/1673.2 *in mourning garments*] This edition; *not in* Q. From *P.A.* (530), following Twine (454). See 17.43/1716 ('And yet we mourne').

17.1/1674 are] Q4; ere Q1

17.3-4/1676-7 The . . . agen] Q. One or both of these lines is presumably corrupt: two tetrameters in sequence are unlikely.

1677 (I) childe] Q4; chidle Q1

17.5/1678 (L) Were . . . world] ROWE; *prose* Q

17.5-6/1678-9 this . . . the] Q; the . . . this G.T. *conj.*

17.6-47/1679-1720 (L) Ide . . . done] MALONE; *prose* Q

17.6/1679 deede, a] MAXWELL (Delius); ~ . O Q. The misreading is only possible in minuscule, which suggests that the heavy punctuation is compositorial.

1681 (I) earth‚] Q4; earth-| Q1

17.12/1685 fact] SINGER 2 (Dyce); face Q

17.13/1686 demaunds] This edition (G.T.); ſhall demaund Q

17.15/1688 is not] This edition (G.T.); it, not Q1; it, nor Q4

17.17/1690 pious] COLLIER (Mason); impious Q1; *not in* Q4. Confirmed by *P.A.*: 'if such a pious innocent as your selfe do not reueale it' (530).

1693 (I) heau'ns] heauens

17.25/1698 cow'd] STEEVENS; coward Q. Q is extrametrical and commonplace. Compare 'it hath Cow'd my better part of man' (*Macbeth* 5.10.18/2089), 'cowish terrer of his spirit' (*History of Lear* 16.12/2118, a scene strikingly similar to this), and 'like a Cow in Iune' (*Antony* 3.10.14/1678; of Cleopatra's flight at Actium)—all late plays.

17.26/1699 euer] Q; euen M.J. *conj.*

17.27/1700 prime] DYCE; prince Q

17.28/1701 sourses] DYCE; courſes Q

17.31/1704 distaine] SINGER (Steevens); diſdaine Q

17.33/1706 Marinas] Q2; *Marianas* Q1

1707 (I) Whilst] whileſt

17.34 malkin] Q (Mawkin)

17.35 through] Q (thorow)

17.37/1710 finde] Q. Perhaps an error for 'fonde' (G.T.), contrasting Dionyza's love with Cleon's lack of it; 'I finde' seems redundant. But an appropriate syntax is difficult to reconstruct.

17.39/1712 your] Q; our DYCE 2 (W. S. Walker)

17.41/1714 And as for] Q; For BROOKS (*conj.*)

1716 (I) And] &

17.43/1716 yet we mourne] Q; even yet ~ MALONE; ~ mourn for her ELZE (*conj.*)

1717 (I) finish'd] MALONE; finiſhed Q

1719 (I) gen'rrall] generrall

17.48-9/1721-2 (L) Which . . . talents] Q4; *prose* Q1

17.48-9/1721-2 Angell . . . Eagle] This edition (G.T.); Angells . . . Eagles Q. For *angel* adjectivally compare *Much Ado* 4.1.163/1808,

LLL 1.1.113/113, Richard III 4.1.68/2295; for *eagle*, Timon 1.1.49/49.

17.49/1722 Ceaze in] This edition (G.T.); ceaze with Q. The syntax is, probably deliberately, entangled: 'betray' belongs with 'Angell face', while 'doest' belongs with 'Ceaze'. No single emendation can alter this interpretation of the syntax, and since it relates to the context it must be regarded as deliberate. The repetition of 'with' might be defended similarly; but it could easily result from inadvertent compositorial or memorial error. The first 'with' is necessary to the conceit: 'by means of' her angel's face, the harpy betrays her victim, thus enabling her to seize it: the face is instrumental to the betrayal and hence the seizure, and an instrumental preposition is therefore appropriate (and metaphorically striking). But the instrumental character of the claws is secondary, and interferes with the metaphor: the angel's face betrays the victim *into* the harpy's claws.

17.49 talons] Q (talents)

17.51-2/1724-5 (L) Doe...aduise] Q4; kills| youle| Q1; one| Gods| know| W. S. WALKER (conj.)

17.51/1724 Doe...Flies] Q. Most editors have regarded this passage as obscure and perhaps corrupt. Maxwell notes that 'sweare too'th Gods' must mean 'take an oath that, testify that [something is true]', in this case that winter kills the flies. Maxwell, followed by Hoeniger, further assumes that 'he who swears is exonerating himself'. But if this were correct one would expect 'killd': 'winter *did* it, not I'. More important, the whole point of the image (self-exoneration) is left unstated; nor has Cleon been engaged in self-exoneration in this scene. One would expect Dionyza's image to refer openly to Cleon's foregoing behaviour: he wishes the deed undone, he calls it impious and ignoble, he asks the heavens to forgive it, he berates his wife. We would gloss 'sweare too'th Gods' as 'inform the gods (in an inappropriately serious manner)' of (a) something they already know, which is (b) trivial, and (c) unavoidable, unalterable, natural. Emendation seems unnecessary.

17.52/1725 Exeunt] ROWE; *not in* Q1; Exit. Q4

Sc. 18] This edition; *not in* Q; Actus Quartus. F3; [ACT IV.] SCENE IV. MALONE

18.0.1/1725.1 Enter Gower] Q4; *not in* Q1

18.1/1726 long] Q1; longest Q4. Most editors adopt Q4, but leagues are of a fixed length: none of Shakespeare's other uses of *leagues* or *longest* encourages the emendation.

18.1/1726 make we] This edition (*conj.* Maxwell); make Q. Sisson and Hoeniger defend the metrical irregularity as deliberate archaizing, but there is nothing archaic—or indicative that the speech is by Gower in particular—in this passage: see Introduction.

18.2 an] Q (and)

18.3/1728 take] HUDSON; take our Q; take your MALONE

1730 (I) pard'ned] Q4; pardoned Q1

1731 (I) seu'rall] feuerall

18.7-8/1732-3 (L) Where...teach you] Q4; 4 lines Q1: liue| beseech you| gappes|

18.7/1732 sceane seemes] MAXWELL; fceanes feemes Q1; fceanes feeme Q4

18.8/1733 ith] MAXWELL (Bullen); with Q1; in Q4; i'the MALONE (Steevens)

1733 (I) teach you,] F4; ~. Q

1734 (I) storie,] F4; ~, Q

18.10/1735 the] Q2; thy Q1

1738 (I) along, behind,] DANIEL (*conj.* in Cambridge); ~, ~, Q

18.14/1739 gouerne, if] This edition (*conj.* Maxwell); ~, it, Q

1739 (I) mind,] MALONE; ~. Q1; ~, Q2

18.16/1741 Tyre] SCHANZER (W. S. Walker); time Q. An easy compositorial misreading and normalization.

18.17/1742 (L) Well...brought] Q4; 2 lines Q1: winds|

18.18/1743 his] MALONE; this Q

1743 (I) thought,] F4; ~, Q

18.19/1744 go one] MAXWELL (Malone); grone Q; grow on MALONE

18.19 on] Q (one)

1745 (I) gone;] F4; ~, Q1

18.21/1746 (L) Like...a while] Q4; 2 lines Q1: them|

18.22.1/1747.1 Dombe shew.] MALONE; *not in* Q

18.22.3/1747.3 in mourning garments] This edition; *not in* Q. See note to 17.0.1/1673.2.

18.22.4/1747.4 drawes the curtaine and] This edition (G.T.); *not in* Q. The tomb must be made visible to an audience between 18.0.1/1725.1 and 18.22.4/1747.4; this seems the most probable method, with the tomb being revealed to Pericles and the audience simultaneously. Editors since MALONE bring the tomb on with Gower, at 18.0.1/1725.1.

18.22.7-8/1747.7-8 followed...doore] This edition (G.T.); *not in* Q; Then CLEON and DIONYZA retire. MALONE; Then exeunt CLEON, DIONYZA, *and the rest* CAMBRIDGE

1748 (I) See] Gowr. See Q

18.24/1749 owde] MAXWELL (anon. *conj.*); olde Q

1751 (I) ore-showr'd,] F4; ~. Q1

18.29/1754 puts] MALONE; put Q

1754 (I) Sea, he beares,] MALONE (*subs.*); ~, ~, Q

1755 (I) teares,] ~. Q1

1756 (I) out.] ~, Q1

1756 (I) wit,] ~ :

18.32-3/1757-8 (L) The...Dionyza] MALONE; *1 line* Q

18.33.1/1758.1 He...tombe] MALONE (*subs.*); *not in* Q

18.34/1759 sweetest, best] MALONE (Steevens); fweeteft, and beft Q; sweet'st, and best STEEVENS (Malone); chastest, and most best P.A. (530)

1760 (I) withred] ROWE (wither'd); withered Q. P.A. has 'wythred' (530).

18.36-7/1761-2 In...good] P.A. (530). For Q's eight lines, see Additional Passages. Maxwell calls Q's alternative 'a shocking piece of fustian (for which one hopes the reporter is largely responsible)'; Hoeniger describes it as 'sheer poetic drivel'. But according to our textual hypothesis, the reporter cannot be held responsible, for Gower's speeches apparently do not derive from the reporter; and Hoeniger notes that the first couplet is based upon Gower. But there can be no doubt that P.A.'s text is much superior, poetically and dramatically, and we have therefore adopted it, assuming either (a) that P.A. represents Shakespeare's revised text, and Q a first shot later cancelled in performance, or (b) that P.A. is a revision (or alternative) by the collaborator Wilkins.

1766 (I) ordered,] Q4; ~ ; Q1

18.42/1767 Sceane] MALONE 2; Steare Q

1768 (I) welladay,] F4; ~. Q

Sc. 19] This edition; *not in* Q; [ACT IV.] SCENE V. MALONE

19.0.1/1770.1 A brothel signe.] This edition; *not in* Q. See note to 16.0.1/1524.2.

19.2/1772 2. GENTLEMAN] '2. Gent.' Q (text), Qb (c.w.); Gower. Qa (c.w.)

19.9/1779 Exeunt] F3; Exit. Q

19.9.1/1779.1 Enter Bawdes] Q. Editors since MALONE mark a new scene here, but it seems likely that the brothel sign remains on stage. Even if it does not, there need be no gap in time, and the place is clearly the same. The gentlemen are leaving the brothel; the bawds are ambiguously in or out of it, and see Lysimachus approaching; one goes in to fetch Marina; Lysimachus asks Marina to 'bring me to some priuate place' (19.97/1868). One tends to assume that the later part of the scene takes place 'in' the brothel, but the Jacobean stage need not have been perturbed by an ambiguous shift of locale in mid-scene.

19.9.1/1779.1 Pander, Bawd, and Boult] MALONE; *not in* Q

19.13/1783 the whole of] This edition (*conj.* Maxwell); a whole Q. In Q 'generation' must mean 'the whole body of individuals born about the same period' (*sb.* 5; never elsewhere in Shakespeare); the sense is possible, but of no special pertinence. 'The whole of procreation' is much more appropriate, especially as a suitably hyperbolic companion to the first half of the sentence; it also permits a Shakespearian pun on *whole* (= 'hole', vagina), supplying the female counterpart to Priapus.

19.21 cavalleria] Q1 (Caualereea); Caualeres Q4

19.24.1/1794.1 *Enter Lysimachus*] This edition; *after* 19.27/1793 Q

19.24.1/1794.1 *disguised*] This edition; *not in* Q

19.26 loon] Q (Lowne)

19.27/1797 custome] This edition; cuſtomers Q. The emendation permits a triple pun on 'customers, business patrons' (*sb.* 5; compare *Shrew* 4.3.99/1978, *Winter's Tale* 5.2.98/2785, and *Pericles* 16.134/1660), 'tradition, conventional practice' (*sb.* 1; here, the normal fate of women, normal practice in a brothel), and 'customary service done by feudal tenants to their lord, customary rent... tax or tribute' (*sb.* 3) or 'impost or duty... *esp.* that levied in the name of the king or sovereign authority upon merchandise... imported into his dominions' (*sb.* 4). The last sense is especially relevant to Marina in relation to Lysimachus.

19.29 to-bless] Q (to blesse)

1801 (I) may$_\wedge$ so,] Q4; ~, ~$_\wedge$ Q1

19.33/1803 iniquitie$_\wedge$ haue you,] Q; iniquity? Have you$_\wedge$ MALONE

19.37/1807 deede] Q5; deedes Q1. Hoeniger's claim that 'the plural form is not unusual' seems unfounded. His citations from *Miseries* and *The Knave in Grain* are irrelevant, because the wording in *Miseries* is 'and yet by light such deeds of darkness may not be', and in *The Knave* 'I defie thee, and thy deeds of darkness'. This is quite different from doing *the* deeds of darkness (M.J.).

19.40/1810 *Exit Pander*] This edition (G.T.); *not in* Q; *Exit Boult* WHITE. White's emendation entails further emendation of speech-prefixes; DYCE has Boult exit at 19.46/1816, where he has little time to re-enter, and exits without particular motive. The Pander, who has nothing else to do hereabouts, can exit on command.

19.45/1815 dignifies] Q4; dignities Q1

19.46/1816 a noble] This edition (M.J.); a number Q; an anchor SINGER; a maiden HUDSON 2; a punk SCHANZER; a pander KINNEAR (*conj.*); a wanton ANON. (*conj.* in Cambridge); a whore TIESSEN (*conj.*). Although Q produces an intelligible sentence, and so has been accepted by most recent editors, the resulting sense is lamentably feeble, and Malone was probably right in thinking Q corrupt. Our emendation assumes that Lysimachus compared his own hypocrisy to that of Boult, and the censor insisted on changing the word. See Introduction.

19.46.1/1816.1 *Enter Pander with Marina*] This edition (G.T.); *not in* Q1; *Enter Marina.* Q4; *Re-enter Boult with Marina.* DYCE (*after* 'you', 19.48/1818). Dyce's postponement of Marina's entrance, despite the implication of the dialogue, was designed to make more plausible his decision that Boult should fetch her.

19.47-8/1817-18 (L) Here... creature] MALONE; *verse* Q: stalke| you|

19.49-50/1819-20 (L) Faith... vs] MALONE; *verse* Q: Sea|

19.50.1/1820.1 *He pays the Bawd*] EDWARDS; *not in* Q

19.51-2/1821-2 (L) I... presently] MALONE; *verse* Q: word|

1821 (I) leaue:] MALONE; ~$_\wedge$ Q. Though Maxwell and Hoeniger retain Q, they can provide no parallels for its expression.

19.56-7/1826-7 honorably know] This edition (M.J.); note Q. Q is sensible but feeble. Marina picks up on 'honorable', saying that she will 'know' him virtuously (not carnally). The reporter repeated the wrong word ('note' instead of 'honorabl(y)').

19.69/1840 hers] This edition (G.T.); her Q. The emendation gives a pun on 'Honor'.

19.69-70/1841 goe thy wayes] Q. MALONE attributed these words to Lysimachus, taking them as a literal injunction to exit; but the phrase is often used metaphorically in reproach or exhortation, and in any case the Bawd might be hurrying her companions off stage.

19.70/1841 *Exit 3. Bawds*] MALONE (*subs.*); *not in* Q1; *Exit Baud* Q4

19.71/1842 Faire] This edition (G.T.); Now prittie Q. Lysimachus repeats 'prettie one' at 19.91/1862, and the Bawd so addresses Marina at 16.65/1589 (where it must be correct). For *faire one(s)* as a vocative, see *Henry V* 5.2.118/2973, *As You Like It* 4.3.76/2163, *Measure* 2.3.20/895, *All's Well* 2.1.99/658, and *Pericles* 21.55/2073.

19.73/1844 I] This edition (M.J.); Why, I Q. The word is metrically superfluous, and Lysimachus uses it again at 19.79/1850 and 19.86/1857 (and, in Q, 19.79/1850).

19.73/1844 name it but] EDWARDS (Hoeniger); name but Q; name't but F3

19.74-5/1845-6 (L) I... name it] ROWE; *1 line* Q

19.75-6/1846-7 (L) How... profession] This edition (*conj.* Brooks); *1 line* Q

19.77-8/1848-9 (L) Did... seuen] This edition (*conj.* Brooks); *prose* Q: gamester | at

19.78/1849 or] This edition (G.T.); or at Q. Superfluous extrametrical repetition.

19.78-9/1849-50 (L) Earlyer... one] This edition (*conj.* Brooks); *1 line* Q

19.79-80/1850-1 (L) Why... sale] This edition (*conj.* Brooks); *prose* Q

19.79/1850 Why] Q (confirmed by *P.A.* 535)

19.80/1851 Proclaimeth] This edition (G.T.); proclaimes Q

19.80/1851 you] This edition (*conj.* Brooks); you to be Q. Anticipation of the following line.

19.80/1851 Creature] Q. A syllable may be missing hereabouts, but *creature* is conceivably trisyllabic.

19.81-4/1852-5 (L) And doe... Prouince] This edition (G.T.); *prose* Q

19.81/1852 And] This edition (*conj.* Brooks); *not in* Q. 'A light syllable seems wanting. The *And* of surprised expostulation would sufficiently combine respect with reproach, and might easily slip the reporter's memory' (Brooks).

19.82/1853 intoo it] This edition (G.T.); intoo't Q

19.83/1854 bloud] This edition (G.T.); parts Q. Q's word could result from memorial substitution or censorship. Lysimachus' vague 'abilities' are not so pertinent here as his social status. Shakespeare often puns on *blood* in the sense 'sexual passion' (or 'sexual emission'), Marina would here declare 'honorable inherited rank', while implying 'instead of dishonorable passion'. Q's 'parts' would be politically innocuous, because a person of any rank might have 'honourable parts'; but 'honourable blood' (*Contention* 4.1.52/2063) specifically alludes to Lysimachus' aristocratic status, which was probably a sore point with the censor.

19.84/1855 whole Prouince] This edition (G.T.); fair town BROOKS (*conj.*); place Q. M.J. notes numerous repetitions of *place*, especially in this scene and Sc. 21; this one is particularly unfortunate, as in context *place* apparently means 'brothel'. Moreover, as with 'parts', Q here offers a vague and politically innocuous word; one suspects that the original was more provocative. For 'Prouince' see 21.50/2068. *P.A.* uses 'whole' of a political entity (city, kingdom, state) 10 times; it seems an appropriate adjective here, to fill out the metre. Marina has been told by the Bawd that Lysimachus is governor of 'this country', not just the 'city'.

19.85/1856 (L) What... am] This edition (G.T.); *prose* Q

19.85/1856 What,] This edition; Why, Q; Why? F3. Of Lysimachus' first seven speeches to Marina, four begin with 'Why', which in one or more of them may be intruded through recollection of the others (Hoeniger). See 19.73/1844. Three of the speeches are exasperated statements, which appropriately begin with 'Why'; only this is a surprised question, for which 'What!' seems more appropriate.

19.85/1856 inform'd] This edition (G.T.); made knowne vnto Q. Q's phrase (*made* or *make known unto*) is unparalleled in the canon; the verb could have been picked up from 22.33/2299 ('Made knowne her selfe...').

19.86-91/1857-62 (L) Why... authoritie] This edition (G.T.); *prose* Q

19.87/1858 seeds of shame, rootes of] This edition (G.T.); ſeeds and rootes of ſhame and Q. Q is unmetrical; a reporter could easily have repeated the wrong word ('and', rather than 'of'), confusing the construction by transposition of the two medial nouns in this group of four.

19.87.1/1858.1 *She weepes*] This edition; *not in* Q. See Twine (457) and *P.A.* (536). Q treats 19.87/1858 as the end of a speech (blank space to the end of the line) and indents 19.88/1859 as though it begins a new speech (though there is no new prefix). Something may be omitted here, which would prompt Lysimachus' change of direction.

19.88/1859 y'haue] This edition (M.J.); you haue Q. For the elision compare *Caesar* 2.1.236/798, *Timon* 5.1.74/2041, *Antony* 2.6.108, 2.7.24/1104, 1156, and Sonnet 120.6 (as well as three occasions in Fletcher's share of *All Is True*).

1859 (I) pow'r] power

19.89/1860 off] This edition (G.T.); *not in* Q. Compare *1 Henry VI* 4.4.21/1880 ('Keepe off aloofe') and *All's Well* 4.2.36-7/1895-6 ('Stand no more off, | But giue thy selfe vnto my sicke desires'), etc.

19.89/1860 alofe] ROWE; aloft Q

19.89/1860 a] This edition (G.T.); *not in* Q. In *P.A.* Lysimachus suspects Marina's tears at this point, thinking they are intended 'to drawe him to a more large expense' (535).

19.91-6/1862-7 can ... ling'ring] This edition; fhall not fee thee, or elfe looke friendly vpon thee, Q. See Introduction. This passage is adapted and versified from *P.A.* 535: 'vrging her, that he was the Gouernour, whose authoritie coulde wincke at those blemishes, her selfe, and that sinnefull house could cast vppon her, or his displeasure punish at his owne pleasure, which displeasure of mine, thy beauty shall not priuiledge thee from, nor my affection, which hath drawen me vnto this place abate, if thou with further lingering withstand me.' *P.A.*'s switch in mid-sentence into direct address strikingly suggests that Wilkins here echoes a dramatic text, and the content—the abuse of power by Lysimachus—is especially likely to have provoked the ire of the censor.

19.91-2/1862-3 can wincke at blemishes] This edition (G.T.); fhall not fee thee Q. See previous note. *P.A.*'s image here is definitely Shakespearian: compare 'the winking of Authoritie' (*K. John* 4.2.212/1833), *Henry V* 2.2.54, 5.2.297/661, 3157, *Macbeth* 1.4.54/287, etc. *P.A.* generalizes in a politically dangerous way; Q is specific ('thee') and innocuous.

19.92/1863 or can on faults looke friendly] This edition (G.T.); or elfe looke friendly vpon thee Q. *P.A.* has nothing corresponding to Q's phrase here. On the evidence of the rest of the passage Q has been censored to substitute an uncontroversial specific ('thee') for a dangerous generalization. Compare *Caesar* 4.2.146/1883: 'A friendly eye could neuer see such faults'. Q's contrast between not seeing (or 'winking') and looking upon in a friendly way seems genuine, and it leads naturally into the rest of the passage in *P.A.*

19.93/1864 at my pleasure] This edition (G.T.); *not in* Q; at his owne pleasure *P.A.*; then at will BULLOUGH (*conj.*). *P.A.*'s symmetry seems too good to destroy.

19.94-5/1865-6 From which displeasure, not thy beauty shall | Priuiledge] This edition (G.T.); *not in* Q; from which displeasure of mine, thy beauty shall not priuiledge thee from *P.A.*; From which thy beauty shall not privilege thee BULLOUGH (*conj.*). Bullough's reorganization of the syntax—omitting 'of mine', and having *from* begin the clause rather than end it, seems irresistible. His omission of *displeasure* is more dubious; if it is retained, the syntax and the verse arrangement are more muscular, and characteristic of Shakespeare's late style. With the exception of the omitted 'of mine', the text here retains *P.A.*'s words, but arranges them as late Shakesperian verse rather than Wilkinsian prose.

19.96/1867 here] This edition (*conj.* Bullough); *not in* Q; vnto this place *P.A.*

19.96/1867 ling'ring] This edition; lingering *P.A.* (535). All Shakespeare's 13 uses of this word mark the elision.

19.97/1868 (L) Come ... come] This edition (*conj.* Brooks); prose Q

19.98-100/1869-71 Let ... your selfe] This edition (G.T.); *not in* Q. These lines are adapted from *P.A.*: 'If as you say (my Lorde) you are the Gouernour, let not your authoritie, which should teach you to rule others, be the meanes to make you mis-gouerne your selfe' (535). Another politically sensitive sentiment. We have not taken over *P.A.*'s conditional clause, because in *Pericles* it is Marina who first identifies him as the Governor: *P.A.* has, under the influence of Twine, confused the exact order of events. (See Taylor, 'Transmission'.)

19.98/1869 not] This edition (*conj.* Bullough); *not in* Q; not your *P.A.*

19.98/1869 teaches] This edition (*conj.* Bullough); *not in* Q; should teach *P.A.*

19.99/1870 gouerne] This edition (G.T.); *not in* Q; rule *P.A.*

19.100/1871 much] This edition (G.T.); *not in* Q, *P.A.* A syllable seems to be missing; compare 'thy much misgouernment' (*Much Ado* 4.1.99/1744).

19.101-3/1872-4 (L) If ... of it] ROWE; prose Q

19.103-13/1874-84 What ... impouerish me] This edition (G.T.); *not in* Q. These lines are adapted from *P.A.*: 'What reason is there in your Iustice, who hath power ouer all, to vndoe any? If you take from mee mine honour, you are like him, that makes a gappe into forbidden ground, after whome too many enter, and you are guiltie of all their euilles: my life is yet vnspotted, my chastitie vnstained in thought. Then if your violence deface this building, the workemanship of heauen, made vp for good, and not to be the exercise of sinnes intemperaunce, you do kill your owne honour, abuse your owne iustice, and impouerish me.' (535).

19.103-113/1874-1884 (L) What ... impouerish me] This edition (*conj.* Bullough); prose *P.A.*

19.103/1874 reason's] This edition (*conj.* Bullough); *not in* Q; reason is there *P.A.*

19.106/1877 y'are] This edition (M.J.); you are *P.A.*. Shakespeare prefers this form of the contraction (53 times, to only 28 of 'you're'—only one in a text from authorial copy).

19.107/1878 whome after] This edition (*conj.* Bullough); *not in* Q; after whome *P.A.*

19.108-9/1879-80 of all their euilles | Your selfe are guiltie] This edition (G.T.); you are guiltie of all their euilles *P.A.* This transposition lets 'all' carry on immediately from 'too many', and postpones 'you are guiltie' to the climax of the sentence, where it is juxtaposed with the completion of the verse line ('*my* life is yet vnspotted'). *P.A.* offers instead normal prose word order.

19.109/1880 Your selfe] This edition (*conj.* Bullough); *not in* Q; you *P.A.* For the emphatic use of *your selfe* meaning 'you' compare *Richard III* 2.1.18/1059 ('your selfe is [Q 'are'] not exempt'), etc.

19.110/1881 eu'n] This edition; *not in* Q, *P.A.*; even BULLOUGH (*conj.*)

19.111/1882 deface] *P.A.* Compare 'his soul's fair temple is defaced' (*Lucrece* 719; of the effect of lust) and 'defacer of Gods handie worke' (*Richard III* 4.4.51/2556).

19.111/1882 building] *P.A.* Shakespeare often uses this word of the human frame (*Macbeth* 2.3.68/682, etc.); it retained a strong verbal sense, as 'a thing built' (*OED*), which leads naturally into the religious image of the next line.

19.112/1883 heau'n, you] This edition (M.J.); heauen, made vp for good, and not to be the exercise of sinnes intemperaunce *P.A.* 'Wilkins habitually pads out his lines with antitheses that elaborate on what something is not; neither the phrasing nor the imagery sounds Shakespearian, and the digression weakens the syntax of the conclusion to this part of her argument' (M.J.). Omitting these phrases produces either an hexameter or an extra stress at the caesura (both acceptable in Shakespeare's late verse).

19.112-13/1883-4 your ... your] This edition (*conj.* Bullough); *not in* Q; your owne ... your owne *P.A.*

19.113/1884 me.] *P.A.* continues: 'Why, quoth *Lysimachus*, this house wherein thou liuest, is euen the receptacle of all mens sinnes, and nurse of wickednesse, and how canst thou then be otherwise then naught, that liuest in it? It is not good, answered *Marina*, when you that are the Gouernour, who should liue well, the better to be bolde to punish euill, doe knowe that there is such a roofe, and yet come vnder it' (535). But this repeats 19.79-82/1850-3, which is essential to the progress of the dialogue (see Taylor, 'Transmission'); the reiteration could be defended as intensive, but neither text has Lysimachus pose this objection twice, and since the repetition is solely the result of conflation it seems to us undesirable. Moreover, *P.A.* also seems here to echo 19.200/1971 ('Olde receptacles . . . of filthe'). We have therefore ignored *P.A.*'s version of this question and answer.

19.114-119/1885-90 (My yet . . . maint'nance] This edition; *not in* Q. Taken from *P.A.*: 'Is there . . .' etc.

19.114/1885 (My] This edition (G.T.); Is there a necessitie *P.A.*; Is there a need BULLOUGH (*conj.*). The whole phrase is otiose, in Wilkins's wordiest prosy manner.

19.115/1886 strait] This edition (*conj.* Bullough); strait then thither *P.A.*

19.115/1886 Suppose] This edition (G.T.); Or if suppose *P.A.*; Or else, suppose BULLOUGH (*conj.*). There are no parallels in the Shakespeare canon for *P.A.*'s phrasing, which looks like Wilkins's syntax; Shakespeare often begins sentences with an imperative *Suppose*.

19.116/1887 too too many feele] The iteration of *too* is characteristic of Shakespeare (seven occurrences, including 'too too oft' and 'too too much'); it does not appear elsewhere in *P.A.*; or in *Miseries*. Collocation of *feel* and *too* occurs at *John* 3.4.59/1364, *All Is True* 1.2.129/387.

19.118/1889 The] This edition (*conj.* Bullough); *not in P.A.*

19.118/1889 it] This edition (*conj.* Bullough); it therefore *P.A.*

1890 (I) maint'nance] This edition (*conj.* Bullough); maintenance *P.A.*

19.120/1891 kneeling] This edition; *not in* Q. See Twine (457-8) and *P.A.*: 'which wordes (being spoken vpon her knees)' (536). In this speech Marina specifically supplicates Lysimachus; in the next, the gods.

19.120-3/1891-4 (L) For . . . Phisicke] MALONE 2; *prose* Q

19.122/1893 frāc't] This edition (G.T.); plac't Q. The fourfold repetition of 'place' in this and Marina's preceding speech in Q (19.81-4/1852-5; see note to 19.84/1855) smacks of error. Compare *Richard III* 4.5.2-3/2976-7: 'in the stye of this most deadlie bore, | My sonne George Stanlie is franckt vp in hold'. Q could result from misreading, facilitated by the three other occurrences of 'place' on this page. Alternatively, one might conjecture 'set' (presuming memorial error).

19.122/1893 Stie] Q; loathsome sty STEEVENS. The emendation was made for metrical reasons, treating 'Fortune . . . Stie' as one line. If an adjective were wanted 'nasty' (as at *Hamlet* 3.4.84/2298) would be more attractive.

19.126/1897 mooued] This edition; *not in* Q. See Twine: 'astonied and mooued with compassion' (457).

19.126-9/1897-1900 (L) I . . . it] ROWE; *prose* Q

19.127.1/1898.1 Hee lifts her vp with his hands] This edition; *not in* Q. From *P.A.* 536 ('. . . lift . . .).

19.128/1899 Though] This edition (G.T.); Had Q. See next note.

19.129/1900 hath] This edition (G.T.); had Q. These two simple alterations change Q's subjunctive sentence into a declarative one, thus producing the same sense as in *P.A.*: 'I hither came with thoughtes intemperate, foule and deformed' (536). Q's text here, in contrast to *P.A.*'s, again presents a sanitized portrait of Lysimachus, and although Q makes the best human sense possible of the resulting situation (see Taylor, 'Transmission'), censorship seems highly probable.

19.129/1900 alter'd] ROWE; altered Q

19.129/1900 He wipes the wet from her eyes] This edition; *not in* Q. See *P.A.*: 'So in steede of willing her to drie her eyes, hee wiped the wet himselfe off, and could haue found in his heart, with modest thoughts to haue kissed her, but that hee feared the offer would offend her' (536). Such a moment of innocent physical intimacy is normal and affecting in performance.

19.129/1900 and my foule thoughtes] This edition (G.T.); *not in* Q. See first note to 19.129/1900 for *P.A.*'s 'thoughtes . . . foule'. Neither *P.A.* nor *Miseries* has any other example of this collocation; Shakespeare has 'foule . . . thoughts' at *Contention* 4.7.100/2558, *Lucrece* 346 (of lust), *Othello* 2.1.258/940 (of lust), and *Antony* 4.10.17/2260.

19.130/1901 Thy . . . white] This edition; *not in* Q. From *P.A.*: 'the which your paines so well hath laued, that they are now white' (536).

19.130/1901 Thy] This edition (G.T.); the which your *P.A. P.A.* normally uses *you*, but in Q Lysimachus uses *thou* consistently from 19.90/1861 (where *P.A.* also switches to *thou*, though it does not keep up the distinction). *P.A.*'s 'the which' is a typical Wilkins construction, superfluous and extrametrical

19.130/1901 teares] This edition (*conj.* Bullough); paines *P.A.* Compare *More* II.C.108 ('Wash your foul minds with tears'), *Much Ado* 4.1.154-5/1799-1800 ('speaking of her foulenesse, | Washt it with teares'); Shakespeare speaks of *tears* 'washing' or 'bathing' something 9 times elsewhere.

19.130/1901 hath] *P.A.*; have BULLOUGH (*unrecorded emendation*)

19.130/1901 lau'd] *P.A.* (laued). This verb appears nowhere else in *P.A.* or *Miseries*; Shakespeare uses it 3 times elsewhere, including *OED*'s first recorded figurative use (*Macbeth* 3.2.34/978), and *Titus* 4.2.101-2/1628-9 ('Can neuer turne the swans blacke legs to white, | Although shee laue them howrely in the flood'). For the image, compare 'Cleanse the foule bodie of th'infected world' (*As You Like It* 2.7.60/983), 'I wash my braine, | And it grow fouler' (*Antony* 2.7.94-5/1227-8).

19.130/1901 that they're now] This edition (G.T.); that they are now *P.A.*; till they are BULLOUGH (*conj.*)

19.131-3/1902-4 I . . . honesty.] This edition (*conj.* Bullough); holde, heeres golde for thee, Q. From *P.A.*: 'and for my parte, who hither came but to haue payd the price, a peece of golde for your virginitie, now giue you twenty to releeue your honesty' (536).

19.131/1902 I came heere meaning but to pay] This edition (G.T.); who hither came but to haue payd *P.A.* The repetition of *hither*—*P.A.* has 'hither came' twice in the same sentence—is unlikely to be Shakespeare's; the rhythmically and syntactically flabby 'but to haue payd' sounds more like Wilkins than Shakespeare. Compare 'but he meanes to pay' (*1 Henry IV* 5.4.42/2839).

1903 (I) golde,] Q (*text*); ~, Q (*c.w.*)

19.132-3/1903-4 thy . . . thine] This edition (G.T.); your . . . your *P.A.* See note to 19.112-13/1883-4.

19.132/1903 virginitie] *P.A.* In *P.A.* (as in Twine) Lysimachus has taken pains to ensure that he is Marina's first customer; he therefore literally pays for her 'virginitie'. In Q he simply arrives on the scene as a regular customer, so that he did not literally come for the explicit purpose of buying her virginity. Nevertheless, he is assured (18.47-8/1817-18) that she is a virgin, before he agrees to pay. In performance this sort of minor contradiction is not noticed, and Shakespeare's plays are full of examples. If emendation were necessary, one might read 'impurity' (G.T.).

19.133/1904 Heeres] This edition (*conj.* Bullough); now giue you *P.A.* The emendation in fact reverts to Q's wording ('holde, heeres golde for thee').

19.134-5/1905-6 (L) Perseuer . . . thee] ROWE; *prose* Q

19.134/1905 Perseuer still] STEEVENS; perfeuer Q. *Persever* is always accented on the second syllable elsewhere, and *clear* never elsewhere disyllabic, so Q is metrically defective: either 'cleare' should be replaced by a disyllabic adjective, or an adverb added after 'perseuer'. The use of *clear* is demonstrably Shakespearian. Of appropriate monosyllabic adverbs, *fast* ('continue fast', *Cymbeline* 1.6.138) seems inappropriate to the 'way' metaphor; for *true* there are no close parallels; but 'continue(s) still' occurs 3 times (*1 Henry VI* 4.1.11/1717 ('still continue'), *Contention* 4.8.17/2699, *Antony* 4.6.29/2178). And see the corresponding speech in *P.A.*: 'continue still to all so . . . It shall become you still to be euen as you are' (536).

19.135/1906 good Gods] Q; gods STEEVENS. 'The' (or 'you') 'good gods' occurs at *Timon* 4.1.37/1373, *Antony* 3.4.15, 5.2.217/1430, 2873, *Coriolanus* 3.1.291, 4.1.57, 5.2.77/1736, 2133, 2876, *Pericles* 11.37/1166, *Cymbeline* 3.2.29/1303 and 5.5.103/2609.

19.136/1907 The] This edition; For me be you thoughten, that I came with no ill intent, for to me Q. Q continues its excuse of Lysimachus' behaviour; its words, whether or not accurately reported, belong to the censored version of the text. As for Q, 'For me' suspiciously repeats the opening of 19.120/1891 (Marina's speech), and is duplicated by 'to me' below. Q1's 'be you thoughten, that' is omitted by Q4; Edwards says of it, 'This is not English, and can hardly be the true reading'. But Deighton noted that participles in -*en* are frequent in Shakespeare; more particularly, for two such participles Shakespeare provides *OED*'s only examples: 'moulten' (*1 Henry IV* 3.1.148/1627) and 'sweaten' (*Macbeth* 4.1.81/1372). *OED* itself notes that *thoughten* here was probably formed by analogy with *boughten*. Unusual word-formation is more characteristic of Shakespeare than of a reporter.

19.137/1908 (L) Fare . . . vertue] This edition (G.T.); *prose* Q. MALONE divided after 'and' (see next notes). A line-divided foot (vilely | Fare).

19.138/1909 The . . . made,] This edition (*conj.* Maxwell); *not in* Q. In *P.A.* this phrase immediately follows 'a peece of goodnesse' and precedes 'and if that any shall inforce you ill, if you but send to me, I am your friend' (536). Compare 'wrought by nature' (*Errors* 1.1.34/34), and 'for a woman wert thou first created, | Till Nature as she wrought thee fell a-doting' (Sonnet 20), and *Cymbeline* 2.4.72-5/1074-7, where a tapestry of Cleopatra is described as 'A peece of Worke . . . so rarely, and exactly wrought'. The juxtaposition of *Nature* and *piece* is equally Shakespearian: see 'Natures peece, 'gainst Fancie' (*Antony* 5.2.98/2754) and 'O ruind peece of nature' (*History of Lear* 20.129/2458). Shakespeare similarly expresses superlative praise in calling Desdemona 'Thou cunning'st patterne of excelling nature' (*Othello* 5.2.11/2908), Helen 'the most virtuous gentlewoman, that euer Nature had praise for creating' (*All's Well* 4.5.9-10/2326-7), and Rosalind as Nature's distillation of the graces of all other women into one body (*As You Like It* 3.2.138-51/1282-95). The collocation 'Nature made' occurs 6 times. Nature is a particularly important concept in Shakespeare's late plays, from *Timon* and *All's Well* to *Cymbeline*. Finally, with this added line Lysimachus' reference to Marina's 'training' follows naturally: he moves from nature to nurture, in a traditional topos.

19.139/1910 (L) And . . . noble] This edition (G.T.); *prose* Q (& . . .). MALONE divides after 'theefe' (as here), but puts 'And' on the previous line.

19.139/1910 not] This edition (G.T.); *not but* Q. *Doubt* can be used with or without 'but', to produce the same meaning; an easy memorial error, which here disrupts the metre. M.J. observes that 'I doubt not but' recurs at 19.209/1980 (in Marina's speech, where it is confirmed by *P.A.*) and at 19.221-2/1992-3; its occurrence here is thus especially likely to be memorial in origin.

19.140/1911 (L) A . . . theefe] ROWE; *prose* Q

19.141/1912 (L) That . . . golde] This edition (G.T.); *prose* Q

19.141/1912 honour] This edition (G.T.); *goodnes* Q. Q's word is suspicious, given 'good' in the next line (which idiomatically must be right); nor is it easy to see how anyone could rob Marina of her *goodness*. Q could easily be a synonym substitution for 'honour', which Shakespeare frequently uses in the sense 'chastity': see especially Giacomo's 'I haue pick't the lock, and ta'ne | The treasure of her Honour' (*Cymbeline* 2.2.41-2/838-9). Despite her *goodness*, Marina's *chastity* could be stolen—as Boult prepares to do when Lysimachus leaves. And in *P.A.* Marina later accuses Boult of trying 'to robbe me of mine honour' (538), which supports the emendation.

19.141/1912 hold, heeres more golde,] This edition (G.T.); hold, heeres more golde for thee, Q (*after* 'noble'). This sentence is of a kind easily misplaced by a reporter, since it could be fitted anywhere in the speech. In Q it interrupts the metrical flow and has to be treated as an isolated mid-speech half-line, and the end of the speech is metrically awkward. Placed after rather than before the sentence ('A curse . . . honour'), it contributes to an acceptable pentameter, with a feminine caesura (the commonest of metrical licences). The omission of 'for thee' seems desirable not only metrically, but because the words are superfluous, and suspiciously repeat 19.132/1903.

19.142/1913 (L) If . . . good] MALONE 2; *prose* Q; me| STEEVENS; dost| DYCE. An acceptable hexameter.

19.142.1-2/1913.1-3 *standing . . . out*] This edition; *not in* Q. From *P.A.* (537), with 'hee' for '*Lysimachus*'. All editors since MALONE add '*Enter Boult*' before this speech, but it seems reasonably clear that Boult is—as his profession requires—simply waiting outside the door; thus, when Lysimachus makes to exit, he opens the door and discovers Boult. Boult would hardly enter without warning, when a woman is entertaining a client.

19.144-6/1915-7 (L) Auaunt . . . Away] ROWE; *prose* Q

1917 (I) ouer-whelme] Q4; ouer-|whelme

19.146/1917 *Exit*] ROWE; *not in* Q

19.151-55/1922-6 come . . . say] Q. Maxwell, noting that the 'substance' of these lines recurs at 19.177-9/1948-51, condemned them as 'suspicious', concluding that the wording 'prob. belongs in the later passage'. But 'weele haue no more Gentlemen driuen away' seems to belong here (Hoeniger) and it is not clear that Boult himself intends to rape Marina here (as Maxwell assumes). Moreover, though Maxwell claims that *P.A.* 'has nothing corresponding to this passage', it has nothing corresponding to 19.147-50/1918-22 either, and as a narrative has less need to allow a reasonable interval before the entrance of the other bawds.

19.154/1925 executioner shal doe] This edition (G.T.); *hāg-man fhal execute* Q. The passage clearly puns on 'maiden-head', as at *Romeo* 1.1.20-5/34-9; but there the head is 'cut off', as we would expect, rather than hung. Q's 'hāg-man' is especially suspicious, not only because it makes poor sense but because—as M.J. notes—'the common hang-man' recurs at 19.201/1972 (Marina's speech), where 'hang-man' seems clearly correct; memorial contamination seems probable. 'Common executioner' occurs at *As You Like It* 3.5.3/1724 and *Measure* 4.2.8-9/1728-9; the reporter might well have used the key word as a verb ('execute') when it should have been a noun ('executioner'), under the influence of 'hang-man'.

19.154/1925 weele] This edition; *come your way, weele* Q. The pointless repetition of this catch-phrase—three times in five lines here, and nine times in the brothel scenes—almost certainly derives in part from the reporter. This instance is particularly suspicious: 19.151/1922 is necessary, and 19.155/1926 a deliberate repetition of the first ('. . . I say'), but the present one serves no purpose, rhymes awkwardly with 'away' and 'say', and separates 'executioner' from 'Gentlemen', thus obscuring the point that if Marina refuses the latter she shall get the former.

19.155.1/1926.1 *Bawd and Pander*] MAXWELL; *Bawdes* Q1; *Bawd* ROWE. Maxwell retains and interprets Q's plural on the grounds that 'it is a pity to edit away any scrap of evidence'. Moreover, *P.A.* has 'the whole swarme of bawdes . . . rushing in hastily vppon' Marina and tells us even more specifically that 'the man and wife (though both bawdes) departed', leaving Marina with Boult (537). These details cannot be taken into *P.A.* from Twine, who has only a single master bawd, and they strongly confirm Q's plural. See 19.166/1937.

19.160/1931 She] ROWE; *He* Q

19.166/1937 PANDER] This edition (G.T.); *Bawd.* Q. Q brings the Pander on stage (see 19.155.1/1926.1), and it seems unlikely that he should remain completely silent. Of the available speeches, 19.156/1927 clearly, and 19.172-6/1943-7 probably ('the way of wemen-kinde'), belong to the Bawd. Such a speech-prefix error would be especially likely after a run of alternating *Bawd/Boult* prefixes. In Twine the Master Bawd (a male) gives Boult this order; in *P.A.* Marina later says that Boult goes about 'to doe an office at their setting on, which thy master himselfe hath more pitty then to attempt' (538), which suggests that the Pander himself gave Boult the order.

19.167/1938 ice] This edition (M.J.); *glaff* Q. Compare 'the yce of chastity' (*As You Like It* 3.4.16/1682), 'chaste as yce' (*Hamlet* 3.1.138/1674), 'Chaste as the Isicle' (*Coriolanus* 5.3.65/2975), 'to breake the ice' (*Shrew* 1.2.267/793), and 'colde as a Snowball' (above). See also the semi-proverbial 'break ice in one place, it will crack in more'—with a sexual meaning (M.J.).

19.176/1947 Exeunt . . . Pander] MAXWELL; not in Q1; Exit. Q4
19.177/1948 catching . . . hand] This edition; not in Q. From *P.A.* (537).
19.186-7/1957-8 (L) Neither . . . commañd] ROWE; *prose* Q
19.186/1957 can be] This edition (G.T.); are Q; are yet ROWE. Rowe recognized that the metre is defective but his addition—which duplicates 'are yet' in 19.202/1973—has nothing to recommend it. 'Can be' sustains the idiom of the question and answer (Canst . . . to be . . . to bee), alliterates, and avoids the lame repetition of 'are . . . art'.
19.188-9/1959-60 (L) Thou . . . thee] This edition (G.T.); *prose* Q; fiend| ROWE
19.188/1959 place] This edition (G.T.); place for which Q. Q's syntax is contorted and confused; metrically, 'for which' forces an awkward enjambment after 'feende'. If we omit these words, the sense is clear, and the line breaks naturally after 'hell'. See 19.189/1960.
19.189/1960 change with thee] This edition (G.T.); change Q. For Shakespearian examples of '*with* before the person with whom the exchange is made' see Schmidt. See 19.188/1959: the reporter seems to have chosen the alternative construction, and then confused it. The recurring and characteristic emphasis on 'thee' is more dramatic than the medial syntactical contortion 'for which'.
19.190/1961 (L) Thou . . . cuſterell] STEEVENS; *prose* Q; every| MALONE
19.190/1961 Thou] This edition (G.T.); Thou art the Q. Q's extra words are redundant, and extrametrical, forcing editors into the grotesque enjambment 'every | cuſterell'; reporters often make explicit such implicit words. At 19.144/1915, moreover, Q has 'thou damned door-keeper' (probably by contamination from this passage).
1961 (I) eu'ry] euery
1961 (I) cuſterell] cuſterell
19.191-2/1962-3 (L) That . . . rogue] MALONE; *prose* Q
19.191/1962 Tib] Q; penny Tib G.T. *conj.* The line is short by a foot, and the only plausible location for an addition is before 'Tib'. For *penny* as a derisive adjective compare 'penny cord' (*Henry V* 3.6.46/1441, *Cymbeline* 5.5.260/2766). *OED* cites examples of *penny* '(of a person) that sells something or does some work for a penny or at a cheap rate; here, engaged in mean or inferior work' (*sb.* 11); examples from this period include 'penny foot-post' (Fletcher, *The Chances*) 'penny Poet' (Kemp, *Nine Daies Wonder*) and 'penny-wits' (H. Hutton, 1619); see also 'Penibag' (*Staple of News*), 'pennie-bench Theatres' (*Satiromastix*, 4.2.53), 'penny-father' (several times in Nashe).
19.192/1963 To th'] This edition; To the Q
19.192/1963 eu'ry] euery Q; each STEEVENS
19.193-4/1964-5 (L) Thy . . . lungs] ROWE; *prose* Q
19.199/1970 (L) Doe . . . emptie] MALONE; *prose* Q; dost| ROWE
19.200-2/1971-3 (L) Olde . . . this] ROWE; *prose* Q; receptacles| HUDSON
19.200/ sew'rs] Q (ſhores)
19.201/1972 publike] This edition (G.T.); common Q. The repetition of this adjective in the same position from the line above is suspicious enough; but Q also has 'common hang-man' at 19.154/1925 (see note). Shakespeare uses *public* as an epithet of contempt elsewhere; synonym substitution, by reporter or compositor, would be easy.
19.202/1973 these] This edition (G.T.); theſe wayes Q. The omitted word is extrametrical and superfluous: 'occupations, offices, employments' are implied, in any case, and 'wayes' does not make 'these' any less vague. M.J. conjectures 'Any employment is yet better than this'.
19.203/1974 (L) For . . . speak] ROWE; *prose* Q
19.204/1975 (L) Would . . . thee] This edition (G.T.); *prose* Q
19.204/1975 deere,] This edition; deere, that the gods wold safely deliuer me from this place: Q. As M.J. notes, Q repeats 19.124/1895 (*that the gods would* set *me free from this* vnhalowed *place*); in the earlier position this exclamation is clearly authoritative, but here it is much more dubious. It produces an unassimilated mid-speech part-line, abruptly changes the subject from Boult to Marina, and interrupts the sequence 'too *dear* . . . *gold* for thee . . . if that thy master would *gain*'. It is also clearly corrupt metrically, and where it differs from 19.124/1895 is undistinguished verbally. *P.A.*, which paraphrases this passage closely, has Marina move from abusing Boult to offering him money; there is nothing comparable to this exclamation (538). Nor does *safely deliver* occur anywhere else in the Shakespeare canon. It seems best to omit the exclamation altogether.
19.204/1975 heers] This edition; here, heers Q; here, here is STEEVENS. Q's first word is extrametrical and superfluous, and the kind of deictic interpolation to which actors are prone. The only comparable juxtaposition occurs at *Troilus* 1.2.177-8/323-4 ('Heere, here, here's an excellent place, here wee may see most brauely'), where *here* is a specific on-stage place, and the repetition characterizes Pandarus.
19.205/1976 (L) If . . . me] MALONE 2; *prose* Q
19.205/1976 make gaine] HUDSON 2; gaine Q; gain aught MALONE; have gain KINNEAR (*conj.*); get gain ANON. (*conj.* in Cambridge). The line is metrically defective; of suggested metrical improvements, only Hudson's is paralleled in Shakespeare (*Othello* 5.1.14/2780, 'makes my gaine').
19.206-8/1977-9 (L) Proclaime . . . teache] ROWE; *prose* Q
19.208/1979 I will] ROWE; will Q
19.209-10/1980-1 (L) I . . . schollers] MALONE; *prose* Q
19.213-14/1984-5 (L) And . . . house] ROWE; *prose* Q ('And . . .')
19.217/1988 women] Q4; woman Q1
1990 (I) but] Q4; But (*first word of line*) Q1
1994.1 *The signe is remoued*] This edition; *not in* Q
Sc. 20] This edition; *not in* Q; ACT V MALONE
2000 (I) berry,] Q4; ~. Q1
2001 (I) ene] euen
2001 (I) Roses,] MALONE; ~ˬ Q1; ~, Q4
2002 (I) Silke, Twine,] Q2; ~ˬ ~, Q1
20.8 twin] Q (Twine)
20.13/2007 Wee] This edition (G.T.); Where wee Q. Q's 'Where' is not only extrametrical but superfluous; it complicates the syntax pointlessly, and contributes to a clutter of repetition in 20.9-15/2005-9 ('here . . . Where . . . there . . . Where . . . Heere where'; see following notes). An easy interpolation in this context, by reporter or compositor.
20.13/2007 waues there him tost] This edition (G.T.); wee there him left Q; we there him lost MALONE. Q is bathetic, and does not rhyme; Malone retrieves a rhyme, but it is difficult to see how the audience has 'lost' Pericles, or why such stress should be placed on a contrast between 'left' and 'loss'. Since the beginning of this line ('wee left him') has clearly contaminated the ending ('wee . . . him left'), the contamination—by reporter or compositor—might have affected the subject as well as the verb. For the collocation of 'Waues . . . tost' see 5.34/524; waves and 'windes' (20.14/2008) are proverbially coupled.
20.14/2008 Whence] STEEVENS; Where Q
20.14/2008 tofore] This edition (G.T.); before Q. Editors regularly note that this line echoes Gower's 'tofore the wynde thei driue' (1615); 'before' for the rare 'tofore' would be an easy substitution for any compositor.
2010 (I) Anchor] Anchor Q
20.20/2014 feruer] Qb; former Qa
2016 (I) *Pericles,*] MALONE (*subs.*); ~ˬ Q
20.22/2016 the] MALONE; his Q
Sc. 21] This edition; *not in* Q; [ACT V.] SCENE I. MALONE
21.0.1-2/2018.1-2 *aboue*; *below, at the first doore enter*] This edition (G.T.); *not in* Q. MALONE added, as a head-note to this scene, 'On board *Pericles' ship, off* Mitylene. *A close Pavilion on deck, with a curtain before it; Pericles within it, reclined on a couch. A barge lying beside the Tyrian vessel*'; moreover, he had Helicanus enter 'to' the Sailors, rather than vice versa (as in Q). The editorial stage directions here and below (21.1/2019, 21.5 and 21.5.1/2023 and 2023.1, 21.6/2024, 21.8.1-2/2026.1-2) attempt both to make the stage action clearer, and to indicate the ways in which Jacobean theatres created the impression of a shipboard scene by

using the permanent features of the stage (rather than through novelistic or scenic devices like those suggested by Malone and other editors). Even by its own standards, Q makes a mess of the action and dialogue of the first portion of this scene, which is full of short speeches and complicated comings and goings—a nightmare for a reporter.

21.0.2-3/2018.2-3   one ... Metaline] MALONE (subs.); not in Q
21.1/2019   SAYLER OF TYRE (to Sayler of Metaline)] MALONE; 1. Say. Q
21.1/2019   Lord ... Sir] This edition (M.J.); Where is Lord Helicanus? hee can refolue you, | O here he is Sir Q
21.2-4/2020-2 (L)   There ... will] STEEVENS; prose Q
21.3/2021   In it] This edition (G.T.); and | in it is Q
21.5/2023   Exit ... doore] This edition (G.T.); not in Q
21.5.1/2023.1   Exit Helicanus aboue] This edition (G.T.); not in Q
21.6/2024   SAYLER OF TYRE] MALONE; 2. Say. Q
21.6/2024   Ho] This edition; Ho Gentlemen Q
21.6/2024   from below] This edition (G.T.); not in Q
21.6/2024   to them enter Helicanus] This edition (G.T.); not in Q
21.6/2024   What is your Lordships pleasure] This edition (G.T.); Doeth your Lordfhip call Q. See Cymbeline 2.3.78/927, 'what's your Lordships pleasure?'
21.7-8/2025-6 (L)   Gentlemen ... fairely] STEEVENS; prose Q
21.7/2025   some] This edition (G.T.); there is fome Q
21.8/2026   you] Q6; not in Q; thee F3; ye ROWE
21.8.1-2/2026.1-2   at ... Metaline] This edition; not in Q; The Gentlemen and the two Sailors descend, and go on board the barge. Enter, from thence, Lysimachus attended; the Tyrian Gentlemen, and the two Sailors. MALONE
21.9/2027   SAYLER OF METALINE] This edition (G.T.); Hell. Qa; 1. Say. Qb; Tyr. Sail. MALONE
21.9/2027 (L)   This ... you] This edition (G.T.); prose Q; Sir| would| MALONE. (See following note.)
21.9/2027   This] This edition; Sir, this Q
21.9/2027   ought] This edition; ought you would Q
21.11-12/2029-30 (L)   And ... doe] MALONE; prose Q
21.11/2029   Syr] MALONE; not in Q. See 21.17/2035.
21.12-16/2030-4 (L)   You ... are] ROWE; prose Q
21.13/2031   I ... Metaline,] This edition (G.T.); Hell. First what is your place? | Ly. I am the Gouernour of this place you lie before. Q. Q places its exchange after 21.16/2034, where it intrudes unnaturally between Lysimachus' question and Helicanus' answer, and rudely implies 'I won't answer you until I know who you are'. Such a tone seems inappropriate to Helicanus' own expressed desire that Lysimachus be greeted 'fairely' (21.8/2026). Moreover, the issue naturally arises as a part of the initial formalities, and Lysimachus' identification of himself leads naturally into the explanation for his visit. Finally, it is nonsensical for Helicanus to ask 'what is thy place' when he has already been informed of it (21.3/2021). A reporter could remember that Lysimachus' rank entered into this exchange, without remembering its exact place or form. (M.J. alternatively conjectures that the whole exchange should be omitted.)
21.13/2031   Metaline] This edition (G.T.); this place you lie before Q. Another of Q's many repetitions of the vague 'place', coupled with a repetition of 'before' from his preceding speech.
21.17/2035   Our] This edition (M.J.); Syr our Q. The reporter appears to have transposed this word from one Helicanus speech to another: here it is extrametrical, but in 21.11/2029 it would rectify Q's otherwise defective metre and balance the 'Syr' in Lysimachus' greeting.
21.17/2035   our King] This edition; the King Q
21.17-20/2035-8   Our ... griefe] STEEVENS; prose Q
21.21/2039   grew] This edition (G.T.); is Q. Q's verb is unidiomatic and flat. Shakespeare often uses grow of the development of mental states: 'from whence his sorrows grow' (Romeo 1.1.151/165), etc. He juxtaposes 'grow' and 'ground' at Richard II 5.3.104/2478, and similarly puns on 'ground' at LLL Add. Pass. A.8, Richard III 3.7.49/2039, and 2 Henry IV 4.1.107-8/1955-6. He also juxtaposes the verb 'grow' with 'tedious' (Measure 2.4.9/928), 'told over' (Dream 5.1.23-6/1723-6: see next note), and 'griefe' (History of Lear 24.213/2996).
2039 (I)   distemp'rature] diftemperature
21.22-4/2040-2 (L)   Twould ... wife] MALONE; prose Q
21.22/2040   tell it ouer] This edition (G.T.); repeat Q. Q is a foot short—especially improbable here, since the next line is also short. Q's verb may have been contaminated by 4.31/414 ('grewe odious to repeat'); 'repeat' here superfluously suggests that Helicanus has had to tell the story before. For 'tell it ouer' compare Dream 5.1.23/1723, Richard III 4.4.39/2544 ('Tell ouer your woes againe'), Othello 3.3.173/1621—all relevant to this passage.
21.23/2041   precious] This edition (G.T.); not in Q. The line is a foot short; MALONE read 'grief of all' (a lame filler). Shakespeare's favourite modifier for loss is dear (7 times); costly (Troilus 4.1.62/2147) is a variant of the same image. He only once juxtaposes grief and loss, as here: 'my griefe in such a precious losse'. (Troilus 4.5.10/2299). Precious, like dear, plays upon the material and spiritual sense of loss; precious is elsewhere juxtaposed with lose or lost (Romeo 1.1.230/244, Lear: History 24.187/2970, Tragedy 5.3.182/2822, Kinsmen 5.3.19/2371), or in similar contexts (Venus 824, Sonnet 30.6, 77.2, Tempest 1.2.242/308, K. John 4.3.40/1931). But the most striking parallel is Winter's Tale 4.2.23-5/1446-7, where Leontes' 'losse of his most precious Queene & Children, are euen now to be a-fresh lamented'.
21.25-7/2043-5 (L)   See ... any] STEEVENS (subs.); prose Q; bootless| MALONE
21.25/2043   See him Sir you may] This edition (G.T.); You may Q. Three syllables seem to be missing; STEEVENS read 'You may indeed, sir'—which is lame, and leaves a defective caesura. More attractive than a vague intensive like 'indeed' would be an emphasis upon the verb see: 'you can see him, but that's all'. See is repeated in single or adjacent lines 78 times in the canon; even if we exclude mere repetitions (see, see; let me see, etc.), there are 54 examples, many involving echo across a question and answer, and/or between speeches (Dream 3.1.109-11/896-8, 5.1.177-8/1877-8, Lear: History 14.80-1/1003-4, Tragedy 3.7.80-1/1982-3, etc.). The echoing by one speaker of the last words of the previous one, and chiasmus, are also characteristic rhetorical devices. Shakespeare juxtaposes sir and may 7 times (Coriolanus 2.3.3, 2.3.147/1187, 1328, Richard III 1.4.95/860, etc.), sir and see 12 times (Antony 3.11.30/1730, Twelfth Night 1.5.106/388, etc.).
2044 (I)   bootlesse,̣ is] Q4; bootleffe. Is Q1
21.26/2044   sight, hee,] Qb; ~,̣ fee, Qa
21.27/2045   any. LYSIMACHUS] Q4; any, Q1
21.27/2045   Let me yet] This edition (G.T.); yet let me Q. Q is metrically anomalous, and could easily arise from transposition (memorial or compositorial). Compare 'O let vs yet' (Henry V 2.2.47/654), 'Let me yet know' (Twelfth Night 2.1.8/593).
21.28/2046   HELICANUS] Q4; Lyf. Q1
21.28/2046   Helicanus ... Pericles] EDWARDS; not in Q; Pericles discovered MALONE
21.28/2046   lying : ... fingers,] This edition; not in Q. Detail from P.A. (541), developed from Twine (462).
21.28/2046   and attired in sacke-cloth] MAXWELL (Wilson); not in Q
21.28-9/2046-7   person,|,Till] Q4; ~. | Hell. ~ Q1
21.29-30/2047-8 (L)   Till ... this] MALONE; prose Q
21.29/2047   of] This edition (conj. Hoeniger); that Q. Q inevitably suggests that he was driven mad on one night; Hoeniger's conjecture more plausibly specifies that the disaster itself—not the madness—occurred on one night (Thaisa's death, leading to his separation from Marina).
21.29/2047   night] MALONE; wight Q
21.31/2049 (L)   Sir ... sir] This edition (M.J.); prose Q; hail| MALONE; you| DYCE
21.31   Sir, King,] ~,̣ ~,̣ Q. Editors usually interpret Q as 'Sir King'; dramatically, it seems more likely that 'Sir' and 'King' are alternative vocatives.
21.31/2049   all haile] This edition (M.J.); all haile, the Gods preferue

you Q. Q repeats 21.10/2028, where the phrase follows 'Hayle reuerent Syr' (as here it precedes 'haile royall sir'). At 21.10/2028 the phrase cannot be disentangled from the dialogue; here it is superfluous, extrametrical, and different in character from the rest of the speech.

21.31.1/2049.1 *Pericles . . . pillow*] This edition; *not in* Q. From *P.A.* 541 ('hee shruncke . . .').

21.33-4/2051-2 (L) Sir . . . him] MALONE 2; *prose* Q

21.34-7/2052-5 (L) Tis . . . ports] MALONE; *prose* Q

21.36/2054 choife] STEEVENS; chofen Q. An easy graphic or memorial error.

21.36/2054 allarum] This edition (G.T.); allure Q. *Allure* seems singularly inappropriate, as though Marina—who has hitherto been remarkable for cooling ardour—were expected to arouse Pericles sexually; it also interrupts the development of imagery from 'harmonie' to 'battrie' and 'defend'. 'Allarum', by contrast, naturally mediates between 'win' and 'battrie', as well as sustaining the aural imagery. Shakespeare elsewhere uses the word figuratively: see *Othello* 2.3.24/1029 ('when she speakes, is it not an alarme to loue?'), *Venus* 424, 'To loues allarmes it will not ope the gate . . . they make no battry'), *Macbeth* 2.1.53/531, *Lear*: *History* 6.52/929, *Tragedy* 2.1.52/929, *Kinsmen* 5.2.13/2297 ('th'allarme to whispers', i.e. incitement to love-talk). The whole sentence plays upon the conceits that war has a harmony, and that love is like both war and music. Shakespeare often thinks of alarums as occurring at night, rousing people from sleep.

21.37 deafened] Q (defend)

21.37/2055 ports] MAXWELL (Steevens); parts Q

21.38-41/2056-9 (L) Which . . . side] This edition (G.T.); *prose* Q; stopp'd| of all| upon| against| MALONE. Malone's arrangement produces a mid-speech part-line, and two adjacent lines ending in prepositions. The alternative is regular, except for a line-divided foot (happie | As).

21.38/2056 in all] This edition (G.T.); is all Q; all as STEEVENS. Steevens's conjecture does nothing to remedy the central difficulty with Q, that Marina can hardly be called 'comprehensively fortunate' or even 'completely contented'. For the idiom *happy in*, meaning 'possessed of, endowed with [an accomplishment or talent]', compare *Two Gentlemen* 4.1.33/1523 and *Cymbeline* 3.4.175/1637. Marina has every desirable talent, as well as beauty—praise much more relevant to this speech than Q.

2057 (I) fair'st] This edition (G.T.); faireft Q. STEEVENS transposed 'of all' to precede 'the fairest', but it is simpler to assume mere failure to mark the required elision.

21.39/2057 among] This edition (G.T.); and Q; and with MALONE; Is, with STEEVENS. However one construes the passage, Lysimachus must mean to say where *both* Marina and her companions can be found. Compare 'among maids' (*Winter's Tale* 4.4.241/1847), 'Among my Maids' (*All Is True* 3.1.74/1384), 'among falce mayds' (*Troilus* 3.2.186/1761).

21.39/2057 maides] Q; maid SCHANZER. Schanzer assumes that Q's 'es' is an error for 'is', thus supplying the usual editorial verb. But why should Lysimachus specify a single particular 'maid' here? Q gives us, more naturally, Marina in the company of a group of young women, one of whom later comes to the ship with her.

21.40/2058 Dwells now i'th'] This edition (G.T.); now vpon the Q; is now upon | The MALONE; now within | The STEEVENS. Q lacks a verb, and is unmetrical; Malone supplies the commonest and least specific of verbs—producing the uncharacteristic flatness of three successive clauses governed by the same lame copula (are . . . is . . . is); and Malone confesses, 'I know not how she could be *upon*' a shelter.

21.41/2059 Goe fetch her hither.] This edition; *not in* Q; *He whispers one of the attendant Lords* MALONE. Edwards suggests that 'a nod would do'. But any such interpolated stage direction is unnecessary, elliptical, potentially confusing, and uncharacteristic of contemporary stagecraft, which abounds in explicit directions for attendants to go fetch things or people. Lysimachus' speech also, however aligned, ends in an incomplete line. Why should he *whisper* 'Go get her', when he could say it aloud? 'Goe fetch him/them hither' occurs at *Measure* 5.1.468/2632, *Shrew* 5.2.108/2509, *Troilus* 4.2.60/2226, *Titus* 5.3.58/2359 ('fetch him hither'), *Cymbeline* 4.2.252/2203. There are also several requests to 'fetch' specific people 'hither': *Othello* 1.3.120/406, *Twelfth Night* 5.1.276/2375, etc.

21.41.1/2059.1 *Exit Lord*] MALONE; *not in* Q

21.42-52/2060-70 (L) Sure . . . sorrow] MALONE; *prose* Q

2061 (I) recou'ries] recoueries

21.48/2066 Gods] DYCE (W. S. Walker); God Q

21.52-3/2070-1 (L) Sit . . . preuented] STEEVENS; *prose* Q; see| MALONE; you| COLLIER

21.52/2070 it] STEEVENS; it to you Q. Superfluous and extrametrical.

21.52.1/2070.1 *Enter . . . maid*] MALONE (subs.), after 'preuented'; *not in* Q

21.54/2072 (I) heer's] Q2; hee'rs Q1

21.55/2073 presenc] MALONE; prefent Q

21.58-9/2076-7 (L) Came . . . wed] Q1; stock| Q4

21.58/2076 of] STEEVENS; of a Q. Q seems unidiomatic; it could have been picked up from 21.57/2075.

21.58/2076 or] This edition (G.T.); and Q. Hoeniger, suspecting corruption in this line, notes that '*gentle kind* and *noble stock* are suspiciously synonymous'. But both collocations are Shakespearian, and seem synonymous only because of Q's conjunction: in fact 'gentle kind' and 'noble stock' can express very different degrees of social rank. Lysimachus would be satisfied, if she were gentry *or* nobility.

21.58/2076 Ide] Q4; I do Q1

21.59/2077 to] This edition (G.T.); and Q

21.59/2077 wed] Q4; to wed Q1. Q1 may represent a bungled press-correction; see previous note.

2078 (I) on,] MALONE; ~ˍ Q

21.60 one] Q (on)

21.60/2078 bountie,] MALONE (Steevens); beautie, Q. Maxwell defended Q, which subsequent editors retain, but the resulting syntax is virtually unintelligible; it also implies that Marina possesses *only* such goodness as resides in beauty. If 'beautie' is correct, perhaps 'Expect' should be 'Express' (G.T.).

2079 (I) ene] euen

21.62 feat] Q (fate)

21.65-8/2083-6 (L) Sir . . . him] MALONE; *prose* Q

21.66/2084 recure] HUDSON 2 (W. S. Walker); recouerie Q. Maxwell objects that 'recure' is not found elsewhere as a substantive in Shakespeare, but he uses it as a verb three times (all verse, all in situations where 'recouer' would fit the sense but not the metre), the substantive is recorded until 1626, and Shakespeare's authentic work always contains a high proportion of *hapax legomena*. The reporter could easily have substituted the commoner, extrametrical word.

21.66-7/2084-5 prouided | That none . . . companion maid] Q (and MALONE); | Provided none . . . companion STEEVENS. Q's 'that' is dispensable, but 'companion maid' is an unusual collocation, unlikely to originate in a reporter; without the second emendation the first seems to little purpose.

2086 (I) suffer'd] MALONE; fuffered Q

21.68/2086 (L) Let . . . her] STEEVENS; *prose* Q

21.68/2086 Let] This edition (conj. Hoeniger); Come, let Q

21.69/2087 prosper her] This edition (G.T.); make her pro-|fperous Q. Q repeats the adjective from 21.62/2080; its formula only appears once elsewhere (*Richard II* 1.3.78/357). The alternative 'god(s) prosper [X]' occurs at *2 Henry IV* 3.2.289/1813, *History of Lear* 14.90, 20.29-30/2013, 2357-8; Folio *Merry Wives* has 'Heauen prosper' (which we emend to 'God prosper') at 3.1.29/1207, 5.2.12/2465.

21.69/2087 *The men withdraw*] MAXWELL (subs.); *not in* Q

21.69.1/2087.1 *The Song*] Q; *Marina sings* MALONE. P.A. (542), here plagiarizing Twine (464), has Marina alone sing; but this moment is the only occasion when Marina's companion could serve any dramatic function, by vocal accompaniment. See also 21.70/2087 ('nor lookt on vs'), where if Marina alone were responsible for the song one would expect 'me'.

21.69/2087 comming forward] This edition; not in Q
21.69/2087 Markt] Q4; Marke Q1
21.70/2088 MAID] This edition (anon. conj. in Cambridge); Mar. Q. An attractive conjecture, based on a simple misreading ('Mai'/'Mar'): see note to 21.69/2087.
21.72.1/2090.1 He roughly repulses her] MAXWELL (Wilson); not in Q; pushing her back HOENIGER (Cambridge). Hoeniger objects that the 'more violent' direction—based on Gower, Twine, and P.A.—is 'not suitable' to Pericles' character in the play, but our only evidence for the action at this moment is the sources and analogues, and our judgement of Pericles' character is itself partly based on this moment.
21.73-85/2091-2103 (L) I ... speake] MALONE; prose Q
21.75/2093 (I) gaz'd] MALONE; gazed Q
2094 (I) endur'd] MALONE; endured Q
21.85/2103 stay] This edition (G.T.); go not Q
21.86-7/2104-5 (L) My ... you] MALONE; prose Q
21.88-9/2106-7 (L) I ... violence] MALONE; prose Q: parentage|
21.89/2107 My Lord] This edition (M.J.); Q places after 'sed'. Misplacement of vocatives is particularly common in memorial texts; in this case, before rather than after the conditional clause.
21.90/2108 (L) I ... me] DYCE; prose Q; do| MALONE; so| STEEVENS
21.90/2108 I do] Q; I HUDSON 2
21.91-2/2109-10 (L) Your ... shores] MALONE; prose Q
21.91 You're] Q (your)
21.91-2/2109-10 woman? | Heere] MALONE (Charlemont); women₍ heare Q1; woman₍ heare Q6
21.92/2110 shores ... shores] MALONE (Charlemont); ſhewes ... ſhewes Q
21.92-4/2110-2 (L) No ... seeme] MALONE; prose Q
21.94/2112 seeme] This edition (G.T.); appeare Q. Apparent substitution of an unmetrical synonym.
21.95-6/2113-4 (L) I ... such] MALONE (subs.); prose Q; woe| wife| such a one| HOENIGER (W. S. Walker)
21.96/2114 such] This edition (M.J.); ſucha one Q. Q repeats 21.57/2075, superfluously and extrametrically.
21.97-106/2115-24 My ... owe] MALONE; prose Q
21.100/ cased] Q (caſte)
2118-9 (I) Iuno, | Who] ~. Who Q1
2121 (I) straunger,] Q6; ~₍ Q1
2121 (I) decke₍] Q6; ~, Q1
21.106-8/2124-6 (L) If ... reporting] This edition (G.T.); prose Q; seem| MALONE; If| lies| MAXWELL. Malone's lineation leaves Pericles' half-line incomplete, and produces an hexameter below. This arrangement is regular except for a defective caesura (of which all Shakespeare's late plays contain a few examples).
21.107/2125 it would] Q; 'Twould STEEVENS
21.108-17/2126-35 (L) Prethee ... discending] MALONE; prose Q
2127 (I) look'st] MALONE; lookeſt Q
2128 (I) seem'st] Q4; ſeemeſt Q1
21.110/2128 Pallas] MALONE (Lillo); Pallas Q. Q's spelling is acceptable as a form of modern 'palace', but the italics indicate compositorial misinterpretation as the Greek goddess. Shakespeare may have intended the pun, but palace seems the primary sense.
2130 (I) And] & (in prose)
21.112/2130 make my senses] Q4; make | ſenſes Q1
21.113/2131 thou show'st] This edition (G.T.); for thou lookeſt Q1; for thou look'ſt Q4. Q repeats 21.109/2127, here extrametrically. For the verb compare Coriolanus 4.5.63/2325, Lear: History 4.261/755, Tragedy 1.4.246/751, Sonnet 126.3.
21.114/2132 (I) lou'd] ROWE; loued Q
21.115/2133 say] MALONE; ſtay Q
21.117/2135 (L) So indeed I did] same type line as end of preceding speech Q
21.118-21/2136-9 (L) Report ... open'd] MALONE; prose Q
2139 (I) open'd] MALONE; opened Q
21.121/2139 Some ... sed] MAXWELL; prose Q
21.122-3/2140-1 (L) And ... likely] COLLIER; prose Q
21.122/2140 circumstance] This edition (M.J.); thoughts Q. The word occurs at about the same point in the scene's development in P.A.: 'Pericles ... by all the circumstances ... ghessed she was his child' (544). The word can mean both 'condition, stage of things' (Two Gentlemen 1.1.36, 37/36, 37, etc.) and 'particulars of evidence, details' (Troilus 3.3.109/1892, etc.). Q repeats 21.120/2138, in a metrically short line.
21.123-33/2141-51 (L) Tell ... at me] MALONE; prose Q
2142 (I) consider'd] MALONE; conſidered Q
21.124 thousandth] Q (thouſand)
2144 (I) suffer'd] MALONE; ſuffered Q
21.129/2147 them?] MALONE; not in Q
21.130.1/2148.1 She sits] This edition; not in Q
21.131/2149 sir,] STEEVENS; not in Q
21.133-9/2151-57 (L) Patience ... cald Marina] STEEVENS; prose Q
21.134/2152 patient:] Q; patient: but G.T. conj.
21.139-41/2157-9 (L) You ... here] MALONE; prose Q
21.142-3/2160-1 Fairie? | Motion as well?] MAXWELL; Fairie? | Motion₍ well, Q; Fairy? | Motion? well, F3; fairy? | No motion?—Well, STEEVENS; fairy—motion? Well, | MALONE 2 (Mason); fairy₍ | Motion? Well, HOENIGER
21.144-5/2162-3 (L) Calld ... sea] MALONE; 1 line Q
21.146/2164 (L) My ... King] MALONE; prose Q
21.147-8/2165-6 (L) Who ... weeping] This edition (M.J.); prose Q; born| oft| MALONE
21.147/2165 when] This edition (M.J.); the minute Q. Q anticipates 21.199/2217, unmetrically here.
21.148/2166 recounted] This edition (G.T.); deliuered Q. Edwards (1952) first stigmatized this repetition of 21.95/2113 as a memorial corruption.
21.149-150/2167-8 (L) O ... withall] Q; little| sleep| MALONE; little| dream| EDWARDS. Q's second line is regular, and its first acceptable (extra initial stress, feminine caesura).
21.149/2167 aside] MALONE; not in Q
21.151-3/2169-71 (L) This ... you] This edition; prose Q; be| bred| story| MALONE; buried| bred| story| EDWARDS. If we accept Q's lineation for the beginning of the speech, the remainder can be divided into three lines (the last with a line-divided foot, and feminine caesura).
21.151/2169 be my daughter,] Q; be. | My daughter's₍ STEEVENS
21.154/2172 (L) You ... ore] Q; me| EDWARDS (W. S. Walker)
21.154/2172 You will] This edition (G.T.); You Q; You'll MALONE. Malone's emendation is difficult to justify: even if 'scorne' is a compositorial misreading (see next note), it need not have led to a sophistication of the preceding word, for 'You'll scorne' makes as much sense as 'You scorne'. Independent compositorial or reporter omission of 'will' seems likelier as a source of error. Shakespeare uses the collocation will scarce 6 times elsewhere, but never elides the preceding auxiliary verb. Metrically, the unelided form simply produces a line-divided foot, or an extra initial stress.
21.154/2172 scarce₍ beleeue me,] MALONE; ſcorne, ~₍ Q. If Marina says 'You scorne', meaning 'You mock me', then 'believe me' is little more than an expletive (= 'I assure you'), whereas the natural inference from Pericles' protestation in reply to her, 'I will belieue you', is that Marina has used 'belieue' in the same way as at 21.139/2157, warning that he'll find her story scarcely credible. The misreading of 'scarce' as 'scorne' would be very easy. (M.J.)
21.155-7/2173-5 (L) I ... bred] MALONE; prose Q; believe you| deliver| parts| EDWARDS
21.160-1/2178-9 (L) Did ... doo't] Q; woo'd| MALONE; woo'd| drawn| BROOKS (conj.)
21.160/2178 wooed] This edition (M.J.); hauing wooed Q. Probably a reporter's anticipation of the next line: omitting it improves syntax and metre.
21.161/2179 the deed] This edition (M.J.); it Q. For collocation of attempt and deed compare Macbeth 2.2.10/552 (of a murder). Q anticipates 'doo't', is vague and metrically deficient.
21.161/2179 hauing] Q; being MALONE
21.162/2180 came and rescued] Q; rescued BROOKS (conj.)
21.163/2181 To Metaline they brought me] This edition (G.T.);

Brought me to *Metaline* Q. The reporter seems to have levelled this line and 22.30/2296 (see note) to almost identical wording.
21.163-4/2181-2 (L) To ... may be] STEEVENS; *Metaline*| Q, *followed by prose*; whither| MALONE
21.164/2182 What wil you of me] This edition (G.T.); whither wil you haue me Q. Q repeats Marina's phrasing at 19.152, 179/1923, 1950.
21.164/2182 It may be] Q; May be G.T. *conj.*
21.165-7/2183-5 (L) You ... be] MALONE; *prose* Q
21.165 impostor] Q (impoſture). See *All's Well* 2.1.155/714.
21.168/2186 PERICLES Hoe] Q4; Hell. Hoe Q1 (*text*); ∧ Hoe Q1 (*c.w.*)
21.168/2186 rising] This edition; *not in* Q. By 21.182/2200 ('Oh come hither') Pericles can no longer be sitting beside Marina (as at 21.130.1/2148.1), and this seems the most natural occasion for him to rise.
21.169/2187 *comming forward*] This edition; *not in* Q
21.171-3/2189-91 (L) Most ... weepe] MALONE; *prose* Q
2189(I) gen'rall] generall
21.173-4/2191-2 (L) I ... *Metaline*] MAXWELL; *prose* Q (*1 line*); but| MALONE
21.173/2191 not] Q; not, I MAXWELL (*conj.*)
21.174/2192 heres] Q; Here is MALONE
21.175/2193 (L) Speakes ... her] MALONE; *prose* Q
21.175-7/2193-5 (L) She ... weepe] MALONE; parentage| Q
21.175/2193 would neuer] STEEVENS; neuer would Q
2194 (I) demaunded∧ that,] Q4, Q1 (MS); ∼, ∼∧ Q1
21.178-82/2196-2200 (L) Oh ... hither] MALONE; *prose* Q
2196 (I) honor'd] MALONE; honored Q
21.182.1/2200.1 *Marina stands*] This edition; *not in* Q
2201 (I) Thou] Q2; thou Q1
2207 (I) For] Q2; for Q1
21.190-1/2208-9 (L) First ... title] STEEVENS; *1 line* Q
21.191-6/2209-14 (L) I ... father] This edition (*conj.* Brooks); my| sayd| kingdomes| Q; I| now| said| kingdomes| MALONE; now| said| kingdoms| STEEVENS
21.193/2211 rest] SINGER (Jackson); reſt ſhe ſayd Q. 'Redundant memorial expansion' (Brooks). It also produces a clash with 'thou' (which Pericles consistently uses to Marina, after 21.183/2201), and 'you', within a single sentence. Such switches are unparalleled in reliable Shakespearian texts (see *Richard III* 3.7.52/2042).
21.194/2212 So proue but true in that, thou art my daughter,] This edition (G.T.); *not in* Q; So be but right in that, thou art my daughter, BROOKS (*conj.*). Since Malone, editors have suspected a lacuna here, but only Brooks has made a plausible conjecture, in part because his rearrangement of the verse allowed him to see that a complete verse line is apparently missing. 'So' and 'in that' are the necessary complements to 'as in the rest' (21.193/2211); 'thou art my daughter' the necessary cue for 'Is it no more | to be your daughter' (21.197/2215). Only Brooks's 'be but right' seems lame and un-Shakespearian. For 'proue but true' compare *Twelfth Night* 3.4.367/1845: 'Proue true imagination, oh proue true' (followed shortly afterwards by 'if it proue, | Tempests are kind, and salt waues fresh in loue').
21.195/2213 life] STEEVENS (Mason); like Q
21.196/2214 kneeling] This edition; *not in* Q. Marina can no longer be sitting (21.182/2200), but she is later commanded to rise (21.200/2218), and she would naturally kneel before her parent, according to Renaissance custom, for his blessing (21.200/2218). In Twine the daughter 'hearing her fathers words, fell down at his feet ... ' (468).
21.196-7/2214-5 (L) Is ... name] This edition (G.T.); *prose* Q; than| MALONE; be| BROOKS (*conj.*). This arrangement, like Brooks's, produces an hexameter, but avoids the harsh line-break.
21.197/2215 name] This edition (*conj.* Brooks); name was *Thaiſa* Q. 'Memorial expansion and duplication' (Brooks).
21.198-9/2216-7 (L) Thaisa ... began] MALONE; *prose* Q
21.200/2218 thou art] Q4; th'art Q1
21.200.1/2218.1 *Marina stands.*] This edition; *not in* Q
21.200.1/2218.1 *He kisses her*] This edition; *not in* Q. Both Twine (467) and *P.A.* (544) repeat this, the latter drawing on several adjacent details in the play; in Gower he takes her in his arms (1740). All three accounts thus agree in a moment of natural physical intimacy here, which balances the unnatural incestuous claspings of Antiochus and his daughter.
21.201-8/2219-26 (L) Giue ... see you] MALONE; *prose* Q
21.202/2220 Not] STEEVENS; ſhee is not Q
21.208-12/2226-30 (L) I ... dout] MALONE; robes| girle| *Marina*| Q
21.208/2226 sir] STEEVENS; *not in* Q
21.209/2227 *He is attired in fresh robes*] This edition; *not in* Q. As Hoeniger notes, a crucial and symbolic stage action, comparable to *Lear*: History 20.80/2408, Tragedy 4.5.80/2287, *Antony* 5.2.277.1/2933.1, and the treatment of Prospero's robe.
21.210/2228 *Celestiall Musicke*] This edition; *not in* Q; *Music* DYCE (*after* 21.218/2236); *Music.* HOENIGER (*after* 'daughter', 21.213/2231). Some editors refuse to supply a stage direction for music, arguing that (*a*) it is heard by Pericles alone among those on stage, and that (*b*) attempts to simulate the heavenly harmonies will inevitably be bathetic. But (*a*) it is surely Pericles' blissful state of mind that the audience is invited to share in this scene, not the normality of Helicanus and Lysimachus, and (*b*) an imaginative musical accompaniment will aid rather than hinder the process of emotional identification. John P. Cutts, *N&Q* 205 (1960), 172-4, cites two King's Men plays of around 1620 in which 'music of the spheres' was certainly played, and compares the 'solemn music' ushering in Posthumus' vision in *Cymbeline* and the music called for in the reanimation of Hermione in *Winter's Tale*. (M.J.)
2228-9 (I) Musicke, | Tell∧] STEEVENS (*subs.*); ∼∧ tell, Q
21.212/2230 dout,] MALONE; doat. Q; doat, Q2
21.213/2231 How∧] Q2; ∼, Q1
21.215/2233 (L) None ... *Marina*] Q; None| MALONE
21.216/2234 *aside to the others*] This edition; *not in* Q
2235 (I) Rar'ſt] This edition (*conj.* W. S. Walker); Rareſt Q. Compare *Cymbeline* 5.5.161/2967.
21.2218-9/2236-7 Lord?] PERICLES I heare∧ most] MAXWELL (Cambridge); Lord? I heare. | *Per.* Moſt Q
2237 (I) heau'nly] heauenly
21.220/2238 raps] COLLIER; nips Q. Modern editors, while acknowledging its strangeness, accept 'nips', which in Maxwell's opinion provides 'a vividly Sh[akespearian] image for the keen attention the music provokes'. Edwards's comment that Q's expression is 'too original for a reporter' is irrelevant, since Collier's emendation assumes an easy minim misreading by the compositor. *Nip* inevitably suggests what is niggling and chilling, an irritant, whereas Pericles experiences rapture, leading to visionary sleep. (It is not 'a nipping and an eager air' that Pericles hears, but celestial harmony.) The transitive verb 'raps' (transports) is used in *Cymbeline* 1.6.52-3/574-5, 'What, deere Sir, | Thus rap's you?' (M.J.)
21.221/2239 eyelids] STEEVENS; eyes Q. The emendation improves both metre and image. Compare *2 Henry IV* 3.1.5-6/1425-6, 'ô sleepe! ô gentle sleep! | ... how haue I frighted thee, | That thou no more wilt weigh my eye-liddes downe'. The collocation of *eyelids* and *hang* occurs in *Much Ado* 4.1.106/1751, 'on my eie-liddes shall Coniecture hang'. (M.J.)
21.221.1/2239.1 *He sleeps*] MALONE; *not in* Q. See *P.A.*: 'he fell into a slumber: in which sweet sleepe of his, hee was by *Diana*, warned ... ' (544).
21.222/2240 A ... friends] This edition (G.T.); A Pillow for his head, ſo leaue him all. | Well my companion friends Q. Editors cast doubt on this speech as 'perhaps the reporter's padding' (Hoeniger) or 'reporter's tack' (Edwards). But the adjectival use of *companion* is rare outside Shakespeare: *OED* cites only *Faustus* Sc. 6.92, *Richard II* 1.3.93/372, and *Pericles* 5.1.67/2085. Shakespeare juxtaposes 'friend and companion' at *Antony* 5.1.44/2623, and 'but ... just' often (*Titus* 4.1.127/1526, *Merchant* 4.1.323/2132, *Much Ado* 5.1.294/2360, *Troilus* 4.7.16/2572, *Measure* 4.2.86/1806, *Cymbeline* 5.1.7/2462). For *remember* = 'reward', see *Macbeth* 2.3.20/634 (*OED*, v. 2b). Verbally, the essentials of the passage seem Shakespearian, and

'If . . . beliefe' is a good pentameter. But the speech does seem to have been memorially corrupted: the repetition of 'well' is pointless, and the lineation anomalous. The first, excrescent 'Well' can be removed; 'my' is equally dispensable, extrametrical, and perhaps picked up from 'my companion maid' at 21.67/2085.

More serious than such verbal tinkering is the dramatic problem. Modern prompt-books regularly omit or abridge this speech: the first line in particular seems a bathetic conclusion to the preceding scene: to which 'leave him all' is the natural culmination. But this difficulty—and the anomalous lineation—is rectified by the simple transposition of 'So leaue him all' to the end of the speech. See following notes.

21.222/2240 Companion friends] Q (subs.); companion-friend SINGER 2 (Malone). Malone conjectured that this sentence belonged to Marina, and was addressed to her 'companion maid'. This seems unlikely, but no more so than Steevens's belief that Lysimachus intends to reward all his followers, out of mere generosity, for his own happiness. But he could address Marina and her companion (who are 'companion-friends' of one another), or address them and the Lord who suggested sending for Marina in the first place. But Marina must be the focus of Lysimachus' thoughts. The speech (so interpreted) serves the useful function of reminding us of Lysimachus' pre-eminence, his noble generosity, and his interest in Marina: 'Ile well remember you' is particularly apposite, in its usual sense, addressed to her.

21.223-4/2241-2 (L) If . . . you] STEEVENS; prose Q

21.224/2242 So leaue him all] This edition (G.T.); ſo leaue him all Q (after 'head', 21.222/2240). See preceding notes.

21.224.1/2242.1 Exeunt all but Pericles] MALONE (subs.); not in Q

21.224.2/2242.2 Diana ⌈discends from the heauens⌉] This edition (G.T.); Diana. Q; Actus Quintus. Diana F3; Diana appearing to Pericles asleep ROWE; [ACT V.] SCENE II. The same. Pericles on deck asleep; Diana appearing to him as in a vision. MALONE. Editors unaccountably continue to print Malone's direction almost verbatim. Diana clearly appears to the audience, as well as to Pericles, probably by means of the same spectacular mechanism used for supernatural entrances in Macbeth, Cymbeline, and Tempest. Such entrances are usually described by the verb descend, and the descent clearly began from the 'heauens' over the stage.

21.225-6/2243-4 (L) My . . . sacrifice] ROWE; Ephesus| Q

21.227/2245 (L) There . . . together] ROWE; prose Q

21.228-9/2246-7 At large . . . voyce,] This edition; not in Q. As previous editors have noted, the absence of a rhyme for 'sacrifice' and the short line 'Before the people all' strongly suggest that a line and a half are missing. STEEVENS, the only editor to attempt to repair the lacuna, conjectured 'Before the people all, in solemn wise | Recount the progress of thy miseries'; the resulting rhyme scheme (ababb) requires alteration of 'call' to 'go'. Gower supports Q, for at this point Shakespeare clearly drew upon his rhymes (sacrifice/wise, all/befalle, wife/life). If we retain Q's and Gower's rhyme, then the lacuna must occur before (rather than after) the word 'before'. Steevens's proposed rhyme with miseries is unfortunate; moreover, the sense seems too explicit, for Pericles in Sc. 22 gives his name and rank, and for the most part recounts good news: his marriage to Thaisa, the birth of his child, her remaining a virgin, her 'better stars' in escaping death, his recovery of her. Steevens's conjecture—accepted by no editor—is no more likely than Q itself to represent what Shakespeare wrote.

Steevens assumed that the missing one and a half lines all belonged to one sentence, but this seems to us improbable. The speech as a whole is staccato; a grammatical heavy stop is required after every second line; formally, a full stop at the end of the first stanza seems desirable. If so, then the four syllables missing in the short line 'Before the people all' are either a short imperative sentence, or an adverbial clause modifying 'Reueale'. The missing line must be a command, completing the sentence 'There, when . . . together'.

'Discourse' is the verb P.A. uses here (544); it also occurs in Twine (473), later on, in the material dramatized in the next scene. 'At large' is more than a metrical filler, meaning both 'publicly' and 'in detail'. For 'at large discourse(d)' compare Errors 5.1.398/1747, Richard II 5.6.10/2657, and Dream 5.1.150/1850 (also 'large discourse' at Hamlet Add. Pass. J.27). The parallel in Errors is especially noteworthy, because it comes from a passage clearly dependent on Gower (the main source for the frame story), in which the Abbess at Ephesus brings the play to a close: 'And heare at large discoursed all our fortunes, | And all that are assembled in this place . . . '. In Gower Pericles is told to make known 'His fortune' (1806), and fortune is a key word in the play. Wise is one of only two words which Shakespeare elsewhere rhymed with sacrifice (22.11-12/2277-8); the other, enterprise (Troilus 1.2.278-9/422-3), cannot plausibly be fitted into this context. Moreover, Gower rhymes sacrifice with wise in this very passage (1803-4), and once earlier (963-4); he uses 'in . . . wise' twice again in the following 25 lines, and 'in this wise' at 379 and 817; in all, Gower uses 'wise' for a rhyme 10 times. Although 'in this wise' occurs nowhere else in Shakespeare (and would here have been used solely for the rhyme), he does use the synonymous 'in this manner' 4 times. Twine has 'With a loude voyce' at this point (471), in both the text and (more conspicuously) the chapter heading; 'with loud voyce' occurs at Contention 1.1.158/158, 'with full voyce' at Coriolanus 3.3.61/1990, and 'so full a voyce' at Henry V 4.4.64/2346.

21.229-35/2247-53 (L) before . . . dreame] ROWE; prose Q

2250 (I) And] & (in prose)

21.232/2250 life] MALONE (Charlemont); like Q

21.233/2251 Performe] MALONE; or performe Q

2251 (I) liu'st] MALONE; li-|ueſt Q

21.234/2252 Doo't] Q; Do it SINGER 2 (Dyce)

21.234/2252 rest] This edition (G.T.); not in Q; be MALONE. Q is metrically defective and syntactically odd. Malone, as elsewhere, supplies the flattest and commonest of verbs. Compare 'Rest you happy' (Antony 1.1.64/64). The senses 'remain' and 'retire, cease from labour' are both relevant; and the imperative followed by an adjective is often used as a formula for farewells (Schmidt).

21.235.1/2253.1 Diana ascends into the heauens] This edition (G.T.); not in Q; Diana disappears MALONE. See 21.224.2/2242.2.

2254 (I) Argentine,] Q2; ~ . Q

21.237/2255 (L) I . . . Sir] 1 type line Q

2255 thee (calling)] This edition; thee, Q1; ~ : Q4

21.237/2255.1 Enter Helicanus, Lysimachus, and Marina] MALONE; not in Q

21.239-41/2257-9 (L) Th'inhospitable . . . sayles] MALONE; first| Q

21.239/2257 Th'] This edition; The Q

21.241-4/2259-62 (L) eftsoones . . . neede] MALONE; prose Q

21.241.1/2259.1 Exit Helicanus] This edition (G.T.); not in Q. Q is completely unreliable about marking exits within a scene; Helicanus should respond at once to the order; he has nothing to do in the rest of the scene, and the final exeunt is symbolically tidier without him.

21.244-5/2262-3 (L) With . . . shuit] This edition (G.T.); a shore| Q

21.244/2262 With all my heart, sir,] STEEVENS; Sir, with all my heart, Q; Sir, | With all my heart, MALONE

21.245/2263 haue a] This edition (G.T.); haue another Q. Lysimachus has no other suit; 'another' is extrametrical; 'I haue a suite' occurs at Merchant 2.2.129-30/673-4, Contention 4.7.3/2458, Othello 3.3.81/1529, All Is True 5.2.194/2617 (perhaps by Fletcher); Q by contrast is unparalleled in the canon.

21.245/2263 shuit] MALONE (suit); ſleight Q. Q's error is easier to understand if the manuscript contained the 'sh-' form of the noun: 'shuit' misread 'sleit' and then normalized by the compositor. (See OED for the spellings of suit and sleight.) Moreover, this form produces a characteristic verbal jingle (a shore . . . a shuit).

21.246-7/2264-5 (L) You . . . her] This edition (G.T.); prose Q; prevail| seems| MALONE. Malone's arrangement leaves an unassimilated part-line; ours presupposes a line-divided foot.

21.248.1-2/2266.1-2 Exit Pericles, with Lysimachus at one arme, Marina at the other] This edition (G.T.); Exeunt. Q

Sc. 22] This edition; not in Q; [ACT V.] SCENE II. STEEVENS

22.0.1/2266.3 Enter Gower] Q4; not in Q1

22.2/2268   dum] Q; dun F4
22.3/2269 (L)   This . . . mee] Q. The line seems to be a foot short, but none of the conjectures—'deign to giue' (DYCE), 'freely giue' (STAUNTON), 'pray you, giue' (HUDSON 2), 'please you giue' (KINNEAR)—is persuasive. G.T. *conj.* 'last and best'.
2274 (I)   Metalin,] Q4; ~. Q1
22.9/2275   well] This edition (*conj.* Brooks); *not in* Q; *has* MALONE. 'The heavy emphasis on *So* seems awkward and improbable' (Brooks). Shakespeare modifies the verb with 'well' 4 times: *Venus* 640, *Richard III* 3.5.96/1968, *Othello* 1.1.53/53, *Timon* 4.3.170/1598.
2278 (I)   sacrifice,] Q4; ~. Q1
2280 (I)   Int'rim] Interim
2280 (I)   pray, you,] MALONE; ~, ~, Q
22.17.1/2283.1   *An alter, Thaysa, and other Vestalls are reuealed*] This edition (G.T.); *not in* Q1; *Enter Pericles, Lysimachus, Hellicanus, Marina, and others.* Q4 (*after* 22.20/2286); SCENE III. *The Temple of Diana at Ephesus; Thaisa standing near the altar, as high priestess; a number of virgins on each side; Cerimon and other inhabitants of Ephesus attending. Enter Pericles with his train; Lysimachus, Helicanus, Marina, and a Lady.* MALONE (*after* 22.20/2286). Absurdly, modern editors continue to accept Malone's staging, although since MAXWELL transposes the first part of Malone's direction ('*the Temple . . . attending*') to precede rather than follow Gower's speech. It is neither necessary nor helpful to have Thaisa etc. standing in the background throughout Gower's speech. All that is absolutely required to establish 'the temple' is an altar (like that in *Kinsmen*) and vestals, whom Gower can dramatically discover on cue; if available, an effigy of Diana would also be appropriate.
22.18.1-2/2284.1   *Enter . . . attendantes*] This edition (G.T.); *not in* Q. See preceding note.
22.20.1/2286.1   *Gower stands aside*] This edition (G.T.); *not in* Q1; *Exit* Q4. Editors follow Q4, but Q1 provides neither an exit here nor an entrance at 22.108/2374, and Gower might appropriately remain on stage for the final episode of his story.
22.21/2287   PERICLES] Q. All editors since MALONE mark a new scene (5.3), although since MAXWELL most editors keep Thaisa and the temple on stage across the scene-break. Even if Gower exits (see preceding note), no break is required. See 22.17.1/2283.1.
22.23-9/2289-95 (L)   Who . . . stars] ROWE; *prose* Q
22.23/2289   espouse] This edition (M.J.); wed Q. Metre requires an iambic synonym for 'wed' and Wilkins supplies one. In *P.A.*, which has several verbal echoes of the play here and adheres quite closely to its events, Pericles at Diana's temple recounts how in youth he had been 'curteously entertained by good *Symonides* king of *Pentapolis*, and after espoused his faire daughter *Thaysa*' (544). Shakespeare uses the verb *espouse* 7 times. Except for one instance in *Henry V*, the examples are all early, but a word with some savour of a discarded poetic diction is appropriate to the formality of Pericles' announcement.
22.24/2290   The faire *Thaisa*, at *Pentapolis*,] MALONE; at *Pentapolis*, the faire *Thaiſa* Q
22.24/2290   *Thaysa startes*] This edition; *not in* Q. *P.A.* continues: 'his faire daughter *Thaysa*. At the naming of whome, she her selfe being by, could not choose but starte' (544-5); *not in* Twine.
22.26/2292   who] F4; whom Q. Q is possible, but uncharacteristic of Shakespeare; and see note to 22.28/2294.
2293 (I)   liurey] liuerey
22.28/2294   whom] TONSON; who Q; her ELZE (*conj.*). Q is awkwardly ambiguous.
22.30/2296   Bore] This edition (G.T.); brought Q. The word suspiciously occurs three times in five lines, and this seems the least appropriate of the three occasions (especially because of the chime with 'sought'). 'Bore' could be used generally of her 'stars' or specifically of the ship (and pirates) which forcibly carried her away: for the verb used of ships, see *Tempest* 1.2.145/211, *Errors* 1.1.102/102 and 5.1.247/1596; *Errors* 5.1.161/1510 contrasts 'brought forth' and 'borne hence'. See note to 21.163/2181.
22.30-1/2296-7 (L)   Bore . . . Barke] ROWE; *prose* Q; shore| MALONE.

Malone's arrangement, followed by editors, produces a pointlessly harsh line-break, and a short line at 23.30/2296.
22.31/2297   our Barke] This edition; vs Q. Q's line is a syllable short, and entails an idiom unparalleled in the canon (and producing an awkward continuation in 'Where'). One would expect a reference to a ship. Of the available nouns, Shakespeare elsewhere uses four in conjunction with 'aboard'. The most frequent—which is also attractive for its alliteration—is 'bark'. Compare 'In few, they hurried us a-boord a Barke, | Bore vs some Leagues to Sea' (*Tempest* 1.2.144/210—of the violent abduction of a prince and his daughter), and 'a Barke of *Epidamnum* | That staies but till her Owner comes aboord' (*Errors* 4.1.85-6/1001-2). Other collocations are 'aboord a new Ship' (*Winter's Tale* 4.4.763/2372), 'Aboord my Gally' (*Antony* 2.6.82/1078), and 'aboard our dauncing Boat' (*Pericles* 20.22/2016). But neither 'galley' (7 times) nor 'boat' (17) is used very often by Shakespeare, and Pericles' ship in Sc. 21 is not called a 'galley' or 'boat' elsewhere in the play. In fact, it is first identified as 'this the Barke' (Sc. 21). For 'our Barke' compare *Duke of York* 5.4.28/2621, *Troilus* 1.1.104/134, and *Timon* 4.2.19/1396 (possibly by Middleton). *Barque* is used of a boat 30 times in Shakespeare—more often than any other noun but *ship*.
22.32-3/2298-9 (L)   Where . . . Daughter] ROWE; *prose* Q
22.33-4/2299-2300 (L)   Voyce . . . Pericles] MALONE; *prose* Q
22.34.1/2300.1   *She falls*] This edition; *not in* Q; *She faints away.* ROWE. *Faint* never appears in the stage directions of the canon, and it seems best to preserve the ambiguity (see 'shee die's', below).
22.35/2301 (L)   What . . . Gentlemen] Q4; *prose* Q1
22.35/2301   nun] COLLIER (*manuscript correction, Capell copy of* Q1); mum Q. Both *P.A.* (545) and Twine (471) describe Thaisa as a 'Nunne', in narrating this episode.
22.36-9/2302-5 (L)   Noble . . . armes] MALONE; *prose* Q
22.39/2305   same] This edition (G.T.); verie Q. Shakespeare uses 'these same' at *Richard II* 5.5.9/2538, *Merchant* 1.1.106/106, *1 Henry IV* 3.1.126/1605, *2 Henry IV* 4.1.339/2187, *Othello* 4.3.24/2686, *Lear: History* 24.274/3057, *Tragedy* 5.3.253/2893, *Coriolanus* 1.9.41/669; 'those same hands' occurs at *K. John* 2.1.319/595. The reporter could easily have substituted the extrametrical synonym 'verie', especially because *very same* was itself a common contemporary collocation.
2306 (I)   warnt] warrant
2307 (I)   oer-joyde] MALONE; ouer-joyde Q
22.42-3/2308-9 (L)   Earlie . . . shore] This edition; *prose* Q; was| MALONE
22.42/2308   on] STEEVENS (Malone); in Q
22.42   one] See preceding note.
22.42/2308   Ladie] Q. The repetition is suspicious, creating as it does a short line.
22.43-5/2309-11 (L)   I . . . temple] MALONE; *prose* Q (*separate paragraph*)
2310 (I)   recouer'd] ROWE; recoue-|red Q
22.47-54/2313-20 (L)   Whither . . . death] MALONE; *prose* Q
22.48/2314   vpon him!] MALONE; *not in* Q
22.56-7/2322-3 (L)   That . . . drownd] This edition (*conj.* Elze); *1 line* Q; I| EDWARDS
22.58/2324   *taking Thaysas hand*] This edition; *not in* Q. This conjectural (but natural) action explains her noticing the ring upon his finger.
2324 (I)   Imortall] Q4; I mortall Q1
22.59-61/2325-7 (L)   Now . . . ring] ROWE; *prose* Q
22.61/2327   ring.] Q; ring. *Shews a ring.* MALONE; ring. *Points to his ring.* HOENIGER. See 22.58/2324.
22.62-67/2328-33 (L)   This . . . bosome] MALONE; *prose* Q
2331   seene,] Q (*c.w.*); ~; (*text*)
22.66/2332   *They embrace, and kisse*] This edition; *not in* Q. *P.A.* describes Pericles 'throwing his head into her bosome . . . he cried aloude, O you heauens! my misfortunes were now againe blessings' (545). In Twine, 'Then did hee most louingly embrace and kisse his ladie . . . and shee likewise requited him' (473-4).
22.66/2332   *kneeling to Thaysa*] MALONE; *not in* Q

22.68-70/2334-6 (L) Looke . . . there] ROWE; *prose* Q (*first line ending* 'Thaiſa')
22.70/2336 embracing Marina] This edition; *not in* Q. *P.A.* describes Pericles 'giuing his daughter to her armes to embrace her as a child' (545). In Twine, 'Then kissed and embraced she her daughter' (474).
22.71/2337 kneeling to Thaysa] This edition; *not in* Q
22.72/2338 PERICLES] Q4; *Hell.* Q1
22.72-81/2338-47 (L) You . . . miracle] ROWE; *prose* Q
2346 (I) preseru'd] preserued
22.82-4/2348-50 (L) Lord . . . you] STEEVENS; *prose* Q
22.82/2348 is the] DYCE 2 (W. S. Walker); *not in* Q
2349 (I) pow'r] power
22.84-5/2350-1 (L) Reuerent . . . officer] ROWE; *prose* Q (*1 line*)
22.86-7/2352-3 (L) More . . . reliues] STEEVENS; *prose* Q
22.87-9/2352-5 (L) I . . . her] MALONE; *prose* Q
2355 (I) her,] Q4 (*subs.*); ~. Q1
22.90/2356 And tolde] This edition (G.T.); *not in* Q. The line is a foot short, and it seems unlikely that Pericles would be 'showne' *how* she was placed in the temple. One must in any case assume some ellipsis, and '[shall be] tolde [you]' is certainly no more difficult an ellipsis than '[and shall be showne you]'.
22.90-1/2356-7 (L) how . . . omitted] ROWE; *prose* Q
22.90/2356 how in this Temple shee came plac'ste] This edition (G.T.); How ſhee came plac'ſte heere in the Temple Q. 'The similarity in wording to [22.44-5/2310-11] suggests cross-contamination of the two passages by the reporter' (Brooks). The emendation is based upon *P.A.*, 'for in this Temple was she placed to be a Nunne, by Lord *Cerimon*' (545). *P.A.* transposes the preposition, to a more unusual position; Q's ordinary position repeats the syntax of 22.44-5/2310-11, from which it also repeats the superfluous 'heere'.
2357 (I) needfull] Q2; needfulll Q1
22.91-2/2357-8 (L) Pure . . . offer] MALONE; *prose* Q (*1 line*)
22.91/2357 Diana] MALONE; *Dian* Q. Both forms are common, both used in this play: an easy memorial confusion.
22.92/2358 I] MALONE; *not in* Q. See next note. It seems safer to suppose simple compositorial omission (frequent enough for this word) than substitution of 'and' for 'I'.
22.92/2358 and] Q; I F3
22.93-4/2359-60 Nightly . . . daughter] STEEVENS; *prose* Q
22.93/2359 Nightly] MAXWELL; Night Q; My night STEEVENS
2359 (I) thee;] Q4; ~. Q1
22.93/2359 belou'd] This edition (G.T.); *not in* Q. Brooks noted that some such word as 'Come' or 'Dear' seems to have dropped out here. But Thaisa was called 'deere' at 22.78/2344, and 'Come' seems pointless. The only adjectives appended to Thaisa's name in *P.A.* are 'faire' (8 times) and 'beloued' (547); the first has been used once already in this scene, and in any case seems less appropriate in a vocative construction. Metrically, a two-syllable adjective is acceptable, assuming only a (common) feminine caesura. Shakespeare uses the word 55 times elsewhere: compare

'Beloued *Regan*' (*Lear*: *History* 7.295/1303, *Tragedy* 2.2.205/1319).
22.95-6/2361-2 At . . . ornament] This edition (G.T.); *prose* Q
22.95/2361 At *Pentapolis* shall marrie her,] This edition (G.T.); ſhall marrie her at *Pentapolis*, Q (*prose*). Q produces an irregular sequence of stresses; as transposed the line is regular, assuming a line-divided foot.
22.96/2362 And now this ornament] Q. HOENIGER obelisks this phrase, marking a lacuna before 'this'. Something may be missing, but it is hard to see what, and the anomalous short line might result from the fact that 'Makes mee looke dismall' is a disguised amphibious section, forming a complete verse line either with the preceding (ROWE) or following (DYCE) phrase.
22.97/2363 (L) Makes . . . forme] DYCE; *prose* Q
22.98-9/2364-5 (L) And . . . beautifie] ROWE; *prose* Q
22.100-1/2366-7 (L) Lord . . . dead] ROWE; *prose* Q
2366 (I) credit,] Q4; ~. Q1
22.101/2367 from *Pentapolis*;] This edition (G.T.); *not in* Q. *P.A.* reports this news when Pericles departs for Tyre, 'taking *Pentapolis* in his way, whome [*sic*: read 'where'] by the death of good *Symonides*' (545); Twine also at this point refers to '*Pentapolis*' (477). Addition of this information completes the verse line, picks up 'At *Pentapolis*' in the preceding speech (22.95/2361), and explains 'there' in the following speech (22.102/2368).
22.102-5/2268-71 (L) Heau'n . . . raigne] ROWE; *prose* Q
22.102/2368 PERICLES Heau'n] This edition; *Per.* Heauens Q (*text*); *Per.* Heauen (*c.w.*). Shakespeare overwhelmingly prefers the singular.
22.107.1/2373.1 Exeunt] Q4; FINIS. Q1
22.107.1/2373.1 all but Gower] This edition; *not in* Q1; Enter Gower. Q4. See 22.201/2286.1.
2376 (I) Pericles,] ROWE; ~ Q
2377 (I) keene,] ~. Q
22.112/2378 preserud] TONSON; preferd Q
22.113/2379 Led] Q2; Lead Q1
2379 (I) heau'n] heauen
22.119/2385 thir] Q4 (their); his Q1
22.119/2385 deede, to th'] MAXWELL (Collier); deede, the Q
22.121/2387 his] Q; her HALLIWELL
2388 (I) seemed] Q4; ſeemde Q1
22.122/2388 so content] Q: to consent EDWARDS. Edwards calls the Q reading difficult, but it surely means 'thereby content'; divine contentment at such a death seems more appropriate to the reality here than mere 'consent'. Edwards's emendation also produces an awkward repetition of 'to'.
22.123/2389 them] MALONE; *not in* Q; crime HUDSON 2 (anon. *conj.*)
22.125.1/2391.1 Exit] *not in* Q

Additional Passage

8 (I) heau'ns] heauens
10 (I) Batt'ry] Battery

QUARTO STAGE DIRECTIONS

1.0.1/0.1 *Enter Gower.*
1.42/42 *Exit.*
1.42.1-2/42.1-2 *Enter Antiochus, Prince Pericles, and fellowers.* (perhaps 'followers')
1.54.1/54.1 *Enter Antiochus daughter.*
1.106.1/106.2 *The Riddle.*
1.163.1/163.1 *Manet Pericles solus.*
1.185/185 *Exit.*
1.185.1/185.1 *Enter Antiochus.*
1.192/192 *Enter Thaliard.*
1.202.1/202.1 *Enter a Messenger.* (after 1.201/201)
2.0.1/213.1 *Enter Pericles with his Lords.*
2.33.1-2/246.1-2 *Enter all the Lords to Pericles.*
2.129.1/342.1 *Exit.*

3.0.1/342.2 *Enter Thaliard solus.*
3.10.1/352.1 *Enter Hellicanus, Escanes, with | other Lords.*
3.41/383 *Exit.*
4.0.1-2/383.1-2 *Enter Cleon the Gouernour of Tharsus, with | his wife and others.*
4.55.1/438.1 *Enter a Lord.*
4.82.1-2/465.1-2 *Enter Pericles with attendants.*
4.107/490.1 *Exeunt.*
5.0.1/490.2 *Enter Gower.*
5.16.1/506.1 *Dombe shew.*
5.16.2-7/506.2-7 *Enter at one dore* Pericles *talking with* Cleon, *all the traine | with them: Enter at an other dore, a Gentleman with a | Letter to* Pericles, Pericles *shewes the Letter to* Cleon; *| Pericles*

PERICLES

giues the Messenger a reward, and Knights *him:* | Exit Pericles *at one dore, and* Cleon *at an other.*

5.38.1/528.1   Enter Pericles wette. (after 5.40/530)

5.51.2-3, 5.55.1-4/541.2, 545.1-4   Enter three Fisher-men. (after 5.51/541)

5.157.1/649.1   *Enter the two Fisher-men, drawing vp a Net.*

6.0.1-2/701.1-2   *Enter* Simonydes, *with attendaunce, and* Thaisa.

6.16.1-3/717.1-3   *The first Knight passes by.*

6.22.3-5/723.3-5   *The second Knight.*

6.28.3-5/729.3-5   *3. Knight.*

6.33.3-5/734.3-5   *4. Knight.*

16.38.3-5/739.3-5   *5. Knight.*

6.43.3-6/744.3-6   *6. Knight.*

6.62.1-2/763.1-2   *Great shoutes, and all cry, the meane Knight.*

7.0.1-4/763.3-6   *Enter the King and Knights from Tilting.*

7.102.1/865.1   *They daunce.*

7.110.1/873.1   *They daunce.*

8.0.1/882.2   *Enter* Hellicanus *and* Escanes.

8.16.1/899.1   *Enter two or three Lords.*

9.0.1-3/956.1-2   *Enter the King reading of a letter at one doore,* | *the Knightes meete him.*

9.19.1/975.1   Enter Pericles. (after the King's speech)

9.62.1/1018.1   *Enter* Thaisa.

9.72/1028   Aside. (opposite 9.97/1053)

9.100/1056   Aside. (opposite 9.101/1057)

9.113.1/1069.1   *Exeunt.*

10.0.1/1069.2   *Enter* Gower.

10.14.2-10/1083.2-10   *Enter* Pericles *and* Symonides *at one dore with attendantes,* | *a Messenger meetes them, kneeles and giues* Pericles *a letter,* | Pericles *shewes it* Symonides, *the Lords kneele to him;* | *then enter* Thaysa *with child, with* Lichorida *a nurse,* | *the King shewes her the letter, she reioyces: she and* Pericles | *take leaue of her father, and depart.*

11.0.1/1129.1   *Enter* Pericles *a Shipboard.*

11.14.1/1143.11   *Enter* Lychorida.

11.37.1/1166.1   *Enter two Saylers.*

11.78.1-3/1207.1-3   *Exit.*

12.0.1-2/1207.4-5   *Enter Lord* Cerymon *with a seruant.*

12.1/1208   *Enter* Phylemon.

12.9/1216   *Enter two Gentlemen.*

12.45.1/1252.1   *Enter two or three with a Chist.*

12.84.1/1291.1   *Enter one with Napkins and Fire.*

12.102/1309   *Shee moues.*

12.108.1/1315.1   *They carry her away. Exeunt omnes.*

13.0.1-2/1315.2-3   *Enter* Pericles, Atharsus, *with* Cleon *and* Dionisa.

14.0.1/1356.1   *Enter* Cerimon, *and* Tharsa.

14.17.1/1373.1   *Exit.*

15.0.1/1373.2   *Enter* Gower.

15.50.1/1423.1   Enter Dioniza, with Leonine. (after 15.52/1425)

15.52/1425   *Exit.*

15.62.1/1435.1-2   Enter Marina with a Basket of flowers. (after 15.64/1437)

15.140.1/1513.1   *Enter Pirats.*

15.144.1/1517   *Exit.*

15.144.2/1517.1   *Enter* Leonine.

15.151.1/1524.1   *Exit.*

16.0.1-2/1524.2-3   *Enter the three Bawdes.*

16.23/1547.1   *Exit.*

16.37.1/1561.1   *Enter* Boult *with the Pirates and* Marina.

16.60/1584   *Exit.*

16.146/1673   *Exit.*

17.0.1/1673.1   *Enter* Cleon, *and* Dioniza.

18.22.2-8/1747.2-8   *Enter* Pericles *at one doore, with all his trayne,* Cleon *and* Dio-|niza *at the other.* Cleon *shewes* Pericles *the tombe, whereat* Pe-|ricles *makes lamentation, puts on sacke-cloth, and in a mighty* | *passion departs.*

18.45/1770   *Exit.*

19.0.1/1770.1   *Enter two Gentlemen.*

19.9/1779   *Exit.*

19.9.1/1779.1   *Enter Bawdes 3.*

19.24.1/1794.1   Enter Lysimachus. (after 19.27/1797)

19.155.1/1926.1   *Enter Bawdes.*

19.223.1/1994.1   *Exeunt.*

20.0.1/1994.2   *Enter* Gower.

20.24/2018   *Exit.*

21.0.1-3/2018.1-3   *Enter* Helicanus, *to him 2. Saylers.*

21.6/2024   *Enter two or three Gentlemen.*

21.8.1-2/2026.1-2   *Enter* Lysimachus.

21.69/2087   *The Song.*

21.224.2/2242.2   Diana.

21.248.1-2/2266.1-2   *Exeunt.*

CORIOLANUS

Coriolanus (BEPD 401) was the first tragedy listed in the block of sixteen unlicensed plays entered in the Stationers' Register by Blount and Jaggard on 18 November 1623. It was subsequently printed in the First Folio (F), where its name heads the tragedies in the catalogue of plays, and the work itself begins the pagination and quire signatures for the tragedies. Though planned as the Folio's first tragedy, it yields place to *Troilus* as a result of *Troilus*' late inclusion. *Coriolanus* was set by Compositor B with assistance from A. The pages containing 2.3.117–3.1.295/1298–1740 and forme-mates 4.2.44–4.6.161/2178–2661, the outer two of the three sheets of quire bb, were printed out of sequence after work had continued on other plays; Hinman (*Printing and Proof-Reading*) supposes that pages first set regularly suffered an accident and had to be replaced. It is possible that the extant pages are wholly or partly a reprint of the first setting.

The Folio text has a high incidence of verse mislineation, but the causes seem to be, for the most part, usual ones. In common with other later plays, *Coriolanus* has many lines divided between speeches; part-lines were evidently often run-on in the copy, enforcing the compositor to introduce line-breaks. Also frequent are verse lines exceeding the usual five feet; these too could be too long for the Folio measure, and so cause further compositorial relining. The most extensive mislineation results from Compositor A's habit of making line-breaks that coincide with breaks in syntax. On occasion Compositor B would split a verse line to help fill up a page of type in accordance with the casting-off mark in his copy. The lineation in F cannot safely be said to reflect any exceptional layout in the copy.

Coriolanus is not noted for the inconsistencies, staging problems, incomplete stage directions, signs of false starts, or volatile speech-prefix forms associated with foul-paper texts. It is often maintained that the play was printed from an authorial fair copy. Certainly there is an authorial basis to the stage directions, which are often remarkably full and 'literary' (for instance, '*Enter two Officers, to lay Cushions, as it were, in the Capitoll.*'). The text also has a recognized Shakespearian spelling: 'Scicinius' (and contractions of it in speech-prefixes) for the character Sicinius, a variant which is consistently found in Compositor A's stints and twice in text evidently set by B. The distinctive 'Sc' spelling is found in Q 2 *Henry IV* for the character Silence, and in the noun *silence* in Hand D's addition to *More* (l. 57) and Q *Troilus* 1703 (where the press-corrector regularized 'scylence' to 'sylence'). Though almost certainly deriving from Shakespeare's hand (and therefore adopted as the standardized speech-prefix form in the original-spelling text of this edition), the 'Sc' spelling of Sicinius does not demonstrate that the compositor's copy was written in that hand. An unfamiliar proper name might prove especially resistant to scribal regularization, just as it did to regularization by one of the compositors.

A number of features, taken together, point firmly away from authorial copy. The form '*Enters*' (1.8.0.1–3/605.1–3 in the stage direction list) does not elsewhere appear in texts thought to be set from Shakespeare's papers (see Introduction to *Contention*). High incidence of apostrophied *ha's* (28, against 7 *has*; see Introduction to *All Is True*) and *do's* (6, against no *dos*; see Introduction to Folio *Lear*), and of parentheses (see Appendix 1 to Taylor's 'Shakespeare and Others'), are not associated with Shakespeare. The favoured spelling 'oh' (40, against 12 'o') runs against Shakespeare's apparent preference. The contraction *a'th* occurs 29 times in *Coriolanus*, but elsewhere just 9 times in *All's Well* (itself anomalously high), 5 times in textually troublesome *Pericles*, and in other plays less or not at all (these figures include *a't* and *a'the*, forms not found in *Coriolanus*). To some extent *a'th* and the alternative *o'th* (16 in *Coriolanus*) are found in clusters which do not follow compositorial stints; in particular the copy for 4.5.21–4.6.131/2285–2631 might have been in a second hand.

F's punctuation is unusually faulty or misleading. The greater reliability of punctuation in Compositor A's stint would suggest that Compositor B was at least partly responsible, but compositorial error is probably not the sole cause. As there are indications of sophisticated pointing in the copy (apostrophes, parentheses, etc.), it cannot be assumed that the compositors were faced with a lightly punctuated manuscript; the manuscript may therefore itself have incorporated misunderstandings of Shakespeare's pointing.

The original stage directions seem to have received annotation. '*A Sennet. Trumpets sound.*' is representative of a group of about eight directions in which the call for music appears to be duplicated. In four entry directions '*the two Tribunes*' stands side by side with their names. At 1.5.13.3/470.3–4 '*Martius followes them to gates, and is shut in*' summarizes action which follows over the next few lines, and is probably authorial; '*Enter the Gati.*', three lines below, an evident error for '*Enter the Gates*', is a duplication at approximately the correct point. Annotation specifying minor participants in the scene would account for the wording of the direction at 1.8.0.1–3/605.1–3 (see stage direction list, and compare the equivalent direction in the text of this edition). Where '*Exeunt*' precedes the fuller '*In this Mutinie, the Tribunes, the Ædiles, and the People are beat in*' (3.1.228.1–2/1673.1–2), the duplication is exposed by misplacement of '*Exeunt*'. It would follow that a good number of Shakespeare's directions have been tidied up or clarified by an annotator, who standardized the original with short notes which emphasized music cues, detailed the names of characters in entries, and affirmed exits. Such annotation is distinctly theatrical.

The relatively full and descriptive directions Shakespeare supplied for *Coriolanus* and other later plays could survive in a prompt-book, and indeed provide a more than usually detailed account of the action. Annotation might therefore have been fairly light. A few theatrical details remain unresolved in F, although one of the more notable, Shakespeare's '*All*' as a prefix for distinct but anonymous characters (see note 1.1.26-7/25-6), may not have required correction. Some speech-prefix errors (for example at 1.1.55/53 and following, and 3.1.231-9/1676-84) look scribal in origin. In certain cases, if the error stood in the fair copy, annotated corrections might not have been acted upon by the Folio compositors (though it should be noted that the two passages cited were set by different compositors). The inaccuracies in speech-prefixes might alternatively indicate that the copy for F was not the prompt-book itself but a transcript of it—in which case the prompt-book may or may not have been based on authorial fair copy.

Coriolanus was evidently written during the period in which the King's Men moved to the Blackfriars (see 'Canon and Chronology'). The cornetts stipulated in directions at 1.10.93.1/721.1 and 2.1.20.1/957.1 might indicate performance in the Blackfriars; larger wind instruments were usual in the open-air theatres (see Lawrence; other directions for trumpets suggest that the play could have been prepared with performance at the Globe in mind as well). Taylor ('Act Intervals') argues that observance of act intervals was a particular convention of the 'private' theatres. F's coherent act divisions, followed in this edition, are probably authorial and—in accordance with the present description of the copy for F—supplied to mark act intervals in performance. There are no scene divisions in F; the present editorial divisions were established by Capell.

A number of readings have been recorded in the textual notes from Charlton Hinman's manuscript notes for the projected Norton edition.

J.J./(S.W.W.)

WORKS CITED

Brockbank, Philip, ed., *Coriolanus*, Arden (1976)
Bulloch, John, *Studies on the Text of Shakespeare. With Numerous Emendations* (1878)
Clayton, Thomas, 'Today We Have Parting of Names: A Preliminary Inquiry into Some Editorial Speech-(be)headings in *Coriolanus*', in *Today*, 15 February 1986
Craig, W. J., and R. H. Case, eds., *Coriolanus*, Arden (1922)
Daniel, P. A., *Shakespeare Notes* (1870)
Gomme, A. H., ed., *Coriolanus* (1969)
Hibbard, G. R., ed., *Coriolanus*, New Penguin (1967)
Honigmann, E. A. J., 'Re-Enter the Stage Direction: Shakespeare and Some Contemporaries', *SSu 29* (1976), 117-25
Lawrence, W. J., *Shakespeare's Workshop* (1928)
Leo, F. A., ed., *Coriolanus* (1864)
Murry, John Middleton, 'A Neglected Heroine of Shakespeare', in *Countries of the Mind: Essays in Literary Criticism* (1922), 31-50
Proudfoot, Richard, 'The Year's Contributions to Shakespearian Study: Textual Studies', *SSu 30* (1977), 203-10
Sanders, Wilbur, 'An Impossible Person: Caius Martius Coriolanus', in Sanders and Harold Jacobson, *Shakespeare's Magnanimity: Four Tragic Heroes, Their Friends and Families* (1978), 136-87
Taylor, Gary, 'Shakespeare and Others' (forthcoming in *Medieval and Renaissance Drama in England*)
—— 'War in Shakespeare' (forthcoming)
Wilson, John Dover, ed., *Coriolanus*, New (1960)

TEXTUAL NOTES

Title *The Tragedy of Coriolanus*] F (*head title and table of contents*); *The Tragedie of Coriolanus*. F (*running title*); *Coriolanus* S.R.
1.1.15 on] F (one). Similarly 1.2.4.
1.1.26-7/25-6 ⌜3 CITIZEN] Against . . . first. |⌜4 CITIZEN] He's] This edition; *All*. Againſt . . . firſt: He's F; *1 Cit⟨izen⟩*. Against . . . first: he's HUDSON (Malone). Honigmann (pp. 120-2) argues that the phrases have separate speakers, who are probably distinct from the identified First and Second Citizens: an interpretation that has also been made in theatrical productions. F gives a Shakespearian formula for dispersed or otherwise anonymous voices. The lines could be spoken together, but are distinct enough in content to suggest separate delivery.
1.1.33/32 5 CITIZEN] This edition; *All*. F; *2 Cit⟨izen⟩*. MALONE. See previous note.
1.1.36-7/35-6 to please . . . partly proud] F; partly to please . . . proud CAPELL. Wilson, following Capell, objects to F as usually interpreted, on the grounds that the Citizen is reinforcing his view that Coriolanus is wholly proud; this objection remains if F is glossed 'partly to be proud'. Previous editors have taken 'he did it . . . proud' as the assertion that comes after the concessive 'though . . . Countrey'. The difficulty in F is resolved if (*a*) 'though' is not forward-referring, but qualifies 'I say . . . end' before it, and (*b*) 'he did it . . . proud' continues what 'soft conscienc'd men' say. Hence the speech may be modernized: 'I say unto you, what he hath done famously, he did it to that end—though soft-conscienced men can be content to say "it was for his country", "he did it to please his mother, and to be partly proud"—which he is even to the altitude of his virtue'.
1.1.43/42 Accusations. He] ROWE; ~, he F
1.1.45 o'th'] F (a'th). F spells similarly 29 times. See Introduction.

1.1.55/53 ⌜1⌝ CITIZEN] CAPELL; *2 Cit⟨izen⟩*. F. Similarly throughout the rest of 1.1. F has been defended by Knight and Sanders, but might arise from misinterpretation of unparticularized or absent prefixes in Shakespeare's manuscript—probably by an annotator or scribe.
1.1.64/62 you. For your wants,] ROWE (*following* F4); ~, for your ~. F1
1.1.66/64 Heauen] F; heavens MASON (*conj*.)
1.1.90/88 stale't] THEOBALD; ſcale't F
1.1.105/103 you:] THEOBALD; ~, F
1.1.108/106 tantingly] F2; taintingly F1
1.1.112/110 What:] THEOBALD; ~, F
116 Foreme] F. Compare 'prithee'.
1.1.124/122 you'st] F; you'll ROWE 3
1.1.134/132 o'th'] F; the RANN (Tyrwhitt)
1.1.135/133 Crankes] F; rankes COLLIER MS
1.1.143 flour] F (Flowre)
1.1.170/168 Geese: you are, no] THEOBALD; ~, you ~ : No F
1.1.198 pitch] F (picke). *OED* describes *pick* (*v*.²) as 'A collateral form of PITCH'.
1.1.199/197 al most] SINGER 2 (Collier MS); almoſt F. The line almost fills the Folio measure, and the 'l' is printed slightly displaced; the error need not, however, be mechanical.
1.1.212 Shouting] F (Shooting)
1.1.215/213, 224 *Velutus*] F. Correctly 'Bellutus'; Shakespeare follows his source, North's Plutarch.
1.1.216/214 vnroo'ft] THEOBALD; vnroo'ſt F. F's apostrophe is both redundant and misplaced. It probably owes its existence to the scribe who prepared the copy (compare 'whil'ſt', 'wer't', etc.).
224 *Iunius*] F4; *Annius* F1

1.1.239/237 Latius] ROWE (Lartius); Lucius F. The spelling 'Latius', found 7 times elsewhere, would more easily be misread than 'Lartius'.
1.1.241/239 LARTIUS] F (Tit⟨us⟩.). Similarly at 1.1.245/243 and 1.5.19/476.
1.1.244, 248/242, 246 ⌈1⌉ SENATOR] F (Sen.)
1.1.247/245 your] F4; you F1. Some editors follow F1, but the construction is extremely strained and error would be especially easy after 'you, right' (see lineation note).
1.1.269/267 of] F; on CAPELL. F could arise from an easy error, and Capell's emendation gives the more usual expression; but F's idiom is found in Henry V 2.3.26/823.
1.2.0.1 Corioles] F (Coriolus). Other variants are 'Corialus' (2, both in stage directions) and 'Carioles' (5, all in dialogue).
1.2.16 Whither] F (Whether)
1.2.27/304 Corioles.] F4 (subs.); ~₍ F1
1.2.28/305 the] F; their HUDSON (Johnson)
1.2.36/313 ALL THE SENATORS] F (All.)
1.3.38/353 thats] F2; that F1
1.3.45/360 Grecian sword₍ Contemning. . . . Tell] LEO; Grecian fword. Contenning, tell F1; Grecian swordes₍ Contending: tell F2; Grecian swords, contemning. Tell SINGER (Collier MS). F1's error of punctuation would be facilitated by copy use of capital 'C', as frequently elsewhere. The italicization looks like a mis-set proof correction whereby 'Grecian' should have been italicized and the literal error corrected in 'Contenning'.
1.3.61 He's] F (ha's)
1.3.83/398 VIRGILIA] F3 (Virg.); Vlug. F1
1.3.86/401 Ithaca] F3; Athica F1. Correctly spelt in Troilus 1.3.69/504.
1.3.106-7/421-2 Ladie: as . . . now, she] POPE (similarly F4); ~, as . . . ~ :| She F1
1.4.14/442 that] F; but JOHNSON
1.4.14/442 lesse] F; more HUDSON
1.4.17/445 vp:] F3 (subs.); ~₍ F1
1.5.0.1/457.3-4 Enter . . . Cursing] This edition; Enter Martius Curfing F. See Taylor, 'War in Shakespeare'. According to the usual conventions for stage battles, a retreat followed by a cleared stage and an entry of the retreating forces indicates a change of location to the place of retreat (the 'Trenches'). There must therefore be a notional mid-scene shift to outside the gates at 1.5.13.1-3/470.1-4. Taylor compares a stage battle in Heywood's 1 Edward IV which apparently influenced Shakespeare's sequence of action.
1.5.2/459 Rome: you₍] F; ~, ~ ! POPE 2 (Hanmer)
1.5.2/459 Heard] F; Herds ROWE. Pope and Hanmer follow Rowe.
1.5.2/459 of—] JOHNSON; ~₍ F; you POPE 1. For the use of the dash, compare 1.7.43/561, etc.
1.5.2 boils] F (Byles)
1.5.13/470 Trenches. Followe] COLLIER 2; ~₍ followes F1; ~₍ followed F2; ~₍ Follow COLLIER 1; ~. Follow me DYCE 2 (Lettsom); Trenches. WILSON (Wright). F1 is weak; it probably combines a contamination from 'followes' in the stage direction (see list) with a typical mispunctuation. The error underlying Collier 2's emendation is easier than that supposed by Wilson. The common editorial addition of 'me' can only be regarded as metrical sophistication; those accepting it must admit three errors in F.
1.5.16.1/473.1 Gates] F2; Gati F1
1.5.18/475 3 SOULDIER] This edition; All. F
1.5.19/476 4 SOULDIER] This edition; All. F
1.5.25/482 stand'st] F; stands ROWE. The implied subject (preceding 'Who') is 'thou'.
1.5.25/482 art lost,] SINGER 2 (Collier); art left, F; artless₍ BULLOCH (conj.); aweless₍ SCHMIDT (conj.). See Wilson's note.
484 Weare] F. Possibly an error influenced by 'Iewell', but OED records the form as a 16th-c. spelling of were (as here, past subjunctive). Compare 'were', [2.1.175]/931, an acceptable 17th-c. spelling of wear.
1.5.28/485 Catoes] THEOBALD (from North's Plutarch); Calues F
1.6.4/494 honors] ROWE 3; hours F. The emendation is especially appropriate after Lartius' comparison of Martius' military worth to a rich jewel.
495 Drachme] F. OED does not record the '-e' termination, which might be an error.
1.6.7/497 them, these] F3 (~, These); ~. Thefe F1
1.6.9/499 him.] F3 (subs.); ~₍ F1
1.7.6/524 The Roman] F; Ye Roman HANMER. The emendation is plausible.
1.7.21 Who's] F (Whofe)
1.7.30/548 woo'd, in heart₍] THEOBALD (Thirlby); ~₍ in ~ ; F
1.7.53/571 Antiats] POPE; Antients F
1.7.70/588 Lesser] F3; Leffen F1
1.7.76/594 O'] SISSON; Oh F; All. O BROOKE (Style). A particularly plausible error, as it is likely that Shakespeare's preferred 'O' for the exclamation repeatedly became 'Oh' in Coriolanus through scribal change.
1.7.84/602 I] HUDSON (Capell); foure F. Wilson posited misreading of 'I' as '4'. The error would be influenced by 'foure' at 1.7.78/596 (and 'A certaine number' at 1.7.80/598).
1.9.15/628 condemned] F; contemned JOHNSON (conj.).
1.10.0.1/628.1 ⌈Flourish.⌉] In F, before 'Alarum'. Probably a misplaced prompt note: the flourish heralds the victorious entry of the Romans.
1.10.32/660 store, of all₍] ROWE; ~₍ of ~, F
1.10.40/668 vpheld] CAPELL; beheld F
1.10.43/671 Courts and] F; camps, as THEOBALD (Warburton)
1.10.46/674 An Ouerture] F (an ~); a coverture STEEVENS 2; An ovator BROCKBANK (Hulme). The relevant sense of overture is 'a formal opening of proceedings; a first indication or hint of something' (OED, sb. 6); F's phrase is an ironic variation of the expression 'an ouerture of peace', as in All's Well 4.3.41/1979 (cited in OED under sb. 3). The later musical sense is irrelevant; the image (both social and theatrical) is of costume as indicative of states of peace or of impending war.
1.10.49 shout] F (fhoot)
1.10.64, 66/692, 694 Marcus Caius] F; Caius Martius ROWE
1.10.64, 66 Martius] F (Marcus)
1.10.67/695 CORIOLANUS] STEEVENS; Mar⟨tius⟩. F. Similarly at 1.10.78, 81, 89/706, 709, and 717.
1.10.82/710 And at] HANMER; At F
1.10.93.1/721.1 A flourish. Cornets.] In F, before the entry beginning 1.11.0.1/721.2. Compare 1.10.0.1/628.1.
1.11.2/723 A SOULDIER] F (Sould.). Similarly at 1.11.16, 29, 33/737, 750, and 754.
1.11.17-18/738-9 valor, poison'd₍ . . . him,] POPE; valors₍ ~, . . . ~ : F
1.11.22 Embargements] F (Embarquements)
755 Agurer] F. Perhaps an error, but compare 'Latius' (914.2, etc.).
2.1.18/772 with all] F3; withall F1
2.1.24/778 how are] F2; ho ware F1
2.1.50/804 vppon,] ROWE; ~, F
2.1.56/810 can not] THEOBALD (can't), CAPELL; can F. Brockbank assumes sarcasm, but Menenius is speaking pointedly directly throughout the speech ('What I think, I vtter, and spend my malice in my breath').
2.1.60/814 you] F; you, you POPE
2.1.63 bisson] F (beefome)
2.1.83-4/839-40 are. When . . . purpose, it] F4 (subs.); ~, when . . . ~. It F1
2.1.105/861 VIRGILIA and VALERIA] F (2. Ladies.)
914.2 Latius] F. The spelling also at 1445.2 and in the following five speech-prefixes for Lartius. All occurrences were set by Compositor A, who also preserved 'Scicinius'. The error 'Lucius' at 237 (see note) further hints at copy 'Latius'.
2.1.161/917 Martius Caius] F; Caius Martius ROWE
2.1.162/918 Coriolanus] STEEVENS; Martius Caius Coriolanus F
2.1.175 wear] F (were)
2.1.177/933 CORIOLANUS] ROWE; Com⟨inius⟩. F
2.1.182/938 begnaw at] CRAIG; begin at F; begnaw the WILSON. The compositor probably read 'beginne at'.
2.1.183/939 You] F2; Yon F1

2.1.214/970 garded] WILSON (Lettsom); gawded F. Minim error after Shakespeare's 'a' is particularly common. Brockbank and others take 'gawded' to refer to cosmetic make-up, but the usage is unparalleled; further, 'the Warre of White and Damaske' refers to changes in natural complexion.

2.1.241/997 Authorities, for an end.] F (~, for an end.); ~. For an end, POPE. The present interpretation ('authority's . . .') originates with Hibbard.

2.1.248/1004 their Warre] F; the war HANMER. Chambers's defence of 'their' as attributing war to the patricians seems unlikely, as 'their Pleaders' and 'their Freedomes' refer to the plebeians. F may be understood as equivalent to *your* in its vague sense 'that you know of' (OED, 5b). Brutus speaks the actual words that should be used in addressing the people, minimally adjusted to indirect speech by substituting the third person. If so, F gives a much stronger reading than Hanmer—though it could, as Brockbank admits, arise from an easy error of anticipation.

2.1.252/1008 touch] HANMER; teach F; reach POPE 2 (Theobald)
2.1.254/1010 his] F; the POPE; as CAPELL
2.2.7/1030 hath] F1; haue F2
2.2.46/1069 Martius Caius] F; Caius Martius ROWE
2.2.47/1070 met] F; meet HANMER
2.2.67, 123, 131/1090, 1146, 1154 ⌈1⌉ SENATOR] F (Senat.)
1104 on ones] F. Neither form is unacceptable, though the combination might suggest an error.
2.2.91 chin] F (Shinne)
2.2.108/1131 tooke: . . . foot,] STEEVENS (Tyrwhitt); ~, . . . ~ : F
2.2.111/1134 he,] This edition (S.W.W.); ~, F. Shakespeare's presumably light punctuation may have been misunderstood by scribe or compositor. 'Painted | With shunlesse destinie' elaborates Coriolanus as 'a thing of Blood'.
2.2.148/1171 thus,] F3; ~, F1
2.2.155/1178 SENATORS] F (Senat.)
2.2.160/1183 heere:] THEOBALD; ~, F
2.3.19 abram] F (Abram). A corruption of *auburn*; here retained as a possible characterizing feature of the Citizen's speech.
2.3.28 wedged] F (wadg'd)
2.3.38/1221 it. I say:] THEOBALD; ~, I ~. F
2.3.42 all together] F (altogether)
2.3.52/1235 tongue] F2; tougne F1
2.3.62/1245 three] F; two ROWE (also adjusting speech-prefixes)
2.3.67/1250 but not] CAMBRIDGE; but F; not F3
2.3.88, 91, 106/1269, 1272, 1287 ⌈4⌉ CITIZEN] CAMBRIDGE; I. F
2.3.104/1285 ⌈5⌉ CITIZEN] CAMBRIDGE; 2. F; Fourth Cit⟨izen⟩. REED
2.3.114/1295 hier] F2 (hire); higher F1
2.3.115/1296 Womanish] This edition; Wooluiſh F; woolish MASON (conj.); foolish LEO (Mason); woolyish WILSON (conj.). The toge is a garment of humility, and can scarcely be wolfish. 'Woolish' or 'woolyish' similarly seems contradicted by 'Naples' (2.1.231/ 987); either suggests a resemblance rather than a fabric, is unexampled elsewhere in Shakespeare, and, especially in combination with 'toge', is quaint if not ridiculous. The beginning and end of the emendation 'Womanish' are the same as those of F's reading; n/u is the simplest misreading. How the middle of the word came to be corrupted is not clear in detail and may involve compound error with 'tongue' (a miscorrection from foul proof?). *Womanish* is disyllabic elsewhere in Shakespeare, and in another Roman tragedy is descriptive of enduring 'Our yoake, and sufferance' (Caesar 1.3.83/481). As well as symbolizing 'Womanish' submission, the toge presumably reminds the manly Coriolanus of a woman's gown.
2.3.115/1296 togue] MALONE (Steevens); tongue F1; gowne F2
2.3.116/1297 does] F1; do F4
2.3.118/1299 things,] POPE; ~, F
2.3.118/1299 doo 't,] THEOBALD; ~ ? F
2.3.132/1313 ⌈6⌉ CITIZEN] CAMBRIDGE; 1. Cit⟨izen⟩. F; 5 Cit⟨izen⟩. REED
2.3.134/1315 ⌈7⌉ CITIZEN] CAMBRIDGE; 2. Cit⟨izen⟩. F; 6 Cit⟨izen⟩. REED
2.3.217 therefor] F (therefore)
2.3.243/1424 And . . . surnam'd,] DELIUS 2; not in F. POPE first supplied a line on the basis of North's Plutarch, which confirms that the sense in F is defective and shows what is missing. Unlike Pope's 'darling of the people', the phrase 'that was so surnam'd' is found in North. The minimum interpolation is 'Censorinus' before 'Nobly nam'd', dividing after 'named so' (SISSON), but it is easier to suppose that eyeskip from 'And Censorinus . . .' to 'And Nobly . . .' led to loss of a whole line.

2.3.244/1425 nam'd, so,] POPE (subs., adding 'for' after 'so'); ~, ~, F
2.3.254/1435 ⌈A CITIZEN⌉ We . . . ⌈ANOTHER CITIZEN⌉ Almost] This edition; All. We . . . almoſt F
3.1.5/1450 raid] F (roade)
3.1.33, 67, 79/1478, 1512, 1524 ⌈1⌉ SENATOR] F (Senat.)
3.1.46/1491 Suppliants,] F4; ~: F1
3.1.50/1495 CORIOLANUS] THEOBALD; Com⟨inius⟩. F. 3.1.49-52/1494-7 is best understood as an exchange of personal insults: Brutus' retort in 3.1.51-2/1496-7 specifically challenges Coriolanus' fitness to wield power.
3.1.61/1506 abus'd, set on:] ROWE; ~ : ſet ~, F; ~.—Set on;— THEOBALD
3.1.94/1539 good,] POPE 2 (Theobald); God! F
3.1.100/1545 he] F; they HANMER. See following note.
3.1.101, 104/1546, 1549 Then . . . īpotance, Let . . . you] F (but reading 'Ignorance' for 'īpotance'); Let . . . you, Then . . . ignorance HANMER. Hanmer's plausible reading could result from misinterpretation of Shakespeare's papers if 'If none . . . if you are not' and 'Then vale your Ignorance' were constituents of a marginal addition, the latter perhaps squeezed in up the side of the leaf. But the transposition is not necessary, and assumes error in 'he' (3.1.100/1545).
3.1.101/1546 īpotance] COLLIER 2 (Collier MS); Ignorance F. Conjecturally, 'īpotance' was misread 'ignorance' under the influence of 'Learn'd' and 'Fooles'. 'Vale your Ignorance' makes doubtful sense and follows with difficulty after 'If he haue power' (see previous note). 'Vale your īpotance' ('debase yourselves in your impotence') is also compressed, but the sense is clarified by the context of 'power' and the similar apparent paradox of 'awake | Your dangerous Lenity'.
3.1.132/1577 Natiue] F; motive CRAIG-CASE (Johnson)
3.1.134/1579 Bosome-multiplied] F; bissom multitude SINGER 2 (Collier MS). *Bissom* gives a sense irrelevant to 'digest'.
3.1.146/1591 Where on] ROWE; Whereon F
3.1.163/1608 the power] F; power HINMAN (MS conj.)
3.1.164-5 He's . . . He's] F (Has . . . Ha's)
3.1.169/1614 Bench: in a Rebellion,] POPE; ~, in a ~ : F
3.1.175/1620 The] F; Ye HINMAN (MS conj.)
3.1.180/1625 ALL ⌈THE PATRICIANS⌉] MALONE (subs.); All. F
3.1.185/1630 ALL ⌈THE CITIZENS⌉] CAPELL; All. F. Similarly 3.1.193, 200, 202, 228, 272, and 282/1638, 1645, 1673, 1717, and 1727.
3.1.185/1630 2 SENATOR] F; Senators, &c. CAMBRIDGE
3.1.186/1631 CITIZENS and PATRICIANS] CAMBRIDGE; not in F. Either the prefix is implied in the stage direction's 'all', or duplication of 'All.' prefixes here and at 3.1.188/1633 led to deletion of the first.
3.1.188/1633 SOME CITIZENS and PATRICIANS] F (All.); Patricians. ALEXANDER; HIBBARD reads MENENIUS (omitting prefix at 3.1.189/1634); ÆDILES This edition conj. In the following lines both citizens and aediles call for peace, but not the patricians as a distinct group. An error for aediles would explain why 'All.' follows lines also evidently spoken by 'All' (see previous note), but F might reflect what Shakespeare actually wrote. North's Plutarch describes some of the citizens favouring restraint: 'When the Ædiles came to laye handes vpon Martius to doe that they were commaunded, diuers of the people them selues thought it to cruell, and violent a dede' (Bullough, v. 523). For Shakespeare's 'All' meaning less than all, see Honigmann.
3.1.190/1635 speake.] F; speak, speak. KEIGHTLEY
3.1.198, 232, 338/1643, 1677, 1783 ⌈1⌉ SENATOR] F (Sena.)
3.1.203/1648 CORIOLANUS] POPE; Com⟨inius⟩. F. Some editors retain F, but the responses 'This deserues Death' (3.1.206/1651) and

'Martius is worthy | Of present Death' (3.1.210-11/1655-6) indicate an error.

3.1.220/1665 poysones] This edition (*conj.* Johnson); poyſonous F. F is defensible, but the equation of an abstract noun ('ways') and a concrete one is highly characteristic of Shakespeare and much more effective than F's weak and weakly qualified epithet. Compare 'It is a minde | That shall remain a poison where it is' (3.1.89-90/1534-5), and 'Dangerous conceits are in their natures poisons' (*Othello* 3.3.330/1778); also 'His Antidotes are poyson' (*Timon* 4.3.434/1862), etc. A form such as 'poysones' could be misunderstood, in which case it is not even necessary to postulate a minor error of misreading.

3.1.224/1669 seene me] F; seen me do KEIGHTLEY; seen HINMAN (MS *conj.*)
3.1.229/1674 your] ROWE; our F
3.1.231/1676 CORIOLANUS] WARBURTON; Com⟨inius⟩. F
3.1.236/1681 COMINIUS] F2; Corio⟨lanus⟩. F1
3.1.237/1682 CORIOLANUS] STEEVENS (Tyrwhitt); Mene⟨nius⟩. F
3.1.239/1684 ⌈MENENIUS⌉ Be] STEEVENS 1 (Tyrwhitt); Be F. Steevens's first arrangement follows F's lineation (see lineation note), but he later (STEEVENS 2) transposed the prefix to before 'Put not'.
3.1.261/1706 A PATRICIAN] F (*Patri.*); 2. Pat⟨rician⟩. MALONE
3.1.272, 282/1717, 1727 ALL ⌈THE CITIZENS⌉] CAPELL; *All.* F
3.1.275 comes't] F (Com'ſt)
3.1.289/1734 our] THEOBALD; one F
3.1.297/1742 Disease:] ROWE; ~ₐ F
3.1.307/1752 SCICINIUS] HANMER (Warburton); Menen⟨ius⟩. F. Some editors have avoided reattribution, THEOBALD conjecturing 'is't' for 'is' (3.1.308/1753) and STEEVENS (2) reading the speech as a rhetorical question.
3.1.326/1771 bring him] POPE; bring him in peace F; bring him in GOMME. F is usually explained as a compositorial anticipation of 3.1.328/1773, but a survival of a false start in Shakespeare's papers is equally likely. PROUDFOOT conjectures retaining 'in peace' but omitting 'go'.
3.2.20/1803 taxings] SISSON; things F; thwartings THEOBALD; crossings HIBBARD
3.2.25/1808 ⌈1⌉ SENATOR] F (*Sen.*)
3.2.31/1814 heard] THEOBALD (Warburton); heart F
3.2.41-2/1824-5 Noble, . . . speake.] F; ~ . . . . ~, HIBBARD
3.2.53/1836 you on] F; on you POPE
3.2.56/1839 roated] F; rooted JOHNSON
3.2.56-7/1839-40 but | Bastards, and] F (*dividing after* 'Tongue' *and* 'Syllables'); but bastards | And CAPELL; thought's bastards, and HUDSON 2 (Badham); thought's bastards, airy STAUNTON (*conj.*). Editors have usually given 'Your . . . syllables' as a verse line, rearranging the previous lines instead, as in this edition, of those which follow (see lineation notes). The metrical irregularity of 'Your . . . syllables' is especially suspect in view of F's incomplete part-line 'The hazard of much blood.' (3.2.61/1844), which is usually retained. As the part-line is 4 lines from the end of a Folio page in the first half of a quire (bb3), Compositor B may have been wasting space. Emendations (Badham's apart) serve primarily to improve the metre; the present lineation renders them unnecessary.
3.2.65-6/1848-9 Sonne, these . . . you,] THEOBALD (Warburton); ~: Theſe . . . ~, F
3.2.78/1861 Wᵗʰ] RANN (Johnson); Which F; While STAUNTON (*conj.*). 'Wᶜʰ' and 'Wᵗʰ' can be virtually indistinguishable.
3.2.78/1861 often] F; offer This edition *conj.* A possible alternative to 'Wᵗʰ'.
3.2.80/1863 or say] F; say HANMER. What follows is the alternative to the gestural silence in which 'Action is eloquence'.
3.2.100/1883 Must I with] F; Must POPE; With WILSON
3.2.101/1884 beare? well,] POPE; ~, ~? F
3.2.102/1885 Plot, to loose,] THEOBALD; ~, to ~, F
3.2.112/1895 turn'd] F; tun'd This edition *conj.* 'Tun'd' would be more specific and would emphasize the Shakespearian image of a played musical instrument, particularly a pipe, as representative of a man whose words are determined by circumstance or expediency. 'Into' in the following line would mean 'unto'.

3.2.115/1898 lull] F; lulls ROWE
3.2.129 sucked'st] F (fuck'ſt)
3.3.33/1962 forth] F2 (for th'); fourth F1
3.3.37/1966 Throng] THEOBALD; Through F
3.3.56/1985 Accents] THEOBALD; Actions F
3.3.71/2000 hell, fould] POPE; ~ . Fould F
3.3.73-5/2002-4 deaths: . . . clutcht, . . . Millions, . . . numbers:] ROWE; ~, . . . ~ : . . . ~, . . . ~ . F
3.3.79/2009 ALL ⌈THE CITIZENS⌉] F (*All.*). Similarly 3.3.109 and 123/2038 and 2052.
3.3.99/2028 Enuei'd] HUDSON 2 (Becket); Enui'd F. *Envy against* is found nowhere else in Shakespeare, and is not sanctioned in *OED*. Shakespeare used *inveigh* once elsewhere (*Lucrece* 1254); it is there followed by 'against'. Medial 'nuei' would easily be misread 'nuie'.
3.3.100/2029 as] F; has HANMER; and HUDSON (*conj.*). See Abbott, 113 and 114.
3.3.103/2032 doth] F1; doe F2
3.3.114/2043 for] THEOBALD; from F
3.3.134/2063 but] F; not CAPELL
3.3.137-8/2066-7 blowes. Despising . . . City, thus] POPE (*adding* 'then' *after* 'Despising'), CAPELL; ~, despiſing . . . ~. Thus F
3.3.143/2072 despight.] CAPELL (*following* F3: ~,); ~, F1
3.3.146/2075 gates, come] F; gates; come, come KEIGHTLEY
4.1.4/2080 Extreamities] F1; Extreamity F2
4.1.5/2081 chances,] F2 (*subs.*); ~. F1. Another punctuation error probably prompted by majuscule 'C' in the copy.
4.1.25 thee] F (the)
4.1.28/2104 My Mother] F; Mother POPE
4.1.35/2111 will thou] F1; will you F2; wilt thou CAPELL
4.1.37 exposure] F (expoſture). This line gives the only known occurrence of *exposture*. *OED* does not record *exposure* before Shakespeare, so 'exposture' cannot be regarded as an error for an established word. Though the alternative forms interestingly illustrate Shakespeare's word-formation, our usual principles of modernization have been applied (compare *fixure*).
4.1.38/2114 VIRGILIA] KEIGHTLEY; Corio⟨lanus⟩. F
4.2.17/2151 VIRGILIA You . . . I would] F; You . . . Vir⟨gilia⟩. I would WARBURTON
4.2.19 this,] F (~,). Either pointed as in this edition or without the comma ('fool' becoming the object of 'Note', the clause being addressed to the others). The latter interpretation seems less likely, and F's punctuation cannot reliably arbitrate.
4.2.23-4/2157-8 words, . . . good.] ROWE (*subs.*); ~ . . . . ~, F
4.2.27-30/2161-4 VIRGILIA . . . Rome] *speech-prefixes as* F. HANMER assigned all to Volumnia; MURRY conjectured that she speaks all but 'Good . . . Rome' (4.2.30/2164), this being Virgilia's; Hinman (MS) anticipated BROCKBANK in assigning 'What then' to Virgilia and the remainder to Volumnia. See Clayton.
4.2.39/2173 let's] F; let us POPE
4.3.9/2199 approu'd] STEEVENS; appear'd F
4.3.32/2222 will] F2; well F1
4.4.13/2252 seeme] F4; ſeemes F1
4.4.23/2262 hate] CAPELL; haue F; leaue PROUDFOOT (*conj.*)
4.5.3 master] F (M.)
4.5.21-2/2285 Prythee . . . him] F. This looks like a cue for an exit. The Third and Second Servingmen remain on stage; nevertheless, only two servingmen participate in 4.5.23-36/2286-2299, and only one thereafter. Confusion in the identity of the servingmen is possible, whereby either the Second should instruct the First to leave here, or the First dismiss the Second, to leave himself at 4.5.36.1/2299. Against this, it will be noted that F is self-consistent: the First Servingman remains on stage throughout the present exchange and the dialogue between Coriolanus and Aufidius, and so becomes one of the two servingmen to overhear that dialogue (assuming, as one probably must, that F's '*Enter*' at 4.5.148.1/2410.2 is misleading). In the theatre, some rationalization might be justified.
4.5.53.1/2315.1 The . . . aside] *not in* F. At 4.5.148.1/2410.2 F has the direction '*Enter two of the Seruingmen*', but it seems from the dialogue that follows that the Servingmen witnessed the en-

counter between Aufidius and Coriolanus. The entry at 4.5.148.1/2410.2 is probably authorial; though apparently explicit, 'Enter' is used imprecisely.

4.5.128/2390 no other] F1; no F3

4.5.132/2394 o're-beart] WHITE (Jackson); o're-beate F; o'er-bear ROWE

4.5.148.1/2410.2 The . . . forward] Enter two of the Seruingmen F. See note to 4.5.53.1/2315.1

4.5.164/2426 is, yet] This edition (S.W.W.); ~ : but F. In other contexts *yet* and *but* would be interchangeable, hence the ease of a substitution. Here 'but', perhaps coupled with a misunderstanding of 'one', seems to have precipitated mispunctuation.

4.5.165/2426 then he,] DYCE; then ~, F. Dyce's altered punctuation was accompanied by the first modernization of 'one' to 'on'. Both changes were resisted by Wilson, who objected to the reading: the "but" . . . rules it out' (see previous note). Brockbank, reading 'on', retained F's comma on the grounds that it maintained ambiguity. But 'you wot on' as an independent clause is unexampled in Shakespeare; 'he' should almost certainly be part of the idiom. F's setting of 'You wot one' as a separate verse line spuriously detaches it, and would further encourage the placing of a comma after 'he'.

4.5.165 on] F (one)

4.5.180 lief] F (liue)

4.5.177, 181/2439, 2442 1 and 2 SERUINGMEN] F (*Both.*). Similarly 4.5.240/2500.

4.5.190-1/2450-1 him, directly, . . . on't, before] F; ~, ~, . . . ~ : before POPE; ~, ~, . . . ~. Before HIBBARD (Smith)

4.5.194/2454 broyld] POPE; boyld F

4.5.205 sowl] F (sole)

4.5.213, 214/2473, 2474 Deiectitude] COLLIER 2 (Collier MS); Directitude F; discreditude MALONE (*conj.*). It is inconceivable why the Third Servingman should coin a word with *direct* as its root. Scribe or compositor, having once committed the error, would assume (correctly) that the second word was the same. Hibbard's claim that 'deiectitude' (a word not in *OED*) would be intelligible to the First Servingman may be dismissed. 'Deiectitude' anticipates 'his Crest vp againe'.

4.5.227/2488 sprightly walking] F; ~, waking POPE

4.5.229/2490 sleepie] F3; fleepe F1

4.5.231/2492 warre] ROWE 3; warres F. Probably contaminated by 'warres' (for 'war's') in the previous line. The singular agrees with 'a Rauisher' and the singular elsewhere in the dialogue; it also gives the truer antithesis to 'peace'.

4.6.2/2502 tame, the] F; tame, i'th THEOBALD; ta'en, the JOHNSON (*conj.*). F favours understanding 'His remedies are tame' as 'our curing ourselves of him is without violent effects', so sustaining the image from earlier scenes of Coriolanus as a diseased limb, but does not rule out the interpretation others prefer, 'the threat of redress from him is weak'.

4.6.4/2504 hurry. Heere do we] F; ~, here, do HUDSON; ~, here, do, WHITE

4.6.14/2514 not] F; not now HINMAN (MS *conj.*)

4.6.33/2533 thinking,] F4; ~, F1

4.6.36/2536 Lamentation] F2; Lamention F1

4.6.37/2537 found] F; find HANMER

4.6.52/2552 hath] F1; haue F4

4.6.60/2560 come] ROWE; comming F; come in MALONE. F is probably contaminated by 'going' at the end of the previous line.

4.6.76/2576 Contrariety] F; contrarieties HANMER

4.6.77/2577 2 MESSENGER] F (*Mes.*)

4.6.99/2599 Flyes] F; sheep CAPELL (*conj.*); pigs LEO (*conj.*)

4.6.100/2600 you, that] F: that POPE

4.6.145/2645 one] F2; oue F1

4.7.15/2683 Haue] F; had POPE

4.7.19/2687 him. Although] CAPELL (*following* Pope: ~ ; though); ~, although F

4.7.37/2705 'twas] F3; 'was F1

4.7.39/2707 defect] F2; detect F1

4.7.49/2717 Vertues,] F2; Vertue, F1

4.7.55/2723 foulter] DYCE; fouler F; founder MALONE (Johnson); fuller HIBBARD

5.1.16/2741 fair] HANMER; for F

5.1.19/2744 lesse] F; least POPE

5.1.60-1/2785-6 him. . . . will,] DYCE 2 (Heath); ~, . . . ~. F

5.1.61/2786 I] F; Ye THEOBALD (*conj.*); You HANMER

5.1.68/2793 He . . . not] F; What he would not, he sent in writing after me JERVIS (*conj.* in Cambridge). Some editors have suspected a missing line or missing part-lines.

5.1.69/2794 hold to his] This edition (*conj.* Solly in Cambridge); yeeld to his F; yield no new JOHNSON (*conj.*); yield to no SINGER. It is strained to take 'Bound' as applying to either the letter itself or Cominius, whilst F gives an improbable reading if Coriolanus is 'Bound'. Brockbank tendentiously glosses *yield* as 'comply', but *OED*'s entry 17, which he cites, indicates eventual compliance with a position at first opposed. 'His' could be a contamination from the line below; 'yeeld to no conditions' is much clearer than F, but might imply that the Romans were in a position to offer conditions to Coriolanus—hence Johnson's more radical suggestion. Solly's convincing 'hold' is strengthened by Wilson's observation that the word could easily be misread 'yeld'.

5.2.19/2817 verified] F; magnified HANMER; notified SINGER; rarefied STAUNTON (*conj.*); amplified HUDSON 2 (Lettsom); vivified BULLOCH (*conj.*); varnished WILSON (Edwards)

5.2.64-7/2863-6 Coriolanus : . . . him, . . . suffering :] HANMER (*see also following note*); ~, . . . ~ : . . . ~, F

5.2.64-5/2863 but by MALONE; but F; by HANMER

5.2.75/2874 our] F4; your F1; yon KEIGHTLEY (*conj.*). A common error. F1 is especially suspicious as the only formal pronoun Menenius uses for Coriolanus in this speech against 11 informal ones, though emendation would be justified in any case.

5.2.87/2886 pitty, note] THEOBALD (Thirlby); ~ : Note F

5.3.15-16/2925-6 accept: . . . more, a] JOHNSON (*subs.*); ~, . . . ~ : A F

5.3.48/2958 prayte] POPE 2 (Theobald); pray F

5.3.63/2973 holpe] POPE; hope F

5.3.66/2976 candied] This edition (*conj.* Daniel); curdied F; curdled ROWE 3. An easy misreading. F is suspect for combining *OED*'s only instance of *curdy* (unless an unusual spelling of *curded* or an error for *curdled*) with a verb which can only with difficulty apply to the formation of an icicle: to *curd* or *curdle* can be glossed as 'congeal', but in the sense 'coagulate' rather than 'freeze, make crystalline'. This would be Shakespeare's only use of a verb based on sb. *curd* which did not apply directly to blood. Compare the emendation with 'Candied with Ice' (*Timon* 4.3.227/1655), where again the image is emblematic.

5.3.73/2983 vnvulnerable] F; invulnerable JOHNSON. A very easy misreading, but as *OED* cites no instance of *invulnerable* before Shakespeare, there was probably no fixed form.

5.3.81/2991 things] CAPELL; thing F. Lack of concord with 'denials' makes F more than plausibly cryptic.

5.3.91/3001 you] F; we ROWE 3

5.3.116/3026 thorough] JOHNSON; through F

5.3.150/3060 fine] JOHNSON; fiue F

5.3.153/3063 charge] THEOBALD; change F

5.3.155 noble man] F (Nobleman)

5.3.170/3080 him with] F2; him with him with F1

5.3.180/3090 this] THEOBALD; his F

5.3.183/3093 He . . . silent] *here in* F; *after* O Mother, Mother! HONIGMANN (*conj.*)

5.4.31/3151 The] F; Ye HINMAN (MS *conj.*)

5.4.41, 46, 61, 62/3161, 3166, 3181, 3182 2 MESSENGER] F (*Mef.* or *Meff.*)

5.4.45/3165 Is't] F; Is it POPE

5.4.49 all together] F (altogether)

5.4.63/3183 Wee'l] F; We will CAPELL

5.5.0.1/3183.1 Enter . . . Citizens] F merely adds 'with other Lords' *after* '*passing ouer the Stage*'. As in *Measure* 5.1/Sc. 16, the scene formally enacts a processional return to the city through the gates; as in *Caesar* 3.1/Sc. 8, the onlookers presumably gather before the procession enters. Citizens seem to be required, though

CORIOLANUS

it is possible that the Senator addresses the audience itself as the supposed bystanders.

5.5.4 Unshout] F (Vnſhoot)
5.6.33/3222 proiects, to accomplish,] F3; ~, to ~, F1
5.6.44-6/3233-5 him.... Lies,] F4 (subs.); ~,... ~; F1
5.6.56-7/3245-6 second:... way, his] THEOBALD (following Rowe); ~,... ~. His F
5.6.102/3291 each at others] F; each at other ROWE; at each other STEEVENS
5.6.116/3305 Flutter'd] F3; Flatter'd F1. OED quotes F3 under Flutter. There is a separate entry for Flatter, 'to float, flutter'; OED's examples show the verb used intransitively; none can be dated afer 1450. F1 almost certainly results from misreading.

5.6.130.2/3319.2 and Conspirators] not in F. See following note.
5.6.133-4/3322-3 him, Masters, | All,] F (but dividing after 'quiet'); him—Masters, all, ROWE. Most editors follow Rowe's emendation which is unnecessary and will not readily accommodate the lineation adopted in this edition (prompted by F's divisions in the previous and following speeches; see lineation note). F's stage direction does not preclude the Conspirators from following the example of Aufidius in treading on the body. 'Be quiet' is perhaps most plausibly addressed to the perpetrators of the violence, and 'put vp your Swords' is certainly not addressed to the citizens.

INCIDENTALS

10 away.] ~, 52 matter,] ~, 101 body. The] ~, the 111 crowned] crown'd 202 Hunger broke] ~-~ 280 proceede.] ~, 352 hand,] ~, 447 off.] ~, 455 fellows.] ~, 472 Fortune,] ~, 515 Martius.] ~, 531 speak'st] ſpeakeſt 561 plague—Tribunes] ~-~ 661 atchieud] atchieued 669 May] Mar. May 778 how are] ho ware 825 Forset-seller] ~-|~ 878 Browes,] ~: 1212 blocke-head] Fb; ~, ~ Fa 1305 suffred] suffered 1425 named] nam'd 1488 ruld] ruled 1575 Valour,] (or ~,) 1620 apprehended.] ~: 1630 weapons.] ~: 1684 Capitoll.] ~: 1709 and] & (see lineation note) 1710 himself.] ~, 1882 vnbarbed] vnbarb'd 1994 so.] ~, 2032 it:] ~. 2136 vexd] vexed 2162 posterity.] ~, 2207 diuision.] ~, 2282 anon.] ~, 2403 waies:] ~, 2438 Rascals.] ~, 2447 him.] ~, 2479 forward?] ~: 2526 Neighbours] Neighhours 2535 assiſtāce.] ~, 2727 lou'd] loued 2748 offred] offered 2775 He] F (text); Hee F (c.w.) 2803 Coriolanus.] ~, 2888 lou'd] loued 2947 And... kin.] &... ~, (see lineation note) 2973 thee.] ~, 3061 Gods,] ~. 3080 knees.] ~, 3093 And... litle.] &... ~, (see lineation note) 3161 preuayl'd,] (or ~.) 3211 watred] watered 3248 Lords.] ~,

FOLIO STAGE DIRECTIONS

1.1.0.1-2/0.1-2 Enter a Company of Mutinous Citizens, with Staues, | Clubs, and other weapons.
1.1.44.1/43.1 Showts within.
1.1.47.1/46.1 Enter Menenius Agrippa. (after 1.1.48/47)
1.1.161/159 Enter Caius Martius.
1.1.221.1/219.1 Enter a Messenger hastily.
1.1.226/224 Enter Sicinius Velutus, Annius Brutus Cominisn, Titus | Lartius, with other Senatours. (after 'Elders'; 'Cominius' with turned 'us' ligature)
1.1.250, 251/248, 249 Exeunt. | Citizens steale away. Manet Sicin. & Brutus. (after 1.1.251/249)
1.1.279/277 Exeunt
1.2.0.1/277.1 Enter Tullus Auffidius with Senators of Coriolus.
1.2.37.1-2/314.1-2 Exeunt omnes.
1.3.0.1-3/314.3-5 Enter Volumnia and Virgilia, mother and wife to Martius: | They set them downe on two lowe stooles and sowe.
1.3.25.1/340.1 Enter a Gentlewoman.
1.3.46/361 Exit Gent.
1.3.49.1/364.1 Enter Valeria with an Vsher, and a Gentlewoman.
1.3.113.1/428.1-3 Exeunt Ladies
1.4.0.1-4/428.4-7 Enter Martius, Titus Lartius, with Drumme and Co-|lours, with Captaines and Souldiers, as | before the City Corialus: to them | a Messenger.
1.4.12.1-2/440.1-2 They Sound a Parley: Enter two Senators with others on | the Walles of Corialus.
1.4.15/443 Drum a farre off.
1.4.19/447 Alarum farre off. (after 'off')
1.4.22.2/450.2 Enter the Army of the Volces.
1.4.29.1-2/457.1-2 Alarum, the Romans are beat back to their Trenches
1.5.0.1-2/457.3-4 Enter Martius Cursing.
1.5.13.2-3/470.2-4 Another Alarum, and Martius followes them to | gates, and is shut in.
1.5.16.1/473.1 Enter the Gati.
1.5.17.1/474.1 Alarum continues (after 'in', 1.5.18/475)
1.5.18.1/475.1 Enter Titus Lartius
1.5.32/489 Enter Martius bleeding, assaulted by the Enemy.
1.5.33.1/490.1 They fight, and all enter the City.

1.6.0.1/490.2 Enter certaine Romanes with spoiles.
1.6.3.2-4/493.1-3 exeunt. | Alarum continues still a-farre off. | Enter Martius, and Titus with a Trumpet.
1.6.28.1/518.1 Exeunt
1.7.0.1/518.2 Enter Cominius as it were in retire, with soldiers.
1.7.9/527 Enter a Messenger. (after 'Newes')
1.7.21/539 Enter Martius.
1.7.75.1-3/593.1-3 They all shout and waue their swords, take him vp in their | Armes, and cast vp their Caps.
1.7.87/605 Exeunt
1.8.0.1-3/605.1-3 Titus Lartius, hauing set a guard vpon Carioles, going with | Drum and Trumpet toward Cominius, and Caius Mar-|tius, Enters with a Lieutenant, other Souldiours, and a | Scout.
1.8.8.1/613.1 Exit
1.9.0.1/613.2 Alarum, as in Battaile.
1.9.0.1-2/613.2-3 Enter Martius and Auffidius at seuerall doores.
1.9.13.1-3/626.1-3 Heere they fight, and certaine Volces come in the ayde | of Auffi. Martius fights til they be driuen in breathles.
1.10.0.1-3/628.1-3 Flourish. Alarum. A Retreat is sounded. Enter at | one Doore Cominius, with the Romanes: At | another Doore Martius, with his | Arme in a Scarfe.
1.10.11/639 Enter Titus with his Power, from the Pursuit.
1.10.40.1-3/668.1-3 A long flourish. They all cry, Martius, Martius, | cast vp their Caps and Launces: Cominius | and Lartius stand bare.
1.10.65.1/693.1 Flourish. Trumpets sound, and Drums.
1.10.93.1/721.1 Exeunt.
1.10.93.1-1.11.0.1/721.2-3 A flourish. Cornets. Enter Tullus Auffidius | bloudie, with two or three Souldiors.
2.1.0.1-2/754.3-4 Enter Menenius with the two Tribunes of the | people, Sicinius & Brutus.
2.1.94.1/850.1 Bru. and Scic. Aside.
2.1.94.2/850.2 Enter Volumina, Virgilia, and Valeria.
2.1.153.1/909.1 A showt, and flourish. (after 'Trumpets')
2.1.158.1-4/914.1-4 A Sennet. Trumpets sound. | Enter Cominius the Generall, and Titus Latius: be-|tweene them Coriolanus, crown'd with an Oaken | Garland, with Captaines and Soul-|diers, and a Herauld.
2.1.163.1/919.1 Sound. Flourish.

599

CORIOLANUS

2.1.168/924 Kneeles.
2.1.201.1-2/957.1-2 Flourish. Cornets. | Exeunt in State, as before. | Enter Brutus and Scicinius.
2.1.256/1012 Enter a Messenger.
2.1.267/1023 Exeunt.
2.2.0.1-2/1023.1-2 Enter two Officers, to lay Cushions, as it were, | in the Capitoll.
2.2.36.1-6/1059.1-5 A Sennet. Enter the Patricians, and the Tribunes of | the People, Lictors before them: Coriolanus, Mene-|nius, Cominius the Consul: Scicinius and Brutus | take their places by themselues: Corio-|lanus stands.
2.2.66/1089 Coriolanus rises, and offers to goe away.
2.2.77/1100 Exit Coriolanus
2.2.132.1/1155.1 Enter Coriolanus.
2.2.155.1-2/1178.1-2 Flourish Cornets. | Then Exeunt. Manet Sicinius and Brutus.
2.3.0.1/1184.1 Enter seuen or eight Citizens.
2.3.40.1-2/1223.1-2 Enter Coriolanus in a gowne of Humility, with | Menenius.
2.3.62/1245 Exit | Enter three of the Citizens. (after 'manner', 2.3.61/1244)
2.3.84-84.1/1265.1-2 Exeunt. Enter two other Citizens.
2.3.124.1/1305.1 Enter three Citizens more.
2.3.138.1/1319.1 Enter Menenius, with Brutus and Scicinius.
2.3.151.1/1332.1 Exeunt Coriol. and Mene.
2.3.154.1/1335.1 Enter the Plebeians.
2.3.255/1436 Exeunt Plebeians.
2.3.263/1445 Exeunt.
3.1.0.1-2/1445.1-2 Cornets. Enter Coriolanus, Menenius, all the Gentry, | Cominius, Titus Latius, and other Senators.
3.1.21.1/1466.1 Enter Scicinius and Brutus.
3.1.175/1620 Enter an Ædile. (after 3.1.174/1619)
3.1.182.1/1627.1 Enter a rabble of Plebeians with the Ædiles.
3.1.185.1/1630.1 They all bustle about Coriolanus.
3.1.222/1667 Corio. drawes his Sword.
3.1.228.1-2/1673.1-2 Exeunt. | In this Mutinie, the Tribunes, the Ædiles, and the | People are beat in.
3.1.253.1/1698.1 Exeunt Coriolanus and | Cominius.
3.1.260/1705 A Noise within.
3.1.262.1/1707.1 Enter Brutus and Sicinius with the rabble againe.
3.1.338.1-2/1783.1-2 Exeunt Omnes.
3.2.0.1/1783.3 Enter Ccriolanus with Nobles.
3.2.6/1789 Enter Volumnia.
3.2.23.1/1806 Enter Menenius with the Senators.
3.2.92/1875 Enter Cominius.
3.2.137.1/1920.1 Exit Volumnia
3.2.146/1929 Exeunt
3.3.0.1/1929.1 Enter Sicinius and Brutus.
3.3.5/1934 Enter an Edile. (after 'come')
3.3.30.1-2/1959.1-2 Enter Coriolanus, Menenius, and Comi-|nius, with others.
3.3.40.1/1969.1 Enter the Edile with the Plebeians.
3.3.139.1-3/2068.1-3 Exeunt Coriolanus, Cominius, with Cumalijs. | They all shout, and throw vp their Caps.
3.3.147/2076 Exeunt.
4.1.0.1-2/2076.1-2 Enter Coriolanus, Volumnia, Virgilia, Menenius, Cominius, | with the yong Nobility of Rome.
4.1.58.1/2134.1 Exeunt
4.2.0.1-2/2134.2-3 Enter the two Tribunes, Sicinius, and Brutus, | with the Edile.
4.2.7.2/2141.2 Enter Volumnia, Virgilia, and Menenius. (after 4.2.8/2142)
4.2.47/2181 Exit Tribunes.
4.2.56/2190 Exeunt
4.2.56.1/2190.1 Exit.
4.3.0.1/2190.2 Enter a Roman, and a Volce.
4.3.50/2239 Exeunt.
4.4.0.1-2/2239.1-2 Enter Coriolanus in meane Apparrell, Dis-|guisd, and muffled.
4.4.6/2245 Enter a Citizen. (after 'sir')

4.4.11.1/2250.1 Exit Citizen
4.4.26/2265 Exit.
4.5.0.1/2265.1 Musicke playes. Enter a Seruingman.
4.5.2.1/2267.1 Enter another Seruingman.
4.5.4/2268.1 Exit
4.5.4.1/2268.2 Enter Coriolanus.
4.5.6.1/2270.1 Enter the first Seruingman.
4.5.8.1/2272.1 Exit
4.5.10.1/2274.1 Enter second Seruant.
4.5.18.1/2282.1 Enter 3 Seruingman, the 1 meets him.
4.5.33.1/2296.1 Pushes him away from him.
4.5.36.1/2299 Exit second Seruingman.
4.5.50.1/2312.1 Beats him away
4.5.50.2/2312.2 Enter Auffidius with the Seruingman.
4.5.148/2410.1 Exeunt
4.5.148.1/2410.2 Enter two of the Seruingmen.
4.5.174.1/2436.1 Enter the third Seruingman.
4.5.240/2500 Exeunt
4.6.0.1/2500.1 Enter the two Tribunes, Sicinius, and Brutus.
4.6.9.1/2509.1 Enter Menenius.
4.6.21.1/2521.1 Enter three or foure Citizens.
4.6.28.1/2528.1 Exeunt Citizens
4.6.39/2539 Enter an Ædile.
4.6.58.1/2558.1 Enter a Messenger.
4.6.76.1/2576.1 Enter Messenger.
4.6.82.1/2582.1 Enter Cominius.
4.6.136/2636 Enter a Troope of Citizens.
4.6.157.1/2657 Exeunt both.
4.6.165.1/2665.1 Exit Cit.
4.6.168/2668 Exeunt Tribunes.
4.7.0.1/2668.1 Enter Auffidius with his Lieutenant.
4.7.57.1/2725.1 exeunt
5.1.0.1-2/2725.2-3 Enter Menenius, Cominius, Sicinius, Brutus, | the two Tribunes, with others.
5.1.62/2787 Exit.
5.1.73/2798 Exeunt
5.2.0.1/2798.1 Enter Menenius to the Watch or Guard.
5.2.59.1/2858.1 Enter Coriolanus with Auffidius.
5.2.94.1/2893.1 Exeunt | Manet the Guard and Menenius.
5.2.107.1/2907 Exit
5.2.110.1/2910 Exit Watch.
5.3.0.1-2/2910.1-2 Enter Coriolanus and Auffidius.
5.3.19/2929 Shout within (after 'this')
5.3.21.1-2/2931.1-2 Enter Virgilia, Volumnia, Valeria, yong Martius, | with Attendants.
5.3.50.1/2960.1 Kneeles
5.3.183/3093 Holds her by the hand silent.
5.3.210/3120 Exeunt.
5.4.0.1/3120.1 Enter Menenius and Sicinius.
5.4.35.1/3155.1 Enter a Messenger.
5.4.40/3160 Enter another Messenger.
5.4.49/3169 Trumpets, Hoboyes, Drums beate, altogether. (after 'you')
5.4.52/3172 A shout within (after 'you')
5.4.58/3178 Sound still with the Shouts. (after 'ioy')
5.4.63/3183 Exeunt.
5.5.0.1-3/3183.1-3 Enter two Senators, with Ladies, passing ouer | the Stage, with other Lords.
5.5.6.1/3189.1 A Flourish with Drummes & Trumpets.
5.6.0.1/3189.2 Enter Tullus Auffidius, with Attendants.
5.6.8/3197 Enter 3 or 4 Conspirators of Auffidius Faction.
5.6.48/3237 Drummes and Trumpets sounds, with great | showts of the people. (after 'hearke')
5.6.58/3247 Enter the Lords of the City. (after 5.6.59/3248)
5.6.70.1-2/3259.1-2 Enter Coriolanus marching with Drumme, and Colours. The | Commoners being with him.
5.6.130.1-2/3319.1-2 Draw both the Conspirators, and kils Martius, who | falles, Auffidius stands on him.
5.6.154.1-2/3343.1-2 Exeunt bearing the Body of Martius. A dead March | Sounded.

THE WINTER'S TALE

The Winter's Tale was first printed in the 1623 Folio, set by Compositors A and B, as the last in the sequence of comedies. Bibliographical evidence suggests that the publishers experienced delay in obtaining a manuscript (Hinman, ii. 521), and that the play was probably set into type in December 1622 (Hinman, i. 363). Malone's transcript of an entry in the office-book of Sir Henry Herbert, now lost, suggests that the prompt-book may have been missing around the time of printing. According to Malone (1790 edition, I. ii. 276) the entry read: 'For the King's players. An olde playe called *Winters Tale*, formerly allowed of by Sir George Bucke, and likewyse by mee on Mr. Hemmings his worde that there was nothing prophane added or reformed, thogh the allowed booke was missinge; and therefore I returned itt without a fee, this 19 of August, 1623.'

Copy for the Folio text was probably a transcript by Ralph Crane (see General Introduction, pp. 20-2). One of Crane's characteristics is the massing at the head of a scene of the names of all who take part in it, regardless of the point at which they enter. This is done in over half the scenes. Also characteristic of Crane is the heavy punctuation, not necessarily always corresponding to Shakespeare's intentions. Apostrophes frequently denote notional words. Paucity of stage directions is another Crane characteristic. At 4.4.639-40/2246-7 and 4.4.643-4/2250-1, Crane appears to use parentheses to mark passages spoken aside. The list of 'The Names of the Actors' printed after the play may also have been prepared by Crane.

As usual, there is little evidence of the nature of the papers that Crane copied. T. H. Howard-Hill has suggested that he transcribed Shakespeare's foul papers to make a prompt-book to replace the lost one, and then made a second transcript from the first, treating the stage directions in a manner different from that required in a prompt-book, to provide printer's copy (*N&Q* 211 (1976), 139-40). But as the Folio had been printed long before Herbert saw the new prompt-book, this seems unlikely. The original prompt-book might even have been lost as a result of being copied by Crane for the Folio. Whatever Crane's copy, it seems to have been in a well-finished state, with few of the loose ends and inconsistencies apparent in, for example, *The Two Gentlemen of Verona*.

One passage has been plausibly interpreted as a late addition of a kind which should not have stood in foul papers. As A. H. Thorndike pointed out (*PMLA* 15 (1900), 114-20), the dance of twelve satyrs at 4.4.340.1/1947.1 performed in part by men who boast to have 'danc'd before the King' is curiously similar to a dance of ten or twelve satyrs in Ben Jonson's *Masque of Oberon*, performed at Court on 1 January 1611. The passage introducing this dance could be omitted without disturbing the dialogue; no one comments upon the dance afterwards; moreover, the Clown's comment that 'My Father, and the Gent. are in sad talke' (4.4.308/1915) would be naturally followed, after the exit of Autolycus and his clients, by Polixenes' 'O Father, you'l know more of that heereafter' (4.4.341/1948), which indicates that they have been carrying on a conversation which we have not heard. Polixenes' comment is not nearly so natural after the satyr dance, since it suggests that he had been talking to the Old Shepherd rather than attending to the dance he had himself insisted upon witnessing. There is no reason to doubt Shakespeare's authorship of the passage introducing the dance, but it could be a late addition; if so, Crane was copying a prompt-book, and the original composition predates January 1611. Textually, however, there seems no reason to exclude the passage.

Obscurity of origin is an effect of Crane's habit of imposing his personal characteristics on the manuscripts that he transcribed. It also results in textual sophistications which, as Howard-Hill points out (*Ralph Crane*, 133), may extend to substantive alteration of copy, undetectable without more evidence.

S.W.W./(G.T.)

WORKS CITED

Moorman, F. W., ed., *The Winter's Tale*, Arden (1912, rev. 1933)
Pafford, J. H., ed., *The Winter's Tale*, Arden (1963)
Ringler, William B., Jr., 'The Number of Actors in Shakespeare's Early Plays', in *The Seventeenth-century Stage*, ed. G. E. Bentley (1968), pp. 110-34

TEXTUAL NOTES

1.1.8/8 vs,] THEOBALD; ~ : F
1.1.27/27 hath] F1. F2's 'have', adopted by many editors, is unnecessary (Abbott, 334).
1.2.0.2/47.2 *Camillo*] F. Ringler (p. 114) states 'it is clear that he does not re-enter until Leontes exclaims "What? *Camillo* there?"' (1.2.210/257). But the ensuing conversation requires Camillo to have observed part, at least, of the earlier action. As Shakespeare has not involved him earlier, he may not have originally intended Camillo to re-enter at the beginning of the scene; there is no other obvious point for him to do so, but, as Leontes' cupbearer, he could come and go. Editors follow Theobald in adding attendants, perhaps rightly, but they have nothing to do, and this is a domestic, not a formal scene.
1.2.106/153 And] F2; A F1. G.T. conjectures 'Or'.
1.2.111 farre] F. See Pafford's note.
1.2.139/186 be—] ROWE; be, F; be? HANMER
1.2.140 Affection, thy] F (Affection? thy). We take the question mark as equivalent to an exclamation mark, indicating a vocative.

1.2.150/197 LEONTES What] F; ˄ What HANMER (Thirlby). The emendation may be correct.
1.2.160/207 Ornament] CAPELL; Ornaments F. Rowe emended F's 'do's' to 'do'; Capell's version seems slightly more appropriate to the sententiousness of the remark. Some editors accept F as an irregularity.
1.2.209/256 they] F2; not in F1
1.2.256/303 forth. In . . . (my Lord)] THEOBALD (Thirlby); forth,˄ in . . . (my Lord.) F
1.2.278/325 Hoby-Horse] ROWE 3; Holy-Horſe F
1.2.462 off hence. Let] F (off, hence: Let). Many editors adopt the alternative interpretation: 'off. Hence!—Let . . .'; but 'bear'st my life off' seems to need some modification.
2.1.2, 5, 14, 16/514, 517, 526, 528 I. LADY] F (Lady.)
2.2.56 let't] F (le't)
2.2.69/782 twixt] POPE; betwixt F
2.3.2/784 weaknesse; if] COLLIER; weakneſſe, if F
2.3.12-13/794-5 Noblenesse. . . . Mother,] F4; ~, . . . ~. F1
2.3.39/821 What] F2; Who F1
2.3.61/843 good, so˄ were] THEOBALD; good˄ ſo, were F
3.2.10/1021 Silence] ROWE; italicized and set as direction F
3.2.32/1043 Who] ROWE; Whom F
3.2.167/1178 certaine] F2; not in F1. F2's addition, though presumably unauthoritative, mends the metre and improves the sense.
3.2.194/1205 the] F; thy This edition conj.
3.3.58/1311 and throughout OLD SHEPHEARD] F (Shep⟨heard⟩.)
3.3.67-8/1320-1 will.) What] THEOBALD; will) what F
3.3.68 bairn] F (Barne). Editors follow F, but that spelling is obsolete; bairn, the Scottish form, survives in northern dialect. Shakespeare's only other direct use is by Lavatch (All's Well 1.3.25/329); he probably regarded it as dialectal. (It also occurs as a pun on 'barnes', Much Ado 3.4.44/1537.)
3.3.75 hallooed] F (hallow'd). OED has hallow for its main entry, halloo as an alternative spelling from the 17th century; modern dictionaries give only halloo.
3.3.117/1371 made] THEOBALD (Thirlby); mad F
4.1.19/1409 himselfe,] F2; ~. F1. Most editors, following Staunton, print 'leaving— | Th'effects of his fond jealousies so grieving | That he shuts up himself—imagine . . .'. The passage is ambiguous.
4.2.4/1426 xvi] HANMER; fifteene F. Most modern editors do not correct the apparent slip (cf. 4.1.6/1396, 5.3.31/2893, 5.3.50/2912), presumably attributing it to Shakespeare; but it could be a compositor's or scribe's misreading of a roman numeral (cf. Measure 1.2.156/237 where, in another Crane play, xiv seems to have been misread as xix).
4.3.10/1486 With heigh, with heigh,] F2; With heigh, F1
4.3.56/1533 offend] F. Many editors adopt F2's 'offends', but this is probably a 'plural by attraction' (to them).
4.4.12/1617 it] F2; not in F1
4.4.13/1618 swound] THEOBALD (Thirlby); ſworne F. F has been defended. The physiological connection between blushing and swooning may support the emendation.
4.4.98/1703 your] F2; you F1
4.4.127 flower-de-luce] F (Flowre-de-Luce). Fleur-de-lis is the modern equivalent, but that is thought of as a French word, whereas the form given here was thoroughly Anglicized.
4.4.148/1753 so] CAPELL (Long MS); not in F
4.4.160/1765 out] THEOBALD (Thirlby); on't F. F is defended by Sisson, and retained by Riverside; either reading offers a strained metaphor, but Theobald's better suggests Perdita's confusion.
4.4.244 kiln-hole] F (kill-hole). F's is a phonetic spelling.
4.4.244 whistle of] F. Hanmer and many later editors modernize to 'whistle off', a term in falconry meaning 'release'; but whistle meaning 'whisper', though not used elsewhere by Shakespeare, is well authenticated by OED.
4.4.246 Clammer] (HUDSON); clamor F. OED's quotations at clam, v.² 2 and clamour, v.² 2 ('better spelt clammer') seem adequate authentication of the meaning 'silence'.

[4.4.294.1]/1901.1 Song] F prints 'Song' before the first line, 'Aut.' before the second.
4.4.308 gentlemen] F (Gent.)
4.4.359/1966 who] F2; whom F1
4.4.406/2013 my] F; any (conj. T. W. Craik privately)
4.4.419/2026 acknowledgd] F2; acknowledge F1
4.4.423/2030 who] F2; whom F1
4.4.428/2035 see] ROWE; neuer ſee F.
4.4.439 hoop] F (hope) (a spelling variant)
4.4.467/2074 your] F2; my F1
4.4.470/2077 sight,˄ as yet,] HANMER (Thirlby); ~, ~˄ F
4.4.499/2106 who] F. Many editors, following F2, emend to 'whom', but this is a common irregularity: OED, 13.
4.4.500/2107 her] F. Theobald's 'our', adopted by many editors, may be right; graphically, 'your' (written 'yr') is a likelier source of the error (G. R. Proudfoot).
4.4.549 there 'Son, forgiveness!'] F (there Sonne forgiueneſſe,). Many editors adopt F3's 'thee the son forgiveness'. Pafford's note puts the arguments fairly.
4.4.589/2197 so] HUDSON (Staunton and Lettsom); not in F
4.4.612/2219 could] GLOBE (Long MS, recorded in Cambridge); would F. Hudson suggests that 'would' means 'could'; Furness, that Autolycus means 'I would have filed them off had I wanted to'. But 'could' is better sense, and the error easy.
4.4.655/2262 eyes] ouer,] MOORMAN (subs.; conj. Schmidt); ~, ~) F. To gloss 'eyes over' as 'overseeing eyes' (Pafford) is strained; the parentheses in this text are probably Crane's.
4.4.705/2313 know not] HANMER (Thirlby); know F
4.4.735/2343 to] CAPELL (Grey MS); at F1; or F2
5.1.12/2465 of, true. | PAULINA Too] F; of. | PAULINA True, too THEOBALD. Almost all editors follow Theobald.
5.1.21/2474 spoke] POPE; ſpoken F
5.1.58-9/2511-12 Stage, | (Where . . . morne) appeare] This edition (G.T.); Stage | (Where . . . now appeare) F. 'Morne' (i.e. 'mourne') could be misread 'nowe'; the usage is paralleled in Sir Thomas More (Add. II.D.137-8/136-7, 'the king . . . is clement yf thoffendor moorne'). 'Mourn' links offenders with 'stage' as 'scaffold' (OED, sb. 4b); the image 'relates to the final scene, when Leontes is taken to a new wife, whom he will see better, at which point Hermione does again possess her corpse, and appear on a stage (not only the theatrical one, but a step or raised platform on which the "statue" appears), where Leontes the offender mourns (the sight of the statue is piercing to his soul, 5.3.34/2896)' (G.T.). As the punctuation is almost certainly Crane's, there is no difficulty in making 'spirit', rather than 'Offendors', the antecedent of 'appeare'.
5.1.61/2514 iust] F3; iuſt ſuch F1
5.1.75/2528 I haue done.] ascribed to Paulina, CAPELL. Modern editors follow Capell; but Knight's dissent (quoted by Furness) is cogent: 'The vehemence of Paulina overbears the interruption of Cleomenes, and he says, "I have done." . . . Paulina . . . is evidently going on, perfectly regardless of any opposition.' Dyce records that John Forster supported a return to the emendation since Paulina's '"Yet" introduces a concession on her part, which properly follows the "I have done".' But Paulina's concession from a position of strength is no less effective, and is consistent with the comedy in her presentation.
5.1.78/2531 your] HUDSON (W. S. Walker); you a F
5.1.159/2612 his,] HANMER; ~˄ F
5.3.5/2867 young contracted] This edition (G.T.); your contracted F; contracted CAMBRIDGE 3 (Staunton)
5.3.18/2880 Lonely] HANMER (Thirlby); Louely F
5.3.67 fixture] F (fixure). Fixture is 'an altered form of FIXURE' (OED); both forms occur during the 17th century, and OED's definitions are in some, though not all, respects identical. It seems clear that the difference is only formal.
5.3.96/2958 Or,˄ those] HANMER; On: thoſe F
5.3.150 This'] (DYCE 2); This F

THE WINTER'S TALE

INCIDENTALS

41 life,] ~.   190 vnreall,]~:   216 Parasite,] ~ₐ   285 neer'st] neereſt   382 (Sir.)] (Sirₐ)   433 th'Disease] the Diſeaſe   492 condemned] condemnd   696 haue] hane   737 gracious] gtacious   745 you.] ~,   749 blister,] ~.   763 presently] presenrly   765 hammerd] hammered   770 good.] ~,   774 (sir.)] (ſir,)   830-1 done, . . . honor)] ~) . . . ~,   832 me.] ~:   855 honest.] ~:   1197 much,] ~.   1211 sweet'st] ~.   1215 eye,] ~ₐ   1281 Thrower-out] Thower-out   1365 borne.] ~,   1390 on't.] ~,   1430 (or] ₐor   1466 cottage.] ~ₐ   1481 *bleaching*] bleachiug   1539 detestable] derestable   1621 ground.] ~ₐ   1645 deerest] deer'ſt   1717 Friend),] (Friend, F1 (*printed above the line*)   1733 of,] of)   1740 disposition.] ~:   1754 Shepherd] Sphepherd   1798 customers] cnſtomers   1808 Beleeue] Beleeee   1842 then] rhen   1854 promis'd] ptomis'd   1861 here.] ~ₐ   1879 things] rhings   1908 *go'st*] *goeſt*   1921 *Cape*] *Crpe*   1986 better.] ~ₐ   2096 gleand] gleaned   2101 (as in] as (in   2338 like] lke   2354 bless'd] bleſſed   2385 Sheepe-whistling] Sheepe-whiſtiing   2448 him:] ~.   2989 the] rhe   2991 time] ttme

FOLIO STAGE DIRECTIONS

F's directions frequently name characters at the opening of the scene rather than at their point of entry. In such cases, the following list does not attempt to indicate the various points of entry.

1.1.0.1/0.1   *Enter Camillo and Archidamus.*
1.1.46/47   *Exeunt.*
1.2.0.1-2/47.1-2   *Enter Leontes, Hermione, Mamillius, Polixenes, | Camillo.*
1.1.351/398   *Exit*
1.2.364/411   *Enter Polixenes.* (after 'Bohemia', 1.2.365/412)
1.2.465/512   *Exeunt.*
2.1.0.1/512.1   *Enter Hermione, Mamillius, Ladies: Leontes, | Antigonus, Lords.*
2.1.201/713   *Exeunt*
2.2.0.1/713.1   *Enter Paulina, a Gentleman, Gaoler, Emilia.*
2.2.69/782   *Exeunt*
2.3.0.1/782.1   *Enter Leontes, Seruants, Paulina, Antigonus, | and Lords.*
2.3.26.1/808.1   *Enter Paulina.*
2.3.130/912   *Exit.*
2.3.192/974   *Exit.*
2.3.193/975   *Enter a Seruant.*
2.2.207/989   *Exeunt.*
3.1.0.1/989.1   *Enter Cleomines and Dion.*
3.1.22/1011   *Exeunt.*
3.2.0.1/1011.1   *Enter Leontes, Lords, Officers: Hermione (as to her | Triall) Ladies: Cleomines, Dion.*
3.2.242/1253   *Exeunt*
3.3.0.1/1253.1-2   *Enter Antigonus, a Marriner, Babe, Sheepe-|heard, and Clowne.*
3.3.14/1267   *Exit*
3.3.57/1310   *Exit pursued by a Beare.*
3.3.76.1/1329.1   *Enter Clowne.*
3.3.135/1390   *Exeunt*
4.1.0.1/1390.1   *Enter Time, the Chorus.*
4.1.32/1422   *Exit.*
4.2.0.1/1422.1   *Enter Polixenes, and Camillo.*
4.2.53.1/1476.1   *Exit*
4.3.0.1/1476.2   *Enter Autolicus singing.*
4.3.30.1/1507.1   *Enter Clowne.*
4.3.117/1596   *Exit.* (after 4.3.116/1595)
4.3.123/1601.1   *Song.*
4.3.126/1605.1   *Exit.*
4.4.0.1-2/1605.2-3   *Enter Florizell, Perdita, Shepherd, Clowne, Polixenes, Ca-|millo, Mopsa, Dorcas, Seruants, Autolicus.*
4.4.166.1/1771.1-2   *Heere a Daunce of Shepheards and | Sheparddesses.*
4.4.181.1/1786.1   *Enter Seruant.*
4.4.218.1-2/1824.1-2   *Enter Autolicus singing.*
4.4.294.1/1901.1   *Song.*
4.4.313/1919.1   *Song.*
4.4.321/1928.1   *Exit*
4.4.340.1/1947.1   *Heere a Dance of twelue Satyres.*
4.4.441/2048   *Exit.*
4.4.462/2069   *Exit.*
4.4.595.2/2202.2   *Enter Autolicus.*
4.4.670.1/2277.1   *Exit.*
4.4.683.1-2/2291.1-2   *Enter Clowne and Shepheard.*
4.4.843/2453   *Exeunt.*
5.1.0.1/2453.1   *Enter Leontes, Cleomines, Dion, Paulina, Seruants: | Florizel, Perdita.*
5.1.84.1/2537.1   *Enter a Seruant.*
5.1.114/2567   *Exit.*
5.1.122.1/2575.1   *Enter Florizell, Perdita, Cleomines, and others.*
5.1.177/2630   *Enter a Lord.*
5.1.232.1/2685   *Exeunt.*
5.2.0.1/2685.1   *Enter Autolicus, and a Gentleman.*
5.2.19.1/2705.1   *Enter another Gentleman.*
5.2.25.1/2711.1   *Enter another Gentleman.*
5.2.111/2799   *Exit.*
5.2.122.1-2/2810.1-2   *Enter Shepheard and Clowne.*
5.2.173/2862   *Exeunt.*
5.3.0.1-2/2862.1-2   *Enter Leontes, Polixenes, Florizell, Perdita, Camillo, | Paulina: Hermione (like a Statue:) Lords, &c.*
5.3.156/3018   *Exeunt.*

[Printed after the play]

The Names of the Actors.

Leontes, King of Sicillia.
Mamillus, yong Prince of Sicillia.
Camillo.
Antigonus.   ⎫ *Foure*
Cleomines.   ⎬ *Lords of Sicillia.*
Dion.   ⎭
Hermione, Queene to Leontes.
Perdita, Daughter to Leontes and Hermione.
Paulina, wife to Antigonus.
Emilia, a Lady.
Polixenes, King of Bohemia.
Florizell, Prince of Bohemia.
Old Shepheard, reputed Father of Perdita.
Clowne, his Sonne.
Autolicus, a Rogue.
Archidamus, a Lord of Bohemia.
Other Lords, and Gentlemen, and Seruants.
Shepheards, and Shepearddesses.

CYMBELINE

Cymbeline first appears in the First Folio; it was entered in the Stationers' Register among the plays in that collection which had not been previously printed. It is evident from the extremely heavy punctuation that the printer's copy was a scribal transcript of some sort. Maxwell summarizes the evidence for scribal copy, some of it compatible with transcription by Ralph Crane; Riverside adds to this evidence the unusual spelling 'dampn'd', present in the uncorrected state of [1.6.105]/627. While it is true, as Maxwell says, that the text does not contain 'all of the peculiarities associated with Crane', the same could be said of the other Folio texts apparently set from Crane transcripts: Maxwell instances in particular the absence of examples of hyphenated verb plus pronominal object; but *Measure* also lacks examples of this idiosyncrasy. The overall proportions of parentheses, hyphens, and apostrophes are consistent with Crane's practice, as documented by Howard-Hill in Crane's manuscripts and the other printed texts apparently set from one of his transcripts. Riverside describes the use of parentheses as 'lighter than usual', but the proportion—one for every 179 words—is higher than in *Barnavelt* and *Measure*. Moreover, aside from one example in *King John*, only the five Crane texts and *Cymbeline* contain parentheses in stage directions ([5.5.123.1, 123.4-5, 123.7]/2629.1-2, 2629.4-5, 2629.7). If Crane was responsible for any text in the Folio other than the five comedies traditionally allotted to him, *Cymbeline* is without doubt the strongest candidate, and it is surprising that it has not received more attention from students of Crane.

Honigmann first suggested, and Jowett and Taylor have confirmed (*Shakespeare Reshaped*, 'With New Additions', Appendix I), that at some stage in its transmission the manuscript of *Cymbeline* was affected by a change of hands between 2.4.152 and 2.5.0.1/1154 and 1154.1. The most striking evidence for this is the abrupt change in the spelling of 'O(h)', which cannot be compositorial in origin; a number of other spellings reinforce this disparity between the two portions of the play. It is, as yet, impossible to be sure whether the change of hands occurred in the Folio copy itself, or in the manuscript from which the Folio copy derived. However, the most prominent features of the Folio text occur in both sections, which suggests that the Folio copy was a Crane transcript of another manuscript of mixed provenance. Moreover, in contrast to *King John*, where the Folio copy seems itself to have been prepared by two different scribes, the break in *Cymbeline* does not affect the spelling of so many words; this is what we would expect if the preferences of another scribe (Crane?) had overlaid the disparities between the two halves of a composite manuscript. We are therefore inclined to the view that the Folio copy was a Crane transcript, itself copied from a manuscript in which a second hand took over at 2.5.0.1/1154.1. It is, through the medium of the Folio compositors and Crane (or a similar, sophisticating scribe), impossible to say much about the nature of the manuscript from which the copy was prepared. The Folio is notable for its omission of necessary sound cues, but this is true of other Crane transcripts, and of other transcripts which appear to be of a literary nature (for instance, the copy for Folio *Othello*). Nothing in the text would rule out derivation from a promptbook; but neither would anything in the text enforce such an ancestry.

The text is clean, and presents few serious difficulties for an editor. It consistently spells the name of the chief female character 'Imogen', a name which first appears in the English language in the Folio text of this play, and which owes its modern popularity (developed during the nineteenth century) entirely to this text. However, as editors have long recognized, this form is an error. The wife of Brute in the portion of Holinshed on which Shakespeare drew for the play was called 'Innogen'; that name also appears in the initial stage direction of *Much Ado*; it is also consistently used in Simon Forman's account of his visit to a performance of *Cymbeline* in 1611 (Bodleian Library, Ashmolean 208). We thus possess evidence for the name 'Innogen' (*a*) in the sources prior to composition, (*b*) in an account of the play after its composition, and (*c*) elsewhere in the author's practice. By contrast, the only evidence for 'Imogen' is the Folio text itself, which could easily be due to the simplest of minim errors. The error could easily originate in the Folio's scribal copy; but it might also originate in the Folio itself, despite the fact that it was set by two compositors: compare Q2 *Hamlet*, where two different compositors consistently commit the error 'Rosencraus'. See also the first edition of Middleton's *Women Beware Women*, where the central character Bianca is consistently called 'Brancha' (in error for 'Beancha'). We have therefore restored the form 'Innogen' throughout the play.

G.T./S.W.W.

WORKS CITED

Brooks, H. F., see Nosworthy
Daniel, P. A., *Notes and Conjectural Emendations of Certain Doubtful Passages in Shakespeare's Plays* (1870)
Dowden, E., ed., *Cymbeline*, Arden (1903)
D'Urfey, Thomas, *The Injured Princess, or the Fatal Wager* (1682)
Furness, H. H., ed., *Cymbeline*, New Variorum (1913)
Gould, George, *Corrigenda and Explanations of the Text of Shakspere* (1881)
Honigmann, E. A. J., 'On the Indifferent and One-Way Variants in Shakespeare', *The Library*, V, 22 (1967), 189-204
Ingleby, C. M., ed., *Cymbeline* (1886)
Maxwell, J. C., ed., *Cymbeline*, New (1960)
Nosworthy, J. M., ed., *Cymbeline*, Arden (1955)

TEXTUAL NOTES

Title *Cymbeline King of Britaine*] F (*table of contents*); THE TRAGEDIE OF CYMBELINE F (*head-title; running titles, alternating with 'Tragedy'*); *Cymbeline* S.R. (*among* 'TRAGEDIES'). One suspects that 'The Tragedie of' was added to the title simply because of its position in the volume. Forman supports the alternative: his note is headed 'Of Cimbalin king of England'. Although 'England' cannot be right—the name never occurs in the play, which refers to Britain(s) or British 51 times—Forman's title has the same form as F's 'Catalogue'. Holinshed also, in the passages which influenced the play, spoke of the 'king of Britaine' or 'of the Britains' (Chap. 18). Finally, this title would have been pertinent to Jacobean politics c.1608–11; as a number of modern critics have remarked, the choice and treatment of the play's subject-matter owe much to the political preoccupations of King James and his court.

1.1.3/3 King] KNIGHT (Tyrwhitt); Kings F
1.1.15/15 of] MAXWELL (Staunton); at F
1.1.30/30 Cassibelan] F2; *Caffibulan* F1. F2 agrees with the sources; an easy misreading.
1.1.70/70 Exeunt] ROWE; *Exeunt | Scena Secunda*. F. Whether or not—as would normally be true—the Queen and the lovers enter before being seen, the exit here and their entrance clearly overlap, with no change of place or time. Compare *Measure* 1.2.107.1/187.1.
1.1.85/85, etc. INNOGEN] This edition; *Imogen* F. See Introduction.
1.1.98/98 Filario's] ROWE; *Filorio's* F
1.1.117 cere] F (*feare*)
1.1.179/179 pray] F (*Pray*); I pray you CAPELL. Brooks conjectures 'pray' has been substituted under the influence of 1.1.177/177 for a disyllable; 'beseech' is the obvious candidate (Maxwell). But, like Capell's emendation, this merely produces an hexameter in place of an extra stress at the caesura. See lineation notes.
1.2.9/190 Steele if he] This edition (*conj.* Brooks); *Steele if it* F
1.3.2/222 question'st] This edition; *queftioned'ft* F; *question'd'st* THEOBALD. Theobald's emendation was designed to rectify the metre, but 'ndst' is an unpronounceable consonant cluster. For euphonic syncopation of the 'ed' in such cases compare *Othello* 3.3.113/1561 ('lik'st' for 'likedst') and *Antony* 3.3.18/1386 ('look'st' for 'lookedst'). F could result from conscious or unconscious scribal or compositorial normalization. Alternatively, 'euery' might be a substitution for 'each'; but such errors are less common. Compare 3.4.48/1510.
1.3.9/229 this] THEOBALD (Warburton); *his* F
1.4.0.1/261.3 *A Table ... it*] This edition; *not in* F. The equivalent scene in *Decameron* and *Frederyke of Jennen* takes place during a meal; see 5.6.156/2962.
1.4.26 Briton] F (*Britaine*)
1.4.46/310 not to] ROWE (D'Urfey); *to* F
1.4.70/336 Britaine] JOHNSON; *Britanie* F. See Maxwell. For comparable transpositions in Compositor E's stints see Werstine, and 'Mistirs' (1.4.78/344), 'preseure' (1.4.134/400), etc.
1.4.72/338 not but] MALONE; *not* F
1.4.81/347 purchase] ROWE (D'Urfey); *purchafes* F. An error characteristic of Compositor E (see Werstine and below).
1.4.101/367 fiue] Fb; *fine* Fa
1.4.110/376 heerein to] F; *hereunto* ANON. (*conj.* in Cambridge)
1.4.125/391 thousand] F3; *thoufands* F1. See 1.4.81/347.
1.4.132/398 a Friend] F; *afraid* THEOBALD (Warburton)
1.4.132/398 therein] F2; *there in* F1
1.5.28/465 factor for] HUDSON 2 (W. S. Walker); *for* F. For the idiom see *Richard III* 3.7.134/2124, *Antony* 2.6.10/1006.
1.5.57/494 worke] F; *worth* WILSON (*conj.* in Maxwell)
1.5.68/505 chance thou changest] F; *change thou chancest* THEOBALD; *chance thou hangest* DANIEL (*conj.*)
1.5.85/522 words Pisanio] This edition (*conj.* Dowden); *words* F
1.6.6–7/530–1 but ... glorious] F; HUDSON (Staunton) places after 'comfort' (1.6.9/533)
1.6.7/531 desire] F2; *defires* F1. See 1.4.81/347.
1.6.17/541 alone,] CRAIG; ~ F

1.6.25/548 truest,] HANMER; *truft.* F
1.6.29/551 takes] POPE; *take* F. See 1.4.81/347.
1.6.37/559 thunnumber'd] THEOBALD; *the number'd* F
1.6.73/595 languish,] STEEVENS; ~: F1; ~, F2
1.6.81/603 count] POPE; *account* F. F could result from an easy synonym substitution, which disrupts the metre.
1.6.102/624 euery] F1; *very* F3
1.6.105/627 Fiering] F1; *Fixing* F2
1.6.110 illustrous] F (*illuftrious*). For forms similar to F's, where the 'i' in the suffix is redundant in modern spelling, see Furness. (On the other hand F would be an easy error.)
1.6.126/648 lend to] This edition; *lend* F. Shakespeare uses 'lend' and 'lend to' interchangeably in such contexts, depending on the metre and the complexity of the syntax. F produces a highly anomalous string of syllables; as emended, the line is a normal hexameter.
1.6.134/656 Liue] F; *Lie* WALKER (*conj.* in Nosworthy)
1.6.163/685 me] Fb; *ma* Fa
1.6.169/691 mens] F2; *men* F1
1.6.170/692 desended] F2; *defended* F1
1.6.183/705 concernes,] ROWE (D'Urfey); ~: F. See Maxwell.
1.6.187/709 Best] POPE; *The beft* F. *The* is one of the most easily and frequently interpolated words.
2.1.23 an] F (*and*)
2.1.26/759 your] F3; *you* F1
2.1.33/766 to night] F2; *night* F1
2.1.60/793 Husband, then] F4; ~. *Then* F1. See next note.
2.1.61/794 make. The] THEOBALD; ~, *the* F. See previous note. As Brooks argues, 'F prints a period and capital T where they are not wanted, and prints neither where they are wanted'; he suggests that a correction has gone wrong. This explanation is even more probable when we recognize that Compositor E—who was especially prone to idiotic misunderstanding of proof-corrections—set this page.
2.1.62/795 Honour:] ROWE (*subs.*); ~. F; ~, NOSWORTHY. A colon leaves it ambiguous whether the imperative 'Keepe' is addressed to the heavens or Innogen; F and Nosworthy impose one or the other interpretation.
2.2.0.1–3/797.1–2 *A Trunke ... Lady*] This edition; *Enter Imogen, in her Bed, and a Lady*. F. The trunk is unlikely to have been 'thrust out'; it might have been pushed up through the trap, which would permit easier entrance and exit for Giacomo, and supply a potent visual image of his ascent from and descent into 'hell'. Arrases appear in other public theatre plays; whether a special one was used for this scene, corresponding to Giacomo's description, cannot be determined, but is possible.
2.2.2/799 houre] Fb; *houe* Fa
2.2.18/815 they doo't] F; *they'd do't* NICHOLSON (*conj.* in Cambridge)
2.2.20/817 lids,] ROWE; ~. F
2.2.22 azure-laced] F (*Azure lac'd*). MAXWELL first inserted the hyphen.
2.2.43/840 riueted] Fb; *riuete* Fa
2.2.49/846 bare] STEEVENS (Theobald); *beare* F
2.2.51.1–2/848.1–2 *the Bed and Trunke are remoued*] This edition; *not in* F; *the Scene closes* ROWE. The bed could be thrust back in; the trunk could sink back through the trap.
2.3.7/855 CLOTEN] F ('*Clot*' *c.w.*); *not in text*
2.3.18.1/867.1 Musicke] This edition (*conj.* Nicholson); *not in* F. See 1.2.15–16/864–5.
2.3.18.2/867.2 MUSITIAN] *not in* F
2.3.19–25/868–74 *Hearke ... arise*] This song also appears in Bodleian MS Don. c. 57. For discussion see Nosworthy's Appendix C, which refers to previous studies, and J. P. Cutts, 'A Bodleian Song-Book', *Music and Letters*, 34 (1953), 192–211.
2.3.19/868 Hearke, hearke] F. The word is repeated five times in MS.
2.3.19/868 Heauen] MS (*subs.*); *Heauens* F. See Sonnet 29.12. F, with the same meaning, creates an awkward consonant cluster,

605

and could easily result from unconscious normalization or substitution, by scribe or compositor.

2.3.20/869 arise] F; to rise MS

2.3.21-2/870-1 His . . . lyes] F; not in MS. W. M. Evans—in *PMLA* 60 (1945), 95-101—conjectures that MS lacks these lines because (*a*) they were a late interpolation in F, or (*b*) the composer deliberately omitted them, to save the singer from their awkward sibilants. Neither explanation seems likely, given the rhymes and the structure of the song; simple transcription error in MS seems probable.

2.3.23/872 And] F; The MS

2.3.24/873 is] F, MS; bin HANMER

2.3.25/874 arise.] a-rise . . . my Lady sweet . . . A-rise MS

2.3.26/875 CLOTEN] DYCE; not in F

2.3.27/876 vyce] ROWE; voyce F

2.3.29/878 amend] F2; amed F1

2.3.41/890 out] F2 (ou't); on't F1

2.3.45/894 solicits] F2; folicity F1

2.3.77/926 Aside] This edition; not in F. DELIUS conjectured that the whole sentence is aside.

2.3.80/929 Aside] This edition (*conj.* Delius); not in F

2.3.98/947 cure] WARBURTON; are F

2.3.118 foil] F (foyle). One might alternatively modernize to *file* (= 'defile'); the spellings, and probably the pronunciation, to a large degree overlapped, and the words are not easily disentangled.

2.3.134/983 Garment] F2; Garments F1. See 1.4.81/347.

2.3.142/991 am:] This edition (?); ~. F1; ~, F4. The punctuation adopted here leaves the grammar ambiguous; F1 and F4 both impose an interpretation, and F1's punctuation is not authorial.

2.3.151/1000 you] F3; your F1

2.4.6/1008 sear'd] TYRWHITT; fear'd F

2.4.6/1008 hopes] F2; hope F1. See 1.4.81/347.

2.4.14 Ere] F (Or)

2.4.18/1020 Legions] THEOBALD; Legion F. See 1.4.81/347 (and 3.7.4/1914).

2.4.24/1026 wing-led] F1; mingled F2; winged CARTWRIGHT (*conj.*); coupled GOULD (*conj.*). Though many editors prefer F2, F1 is undoubtedly the rarer, more difficult reading, and cannot result from mechanical inadvertence; a scribe or compositor, facing '[minims]ingled', will hardly see the extraordinary compound 'wing-led' instead of the common verb 'mingled'. If F1 is wrong, F2 is not right.

2.4.24/1026 courage] DYCE; courages F. A typical Compositor E error (see 1.4.81/347), which here disrupts both the metre and the symmetry with 'discipline'.

2.4.32/1034 One of the] F1; one the STEEVENS; of the POPE. See lineation notes.

2.4.34/1036 through] ROWE; thorough F

2.4.37/1039 PHILARIO] CAPELL; *Poft.* F

2.4.41/1043 had] SINGER (D'Urfey); haue F

2.4.43/1045 Ile] F; Ild NOSWORTHY (*conj.*)

2.4.47/1049 not] F2; note F1

2.4.57/1059 you] F2; yon F1

2.4.60/1062 leaues] ROWE; leaue F. See 1.4.81/347.

2.4.76/1078 Such] SINGER 2 (Mason); Since F. An easy misreading: minims and e/h.

2.4.76/1078 on't was.] HANMER; ~ — F; was out on't. MAXWELL (anon. *conj.*). Maxwell supposes omission followed by transposition and repunctuation. In manuscripts speeches often have no terminal punctuation; the dash could easily be compositorial.

2.4.116/1118 her woman] her women F1; of her women F2

2.4.135/1137 the] ROWE; her F. Easily assimilated to the previous phrase.

2.4.151/1153 follow] This edition; follow him F. Compare *Shrew* 5.1.132/2392, *Hamlet* 1.4.65, 4.7.164, 167/614, 2968, 2971. The pronoun is easily interpolated after the verb, but is superfluous and extrametrical here.

2.5.2/1156 Bastards all] POPE; all Baftards F. F has the commoner, and less metrical, word-order.

2.5.16 German one] F (Iarmen on)

2.5.27/1181 man can name] This edition (*conj.* W. S. Walker); name F1; may be nam'd F2; have a name INGLEBY (Dyce); man may name CRAIG (W. S. Walker). Also possible would be 'earth can name' (*earth*, as often, contrasting with *hell*): see 'earthie name' (*K. John* 3.1.73/1022 'on earth vsurpt his name' (*Venus* 794) 'earthly faults', (*Measure* 5.1.482/2646), and 'known the earth so full of faults' (*Caesar* 1.3.45/443).

3.1.0.1, 3.1.85/1189.1, 1274 Flourish.] This edition; not in F. Such musical accompaniment is virtually mandatory for formal royal entrances and exits; F—like some other scribal texts—has no music cues at all.

3.1.5, 30, 41/1194, 1219, 1230 Cassibelan] F2; *Caffibulan* F1. See 1.1.30/30.

3.1.11/1200 There will] This edition; There F; There'll WARBURTON (*conj.*). The future tense seems required by 'Ere'; metrically, the emendation produces an extra unstressed syllable at the caesura, the commonest licence (especially when the line is divided between two speakers).

3.1.13/1202 By] F; Vnto This edition *conj.* For 'unto itself', compare *Coriolanus* 4.7.51/2719.

3.1.19/1208 ribb'd, and pal'd] F; ribbed and paled ROWE 3; were ribb'd and paled NOSWORTHY (*conj.*).

3.1.20/1209 bākes] This edition (S.W.W.); Oakes F; rocks HANMER (Theobald). Editors agree in rejecting F; but *banks* seems preferable to *rocks* in suggesting both 'sea-coast' (*sb.*[1] 9, citing *Contention* 3.2.83/1647) and 'an artificial earthwork, an embankment, for military use' (*sb.*[1] 3).

3.1.53/1242 be, we do, say] MALONE; ~, we do. Say F; ~. | Clo⟨ten⟩ *and Lords.* We do. | *Cym*⟨*beline*⟩. Say GLOBE

3.2.2/1276 accuser] CAPELL; *accufe* F

3.2.10/1284 to hers] HANMER; to her F. Nosworthy defends F, glossing 'compared to her'; but 'hers' produces better symmetry, not only with 'Thy mind' but with 'Thy Fortunes' (which are 'as lowe', by comparison with 'hers'). The line was set by Compositor E (see 1.4.81/347).

3.2.14/1288 to do good] Fb; to go do od Fa

3.2.21/1295 Feodarie] CAPELL; *Fœdarie* F. If Capell is right, F is a compound error (transposition, followed by provision of a ligature for the resulting 'oe'). Alternatively, if 'Federarie' at *Winter's Tale* 2.1.92/604 is correct, one might presume simple haplography here, and read 'Fœdarerie'.

3.2.22/1296 here] Fb; her Fa

3.2.46/1320 Loue,] CAPELL (Tyrwhitt); ~. F

3.2.64/1337 Till] POPE; And F; To CAPELL

3.2.67/1340 score] F2; ftore F1

3.2.67/1340 ride] F2; rid F1

3.2.78/1351 nor heere, nor] F2; nor heere, not F1; not here, nor CHAMBERS

3.3.0.1/1355.1 *followed by*] This edition; *not in* F

3.3.0.2/1355.2 *from a Caue in the Woods*] This edition; *not in* F. The woods ('wods') are mentioned twice in Forman's account; 'trees' could clearly be approximated on the Jacobean stage; and in any event readers may if they wish take these 'woods' as literary rather than theatrical.

3.3.2/1357 Stoope] HANMER; Sleepe F. See Nosworthy's note.

3.3.15-16/1370-1 Warre; | That] This edition; ~. | This F. F makes sense, 'This' being interpreted vaguely as a reference to the activities common in 'Courts' and 'Warre'; but it is unfortunately ambiguous, suggesting 'This service' [that we now perform]. 'That' would, without confusion, allow a reference to the preceding line ('services of that kind'), but also permit a more general construction: 'then revolve . . . that service [of any kind] is not service. . . .' Compositorial or scribal substitution of 'This' for 'That' would be easy.

3.3.23/1378 Bable] ROWE; Babe F; Bribe HANMER; robe NOSWORTHY (Bulloch). Unlike 'bauble', 'check', and 'unpaid-for silk', there is nothing self-evidently undesirable or foolish about a 'robe' as the reward for a courtier's devotion. For dropped letters in Compositor E's stints compare 'Spectacles' (1.6.38/560), 'oppos'd' (1.6.45/567), 'expulsion' (2.1.59/792), etc.

3.3.25/1380 em] CAPELL; him F

3.3.28/1383 know] F2; knowes F1. See 1.4.81/347.

3.3.33 travelling abed] F (trauailing a bed). Though there is a pun—'travail a-bed' would be a mother's birth pangs—the primary sense seems to be 'travelling in dreams, or lazy day-dreams'.

3.3.34/1389 Prison, for] POPE; Prifon, or F; prison, of VAUGHAN (conj.). Either a substitution, or another dropped letter by Compositor E.

3.3.83/1438 wherein they Bowe,] WARBURTON; whereon the Bowe, F

3.3.86/1441 Polidour] ROWE; Paladour F

3.3.98, 107/1453, 1462 A Hunting Horn sounds] This edition (conj. Collier); not in F

3.3.99–107/1454–1462 Oh . . . vp.] F. Ingram (see Furness) conjectures that these lines are a non-Shakespearian interpolation. There is no particular reason to doubt Shakespeare's authorship, but they do look like an afterthought: they provide a huddle of narrative information, not integrated into the speech, and 'The Game is vp' (3.3.107/1462) repeats 'the Game is rows'd' (3.3.98/1453)—a form of ring composition which Honigmann has noted as characteristic of Shakespearian additions in revision ('Shakespeare's Revised Plays').

3.3.106/1461 Morgan] ROWE; Mergan F

3.4.0.1/1462.1 in a Riding Suit] This edition; not in F. The 'Riding Suit' is specified at 3.2.76/1349.

3.4.48/1510 look'st] This edition; look'dft F. F is the only occurrence of that form in the canon, and looks like grammatical sophistication. See 1.3.2/222.

3.4.79/1541 a-fort] ROWE; a-foot F

3.4.85/1547 Teachers] F; Treachers NOSWORTHY (conj.)

3.4.89/1551 make] MALONE; makes F

3.4.101/1563 out] INGLEBY (Johnson); not in F

3.4.133/1595 churlish noble] This edition; noble F; feeble, noble MAXWELL. Of many other attempts to rectify the sense and metre of this line, only Maxwell's is plausible; but although it provides an explanation for the apparent error (homoeoteleuton before 'noble'), *feeble* is not a compelling antithesis to either *harsh* or *noble*, and the triple iteration of termination in 'feeble, noble, simple' is unattractive. By contrast, 'churlish' is equally plausible in explaining the error (homoeoteleuton after 'harsh'); but *churlish* and *noble* are a natural oxymoron (like *simple* and *nothing*), appropriate to Cloten. Moreover, Shakespeare elsewhere juxtaposes *harsh* and *churlish* (*Venus* 134), and uses 'churlish' in the oxymoronic description of Ajax (*Troilus* 1.2.20/166), who is like Cloten in his compounding of incompatible characteristics.

3.5.0.1/1656.2 Flourish.] This edition; not in F. See note at 3.1.0.1/1189.1.

3.5.32/1688 lookes] F2; looke F1

3.5.40/1696 strokes;] F2; ftroke; , F1

3.5.44/1700 lowdst of] CAPELL; lowd of F; loudest ROWE. Nosworthy calls Rowe's emendation 'bibliographically more tenable' than Capell's, presumably assuming misreading (eft to of); but compositorial omission of a single ft ligature could account for the F reading equally well.

3.5.86/1742 tongue] This edition; heart F. Nosworthy conjectures 'mouth' or 'lips' but Shakespeare never elsewhere contrasts these with 'heart'; the tongue/heart contrast occurs at least 28 times elsewhere (*Shrew* 4.1.6–7, 4.3.77/1564–5, 1956, *Contention* 3.1.269/1450, etc.).

3.6.27.1/1844.1 Enter] F here marks 'Scena Septima'; but in an identical situation at 4.2.102/2053—where the stage is cleared, but the 'Cave' apparently remains visible—it marks no such division. See Introduction.

3.6.68 Ay,] F (I). DOWDEN conjectured that this word should be omitted, and NOSWORTHY that it be replaced by 'And', in order to have 'bid' governed by 'I should' (3.6.67); this simple modernization achieves the same effect.

3.6.68/1885 Ide] JOHNSON (Tyrwhitt); I do F

3.6.74 price] F (prize). The two words were not distinguished in Shakespeare's day, and 'price' seems the primary sense, though there is a pun on 'prize' (as though a merchant ship, seized as booty).

3.7.9 commends] F (commands). For evidence that this is a spelling variant, see Nosworthy.

3.7.14 supplyant] F (fuppliant)

4.1.14 imperceiverant] F (imperfeuerant). See OED.

4.2.2/1953 from] This edition; after F. F is metrically anomalous, and could result from synonym substitution: compare 'comes from hunting' (*Timon* 2.2.8/581), 'returnes from hunting' (*History of Lear* 3.7/476).

4.2.22 bier] F (Beere). 'Bear' is perhaps an alternative modernization, in the Welsh woods.

4.2.35/1986 breeds] F1; breed F2

4.2.47/1998 appeares] F; approues NOSWORTHY (conj.)

4.2.47/1998 hath] This edition; he hath F. F is metrically anomalous; it could easily arise from sophistication of the contraction *hath* for 'he hath' (*All Is True* 5.1.50/2296, etc.).

4.2.51/2002 BELARIUS] This edition; Arui⟨ragus⟩. F; not in CAPELL. Though Capell's solution has been popular, it leaves F's error—and its line-division—unexplained, and produces a fourteener ('But . . . Charracters'). It seems more likely that '*Arui*' has replaced some other prefix (a species of error which occurs elsewhere), and Belarius is the only candidate. Belarius joins in their praises elsewhere; indeed, he initiates this topic of conversation (4.2.46-8/1997-9).

4.2.59/2010 him] POPE; them F. Nosworthy defends 'them' as the smile and sigh of 4.2.54/2005; but while both grief and patience are clearly rooted in Innogen herself, it is harder to see how the smile expresses grief and the sigh patience. The proposed error is a common one.

4.2.60/2011 patienc] THEOBALD; patient F

4.2.112/2063 defect] F; th'effect THEOBALD. There is no need for emendation if we recognize that this speech refers to Guiderius, not Cloten: Guiderius' good judgement prevents him from being afraid.

4.2.123/2074 thanks ye] JOHNSON; thanks the F1; thanks to the F3; thank the STEEVENS. Misinterpretation of 'ye' as 'ye' is common; Compositor B commits relatively few terminal 's' errors.

4.2.133/2084 Humor] THEOBALD; Honor F

4.2.155 reck] F (reake). See OED.

4.2.171/2122 how] POPE; thou F

4.2.187 ingenious] F (ingenuous)

4.2.203/2154 not] ROWE 3; not the F. An easy interpolation, which in this instance may be related to the preceding 'thee'.

4.2.206/2157 crare] STEEVENS (Sympson); care F

4.2.207/2158 Might] F2; Might'ft F1

4.2.207/2158 easilest] F1; easiliest F4; easliest HOWARD-HILL (*in Oxford Concordance*). Although Shakespeare elsewhere elides *easily* to *easlie* (*LLL* 5.2.189/1939, *John* 2.1.516/792), Howard-Hill's emendation involves more than a simple transposition: for an intended 'eaflieft' to become 'eaflieft', the compositor would have to set the wrong ligature (fi in place of fl) and then the correspondingly wrong letter ('l' in place of 'i'). This is not impossible; but neither is it simple. For F's form compare 'maidenlest' (*History of Lear* 2.127/424) and 'busielest' (*Tempest* 3.1.15/1111).

4.2.219/2170 to thee] F; there CAPELL

4.2.225/2176 Ruddocke] HANMER; Raddocke F. See Maxwell.

4.2.229/2180 besides, when] THEOBALD; ~ . When F

4.2.230/2181 winter-goune] THEOBALD (Warburton); winter-ground F; winter-green VERPLANCK (Douce). Steevens's defence of F is, like other of his nonce glosses, unsubstantiated. Wilson (in MAXWELL) prefers 'winter-green', but as a noun this compound refers to 'various plants . . . whose leaves remain green in winter'; its familiarity (OED gives examples from 1548 on) would make it less likely to cause a compositor or scribe trouble. Palaeographically, 'greene'—involving the misreading of 'e' as three different letters—is much less likely than 'goune'.

4.2.238/2189 once] POPE; once to F. F's preposition, superfluous both syntactically and metrically, could easily have resulted from the influence of the preceding phrase.

4.2.239–44/2190–95 *Fidele*. . . . BELARIUS] If anything in the canon is a theatrical interpolation due to exigencies of casting, these

4.2.255/2206 lines are a chief candidate. Quite apart from their evident excusing of a bad voice, they are contradicted by the direction 'SONG' at 4.2.258/2009.

4.2.255/2206   say] F; sing This edition *conj.* See preceding note.
4.2.258/2209   begin.] This edition; begin. | SONG. F
4.2.286/2237   therths Face.] This edition; their Faces. F. Editors are virtually unanimous in decrying F's text and retaining it. After 'on them' (4.2.285/2236), contamination to 'vpon their' would be easy, and after 'their' the following noun would—at some stage—naturally be 'corrected' to a plural. The punctuation is, here as elsewhere, scribal or compositorial. Compare 'the Earths cold face' (*Duke of York* 2.3.35/1003) and 'my could corps on the earths cold face' (*Richard III* 5.5.220/3311). Shakespeare repeatedly juxtaposes 'cold' (4.2.285/2236) with 'earth'.
4.2.288   strow] F (ſtrew)
4.2.289/2240   knees‸] This edition (*conj.* Keightley); ∼: F. As the preceding and following lines rhyme, it is natural to assume that a line has been omitted; in a play of this length, by normal standards the compositors alone could be expected to omit more than one. One also expects a contamination of the sentence beginning 'apart vpon our knees [we'll pray, etc.]'; otherwise 'apart' is being used as an imperative.
4.2.292/2243   is] POPE; are F
4.2.325/2276   thy] HANMER; this F
4.2.338/2289   are hence] This edition; are heere F1; are F2. Almost all editors follow F2, and the repetition of 'heere' is suspicious; but assimilation is a commoner error than interpolation.
4.2.375/2326   many, all] F; many, and all JOHNSON; many men, all ANON. (*conj.* in Cambridge). 'Men' would be especially appropriate, given Innogen's situation and frame of mind.
4.2.378/2329   Maister in] F; Master POPE; master in his STAUNTON (*conj.*)
4.2.381/2332   pardon it] F; pardon't HANMER
4.2.392/2343   wild-wood leaues] NEILSON-HILL (Cambridge); wild wood-leaues F. See *OED wildwood*: 'forest of natural growth... uncultivated or unfrequented wood'. The hyphens in this text must be largely or wholly scribal in origin; the error would be easy.
4.2.401/2352   hee is] F2; hee's F1
4.3.16/2371, 4.3.23/2378   A LORD] Lord. F; 1. L. CAPELL. Capell's identification as 'First Lord', accepted by subsequent editors, creates an unnecessary identity with the 'First Lord' of Act 1.
4.3.28/2383   A LORD] Lord. F; 2. L. CAPELL; 1. lord. MALONE. See previous note.
4.3.40   betid] F (betide)
4.4.2/2403   finde we] F2; we finde F1
4.4.17/2418   the] ROWE; their F
4.4.18/2419   Files] RANN; Fires F. An easy misreading; the 'Files' and 'horses' suggest an imminent attack; 'Fires' by contrast merely implies a Roman camp.
4.4.27   hard] F (heard). See *OED*.
4.4.35/2436   is't] F1; is it F2
5.1.1/2456   onc wisht] This edition (*conj.* Kellner); am wiſht F; wish'd POPE; am whisht CHAMBERS. For Kellner's conjecture see *Anglica, Untersuchungen... Alois Brandl... überreicht* (1925), ii. 168. Maxwell rejects it on metrical grounds, but an extra unstressed syllable after the caesura is a common metrical licence (see 4.3.30/2385, etc.). Pope's emendation, almost always adopted, leaves F's error unexplained; Chambers's *whisht* (meaning 'hushed') makes poor sense.
5.1.15/2470   dread it] This edition; dread it F; dreaded THEOBALD. The line has provoked much emendation and conjecture; 'it' has been defended only as a 'rather vague' allusion to 'this accumulation' or 'sin'. The misreading proposed here would be easy; for the spelling, see *OED*. (The form 'illes' in the preceding line is almost certainly scribal.)
5.1.16/2471   blest] This edition (*conj.* Johnson); beſt F. The emendation is supported by 'sacred wil's' (*Winter's Tale* 3.3.7/1260), as well as symmetry. For omitted letters in Compositor B's work compare 'amed' (2.3.29/878), 'inſulment' (3.5.141/1797), 'ſtopt' (5.5.42/2548), etc.

5.1.20/2475   Mistris-peace] This edition (*conj.* Staunton, *Athenaeum* (14 June 1873), 761–2); Mistris: Peace F. It is not clear why Posthumus should say 'Peace' to 'Britaine'; F could easily arise from misinterpretation of an unusual compound (see *OED*). *Piece* could be spelled 'peace' in this period.
5.1.20   mistress-piece] See preceding note.
5.1.32-3/2487-8   begin‸ | The fashion,] THEOBALD; ∼, ∼‸
5.2.0.1/2488.1   A March.] This edition; *not in* F. F characteristically omits the music cues from this direction.
5.2.0.4/2488.4   Alarums.] This edition; *not in* F. See preceding note.
5.3/Sc. 25]   This edition; *not in* F. Either Giacomo's '*Exit*' is incorrect, or the stage is cleared and a new scene should be marked (as in many other battle sequences identical to this one).
5.3.0.1-2/2498.1-2   Alarums... Retreat] This edition; *not in* F. (The practical implications of F's '*The Battaile continues*'.)
5.4/Sc. 26]   This edition; *not in* F. See 5.3/Sc. 25.
5.4.0.1/2501.3   *The Trumpets sound a Retreat*] This edition; *not in* F. See 5.2.0.1/2488.1.
5.5.2/2508   I] This edition (*conj.* Craig; I did F. F's repetition is extrametrical, and could easily arise from assimilation to the preceding line. 'I' is also usefully ambiguous: 'ay' or 'I?' or 'I—'.
5.5.24/2530   harts] POPE 2 (Theobald); hearts F
5.5.24/2530   her] THIRLBY; our F
5.5.42/2548   stoopt] ROWE; ſtopt F
5.5.43/2549   they] THEOBALD; the F
5.5.53/2559   do not] F; do but THEOBALD; do you INGLEBY. See next note.
5.5.53/2559   yet you] This edition; you F; tho' you HANMER; but you CAPELL (*conj.*). The emendation serves the same purpose as the 18th-c. conjectures, but better explains the alleged error (eyeskip from one 'y' to the next). As Johnson explained, 'Posthumus first bids him not wonder, then tells him in another mode of reproach, that wonder is all that he was made for'. But this sense is difficult to convey without a conjunction—especially as this conjunction is the pivot of Posthumus' whole attitude toward his interlocutor.
5.5.64/2570   This] This edition (*conj.* Ritson); This is F. F's extrametrical 'is' adds nothing, since 'This' could be used as a contraction of 'This is'.
5.5.72/2578   words] F; viands VAUGHAN (*conj.*). Vaughan supposes an easy misreading, supported by 5.6.157/2963.
5.5.74/2580   For] F; Fortune INGLEBY (Brae)
5.5.75/2581   a Britaine] This edition; a Britaine I This edition *conj.* The addition would make the syntax of this difficult passage more comprehensible; F could easily arise from haplography.
5.5.75/2581   haue resum'd] F; here resume This edition *conj.* Posthumus must be dressed as a Briton earlier in the scene, and the first part of his soliloquy gives no clue or cue to a change in costume—and it is hard to see how he can resume his role as an Italian without some corresponding visual gesture.
5.5.94.1/2600.1   Flourish.] This edition; *not in* F. See Introduction.
5.5.94.5/2600.5   Exeunt] THEOBALD (subs.); *not in* F. See next note.
5.5.94.5/2600.5   Manet] This edition; *Scena Quarta.* | *Enter* F. F as it stands is clearly wrong in some way: it calls for Posthumus and a Jailer to enter, when they are still on stage. Hanmer solved this problem by adding an '*Exeunt*' at 5.5.94/2600 and omitting 5.5.94.1-5/2600.1-5; other editors, following Theobald, add an '*Exeunt omnes*' after 5.5.96/2602. But Hanmer's solution is at least logical, in that it recognizes that the extended direction at 5.5.94.1-5/2600.1-5 and the entrance at 5.5.94.5/2600.5 are incompatible; for the dumb show serves only as a transition for Posthumus from one set of custodians to another, making the (editorially interpolated) mass exeunt not only superfluous but nonsensical. This contradiction in F might be resolved by presuming that the dumb show is an interpolation (Hanmer); but it would be simpler to suppose a misunderstanding in 5.5.94.5/2600.5 (as in this edition).
5.5.94.5-6/2600.5-6   who... legges] This edition; *not in* F
5.5.95/2601   GAOLER] F (*Gao.*). Editors since ROWE change the prefix to '*1. Gaoler*'; although this is undoubtedly the sense, and

appropriate in a modernized text, it seems probable that 'Gaoler' (like 'Messenger') means 'First Gaoler', and that the numeral is only added for a second such character. See 5.5.245/2751.

5.5.110/2616 maine part] F; mainport NOSWORTHY (Walker)
5.5.121/2627 make] HUDSON 2 (Daniel); take F. Nosworthy defends F as 'the operative verb throughout the second half of the speech, being used six times'; but this very repetition would make the proposed error exceptionally easy. Shakespeare never elsewhere uses *take* with *audit*; *make . . . audit* occurs at *Macbeth* 1.6.27/392, and *Coriolanus* 1.1.142/140.
5.5.161/2667 gecke] CAPELL; geeke F
5.5.163/2669 come] DYCE 2 (W. S. Walker); came F. See Maxwell.
5.5.175/2681 looke] F2; looke, | looke F1
5.5.212 Preens] F (Prunes)
5.5.212 claws] F (cloyes). *OED* lists this passage as its only example of *cloy*, v.²; but the form seems clearly related to *cly*, *clye*, *clee*, *cloy* (v.¹), and *claw*, each in a range of spellings, all with variants of the same sense, and all but *claw* now obsolete.
5.5.244.1/2750.1 Gaoler] F; *Re-enter Jailers.* CAPELL
5.5.245/2751, etc. GAOLER] F (*Gao.*). As F gives no indication of a second jailer's presence, there seems no need to specify '1. GAOLER' in all the prefixes here (as editors who follow Capell's stage directions do).
5.5.253/2759 are as] MAXWELL (Collier); are F
5.5.259/2765 Of] GLOBE; Oh, of F
5.5.263/2769 Sir] F2; Sis F1
5.5.274/2780 or take] CAPELL (Heath); or to take F
5.5.278 on] F (one)
5.5.300/2806 Exeunt.] F1; *Exit* F2. F2 has an '*Exeunt*' after 5.5.291/2797, which editors traditionally accept, taking it to mean '*Exeunt all but the First Gaoler*'. But the Messenger tells the Jailer himself to 'bring' his prisoner to the King. The Jailer's final speech can be spoken partly to Posthumus, partly aside, partly to the messenger, as he is unlocking Posthumus' leg-irons.
5.6.0.1/2806.1 Flourish.] This edition; *not in* F
5.6.5 targs] F (targes). This spelling makes it clear that the word is a monosyllable. See *Antony* 2.6.39/1035.
5.6.55/2860 and in fine] This edition; and in time F; yes and in time F2; and in due time KEIGHTLEY (W. S. Walker); and so in time HUDSON 2 (Jervis); and thus in time HERTZBERG (cited in Nosworthy). Though F2 initiated a tradition of metrical emendation, F1 is metrically acceptable as a defective caesura. More suspicious is the lame repetition of 'in . . . time', some lines above; one expects some sense of culmination (which the emendations of Keightley, Hudson, and Hertzberg all attempt to supply). This is most easily provided by 'in fine' (meaning 'in the end'), an idiom Shakespeare uses 8 times elsewhere. Under the influence of 5.6.53/2858, and aural similarity, a scribe or compositor could easily substitute 'in time' for 'in fine' (which also alliterates with 'fitted' 5.6.56/2861). The same sense, and a normalization of the metre, would be achieved by 'in conclusion', which is equally common in Shakespeare's work; but the Folio error would be rather less easy to explain.

5.6.56/2861 fit] HUDSON 2 (W. S. Walker); fitted. F's termination is extrametrical and superfluous: see Abbott, 341, 342.
5.6.63/2868 LADIES] CAMBRIDGE; *La.* F1; *Lady.* F4
5.6.65/2870 heard] F3; heare F1
5.6.122/2928 resembles: . . . Lad,] JOHNSON; ∼, . . . ∼ : F
5.6.135 On] F (One)
5.6.143/2949 Torments] HUDSON 2 (Ritson); Which torments F
5.6.165 straight-pitched] F (ftraight-pight)
5.6.178 cracked] F (crak'd)
5.6.206/3012 got it] F2; got F1
5.6.226/3032 villain] MAXWELL; villany F
5.6.234/3040 comes] F1; come ROWE
5.6.262/3068 frō] ROWE; fro F
5.6.263/3069 locke] NEILSON-HILL (Dowden); Rocke F
5.6.275 truth] F (troth)
5.6.278/3084 was] F; had This edition *conj.* Substitution of auxiliary verbs is a common error; 'had' permits elision ('sh'd'), where 'was' does not (being indistinguishable, if elided, from 'she is').
5.6.304/3110 boy] This edition; man F; youth KEIGHTLEY. Keightley suspected that F's lame 'man' is a substitution for some other noun, caused by contamination from the other 'man' in the line. But 'boy' is much more likely than 'youth' to be the original noun. Belarius calls Arviragus and Guiderius 'boys' 10 times, 'youths' never; 'boy' better alliterates; and Shakespeare contrasts 'boy' with 'man' at least 18 times elsewhere, including: 'If thou kil'st me, boy, thou shalt kill a man' (*Much Ado* 5.1.79/2143), 'His disgrace is to be called Boy, but his glorie is to subdue men' (*LLL* 1.2.171-2/472-3), and—in *Cymbeline* itself—'The Boy hath taught vs manly duties' (4.2.398/2349) and 'Two Boyes, an Oldman (twice a Boy)' (5.5.57/2563).
5.6.313 on's] F (one's)
5.6.336/3142 meere] RANN (Tyrwhitt); neere F
5.6.337/3143 Treason:] POPE; ∼, F
5.6.353/3159 like] F2; liks F1
5.6.360.1/3166.1 *Guiderius kneeles*] This edition; *not in* F. The subsequent directions for Arviragus (5.6.362.1/3168) and both (5.6.374/3180) are also editorial. It seems natural for both, when presented to their father/king, to kneel; he in turn blesses them.
5.6.380/3186 ye] ROWE; we F
5.6.388/3194 Brothers] ROWE; Brother F
5.6.394/3200 Intergatories] MALONE (Tyrwhitt); Interrogatories F
5.6.407/3213 so] F2; no F1
5.6.448/3253 thy] F; this This edition *conj.*
5.6.451/3256 this] F; thy CAPELL. If one assumes that the difficulty in 5.6.451/3256 is related to that in 5.6.448/3253, the entire speech can be addressed to Posthumus (whose tablet the Soothsayer is interpreting).
5.6.471/3276 this yet] F3; yet this F1
5.6.487.1/3292.1 Flourish.] This edition; *not in* F
5.6.487.1/3292.1 *in Triumph*] This edition; *not in* F

INCIDENTALS

2 Courtiers,] ∼ :   58 eld'st] eldeft   58 old;] ∼ˬ   59 cloathesˬ the other,] ∼, ∼ˬ   140 bless'd] bleſſed   320-1 Country-Mistresses] ∼-| 336 others,] ∼.   344 Mistris] Miſtirs   381 that] rhat   387 Estate] Fſtate   388 spoke.] ˬ,   391 safe.] Fb; ∼, Fa   396 my] Fa; My Fb   400 preserue] pre-|ſeure   555 mad?] Fb; ∼. Fa   559 Beach,] Fb; ∼ˬ Fa   560 Spectacles] Spectales   567 oppos'd] Fb; opos'd Fa   569 allur'd] allur,d   577 abode] Fb; aboed Fa   579 Continews] Continwes Fa; Continues Fb   586 knowing] knowiug   595 be:] Fb; ∼■ Fa   603 Tallents] Fa; Talents Fb   614 your—] Fb; ∼ : Fa   625 loyalty:] ∼.   627 dampn'd] Fa; damn'd Fb   628 Slauer] F (*c.w.*); Slauuer F (*text*). (*OED* does not record 'slauuer'.)   635 Encounter] Fb; Eneounter Fa   635 feare,] Fa; ∼ˬ Fb   636 IACHIMO] Fb (*Iach.*); Iacb. Fa   788 And] Aud   792 expulsion] Fb; expuſion Fa   820 designe?] Fa; ∼. Fb   823 adornement] Fb; adornement Fa   872 eyes:] ∼ˬ   875 penetrate] pen trate   884 daughter?] ∼.   944 kindnesse] kinduesſe   947 Fooles] Fooies (?)   974 Enuie,] ∼.   979 meanest] mean'ft   1002 meanest] mean'ft   1034 fayr'st] fayreſt   1102 that:] ∼ˬ   1130 deerly.] ∼ˬ   1182 rather all.] ∼ˬ   1269 Salt-water-Girdle] Salt-|water-Girdle   1291 So much] Fb; Somuch Fa   1291 Doo't: The Letter,] Doo't: The Letter.   1294 Incke] Fa; Inke Fb   1313.1 *She . . . Letter*] (Fb *here has a blank line*; Fa *places the blank line instead between* - .)   1320 Leonatus-Posthumus] Fa (*roman*); ∼ˬ ∼ Fb (*roman*)   1333 Wales,] Fb; ∼ : Fa

CYMBELINE

1335 and] Fb; ₐnd Fa   1337 get] ger   1343 Execution] Excution   1351 (Man);] (Man)ₐ   1351 heere,] ~;
1483 INNOGEN (reades)] Imogen reades. (indented as stage direction)   1502 false] falſe   1630 one.] ~,   1631 this,] ~.
1797 insultment] inſulment   1889 Friends,] ~?   1956 sicke.] ~,   1992 answer] auſwer   2035 Grandfather:] ~?
2151 Age,] Agₐe (very faint inking of a fragment in some copies)   2173 face,] ~.   2356 bring] hring   2409 vs] v.   2420 And] Aud   2537 nothing:] ~.   2650 deseru'd] dₐſeru'd   2655 or] Or   2813 Our] Onr   2931 forbeare,] ~ₐ
2957 strength,] ~ₐ   3004 operate] operare   3047 PISANIO] Piſæ.   3052 If Pisanio] If Paſanio   3108 Lord.] ~ₐ
3167 Aruiragus,] ~.   3195 whether? these,] ~ₐ ~?   3203 Me,] ~:

FOLIO STAGE DIRECTIONS

1.1.0.1/0.1   Enter two Gentlemen.
1.1.68.1/68.1   Enter the Queene, Posthumus, and Imogen.
1.1.70/70   Exeunt
1.1.84/84   Exit
1.1.102/102   Enter Queene.
1.1.125/125   Enter Cymbeline, and Lords.
1.1.131/131   Exit.
1.1.151/151   Enter Queene.
1.1.159/159   Exit.
1.1.159.1/159.1   Enter Pisanio. (after 'Folly', 1.1.159/159)
1.1.181/181   Exeunt.
1.2.0.1/181.1   Enter Clotten, and two Lords.
1.2.40/220   Exeunt.
1.3.0.1/220.1   Enter Imogen, and Pisanio.
1.3.38/258   Enter a Lady.
1.3.41.1/261.1   Exeunt.
1.4.0.1-3/261.3-5   Enter Philario, Iachimo: a Frenchman, a Dutch-|man, and a Spaniard.
1.4.25.1/288.1   Enter Posthumus.
1.4.169/437   Exeunt
1.5.0.1/437.1   Enter Queene, Ladies, and Cornelius.
1.5.3/440   Exit Ladies.
1.5.26.1/463.1   Enter Pisanio.
1.5.45/482   Exit.
1.5.75/512   Exit Pisa. (after 1.5.74/511)
1.5.82/519   Enter Pisanio, and Ladies.
1.5.85.1/522.1   Exit Qu. and Ladies (after 'words', 1.5.85/522)
1.5.87/524   Exit.
1.6.0.1/524.1   Enter Imogen alone.
1.6.9/533   Enter Pisanio, and Iachimo. (after 'Fye')
1.6.22/546   Imogen reads.
1.6.57/579   Exit.
1.6.211.1/733.1   Exeunt.
1.7.0.1/733.2   Enter Clotten, and the two Lords.
2.1.50.1/783.1   Exeunt.
2.1.64/797   Exit.
2.2.0.1-3/797.1-2   Enter Imogen, in her Bed, and a Lady.
2.2.10.1/807   Sleepes.
2.2.10.2/807.1   Iachimo from the Trunke.
2.2.50.1/847.1   Clocke strikes
2.2.51.1/848.1   Exit.
2.3.0.1/848.3   Enter Clotten, and Lords.
2.3.12.1/861.1   Enter Musitians.
2.3.19/867.2   SONG.
2.3.29.2/878.2   Enter Cymbaline, and Queene.
2.3.61.1/910.1   Exeunt.
2.3.74.1/923.1   Knockes.
2.3.74.1/923.1   Enter a Lady.
2.3.83/932   Enter Imogen. (after 'Princesse')
2.3.133.1/982.1   Enter Pisanio.
2.3.152/1001   Exit.
2.3.153/1002   Exit.
2.4.0.1/1002.1   Enter Posthumus, and Philario.
2.4.26/1028   Enter Iachimo.
2.4.149/1151   Exit.
2.4.152/1154   Exeunt.
2.5.0.1/1154.1   Enter Posthumus.
2.5.35/1189   Exit.
3.1.0.1-3/1189.1-3   Enter in State, Cymbeline, Queene, Clotten, and Lords at | one doore, and at another, Caius, Lucius, | and Attendants.

3.1.85/1274   Exeunt.
3.2.0.1/1274.1   Enter Pisanio reading of a Letter.
3.2.22/1296   Enter Imogen. (after 'comes')
3.2.82/1355   Exeunt.
3.3.0.1-2/1355.1-2   Enter Belarius, Guiderius, and Aruiragus.
3.3.78.1/1433.1   Exeunt.
3.3.107/1462   Exit.
3.4.0.1/1462.1   Enter Pisanio and Imogen.
3.4.21/1483   Imogen reades.
3.4.194.1/1656.1   Exeunt.
3.5.0.1-2/1656.2-3   Enter Cymbeline, Queene, Cloten, Lucius, | and Lords.
3.5.17.1/1673.1   Exit Lucius, &c
3.5.41/1697   Enter a Messenger.
3.5.53/1709   Exit.
3.5.55.1/1711.1   Exit. (after 'dayes')
3.5.65.1/1721.1   Enter Cloten.
3.5.69.1/1725.1   Exit Qu.
3.5.80/1736   Enter Pisanio.
3.5.129/1785   Exit.
3.5.145.1/1802.1   Enter Pisanio.
3.5.154/1811   Exit
3.5.160/1817   Exit
3.6.0.1/1817.1   Enter Imogen alone.
3.6.27/1844   Exit.
3.6.27.1/1844.1   Enter Belarius, Guiderius, and Aruiragus.
3.6.44/1861   Enter Imogen.
3.6.93/1910   Exeunt.
3.7.0.1/1910.1   Enter two Roman Senators, and Tribunes.
3.7.16/1926.1   Exeunt.
4.1.0.1/1926.2   Enter Clotten alone.
4.1.25/1951   Exit.
4.2.0.1-2/1951.1-2   Enter Belarius, Guiderius, Aruiragus, and | Imogen from the Caue.
4.2.46/1997   Exit.
4.2.63.1/2014.1   Enter Cloten.
4.2.102/2053   Fight and Exeunt.
4.2.102/2053   Enter Belarius and Aruiragus.
4.2.113/2064   Enter Guiderius.
4.2.155/2106   Exit.
4.2.170/2121   Exit.
4.2.184/2135   Enter Guidereus.
4.2.187/2138   Solemn Musick.
4.2.196/2147   Enter Aruiragus, with Imogen dead, bearing | her in his Armes.
[4.2.258.1/2209.1]   SONG.
4.2.282.1/2233.1   Enter Belarius with the body of Cloten.
4.2.292.1/2243.1   Exeunt.
4.2.293/2244   Imogen awakes.
4.2.334.2/2285.2   Enter Lucius, Captaines, and a Soothsayer.
4.2.404.1/2355.1   Exeunt
4.3.0.1/2355.2   Enter Cymbeline, Lords, and Pisanio.
4.3.35.1/2390.1   Exeunt
4.3.46.1/2401.1   Exit.
4.4.0.1/2401.2   Enter Belarius, Guiderius, & Aruiragus.
4.4.54/2455   Exeunt.
5.1.0.1/2455.1   Enter Posthumus alone.
5.1.33/2488   Exit.
5.2.0.1-7/2488.1-7   Enter Lucius, Iachimo, and the Romane Army at one doore: | and the Britaine Army at another: Leonatus Posthumus |

CYMBELINE

following like a poore Souldier. They march ouer, and goe | out. Then enter againe in Skirmish Iachimo and Posthu-|mus: he vanquisheth and disarmeth Iachimo, and then | leaues him.

5.2.10/2498   *Exit.*

5.3.0.1-4/2498.1-4   *The Battaile continues, the Britaines fly, Cymbeline is | taken: Then enter to his rescue, Bellarius, Guiderius, | and Aruiragus.*

5.3.1-2/2501.1-2   *Enter Posthumus, and seconds the Britaines. They Rescue | Cymbeline, and Exeunt.*

5.4.0.1-2/2501.3-4   *Then enter Lucius, Iachimo, and Imogen.*

5.4.5/2506   *Exeunt*

5.5.0.1-2/2506.1-2   *Enter Posthumus, and a Britaine Lord.*

5.5.63.1/2569.1   *Exit.*

5.5.83.1/2589.1   *Enter two Captaines, and Soldiers.*

5.5.94.1-4/2600.1-4   *Enter Cymbeline, Belarius, Guiderius, Aruiragus Pisanio, and | Romane Captiues. The Captaines present Posthumus to | Cymbeline, who deliuers him ouer to a Gaoler.*

[5.5.94.5/2600.5]   *Enter Posthumus, and Gaoler.*

5.5.123.1-9/2629.1-9   *Solemne Musicke. Enter (as in an Apparation) Sicillius Leo-|natus, Father to Posthumus, an old man, attyred like a war-|riour, leading in his hand an ancient Matron (his wife, & | Mother to Posthumus) with Musicke before them. Then | after other Musicke, followes the two young Leonati (Bro-|thers to Posthumus) with wounds as they died in the warrs. | They circle Posthumus round as he lies sleeping.*

5.5.186.1-3/2692.1-3   *Iupiter descends in Thunder and Lightning, sitting vppon an | Eagle: hee throwes a Thunder-bolt. The Ghostes fall on | their knees.*

5.5.207.1/2713.1   *Ascends*

5.5.216.1/2722.1   *Vanish*

5.5.231.1/2738   *Reades.*

5.5.244.1/2750.1   *Enter Gaoler.*

5.5.284.1/2790.1   *Enter a Messenger.*

5.5.300/2806   *Exeunt.*

5.6.0.1-2/2806.1-2   *Enter Cymbeline, Bellarius, Guiderius, Arui-|ragus, Pisanio, and Lords.*

5.6.23.2/2828.2   *Enter Cornelius and Ladies.*

5.6.69.1-2/2874.1-2   *Enter Lucius, Iachimo, and other Roman prisoners, | Leonatus behind, and Imogen.*

5.6.437/3243   *Reades.*

5.6.487.1/3292.1   *Exeunt.*

THE TEMPEST

The Tempest (BEPD 390) was one of sixteen plays in the First Folio to be first entered in the Stationers' Register on 8 November 1623. Perhaps partly because it was Shakespeare's last work of single authorship, it was printed to appear as the first play in the Folio, giving the only authoritative printed text (F). As befits the opening play in such a volume, it was prepared with care; the compositors were B, C, and D. A variety of features indicate that the copy for F was a transcript by Ralph Crane (see General Introduction, Howard-Hill, and Roberts, 'Ralph Crane'). The transcript might have been prepared specifically to provide copy for F. As in three other of the five acknowledged Crane texts, a list of characters ('*Names of the Actors*') is printed at the end of the play. Some stage directions set characters' names in roman letters, preserving a feature of the transcript also found in extant manuscripts in Crane's hand. Many incidentals reflect Crane's recognized scribal characteristics; his intervention as a sophisticating scribe means that the incidentals generally are of little authority.

In *The Tempest* Crane did not, as in several other plays, introduce massed stage directions, though twice he appears to have run together directions which should be separated by a few lines of text. He was apparently influenced by his experience of the play on stage. Jowett argues that he probably elaborated upon Shakespeare's directions, emphasizing visual aspects of the play as seen in the theatre and recording them in a descriptive, complimentary, literary manner, in terms which aid the reader's appreciation of the play but which are unlikely to have been used by a dramatist instructing the players. Examples of words and phrases that might have been introduced by Crane are '*A tempestuous noise*' (1.1.0.1/0.1), '*confused*' (1.1.57/59), '*dispersedly*' (1.2.385/451), '*shapes*' (3.3.18.1/1366.1 and 3.3.82.2/1429.2), '*with gentle actions of salutations*' (3.3.18.2–3/1366.2–3), '*with a quient device*' (3.3.52.3–4/1399.3–4), '*properly habited*' (4.1.138.1/1594.1), and '*a strange hollow and confused noyse*' (4.1.142.1/1598.1). Wilson suggested that Shakespeare was writing such directions himself as a substitute for verbal instructions because he was working from semi-retirement in Stratford; the non-dramatic and sometimes theatrically misleading qualities of these directions rather suggest their origin in a self-consciously 'literary' transcript.

Crane was often careful to mark part-lines of verse on a separate manuscript line, but is likely to have contributed to the confusion of verse and prose in scenes where they are mixed (though in one case at least—at the foot of A6^v, 3.2.155/1347—Compositor B evidently split lines to lose space). A complicating factor is Shakespeare's extensive use of semi-verse or metrical prose in some scenes. Chambers demonstrated that most of the first scene's prose could be rearranged as approximate verse.

One of the most serious textual problems is internal to the masque, and is not touched by the controversy as to whether the masque as a whole was interpolated. In F the direction '*Iuno descends.*' appears some thirty lines before Juno arrives on the stage. Kermode follows many editors in regarding the direction as misplaced, arguing that it is an anticipatory direction which indicates that Crane's copy was a theatrical manuscript. But it seems to us unlikely that Crane would have preserved a direction inconsistent with performance and, by coincidence, eliminated the appropriate direction (which he could have recognized as necessary and might even be expected to elaborate). An alternative explanation is that foul papers underlie the transcript, and that these contained only sketchy or provisional directions for the masque scene. The direction may be accurate in its content and its position, but lacking subsequent supporting directions to explicate the action. The sophisticated and elegant stage direction which rounds off the masque shows strong signs of having been rewritten by Crane, and may give a false impression of an underlying manuscript whose stage directions for the masque were incomplete. The staging of the masque given in this edition is not without possible modifications, but if '*Iuno descends.*' is retained where it is marked in F, the range of plausible interpretations consistent with Jacobean stagecraft is limited.

F's act divisions were probably supplied as theatrical act-breaks; they are followed in this edition, as are F's scene divisions. The wording of stage directions is retained where Crane is thought to have intervened except where the result is misleading: the two strata of directions cannot be clinically separated and the elaborated phrases usually either embellish necessary directions or provide helpful information in their own right.

Most of the songs in *The Tempest* are preserved in early to mid seventeenth-century manuscripts. These fall into two groups:

(*a*) BL, Egerton MS 2421, fols. 6–7 ('Full Fathom Five', 'The Master, the Swabber', 'No more Dams', 'Honours, Riches', 'Where the Bee Sucks')

(*b*) A number of music manuscripts which evidently derive from a single source, Robert Johnson's settings, as arranged by John Wilson:

    (i) Birmingham Reference Library, Acc. No. 57316, Location No. 5747.01 ('Full Fathom Five', 'Where the Bee Sucks')

    (ii) Bodleian, MS Don. C. 57, fol. 75 ('Where the Bee Sucks')

    (iii) Bodleian, MS Mus. d. 238, pp. 87–8 ('Full Fathom Five', 'Where the Bee Sucks')

    (iv) Folger, MS V.a. 411, fols. 9^v, 10, 11, 12^v ('Full Fathom Five') and fols. 9^v, 10^v, 11^v, 13^v ('Where the Bee Sucks')

(v) New York Public Library, MS Drexel 4041, No. 90, fols. 67ᵛ-68 ('Full Fathom Five')

(vi) Yale Music Library, Misc. MS 170, Filmer MS 4, fols. 14, 20, 20ᵛ ('Full Fathom Five') and fols. 15, 20ᵛ, 21 ('Where the Bee Sucks').

The Egerton MS has a number of plausible variants, but there are reasons for doubting that the manuscript has independent authority. The variants are in themselves inconclusive. If the manuscript's calls for repeated refrains at 1.2.408/473 and 2.2.54/961 hints at an independent source, the error shared with F of a missing speech-prefix for Ceres at 4.1.110/1566 indicates the opposite. Details of layout suggest that the Egerton texts are derivative either from F or from a closely related manuscript such as Crane's transcript. Even in the latter case, the more interesting variants are unlikely to be the result of compositorial error in F. None of the Egerton verbal variants appears in the music manuscripts; these presumably derive ultimately from a music manuscript in Shakespeare's theatre. Though it is just possible that an underlying music manuscript and F were collated, it seems more likely that the Egerton manuscript has been sophisticated during transmission. The refrain need only indicate that a scribe was familiar with musical settings. In the absence of plausible verbal variants in the music manuscripts, both groups of manuscripts are of most use for their indications of repeats and refrains, which have been accepted in the text of this edition.

J.J./(S.W.W.)

WORKS CITED

Allen, George, 'Notes of Studies on *The Tempest*', in *Minutes of the Shakspere Society of Philadelphia for 1864-65* (1866)

Chambers, E. K., *Shakespearian Gleanings* (1944)

Falconer, Alexander Frederick, *Shakespeare and the Sea* (1964)

Grigson, Geoffrey, *The Englishman's Flora* (1958)

Holt, John, *An Attempt to Rescue that Auncient English Poet [etc.]* (1749)

Jowett, John, 'New Created Creatures: Ralph Crane and the Stage Directions in *The Tempest*', *SSu* 36 (1983), 107-20

Kermode, Frank, ed., *The Tempest*, Arden (1954)

Orgel, Stephen, ed., *The Tempest*, Oxford (1987)

Roberts, Jeanne Addison, ' "Wife" or "Wise"—*The Tempest* l. 1786', *SB* 31 (1978), 203-8

—— 'Ralph Crane and the Text of *The Tempest*', *SSt* 13 (1980), 213-33

Smith, Irwin, *Shakespeare's Blackfriars Playhouse: Its History and its Design* (1964)

—— 'Ariel and the Masque in *The Tempest*', *SQ* 21 (1970), 213-22

Wilson, John Dover, and Sir Arthur Quiller-Couch, eds., *The Tempest*, New (1948)

TEXTUAL NOTES

Title *The Tempest*] F, S.R.

1.1.7.2/8.2 *and others*] F. See note to 2.1.0.2/573.2.

1.1.20 councillor] F (Counfellor)

1.1.21/22 worke peace] This edition; worke the peace F. The difficulty in F is that the article leads one to understand 'the peace of the present' as an object noun-phrase whereas 'of the present' must function as a complement. F's error would be a dittography anticipating 'the present'.

1.1.21/22 present] F; presence KERMODE (Maxwell). The emendation depends upon 'the peace of the presence' being recognized as a set phrase; Kermode finds no evidence that this would be the case.

1.1.32/33 *Exeunt ⌈Courtiers⌉*] *Exit.* F. It is doubtful if there should be a cleared stage; one should rather envisage that the Mariners are constantly toing and froing. Wilson avoids clearing the stage by stipulating '*BOATSWAIN comes aft: courtiers retreat before him to their cabins*'.

1.1.34/35 to,] F; ~ ; WHITE

1.1.34 wi'th'] F (with)

1.1.35/36 plague,] CAPELL; ~ — F. The direction '*A cry within.*' and the entry of Sebastian, Antonio, and Gonzalo follow in F. The layout led to scribe or compositor inferring an interrupted speech.

1.1.47/49 courses,] STEEVENS (Holt); ~, F

1.1.51 prayers!] F (~,). The common interpretation retaining F's comma, 'the King and Prince being at prayers', lacks urgency. The exclamation derives from Pope.

1.1.52 I'm] F (I'am)

1.1.57-8/59-60 Mercy...split] The unambiguous verse lineation in F is in apparent conflict with the direction for '*confused noyse*', which suggests mixed and therefore non-metrical articulations. The entire scene is laced with verse rhythms, and a less realistic effect may be indicated. The '*confused noyse*' may be distinct from the cries, but we cannot be sure that the direction is Shakespeare's.

1.1.60 wi'th'] F1 (with')

1.1.62/64 Long] F; ling HANMER. See Kermode's defence of F.

1.1.62/64 Broume,] HANMER; Browne, F

1.1.62 furze] F (firrs)

1.2.7/73 creature] F; creatures THEOBALD

1.2.29/95 soule] F; soul lost POPE; soil JOHNSON; loss CAPELL

1.2.50 abyss] F (Abifme). See Sonnet 112.9.

1.2.59/125 And] F; A POPE

1.2.92 O'er-priced] F (Ore-priz'd)

1.2.95 falsehood,...contrary,] F (~,...~,)

1.2.100/166 oft] WARBURTON; of it F; 't oft HANMER (Theobald). F's 'it' would have to refer to 'his own lie', but inevitably seems to indicate 'truth'. The emendation permits a suitable transition from 'truth' to 'lie'. The 'telling' is necessarily repeated, and the meaning of these difficult lines is more apparent if this is spelt out. Crane might easily have misunderstood 'oft' as 'of't' and expanded: such interference would be quite typical of him.

1.2.112 wi'th'] F (with). Compare 1.1.60.

1.2.133/199 out] F; on't THEOBALD

1.2.135/201 sitting] not in F. Prospero later says 'Now I arise' (1.2.170/236), which is probably not merely figurative. Any attempt to locate when Prospero sits must be tentative, but 1.2.135/201 does mark a change in the mood of Prospero's story as he begins to recall Miranda's part in it: Prospero has been brought low, and shares in vulnerability with his young daughter.

1.2.146/212 Butt] F; boat ROWE; buss FALCONER (*conj.*)

1.2.153 wast] F (was't)

1.2.160 diuine.] F (~,)

1.2.174 princes] F (Princeffe). Roberts ('Ralph Crane') shows that Crane used 'Princesse' as a plural form of *Prince*.

1.2.176/242 Heuens] It used to be thought that there was a press variant, 'Heuen', but this has been shown to be a reading apparent only in the Lee facsimile; the '-s' is visible in the F copy from which it was taken.

1.2.188/254 I am] F. Metre suggests that Crane might have expanded copy 'I'm'.

1.2.191-3 pleasure. Be't...clouds,] This follows the Cambridge edition's interpretation of F's 'pleasure; be't...clouds:'. The intervening phrases are sometimes understood to qualify 'I come...pleasure'.

1.2.201 bowsprit] F (Bore-ſpritt)
1.2.202/268 Lightning] F; lightnings THEOBALD A quasi-collective noun for all the individual flashes ('precursors'). Compare 'hony-combe' (1.2.332/398), which similarly attracts a plural pronoun because it suggests many individual cells.
1.2.212-13/278-9 vessell, ... me;] ROWE; ~ ; ... ~, F
1.2.230 Bermudas] F (Bermoothes)
1.2.235 float] F (Flote)
1.2.250/316 did] F1; didst F3
1.2.262, 267 Algiers] F (Argier)
1.2.284/350 she] ROWE; he F
1.2.304/370 like to] F2; like F1
1.2.307-8/373-4 with ... Awake] F (With diligence. *Exit.* | *Pro⟨spero⟩. Awake*) The redundant prefix may merely compensate for the ambiguity of the exit; but it is at least possible that there is a part-line spoken by Ariel missing. Compare 4.1.187/1643, where F has 'For stale to catch these theeues. *Ar.* I go, I goe. *Exit.* | *Pro.*'.
1.2.330/396 forth at] This edition (White); for that F. F gives a problematic reading, one in which 'that they may worke' lacks point and the repeated 'that' is awkward; moreover the intransitive use of *exercise* in the required sense (OED, 6b) is rare, with the present line the first recorded instance. The emendation gives strong and clear sense, and restores the phrasing implied by F's punctuation by reading 'exercise' as the object of 'worke'.
1.2.342/408 Curs'd] F; Cursed STEEVENS
1.2.349 human] F (humane)
1.2.354/420 MIRANDA] F; *Pros⟨pero⟩.* THEOBALD (following Dryden/Davenant)
1.2.380/446 kist:] HALLIWELL (following Dryden/Davenant); ~, F. F would have to imply that the waves themselves are kissed into silence. This sense is not only excessively conceited; it is also practically incommunicable in a song. Kissing partners as a preliminary to a dance may be unconventional but is quite plausible for imagined spirits.
1.2.383 sprites] F (Sprights). Ariel's attendants may be described as 'spirits' or 'sprites'. Impish mannikins are appropriate here, and the metre requires a monosyllable. At 2.2.114 'sprights' is regularized to 'spirits', where the context suggests human-sized phantasms.
1.2.385-8/451-5 SPIRITS ... ARIELL ... SPIRITS ... ARIELL] *speech distribution as* CAPELL; 'Burthen dispersedly' *after* 'the burthen' (1.2.384/450) *and* '*Ar.*' *before* 'Hark, hark, I heare' (1.2.388/454) *in* F. F's direction is positioned for convenience of spacing and does not necessarily indicate that all that follows as far as the Ariel prefix is the 'Burthen'.
1.2.390 cock-a-diddle-dow] F (cockadiddle-dowe). Not modernized to *cock-a-doodle-doo* because the form is mimetic and contrived to rhyme with 'bow-wow' ('bowgh-wawgh' F).
1.2.394/460 wracke,] POPE; ~. F
1.2.407/473 SPIRITS ... dong] F (Burthen ding dong). The Egerton MS resembles F. F is ambiguous: it might indicate either that the Spirits sing 'ding dong' at this point or that 'ding dong' etc., as printed two lines below, is the burden. The first interpretation is adopted here, despite the roman type of 'ding dong' where the song is italic. It is logical for 'ding dong' to be heard before Ariel responds to it. Furthermore, the Birmingham Public Library MS indicates an accompaniment of notes representing the 'ding dong' refrain which begins before Ariel's 'Harke'; this might derive from the Spirits' refrain in the original version.
1.2.407/473 SPIRITS (*within*)] *not in* F
1.2.408/474 *etc.*] ROBERT JOHNSON SETTING (*by specifying the refrain*), EGERTON MS; *not in* F. If textually unauthoritative, the Egerton MS may nevertheless reflect experience of the song in performance. The Johnson setting gives a good indication that the words were indeed repeated in Shakespeare's theatre.
1.2.413 What is't?] F has no punctuation after 'What' or 'is't', and thereby also permits the interpretation 'What! is't a spirit?' (Daniel). This edition substantively follows Capell.
1.2.431/497 Mayd] F1; made F4
1.2.470/536 power] THEOBALD; pow'r F. Probably a spurious Crane elision: it is unlikely that the apostrophe authoritatively indicates a defective caesura.
1.2.492/558 nor] F; and ROWE; or CAPELL; nay KEIGHTLEY (*conj.*)
1.2.493/559 are but] F; are CARTWRIGHT
2.1.0.2/572.2 Francisco] This edition; *Franciſco and others* F. F also adds '&c.' at 3.3.0.2/1347.3, but has no such stipulation at 5.1.57.4/1776.4. Shakespeare may have changed his mind about supernumeraries as he wrote. Other lords or attendants are unnecessary to the play in performance and would obstruct the carefully observed symmetry of the 5.1 direction. The decision to create consistency need not be extended to 1.1.7.2/8.2.
2.1.38, 39/610, 611 ANTHONIO ... SEBASTIAN] WHITE; *Seb⟨astian⟩. ... Ant⟨onio⟩.* F
2.1.63, 65 rarity ... rarities] F (rariety ... rarieties)
2.1.131 loose] F. F can be modernized to 'loose' or 'lose'; both meanings are present, but 'loose' is the more particular.
2.1.133/706 wet,] F. The usage of *wet* may be explained as meaning 'add tears to' or as an analogous substitute for *weep*. However, 'wet' could be intransitive, with 'the greefe on't' expanding the 'cause'; if this were so, a comma might follow 'wet'.
2.1.136-7/709-10 Waigh'd ... bow] The difficulty is probably one of compression rather than corruption. 'Waigh'd ... at' can be understood as 'weighted ... to find out'. Proposed emendations have not notably improved the sense, and the criticism that the image is imperfectly realized is not fully justified.
2.1.136/709 at] F; as COLLIER
2.1.137/710 should] F; she'ld CAPELL
2.1.139 More] F (Mo)
2.1.146 chirurgeonly] F (Chirurgeonly). 'Very well' is amphibious, giving a possible verse-line with 'And ... chirurgeonly', beginning in a line-divided foot. The modernization 'surgeonly' destroys the metre.
2.1.156/729 Riches, pouerty] F; poverty, riches CAPELL
2.1.175 And—] F (~,)
2.1.208/781 consent,] CAMBRIDGE (*subs.*); ~, F
2.1.211-12/784-5 face: ... be,] This edition; ~, ... ~: F. F's punctuation gives a double subject to 'see' and an awkward expression in 'th' occasion speaks thee'. The details of punctuation in F depend upon both Crane's interpretation of his copy and the sophisticating Compositor B's interpretation of his copy.
2.1.255/828 that from] F; for POPE
2.1.257/830 by that] F; that by JOHNSON
2.1.262 every] F (eu'ry). F marks a redundant elision, *every* being usually disyllabic in Shakespeare, as in modern usage.
2.1.301.1/874.1 with Musicke] This edition; *with Muſicke and Song* F. Ariel surely does not enter singing. The words '*and Song*' are a redundant anticipation of '*Sings in Gonzaloes eare*', which is correctly placed and Shakespearian in expression. This suggests a Crane addition, perhaps on the analogy of '*playing and singing*' (1.2.377.2-3/443.3). Such an addition might include '*with Musicke*' itself.
2.1.303/876 you (his friend)] F; these his friends JOHNSON (*conj.*); you his friends WHITE
2.1.304/877 them] F; you HANMER; thee HALLIWELL
2.2.49/956 tang] F; twange EGERTON MS
2.2.54/961 *Then to Sea, etc.*] EGERTON MS; *not in* F. The Egerton MS's refrain presumably derives from a musical tradition.
2.2.58 savages] F (Saluages). 'Saluage' was a form sometimes used in the expression *salvage man*, 'the conventional representation of a savage in heraldry and pageants; a human figure naked or enveloped in foliage' (OED). Excepting this set expression, 'Saluage' is no more than a common spelling variant that Crane is known to have used regularly. The context suggests that Stefano is referring not to a heraldic or pageant figure, but to real (and topical) 'savages'.
2.2.114 spirits] F (sprights). See note to 1.2.38.
2.2.127 Swum] F (Swom)
2.2.171/1080 Seamels] HANMER (Theobald); Scamels F; Staniels HUDSON (Theobald). 'Seamels' and 'Staniels' are almost equally attractive emendations. *Staniel* appears in *Twelfth Night* 2.5.112/1098 (misread 'stallion' in F), and is orthographically plausible.

'Seamels' would be corrupted through the compositor's confusion of literals 'e' and 'c'; other examples in F include *As You Like It* 5.1.17, 5.4.172/2287, 2669; *Shrew* 3.1.28, 4.2.66/1248, 1823; *All's Well* 4.3.34, 4.3.281, 5.2.48/1973, 2220, 2512. The suffix '-mel' is not recorded elsewhere, but may be taken as a variant of '-mall' (compare also *dotterel, petrel*, etc.). Alternatively we might see in F a miscorrection after proof-reading of 'Scamals'. 'Seamels' contextually gives the more plausible reading, and attractively adds to the list of *sea-* compounds in *The Tempest*.

2.2.171 seamews] The old-spelling reading 'Seamels' has been supported by a 1688 reference to the *Sea Mall* as a species distinct from the *Seamew*. This distinction between etymologically related forms is unreliable and of little or no value.

2.2.182/1091 trenchering] F; trenchers EGERTON MS; trencher POPE
3.1.2/1098 sets] ROWE; ſet F.
3.1.15/1111 busielest] KERMODE (Bulloch); buſie left F; busie least F2; busie less THEOBALD; busiest SINGER 2 (Holt). See Kermode. To his parallel of 'easilest' (*Cymbeline* 4.2.207/2158) may be added 'maidenlest' in Q1 *History of Lear* 2.127/424 (F 'maidenliest').
3.1.47/1143 peerlesse] F2; peetleſſe F1
3.2.15/1207 light,] F; ~. CAPELL
3.2.26 debauched] F (debolh'd)
3.2.32/1224 TRINCULO] F (*text*) (*Trin.*); Cal⟨iban⟩. F (*c.w.*)
3.2.53/1245 Isle.] THEOBALD; ~, F
3.2.79-81/1271-3 I . . . doo] F's layout suggests doggerel (see lineation note). Crane or compositor may have interpreted thus, but the rhyme (emphasized by the spelling 'doo') is probably accidental.
3.2.123/1315 cout] F; scout ROWE. *Cout* is improbable as a misreading of 'scout'; and a dropped first letter is not an error typical of Compositor B. The dialect form of *colt* is appropriate to a song of popular anti-authoritarian sentiment. There are no other pre-19th-c. examples of *cout*, but this is unsurprising of a form which merely represents a pronunciation variant of a verb not in itself particularly common.
3.3.0.2/1347.3 Francisco] This edition; Franciſco, &c. F. See note to 2.1.0.2/572.2.
3.3.2/1349 ake] F2; akes F1. An easy terminal '-s' error, especially as the following word (as well as the preceding) ends in '-s'.
3.3.15 travel] F (trauaile)
3.3.29/1376 Islanders] F2; Iſlands F1
3.3.32 gentle-kind] F (~, ~)
3.3.33 human] F (humaine)
3.3.36/1383 muse:] F4 (*subs.*); ~, F1. Shakespeare does not elsewhere use *muse* transitively.
3.3.52.2/1399.2 Ariell ⌈descends⌉] Enter Ariell F. The theatrical impact of the harpy as a bird-monster and an agent of Fate depends upon an aerial 'flight'; this is not indicated in F, and modern texts apparently assume a normal entry. As 'Thunder' of 3.3.82.1/1429.1 would come from the heavens, '*vanishes in thunder*' is tantamount to '*vanishes into the heavens*' and implies a flight. Machinery for such a spectacle would be available at both Globe and Blackfriars theatres.
3.3.65 plume] F (plumbe). Similar spellings (on the analogy of 'comb' etc.) are found elsewhere in Shakespeare's works (Cercignani, 312).
3.3.82.1/1429.1 ⌈ascends and⌉ vanishes] vaniſhes F. See note to 3.3.52.2/1399.2.
3.3.99 bass] F (baſe)
3.3.106/1453 the] F; their ALLEN (*conj.*)
4.1.3/1459 third] F; thread THEOBALD. 'Thread' is plausible in that *third* could be spelt 'thred'. However, Prospero similarly apportions his future life in thirds at 5.1.315/2035. 'A kind of pun' (Kermode) seems unlikely.
4.1.9/1465 of her] ORGEL; her of F; hereof WILSON. Editors usually follow F, modernizing to 'her off', but to show, boast, etc. *off* were not current idioms.
4.1.13/1469 guift] ROWE; gueſt F
4.1.17 rite] F (right)

4.1.23/1479 Lamps] F; lamp WILSON (Elze)
4.1.25/1481 loue, as 'tis now,] ROWE; ~, as 'tis ~, F
4.1.52 rein] F (raigne). F's spelling is probably Crane's, and is used elsewhere by him to denote *rein*.
4.1.53 abstemious] F (abſtenious)
4.1.61 vetches] F (Fetches)
4.1.61 peas] F (Peaſe)
4.1.64 peonied] F (pioned). F gives an acceptable period spelling. *Pioned* as 'dug out, excavated' is a highly conjectural sense, though editors have often accepted it.
4.1.66 groves] F. *Greaves* ('thickets') are almost certainly what is indicated. As the main distinction between a grove and a greave is one of size, and in view of the similar word-forms, there may have been some overlap in usage. Here 'groues' is retained for the rhyme with 'loues' and for its contribution to the mannered diction of the masque.
4.1.72.1/1528.1 Iuno ⌈appears in the ayre⌉] Iuno deſcends. F. There are no reasons for following Theobald's relocation to 4.1.101/1557, so supposing that the direction has been transposed by almost 30 lines, or for postulating no descent at all in the Blackfriars or Globe (as does Smith, *Shakespeare's Blackfriars Playhouse*, 416-17); nor, in view of its wording, and in the absence of other evident playhouse annotations and of a later direction for descent, is F's plausibly an anticipatory direction. A long, slow descent is theatrically awkward. Shakespeare's conception of the spectacular descent may have been less fully formed than that of stage business elsewhere; the direction can nevertheless be interpreted in the light of theatrical practice elsewhere. Dramatists often used '. . . *descends*' to signify an appearance in the air rather than a descent to the stage. 'Her Peacocks flye amaine' gains significance if Juno becomes visible. See Jowett, 115-18.
4.1.74/1530 her] ROWE; here F
4.1.75.1/1531.1 Ariell as] See 4.1.167/1623. The interpretation is not absolutely certain, but Ceres has the main singing role in the masque as Ariel does in the play; it is difficult to believe that Ariel means merely that he arranged the masque in which Ceres was presented.
4.1.81 bosky] F (boskie). This might be modernized 'bushy'; but Shakespeare appears to be using a deliberate archaism as part of the masque's obscure agricultural vocabulary.
4.1.83 short-grassed] F (short gras'd). Collier modernized to 'short-graz'd', which gives a possible sense.
4.1.96 bed-right] F. 'Right' is a common Shakespearian spelling for *rite*, though here 'right' best accords with 'paid'.
4.1.101/1557 Musicke.] not in F. Music is usual for descents; it is needed to create a space in the text for the spectacle and covers the noise of machinery. The accompaniment for the descent may become the accompaniment for the song four lines later.
4.1.101/1557 Iuno . . . stage] See note to 4.1.72.1/1528.1.
4.1.106 marriage-blessing] F (*marriage, bleſſing*). F, though somewhat misleading in the context of sophisticated Jacobean punctuation, gives an acceptable equivalent to a hyphen (compare F's 'gentle, kinde', 3.3.32). The Egerton MS has no punctuation mark.
4.1.110/1566 CERES] THEOBALD; not in F, EGERTON MS
4.1.110/1566 and] EGERTON MS, F2; not in F1. F2 is unauthoritative; the Egerton MS may belong to an independent textual group but probably has no authority. The reading is nevertheless attractive. Cercignani's defence of F1 (p. 287) carries little conviction. He supports disyllabic genitive 'earths', but (*a*) other examples are from much earlier in the canon, (*b*) this reading retains a metrical anomaly, an inversion of Shakespeare's usual stress on the second syllable of sb. *increase*. If 'earths' is taken as monosyllabic, the anomaly is a defective caesura. This would be acceptable licence in spoken pentameter, but is especially awkward in a ceremonious and otherwise metrically regular song.
4.1.117/1573 blessing so is] F; blessings so be EGERTON MS. In either direction the error is presumably two-stage, probably (*a*) terminal '-s' error introducing lack of concord, (*b*) correction introducing

the wrong mood. In that subjunctive 'be' is a 'marked' form and a less obvious correction of 'is' than 'are' would be, F is more easily explained as a corruption than is the MS. If the MS had independent authority, the reading should be preferred, especially as 'blessings' agrees with 4.1.109/1565 and 'be' with 4.1.108/1564.

4.1.123/1579 wise] F2; wife F1. F1 was often taken to read 'wife' until Roberts ('"Wife" or "Wise"') showed that there was progressive damage to the crossbar of 'f' during printing. Error is none the less so easy that the matter does not end there. Whereas previous critics were divided as to what F actually read, almost all preferred 'wise' as the more convincing reading. F's pararhyme is suspicious; *wise/paradise* is a Shakespearian rhyme. 'Wife' gives trite sense and demands two grammatical licences: that 'So rare a wondred' is extended to qualify 'a wife', and that 'Makes' has a plural subject.

4.1.128/1584 windring] F; winding ROWE; wandring STEEVENS
4.1.136 holiday] F (holly day)
4.1.180 gorse] F (goſſe)
4.1.193/1649 them on] ROWE; on them F
4.1.193, 234 lime] F (line). The property indicated must be a tree, not a clothes-line, as there are no references to clothes-lines in the period. Editors usually retain 'line'. This facilitates word-play in 4.1.234-9, but makes the primary sense obscure.
4.1.230/1686 let't alone] HANMER (Let it alone), RANN; let's alone F; let's along THEOBALD. Terminal '-t' and '-s' were more easily confused than Theobald's 'e' and 'g'.
4.1.247/1702 to Apes] F; apes POPE
5.1.10 lime-grove] F (*Line-groue*)
5.1.16/1735 run] F2; runs F1. Compare 3.3.2.
5.1.23/1742 sharpely,] F3; ~, F1
5.1.60/1779 boild] ROWE; boile F
5.1.72/1791 Didst] F (*c.w.*); Did F (*text*)
5.1.75/1794 entertaind] F2; entertaine F1
5.1.81-2/1800-1 shores ... ly] MALONE; ſhore ... ly F1; shore ... lies F3. 'Shores' is more appropriate than 'lies', as the metaphor refers to plural subjects.
5.1.89/1808 a] F; the BODLEIAN MS DON.
5.1.89/1808 bell] F; bath EGERTON MS. The Egerton MS is not necessarily an error. Dialect terms for the cowslip recorded by Grigson include 'Fairy's baisins' as well as 'Fairy bells'.
5.1.90/1809 I cowch] F1; couch I EGERTON MS; I crowch F3. The Egerton MS gives an attractive alternative reading whereby the line is split into a couplet.

5.1.91/1810 the] F; a YALE MS
5.1.92/1811 Sommer] F; sunset THEOBALD
5.1.93-6/1812-15 Merrily ... Bow] ROBERT JOHNSON SETTING; *lines not repeated in* F
5.1.93/1812 I] F, YALE MS (fol. 20ᵛ); wee YALE MS (fols. 15 and 21)
5.1.113 Whe'er] F (Where)
5.1.126/1844 not] F3; nor F1
5.1.158/1877 Truth: Theis] CAPELL (*subs.*); ~ : Their F; ~ . These WILSON. Prospero claims that Antonio and Sebastian refuse to use reason and acknowledge truth; he goes on to insist on the verity of his words. Capell's emendation is consistent with these ideas where F is not. F is especially inappropriate as the lords have scarcely spoken. The misreading 'Their words' would easily follow the reading 'Their eies'. Wilson's interpretation of 'These ... breath' as a separate sentence is undermined by the force of the following 'But'.
5.1.177 kingdoms,] F (~,). Johnson modernized by supplying a full-stop.
5.1.178 An] F (And). Editors retain 'And', which is best defended by following Johnson's punctuation in 5.1.177.
5.1.202/1921 remembrance] ROWE 3; remembrances F. A simple error after 'our' leading to a metrically anomalous line.
5.1.230/1949 euents] F(b); euens F(a)
5.1.233/1952 of sleepe] F; a-sleep POPE. A possible corruption, as *a'* (as in *a'th*) was a common Jacobean contraction of *of*.
5.1.237 more] F (mo)
5.1.237/1956 horrible,] ROWE; ~.F
5.1.239 her] THEOBALD (Thirlby); our F
5.1.251/1970 shortly) single,] ROWE 3; ~, ~) F. Kermode defends F, *single* meaning 'continuous'. Such usage is rare (see *OED*) and is not Shakespearian. Most pertinently, 'single' would be contradicted by 'pick'd'. As elsewhere, the parenthesis is probably Crane's.
5.1.288/2007 Why] Fb; Who Fa
5.1.292/2012 a strange] F; as strange a CAPELL
5.1.322.1/2042.1 Exeunt [*all but Prospero*]] Exeunt omnes. F. The emendation is made for the practical reason that if Prospero leaves the stage, a moment of dramatic indeterminacy is created; an audience, thinking the play ended, may supply the applause for which Prospero appeals in the Epilogue. An exeunt does not invariably mean that all characters leave the stage, and '*omnes*' could be a Crane addition; but F's 'Epilogue, spoken by *Prospero*' could be reasonably interpreted as 'Manet Prospero'.

INCIDENTALS

43-4 Noyse-maker] ~-|~   62 King.] ~,   84 art,] ~.   95 ordred] ordered   131 farther.] ~;   175 Millaine] Fb; Millanie Fa   178 (So] (ſo   179-80 homage, ... Coronet,] ~, ... ~,   182 heauens.] ~:   300 (Which] F (*text*); ,~ F (*c.w.*)   313 more.] ~:   328 me.] ~,   374 Awake] *Pro.* Awake   554 againe,] ~.   697 kept,] ~.   745 knaues.] ~,   1029 o're-boord] ~-|~   1094-5 freedome high-day] freedome ~-|~   1117 Hee's] F (*text*); He's F (*c.w.*)   1522 broome-groues] ~-|(~ (*turn-down*)   1527 I,] ~.   1828 Millaine] Fb; Mailaine Fa   1834 beene] Fb; beenee Fa   1845 Isle] Fb (Iſle); Iſlle Fa   1980 Coragio] Coraſio   2033 deere-beloued] deere-belou'd   2044 owne,] ~.

FOLIO STAGE DIRECTIONS

1.1.0.1-2/0.1-3 *A tempestuous noise of Thunder and Lightning heard: En-|ter a Ship-master, and a Boteswane.*
1.1.4/4.1 *Exit.*
1.1.4.1/4.2 *Enter Mariners.*
1.1.7.1-2/8.1-2 *Enter Alonso, Sebastian, Anthonio, Ferdinando, | Gonzalo, and others.*
1.1.26/27 *Exit.*
1.1.32/33 *Exit.*
1.1.32.1/33.1 *Enter Boteswaine.*
1.1.34.1, 36.1/35.1, 37.1 *A cry within. Enter Sebastian, Anthonio & Gonzalo.* (after 'plague', 1.1.35/36)

1.1.48.1/50.1 *Enter Mariners wet.*
1.1.57/59 *A confused noyse within.*
1.1.60.1/62.1 *Exit.*
1.1.64/66 *Exit.*
1.2.0.1-2/66.1-2 *Enter Prospero and Miranda.*
1.2.189.1/255.1 *Enter Ariel.*
1.2.307.1/373.1 *Exit.*
1.2.317/383 *within.*
1.2.319.1/385.1 *Enter Ariel like a water-|Nymph.* (opposite 1.2.319-20/385-6)
1.2.321/387 *Exit.*

THE TEMPEST

1.2.323.1/389.1 Enter Caliban.
1.2.377.1/443.1 Exit Cal.
1.2.377.2-3/443.2-3 Enter Ferdinand & Ariel, inuisible playing & singing.
1.2.377.5/443.5 Song. (after speech-prefix, 1.2.378/444)
1.2.385/451 Burthen dispersedly. (after 'burthen', 1.2.384/450)
1.2.399.1/465.1 Song. (after speech-prefix, 1.2.400/466)
1.2.407/473 Burthen: ding dong. (equivalent to ⌈SPIRITS⌉ (within) Ding dong.')
1.2.470/536 He drawes, and is charmed from mouing.
1.2.506/572 Exeunt.
2.1.0.1-2/572.1-2 Enter Alonso, Sebastian, Anthonio, Gonzalo, Adrian, | Francisco. and others.
2.1.189.1/762.1 Enter Ariell playing solemne Musicke.
2.1.301.1/874.1 Enter Ariell with Musicke and Song.
2.1.304.1/877.1 Sings in Gonzaloes eare.
2.1.330, 332/903.1, 905 Exeunt. (after 2.1.332/903)
2.2.0.1-2/905.1-2 Enter Caliban, with a burthen of Wood (a noyse | of Thunder heard.)
2.2.14/919 Enter | Trinculo. (opposite 2.2.14-15/917-18)
2.2.40.2-3/947.2-3 Enter Stephano singing.
2.2.44.1/951.1 Drinkes. | Sings.
2.2.55.1/962.1 drinks.
2.2.176/1085 Caliban Sings drunkenly.
2.2.187/1096 Exeunt.
3.1.0.1/1096.1 Enter Ferdinand (bearing a Log.)
3.1.15/1111 Enter Miranda | and Prospero. (opposite 'it' and 'you')
3.1.92.1/1188.1 Exeunt.
3.1.97/1193 Exit.
3.2.0.1/1193.1 Enter Caliban, Stephano, and Trinculo.
3.2.41-2/1233.2 Enter Ariell invisible.
3.2.123/1315 Sings.
3.2.126.1/1318.1 Ariell plaies the tune on a Tabor and Pipe.
3.2.155.1/1347.1 Exeunt.
3.3.0.1-2/1347.2-3 Enter Alonso, Sebastian, Anthonio, Gonzallo, | Adrian, Francisco, &c.
3.3.17.1-2, 19.1-4/1364.1-2, 1366.1-4 Solemne and strange Musicke: and Prosper on the top (inui-|sible:) Enter seuerall strange shapes, bringing in a Banket; | and dance about it with gentle actions of salutations, and | inuiting the King, &c. to eate, they depart. (after 'fresh', 3.3.17/1362)
3.3.52.2-4/1399.2-4 Thunder and Lightning. Enter Ariell (like a Harpey) claps | his wings vpon the Table, and with a quient deuice the | Banquet vanishes.
3.3.82.1-3/1429.1-4 He vanishes in Thunder: then (to soft Musicke.) Enter the | shapes againe, and daunce (with mockes and mowes) and | carrying out the Table.
3.3.102/1449 Exit.
3.3.103.1/1450.1 Exeunt.
3.3.109/1456.1 Exeunt omnes.
4.1.0.1/1456.2 Enter Prospero, Ferdinand, and Miranda.
4.1.33.1/1489.1 Enter Ariell.
4.1.50/1506 Exit.
4.1.58.1/1514.1 Soft musick.
4.1.59.1/1515.1 Enter Iris.
4.1.72.1/1528.1 Iuno | descends. (opposite 4.1.72-3/1526-7)
4.1.75.1/1531.1 Enter Ceres.
4.1.105.1/1561.1 They Sing.
4.1.124/1580 Iuno and Ceres whisper, and send Iris on employment. (after 'mar'd', 4.1.127/1583)
4.1.133.1/1589.1 Enter Certaine Nimphes.
4.1.138.1-3, 142.1-2/1594.1-3, 1598.1-2 Enter certaine Reapers (properly habited:) they ioyne with | the Nimphes, in a gracefull dance, towards the end where-|of, Prospero starts sodainly and speakes, after which to a | strange hollow and confused noyse, they heauily vanish. (after 4.1.138/1594).
4.1.163.1/1619.1 Exit.
4.1.164.1/1620.1 Enter Ariell.
4.1.187/1643 Exit.
4.1.193, 193.3/1649, 1649.3 Enter Ariell, loaden with glistering apparell, &c. Enter | Caliban, Stephano, and Trinculo, all wet. (after 'line')
4.1.253.2-4/1708.2-4 A noyse of Hunters heard. Enter diuers Spirits in shape | of Dogs and Hounds, hunting them about: Prospero | and Ariel setting them on.
4.1.264/1719 Exeunt
5.1.0.1/1719.1 Enter Prospero (in his Magicke robes) and Ariel.
5.1.32/1751 Exit.
5.1.57.1-6/1776.1 Solemne musicke. | Heere enters Ariel before: Then Alonso with a franticke ge-|sture, attended by Gonzalo. Sebastian and Anthonio in |like manner attended by Adrian and Francisco: They all | enter the circle which Prospero had made, and there stand | charm'd: which Prospero obseruing, speakes.
5.1.87.1/1806.1 Ariell sings, and helps to attire him.
5.1.105/1824 Exit.
5.1.173.1-2/1892.1-2 Here Prospero discouers Ferdinand and Miranda, play-|ing at Chesse.
5.1.218.1-2/1937.1-2 Enter Ariell, with the Master and Boatswaine | amazedly following.
5.1.258.1-2/1977.1-2 Enter Ariell, driuing in Caliban, Stephano, and | Trinculo in their stolne Apparell.
5.1.322.1/2042.1 Exeunt omnes.
Epi. 20.1/2062.1 Exit.

[Printed after the play]

The Scene, an vn-inhabited Island

Names of the Actors.

Alonso, K. of Naples:
Sebastian his Brother.
Prospero, the right Duke of Millaine.
Anthonio his brother, the vsurping Duke of Millaine.
Ferdinand, Son to the King of Naples.
Gonzalo, an honest old Councellor.
Adrian, & Francisco, Lords.
Caliban, a saluage and deformed slaue.
Trinculo, a Iester.
Stephano, a drunken Butler.
Master of a Ship.
Boate-Swaine.
Marriners.
Miranda, daughter to Prospero.
Ariell, an ayrie spirit.
Iris ⎫
Ceres ⎪
Iuno ⎬ Spirits.
Nymphes ⎪
Reapers ⎭

ALL IS TRUE

OUR only authority for this play is the text of the First Folio where, with the title 'The Famous Hiſtory of the Life of | King HENRY the Eight', it was first printed; it was included ('Henry the eight') in the Stationers' Register entry for plays new to that volume. From a variety of contemporary references, however, it seems most probable that 'All is true' was the play's original title, and that the Folio alternative was either a subtitle, or, more likely, an unauthoritative one imposed by the compilers of that volume (see the 'title' textual note, below, and the General Introduction, p. 28).

James Spedding (1850) was the first to develop the view that Shakespeare wrote *All Is True* in collaboration with John Fletcher. (See 'Canon and Chronology'.) The most recent detailed attempt to assign responsibility is by Cyrus Hoy, who divides the play as follows:

Prologue	no view expressed; Spedding tentatively assigned to Fletcher
1.1, 1.2	Shakespeare
1.3, 1.4	Fletcher
2.1, 2.2	principally Shakespeare, touched up by Fletcher
2.3, 2.4	Shakespeare
3.1	Fletcher
3.2.1–203/1494–1697	Shakespeare
3.2.204–460.1/1697–1953.1, 4.1, 4.2	principally Shakespeare, touched up by Fletcher
5.1	Shakespeare
5.2, 5.3, 5.4	Fletcher
Epilogue	no view expressed; Spedding tentatively assigned to Fletcher

Spedding's principal aim was to identify what is not by Shakespeare; Hoy's, on the other hand, was to identify, by means of a well-tested thumb-print of identifiable linguistic forms, those portions of the play which are by Fletcher. His assumption that portions not bearing that thumb-print are by Shakespeare has been questioned (e.g. by Schoenbaum), and a third hand, perhaps Beaumont's, may be present.

The Folio text is a clean one, presenting few editorial problems. It is generally agreed that it was set from a carefully prepared manuscript in a single hand; two features of the text powerfully suggest that this manuscript was a scribal transcript and not the authors' papers.

The word *has* occurs in the play a total of 44 times (this excludes from consideration any occurrences as part of contractions of, for example, *he has*): 35 of these occur in parts of the play which Hoy ascribes either partly or wholly to Shakespeare; 9 in parts he assigns to Fletcher (or 13 Shakespeare, and 31 Fletcher, by the traditional division). Excluding Q *Othello*, which was itself set from a scribal transcript, the good quartos seem to indicate that Shakespeare preferred the form without apostrophe (74 'has' versus 3 'ha's'); we do not have figures for Fletcher, but we have observed that of the 34 occurrences of *has* in his share of *Kinsmen*—a play which we believe was probably set from his and Shakespeare's own papers—all are without apostrophe. It seems unlikely from what we know, therefore, that the high proportion of the form with apostrophe in *All Is True* derives from a manuscript in either Shakespeare's or Fletcher's hand. Neither does it seem probable that the compositors of the play were responsible. Of the 44 occurrences of *has* in *All Is True*, Compositor I set 24 (6 'has'; 19 'ha's') and Compositor B set 19 (2 'has'; 17 'ha's'). Compositor I's total share of the Folio is too small for one to draw any firm conclusions from his practice here (he sets the word only once elsewhere—in *Hamlet*—and there he uses 'ha's'), but we can say with some confidence that B here is at variance with his evident preference for 'has' (or for his willingness to follow copy 'has') elsewhere in the Folio. First, we should observe that in the whole of the Folio, with but two exceptions, the word *has* is spelt either 'has' or 'ha's' (these exceptions are the two occurrences of 'haz' in *1 Henry IV*, which derive from Q4 (1604): TLN 2058 set by J and TLN 2241 set by B). In *All Is True* B sets 17 out of 19 occurrences of the word with an apostrophe (89%). The only other of his stints containing a reasonable number of occurrences of *has* (say, 8 or more) in which he comes near this figure are:

	has	% with apostrophe
Coriolanus	21	71
Macbeth	15	87
Hamlet	13	77

Folio *Hamlet* and *Macbeth* were certainly set from scribal copies; so too, probably, was *Coriolanus*. All of the other Folio plays (which we list here in the order in which they were set) in which B sets 8 or more occurrences of *has* exhibit a decided preference for the form without apostrophe:

	has	% with apostrophe
Merry Wives	8	0
All's Well	23	35
Twelfth Night	16	12.5
Winter's Tale	9	22
Lear	8	25
Timon	25	32
Antony	19	42

Given that in *All Is True* the form with apostrophe is more or less evenly distributed between both compositors' stints, and that it does not derive from Shakespeare or Compositor B, and probably not from Fletcher (we can say nothing about Compositor I), it seems reasonable to conclude that it was present in the compositors' copy, and that that copy was not in the handwriting of either of the authors.

The second feature of the Folio text of *All Is True* which

suggests that its copy was a scribal transcript is the unusually great number of round brackets, set across both authors' shares and both compositors' stints. Taylor ('Shakespeare and Others') has shown that round brackets do not appear to have been a mark of punctuation which Shakespeare frequently used (again, we do not have figures for Fletcher, but can observe that none occur in his share of *Kinsmen*). Taylor has also shown, however, that Compositor B seems to have regularly added some round brackets to his copy. But B's average of 176 words per pair of brackets in *All Is True* is far higher than for any quarto or Folio text set from authorial copy in the stints of B himself or any other compositor, and is closest to the figures in several indubitably scribal texts (*Two Gentlemen*, for example, contains an average of 142 words per pair of brackets; *Cymbeline*, 178; *The Tempest*, 193). The frequency of 'ha's' in *All Is True*, along with the round brackets, when taken together, strongly suggest that a scribal transcript served as copy for F.

What may be a duplicated music direction at 2.4.0.1/ 1072.2 (and possibly another at 4.1.36.11/1989.8) suggests that either the transcript itself, or the authorial manuscript which lay behind it, may have undergone some theatrical annotation.

The Folio regularly, and in our view, correctly, divides the play into acts and scenes, though some editors have introduced an additional scene to Act 5, at 5.2.34.3/2457.3.

We wish to thank Fredson Bowers for lending us the typescript of the textual notes to his forthcoming edition of this play.

W.L.M./(S.W.W.)

WORKS CITED

Berdan, John M., and Tucker Brooke, eds., *The Life of King Henry the Eighth*, Yale (1925)

Bowers, Fredson, ed., *Henry VIII*, in *The Dramatic Works in the Beaumont and Fletcher Canon*, gen. ed. Fredson Bowers, vol. vii (forthcoming)

Foakes, R. A., ed., *King Henry VIII*, Arden (1957)

Hoy, Cyrus, 'The Shares of Fletcher and his Collaborators in the Beaumont and Fletcher Canon (VII)', *SB* 15 (1962), 71–90

Humphreys, A. R., ed., *King Henry the Eighth*, New Penguin (1971)

Maxwell, J. C., ed., *King Henry the Eighth*, New (1962)

Pooler, C. Knox, ed., *The Famous History of the Life of King Henry VIII*, Arden (1915)

Schoenbaum, S., ed., *The Life of King Henry the Eighth*, Signet (1967)

S[pedding], J[ames], 'Who Wrote Shakespeare's Henry VIII?' *The Gentleman's Magazine*, NS 34 (August 1850), 115-23

Taylor, Gary, 'Shakespeare and Others: The Authorship of *1 Henry VI*', Appendix 1 (forthcoming in *Medieval and Renaissance Drama in England*)

Wright, William Aldis, ed., *King Henry the Eighth*, in *Shakespeare: Select Plays*, Clarendon (1895)

TEXTUAL NOTES

Title *All is true*] This edition; All is true (Matthew Page, almanac, 29 June 1613); the play of Hen: 8 (Thomas Lorkin, letter, 30 June 1613); *All is true* (Henry Wotton, letter, 2 July 1613); all is triewe (Henry Bluett, letter, 4 July 1613); the play, viz. of *Henry* the 8. (Edmond Howes, 1614 addition to Stow's *Chronicles and Annals*, STC 23338, p. 926b); Henry the eight S.R.; The Famous Hiſtory of the Life of | King HENRY the Eight F (main title); *The Life of King Henry the Eight* F (running title); all this is true (from the refrain of a 17th-c. ballad 'A Sonnett vpon the pittifull burneing of the Globe-playhowse in London'). See the General Introduction, p. 28.

Pro.0.1-Pro.1/0.1-1 Enter Prologue | PROLOGUE] This edition; THE PROLOGVE. F

Pro.11/11 *paſſe, if*] JOHNSON (Pope); *paſſe: If* F

Pro.32/32 Exit] This edition; not in F

1.1.0.1/32.1 *A Cloth of State throughout the Play*] This edition; *not in* F. The Folio stage directions frequently take for granted the presence on stage of a seat (3.2.136, 5.2.147.1-2/1629, 2570.1-2) or state (1.2.0.3-4/259.6-7) for the King; once there is a specific reference to 'the Cloth of State' under which he 'takes place' (2.4.0.14-15/1072.15-16). Wolsey once 'takes his State' (1.4.35.1-2/575.1-2); that a canopy of some kind is meant here is made clear earlier in the scene when 'A ſmall Table' is directed to be placed 'vnder a State for the Cardinall' (1.4.0.1-3/ 540.2-4). Wolsey later relinquishes 'this place' of honour to the King (1.4.80-4/620-4). Probably the state remained on stage throughout the play, but of this we cannot be certain.

The stage, moreover, seems to have been covered with some kind of matting for all or part of the play (see Illustration 12, line 13, in the General Introduction).

1.1.7 Ardres] F (Andren)

1.1.7 Guisnes] F (Guynes)

1.1.7 Ardres] F (Arde)

1.1.23 mesdames] F (Madams)

1.1.42 to] F (too)

1.1.42/74 All] THEOBALD; |Buc. All F

1.1.45/77 Function. | BUCKINGHAM Who] THEOBALD (subs.); Function: who F

1.1.47-8/79-80 together, as you guesse? | NORFOLKE] F4 (subs.); together? | *Nor.* As you gueſſe:| F1

1.1.63/95 Selfe-drawing] F; self-drawn ROWE 2

1.1.63/95 Web, a] CAMBRIDGE 2 (Capell); Web. O F; web, he CAPELL; web, O, FOAKES. Foakes rejects Capell's conjecture largely on the basis that 'a' (=*he*) occurs nowhere else in the play. But either the scribe or the Folio Compositor may have altered other occurrences of 'a' to 'he'. Generally, very few instances of 'a' survive in the Folio, though we know from Q texts that Shakespeare used the form. Alternatively, the misreading o/a would be easy.

1.1.64/96 way;] THEOBALD; ~ˏ F

1.1.69-70/101-2 that? | If not from Hell, the] THEOBALD (subs.); that, | If not from Hell? The F

1.1.78/110 Letter,] POPE (subs.); ~ˏ F

1.1.79/111 Councell, out,] POPE (subs.); ~, ~ˏ F

1.1.116, 117/148, 149 SECRETARY] F (Secr.). We cannot be certain which secretary speaks which lines (two entered with Wolsey).

1.1.120/152 venome-mouth'd] ROWE; venom'd-mouth'd F

1.1.154/186 Iuly] F2; Inly F1

1.1.167 rinsing] F (wrenching). Compare *Kinsmen* 1.1.155/187.

1.1.172/204 Count-Cardinall] F; Court-Cardinal POPE. Compare 'King-Cardinall', 2.2.19/839, and see Maxwell's note to 2.2.18.

1.1.183/215 Priuily he] This edition; Priuily F1; He Privily F2

1.1.194/226 he] F1; you F4; ye This edition *conj*. It would not be difficult to mistake manuscript 'y' for 'h' in secretary hand.

1.1.200/232 Hereford] CAPELL (Vaughan); Hertford F

1.1.211 Abergavenny] F (*Aburgany*). Though the place name is now pronounced with 5 syllables, the personal name continues to be pronounced with 4. The unelided form is therefore a metrically acceptable modern spelling.

1.1.218/250 Car] F; Court THEOBALD 2. Theobald's emendation, which derives from Holinshed (see the note to 1.2.165/423), fails to notice that elsewhere Holinshed refers to the man as 'maister Iohn de la Car *alias* de la Court' (Bullough, iv. 459). 'Car' is consistently used in F (1.2.163, 2.1.21/421, 673).

1.1.219/251 *Perke*] FOAKES (subs.); *Pecke* F. Holinshed and Hall both read *Perke* (erroneously, as Wright observes), and this probably is what Shakespeare wrote. F's error, c/r, is an easy one, and may be either scribal or compositorial in origin. See 2.1.21/673.

1.1.219/251 *Chancellour*] POPE 2 (Theobald); *Councellour* F. Theobald's conjecture derives from Holinshed.

1.1.221/253 *Nicholas*] POPE 2 (Theobald); *Michaell* F. The emendation derives from Holinshed. Manuscript 'nich' could easily have been misread as 'mich', and so mistakenly expanded. The Christian name is correctly given at 1.2.148/406. See the note to 1.2.148, 149/406, 407.

1.1.227/259 *Lord*] ROWE; *Lords* F

1.2.0.3-4/259.6-7 *the King takes his Seate*] This edition; *not in* F. See the note to 1.1.0.1/32.1.

1.2.5 *Buckingham's. In person*ˌ] F (~, ~,). This interpretation of F is JOHNSON'S; ROWE read '~ˌ ~;'.

1.2.9 ⌜CRIER⌝ (*within*)] F (*A noyse within crying*)

1.2.14/272 *Maiesty.*] F4; ~ˌ F1

1.2.33 *many*] F; *meiny* JOHNSON

1.2.37 *to*] F (*too*)

1.2.38/296 *serues*] F; *swerues* G.T. *conj.*; *scoures* G.T. *conj.*

1.2.68/326 *busenesse*] HANMER (Warburton, *subs.*); *basenesse* F. The proposed misreading, u/a, is an easy one.

1.2.83/341 *once*] F; *or(e)* This edition *conj.* Manuscript 'or(e)' may have been mistaken as 'ōc(e)', and so erroneously expanded.

1.2.84/342 *oft,*] CAPELL; ~ˌ F

1.2.98/356 *roote*] THEOBALD (Warburton); ~ˌ F

1.2.112/370 *and a*] F; *a* POPE

1.2.140/398 *His*] POPE; *This* F

1.2.148, 149/406, 407 *Hopkins*] POPE 2 (Theobald); *Henton* F. The error is probably authorial, and, as Maxwell observes (his note to 1.2.147), in all likelihood derives from a careless reading of Holinshed: 'Nicholas Hopkins, a monke of an house of the Chartreux order beside Bristow, called Henton' (Holinshed 863.a.6-8; repr. Bullough, iv. 458). Emendation is necessary to achieve internal consistency: see 1.1.221/253. Sisson, however, believes the inconsistency deliberate (*New Readings*, ii. 99), and that 'Nicholas [of] Henton' may have been an alternative way of referring to the monk.

1.2.157/415 *feard*] POPE (*subs.*); *feare* F

1.2.165/423 *Confessions*] THEOBALD; *Commissions* F. Theobald derives the emendation from Holinshed (863.b.53-55): 'to bind his chapleine Iohn de la Court, vnder the seale of confession, to keepe secret such matter'. Foakes suggests the mistake is the result of the frequent occurrence of 'commission' earlier in the scene.

1.2.171/429 *win*] SISSON (White); *not in* F1; *gain* F4; *purchase* BOWERS (after Holinshed). Maxwell (his note to 1.2.170) observes that Shakespeare seems to have conflated two phrases in Holinshed: 'to win the fauour of the people' (863.a.10-11) and 'to purchase the good wils of the communaltie of England' (864.b.34-5).

1.2.181/439 *To*] MAXWELL (anon. *conj.* in Cambridge); *For this to* F; *For him to* ROWE. 'For this' is probably an undeleted false start.

1.2.191/449 *Bulmer*] WRIGHT; *Blumer* F. Both Holinshed and Hall read 'Bulmer'.

1.2.191/449 *remember*] This edition; *remember of* F. The F line is unmetrical, and, as Wright observes, Shakespeare nowhere else uses the collocation *remember of*.

1.3.12/485 *see*] F; *saw* POPE. See *LLL* 4.1.69/1000.

1.3.13/486 *Or*] DYCE (Collier); *A* F; *And* POPE. (Collier's conjecture appears among the list of notes and emendations made to his copy of F2. This list was appended to Coleridge's *Seven Lectures on Shakespeare and Milton* (1856), p. 231.)

1.3.21 *messieurs*] F (*Monsieurs*)

1.3.34 *oui*] F (*wee*); *weare* F2

1.3.59 *he's*] F (*ha's*). F uses the form 'ha's' for both *he's* (meaning, as here, *he has*), and *has*. See the note to 3.1.118 and the Introduction.

1.3.59/532 *wherewithall; in him*ˌ] THEOBALD (Thirlby); ~ˌ ~ ~;   F

1.4.6/546 *feast*] STAUNTON; *first* F

1.4.25/565 *He ... another*] This edition; *not in* F

2.1.19/671 *him*] F1; *have* F4

2.1.21/673 *Perke*] FOAKES; *Pecke* F. See the first note to 1.1.219/251.

2.1.42 *attainder*] F (*Attendure*)

2.1.43-4/695-6 *remou'd, ... Surrey*ˌ] F2; ~ˌ ... ~, F1

2.1.54/706 *William*] THEOBALD (after Holinshed); *Walter* F. The slip may be the author's, or it may result from an erroneous expansion of an authorial 'W' by either the scribe or the compositor. This is the only time in the play that Sands's Christian name occurs.

2.1.79 *i'*] F (*a*). See *OED a, prep.*¹.

2.1.87/739 *marke*] HANMER (Warburton); *make* F. This emendation supposes that either the scribe or the compositor dropped the 'r'. The error may instead derive from a misreading: in this case we would suppose something like authorial 'marc' being mistaken as 'mace' and transcribed (or set) as 'make'.

2.2.0.1-2.2.1/821.1-822 *Enter Lord Chamberlaine | CHAMBERLAINE (reading this Letter)*] F (*Enter Lord Chamberlaine, reading this Letter*)

2.2.85/905 *one,*ˌ] BOSWELL; ~ ; F

2.2.93/913 (*I ... ones*ˌ ... *Kingdomes*)] F; ,~ ... ~, ... ~, THEOBALD; (~ ... ~) ... ~ˌ BOWERS (after Theobald). However, given the general unreliability of the round brackets in this text (see the Introduction), Bowers may well be right; see his textual note.

2.2.105/925 *commanding, you*] F4; ~. *You* F1

2.3.14/978 *quarrell, Fortune, do*] F2; *quarrell. Fortune, do* F1; *quarr'ler fortune do* HANMER; *quarrel fortune to* STEEVENS (*conj.*); *quarrel & fortune do* FOAKES (*conj.*, after Upton in Cambridge). As Johnson first observed, this is probably an instance of the abstract (*quarrel*) used for the concrete (*quarreller*). See *Antony* 2.2.51/625 (*reports* for *reporters*) and 4.13.16/2305 (*charm* for *charmer*). But Steevens's conjecture (with 'Fortune' a verb) remains a possibility, as do those of Foakes and Hanmer. F1's erroneous full stop may derive, as Foakes points out, from either a hurriedly written mark of abbreviation or ampersand. Staunton's conjecture (*squirrel* for *quarrel*), which Foakes finds attractive, observing that *squirrel* can mean *strumpet*, is most implausible. Shakespeare uses *squirrel* only three times: each use is in a relatively early play (*Two Gentlemen*, *Dream*, and *Romeo*), and none carries the sense *strumpet*.

2.3.47/1011 *emballing*] F; *empalling* MALONE (*conj.*); *embalming* WHALLEY (*conj.* in Cambridge); *empaling* COLLIER 2 (*conj.*); *embailing* KELLNER (*conj.*)

2.3.59 *note's*] F (*notes*)

2.3.61/1025 *of you*] CAPELL; *of you, to you* F. *To you* was probably caught from the following line.

2.3.87/1051 *fye, fye*] POPE; *fye, fye, fye* F. Pope's reading is metrically superior; F's dittography would be an easy error for either a scribe or compositor.

2.4.0.1/1072.1 *Trumpets: Sennet. Cornets*] This edition (S.W.W.); *Trumpets, Sennet, and Cornets* F. A sennet is a call, not an instrument, and one which customarily was sounded by trumpets. The form of the F direction suggests that '*Trumpets*' may be a playhouse marginal annotation which either the scribe or the compositor incorporated in the main direction.

2.4.7, 10/1079, 1082 *come into the Court*] HUMPHREYS; &c. F

2.4.10.3-2.4.11/1082.3-1083 QUEENE KATHERINE *Sir*] WARBURTON; *Sir* F

2.4.27/1099 *Or which*] F; *Which* POPE

2.4.38-9/1110-11 *Dutie*ˌ *| Against*] F; ~, | ~ MALONE. *OED* confirms that *against* may mean *towards*. This is the sense F's punctuation seems to require, but, as Maxwell observed (in his note to 2.4.40), it is perhaps a little harsh in juxtaposition with *against* in its more usual sense in 2.4.37/1109. Malone's slightly awkward arrangement may be the correct one.

2.4.124/1196 GRIFFITH] MALONE (subs.); Gent. Vſh. F. See the note to 3.1.14.1/1324.1 and line 4.2.0.2/2072.3 of the play.
2.4.125-6 way. . . . called, return] F (way, . . . cald, returne); alternatively way, . . . called, return
2.4.145/1217 At once] F; Atton'd HANMER (Warburton)
2.4.161/1233 oft,] F4; ~, F1
2.4.171/1243 A] ROWE 3; And F
2.4.180/1252 spitting] F1; splitting F2
2.4.183 prest] F. Usually modernized to 'pressed'; but see OED prest, v.³ (Obs. rare. . . . b. To make haste, hasten).
2.4.188/1260 does yeeld to th'] This edition (G.T.); does to th' F; does to the ROWE 3
2.4.196 throe] F (throw)
2.4.216/1288 Summons. Vnsolicited,] THEOBALD (subs.) ~, vnſolicited. F
2.4.227/1299 o'th'] F; i'th' POPE
2.4.236/1308 returne: with thy approch,] F4 (returne; . . .); returne, with thy approch: F1
3.1.3/1313 WOMAN] HUMPHREYS (subs.); not in F
3.1.14.1/1324.1 Griffith] This edition; not in F. This part of the play is by Fletcher: it seems reasonable to suppose that this gentleman is the same as the 'Gent. Vſh.' in Shakespeare's share, earlier (2.4.124/1196), which editors since Malone have identified with 'Griffith, her Gentleman Vsher' below (4.2.0.2/2072.3), in a part of the play probably by Shakespeare, and only touched up by Fletcher.
3.1.16, 18/1326, 1328 GRIFFITH] This edition; Gent. F. See the previous note.
3.1.19/1329 Exit] CAPELL; not in F. Maxwell (in his notes to 3.1.19 and 4.2.108) observes that the Gentleman need not exit in order to usher in the two cardinals (he may simply go to the door) and compares this staging with that of 4.2.109/2181. Maxwell may be right. Also compare 5.1.83.1/2329.1.
3.1.21/1331 comming, now I thinke on't;] CAPELL (subs.); ~ ; . . . ~, F. See Sisson, New Readings, ii. 101.
3.1.23/1333 vsher'd by Griffith] This edition; not in F
3.1.51/1361 And] F; In KINNEAR (conj.)
3.1.60/1370 your] F2; our F1
3.1.68/1378 (pray God ye proue so)] F. Possibly an aside.
3.1.82/1392 profit:] F2; ~, F1
3.1.89/1399 other comforts] F; other comforts are ROWE 3; comforts are POPE
3.1.89/1399 far] F; from S.W.W. conj.
3.1.118 he's] F (ha's). See the note to 1.3.59.
3.1.119 love, too, long] F (Loue, too long); alternatively love, too long
3.1.123/1433 acurst] This edition (Foakes); a Curſe F. The misreading e/t would be easy, and may have been made either by the scribe or by the compositor. The author may have written it as two words.
3.1.174-5/1484-5 me; . . . vnmannerly,] F1; ~, . . . ~ ; F4
3.2.58 Has] F (Ha's); alternatively He's. See the note to 1.3.59.
3.2.76/1569 gau't] F; gaue it G.T. conj.
3.2.124/1617 There (on my Conscience, . . . vnwittingly)] F; There; on my conscience, . . . unwittingly? CAPELL
3.2.125/1618 importing,] F; ~ ; THEOBALD
3.2.137/1630 To the King] This edition; not in F. Wolsey's previous line may also be to the King, or it may be an exclamation to himself denoting annoyance with himself for not noticing the King's presence earlier.
3.2.143/1636 glad] F2; gald F1
3.2.161/1654 aside] ROWE; not in F. Possibly 'to the other Nobles'.
3.2.172 filed] F (fill'd). Hanmer's interpretation of F, meaning kept pace with, is widely accepted. Sisson (New Readings, ii. 101), however, argued for filled in the sense of 'fulfilled (to the best of my abilities)'. He may be right, but parallels have proved elusive.
3.2.234/1727 Commission, Lords?] ROWE; ~ ? ~, F
3.2.273/1766 That in the] F; That I, i'th' THEOBALD; ⌈. . .⌉ | That in the W. S. WALKER (conj.); I that in the J.J. conj.
3.2.194-7 be— | Though . . . horrid—yet] F ('be | (Though . . . horrid) yet'). Bowers argues forcefully for Berdan and Brooke's modernization of this passage ('be. | Though . . . horrid, yet'); given the probable spuriousness of the round brackets in the F text generally (see the Introduction), he may well be right that they here ought not to be taken seriously.
3.2.293/1786 Whom] F1; Who F2. Most editors follow F2 and emend to the currently acceptable form. But OED (whom, pron. 11) records confusion of these two forms in the 17th c. Whom, though clearly unacceptable to the editors of F2, was apparently acceptable to those of F1, and may well not have been recognized by the author as an error.
3.2.315 et] F (&)
3.2.326/1819 to be] F; be G.T. conj.
3.2.340/1833 Legātine] F4 (Legantine); Legatiue F1; Legatine ROWE 2. F1 and Rowe are each perfectly acceptable here, both meaning of or pertaining to a legate, though Rowe's appears to be the newer form (from 1611, versus 1537 for F1). But Holinshed (Bullough, iv. 472) uses legantine (which OED records as an incorrect synonym of legatine), and this part of the scene closely follows Holinshed. The proposed misreading, 'Legatiue' for 'Legātine', would be very easy, and seems on the whole more probable than a deliberate authorial alteration of the source.
3.2.344/1837 Cattles] THEOBALD (Chattels); Caſtles F. Holinshed (909.b.48) uses 'cattels', meaning chattels or possessions, for which F would be an easy error. But Foakes observes that '"Castles" may be defended as a climax to "goods, lands, tenements . . .", and as an allusion to the notoriety Wolsey suffered for his building palaces such as Hampton Court and York Place' (Foakes's note to 3.2.342-3). Compare 4.1.96-9/2049-52.
3.2.362/1855 depth: my] F; depth, my This edition conj. The incidentals of F, deriving as it does from a transcript, are suspect.
3.2.452-3 haue: | To the last penny] F (haue, | To the laſt peny,). An alternative interpretation would be 'have, | . . . penny:'.
3.2.460/1953 do] F; now G.T. conj.
4.1.20/1973 2. GENTLEMAN] F4 (subs.); 1, F1
4.1.32/1985 these] F; those G.T. conj.
4.1.35.1/1988.1 Flourish of Trumpets within] CAPELL (Trumpets.); not in F. Capell deletes F's Ho-boyes after the next line. His direction here may duplicate the first item under 'The Order of the Coronation'.
4.1.36.11-12 with them, musicians playing] F (Muſicke.). While the F direction may simply be a call for off-stage music, the third gentleman's comment that 'the Quire | With all the choysest Muſicke of the Kingdome, | Together sung Te Deum' (4.1.92-4/2045-7) suggests that we here, also, should interpret 'Muſicke' to mean 'musicians playing'.
4.1.55-6/2008-9 indeed. | ⌈1. GENTLEMAN⌉ And] DYCE 2 (W. S. Walker); indeed, | And F
4.1.56/2009 2. GENTLEMAN] F1 (subs.); 1. F3
4.1.56.3/2009.3 in a sweate] This edition; not in F. The dialogue immediately following the third gentleman's entrance would seem to require that he enter sweating.
4.1.57/2010 1. GENTLEMAN God] F1 (subs.); , God F3; 2. G⟨entleman⟩. God CAPELL
4.1.103/2056 Stokesley] F4; Stokeley F. Holinshed, p. 909, reads 'Stokesleie'. The error may scribal, compositorial (ſ instead of ſl), or a slip on the part of the author.
4.1.119/2072 1. and 2. GENTLEMEN] F (Both.)
4.2.0.1/2072.2 Three Chaires] This edition; not in F
4.2.5 led'st] F (lead'ſt)
4.2.7/2079 thinke] F2; thanke F1
4.2.19 convent] F (Couent)
4.2.50/2122 Honor. From his Cradle,] F; honour, from his cradle; THEOBALD. Theobald's emendation is frequently adopted, and may be right. But F offers the more difficult reading, and seems, moreover, to have some foundation in Holinshed: 'This Thomas Wolseie was a poore mans sonne of Ipswich, in the countie of Suffolke, & there borne, and being but a child, verie apt to be learned, by the meanes of his parents he was conueied to the vniuersitie of Oxenford, where he shortlie prospered so in learning, as he was made bachellor of art, when he passed not fiftéene

yeares of age, and was called most commonlie thorough the vniuersitie the boie bachellor' (917.b.52 ff.; repr. Bullough, iv. 477)

4.2.99/2171 color] DYCE 2 (W. S. Walker); cold F. See Sisson, *New Readings*, ii. 102.

4.2.99/2171 Marke] F; Mark you CAPELL

4.2.109/2181 *Enter . . . Griffith*] This edition; *Enter Lord Capuchius* F. See the note to 3.1.19/1329.

4.2.109, etc. *Caputius*] F (*Capuchius*). F represents a quasi-phonetic spelling of the Latinized form of *Chapuys*, the historical character's name. See the note to *Shrew* 1.2.0.1/252.

5.1.0.1/2246.3 *Enter*] F ('*Actus Quintus. Scena Prima. | Enter*' text); *Scena* (c.w.)

5.1.37/2283 time] F4; Lime F1

5.1.42/2288 you I thinke)] JOHNSON ('you, I think,'); you) I thinke F. Round brackets are, throughout the play, particularly suspect, because they appear to have been added frequently by the scribe. See the Introduction.

5.1.50/2296 hath] F; he hath POPE

5.1.83.1/2329.1 *Exit Denny*] ROWE; *not in* F. F marks Denny's entrance, though, with Cranmer at 5.1.85.1/2331.1. See the note to 3.1.19/1329.

5.1.95.1/2341.1 *Cranmer rises. They walke*] This edition; *not in* F

5.1.123/2369 good] F; ground RANN (Johnson). Johnson's conjecture is a plausible one: *OED* verifies, for the 14th century to the 16th, the form 'grond', and either this, or 'grŏd' may have been mistaken by either scribe or compositor as 'good'. But F provides the superior reading.

5.1.140/2386 Precepic] F2 (Precepice); Precepit F1. The proposed misreading, c/t, is both easy and common.

5.1.141 woo] F (woe)

5.1.158/2404 ⌈LOUELL⌉ (*within*)] HUMPHREYS; *Gent. within.* F

5.2.7/2430 Peece] F2 (Peice); Peere F1

5.2.119/2542 CHANCELLOUR] CAPELL; *Cham.* F

5.2.121/2544 CHANCELLOUR] CAPELL (Theobald); *Cham.* F

5.2.126/2549 ALL THE COUNCELL] This edition; *All.* F

5.2.147.1-2/2570.1-2 *Enter . . . Seate*] F. Sisson places after 'burnes ye:' in the previous line.

5.2.159/2582 base] F; bare SINGER (Malone)

5.2.164/2587 proudest,] COLLIER; ~ˌ F

5.2.167/2590 this] F4; his F1

5.2.192/2615 embrace him] F; embrace JOHNSON. F's 'him' may have been caught from the previous line.

5.2.206/2629 Brother-loue] MALONE; Brother; loue F1; Brothers love F2

5.2.208/2631 heart] F2; hearts F1

5.3.0.1/2638.1-2 *with Rushes*] This edition; *not in* F. This property, or something like it, would seem to be required by lines 5.3.7-8/2645-6. Compare *2 Henry IV* 5.5.0.1-5.5.4/3088.1-3092.

5.3.0.2/2638.2 *with a broken Cudgell*] This edition; *not in* F. This property would seem to be required by lines 5.3.19-20/2656-7.

5.3.2 Paris] F (Pariſh)

5.3.4, 27/2642, 2665 ONE (*within*)] FOAKES; *Within.* F

5.3.45/2683 blow vs] F1; blow us up F3

5.3.53/2692 to me] F; with me POPE

5.3.82/2721 a way] F2; away F1

5.3.84.1/2723.1 *As . . . within*] This edition; *not in* F. But see J. W. Saunders, 'Vaulting the Rails', *SSu* 7 (1954), 70-1.

5.4.37/2764 ways] F4; way F1

5.4.70/2797 your] THEOBALD (Thirlby); you F

5.4.75/2802 He's] F ('Has)

5.4.76.1/2803.1 *Flourish*] This edition (G.T.); *not in* F. The allusion to 'Trumpets' at Epi.4/2807 may be to this final exit.

Epi.0.1-Epi.1/2803.2-2804 *Enter Epilogue* | EPILOGUE] This edition; THE EPILOGVE. F

Epi.14/2817 *Exit*] This edition; *not in* F

INCIDENTALS

10 agree] a gree   236 practise.] ~:   274 vnconsidred] vnconſidered   310 or] er   314 patience;] (*possibly* ~,)   488 Christendome] Chiſtendome   507 Priuilegio] Pruiilegio   571 Gentlemen] Gntlemen   623 and] aud   678 could not] couldnot   698 one.] ~,   973 Proceſſe,ˌ] ~.   1097 inclin'd.] ~?   1158 wrong.] ~ˌ   1177 cunning] eunning   1177 humble-mouth'd:] ~ˌ   1219 which] whi h   1273 feele] (*possibly* ſeele)   1299 World.] ~,   1312 working.] (*possibly* ~:)   1360 should] ſhoul   1397 afflictions] afflliĉtions   1409 Iudge,] ~.   1584 Pembroke] Penbroke   1651 kept] (*possibly* kept)   1676 contrary] (*possibly* contrarv)   1727 Words] words   1781 to'th'Pope] (*possibly* to'thˌPope)   1838 of] oſ   2086 sorely] ſorcly   2099 Repentance] (*possibly* Repentanee)   2239 You] Vou   2264 Labor,] ~ˌ   2345 greeuous,] (*possibly* ~.)   2432 Buts,] ~.   2433 Physitian. As] ~, as   2502 your,ˌ] (*possibly* ~,)   2532 faulty] faulty   2560 'Tis] 'Ts   2709 friends] ſtiends   2769 selfe,] ~.   2807 Trumpets] Tumpets   2811 heare,ˌ] ~.

FOLIO STAGE DIRECTIONS

1.1.0.1-3/32.1-3 *Enter the Duke of Norfolke at one doore. At the other, | the Duke of Buckingham, and the Lord | Aburgauenny.*

1.1.114.1-5/146.1-5 *Enter Cardinall Wolsey, the Purse borne before him, certaine | of the Guard, and two Secretaries with Papers: The | Cardinall in his passage, fixeth his eye on Buck-|ham, and Buckingham on him, | both full of disdaine.*

1.1.119/151.1 *Exeunt Cardinall, and his Traine.*

1.1.197.1-2/229.1-2 *Enter Brandon, a Sergeant at Armes before him, and | two or theee of the Guard.*

1.1.227.1/259.1 *Exe.*

1.2.0.1-6/259.4-8 *Cornets. Enter King Henry, leaning on the Cardinals shoul-|der, the Nobles, and Sir Thomas Louell: the Cardinall | places himselfe vnder the Kings feete on | his right side.*

1.2.9-1.2.9.3/267.1-4 *A noyse within crying roome for the Queene, vsher'd by the | Duke of Norfolke. Enter the Queene, Norfolke and | Snffolke: she kneels. King riseth from his State, | takes her vp, kisses and placeth | her by him.*

1.2.109/367 *Exit Secret.*

1.2.109.1/367.1 *Enter Surueyor.*

1.2.215/473 *Exeunt.*

1.3.0.1/473.1 *Enter L. Chamberlaine and L. Sandys.*

1.3.15/488 *Enter Sir Thomas Louell.* (after 'Louell', 1.3.16/499)

1.3.67.1/540.1 *Exeunt.*

1.4.0.1-6/540.2-7 *Hoboies. A small Table vnder a State for the Cardinall, a | longer Table for the Guests. Then Enter Anne Bullen, | and diuers other Ladies, & Gentlemen, as Guests | at one Doore; at an other Doore enter | Sir Henry Guilford.*

1.4.7/547 *Enter L. Chamberlaine L. Sands, and Louell.*

1.4.35.1-2/575.1-2 *Hoboyes. Enter Cardinall Wolsey, and takes his State.*

1.4.50/590 *Drum and Trumpet, Chambers discharg̣d.* (after 1.4.49/589)

1.4.53.1/593.1 *Enter a Seruant.*

1.4.61.2/601.2 *All rise, and Tables remou'd.*

1.4.64.1-4/604.1-4 *Hoboyes. Enter King and others as Maskers, habited like | Shepheards, vsher'd by the Lord Chamberlaine. They | passe directly before the Cardinall and gracefully sa-|lute him.*

ALL IS TRUE

1.4.75.1-2/615.1   *Choose Ladies, King and An Bullen.*
1.4.77.1/617.1   *Musicke, Dance.*
1.4.84.1/624.1   *Whisper.* (after 'it')
1.4.112.1/652.1   *Exeunt with Trumpets.*
2.1.0.1/652.2   *Enter two Gentlemen at seuerall Doores.*
2.1.54/706   *Enter Buckingham from his Arraignment, Tipstaues before | him, the Axe with the edge towards him, Halberds on each | side, accompanied with Sir Thomas Louell, Sir Nicholas | Vaux, Sir Walter Sands, and common people, &c.*
2.1.136.1/788.1   *Exeunt Duke and Traine.*
2.1.169/821   *Exeunt.*
2.2.0.1-2.2.1/821.1-822   *Enter Lord Chamberlaine, reading this Letter.*
2.2.11.1-2/831.1-2   *Enter to the Lord Chamberlaine, the Dukes of Nor-|folke and Suffolke.*
2.2.62.1-3/882.1-3   *Exit Lord Chamberlaine, and the King drawes the Curtaine | and sits reading pensiuely.*
2.2.73.1-2/893.1-2   *Enter Wolsey and Campeius with a Commission.*
2.2.85.1/905.1   *Exeunt Norfolke and Suffolke.*
2.2.117.1/937.1   *Enter Gardiner.*
2.2.121.1/941.1   *Walkes and whispers.*
2.2.137/957.1   *Exit Gardiner.*
2.2.144/964   *Exeunt.*
2.3.0.1/964.1   *Enter Anne Bullen, and an old Lady.*
2.3.49.1/1013.1   *Enter Lord Chamberlaine.*
2.3.81/1045   *Exit Lord Chamberlaine.* (after 2.3.80/1044)
2.3.108.1/1072.1   *Exeunt.*
2.4.0.1-22/1072.2-23   *Trumpets, Sennet, and Cornets. | Enter two Vergers, with short siluer wands; next them two | Scribes in the habite of Doctors; after them, the Bishop of | Canterbury alone; after him, the Bishops of Lincolne, Ely, | Rochester, and S. Asaph: Next them, with some small | distance, followes a Gentleman bearing the Purse, with the | great Seale, and a Cardinals Hat: Then two Priests, bea-|ring each a Siluer Crosse: Then a Gentleman Vsher bare-|headed, accompanyed with a Sergeant at Armes, bearing a | Siluer Mace: Then two Gentlemen bearing two great | Siluer Pillers: After them, side by side, the two Cardinals, | two Noblemen, with the Sword and Mace. The King takes | place vnder the Cloth of State. The two Cardinalls sit | under him as Iudges. The Queene takes place some di-|stance from the King. The Bishops place themselues on | each side the Court in manner of a Consistory: Below them | the Scribes. The Lords sit next the Bishops. The rest of the | Attendants stand in conuenient order about the Stage.*
2.4.10.1-3/1082.1-3   *The Queene makes no answer, rises out of her Chaire, goes about the Court, comes to the King, and kneeles at | his Feete. Then speakes.*
2.4.119/1191   *She Curtsies to the King, and offers to depart.*
2.4.130/1202   *Exit Queene, and her Attendants.*
2.4.238/1310   *Exeunt, in manner as they enter'd.*
3.1.0.1/1310.1   *Enter Queene and her Women as at worke.*
3.1.3/1312.1   *Song.*
3.1.14.1/1324.1   *Enter a Gentleman.*
3.1.23/1333   *Enter the two Cardinalls, Wolsey & Campian.*
3.1.183/1493.1   *Exeunt*
3.2.0.1-2/1493.2-3   *Enter the Duke of Norfolke, Duke of Suffolke, Lord Surrey, | and Lord Chamberlaine.*
3.2.74.1/1567.1   *Enter Wolsey and Cromwell.*
3.2.85/1578   *Exit Cromwell.*
3.2.105.1/1598.1   *Enter King, reading of a Scedule.*
3.2.136/1629   *King takes his Seat, whispers Louell, who goes | to the Cardinall.*
3.2.204/1697   *Exit King, frowning vpon the Cardinall, the Nobles | throng after him smiling, and whispering.*
3.2.228.1-2/1721.1-3   *Enter to Woolsey, the Dukes of Norfolke and Suffolke, the | Earle of Surrey, and the Lord Chamberlaine.*
3.2.350.1/1843.1   *Exeunt all but Wolsey.*
3.2.373/1866   *Enter Cromwell, standing amazed.*
3.2.460.1/1953.1   *Exeunt.*
4.1.0.1/1953.2   *Enter two Gentlemen, meeting one another.*
4.1.36.1-2/1989.1-2   *first passing ouer the Stage in Order and State,* (after 'Exeunt,', which in F follows 4.1.36.36/1989.33). See 4.1.56.1-2/2009.1-2.
4.1.36.2/1989.2   *Ho-boyes.*
4.1.36.4/1989.4   *The Order of the Coronation.*
4.1.36.5-6/1989.5   1 *A liuely Flourish of Trumpets.*
4.1.36.7/1989.6   2 *Then, two Iudges.*
4.1.36.8-10/1989.7   3 *Lord Chancellor, with Purse and Mace before him.*
4.1.36.11-12/1989.8   4 *Quirristers singing. Musicke.*
4.1.36.13-15/1989.9-11   5 *Maior of London, bearing the Mace. Then Garter, in | his Coate of Armes, and on his head he wore a Gilt Copper | Crowne.*
4.1.36.16-21/1989.12-16   6 *Marquesse Dorset, bearing a Scepter of Gold, on his head, | a Demy Coronall of Gold. With him, the Earle of Surrey, | bearing the Rod of Siluer with the Doue, Crowned with an | Earles Coronet. Collars of Esses.*
4.1.36.22-6/1989.17-21   7 *Duke of Suffolke, in his Robe of Estate, his Coronet on his | head, bearing a long white Wand, as High Steward. With | him, the Duke of Norfolke, with the Rod of Marshalship, | a Coronet on his head. Collars of Esses.*
4.1.36.27-31/1989.22-6   8 *A Canopy, borne by foure of the Cinque-Ports, vnder it | the Queene in her Robe, in her haire, richly adorned with | Pearle, Crowned. On each side her, the Bishops of London, | and Winchester.*
4.1.36.32-4/1989.27-9   9 *The Olde Dutchesse of Norfolke, in a Coronall of Gold, | wrought with Flowers bearing the Queenes Traine.*
4.1.36.35-6/1989.30-1   10 *Certaine Ladies or Countesses, with plaine Circlets of | Gold, without Flowers.*
4.1.56.1-2/2009.1-2   *Exeunt, . . . and | then, A great Flourish of Trumpets.* (after 4.1.36.36/1989.33). See 4.1.36.1-2/1989.1-2.
4.1.56.3/2009.3   *Enter a third Gentleman.*
4.1.119.1/2072.1   *Exeunt.*
4.2.0.1-3/2072.2-4   *Enter Katherine Dowager, sicke, lead betweene Griffith, | her Gentleman Vsher, and Patience | her Woman.*
4.2.80.1/2152.1   *Sad and solemne Musicke.*
4.2.82.2-19/2154.2-20   *The Vision. | Enter solemnely tripping one after another, six Personages, | clad in white Robes, wearing on their heades Garlands of | Bayes, and golden Vizards on their faces, Branches of Bayes | or Palme in their hands. They first Conge vnto her, then | Dance: and at certaine Changes, the first two hold a spare | Garland ouer her Head, at which the other foure make re-|uerend Curtsies. Then the two that held the Garland, deli-|uer the same to the other next two, who obserue the same or-|der in their Changes, and holding the Garland ouer her | head. Which done, they deliuer the same Garland to the | last two: who likewise obserue the same Order. At which | (as it were by inspiration) she makes (in her sleepe) signes of | reioycing, and holdeth vp her hands to heauen. And so, in | their Dancing vanish, carrying the Garland with them. | The Musicke continues.*
4.2.96/2168   *Musicke ceases.*
4.2.100.1/2172.1   *Enter a Messenger.*
4.2.109/2181   *Exit Messeng.*
4.2.109/2181   *Enter Lord Capuchius.*
4.2.174.1-2/2246.1-2   *Exeunt leading Katherine.*
5.1.0.1-2, 5.1.5/2246.3-4, 2251   *Enter Gardiner Bishop of Winchester, a Page with a Torch | before him, met by Sir Thomas Louell.* (begins scene)
5.1.55.1/2301.1   *Exit Gardiner and Page.* (after 5.1.54/2300)
5.1.55/2301.2   *Enter King and Suffolke.*
5.1.78.1/2324.1   *Exit Suffolke.*
5.1.78.2/2324.2   *Enter Sir Anthony Denny.* (after 5.1.79/2325)
5.1.85.1/2331.1   *Enter Cranmer and Denny.*
5.1.86.1/2332.1   *Louel seemes to stay.*
5.1.88/2334   *Exeunt Louell and Denny.*
5.1.157/2403   *Exit Cranmer.*
5.1.158/2404   *Enter Olde Lady.*
5.1.171/2417.1   *Exit King.*
5.1.177/2423   *Exit Ladie.*
5.2.0.1-2/2423.1-2   *Enter Cranmer, Archbyshop of Canterbury.*
5.2.4/2427   *Enter Keeper.* (after 'me?')

ALL IS TRUE

5.2.5.1/2428.1 Enter Doctor Buts. (after 5.2.6/2429)
5.2.9/2432 Exit Buts
5.2.18.1-2/2441.1 Enter the King, and Buts, at a Windowe | aboue.
5.2.34.4-13/2457.4-12 A Councell Table brought in with Chayres and Stooles, and | placed vnder the State. Enter Lord Chancellour, places | himselfe at the vpper end of the Table, on the left hand: A | Seate being left void aboue him, as for Canterburies Seate. | Duke of Suffolke, Duke of Norfolke, Surrey, Lord Cham-|berlaine, Gardiner, seat themselues in Order on each side. | Cromwell at lower end, as Secretary.
5.2.41.1/2464.1 Cranmer approches the Councell Table.
5.2.129/2552 Enter the Guard.
5.2.147.1-2/2570.1-2 Enter King frowning on them, takes his Seate.
5.2.215/2638 Exeunt.
5.3.0.1-2/2638.1-2 Noyse and Tumult within: Enter Porter and | his man.
5.3.64.1/2703.1 Enter Lord Chamberlaine.
5.3.88/2727 Exeunt.
5.4.0.1-12/2727.1-11 Enter Trumpets sounding: Then two Aldermen, L. Maior, | Garter, Cranmer, Duke of Norfolke with his Marshals | Staffe, Duke of Suffolke, two Noblemen, bearing great | standing Bowles for the Christening Guifts: Then foure | Noblemen bearing a Canopy, vnder which the Dutchesse of | Norfolke, Godmother, bearing the Childe richly habited in | a Mantle, &c. Traine borne by a Lady: Then followes | the Marchionesse Dorset, the other Godmother, and La-|dies. The Troope passe once about the Stage, and Gar-|ter speakes.
5.4.3.1/2730.1 Flourish. Enter King and Guard.
5.4.76.1/2803.1 Exeunt.

THE TWO NOBLE KINSMEN

The Two Noble Kinsmen (*BEPD* 492) was entered in the Stationers' Register on 8 April 1634:

M.^r Io: Waterſon   Entred for his Copy vnder the hands of Sr Hen: Herbert & m.^r Aſpley warden a TragiComedy called the two noble kinſmen by Io: Fletcher & Wm Shakeſpeare

That year the only substantive text was printed, in quarto, for Waterson by Thomas Cotes (Q); all subsequent editions derive from this. Forty-five copies of this edition are known; after a collation of eighteen of these, G. R. Proudfoot has isolated eight substantive press variants distributed among six formes: C inner, E outer, G inner, H outer, K outer, and M inner. Proudfoot observes that the variants resulting from stop-press correction are few and sporadic, suggesting that they represent only a final round of correction, carried out piecemeal during working off of the sheets.

Paul Werstine, in a forthcoming article which he has kindly shown us, argues on the evidence of spacings, punctuation, catchwords, and marginal stage directions that two compositors set the 1634 quarto. His findings agree in large part with those of F. O. Waller (1957), and Fredson Bowers's analysis of damaged type in Q (in the Introduction to his forthcoming edition of *Kinsmen*, which he, too, kindly showed us) corroborates Waller-Werstine. A consensus appears to be emerging, which we here summarize:

Pro.0.1–Pro.32.1/ 0.1–32.1	A1^v	B
1.1.0.1–1.1.12/ 32.2–44	B1^r	A (?)
1.1.13–1.2.42/ 45–307 ('...Monsters')	B1^v–C1^r	A
1.2.42–76/ 307–41 ('Tis...')	C1^v	B (?)
1.2.77–107/ 342–72 ('...defier')	C2^r	A (?)
1.2.107–2.4.28/ 372–996 ('Lets...')	C2^v–E4^r	A
2.4.29–3.1.85/ 997–1189	E4^v–F3^r	B
3.1.86–3.5.72/ 1190–1417	F3^v–G2^v	A
3.5.73–3.6.16/ 1418–1521	G3^r–4^r	B
3.6.17–48/ 1522–53	G4^v	A (?)
3.6.49–295/ 1554–1800	H1^r–4^v	B
3.6.296–4.2.44/ 1801–2007	I1^r–4^r	A
4.2.45–4.3.54.1/ 2008–2173.1	I4^v–K2^v	B
4.3.55–93/ 2174–2212 ('...and')	K3^r	A (?)
4.3.93–5.4.92/ 2212–2481 ('regiment...')	K3^v–L3^v	B
5.4.93–5.5.0.1/ 2482–2502.1 ('...Florish')	L4^r	A (?)
5.5.0.1–5.6.9/ 2502.1–2658 ('Enter...')	L4^v–M2^v	A
5.6.10–137/ 2659–2786	M3^r–4^v	B
Epi.1–18.1/ 2787–2804.1	N1^r	A (?)

Waller and Werstine agree on all assignments except four: Waller assigns B1^r and L4^r to Compositor A, Werstine to Compositor B; Waller gives C2^r and N1^r to Compositor B, Werstine to Compositor A. Bowers favours Compositor A for both L4^r and N1^r; B1^r and C2^r, he observes, 'remain in legitimate doubt', but from pattern alone he assigns both to Compositor A. The remaining three queries (C1^v, G4^v, and K3^r) reflect Bowers's reservations about either compositor setting a single page in isolation.

The title-page of Q describes the play as having been

> Written by the memorable Worthies
> of their time;
> { Mr *John Fletcher*, and } Gent.
> { Mr *William Shakſpeare*. }

Most recent scholarship endorses the statement that the play was a collaboration of Shakespeare and Fletcher; a few have argued that Q represents Fletcher's revision of a Shakespearian fragment; a few others (including Paul Bertram) believe the play to be wholly Shakespeare's. Among the majority who believe the play to have been a joint effort there is general agreement regarding the two authors' shares of the composition:

Prologue	Fletcher (?)
1.1–2.1	Shakespeare (some doubt about 1.4, 1.5)
2.2–2.6	Fletcher
3.1–3.2	Shakespeare (some doubt about 3.2)
3.3–5.1.33/2250	Fletcher (some doubt about 4.2 and 5.1.1–33/2218–50)
5.1.34/2251–5.3	Shakespeare
5.4	Fletcher
5.5–5.6	Shakespeare
Epilogue	Fletcher (?)

The names 'Curtis' and 'T. Tucke', which appear in stage directions in Q (see the stage directions list 4.2.69.1/2032.1, 5.5.0.1-2/2502.1-2), have been identified with Curtis Greville and Thomas Tuckfield, actors believed to have overlapped as members of the King's Men only from 1625 until, at the latest, the summer of 1626; these dates, coupled with the severe bout of plague in London during most of 1625, have given rise to the theory of a revival during the winter of 1625 or the spring of 1626. Several warning notes and stage directions are printed marginally, occasionally making good deficiencies in the directions of the text. Some, at least, of these, because they are punctuated with colons, a feature associated with Edward Knight (Greg, *Folio*, 78-9, 98), are believed to have been added by him at the time of this revival (see General Introduction, p. 22). There may have been an earlier revival, c.1619-20, at Court: four lists of plays written on what appears to be waste paper from the Revels Office survive in the British Library as part of Cotton MS Tiberius E. x; fol. 70^v (reproduced by Marcham) names, among other titles, 'The 2. Noble Kinesmen'. Chambers (*RES* 1 (1925), 479-84; *Shakespeare*, ii. 346) proposes that these lists represent plays which the Revels Office considered for performance at Court; a variety of evidence leads him to suggest 1619 or 1620. No record survives of the play's original performances.

Revision of the Underlying Manuscript

The manuscript from which Q was printed had almost certainly undergone some revision. The first eight lines of the Prologue, which develop an analogy between maids and new plays—maids recently deflowered, like new plays performed, if virtuous ('good'), afterwards retain their appeal—have suggested to some that it is a late addition, made after the play had lost its own 'maidenhead' at its initial performance, probably, the argument goes, for some revival, possibly that of c.1625-6. This interpretation of the Prologue conditions one's view of subsequent allusions—'first sound' (line 16) becomes not 'first sound ever' but 'first sound at this performance', 'a wrighter' (line 19) becomes an indication that the play's dual authorship has, with the passage of time, been overlooked or forgotten, and 'our losses' (line 32), if we accept the revival to have been that of c.1625-6, may refer to the deaths of James I and Fletcher (both in 1625) and perhaps also to the 1625 plague victims. In this context, 'us' (line 31) may be taken to mean 'all of us who work in the theatre' and the worry expressed in this and the subsequent line to be tied up with the actors' fear of closure as a result of worsening plague. However, there is nothing in the Prologue which requires us to take this view: the crucial opening eight lines may as plausibly be read as expressing the hope that, like a maid, this new play will retain its attractions after its initial performance. 'First sound' is thus read as 'first sound ever' and 'a wrighter | That' as 'any writer who'. 'Our losses' may refer to the Globe fire of 1613, or it may be an untraceable allusion.

A more probable instance of revision involves Emilia's soliloquy in 4.2. The scene opens with the direction 'Enter Emilia alone, with 2. Pictures'; a soliloquy ensues in which she compares the two suitors; this, in turn, is immediately followed by the direction 'Enter Emil. and Gent.' Emilia's duplicated entrance may be explained (1) by supposing the soliloquy is an authorial addition (for it appears to be by Fletcher) which was inserted without altering the original dual entrance direction, or (2) by supposing it is part of the original draft, but a part which at some stage, and probably by means of a marginal indication, was cut by someone who at the same time inserted 'Emil. and' into the already present direction, 'Enter Gent.', or (3) by supposing, with Werstine, that the soliloquy was always an integral part of the play and that the second direction results from compositorial error. Arguments can be adduced in support of each of these hypotheses.

The first requires us to suppose that after setting an added soliloquy for Emilia, the compositor failed to excise 'Emil. and' from the following entrance direction. The soliloquy, though, is a long one, extending over three pages (I3^v-I4^v) and two formes: Werstine believes that the last of these, I4^v, part of the outer forme of this sheet, was set by one compositor (B), while the first two (I3^v-I4^r), part of the sheet's inner forme, were set by another (A). If he is right, we need only suppose that 'Emil. and' had been inadequately marked for deletion in the manuscript to understand why it is retained in Q. The compositor who set it did not know that it followed a speech by Emilia. But even if Werstine is wrong and a single compositor set all three pages, that compositor might easily have forgotten by the time he reached the end of the soliloquy who its speaker was, and so have overlooked the duplicated entrance. Indeed, if the book was set by formes, the usual practice would have been to set the outer forme, and thus the end of the speech, before the inner, thereby increasing the chances that even a lone compositor would not have noticed the inconsistency. This hypothesis, if accepted by an editor concerned with reproducing the latest authorial version of the text, would require him to retain the speech and emend the direction.

The second hypothesis, on the other hand, if accepted by an editor with the same aim, would require him to delete Emilia's initial entry direction and her soliloquy and retain the second direction, for this hypothesis proposes that the entire soliloquy, itself a part of the original draft, was marked, probably marginally, for deletion, that 'Emil. and' was inserted between 'Enter' and 'Gent.' in the direction which followed it, and that the mark of deletion was overlooked by the compositor but the two-word addition caught. This, too, is plausible if we can point to a good reason for making the deletion. The soliloquy—by Fletcher, remember—duplicates an episode treated by Shakespeare later in the play (5.5.41/2544 ff.), but in a manner which conflicts with Shakespeare's characterization of Emilia—in particular, her desire for chastity—in Acts 1 and 5. The inconsistency could easily have occurred if the two authors wrote their shares separately—Fletcher would not then be aware precisely how Shakespeare had handled Emilia—and the soliloquy could then have been cut, either by one or the other author or by someone in the theatre (probably with the author's acquiescence), when the two shares were brought together and the contradiction became apparent. The inconsistency of Emilia's soliloquy being followed by an entry direction for her would as probably have gone unnoticed by the compositor(s) under these circumstances, and for the same reasons, as under those we previously discussed. However, a late addition of the kind proposed by the first hypothesis could also have introduced inconsistency in characterization.

The third hypothesis requires us merely to conjecture that Compositor B, who would have been unaware that Emilia spoke the first ten lines of I4ᵛ because he did not set the earlier part of her soliloquy, interpolated 'Emil. and' into the 'Enter Gent.' direction when he saw that the Gentleman's entry was followed by an exchange between him and Emilia. This hypothesis does not propose revision, and, for the editor to arrive at the latest authorial version of the passage, it requires him merely to remove the compositor's interpolated 'Emil. and'.

In the absence of decisive arguments in favour of any one of these three hypotheses, we adopt a conservative editorial approach and accept the first hypothesis (or the third—both lead to the same editorial decision): we retain the speech, and emend the direction. Tilting us slightly in favour of the first hypothesis—which argues that the soliloquy is a late addition—rather than the third is an anomalous double exit for the Jailer's Daughter later in the play, which we believe probably also results from a late addition.

In 4.3 two exit directions for the Daughter follow one another without an intervening indication of entrance. At 4.3.36/2155, immediately following one of her speeches, is the direction 'Exit'; her next speech, which dwells on licentiousness at court, begins two lines later (4.3.38/2157), and her next speech after that, which deals with proud ladies, is followed by the direction 'Exit. Daugh.' (4.3.54.1/2173.1).

This anomaly could be explained by assuming that an intervening entrance direction has been omitted: since she is mad, for her to exit and immediately re-enter would make theatrical sense. It is also possible that someone added the first of the two exit directions with the intention that she should not stay to deliver her denunciation of adulterous courtiers and proud ladies. Similar material is cut by the censor in the manuscripts of *The Second Maiden's Tragedy* and *The Honest Man's Fortune*.

The lineation of the scene in Q, however, suggests that the manuscript was in two hands, one of which wrote the daughter's denunciation, the other, the rest of the scene. The whole of 4.3 is in prose, but with the exception of this one passage, which is correctly set, the scene is set in Q as if it were verse. Proudfoot has suggested to us in conversation that the mislineation in this scene, and possibly that in the other prose scene mis-set as verse (2.1), may result not from compositorial use of cast-off copy, as he originally believed, but from some feature of the manuscript which led the compositor to mistake these lines as verse. He has observed that in 4.3, and to a lesser extent in 2.1, the first line in mis-set speeches frequently fills the compositor's measure, and occasionally terminates in a turned word; this reminds him of work on mislineation in Rowley by George Cheatham, who interpreted a similar phenomenon there as evidence that the compositor was slavishly following the lineation of his copy, unable to distinguish from that copy whether what he was setting was intended as prose or verse. If this is so here, if the mislineation of this scene in Q reflects the lineation of the manuscript, then the fact that the daughter's denunciation alone is correctly set as prose strongly suggests that there was something different about that part of the manuscript—that whatever feature of the manuscript had misled the compositor in the earlier and later parts of the scene to line as verse was absent from the denunciation. The most probable explanation is that this passage was in a different hand from the rest of the scene. This points to the conclusion that the first of the daughter's two exits was the original, and that in the original draft the scene continued, in the same (scribal?) hand, from that point directly to the point following her second exit in Q; at some subsequent time the alternative hand (the author's?) introduced the lines of denunciation and the second exit without adequately marking for deletion the original, earlier exit.

We recast both mis-set scenes (2.1, 4.3) as prose. Occasionally in Q verse is mislined or set as prose (see Werstine, who suggests that much of the play's mislineation may be viewed as evidence for the hand of a scribe). We closely follow Proudfoot in our correction of Q's mislineation.

The quarto is regularly, though not always correctly, divided into acts and scenes. Two scenes are marked '4' in Act 2; the second of these is followed by Scene 6. In Act 3, Scene 4 is followed by Scene 6 and Scene 7. Since the scene divisions were probably marked in the manuscript, some scholars have thought that these misnumberings suggest anomalies in the copy. They consider it significant that the first 2.4, 2.6, and 3.4 are all short scenes featuring only the Jailer's Daughter and suggest that these three scenes, and perhaps others, at a late stage in the composition or perhaps even after it, were somehow revised or rearranged. Werstine's assignment of the first Scene 4 in Act 2 (on E4ʳ) to Compositor A and the second (on E4ᵛ) to Compositor B explains why this duplication may not have been caught in the typesetting, and leaves open the possibility that each compositor was following copy. However, the second error in scene numbering is not illuminated by compositorial analysis—Compositor A set (on G1ᵛ) 'Scæna 4' in Act 3 and he followed it (on G2ʳ) with 'Scæna 6'; Compositor B set (on G4ʳ) the sequent 'Scæna 7'. Werstine tentatively concludes, and we incline to agree with him, that here Compositor A was probably following his copy, and reflecting an anomaly in it. Perhaps a fifth scene was present in the manuscript but had been marked for deletion, and, though the deletion was observed, the necessary renumbering of scenes was forgotten about. We follow the usual editorial practice: the second 2.4 becomes our 2.5, and 3.6 and 3.7 become our 3.5 and 3.6. We also introduce two additional scene divisions into Act 5, between Q 5.1 and 5.2, at points at which the stage is cleared and a shift of locality occurs (see the note to 5.2/Sc. 22). The later three scenes in Act 5 are accordingly renumbered: 5.2 becomes our 5.4, 5.3 becomes our 5.5, and 5.4 becomes our 5.6.

The Nature of the Copy for Q

Two principal hypotheses have been advanced since the mid-1950s to identify the copy for the 1634 quarto. F. O. Waller (1958) proposed that authorial foul papers, or a very literal transcript of them (or perhaps of only Fletcher's share), lay behind Q. Having found features in the text which he believed indicative of foul papers, Waller had to reconcile this observation with the lower-than-average occurrence of what Cyrus Hoy had shown to be Fletcher's characteristic *ye*. Waller ruled out compositorial interference, and suggested instead a transcript, at least of Fletcher's episodes, which carefully preserved most features of the authorial original, but which frequently altered *ye* to *you*.

At the time of the 1625 revival, Waller went on to argue, Edward Knight, then prompter of the King's Men, on discovering that the prompt-book for the original production had been lost, found these partly transcribed foul papers in the company archives and annotated them, probably with the intention that they serve as copy for a new official prompt-book. It was this annotated document, Waller argued, which the company handed over to Waterson and which served as copy for Q.

Bertram (1965), on the other hand, took the view that the manuscript was a fair copy in a single hand, that this hand was Shakespeare's, that this Shakespearian fair copy had been thoroughly annotated—indeed remarkably so—by the company prompter and constituted the original official prompt-book, and that at the time of the 1625 revival Edward Knight added to it a few annotations of his own. Subsequent editors have, on the whole, accepted Bertram's refutation of Waller's foul-paper argument, and endorsed the view that the Q copy probably was the official company prompt-book, a fair copy in a single hand, though none have gone so far as to accept that the hand was Shakespeare's.

Our view is very close to Waller's: we believe (1) that the manuscript which lay behind Q probably was in the hands of its two authors and (2) that these authors' papers probably contained several layers of theatrical annotation. Unlike Waller, we do not think it necessary to argue that part of these holograph papers had been transcribed prior to their use as copy for Q, though this remains a possibility.

Certainly there has been some editorial intervention between the authors' papers and the printed text, but whether this intervention was that of a scribe, or occurred in the printing house, or resulted partly from one, and partly from the other of these agencies is uncertain. The evidence for intervention is this: (1) the old i/j, u/v conventions, which both Shakespeare and Fletcher would certainly have used, are frequently modernized in Q; (2) the incidence of *ye* relative to *you* is much lower than is usual in Fletcher's share of the play. However, any hypothesis of copy must also take account of the fact that *Pirithous* and *Jailer* both appear in Q in two forms ('Perithous', 'Pirithous'; 'Iailor', 'Iaylor'), and the distribution of these forms within the play reflects the traditional division of authorship as we earlier described it. Pirithous is mentioned 55 times: 36 times in Fletcher's share, and 19 times in Shakespeare's. Fletcher uses the 'Per-' form 32 times, and the 'Pir-' form only 4 times; Shakespeare, on the other hand, uses 'Pir-' 14 times, 'Pyr-' twice, and 'Per-' only 3 times. Similarly, the Jailer is mentioned 63 times (excluding the 22 aberrant Fletcherian references to him as 'Keeper', all but one in 2.2): 50 times by Fletcher and 13 times by Shakespeare. Fletcher uses 'Iay-' 46 times, and 'Iai-' only 4 times; Shakespeare uses 'Iay-' 4 times and 'Iai-' 9 times. It is certainly possible to imagine a scribe who in copying the play modernized both i/j and u/v and frequently altered Fletcher's *ye* to *you*, perhaps feeling *ye* to be somehow old-fashioned (*OED you* confirms that by 1600 *ye* had been supplanted in normal use by *you*). Such a scribe, too, might well have retained more or less intact the variant forms of *Pirithous* he found in the authors' papers: variant forms of unfamiliar proper names often survive in scribal transcripts. It less easy to suppose that this hypothetical scribe would not have ironed out the inconsistency of the two forms of the common noun *Jailer*, but this, too, is possible; the evidential value of the variant forms of *Jailer* is in any case weaker than that of *Pirithous* because Shakespeare uses the word much less often than Fletcher, and a preference for one form over the other is not so clear-cut. This is the position—that is, that there was such an intermediate scribe—favoured by both Werstine and Bowers.

An alternative hypothesis, which we favour, places within Cotes's printing house the editorial intervention which both modernized the i/j, u/v practice and frequently substituted *you* for Fletcher's *ye*. We know from, for example, Black and Shaaber that the modernization of spelling, punctuation, and even word form was usual among seventeenth-century printers. We can observe this in the Shakespeare First Folio by comparing some of its texts with their earlier quarto copy, and we can observe it in each successive edition of the Folio when we compare it with its immediate predecessor (which invariably served as copy). By the Second Folio (1632)—which was printed by Cotes—the transformation of i/j, u/v to modern practice was well under way, and we can observe by way of parallel that Simmes, in the second quarto edition of *The First Part of the Contention* (1600), which he set from Creede's first quarto edition, systematically replaced all twenty-one instances of 'I' meaning *yes* with 'yea'. We suggest that a Cotes house style similarly dictated the modernization of i/j and u/v in the 1634 *Kinsmen*, and that this process of modernization extended to the frequent substitution of *you* for Fletcher's *ye*. The variant forms of *Pirithous* and *Jailer* would be unaffected by such a policy, and—except perhaps for occasional compositorial interference—would be expected to survive as the authors left them.

Before any such hypothesis could be advanced with confidence, a more thorough study than has yet been undertaken of Cotes's work would need to be made. However, in each of the three plays partly or wholly by Fletcher printed by Cotes from manuscript copy (*Wit Without Money* (1631), BEPD 563a; *Kinsmen*; *The Night Walker* (1640), BEPD 574a) Cyrus Hoy observed a strikingly low incidence of *ye*. (The only other Fletcher play which Cotes printed, *The Faithful Shepherdess* (1629, BEPD 287b), seems to have been written by Fletcher with a lower than usual incidence of *ye*, and so, like Hoy (I, 142), we exclude it from consideration.) *The Night Walker*, we know from external evidence, was revised by James Shirley. Hoy (IV) finds a number of linguistic features clearly characteristic of Shirley in the printed text of this play, and ascribes the low incidence of *ye*, also, to the revising hand. But it is far from clear that Shirley's aversion to *ye* was so great that he would systematically have removed it in revision—even Hoy, who examined only four plays by Shirley, concludes merely that this playwright 'had no great regard for pronominal *ye*, though he occasionally employed forms in *y*'' (IV, 110). Hoy believes that *Wit Without Money* also was revised by someone after Fletcher had completed it, and with this view Hans Walter Gabler concurs. But the only evidence of revision here (unlike *Walker*, which clearly exhibits other linguistic features which one can confidently associate with Shirley) is the absence of *ye*; 'In every other respect,' writes Hoy, 'the linguistic pattern of *Wit Without Money* is as typically Fletcherian as is to be found' (IV, 110).

In short, Cyrus Hoy observed that the three Fletcher plays printed by Cotes—*Wit Without Money*, *Kinsmen*, and *The Night Walker*—share a markedly lower incidence of *ye* than is usual for Fletcher. Rather than postulate separate agencies for each (an unidentified reviser or scribe for *Wit Without Money*, another scribe for *Kinsmen*, and Shirley for *The Night Walker*), we suggest, provisionally, that the removal of Fletcher's *ye* in each case was by the same agency, and that that agency was a policy of modernization within Cotes's printing house which extended to the frequent substitution of *you* for *ye*.

Waller ('Printer's Copy', p. 78, n. 26) seems to have anticipated this suggestion, though he did not find it an attractive one. Against it he correctly observes that Cotes's Second Folio edition of *Henry VIII* 'reproduces all the *ye*'s from the First Folio text, in the scenes assigned to Fletcher'. This is a valid objection: it may be that Cotes's practice varied depending on whether his copy was printed or manuscript, but in the absence of a detailed study of Cotes's output, we can say little with assurance. Waller also—and rather enigmatically—observes that the 'variations in the linguistic patterns of the three plays [*Wit Without Money*, *Kinsmen*, and *Night Walker*] also remove the printing house as a likely factor in the diminution of Fletcher's *ye*'s', but he does not explain what he has in mind (though we have not had the opportunity to consult his doctoral thesis, which may expand on this matter). He usefully reminds us, however, that the low incidence of *ye* in *Kinsmen* on the one hand and in *Wit Without Money* and *The Night Walker* on the other cannot be attributed to their sharing a common scribal background, for they were the property of different companies (*Kinsmen* was King's; *Wit* and *Walker* were Lady Elizabeth's (?)/Queen's); moreover, *The Night Walker*, certainly, had been revised by Shirley.

Though other evidence has been cited in support of the hypothesis that the copy for *Kinsmen* was a scribal transcript (see Werstine, and our own observations, above, on the misset scene 4.3), the most compelling has always been the paucity of *ye* in Fletcher's share of the play. The hypothesis we have advanced accounts for this, without having to postulate an intermediate transcript between the authors' papers and the printer, though such a transcript is not incompatible with our hypothesis. Pending further investigation of Cotes's other work, we act on the hypothesis that the copy for Q was holograph.

Q contains a fair number of marginally placed stage directions. Most critics agree that these reflect similarly placed theatrical annotations made to the manuscript which served as copy for Q. Indeed, Werstine persuasively argues that the manuscript actually may have had far more of these marginal annotations than were printed in Q: some, he suggests, were moved by the compositors into the body of the text (and sometimes to the wrong place), while others—chiefly those of an 'advisory' or 'warning' nature—the compositors began setting but soon discontinued doing so. The theatrical annotations made to the manuscript, most agree, are in at least two layers, representing the work of at least two book-keepers. The later of these, those annotations made probably by Edward Knight at the time of the 1625-6 revival, we have already briefly discussed in connection with our consideration of the circumstances of that revival. There probably also was an earlier, and, Bowers suggests, a lighter, layer of theatrical annotation, however, perhaps dating back to the original production of *c.*1613.

Far less clear is whether this annotated manuscript was itself the original official prompt-book (or, indeed, Knight's prompt-book for the revival), or whether it was intended to serve as copy for a prompt-book. Bowers summarizes a number of inconsistencies and shortcomings in what he identifies as the pre-Knight layer of directions which he believes tell against the manuscript having been itself used as the original prompt-book, but these are not, we think, sufficient to warrant the dismissal of this possibility. On the contrary, the presence of theatrical annotations of the kind we find in Q seems to us powerful evidence that the document which served as its copy *had* been used as a prompt-book.

Summary

We conclude, provisionally, that the manuscript from which Q was set (1) was a revised holograph (or perhaps a scribal transcript to which revisions were made), (2) was annotated by a book-keeper, *c.*1613, and (3) that this document was further annotated, probably by Edward Knight, in preparation for a revival *c.*1625-6.

G. R. Proudfoot has kindly lent us a typescript of the text of *The Two Noble Kinsmen* which originally formed part of a projected edition of the Shakespeare Apocrypha. Where we wish to record readings originating with this edition, we do so with PROUDFOOT 2.

W.L.M./(G.T.)

WORKS CITED

Bawcutt, N. W., ed., *The Two Noble Kinsmen*, New Penguin (1977)
Bertram, Paul, *Shakespeare and 'The Two Noble Kinsmen'* (1965)
Black, M. W. and M. A. Shaaber, *Shakespeare's Seventeenth-Century Editors* (1937)
Bowers, Fredson, ed., *The Two Noble Kinsmen*, in *The Dramatic Works in the Beaumont and Fletcher Canon*, gen. ed. Fredson Bowers, vol. vii (forthcoming)
Cheatham, George, 'Confused Lineation: An Indication of Rowley's Hand in Collaboration', *The Library*, VI, 7 (1985), 16-37
Colman, George, ed., *The Two Noble Kinsmen*, in *The Dramatick Works of Beaumont and Fletcher* (1778), x. 1-124
Dessen, Alan C., *Elizabethan Stage Conventions and Modern Interpreters* (1984)
Dyce, Alexander, ed., *The Two Noble Kinsmen*, in *The Works of Beaumont and Fletcher* (1846), xi. 325-438
Gabler, Hans Walter, 'Textual Introduction', *Wit Without Money*, in *The Dramatic Works in the Beaumont and Fletcher Canon*, gen. ed. Fredson Bowers, vol. vi (1985), 3-8
Hoy, Cyrus, 'The Shares of Fletcher and His Collaborators in the Beaumont and Fletcher Canon (I)', *SB* 8 (1956), 129-46
—— 'The Shares of Fletcher and His Collaborators in the Beaumont and Fletcher Canon (IV)', *SB* 12 (1959), 91-116
—— 'The Shares of Fletcher and His Collaborators in the Beaumont and Fletcher Canon (VII)', *SB* 15 (1962), 71-90
Lamb, Charles, ed., *The Two Noble Kinsmen* [part of 1.1, 1.3, and 2.2], *Specimens of English Dramatic Poets, who Lived about the time of Shakespeare* (1808)
Leech, Clifford, ed., *The Two Noble Kinsmen*, Signet (1966)
Littledale, Harold, ed., *The Two Noble Kinsmen: A Revised Edition from the Quarto of 1634*, New Shakspere Society (1876, 1885)
Marcham, Frank, *The King's Office of the Revels, 1610-22* (1925)
Mason, J. Monck, *Comments on the Plays of Beaumont and Fletcher* (1789)
Proudfoot, G. R., ed., *The Two Noble Kinsmen*, Regents Renaissance Drama Series (1970)
Seward, Thomas, principal editor, with John Sympson and Lewis Theobald, contributing editors, *The Two Noble Kinsmen*, in *The Works of Mr. Francis Beaumont and Mr. John Fletcher* (1750), x. 1-118
Skeat, Walter W., ed., *The Two Noble Kinsmen* (1875)

Smith, Irwin, *Shakespeare's Blackfriars Playhouse: Its History and Design* (1964)
Sympson, *see* Seward
Theobald, *see* Seward
Waller, F. O., 'A Critical, Old-spelling Edition of *The Two Noble Kinsmen*' (unpublished doctoral dissertation, University of Chicago, 1957)
—— 'Printer's Copy for *The Two Noble Kinsmen*', SB 11 (1958), 61-84

Weber, Henry, ed., *The Two Noble Kinsmen*, in *The Works of Beaumont and Fletcher* (1812), xiii. 1-169
Werstine, Paul, 'On the Compositors of *The Two Noble Kinsmen* (1634)' (forthcoming)
1679, *The Two Noble Kinsmen*, in *Fifty Comedies and Tragedies* [The Beaumont and Fletcher Second Folio], 425-49
1711, *The Two Noble Kinsmen*, in *The Works of Mr. Francis Beaumont, and Mr. John Fletcher*, x. 3604-95

TEXTUAL NOTES

Title *The Two Noble Kinsmen*] Q; a TragiComedy called the two noble kinſmen S.R.
Pro.0.1-Pro.1/0.1-1 *Enter Prologue* | PROLOGUE] This edition; PROLOGVE. Q
Pro.4-5/4-5 his . . . his] Q; hir . . . hir G.T. *conj.*
Pro.26 tack] Q (take)
1.1.0.7/32.8 Pirithous] SEWARD (Theobald); Theſeus Q
1.1.1/33 BOY] DYCE; *not in* Q. That the boy sings the song may be inferred from the opening stage direction.
1.1.7/39 borne‸] 1711; ~, Q
1.1.9/41 harbels] SKEAT; her bels Q
1.1.13/45 children‸ sweete: | Ly] 1679; ~: ſweete-|Ly Q
1.1.14.1/46.1 He strews] Q (Strew). Again, this is confirmed by the opening stage direction.
1.1.16 angel] Q (angle)
1.1.20/52 Chough hor,] SEWARD; Clough hee‸ Q
78 Phœbus] Q. In Elizabethan Latin, *ae*, *oe*, and sometimes *e* are treated as indifferent alternatives (Binns, p. 120).
1.1.59/91 Lord:] 1711 (*subs.*); ~‸ Q
1.1.68/100 Nemean] SEWARD; Nenuan Q
1.1.74.1/106.1 *The 1. Queene rises*] This edition; *not in* Q
1.1.90/122 thy] SEWARD; the Q
1.1.106/138 *The 2. Queene rises*] This edition; *not in* Q
1.1.112/144 glassie] SEWARD; glaſſe Q. Q's reading could arise from ligature confusion (ſſ for ſſi) or misreading (-e for -y).
1.1.113/145 *The 3. Queene rises*] This edition; *not in* Q
1.1.123/155 greefe,] PROUDFOOT; ~‸ Q
1.1.132/164 longer] SEWARD; long Q
1.1.138/170 mooves] 1679; mooues Q
1.1.142/174 drams,] SEWARD (Sympson); ~‸ Q. See Bowers's note for a detailed discussion of this crux.
1.1.155 Rinsing] Q (Wrinching). See *OED*.
1.1.158/190 Artesius] SEWARD; Arteſuis Q. Q probably represents what the compositor believed he saw in the manuscript, since he has not used the '*ſi*' ligature, but has employed the '*is*' ligature. The manuscript may itself have been in error, or the compositor may have misread 'iu' as 'ui', a very easy error.
1.1.166/198 ALL 3. QUEENES] WEBER (*subs.*); *All.* Q
1.1.171/203 war] SEWARD (Theobald); was Q
1.1.177 twinning] Q (twyning)
1.1.211/243 Aulis] SEWARD (Theobald); Anly Q
1.2.42/307 be,] LITTLEDALE (Nicholson); ~‸ Q
1.2.55 canon] Q (Cannon)
1.2.65/330 power,] SEWARD (Sympson, *subs.*); ~: Q
1.2.65/330 nothing:] SEWARD (Sympson, *subs.*); ~, Q
1.2.69/334 mens service] SEWARD; men ſervice Q. One can certainly say 'commands . . . service', but the parallel with 'boot' and 'glory' would be easier if 'service', rather than being a verb, were the object of a possessive noun; assimilation would be very easy, with 'mens service'.
1.2.70/335 glory; on‸] LITTLEDALE (Ingram); ~‸ ~, Qa; ~‸ ~; Qb
1.2.70 one] Q (on)
1.3.4 an't] Q (and't)
1.3.31/412 one] WEBER (Mason); ore Q
1.3.54/435 a leven] 1679 (*subs.*: eleven); a eleven Q. A similar compositorial error is made in *Romeo* 1.3.37/377: Q2-4 (Q2 deriving from Shakespeare's foul papers) all read 'a leuen' while F, which was set from Q3, reads 'a eleuen'. Hand D in *More* (line 2) writes 'a leuenpence'

1.3.54/435 Flauina] SEWARD (*subs.*); Flauia Q
1.3.73 wear] Q (were)
1.3.75 one] Q (on)
1.3.79/460 sely innocenc] This edition (G.T.); fury-innocent Q; surely Innocence SEWARD (Sympson); every innocent LAMB; sorry innocence BERTRAM (*conj.*); story innocence PROUDFOOT 2. Q does not make sense. Innocent/innocenc is an easy misreading: the difficulty is with the first word. The e/f misreading necessary to Lamb's proposal, the usual emendation, is virtually impossible. A u/o misreading (Bertram, Proudfoot) in Shakespeare is not probable, nor is it easy to explain how the additional letters necessary to Seward's proposal were left out by the compositor. 'Sely' = *seely* (*OED*, 13th-17th c.) = 'helpless, harmless, foolish', on the other hand, is often used by Shakespeare and might plausibly have been misread as 'fury'. To mistake manuscript 'ſ' as 'f' is easy (see, for example, 5.4.104/2493), and it is not uncommon in Shakespeare to misread e/u and l/r.
1.3.82/463 dividuall] SEWARD (Sympson); individuall Q
1.3.82/463 out] 1679; ont Q
1.4.18/497 smeard] Qb; ſuccard Qa
1.4.22/501 Wi leave] DYCE; We leave Q; We 'lieve LITTLEDALE (*conj.*)
1.4.39/518 doe:] SEWARD (*subs.*); ~‸ Q
1.4.40/519 friends,] WEBER (friends'); ~‸ Q
1.4.41/520 Loves,] WEBER (Love's); ~‸ Q
1.4.45 O'er-wrestling] Q (Or wraſtling)
1.4.49 fore] Q (for)
1.5.0.2/528.2-3 *with Attendants*] BAWCUTT; *&c.* Q
1.5.0.3/528.4 *Song*] SKEAT; *not in* Q
1.5.9-10/537-8 woes. | We . . . woes.] BAWCUTT; woes. We convent, &c. Q. It is possible that more than the repeated high-line is intended by Q's '*&c.*'
2.1.17/562 that‸ now;] SEWARD; that. | Now, Q
2.1.28 grece] Q (greiſe). See the note to *Twelfth Night* 3.1.123.
2.1.47.1-2.2.0.2/590.1-599.2] This scene division is directly related to the staging. The problem is that near the end of 2.1 Palamon and Arcite are directed to enter above; they do not speak, but are observed from the main stage; then immediately following a general exeunt, they are directed to enter 'in prison', which, presumably, must also be above, because of the later entrance—clearly separated—of Emilia and her woman. Most editions assume 2.1 and 2.2 constitute essentially a single scene (though the division is frequently retained for ease of reference): Palamon and Arcite are usually directed to remain on stage, above, when the others leave at the end of 2.1.

However, it is difficult to disregard explicit stage directions in a text, like this one, set from a manuscript which had so obviously been prepared for the stage. Palamon and Arcite's first appearance is pretty clearly at a window: one of them 'lookes out', and of the other only 'a part' is seen: neither speaks. To clarify this point, a relatively uncontroversial one, we have altered the directions at 2.1.47.1/590.1. from '*Enter Palamon, and Arcite*' to '*Palamon, and Arcite appear ⌈at a window⌉*'. Their second appearance, though possibly visible through a window (Smith), but improbably set on the lower inner stage (Bertram), would most likely have occurred on the principal upper stage. This would make sense of Q's stage direction: they 'enter . . . in prison' at 2.2.0/599.1, whereas before they had only been observed to be within the prison from without it. In other words, the setting of 2.1 is outside the prison; the locale then shifts, by an exeunt and an entrance, to within it (2.2). We have, therefore, retained the general exeunt at the end of 2.1, the scene division, and Palamon and Arcite's immediate re-entrance.

2.2.3/602 warre, yet,] BROOKE; ~ ~, Q
2.2.21/620 wore] SEWARD; were Q
2.2.22/621 Ravishd] SEWARD; Braviſhd Q
2.2.51/650 Strucke] Q; Stuck DYCE (conj.)
2.2.64 twined] Q (twyn'd). Compare Fletcher's lines in *Sir John Van Olden Barnavelt* (MSR 1577-8), to which Bowers has drawn our attention: 'Our bodies are the earthes, that's their dyvorsse, | But our immortall names shall twyn togeather', and see Bowers's note on this line. However, 'twinned' remains a possible alternative modernization.
2.2.91/690 Crave] Q. Skeat's emendation, 'Grave', i.e. 'bury', requires us to identify 'acquaintance' with the kinsmen's friendship: but 2.2 makes clear that theirs is an extraordinarily close bond, while *OED* records 'acquaintance' to be a less than familiar or intimate friendship.

Additionally, however, *acquaintance* can mean 'knowledge of something gained by intercourse or experience', and Q's 'Crave' seems to require no more than these two senses: 'we might come to be contaminated (*a*) by (our) envy of ill men or (*b*) by the malice (*envy*) of such ill men as a result of our regular contact with such ill men or malice'. We retain Q 'Crave'.
2.2.115.1/714.1 below] WEBER; not in Q
2.2.118-19/717-18 EMILIA This ... in't. | What] SEWARD; This ... in't. | *Emil.* What Q
2.2.132/731 was I] This edition; I was Q. Transposition of this kind is an easy compositorial error.
2.2.150/749 close] This edition (G.T.); neere Q. Q's repetition ('neere ... neere') is suspicious, and could easily have resulted from compositorial eyeskip. Our reading, besides being alliterative, means both 'near' (modifying 'come') and 'secret' (modifying 'Art').
2.2.182/781 love her] HUDSON 2 (W. S. Walker); love Q
2.2.189/788 your blood] 1679; you blood Q
2.2.204/803 be,] 1711; ~. Q
2.2.264 to] Q (too). Though Q may be a compositorial error, misinterpreting manuscript 'to' as a variant spelling of 'too' ('also'), and so expanding it, it equally may be itself a variant spelling of 'to'. Compare *All's Well* 4.5.58/2375 'let my horses be wel look'd too'.
2.2.272/871 you] 1679; yon Q
2.3.6/886 sins] Qb; fins Qa
2.3.24.2/904.1 Garlond] Garlon Qa; garlond Qb. The change to lower case is probably occasioned by the need to justify the expanded line.
2.3.40/920 yee] SEWARD; yet Q
2.3.56/935 sed] This edition; fees Q; says SEWARD. The form occurs earlier, in Shakespeare's probable share, at 1.2.104/369, and later, in Fletcher's, at, e.g., 3.5.69-71/1414-16.
2.3.67/947 Yet,] This edition (G.T.); Yes, Q
2.3.81/961 Well,] SEWARD; ~, Q
2.4.33 night; ere tomorrow,] This edition; night, or to morrow,. Editors understand her to say that she will free him 'this night or tomorrow', and punctuate accordingly; Q instead breaks the sentence only after 'night', making it probable that 'or' is the obsolete preposition now spelled 'ere', and that she means 'I will free him tonight; before tomorrow he shall love me'.
2.5] SEWARD; Scæna 4 Q
2.5.0.1/1001.1 Short] This ſhort Q. The whole sentence ('This short ... within') is in roman type in the left margin, opposite lines 2.5.0.1-2.5.3/1001.1-1004. There is no reference or explanation for 'This'; it may be an error for some other word ('Here'?), or have arisen from some accretion of marginal markings and alterations.
2.5.0.3/1001.3 and Attendants] PROUDFOOT; &c. Q
2.5.28/1029 For] 1679; Fo Q
2.6.3/1068 him:] PROUDFOOT (subs.); ~, Q

2.6.4/1069 hence,] Q; ~; SEWARD
2.6.33/1098 patch] LITTLEDALE (Ingleby); path Q
3.1.0.1/1104.2 *A Bush in place*] This edition; not in Q. Palamon is directed later in the scene to emerge 'as out of a Bush'—if a property bush was used, it could easily have been supplied during the act-break. A bush is called for only in this act, but here it is mentioned several times (once in 3.1, twice in 3.6). See, however, Dessen's discussion of 'as from' directions.
3.1.2 laund] Q (land)
3.1.10/1114 pace] Q; place SEWARD. See *OED*, sb.¹ 10 ('a passage, narrow way; esp. a pass through ... woods') and 11 ('In a church: A passage between the seats'). The latter is significant as an associative link with 'blest' and 'sole presence'.
3.1.11-12/1115-16 With ... rumination] This edition (G.T.); *as 1 line with no lacuna marked* Q. The difficulty in Q appears to be in the transition—or lack of transition—between 'presence' and what follows. We suggest the cause of this difficulty to have been an instance of compositorial eyeskip from the middle of one verse line to the middle of the next. We favour the lacuna immediately before 'rumination', rather than either of the other possibilities (i.e. before 'in' or after 'rumination'), because this helps to explain the awkwardness of 'coming between [thy rumination]', where one would expect a plural.
3.1.37/1141 lookd,] SEWARD (subs.); ~, Q
3.1.37/1141 voyd'st] SEWARD (Sympson, subs.); voydes Q. This traditional emendation has two problems. Firstly, its best justification—that Q represents a foul-case substitution of short 's' for the required 'ſt' ligature—is difficult to explain: short 's' not only does not look very much like 'ſt', but, according to Moxon, the two typepieces would normally have been kept in separate cases—'s' in the lower, 'ſt' in the upper. Secondly, on practice elsewhere, if 'voydest' was meant to be elided, as the metre here requires, it probably would have been written 'voy'ſt', which makes the alleged error even harder to explain. Nevertheless, the rhetorical pattern of the preceding and following clauses encourages a superlative here, linking 'honour' with 'gentle token'.
3.1.43/1147 Not] BAWCUTT (Littledale); Nor Q
3.1.96.1/1200.1 *of: Cornets*] LEECH (Bertram); ~, ~ Q. Q's '*Cornets*' is probably a playhouse addition.
3.1.96.1 *within*] Q has 'of' = 'off', meaning 'off stage'.
3.1.98/1202 Muſitte] KNIGHT (musit); Muſicke Q
3.1.108/1212 not] 1679; nor Q
3.1.113/1217 Tis] PROUDFOOT 2; If Q; I've SEWARD
3.1.123/1227 enjoy it] SEWARD; enjoy't Q
3.2.1/1229 mistooke,] SEWARD; ~; Q
3.2.1/1229 Brake] WEBER (Theobald); Beake Q; Beck SEWARD; Brook SYMPSON (conj.)
3.2.7 reck] Q (wreake)
3.2.19/1247 fedd] 1679 (subs.); feed Q
3.2.28/1256 brine] 1711; bine Q
3.3.12/1278 Sʳ] PROUDFOOT 1; &c Q
3.3.23/1289 them] 1679; then Q
3.3.34/1300 What] Q; *Arcite.* What PROUDFOOT 2
3.3.35/1301 ARCITE] Q; *Palamon.* PROUDFOOT 2
3.3.35/1301 PALAMON Made] Q; made PROUDFOOT 2
3.3.52/1318 Sirha] SEWARD; Sir ha Q
3.4.9/1328 Open] RIVERSIDE (John Freehafer, 'A Textual Crux in *The Two Noble Kinsmen*', *Modern Language Notes*, 7 (1979), 254-7); Vpon Q; Up with SEWARD (Sympson); Spoom WEBER (Theobald, subs.); Run SKEAT; Boom BERTRAM (conj.)
3.4.10 tack] Q (take)
3.4.19/1338 a foote] 1711; afoote Q
3.5.8/1353 jane] DYCE; jave Q
3.5.8 jean] Q (jane)
3.5.21/1366 figure, trace,] SEWARD (subs.); ~, ~, Q
3.5.25/1370 theis] PROUDFOOT 1 (subs.); their Q. Q, however, may be right.
3.5.47 an] Q (and)
3.5.60/1405 DAUGHTER ... The] 1679; Q *prints the speech-prefix in*

the margin, next to line 61 (*which begins with* 'The coast . . .'; *see the lineation notes*). *The direction is editorial.*

3.5.67/1412 I] 1711; *not in* Q; We WEBER

3.5.68/1413 There . . . howlet:] LEECH; There . . . howlet‸ Q. Q's italics appear to derive from the compositor mistakenly interpreting this line as part of the song.

3.5.69/1414 he] BAWCUTT; *not in* Q

3.5.96/1441 THESEUS] 1679; Per⟨ithous⟩. Q

3.5.101.1/1446.1 *They . . . stooles*] This edition; *not in* Q. The direction is suggested by Q's marginal note, 'Chaire and | ſtooles out' on G2ᵛ, to the left of lines 65-6/1410-11.

3.5.120 Moor] Q (Morr)

3.5.121 Ice] Q (Is)

3.5.125 tenor] Q (tenner). We find Eugene Waith's suggestion that Q means 'tenner', in the sense of a ten-syllable line, exceedingly attractive; we probably would have adopted this modernization had the suggestion reached us in time.

3.5.133 beest-eating] Q (beaſt eating). See H. Kökeritz, 'The Beast-Eating Clown, *The Two Noble Kinsmen*, 3.5.151', *Modern Language Notes*, 61 (1964), 532-5.

3.5.138/1483 SCHOOLEMASTER (*knocke for the Dance*)] This edition. Q omits the speech-prefix, but prints in the left margin 'Knocke for | Schoole. Enter | The Dance'. We suggest that in the manuscript's margin was actually 'Knocke for Schoole. | The Dance', where 'Knocke for | The Dance' represents the marginal direction, and 'Schoole.' (or perhaps 'Sch.') the speech-prefix. The compositor, misinterpreting this, interpolated 'Enter' and set the whole thing as a marginal direction. Following the preceding line, in the more usual right-justified position, Q prints '*Muſicke Dance.*': this probably represents the genuine entry direction for the Dance. It is early, but this is not uncommon in Q.

3.5.138.1/1483.1 *He flings up his Cap*] This edition; *not in* Q. This direction is suggested by the schoolmaster's earlier remarks (3.5.17/1362).

3.5.138.1-13/1483.1-13 *Musicke . . . morris*] This edition (G.T.); *Muſicke Dance* Q. In Q the direction follows line 3.5.137/1482. The Schoolmaster names six male parts to the dance, but only three female parts (3.5.127-34/1472-9). We know, however, from the earlier dialogue (3.5.38/1383 ff.) that, if we include the Jailer's Daughter, there are an equal number of male and female dancers. Since the nine parts he has mentioned correspond with the six male and three of the six female dancers in the second anti-masque of Beaumont's *Masque of the Inner Temple* from which this morris, it is generally agreed, derives, we suggest that the remaining three women here, like in Beaumont, play female counterparts to the Clown, the Babion, and the Fool. We further suggest that the Jailer's Daughter, in her distracted state, danced the She Fool. Our direction is an adaptation of lines in Beaumont's masque (*The Masque of the Inner Temple and Gray's Inn*, ed. Fredson Bowers, *The Dramatic Works in the Beaumont and Fletcher Canon*, gen. ed. Fredson Bowers, vol. i (Cambridge, 1966), p. 133).

3.5.139-48/1484-93 Ladies . . . rout] LITTLEDALE; *italic* Q. The compositor, possibly misinterpreting the '*Musicke*' direction, set this speech as if it were a song.

3.5.140/1485 yee] SEWARD; *thee* Q. An easy misreading, though here it may possibly be an instance of Cotes's widespread elimination of the Fletcherian *ye* gone wrong. 'Ladies' makes the plural, 'ye' (or 'you'), necessary. See the Introduction.

3.5.143/1488 thee] 1679; three Q

3.5.152/1497 you] 1679; yon Q

3.5.158.1/1503.1-2 *Exeunt . . . within*] Q prints '*Winde Hornes*' after '*made*', line 3.5.159/1504, and omits '*Exeunt . . . traine*' and '*within*'.

3.5.159 deaeque] Q (Deæq;)

3.6.110/1615 safely] Q; safety SEWARD (Theobald)

3.6.112/1617 dye;] This edition; ~‸ Q

3.6.131.3/1636.3 [*Theseus*] . . . *Arcite*] This edition; *not in* Q. It is reasonably certain that someone in Theseus' party separates the two combatants: in Chaucer this is clearly done by Theseus himself, and Theseus' comment near the end of the play, 'ev'n very here | I sundred you' (5.6.99-100/2748-9), strongly suggests that he does so in this play, as well.

3.6.145/1650 thīe] SKEAT (subs.); this Q; thy DYCE

3.6.175/1680 valiant,] SEWARD; ~ ; Q

3.6.236 fail] Q (fall)

3.6.240/1745 name, Opinion;] SEWARD (subs.); ~ ; ~, Q; name's opinion KNIGHT (Theobald); name, or person; (PROUDFOOT conj. in conversation)

3.6.272/1777 must] 1679; muff Q

3.6.273/1778 the other] SEWARD; th'other Q

3.6.279, 280/1784, 85 PALAMON *and* ARCITE] This edition; *Both* Q

3.6.285/1790 excellent:] 1711; ~‸ Q

3.6.307.1/1812.1 *In . . . remooved*] This edition (G.T.); *not in* Q. If a property bush is employed for Palamon's entrances and exits, its presence on stage is probably confined to Act 3. Our direction for its removal is adapted from the Act 3 opening stage direction of *The Changeling* (1622), D3ᵛ. See Taylor, 'Act Intervals'.

4.1.11/1823 oth] 1679; o'th Q

4.1.20/1832 hee scapt] 1679; he escapt Q. This scene regularly uses *scape*, and here the line seems to require the monosyllable.

4.1.26/1838 nev'r] Q; never SEWARD

4.1.45/1857 Well . . . Not well] PROUDFOOT 2; Well Sir. | 1. Fr⟨iend⟩. Not right? | 2. Fr⟨iend⟩. Not well?—*Wooer*, No Sir not well. Q; Well Sir. WOOER No Sir not well. 2. FRIEND Not well? 1. FRIEND Not right? W.L.M. *conj.*

4.1.63 sung] Q (song)

4.1.84/1896 wreath] SEWARD; wreake Q

4.1.86/1898 she appeard me thought] This edition (G.T.); me thought she appeard Q. This simple transposition produces a much more regular line.

4.1.104 light . . .] Q (light, *&c*). The song from which this line comes has not been identified; Q's '*&c*' seems to indicate that more than this single line was sung.

4.1.110/1922 rarely] Q; early SEWARD. Q's 'rarely' means 'early' (*OED* rare, *a.*³ + *-ly*, suffix²). Seward's emendation is not necessary.

4.1.113 sweet . . .] Q (sweete, *&c*). The seventh of Sidney's *Certain Sonnets* (1598), a song, begins each of its four stanzas with the lines 'O fair, ô sweet, when I do looke on thee, | In whom all ioyes so well agree, | Heart and soule do sing in me.' Q's '*&c*' seems to indicate that more than this single line was sung: if the snatch is from Sidney's song, perhaps the Daughter sang all four lines of the refrain.

4.1.118/1930 meane] Q; means COLMAN. Q is acceptable (*OED* mean, *sb.*² 10a), though the error would be an easy one.

4.1.119 Far] Q (For)

4.1.133/1945 BROTHER] PROUDFOOT; *Daugh*⟨*ter*⟩. Q

4.1.140/1952 2.] 1679; 1. Q

4.1.144-5/1956-7 cheerely‸ all. | Owgh] LEECH; cheerely. | *All.* Owgh Q

4.1.145 Uff, uff, uff] Q (Owgh, owgh, owgh). These appear to represent three grunts, or heaves, of exertion.

4.1.148/1960 Vp to the top boy] Q. Citing Heywood's *Fortune by Land and Sea* (1609) 6.410-18, G.T. suggests that, at this order, the Second Friend climbs to the area above, thereby exploiting a recognized convention in the staging of sea scenes. See Dessen, 14.

4.1.150 Tack] Q (Take)

4.1.151 light . . .] Q (light, *&c*). The song from which this snatch is taken has not been identified, though Thomas Sackville's 'Tragedy of Henry Duke of Buckingham' in *The Mirror for Magistrates* (1563) contains the line 'And pale Cinthea with her borrowed light' (line 43). Q's '*&c*' suggests that more than the single line was sung.

4.2.16/1979 love] SEWARD; Love Q

4.2.16/1979 once] This edition; with Q

4.2.54.1/2017.1 *a*] 1711; *Emil*⟨*ia*⟩. *and* Q. For alternative explanations of this displaced entrance, see Introduction. We do not find convincing Bertram's hypothesis that Q is correct as it stands and that Emilia is meant to deliver her soliloquy on the inner stage, and then 'enter', i.e. come forward, to the main stage, where she meets the Gentleman.

4.2.55/2018 How] *Emil⟨ia⟩.* How Q. See the previous note.

4.2.69.1/2032.1 *Messenger*] 1679; *Meſſengers. Curtis.* Q. G.T. suggests that the Q passage extending from here through 4.2.122/2085 represents a revision, consisting chiefly of speech reassignments, made at the time of the 1625-6 revival. Two points suggest this hypothesis: (*a*) why would the Q direction be in the plural, and (*b*) why should Pirithous, who enters with Theseus, report on the knights? G.T. suggests that perhaps originally several messengers entered to describe the trains, then later their speeches were reassigned to a single messenger and Pirithous, presumably to pad out the latter's role. Since this change seems to be connected with the singular *Curtis*, added opposite the plural *Messengers*, the change would appear to date from the 1626 revival, that is, after the deaths of Shakespeare and Fletcher, and is therefore of doubtful authority. These suspicions are also encouraged by the dialogue just after the '*Messengers*' direction. It is odd that the entrance is not, at such a juncture, immediately followed by Theseus' 'From whence come you, Sir' (or 'Sirs', if it had originally been plural). But if Pirithous were to take over the role of one of the messengers, an explanation had to be provided for his having seen the knights, *despite* the fact that he enters with Theseus. Hence the single verse line welded between the entrance direction and the response to it ('Who saw 'em?'—'I a while'—'And I'). The Gentleman's 'And I' seems designed to complete the verse line, make the whole thing more plausible, and provide a number of people who could speak (although he appears not to have been used). But earlier the Gentleman said he had been sent from the Duke to tell Emilia about the knights' arrival, and he shows to her no special knowledge beyond that; if he had seen the knights before Theseus sent him, why did not Theseus question him then?

To accept this hypothesis we would also have to accept that at the time of the revision two vocatives were altered, for neither Theseus' 'friend' (4.2.92/2055) nor the Messenger's 'my lord' (4.2.121/2084) could ever have referred to a simple messenger (unless, of course, we imagine the messengers to have been nobles).

4.2.76/2039 first] 1679; fitſt Q
4.2.81/2044 fire] DYCE (Heath); faire Q
4.2.105/2068 tods] LITTLEDALE; tops Q.
4.2.110/2073 court] LITTLEDALE; corect Q
4.3.21/2141 spirits, ar:] WEBER (Mason, *subs.*); ſpirits, as, Q
4.3.29/2149 i'th tother] BAWCUTT; i'th | Thother Q; i'thother 1679
4.3.36/2155 enough] Q; done enough G.T. *conj.* Enough can, at this time, mean 'cooked sufficiently'; see *OED* done, *adv.*, B.1c.
4.3.36/2155 enough] enough. Exit. Q. See the Introduction.
4.3.46 engrafted] Q (engraffed). See *As You Like It* 3.2.115/1259.
4.3.49 an] Q (and)
4.3.50/2169 th'other] DYCE; another Q
4.3.51/2170 behind] Qb; behold Qa
4.3.54 fate...] Q (*fate, &c.*). Though the song from which this line comes has not been identified, Q's *&c.* seems to indicate that more than the single line was sung.
4.3.84/2203 carve] 1679; crave Q
5.1.0.1/2217.2 *An Altar prepared.*] This edition; *not in* Q. Clearly necessary, this may have been concealed on the inner stage until after Theseus', and possibly Palamon's, departure. It is only required for the first three scenes of the act (see the head-note to 5.2), and may have been concealed again at the end of 5.3.

2217.2 *Thesius*] Q. This spelling must be intentional, for instead of the two typepieces 'ſ' and 'e' the compositor used the single 'ſi' ligature. Since e/i is a difficult misreading, we must suppose that the compositor is following the manuscript here.

5.1.37/2254 father off] WEBER (Theobald, *subs.*); farther off Q; furth'rer of PROUDFOOT
5.1.37 of] Q (off)
5.1.44/2261 me] PROUDFOOT 1 (Littledale); *not in* Q
5.1.49-50/2266-7 purple, ... prewarne] PROUDFOOT 2; purple. | Comets prewarne, whoſe havocke in vaſte Feild Q; purple; whose Approach | Comets prewarn, whose havoc in vast Field SEWARD
5.1.53/2270 armypotent] SEWARD (*subs.*); armenypotent Q
5.1.67/2284 designe,] 1711 (*subs.*); ~ ; Q
5.1.67/2284 boldly;] 1711; ~ , Q
5.2] WEBER; Q *continues as part of* 5.1. It seems more probable that a single on-stage altar did triple duty than that there were three separate altars. When, therefore, Palamon and his knights enter to pray to Venus, it is probably before the same altar at which Arcite had prayed to Mars; similarly, when Emilia prays to Diana, she probably also does so before the same altar. In each case a shift of locale has occurred, and in each case there is no reason to suppose temporal continuity (indeed, the three episodes may be meant to be occurring simultaneously), and in each case the shift is signalled in Q by a general exeunt and an entrance direction. We therefore treat each as a separate scene.
5.2.8.1-2/2292.1-2 *Here ... againe*] Here they kneele as formerly Q. The direction at 5.2.61.1-2/2345.1-2 makes clear that earlier in the scene Palamon and his knights had prostrated themselves. This is one of two possible points at which they did so: the other is at 5.2.0.1-2/2284.1-2, 'with the former observance'.
5.2.23/2307 his;] SEWARD; ~ , Q
5.2.50/2334 briefe,] SEWARD (*subs.*: ~ ;); ~ , Q
5.2.51/2335 done, ... Companion;] SEWARD (*subs.*: ~ , ... ~ ;); ~ ; ... ~ , Q
5.2.52/2336 not, ... defyer;] SEWARD (*subs.*: ~ , ... ~ ;); ~ ; ... ~ , Q
5.2.53/2337 cannot, ... Rejoycer;] SEWARD (*subs.*: ~ , ... ~ .); ~ ; ... ~ , Q
5.3] WEBER; Q *continues as part of* 5.1. See the head-note to 5.2.
5.3.18/2370 election;] DYCE (*subs.*); ~ , Q
5.3.36/2388 *To her women*] This edition; *not in* Q. These last words of Emilia may be an aside, however.
5.4] WEBER; Scæna 2 Q
5.4.29 An] Q (And)
5.4.36/2425 Yes] 1679; Yet Q
5.4.39.1/2428.1 *Madde*] This edition (S.W.W.); *Maide* Q. All previous editors have accepted that Q refers to a silent maidservant attending the Jailer's Daughter. It seems unlikely, however, that a jailer's daughter would have a personal servant, and, indeed, the presence of such a servant would become theatrically awkward in the latter part of the scene, during the intimate conversation between the Daughter and the Wooer. A direction for one to enter 'mad' would be acceptable at the time, and would imply, for a woman, dishevelled clothes and loosely hanging hair. The error would be an easy one.
5.4.40/2429 humour] SEWARD; honour Q
5.4.54/2443 tune] SEWARD (Theobald); turne Q
5.4.85 two] Q (too)
5.4.104/2493 loose the sight] DYCE (*subs.*); loose the Fight Q. Though according to *OED* Q's 'loose' (i.e. 'lose') can mean 'fail to apprehend by sight or hearing' (*v.*¹, 7.b), Dyce's emendation seems desirable from the parallels at 5.4.100/2489, 5.5.1/2503, and (though less close) 5.5.10/2512. For the compositor to misread manuscript 'ſ' as 'f', which he then capitalized to 'F', would be easy.
5.4.106/2495 *Exit Iaylor with Messenger*] This edition; *not in* Q. This enables the Doctor to speak openly to the Wooer at 5.4.111/2500. When they spoke at length previously about the Wooer sleeping with the Daughter, it was after the Jailer's exit (5.4.27.1/2416.1).
5.5] WEBER; Scæna 3 Q
5.5.40/2542.1 *and Attendants*] SKEAT (*subs.*); *&c.* Q
5.5.40.1-2/2542.3-4 *Emilia ... left*] This edition; *not in* Q. We know from 4.2.0.1/1963.2 that Emilia possesses pictures of Palamon and Arcite. It seems probable that she here once again looks at them as she speaks; later in this scene, at line 72/2574, she almost certainly does so. We know from that later speech that she always wears Arcite's picture on her right side, and Palamon's on her left.
5.5.72/2574 *She ... hand*] This edition; *not in* Q

THE TWO NOBLE KINSMEN

5.5.78/2580 the end] SEWARD; th'end Q
5.5.111/2613 Emilia] SEWARD; Emily Q
5.5.121/2624 all,] SEWARD; ~ ; Q
5.5.139/2642 your] 1679; you Q
5.6] WEBER; Scæna 4 Q
5.6.0.3/2649.2 with Blocke and Axe] This edition; &c. Q
5.6.1/2650 PALAMON] 1711; not in Q
5.6.10/2659 unwapper'd, not,] 1711; ~, ~ , Q
5.6.39/2688 2. and 3.] LITTLEDALE; 1. 2. Q
5.6.47/2696 rarly] PROUDFOOT 1 (Sympson, subs.); early Q; dearly SEWARD
5.6.77/2726 On end he stands] Q begins this line half-way across the measure and with a lower-case letter. It appears to represent a faithful compositorial transcription of an interlinear or marginal addition, which possibly had been inserted as an alternative to 'on his hind hoofes' (line 76/2725). Since this arrangement is invariant in both states of this sheet—i.e. it passed through press correction without alteration—it may be regarded as accurately reflecting compositional wish.

5.6.79/2728 victors] Qb; victoros Qa
5.6.101/2750 Our] Q; Your DYCE
5.6.104 arrouse] Q (arowze)
5.6.107/2756 Hath] DYCE; Haft Q
5.6.109/2758 Exeunt . . . Body] This edition (S.W.W.); not in Q.
5.6.133/2782 sorry, still,] WEBER (Mason, subs.); ~, ~ , Q
Epi.0.1-Epi.1/2786.1-2787 Enter Epilogue | EPILOGUE] This edition; EPILOGVE. Q (text); Epilogue. Q (c.w.)

INCIDENTALS

60 me.] ~ ,   109 Honour'd] Honoured   121 his,] ~ ,   144 peebles] peobles   145 'em.] ~ ,   166 eare,] ~ ,   167 more,] ~ .   178 Ly] Q (text); Lie (c.w.)   179 true,] ~ . (possibly ~ ,)   181 Creon.] Creou;   196 hands:] ~ ,   200 unpang'd] unpanged   242 Soldier:] ~ ,   260 mak'st] makest   347 not,] ~ :   348 Valerius.] ~ ,   370 motion,] ~ ,   397 advis'd] advised   409 skill] skilll   435 Yes:] ~ ,   438 Iudgement,] ~ .   447 plucke] plncke   454 careles,] ~ ,   457 musicall] mificall   460 well,] ~)   461 bastard)] ~ ,   464 high-speeded-pace] high,~   477 Pirithous] Pirothous   492 What] what   501 enquir'd] enquired   502 Palamon.] ~ ,   502 those.] ~ ,   506 recover'd] recovered   507 'em:] ~ ,   509 All] all   531 dying.] ~ ,   550 appeare,] ~ ,   555 promised.] ~ ,   673 Conversation,] ~ ,   674 spirits,] ~ ;   726 worke] Q (probably not 'work:', which it resembles, on the evidence of 'performe', 944 (D3ᵛ 14), which uses the same typepiece for the medial 'e')   730 Cosen, Cosen] Gofen ~   734 Flowres,] ~ . (possibly ~ ,)   752 Madam.] ~ ,   771 mankinde] mankindc   771 her,] ~ .   795 No;] (possibly ~ ,)   823 Gentlemen.] (possibly ~ :)   837 bright] brighr   837 ye,] ~ .   847 Arcite?] ~ ,   855 battle] batrle   863 too,] ~ .   944 performe] (probably not 'p:rforme': see 726)   945 goe] (possibly 'goc')   955 Boyes.] ~ ,   957 for't.] ~ ,   983 Extreamely] Extreame!y   1026 Theseus,] ~ .   1044 and] aud   1062 else.] ~ ,   1077 it:] ~ ,   1080 Dirge,] ~ .   1102 Father,] (possibly ~ ;)   1104 him.] ~ :   1140 perfidious] perfidious   1141 lookd,] ~ ,   1141 honour,] ~ ,   1206 certaine] crtaine (possibly 'creaine')   1210 reason.] ~ ,   1224 strength,] ~ ,   1282 shall] fha!l   1289 Cosen?] ~ ,   1291 see.] ~ ,   1298 Arcite,] ~ .   1311 You] you   1313 now.] ~ :   1316 all.] ~ ,   1318 nought.] ~ ;   1339 lockes,] ~ ;   1345 sleepe] (possibly 'fleepe')   1351 And] &   1383 wanting.] ~ ,   1387 labour'd] laboured   1397 position.] ~ ,   1404 thee.] ~ ,   1408 a.] ~ ,   1410 a?] ~ ,   1412 a.] ~ ,   1425 Buz.] ~ ,   1465 waight—] ~ ,   1466 Is,] ~ —   1480 alijs] aliijs ~ ,   1522 kinesman.] ~ ,   1553 deceiv'd] deceived   1553 Soldier,] ~ ,   1554 it.] ~ ,   1574 Cosen] Gofen   1611 Cosen.] ~ ,   1689 sleepe] Qb; fleepe Qa   1726 you] yov   1744 how,] (possibly ~ .)   1765 and] aud   1830 welcome.] ~ ,   1850 answer'd] answered   1851 childishly,] ~ . (possibly ~ ,)   1856 her.] ~ :   1857 well?] ~ ?—   1891 sung] fnng   1918 can.] ~ ,   1921 Yes.] ~ ,   1926 true.] ~ ,   1954 course] conrfe   1960 Heere.] ~ ,   1988 such] fueh   2003 'em?] ~ ,   2007 Gipsey,] ~ .   2012 Sister,] ~ ;   2012 Palamon;] ~ ,   2032 untimely.] ~ ,   2052 him.] ~ ,   2125 another] anorher   2170 arras,] ~ . (possibly ~ ,)   2210 falsehoods] fafehoods   2212 regiment;] Q ('Regiment;' text); ~, (c.w.)   2254 it;] (possibly ~ ,)   2266 Neptune] Nepture   2266 purple,] ~ ,   2346 O] Pal. O   2392 kept] hept   2418 that.] ~ :   2427 her.] ~ , (possibly ~ ,)   2471 businesse:] ~ ,   2490 are:] ~ ,   2491 straight,] ~ ,   2505 decision; ev'ry,] ~ , ~ ;   2520 winke.] ~ ,   2576 left] leff   2590 (values shortnes)] ,~ ,   2613 decay.] ~ ;   2662 kinsmen,] ~ .   2687 couragious] couragiour   2692 life,] ~ .   2735 alliance:] ~ ,   2752 and,] ~ ,   2799 ye,] ~)

QUARTO STAGE DIRECTIONS

Pro.0.1/0.1 Florish. (marginal)
Pro.32.1/32.1 Florish.
1.1.0.1/32.2 Musike. (after 1.1.1/32.12)
1.1.0.1-9/32.2-10 Enter Hymen with a Torch burning: a Boy, in a white | Robe before singing, and strewing Flowres: After Hymen, | a Nimph, encompast in her Tresses, bearing a wheaten Gar-|land. Then Theseus betweene two other Nimphs with | wheaten Chaplets on their heades. Then Hipolita the Bride, | lead by Theseus, and another holding a Garland over her | head (her Tresses likewise hanging.) After her Emilia hol-|ding up her Traine.
1.1.1/32.12 The Song,
1.1.14.1/46.1 Strew | Flowers. (opposite 1.1.14-15/46-7)
1.1.24.1-4/56.1-4 Enter 3. Queenes in Blacke, with vailes staind, with impe-|riall Crownes. The 1. Queene fals downe at the foote of | Theseus; The 2. fals downe at the foote of Hypolita. The | 3. before Emilia.
1.1.76.1/108.1 turnes away.
1.1.106/138 kneele to Emilia.

1.1.224.1-2/256.1-2 Exeunt towards the Temple.
1.1.233.1/265.1 Florish. (after 1.1.232/255)
1.1.233.1/165.1 Exeunt.
1.2.0.1/265.2 Enter Palamon, and Arcite.
1.2.82.1/347.1 Enter Va-|lerius.
1.2.116/381 Exeunt.
1.3.0.1/381.1 Enter Pirithous, Hipolita, Emilia.
1.3.26/407 Exit Pir.
[1.3.58-64/439-45] 2. Hearses rea-|dy with Pala-|mon: and Arci-|te: the 3. | Queenes. | Theseus: and | his Lordes | ready. (marginal)
1.3.98/479 Exeunt.
1.4.0.1/479.1 Cornets.
1.4.0.1-3/479.1-4 A Battaile strooke withim: Then a Retrait: Florish. | Then Enter Theseus (victor) the three Queenes meete | him, and fall on their faces before him.
1.4.13/492 Exeunt Queenes. (after 'those')
[1.4.26-7/505-6] 3. Hearses rea-|dy. (marginal)
1.4.49/528 Florish. (after 1.4.48/527)

THE TWO NOBLE KINSMEN

1.4.49/528 Exeunt.
1.5.0.1/528.1 Musicke.
1.5.0.1-2/528.1-3 Enter the Queenes with the Hearses of their | Knightes, in a Funerall Solempnity, &c.
1.5.16.1/544 Exeunt severally.
2.1.0.1/544.1 Enter Iailor, and Wooer.
2.1.13.1/557.1 Enter Daughter.
2.1.47.1/590.1 Enter Palamon, and Arcite, above.
2.1.55/599 Exeunt,
2.2.0.1/599.1 Enter Palamon, and Arcite in prison.
2.2.115.1/714.1 Enter Emilia and her woman.
2.2.153.1/752.1 Exeunt Emilia and woman.
2.2.220.1/819.1 Enter Keeper.
2.2.228/827 Exeunt Arcite, and Keeper.
2.2.246.1/845.1 Enter Keeper.
2.2.281.1/880.1 Exeunt Palamon, and Keeper.
2.3.0.1/880.2 Enter Arcite.
2.3.24.1-2/904.1-2 Enter .4. Country people, & one with a garlond before them.
2.3.79.1/959.1 Exeunt 4.
2.3.88/968 Exit Arcite,
2.4.0.1/968.1 Enter Iailors Daughter alone.
2.4.33/1001 Exit.
2.5.0.1/1001.1 This short flo-|rish of Cor-|nets and | Showtes with-|in. (marginal, opposite 2.5.0.1-2.5.3/1001.1-1004)
2.5.0.1-3/1001.1-3 Enter Theseus, Hipolita, Pirithous, | Emilia: Arcite with a Garland, &c.
2.5.64.1/1065.1 Florish. (after 'wise')
2.5.64.1/1065.1 Exeunt omnes.
2.6.0.1/1065.2 Enter Iaylors Daughter alone.
3.1.0.1-2/1104.2-3 Cornets in | sundry places. | Noise and | hallowing as | people a May-|ing: (marginal, opposite 'Actus Tertius.' which in Q is printed after 2.6.39/1104)
3.1.0.3/1104.4 Enter Arcite alone.
3.1.31/1135 Enter Palamon as out of a Bush, with his Shackles: bends | his fist at Arcite.
3.1.96.1/1200.1 Winde hornes of Cornets.
3.1.107.1/1211.1 Winde hornes.
3.1.124.1/1228.1 Exeunt.
3.2.0.1/1228.2 Enter Iaylors daughter alone.
3.2.38/1266 Exit.
3.3.0.1-2/1266.1-2 Enter Arcite, with Meate, Wine, and Files.
3.3.1.1/1267.1 Enter Palamon.
3.3.53/1319 Exit.
3.3.53.1/1319.1 Exit
3.4.0.1/1319.2 Enter Iaylors daughter.
3.4.18.1/1337.1 Sing. (marginal)
3.4.26.1/1345.1 Exit.
3.5.0.1-3/1345.2-4 Enter a Schoole master .4. Countrymen: and | Baum 2. or 3. wenches, with a Taborer.
3.5.59.1/1404.1 Enter Iaylors daughter.
[3.5.65-66/1410-11] Chaire and | stooles out. (marginal)
3.5.93/1438 (Winde Hornes: (after 3.5.91/1436)
3.5.95/1440 Ex. all but Schoolemaster.
3.5.95.1-2/1440.1-2 Enter Thes. Pir. Hip. Emil. Arcite: and traine.
3.5.138.1-13/1483.1-13 Musicke Dance. (follows 3.5.137/1482; see textual note to 3.5.138/1483 and 3.5.138.1-13/1483.1-13)
3.5.138/1483 Knocke for | Schoole. Enter | The Dance. (marginal, opposite 3.5.138-40/1483-5; see the textual note)
3.5.158.1/1503.1-2 Winde Hornes. (after 'made', 3.5.159/1504)
3.5.160/1505 Exeunt.
3.6.0.1/1505.1 Enter Palamon from the Bush.
3.6.16/1521 Enter Arcite with Armors and Swords. (after 'morrow')
3.6.93/1598 They bow se-|verall wayes: | then advance | and stand. (marginal, opposite 3.6.93-6/1598-1601; placement in our edition determined by the asterisk which, in Q, follows 'love' 3.6.93/1598)
3.6.106.1/1611.1 Fight. | Hornes within: they stand.
3.6.131.1-2/1636.1-2 Fight againe. Hornes.

3.6.131.2-3/1636.2-3 Enter Theseus, Hipolita, Emilia, Perithous and traine.
3.6.307.1/1812.1 Exeunt.
4.1.0.1/1812.2 Enter Iailor, and his friend.
4.1.16/1828 Enter 2. Friend.
4.1.31/1843 Enter Wooer.
4.1.102.1-2/1914.1 Enter Brother, Daughter, and others.
4.1.113/1925 Singes. (after 'sweete, &c.')
4.1.151/1963 Singes.
4.1.151.1/1963.1 Exeunt.
4.2.0.1/1963.2 Enter Emilia alone, with 2. Pictures.
4.2.54.1/2017.1 Enter Emil. and Gent.
4.2.64/2027 Enter Theseus, Hipolita, Perithous and attendants.
4.2.69.1/2032.1 Enter Messengers. Curtis.
4.2.157/2120 Exeunt.
4.3.0.1/2120.1 Enter Iailor, Wooer, Doctor.
4.3.7.1/2127.1 Enter Daughter.
[4.3.36/2155] Exit. (after 'enough')
4.3.54/2173 Sings.
4.3.54.1/2173.1 Exit. Daugh.
4.3.98.1/2217.1 Exeunt.
5.1.0.1/2217.2 Florish. (after 4.3.98/2217)
5.1.0.1-2/2217.2-3 Enter Thesius, Perithous, Hipolita, attendants.
5.1.5.1/2222.1 Florish of Cornets.
5.1.7/2224 Enter Palamon and Arcite, and their Knights.
5.4.17.1/2234.1 Exit Theseus, and his traine.
5.4.33.1/2250.1 Exeunt Palamon and his Knights.
5.1.48/2265 They kneele.
5.4.60.1-4/2277.1-4 Here they fall on their faces as formerly, and there is heard | clanging of Armor, with a short Thunder as the burst of | a Battaile, whereupon they all rise and bow to the Altar.
5.1.67.1/2284 Exeunt.
5.2.0.1-2/2284.1-2 Enter Palamon and his Knights, with the former obser-|vance.
5.2.8.1-2/2292.1-2 Here they kneele as formerly.
5.2.61.1-2/2345.1-2 Here Musicke is heard, Doves are seene to flutter, they | fall againe upon their faces, then on their knees.
5.2.68/2352 They bow. (after 5.2.66/2350)
5.2.68/2352 Exeunt.
5.3.0.1-7/2352.1-8 Still Musicke of Records. | Enter Emilia in white, her haire about her shoulders, a whea-|ten wreath: One in white holding up her traine, her haire | stucke with flowers: One before her carrying a silver | Hynde, in which is conveyd Incense and sweet odours, | which being set upon the Altar her maides standing a | loofe, she sets fire to it, then they curtsey and kneele.
5.3.26.1-2/2378.1-3 Here the Hynde vanishes under the Altar: and in the | place ascends a Rose Tree, having one Rose upon it.
5.3.32.1-2/2384.1-2 Here is heard a sodaine twang of Instruments, and the | Rose fals from the Tree.
5.3.37/2389 They curtsey and Exeunt.
5.4.0.1-2/2389.1-2 Enter Doctor, Iaylor and Wooer, in habite of | Palamon.
5.4.27.1/2416.1 Exit Iaylor.
5.4.39.1/2428.1 Enter Iaylor, Daughter, Maide.
5.4.99.1/2488.1 Enter a Messenger.
5.4.113/2502 Exeunt.
5.5.0.1/2502.1 Florish (after 'cry' 5.4.113/2502)
5.5.0.1-2/2502.1-2 Enter Theseus, Hipolita, Emilia, Perithous: and | some Attendants, T. Tucke: Curtis.
5.5.40/2542.1-2 Exeunt Theseus, Hipolita, Perithous, &c.
5.5.55.1/2557.1 Cornets. Trompets sound as to a charge.
5.5.64.1-2/2566.1-2 (Cornets. a great cry and noice within crying a Palamon.)
5.5.66/2568 Enter Servant. (after 'chance')
5.5.71/2573 Showt, and Cornets: Crying a Palamon.
5.5.75.1/2577.1 Another cry, and showt within, and Cornets.
5.5.78.1/2580.1 Enter Servant.
5.5.89/2591 Cornets. Cry within, Arcite, Arcite. (after 5.5.88/2590)
5.5.91.1/2593.1 Cornets. a great showt and cry, Arcite, victory.
5.5.104.2-3/2606.2-3 Cornets. | Enter Theseus, Hipolita, Pirithous, Arcite as victor, and | attendants, &c.

635

5.5.138/2641 *Florish.*
5.5.146/2649 *Exeunt.*
5.6.0.1-3/2649.1-2 *Enter Palamon and his Knightes pyniond: Iaylor, | Executioner &c. Gard.*
5.6.35.1/2684.1 *They give their purses.*
5.6.38/2687 *Lies on the Blocke.*

5.6.39.1/2688.1 *A great noise within crying, run, save hold:*
5.6.39.2/2688.2 *Enter in hast a Messenger.*
5.6.40.1/2689.1 *Enter Pirithous in haste.*
5.6.85.1-2/2734.1 *Enter Theseus, Hipolita, Emilia, Arcite, in a chaire.*
5.6.137/2786 *Florish. Exeunt.*
Epi.18.1/2804.1 *Florish.*

LINEATION NOTES

EDITORS have emended the lineation of Shakespeare's early texts since the beginning of the eighteenth century, but the editorial problems created by the distinction between verse and prose, and the principles which should govern editorial practice, have only recently begun to be discussed systematically. The arrangement of words in a text, like the words themselves, may be disturbed in the course of the text's transmission. An author's intentions sometimes fell victim to simple mechanical restraints in the printing house. Full verse lines often would not fit on a single type line of the Folio, with its narrow columns—particularly when such lines occurred at the beginning of a speech, so that room had to be found not only for the verse line but also for an indented speech-prefix. Faced with more verse than the column could accommodate, Folio compositors often simply cut such a line in two, producing two short lines in the place of one long one. Such split lines occur far more often in the Folio than in the quartos (which usually had a wider measure), and they can almost always be attributed to real or anticipated difficulties of justification. What happened on a small scale with individual lines might happen on a larger scale with whole pages: if someone had made an error in casting off the amount of manuscript text that should be fitted on to a given page of type the compositor might find that he had too much or too little text, and in such circumstances the text might be artificially compressed or stretched by rearranging it: turning verse into prose, or prose into verse, or regular into irregular verse. Just as problems of justification can easily be identified by measuring the words against the space available, so problems of casting off can easily be identified because they will occur on certain pages of a quire, and because the suspected rearrangements will waste or save a certain number of type lines. A large proportion of the emendations of lineation recorded below arise from such evident causes.

But compositors could also make mistakes that are not excused or explained by exigencies of the printing process. In the most important and thorough study of mislineation in English Renaissance texts ('Line Division in Shakespeare's Dramatic Verse: An Editorial Problem', *AEB* 8 (1984), 73-125), Paul Werstine has demonstrated that Folio compositors occasionally made errors of almost every kind when setting from known and unambiguous printed copy. Moreover, some compositors were particularly prone to certain kinds of error. Compositor A, for instance, had a regrettable tendency to rearrange normal blank verse into a succession of irregular lines. Usually this errant behaviour was prompted by a single long line which would not fit his measure; rather than simply divide the offending line in two, he would begin redistributing line-breaks in a whole sentence or speech, producing a pattern less obtrusively anomalous visually, but maddeningly inaccurate metrically. Compositor B, on the other hand, had a tendency to set up prose as though it were verse, sometimes for no discernible reason. No doubt the compositors who worked on quarto editions were just as susceptible to occasional or idiosyncratic error.

If compositors can commit irrational or habitual errors, so, theoretically, can scribes. Howard-Hill (*Crane*, p. 59) notes that Ralph Crane apparently relined his copy ten times in preparing his transcript of Fletcher's *Demetrius and Enanthe*. More generally, the characteristic layout of a Crane page could create ambiguities about the distinction between verse and prose: for instance, most of the lineation errors in *Two Gentlemen* involve prose mistakenly set as verse—errors that occur in the work of three different compositors, and are almost certainly attributable to ambiguity in the underlying manuscript. Unfortunately, most of the scribes who prepared printer's copy for Shakespeare editions have not been identified, and we can only guess what kind and quantity of lineation error should be attributed to them.

Authors could also occasionally arrange the text in ways that were ambiguous, misleading, or positively 'wrong'. We emend the lineation of Hand D's addition to *Sir Thomas More* on seven occasions. Two of these occur, one after the other, at the end of a manuscript page; the author crammed three and a half verse lines into two manuscript lines, in order to finish the speech on that page (Add.II.D.104-7/103-6). In another place (Add.II.D.125-6/124-5), Hand D made an interlinear insertion of five words ('In, in, to your obedience!'), apparently intended to fall between the two halves of an existing verse line; its intended relationship to the verse structure is unclear. It could be (*a*) a tetrameter—assuming that 'obedience' was pronounced as four syllables—interposed between two mid-speech part-lines, or (*b*) the second half of a hexameter verse line, with a feminine caesura and a feminine ending—assuming that 'obedience' was pronounced as three syllables—followed by a part-line, or (*c*) the first half of a hexameter—assuming that 'even' was pronounced as a monosyllable—preceded by a part-line. From such examples we might deduce that authorial changes of mind during the process of composition, or the distribution of speeches on (irrecoverable) manuscript pages, might occasionally disturb the pattern of lineation in a printed book. In all of the other four examples of amended lineation in Hand D's pages a line and a half of verse is fitted on to a single line of manuscript. Such 'errors', in which a floating part-line of verse is attached to an adjacent complete line, occur sporadically in both quarto and Folio texts set from authorial copy, and apparently reflect Shakespeare's own practice, at least fitfully. The same paper-saving frugality can be seen in songs, where very short rhyming lines are usually run together in the early texts. The consistency of this practice, in texts set in different decades in different shops, demonstrates that it reflects the author's own material intentions, just as clearly as we can see Hand D's material intentions in the manuscript pages that survive. Shakespeare also usually, and perhaps invariably, wrote out the speeches of Pistol as prose, even though they fall into patterns of obtrusively old-fashioned verse. In such cases editors must make a choice between reproducing the known or inferred layout of an authorial manuscript or creating a layout which more intelligibly communicates the author's rhythmical intentions. The editors of classical Greek drama, for instance, know that the choric odes were originally written out as prose, and that the strophic arrangements which govern their structure were first visually displayed by Alexandrian editors; they nevertheless continue to reproduce the Alexandrian layout, which is more helpful for readers. On the same principle we have—like earlier editors—emended Hand D's lineation, the layout of songs, the arrangement of Pistol's speeches, and some other anomalies of lineation which probably reflect the state of Shakespeare's own manuscript. Certain readers, and certain editors, might prefer to revert to the authorial habit in such cases.

When a verse line was split between two or more speakers, Shakespeare probably did not attempt to place the separate part-lines on a single manuscript line, but instead began each new speech on a new line. Some dramatists of the period did consistently insist that the verse structure of such divided lines be physically reflected in the manuscript or printed text; but such niceties are seldom preserved in the Shakespeare canon. When they do occur—as in *1 Henry IV*, sporadically— they probably reflect the practice of a scribe, not Shakespeare; in other cases—as in *The History of King Lear*—they appear to be no more than an expedient for saving space, not accurately reflecting either the structure of the verse or the layout of the manuscript. (We record among the notes below all instances of dialogue spoken by two or more characters set on a single type line.) Like most editors since the late eighteenth century, we have nevertheless sought, for the convenience of readers, to make the structure of Shakespeare's verse visible by indicating the relationship between such part lines. In the Renaissance, printers usually placed such linked part-lines (and the abbreviated speech-prefixes which accompany them) on a single part-line; most Shakespeare editors since Steevens have, instead, begun each speech on a new type line, but indented the words of the speech itself so that it begins immediately below the point where the previous part-line ends. We have adopted Steevens's procedure. All such indentations are editorial unless recorded below.

In the overwhelming majority of cases such indentation creates no editorial problem and obscures no authorial ambiguity. But Shakespeare sometimes wrote three half-lines in a row, in such a way that the second could form a complete verse line with either the first or the third. Such 'amphibious' part-lines create a metrical ambiguity, in the same way that certain spellings create lexical ambiguity. In the past editors have, nevertheless, attached such part-lines to one or the other of their neighbours. It seems better to leave the ambiguity intact by not indenting any of the part-lines in such cases, but simply printing each short speech immediately to the right of its speech prefix. This procedure makes such amphibious part-lines visually indistinguishable from short prose speeches; but the resulting uncertainty about whether Shakespeare intended prose or verse merely reflects an ambiguity inherent in the material. When Shakespeare moves in and out of verse, or mixes rhythmical prose with irregular verse, or writes a succession of short speeches, his metrical intentions become obscure, as can be seen by the disagreements among editors. When it is clear that Shakespeare intended two or more part-lines to form a single verse line, we make that structure visually available to readers (and actors); when Shakespeare's intentions are not clear, we leave them unclear, rather than imposing upon them an arbitrary editorial clarity.

Fredson Bowers has tried to reduce the number of such ambiguous cases by developing a set of rules to guide editorial practice in indenting part-lines ('Establishing Shakespeare's Text: Notes on Short Lines and the Problem of Verse Division', *SB* 33 (1980), 74-130). Bowers makes a number of important observations about the frequency of part-lines in different positions in unambiguous contexts: part-lines occur much less often at the beginning of a speech than at the end, for instance, and knowledge of this fact can be of assistance when editors are forced to rearrange verse lines mis-set as prose. But Bowers's principles become so complex in their application that different editors applying the same rules may reach different decisions; Shakespeare's practice remains erratic, and hence unpredictable. Moreover, Bowers sets out to find ways around an ambiguity for which Shakespeare himself is undoubtedly responsible; it seems preferable to submit to the fluidity of the medium, and recognize that Shakespeare made use of such lines as one of many techniques for melting down the rigidity of early blank verse.

We have accordingly not attempted to sort one set of amphibious part-lines from another, but have simply treated as ambiguously amphibious any part-line which makes an acceptable verse line with both the preceding and the following part-line. In some cases one option will create a more regular or common verse line than the alternative; in some cases one option will produce a verse line more unified in matter or manner than the alternative; but Shakespeare's works contain many verse lines which are irregular in metre or manner or matter, and we have tried to resist the itch to insist that some verse lines are more equal than others.

Nevertheless, in making unavoidable decisions about whether a sustained passage is in verse or prose, or about how a mislined passage should be relined, an editor must entertain some hypothesis about the nature of Shakespeare's verse. We have assumed that most of Shakespeare's dramatic verse—with the exception of certain clearly signalled, formally distinct interludes—is written in iambic pentameters, enlivened by a limited variety of predictable deviations: hexameters, tetrameters, unassimilated part-lines, feminine endings (an extra unstressed syllable at the end of a line), feminine caesurae (an extra unstressed syllable before the caesura), an extra stressed syllable at the end of the line or after the caesura. Sometimes a line with a feminine ending is followed by a line that begins with an extra stressed syllable (or that lacks its initial unstressed syllable), thus producing a two-syllable iambic 'foot' divided between two verse lines. Such 'line-divided feet' contribute—as do amphibious part-lines—to one of the most important characteristics of Shakespeare's late verse: the caesura and the line-break are treated, to an increasing degree, as interchangeable. The same metrical licences that occur in one position can occur in the other. The practice of writing a line and a half of verse on a single manuscript line may have encouraged, or may simply reflect, this development. At times Shakespeare himself seems to have lost track, in the middle of a speech, of whether he had reached a caesura or the end of a line. Sometimes whole passages can be legitimately arranged in two different ways, depending on which pauses we take as caesurae and which as line-breaks.

The possibility of authorial mislineation makes it difficult to be confident that major problems in the arrangement of verse necessarily result from interference in transmission. Werstine convincingly demonstrates (*a*) that much Folio mislineation can be blamed on particular compositors, and (*b*) that the mislineation evident in some plays—*Coriolanus* and *Antony*, for instance—cannot be blamed on the compositors alone. He attributes problems of lineation in these two late plays to scribal copy, and we have independently offered other evidence for scribal copy in both plays. But we are less sure than Werstine that such problems have no basis in the evolution of Shakespeare's verse style. The fact that not all late plays share such severe lineation problems might simply be due to the fact that those texts derive from authorial fair copies, in which Shakespeare himself visually clarified ambiguities in his foul papers; plays where something goes seriously wrong with lineation might have been set either from foul papers, or from transcripts prepared by scribes working from (and bewildered by) foul papers. In this scenario, some but not all of Shakespeare's late plays would—depending upon their derivation—display a messiness and ambiguity in verse arrangement generated in part by Shakespeare's own working methods. If massive mislineation simply testifies to scribal incompetence, why does such incompetence not affect any early plays? Why do all the clearest examples come from the second half of Shakespeare's career? Even the differences between compositors might in certain situations reflect only their individual habits in dealing with ambiguous manuscript material, with one compositor tending to interpret it 'correctly' and another interpreting it 'incorrectly'. Is it mere coincidence that Compositor B, whom Werstine regards as the more faithful to verse arrangements in his copy, also has a tendency to transform prose into verse—that is, to 'see' verse patterns, and put them into type, even when they are *not* there? Though Werstine's work represents a quantum leap over all previous studies, it has not yet solved all our problems.

Because they seldom impinge directly upon one's understanding of the text, and because anyone interested in them may best evaluate them as a group, we have pooled alterations in the arrangement of verse and prose into the following separate lists. Where emendations affect the lineation, or where the lineation affects emendations, we have provided cross-references in or to the relevant textual notes. As this list records only matters of lineation, it differs from the other collations in this volume in a few details of presentation. Both in the lemma and in quotations to the right of the bracket, punctuation is ignored and spelling modernized. Editorial emendations are not attributed unless we believe that we are the first edition to adopt them. The first word of the lemma is usually the first word of the first line realigned; the last word of the lemma is usually the last word of the first line in which our line-breaks again begin to coincide with those of the control-text.

Most emendations fall into a small number of simple categories, and our collations have been designed to facilitate recognition of those categories. When the control-text sets as prose a passage that we believe to be verse, the italicized word '*prose*' appears to the right of the bracket (see the first note to *Shrew*, below). When the control-text sets as verse a passage that we believe to be prose, the italicized word '*verse*' appears to the right of the bracket, followed by a colon; after the colon we list the last word of each verse line in the control-text, followed by a vertical rule (see the second, third, and fourth notes to *Two Gentlemen*, below). When the control-text sets a line and a half of verse on a single type line, '*1 line*' appears in italics to the right of the bracket (see the first note of *Errors*, below). When '*2 lines*' occurs in italics to the right of the bracket, it means that the control-text divides what we regard as a single verse line into two part-lines; after a colon, we quote the last word that occurs before the control-text's intruded line-break, followed by a vertical rule (see the first note to *1 Henry VI*, below). When the control-text correctly identifies a passage as verse but (in our judgement) arranges it incorrectly, then to the right of the bracket we quote the last word of each verse line in the control-text's arrangement, each followed by a vertical rule (see the first note to *Richard II*, below). If in such circumstances our arrangement results in a different number of line-ends from that of the control-text, we precede our record of the control-text's lineation with a note of how many line-ends that lineation produced (see *Macbeth* 3.1.87–92/888–93).

Compositor A of the Folio, and to a lesser extent other compositors, sometimes set verse speeches consisting of a single long line in a way that might be misinterpreted as prose. When the last word or words would not fit on the line, rather than create an obtrusive turn-over or turn-up the compositor simply carried the remaining word or words of the speech on to the next line. Sometimes the compositor would slightly indent the resulting second line, in order to indicate its status; but in other cases he did not, thus making it visually indistinguishable from prose. Such 'unindented flow-overs' were almost certainly treated in the manuscript, regarded by the compositor, and interpreted by contemporary readers, as verse; we have not recorded them unless they have been regarded as genuinely ambiguous.

In some cases, because of an ambiguity in the context, it is more convenient to indicate a copy-text line-break by means of the word which occurs *after* the break, rather than the word which occurs before it; in those circumstances, the vertical rule is placed before the word quoted (see the first note to *Two Gentlemen*).

In general, the following notes only record departures from the lineation of the control text. Where the relevant Folio text is essentially a mere reprint of a more authoritative quarto (as in *Titus Andronicus*), we have not recorded variant lineation in the derivative text unless we adopt it. But where we possess two substantive collateral texts (*2 Henry IV*, *Hamlet*, *Troilus*, *Othello*), we have recorded all departures from the lineation of the control-text and all variants in the lineation of the secondary text.

We have commented upon very few of the emendations recorded here, because the overwhelming bulk are traditional; they require no defence beyond a glance at the context. However, earlier editors had little understanding of the causes of error in matters of lineation; they tended also to adopt an anachronistic attitude towards the kinds of metrical licence permissible in Shakespeare's verse. We have examined afresh problems of lineation throughout the canon, and have sometimes departed from previous editorial practice. The editor primarily responsible for each individual work (noted elsewhere in this volume) is also individually responsible for the relevant lineation notes below; Gary Taylor has served as a secondary editor scrutinizing and advising upon all editorial decisions affecting lineation.

G.T./(W.L.M.)

The Two Gentlemen of Verona

1.1.111-2/111-2 You ... Ay] *verse*: |and you|
1.1.119-20/119-20 Marry ... pains] *verse*: orderly|
1.1.131-5/132-6 Sir ... steel] *verse*: her| letter| mind| mind|
1.1.137-40/138-41 No ... master] *verse*: pains| me| letters your|
1.2.88/235 Let's ... minion] *2 lines*: song|
2.1.51-2/430-1 I ... infinite] *verse*: exquisite|
2.1.63-4/442-3 I have ... beautiful] *verse*: saw her|
2.1.74-5/455-6 Belike ... shoes] *verse*: morning|
2.1.82-3/463-4 Last ... loves] *verse*: me|
2.1.87-8/468-9 No ... comes] *verse*: them|
2.1.89-90/470-1 O ... her] *verse*: puppet|
2.1.114/495 What ... it] *2 lines*: ladyship|
2.1.132/513 That ... letter] *2 lines*: scribe|
2.1.133-4/514-5 How ... yourself] *verse*: sir|
2.1.143-4/524-5 What ... jest] *verse*: need she | yourself
2.1.146-7/527-8 No ... earnest] *verse*: sir|
2.1.159-60/539-40 All ... dinner-time] *verse*: it|
2.2.6/551 Why ... this] *2 lines*: exchange|
2.4.36-8/659-61 Yourself ... company] *verse*: fire| looks|
2.4.41-4/664-7 I ... words] *verse*: of| followers| liveries|
2.4.45-6/668-9 No ... father] *verse*: |Here
3.1.191-2/1210-11 Him ... Valentine] *verse*: find|
3.1.302-3/1321-2 What ... stock] *verse*: wench|
3.1.325-7/1345-7 O ... virtue] *verse*: vices| only virtue|
3.1.329-50/1349-50 Out ... her] *verse*: too|
3.1.356-8/1377-9 Why ... impossible] *verse*: gracious| is|
4.2.59-60/1623-4 Not ... heart-strings] *verse*: yet|
4.2.69-71/1633-5 I ... gentlewoman] *verse*: thing| on|
4.2.72-3/1636-7 I ... nick] *verse*: me|
4.2.134-5/1698-9 Marry ... day] *verse*: house|
4.4.42/1790 I ... peasant] *2 lines*: wilt|
4.4.50-1/1798-9 No ... again] *verse*: not|
4.4.53-6/1801-4 Ay ... greater] *verse*: me| place| dog|
5.3.1/2017 Come ... captain] *2 lines*: patient|

The Taming of the Shrew

Ind.1.29/29 What's ... breathe] *prose*
Ind.1.30-31/30-31 He ... soundly] *prose*
Ind.1.77/77 Bid ... welcome] *2 lines*: near|
Ind.2.99-100/235-6 Marry ... wife] enough|
Ind.2.133-4/269-70 Marry ... trick] *prose*
Ind.2.137-8/273-4 Well ... younger] *3 lines*: see't| side|
1.1.59/333 Mates ... for you] *2 lines*: that|
1.1.78-9/352-3 A ... why] *prose*
1.1.102-4/376-8 Why ... Ha] *verse*: not| though| take|
1.1.237-42/511-16 So ... Lucentio] *prose*
1.2.13/539 My ... first] *2 lines*: quarrelsome|
1.2.34-5/560-1 Whom ... worst] *prose*
1.2.162-3/688-9 Trow ... Minola] *1 line*
1.2.218-20/744-6 Gentlemen ... Minola] *verse*: bold| way|
2.1.41-2/850-1 And ... virtuous] *prose*
2.1.71-3/879-81 Saving ... forward] *prose*
2.1.75/883 I ... wooing] curse|
2.1.76-83/884-91 Neighbour ... service] *verse*: gift| express| been| any| hath| cunning| languages| mathematics|
2.1.213-14/1021-2 Who ... tail] *prose*
2.1.388-9/1196-7 Well ... know] resolved|
3.1.27-9/1242-4 Here ... *senis*] *prose*
3.2.80-4/1387-91 Nay ... many] *prose*
3.3.40-56/1474-90 Trembled ... play] *prose*
3.3.80/1513 Nay ... today] *2 lines*: then|
4.1.127-8/1687-8 Where ... Soud, soud, soud, soud] Kate|
4.1.168-73/1728-33 In ... hither] *prose*
4.3.107/1986 O ... thimble] *2 lines*: arrogance|
4.3.159-61/2038-40 O ... fie, fie, fie] *verse*: for| use|
4.4.61-2/2134-5 It ... straight] well|
5.2.88-9/2489-90 How ... answer] *prose*
5.2.91-2/2492-3 Sirrah ... forthwith] *prose*
5.2.98-9/2299-2500 Worse ... endured] come|
5.2.135-6/2536-7 Katherine ... husbands] *prose*

Additional Passages

A.3-4 Gi's ... things] *verse*: where's|
C.3-5 I ... prison] *verse*: sending| Vary|
C.6 No ... away] *verse*: Lord|
C.7-8 Are ... again] *verse*: well|
E.8-9 Sim ... lord] *verse*: the|

The First Part of the Contention

1.1.60-7/60-7 They ... Warwick] F; *prose* Q
1.1.207/207 And ... cause] *2 lines* F: York|
1.1.208/208 Then ... main] Q; *2 lines* F: away|. See textual notes.
1.1.209/209 Unto ... lost] Q; *2 lines* F: main|
1.3.224-6/590-3 Away ... away] *prose* F. See the first textual note to 1.3.225/591.
1.4.25-8/617-20 Asnath ... hence] God| at| speak| F
1.4.36-7/628-9 Let ... stand] *3 lines* F: castles| plains|. The metre is rough here, however arranged; but it is especially unlikely that one irregular verse line stood between two incomplete lines. As rearranged, one regular line is followed by a hexameter with an extra syllable after the caesura. See also 2.1.188-9/850-1.
1.4.58-9/650-1 Why ... posse] *1 line*
1.4.64/656 Thither ... them] *2 lines*: news|
1.4.68/660 At ... ho] *2 lines*: lord|
2.1.23/685 What ... peremptory] *2 lines*: Cardinal|
2.1.24-5/686-7 Tantaene ... malice] *2 lines*: hot|
2.1.32-3/694-5 I ... peers] Queen|
2.1.38-9/700-70 Dare ... the dare] *prose* Q
2.1.40-1/702-3 I ... Gaunt] *prose* Q
2.1.46-7/708-9 Ay ... grove] *3 lines*: peep| evening|
2.1.50/712 We ... sword] *2 lines*: sport|
2.1.51-2/713-14 True ... grove] *2 lines*: advised|. See textual note to 2.1.52-3/714-15.
2.1.55/717 Now ... this] *2 lines*: priest|
2.1.56-7/718-19 Medice ... yourself] protect | yourself (*prose? overflow?*)
2.1.58/720 The ... lords] Q; *2 lines* F: high|
2.1.83-4/745-6 Hadst ... told] Q; *prose? overflow?* F (have | told)
2.1.85/747 At ... grace] your | grace (*prose? overflow?*)
2.1.86/748 Poor ... thee] *2 lines*: soul|
2.1.89-90/751-2 Tell ... shrine] *3 lines*: fellow| devotion|
2.1.91-4/753-6 God ... thee] *5 lines*: devotion| oft'ner| Alban| shrine|
2.1.95-6/757-8 Most ... so] *3 lines*: forsooth| voice|
2.1.103/765 Mass ... so] *prose* (*overflow?*)
2.1.104-5/767-8 Alas ... life] *prose*

640

LINEATION NOTES

2.1.111/773 Say'st . . . of] *prose* (*or perhaps overflow*: cloak|)
2.1.113–14/775–6 And . . . hose] *1 line* Q
2.1.130–8/792–800 Then . . . again] *prose* Q; *11 lines* F: there| Christendom| blind| names| wear| colours| all| impossible| miracle| great|
2.1.140–1/802–3 My . . . whips] *3 lines* Q, F: Albans| town|
2.1.145–7/807–9 Bring . . . away] This edition; *1 verse line* Q, F: (. . . by and by|), followed by *prose*. See textual notes.
2.1.147–8/809–10 Alas . . . alone] *1 line* Q, F. See textual notes.
2.1.150–1/812–13 Well . . . stool] Q; F's intentions are unclear: it divides after 'legs.', but the line in any case fills the measure; 'stool' flows over, but might have been intended as verse.
2.1.153/815 Come . . . quickly] F; *prose* Q
2.1.188–9/850–1 Let . . . stand] *3 lines*: castles| plains|. See the lineation note to 1.4.36–7/628–9.
2.2.34–5/913–14 The . . . daughter] *3 lines*: Clarence| crown|
2.2.45–6/924–5 Marrièd . . . fifth son] *3 lines*: Cambridge| Langley|. See textual note to 2.2.45/924.
2.2.47–50/926–9 By . . . Clarence] *5 lines*: kingdom| March| Mortimer| daughter|
2.2.64–5/943–5 We . . . stained] *3 lines*: lord| crowned|
2.3.1/962 Stand . . . wife] *2 lines*: Cobham|
2.3.22–5/983–6 Stay . . . feet] *5 lines*: Gloucester| staff| be| guide|
2.3.64–6/1025–7 Here's . . . man] F; *verse* Q: drink|
2.3.67–8/1028–9 Let . . . Peter] F; *verse* Q: all|
2.3.73–5/1034–6 And here's . . . prentices] *verse* Q: Peter|; F, *also verse, omits* 'And here's . . . and' *and divides* master|
2.4.72/1142 holden . . . month] *verse* (?)
2.4.84–5/1154–5 And . . . farewell] her| ; F; live| her| Q
2.4.106–7/1176–7 Madam . . . sheet] *2 lines*: done|
3.1.104/1285 'Tis . . . France] *2 lines*: lord|
3.1.107/1288 Is . . . it] *2 lines*: so|
3.1.223/1404 Free . . . beams] *2 lines*: lords|
3.2.238/1801 Why . . . drawn] *2 lines*: lords|
4.1.70/2081 Strike . . . own] *1 type line*
4.1.116–17/2127–8 CAPTAIN . . . death] *prose*; CAPTAIN . . . thee *1 type line*. See the textual note.
4.1.118–19/2129–30 Paene . . . fear] *1 line*
4.2.134–5/2296–7 Marry . . . not] Q; *prose* F (?): March | married
4.2.149–50/2311–12 And . . . what] *prose* F (?): words | that
4.2.153/2315 He . . . myself] *prose* F
4.2.188–9/2350–1 But . . . forward] *prose*
4.4.7/2375 What . . . supplication] This edition; *prose* F (?): rebels' | supplication. The rest of the scene is verse, and this line is an acceptable hexameter, if (as elsewhere) 'to the' is elided.
4.4.20–1/2388–9 How . . . death] This edition; madam| F. See textual note to 4.4.19–24.1/2387–92.1.
4.5.2–6/2429–33 No . . . rebels] *verse* Q, F: slain| bridge| them| Tower|. See the textual notes.
4.6.1–6/2441–6 Now . . . Lord Mortimer] *verse*: city| Stone| cost| wine| reign| any|
4.6.13–15/2453–5 Come . . . away] *verse* Q, F: them| fire| too|
4.7.1–2/2456–7 So . . . all] *verse* Q (. . . Savoy, | Others . . .); *verse* F? (. . . Savoy: | Others . . .)
4.7.15–16/2471–2 Then . . . out] *verse*: statutes|
4.7.130–2/2589–91 Why . . . house] *verse* Q: me|
4.7.133–40/2592–9 Dick . . . mace] *verse* Q: place| you'll| pence| dinner| mouth| cogging| conclude|
4.7.141/2600 My lord, when| My lord, | When F
4.7.143–6/2602–5 He . . . smock] *verse* Q: it| following|
4.7.148–54/2607–13 But . . . Away] *verse*: braver| well| again| up| Soldiers| night| maces| corner|. See textual note to 4.7.141/2600.
4.7.157–8/2616–17 What . . . kill] *verse*: hear| parley|. See textual notes.
4.7.187–8/2646 We'll . . . Cade] *verse*: Cade | We'll
4.7.208–9/2666–7 A . . . and Clifford] *verse*: a Clifford|
4.8.42/2724 My . . . willingly] *2 lines*: lord|. See textual notes.

Additional Passages

D.1 What . . . pause] *2 lines* F: York|

Richard Duke of York

1.1.113/113 You . . . lose] O; *2 lines* F: now|
1.1.116/116 Good . . . arms] O; *2 lines* F: brother|
1.1.156/156 Thou . . . power] O; *2 lines*: deceived|
1.1.212/212 Here . . . anger] *2 lines*: queen|
1.1.265/265 Poor . . . son] *2 lines*: Queen|
1.2.49/323 The . . . lords] *2 lines*: Queen|
1.2.53/327 Ay . . . them] *2 lines*: sword|
1.2.69/343 I . . . order] *2 lines*: drums|
1.3.22–3/371–2 In . . . enter] *3 lines*: boy| passage|
1.4.112/513 She-wolf . . . wolves of France] O; *2 lines* F: |but
1.4.121/522 Were . . . shameless] O; *2 lines* F: thee|
1.4.153–4/554–5 That . . . blood] O; *3 lines* F: his| touched|
2.1.33/615 'Tis . . . of] *2 lines*: strange|
2.1.41/623 Nay . . . it] *2 lines*: Daughters|
2.2.101/892 What . . . crown] O; *2 lines* F: Henry|
2.3.44/1012 Brother . . . Warwick] *2 lines*: Brother|
2.3.48/1016 Away . . . farewell] O; *2 lines* F: away|
2.6.68/1244 If . . . words] *2 lines*: think'st|
2.6.76/1252 They . . . wont] O; *2 lines* F: *Clifford*|
3.1.93/1379 We . . . Edward] *2 lines*: king | king
3.2.101/1487 No . . . mother] *2 lines*: Daughters|
3.3.16–18/1597–9 And . . . mischance] *4 lines*: side| yoke| triumph|
3.3.21/1602 Those . . . thoughts] *2 lines*: words|
3.3.38/1619 Renowned . . . storm] *2 lines*: Queen|
3.3.59/1640 And . . . behalf] O; *2 lines* F: madam|
3.3.134/1715 Then . . . Edwards] *2 lines*: thus|
3.3.163/1744 My . . . you] O; *2 lines* F: ambassador|
3.3.166/1747 And . . . not] O; *2 lines* F: you|
3.3.169–70/1750–1 Nay . . . best] *prose*
3.3.171/1752 Warwick . . . queen] *2 lines*: news|
3.3.199/1780 Warwick . . . love] *2 lines*: Warwick|
3.3.234/1815 But . . . men] *2 lines*: Warwick|
4.1.9/1855 Now . . . choice] *2 lines*: Clarence|
4.1.11/1857 As . . . Warwick] *2 lines*: France|
4.1.20/1866 Not . . . severed] This edition (G.T.); *2 lines* F: no| ; *2 lines* CAPELL : Not I|. Hexameters are acceptable: the full line would not fit F's measure.
4.1.21–2/1867–8 Whom . . . well together] *3 lines*: together| them|
4.1.28–30/1874–6 Then . . . Bona] *4 lines*: opinion| enemy| marriage|
4.1.60/1906 In . . . judgement] *2 lines*: yourself|
4.1.87–8/1933–4 Go . . . them] *3 lines*: thee| words|
4.1.102/1948 Tell . . . done] *2 lines*: she|
4.1.114/1960 Ay . . . friendship] O; *2 lines* F: sovereign|
4.1.116/1962 Belike . . . younger] *2 lines*: elder|
4.1.122/1968 Not . . . matter] *2 lines*: I|
4.4.3/2051 The . . . parted] O; *2 lines* F: duke|
4.4.14/2062 Yea . . . too] *2 lines*: Clarence|
4.5.4/2089 What . . . Warwick] O; *2 lines* F: battle|
4.5.25/2110 But . . . become] *2 lines*: madam|
4.6.14/2134 This . . . game] *2 lines*: lord|
4.6.15/2135 Nay . . . stand] *2 lines*: man|
4.6.26/2146 Huntsman . . . along] *2 lines*: thou|
4.6.29/2149 Bishop . . . frown] *2 lines*: farewell|
4.7.68–9/2218–19 Come . . . thoughts] *3 lines*: hope| truth|
4.8.10/2262 The . . . this] *2 lines*: Brother|
4.8.17/2269 My . . . coming] O; *2 lines* F: lords|
4.8.45–7/2297–9 Thanks . . . rest] *4 lines*: Montgomery| crown| dukedom|
4.8.59/2311 When . . . claim] *2 lines*: stronger|
4.8.76/2328 Thanks . . . all] *2 lines*: Montgomery|
5.1.48/2451 Come . . . down.] *2 lines*: Warwick|
5.1.53/2456 Sail . . . friend] *2 lines*: canst|
5.1.110/2513 What . . . fight] *2 lines*: Warwick|
5.2.48/2567 Sweet . . . yourselves] O; *2 lines* F: soul|
5.6.57/2821 I'll . . . speech] *2 lines*: more|

641

Titus Andronicus

1.1.286-7/286-7	What...Rome]	*1 line*
2.1.79-80/570-1	Aaron...love]	propose|
2.2.16-17/643-4	I say...more]	F; *1 line* Q
3.2.65/1380	Came...him]	*2 lines* F: merry|
3.2.66/1381	Pardon...fly]	*2 lines* F: sir|
4.2.20-1/1547-8	*Integer...arcu*]	*1 line*
4.2.64-5/1591-2	Why...issue]	*1 line*
4.2.168-9/1695-6	Aaron...secrets]	*1 line*
4.3.4-8/1710-14	*Terras...sea*]	*4 lines*: Marcus| tools| ocean|
4.3.77/1783	News...come]	*2 lines*: heaven|
4.3.84-5/1790-1	Alas...life]	*verse*: Jupiter|
4.3.89/1795	From...there]	*1 line of verse*
4.3.98-9/1804-5	Give...supplication]	ink|
5.1.95-6/2027-8	Why...it]	trimmed|

Henry VI Part One

1.1.33/33 The...prayed] *2 lines*: it|
1.3.16/214 Let's...slaves] *2 lines*: town|
1.5.16-17/432-3 And...longer] CAIRNCROSS (Vaughan); *3 lines* F: watched| watch|; *3 lines* MALONE: watched| them|. See textual notes. If 'And...them' had stood in the manuscript as a single line, it would not have fitted into F's column; in the circumstances Compositor A sometimes carried over part of a long line, and relined subsequent verse accordingly.
1.8.11/576 Why...town] *2 lines*: aloud|
2.3.27/764 What...goes] *2 lines*: now|
2.3.43/780 Laughest...moan] *2 lines*: wretch|
2.4.1/820 Great...silence] *2 lines*: gentlemen|
3.5.10-11/1334-5 What...chair] *3 lines*: graybeard| death|
3.7.78/1498 I...hers] *2 lines*: vanquishèd|
3.7.90/1510 Now...powers] *2 lines*: lords|
3.8.38/1549 Villain...such] *2 lines*: knowest|
4.1.133/1689 It...friends] *2 lines*: highness|
5.6.165/2556 How...stand] *2 lines*: Charles|

Richard III

1.1.41/41 Dive...comes] F; *2 lines* Q: soul|
1.1.43-5/43-5 His...Tower] *2 lines* Q: appointed|; *2 lines* F: safety|
1.1.94-5/94-5 A cherry...tongue] *1 line* QF
1.1.99-101/99-101 Naught...alone] Q; Shore| her| F
1.1.104-5/104-5 I...Duke] forbear| Q; *3 lines* F: grace| forbear|
1.2.39/201 Unmannered...command] Q; *2 lines* F: dog|
1.2.50/212 Foul...not] Q; *2 lines* F: devil|
1.2.83-4/245 Fouler...thyself] Q; thee| current| F
1.2.93/255 In...saw] Q; *2 lines* F: liest|
1.2.101/263 Didst...ye] *1 type line* Q
1.2.102/264 Dost...too] Q; *2 lines* F: hedgehog|
1.2.111/273 LADY ANNE...bedchamber] *1 type line* Q
1.2.132/294 Curse...both] Q; *2 lines* F: creature|
1.2.142/304 LADY ANNE...Plantagenet] *1 type line* Q
1.2.144/306 Here...me] *2 lines* QF: Here|
1.2.225/387 And...Ha] Q; *2 lines* F: nothing|
1.3.117/529 'Tis...forgot] Q; *2 lines* F: speak|
1.3.118/530 Out...well] Q; *2 lines* F: devil|
1.3.121/533 Ere...king] Q; *2 lines* F: queen|
1.3.126/538 Ay...thine] Q; *2 lines* F: blood|
1.3.232/644 QUEEN MARGARET Richard...Ha] *1 type line* QF
1.3.295/707 What...counsel]] Q; *2 lines* F: me|
1.4.81/846 What...hither] Q; *prose* F
1.4.85-7/850-2 'Tis...more] *prose* QF
1.4.95-6/860-1 You...well] *verse* F: wisdom|
1.4.98-9/863-4 No...wakes] F; *verse* Q: cowardly|
1.4.104-5/868-9 The...me] F; *verse* Q: bred|

1.4.107-9/871-3 Not...me] *verse* Q: damned|; *verse* F: warrant| which|
1.4.114-16/878-80 Nay...twenty] *verse* Q: will|; *verse* F: little| change|
1.4.126-7/889-90 When...out] F; *verse* Q: reward|
1.4.131-41/894-904 I'll...without it] F; *verse* Q: with it, it is a dangerous thing| steal| checks him| detects| mutinies| obstacles| found| out of all| every| to trust to|
1.4.142-3/905-6 'Swounds...Duke] F; *verse* Q: me|
1.4.144-6/907-9 Take...sigh] *verse* QF|
1.4.149-50/912-13 Spoke...work] *verse* QF(?): reputation|
1.4.151-3/914-16 Take...room] F; *verse* Q: sword|
1.4.169/932 CLARENCE To...Ay, ay] *1 type line* Q
1.4.198-9/961-2 Thou...Lancaster] F; sacrament| Q
1.4.227/990 You...you] *2 lines* F: deceived|
1.4.237/1000 As...yourself] Q; *2 lines* F: harvest|
1.4.269-70/1032-3 How...been] Q; *prose* F. If set as verse, both these lines would have required turn-overs; and, as there was no possibility of turning up into the cramped 1.4.268/1030, to fit them onto the page B had to set them as prose. See textual notes.
2.1.25/1066 Dorset...Marquis] *2 lines* F: him|
2.1.56-7/1097-8 Hold...rage] *1 line* QF
2.1.82/1123 Who...is?] Q; *2 lines* F: dead|
2.1.134-5/1175-6 Come...Clarence] F; *1 line* Q
2.4.26/1380 How...it] Q; *2 lines* F: York|
2.4.37-8/1391-2 Here...Marquis] Q; *1 line* F. See textual notes.
2.4.38-9/1392-3 Such...report] *1 line* QF
2.4.41-2/1395-6 Lord...prisoners] Q; *3 lines* F: Gray| them|
2.4.43-4/1397-8 The...Buckingham] *1 line* QF
2.4.61-2/1415-16 Make...preposterous] F; against blood| Q
3.1.1/1427 Welcome...chamber] Q; *2 lines* F: London|
3.1.16/1442 God...none] Q; *2 lines* F: friends|
3.1.124-5/1550-1 RICHARD...Little] *1 type line* Q
3.1.156-7/1582-3 Well...intend] Catesby| QF. The first line would not have fit the measure in Q or F.
3.1.168-70/1594-6 Well...purpose] *4 lines* Q: this| off| affected|; *4 lines* F: this| off| Hastings|
3.1.188/1614 My...perceive] Q; *2 lines* F: lord|
3.1.190/1616 Chop...determine] Q; *2 lines* F: head|
3.2.38/1661 How...crown] Q; *2 lines* F: garland|
3.2.86/1709 Come...lord] *2 lines* F: you|
3.3.16/1757 Then...Buckingham] Q; *2 lines* F: Richard|
3.4.10-12/1775-7 We...you of mine] F; faces| more of mine| Q
3.4.46-7/1811-12 Where...strawberries] F; *1 line* Q
3.4.76-8/1841-3 Off...done] F; Paul| swear| Q. See textual notes.
3.5.1/1873 Come...colour] Q; *2 lines* F: cousin|
3.5.32-4/1904-6 The...preservation] *4 lines* F: traitor| lived| believe|; *3 lines* Q: traitor| imagined|
3.5.68-9/1940-1 Yet...farewell] F; *1 line* Q
3.6.10-11/1986-7 Here's...device] Q; while| F
3.7.42/2032 What...speak] Q; *2 lines* F: | would
3.7.82-3/2072-3 I fear...grace] F; now Catesby| Q
3.7.114/2104 You...grace] Q; *2 lines* F: | would
4.1.1/2228 Who...Plantagenet] Q; *2 lines* F: here|
4.1.5-6/2232-3 God...day] happy| F
4.1.33-5/2260-2 Ah...news] Q; asunder| beat| F. F was set by Compositor A, prone to such erratic mislineation; initial part-lines (F) are much less common than terminal part-lines (Q).
4.2.3-5/2326-8 Give...seated] Q; hand| assistance| F
4.2.42/2365 I...boy] hither| F
4.2.48-51/2371-4 Know...abides] This edition; *3 lines* F: Dorset| Richmond|; *2 lines* Q: Dorset| (*leaving 'abides' indented on a line on its own, and not capitalized*). See textual note.
4.2.72/2395 Please...enemies] Q; *2 lines* F: you|. There is no difficulty with a hexameter here, and F's lineation may result merely from the ambiguous placement of the marginal insertions.
4.2.79/2402 Thou...Tyrrell] Q; *2 lines* F: music|
4.4.125/2630 Thy...mine] Q; *2 lines* F: sharp|
4.4.145/2650 Thou...Clarence] Q; *2 lines* F: | where
4.4.176/2681 Faith...grace] Q; *2 lines* F: | that

LINEATION NOTES

4.4.452-4/2957-9   The Breton . . . banks] F; Dorsetshire| Q
5.3.5/3052   Norfolk . . . not] Q; *2 lines* F: knocks|
5.4.20/3085   Good night . . . gentlemen] *2 lines* F: Blunt|
5.5.18-19/3109-10   Look . . . Ratcliffe] *1 line* QF
5.6.6-7/3321-2   Tell . . . today] there| QF
5.6.10-11/3325-6   A . . . Ratcliffe] *1 line* QF

Additional Passages

E.1   Why . . . Buckingham] *2 lines* F: train|

The Comedy of Errors

60-1.1.60-1/60-1   Unwilling . . . aboard] *1 line*
2.1.50/313   Spake . . . meaning] *prose*
2.1.58/321   I . . . stark made] *2 lines* : cuckold mad|
2.1.69-73/332-6   Quoth my . . . there] *prose*
2.2.45-6/423-4   Why . . . me] *prose* (?): wherefore,| for
2.2.47-9/425-7   Was . . . you] *prose*
2.2.158-9/536-7   SYRACUSIAN ANTIPHOLUS By . . . me] *1 type line*
3.1.49-50/649-50   Faith . . . master] *1 line*
3.1.50-1/650-1   O . . . staff] *proverb*|
3.2.60-1/784-5   No . . . part] *1 line*
3.2.71-80/795-804   Why . . . how besides thy self] *verse* (each speech 1 verse line)
4.2.44-6/1073-5   I . . . desk] *prose*
4.2.55-7/1084-6   O . . . season] *prose*
4.3.15/1109   What . . . mean] *prose* (?)
4.3.34-6/1128-30   Well . . . gone] *verse*: foolery|
4.3.51-2/1145-6   Nay . . . again] *1 verse line*
4.3.72-6/1166-70   A rush . . . it] *prose*
4.3.80/1174   Fly . . . know] *prose* (?)
4.4.111-12/1301-2   I . . . rescue] *prose* (?), *or 1 verse line* (run-over 'res-|cue')
4.4.112-13/1302-3   Masters . . . him] *prose*
4.4.128-9/1318-19   Will . . . devil] *prose*
4.4.146-7/1336-7   And . . . again] swords|
5.1.196-7/1545-6   Unless . . . Dromio] *prose*

Love's Labour's Lost

Unattributed lineation to the right of the square bracket may be assumed to be QF.

2.1.105-6/582-3   'Tis . . . it] F; *1 line* Q
2.1.116-17/593-4   How . . . question] *1 line*
2.1.204-5/681-2   Good . . . Fauconbridge] F; *1 line* Q
2.1.206-7/683-4   Nay . . . lady] F; *1 line* Q
3.1.56-7/789-90   The . . . slow] *prose*
3.1.157-8/889-90   It . . . this] afternoon|
3.1.170-1/901-2   A . . . constable] *1 line* Q; critic| F
3.1.172-3/903-4   A . . . magnificent] F; *1 line* Q
4.1.53/984   I . . . Rosaline] *2 lines* : Biron|
4.1.126-7/1058-9   An . . . can] F; *1 line* Q
4.2.22-3/1101-2   Twice-sod . . . look] *prose*
4.2.28-9/1107-8   And . . . be] *prose*
4.2.57-62/1135-40   The . . . more 'l'] *12 lines*: pricked| pricket| not a sore| shooting| sore| thicket| sorel| a-hooting| to 'sore'| sore 'l'| make|
4.2.96-7/1174-5   Venezia . . . prezia] *prose*
4.3.1-2/1242-3   The . . . myself] *verse*: deer|
4.3.181-4/1423-6   In . . . limb] *prose*
4.3.209-10/1451-2   True . . . gone] *1 line*
5.2.3-4/1753-4   A . . . King] *prose*
5.2.15-18/1765-8   And . . . long] *prose*
5.2.47/1797   But . . . Dumaine] *2 lines* : you|
5.2.159-60/1909-10   A . . . views] *prose*
5.2.174/1924   What . . . Boyet] *2 lines* : strangers|
5.2.234-5/1984-5   Seventh . . . with you] cog|

5.2.239-40/1989-90   Say . . . lady] *1 line*
5.2.240-1/1990-1   Please . . . adieu] *1 line*
5.2.312-3/2061-2   Gone . . . thither] *prose* Q; |tent F
5.2.440-1/2189-90   Peace . . . forswear] F; *prose* Q
5.2.482-3/2231-2   Full . . . run] *prose*
5.2.491-2/2240-1   You . . . thrice, sir] *prose*
5.2.534-5/2284-5   And . . . five] *prose*
5.2.552-3/2302-3   If . . . done] *1 line of verse*
5.2.638-9/2390-1   The . . . gift] *prose*
5.2.654-6/2406-8   The . . . man] *verse*: rotten| buried|
5.2.710-11/2462-3   Welcome . . . merriment] *prose*
5.2.712-13/2464-5   I . . . father] *prose*

A Midsummer Night's Dream

Unattributed lineation to the right of the square bracket may be assumed to be QF.

1.1.53/53   So . . . he is] *1 type line* Q
1.2.27-34/278-85   The . . . Fates] *prose*
1.2.53-4/304-5   BOTTOM . . . tailor] *1 type line* Q
1.2.57/308   Tom . . . Tinker] Q1; indented on new line in F; *first line of a new page* Q2: (*previous line does not fill measure*)
2.1.2-9/357-64   Over hill . . . green] *4 lines* QF: brier| fire| sphere|
2.1.42-3/397-8   Thou . . . night] F; *1 line* Q
2.1.59/414   And . . . gone] *2 lines* F: mistress|
2.1.60/415   Ill . . . Titania] *2 lines* F: moonlight|
2.1.115-16/470-1   And . . . dissension] F2; evils| Q, F1
2.1.175-6/530-1   I'll . . . minutes] *1 line*
2.2.16-17/639-40   Never . . . charm] *1 line*
3.1.92-5/879-82   Ninus' . . . cue] Q2; *verse* Q1: |that |all
3.2.48-9/1029-30   Being . . . too] *1 line*
3.2.80-1/1061-2   And . . . or no] no more|
3.2.258-9/1239-40   No . . . follow] Q1; loose| Q2, F. See textual note.
3.2.263-4/1244-5   Why . . . love] rude| Q2, F
3.2.397-400/1378-81   Up . . . down] *2 lines* (*justified*) Q1: |I am; *prose* Q2, F
3.2.401/1382   Here comes one] Q1; *prose* Q2, F
3.2.402/1383   Where . . . now] *2 lines* F: Demetrius|
3.2.404-5/1385-6   Follow . . . ground] *1 line*
3.3.37-8/1431-2   I'll . . . remedy] *1 line*
3.3.40-1/1434-5   True . . . eye] *1 line*
3.3.45-6/1439-40   Jack . . . ill] *1 line*
4.1.19-20/1460-1   Give . . . good monsieur] *verse* Q2, F: |Pray
4.1.27/1468   What . . . love] *prose*
4.1.34-5/1475-6   I . . . nuts] hoard| Q1; *3 lines* Q2, F: fairy| hoard|
4.1.45/1486   Welcome . . . sight] *2 lines* F: Robin|
4.1.164-6/1605-7   But . . . gaud] love| snow|
4.1.184-5/1625-6   We'll . . . Hippolyta] Q2, F; *1 line* Q1
4.1.196-7/1637-8   Why . . . dreams] *prose*
4.2.21/1679   hanged. He] Q2, F; Q1 does not drive out the line to its measure, but leaves a gap after 'hang'd'; 'He' begins a new line.
5.1.5-6/1705-6   Such . . . More] *1 line*
5.1.6-8/1706-8   than . . . compact] Q2, F; *2 lines* Q1: lunatic|
5.1.12-13/1712-13   The . . . glance] *1 line*
5.1.13-14/1713-14   from . . . as] Q2, F; *1 line* Q
5.1.14-18/1714-18   imagination . . . imagination] *4 lines*: things| shapes| habitation|
5.1.29-30/1729-30   Joy . . . hearts] F2; days| Q, F1
5.1.30-1/1730-1   More . . . bed] F2; *prose* Q, F1
5.1.33-8/1733-8   To . . . Egeus] Q2, F; *4 lines* Q1: Between| manager| play|
5.1.58-60/1758-60   'Merry' . . . discord] ice| concord| Q1; *prose* Q2, F
5.1.66-70/1766-70   And . . . shed] F2; *5 lines* Q, F1: Pyramus| saw| water| laughter|
5.1.76-8/1776-8   No . . . world] *2 lines* : heard|

643

LINEATION NOTES

5.1.81-3/1781-3 I...it] *2 lines*: anything|
5.1.91-2/1791-2 And...merit] respect| QF. Whether or not something has been omitted, it seems most unlikely that Shakespeare intended a hexameter followed by a part-line, especially when the hexameter has a reversed stress after the caesura and a strong enjambment.
5.1.182-6/1882-6 No...comes] *verse*: is| spy| fall|
5.1.192-3/1892-3 To...Thisbe?] *1 line*
5.1.239-40/1940-1 This...be] *prose* F
5.1.244-5/1945-6 He...snuff] *verse* Q2, F: candle|
5.1.262-3/1963-4 Well...grace] *verse* F:| Truly
5.1.271-81/1972-82 But...thrum] *6 lines*: knight| here| be| dear| blood|
5.1.283-4/1984-5 This...sad] *verse* F: friend|
5.1.290-300/1991-2001 Come...flight] *6 lines*: wound| Pyramus| hop| thus.| sky|
5.1.307-8/2008-9 How...lover] *verse* Q2, F: before|
5.1.309-10/2010-11 She...play] *verse* F: starlight|. See textual notes.
5.1.319-341/2020-2042 Asleep...ends] *15 lines*: dove| arise| tomb| eyes| nose| cheeks| moan| leeks| me| milk| shore| silk| sword| imbrue|
5.2.25-6/2089-90 And...trippingly] *1 line*

Romeo and Juliet

1.1.225-6/239-40 'Tis...more] *1 line*
1.2.64-72/313-21 Signor...Helena] *prose*
1.3.2-4/354-6 Now...Juliet] *prose*
1.3.8-11/360-3 This...age] *prose*
1.3.18-50/370-402 Even...Ay] *prose*
1.3.52-59/404-11 Yes...Ay] *prose*
1.3.61-64/413-16 Peace...wish] *prose*
1.3.69-70/421-2 An...teat] *prose*
1.3.77-8/429-30 A...wax] *world*
1.4.56-92/514-50 She...bodes] *verse arrangement after* Q1; *prose* Q2. See textual notes.
1.5.3-5/576-8 When...thing] *verse*? ('When...hands' *justified*; 'and' *capitalized*)
1.5.13-15/587-89 We...all] *verse*: boys|
2.1.27-8/758-9 That...name] spite|
2.1.41-2/772-3 Go then...found] here|
2.1.52-3/783-4 It...were] *1 line*
2.1.95-6/826-7 By...am] F; *1 line* Q2 (*with* am *turned up*)
2.1.190-1/921-2 And...Madam] *1 type line with no speech-prefix*
2.1.193-5/924-6 I...come] *1 type line with no speech-prefix*; 'Madam.' *placed after* 'By and by I come'
2.1.229-30/960-1 Good...morrow] Q1; *2 lines* Q2: |Parting. See textual note to 2.1.229-32/960-3.
2.3.6-7/1065-6 Tybalt...house] Q1; *prose* Q2
2.3.169-70/1232-3 Bid...afternoon] *1 line*
2.3.185-6/1248-9 Is...away] *prose*
2.3.188-98/1251-61 Well...letter] *prose*. See textual note.
2.4.15-16/1285-6 And...dead] *1 line*
2.4.58-9/1328-9 Where...repliest] be|
3.1.3-4/1388-9 And...stirring] *prose*
3.3.68/1793 Then...hair] Q1; *2 lines* Q2: speak|
3.3.83/1808 There...drunk] Q1; *2 lines* Q2: ground|
3.3.101-2/1826-7 As...gun] *1 line*
3.4.33-5/1933-4 Afore...night] Afore...and by| *justified*
3.5.128-9/2062-3 It...tears] Q4, F; *1 line* Q2
3.5.176/2110 God's...play] *2 lines*: mad|. See textual note to 3.5.176-7/2110-11.
3.5.212-3/2146-7 Faith...nothing] *1 line*
4.2.9-10/2311-12 Go...time] *1 line*
4.4.26-7/2433-4 Make...say] F; *1 line* Q2
4.4.128-9/2534-5 Musicians...play 'Heart's ease'] *verse*: ease'; |O
4.4.131-3/2537-9 O...me] *verse*: full|

4.4.140-1/2545-6 No...minstrel] *verse*: gleek|
4.4.143/2548-50 Then...me] Q4, F; *verse* Q2: pate| fa|
4.4.147-9/2552-4 Pray...my wit] *verse*: your wit|. See textual note to 4.4.149/2554.
4.4.149-51/2554-6 I...men] *verse*: dagger|
4.4.152-4/2557-9 When...sound] *1 line*
4.4.155-6/2560-1 Why...Minikin] *1 verse line*
4.4.164-6/2568-70 O...sounding] Q1; *verse* Q2: singer| sound|
4.4.167-8/2571-2 Then...redress] *1 line*
5.3.264-7/2954-7 All...time] *3 lines*: privy| fault|

Richard II

1.3.123-4/402 Draw...done] list|
2.1.187-9/801-3 Why...all] matter| please| Q; *4 lines* F: uncle| matter| not|
2.1.285-6/899-900 Sir...Quoint] *1 line*
2.2.50-1/966-7 And...Ravenspurgh] F; *1 line* Q
2.2.60-1/976-7 And...Bolingbroke] *1 line*
2.2.117-18/1033-4 I'll...men] *1 line*. See textual note to 2.2.119.
2.2.121-2/1037-8 All...seven] *1 line*
2.3.28-9/1103-4 The...together] F; resolved| Q
3.2.129-30/1432-3 Would...offence] F; hell|. Q. See textual note.
3.3.11-13/1528-30 The...you] F; *2 lines* Q: him|. See textual note.
3.3.22-3/1539-49 Royally...king] *1 line*
3.3.34-5/1551-2 Henry...hand] *1 line* Q; kiss| (*then* allegiance| come|) F. See textual note.
3.4.55-8/1779-82 They...year] *5 lines* Q: dead| are| king| trimmed|. See textual note.
4.1.16-18/1848-50 Than...lords] *4 lines* Q: withal| death| lords|
4.1.56-7/1888-9 Surrey...sword] F; *3 lines* Q: liest| sword|
4.1.309-10/2141-2 On...yourselves] F; *3 lines* Q: next| coronation|. See textual note.
4.1.322-3/2154-5 Come...day] plot|
5.2.99-100/2356-7 He...him] F; here| Q
5.3.11-12/2385-6 Takes...crew] F; *1 line* Q
5.3.44-5/2418-19 What...danger] breath|
5.5.14-15/2543-4 Against...again] *1 line*

King John

1.1.160/160 From...bear'st] *2 lines*: name|
2.1.133/409 There's...thee] *2 lines*: boy|
2.1.288-9/564-5 Saint...door] dragon|
3.1.235-8/1184-7 O...heaven] *3 lines*: kneeling| Dauphin|
4.2.165-6/1786-7 Of...suggestion] *1 line*
4.3.78/1969 I...law] *1 type line with* 'the law' *turned up*
4.3.117-19/2008-10 Beyond...Hubert] *2 lines*: mercy|

The Merchant of Venice

Q fourteen times indents isolated lines of dialogue well into the measure. Each of these indentations occurs within the stints of Brown's Compositor Y. We record them thus among the following notes: 'last word of line'| *indent* 'first word of indented line'.

1.1.5-6/5-6 I...me] sadness| *indent* makes
1.2.1-2/186-7 By...world] this| *indent* great
1.2.117-8/303-4 I...praise] *verse*: of| *indent* thy
1.2.129-31/315-17 Come...door] *prose*
1.3.4-5/321-2 For...bound] you| *indent* Antonio
1.3.7-8/324-5 May...answer] me?| *indent* Shall
1.3.9-10/326-7 Three...bound] months| *indent* and
1.3.95-6/412-13 I...signor] fast| *indent* But
1.3.139-40/456-7 Of...offer] me| *indent* This
1.3.176-7/493-4 Hie...kind] turn|

2.4.2-3/765-6   Disguise...hour] *1 line*
2.4.21-3/784-6   Go...torchbearer] *2 lines*: tonight|
2.4.25-6/788-9   Meet...hence] lodging|
2.5.8-9/810-11   Your...bidding] me| *indent* I
2.5.19-20/821-2   I...reproach] master| *indent* doth
2.5.40-1/842-3   Mistress...by] this| *indent* There
2.5.52-3/854-5   Do...find] *1 line*
2.6.45-6/903-4   Even...once] *1 line*
2.7.62-4/987-9   O...writing] death| scroll|
2.8.25-6/1029-30   Let...this] day| *indent* Or
3.2.65-6/1345-6   How...reply] *1 line*. See the textual note.
3.2.71/1351   I'll...bell] *2 lines*: it|
3.2.154-5/1434-5   A...account] times|
3.2.296-7/1576-7   What...bond] *1 line*
3.3.18-19/1622-3   It...men] cur| *indent* That
3.3.24-5/1628-9   I...hold] grant| *indent* this
3.4.45-6/1685-6   Now...honest-true] *1 line*

1 Henry IV

1.1.55-6/55-6   At...hour] spend|
1.1.75-6/75-6   A...of] it is|. See the textual note.
1.1.102-3/102-3   Cousin...lords] hold|
1.3.13/330   Have...lord] *1 type line*
1.3.113-14/430-1   He...alone] Glyndŵr|
1.3.211-12/528-9   Those...prisoners] F; *1 line* Q
1.3.246/563   NORTHUMBERLAND...true] *1 type line*
2.3.12-18/811-17   Got...him] *prose*
2.4.70-2/890-2   That...park] *prose*
2.4.74-5/894-5   Why...horse] *1 line*
2.4.75-81/895-901 Out...go] *prose*
2.4.83-6/903-6   Come...true] *prose*
2.5.483-5/1411-13 Banish...world] *prose*
2.5.513-14/1439-40 First...house] *prose*
2.5.516-17/1442-3 One...man] *prose*
2.5.532-3/1458-9   This...forth] *prose*
2.5.533-4/1459-60 Oldcastle...horse] *prose*
3.1.3-5/1482-4   Lord...map] *prose*
3.1.6-10/1485-9   No...heauen] F; *prose* Q
3.1.10-11/1489-90 And...of] *prose*
3.1.16-18/1495-7   Why...born] *prose*
3.1.104-5/1583-4   Yea...side] *prose*
3.1.106-7/1585-6   Gelding...you] F; *prose* Q
3.1.194/1673   She...here] *verse line*
3.1.194-5/1673-4   a...upon] F (|A...harlotry|); *prose* Q
3.1.246/1726   As...day] *verse line begins* God
3.2.71-2/1812-13   They...little] loathe|
3.2.93/1834   Be...world] *1 type line*
3.2.175-6/1916-17 Our...account] *3 lines*: meeting| march|
3.3.92-3/2011-12   What...man] *prose*
4.1.12-13/2136-7   Do...you] there|
4.1.53-5/2177-9   Faith...in] should| reversion|
4.2.79-81/2339-41 Well...guest] *prose*
4.3.13-14/2354-5   Let...fears] F; *1 line* Q
4.3.15-16/2356-7   DOUGLAS...Content] *1 type line*
4.3.18-19/2359-60 Come...are] be|
4.4.6-7/2462-3   My...tenor] *1 line*
4.4.21-2/2477-8   Why...Mortimer] fear|
5.1.121-2/2617-18 Hal...friendship] *verse*: battle|
5.1.123-4/2619-20 Nothing...farewell] *verse*: friendship|
5.2.26-7/2662-3   Deliver...cousin] F; *1 line* Q
5.2.92-3/2728-9   Let...stain] sword|
5.3.1-3/2737-9   What...head] *2 lines*: me|
5.3.17-18/2753-4   HOTSPUR...Here] *1 type line*
5.3.28/2764   Until...away] *1 type line*
5.3.43-4/2779-80   Whose...sword] *prose*
5.3.45-8/2781-4   O...sure] *prose*
5.3.48-50/2784-6   He...sword] *2 lines*: thee|
5.3.50-2/2786-8   Nay...wilt] *prose*

5.4.6-7/2803-4   I...tent] *1 line*
5.4.60-1/2857-8   Why...name] *1 line*

The Merry Wives of Windsor

1.1.4-5/4-5   In...Coram] *1 line, with turn-up*
1.1.108-9/107-8   I will...answered] *verse*: this|
1.1.147-50/146-9   Ha...liest] *prose*
1.1.220-1/219-20   That...her] *verse*: must|
1.3.80-1/383-4   Let...poor] *prose* (gourd and | fullam)
1.3.84/387   I...revenge] *2 lines*: operations|
1.3.96-7/399-400   Thou...on] *prose*
1.4.44/445   Ay...you] *verse line*
1.4.63-4/464-5   O...rapier] *verse*: closet|
2.1.13-18/573-8   By me...Falstaff] *3 lines*: night| might|
2.1.20-2/580-2   One...i'th'] *verse*: age| unweighed|
2.1.22-7/582-7   th'...down] *verse?*: dares| thrice| then| I'll|. These five lines are justified in F, but they all begin with upper case letters.
2.1.108-10/668-70 He...perpend] *prose*
2.1.113-15/673-5   Or...name] with|
2.1.120/680   Away...sense] *2 lines*: Nim|
2.1.143-4/702-3   I...go] *verse*: |Get
2.1.145-6/704-5   Faith...Page] *verse?*: head|. 'Faith...head' is justified; 'now' begins with a capital letter.
2.1.169-70/728-9   I...Garter] *verse*: that|
2.2.15/799   Didst...pence] *prose*
2.2.37-8/821-2   I'll...born] *verse*: sworn|
2.2.91-2/874-5   Ten...fail her] *verse (across page-break)*: eleven|
3.1.16-20/1194-8   To...To shallow] *prose*
3.1.21-5/1200-3   Melodious...shallow] *prose*
3.1.28/1206   To...falls] *prose*
3.1.41-2/1219-20   What...Parson] *verse*: word|
3.1.92-3/1271-3   Peace...Machiavel] *verse*: Garter|
3.2.7-8/1301-2   O...courtier] *1 line, with turn-up*
3.2.48-50/1342-4   And...of] *verse*: sir| Anne| money|
3.2.55-7/1349-50   You...altogether] *verse*: wholly for you|
3.2.76-7/1369-70   Well...Page's] *verse*: well|
3.3.16-17/1394-5   I...direction] *1 line, with turn-up (at page-break)*
3.3.19-20/1397-8   How...you] *1 line, with turn-up*
3.3.21-2/1399-1400 My...company] *verse*: door|
3.3.54-5/1432-3   A...neither] *verse*: John|
3.3.75-6/1453-4   Well...it] *verse*: you|
3.3.78-9/1456-7   Nay...mind] *verse*: do|
3.3.88-90/1465-6   O...ever] *verse*: done|
3.3.96-7/1472-3   What...in you] *verse*: upon you|
3.3.127-9/1504-6   Let...counsel, I'll in] *verse*: see't|
3.3.143-6/1520-3   Pray...this] *verse*: cause| jest|
3.3.151-2/1528-9   Buck...appear] *verse*: the buck| you buck|
3.3.158-9/1535-6   Good...much] *verse*: contented|
3.3.160-1/1537-8   True...me, gentlemen] *verse*: up, gentlemen| anon| (*with page-break after* anon)
3.3.163-4/1540-1   By...in France] *verse*: of France|
3.3.168-9/1545-6   I...John] *verse*: better|
3.4.22-3/1628-9   Break...himself] *verse*: Quickly|
3.4.24-5/1630-1   I'll...venturing] *1 line, with turn-up*
3.4.33-4/1639-40   And...you] *verse*: Fenton|
3.4.35-6/1641-2   She's...father] *verse*: coz|
3.4.88-9/1694-5   Come...enemy] Master| (*first line justified*)
3.4.97/1703   Look...doing] *verse line*
3.5.3/1718   Go...in't] *verse line*
3.5.24-5/1739-40   By...morrow] *verse*: mercy|
3.5.26-7/1741-2   Take...finely] *verse*: chalices|
3.5.39-40/1754-5   So...promise] *1 line, with turn-up*
3.5.56/1771   By...comes] *verse line*
3.5.58-9/1773-5   Now...wife] *verse*: know|
3.5.61-2/1776-7   Master...me] *verse*: you|
3.5.114-16/1829-31 In...more] *verse (?)*: this|
4.1.78-80/1933-5   Adieu...long] *verse*: Hugh|

LINEATION NOTES

4.2.42-3/1977-8 No . . . come] *verse*: basket|
4.2.92-3/2028-9 Hang . . . enough] *verse*: varlet|
4.3.175-6/2111-12 Are . . . woman] *verse*: ashamed|
4.3.186-7/2122-3 Let's . . . gentlemen] *verse*: further|
4.4.10-11/2169-70 Be . . . offence] *1 line*
4.4.17-18/2176-7 How . . . come] *prose*
4.4.27-8/2186-7 There . . . forest] the|
4.4.69/2228 That . . . vizards] *2 lines*: excellent|
4.4.70-1/2229-30 My . . . white] the|
4.4.79-80/2238-9 Let's . . . knaveries] *verse*: about it|
4.6.25-6/2395-6 Immediately . . . match] sir|
4.6.45/2415 Which . . . mother] *prose*
5.5.16-17/2512-13 Sir . . . male deer] *verse*: my deer|
5.5.33-5/2529-31 I . . . thus] *verse*: damned| fire|
5.5.82/2578 Vile . . . birth] *prose*
5.5.92-3/2588-9 Fie . . . desire] *2 lines*: luxury|
5.5.98-9/2594-5 Pinch . . . villainy] *1 line*
5.5.102-3/2598-9 Nay . . . turn] *prose*
5.5.108-10/2604-6 Now . . . Brooke] *verse*: now| knave|
5.5.120/2616 And . . . fairies] *verse line*
5.5.172/2668 Doctors doubt that] *verse line*
5.5.175-6/2671-2 Son? How . . . dispatched] *verse*: now, son|
5.5.191-2/2687-8 Why . . . garments] *verse*: folly| daughter|
5.5.210/2706 Now . . . Slender] *2 lines*: Mistress|
5.5.228-9/2724-5 Well . . . embraced] *prose*

2 Henry IV

1.1.1/41 Who . . . Earl] *2 lines* F: ho|
1.1.48/88 Staying . . . Again] *1 type line*
1.3.78-80/579-81 If . . . that] Q; *prose* F. See textual notes.
2.1.185-6/793-4 I . . . John] F; *verse* Q: here|
2.1.187-9/795-6 Sir . . . go] F; *verse* Q: long| up|
2.4.61-2/1099-1100 in him . . . hold] *unjustified type line*
2.4.151-5/1185-90 To . . . here] *prose*
2.4.160-6/1194-200 Shall . . . toys] *prose*
2.4.171-2/1204-5 Die . . . here] *prose*
2.4.176-81/1209-14 Then . . . nothings] *prose*
2.4.193-6/1226-9 What . . . say] *prose*
2.4.364/1399 Give . . . night] Q; *2 lines* F: cloak|
3.2.140/1666 Shall . . . John] Q; *verse* F: | Sir
3.2.146/1672 Francis Feeble] Q; *verse* F
3.2.151/1677 You may] Q; *verse line* F
4.1.2/1850 Tis . . . grace] Q; *prose* F
4.1.30-1/1878-9 Then . . . address] F; *1 line* Qc; Then my Lord *not in* Qa, Qb
4.1.100-1/1948-9 To . . . honours] *1 line* F
4.1.221-2/2069-70 Be . . . Westmorland] F; *1 line* Q
4.1.225/2073 Your . . . forward] Q; *prose* F
4.1.276/2124 You . . . Much too shallow] Q; *2 lines* F: Hastings|
4.1.297/2145 I . . . captain] Q; *2 lines* F: them|
4.1.299-300/2147-8 I . . . peace] Q; *3 lines* F: Grace| bestowed|
4.1.313/2161 The . . . shout] Q; *prose* F
4.2.3-4/2200-1 I . . . Dale] Q; *verse* F: sir|
4.2.66-8/2264-6 I . . . for thee] *prose*
4.2.78-80/2276-8 My . . . report] *prose*
4.2.81-2/2279-80 Fare . . . deserve] F; *prose* Q
4.3.12-13/2337-8 Humphrey . . . brother] *prose*
4.3.14/2339 I . . . Windsor] Q; *prose* F
4.3.16/2341 Is . . . him] Q; *prose* F
4.3.50/2375 Why . . . Thomas] Q; *prose* F
4.3.51/2376 He . . . London] Q; *prose* F
4.3.52/2377 And . . . that] Q (*omitting* Canst . . . that); *prose* F
4.3.53/2378 With . . . followers] Q; *prose* F
4.3.102/2427 And . . . sick] Q; *2 lines* F: news|
4.3.113/2438 My . . . up] Q; *prose* F
4.3.116/2441 Stand . . . well] Q; *2 lines* F: air|
4.3.129/2454 Speak . . . recovers] Q; *prose* F
4.3.140-1/2466-7 How . . . King] Q; *prose* F
4.3.143/2468 Heard . . . him] Q; *2 lines* F: yet|
4.3.145-6/2470-1 If . . . physic] Q; *verse* F: joy|
4.3.147-8/2472-3 Not . . . sleep] Q; *prose in 3 lines* F: lords| low|
4.3.175-8/2500-3 Which . . . me] Q; *5 lines* F: guard| arm| me| leave|
4.3.180/2505 What . . . Grace] Q (*omitting* How . . . Grace); *prose* F
4.3.182-3/2507-8 We . . . you] F; *prose* Q
4.3.184/2509 The . . . him] *prose*
4.3.186/2511 He . . . stayed] Q; *prose* F
4.3.187/2512 Where . . . pillow] Q; *prose* F
4.3.188/2513 When . . . here] Q; *prose* F
4.3.189/2514 The . . . out] Q; *2 lines* F: hence|
4.3.190-4/2515-19 Is . . . are] *as* Q *except* 4.3.190-1/2515-16 (*1 line* Q); suppose| Warwick| conjoins| me| F
4.3.198-204/2523-9 Have . . . flower] thoughts| industry| up| gold| invest| exercises|
4.3.204/2529 The virtuous sweets] *verse line* F; *not in* Q
4.3.204-8/2529-33 the . . . father] Q (*omitting* the virtuous sweets); wax| hive| pains| engrossments| F
4.3.267/2592 O . . . tears] Q; *2 lines* F: liege|
4.3.293/2618 Hast . . . liege] Q; *2 lines* F: up|
4.3.324/2649 Wounding . . . fears] Q; *2 lines* F: peace|
4.3.341/2666 Too . . . Harry] Q; *2 lines* F: state|
4.3.354/2679 Look, look . . . Lancaster] Q; *2 lines* F: Look, look|
4.3.355/2680 Health . . . father] Q; *2 lines* F: happiness|
4.3.356/2681 Thou . . . John] Q; *2 lines* F: peace|
4.3.364/2687 Laud . . . end] Q; *2 lines* F: heaven (*for* God)|
5.1.6/2698 Why, Davy] Q; *verse line* F
5.1.16-17/2707-8 Yes . . . plough-irons] Q; *verse* F: sir| shoeing|
5.1.18/2709 Let . . . shall] Q; *unjustified line* F
5.1.22/2714 A . . . it] Q; *verse line* F
5.1.26/2718 Yea, Davy] Q; *verse line* F
5.1.45-8/2737-40 Go . . . Bardolph] Q; *verse* F: too| Davy| boots|
5.1.52/2743-4 Come, Sir John] Q; *verse line* F
5.2.1/2772 How . . . away] Q; *prose* F
5.2.3/2775 Exceeding . . . ended] Q; *2 lines* F: cares|
5.3.17-22/2936-42 Do . . . merrily] *prose*
5.3.33-5/2953-5 Be . . . all] F; *prose* Q
5.3.36-7/2956-7 And . . . merry, be merry] *prose in single verse line* F
5.3.46-9/2966-9 A . . . long-a] *prose*
5.3.74-6/2994-6 Do . . . Samingo] *prose*
5.3.93-7/3012-16 Puff . . . price] *prose*
5.3.100-1/3019-20 A . . . joys] F; *prose* Q
5.3.102-3/3021-2 O . . . thereof] F; *prose* Q
5.3.105-7/3024-6 Shall . . . lap] F; *prose* Q
5.3.108/3027 Honest . . . breeding] Q; *verse* F: gentleman|
5.3.110/3029 Give . . . sir] Q; *verse line* F
5.3.114/3033 Under . . . die] Q; *2 lines* F: king|
5.3.116-20/3035-9 A . . . Spaniard] F; *prose* Q
5.3.121/3040 As . . . just] Q; *2 lines* F: door|
5.3.121-4/3041-3 Away . . . dignities] Q; *verse* F: horse| wilt| thee|
5.3.125-6/3044-5 O . . . fortune] F; *prose* Q
5.3.138-40/3057-9 Let . . . days] F; *prose* Q
5.4.25-6/3084 Come you . . . justice] Q; *verse* F: rogue, come|
5.4.30/3088 Come, you thin . . . rascal] Q; *verse* F: thing|
5.5.20-2/3109-11 As . . . me] Q; *verse* F: night| remember|
5.5.31-8/3120-7 My . . . truth] *prose*
5.5.40/3129 There . . . sounds] Q; *prose* F
5.5.42/3131 The . . . fame] *prose*
5.5.44/3133 My . . . man] Q; *prose* F
5.5.45/3134 Have . . . speak] Q; *2 lines* F: wits|
5.5.86-8/3176-8 Fear . . . night] *verse*: dinner| Bardolph|
5.5.92-3/3182-3 I . . . away] F; *prose* Q
5.5.101/3191 The . . . lord] Q; *2 lines* F: parliament|

Much Ado About Nothing

1.1.273/274 My . . . good] *prose*
1.3.36-8/373-5 I . . . Borachio] *verse*: only|

2.1.88/494   My . . . Jove] *prose*
3.1.104/1181   She's . . . madam] *2 lines*: you|
4.1.50-1/1695-6   And . . . Leonato] *1 line*
4.1.95-6/1740-1   Fie . . . of] lord|
4.1.144-6/1789-91   Sir . . . say] *prose*
4.1.156-60/1801-5   Hear . . . marked] *prose*
5.1.237/2303   Runs . . . blood] *prose*
5.1.321-2/2388-9   Bring . . . fellow] *prose*
5.2.25-8/2415-8   The . . . deserve] *prose*
5.3.16-17/2501-2   Midnight . . . groan] *1 line*
5.3.22-3/2507-8   Now . . . rite] *1 line*

Henry V

Unattributed lineation to the right of the square bracket may be assumed to be F's.

1.2.167-8/300-1   If . . . begin] Q; *1 line* F
2.1.29-30/514-15   Base . . . lodgers] TAYLOR; *prose* F; *3 lines* Q: host| term|
2.1.44-51/529-36   Solus . . . follow] *prose*
2.1.65-6/550-1   Give . . . tall] *prose*
2.1.69/554   Couple a gorge] *prose* F; *as part of the following line* Q
2.1.70-77/555-62   That . . . to] *prose*
2.1.102-8/587-93   A . . . hand] Q; *prose* F
2.1.118-19/603-4   Nim . . . corroborate] *prose* F; *not in* Q
2.2.164-6/771-3   Joined . . . death] TAYLOR; *2 lines* F: coffers|; *2 lines* Q: fixed|
2.3.3-6/800-3   No . . . therefore] *prose*
2.3.44-52/842-50   Come . . . blood to suck] *after* Q; *prose* F
2.4.67/923   We'll . . . bring them] *2 lines*: audience|
2.4.129-30/985-6   Nothing . . . vanity] England|
3.0.2-3/1004-5   In . . . seen] thought|
3.1.1/1038   Once . . . once more] *2 lines*: breach|
3.2.7-11/1077-81   The . . . fame] *prose*
3.2.14-17/1084-7   And . . . high] *prose*
3.2.18-20/1088-90   As . . . bough] *prose*
3.2.23-4/1093-4   Be . . . manly rage] *prose*
3.2.25-6/1095-6   Abate . . . chuck] TAYLOR; *prose* F
3.3.109-10/1237-8   As . . . Harfleur] ashore|
3.6.20-1/1414-15   Captain . . . well] Q; *prose* F
3.6.24-6/1418-20   Bardolph . . . wheel] *prose*
3.6.27/1421   That . . . stone] Q; *prose* F
3.6.38/1433   For . . . be] Q; *prose* F
3.6.39-41/1434-6   A . . . suffocate] *prose* F
3.6.42-7/1437-42   But . . . requite] Q; *prose* F
3.6.59/1454   I . . . maw] Q; *not in* F; *2 lines* TAYLOR: fig|
3.6.90/1485   How . . . bridge] TAYLOR; *prose (?)* F
3.6.116/1512   Well . . . thee] TAYLOR; *prose (?)* F
3.6.117/1513   Thus . . . King] TAYLOR; *prose* F
3.6.136/1532   So . . . office] TAYLOR; *prose* F
4.1.38-9/1818-19   Discuss . . . popular] Q; *prose* F
4.1.45-9/1825-9   The . . . name] Q; *prose* F
4.1.55-6/1835-6   Tell . . . day] *prose*
4.1.227-8/2008-9   Upon . . . wives] TAYLOR; souls| F
4.1.230-4/2011-15   We . . . enjoy] *6 lines*: all| greatness| sense| wringing| neglect|
4.1.283-5/2064-6   Good . . . thee] *2 lines*: together|
4.1.297-9/2078-80   Toward . . . do] blood| chantries| still|
4.2.56/2142   They . . . death] *2 lines*: prayers|
4.2.60-1/2146-7   I . . . take] guidon|
4.3.122/2271   Will . . . labour] *2 lines*: levied|
4.4.4-5/2286-7   Qualité . . . Discuss] *prose*
4.4.7-11/2289-93   O . . . ransom] *prose*
4.4.13-15/2295-7   Moy . . . blood] *prose*
4.4.18/2300   Brass . . . goat] TAYLOR; *prose* F
4.4.21-3/2303-5   Sayst . . . name] *prose*
4.4.36-8/2318-20   Oui . . . sword] *prose*
4.4.46/2328   Tell . . . take] *prose*

4.4.61-2/2343-4   As . . . me] Q; *prose* F
4.8.40-1/2635-6   Give . . . it] soldier|
4.8.106/2701   But . . . here] *2 lines*: twenty| indent O God
5.1.18/2785   Ha . . . Trojan] *prose* F; *2 lines* Q: bedlam|
5.1.19-20/2786-7   To . . . leek] Q; *prose* F
5.1.77-8/2847-8   News . . . France] TAYLOR; *prose* F
5.1.79-83/2849-53   And . . . I'll steal] *prose*
5.2.15-16/2870-1   Your . . . bent] F2; borne| F1
5.2.75-6/2930-1   Well . . . answer] *2 lines*: urged|

Julius Caesar

1.1.32/32   Wherefore . . . home] *2 lines*: rejoice|
1.2.54-5/129-30   No . . . things] *3 lines*: Cassius| reflection|
1.2.60/135   That . . . heard] *2 lines*: shadow|
1.2.65/140   Into . . . Cassius] *2 lines*: you|
1.2.81-2/156-7   What . . . King] *3 lines*: shouting| Caesar|
1.2.176-8/251-3   I . . . Brutus] *2 lines*: words|
1.2.179/254   The . . . returning] *2 lines*: done|
1.2.180/255   As . . . sleeve] *2 lines*: by|
1.2.303/379   And . . . you] *2 lines*: is|
1.3.39-40/437-8   Good . . . in] Casca|
1.3.42/440   Your . . . this] *2 lines*: good|
1.3.45/443   Those . . . faults] *prose*
1.3.57-60/455-8   You . . . wonder] *5 lines*: Casca| Roman| not| fear|
1.3.71-2/469-701   Unto . . . night] *3 lines*: state| man|
1.3.78/476   'Tis . . . Cassius] *2 lines*: mean|
1.3.130/528   Stand . . . haste] *prose*
1.3.133/531   To . . . Cimber] *prose*
1.3.136/534   I . . . this] *2 lines*: on't|
1.3.139-41/537-9   Yes . . . party] Cassius| Brutus|
2.1.96/658   This . . . Cimber] *prose*
2.1.100/662   Here . . . here] *prose*
2.1.208/770   He . . . work] *2 lines*: flattered|
2.1.220/782   The . . . Brutus] *2 lines*: upon's|
2.1.326/888   A . . . whole] *2 lines*: work|
2.2.1/896   Nor . . . tonight] *2 lines*: earth|
2.4.33/1072   Why . . . him] *prose? (divided* to-|words, *but not justified)*
2.4.34/1073   None . . . chance] *2 lines*: be|
2.4.41/1080   I . . . thing] *2 lines*: in|
3.1.47-8/1134-5   Know . . . satisfied] without cause|. See textual note.
3.1.148/1236   But . . . Mark Antony] *2 lines*: comes Antony|
3.1.290/1376   Post . . . chanced] *2 lines*: speed|
3.2.53/1440   We'll . . . clamours] *2 lines*: house|
3.2.111-12/1497-8   Has . . . place] *1 line*. See textual notes.
3.2.162-3/1548-9   A . . . round] *1 line*
3.2.199-200/1585-6   We . . . slay] Revenge|. See the textual note to these lines.
4.2.111/1848   You wrong me every . . . Brutus] *2 lines*: way|
4.2.217/1954   Come . . . Messala] *2 lines*: Titinius|
4.2.233-4/1970-1   Ay . . . proscription] *1 line (omitting* Ay)
4.2.239/1976   Why . . . yours] *2 lines*: ask you|
4.2.278-9/2015-16   Then . . . Philippi] along|
4.2.302/2039   So . . . pleasure] *2 lines* stand
4.2.347/2084   Didst . . . out] *prose*
5.1.42/2139   You . . . hounds] *2 lines*: apes|
5.1.67/2164   Why . . . bark] *2 lines*: billow|
5.1.70-1/2167-8   Messala . . . very day] *1 line*
5.3.46/2275   So . . . been] *2 lines*: free|
5.5.1/2371   Come . . . rock] *prose*

As You Like It

1.2.139-40/305-5   Come . . . forwardness] *verse*: entreated|
1.2.144-5/309-10   How . . . wrestling] *verse*: cousin|
1.2.205-10/379-75   No . . . man] *prose*

LINEATION NOTES

2.4.93-4/841-2 And . . . it] *3 lines*: wages| could|
2.5.6-7/853-4 Here . . . enemy] *1 line*
2.6.11-12/858-60 I thank . . . prithee, more] *verse*: more| song|
2.6.15-17/862-4 I do not . . . stanzas] *verse*: me| sing|
2.6.31-4/878-81 And . . . come] *verse*: him| company| give| them|
2.6.47-8/894-5 If . . . ass] *1 line*
2.6.52-3/899-900 Here . . . he] *1 line*
2.6.59/906 And . . . prepared] *verse*: Duke|
2.6.1-3/907-9 Dear . . . master] *verse*: further| down|
2.6.4-17/910-923 Why . . . good Adam] *verse*: thee| thyself a little| savage| thee| powers| a while| presently| eat| diest| labour| cheerly| liest| thee| die| dinner| desert|
2.7.102-3/1025-6 What . . . gentleness] *3 lines*: have| force|
2.7.167-8/1090-1 Welcome . . . feed] *prose*
2.7.176-9/1099-1102 Thou . . . seen] *2 lines*: ingratitude|
2.7.185-9/1108-1112 Freeze . . . sharp] *3 lines*: nigh| forgot|
3.1.31-2/1176-9 Such . . . shepherd] *verse*: philosopher|
3.2.250-1/1394-5 And . . . society] *verse*: sake|
3.3.85/1653 Go . . . counsel thee] *verse*: me|
3.3.88-95/1656-63 Farewell . . . with thee] *prose*
3.4.5/1671 As . . . weep] *verse*: desire|
3.4.6/1672 His . . . colour] *verse*: hair|
3.4.7-8/1673-4 Something . . . children] *verse*: Judas's|
3.4.10-11/1676-7 An . . . only colour] *verse*: excellent colour|
3.4.12-13/1678-9 And . . . bread] *verse*: sanctity|
3.5.67-71/1788-92 He's . . . me] *verse*: she'll| fast| sauce|
4.1.83/1945 Am . . . Rosalind] *as a separate line*
4.3.1-2/2088-9 How . . . Orlando] *verse (?)*: o'clock|
4.3.3-6/2090-3 I . . . here] *verse (first line justified)*: brain| forth|
4.3.165-6/2252-3 Be . . . heart] *verse*: man|
4.3.167/2254 I do . . . it] *as a separate line*
5.1.61-2/2331-2 Trip . . . attend, I attend.] *verse*: attend,|
5.2.13-16/2345-8 You . . . Rosalind] *verse*: consent| I| followers| look you|
5.4.118-19/2615-16 If . . . adieu] *1 line*

Hamlet

1.1.8-10/8-10 Well . . . haste] Q2; *prose* F
1.1.38/38 Peace . . . again] Q2; *2 lines* F: Peace, break thee off: Enter the Ghost. | Look . . .
1.1.110-11/110-11 Speak . . . done] *1 line* Q2, F
1.1.112-13/112-13 That . . . me] Q1-2; *1 line* F
1.1.115-16/115-16 Which . . . speak] Q2; *1 line* F, Q1
1.2.57/213 Have . . . Polonius] Q2; *2 lines* F: leave|
1.2.87/243 'Tis . . . Hamlet] Q2; *2 lines* F: commendable|
1.2.120/276 I . . . madam] Q2; *2 lines* F: best|
1.2.160-1/316-17 I . . . myself] F; *1 line* Q2
1.2.162/318 The . . . ever] Q2; *2 lines* F: lord|
1.2.163/319 Sir . . . you] Q2; *2 lines* F: friend|
1.2.229-30/385-6 A . . . anger] *1 line* QF
1.2.241-2/397-8 I'll . . . again] *1 line* F, Q1; tonight| Q2
1.3.9-10/422-3 The . . . more] Q2; *1 line* F (*omitting* 'perfume and')
1.3.113-14/526-7 And . . . heaven] speech| Q2, F
1.4.56/605 It . . . thee] F; *2 lines* Q2: still|
1.5.29/646 Haste . . . swift] Q2; *2 lines* F: it|
1.5.52-3/669-70 To . . . moved] *1 line* Q2, F
1.5.56-7/673-4 Will . . . garbage] Q2; *1 line* F
1.5.107-8/724-5 My . . . down] This edition; *1 line* F. See textual notes.
1.5.112-13/729-30 It . . . sworn't] Q2; *1 line* F
1.5.127/744 There's . . . Denmark] F, Q1; *2 lines* Q2: villain|
1.5.129-30/746-7 There . . . this] Q2; *prose?* F: |grave
1.5.152-3/769-70 Ah ha . . . cellarage] Q2; *prose* F
1.5.181/798 So . . . swear] This edition; *2 lines* F: you|. F might have set 'Sweare' on a line of its own because the line to which it properly belonged already filled the column measure; hexameters are common.
2.1.6/814 Marry . . . sir] Q2; *2 lines* F: |very

2.1.35-6/843-4 A . . . assault] Q2; *1 line* F
2.1.37-8/845-6 Ay . . . that] *1 line* Q2, F
2.1.49-51/857-9 And . . . leave] This edition; *verse* Q2: |By |Where; *verse* F: |a does |By
2.1.52-3/860-1 At 'closes . . . gentleman] consequence| F
2.1.61/869 Videlicet . . . now] *1 line* Q2, F
2.1.75/883 Farewell . . . matter] Q2; *2 lines* F: Farewell|
2.1.86-7/894-5 My . . . it] Q2; *1 line* F
2.2.36/964 My . . . ye] Q2; *2 lines* F: son|
2.2.105-6/1033-4 Thus . . . Perpend] Q2; *1 line* F
2.2.128-9/1057-8 But . . . love] *1 line* Q2, F
2.2.161-2/1090-1 You . . . lobby] Q2; *3 lines* F: sometimes| Here|
2.2.169/1098 But . . . reading] Q2; *2 lines* F: wretch|
2.2.171-2/1100-1 I'll . . . Hamlet] Q2; F *divides after* 'presently', *with the direction* 'Exit King & Queen' *in the right margin*
2.2.179-80/1108-9 Ay . . . thousand] F; *verse* Q1-2: goes|
2.2.183/1112 have . . . daughter] Q2; *separate line*
2.2.185-7/1114-16 Let . . . to't] F; *verse* Q2: blessing|
2.2.206-7/1136-8 Though . . . lord] Q2; *verse* F: madness| walk|
2.2.209-15/1140-6 Indeed . . . you] Q2; *verse* F: air| are| happiness| on| not| of| him| meeting| daughter| |take. See textual note to 2.2.214/1145.
2.2.225-7/1156-7 My . . . both] F; *verse* Q2: Guildenstern|
2.2.229-30/1159-60 Happy . . . button] cap| Q2; *prose* F
2.2.236-7/1166-7 In . . . news] F; *verse* Q2: strumpet|
2.2.240-1/1170-1 Then . . . true] F; *1 verse line* Q2
2.2.270-1/1200-1 But . . . Elsinore] F; *1 verse line* Q2
2.2.391-2/1321-2 My . . . Rome] Q2; *verse* Q1-2: you|
2.2.406/1337 Why] *continues into rest of speech* QF
2.2.407-8/1338-9 One . . . well] F, Q1; *prose* Q2
2.2.416-20/1347-51 As by . . . was] *prose* Q2, F
2.2.452-3/1382-3 The . . . Pyrrhus] *prose* Q2, F
2.2.454/1384 The . . . arms] F; *prose* Q2
2.2.466-7/1396-7 Old . . . you] Q1; *1 verse line* Q2
2.2.483-4/1413-14 And . . . nothing] Q2; *1 line* F
2.2.507/1437 Run . . . flames] Q2; *2 lines* F: down|
2.2.523-4/1453-4 'Tis . . . soon] *1 verse line* Q2
2.2.588-90/1518-20 And . . . play] F, Q1; foh| heard| Q2
3.1.15-16/1551-2 Did . . . pastime] *1 line* QF
3.1.25-8/1561-4 With . . . delights] F; heart| me| inclined| edge| Q2
3.1.33-4/1569-70 Affront . . . espials] *1 line* F; *1 line* Q2 (which does not contain 'lawful espials')
3.1.111-12/1647-8 Could . . . honesty] F; *verse* Q2: commerce|
3.1.134-5/1670-1 Let . . . Farewell] F; *verse* Q2: him| house|
3.1.177-8/1713-14 Whereon . . . on't] F; *3 lines* Q2: beating| himself|
3.1.179-80/1715-16 It . . . grief] F; well| Q2
3.2.46-7/1773-4 How . . . work] *verse* F: lord|
3.2.90-1/1817-18 Excellent . . . so] F; *verse* Q2: i'faith| air|
3.2.92-3/1819-20 I . . . mine] F; *verse* Q2: Hamlet|
3.2.94-5/1821-2 No . . . say] F; *verse* Q2: lord|
3.2.99-100/1826-7 I . . . me] F; *verse* Q2: Capitol|
3.2.101-2/1828-9 It . . . ready] F; *verse* Q2: there|
3.2.134-5/1862-3 We . . . all] F; *verse* Q2: fellow|
3.2.214/1942 'Tis . . . a while] Q1-2; *2 lines* F: sworn|
3.2.234-5/1962-3 I . . . dallying] F, Q1; *verse* Q2: love|
3.2.239/1968 So . . . husbands] Q1-2; F *sets off as a separate line*
3.2.243/1972 Thoughts . . . agreeing] Q1-2; *2 lines* F: apt|
3.2.262/1991 So . . . away] F; *prose* Q2
3.2.270-1/1999-2000 This . . . here] Q2; himself| F
3.2.295-6/2024-5 Good . . . affair] F; *verse* Q2: frame|
3.2.371-3/2099-2101 Then . . . come by and by] *verse* Q2, F: and by| Q2; and by| bent| F
3.2.375-6/2103-4 By . . . friends] For Q2 see textual note. F sets as one line which fills the measure, and is thus ambiguous.
3.3.11/2127 The . . . bound] Q2; *2 lines* F: single|
2.2.78-9/2194-5 To . . . revenge] Q2; *1 line* F
3.3.86-7/2202-3 When . . . No] Q2; *1 line* F
3.4.1/2215 A . . . him] Q2; *2 lines* F: straight|
3.4.7/2221 I'll . . . coming] HIBBARD; *2 lines* Q2, F: not|. In Q2

the speech is divided because the first half completes 'Pray you be round' (3.4.5/2219); in F, the full line would not fit the measure. F has a sequence of five consecutive trimeters; their arrangement is problematic.

3.4.50-1/2264-5 Ay . . . index] Q2; *prose* F
3.4.99-100/2313-14 Th'important . . . say] *1 line* Q2, F
3.4.129-30/2343-4 This . . . in] *1 line* Q2, F
3.4.147/2361 O . . . twain] Q2; *2 lines* F: Hamlet|
3.4.151-2/2365-6 Assume . . . tonight] HIBBARD; *1 line* F
3.4.183-4/2397-8 I . . . that] This edition; *1 line* Q2, F
3.4.184-5/2398-9 Alack . . . on] Q2; *1 line* F
4.1.1/2406 There's . . . heaves] Q2; *2 lines* F: sighs|. F's mislineation is probably compositorial, since the full line would not fit its measure; its mispunctuation—with a break after 'sighes' rather than 'heaues'—is probably related, since Composition B liked to break lines at a semantic break.
4.2.3/2448 What . . . come] This edition; *2 lines* Q2, F: Hamlet|. Q2's division is correct on its own terms: 'Safely ſtowd, but ſoft, what noyſe, who calls on *Hamlet*?' is an acceptable pentameter, with an extra initial stress and a feminine ending. F divides and rewrites this speech: 'What noiſe? Who cals on *Hamlet*? Oh heere they come' is an acceptable pentameter, with a feminine caesura; but it would not fit F's column measure, and so was characteristically split by Compositor B at the main break in the sense.
4.3.50-1/2527-8 I . . . mother] F; *verse* Q2: England|
4.3.53-5/2530-2 My . . . England] F; *verse* Q2: wife,|man . . . mother|
4.3.56/2533 Follow . . . aboard] *2 lines* Q2, F: foot|. Q2's division continues the mislineation of 4.3.50-5/2527-32; F's reflects the narrowness of its column.
4.5.1-2/2557-8 She . . . pitied] Q2; *prose* F
4.5.14-16/2570-2 'Twere . . . in] Q2; with| conjectures| F
4.5.23-6/2579-82 How . . . shoon] Q1; *2 lines* Q2, F: one|
4.5.29-32/2585-8 He . . . stone] *2 lines* Q2, F: gone | At
4.5.34-5/2590-1 Pray . . . snow] F; *1 line* Q2
4.5.43/2599 God be at your table] F; *on a separate line* Q2
4.5.47-50/2603-6 Tomorrow . . . Valentine] Q1-2; *2 lines* F: betime|
4.5.51-4/2607-10 Then . . . more] Q1; *2 lines* Q2, F: door|
4.5.62-3/2618-19 Quoth . . . wed] F, Q1; *1 line* Q2
4.5.71-2/2627-8 sweet . . . night, good night] F; *separate line* Q2
4.5.73/2629 Follow . . . you] Q2; *2 lines* F: close|
4.5.74-5/2630-1 O . . . Gertrude, Gertrude] F; *prose* Q2
4.5.95-6/2651-2 Where . . . matter] Q2; Switzers| F
4.5.114-15/2670-1 I . . . father] Q2; door| F
4.5.116/2672 That . . . bastard] Q2; *2 lines* F: calm|
4.5.138-9/2694-5 Good . . . certainty] F; *1 line* Q2
4.5.169-70/2725-6 Hadst . . . thus] Q2; *prose* F
4.5.171-3/2727-9 You . . . daughter] F; *verse* Q2: a-down| it|
4.5.178/2733 A . . . fitted] Q; *prose* F
4.5.190-1/2745-6 No . . . death-bed] *1 line* Q2, F
4.5.195-6/2750-1 He . . . moan] *1 line* Q1-2, F
4.5.198/2753 And . . . ye] *verse*: souls| Q2; pray God| F, Q1
4.7.30/2834 Break . . . think] Q2; *2 lines* F: that|
4.7.36/2840 Letters . . . Hamlet] *prose* F
4.7.37/2841 This . . . Queen] Q2; *prose* F
4.7.41/2845 Laertes . . . us] Q2; *2 lines* F: them|
4.7.50-2/2854-6 'Tis . . . me] *prose* F; Naked| Alone| Q2
4.7.56-8/2860-2 If . . . me] Q2; so| how F
4.7.120-1/2924-5 With . . . death] F; *1 line* Q2
5.1.116-17/3087-8 Mine . . . made] F; *1 line* Q2
5.1.171-2/3142-3 A . . . think it was] Q2; *verse* F: |Whose
5.1.190-1/3162 Prithee . . . thing] F; *on a separate line* Q2
5.1.257-8/3227-8 Thou . . . throat] F; *1 line* Q2
5.2.74-6/3341-3 It . . . Horatio] short| more| F
5.2.83-4/3350-1 I . . . water-fly] F; *verse* Q2: sir|
5.2.173-6/3441-4 But . . . done] F; *3 lines* Q2: knows| punished|; *4 lines* ROWE: gentleman| heard| distraction|
5.2.198-9/3466-7 I . . . play] F; *prose* Q2
5.2.206-7/3474-5 Give . . . wager] Q2; Osric| F
5.2.209/3477 I . . . both] Q2; *2 lines* F: it|
5.2.211/3479 This . . . another] Q2; *2 lines* F: heavy|
5.2.212/3480 This . . . length] Q2; *2 lines* F: well|
5.2.221/3489 In . . . cups] Q2; *2 lines* F: worn|. This line bridges a page and quire-break (pp6ᵛ-qq1), and F's error does not seem attributable to justification problems; it may therefore reflect error or ambiguity in the manuscript.
5.2.234/3502 Stay . . . thine] Q2; *2 lines* F: drink|
5.2.237/3505 What say you?] In Q2 these words are separated from the rest of the speech by a 1.5 cm space.
5.2.244/3511 I will . . . me] Q2; *2 lines* F: lord|
5.2.246/3513 I . . . and by] Q2; *2 lines* F: madam|
5.2.251/3518 Come . . . dally] Q2; *2 lines* F: third|. F's repunctuation of this speech ('third. *Laertes,*') is probably a consequence of its deliberate mislineation.
5.2.259/3526 Why . . . Osric] Q2; *2 lines* F: woodcock|
5.2.262-3/3529-30 No . . . poisoned] Q2; *3 lines* F: |O |I
5.2.266/3533 It . . . slain] Q2; *2 lines* F: Hamlet|Hamlet
5.2.274/3541 The . . . work] Q2; *2 lines* F: too|
5.2.277/3544 Here . . . Dane] Q2; *2 lines* F: murd'rous|
5.2.279-80/3546-7 He . . . himself] F; *1 line* Q2
5.2.294-5/3561-2 As . . . ha't] Q2; cup| F
5.2.303-4/3570-1 To . . . volley] *1 line* Q2, F
5.2.312/3579 Now . . . prince] Q2; *2 lines* F: heart|
5.2.344/3611 Which . . . me] Q2; *2 lines* F: doth|. F expands its text here to balance the two short columns on qq1ᵛ.
5.2.346/3613 And . . . more] Q2; *2 lines* F: mouth|
5.2.348/3615 Even . . . mischance] Q2; *2 lines* F: wild|
5.2.352/3619 To . . . passage] Q2; *2 lines* F: royally|

Twelfth Night

1.2.22-3/62-3 A . . . name] *1 line*
1.5.203-4/487-8 Yet . . . would you] *verse*: are you|
1.5.209-11/493-5 Give . . . text] *verse*: alone|
2.4.54-7/914-17 My . . . share it] *2 lines*: prepare it|
2.4.62-5/922-5 A . . . there] *2 lines*: where|
2.5.95-8/1081-4 Jove . . . know] *prose*
2.5.99-101/1085-7 The . . . Malvolio] *verse*: know|
2.5.103-6/1089-92 I . . . life] *2 lines*: knife|
3.4.4-5/1480-1 I . . . civil] *1 line*
3.4.8-9/1484-5 He's . . . possessed, madam] *verse*: |but
3.4.19-21/1495-7 Sad . . . that] *verse*: be sad| blood|
3.4.23/1499 Why . . . thee] *verse*: man|
3.4.33-4/1510-11 At . . . daws] *verse*: request|
3.4.201-2/1677-8 With . . . griefs] bears|
3.4.273-4/1750-1 Ay . . . yonder] *verse*: pacified|
3.4.363/1841 The . . . sir] *2 lines*: him|
4.1.9-10/1875-6 I . . . me] *prose*
4.1.17-19/1883-5 I . . . payment] *prose*
4.2.73-4/2004-5 Hey . . . does] *prose*
4.2.80-1/2011-12 She . . . ha] *1 line*
4.2.123-34/2054-65 I . . . devil] *8 lines*: anon, sir| again| Vice| sustain| wrath| devil| dad|
5.1.324-5/2423-4 Ay . . . Malvolio] *1 line*

Troilus and Cressida

1.1.84-5/114-15 TROILUS . . . I] *1 type line* QF
1.2.11/157 In . . . anger] *1 type line* Q
1.2.14/160 They . . . him] *1 type line* Q
1.2.15-16/161-2 They . . . alone] *1 line* QF
1.2.16-17/162-3 So . . . legs] This edition; *prose* QF
1.2.43-4/189-90 you . . . uncle] *1 type line* Q
1.2.51-2/197-8 PANDARUS . . . here] *1 type line* Q
1.2.65-6/211-12 Then . . . Hector] This edition; *prose* Q
1.2.77-8/223-4 CRESSIDA . . . elder] *1 type line* Q
1.2.85-6/231-2 CRESSIDA . . . beauty] *1 type line* Q

1.2.95-6/241-2 CRESSIDA ... has] *1 type line* Q
1.2.117/264 Why ... dimpled] *separate line* QF
1.2.275-6/419-20 CRESSIDA ... Troilus] *1 type line* Q
1.3.1/436 Princes ... cheeks] Q; Princes] F (justification)
1.3.46/481 In ... brightness] Q; *2 lines* F: Fortune|
1.3.50/485 And ... courage] Q; *2 lines* F: then|
1.3.124/559 And ... Agamemnon] *2 lines* QF: himself|
1.3.212-13/647-8 What ... Menelaus] This edition; *1 line* QF
1.3.227-8/662-3 Modest ... Phoebus] F; *1 line* Q
1.3.246/681 He ... Troy] Q; *2 lines* F: privately|
1.3.301/736 Fair ... hand] Q; *2 lines* F: Aeneas|
1.3.307-9/742-4 I have ... shape] This edition; *2 lines* QF: brain|
1.3.307/742 ULYSSES ... Ulysses] *1 type line* Q
1.3.314/749 To ... how] *1 type line* Q
1.3.324-5/759-60 I ... him] F; *1 line* Q
1.3.350-5/785-90 Give ... consent] F; meet| merchants| sell| better shall exceed] Q
1.3.357-8/792-3 For ... followers] F; *prose* Q
2.2.9/958 As ... Priam] QF; *2 lines* COLLIER: particular|. OED supports a trisyllabic pronunciation of *particular*, which is required in most of the word's Shakespearian uses.
2.2.50-1/999-1000 Brother ... holding] *prose* Q; worth| F
2.2.96-9/1045-8 CASSANDRA ... Cassandra] *1 type line* Q
2.3.102-3/1264-5 Here ... him] *1 type line* Q (probably intended as verse)
2.3.104-5/1266-7 The ... flexure] *verse* QF: courtesy|
2.3.176/1338-9 Cry ... him] *1 type line* Q
2.3.191-2/1353-4 As ... to Achilles] *1 line* Q
2.3.200-1/1362-3 If ... face] *prose* QF
2.3.202-3/1364-5 An ... him] Q; *prose* F
2.3.226-7/1388-9 Here ... silent] F; *1 line* Q
2.3.251/1413 But ... father] *1 type line* Q
3.1.48-9/1470-1 You ... music] F; *verse* Q: Queen|
3.1.65-6/1487-8 Go ... you] *verse* QF: |commends
3.1.67-8/1489-90 You ... head] *verse* QF: melody|
3.1.212-13/1534-5 For ... do] F; *1 line* Q
3.1.114-15/1536-7 The ... wounds] *1 line* QF
3.1.131/1553 Sweet ... today] *as a separate line* QF
3.1.134-5/1556-7 How ... not] *as a separate line* QF
3.1.139-40/1561-2 You'll ... excuse] *as a separate line* QF
3.2.38/1615 Come ... blush] *as a separate line* QF
3.2.71-2/1648-9 O ... monster] *verse* QF: fear|
3.2.111-12/1687-8 Prince ... months] *prose* QF
3.2.140/1716 CRESSIDA ... lady] *1 type line* QF
3.2.167/1743 CRESSIDA ... fight] *1 type line* QF
3.3.58-62/1842-6 Would ... morrow] This edition's *lineation*; not indented QF
3.3.67-8/1851-2 To come ... altars] *1 line* QF
3.3.80-1/1864-5 Doth ... me] F; fall| Q
3.3.120-2/1904-5 The ... are] F; there|what| Q
3.3.136-9/1920-3 I do ... forgot] QF; by me| to me| CAPELL
3.3.139-42/1923-6 Time ... past] This edition; back| oblivion| ingratitudes| QF
3.3.164-5/1948-9 Remuneration ... wit] *1 line* QF
4.1.34-5/2120-1 The noblest ... early] F; *prose* Q
4.1.45-6/2131-2 With ... unwelcome] F; wherefore|
4.1.46-8/2132-4 That ... from Troy] F; *prose* Q
4.1.50/2136 Will have it so] This edition; *as part of preceding line* QF; *as part of following line* POPE
4.1.80-1/2166-7 We'll ... way] F; *prose* Q
4.2.25-7/2192-4 How ... Cressid] *verse* QF: maidenheads|
4.2.30-1/2197-8 To ... you to do] *verse* QF: say what|
4.2.32-3/2199-200 Come ... others] *prose* QF (Q divided as here)
4.2.37-8/2204-5 Did ... see] Q; *prose* F
4.2.49-50/2216-17 Who's ... early] *prose* QF
4.2.57-60/2224-7 Whoa ... Go] This edition; *prose* QF; then| ware| false to him| CAPELL
4.5.15-16/2305-6 O ... breaking] *prose* QF
4.5.18-19/2308-9 Because ... speaking] *prose* QF
4.5.65-6/2355-6 My ... thee] F; *1 line* Q
4.5.69/2359 And ... sleeve] Q; *2 lines* F: danger|
4.5.70/2360 And ... you] Q; *2 lines* F: glove|
4.5.72-3/2362-3 To ... true] F; *1 line* Q
4.5.77-8/2367-8 nature flowing, | And swelling] PALMER; nature, | Flawing and swelling F. See textual note.
4.6.5-6/2443-4 May ... hither] F; *prose* Q
4.6.21-2/2459-60 Yet ... general] *prose* QF
4.6.23-4/2461-2 And ... Nestor] *prose* QF
4.6.39-40/2477-8 The ... no kiss] *1 line* Q; *prose* F
4.6.49/2487 CRESSIDA ... it] *1 type line* Q
4.6.72-3/2510-11 By ... ask] *1 line* QF
4.6.77-8/2515-16 If ... name] *1 line* QF
4.6.98/2536 The ... knight] Q; *2 lines* F: Priam|
4.7.92-3/2649-50 Ha ... time] Q; *prose* F
4.7.108-9/2655-6 And ... it] F; *1 line* Q
4.7.115-16/2672-3 I ... joint] F; *1 line* Q
4.7.117-18/2674-5 HECTOR ... am Achilles] *1 type line* Q
4.7.151-2/2708-9 We ... cause] F; *1 line* Q
4.7.153-4/2710-11 Tomorrow ... friends] F; *1 line* Q
5.1.6-7/2740-1 Why ... thee] F; *verse* Q: idol|
5.1.14-15/2747-8 Prithee ... varlet] F; *verse* Q: talk|
5.1.43-4/2776-7 This ... Patroclus] F; *1 line* Q
5.1.64-5/2797 No ... light] *1 line* QF
5.1.65-6/2798-9 HECTOR ... whit] *1 type line* Q
5.1.74-5/2807-8 Good ... tarry] *prose* QF (F divided as here)
5.1.75-6/2808-9 tarry ... night] *1 type line* Q
5.1.82-3/2815-16 Follow ... company] F; *prose* Q
5.1.83/2816 TROILUS ... me] *same type line as end of preceding speech* Q
5.2.15-16/2842-3 Nay ... words] *prose* QF
5.2.30/2857 ULYSSES ... Diomed] *1 type line* Q
5.2.44-5/2871-2 Doth ... truth] *1 line* QF
5.2.45-6/2872-3 By ... patient] *1 line* QF
5.2.47-8/2874-5 CRESSIDA ... palter] *1 type line* Q
5.2.50-1/2877-8 You ... out] *prose* QF
5.2.51/2878 TROILUS ... come] *1 type line* Q
5.2.79-80/2906-7 CRESSID ... that] *1 type line* Q
5.2.84-5/2911-12 And ... thee] F; *1 line* Q
5.2.101-4/2928-31 Why ... you] F; *prose* Q
5.2.105-6/2932-3 Nor ... best] *prose* QF
5.2.117/2944 ULYSSES ... is] *1 type line* Q
5.2.126-7/2953-4 Created ... here] F; *1 line* Q
5.2.177-9/3004-6 Shall ... Diomed] F; *2 lines* Q: descent|
5.3.39/3064 What ... it] F; *prose* Q
5.3.95/3120 Go ... fight] F; *2 lines* Q: town|
5.4.18-19/3162-3 Fly ... after] F; *prose* Q
5.4.21/3165 Withdrew ... thee] Q; *2 lines* F: multitude|. Editors follow F; but the full Q line would not fit F's measure, and hexameters are common.
5.4.22-3/3166-7 Hold ... sleeve] F; *verse* Q: Trojan|
5.5.41-2/3218-19 As ... all] Q; *1 line* F
5.6.4/3230 Were ... office] Q; *2 lines* F: general|
5.6.6/3232 O ... thou traitor] Q; *2 lines* F: Diomed|
5.6.27/3253 Stand ... mark] Q; *2 lines* F: Greek|
5.10.1-2/3303-4 Achilles ... Achilles.] *1 line* QF

Various Poems: A Song

Y divides each stanza into four lines, with breaks after the third, sixth, and eighth lines as arranged in our text. See the Introduction.

10 I retire ... never] This edition; *2 lines* B: despair|
20 I ... venture] This edition; *2 lines* B: hope|
30 Her ... duty] This edition; *2 lines* B: him|
38 We ... pleasure] This edition; *2 lines* B: us|
40 Arms ... treasure] This edition; *2 lines* B: bind|

Sir Thomas More

Add.II.D.22-3/22-3 What ... it] *1 line*
Add.II.D.27-8/27-8 You ... question] *1 line*

LINEATION NOTES

Add.II.D.104-5/103-4   Which ... authority] *1 line*
Add.II.D.106-7/105-6   And ... God] *1 line*
Add.II.D.125-6/124-5   Whose ... hurly] *1 line* (see Introduction)
Add.II.D.127-8/126-7   Cannot ... captain] *1 line*
Add.II.D.136-7/135-6   To ... King] This edition (*conj.* Melchiori);
    1 line MS
Add.II.D.163-4/162-3   And .. it] *1 line*

Measure for Measure

1.2.43-5/126-8   I ... to] *verse*: roof|
1.2.130/211   One ... you] *2 lines*: friend|
1.2.131-2/212-13   A ... after] hundred|
1.4.69-70/386-7   To ... brother] business|
1.4.71/388   Doth ... life] *2 lines*: so|
2.1.44/451   How ... matter] *prose*
2.1.57/464   Why ... Elbow] *verse line*
2.1.133/539   I ... lordship] *prose*
2.1.244/652   Whip ... jade] *prose*
2.2.65-6/748-9   As ... he] *1 line*
2.2.85/768   Tomorrow ... him, spare him] *2 lines*: sudden|
2.2.116-17/799-800   Would ... heaven] for thunder|
2.4.119/1037   To ... mean] *2 lines*: would have|
3.1.3-4/1108-9   But ... die] *verse*
3.1.45/1150   Who's ... welcome] *prose*
3.1.49/1154   And ... sister] *prose*
3.1.51/1156   Bring ... concealed] *prose*
3.1.33/1158   Why ... indeed] *2 lines*: Why|
3.1.296-7/1403-4   Indeed ... prove] *verse*: sir|
3.1.343/1449   Adieu ... friar] *verse*: Pompey|
3.1.351-2/1457-8   Go ... Duke] *verse*: go|
3.1.490-1/1597-8   One ... himself] *verse*: Strifes|
3.1.512-13/1619-20   If ... proceeding] *verse*: life|
4.1.33-5/1679-81   There ... him] *2 lines*: upon the|
4.2.3-5/1722-4   If ... woman's head] *verse*: can| wife's head|
4.2.104-8/1823-7   My . . . day] *verse*: note| charge| it| circumstance|
4.2.117-20/1836-9   I ... before] *verse*: you| remiss| me| strangely|
4.2.132-3/1851-2   A ... old] *verse* (?): bred| (*but* PROVOST ... bred *justified*)
4.2.137/1856   His ... him] *verse line*
4.2.170-2/1889-91   By ... Angelo] *verse*: you| guide| executed|
4.2.173-4/1892-3   Angelo ... favour] *verse*: both|
4.3.20-1/1949-50   Master ... Barnardine] *verse*: hanged|
4.3.25-6/1954-5   Your ... death] *verse*: hangman|
4.3.28/1957   Tell ... too] *verse*: awake|
4.3.36-7/1965-6   How ... you] *verse*: Abhorson|
4.3.40-1/1969-70   You ... for't] *verse*: night|
4.3.49/1978   comfort ... with you] *verse line*
4.3.109/2038   Good ... daughter] *prose*
4.3.159-60/2089-90   Nay ... Duke] *verse*: with thee|
4.4.13-16/2115-18   Well ... him] *prose*
4.6.13/2161   He ... sounded] *2 lines*: you|
4.6.16/2164   The ... away] *2 lines*: entering|
5.1.19/2183   Now ... him] *2 lines*: time|
5.1.26/2190   Relate ... brief] *2 lines*: wrongs|
5.1.32/2196   Or ... me hear] *2 lines*: reason|
5.1.68/2232   Have ... say] *2 lines*: reason|
5.1.80-2/2244-6   I ... perfect] then| have| then|
5.1.90-1/2254-5   Mended ... proceed] *1 line*
5.1.126/2290   A ... Lodowick] *2 lines*: belike|
5.1.278-9/2442-3   Come ... said] *verse*: gentlewoman|
5.1.280-1/2444-5   My ... provost] *verse*: of|
5.1.310-11/2473-4   Be ... he] dare|
5.1.447-8/2610-11   For ... intent] *1 line*
5.1.521-2/2684-5   Marrying . . . hanging] *verse* (?): death|
    (LUCIO ... death *justified*)

Othello

Unattributed lineation to the right of the square bracket may be taken to be QF.

1.1.4-5/4-5   'Sblood ... me] Q; dream| F
1.1.6/6   Thou ... hate] Q; *2 lines* F: me|
1.1.7-8/7-8   Despise ... city] F; *1 line* Q
1.1.16-17/16-17   I ... he] *1 line*
1.1.34/34   Why ... service] *2 lines*: remedy|
1.1.37/37   Stood ... yourself] F; *2 lines* Q: first|
1.1.49-52/49-52   Whip ... lords] F; *5 lines* Q: knaves| forms| hearts| throwing|
1.1.53-4/53-4   Do ... soul] *4 lines*: 'em| coats| homage|
1.1.59-60/59-60   Heaven ... end] F; *3 lines* Q: I| so|
1.1.65/65   For ... what I am] F; *2 lines* Q: at|
1.1.79/79   Awake . . . thieves, thieves, thieves] F; *2 lines* Q: Brabanzio|. F repeats 'thieves' only twice.
1.1.82-3/82-3   What ... there] Q; terrible| F
1.1.91-2/91-2   Or ... say] F; *1 line* Q
1.1.107-8/107-8   What ... grange] Q; robbing| F
1.1.159-60/160-1   Which ... search] F; surely| Q
1.1.171/172   O heaven ... blood] Q; *2 lines* F: out|
1.2.5/191   I ... ribs] F; *2 lines* Q: here|
1.2.8-9/194-5   Against ... have] *1 line*
1.2.28/214   For ... yond] F; *2 lines* Q: worth|
1.2.34/220   The ... lieutenant] Q; *2 lines* F: Duke|
1.2.48-9/234-5   I ... you] F; *1 line* Q
1.2.60-2/246-8   Keep ... weapons] Q; *prose* F
1.2.63/249   O ... daughter] Q; *2 lines* F: thief|
1.3.18-19/304-5   This ... pageant] F; reason| Q
1.3.46/332   Write ... Dispatch] Q; *2 lines* F: us|
1.3.91/377   Of ... charms] Q; *2 lines* F: love|
1.3.94-5/380-1   A ... motion] F; spirit| Q
1.3.121/407   Ensign ... place] Q; *2 lines* F: them|
1.3.169/455   Here ... it] F; *2 lines* Q: lady|
1.3.171-2/457-8   Good ... best] *1 line*
1.3.198/484   Let ... sentence] Q; *2 lines* F: yourself|
1.3.306-7/592-3   If ... gentleman] F; *verse* Q: |why
1.3.373-4/659-60   Go ... Roderigo] This edition; *1 line*
1.3.393-4/679-80   And ... are] F; *1 line* Q
2.1.22-3/704-5   That ... sufferance] F; seen| Q
2.1.31/713   I ... governor] Q; *2 lines* F: on't|
2.1.37/719   Like ... ho] F; *2 lines* Q: soldier|
2.1.75/757   She ... captain] Q; *2 lines* F: of|
2.1.82/764   Give ... spirits] F; *2 lines* Q: fire|
2.1.92/774   O ... company] Q; *2 lines* F: fear|
2.1.112-15/794-7   Come on, come ... beds] Q; *prose* F
2.1.120/802   What ... praise me] F; *2 lines* Q: me| (*prose*?)
2.1.123/805   Come ... harbour] Q; *2 lines* F: essay|
2.1.128-31/810-13   I ... delivered] Q; *prose* F
2.1.134/816   Well ... witty] Q; *2 lines* F: praised|
2.1.140-3/822-5   These ... foolish] Q; *prose* F
2.1.164-7/846-9   O . . . counsellor] F; *verse* Q: conclusion| husband| liberal|
2.1.168-9/850-1   He ... scholar] F; *verse* Q: him|
2.1.181/862   The ... trumpet] F; *prose* Q
2.1.185/866   To ... joy] Q; *2 lines* F: me|
2.1.195/876   But ... increase] Q; *2 lines* F: |loves
2.1.200-2/881-3   O ... am] Q; *prose* F
2.1.203/884   News ... drowned] Q; *2 lines* F: done|
2.3.21-2/1026-7   What ... provocation] *verse*: has|
2.3.23/1028   An ... modest] *1 line* Q; *2 lines* F: eye|
2.3.24/1029   And ... love] *1 line* Q; *2 lines* F: speaks|
2.3.47/1053   As ... Roderigo] Q; *2 lines* F: dog|
2.3.57/1063   That ... come] F; *2 lines* Q: isle|
2.3.61-2/1067-8   Good ... soldier] Q; *prose* F. 'As ... ho' *1 type line* Q.
2.3.65-6/1071-2   A ... span] *1 line*
2.3.112/1118   To ... watch] Q; *prose* F
2.3.123-4/1129-30   It ... it] F; *1 line* Q

LINEATION NOTES

2.3.133-4/1139-40 It . . . Moor] F; *1 line* Q
2.3.141-2/1146-7 A . . . bottle] Q; *verse (?)* F: the|
2.3.145-6/1151-2 Nay . . . hand] Q; *verse* F: lieutenant|
2.3.147/1153 Let . . . mazard] Q; *verse* F: sir|
2.3.256-9/1262-5 Reputation . . . Iago, my reputation] F; *verse* Q: my reputation| myself| reputation|
2.3.278-9/1284-5 What . . . you] F; *verse* Q: sword|
2.3.324-5/1333-4 You . . . watch] F; *verse* Q: night|
2.3.327/1336 And . . . villain] Q; *2 lines* F: then|
2.3.330/1339 To . . . easy] Q; *2 lines* F: again|
2.3.353/1362 That . . . Roderigo] *2 lines* F: all|
2.3.372/1381 Nay . . . done] Q; *2 lines* F: gone|
2.3.374-5/1383-4 I'll . . . apart] Q; *1 line* F
3.1.22/1409 No . . . you] Q; *verse* F: friend|
3.1.30-3/1418-21 Why . . . Desdemona] *3 lines* Q: parted| her|; *3 lines* F: parted| wife|
3.1.38-9/1426-7 I . . . honest] knew|
3.3.3/1451 Good . . . husband] Q; *2 lines* F: do|
3.3.96-7/1544-5 Did . . . love] Q; Cassio| F
3.3.98/1546 He . . . ask] Q; *2 lines* F: last|
3.3.106/1554-5 IAGO . . . Ay, honest] F; *1 type line* Q
3.3.162/1610 Who . . . nothing] Q; *2 lines* F: trash|
3.3.207/1655 They . . . conscience] Q; *2 lines* F: husbands|
3.3.212/1660 She . . . most] F; *1 type line* Q
3.3.215/1663 He . . . blame] Q; *2 lines* F: witchcraft|
3.3.221/1669 Comes . . . moved] Q; *2 lines* F: love|
3.3.228/1676 Which . . . friend] Q; *2 lines* F: not|
3.3.231/1679 Long . . . so] Q; *2 lines* F: she so|
3.3.233/1681 Ay . . . you] Q; *2 lines* F: point|
3.3.243-4/1691-2 Farewell . . . know more] F; |thou Q. Q has only one 'Farewell'.
3.3.245/1693 Set . . . Iago] *2 lines* F: observe|; *2 lines* Q: on|. In Q, 'thou . . . on' is one line. See the previous note.
3.3.247/1695 Why . . . doubtless] Q; *2 lines* F: marry|
3.3.306/1754 You . . . common thing] Q; *2 lines* F: me|
3.3.319-20/1767-8 What . . . it] been] Q; *prose* F
3.3.324/1772 Be . . . me] Q; *2 lines* F: on't|
3.3.377-8/1824-5 For . . . that] F; *1 line* Q
3.3.419-20/1866-7 And . . . men] F; sleep| Q
3.3.421-2/1868-9 So . . . Cassio] mutter| F; *3 lines* Q: soul| affairs|. In Q, 'There . . . soul' is one line. See the previous note.
3.3.428-30/1875-7 That . . . Moor] F; leg| then| Q
3.3.477/1924 'Tis . . . live] Q; *2 lines* F: request|
3.3.478/1925 Damn . . . her, damn her] Q; *2 lines* F: minx|
3.3.481/1928 For . . . lieutenant] Q; *2 lines* F: devil|
3.4.23/1952 Where . . . Emilia] Q; *prose (?)* F (Æ-|milia)
3.4.32-3/1961-2 I . . . lord] now| Q; Be| F
3.4.36/1965 Give . . . lady] Q; *2 lines* F: your hand|
3.4.48/1977 I . . . promise] Q; *2 lines* F: this|
3.4.89/2018 Fetch . . . misgives] Q; *2 lines* F: handkerchief|
3.4.143-6/2072-5 Though . . . gods] F; *5 lines* Q: object| ache| members| think|
3.4.152-4/2081-3 Pray . . . concerning you] F; think| toy| Q
3.4.185/2114 I . . . chamber] Q; *2 lines* F: sweet|
4.1.33/2160 OTHELLO What, what . . . Lie] F; *1 type line* Q ('Oth. But what?')
4.1.43/2170 Work . . . caught] *prose* Q; *2 lines* F: on|
4.1.44-5/2171-2 And . . . lord] F; *prose* Q
4.1.46/2173 My . . . Cassio] *prose* Q; *2 lines* F: Othello|
4.1.113-14/2240-1 Now . . . said, well said] F; o'er| Q
4.1.118-20/2245-7 I . . . Ha, ha, ha!] *verse* Q: wit|; *verse* F: bear| it|
4.1.126-8/2253-5 This . . . promise] Q; *verse* F: out| her|
4.1.136-7/2263-4 So . . . ha, ha, ha] Q; *2 lines* F: upon me|
4.1.138-40/2265-7 Now . . . to] F; *verse* Q: chamber|
4.1.154/2281 How . . . now?] Q; *verse* F: Bianca|
4.1.174-5/2301-2 I . . . sweet woman] Q; *verse* F: a-killing|
4.1.188-9/2315-16 O . . . condition] Q; *2 lines* F: times|
4.1.191-2/2318-19 Nay . . . Iago, the pity of it, Iago] Q; *verse* F: certain|
4.1.202-3/2330-1 Do . . . contaminated] Q; *verse* F: her bed|

4.1.204/2332 Good . . . very good] Q; *2 lines* F: |the
4.1.205-6/2333-4 And . . . midnight] Q; *verse* F: undertaker|
4.1.207-8/2335-6 Excellent . . . same] F (*1 line*); *verse* Q: good|
4.1.209-11/2337-9 I . . . him] This edition; *verse* Q: Lodovico|; *verse* F: Venice| Duke|
4.1.218-19/2346-7 I . . . Cyprus] Q; *verse* F: signor|
4.1.265/2392 You . . . monkeys] Q; *2 lines* F: Cyprus
4.2.26-7/2437-8 Let . . . face] *1 line*
4.2.37-40/2448-51 Come . . . honest] Q; *prose* F
4.2.42/2453 To . . . false] Q; *2 lines* F: lord|
4.2.69-70/2480-1 That . . . sweet] F; *3 lines* Q: blowing| fair|
4.2.71/2482 That . . . born] *2 lines*: thee|. In Q, 'thou smell'st [and smell'st *in this edition*] . . . thee' is one line. See the previous note.
4.2.113/2524 What . . . you] *2 lines*: madam|
4.2.132-3/2543-4 Beshrew . . . him] F; *1 line* Q
4.2.140-2/2551-3 A . . . likelihood] Q; *5 lines* F: him| bones| whore| company| time|
4.2.178/2589 I . . . me] Q; *2 lines* F: find|
4.2.180-5/2591-6 Every . . . suffered] F; *verse* Q: Iago| me| least| it| already|
4.2.187-8/2598-9 Faith . . . together] F; *verse* Q: words|
4.2.225-6/2636-7 Sir . . . place] F; *verse* Q: Venice|
4.2.227-8/2638-9 Is . . . Venice] Q; *verse* F: Desdemona|
4.2.229-32/2640-3 O . . . Cassio] F; *verse* Q: him| lingered| so|
4.2.234-5/2645-6 Why . . . brains] F; *verse* Q: place|
4.3.4-5/2665-6 Will . . . Desdemona] *1 line*
4.3.45-8/2707-10 Sing . . . anon] *2 lines* F: these|; *not in* Q
4.3.56-7/2718-19 So . . . weeping] F; *2 lines* Q: night|
4.3.64-5/2726-7 Nor . . . dark] *verse*: light|
4.3.67-8/2729-30 The . . . vice] *verse* Q: price|; *verse* F: thing|
4.3.83-4/2745-6 Yes . . . for] *prose*
4.3.103/2765 Good . . . send] Q; *2 lines* F: night, good night|
5.1.1/2767 Here . . . come] Q; *2 lines* F: bulk|
5.1.27/2793 I . . . murder, murder] Q; *2 lines* F: ever|
5.1.38/2804 What . . . Murder, murder] Q; *2 lines* F: passage|
5.1.40-1/2806-7 CASSIO . . . Hark] F; *1 type line* Q
5.1.49/2815 Who's . . . murder] Q; *2 lines* F: there|
5.1.57/2823 O . . . this] Q; *2 lines* F: lieutenant|
5.1.65/2831 Kill . . . thieves] Q; *2 lines* F: dark|
5.1.77-8/2843-4 O . . . Cassio, Cassio] F; *1 line* Q
5.1.82/2848 I am . . . seek you] Q; *2 lines* F: thus|
5.1.87-8/2853-4 To . . . Come, come] F; *1 line* Q (which omits 'Come, come')
5.1.100/2866 He . . . chair] Q; *2 lines* F: 'tis he|
5.1.111-12/2877-8 Do . . . use] Q; speak| F
5.1.113/2879 Alas . . . husband] Q; *2 lines* F: matter | What
5.1.126/2892 Kind . . . dressed] Q; *2 lines* F: gentlemen|
5.2.13/2910 That . . . rose] Q; *2 lines* F: relume|
5.2.31/2928 Alack . . . that] Q; *2 lines* F: lord|
5.2.40/2937 When . . . not] Q; *2 lines* F: so|
5.2.50-1/2947-8 That . . . Cassio] F; thee| Q
5.2.52-3/2949-50 No . . . him] F; soul| Q
5.2.63-4/2960-1 And . . . Cassio] F; too| Q
5.2.81-2/2978-9 Had . . . all] F; lives| Q
5.2.94/2991 My . . . ho, my lord, my lord] Q; *2 lines* F: ho|
5.2.97-8/2994-5 I . . . so, so] F; *1 line* Q
5.2.110-11/3007-8 I . . . lord] F; *1 line* Q
5.2.121-2/3018-19 Cassio . . . Roderigo] Q; killed| F
5.2.122-3/3019-20 Roderigo . . . Cassio killed] Q; *1 line* F
5.2.140/3037 O . . . devil] F (black-|er devil); *2 lines* Q: she|
5.2.143-4/3040-1 Thou . . . true] Q; say| F
5.2.157/3054 What . . . husband] Q; Woman| F
5.2.158/3055 O . . . love] *2 lines* F: mistress|; *not in* Q
5.2.183/3080 I told . . . more] Q; *2 lines* F: thought|
5.2.185/3082 But . . . false] Q; *2 lines* F: him|
5.2.189/3086 She . . . say with Cassio] Q; *2 lines* F: |Did
5.2.190/3087 With . . . tongue] Q; *2 lines* F: mistress|
5.2.191/3088 I will . . . speak] Q; *2 lines* F: tongue|
5.2.195/3092 Nay . . . indeed] *2 lines* F: masters|; *not in* Q
5.2.201/3098 What . . . home] Q; *2 lines* F: mad|
5.2.211/3108 Poor . . . dead] Q; *2 lines* F: Desdemon|

LINEATION NOTES

5.2.232/3129   O . . . of] Q; *2 lines* F: Moor|
5.2.242/3139   But . . . villain] Q; *2 lines* F: thunder|
5.2.243/3140   The . . . wife] Q; *2 lines* F: falls|
5.2.291/3188   Where . . . forth] Q; *2 lines* F: viper|
5.2.314/3211   Sir . . . befall'n] Q; *2 lines* F: Sir|
5.2.318-19/3215-16   The . . . Roderigo] F; *1 line* Q
5.2.352/3249   Nor . . . speak] Q; *2 lines* F: malice|
5.2.374/3271   This . . . sight] Q; *2 lines* F: work|

All's Well That Ends Well

1.1.183/186   Monsieur . . . you] *2 lines*: Paroles|
1.1.198/201-2   So . . . safety] *verse*: away| safety|
1.3.16-17/320-1   No . . . many] *verse*: madam|
1.3.60-3/364-7   For . . . kind] *prose*
1.3.74-7/378-81   And . . . ten] *prose*
1.3.133-4/437-8   You . . . you] *1 line*
1.3.135-6/439-40   Nay . . . said 'a mother'] *1 line*
1.3.189-90/493-4   That . . . son] *1 line*
1.3.228-8/532-3   This . . . speak] *1 line*
2.1.29/588   And . . . bravely] *2 lines*: boy|
2.1.36-7/595-6   I . . . body] *1 line*
2.1.66-8/625-7   Good . . . infirmity] *2 lines*: thus|
2.1.68-71/627-30   O . . . medicine] *3 lines*: fox| if|
2.1.100/659   Ay . . . father] *2 lines* F: lord|
2.3.64-5/902-3   Gentlemen . . . health] *prose*
2.3.79/917-18   I . . . life] *verse (?)*: throw|
2.3.106/944   Why . . . wife] *prose*
2.3.109-12/947-50   Know'st . . . bed] *prose*
2.3.266-7/1106-7   Although . . . her] *prose*
2.3.273-4/1113-14   There's . . . yet] *prose*
2.3.275/1115   Ay . . . wars] *prose*
2.4.6-7/1143-4   If . . . very well] *prose*
2.4.14-15/1151-2   I . . . fortunes] *prose*
2.4.53-4/1191-2   In . . . will] *1 line*
2.5.76-7/1271-2   Let . . . home] Farewell|
3.2.62-3/1370-1   Brought . . . pains] *prose*
3.2.78-9/1386-7   'Tis . . . to] This edition; *prose*
3.2.85-6/1393-4   A . . . known] *prose*
3.2.91-8/1399-1406   Indeed . . . affairs] *prose*
3.5.1-15/1493-1507   Nay . . . companion] *verse*: come| city| sight| done| service| reported| commander| slew| labour| hark| trumpets| again| it| earl| name| rich| honesty| neighbour| gentleman|
3.5.33/1525   God . . . bound] *prose*
3.5.37-9/1529-31   Ay . . . by] This edition; way| pilgrim| by|
3.5.81-2/1573-4   He . . . gentleman] *1 line*
3.5.84-7/1576-9   'Tis . . . rascal] This edition; knave| lady|
3.5.87-8/1579-80   That . . . melancholy] This edition; *prose*
3.5.91-2/1583-4   He's . . . us] This edition; *prose*
3.5.94-5/1586-7   bring you | Where] bring | you, Where
3.6.7/1601   Do . . . him] *verse*: far|
3.6.82-3/1677-8   I . . . Farewell] *verse*: valiant| soldiership|
3.6.107/1703   I . . . caught] *2 lines*: twigs|
4.1.68/1830   O . . . eyes] *2 lines*: |do
4.1.75-9/1837-41   Boskos . . . pray] *prose*
4.3.315/2254   So . . . here] *as a separate line (without intervening stage direction)*
4.5.98-102/2416-20   A . . . soldier] *verse*: got| honour| that| face| see| talk|
5.1.39-41/2462-4   And . . . provide] *prose*
5.3.28/2546   What . . . spoke] *2 lines*: daughter|
5.3.30-1/2548-9   Then . . . fame] *prose*
5.3.245/2763   Come . . . woman] *prose*
5.3.272/2790   This . . . yours] *prose continued*
5.3.323/2841-2   Good . . . handkerchief] *1 verse line*

Timon of Athens

1.1.7/7   Hath . . . merchant] *2 lines*: attend|
1.1.19-20/19-20   You . . . lord] *prose*
1.1.65/65   Feigned . . . mount] *2 lines*: throned|
1.1.146/146   This . . . long] *2 lines*: mine|
1.1.152/152   My . . . promise] *2 lines*: thee|
1.1.156/156   Vouchsafe . . . lordship] *2 lines*: labour|
1.1.179-80/179-80   Look . . . chid] *1 line*
1.1.183/183   Good . . . Apemantus] *2 lines*: thee|
1.1.186/186   Why . . . not] *prose*
1.1.210/210-11   O . . . bellies] *verse*: lords|
1.1.212/213   So . . . labour] *2 lines*: |take
1.1.225/226   Then thou liest] *verse*
1.1.237-8/238-9   That . . . merchant] *verse*: lord|
1.1.251-5/252-6   So . . . monkey] *prose*
1.1.259/260   In . . . in] *2 lines*: pleasures|
1.1.271-2/272-3   No . . . friend] *verse*: bidding|
1.1.273-4/274-5   Away . . . hence] *verse*: dog|
1.1.276/277   He's . . . in] *2 lines*: humanity|
1.2.1-2/288-9   Most . . . peace] *3 lines*: Timon| age|
1.2.13-19/300-1   Nay . . . first] *1 line*
1.2.22-3/309-10   No . . . welcome] *1 line*
1.2.34-6/321-3   I . . . silent] *prose*
1.2.50-1/337-8   Lest . . . throats] *prose*
1.2.72/359   Captain . . . now] *verse*: Captain|
1.2.79-80/366-7   Would . . . to 'em] *prose*
1.2.113-14/400-1   Please . . . admittance] *verse*: ladies|
1.2.119-22/406-9   Hail . . . bosom] *prose*
1.2.122-3/409-10   Th'ear . . . rise] *1 line*
1.2.125-6/412-13   They're . . . welcome] *prose*
1.2.128/415   Hey-day . . . way] *2 lines*: Hey-day|
1.2.142/429   You . . . ladies] *2 lines*: pleasures|
1.2.166-7/453-4   O . . . lord] friends|
1.2.185/472   Be . . . news] *2 lines*: entertained|
1.2.190-1/477-8   I'll . . . reward] him|
1.2.192-3/479-80   He . . . coffer] *1 line*
1.2.198-202/485-9   That . . . out] *4 lines*: word| for't| were|
1.2.205-6/492-3   You . . . merits] wrong|
1.2.208/495   With . . . it] *2 lines*: thanks|
1.2.214-17/501-4   You . . . to you] *prose*
1.2.233-6/520-3   What . . . 'em] *prose*
1.2.236/523   Friendship's . . . dregs] *1 line*
1.2.248/536   Farewell . . . music] *prose*
1.2.248-50/536-8   So . . . thee] *prose*
1.2.250/538   O . . . be] *1 line*
2.2.29/602   From . . . payment] *prose*
2.2.31/604   'Twas . . . past] *prose*
2.2.43-4/616-17   Do . . . entertained] *1 line*
2.2.45-6/618-19   Stay . . . 'em] *prose*
2.2.66-7/639-40   Gramercies . . . mistress] *verse*: fool|
2.2.73/646   How . . . Apemantus] *verse line*
2.2.85/657   Answer . . . gone] *verse line*
2.2.89-90/661-2   If . . . usurers] *verse*: home|
2.2.92-3/664-5   So . . . thief] *verse*: I|
2.2.113-14/686-7   Nor . . . lack'st] *verse*: man|
2.2.120/693   Pray . . . anon] *2 lines*: near|
2.2.180-1/753-4   Shall . . . friends] *3 lines*: perceive| fortunes|
2.2.184-9/757-62   You . . . talents] *prose*
2.2.228/801   I . . . foe] *2 lines*: it|
3.1.55-6/858-9   I . . . him]|has
3.2.65/930   Why . . . piece] *2 lines*: soul|
3.2.77-8/942-3   For . . . life] *1 line*
3.3.1/954   Must . . . others] *2 lines*: Hmh|
3.4.7/1001   Welcome . . . hour] *2 lines*: brother|
3.4.15-16/1009-10   Is . . . fear] *1 line*
3.4.17-18/1011-12   'Tis . . . little] *prose*
3.4.29/1023   I'm . . . witness] *2 lines*: charge|
3.4.32/1026   Yes . . . yours] *2 lines*: crowns|
3.4.36-7/1030-1   Flaminius . . . forth] *prose*
3.4.39-40/1033-4   We . . . much] *1 line*

LINEATION NOTES

3.4.40-1/1034-5 I . . . diligent] *1 line*
3.4.47-8/1041-2 Ay . . . waiting] *1 line*
3.4.61-2/1055-6 How . . . worship] *unjustified type line*
3.4.88/1082 Knock . . . girdle] *prose*
3.4.93/1087 Five . . . And yours] *2 lines*: that|
3.5.1-2/1094-5 They . . . Devils] *prose*
3.5.9-12/1102-5 O . . . table] *prose*
3.6.1/1108 My . . . bloody] *2 lines*: to't|
3.6.14-15/1121-2 He . . . virtues] *1 line*
3.6.32/1139 The . . . outsides] *2 lines*: breathe|
3.6.49-50/1156-7 And . . . judge] lion|
3.6.78-9/1185-6 And . . . security] *1 line*
3.6.98-9/1205-6 If . . . judgement] thee|
3.6.100-1/1207-8 And . . . presently] spirit|
3.6.102/1209 Now . . . live] *2 lines*: enough|
3.7.46-7/1268-9 Let . . . together] *verse*: remembrance|
3.7.68-9/1291 The . . . thanks] *verse line*
4.3.45/1473 Do . . . quick] *2 lines*: nature|
4.3.73/1501 Promise . . . none] *verse line*
4.3.82-3/1510-11 TIMON . . . Yes] *1 type line*
4.3.84-8/1512-16 Be . . . diet] *prose*
4.3.130-1/1558-9 Hast . . . counsel] *prose*
4.3.132/1560 Dost . . . thee] *prose*
4.3.145-7/1573-5 Be . . . still] *4 lines (near foot of page)*: thatch| dead| matter|
4.3.167/1595 More . . . Timon] *prose*
4.3.168/1596 More . . . earnest] *prose*
4.3.169-70/1597-8 Strike . . . again] *prose*
4.3.280-1/1708-9 I . . . prodigal] *1 line*
4.3.295-6/1723-4 Under . . . Apemantus] *verse*: me|
4.3.348-50/1776-8 If . . . beasts] *verse*: please me| mightst| here| become|
4.3.353-6/1781-4 Yonder . . . again] *verse*: painter| thee| way| do|
4.3.357-9/1785-7 When . . . Apemantus] *verse*: thee| welcome| dog|
4.3.360/1788 Thou . . . alive] *2 lines*: cap|
4.3.361/1789 Would . . . upon] *2 lines*: enough|
4.3.362/1790 A . . . curse] *2 lines*: thee|
4.3.363/1791 All . . . pure] *2 lines*: villains|
4.3.364/1792 There . . . speak'st] *2 lines*: leprosy|
4.3.365-6/1793-4 If . . . hands] beat thee|
4.3.367/1795 I . . . off] *2 lines*: tongue|
4.3.369-70/1797-8 Choler . . . thee] me|
4.3.372-73/1800-1 Away . . . thee] *prose?* (Away . . . shall *as unjustified type line*)
4.3.389/1817 That . . . god] *2 lines*: lap|
4.3.400/1828 More . . . them] *2 lines*: men|
4.3.405/1833 It . . . treasure] *verse*: noised|
4.3.409/1837 True . . . hid] *verse*: him|
4.3.417/1845 We . . . want] *2 lines*: men|
4.3.456-7/1884-5 I'll . . . trade] *verse*: enemy|
4.3.471-3/1899-1901 He's . . . life] *prose*
4.3.473/1901 My dearest master] *verse line*
4.3.476/1904 Then . . . thee] *2 lines*: man|
4.3.478-80/1906-8 Then . . . villains] not| all|
4.3.483/1911 What . . . thee] *2 lines*: weep|
4.3.534-5/1962-3 O . . . master] *1 line*
5.1.3-4/1968-9 What's . . . gold] *verse*: him| true|
5.1.5-8/1970-3 Certain . . . sum] *verse*: Certain| Timandra| enriched| quantity| steward|
5.1.9-10/1974-5 Then . . . friends] *verse*: of his|
5.1.11-16/1976-82 Nothing . . . having] *verse*: else| again| highest| loves| his| us| purposes| for| goes|
5.1.17/1983 What . . . him] *verse*: now|
5.1.18-19/1984-5 Nothing . . . piece] *verse*: time| him|
5.1.20-1/1986-7 I . . . him] *verse*: too|
5.1.22-9/1988-95 Good . . . it] *verse*: best| time| expectation| act| people| use| fashionable| testament| judgement|
5.1.30-1/1996-7 Excellent . . . thyself] *verse*: workman| bad|
5.1.32-5/1998-2002 I . . . opulency] *verse*: thinking| him| himself| prosperity| flatteries|

5.1.36-8/2003-5 Must . . . thee] *verse*: needs| work| men|
5.1.46-8/2013-15 I'll . . . feed] turn| worshipped|
5.1.55/2022 Have . . . men] *2 lines*: lived|
5.1.56/2023 Sir . . . tasted] *2 lines*: Sir|
5.1.65/2032 Let . . . better] *2 lines*: go|
5.1.70/2037 We . . . service] *2 lines*: come|
5.1.71/2038 Most . . . you] *2 lines*: men|
5.1.73/2040 What . . . service] *2 lines*: can do|
5.1.74/2041 You're . . . gold] *2 lines*: men|
5.1.94/2061 Ay . . . dissemble] *2 lines*: cog|
5.1.100/2067 Look . . . gold] *2 lines*: Look you|
5.1.105/2072 You . . . company] *2 lines*: this|
5.2.16/2097 Thou . . . hanged] *2 lines*: burn|
5.2.20/2101 Of . . . Timon] *2 lines*: as you|
5.2.22/2103 I . . . plague] *2 lines*: thank them|
5.2.80/2161 These . . . them] *prose*
5.2.98/2179 Trouble . . . find him] *2 lines*: shall|
5.2.109-10/2190-1 His . . . nature] *1 line*
5.3.3-4/2197-8 Besides . . . approach] *1 line*
5.4.71-8/2290-7 Here . . . gait] *4 lines*: bereft| left| hate|

The History of King Lear

1.63-4/63-4 Sir . . . is] BLAYNEY; *1 line* Q
1.66-8/66-8 I find . . . joys] F; *2 lines* Q: short|
1.70-1/70-1 And . . . love] F; *1 line* Q
1.71-3/71-3 Then . . . tongue] F; *2 lines* Q: sure|
1.83-5/83-5 Unhappy . . . less] F; *prose* Q
1.91-5/91-5 Why . . . sisters] F; all| hand| him| never| Q
1.136-9/136-9 Let . . . speak] F; *5 lines* Q: rather| heart| mad| duty|
1.140/140 When . . . bound] *2 lines* QF: bows|
1.141-3/141-3 When . . . judgement] F; *4 lines* Q: folly| consideration| life|
1.179-83/179-83 My . . . love] F; *4 lines* Q: you| daughter| present|
1.183-5/183-5 Royal . . . less] F; *2 lines* Q: what|
1.185-9/185-9 Right . . . pieced] F; *4 lines* Q: us| fallen| little|
1.195-6/195-6 Pardon . . . conditions] F; up| Q
1.208-10/208-10 So . . . degree] F; *2 lines* Q: favour|
1.225-6/225-6 Go . . . better] This edition; born| Q
1.228-31/228-31 That often . . . stands] F; *3 lines* Q: do| lady|
1.233-6/233-6 Royal . . . Burgundy] F; *3 lines* Q: portion| Cordelia|
1.253-4/253-4 Thou . . . see] F; thine| Q
1.256-7/256-7 Without . . . Burgundy] F; *1 line* Q
1.258-61/258-61 Ye . . . father] F; our father| are| faults| Q
1.267-9/267-9 Let . . . scanted] F; lord| alms| Q
1.274-6/274-6 Sister . . . tonight] *verse* QF: say| both|
2.1-8/299-306 Thou . . . true] F; *prose* Q
2.9-10/307-8 As . . . bastardy] BLAYNEY; *prose* Q
2.11-12/309-10 Who . . . quality] F; *prose* Q
2.13-14/311-12 Than . . . fops] This edition; *prose* Q
2.15-17/313-15 Got . . . Edmund] F; *prose* Q
2.18-21/316-19 As . . . bastards] This edition; *prose* Q
2.22-5/320-23 Kent . . . news] F; *prose* Q
3.1-2/470-1 Did . . . fool] This edition; *prose* QF
3.3-4/472-3 By . . . other] F; me| Q
3.12-15/481-4 Put . . . one] F; *prose* Q
3.16-20/485-9 Not . . . abused] F; *prose* Q
3.21/490 Remember . . . you] F; *prose* Q
3.22-6/491-5 And . . . dinner] *prose* QF
4.1-5/496-500 If . . . condemned] F; *prose* Q
4.6/501 Thy . . . labour] F; *prose* Q
4.114-23/608-17 Have . . . score] F; *prose* Q
4.135-142/629-36 That . . . there] *4 lines* Q: land| stand| appear|
4.168/662 Then they] *prose* QF
4.168-71/662-5 for . . . among] F; *prose* Q
4.191-2/685-6 Mum . . . crumb] *1 line* QF
4.193-4/687-8 Weary . . . peascod] *1 line* QF
4.195-7/689-91 Not . . . forth] F; *prose* Q

4.198-9/692-3 In . . . you] This edition; *prose* Q; Sir| F
4.200-8/694-702 To . . . proceedings] F; *prose* Q
4.210-11/704-5 The hedge-sparrow . . . young] *prose* QF
4.214-17/708-11 Come . . . are] F; *prose* Q
4.220-2/714-6 Doth . . . discernings] F; *prose* Q; *5 lines* BLAYNEY: me| walk| speak thus| notion|. Part-lines are commoner within speeches than at the beginning of them.
4.223-4/717-8 Are . . . so] This edition; *prose* Q
4.225/719 Who . . . am] F; *prose* Q
4.226-8/720-2 Lear's . . . daughters] *prose* Q
4.230/724 Come, sir] *prose* Q
4.231-7/725-31 This . . . manners] F; *prose* Q
4.238-9/732-3 Shows . . . brothel] BLAYNEY; *prose* Q; lust| F
4.250-1/744-5 You . . . betters] *prose* (?) F: rabble|; *prose* Q
4.252-5/746-9 We . . . child] F; *prose* Q
4.256/750 Than . . . liest] BLAYNEY
4.257-66/751-60 My train . . . people] F; *prose* Q
4.268-70/762-4 It . . . fruitful] BLAYNEY; *prose* Q; *4 lines* F: lord| goddess [hear]| intend|
4.271-80/765-74 Into . . . feel] F; *prose* Q
4.281/775 That she may feel] This edition; *prose* Q
4.282-3/776-7 How . . . people] F; *prose* Q
4.285-7/779-81 Never . . . it] F; *prose* Q
4.288-9/782-3 What . . . fortnight] F; *prose* Q
4.290/784 I'll . . . ashamed] *prose* Q; *2 lines* F: thee|
4.291-2/785-6 That . . . perforce] F; *prose* Q
4.293/787 And . . . upon thee] ROWE; *prose* Q; *2 lines* F: |blasts.
4.294-7/788-91 Untented . . . make] F; *prose* Q
4.298-9/792-3 To . . . this] This edition; *prose* Q. Any decision on where to place Q's amphibious part-line ('yea, i'st come to this') is arbitrary; this one requires the fewest metrical licences.
4.299-304/793-8 Yet . . . ever] F; *prose* Q
4.304/798 thou . . . thee] *prose* Q
4.306-7/800-1 I . . . you] F; *prose* Q
4.307-8/801-2 Come . . . master] BLAYNEY; *prose* Q
4.311-15/805-9 A . . . after] F; *prose* Q
4.316-17/810-11 What . . . madam] *1 type line* Q
4.320-8/814-22 Take . . . mildness] F; *2 lines* Q: top|
4.329-30/823-4 How . . . well] F; *prose* Q
4.331-2/825-6 Nay . . . event] *1 type line* Q
5.32-3/858-9 I . . . ready] *prose* Q
5.45-6/871-2 O . . . mad] This edition; *prose* QF
5.47-8/873-4 Keep . . . ready] *prose* QF
6.14-27/891-904 The Duke . . . you] F; *prose* Q
6.28-9/905-6 I . . . you] F; *prose* Q
6.30/907 Seem . . . well] *prose* Q; *2 lines* F: [Draw,] seems . . . yourself|
6.31-6/908-13 Yield . . . help] F; *prose* Q
6.37-9/914-16 Here . . . mistress] F; *prose* Q
6.39/916 GLOUCESTER But . . . he] *same type line as the end of the preceding speech* Q
6.43-54/920-31 Persuade . . . made] F; *prose* Q
6.56/933 But . . . fled] F; *prose* Q
6.56-63/933-40 Let . . . death] F; *prose* Q
6.64-77/941-54 When . . . it] F; *prose* Q
6.77-85/954-62 Strong . . . capable] F; *prose* Q
6.86-7/963-4 How . . . news] F; *prose* Q
6.88-9/965-6 If . . . lord] F; *prose* Q
6.91-2/968-9 What . . . Edgar] F; *prose* Q
6.94-5/971-2 Was . . . father] F; *prose* Q
6.103-4/980-1 That . . . there] F; *1 line* Q
6.104-6/981-3 Nor . . . office] F; *prose* Q
6.109/986 CORNWALL . . . lord] *1 type line* Q
6.110-16/987-93 If . . . on] F; *prose* Q
6.116-17/993-4 I . . . else] *1 line* QF
6.126-8/1003-5 Lay . . . use] F; *2 lines* Q: counsel|
6.129-30/1006-7 I . . . welcome] F; *1 line* Q
7.2-3/1009-10 KENT . . . horses] *1 type line* Q
7.4-5/1011-12 KENT . . . tell me] *1 type line* Q
7.6-7/1013-14 KENT . . . for thee] *1 type line* Q

7.40/1044 OSWALD . . . murder, help] *on the same type line as the end of the preceding speech* Q
7.71-2/1078-9 That . . . twain] these| QF
7.78-80/1085-7 Knowing . . . fool] Q2, F; *2 lines* Q1: epileptic|
7.85-6/1092-3 Why . . . offence] F; *1 line* Q
7.91-100/1098-1107 This . . . nicely] F; *9 lines* Q: praised| roughness| nature| plain| so| know| craft| silly-ducking|
7.110-12/1117-19 I . . . misconstruction] F; *2 lines* Q: master|
7.119-20/1126-7 None . . . fool] F; *1 line* Q
7.122-31/1129-31 I . . . you] F; *2 lines* Q: me|
7.127-8/1134-5 Fetch . . . noon] F; honour| Q
7.130-1/1137-8 Why . . . so] F; *prose* Q
7.137-9/1144-6 Is . . . with] *2 lines* Q: pilf'rings |
7.139-41/1146-8 The King . . . restrained] F; *2 lines* Q: valued|
7.189-91/1196-8 As . . . remove] F; *2 lines* Q: as|
7.193-6/1200-4 Ha . . . nether-stocks] F; *verse* Q: garters| bears| men| legs|
7.197-8/1205-6 What's . . . here] *prose* Q
7.198-9/1206-7 It . . . daughter] F; *1 line* Q
7.199/1207 LEAR No . . . yes] *1 type line* Q
7.199-200/1207-8 LEAR No, I . . . yea] *1 type line* Q
7.200/1208 LEAR No, no . . . have] *1 type line* Q
7.215-16/1223-4 Commanded . . . looks] F; leisure| Q
7.257-60/1265-8 My . . . course] F; *prose* Q
7.260/1268 Vengeance . . . confusion] F; *prose* Q
7.261-2/1269-70 What . . . wife] This edition; *prose* Q; Gloucester, Gloucester| F
7.268-71/1276-9 Infirmity . . . forbear] *3 lines* Q: health| oppressed|
7.273-4/1281-2 To . . . man] F; *1 line* Q
7.274-5/1282-3 Death . . . here] *1 line* Q
7.275-6/1283-4 This . . . her] F; *1 line* Q
7.281-2/1289-90 I . . . you] This edition; *1 line* QF
7.305-9/1313-17 Nature . . . return] F; *4 lines* Q: confine| discretion| yourself|
7.320-2/1328-30 All . . . lameness] F; *2 lines* Q: top|
7.326-7/1334-5 O . . . mood] F; me| Q
7.329-32/1337-40 Thy . . . train] F; *3 lines* Q: o'er| burn| Q
7.348-50/1356-8 If you . . . part] F; Allow| cause| Q
7.370-1/1378-9 Why . . . brought] F; dowerless| Q
7.382-3/1390-1 A . . . thee] F; my| Q
7.389-92/1397-1400 Not . . . passion] F; yet| welcome| those| Q
7.442-4/1450-2 No . . . flaws] *2 lines* QF: weeping|
7.448/1456-7 'Tis . . . folly] This edition; rest| QF
7.458-9/1466-7 Do . . . bush] F; *1 line* Q
8.1-2/1475-6 One . . . unquietly] This edition; *1 line* QF
8.22-6/1496-1500 Into . . . far] *4 lines* Q: negligence| ports| banner|
8.32-3/1506-7 And . . . you] assurance| Q
8.42-3/1516-17 Give . . . say] F; *1 line* Q
8.43-4/1517-18 Few . . . King] This edition; yet| QF
8.45-6/1519-20 I'll . . . other] This edition; lights| Q; him| F
9.2-9/1522-9 You . . . man] F; drenched| and| to| head| flat| nature's| make| Q
9.10-13/1530-3 O . . . fool] F; *verse* Q: house| door| blessing|
9.18-24/1538-44 You . . . foul] F; *6 lines* Q: pleasure| and| servile| joined| white|
9.25-36/1545-56 He . . . glass] CAPELL; *prose* Q. F treats as Capell, but divides the verse into four lines instead of eight.
9.42-49/1562-69 Alas . . . force] F; *9 lines* Q: here| these| of the| caves| fires| groans of| remember| carry|
9.49-56/1569-76 Let . . . covert] F; *7 lines* Q: dreadful| now| thee| justice| and| incestuous|
9.56-8/1576-8 and . . . guilts] This edition; *2 lines* Q: life|; *2 lines* F: seeming|
9.61-8/1581-88 Alack . . . courtesy] F; *prose* Q
9.71-3/1591-3 The . . . heart] F; can| Poor| Q
9.75-8/1595-8 He . . . day] F; *prose* Q
10.8-20/1607-18 Go . . . careful] F; *verse* Q: Dukes| received| spoken| injuries| home| landed| and| talk| him| gone| me| is|
10.21-5/1619-23 This . . . fall] F; *4 lines* Q: now| deserving| less|

LINEATION NOTES

11.1-3/1624-6 Here ... endure] F; *prose* Q
11.3-4/1626-7 LEAR Let ... here] *1 type line* Q
11.18-21/1641-4 In ... that] F; this| father| lies| Q
11.38-9/1661-2 What ... forth] Q1 (*not capitalizing* 'come'); *prose* Q2, F
11.43-4/1666-7 Hast .. this] *prose* QF
11.67-8/1690-91 Judicious ... daughters] F; flesh| Q
11.109-13/1732-6 Swithin ... thee] *prose* Q
11.125/1748 Horse ... wear] F; *prose* Q
11.131-2/1753-4 The Prince ... Mahu] *prose* QF. Edgar's next two speeches appear to be verse, and there is a particular appropriateness in his adopting verse immediately after Gloucester's jibe about 'better company'.
11.133-4/1755-6 Our ... gets it] *prose* QF
11.135-40/1757-62 Go ... ready] F; *prose* Q
11.142-3/1764-5 My ... house] *1 line* Q
11.144-5/1766-7 I'll ... study] *prose* Q
11.148-9/1770-1 Importune ... unsettle] F; *1 line* Q
11.157-8/1779-80 The ... grace] F; wits| Q
11.158-9/1780-1 O ... company] F; *1 line* Q
11.161-2/1783-4 With ... philosopher] F; *1 line* Q
13.11-12/1827-8 A king, a ... them] This edition; *prose* Q
13.21/1837 Come ... me] *prose* Q
13.22-3/1838-9 Her ... speak] *1 line* Q
13.25-7/1841-3 The foul ... herring] Q2; *verse* Q1: nightingale|
13.27-8/1843-4 Croak ... thee] *1 verse line* Q
13.29-30/1845-6 How ... cushions] *prose* Q
13.31-5/1847-51 I'll ... too] *prose* Q
13.37-40/1853-6 Sleepest ... harm] *prose* Q
13.58-9/1874 Tom ... curs] *1 verse line*
13.60-5/1875-80 Be ... wail] F; *3 lines* Q: bite| him|. Shakespeare apparently often wrote two adjoining short rhymed lines as one manuscript line; F abandons this practice because of the narrowness of its column; we accept F's (the traditional) arrangement because it clarifies the form.
13.66-9/1881-4 For ... dry] F; *prose* Q (*though* 'For' *is capitalized at the beginning of the line, after a comma*)
13.70-5/1885-90 Then ... changed] F; *verse* Q: her| hardness| hundred| say|
13.77-8/1892-3 Make ... morning. So, so, so] F; *verse* Q: |We'll
13.83-5/1898-1900 There ... master] F; *2 lines* Q: friend|
13.86-9/1901-4 If ... provision] F; *3 lines* Q: thine| losse|
13.92-4/1907-9 Which ... behind] *2 lines* Q: cure| Q
13.95-6/1910-11 When ... foes] Q2; *prose* Q1
14.1-3/1924-6 Post ... Gloucester] BLAYNEY; *2 lines* Q: letter|; *prose* F
14.4-5/1927-8 Leave ... company] BLAYNEY; *1 line* Q1; *prose* Q2, F
14.6-9/1929-32 The ... like] Q2; *verse* Q1: father| going|
14.9-10/1932-3 Our ... us] *prose* F; *one line of verse* Q
14.14-18/1937-41 Some ... friends] F; *prose* Q (*though* 'Some' *is capitalized at the beginning of a line, after a comma*)
14.25-6/1948-9 Shall ... traitor] F; blame| Q
14.33-4/1956-7 By ... beard] F; *prose* Q
14.35/1958 REGAN ... traitor] *same type line as the end of the preceding speech* Q
14.36-7/1959-60 Naughty ... chin] *1 line* Q
14.43-4/1966-7 And ... kingdom] *prose* QF
14.44-5/1967-8 To ... Speak] F; *prose* Q
14.48/1971 CORNWALL ... false] *1 type line* Q
14.49/1972 CORNWALL ... Dover] *1 type line* Q
14.72-3/1995-6 But ... hold] F; *1 line* Q
14.74-5/1997-8 If ... mean] *prose* Q
14.79-80/2002-3 O ... O] F; *prose* Q
14.84-5/2007-8 Edmund ... act] F; *1 line* Q
14.85-8/2008-11 Out ... thee] F; *prose* Q
14.91-2/2014-15 Go ... you] F; *prose* Q
14.94-6/2017-9 Turn ... arm] F; upon| untimely| Q
14.98-100/2021-3 If she ... monsters] *prose* Q
14.104-5/2027-8 Go ... him] *prose* Q
15.9-11/2037-9 O ... fourscore] *prose* Q

15.36-8/2064-6 How ... master] F; *prose* Q
15.54-6/2082-4 Both ... fiend] F; *verse* Q: footpath| wits|
15.56-61/2084-9 Five ... master] *verse* Q: once| dumbness| Flibbertigibbet of| chambermaids|
15.63-4/2091-2 Have ... still] F; thee| Q
15.75-6/2103-4 With ... need] F; me| Q
15.77-8/2105-6 Give ... thee] F; *1 line* Q
16.3-11/2109-17 Madam ... offensive] F; *prose* Q
16.26-7/2132-3 My ... due] *1 line* Q
16.29-30/2135-6 O ... wind] F; *1 line* Q
16.46-7/2152-3 Send ... come] *1 line* Q
16.48-9/2154-5 Humanity ... deep] *1 line* Q
16.51-5/2157-61 Who ... land] *4 lines* Q: honour| pity| mischief|
16.58-60/2164-6 See ... woman] F; *prose* Q
16.69-71/2175-7 O ... Gloucester] F; *prose* Q
16.77-80/2183-6 This ... eye] F; *3 lines* Q: justicers| venge|
16.80-1/2186-7 Both ... answer] F; *1 line* Q
16.82/2188 'Tis ... well] *1 type line* Q
16.85-6/2191-2 Upon ... answer] F; took| Q
16.88/2194 [SECOND] GENTLEMAN ... here] *1 type line* Q
16.93-4/2199-2200 Gloucester ... King] F; *1 line* Q
17.3-7/2205-9 Something ... necessary] STEEVENS; *prose* Q (*but reading* 'So' *after a comma, at the beginning of a type line*). Except for the required elision of 'to the' and the line-divided foot created by 'danger | That', this is regular verse.
17.10-11/2212-13 Did ... grief] *1 verse line* Q ('of grief' *turned up*)
17.14-16/2216-18 Her ... o'er her] *2 lines* Q: passion|
17.33-4/2235-6 It ... conditions] *1 line* Q
17.37-8/2239-40 [FIRST] GENTLEMAN ... returned] *1 type line*
17.41-2/2243-4 What ... daughter] *1 line* Q
17.46-8/2248-50 To ... Cordelia] *2 lines* Q: mind|
17.55-6/2257-8 Lending ... me] JENNENS; *1 line* Q. The line-break thus produced is awkward; it might be better to divide after 'aright' and 'acquaintance'.
18.9-10/2267-8 In ... him] This edition; *1 line* QF. Shakespeare probably wrote this fourteener on one manuscript line. Editors follow Pope in marking 'He ... worth' one line, but F emends *can helpe* to *helpes*, which makes this metrically acceptable. Since either arrangement leaves us with one unassimilated part-line, it seems best to adopt an arrangement which leaves Q's extra syllable at a line-break instead of in the middle of a line.
18.16-17/2274-5 All ... earth] F; *1 line* Q
18.21-2/2279-80 News ... hitherward] F; *1 line* Q
18.25-6/2283-4 It ... France] *1 line* Q
19.1-2/2289-90 OSWALD Ay ... person] *1 type line* Q
19.2-3/2290-1 Madam ... soldier] F; *1 line* Q
19.12-14/2300-2 In ... army] F; *2 lines* Q: life|
19.12-13/2300-1 In ... life] BLAYNEY; *1 line* Q. F treats 'His ... descry' as one line; see 18.9-10/2267-8, above.
19.17-18/2305-6 I ... business] F; *prose* Q
19.35-6/2323-4 I ... farewell] F; *1 line* Q
20.3-4/2331-2 Horrible ... sea] F; *1 line* Q
20.33-4/2361-2 Why ... it] F; *1 line* Q
20.41-8/2369-76 Gone ... sir] F; *prose* Q
20.81-2/2409-10 The ... thus] F; *1 line* Q
20.83-4/2411-12 No ... himself] *prose* Q2, F; *1 verse line* Q2; *verse* BLAYNEY: I|
20.104-5/2433-4 The ... King] F; *prose* Q
20.105-9/2434-8 Ay ... fly] F; *prose* Q
20.110-12/2439-41 Does ... daughters] *prose* Q; thrive| father| F
20.113-14/2442-3 Got ... dame] *prose* Q; *3 lines* F: sheets| soldiers|
20.115-127/2444-56 Whose ... thee] *prose* QF. Q capitalizes 'Give' (20.125/2454), though this follows a comma in the middle of a line.
20.129/2458 O ... world] F; *prose* Q
20.130/2459 Shall ... me] *prose* Q; *2 lines* F: naught|
20.133-4/2462-3 No ... of't] *prose* QF
20.136-7/2465-6 I ... it] *prose* Q; report| F
20.137-9/2466-8 And ... eyes] Q, which sets Edgar's speech as prose, sets 'breaks ... case' on one type line; this produces a regular pentameter, but makes the preceding line unmetrical.

LINEATION NOTES

20.154-162/2483-91   Thou . . . So] *prose* QF
20.163-4/2492-3   O . . . madness] F; *1 line* Q
20.165-9/2494-8   If . . . me] *prose* Q
20.171-3/2500-2   When . . . shoe] F; *prose* Q
20.174-5/2503-4   A . . . kill, kill, kill, kill, kill, kill] This edition; *prose* Q; F adds 'I'll put't in proof' after 'felt', and divides after 'proof' and 'son-in-laws'
20.176-7/2505-6   O . . . dear] F; *1 line* Q
20.178-81/2507-10   No . . . brains] F; *prose* Q
20.183-4/2512-13   No . . . salt] F; *prose* Q
20.185/2514   To . . . waterpots] *prose* Q
20.186/2515   Ay . . sir] *1 type line* Q2
20.187-9/2516-8   I . . . that] This edition; *prose* Q; what| king| POPE
20.193-6/2522-5   A . . . to] F; *prose* Q
20.202-3/2530-1   But . . . army] F; *1 line* Q
20.207/2535   Her . . . sir] *1 type line* Q
20.210-11/2538-9   To . . . father] *1 type line* Q
20.216-18/2544-6   Hearty . . . boot] F; *prose* Q (*though Qb divides after* 'heauen')
20.218-22/2546-50   A . . . thee] F; *prose* Q
20.222-3/2550-1   Now . . . to't] F; *1 line* Q
20.223-6/2551-4   Wherefore . . . arm] F; *prose* Q
20.241-2/2569-70   To . . . death! Death] F; upon| Q
20.244-5/2572-3   As . . . desire] Q2, F; *1 line* Q
20.247-51/2575-9   Sit . . . not] *4 lines* Q: pockets| friends| deathsman|
20.277-8/2603-4   Give . . . drum] Q2, F; *1 line* Q1
21.1-2/2606-7   O . . . goodness] Q2; *1 line* Q1. Editors usually adopt Rowe's arrangement, dividing after 'work'; but this requires alteration of Q's next line as well, and in any case leaves the speech with an unassimilated part-line. Q1's arrangement (turning 'thy goodness' up into the line above, opposite the entrance direction) strongly suggests that 'O . . . goodness' was written as one line in the manuscript, and this is most easily explained on the assumption that 'O thou good Kent' was regarded as a separate part-line.
21.6-8/2611-13   Be . . . off] Q2, F; *2 lines* Q1: those|
21.11-12/2616-7   Then . . . King] F; *1 line* Q
21.12-13/2617-8   O . . . nature] Q2, F; *1 line* Q1
21.15-16/2620-1   So . . . long] F; king| Q
21.24-6/2629-31   O . . . sisters] F; *2 lines* Q: lips|
21.54-5/2659-60   I feel . . . condition] F; *1 line* Q
21.55-7/2660-2   O . . . kneel] Q2, F; *prose* Q1
21.67/2672   To . . . am] *1 type line* Q
21.72-3/2677-8   CORDELIA . . . France] *1 type line* Q
21.76-7/2681-2   Be . . . in him] F; *1 line* Q
21.77-80/2682-5   and yet . . . settling] *prose* Q
21.81/2686   CORDELIA . . . walk] *same type line as end of preceding speech* Q
21.82-4/2687-9   You . . . foolish] This edition; Q1 *divides after* 'forgive' (*it is unclear whether verse or prose is intended*); Q2 *and* F *divide after* 'me' *and* 'forgive'. The speech might be prose, but the fact that the preceding scene has been entirely verse, and that what follows easily scans as verse, tell against this. But Q1's line-ending 'and for*give*' would be unparalleled; an ionic ('and for*giue, I*') is much more acceptable, and also lends to a more regular interpretation of the following speech (see next note).
21.84-5/2689-90   Holds . . . slain] This edition; *1 line*. Capell divided after 'sir', omitting 'that'; most editors treat as prose. This division produces regular lines before and after.
21.86-7/2691-2   As . . . Gloucester] CAPELL; *1 line* Q. Capell unnecessarily omitted 'As'; hexameters are common.
21.87-9/2692-4   They . . . Germany] *prose* Q
21.89-91/2694-6   Report . . . apace] *2 lines* Q: about|
21.91-2/2696-7   The . . . sir] This edition; *1 line* Q. Capell emended and divided after 'And the arbitrement'; most editors leave the speech undivided, as in Q, and regard it as prose. But although Shakespeare twice accentuates 'arbitrement' on the second syllable (*1 Henry IV* 4.1.70/2194, *Kinsmen* 5.5.107/2609), his usage at *Richard III* 5.5.42/3133 is ambiguous, and *The Jew of Malta* 5.2.52-3 testifies to the currency of an alternative accentuation ('Thou seest thy life, and *Malta's* happinesse, | Are at my Arbitrament; and *Barabas*'). For the general phenomenon of primary accent on the first syllable of tetrasyllabic words, see Cercignani, 42-3; other words formed on the *arbit-* root are, of course, accented on the first syllable, and there is nothing unusual about Shakespearian inconsistency on how to accent a word (or about a one-and-a-half-line speech being set as one line).

22.9/2708   Do . . . honoured love] *1 type line* Q
22.11-12/2710-11   To . . . you] *1 type line* Q
22.13-15/2712-14   I . . . hers] This edition; *prose* Q1; *2 lines* Q2: conjunct| Q2. Q2's arrangement produces a line which begins (anomalously) with two reversed feet. Our arrangement, taking 22.13/2712 as an amphibious section, instead produces an (acceptable) defective caesura.
22.16-17/2715-16   I . . . her] F; *1 line* Q
22.18-19/2717-18   Fear . . . husband] *1 line* QF
22.20-21/2719-20   I . . . me] *prose* Q
22.30/2729   EDMUND . . . reasoned] *1 type line* Q
22.34-5/2733-4   Let . . . proceedings] F; *prose* Q1; determine| Q2. Editors almost always follow Q2. But Q2's arrangement is without authority, and was altered by F (set from Q2 copy); it produces an (anomalous) anapaest at the end of Edmund's next speech. Our arrangement produces an (acceptable) hexameter, or even a pentameter, depending on whether one reads 'with th'ensign' or 'with the ensign'.
22.35-6/2734-5   EDMUND . . . tent] This edition; *same type line as the end of the preceding speech* Q. See preceding note. Defective caesurae in lines broken between two speeches occur elsewhere.
22.36-7/2735-6   REGAN . . . No] *1 type line* Q
22.50-2/2749-51   I . . . again] Q2, F; *prose* Q1
22.53-4/2752-3   Why . . . paper] *1 line* QF
22.57-8/2756-7   By . . . you] F; *1 line* Q
22.60-2/2759-61   Each . . . enjoyed] F; *2 lines* Q: adder|
23.3-4/2775-6   If . . . comfort] Q2, F; *1 line* Q1
24.3-5/2786-8   We . . . down] Q2, F; *2 lines* Q1: incurred|
24.37-8/2820-1   I . . . do't] This edition; oats| Q
24.45-6/2828-9   To . . . guard] F; *1 line* Q
24.51-3/2834-6   My . . . session] F; tomorrow| hold| Q
24.53-6/2836-9   At . . . sharpness] *3 lines* Q: bleed| quarrels|
24.59-60/2842-3   I . . . brother] F; *1 line* Q
24.65-6/2848-9   Not . . . himself] F; *prose* Q
24.67-8/2850-51   In . . . best] F; *1 line* Q
24.70-1/2853-4   Holla . . . asquint] F; *1 line* Q
24.100-1/2883-4   ALBANY . . . ho, a herald] *1 type line* Q
24.103-4/2886-7   All . . . discharge] F; *1 line* Q
24.107-8/2890-1   And . . . trumpet] *1 type line* Q
24.116-18/2899-2901   What . . . summons] F; *2 lines* Q: quality|
24.119/2902   By . . . canker-bit] Q2, F; tooth| Q1
24.120-1/2903-4   Yet . . . withal] F; move't| Q
24.124-5/2907-8   That . . . mine] F; arm| Q
24.136-8/2919-21   This . . . liest] F; *2 lines* Q: spirits|
24.147-50/2930-3   This . . . beguiled] F; *3 lines* Q: arms| opposite|
24.150-3/2933-6   Stop . . . know't] F; *prose* Q
24.154-5/2937-8   Say . . . for't] F; *1 line* Q
24.155-6/2938-9   Most . . . paper] *1 line* QF
24.167-9/2950-2   Make . . . eyes] F; *2 lines* Q: vicious|
24.169-70/2952-3   Thou . . . here] Q2, F; come| Q1 (*but* 'full' *is not capitalized*)
24.173-4/2956-7   Let . . . father] This edition; *1 line* Q
24.178-86/2961-69   By . . . rings] F; lord| told| proclamation| near| death| once| rags| disdained| Q
24.200-1/2983-4   For . . . this] Q2, F; *1 line* Q1
24.201-4/2984-7   This . . . extremity] *3 lines* Q: such | much|
24.218-9/3001-2   What kind . . . knife] F; *1 line* Q
24.219-20/3002-3   It's . . . of] *1 line* Q
24.227/3010   Touches . . . sir] *1 type line* Q
24.230-1/3013-14   I . . . night] F; *1 line* Q
24.238/3021   And . . . faces] *1 type line* Q
24.243/2026   Nay . . . O run] *1 type line* Q

24.247/3030 Give . . . life] *1 type line* Q
24.249-50/3032-3 To . . . despair] F; lay| Q
24.259/3042 Why . . . end] *1 type line* Q
24.260/3043 EDGAR . . . cease] *1 type line* Q
24.263/3046 That . . . master] *1 type line* Q
24.264/3047 LEAR . . . friend] *1 type line* Q
24.271-3/3054-6 Did . . . now] F; day| would| Q
24.277/3060 One . . . Kent] *1 type line* Q
24.284/3067 Have . . . hither] *1 type line* Q
24.287/3070 And . . . too] *1 type line* Q
24.289/3072 That . . . bootless] *1 type line* Q
24.290-6/3073-79 That's . . . honours] F; *prose* Q (*but capitalizing* 'Know' *at the beginning of its second prose line*)
24.297/3080 Have . . . taste] *prose* Q
24.298-9/3081-2 The . . . see, see] F; *prose* Q
24.300-2/3083-5 And . . . more] F; *prose* Q
24.303-4/3086-7 Never . . . O, O, O, O] *This edition*; *prose* Q
24.305/3088 EDGAR . . . , my lord] *same type line as end of preceding speech* Q
24.306-7/3089-90 LEAR . . . lord] *1 type line* Q
24.308-10/3091-3 Vex . . . longer] pass| rack| Q
24.313-15/3096-8 Bear . . . sustain] QF; *4 lines G.T. conj.*: hence| woe| kingdom|

The Tragedy of King Lear

1.1.26-7/27-8 My . . . friend] Q; *verse* F: Kent|
1.1.148/149 When . . . bound] *2 lines* F: bows|
1.1.160/161 Now . . . vain] Q; *2 lines* F: King|
1.1.233-4/234-5 Better . . . better] Hadst| F; born| Q
*1.1.283-5/284-6 Sister . . . tonight] *verse* QF: say| both|
1.1.286-7/287-8 That's . . . us] *verse* F, *with* 'with us' *turned up*
1.2.42-3/349-50 I shall . . . blame] Q; *verse* F: it| them|
1.3.1-2/484-5 Did . . . fool] *prose* QF
1.3.17-18/500-1 And . . . so] *prose* QF
1.3.19-20/502-3 I'll . . . dinner] *This edition*: *prose* QF. *See textual notes.*
1.4.80-1/584-5 I am . . . pardon] Q; *verse* F: lord|
1.4.86-7/590-1 I . . . thee] *verse* F: fellow|
1.4.131/636 Why . . . of nothing] *verse* F: boy|
1.4.156/661 Then they] *prose* QF (F *begins song with* 'For')
1.4.171-2/676-7 How . . . frown] *verse* F
1.4.179-80/684-5 Mum . . . crumb] *1 line* QF
1.4.181-2/686-7 Weary . . . peascod] *1 line* QF
1.4.198-9/703-4 The . . . young] *prose* QF
1.4.208/713 Does . . . Lear] *2 lines* F: me|; *prose* Q (*which has* 'why this')
1.4.234-5/739-40 You . . . betters] *prose* QF
1.4.270/775 Now . . . this] Q; *2 lines* F: adore|
1.4.276/781 I'll . . . ashamed] *2 lines* F: thee|; *prose* Q
1.4.279/784 Should . . . upon thee] *2 lines* F: them|; *prose* Q (*which has* 'worst' *for* 'worth them')
1.4.294-5/800-1 Nuncle . . . thee] F; *prose* Q. *Always emended to prose, but F's arrangement neither saves nor wastes space, and the omission of Q's* and *produces a strong lyric rhythm.*
1.4.301/807 This . . . knights] *2 lines* F: counsel|
1.5.33-4/866-7 I . . . ready] *prose* QF
1.5.45-7/879-81 O . . . ready] *prose* QF (F *dividing first line after* 'heaven')
2.1.2-4/886-8 And . . . night] Q; *verse* F: been| notice| duchess|
2.1.10-11/894-5 Have . . . Albany] Q1; *not in* Q2; *verse* F: toward|
2.1.13/897 You . . . sir] *verse* F: time|
2.1.30/914 Draw . . . well] *2 lines* F: yourself|
2.1.115-16/999-1000 I . . . else] *1 line* QF
2.2.46-7/1059-60 Keep . . . matter] *prose* QF
2.2.68-9/1081-2 Peace . . . reverence] F; *1 line* Q. *Even with Q's* 'sir' *in place of F's* 'sirrah', *Cornwall's speech would not have fitted Compositor E's measure; Q may be right.*
2.2.150/1163 The . . . taken] Q; *2 lines* F: this|

2.2.194/1208 What's . . . mistook] *2 lines* F: he|
2.2.222/1236 Winter's . . . way] *1 line of verse* F
2.2.223-8/1237-42 Fathers . . . poor] *3 lines* F: blind| kind|
2.2.235/1249 Made . . . of] Q; *2 lines* F: offence|
2.2.261/1275 Deny . . . weary] Q; *2 lines* F: me|
2.2.273/1287 The King . . . father] Q; *2 lines* F: Cornwall|
2.2.362/1376 Thou . . . heavens] *2 lines* F: on't|. *See* 'Folio Compositors', 24.
2.2.371/1385 Will . . . stocks] Q; *2 lines* F: hold|
2.2.418/1432 Why . . . ye] Q; *2 lines* F: lord|
2.2.462-3/1476-8 'Tis . . . folly] *This edition*; *2 lines* QF: rest|
3.1.1-2/1496-7 One . . . unquietly] *This edition*; *1 line* QF
3.1.29/1524 Give . . . say] Q; *2 lines* F: hand|
3.2.27-34/1555-62 The . . . wake] *4 lines* F: any| many| make|
3.2.79-80/1607-8 This . . . go] *verse* F: courtesan|
3.2.85-6/1613-14 Then . . . confusion] *1 line* F
3.2.95-6/1623-4 This . . . time] *1 line of verse* F
3.4.5/1653 I . . . enter] Q; *2 lines* F: own|
3.4.42-3/1690-1 What . . . forth] Q1 (*but with* 'come' *not capitalized*); *prose* Q2, F
3.4.43/1691 Away . . . me] BLAYNEY; *prose* QF
3.4.46-7/1694-5 Didst . . . this] *prose* QF
3.4.115-16/1765-6 Bid . . . plight] *1 line* QF
*3.4.134-5/1784-5 The . . . Mahu] *prose* QF
3.4.136-7/1786-7 Our . . . gets it] *prose* QF
3.4.146/1796 Good . . . house] *2 lines* F: offer|
3.4.166/1816 Good . . . fellow] *2 lines* F: soothe him|
3.6.24/1871 Be . . . white] Q (*separating* 'Tom . . . curs' *from remainder of speech*); *prose continued* F. *See* 'Folio Compositors', 24-5.
3.6.32-3/1879-80 Do . . . dry] F; *prose* Q. *Editors usually reject F, but F's variants produce a regular hexameter and pentameter; moreover, since* 3.4.134-5/1784-5 *Edgar has (in F) spoken verse except at* 3.6.6-8/1853-5 *and (ambiguously)* 3.6.22-3/1869-70.
3.6.44/1891 Come . . . master] Q; *2 lines* F: friend|
3.7.1-3/1903-5 Post . . . Gloucester] BLAYNEY; *prose* F; *2 lines* Q: letter|
3.7.4-5/1906-7 Leave . . . company] BLAYNEY; *1 line* Q1; *prose* Q2, F
3.7.28-9/1931-2 What . . . friends] Q; *3 lines* F: graces| guests|
3.7.32/1935 To . . . find] Q; *2 lines* F: him|
3.7.41/1944 Come . . . France] Q; *2 lines* F: sir|
3.7.43-4/1946-7 And . . . kingdom] *prose* QF
3.7.50/1953 Wherefore . . . peril] Q; *2 lines* F: Dover|
3.7.52/1955 I am . . . course] Q; *2 lines* F: stake|
3.7.83/1986 All . . . Edmond] Q; *2 lines* F: comfortless|
3.7.92/1995 His . . . you] Q; *2 lines* F: Dover|
4.1.9-10/2008-9 Owes . . . O world] *3 lines* F: blasts| led|
4.1.12-14/2011-13 O . . . years] *2 lines* F: tenant|; *prose* Q. *F's error might arise from the compositor's unassisted attempt to versify prose copy.*
4.1.36/2035 Was . . . since] Q; *2 lines* F: him|
4.1.47/2046 'Tis . . . blind] Q; *2 lines* F: plague|
4.2.56/2129 Where . . . eyes] Q; *2 lines* F: son|
4.3.9-10/2147-8 In . . . worth] him| QF
4.3.24-5/2162-3 It . . . France] *1 line* QF
4.4.19-20/2186-7 Why . . . Belike] Q; Edmond| F
4.5.11/2218 Come . . . fearful] Q; *2 lines* F: sir|
4.5.25-7/2232-4 Give . . . upright] Q; hand| verge| F
4.5.49/2256 Hadst . . . air] Q; *2 lines* F: aught|
4.5.113-16/2320-3 For . . . soldiers] *prose* Q; *3 lines* F: father| sheets|
4.5.116-24/2323-31 Behold . . . darkness] *prose* QF
4.5.129/2336 Let . . . mortality] Q; *2 lines* F: first|
4.5.131/2338 Shall . . . me] *prose* Q; *2 lines* F: naught|
4.5.134-5/2341-2 No . . . it] *prose* QF
4.5.137-8/2344-5 I . . . it] *prose* Q; report| F
4.5.156-61/2363-8 Thou . . . all] *prose* QF
4.5.161-6/2368-73 Plate . . . lips] *prose* F
4.5.166-9/2373-6 Get . . . So] *prose* QF

LINEATION NOTES

4.5.193-6/2400-3 To ... that] *prose* Q; *3 lines* F: bravely| jovial|
4.5.198-9/2405-6 Then ... Sa, sa, sa, sa] Q; *verse* F: get it,|
4.5.207-8/2414-15 Most ... sound] Q; *2 lines* F: vulgar| F
4.5.234/2441 'Chill ... 'cagion] *verse* F: zir|
4.5.279/2485 The ... sense] Q; *2 lines* F: mad|
4.6.1-3/2493-5 O ... me] *2 lines* Q1: goodness|; Kent| goodness| Q2; *4 lines* F: Kent| work| goodness| short|. See 'Folio Compositors', 25-6.
4.6.30-1/2522-3 Mine ... father] This edition; *3 lines* Q: dog| night|; *3 lines* F: me| fire|. Q's arrangement of course reflects the original intention, before F's cut of the three and a half preceding lines: conflated texts naturally adopt it. But that cut could hardly have obscured the line-arrangement in Compositor E's printed copy, and such a rearrangement on his own initiative would be highly untypical of E. It saves no space either. We must therefore assume that the manuscript did not have Q's pattern of line-breaks. F as it stands, however, simply moves down the part-line which resulted from the cut, to no discernible purpose, and at the cost of creating a line-divided foot. We have therefore assumed that the manuscript marked only two lines, both hexameters, and that F's arrangement results from the fact that neither manuscript line (marked by the annotator on Q2 copy) would have fitted F's column.
4.6.37/2529 How ... majesty] Q; *2 lines* F: lord|
4.6.44/2536 He's ... a while] Q; *2 lines* F: awake|
4.6.45/2537 Where have ... daylight] Q; *2 lines* F: been|
*4.6.55/2547 Not ... plainly] Q; *2 lines* F: less|. Editors sometimes adopt Knight's combination of TLN 2815-16 (Fourscore ... less) rather than Rowe's of TLN 2816-17 as here.
4.6.64/2556 Be ... not] Q; *2 lines* F: wet|
*4.6.76-7/2568-9 You ... foolish] This edition; forgive| Q1; *3 lines* Q2; F: me| forgive|. See Q. F's added 'you' after 'Pray', and the fact that it ends the following dialogue, suggest that the revised version's lineation differed from the original's; F simply reproduces its Q2 copy.
5.1.14-15/2583-4 Fear ... husband] *1 line* QF
5.2.9/2638 What ... endure] Q; *2 lines* F: again|
5.3.21/2661 The ... thee] Q; *2 lines* F: incense|
5.3.25/2665 Ere ... Come] Q; *2 lines* F: weep|
5.3.44-5/2684-5 To ... retention] Q2; *1 line* Q1, F. See textual note to 5.3.45/2685.
5.3.83/2723 Thou ... sound] *2 lines* F: Gloucester|
5.3.146-7/2786-7 Or ... evil] This edition; sir| F. F's line 5.3.146/2786 would not have fitted the column, if 'Hold, sir' were placed at the beginning of it (as here); but it would easily fit the end of 5.3.145/2785. It seems better to make the sentence-break and change of addressee coincide with the line-break, especially as 'worse than any *name*' seems to develop from 'sir'; metrically the resulting hexameter is as acceptable at 5.3.147/2787 as at 5.3.146/2786.
5.3.150-1/2790-1 Most ... paper] This edition; *1 line* QF; O| CAPELL. A line-divided foot, allowing the sentence-break and change of addressee to coincide with the line-break. See textual note.
5.3.153/2793 What ... done] Q; *2 lines* F: with|
5.3.198-9/2838-9 'Tis ... dead] *prose* F; *1 line* Q (*ending* 'of—'). If 'O she's dead' were added by an annotator in the margin of Q, Compositor E could easily have misinterpreted the speech as prose.
5.3.223-4/2863-4 To ... reprieve] Q1; office| Q2, F
5.3.256-7/2896-7 This' ... Kent] This edition (*conj.* Walker); *1 line* F. See 'Folio Compositors', 28.
5.3.266/2906 Nor ... deadly] Q; *2 lines* F: else|
5.3.278-9/2918-19 Have ... foes] shall| F; *prose* Q

Macbeth

1.1.9-10/9-10 Paddock ... fair] *1 line*
1.2.19-20/30-1 Like ... slave] passage|
1.2.34/45 Dismayed ... Banquo] F; *2 lines* POPE: this|
1.2.35/46 Yes ... lion] This edition; *2 lines* F: Eagles|. POPE divided after 'Yes', but lines with an extra initial syllable are common (especially as here, completing a line-divided foot). The full hexameter would not fit F's column.
1.2.41-2/52-3 I ... help] faint|
1.2.46-7/57-8 What ... strange] eyes|
1.2.58-9/69-70 That ... composition] King|
1.3.4/82 And ... I] *2 lines*: munched|
1.3.76/154 With ... you] *2 lines*: greeting|
1.3.80/158 Melted ... stayed] *2 lines*: wind|
1.3.106-7/184-5 The ... robes] lives|
1.3.109-12/187-90 Which ... not] *5 lines*: lose| Norway| help| laboured|
1.3.130-1/208-9 Cannot ... success] good|
1.3.139-41/217-9 Shakes ... not] man| surmise|
1.3.142/220 If ... crown me] *2 lines*: king|
1.3.148-152/226-30 Give ... time] *7 lines*: favour| forgotten| registered| leaf| them| upon|
1.3.156/234 Till ... friends] *2 lines*: enough|
1.4.1-2/235-6 Is ... returned] Cawdor|
1.4.2-8/236-42 My ... died] back| die| he| pardon| repentance| him|
1.4.23-7/257-61 In ... honour] *6 lines*: itself| receive our duties| state| should| love|
1.5.21-2/314-15 And ... it] *3 lines*: win| cries|
1.5.29/322 To ... tidings] *2 lines*: withal|
1.5.37/330 He ... hoarse] *2 lines*: news|
1.5.53/346 To ... Cawdor] *2 lines*: hold, hold|
1.6.1-2/366-7 This ... itself] seat|
1.6.17-20/382-5 Against ... hermits] broad| house| dignities|
1.7.28/424 And ... news] *2 lines*: th'other|
2.1.4/482 Hold ... heaven] *2 lines*: sword|
2.1.7-9/485-7 And ... repose] sleep| thoughts|
2.1.12-13/490-1 He ... offices] pleasure|
2.1.15-16/493-4 By ... content] hostess|
2.1.24-5/502-3 If ... for you] consent|
2.2.2-6/544-8 What ... possets] *6 lines*: fire| shrieked | good-night| open| charge|
2.2.13/555 My father ... husband] *2 lines*: done't|
2.2.14/556 I ... noise] *2 lines*: deed|
2.2.20-3/562-5 There's ... sleep] in's sleep| other| prayers|
2.2.30-1/572-3 I ... throat] *1 line*
2.2.63-4/605-6 To ... chamber] *3 lines*: white| entry|
2.2.71-2/613-14 To ... couldst] *4 lines*: deed| myself| knocking|
2.3.23-4/637-8 Faith ... things] *verse* (?): cock|
2.3.50-1/664-5 I'll ... service] *prose*
2.3.53-5/667-9 The ... death] *4 lines*: unruly| down| air|
2.3.58-60/672-4 New-hatched ... shake] *4 lines*: time| night| feverous|
2.3.85-6/699-700 O Banquo ... murdered] *1 line*
2.3.121-3/735-7 What ... brewed] *4 lines*: here| hole| away|
2.3.134/748 What ... them] *2 lines*: do|
2.3.136/750 Which ... England] *2 lines*: easy|
2.3.137-40/751-4 To Ireland ... bloody] I| safer| smiles|
2.4.14/773 And ... certain] *2 lines*: horses|
2.4.19-20/778-9 They ... Macduff] *3 lines*: so| upon't|
3.1.36-7/837-8 Craving ... with you] *3 lines*: horse| night|
3.1.44-5/845-6 The ... you] *3 lines*: welcome| alone|
3.1.49-52/850-3 Bring ... dares] *5 lines*: us| thus| deep| that|
3.1.73/874 And ... there] *2 lines*: th'utterance|
3.1.76-81/877-82 Well ... with you] *7 lines*: then| speeches| past| fortune| self| conference|
3.1.82-3/883-4 How ... might] *3 lines*: crossed| them|
3.1.86/887 I ... now] *2 lines*: so|
3.1.87-92/888-93 Our point ... ever] *7 lines*: meeting| predominant| go| man| hand| beggared|
3.1.111-12/912-13 Hath ... world] do|
3.1.115-16/916-17 Both ... enemy] *1 line*
3.1.129/930 Your ... most] *2 lines*: you|
3.2.18/962 But ... suffer] *2 lines*: disjoint|

659

3.2.24/968 In . . . grave] *2 lines*: ecstasy|
3.2.28-30/972-4 Come . . . tonight] on| looks|
3.2.30-4/974-8 So . . . streams] you| Banquo| tongue| lave|
3.2.51-2/995-6 Which . . . wood] thickens|
3.3.9-10/1010-11 Then . . . expectation] he|
3.3.17/1018 O . . . fly, fly, fly] *2 lines*: treachery|
3.3.22/1023 We . . . affair] *2 lines*: lost|
3.4.1-2/1025-6 You . . . welcome] down|
3.4.4-5/1028-9 And . . . welcome] This edition; *3 lines*: host| time|
3.4.16-18/1040-2 Thou . . . nonpareil] cut-throats| Fleance|
3.4.20/1044 Then . . . perfect] *2 lines*: again|
3.4.47/1071 Here . . . highness] *2 lines*: lord|
3.4.68/1092 Prithee . . . you] *2 lines*: there|
3.4.108-9/1132-3 You . . . disorder] mirth|
3.4.121/1145 It . . . Blood will have blood] *2 lines*: say|
3.5.52/1219 O . . . news] *2 lines* WITCH: come|
3.5.54/1221 Either . . . refuse, refuse] *2 lines* WITCH: else|
3.5.74/1241 Come . . . again] *2 lines*: be|
3.6.1/1242 My . . . thoughts] *2 lines*: speeches|
4.1.87/1378 Macbeth, Macbeth, Macbeth . . . Macduff] *2 lines*: |beware
4.1.95/1386 Be . . . scorn] *2 lines*: resolute|
4.1.102-3/1393-4 What . . . king] *1 line*
4.1.149/1440 Where . . . hour] *2 lines*: Gone|
4.2.27/1490 Fathered . . . fatherless] *2 lines*: is|
4.2.34/1497 Poor . . . lime] *2 lines*: bird|
4.2.36/1499 Why . . . for] *2 lines*: mother|
4.2.38-9/1501 Yes . . . father] *verse*: dead|
4.2.43-4/1505-6 Thou . . . thee] *verse*: wit|
4.2.50-1/1512-13 Everyone . . . hanged] *verse*: traitor|
4.2.60-1/1521-2 Now . . . father] *verse*: monkey|
4.2.80/1541 To . . . faces] *2 lines*: harm|
4.3.26/1573 Perchance . . . doubts] *2 lines*: there|
4.3.103-4/1650-1 Fit . . . miserable] *1 line*
4.3.141/1688 Well . . . you] *2 lines*: forth|
4.3.174-5/1721-2 O . . . true] *1 line*
4.3.212-13/1759-60 Wife . . . found] *1 line*
4.3.213-14/1760-1 And . . . too] *1 line*
5.1.25-6/1815-16 What . . . hands] *verse*: now|
5.1.44-5/1834-5 Go . . . not] *verse*: |You have
5.1.49-50/1839 O, O, O] *on a separate line*
5.5.27-28/2008-9 Thou . . . quickly] This edition; *1 line* F
5.6.1/2032 Now . . . down] *2 lines*: enough|
5.11.20/2125 Hail . . . stands] *2 lines*: art|

Antony and Cleopatra

1.1.4/4 Have . . . turn] *2 lines*: Mars|
1.1.17/17 Then . . . earth] *prose*
1.1.44-5/44-5 I'll . . . himself] *1 line*
1.1.54-5/54-5 No . . . note] Tonight|
1.1.61-4/61-4 I . . . happy] *prose*
1.2.4-5/68-9 O . . . garlands] *prose*
1.2.8-9/72-3 In . . . read] *prose*
1.2.11-12/75-6 Bring . . . drink] This edition; F *divides* enough|
1.2.15-16/78-9 You . . . are] *1 line*
1.2.29-30/93-4 You . . . approach] *prose*
1.2.33-4/97-8 If . . . million] *prose*
1.2.77/142 A . . . Enobarbus] *2 lines*: him|
1.2.80/145 Here . . . approaches] *2 lines*: service|
1.2.81/146 We . . . us] *2 lines*: him|
1.2.82/147 Fulvia . . . field] *2 lines*: wife|
1.2.84/149 Ay . . . state] *2 lines*: end|
1.2.92-8/158-63 Labienus . . . whilst] *5 lines*: news| force| conquering| Lydia|
1.2.99-100/164-5 Speak . . . Rome] *3 lines*: home| Name|
1.2.108/173 The . . . Sicyon] *1 line*
1.2.108/173 Is . . . one] *1 line*. See textual note: F omits the speech-prefix.

1.2.113-14/177-9 In . . . serious] sickness|
1.2.169/234 No . . . officers] *2 lines*: answers|
1.3.2/256 See . . . does] *2 lines*: is|
1.3.29/283 Who . . . madness] *2 lines*: Fulvia|
1.3.33/287 But . . . staying] *2 lines*: go|
1.4.8-9/367-8 Or . . . faults] You|
1.4.10-11/370-1 I . . . goodness] think|
1.4.43/403 And . . . love] *2 lines*: man|
1.4.80-1/440-1 Till . . . Farewell] *1 line*
1.5.37-8/482-3 With . . . Antony] This edition; thee|
1.5.62-6/507-11 Who's . . . so] *prose*
1.5.76-7/521-2 He . . . Egypt] *prose*
2.1.2-3/524-5 Know . . . deny] *prose*
2.1.4-5/526-7 Whiles . . . for] *prose*
2.1.17-18/538-9 Caesar . . . carry] field|
2.2.8-9/582-3 'Tis . . . stomaching] *1 line*
2.2.9-10/583-4 Every . . . in't] *prose*
2.2.12-14/586-8 Your . . . Antony] *2 lines*: stir|
2.2.16/590-1 I . . . Agrippa] *1 line*
2.2.34-5/608-9 I . . . I] *1 line*
2.2.58-60/632-4 You praise . . . excuses] *prose*
2.2.75-6/649-50 I . . . you] *1 line*
2.2.85-7/659-61 You . . . with] *prose*
2.2.93-4/667-8 To . . . denied] *prose*
2.2.114/689 You . . . more] *prose*
2.2.124-6/699-701 Thou . . . widower] *prose*
2.2.126-8/701-3 Say . . . rashness] *prose*
2.2.129-30/704-5 I . . . speak] *prose*
2.2.135-6/710-11 No . . . speak] Whose|
2.2.168-9/743-4 What . . . land] *1 line*
2.2.169-70/744-5 Great . . . master] increasing|
2.2.175-6/750-1 Let . . . company] *1 line*
2.2.176-7/751-2 Noble . . . me] *prose*
2.2.201/776 The winds . . . silver] *2 lines*: love-sick|
2.2.239-40/814-15 Now . . . utterly] *1 line*
2.2.249-51/824-6 Let . . . here] *prose*
2.3.1-2/827-8 The . . . bosom] will|
2.3.2-4/829-30 All . . . you] *prose*
2.3.11-12/837-8 Would . . . thither] *prose*: you | thither. See textual notes.
2.3.14-15/840-1 Say . . . mine] This edition; *prose or verse unclear*: higher|
2.4.1-2/867-8 Trouble . . . after] *prose*
2.4.2-3/868-9 Sir . . . follow] *prose*
2.4.5-7/871-3 We . . . Lepidus] *prose*
2.4.7-9/873-5 Your . . . me] *prose*
2.5.1-2/877-8 Give . . . love] *prose*: food|
2.5.5-6/881-2 As . . . sir] *prose*
2.5.8/884 And . . . short] *2 lines*: showed|
2.5.15-18/891-4 'Twas . . . up] *prose*
2.5.26-8/902-4 Antonio's . . . here] *4 lines*: dead| mistress| him|
2.5.31/907 Why . . . use] *2 lines*: gold|
2.5.93/969 The . . . still] *2 lines*: thee|
2.5.106-7/982-3 Are . . . 'em] me|
2.5.110/986 I . . . hence] F. Editors divide after *now* (CAPELL) or *faint* (W. S. Walker); but F is regular if a line-divided foot (mád-am | Í) is understood.
2.6.2-3/998-9 Most . . . have we] words|
2.6.32-3/1028-9 Which . . . embraced] to|
2.6.33-4/1029-30 And . . . fortune] *1 line*
2.6.39-40/1035-6 Know . . . prepared] here|
2.6.52-3/1048-9 Since . . . you] *1 line*
2.6.63-6/1059-62 No . . . there] *prose*
2.6.81/1077 Enjoy . . . thee] This edition; *2 lines*: plainness|
2.6.84/1080 Thy . . . treaty] This edition; *prose*
2.7.57-8/1190-1 Thou . . . lords] *prose*
2.7.61/1194 Wilt . . . twice] *2 lines*: world|
2.7.62-4/1195-7 But . . . world] *prose*
2.7.80-2/1213-15 For . . . more] This edition; *2 lines*: follow|
2.7.83/1216 Bear . . . Pompey] *2 lines*: ashore|
2.7.87-9/1220-2 A . . . wheels] *prose*

LINEATION NOTES

2.7.93-5/1226-8   I . . . fouler] *prose*
2.7.97-9/1230-2   Possess . . . one] *prose*
2.7.99-101/1232-4   Ha . . . drink] *prose*
2.7.116/1249   What . . . Good-brother] *2 lines:* more|
2.7.124-5/1250-1   O . . . friends] house|
2.7.128/1261   No . . . what] This edition; *2 lines:* drums|
3.1.27-9/1291-3   Thou . . . Antony] *prose*
3.2.16/1317   Hoo . . . cannot] *2 lines:* figures|
3.2.33-4/1334-5   Make . . . distrust] *1 line*
3.2.48/1349   Her . . . feather] *2 lines:* tongue|
3.2.53-4/1354-5   He . . . man] *prose*
3.3.2-4/1370-2   Good . . . pleased] *prose*
3.3.4-6/1372-4   That . . . near] *prose*
3.3.7-8/1375-6   Didst . . . Octavia] *1 line*
3.3.8-10/1376-8   Madam . . . Antony] *prose*
3.3.12/1380   Didst . . . low] *2 lines:* speak|
3.3.18-19/1386-7   She . . . one] *1 line*
3.3.22-3/1390-1   Three . . . note] *1 line*
3.3.23-4/1391-2   He's . . . yet] perceive't|
3.3.26-7/1394-5   Madam . . . widow] *1 line*
3.3.31-2/1399-1400   For . . . colour] *prose*
3.3.41/1409   The . . . know] *prose*
3.3.42-3/1410-11   Hath . . . long] *prose*
3.3.44-6/1412-14   I . . . enough] *prose*
3.5.12-14/1465-7   Then . . . Antony] *prose:* more| they'll|
3.5.21-2/1474-5   'Twill . . . Antony] *1 line*
3.6.10-11/1485-6   Of . . . queen] *1 line*
3.6.28-30/1503-5   That . . . revenue] *2 lines:* deposed|
3.6.36-7/1511-12   And . . . like] *1 line*
3.6.63-4/1538-9   And . . . now] *1 line*
3.6.78-9/1553-4   Welcome . . . forth] *1 line*
3.6.90/1565   And . . . lady] *1 type line*
3.7.5-6/1578-9   Is't . . . person] *prose*
3.7.6-9/1579-82   Well . . . horse] *prose*
3.7.19-20/1592-3   Nay . . . Emperor] *1 line*
3.7.70-1/1643-4   You . . . not] *prose*
3.7.80-1/1653-4   With . . . some] labour|
3.8.3/1657   Strike . . . battle] *2 lines:* land|
3.10.4-5/1668-9   Gods . . . them] *1 line*
3.10.29/1693   Ay . . . indeed] This edition; *prose* F: |indeed; *verse* HANMER: |Indeed
3.10.31-2/1695-6   'Tis . . . comes] to't|
3.11.43-5/1743-5   Go . . . shame] CAPELL; F *divides* |He's
3.11.71-2/1771-2   Even . . . wine] This edition; me| back|
3.13.13/1823   ANTONY . . . lord] *1 type line*
3.13.14-15/1824-5   The . . . up] courtesy|
3.13.15-17/1825-7   Let . . . brim] *prose*
3.13.60-2/1870-2   He . . . merely] god| honour|
3.13.62-3/1872-3   To . . . leaky] Antony|
3.13.71-2/1881-2   And . . . landlord] *1 line*
3.13.85-6/1895-6   Favours . . . fellow] *1 line*
3.13.92-3/1902-3   And . . . him] ears|
3.13.156-8/1966-8   Alack . . . Antony] *2 lines:* eclipsed|
3.13.192-3/2002-3   Do . . . queen] *3 lines:* them| force| scars|
4.1.10-11/2023-4   Let . . . battles] Know|
4.3.9-10/2083-4   'Tis . . . purpose] *1 line*
4.3.12-13/2086-7   Peace . . . mean] *1 line*
4.3.16-17/2090-1   How now? . . . this] *1 line*
4.4.8-10/2102-4   Well . . . defences] *2 lines:* now|
4.4.21-3/2115-17   A . . . you] *2 lines:* their|
4.5.10-11/2142-3   Sir, his . . . him] *1 line*
4.6.6-7/2155-6   Antony . . . field] *1 line*
4.9.1-2/2205-6   We . . . Tomorrow] one|
4.9.19/2223   We . . . grey] *2 lines:* beds|
4.10.29-32/2272-5   Hark . . . out] *3 lines:* sleepers| note|
4.13.1-3/2290-2   Yet . . . go] joined| all|
4.14.3-4/2341-2   To th' . . . dead] yourself|
4.15.7/2355   And . . . signs] *2 lines:* air|
4.15.22-3/2370-1   O . . . sword] *1 line*
4.15.25-6/2373-4   Hence . . . death] me|

4.15.65-9/2413-17   Th'inevitable . . . cheek] *4 lines:* horror| kill me| not me|
4.15.94-5/2442-3   Why . . . death] then|
4.15.105-6/2453-4   I . . . begun] friends|
4.15.107-8/2455-6   Alas . . . woe] This edition; *1 line*
4.15.114/2462   Art . . . me] *2 lines:* Diomed|
4.15.127-8/2475-6   What . . . calls] Emperor's guard|
4.16.11-14/2497-500   The . . . hither] This edition; *3 lines* F: |Help Charmian |below; *3 lines* MALONE: O Antony| Iras, help|; *3 lines* CAPELL: O Antony| Iras|
4.16.14-16/2500-2   Peace . . . itself] This edition (*conj.* W. S. Walker); Peace| Antony|
4.16.33/2519   Here's . . . lord] *2 lines:* indeed|
5.1.2-3/2581-2   Being . . . makes] him|
5.1.11-12/2590-1   I'll . . . life] *1 line*
5.1.30-1/2609-10   His . . . him] *1 line*
5.1.47-8/2626-7   Unreconciliable . . . friends] this|
5.1.59-60/2638-9   Determine . . . ungentle] *1 line*
5.1.69-70/2648-9   Gallus . . . Proculeius] *prose*
5.2.40-1/2666-7   What . . . languish] *1 line*
5.2.41-2/2667-8   Cleopatra . . . by] *1 line*
5.2.111-13/2767-9   Sir . . . obey] *2 lines:* thus|
5.2.187-8/2843-4   He . . . Charmian] *3 lines:* me| myself|
5.2.200-1/2856-7   Dolabella . . . debtor] *1 line*
5.2.203/2859   Farewell . . . thou] *2 lines:* thank|
5.2.220-2/2876-8   Why . . . intents] *2 lines:* preparation|
5.2.238-9/2894-5   Hast . . . not] there|
5.2.302-3/2958-9   That . . . unpolicied] *1 line*
5.2.318/2974   Approach . . . beguiled] *2 lines:* ho|
5.2.320/2976   What . . . done] *2 lines:* Charmian|
5.2.344-6/3000-2   This . . . Nile] F; JOHNSON *divides* fig-leaves| leaves|

Pericles

The lineation notes to our reconstructed text of *Pericles* are incorporated in the main body of textual notes to that play, where they are flagged '(L)'.

Coriolanus

1.1.53-4/51-2   What . . . you] *3 lines:* hand| matter|
1.1.60-1/58-9   Why . . . yourselves] *prose*
1.1.91-3/89-91   Well . . . deliver] *verse:* Well| think| tale|
1.1.117-18/115-16   What . . . then? What then] speaks|
1.1.233-4/231-2   Were . . . make] *prose*
1.1.245-7/243-5   Lead . . . priority] *prose*
1.1.259-63/257-61   Such . . . Cominius] *prose*
1.1.272-3/270-1   Come . . . Martius] *1 line*
1.3.73/388   No . . . doors] *verse:* madam|
1.3.106-7/421-2   Let . . . mirth] *verse:* now|
1.3.108-10/423-5   In . . . us] *verse:* would| lady| door|
1.3.111-12/426-7   No . . . mirth] *verse:* No| not|
1.4.1/429   Yonder . . . met] *2 lines:* news|
1.4.25/453   With . . . Titus] *2 lines:* shields|
1.6.19-20/509-10   Than . . . fight] *1 line* (and fight *turned down*)
1.7.57/575   By . . . made] *2 lines:* together|
1.9.6-7/619-20   If . . . hare] *1 line*
1.10.13-14/641-2   Pray . . . blood] more|
1.10.15-17/643-5   When . . . country] grieves me| can|
1.10.19-22/647-50   You . . . traducement] deserving| own| theft|
1.10.44-50/672-8   Made . . . hyperbolical] soothing| silk| wars| washed| wretch| done|
1.10.64-5/692-3   Martius . . . ever] *1 line*
1.10.78-80/706-8   The . . . general] me| gifts|
2.1.109-10/865-6   I . . . me] *verse:* tonight|
2.1.155-6/911-12   These . . . tears] *verse:* Martius| noise|
2.1.161-2/917-18   With . . . Coriolanus] Caius|

LINEATION NOTES

2.1.165-6/921-2 No ... more] *prose*
2.1.166-8/922-4 O ... prosperity] *prose*
2.1.178-9/934-5 I ... all] *3 lines*: turn| general|
2.1.180-1/936-7 A ... welcome] *3 lines*: welcomes| laugh|
2.1.183-6/939-42 That ... warriors] *6 lines*: thee| on| have| home| relish|
2.1.187-8/943-4 We ... folly] nettle|
2.1.197-9/953-5 And ... thee] *4 lines*: fancy| wanting| Rome|
2.1.207-8/963-4 Clamb'ring ... horsed] *3 lines*: him| up|
2.1.213-14/969-70 Commit ... spoil] damask|
2.1.218-19/974-5 On ... consul] *1 line*
2.1.219-20/975-6 Then ... sleep] *prose*
2.1.226-7/982-3 With ... question] honours|
2.1.234-5/990-1 It ... him] *3 lines*: word| carry it|
2.1.236-8/992-4 I ... execution] *prose*
2.1.239-40/995-6 It ... destruction] *prose*
2.1.257-60/1013-16 You ... gloves] Capitol| consul| see him|
2.2.37-8/1060-1 Having ... remains] Volsces|
2.2.40-1/1063-4 To ... you] Hath|
2.2.54-7/1077-80 We ... assembly] *prose*
2.2.57-60/1080-3 Which ... at] *prose*
2.2.60-2/1083-5 That's ... speak] *prose*
2.2.62-4/1085-7 Most ... it] *prose*
2.2.64-6/1087-9 He ... speak] *prose*
2.2.70-1/1093-4 Sir ... not] *1 line*
2.2.84-5/1107-8 That ... be] virtue|
2.2.119-20/1142-3 Run ... called] 'Twere|
2.2.123-4/1146-7 He ... him] *prose*
2.2.127-8/1150-1 Than ... content] deeds|
2.2.129-30/1152-3 He's ... for] *1 line*
2.2.133-4/1156-7 The ... consul] *prose*
2.2.134-5/1157-8 I ... services] *1 line*
2.2.135-6/1158-9 It ... people] *prose*
2.2.140-2/1163-5 Sir ... ceremony] *2 lines*: voices|
2.2.143-4/1166-7 Pray ... have] custom|
2.2.145-7/1168-70 It ... people] *2 lines*: acting|
2.3.50-1/1233-4 What ... bring] sir|
2.3.55-7/1238-40 O ... you] *2 lines*: that|
2.3.129-31/1310-12 I ... consul] for your voices| more|
2.3.139-42/1320-3 You ... senate] limitation| voice| invested|
2.3.153-4/1334-5 With ... people] weeds|
2.3.166/1347 He ... private] *2 lines*: wounds|
2.3.188-9/1369-70 Would ... love] voices|
2.3.205-8/1386-9 Have ... tongues] *3 lines*: asker| mock|
2.3.217-19/1398-1400 Let ... pride] *3 lines*: judgement|
2.3.226-9/1407-10 Lay ... him] *3 lines*: tribunes| between|
2.3.229-32/1410-13 Say ... do] *3 lines*: commandment| that|
2.3.254-5/1435-6 We ... election] *1 line*. See textual note.
3.1.34-5/1479-80 Stop ... broil] *1 line*
3.1.51-2/1496-7 Not ... yours] *1 line*
3.1.64-5/1509-10 Tell ... again] speech|
3.1.68-9/1513-14 Now ... pardons] will|
3.1.89-91/1534-6 It ... further] *2 lines*: poison|
3.1.93-4/1538-9 Shall ... why] *1 line*
3.1.120-1/1565-6 First ... state] *1 line*
3.1.183-4/1628-9 Here's ... power] *prose*
3.1.191-2/1636-7 To ... Sicinius] *1 line*
3.1.196-7/1641-2 Fie ... quench] *prose*
3.1.199-200/1644-5 True ... city] *1 line*
3.1.200-1/1645-6 By ... magistrates] *prose*
3.1.214-15/1659-60 Hear ... word] *prose*
3.1.225/1670 Down ... while] *prose*
3.1.226-7/1671-2 Help ... old] *prose*
3.1.239-40/1684-5 Be ... tongue] *1 line*. See textual note.
3.1.241-2/1686-7 On ... them] *1 line*
3.1.242-3/1687-8 I could myself ... tribunes] *prose*
3.1.264-5/1709-10 That ... himself] *1 line*
3.1.270-2/1715-17 He ... hands] *2 lines*: are|
3.1.272-3/1717-18 MENENIUS ... Peace] *1 type line*
3.1.275-6/1720-1 Sir ... rescue] holp|
3.1.276-8/1721-3 Hear ... faults] *2 lines*: know|

3.1.283/1728 If ... people] *2 lines*: leave|
3.1.306-7/1751-2 Merely ... him] awry|
3.1.331-2/1776-7 Noble ... officer] *1 line*
3.2.24-5/1807-8 Come ... it] *prose*
3.2.53/1836 Because ... people] *2 lines*: that|
3.2.56-61/1839-44 That ... blood] *7 lines*: tongue| syllables| truth| all| words| and|
3.2.96-7/1879-80 I ... spirit] *prose*
3.9.9-10/1938-9 Of ... poll] *1 line* (poll *turned up*)
3.3.34/1963 Will ... gods] *2 lines*: volume|
3.3.52-3/1981-2 Scratches ... only] move|
3.3.87-8/2016-17 But ... Rome] *1 line*
3.3.109-11/2038-40 It ... so] *2 lines*: away|
4.2.5-7/2139-41 Bid ... strength] *2 lines*: gone|
4.2.7-8/2141-2 Dismiss ... mother] *1 line*
4.2.13-14/2147-8 O ... love] met|
4.2.27-8/2161-2 What then? | He'd ... posterity] *1 line*
4.4.7-8/2246-7 Direct ... Antium] *prose*
4.4.9-10/2248-9 He ... night] *prose*
4.5.5-6/2269-70 A ... guest] house|
4.5.9-10/2273-4 I ... Coriolanus] *prose*
4.5.13/2277 Pray ... out] *verse line*
4.5.33/2296 Follow ... bits] *prose*
4.5.55-8/2317-20 If ... myself] *prose*
4.5.164-5/2426-7 I ... on] *verse*: he|
4.5.179-80/2440-1 I ... man] *verse*? (*unjustified line break* as|)
4.6.12-13/2512-13 Hail, sir ... both] *1 type line*
4.6.14-16/2514-16 Your ... it] *prose*
4.6.17-18/2517-18 All's ... temporized] *prose*
4.6.34-5/2534-5 And ... assistance] *1 line*
4.6.57-8/2557-8 Tell ... be] *1 line*
4.6.120-1/2620-1 'Tis ... brand] *1 line*
4.6.128-9/2628-9 How ... nobles] him|
4.6.139-40/2639-40 Your ... coming] hooting|
4.7.14-16/2682-4 Joined ... solely] *2 lines*: borne|
5.1.21-2/2746-7 Very ... less] *1 line*
5.2.3-5/2801-3 You ... Coriolanus] *2 lines*: leave|. Both lines are justified; perhaps prose.
5.2.6-7/2804-5 FIRST ... Rome] *1 type line*
5.2.7-8/2805-6 You ... thence] *prose*
5.2.52-3/2851-2 Sirrah ... estimation] *verse*: here|
5.2.96-7/2895-6 'Tis ... again] *verse*: power|
5.2.109-10/2909-10 The ... wind-shaken] *verse*: rock|
5.3.4-7/2914-17 Only ... friends] *3 lines*: respected| Rome|
5.3.36-7/2946-7 As ... kin] *1 line (justified)*
5.3.40-2/2950-2 Like ... flesh] *2 lines*: part|
5.3.56-7/2966-7 What's ... son] me|
5.3.62-3/2972-3 Thou ... lady] thee|
5.3.126-8/3036-8 Ay ... time] *2 lines*: boy|
5.3.128-9/3038-9 A ... fight] away|
5.3.182-3/3092-3 I ... little] *1 line (justified)*
5.3.203-4/3113-14 Ay ... bear] together|
5.4.1-2/3121-2 See ... corner-stone] *verse line* (stone *turned up*)
5.4.44-5/3164-5 Friend ... certain] true|
5.4.59-60/3179-80 First ... thankfulness] tidings|
5.6.9-11/3198-3200 Even .... slain] *prose*
5.6.11-13/3200-2 Most ... deliver you] *2 lines*: intent|
5.6.58-9/3247-8 Say ... lords] *1 line*
5.6.128-9/3317-18 O ... sword] more|
5.6.133-4/3322-3 Tread ...swords] quiet|

The Winter's Tale

1.2.149-50/197-8 What ... distraction] Brother|
1.2.344/391 My ... clear] *2 lines*: Lord|
2.1.27-8/539-40 A ... goblins] Winter|
2.1.38-9/545-6 Yon ... ear] it|
2.1.171-2/683-4 The ... ours] on't|
2.1.9-11/722-4 I ... from] Madam| commandment|

LINEATION NOTES

2.3.10-11/792-3 He...discharged] hoped|
2.3.60/842 Good Queen...Queen] *2 lines*: good Queen|
3.2.8-9/1019-20 It...court] Queen|
4.4.423-4/2030-31 I...piece] can|
4.4.631-2/2238-9 How...thee] *verse*: Fellow| man|
5.1.8/2613 Most...daughter] *2 lines*: Sir|

Cymbeline

1.1.1-2/1-2 You...courtiers] *3 lines*: frowns| heavens|
1.1.53-4/53-4 By...is] *1 line*
1.1.54-6/54-6 I...king] *2 lines*: report|
1.1.139/139 That...queen] *2 lines*: had|
1.1.142-3/142-3 Thou...baseness] *prose* (?): my | Throne
1.1.143-4/143-4 No...it] *1 line*
1.1.179/179 About...me] *2 lines*: hence|. The full line would not fit F's column; there is no need to suppose more extensive corruption.
1.2.5-6/186-7 If...him] *verse*: it|
1.2.31-2/211-12 She...her] *verse*: reflection|
1.3.17-18/237-8 I...diminution] eye-strings|
1.4.168-9/436-7 Signor...'em] *verse*: it|
1.5.1/438 Whiles...flowers] *2 lines*: ground|
1.5.46/483 Weeps...time] *2 lines*: sayst thou|
1.6.77-8/599-600 And...blame] Frenchman|
1.6.79/601 Not...might] *2 lines*: he|
1.6.180/702 All's...yours] *2 lines*: sir|
2.2.3/800 I...weak] *2 lines*: then|
2.3.61/910 T'employ...queen] *2 lines*: Roman|
2.3.79-80/928-9 Ay...chamber] *1 line*
2.4.31-2/1033-4 Your...upon] This edition (*conj*. Ingleby); lady| F. This rearrangement resolves the metrical problems in 2.4.32/1034, produces an acceptable two-speaker hexameter in 2.4.31/1033, and encourages an appropriate emphasis on 'is' (Giacomo conceding, 'she *is* beautiful, as you claimed, but...').
2.5.12/1166 Might...her] *2 lines*: Saturn|
2.5.28-9/1182-3 Why...vice] *1 line*
3.3.78/1433 In...valleys] *2 lines*: state|
3.3.82/1437 They...meanly] *2 lines*: mine|
3.5.79-80/1735-6 To...sirrah] shall|
3.6.91/1908 The...welcome] *2 lines*: owl|
4.2.32/1983 These...heard] *2 lines*: creatures|
4.2.191/2142 What...mother] *2 lines*: mean|
4.2.283/2234 We...down] *2 lines*: obsequies|
5.5.95/2601 You shall...upon you] *2 lines*: stol'n|
5.5.124-86/2630-92 No...fly] These fourteeners create the same problem for modern editors as they did for F: they are too long to fit the printer's measure, and are most conveniently broken into alternating lines of eight and six syllables. Whether or not this reflects the visual arrangement in Shakespeare's manuscript, it does indicate the metrical structure accurately.
5.5.124-5/2630-1 No...flies] thunder-master|
5.5.126-7/2632-3 With...adulteries] *1 line*
5.5.150-1/2656-7 In...dignity] deem|
5.5.154-5/2660-1 From...one] her|
5.5.157-8/2663-4 Why...Italy] *1 line*
5.5.159-60/2665-6 To...jealousy] *1 line*
5.5.161-2/2667-8 And...villainy] *1 line*
5.5.167-8/2673-4 Our...maintain] *1 line*
5.5.171-2/2677-8 Then...adjourned] *1 line*
5.5.173-4/2679-80 The...turned] *1 line*
5.5.175-6/2681-2 Thy...exercise] look, | look out. See textual notes.
5.5.177-8/2683-4 Upon...injuries] *1 line*
5.5.183-4/2689-90 To...deity] *1 line*
5.6.169-70/2975-6 I...matter] *1 line*
5.6.260-1/3066-7 My...error] *1 line*
5.6.287-8/3093-4 Let...there] *1 line*
5.6.301-2/3107-8 That...lord] *1 line*

5.6.319-20/3125-6 What...traitor] *1 line*
5.6.341-2/3147-8 Could...Euriphile] F; as| JOHNSON. Johnson's rearrangement is unnecessary, if we presume a line-divided foot.
5.6.405-6/3211-12 My...service] *1 line*

The Tempest

1.1.54-5/56-7 This...tides] *prose*
1.2.252/318 From...No] *1 type line*
1.2.269-70/335-6 They...sir] *1 type line*
1.2.304-5/370-1 Go...invisible] subject|
1.2.307/373 And...diligence] *2 lines*: hence|
1.2.312-13/378-9 'Tis...on] *1 line*
1.2.364-5/430-1 Deservedly...prison] hadst|
1.2.382-3/448-9 Foot...bear] *1 line*
1.2.383-6/450-2 Hark, hark. | Bow-wow! | The...bark] *1 line* (*without speech-prefixes*)
1.2.388-9/454-5 Hark...Chanticleer] *1 line*
1.2.408/474 Hark...bell] *1 type line* (*without speech-prefixes*)
2.1.13-14/585-6 Look...strike] *verse*: wit|
2.1.17-18/589-90 When...entertainer] entertained|
2.1.30-1/602-3 Which...crow] *verse*: wager|
2.1.57-8/629-30 How...green] *verse*: looks|
2.1.84-5/656-7 What...it] *verse*: too|
2.1.89-90/661-2 ADRIAN...you, Carthage] *1 type line*
2.1.99-100/672-3 GONZALO...time] *1 type line*
2.1.112-13/685-7 You...never] *prose* (*first type line ending against*)
2.1.140/713 Than...own] *2 lines*: them|
2.1.145-6/718-19 SEBASTIAN...chirurgeonly] *1 type line*
2.1.148/722 SEBASTIAN...foul] *1 type line*
2.1.174-5/747-8 SEBASTIAN...Gonzalo] *1 type line*
2.1.197-8/770-1 Would...sir] thoughts|
2.1.200-1/773-4 It...comforter] *1 line* (*at foot of page*)
2.1.201-3/774-6 We...safety] *2 lines*: person|
2.1.249-50/822-3 Then...Naples] *1 line*
2.1.311-12/884-5 Now...King] *1 line*
2.2.41-2/948-9 I...ashore] *1 line*
2.2.43-4/950-1 This...comfort] *verse*: man's|
2.2.55/962 This...comfort] *verse*: too|
2.2.57/964 What's...here] *verse*: matter|
2.2.87/995 I...be] *verse*: voice|
2.2.114-16/1023-5 These...him] *prose*
2.2.117-18/1026-7 How...hither] *verse*: scape|
2.2.129/1038 Here...book] *verse line*
2.2.135/1044 How...ague] *verse line*
2.2.144-6/1053-5 The...sooth] *verse*: Moon| credulous monster|
2.2.147-8/1056-7 I'll...god] *prose*
2.2.157-8/1066-7 But...monster] *verse*: drink|
2.2.159-60/1068-9 I'll...enough] *prose*
2.2.162-3/1071-2 I'll...man] *prose*
2.2.166-71/1075-80 I...me] *prose*
2.2.180-1/1089-90 Nor...requiring] *1 line*
3.2.38-9/1230-1 I...thee] *prose* (*first type line ending* pleased)
3.2.40-1/1232-3 Marry...Trinculo] *verse*: it|
3.2.42-4/1234-6 As...island] *verse*: tyrant| me|
3.2.49-50/1241-2 Trinculo...teeth] *verse*: tale|
3.2.59-60/1251-2 How...party] *verse*: compassed|
3.2.69/1262 Trinculo...danger] *verse line*
3.2.73-4/1265-6 Why...off] *verse*: nothing|
3.2.77-8/1269-70 Do...time] *verse*: that|
3.2.80-1/1272-3 A...do] *verse line* (*with* hearing too *as an unjustified type line*)
3.2.109-10/1301-2 Dost...Trinculo] *verse line*
3.2.112/1304-5 Give...head] *verse*: thee|
3.2.121-2/1313-14 At...sing] *verse*: reason|
3.2.122-4/1315-16 Flout...flout 'em] *1 line*
3.2.134-5/1326-7 He...us] *verse*: thee|
3.2.147-8/1339-40 This...nothing] *verse*: me|

663

3.2.150/1342   That . . . story] verse: and by|
3.2.151-2/1343-4   The . . . work] verse: work|
3.2.153-4/1345-6   Lead . . . on] verse: monster| taborer|
3.2.155/1347   Wilt . . . Stefano] verse: come|
3.3.13-14/1360-1   The . . . throughly] 1 line
4.1.165-6/1621-2   Spirit . . . Caliban] 1 line
4.1.187/1643   For . . . Exit] 1 type line
4.1.194-5/1650-1   Pray . . . cell] prose
4.1.196-8/1652-3   Monster . . . us] verse: fairy|
4.1.199-200/1654-5   Monster . . . indignation] verse: which|
4.1.201-2/1656-7   So . . . look you] verse: should|
4.1.211-12/1666-7   That's . . . monster] verse: wetting|
4.1.213-14/1668-9   I . . . labour] verse: bottle|
4.1.221-2/1676-8   O King . . . thee] verse: Stefano| (but O . . . Stefano justified)
5.1.97-8/1816-17   Why . . . so, so, so] miss|
5.1.223/1942   Hast . . . news] 2 lines: land|
5.1.259-61/1978-80   Every . . . Coragio] verse: let| is|
5.1.267/1986   Ha . . . Antonio] 2 lines: Ha, ha|
5.1.281/2000   He . . . wine] 2 lines: now|
5.1.285-7/2004-6   I . . . fly-blowing] verse: last| bones|

All Is True

1.1.11/43   Which . . . weighed] 2 lines: they|
1.2.177-8/435-6   Let . . . forward] 1 line
1.2.191-2/449-50   I . . . servant] 1 line. See the textual note.
1.3.11/484   They . . . it] 2 lines: legs|
1.3.21/494   I'm . . . messieurs] 2 lines: there|
1.3.42/515   The . . . going] 2 lines: 'em|
1.3.55/528   That . . . indeed] 2 lines: churchman|
1.3.59/532   He . . . him] 2 lines: lord|
1.3.63/536   But . . . stays] 2 lines: ones|
1.4.1/541   Ladies . . . grace] 2 lines: Ladies|
1.4.74-5/614-15   They . . . pleasures] 3 lines: grace| thanks|
1.4.95-6/635-6   An't . . . women] 3 lines: grace| Rochford|
2.1.8/660   Yes . . . upon't] 2 lines: he|
2.1.72/724   More . . . me] 2 lines: faults|
2.1.79/731   And . . . name] 2 lines: heaven|
2.1.86-7/738-9   'Gainst . . . grace] 3 lines: with| grave|
2.1.136/788   Speak . . . me] 2 lines: fell|
2.1.165/817   I . . . cruel] 2 lines: think|
2.2.10-11/830-1   I . . . think] prose
2.2.22/842   Pray . . . else] 2 lines: do|
2.2.84-5/904-5   If . . . have-at-him] 1 line
2.4.9/1081   Say . . . court] This edition; 2 lines F: England|
2.4.66-7/1138-9   Lord . . . speak] 1 line
2.4.67-8/1139-40   Sir . . . that] 1 line
2.4.164/1236   And . . . to't] 2 lines: him|
3.1.1/1311   Take . . . troubles] 2 lines: wench|
3.1.80/1390   Madam . . . fears] 2 lines: Madam|
3.1.137/1447   Madam . . . at] 2 lines: good|
3.1.138/1448   My . . . guilty] 2 lines: lord|
3.1.167/1477   Madam . . . virtues] 2 lines: so|
3.1.174/1484   Do . . . me] 2 lines: lords|
3.2.76/1569   The . . . King] 2 lines: Cromwell|
3.2.77-8/1570-1   Looked . . . paper] 1 line
3.2.82-3/1575-6   Is . . . abroad] 1 line
3.2.95/1588   The . . . daughter] 2 lines: gentlewoman|
3.2.229/1722   Hear . . . you] 2 lines: Cardinal|
3.2.277/1770   Your . . . feel] 2 lines: you|
3.2.310/1803   I . . . you] 2 lines: head|
3.2.387/1880   I . . . it] 2 lines: grace|
3.2.388/1881   I . . . methinks] 2 lines: have|
3.2.408/1901   There . . . Cromwell] 2 lines: down|
4.1.36/1989   The . . . coming] 2 lines: close|
4.2.31/2103   So . . . him] 2 lines: rest|
4.2.92-3/2164-5   I . . . Assuredly] 1 line
4.2.114/2186   With . . . pray you] 2 lines: |But

4.2.139/2211   Heaven . . . petition] 2 lines: dearly|
5.1.90-1/2336-7   How . . . you] 3 lines: lord| wherefore|
5.1.95/2341   I . . . hand] 2 lines: you|
5.1.157-8/2403-4   He . . . tears] 1 line
5.1.171/2417   Give . . . Queen] 2 lines: marks|
5.2.17/2440   'Mong . . . pleasures] 2 lines: lackeys|
5.2.148/2571   Dread . . . heaven] 2 lines: sovereign|
5.3.1-3/2639-41   You'll . . . gaping] prose
5.3.5-10/2643-48   Belong . . . rascals] prose
5.3.28-29/2666-7   I . . . sirrah] puppy] (possibly prose)
5.4.1-3/2728-30   Heaven . . . Elizabeth] verse: Heaven| life| mighty|
5.4.32/2759   And . . . her] 2 lines: sorrow|

Two Noble Kinsmen

1.1.76/108   And . . . am] 2 lines: soldier|
1.1.95-6/127-8   As . . . knee] 1 line
1.1.147-8/179-80   It . . . graves] comfort|
1.3.197-8/478-9   I . . . mine] faith|
2.1.1-56/545-99   I . . . men] verse: thing I| I| seldom| number| lined| true| am| it what| at| death| offer| what I| promised| solemnity| hen| consent| comes| name| that| will| tenderly| princes| they| I| adversity| and| chamber| men| they| report| doers| I| been| enforce| their| at| so| their| eat| things| disasters| 'twere| them| rebuke| chide| comforted| 'em| night| I| that's| out| the| part| him| not| sight| the|
2.2.169/768   Not . . . me] 2 lines: all|
2.2.181-2/780-1   I . . . maintain] 1 line
2.3.17-18/897-8   Tempests . . . come] 1 line
2.3.34-5/914-15   Ay . . . see her] 1 line
2.3.39-43/919-23   And . . . all ye know] verse: Sennois| tree| ha| touch|
2.3.59-62/939-42   We'll . . . on't]? verse: and| before| what|
2.3.65/945   By . . . you] prose
2.3.67-8/947-8   Yet . . . not] 1 line
3.1.121-2/1226-7   That . . . till] these|
3.3.18-19/1284-5   Stay . . . more] 1 line
3.3.19-20/1285-6   Spare . . . now] 1 line
3.3.20-1/1286-7   I . . . stomach] 1 line
3.3.21-2/1287-8   I . . . to't] 1 line
3.3.22-3/1288-9   Is't . . . cousin] 1 line
3.3.23-4/1289-90   Yes . . . consciences] 1 line
3.3.24-5/1290-1   How . . . see] 1 line
3.3.26-7/1292-3   But . . . this] 1 line
3.3.34-6/1301-2   Something . . . ten] sir|. See the textual note.
3.3.41-2/1307-8   And . . . ho] 1 line
3.3.45-6/1311-12   By . . . honest] 1 line
3.3.46-7/1312-13   Then . . . now] 1 line
3.4.25-6/1344-5   O . . . else] breast|
3.5.1-21/1346-66   Fie . . . boys] prose
3.5.160-1/1405-6   The . . . a] south, from|
3.5.66-7/1411-12   O . . . a] 1 line
3.5.71-2/1416-17   The third . . . away] 1 line
3.5.73-6/1418-21   There's . . . gambols] prose
3.5.84-5/1429-30   Dii . . . damsel] 1 line
3.5.85-6/1430-1   Or . . . play] 1 line
3.5.87-8/1432-3   Go . . . peace] 1 line
3.5.94-5/1439-40   I . . . me] 3 lines: some| cue|
3.5.150-1/1495-6   'Twas . . . preface] 1 line
3.5.158-60/1503-5   And . . . wenches] 2 lines: made|
3.6.201-2/1706-7   Nay . . . dangers] 1 line
3.6.255-6/1760-1   Wherever . . . another] 1 line
4.1.19-20/1831-2   And . . . daughter's] discovered|
4.1.34-5/1846-7   Was . . . sleep] This edition; 1 line Q; health, sir?| COLMAN
4.1.42-3/1854-5   Nothing . . . me] 1 line
4.1.45/1857   WOOER . . . Not well] 1 type line. See the textual note.
4.1.145-6/1957-8   Uff . . . master] 3 lines: top the| your|
4.1.149-50/1961-2   Bear . . . about] 1 line

LINEATION NOTES

4.2.64-5/2027-8 Bring . . . see 'em] quickly|
4.3.1-2/2121-2 Her . . . not] *verse*: moon|
4.3.3-9/2122-9 She . . . behaviour] *verse*: sleeps| drinking| what| name| business| where|
4.3.10-15/2130-5 I . . . Aeneas] *verse*: down| than| as| legs| and|
4.3.18-25/2138-45 Now . . . then] *verse*: must| tongue| where| maids| with| long| make|
4.3.27-36/2147-55 Faith . . . enough] *verse*: break| i'th| hissing| shrewd| hang or| bless| of| of| bacon|
4.3.59-60/2178-9 Understand . . . Palamon] *verse*: ere|
4.3.61-2/2180-1 I . . . friend] *verse*: her|
4.3.63-6/2182-5 I . . . terms] *verse*: great| both| the|
4.3.67-98/2186-217 That . . . comfort] *verse*: the| to| are| you| light| take| of| and to| for| are| pranks| green| in| the| addition of| the| can| desire| still| acceptance| been her| to| appear with| falsehood| combatted| what's| and| times| have| of| us| not|
5.1.48-9/2265-6 Thou . . . purple] This edition; turned| Q
5.4.3-7/2392-6 O . . . twice] *verse*: company| this| I| told her|
5.4.25/2414 Pray . . . is] *2 lines*: in|
5.4.26-7/2415-16 I . . . still] *3 lines*: tell her| doctor|
5.4.67/2456 A . . . her] *2 lines*: mare|
5.6.36/2685 The . . . thankful] *2 lines*: all|

INDEX TO NOTES ON MODERNIZATION

This index lists words whose modernization is discussed in the textual notes at the point indicated.

a 'auld grey doe', *LLL* 4.2.12, 20
Abergavenny, *All Is True* 1.2.211
Abraham, *Romeo* 1.1.30.1
abram, *Coriolanus* 2.3.19
accosting, *Troilus* 4.6.60
Aeschines, *Pericles* 8.0.1
ah, *Troilus* 2.2.110
Alençon's, *LLL* 2.1.61
All Hallow Eve, *Measure* 2.1.121
all together, *1 Henry VI* 2.1.29
allons, allons!, *LLL* 4.3.359
a-mending, *Troilus* 1.3.159
angerly, *Two Gentlemen* 1.2.62
antique, *Hamlet* 2.2.471
Ardenne, *As You Like It* 1.1.109, etc.
artere, *Hamlet* 1.4.59
askance, *Shrew* 2.1.242
asnico, *Troilus* 2.1.46
attainture, *Richard III* 3.5.31
ay, *Cymbeline* 3.6.68
ay, faith, *Troilus* 3.1.70

bairn, *Winter's Tale* 3.3.68
bauble, *Two Gentlemen* 1.2.99
bear, *History of Lear* 20.80
bearherd, *Contention* 5.1.147; *Much Ado* 2.1.35
bed-right, *Tempest* 4.1.96
beest-eating, *Kinsmen* 3.5.133
beholden, *Two Gentlemen* 4.4.170
bier, *Cymbeline* 4.2.22
Biron, *LLL* 1.1.0.1
blood-baltered, *Macbeth* 4.1.139
Bois, *As You Like It* 1.1.54
bore, *Richard III* 2.1.90
born, *K. John* 3.4.149
bosky, *Tempest* 4.1.81
braggartism, *Two Gentlemen* 2.4.162
bye, *Duke of York* 5.1.68

canon, *Duke of York* 5.2.44
capriccio, *All's Well* 2.3.290
Caputius, *All Is True* 4.2.109
catalogue, *Two Gentlemen* 3.1.271
Cathayan, *Twelfth Night* 2.3.72
cavaliery, *Dream* 4.1.22
cessez, *Tragedy of Lear* 3.4.93
chapped, *As You Like It* 2.4.47
charnel, *Richard III* 4.4.56
chevaliers, *K. John* 2.1.287
chirurgeonly, *Tempest* 2.1.146
christen, *1 Henry IV* 2.5.8
cinquepace, *Twelfth Night* 1.3.125
clammer, *Winter's Tale* 4.4.246
claws, *Cymbeline* 5.5.212

coast, *Duke of York* 1.2.269
cock-a-diddle-dow, *Tempest* 1.2.390
co-leaguèd, *Hamlet* 1.2.21
Colum's, *Macbeth* 1.2.61
comfit, *Much Ado* 4.1.317
commends, *Cymbeline* 3.7.9
competent, *Twelfth Night* 3.4.240
Compiègne, *1 Henry VI* 1.1.60
construe, *LLL* 5.2.342
copintank, *Shrew* 5.1.60
Corioles, *Coriolanus* 1.2.0.1
cot, *As You Like It* 2.4.82, etc.
count, *Macbeth* 1.6.26
'countable, *Twelfth Night* 1.5.168
courtesy, *Dream* 4.1.20
Cush, *Merchant* 3.2.283

dammed, *All's Well* 2.3.141
dauphin, *1 Henry VI* 1.6.85
dear, *Twelfth Night* 5.1.67
denier, *Richard III* 1.2.238
Denis, *As You Like It* 1.1.83
desertless, *Much Ado* 3.3.8
dilated, *Hamlet* 1.2.38
distraught, *Caesar* 4.2.209
dizzy, *Hamlet* Add. Pass. N.8
doffed . . . doff, *Much Ado* 2.3.163
dolphin, *All's Well* 2.3.27
domicella-virgin, *LLL* 4.2.127–8
douts, *Hamlet* 4.7.164
Drop-hair, *Measure* 4.3.14
drover, *Much Ado* 2.1.183
drudges, *Timon* 4.3.255
due, *1 Henry VI* 4.2.34
Dumaine, *LLL* 1.1.0.2

eat, *Antony* 2.2.233
eche, *Pericles* 10.13
e'en, *Troilus* 4.1.10
embosked, *All's Well* 3.6.99
embowelled, *1 Henry IV* 5.4.108, 110
employ, *2 Henry IV* 4.1.250
endowed, *Two Gentlemen* 5.4.151
engineer, *Othello* 2.1.66
engrafted, *Kinsmen* 4.3.46
ensign, *Duke of York* 2.1.94.2
ere, *History of Lear* 24.120
every, *Tempest* 2.1.262
exposure, *Coriolanus* 4.1.37

facinerous, *All's Well* 2.3.30
Falconbridge, *K. John* 1.1.49
far, *Richard II* 1.3.186
farre, *Winter's Tale* 1.2.111
Fastolf, *1 Henry VI* 1.1.131

federy, *Measure* 2.4.123
fery, *Merry Wives* 1.1.45
figure, *Titus* 4.2.107
filed, *All Is True* 3.2.172
Fitzwalter, *Richard II* 4.1.42
fixture, *Troilus* 1.3.101; *Winter's Tale* 5.3.67
flee, *1 Henry VI* 1.2.21
flower-de-luce, *Winter's Tale* 4.4.127
flow'n, *All's Well* 2.1.138
flow'rets, *Dream* 4.1.54
foal, *Tragedy of Lear* 3.4.114
foil, *Cymbeline* 2.3.118
fool-born, *2 Henry IV* 5.5.55
foolhardy, *Richard II* 5.3.41
fore, *Shrew* 1.1.3; *Measure* 5.1.291
freight, *Twelfth Night* 5.1.57

galloglasses, *Macbeth* 1.2.13
gambol, *Shrew* Ind.2.134
gentleman, *All's Well* 5.3.248
Gérard, *All's Well* 1.1.25
ghasted, *History of Lear* 6.54
gild'st, *Sonnet* 28.12
glisten, *K. John* 5.1.54
Glyndŵr, *1 Henry IV* 1.1.40
Goliath, *Merry Wives* 5.1.22
good-brother, *Antony* 2.7.116
good-mother, *Hamlet* 1.2.77
graft, *As You Like It* 3.2.115
grainèd, *Hamlet* 3.4.80
Gratii . . . Bentii, *All's Well* 4.3.168–70
grece, *Twelfth Night* 3.1.123
gripple, *K. John* 5.2.36
groves, *Tempest* 4.1.66
guerdon, *LLL* 3.1.165

ha!, *History of Lear* 20.91
had, *Twelfth Night* 5.1.399
half-cheeked, *Shrew* 3.2.55–6
hallooed, *Winter's Tale* 3.3.75
hallowed, 'Complaint' 228
handkerchief, *As You Like It* 4.3.98, 5.2.26
hard, *Cymbeline* 4.4.27
Harlechy, *Richard II* 3.2.1
has, *All Is True* 3.2.58
he's, *All Is True* 1.3.59
hissing, *History of Lear* 13.12
Holmedon, *1 Henry IV* 1.1.55
hushed, *Richard II* 1.1.53
hyena, *As You Like It* 4.1.147

i', *All Is True* 2.1.79
ice-brook's, *Othello* 5.2.260
illustrous, *Cymbeline* 1.6.110
imperceiverant, *Cymbeline* 4.1.14

666

INDEX TO NOTES ON MODERNIZATION

important, *All's Well* 3.7.21
impostor, *Pericles* 21.165; *All's Well* 2.1.155
inbarqued, *Hamlet* 1.3.1
indices, *Troilus* 1.3.337
ingenuously, *Timon* 2.2.217
intertalk, *1 Henry VI* 3.1.64

Jaques, *As You Like It* 2.1.26
Jarteer, *Merry Wives* 1.4.114
Jewës, *Merchant* 2.5.42
Jordan, *Contention* 1.2.75
jostle, *LLL* 5.2.741
Julietta, *Measure* 1.2.71
juvenal, *LLL* 1.2.8
juvenile, *Dream* 3.1.89

Katherine, *Shrew* 1.1.47.1
kiln-hole, *Winter's Tale* 4.4.244

la pauvre gens, *1 Henry VI* 3.2.13
laager, *All's Well* 3.6.27
Lance, *Two Gentlemen* 2.3.0.1
lanced, *History of Lear* 6.51
leopard's, *LLL* 5.2.543
Lestrelles, *Henry V* 3.5.45
Licio, *Shrew* 2.1.60
lime, *Tempest* 4.1.193, 234
Longueville, *LLL* 1.1.0.2
loose, *Tempest* 2.1.131
lose, *Sonnet* 5.14
lustig, *All's Well* 2.3.42

maidenliest, *History of Lear* 2.127
majesté, *Henry V* 5.2.216, 263
manège, *As You Like It* 1.1.11
maréchal, *1 Henry VI* 4.7.70; *History of Lear* 17.9
marriage-blessing, *Tempest* 4.1.106
Marseilles, *Shrew* 2.1.371
marvellous, *2 Henry IV* 5.1.30
masque, *Troilus* 1.3.83
master, *LLL* 1.2.154; *Merry Wives* 1.1.98; *Twelfth Night* 4.2.86; *All's Well* 5.2.1
matter-a, *Merry Wives* 1.4.111
Mediterraneum, *LLL* 5.1.55
melancholy, *LLL* 4.3.12, 14
metamorphosed, *Two Gentlemen* 1.1.66
mets-le, *Merry Wives* 1.4.50
mi perdonate, *Shrew* 1.1.25
minimus, *Dream* 3.2.330
mis-shape, 'A Song' (Various Poems) 77
mistress-piece, *Cymbeline* 5.1.20
model, *All's Well* 4.3.102
monstruosity, *Troilus* 3.2.78
Moorish, *Errors* 4.3.27
Moscows, *All's Well* 4.1.70
Moses, *Two Gentlemen* 5.3.7
Mote, *LLL* 1.2.0.1; *Dream* 3.1.154
Mrs, *Richard III* 1.1.73
mustachio, *LLL* 5.1.99

Narbonne, *All's Well* 1.1.25
noble man, *1 Henry IV* 5.3.41
non point, *LLL* 2.1.190, 5.2.277
nurse, *Contention* 3.1.348

o'er, *Contention* 4.9.6; *Dream* 4.1.72
on, *Richard III* 1.3.302

or, *Lucrece* 56
ostriches, *1 Henry IV* 4.1.98
o'th', *Coriolanus* 1.1.45
overdaub, *Hamlet* Add. Pass. B.21
overshoot, *Venus* 680

pallid, 'Complaint' 198
Paroles, *All's Well* 1.1.97.1
passy-measures pavan, *Twelfth Night* 5.1.198
pavan, *Twelfth Night* 5.1.198
peonied, *Tempest* 4.1.64
Périgord, *LLL* 2.1.41
persevere, *As You Like It* 5.2.4
Petruccio, *Shrew* 1.2.0.1
pheezer, *Merry Wives* 1.3.9
phthisic, *Troilus* 5.3.104
phys'namy, *All's Well* 4.5.40
pish, *Much Ado* 5.1.38
pitch, *Coriolanus* 1.1.198
plume, *Tempest* 3.3.65
point's, *Errors* 5.1.119
Poitou, *K. John* 1.1.11
pother, *Tragedy of Lear* 3.2.50
pottage, *Merry Wives* 3.1.59
preambulate, *LLL* 5.1.76
prest, *All Is True* 2.4.183
price, *Troilus* 1.2.285; *Cymbeline* 3.6.74
princes, *Tempest* 1.2.174
pruning, *LLL* 4.3.181
Pucelle or pucelle, *1 Henry VI* 1.6.85
pueritia, *LLL* 5.1.47
puny, *As You Like It* 3.4.39
puts, *Timon* 4.3.43

quart d'écu, *All's Well* 4.3.281
quote, *Romeo* 1.4.31

racked, *Richard III* 4.1.96
ragged, *Two Gentlemen* 1.2.122
Ragusine, *Measure* 4.3.68
rain, *Merchant* 3.2.112
reck, *Cymbeline* 4.2.155
rein, *Tempest* 4.1.52
René, *1 Henry VI* 1.2.0.2, etc.
renegade, *Richard III* 4.4.395
resides, *Troilus* 1.3.117
reverend'st, *Timon* 5.2.67
Reynaldo, *All's Well* 3.4.19
rinsing, *Kinsmen* 1.1.155; *All Is True* 1.1.167
roast, *Contention* 1.1.106
roundure, *K. John* 2.1.259
runnion, *Merry Wives* 4.2.173

Santrailles, *1 Henry VI* 1.6.6
savages, *Tempest* 2.2.58
'schew, *Pericles* 1.179
scramble, *K. John* 4.3.147
sea-mews, *Tempest* 2.2.171
seize, *Antony* 3.11.47
self-willed, *Troilus* 1.3.188
señor, *LLL* 1.1.185, 1.2.10, 11, 16
sewer, *Troilus* 2.2.70
shamefaced, *Richard III* 1.4.135
shekels, *Measure* 2.2.153
shoal, *Macbeth* 1.7.6
short-grassed, *Tempest* 4.1.83
shot, *Two Gentlemen* 2.5.8
shout, *LLL* 4.1.147.1

shut, *Romeo* 3.2.49
Sienese, *All's Well* 1.2.1
simular, *History of Lear* 9.54
sire, *Troilus* 5.3.75
sleekly, *Shrew* 4.1.81
smilingly, *History of Lear* 24.196
sole, *1 Henry IV* 4.1.50
spat, *Merchant* 1.3.124
spay, *Measure* 2.1.220
spit, *Merchant* 1.3.111
spoil, *History of Lear* 9.8
sprites, *Tempest* 1.2.383
struck, *Richard III* 1.4.217
swam, *Two Gentlemen* 1.1.26
succour, *Richard II* Add. Pass. D.4
sue, 'A Song' (Various Poems) 5
suitor, *LLL* 4.1.107
summit, *Hamlet* 3.3.18
sun set, *K. John* 3.1.36

targs, *Cymbeline* 5.6.5
tatt'ring, *K. John* 5.5.7
tender-hafted, *Tragedy of Lear* 2.2.344
tenor, *Kinsmen* 3.5.125
thee, *Contention* 1.1.190
there, *LLL* 5.2.517
these, *2 Henry IV* 4.1.348; *Troilus* 5.1.12
thills, *Troilus* 3.2.44
this, *Romeo* 4.3.39; *1 Henry IV* 4.1.127
thou'lt, *Hamlet* 5.1.272
throws, *Antony* 3.7.80
till, *Hamlet* 2.2.547
tiny, *History of Lear* 9.75
tithe-soul, *Troilus* 2.2.18
title, *All's Well* 2.4.25
to, *Kinsmen* 2.2.264
togaed, *Othello* 1.1.24
torment'st, *Richard II* 4.1.260
trait'rous, *Contention* 4.4.42
travelling abed, *Cymbeline* 3.3.33
two, *Shrew* 5.2.47

vagrom, *Much Ado* 3.3.24
vial, *Pericles* 12.87
vice, *Merchant* 3.2.81
vinaigre, *All's Well* 2.3.45
'visaments, *Merry Wives* 1.1.35
visor, *Richard III* 2.2.28
visors, *1 Henry IV* 1.2.126
vizier, *1 Henry VI* 1.4.29
voluble, *LLL* 3.1.64

wafture, *Caesar* 2.1.245
waned, *Antony* 2.1.21
warr'nt, *As You Like It* 4.1.72
we, *Dream* 5.2.13
where, *Contention* 4.7.58
whew!, *Tragedy of Lear* 4.5.92
whilst, *Hamlet* 1.3.49
whirling, *Hamlet* 1.5.137
whistle of, *Winter's Tale* 4.4.244
whoa, *Troilus* 4.2.57
who's, *K. John* 4.3.16
wiped, *1 Henry VI* 2.4.117
wi'th', *Shrew* Ind.2.52; *Tempest* 1.2.112
withal, *Merchant* 2.7.12
world's, *K. John* 3.4.110
wreck, *Twelfth Night* 5.1.75

A SELECTIVE INDEX

This index aims to provide guidance to the more important primary topics treated in the General Introduction, the section on Canon and Chronology, and the Textual Introductions, but not to the Textual Notes. The section on Canon and Chronology provides (pp. 109-134) individual entries on the authorship and date of each of Shakespeare's works.

abridgement, 231, 340, 351, 543
'act' (i.e. act interval), 279
act-breaks, 16, 318, 468-9, 530, 594, 612
act divisions, 39, 209, 352, 476-7, 492
act-scene division, 170, 178, 199, 218, 231-2, 266, 271, 279-80, 290, 306, 317-18, 324, 331-2, 340, 353, 371, 377, 387-8, 392, 399, 402, 421, 426, 469, 493, 502, 510, 530, 544, 549, 559-60, 612, 619, 627
actors as reporters, 26-8, 175-6, 197, 228, 340, 398, 557
actors' names in prompt-books, 12
actors' names in text, 169, 176, 197, 371
adaptation, theatrical, 15, 73-4, 129, 340, 375, 468-9, 544 (*see also* abridgement)
additions, *see* interpolation
Admiral's Men, Lord, 169
Alexander, Peter, 56, 58
All Is True, 28, Ill. 9-12
Allde, Edward, 288
Alston, Tobias, 451
amphibious sections, 638
Amurath, 120
'and', frequency of, 114
'and', use of in stage directions, 329-30
annotated quarto copy, 306, 331
annotation, theatrical, 169, 176, 217-18, 289, 317, 323, 331, 386, 492, 593-4, 619
anti-theatrical prejudice, 19
apocrypha, the Shakespeare, 53
apostrophes denoting notional words, 601
apostrophes, incidence of, 604
apostrophes, scribal, 22
Archer, Edward, 135
Arden of Faversham, 88
Armin, Robert, 121; *The Italian Tailor and His Boy*, 131; *The Time Triumphant*, 126
asides, indicated by parentheses, 601
Aspinall, Alexander, 455
Aspley, William, 36, 351, 371
'a'th', incidence of, 593
attributions, manuscript, 74-5
Aubrey, John, 450, 458
authorial copy, characteristics of, 197, 266 (*see also* foul papers)
ay/yea, 329

bad quartos, 85, 175, 197, 228-9, 270, 340, 375, 398, 556, 559 (*see also* reported texts)
Barenz, William, 123
Barker, Robert, 459
Barnes, Barnaby, *The Devil's Charter*, 129
Barnett, William, 38

Barnfield, Richard, 455
Beaumarchais, Pierre Augustin Caron de, *Le Mariage de Figaro*, 23
Beaumont, Francis, 618; *Inner Temple and Gray's Inn Masque*, 134; Beaumont, Francis, and John Fletcher, *The Knight of the Burning Pestle*, 128; *Philaster*, 132, 477
Bedford, Earls of, 331
Benson, John, 38, 444, 449, 457
Berners, Lord, 136
between/betwixt, 329
Binns, J. W., 271
biographical evidence of authorship, 77
biographical evidence of date, 95-7
blocking entry, 396, 558 (*see also* staying entry)
Blount, Edward, 36, 386, 468, 549, 556, 593
Bonian (also Bonion), Richard, 52, 424
book-keeper, 12, 23, 125
Boswell, James, the younger (edition), 53, 55
Bowers, Fredson, 7, 12, 57
Bradock, Richard, 279
Brainerd, B., 101, 107
Brathwait, Richard, *Remains after Death*, 458
Breton, Nicholas, *The Will of Wit*, 135
Brooke, Arthur, *Romeus and Juliet*, 109
Brooke family, 341
Brooke, Henry, Lord Cobham, 120
Brooke, William, Lord Cobham, 120
Buc, Sir George, 26, 53, 71, 138
Burbage, Richard, 19, 69, 124
Burby, Cuthbert, 169, 270, 288
Burgh, Nicholas, 457-8
Busby, John, 340, 375, 509
Butter, Nathaniel, 52, 509

Cambridge edition (1863-6), 56-8
Camden, William, *Remains*, 131
Canterbury, Archbishop of, 34
Capell, Edward, 37, 53, 55
casting-off of copy, 39-41, 198, 288, 306, 329, 353, 376, 386, 501, 549, 556, 612, 637
Caxton, William, 31
Cecil, Sir Robert, 93, 117
censorship, 15-16, 34, 120, 176, 209, 307, 323, 330-1, 341, 351, 558 (*see also* expurgation)
Chamberlain's Men, Lord, 69, 72, 91, 169, 288, 371, 396 (*see also* King's Men)
Chapman, George, *Seven Books of the Iliads*, 121, 123
Chester, Robert, *Love's Martyr*, 457
Chettle, Henry, 139, 288-9; *Hoffman*, 125

chronological evidence of authorship, 78
chronology of Shakespeare's works, 36-7, 69-142 *passim*
Chute, Antony, *Beauty Dishonoured*, 110
Clark, W. G., 56
Cobham, the Lords, 330, 341 (*see also* Brooke, Henry, *and* Brooke, William)
Cokayne, Aston, 70
collaboration, 72-4, 111, 114-15, 127, 133, 135, 198, 217-18, 501, 557 ff.
Collier, John Payne, 7, 450, 456; edition, 56
colloquial contractions, 332
colloquialism in verse, 101-6
colloquialisms, expansion of, 477
comma as hyphen, 492
composition, Shakespeare's patterns of, 92-3
compositor, functions of, 43-7
compositor identification, 41-3
Compositor A (Creede), 375
Compositor A (Eld), 424, 426
Compositor A (Folio), 307, 331, 386, 593, 637, 639
Compositor A (Simmes), 306, 351, 371
Compositor B (Eld), 424, 426
Compositor B (Folio), 41-2, Ill. 18, 331, 352-3, 399, 421, 492-3, 501, 529, 531, 593, 618-19, 637, 639
Compositor C (Eld), 424, 426
Compositor C (Folio), 492-3
Compositor E (Folio), 399, 477, 529, 531
Compositor I (Folio), 618
Compositor S (Simmes), 306
concurrent printing, 288
Condell, Henry, 19, 36, 69-73
conflation, 509
Cope, Walter, 93
copy-editing, 34, 36
copyright, 34, 425
cornetts, 492, 594
correction, stop-press, 489
Cotes, Thomas, 625, 628-9
court performance, 93, 120, 129, 266, 279, 341
Cowley, Richard, 371
Crane, Ralph, 20-2, Ill. 6, 36, 39, 127, 166, 340, 352, 468, 531, 543, 601, 604, 612, 637
Creede, Thomas, 175, 288, 340, 375, 556
Curtis, *see* Greville, Curtis

Daniel, Samuel, *Civil Wars*, 117, 120; *Cleopatra*, 129; *Complaint of Rosamund*, 118; *Hymen's Triumph*, 119; *Musophilus*, 121
Danter, John, 113, 118, 209, 288
Davenant, Robert, 449-50

668

A SELECTIVE INDEX

Davenant, William, 53, 449-50, 543
Davies, Sir John, *Nosce Teipsum*, 121
Day, John, 9
dedications, Shakespeare's, 2
Dekker, Thomas, 124-5, 138-9; *The Honest Whore*, 126; *Satiromastix*, 122-3
Deloney, Thomas, *Garland of Good Will*, 455
Der Bestrafte Brudermord, 398
Derby's Men, *see* Strange's Men
Dering, Sir Edward, 329
difficilior lectio, 60
Digby, Sir Kenelm, 136
Digges, Leonard, 36, 70, 72
Dobyns, Robert, 458
does/do's, 530-1, 593
doubling of parts, 317, 331, 340, 375, 386
Dowland, John, 450
Drayton, Michael, 140
Dryden, John, 36
du Bartas, Guillaume Saluste, 118
Dugdale, Sir William, 457
duplication, 468

Eastward Ho, 128, 559
Ecclestone, William, 492
echoes as evidence of date, 93
-ed syllabic endings, 209, 307, 371
editions, derivative, 33
editions, substantive, 33
editors, ideal, 6-7
Edmond Ironside, 88
Edward III, 88, 100
Edwards, Thomas, *The Canons of Criticism*, 54
Eld, George, 424, 426, 444
'element', an overworn word, 123
Eliot, John, *Ortho-epia Gallica*, 118
Elizabeth I, Queen, 341
'em' (for 'them'), 478
emendation, 58-60
England's Helicon, 270, 455
'enters' in stage directions, 177, 593
error, compositorial, 43-7
Essex, Earl of, 424
-eth inflection, 329
Evans, G. Blakemore, 58
expurgation, 39, 230-1, 306, 317, 323, 331, 340-1, 375, 399, 476-8 (*see also* censorship)

facsimiles, photographic, 4
fair copy, 9, 14, 351, 426, 628
Faithful Friends, The, 'plot' of, 9
false starts, 176, 288
Fane, Sir Francis, 455, 458, 460
Farmer, Richard, 37
Fel. (actor's name?), 169
feminine verse endings, 114
Field, Richard, 2, 264-5
Fisher, Thomas, 279
Fletcher, John, 72, 88, 133-4, 329, 468, 618-19, 265-9; *Bonduca*, 492; *Demetrius and Enanthe*, 637; *The Mad Lover*, 492; *The Maid's Tragedy*, 477; *Rollo, Duke of Normandy*, 468; *Women Pleased*, 110, 170; *The Woman's Prize*, 111
Florio, John, 122
Folio (1623), act divisions in, 39
—— authenticity of contents, 70-1, 74
—— commendatory verses in, 36
—— contents of, 36
—— copy-editing in, 36
—— editing of, 36
—— exclusion of poems, 38, 74
—— expurgation in, 39
—— heavy punctuation in, 39
—— kinds of copy in, 39
—— make-up of, 40, Ill. 16
—— modernization in, 39
—— organization of, 36-9
—— title of, 37-8
—— use of annotated copy in, 51-2
Folio, Second (1632), 53
Folio, Third (1663-4), 53
Folio, Fourth (1685), 53
Forman, Simon, 28, 128, 131-2, 543-4, 604
foul-case errors, 45
foul papers, 9, 14, 166, 176, 198, 217, 229-30, 266, 270, 279, 288-9, 306, 351, 371, 375, 425, 476-9, 492, 501, 510, 549, 593, 627-8
function words as evidence of authorship, 80-9
function words in bad quartos, 85
Furnivall, F. J., 7

Gabriel (actor's name), 197
Garrick, David, 53
Garter, Order of the, 341
Gascoigne, George, 118
Gerard, John, *Herbal*, 270
ghost characters, 371, 492, 549
Globe edition, 56
Globe Theatre, motto of, 121, 449
Glover, J., 56
Goodal, Thomas, 125
Gosson, Henry, 556
Gough, Robert, 492
Gower, John, 558
Greene, Robert, 95-7, 217; *Groatsworth of Wit*, 112; *Menaphon*, 110, 137
Greg, W. W., 7, 28-31, 49, 57-9
Greville, Curtis, 626
Griffin, Bartholomew, 455
Gutenberg, Johannes, 31

'ha' (for 'have'), 478
Halliwell, J. O., 7
Hand D (*Sir Thomas More*), characteristics of, 9-10
handwriting, Shakespeare's, 9-10
Hanmer, Sir Thomas (edition), 53-4
Harington, Sir John, 2
Harrison, John, 264-5
Harsnett, Samuel, *A Declaration of Egregious Popish Impostures*, 128
Harvey, Gabriel, 70, 122, 138, 330-1
has/h'as, 531, 593, 618-19
has/hath, 478
Hathway, Richard, 140
Hayes, Thomas, 323
Heminges, John, 19, 36, 69-73, 601
2 *Henry IV*, 170; second issue, 49-50, Ill. 22
Henslowe, Philip, 91, 169, 398
Herbert, Sir Henry, 22, 53, 601
'here' in stage directions, 112
Heywood, Thomas, 25, 33, 74, 124, 455
Hilton, John, 392
Hinman, Charlton, 57, 59
Hoby, Sir Edward, 117
Holinshed, Raphael, *Chronicles*, 112, 117, 119, 132, 135
Holland, Hugh, 36
Holland, John, 176
Honest Man's Fortune, The, 559, 627
'houses' indicated on stage, 266
Housman, A. E., 31, 56, 59
Humfrey (actor's name), 197
Hunsdon's Men, Lord, 288
hyphens, incidence of, 604
hyphens, scribal, 22

'if' for 'an', 478
imagery as evidence of authorship, 78
inconsistencies, 127, 166, 198, 218, 266, 279, 501
Inns of Court, 266, 424
interpolation, 122, 131-2, 351, 375, 425, 626
interpolation, actors', 399-400
i'the, 478

Jackson, Richard, 450
Jackson, Roger, 38
Jaggard, Isaac and William, 34-6, 47, 197, 323, 376, 386, 425-6, 468, 509, 593
James I, King, 341, 459, 626
James, Richard, 70
Jewell, Simon, 110
Johnson, Arthur, 340
Johnson, Robert, 612
Johnson, Samuel, 7; edition, 53-5
Jones, Robert, *First Book of Songs or Airs*, 123
Jonson, Ben, 28, 36-8, 70, 72, 387, 480; *Bartholomew Fair*, 114, 134; *Cynthia's Revels*, 559; *Epicoene*, 131; *Every Man Out of his Humour*, 120-1; *Poetaster*, 123; *Masque of Oberon*, 601; *Masque of Queens*, 129; *Volpone*, 558
Jourdain, Sylvester, *Discovery of the Bermudas*, 132
justification of type, 46

Kempe (also Kemp), William, 69, 120, 371
kerning, 45
A King and No King, 477
King's Men, 134, 279, 317, 396, 468-9, 477, 492, 557-8, 594, 626 (*see also* Chamberlain's Men)
King's Men, dissolution of, 53
Knack to Know a Knave, A, 110, 113
Knight, Charles (edition), 56
Knight, Edward, 22, 36, 626, 627-8
Knolles, Richard, *History of the Turks*, 126
Kyd, Thomas, 138, 398; *The Spanish Tragedy*, 110

Lachmann, Karl, 56
Latin, printing of, 271
Law, Matthew, 52, 306, 329
Legate, Bartholomew, 132
licensing of plays for performance, 10
licensing of plays for publication, 34
ligatures, 45-6
lineation, 128, 637-40
Ling, Nicholas, 289, 396-7
linguistic evidence of authorship, 80
linguistic evidence of date, 101
location directions, 266

Locrine, 112, 217
Lodge, Thomas, *Rosalynde*, 121; *Wit's Misery*, 137, 398
London, Bishop of, 34, 307, 351
London Prodigal, The, 70
Lord Admiral's Men, *see* Admiral's Men
Lord Chamberlain's Men, *see* Chamberlain's Men
Lord Hunsdon's Men, *see* Hunsdon's Men
Lord Strange's Men, *see* Strange's Men
Lucrece, 2
Love's Labour's Won, 71-2
lower case letters, initial, in verse, 324
Lyly, John, *Endymion*, 135; *Midas*, 109

McKerrow, R. B., 3, 57, 59, 178, 199, 219, 232, 266, 290
Macklin, Charles, *Love à-la-Mode*, 23
Mabbe, James, 36
Malone, Edmond, 37, 95; edition, 53, 55
manent, 329
Manningham, John, 123
manuscripts, dramatic, 10
manuscripts, Shakespeare's, 4-6, 52-3
Marlowe, Christopher, 455; *Dr Faustus*, 110; *Edward II*, 116; *Hero and Leander*, 121; *Tamburlaine*, 111
Marston, John, *Antonio's Revenge*, 122; *The Malcontent*, 170
massed entries, 22, 340
Massinger, Philip, 131; *Believe as you List*, 71
Master of the Revels, 10, 12, 26
Melbourne manuscript, 9, Ill. 2
memorial reconstruction, 23-8, 122, 398 (*see also* bad quartos)
Meres, Francis, 23, 70, 74, 90-1, 112, 398, 444
metrical emendation, 59-60
metrical evidence of authorship, 79
metrical tests as evidence of date, 106
mislineation, 279, 307, 399, 510, 556, 593, 627
misreadings, 9-10
Middleton, Hugh, 131
Middleton, Thomas, 73, 86, 126, 128, 140, 468-9, 501; *The Black Book*, 139; *A Game at Chess*, 20; *The Witch*, 20-2, 129, 543; *Women Beware Women*, 604
Millington, Thomas, 175, 177, 197, 199, 375
Milton, John, 37, 136
modernization, 58
Mommsen, Tycho, 56
Mömpelgard, Count, 341
Montaigne, *Essays*, 122
Moorditch, 125
Morley, Thomas, 392; *First Book of Airs*, 121
Mosse, Miles, *The Arraignment and Conviction of Usury*, 119
'Mr', expansion of, 392
Muhammad III, 120
Munday, Anthony, 124-5, 140; *The Heaven of the Mind*, 139; *John a Kent and John a Cumber*, 139
music cues, 198, 317, 323, 477, 593
musicians, 279

Nashe, Thomas, 34, 137, 217; *Have With You to Saffron Walden*, 118; *Pierce Penniless*, 112, 122

'ne' in Henslowe, 92
Neville, Sir Henry, 477
New Academy of Compliments, 449
Newcombe, Henry, 460
Nicke (actor's name?), 169
Nieuport, Battle of, 122

oaths, 140
oaths and exclamations as evidence of authorship, 78
oh/o spellings, 112, 169, 228, 306, 317, 399, 468, 477, 549, 593, 604
Okes, Nicholas, 476, 509-10
Oldcastle, Sir John, 120, 330-1, 351
Oldys, William, 449
omission in early texts, 59
omissions, 169, 306-7, 399-400, 469
Oras pause tests, 107
Orwell, George, 7
Ostend, Siege of, 122
Overbury, Sir Thomas, 140
Oxford edition (1986), limitations of, 60-2; particular aims of, 61

Painter, William, *The Palace of Pleasure*, 127, 136
palaeographical evidence of authorship, 77
Par. (actor's name?), 169
parentheses, incidence of, 22, 352, 477, 593, 604, 618
parentheses, scribal, 22
parts, actors', 12
Passionate Pilgrim, The, 74, 123, 270, 444
Pavier, Thomas, 34-6, 121, 139, 175, 197, 279, 323, 375-6, 509, 559
Peck, Francis, 449
Peele, George, 114-15, 217; *Edward I*, 129
Pembroke's Men, 110, 113-14, 169, 288-9
performance, records of, 91-2
Phillips, Edward, 449
Phoenix' Nest, The, 139
piracy, 396
'plat', 12 (*see also* 'plot')
Platter, Thomas, 121
Players' Quartos, 53, 396
Playford, John, 449
plays, publication of, 33-4
'plot', 9 (*see also* 'plat')
Plume, Archbishop Thomas, 457
Plutarch, *Lives*, 121
Poems (1640), 469 (*see also* Shakespeare's Poems)
Pollard, A. W., 49
Pope, Alexander, 509; edition, 53-4
praestat insolitior lectio, 60
pray thee/prithee, 329-30
press corrections, 166
press variants, 49, 386, 424, 444, 478, 510, 529, 549
Prince d'Amour, 449
printing, 47-9
printing, shared, 556
private performance, 129, 266, 424
profanity, 15-16, 125, 166, 230-1, 279, 317-18, 331, 340-1, 351-2, 375, 399, 468, 476-8 (*see also* expurgation)
prompt-book, 10-12, 52-3, 169, 266, 279, 392, 399, 601
proof corrections, 549
proof, foul, 47

proof-reading, authorial, 47
properties, stage, 217
provincial performance, 289, 341
publication, records of, 92
Pudsey, Edward, 28
punctuation, 22, 324, 399, 444, 477, 492, 593, 601, 604
Puritan, The, 128

quartos, misdated, 49
Queen's Men, 97
question marks, superfluity of, 324
quotations as evidence of date, 93

Ralegh, Sir Walter, 455
Ravenscroft, Edward, 114
recurring type, 371
re-entry, law of, 209
Register, Stationers', 34
reported texts, 307, 557 (*see also* bad quartos)
Revels Accounts (1604-5), 71
Revels, Master of the, *see* Master of the Revels
revision, 16-18, 169-70, 176-7, 198, 209, 217, 228-9, 270-1, 279, 306-7, 317, 330, 332, 341, 351, 353, 375, 386-7, 399-402, 421, 426, 468-9, 476-8, 509, 626
rhyme, 95, 119
Richard, Duke of York, 170
Robert, Earl of Huntington, 199
Roberts, James, 279, 323, 396, 424
Rowe, Nicholas, 449; edition, 53-4
Rowlands, S., *A Whole Crew of Kind Gossips*, 110
Rowley, William, 135
Russell, Dowager Lady, 331
Russell, Sir John, 330-1, 351
Russell, Thomas, 70
Rutland, Earl of, 124

Sampson, William, 75
Satchell, Thomas, 41, 43
Schoenbaum, S., 266
Scoloker, Anthony, *Daiphantus*, 122
Scot, Reginald, *The Discovery of Witchcraft*, 129
scribal characteristics, 352
scribal copy, 169, 329
scribal corruption, 341
scribal practice, 317
season, the London theatrical, 90-2
Second Maiden's Tragedy, The, 12, 22, 559, 627
setting by formes, 288
Seven Deadly Sins, The, 170
'severally', 530
Shakespeare's name on title pages, 70
Shakespeare's Poems (1640), 34 (*see also* Benson, John, *and* Poems)
Sharpham, Edward, *The Fleer*, 128, 279
Sheridan, Richard, *The Duenna* 23; *The School for Scandal*, 23
Sherley, Sir Anthony, 123
Shirley, James, 628
Short, Peter, 169, 197, 228, 329
shorthand, 26
Sidney, Sir Philip, *Astrophil and Stella*, 123
Simmes, Valentine, 175, 228, 306, 329, 351, 371, 396, 628

A SELECTIVE INDEX

Simon (actor's name?), 110
Sincklo (also Sinclo, Sinklo), John, 110-11, 169, 170, 197
Singer, John, 125
1 Sir John Oldcastle, 70, 121
Sir John van Olden Barnavelt, 12
Sir Thomas More, 1, 9-10, Ill. 4, 17, 169
Sir Thomas Wyatt (Webster and Dekker), 559
size of cast as evidence of date, 95
Slater, Eliot, 100-1
Smethwick, John, 36, 289, 396-7
Smith, Wentworth, 75
Smith, William, 75, 123, 139
Snelling, William, 75
songs in plays, 73
sophistication, compositorial, 166, 231, 376, 425, 530
sophistication, scribal, 317, 332, 340, 352, 399, 478, 601
Sorevin, Thomas, 124
Soto, 110-11
sources as evidence of date, 94
Southampton, Henry Wriothesley, third Earl of, 2, 118, 331
Spedding, James, 133
speech-prefixes, 169, 270-1, 317, 323-4, 351, 371, 387, 476, 492-3, 501, 549
spelling, 628
spelling, Elizabethan, 3
spelling in printed works, 45
spellings, Shakespearian, 279, 375, 461, 492, 593
spellings, variant, 628
Spenser, Edmund, *The Faerie Queene*, 111-12, 115
stage directions, 22-3, 80, 112, 177, 230, 306, 317, 329-30, 340, 352, 386, 476-7, 492, 530, 549, 593, 601, 612, 626
Stanley, William, sixth Earl of Derby, 75
staying entry, 324, 371, 375 (*see also* blocking entry)

Steevens, George (edition), 53, 55
Stonehouse, Walter, 75
Stow, John, 458
Strachey, William, 75, 140; *A True Repertory* . . ., 132
Strange's Men, 69, 113, 137, 139
Strode, William, 75, 449, 451
structural parallels as evidence of authorship, 76
stylometry, 80, 134
Sussex's Men, 113-14

Tailor, Robert, *The Hog Hath Lost His Pearl*, 26
Taming of A Shrew, The, 169-70
Tawyer, William, 279-80
theatrical provenance as evidence of authorship, 77
theatrical provenance as evidence of date, 93
Theobald, Lewis, 509; edition, 53-4; *The Double Falsehood*, 133
'they' misprinted 'their', 444
Thierry and Theodoret, 477
Thirlby, Styan, 54
Thorpe, Thomas, 38, 444
Tiger, The (ship), 128
Tilney, Sir Edmund, 71, 124-5, 139
Titus Andronicus (1600), 34
topical allusions, 94, 116-17, 121-8, 131-2, 134, 140, 341, 626
transcripts, 12-14, 19-21, 23, 230, 317, 331, 387, 392, 399, 421, 425, 444, 476-7, 593-4, 604, 612, 618-19, 628
Trinity College, Cambridge, 56-7
Troublesome Reign of John, King of England, The, 70, 97, 317
Trundell, John 396
Tucke, *see* Tuckfield, Thomas
Tuckfield, Thomas, 626
Twine, Laurence, *Pattern of Painful Adventures*, 557-8
Two Noble Ladies, The, 386

two-part plays, 199
type shortage, 324, 425, 510

Ule, Louis, 100-1

variorum editions, 4
de Vega, Lope, 23
Venus and Adonis, 2
verbal parallels as evidence of authorship, 78-9
verbal parallels as evidence of date, 106
verbal variation, 401
Vincent, Thomas, 23, 125
vocabulary as evidence of authorship, 78
vocabulary as evidence of date, 100-1

Walker, Alice, 3, 59, 178, 199, 219, 266, 324
Walkley, Thomas, 476-7
Walley (also Walleys), Henry, 52, 424
Warburton, William (edition), 53-4
Waterson, John, 625
Webster, John, 124-5
Weelkes, Thomas, 455
Weever, John, 70
White, William, 197, 270, 556
Wightman, Edward, 131
Wilkins, George, 138, 557-8; *The Miseries of Enforced Marriage*, 128, 130; *The Painful Adventures of Pericles, Prince of Tyre*, 130
Wilson, Jack, 371
Wilson, John, 449, 469, 612
Wilson, Robert, 140
Wise, Andrew, 228, 306, 329, 351, 371
Wright, James, 90
Wright, W. A., 56-8
W.S., ascriptions to, 75-6, 449-50, 456

'ye', incidence of, 112, 329
ye/you, 627-9
Yorkshire Tragedy, A, 70, 76-7

zounds, 230